THE EUROPEAN FOOTBALL 99/00 YEARBOOK

General Editor **MIKE HAMMOND**   Published by **SPORTS PROJECTS LTD**

www.sportsprojects.com

ICELAND

Arctic Circle

FAROE
ISLANDS

N O R W A Y

S W E D E N

F I N L A N D

ESTONIA

LATVIA

LITHUANIA

RUSSIA

SCOTLAND

NORTHERN
IRELAND

REPUBLIC OF
IRELAND

WALES

ENGLAND

HOLLAND

BELGIUM

North
Sea

DENMARK

Baltic
Sea

BELAR

POLAND

LUXEMBOURG

GERMANY

CZECH
REPUBLIC

SLOVAKIA

Bay of
Biscay

F R A N C E

LIECHTENSTEIN

SWITZERLAND

AUSTRIA

HUNGARY

ROMAN

SLOVENIA

CROATIA

MONACO

I T A L Y

SAN MARINO

BOSNIA-
HERZEGOVINA

YUGOSLAVIA

PORTUGAL

S P A I N

ANDORRA

CORSICA (Fr)

BULGA

MACE-
DONIA

ALBANIA

SARDINIA (It)

GREECE

M e d i t e r r a n e a n

SICILY

MALTA

S e a

THE EUROPEAN FOOTBALL YEARBOOK 1999/2000

RUSSIA

KRAINE

Caspian Sea

Black Sea

GEORGIA

AZERBAIJAN

ARMENIA

TURKEY

CYPRUS

ISRAEL

ACKNOWLEDGEMENTS

The European Football Yearbook 1999/2000
First Published in Great Britain by Sports Projects Ltd
October 1999

Copyright Sports Projects Ltd
188 Lightwoods Hill, Smethwick, Warley, West Midlands,
B67 5EH, England
website: www.sportsprojects.com
email: info@sportproject.u-net.com

ISBN 0 946866 53 8 (paperback)
ISBN 0 946866 52 X (hardback)

Printed in Great Britain

General Editor
Mike Hammond

Editorial and Research Co-ordinators
Lakis Avraamides, Mert Aydin, Nikolai Belov, José Del Olmo,
Tamás Dénes, Gerry Desmond, Dimcho Dimitrov Ivanov,
Marshall Gillespie, Miron Goihman, Andriy Grechylo,
Michael Hansen, Peter Hekkema, Romeo Ionescu, Valery Karpoushkin,
Daniel Kolbusch, Jean-Paul Kolbusch, Zsolt Kormanik,
Yeorgos Kousounelos, Dragan Krstic, Zdenek Kucera,
Esko S. Lahtinen, Tarmo Lehiste, Dag Lindholm, Kevin McNamara,
Fatmir Meneri, Kazimierz Oleszek, Alexander Pauk,
Humberto M. Pereira Silva, Zdravko Reic, Mike Ritter,
Revaz Shengelia, Vídir Sigurdsson, Mikhail Sipovich, Andrej Stare,
Algis Staskevicius, Edouard Stutz, Matej Széher, Natan Tamari,
Mel ap ior Thomas, Serge Van Hoof, Victor Vassallo, Stefan Welte,
Jacob Zelazo, Luciano Zinelli.

Special thanks to
Susan Hammond

Photographs:
Empics Ltd and courtesy of featured clubs

Design, layout and graphics:
Nadine Goldingay, Phil Lees and Vic Millward, Mikhail Sipovich

Cover design:
Bernard Gallagher

INTRODUCTION

'European Superleague' was the phrase on everyone's lips when I penned the introduction to last season's edition of the European Football Yearbook.

As is always the case in football, however, much can happen in a year. UEFA acted quickly to prevent a breakaway by the continent's most glamorous clubs, producing a revamped programme of European competition this season.

While the Cup-winners' Cup has left us, what remains is a huge competitive structure that only confirms the increasing pre-eminence of European competition.

Once again, we offer the *European Football Yearbook* as your definitive guide to football around the continent.

Now in its 10th edition, it continues to place at your fingertips the facts and figures on last season for top-flight club sides from Albania to Yugoslavia.

A full-colour supplement provides a rundown of team strips and club and national emblems. There's also a review of domestic and continental competition in all European nations, as well as a look at the summer's transfer activity.

Your comments are always welcome as we strive to maintain the high standard of this football 'bible', which is in demand not only in Europe but around the world. Queries or suggestions can be e-mailed to us via our website at **www.sportsprojects.com** where further copies of this book can also be ordered.

BERNARD GALLAGHER

Publisher

COMMENT

No room to breathe in football's crowded house

Football is a phenomenon, a powerful, emotional, life-enhancing force. It is one of the 20th century's greatest success stories. No other sport shares its widespread appeal to participants and spectators alike. And as the new millennium approaches, it can be said without fear of exaggeration that the game has never been followed with so much affection, enthusiasm and goodwill.

But while football is indestructible and will always be with us, it cannot afford to take its present level of popularity for granted. Though largely resistant to the vagaries of fashion, the professional game still has duties and responsibilities. No matter how much money is pumped in by sponsors, television companies and sundry other external supply lines, the game's powerbrokers must never lose sight of the fact that football's success relies first and foremost on those who play it and those who watch it.

The quality of the product is determined by the players, and, generally, if this meets with the approval of the fans, they will pay what it takes and go to the stadium to watch the players perform. It doesn't matter how much that product is glossed up, branded and marketed, the basic premise of professional spectator sport remains the same. Therefore, the key to sustained success is in maintaining and improving the standard of the football.

Yet, how is that possible given the huge demands that are currently being placed on the game's top players? The danger of burn-out is clear and present, yet no significant attempt has been made to reduce the workload of the men whose health, fitness and vitality are paramount.

Rather, the opposite is true. In the rush to cash in on football's increasingly magnetic appeal, the game's authorities have done their best to bring the international football calendar to a state of gridlock. New competitions have been proposed, old ones have been expanded, and there has even been a concerted effort by FIFA's top man, president Sepp Blatter, to tamper with the birthright of the World Cup, proposing that the game's greatest

showpiece, the jewel in its crown, be held every two years instead of four.

This is sheer, unabashed greed. It is the footballing equivalent of snacking between meals. It would spoil the anticipation. "All good things come to those who wait" is no idle proverb. It is a fact of life. The treasures we prize and value the most are those which are rare. The World Cup is what it is because of the great expectation that precedes it and the grandeur and majesty that surround it. Doubling its frequency would probably halve its appeal.

The same goes for the Olympic Games. Perhaps Blatter should have listened in to those gold-medal winners at the biennial World Athletics Championships in Seville, almost all of whom talked of their triumphs as mere stepping stones towards the ultimate target of Olympic gold in Sydney. The Copa América, the former South American Championship, is another big sporting occasion that has been considerably devalued since switching from a four-yearly to a two-yearly timetable. With the exception of Brazil, all of the major countries appearing at the 1999 tournament in Paraguay chose to rest a number of their leading players, who were tired out after a long, gruelling season in Europe. Would the FIFA president really like to see that happening in the World Cup? Does he not subscribe to that other proverbial nugget of wisdom that warns of familiarity breeding contempt?

International football overkill has also seen the Blatter-approved introduction of time-wasting, tarted-up non-events such as the Confederations' Cup and the World Team Championship. World champions France didn't want to compete in the former and just about got away with it, but there was no such freedom for Manchester United, the new club champions of Europe, who were largely bullied into competing in the latter by a British government desperate to curry favour with the high-ranking suits of FIFA with a view to the attribution of hosting rights for the 2006 World Cup.

The UEFA Champions' League trophy against a backdrop of the 1999/2000 draw.

COMMENT

In consequence, United felt compelled, for whatever reason, though perhaps partly - let's give them the benefit of the doubt - through respect for the condition of their players, to withdraw from the FA Cup, a trophy they should have had an obligation to defend.

United have largely been derided for their action, and while it must be especially galling for supporters of the club who have been brought up to love and respect the traditions and values of the FA Cup, the oldest ongoing knockout tournament in existence, in the long run United might ultimately be revered for having taken a deliberate and high-profile stand against the perils of too much competition.

Only those who inhabit professional football clubs can fully appreciate the demands that are made on today's players. While diet, medicine and training techniques are far more advanced now than they once were and can considerably extend and improve a top-class footballer's career, there is only so much that the human body, *any* human body, can take. While championship boxers generally go several months between big fights, more often than not the world's finest footballers are asked to play three times in eight days, which, when added to training and travel and repeated over and over in a continuous cycle for months on end, will inevitably lead to frustration, fatigue and a reduction in performance levels. Even today's modern super-athletes, pampered and protected as they are, occasionally need a break.

The fact is you *can* have too much of a good thing, and spectators, like players, would rather have less of more than more of less. Quality and quantity do not necessarily move in opposite directions, but they rarely travel hand in hand. This is an inherent danger for UEFA's new, enlarged Champions' League.

The new structure of European football's biggest, most prestigious and most lavishly-sponsored club competition does have a certain glamorous, gluttonous appeal. And everybody knows that UEFA were forced into drawing up such an elaborate blueprint in response to the considerable threat to their sovereignty posed by the jackals of the alternative 'European Super League'. But can the new Champions' League co-exist peacefully and harmoniously with Europe's domestic championships? Will the players be able to cope with the punishing schedule? And what will the fans make of it all? How much more football can they take in before infatuation leads to overdose?

These are questions which will all be answered in time, but one wonders whether any of them were properly considered and addressed at the time of conception. Let us hope that UEFA's new baby grows up to be happy and wise as well as wealthy. Its first annual

Senes Erzik (right) and Jean Fournet-Fayard of the UEFA Club Competitions Committee make the 1999/2000 UEFA Champions' League draw in Monaco.

check-up should be interesting. That will come at the finals of the European Championship in Holland and Belgium next June, where many jaded, leg-weary Champions' League participants will be expected to produce their very best form for their respective countries.

Reaching peak condition at a major tournament is no guarantee for a footballer at the best of times, no matter how great his talent and commitment, but asking him to perform to maximum potential after nine months of hard slog for his club, during which he might have totted up 60 or more matches in three or four different competitions, is not fair or realistic.

Professional footballers are often accused of living the easy life. Those in the top bracket are paid exorbitant - some would say obscene - salaries for what, essentially, is a pleasurable, rewarding, diverting occupation, so clearly they should be expected to work hard, very hard, for their money.

But, jealousies aside, what is the point of flogging them to the verge of exhaustion? It serves the interests of nobody. The fabric of the game is dependent on the quality of the yarns and fibres which the teams and players supply to it. Sub-standard footballers make sub-standard teams. Sub-standard teams play sub-standard football. And sub-standard football is no good to anyone.

MIKE HAMMOND

EURO 2000 FINALS SCHEDULE

FIRST ROUND

Date	Venue	Teams	Kick-Off
GROUP A			
Mon, 12 June	Liège	A1 v A2	18.00
Mon, 12 June	Eindhoven	A3 v A4	20.45
Sat, 17 June	Arnhem	A2 v A3	18.00
Sat, 17 June	Charleroi	A4 v A1	20.45
Tue, 20 June	Charleroi	A4 v A2	20.45
Tue, 20 June	Rotterdam	A3 v A1	20.45
GROUP B			
Sat, 10 June	Brussels	B1 v B2	20.45
Sun, 11 June	Arnhem	B3 v B4	14.30
Wed, 14 June	Brussels	B4 v B1	20.45
Thu, 15 June	Eindhoven	B2 v B3	20.45
Mon, 19 June	Brussels	B3 v B1	20.45
Mon, 19 June	Eindhoven	B4 v B2	20.45
GROUP C			
Tue, 13 June	Rotterdam	C1 v C2	18.00
Tue, 13 June	Charleroi	C3 v C4	20.45
Sun, 18 June	Amsterdam	C4 v C1	18.00
Sun, 18 June	Liège	C2 v C3	20.45
Wed, 21 June	Bruges	C3 v C1	18.00
Wed, 21 June	Arnhem	C4 v C2	18.00
GROUP D			
Sun, 11 June	Bruges	D3 v D4	18.00
Sun, 11 June	Amsterdam	D1 v D2	20.45
Fri, 16 June	Bruges	D2 v D3	18.00
Fri, 16 June	Rotterdam	D4 v D1	20.45
Wed, 21 June	Liège	D4 v D2	20.45
Wed, 21 June	Amsterdam	D3 v D1	20.45

QUARTER-FINALS

Sat, 24 June	Amsterdam	2B v 1A (*1)	18.00
Sat, 24 June	Brussels	1B v 2A (*2)	20.45
Sun, 25 June	Rotterdam	1D v 2C (*3)	18.00
Sun, 25 June	Bruges	1C v 2D (*4)	20.45

SEMI-FINALS

Wed, 28 June	Brussels	Winner *1 v Winner *4	20.45
Thu, 29 June	Amsterdam	Winner *2 v Winner *3	20.45

FINAL

Sun, 2 July	Rotterdam		18.00

Czech Republic's Patrik Berger and Pavel Nedved tackle Scotland's Eoin Jess in the match in Prague, a victory for the Czech Republic which comfirmed their qualification for the finals.

EURO 2000 VENUES

HOLLAND
Amsterdam Arena, Amsterdam (51,200)
Gelredome, Arnhem (30,000)
Philips Stadion, Eindhoven (30,200)
Feyenoord Stadion (De Kuip), Rotterdam (51,086)

BELGIUM
Jan Breydelstadion, Bruges (30,000)
Stade Roi Baudouin, Brussels (50,000)
Stade Communal, Charleroi (30,200)
Stade de Sclessin, Liège (30,000)

PREVIOUS WINNERS

1960	USSR
1964	SPAIN
1968	ITALY
1972	WEST GERMANY
1976	CZECHOSLOVAKIA
1980	WEST GERMANY
1984	FRANCE
1988	HOLLAND
1992	DENMARK
1996	GERMANY

EURO 2000 QUALIFYING GROUP ONE

Italians off to a flier under new boss Zoff

The Euro 2000 qualifying competition got underway less than two months after the end of the 1998 World Cup. But while several other France '98 participants made a very poor start, Italy, reinvigorated by the arrival of a new coach, former World Cup-winning captain and goalkeeper Dino Zoff, set about their business in impressive style.

Their first fixture, away to Wales (but staged in England, at Liverpool's Anfield ground), took place before the new Italian league season had even begun. That, however, had no adverse effect on the *Azzurri*, who collected a comfortable 2-0 win. Wales gifted them the first goal, slotted home by Diego Fuser after a schoolboy error from Welsh centre-back Chris Coleman, but the decisive second, scored 13 minutes before the end by Christian Vieri, was the result of a wonderful build-up involving débutant Eusebio Di Francesco and veteran Roberto Baggio.

There was no turning back for the Italians after that positive start. Their next match, at home to Switzerland in Zoff's native Udine, also ended 2-0, with Alessandro Del Piero emerging as the star of the show with his first two competitive goals for Italy. His first came after he burst through the centre of the Swiss defence to meet De Francesco's slide-rule pass; his second was a trademark free-kick.

Fabio Connavaro, Italy (left) and Ryan Giggs, Wales battle for the ball.

A month later in the same stadium Del Piero was to suffer a terrible knee injury that ruled him out of action for the remainder of the season. However, the *Azzurri* showed they could cope without him, taking another eight points from their four matches in the spring to stretch their lead at the top of the table to an almost unassailable six points. Nevertheless, the Italians were quite fortunate to win 2-1 in Denmark and extremely lucky to get a point at home to Belarus. Their equaliser in Ancona came from a hotly disputed penalty, and Belarus had a perfectly good goal cancelled out with the score at 1-1.

Italy were back to their best a couple of months later when they pulverised Wales 4-0 in Bologna. Despite playing in a half-empty stadium Zoff's men tore into their feeble opponents right from the off.

TOP SCORERS

3   Filippo INZAGHI (Italy)
    Stéphane CHAPUISAT
    (Switzerland)

2   Alessandro DEL PIERO (Italy)
    Christian VIERI (Italy)
    Valentin BELKEVICH (Belarus)

GROUP ONE TABLE

GROUP ONE TABLE (at 30/06/99)

			Home				Away				Total					
		Pd	W	D	L	F	A	W	D	L	F	A	W	D	L	F	A	Pt	GD
1	Italy	6	2	1	0	7	1	2	1	0	4	1	4	2	0	11	2	14	+9
2	Denmark	6	1	0	2	3	4	1	2	0	3	1	2	2	2	6	5	8	+1
3	Switzerland	5	1	2	0	3	1	1	0	1	1	2	2	2	1	4	3	8	+1
4	Wales	6	1	0	2	3	6	1	0	2	2	7	2	0	4	5	13	6	-8
5	Belarus	5	0	1	1	0	1	0	1	2	3	5	0	2	3	3	6	2	-3

EURO 2000 QUALIFYING GROUP ONE

1998/99 MATCH DETAILS

05/09/98, Minsk
BELARUS 0
DENMARK 0
referee - Dardenne (GER)
BELARUS - Satsunkevich; Yakhimovich, Ostrovskiy, Shtanyuk, Romashchenko My. (Gerashchenko 40), Gurenko, Khatskevich, Baranov, Lavrik, Belkevich, Makovskiy V. (Romashchenko Ma. 89).
DENMARK - Schmeichel; Tobiasen, Rieper, Høgh, Heintze, Helveg, Nielsen A., Thomsen, Tomasson (Frederiksen 80), Jørgensen (Andersen 66), Møller (Gravesen 66).

05/09/98, Liverpool
WALES 0
ITALY 2 Fuser (19), Vieri (77)
referee - Hauge (NOR)
WALES - Jones; Robinson, Barnard, Symons, Williams, Coleman, Speed, Johnson, Blake (Saunders 65); Hughes (Savage 80), Giggs.
ITALY - Peruzzi; Panucci, Pessotto, Albertini (Di Biagio 66), Cannavaro, Iuliano, Fuser, Baggio D., Vieri, Del Piero (Baggio R. 75), Di Francesco (Serena 85).

10/10/98, Copenhagen
DENMARK 1 Frederiksen (58)
WALES 2 Williams (59), Bellamy (86)
referee - Pillér (HUN)
DENMARK - Krogh; Tobiasen, Rieper, Høgh, Heintze, Helveg, Frandsen (Gravesen 76), Nielsen B.S., Jørgensen, Frederiksen, Beck (Sand 66).
WALES - Jones; Savage, Barnard, Williams, Symons, Coleman, Saunders (Robinson 80), Blake (Bellamy 69), Hughes, Johnson (Pembridge 54), Speed.

10/10/98, Udine
ITALY 2 Del Piero (19, 61)
SWITZERLAND 0
referee - Sars (FRA)
ITALY - Buffon; Panucci, Cannavaro, Maldini, Torricelli, Fuser, Baggio D., Albertini, Di Francesco (Bachini 61), Inzaghi, Del Piero (Totti 70).
SWITZERLAND - Hilfiker; Wolf (Chassot 65), Vega, Henchoz, Vogel, Wicky (Celestini 86), Sforza, Rothenbühler, Sesa, Chapuisat, Müller.

14/10/98, Zürich
SWITZERLAND 1 Chapuisat (58)
DENMARK 1 Tobiasen (90)
referee - Radoman (YUG)
SWITZERLAND - Hilfiker; Jeanneret (Rothenbühler 76), Sforza, Henchoz, Vogel, Wicky, Sesa (Haas 90), Fournier, Celestini, Chapuisat, Müller (Di Jorio 77).
DENMARK - Krogh; Tobiasen, Rieper, Høgh, Heintze, Helveg, Frandsen (Colding 59), Nielsen B.S., Tomasson (Beck 78), Frederiksen (Sand 61), Jørgensen.

14/10/98, Cardiff
WALES 3 Robinson (14), Coleman (53), Symons (84)
BELARUS 2 Gurenko (20), Belkevich (48)
referee - Sammut (MLT)

WALES - Jones; Robinson, Barnard, Savage, Symons, Coleman, Saunders, Johnson, Blake, Hughes, Pembridge.
BELARUS - Satsunkevich; Yakhimovich, Ostrovskiy, Lavrik, Shtanyuk, Baranov (Gerasimets 69), Khatskevich, Gerashchenko (Romashchenko Ma. 88), Gurenko, Belkevich, Makovskiy V. (Kachuro 72).

27/03/99, Minsk
BELARUS 0
SWITZERLAND 1 Fournier (72)
referee - Sarvan (TUR)
BELARUS - Tumilovich; Lavrik, Lukhvich, Yakhimovich, Gurenko, Khatskevich, Belkevich, Gerashchenko (Skripchenko 85), Baranov (Chaika 59), Romashchenko Ma., Makovskiy V. (Ostrovskiy 86).
SWITZERLAND - Brunner; Hodel, Henchoz, Vogel, Fournier, Jeanneret, Wicky (Müller 66), Sforza, Sesa (De Napoli 74), Chapuisat, Comisetti.

27/03/99, Copenhagen
DENMARK 1 Sand (56)
ITALY 2 Inzaghi (1), Conte (68)
referee - López Nieto (ESP)
DENMARK - Schmeichel; Helveg, Henriksen, Høgh, Heintze, Goldbaek (Colding 83), Thomsen, Nielsen A. (Tøfting 77), Grønkjaer (Molnar 53), Jørgensen, Sand, **ITALY** - Buffon; Panucci, Nesta, Cannavaro, Maldini, Fuser (Conte 46), Baggio D., Di Biagio, Di Francesco, Inzaghi, Chiesa (Totti 63).

31/03/99, Ancona
ITALY 1 Inzaghi (31p)
BELARUS 1 Belkevich (24)
referee - Piraux (BEL)
ITALY - Buffon; Panucci, Nesta, Cannavaro, Maldini, Conte, Baggio D. (Giannichedda 46), Di Biagio, Totti (Di Francesco 46), Inzaghi, Chiesa (Baggio R. 64).
BELARUS - Tumilovich; Lavrik, Lukhvich, Yakhimovich, Gurenko, Orlovskiy, Belkevich, Ostrovskiy, Baranov, Romashchenko Ma., Makovskiy V..

31/03/99, Zürich
SWITZERLAND 2 Chapuisat (4, 70)
WALES 0
referee - Liba (CZE)
SWITZERLAND - Brunner; Jeanneret, Henchoz, Wolf, Müller, Vogel, Sforza, Fournier, Wicky, Chapuisat, Comisetti (Bühlmann 68).
WALES - Jones (Crossley 26); Robinson, Pembridge, Symons, Coleman, Johnson, Saunders, Savage, Blake (Hartson 64), Hughes (Bellamy 75), Speed.

05/06/99, Copenhagen
DENMARK 1 Heintze (23)
BELARUS 0
referee - Baptista (POR)
DENMARK - Schmeichel; Colding, Henriksen, Høgh, Heintze, Goldbaek, Nielsen A., Tøfting (Nielsen B.S. 67), Grønkjaer, Jørgensen, Sand (Molnar 78).
BELARUS - Tumilovich; Lavrik, Lukhvich, Yakhimovich, Gurenko, Orlovskiy, Belkevich, Khatskevich (Kulchiy 70), Ostrovskiy (Romashchenko Ma. 46),

EURO 2000 QUALIFYING GROUP ONE

1998/99 MATCH DETAILS

Baranov, Makovskiy V. (Ryndyuk 85).

05/06/99, Bologna
ITALY 4 Vieri (7), Inzaghi (37), Maldini (40), Chiesa (89)
WALES 0
referee - Steinborn (GER)
ITALY - Buffon; Panucci, Maldini, Fuser (Di Livio 69), Negro, Cannavaro, Conte, Albertini, Vieri (Montella 46), Inzaghi (Chiesa 80), Di Francesco.
WALES - Jones; Robinson (Jenkins 78), Barnard, Page, Melville, Williams, Giggs, Bellamy (Pembridge 78), Saunders (Hartson 46), Hughes, Speed.

09/06/99, Lausanne
SWITZERLAND 0
ITALY 0
referee - Poll (ENG)
SWITZERLAND - Huber; Wicky (Haas 70), Müller, Hodel, Jeanneret (Di Jorio 78), Vogel, Sforza, Rothenbühler, Sesa, Chapuisat, Comisetti (Celestini 56).
ITALY - Buffon; Panucci (Pancaro 69), Negro, Cannavaro, Maldini (Di Livio 69), Albertini, Conte, Vieri (Chiesa 60), Inzaghi, Di Francesco.

09/06/99, Liverpool
WALES 0
DENMARK 2 Tomasson (84), Tøfting (90p)
referee - Ancion (BEL)
WALES - Jones; Jenkins, Barnard (Legg 90), Robinson (Pembridge 87), Melville, Coleman, Speed, Saunders, Hartson (Bellamy 89), Hughes, Giggs.
DENMARK - Schmeichel; Colding, Heintze, Grønkjaer, Høgh, Henriksen, Goldbaek, Nielsen A. (Tøfting 83), Jørgensen (Frandsen 90), Sand, Molnar (Tomasson 70).

GROUP ONE

1999/2000 FIXTURES

04/09/99	Belarus v Wales
	Denmark v Switzerland
08/09/99	Switzerland v Belarus
	Italy v Denmark
09/10/99	Belarus v Italy
	Wales v Switzerland

Wales' John Hartson leaps above Denmark's René Henriksen.

The result was never in doubt from the moment that Christian Vieri headed his team in front, and had it not been for Welsh goalkeeper Paul Jones the humiliation for his team would have been much more severe. As it was, Wales boss Bobby Gould decided he had seen enough and resigned immediately after the game.

It was not quite curtains for Wales but when they lost again four days later, against Denmark at Anfield, there seemed no way back - despite the failure of any of the other teams in the group to stake a significant claim for the runners-up spot behind Italy.

Denmark certainly did their cause no harm with that 2-0 victory in Liverpool, which was delayed until a few minutes from time thanks to another outstanding display from Paul Jones, who had also been the man of the match when Wales surprisingly won 2-1 in Copenhagen earlier in the campaign. The Danes, quarter-finalists at the 1998 World Cup, had made a wretched start, but two wins in four days breathed new life into their chances of qualification.

Switzerland, too, managed to stay in touch for the play-off place by holding Italy to a rather dull and uneventful 0-0 draw in Lausanne. Like the Danes, the Swiss had made a faltering start, but two victories within the space of a few days against Belarus and Wales (at the end of March) rekindled their hopes. The draw with the Italians meant that they had gone three successive games without conceding a goal, and with Stéphane Chapuisat firing on all cylinders, Switzerland went into the summer recess still feeling genuinely optimistic about their chances...

EURO 2000 QUALIFYING GROUP TWO

Home advantage counts for nothing

Norway could hardly have asked for an easier group as they sought to reach the European Championship finals for the first time. Yet they made such a sluggish and wayward start under their new coach Nils Johan Semb (the former assistant to Egil Olsen) that for a while it looked as if they might struggle to finish on top of the table.

Slowly but surely, however, the Norwegians

took charge, and by the end of the season the memories of their first two outings in Oslo (a 1-3 defeat by Latvia and a 2-2 draw against Albania, which could have been much worse but for a brave late fightback) had largely been forgotten. Norway proved to be outstanding travellers, taking maximum points from their four away games.

The run actually started in the autumn when skipper Kjetil Rekdal's late winner enabled them to come from a goal behind to beat Slovenia 2-1 in Ljubljana. In the spring they really found their rhythm and took maximum points in Athens, Tbilisi and Tirana, with their English-based attacking trio of Tore André Flo, Steffen Iversen and Ole Gunnar Solskjaer accounting for seven of the eight goals scored in those three games (the other was an own-goal which some sources also credited to Iversen).

Solskjaer's double in the 2-0 victory over Greece was particularly significant, because it enabled Norway to win a game which could easily have gone the other way. Greece dominated possession and created several chances but the Manchester United striker showed the home side how to finish with two typically opportunistic strikes at the end of each half. That victory effectively swung the balance of the group towards the Norwegians and gave them the push they needed for their busy programme in April, May and June.

Greece were expected to provide the strongest challenge to the Scandinavians but they,

TOP SCORERS

6   Zlatko ZAHOVIC (Slovenia)
4   Tore André FLO (Norway)
3   Nikos MAHLAS (Greece)
    Ole Gunnar SOLSKAER
    (Norway)
2   Kjetil REKDAL (Norway)
    Steffen IVERSEN (Norway)
    Kostas FRANTZESKOS
    (Greece)
    Marian PAKHAR (Latvia)
    Andrey SHTOLCERS (Latvia)
    Mikhail ZEMLINSKY (Latvia)
    Zaza JANASHIA (Georgia)
    Igli TARE (Albania)

GROUP TWO

1999/2000 FIXTURES

18/08/99	Slovenia v Albania
04/09/99	Norway v Greece
	Albania v Latvia
	Slovenia v Georgia
08/09/99	Greece v Albania
	Georgia v Latvia
	Norway v Slovenia
09/10/99	Slovenia v Greece
	Latvia v Norway
	Albania v Georgia

GROUP TWO TABLE

GROUP TWO TABLE (at 30/06/99)

			Home				Away				Total					
		Pd	W	D	L	F	A	W	D	L	F	A	W	D	L	F	A	Pt	GD
1	Norway	7	1	1	1	4	5	4	0	0	10	3	5	1	1	14	8	16	+6
2	Slovenia	6	1	0	1	2	2	2	2	0	6	4	3	2	1	8	6	11	+2
3	Latvia	7	1	2	1	2	2	2	0	1	5	3	3	2	2	7	5	11	+2
4	Greece	7	1	1	2	6	6	1	2	0	2	1	2	3	2	8	7	9	+1
5	Georgia	7	1	1	2	4	7	0	0	3	0	5	1	1	5	5	4	12	4	-8
6	Albania	6	0	1	2	1	3	0	2	1	2	3	0	3	3	3	6	3	-3

EURO 2000 QUALIFYING GROUP TWO

1998/99 MATCH DETAILS

05/09/98, Tbilisi
GEORGIA 1 Arveladze A. (65)
ALBANIA 0
referee - Detruche (SUI)
GEORGIA - Gvaramadze; Kaladze, Tskitishvili, Silagadze (Kiknadze 43), Tsereteli, Kobiashvili, Nemsadze, Jamarauli, Ketsbaia (Janashia Z. 54), Kinkladze, Iashvili (Arveladze A. 62).
ALBANIA - Strakosha; Lala, Shulku, Xhumba, Vata, Pinari, Haxhi, Bushi (Gallo 74), Kola, Rrakli, Tare (Peço 68; Maxhuni 86).

06/09/98, Athens
GREECE 2 Mahlas (54p), Frantzeskos (58)
SLOVENIA 2 Zahovic (19, 73)
referee - Trentalange (ITA)
GREECE - Atmatsidis; Kalitzakis, Ouzounidis, Dabizas, Borbokis (Liberopoulos 83), Markos, Zagorakis, tsartas (Frantzeskos 46), Kasapis (Yeorgatos 78), Mahlas, Nikolaidis.
SLOVENIA - Simeunovic; Milanic, Galic, Knavs, Novak (Englaro 46), Ceh, Zahovic, Pavlin, Rudonja, Udovic, Osterc (Siljak 60; Acimovic 62).

06/09/98, Oslo
NORWAY 1 Solbakken (17)
LATVIA 3 Pakhar (11), Shtolcers (53), Zemlinsky (65p)
referee - Shmolik (BLS)
NORWAY - Baardsen; Heggem (Berg 61), Bjørnebye, Johnsen, Hoftun, Rekdal, Rudi (Flo H. 80), Solbakken, Strandli, Flo T.A., Solskjaer (Flo J. 63).
LATVIA - Karavayev; Laizans (Lukashevich 51), Lobanyov, Zemlinsky, Ivanov, Bleidelis, Zakreshevsky, Babichev, Sharando (Boulders 73), Pakhar (Isakov 81), Shtolcers.

10/10/98, Riga
LATVIA 1 Shtolcers (2)
GEORGIA 0
referee - Zotta (ROM)
LATVIA - Karavayev; Lukashevich, Zemlinsky, Lobanyov, Sharando, Ivanov, Astafyev (Isakov 75), Bleidelis (Laizans 51), Babichev, Pakhar (Boulders 89), Shtolcers.
GEORGIA - Gvaramadze; Kaladze, Shekiladze, Kavelashvili, Gakhokidze (Demetradze 60), Kobiashvili, Nemsadze, Jamarauli, Ketsbaia, Kinkladze, Arveladze S.

10/10/98, Ljubljana
SLOVENIA 1 Zahovic (24)
NORWAY 2 Flo T.A. (45), Rekdal (80)
referee - Schluchter (SUI)
SLOVENIA - Simeunovic; Galic, Milanic, Knavs, Rudonja, Novak, Ceh, Zahovic, Pavlin, Osterc (Englaro 46), Udovic (Acimovic 46).
NORWAY - Grodås; Håland, Berg, Hoftun, Bjørnebye, Heggem (Riseth 86), Strand (Berg Hestad 78), Rekdal, Solbakken, Flo J., Flo T.A. (Rushfeldt 90).

14/10/98, Athens
GREECE 3 Mahlas (13), Liberopoulos (15), Ouzounidis (36)
GEORGIA 0
referee - Ouzounov (BUL)
GREECE - Atmatsidis; Kalitzakis, Ouzounidis, Dabizas, Zagorakis, Markos,

Poursanidis, Frantzeskos (Tsartas 74), Yeorgatos, Liberopoulos (Yanakopoulos 68), Mahlas (Mavroyenidis 84).
GEORGIA - Togonidze; Kobiashvili, Kaladze, Shelia, Nemsadze, Shekiladze, Ketsbaia, Jamarauli, Kinkladze, Kavelashvili (Gakhokidze 59), Arveladze S..

14/10/98, Oslo
NORWAY 2 Rekdal (82p), Berg (88)
ALBANIA 3 Bushi (38), Tare (52)
referee - Grabher (AUT)
NORWAY - Grodås; Håland (Iversen 57), Berg, Hoftun, Bjørnebye, Heggem, Strand, Rekdal, Solbakken (Rushfeldt 90), Flo J. (Solskjaer 57), Flo T.A..
ALBANIA - Strakosha; Shulku, Lala, Xhumba, Haxhi, Bushi (Halili 84), Vata, Kola (Dalipi 89), Fakaj, Tare, Rrakli.

14/10/98, Maribor
SLOVENIA 1 Udovic (85)
LATVIA 0
referee - Nalbandyan (ARM)
SLOVENIA - Simeunovic; Galic, Milanic, Knavs (Gliha 46), Novak, Istenic (Acimovic 65), Pavlin, Englaro, Zahovic, Udovic (Milinovic 87), Rudonja.
LATVIA - Karavayev; Lukashevich, Zemlinsky, Ivanov (Rimkus 87), Lobanyov, Sharando, Bleidelis (Mikholap 51), Astafyev (Boulders 79), Isakov, Pakhar, Shtolcers.

18/11/98, Tirana
ALBANIA 0
GREECE 0
referee - Esquinas Torres (ESP)
ALBANIA - Strakosha; Dalipi (Halili 50), Haxhi, Vata, Xhumba, Shulku, Fakaj, Kola, Bushi, Rrakli, Tare.
GREECE - Atmatsidis; Dabizas (Vokolos 89), Ouzounidis, Kalitzakis, Zagorakis, Poursanidis, Frantzeskos (Liberopoulos 46), Yeorgatos, Mahlas, Nikolaidis (Konstantinidis 69), Markos.

27/03/99, Tbilisi
GEORGIA 1 Janashia Z. (42)
SLOVENIA 1 Knavs (52)
referee - Hamer (LUX)
GEORGIA - Grishikashvili; Kaladze, Balashvili, Chkhaidze, Tsereteli, Aleksidze (Kinkladze 46), Nemsadze, Jamarauli (Daraselia 82), Kobiashvili, Janashia Z., Demetradze (Kavelashvili 74).
SLOVENIA - Simeunovic; Karic, Milanic, Knavs, Rudonja (Mitrakovic 90), Bulajic, Milinovic, Ceh, Pavlin (Istenic 78), Udovic (Acimovic 60), Zahovic.

27/03/99, Athens
GREECE 0
NORWAY 2 Solskjaer (38, 87)
referee - Irvine (NIR)
GREECE - Atmatsidis; Dabizas, Ouzounidis, Anatolakis, Zagorakis (Mavroyenidis 46), Yanakopoulos, Poursanidis, Markos (Mahlas 55), Yeorgatos, Liberopoulos (Frantzeskos 76), Nikolaidis.
NORWAY - Myhre; Heggem, Berg, Johnsen, Bergdølmo (Halle 66), Iversen, Strand (Bohinen 60), Solbakken, Mykland, Rudi, Solskjaer (Carew 89).

EURO 2000 QUALIFYING GROUP TWO

1998/99 MATCH DETAILS

31/03/99, Riga
LATVIA 0
GREECE 0
referee - Fisker (DEN)
LATVIA - Karavayev; Lukashevich, Astafyev, Zemlinsky, Lobanyov, Ivanov (Isakov 27), Sharando (Stepanov 62), Mikholap (Boulders 46), Blagonadezhdin, Pakhar, Shtolcers.
GREECE - Atmatsidis; Kasapis, Ouzounidis, Dabizas, Poursanidis, Mavroyenidis, Yanakopoulos (Zagorakis 74), Liberopoulos, Yeorgatos (Frantzeskos 74), Mahlas (Anastasiou 80), Nikolaidis.

28/04/99, Tbilisi
GEORGIA 1 Janashia Z. (58)
NORWAY 4 Shekiladze (16og), Flo T.A. (26, 38), Solskjaer (35)
referee - Puhl (HUN)
GEORGIA - Togonidze; Shekiladze (Popkhadze 46), Didava, Tsereteli, Kaladze, Nemsadze, Rekhviashvili (Kiknadze 81), Jamarauli, Kobiashvili, Janashia Z., Ketsbaia (Demetradze 46).
NORWAY - Myhre; Håland, Pedersen, Hoftun, Bergdølmo, Solskjaer (Strand 46), Iversen, Solbakken, Mykland, Rudi (Riseth 81), Flo T.A. (Carew 87).

28/04/99, Riga
LATVIA 0
ALBANIA 0
referee - Romain (BEL)
LATVIA - Karavayev; Stepanov (Sharando 84), Isakov, Lukashevich, Lobanyov, Blagonadezhdin, Ivanov, Boulders, Rubins, Mikholap (Dobretsov 70), Shtolcers (Laizans 60).
ALBANIA - Strakosha; Lala, Shulku, Xhumba, Vata (Jupi 78), Fakaj, Haxhi, Bushi (Halili 86), Kola, Rrakli (Dalipi 82), Tare.

30/05/99, Oslo
NORWAY 1 Iversen (4)
GEORGIA 0
referee - Huyghe (BEL)
NORWAY - Olsen; Heggem, Pedersen, Hoftun, Bergdølmo, Iversen (Dahlum 85), Leonhardsen (Rudi 46), Solbakken, Mykland, Riseth (Rekdal 71), Flo T.A..
GEORGIA - Gvaramadze; Guchua (Chichveishvili 63), Kaladze, Didava (Popkhadze 46), Tsereteli, Tskitishvili, Nemsadze, Ketsbaia, Jamarauli, Kavelashvili, Demetradze (Ashvetia 78).

05/06/99, Tirana
ALBANIA 1 Tare (15)
NORWAY 2 Iversen (3), Flo T.A. (83)
referee - Stoica (ROM)

ALBANIA - Strakosha; Lala, Shulku, Xhumba, Vata, Haxhi, Bushi, Kola (Duro 69), Fakaj (Bellai 62), Tare, Rrakli (Bogdani 80).
NORWAY - Olsen; Håland, Pedersen (Bragstad 62), Hoftun, Bergdølmo, Iversen, Solbakken (Riseth 89), Rekdal, Mykland, Rudi (Dahlum 78), Flo T.A..

05/06/99, Tbilisi
GEORGIA 1 Ketsbaia (55)
GREECE 2 Frantzeskos (88), Mahlas (90)
referee - Young (SCO)
GEORGIA - Gvaramadze; Chichveishvili (Didava 10), Khizaneishvili (Khizanishvili 65), Tsereteli, Tskitishvili (Aleksidze 56), Nemsadze, Ketsbaia, Jamarauli, Ashvetia, Kobiashvili.
GREECE - Atmatsidis; Mavroyenidis, Ouzounidis, Anatolakis, Kasapis, Konstantinidis (Frousos 46), Poursanidis, Zagorakis (Frantzeskos 79), Niniadis, Yeorgatos (Anastasiou 61), Mahlas.

05/06/99, Riga
LATVIA 1 Pakhar (18)
SLOVENIA 2 Zahovic (27, 42p)
referee - Brito Arceo (ESP)
LATVIA - Kolinko; Lukashevich, Astafyev (Rubins 41), Zemlinsky, Lobanyov (Korablyov 43), Sharando (Bleidelis 59), Laizans, Shtolcers, Pakhar, Babichev, Mikholap.
SLOVENIA - Simeunovic; Rudonja (Osterc 86), Milinovic, Karic, Galic, Knavs, Novak, Ceh, Udovic (Acimovic 66), Zahovic, Pavlin (Istenic 80).

09/06/99, Tirana
ALBANIA 0
SLOVENIA 1 Zahovic (25p)
referee - Stoica (ROM)
ALBANIA - Strakosha; Lala, Shulku, Xhumba, Vata, Duro, Bushi, Bellai, Bogdani (Dalipi 74), Rrakli (Halili 46), Tare.
SLOVENIA - Simeunovic; Galic, Knavs, Osterc, Milinovic, Karic, Novak, Ceh, Udovic (Acimovic 63), Pavlin, Zahovic.

09/06/99, Athens
GREECE 1 Niniadis (38p)
LATVIA 2 Verpakovsky (25), Zemlinsky (90p)
referee - Pucek (CZE)
GREECE - Atmatsidis; Mavroyenidis, Ouzounidis, Anatolakis, Kasapis, Zikos, Zagorakis, Frantzeskos (Anastasiou 60), Niniadis (Frousos 79), Yeorgatos (Markos 73), Mahlas.
LATVIA - Kolinko; Lukashevich, Astafyev (Bleidelis 54), Zemlinsky, Rubins (Zhizhmanov 64), Pakhar, Babichev, Laizans, Verpakovsky (Mikholap 46), Korablyov, Lobanyov.

too, made a mess of their home fixtures. They squandered two points in their opening game, against Slovenia, and experienced another night of sheer frustration in their last fixture of the season, against Latvia, which resulted in a shock 2-1 victory for their opponents thanks to a last-minute penalty from Mikhail Zemlinsky.

That was a massive win for Latvia and kept them in the

hunt. But with Slovenia having taken a leaf out of Norway's book and put together two successive away wins (in Latvia and Albania), it was they, inspired by new coach Srecko Katanec and six-goal skipper Zlatko Zahovic, who entered the summer break feeling more optimistic about their chances - perhaps not of catching Norway but certainly of reaching the play-offs.

EURO 2000 QUALIFYING GROUP THREE

Defending champions recover from early shock

Northern Ireland's Danny Griffin (right) tangles with Moldova's Serghei Dinov (left).

Germany, the 1996 winners, began their European Championship defence in turmoil. While most of the other teams in the competition were getting their campaign underway in early September, the Germans were in the process of parting company with their coach.

Berti Vogts' eight-year tenure as *Nationaltrainer* ended when he caved in to press criticism following a couple of miserable performances from his new-look team on a mini-tour to Malta. With so many leading German internationals having chosen to end their international careers after the World Cup in France, there was considerable relief in Germany that their team had been handed a straightforward qualifying group. With only Turkey, Finland, Northern Ireland and Moldova standing between them and the finals in neighbouring Holland and Belgium, there was surely no way that Germany - even a wounded, depleted Germany - could fail to qualify.

Or was there? New coach Erich Ribbeck was given a very painful jolt when his team lost their opening match, 1-0 in Turkey. In fairness, Germany did not play too badly. They certainly created more clear-cut chances than their hosts. But newly-appointed captain Oliver

Bierhoff had a rare off-night in front of goal, and while the Germans drew a blank, Turkey managed to put the ball in the net. The goal was an odd one. It was officially credited to Hakan Sükür but strictly speaking it was an own-goal by German goalkeeper Oliver Kahn, who redirected the ball into the net after Hakan's header had hit the foot of the post.

The Turks were none too concerned with the identity of the scorer. They were just elated to get a goal. A typical German comeback seemed inevitable, but this time, for once, it did not happen - despite the Turks being reduced to ten men a minute after their goal following the harsh dismissal of Tayfun for an innocuous tackle on Jörg Heinrich.

Turkey's win, their first over Germany for 47 years, took them to six points from two games played. They had opened their campaign with a handsome 3-0 victory at home to Northern Ireland, a game in

GROUP THREE TABLE

GROUP THREE TABLE (at 30/06/99)

		Pd	Home W	D	L	F	A	Away W	D	L	F	A	Total W	D	L	F	A	Pt	GD
1	Turkey	5	3	0	1	7	3	1	0	0	4	2	4	0	1	11	5	12	+6
2	Germany	5	2	0	0	8	1	2	0	1	6	2	4	0	1	14	3	12	+11
3	Finland	6	1	0	1	5	6	1	1	2	3	4	2	1	3	8	10	7	-2
4	Northern Ireland	5	1	1	1	3	5	0	1	1	0	3	1	2	2	3	8	5	-5
5	Moldova	7	0	2	1	1	3	0	1	3	5	13	0	3	4	6	16	3	-10

EURO 2000 QUALIFYING GROUP THREE

1998/99 MATCH DETAILS

05/09/98, Helsinki
FINLAND 3 Kolkka (8), Johansson (44), Paatelainen (63)
MOLDOVA 2 Oprea (10, 12)
referee - Barber (ENG)
FINLAND - Niemi; Ylönen, Tuomela, Hyypiä, Turpeinen (Reini 46), Wiss,
Kautonen, Litmanen, Johansson (Sumiala 80), Paatelainen, Kolkka (Mahlio 72).
MOLDOVA - Coselev; Fistican (Tabanov 76), Rebeja (Pusca 46), Testimitanu,
Guzun, Stroenco, Oprea, Gaidamasciuc, Epureanu (Suharev 71), Curtianu,
Clescenco.

05/09/98, Istanbul
TURKEY 3 Oktay (19, 59), Tayfur (50p)
NORTHERN IRELAND 0
referee - Wojcik (POL)
TURKEY - Rüstü; Saffet, Mert, Alpay, Okan (Arif 88), Sergen, Tayfur, Tugay
(Oguz 75), Abdullah, Oktay (Hami 80), Hakan Sükür.
NORTHERN IRELAND - Fettis; Hughes A., Horlock, Mulryne, Hill, Morrow,
Gillespie (Whitley Ji. 73), Lennon, Dowie, Rowland (Quinn 46), Hughes M..

10/10/98, Belfast
NORTHERN IRELAND 1 Rowland (31)
FINLAND 0
referee - Arsic (YUG)
NORTHERN IRELAND - Fettis; Hughes A., Horlock, Mulryne, Morrow,
Patterson, Gillespie (McCarthy 70), Lennon, Dowie (O'Boyle 79), Rowland (Quinn
88), Hughes M..
FINLAND - Niemi; Ylönen, Ilola, Hyypiä, Kautonen, Reini, Riihilahti (Litmanen
75), Valakari, Kolkka, Paatelainen, Johansson.

10/10/98, Bursa
TURKEY 1 Hakan Sükür (70)
GERMANY 0
referee - Dallas (SCO)
TURKEY - Rüstü; Fatih, Ogün (Hakan Ünsal 89), Alpay, Tayfun, Tayfur, Tugay
(Oktay 61), Abdullah, Mert, Sergen (Saffet 81), Hakan Sükür.
GERMANY - Kahn; Babbel, Nowotny, Rehmer, Ricken (Bode 81), Ramelow,
Beinlich, Jeremies, Heinrich (Neuville 76), Bierhoff, Kirsten.

14/10/98, Chisinau
MOLDOVA 1 Guzun (6)
GERMANY 3 Kirsten (19, 36), Bierhoff (38)
referee - Fernández Marín (ESP)
MOLDOVA - Coselev; Fistican, Stroenco, Testimitanu, Gaidamasciuc, Rebeja,
Guzun, Oprea, Curtianu (Suharev 52), Clescenco, Epureanu.
GERMANY - Kahn; Babbel, Nowotny, Rehmer, Ricken (Neuville 53), Ramelow,
Beinlich (Wosz 83), Nerlinger, Tarnat, Kirsten (Jancker 74), Bierhoff.

14/10/98, Istanbul
TURKEY 1 Ogün (74)
FINLAND 3 Paatelainen (6), Johansson (52), Litmanen (90)
referee - Krondl (CZE)

TURKEY - Rüstü; Alpay, Ogün, Fatih, Mert (Hami 46), Tugay (Okan 46), Sergen
(Hasan Sas 84), Tayfur, Abdullah, Hakan Sükür, Oktay.
FINLAND - Niemi; Reini, Ylönen, Hyypiä, Kautonen, Tuomela, Riihilahti (Valakari
76), Litmanen, Ilola, Johansson (Saastamoinen 90), Paatelainen (Kolkka 46).

18/11/98, Belfast
NORTHERN IRELAND 2 Dowie (49), Lennon (63)
MOLDOVA 2 Gaidamasciuc (23), Testimitanu (58)
referee - Hrinak (SVK)
NORTHERN IRELAND - Fettis; Griffin, Kennedy, Lomas, Patterson, Morrow,
Gillespie (McCarthy 88), Lennon, Dowie, Rowland (Gray 77), Hughes M..
MOLDOVA - Dinov; Fistican, Guzun (Pusca 71), Stroenco, Rebeja, Curtianu,
Stratulat (Suharev 50), Tetsimitanu (Maievici 85), Epureanu, Gaidamasciuc,
Clescenco.

27/03/99, Belfast
NORTHERN IRELAND 0
GERMANY 3 Bode (11, 43), Hamann (62)
referee - Cesari (ITA)
NORTHERN IRELAND - Taylor; Patterson, Horlock, Lomas, Williams, Morrow,
Gillespie (McCarthy 83), Lennon (Sonner 68), Dowie, Rowland (Kennedy 68),
Hughes M.
GERMANY - Kahn; Babbel, Wörns, Jeremies, Matthäus (Nowotny 46), Strunz,
Heinrich, Hamann, Bierhoff, Neuville (Jancker 68), Bode (Preetz 78).

27/03/99, Istanbul
TURKEY 2 Hakan Sükür (35), Sergen (90)
MOLDOVA 0
referee - Plautz (AUT)
TURKEY - Rüstü; Fatih, Ogün, Alpay, Okan, Tugay (Ayhan 86), Sergen, Tayfur,
Abdullah, Hakan Sükür, Oktay (Hami 25; Arif 75).
MOLDOVA - Dinov; Fistican, Rebeja, Tabanov, Guzun, Stroenco, Sischin,
Stratulat, Gaidamasciuc, Epureanu, Clescenco (Suharev 80).

31/03/99, Nuremberg
GERMANY 2 Jeremies (31), Neuville (36)
FINLAND 0
referee - Khusainov (RUS)
GERMANY - Kahn; Babbel, Matthäus, Wörns, Strunz, Hamann (Nowotny 72),
Jeremies, Heinrich, Neuville (Kirsten 65), Bierhoff, Bode (Jancker 76).
FINLAND - Niemi; Reini (Lehkosuo 88), Hyypiä, Ylönen, Kautonen (Kolkka 70),
Kinnunen, Riihilahti, Litmanen, Ilola, Johansson, Paatelainen (Saastamoinen 46).

31/03/99, Chisinau
MOLDOVA 0
NORTHERN IRELAND 0
referee - Trivkovic (CRO)
MOLDOVA - Dinov; Fistican, Stroenco, Sosnovschi, Oprea (Stratulat 90),
Gaidamasciuc, Epureanu, Rebeja, Guzun, Clescenco, Suharev.
NORTHERN IRELAND - Taylor; Patterson (Hughes A. 63), Horlock, Lomas,
Williams, Morrow, Gillespie, Lennon, Dowie, Robinson, Hughes M..

EURO 2000 QUALIFYING GROUP THREE

1998/99 MATCH DETAILS

04/06/99, Leverkusen
GERMANY 6 Bierhoff (2, 56, 82), Kirsten (27), Bode (38), Scholl (71)
MOLDOVA 1 Stratulat (76)
referee - Monteiro Coroado (POR)
GERMANY - Kahn; Nowotny, Matthäus (Babbel 74), Strunz, Hamann, Jeremies (Scholl 46), Heinrich, Neuville, Bierhoff, Kirtsen (Ramelow 54), Bode.
MOLDOVA - Dinov; Fistican, Maievici (Stratulat 55), Stroenco, Rebeja, Gaidamasciuc (Belous 75), Epureanu, Guzun, Curtianu, Oprea, Clescenco (Sischin 81).

05/06/99, Helsinki
FINLAND 2 Tihinen (10), Paatelainen (14)
TURKEY 4 Tayfur (26, 85), Hakan Sükür (35, 87)
referee - Jol (HOL)
FINLAND - Niemi; Ylönen, Hyppiä, Kuivasto, Tihinen, Riihilahti, Valakari, Litmanen, Kolkka, Paatelainen, Johansson.
TURKEY - Rüstü; Fatih, Ali Eren, Alpay, Saffet, Sergen (Ümit 89), Tayfur, Abdullah (Hakan Ünsal 89), Tayfun, Hakan Sükür, Ayhan (Tugay 75).

09/06/99, Chisinau
MOLDOVA 0
FINLAND 0
referee - Treossi (ITA)
MOLDOVA - Dinov; Fistican, Stratulat, Stroenco, Rebeja, Sischin (Belous 75), Guzun, Epureanu, Curtianu, Oprea (Gaidamasciuc 79), Suharev (Chirilov 89).
FINLAND - Niemi; Ylönen, Reini (Lehkosuo 86), Hyypiä, Tihinen (Kautonen 46), Riihilahti, Valakari, Paatelainen, Kolkka, Ilola, Johansson (Forssell 61).

GROUP THREE

1999/2000 FIXTURES

04/09/99	Northern Ireland v Turkey
	Finland v Germany
08/09/99	Germany v Northern Ireland
	Moldova v Turkey
09/10/99	Finland v Northern Ireland
	Germany v Turkey

in the goal charts with Turkey's Hakan, who scored twice as his team avenged their home defeat against the Finns by winning 4-2 in Helsinki. They had been 0-2 down early on, but knowing that they had to keep winning in order to stay abreast with the Germans at the top of the table, they dug deep and staged a thrilling comeback. The result effectively killed off Finland's qualification hopes but reawakened Turkey's ambitions of reaching their second European Championship finals in succession.

which Besiktas striker Oktay twice re-affirmed his reputation as a scorer of spectacular international goals. But four days after overcoming Germany the Turks crashed back down to earth when they were beaten 3-1 in Istanbul by Finland. It was something of a freak result. Turkey had almost all of the game, but Finland counter-attacked brilliantly and they also possessed a goalkeeper who could do no wrong. Antti Niemi stopped everything the Turks threw at him, making at least three world-class saves to deny the home side a dserved equaliser after Ogün had beaten him with a scintillating long-range shot that ricocheted in off the post.

While Turkey lost, Germany won, 3-1 in Moldova - but not before they had survived the scare of conceding an early goal. That was to be the first of four consecutive wins for the defending champions. They were much improved in the spring, easily beating their one-time *bête noire* Northern Ireland 3-0 in Belfast before claiming maximum points against Finland in Nuremberg (2-0) and Moldova in Leverkusen (6-1).

Bierhoff scored a hat-trick against the Moldovans, but Germany's Euro '96 final hero could only share top spot

Finland's Joonas Kolkka (right) gets away from Northern Ireland's Keith Gillespie.

EURO 2000 QUALIFYING GROUP FOUR

World champions locked in four-way tussle

It was never going to be easy for France. The newly-crowned world champions had been drawn against two formidable opponents in Russia and Ukraine. They also had to adapt quickly to a new coach (Roger Lemerre instead of Aimé Jacquet), and they were still hung over from their World Cup win when they opened their Euro 2000 campaign in Iceland.

It proved to be a fairly traumatic experience. They could manage only a 1-1 draw and even fell behind -

albeit for only a few minutes - when an error from goalkeeper Fabien Barthez enabled Iceland's Ríkhardur Dadason to find the net with a looping header.

There was a considerable improvement from *Les Bleus* in their next game, a month later, when they claimed their first-ever victory in Moscow, beating Russia 3-2 in the Luzhniki stadium. A late winning goal from Parma midfielder Alain Boghossian gave the French the three points after they had allowed the Russians to come back from a 0-2 deficit. World Cup final hero Zinedine Zidane orchestrated the victory. He took charge in the closing stages, twice almost scoring himself before setting up Boghossian's goal and then earning a last-minute penalty which Laurent Blanc struck against the bar.

While that victory put the French firmly back on track, it was a devastating blow for the Russians, who had also lost 3-2 in their opening game, away to Ukraine. When they subsequently went down 1-0 to Iceland, it looked all over. But a change of coach - Oleg Romantsev for the luckless Anatoliy Byshovets - had a remarkable effect, and in the spring they followed up their opening three defeats with four successive wins, which miraculously brought them back into the qualifying frame.

The Russians' most important victory was away to France in early June. They simply had to win to stay in contention and did so thanks to two goals from newcomer Aleksandr Panov and a late winner from midfielder Valeriy Karpin. The 3-2 win meant that their head-to-head record with the French was identical, but the Russians

TOP SCORERS

4 Valeriy KARPIN (Russia)
3 Serhiy REBROV (Ukraine)
   Vladimir BESCHASTNYKH (Russia)
2 Andriy GUSIN (Ukraine)
   Serhiy POPOV (Ukraine)
   Serhiy SKACHENKO (Ukraine)
   Christophe DUGARRY (France)
   Sylvain WILTORD (France)
   Viktor ONOPKO (Russia)
   Aleksandr PANOV (Russia)
   Rikhardur DADASON (Iceland)

GROUP FOUR

1999/2000 FIXTURES

04/09/99	Ukraine v France
	Russia v Armenia
	Iceland v Austria
08/09/99	Armenia v France
	Iceland v Ukraine
	Andorra v Russia
09/10/99	France v Iceland
	Russia v Ukraine
	Andorra v Armenia

GROUP FOUR TABLE

GROUP FOUR TABLE (at 30/06/99)

			Home					Away					Total						
		Pd	W	D	L	F	A	W	D	L	F	A	W	D	L	F	A	Pt	GD
1	Ukraine	7	3	1	0	10	3	1	2	0	2	0	4	3	0	12	3	15	+9
2	France	7	2	1	1	6	3	2	1	0	5	3	4	2	1	11	6	14	+5
3	Russia	7	2	0	1	9	4	2	0	2	8	6	4	0	3	17	10	12	+7
4	Iceland	7	2	1	0	4	1	1	2	1	3	2	3	3	1	7	3	12	+4
5	Armenia	7	1	2	1	3	4	0	0	3	0	6	1	2	4	3	10	5	-7
6	Andorra	7	0	0	3	0	5	0	0	4	2	15	0	0	7	2	20	0	-18

EURO 2000 QUALIFYING GROUP FOUR

ended the season with the better goal-difference chiefly as a result of France's sorry attempts to penetrate the defence of Andorra. They could beat them only 2-0 at home and 1-0 away, the latter courtesy of a very generous penalty award just a few minutes from time.

Ukraine were the only unbeaten team after seven games and they led the table by a point from the French, with whom they shared a goalless draw at the Stade de France. The Ukrainians should really have won that game but

golden boy Andriy Shevchenko missed a wonderful opportunity ten minutes from time. The Ukrainians also squandered other points at home to Iceland and away to Armenia, and although they were parked at the top of the table, their three remaining matches were all tough ones. It looked as if they would have to retain their unbeaten record right through to the close of play if they were to qualify for their first major tournament.

1998/99 MATCH DETAILS

05/09/98, Yerevan
ARMENIA 3 Avalyan (40), Yesayan (71, 90)
ANDORRA 1 Lucendo (86p)
referee - O'Hanlon (IRL)
ARMENIA - Berezovski; Sukiasyan, Krbashyan, Hovsepyan, Hovhannisyan T. (Khodgoyan 83), Vardanyan, Sarkisyan, Adamyan Ara. (Gsepyan 86), Adamyan Art., Shahgeldyan, Avalyan (Yesayan 69).
ANDORRA - Koldo; Ramírez, Txema, Martin, Lima A., Escurza, Garcia, Sonejee, Sánchez, Lucendo, Ruiz.

05/09/98, Reykjavik
ICELAND 1 Dadason (33)
FRANCE 1 Dugarry (36)
referee - Blareau (BEL)
ICELAND - Kristinsson B.; Helgason, Sigurdsson L., Sverrisson E., Marteinsson, Hreidarsson, Kolvidsson, Gudjónsson Th., Kristinsson R., Dadason, Gunnlaugsson A. (Thórdarson 69).
FRANCE - Barthez; Karembeu, Thuram, Leboeuf, Lizarazu, Dugarry (Henry 67), Deschamps, Djorkaeff, Zidane, Pires, Laslandes.

05/09/98, Kiev
UKRAINE 3 Popov (14), Skachenko (25), Rebrov (74p)
RUSSIA 2 Varlamov (66), Onopko (87)
referee - Merk (GER)
UKRAINE - Shovkovskyi; Gusin, Mykytyn, Holovko, Vashchuk, Dmitrulin, Skachenko (Kalitvintsev 46), Popov, Kovalev (Kriventsov 87), Shevchenko, Rebrov.
RUSSIA - Kharin; Minko, Chugainov, Kovtun, Yanovskiy, Semak (Cherchesov 74), Onopko, Alenichev (Mostovoi 64), Kanchelskis (Karpin 70), Kolyvanov, Varlamov.

10/10/98, Andorra La Vella
ANDORRA 0
UKRAINE 2 Kosovskyi (31), Rebrov (43)
referee - Getsov (BUL)
ANDORRA - Koldo; Ramírez, Txema, Garcia, Lima A., Lima I., Pol, Sonejee, González, Sánchez (Jiménez 89), Ruiz.
UKRAINE - Shovkovskyi; Luzhnyi, Holovko, Vashchuk, Mykytyn (Kovalev 46), Popov, Maximov (Kriventsov 53), Gusin, Kosovskyi, Shevchenko (Mykhailenko 69), Rebrov.

10/10/98, Yerevan
ARMENIA 0
ICELAND 0
referee - Norman (SWE)
ARMENIA - Berezovski; Sukiasyan, Vardanyan, Khachatryan, Hovsepyan, Sarkisyan, Petrosyan A. (Hovhannisyan T. 40), Adamyan Art., Shahgeldyan, Mikaelyan, Assadourian (Yesayan 61).

ICELAND - Kristinsson B.; Jónsson, Hreidarsson, Adolfsson, Helgason, Kristinsson R., Kolvidsson, Gunnlaugsson A., Dadason, Gudjónsson Th., Sigurdsson L..

10/10/98, Moscow
RUSSIA 2 Yanovskiy (45), Mostovoi (55)
FRANCE 3 Anelka (13), Pires (29), Boghossian (82)
referee - Ceccarini (ITA)
RUSSIA - Ovchinnikov; Onopko, Varlamov, Khlestov, Karpin, Yanovskiy, Alenichev (Semak 70), Mostovoi, Tikhonov, Titov, Beschastnykh (Gerasimenko 60).
FRANCE - Lama; Thuram, Blanc, Desailly, Lizarazu, Deschamps, Petit (Boghossian 46), Pires, Zidane, Djorkaeff (Vieira 54), Anelka (Vairelles 88).

14/10/98, Saint-Denis
FRANCE 2 Candela (53), Djorkaeff (59)
ANDORRA 0
referee - Koren (ISR)
FRANCE - Lama; Candela, Leboeuf, Blanc, Lizarazu, Deschamps, Zidane, Djorkaeff (Boghossian 83), Dugarry (Pires 69), Trezeguet (Anelka 69), Vairelles.
ANDORRA - Koldo; Ramírez (Sánchez 80), Txema, Martin, Lima A., Lima I., Pol, Sonejee, Lucendo (Jiménez 88), Ruiz, González.

14/10/98, Reykjavik
ICELAND 1 Kovtun (86og)
RUSSIA 0
referee - Temmink (HOL)
ICELAND - Kristinsson B.; Jónsson, Hreidarsson, Adolfsson, Helgason, Kristinsson R., Kolvidsson (Thórdarson 84), Gunnlaugsson A., Dadason, Sigurdsson L., Gudjónsson Th. (Sigurdsson H. 4).
RUSSIA - Cherchesov; Kovtun, Onopko, Smertin, Yanovskiy, Shalimov, Varlamov (Khokhlov 59), Mostovoi, Tikhonov (Igonin 13), Karpin (Khokhlov 59), Titov.

14/10/98, Kiev
UKRAINE 2 Skachenko (32), Gusin (80)
ARMENIA 0
referee - Lica (ROM)
UKRAINE - Shovkovskyi; Luzhnyi, Holovko, Vashchuk, Popov (Maximov 75), Skachenko (Kovalev 59), Gusin, Kosovskyi, Shevchenko (Kriventsov 80), Rebrov.
ARMENIA - Berezovski; Sukiasyan, Vardanyan, Khachatryan, Hovsepyan, Krbashyan (Hovhannisyan T. 85), Petrosyan A., Adamyan Ara., Shahgeldyan, Mikaelyan (Avalyan 68), Assadourian (Yesayan 74).

27/03/99, Andorra La Vella
ANDORRA 0
ICELAND 2 Sverrisson E. (57), Adolfsson (66)
referee - Agius (MLT)
ANDORRA - Koldo; Ramírez (González 76), Txema, Martín, Lima A., Lima I., Pol,

EURO 2000 QUALIFYING GROUP FOUR

1998/99 MATCH DETAILS

Sonejee, Jiménez (Sánchez 63), Lucendo, Ruiz (Imbernon 82).
ICELAND - Kristinsson B.; Jónsson, Gunnarsson (Hreidarsson 71), Adolfsson, Helgason, Kristinsson R., Thórdarson, Gunnlaugsson A. (Gudmundsson 80), Sverrisson E. (Grétarsson 60), Sigurdsson H., Gudjónsson Th..

27/03/99, Yerevan
ARMENIA 0
RUSSIA 3 Karpin (7, 63p), Beschastnykh (89)
referee - Hauge (NOR)
ARMENIA - Berezovski; Mkrchyan, Hovsepyan, Hovhannisyan S., Krbashyan (Harutyunyan 64), Vardanyan, Petrosyan A., Voskanyan (Kakosyan 78), Sarkisyan, Shahgeldyan, Mikaelyan (Yesayan 81).
RUSSIA - Filimonocv; Khlestov, Onopko, Drozdov, Tsymbalar, Karpin, Alenichev (Tikhonov 65), Yanovskiy, Titov, Yuran (Khokhlov 84), Panov (Beschastnykh 46).

27/03/99, Saint-Denis
FRANCE 0
UKRAINE 0
referee - Benkö (AUT)
FRANCE - Barthez; Thuram, Lizarazu, Deschamps, Blanc, Desailly, Pires (Dhorasoo 84), Djorkaeff, Petit (Boghossian 78), Anelka, Dugarry (Wiltord 68).
UKRAINE - Shovkovskyi; Luzhnyi, Vashchuk, Holovko, Mykytyn, Gusin (Skrypnyk 85), Popov, Kovalev (Kosovskyi 54), Rebrov, Skachenko (Maximov 68), Shevchenko.

31/03/99, Saint-Denis
FRANCE 2 Wiltord (2), Dugarry (45)
ARMENIA 0
referee - Bikas (GRE)
FRANCE - Barthez; Thuram (Karembeu 79), Blanc, Desailly, Deschamps, Vieira, Djorkaeff (Pires 69), Boghossian, Anelka, Wiltord, Dugarry (Trezeguet 46).
ARMENIA - Berezovski; Sukiasyan (Khachatryan 40), Mkrchyan, Vardanyan, Hovsepyan, Hovhannisyan S., Petrosyan A., Voskanyan (Hairapetyan 77), Sarkisyan, Shahgeldyan (Yesayan 53), Mikaelyan.

31/03/99, Moscow
RUSSIA 6 Titov (8), Beschastnykh (12, 62), Onopko (43), Tsymbalar (50), Alenichev (90)
ANDORRA 1 Sánchez (73)
referee - Vuorela (FIN)
RUSSIA - Filimonov; Khlestov, Smertin, Tsymbalar, Yevseyev (Tikhonov 46), Alenichev, Onopko, Karpin, Titov, Shirko, Beschastnykh.
ANDORRA - Koldo; Alonso (González 57), Txema, Martin, Lima A., Lima I., Pol, Sonejee, Jiménez, Lucendo (Sánchez 65), Ruiz.

31/03/99, Kiev
UKRAINE 1 Vashchuk (59)
ICELAND 1 Sigurdsson L. (66)
referee - Koren (ISR)
UKRAINE - Shovkovskyi; Luzhnyi, Vashchuk, Holovko, Mykytyn, Gusin, Popov (Kalitvintsev 76), Kosovskyi, Rebrov, Skachenko (Maximov 46), Shevchenko.
ICELAND - Kristinsson B.; Jónsson, Gunnarsson, Adolfsson, Helgason, Kristinsson R. (Kolvidsson 78), Sigurdsson L., Hreidarsson, Sverrisson E., Sigurdsson H. (Sverrisson S. 82), Gudjónsson Th..

05/06/99, Saint-Denis
FRANCE 2 Petit (48), Wiltord (54)
RUSSIA 3 Panov (38, 75), Karpin (86)

referee - Durkin (ENG)
FRANCE - Barthez; Thuram, Blanc, Desailly, Candela (Pires 88), Deschamps, Petit, Djorkaeff (Boghossian 90), Dugarry (Vieira 59), Anelka, Wiltord.
RUSSIA - Filimonov; Khlestov, Onopko, Smertin, Varlamov, Karpin, Semak (Beschastnykh 60), Mostovoi (Khokhlov 26), Titov, Tikhonov (Tsymbalar 72), Panov.

05/06/99, Reykjavik
ICELAND 2 Dadason (30), Kristinsson R. (46)
ARMENIA 0
referee - Peltola (FIN)
ICELAND - Kristinsson B.; Helgason (Kolvidsson 71), Hreidarsson, Jónsson, Marteinsson, Gunnarsson, Kristinsson R., Sverrisson E., Sigurdsson H. (Danielsson 80), Gudjónsson Th., Dadason (Helguson 69).
ARMENIA - Berezovski; Sukiasyan (Mkrchyan 65), Khachatryan, Hovsepyan, Voskanyan (Grigoryan 84), Vardanyan, Petrosyan A. (Hairapetyan 75), Harutyunyan, Sarkisyan, Shahgeldyan, Mikaelyan.

05/06/99, Kiev
UKRAINE 4 Popov (36), Rebrov (41), Dmitrulin (56), Gusin (90)
ANDORRA 0
referee - Georgiou (CYP)
UKRAINE - Vorobiov; Luzhnyi, Mykytyn (Mizin 69), Holovko, Vashchuk, Dmitrulin (Maxymyuk 80), Tsykhmeistruk, Popov, Gusin, Shevchenko (Skachenko 74), Rebrov.
ANDORRA - Koldo; Pol, Martin (Lucendo 53), Txema, Lima A., Lima I., González, Sonejee, Ramírez, Sánchez, Ruiz.

09/06/99, Barcelona
ANDORRA 0
FRANCE 1 Leboeuf (86p)
referee - Ross (NIR)
ANDORRA - Koldo; Pol, Ramirez, Lima A., Lima I., Txema (Jonas 70), González, Sonejee, Ruiz, Jiménez (García 89), Lucendo (Martin 78).
FRANCE - Ramé; Karembeu, Candela, Boghossian, Leboeuf, Desailly, Wiltord, Dugarry, Anelka, Petit (Vieira 56), Dhorasoo (Pires 61).

09/06/99, Yerevan
ARMENIA 0
UKRAINE 0
referee - Boggi (ITA)
ARMENIA - Berezovski; Petrosyan T. (Grigoryan 66), Khachatryan, Hovsepyan, Hovhannisyan S. (Harutyunyan 46), Vardanyan, Petrosyan A., Voskanyan, Sarkisyan, Shahgeldyan, Mikaelyan (Mkrchyan 46).
UKRAINE - Vorobiov; Luzhnyi, Mykytyn, Holovko, Vashchuk, Dmitrulin, Tsykhmeistruk, Popov (Konovalov 37), Gusin, Shevchenko (Kardash 82), Rebrov (Skachenko 71).

09/06/99, Moscow
RUSSIA 1 Karpin (44)
ICELAND 0
referee - Tokat (TUR)
RUSSIA - Filimonov; Khlestov, Varlamov (Yanovskiy 56), Onopko, Semak (Bulatov 46), Smertin, Karpin, Khokhlov, Tikhonov, Beschastnykh (Tsymbalar 72), Panov.
ICELAND - Kristinsson B.; Helgason, Hreidarsson (Adolfsson 58), Jónsson (Kolvidsson 46), Marteinsson, Kristinsson R., Gunnarsson (Helguson 82), Sverrisson E., Sigurdsson L., Gudjónsson Th., Dadason

EURO 2000 QUALIFYING GROUP FIVE

England left behind as Sweden stride clear

England's Paul Ince gets a foot in ahead of Sweden's Johan Mjällby.

None of the five teams in this evenly-balanced group could come to a mutually satisfactory fixture arrangement, so the schedule was determined independently by UEFA. England were the big losers. Not only did they have to play three of their matches in September - historically a poor month for them - but they were also obliged to end their campaign before all of the others, which left them open to devious manipulation from their rivals.

A tough ordeal for Glenn Hoddle's team became even tougher when they lost their opening game away to Sweden. They failed to capitalise on a bright start, during which Alan Shearer scored from a free-kick, and eventually went to pieces as the home side twice profitted from some unfortunate deflections in the England box to turn the game on its head within the space of a couple of minutes. Paul Ince's sending-off midway through the second half merely added to England's woes, although Shearer had a very strong case for a penalty in the dying seconds that was ignored by Italian referee Pierluigi Collina.

Sweden's 2-1 win was a repeat of

their triumph at the Euro '92 finals and it set the pattern for the remainder of the campaign. While the Swedes went on from there, picking up victories in each of their next three games - including crucial ones in Bulgaria and Poland - and not conceding any goals in the process, England went from bad to worse. Their next fixture, at home to Bulgaria, ended 0-0 and produced one of the worst England performances in living memory. The Bulgarians, who, shorn of most of their best players, had been beaten 3-0 at home by Poland in their opening match, came to Wembley with a new coach, Dimitar Dimitrov. His tactics were all-out defence, and they worked, with England mustering just one effort on target in the entire 90 minutes.

England got their first win, 3-0 away to Luxembourg (after the home side had missed a penalty), but that was Hoddle's

GROUP FIVE TABLE

GROUP FIVE TABLE (at 30/06/99)

			Home				Away				Total					
		Pd	W	D	L	F	A	W	D	L	F	A	W	D	L	F	A	Pt	GD
1	Sweden	5	2	0	0	4	1	2	1	0	2	0	4	1	0	6	1	13	+5
2	Poland	6	2	0	1	5	1	2	0	1	7	5	4	0	2	12	6	12	+6
3	England	6	1	2	0	3	1	1	1	1	5	3	2	3	1	8	4	9	+4
4	Bulgaria	6	0	1	2	1	5	1	1	1	2	2	1	2	3	3	7	5	-4
5	Luxembourg	5	0	0	3	2	8	0	0	2	0	5	0	0	5	2	13	0	-11

EURO 2000 QUALIFYING GROUP FIVE

1998/99 MATCH DETAILS

05/09/98, Solna
SWEDEN 2 Andersson A. (30), Mjällby (33)
ENGLAND 1 Shearer (2)
referee - Collina (ITA)
SWEDEN - Hedman; Nilsson, Andersson P., Björklund, Kåmark (Lucic 82), Schwarz, Andersson A. (Andersson D. 89), Mjällby, Ljungberg, Larsson, Pettersson.
ENGLAND - Seaman; Anderton (Lee 42), Le Saux, Southgate, Adams, Campbell (Merson 74), Redknapp, Ince, Shearer, Owen, Scholes (Sheringham 86).

06/09/98, Bourgas
BULGARIA 0
POLAND 3 Czereszewski (19, 45), Iwan (48)
referee - Batta (FRA)
BULGARIA - Zdravkov; Ginchev, Zagorcic (Petkov I. 50), Yordanov, Petkov M. (Trendafilov 46), Sirakov, Kishishev, Bachev, Borimirov (Gruev 46), Stoichkov, Donev.
POLAND - Sidorczuk; Bak, Zielinski, Lapinski, Siadaczka, Hajto (Klos 67), Brzeczek, Czereszewski, Swierczewski (Michalski 68), Iwan, Trzeciak (Juskowiak 80).

10/10/98, Wembley
ENGLAND 0
BULGARIA 0
referee - Vágner (HUN)
ENGLAND - Seaman; Anderton (Batty 67), Hinchcliffe (Le Saux 34), Neville G., Southgate, Campbell, Lee, Scholes (Sheringham 77), Shearer, Owen, Redknapp.
BULGARIA - Zdravkov; Yordanov, Zagorcic, Kirilov, Kishishev, Iliev (Gruev 63), Yankov, Petkov M., Naidenov, Stoichkov (Bachev 60), Hristov (Ivanov 90).

10/10/98, Warsaw
POLAND 3 Brzeczek (18), Juskowiak (33), Trzeciak (63)
LUXEMBOURG 0
referee - Pregia (ALB)
POLAND - Matysek; Zielinski, Lapinski, Ratajczyk (Siadaczka 69), Hajto (Majak 62), Czereszewski (Bak 75), Iwan, Brzeczek, Swierczewski, Juskowiak, Trzeciak.
LUXEMBOURG - Koch; Ferron, Birsens, Funck, Strasser, Holtz (Afrika 71), Theis (Deville F. 46), Saibene, Cardoni, Deville L., Christophe (Thill 65).

14/10/98, Bourgas
BULGARIA 0
SWEDEN 1 Larsson (62)
referee - Heynemann (GER)
BULGARIA - Zdravkov; Zagorcic, Yordanov, Kirilov (Parushev 18), Naidenov (Ivanov 69), Iliev (Bachev 60), Yankov, Petkov M., Petkov I., Stoichkov, Hristov.
SWEDEN - Hedman; Nilsson, Andersson P., Björklund, Lucic (Sundgren 76), Ljungberg, Mild, Mjällby, Schwarz, Larsson (Erlingmark 88), Åslund (Blomqvist 71).

14/10/98, Luxembourg
LUXEMBOURG 0
ENGLAND 3 Owen (19), Shearer (39p), Southgate (89)
referee - Vorgias (GRE)

LUXEMBOURG - Koch; Ferron, Deville L., Funck, Deville F. (Alverdi 84), Theis (Holtz 61), Saibene, Strasser, Posing, Cardoni, Christophe (Amodio 78).
ENGLAND - Seaman; Anderton (Lee 63), Neville P., Southgate, Ferdinand, Campbell, Beckham, Batty, Shearer, Owen, Scholes (Wright 76).

27/03/99, Wembley
ENGLAND 3 Scholes (11, 21, 70)
POLAND 1 Brzeczek (28)
referee - Melo Pereira (POR)
ENGLAND - Seaman; Neville G., Le Saux, Sherwood, Keown, Campbell, Beckham (Neville P. 78), Scholes (Redknapp 83), Shearer, Cole, McManaman (Parlour 70).
POLAND - Matysek; Hajto, Zielinski, Lapinski, Ratajczyk, Swierczewski (Klos 46), Bak, Brzeczek, Siadaczka (Kowalczyk 46), Iwan, Trzeciak (Juskowiak 83).

27/03/99, Gothenburg
SWEDEN 2 Mjällby (34), Larsson (86)
LUXEMBOURG 0
referee - Melnichuk (UKR)
SWEDEN - Hedman; Kåmark (Lucic 68), Andersson P., Björklund, Sundgren, Schwarz, Alexandersson, Mjällby, Ljungberg (Andersson D. 78), Larsson, Andersson K..
LUXEMBOURG - Felgen; Ferron, Funck, Birsens, Strasser, Theis (Holtz 69), Vanek, Saibene (Deville F. 88), Cardoni, Deville L., Christophe (Zaritski 80).

31/03/99, Luxembourg
LUXEMBOURG 0
BULGARIA 2 Stoichkov (17), Yordanov (38)
referee - Mitrovic (SLO)
LUXEMBOURG - Felgen; Ferron (Holtz 75), Vanek, Strasser, Deville L., Saibene, Birsens, Theis (Deville F. 89), Posing (Zaritski 46), Cardoni, Christophe.
BULGARIA - Zdravkov; Kishishev, Yankov, Stoianov (Petkov I. 46), Petkov M., Markov, Yordanov, Petrov S., Iliev, Yovov (Ivanov 77), Stoichkov (Todorov 78).

31/03/99, Chorzow
POLAND 0
SWEDEN 1 Ljungberg (36)
referee - Merk (GER)
POLAND - Sidorczuk; Waldoch, Lapinski, Zielinski, Siadaczka (Adamczuk 81), Iwan, Michalski (Bak 88), Brzeczek, Majak (Kowalczyk 69), Juskowiak, Trzeciak.
SWEDEN - Hedman; Kåmark, Andersson P., Björklund, Lucic, Mild (Alexandersson 73), Schwarz, Mjällby, Ljungberg, Larsson (Pettersson 89), Andersson K..

04/06/99, Warsaw
POLAND 2 Hajto (16), Iwan (62)
BULGARIA 0
referee - Braschi (ITA)
POLAND - Matysek; Waldoch, Lapinski, Zielinski, Hajto (Majak 80), Nowak (Brzeczek 74), Michalski, Iwan, Siadaczka, Wichniarek (Frankowski 59), Trzeciak.

EURO 2000 QUALIFYING GROUP FIVE

1998/99 MATCH DETAILS

BULGARIA - Ivankov; Kirilov, Zagorcic, Markov, Kishishev, Petrov S., Stoilov, Petkov M., Petkov I. (Iliev 80), Stoichkov (Ivanov 63), Yovov (Bachev 46).

05/06/99, Wembley
ENGLAND 0
SWEDEN 0
referee - García Aranda (ESP)
ENGLAND - Seaman; Neville P., Le Saux (Gray 46), Batty, Keown (Ferdinand 34), Campbell, Beckham (Parlour 75), Sherwood, Shearer, Cole, Scholes.
SWEDEN - Hedman; Nilsson, Kämark, Schwarz, Andersson P., Björklund, Mild (Alexandersson 6), Mjällby (Andersson D. 82), Andersson K., Larsson (Svensson 69), Ljungberg.

09/06/99, Sofia
BULGARIA 1 Markov (18)
ENGLAND 1 Shearer (15)
referee - Van der Ende (HOL)
BULGARIA - Ivankov; Kirilov, Stoilov, Kishishev, Zagorcic, Markov, Petrov S., Iliev (Borimirov 60), Petkov M., Stoichkov (Bachev 73), Yovov (Petrov M. 46).
ENGLAND - Seaman; Neville P., Gray, Southgate, Woodgate (Parlour 64), Campbell, Redknapp, Batty, Shearer, Fowler (Heskey 81), Sheringham.

09/06/99, Luxembourg
LUXEMBOURG 2 Birsens (76), Vanek (83)
POLAND 3 Siadaczka (21), Wichniarek (45), Iwan (68)
referee - Ivanov (RUS)
LUXEMBOURG - Felgen; Vanek, Funck, Birsens, Strasser, Saibene (Alverdi 85), Theis (Schneider 46), Deville F., Cardoni, Christophe, Zaritski (Posing 65).
POLAND - Matysek; Waldoch, Lapinski, Klos, Hajto (Brzeczek 66), Nowak, Michalski, Iwan, Siadaczka, Wichniarek (Majak 87), Trzeciak.

GROUP FIVE

1999/2000 FIXTURES

04/09/99	Sweden v Bulgaria
	England v Luxembourg
08/09/99	Poland v England
	Luxembourg v Sweden
09/10/99	Sweden v Poland
10/10/99	Bulgaria v Luxembourg

have sewn everything up at Wembley after England were reduced to ten men following the 51st-minute dismissal of Scholes (who thus became the first England international ever sent off at Wembley) but they were interested only in the draw, which they obtained with ease.

The battle for second place was between England and Poland. Like the English, the Poles had not done a great deal to impress but they had taken six points off Bulgaria, adding a 2-0 victory in Warsaw to their earlier 3-0 triumph in Bourgas, and that was enough to give them a three-point advantage over England, who had managed just two points against the same opponents. Everything was set up for a decisive head-to-head encounter in Warsaw at the beginning of September. Victory for either side would ensure their progress to the play-offs whereas a draw would leave the Poles requiring a draw away to Sweden in their final match, in which case England, victims of the fixture schedule, could only sit, hope and pray..

last competitive game as England manager. When the next qualifier came around, in March, Kevin Keegan was the new man in charge. He started promisingly, with Paul Scholes scoring a hat-trick to give England a 3-1 victory at home to Poland. But the bad times returned in early June when Keegan's jaded, uninspired team could only draw 0-0 at Wembley against Sweden and 1-1 in Sofia against Bulgaria.

The point earned by the Swedes at Wembley effectively ensured that they would go on to win the group. They led the table by a point, had a game in hand on both Poland and England and were faced with a relatively straightforward end to their programme - two home games and a trip to Luxembourg. They could

England v Poland - Poland's Jacek Zielinski passes the ball.

EURO 2000 QUALIFYING GROUP SIX

Rampant Raúl leads Spanish goal romp

Group Six opened with one of the biggest upsets in European Championship history when Spain, still licking their wounds after World Cup failure, plummeted to a new low with a humiliating 3-2 defeat in Cyprus.

It was no fluke, either, as the Cypriots, aided and abetted by two nationalised Serbs, Sinisa Gogic and Milenko Spoljaric, matched the Spaniards in every department, scoring three top-quality goals. The first, from man of the match Yotis Engomitis, was a sumptuous lob on the run that any of the world's leading strikers would have been proud of. The win was the best in Cyprus's history and was celebrated accordingly.

For Spain, defeat signalled the end of Javier Clemente's six-year reign as coach. He was replaced by José Antonio Camacho, who made an immediately positive impression in his first game, which Spain deservedly won 2-1 in Israel after a tremendous second-half fightback, during which Fernando Hierro levelled with a blistering 35-yard shot and Joseba Etxeberria stole the points with a late header.

That victory was particularly important for Spain because it prevented the

Israelis from establishing a bridgehead at the top of the table. Instead the group remained very open, with Austria, thanks to a 3-0 victory away to one-game wonders Cyprus, also getting involved in the scrap for group leadership.

But any ambitions the Austrians had of finishing ahead of Spain were flattened in the first qualifier of 1999 when they went to Valencia and were demolished 9-0. It was a truly incredible scoreline and an equally remarkable display by the Spaniards who were simply unstoppable. Camacho had freed the team from the tactical constraints of the Clemente era and they crushed the Austrians with an incessant onslaught that brought goals of every type and description. Raúl, the Real Madrid superstar, scored four of them and also supplied three assists. A few days later he added another three goals to his total as Spain won 6-0 in San Marino.

The matches in the spring were all one-sided affairs embroidered with plenty of goals. Austria recovered from their mauling by hammering San Marino 7-0 in Graz - their first game under new coach Otto Baric, who had replaced Herbert Prohaska - and then Spain went into overdrive yet again with another nine-goal attack on the hapless Sammarinesi in Villarreal to forge clear at the top of the table. They had won four games in a row, scoring 26 goals in the process. The opening-day embarrassment in Cyprus had now been well and truly forgotten.

The season ended with perhaps the most astonishing scoreline of all as Israel, responding to a magnificent atmosphere

TOP SCORERS

9	RAUL González (Spain)
4	Joseba ETXEBERRIA (Spain)
	Alon MIZRAHI (Israel)
	Ivica VASTIC (Austria)
3	Fernando HIERRO (Spain)
	LUIS ENRIQUE (Spain)
	Ismael URZAIZ (Spain)
	Avi NIMNI (Israel)
	Christian MAYRLEB (Austria)
2	FRAN (Spain)
	Haim REVIVO (Israel)
	Eyal BERKOVIC (Israel)
	Najwan GHRAYEB (Israel)
	Harald CERNY (Austria)
	Hannes REINMAYR (Austria)
	Michalis CONSTANDINOU (Cyprus)
	Milenko SPOLJARIC (Cyprus)

GROUP SIX TABLE

GROUP SIX TABLE (at 30/06/99)

			Home				Away				Total					
		Pd	W	D	L	F	A	W	D	L	F	A	W	D	L	F	A	Pt	GD
1	Spain	5	2	0	0	18	0	2	0	1	10	4	4	0	1	28	4	12	+24
2	Israel	5	2	0	1	9	2	1	1	0	6	1	3	1	1	15	3	10	+12
3	Austria	6	1	1	0	8	1	2	0	2	7	15	3	1	2	15	16	10	-1
4	Cyprus	5	2	0	1	7	5	1	0	1	1	3	3	0	2	8	8	9	0
5	San Marino	7	0	0	4	1	16	0	0	3	0	20	0	0	7	1	36	0	-35

EURO 2000 QUALIFYING GROUP SIX

1998/99 MATCH DETAILS

05/09/98, Vienna
AUSTRIA 1 Reinmayr (7)
ISRAEL 1 Nimni (68p)
referee - Frisk (SWE)
AUSTRIA - Wohlfahrt; Schöttel (Hiden 72), Feiersinger, Pfeffer, Cerny (Stöger 74), Kühbauer, Mählich, Reinmayr, Amerhauser, Vastic, Haas (Mayrleb 71).
ISRAEL - Cohen; Harazi A., Shelach (Nimni 46), Ben Shimon, Amsalem, Abuksis (Mizrahi 46), Berkovic, Revivo, Benado, Harazi R. (Ghrayeb 60), Badir.

05/09/98, Larnaca
CYPRUS 3 Engomitis (44), Gogic (48), Spoljaric (77)
SPAIN 2 Raúl (71), Morientes (85)
referee - Khusainov (RUS)
CYPRUS - Panayiotou N.; Costa, Ioannou D. (Ioakim 85), Charalambous M., Pittas, Melanarkitis, Spoljaric, Christodoulou M., Engomitis, Gogic (Agathocleous 61), Malekkos (Pounas 55).
SPAIN - Cañizares; Míchel Salgado, Nadal (Amor 65), Alkorta, Sergi, Etxeberria (Ezquerro 60), Hierro, Raúl, Luis Enrique, Alfonso (Kiko 39), Morientes.

10/10/98, Larnaca
CYPRUS 0
AUSTRIA 3 Cerny (53, 61), Reinmayr (75)
referee - Meese (BEL)
CYPRUS - Panayiotou N.; Engomitis, Ioannou D., Costa, Charalambous M., Pittas (Georgiou 67), Spoljaric, Melanarkitis (Constandinou M. 68), Christodoulou M., Agathocleous (Okkas 46), Gogic.
AUSTRIA - Wohlfahrt; Hiden, Schöttel, Pfeffer, Cerny, Kühbauer, Mählich, Reinmayr (Stöger 79), Wetl, Vastic (Glieder 82), Haas (Mayrleb 79).

10/10/98, Serravalle
SAN MARINO 0
ISRAEL 5 Revivo (15), Nimni (17, 57), Mizrahi (31), Ghrayeb (82)
referee - Khudiev (AZB)
SAN MARINO - Gasperoni F.; Gennari, Guerra, Valentini M., Bacciocchi S. (Valentini V. 59), Marani, Montagna (Gualtieri 76), Muccioli, Della Valle (Francini 68), Matteoni, Selva A..
ISRAEL - Cohen; Harazi A., Ben Shimon, Telasnikov, Badir, Benado (Shelach 67), Nimni (Banin 59), Ghrayeb, Revivo, Berkovic (Shitrit 71), Mizrahi.

14/10/98, Tel Aviv
ISRAEL 1 Hazan (63)
SPAIN 2 Hierro (65), Etxeberria (77)
referee - Elleray (ENG)
ISRAEL - Cohen; Harazi A., Ben Shimon, Benado, Hazan (Banin 75), Badir, Telasnikov (Mizrahi 59), Ghrayeb, Nimni, Revivo, Berkovic.
SPAIN - Cañizares; Míchel Salgado, Hierro, Alkorta, Aranzábal, Luis Enrique, Engonga, Alkiza, De Pedro (Etxeberria 72), Kiko (Urzaiz 88), Raúl (Vales 90).

14/10/98, Serravalle
SAN MARINO 1 Selva A. (80p)
AUSTRIA 4 Vastic (59), Mayrleb (64), Hiden (69), Glieder (76)
referee - Onufer (UKR)

SAN MARINO - Gasperoni F.; Gennari, Guerra, Valentini M. (Della Valle 79), Bacciocchi S., Marani, Muccioli, Francini (Valentini V. 61), Ugolini (Montagna 61), Matteoni, Selva A..
AUSTRIA - Wohlfahrt; Hiden, Schöttel, Pfeffer, Cerny, Kühbauer. Heraf, Reinmayr (Mayrleb 46), Wetl, Vastic (Stöger 71), Haas (Glieder 66).

18/11/98, Serravalle
SAN MARINO 0
CYPRUS 1 Spoljaric (40)
referee - McDermott (IRL)
SAN MARINO - Gasperoni F.; Gennari, Valentini M., Guerra, Valentini V., Marani, Gasperoni B., Muccioli (Mularoni 83), Matteoni (Francini 75), Montagna (Bacciocchi N. 67), Ugolini.
CYPRUS - Panayiotou N.; Pittas, Panayiotou Y., Charalambous M., Sophocleous, Engomitis, Melanarkitis, Spoljaric, Agathocleous (Constandinou M. 72), Malekkos (Ioannou Y. 72), Gogic (Okkas 85).

10/02/99, Nicosia
CYPRUS 4 Melanarkitis (18), Constandinou M. (32, 45), Christodoulou M. (88)
SAN MARINO 0
CYPRUS - Panayiotou N.; Theodotou, Christodoulou M., Ioakim, Charalambous M., Pittas, Melanarkitis, Spoljaric, Gogic (Ioannou Y. 80), Constandinou M. (Okkas 80), Malekkos (Aristocleous 89).
SAN MARINO - Gasperoni F.; Gennari, Marani (Vannucci 84), Gobbi, Valentini V., Guerra, Zonzini, Della Valle (Manzaroli 69), Ugolini (Bacciocchi N. 46), Mularoni, Selva A..

27/03/99, Valencia
SPAIN 9 Raúl (5, 16, 47, 73),Urzaiz (29, 45), Hierro (34p), Wetl 7(6og), Fran (83)
AUSTRIA 0
referee - Veissière (FRA)
SPAIN - Cañizares; Míchel Salgado, Hierro, Marcelino, Sergi, Etxeberria (Dani 83), Guardiola, Valerón (Mendieta 70), Fran, Raúl, Urzaiz (Munitis 60).
AUSTRIA - Wohlfahrt; Schöttel, Feiersinger (Kogler 54), Pfeffer, Cerny, Mählich, Neukirchner, Prosenik (Reinmayr 58), Wetl, Herzog, Haas (Mayrleb 69).

28/03/99, Tel-Aviv
ISRAEL 3 Banin (11), Mizrahi (47, 53)
CYPRUS 0
referee - Lica (ROM)
ISRAEL - Davidovich; Harazi A., Ghrayeb, Shelach, Badir (Talker 46), Banin, Benado, Berkovic, Revivo (Tikva 85), Harazi R. (Mizrahi 46), Nimni.
CYPRUS - Panayiotou N.; Theodotou, Pittas, Ioannou D., Charalambous M., Constandinou M. (Okkas 66), Melanarkitis, Spoljaric (Agathocleous 79), Malekkos (Nicolaou Ch. 46), Sophocleous, Christodoulou M..

31/03/99, Serravalle
SAN MARINO 0
SPAIN 6 Fran (20), Raúl (45, 59, 67), Urzaiz (49), Etxeberria (72)
referee - Maric (CRO)

EURO 2000 QUALIFYING GROUP SIX

1998/99 MATCH DETAILS

SAN MARINO - Gasperoni F.; Gennari, Marani, Valentini V., Zonzoni, Valentini M., Manzaroli, Gasperoni B. (Muccioli 75), Gobbi (Della Balda 51), Selva A., Montagna (Gualtieri 59).
SPAIN - Cañizares; Michel Salgado, Marcelino, Paco, Sergi, Etxeberria, Guardiola (Engonga 69), Valerón (Helguera 76), Fran, Raúl, Urzaiz (Dani 62).

28/04/99, Graz
AUSTRIA 7 Mayrleb (24, 53), Vastic (42, 44, 84), Amerhauser (71), Herzog (82p)
SAN MARINO 0
referee - Vasaros (GRE)
AUSTRIA - Wohlfahrt; Winklhofer (Rohseano 81), Feiersinger, Neukirchner, Cerny (Kitzbichler 72), Schopp (Glieder 72), Herzog, Prosenik, Amerhauser, Mayrleb, Vastic.
SAN MARINO - Gasperoni F.; Gennari (Bacciocchi S. 46), Della Balda, Guerra, Gobbi, Vannucci, Gasperoni B. (Manzaroli 15), Zonzini, Muccioli, Selva A., Montagna (Selva R. 84).

05/06/99, Villarreal
SPAIN 9 Hierro (8p), Luis Enrique (22, 71, 75), Etxeberria (24, 45), Raúl (61), Gennari (89og), Mendieta (90)
SAN MARINO 0
referee - Perry (IRL)
SPAIN - Cañizares; Michel Salgado (Munitis 67), Marcelino, Hierro, Aranzábal, Etxeberria, Guardiola, Guerrero (Mendieta 80), Luis Enrique, Raúl (Urzaiz 67), Morientes.
SAN MARINO - Gasperoni F.; Gennari (Vannucci 84), Marani, Della Balda, Gobbi, Guerra, Bacciocchi N., Della Valle, Zonzini, Manzaroli (Valentini V. 74), Montagna (Ugolini 59).

06/06/99, Tel-Aviv
ISRAEL 5 Berkovic (26, 47), Revivo (45), Mizrahi (54), Ghrayeb (75)
AUSTRIA 0
referee - Michel (SVK)
ISRAEL - Davidovich; Shelach, Benado, Harazi A., Ghrayeb, Banin, Abuksis (Tal 82), Hazan, Mizrahi (Tikva 78), Berkovic (Sivilia 77), Revivo.
AUSTRIA - Wohlfahrt; Winklhofer, Barisic, Kogler, Cerny, Mählich, Herzog, Neukirchner, Amerhauser (Prosenik 46), Mayrleb (Haas 67), Vastic (Glieder 57).

GROUP SIX

1999/2000 FIXTURES

04/09/99	Austria v Spain
05/09/99	Cyprus v Israel
08/09/99	Spain v Cyprus
	Israel v San Marino
09/10/99	Spain v Israel
10/10/99	Austria v Cyprus

4-0 before full-back Najwan Ghrayeb sealed a comprehensive win with a close-range strike after more trickery from Revivo and Berkovic had opened up a woeful Austrian defence.

Austria had been shellshocked again, and there appeared to be no way back for them. Israel, however, were buoyant, and although the revitalised Spaniards appeared to be out of their reach, the non-Europeans certainly had every reason to believe that they could reach their first European Championship finals by way of the play-offs. If they played again like they did against Austria, they could beat anybody...

in the Ramat-Gan stadium, destroyed Austria 5-0. It was a breathtaking display by Shlomo Sharf's team, arguably the best ever by an Israeli side in international competition. The team's two exiled stars, Eyal Berkovic and Haim Revivo, were in awesome form. Berkovic scored twice while Revivo netted the goal of the game with a stunning free-kick just before half-time. Alon Mizrahi added his fourth goal of the competition to make it

Alon Mizrahi - Israel's leading scorer in the qualifying group.

EURO 2000 QUALIFYING GROUP SEVEN

Portugal and Romania engaged in private battle

It was always anticipated that Portugal and Romania would be too strong for the opposition in this group, and so it proved. By the end of the season, with all teams having played seven matches, Portugal led the table with six victories and one defeat while Romania were just one point adrift with an unbeaten record.

It was anybody's guess which of the two front-runners would emerge to win the race for first place. While the Portuguese had a slight advantage, they still had to travel to Bucharest - where the Romanians would be bidding to complete the 'double' over them following their

earlier smash-and-grab victory in Oporto.

That match, played early on in the campaign, threatened to leave a lasting impression on the group. Portugal really should have won it. They peppered the Romanian goal all night long but ultimately had only themselves to blame for not securing victory. The team's age-old problem of not taking their chances returned to haunt them, most notably in the first half when Paulinho Santos missed a penalty. Romania defended well and would have been happy with one point, but with the game entering injury-time they succeeded in collecting all three when veteran campaigner Dorinel Munteanu curled in a free-kick.

Portugal were entitled to lament their bad luck but four days later they gave themselves the perfect pick-me-up when they went to Bratislava and beat Slovakia 3-0. Here the goals did come, with João Pinto scoring twice in the first half and Abel Xavier securing a decisive victory with a low drive 20 minutes from time. It was Portugal's second important away win. They had opened their campaign with an impressive 3-1 victory in Hungary, coming from behind to win thanks to two goals from striker Sá Pinto, available again after a one-year suspension.

Romania could not emulate Portugal's feat in Budapest, where they were held 1-1 as a result of János Hrutka's fabulous 35-yard free-kick. And when, in the spring, Victor Piturca's team dropped two further points, in a goalless draw at home to Slovakia, the advantage they had gained over the Portuguese with that victory in Oporto had been totally nullified.

Portugal went goal-crazy against Liechtenstein and Azerbaijan but they only just sneaked a 1-0 home win against the Slovakians, with skipper Luís Figo setting up the winning goal for

GROUP SEVEN

1999/2000 FIXTURES

03/09/99	Azerbaijan v Portugal
04/09/99	Liechtenstein v Hungary
	Slovakia v Romania
08/09/99	Slovakia v Liechtenstein
	Romania v Portugal
	Hungary v Azerbaijan
09/10/99	Liechtenstein v Romania
	Azerbaijan v Slovakia
10/10/99	Portugal v Hungary

GROUP SEVEN TABLE

GROUP SEVEN TABLE (at 30/06/99)

		Pd	W	D	L	F	A	W	D	L	F	A	W	D	L	F	A	Pt	GD
1	Portugal	7	3	0	1	16	1	3	0	0	11	1	6	0	1	27	2	18	+25
2	Romania	7	3	1	0	13	0	2	1	0	3	1	5	2	0	16	1	17	+15
3	Slovakia	7	1	1	1	3	3	2	1	1	5	1	3	2	2	8	4	11	+4
4	Hungary	7	1	1	2	7	5	1	1	1	4	2	2	2	3	11	7	8	+4
5	Azerbaijan	7	1	0	2	4	5	0	0	4	1	16	1	0	6	5	21	3	-16
6	Liechtenstein	7	1	0	2	2	10	0	0	4	0	24	1	0	6	2	34	3	-32

EURO 2000 QUALIFYING GROUP SEVEN

1998/99 MATCH DETAILS

02/09/98, Bucharest
ROMANIA 7 Popescu Gh. (17), Munteanu C. (29), Ilie (31, 44, 51), Moldovan (54), Haas (59og)
LIECHTENSTEIN 0
referee - Prolic (BOS)
ROMANIA - Stelea (Lobont 82); Petrescu, Batrânu, Popescu Gh., Contra, Petre, Gâlca, Munteanu C. (Sabau 71), Munteanu D., Moldovan, Ilie (Mihalcea 68).
LIECHTENSTEIN - Oehry; Hefti, Hanselmann, Stocklasa Mi., Telser M. (Ender 89), Ritter, Zech, Lingg (Büchel 62), Beck T., Oehri, Haas (Stocklasa Ma. 63).

05/09/98, Kosice
SLOVAKIA 3 Fabus (17), Dubovsky (26p), Moravcik (39)
AZERBAIJAN 0
referee - Snoddy (NIR)
SLOVAKIA - Vencel; Varga, Tomaschek, Tittel, Spilar, Kinder, Sovic, Moravcik, Fabus (Jancula 62), Majoros (Ujlaky 82), Dubovsky (Zvara 62).
AZERBAIJAN - Kramarenko; Gaysumov, Abushev, Jabbarov, Agaev, Lychkin, Kasumov, Asadov, Sirkhaev, Suleymanov (Kuliev 46), Kurbanov K. (Rzaev 66).

06/09/98, Budapest
HUNGARY 1 Horváth (32)
PORTUGAL 3 Sá Pinto (56, 76), Rui Costa (84)
referee - Meier (SUI)
HUNGARY - Király; Fehér C. (Korsós G. 78), Lakos, Hrutka, Mátyus, Lisztes (Dárdai 46), Halmai, Illés, Dombi (Kovács 78), Horváth, Hamar.
PORTUGAL - Vitor Baia; Secretário, Jorge Costa, Paulo Madeira, Dimas, Figo, Paulo Bento, Rui Costa, Paulinho Santos, João Pinto, Sá Pinto.

10/10/98, Baku
AZERBAIJAN 0
HUNGARY 4 Dárdai (58), Illés (84p), Pisont (88), Fehér M. (90)
referee - Bré (FRA)
AZERBAIJAN - Kramarenko (Zhidkov 59); Gaysumov, Agaev, Abushev, Kerimov, Asadov (Mamedov 51), Lychkin, Sirkhaev, Rzaev, Kambarov (Kasumov 56), Kurbanov K..
HUNGARY - Király; Sebök V. (Korsós G. 65), Fehér C., Hrutka, Mátyus, Dárdai, Pisont, Illés, Lisztes (Dombi 75), Horváth (Fehér M. 6), Hamar.

10/10/98, Vaduz
LIECHTENSTEIN 0
SLOVAKIA 4 Sovic (3), Dubovsky (13), Tomaschek (36, 61)
referee - Antonov (MOL)
LIECHTENSTEIN - Oehry; Ritter, Hanselmann, Zech, Hefti (Lingg 76), Haas (Stocklasa Ma. 33), Oehri (Ospelt 46), Hasler, Stocklasa Mi., Frick M., Telser M..
SLOVAKIA - Vencel; Varga (Timko 65), Tittel, Spilar, Sovic, Tomaschek, Moravcik, Dubovsky, Kinder (Kozak 30), Majoros, Fabus (Jancula 61).

10/10/98, Oporto
PORTUGAL 0
ROMANIA 1 Munteanu D. (90)
referee - Krug (GER)
PORTUGAL - Vitor Baia; Abel Xavier (Dani 85), Jorge Costa, Fernando Couto, Dimas, Figo, Paulo Bento (Sérgio Conceição 69), Rui Costa, Paulinho Santos, João Pinto (Nuno Gomes 78), Sá Pinto.
ROMANIA - Stelea; Petrescu (Contra 85), Filipescu, Popescu Gh., Ciobotariu, Petre,

Munteanu C. (Lupescu 62), Gâlca, Munteanu D., Rosu, Moldovan (Mihalcea 90).

14/10/98, Budapest
HUNGARY 1 Hrutka (83)
ROMANIA 1 Moldovan (50)
referee - Nielsen (DEN)
HUNGARY - Király; Fehér C., Sebök V., Hrutka, Mátyus, Pisont, Dárdai, Illés, Egressy (Lisztes 78), Fehér M. (Hámori 75), Hamar (Tóth 69).
ROMANIA - Stelea; Petrescu, Filipescu, Popescu Gh., Ciobotariu, Petre (Serban 69), Gâlca, Lupescu, Munteanu D., Moldovan (Mihalcea 80), Craioveanu (Munteanu C. 75).

14/10/98, Vaduz
LIECHTENSTEIN 2 Frick M. (47p), Telser M. (49)
AZERBAIJAN 1 Kurbanov K. (59)
referee - Barr (NIR)
LIECHTENSTEIN - Jehle; Ritter, Zech, Hasler, Stocklasa Ma., Bicker (Ospelt 67), Lingg, Stocklasa Mi., Beck T. (Büchel 74), Frick M., Telser M..
AZERBAIJAN - Zhidkov; Yaddulayev, Gaysumov, Agaev, Kerimov, Abushev (Kuliev 79), Kurbanov M. (Suleymanov 25), Rzaev, Kambarov (Mamedov 51), Kurbanov K., Sirkhaev.

14/10/98, Bratislava
SLOVAKIA 0
PORTUGAL 3 João Pinto (16, 33), Abel Xavier (69)
referee - Sarvan (TUR)
SLOVAKIA - Vencel; Spilar, Kinder (Kozak 46), Tittel, Varga, Sovic (Pinte 83), Tomaschek, Fabus (Nemeth 57), Moravcik, Majoros, Dubovsky.
PORTUGAL - Vitor Baia; Abel Xavier, Jorge Costa, Fernando Couto, Dimas, Figo (Capucho 90), Paulo Bento, Rui Costa (Da Costa 67), Paulinho Santos, João Pinto (Sérgio Conceição 46), Sá Pinto.

26/03/99, Guimarães
PORTUGAL 7 Sá Pinto (28), João Pinto (36, 71), Paulo Madeira (68), Sérgio Conceição (75), Pauleta (82, 83)
AZERBAIJAN 0
referee - Granat (POL)
PORTUGAL - Vitor Baia (Pedro Espinha 77); Secretário, Paulo Madeira, Fernando Couto, Dimas, Paulo Sousa, Rui Costa (Pedro Barbosa 83), Sérgio Conceição, Figo (Pauleta 73), Sá Pinto, João Pinto.
AZERBAIJAN - Kramarenko; Agaev, Asadov, Akhmedov, Stukas, Abushev, Kambarov (Vasilyev 72), Musayev (Rzaev 67), Sirkhaev, Lychkin, Kurbanov K..

27/03/99, Budapest
HUNGARY 5 Sebök J. (17), Sebök V. (33, 41, 86), Illés (74)
LIECHTENSTEIN 0
referee - Kapitanis (CYP)
HUNGARY - Király; Hrutka (Somogyi 78), Sebök V., Korsós G., Mátyus, Halmai, Sebök J. (Dombi 71), Pisont, Illés, Fehér J., Tóth (Hamar 76).
LIECHTENSTEIN - Jehle; Hanselmann (Hefti 46), Stocklasa Ma., Lingg, Ritter, Stocklasa Mi., Wohlwend, Frick M., Hasler, Telser M., Beck M. (Ospelt 78).

27/03/99, Bucharest
ROMANIA 0
SLOVAKIA 0
referee - Barber (ENG)

EURO 2000 QUALIFYING GROUP SEVEN

substitute Capucho with a fantastic run and pass. On the same night, in Bucharest, Romania rediscovered their very best form thanks to the return from international retirement of national hero Gheorghe Hagi, who gave a virtuoso performance in the first half, repeatedly puncturing the Hungarian defence with his whiplash shooting and slide-rule passing. Goals from Adrian Ilie and Dorinel Munteanu gave Romania their first win over neighbours Hungary for 63 years and kept them very much within striking distance of the Portuguese at the top of the table.

1998/99 MATCH DETAILS

ROMANIA - Stelea; Petrescu, Batrânu, Popescu Gh., Rosu, Petre, Gâlca, Munteanu C. (Lupescu 68), Munteanu D., Moldovan (Craioveanu 72), Ilie.
SLOVAKIA - König; Varga, Zeman, Karhan, Kratochvil, Zatek (Dzurik 77), Tomaschek, Balis, Labant, Dubovsky (Suchancok 87), Majoros (Slicho 71).

31/03/99, Baku
AZERBAIJAN 0
ROMANIA 1 Petre (49)
referee - Luinge (HOL)
AZERBAIJAN - Magomedov; Kerimov, Poshekhontsev, Asadov, Agaev (Kuliev 77), Tagizade (Kambarov 69), Kurbanov M. (Rzaev 65), Akhmedov, Lychkin, Sirkhaev, Kurbanov K..
ROMANIA - Lobont; Contra, Filipescu, Ciobotariu, Munteanu D., Petre, Gâlca, Lupescu, Rosu (Florea 74), Moldovan, Craioveanu (Mihalcea 89).

31/03/99, Vaduz
LIECHTENSTEIN 0
PORTUGAL 5 Rui Costa (15p, 79), Figo (49), Paulo Madeira (54, 60)
referee - Orrason (ISL)
LIECHTENSTEIN - Jehle; Lingg, Hasler, Stocklasa Ma., Ritter, Hanselmann (Ospelt 84), Telser, Frick C., Stocklasa Mi. (Beck M. 65), Wohlwend (Burgmeier 82), Frick M..
PORTUGAL - Vítor Baía; Secretário, Paulo Madeira, Fernando Couto, Dimas, Sérgio Conceição (Capucho 87), Paulo Sousa, Rui Costa, Figo, Sá Pinto (Pauleta 61), João Pinto (Nuno Gomes 75).

31/03/99, Bratislava
SLOVAKIA 0
HUNGARY 0
referee - Colombo (FRA)
SLOVAKIA - König; Kratochvil, Zeman (Dzurik 14), Varga, Karhan, Balis, Tomaschek, Dubovsky, Zatek (Hrncar 79), Majoros, Pinte (Slicho 83).
HUNGARY - Király; Korsós G., Sebök V., Hrutka, Mátyus, Pisont, Halmai, Illés, Sebök J. (Dombi 55), Fehér M. (Hamar 64), Tóth.

05/06/99, Baku
AZERBAIJAN 4 Kurbanov K. (16), Lychkin (42), Tagizade (60), Isaev (73)
LIECHTENSTEIN 0
referee - Stadsgaard (DEN)
AZERBAIJAN - Kramarenko; Agaev, Yadullayev, Akhmedov, Kerimov, Kurbanov M., Tagizade (Isaev 68), Vasilyev (Khankishiev 61), Sirkhaev, Lychkin (Stukas 74), Kurbanov K..
LIECHTENSTEIN - Jehle; Lingg, Hasler, Zech, Stocklasa Ma., Ritter, Telser, Stocklasa Mi. (Wohlwend 74), Frick C., Bicker (Beck M. 59), Benz (Beck T. 46).

05/06/99, Lisbon
PORTUGAL 1 Capucho (62)
SLOVAKIA 0
referee - Larsen (DEN)

PORTUGAL - Vítor Baía; Abel Xavier (Sérgio Conceição 31), Fernando Couto, Paulo Madeira, Dimas, Paulo Sousa, Paulo Bento, Rui Costa, Figo (Pedro Barbosa 90), João Pinto (Capucho 61), Sá Pinto.
SLOVAKIA - König; Varga, Timko, Karhan, Kratochvil, Zvara (Valachovic 31), Tomaschek, Pinte (Slicho 66), Labant, Dubovsky, Majoros (Kozuch 85).

05/06/99, Bucharest
ROMANIA 2 Ilie (3), Munteanu D. (15)
HUNGARY 0
referee - Pedersen (NOR)
ROMANIA - Lobont; Petrescu, Filipescu, Popescu Gh., Nanu, Petre, Hagi (Lupescu 46), Gâlca, Munteanu D., Moldovan (Ganea 60), Ilie (Craioveanu 87).
HUNGARY - Király; Sebök V., Hrutka, Mátyus, Korsós G., Dárdai, Halmai, Illés (Preisinger 83), Egressy, Sebök J. (Herczeg 76), Fehér M. (Pisont 46).

09/06/99, Győr
HUNGARY 0
SLOVAKIA 1 Fabus (53)
referee - Díaz Vega (ESP)
HUNGARY - Király; Sebök V., Hrutka, Mátyus, Korsós G., Dárdai, Halmai (Pisont 73), Illés, Egressy (Dombi 60), Sebök J., Somogyi (Preisinger 78).
SLOVAKIA - König; Varga, Timko, Karhan, Kratochvil, Zvara (Dzurik 81), Valachovic, Pinte, Labant, Nemeth, Fabus.

09/06/99, Coimbra
PORTUGAL 8 Sá Pinto (22, 44, 51), João Pinto (40, 59, 68), Rui Costa (80, 90p)
LIECHTENSTEIN 0
referee - Drabek (AUT)
PORTUGAL - Vítor Baía; Secretário (Capucho 14), Fernando Couto, Paulo Madeira, Dimas, Paulo Sousa (Pedro Barbosa 64), Sérgio Conceição, Rui Costa, Figo, João Pinto, Sá Pinto.
LIECHTENSTEIN - Jehle; Zech, Hasler, Ospelt, Ritter, Telser D. (Lingg 52), Stocklasa Mi. (Burgmeier 66), Wohlwend, Telser M. (Büchel 75), Bicker, Beck T..

09/06/99, Bucharest
ROMANIA 4 Ganea (35), Munteanu D. (44p), Vladoiu (48), Rosu (90)
AZERBAIJAN 0
referee - Siric (CRO)
ROMANIA - Lobont; Petrescu, Filipescu, Popescu Gh., Nanu, Petre (Moldovan 66), Gâlca, Lupescu, Munteanu D., Ganea (Craioveanu 60), Vladoiu (Rosu 77).
AZERBAIJAN - Kramarenko; Agaev (Getman 71), Yadullayev, Akhmedov, Lychkin (Vasilyev 82), Kerimov, Kurbanov M. (Musayev 59), Tagizade, Kurbanov K., Poshekhontsev, Sirkhaev.

EURO 2000 QUALIFYING GROUP EIGHT

Politics and war overshadow the football

Malta's Nicky Saliba (centre) tries to sheild the ball from Yugoslavia's Albert Nadj (left) and Dejan Stankovic (right).

With three countries from the former Yugoslavia in this five-team group, it was almost inevitable that there would be interference of a non-footballing nature. The conflict in Kosovo ensured that would be the case, with only 11 of the original 15 fixtures scheduled for the 1998/99 season actually taking place. Between November and June only one match went ahead as planned. The remainder were all postponed as a result of the war in the Balkans.

The Football Association of Ireland were unwittingly drawn into the world of international politics when they refused to comply with UEFA instructions to stage their scheduled fixture at home to Yugoslavia in early June. They did, however, rearrange a home fixture with Macedonia for a few days later and the Irish won that, 1-0, to maintain a 100 per cent home record that gave them every chance of going on to top the group or, failing that, qualify for the play-offs.

Mick McCarthy's men got off to the perfect start, beating a World Cup-weary and indisciplined Croatia 2-0 at Lansdowne Road through two early goals from Manchester United duo Denis Irwin (a penalty) and Roy Keane (a close-range

TOP SCORERS

3   Savo MILOSEVIC
    (Yugoslavia)
    Davor SUKER (Croatia)
2   Predrag MIJATOVIC
    (Yugoslavia)
    Albert NADJ (Yugoslavia)
    Robbie KEANE (Rep. Ireland)
    Roy KEANE (Rep. Ireland)
    Niall QUINN (Rep. Ireland)
    Zvonimir BOBAN (Croatia)
    Davor VUGRINEC (Croatia)
    Risto BOZINOV (Macedonia)
    Artim SAKIRI (Macedonia)

header). The latter was on target again the following month, and so too was his teenaged namesake Robbie, who struck twice to become his country's youngest-ever goalscorer as the Irish easily beat Malta 5-0 at the same venue. They had been supposed to play Yugoslavia four days prior to that game, but, with tensions mounting in the Balkans, they had to wait a month until it was safe to fly to Belgrade. When they got there, they put up a decent defensive performance and ensured a fairly sterile and uneventful game, but a defensive mix-up involving Gary Breen and Steve Staunton enabled Predrag Mijatovic to slide home the winner midway through the second half.

Yugoslavia went on to play just two more fixtures during the season, both of them against Malta. As expected, they were victorious on both occasions. Midfielder

GROUP EIGHT TABLE

GROUP EIGHT TABLE (at 30/06/99)

			Home				Away				Total					
		Pd	W	D	L	F	A	W	D	L	F	A	W	D	L	F	A	Pt	GD
1	Yugoslavia	3	2	0	0	5	1	1	0	0	3	0	3	0	0	8	1	9	+7
2	Rep. Ireland	4	3	0	0	8	0	0	0	1	0	1	3	0	1	8	1	9	+7
3	Croatia	4	1	0	0	3	2	1	1	1	5	4	2	1	1	8	6	7	+2
4	Macedonia	5	1	1	0	5	1	1	0	2	4	5	2	1	2	9	6	7	+3
5	Malta	6	0	0	3	2	9	0	0	3	1	13	0	0	6	3	22	0	-19

EURO 2000 QUALIFYING GROUP EIGHT

1998/99 MATCH DETAILS

05/09/98, Dublin
REPUBLIC OF IRELAND 2 Irwin (2p), Keane Roy (15)
CROATIA 0
referee - Melo Pereira (POR)
REPUBLIC OF IRELAND - Given; Irwin, Staunton, McAteer, Cunningham, Babb, Kinsella, Keane Roy, O'Neill (Cascarino 5), Keane Rob. (Carsley 61), Duff (Kenna 46).
CROATIA - Ladic; Soldo (Tokic 77), Stimac, Simic D., Tudor (Krpan 65), Jurcic, Boban, Asanovic, Jarni, Stanic, Maric (Pamic 46).

06/09/98, Skopje
MACEDONIA 4 Bozinov (20, 48), Sakiri (75, 80)
MALTA 0
referee - Wegereef (HOL)
MACEDONIA - Milosevski; Lazarevski, Stojkovski (Gosev 80), Nikolovski (Sainovski 78), Sedloski, Micevski, Stojanoski (Sakiri 70), Trenevski, Zaharievski, Stavrevski, Bozinov.
MALTA - Muscat; Said, Magri Overand, Debono, Chetcuti, Turner, Agius (Suda 70), Brincat, Zahra (Carabott 78), Busuttil, Camilleri.

10/10/98, Ta' Qali
MALTA 1 Suda (29p)
CROATIA 4 Simic D. (54), Vugrinec (67, 74), Suker (80)
referee - Benedik (SVK)
MALTA - Muscat; Buttigieg, Spiteri, Debono, Chetcuti, Suda (Turner 57), Agius (Zammit 54), Brincat, Zahra (Sixsmith 77), Busuttil, Camilleri.
CROATIA - Ladic; Simic D. (Tokic 81), Soldo, Tudor, Saric, Maric, Boban, Asanovic, Jarni (Cvitanovic 87), Suker, Vucko (Vugrinec 16).

14/10/98, Zagreb
CROATIA 3 Suker (16), Boban (45, 70)
MACEDONIA 2 Cirlc (2), Sainovski (55)
referee - Levnikov (RUS)
CROATIA - Ladic; Tudor, Stimac, Simic D., Stanic (Jurcic 80), Soldo, Boban, Asanovic (Saric 62), Jarni, Maric, Suker.
MACEDONIA - Milosevski; Sedloski, Stavrevski, Nikolovski (Stojanoski 77), Sainovski, Zaharievski, Micevski (Gosev 46), Lazarevski (Bozinov 60), Trenevski, Sakiri, Ciric.

14/10/98, Dublin
REPUBLIC OF IRELAND 5 Keane Rob. (16, 18), Keane Roy (54), Quinn (63), Breen (82)
MALTA 0
referee - Olsen (NOR)
REPUBLIC OF IRELAND - Given; Kenna, Staunton, McAteer (Carsley 84), Cunningham, Breen, Kinsella, Keane Roy, Quinn (Cascarino 74), Keane Rob. (Kennedy 83), Duff.
MALTA - Cini; Debono, Buttigieg, Spiteri, Carabott, Brincat, Zahra (Zammit 70), Sixsmith (Camilleri 77), Chetcuti, Turner, Suda (Agius 65).

18/11/98, Ta' Qali
MALTA 1 Sixsmith (69)
MACEDONIA 2 Nikolovski (49), Zaharievski (62)
referee - Shmolik (BLS)
MALTA - Muscat; Sixsmith, Camilleri, Buttigieg, Spiteri, Debono, Busuttil, Saliba (Turner 68), Brincat, Nwoko (Carabott 56), Cutajar (Agius 60).
MACEDONIA - Milosevski; Veselinoski, Nikolovski, Sedloski, Babunski, Stavrevski, Zaharievski, Micevski, Sainovski, Bozinov (Trenevski 65), Sakiri.

18/11/98, Belgrade
YUGOSLAVIA 1 Mijatovic (63)
REPUBLIC OF IRELAND 0
referee - Nilsson (SWE)
YUGOSLAVIA - Kralj; Djukic, Djorovic, Mihajlovic, Jokanovic, Jugovic (Grodzic 84), Stojkovic (Kovacevic 46), Stankovic J., Stankovic D., Mijatovic, Milosevic (Drulovic 77).
REPUBLIC OF IRELAND - Given; Cunningham, Irwin, McLoughlin (Connolly 73), Breen, Staunton, Kinsella, Keane Roy, Quinn (Cascarino 73), McAteer (O'Neill 82), Duff.

10/02/99, Ta' Qali
MALTA 0
YUGOSLAVIA 3 Nadj (22, 56), Milosevic (90)
referee - Garibian (FRA)
MALTA - Barry; Said, Turner, Spiteri, Camilleri (Sixsmith 72), Buttigieg, Busuttil, Saliba, Carabott, Nwoko (Cutajar 81), Agius (Bencini 58).
YUGOSLAVIA - Kralj; Mirkovic, Djorovic, Jokanovic, Djukic, Mihajlovic, Stankovic J. (Tomic 75), Nadj, Stankovic D. (Grodzic 88), Mijatovic, Kovacevic D. (Milosevic 70).

05/06/99, Skopje
MACEDONIA 1 Hristov (80)
CROATIA 1 Suker (19)
referee - Dallas (SCO)
MACEDONIA - Milosevski; Nikolovski, Stojanoski, Stavrevski, Babunski (Zaharievski 75), Sainovski, Micevski, Trenevski (Bozinov 46), Trajcov (Hristov 75), Sakiri, Ciric.
CROATIA - Ladic; Juric, Simic D., Soldo, Saric, Boban, Asanovic, Vugrinec (Vlaovic 64), Jarni, Suker, Boksic (Rapaic 19).

08/06/99, Salonika (Greece)
YUGOSLAVIA 4 Mijatovic (33), Milosevic (47, 90), Kovacevic D. (74)
MALTA 1 Saliba (6)
referee - Ståhl (SWE)
YUGOSLAVIA - Kralj; Mirkovic, Djukic, Djorovic, Saveljic, Stojkovic (Drulovic 77), Nadj (Milosevic 46), Jokanovic, Stankovic D. (Grozdic 61), Mijatovic, Kovacevic.
MALTA - Barry; Buhagiar (Cutajar 80), Said, Debono, Chetcuti, Buttieg, Saliba, Camilleri (Brincat 64), Carabott, Busuttil, Nwoko (Sultana 83).

EURO 2000 QUALIFYING GROUP EIGHT

1998/99 MATCH DETAILS

09/06/99, Dublin
REPUBLIC OF IRELAND 1 Quinn (67)
MACEDONIA 0
referee - Meier (SUI)
REPUBLIC OF IRELAND - Kelly A,; Carr, Irwin, Duff (Kilbane 63),
Cunningham, Breen, Kennedy, Kinsella, Quinn (Connolly 81), Keane Rob.
(Cascarino 68), Carsley.
MACEDONIA - Milosevski; Stavrevski, Babunski, Stojanoski, Trajcov
(Memedi 46), Micevski, Trenevski (Hristov 77), Sainovski (Sedloski 70),
Nikolovski, Ciric, Sakiri.

GROUP EIGHT

1999/2000 FIXTURES

18/08/99	Yugoslavia v Croatia
28/08/99	Croatia v Malta
01/09/99	Rep. Ireland v Yugoslavia
04/09/99	Croatia v Rep. Ireland
05/09/99	Yugoslavia v Macedonia
08/09/99	Malta v Rep. Ireland
	Macedonia v Yugoslavia
10/10/99	Croatia v Yugoslavia
	Macedonia v Rep. Ireland

Albert Nadj was an unlikely two-goal match-winner on their visit to the Mediterranean island in February, and there was considerable consternation in the Yugoslav camp during the first half of the return fixture, played in neutral Salonika, until substitute Savo Milosevic turned the game around in their favour after the interval.

Yugoslavia's 4-1 win over Malta was a repeat of Croatia's victory by the same scoreline in Ta' Qali eight months earlier, when they had also had to come from behind to win. Miroslav Blazevic's side, third at the World Cup in France, appeared to be heading for disaster until a late goal-flurry got them out of jail. They also fell behind at home to Macedonia four days later before old reliables Davor Suker and Zvonimir Boban rescued them. Boban, the Croatian captain, had a particularly memorable night, scoring two exquisite goals. The free-kick which won the match 20 minutes from time could not have been struck more precisely. It curled right into the top corner, leaving Macedonian 'keeper Petar Milosevski rooted helplessly to the spot.

The Croatians had to wait another eight months until they took the field again. Once more their opponents were

Macedonia, and once more they were to find things much more difficult than expected. Davor Suker's 41st international goal (on his 49th appearance) gave them an early lead, but Macedonia, urged on by a passionate crowd, came back strongly in the second half and deservedly equalised, through Georgi Hristov's well-placed shot, ten minutes from the end.

The Macedonian crowd were cock-a-hoop at the final whistle, but their 1-0 defeat in Dublin four days later effectively ended their qualifying hopes. With so many matches still to play, including both mammoth confrontations between Yugoslavia and Croatia, it was impossible to predict at the close of the season how the group would end up. But there was a strong possibility that neither first or second place would be resolved until the final set of matches scheduled for the beginning of October, with Croatia hosting the Yugoslavs and Ireland travelling to Macedonia...

Republic of Ireland's Jeff Kenna (right) battles against Croatia's Igor Pamic (left).

EURO 2000 QUALIFYING GROUP NINE

Perfect Czechs qualify for finals in style

The Czech Republic may not have qualified for the World Cup finals in France but their second-place finish at Euro '96, coupled with the luck of the draw, rewarded them with a very easy Euro 2000 qualifying group. They were not expected to have any difficulty finishing first in a section that comprised Scotland, Lithuania, Bosnia-Herzegovina,

Estonia and the Faroe Islands, and by the end of the season, with seven wins out of seven, they duly celebrated their second successive qualification for the European Championship finals.

The match that confirmed the Czechs' presence in Belgium and Holland, against Scotland in Prague, showed just how accomplished and resilient a team they had become under their popular new coach Jozef Chovanec. 0-2 down to a surprisingly attack-minded Scottish team after just over an hour's play, they came back brilliantly to win 3-2, with substitutes Pavel Kuka and Jan Koller adding to defender Tomas Repka's first international goal amid scenes of delirium in the Letna stadium.

To become the first qualifiers for the finals was one thing; to do it with a perfect record was quite another. The Czechs simply never dropped their guard. A hint of controversy overshadowed their first victory, 1-0 away to the Faroe Islands, but they were in top form for their next two matches, away to Bosnia-Herzegovina and at home to Estonia. Patrik Berger's two free-kick goals in the 4-1 win against the Estonians in Teplice were extra special, and the Liverpool schemer was on target again in the same stadium five months later when the Czechs continued their winning sequence with a 2-0 triumph over Lithuania.

By this stage the other teams in the group were beginning to fear the worst, and when Chovanec's men claimed victory number five, away to Scotland at Celtic Park, it was obvious that they would go on to win the

TOP SCORERS

4 Patrik BERGER
   (Czech Republic)
3 Vladimir SMICER
   (Czech Republic)
   Billy DODDS (Scotland)
   Elvir BOLIC
   (Bosnia-Herzegovina)
   Valdas IVANAUSKAS
   (Lithuania)
   Sergei TEREHHOV (Estonia)
2 Jan KOLLER (Czech Republic)
   Pavel KUKA (Czech Republic)
   Allan JOHNSTON (Scotland)
   Elvir BALJIC
   (Bosnia-Herzegovina)
   Andres OPER (Estonia)
   Uni ARGE (Faroe Islands)

GROUP NINE

1999/2000 FIXTURES

04/09/99	Bosnia-Herzegovina v Scotland
	Faroe Islands v Estonia
	Lithuania v Czech Republic
08/09/99	Estonia v Scotland
	Faroe Islands v Lithuania
	Czech Republic v
	Bosnia-Herzegovina
05/10/99	Scotland v Bosnia-Herzegovina
09/10/99	Czech Republic v Faroe Islands
	Scotland v Lithuania
	Estonia v Bosnia-Herzegovina

GROUP NINE TABLE

GROUP NINE TABLE (at 30/06/99)

| | | | Home | | | | Away | | | | Total | | | | | | |
		Pd	W	D	L	F	A	W	D	L	F	A	W	D	L	F	A	Pt	GD
1	Czech Republic	7	3	0	0	9	3	4	0	0	8	2	7	0	0	17	5	21	+12
2	Scotland	6	2	0	1	6	5	0	2	1	3	4	2	2	2	9	9	8	0
3	Bosnia-Herzegovina	6	2	1	1	5	4	0	1	1	4	6	2	2	2	9	10	8	-1
4	Lithuania	7	1	2	1	5	4	1	0	2	2	5	2	2	3	7	9	8	-2
5	Estonia	7	1	0	2	6	4	1	1	2	6	9	2	1	4	12	13	7	-1
6	Faroe Islands	7	0	2	1	3	4	0	1	3	1	8	0	3	4	4	12	3	-8

EURO 2000 QUALIFYING GROUP NINE

1998/99 MATCH DETAILS

Previous result
ESTONIA 5, FAROE ISLANDS 0

19/08/98, Sarajevo
BOSNIA-HERZEGOVINA 1 Baljic (65)
FAROE ISLANDS 0
referee - Mikulski (POL)
BOSNIA-HERZEGOVINA - Dedic; Kapetanovic, Barbarez (Mujdza 75), Konjic,
Varesanovic, Hibic, Bolic (Mujcin 65), Halilovic, Kodro, Salihamidzic (Sabic 81),
Baljic.
FAROE ISLANDS - Mikkelsen; Hansen H.F., Hansen J.K., Thorsteinsson,
Johannesen, Jarnskor H., Joensen S., Johnsson, Mørkøre, Arge (Borg 78), Petersen.

05/09/98, Sarajevo
BOSNIA-HERZEGOVINA 1 Barbarez (75p)
ESTONIA 1 Hibic (29og)
referee - Agius (MLT)
BOSNIA-HERZEGOVINA - Dedic; Varesanovic, Konjic, Hibic, Kapetanovic,
Salihamidzic, Katana (Mujcin 60), Halilovic (Bolic 77), Mujdza (Sabic 67),
Barbarez, Baljic.
ESTONIA - Poom; Rooba (Meet 81), Kirs, Hohlov-Simson, Reim, Smirnov,
Terehhov, Kristal, Alonen, Zelinski (Viikmäe 81), Oper.

05/09/98, Vilnius
LITHUANIA 0
SCOTLAND 0
referee - Zotta (ROM)
LITHUANIA - Stauce; Sugzda (Buitkus 63), Semberas, Zutautas R., Zvirgzdauskas,
Mikulenas (Slekys 90), Skerla, Baltusnikas, Preiksaitis, Jankauskas, Skarbalius.
SCOTLAND - Leighton; Dailly, Boyd, Elliott, Hendry, Calderwood (Davidson 71),
Lambert, Gallacher, McCoist (McCann 83), Jackson (Ferguson 57), Collins.

06/09/98, Toftir
FAROE ISLANDS 0
CZECH REPUBLIC 1 Smicer (85)
referee - Hirviniemi (FIN)
FAROE ISLANDS - Mikkelsen; Johannesen, Hansen J.K., Thorsteinsson, Hansen
H.F., Jarnskor H., Arge (Jarnskor M. 79), Johnsson, Mørkøre, Jonsson, Petersen.
CZECH REPUBLIC - Postulka; Rada, Bejbl (Latal 81), Suchoparek, Votava, Cizek
(Berger 55), Nemec, Nedved, Lokvenc, Poborsky (Sloncik 81), Smicer.

10/10/98, Sarajevo
BOSNIA-HERZEGOVINA 1 Topic (88)
CZECH REPUBLIC 3 Baranek (12), Smicer (59), Kuka (90)
referee - Messina (ITA)
BOSNIA-HERZEGOVINA - Dedic; Varesanovic, Konjic, Hibic, Kapetanovic,
Salihamidzic (Demirovic 65), Katana, Halilovic, Mujcin (Topic 63), Barbarez, Baljic
(Besirevic 71).
CZECH REPUBLIC - Postulka; Baranek (Rada 71), Repka, Suchoparek, Latal,
Votava, Nemec, Bejbl, Lokvenc (Kuka 79), Smicer (Sloncik 86), Berger.

10/10/98, Vilnius
LITHUANIA 0
FAROE ISLANDS 0

referee - Schaack (LUX)
LITHUANIA - Stauce; Skerla, Mikalajunas (Zvingilas 74), Zutautas R., Baltusnikas,
Zvirgzdauskas, Mikulenas (Buitkus 46), Ivanauskas, Skarbalius, Preiksaitis,
Jankauskas.
FAROE ISLANDS - Mikkelsen; Johannesen, Hansen J.K., Thorsteinsson, Hansen
H.F., Joensen S., Jarnskor H., Johnsson, Arge (Borg 87), Jonsson, Petersen.

10/10/98, Edinburgh
SCOTLAND 3 Dodds (70, 85), Hohlov-Simson (78og)
ESTONIA 2 Hohlov-Simson (35), Smirnov (76)
referee - Bento Marques (POR)
SCOTLAND - Leighton; Weir, Davidson, Calderwood (Donnelly 57), Hendry, Boyd,
McKinlay, Durrant, McCoist (Dodds 69), Gallacher (Jackson 18), Johnston.
ESTONIA - Poom; Kirs, Hohlov-Simson, Reim, Rooba, Kristal, Smirnov, Alonen,
Terehhov, Zelinski (Viikmäe 88), Oper.

14/10/98, Teplice
CZECH REPUBLIC 4 Nedved (9), Berger (22, 42), Lokvenc (45))
ESTONIA 1 Arbeiter (90)
referee - Olafsson (ISL)
CZECH REPUBLIC - Postulka; Latal, Suchoparek, Repka, Votava (Rada 53),
Nedved, Nemec, Bejbl (Cizek 80), Berger, Lokvenc (Kuka 61), Smicer.
ESTONIA - Poom; Smirnov (Nõmmik 46), Meet, Hohlov-Simson, Rooba, Alonen,
Terehhov (O'Konnel-Bronin 63), Oper, Viikmäe (Arbeiter 46), Reim, Zelinski.

14/10/98, Vilnius
LITHUANIA 4 Ivanauskas (10, 67, 75), Baltusnikas (90)
BOSNIA-HERZEGOVINA 2 Konjic (5), Baljic (68)
referee - Schüttengruber (AUT)
LITHUANIA - Stauce; Skerla, Mikalajunas (Baltusnikas 87), Zutautas R.,
Gleveckas, Zvirgzdauskas, Semberas, Ivanauskas, Skarbalius (Zvingilas 62),
Preiksaitis, Jankauskas (Danilevicius 79).
BOSNIA-HERZEGOVINA - Dedic; Varesanovic, Konjic, Ramcic, Kapetanovic
(Mujdza 80), Salihamidzic, Katana (Topic 75), Halilovic, Mujcin (Besirevic 80),
Barbarez, Baljic.

14/10/98, Aberdeen
SCOTLAND 2 Burley (22), Dodds (45)
FAROE ISLANDS 1 Petersen (86p)
referee - Kapitanis (CYP)
SCOTLAND - Sullivan; Weir, Davidson, Elliott, Hendry, Boyd, McKinlay (Durrant
46), Donnelly, Dodds, Burley, Johnston (Glass 79).
FAROE ISLANDS - Mikkelsen; Hansen H.F., Johannesen, Hansen J.K.,
Thorsteinsson, Petersen, Joensen S., Johnsson, Jarnskor H. (Hansen J. 81), Arge
(Borg 69), Jonsson.

27/03/99, Teplice
CZECH REPUBLIC 2 Hornak (10), Berger (74p)
LITHUANIA 0
referee - Juhás (HUN)
CZECH REPUBLIC - Srnicek; Repka, Suchoparek, Hornak, Poborsky (Kuka 63),
Hasek, Nemec, Berger, Nedved, Lokvenc (Koller 71), Smicer (Baranek 80).
LITHUANIA - Stauce; Skerla, Zvirgzdauskas, Zutautas D., Semberas, Vainoras,
Preiksaitis, Skarbalius, Mikalajunas (Mikulenas 78), Ivanauskas (Buitkus 83),

EURO 2000 QUALIFYING GROUP NINE

group. The Scots had not lost a qualifying match at home for 12 years - a span of 26 matches - but the Czechs rocked them with two sucker-punches in the first half and might even have extended their lead after the interval when man of the match Berger twice went close to scoring. Eoin Jess's goal for Scotland served as a mere consolation. The Czechs were worthy winners.

Another victory in Estonia followed by that 3-2 triumph over the Scots in Prague completed the Czechs' magnificent season and clinched the sole automatic qualifying spot,

but for the other teams in the group there was still plenty at stake. The play-off place was very much up for grabs, with Scots, Bosnians, Lithuanians and Estonians all still harbouring realistic ambitions of claiming it.

As things stood at the end of the season, Scotland, despite their two defeats by the Czechs and an embarrassing 1-1 draw in the Faroe Islands, still looked favourites to finish runners-up. They still had two matches to play against Bosnia-Herzegovina, and they had the advantage of playing their last two fixtures at home.

1998/99 MATCH DETAILS

Jankauskas (Zvingilas 67).

31/03/99, Vilnius
LITHUANIA 1 Fomenka (83)
ESTONIA 2 Terehhov (49, 78)
referee - Trentalange (ITA)
LITHUANIA - Stauce; Skerla, Zutautas R., Zvirgzdauskas, Semberas, Vainoras, Preiksaitis, Maciulevicius, Mikalajunas, Skarbalius (Gleveckas 37; Buitkus 56), Mikulenas (Fomenka 46).
ESTONIA - Poom; Lemsalu, Kirs, Hohlov-Simson, Saviauk, Svets (Kristal 68), Terehhov, Oper (Zelinski 66) Viikmäe, Smirnov (Alonen 90), Reim.

31/03/99, Glasgow
SCOTLAND 1 Jess (68)
CZECH REPUBLIC 2 Elliott (27og), Smicer (36)
referee - Nielsen (DEN)
SCOTLAND - Sullivan; Hopkin, Davidson (Johnston 52), Elliott, Boyd, Weir, Burley, Lambert, McCann, McAllister (Hutchison 64), Jess.
CZECH REPUBLIC - Srnicek; Hornak, Votava, Suchoparek, Poborsky (Rada 76), Hasek, Nedved, Berger, Nemec, Smicer (Baranek 84), Lokvenc (Kuka 70).

05/06/99, Sarajevo
BOSNIA-HERZEGOVINA 2 Kodro (26p), Bolic (90)
LITHUANIA 0
referee - Ibañez (ESP)
BOSNIA-HERZEGOVINA - Dedic; Smajic, Kapetanovic, Varesanovic, Hibic, Repuh (Bolic 87), Besirevic, Sabic, Topic (Turkovic 90), Kodro (Mujcin 79), Salihamidzic.
LITHUANIA - Leusas; Skerla, Skinderis, Gvildys, Kancelskis, Mikalajunas, Zvirgzdauskas, Semberas (Mikulenas 64), Maciulevicius (Fomenka 46), Ivanauskas, Preiksaitis.

05/06/99, Tallinn
ESTONIA 0
CZECH REPUBLIC 2 Berger (45), Koller (83)
referee - Roca (ESP)
ESTONIA - Poom; Lemsalu, Kirs, Hohlov-Simson, Saviauk, Alonen (Smirnov 65; O'Konnel-Bronin 74), Terehhov (Shvets 80), Kristal, Oper, Reim, Viikmäe.
CZECH REPUBLIC - Srnicek; Suchoparek, Repka, Hornak, Poborsky, Hasek, Nedved (Galasek 85), Berger, Nemec, Smicer (Kuka 65), Lokvenc (Koller 70).

05/06/99, Toftir
FAROE ISLANDS 1 Hansen H.F. (90)
SCOTLAND 1 Johnston (38)
referee - Kalt (FRA)
FAROE ISLANDS - Mikkelsen; Johannesen, Hansen H.F., Thorsteinsson, Hansen Ø. (Hansen J. 85), Johnsson, Joensen J. (Borg 70), Joensen S., Jonsson, Mørkøre, Petersen (Arge 82).
SCOTLAND - Sullivan; Weir, Davidson, Elliott, Calderwood, Boyd, Durrant (Cameron 46), Gallacher (Jess 89), Dodds, Lambert, Johnston (Gemmill 86).

09/06/99, Prague
CZECH REPUBLIC 3 Repka (65), Kuka (75), Koller (87)
SCOTLAND 2 Ritchie (30), Johnston (62)
referee - Krug (GER)
CZECH REPUBLIC - Srnicek; Poborsky (Kuka 69), Berger, Hornak, Suchoparek, Repka, Nedved, Hasek (Baranek 61), Nemec, Lokvenc (Koller 69), Smicer.
SCOTLAND - Sullivan; Johnston, Davidson, Weir, Boyd, Ritchie, Lambert, Calderwood, Gallacher, Dodds, Durrant (Jess 71).

09/06/99, Tallinn
ESTONIA 1 Oper (10)
LITHUANIA 2 Ramelis (51), Maciulevicius (56)
referee - Albrecht (GER)
ESTONIA - Poom; Lemsalu, Kirs, Kaal, Viikmäe, Alonen, Terehhov (O'Konnel-Bronin 75), Kristal (Shvets 81), Oper, Reim, Zelinski.
LITHUANIA - Leusas; Skerla, Skinderis, Zutautas D. (Maciulevicius 46), Zutautas R., Mikalajunas, Zvirgzdauskas, Ramelis, Razanauskas, Skarbalius, Ivanauskas (Preiksaitis 87).

09/06/99, Toftir
FAROE ISLANDS 2 Arge (38, 47)
BOSNIA-HERZEGOVINA 2 Bolic (13, 50)
referee - Jones (ENG)
FAROE ISLANDS - Mikkelsen; Johannesen, Joensen S., Thorsteinsson, Hansen Ø. (Jarnskor H. 65), Johnsson, Hansen H.F., Arge (Joensen J. 87), Mørkøre, Jonsson, Petersen.
BOSNIA-HERZEGOVINA - Dedic; Smajic, Besirevic, Varesanovic, Hibic, Repuh (Osmanhodzic 78), Sabic, Topic (Muratovic 85), Turkovic (Joldic 63), Bolic, Mujcin.

UEFA CHAMPIONS' LEAGUE

UEFA's grand designs for Champions' League expansion were put on hold for a year as, for once, their blue riband event retained the same shape and dimensions as the previous year's model.

UEFA had been forced into a charm offensive by the lurking menace of the alternative 'European Super League', but their efforts to entrance Europe's leading clubs into remaining loyal to the UEFA family were confined to the theoretical in 1998/99. The big, revolutionary changes would not be applied until 1999/2000.

Even so, UEFA already knew they were onto a winner.

Interest in their premier club competition had evolved to such an extent that for most of the Continent's richest and most celebrated clubs the Champions' League was the only place to be. It had got to the point where qualifying for the Champions' League had actually become more important than winning the domestic championship, which, of course, in the case of a select few countries, could be achieved merely by finishing second.

Once again, the eight runners-up from the highest-ranked UEFA member nations took their place in the qualifying round. Before the arrival of the aristocrats,

PRELIMINARY ROUND RESULTS

(July 22/29, 1998)

Beitar Jerusalem 4 (Shitrit 2, Sallói 9, 45, 78), **B36 1** (Petersen 73p)
B36 0, Beitar Jerusalem 1 (Hamar 68)
(Beitar Jerusalem 5-1)

Celtic 0, St. Patrick's Athletic 0
St. Patrick's Athletic 0, Celtic 2 (Brattbakk 12, Larsson 72)
(Celtic 2-0)

Cliftonville 1 (Flynn 45),
1.FC Kosice 5 (Zvara 22, 28, Nemeth 35, Lyubarskyi 65, Prohaszka 78)
1.FC Kosice 8 (Kozak 1. 4, Janocko 14, 54, Nemeth 32, Prohaszka 59, 72, Lyubarskyi 67, Kozlej 84), **Cliftonville 0**
(1.FC Kosice 13-1)

Dinamo Tbilisi 1 (Khomeriki 53), **Vllaznia Shkodër 0** (awarded 3-0)
Vllaznia Shkodër 3 (Cungu 14, Miloti 86, Noga 90p),
Dinamo Tbilisi 1 (Ashvetia 89)
(Dinamo Tbilisi 4-3)

Dynamo Kyiv 8 (Rebrov 9, 16, 37, 82, Shevchenko 34, 60, Gerasimenko 48, Belkevich 65), **Barry Town 0**
Barry Town 1 (Williams 30),
Dynamo Kyiv 2 (Mykhailenko 11, Venhylynskyi 50)
(Dynamo Kyiv 10-1)

Grasshopper-Club Zürich 6 (N'Kufo 6, 51, Kavelashvili 29, Cabanas 41, Tikva 65p, Tararache 90), **Jeunesse Esch 0**
Jeunesse Esch 0, Grasshopper-Club Zürich 2 (Esposito 37p, Türkyilmaz 44)
(Grasshopper-Club Zürich 8-0)

HJK 2 (Wiss 50, Kuqi 85), **FK Yerevan 0**
FK Yerevan 0, HJK 3 (Lehkosuo 1, 81p, Jäväjä 27)
(HJK 5-0)

Kareda Siauliai 0, Maribor Teatanic 3 (Gajser 42, 87, Filipovic 70)
Maribor Teatanic 1 (Balajic 78), **Kareda Siauliai 0**
(Maribor Teatanic 4-0)

Liteks Lovech 2 (Bushi 8, Yurukov 90), **Halmstads BK 0**
Halmstads BK 2 (Sakiri 39, Arvidsson 43),
Liteks Lovech 1 (Yurukov 77)
(Liteks Lovech 3-2)

LKS Lodz 4 (Cebula 12, Trzeciak 50p, 76p, Wieszczycki 73),
Kapaz Ganja 1 (Suleymanov 82)
Kapaz Ganja 1 (Smirnov 55),
LKS Lodz 3 (Trzeciak 44, 49, Wieszczycki 81)
(LKS Lodz 7-2)

Obilic Beograd 2 (Juksic 18, Grozdic 65), **ÍBV 0**
ÍBV 1 (Haflidason 22), **Obilic Beograd 2** (Vasiljevic 65, Grozdic 87)
(Obilic Beograd 4-1)

Sileks Kratovo 0, Club Brugge KV 0
Club Brugge KV 2 (Vermant 13, Claessens 30), **Sileks Kratovo 1** (Bozinov 76)
(Club Brugge KV 2-1)

Skonto Riga 0, Dinamo Minsk 0
Dinamo Minsk 1 (Osipovich 26),
Skonto Riga 2 (Astafyev 45, Novikov 72)
(Skonto Riga 2-1)

Steaua Bucuresti 4 (Ciocoiu 12, 40, Serban 77p, Danciulescu 89),
FC Flora Tallinn 1 (Terehhov 40)
FC Flora Tallinn 3 (Smirnov 42, Zelinski 46, Oper 81),
Steaua Bucuresti 1 (Danciulescu 71)
(Steaua Bucuresti 5-4)

Valletta 0, Anorthosis Famagusta 2 (Elia 50, Okkas 78)
Anorthosis Famagusta 6 (Ciric 16, Charalambous 18, Andreou 45p, Sotiriou 51, 90, Okkas 75), **Valletta 0**
(Anorthosis Famagusta 8-0)

Zimbru Chisinau 1 (Kulik 11p), **Újpest FC 0**
Újpest FC 3 (Miriuta 17, Kovács 72, 90), **Zimbru Chisinau 1** (Kulik 18)
(Újpest FC 3-2)

UEFA CHAMPIONS' LEAGUE

however, it was necessary to clear away the riff-raff. That procedure took place in the preliminary round, scheduled out of season in the last two weeks of July.

PRELIMINARY ROUND

With the draw for the qualifying round already made, the 32 teams entering the preliminary round knew which opponents were waiting for them if they made it through. For some, the prize on offer was a guaranteed pay-day against one of Europe's top teams. For all, the incentive to win was great, because qualification ensured participation in either the Champions' League or, for the qualifying-round losers, the first round proper of the UEFA Cup. The preliminary-round losers, on the other hand, would be out of Europe for good.

UEFA's co-efficient and seeding system is elaborate and complex, but it cannot be considered as scrupulously fair. Otherwise Dynamo Kiev, the previous season's quarter-finalists, would not have found themselves forced to do battle in the preliminary round with League of Wales champions Barry Town for the second year running. In the event, the Ukrainians were probably pleased to have the practice. They destroyed their opponents 8-0 at home in the first leg, with Serhiy Rebrov scoring four goals and his strike-partner Andriy Shevchenko supplying two more.

Most of the favoured teams came through, although some were pressed rather harder than they might have imagined. Former winners Celtic, for instance, could only draw 0-0 in front of a huge crowd of 56,864 at home to League of Ireland minnows St. Patrick's Athletic before dominating the second leg in Dublin. Belgian champions Bruges were also made to live on their nerves against Sileks Kratovo of Macedonia, while Steaua Bucharest, another one-time winner of the trophy, were grateful for their 4-1 first-leg advantage against Flora Tallinn of Estonia.

Dinamo Tbilisi were extremely lucky to get past Vllaznia Shkodër. The Georgians won their home leg 1-0 but the result was later changed to 3-0 when it emerged that the Albanians had fielded an ineligible player. Vllaznia made a valiant effort to rectify the error in the home leg but the deficit proved just too great.

The Baltic confrontation between Skonto Riga and Dinamo Minsk was another evenly-balanced contest. Minsk seemed to hold the advantage after drawing the away leg 0-0 but the Latvians came back at them well in the return, winning 2-1 to book themselves a high-profile clash with the Italians of Inter in the next round.

QUALIFYING ROUND

Inter, the Serie A runners-up, joined seven other non-champions at this stage of the competition. All eight had had the opportunity to study their opponents twice during the preliminary round so they knew what to expect. Given the benefits they enjoyed, it was widely anticipated that they would all qualify for the Champions' League.

In fact, only seven of them made it. French side FC Metz were calamitously bundled out by Finnish champions HJK, 2-1 on aggregate. The Finns were not the only survivors from the preliminary round. There was one other - Dynamo Kiev, who were extremely fortunate to progress at the expense of Czech champions Sparta Prague. Beaten 1-0 at home, the Ukrainians did not get back into the tie until one minute from the end of the second leg when a scrappy own-goal, initiated by Shevchenko, saved them. The outcome was resolved by a penalty shoot-out, which Kiev won 3-1.

Most of the fancied teams did enough in the first legs to ensure a smooth passage. Inter and Bayern Munich both ran up problem-free 4-0 victories at home. Inter were inspired by Roberto Baggio, who celebrated his official début for the club, against Skonto Riga, by creating all three first-half goals before scoring himself after the interval. Bayern were struggling to make headway against Yugoslavia's Obilic Belgrade until a scrambled goal, credited to new signing Stefan Effenberg, set up a second-half goal onslaught. Benfica did even better, hitting Beitar Jerusalem for six, while Spartak Moscow scored five times in the second half away to Liteks Lovech. Their 6-2 victory in Moscow two weeks later completed an 11-2 rout, with five Spartak players all helping themselves to two goals apiece over the tie.

Manchester United were far superior to LKS Lodz but could manage only two goals at Old Trafford before settling for a bore draw in Poland. Celtic scraped a 1-0 home win against Croatia Zagreb but were torn apart in the return, with two-goal Robert Prosinecki inspiring the Croatian champions to a 3-0 victory. Athletic Bilbao also came back from a first-leg defeat, 2-1 against Dinamo Tbilisi, to go through on the away-goals rule and ensure a trio of Spanish teams in the group phase.

The most exciting fightback, however, came from PSV. Beaten 2-1 in Slovenia by Maribor, they fell further behind when a defensive error allowed Dalibor Filipovic to lob 'keeper Patrik Lodewijks. Ruud van Nistelrooy quickly equalised for the home side but with an hour gone Maribor came within inches of settling the tie when Damjan Gajser struck an upright. That was the Slovenians'

UEFA CHAMPIONS' LEAGUE

QUALIFYING ROUND RESULTS

(August 12/26, 1998)

FC Bayern München 4 (Effenberg 59, Elber 63, Zickler 65, Fink 76),
Obilic Beograd 0

Obilic Beograd 1 (Sarac 67), **FC Bayern München 1** (Matthäus 89)
(FC Bayern München 5-1)

SL Benfica 6 (Pembridge 24, 82, Deane 29, Calado 63p, Shelach 80og, Nuno Gomes 86p), **Beitar Jerusalem 0**

Beitar Jerusalem 4 (Hamar 24, Sallói 26, Shitrit 51, Abuksis 79),
SL Benfica 2 (Nuno Gomes 17p, João Pinto 89)
(SL Benfica 8-2)

Celtic 1 (Jackson 51), **Croatia Zagreb 0**

Croatia Zagreb 3 (Maric 23, Prosinecki 44p, 69), **Celtic 0**
(Croatia Zagreb 3-1)

Dinamo Tbilisi 2 (Khomeriki 15, Tskitishvili 30), **Athletic Bilbao 1** (Imaz 47)

Athletic Bilbao 1 (Etxeberria J. 51), **Dinamo Tbilisi 0**
(2-2; Athletic Bilbao on away goal)

Dynamo Kyiv 0, Sparta Praha 1 (Baranek 5)

Sparta Praha 0, Dynamo Kyiv 1 (Votava 89og) (aet)
(1-1; Dynamo Kyiv 3-1 on pens.)

Galatasaray 2 (Hagi 59p, Hakan Sükür 67),
Grasshopper-Club Zürich 1 (Vogel 87)

Grasshopper-Club Zürich 2 (Türkyilmaz 45, Vogel 71p),
Galatasaray 3 (Hakan Sükür 18, 45, Hagi 64p)
(Galatasaray 5-3)

HJK 1 (Riihilahti 72), **FC Metz 0**

FC Metz 1 (Meyrieu 79p), **HJK 1** (Vasara 69)
(HJK 2-1)

Inter 4 (Zamorano 4, Simeone 10, Ventola 20, Baggio 59), **Skonto Riga 0**

Skonto Riga 1 (Mikholap 22),
Inter 3 (Zamorano 8, Galante 54, Djorkaeff 70)
(Inter 7-1)

1.FC Kosice 0, Brondby IF 2 (Daugaard 54, Thygesen 85)

Brondby IF 0, 1.FC Kosice 1 (Lapsansky 39)
(Brøndby IF 2-1)

Liteks Lovech 0,
Spartak Moskva 5 (Pisarev 55, 86, Titov 67, Samarone 77, Tsymbalar 90)

Spartak Moskva 6 (Tikhonov 8, 32, Titov 37, Tsymbalar 49, Robson 56, 90),
Liteks Lovech 2 (Beliakov 27, Bushi 70)
(Spartak Moskva 11-2)

Manchester United 2 (Giggs 16, Cole 81), **LKS Lodz 0**

LKS Lodz 0, Machester United 0
(Manchester United 2-0)

Maribor Teatanic 2 (Filipovic 14, Breznik 85), **PSV 1** (Marcos 61)

PSV 4 (Van Nistelrooy 8, Bruggink 70, Rommedahl 100, De Bilde 103),
Maribor Teatanic 1 (Filipovic 4) (aet)
(PSV 5-3)

Olympiakos 2 (Yannakopoulos 11, Luciano 32),
Anorthosis Famagusta 1 (Mihajlovic 68)

Anorthosis Famagusta 2 (Mihajlovic 36, Krcmarevic 80),
Olympiakos 4 (Yorgatos 47, Djordjevic 57, 85, Gogic 90)
(Olympiakos 6-3)

Rosenborg BK 2 (Rushfeldt 61, Skammelsrud 81), **Club Brugge KV 0**

Club Brugge KV 4 (Fadiga 22, Claessens 47, 85, Schockaert 78),
Rosenborg BK 2 (Rushfeldt 43, 71)
(4-4; Rosenborg BK on away goals)

Steaua Bucuresti 2 (Serban 9, Szekely 75),
Panathinaikos 2 (Asanovic 5, Liberopoulos 68)

Panathinaikos 6 (Milojevic 8p, Lincar 27og, Liberopoulos 34, Warzycha 59, 67, Asanovic 87), **Steaua Bucuresti 3** (Rachita 13, 17, Belodedici 61)
(Panathinaikos 8-5)

SK Sturm Graz 4 (Vastic 7, 70, Neukirchner 82, Haas 89), **Újpest FC 0**

Újpest FC 2 (Kovács 36, Jenei 72),
SK Sturm Graz 3 (Haas 8, Reinmayr 51, 57)
(SK Sturm Graz 7-2)

---

last chance. Soon afterwards Arnold Bruggink volleyed PSV into the lead on the night, and two goals in three extra-time minutes were enough to put Bobby Robson's team through to join Europe's élite in the next round.

GROUP A

Qualifiers Olympiakos and Croatia Zagreb joined exempt clubs Ajax and FC Porto in this nicely-balanced group. All four teams had it in them to reach the knockout phase, although only Ajax and Porto had been there before.

Croatia Zagreb had impressed in knocking out Celtic, but their first-ever Champions' League encounter, at home to Ajax, failed to live up to expectations. Despite the fervour of their support, they could do no more than draw 0-0. The other opening encounter also finished with honours even, although Olympiakos certainly emerged the far happier team after scoring twice late on to rescue a point away to FC Porto.

The next round of matches saw the Greeks go to the top of the table. They were good value for their 2-0 win at

UEFA CHAMPIONS' LEAGUE

CHAMPIONS' LEAGUE GROUP A

(September 16, 30, October 21, November 4, 25, December 9, 1998)

RESULTS

Croatia Zagreb 0, Ajax 0

FC Porto 2 (Zahovic 64, Jardel 81),
Olympiakos 2 (Yanakopoulos 79, Gogic 90)

Ajax 2 (Rudy 57, Litmanen 86p), **FC Porto 1** (Zahovic 69)

Olympiakos 2 (Alexandris 21, Gogic 80), **Croatia Zagreb 0**

Olympiakos 1 (Alexandris 38), **Ajax 0**

FC Porto 3 (Drulovic 33, Zahovic 43, 76), **Croatia Zagreb 0**

Ajax 2 (Witschge 33, Gorré 88), **Olympiakos 0**

Croatia Zagreb 3 (Mikic 7, Rukavina 37, Mujcin 61),
FC Porto 1 (Jardel 38)

Ajax 0, Croatia Zagreb 1 (Simic J. 58)

Olympiakos 2 (Gogic 18, Djordjevic 54), **FC Porto 1** (Zahovic 80)

Croatia Zagreb 1 (Jelicic 35), **Olympiakos 1** (Yanakopoulos 64)

FC Porto 3 (Zahovic 53, 71, Drulovic 79), **Ajax 0**

FINAL TABLE			Home			Away					Total					
		Pd	W	D	L	F	A	W	D	L	F	A	W	D	L	F	A	Pt	GD
1	Olympiakos	6	3	0	0	5	1	0	2	1	3	5	3	2	1	8	6	11	+2
2	Croatia Zagreb	6	1	2	0	4	2	1	0	2	1	5	2	2	2	5	7	8	-2
3	FC Porto	6	2	1	0	8	2	0	0	3	3	7	2	1	3	11	9	7	+2
4	Ajax	6	2	0	1	4	2	0	1	2	0	4	2	1	3	4	6	7	-2

home to Croatia Zagreb, while Ajax could count them-selves extremely lucky to take the three points at home to Porto. Although their first goal, struck venomously from long range by Andrzej Rudy, was a beauty, the one which won the game, four minutes from time, was highly con-tentious, with Jari Litmanen converting from the penalty spot after substitute Gerald Sibon went sprawling in the area.

Olympiakos and Ajax faced each other in the next two matchdays, and they were to claim a home win each. The Greeks took the points in front of nearly 80,000 in Athens thanks to a splendid volley hooked home by Alexandros Alexandris from Grigoris Yeorgatos's left-wing cross. But Ajax gained their revenge a fortnight later with goals from Richard Witschge and Dean Gorré. The latter's delight-ful lob in the 88th minute had added significance because it put Ajax top of the group courtesy of their superior head-to-head record.

Porto and Croatia Zagreb also traded home wins. Slovenian Zlatko Zahovic maintained his record of scoring in every game when he netted a brace in the Das Antas stadium to add to a stunning 35-yard free-kick goal from Doriva. The Croatians finally ended their goal drought in the return match, winning 3-1 to put themselves back in with a chance of qualification.

Zagreb's hopes rose dramatically when, to general astonishment, they won 1-0 away to Ajax in their next

Jari Litmanen of Ajax (right) celebrates scoring the winner against FC Porto.

UEFA CHAMPIONS' LEAGUE

game. They had to win to stay alive, and they did their duty thanks to a finely judged lob from young substitute striker Josip Simic. With Olympiakos simultaneously completing their third home win out of three - 2-1 against Porto after Ljubinko Drulovic had missed a penalty - it meant that with one game left Ajax had blown their chances of winning the group. Olympiakos were clear favourites to reach the quarter-finals. Porto were already out.

To guarantee a first-place finish the Greeks had to win or draw their final game, in Zagreb. They could also afford to lose the match by up to three goals and still top the group on the condition that Ajax did not win in Oporto. But if Ajax won - and they still had a remote chance of taking one of the best runners-up spots - a defeat by any scoreline would be good enough for Croatia Zagreb.

By half-time of the final encounters, all permutations remained open. Olympiakos were being beaten 1-0 on a frost-bound pitch in Zagreb, while Ajax were having the better of a goalless draw in Oporto. In the second 45 minutes, however, eveything changed. Zlatko Zahovic, twice served by his forward partner Jardel, scored his sixth and seventh goals of the competition (the best total in all six groups) to see off Ajax, while Olympiakos found the net with their first chance of the game, Stelios Yanakopoulos stooping to head home from a corner.

It finished 3-0 in Oporto, with Drulovic adding a late solo goal, and 1-1 in Zagreb. Olympiakos were therefore the clear group winners and went through to the Champions' Cup quarter-finals for the first time in their history.

GROUP B

There was no doubt who the favourites were in this group. Juventus, who had reached the previous three Champions' Cup finals, were expected to sail through a section containing experienced but hardly formidable opposition. After the draw the Italians were installed as 3-1 favourites to win the tournament.

There was a shock for Marcello Lippi's men on opening night, however, as they were held 2-2 in the Stadio delle Alpi by Galatasaray. It all started well enough for the *Bianconeri* when Pippo Inzaghi put them ahead with a sumptuous overhead kick after 16 minutes. But the sending-off of goalkeeper Angelo Peruzzi after half an hour (for handling outside his area) sent panic waves through the team and by the end they were grateful to take the 2-2 draw.

There was another upset in the other tie, with Rosenborg grabbing a useful 1-1 draw in Bilbao courtesy of a beautifully struck shot by Roar Strand. Things got even worse for the Spaniards when they lost their next fixture, away to Galatasaray. They were undone in stoppage-time by a typically ferocious left-foot drive from veteran Romanian schemer Gheorghe Hagi. His goal put Galatasaray on top of the group, because Rosenborg and Juventus drew 1-1 in Trondheim. Once again Inzaghi gave the Italians an early advantage, but the Norwegians, always strong at home, came back to equalise through a Bent Skammelsrud penalty. Shortly afterwards, however, Skammelsrud went from hero to villain when he missed a second effort from the spot.

Juventus had been let off the hook in their first two

CHAMPIONS' LEAGUE GROUP B

(September 16, 30, October 21, November 4, 25, December 2/9, 1998)

RESULTS

Athletic Bilbao 1 (Etxeberria J. 5), **Rosenborg BK 1** (Strand 66)

Juventus 2 (Inzaghi 16, Birindelli 67), **Galatasaray 2** (Hakan Sükür 44, Ümit 63)

Galatasaray 2 (Okan 16, Hagi 90), **Athletic Bilbao 1** (Urzaiz 17)

Rosenborg BK 1 (Skammelsrud 69p), **Juventus 1** (Inzaghi 27)

Athletic Bilbao 0, Juventus 0

Rosenborg BK 3 (Rushfeldt 69, 86, 90), **Galatasaray 0**

Juventus 1 (Laso 69og), **Athletic Bilbao 1** (Guerrero 45)

Galatasaray 3 (Hakan Sükür 55, 74, Arif 66), **Rosenborg BK 0**

Rosenborg BK 2 (Sørensen 2, 50), **Athletic Bilbao 1** (Pérez 90)

Galatasaray 1 (Suat 90), **Juventus 1** (Amoruso 78)

Athletic Bilbao 1 (Guerrero 43), **Galatasaray 0**

Juventus 2 (Inzaghi 16, Amoruso 36), **Rosenborg BK 0**

FINAL TABLE		Home					Away					Total						
		Pd	W	D	L	F	A	W	D	L	F	A	W	D	L	F	A	Pt	GD
1	Juventus	6	1	2	0	5	3	0	3	0	2	2	1	5	0	7	5	8	+2
2	Galatasaray	6	2	1	0	6	2	0	1	2	2	6	2	2	2	8	8	8	0
3	Rosenborg BK	6	2	1	0	6	2	0	1	2	1	6	2	2	2	7	8	8	-1
4	Athletic Bilbao	6	1	2	0	2	1	0	1	2	3	5	1	3	2	5	6	6	-1

UEFA CHAMPIONS' LEAGUE

encounters, and they were even luckier in their next two games, both against Athletic Bilbao. The first match, in the Basque country, was pretty much one-way traffic in the direction of the Juventus goal, but Peruzzi, back from his suspension, had an inspired evening, making save after save to thwart the Bilbao attack. 0-0 at the final whistle, Juve could be pleased with a job well done, but that first victory remained elusive. It seemed they would have to win the return in Turin to keep their hopes alive, but once again they could only draw. For the second successive home match they had to come from behind even to get a point, and the goal which cancelled out Julen Guerrero's opener was as inelegant as they come, Mikel Lasa bundling the ball over his own goalline after a scramble induced by Paolo Montero's goalbound header.

Juve's position was helped by the fact that Rosenborg and Galatasaray cancelled each other out, each winning 3-0 at home. The Norwegians got in the first blows, with Sigurd Rushfeldt claiming a 21-minute hat-trick in the latter stages of the first encounter in Trondheim. Galatasaray also waited until the second half two weeks later before asserting their supriority in Istanbul. This time it was the turn of Galatasaray's prolific striker, Hakan Sükür, to take centre stage.

With seven points from four games, Galatasaray led the group, but their eagerly-anticipated home match with Juventus, scheduled for matchday five, had to be postponed because of a diplomatic crisis between Turkey and Italy over the extradition of Kurdish separatist guerilla leader Abdullah Ocalan. Juventus, trying to take advantage of the situation, requested that the game be staged at a neutral venue, but in the end it was merely delayed by a week, during which time Rosenborg had leapfrogged into first place with another convincing home win, 2-1 against Bilbao, who were thus eliminated.

The Italian players were none too happy to be forced to travel to Istanbul in such a hostile climate. However, the Turkish authorities took no security risks, and the match was played against a backdrop of armed policemen and soldiers. Juventus had to go for the win, and they so nearly got what they wanted when Nicola Amoruso put them ahead 12 minutes from time. But the Turks refused to throw in the towel and in the dying seconds they found the equaliser that enabled them to join Rosenborg at the top of the table, with Juve still three points adrift.

It looked grim for the Italians, but in fact the odds still favoured them to reach the quarter-finals. This was because the final two fixtures had them up against Rosenborg in the Stadio delle Alpi, with Bilbao entertaining

Galatasaray in the San Mamés. Both the Norwegians and the Turks were notoriously poor travellers, and if the two matches both resulted in home wins, Juventus would qualify on account of their better three-way head-to-head record with Galatasaray and Rosenborg.

And so it transpired. Juventus secured their victory early, through Inzaghi and Amoruso, while Bilbao offered them a helping hand, beating Galatasaray with a solitary goal from Julen Guerrero. The Turks should have provided a final twist to the tale but midfielder Okan failed to convert a simple header right at the death. Juventus could hardly believe their luck, and there were a fair few fans from teams in other groups shaking their heads in disbelief at the way the Italians had staged their second great Champions' League escape in successive years. They had just eight points and one win from their six games, but they were in the quarter-finals, and that was all that mattered.

GROUP C

Two of the tournament favourites found themselves pitched together in this section. Real Madrid and Inter were both European trophy-holders, of Champions' Cup and UEFA Cup respectively. With those two super-heavyweights to contend with, the prospects did not look good for either Spartak Moscow or Sturm Graz, the two pre-qualifiers.

The fixture schedule seemed to favour Inter. Although their first match was away to Real, it coincided with the holders' one-match stadium ban - a legacy of the farcical broken goalposts episode in the previous season's semi-final. So instead of entering the den of the Bernabéu, the Italians took on the holders in Seville. The game did not live up to pre-match hype, and the two sides both looked out of condition, but the points went to Real thanks to a couple of refereeing decisions in their favour. Scotsman Hugh Dallas sent off Inter defender Salvatore Fresi and then awarded a controversial late penalty to the Spaniards, which skipper Fernando Hierro converted. Clarence Seedorf's last-minute goal was simply the icing on the cake as the holders completed an important but unconvincing victory.

With Spartak Moscow also winning 2-0, away to Sturm Graz, group leadership was at stake when Real travelled to Moscow for their second fixture. Despite the wretched state of the Russian economy, 80,000 Muscovites turned up at the Luzhniki stadium. They were to go home in raptures as Spartak came from a goal behind (a header from Raúl) to clinch victory with two wonderful late strikes from midfielders Ilya Tsymbalar and Yegor Titov - their two scorers also from the first game in Graz.

UEFA CHAMPIONS' LEAGUE

With that win Spartak became the only one of the 24 Champions' League sides to take maximum points from their opening two fixtures. But they could not afford to be too euphoric because their next two games were both against Inter, the team that had dumped them out of the UEFA Cup semi-finals six months earlier. Inter were back in contention themselves but only as a result of a lucky 1-0 win against Sturm Graz in the San Siro. Their winning goal arrived from Youri Djorkaeff in the fifth minute of stoppage-time. Sturm looked down and out after that cruel setback, and in their next two games the Austrians were no more than cannon fodder for Real Madrid, who made the most of their Bernabéu homecoming with a 6-1 victory, which was then followed by another slaughter in the Arnold Schwarzenegger stadium in a match delayed 24 hours because of a waterlogged pitch.

The real intrigue lay elsewhere. In Milan, Inter had some very sticky moments before they eventually saw off Spartak with a 2-1 win, the decisive goal coming from Ronaldo in his comeback match after youngster Nicola Ventola had opened the scoring with a superb free-kick. In Moscow, with another massive crowd in attendance despite the chilly temperatures, it was Spartak who did most of the running. They looked to be heading for another famous win when Andrei Tikhonov's long-range strike entered the net via Inter 'keeper Gianluca Pagliuca's back after hitting the post, but with just one minute left poor marking at a free-kick allowed Diego Simeone to find the net with one of his trademark headers and steal a potentially priceless point for the Italians.

Spartak still remained in contention, but it was imperative for them to win their next home game against pointless Sturm. That they didn't was down to a phenomenal performance from Sturm's Polish goalkeeper Kazimierz Sidorczuk, who effectively blocked Spartak's route to the quarter-finals by forcing a 0-0 draw.

That result left Inter and Real to slug it out for group leadership. The Italians were going through a difficult patch at home and for much of the match in the San Siro they looked uninspired and heavy-legged. But cometh the hour, cometh the man, and Roberto Baggio, the scourge of Spain at the 1994 World Cup, came off the bench to break Spanish hearts once again, twice finding the target in the last four minutes to secure the victory that enabled Inter to overtake Real and move to the top of the table.

By the time Inter went to freezing Graz for their final fixture they had a different coach, Romanian Mircea Lucescu. His first important mission was to steer the team to the victory in Austria that would ensure their safe passage through to the quarter-finals. Although the conditions were less than ideal, Inter were too good for their opponents, and two excellent second-half goals from Javier Zanetti and - that man again - Baggio completed a very successful first Champions' League for the Nerazzurri.

Real, though unable to finish first, had to beat Spartak in the Bernabéu to secure one of the two best runners-up berths. They were all over the Russians in the first half, with Raúl's header giving them scant reward for their supremacy. Another headed goal from Sávio midway through the second period ended the match as a contest before

CHAMPIONS' LEAGUE GROUP C

(September 16, 30, October 21, November 4, 25, December 9, 1998)

RESULTS

Real Madrid 2 (Hierro 79p, Seedorf 90), Inter 0

SK Sturm Graz 0, Spartak Moskva 2 (Titov 60, Tsymbalar 63)

Inter 1 (Djorkaeff 90), SK Sturm Graz 0

Spartak Moskva 2 (Tsymbalar 72, Titov 77), Real Madrid 1 (Raúl 63)

Real Madrid 6 (Sávio 13, 90, Raúl 22, Jarni 61, 78, Popovic 67og), SK Sturm Graz 1 (Vastic 8)

Inter 2 (Ventola 32, Ronaldo 58), Spartak Moskva 1 (Tsymbalar 65)

Spartak Moskva 1 (Tikhonov 68), Inter 1 (Simeone 90)

SK Sturm Graz 1 (Haas 3),
Real Madrid 5 (Panucci 8, 61, Mijatovic 34, Seedorf 57, Suker 74)

Inter 3 (Zamorano 50, Baggio 86, 90), Real Madrid 1 (Seedorf 58)

Spartak Moskva 0, SK Sturm Graz 0

Real Madrid 2 (Raúl 34, Sávio 66), Spartak Moskva 1 (Khlestov 89)

SK Sturm Graz 0, Inter 2 (Zanetti J. 63, Baggio 80)

FINAL TABLE				Home						Away						Total					
		Pd	W	D	L	F	A	W	D	L	F	A	W	D	L	F	A	Pt	GD
1	Inter	6	3	0	0	6	2	1	1	1	3	3	4	1	1	9	5	13	+4
2	Real Madrid	6	3	0	0	10	2	1	0	2	7	6	4	0	2	17	8	12	+9
3	Spartak Moskva	6	1	2	0	3	2	1	0	2	4	4	2	2	2	7	6	8	+1
4	SK Sturm Graz	6	0	0	3	1	9	0	1	2	1	7	0	1	5	2	16	1	-14

UEFA CHAMPIONS' LEAGUE

Spartak bowed out of the competition with a late consolation goal.

Real had finished second, but the holders had no need to feel any shame. With 12 points collected from a possible 18, their total was superior to that of four group winners. They, like Inter, thoroughly deserved their place in the last eight.

GROUP D

No doubt about it, this was the toughest of the six Champions' League groups. While Brøndby had every reason to lick their lips at the prospect of three sell-out home fixtures against Bayern Munich, Manchester United and Barcelona, the Danes' chances of reaching the next round were virtually nil. But which of the three giants would rule the roost? The contest was wide open, but great football seemed guaranteed.

Manchester United and Barcelona combined to produce a rip-roaring spectacle at Old Trafford in the opening game. It was thrill-a-minute stuff as the Spaniards came back twice, from 2-0 and 3-2 down, to force a 3-3 draw. United took command with a headed goal from Ryan Giggs and a close-range effort from Paul Scholes but Barça ended the first half strongly and made an even better start to the second when Sonny Anderson latched on to a lucky ricochet to make it 2-1. The scores were level after an hour when Giovanni crashed in a penalty awarded for a foul by Jaap Stam on Rivaldo. But a brilliant free-

kick by David Beckham - a carbon copy of his strike for England against Colombia at the World Cup - put United back in front. The lead did not last long. Nicky Butt handled on the goal-line. He was sent off and Luis Enrique scored the penalty. 3-3. United were down to ten men, and for the last 19 minutes Barcelona swarmed all over their goal, but there was no further scoring, and in the end the draw was a fair and appropriate result, even if both teams probably felt that they should have won.

The mood in both camps no doubt lifted when news filtered through of Bayern Munich's dramatic defeat away to Brøndby. The Germans appeared to be on their way to victory when Markus Babbel headed in Stefan Effenberg's free-kick, but sensationally the Danes came storming back, equalising with an own-goal from Bayern skipper Thomas Helmer and then bringing the house down with a fantastic solo goal from midfielder Allan Ravn.

Brøndby could not repeat their heroic deeds in the Nou Camp two weeks later. Two Anderson goals brought Barcelona a straightforward 2-0 win. In Munich, however, there was more last-minute drama as Bayern stole a late goal themselves to draw 2-2 with Manchester United. Alex Ferguson's team were denied a famous victory when goalkeeper Peter Schmeichel made a crass error of judgment in trying to collect a long throw. The goal was credited to Bayern striker Elber but appeared to go in off the head of United's Teddy Sheringham. Goals from Dwight Yorke and Paul Scholes had put United in a commanding

CHAMPIONS' LEAGUE GROUP D

(September 16, 30, October 21, November 4, 25, December 9, 1998)

RESULTS

Brøndby IF 2 (Helmer 87og, Ravn 89), **FC Bayern München 1** (Babbel 77)

Manchester United 3 (Giggs 17, Scholes 24, Beckham 64),
FC Barcelona 3 (Anderson 47, Giovanni 60p, Luis Enrique 71p)

FC Barcelona 2 (Anderson 43, 84), **Brøndby IF 0**

FC Bayern München 2 (Elber 11, 90),
Manchester United 2 (Yorke 29, Scholes 49)

Brøndby IF 2 (Daugaard 35, Sand 90), **Manchester United 6**
(Giggs 2, 21, Cole 28, Keane 55, Yorke 59, Solskjaer 62)

FC Bayern München 1 (Effenberg 45), **FC Barcelona 0**

FC Barcelona 1 (Giovanni 28p),
FC Bayern München 2 (Zickler 47, Salihamidzic 87)

Manchester United 5 (Beckham 7, Cole 13, Neville P. 16, Yorke 28, Scholes 62), **Brøndby IF 0**

FC Barcelona 3 (Anderson 1, Rivaldo 56, 72),
Manchester United 3 (Yorke 25, 68, Cole 53)

FC Bayern München 2 (Jancker 51, Basler 57), **Brøndby IF 0**

Manchester United 1 (Keane 43), **FC Bayern München 1** (Salihamidzic 56)

Brøndby IF 0, FC Barcelona 2 (Figo 5, Rivaldo 35)

FINAL TABLE				Home					Away					Total					
		Pd	W	D	L	F	A	W	D	L	F	A	W	D	L	F	A	Pt	GD
1	FC Bayern München	6	2	1	0	5	2	1	1	1	4	4	3	2	1	9	6	11	+3
2	Manchester United	6	1	2	0	9	4	1	2	0	11	7	2	4	0	20	11	10	+9
3	FC Barcelona	6	1	1	1	6	5	1	1	1	5	4	2	2	2	11	9	8	+2
4	Brøndby IF	6	1	0	2	4	9	0	0	3	0	9	1	0	5	4	18	3	-14

UEFA CHAMPIONS' LEAGUE

position after losing an early (offside) goal to the Germans, but although Bayern rallied strongly in the last half-hour, United resisted well and were unfortunate not to take all three points.

United's next trip was to Copenhagen. After two draws they needed a win, and although David Beckham and Nicky Butt were suspended, they fancied their chances against Peter Schmeichel's old club. Two early Ryan Giggs goals sent them on their way, and when Andy Cole grabbed a third soon afterwards, the three points were secure. United eventually romped to a 6-2 victory, with Roy Keane, Dwight Yorke and Ole Gunnar Solskjaer all adding their names to the scoresheet in the second half. Brøndby appeared to have learned no lessons from the thrashing because a fortnight later United set hungrily about them again and came away with another big win, with five different goalscorers contributing to the 5-0 rout.

Meanwhile, Bayern Munich were also claiming an impressive 'double' themselves, adding a 2-1 victory over Barcelona in the Nou Camp to a 1-0 win in the Olympiastadion. Stefan Effenberg swept home the only goal in the first encounter, but goalkeeper Oliver Kahn was the man of the match as he kept out the Brazilian trio of Rivaldo, Giovanni and Anderson with a string of fine saves. Giovanni did get the ball past him in the rematch at the Nou Camp - from a harshly conceded penalty - but Bayern dug deep and emerged victorious once again, with Bosnian striker Hasan Salihamidzic muscling his way past a weak challenge from Sergi and slipping the ball into the far corner to give the Germans victory three minutes from the end. It was the second time in three years that Bayern had beaten Barcelona 2-1 in the Nou Camp.

With their Champions' League future hanging by a thread, Barcelona faced Manchester United at home fully aware that anything less than a victory would bring elimination at the group stage of the competition for the second year running. United, equally, knew that, with Bayern facing an easy home game with Brøndby, they too would probably have to win to remain top of the group. With both teams committed to attack, excitement was guaranteed.

Barcelona struck within fifty seconds of the start. Poor United defending allowed Anderson to score his fourth goal of the competition, and there must have been a fear swelling up in the English team's ranks that they would be in for another mauling like the one a few years earlier, when Barcelona tanned them 4-0. But this United side was made of sterner stuff. They scored with almost their first attack, Dwight Yorke rifling a low right-foot shot beyond Ruud Hesp to bring his team level. It was a tremendous

first half but the quality of play got even better after the interval. United went ahead with a truly outstanding second goal, Andy Cole finding the net after some wonderful combination play with Yorke. But another Schmeichel error gifted Barça an equaliser, from Rivaldo's free-kick. The action was fast and furious now and when Yorke, playing out of his skin, restored United's lead with a free header from a perfect David Beckham cross, the balance again tipped in the visitors' favour. But while Yorke's performance was world-class, so too was Rivaldo's, and the Brazilian made it 3-3 with a crafty overhead kick before sending another fierce left-foot drive crashing against the crossbar. The last 15 minutes were hyperactive, with good chances being created at both ends. But neither team could snatch the winner they needed. When the final whistle sounded, both teams looked disconsolate - despite the ovation they received from the crowd. The second 3-3 thriller between the two teams meant that United no longer held first place and Barcelona were out.

Bayern Munich had duly risen to the top of the table by beating Brøndby 2-0 - their third win in a row. It left them requiring just a draw against Manchester United at Old Trafford to finish above their only remaining rivals for group leadership. United knew that a victory was their only guarantee to reach the quarter-finals but that they were in a strong position to qualify as one of the best two runners-up with a draw.

As expected, it was a very even contest. United took the lead just before half-time when Roy Keane smashed in a low right-foot shot on the run. The goal was perfectly executed and perfectly timed, but United were to pay for a horrible double miss by Ronny Johnsen just after the interval. A goal then would have put them in the clear but Bayern began to take charge and although their equaliser, through Hasan Salihamidzic, was the consequence of poor defending, it was well deserved. At 1-1 United began to concern themselves with results elsewhere, and as the news filtered through that a draw would probably be enough, it became obvious from the action of both sets of players that a mutually beneficial draw had been agreed upon. In fact, when all the final scores from the other groups were gathered together, it emerged that any scoreline at Old Trafford would have enabled both Bayern and United to qualify. It had all been a phoney war...

GROUP E

This was the only group without a former winner. Lens, of France, were the weakest seeds, but that was levelled out

UEFA CHAMPIONS' LEAGUE

by the presence of Dynamo Kiev, the most dangerous of all the floaters.

English champions Arsenal were especially delighted to draw Lens because it meant that Dennis Bergkamp, who refuses to set foot on an aeroplane, could travel comfortably over land and sea to the away leg. That was the first match of the programme and it was one Arsenal really should have won. They were much the better side, but Bergkamp and his French strike-partner Nicolas Anelka missed a succession of good chances, and with just one goal in the bag, from Marc Overmars, they paid the price for their profligacy in the second minute of injury-time when the home side bundled in an equaliser from a corner.

There was a surprise in the other opening tie when Panathinaikos came from behind to beat Dynamo Kiev 2-1 in Athens, with the Ukrainian defence twice being exposed in the air. The Greeks' next game was at Wembley Stadium, where Arsenal had chosen to hold their Champions' League matches in order to meet ticket demand. The stadium was full to capacity and Arsenal treated the big crowd to another confident performance. Still, however, the goals would not come, and it was left to centre-backs Tony Adams and Martin Keown to break the deadlock midway through the second half. Meanwhile, in Kiev, Dynamo Kiev's poor start continued when they could only draw 1-1 at home to Lens, Tony Vairelles equalising for the French champions barely a minute after

Andriy Shevchenko had headed the home side in front.

The Ukrainians could afford no more false moves and they came to Wembley with the firm objective of taking the three points. They more than matched Arsenal in the first half and were considerably superior in the second. There was a terrible miscarriage of justice when Shevchenko put the visitors in front after a defence-splitting one-two, only to be wrongly flagged offside. It looked like it was going to be one of those nights for Kiev when, just a minute later, Dennis Bergkamp headed in a spectacular goal from Lee Dixon's measured cross. Marc Overmars should have made it 2-0 after 87 minutes but his goalbound shot was brilliantly cleared off the line by Oleh Luzhnyi. It proved an important stop because three minutes later Kiev got an equaliser, Serhiy Rebrov slotting the ball into the net from close range. Once again Arsenal had conceded a last-minute equaliser. It had become a very costly habit.

Arsenal now shared first place with Lens, who won 1-0 at home to Panathinaikos. But the fourth matchday was to turn everything on its head. Panathinaikos gave Lens a taste of their own medicine in Athens, reciprocating with a 1-0 victory courtesy of a late goal, while Dynamo Kiev at long last registered their first victory, at the expense of Arsenal. In truth, the English champions went to Kiev with only half a team. With Bergkamp grounded and Adams, Overmars and Anelka all injured, it was very much a damage-limitation mission for Arsène

CHAMPIONS' LEAGUE GROUP E

(September 16, 30, October 21, November 4, 25, December 9, 1998)

RESULTS

RC Lens 1 (Keown 90og), **Arsenal** 1 (Overmars 51)

Panathinaikos 2 (Mykland 57, Liberopoulos 69), **Dynamo Kyiv** 1 (Rebrov 31)

Arsenal 2 (Adams 63, Keown 73), **Panathinaikos** 1 (Mauro 88)

Dynamo Kyiv 1 (Shevchenko 61), **RC Lens** 1 (Vairelles 62)

Arsenal 1 (Bergkamp 73), **Dynamo Kyiv** 1 (Rebrov 90)

RC Lens 1 (Eloi 81), **Panathinaikos** 0

Dynamo Kyiv 3 (Rebrov 27p, Holovko 62, Shevchenko 72), **Arsenal** 1 (Hughes 83)

Panathinaikos 1 (Vokolos 83), **RC Lens** 0

Arsenal 0, **RC Lens** 1 (Debève 72)

Dynamo Kyiv 2 (Rebrov 72, Basinas 80og), **Panathinaikos** 1 (Lagonikakis 36)

Panathinaikos 1 (Sypniewski 74), **Arsenal** 3 (Mendez 66, Anelka 78, Boa Morte 85)

RC Lens 1 (Smicer 77), **Dynamo Kyiv** 3 (Kaladze 60, Vashchuk 76, Shevchenko 85)

FINAL TABLE

			Home				Away				Total						
		Pd	W	D	L	F	A	W	D	L	F	A	W	D	L	F	A	Pt	GD
1	Dynamo Kyiv	6	2	1	0	6	3	1	1	1	5	4	3	2	1	11	7	11	+4
2	RC Lens	6	1	1	1	3	4	1	1	1	2	2	2	2	2	5	6	8	-1
3	Arsenal	6	1	1	1	3	3	1	1	1	5	5	2	2	2	8	8	8	0
4	Panathinaikos	6	2	0	1	4	4	0	0	3	2	5	2	0	4	6	9	6	-3

UEFA CHAMPIONS' LEAGUE

Wenger's side. To their credit, they gave it their best shot and created enough chances to get something out of the game, but the luck they had enjoyed at Wembley deserted them and in any case Kiev proved themselves once more to be a very strong side, capping a solid 3-1 victory with a splendid free-kick from the excellent Shevchenko.

Kiev's next opponents were new group leaders Panathinaikos. A victory would send the Ukrainians to the top of the group. They needed it badly but they played poorly and were fortunate to take the three points through a farcical own-goal ten minutes from time. Arsenal and Lens both required a victory to join Kiev on eight points. They met at Wembley, where, once again, the Londoners were unable to field a full-strength side. Emmanuel Petit was suspended while Vieira and Bergkamp were both injured. Even so, Arsenal created enough chances to take the lead and build on it, but once again Anelka and co. left their shooting boots in the dressing room. Lens, too, made incursions into the Arsenal defence and after 72 minutes they scored. Michaël Debève managed to find space at the far post to convert Vladimir Smicer's low cross. There was a suspicion of offside but the flag stayed down. Arsenal now faced elimination, but rather than go out gracefully they lost their nerve. Ray Parlour was sent off in the 90th minute and a disgraceful piece of play-acting from Lee Dixon duped the Swedish referee into sending off Lens's Tony Vairelles, who seemingly had done nothing.

Lens appealed against Vairelles' subsequent suspension but UEFA sided with the referee, which meant that the French side's top striker was unavailable for the death-or-glory final showdown at home to Dynamo Kiev. The situation with one game left was intriguing. A victory for either Lens or Kiev would enable them to win the group, but if they drew and Panathinaikos defeated already-eliminated Arsenal in Athens, the Greeks would go through. Alternatively, if Panathinaikos failed to win, a score draw would favour the Ukrainians while a goalless draw would suit Lens.

Those were the battle lines at the outset, and with an hour gone they were still in place. Neither match had produced a goal. But then came the deluge. Georgian defender Kakhi Kaladze headed Kiev in front in France while Alberto Mendez, one of several reserves in an experimental Arsenal side, put the Londoners ahead in Athens. Both visiting teams subsequently went on to win 3-1. Arsenal's triumph was academic but not Kiev's. The Ukrainians had undone Lens with their ability on the counter-attack, and with three wins on the trot they were through to the Champions' League quarter-finals for the second year in a row.

GROUP F

To most neutrals, Group F was the least attractive section. Kaiserslautern were the German champions but lacked international appeal. PSV and Benfica were fallen giants

CHAMPIONS' LEAGUE GROUP F

(September 16, 30, October 21, November 4, 25, December 9, 1998)
RESULTS

1.FC Kaiserslautern 1 (Wagner 41), **SL Benfica 0**

PSV 2 (Ouijer 57, Bruyyink 90), **HJK 1** (Kottilu 32)

SL Benfica 2 (Nuno Gomes 46, João Pinto 76), **PSV 1** (Rommedahl 71)

HJK 0, 1.FC Kaiserslautern 0

HJK 2 (Lehkosuo 20p, Kottila 70), **SL Benfica 0**

PSV 1 (Khokhlov 78), **1.FC Kaiserslautern 2** (Riedl 67, Rische 80)

SL Benfica 2 (Nuno Gomes 78, Calado 80), **HJK 2** (Minto 3og, Luiz António 85)

1.FC Kaiserslautern 3 (Rische 68, Reich 77, Hristov 90), **PSV 1** (Van Nistelrooy 18)

SL Benfica 2 (Nuno Gomes 39, João Pinto 69), **1.FC Kaiserslautern 1** (Rische 90)

HJK 1 (Lehkosuo 70p), **PSV 3** (Van Nistelrooy 30, 67, 81p)

1.FC Kaiserslautern 5 (Rösler 43, 61, 80, Marschall 49, Rische 85), **HJK 2** (Ilola 29, Luiz António 68)

PSV 2 (Khokhlov 41, Van Nistelrooy 89), **SL Benfica 2** (Nuno Gomes 47p, 63)

FINAL TABLE

				Home				Away				Total					
		Pd	W	D	L	F	A	W	D	L	F	A	W	D	L	F	A	Pt	GD
1	1.FC Kaiserslautern	6	3	0	0	9	3	1	1	1	3	3	4	1	1	12	6	13	+6
2	SL Benfica	6	2	1	0	6	4	0	1	2	2	5	2	2	2	8	9	8	-1
3	PSV	6	1	1	1	5	5	1	0	2	5	6	2	1	3	10	11	7	-1
4	HJK	6	1	1	1	3	3	0	1	2	5	9	1	2	3	8	12	5	-4

UEFA CHAMPIONS' LEAGUE

who together had contributed to one of the most boring Champions' Cup finals of all time, in 1988. As for HJK of Helsinki, they had surpassed themselves simply by getting this far.

The strength of the underdog, of course, is the element of surprise they bring to the contest, and PSV were certainly caught napping by the Finns in the opening encounter in Eindhoven. HJK had the temerity to take the lead in the Philips stadium and were within seconds of grabbing a well-deserved draw when a catastrophic goalkeeping error allowed Arnold Bruggink to fire home a 93rd-minute winner. The other opening match also resulted in a home win, with Kaiserslautern beating Benfica 1-0 thanks to a 41st-minute volley from Martin Wagner.

HJK continued to defy predictions in their second match, at home to Kaiserslautern. The Finns were lively throughout and deserved more than a 0-0 draw. The victory would have been theirs had it not been for some heroic interventions by Kaiserslautern 'keeper Andreas Reinke. In Lisbon, Benfica became the third team to win at home when João Pinto made up for an earlier missed penalty from his strike partner Nuno Gomes by scoring an excellent late winner.

After two games the group had a fairly even feel to it, but that was to change in rounds three and four as Kaiserslautern stepped up their bid to reach the quarter-finals by doing the 'double' over PSV. Their 2-1 win in Eindhoven was tainted with controversy, with the home side claiming that Jürgen Rische's winning goal had not crossed the line. It was an extremely close call, and even video stills could not determine the truth. The Germans profited from an even more contentious refereeing decision in the second game, with PSV 'keeper Lodewijks being red-carded by Englishman David Elleray for supposedly handling outside his area. The referee was so sure of his judgment that he failed to consult his linesman. TV pictures, however, proved him wrong. 1-0 up at the time through Ruud van Nistelrooy's early goal, PSV had to send on third-choice 'keeper Wilbert Need for his competitive début. It was not a happy one. Kaiserslautern made their one-man advantage count in the second half, scoring three times without reply to romp into a five-point lead at the top of the table.

The Germans had HJK to thank for the extent of the gap at the top. While they were in the process of eliminating PSV, the Finns were causing more merriment and mayhem by taking four points off Benfica. They were comprehensive 2-0 winners in Helsinki and led for most of the return match in Lisbon until Benfica turned the game

around with two goals in three minutes near the end. HJK's resolve didn't slacken, though, and they silenced the locals with a superb equaliser from their Brazilian striker Luíz António.

Kaiserslautern duly booked their place in the quarter-finals in their next match, but they did so despite going down to their first defeat of the competition, in Lisbon. A last-minute 'consolation' goal from Jürgen Rische was crucial as it gave them a better head-to-head record against Benfica, who were now in second place. HJK, sadly, had slumped to the bottom of the table after being gunned down by new Dutch striking sensation Ruud van Nistelrooy, who scored all three PSV goals in a 3-1 win in Helsinki.

It was Van Nistelrooy who also killed off Benfica's last lingering hopes of a quarter-finals spot (as one of the best runners-up) when he netted a brilliant late volley to earn PSV a 2-2 draw against the Portuguese side in Eindhoven. As for Kaiserslautern, they treated their fans to a last-day goal-fest in the Fritz Walter stadium, beating HJK 5-2, with Uwe Rösler scoring a splendid hat-trick of headers.

QUARTER-FINALS

There was a familiar look to the quarter-final line-up. Five of the eight teams had reached the same stage the previous season, while another, Inter, were the reigning UEFA Cup holders. Only Olympiakos and Kaiserslautern looked as if they might be out of their depth, but they had been the clearest group winners, so nothing could be taken for granted.

It was a free draw with just a couple of notable provisos.

QUARTER-FINAL RESULTS

(March 3 & 17, 1999)

Real Madrid 1 (Mijatovic 66), **Dynamo Kyiv 1** (Shevchenko 54)
Dynamo Kyiv 2 (Shevchenko 63, 80), **Real Madrid 0**
(Dynamo Kyiv 3-1)

Juventus 2 (Inzaghi 37, Conte 78), **Olympiakos 1** (Niniadis 90p)
Olympiakos 1 (Gogic 12), **Juventus 1** (Conte 85)
(Juventus 3-2)

Manchester United 2 (Yorke 6, 45), **Inter 0**
Inter 1 (Ventola 63), **Manchester United 1** (Scholes 88)
(Manchester United 3-1)

FC Bayern München 2 (Elber 31, Effenberg 35),
1.FC Kaiserslautern 0
1.FC Kaiserslautern 0,
FC Bayern München 4 (Effenberg 9p, Jancker 22, 39, Basler 56)

UEFA CHAMPIONS' LEAGUE

The two best runners-up, i.e. Real Madrid and Manchester United, were kept apart both from each other and the winners of their respective groups. Also, they were obliged to play the first leg at home.

United could hardly have been given a tougher task. They were paired with Inter. Although the Italians were having a poor time of it in Serie A, they were formidable opposition, and it had long been documented that United had never beaten an Italian side in European competition over two legs.

The good news for Alex Ferguson was that he was able to field a full-strength side for the first leg at Old Trafford. Inter, on the other hand, were missing Ronaldo, who was still recovering from injury. The atmosphere at Old Trafford was tremendous and the United fans were sent into ecstasy after just seven minutes when Dwight Yorke headed in a magnificent first-time cross from David Beckham. United dominated the remainder of the half, with Beckham's crossing ability giving the Inter defence constant concern. Just on the stroke of half-time the young England star swung in another centre and Yorke headed it down and in to put United 2-0 up. With the goals in the bag, the priority for Alex Ferguson's team was to make sure they kept a clean

Alessio Tacchinardi of Juventus (right) holds off a challenge against Olympiakos.

sheet. Diego Simeone, booed throughout as a result of his World Cup altercation with Beckham, appeared to score after 65 minutes when he headed in a Roberto Baggio corner but the goal was disallowed. In the closing minutes Inter came even nearer to getting that vital away goal. Inspired by substitute Nicola Ventola, they created three clear chances, but Peter Schmeichel saved two of them and the third was brilliantly cleared off the line by Henning Berg. The final whistle was greeted by an audible gasp of relief.

Almost 80,000 spectators packed the San Siro for the return leg. United were clearly in the driving seat at 2-0, but Inter had come back from similar reverses before - and Ronaldo was back in the team. It was fairly obvious, however, that the Brazilian was well short of full fitness. United coped very well defensively for the first hour and might even have finished the tie but for some errant finishing. Ventola eventually replaced Ronaldo and once again made an immediate impact, converting Benoît Cauet's pass after a rare error from Roy Keane. After that pressure intensified on the United goal, but relief eventually came to the travelling support when Paul Scholes prodded the ball home two minutes from time after Cole had headed Gary Neville's high cross back into his path. The tie was over. United had finally freed themselves of their Italian jinx.

Juventus, whose name increasingly appeared to be 'on the Cup', appeared to have the luck of the draw when they were paired with Olympiakos. They were totally dominant in the first leg at the Stadio delle Alpi. Pippo Inzaghi missed a number of early chances before he finally converted the most difficult of them all - an acrobatic volley - to give Juve the lead. Greek goalkeeper Eleftheropoulos was in good form and made one incredible treble-save to deny Fonseca, Conte and Inzaghi, but Conte beat him soon afterwards with a low left-footed drive, and that seemed to be that. In the very last minute, however, Olympiakos were awarded a controversial penalty and substitute Andreas Niniadis slotted it coolly past Peruzzi.

When Serb/Cypriot striker Sinisa Gogic headed in a Yeorgatos cross after just 12 minutes in Athens, Olympiakos could suddenly see the semi-finals on the horizon. The match, played in driving rain, was intense and absorbing, but with defences on top, few chances were created. There were just a few minutes left when Alessandro Birindelli sent a hanging cross into the Olympiakos area. It should have been a formality for the hitherto excellent Eleftheropoulos but he completely misjudged the flight and Conte, the Juve skipper, gleefully tapped the loose ball into the net. The Italians, once again,

UEFA CHAMPIONS' LEAGUE

had left it late, but they were through to their fourth successive Champions' Cup semi-final.

Real Madrid, however, were unable to join them. They could only manage a 1-1 draw at home to Dynamo Kiev and were then beaten 2-0 in the return leg. The star of the tie was Kiev striker Andriy Shevchenko, who scored all three of his team's goals. He put his side in front in the Bernabéu with a typically decisive finish after a lovely flick-on by his trusty sidekick Serhiy Rebrov. Predrag Mijatovic later levelled the scores with a free-kick to ensure that Real's new coach, John Toshack, retained his record of never having lost a match in the Bernabéu (this was his first match of a second spell in charge). But in Kiev two weeks later, with 80,000 fans huddled together in sub-zero temperatures, Shevchenko stole the show again. He was brought down cynically by Real 'keeper Bodo Illgner after a typical burst through the middle. The German should have been red-carded but stayed on the field to save Shevchenko's spot-kick, but justice was done when the Kiev striker blasted home the rebound. Shevchenko's second goal, ten minutes from time, was altogether more aesthetic - another fine finish after superb link-up play with Rebrov. Real, who had dominated the game for large periods, simply had no answer to Shevchenko, who had now become the star of the entire competition.

Joining the holders on the quarter-final scrapheap were Kaiserslautern, who were completely outclassed over the two legs by their Bundesliga brethren from Bayern Munich. The Bavarians took an early hold on the tie in the home leg with two goals in quick succession from Elber and Effenberg and in the return they simply demolished the reigning Bundesliga champions, winning 4-0. Their task was made straightforward by a penalty awarded to them in the ninth minute when Bayern striker Carsten Jancker fell theatrically in the area after a slight tug from 'Lautern defender János Hrutka, who was subsequently red-carded. Effenberg converted the spot-kick, Jancker added another couple of first-half goals and then Mario Basler completed the rout with a deflected free-kick.

SEMI-FINALS

Having disposed of one Italian club, Manchester United were pitted against another in the semi-finals. Juventus were familiar foes. The two teams had played each other in the group phase in each of the previous two years, and it was Juve who had the better record, winning three games to United's one.

As against Inter, United were at home first and had everybody fit and available. Juventus made a very impres-

sive start. Their skill in retaining possession and working the spaces stifled United's normal high-tempo style. Inzaghi brought the best out of Schmeichel with a good low shot before Conte, with his third goal in as many Champions' League matches, latched onto Edgar Davids' astute pass and drove the ball into the far corner. There were further first-half chances for the Italians and at the interval they were thoroughly in command of the tie. In the second half Juve reverted to stereotypical Italian absorb-and-counter tactics, preferring to hold onto what they had rather than ramming home a decisive advantage. This allowed the home side to regain the initiative and for the last quarter of the match they put the Juve defence under incessant pressure. The last few minutes were frantic, with Teddy Sheringham having a header disallowed for offside and Paul Scholes twice coming close. All hope appeared to be lost, but with the match into its third minute of added time Ryan Giggs arrived at the far post to despatch a half-volley into the roof of net and bring the tie level.

And so to Turin. United had never previously won a competitive match on Italian soil and after 11 minutes it looked as if the drought would continue. Juventus got off to a whirlwind start, with Inzaghi snatching two quick goals, the first a close-range tap-in, the second a deflected left-footer after he had skilfully turned United's Dutch centre-back Jaap Stam.

But where previous United teams might have panicked, this one remained serene. They should have been awarded a penalty when Dwight Yorke was fouled by Ciro Ferrara, but a couple of minutes later United were back in the game, skipper Keane glancing in a header from a Beckham corner. The visitors then had a lucky escape when Stam cleared off the line following a Schmeichel error but five minutes later United's deadly forward combination struck as Yorke headed in a finely-judged centre from Andy Cole. The fightback was now complete.

UEFA CHAMPIONS' LEAGUE

At 2-2 United had the away-goal advantage - but there was still almost an hour to go.

Juve turned up the heat in the second half, but United defended superbly, and on 71 minutes Denis Irwin was desperately unlucky not to score when his shot cannoned back off the inside of the post. As the game opened up, so United created as many chances as their hosts and with five minutes remaining they scored the crucial winning goal. This time it was Yorke who set it up and Cole who finished it, tucking the ball in from an acute angle after his strike-partner had burst into the area and fallen to the ground from Peruzzi's challenge. It was probably a penalty but Cole did the right thing by making sure.

Juventus were stunned. They were not accustomed to losing semi-finals, let alone being beaten at home on such a big occasion. But United had played quite brilliantly. They had won a memorable match by keeping their patience and their shape and making the most of their chances. In short, Alex Ferguson's team had come of age. The club's first Champions' Cup final in 31 years now beckoned.

The other semi-final, between Dynamo Kiev and Bayern Munich, was every bit as entertaining, especially in the first leg in the Ukrainian capital. Another glorious goal from the sensational Shevchenko set the scene for a riveting encounter. 16 minutes in he latched onto a brilliant pass from Valentin Belkevich and beat Oliver Kahn with a nerveless finish. The Kiev 'number ten' was on the score-sheet again just before half-time when his free-kick from the left eluded everybody before nestling in the net at the far post. But just as Kiev looked certain to go in at half-time with a two-goal advantage they dropped their guard for a moment and the Germans punished them, Michael Tarnat's skimming 35-yard free-kick somehow eluding defenders and goal-keeper before lodging itself in the corner of the Kiev net.

Dynamo's two-goal cushion was restored shortly after the break when Vitaliy Kosovskyi exploited an error by Sammy Kuffour in the Bayern defence to volley his team spectacularly into a 3-1 lead. The same player had another wonderful chance a few minutes later but he lifted his shot just over the bar. Kiev's football was a joy to watch, but the threat of a Bayern comeback was

ever-present, and sure enough, in time-honoured German fashion, they kept going and succeeded in turning the tie back in their favour with two late goals. The first was an outrageous but brilliant free-kick from Stefan Effenberg, and the blond schemer was also responsible for setting up Bayern's equaliser, turned in by Carsten Jancker two minutes from time.

That was Kiev's chance virtually gone. They had an early opportunity in Munich to take the lead again when Belkevich raced free, but Oliver Kahn's superb one-handed save proved crucial and when Mario Basler scored for Bayern with a brilliant dipping left-foot shot after 35 minutes, the Ukrainians were left with too much to do. They never gave up, but Kahn was in outstanding form and kept out everything Shevchenko and co. could throw at him.

So, Bayern Munich and Manchester United were set to meet again. They had come through the same group, drawing twice, and had both won their semi-finals 4-3 on aggregate. There was clearly little to choose between them. It promised to be a classic final...

FINAL

Manchester United were severely handicapped in Barcelona by the absence through suspension of their two first-choice central midfielders. Roy Keane and Paul Scholes had both picked up second yellow cards in Turin, which meant that United were without not just their entire midfield engine-room but also two players who had scored against Bayern Munich in the group games. To balance that Bayern lacked their two long-term injury victims, Frenchman Bixente Lizarazu and Brazilian Giovane Elber. There were ten Germans in the Bayern starting line-up but only four Englishmen on show for United.

The stakes could not have been higher. Both Bayern and United were chasing historic 'trebles'. United had already captured parts one and two of theirs, while Bayern still had the German Cup final to play. It had been a long time since either club had been crowned kings of Europe. United had won the Champions' Cup just once before, in 1968, while Bayern were still

TOP SCORERS

(excluding Preliminary/Qualifying rounds)

8   Andriy SHEVCHENKO (Dynamo Kyiv)
    Dwight YORKE (Manchester United)
7   Zlatko ZAHOVIC (FC Porto)
6   Filippo INZAGHI (Juventus)
5   Ruud VAN NISTELROOY (PSV)
    NUNO GOMES (SL Benfica)
4   ANDERSON (FC Barcelona)
    Jürgen RISCHE (1.FC Kaiserslautern)
    Serhiy REBROV (Dynamo Kyiv)
    Sinisa GOGIC (Olympiakos)
    Andy COLE (Manchester United)
    Ryan GIGGS (Manchester United)
    Paul SCHOLES (Manchester United)
    Mario BASLER (FC Bayern München)
    Stefan EFFENBERG (FC Bayern München)

UEFA CHAMPIONS' LEAGUE

waiting to lift it for a fourth time after a hat-trick of victories in the mid-'70s.

The Nou Camp was full. And it was the German section of the crowd that rose as one just six minutes in when Mario Basler curled a low free-kick around the wall, leaving Peter Schmeichel flat-footed and helpless. United were rocked. It would have to be Turin all over again for Alex Ferguson's team. But without captain Keane they looked misshapen and disorganised. The United boss had decided to compensate for the loss of Keane and Scholes by moving David Beckham into the centre and Ryan Giggs to a very unfamilar rôle on the right wing, with Jesper Blomqvist getting the nod on the left.

Although Beckham looked the part, spraying his finely-judged passes to all areas of the field, there was little harmony to the team's play and no cutting edge.

The pattern of the match had been set by Basler's early goal. Bayern defended and United attempted to find an opening in their well-manned and disciplined rearguard. Chances were few and far between. Cole and Yorke looked especially ineffective, and when United did manage to carve a good opportunity it was wasted by the totally out-of-sorts Blomqvist.

Bayern moved in for the kill. On 73 minutes Stefan Effenberg forced a superb tip-over from Schmeichel. Six minutes later Mehmet Scholl, a Bayern substitute, seized

FINAL

May 26, 1999, Barcelona

MANCHESTER UNITED 2 Sheringham (90), Solskjaer (90)
FC BAYERN MÜNCHEN 1 Basler (6)

referee - Collina (ITA)

MANCHESTER UNITED - Schmeichel; Neville G., Stam, Johnsen, Irwin; Giggs, Beckham, Butt, Blomqvist (Sheringham 66); Yorke, Cole (Solskjaer 80).

FC BAYERN MÜNCHEN - Kahn; Linke, Matthäus (Fink 80), Kuffour; Babbel, Jeremies, Effenberg, Tarnat; Basler (Salihamidzic 89), Jancker, Zickler (Scholl 71).

possession after Basler's superb solo run and deceived Schmeichel with a chip but could only watch in agony as the ball came back off the post. Bayern hit the woodwork again shortly afterwards when Carsten Jancker's overhead-kick smacked against the crossbar. But by now United were coming forward themselves. The introduction of Ole Gunnar Solskjaer for Cole acted as a spark and in the last ten minutes United gradually applied more and more pressure on the Bayern defence.

Then came stoppage-time...and the most incredible and dramatic two minutes ever seen in the history of this great competition.

A corner was swung in from the left. Bayern made a hash of clearing it. The ball fell on the edge of the area to Giggs. He swung his right boot at it, managing to send the ball goalwards. And there was Teddy Sheringham, unmarked six yards out. He swivelled and redirected the ball into the corner of the net with Bayern appealing vainly for offside. 1-1.

United might have left it at that and taken their chances in 'golden goal' extra-time. But they scented victory. Another corner, another pin-point Beckham delivery, and there was Sheringham again, rising above the Bayern defence to deflect the ball across goal, where Solskjaer, the arch-poacher, raised a leg and clipped the ball into the roof of the net.

Seconds later referee Collina blew the final whistle. The shockwaves were everywhere. Bayern were distraught, inconsolable. United were utterly euphoric. They had achieved the impossible dream, and done so in the most exciting and spectacular manner possible. The Premiership. The FA Cup. And now this - the European Champions' Cup, the prize they had coveted for so long. Their time had come. The 'treble' had been completed. The finest team in England were now also the Champions of Europe.

Manchester United captain Peter Schmeichel holds the Champions' Cup with manager Alex Ferguson and the rest of the team.

CUP-WINNERS' CUP

This was the 39th and last European Cup-winners' Cup. UEFA, understandably, had taken the decision to scrap a competition that had become very much the poor relation of European club football. The ever-expanding Champions' League was responsible for its demise. With places in UEFA's money-spinning, sponsor-driven flagship competition at a premium, the big clubs had no great desire to compete in the Cup-winners' Cup, which had effectively become a minor trophy with no real part to play in the football calendar of the 21st century.

The field in 1998/99 was as weak as it had been the previous year. Most of the Continent's bigger names had hitched a ride on the Champions' League juggernaut or had settled for a place in the UEFA Cup. Germany, England, Spain and Portugal, for example, were all represented by teams who had not won their domestic Cup, while Holland's entry was a team which had not even reached their own Cup final.

As in 1997/98, there were only three previous European trophy-winners in the field - the English duo of Newcastle United and Chelsea (the holders), plus the 1996 winners and 1997 beaten finalists Paris Saint-Germain. The only other one of the 49 teams on the starting grid with the look of potential trophy-winners was Italian Cup winners and 1998 UEFA Cup finalists Lazio, who, as a result of their £70m summer spending spree, were installed as the pre-tournament favourites.

QUALIFYING ROUND

The summer scramble to join the seeded élite began in mid-August. 17 qualifying-round ties were required to bring the total number of participants down to 32 for the first round proper, and on the whole the results were very predictable, with not one major shock to report.

Even though this round was the last stop in Europe for many countries, whose other teams had already gone to ground the previous month in the other two competitions, very little excitement was generated. Only two ties drew five-figure crowds to both games, and they were the all-Eastern European clashes between Partizan Belgrade and Dinamo Batumi and Vardar Skopje and Spartak Trnava.

Partizan v Batumi was one of the few ties which remained in the balance until the final whistle of the second leg, with the Yugoslavs just managing to hang on to their 2-0 first-leg lead. Ekranas Panevezys v Apollon Limassol was quite a thriller, with the tie fluctuating one way and then the other until a late penalty sealed it in the Cypriots' favour.

There were several one-sided match-ups, with Danish

side FC Copenhagen running up the best aggregate score (10-0 v Karabakh Agdam), followed closely by MTK (10-1 v Gİ), Genk (9-1 v Apolonia Fier) and Levski Sofia (9-2 v Lokomotiv '96 Vitebsk). The best individual scoring performance came from Fabio Celestini of Lausanne, who struck four of his team's five goals at home to Tsement Ararat. Other hat-trick heroes were Rolands Boulders of Metalurgs Liepaya and Georgi Borisov of Levski Sofia, while Maccabi Haifa striker Alon Mizrahi scored all three of his team's goals in their two matches with Glentoran.

For all but one of the countries whose teams were eliminated in this round, it meant the end of the European road. Only Georgia still had representation in another competition (Dinamo Tbilisi in the UEFA Cup). Those nations bidding an *au revoir* to Europe and an adieu to the Cup-winners' Cup were (in alphabetical order) Albania, Armenia, Azerbaijan, Belarus, Estonia, the Faroe Islands, Iceland, Liechtenstein, Lithuania, Luxembourg, Macedonia, Malta, Moldova, Northern Ireland, the Republic of Ireland and Wales.

The minnows were out. Now it was time for the big fish to dive in...

FIRST ROUND

Tha lack of upsets in the qualifying round was counter-balanced by a rash of unlikely results in the first legs of the first round, with all of the more fancied teams struggling to impose themselves at home.

The two English sides, Newcastle and Chelsea, both sneaked narrow victories against Partizan Belgrade and Helsingborg, respectively, while Lazio, Paris Saint-Germain and MSV Duisburg could do no better than draw 1-1 at home turf. Remarkably, only two of the five teams, Chelsea and Lazio, were to redress the balance in the second legs, and even they only made it through after a struggle.

Newcastle against Partizan was the most attractive-looking tie of the round. The battle of the black-and-white stripes began well for the English side, newly managed by Ruud Gullit, when Alan Shearer applied an excellent finish to a move set up by England colleagues Robert Lee and Stuart Pearce. But the Geordies could not build on that lead and then shot themselves in the foot in the second half when French defender Laurent Charvet lunged recklessly in the area and conceded a penalty, which was coolly despatched by Partizan defender Vuk Rasovic. Newcastle replied immediately with a looping header from Greek centre-back Nikos Dabizas, but the away-goal was to prove fatal. Two weeks later in Belgrade, Partizan were

CUP-WINNERS' CUP

gifted another penalty after a silly challenge from David Batty, who was playing his first match since his penalty shoot-out horror for England in the World Cup. Rasovic was on the mark again to put the Yugoslavs into the next round.

A crowd of 35,000 Parisians were stunned when PSG conceded a late equaliser in their home tie with Maccabi Haifa, Israeli teenage sensation Yossi Benayoun finding the net shortly after a Marco Simone penalty had put the

French Cup winners in front. The return leg, watched by a sell-out crowd in Haifa, had an equally dramatic ending. PSG were twice behind in the second half but appeared to have saved themselves from the embarrassment of a first-round exit when their record signing Jay-Jay Okocha poached an equaliser four minutes from time. But with the match in stoppage-time the ever-dependable Alon Mizrahi fired in a shot that was deflected into the net off PSG defender Alain Goma. There was bedlam in the crowd,

QUALIFYING ROUND RESULTS

(August 13/27, 1998)

Amica Wronki 4 (Kryszalowicz 36, Przerada 56, Sobocinski 63, 75), **Hibernians 0**
Hibernians 0, Amica Wronki 1 (Kryszalowicz 70)
(Amica Wronki 5-0)

Apolonia Fier 1 (Vangronsveld 26og),
KRC Genk 5 (Strupar 33, Oulare 37p, 68, Hendrickx 40, Horváth 80)
KRC Genk 4 (Oulare 5, N'Sumbu 86, Strupar 87, 90), **Apolonia Fier 0**
(KRC Genk 9-1)

Bangor City 0, FC Haka 2 (Niemi 40, Salli 59)
FC Haka 1 (Ruhanen 28), **Bangor City 0**
(FC Haka 3-0)

Cork City 2 (Flanagan 20p, Coughlan 31), **CSKA Kyiv 1** (Revut 90)
CSKA Kyiv 2 (Tsykhmeistruk 41, Leonenko 56), **Cork City 0**
(CSKA Kyiv 3-2)

Ekranas Panevezys 1 (Stumbrys 38),
Apollon Limassol 2 (Cârstea 17, Pittas 89)
Apollon Limassol 3 (Spoljaric 51, 89, Kavazis 60),
Ekranas Panevezys 3 (Vileniskis 6, 9, Varnas 90)
(Apollon Limassol 5-4)

GÍ 1 (Olsen Su. 8),
MTK Hungária FC 3 (Kenesei 18, Preisinger 19, Szekeres 90)
MTK Hungária FC 7 (Kenesei 16, 71, 76, Preisinger 34, Halmai 37, Illés 63, Balaskó 72), **GÍ 0**
(MTK Hungária FC 10-1)

Glentoran 0, Maccabi Haifa 1 (Mizrahi 22)
Maccabi Haifa 2 (Mizrahi 16p, 79p), **Glentoran 1** (Batey 42)
(Maccabi Haifa 3-1)

CS Grevenmacher 2 (Krahen 38, 70), **Rapid Bucuresti 6** (Sabau 13, Pancu 62, Dulca 65, Stanciu 70, Lupu 76p, Mutica 82)
Rapid Bucuresti 2 (Pancu 54, 88), **CS Grevenmacher 0**
(Rapid Bucuresti 8-2)

FC København 6 (Nielsen Ma. 2, Thorninger 6, Nielsen P. 12, 40, Goldbaek 19, Falch 25), **Karabakh Agdam 0**
Karabakh Agdam 0, FC København 4 (Jensen N. 64, Nielsen P. 70, Nielsen D. 75, 84)
(FC København 10-0)

FC Lantana Tallinn 0, Heart of Midlothian 1 (Makel 20)
Heart of Midlothian 5 (Hamilton 18, Fulton 29, McCann 41, Flögel 75, Holmes 90), **FC Lantana Tallinn 0**
(Heart of Midlothian 6-0)

Lausanne-Sports 5 (Celestini 28p, 47, 58, 71, Cavin 87),
Tsement Ararat 1 (Hovhannisyan T. 35)
Tsement Ararat 1 (Asatryan 40),
Lausanne-Sports 2 (Douglas 66, Hottiger 89)
(Lausanne-Sports 7-2)

Levski Sofia 8 (Ivanov 8, 32, Borisov 23, 44, 88, Donev 42, Radukanov 52, Todorov 85), **Lokomotiv-96 Vitebsk 1** (Demenkovets 48p)
Lokomotiv-96 Vitebsk 0 (Sivkov 90), **Levski Sofia 1** (Lazarov 50)
(Levski Sofia 9-2)

Metalurgs Liepaya 4 (Boulders 61, 85, 88, Magdishauskas 86),
Keflavík 2 (Kristjánsson 60, Gylfason 90)
Keflavík 1 (Hauksson 58), **Metalurgs Liepaya 0**
(Metalurgs Liepaya 4-3)

Partizan Beograd 2 (Bjekovic 17, Ilic 34), **Dinamo Batumi 0**
Dinamo Batumi 1 (Sichinava 28), **Partizan Beograd 0**
(Partizan Beograd 2-1)

Rudar Velenje 2 (Vidojevic 32, Sumnik 90), **Constructorul Chisinau 0**
Constructorul Chisinau 0, Rudar Velenje 0
(Rudar Velenje 2-0)

FC Vaduz 0, Helsingborgs IF 2 (Stavrum 9, Wibrån 70)
Helsingborgs IF 3 (Wibrån 44, Edman 58, Powell 68), **FC Vaduz 0**
(Helsingborgs IF 5-0)

Vardar Skopje 0, Spartak Trnava 1 (Ujlaky 76)
Spartak Trnava 2 (Tittel 82, Gomes 86), **Vardar Skopje 0**
(Spartak Trnava 3-0)

CUP-WINNERS' CUP

and the victory was hailed in the local press as the best-ever in Europe by an Israeli team.

Lazio's excuse for their home draw with Lausanne was the sending-off after just two minutes of new signing Dejan Stankovic for handling deliberately in the area. The Italians were reprieved when Lausanne's qualifying-round hero Celestini missed the ensuing penalty, and there was another let-off later on when Slovenian international Saso Udovic headed against a post. But although Pavel Nedved gave Lazio the lead, heading in Marcelo Salas's cross, the Swiss got their just reward with an equaliser from Philippe Douglas early in the second half. The second leg in

Lausanne also ended all square, which gave Lazio their fifth successive draw of the season. Fortunately the score was 2-2, which enabled them to go through on away goals - but not before they had endured a hairy last few minutes of Lausanne pressure.

Chelsea's defence of the trophy got off to a low-key start with a 1-0 aggregate victory over Sweden's last remaining European representative, Helsingborg. The only goal of the tie came at the end of the first half at Stamford Bridge from a Frank Leboeuf free-kick.

The scoreline of the round was undoubtedly Genk 5 MSV Duisburg 0. The Belgian Cup winners, making their

FIRST ROUND RESULTS

(September 17, October 1, 1998)

Apollon Limassol 2 (Kavazis 45, Cârstea 67), **FK Jablonec 97 1** (Fukal 39)
FK Jablonec 97 2 (Prochazka 24, 45),
Apollon Limassol 1 (Themistocleous 58) (aet)
(3-3; Apollon Limassol 4-3 on pens.)

Besiktas 3 (Mehmet 10, Oktay 21, Ohen 49), **Spartak Trnava 0**
Spartak Trnava 2 (Formanko 50, Timko 71), **Besiktas 1** (Oktay 45)
(Besiktas 4-2)

Chelsea 1 (Leboeuf 43), **Helsingborgs IF 0**
Helsingborgs IF 0, Chelsea 0
(Chelsea 1-0)

CSKA Kyiv 0, Lokomotiv Moskva 2 (Kharlachyev 24, Janashia 51)
Lokomotiv Moskva 3 (Bulykin 19, 53, Janashia 70),
CSKA Kyiv 1 (Bezhenar 13)
(Lokomotiv Moskva 5-1)

MSV Duisburg 1 (Wedau 83), **KRC Genk 1** (Reini 61)
KRC Genk 5 (Oulare 13, 49, Strupar 32, Gudjónsson 73, 80),
MSV Duisburg 0
(KRC Genk 6-1)

Heart of Midlothian 0, RCD Mallorca 1 (Marcelino 17)
RCD Mallorca 1 (López 48), **Heart of Midlothian 1** (Hamilton 75)
(RCD Mallorca 2-1)

SC Heerenveen 3 (Talan 38, Mitrita 45, Pahlplatz 66),
Amica Wronki 1 (Krol 64)
Amica Wronki 0, SC Heerenveen 1 (De Nooijer D. 30)
(SC Heerenveen 4-1)

Lazio 1 (Nedved 37), **Lausanne-Sports 1** (Douglas 55)
Lausanne-Sports 2 (Douglas 10, Rehn 84),
Lazio 2 (Salas 7, Sérgio Conceição 25)
(3-3; Lazio on away goals)

Levski Sofia 0, FC Kobenhavn 2 (Goldbaek 34, Thorninger 76)
FC Kobenhavn 4 (Nielsen Ma. 17, Nielsen L.H. 49, Thorninger 58, 76),
Levski Sofia 1 (Lazarov 85)
(FC Kobenhavn 6-1)

Metalurgs Liepaya 0, SC Braga 0
SC Braga 4 (Bruno 13p, 61, Karoglan 35, Silva 86),
Metalurgs Liepaya 0
(SC Braga 4-0)

Newcastle United 2 (Shearer 12, Dabizas 71),
Partizan Beograd 1 (Rasovic 70p)
Partizan Beograd 1 (Rasovic 53p), **Newcastle United 0**
(2-2; Partizan Beograd on away goal)

Panionios 2 (Haylock 36, Robins 53), **FC Haka 0**
FC Haka 1 (Popovits 74),
Panionios 3 (Fissas 33, Kouvalis 45, Sapountzis 57)
(Panionios 5-1)

Paris Saint-Germain 1 (Simone 83p), **Maccabi Haifa 1** (Benayoun 87)
Maccabi Haifa 3 (Keissy 60, Mizrahi 78, 90),
Paris Saint Germain 2 (Ouédec 72, Okocha 84)
(Maccabi Haifa 4-3)

Rapid Bucuresti 2 (Sumudica 52, Bundea 76),
Vålerenga IF 2 (Carew 52, 88)
Vålerenga IF 0, Rapid Bucuresti 0
(2-2; Vålerenga IF on away goals)

SV Ried 2 (Strafner 19, Brunmayr 64), **MTK Hungária FC 0**
MTK Hungária FC 0, SV Ried 1 (Strafner 11)
(SV Ried 3-0)

Rudar Velenje 0, Varteks Varazdin 1 (Matas 90)
Varteks Varazdin 1 (Kamberovic 7), **Rudar Velenje 0**
(Varteks Varazdin 2-0)

CUP-WINNERS' CUP

European début, had drawn the first leg 1-1 on a rainy night in Germany despite being down to ten men for most of the second half and surviving two late Dusiburg efforts against the woodwork. But at home they regally disposed of their supposedly superior opponents, with their exciting, in-form front trio of Souleymane Oulare, Branko Strupar and Thórdur Gudjónsson all getting among the goals.

Mallorca were another team playing in European competition for the first time. They started with a victory, 1-0 away to Hearts courtesy of a freak goal from defender Marcelino, but had to survive a late scare in the home leg after the Scottish Cup winners equalised 15 minutes from time. Hearts subsequently raised a protest about the dimensions of the goalposts in the Mallorca stadium, but their pleas fell on deaf ears at UEFA.

SECOND ROUND

Holders Chelsea were drawn against Scandinavian opposition once more, with the first leg again being scheduled for Stamford Bridge. A poor crowd of just 21,207 came to watch, and it proved to be a frustrating night for all concerned as FC Copenhagen, who had racked up 16 goals in their previous two rounds, showed commendable resistance to keep the Londoners at bay. Gianfranco Zola and Gustavo Poyet both had good chances deflected onto the post, and there was a collective shriek of disbelief nine minutes from time as Danish international midfielder Bjarne Goldbaek took advantage of an error by Chelsea skipper Dennis Wise to drill a right-foot shot into the corner of the net. Chelsea's unbeaten European home record was in peril, but Gianluca Vialli's side launched a late siege on the Danish goal and were finally rewarded when defender Marcel Desailly toe-poked a loose ball in off the post to bring Chelsea level. It was the French World Cup winner's first goal for the club, and it could not have come at a more opportune moment.

The second leg, in Copenhagen, promised much, and further intrigue was added to the contest by the news that Chelsea's Brian Laudrup was about to play his last game for the club and return to Denmark to join...FC Copenhagen. How ironic, then, that it should be Laudrup who provided the winning goal, his close-range header in the 32nd minute proving to be the difference in a tight, absorbing contest that could have gone either way. Both teams were guilty of some incredible misses in the second half, with Chelsea's Tore André Flo being especially relieved to hear the final whistle after missing a sitter near the end.

Lazio also needed a victory away from home in the second leg to make it through to the quarter-finals. The first leg of their tie with Partizan Belgrade ended goalless in Rome, but Marcelo Salas returned from injury to play in the second leg and the Chilean striker proved to be the key man in the tie, for reasons good and bad.

Partizan were leading through a splendid early strike from defender Mladen Krstajic when, just before half-time,

(October 22, November 5, 1998)

Chelsea 1 (Desailly 90), **FC Kobenhavn 1** (Goldbaek 81)
FC Kobenhavn 0, Chelsea 1 (Laudrup 32)
(Chelsea 2-1)

KRC Genk 1 (Oulare 71), **RCD Mallorca 1** (Dani 55)
RCD Mallorca 0, KRC Genk 0
(1-1; RCD Mallorca on away goal)

SC Heerenveen 2 (De Nooijer D. 56, Hansma 89),
Varteks Varazdin 1 (Mumlek 63)
Varteks Varazdin 4 (Mumlek 67, 117, Kamberovic 82, 98),
SC Heerenveen 2 (Samardzic 18, De Visser 114) (aet)
(Varteks Varazdin 5-4)

Lazio 0, Partizan Beograd 0
Partizan Beograd 2 (Krstajic 18, Ilijev 85),
Lazio 3 (Salas 43p, 75, Stankovic 66)
(Lazio 3-2)

Lokomotiv Moskva 3 (Bulykin 21, 35, Chugainov 59p),
SC Braga 1 (Odair 47)
SC Braga 1 (Karoglan 11), **Lokomotiv Moskva 0**
(Lokomotiv Moskva 3-2)

Panionios 3 (Sapountzis 25, Haylock 40, Robins 57),
Apollon Limassol 2 (Spoljaric 14, 42)
Apollon Limassol 0, Panionios 1 (Sapountzis 18)
(Panionios 4-2)

SV Ried 2 (Sliwowski 23, Strafner 88), **Maccabi Haifa 1** (Mizrahi 14)
Maccabi Haifa 4 (Mizrahi 33, Keissy 62, Benayoun 74, Duro 90),
SV Ried 1 (Anicic 70)
(Maccabi Haifa 5-3)

Vålerenga IF 1 (Levernes 49), **Besiktas 0**
Besiktas 3 (Oktay 8, 43, Tayfur 40),
Vålerenga IF 3 (Haraldsen 64, Kaasa 67, Carew 73)
(Vålerenga IF 4-3)

CUP-WINNERS' CUP

Salas took a theatrical dive in the area, for which he was awarded a highly contentious penalty. He converted the kick and from that moment on Lazio were in control. They dominated the second half and scored two further goals - the first from substitute Dejan Stankovic who, because of his allegiances with Partizan's rivals Red Star, was whistled at every touch; the second from Salas, with a rare right-foot shot. The vociferous Partizan fans had something else to get excited about when Ivica Ilijev headed in a consolation goal five minutes from time, but it was too late to matter.

Mallorca and Genk, European first-timers both, engaged in a very competitive tie that was only settled in the Spaniards' favour on the away-goals rule. The first leg, transported to the King Baudouin stadium in Brussels, was the more eventful of the two, with a second-half header apiece from Dani and Oulare producing a fair result. Genk tried valiantly to rescue the tie in the return but Mallorca's defence, which had been the talk of the Spanish league, held firm once again.

Goals were not in short supply in the other tie involving two European débutants - Herrenveen v Varteks Varazdin. A last-gasp winner gave the Dutch side a slender advantage from the home leg, but the real excitement came two weeks later, in the second leg, when the Croatian underdogs came from behind not once but twice before scoring the deciding goal three minutes from the end of an extra-time thriller.

There was an even more astonishing comeback from Norwegian side Vålerenga, who appeared to be down and out in their tie with Besiktas after going in at half-time in the second leg trailing 3-0 on the night and 3-1 on aggregate. The Turks had been brilliant in the first 45 minutes, scoring three quality goals, but after skipper Mehmet missed an easy chance to make it 4-0 just after the interval the Norwegians suddenly woke up. With former Norwegian national coach Egil Olsen encouraging them from the sidelines, Vålerenga put themselves back into contention with a header from defender Knut Haraldsen and then stole the tie with two fine breakaway goals from Kjell Kaasa and John Carew.

The quarter-final line-up was completed by Lokomotiv Moscow, who narrowly defeated Portugal's Sporting Braga, Panionios, who disposed of Cyprus's Apollon Limassol, and Maccabi Haifa, who carried on where they had left off against PSG, with the prolific Alon Mizrahi leading them to a goal spree against Austria's SV Ried. With their victory, Maccabi made history by becoming the first Israeli side to reach a European quarter-final.

QUARTER-FINALS

Another round, another trip to Scandinavia, another first-leg tie at Stamford Bridge. Chelsea's Cup-winners' Cup campaign was becoming rather repetitive. After knocking out teams from Sweden and Denmark in the autumn, they now had to do battle with the Norwegians of Vålerenga.

For the first time in the competition Gianluca Vialli's men played in front of a capacity home crowd. And it seemed to encourage them because for the first 45 minutes Chelsea played their best football of the tournament. Two exquisite left-footed strikes from Celestine Babayaro and Gianfranco Zola put them in command, and although the Norwegians defended with great discipline, they could not prevent a third goal, from Dennis Wise, five minutes from time.

The talk between the two legs focussed on Vålerenga's comeback from three goals down in the previous round against Besiktas, but Chelsea were in a different class, and they felt comfortable enough to rest a number of key players for the second leg in Oslo. Once again the first 45 minutes were tremendously entertaining, with the two teams sharing five goals - three for Chelsea, two for Vålerenga - before the whole tie petered out into a second-half non-event.

Lazio had an even easier passage to the semi-finals than Chelsea. They were far too good for struggling Greek side Panionios. Once Dejan Stankovic volleyed the Italians into the lead after just three minutes in Athens, the die was cast. Marcelo Salas was once again Lazio's key man away

CUP-WINNERS' CUP

Chelsea's Tore André Flo gets in a tangle with Vålerenga's Fredrik Kjølner.

from home. Although he failed to put his own name on the scoresheet, the Chilean was responsible for setting up each of the other three goals which brought the visitors a comprehensive 4-0 victory. The return in Rome was a formality, with barely 15,000 fans bothering to turn up to witness Lazio's inevitable progress into the last four. Those who did saw a virtuoso performance from the 'forgotten man' of Lazio, Iván de la Peña. The little Spaniard marked a rare appearance in the starting line-up by setting up two goals for Stankovic and Nedved before collecting one for himself and completing his team's 7-0 aggregate triumph.

Mallorca travelled to Croatia for the first leg of their quarter-final and had to cope with a swirling wind as well as a small stadium packed to the rafters with enthusiastic home supporters. They emerged from the ordeal with a 0-0 draw and in fact had the better chances to score, but Varteks' new signing, Croatian international goalkeeper Marijan Mrmic, had a night to remember, making several terrific saves. One in particular, from a point-blank Dani header, was quite astonishing.

Mrmic was kept even busier in the return leg. He managed to keep his goal intact for the entire first half, seeing one effort from Dani hit the bar, the goalline and the post before bouncing away to safety. But early in the second period the Spaniards made the decisive breakthrough, scoring two goals in quick succession, the first a cross from Ibagaza which was allowed to drift all the way into the net, the second a much more elaborately constructed effort from Veljko Paunovic after an excellent one-two with Dani. The latter got the goal he deserved later on, beating Mrmic with a well-placed shot, before Varteks bowed out of the competition with a late consolation goal from Andrija Balajic.

Georgian international striker Zaza Janashia was the decisive figure in the quarter-final between Lokomotiv Moscow and Maccabai Haifa. The first leg, in the Russian capital, was played in freezing conditions. The Israelis, kitted out for the occasion in their thermals and woollens, held out until half-time, but Janashia stole the show in the second half with a superb hat-trick. Haifa 'keeper Nir Davidovich made a hash of the spectacular long-range strike that gave the Georgian his first goal and was also partly at fault for the late goal that enabled Janashia to complete his hat-trick. Although the temperature was considerably higher for the second match in Haifa, there was no way back for the Israelis. Lokomotiv confirmed their second successive qualification for the Cup-winners' Cup semi-finals with another victory courtesy of defender Igor Chugainov's second-half penalty.

SEMI-FINALS

The two favourites, Lazio and Chelsea, managed to avoid each other in the semi-final draw, which raised the prospect that the last-ever Cup-winners' Cup final would be a high-profile event fit for the occasion. Mallorca and Lokomotiv Moscow had plans of their own, of course. Neither club had ever participated in a European final before and they were aware that in future it would be very difficult for either of them to get into a similar position again in the Champions' League or the new, improved UEFA Cup.

Mallorca were paired with Chelsea, whose own ambition was to become the first (and last) club to make a successful defence of the Cup-winners' Cup. Once again the Londoners were drawn at home first, so the onus was on them to wrest control of the tie in the first leg. Roared on by a capacity crowd, Chelsea went at Mallorca right from the off. But with the Spaniards defending deep and with great discipline, they found it difficult to create any clear chances. The best of them fell to Celestine Babayaro, but he could only direct his shot straight at goalkeeper

SEMI-FINAL RESULTS
(April 8 & 22, 1999)
Chelsea 1 (Flo 50), **RCD Mallorca 1** (Dani 32)
RCD Mallorca 1 (Biagini 14), **Chelsea 0**
(RCD Mallorca 2-1)
Lokomotiv Moskva 1 (Janashia 60), **Lazio 1** (Boksic 77)
Lazio 0, Lokomotiv Moskva 0
(1-1; Lazio on away goal)

CUP-WINNERS' CUP

Carlos Roa, the bane of England in the previous year's World Cup.

A ghastly hush descended over Stamford Bridge when, after 31 minutes and totally against the run of play, Mallorca scored. It was a lovely goal, scored in fine style by Dani after a brilliant through-ball from Paunovic. It was also Mallorca's only shot of the entire half. Chelsea had to respond, and five minutes after the interval they were deservedly back on level terms when Tore André Flo, who had just come on as a substitute, blasted in a right-foot shot following a rare error from Mallorca's Spanish international centre-back Marcelino. A few minutes later the same defender was involved in a bizarre off-the-ball incident when Dennis Wise, who had just missed a good chance to put Chelsea ahead, appeared to take a bite of his shoulder. Further Chelsea pressure could not produce a second goal, and in the end they simply had to take their hats off to Mallorca's excellent defence and hope for the best in the return.

There was a surprise in the Chelsea line-up at Mallorca's Luis Sitjar stadium when player-coach Glianluca Vialli, who had played the full 90 minutes of the first leg, decided to exclude himself both from the starting XI and the substitutes' bench. On the other hand, Mallorca welcomed back Yugoslav left-winger Jovan Stankovic, who had been suspended at Stamford Bridge, and he was to cause the Chelsea defence untold problems in the early minutes, creating one great chance for Dani, which he headed wide, and then another for Leonardo Biagini, who found the target and watched as Chelsea 'keeper Ed de Goey could only paw the ball into the net. Now Chelsea had to show what they were made of. They came forward repeatedly but could only fashion a couple of half-chances in a very even first half.

The second period saw Mallorca retreat into the blanket defensive formation which had so frustrated the holders in the first leg, and once again Chelsea lacked the guile to find a way through. They had all the possession but were clueless when they got near the penalty area. It was not until the very last minute of the match that they finally fashioned a proper chance, but Wise, meeting Zola's perfectly flighted cross, made a pig's ear of his header, sending it down and wide of the target when it seemed easier to score. So, that was that. Mallorca, having fully confirmed their reputation as an outstanding defensive side, were into the final, in their first European campaign, while Chelsea were out, the latest and last Cup-

---

TOP SCORERS

(excluding Qualifying round)

6 Zaza JANASHIA (Lokomotiv Moskva)
4 OKTAY Derelioglu (Besiktas)
   DANI (RCD Mallorca)
   Dmitriy BULYKIN (Lokomotiv Moskva)
   Pavel NEDVED (Lazio)
   Dejan STANKOVIC (Lazio)
   John CAREW (Vålerenga IF)

---

winners' Cup holders thwarted in their attempt to defend the trophy.

Lazio travelled to Moscow for the first leg of their semi-final against Lokomotiv with a commanding lead in their domestic championship. They were chasing glory on two fronts and bidding to reach a European final for the second year in a row. For the first hour or so against the Russians, however, they looked very edgy and uncomposed, and it was only right that Lokomotiv should be the first to score. Their goal was a peach. Quarter-final hero Zaza Janashia latched onto a through-ball, rounded the goalkeeper and, after appearing to take it too wide, readjusted his position and hooked the ball brilliantly into the empty net for his sixth goal of the competition.

Lazio were roused into action but it took the introduction of two substitutes, Roberto Mancini and Alen Boksic, to put them back in the tie, with Mancini flicking on a Stankovic cross for Boksic to stab home on the run. It was quite a comeback for the Croatian, who had been absent for many months. He might even have had a second goal as the Italians came on strong at the end, although the very best chance fell to the Russians in stoppage-time as substitute Borodyuk deflected a left-wing cross inches wide of the post. The 1-1 result meant that none of the six European semi-final first legs had been won by the home team.

Two weeks later, in Rome, Lazio were in crisis. They had suffered back-to-back 1-3 defeats in Serie A and were now under considerable pressure to make certain of their place in the Cup-winners' Cup final as an insurance against further woes in the Italian league. There were many empty seats in the Stadio Olimpico, and although Lazio tried hard to enhance their position, they met with stout Russian resistance and could not score. Christian Vieri came close on a number of occasions but his sights were off beam. Fortunately for the Italians, Lokomotiv had very little to offer in reply and the game tailed off into a stalemate. That, of course, was all Lazio needed to progress into the final, but it was with relief more than joy that players and fans celebrated their qualification.

FINAL

Villa Park in Birmingham was the venue chosen for the last European Cup-winners' Cup final. The absence of Chelsea did nothing to dampen the enthusiasm of the locals, and, contrary to expectations, the stadium was virtually full,

CUP-WINNERS' CUP

with approximately 10,000 Lazio fans having made the journey, either from Rome or from various parts of England.

Although light-blue was very much the prominent colour in the crowd, Lazio had chosen to wear their 'lucky' all-yellow kit for the occasion. As for Mallorca, not short of support themselves, they were decked out in their traditional red shirts and black shorts. Both teams were bidding to make history as neither had previously won a European trophy. Another thing they had in common was a midfielder called Stankovic, with Dejan playing for Lazio and Jovan, his Yugoslav international colleague, for Mallorca.

There was a breathtaking opening to the match. After seven minutes a long, diagonal cross from the right touch-line tempted Mallorca 'keeper Roa to stray from his goal-line, but he was never going to reach the ball. Christian Vieri did, with a tremendous header, and all the Argentine could do was help it on its way into the net. The Lazio fans in the Holte End behind that goal were exultant, but just a few minutes later it was the turn of the Mallorca fans up at the other end to raise their voices in celebration as Dani, eluding his markers, calmly sidefooted Jovan Stankovic's low cross into the net through Lazio 'keeper Luca Marchegiani's legs. Game on!

The remainder of the first half was highly entertaining, although chances were few and far between. Vieri, making up for the poor form of his attacking accomplices

Lazio captain Alessandro Nesta lifts the trophy.

Mancini and Salas, was at the centre of everything and had to leave the field for a while with a head injury... only to return, swathed in bandages, and force a fine save from Roa before getting himself booked for a deliberate hand-ball. It was a very even contest, with two well-organised and talented teams both playing well but without over-exerting themselves.

The second half was less appealing. As the two teams' mutual respect grew, so the excitement level dropped. Lauren, Mallorca's Cameroonian winger, forced a good save from Marchegiani, and Lazio skipper Alessandro Nesta headed over from a Dejan Stankovic cross, but it looked odds-on that the match would have to go into 'golden goal' extra-time and maybe penalties.

But then, completely out of the blue, Lazio scored. Pavel Nedved, who was badly winded just a few moments earlier and seemed set to be called off, was presented with a loose ball on the egde of the area. Instinctively he took aim with his right foot and sent a superb shot beyond Roa into the net. It was a splendid strike, although Mallorca's protests that Vieri had caused a foul in winning the aerial challenge that set the chance up could not entirely be dismissed.

There was no way back for the Spaniards. The goal had arrived with just nine minutes left, and Lazio were too canny to let their lead slip. It had been a close contest, but Lazio had just had that little bit extra. They were worthy winners.

Vieri was voted official Man of the Match and Lazio had their first European trophy, although by the time skipper Nesta went up to lift the Cup there were no medals left for him to hang around his neck. It was an obvious embarrassment for the UEFA officials but Nesta did not seem over-concerned. In his hand was the trophy, and it would forever be his honour and privilege to be remembered as the last winning captain to hoist the European Cup-winners' Cup to the skies.

UEFA CUP

PRELIMINARY ROUND RESULTS

(July 22/29, 1998)

FC Arges Dacia Pitesti 5 (Emirbekov 3og, Barbu 9, 78p, Bârdes 27, Jilaveanu 88), **Dinamo Baku 1** (Aliev 36p)
Dinamo Baku 0, FC Arges Dacia Pitesti 2 (Mutu 52, Jilaveanu 90)
(FC Arges Dacia Pitesti 7-1)

Belshina Bobruisk 0, CSKA Sofia 0
CSKA Sofia 3 (Petrov M. 6, Naidenov 38, Stanchev 90),
Belshina Bobruisk 1 (Balashov 50)
(CSKA Sofia 3-1)

Ferencvearos 6 (Fülöp 25, Selimi 42, Schultz 48, 75p, Vámosi 63, Mátyus 90), **CE Principat 0**
CE Principat 1 (Pasqui 24), **Ferencváros 8** (Selimi 18, 74, Kovács 23, 83, Kriston 51, Nagy 52, Jagodics 58, Schultz 84))
(Ferencváros 14-1)

KFC Germinal Ekeren 4 (Van Ankeren 25, Morhaye 28, 89, Kovács 41),
FK Sarajevo 1 (Ferhatovic 59)
FK Sarajevo 0, KFC Germinal Ekeren 0
(KFC Germinal Ekeren 4-1)

Hapoel Tel-Aviv 3 (Cimerotic 31, Tubi 53, Tikva 63),
FinnPa 1 (Hautala 45)
FinnPa 1 (Geagea 88), **Hapoel Tel-Aviv 3** (Tikva 5, 18, Tubi 74)
(Hapoel Tel-Aviv 6-2)

HB 2 (Johannesen S.F. 28, 73), **VPS 0**
VPS 4 (Suoste 3, 17, Tarkkio 72, Nygård 90), **HB 0**
(VPS 4-2)

ÍA 3 (Adolfsson 41, Eyjólfsson 61, Ivsic 86),
Zalgiris Vilnius 2 (Skinderis 11, Vasilauskas 72)
Zalgiris Vilnius 1 (Stesko A. 15), **ÍA 0**
(3-3; Zalgiris Vilnius on away goals)

Inter Bratislava 2 (Suchancok 14, Miklus 58), **SK Tirana 0**
SK Tirana 0, Inter Bratislava 2 (Babnic 54, Miklos 80)
(Inter Bratislava 4-0)

Kolkheti 1913 Poti 0,
Crvena zvezda Beograd 4 (Ognjenovic 20, Acimovic 57, 73, Pantelic 63)
Crvena zvezda Beograd 7 (Pantelic 28, Ognjenovic 45p, 47, Gojkovic 54, Micic 57, 69, 90), **Kolkheti 1913 Poti 0**
(Crvena zvezda Beograd 11-0)

Mura Murska Sobota 6 (Cifer 5, 31, Lukic 16, 88, Cipot 30, Galic 39),
Daugava Riga 1 (Ridny 75)
Daugava Riga 1 (Sharando 69),
Mura Murska Sobota 2 (Vogrincic 58, Ristic 66)
(Mura Murska Sobota 8-2)

Newtown 0, Wisla Krakow 0
Wisla Krakow 7 (Kulawik 28, 47, 51, Sunday 35, Dubicki 54, Pater 61, 66),
Newtown 0
(Wisla Krakow 7-0)

Omonia Nicosia 5 (Kitanov 40, 61, Rauffmann 43p, Panayiotou 64, Kondolefteros 88), **Linfield 1** (Ferguson 73)
Linfield 5 (Feeney 19, Gorman 35, 48, McDonald 45, Campbell 73),
Omonia Nicosia 3 (Marangos 2, Kitanov 35, 43)
(Omonia Nicosia 8-6)

Otelul Galati 3 (Stefan 30, Mihalache 41, Males 90p),
Sloga Jugomagnat Skopje 0
Sloga Jugomagnat Skopje 1 (Stankovski 42),
Otelul Galati 1 (Mihalache 59)
(Otelul Galati 4-1)

Shakhtar Donetsk 2 (Seleznev 62, Kriventsov 69p),
Birkirkara 1 (Zammit 75)
Birkirkara 0,
Shakhtar Donetsk 4 (Seleznev 39, Kriventsov 49p, Kovalev 82, 90)
(Shakhtar Donetsk 6-1)

Shelbourne 3 (Porrini 7og, Rutherford 41, Morley 58),
Rangers 5 (Albertz 59p, 85p, Amato 72, 81, Van Bronckhorst 74)
Rangers 2 (Johansson 4, 89), **Shelbourne 0**
(Rangers 7-3)

Shirak Gyumri 0, Malmö FF 2 (Pavlovic 55, Ohlsson 68)
Malmö FF 5 (Thylander 19, Kindvall 33, 45, 77, Gudmundsson 68),
Shirak Gyumri 0
(Malmö FF 7-0)

Tallinna Sadam 0, Polonia Warszawa 2 (Olisadebe 34, Bak 80)
Polonia Warszawa 3 (Moskal 8, Wedzynski 16, Bak 21),
Tallinna Sadam 1 (Krölov 3)
(Polonia Warszawa 5-1)

Tiligul Tiraspol 0, RSC Anderlecht 1 (Staelens 56)
RSC Anderlecht 5 (Stoica 32, De Boeck 42, Dheedene 56, Taument 60, Årst 76), **Tiligul Tiraspol 0**
(RSC Anderlecht 6-0)

Union Luxembourg 0,
IFK Göteborg 3 (Ekström 58, Nilsson 63p, Hermansson 86)
IFK Göteborg 4 (Ekström 17, 50, 79, Henriksson 71),
Union Luxembourg 0
(IFK Göteborg 7-0)

Zeljeznicar Sarajevo 1 (Vazda 63), **Kilmarnock 1** (McGowne 55)
Kilmarnock 1 (Mahood 31), **Zeljeznicar Sarajevo 0**
(Kilmarnock 2-1)

UEFA CUP

The 1998/99 UEFA Cup retained the format of the previous season, with two summer preliminary rounds being required in order to reduce the field to 64 at the first-round stage in September.

The original entry was 84 teams, but with 16 repêchage entries from the Champions' League and three InterToto qualifiers being added in the first round, it meant that of the 60 clubs obliged to enter at one or other of the two preliminary rounds, only 20 would remain in the field to join the new arrivals from other competitions plus the 25 exempt teams from UEFA's highest-ranking countries.

Although the UEFA Cup still has considerable prestige, it was significant that of the 16 clubs proposed for full membership of the UEFA-alternative 'European Super League', only two - Liverpool and Marseille - were among the UEFA Cup starting contingent. Of the others, 11 were in the Champions' League, one competed in the Cup-winners' Cup, and two were not involved in European competition at all.

Even so, the UEFA Cup field had a strong and balanced look to it, with impressive block representations from all of Europe's major leagues, including Italy's Serie A, which had provided no fewer than seven winners and six runners-up in the previous decade.

PRELIMINARY ROUND

40 teams from UEFA's lesser-ranked nations set the competition in motion in July. Two national champions were among them.

Neither Andorra's CE Principat or Bosnia-Herzegovina's Zeljeznicar Sarajevo had been granted Champions' League access, which seemed rather unfair. But, as latecomers to European competition, they were informed that there was no room for them in the bigger tournament. The alternative was a place in the opening round of the UEFA Cup, and they could take it or leave it.

Principat might have been better advised to go down the latter route. They were pummelled mercilessly into submission by Ferencváros, who beat them 6-0 in Hungary and 8-1 in Andorra. Zeljeznicar fared a lot better, making a real fight of their tie with Scottish qualifiers Kilmarnock before losing out narrowly 2-1 on aggregate in front of two five-figure crowds.

That was a rare competitive tussle among a welter of mismatches. The only other tie which finished with a victory margin of less than two goals was the one

between ÍA and Zalgiris Vilnius, which went the way of the Lithuanians on the away-goals rule.

At one stage, however, it looked as if Rangers, one of five previous European trophy-winners obliged to compete at this stage, would be pushed to the limit by League of Ireland side Shelbourne. Incredibly, they fell three goals behind in the first leg, switched to the ground of English club Tranmere Rovers, before a sudden surge of second-half goals rescued them from complete humiliation. Another Irish side, Linfield from the North, enjoyed a rare bout of goalscoring, at home to the Cypriots of Omonia Nicosia. But their 5-3 victory at Windsor Park was only ever going to be academic after they lost the first leg 5-1 in the Cypriot capital.

There were no real surprises. All 20 of the higher-seeded teams came safely through, and they included the likes of Red Star Belgrade, IFK Gothenburg and Anderlecht - all clubs which would not normally have expected to be participating in Europe at this early juncture of the season.

QUALIFYING ROUND

The second process of elimination brought the 20 preliminary-round qualifiers together with another 20 clubs from the middle band of UEFA's ranking table. The draw produced some interesting pairings, but when all the matches had been played, there were a mere six survivors from the preliminary round.

Those happy half-dozen were Anderlecht, Rangers, Wisla Krakow, Red Star Belgrade, CSKA Sofia and, most surprisingly of all, FC Arges Dacia Pitesti.

The Romanians caused quite a stir by eliminating Istanbulspor of Turkey on away goals. There was an even heavier defeat for another Turkish side, Trabzonspor, who felt the full force of ambitious, big-spending Polish side Wisla Krakow, losing 5-1 in Poland and 2-1 at home. Fortunately, Fenerbahçe prevented a Turkish whitewash by overcoming IFK Gothenburg in perhaps the most fiercely-contested and certainly one of the best-attended ties of the round.

Swedish woe was complete with the elimination of Malmö FF, who lost out to Hajduk Split for the second season running. Malmö did well to get a draw away from home in the first leg, but they were no match for the Croatians in the return. Osijek almost made it a Croatian double but they lost out on away goals to Anderlecht after building an impressive 3-1 lead in the home leg. It was the same story in the tie between

UEFA CUP

QUALIFYING ROUND RESULTS

(August 11/25, 1998)

FC Arges Dacia Pitesti 2 (Mutu 31, Barbu 45), **Istanbulspor 0**
Istanbulspor 4 (Saffet 14, Sergen 20, Mehmet 79, Aykut 86),
FC Arges Dacia Pitesti 2 (Mutu 52, Barbu 73)
(4-4; FC Arges Dacia Pitesti on away goals)

SK Brann 1 (Kvisvik 75p), **Zalgiris Vilnius 0**
Zalgiris Vilnius 0, SK Brann 0
(SK Brann 1-0)

Crvena zvezda Beograd 2 (Skoric 61p, Ognjenovic 90p),
Rotor Volgograd 1 (Abramov 66)
Rotor Volgograd 1 (Zernov 59),
Crvena zvezda Beograd 2 (Ognjenovic 74, Dudic 81)
(Crvena zvezda Beograd 4-2)

Ferencváros 4 (Selimi 9, Lendvai 28, Nyilas 55p, Vincze 83),
AEK 2 (Nikolaidis 87, Sebwe 89)
AEK 4 (Nikolaidis 8, 12p, 25, Donis 62), **Ferencváros 0**
(AEK 6-4)

KFC Germinal Ekeren 1 (Morhaye 85),
Servette FC Genève 4 (Rey 20p, 51, Wolf 35, Durix 78)
Servette FC Genève 1 (Rey 83p),
KFC Germinal Ekeren 2 (Fournier 18og, Karagiannis 43)
(Servette FC Genève 5-3)

IFK Göteborg 2 (Hermansson 37, Persson J. 74),
Fenerbahçe 1 (Kemalettin 49)
Fenerbahçe 1 (Baljic 64), **IFK Göteborg 0**
(2-2; Fenerbahçe on away goal)

Hajduk Split 1 (Brajkovic 44), **Malmö FF 1** (Bjarnason 72)
Malmö FF 1 (Ohlsson 90), **Hajduk Split 2** (Vucko 40, 55)
(Hajduk Split 3-2)

Hapoel Tel-Aviv 1 (Tubi 75), **Stromsgodset IF 0**
Stromsgodset IF 1 (Michelsen 42), **Hapoel Tel-Aviv 0** (aet)
(1-1, Stromsgodset IF 4-2 on pens.)

Molde FK 0, CSKA Sofia 0
CSKA Sofia 2 (Petkov 39, Stanchev 60), **Molde FK 0**
(CSKA Sofia 2-0)

Mura Murska Sobota 0, Silkeborg IF 0
Silkeborg IF 2 (Sørensen 63, Larsen T.R. 64),
Mura Murska Sobota 0
(Silkeborg IF 2-0)

Omonia Nicosia 3 (Rauffmann 42, 58, Malekkos 46),
SK Rapid Wien 1 (Wagner 22)
SK Rapid Wien 2 (Heraf 9, Wagner 70),
Omonia Nicosia 0
(3-3; SK Rapid Wien on away goal)

Osijek 3 (Krpan 29, Prisc 53, Vranjes J. 81),
RSC Anderlecht 1 (Claeys 80)
RSC Anderlecht 2 (Årst 4, Stoica 84), **Osijek 0**
(3-3; RSC Anderlecht on away goal)

Polonia Warszawa 0, Dinamo Moskva 1 (Gusev 54)
Dinamo Moskva 1 (Teryokhin 90),
Polonia Warszawa 0
(Dinamo Moskva 2-0)

Rangers 2 (Kanchelskis 55, Wallace 68), **PAOK 0**
PAOK 0, Rangers 0
(Rangers 2-0)

Sigma Olomouc 2 (Krohmer 27, König 79), **Kilmarnock 0**
Kilmarnock 0, Sigma Olomouc 2 (Heinz 13, Mucha 20)
(Sigma Olomouc 4-0)

Slavia Praha 4 (Vagner 22, 90, Kozel 55, Skala 71),
Inter Bratislava 0
Inter Bratislava 2 (Babnic 12, Ovad 52), **Slavia Praha 0**
(Slavia Praha 4-2)

Vejle BK 3 (Wael 31, 42, Søgaard 62), **Otelul Galati 0**
Otelul Galati 0, Vejle BK 3 (Jung 22, Graulund 36, Wael 53)
(Vejle BK 6-0)

VPS 0, Grazer AK 0
Grazer AK 3 (Luhovy 51, Grimm 54, Drechsel 90), **VPS 0**
(Grazer AK 3-0)

Wisla Krakow 5 (Dubicki 3, Kulawik 33, 71, 80, Zajac B. 89),
Trabzonspor 1 (Vugrinec 66)
Trabzonspor 1 (Hüseyin 67),
Wisla Krakow 2 (Sunday 54, Kulawik 63)
(Wisla Krakow 7-2)

FC Zürich 4 (Sant'Anna 1, Djordjevic 61, Chassot 71, Tarone 88),
Shakhtar Donetsk 0
Shakhtar Donetsk 3 (Orbu 24, 69, Shtolcers 90),
FC Zürich 2 (Bartlett 19, 28)
(FC Zürich 6-3)

UEFA CUP

Omonia Nicosia and Rapid Vienna, with the Austrians surviving on away goals thanks to a 2-0 second-leg win in Vienna.

The biggest two crowds of the round came to see the tie between Rangers and PAOK, with an aggregate attendance of around 70,000 being reached. The Scots deservedly went through, scoring twice without reply at Ibrox and then defending calmly and intelligently in Salonika to ensure their passage to the next round. There was no such joy for the other Scottish team, Kilmarnock, who were convincingly beaten home and away by Sigma Olomouc. Slavia Prague were another Czech side to get through, winning the 'derby' against the Slovakians of Inter Bratislava - the first competitive confrontation of two teams from different 'sides' of the former Czechoslovakia.

The comeback of the round was undoubtedly that of AEK Athens. Trailing 4-0 in their first leg away to Ferencváros, they scored two late away goals in Budapest and put the Hungarians to the sword in Athens, with Themistoklis Nikolaidis scoring a hat-trick to add to the goal he scored in the first leg.

FIRST ROUND

16 outcasts from the Champions' League were added to the UEFA Cup field, but the vast majority were to have a brief stay. Only three - Grasshopper, Celtic and Bruges - managed to prolong their European involvement. The other 13 all lost a European tie for the second round in succession.

There were better fortunes, however, for the three InterToto qualifiers - Valencia, Bologna and Werder Bremen - all of whom progressed. Valencia enjoyed themselves immensely against Romanian champions Steaua Bucharest, winning 4-3 away, with Adrian Ilie notching two goals against his former club, and 3-0 at home. Bologna comprehensively beat Sporting of Portugal, but Bremen had to stage a grand extra-time recovery at home before seeing off the Norwegians of SK Brann.

An even better second-leg fightback was staged by VfB Stuttgart, the previous season's Cup-winners' Cup finalists. Trounced 3-1 at home by Feyenoord in the first leg, they somehow contrived to turn the tie around in Rotterdam, with Fredi Bobic squeezing home the decisive goal through a crowded goalmouth in the very last minute. All had seemed lost for Stuttgart a minute earlier when Bobic hit the post, but, not for the

first time, German perseverance ultimately bore fruit.

Another German side, 1997 winners Schalke, were forced into extra-time in their tie with Slavia Prague but no goals ensued and it was the Czechs who eventually prevailed in the shoot-out, dispelling the myth that the Germans never lose penalty competitions. Some English teams do occasionally win them, too, as Leeds United showed in overcoming Marítimo in that manner after the two teams had each posted 1-0 home wins. The triumph in Madeira enabled Leeds' manager George Graham to bow out on a winning note - it was his last match before he departed to join Tottenham.

The only one of the four English teams to go out were Blackburn Rovers, whose poor record in Europe continued when they went down 3-2 on aggregate against Lyon. In truth, they did not deserve to lose, but after conceding a magnificent 35-yard shot from Polish defender Jacek Bak to lose the home leg, they were always up against it in the return, especially with all four first-choice strikers missing through injury. They bravely battled for a 2-2 draw in the Stade Gerland and almost nicked a famous victory right at the end.

Aston Villa were in great peril at one stage at home to Strømsgodset before an incredible late goal-flurry, inspired by youngster Darius Vassell, gave them an improbable 3-2 victory. The mercurial Stan Collymore did the rest in the return, scoring a fine hat-trick. Liverpool had less trouble, annihilating Slovakian champions Kosice 8-0 on aggregate.

Like Germany and England, Italy also lost one representative, with Udinese losing narrowly to Bayer Leverkusen in the tie of the round. A goal from newly-capped German international midfielder Stefan Beinlich was enough to finish off the Serie A side in the second leg after they had been forced to chase the tie following Ulf Kirsten's early goal in Udine.

Parma also came close to going out. They lost the first leg of their tie with Fenerbahçe, 1-0 in Istanbul, and were heading for an early exit on away goals when French World Cup winner Alain Boghossian scored a brilliant late goal to give them a 3-1 home win. Fiorentina joined them in round two after a classic Italian all-out defensive performance away to Hajduk Split. That enabled them to preserve the slender 2-1 advantage given them by Brazilian striker Edmundo in the first leg - a game which had been switched to Bari as punishment for crowd disturbances in Florence at the 1997 Cup-winners' Cup semi-final against Barcelona.

UEFA CUP

(September 15 & 29, 1998)

RSC Anderlecht 0, Grasshopper-Club Zürich 2 (Comisetti 54, Tikva 84)
Grasshopper-Club Zürich 0, RSC Anderlecht 0
(Grasshopper-Club Zürich 2-0)

FC Arges Dacia Pitesti 0, RC Celta 1 (Sánchez 25)
RC Celta 7 (Penev 5, 13, 26, Mazinho 16, Sánchez 69, Tomás 78. 89),
FC Arges Dacia Pitesti 0
(RC Celta 8-0)

Atlético Madrid 2 (Juninho 15, José Mari 53), **Obilic Beograd 0**
Obilic Beograd 0, Atlético Madrid 1 (Kiko 54)
(Atlético Madrid 3-0)

Aston Villa 3 (Charles 83, Vassell 89, 90),
Stromsgodset IF 2 (Michelsen 22, George 23)
Stromsgodset IF 0, Aston Villa 3 (Collymore 11, 24, 64)
(Aston Villa 6-2)

Beitar Jerusalem 1 (Abuksis 17p), **Rangers 1** (Albertz 82)
Rangers 4 (Gattuso 1, Porrini 25, Johansson 59, Wallace 63),
Beitar Jerusalem 2 (Sallói 35, Ohana 80p)
(Rangers 5-3)

Blackburn Rovers 0, Olympique Lyonnais 1 (Bak 85)
Olympique Lyonnais 2 (Caveglia 3, Grassi 36p),
Blackburn Rovers 2 (Perez 26, Flitcroft 56)
(Olympique Lyonnais 3-2)

Girondins de Bordeaux 1 (Hatz 23og), **SK Rapid Wien 1** (Freund 65)
SK Rapid Wien 1 (Wagner 42),
Girondins de Bordeaux 2 (Alicarte 28, Diabaté 87)
(Girondins de Bordeaux 3-2)

SK Brann 2 (Moen 29, Løvvik 56), **SV Werder Bremen 0**
SV Werder Bremen 4 (Wicky 33, Wiedener 70, Maximov 107, Гlo 110),
SK Brann 0 (aet)
(SV Werder Bremen 4-2)

Crvena zvezda Beograd 2 (Ognjenovic 3, Drulic 12),
FC Metz 1 (Rodriguez 90)
FC Metz 2 (Kastendeuch 38, Meyrieu 68p),
Crvena zvezda Beograd 1 (Marinovic 18) (aet)
(3-3; Crvena zvezda Beograd 4-3 on pens.)

Dinamo Moskva 2 (Golovskoi 2, Ostrovskiy 69),
Skonto Riga 2 (Mikholap 39, Pakhar 49)
Skonto Riga 2 (Pakhar 75, 89),
Dinamo Moskva 3 (Gusev 17, Golovskoi 51, Teryokhin 76)
(Dinamo Moskva 5-4)

Fenerbahçe 1 (Moldovan 23), **Parma 0**
Parma 3 (Saffet 14og, Crespo 45, Boghossian 73),
Fenerbahçe 1 (Baljic 59)
(Parma 3-2)

Fiorentina 2 (Edmundo 51, 82), **Hajduk Split 1** (Vucko 45)
Hajduk Split 0, Fiorentina 0
(Fiorentina 2-1)

1.FC Kosice 0, Liverpool 3 (Berger 19, Riedle 23, Owen 59)
Liverpool 5 (Redknapp 23, 55, Ince 52, Fowler 53, 90), **1.FC Kosice 0**
(Liverpool 8-0)

Leeds United 1 (Hasselbaink 84), **CS Marítimo 0**
CS Marítimo 1 (Jorge Soares 45), **Leeds United 0** (aet)
(1-1; Leeds United 4-1 on pens.)

Liteks Lovech 1 (Stoilov 60), **Grazer AK 1** (Lipa 56)
Grazer AK 2 (Golombek 7, Akwuegbu 82), **Liteks Lovech 0**
(Grazer AK 3-1)

LKS Lodz 1 (Matys 9),
AS Monaco 3 (Bendkowski 57og, Trezeguet 68p, Spehar 84)
AS Monaco 0, LKS Lodz 0
(AS Monaco 3-1)

Maribor Teatanic 0, Wisla Krakow 2 (Frankowski 22, Pater 45)
Wisla Krakow 3 (Zajac M. 85, 89, Kulawik 90), **Maribor Teatanic 0**
(Wisla Krakow 5-0)

FC Schalke 04 1 (Wilmots 40), **Slavia Praha 0**
Slavia Praha 1 (Dostalek 18), **FC Schalke 04 0** (aet)
(1-1; Slavia Praha 5-4 on pens.)

Servette FC Genève 2 (Pizzinat 85, Melunovic 89),
CSKA Sofia 1 (Stanchev 45)
CSKA Sofia 1 (Stanchev 9), **Servette FC Genève 0**
(2-2; CSKA Sofia on away goal)

Sigma Olomouc 2 (Heinz 35, 41),
Olympique Marseille 2 (Ravanelli 27, Roy 82)
Olympique Marseille 4 (Dugarry 18, 75, Pires 22, 83), **Sigma Olomouc 0**
(Olympique Marseille 6-2)

Silkeborg IF 0, Roma 2 (Totti 62, Alenichev 70)
Roma 1 (Delvecchio 53), **Silkeborg IF 0**
(Roma 3-0)

Sparta Praha 2 (Cizek 31, Lokvenc 40),
Real Sociedad 4 (Kovacevic 7, 57, Aldeondo 47, De Pedro 80)
Real Sociedad 1 (Kovacevic 50), **Sparta Praha 0**
(Real Sociedad 5-2)

UEFA CUP

FIRST ROUND RESULTS (CONTINUED)

Sporting CP 0, Bologna 2 (Nervo 16, Eriberto 90)

Bologna 2 (Nervo 78, Signori 90p), **Sporting CP 1** (Leandro 64)

(Bologna 4-1)

Steaua Bucuresti 3 (Lincar 29, Rosu 60, Dumitrescu 85),
Valencia CF 4 (Ilie 11, 24, Angulo 74, 85)

Valencia CF 3 (Roche 52, López 56, Lucarelli 86), **Steaua Bucuresti 0**

(Valencia CF 7-3)

VfB Stuttgart 1 (Bobic 31), **Feyenoord 3** (Van Gastel 19, Tomasson 22, 33)

Feyenoord 0, VfB Stuttgart 3 (Balakov 34, Djordjevic 69, Bobic 90)

(VfB Stuttgart 4-3)

Udinese 1 (Walem 82), **Bayer 04 Leverkusen 1** (Kirsten 12)

Bayer 04 Leverkusen 1 (Beinlich 77), **Udinese 0**

(Bayer 04 Leverkusen 2-1)

Újpest FC 0,
Club Brugge KV 5 (Jankauskas 12, Ilic 25, Vermant 42, Anic 50, Ekakia 89)

Club Brugge KV 2 (Borkelmans 32, Vermant 70),
Újpest FC 2 (Kopunovic 50, Szanyó 90p)

(Club Brugge KV 7-2)

Vejle BK 1 (Graulund 86), **Real Betis 0**

Real Betis 5 (Iván 1, 20, 87, Finidi 70, Gálvez 71), **Vejle BK 0**

(Real Betis 5-1)

Vitesse 3 (Laros 48, Perovic 51, Mahlas 89), **AEK 0**

AEK 3 (Nikolaidis 14, 76, Kopitsis 67), **Vitesse 3** (Mahlas 13, 17, Reuser 54)

(Vitesse 6-3)

Vitória Guimarães 1 (Geraldo 86), **Celtic 2** (Larsson 1, Donnelly 69)

Celtic 2 (Stubbs 39, Larsson 90), **Vitória Guimarães 1** (Söderström 86)

(Celtic 4-2)

Willem II 3 (Ramzi 73, Arts 79, Schenning 85), **Dinamo Tbilisi 0**

Dinamo Tbilisi 0, Willem II 3 (Valk 18, Ceesay 81, Ramzi 90)

(Willem II 6-0)

FC Zürich 4 (Nixon 35, Hodel 58, Bartlett 69, Chassot 81),
Anorthosis Famagusta 0

Anorthosis Famagusta 2 (Fischer 45og, Krcmarevic 71),
FC Zürich 3 (Sant'Anna 12, Bartlett 38, 62)

(FC Zürich 7-2)

France, like Italy, carried four teams through to the next round, losing just Metz, whose miserable start to the season continued when they were beaten on penalties by Red Star Belgrade. But the best collective performance was that of Spain, whose five teams all made further progress, four of them having won both of their matches. The only defeat by a Spanish team was Betis's 0-1 reverse away to Vejle, but they made up for that with a thumping 5-0 win in Seville. Remarkably, all five Spanish sides won their second leg matches without conceding a goal, with Celta's 7-0 victory over Arges Pitesti ranking as the biggest win of the round. Bulgarian striker Liuboslav Penev was the star of the show, destroying the Romanians with a 20-minute first-half hat-trick.

SECOND ROUND

The second round first-leg ties threw up a major imbalance, with only two of the 16 teams drawn at home first managing to record a victory. Both of those were Italians, with Roma beating Leeds 1-0 and Bologna overcoming Slavia Prague 2-1.

In both cases that home advantage proved sufficient, although Roma made life difficult for themselves when they went down to ten men just before half-time at

Elland Road following the expulsion of left-back Pierre Wome. Leeds, though, lacked the knowhow to penetrate the well-staffed Italian rearguard and created very few chances to score.

Of those 14 teams who did not carve out a first-leg

Celta Vigo's Tomás heads clear from Aston Villa's Julian Joachim (right).

THE EUROPEAN FOOTBALL YEARBOOK 1999-2000

UEFA CUP

SECOND ROUND RESULTS

(October 20/22, November 3/5, 1998)

Bayer 04 Leverkusen 1 (Reichenberger 90),
Rangers 2 (Van Bronckhorst 45, Johansson 64)
Rangers 1 (Johansson 56), **Bayer 04 Leverkusen 1** (Kirsten 79)
(Rangers 3-2)

Bologna 2 (Signori 51, Ingesson 84), **Slavia Praha 1** (Dostalek 68)
Slavia Praha 0, Bologna 2 (Signori 79, Cappioli 85)
(Bologna 4-1)

RC Celta 0, Aston Villa 1 (Joachim 14)
Aston Villa 1 (Collymore 27p),
RC Celta 3 (Sánchez 26, Mostovoi 33, Penev 48)
(RC Celta 3-2)

Celtic 1 (Brattbakk 22), **FC Zürich 1** (Fischer 76)
FC Zürich 4 (Del Signore 52, Chassot 56, Bartlett 61, Sant'Anna 75),
Celtic 2 (O'Donnell 57, Larsson 72)
(FC Zürich 5-3)

Crvena zvezda Beograd 1 (Skaric 58p),
Olympique Lyonnais 2 (Grassi 70, Kanoute 84)
Olympique Lyonnais 3 (Caveglia 17, 44, Cocard 41),
Crvena zvezda Beograd 2 (Bunjevcevic 31, Acimovic 90)
(Olympique Lyonnais 5-3)

CSKA Sofia 2 (Genchev 53, Naidenov 84),
Atlético Madrid 4 (Torrisi 40, Kiko 42, 87, Roberto 73)
Atlético Madrid 1 (Juninho 45p), **CSKA Sofia 0**
(Atlético Madrid 5-2)

Dinamo Moskva 2 (Nekrasov 72, 73),
Real Sociedad 3 (Kovacevic 3, 10, De Pedro 35p)
Real Sociedad 3 (Kovacevic 57, 75, De Paula 69), **Dinamo Moskva 0**
(Real Sociedad 6-2)

Grasshopper-Club Zürich 0, Fiorentina 2 (Batistuta 20, Robbiati 47)
Fiorentina 2 (Oliveira 12, 38), **Grasshopper-Club Zürich 1** (Gren 29)
(match abandoned; awarded 0-3)
(Grasshopper-Club Zürich 3-2)

Grazer AK 3 (Akwuegbu 28, 57, Ehmann 90),
AS Monaco 3 (Spehar 17, 60, Giuly 78)
AS Monaco 4 (Gava 8, 67, Spehar 16, Diawara 55), **Grazer AK 0**
(AS Monaco 7-3)

Liverpool 0, Valencia CF 0
Valencia CF 2 (López 45, 90), **Liverpool 2** (McManaman 80, Berger 86)
(2-2; Liverpool on away goals)

Roma 1 (Delvecchio 18), **Leeds United 0**
Leeds United 0, Roma 0
(Roma 1-0)

VfB Stuttgart 1 (Akpoborie 8), **Club Brugge KV 1** (Vermant 70)
Club Brugge KV 3 (De Cock 60, Claessens 105, Ilic 116),
VfB Stuttgart 2 (Verlaat 76, Bobic 109) (aet)
(Club Brugge KV 4-3)

Vitesse 0, Girondins de Bordeaux 1 (Wiltord 45)
Girondins de Bordeaux 2 (Micoud 9, Wiltord 63), **Vitesse 1** (Jochemsen 8)
(Girondins de Bordeaux 3-1)

SV Werder Bremen 1 (Herzog 69), **Olympique Marseille 1** (Maurice 67)
Olympique Marseille 3 (Maurice 35, Issa 52, Dugarry 78),
SV Werder Bremen 2 (Eilts 47, Herzog 83)
(Olympique Marseille 4-3)

Willem II 1 (Bombarda 85), **Real Betis 1** (Alexis 84)
Real Betis 3 (Finidi 30, Benjamin 55, Fernando 90), **Willem II 0**
(Real Betis 4-1)

Wisla Krakow 1 (Kulawik 68), **Parma 1** (Chiesa 2)
Parma 2 (Fiore 21, Zajac B. 47og), **Wisla Krakow 1** (Zajac B. 90)
(Parma 3-2)

advantage at home, only three succeeded in making up for it in the away leg. One of those was Celta, who, after succumbing to a rare home defeat by English table-toppers Aston Villa, reaped their revenge in some style at Villa Park, winning 3-1. There was another reversal of fortunes in the other Anglo-Spanish clash, between Liverpool and Valencia. This was to be arguably the tie of the round, even though the first leg at Anfield failed to produce any goals.

Valencia should have won that match. In the second half they gave Liverpool the runaround, slicing them apart with rapid, beautifully choreographed counterattacks. But a mixture of poor finishing and accomplished goalkeeping from David James prevented the Spaniards from scoring a deserved away goal. Liverpool controversially chose to omit Michael Owen and the gamble did not pay off. Throughout the 90 minutes they barely posed any danger other than at the odd set-piece.

The second leg saw Owen restored and he was even-

UEFA CUP

tually to play a major part in Liverpool's qualification for the next round, setting up an equalising goal for Steve McManaman with a superb run and cross just when it seemed as if Valencia had dome enough to win through Claudio López's goal on the stroke of half-time. In fact, the last few minutes were to produce some of the most incident-packed football seen anywhere in Europe during the season. First, Patrik Berger put Liverpool ahead with a magnificent solo goal, but Valencia refused to give up, and when McManaman and Paul Ince were both sent off (along with Valencia's Amedeo Carboni) after a ridiculous altercation in stoppage-time, there was still time for López to crash in a free-kick off David James' back and provide the visitors with an anxious few final seconds. Liverpool were mightily relieved to hear the final whistle, and so was English football in general, otherwise there would have been no Premiership sides left in the competition.

As for Germany, they *did* lose their entire complement. Werder Bremen, Stuttgart and Bayer Leverkusen all paid the price for failing to win their home matches. They battled with great valour in the return legs but none of them could repair the damage. Stuttgart were desperately unfortunate to lose an extra-time thriller away to Bruges, scoring twice after they had been reduced to nine men and only conceding defeat in the 116th minute when Bruges defender Aleksandar Ilic headed in unmarked from a free-kick. Bremen were always behind away to Marseille, but a late goal from Austrian Andy Herzog made for a very nervous final few minutes for the in-form French side. Likewise Bayer Leverkusen, who, having fallen to a shock 1-2 home defeat by an inspired Rangers, laid siege to the Glaswegians' goal for almost 90 minutes at Ibrox, eventually scoring late on through Ulf Kirsten and coming close several times afterwards.

Marseille's win completed a clean sweep for France, with Monaco, Lyon and Bordeaux all coming through without undue stress to join them in the third round. Italy should also have made it four qualifiers out of four. In addition to Roma and Bologna, Parma managed to see off Polish league leaders Wisla Krakow in a tie that was overshadowed by a frightening incident that occurred ten minutes from time in the first leg in Poland when midfielder Dino Baggio fell to the ground after being struck on the head by a knife thrown from the stands. The Italian international required five stitches, and Wisla were subsequently handed a one-year ban by UEFA.

There was also major controversy at the tie involving the other remaining Italian club, Fiorentina. The *Viola* were comfortably beating Grasshopper 4-1 on aggregate at half-time in the second leg, which had been switched to Salerno as part of the continuing home-ground ban being served on the Italian club. But as the players and officials marched off to the dressing-rooms in the corner of the pitch, an idiot in the crowd hurled an explosive device onto the pitch. The fourth official was injured on the leg and a number of players suffered temporary deafness. The referee had no alternative but to abandon the match there and then. Fiorentina awaited their fate but were understandably dismayed when they discovered that they had been ejected from the competition. They pleaded that the person responsible for the outrage was a fan of local club Salernitana, but UEFA retorted that it was Fiorentina's responsibility to ensure safety - even if it was a stadium that they were borrowing for just the one night.

Spain maintained a very strong southern European presence in the last 16 by winning four of their five ties. Although Valencia dropped out, Betis, Atlético Madrid and Real Sociedad all joined Celta in the third round. Once again, Atlético and Real Sociedad won both home and away, while Betis relied upon their second-leg prowess in Seville. The best individual performance of the round came from Real Sociedad's Yugoslav striker Darko Kovacevic, who scored twice in each of his team's victories against Dinamo Moscow, which, added to his three goals in the first round, made him the top scorer of the competition (preliminary rounds excluded) with seven goals.

THIRD ROUND

In contrast to the chain of events in the previous round, none of the teams drawn at home first this time were beaten. In fact, of the 16 matches played over the two legs, only a couple resulted in away victories.

The two teams who lost at home were Club Bruges and Liverpool. Bruges, the last remaining Champions' League survivors, went into their second leg in a reasonably confident frame of mind after losing by just a single goal away to Lyon, but they failed to reckon with the prolific goalscoring of Lyon skipper Alain Caveglia, who won the game - and the tie - for the French side with a classic poacher's hat-trick.

As for Liverpool, they went the way of Aston Villa, losing out to an outstanding Celta Vigo side, who had

UEFA CUP

Real Sociedad's Agustín Aranzábal leaps for a header against Atlético Madrid.

made their best-ever start to the Spanish league and were coached by Víctor Fernández, the man who had led Real Zaragoza to victory over Arsenal in the 1995 Cup-winners' Cup final. It looked as if, for once, an English side might finally get the better of him when Michael Owen put Liverpool 1-0 up in Vigo with a typical counter-attacking strike. But the Galicians made mincemeat of the Merseysiders in the second half, with the comedy capers of the Liverpool defence helping them to turn a 0-1 deficit into a 3-1 lead.

Two weeks later, at Anfield, the pressure was on Gérard Houllier's team to keep English interest in the competition alive, but with four players suspended, the task proved beyond them. Never at any stage did they look like getting the two goals they needed, and the final nail in their coffin was provided by Israeli striker Haim Revivo, who silenced the crowd with a fine individual goal early in the second half. It was the first time

Liverpool had ever lost a European tie to a Spanish club.

Because of the proliferation of survivors from France, Italy and Spain, it was always likely that the draw would place together a couple of teams from the same country. In fact, there were two such ties, with Spain's Real Sociedad and Atlético Madrid going head-to-head in one and France's Monaco and Marseille in another.

The all-Spanish clash, the 13th of its kind in Europe, was, alas, utterly overshadowed by the fatal stabbing of a 28-year-old Real Sociedad fan prior to the second leg in Madrid. On the field the two teams went at each other hammer and tongs, with fouls littering the play and the match officials being forced to keep a beady eye on proceedings throughout. The Basques won the first leg in San Sebastián, but although they trailed to a brilliant goal from Juninho early on, they had enough chances to carve out a more handsome lead than 2-1. After 90 minutes in the Vicente Calderón that scoreline was reversed, which meant an extra half-hour was necessary to separate the two sides. It was Atlético who then took command. Inspired by their Uruguayan striker Correa, the home side scored twice, through Santi and José Mari, to book their quarter-final place for the second year in succession. It was midnight local time before the final whistle sounded.

No two French teams had ever previously met in Europe, but Monaco and Marseille were very familiar foes. Refereeing blunders scarred the first game, in the Stade Louis II, with Monaco being awarded a very controversial penalty and Maurice, of Marseille, and Dumas, of Monaco, both being red-carded for very minor offences. It finished 2-2, which was more beneficial to Marseille, who duly finished off the job in front of 60,000 in the Stade Vélodrome a fortnight later thanks to a single goal from Guinean striker Titi Camara.

Bordeaux, Marseille's French title challengers, also progressed to the quarter-finals, albeit with a nervy away-goals win against Grasshopper. Two goals in Zürich from their in-form striker Sylvain Wiltord paved the way for their qualification, which ensured a new French record, with three of their teams reaching the UEFA Cup quarter-finals in the same season for the first time.

Grasshopper's elimination completed an unfortunate double for the Swiss city as FC Zürich also went out, losing narrowly to Roma, for whom skipper Francesco Totti scored in the last minute of each match. There was

UEFA CUP

huge controversy over his last-gasp winner in the first leg, in Rome, when he took a dive in the area and duped the referee into giving a penalty, which he then converted.

Bologna, the InterToto qualifiers, equalled their best-ever European result with a 4-1 home win en route to knocking out Betis, while Parma ensured a three-strong Italian presence in the last eight by disposing of Rangers. They were the better team in a 1-1 draw at Ibrox but found themselves having to chase the game at home after an excellent individual goal by German midfielder Jörg Albertz had put Rangers in front. However, the Scottish side were betrayed by their two Italian defenders. Sergio Porrini stupidly got himself sent off in first-half stoppage-time, and with the score at 2-1, after goals from Balbo and Fiore, Lorenzo Amoruso nonsensically handled the ball in his own area, which enabled Parma to score the decisive goal from the penalty spot.

With three French, three Italian and two Spanish sides left in the competition, the UEFA Cup had turned into a private southern convention.

THIRD ROUND RESULTS

(November 24, December 8, 1998)

Bologna 4 (Fontolan 25, 73, Kolyvanov 52, Eriberto 58), **Real Betis 1** (Benjamín 63)
Real Betis 1 (Oli 4), **Bologna 0**
(Bologna 4-2)

RC Celta 3 (Mostovoi 49, Karpin 55, Gudelj 90), **Liverpool 1** (Owen 35)
Liverpool 0, RC Celta 1 (Revivo 56)
(RC Celta 4-1)

Grasshopper-Club Zürich 3 (Kavelashvili 21, Türkyilmaz 33, Comisetti 53), **Girondins de Bordeaux 3** (Wiltord 6, 74, Micoud 20)
Girondins de Bordeaux 0, Grasshopper-Club Zürich 0
(3-3; Girondins de Bordeaux on away goals)

Olympique Lyonnais 1 (Bak 45), **Club Brugge KV 0**
Club Brugge KV 3 (De Brul 63, De Cock 69, Anic 72), **Olympique Lyonnais 4** (Caveglia 16, 55, 71, Dhorasoo 76)
(Olympique Lyonnais 5-3)

AS Monaco 2 (Trezeguet 17p, Giuly 56), **Olympique Marseille 2** (Pires 9, Camara 39)
Olympique Marseille 1 (Camara 71), **AS Monaco 0**
(Olympique Marseille 3-2)

Rangers 1 (Wallace 68), **Parma 1** (Balbo 51)
Parma 3 (Balbo 48, Fiore 63, Chiesa 68p), **Rangers 1** (Albertz 28)
(Parma 4-2)

Real Sociedad 2 (Kovacevic 45, Roberto 85og), **Atlético Madrid 1** (Juninho 3)
Atlético Madrid 4 (Jugovic 17, 46p, Santi 94, José Mari 100), **Real Sociedad 1** (Gracia 50) *(aet)*
(Atlético Madrid 5-3)

Roma 1 (Totti 90p), **FC Zürich 0**
FC Zürich 2 (Bartlett 60, 81), **Roma 2** (Delvecchio 13, Totti 90)
(Roma 3-2)

QUARTER-FINALS

Given the content of the last eight, it was quite a surprise that there were no more match-ups between clubs from the same country. The draw did, however, throw up two Franco-Italian ties, the most appealing of which had favourites Parma paired with in-form Bordeaux.

At the time of their first encounter, at Bordeaux's Parc Lescure, both teams were lying second in their respective leagues. It certainly looked as though Parma boss Alberto Malesani had more important things on his mind when he opted to leave out three key players, Baggio, Chiesa and Crespo. It seemed a needless gamble, and during the first half it was obvious which team had the scent of victory in their nostrils. Bordeaux pressed and pressed and just before half-time were

QUARTER-FINAL RESULTS

(March 2 & 16, 1999)

Olympique Marseille 2 (Maurice 33, 67), **RC Celta 1** (Mostovoi 63)
RC Celta 0, Olympique Marseille 0
(Olympique Marseille 2-1)

Bologna 3 (Signori 9, 49, Binotto 55), **Olympique Lyonnais 0**
Olympique Lyonnais 2 (Caveglia 16, Job 40), **Bologna 0**
(Bologna 3-2)

Girondins de Bordeaux 2 (Micoud 40, Wiltord 45), **Parma 1** (Crespo 84)
Parma 6 (Crespo 37, 67, Chiesa 43, 60, Sensini 49, Balbo 89p), **Girondins de Bordeaux 0**
(Parma 7-2)

Atlético Madrid 2 (José Mari 13, Roberto 46), **Roma 1** (Di Biagio 75)
Roma 1 (Delvecchio 32), **Atlético Madrid 2** (Aguilera 57, Roberto 89)
(Atlético Madrid 4-2)

UEFA CUP

rewarded for their incessant adventure with two goals. Johan Micoud, Bordeaux's punkish playmaker, scored the first of them, crashing in a header off the underside of the bar, and he was heavily involved in the lavish build-up to the second, lashed in fiercely by Wiltord for his fifth goal of the competition.

In the second half Bordeaux remained in control, their offside trap working a treat to keep Parma's ersatz strike-force of Asprilla and Balbo in check. When full-back Antonio Benarrivo was sent off for dissent with nine minutes left, it looked as if the Italians would have to go home with at best a 0-2 deficit to make up, but the dismissal seemed to lull Bordeaux into a false sense of security and they were punished five minutes from time when the belatedly introduced Chiesa and Crespo combined to score a potentially decisive away goal, exquisitely flicked in by the Argentinian at the near post. In stoppage-time Parma even had a great chance to level but Chiesa could only manage an embarrassing 'airshot' after a great run and cross by Lilian Thuram.

If that miss haunted Chiesa, it certainly didn't show, for two weeks later he and Crespo were both in world-class form. Where the Bordeaux offside ploy had functioned almost to perfection in the first game, it was to be utterly demolished in the Ennio Tardini stadium. Once the Parma strikers had broken it - just - to score the first goal, they were all over the Bordeaux defence. Chiesa and Crespo helped themselves to two goals apiece, with Juan Verón also weighing in with a free-kick from the left touchline that flew, undeflected, into the net. A late penalty from substitute Abel Balbo completed the rout after Bordeaux defender Nisa Saveljic, clearly driven to distraction, caught the ball for no apparent reason in his own area.

Bologna against Lyon was more closely contested. The InterToto refugees recorded their seventh successive European home win of the season to take command in the first leg, with Giuseppe Signori scoring twice (the first a magnificent volley) and then setting up another goal for Jonatan Binotto in a comprehensive 3-0 win. Lyon had to stage a Parma-like comeback in the second leg, and with two goals in the first half, the opener from Alain Caveglia, now on seven for the competition, it looked as if they could actually do it. The atmosphere in the Stade Gerland was tremendous as Lyon strove to get a third goal in the second half. But with Bologna sitting back, the openings became less and less frequent and eventually the French fire burned out.

Roma had the chance to make it three Italian successes out of three when captain Luigi Di Biagio fired in a stunning 30-yard free-kick to bring his team back from a two-goal deficit in the first leg away to Atlético Madrid. That goal got the Italians out of jail after they had been shackled for more than an hour by an Atlético side that showed no sign of the turmoil they were going through in the Spanish league.

Di Biagio's goal from nowhere threatened to undermine the Spanish club's bid to reach the semi-finals for the second successive year, and when Marco Delvecchio opened the scoring in the second leg at the Stadio Olimpico, the odds were on another Italian triumph. However, a second red card of the competition for Roma's Cameroonian defender Pierre Wome offered Atlético renewed hope, and when Carlos Aguilera volleyed home Michele Serena's high cross early in the second half, the Spaniards were back in control. Delvecchio had a goal contentiously disallowed for pushing, and Dutch refereee Mario van der Ende, a major figure on the same ground 18 months earlier when Italy drew 0-0 with England in a key World Cup qualifier, aggravated the home fans further when he refused Roma a penalty. There was even worse to come, in the final minute, when Roma captain Totti was sent off by the Dutchman for his second bookable offence. By then the tie was over, however, with Atlético having finished the Italians off thanks to a late strike from Roberto.

Celta, Spain's other remaining representative, had to beat a third former Champions' Cup winner in a row in order to join Atlético in the semi-finals. After Aston Villa and Liverpool, they were up against Marseille. The first leg took place in the Stade Vélodrome, where a strong wind greeted both teams. Marseille looked the better, more constructive team in the first half and gained a deserved lead when Florian Maurice clipped a fine shot into the top corner. But with the wind at their backs in the second half, the Spaniards made a much more positive impression, and it was no surprise when they grabbed an equaliser, Russian schemer Aleksandr Mostovoi sliding in to score from close range after 'keeper Stéphane Porato mishandled a cross from Haim Revivo. Marseille's reply was immediate, however, and it was Maurice who again supplied the perfect finish after some excellent build-up play from Robert Pires.

2-1 was a fair result, and it left everything to play for in the second leg in Vigo. The atmosphere in the

UEFA CUP

Balaídos stadium was everything that the two teams had experienced in Marseilles. Celta dominated the first half but could not penetrate a very disciplined Marseille defence. It was the same story after the interval, with the French side continuing to frustrate their opponents and also the crowd. As so often happens in such stalemates, the best chance of all arrived in stoppage-time, but nobody could touch in Goran Djorovic's low cross, so Marseille held out for the goalless draw that saw them through the semi-finals. They had played a dangerous game, but it had paid off.

SEMI-FINALS

And then there were four... one from France, one from Spain and two from Italy. The prospect of yet another all-Italian UEFA Cup final - the fifth of the decade - was maintained when Parma and Bologna avoided each other in the draw. Parma, paired with Atlético Madrid, appeared to be blessed as for the fifth round in a row they were drawn to play the second leg at home. Bologna, bidding to match Bordeaux's 1995/96 feat of going all the way from the InterToto to the UEFA Cup final, were also given home advantage in the return match, but first they had to visit the cauldron of the Stade Vélodrome - a place where Marseille had been victorious in all of their previous games.

The noise, colour and spectacle offered by the sell-out crowd should have inspired Marseille to their best form, but from the start they looked edgy and disoriented. Twice within the opening moments Bologna might have taken a shock lead when Davide Fontolan went close, and throughout the first half Marseille's Porato was the busier of the two goalkeepers. Little changed after the interval. The game was open and free-flowing but very few chances were created and the two defences were most definitely on top. Marseille had all four of their highly-rated forwards on the pitch - Pires, Dugarry, Maurice and Ravanelli - but Bologna's rearguard withstood eveything they could throw at them, and the end result was a 0-0 stymie.

Being held goalless at home is never a bad first-leg result in Europe, but with Bologna's outstanding record in the Renato Dall'Ara stadium and a full house guaranteed, Marseille knew that by failing to claim an advantage at home, they had become the second-favourites to reach the final. That feeling was enhanced after 18 minutes when Bologna defender and stand-in captain Michele Paramatti put his team in front after the

Marseille defence had failed to clear a free-kick. There was relatively little goalmouth activity during a dull first 45 minutes but the game livened up considerably after the break - although much of it was down to a succession of fouls, for which Marseille trio Gallas, Ravanelli and Luccin all collected yellow cards that would keep them out of the final.

First, of course, Marseille had to get there, and with five minutes left they were presented wth the perfect opportunity to book their place in Moscow when Maurice went down under a rash challenge from Bologna 'keeper Francesco Antonioli and the German referee pointed to the spot. Laurent Blanc struck the penalty into the centre of the goal... but the referee disallowed it for encroachment. He had to try again. Requiring nerves of steel, the tall centre-back stepped forward... and found the bottom corner. 1-1. There was still time for Beppe Signori to miss a golden chance, which Porato brilliantly saved with his legs, but soon afterwards the final whistle sounded. Marseille had made it to the final on away goals.

But that was not the end of the tale. As the two teams walked off, a brawl broke out in the tunnel. Players, fans and riot police all got involved. Tempers flared, fists flew, and it was a miracle that nobody had to be carted off to hospital with a serious injury. Both clubs were later censured by UEFA, with Marseille's Christophe Dugarry being singled out as one of the ringleaders and handed a lengthy ban, which added to the list of Marseille absentees for the final.

Parma had gone through the first four rounds of the competition without winning a single match away from home, but that run ended in the first leg of the semi-final when the Italians cruised to an impressive 3-1 victory away to Atlético Madrid. Enrico Chiesa was once again the leading man for the Italians. He scored twice in the

---

SEMI-FINAL RESULTS

(April 6 & 20, 1999)

Olympique Marseille 0, Bologna 0
Bologna 1 (Paramatti 18), **Olympique Marseille 1** (Blanc 86p)
(1-1; Olympique Marseille on away goal)

Atlético Madrid 1 (Juninho 21p), **Parma 3** (Chiesa 14, 41, Crespo 62)
Parma 2 (Balbo 35, Chiesa 84), **Atlético Madrid 1** (Roberto 62)
(Parma 5-2)

UEFA CUP

first half, sandwiching a penalty from Juninho, and when Hernán Crespo added a third for the Italians in the second half, the final beckoned. Atlético, back under the guidance of Radomir Antic, who had belatedly arrived to replace the departed Arrigo Sacchi, had two great chances to level the tie in the closing stages, but Juninho, who was being whistled by his own fans, wasted both of them. The first came from the penalty spot, the second from an even easier chance served to him on a plate just a few yards out from goal.

At 3-1 up, Parma were virtually home and dry. That was certainly the feeling of their fans, who chose to boycott the second leg in their thousands, leaving huge empty spaces on both sides of the ground. That complacency also seemed to get to the Parma players, who were pretty much overrun for the first 45 minutes yet still managed to extend their aggregate lead. Atlético had all the chances but could not finish them, whereas Abel Balbo had just once opportunity and buried it, latching onto Verón's wonderful through-ball, strolling around the 'keeper and clipping in an excellent finish with his left foot. After that both sides simply went through the motions. There were further chances, and indeed further goals - one per side, a header from Roberto, another classy strike from Chiesa - but the outcome had long been settled. For the second year running Atlético's UEFA Cup dream had been crushed in the semi-finals by Italian opposition. As for Parma, they had supplied further evidence over the two legs that they were the best side in the competition. Now all they had to do was go out and prove it once and for all in the final, against Marseille.

FINAL

There had been a suggestion that UEFA would be forced to move the UEFA Cup final from Moscow's Luzhniki stadium had two Italian teams qualified. But Marseille's victory over Bologna erased the issue from debate. Thus, Eastern Europe staged its first major showpiece final. A reported 61,000 tickets were sold, but far fewer than that figure actually turned up. Perhaps they were put off by the freezing temperatures (even in early May, it

Parma players celebrate with the Cup after their 3-0 victory over Marseille.

can be very cold in Moscow) or the late-night kick-off time, which, for the purpose of Western European TV, had been put back to the local bedtime hour of 10pm.

Marseille had the greater travelling support but the French team, the first from their country to reach a UEFA Cup final, were the clear outsiders. They were decimated by the suspensions incurred in the semi-final second leg at Bologna and had been going through a sticky patch at home, taking just one point from three French First Division games. Parma, on the other hand, were at full strength and feeling hyper-confident, having lifted the Italian Cup a week earlier.

There was a typically cagey opening to the encounter, but while this seemed a deliberate policy from the Italians, Marseille really struggled to get into any sort of rhythm. They did not look up for the challenge and seemed resigned to defeat right from the opening whistle. Even so, it was sad and unexpected that Laurent Blanc, their semi-final hero, should be responsible for making the error that presented Parma with the opening goal. The French international made a terrible hash of a routine backheader to his goalkeeper, and Hernán Crespo rushed in to seize possession and plant a delightful lob over Stéphane Porato's head. It was an awful mistake, but a wonderful finish.

Marseille's task became virtually

TOP SCORERS

(excluding Preliminary and Qualifying rounds)

8 Enrico CHIESA (Parma)

7 Alain CAVEGLIA (Olympique Lyonnais)
   Darko KOVACEVIC (Real Sociedad)

6 Hernán CRESPO (Parma)
   Shaun BARTLETT (FC Zürich)

5 Giuseppe SIGNORI (Bologna)
   Sylvain WILTORD (Girondins de Bordeaux)

4 Stan COLLYMORE (Aston Villa)
   JUNINHO (Atlético Madrid)
   ROBERTO Fresnedoso (Atlético Madrid)
   Florian MAURICE (Olympique Marseille)
   Robert SPEHAR (AS Monaco)
   Abel BALBO (Parma)
   Marco DELVECCHIO (Roma)
   Liuboslav PENEV (RC Celta)

UEFA CUP

impossible ten minutes later when Paolo Vanoli, who had scored a header in Parma's Coppa Italia triumph a week earlier, did it again, brilliantly despatching Diego Fuser's excellent right-wing cross into the top corner after Blanc had again been at fault, playing Parma onside in the build-up.

That was game over. Marseille were being outplayed and they could do nothing to stop it. Things got even worse for them ten minutes after the interval when Parma scored a third goal. And what a goal it was! Lilian Thuram raced down the right, Juan Verón chipped the ball in from the right touchline, Crespo dummied and Chiesa, holding nothing back, crashed a fantastically powerful right-foot shot high into the roof of the net. It was a goal fit to grace any final, even one as utterly one-sided as this. And it also enabled Chiesa to become the outright top scorer of the competition with a total of eight goals.

From then on Parma were happy to allow Marseille to enjoy the bulk of the possession while they sat back and revelled in their impregnable lead, occasionally making the odd raid into their opponents' half. Only once, when substitute Camara blasted badly wide from a Maurice knock-down, did Marseille look

FINAL
12/05/99, Moscow
PARMA 3 Crespo (26), Vanoli (36), Chiesa (55)
OLYMPIQUE MARSEILLE 0
referee - Dallas (SCO)
PARMA - Buffon; Thuram, Sensini, Cannavaro; Fuser, Baggio, Boghossian, Vanoli; Verón (Fiore 77); Chiesa (Balbo 72), Crespo (Asprilla 84).
OLYMPIQUE MARSEILLE - Porato; Blondeau, Domoraud, Blanc, Issa, Edson (Camara 46); Brando, Bravo, Gourvennec, Pires; Maurice.

likely to reduce the deficit. But Parma were so comfortably superior that they would probably have been able to respond immediately with another goal themselves had the situation demanded it. As it was, Abel Balbo nearly made it 4-0 when he curled a free-kick against the post nine minutes from time.

Parma were happy to leave it at 3-0 - the same scoreline as the Inter v Lazio final of 1998. Italy's domination of the UEFA Cup remained unthreatened. Parma, who had won the trophy once before, in 1995, became the eighth Serie A winners of the competition in 11 years. Quite a record. Quite a team.

EUROPEAN CUP QUALIFIERS 1999/2000

COUNTRY	CHAMPIONS' CUP	UEFA CUP
ALBANIA	SK Tirana	Vllaznia Shkodër, Bylis Ballsh
ANDORRA		CE Principat
ARMENIA	Tsement Ararat	Shirak Gyumri, FK Yerevan
AUSTRIA	SK Sturm Graz, SK Rapid Wien	LASK Linz, Grazer AK
AZERBAIJAN	Kapaz Ganja	Neftchi Baku, Shamkir
BELARUS	Dnepr-Transmash Mogilev	Belshina Bobruisk, BATE Borisov
BELGIUM	KRC Genk	Club Brugge KV, RSC Anderlecht, K Lierse SK
BULGARIA	Liteks Lovech	CSKA Sofia, Levski Sofia
CROATIA	Croatia Zagreb, Rijeka	Osijek, Hajduk Split
CYPRUS	Anorthosis Famagusta	APOEL Nicosia, Omonia Nicosia
CZECH REPUBLIC	Sparta Praha, FK Teplice	Slavia Praha, Sigma Olomouc
DENMARK	AaB, Brøndby IF	AB, Lyngby FC
ENGLAND	Manchester United, Arsenal, Chelsea	Newcastle United, Tottenham Hotspur, Leeds United, * West Ham United
ESTONIA	FC Flora Tallinn	Levadia Maardu, FC Lantana Tallinn. Tulevik Viljandi
FAROE ISLANDS	HB	KÍ, B36
FINLAND	FC Haka	HJK, VPS
FRANCE	Girondins de Bordeaux, Olympique Marseille, Olympique Lyonnais	RC Lens, FC Nantes, AS Monaco, * Montpellier HSC
GEORGIA	Dinamo Tbilisi	Torpedo Kutaisi, Lokomotivi Tbilisi
GERMANY	FC Bayern München, Bayer 04 Leverkusen, Hertha BSC Berlin, Borussia Dortmund	SV Werder Bremen, 1.FC Kaiserslautern, VfL Wolfsburg
GREECE	Olympiakos, AEK	Panathinaikos, PAOK, Ionikos, Aris
HOLLAND	Feyenoord, Willem II, PSV	Ajax, Vitesse, Roda JC
HUNGARY	MTK Hungária FC	DVSC-Epona, Ferencváros, Újpest FC
ICELAND	ÍBV	Leiftur, KR
ISRAEL	Hapoel Haifa	Hapoel Tel-Aviv, Maccabi Tel-Aviv

EUROPEAN CUP QUALIFIERS 1999/2000

COUNTRY	CHAMPIONS' CUP	UEFA CUP
ITALY	Milan, Lazio, Parma, Fiorentina	Roma, Udinese, Bologna, * Juventus
LATVIA	Skonto Riga	FK Riga, Metalurgs Liepaya
LIECHTENSTEIN		FC Vaduz
LITHUANIA	Kareda Siauliai	FBK Kaunas, Zalgiris Vilnius
LUXEMBOURG	Jeunesse Esch	FC Mondercange, F91 Dudelange
MACEDONIA	Sloga Jugomagnat Skopje	Vardar Skopje, Sileks Kratovo
MALTA	Valletta	Birkirkara, Sliema Wanderers
MOLDOVA	Zimbru Chisinau	Constructorul Chisinau, Sheriff Tiraspol
N. IRELAND	Glentoran	Portadown, Linfield
NORWAY	Rosenborg BK, Molde FK	Stabaek IF, Viking FK, FK Bodø/Glimt
POLAND	Widzew Lodz	Amica Wronki, Legia Warszawa, Lech Poznan
PORTUGAL	FC Porto, Boavista FC	SC Beira Mar, Sporting CP, SL Benfica, Vitória Setúbal
REP. IRELAND	St. Patrick's Athletic	Bray Wanderers, Cork City
ROMANIA	Rapid Bucuresti	Dinamo Bucuresti, Steaua Bucuresti
RUSSIA	Spartak Moskva, CSKA Moskva	Zenit Sankt-Peterburg, Lokomotiv Moskva
SCOTLAND	Rangers	Celtic, St. Johnstone, Kilmarnock
SLOVAKIA	Slovan Bratislava	Dukla Banska Bystrica, Inter Bratislava, Spartak Trnava
SLOVENIA	Maribor Teatanic	SCT Olimpija Ljubljana, HIT Gorica
SPAIN	FC Barcelona, Real Madrid, RCD Mallorca, Valencia CF	Atlético Madrid, RC Celta, RC Deportivo
SWEDEN	AIK	IFK Göteborg, Helsingborgs IF
SWITZERLAND	Servette FC Genève	Grasshopper-Club Zürich, Lausanne-Sports, FC Zürich
TURKEY	Galatasaray, Besiktas	Ankaragücü, Fenerbahçe
UKRAINE	Dynamo Kyiv	Karpaty Lviv, Shakhtar Donetsk, Kryvbas Kryvyi Rih
WALES	Barry Town	Inter Cardiff, Cwmbran Town
YUGOSLAVIA	Partizan Beograd	Crvena zvezda Beograd, Vojvodina Novi Sad

N.B. * = InterToto qualifiers.

MISCELLANEOUS

EUROPEAN FOOTBALLER OF THE YEAR 1998

Pts	Player/Club/Nationality
244	Zinedine ZIDANE (Juventus/FRANCE)
68	Davor SUKER (Real Madrid/CROATIA)
66	RONALDO (Inter/BRAZIL)
51	Michael OWEN (Liverpool/ENGLAND)
45	RIVALDO (FC Barcelona/BRAZIL)
43	Gabriel BATISTUTA (Fiorentina/ARGENTINA)
36	Lilian THURAM (Parma/FRANCE)
28	Dennis BERGKAMP (Arsenal/HOLLAND)
	Edgar DAVIDS (Juventus/HOLLAND)
19	Marcel DESAILLY (Milan/Chelsea/FRANCE)
17	Frank DE BOER (Ajax/HOLLAND)
16	Emmanuel PETIT (Arsenal/FRANCE)
13	ROBERTO CARLOS (Real Madrid/BRAZIL)
11	Fabien BARTHEZ (AS Monaco/FRANCE)
	Laurent BLANC (Olympique Marseille/FRANCE)

10	Alessandro DEL PIERO (Juventus/ITALY)
	Predrag MIJATOVIC (Real Madrid/YUGOSLAVIA)
9	Oliver BIERHOFF (Udinese/Milan/GERMANY)
	Didier DESCHAMPS (Juventus/FRANCE)
6	Michael LAUDRUP (Ajax/DENMARK)
4	Ronald DE BOER (Ajax/HOLLAND)
	RAUL González (Real Madrid/SPAIN)
3	Brian LAUDRUP (Rangers/Chelsea/DENMARK)
	Marc OVERMARS (Arsenal/HOLLAND)
	Clarence SEEDORF (Real Madrid/HOLLAND)
2	Fernando HIERRO (Real Madrid/SPAIN)
	Christian VIERI (Atlético Madrid/Lazio/ITALY)
1	David BECKHAM (Manchester United/ENGLAND)
	LUIS ENRIQUE Martínez (FC Barcelona/SPAIN)
	Bixente LIZARAZU (FC Bayern München/FRANCE)
	Nikos MAHLAS (Vitesse/GREECE)

N.B. The following players were pre-selected for the poll but did not receive any votes:

Tony ADAMS (Arsenal/ENGLAND)
Roberto BAGGIO (Bologna/Inter/ITALY)
Zvonimir BOBAN (Milan/CROATIA)
Fabio CANNAVARO (Parma/ITALY)
Andriy SHEVCHENKO (Dynamo Kyiv/UKRAINE)
DENÍLSON (FC São Paulo/Real Betis/BRAZIL)
Tore André FLO (Chelsea/NORWAY)
Adrian ILIE (Valencia CF/ROMANIA)
Filippo INZAGHI (Juventus/ITALY)
Robert JARNI (Real Betis/Real Madrid/CROATIA)
Hidetoshi NAKATA (Bellmare Hiratsuka/Perugia/JAPAN)
Pavel NEDVED (Lazio/CZECH REPUBLIC)
Sunday OLISEH (Ajax/NIGERIA)
Ariel ORTEGA (Valencia CF/Sampdoria/ARGENTINA)
Gianluca PAGLIUCA (Inter/ITALY)
Marcelo SALAS (River Plate/Lazio/CHILE)
David SEAMAN (Arsenal/ENGLAND)
Juan Sebastián VERON (Sampdoria/Parma/ARGENTINA)
Iván ZAMORANO (Inter/CHILE)

MISCELLANEOUS

WORLD CLUB CUP 1998

01/12/98, Tokyo
REAL MADRID 2 Naza (26og), Raúl (83)
VASCO DA GAMA 1 Juninho (57)
referee - Yanten (CHL)
REAL MADRID - Illgner; Panucci, Sanchis, Sanz, Hierro, Roberto Carlos; Raúl, Redondo, Seedorf; Sávio (Suker 90), Mijatovic (Jarni 81).
VASCO DA GAMA - Germano; Mauro Galvão, Odvan, Felipe, Luizinho (Guilherme 85); Naza, Ramón (Valver 88), Vagner (Vitor 81), Juninho; Donizete, Luizão.

EUROPEAN SUPER CUP 1998

28/08/98, Monaco
REAL MADRID 0
CHELSEA 1 Poyet (83)
referee - Batta (FRA)
REAL MADRID - Illgner; Panucci, Sanchis, Hierro, Roberto Carlos; Karembeu (Morientes 58), Seedorf, Redondo, Sávio; Mijatovic (Jarni 74), Raúl.
CHELSEA - De Goey; Ferrer, Leboeuf, Desailly, Le Saux; Duberry, Wise, Di Matteo (Poyet 63), Babayaro; Zola (Laudrup 83), Casiraghi (Flo 90).

Left: Vasco da Gama's Naza (right) gets the better of Real Madrid's Clarence Seedorf (left).

Right: Real Madrid's Karembeu tries to tackle Chelsea's French defender, Frank Leboeuf.

For The **Best** **European** Football **Photography**

e m p i c s

http://www.empics.co.uk

INTRODUCTION TO NATIONS/CLUBS

The following pages contain individual reviews of each of the UEFA nations, including Statistics, a General Review, Photographs, Players of the Season and, in a separate section, Colour Team Strips and Emblems.

As a general guide, all Clubs are referred to by the names of their original language in statistical tables and headings. In narrative text, however, some will be referred to by their English names (e.g. Crvena zvezda Beograd = Red Star Belgrade).

The abbreviations and explanations below should act as a guide to assist the reader in understanding and appreciating the various items of information.

NATIONAL SECTION
LEAGUE CHAMPIONSHIP RESULTS
Home teams are listed, together with numbers, in the left-hand column. Away teams are ranged horizontally across the top of the table, with the team's corresponding number as reference. Teams are listed alphabetically.

LEAGUE CHAMPIONSHIP FINAL TABLE
This is the final table of the country's First, or Premier, Division championship, with clubs listed in official classification order. Home, Away and Total performance records are shown in separate columns.

KEY:
Pd = Played
W = Won
D = Drawn
L = Lost
F = Goals for
A = Goals against
Pt = Points
GD = Goal Difference

An unbroken line (——————) indicates the relegation zone.
A dotted line (··················) indicates the play-off zone.

Any irregularities from the standard formula of 3 points for a win, 1 point for a draw and 0 points for a defeat are stipulated at the foot of the table.

TOP SCORERS
These refer to league goals only.

DOMESTIC CUP
The rounds included are those in which the First, or Premier, Division clubs are involved.
For two-legged ties, the aggregate scores and qualifiers are shown in brackets.
(aet) = after extra-time
(asd) = after sudden-death

NATIONAL TEAM RESULTS
This covers all the official full international matches played by the country's national team from July 1998 to June 1999.

KEY:
(ECQ) = European Championship Qualifier
H = Home
A = Away
N = Neutral
p = penalty
og = own-goal

NATIONAL TEAM APPEARANCES
This lists all the players who have appeared in their national team during the 1998/99 season, together with date of birth, club(s), match-by-match appearances and all-time appearance and goal totals.

KEY:
G = Goalkeeper
D = Defender
M = Midfielder
A = Attacker
s = substitute

The number after the letter indicates the time of substitution.

Cps = Total full international caps gained at the end of the season.

Gls = Total full international goals scored at the end of the season.

Three-letter codes have been used as column headings to indicate opponents. These are as follows:

EUROPE
ALB = Albania
AND = Andorra
ARM = Armenia
AUT = Austria
AZB = Azerbaijan
BLS = Belarus
BEL = Belgium
BOS = Bosnia-Herzegovina
BUL = Bulgaria
CRO = Croatia
CYP = Cyprus
CZE = Czech Republic
DEN = Denmark
ENG = England
EST = Estonia
FAR = Faroe Islands
FIN = Finland
FRA = France
GEO = Georgia
GER = Germany
GRE = Greece
HOL = Holland
HUN = Hungary
ISL = Iceland
ISR = Israel
ITA = Italy
LAT = Latvia
LIE = Liechtenstein
LIT = Lithuania
LUX = Luxembourg
MAC = Macedonia
MLT = Malta
MOL = Moldova
NIR = Northern Ireland
NOR = Norway
POL = Poland
POR = Portugal
IRL = Republic of Ireland
ROM = Romania
RUS = Russia
SMR = San Marino
SCO = Scotland
SVK = Slovakia
SLO = Slovenia
ESP = Spain
SWE = Sweden
SUI = Switzerland

INTRODUCTION TO NATIONS/CLUBS

TUR = Turkey
UKR = Ukraine
WAL = Wales
YUG = Yugoslavia

NON-EUROPE
ALG = Algeria
ANG = Angola
ARG = Argentina
AUS = Australia
BER = Bermuda
BOL = Bolivia
BRA = Brazil
BFA = Burkina Faso
BUR = Burundi
CMR = Cameroon
CAN = Canada
CAF = Central African Republic
CHD = Chad
CHL= Chile
COL = Colombia
CON = Congo
CRC = Costa Rica
DRC = Democratic Republic of Congo
EGY = Egypt
GAB = Gabon
GAM = Gambia
GHA = Ghana
GUI = Guinea
IRN = Iran
IRQ = Iraq
CIV = Ivory Coast
JAM = Jamaica
JOR = Jordan
JPN = Japan
KAZ = Kazakhstan
KEN = Kenya
LIB = Liberia
MAD = Madagascar
MLI = Mali
MWI = Malawi
MEX = Mexico
MAR = Morocco
MOZ = Mozambique
NAM = Namibia
NZL = New Zealand
NIG = Nigeria
OMN = Oman

PAN = Panama
PAR = Paraguay
PER = Peru
PHI - Philippines
ROW = Rest of the World
RWA = Rwanda
STV = St. Vincent
SAU = Saudi Arabia
SEN = Senegal
SRL = Sierra Leone
SAF = South Africa
KOR = South Korea
SYR = Syria
TAD = Tadjikistan
TOG = Togo
TRI = Trinidad & Tobago
TUN = Tunisia
UGA = Uganda
UAE = United Arab Emirates
USA = United States
URU = Uruguay
UZB = Uzbekistan
VEN = Venezuela
ZAM = Zambia
ZIM = Zimbabwe

EUROPEAN CUPS

Results, goalscorers, goal-times and full line-ups
are included

KEY:
H = Home
A = Away

The three-letter country codes used are the same
as those shown above.

CLUB SECTION
LEAGUE RESULTS

This lists each club's league matches in
chronological order, giving Date, Opponent,
Venue, Result and Goalscorer(s)

KEY:
H = Home
A = Away
p = penalty
og = own-goal

APPEARANCES

The figures refer to league games only.

KEY:
P = Position
Ap = Number of appearances in starting
line-up
(s) = Number of appearances as
a substitute
Gls = Number of goals scored
G = Goalkeeper
D = Defender
M = Midfielder
A = Attacker

Foreign players are indicated using the same
three-letter codes as shown above.

DIRECTORIES

Where more than one Coach/Manager has been
used during the course of the season, these are
all indicated. New Coaches/Managers for the
1999/2000 season have been added where
known at the time of going to press.

PROMOTED CLUBS

The clubs promoted to the First, or Premier,
Division at the end of the 1998/99 season are
presented at the back of each national section,
together with Second, or First, Division tables and
Promotion/Relegation Play-off details. These
tables use the same abbreviations as the LEAGUE
CHAMPIONSHIP FINAL TABLE (see above),
except that no Home and Away performance
records are shown.

An unbroken line (————) at the top
of the table indicates the promotion zone.

A dotted line (··········) at the top of
the table indicates the promotion play-off zone.

An unbroken line (————) at the
bottom of the table indicates the relegation zone.

A dotted line (··········) at the bottom
of the table indicates the relegation play-off zone.

N.B. Where reference is made to the 1998/99
domestic season, this should be understood as
the 1998 season for Armenia, Belarus, Estonia,
the Faroe Islands, Finland, Iceland, Latvia,
Norway, Russia and Sweden.

ALBANIA

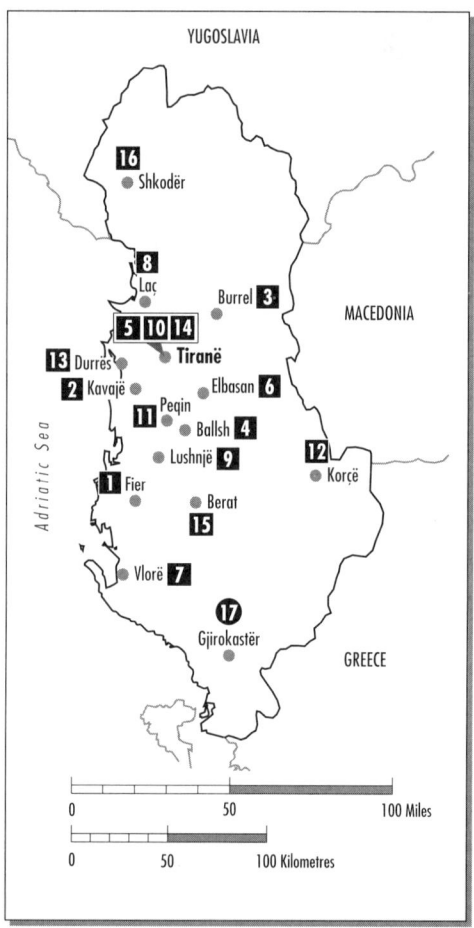

1	APOLONIA FIER	85
2	BESA KAVAJË	86
3	BURRELI	87
4	BYLIS BALLSH	88
5	DINAMO TIRANË	89
6	ELBASANI	90
7	FLAMURTARI VLORË	91
8	LAÇI	92
9	LUSHNJA	93

10	PARTIZANI TIRANË	94
11	SHKUMBINI PEQIN	95
12	SKËNDERBEU KORÇË	96
13	TEUTA DURRËS	97
14	SK TIRANA	98
15	TOMORI BERAT	99
16	VLLAZNIA SHKODËR	100
Promoted club		
17	SHQIPONJA GJIROKASTËR	101

TWO TROPHIES FOR SK TIRANA

International football back on the agenda

FEDERATION DIRECTORY

Federata Shqiptarë e Futbollit
Rruga Dervish Hima Nr. 31, Tiranë

tel - (42) 50275/6/7
fax - (42) 27877

Year of Formation - 1930
President - Miço Papadhopulli
Secretary - Sulejman Starova

Stadium - Qemal Stafa, Tirana (18,000)

Despite the horrific slaughter in nearby Kosovo and the ever-present threat of violence in all but the central region of the country, Albanian football carried on pretty much as normal in 1998/99.

There was no threat to the championship or the Cup, not even an enforced break in the schedule. Furthermore, Albanian clubs were re-admitted to European competition after a one-year absence and the national team were granted permission once more to play their home internationals in Tirana.

A few flies did, however, crop up in the ointment. Pitch-brawling was a rather too familiar sight, and one club, Skënderbeu Korçë, even threatened to quit the league after having a 3-2 home win over defending champions Vllaznia Shkodër overturned into a 0-2 defeat for that very reason. Even more exasperated by the treatment they received from the disciplinary commission were the players of newly-promoted side Burreli, who decided to go on a hunger-strike in protest at the four-match home-ground ban imposed on them after crowd disturbances during a 0-0 draw against Tirana.

Being deprived of home advantage is a serious issue in Albania. A look at the league table shows a remarkable home-team bias. Burreli ultimately finished bottom of the pile with 26 points, but 25 of those were claimed at home, where, in common with all the other 15 teams in the division (even the other two relegated sides Besa and Laçi), they won more games than they lost.

The only team to show a positive balance from their away schedule were SK Tirana, who, not surprisingly, finished top of the table to win their fourth title in five years and a record-extending 18th in all.

The season did not begin as Tirana would have liked. First up was the club's return to Europe, in the UEFA Cup, a misadventure that brought a pair of 0-2 defeats by the Slovakians of Inter Bratislava. And there was a none too promising start in the league, either, with the players voicing their wholehearted disapproval of new coach Ali Mema, who was sacked after a stunning 6-1 defeat by Lushnja. Slowly but surely, however, Tirana picked up the pace under their new leader Sulejman Mema and by the time the half-way point of the season had been reached, they were sitting proudly on top of the table - despite having lost an important fixture away to their closest pursuers, Vllaznia.

The title-holders from the north were to step up their challenge in the second half of the

LEAGUE CHAMPIONSHIP RESULTS 98/99

		1	2	3	4	5	6	7	8	9	10	11	12	13	14	15	16
1	Apolonia Fier		1-0	2-0	1-0	2-0	2-1	1-0	2-1	1-1	1-0	1-1	4-2	2-1	0-1	0-0	0-0
2	Besa Kavajë	1-0		4-1	0-1	1-0	0-0	2-1	2-0	1-0	2-1	1-0	2-1	0-0	1-1	1-1	0-0
3	Burreli	2-0	2-3		1-2	4-4	2-0	0-2	1-3	4-1	2-3	3-0	4-2	3-0	0-0	2-1	1-0
4	Bylis Ballsh	4-1	2-1	5-1		1-0	3-0	4-0	4-1	1-0	2-0	2-0	5-0	3-0	2-1	2-0	2-2
5	Dinamo Tiranë	3-1	1-0	0-0	2-1		2-1	3-1	3-1	2-0	2-2	1-0	1-0	1-2	0-3	0-0	0-1
6	Elbasani	1-0	4-1	3-1	1-0	0-0		2-1	3-0	1-0	1-2	1-0	3-0	2-0	0-0	2-1	1-1
7	Flamurtari Vlorë	1-1	4-0	2-1	0-0	2-0	1-1		3-0	3-1	0-0	2-0	3-0	3-0	1-0	3-2	0-0
8	Laçi	4-1	1-0	2-1	0-0	2-1	1-0	4-2		0-2	2-3	1-1	5-3	2-0	3-3	0-0	0-1
9	Lushnja	3-1	4-0	3-0	0-2	1-1	2-0	3-2	3-1		3-0	3-0	5-1	2-0	6-1	1-0	1-2
10	Partizani Tiranë	2-2	2-1	3-1	1-2	2-2	1-1	3-2	3-0	2-1		1-0	0-0	1-1	1-2	1-0	1-1
11	Shkumbini Peqin	2-1	0-0	1-0	1-0	1-0	1-0	3-0	5-0	2-1	2-0		1-0	4-1	1-2	1-0	1-0
12	Skënderbeu Korçë	2-0	1-0	2-1	1-0	2-3	2-0	4-1	4-1	2-1	4-0	3-1		5-0	0-1	2-0	0-2
13	Teuta Durrës	1-1	2-0	3-0	2-1	3-2	1-0	2-0	1-0	1-2	2-0	2-0	1-1		0-5	1-0	1-0
14	SK Tirana	2-0	2-0	3-0	0-0	1-0	1-0	1-0	0-0	3-0	2-2	4-1	2-0	3-0		3-0	1-0
15	Tomori Berat	2-1	2-1	2-1	1-0	1-0	1-0	1-1	3-2	3-0	4-0	2-0	2-0	1-0			1-0
16	Vllaznia Shkodër	4-2	5-0	4-1	2-0	1-3	3-1	8-0	2-0	3-0	2-0	4-1	4-0	3-0	1-0	1-0	

LEAGUE CHAMPIONSHIP FINAL TABLE 98/99

			Home					Away					Total						
		P	W	D	L	F	A	W	D	L	F	A	W	D	L	F	A	P	GD
1	SK Tirana	30	12	3	0	28	3	6	4	5	20	17	18	7	5	48	20	61	+28
2	Vllaznia Shkodër	30	14	0	1	47	8	4	6	5	10	10	18	6	6	57	18	60	+39
3	Bylis Ballsh	30	14	1	0	42	7	4	4	7	9	12	18	5	7	51	19	59	+32
4	Tomori Berat	30	13	2	0	26	6	0	5	10	5	19	13	7	10	31	25	46	+6
5	Lushnja	30	12	1	2	40	11	2	1	12	12	29	14	2	14	52	40	44	+12
6	Dinamo Tiranë	30	9	3	3	21	13	2	4	9	16	24	11	7	12	37	37	40	0
7	Shkumbini Peqin	30	12	2	1	25	5	0	2	13	5	33	12	4	14	30	38	40	-8
8	Teuta Durrës	30	11	2	2	23	12	1	2	12	5	36	12	4	14	28	48	40	-20
9	Elbasani	30	11	3	1	25	7	0	3	12	5	23	11	6	13	30	30	39	0
10	Partizani Tiranë	30	7	6	2	24	16	3	3	9	13	30	10	9	11	37	46	39	-9
11	Flamurtari Vlorë	30	10	5	0	28	6	1	0	14	12	41	11	5	14	40	47	38	-7
12	Skënderbeu Korçë	30	12	0	3	34	11	0	2	13	10	42	12	2	16	44	53	38	-9
13	Apolonia Fier	30	10	4	1	20	8	0	3	12	12	34	10	7	13	32	42	37	-10
14	Besa Kavajë	30	9	5	1	18	7	1	1	13	7	33	10	6	14	25	40	36	-15
15	Laçi	30	8	4	3	27	18	1	2	12	9	37	9	6	15	36	55	33	-19
16	Burreli	30	8	2	5	31	21	0	1	14	9	39	8	3	19	40	60	27	-20

campaign, buoyed by a brilliant 8-0 demolition of southerners Flamurtari in their first game back - the highest scoreline of the season. They largely kept pace with Tirana, and when the two teams faced each other head-to-head three matches from the end, they were both exactly level on 54 points apiece.

Once more, however, the home team made the most of their advantage, Tirana beating Vllaznia 1-0 with a goal from their top scorer Devi Muka, a young striker who had joined the club at the start of the season from cash-

PLAYER OF THE SEASON

ALBAN BUSHI

Although the official title of Albanian Footballer of the Year went to national team goalkeeper Foto Strakosha of European Cup-winners' Cup quarter-finalists Panionios, the only Albanian players who actually won any silverware with their foreign clubs in 1998/99 were Liteks Lovech duo Alban Bushi and Altin Haxhi, who captured the Bulgarian title. For Bushi, the younger and more prominent of the pair, it was a second consecutive title, and he played a major part in the team's success, scoring ten goals, many of them significant, to become Liteks' second highest scorer. The 26-year-old midfielder also chipped in with an important goal for Albania in the Euro 2000 qualifier away to Norway and went on to start all eight of the internationals played by Albania during the season.

EUROPEAN CUPS 98/99

CHAMPIONS' CUP
● VLLAZNIA SHKODËR
Preliminary round DINAMO TBILISI (GEO)
A 0-1   (awarded as 0-3)
Grima; Zmijani (Jahja 83), Lici, Premçi, Shkabari, Noga, Xhahysa (Shllaku 62), Sinani, Cungu, Kaçaj, Miloti (Bizi 90).
H 3-1   Cungu (14), Miloti (86), Noga (90p)
Grima; Zmijani, Lici (Bizi 63), Premçi, Shkabari (Jahja 54), Noga, Xhahysa, Sinani, Cungu, Kaçaj, Miloti.

CUP WINNERS' CUP
● APOLONIA FIER
Qualifying round KRC GENK (BEL)
H 1-5   Vangronsveld (26og)
Sinani; Bita, Çobani (Sulaj 58), Poçi A., Buziu (Demiri 45), Nuredini (Ruko 89), Zeqo, Bare, Poçi D., Haxhiaj, Jahiqi.
A 0-4
Sinani; Bita, Çobani (Ruko 68), Poçi A., Demiri, Nuredini, Zeqo, Sulaj, Poçi D , Haxhiaj, Jahiqi (Yzeiri 83).

UEFA CUP
● SK TIRANA
Preliminary round INTER BRATISLAVA (SVK)
A 0-2
Nallbani; Dabulla, Zere, Osmani, Alimehmeti, Ruhi, Tafaj (Stërmasi 62), Bulku, Dalipi, Jupi (Ristami 46), Çoçlli (Liti 55).
H 0-2
Nallbani; Dabulla, Zere, Osmani, Alimehmeti, Ruhi, Tafaj (Ohri 56), Bulku, Dalipi, Jupi (Stërmasi 77), Çoçlli (Liti 51).

INTERNATIONAL HONOURS

None

DOMESTIC CUP 98/99

1/8 FINALS

Besa Kavajë v Partizani Tiranë 2-1; 1-2
(3-3; Partizani Tiranë 4-3 on pens.)

Byllis Ballsh v Lushnja 2-2; 0-0
(2-2; Lushnja on away goals)

Dinamo Tiranë v Teuta Durrës 0-0; 1-5
(Teuta Durrës 5-1)

Flamurtari Vlorë v Shkumbini Peqin 3-0; 1-3
(Flamurtari Vlorë 4-3)

Tomori Berat v Vllaznia Shkodër 1-1; 1-5
(Vllaznia Shkodër 6-2)

Shqiponja Gjirokastër v Elbasani 2-2; 2-1
(Shqiponja Gjirokastër 4-3)

Burreli v Apolonia Fier 1-3; 0-2
(Apolonia Fier 5-1)

Sjënderbeu Korçë v SK Tirana 0-0; 1-2
(SK Tirana 2-1)

QUARTER-FINALS

Flamurtari Vlorë 1 (Xhafa F.), Teuta Durrës 0
Teuta Durrës 2 (Begeja, Haxhiu og),
Flamurtari Vlorë 1 (Ruko)
(2-2; Flamurtari Vlorë on away goal)

Apolonia Fier 2 (Fejzullahi, Gurguri), Partizani Tiranë 0
Partizani Tiranë 2 (Riza, Tiko),
Apolonia Fier 1 (Yzeiri)
(Apolonia Fier 3-2)

Lushnja 1 (Bano p), SK Tirana 1 (Alimehmeti p)
SK Tirana 1 (Gallo), Lushnja 1 (Manko)
(2-2; SK Tirana 2-1 on pens.)

Shqiponja Gjirokastër 0,
Vllaznia Shkodër 2 (Lici, Sinani)
Vllaznia Shkodër 2, Shqiponja Gjirokastër 0 (w/o)
(Vllaznia Shkodër 4-0)

SEMI-FINALS

Vllaznia Shkodër 5 (Xhahysa, Sinani 2, Noga 2),
Apolonia Fier 0

Apolonia Fier 4 (Marini 2, Bare 2),
Vllaznia Shkodër 2 (Xhahysa, Perloshi)
(Vllaznia Shkodër 7-4)

Flamurtari Vlorë 1 (Xhafa D.),
SK Tirana 2 (Muka, Dede)
SK Tirana 2 (Gallo, Prenga), Flamurtari Vlorë 0
(SK Tirana 4-1)

FINAL

22/05/99, Tirana
SK TIRANA 0
VLLAZNIA SHKODËR 0
(aet; 3-0 on pens.)
referee - Velçani

SK TIRANA - Nallbani; Alimehmeti, Dede, Dabulla,
Sina, Tafaj, Malko (Duro 74), Prenga (Zeqo 74),
Mema, Merkoçi (Bulku 98), Muka.

VLLAZNIA SHKODËR - Gjeloshi; Zmijani, Lici, Premçi,
Kotrri, Noga, Ymeri (Jahja 83), Xhahysa, Sinani,
Cungu (Osmani 105), Miloti.

---

crippled Partizani and become one of the team's most effective players along with two other rookies, 21-year-old Eldorado Merkoçi and 19-year-old Rezart Dabulla. All of the trio earned début call-ups for the Albanian national team during the season.

Tirana's lead over Vllaznia was reduced to just a single point when they could only draw their penultimate game away to Besa, but there was never any doubt that they would beat bottom club Burreli at home in their final fixture. 3-0 was the final score, enabling them to complete the season as one of four clubs with an unbeaten home record, winning 12 and drawing three of their 15 matches in the new, smaller-sized 16-team First Division.

A further reduction to 14 clubs in 1999/2000 meant that only one club was promoted. As in the previous year,

the Second Division winners were determined by a series of play-offs, and it was Shqiponja Gjirokastër, relegated only the year before, who regained their place in the top flight thanks to a fine record of 15 victories in 17 matches. No away-day panic here.

A week after clinching the title at Vllaznia's expense, Tirana came face to face with their rivals once again in the final of the Albanian Cup. With the game taking place in Tirana, rather than in a neutral city, the newly-crowned champions had the significant advantage of playing on home soil. But Vllaznia made a gallant fight of it, taking the contest to a penalty shoot-out before they finally caved in, missing all three of their spot-kicks (all saved by Tirana 'keeper Blendi Nallbani) and thus allowing their deliriously happy opponents to celebrate their second domestic 'double' in four seasons.

NATIONAL TEAM RESULTS 98/99

19/08/98	Cyprus	A	Nicosia	2-3	Haxhi (56), Bushi (57)
05/09/98	Georgia (ECQ)	A	Tbilisi	0-1	
14/10/98	Norway (ECQ)	A	Oslo	2-2	Bushi (38), Tare (52)
18/11/98	Greece (ECQ)	H	Tirana	0-0	
10/02/99	Macedonia	H	Tirana	2-0	Vata (48), Bogdani (90)
28/04/99	Latvia (ECQ)	A	Riga	0-0	
05/06/99	Norway (ECQ)	H	Tirana	1-2	Tare (15)
09/06/99	Slovenia (ECQ)	H	Tirana	0-1	

TOP SCORERS

22	Artan BANO (Lushnja)
19	Rigels QOSA (Shkumbini Peqin)
14	Vjoresin SINANI (Vllaznia Shkodër)
12	Bardhyl ELEZI (Lushnja)
	Klodian ASLLANI (Bylis Ballsh)
11	Fjodor XHAFA (Flamurtari Vlorë)
	Hekuran JAKUPI (Bylis Ballsh)
10	Daniel XHAFA (Flamurtari Vlorë)
	Vladimir GJONI (Burreli)
	Fatjon YMERI (Dinamo Tiranë)

NATIONAL TEAM APPEARANCES 98/99

Coach - Astrit HAFIZI	CYP	GEO	NOR	GRE	MAC	LAT	NOR	SLO	Cps	Gls
Foto STRAKOSHA (29/03/65) - Panionios (GRE)	G80	G	G	G	G81	G	G	G	37	-
Ilir SHULKU (02/01/69) - Eintracht Nordhorn (GER)	D	D	D	D		D	D	D	38	1
Altin LALA (18/02/74) - Hannover 96 (GER)	D	D	D			D	D	D	10	-
Oltion OSMANI (20/05/72) - Bylis Ballsh	D64								1	-
Luan PINARI (27/10/77) - Dinamo Tiranë	D65	D			D				3	-
Rudi VATA (13/02/69) - Energie Cottbus (GER)	M	M	M	M	M	M78	M	M	44	3
Altin HAXHI (07/06/65) - Liteks Lovech (BUL)	M	M	M	M	M	M	M		17	2
Alban BUSHI (24/08/73) - Liteks Lovech (BUL)	M76	M74	M84	M	A	M86	M	M	21	4
Bledar KOLA (01/08/72) - Panathinaikos (GRE)	M	M	M89	M	M78	M	M70		25	4
Altin RRAKLI (17/07/70) - SpVgg Unterhaching (GER)	A46	A	A	A		A82	A80	A46	37	7
Igli TARE (25/07/73) - Fortuna Düsseldorf (GER)	A72	A68	A	A	A	A	A	A	18	3
Edvin MURATI (12/11/75) - Fortuna Düsseldorf (GER)	s46								1	-
Alpin GALLO (12/01/74) - SK Tirana	s64	s74							9	-
Johan DRIZA (20/09/76) - Flamurtari Vlorë	s65								1	-
Erjon BOGDANI (14/04/75) - Dinamo Tiranë/Zagreb (CRO)	s72				s78		s80	M74	5	1
Devi MUKA (21/12/76) - SK Tirana	s76				s46				2	-
Armir GRIMA (16/06/74) - Ethnikos Piraeus (GRE)	s80								3	-
Arian XHUMBA (07/09/68) - Paralimni (CYP)		D	D	D	D		D	D	25	-
Arian PEÇO (21/04/75) - SR Delémont (SUI)		s68							10	-
		/86								
Artur MAXHUNI (27/10/72) - FC St. Pauli (GER)		s86							1	-
Ervin FAKAJ (15/07/76) - CD Toledo (ESP)/Hannover 96 (GER)			D	D		D	D63		12	-
Mahir HALILI (30/06/75) - SR Delémont (SUI)			s84	s50	M46	s86		s46	12	1
Edmond DALIPI (03/03/72) - Apollon (GRE)			s89	M50	M74	s82		s74	11	-
Redi JUPI (31/05/74) - Partizani Tiranë					M61	s78			4	-
Rezart DABULLA (24/10/79) - SK Tirana					s61				1	-
Eldorado MERKOÇI (06/01/78) - SK Tirana					s74				1	-
Arian BEQAJ (20/08/75) - OFI (GRE)					s81				3	-
Arian BELLAI (11/03/70) - Yannina (GRE)							s63	M	12	1
Albert DURO (12/06/78) - Elbasani							s70	M	2	-

For Vllaznia, the season ended as bitterly as it had begun. The first leg of their Champions' Cup qualifying tie away to Dinamo Tbilisi ended with a satisfactory 0-1 defeat, but the scoreline was later changed to 0-3 after it emerged that Vllaznia had made a basic and banal administrative error, fielding a substitute who had not figured on the official teamsheet. Vasil Bici's team made a heroic attempt to claw back the deficit in the return leg, but their 3-1 victory was not enough, so out they went, to be joined as first-hedge fallers by Tirana in the UEFA Cup and, later, Apolonia Fier in the Cup-winners' Cup.

There were happier tidings to report from the international excursions of the Albanian national team. Although they, like Vllaznia, began their European campaign with a 0-1 defeat in Tbilisi, the manner of that narrow reverse encouraged Astrit Hafizi's troops to go 2-0 up away to France '98 qualifiers Norway in their next match before eventually having to settle for a 2-2 draw. There then followed a couple of goalless draws at home to Greece - the first international staged in Tirana for three years, albeit a month later than planned - and away to Latvia, plus, in between, a 2-0 victory in a friendly at home to Macedonia.

Unfortunately, the conflict in Kosovo meant that the home qualifying ties against Latvia and Slovenia had to be postponed. But by early June, UEFA had given Albania permission, under NATO supervision, to stage their two home fixtures against Norway and Slovenia. There was optimism from the Albanian fans that they might see their team record their first victory, but, sadly, both matches ended in defeat, making it unlikely that Albania would end their campaign anywhere other than in bottom place.

APOLONIA FIER

Klubi Sportiv Apolonia
Rruga 1 Maji, nr.73
Fier
tel - (42) 2183
Year of Formation - 1925
Secretary - Besnik Veliu
Coach - Dhimitër Papuçiu
Stadium - Loni Papuçiu (6,000)

MAJOR HONOURS
Domestic Cup - (1) 1998.

	P	Ap	(s)	Gls
Artan BARE	M	23		1
Dashnor BITA	D	21		4
Gëzim BUZIU	D	13		
Elidon ÇOBANI	A	17	(3)	1
Elidon DEMIRI	D	25		1
Blenard FEJZULLAHU	M	17	(6)	2
Romeo HAXHIAJ	A	13		4
Arben JAHIQI	M	6	(1)	
Aurel MALAJ	M	18	(1)	
Jurgen MALI	A	26	(2)	2
Edis MARINI	A	8		4
Robert NUREDINI	D	7		
Kudret OSMANI	G	15		
Artan POÇI	D	26		2
Dashnor POÇI	M	20	(1)	3
Vaskë RUKO	A	6	(5)	1
Arben SINANI	G	15		
Fatos SULAJ	M	25	(1)	
Endri YZEIRI	M	24	(3)	6
Alket ZEQO	A	5		1

29/08/98	Tomori Berat	H	0-0	
12/09/98	Vllaznia Shkodër	A	2-4	Bita (p), Zeqo
19/09/98	Besa Kavajë	H	1-0	Haxhiaj
26/09/98	Burreli	A	0-2	
03/10/98	SK Tirana	H	0-1	
17/10/98	Elbasani	A	0-1	
24/10/98	Lushnja	H	1-1	Poçi D.
31/10/98	Flamurtari Vlorë	A	1-1	Ruko
07/11/98	Partizani Tiranë	H	1-0	Bare (p)
11/11/98	Laçi	H	2-1	Poçi D., Haxhiaj
25/11/98	Bylis Ballsh	A	1-4	Haxhiaj
28/11/98	Skënderbeu Korçë	H	4-2	Poçi A., Fejzullahu 2, Haxhiaj
05/12/98	Dinamo Tiranë	A	1-3	Mali
12/12/98	Shkumbini Peqin	H	1-1	Yzeiri
19/12/98	Teuta Durrës	A	1-1	Yzeiri
06/02/99	Tomori Berat	A	1-2	Yzeiri
13/02/99	Vllaznia Shkodër	H	0-0	
20/02/99	Besa Kavajë	A	0-1	
27/02/99	Burreli	H	2-0	Çobani, Bita (p)
06/03/99	SK Tirana	A	0-2	
13/03/99	Elbasani	H	2-1	Poçi D., Demiri
20/03/99	Lushnja	A	1-3	Bita (p)
27/03/99	Flamurtari Vlorë	H	1-0	Marini
03/04/99	Partizani Tiranë	A	2-2	Yzeiri, Mali
10/04/99	Laçi	A	1-4	Marini
17/04/99	Bylis Ballsh	H	1-0	Bita (p)
01/05/99	Skënderbeu Korçë	A	0-2	
08/05/99	Dinamo Tiranë	H	2-0	Yzeiri, Marini
12/05/99	Shkumbini Peqin	A	1-2	Poçi A.
15/05/99	Teuta Durrës	H	2-1	Marini, Yzeiri

BESA KAVAJË

CLUB DIRECTORY

Klubi Sportiv Besa
Rruga Vangjel Thanasi, nr.7
Kavajë
tel - (57) 42617
Year of Formation - 1925
President - Taip Dedej
Secretary - Haki Arkaxhiu
Coach - Shkëlqim Muça
Stadium - Besa (8,000)

APPEARANCES 98/99

	P	Ap	(s)	Gls
Neritan BAJAZITI	A	27		4
Egert BAKALLI	A	15		1
Aranit BALLHYSA	G	11		
Gentian BRATJA	D	18	(3)	
Dorian BUBEQI	A	27		9
Klodian BYGJYMI	D	4	(13)	1
Artan ÇIÇIKU	M	8	(1)	1
Armand DAIU	M	22	(3)	
Përparim DAIU	D	14		
Indrit DOKA	D	25	(1)	
Sparti DOMI	D	25		2
Artan DUKA	M	26	(1)	
Devis ISMAILI	D	12		2
Bekim KULI	A	6	(10)	2
Alket MEÇE	A	16	(2)	
Bujar MUÇA	M	13		1
Altin RRICA	M	11		
Kujtim SHTAMA	G	19		
Altin SIMAKU	A	4	(13)	1
Arben YMERI	D	9		
Enkelejd ZYLA	M	18		1

LEAGUE RESULTS 1998/99

29/08/98	Lushnja	A	0-4	
12/09/98	Flamurtari Vlorë	H	2-1	Bubeqi, Domi
19/09/98	Apolonia Fier	A	0-1	
26/09/98	Laçi	H	2-0	Bubeqi 2 (1p)
03/10/98	Bylis Ballsh	A	1-2	Bubeqi
17/10/98	Skënderbeu Korçë	H	2-1	Bubeqi (p), Simaku
24/10/98	Dinamo Tiranë	A	0-1	
31/10/98	Shkumbini Peqin	H	1-0	Bajaziti
07/11/98	Teuta Durrës	A	0-2	
11/11/98	Tomori Berat	H	1-1	Bubeqi
25/11/98	Vllaznia Shkodër	A	0-5	
28/11/98	Partizani Tiranë	A	1-2	Çiçiku
05/12/98	Burreli	H	4-1	Bajaziti, Kuli, Bubeqi, Bygjymi
12/12/98	SK Tirana	A	0-2	
19/12/98	Elbasani	H	0-0	
06/02/99	Lushnja	H	1-0	Ismaili
13/02/99	Flamurtari Vlorë	A	0-4	
20/02/99	Apolonia Fier	H	1-0	Bubeqi
27/02/99	Laçi	A	0-1	
06/03/99	Bylis Ballsh	H	0-1	
13/03/99	Skënderbeu Korçë	A	0-1	
20/03/99	Dinamo Tiranë	H	1-0	Zyla
03/04/99	Teuta Durrës	H	0-0	
10/04/99	Tomori Berat	A	1-2	Ismaili
17/04/99	Vllaznia Shkodër	H	0-0	
01/05/99	Partizani Tiranë	H	2-1	Kuli, Muça
08/05/99	Burreli	A	3-2	Bubeqi, Bajaziti 2
12/05/99	SK Tirana	H	1-1	Domi
15/05/99	Elbasani	A	1-4	Bakalli
27/03/99	Shkumbini Peqin	A	0-0	

BURRELI

Klubi Sportiv Burreli
Burrel
Year of Formation - 1960
President - Dëfrim Çupi
Secretary - Lekë Sulkaj
Coach - Baftiar Punavia
Stadium - Burreli (4,000)

	P	Ap	(s)	Gls
Besnik BEQIRI	G	7	(4)	
Bledar ÇULIQI	D	22	(4)	
Kastriot FARUKU	M	20	(1)	5
Leonard FARUKU	D	13		
Xhelal FARUKU	M	21	(2)	9
Dritan GJOKA	D	22		1
Vladimir GJONI	A	27		10
Lulzim KOLA	D	27		
Paulin KOLAVERI	M	27	(1)	1
Arben LIKA	M	21	(6)	2
Iefik MUKA	D	10	(3)	
Kasem NDREU	M	17	(5)	
Sajmir PATUSHI	M	13		2
Kastrot RAMA	G	21	(1)	
Alfred STAFASANI	M	3	(6)	
Sajmir XHETANI	A	26	(5)	7
Roland ZEQIRI	M	11	(2)	

29/08/98	Elbasani	A	1-3	Faruku K. (p)
12/09/98	Lushnja	H	4-1	Patushi 2, Faruku X., Xhetani
19/09/98	Flamurtari Vlorë	A	1-2	Lika
26/09/98	Apolonia Fier	H	2-0	Gjoni, Xhetani
03/10/98	Laçi	A	1-2	Gjoni
17/10/98	Bylis Ballsh	H	1-2	Faruku X. (p)
24/10/98	Skënderbeu Korçë	A	1-2	Gjoni
31/10/98	Dinamo Tiranë	H	4-4	Gjoni 2, Faruku X. 2 (1p)
07/11/98	Shkumbini Peqin	A	0-1	
11/11/98	Teuta Durrës	H	3-0	Faruku X. (p), Kolaveri, og (Karaj)
25/11/98	Tomori Berat	A	1-2	Gjoni
28/11/98	Vllaznia Shkodër	H	1-0	Xhetani
05/12/98	Besa Kavajë	A	1-4	Gjoka
12/12/98	Partizani Tiranë	A	1-3	Faruku K.
19/12/98	SK Tirana	H	0-0	
06/02/99	Elbasani	H	2-0	(w/o)
13/02/99	Lushnja	A	0-3	
20/02/99	Flamurtari Vlorë	H	0-2	(w/o)
27/02/99	Apolonia Fier	A	0-2	
06/03/99	Laçi	H	1-3	Faruku K.
13/03/99	Bylis Ballsh	A	1-5	Faruku K.
20/03/99	Skënderbeu Korçë	H	4-2	Faruku X. 3 (1p), Lika
27/03/99	Dinamo Tiranë	A	0-0	
03/04/99	Shkumbini Peqin	H	3-0	Xhetani 2, Faruku X.
10/04/99	Teuta Durres	A	0-3	
17/04/99	Tomori Berat	H	2-1	Xhetani, Gjoni
01/05/99	Vllaznia Shkodër	A	1-4	Gjoni
08/05/99	Besa Kavajë	H	2-3	Gjoni 2
12/05/99	Partizani Tiranë	H	2-3	Faruku K., Xhetani
15/05/99	SK Tirana	A	0-3	

BYLIS BALLSH

CLUB DIRECTORY

Klubi Sportiv Bylis
Bashkia
Ballsh
Year of Formation - 1972
President - Ismet Beqiri
Secretary - Besnik Sulaj
Coach - Vangjel Capo; Hysen Dedja
Stadium - Ballshi (6,500)

APPEARANCES 98/99

	P	Ap	(s)	Gls
Julian AHMATAJ	M	18	(1)	2
Klodian ASLLANI	M	27	(1)	12
Luan ASLLANI	D	26	(1)	
Lorenc BASHA	D	8	(6)	
Sajmir BENDO	D	26		2
Ferdinand BILALI	M	24	(2)	8
Luan BRAÇE	A	7	(7)	2
Gazmend ÇANAKU	A	19	(7)	
Bledar DEVOLLI	M	9		1
Dashnor DUME	D	26		1
Arben HYSKO	M	14		1
Hekuran JAKUPI	A	26	(1)	11
Adriatik KANANI	D	9		
Edmond KRAJA	M	8	(6)	2
Ardian NINI	M	6	(6)	1
Oltion OSMANI	D	12		1
Nuri REXHA	M	25	(2)	3
Orges SHEHI	G	29		

LEAGUE RESULTS 1998/99

29/08/98	Shkumbini Peqin	H	2-0	Bendo, Jakupi
12/09/98	Teuta Durrës	A	1-2	Jakupi
19/09/98	Tomori Berat	H	2-0	Asllani L. (p), Bendo
26/09/98	Vllaznia Shkodër	A	0-2	
03/10/98	Besa Kavajë	H	2-1	Jakupi, Asllani K.
17/10/98	Burreli	A	2-1	Jakupi, Rexha
24/10/98	SK Tirana	H	2-1	Asllani K., Bilali
31/10/98	Elbasani	A	0-1	
07/11/98	Lushnja	H	1-0	Bilali
11/11/98	Flamurtari Vlorë	A	0-0	
25/11/98	Apolonia Fier	H	4-1	Asllani K. 4
28/11/98	Laçi	A	0-0	
05/12/98	Partizani Tiranë	H	2-0	Hysko, Bilali
12/12/98	Skënderbeu Korçë	H	5-0	Braçe, Bilali 3, Ahmataj
19/12/98	Dinamo Tiranë	A	1-2	Jakupi
06/02/99	Shkumbini Peqin	A	0-1	
13/02/99	Teuta Durrës	H	3-0	Asllani K. 2, Bilali
20/02/99	Tomori Berat	A	0-0	
27/02/99	Vllaznia Shkodër	H	2-2	Jakupi, Osmani (p)
06/03/99	Besa Kavajë	A	1-0	Rexha
13/03/99	Burreli	H	5-1	Devolli, Kraja, Ahmataj, Rexha, og (Faruku X.)
20/03/99	SK Tirana	A	0-0	
27/03/99	Elbasani	H	3-0	Asllani K. 2, Jakupi
03/04/99	Lushnja	A	2-0	(w/o)
10/04/99	Flamurtari Vlorë	H	4-0	Nini, Jakupi 2, Bilali
17/04/99	Apolonia Fier	A	0-1	
01/05/99	Laçi	H	4-1	Jakupi 2, Dume, Kraja
08/05/99	Partizani Tiranë	A	2-1	Asllani K. 2
12/05/99	Skënderbeu Korçë	A	0-1	
15/05/99	Dinamo Tiranë	H	1-0	Braçe

DINAMO TIRANË

Klubi Sportiv Dinamo
Rruga Dervish Hima, nr. 30
Tiranë
tel - (42) 23662
Year of Formation - 1950
President - Besnik Sulo
Secretary - Sokol Morina
Coach - Faruk Sejdini
Stadium - Selman Stërmasi (12,000)

MAJOR HONOURS
League Championship - (15) 1950, 1951, 1952,
1953, 1955, 1956, 1960, 1967, 1973, 1975,
1976, 1977, 1980, 1986, 1990.
Domestic Cup - (12) 1950, 1951, 1952, 1953,
1954, 1960, 1971, 1974, 1978, 1982, 1989,
1990.

	P	Ap	(s)	Gls
Ergert BAKALLI	M	13		1
Ardian BOGDANI	G	12		
Erjon BOGDANI	M	6		2
Edmond DALIPI	M	15		3
Elton DALIPI	A	6	(4)	
Paulin DHEMBI	A	11	(3)	
Genti GJONDEDA	M	8	(3)	
Robert GUCE	D	10	(3)	
Gentian HAJDARI	D	24	(2)	
Elton HASANI	A	7	(7)	2
Blendi HAXHIAJ	D	26		
Redi HOXHA	M	21	(4)	2
Saimir ILIAZI	D	7	(2)	
Shpëtim IMERAJ	M	27		
Xhevahir KAPLLANI	G	6		
Ilir KURTI	D	20		
Erjon MATRAKU	M	29	(1)	6
Genc NASTASI	A	15	(1)	3
Luan PINARI	D	25	(1)	7
Andi SHTREPI	A	2	(8)	1
Bashkim TOSKA	G	12	(1)	
Fatjon YMERI	A	28		10

29/08/98	Skënderbeu Korçë	A	3-2	Dalipi Ed., Ymeri 2
12/09/98	Partizani Tiranë	A	2-2	Pinari (p), Ymeri
19/09/98	Shkumbini Peqin	H	1-0	Bakalli
26/09/98	Teuta Durrës	A	2-3	Bogdani E., Pinari (p)
03/10/98	Tomori Berat	H	0-0	
17/10/98	Vllaznia Shkodër	A	3-1	Bogdani E., Nastasi, Hoxha
24/10/98	Besa Kavajë	H	1-0	Dalipi Ed.
31/10/98	Burreli	A	4-4	Pinari, Ymeri, Nastasi 2
07/11/98	SK Tirana	H	0-3	
11/11/98	Elbasani	A	0-0	
25/11/98	Lushnja	H	2-0	Ymeri, Matraku
28/11/98	Flamurtari Vlorë	A	0-2	
05/12/98	Apolonia Fier	H	3-1	Ymeri 2, Pinari (p)
12/12/98	Laçi	A	1-2	Dalipi Ed.
19/12/98	Bylis Ballsh	H	2-1	Hoxha, Matraku
06/02/99	Skënderbeu Korçë	H	1-0	Matraku
13/02/99	Partizani Tiranë	H	2-2	Pinari (p), Ymeri
20/02/99	Shkumbini Peqin	A	0-1	
27/02/99	Teuta Durrës	H	1-2	Shtrepi
06/03/99	Tomori Berat	A	0-1	
13/03/99	Vllaznia Shkodër	H	0-1	
20/03/99	Besa Kavajë	A	0-1	
27/03/99	Burreli	H	0-0	
03/04/99	SK Tirana	A	0-1	
10/04/99	Elbasani	H	2-1	Matraku (p), Pinari
17/04/99	Lushnja	A	1-1	Ymeri
01/05/99	Flamurtari Vlorë	H	3-1	Pinari (p), Matraku, Hasani
08/05/99	Apolonia Fier	A	0-2	
12/05/99	Laçi	H	3-1	Hasani, Matraku, Ymeri
15/05/99	Bylis Ballsh	A	0-1	

ELBASANI

CLUB DIRECTORY

Klubi i Futbollit Elbasani
Bulevardi Qemal Stafa
Stadiumi KF Elbasani
Elbasan
tel - (42) 53253
Year of Formation - 1923
Secretary - Zamir Arapi
Coach - Astrit Sejdini
Stadium - Elbasani (13,500)

MAJOR HONOURS
League Championship - (1) 1984.
Domestic Cup - (2) 1975, 1992.

APPEARANCES 98/99

	P	Ap	(s)	Gls
Julian AHMATAJ	A	6		1
Taulant BAKIU	D	27		1
Dorian BYLYKBASHI	A	20		4
Gentian BYLYKBASHI	M	22	(2)	3
Muharrem DOSTI	G	29		
Albert DURO	M	12		1
Ilirian FILE	D	17		
Gjergj GJIKA	M	16	(1)	
Gentian GRABOCKA	A	20	(2)	3
Isuf IBËRSHIMI	M	26	(6)	7
Eriol MERXHA	M	8	(15)	
Bujar MUÇA	D	12	(1)	4
Arian PISHA	D	27		1
Ilir QORRI	D	28		3
Saimir SHENGJERGJI	D	26	(1)	
Armand STAMBOLLXHIU	A	9	(8)	1
Gentian STOJKU	D	3		1
Elton VERÇANI	D	11	(11)	

LEAGUE RESULTS 1998/99

29/08/98	Burreli	H	3-1	Muça 2, Duro
12/09/98	SK Tirana	A	0-1	
19/09/98	Partizani Tiranë	H	1-2	Bylykbashi G.
26/09/98	Lushnja	H	1-0	Grabocka
03/10/98	Flamurtari Vlorë	A	1-1	Muça
17/10/98	Apolonia Fier	H	1-0	Bylykbashi D.
24/10/98	Laçi	A	0-1	
31/10/98	Bylis Ballsh	H	1-0	Ahmataj
07/11/98	Skënderbeu Korçë	A	0-2	
11/11/98	Dinamo Tiranë	H	0-0	
25/11/98	Shkumbini Peqin	A	0-1	
28/11/98	Teuta Durrës	H	2-0	Qorri, Muça
05/12/98	Tomori Berat	A	0-1	
12/12/98	Vllaznia Shkodër	H	1-1	Stojku
19/12/98	Besa Kavajë	A	0-0	
06/02/99	Burreli	A	0-2	(w/o)
13/02/99	SK Tirana	H	0-0	
20/02/99	Partizani Tiranë	A	1-1	Bylykbashi D.
27/02/99	Lushnja	A	0-2	
06/03/99	Flamurtari Vlorë	H	2-1	Stambollxhiu, Grabocka
13/03/99	Apolonia Fier	A	1-2	Ibërshimi
20/03/99	Laçi	H	3-0	Qorri, Bylykbashi D., Ibërshimi
27/03/99	Bylis Ballsh	A	0-3	
03/04/99	Skënderbeu Korçë	H	3-0	Grabocka, Bakiu, Ibërshimi
10/04/99	Dinamo Tiranë	A	1-2	Bylykbashi G.
17/04/99	Shkumbini Peqin	H	1-0	Ibërshimi
01/05/99	Teuta Durrës	A	0-1	
08/05/99	Tomori Berat	H	2-1	Bylykbashi D., Bylykbashi G.
12/05/99	Vllaznia Shkodër	A	1-3	Ibërshimi
15/05/99	Besa Kavajë	H	4-1	Qorri (p), Pisha, Ibërshimi 2

FLAMURTARI VLORË

CLUB DIRECTORY

Klubi Sportiv Flamurtari
Rruga Perlat Rexhëpi, nr.41
Vlorë
tel - (63) 24563
Year of Formation - 1923
President - Shkëlqim Selami
Secretary - Mallëngjim Skënderaj
Coach - Vasil Ruci
Stadium - Flamurtari (8,200)

MAJOR HONOURS
League Championship - (1) 1991.
Domestic Cup - (2) 1985, 1988.

APPEARANCES 98/99

		P	(s)	Gls
Ilir ALLIU	D	6		
Alven BEJLERI	G	29		
Taulant ÇERÇIZI	D	11	(4)	
Arnold ÇIPI	A	14	(1)	
Geri ÇIPI	D	16		
Jorgaq DIAMANTI	D	11	(1)	
Dritan HALIBI	M	8	(3)	
Sajmir HAXHIU	A	25		1
Gentian IBRAHIMI	M	5	(12)	2
Sherif IDRIZI	M	7	(8)	
Besnik KOLA	D	11		
Bledar LALA	M	15	(1)	
Klodian LIÇAJ	M	13	(6)	2
Edmond LILAJ	D	11	(2)	
Fation MALAJ	M	15		
Gentian MEZINI	D	8		
Roland NENAJ	A	20	(3)	2
Robert NUREDINI	M	10	(3)	1
Dritan RESULI	M	12	(1)	1
Elion RUKA	M	8	(3)	2
Alven SHEHAJ	M	6		1
Anesti VITO	A	10	(3)	5
Daniel XHAFA	A	22	(1)	10
Fjodor XHAFA	A	26	(1)	11

LEAGUE RESULTS 1998/99

29/08/98	Vllaznia Shkodër	H	0-0	
12/09/98	Besa Kavajë	A	1-2	Xhafa D.
19/09/98	Burreli	H	2-1	Xhafa F., Xhafa D.
26/09/98	SK Tirana	A	0-1	
03/10/98	Elbasani	H	1-1	Liçaj (p)
17/10/98	Lushnja	A	2-3	Xhafa F. 2
24/10/98	Partizani Tiranë	H	0-0	
31/10/98	Apolonia Fier	H	1-1	Nenaj
07/11/98	Laçi	A	2-4	Liçaj, Xhafa F.
11/11/98	Bylis Ballsh	H	0-0	
25/11/98	Skënderbeu Korçë	A	1-4	Xhafa F.
28/11/98	Dinamo Tiranë	H	2-0	Xhafa D. (p), Xhafa F.
05/12/98	Shkumbini Peqin	A	0-3	
12/12/98	Teuta Durrës	H	3-0	Xhafa D. 2 (1p), Nenaj
19/12/98	Tomori Berat	A	0-1	
06/02/99	Vllaznia Shkodër	A	0-8	
13/02/99	Besa Kavajë	H	4-0	Ruka, Xhafa F., Xhafa D., Vito
20/02/99	Burreli	A	2-0	(w/o)
27/02/99	SK Tirana	H	1-0	Xhafa F.
06/03/99	Elbasani	A	1-2	Haxhiu
13/03/99	Lushnja	H	3-1	Xhafa D., Shehaj, Vito
20/03/99	Partizani Tiranë	A	2-3	Xhafa D., Vito
27/03/99	Apolonia Fier	A	0-1	
03/04/99	Laçi	H	3-0	Ruka, Nuredini, Xhafa D.
10/04/99	Bylis Ballsh	A	0-4	
17/04/99	Skënderbeu Korçë	H	3-0	Vito, Xhafa D., Ibrahimi
01/05/99	Dinamo Tiranë	A	1-3	Resuli
08/05/99	Shkumbini Peqin	H	2-0	Xhafa F. 2
12/05/99	Teuta Durrës	A	0-2	
15/05/99	Tomori Berat	H	3-2	Xhafa F., Ibrahami, Vito

LAÇI

CLUB DIRECTORY

Klubi i Futbollit Laçi
Laç
tel - (42) 288
Year of Formation - 1938
President - Filip Gjoka
Secretary - Kujtim Ceka
Coach - Luigj Dodaj
Stadium - Laçi (5,000)

APPEARANCES 98/99

	P	Ap	(s)	Gls
Altin BIBA	D	18	(9)	
Luan BICI	M	13	(6)	
Kliton ÇAFI	M	6		2
Artan ÇIÇIKU	M	10	(4)	1
Ded DEDA	D	21		3
Afrim DELIU	D	11		1
Valentin GJETJA	D	13		4
Martin GJINI	M	2		1
Eno GJOKA	M	17	(3)	
Shpëtim GRUDA	D	10		9
Besnik HASA	D	13		1
Eris HOXHA	M	9	(13)	
Thoma KOKURI	G	29		
Përparim KRAJA	M	5	(1)	1
Sajmir MALOKU	A	11		3
Sabah MICI	A	22	(1)	5
Artan PALOKA	D	22		
Elvis PLORI	A	13		
Shkëlzen RUSTAMI	D	21	(2)	3
Oltion SINANI	M	13	(9)	
Indrit TUÇI	D	11	(12)	
Roland TUNA	D	12		
Alban VOLUMI	M	8		2
Roland ZEQIRI	M	9	(1)	

LEAGUE RESULTS 1998/99

29/08/98	Teuta Durrës	H	2-0	Gjetja, Rustami
12/09/98	Tomori Berat	A	1-1	Rustami
19/09/98	Vllaznia Shkodër	H	0-1	
26/09/98	Besa Kavajë	A	0-2	
03/10/98	Burreli	H	2-1	Kraja, Maloku
17/10/98	SK Tirana	A	0-0	
24/10/98	Elbasani	H	1-0	Maloku
31/10/98	Lushnja	A	1-3	Gjetja
07/11/98	Flamurtari Vlorë	H	4-2	Mici 2, Maloku, Deda
11/11/98	Apolonia Fier	A	1-2	Gjetja
25/11/98	Partizani Tiranë	H	2-3	Gjetja, Deliu
28/11/98	Bylis Ballsh	H	0-0	
05/12/98	Skënderbeu Korçë	A	1-4	Hasa (p)
12/12/98	Dinamo Tiranë	H	2-1	Çafi 2
19/12/98	Shkumbini Peqin	A	0-5	
06/02/99	Teuta Durrës	A	0-1	
13/02/99	Tomori Berat	H	0-0	
20/02/99	Vllaznia Shkodër	A	0-2	
27/02/99	Besa Kavajë	H	1-0	Mici
06/03/99	Burreli	A	3-1	Gruda, Volumi, Rustami
13/03/99	SK Tirana	H	3-3	Mici, Gruda 2
20/03/99	Elbasani	A	0-3	
27/03/99	Lushnja	H	0-2	(w/o)
03/04/99	Flamurtari Vlorë	A	0-3	
10/04/99	Apolonia Fier	H	4-1	Deda, Gruda 2, Çiçiku
17/04/99	Partizani Tiranë	A	0-3	
01/05/99	Bylis Ballsh	A	1-4	Deda
08/05/99	Skënderbeu Korçë	H	5-3	Gruda 3, Volumi, Mici
12/05/99	Dinamo Tiranö	A	1-3	Gruda
15/05/99	Shkumbini Peqin	H	1-1	Gjini

LUSHNJA

CLUB DIRECTORY

Klubi Sportiv Lushnja
Lagjja Xh. Nepravishta
Lushnjë
tel - (42) 300
Year of Formation - 1927
Secretary - Genci Tufa
Coach - Ilir Gjyla
Stadium - Roza Haxhiu (12,000)

APPEARANCES 98/99

	P	Ap	(s)	Gls
Devis AJAZI	A	13	(5)	
Artan BANO	A	22	(1)	22
Arben ÇELA	A	27		5
Dritan ÇUKO	M	24		6
Enik DHIMA	M	9	(6)	
Aurel DUSHI	A	20	(4)	
Bardhyl ELEZI	A	24	(1)	12
Judmir GAZHELI	D	19	(5)	
Argenc GJERJOVA	A	13	(2)	
Blerim HASALLA	D	25		1
Altin HYSKO	M	20	(1)	
Arben HYSKO	M	7		1
Eduart KAPLLANI	A	7	(5)	1
Bledar MANKO	D	17		
Orgert MUKA	M	16	(3)	2
Hektor PREMÇE	G	27		
Armir SALLAKU	G	1		
Maksim TAULLAI	M	10	(3)	
Admir TOSHKELLARI	D	7		

LEAGUE RESULTS 1998/99

29/08/98	Besa Kavajë	H	4-0	Bano 2, Çela, Elezi
12/09/98	Burreli	A	1-4	Bano
19/09/98	SK Tirana	H	6-1	Çuko 2, Elezi, Bano 2 (1p), Çela
26/09/98	Elbasani	A	0-1	
03/10/98	Partizani Tiranë	H	3-0	Muka, Çuko, Bano
17/10/98	Flamurtari Vlorë	H	3-2	Bano 3
24/10/98	Apolonia Fier	A	1-1	Hasalla
31/10/98	Laçi	H	3-1	Bano, Çuko, Elezi
07/11/98	Bylis Ballsh	A	0-1	
11/11/98	Skënderbeu Korçë	H	5-1	Bano, Çuko, Elezi 2, Çela
25/11/98	Dinamo Tiranë	A	0-2	
28/11/98	Shkumbini Peqin	H	3-0	Kapllani, Bano, Elezi
05/12/98	Teuta Durrës	A	2-1	Çela, Elezi
12/12/98	Tomori Berat	H	1-0	Bano
19/12/98	Vllaznia Shkodër	A	0-3	
06/02/99	Besa Kavajë	A	0-1	
13/02/99	Burreli	H	3-0	Muka, Çela (p), Elezi
20/02/99	SK Tirana	A	0-3	
27/02/99	Elbasani	H	2-0	Hysko Ar., Bano (p)
06/03/99	Partizani Tiranë	A	1-2	Bano
13/03/99	Flamurtari Vlorë	A	1-3	Bano (p)
20/03/99	Apolonia Fier	H	3-1	Bano 3 (1p)
27/03/99	Laçi	A	2-0	(w/o)
03/04/99	Bylis Ballsh	H	0-2	(w/o)
10/04/99	Skënderbeu Korçë	A	1-2	Elezi
17/04/99	Dinamo Tiranë	H	1-1	Elezi
01/05/99	Shkumbini Peqin	A	1-2	Elezi
08/05/99	Teuta Durrës	H	2-0	Bano, Çuko
12/05/99	Tomori Berat	A	2-3	Bano, Elezi
15/05/99	Vllaznia Shkodër	H	1-2	Bano

PARTIZANI TIRANË

CLUB DIRECTORY

Klubi Sportiv Partizani
Rruga Frosina Plaku, nr.31
Tiranë
tel - (42) 25138
Year of Formation - 1946
President - Antonio De Simone
Secretary - Bujar Labinoti
Coach - Edmond Gëzdari
Stadium - Selman Stërmasi (12,000)

MAJOR HONOURS

League Championship - (15) 1947, 1948, 1949,
1954, 1957, 1958, 1959, 1961, 1963, 1964,
1971, 1979, 1981, 1987, 1993.
Domestic Cup - (14) 1948, 1949, 1957, 1958,
1961, 1964, 1966, 1968, 1970, 1973, 1980,
1991, 1993, 1997.

APPEARANCES 98/99

	P	Ap	(s)	Gls
Ervin BARDHI	M	16		
Fatmir BEGA	M	6	(12)	2
Astrit BEQIRI	D	2	(1)	1
Gentian BRATJA	D	19		1
Ledio CAPO	G	8		
Adriatik GJONI	D	17		
Redi JUPI	M	25		2
Maringlen KAPAJ	D	13	(7)	
Edmond KODRA	A	19	(5)	3
Gugash MAGANI	M	19		3
Artan MERGJYSHI	D	15		
Erman MERGJYSHI	G	22	(1)	
Sulior MULLETI	A	11		
Erjon NOVAKU	M	28		3
Alban REXHA	A	14	(7)	7
Florian RIZA	A	11	(2)	5
Altin RRICA	M	11	(1)	2
Jani RUÇO	D	8	(1)	
Arjan SHETA	D	9	(12)	
Ilir SHULKU	D	5		
Alban THAÇI	M	10	(10)	2
Ligoraq TIKO	A	26		6
Rigels TURTULLI	M	16	(3)	

LEAGUE RESULTS 1998/99

29/08/98	SK Tirana	A	2-2	Tiko, Kodra
12/09/98	Dinamo Tiranë	H	2-2	Magani, Rexha
19/09/98	Elbasani	A	2-1	Bratja, Kodra
26/09/98	Shkumbini Peqin	H	1-0	Kodra
03/10/98	Lushnja	A	0-3	
17/10/98	Teuta Durrës	H	1-1	Rexha
24/10/98	Flamurtari Vlorë	A	0-0	
31/10/98	Tomori Berat	H	1-0	Magani
07/11/98	Apolonia Fier	A	0-1	
11/11/98	Vllaznia Shkodër	H	1-1	Rexha
25/11/98	Laçi	A	3-2	Tiko, Novaku 2
28/11/98	Besa Kavajë	H	2-1	Jupi, Magani
05/12/98	Bylis Ballsh	A	0-2	
12/12/98	Burreli	H	3-1	Rexha, Tiko, Novaku
19/12/98	Skënderbeu Korçë	A	0-4	
06/02/99	SK Tirana	H	1-2	Rexha
13/02/99	Dinamo Tiranë	A	2-2	Bega, Thaçi
20/02/99	Elbasani	H	1-1	Riza
27/02/99	Shkumbini Peqin	A	0-2	
06/03/99	Lushnja	H	2-1	Riza (p), Rrica
13/03/99	Teuta Durrës	A	0-2	
20/03/99	Flamurtari Vlorë	H	3-2	Riza 2 (1p), Tiko
27/03/99	Tomori Berat	A	0-3	
03/04/99	Apolonia Fier	H	2-2	Tiko, Rrica
10/04/99	Vllaznia Shkodër	A	0-2	
17/04/99	Laçi	H	3-0	Beqiri, Tiko, Riza
01/05/99	Besa Kavajë	A	1-2	Thaçi
08/05/99	Bylis Ballsh	H	1-2	Jupi
12/05/99	Burreli	A	3-2	Bega, Rexha 2
15/05/99	Skënderbeu Korçë	H	0-0	

SHKUMBINI PEQIN

Klubi Sportiv Shkumbini
Pranë Bashkisë
Peqin
tel - (73) 4234
Year of Formation - 1924
Secretary - Sokol Branica
Coach - Agustin Kola; Luan Deliu
Stadium - Peqin (5,000)

APPEARANCES 98/99

	P	Ap	(s)	Gls
Ardian ALIU	A	7	(1)	
Elson BAHITI	M	11		
Aranit BALLHYSA	G	3	(2)	
Elton CENO	A	7		7
Daniel DALIPI	M	13	(8)	2
Klodian DERVISHI	D	29	(1)	1
Roland DERVISHI	A	2	(2)	2
Drinush ELEZI	A	21	(4)	5
Klodian ELEZI	G	23		
Klevis JANI	M	20	(5)	
Gentian KAJA	D	27	(1)	
Kujtim KRYEMADHI	G	4	(1)	
Gerti KURTI	M	6	(1)	1
Shkëlqim LESHANAKU	M	15	(7)	
Dashamir MUÇA	D	26		
Astrit NEXHA	M	24	(1)	5
Dritan OMERI	M	27	(1)	3
Lorenc PASHA	M	29		1
Alfred SALLIU	M	11	(12)	1
Erion STAVRE	D	25		

LEAGUE RESULTS 1998/99

29/08/98	Bylis Ballsh	A	0-2	
12/09/98	Skënderbeu Korçë	H	1-0	Ceno
19/09/98	Dinamo Tiranë	A	0-1	
26/09/98	Partizani Tiranë	A	0-1	
03/10/98	Teuta Durrës	H	4-1	Omeri, Ceno 2, Nexha
17/10/98	Tomori Berat	A	0-4	
24/10/98	Vllaznia Shkodër	H	1-0	Ceno
31/10/98	Besa Kavajë	A	0-1	
07/11/98	Burreli	H	1-0	Ceno
11/11/98	SK Tirana	A	1-4	og (Mema)
25/11/98	Elbasani	H	1-0	Ceno
28/11/98	Lushnja	A	0-3	
05/12/98	Flamurtari Vlorë	H	3-0	Elezi D. 2, Ceno
12/12/98	Apolonia Fier	A	1-1	Nexha
19/12/98	Laçi	H	5-0	Elezi D., Nexha 2, Dalipi 2
06/02/99	Bylis Ballsh	H	1-0	Nexha
13/02/99	Skënderbeu Korçë	A	1-3	Elezi D.
20/02/99	Dinamo Tiranë	H	1-0	Omeri
27/02/99	Partizani Tiranë	H	2-0	Kurti, Omeri
06/03/99	Teuta Durrës	A	0-2	
13/03/99	Tomori Berat	H	0-0	
20/03/99	Vllaznia Shkodër	A	1-4	Elezi D.
27/03/99	Besa Kavajë	H	0-0	
03/04/99	Burreli	A	0-3	
10/04/99	SK Tirana	H	1-2	Dervishi K.
17/04/99	Elbasani	A	0-1	
01/05/99	Lushnja	H	2-1	Pasha, Dervishi R.
08/05/99	Flamurtari Vlorë	A	0-2	
12/05/99	Apolonia Fier	H	2-1	Salliu, og (Bita)
15/05/99	Laçi	A	1-1	Dervishi R.

SKËNDERBEU KORÇË

CLUB DIRECTORY

Klubi Sportiv Skënderbeu
Rruga Gjergj Kastrioti
Korçë
tel - (824) 2241
Year of Formation - 1909
President - Vasfi Haruni
Secretary - Gjergj Ballço
Coach - Gjergji Ballço
Stadium - Skënderbeu (8,000)

MAJOR HONOURS
League Championship - (1) 1933.

APPEARANCES 98/99

		P	Ap	(s)	Gls
Ylli ÇEKIÇI	A	13	(2)	5
Roland DEMBO	D	23		1
Bardhyl DOSKU	G	27		
Festim FETOLLARI	M	22		2
Olsi GJOKA	A	18	(1)	2
Bledi KADIU	M	19	(6)	2
Besnik KOLA	M	6		1
Edi KOLECI	M	13	(5)	4
Ervin KOTOMELO	M	22	(2)	1
Stavrion LAKO	D	24		
Gentian LIÇI	M	17		2
Genc LLUKA	D	7	(3)	
Rigels QOSA	A	22	(3)	19
Jani RUÇO	M	6	(2)	
Roland SHEHU	D	12	(1)	
Bledi SHKËMBI	M	23	(1)	2
Gentian SPAHIU	A	9	(4)	
Bledar VILA	D	24	(6)	2
Fjoralb ZGURRO	G	1	(1)	

LEAGUE RESULTS 1998/99

29/08/98	Dinamo Tiranë	H	2-3	Kola, Çekiçi (p)
12/09/98	Shkumbini Peqin	A	0-1	
19/09/98	Teuta Durrës	H	5-0	Gjoka, Qose, Liçi 2, Vila
26/09/98	Tomori Berat	A	0-2	
03/10/98	Vllaznia Shkodër	H	0-2	(w/o)
17/10/98	Besa Kavajë	A	1-2	Dembo
24/10/98	Burreli	H	2-1	Koleci, Kadiu
31/10/98	SK Tirana	A	0-2	(w/o)
07/11/98	Elbasani	H	2-0	Gjoka, Çekiçi
11/11/98	Lushnja	A	1-5	Qose
25/11/98	Flamurtari Vlorë	H	4-1	Fetollari, Shkëmbi (p), Qose 2
28/11/98	Apolonia Fier	A	2-4	Qose, Koleci
05/12/98	Laçi	H	4-1	Koleci, Çekiçi (p), Qose 2
12/12/98	Bylis Ballsh	A	0-5	
19/12/98	Partizani Tiranë	H	4-0	Qose 2 (1p), Koleci, Çekiçi
06/02/99	Dinamo Tiranë	A	0-1	
13/02/99	Shkumbini Peqin	H	3-1	Qose 2 (1p), Fetollari
20/02/99	Teuta Durrës	A	1-1	Kadiu
27/02/99	Tomori Berat	H	2-0	Çekiçi, Qosa
06/03/99	Vllaznia Shkodër	A	0-4	
13/03/99	Besa Kavajë	H	1-0	Qosa
20/03/99	Burreli	A	2-4	Qosa, og (Faruku K.)
27/03/99	SK Tirana	H	0-1	
03/04/99	Elbasani	A	0-3	
10/04/99	Lushnja	H	2-1	Qose 2
17/04/99	Flamurtari Vlorë	A	0-3	
01/05/99	Apolonia Fier	H	2-0	Kotomelo, Shkëmbi
08/05/99	Laçi	A	3-5	Qose 3
12/05/99	Bylis Ballsh	H	1-0	Vila
15/05/99	Partizani Tiranë	A	0-0	

TEUTA DURRËS

CLUB DIRECTORY

Klubi Sportiv Teuta
Rruga Mujo Ulqinaku, nr.19
Lagja 12, Durrës
tel - (52) 23631
Year of Formation - 1920
President - Edmond Hasanbelliu
Secretary - Maksut Leshteni
Coach - Enver Shehu; Hasan Lika
Stadium - Niko Dovana (12,000)

MAJOR HONOURS
League Championship - (1) 1994.
Domestic Cup - (1) 1995.

APPEARANCES 98/99

	P	Ap	(s)	Gls
Klement AVRAMI	G	7		
Neritan BABAMUSTA	M	26		2
Gentian BEGEJA	A	25		8
Justin BESPALLA	A	22	(3)	1
Qazim BUNA	M	25		2
Përparim DAIU	M	10		
Indrit ESTREFI	D	20	(3)	
Artur KALLÇO	A	10	(4)	3
Xhevahir KAPLLANI	G	23		
Ervin KARAJ	A	17	(2)	1
Oert KOTE	D	11	(7)	2
Fatos KUCI	D	24		
Kreshnik MANÇE	A	17	(3)	
Habib REXHEPI	M	23	(1)	3
Dritan SPAHIU	D	9	(3)	
Gentian STOJKU	D	12		4
Afrim TOLE	A	12		
Kastriot TOSKU	D	15	(5)	
Agron XHAFA	A	5	(13)	2
Marenglen XHAI	M	17		

LEAGUE RESULTS 1998/99

29/08/98	Laçi	A	0-2	
12/09/98	Bylis Ballsh	H	2-1	Begeja, Rexhepi
19/09/98	Skënderbeu Korçë	A	0-5	
26/09/98	Dinamo Tiranë	H	3-2	Kallço 2, Bespalla
03/10/98	Shkumbini Peqin	A	1-4	Buna
17/10/98	Partizani Tiranë	A	1-1	Begeja
24/10/98	Tomori Berat	H	1-0	Rexhepi
31/10/98	Vllaznia Shkodër	A	0-3	
07/11/98	Besa Kavajë	H	2-0	Karaj, Begeja
11/11/98	Burreli	A	0-3	
25/11/98	SK Tirana	H	0-5	
28/11/98	Elbasani	A	0-2	
05/12/98	Lushnja	H	1-2	Begeja
12/12/98	Flamurtari Vlorë	A	0-3	
19/12/98	Apolonia Fier	H	1-1	Buna (p)
06/02/99	Laçi	H	1-0	Kote
13/02/99	Bylis Ballsh	A	0-3	
20/02/99	Skënderbeu Korçë	H	1-1	Begeja (p)
27/02/99	Dinamo Tiranë	A	2-1	Kote, Stojku
06/03/99	Shkumbini Peqin	H	2-0	Stojku, Xhafa
13/03/99	Partizani Tiranë	H	2-0	Babamusta 2
20/03/99	Tomori Berat	A	0-2	
27/03/99	Vllaznia Shkodër	H	1-0	Stojku
03/04/99	Besa Kavajë	A	0-0	
10/04/99	Burreli	H	3-0	Rexhepi, Begeja, Stojku
17/04/99	SK Tirana	A	0-3	
01/05/99	Elbasani	H	1-0	Begeja (p)
08/05/99	Lushnja	A	0-2	
12/05/99	Flamurtari Vlorë	H	2-0	Begeja, Xhafa
15/05/99	Apolonia Fier	A	1-2	Kallço

SK TIRANA

CLUB DIRECTORY

Klubi Sportiv SK Tirana
Stadiumi Selman Stërmasi
Tiranë
tel - (42) 33299
Year of Formation - 1920
President - Lufti Nuri
Secretary - Sulejman Mema
Coach - Ali Mema; Ramadan Shehu; Shkëlqim Muça
Stadium - Selman Stërmasi (12,000)

MAJOR HONOURS

League Championship - (18) 1930, 1931, 1932, 1934, 1936, 1965, 1966, 1967, 1968, 1970, 1982, 1985, 1988, 1989, 1995, 1996, 1997, 1999.
Domestic Cup - (9) 1963, 1976, 1977, 1983, 1984, 1986, 1994, 1996, 1999.

APPEARANCES 98/99

	P	Ap	(s)	Gls
Krenar ALIMEHMETI	D	26		4
Ervin BULKU	D	6	(7)	
Sokol BULKU	M	9	(5)	
Nikolin ÇOÇLLI	M	12	(11)	
Rezart DABULLA	D	25	(1)	1
Nevil DEDE	D	9	(2)	
Klodian DURO	M	18	(9)	1
Isli HIDI	G	4		
Sokol ISHKA	A		(10)	1
Saimir MALKO	D	26		3
Ardian MEMA	M	24		3
Eldorado MERKOÇI	A	22		7
Devi MUKA	A	23		9
Blendi NALLBANI	G	25		
Sokol PRENGA	M	22		6
Elvis SINA	D	28		1
Taulant STERMASI	A	3	(1)	1
Alban TAFAJ	D	26	(1)	2
Alket ZEQO	A	11	(8)	6

LEAGUE RESULTS 1998/99

29/08/98	Partizani Tiranë	H	2-2	Alimehmeti 2 (2p)
12/09/98	Elbasani	H	1-0	Stërmasi
19/09/98	Lushnja	A	1-6	Alimehmeti (p)
26/09/98	Flamurtari Vlorë	H	1-0	Alimehmeti (p)
03/10/98	Apolonia Fier	A	1-0	Muka
17/10/98	Laçi	H	0-0	
24/10/98	Bylis Ballsh	A	1-2	Prenga
31/10/98	Skënderbeu Korçë	H	2-0	(w/o)
07/11/98	Dinamo Tiranë	A	3-0	Merkoçi, Muka, Ishka
11/11/98	Shkumbini Peqin	H	4-1	Mema, Merkoçi, Zeqo 2
25/11/98	Teuta Durrës	A	5-0	Muka 2, Zeqo, Prenga, og (Karaj)
28/11/98	Tomori Berat	H	3-0	Prenga, Malko, Muka
05/12/98	Vllaznia Shkodër	A	0-1	
12/12/98	Besa Kavajë	H	2-0	Mema, Tafaj
19/12/98	Burreli	A	0-0	
06/02/99	Partizani Tiranë	A	2-1	Sina, Malko
13/02/99	Elbasani	A	0-0	
20/02/99	Lushnja	H	3-0	Merkoçi 2, Duro
27/02/99	Flamurtari Vlorë	A	0-1	
06/03/99	Apolonia Fier	H	2-0	Merkoçi, Prenga
13/03/99	Laçi	A	3-3	Zeqo 2, Prenga
20/03/99	Bylis Ballsh	H	0-0	
27/03/99	Skënderbeu Korçë	A	1-0	Zeqo
03/04/99	Dinamo Tiranë	H	1-0	Muka
10/04/99	Shkumbini Peqin	A	2-1	Malko (p), Merkoçi
17/04/99	Teuta Durrës	H	3-0	Prenga, Muka, Merkoçi
01/05/99	Tomori Berat	A	0-1	
08/05/99	Vllaznia Shkodër	H	1-0	Muka
12/05/99	Besa Kavajë	A	1-1	Muka
15/05/99	Burreli	H	3-0	Mema, Dabulla, Tafaj

TOMORI BERAT

CLUB DIRECTORY

Klubi Sportiv Tomori
Lagjja 30 vjetori
Stadiumi Tomori
Berat
tel - (623) 2627
Year of Formation - 1923
Secretary - Andrea Karaj
Coach - Theodhori Arbri
Stadium - Tomori (14,750)

APPEARANCES 98/99

	P	Ap	(s)	Gls
Eduart ALIAJ	D	26		1
Klodian ARBRI	A	27		7
Afrim ÇALA	M	24	(1)	
Altin ÇUKO	A	10	(6)	1
Altin ÇULLHAJ	M	15	(6)	
Afrim DELIU	D	13		1
Klodian DINO	D	25	(1)	2
Arben DURO	G	6		
Elton FANI	D	14	(3)	
Gëzim GEGA	M	21		
Edmond GJATA	A	19	(1)	7
Ergen GJONI	M	10	(2)	1
Ilir KAPO	D	11	(2)	
Blendi KATORI	M	9	(1)	1
Gentian LAKO	D	27		3
Sajmir MALOKU	A	12		2
Madrit MUZHAJ	G	12		1
Elijon NUSHI	M	14	(7)	3
Arben SINANI	G	12		
Armir TABAKU	M	12	(12)	
Arjan ZERE	M	11		1

LEAGUE RESULTS 1998/99

29/08/98	Apolonia Fier	A	0-0	
12/09/98	Laçi	H	1-1	Gjata
19/09/98	Bylis Ballsh	A	0-2	
26/09/98	Skënderbeu Korçë	H	2-0	Nushi, Lako
03/10/98	Dinamo Tiranë	A	0-0	
17/10/98	Shkumbini Peqin	H	4-0	Lako, Arbri 2, Muzhaj
24/10/98	Teuta Durrës	A	0-1	
31/10/98	Partizani Tiranë	A	0-1	
07/11/98	Vllaznia Shkodër	H	1-0	Arbri
11/11/98	Besa Kavajë	A	1-1	Gjata
25/11/98	Burreli	H	2-1	Arbri, Dino
28/11/98	SK Tirana	A	0-3	
05/12/98	Elbasani	H	1-0	Dino
12/12/98	Lushnja	A	0-1	
19/12/98	Flamurtari Vlorë	H	1-0	Gjoni
06/02/99	Apolonia Fier	H	2-1	Aliaj (p), Zere
13/02/99	Laçi	A	0-0	
20/02/99	Bylis Ballsh	H	0-0	
27/02/99	Skënderbeu Korçë	A	0-2	
06/03/99	Dinamo Tiranë	H	1-0	Gjata
13/03/99	Shkumbini Peqin	A	0-0	
20/03/99	Teuta Durrës	H	2-0	Gjata, Arbri
27/03/99	Partizani Tiranë	H	3-0	Maloku, Nushi, Çuko
03/04/99	Vllaznia Shkodër	A	0-1	
10/04/99	Besa Kavajë	H	2-1	Gjata 2
17/04/99	Burreli	A	1-2	Nushi
01/05/99	SK Tirana	H	1-0	Deliu
08/05/99	Elbasani	A	1-2	Lako
12/05/99	Lushnja	H	3-2	Arbri 2, Maloku
15/05/99	Flamurtari Vlorë	A	2-3	Gjata (p), Katori

VLLAZNIA SHKODËR

CLUB DIRECTORY

Klubi Sportiv Vllaznia
Lagja Kongresi i Përmetit
Shkodër
tel - (22) 4233305
Year of Formation - 1919
President - M. Çela
Secretary - Sabah Bizi
Coach - Vasil Bici
Stadium - Loro Boriçi (15,000)

MAJOR HONOURS
League Championship - (8) 1945, 1946, 1972,
1974, 1978, 1983, 1992, 1998.
Domestic Cup - (5)
1965, 1972, 1979, 1981, 1987.

APPEARANCES 98/99

	P	Ap	(s)	Gls
Armando CUNGU	M	12	(5)	1
Ilir DIBRA	A	26	(3)	4
Julian GJELOSHI	G	23		
Romeo HAXHIAJ	M	13		3
Luan JAHJA	M	6		
Salvador KAÇAJ	M		(3)	1
Uliks KOTRRI	M	23	(1)	1
Suad LICI	D	23		6
Pjerin MARTINI	G	2		
Auron MILOTI	A	26		8
Arjan MUSTAFA	G	4	(4)	
Alban NOGA	D	26	(2)	6
Kreshnik OSMANI	A	6	(9)	1
Leonard PERLOSHI	D	20		3
Astrit PREMÇI	D	27		
Armando SHLLAKU	A	8		1
Vjoresin SINANI	A	27		14
Alban VOLUMI	A	3	(7)	2
Altin XHAHYSA	M	14	(7)	4
Ilir YMERI	D	6		
Luan ZMIJANI	D	24	(7)	

LEAGUE RESULTS 1998/99

29/08/98	Flamurtari Vlorë	A	0-0	
12/09/98	Apolonia Fier	H	4-2	Sinani 2, Shllaku, Noga (p)
19/09/98	Laçi	A	1-0	Xhahysa
26/09/98	Bylis Ballsh	H	2-0	Dibra 2
03/10/98	Skënderbeu Korçë	A	2-0	(w/o)
17/10/98	Dinamo Tiranë	H	1-3	Perloshi
24/10/98	Shkumbini Peqin	A	0-1	
31/10/98	Teuta Durrës	H	3-0	Lici 2, Volumi
07/11/98	Tomori Berat	A	0-1	
11/11/98	Partizani Tiranë	A	1-1	Dibra
25/11/98	Besa Kavajë	H	5-0	Miloti 2, Sinani, Volumi, Kaçaj
28/11/98	Burreli	A	0-1	
05/12/98	SK Tirana	H	1-0	Noga (p)
12/12/98	Elbasani	A	1-1	Noga (p)
19/12/98	Lushnja	H	3-0	Miloti, Noga (p), Lici
06/02/99	Flamurtari Vlorë	H	8-0	Lici 3, Miloti 2, Sinani, Xhahysa, Haxhiaj
13/02/99	Apolonia Fier	A	0-0	
20/02/99	Laçi	H	2-0	Kotrri, Sinani
27/02/99	Bylis Ballsh	A	2-2	Perloshi, Miloti
06/03/99	Skënderbeu Korçë	H	4-0	Sinani, Xhahysa, Miloti, Haxhiaj
13/03/99	Dinamo Tiranë	A	1-0	Noga (p)
20/03/99	Shkumbini Peqin	H	4-1	Perloshi, Noga (p), Miloti, Sinani
27/03/99	Teuta Durrës	A	0-1	
03/04/99	Tomori Berat	H	1-0	Dibra
10/04/99	Partizani Tiranë	H	2-0	Cungu, Sinani
17/04/99	Besa Kavajë	A	0-0	
01/05/99	Burreli	H	4-1	Haxhiaj, Sinani 2 (1p), Osmani
08/05/99	SK Tirana	A	0-1	
12/05/99	Elbasani	H	3-1	Sinani 3
15/05/99	Lushnja	A	2-1	Xhahysa, Sinani

PROMOTED CLUB

SECOND DIVISION FINAL TABLES 98/99

GROUP A

		Pd	W	D	L	F	A	Pt	GD
1	Besëlidhja	15	14	1	0	35	7	43	+28
2	Porto	15	11	2	2	33	12	35	+21
3	Shkodra	15	7	3	5	29	24	24	+5
4	Kukësi	15	2	5	8	10	23	11	-13
5	Korabi	15	1	5	9	11	29	8	-18
6	Iliria	15	1	2	12	10	33	5	-23

GROUP B

		Pd	W	D	L	F	A	Pt	GD
1	Albpetrol	15	11	1	3	40	13	34	+27
2	Albanët	15	9	3	3	33	13	30	+20
3	Kastrioti	15	9	3	3	36	20	30	+16
4	Durrësi	15	2	6	7	14	27	12	-13
5	Erzeni	15	2	4	9	23	41	10	-18
6	Eurest	15	2	3	10	19	51	9	-32

GROUP C

		Pd	W	D	L	F	A	Pt	GD
1	Naftëtari	15	10	3	2	30	14	33	+16
2	Sopoti	15	9	2	4	21	16	29	+5
3	Pogradeci	15	7	3	5	28	21	24	+7
4	Egnatia	15	5	5	5	25	24	20	+1
5	Plugu	15	4	3	8	18	27	15	-9
6	Divjaka	15	0	4	11	16	36	4	-20

GROUP D

		Pd	W	D	L	F	A	Pt	GD
1	**Shqiponja**	**15**	**13**	**1**	**1**	**30**	**4**	**40**	**+26**
2	Tepelena	15	11	1	3	43	14	34	+29
3	Memaliaj	15	6	1	8	14	16	19	-2
4	Delvina	15	3	4	8	8	18	13	-10
5	Butrinti	15	3	3	8	11	32	12	-21
6	Erseka	15	2	2	10	13	35	8	-22

PROMOTION PLAY-OFFS

Shqiponja 2, Besëlidhja 1
Naftëtari 0, Albpetrol 1

Shqiponja 1, Albpetrol 0

CLUB DIRECTORY

Klubi Sportiv Shqiponja
Lagja 18 shtatori
Gjirokastër
tel - (726) 63647
Year of Formation - 1930
Secretary - Çaush Begaj
Coach - Mustafa Hysi
Stadium - Gjirokastra (8,400)

ANDORRA

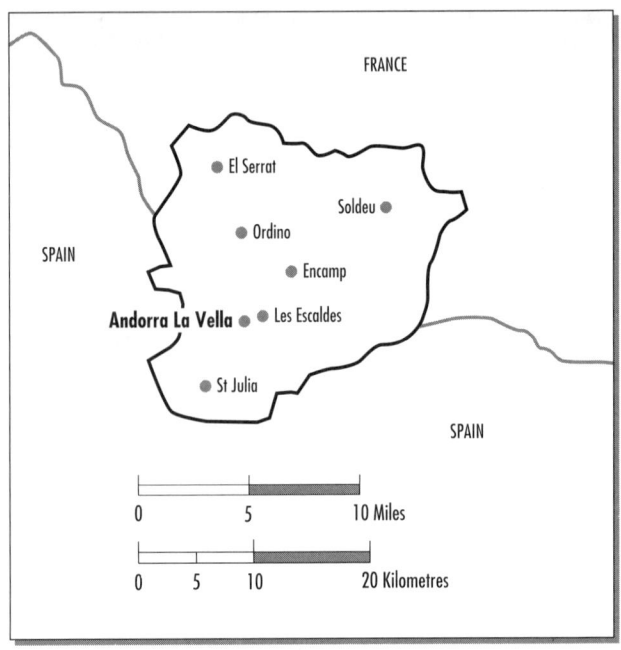

PRINCIPAT COAST TO ANOTHER TITLE

World champions embarrassed - twice!

FEDERATION DIRECTORY

Federació Andorrana de Futbol
C/ Sant Salvador 10 - 2 - 5, Edifici Galerias Plaza, Andorra La Vella
tel - (00376) 862003   Year of Formation - 1994
fax - (00376) 862006   President - Francesc Vila Circuns
                            Secretary - Gea Tomás
Stadium - Coronal, Andorra La Vella (1,400)

The Principality of Andorra's first season of bona fide international competition ended, as expected, with defeats in all seven of their European Championship qualifiers. But what a miracle they nearly produced when, in the last of those games, they came within just four minutes of holding world champions France to a goalless draw.

The match, which had been transferred to the neutral venue of Barcelona's Montjuic Olympic Stadium, was cruelly lost when the French were awarded a highly contentious late penalty - which Franck Leboeuf only just converted, via the fingertips of Andorra's goalkeeper and man of the match, Koldo Alvarez. It could scarcely have been crueller on the Andorrans, who had given absolutely everything to keep the French at bay in their brave attempt to win a first European Championship point. How the Northern Irish referee who gave the penalty can live with himself, Lord only knows.

It was the second scare Andorra had given the French.

LEAGUE CHAMPIONSHIP RESULTS 98/99

		1	2	3	4	5	6	7	8	9	10	11	12
1	CE Benito		1-3	1-2	3-0	1-1	0-0	4-0	2-0	1-4	1-3	2-3	0-0
2	Constellacio Esportiva	1-0		2-3	2-1	1-3	4-0	6-0	6-1	0-3	1-2	0-2	5-0
3	Construccions Modernes	2-0	0-0		3-1	1-2	0-0	2-3	4-1	0-0	1-0	1-2	4-0
4	Deportivo La Massana	0-2	0-6	1-5		1-4	0-3	1-2	4-0	0-10	1-3	0-2	2-2
5	FC Encamp	1-2	3-1	1-1	3-0		0-2	9-0	5-1	0-1	5-2	3-1	3-0
6	FC Engolaster	0-2	0-2	1-3	0-0	1-1		0-3	4-1	1-4	1-1	0-3	0-3
7	Frankfurt Cerni	0-2	3-2	0-5	0-2	1-5	2-5		3-2	0-9	0-4	0-1	1-2
8	Gimnastic Valira	0-2	3-5	1-3	1-5	1-6	3-1	3-3		0-11	0-3	0-2	2-2
9	CE Principat	3-2	3-0	4-1	16-0	5-1	4-0	4-0	10-1		5-0	0-0	1-0
10	UE Sant Iuliá	1-1	1-1	0-4	6-1	4-4	6-1	6-1	3-0	2-5		0-3	0-0
11	FC Santa Coloma	4-1	2-1	1-1	5-1	3-1	3-2	6-0	10-1	0-2	5-1		2-2
12	Sporting D'Escaldes	1-3	1-3	1-0	4-1	0-1	4-2	3-1	2-1	1-6	1-2	0-4	

LEAGUE CHAMPIONSHIP FINAL TABLE 98/99

			Home					Away					Total						
		Pd	W	D	L	F	A	W	D	L	F	A	W	D	L	F	A	Pt	GD
1	CE Principat	22	10	1	0	55	5	10	1	0	55	5	20	2	0	110	10	62	+100
2	FC Santa Coloma	22	8	2	1	41	13	9	1	1	23	6	17	3	2	64	19	54	+45
3	FC Encamp	22	7	1	3	33	11	6	3	2	29	19	13	4	5	62	30	43	+32
4	Construccions Modernes	22	5	3	3	18	9	7	2	2	28	13	12	5	5	46	22	41	+24
5	Constellacio Esportiva	22	6	0	5	28	15	5	2	4	24	17	11	2	9	52	32	35	+20
6	UE Sant Juliá	22	4	4	3	29	21	6	1	4	21	21	10	5	7	50	42	35	+8
7	CE Benito	22	3	3	5	16	16	6	1	4	17	13	9	4	9	33	29	31	+4
8	Sporting D'Escaldes	22	5	0	6	18	24	2	5	4	11	20	7	5	10	29	44	26	-15
9	Frankfurt Cerni	22	2	0	9	10	39	3	1	7	13	44	5	1	16	23	83	16	-60
10	FC Engolaster	22	1	3	7	8	23	3	2	6	16	26	4	5	13	24	49	14	-25
11	Deportivo La Massana	22	1	1	9	10	39	2	1	8	12	43	3	2	17	22	82	11	-60
12	Gimnastic Valira	22	1	2	8	14	43	0	0	11	9	53	1	2	19	23	96	5	-73

NATIONAL TEAM APPEARANCES 98/99

Coach - Manuel MILUIR; David RODRIGO	ARM	UKR	FRA	FAR	ISL	RUS	UKR	FRA	Cps	Gls
Jesús Luis ALVAREZ DE FULATE, "KOLDO" (04/09/70) - FC Andorra (ESP)	G	G	G	G	G	G	G	G	13	-
Francisco Javier RAMIREZ PALOMO (07/09/76) - FC Andorra (ESP)	D	D	D80		D76		D	D	8	-
José Manuel GARCIA LUENA, "TXEMA" (04/12/74) - FC Andorra (ESP)	D	D	D	D62	D	D	D	D70	14	-
Angel MARTIN GARCIA (25/11/78) - FC Andorra (ESP)	D		D	D89	D	D	D53	s78	14	-
Antonio LIMA SOLA (22/09/70) - União Madeira (POR)	D	D	D		D	D	D	D	13	1
Jordi ESCURA AIXAS (19/04/80) - CE Europa (ESP)	D								2	-
Genis GARCIA ISCLA (18/05/78) - FC Andorra (ESP)	M	M		s89				s89	7	-
Oscar SONEJEE MASAND (26/03/76) - FC Andorra (ESP)	M	M	M	M	M	M	M	M	13	-
Jesús Julián LUCENDO HEREDIA (19/04/70) - FC Andorra (ESP)	M		M88	M	M	M65	s53	M78	14	2
Justo RUIZ GONZALEZ (31/08/69) - União Madeira (POR)	M	M	M		M82	M	M	M	12	-
Julí SANCHEZ SOTO (20/06/78) - FC Andorra (ESP)	A	A89	s80		s63	s65	A		13	1
Agusti POL PEREZ (13/01/77) - CE Sant Andreu		D	D	D	D	D	D	D	14	1
Ildefons LIMA SOLA (10/12/79) - RCD Espanyol B (ESP)/FC Andorra (ESP)		M	M	M	M	M	M	M	13	-
Emiliano GONZALEZ ARQUEZ (20/09/69) - FC Andorra (ESP)		A	A	A	s76	s57	A	A	7	-
Manuel JIMENEZ SORIA (12/08/76) - Constellacio Esportiva		s89	s88	A80	A63	A		A89	9	-
ALONSO JUNAS				D		D57			2	-
Carlos GOMEZ - CE Principat				D68					1	-
Gerard JUANES CALVET (12/09/76) - FC Seu d'Urgell (ESP)				s62					2	-
Jordi BARRA CABELLO (10/07/78) - FC Andorra (ESP)				s68					3	-
Oriol ABELLA (1981) - Constellacio Esportiva				s80					1	-
Richard IMBERNON RIOS (21/12/75) - CE Principat						s82			2	-
Roberto JONAS								s70	1	-

The first encounter, played eight months earlier in the Stade de France - in front of a crowd larger than Andorra's entire population - had also ended honourably for the minnows, who actually went in level at half-time before losing only 2-0. Other results were not quite so good, although the team did manage to score two goals - a penalty away to Armenia by skipper Jesús Julián Lucendo Hereda and one from open play against Russia by young striker Julí Sánchez Soto.

There was no change in Andorra's domestic league, where CE Principat took their fourth successive title, winning it by some distance and without a single defeat.

Principat shrugged off the humiliation of going down 14-1 on aggregate to Ferencváros in the UEFA Cup by winning 20 of their 22 league matches and drawing the other two. They finished up with identical home and away records and a massive haul of 110 goals - an average of five per game. Their reward was a return to the UEFA Cup rather than a place in the Champions' League, which for reasons best known to UEFA, remains closed to the champion club of Andorra but no other.

NATIONAL TEAM RESULTS 98/99

05/09/98	Armenia (ECQ)	A	Yerevan	1-3	Lucendo Heredia (86p)
10/10/98	Ukraine (ECQ)	H	Andorra La Vella	0-2	
14/10/98	France (ECQ)	A	Saint-Denis	0-2	
03/03/99	Faroe Islands	H	San Fernando	0-0	
27/03/99	Iceland (ECQ)	H	Andorra La Vella	0-2	
31/03/99	Russia (ECQ)	A	Moscow	1-6	Sánchez Soto (72)
05/06/99	Ukraine (ECQ)	A	Kiev	0-4	
09/06/99	France (ECQ)	H	Barcelona	0-1	

DOMESTIC CUP 98/99

FINAL - CE Principat 3, FC Santa Coloma 1

EUROPEAN CUPS 98/99

UEFA CUP
● **CE PRINCIPAT**
Preliminary round FERENCVAROS (HUN)
A 0-6
Iñaki; Pablo, Luis, Coto, Cañito, Imbernon, Laorenza, Alvarez (Mario 46), Patri, Lamelas (Emiliano 61), Sandro (Delfin 81).
H 1-8 Pasqui (24)
Esprot; Pablo, Luis, Coto, Cristian, Imbernon (Alvarez 78), Laorenza, Patri, Lamelas (Felix 63), Vicente, Pasqui.

ARMENIA

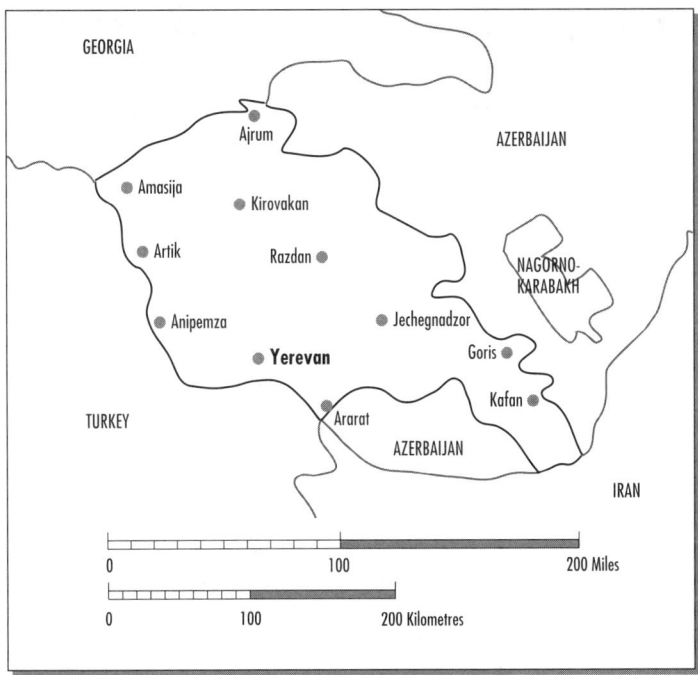

GEORGIA

Ajrum

AZERBAIJAN

Amasija

Kirovakan

Artik

Razdan

NAGORNO-
KARABAKH

Anipemza

Jechegnadzor

Yerevan

Goris

Kafan

TURKEY

Ararat

AZERBAIJAN

IRAN

0   100   200 Miles

0   100   200 Kilometres

SHIRAK GYUMRI TWICE RUNNERS-UP

Two trophies for Tsement Ararat

FEDERATION DIRECTORY

Football Federation of Armenia
19a Koryun Str., 375009 Yerevan

tel - (3742) 533010   Year of Formation - 1934
fax - (3742) 151573   President - Suren Abrahamyan
   Secretary - Arman Hovhannisyan

Stadium - Razdan, Yerevan (69,500)

Prior to 1998 Tsement Ararat had never won a thing. But by mid-1999 they had captured three trophies in a row. They started off by winning the 1998 Cup and concluded the calendar year by lifting their first Armenian national title. Then, the following spring, they completed their stunning hat-trick by retaining the Cup, beating league runners-up Shirak Gyumri 3-2 in a thrilling final.

The championship triumph was, of course, what mattered most to coach Varuzhan Sukiasyan and his players. The newly-structured league, which had reverted to the spring-autumn fixture planner, was split into two halves. The first phase was played in the traditional way,

but after 16 matches the top six teams went through to a second phase, maintaining their previous records, while the others played-off to avoid relegation.

There should have been ten teams in at the start but Kotayk Abovyan were excluded because they did not have sufficient funds to pay the tax required by Armenian law to compete in the national league. Thus, the relegation group in the second half of the campaign was made up of just three teams and they had little to play for because Shirak Gyumri's reserve side were already effectively condemned to the relegation play-off spot having taken just one point from their first 16 matches. Surprisingly, they retained their top-flight status by beating Lori Vanadzor 3-2 in the play-off. Second Division champions Zvartnots Yerevan were thus the only team promoted, which meant that the 1999 season kicked-off with six teams from the capital.

However, there were no Yerevan teams involved in the race for the title. Tsement and Shirak forged ahead of the rest during phase one, and that superiority was re-emphasised during phase two. The most important match of the season took place in the penultimate round when Tsement met Shirak head-on. Tsement held a three-point lead so a victory would give them the title. They had not beaten Shirak in any of their previous meetings (Shirak had won once and there had been two draws), but when it mattered most, they came up with the goods, a 37th-minute strike from midfielder Gagik Manukyan giving them the three points that wrapped up the title. Midfield was Tsement's strong point, with Manukyan being supported superbly by Haik Harutyunyan, Tigran Hovhannisyan and especially Artur Voskanyan, the team's young playmaker, who was voted 1998 Armenian Player of the Year.

The two championship front-runners were to

LEAGUE CHAMPIONSHIP FINAL TABLE 1998

FIRST PHASE		Pd	W	D	L	F	A	Pt	GD
1	Shirak Gyumri	16	13	3	0	42	9	42	+33
2	Tsement Ararat	16	12	3	1	44	11	39	+33
3	FK Yerevan	16	8	3	5	26	17	27	+9
4	Erebuni-Homenmen Yerevan	16	7	4	5	19	13	25	+6
5	Ararat Yerevan	16	5	5	6	16	20	20	-4
6	Pyunik Yerevan	16	5	3	8	18	29	18	-11
7	Dvin Artashat	16	4	5	7	22	27	17	-5
8	Karabakh Yerevan	16	2	5	9	15	29	11	-14
9	Shirak-2 Gyumri	16	0	1	15	6	53	1	-47

CHAMPIONSHIP GROUP		Pd	W	D	L	F	A	Pt	GD
1	Tsement Ararat	26	20	4	2	70	22	64	+48
2	Shirak Gyumri	26	19	4	3	72	25	61	+47
3	FK Yerevan	26	15	3	8	47	30	48	+17
4	Ararat Yerevan	26	10	5	11	40	40	35	0
5	Erebuni-Homenmen Yerevan	26	9	4	13	39	44	31	-5
6	Pyunik Yerevan	26	6	3	17	27	68	21	-41

RELEGATION GROUP		Pd	W	D	L	F	A	Pt	GD
7	Dvin Artashat	20	8	5	7	41	36	29	+5
8	Karabakh Yerevan	20	4	5	11	24	37	17	-13
9	Shirak-2 Gyumri	20	0	1	19	10	68	1	-58

PROMOTION/RELEGATION PLAY-OFF
Shirak-2 Gyumri 3, Lori Vanadzor 2

NATIONAL TEAM APPEARANCES 98/99

Coach - Suren BARSEGYAN	AND	ISL	UKR	EST	POL	RUS	FRA	ISL	UKR	Cps	Gls
Roman BEREZOVSKI (05/08/74) - Zenit Sankt-Peterburg (RUS)	G	G	G		G	G	˙G	G	G	16	-
Yervand SUKIASYAN (20/01/67) - BV Klopenburg (GER)	D	D	D	D	D		D40	D65		23	-
Yervand KRBASHYAN (01/10/71) - Torpedo Moskva (RUS)	D		D85			D64				15	-
Sarkis HOVSEPYAN (02/11/72) - Zenit Sankt-Peterburg (RUS)	D	D	D		D	D	D	D	D	37	-
Harutyun VARDANYAN (05/12/70)											
- Lausanne-Sports (SUI)/Fortuna Köln (GER)	D	D	D		D	D	D	D	D	32	1
Tigran HOVHANNISYAN (05/12/74) - Tsement Ararat	M83	s81	s85							3	-
Albert SARKISYAN (15/05/75) - Lokomotiv Moskva (RUS)	M	M				M	M	M	M	12	-
Artak ADAMYAN (11/07/74) - Kristall Smolensk (RUS)	M86	M								2	-
Ara ADAMYAN (06/06/73) - Shirak Gyumri	M		M		M66					7	-
Armen SHAHGELDYAN (28/08/73) - Lausanne-Sports (SUI)	A	M	M	s46	A79	A	M53	A	A	22	2
Garnik AVALYAN (06/09/62) - Krylya Sovetov Samara (RUS)	A69		s68							6	2
Tigran YESAYAN (02/06/72) - FK Yerevan/Torpedo Zaporizhzhya (UKR)	s69	s61	s74	A85	A	s81	s53			17	3
Felix KHODGOYAN (22/12/75) - Shirak Gyumri	s83			D						6	1
Tigran GSPEYAN (12/10/69) - Tsement Ararat	s86									12	-
Vardan KHACHATRYAN (29/10/68) - FK Yerevan/Shinnik Yaroslavl (RUS)		D	D				s40	D	D	23	-
Artur PETROSYAN (17/12/71) - Maccabi Petach-Tikva (ISR)		M81	M	M72	M	M	M	M75	M	37	2
Eric ASSADOURIAN (24/06/66) - AS Beauvais-Oise (FRA)		A61	A74							12	3
Karapet MIKAELYAN (27/09/69) - Krylya Sovetov Samara		A	A68	A66		A81	A	A	A46	17	1
Harutyun ABRAHAMYAN (28/08/71) - FK Yerevan				G						15	-
Artur MKRCHYAN (09/08/73) - FK Yerevan/Torpedo Moskva (RUS)			D	D		D	D	s65	s46	8	-
Karen SIMONYAN (06/07/70) - Erebuni-Homenmen Yerevan				D						1	1
Karen BARSEGYAN (15/03/75) - Ararat Yerevan				M61						1	1
Vardan MINASYAN (05/01/74) - Pyunik Yerevan				M46						9	-
Armen MARKOSYAN (23/08/78) - FK Yerevan				M66	M46					2	-
Kolya YEPRANOSYAN (29/10/75) - Shirak Gyumri				s61						1	-
Ara HAKOPYAN (04/11/80) - Dvin Artashat				s66						1	-
Arshak AMIRYAN (11/09/77) - Ararat Yerevan				s66						1	-
Henrik BADIKYAN (12/02/77) - Shirak Gyumri				s72						1	-
Haik HAKOPYAN (26/12/80) - Dvin Artashat				s85						1	-
Armen SHAKHALYAN (26/12/69) - FK Yerevan					M63					1	-
Tigran PETROSYAN (23/12/73) - Krylya Sovetov Samara (RUS)					s46				M66	2	-
Sarkis HOVHANNISYAN (17/08/68) - Lokomotiv Moskva (RUS)					s63	D	D		D46	14	-
Manuk KAKOSYAN (01/08/74) - Zhemchuzhina Sochi (RUS)					s66	s78				2	-
Aram HAIRAPETYAN (17/06/75) - Tsement Ararat					s79		s77	s75		3	-
Artur VOSKANYAN (13/08/76) - Tsement Ararat						M78	M77	M84	M	4	-
Haik HARUTYUNYAN (10/12/74) - Tsement Ararat						s64		D	s46	4	-
Karen GRIGORYAN (23/08/74) - FK Yerevan								s84	s66	2	-

meet again in the Armenian Cup final several months later, and once more it was Tsement who came out on top, winning an exciting match 3-2. Unfortunately there were barely 2,500 spectators there to watch Tsement retain their trophy and complete the 'double'.

Armenian fans are not exactly smitten by the football they see in their domestic competitions but they do turn out in reasonable numbers when the Armenian national team is in town. There were 20,000 crowds for both of the European Championship qualifying games at home to Russia and Ukraine in the spring. Unfortunately the locals didn't have a home goal to cheer, although the 0-0 draw against the Ukrainians, the Group Four leaders, was hailed as a very positive result.

The team's most prominent individual that day, as on so many other previous occasions, was goalkeeper Roman Berezovski. He is perhaps the only current Armenian footballer of true international class. Like many of his compatriots, he plays his club football in Russia, but none of the outfield players have enjoyed the same sort of praise or success that has come the way of the 25-year-old Zenit St. Petersburg 'keeper. Until there are more like him, Armenia will always struggle to make headway in international competition.

DOMESTIC CUP 98/99

1/8 FINALS
Fima Yerevan v Shirak Gyumri 1-8; 0-2
(Shirak Gyumri 10-1)
Zvartnots Yerevan v Karabakh-2 Stepanakert 2-0; 2-1
(Zvartnots Yerevan 4-1)
Kilikia Yerevan v Lori Vanadzor 4-1; 1-0
(Kilkia Yerevan 5-1)
Kasakh Ashtarak v FK Yerevan 0-1; 0-3
(FK Yerevan 4-0)
Karabakh Stepanakert v Ararat Yerevan 0-2; 0-3
(w/o) (Ararat Yerevan 5-0)
Alashkert Martuni v Erebuni Yerevan 0-4; 0-3 (w/o)
(Erebuni Yerevan 7-0)
FK Gyumri v Dvin Artashat 1-2; 1-4
(Dvin Artashat 6-2)
Dinamo Yerevan v Tsement Ararat 0-7; 0-4
(Tsement Ararat 11-0)

QUARTER-FINALS
Dvin Artashat v Tsement Ararat 0-4; 0-2
(Tsement Ararat 6-0)
FK Yerevan v Kilikia Yerevan 1-0; 1-2
(2-2; FK Yerevan on away goal)
Ararat Yerevan v Erebuni Yerevan 1-1; 0-1
(Erebuni Yerevan 2-1)
Zvartnots Yerevan v Shirak Gyumri 2-1; 0-1
(2-2; Shirak Gyumri on away goal)

SEMI-FINALS
Erebuni Yerevan v Tsement Ararat 2-4; 2-3
(Tsement Ararat 7-4)
Shirak Gyumri v FK Yerevan 3-1; 0-1
(Shirak Gyumri 3-2)

FINAL
29/05/99, Yerevan
TSEMENT ARARAT 3 Hakopyan H. (3, 16), Hakopyan
A. (43)
SHIRAK GYUMRI 2 Bernetsyan (5), Artoyan (76)
referee - Kazaryan
TSEMENT ARARAT - Hovhannisyan K. (Dadamyan 29);
Hairapetyan, Khachatryan (Grigoryan 61),
Hovhannisyan T.L.; Asatryan, Hokhoyan, Hakopyan A.
(Nazaryan 79), Harutyunyan, Simonyan, Voskanyan,
Hakopyan H..
SHIRAK GYUMRI - Hovhannisyan A.; Adamyan,
Markaryan (Batikyan 46), Aleksanyan, Artoyan,
Nikolyan, Petrosyan, Tamazyan, Yepranosyan,
Harutyunyan (Hovhannisyan T. 80), Bernetsyan
(Tumasyan 71).

EUROPEAN CUPS 98/99

CHAMPIONS' CUP
● FK YEREVAN
Preliminary round HJK (FIN)
A 0-2
Abrahamyan; Khachatryan (Grigoryan 73), Tonoyan, Mkrchyan,
Stepanyan, Shakhalyan (Sahakyan 66), Nigoyan,
Yesayan (Markosyan 78), Cecutti, Garault, Barraud.
H 0-3
Abrahamyan; Khachatryan, Tonoyan, Mkrchyan (Grigoryan 40),
Stepanyan, Shakhalyan (Markosyan 34), Nigoyan, Yesayan, Cecuttu,
Garault, Barraud (Karapetyan 56).

CUP WINNERS' CUP
● TSEMENT ARARAT
Qualifying round LAUSANNE-SPORTS (SUI)
A 1-5   Hovhannisyan T. (35)
Hovhannisyan G.; Arzumanyan, Gspeyan, Hokhoyan (Hayrapetyan 59),
Manukyan, Harutyunyan (Asatryan 75), Sargsyan Aram (Sargsyan Armen
63), Sarikyan, Voskanyan, Hovnahhisyan T., Hovhannisyan V..

H 1-2   Asatryan (40)
Dadamyan; Hayrapetyan (Manukyan 46), Arzumanyan, Gspeyan,
Sargsyan Aram (Harutyunyan 57), Sarikyan, Hovhannisyan T., Voskanyan,
Hovhannisyan V., Asatryan, Jenebyan (Abrahamyan 75).

UEFA CUP
● SHIRAK GYUMRI
Preliminary round MALMÖ FF (SWE)
H 0-2
Hovhannisyan A.; Khodogoyan, Margaryan, Demirtshyan, Tamazyan,
Yepranosyan, Adamyan Artak (Adamyan Arayik 46), Aleksanyan
(Bernetsyan 77), Badikyan, Avanesyan, Nikolyan.

A 0-5
Zadryan; Khodogoyan, Margaryan (Adamyan Artak 46), Demirtshyan,
Artoyan, Nikolyan, Tamazyan (Bichakhchyan 65), Yepranosyan,
Bernetsyan, Harutyunyan, Avanesyan.

NATIONAL TEAM RESULTS 98/99

05/09/98	Andorra (ECQ)	H	Yerevan	3-1	Avalyan (40), Yesayan (71, 90)
10/10/98	Iceland (ECQ)	H	Yerevan	0-0	
14/10/98	Ukraine (ECQ)	A	Kiev	0-2	
21/11/98	Estonia	H	Abovyan	2-1	Barsegyan (8), Simonyan (17)
03/03/99	Poland	A	Warsaw	0-1	
27/03/99	Russia (ECQ)	H	Yerevan	0-3	
31/03/99	France (ECQ)	A	Saint-Denis	0-2	
05/06/99	Iceland (ECQ)	A	Reykjavik	0-2	
09/06/99	Ukraine (ECQ)	H	Yerevan	0-0	

TOP SCORERS

20	Ara HAKOPYAN (Dvin Artashat)
13	Ara ADAMYAN (Shirak Gyumri)
12	Artur PETROSYAN (Shirak Gyumri)
	Shirak SARIKYAN (Tsement Ararat)
11	Mher AVANESYAN (Shirak Gyumri)
	Haik HAKOPYAN (Dvin Artashat)
10	Tigran YESAYAN (FK Yerevan)
	Tigran HOVHANNISYAN (Tsement Ararat)
	Aram VOSKANYAN (Ararat Yerevan)

INTERNATIONAL HONOURS
None

AUSTRIA

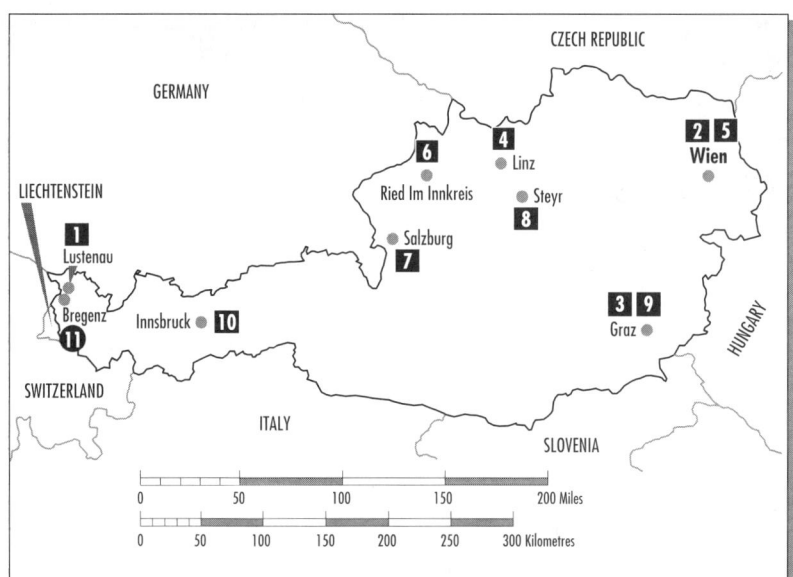

1	SC AUSTRIA LUSTENAU	116	7	SV SALZBURG	122
2	FK AUSTRIA WIEN	117	8	SK VORWÄRTS STEYR	123
3	GRAZER AK	118	9	SK STURM GRAZ	124
4	LASK LINZ	119	10	FC TIROL INNSBRUCK	125
5	SK RAPID WIEN	120	**Promoted club**		
6	SV RIED	121	11	SW BREGENZ	126

PROHASKA GOES AFTER 9-0 DRUBBING

Order maintained as Sturm strike again

FEDERATION DIRECTORY

Österreichischer Fussball-Bund
Ernst Happel Stadion
Meiereistrasse 7, 1020 Wien

tel - (01) 72718-0
fax - (01) 72816-32

Year of Formation - 1904
President - Beppo Mauhart
Secretary - Alfred Ludwig

Stadium - Ernst-Happel-Stadion, Wien (47,500)

The 1998/99 Austrian Bundesliga was little more than an action replay of what had taken place the season before. Incredibly, the final table showed all ten teams occupying precisely the same positions that they had filled 12 months earlier, the only exception being the identity of the team in the relegation zone, with Vorwärts Steyr taking the place of Admira Wacker Mödling.

Although there was no change in the final order of classification, there was at least some excitement in the race for the championship. In 1997/98 Sturm Graz had been virtually unchallenged, concluding their procession to a first-ever title with a 19-point victory margin. This time, however, they had to fend off approaches from two clubs - first city rivals Grazer AK, then Rapid Vienna - before they could drink from the victory chalice once again.

Sturm, still under the influence of their cunning Bosnian coach Ivica Osim, started the season by destroying their Cup final conquerors of the previous campaign, SV Ried, 4-0 to win the Austrian Super Cup. But they suffered a major setback to their title hopes when they lost three league matches in a row, the first at home to GAK, the second away to Rapid. From then on they knew that the road to the title would be a lot bumpier than it had been the year before. They also had to contend with the distraction of the Champions' League.

Having qualified for Europe's glamour tournament with ease at the expense of Hungarian champions Újpest, Sturm were always up against it in a group that contained Real Madrid, Inter and Spartak Moscow, and when they began by losing 0-2 at home to Spartak in what was generally considered to be their least difficult fixture, the whole campaign became simply an exercise in damage limitation. Destroyed home and away by Real, they were unlucky losers, to a stoppage-time winner, in the San Siro against Inter and secured their only point with a goalless draw in Moscow.

But while Sturm took the punishment in Europe, the experience of competing against the best clearly had a positive effect on their domestic form, because from mid-September onwards they won nine Bundesliga matches in succession to take command at the top of the table. The victory that took them there could hardly have been more comprehensive - a 5-0 hammering of leaders GAK in the Arnold-Schwarzenegger-Stadion. By the winter

LEAGUE CHAMPIONSHIP RESULTS 98/99

		1	2	3	4	5	6	7	8	9	10
1	SC Austria Lustenau		1-1	0-3	0-4	2-0	0-2	1-1	1-1	1-2	2-2
			0-0	2-1	0-1	2-0	0-0	0-0	1-1	1-2	0-3
2	FK Austria Wien	1-1		0-0	2-0	0-1	1-0	3-2	4-1	0-3	1-1
		2-1		0-3	2-0	1-1	3-0	3-1	4-1	1-0	1-1
3	Grazer AK	4-0	0-0		0-2	1-1	1-0	3-1	2-0	0-5	2-0
		2-0	3-0		2-1	0-1	1-0	1-4	1-0	1-2	0-1
4	LASK Linz	3-0	1-3	0-1		0-0	3-1	3-1	2-1	0-0	3-2
		2-0	0-0	0-0		1-3	6-1	3-2	2-0	1-2	0-1
5	SK Rapid Wien	1-0	3-1	0-2	5-0		1-1	1-0	5-1	2-0	1-0
		2-1	0-0	1-0	2-0		1-0	1-1	2-1	2-0	1-1
6	SV Ried	3-1	2-1	0-1	0-0	0-1		0-0	0-0	0-1	0-1
		1-0	2-1	0-2	1-2	0-0		1-1	1-0	0-3	2-0
7	SV Salzburg	1-2	2-0	1-0	1-3	1-1	3-2		5-2	1-1	1-1
		1-0	3-0	3-0	2-0	0-0	0-0		1-0	3-1	2-2
8	SK Vorwärts Steyr	1-1	0-1	0-1	1-4	1-2	0-3	0-1		0-1	2-1
		2-0	1-3	0-3	1-1	3-3	2-0	1-3		1-4	0-1
9	SK Sturm Graz	3-0	2-0	2-3	0-1	2-1	4-0	2-0	5-2		2-0
		5-2	0-0	0-1	2-0	1-1	4-2	1-2	5-0		3-0
10	FC Tirol Innsbruck	3-1	3-0	1-1	1-4	1-3	1-0	1-1	3-2	0-1	
		0-0	4-1	1-0	4-0	0-0	1-0	0-3	4-0	3-1	

LEAGUE CHAMPIONSHIP FINAL TABLE 98/99

				Home					Away					Total						
		P	W	D	L	F	A	W	D	L	F	A	W	D	L	F	A	P	GD
1	SK Sturm Graz	36	12	2	4	43	15	11	2	5	29	17	23	4	9	72	32	73	+40
2	SK Rapid Wien	36	13	4	1	31	9	6	9	3	19	16	19	13	4	50	25	70	+25
3	Grazer AK	36	10	2	6	24	18	10	3	5	22	11	20	5	11	46	29	65	+17
4	SV Salzburg	36	10	6	2	31	15	5	6	7	24	25	15	12	9	55	40	57	+15
5	LASK Linz	36	9	4	5	30	18	8	2	8	23	26	17	6	13	53	44	57	+9
6	FC Tirol Innsbruck	36	10	4	4	31	18	5	6	7	18	23	15	10	11	49	41	55	+8
7	FK Austria Wien	36	10	5	3	29	17	3	6	9	12	27	13	11	12	41	44	50	-3
8	SV Ried	36	6	5	7	13	15	2	3	13	12	32	8	8	20	25	47	32	-22
9	SC Austria Lustenau	36	3	8	7	14	24	1	3	14	10	37	4	11	21	24	61	23	-37
10	SK Vorwärts Steyr	36	3	3	12	16	33	0	3	15	13	48	3	6	27	29	81	12	-52

N.B. SK Vorwärts Steyr deducted 3pts.

break Sturm led the way and were once again the team to beat.

Come the spring, however, Osim's team looked jaded and sluggish. The entertainment factor of the previous year was missing, and they began to drop silly points, allowing Rapid to come right back into contention. However, the players remained resilient, and when the big games arrived thick and fast in mid-May, Sturm stood up to be counted in impressive fashion. They drew 1-1 in the home game against Rapid to keep their noses out in front and three days later captured the Austrian Cup, beating LASK Linz on penalties in the final. Four days after that they won 2-1 away to GAK, and after a welcome week's rest they completed an unprecedented 'double' with a 3-0 home win over FC Tirol Innsbruck.

The season could hardly have had a sweeter finish for Sturm and their fans, although there was a bitter aftertaste when it was

announced that top scorer Mario Haas was being sold to French club Strasbourg. For the second season running he and his attacking accomplices Ivica Vastic and Hannes Reinmayr had been the major attraction of the championship. The so-called 'magic triangle' contributed 42 of Sturm's 72 goals, giving the Styrians by far the best attack in the league.

As Sturm marked their 90th birthday with the first 'double' in their history, Rapid Vienna had nothing to celebrate in their centenary year except a consolation place in the Champions' League qualifying round. Although Rapid pushed Sturm hard for the title, remaining undefeated for six months until a shock 0-2 defeat by lowly Austria Lustenau blew them off course, they were a team without flair. Coach Heribert Weber constructed a team in his own image, in which hard work,

TOP SCORERS

22	Eduard GLIEDER (SV Salzburg)
17	Mario HAAS (SK Sturm Graz)
16	Christian MAYRLEB (FK Austria Wien)
14	Ivica VASTIC (SK Sturm Graz)
11	Hannes REINMAYR (SK Sturm Graz)
10	Geir FRIGÅRD (LASK Linz)
	René WAGNER (SK Rapid Wien)
8	Radoslaw GILEWICZ (FC Tirol Innsbruck)
	Michael WAGNER (FK Austria Wien)
7	Marcus PÜRK (SK Rapid Wien)
	Gerald STRAFNER (SV Ried)
	Samuel KOEJOE (SV Salzburg)

NATIONAL TEAM RESULTS 98/99

19/08/98	France	H	Vienna	2-2	Haas (41), Vastic (76p)
05/09/98	Israel (ECQ)	H	Vienna	1-1	Reinmayr (7)
10/10/98	Cyprus (ECQ)	A	Nicosia	3-0	Cerny (53, 61), Reinmayr (75)
14/10/98	San Marino (ECQ)	A	Serravalle	4-1	Vastic (59), Mayrleb (64), Hiden (69), Glieder (76)
10/03/99	Switzerland	A	St. Gallen	4-2	Herzog (4, 57p), Neukirchner (33), Reinmayr (44)
27/03/99	Spain (ECQ)	A	Valencia	0-9	
28/04/99	San Marino (ECQ)	H	Graz	7-0	Mayrleb (24, 53), Vastic (42, 44, 84), Amerhauser (71), Herzog (82p)
06/06/99	Israel (ECQ)	A	Tel-Aviv	0-5	

NATIONAL TEAM APPEARANCES 98/99

Coach - Herbert PROHASKA; Otto BARIC	FRA	ISR	CYP	SMR	SUI	ESP	SMR	ISR	Cps	Gls
Michael KONSEL (06/03/62) - Roma (ITA)	G21								43	-
Peter SCHÖTTEL (26/03/67) - SK Rapid Wien	D	D72	D	D	D	D			62	-
Wolfgang FEIERSINGER (30/01/65) - Borussia Dortmund (GER)	D	D			D	D54	D		46	-
Anton PFEFFER (17/08/65) - FK Austria Wien	D	D	D	D		D			63	1
Markus SCHOPP (22/02/74) - SK Sturm Graz	M46				s58		M72		21	1
Dietmar KÜHBAUER (04/04/71) - Real Sociedad (ESP)	M46	M	M	M					34	4
Roman MÄHLICH (17/09/71) - SK Sturm Graz	M	M	M		M	M		M	18	-
Hannes REINMAYR (23/08/69) - SK Sturm Graz	M79	M	M79	M46	M74	s58			14	4
Arnold WETL (02/02/70) - SK Rapid Wien	M79		M	M		M			21	4
Mario HAAS (16/09/74) - SK Sturm Graz	A73	A71	A79	A66	A46	A69		s67	14	2
Ivica VASTIC (29/09/69) - SK Sturm Graz	A	A	A82	A71			A	A57	22	8
Franz WOHLFAHRT (01/07/64) - VfB Stuttgart (GER)	s21	G	G	G	G	G	G	G	44	-
Martin HIDEN (11/03/73) - Leeds United (ENG)	s46	s72	D	D					7	1
Peter STÖGER (11/04/66) - LASK LInz/FK Austria Wien	s46	s74	s79	s71	s74				65	15
Christian MAYRLEB (08/06/72) - FK Austria Wien	s73	s71	s79	s46	s46	s69	A	A67	8	3
Günther NEUKIRCHNER (02/12/71) - SK Sturm Graz	s79				M58	M	D	M	5	1
Heimo PFEIFENBERGER (29/12/66) - SV Salzburg	s79								40	9
Harald CERNY (13/09/73) - TSV 1860 München (GER)		M74	M	M	M	A	M72	M	32	3
Martin AMERHAUSER (23/07/74) - SV Salzburg		M					M	M46	6	2
Eduard GLIEDER (28/01/69) - SV Salzburg			s82	s66			s72	s57	4	1
Andreas HERAF (10/09/67) - SK Rapid Wien				M					11	1
Walter KOGLER (12/12/67) - FC Tirol Innsbruck					D	s54		D	25	1
Christian PROSENIK (07/06/68) - SK Rapid Wien					M	M58	M	s46	24	1
Andreas HERZOG (10/09/68) - SV Werder Bremen (GER)					A	M	M	M	75	17
Thomas WINKLHOFER (30/12/70) - SV Salzburg							D81	D	6	-
Richard KITZBICHLER (12/01/74) - SV Salzburg							s72		2	-
Klaus ROHSEANO (08/09/67) - LASK Linz							s81		1	-
Zoran BARISIC (22/03/70) - FC Tirol Innsbruck								D	1	-

discipline and solid organisation were the watchwords. The loss through injury of key players Arnold Wetl (knee ligaments) and Krzysztof Ratajczyk (Achilles) in the spring eventually proved costly, as did the team's concession of far too many points to the clubs at the wrong end of the table. On the positive side, Rapid were the strongest side at home and their Czech import Ladislav Maier was the outstanding goalkeeper in the league, playing every minute of every match in his first season at the club following a summer move from Slovan Liberec.

Grazer AK achieved their pre-season objective of winning a place in the UEFA Cup, but for a long time it looked as if they might have the wherewithal to claim the bigger prize of the championship - something they had never managed before. But their good early form eventually deserted them and with skipper Didi Ramusch suffering a long-term injury and mid-season signing Igor Pamic failing to do himself justice, GAK struggled in the goals department. Their two leading indivisual scorers managed just six goals apiece, which just about said it all.

While GAK faded in the spring, Salzburg, coached by one of Austria's greatest-ever footballers, Hans Krankl, found their best form after the winter break to move up to fourth. Striker Eduard Glieder also collected the Bundesliga Golden Boot prize with his tally of 22 goals - just one short of the club record held by German superstar Oliver Bierhoff.

EUROPEAN CUPS 98/99

CHAMPIONS' CUP
● SK STURM GRAZ
Qualifying round ÚJPEST FC (HUN)
H 4-0 Vastic (7, 70), Neukirchner (82), Haas (89)
Sidorczuk; Schupp; Milanic, Posch; Schopp, Mählich, Reinmayr (Bardel 73), Angibeaud, Neukirchner (Martens 83); Vastic, Haas.
A 3-2 Haas (8), Reinmayr (51, 57)
Sidorczuk; Schupp; Popovic, Posch; Schopp (Foda 76), Mählich (Bardel 84), Reinmayr, Angibeaud (Minavand 76), Neukirchner; Vastic, Haas.

Champions' League
1st match SPARTAK MOSKVA (RUS)
H 0-2
Sidorczuk; Neukirchner; Milanic, Popovic; Schopp, Schupp, Mählich, Reinmayr (Angibeaud 60); Posch; Vastic, Haas.

2nd match INTER (ITA)
A 0-1
Sidorczuk; Foda; Neukirchner, Milanic (Angibeaud 79); Schopp (Popovic 59), Mählich, Reinmayr (Minavand 90), Schupp, Posch; Vastic, Haas.

3rd match REAL MADRID (ESP)
A 1-6 Vastic (8)
Sidorczuk; Foda; Neukirchner (Kocijan 68), Popovic; Schopp, Posch, Schupp (Martens 89), Mählich, Reinmayr; Vastic, Haas.

4th match REAL MADRID (ESP)
H 1-5 Haas (3)
Sidorczuk; Foda; Milanic, Popovic (Babalade 71); Neukirchner, Schupp, Minavand, Reinmayr (Kocijan 71); Posch; Vastic, Haas (Martens 75).

5th match SPARTAK MOSKVA (RUS)
A 0-0
Sidorczuk; Popovic; Milanic, Posch; Schopp, Schupp, Mählich, Kocijan (Martens 57); Prilasnig; Vastic, Haas (Babalade 90).

6th match INTER (ITA)
H 0-2
Sidorczuk; Foda; Milanic (Martens 46), Popovic; Schopp, Schupp, Kocijan (Wallner 84), Neukirchner (Prilasnig 77), Posch; Haas, Reinmayr.

CUP WINNERS' CUP
● SV RIED
1st round MTK HUNGÁRIA FC (HUN)
H 2-0 Strafner (19), Brunmayr (64)
Unger; Kitka; Steininger, Glasner; Rothbauer, Angerschmid (Hartl 61), Stanisavljevic, Anicic (Berensztajn 73), Zeller; Brunmayr (Sliwowski 82), Strafner.
A 1-0 Strafner (11)
Unger; Kitka; Steininger, Glasner, Zeller (Hacker 81); Rothbauer (Jank 60), Angerschmid, Stanisavljevic, Anicic; Brunmayr (Sliwowski 68), Strafner.

2nd round MACCABI HAIFA (ISR)
H 2-1 Sliwowski (23), Strafner (88)
Unger; Steininger, Kitka, Glasner (Jank 67), Zeller; Rothbauer, Angerschmid (Hacker 80), Stanisavljevic, Anicic; Strafner, Sliwowski (Brunmayr 71).
A 1-4 Anicic (70)
Oraze; Kitka; Steininger, Glasner, Rothbauer (Hujdurovic 79); Angerschmid, Stanisavljevic, Anicic, Zeller (Hacker 81); Strafner, Sliwowski (Brunmayr 76).

UEFA CUP
● GRAZER AK
Qualifying round VPS (FIN)
A 0-0
Almer; Vukovic; Ehmann, Akoto (Grimm 74); Hartmann, Ramusch, Ceh (Kulovits 80), Sick, Drechsel (Dmitrovic 69); Akwuegbu, Luhovy.
H 3-0 Luhovy (51), Grimm (54), Drechsel (90)
Almer; Vukovic; Lipa, Grimm, Hartmann; Ramusch, Kulovits, Radovic (Drechsel 71), Dmitrovic; Akwuegbu, Luhovy (Brenner 79).

1st round LITEKS LOVECH (BUL)
A 1-1 Lipa (56)
Almer; Vukovic; Lipa, Ehmann, Hartmann; Ramusch, Ceh, Kulovits (Sick 61), Dmitrovic; Luhovy (Wieger 67), Akwuegbu (Radovic 90).
H 2-0 Golombek (7), Akwuegbu (82)
Almer; Vukovic; Pötscher, Grimm, Golombek; Ramusch, Ehmann, Kulovits, Dmitrovic (Drechsel 67); Luhovy (Brenner 71), Akwuegbu (Sick 90).

2nd round AS MONACO (FRA)
H 3-3 Akwuegbu (28, 57), Ehmann (90)
Tomic, Vukovic, Pötscher (Lipa 71), Grimm, Hartmann; Ramusch, Sick (Ehmann 78), Ceh, Dmitrovic; Luhovy (Brenner 64), Akwuegbu.
A 0-4
Tomic; Pötscher; Vukovic, Akoto, Hartmann; Ramusch, Sick (Luhovy 54), Ehmann, Drechsel (Radovic 59), Dmitrovic; Akwuegbu (Brenner 75).

● SK RAPID WIEN
Qualifying round OMONIA NICOSIA (CYP)
A 1-3 Wagner (22)
Maier; Zingler; Schöttel, Ratajczyk; Wimmer, Braun, Heraf, Wetl, Prosenik; Wagner (Pürk 46), Penksa (Saler 46).
H 2-0 Heraf (9), Wagner (70)
Maier; Zingler; Schöttel, Ratajczyk (Hatz 63); Wimmmer, Heraf, Freund, Penksa, Prosenik; Pürk (Saler 79), Vier (Wagner 46).

1st round GIRONDINS DE BORDEAUX (FRA)
A 1-1 Freund (65)
Maier; Zingler; Hatz, Schöttel; Prosenik, Heraf (Saler 61), Freund, Ratajczyk, Wetl (Wimmer 71); Penksa, Wagner (Pürk 80).
H 1-2 Wagner (42)
Maier; Zingler; Hatz, Schöttel (Braun 46); Prosenik (Saler 46), Heraf, Wetl, Freund, Ratajczyk; Wagner, Pürk.

FC Tirol also came good in the second half of the season after a terrible start, with Polish mid-season signing Radoslaw Gilewicz single-handedly solving the team's goalscoring problems and experienced Austrian international Walter Kogler successfully stabilising the defence. Tirol thus ended up in mid-table with LASK and Austria Vienna, two teams who delivered considerably less than they promised and were subjected to disruptive manoeuvres on the coaching and management front.

INTERNATIONAL HONOURS

World Cup Finals appearances: 1934 (4th), 1954 (3rd), 1958, 1978 (2nd phase), 1982 (2nd phase), 1990, 1998
European Championship appearances (last 8): 1960.

LASK's season was sent into turmoil following the disappearance and subsequent arrest, for fraud, of club president Wolfgang Rieger. Consequently, the 'Athletiker' were forced to sell just about all of their best players - Vidar Riseth, Peter Stöger, Jerzy Brzeczek, Geir Frigård, Walter Kogler - and they also lost star coach Otto Baric, who refused to carry on in circumstances that he considered unworkable. His assistant, fellow Croat Marinko Koljanin, did extremely well to take the much-depleted, rejuvenated side into the Cup final, and both he and his players emerged with great credit after losing unluckily on penalties to Sturm at the end of one of the best finals for years.

Austria Vienna, one of just two clubs from the capital left in the top division, never accepted their new Slovenian coach Zdenko Verdenik, and their sorry sequence of winless matches against old rivals Rapid entered a fourth year. The only good news for the long-suffering *Violetten*

DOMESTIC CUP 98/99

SECOND ROUND
ASK Klingenbach 1, SV Spittal/Drau 3
SAK Klagenfurt 1, Grazer AK 5
SV Salzburg Amateure 0, LASK Linz 2
SK Sturm Amateure/LUV 0, SV Braunau 3
SV Kapfenberg 0, Casino Vienna 4
SC Untersiebenbrunn 3, SC Himberg 1
WSC Wattens 0, VfB Admira Wacker Mödling 4
TSV Pöllau 1, ASK Kottingbrunn 1 (aet; 4-5 on pens.)
SC Eisenstadt 2, SK Vorwärts Steyr 1
SC Zwettl 3, FCN St. Pölten 4
ASKÖ Pasching 0, SK Eintracht Wels 1
SV Mattersburg 2, FC Tirol Innsbruck 1
SV Bad Schallerbach 1, SV Ried 2
ASKÖ Donau Linz 0, SC Austria Lustenau 2 (aet)
ESK/GAK Amateure 0, SK Sturm Graz 4
FC Zeltweg 0, SV Wörgl 2
SV Oberndorf 0, SK Rapid Wien 8
FC Hard 2, SV Stockerau 2 (aet; 3-5 on pens.)
SV Lendorf 1, DSV Leoben 6
FAC avanti 0, SV Salzburg 3
SK Rum 1, SW Bregenz 3
SCR Altach 1, FK Austria Wien 1 (aet; 4-3 on pens.)
SV Schwechat 3, SK Rapid Lienz 1
FC Deutschkreuz 2, SVG Reichenau 4
SVG Bleiburg 2, SV Grieskirchen 1
Union St. Florian 2, TSV Hartberg 1
SV Leibnitz 4, EPSV Gmünd 1
LAC Nettig 2, FC Austria Klagenfurt 8
Sturm FC St. Pölten 3, FC Lustenau 1907 4
FC Tulln 2, ATSV Sattledt 1
SV Horn 4, Union Esternberg 0
FC Waidhofen/Ybbs 3, FC Würmla 2 (aet)

THIRD ROUND
SC Eisenstadt 1, Grazer AK 6
SC Untersiebenbrunn 1, SW Bregenz 3
Union St. Florian 2, VfB Admira Wacker Mödling 2 (aet; 3-4 on pens.)
SV Leibnitz 1, SC Austria Lustenau 3
SCR Altach 1, SV Austria Braunau 2 (aet)
SVG Bleiburg 0, SV Salzburg 5
FC Waidhofen/Ybbs 0, SK Ried 2 (aet)
ASK Kottingbrunn 0, SV Wörgl 4
FC Tulln 0, FCN St. Pölten 2
SV Mattersburg 3, SK Rapid Wien 5
SK Eintracht Wels 0, SV Spittal/Drau 0 (aet; 4-5 on pens.)
SVG Reichenau 0, SK Sturm Graz 5
SV Stockerau 0, LASK Linz 2
SV Horn 7, FC Austria Klagenfurt 1
SV Schwechat 1, Casino Vienna 0
FC Lusteenau 1907 1, DSV Leoben 3 (aet)

FOURTH ROUND
SV Horn 0, SV Ried 3
SV Spittal/Drau 0, LASK Linz 1
SV Schwechat 0, SV Austria Braunau 4
SK Rapid Wien 3, SV Wörgl 0
SK Sturm Graz 2, SW Bregenz 1
SC Austria Lustenau 3, DSV Leoben 1 (aet)
VfB Admira Wacker Mödling 2, SV Salzburg 2 (aet; 2-4 on pens.)
FCN St. Pölten 0, Grazer AK 4

QUARTER-FINALS
SV Austria Braunau 0, SV Ried 1 (Anicic 9)
Grazer AK 1 (Lipa 16),
SK Sturm Graz 2 (Vastic 66p, Martens 73)
SK Rapid Wien 4 (Vier 1, Adzic 14, 63, Wagner 78),
SV Salzburg 1 (Kitzbichler 74)
SC Austria Lustenau 0, LASK Linz 1 (Pichorner 27)

SEMI-FINALS
SK Rapid Wien 0,
LASK Linz 2 (Panis 5, Stumpf 79)
SK Sturm Graz 5 (Kocijan 4, Minavand 7, Vastic 45, Schopp 54, Prilasnig 88), SV Ried 0

FINAL
18/05/99, Vienna
SK STURM GRAZ 1 Haas (60)
LASK LINZ 1 Vastic (36og)
(aet; 4-2 on pens.)
referee - Sedlacek

SK STURM GRAZ - Sidorczuk; Foda; Neukirchner, Popovic; Martens (Berco 105), Schupp, Mählich, Reinmayr (Milanic 110), Minavand (Bochtler 97); Vastic, Haas.

LASK LINZ - Pavlovic; Muhr; Milinovic, Ba (Mehlem 56); Grassler, Rohseano, Pichorner, Kauz, Augustine (Weissenberger 64); Panis; Dadi (Stumpf 93).

PLAYERS OF THE SEASON

MARIO HAAS

25-year-old Mario Haas is not only Austria's fastest striker. He is now also the most expensive Austrian footballer of all time following his summer transfer from Sturm Graz to Strasbourg. He left for France having won the Austrian league and Cup 'double' and finished as Sturm's top scorer in the league. For the second season running his 17-goal tally placed him second in the overall Bundesliga standings. Having received a last-minute call-up to Austria's national squad at the 1998 World Cup, he began the new campaign by scoring the first goal conceded by new world champions France, in a 2-2 draw in Vienna. Although he has now left Sturm it is to be hoped that his fabulous understanding with Ivica Vastic and Hannes Reinmayr will continue to reap dividends for the national team.

EDUARD GLIEDER

After spending a decade of relative anonymity in the Austrian Bundesliga during two spells each with Grazer AK and Salzburg, Eduard "Edi" Glieder discovered his best form in his 30th year as he raced to the top of the goalscorer listings and stayed

there through to the end of the season, notching a final total of 22 goals. He put his improvement down to a better mental approach and the fact that he was able to focus solely on attacking whereas before he had been asked to fill a variety of positions, even in defence. He made his national team début for Austria in October 1998 against Cyprus and scored his first international goal four days later in a 4-1 victory away to San Marino.

RICHARD KITZBICHLER

This 25-year-old Tyrolean is one player expected to figure prominently in the rebuilding of the Austrian national team by new coach Otto Baric. By the end of the 1998/99 season he had earned only two international caps, but his brilliant performances for Salzburg during the second half of the season deserved greater recognition. An attacking midfielder who makes things happen when he is on the ball and running at the opposition, "Kitz" joined Salzburg in 1997 after two good years with his local side FC Tirol Innsbruck, where he picked up many good habits from the influential tuition of former Austrian national team boss Didi Constantini.

fans was the return of their old flame, Herbert Prohaska, but even his arrival was fanfare-free given what he had just experienced in his final match in charge of the Austrian national team.

Prohaska's move from one Austria to another followed one of the most humiliating defeats ever suffered by the national team. Despite having served in the job for six years - longer than any other post-war Austrian national coach - Prohaska's position became untenable after his side were routed 9-0 by Spain in a European Championship qualifier.

The sense of shock and embarrassment felt by the Austrian fans was doubly deep because there had been no warning signs beforehand. Prohaska's men travelled to Valencia in a relatively confident mood, having maintained an unbeaten five-match run since the World Cup. Second-half goal sprees against Cyprus and San Marino had given them six Euro 2000 qualifying points to add to the one earned at home to Israel, and only a couple of weeks before the trip to Spain the Austrians had won 4-2 away to neighbours Switzerland in a friendly.

But what transpired in the Mestalla stadium left Prohaska lost for words. The Austrian players simply made

fools of themselves as they spinelessly surrendered to the sparkling Spaniards. The only positive aspect of the evening was that they prevented their opponents from taking their goal tally into double figures.

The search for a successor to Prohaska took longer than expected, with ex-German boss Berti Vogts even being touted as a prospective candidate. Eventually the job was given to the now out-of-work ex-LASK Linz boss Otto Baric. He was a popular choice. Not only had he won enough Austrian domestic trophies to fill a treasure-chest; he had also guided both Rapid Vienna and Salzburg to European finals. His first match, at home to San Marino, could end only one way, but there was a bumper feast for the crowd in Graz as Austria rattled in seven goals, with local hero Ivica Vastic helping himself to a hat-trick.

But the ecstasy soon turned to agony as in Baric's second game, away to Israel, the team were annihilated once again. Israel played brilliantly, but Austria were woeful. The 5-0 defeat all but killed off their hopes of reaching the European Championship finals for the first time, and, not surprisingly, Baric reacted by announcing that there would be wholesale changes in the team for future games...

SC AUSTRIA LUSTENAU

CLUB DIRECTORY

SC Austria Memphis Lustenau
Kaiser-Franz-Josef-Str. 1
6890 Lustenau
tel - (05577) 86250
fax - (05577) 85689
Year of Formation - 1914
President - Hubert Nagel
Secretary - Christian Ortner
Coach - Edmund Stöhr (99/00 - Klaus Scheer)
Stadium - Reichshof-Stadion (11,750)

APPEARANCES 98/99

		P	Ap	(s)	Gls
Armand BENNEKER (HOL)	D		11		
Michael BUTREJ (GER)	M		24	(5)	2
Harald DÜRR	D		11	(5)	
Panayotis EFTHIMIADIS (GRE)	D		5	(3)	
Marcus ENZENEBNER	D		18	(6)	
Theo GRÜNER	M		28	(2)	
Patrick JOVANOVIC	D		28		
Matthias KECK	M		3	(2)	
KLÉBER dos Santos (BRA)	A		7	(13)	1
Johann KLEER	M		32	(1)	3
Petar KOSTURKOV (BUL)	M		6	(5)	1
Mario KRASSNITZER	G		16		
Ivan KRISTO	A		9	(11)	3
Peter LETOCHA	M		25	(2)	
Joachim MOITZI	A		13	(10)	2
Michael Jide OLUGBODI (NIG)	M			(5)	
Richard PADMORE (GHA)	D		7		
Marcelo PAVÃO Moreira (BRA)	M		20	(5)	1
Roger PRINZEN (GER)	D		29		3
Hendrik Jan REGTOP (HOL)	A		26	(1)	3
Harald SCHROLL	M		16	(9)	
Christian SWOBODA	D		11	(3)	
Tamás TIEFENBACH (HUN)	A		26	(1)	5
Martin UNGER	G		20		
Zoran VUJIC (YUG)	A		3	(4)	
Thomas WEISSENBERGER	A		2	(3)	

LEAGUE RESULTS 1998/99

29/07/98	LASK Linz	A	0-3	
01/08/98	FC Tirol Innsbruck	H	2-2	Tiefenbach (p), Prinzen
04/08/98	SK Sturm Graz	A	0-3	
08/08/98	FK Austria Wien	H	1-1	Kleer (p)
15/08/98	SV Ried	A	1-3	Kosturkov
29/08/98	SK Vorwärts Steyr	H	1-1	Kleer
09/09/98	SV Salzburg	H	1-1	Kleer (p)
19/09/98	Grazer AK	A	0-4	
23/09/98	SK Rapid Wien	H	2-0	Regtop, Kléber
26/09/98	SK Rapid Wien	A	0-1	
03/10/98	LASK Linz	H	0-4	
17/10/98	FC Tirol Innsbruck	A	1-3	Prinzen
24/10/98	SK Sturm Graz	H	1-2	Tiefenbach
28/10/98	FK Austria Wien	A	1-1	Moitzi
08/11/98	SV Ried	H	0-2	
14/11/98	SV Salzburg	A	2-1	Tiefenbach 2
21/11/98	Grazer AK	H	0-3	
01/12/98	SK Vorwärts Steyr	H	1-1	Prinzen
05/12/98	SV Salzburg	A	0-1	
06/03/99	SK Vorwärts Steyr	A	1-1	Prinzen
09/03/99	SV Ried	H	0-0	
13/03/99	SK Rapid Wien	A	1-2	Tiefenbach
16/03/99	Grazer AK	H	2-1	Butrej, Pavão
20/03/99	FC Tirol Innsbruck	A	0-0	
31/03/99	LASK Linz	A	0-2	
03/04/99	FK Austria Wien	H	0-0	
09/04/99	SK Sturm Graz	A	2-5	Regtop, Kristo
13/04/99	SK Sturm Graz	H	1-2	Kristo
17/04/99	SV Ried	A	0-1	
24/04/99	SV Salzburg	H	0-0	
01/05/99	SK Vorwärts Steyr	A	0-2	
08/05/99	SK Rapid Wien	H	2-0	Regtop, Butrej
11/05/99	Grazer AK	A	0-2	
16/05/99	FC Tirol Innsbruck	H	0-3	
24/05/99	LASK Linz	H	0-1	
29/05/99	FK Austria Wien	A	1-2	Moitzi

FK AUSTRIA WIEN

CLUB DIRECTORY

FK Austria-Memphis Wien
Ernst Happel Stadion
Meiereistrasse 7, Sektor D, 1020 Wien
tel - (01) 27788   fax - (01) 7283178
Year of Formation - 1911
President - Rudolf Streicher
Secretary - Markus Kraetschmer
Coach - Zdenko Verdenik; Friedl Koncilia
(99/00 - Herbert Prohaska)
Stadium - Horr (10,459)

MAJOR HONOURS
League Championship - (21)
1924, 1926, 1949, 1950, 1953, 1961, 1962,
1963, 1969, 1970, 1976, 1978, 1979, 1980,
1981, 1984, 1985, 1986, 1991, 1992, 1993.
Domestic Cup - (22) 1921, 1924, 1925, 1926,
1933, 1935, 1936, 1948, 1949, 1960, 1962,
1963, 1967, 1971, 1974, 1977, 1980, 1982,
1986, 1990, 1992, 1994.

APPEARANCES 98/99

	P	Ap	(s)	Gls
Thomas DARASZ	A	10	(7)	1
Ernst DOSPEL	D	18	(7)	
Ludwig ERNSTSSON (SWE)	A	17	(8)	4
René GLATZER	M	2	(2)	
Michael GRUBER	M	11	(2)	
Wolfgang HOPFER	M	23	(1)	
Shay HOLTSMAN (ISR)	A	9	(9)	2
Christian KELLNER	M		(2)	
Wolfgang KNALLER	G	31		
Günter KREISSL	G	5	(2)	
Gernot KRINNER	A		(1)	
Jürgen LEITNER	M	24	(9)	1
Alexander LEZ	A		(3)	
Christian MAYRLEB	A	35		16
Anton PFEFFER	D	21		
Gernot PLASSNEGGER	M	27	(5)	3
Rashid RAKHIMOV (RUS)	M	17	(2)	2
Manfred ROSENEGGER	A	7	(10)	1
Paul SCHARNER	M	1	(3)	
Gerald SCHEIBLEHNER	M		(1)	
Günter SCHIESSWALD	D	19	(6)	1
Manfred SCHMID	M	27		
Christian SCHREIBER	M	2	(5)	
Rafal SIADACZKA (POL)	M	15		
Julius SIMON (SVK)	M	10	(3)	1
Peter STÖGER	M	10		
Michael STREITER	D	27		1
Christian TAMANDL	D		(1)	
Michael WAGNER	M	28		8

LEAGUE RESULTS 1998/99

28/07/98	SK Sturm Graz	A	0-2	
01/08/98	SK Vorwärts Steyr	H	4-1	Mayrleb 2, Rosenegger, Plassnegger
05/08/98	SV Ried	H	1-0	Mayrleb
08/08/98	SC Austria Lustenau	A	1-1	Mayrleb
15/08/98	SV Salzburg	H	3-2	Wagner 2, Simon
28/08/98	Grazer AK	A	0-0	
08/09/98	SK Rapid Wien	H	0-1	
18/09/98	LASK Linz	A	3-1	Ernstsson 2, Mayrleb
23/09/98	FC Tirol Innsbruck	H	1-1	Wagner
27/09/98	FC Tirol Innsbruck	A	0-3	
03/10/98	SK Sturm Graz	H	0-3	
17/10/98	SK Vorwärts Steyr	A	1-0	Schiesswald
25/10/98	SV Ried	A	1-2	Mayrleb
28/10/98	SC Austria Lustenau	H	1-1	Holtsman
07/11/98	SV Salzburg	A	0-2	
11/11/98	Grazer AK	H	0-0	
15/11/98	SK Rapid Wien	A	1-3	Mayrleb
22/11/98	LASK Linz	H	2-0	Ernstsson, Mayrleb
28/11/98	SK Sturm Graz	H	1-0	Mayrleb
27/02/99	SV Ried	A	1-2	Wagner
06/03/99	SV Salzburg	H	3-1	Mayrleb 2, Rakhimov
13/03/99	SK Vorwärts Steyr	A	3-1	Wagner 2, Mayrleb
16/03/99	SK Rapid Wien	H	1-1	Wagner
20/03/99	Grazer AK	A	0-3	
31/03/99	FC Tirol Innsbruck	H	1-1	Mayrleb
03/04/99	SC Austria Lustenau	A	0-0	
11/04/99	LASK Linz	H	2-0	Streiter, Plassnegger
14/04/99	LASK Linz	A	0-0	
18/04/99	SK Sturm Graz	A	0-0	
24/04/99	SV Ried	H	3-0	Wagner (p), Mayrleb 2
01/05/99	SV Salzburg	A	0-3	
08/05/99	SK Vorwärts Steyr	H	4-1	Leitner, Darasz, Ernstsson, Plassnegger
11/05/99	SK Rapid Wien	A	0-0	
14/05/99	Grazer AK	H	0-3	
23/05/99	FC Tirol Innsbruck	A	1-4	Rakhimov
29/05/99	SC Austria Lustenau	H	2-1	Mayrleb, Holtsman

GRAZER AK

CLUB DIRECTORY

Liebherr Grazer Athletik-Klub
Stadionplatz 1
8040 Graz
tel - (0316) 4830300
fax - (0316) 4830309
Year of Formation - 1902
President - Peter Svetits
Secretary - Andreas Kindlinger
Coach - Klaus Augenthaler
Stadium - Arnold Schwarzenegger-Stadion (15,428)

MAJOR HONOURS
Domestic Cup - (1) 1981.

APPEARANCES 98/99

		P	Ap	(s)	Gls
Eric AKOTO (GHA)	D	14		(2)	
Benedict AKWUEGBU (NIG)	A	29		(2)	6
Franz ALMER	G	32			
Ewald BRENNER	A	9		(19)	3
Ales CEH (SLO)	M	29			1
Boban DMITROVIC (YUG)	M	28		(4)	4
Herwig DRECHSEL	M	13		(7)	3
Anton EHMANN	D	15		(4)	
Andreas GOLOMBEK (GER)	D	8		(5)	1
Marco GRIMM (GER)	D	22		(4)	2
Jürgen HARTMANN	D	24		(1)	
Enrico KULOVITS	M	21		(5)	4
Andreas LIPA	D	25		(4)	5
Lubomir LUHOVY (SVK)	A	13		(8)	3
Igor PAMIC (CRO)	A	11			1
Gregor PÖTSCHER	D	5		(6)	
Thomas RADLSPECK (GER)	M	9		(5)	
Zeljko RADOVIC	A	13		(12)	6
Dieter RAMUSCH	M	24		(1)	3
Andreas SCHRANZ	G	1			
Gernot SICK	M	11		(9)	
Joachim STANDFEST	A			(3)	
STÜCKLER	D			(1)	
Tomas TOMIC (GER)	G	3			
Zeljko VUKOVIC	D	35			3
Herbert WIEGER	A	2		(2)	

LEAGUE RESULTS 1998/99

29/07/98	SK Vorwärts Steyr	A	1-0	Akwuegbu
02/08/98	SK Rapid Wien	H	1-1	Kulovits
05/08/98	LASK Linz	A	1-0	Radovic
08/08/98	FC Tirol Innsbruck	H	2-0	Akwuegbu, Dmitrovic
15/08/98	SK Sturm Graz	A	3-2	Kulovits, Ramusch, Brenner
28/08/98	FK Austria Wien	H	0-0	
09/09/98	SV Ried	A	1-0	Dmitrovic
19/09/98	SC Austria Lustenau	H	4-0	Grimm, Brenner, Radovic, Luhovy (p)
22/09/98	SV Salzburg	A	0-1	
25/09/98	SV Salzburg	H	3-1	Ceh, Grimm, Radovic
03/10/98	SK Vorwärts Steyr	H	2-0	Radovic, Lipa
17/10/98	SK Rapid Wien	A	2-0	Luhovy, Ramusch
23/10/98	LASK Linz	H	0-2	
28/10/98	FC Tirol Innsbruck	A	1-1	Brenner
08/11/98	SK Sturm Graz	H	0-5	
11/11/98	FK Austria Wien	A	0-0	
14/11/98	SV Ried	H	1-0	Lipa
21/11/98	SC Austria Lustenau	A	3-0	Drechsel 2, Dmitrovic
28/11/98	SK Vorwärts Steyr	H	1-0	Vukovic
06/12/98	SK Rapid Wien	A	0-1	
05/03/99	LASK Linz	A	0-0	
12/03/99	FC Tirol Innsbruck	H	0-1	
16/03/99	SC Austria Lustenau	A	1-2	Akwuegbu
20/03/99	FK Austria Wien	H	3-0	Akwuegbu, og (Dospel), Kulovits
30/03/99	SK Sturm Graz	A	1-0	Pamic (p)
03/04/99	SV Ried	H	1-0	Akwuegbu
10/04/99	SV Salzburg	A	0-3	
14/04/99	SV Salzburg	H	1-4	Golombek
17/04/99	SK Vorwärts Steyr	A	3-0	Drechsel, Lipa, Radovic
24/04/99	SK Rapid Wien	H	0-1	
01/05/99	LASK Linz	H	2-1	Vukovic, Lipa
07/05/99	FC Tirol Innsbruck	A	0-1	
11/05/99	SC Austria Lustenau	H	2-0	Lipa, Kulovits
14/05/99	FK Austria Wien	A	3-0	Ramusch, Akwuegbu, Radovic
22/05/99	SK Sturm Graz	H	1-2	Dmitrovic (p)
29/05/99	SV Ried	A	2-0	Vukovic (p), Luhovy

LASK LINZ

CLUB DIRECTORY

LASK Linz
Stadion der Stadt Linz
Ziegeleistrasse, 4020 Linz
tel - (0732) 603332
fax - (0732) 6033329
Year of Formation - 1908
President - Manfred Reitinger
Secretary - Gottfried Leeb
Coach - Otto Baric; Marinko Koljanin
Stadium - Linzer Stadion (25,000)

MAJOR HONOURS
League Championship - (1) 1965.
Domestic Cup - (1) 1965.

APPEARANCES 98/99

		P	Ap	(s)	Gls
Brendan AUGUSTINE (SAF)	M	5	(10)	1
Cheikh Sidy BA (SEN)	D	29	(1)	
Jerzy BRZECZEK (POL)	M	14	(6)	2
Eugène DADI (FRA)	A	9	(11)	3
DEMIR	D		(1)	
Geir FRIGÅRD (NOR)	A	20		10
Herbert GRASSLER	M	31	(2)	1
Jürgen KAUZ	M	25	(1)	1
Johann KOGLER	M	10	(4)	1
Walter KOGLER	D	19		4
Armin LEITNER	A		(2)	
Christoph LICHTENWAGNER	M	1	(6)	3
Michael MEHLEM	M	6	(10)	
Zeljko MILINOVIC (SLO)	D	29	(4)	4
Bernhard MUHR	D	15	(4)	
Pascal ORTNER	M		(4)	
Jürgen PANIS	M	16	(3)	1
Zeljko PAVLOVIC (CRO)	G	30		
Peter PAWLOWSKI	A	6	(17)	6
Jürgen PICHORNER	M	16	(10)	1
Vidar RISETH (NOR)	A	7		
Klaus ROHSEANO	M	34		1
Josef SCHICKLGRUBER	G	4		
Peter STÖGER	M	19		3
Christian STUMPF	A	12	(2)	4
Rune TANGEN (NOR)	D	9	(5)	1
Markus WEISSENBERGER	A	28	(1)	6

LEAGUE RESULTS 1998/99

29/07/98	SC Austria Lustenau	H	3-0	Frigård, Kogler W., Pawlowski
01/08/98	SV Salzburg	A	3-1	Kogler J., Frigård, Pawlowski
05/08/98	Grazer AK	H	0-1	
08/08/98	SK Rapid Wien	A	0-5	
15/08/98	SK Vorwärts Steyr	A	4-1	Pawlowski, Kogler W., Dadi, Weissenberger
29/08/98	FC Tirol Innsbruck	H	3-2	Frigård 2, Weissenberger
09/09/98	SK Sturm Graz	A	1-0	Panis
18/09/98	FK Austria Wien	H	1-3	Frigård
23/09/98	SV Ried	A	0-0	
26/09/98	SV Ried	H	3-1	Kogler W., Frigård, Pawlowski
03/10/98	SC Austria Lustenau	A	4-0	Kogler W., Weissenberger, Brzeczek, Stöger
18/10/98	SV Salzburg	H	3-1	Weissenberger, Stöger, Pawlowski
23/10/98	Grazer AK	A	2-0	Frigård 2
27/10/98	SK Rapid Wien	H	0-0	
08/11/98	SK Vorwärts Steyr	H	2-1	Stöger, Frigård
11/11/98	FC Tirol Innsbruck	A	4-1	Milinovic, Brzeczek, Frigård, Weissenberger
15/11/98	SK Sturm Graz	H	0-0	
22/11/98	FK Austria Wien	A	0-2	
29/11/98	SK Rapid Wien	H	1-3	Milinovic
04/12/98	SK Sturm Graz	A	0-2	
05/03/99	Grazer AK	H	0-0	
13/03/99	SV Ried	A	2-1	Stumpf (p), Augustine
16/03/99	FC Tirol Innsbruck	H	0-1	
19/03/99	SV Salzburg	A	0-2	
31/03/99	SC Austria Lustenau	H	2-0	Pawlowski, Weissenberger
03/04/99	SK Vorwärts Steyr	A	1-1	Stumpf
11/04/99	FK Austria Wien	A	0-2	
14/04/99	FK Austria Wien	H	0-0	
17/04/99	SK Rapid Wien	A	0-2	
23/04/99	SK Sturm Graz	H	1-2	Kauz
01/05/99	Grazer AK	A	1-2	Rohseano
08/05/99	SV Ried	H	6-1	Milinovic 2, Stumpf, Tangen, Dadi, Pichorner
11/05/99	FC Tirol Innsbruck	A	0-4	
15/05/99	SV Salzburg	H	3-2	Lichtenwagner 2, Dadi
24/05/99	SC Austria Lustenau	A	1-0	Stumpf (p)
29/05/99	SK Vorwärts Steyr	H	2-0	Grassler, Lichtenwagner

SK RAPID WIEN

CLUB DIRECTORY

Sportklub Rapid Wien
Keisslergasse 6
1140 Wien
tel - (01) 91001
fax - (01) 9111906
Year of Formation - 1899
President - vacant
Secretary - Werner Kuhn
Coach - Heribert Weber
Stadium - Gerhard-Hanappi (19,600)

MAJOR HONOURS

League Championship - (30) 1912, 1913, 1916,
1917, 1919, 1920, 1921, 1923, 1929, 1930,
1935, 1938, 1940, 1941, 1946, 1948, 1951,
1952, 1954, 1956, 1957, 1960, 1964, 1967,
1968, 1982, 1983, 1987, 1988, 1996.
Domestic Cup - (14)
1919, 1920, 1927, 1946, 1961, 1968, 1969,
1972, 1976, 1983, 1984, 1985, 1987, 1995.

APPEARANCES 98/99

		P	Ap	(s)	Gls
Ivan ADZIC (YUG)	M		22		2
Martin BRAUN (GER)	M		24	(7)	1
Oliver FREUND (GER)	D		32		2
Michael HATZ	D		14	(13)	
Andreas HERAF	M		27	(2)	4
Ladislav MAIER (CZE)	G		36		
René MITTEREGGER	M			(1)	
Marek PENKSA (SVK)	A		31	(4)	4
Christian PROSENIK	M		33	(1)	6
Marcus PÜRK	A		16	(19)	7
Krzysztof RATAJCZYK (POL)	D		15		2
Jürgen SALER	M		7	(19)	2
Peter SCHÖTTEL	D		35		
Florian SCHWARZ	A			(2)	
Angelo VIER (GER)	A		9	(12)	3
René WAGNER (CZE)	A		26	(7)	10
Arnold WETL	M		19	(2)	2
Gerd WIMMER	M		26	(6)	2
Charles WITTL	M		5	(4)	
Thomas ZINGLER	D		19		2

LEAGUE RESULTS 1998/99

Date	Opponent		Score	Scorers
02/08/98	Grazer AK	A	1-1	Zingler
05/08/98	SK Vorwärts Steyr	A	2-1	Penksa, Wetl
08/08/98	LASK Linz	H	5-0	Penksa, Pürk, Prosenik (p), Ratajczyk, Wagner
14/08/98	FC Tirol Innsbruck	A	3-1	Heraf 2, Pürk
30/08/98	SK Sturm Graz	H	2-0	Prosenik (p), Saler
08/09/98	FK Austria Wien	A	1-0	Wagner
20/09/98	SV Ried	H	1-1	Heraf
23/09/98	SC Austria Lustenau	A	0-2	
26/09/98	SC Austria Lustenau	H	1-0	Wagner
02/10/98	SV Salzburg	A	1-1	Wagner
17/10/98	Grazer AK	H	0-2	
24/10/98	SK Vorwärts Steyr	H	5-1	Prosenik 2 (1p), Heraf, Vier, Adzic
27/10/98	LASK Linz	A	0-0	
03/11/98	SV Salzburg	H	1-0	Zingler
06/11/98	FC Tirol Innsbruck	H	1-0	Prosenik
11/11/98	SK Sturm Graz	A	1-2	Wagner
15/11/98	FK Austria Wien	H	3-1	Penksa, Prosenik (p), Wagner
21/11/98	SV Ried	A	1-0	Wagner
29/11/98	LASK Linz	A	3-1	Freund, Wagner, og (Ba)
06/12/98	Grazer AK	H	1-0	Pürk
06/03/99	FC Tirol Innsbruck	A	0-0	
13/03/99	SC Austria Lustenau	H	2-1	Ratajczyk, Pürk
16/03/99	FK Austria Wien	A	1-1	Wagner
21/03/99	SK Sturm Graz	H	2-0	Wetl, Pürk
31/03/99	SV Ried	A	0-0	
03/04/99	SV Salzburg	H	1-1	Penksa
10/04/99	SK Vorwärts Steyr	A	3-3	Braun, Vier, Wimmer
14/04/99	SK Vorwärts Steyr	H	2-1	Pürk, Vier
17/04/99	LASK Linz	H	2-0	Pürk, Wagner
24/04/99	Grazer AK	A	1-0	Adzic
01/05/99	FC Tirol Innsbruck	H	1-1	Freund
08/05/99	SC Austria Lustenau	A	0-2	
11/05/99	FK Austria Wien	H	0-0	
15/05/99	SK Sturm Graz	A	1-1	Wimmer
22/05/99	SV Ried	H	1-0	Saler
29/05/99	SV Salzburg	A	0-0	

SV RIED

SV Josko Ried im Innkreis
Bahnhofstrasse 19
4910 Ried/Innkreis
tel - (07752) 81100
fax - (07752) 81102
Year of Formation - 1912
President - Wenzel Schmidt
Secretary - Stefan Reiter
Coach - Klaus Roitinger (99/00 - Heinz Hochhauser)
Stadium - Rieder Stadion (10,200)

MAJOR HONOURS
Domestic Cup - (1) 1998.

	P	Ap	(s)	Gls
Michael ANGERSCHMID	M	28	(1)	1
Michael ANICIC (YUG)	M	30		2
Jacek BERENSZTAJN (POL)	M	4	(6)	
Mario BROSER	M	3	(2)	
Ronald BRUNMAYR	A	18	(10)	1
Oliver GLASNER	D	31		1
Oliver GRAF	M	2	(3)	
Wolfgang HACKER	M	7	(13)	
Stefan HARTL	M	10	(13)	1
Faruk HUJDUROVIC (BOS)	D	26	(6)	2
Alexander JANK	D	15	(11)	1
Boris KITKA (SVK)	D	23		
Josef LITZLBAUER	D	1	(3)	
Milan ORAZE	G	20		
Manfred ROTHBAUER	M	23	(9)	3
Julius SIMON (SVK)	M	3	(3)	
Maciej SLIWOWSKI (POL)	A	18	(10)	3
Goran STANISAVLJEVIC (YUG)	M	30		2
Günter STEININGER	D	27	(1)	
Gerald STRAFNER	A	34		7
Ronald UNGER	G	16	(1)	
Helmut ZELLER	M	23	(4)	
Goran ZIVADINOVIC (YUG)	D	4	(6)	

29/07/98	FC Tirol Innsbruck	A	0-1	
01/08/98	SK Sturm Graz	H	0-1	
05/08/98	FK Austria Wien	A	0-1	
08/08/98	SK Vorwärts Steyr	H	0-0	
15/08/98	SC Austria Lustenau	H	3-1	Stanisavljevic (p), Sliwowski, Brunmayr
29/08/98	SV Salzburg	A	2-3	Strafner, Hartl
09/09/98	Grazer AK	H	0-1	
20/09/98	SK Rapid Wien	A	1-1	Rothbauer
23/09/98	LASK Linz	H	0-0	
26/09/98	LASK Linz	A	1-3	Strafner
04/10/98	FC Tirol Innsbruck	H	0-1	
17/10/98	SK Sturm Graz	A	0-4	
25/10/98	FK Austria Wien	H	2-1	Strafner, Sliwowski
28/10/98	SK Vorwärts Steyr	A	3-0	Sliwowski, og (Metlitski), Rothbauer
08/11/98	SC Austria Lustenau	A	2-0	Strafner 2
11/11/98	SV Salzburg	H	0-0	
14/11/98	Grazer AK	A	0-1	
21/11/98	SK Rapid Wien	H	0-1	
27/02/99	FK Austria Wien	H	2-1	Anicic, Stanisavljevic (p)
06/03/99	SK Sturm Graz	A	2-4	Anicic, Hujdurovic
09/03/99	SC Austria Lustenau	A	0-0	
13/03/99	LASK Linz	H	1-2	Innk
16/03/99	SV Salzburg	H	1-1	Hujdurovic
20/03/99	SK Vorwärts Steyr	A	0-2	
31/03/99	SK Rapid Wien	H	0-0	
03/04/99	Grazer AK	A	0-1	
10/04/99	FC Tirol Innsbruck	H	2-0	Strafner, Glasner
14/04/99	FC Tirol Innsbruck	A	0-1	
17/04/99	SC Austria Lustenau	H	1-0	Strafner
24/04/99	FK Austria Wien	A	0-3	
01/05/99	SK Sturm Graz	H	0-3	
08/05/99	LASK Linz	A	1-6	Angerschmid
11/05/99	SV Salzburg	A	0-0	
15/05/99	SK Vorwärts Steyr	H	1-0	Rothbauer
22/05/99	SK Rapid Wien	A	0-1	
29/05/99	Grazer AK	H	0-2	

SV SALZBURG

CLUB DIRECTORY

SV Wüstenrot Salzburg
Schumacherstrasse 14
5020 Salzburg
tel - (0662) 433332
fax - (0662) 430216
Year of Formation - 1933
President - Rudolf Quehenberger
Secretary - Harald Böhacker
Coach - Johann Krankl
Stadium - Lehen (14,457)

MAJOR HONOURS
League Championship - (3) 1994, 1995, 1997.

APPEARANCES 98/99

	P	Ap	(s)	Gls
Franz AIGNER	M	24	(3)	1
Martin AMERHAUSER	M	27	(2)	2
René AUFHAUSER	M	25	(3)	2
Amir BRADARIC	M	6	(7)	1
Gerhard BREITENBERGER	M		(1)	
Markus FÜRSTALLER	D	1	(2)	
Eduard GLIEDER	A	34		22
Roman HUPF	D		(2)	
Adolf HÜTTER	M	31	(2)	2
Robert IBERTSBERGER	M	19	(12)	
Valdas IVANAUSKAS (LIT)	A	3	(6)	1
Nikola JURCEVIC (CRO)	A	4	(2)	
Richard KITZBICHLER	M	31	(3)	6
Samuel KOEJOE (HOL)	A	16	(18)	7
Heiko LAESSIG (GER)	M	31	(1)	
Péter LIPCSEI (HUN)	M	13		2
Sladjan NIKOLIC (YUG)	M	9	(6)	1
Manfred PAMMINGER	D	4	(5)	
Stefan PARTINGER	D	2		
Heimo PFEIFENBERGER	A	12	(3)	2
Herfried SABITZER	A	16	(13)	5
Szabolcs SÁFÁR (HUN)	G	36		
Thomas SCHMIEDHUBER	M		(1)	
Robert SPIRIC	A		(1)	
Roman SZEWCZYK (POL)	D	22		1
Bernd WINKLER	A		(2)	
Thomas WINKLHOFER	D	28		
Uwe WOLF (GER)	D	2	(1)	

LEAGUE RESULTS 1998/99

01/08/98	LASK Linz	H	1-3	Sabitzer
08/08/98	SK Sturm Graz	H	1-1	Kitzbichler
15/08/98	FK Austria Wien	A	2-3	Hütter, Pfeifenberger
29/08/98	SV Ried	H	3-2	Glieder 3
09/09/98	SC Austria Lustenau	A	1-1	Glieder
16/09/98	FC Tirol Innsbruck	A	1-1	Glieder
19/09/98	SK Vorwärts Steyr	H	5-2	Glieder 2, Aufhauser, Nikolic, Koejoe
22/09/98	Grazer AK	H	1-0	Glieder
25/09/98	Grazer AK	A	1-3	Aufhauser
02/10/98	SK Rapid Wien	H	1-1	Glieder
18/10/98	LASK Linz	A	1-3	Hütter
25/10/98	FC Tirol Innsbruck	H	1-1	Ivanauskas
28/10/98	SK Sturm Graz	A	0-2	
03/11/98	SK Rapid Wien	A	0-1	
07/11/98	FK Austria Wien	H	2-0	Glieder, Koejoe
11/11/98	SV Ried	A	0-0	
14/11/98	SC Austria Lustenau	H	1-2	Pfeifenberger
21/11/98	SK Vorwärts Steyr	A	1-0	Koejoe
27/11/98	FC Tirol Innsbruck	A	3-0	Koejoe 2, Glieder
05/12/98	SC Austria Lustenau	H	1-0	Glieder
06/03/99	FK Austria Wien	A	1-3	Kitzbichler
13/03/99	SK Sturm Graz	H	3-1	Lipcsei, Glieder 2
16/03/99	SV Ried	A	1-1	Glieder
19/03/99	LASK Linz	H	2-0	Kitzbichler, Sabitzer
31/03/99	SK Vorwärts Steyr	H	1-0	Glieder (p)
03/04/99	SK Rapid Wien	A	1-1	Kitzbichler
10/04/99	Grazer AK	H	3-0	Aigner, Lipcsei, Sabitzer
14/04/99	Grazer AK	A	4-1	Amerhauser, Kitzbichler, Glieder, Sabitzer
17/04/99	FC Tirol Innsbruck	H	2-2	Glieder, Koejoe
24/04/99	SC Austria Lustenau	A	0-0	
01/05/99	FK Austria Wien	H	3-0	Koejoe, Glieder, Bradaric
08/05/99	SK Sturm Graz	A	2-1	Szewczyk, Sabitzer
11/05/99	SV Ried	H	0-0	
15/05/99	LASK Linz	A	2-3	Glieder 2
22/05/99	SK Vorwärts Steyr	A	3-1	Glieder, Kitzbichler, Amerhauser
29/05/99	SK Rapid Wien	H	0-0	

SK VORWÄRTS STEYR

CLUB DIRECTORY

SK Vorwärts Steyr
Volksstr.
4400 Steyr
tel - (07252) 54119
fax - (07252) 46195
Year of Formation - 1919
President - Manfred Polster
Secretary - Alois Radlspäck
Coach - Rudolf Eggenberger; Jürgen Sundermann
Stadium - Steyr (8,500)

APPEARANCES 98/99

	P	Ap	(s)	Gls
Enver ADROVIC (SLO)	D	11		
Dirk ANDERS (GER)	M	12	(4)	
Amir BRADARIC	M	11		4
Gordan CUPAK (CRO)	M	2	(7)	
George DATORU (NIG)	A	23	(8)	3
Thomas ENGELMAIER	G	7	(1)	
Andreas FADING	A	10	(4)	
Didier FRENAY (BEL)	M	8		
Slobodan GRUBOR (CRO)	D	32		3
Oliver HEIML	M	4	(2)	
Thomas HICKERSBERGER	D	7		1
Markus HOLFMAR	M	3	(9)	
Markus HUBICH	A	10	(7)	3
Patrik IPAVEC (SLO)	A	9	(2)	2
Karl IRNDORFER	D	11	(10)	
Christoph JANK	D	19	(1)	
Leo KIESENHOFER	D	26	(3)	
C LACKENBAUER	G		(1)	
Alexander LÖBE (GER)	A	12		2
Daniel MADLENER	M	18	(7)	
Aleksandr METLITSKI (BLS)	M	27		3
Dragan MISIMOVIC	M	2	(2)	
Nikica PAVLEK (CRO)	M	18	(8)	3
Elvir RAHIMIC (BOS)	M	6		1
Thomas REICHHOLD	D	6	(2)	
Franck ROLLING (FRA)	D	7	(4)	
Markus SCHNEIDHOFER	D	15	(8)	1
Christian SCHRAMMEL	M	27		1
Jan SOPKO (CZE)	D	12		
Herwig WALKER	G	29		
Johannes WOLDEAB (GER)	M	3	(6)	1
Denis ZOVKO (CRO)	D	9	(4)	1

LEAGUE RESULTS 1998/99

29/07/98	Grazer AK	H	0-1	
01/08/98	FK Austria Wien	A	1-4	Metlitski
05/08/98	SK Rapid Wien	H	1-2	Metlitski
08/08/98	SV Ried	A	0-0	
15/08/98	LASK Linz	H	1-4	Hickersberger
29/08/98	SC Austria Lustenau	A	1-1	Datoru
09/09/98	FC Tirol Innsbruck	H	2-1	Bradaric, Schrammel
19/09/98	SV Salzburg	A	2-5	Ipavec, Bradaric
23/09/98	SK Sturm Graz	A	2-5	Ipavec, Bradaric
26/09/98	SK Sturm Graz	H	0-1	
03/10/98	Grazer AK	A	0-2	
17/10/98	FK Austria Wien	H	0-1	
24/10/98	SK Rapid Wien	A	1-5	Hubich
28/10/98	SV Ried	H	0-3	
08/11/98	LASK Linz	A	1-2	Hubich
14/11/98	FC Tirol Innsbruck	A	2-3	Hubich, Bradaric
21/11/98	SV Salzburg	H	0-1	
28/11/98	Grazer AK	A	0-1	
01/12/98	SC Austria Lustenau	H	1-1	Rahimic
02/03/99	FC Tirol Innsbruck	H	0-1	
06/03/99	SC Austria Lustenau	A	1-1	Pavlek
13/03/99	FK Austria Wien	H	1-3	Grubor
16/03/99	SK Sturm Graz	A	0-5	
20/03/99	SV Ried	H	2-0	Pavlek 2
31/03/99	SV Salzburg	A	0-1	
03/04/99	LASK Linz	H	1-1	Schneidhofer
10/04/99	SK Rapid Wien	H	3-3	Datoru, Grubor, Zovko
14/04/99	SK Rapid Wien	A	1-2	Metlitski
17/04/99	Grazer AK	H	0-3	
24/04/99	FC Tirol Innsbruck	A	0-4	
01/05/99	SC Austria Lustenau	H	2-0	Grubor, Löbe
08/05/99	FK Austria Wien	A	1-4	Datoru
11/05/99	SK Sturm Graz	H	1-4	Woldeab (p)
15/05/99	SV Ried	A	0-1	
22/05/99	SV Salzburg	H	1-3	Löbe (p)
29/05/99	LASK Linz	A	0-2	

SK STURM GRAZ

CLUB DIRECTORY

SK Puntigamer Sturm Graz
Eggenbergergürtel 9
8020 Graz
tel - (0316) 771771
fax - (0316) 724811
Year of Formation - 1909
President - Hannes Kartnig
Secretary - Heinz Schilcher
Coach - Ivica Osim
Stadium - Arnold Schwarzenegger-Stadion (15,428)

MAJOR HONOURS
League Championship - (2) 1998, 1999.
Domestic Cup - (3) 1996, 1997, 1999.

APPEARANCES 98/99

	P	Ap	(s)	Gls
Didier ANGIBEAUD (CMR)	M	9	(5)	1
Ajibade BABALADE (NIG)	D	3	(7)	
Georg BARDEL	A		(8)	
Abioudun BARUWA (NIG)	G	1		
Victor BERCO (MOL)	M		(10)	
Michael BOCHTLER (GER)	D		(8)	
Ferdinand FELDHOFER	D		(3)	
Franco FODA (GER)	D	26	(1)	1
Mario HAAS	A	32		17
Wolfgang HOPFER	M	1	(2)	
Alexander KNEZEVIC	G		(1)	
Tomislav KOCIJAN	M	11	(7)	1
Roman MÄHLICH	M	30	(1)	4
Jan-Pieter MARTENS (BEL)	M	9	(16)	5
Darko MILANIC (SLO)	D	28	(2)	1
Mehrdad MINAVAND (IRN)	M	2	(15)	
Günther NEUKIRCHNER	D	32		5
Ranko POPOVIC (YUG)	D	21	(4)	3
Mario POSCH	D	18		
Gilbert PRILASNIG	M	14	(9)	3
Hannes REINMAYR	M	30	(1)	11
Josef SCHICKLGRUBER	G	1		
Markus SCHOPP	M	30		4
Markus SCHUPP (GER)	M	34		1
Kazimierz SIDORCZUK (POL)	G	34		
Ivica VASTIC	A	30		14

LEAGUE RESULTS 1998/99

28/07/98	FK Austria Wien	H	2-0	Vastic 2
01/08/98	SV Ried	A	1-0	Vastic
04/08/98	SC Austria Lustenau	H	3-0	Reinmayr 2, Martens
08/08/98	SV Salzburg	A	1-1	Haas
15/08/98	Grazer AK	H	2-3	Vastic, Reinmayr
30/08/98	SK Rapid Wien	A	0-2	
09/09/98	LASK Linz	H	0-1	
19/09/98	FC Tirol Innsbruck	A	1-0	Haas
23/09/98	SK Vorwärts Steyr	H	5-2	Reinmayr 2, Neukirchner, Haas, og (Grubor)
26/09/98	SK Vorwärts Steyr	A	1-0	Milanic
03/10/98	FK Austria Wien	A	3-0	Mählich 2, Foda
17/10/98	SV Ried	H	4-0	Haas 2, Vastic, Angibeaud
24/10/98	SC Austria Lustenau	A	2-1	Schopp, Haas
28/10/98	SV Salzburg	H	2-0	Reinmayr, Haas
08/11/98	Grazer AK	A	5-0	Haas 2, Vastic, Reinmayr, Popovic
11/11/98	SK Rapid Wien	H	2-1	Neukirchner 2
15/11/98	LASK Linz	A	0-0	
20/11/98	FC Tirol Innsbruck	H	2-0	Popovic, Prilasnig
28/11/98	FK Austria Wien	A	0-1	
04/12/98	LASK Linz	H	2-0	Vastic (p), Reinmayr
06/03/99	SV Ried	H	4-2	Schopp, Haas, Reinmayr, Martens
13/03/99	SV Salzburg	A	1-3	Haas
16/03/99	SK Vorwärts Steyr	H	5-0	Haas 2 (1p), Mählich, Kocijan, Reinmayr
21/03/99	SK Rapid Wien	A	0-2	
30/03/99	Grazer AK	H	0-1	
03/04/99	FC Tirol Innsbruck	A	1-3	Vastic
09/04/99	SC Austria Lustenau	H	5-2	Neukirchner 2, Schopp, Haas, Vastic (p)
13/04/99	SC Austria Lustenau	A	2-1	Reinmayr, Vastic
18/04/99	FK Austria Wien	H	0-0	
23/04/99	LASK Linz	A	2-1	Martens, Vastic
01/05/99	SV Ried	A	3-0	Prilasnig, Vastic 2
08/05/99	SV Salzburg	H	1-2	Popovic
11/05/99	SK Vorwärts Steyr	A	4-1	Mählich, Prilasnig, Schupp, Haas
15/05/99	SK Rapid Wien	H	1-1	Schopp
22/05/99	Grazer AK	A	2-1	Vastic, Martens
29/05/99	FC Tirol Innsbruck	H	3-0	Haas 2, Martens

FC TIROL INNSBRUCK

CLUB DIRECTORY

FC Tirol Milch Innsbruck
Resselstrasse 18/II
6020 Innsbruck
tel - (0512) 33432
fax - (0512) 393288
Year of Formation - 1913
President - Martin Kerscher
Secretary - Siegmund Feistmantl
Coach - Frantisek Cipro; Kurt Jara
Stadium - Tirol Milch-Stadion (14,680)

MAJOR HONOURS
League Championship - (7)
1971, 1972, 1973, 1975, 1977, 1989, 1990.
Domestic Cup - (7)
1970, 1973, 1975, 1978, 1979, 1989, 1993.

APPEARANCES 98/99

		P	Ap	(s)	Gls
Markus ANFANG (GER)	M	27	(7)	2
Zoran BARISIC	M	15	(7)	4
Michael BAUR	M	21	(6)	4
Bülent-Kaan BILGEN	D		(4)	1
Stanislav CHERCHESOV (RUS)	G	35	
Christoph DAMM	A		(4)	
Mahmoud Abou EL DAHAB (EGY)	D	4	
FOIDEL	M		(1)	
Abdol EL SABRY (EGY)	M	9	(9)	2
Radoslaw GILEWICZ (POL)	A	12		8
Alfred HÖRTNAGL	M	29	(1)	3
Patrik JEZEK (CZE)	M	30	(2)	5
Hannes JOCHUM	M	2	(5)	
Roland KIRCHLER	M	31		4
Aleksander KNAVS (SLO)	D	16	(5)	1
Stefan KÖCK	D	13	(6)	
Walter KOGLER	D	14		1
Roland KOLLMANN	A		(8)	1
Wolfgang MAIR	A	1	(8)	
Stefan MARASEK	M	27		1
Oliver PRUDLO	D	28	(3)	
Markus SCHARRER	M	29	(6)	5
STURM	M		(2)	
Mathias SVENSSON (SWE)	A	6		1
Karel VACHA (CZE)	A	21	(5)	5
Robert WAZINGER	D	25	(2)	
Heinz WEBER	G	1		

LEAGUE RESULTS 1998/99

29/07/98	SV Ried	H	1-0	Svensson
01/08/98	SC Austria Lustenau	A	2-2	Baur (p), Scharrer
08/08/98	Grazer AK	A	0-2	
14/08/98	SK Rapid Wien	H	1-3	Kollmann
29/08/98	LASK Linz	A	2-3	Knavs, Barisic
09/09/98	SK Vorwärts Steyr	A	1-2	Vacha
16/09/98	SV Salzburg	H	1-1	Vacha
19/09/98	SK Sturm Graz	H	0-1	
23/09/98	FK Austria Wien	A	1-1	Baur (p)
27/09/98	FK Austria Wien	H	3-0	Vacha 2, Anfang
04/10/98	SV Ried	A	1-0	El Sabry
17/10/98	SC Austria Lustenau	H	3-1	Hörtnagl, Jezek 2
25/10/98	SV Salzburg	A	1-1	Scharrer
28/10/98	Grazer AK	H	1-1	Scharrer (p)
06/11/98	SK Rapid Wien	A	0-1	
11/11/98	LASK Linz	H	1-4	Kirchler
14/11/98	SK Vorwärts Steyr	H	3-2	El Sabry, Hörtnagl, Jezek
20/11/98	SK Sturm Graz	A	0-2	
27/11/98	SV Salzburg	H	0-3	
02/03/99	SK Vorwärts Steyr	A	1-0	Gilewicz
06/03/99	SK Rapid Wien	H	0-0	
12/03/99	Grazer AK	A	1-0	Gilewicz
16/03/99	LASK Linz	A	1-0	Barisic
20/03/99	SC Austria Lustenau	H	0-0	
31/03/99	FK Austria Wien	A	1-1	Hörtnagl
03/04/99	SK Sturm Graz	H	3-1	Vacha, Jezek 2
10/04/99	SV Ried	A	0-2	
14/04/99	SV Ried	H	1-0	Baur
17/04/99	SV Salzburg	A	2-2	Scharrer, Kirchler
24/04/99	SK Vorwärts Steyr	H	4-0	Barisic, Gilewicz 3
01/05/99	SK Rapid Wien	A	1-1	Kirchler
07/05/99	Grazer AK	H	1-0	Baur (p)
11/05/99	LASK Linz	H	4-0	Gilewicz, Marasek (p), Anfang,
				Kirchler
16/05/99	SC Austria Lustenau	A	3-0	Barisic, Scharrer, og (Benneker)
23/05/99	FK Austria Wien	H	4-1	Kogler, Gilewicz 2, Bilgen
29/05/99	SK Sturm Graz	A	0-3	

PROMOTED CLUB

SECOND DIVISION FINAL TABLE 98/99

		Pd	W	D	L	F	A	Pt	GD
1	**SW Bregenz**	**36**	**20**	**9**	**7**	**66**	**48**	**69**	**+18**
2	FCN St. Pölten	36	16	10	10	54	41	58	+13
3	VfB Admira Wacker Mödling	36	14	12	10	44	42	54	+2
4	First Vienna FC 1894	36	15	7	14	51	43	52	+8
5	SV Austria Braunau	36	13	9	14	31	34	48	-3
6	FC Austria Kärnten	36	11	12	13	41	41	45	0
7	SV Wörgl	36	12	9	15	46	56	45	-10
8	DSV Leoben	36	12	8	16	47	44	44	+3
9	SV Spittal	36	10	10	16	33	40	40	-7
10	SV Stockerau	36	9	10	17	35	59	37	-24

CLUB DIRECTORY

Casino SW Bregenz
Postfach 261
6901 Bregenz
tel - (05574) 42795
fax - (05574) 53621
Year of Formation - 1921
President - Josef Fitz
Secretary - Markus Feldkircher
Coach - Srdjan Gemaljevic
Stadium - Casinostadion (13,000)

AZERBAIJAN

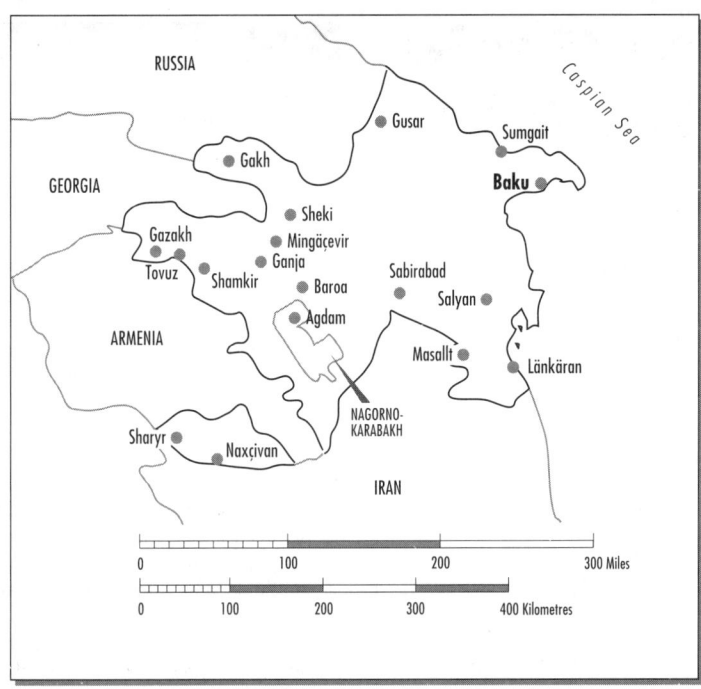

SIX EURO DEFEATS OUT OF SEVEN

Kapaz Ganja top the table - not once but twice

FEDERATION DIRECTORY

Azärbaycan Futbol Federasiyalari Assosiasiyasi
42 Hüsü Haciyev küç., 370009 Baku

tel - (12) 944916　　Year of Formation - 1992
fax - (12) 989393　　President - Fuad Musaev
　　　　　　　　　　Secretary - Cingiz Ismayilov

Stadium - Tofig Bahramov, Baku (54,000)

LEAGUE CHAMPIONSHIP TABLES 98/99

FIRST PHASE		Pd	W	D	L	F	A	Pt	GD
1	Kapaz Ganja	26	18	4	4	76	14	58	+62
2	Karabakh Agdam	26	17	3	6	40	16	54	+24
3	Dinamo Baku	26	16	4	6	36	16	52	+20
4	Neftchi Baku	26	15	7	4	47	17	52	+30
5	Shamkir	26	16	2	8	39	23	50	+16
6	Baki Fehlesi Baku	26	15	5	6	37	21	50	+16
7	Turan Tovuz	26	14	7	5	41	20	49	+21
8	Vilash Masalli	26	14	4	8	31	20	46	+11
9	Bakili Baku	26	7	7	12	14	27	28	-13
10	SKA Baku	26	6	8	12	18	24	26	-6
11	Kimyachi Sumgayit	26	5	1	20	19	58	16	-39
12	Shafa Baku	26	3	5	18	19	49	14	-30
13	Shahdag Kusari	26	2	4	20	17	81	10	-64
14	Neftgaz Baku	26	2	3	21	13	61	9	-48

CHAMPIONSHIP GROUP		Pd	W	D	L	F	A	Pt	GD
1	Kapaz Ganja	10	8	1	1	17	7	25	+10
2	Shamkir	10	5	1	4	10	10	16	0
3	Neftchi Baku	10	4	3	3	11	7	15	+4
4	Karabakh Agdam	10	3	3	4	5	8	12	-3
5	ANS Pivani	10	2	3	5	5	8	9	-3
6	Dinamo Baku	10	2	1	7	6	14	7	-8

MIDDLE GROUP		Pd	W	D	L	F	A	Pt	GD
7	Turan Tovuz	6	4	2	0	17	6	14	+11
8	Vilash Masalli	6	2	3	1	16	12	9	+4
9	SKA Baku	6	2	3	1	8	7	9	+1
10	Bakili Baku	6	0	0	6	0	16	0	-16

RELEGATION GROUP		Pd	W	D	L	F	A	Pt	GD
11	Shafa Baku	4	3	1	0	12	3	10	+9
12	Kimyachi Sumgayit	4	1	2	1	9	9	5	0
13	Neftgaz Baku	4	0	1	3	3	12	1	-9

N.B. Shahdag Kusari withdrew after First Phase and were relegated.

There was a new twist to the Azerbaijani national championship in 1998/99. In their wisdom the Federation decided to introduce a new two-tiered structure, with a regular season and play-offs, similar in its framework to the type of system that had been tried out in a number of other European leagues...but with one significant difference.

The Azerbaijani model did not reward teams for their classification in the first part of the campaign. There was no carrying forward of points totals. In effect, the first 26-match, stage was used merely as a preliminary tournament in order to separate the wheat from the chaff. It did not matter whether a team finished first or sixth. They would make it to the leading group of the second phase as long as they remained in sixth spot or above. After that everything started again from scratch.

There were no surprises in the composition of the 'lucky six' who went forward to contest the title. They were the same half-dozen which had filled those positions in the 1997/98 final table. In first place were the defending champions Kapaz Ganja, albeit with 12 points fewer than a year before (when every point had actually counted). They could only draw their first match of the play-offs away to Shamkir, but after that they put their foot down and scorched ahead of the field with six wins on the trot. That was enough to put them well clear in a mere ten match contest, and although they lost match number eight 0-3 to Neftchi Baku, a 3-1 victory at home to Dinamo Baku in their next fixture was sufficient to seal their second successive championship win.

Shamkir were a distant second, but they collected enough points to earn a UEFA Cup place, finishing one position and one point ahead of Neftchi. Both of those teams reached the Azerbaijani Cup final. It was a pretty dull affair, with Neftchi eventually prevailing 5-4 on penalties after a two-hour stalemate to lift the trophy for the third time, after previous successes in 1995 and 1996.

Azerbaijan continued to be a small-time player in international football. Once again the three teams assigned

DOMESTIC CUP 98/99

FINAL
28/05/99, Baku
NEFTCHI BAKU 0
SHAMKIR 0
(aet; 5-4 on pens.)
referee - Mamedov
NEFTCHI BAKU - Gasanzade; Getman, Stukas, Akhmedov, Poshekhontsev,
Guliyev, Rakhmanov, Ismailov (Niftaliyev 78), Kalfa (Kambarov 46), Mamedov
I., Musayev (Yadullayev 103).
SHAMKIR - Mehtiyev; Mamedov A., Yunusov, Mamedov R., Ocagverdiyev,
Veliyev, Kakuvava, Ibragimov, Gabisonia (Kerimov 46), Akhmedov,
Kvaratskhelia.

to the European club competitions all lost home and away
in the preliminary round. There was a modicum of
improvement on the previous season, if only because this
time two of the teams actually scored a goal. In fact, Kapaz
scored in each of their two matches with Polish champions
LKS Lodz, but unfortunately their opponents scored seven
over the tie to go forward and meet Manchester United
in the next round.

One defeat followed another in Azerbaijan's Euro
2000 qualifying campaign. Vagif Sadigov made bold
predictions before the tournament began that the team
would do considerably better than in the previous World
Cup qualifying campaign, but after three games he was
left with egg on his face and out of a job. A 0-4 home
defeat by Hungary was bad. But losing in Liechtenstein
four days later was intolerable.

Akhmed Alekserov was appointed as the new team
chief, and although he got off to a painful start in his first
qualifying match with a 0-7 defeat in Portugal, there was
a distinct improvement in the narrow 0-1 home loss to
Romania, which was followed at the
beginning of June by a 4-0 'revenge'
victory over Liechtenstein in Baku. At
last Azerbaijan were off the mark, and
off the bottom of the table - to the
considerable relief of all concerned.

INTERNATIONAL HONOURS

None

TOP SCORERS

24 Asay BAHRAMOV (Vilash Masalli)
19 Vadim VASILYEV (ANS Pivani)
18 Vidadi RZAEV (Kapaz Ganja)

EUROPEAN CUPS 98/99

CHAMPIONS' CUP
● KAPAZ GANJA
Preliminary round LKS LODZ (POL)
A 1-4 Suleymanov (82)
        Magamedov; Allakhverdiev, Jabbarov, Kurbanov M., Mardanov,
        Smirnov (Parvarov 58), Kvaratskhelia (Suleymanov 58), Lychkin,
        Guseinov, Rzayev, Kerimov.
H 1-3 Smirnov (55)
        Magamedov; Allakhverdiev, Jabbarov, Kurbanov M. (Tanriverdiev 67),
        Mardanov, Smirnov, Mamedov, Kvaratskhelia (Kerdzevadze 61),
        Guseinov, Rzayev, Kerimov.

CUP WINNERS' CUP
● KARABAKH AGDAM
Qualifying round FC KØBENHAVN (DEN)
A 0-6
        Aliev D.; Akhmedov, Nuriev, Karaev, Kuliev (Azimov 59),
        Isaev (Aliev S. 80), Hasanov, Guseinov M., Musaev, Abdashev,
        Pashayev.
H 0-4
        Aliev D.; Aliev S., Akhmedov, Karaev, Kuliev, Isaev (Makhmudov 79),
        Azimov, Hasanov, Guseinov M. (Bagirov 68), Pashayev, Guseinov V.

UEFA CUP
● DINAMO BAKU
Preliminary round FC ARGES DACIA PITESTI (ROM)
A 1-5 Aliev (36)
        Shukurov; Khairov, Mamedov, Gasanov, Kuliyev,
        Amirov (Musaev 53), Askerov (Kurbanov 72), Sultanov, Aliev,
        Ismailov, Amirbekov.
H 0-2
        Salamov; Khairov, Mamedov, Gasanov (Ragimov 87), Kuliyev, Amirov
        (Guseinov 64), Askerov (Musaev 64), Sultanov, Aliev, Ismailov,
        Kurbanov.

NATIONAL TEAM RESULTS 98/99

Date	Opponent	H/A/N	Venue	Score	Scorers
12/08/98	Georgia	H	Ganja	1-0	Agaev (49)
05/09/98	Slovakia (ECQ)	A	Bratislava	0-3	
10/10/98	Hungary (ECQ)	H	Baku	0-4	
14/10/98	Liechtenstein (ECQ)	A	Vaduz	1-2	Kurbanov K. (59)
28/11/98	Estonia	H	Ganja	2-1	Sultanov (81), Mamedov K. (87p)
06/03/99	Estonia	N	Larnaca	2-2	Kurbanov K. (1), Lychkin (30p)
26/03/99	Portugal (ECQ)	A	Guimarães	0-7	
31/03/99	Romania (ECQ)	H	Baku	0-1	
05/06/99	Liechtenstein (ECQ)	H	Baku	4-0	Kurbanov K. (16), Lychkin (42), Tagizade (60), Isaev (73)
09/06/99	Romania (ECQ)	A	Bucharest	0-4	

NATIONAL TEAM APPEARANCES 98/99

Coach - Vagif SADIGOV; Akhmed ALESKEROV	GEO	SVK	HUN	LIE	EST	EST	POR	ROM	LIE	ROM
Gusein MAGOMEDOV (22/08/74) - Kapaz Ganja	G							G		
Faik JABBAROV (26/06/72) - Kapaz Ganja	D	D								
Deni GAYSUMOV (06/02/68) - CSKA Moskva (RUS)	D	D	D	D						
Ermin AGAEV (16/07/73) - Torpedo Zil (RUS)	D	D	D	D		D	D	D77	D	D71
Aslan KERIMOV (01/01/73) - Kapaz Ganja/Baltika Kaliningrad (RUS)	D		D	D				D	D	D
Vyacheslav LYCHKIN (30/09/73) - Kapaz Ganja/Spartak Moskva (RUS)	M	D	M			M71	D	M	M74	M82
Rasim ABUSHEV (15/10/63) - Dinamo Stavropol (RUS)	M75	M	M	M79			M			
Arif ASADOV (18/08/70) - FK Tyumen (RUS)	M87	M	D51			D51	D	D		
Makhmud KURBANOV (10/05/73) - Kapaz Ganja	M58			M25		s71		M65	M	M59
Kurban KURBANOV (13/04/72) - Baltika Kaliningrad (RUS)	A71	A66	A	A		A23	A	A	A	A
Velli KASUMOV (04/10/68) - Vitória Setúbal (POR)	A81	A	s56							
Yunis GUSEYNOV (01/02/65) - Neftchi Baku	s58									
Vidadi RZAEV (04/09/67) - Kapaz Ganja	s71	s66	M	M		M	s67	s65		
Khalid MARDANOV (31/03/71) - Kapaz Ganja	s75									
Nazim SULEYMANOV (17/02/65) - Zhemchuzhina Sochi (RUS)	s81	A46		s25						
Farrukh ISMAILOV - Dinamo Baku	s87				s74					
Dmitriy KRAMARENKO (12/09/74) - Dinamo Moskva (RUS)		G	G59			G	G		G	G
Narvik SIRKHAEV (16/03/74) - CSKA Moskva (RUS)		M	M	M			M	M	M	M
Rufat KULIEV (04/12/72) - Karabakh Agdam/Shafa Baku		s46		s79		s51		s77		
Elshan KAMBAROV (1972) - Novbakhov Namangan (UZB)			M56	M51		M78	M72	s69		
Ilkhan MAMEDOV (01/01/70) - Kapaz Ganja/Neftchi Baku			s51	s51		M74				
Alexander ZHIDKOV (04/04/65) - Zafririm Holon (ISR)			s59	G						
Ilgham YADULLAYEV (17/09/75) - Neftchi Baku					M	M	M		M	M
Jangiv GASANADZE - Neftchi Baku					G					
F MAMEDOV					D					
Rinat ABDASHEV - Karabakh Agdam					D					
M KAMBAROV					D89					
Mushviq SHUKUROV					D					
A KURBANOV					M					
Khagani MAMEDOV					M					
R MUSAYEV					M74					
Elkhim RAKHMANOV (18/01/79) - Neftchi Baku					A					
Zaur TAGIZADE (21/02/79) - Neftchi Baku					A74			M69	M68	M
Seykhun SULTANOV - Dinamo Baku					s74					
GASHIMOV					s89					
Tarlan AKHMEDOV (17/11/71) - Neftchi Baku						D	D	D	D	D
Vadim VASILYEV (17/05/72) - ANS Pivani						s23	s72		M61	s82
Igor GETMAN (06/07/71) - Neftchi Baku						s74				s71
Mirbagir ISAEV (13/03/74) - Karabakh Agdam						s78		s68		
Alexei STUKAS (17/02/79) - Neftchi Baku							D	s74		
Bakhtiyar MUSAYEV (04/08/73) - Neftchi Baku							M67			s59
Vladimir POSHEKHONTSEV (23/05/67) - Neftchi Baku									M	M
Elmir KHANKISHIEV (1974)									s61	

BELARUS

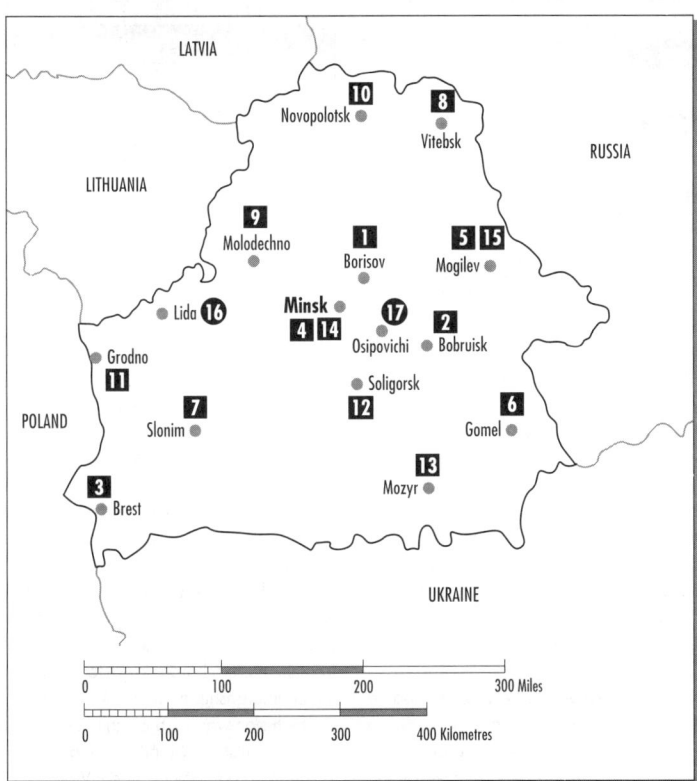

LATVIA

10 Novopolotsk ●

8 Vitebsk ●

RUSSIA

LITHUANIA

9 Molodechno ●

1 Borisov ●

5 15 Mogilev ●

Minsk ●
4 14 Osipovichi ●

17

2 Bobruisk ●

● Lida **16**

● Grodno
11

● Soligorsk
12

6 Gomel ●

POLAND

7 Slonim ●

13 Mozyr ●

3 ● Brest

UKRAINE

0	100	200	300 Miles

0	100	200	300	400 Kilometres

1	BATE BORISOV	136
2	BELSHINA BOBRUISK	137
3	DINAMO BREST	138
4	DINAMO MINSK	139
5	DNEPR-TRANSMASH MOGILEV	140
6	FC GOMEL	141
7	KOMMUNALNIK SLONIM	142
8	LOKOMOTIV-96 VITEBSK	143
9	FC MOLODECHNO	144

10	NAFTAN-DEVON NOVOPOLOTSK	145
11	NEMAN GRODNO	146
12	SHAKHTER SOLIGORSK	147
13	SLAVIYA MOZYR	148
14	TORPEDO MINSK	149
15	TORPEDO ATF-KADINO MOGILEV	150
Promoted clubs		
16	FC LIDA	151
17	SVISLOCH-KROVLYA OSIPOVICHI	151

FINANCIAL CRISIS HITS DINAMO MINSK

Instant success for Mogilev merger club

FEDERATION DIRECTORY

The Belarussian Football Federation
ul. S. Kirov 8/2, 220060 Minsk

tel - (0172) 2272920/2272325/
2204540
fax - (0172) 2272920

Stadium - Dinamo, Minsk (42,375)

Year of Formation - 1992
President - Grigoriy Fedorov
Secretary - Viktor Novikov

Out with the old, in with the new.

That, in a nutshell, was the story of the 1998 season in Belarus - a season in which Dinamo Minsk, the nation's traditional top dogs, were led astray and almost had to be put down, while the new cross-breeds of Dnepr-Transmash Mogilev raced away from the field to take the championship at the first attempt.

The dramatic decline of Dinamo, the defending champions, was induced by crippling finances - a legacy of former president Yevgeniy Khvastovich's mismanagement of the club he presumed to own in conjunction with three others - FC Molodechno, Ataka Minsk and Dinamo's nursery team, Dinamo '93.

Ataka went out of existence before the 1998 campaign had even begun, and Dinamo '93 were excluded from the championship and disbanded midway through it after failing to fulfil a couple of fixtures due to a strike by the team's players, who had not been paid. All the club's results were subsequently declared null and void.

As for Dinamo themselves, the season proved to be a long, hard struggle. Shorn of their best players, almost all of whom had been sold abroad, they could finish no better than eighth in the final table, losing as many games as they won. With no private backers willing to come forward and clear the club's debts, they were rescued from extinction only by the intervention of the state, who officially nationalised the club in a move that was reminiscent of former communist times.

With the former giants of the domestic scene out of the way, there was ample opportunity for others to shine. Dnepr-Transmash Mogilev, the newly-formed merger club from the eastern border town, took full advantage, winning the championship in impressive style.

The fusion was the brainchild of long-time Dnepr coach Valeriy Strelstsov, Mogilev mayor Dmitriy Savitskiy and Transmash company president Valeriy Chertkov. The joint ambition of the three was to pool all of their resources together and give the town one powerful club that could

LEAGUE CHAMPIONSHIP RESULTS 1998

	Team	1	2	3	4	5	6	7	8	9	10	11	12	13	14	15
1	BATE Borisov		1-0	6-0	3-0	1-0	1-1	1-0	1-3	3-0	2-1	3-0	2-0	2-0	0-1	4-1
2	Belshina Bobruisk	4-0		2-0	4-2	1-1	2-0	5-1	1-0	1-0	6-0	0-0	2-1	4-4	1-0	2-1
3	Dinamo Brest	0-3	0-3		0-1	2-0	2-1	0-0	0-1	6-3	1-0	1-2	5-0	1-2	4-0	1-1
4	Dinamo Minsk	2-0	0-0	0-5		2-1	2-2	3-0	1-1	0-0	1-2	1-2	1-2	3-1	0-0	2-1
5	Dnepr-Transmash Mogilev	1-0	1-0	2-0	3-1		3-0	4-0	2-0	5-0	2-0	3-0	4-0	1-1	1-0	2-2
6	FC Gomel	0-0	1-0	1-0	4-3	1-2		2-1	3-0	1-0	2-0	2-1	0-0	2-1	0-0	
7	Kommunalnik Slonim	1-3	1-1	1-0	1-0	0-5	0-3		2-3	3-1	0-0	1-2	0-0	0-2	0-0	0-2
8	Lokomotiv-96 Vitebsk	0-0	1-0	0-1	1-0	0-1	2-1	2-0		1-2	2-1	3-0	1-2	3-0	1-0	1-1
9	FC Molodechno	1-2	0-1	0-2	0-3	1-2	0-0	5-2	1-2		0-0	1-2	0-1	0-1	0-1	1-2
10	Naftan-Devon Novopolotsk	0-1	0-1	1-3	0-2	0-1	2-0	4-0	1-1	5-1		5-2	4-4	0-1	1-5	3-1
11	Neman Grodno	1-2	0-2	2-1	1-4	0-1	1-1	2-0	0-0	2-0	1-0		2-3	1-1	0-0	1-3
12	Shakhter Soligorsk	3-5	0-1	1-3	0-1	1-3	1-2	2-0	1-1	1-0	2-0	1-0		2-2	0-3	3-1
13	Slaviya Mozyr	2-2	1-0	1-2	0-0	1-3	1-1	2-0	2-1	1-2	3-2	3-2	4-1		0-2	2-1
14	Torpedo Minsk	0-1	1-1	5-0	3-4	0-0	3-1	6-0	0-1	1-1	2-0	3-1	4-0	0-0		2-2
15	Torpedo ATF-Kadino Mogilev	3-1	0-2	1-0	1-0	0-1	2-2	3-0	0-3	0-1	0-1	0-0	1-1	0-3	0-1	

LEAGUE CHAMPIONSHIP FINAL TABLE 1998

			Home				Away				Total						
		P	W	D	L	F	A	W	D	L	F	A	W	D	L	F	A	P	GD
1	Dnepr-Transmash Mogilev	28	12	2	0	34	4	9	2	3	21	10	21	4	3	55	14	67	+41
2	BATE Borisov	28	11	1	2	30	7	7	3	4	20	18	18	4	6	50	25	58	+25
3	Belshina Bobruisk	28	11	3	0	35	10	6	3	5	12	7	17	6	5	47	17	57	+30
4	Lokomotiv-96 Vitebsk	28	8	2	4	18	9	6	4	4	17	15	14	6	8	35	24	48	+11
5	FC Gomel	28	10	3	1	21	8	2	6	6	15	22	12	9	7	36	30	45	+6
6	Slaviya Mozyr	28	7	3	4	23	19	5	6	3	18	17	12	9	7	41	36	45	+5
7	Torpedo Minsk	28	6	5	3	30	12	6	3	5	14	10	12	8	8	44	22	44	+22
8	Dinamo Minsk	28	5	5	4	18	17	6	1	7	21	21	11	6	11	39	38	39	+1
9	Dinamo Brest	28	6	2	6	23	17	6	0	8	17	23	12	2	14	40	40	38	0
10	Neman Grodno	28	4	4	6	14	18	4	3	7	13	26	8	7	13	27	44	31	-17
11	Shakhter Soligorsk	28	4	3	7	17	22	4	3	7	16	32	8	6	14	33	54	30	-21
12	Torpedo ATF-Kadino Mogilev	28	4	3	7	11	16	3	5	6	19	24	7	8	13	30	40	29	-10
13	Naftan-Devon Novopolotsk	28	5	2	7	26	23	2	2	10	7	24	7	4	17	33	47	25	-14
14	FC Molodechno	28	1	2	11	10	21	3	2	9	11	30	4	4	20	21	51	16	-30
15	Kommunalnik Slonim	28	3	4	7	10	22	0	1	13	4	41	3	5	20	14	63	14	-49

N.B. Where two or more teams are level on points, classification is determined by the results of the matches between them.

compete on an equal footing with those from Minsk and elsewhere.

The concept was matched by sound planning and investment, and the new team blossomed in double-quick time, taking over at the top of the table after seven rounds and pressing home their superiority with an astonishing 15-match winning run from early June through to mid-September that killed off any would-be challengers. The team were physically and mentally very strong, with an outstanding defence and midfield. During the course of the campaign they became noted for their ability to squeeze all the energy out of their opponents before finishing them off in the second half. Coach Streltsov proved to be an expert tactician, while Ukrainian Ihor Chumachenko, back at his former club after a spell in his homeland with Chornomorets Odesa, proved to be the team's leading light on the field, playing the role of midfield conductor (and goalscorer) to perfection.

Dnepr-Transmash were able to drop seven points in their final three games and still take the title by nine points from runners-up BATE Borisov, the other surprise package in the championship. The newly-promoted club were inspired by

EUROPEAN CUPS 98/99

CHAMPIONS' CUP
● DINAMO MINSK
Preliminary round SKONTO RIGA (LAT)
A 0-0
    Satsunkevich; Makarenko, Rodnenok (Mishchishin 46), Khrapkovskiy, Yermolenko, Ostrikov, Shilo, Chernyavskiy, Volodenkov, Osipovich, Vyazhevich.
H 1-2 Osipovich (26)
    Satsunkevich; Makarenko, Mishchishin, Khrapkovskiy, Yermolenko, Ostrikov (Lobanov 52), Shilo, Chernyavskiy (Rodnenok 57), Volodenkov, Osipovich, Vyazhevich (Lagodich 87).

CUP WINNERS' CUP
● LOKOMOTIV-96 VITEBSK
Qualifying round LEVSKI SOFIA (BUL)
A 1-8 Demenkovets (18p)
    Lyubchenko; Dyatlov (Yeremeyev 56), Kulanin, Kashkar, Konoplev (Sigov 46), Chernyshov, Sivkov (Malyavko 46), Rogozhkin, Demenkovets, Gormash, Vekhtev.

H 1-1 Sivkov (90)
    Lyubchenko; Dyatlov, Kulanin, Kashkar, Malyavko, Chernyshov, Rogozhkin, Yeremeyev, Demenkovets (Soldatov 63), Sivkov, Vekhtev.

UEFA CUP
● BELSHINA BOBRUISK
Preliminary round CSKA SOFIA (BUL)
H 0-0
    Zhemchugov; Kovalevich, Razumovich, Khripach, Timofeyev, Gradoboyev I., Gradoboyev E. (Levitskiy 41), Smirnykh, Balashov (Derban 80), Khlebosolov, Turchinovich (Ulezlo 61).
A 1-3 Balashov (50)
    Zhemchugov; Kovalevich, Razumovich, Khripach, Timofeyev, Gradoboyev I., Smirnykh (Derban 74), Balashov, Levitskiy (Gradoboyev E. 46), Khlesbosolov (Ulezlo 57), Turchinovich.

TOP SCORERS

19	Sergei YAROMKO (Torpedo Minsk)
16	Roman VASILYUK (Dinamo Brest)
	Valeriy STRIPEIKIS (Naftan-Devon Novopolotsk)
14	Dmitriy BALASHOV (Belshina Bobruisk)
12	Dmitriy OGORODNIK (Dnepr-Transmash Mogilev)
9	Ihor CHUMACHENKO (Dnepr-Transmash Mogilev)
	Sergei VEKHTEV (Lokomotiv-96 Vitebsk)
	Dmitriy DENISYUK (Slaviya Mozyr)
	Oleg KONONOV (Torpedo Minsk)

NATIONAL TEAM RESULTS 98/99

19/08/98	Lithuania	A	Vilnius	3-0	Ostrovskiy (43), Makovskiy V. (44), Romashchenko Max. (76)
05/09/98	Denmark (ECQ)	H	Minsk	0-0	
14/10/98	Wales (ECQ)	A	Cardiff	2-3	Gurenko (20), Belkevich (48)
09/02/99	Israel	A	Haifa	1-2	Baranov (28)
27/03/99	Switzerland (ECQ)	H	Minsk	0-1	
31/03/99	Italy (ECQ)	A	Ancona	1-1	Belkevich (24)
19/05/99	Russia	A	Tula	1-1	Tarlovskiy (47)
05/06/99	Denmark (ECQ)	A	Copenhagen	0-1	

the ambition of their young president Anatoliy Kapskiy, whose fervent attempt to put the club on the map included the building of a fine new stadium and a commitment to the development of young talent. Goalkeeper Vasiliy

Khomutovskiy is one rookie being tipped for a particularly fine future.

Belshina Bobruisk, unlucky runners-up in 1997, finished in third place a point behind BATE Borisov. They began

DOMESTIC CUP 98/99

1/16 FINALS
Svisloch-Krovlya Osipovichi 0, Belshina Bobruisk 3
Dinamo-Energogaz Vitebsk 3, Naftan-Devon Novopolotsk 3 (aet; 3-4 on pens.)
Polesiye Kozenki 0, Torpedo Minsk 1
FC Rogachev 0, FC Gomel 1
Kommunalnik Svetlogorsk 0, Kommunalnik Slonim 0 (aet; 4-3 on pens.)
Vedrich-97 Rechitsa 0, BATE Borisov 9
ZLIN Gomel 0, Dnepr-Transmash Mogilev 4
Veras Nesvizh 0, Slaviya Mozyr 2
Torpedo Zhodino 2, Dinamo Minsk 3
Belkard Grodno 0, Torpedo ATF-Kadino Mogilev 3
FC Lida 0, FC Molodechno 1
FC Bereza 1, Neman Grodno 2 (aet)
Zvezda-VA-BGU Minsk 2, Dinamo-93 Minsk 2 (aet; 5-4 on pens.)
FC Pinsk-900 1, Shakhter Soligorsk 2
Veino Mogilevskiy r-n 0, Lokomotiv-96 Vitebsk 4
Dinamo-Yuni Minsk 0, Dinamo Brest 1

1/8 FINALS
FC Molodechno 1, Shakhter Soligorsk 1 (aet; 8-7 on pens.)
BATE Borisov 7, Zvezda-VA-BGU Minsk 1
Torpedo Minsk 2, Kommunalnik Svetlogorsk 1
Dinamo Minsk 2, Slaviya Mozyr 4
Dnepr-Transmash Mogilev 2, Naftan-Devon Novopolotsk 0
Dinamo Brest 0, FC Gomel 2
Belshina Bobruisk 3, Lokomotiv-96 Vitebsk 0
Torpedo ATF-Kadino Mogilev 0, Neman Grodno 2

QUARTER-FINALS
BATE Borisov 2 (Klimovich 15og, Doroshkevich 67), Dnepr-Transmash Mogilev 1 (Ogorodnik 12)
Neman-Belcard Grodno 0, Belshina Bobruisk 1 (Gamanovich 81)
FC Gomel 0, Slaviya Mozyr 1 (Stripeikis 41)
FC Molodechno 1 (Yevseyenko 52), Torpedo-MAZ Minsk 3 (Yaromko 3, Shydakov 46, Kononov 72)

SEMI-FINALS
Slaviya Mozyr 2 (Malyukov 33, Matveichik 46), BATE Borisov 1 (Tikhomirov 67)
Belshina Bobruisk 1 (Borisik 68), Torpedo-MAZ Mogilev 0

FINAL
29/05/99, Minsk
BELSHINA BOBRUISK 1 Khlebosolov (9)
SLAVIYA MOZYR 1 Stripeikis (48)
(aet; 4-2 on pens.)
BELSHINA BOBRUISK - Shalai (Zhemchugov 46); Razumovich, Timofeyev, Shustikov, Barul (Gamanovich 54), Gradoboyev I., Gradoboyev E., Khripach (Mikhalev 74), Borisik, Khlebosolov, Turchinovich.
SLAVIYA MOZYR - Sinitsyn S.; Balin, Lukashenko, Apanas, Malyukov (Danilyuk 31), Chalei (Denisyuk 46), Antonovich (Kushnir 70), Karsakov, Somotov, Matveichik, Stripeikis.

PLAYER OF THE SEASON

ALEXANDER KHATSKEVICH
It was no surprise that the 1998 Belarus Footballer of the Year prize should go to a player no longer performing in the domestic league. In fact, the top three places in the poll were all occupied by exiles, with Dynamo Kiev's Alexander Khatskevich beating Spartak Moscow's Vasiliy Baranov and Lokomotiv Moscow's Sergei Gurenko into second and third place, respectively. Khatskevich, a muscular

midfielder, enjoyed an excellent season both for the Belarus national team and his club, returning from a five-match suspension to play a leading role in Kiev's passage to the semi-finals of the European Champions' Cup as well as assisting in their retention of the Ukrainian domestic 'double'. A classy all-rounder, he is always prepared to sacrifice individual glory for the benefit of the team and has a burning desire to win every game he plays.

poorly but managed eight wins and two draws in their final ten games, and that excellent form was carried forward into 1999, when they lifted the national Cup for the second time in three years courtesy of a penalty shoot-out victory in the final against Slaviya (ex-MPKC) Mozyr.

It was an early elimination from the UEFA Cup, by CSKA Sofia, which seemed to kick-start Belshina's campaign, and it was a similar story for Lokomotiv-96 Vitebsk, who also responded positively to being dismissed in Europe by Bulgarian opposition. The 1998 Cup-winners succeeded in climbing up the table into fourth place thanks to seven victories in their last ten fixtures.

The Belarus national team, coached by new Dinamo Minsk supremo Mikhail Vergeyenko, registered one of their best ever results when they drew 1-1 away to Italy in a Euro 2000 qualifier in March 1999. Unfortunately, that was just one of two points garnered from their first five qualifying matches, but the truth was that they performed satisfactorily in each and every game. The general verdict of the local press was that the team had shown that they could play but now had to prove that they could also win.

The fact that almost every national team player is currently exiled in neighbouring Russia and Ukraine, where the quality of football is considerably higher, serves to explain the improvements being made. And talented wing-back Sergei Gurenko's summer transfer from Lokomotiv Moscow to Roma can only further the reputation of Belarussian football - especially if he does himself justice in the hard, professional world of Italy's Serie A.

INTERNATIONAL HONOURS

None

NATIONAL TEAM APPEARANCES 98/99

Coach - Mikhail VERGEYENKO	LIT	DEN	WAL	ISR	SUI	ITA	RUS	DEN	Cps	Gls
Andrei SATSUNKEVICH (18/03/66) - Dinamo Minsk	G	G	G	s46					18	-
Erik YAKHIMOVICH (06/12/68) - Dinamo Moskva (RUS)	D	D	D	D	D	D	D	D	20	-
Andrei OSTROVSKIY (13/09/73) - Dinamo Moskva (RUS)	D53	D	D	D	s86	D	D	D46	19	1
Sergei SHTANYUK (13/08/73) - Dinamo Moskva (RUS)	D	D	D						18	1
Sergei GURENKO (30/09/72) - Lokomotiv Moskva (RUS)	D	D	D	D	D	D	D	D	34	2
Vyacheslav GERASHCHENKO (25/07/72) - Chernomorets Novorossiisk (RUS)	M	s40	M88	M56	M85		M26		13	-
Alexandr KHATSKEVICH (19/10/73) - Dynamo Kyiv (UKR)	M	M	M	M				M70	15	-
Vasiliy BARANOV (05/10/72) - Spartak Moskva (RUS)	M51	M	M69	M	M59	M	M	M	17	2
Valentin BELKEVICH (27/01/73) - Dynamo Kyiv (UKR)	M66	M	M		M	M		M	28	5
Sergei GERASIMETS (13/10/65) - Zenit Sankt-Peterburg (RUS)	M50		s69						24	7
Vladimir MAKOVSKIY (23/04/77) - Dynamo Kyiv (UKR)	A67	A89	A72	A74	A86	A	A73	A85	21	4
Alexandr CHAIKA (27/01/76) - Alania Vladikavkaz (RUS)	s50			M46	s59		s84		11	-
Radislav ORLOVSKIY (09/03/70) - Torpedo Moskva (RUS)	s51					M	M	M	18	2
Alexandr KULCHIY (01/11/73) - Dinamo Moskva (RUS)	s53			s56			s26	s70	18	2
Maxym ROMASHCHENKO (31/07/76) - Dinamo Moskva (RUS)	s66	s89	s88	A	A	A	A84	s46	9	2
Vasiliy MAZUR (11/03/72) - FC Gomel	s67			s74					3	-
Andrei LAVRIK (07/12/74) - Lokomotiv Moskva (RUS)		D	D	D	D	D	D		11	-
Myroslav ROMASHCHENKO (16/12/73) - Spartak Moskva (RUS)		M40							15	1
Petr KACHURO (02/08/72) - Sheffield United (ENG)			s72						23	4
Valeriy SHANTALOSOV (15/03/66) - Lokomotiv Nizhniy Novgorod (RUS)				G46					21	-
Igor TARLOVSKIY (21/09/74) - Alania Vladikavkaz (RUS)				M46			s46		2	1
Vadim SKRIPCHENKO (26/11/75) - BATE Borisov				s46	s85		D46		4	1
Dmitriy BALASHOV (08/01/74) - Belshina Bobruisk				s46					6	-
Gennadiy TUMILOVICH (03/09/71) - Zhemchuzhina Sochi (RUS)					G	G	G	G	5	-
Alexandr LUKHVICH (21/02/70) - Torpedo Moskva (RUS)					D	D		D	4	-
Nikolai RYNDYUK (02/02/78) - Lokomotiv Moskva (RUS)							s73	s85	3	1

BATE BORISOV

CLUB DIRECTORY

BATE Borisov
boulevard Komarov 28
222120 Borisov
tel - (01777) 254410
Year of Formation - 1996
President - Anatoliy Kapskiy
Coach - Yuriy Puntus
Stadium - City (4,000)

APPEARANCES 1998

	P	Ap	(s)	Gls
Alexei ADAMITSKIY	D	3	(1)	
Dmitriy AKULICH	M	8	(6)	1
Alexandr ARZAMASTSEV	M	11	(10)	
Alexei BAGA	M		(1)	
Alexandr Va. BARANOV	M	28		8
Anatoliy BUDAYEV	D	5		
Yuriy DOROSHKEVICH	M	23	(2)	8
Alexandr FEDOROVICH	G	17		
Viktor GONCHARENKO	M	19	(4)	
Artem GONCHARIK	A	1	(2)	
Dmitriy KAPELYAN	D	3		
Vasiliy KHOMUTOVSKIY	G	11		
Sergei KOZLOVSKIY	D	4		
Sergei KUKALEVICH	M	4	(3)	
Vitaliy KUTUZOV	A	9	(17)	5
Leonid LAGUN	M	6	(12)	3
Alexandr LISOVSKIY	M	19	(1)	7
Yevgeniy LOSHANKOV	M	11	(5)	2
Sergei MIROSHKIN	D	23	(1)	1
Vladimir NEVINSKIY	A	28		7
Kirill SAVOSTIKOV	M	13		1
Sergei SERGEL	A		(14)	2
Vitaliy SHIMKO	A	1	(2)	
Vadim SKRIPCHENKO	M	26		1
Yuriy TIKHOMIROV	D	16	(1)	3
Alexandr YERMAKOVICH	M	19	(1)	1

LEAGUE RESULTS 1998

12/04/98	FC Molodechno	A	2-1	Nevinskiy, Tikhomirov
18/04/98	Kommunalnik Slonim	A	3-1	Tikhomirov 2 (1p), Kutuzov
25/04/98	Naftan-Devon Novopolotsk	H	2-1	Miroshkin, Kutuzov
04/05/98	Dinamo Minsk	A	0-2	
09/05/98	Neman Grodno	H	3-0	Baranov 2, Lagun
18/05/98	Slaviya Mozyr	A	2-2	Lisovskiy, Kutuzov
22/05/98	FC Gomel	H	1-1	Baranov
03/06/98	Torpedo Minsk	H	0-1	
10/06/98	Torpedo ATF-Kadino Mogilev	A	1-3	Baranov
14/06/98	Belshina Bobruisk	H	1-0	Doroshkevich
18/06/98	Dinamo Brest	H	6-0	Doroshkevich 2, Lisovskiy 3, Kutuzov
25/06/98	Shakhter Soligorsk	A	5-3	Nevinskiy 2, Doroshkevich, Lagun, Sergel
01/07/98	Lokomotiv-96 Vitebsk	H	1-3	Nevinskiy
08/07/98	Dnepr-Transmash Mogilev	A	0-1	
25/07/98	FC Molodechno	H	3-0	Nevinskiy 2 (1p), Lagun
01/08/98	Kommunalnik Slonim	H	1-0	Loshankov
08/08/98	Naftan-Devon Novopolotsk	A	1-0	Yermakovich
15/08/98	Dinamo Minsk	H	3-0	Doroshkevich, Savostikov, Kutuzov
21/08/98	Neman Grodno	A	2-1	Baranov, Sergel
25/08/98	FC Gomel	A	0-0	
29/08/98	Slaviya Mozyr	H	2-0	Doroshkevich, Loshankov
13/09/98	Torpedo Minsk	A	1-0	Baranov
19/09/98	Torpedo ATF-Kadino Mogilev	H	4-1	Baranov, Skripchenko, Doroshkevich, Nevinskiy (p)
27/09/98	Belshina Bobruisk	A	0-4	
04/10/98	Dinamo Brest	A	3-0	Baranov, Lisovskiy, Akulich
17/10/98	Shakhter Soligorsk	H	2-0	Lisovskiy, Doroshkevich
24/10/98	Lokomotiv-96 Vitebsk	A	0-0	
31/10/98	Dnepr-Transmash Mogilev	H	1-0	Lisovskiy

BELSHINA BOBRUISK

CLUB DIRECTORY

FC Belshina Bobruisk
ul. Uyanovskaya 94A
213800 Bobruisk
tel - (02251) 40056/26705
Year of Formation - 1996
President - Arkadiy Polyakov
Coach - Igor Belov; Oleg Volokh; Lindas Rumbutis
Stadium - Spartak (4,800)

MAJOR HONOURS
Domestic Cup - (2) 1997, 1999.

APPEARANCES 1998

		P	Ap	(s)	Gls
Dmitriy BALASHOV	M	26	(2)	14
Alexandr BORISIK	A	1	(8)	
Vyacheslav DERBAN	M	5	(7)	
Eduard GRADOBOYEV	M	16	(7)	
Igor GRADOBOYEV	M	24		
Gennadiy KARASEV	M	1	(5)	
Andrei KHLEBOSOLOV	A	23		8
Andrei KHRIPACH	D	26		2
Igor KOVALEVICH	D	21		1
Roman LEVITSKIY	M	21	(7)	3
Dmitriy MIGAS	M	5	(11)	
Sergei RAZUMOVICH	D	21	(2)	1
Sergei SHALAI	G	12	(1)	
Igor SHUSTIKOV	D	14	(2)	
Vasiliy SMIRNYKH	M	22	(2)	3
Alexandr SYSOI	D	1	(2)	
Yevgeniy TIMOFEYEV	D	27		3
Andrei TURCHINOVICH	A	22	(2)	7
Sergei ULEZLO	A	4	(19)	5
Sergei ZHEMCHUGOV	G	16		

LEAGUE RESULTS 1998

12/04/98	Slaviya Mozyr	A	0-1	
18/04/98	Lokomotiv-96 Vitebsk	H	1-0	Levitskiy
25/04/98	FC Gomel	A	0-1	
04/05/98	Dnepr-Transmash Mogilev	H	1-1	Khlebosolov
18/05/98	FC Molodechno	H	1-0	Turchinovich
22/05/98	Torpedo Minsk	A	1-1	Timofeyev
30/05/98	Kommunalnik Slonim	H	5-1	Levitskiy 2, Balashov 2, Ulezlo
03/06/98	Torpedo ATF-Kadino Mogilev	A	2-0	Timofeyev (p), Smirnykh
10/06/98	Naftan-Devon Novopolotsk	H	6-0	Khlebosolov, Balashov 3, Ulezlo 2
14/06/98	BATE Borisov	A	0-1	
25/06/98	Dinamo Brest	H	2-0	Turchinovich, Balashov
01/07/98	Neman Grodno	H	0-0	
08/07/98	Shakhter Soligorsk	A	1-0	Khlebosolov
12/07/98	Dinamo Minsk	H	4-2	Khlebosolov, Timofeyev, Turchinovich, Ulezlo
25/07/98	Slaviya Mozyr	H	4-4	Khlebosolov 2, Smirnykh, Turchinovich
02/08/98	Lokomotiv-96 Vitebsk	A	0-1	
07/08/98	FC Gomel	H	2-0	Balashov 2
15/08/98	Dnepr-Transmash Mogilev	A	0-1	
25/08/98	Torpedo Minsk	H	1-0	Balashov
29/08/98	FC Molodechno	A	1-0	Smirnykh
09/09/98	Kommunalnik Slonim	A	1-1	Razumovich
13/09/98	Torpedo ATF-Kadino Mogilev	H	2-1	Balashov, Khlebosolov
19/09/98	Naftan-Devon Novopolotsk	A	1-0	Khlebosolov
27/09/98	BATE Borisov	H	4-0	Kovalevich, Balashov 3
04/10/98	Dinamo Minsk	A	0-0	
17/10/98	Dinamo Brest	A	3-0	Turchinovich 2, Balashov
24/10/98	Neman Grodno	A	2-0	Khripach, Ulezlo
31/10/98	Shakhter Soligorsk	H	2-1	Turchinovich, Khripach

DINAMO BREST

CLUB DIRECTORY

Dinamo Brest
ul. N. Gogol 9
224000 Brest
tel - (0162) 264283/265221
fax - (0162) 264283
Year of Formation - 1976
President - Nikolai Shirinskiy
Coach - Alexandr Razin
Stadium - Dinamo (15,000)

APPEARANCES 1998

	P	Ap	(s)	Gls
Andrei ASHIKHMIN	G	5	(1)	
Alexandr GERASIMUK	M	14	(1)	2
Denis GOLUBOVSKIY	A	5	(8)	
Sergei GRIB	D	23	(2)	1
Yuriy KHOMKO	D	23	(2)	1
Sergei P. KOVALCHUK	M	3	(4)	
Sergei KOVALYUK	A		(3)	
Vadim LASOVSKIY	D	14		
Mikhail LITVINCHUK	A	8	(2)	
Andrei OLSHEVSKIY	D	5	(1)	
Andrei PROKOPYUK	A	23	(1)	2
Andrei RAZIN	A		(14)	3
Vadim SAVCHUK	D	22	(2)	4
Maxim SHCHERBIN	M	16		4
Dmitriy SIIKINDERUK	M		(1)	
Andrei SLADINSKIY	D		(6)	
Vladimir SOROCHINSKIY (KAZ)	D	17	(4)	
Andrei SOSNITSKIY	D	6		2
Dmitriy STRACHKO	D	27		
Oleg STRAKHANOVICH	M	20	(4)	4
Viktor SYCHIK	D	5	(3)	
Andrei VASILIYEV	M	26		
Roman VASILYUK	A	23	(5)	16
Dmitriy VIRKO	G	23	(1)	

LEAGUE RESULTS 1998

12/04/98	Dnepr-Transmash Mogilev	H	2-0	Sosnitskiy, Vasilyuk
18/04/98	FC Molodechno	A	2-0	Gerasimuk, Strakhanovich
25/04/99	Kommunalnik Slonim	H	0-0	
04/05/98	Naftan-Devon Novopolotsk	A	3-1	Vasilyuk, Savchuk, Sosnitskiy
09/05/98	Dinamo Minsk	H	0-1	
18/05/98	Neman Grodno	A	1-2	Strakhanovich
22/05/98	Slaviya Mozyr	H	1-2	Savchuk
30/05/98	FC Gomel	A	0-1	
09/06/98	Torpedo Minsk	A	0-5	
14/06/98	Torpedo ATF-Kadino Mogilev	A	0-1	
18/06/98	BATE Borisov	A	0-6	
25/06/98	Belshina Bobruisk	A	0-2	
01/07/98	Shakhter Soligorsk	H	5-0	Strakhanovich, Vasilyuk, Shcherbin 2, Khomko
08/07/98	Lokomotiv-96 Vitebsk	A	1-0	Vasilyuk
25/07/98	Dnepr-Transmash Mogilev	A	0-2	
01/08/98	FC Molodechno	H	6-3	Strakhanovich, Vasilyuk 3, Razin, Gerasimuk (p)
08/08/98	Kommunalnik Slonim	A	0-1	
15/08/98	Naftan-Devon Novopolotsk	H	1-0	Vasilyuk
21/08/98	Dinamo Minsk	A	5-0	Prokopyuk, Savchuk, Vasilyuk 2, Razin
25/08/98	Slaviya Mozyr	A	2-1	Grib, og (Polyakov)
29/08/98	Neman Grodno	H	1-2	Razin
09/09/98	FC Gomel	H	2-1	Vasilyuk 2 (1p)
19/09/98	Torpedo Minsk	H	4-0	Prokopyuk, Savchuk, Vasilyuk 2
27/09/98	Torpedo ATF-Kadino Mogilev	H	1-1	Vasilyuk
04/10/98	BATE Borisov	H	0-3	
17/10/98	Belshina Bobruisk	H	0-3	
24/10/98	Shakhter Soligorsk	A	3-1	Shcherbin 2, Vasilyuk
31/10/98	Lokomotiv-96 Vitebsk	H	0-1	

DINAMO MINSK

Dinamo Minsk
4j-Zagorodnyi per. 58-B
220079 Minsk
tel - (0172) 2282944/2282945
fax - (0172) 2261694/2102416
Year of Formation - 1927
President - Mikhail Vergeyenko
Secretary - Leonid Vasilevskiy
Coach - Vladimir Kurnev; Mikhail Vergeyenko
Stadium - Dinamo (42,375)

MAJOR HONOURS
League Championship (USSR) - (1) 1982.
League Championship - (6) 1992, 1993, 1994,
1995 (spring), 1995 (autumn), 1997.
Domestic Cup - (1) 1992, 1994.

		P	Ap	(s)	Gls
Ruslan AZARENOK	M	3	(2)	1
Anatoliy BAIDACHNYI	M	8	(10)	1
Alexei BELOUSOV	D	8	(2)	
Oleg CHERNYAVSKIY	M	14	(1)	1
Sergei DEMIDCHIK	M		(1)	
Alexei DENISENYA	A	6	(4)	1
Pavel DOVGULEVETS	A	5	(2)	1
Andrei DOVNAR	D	9	(1)	1
Alexandr KHRAPKOVSKIY	D	13	(7)	2
Sergei KOVALCHUK	D	14	(1)	4
Yuriy LAGODICH	A	9	(5)	4
Andrei LOBANOV	A	3	(10)	6
Dmitriy MAKARENKO	M	21	(5)	
Vyacheslav MARCHENKO	M	4	(1)	1
Alexandr MISHCHISHIN	D	14	(3)	
Alexandr OSIPOVICH	M	17	(7)	1
Vladimir OSTRIKOV	M	16	(3)	3
Dmitriy PODREZ	M	6	(2)	1
Pavel RODNENOK	D	24	(1)	
Andrei SATSUNKEVICH	G	22		
Andrei SHILO	D	26	(1)	
Sergei SHUSHKEVICH	A	6	(2)	
Andrei VETELKIN	A	6	(3)	2
Vitaliy VOLODENKOV	M	22		1
Alexandr VYAZHEVICH	A	20	(3)	7
Dmitriy YEKIMOV	G	4		
Sergei YERMOLENKO	D	6		
Vladimir YURKEVICH	G	2		

18/04/98	Torpedo Minsk	H	0-0	
25/04/98	Torpedo ATF-Kadino Mogilev	A	0-1	
04/05/98	BATE Borisov	H	2-0	Lobanov, Chernyavskiy
09/05/98	Dinamo Brest	A	1-0	Dovgulevets
18/05/98	Shakhter Soligorsk	H	1-2	Podrez
22/05/98	Lokomotiv-96 Vitebsk	A	0-1	
30/05/98	Dnepr-Transmash Mogilev	H	2-1	Lobanov 2
03/06/98	FC Molodechno	A	3-0	Lagodich, Vyazhevich, Lobanov
10/06/98	Kommunalnik Slonim	H	3-0	Volodenkov, Lobanov, Lagodich
14/06/98	Naftan-Devon Novopolotsk	A	2-0	Baidachnyi, Vyazhevich
25/06/98	Neman Grodno	H	1-2	Lagodich
01/07/98	Slaviya Mozyr	A	0-0	
08/07/98	FC Gomel	H	2-2	Dovnar, Lobanov
12/07/98	Belshina Bobruisk	A	2-4	Vyazhevich, Osipovich (p)
02/08/98	Torpedo Minsk	A	4-3	Azarenok, Marchenko,
				Vyazhevich, Vetelkin
07/08/98	Torpedo ATF-Kadino Mogilev	H	2-1	og (Maximenko), Kovalchuk
15/08/98	BATE Borisov	A	0-3	
21/08/98	Dinamo Brest	H	0-5	
30/08/98	Shakhter Soligorsk	A	1-0	Vyazhevich
09/09/98	Dnepr-Transmash Mogilev	A	1-3	Vyazhevich
13/09/98	FC Molodechno	H	0-0	
19/09/98	Kommunalnik Slonim	A	0-1	
27/09/98	Naftan-Devon Novopolotsk	H	1-2	Khrapkovskiy
04/10/98	Belshina Bobruisk	H	0-0	
17/10/98	Neman Grodno	A	4-1	Ostrikov 2, Lagodich,
				Khrapkovskiy
21/10/98	Lokomotiv-96 Vitebsk	H	1-1	Ostrikov
24/10/98	Slaviya Mozyr	H	3-1	Kovalchuk 2, Vetelkin
31/10/98	FC Gomel	A	3-4	Vyazhevich, Kovalchuk, Denisenya

DNEPR-TRANSMASH MOGILEV

CLUB DIRECTORY

Dnepr-Transmash Mogilev
Zadorozhnoye shosse 21
212026 Mogilev
tel - (0222) 263009/263485
fax - (0222) 263485
Year of Formation - 1998
President - Valeriy Chertkov
Secretary - Igor Genisev
Coach - Valeriy Streltsov
Stadium - Spartak (11,200)

MAJOR HONOURS
League Championship - (1) 1998.

APPEARANCES 1998

	P	Ap	(s)	Gls
Sergei ASTAPCHIK	G	23		
Alexandr Vl. BARANOV	D	17	(3)	2
Eduard BOLTRUSHEVICH	D	28		4
Vitaliy BULYGA	A		(1)	
Ihor CHUMACHENKO (UKR)	M	27	(1)	9
Dmitriy KALACHEV	M	14	(12)	4
Yevgeniy KAPOV	M	4	(12)	
Igor KHARLAN	G	5	(3)	
Vladimir KLIMOVICH	D	27		
Yevgeniy KOZLOV	A	9	(13)	8
Vitaliy LANKO	M	14	(13)	8
Dmitriy LIKHTAROVICH	M	25	(2)	2
Alexei LITVINKO	M		(1)	
Yuriy LUKASHOV	M	25	(1)	1
Viktor MASYUK (UKR)	M	5	(1)	
Dmitriy OGORODNIK	A	20	(8)	12
Vladimir SHUNEIKO	D	27		
Vladimir SOLODUKHIN	A	10	(5)	3
Yaroslav SVERDLOV	M	27	(1)	1
Alexandr VOLSKIY	D	1	(2)	
Viktor VRUBLEVSKIY	M		(2)	

LEAGUE RESULTS 1998

12/04/98	Dinamo Brest	A	0-2	
18/04/98	Shakhter Soligorsk	H	4-0	Baranov 2, Solodukhin, Ogorodnik
25/04/98	Lokomotiv-96 Vitebsk	A	1-0	Solodukhin
04/05/98	Belshina Bobruisk	A	1-1	Boltrushevich
09/05/98	FC Molodechno	H	5-0	Boltrushevich, Ogorodnik 2, Kozlov 2
18/05/98	Kommunalnik Slonim	A	5-0	Chumachenko, Boltrushevich (p), Kozlov 3
22/05/98	Naftan-Devon Novopolotsk	H	2-0	Lanko 2
30/05/98	Dinamo Minsk	A	1-2	Lanko
04/06/98	Neman Grodno	H	3-0	Chumachenko, Lanko, Ogorodnik
10/06/98	Slaviya Mozyr	A	3-1	Chumachenko, Boltrushevich (p), Solodukhin
14/06/98	FC Gomel	H	3-0	Kozlov 2, Chumachenko
24/06/98	Torpedo Minsk	H	1-0	Likhtarovich
01/07/98	Torpedo ATF-Kadino Mogilev	A	1-0	Lanko
08/07/98	BATE Borisov	H	1-0	Ogorodnik
25/07/98	Dinamo Brest	H	2-0	Lanko 2
01/08/98	Shakhter Soligorsk	A	3-1	Sverdlov, Ogorodnik 2
08/08/98	Lokomotiv-96 Vitebsk	H	2-0	Kozlov, Chumachenko
15/08/98	Belshina Bobruisk	H	1-0	Chumachenko
21/08/98	FC Molodechno	A	2-1	Ogorodnik, Lukashov
25/08/98	Naftan-Devon Novopolotsk	A	1-0	og (Bitikin)
29/08/98	Kommunalnik Slonim	H	4-0	Chumachenko, Ogorodnik 2, Kalachev
09/09/98	Dinamo Minsk	H	3-1	Chumachenko, Kalachev, Lanko
13/09/98	Neman Grodno	A	1-0	Kalachev
19/09/98	Slaviya Mozyr	H	1-1	Ogorodnik
27/09/98	FC Gomel	A	2-1	Kalachev, Chumachenko
16/10/98	Torpedo Minsk	A	0-0	
24/10/98	Torpedo ATF-Kadino Mogilev	H	2-2	Ogorodnik, Likhtarovich
31/10/98	BATE Borisov	A	0-1	

FC GOMEL

CLUB DIRECTORY

FC Gomel
ul. Bogdanova 7
246031 Gomel
tel - (0232) 507773/524019
fax - (0232) 504418
Year of Formation - 1995
President - Semen Voronchuk
Secretary - Sergei Vershinin
Coach - Valeriy Yanochkin
Stadium - Centralnyi (10,000)

APPEARANCES 1998

	P	Ap	(s)	Gls
Alexandr AFANASENKO	A	2	(16)	
Vladimir BLAGODAROV	M		(2)	
Viktor BOREL	A	18	(5)	8
Dmitriy BORISOV (RUS)	M	1	(2)	
Igor DOLINOV	D	8	(14)	
Vasiliy DROZDOV	D	23	(3)	
Sergei FEDOROVICH	D	26	(2)	2
Igor FROLOV	A	1	(7)	1
Andrei KLIMENOK	D	12	(5)	
Vyacheslav LEVCHUK	D	25	(2)	
Vasiliy MAZUR	A	28		5
Alexei MERKULOV	G	14		
Yevgeniy NEDUGOV	A		(2)	
Sergei NIKITENKO	M	21	(5)	2
Serhiy NYKONCHUK (UKR)	A	22	(6)	5
Vladimir RYZHCHENKO	G	14		
Fedor SIKORSKIY	M	24		
Oleg SYSOYEV	D	28		4
Sergei TERIKHOV	M	16	(7)	1
Andrei YUSIPETS	M	25		7
Dmitriy ZALESSKIY	A		(1)	

LEAGUE RESULTS 1998

12/04/98	Neman Grodno	H	2-0	Yusipets, Sysoyev
18/04/98	Slaviya Mozyr	A	1-1	Nykonchuk
25/04/98	Belshina Bobruisk	H	1-0	Nykonchuk
10/05/98	Torpedo Minsk	A	1-3	Nikitenko
18/05/98	Torpedo ATF-Kadino Mogilev	H	0-0	
22/05/98	BATE Borisov	A	1-1	Borel
30/05/98	Dinamo Brest	H	1-0	Mazur
03/06/98	Shakhter Soligorsk	A	2-1	Borel 2
09/06/98	Lokomotiv-96 Vitebsk	H	3-0	Borel, Yusipets, Nykonchuk
14/06/98	Dnepr-Transmash Mogilev	A	0-3	
18/06/98	FC Molodechno	H	1-0	Nykonchuk
25/06/98	Kommunalnik Slonim	A	3-0	Borel, Terikhov, Yusipets
01/07/98	Naftan-Devon Novopolotsk	H	2-0	Sysoyev, Yusipets
08/07/98	Dinamo Minsk	A	2-2	Sysoyev, Mazur
25/07/98	Neman Grodno	A	1-1	Borel
01/08/98	Slaviya Mozyr	H	0-0	
07/08/98	Belshina Bobruisk	A	0-2	
21/08/98	Torpedo Minsk	H	2-1	Yusipets, Nykonchuk
25/08/98	BATE Borisov	H	0-0	
29/08/98	Torpedo ATF-Kadino Mogilev	A	2-2	Nikitenko, Fedorovich
09/09/98	Dinamo Brest	A	1-2	Mazur
13/09/98	Shakhter Soligorsk	H	2-1	og (Tishkov), Borel
19/09/98	Lokomotiv-96 Vitebsk	A	1-2	Yusipets (p)
27/09/98	Dnepr-Transmash Mogilev	H	1-2	Yusipets (p)
04/10/98	FC Molodechno	A	0-0	
17/10/98	Kommunalnik Slonim	H	2-1	Frolov, Sysoyev
24/10/98	Naftan-Devon Novopolotsk	A	0-2	
31/10/98	Dinamo Minsk	H	4-3	Fedorovich, Borel, Mazur 2

KOMMUNALNIK SLONIM

CLUB DIRECTORY

Kommunalnik Slonim
ul. A. Pushkina 57 A
231800 Slonim
tel - (01562) 25776/25176/23933
fax - (01562) 23429/25358
Year of Formation - 1996
President - Oleg Laktyushin
Coach - Alexei Shubenok; Yakov Shapiro;
Alexei Shubenok
Stadium - Yunost (5,000)

APPEARANCES 1998

	P	Ap	(s)	Gls
Alexei ADAMITSKIY	D	13		
Andrei ADAMITSKIY	M	1		
Alexei BAL	M	23		
Alexandr BULOICHIK	D	1	(2)	
Yuriy DANILEVICH	A	1	(1)	
Anatoliy DEGIL	M	27		2
Valentin DEGIL	M	7	(8)	
Andrei DIVAKOV	M	13	(1)	1
Nikolai DYM	D	12	(5)	
Gennadiy FEOKTISTOV	M	2	(3)	
Sergei KAPANETS	D	9	(1)	
Dmitriy KAPELYAN	D	13		
Andrei KHMELEV	D	4		
Oleg KIRENYA	M	12	(9)	
Igor KIRKIZH	G	26		
Valeriy KOLYADCHIK	M	7	(2)	
Sergei KOZLOVSKIY	D	13	(1)	
Nikita MALYI	A	5	(5)	
Alexei PANKOVETS	M		(5)	
Sergei PASHKEVICH	D	11		
Andrei POGOTSKIY	M	3	(1)	
Oleg SAVITSKIY	A	19	(5)	3
Yevgeniy SAVON	A	15	(4)	2
Vladimir SHUPILOV	M	15	(5)	2
Georgi TATARASHVILI (GEO)	A	16	(10)	4
Andrei TOLMACH	A	3	(4)	
Viktor TRUSILO	G	2	(1)	
Andrei TSYBULKO	D	14	(3)	
Alexandr VORONIN	D	13		
Sergei VRUBLEVSKIY	M		(3)	
Vladimir YANKOVSKIY	D	8		

LEAGUE RESULTS 1998

12/04/98	Torpedo ATF-Kadino Mogilev	A	0-3	
18/04/98	BATE Borisov	H	1-3	Tatarashvili
25/04/98	Dinamo Brest	A	0-0	
04/05/98	Shakhter Soligorsk	H	0-0	
09/05/98	Lokomotiv-96 Vitebsk	A	0-2	
18/05/98	Dnepr-Transmash Mogilev	H	0-5	
22/05/98	FC Molodechno	A	2-5	Savon, Tatarashvili
30/05/98	Belshina Bobruisk	A	1-5	Savon
03/06/98	Naftan-Devon Novopolotsk	H	0-0	
10/06/98	Dinamo Minsk	A	0-3	
14/06/98	Neman Grodno	H	1-2	Degil A.
18/06/98	Slaviya Mozyr	A	0-2	
25/06/98	FC Gomel	H	0-3	
08/07/98	Torpedo Minsk	H	0-0	
25/07/98	Torpedo ATF-Kadino Mogilev	H	0-2	
01/08/98	BATE Borisov	A	0-1	
08/08/98	Dinamo Brest	H	1-0	Divakov (p)
15/08/98	Shakhter Soligorsk	A	0-2	
21/08/98	Lokomotiv-96 Vitebsk	H	2-3	Shupilov, Tatarashvili
25/08/98	FC Molodechno	H	3-1	Degil A., Shupilov, Savitskiy
29/08/98	Dnepr-Transmash Mogilev	A	0-4	
09/09/98	Belshina Bobruisk	H	1-1	Savitskiy
13/09/98	Naftan-Devon Novopolotsk	A	0-4	
19/09/98	Dinamo Minsk	H	1-0	Tatarashvili
27/09/98	Neman Grodno	A	0-2	
04/10/98	Slaviya Mozyr	H	0-2	
17/10/98	FC Gomel	A	1-2	Savitskiy
31/10/98	Torpedo Minsk	A	0-6	

LOKOMOTIV-96 VITEBSK

CLUB DIRECTORY

Lokomotiv-96 Vitebsk
ul. Karl Marx 2A
210001 Vitebsk
tel - (0212) 378574
Year of Formation - 1996
President - Igor Lobanov
Secretary - Eduard Verkhovskiy
Coach - Vyacheslav Akshayev
Stadium - Dinamo (5,500)

MAJOR HONOURS
Domestic Cup - (1) 1998.

APPEARANCES 1998

	P	Ap	(s)	Gls
Vitaliy ALESHCHENKO	M	1	(6)	2
Vyacheslav BELEI	D	1	(2)	
Sergei CHERNYSHOV	M	21	(2)	1
Eduard DEMENKOVETS	M	27		4
Vasiliy DYATLOV	D	26	(1)	
Vyacheslav GORMASH	A	24	(4)	7
Gennadiy KASHKAR	D	21	(3)	
Yuriy KONOPLEV	D	10		
Artem KOSAK	D	4	(3)	
Sergei KULANIN	D	20	(3)	1
Andrei LYUBCHENKO	G	15	(1)	
Viktor MALYAVKO	A	10	(13)	
Maxim RAZUMOV	A	12	(1)	2
Vitaliy ROGOZHKIN	M	26	(1)	3
Vladimir SELKIN	G	13		
Vitaliy SIGOV	D	10	(4)	
Andrei SIVKOV	A	26	(1)	2
Alexei SOLDATOV	M	1	(6)	
Igor TRUKHOV	M		(3)	
Sergei VEKHTEV	A	17	(9)	9
Oleg VOROPAYEV	D	13	(5)	
Sergei YEREMEYEV	M	10	(8)	3

LEAGUE RESULTS 1998

12/04/98	Shakhter Soligorsk	A	1-1	Demenkovets
18/04/98	Belshina Bobruisk	A	0-1	
25/04/98	Dnepr-Transmash Mogilev	H	0-1	
04/05/98	FC Molodechno	A	2-1	Gormash, Razumov
09/05/98	Kommunalnik Slonim	H	2-0	Rogozhkin 2
18/05/98	Naftan-Devon Novopolotsk	A	1-1	Kulanin (p)
22/05/98	Dinamo Minsk	H	1-0	Gormash
30/05/98	Neman Grodno	A	0-0	
03/06/98	Slaviya Mozyr	H	3-0	Vekhtev 2 (1p), Gormash
09/06/98	FC Gomel	A	0-3	
17/06/98	Torpedo Minsk	A	1-0	Razumov
24/06/98	Torpedo ATF-Kadino Mogilev	H	1-1	Rogozhkin
01/07/98	BATE Borisov	A	3-1	Vekhtev 2, Yeremeyev
08/07/98	Dinamo Brest	H	0-1	
25/07/98	Shakhter Soligorsk	H	1-2	Vekhtev
02/08/98	Belshina Bobruisk	H	1-0	Vekhtev
08/08/98	Dnepr-Transmash Mogilev	A	0-2	
17/08/98	FC Molodechno	H	1-2	Yeremeyev
21/08/98	Kommunalnik Slonim	A	3-2	Chernyshov, Gormash 2
31/08/98	Naftan-Devon Novopolotsk	H	2-1	Vekhtev 2
09/09/98	Neman Grodno	H	3-0	Demenkovets 2 (1p), Gormash
13/09/98	Slaviya Mozyr	A	1-2	Aleshchenko
19/09/98	FC Gomel	H	2-1	Demenkovets, Aleshchenko
04/10/98	Torpedo Minsk	H	1-0	Vekhtev
17/10/98	Torpedo ATF-Kadino Mogilev	A	3-0	Sivkov, Yeremeyev, Gormash
21/10/98	Dinamo Minsk	A	1-1	Sivkov
24/10/98	BATE Borisov	H	0-0	
31/10/98	Dinamo Brest	A	1-0	og (Khomko)

FC MOLODECHNO

FC Molodechno
ul. M. Masherov 6 A
223310 Molodechno
tel - (01773) 52444
fax - (01773) 54582
Year of Formation - 1993
President - Yuriy Lukin
Coach - Vladimir Golubko; Yuriy Lukin;
Leonid Kuchuk
Stadium - Metallurg (5,500)

APPEARANCES 1998

	P	Ap	(s)	Gls
Nikolai ABRAMOVICH	G	15	(1)	
Alexandr ANDROSIK	D	25	(1)	
Sergei DEMIDCHIK	A	8	(1)	2
Dmitriy DROZHZHA	M	4	(4)	
Alexandr GAVLUSH	A	8	(4)	
Alexandr GUKAILO	M		(1)	
Dmitriy KABELSKIY	D	1	(3)	
Sergei KABELSKIY	D	26		2
Sergei KAPANETS	D		(2)	
Dmitriy KAPLENKO	D	3	(4)	1
Alexandr KLIMOVICH	D	27	(1)	1
Dmitriy KOLTOVICH	M	19	(8)	2
Sergei KOLTUNOVSKIY	D	19	(2)	
Vladimir KORYTKO	M	2	(5)	
Vladimir KOZLOV	A	5	(4)	1
Vitaliy KOZYAK	M	23	(1)	2
Alexei KRIVITSKIY	M	15	(7)	
Alexandr LEBEDEV	D	25	(2)	
Viktor LEDOVSKICH	A	1	(2)	
Vladimir LIS	D	9	(4)	
Alexandr MAKEI	A	1	(2)	
Vitaliy MAKRITSKIY	A		(1)	
Nikita MALYI	A	7	(4)	5
Vitaliy MIKHALEV	D	25	(3)	1
Pavel MIRONCHIK	M	6	(1)	
Dmitriy NEDELKO	M	2		
Ruslan NOSKOV	A		(3)	
Alexandr OSTRIKOV	M	1	(6)	
Maxim PESETSKIY	G	6		
Sergei PONOMAREV	G	1		
Taras SHAMSHORIK	M	13	(1)	3
Alexandr SINKOVETS	D	5		1
Stanislav TISHCHENKO (RUS)	G	6		

LEAGUE RESULTS 1998

12/04/98	BATE Borisov	H	1-2	Malyi
18/04/98	Dinamo Brest	H	0-2	
25/04/98	Shakhter Soligorsk	A	0-1	
04/05/98	Lokomotiv-96 Vitebsk	H	1-2	Malyi
09/05/98	Dnepr-Transmash Mogilev	A	0-5	
18/05/98	Belshina Bobruisk	A	0-1	
22/05/98	Kommunalnik Slonim	H	5-2	Malyi 3, Kaplenko, Koltovich (p)
30/05/98	Naftan-Devon Novopolotsk	A	1-5	Kozyak
03/06/98	Dinamo Minsk	H	0-3	
10/06/98	Neman Grodno	A	0-2	
14/06/98	Slaviya Mozyr	H	0-1	
18/06/98	FC Gomel	A	0-1	
30/06/98	Torpedo Minsk	A	1-1	Shamshorik
08/07/98	Torpedo ATF-Kadino Mogilev	H	1-2	Kabelskiy S.
25/07/98	BATE Borisov	A	0-3	
01/08/98	Dinamo Brest	A	3-6	Demidchik, Shamshorik 2
08/08/98	Shakhter Soligorsk	H	0-1	
17/08/98	Lokomotiv-96 Vitebsk	A	2-1	Sinkovets, Kozyak
21/08/98	Dnepr-Transmash Mogilev	H	1-2	Koltovich (p)
25/08/98	Kommunalnik Slonim	A	1-3	Demidchik
29/08/98	Belshina Bobruisk	H	0-1	
09/09/98	Naftan-Devon Novopolotsk	H	0-0	
13/09/98	Dinamo Minsk	A	0-0	
19/09/98	Neman Grodno	H	1-2	Mikhalev
27/09/98	Slaviya Mozyr	A	2-1	Kozlov, Klimovich
04/10/98	FC Gomel	H	0-0	
24/10/98	Torpedo Minsk	H	0-1	
31/10/98	Torpedo ATF-Kadino Mogilev	A	1-0	Kabelskiy S.

NAFTAN-DEVON NOVOPOLOTSK

CLUB DIRECTORY

Naftan-Devon Novopolotsk
ul. Molodezhnaya 49 A
211440 Novopolotsk
tel - (02144) 57740/50605
Year of Formation - 1995
President - Anatoliy Artyukh
Coach - Alexandr Traiduk
Stadium - Atlant (7,000)

APPEARANCES 1998

	P	Ap	(s)	Gls
Sergei ALANTSOV	M		(1)	
Lev BARABANOV	D	28		
Igor BATURIN	G	3	(2)	
Valeriy BITKIN (RUS)	M	4	(9)	1
Vyacheslav BOGUSH	A		(7)	1
Alexandr CHAPKOVSKIY	D	18	(1)	1
Vitaliy GAMANOVICH	M	27	(1)	6
Vladimir GAVRILENKO	D	1	(5)	
Ruslan GNEDKOV	D	11	(7)	
Andrei GORNOSTAYEV	A	21	(3)	2
Viktor IGNATIYEV	G	21		
Dmitriy KURAKIN	A	1	(5)	
Andrei KUZMIN	G	4		
Vladimir LOMAKO	D	7	(2)	
Anatoliy MIKHNEVICH	D		(7)	
Yuriy NIKITOCHKIN	A	7	(3)	1
Sergei SALYGO	D	27		
Sergei SHEVCHENKO	A	15	(3)	1
Oleg SIDORENKOV	D	1	(1)	
Alexandr SOKOLOV	M	5		
Igor SOROKA	M	11	(13)	
Vitaliy STRIPEIKIS	A	27		16
Vitaliy TARAKANOV	M	28		2
Vitaliy TIKHOMIROV	M	22		2
Dmitriy TIMOFEYEV	M		(1)	
Andrei YEROKHIN	M	19	(3)	

LEAGUE RESULTS 1998

Date	Opponent	H/A	Score	Scorers
13/04/98	Torpedo Minsk	A	0-2	
18/04/98	Torpedo ATF-Kadino Mogilev	H	3-1	Shevchenko, Gamanovich 2 (2p)
25/04/98	BATE Borisov	A	1-2	Gamanovich
04/05/98	Dinamo Brest	H	1-3	Stripeikis
09/05/98	Shakhter Soligorsk	A	0-2	
18/05/98	Lokomotiv-96 Vitebsk	H	1-1	Tikhomirov
22/05/98	Dnepr-Transmash Mogilev	A	0-2	
30/05/98	FC Molodechno	H	5-1	Gornostayev, Stripeikis 3 (1p), Bogush
03/06/98	Kommunalnik Slonim	A	0-0	
10/06/98	Belshina Bobruisk	A	0-6	
14/06/98	Dinamo Minsk	H	0-2	
18/06/98	Neman Grodno	A	0-1	
25/06/98	Slaviya Mozyr	H	0-1	
01/07/98	FC Gomel	A	0-2	
25/07/98	Torpedo Minsk	H	1-5	Stripeikis (p)
01/08/98	Torpedo ATF-Kadino Mogilev	A	1-0	Gamanovich
08/08/98	BATE Borisov	H	0-1	
15/08/98	Dinamo Brest	A	0-1	
21/08/98	Shakhter Soligorsk	H	4-4	Bitkin, Tikhomirov, Stripeikis 2
25/08/98	Dnepr-Transmash Mogilev	H	0-1	
31/08/98	Lokomotiv-96 Vitebsk	A	1-2	Gornostayev
09/09/98	FC Molodechno	A	0-0	
13/09/98	Kommunalnik Slonim	H	4-0	Stripeikis 3 (2p), Chapkovskiy
19/09/98	Belshina Bobruisk	H	0-1	
27/09/98	Dinamo Minsk	A	2-1	Tarakanov 2
04/10/98	Neman Grodno	H	5-2	Gamanovich 2, Stripeikis 3 (1p)
17/10/98	Slaviya Mozyr	A	2-3	Stripeikis 2
24/10/98	FC Gomel	H	2-0	Nikitochkin, Stripeikis (p)

NEMAN GRODNO

CLUB DIRECTORY

Neman Grodno (now - Neman-Belcard Grodno)
ul. Kommunalnaya 3
230023 Grodno
tel - (0152) 453799/470971/723799
Year of Formation - 1964
President - Vasiliy Pirozhnik
Secretary - Stanislav Ulasevich
Coach - Vyacheslav Sivakov; Sergei Solodovnikov
Stadium - Neman (14,000)

MAJOR HONOURS
Domestic Cup - (1) 1993

APPEARANCES 1998

		P	Ap	(s)	Gls
Pavel BATYUTO	M	7		(7)	
Dmitriy BORISEIKO	A	22		(3)	4
Alexandr DAVIDOVICH	A	5		(14)	1
Sergei DOMASHEVICH	D	10		(1)	
Anatoliy DRACHILOVSKIY	D	6			2
Vladimir KASYUK	D	26			
Gennadiy KARASEV	M	9		(3)	2
Sergei KOROZA	M	1		(1)	
Artur KRIVONOS	M	22		(3)	1
Sergei LAGUTKO	A	5		(6)	2
Gennadiy MARDAS	D	26			
Yuriy MAZURCHIK	A	8		(15)	3
Vladimir MOZOLOVSKIY	D	22		(3)	3
Vitaliy NADIYEVSKIY	D	1			
Vladimir PETROV	M	17		(5)	1
Pavel PUZYNA	M	17		(5)	
Oleg RADUSHKO	D	23		(1)	
Dmitriy ROVNEIKO	D	8		(1)	
Albert RYBAK	G	24			
Dmitriy SAFRONOV	A	1			
Vitaliy TARASHCHIK	M	21		(4)	1
Sergei TSYBUL	A	22		(6)	7
Vladimir VASILEVSKIY	G	4			
Alexandr ZHILYUK	D	1		(2)	

LEAGUE RESULTS 1998

12/04/98	FC Gomel	A	0-2	
25/04/98	Torpedo Minsk	A	1-3	Mozolovskiy
04/05/98	Torpedo ATF-Kadino Mogilev	H	1-3	Petrov
09/05/98	BATE Borisov	A	0-3	
18/05/98	Dinamo Brest	H	2-1	Lagutko, Mozolovskiy
22/05/98	Shakhter Soligorsk	A	0-0	
30/05/98	Lokomotiv-96 Vitebsk	H	0-0	
04/06/98	Dnepr-Transmash Mogilev	A	0-3	
10/06/98	FC Molodechno	H	2-0	Tsybul, Mozolovskiy
14/06/98	Kommunalnik Slonim	A	2-1	Davidovich, Tsybul
18/06/98	Naftan-Devon Novopolotsk	H	1-0	Tsybul
25/06/98	Dinamo Minsk	A	2-1	Tsybul, Lagutko
01/07/98	Belshina Bobruisk	A	0-0	
08/07/98	Slaviya Mozyr	H	1-1	Krivonos
25/07/98	FC Gomel	H	1-1	Boriseiko
08/08/98	Torpedo Minsk	H	0-0	
14/08/98	Torpedo ATF-Kadino Mogilev	A	0-0	
21/08/98	BATE Borisov	H	1-2	Mazurchik
25/08/98	Shakhter Soligorsk	H	2-3	Boriseiko 2
29/08/98	Dinamo Brest	A	2-1	Karasev 2
09/09/98	Lokomotiv-96 Vitebsk	A	0-3	
13/09/98	Dnepr-Transmash Mogilev	H	0-1	
19/09/98	FC Molodechno	A	2-1	Mazurchik, Tarashchik
27/09/98	Kommunalnik Slonim	H	2-0	Boriseiko, Tsybul
04/10/98	Naftan-Devon Novopolotsk	A	2-5	Tsybul, Mazurchik
17/10/98	Dinamo Minsk	H	1-4	Tsybul
24/10/98	Belshina Bobruisk	H	0-2	
31/10/98	Slaviya Mozyr	A	2-3	Drachilovskiy 2

SHAKHTER SOLIGORSK

CLUB DIRECTORY

Shakhter-Belaruskaliy Soligorsk
ul. Maxim Gorkiy 1
Sportkomplex
223710 Soligorsk
tel - (01710) 20621
Year of Formation - 1963
President - Ivan Tupolskiy
Secretary - Sergei Cherevako
Coach - Ivan Shchekin
Stadium - Shakhter (5,000)

APPEARANCES 1998

	P	Ap	(s)	Gls
Vadim ARTAMONOV	M	6		2
Ruslan BELASH	A	3	(5)	
Dmitriy BESPANSKIY	M	12		2
Vadim BRAZOVSKIY	D	12	(1)	
Anatoliy BUDAYEV	D	12		
Andrei DROZD	G	16	(1)	
Alexandr KARPILENKO	D	4	(1)	
Vladimir KAVALENYA	M	2	(3)	
Vitaliy KIRIK	D	7	(7)	
Vitaliy KIRILKO	A	1	(4)	
Yuriy KROT	M	17	(3)	3
Ruslan LUKIN	A	1	(3)	
Andrei LYUBCHUK	M	28		1
Oleg MANCHAK	M		(1)	
Andrei MILEVSKIY	M	6	(8)	2
Vadim NARUSHEVICH	D	14	(2)	
Sergei NIKIFORENKO	A	10	(14)	4
Alexandr NOVIK	A	18	(8)	
Sergei PAVLYUCHUK	D	24		
Dmitriy PODREZ	M	13		2
Pavel SHAVROV	A	13		7
Sergei SHIROKIY	D	7	(3)	
Anatoliy TIKHONCHIK	A	23	(4)	4
Alexandr TISHKOV	D	9	(4)	1
Oleg VERAXA	D	4		
Vladimir VORONOV	D	16	(3)	1
Alexandr YEVNEVICH	G	12		
Sergei ZHURAVSKIY	M	18	(2)	3

LEAGUE RESULTS 1998

12/04/98	Lokomotiv-96 Vitebsk	H	1-1	Milevskiy
18/04/98	Dnepr-Transmash Mogilev	A	0-4	
25/04/98	FC Molodechno	H	1-0	Tikhonchik
04/05/98	Kommunalnik Slonim	A	0-0	
09/05/98	Naftan-Devon Novopolotsk	H	2-0	Zhuravskiy, Krot
18/05/98	Dinamo Minsk	A	2-1	Nikiforenko 2
22/05/98	Neman Grodno	H	0-0	
30/05/98	Slaviya Mozyr	A	1-4	Zhuravskiy
03/06/98	FC Gomel	H	1-2	Tikhonchik
13/06/98	Torpedo Minsk	H	0-3	
18/06/98	Torpedo ATF-Kadino Mogilev	A	1-1	Tikhonchik
25/06/98	BATE Borisov	H	3-5	Voronov, Nikiforenko 2
01/07/98	Dinamo Brest	A	0-5	
08/07/98	Belshina Bobruisk	H	0-1	
25/07/98	Lokomotiv-96 Vitebsk	A	2-1	Artamonov, Zhuravskiy
01/08/98	Dnepr-Transmash Mogilev	H	1-3	Shavrov
08/08/98	FC Molodechno	A	1-0	og (Klimovich)
15/08/98	Kommunalnik Slonim	H	2-0	Bespanskiy, Krot (p)
21/08/98	Naftan-Devon Novopolotsk	A	4-4	Artamonov, Lyubchuk, Podrez, Shavrov
25/08/98	Neman Grodno	A	3-2	Shavrov 2, Tishkov
30/08/98	Dinamo Minsk	H	0-1	
09/09/98	Slaviya Mozyr	H	2-2	Krot, Podrez
13/09/98	FC Gomel	A	1-2	Tikhonchik
27/09/98	Torpedo Minsk	A	0-4	
04/10/98	Torpedo ATF-Kadino Mogilev	H	3-1	Shavrov 3
17/10/98	BATE Borisov	A	0-2	
24/10/98	Dinamo Brest	H	1-3	Bespanskiy (p)
31/10/98	Belshina Bobruisk	A	1-2	Milevskiy

SLAVIYA MOZYR

CLUB DIRECTORY

Slaviya Mozyr
ul. Yanko Kupaly 26 A
247760 Mozyr
tel - (02315) 20194
fax - (02315) 23881
Year of Formation - 1995
President - Nikolai Yashchenko
Coach - Alexandr Bubnov; Alexandr Kuznetsov
Stadium - Yunost (7,500)

MAJOR HONOURS
League Championship - (1) 1996.
Domestic Cup - (1) 1996.

APPEARANCES 1998

		P	Ap	(s)	Gls
Valeriy APANAS	D	26			
Igor BALIN	D	20	(4)		
Levan BERISHVILI (GEO)	A	5	(7)		
Sergei BOIKO	M		(1)		
Dmitriy CHALEI	M	10	(4)	3	
Ruslan DANILYUK	D	9	(4)	1	
Dmitriy DENISYUK	M	19	(9)	9	
Alexandr DERINGOVSKIY	M		(1)		
Vladimir GAYEV	G	16			
Dmitriy KARSAKOV (RUS)	M	27		4	
Georgiy KONDRATIYEV	A	9	(2)	2	
Vasiliy KUSHNIR	A	1	(12)	2	
Vladislav LEMISH	A	3		1	
Yevgeniy LOVCHEV (RUS)	M		(3)		
Fedor LUKASHENKO	M	15		1	
Andrei LUKASHEVICH	D	18	(6)		
Yuriy MALEYEV	M	16	(1)	4	
Artur MATVEICHIK	M	26	(1)	1	
Sergei POLYAKOV	D	21	(1)	7	
Serei SINITSYN	G	12			
Igor SLESARCHUK	M	21	(6)	3	
Andrei SOSNITSKIY	D	6			
Maxim SUKHOVEYEV	M	3	(7)	2	
Mikhail VAVILOV	D	15	(4)		
Malkhaz VOSKANOV (GEO)	M	6	(1)		
Valeriy VYSOKOS (UKR)	M	4	(5)	1	

LEAGUE RESULTS 1998

12/04/98	Belshina Bobruisk	H	1-0	Lemish
18/04/98	FC Gomel	H	1-1	Polyakov
04/05/98	Torpedo Minsk	H	0-2	
09/05/98	Torpedo ATF-Kadino Mogilev	A	3-0	Kondratiyev, Maleyev, Denisyuk
18/05/98	BATE Borisov	H	2-2	Karsakov, Denisyuk
22/05/98	Dinamo Brest	A	2-1	Denisyuk, Matveichik
30/05/98	Shakhter Soligorsk	H	4-1	Karsakov, Denisyuk 2,
				Kondratiyev
03/06/98	Lokomotiv-96 Vitebsk	A	0-3	
10/06/98	Dnepr-Transmash Mogilev	H	1-3	Polyakov
14/06/98	FC Molodechno	A	1-0	Sukhoveyev
18/06/98	Kommunalnik Slonim	H	2-0	Sukhoveyev, Denisyuk
25/06/98	Naftan-Devon Novopolotsk	A	1-0	Kushnir
01/07/98	Dinamo Minsk	H	0-0	
08/07/98	Neman Grodno	A	1-1	Chalei
25/07/98	Belshina Bobruisk	A	4-4	Denisyuk, Lukashenko,
				Slesarchuk, Polyakov
01/08/98	FC Gomel	A	0-0	
15/08/98	Torpedo Minsk	A	0-0	
21/08/98	Torpedo ATF-Kadino Mogilev	H	2-1	Polyakov, Chalei
25/08/98	Dinamo Brest	H	1-2	Danilyuk
29/08/98	BATE Borisov	A	0-2	
09/09/98	Shakhter Soligorsk	A	2-2	Chalei, Karsakov (p)
13/09/98	Lokomotiv-96 Vitebsk	H	2-1	Maleyev, Polyakov (p)
19/09/98	Dnepr-Transmash Mogilev	A	1-1	Vysokos
27/09/98	FC Molodechno	H	1-2	Slesarchuk
04/10/98	Kommunalnik Slonim	A	2-0	Karsakov (p), Polyakov
17/10/98	Naftan-Devon Novopolotsk	H	3-2	Maleyev 2, Slesarchuk
24/10/98	Dinamo Minsk	A	1-3	Denisyuk
31/10/98	Neman Grodno	H	3-2	Polyakov, Kushnir, Denisyuk

TORPEDO MINSK

FC Torpedo-MAZ Minsk
ul. Kotovskogo 2
220021 Minsk
tel - (0172) 429949/430771
fax - (0172) 430811
Year of Formation - 1947
President - Viktor Bogmolov
Secretary - Valentina Lazebnaya
Coach - Anatoliy Yurevich
Stadium - Torpedo (7,000)

APPEARANCES 1998

	P	Ap	(s)	Gls
Oleg AVGUL	D	3	(3)	
Oleg CHEREPNEV	D	25	(1)	
Andrei DOVNAR	D	11	(1)	2
Ivan GALYUKHIN	A	8	(6)	3
Vladimir GOLMAK	D	28		
Boris GOROVOI	M	27		1
Alexandr GUKAILO	M		(1)	
Peter KAIE (NIG)	M	15	(10)	1
Oleg KAMYSHOV (RUS)	A	2	(8)	
Oleg KONONOV	D	27		9
Vladimir KONOVALOV	A	25	(2)	1
Viktor KUKAR	M	27		2
Vitaliy LESUN	A	1	(4)	1
Alexandr NOVASH	M		(2)	
Sergei PAVLYUKOVICH	M	16	(6)	2
Mohammed SANI (NIG)	M	8	(8)	
Nikolai SHVYDAKOV	M	2	(20)	1
Andrei SVIRKOV	G	18		
Yuriy SVIRKOV	G	10		
Dmitriy TROSKO	M	27		2
Sergei YAROMKO	A	28		19
Yevgeniy ZHUK	M		(5)	

LEAGUE RESULTS 1998

12/04/98	Naftan-Devon Novopolotsk	H	2-0	Trosko, Gorovoi
18/04/98	Dinamo Minsk	A	0-0	
25/04/98	Neman Grodno	H	3-1	Kononov, Yaromko (p), Shvydakov
04/05/98	Slaviya Mozyr	A	2-0	Konovalov, Yaromko
10/05/98	FC Gomel	H	3-1	Kononov, Yaromko 2
22/05/98	Belshina Bobruisk	H	1-1	Yaromko (p)
29/05/98	Torpedo ATF-Kadino Mogilev	H	2-2	Kononov, Yaromko (p)
03/06/98	BATE Borisov	A	1-0	Kononov
09/06/98	Dinamo Brest	H	5-0	Yaromko 3, Kononov, Lesun
13/06/98	Shakhter Soligorsk	A	3-0	Yaromko, Trosko, Kononov
17/06/98	Lokomotiv-96 Vitebsk	H	0-1	
24/06/98	Dnepr-Transmash Mogilev	A	0-1	
30/06/98	FC Molodechno	H	1-1	Yaromko (p)
08/07/98	Kommunalnik Slonim	A	0-0	
25/07/98	Naftan-Devon Novopolotsk	A	5-1	Galyukhin 2, Kononov, Kukar, Yaromko
02/08/98	Dinamo Minsk	H	3-4	Yaromko 2, Kaie
08/08/98	Neman Grodno	A	0-0	
15/08/98	Slaviya Mozyr	H	0-0	
21/08/98	FC Gomel	A	1-2	Pavlyukovich
25/08/98	Belshina Bobruisk	A	0-1	
08/09/98	Torpedo ATF-Kadino Mogilev	A	1-0	Yaromko
13/09/98	BATE Borisov	H	0-1	
19/09/98	Dinamo Brest	A	0-4	
27/09/98	Shakhter Soligorsk	H	4-0	Kononov 2, Yaromko 2 (1p)
04/10/98	Lokomotiv-96 Vitebsk	A	0-1	
16/10/98	Dnepr-Transmash Mogilev	H	0-0	
24/10/98	FC Molodechno	A	1-0	Pavlyukovich
31/10/98	Kommunalnik Slonim	H	6-0	Dovnar 2, Kukar, Yaromko 2 (1p), Galyukhin

TORPEDO ATF-KADINO MOGILEV

CLUB DIRECTORY

Torpedo ATF-Kadino Mogilev
Avenue Vitebsk 43
212004 Mogilev
tel - (0222) 422447
fax - (0222) 422894
Year of Formation - 1974
President - Alexandr Lakizo
Secretary - Vadim Krasnov
Coach - Mikhail Bass
Stadium - Torpedo (7,000)

APPEARANCES 1998

		P	Ap	(s)	Gls
Dmitriy BAIDA	A	11	(10)		5
Vyacheslav BANUL	M	27			1
Vitaliy BRONSKYI (UKR)	M		(3)		
Christopher CHE (CMR)	D	7	(1)		
Serhiy DEMUSHKIN (UKR)	D	12			
Yuriy FENIN (UKR)	A	6	(4)		1
Igor GORBACHEV	M	13	(1)		1
Vyacheslav KANASHEVICH	G	6			
Dmitriy KISELEV	D	5	(2)		
Igor KUTSENKO	A	4	(9)		1
Oleg KUZMENOK	M	20	(4)		5
Sergei KUZMINICH	M	9	(11)		
Alexandr LEPEKHO	M	19	(2)		1
Alexei MAXIMENKO	D	23	(2)		
Vyacheslav MIZYUK	M		(1)		
Andrei PAIOS	D	8	(2)		1
Valeriy PALAMARCHUK (UKR)	G	22			
Ruslan POKAZATSKIY	M	2	(4)		
Vladislav SAVCHUK	D	25	(2)		1
Andrei SKOROBOGATKO	M	19	(2)		5
Sergei TEPLYAKOV	D	9	(9)		
Vladimir TERESHCHENKO	A	3			1
Pavlo TSISLEVSKYI (UKR)	M	12	(2)		
Sergei VOITOVICH	D	24			3
Sergei ZAKHAROV (RUS)	D	11			
Sergei ZELINSKIY	D	11	(11)		3

LEAGUE RESULTS 1998

12/04/98	Kommunalnik Slonim	H	3-0	Baida 2 (1p), Skorobogatko
18/04/98	Naftan-Devon Novopolotsk	A	1-3	Kuzmenok
25/04/98	Dinamo Minsk	H	1-0	Lepekho (p)
04/05/98	Neman Grodno	A	3-1	Kuzmenok 2, Zelinskiy
09/05/98	Slaviya Mozyr	H	0-3	
18/05/98	FC Gomel	A	0-0	
29/05/98	Torpedo Minsk	A	2-2	Voitovich, Skorobogatko
03/06/98	Belshina Bobruisk	H	0-2	
10/06/98	BATE Borisov	H	3-1	Paios, og (Goncharenko), Baida
14/06/98	Dinamo Brest	H	1-0	Voitovich
18/06/98	Shakhter Soligorsk	H	1-1	Zelinskiy
24/06/98	Lokomotiv-96 Vitebsk	A	1-1	Barul
01/07/98	Dnepr-Transmash Mogilev	H	0-1	
08/07/98	FC Molodechno	A	2-1	Tereshchenko, Baida
25/07/98	Kommunalnik Slonim	A	2-0	Skorobogatko 2
01/08/98	Naftan-Devon Novopolotsk	H	0-1	
07/08/98	Dinamo Minsk	A	1-2	Zelinskiy
14/08/98	Neman Grodno	H	0-0	
21/08/98	Slaviya Mozyr	A	1-2	Fenin
29/08/98	FC Gomel	H	2-2	Gorbachev, Savchuk
08/09/98	Torpedo Minsk	H	0-1	
13/09/98	Belshina Bobruisk	A	1-2	Baida
19/09/98	BATE Borisov	A	1-4	Kuzmenok
27/09/98	Dinamo Brest	A	1-1	Skorobogatko
04/10/98	Shakhter Soligorsk	A	1-3	Kuzmenok
17/10/98	Lokomotiv-96 Vitebsk	H	0-3	
24/10/98	Dnepr-Transmash Mogilev	A	2-2	Voitovich, Kutsenko
31/10/98	FC Molodechno	H	0-1	

PROMOTED CLUBS

SECOND DIVISION FINAL TABLE 1998

		Pd	W	D	L	F	A	Pt	GD
1	FC Lida	30	23	5	2	65	19	74	+46
2	Svisloch-Krovlya Osipovichi	30	18	6	6	63	27	60	+36
3	FC Pinsk-900	30	17	8	5	54	22	59	+32
4	Dinamo-Yuni Minsk	30	17	5	8	61	36	56	+25
5	Torpedo Zhodino	30	15	10	5	58	31	55	+27
6	Vedrich-97 Rechitsa	30	13	6	11	42	37	45	+5
7	ZLIN Gomel	30	12	8	10	42	41	44	+1
8	Belkard Grodno	30	11	7	12	36	37	40	-1
9	Kommunalnik Svetlogorsk	30	9	11	10	41	27	38	+14
10	FC Rogachev	30	8	11	11	26	42	35	-16
11	Polesiye Mozyrskiy r-n	30	10	4	16	41	54	34	-13
12	FC Bereza	30	8	8	14	37	48	32	-11
13	Dinamo-Energogaz Vitebsk	30	7	10	13	32	53	31	-21
14	FC Orsha	30	5	8	17	23	59	23	-36
15	Veino Mogilevskiy r-n	30	5	5	20	31	83	20	-52
16	Belemergostroi Beloozersk	30	2	8	20	20	56	14	-36

CLUB DIRECTORY

FC Lida
ul. S. Kirova 32 A
231300 Lida
tel - (01561) 29761
Year of Formation - 1997
President - Vladimir Malets
Coach - Ivan Prokhorov
Stadium - City (4,500)

CLUB DIRECTORY

Svisloch-Krovlya Osipovichi
ul. V. Chapayev 11
213760 Osipovichi
tel - (02235) 22190/24635
fax - (02235) 24002
Year of Formation - 1994
President - Alexandr Konchits
Secretary - Vladimir Zavadskiy
Coach - Vasiliy Senkevich
Stadium - Yunost (2,200)

BELGIUM

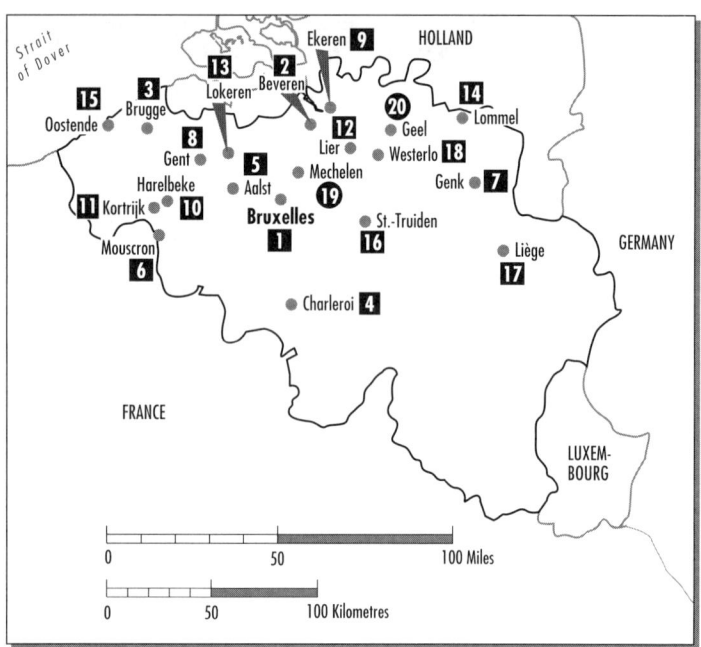

1	RSC ANDERLECHT	160
2	KSK BEVEREN	161
3	CLUB BRUGGE KV	162
4	RSC CHARLEROI	163
5	KSC EENDRACHT AALST	164
6	R EXCELSIOR MOUSCRON	165
7	KRC GENK	166
8	KAA GENT	167
9	KFC GERMINAL EKEREN	168
10	KRC HARELBEKE	169
11	KV KORTRIJK	170

12	K LIERSE SK	171
13	KSC LOKEREN	172
14	KFC LOMMELSE SK	173
15	KV OOSTENDE	174
16	K ST.-TRUIDENSE VV	175
17	R STANDARD LIEGE	176
18	KVC WESTERLO	177
Promoted clubs		
19	KV MECHELEN	178
20	FC VERBROEDERING GEEL	178

GENK HOLD NERVE TO LIFT FIRST TITLE

Shame and suffering for Euro 2000 co-hosts

FEDERATION DIRECTORY

Union Royale des Sociétés de Football Association
Houba de Strooperlaan 145, 1020 Bruxelles
tel - (02) 4771211   Year of Formation - 1895
fax - (02) 4782391   President - Michel D'Hooghe
                            Secretary - Alain Courtois
Stadium - Roi Baudouin, Bruxelles (40,000)

The summer of 2000 will see Belgium present at their first European Championship finals for 16 years. But were it not for the fact that they are the tournament co-hosts, they would surely not be taking part. The form of the Red Devils during 1998/99 was so pitiful that if they had been competing in the Euro 2000 qualifying competition, they would have been eliminated long before the season was out. Bereft of quality and character, Georges Leekens' team began their two-year countdown to the European finals with a goalless draw in Luxembourg. That, amazingly, was to prove one of the better results of a nightmare season, during which they were beaten 1-0 in five successive matches, three of them at home.

The only comforting aspect for the Belgian fans was that all burdens of expectation had been lifted. Interest in the team had virtually expired by the time the end-of-season trip to the Far East came around, but a couple of draws in the Kirin Cup, against Peru and Japan, and then, at last, a victory, 2-1 in Seoul against South Korea, managed to rekindle a certain enthusiasm with one year to go until the Big Kick-Off.

Leekens, however, will not be leading Belgium at Euro 2000. Although the Belgian FA stood by him through all the grim, goalless defeats, they finally surrendered to public opinion in August and sent him packing, with veteran coach Robert Waseige (ex-Liège, Standard,

LEAGUE CHAMPIONSHIP RESULTS 98/99

		1	2	3	4	5	6	7	8	9	10	11	12	13	14	15	16	17	18
1	RSC Anderlecht		3-1	2-3	1-1	2-1	1-1	3-2	4-0	2-0	3-1	3-1	2-0	1-1	3-0	3-0	1-1	0-1	3-2
2	KSK Beveren	2-1		1-2	1-2	0-2	1-4	1-0	0-3	2-1	0-3	2-2	1-3	1-2	0-0	5-0	0-1	0-6	1-0
3	Club Brugge KV	2-0	3-1		3-2	0-0	0-0	2-0	1-0	2-1	1-0	3-0	3-1	4-0	0-1	2-0	3-2	1-1	5-3
4	RSC Charleroi	0-2	1-2	1-2		0-1	1-3	1-1	1-1	2-2	2-1	2-1	5-0	2-1	1-1	1-1	2-1	1-0	1-3
5	KSC Eendracht Aalst	0-0	0-1	0-2	2-2		1-4	1-2	0-2	5-0	2-2	1-1	1-4	3-3	3-1	4-0	1-3	1-0	3-2
6	R Excelsior Mouscron	2-3	1-0	2-0	3-2	3-1		3-5	7-1	2-2	2-2	3-1	0-0	5-1	2-0	2-1	5-1	1-5	2-1
7	KRC Genk	2-5	1-0	1-1	2-1	2-0	3-0		1-0	3-2	2-2	3-1	3-1	3-1	6-0	3-0	4-1	2-1	3-0
8	KAA Gent	3-2	4-1	0-4	1-1	2-2	3-0	0-1		1-3	0-0	3-1	1-0	2-1	2-2	1-1	1-1	3-2	2-0
9	KFC Germinal Ekeren	0-3	1-0	2-0	2-0	1-0	1-1	0-2	8-1		0-2	2-1	1-1	1-1	1-0	2-0	1-0	0-1	0-3
10	KRC Harelbeke	1-2	1-1	0-2	1-1	5-1	0-4	1-2	2-2	0-4		1-0	3-1	3-2	1-1	2-1	1-1	1-1	1-2
11	KV Kortrijk	0-4	1-0	2-4	2-2	3-4	2-2	1-3	3-4	1-2	0-0		3-2	0-6	4-1	2-0	2-2	1-3	4-2
12	K Lierse SK	0-0	3-0	5-2	4-0	3-1	1-2	1-1	1-2	1-0	3-1	5-1		2-3	2-1	4-2	6-0	3-0	5-1
13	KSC Lokeren	2-3	4-3	2-0	3-1	6-2	0-0	2-0	1-4	1-1	1-0	2-1	2-0		2-1	1-2	2-1	4-1	3-0
14	KFC Lommelse SK	2-2	2-1	2-1	2-1	0-3	2-3	0-3	0-1	1-2	0-1	3-1	0-0	1-2		3-0	0-1	3-0	0-1
15	KV Oostende	0-2	1-1	1-4	0-0	4-1	2-4	1-1	2-2	0-1	1-0	1-3	0-6	0-0	1-1		0-1	2-1	1-1
16	K St.-Truidense VV	1-4	1-1	1-1	1-0	2-0	0-2	2-2	1-0	2-0	1-0	2-2	3-0	7-0	2-1	5-0		0-1	0-0
17	R Standard Liège	0-6	1-2	3-0	2-0	3-0	2-0	2-4	2-0	1-0	0-2	2-1	2-2	2-4	1-0	3-0	2-0		2-0
18	KVC Westerlo	6-0	0-0	1-2	1-0	1-1	1-1	1-1	3-3	2-4	0-3	2-0	0-2	4-3	2-1	7-0	1-4	3-1	

LEAGUE CHAMPIONSHIP FINAL TABLE 98/99

			Home				Away					Total						
		P	W	D	L	F	A	W	D	L	F	A	W	D	L	F	A	P	GD
1	KRC Genk	34	14	2	1	44	16	8	5	4	30	22	22	7	5	74	38	73	+36
2	Club Brugge KV	34	13	3	1	35	12	9	2	6	30	26	22	5	7	65	38	71	+27
3	RSC Anderlecht	34	11	4	2	37	16	10	3	4	39	23	21	7	6	76	39	70	+37
4	R Excelsior Mouscron	34	11	3	3	45	26	8	6	3	31	21	19	9	6	76	47	66	+29
5	KSC Lokeren	34	11	2	3	34	19	6	4	8	35	42	17	6	11	69	61	57	+8
6	R Standard Liège	34	11	1	5	30	21	6	2	9	25	26	17	3	14	55	47	54	+8
7	K Lierse SK	34	12	1	3	49	17	4	4	9	24	27	16	6	12	73	44	54	+29
8	KAA Gent	34	8	6	3	29	22	6	4	7	26	37	14	10	10	55	59	52	-4
9	K St.-Truidense VV	34	9	5	3	31	14	5	4	8	21	32	14	9	11	52	46	51	+6
10	KFC Germinal Ekeren	34	8	4	5	23	18	6	3	8	25	28	14	7	13	48	46	49	+2
11	KRC Harelbeke	34	5	6	6	24	28	5	5	7	20	18	10	11	13	44	46	41	-2
12	KVC Westerlo	34	7	5	5	35	26	4	2	11	21	36	11	7	16	56	62	40	-6
13	KSC Eendracht Aalst	34	5	5	7	28	29	4	3	10	20	37	9	8	17	48	66	35	-18
14	RSC Charleroi	34	6	5	6	21	24	1	6	10	16	31	7	11	16	37	55	32	-18
15	KSK Beveren	34	5	2	10	18	32	3	4	10	15	28	8	6	20	33	60	30	-27
16	KFC Lommelse SK	34	6	2	9	21	23	1	5	11	12	33	7	7	20	33	56	28	-23
17	KV Kortrijk	34	5	4	7	30	38	1	3	14	19	43	6	7	21	49	81	25	-32
18	KV Oostende	34	3	7	7	17	29	1	3	13	10	50	4	10	20	27	79	22	-52

N.B. Where teams are level on points, classification is determined by the number of victories.

Charleroi) rather unenviably being asked to step into the breach.

The most that can be asked of Waseige is to try to make the best of a bad job. Despite their home advantage it is obvious that Belgium will not win Euro 2000. In fact, given their recent results, it would be something of a minor miracle if they were to qualify from their first-round group. Their problem is an almost total lack of proven international-quality players. Of those Belgians who once belonged in that category, Enzo Scifo and Luc Nilis both retired from international football after France '98, Franky Van der Elst has now hung his boots up altogether, and Luís Oliveira rarely plays as an out-and-out striker at club level. Leekens was not afraid to experiment in a bid to reconstruct - he gave first caps to 17 players during the 1998/99 season alone - but by the end of his tenure he was no nearer finding a settled side than he was 12 months earlier. Now the baton has been passed on to Waseige, but time is running out fast.

Belgium's standing in the international game has probably never been so low. It is almost unheard of for a nation hosting a major championship to enter its final season of preparation in such turmoil. But international failings have been rather too familiar for Belgian fans in recent years. The country's top club sides, once respected throughout Europe, now regularly find their participation in the UEFA club competitions restricted to just a couple of rounds at the start of the season.

Once again, in 1998/99, Belgium's clubs failed to leave a lasting impression in Europe. Each of them had their moments, but overall it was another season of failure, with no team getting through to the latter stages. Club Bruges went the furthest, but that was in the UEFA Cup, their bid to reach the group phase of the Champions' League having been ended by an away-goals defeat against Rosenborg. The highlight of Bruges's European season was a

TOP SCORERS

24	Jan KOLLER (KSC Lokeren)
18	Branko STRUPAR (KRC Genk)
17	Souleymane OULARE (KRC Genk)
16	Zoran BAN (R Excelsior Mouscron)
15	Filip FIERS (K St.-Truidense VV)
	Jochen JANSSEN (KVC Westerlo)
	Tomasz RADZINSKI (RSC Anderlecht)
14	Eric VAN MEIR (K Lierse SK)
13	Gordan VIDOVIC (R Excelsior Mouscron)
	Jurgen CAVENS (K Lierse SK)
	Salif KEITA (KV Kortrijk)

NATIONAL TEAM APPEARANCES 98/99

Coach - Georges LEEKENS	LUX	CYP	GRE	CZE	BUL	EGY	ROM	PER	JPN	KOR	Cps	Gls
Ronny GASPERCIC (09/05/69) - CF Extremadura (ESP)	G	G			G	G					4	-
Eric DEFLANDRE (02/08/73) - Club Brugge KV	D73		D		s76		D				15	-
Gordan VIDOVIC (23/06/68) - R Excelsior Mouscron	D		D		D	D	D	D28			16	-
Glen DE BOECK (22/08/71) - RSC Anderlecht	D	s25	D	D	D	D	D	s81	s28	s83	21	-
Nico VAN KERCKHOVEN (14/12/70) - FC Schalke 04 (GER)	D59	D46									18	2
Philippe CLEMENT (22/03/74) - Coventry City (ENG)	M	M81									9	-
Chris JANSSENS (12/06/69) - KSC Lokeren	M	M	s64		s51	M46			s90	s88	7	-
Johan WALEM (01/02/72) - Udinese (ITA)	M	M		M	M	M	M				14	-
Sven VERMANT (04/04/73) - Club Brugge KV	M										2	-
Bob PEETERS (10/01/74) - Roda JC (HOL)	A59										2	-
Gert CLAESSENS (21/02/72) - Club Brugge KV (BEL)	A82										4	1
Davy OYEN (17/07/75) - PSV (HOL)	s59		M64								2	-
Mbo MPENZA (04/12/76) - R Standard Liège	s59	A63	s64		s81	s61			s65	s82	14	-
Tjörven DE BRUL (22/06/73) - Club Brugge KV	s73	D	D56	D				s86	D	D	9	-
Toni BROGNO (19/07/73) - KVC Westerlo	s82							s83			2	-
Lorenzo STAELENS (30/04/64) - RSC Anderlecht		D25	M	M			M	D	D	D	60	6
Eric VAN MEIR (28/02/68) - K Lierse SK		D	D								16	1
David BROCKEN (18/02/71) - K Lierse SK		D									1	-
Lokonda MPENZA (04/07/78) - R Standard Liège		A	s80	A46	A81	A	A58				19	3
Bart GOOR (09/04/73) - RSC Anderlecht		s46	M	M		s74	M	M	M	M	8	-
Frédéric PIERRE (23/02/74) - R Excelsior Mouscron		s63	A64	A			s58				8	-
Wilfried DELBROEK (25/08/72) - KRC Genk		s81	M	M					M81	M90	5	-
Geert DE VLIEGER (16/10/71) - KRC Harelbeke		G	G							G	3	-
Daniel KIMONI (18/01/71) - KRC Genk		D	s56			s65					3	-
Gilles DE BILDE (09/06/71) - PSV (HOL)			A80	s46							17	1
Régis GENAUX (30/08/73) - Udinese (ITA)				D77	D76	D					19	-
Stefaan TANGHE (15/01/72) - R Excelsior Mouscron				s77		s61	M58	M	M	M88	6	1
Philippe LEONARD (14/02/74) - AS Monaco (FRA)				D	D74						13	-
Walter BASEGGIO (19/08/78) - RSC Anderlecht					M51		M65				2	-
Marc WILMOTS (22/02/69) - FC Schalke 04 (GER)					M	M61					39	13
Sandy MARTENS (23/12/72) - KAA Gent					M	M		A83	A65	A83	5	2
Luís OLIVEIRA (24/03/69) - Fiorentina (ITA)					A81	A61					31	7
Peter VAN HOUDT (04/11/76) - Roda JC (HOL)					s81			s75			2	-
Didier ERNST (15/09/71) - R Standard Liège					s46						1	-
Filip DE WILDE (05/07/64) - RSC Anderlecht						G	G19				27	-
Danny BOFFIN (10/07/65) - FC Metz (FRA)						M					41	1
Jurgen CAVENS (19/08/78) - K Lierse SK						s58		s65	A82		3	-
Bertrand CRASSON (05/10/71) - RSC Anderlecht						D			s85		21	1
Yves VANDERHAEGHE (30/01/70) - R Excelsior Mouscron								M	M	M	3	-
Marc HENDRICKX (02/07/74) - KRC Genk								M86	D	D85	3	-
Gert VERHEYEN (20/09/70) - Club Brugge KV								A75	A65	A	20	2
Philippe VANDE WALLE (22/12/61) - KSC Eendracht Aalst								s19		G	6	-
Carl HOEFKENS (06/10/78) - K Lierse SK										D	1	-

DOMESTIC CUP 98/99

1/16 FINALS
K Lierse SK 8, RWD Molenbeek 1
Denderhoutem 2, KSV Waregem 1
SK Tongeren 2, Excelsior Mouscron 3
K St.-Truidense VV 1, KSK Deinze 1 (aet; 3-1 on pens.)
KFC Lommelse SK 3, FC Kapellen 1
KSK Beveren 0, KVC Westerlo 0 (aet; 3-4 on pens.)
KSV Cercle Brugge 2, SK Roeselare 1
KFC Germinal Ekeren 1, KSC Lokeren 2
KV Kortrijk 5, KAA Gent 2
AA La Louvière 4, R Standard Liège 4 (aet; 3-4 on pens.)
KRC Harelbeke 3, KV Oostende 1
Maasland 0, SV Ingelmunster 4
FC Denderleeuw 3, RSC Anderlecht 3 (aet; 4-2 on pens.)
KSC Eendracht Aalst 4, RSC Charleroi 3
KRC Genk 6, Zultse VV 2
RTFC Liégeois 3, Club Brugge KV 2

1/8 FINALS
SV Ingelmunster 4, RTFC Liégeois 0
KFC Lommelse SK 2, K St.-Truidense VV 3
K Lierse SK 2, Denderhoutem 0
KSC Lokeren 2, FC Denderleeuw 0
KSC Eendracht Aalst 0, R Standard Liège 3

KSV Cercle Brugge 0, KV Kortrijk 0 (aet; 1-3 on pens.)
KVC Westerlo 2, KRC Harelbeke 2 (aet; 3-2 on pens.)
KRC Genk 4, Excelsior Mouscron 3 (aet)

QUARTER-FINALS
KSC Lokeren 3
(Koller 22, Van Geneugden 41, Budka 90),
KVC Westerlo 0
SV Ingelmunster 1 (Vanderdonck 32p),
R Standard Liège 3 (Folha 42, Cruz 76, De Condé 88)
KV Kortrijk 0,
K Lierse SK 6 (Poorters 30, Somers 32, Brocken 53,
Van de Weyer 73, Huysmans 80, Huistra 89)
K St.-Truidense VV 0,
KRC Genk 1 (Van Oekelen 90og)

SEMI-FINALS
KRC Genk 2 (Strupar 77p, Oulare 88),
K Lierse SK 4 (Daems 8, 62, Van de Weyer 48,
Cavens 83)
K Lierse SK 1 (Cavens 90),
KRC Genk 1 (Strupar 46)
(K Lierse 5-3)

KSC Lokeren 0,
R Standard Liège 2 (Mpenza L. 49, Ernst 51)
R Standard Liège 3
(Mornar 47, Cruz 57, Mpenza M. 60),
KSC Lokeren 0
(R Standard Liège 5-0)

FINAL
30/05/99, Brussels
K LIERSE SK 3 Spiteri (17), Cavens (54, 90)
R STANDARD LIEGE 1 Lukunku (64)
referee - Meese

K LIERSE SK - Menzo; Brocken, Van Meir,
Hoefkens, Poorters, Laeremans, Leen, Zdebel, Daems
(Shekiladze 84), Spiteri (Van de Weyer 76), Cavens
(Huysmans 90).

R STANDARD LIEGE - Runje; Afolabi, Hellers, Ernst,
Cruz, Renier, Remacle (De Condé 58) Thys (Blay 74),
Folha, Mpenza M., Lukunku (Godfroid 77).

---

thrilling extra-time victory over VfB Stuttgart. That was preceded a month earlier by an even more memorable Belgian victory over German opposition when Genk thrashed MSV Duisburg 5-0 in Brussels in the Cup-winners' Cup. But those were rare highlights, and both Genk and Bruges were eliminated one round later to join earlier fallers Germinal Ekeren and Anderlecht - both knocked out of the UEFA Cup after losing at home to teams from Switzerland.

For all the doom and gloom that accompanies Belgian teams into the international arena, the domestic Eerste Klasse remains one of the more open and competitive top divisions in Europe. Also, the football is generally entertaining and exciting, if not exactly five-star quality.

There were all sorts of crazy goings-on during the 1998/99 season. Anderlecht suffered their heaviest defeat in 60 years when they were sensationally beaten 6-0 by Westerlo. Sint-Truiden beat Lokeren 7-0 and then lost 6-0 to Lierse a week later. And Gent lost 7-1 away to

Excelsior Mouscron, a team they had comfortably beaten 3-0 at home in their earlier meeting.

The race for the championship remained gripping and undecided right until the final whistle of the last match. There were two main contenders - defending champions Club Bruges and 1997/98 runners-up and Cup winners Genk. Bruges were coached by Eric Gerets, who was seeking a hat-trick of Eerste Klasse titles before departing

NATIONAL TEAM RESULTS 98/99

18/11/98	Luxembourg	A	Luxembourg	0-0	
03/02/99	Cyprus	A	Limassol	1-0	Mpenza L. (75)
05/02/99	Greece	N	Nicosia	0-1	
09/02/99	Czech Republic	H	Brussels	0-1	
27/03/99	Bulgaria	H	Bruges	0-1	
30/03/99	Egypt	H	Liège	0-1	
28/04/99	Romania	A	Bucharest	0-1	
30/05/99	Peru	N	Kyoto	1-1	Tanghe (28)
03/06/99	Japan	A	Tokyo	0-0	
05/06/99	South Korea	A	Seoul	2-1	Martens (23, 32)

EUROPEAN CUPS 98/99

CHAMPIONS' CUP
● CLUB BRUGGE KV
Preliminary round SILEKS KRATOVO (MAC)
A 0-0
    Verlinden; Deflandre, De Brul, Ilic, Borkelmans, Anic, Van der Elst, Addo,
    Claessens (Vermant 70), Jankauskas (Schockaert 84), Fadiga (Sillah 81).
H 2-1 Vermant (3), Claessens (30)
    Verlinden; Deflandre, De Brul, Lesnjak, Ilic (Borkelmans 40), Anic
    (Sillah 46), Van der Elst, Addo, Claessens, Vermant, Jankauskas (Ekakia 78).

Qualifying round ROSENBORG BK (NOR)
A 0-2
    Verlinden; Deflandre, De Brul, Ilic, Borkelmans, Vermant (Schockaert 62),
    Van der Elst, Addo (Jankauskas 70), Claessens (Sillah 84), Vermant,
    Ekakia.
H 4-2 Fadiga (22), Claessens (47, 85), Schockaert (78)
    Verlinden; Deflandre, Lesnjak, De Brul, Borkelmans, Van der Elst,
    Addo (Vermant 59), Claessens, Ekakia (Verjans 70), Jankauskas
    (Schockaert 59), Fadiga.

CUP WINNERS' CUP
● KRC GENK
Qualifying round APOLONIA FIER (ALB)
A 5-1 Strupar (33), Oulare (37p, 68), Hendrickx (40), Horváth (80)
    Brockhauser; Hendrickx (Origi 46), Kimoni, Olivieri, Vangronsveld,
    Rogério, Gudjónsson Th., Hasi, Delbroek, Strupar (Dos Santos 83),
    Oulare (Horváth 75).
H 4-0 Oulare (5), N'Sumbu (86), Strupar (87, 90)
    Brockhauser; Reini (Origi 58), Kimoni, Vangronsveld, Van Geem
    (N'Sumbu 62), Hendrickx, Hasi, Delbroek, Gudjónsson Th., Strupar, Oulare
    (Horváth 73).

1st round MSV DUISBURG (GER)
A 1-1 Reini (61)
    Brockhauser; Reini, Olivieri, Kimoni, Van Geem, Hendrickx, Delbroek, Hasi,
    Gudjónsson Th., Oulare (Origi 84), Strupar (Vangronsveld 00).
H 5-0 Oulare (13, 49), Strupar (32), Gudjónsson 1h. (73, 80)
    Brockhauser; Reini, Kimoni, Delbroek, Olivieri, Hasi, Oulare (Horváth 85),
    Gudjónsson Th. (Origi 89), Strupar (Vangronsveld 87), Van Geem, Rogério.

2nd round RCD MALLORCA (ESP)
H 1-1 Oulare (71)
    Brockhauser; Kimoni, Olivieri, Van Geem, Reini, Delbroek, Hasi, Origi,
    Rogério (N'Sumbu 60), Strupar, Oulare.
A 0-0
    Brockhauser; Reini, Kimoni, Olivieri, Van Geem, Rogério (N'Sumbu 72),
    Gudjónsson Th., Origi, Delbroek, Strupar (Dos Santos 83), Oulare.

UEFA CUP
● KFC GERMINAL EKEREN
Preliminary round FK SARAJEVO (BOS)
H 4-1 Van Ankeren (25), Morhaye (28, 89), Kovács (41)
    Moons; Schaessens, Verstraeten, Siquet (Camerman 65), Herreman,
    Milosevic, Kovács, Karagiannis, Hofmans, Van Ankeren, Morhaye.
A 0-0
    Moons; Schaessens, Verstraeten, Siquet, Herreman, Karagiannis, Kovács,
    Milosevic, Hofmans, Van Ankeren (Vandervee 87), Morhaye.

Qualifying round SERVETTE FC GENEVE (SUI)
H 1-4 Morhaye (85)
    Moons (Andrews 56); Siquet (Sonck 65), Kovács, Verstraeten, Herreman,
    Schaessens, Karagiannis, Milosevic, Morhaye, Hofmans, Van Ankeren
    (Vandervee 71).
A 2-1 Fournier (18og), Karagiannis (43)
    Andrews; Vandervee, Kovács, Budts, Bartholomeeussen, Herreman,
    Schaessens (Sonck 32), Milosevic, Karagiannis, Hofmans, Morhaye.

● RSC ANDERLECHT
Preliminary round TILIGUL TIRASPOL (MOL)
A 1-0 Staelens (56)
    De Wilde; Crasson (Stassin 85), De Boeck, Staelens, Dheedene,
    Van Diemen, Zetterberg, Scifo (Claeys 70), Taument, Årst (Goor 75),
    Stoica.
H 5-0 Stoica (32), De Boeck (42), Dheedene (56), Taument (60), Årst (76)
    De Wilde; Crasson, De Boeck, Doll, Dheedene, Van Diemen, Zetterberg
    (Årst 75), Baseggio (Soetaers 67), Taument, Goor, Stoica.

Qualifying round OSIJEK (CRO)
A 1-3 Claeys (80)
    De Wilde; Crasson, De Boeck (Claeys 76), Doll, Dheedene, Taument,
    Baseggio, Van Diemen, Zetterberg, Stoica (Årst 65), Goor.
H 2-0 Arst (4), Stoica (84)
    De Wilde; Crasson, Doll, Stassin, Dheedene, Taument (Yashchuk 75),
    Van Diemen (Claeys 85), Zetterberg, Stoica, Goor (Baseggio 80), Årst.

1st round GRASSHOPPER-CLUB ZÜRICH (SUI)
H 0-2
    De Wilde; Crasson, Stassin, Doll, Dheedene, Van Diemen (Taument 46),
    Baseggio, Zetterberg, Goor (Stoica 77), Yashchuk, Årst (Scifo 46).
A 0-0
    De Wilde; Crasson, Doll, De Boeck (Stoica 64), Dheedene, Scifo, Zetterberg,
    Staelens, Van Diemen, Goor, Yashchuk (Årst 46).

● CLUB BRUGGE KV
1st round ÚJPEST FC (HUN)
A 5-0 Jankauskas (12), Ilic (25), Vermant (42), Anic (50), Ekakia (89)
    El Sayed; Deflandre (De Cock 77), De Brul, Lesnjak, Ilic, Borkelmans,
    Van der Elst (Verjans 54), Anic, Vermant, Ekakia, Jankauskas (Addo 64).
H 2-2 Borkelmans (32), Vermant (70)
    El Sayed; Deflandre (De Cock 46), Lesnjak, Ilic (Lembi 65), Addo, Verjans,
    Anic, Borkelmans, Vermant, Jankauskas, Fadiga (Sillah 59).

2nd round VFB STUTTGART (GER)
A 1-1 Vermant (70)
    El Sayed; De Cock, Lembi, Van der Elst, Ilic, Borkelmans, Deflandre, Addo,
    Anic, Vermant (Schockaert 83), Jankauskas (Ekakia 82).
H 3-2 De Cock (60), Claessens (105), Ilic (116)
(aet) El Sayed; Addo, Ilic, Lembi, De Cock, Deflandre (Fadiga 81), Van der Elst
    (Lesnjak 108), Anic (Claessens 72), Borkelmans, Vermant, Jankauskas.

3rd round OLYMPIQUE LYONNAIS (FRA)
A 0-1
    El Sayed; Lesnjak, Ilic, Addo, De Cock, Deflandre, Van der Elst, Claessens,
    Fadiga (Ekakia 55), Vermant, Jankauskas.
H 3-4 De Brul (63), De Cock (69), Anic (72)
    El Sayed; De Brul, Van der Elst, Ilic, De Cock, Lembi, Anic, Borkelmans,
    Vermant (Fadiga 46), Jankauskas (Schockaert 66), Claessens (Ekakia 71).

for PSV Eindhoven at the end of the campaign, while Genk were led by Aimé Anthuenis, who midway through the season announced that he, too, would be moving to pastures new in the summer, having agreed a three-year deal with Anderlecht.

So the second half of the season was all about two coaches trying to give their respective clubs the perfect farewell gift. Gerets' side led at halfway, proclaiming themselves 'autumn champions' for the fourth season running with a 2-1 victory away to Westerlo - sealed by a penalty from veteran left-back Vital Borkelmans on his 300th appearance for the club. But Genk, who trailed by five points at that stage, made their move in the New Year, stringing six successive victories together to take over at the top as Bruges began to suffer from the yips away from home.

Once in front, Genk showed tremendous nerve and courage to stay there. A shock defeat at lowly Beveren halted them in their tracks but they responded with a brilliant 3-0 victory at home to in-form Mouscron and then gained probably their most important result of the entire season when they came from behind to draw 1-1 in the top-of-the-table clash at home to Bruges. Victories for both challengers in their next three matches allowed Genk to retain a two-point lead going into the last two games. Then came the big twist. While Bruges lost away from home yet again, to Mouscron, Genk's unbeaten home record was destroyed by a 5-2 pummelling from Anderlecht, who now, incredibly, after a brilliant run of ten wins in 12 matches, were just three points behind - with one game to go.

Had Genk beaten Anderlecht, the title would have been theirs. But all of a sudden they faced not one but two challengers. Clearly, with their two-point lead still intact, they remained the favourites, but their last match was a tricky fixture away to Harelbeke, whereas Bruges and Anderlecht both had relatively easy games at home. And because of the Belgian league rule whereby the number of victories determines classification if two teams finish equal on points, Genk knew that they were vulnerable to both of their challengers unless they won in Harelbeke.

Bruges and Anderlecht duly claimed their victories, but Genk and their fans were subjected to an afternoon of high tension and anxiety. Souleymane Oulare, the team's outstanding African striker, opened the scoring in the first half and Icelandic international Thórdur Gudjónsson made it 2-0 midway through the second. But a goal for Harelbeke with seven minutes to go set up a desperate, nail-biting finale. The final whistle brought utter joy and relief, not just for Genk and their fans but for most neutrals up and down the country who had been rooting for the underdogs to succeed.

Genk thus became the 15th different club to win the Belgian championship but the very first from the province of Limburg. The club's maiden triumph was achieved with a settled, cosmopolitan side that featured players from Hungary, Croatia, Iceland, Guinea, Kenya, Italy, Finland and the Democratic Republic of Congo as well as Belgium. As in the previous season, Genk's great strength was the attacking threesome of Oulare, Gudjónsson and Branko Strupar. The latter, a Croatian by birth, took out Belgian citizenship and looked a class above any other candidate for the centre-forward spot in the Belgian national team. He was deservedly voted Footballer of the Year and finished second behind Lokeren's Czech striker Jan Koller in the top-scorer charts, scoring 18 goals and also providing a league-best total of 20 assists.

Genk coach Aimé Anthuenis, who had masterminded the club's remarkable three-year rise from the Second Division to the championship, must have had mixed feelings about leaving, but, equally, the way his new club Anderlecht had ended the season could only have whetted his appetite. The Brussels side had begun the campaign in such a lamentable state, dropping to bottom place after five matches, that nobody could possibly have forecast that by the last game they would actually be in a position to win the title.

Arie Haan could not survive the early disasters, which also included swift exits from the UEFA Cup and Belgian Cup (the latter on penalties against little Denderleeuw). His place was taken by assistants Jean Dockx and Franky Vercauteren, and the effect this pair had on morale and confidence was illustrated by the team's incredible rise up the table from November to May, climaxing in that brilliant 5-2 victory at the fortress of the future champions. Everybody was in agreement that if the championship had been extended by a couple of matches, Anderlecht would have won it.

There was also a common consensus that Anderlecht had not played with such style and swagger for years.

INTERNATIONAL HONOURS

World Cup Finals appearances: 1930, 1934, 1938, 1954, 1970, 1982 (2nd phase), 1986 (4th), 1990 (2nd round), 1994 (2nd round), 1998

European Championship appearances (last 8): 1972 (3rd), 1976, 1980 (runners-up), 1984

European Club Competitions

Cup-winners' Cup	RSC Anderlecht (1976, 1978)
	KV Mechelen (1988)
UEFA Cup	RSC Anderlecht (1983)
Super Cup	RSC Anderlecht (1976, 1978)

With Anthuenis at the command controls and the likes of Tomasz Radzinski, Bart Goor, Walter Baseggio and Enzo Scifo still on board, there was no doubt which club began the 1999/2000 season as title favourites.

Bruges appointed assistant coach René Verheyen as the successor to Eric Gerets. The bearded wonder had come close to his third successive title but not close enough. His was not the only significant departure.

Veteran midfielder Frank Van der Elst also called it a day, leaving the club after 15 unbroken seasons to become the coach of newly-formed Germinal Beerschot Antwerp, or GBA for short - a merger club formed from Germinal Ekeren and Third Division side Beerschot from the Antwerp suburbs.

Royal Antwerp, rather more established at 119 years old, seemed set to return to the top flight after just a season away but they came badly unstuck in the final weeks of the season and allowed KV Mechelen to overtake them and snap up the one automatic promotion place. Antwerp carried that poor form into the play-offs as well and finished up eight points shy of winners Verbroedering Geel, who thus celebrated the first top-flight promotion in their history. Vacating the space for Mechelen and Geel were the two teams promoted 12 months earlier, Kortrijk and Oostende, the latter failing to gain inspiration from legendary Belgian international goalkeeper Jean-Marie Pfaff during his 100-day stint as coach.

PLAYERS OF THE SEASON

SOULEYMANE OULARE

The Belgian league is awash with foreigners, but very few of them are of sufficient quality to make a real difference to the fortunes of the club they represent. Souleymane Oulare, from the African state of Guinea, is one of those exceptions. The two-goal Cup final hero of Genk in 1997/98, he came to even greater prominence in 1998/99, scoring 17 goals in the league to play a crucial rôle in the Limburg club's first Belgian championship triumph. Although his attacking partner Branko Strupar scored one goal more, Oulare had a habit of finding the net at crucial times. He came alive in the big games, notably in the two victories over Mouscron, the Cup-winners' Cup mauling of MSV Duisburg and the decisive last-day win at Harelbeke. Second to Strupar in the Belgian Footballer of the Year vote, he pipped his team-mate to the Players' Player of the Year prize. Genk wanted to keep him and they almost did after a move to French club Metz fell through, but in late summer he was on his way, making the long trip to Istanbul to join Fenerbahçe.

JURGEN CAVENS

The young guns of Lierse came to the fore in 1998/99. Walter Meeuws' youthful team claimed a few notable scalps in the league and also won the Belgian Cup, for the first time in 30 years, beating Standard Liège 3-1 in the final. Their star was 21-year-old striker Jurgen Cavens, who notched 13 goals in the league and another nine in the Cup,

including two in the final. Named 'Rookie of the Year' by the country's leading football magazine, he graduated to the Belgian national team and earned his début as a substitute against Romania before making his first start a few weeks later in the impressive setting of Seoul's Olympic Stadium. One of the few Belgian players with genuine international promise, he leads the line well and has a tremendous left foot. Another good season in 1999/2000 should see him rewarded with a place in Belgium's European Championship squad.

STEFAAN TANGHE

Viewed over the whole season, Excelsior Mouscron played arguably the most entertaining football in Belgium's Eerste Klasse in 1998/99, and their most valuable player was undoubtedly 27-year-old Stefaan Tanghe. In previous seasons he had done little to commend himself but he made up for lost time with a series of outstanding performances that catapulted Mouscron into fourth place. He scored 12 goals and set up a similar number for his team-mates, notably Croatian striker Zoran Ban. His speciality is arriving late in the opposition's box, and his goals-per-chances ratio is exceptionally high for a midfielder. He ended almost 500 goalless minutes for the Belgian national team when, on only his fourth appearance, he blasted home a powerful shot to give the Red Devils a 1-1 draw against Peru in the Kirin Cup. He is another newcomer set to figure prominently for Belgium at Euro 2000.

RSC ANDERLECHT

CLUB DIRECTORY

RSC Anderlecht
Avenue Théo Verbeeck 2
Anderlecht, 1070 Bruxelles
tel - (02) 5229400 / fax - (02) 5200740
Year of Formation - 1908
President - Roger Vanden Stock
Manager - Michel Verschueren
Secretary - Philippe Collin
Coach - Arie Haan; Franky Vercauteren &
Jean Dockx (99/00 - Aimé Antheunis)
Stadium - Constant Vanden Stock (28,063)

MAJOR HONOURS

League Championship - (24) 1947, 1949, 1950,
1951, 1954, 1955, 1956, 1959, 1962, 1964,
1965, 1966, 1967, 1968, 1972, 1974, 1981,
1985, 1986, 1987, 1991, 1993, 1994, 1995.
Domestic Cup - (8) 1965, 1972, 1973, 1975,
1976, 1988, 1989, 1994.
European Cup-winners' Cup - (2) 1976, 1978.
UEFA Cup - (1) 1983.
European Super Cup - (2) 1976, 1978.

APPEARANCES 98/99

		P	Ap	(s)	Gls
Ole Martin ÅRST (NOR)	A	10	(8)	1	
Ioanis ANASTASIOU (GRE)	A	10	(3)	5	
Walter BASEGGIO	M	24	(1)	4	
Didier CALVO	M		(1)		
Geoffrey CLAEYS	M	8	(6)		
Bertrand CRASSON	D	29	(1)	1	
Glen DE BOECK	D	25	(1)	2	
Filip DE WILDE	G	33			
Didier DHEEDENE	D	15	(7)		
Olivier DOLL	D	14	(2)	1	
Bart GOOR	A	33		7	
Zvonko MILOJEVIC (YUG)	G	1	(1)		
Tomasz RADZINSKI (CAN)	A	21	(1)	15	
Enzo SCIFO	M	26	(1)	8	
Tibor SELYMES (ROM)	D	11		1	
Tom SOETAERS	A		(4)		
Lorenzo STAELENS	D	23	(1)	6	
Stéphane STASSIN	D	11	(5)		
Alin STOICA (ROM)	A	6	(20)	1	
Gaston TAUMENT (HOL)	A	4			
Patrick VAN DIEMEN (HOL)	M	32		5	
Oleh YASHCHUK (UKR)	A	16	(11)	11	
Pär ZETTERBERG (SWE)	M	22	(2)	7	

LEAGUE RESULTS 1998/99

22/08/98	RSC Charleroi	H	1-1	Zetterberg
29/08/98	KSK Beveren	A	1-2	Goor
02/09/98	R Excelsior Mouscron	H	1-1	Årst
05/09/98	KVC Westerlo	A	0-6	
09/09/98	Club Brugge KV	H	2-3	Zetterberg (p), Yashchuk
12/09/98	KFC Germinal Ekeren	A	3-0	Yashchuk 2, Doll
19/09/98	K St.-Truidense VV	H	1-1	Scifo
26/09/98	KFC Lommelse SK	A	2-2	Van Diemen, Zetterberg (p)
04/10/98	KSC Eendracht Aalst	A	0-0	
10/10/98	KRC Harelbeke	H	3-1	Staelens, Van Diemen, Scifo
23/10/98	KSC Lokeren	A	3-2	Zetterberg, De Boeck 2
31/10/98	K Lierse SK	H	2-0	Scifo, Goor
07/11/98	KV Oostende	A	2-0	Zetterberg, Goor
15/11/98	R Standard Liège	H	0-1	
21/11/98	KAA Gent	A	2-3	Crasson, Staelens
28/11/98	KRC Genk	H	3-2	Staelens 2, Radzinski
06/12/98	KV Kortrijk	A	4-0	Staelens 2, Goor, Yashchuk
19/12/98	KSK Beveren	H	3-1	Radzinski, Scifo (p), Yashchuk
15/01/99	R Excelsior Mouscron	A	3-2	Radzinski, Goor, og (Besengez)
23/01/99	KVC Westerlo	H	3-2	Anastasiou, Radzinski 2
29/01/99	Club Brugge KV	A	0-2	
20/02/99	KFC Germinal Ekeren	H	2-0	Anastasiou, Van Diemen
27/02/99	K St.-Truidense VV	A	4-1	Baseggio, Yashchuk 2, Goor
06/03/99	KFC Lommelse SK	H	3-0	Selymes, Scifo, Radzinski
13/03/99	KSC Eendracht Aalst	H	2-1	Baseggio, Yashchuk
21/03/99	KRC Harelbeke	A	2-1	Yashchuk, Baseggio
02/04/99	KSC Lokeren	H	1-1	Scifo (p)
09/04/99	RSC Charleroi	A	2-0	Radzinski, Goor
17/04/99	K Lierse SK	A	0-0	
24/04/99	KV Oostende	H	3-0	Van Diemen, Anastasiou, Zetterberg (p)
02/05/99	R Standard Liège	A	6-0	Scifo, Baseggio, Radzinski 3, Yashchuk
05/05/99	KAA Gent	H	4-0	Radzinski 3, Anastasiou
09/05/99	KRC Genk	A	5-2	Yashchuk, Stoica, Anastasiou, Radzinski 2
16/05/99	KV Kortrijk	H	3-1	Van Diemen, Scifo, Zetterberg (p)

KSK BEVEREN

CLUB DIRECTORY

KSK Beveren
Klapperstraat 151 bis
9120 Beveren
tel - (03) 7759000/7759697
fax - (03) 7750800
President - Frans Van Hoof
Manager - Marc Pinson
Coach - Stani Gzil
Stadium - Freethiel (13,290)

APPEARANCES 98/99

	P	Ap	(s)	Gls
Riccardo BONETTO (ITA)	A	9		1
David DAMMAN	D	8		
Bert DHONT	M	26		3
Gidéon IMAGBUDU (NIG)	M	24	(1)	
Mohammed KANU (SRL)	M	9	(1)	
Erwin LEMMENS	G	32		
Frank MAGERMAN	M		(1)	
Arben NUHIJU (MAC)	A	13	(13)	3
Sunny NWACHUKWU (NIG)	A	3	(9)	
Tristan PEERSMAN	G	1		
Gábor PUGLITS (HUN)	D	30		1
Eric SCALIA (FRA)	D	29		1
Werry SELS	M	16	(14)	1
Didier SIMBA-EKANZA (DRC)	A	7	(9)	
Jimmy SMET	D	29		
Lambert SMID (CZE)	M	15		3
Davy THEUNIS	M	12	(5)	
Remco TORKEN (HOL)	A	8	(10)	5
Bart VAN DEN EEDE	A	27	(1)	6
Martin VAN OPHUIZEN (HOL)	D	11		
Johan VAN RUMST	D		(1)	
Roland VELKENEERS	G	1	(2)	
Andy VEREERTBRUGGHEN	D	2	(1)	
Stijn VLAMINCK	D	15	(10)	
Marcin ZEWLAKOW (POL)	A	23		8
Michal ZEWLAKOW (POL)	M	24		1

LEAGUE RESULTS 1998/99

22/08/98	KFC Lommelse SK	A	1-2	Dhont
29/08/98	RSC Anderlecht	H	2-1	Dhont, Van den Eede
02/09/98	KRC Harelbeke	A	1-1	Torken
05/09/98	KSC Lokeren	H	1-2	Dhont
09/09/98	K Lierse SK	A	0-3	
12/09/98	KV Oostende	H	5-0	Torken 2, Nuhiju, Smid (p), Scalia
19/09/98	R Standard Liège	A	2-1	Van den Eede, Nuhiju
26/09/98	KAA Gent	H	0-3	
04/10/98	KRC Genk	A	0-1	
10/10/98	KV Kortrijk	H	2-2	Zewlakow Ma. 2
24/10/98	RSC Charleroi	A	2-1	Puglits (p), Zewlakow Ma.
31/10/98	KSC Eendracht Aalst	H	0-2	
07/11/98	R Excelsior Mouscron	H	1-4	Zewlakow Ma.
14/11/98	KVC Westerlo	A	0-0	
21/11/98	Club Brugge KV	H	1-2	Torken
29/11/98	KFC Germinal Ekeren	A	0-1	
12/12/98	KFC Lommelse SK	H	0-0	
19/12/98	RSC Anderlecht	A	1-3	Zewlakow Mi.
16/01/99	KRC Harelbeke	H	0-3	
23/01/99	KSC Lokeren	A	3-4	Sels, Van den Eede 2
30/01/99	K Lierse SK	H	1-3	Torken
06/02/99	K St.-Truidense VV	H	0-1	
14/02/99	KV Oostende	A	1-1	Nuhiju
27/02/99	R Standard Liège	H	0-6	
06/03/99	KAA Gent	A	1-4	Van den Eede
13/03/99	KRC Genk	H	1-0	Smid (p)
21/03/99	KV Kortrijk	A	0-1	
03/04/99	RSC Charleroi	H	1-2	Zewlakow Ma.
17/04/99	KSC Eendracht Aalst	A	1-0	Zewlakow Ma.
24/04/99	R Excelsior Mouscron	A	0-1	
01/05/99	KVC Westerlo	H	1-0	Bonetto
05/05/99	Club Brugge KV	A	1-3	Zewlakow Ma.
09/05/99	KFC Germinal Ekeren	H	2-1	Zewlakow Ma., Smid (p)
16/05/99	K St.-Truidense VV	A	1-1	Van den Eede

CLUB BRUGGE KV

CLUB DIRECTORY

Club Brugge KV
Olympialaan 74
8200 Brugge
tel - (050) 402121
fax - (050) 381023
Year of Formation - 1894
President - Michel Van Maele
Secretary - Jacques De Nolf
Coach - Eric Gerets (99/00 - René Verheyen)
Stadium - Jan Breydel (14,500)

APPEARANCES 98/99

	P	Ap	(s)	Gls
Eric ADDO (GHA)	M	14	(4)	1
Darco ANIC (YUG)	M	20	(4)	4
Vital BORKELMANS	D	28	(6)	1
Gert CLAESSENS	A	20	(2)	10
Tjörven DE BRUL	D	30		8
Olivier DE COCK	D	11	(4)	1
Eric DEFLANDRE	D	31	(2)	1
Elonga Elos EKAKIA (DRC)	A	15	(5)	2
Nader Ibrahim EL SAYED (EGY)	G	20		
Khalilou FADIGA (SEN)	A	16	(5)	4
Aleksandar ILIC (YUG)	D	31	(1)	4
Edgaras JANKAUSKAS (LIT)	A	21	(1)	5
Nordin JBARI	A	6	(7)	5
Nzelo LEMBI (DRC)	D	12	(9)	4
Milan LESNJAK (YUG)	D	9	(3)	1
Dalibor MITROVIC (YUG)	M	2	(5)	
Koen SCHOCKAERT	A	1	(6)	1
Ebou SILLAH (GAM)	A	1	(4)	
Franky VAN DER ELST	M	30		1
Gert VERHEYEN	M	14	(1)	5
Gunther VERJANS	M	2	(10)	
Dany VERLINDEN	G	14		
Sven VERMANT	M	26	(5)	7

LEAGUE RESULTS 1998/99

23/08/98	KSC Eendracht Aalst	A	2-0	Claessens 2
29/08/98	KFC Germinal Ekeren	H	2-1	Claessens 2
02/09/98	K St.-Truidense VV	A	1-1	Addo
09/09/98	RSC Anderlecht	A	3-2	Anic, Deflandre, Lesnjak
13/09/98	KRC Harelbeke	H	1-0	Jankauskas
18/09/98	KSC Lokeren	A	0-2	
23/09/98	KFC Lommelse SK	H	0-1	
26/09/98	K Lierse SK	H	3-1	Jbari 2, Vermant
03/10/98	KV Oostende	A	4-1	Lembi, Jbari, Anic, Vermant
10/10/98	R Standard Liège	H	1-1	De Brul
24/10/98	KAA Gent	A	4-0	De Brul 3, Schockaert
30/10/98	KRC Genk	H	2-0	Vermant, Ekakia
08/11/98	KV Kortrijk	A	4-2	Claessens 2, De Cock, Vermant
15/11/98	RSC Charleroi	H	3-2	Claessens, De Brul, Ilic
21/11/98	KSK Beveren	A	2-1	Claessens, Fadiga
29/11/98	R Excelsior Mouscron	H	0-0	
04/12/98	KVC Westerlo	A	2-1	Lembi, Borkelmans (p)
13/12/98	KSC Eendracht Aalst	H	0-0	
20/12/98	KFC Germinal Ekeren	A	0-2	
17/01/99	K St.-Truidense VV	H	3-2	De Brul, Verheyen, Claessens
23/01/99	KFC Lommelse SK	A	1-2	Fadiga
29/01/99	RSC Anderlecht	H	2-0	De Brul 2
14/02/99	KRC Harelbeke	A	2-0	Vermant, Verheyen
26/02/99	KSC Lokeren	H	4-0	Fadiga, Jankauskas, Ilic, Vermant
07/03/99	K Lierse SK	A	2-5	Jbari 2
14/03/99	KV Oostende	H	2-0	Verheyen, Fadiga
19/03/99	R Standard Liège	A	0-3	
03/04/99	KAA Gent	H	1-0	Vermant (p)
18/04/99	KRC Genk	A	1-1	Jankauskas
25/04/99	KV Kortrijk	H	3-0	Verheyen, Jankauskas 2
30/04/99	RSC Charleroi	A	2-1	Lembi, Verheyen
05/05/99	KSK Beveren	H	3-1	Anic, Lembi, Ilic
09/05/99	R Excelsior Mouscron	A	0-2	
16/05/99	KVC Westerlo	H	5-3	Ilic, Ekakia, Anic, Claessens, Van der Elst (p)

RSC CHARLEROI

CLUB DIRECTORY

Royal Charleroi Sporting Club
Boulevard Zoë Drion 19
6000 Charleroi
tel - (071) 328734/319126
fax - (071) 327514
Year of Formation - 1904
President - Jean-Paul Spaute
Secretary - Pierre-Yves Hendrickx
Coach - Robert Waseige (99/00 - Luka Peruzovic)
Stadium - Mambourg (10,000)

APPEARANCES 98/99

	P	Ap	(s)	Gls
Enzo BIONDO	M	1		
Dante BROGNO	M	19	(2)	9
Carlo CAMILLERI	M	2	(4)	
Ray Luciano DJIM (CAF)	A	11	(16)	2
Serge EPUTA	M		(1)	
Mario FASANO (ITA)	D	9	(1)	
Franky FRANS	G	34		
Roch GERARD	D	3	(2)	
Adama GUEYE (SEN)	A	22	(1)	7
Róbert JÓVAN (HUN)	A	3	(3)	
Mamadou KERE	M	4	(1)	
Kaba MANE	A	4	(6)	1
Geoffrey N'GORAN (CIV)	A	7	(1)	1
Serhiy OMELIANOVICH (UKR)	M	16	(4)	
Alassane OUEDRAOGO (BFA)	A	14	(10)	2
Frédéric PEIREMANS	D	23	(1)	1
Aziz RABBAH (MAR)	M	30		1
Samuel REMY	M	19	(6)	4
Dandou SELENGE (DRC)	D	19	(2)	
Sandro SOUZA	A	10	(1)	2
Alexandre TEKLAK	D	33		1
Bertin TOKENE (CMR)	D	26		1
Jacky ULLRICH (FRA)	D	4	(3)	
Daniel VAN BUYTEN	M	12	(7)	1
Christophe VANDENBERGH	M	3	(3)	
Maurice VAN HAM (HOL)	M	19	(4)	1
Laurent WUILLOT	D	27		2

LEAGUE RESULTS 1998/99

22/08/98	RSC Anderlecht	A	1-1	Gueye
30/08/98	KRC Harelbeke	H	2-1	Ouedraogo, Rabbah
02/09/98	KSC Lokeren	A	1-3	og (Van Dender)
09/09/98	KV Oostende	A	0-0	
12/09/98	R Standard Liège	H	1-0	Van Ham
19/09/98	KAA Gent	A	1-1	Gueye
22/09/98	K Lierse SK	H	2-1	Gueye, Remy
26/09/98	KRC Genk	H	1-1	Tokene
04/10/98	KV Kortrijk	A	2-2	Gueye, Peiremans
10/10/98	KSC Eendracht Aalst	H	0-1	
24/10/98	KSK Beveren	H	1-2	N'Goran
30/10/98	R Excelsior Mouscron	A	2-3	Gueye 2
07/11/98	KVC Westerlo	H	1-3	Gueye
15/11/98	Club Brugge KV	A	2-3	Brogno 2
21/11/98	KFC Germinal Ekeren	H	2-2	Remy, Djim
28/11/98	K St.-Truidense VV	A	0-1	
05/12/98	KFC Lommelse SK	H	1-1	Remy
20/12/98	KRC Harelbeke	A	1-1	Djim
16/01/99	KSC Lokeren	H	2-1	Ouedraogo, Brogno
23/01/99	K Lierse SK	A	0-4	
30/01/99	KV Oostende	H	1-1	Wuillot
13/02/99	R Standard Liège	A	0-2	
27/02/99	KAA Gent	H	1-1	Brogno
06/03/99	KRC Genk	A	1-2	Souza
13/03/99	KV Kortrijk	H	2-1	Mané, Brogno (p)
21/03/99	KSC Eendracht Aalst	A	2-2	Van Buyten, Wuillot
03/04/99	KSK Beveren	A	2-1	Teklak, Remy
09/04/99	RSC Anderlecht	H	0-2	
17/04/99	R Excelsior Mouscron	H	1-3	Brogno
24/04/99	KVC Westerlo	A	0-1	
30/04/99	Club Brugge KV	H	1-2	Brogno
05/05/99	KFC Germinal Ekeren	A	0-2	
09/05/99	K St.-Truidense VV	H	2-1	Brogno 2 (1p)
16/05/99	KFC Lommelse SK	A	1-2	Souza

KSC EENDRACHT AALST

CLUB DIRECTORY

KSC Eendracht Aalst
Bredestraat 10
9300 Aalst
tel - (053) 769110
fax - (053) 779878
Year of Formation - 1919
President - Gilbert De Jonge
Secretary - Jean-Pierre Van Drogenbroeck
Coach - Barry Hulshoff
Stadium - Pierre Cornelis (10,683)

APPEARANCES 98/99

		P	Ap	(s)	Gls
Kingsley AMUNIKE (NIG)	D		8	(1)	
Eric BONGUMBA	M		1	(3)	
Davy COOREMAN	M		28	(3)	8
Steve COOREMAN	D		18	(9)	
Dirk DAELMANS	D		14	(11)	
José DE OLIVEIRA Alexandre (BRA)	A		22	(4)	6
Altair DOS SANTOS (BRA)	A		1	(3)	
Daniel GARCIA (ESP)	A		2	(5)	
Johan GEERAERTS	M			(3)	
Jonny HANSSEN (NOR)	M		7	(6)	
Peter LASSEN (DEN)	A		1		1
Christophe LAUWERS	A		9	(4)	2
Harald MEYSSEN	M		24	(5)	5
Ljubodrag MILOSEVIC (MAC)	D		5	(1)	
Jean-Claude MUKANYA (DRC)	D		24	(3)	
Peter QUINTELIER	M		13	(5)	
Cosimó SARLI (ITA)	A		9	(1)	7
Kris TEMMERMAN	M		15	(5)	1
Gunter THIEBAUT	A		21	(9)	7
Florián URBÁN (HUN)	D		18	(2)	3
Sammy VAN DEN BOSSCHE	A		32		
Peter VAN DER HEYDEN	D		29		4
Philippe VANDE WALLE	G		34		
David VAN HOYWEGHEN	D		26		2
Jan VAN STEENBERGHE	G			(1)	
Stijn VERGEYLEN	D		13	(5)	

LEAGUE RESULTS 1998/99

23/08/98	Club Brugge KV	H	0-2	
29/08/98	R Standard Liège	A	0-3	
02/09/98	KFC Germinal Ekeren	H	5-0	Lassen, Cooreman D., Van der Heyden, De Oliveira, Urbán
05/09/98	KAA Gent	A	2-2	Cooreman D., Thiebaut
09/09/98	K St.-Truidense VV	H	1-3	Meyssen
12/09/98	KRC Genk	A	0-2	
20/09/98	KFC Lommelse SK	H	3-1	Van der Heyden, Meyssen (p), Cooreman D.
27/09/98	KV Kortrijk	A	4-3	Cooreman D., Lauwers, Meyssen, Thiebaut
04/10/98	RSC Anderlecht	H	0-0	
10/10/98	RSC Charleroi	A	1-0	Thiebaut
25/10/98	KRC Harelbeke	H	2-2	Thiebaut, De Oliveira
31/10/98	KSK Beveren	A	2-0	Temmerman, Thiebaut
08/11/98	KSC Lokeren	H	3-3	De Oliveira, Van der Heyden, Urbán (p)
14/11/98	R Excelsior Mouscron	A	1-3	Urbán
22/11/98	K Lierse SK	H	1-4	Cooreman D.
29/11/98	KVC Westerlo	H	3-2	Meyssen, Lauwers, Van Hoywegen
05/12/98	KV Oostende	A	1-4	De Oliveira
13/12/98	Club Brugge KV	A	0-0	
20/12/98	R Standard Liège	H	1-0	Van der Heyden
17/01/99	KFC Germinal Ekeren	A	0-1	
24/01/99	KAA Gent	H	0-2	
30/01/99	K St.-Truidense VV	A	0-2	
13/02/99	KRC Genk	H	1-2	Thiebaut
28/02/99	KFC Lommelse SK	A	3-0	og (Simons), Sarli, De Oliveira
07/03/99	KV Kortrijk	H	1-1	Cooreman D.
13/03/99	RSC Anderlecht	A	1-2	Sarli
21/03/99	RSC Charleroi	H	2-2	Sarli 2
03/04/99	KRC Harelbeke	A	1-5	Sarli
17/04/99	KSK Beveren	H	0-1	
24/04/99	KSC Lokeren	A	2-6	Meyssen, Sarli
02/05/99	R Excelsior Mouscron	H	1-4	og (De Vleeschauwer)
05/05/99	K Lierse SK	A	1-3	Cooreman D.
08/05/99	KVC Westerlo	A	1-1	Thiebaut
16/05/99	KV Oostende	H	4-0	Cooreman D., Van Hoyweghen, De Oliveira, Sarli

R EXCELSIOR MOUSCRON

CLUB DIRECTORY

Royal Excelsior Mouscron
Rue du Stade 33
7700 Mouscron
tel - (056) 860600
fax - (056) 860550
Year of Formation - 1964
President - Jean-Pierre Doutremmerie
Manager - Jacques Vandewalle
Coach - Hugo Broos
Stadium - Le Canonnier (8,199)

APPEARANCES 98/99

		P	Ap	(s)	Gls
Matthieu ASSOU	M			(3)	
Zoran BAN (CRO)	A	24		(4)	16
Olivier BESENGEZ	D	30			3
Marco CASTO	M	24		(6)	4
Thomas DEBENEST	M			(1)	
Koen DE VLEESCHAUWER	D	14			
Steve DUGARDEIN	M	33			2
Mustapha EL IDRISSI (FRA)	A	5		(18)	3
Lionel LADON	M			(4)	
Axel LAWAREE	A	8			2
Damir LESJAK (CRO)	D	7		(6)	1
Tonci MARTIC (CRO)	M	28		(2)	2
Olivier NZUZI (DRC)	A			(2)	
Frédéric PIERRE	A	22			6
Giovanni SEYNHAEVE	D	14		(3)	
Stefaan TANGHE	M	31		(1)	12
Franck VANDENDRIESSCHE	G	34			
Yves VANDERHAEGHE	M	31			3
Gonzague VAN DOOREN	A	22		(10)	4
Donald VAN DURME	D	5		(3)	1
Claude VERSPAILLE	D	4		(8)	
Gordan VIDOVIC	D	30			13
Marc WUYTS	A	8		(2)	3

LEAGUE RESULTS 1998/99

22/08/98	K St.-Truidense VV	A	2-0	Ban, El Idrissi
29/08/98	KFC Lommelse SK	H	2-0	Vidovic (p), Besengez
02/09/98	RSC Anderlecht	A	1-1	Vidovic (p)
05/09/98	KRC Harelbeke	H	2-2	Lawarée, Ban
09/09/98	KSC Lokeren	A	0-0	
12/09/98	K Lierse SK	H	0-0	
19/09/98	KV Oostende	A	4-2	Lawarée, Vidovic (p), Vanderhaeghe, Ban
25/09/98	R Standard Liège	H	1-5	Van Dooren
02/10/98	KAA Gent	A	0-3	
11/10/98	KRC Genk	H	3-5	Pierre, Ban, Van Durme
25/10/98	KV Kortrijk	A	2-2	Ban, Pierre
30/10/98	RSC Charleroi	H	3-2	Dugardein, Vanderhaeghe, Tanghe
07/11/98	KSK Beveren	A	4-1	Ban, El Idrissi, Casto, Vidovic (p)
14/11/98	KSC Eendracht Aalst	H	3-1	Tanghe 2, Pierre
21/11/98	KVC Westerlo	H	2-1	Ban, Besengez
29/11/98	Club Brugge KV	A	0-0	
05/12/98	KFC Germinal Ekeren	H	2-2	Vanderhaeghe, Van Dooren
12/12/98	K St.-Truidense VV	H	5-1	og (Fiers), Vidovic, Pierre, Lesjak, Van Dooren
19/12/98	KFC Lommelse SK	A	3-2	Ban 2 (1p), Martic
16/01/99	RSC Anderlecht	H	2-3	Casto, Tanghe
24/01/99	KRC Harelbeke	A	4-0	Besengez, Vidovic (p), Wuyts 2
30/01/99	KSC Lokeren	H	5-1	Vidovic 2 (1p), Tanghe, Casto, El Idrissi
12/02/99	K Lierse SK	A	2-1	Pierre, Tanghe
27/02/99	KV Oostende	H	2-1	Casto, Van Dooren
05/03/99	R Standard Liège	A	0-2	
12/03/99	KAA Gent	H	7-1	Dugardein, Tanghe, Ban 2, Vidovic 2 (1p), Wuyts
20/03/99	KRC Genk	A	0-3	
03/04/99	KV Kortrijk	H	3-1	Vidovic 2, Tanghe
17/04/99	RSC Charleroi	A	3-1	Ban 2, Martic
24/04/99	KSK Beveren	H	1-0	Ban
02/05/99	KSC Eendracht Aalst	A	4-1	Tanghe 3, Pierre
05/05/99	KVC Westerlo	A	1-1	Tanghe
09/05/99	Club Brugge KV	H	2-0	Ban 2
16/05/99	KFC Germinal Ekeren	A	1-1	Vidovic (p)

KRC GENK

CLUB DIRECTORY

KRC Genk
Stadionplein 4
3600 Genk
tel - (089) 841608
fax - (089) 841708
Year of Formation - 1988
President - Edgard Troonbeeckx
Manager - Paul Heylen
Coach - Aimé Anthuenis (99/00 - Jos Heyligen)
Stadium - Thyl Gheyselinck (16,570)

MAJOR HONOURS
League Championship - (1) 1999.
Domestic Cup - (1) 1998.

APPEARANCES 98/99

	P	Ap	(s)	Gls
István BROCKHAUSER (HUN)	G	33		
Wilfried DELBROEK	M	32		1
Edmilson DOS SANTOS (BRA)	A		(2)	
Gert DOUMEN	G	1		
Bjarni GUDJÓNSSON (ISL)	M	4	(3)	
Johannes GUDJÓNSSON (ISL)	M		(5)	
Thórdur GUDJÓNSSON (ISL)	M	28		9
Besnik HASI (CRO)	M	32		2
Marc HENDRICKX	M	27	(4)	4
Ferenc HORVÁTH (HUN)	A	1	(6)	3
Daniel KIMONI	D	31		
Ngoy N'SUMBU (DRC)	A	2	(21)	4
Domenico OLIVIERI (ITA)	D	26		
Mike ORIGI (KEN)	M	24	(8)	12
Souleymane OULARE (GUI)	A	30	(1)	17
Juha REINI (FIN)	D	21	(5)	
ROGÉRIO de Oliveira (BRA)	A	5	(11)	1
Branko STRUPAR	A	33		18
Stefan TEELEN	M		(5)	
Chris VAN GEEM	D	31		1
Marc VANGRONSVELD	D	13	(9)	

LEAGUE RESULTS 1998/99

23/08/98	KSC Lokeren	A	0-2	
30/08/98	K Lierse SK	H	3-1	Delbroek, Oulare, Horváth
06/09/98	R Standard Liège	H	2-1	N'Sumbu, Origi
09/09/98	KAA Gent	A	1-0	Gudjónsson Th.
12/09/98	KSC Eendracht Aalst	H	2-0	Gudjónsson Th., Horváth
20/09/98	KV Kortrijk	H	3-1	Oulare, Strupar, Origi
23/09/98	KV Oostende	A	1-1	Oulare
26/09/98	RSC Charleroi	A	1-1	Strupar
04/10/98	KSK Beveren	H	1-0	Horváth
10/10/98	R Excelsior Mouscron	A	5-3	Rogério, Strupar, Oulare 3
25/10/98	KVC Westerlo	H	3-0	Origi 2, Oulare
30/10/98	Club Brugge KV	A	0-2	
08/11/98	KFC Germinal Ekeren	H	3-2	Origi, Oulare, Hendrickx
14/11/98	K St.-Truidense VV	A	2-2	Strupar, Origi
21/11/98	KFC Lommelse SK	H	6-0	Strupar 4, Hasi, Oulare
28/11/98	RSC Anderlecht	A	2-3	Strupar, Oulare
06/12/98	KRC Harelbeke	H	2-2	Gudjónsson Th., N'Sumbu
13/12/98	KSC Lokeren	H	3-1	Origi, og (Staelens), Oulare
18/12/98	K Lierse SK	A	1-1	Van Geem
18/01/99	KV Oostende	H	3-0	Origi, Gudjónsson Th., N'Sumbu
27/01/99	R Standard Liège	A	4-2	Strupar 2, Gudjónsson Th., Oulare
30/01/99	KAA Gent	H	1-0	Origi
13/02/99	KSC Eendracht Aalst	A	2-1	Strupar 2
06/03/99	RSC Charleroi	H	2-1	Oulare, Gudjónsson Th.
10/03/99	KV Kortrijk	A	3-1	Strupar, Oulare, Gudjónsson Th.
13/03/99	KSK Beveren	A	0-1	
20/03/99	R Excelsior Mouscron	H	3-0	Oulare 2 (1p), og (Besengez)
03/04/99	KVC Westerlo	A	1-1	N'Sumbu
18/04/99	Club Brugge KV	H	1-1	Origi
24/04/99	KFC Germinal Ekeren	A	2-0	Hendrickx, Hasi
02/05/99	K St.-Truidense VV	H	4-1	Gudjónsson Th., Origi 2, Strupar (p)
05/05/99	KFC Lommelse SK	A	3-0	Strupar, Hendrickx 2
09/05/99	RSC Anderlecht	H	2-5	Strupar 2 (2p)
16/05/99	KRC Harelbeke	A	2-1	Oulare, Gudjónsson Th.

KAA GENT

CLUB DIRECTORY

KAA Gent
Bruiloftstraat 42
9050 Gentbrugge-Gent
tel - (09) 2306610
fax - (09) 2302010
Year of Formation - 1898
President - Jean Van Milders
Manager - Michel Louwagie
Coach - Johan Boskamp; Herman Vermeulen;
Trond Sollied
Stadium - Jules Ottenstadion (18,215)

MAJOR HONOURS
Domestic Cup - (2) 1964, 1984.

APPEARANCES 98/99

		P	Ap	(s)	Gls
Mohammed BARKA	M	20	(3)	6
Thomas CAERS	D	18	(4)	1
Daniel CAMUS	D	8	(9)	
Thomas CHATELLE	A	8	(10)	1
Pieter COLLEN	D	30		2
Frank DAUWEN	M	9	(1)	
Tom DECRAEKE	A	3		1
Marc DEGRYSE	M	28	(1)	10
Laurent DELORGE	A	9	(1)	5
Gunter DE MEYER	M		(2)	
Stefaan DE PUYDT	M		(1)	
Ivica DRAGUTINOVIC (YUG)	D	31		2
Abdelkarim ERMOUKI	M	3	(1)	
Ronald FOGUENNE	M	25	(2)	4
Frédéric HERPOEL	G	34		
Sandy MARTENS	A	27	(1)	8
Carl MASSAGIE	D	10	(4)	
Sylvain N'DIAYE	M	5	(6)	
Anders NIELSEN (DEN)	A	21	(5)	6
Edin RAMCIC (BOS)	D	30		
Cédric ROUSSEL	A	19	(12)	8
Ben SASSI	M		(1)	
Krystof SNELDERS	M		(1)	
Tomas VASOV (YUG)	D	8	(1)	
Stijn VREVEN	D	27	(1)	
Evan WHITFIELD	M	1	(1)	

LEAGUE RESULTS 1998/99

22/08/98	K Lierse SK	A	2-1	Degryse, Roussel
29/08/98	KV Oostende	H	1-1	Delorge
02/09/98	R Standard Liège	A	0-2	
05/09/98	KSC Eendracht Aalst	H	2-2	Roussel, Delorge
09/09/98	KRC Genk	H	0-1	
13/09/98	KV Kortrijk	A	4-3	Delorge, Dragutinovic, Foguenne, Nielsen
19/09/98	RSC Charleroi	H	1-1	Roussel (p)
26/09/98	KSK Beveren	A	3-0	Delorge, Martens, Roussel (p)
02/10/98	R Excelsior Mouscron	H	3-0	Martens, Degryse, Nielsen
10/10/98	KVC Westerlo	A	3-3	Nielsen, Delorge, Roussel (p)
24/10/98	Club Brugge KV	H	0-4	
31/10/98	KFC Germinal Ekeren	A	1-8	Nielsen
07/11/98	K St.-Truidense VV	H	1-1	Degryse
14/11/98	KFC Lommelse SK	A	1-0	Caers
21/11/98	RSC Anderlecht	H	3-2	Degryse, Collen, Martens
29/11/98	KRC Harelbeke	A	2-2	Barka, Dragutinovic
05/12/98	KSC Lokeren	H	2-1	Barka, Martens
12/12/98	K Lierse SK	H	1-0	Barka (p)
19/12/98	KV Oostende	A	2-2	Degryse, Barka (p)
16/01/99	R Standard Liège	H	3-2	Martens, Barka 2
24/01/99	KSC Eendracht Aalst	A	2-0	Degryse, Martens (p)
30/01/99	KRC Genk	A	0-1	
13/02/99	KV Kortrijk	H	3-1	Foguenne 3
27/02/99	RSC Charleroi	A	1-1	Degryse
06/03/99	KSK Beveren	H	4-1	Degryse 2, Martens, Nielsen
12/03/99	R Excelsior Mouscron	A	1-7	Roussel
20/03/99	KVC Westerlo	H	2-0	Martens, Chatelle
03/04/99	Club Brugge KV	A	0-1	
17/04/99	KFC Germinal Ekeren	H	1-3	Roussel
24/04/99	K St.-Truidense VV	A	0-1	
01/05/99	KFC Lommelse SK	H	2-2	Roussel, Nielsen
05/05/99	RSC Anderlecht	A	0-4	
09/05/99	KRC Harelbeke	H	0-0	
16/05/99	KSC Lokeren	A	4-1	og (Zéré), Degryse, Collen, Decraeke

KFC GERMINAL EKEREN

CLUB DIRECTORY

KFC Germinal Ekeren (now - Germinal Beerschot
Antwerpen)
De Geyterstraat 133
2020 Antwerpen
tel - (03) 2484845
fax - (03) 2484846
Year of Formation - 1999
President - Jos Verhaegen
Manager - Louis De Vries
Coach - Herman Helleputte
(99/00 - Franky Van der Elst)
Stadium - Olympisch Stadion (10,300)

MAJOR HONOURS
Domestic Cup - (1) 1997.

APPEARANCES 98/99

		P	Ap	(s)	Gls
Matthew ANDREWS (ENG)	G	1			
Ian BAKALA	M		(1)		
Joël BARTHOLOMEEUSSEN	M	9	(8)	2	
Mario DA GRACA	M		(2)		
Nick DESCAMPS	D	5	(1)		
Tony HERREMAN	D	30	(2)	2	
Gunther HOFMANS	M	31	(1)	8	
Manu KARAGIANNIS	M	31		2	
Ervin KOVÁCS (HUN)	D	20	(3)	1	
Cvijan MILOSEVIC (BOS)	M	23	(2)	3	
Jan MOONS	G	33			
Kurt MORHAYE	A	23	(7)	6	
Justice SANDJON (CMR)	D	20			
Marc SCHAESSENS	D	11	(10)		
Francis SEVEREYNS	A	11	(4)	6	
Thierry SIQUET	D	24	(3)		
Rudi SMIDTS	D	32		2	
Wesley SONCK	A	15	(17)	7	
Edwin VAN ANKEREN (HOL)	A	20	(4)	7	
Tom VANDERVEE	D	25	(4)	1	
Alain VAN MIEGHEM	M	1	(5)		
Bart VAN ZUNDERT	M		(3)		
Mike VERSTRAETEN	D	9	(1)		

LEAGUE RESULTS 1998/99

22/08/98	KVC Westerlo	H	0-3	
29/08/98	Club Brugge KV	A	1-2	Herreman
02/09/98	KSC Eendracht Aalst	A	0-5	
05/09/98	K St.-Truidense VV	H	1-0	Sonck
09/09/98	KFC Lommelse SK	A	2-1	Hofmans, Sonck
12/09/98	RSC Anderlecht	H	0-3	
18/09/98	KRC Harelbeke	A	4-0	Van Ankeren 3, Morhaye
26/09/98	KSC Lokeren	H	1-1	Morhaye
03/10/98	K Lierse SK	A	0-1	
10/10/98	KV Oostende	H	2-2	Van Ankeren, Smidts
24/10/98	R Standard Liège	A	0-1	
31/10/98	KAA Gent	H	8-1	Van Ankeren, Smidts, og (Vreven), Hofmans, Milosevic, Sonck 2, Morhaye
08/11/98	KRC Genk	A	2-3	Hofmans, Morhaye
15/11/98	KV Kortrijk	H	2-1	Milosevic, Van Ankeren
21/11/98	RSC Charleroi	A	2-2	Hofmans 2
29/11/98	KSK Beveren	H	1-0	Milosevic
05/12/98	R Excelsior Mouscron	A	2-2	Morhaye, Sonck
12/12/98	KVC Westerlo	A	4-2	Herreman, Sonck, Hofmans 2
20/12/98	Club Brugge KV	H	2-0	Karagiannis, Sonck
17/01/99	KSC Eendracht Aalst	H	1-0	Hofmans
23/01/99	K St.-Truidense VV	A	0-2	
31/01/99	KFC Lommelse SK	H	1-0	Morhaye
20/02/99	RSC Anderlecht	A	0-2	
28/02/99	KRC Harelbeke	H	0-2	
06/03/99	KSC Lokeren	A	1-1	Vandervee (p)
13/03/99	K Lierse SK	H	1-1	Kovács
21/03/99	KV Oostende	A	1-0	Severeyns
03/04/99	R Standard Liège	H	0-1	
17/04/99	KAA Gent	A	3-1	Van Ankeren, Severeyns, Bartholomeeussen
24/04/99	KRC Genk	H	0-2	
02/05/99	KV Kortrijk	A	2-1	Severeyns, Bartholomeeussen
05/05/99	RSC Charleroi	H	2-0	Severeyns, Karagiannis
09/05/99	KSK Beveren	A	1-2	Severeyns
16/05/99	R Excelsior Mouscron	H	1-1	Severeyns

KRC HARELBEKE

CLUB DIRECTORY

KRC Harelbeke
Stasegemsesteenweg 23
8530 Harelbeke
tel - (056) 739170
fax - (056) 718135
Year of Formation - 1930
President - Geert Sustronck
Secretary - José Debrabandere
Coach - Henk Houwaart
Stadium - Forestiers (9,737)

APPEARANCES 98/99

	P	Ap	(s)	Gls
Aziz ANSAH (GHA)	M	1	(1)	1
Olivier BAUDRY (FRA)	M	24	(3)	6
Bafodé CAMARA (GUI)	A	6	(6)	3
Kurt DELTOUR	D	4	(9)	
Joris DE TOLLENAERE	A	28	(1)	3
Geert DE VLIEGER	G	33		
Ivan DE WILDE	G		(1)	
Andrei DIATEL	M	6	(2)	1
Ronny GASPERCIC	G	1		
Nordne HAMEG (ALG)	D	15		
Ali IBRAHIM (GHA)	A	7	(5)	
René KLOMP (HOL)	M	14	(10)	1
Arkadiusz KUBIK (POL)	M	29	(3)	1
Lukasz KUBIK (POL)	D	23	(1)	1
Martinius LAAMERS (HOL)	M	31		1
Daniel MAES	D	28	(1)	1
Dimitri MITCHKOV	A	4		2
Alex PASTOOR (HOL)	D	10	(2)	
David PAAS	A	14		4
Daniel SCAVONE	D	10		
Dragan TADIC (CRO)	M	4	(12)	
Ludwin VANNIEUWENHUYZE	D	3	(2)	
Kenny VERHOENE	D	21	(4)	3
Jeffrey VERHOEVEN	M	1		1
Hans VISSER (HOL)	M	25	(5)	4
Steven WOSTIJN	M	15	(13)	7
Rafael ZANGIONOV (RUS)	M	8	(5)	2
Rimantas ZVINGILAS (LIT)	A	9		1

LEAGUE RESULTS 1998/99

23/08/98	KV Kortrijk	H	1-0	Baudry
30/08/98	RSC Charleroi	A	1-2	Camara
02/09/99	KSK Beveren	H	1-1	Verhoene
05/09/98	R Excelsior Mouscron	A	2-2	De Tollenaere, Visser
09/09/98	KVC Westerlo	H	1-2	De Tollenaere
13/09/98	Club Brugge KV	A	0-1	
18/09/98	KFC Germinal Ekeren	H	0-4	
26/09/98	K St.-Truidense VV	A	0-1	
04/10/98	KFC Lommelse SK	H	1-1	Verhoene
10/10/98	RSC Anderlecht	A	1-3	Camara (p)
25/10/98	KSC Eendracht Aalst	A	2-2	Laamers, Baudry
31/10/98	KSC Lokeren	H	3-2	Baudry, Visser (p), Wostijn
07/11/98	K Lierse SK	A	1-3	Zangionov
15/11/98	KV Oostende	H	2-1	Visser, Wostijn
21/11/98	R Standard Liège	A	2-0	Klomp, Baudry
29/11/98	KAA Gent	H	2-2	Wostijn, Verhoene
06/12/98	KRC Genk	A	2-2	Wostijn, Camara
13/12/98	KV Kortrijk	A	0-0	
20/12/98	RSC Charleroi	H	1-1	De Tollenaere
16/01/99	KSK Beveren	A	3-0	Paas, Maes, Zangionov
24/01/99	R Excelsior Mouscron	H	0-4	
30/01/99	KVC Westerlo	A	3-0	og (Franken), Baudry, Ansah
14/02/99	Club Brugge KV	H	0-2	
28/02/99	KFC Germinal Ekeren	A	2-0	Paas, Baudry
07/03/99	K St.-Truidense VV	H	1-1	Zvingilas
13/03/99	KFC Lommelse SK	A	1-0	Verhoeven
21/03/99	RSC Anderlecht	H	1-2	Paas (p)
03/04/99	KSC Eendracht Aalst	H	5-1	Mitchkov 2, Kubik L., Wostijn, Paas
17/04/99	KSC Lokeren	A	0-1	
25/04/99	K Lierse SK	H	3-1	Wostijn 2, Visser
02/05/99	KV Oostende	A	0-1	
05/05/99	R Standard Liège	H	1-1	Diatel
09/05/99	KAA Gent	A	0-0	
16/05/99	KRC Genk	H	1-2	Kubik A.

KV KORTRIJK

CLUB DIRECTORY

KV Kortrijk
Meensesteenweg 84a
8500 Kortrijk
tel - (056) 350560
fax - (056) 355824
Year of Formation - 1971
President - Jacques Laverge
Manager - Gino Gylain
Coach - Michel De Wolf; Luc Vanderschommen
Stadium - Gulden Sporen (11,761)

APPEARANCES 98/99

	P	Ap	(s)	Gls
Nico BOONE	D	29	(1)	2
Koen DEBRABANDERE	M	3	(10)	2
Erik DE KOEYER (HOL)	G	19	(1)	
Andrei DEMKIN (RUS)	A	27	(6)	10
Andy DE PRE	M	2	(3)	
Farid DIFFALAH	D	3	(4)	
Stefano GHIRO (ITA)	A	1		
Jurgen HEYMANS	M	27	(2)	5
Peter JACOBS	D	11	(6)	
Eric JOLY (FRA)	M	24		2
Salif KEITA	A	28		13
Bert LAMAIRE	D	14	(9)	
Stefan LELEU	D	30		
Stijn MEERT	A	25	(6)	4
William PRUNIER (FRA)	D	14		3
Kevin REYNS	A	3	(3)	
Axel SMEETS	D	23		1
Fabrice STAELENS	D	16	(5)	2
Branko STOJANOVIC (YUG)	M	10	(3)	3
Ben SYLLA	M	1	(1)	
Piet TIMMERMAN	D	3	(2)	
Marc VAN BRITSOM	M	30		2
Jude VANDELANOITTE	D	14	(5)	
Kurt VANDOORNE	G	15	(1)	
Bart VANMARSENILLE	A	2		
Christophe VERBEEREN	D		(1)	

LEAGUE RESULTS 1998/99

23/08/98	KRC Harelbeke	A	0-1	
30/08/98	KSC Lokeren	H	0-6	
02/09/98	K Lierse SK	A	1-5	Meert
06/09/98	KV Oostende	H	2-0	Keita 2
09/09/98	R Standard Liège	A	1-2	Debrabandere
13/09/98	KAA Gent	H	3-4	Keita 2, Debrabandere
20/09/98	KRC Genk	A	1-3	Keita
27/09/98	KSC Eendracht Aalst	H	3-4	Keita 2, Van Britsom
04/10/98	RSC Charleroi	H	2-2	Meert, Boone
10/10/98	KSK Beveren	A	2-2	Heymans, Keita
25/10/98	R Excelsior Mouscron	H	2-2	Keita (p), Prunier
31/10/98	KVC Westerlo	A	0-2	
08/11/98	Club Brugge KV	H	2-4	Demkin, Heymans
15/11/98	KFC Germinal Ekeren	A	1-2	Keita
22/11/98	K St.-Truidense VV	H	2-2	Demkin, Meert
28/11/98	KFC Lommelse SK	A	1-3	Demkin
06/12/98	RSC Anderlecht	H	0-4	
13/12/98	KRC Harelbeke	H	0-0	
19/12/98	KSC Lokeren	A	1-2	Demkin
17/01/99	K Lierse SK	H	3-2	Boone, Demkin, Heymans
23/01/99	KV Oostende	A	3-1	Heymans, Stojanovic 2
31/01/99	R Standard Liège	H	1-3	Prunier
13/02/99	KAA Gent	A	1-3	Keita
07/03/99	KSC Eendracht Aalst	A	1-1	Staelens
10/03/99	KRC Genk	A	1-3	Stojanovic
13/03/99	RSC Charleroi	A	1-2	Joly (p)
21/03/99	KSK Beveren	H	1-0	Demkin
03/04/99	R Excelsior Mouscron	A	1-3	Keita
11/04/99	K St.-Truidense VV	A	2-2	Keita, Demkin
18/04/99	KVC Westerlo	H	4-2	Demkin (p), Van Britsom, Smeets (p), Meert
25/04/99	Club Brugge KV	A	0-3	
02/05/99	KFC Germinal Ekeren	H	1-2	Joly
09/05/99	KFC Lommelse SK	H	4-1	Prunier, Heymans, Demkin, Staelens
16/05/99	RSC Anderlecht	A	1-3	Demkin

K LIERSE SK

CLUB DIRECTORY

K Lierse SK
Voetbalstraat 4
2500 Lier
tel - (03) 4801370
fax - (03) 4880659
Year of Formation - 1906
President - Freddy Van Laer
Manager - Corneel De Ceulaer
Coach - Walter Meeuws
Stadium - Herman Vanderpoorten (14,000)

MAJOR HONOURS
League Championship - (4)
1932, 1942, 1960, 1997.
Domestic Cup - (2) 1969, 1999.

APPEARANCES 98/99

	P	Ap	(s)	Gls
David BROCKEN	D	29		5
Jurgen CAVENS	A	29	(4)	13
Filip DAEMS	D	27		1
Tim DE KEYSER	D	2	(3)	
Patrick DEMAN	G	8	(2)	
Filip HAAGDOREN	A	16	(14)	5
Carl HOEFKENS	D	29	(1)	
Pieter HUISTRA (HOL)	A	15	(7)	
Stijn HUYSEGEMS	D		(3)	
Dirk HUYSMANS	A	20	(9)	11
Steve LAEREMANS	D	21	(9)	1
Frank LEEN	M	29	(1)	1
Stanley MENZO (HOL)	G	26		
Jerry POORTERS	D	13	(2)	
Yves SERNEELS	D	11	(15)	
Gela SHEKILADZE (GEO)	D	7	(2)	
Hans SOMERS	M	21	(3)	8
Joe SPITERI (AUS)	A	3	(4)	3
Robby VAN DE WEYER	A	10	(14)	7
Eric VAN MEIR	D	32		14
Thomas ZDEBEL (GER)	M	26	(2)	3

LEAGUE RESULTS 1998/99

22/08/98	KAA Gent	H	1-2	Van Meir
30/08/98	KRC Genk	A	1-3	Cavens
02/09/98	KV Kortrijk	H	5-1	Van Meir, Somers, Huysmans 3
09/09/98	KSK Beveren	H	3-0	Van Meir, Somers 2
12/09/98	R Excelsior Mouscron	A	0-0	
19/09/98	KVC Westerlo	H	5-1	Somers, Leen, Brocken, Van Meir 2 (2p)
23/09/98	RSC Charleroi	A	1-2	Cavens
26/09/98	Club Brugge KV	A	1-3	Van Meir (p)
03/10/98	KFC Germinal Ekeren	H	1-0	Somers
10/10/98	K St.-Truidense VV	A	0-3	
24/10/98	KFC Lommelse SK	H	2-1	Brocken, Huysmans
31/10/98	RSC Anderlecht	A	0-2	
07/11/98	KRC Harelbeke	H	3-1	Van Meir 2, Cavens
14/11/98	KSC Lokeren	A	0-2	
22/11/98	KSC Eendracht Aalst	A	4-1	Haagdoren, Huysmans, Brocken, og (Temmerman)
28/11/98	KV Oostende	H	4-2	Haagdoren, Brocken 2, Cavens
12/12/98	KAA Gent	A	0-1	
18/12/98	KRC Genk	H	1-1	Van Meir
13/01/99	R Standard Liège	A	2-2	Cavens, Van Meir (p)
17/01/99	KV Kortrijk	A	2-3	Van de Weyer 2
23/01/99	RSC Charleroi	H	4-0	Cavens 2, Van Meir (p), Huysmans
30/01/99	KSK Beveren	A	3-1	Huysmans 2, Zdebel
12/02/99	R Excelsior Mouscron	H	1-2	Haagdoren
27/02/99	KVC Westerlo	A	2-0	Laeremans, Van Meir
07/03/99	Club Brugge KV	H	5-2	Somers 2, Cavens, Van de Weyer 2
13/03/99	KFC Germinal Ekeren	A	1-1	Huysmans
20/03/99	K St.-Truidense VV	H	6-0	Van de Weyer, Daems, Cavens 2, Zdebel 2
03/04/99	KFC Lommelse SK	A	0-0	
17/04/99	RSC Anderlecht	H	0-0	
25/04/99	KRC Harelbeke	A	1-3	Van Meir
01/05/99	KSC Lokeren	H	2-3	Van Meir (p), Huysmans
05/05/99	KSC Eendracht Aalst	H	3-1	Van de Weyer, Cavens 2
09/05/99	KV Oostende	A	6-0	Haagdoren 2, Huysmans, Somers, Van de Weyer, Spiteri
16/05/99	R Standard Liège	H	3-0	Spiteri 2, Cavens

KSC LOKEREN

KSC Lokeren
Daknamstraat 91
9160 Lokeren
tel - (09) 3483905
fax - (09) 3491243
Year of Formation - 1970
President - Roger Lambrecht
Secretary - Romain Van Schnoor
Coach - Willy Reynders
Stadium - Daknam (15,609)

APPEARANCES 98/99

	P	Ap	(s)	Gls
Dominique-Sam ABOUO	M	4	(1)	
Jean-Paul Gauthier BOEKA-LISASI (DRC)	A	17	(9)	9
Rigo BUAYI-KIDODA (DRC)	A		(1)	
Vaclav BUDKA (CZE)	M	8	(11)	1
Steven DE GEEST	D		(1)	
Danny D'HONDT	G	26		
Pascal DIAS (FRA)	A	18	(14)	6
Sinisa DOBRASINOVIC (YUG)	M		(3)	
Davy GIJSBRECHTS	D	9	(5)	
Chris JANSSENS	M	24	(3)	5
Jan KOLLER (CZE)	A	33		24
Jan KOZAK (SVK)	M	1	(3)	
Bart PEETERS	G		(1)	
Martin PENICKA (CZE)	D	22	(8)	3
Jurgen SIERENS	G	8		
Karel SNOECKX	M	19	(10)	2
Stefaan STAELENS	D	29	(3)	1
Branko STOJANOVIC (YUG)	A		(3)	
Jan VAN DAMME	D		(1)	
Stefan VAN DENDER	D	28	(1)	
Ronny VAN GENEUGDEN	M	29	(4)	5
Hein VANHAEZEBROUCK	D	22	(1)	1
Arnar VIDARSSON (ISL)	M	19	(2)	1
Roman VONASEK (CZE)	M	28		9
Patrice ZERE (CIV)	D	30		2

LEAGUE RESULTS 1998/99

23/08/98	KRC Genk	H	2-0	Vanhaezebrouck, Dias
30/08/98	KV Kortrijk	A	6-0	Penicka 2, Vonasek 2, Janssens, Koller
02/09/98	RSC Charleroi	H	3-1	Penicka, Koller, Van Geneugden
05/09/98	KSK Beveren	A	2-1	Janssens, Koller
09/09/98	R Excelsior Mouscron	H	0-0	
12/09/98	KVC Westerlo	A	3-4	Janssens, Staelens, Dias
18/09/98	Club Brugge KV	H	2-0	Dias, Koller
26/09/98	KFC Germinal Ekeren	A	1-1	Koller
03/10/98	K St.-Truidense VV	H	2-1	Vonasek 2
10/10/98	KFC Lommelse SK	A	2-1	Vonasek, Koller
23/10/98	RSC Anderlecht	H	2-3	Janssens, Koller
31/10/98	KRC Harelbeke	A	2-3	Koller, Janssens
08/11/98	KSC Eendracht Aalst	A	3-3	Koller, Van Geneugden (p), Dias
14/11/98	K Lierse SK	H	2-0	Koller 2
21/11/98	KV Oostende	A	0-0	
27/11/98	R Standard Liège	A	4-1	Snoeckx 2, Boeka-Lisasi, Koller
05/12/98	KAA Gent	A	1-2	Koller
13/12/98	KRC Genk	A	1-3	Boeka-Lisasi
19/12/98	KV Kortrijk	H	2-1	Van Geneugden, Zéré
16/01/99	RSC Charleroi	A	1-2	Vonasek
23/01/99	KSK Beveren	H	4-3	Dias, Van Geneugden, Vonasek, Koller
30/01/99	R Excelsior Mouscron	A	1-5	Koller
26/02/99	Club Brugge KV	A	0-4	
06/03/99	KFC Germinal Ekeren	H	1-1	Koller
10/03/99	KVC Westerlo	H	3-0	Boeka-Lisasi, Koller, Dias
13/03/99	K St.-Truidense VV	A	0-7	
20/03/99	KFC Lommelse SK	H	2-1	Koller, Vidarsson
02/04/99	RSC Anderlecht	A	1-1	Koller
17/04/99	KRC Harelbeke	H	1-0	Van Geneugden
24/04/99	KSC Eendracht Aalst	H	6-2	Vonasek, Zéré, Boeka-Lisasi, Koller 3 (1p)
01/05/99	K Lierse SK	A	3-2	Vonasek, Boeka-Lisasi 2
05/05/99	KV Oostende	H	1-2	Koller
09/05/99	R Standard Liège	A	4-2	Boeka-Lisasi 3, Budka
16/05/99	KAA Gent	H	1-4	Koller

KFC LOMMELSE SK

CLUB DIRECTORY

KFC Lommelse SK
Gemeentelijk Sportcentrum
Speelpleinstraat 20
3920 Lommel
tel - (011) 559090
fax - (011) 559099
Year of Formation - 1932
President - Dirk Vanden Boer
Manager - Gaston Peeters
Coach - Leo Clijsters; Jos Daerden
Stadium - Gemeentelijk Sportcentrum (12,500)

APPEARANCES 98/99

	P	Ap	(s)	Gls
Ismail AYAZ (TUR)	A	1	(4)	
Zsolt BÁRÁNYOS (HUN)	M	13	(6)	
Eddy BEMBUANA-KEVE (DRC)	A	3	(13)	1
Gert CANNAERTS	A	14	(3)	4
Dieter DEKELVER	A	15	(11)	7
Robert ESHUN (GHA)	A	23	(8)	6
Jacky MATTHIJSSEN	G	6		
Wim MENNES	M	17	(4)	1
Daniel NASSEN	D	23		1
Patrick NIJS	G	28	(1)	
Michel NOBEN	D	8	(8)	
Didier SEGERS	D	21	(2)	
Timmy SIMONS	D	32		1
Dariusz SZUBERT (POL)	M	6	(5)	2
Fenad TIGANJ	M	3	(1)	
Wim VAN DIEST	D	23	(1)	1
Eric VAN KESSEL (HOL)	D	23	(1)	
Dominique VANMAELE	M	5		
Harm VANVELDHOVEN	M	28		
Nivaldo Lima VIEIRA (BRA)	M	12	(2)	
Kris VINCKEN	D	18	(3)	
Miroslaw WALIGORA (POL)	A	22	(8)	5
Karim ZOUAOUI (FRA)	M	30	(1)	3

LEAGUE RESULTS 1998/99

22/08/98	KSK Beveren	H	2-1	Zouaoui, Cannaerts
29/08/98	R Excelsior Mouscron	A	0-2	
02/09/98	KVC Westerlo	H	0-1	
09/09/98	KFC Germinal Ekeren	H	1-2	Waligora (p)
12/09/98	K St.-Truidense VV	A	1-2	Szubert
20/09/98	KSC Eendracht Aalst	A	1-3	Bembuana-Keve
23/09/98	Club Brugge KV	A	1-0	Cannaerts
26/09/98	RSC Anderlecht	H	2-2	Waligora 2
04/10/98	KRC Harelbeke	A	1-1	Van Diest
10/10/98	KSC Lokeren	H	1-2	Eshun
24/10/98	K Lierse SK	A	1-2	Waligora
31/10/98	KV Oostende	H	3-0	Nassen, Zouaoui, Szubert
07/11/98	R Standard Liège	A	0-1	
14/11/98	KAA Gent	H	0-1	
21/11/98	KRC Genk	A	0-6	
28/11/98	KV Kortrijk	H	3-1	Cannaerts, Zouaoui, Dekelver
05/12/98	RSC Charleroi	A	1-1	Mennes
12/12/98	KSK Beveren	A	0-0	
19/12/98	R Excelsior Mouscron	H	2-3	Waligora, Cannaerts
16/01/99	KVC Westerlo	A	1-2	Simons
23/01/99	Club Brugge KV	H	2-1	Dekelver, Eshun
31/01/99	KFC Germinal Ekeren	A	0-1	
13/02/99	K St.-Truidense VV	H	0-1	
28/02/99	KSC Eendracht Aalst	H	0-3	
06/03/99	RSC Anderlecht	A	0-3	
13/03/99	KRC Harelbeke	H	0-1	
20/03/99	KSC Lokeren	A	1-2	Dekelver
03/04/99	K Lierse SK	H	0-0	
17/04/99	KV Oostende	A	1-1	Eshun
24/04/99	R Standard Liège	H	3-0	og (Remacle), Eshun, Dekelver
01/05/99	KAA Gent	A	2-2	Dekelver 2
05/05/99	KRC Genk	H	0-3	
09/05/99	KV Kortrijk	A	1-4	Eshun
16/05/99	RSC Charleroi	H	2-1	Dekelver, Eshun

KV OOSTENDE

CLUB DIRECTORY

KV Oostende
Leopold Van Tyghemlaan 62
8400 Oostende
tel - (059) 703610
fax - (059) 514698
Year of Formation - 1981
President - Eddy Vergeylen
Manager - Luc Devroe
Coach - Dennis van Wijk; Jean-Marie Pfaff; Ronni
Brackx (99/00 - Leo Van der Elst)
Stadium - Albertpark (9,940)

APPEARANCES 98/99

	P	Ap	(s)	Gls
Frederik ANNYS	M	1	(3)	
Didier BAPUPA (DRC)	D	25	(2)	
Sven BROUCKMEERSCH	M	1	(1)	
Wim CUFFEZ	M	30	(3)	2
Laurent DAUWE	M	8	(3)	
Ivan DE CORTE	G	11		
Thibault DELIENS	M		(1)	
Björn DERYCKE	M	10	(4)	
Kenny DE VUYST	D	18	(6)	2
Virgil DE WINDT	G	1		
Paulo da Silva EDMILSON (BRA)	M	9	(1)	3
Haysam HAMOUCH (MAR)	A	4	(6)	1
Thierry FLIES	A	10	(10)	1
Noureddine HAMOUCH (MAR)	A	4	(6)	1
Antoine KABEMBA (DRC)	A	7	(8)	1
Lorenz KINDTNER (AUS)	M	26		3
Sidney LAMMENS	D	34		
Roger LUKAKU (DRC)	A	15	(5)	2
Johny NIERYNCK	D	30		
Bruno PARMENTIER	D	21	(7)	
Djörn PLETTINCK	D	3	(2)	
Ronny PRINS (HOL)	M	5	(2)	
Björn RENTY	M	7	(3)	
Gregorio SALHI	M	1		
Björn SMITS	M	27		4
Saïd TAHIRI	M	3	(2)	
Joey VAN ACKER	M		(1)	
Bart VAN DEN EECKHOUTE	M		(1)	
Kris VAN DE PUTTE	G	22		
Stefaan VAN RIEL	D	13		2
Kris WINDELS	A	21	(7)	5
Rachide YACHOU (MAR)	A	6	(2)	

LEAGUE RESULTS 1998/99

21/08/98	R Standard Liège	H	2-1	Kindtner 2
29/08/98	KAA Gent	A	1-1	Kindtner
06/09/98	KV Kortrijk	A	0-2	
09/09/98	RSC Charleroi	H	0-0	
12/09/98	KSK Beveren	A	0-5	
19/09/98	R Excelsior Mouscron	H	2-4	De Vuyst, Hamouch
23/09/98	KRC Genk	H	1-1	Smits
26/09/98	KVC Westerlo	A	0-7	
03/10/98	Club Brugge KV	H	1-4	Windels
11/10/98	KFC Germinal Ekeren	A	2-2	Windels, Lukaku
24/10/98	K St.-Truidense VV	H	0-1	
31/10/98	KFC Lommelse SK	A	0-3	
07/11/98	RSC Anderlecht	H	0-2	
15/11/98	KRC Harelbeke	A	1-2	Lukaku
21/11/98	KSC Lokeren	H	0-0	
28/11/98	K Lierse SK	A	2-4	Smits, De Vuyst
05/12/98	KSC Eendracht Aalst	H	4-1	Windels, Van Riel, Smits, Flies
12/12/98	R Standard Liège	A	0-3	
19/12/98	KAA Gent	H	2-2	Van Riel, Cuffez
18/01/99	KRC Genk	A	0-3	
23/01/99	KV Kortrijk	H	1-3	Edmilson
30/01/99	RSC Charleroi	A	1-1	Edmilson (p)
14/02/99	KSK Beveren	H	1-1	Windels
27/02/99	R Excelsior Mouscron	A	1-2	Windels
06/03/99	KVC Westerlo	H	1-1	Edmilson
14/03/99	Club Brugge KV	A	0-2	
21/03/99	KFC Germinal Ekeren	H	0-1	
03/04/99	K St.-Truidense VV	A	0-5	
17/04/99	KFC Lommelse SK	H	1-1	og (Van Kessel)
24/04/99	RSC Anderlecht	A	0-3	
02/05/99	KRC Harelbeke	H	1-0	Cuffez
05/05/99	KSC Lokeren	A	2-1	Smits, Kabemba
09/05/99	K Lierse SK	H	0-6	
16/05/99	KSC Eendracht Aalst	A	0-4	

K ST.-TRUIDENSE VV

CLUB DIRECTORY

K Sint-Truidense VV
Tiensesteenweg 170
3800 Sint-Truiden
tel - (011) 683829
fax - (011) 692380
Year of Formation - 1924
President - Léon Schepers
Secretary - Fernand Knaepen
Coach - Poll Peters
Stadium - Staaien (14,785)

APPEARANCES 98/99

	P	Ap	(s)	Gls
Samuel AERTS	D	2	(5)	
Dusan BELIC (YUG)	G	25		
Kris BUVENS	M	1	(4)	
Robrecht DECKERS	D		(1)	
Robbie DELLO	D	2	(2)	
Peter DELORGE	M		(1)	
Eddy DIERICKX	M	32		1
Rudy DUCOULOMBIER	D	17	(3)	1
Gaëtan ENGLEBERT	M	32		3
Filip FIERS	A	33		15
Gunthyer GRAMMET	M	2	(1)	
ISAÍAS (BRA)	M	25	(6)	3
Philippe LENGLOIS	D	31	(1)	
Kurt MERTENS	A	15	(12)	4
Steven NIJS	D	9		
René PETERSEN (DEN)	M	5	(7)	1
Mladen RUDONJA (SLO)	A	24	(5)	10
Patrick TEPPERS	M	32		9
Bram VANGEEL	A	1	(5)	
Dirk VAN OEKELEN	D	32		2
Peter VOETS	D	33		1
Robert VOLK (SLO)	G	9	(1)	
Wouter VRANCKEN	D	12	(8)	2

LEAGUE RESULTS 1998/99

22/08/98	R Excelsior Mouscron	H	0-2	
29/08/98	KVC Westerlo	A	4-1	Fiers, Teppers (p), Rudonja, Mertens
02/09/98	Club Brugge KV	H	1-1	Teppers (p)
05/09/98	KFC Germinal Ekeren	A	0-1	
09/09/98	KSC Eendracht Aalst	A	3-1	Petersen, Fiers, Englebert
12/09/98	KFC Lommelse SK	H	2-1	Englebert, Fiers
19/09/98	RSC Anderlecht	A	1-1	Rudonja
26/09/98	KRC Harelbeke	H	1-0	Fiers
03/10/98	KSC Lokeren	A	1-2	Voets
10/10/98	K Lierse SK	H	3-0	Isaías, Mertens, Van Oekelen
24/10/98	KV Oostende	A	1-0	Rudonja
31/10/98	R Standard Liège	H	0-1	
07/11/98	KAA Gent	A	1-1	Englebert
14/11/98	KRC Genk	H	2-2	Teppers (p), Fiers
22/11/98	KV Kortrijk	A	2-2	Teppers, Fiers
28/11/98	RSC Charleroi	H	1-0	Fiers
12/12/98	R Excelsior Mouscron	A	1-5	Rudonja
19/12/98	KVC Westerlo	H	0-0	
17/01/99	Club Brugge KV	A	2-3	Teppers 2 (1p)
23/01/99	KFC Germinal Ekeren	H	2-0	Fiers, Isaías
30/01/99	KSC Eendracht Aalst	H	2-0	Vrancken, Fiers
06/02/99	KSK Beveren	A	1-0	Van Oekelen
13/02/99	KFC Lommelse SK	A	1-0	Fiers
27/02/99	RSC Anderlecht	H	1-4	Mertens
07/03/99	KRC Harelbeke	A	1-1	Ducoulombier
13/03/99	KSC Lokeren	H	7-0	Fiers 3, Teppers, Mertens, Rudonja, Dierickx
20/03/99	K Lierse SK	A	0-6	
03/04/99	KV Oostende	H	5-0	Isaías, Fiers, Teppers (p), Rudonja 2
11/04/99	KV Kortrijk	H	2-2	Rudonja 2
17/04/99	R Standard Liège	A	0-2	
24/04/99	KAA Gent	H	1-0	Fiers
02/05/99	KRC Genk	A	1-4	Teppers
09/05/99	RSC Charleroi	A	1-2	Rudonja
16/05/99	KSK Beveren	H	1-1	Vrancken

R STANDARD LIEGE

CLUB DIRECTORY

Royal Standard de Liège
Rue de la Centrale 2
4200 Liège
tel - (04) 2522122
fax - (04) 2521469
Year of Formation - 1900
President - André Duchêne
Secretary - Francis Nicolay
Coach - Tomislav Ivic
Stadium - Sclessin (25,998)

MAJOR HONOURS
League Championship - (8) 1958, 1961, 1963,
1969, 1970, 1971, 1982, 1983.
Domestic Cup - (5)
1954, 1966, 1967, 1981, 1993.

APPEARANCES 98/99

	P	Ap	(s)	Gls
Rabiu AFOLABI (NIG)	D	26		1
Adrian ALIAJ (ALB)	M	16		1
Theophilius AMUZU	A		(1)	
Josko BILIC (CRO)	D	19	(2)	2
Robert BISCONTI	M	8	(2)	3
George BLAY (GHA)	D	18	(7)	2
Frédéric COLLARD	M		(1)	
André CRUZ (BRA)	D	9	(1)	1
Dimitri DE CONDE	M	29	(4)	5
Didier ERNST	D	31		
Laurent FASOTTE	M	2	(5)	
António FOLHA (POR)	A	23	(2)	3
Jean-François GILLET	G		(1)	
Emmanuel GODFROID	M	13	(15)	5
Stijn HAELDERMANS	M	12	(9)	4
Guy HELLERS (LUX)	M	18		1
Sasha JAKOBIA	A		(2)	
Ali LUKUNKU (FRA)	A	13	(4)	3
Dirk MEDVED	D	12		
Roberto MONES	M		(1)	
Ivica MORNAR (CRO)	A	12	(3)	3
Lokonda MPENZA	A	15	(2)	10
Mbo MPENZA	A	14	(3)	6
Gauthier REMACLE	D	20	(9)	3
Pascal RENIER	D	16		1
Vedran RUNJE (CRO)	G	34		
Bernd THIJS	D	14	(5)	
Reza TORABIAN	M		(1)	

LEAGUE RESULTS 1998/99

21/08/98	KV Oostende	A	1-2	Aliaj
29/08/98	KSC Eendracht Aalst	H	3-0	Bisconti, Renier, Blay
02/09/98	KAA Gent	H	2-0	De Condé, Bisconti
06/09/98	KRC Genk	A	1-2	Remacle
09/09/98	KV Kortrijk	H	2-1	Haeldermans (p), Mornar
12/09/98	RSC Charleroi	A	0-1	
19/09/98	KSK Beveren	H	1-2	Godfroid
25/09/98	R Excelsior Mouscron	A	5-1	og (Besengez), Haeldermans,
				Mornar, De Condé, Remacle
03/10/98	KVC Westerlo	H	2-0	Haeldermans (p), De Condé
10/10/98	Club Brugge KV	A	1-1	Remacle
24/10/98	KFC Germinal Ekeren	H	1-0	Godfroid
31/10/98	K St.-Truidense VV	A	1-0	Bilic (p)
07/11/98	KFC Lommelse SK	H	1-0	Godfroid
15/11/98	RSC Anderlecht	A	1-0	Mpenza M.
21/11/98	KRC Harelbeke	H	0-2	
27/11/98	KSC Lokeren	A	1-4	Mpenza L.
12/12/98	KV Oostende	H	3-0	Hellers, Lukunku, Folha
20/12/98	KSC Eendracht Aalst	A	0-1	
13/01/99	K Lierse SK	H	2-2	Lukunku, Afolabi
16/01/99	KAA Gent	A	2-3	Mpenza L., Folha
27/01/99	KRC Genk	H	2-4	Mpenza L., Blay
31/01/99	KV Kortrijk	A	3-1	Bilic, De Condé, Mpenza L.
13/02/99	RSC Charleroi	H	2-0	Folha, Mpenza L.
27/02/99	KSK Beveren	A	6-0	Godfroid 2, De Condé,
				Mpenza L. 3
05/03/99	R Excelsior Mouscron	H	2-0	Mpenza M., Mpenza L.
13/03/99	KVC Westerlo	A	1-3	Bisconti
19/03/99	Club Brugge KV	H	3-0	Cruz, Mpenza M. 2
03/04/99	KFC Germinal Ekeren	A	1-0	Mornar
17/04/99	K St.-Truidense VV	H	2-0	Mpenza M. 2
24/04/99	KFC Lommelse SK	A	0-3	
02/05/99	RSC Anderlecht	H	0-6	
05/05/99	KRC Harelbeke	A	1-1	Mpenza L.
09/05/99	KSC Lokeren	H	2-4	Lukunku, Haeldermans
16/05/99	K Lierse SK	A	0-3	

KVC WESTERLO

CLUB DIRECTORY

KVC Westerlo
De Merodedreef 189
2260 Westerlo
tel - (014) 545288
fax - (014) 542331
Year of Formation - 1933
President - René Gijbels
Manager - Herman Wijnants
Coach - Jos Heyligen (99/00 - Jan Ceulemans)
Stadium - 't Kuipje (10,606)

APPEARANCES 98/99

	P	Ap	(s)	Gls
Toni BROGNO	A	27		11
Coen BURG	M	26		4
Marc COX	D	16	(2)	
Laurent DAUWE	M	10	(3)	2
Björn DE CONINCK	D	14	(8)	
Sallou DIALLO (GUI)	G	8	(1)	
António DOS SANTOS (BRA)	M	1	(1)	
Allan FERREIRA (BRA)	A	5	(12)	3
Paul FRANKEN	D	17	(11)	1
Jochen JANSSEN	A	32		15
Rudi JANSSENS	M	33		2
Dimitri LECONTE	D	11	(1)	1
Sergio LA VALLE	A		(1)	
Frank MACHIELS	D	28	(3)	1
John MAISANO (AUS)	M	1	(9)	
Stefaan MARIEN	M		(1)	
Dejan MITROVIC (YUG)	A	19	(8)	6
Sedran PELIC (YUG)	A		(3)	
Krist PORTE	M	23	(1)	5
Patrick RONDAGS	G	26		
Yurika SILJANOSKI (MAC)	A	5	(2)	1
Benoît THANS	M	31		2
Dirk THOELEN	D	26	(1)	1
Mario VERHEYEN	D	15	(6)	
Bart WILMSSEN	M		(3)	

LEAGUE RESULTS 1998/99

22/08/98	KFC Germinal Ekeren	A	3-0	Porte, Burg, Ferreira
29/08/98	K St.-Truidense VV	H	1-4	Dauwe
02/09/98	KFC Lommelse SK	A	1-0	Janssen
05/09/98	RSC Anderlecht	H	6-0	Burg, Janssen, Thans, Machiels, Brogno 2
09/09/98	KRC Harelbeke	A	2-1	Dauwe, Porte
12/09/98	KSC Lokeren	H	4-3	Janssen 3, Leconte
19/09/98	K Lierse SK	A	1-5	Brogno
26/09/98	KV Oostende	H	7-0	Brogno, Janssen 3, Janssens, Franken, Burg
03/10/98	R Standard Liège	A	0-2	
10/10/98	KAA Gent	H	3-3	Janssen, Brogno, Porte (p)
24/10/98	KRC Genk	A	0-3	
31/10/98	KV Kortrijk	H	2-0	Brogno, Porte (p)
07/11/98	RSC Charleroi	A	3-1	Burg, Porte, Mitrovic
14/11/98	KSK Beveren	H	0-0	
21/11/98	R Excelsior Mouscron	A	1-2	Brogno
29/11/98	KSC Eendracht Aalst	A	2-3	Brogno 2
04/12/98	Club Brugge KV	H	1-2	Thans
12/12/98	KFC Germinal Ekeren	H	2-4	Janssen 2 (1p)
19/12/98	K St.-Truidense VV	A	0-0	
16/01/99	KFC Lommelse SK	H	2-1	Janssen, Brogno
23/01/99	RSC Anderlecht	A	2-3	Mitrovic 2
30/01/99	KRC Harelbeke	H	0-3	
27/02/99	K Lierse SK	H	0-2	
06/03/99	KV Oostende	A	1-1	Janssens
10/03/99	KSC Lokeren	A	0-3	
13/03/99	R Standard Liège	H	3-1	og (Afolabi), Janssen, Brogno
20/03/99	KAA Gent	A	0-2	
03/04/99	KRC Genk	H	1-1	Mitrovic
18/04/99	KV Kortrijk	A	2-4	Janssen, Ferreira
24/04/99	RSC Charleroi	H	1-0	Janssen
01/05/99	KSK Beveren	A	0-1	
05/05/99	R Excelsior Mouscron	H	1-1	Ferreira
08/05/99	KSC Eendracht Aalst	H	1-1	Mitrovic
16/05/99	Club Brugge KV	A	3-5	Mitrovic, Siljanoski, Thoelen

PROMOTED CLUBS

SECOND DIVISION FINAL TABLES 98/99

		Pd	W	D	L	F	A	Pt	GD
1	**KV Mechelen**	34	21	8	5	79	30	71	+49
2	Royal Antwerp FC	34	20	9	5	58	32	69	+26
3	KFC Verbroedering Geel	34	18	10	6	58	35	64	+23
4	AA La Louvière	34	16	13	5	56	31	61	+25
5	FC Turnhout	34	17	9	8	81	47	60	+34
6	SK Roeselaere	34	16	10	8	76	48	58	+28
7	RWD Molenbeek	34	17	5	12	53	41	56	+12
8	FC Denderleeuw	34	14	14	6	57	41	56	+16
9	KSV Cercle Brugge	34	11	9	14	49	58	42	-9
10	Visé	34	9	13	12	45	69	40	-24
11	FC Herentals	34	11	6	17	62	71	39	-9
12	Maasland	34	10	7	17	42	58	37	-16
13	Dessel Sport	34	10	7	17	35	55	37	-20
14	RTFC Liégeois	34	8	10	16	38	60	34	-22
15	FC Kapellen	34	9	6	19	48	70	33	-22
16	KSK Deinze	34	7	9	18	43	68	30	-25
17	KSV Waregem	34	6	8	20	45	71	26	-26
18	St.-Niklaas SK	34	5	9	20	43	83	24	-40

PROMOTION PLAY-OFFS FINAL TABLE

		Pd	W	D	L	F	A	Pt	GD
1	**KFC Verbroedering Geel**	6	4	1	1	12	7	13	+5
2	FC Turnhout	6	2	2	2	8	9	8	-1
3	AA La Louvière	6	2	1	3	5	11	7	-6
4	Royal Antwerp FC	6	1	2	3	9	7	5	+2

CLUB DIRECTORY

KV Mechelen
Kleine Nieuwedijkstraat 53
2800 Mechelen
tel - (015) 218230
fax - (015) 219033
Year of Formation - 1904
President - Willy Van den Wijngaert
Manager - Ivan Buskens
Coach - Gunter Jacob
Stadium - Achter de Kazerne (14,164)

MAJOR HONOURS
League Championship - (4)
1943, 1946, 1948, 1989.
Domestic Cup - (1) 1987.
European Cup-winners' Cup - (1) 1988.
European Super Cup - (1) 1989.

CLUB DIRECTORY

KFC Verbroedering Geel
Rauwelkoven 43
2440 Geel
tel - (014) 580126
fax - (014) 591097
Year of Formation - 1924
President - Vic Keersmakers
Manager - Rudy Laermans
Coach - Paul Put
Stadium - De Leunen (11,500)

BOSNIA-HERZEGOVINA

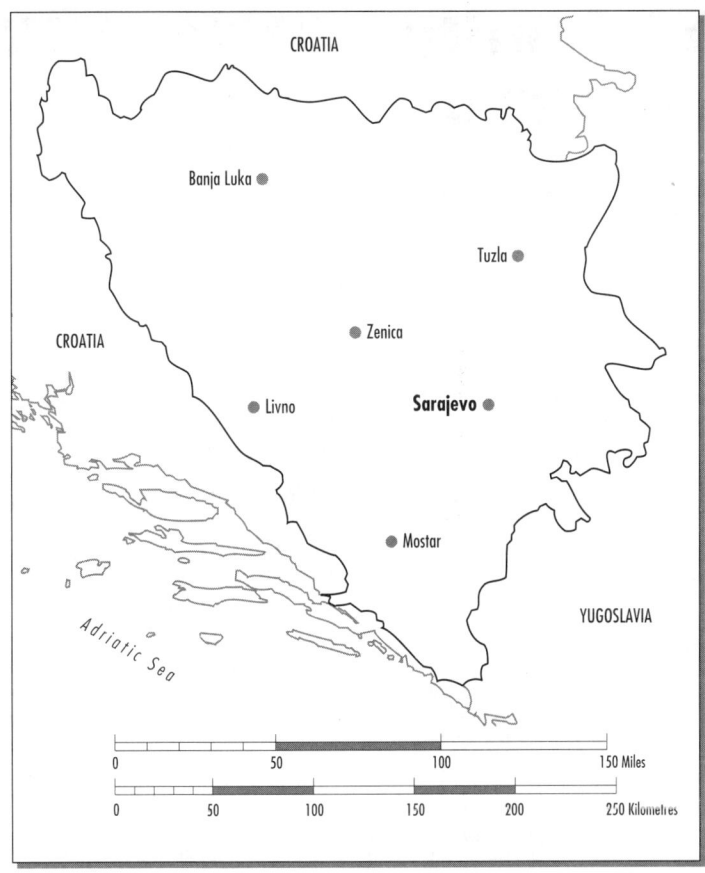

HADZIBEGIC TAKES OVER NATIONAL TEAM

Lack of unity brings UEFA disapproval

FEDERATION DIRECTORY

Nogometni savez Bosne i Hercegovine
Sirne Milutinovic e- Sarajlije 12, 71000 Sarajevo

tel - (071) 213881/440644   Year of Formation - 1992
fax - (071) 447562/444332   President - Jusuf Pusina
                             Secretary - Munib Usanovic

Stadium - Kosevo, Sarajevo (20,000)

Bosnia and Herzegovina were entitled to enter two teams in the 1998/99 UEFA Cup. However, the country's first dabble in the waters of international club competition was to be all too brief. Not only did both Sarajevo and Zeljeznicar fall at the first hurdle, but, worse still, UEFA decided that there would be no repeat participation in 1999/2000.

This was because the three leagues which make up the national football grid - those from the Muslim, Serbian and Croatian communities - could not come to agreement over the venue for the scheduled end-of-season play-offs. As a result, the play-offs were cancelled, and, with no official unified champions being declared, UEFA stepped in to withdraw the country's passport to Europe.

Unless a solution can be found to unite the different factions, it is unlikely that UEFA's stance will alter. There is no threat, however, to the continued participation of the Bosnia and Herzegovina national team in European Championships and World Cups. This is essentially an all-Muslim team, with the vast majority of the players earning their living abroad.

The national team had their second new coach in a year when Faruk

LEAGUE CHAMPIONSHIP RESULTS 98/99

MUSLIM LEAGUE	1	2	3	4	5	6	7	8	9	10	11	12	13	14	15	16
1 Bosna Visoko		3-0	4-0	1-0	3-1	3-0	2-0	2-0	1-0	1-0	4-1	6-1	4-0	1-0	3-1	3-0
2 Buducnost Banovici	2-0		2-0	0-1	0-0	1-0	2-0	1-0	0-0	1-0	0-1	0-0	2-0	1-2	2-0	2-1
3 Celik Zenica	2-1	1-0		3-1	3-1	4-0	2-0	1-0	2-0	1-3	3-2	0-2	4-1	1-1	1-1	6-1
4 Drina Zvornik Zivinice	1-2	0-0	1-0		1-1	1-2	1-1	2-1	0-0	1-3	0-0	2-0	2-0	0-0	2-2	1-0
5 Gradina Srebrnik	1-0	0-0	0-2	0-0		2-0	1-0	1-1	0-0	0-0	0-2	0-0	2-0	2-1	1-1	2-0
6 Iskra Bugojno	2-0	0-0	2-0	0-1	2-2		1-0	2-0	0-0	0-0	0-0	1-4	2-0	1-0	0-0	7-0
7 Jedinstvo Bihac	1-0	1-0	4-2	3-1	1-0	1-0		4-1	3-1	2-1	1-0	1-1	2-0	1-1	2-1	3-0
8 Lukavac	1-0	1-0	3-0	0-1	1-0	1-0	1-1		2-0	2-0	0-2	1-0	4-0	1-0	3-0	4-1
9 Rudar Kakanj	1-0	4-0	2-0	3-2	2-1	1-0	3-0	2-0		2-0	0-2	2-2	2-1	1-0	5-1	3-1
10 Sarajevo	1-0	4-1	2-1	3-1	1-0	5-0	3-0	4-0	2-1		2-0	2-0	3-2	3-1	2-1	1-0
11 Sloboda Tuzla	0-1	3-1	2-0	1-0	0-0	3-1	4-0	3-2	1-2	0-2		2-0	3-0	1-0	0-1	5-5
12 Velez Mostar	1-0	3-0	5-3	2-1	2-2	3-2	2-2	3-2	3-0	1-3	3-1		3-0	0-0	1-0	1-0
13 Vrbanjusa Sarajevo	1-4	0-1	1-2	0-0	1-0	2-1	1-1	0-3	0-0	0-1	0-0	2-1		2-2	1-0	3-2
14 Zeljeznicar Sarajevo	2-0	2-0	2-1	1-1	5-2	2-0	3-1	1-1	1-2	1-2	1-2	2-0	1-1		5-2	2-0
15 Zenica	1-1	0-3	1-1	3-2	0-1	1-1	2-1	1-0	1-0	1-0	1-1	0-1	3-2	0-3		1-3
16 Zmaj od Bosne Tuzla	0-0	0-1	2-1	2-1	3-0	2-2	2-0	0-0	0-0	0-2	2-3	0-1	2-1	0-1	5-0	

NATIONAL TEAM RESULTS 98/99

19/08/98	Faroe Islands (ECQ)	H	Sarajevo	1-0	Baljic (65)
05/09/98	Estonia (ECQ)	H	Sarajevo	1-1	Barbarez (75p)
10/10/98	Czech Republic (ECQ)	H	Sarajevo	1-3	Topic (88)
14/10/98	Lithuania (ECQ)	A	Vilnius	2-4	Konjic (5), Baljic (68)
27/01/99	Malta	A	Ta' Qali	1-2	Salihamidzic (29)
10/03/99	Hungary	A	Budapest	1-1	Kodro (31)
05/06/99	Lithuania (ECQ)	H	Sarajevo	2-0	Kodro (26p), Bolic (90)
09/06/99	Faroe Islands (ECQ)	A	Toftir	2-2	Bolic (13, 50)

INTERNATIONAL HONOURS

None

LEAGUE CHAMPIONSHIP FINAL TABLES 98/99

MUSLIM LEAGUE		Pd	W	D	Home L	F	A	W	D	Away L	F	A	W	D	Total L	F	A	Pt	GD
1	Sarajevo	30	15	0	0	38	8	7	2	6	17	13	22	2	6	55	21	68	+34
2	Bosna Visoko	30	15	0	0	41	4	3	2	10	9	17	18	2	10	50	21	56	+29
3	Rudar Kakanj	30	13	1	1	33	10	2	6	7	6	16	15	7	8	39	26	52	+13
4	Velez Mostar	30	11	3	1	33	16	4	4	7	13	21	15	7	8	46	37	52	+9
5	Sloboda Tuzla	30	9	2	4	28	15	6	4	5	17	17	15	6	9	45	32	51	+13
6	Jedinstvo Bihac	30	13	2	0	30	9	0	4	11	7	30	13	6	11	37	39	45	-2
7	Zeljeznicar Sarajevo	30	9	3	3	31	15	3	5	7	12	15	12	8	10	43	30	44	+13
8	Lukavac	30	12	1	2	25	5	1	3	11	11	27	13	4	13	36	32	43	+4
9	Celik Zenica	30	11	2	2	34	14	2	1	12	13	33	13	3	14	47	47	42	0
10	Buducnost Banovici	30	9	3	3	16	5	3	3	9	7	22	12	6	12	23	27	42	-4
11	Drina Zvornik Zivinice	30	5	7	3	15	12	3	3	9	13	22	8	10	12	28	34	34	-6
12	Gradina Srebrnik	30	6	7	2	12	7	1	5	9	12	25	7	12	11	24	32	33	-8
13	Iskra Bugojno	30	7	6	2	20	7	1	2	12	9	32	8	8	14	29	39	32	-10
14	Zenica	30	6	4	5	16	21	1	4	10	11	33	7	8	15	27	54	29	-27
15	Zmaj od Bosne Tuzla	30	6	4	5	20	13	1	1	13	14	44	7	5	18	34	57	26	-23
16	Vrbanjusa Sarajevo	30	5	5	5	14	18	0	1	14	8	39	5	6	19	22	57	21	-35

SERBIAN LEAGUE		Pd	W	D	L	F	A	Pt	GD
1	Radnik Bijeljina	34	23	5	6	71	30	74	+41
2	Rudar Ugljevik	34	22	7	5	80	25	73	+55
3	Boksit Milici	34	22	3	9	60	34	69	+26
4	Kozara Gradiska	34	17	8	9	58	36	59	+22
5	Sloga Trn	34	18	4	12	66	40	58	+26
6	BSK Banja Luka	34	19	1	14	57	41	58	+16
7	Drina Zvornik	34	15	5	14	58	49	50	+9
8	Sloboda Novi Grad	34	15	4	15	54	39	49	+15
9	Glasinac Sokolac	34	15	3	16	57	56	48	+1
10	Leotar Trebinje	34	14	5	15	43	46	47	-3
11	Ljubic Prnjavor	34	13	7	14	59	58	46	+1
12	Borac Banja Luka	34	13	6	15	44	39	45	+5
13	Famos Vojkovici	34	13	5	16	35	54	44	-19
14	Rudar/Prijedor	34	12	6	16	39	46	42	-7
15	Borac Samac	34	13	2	19	37	64	41	-27
16	Jedinstvo Brcko	34	11	5	18	43	70	38	-27
17	Omladinac Banja Luka	34	7	4	23	35	76	25	-41
18	Sarajevo Srpsko Sarajevo	34	4	0	30	20	113	12	-93

CROATIAN LEAGUE		Pd	W	D	L	F	A	Pt	GD
1	Posusje	26	17	7	2	53	14	58	+39
2	Siroki Brijeg	26	16	5	5	65	25	53	+40
3	Zrinjski Mostar	26	16	4	6	44	21	52	+23
4	Brotnjo Citluk	26	14	5	7	53	26	47	+27
5	Orasje	26	13	5	8	39	25	44	+14
6	Troglav Livno	26	12	1	13	36	31	37	+5
7	Dragovoljac Kiseljak	26	9	5	12	30	35	32	-5
8	Vitez	26	10	1	15	24	40	31	-16
9	Stolac	26	9	4	13	20	42	31	-22
10	Ljubuski	26	8	6	12	26	37	30	-11
11	GOSK Gabela	26	9	3	14	30	54	30	-24
12	Redarstvenik Mostar	26	8	5	13	27	36	29	-9
13	Odzak 102	26	8	5	13	38	53	29	-15
14	Sloga Uskoplje	26	2	6	18	16	62	12	-46

DOMESTIC CUP 98/99

MUSLIM SECTION
QUARTER-FINALS
Travnik v Bosna Visoko 2-1; 0-3
(Bosna Visoko 4-2)
Zrnaj od Bosne Tuzla v Sarajevo 0-0; 0-3
(Sarajevo 3-0)
Zeleznicar Sarajevo v Celik Zenica 0-0; 0-0
(0-0; Zeljeznicar Sarajevo 4-3 on pens.)

Sloboda Tuzla v Zenica 1-0; 0-1
(1-1; Sloboda Tuzla 4-2 on pens.)

SEMI-FINALS
Sarajevo v Zeljeznicar Sarajevo 1-0; 0-1
(1-1; Sarajevo 3-1 on pens.)
Sloboda Tuzla v Bosna Visoko 3-0; 0-3
(3-3; Bosna Visoko 4-3 on pens.)

FINAL
Bosna Visoko 1, Sarajevo 0

CROATIAN SECTION – FINAL
Brotnjo 1, Siroki Brijeg 1 (5-4 on pens.)

SERBIAN SECTION – FINAL
Rudar Ugljevik 0, Sloga Trn 0 (4-3 on pens.)

Hadzibegic, the former Yugoslav international sweeper, replaced Dzemaludin Musovic as team chief in February 1999. Musovic's last stand was a shock 2-1 defeat in Malta but his departure was on the cards before then. The team had started the Euro 2000 campaign poorly and Musovic had fallen out with a number of senior players. Among those were strikers Meho Kodro and Elvir Bolic, who returned in June to score the goals against Lithuania and the Faroe Islands that kept the team in with a chance of reaching the play-offs.

TOP SCORER

(Muslim League)
19   Nermin VAZDA (Zeljeznicar Sarajevo)

EUROPEAN CUPS 98/99

UEFA CUP
● **SARAJEVO**
Preliminary round KFC GERMINAL EKEREN (BEL)
A 1-4   Ferhatovic (59)
Dedic; Suljagic, Duro, Hadispahic, Begic, Hosic, Dzdic (Gogalic 33), Granov, Zahirovic, Ihtijarevic (Ferhatovic 46), Smjecanin (Noukeu 54).
H 0-0
Dedic; Suljagic, Hadispahic, Begic, Hosic (Zukic 35), Gogalic (Alic 65), Granov, Ferhatovic, Selimovic (Memisevic 46), Noukeu, Smjecanin.

● **ZELJEZNICAR SARAJEVO**
Preliminary round KILMARNOCK (SCO)
H 1-1   Vazda (66)
Guso; Biscevic, Mulalic, Kunic (Pehlivancic 88), Gredic (Cenan 81), Fatic, Vazda, Muharemovic, Mulaosmanovic, Burek, Zeric (Selimovic 46).
A 0-1
Guso; Biscevic, Mulalic, Selimovic, Kunic, Gredic (Zeric 64), Fatic (Cenan 51), Vazda, Muharemovic, Mulaosmanovic, Burek.

NATIONAL TEAM APPEARANCES 98/99

Coach - Dzemaludin MUSOVIC; Faruk HADZIBEGIC	FAR	EST	CZE	LIT	MLT	HUN	LIT	FAR	Cps	Gls
Mirsad DEDIC (04/02/68) - Sarajevo	G	G	G	G	s66	G	G	G	23	-
Muhamed KONJIC (04/05/70) - AS Monaco (FRA)/Coventry City (ENG)	D	D	D	D	D	D			16	1
Mirsad VARESANOVIC (31/05/72) - Bursaspor (TUR)	D	D	D	D	D		D	D	13	-
Mirsad HIBIC (11/10/73) - Sevilla FC (ESP)	D	D	D			D	D	D	10	-
Sead KAPETANOVIC (21/01/72) - VfL Wolfsburg (GER)	M	M	M	M80	D81		D		11	-
Sead HALILOVIC (16/03/69) - Karabükspor (TUR)	M	M77	M	M	M				13	-
Hasan SALIHAMIDZIC (01/01/77) - FC Bayern München (GER)	M81	A	A65	A	A		A		15	4
Sergej BARBAREZ (17/09/71) - Borussia Dortmund (GER)	M75	M	M	M					5	1
Elvir BALJIC (08/07/74) - Fenerbahçe (TUR)	M	A	A71	A					13	2
Elvir BOLIC (10/10/71) - Fenerbahçe (TUR)	A65	s77					s87	A	16	9
Meho KODRO (12/01/67) - CD Tenerife (ESP)	A					A46	A79		10	3
Edin MUJCIN (14/01/70) - Croatia Zagreb (CRO)	s65	s60	M63	M80		M73	s79	M	12	1
Jasmin MUJDZA (02/03/74) - Hajduk Split (CRO)	s75	M67		s80	D	D			7	-
Nermin SABIC (21/12/73) - Croatia Zagreb (CRO)	s81	s67				s88	M	M	16	-
Suad KATANA (06/04/69) - Adanaspor (TUR)		D60	D	D75					10	-
Marko TOPIC (01/01/76) - Monza (ITA)			s63	s75		M85	M90	M85	7	1
Enes DEMIROVIC (13/06/72) - Adanaspor (TUR)			s65						8	-
Bakir BESIREVIC (03/11/65) - Osijek (CRO)			s71	s80			M	D	14	-
Edin RAMCIC (01/08/70) - KAA Gent (BEL)			D						6	-
Nihad PEJKOVIC (23/10/68) - SCT Olimpija Ljubljana (SLO)						G			2	-
Munever RIZVIC (04/11/73) - Olimpik Sarajevo						M			1	-
Dzenan ZAIMOVIC (25/09/73) - Velez Mostar						M			1	-
Senad REPUH (18/11/72) - Bursaspor (TUR)						M66	M	M87	M78	12	1
Admir HASANCIC (29/11/70) - Rijeka (CRO)						A58			2	-
Samir MURATOVC (25/02/76) - Zrnaj od Bosne Tuzla						s58	s46		s85	3	-
Faruk IHTIJAREVIC (01/05/76) - Sarajevo						s81	M			2	-
Edin SMAJIC (30/08/71) - Iskra Bugojno						D55	D	D	3	-
Almir TURKOVIC (03/11/70) - Zadarkomerc Zadar (CRO)						M88	s90	M63	10	-
Edis MULALIC (25/10/5) - Zeljeznicar Sarajevo						s55			1	-
Omer JOLDIC (01/01/77) - Sloboda Tuzla						s73		s63	6	-
Alen AVDIC (03/04/77) - Sarajevo						s85			1	-
Adnan OSMANHODZIC (24/05/71) - Sloboda Tuzla								s78	1	-

BULGARIA

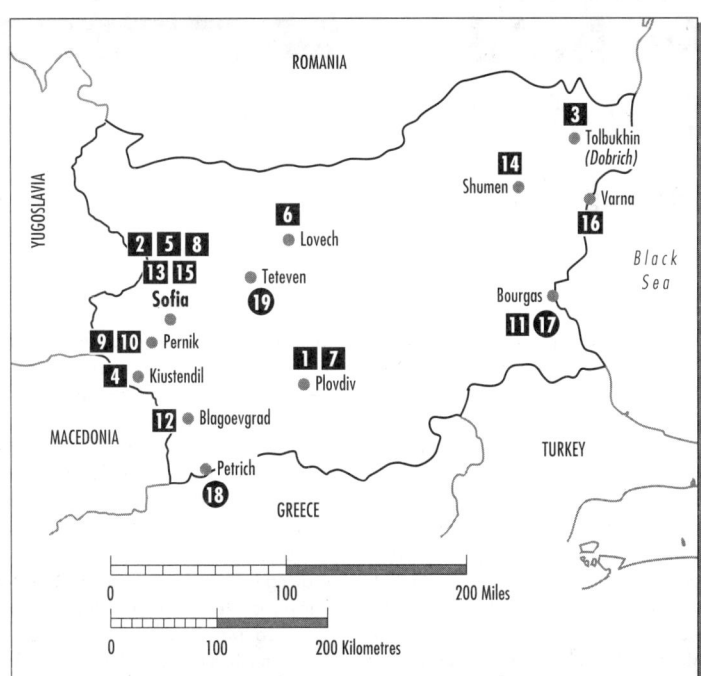

1	**BOTEV PLOVDIV**	190
2	**CSKA SOFIA**	191
3	**DOBRUDZHA DOBRICH**	192
4	**LEVSKI KIUSTENDIL**	193
5	**LEVSKI SOFIA**	194
6	**LITEKS LOVECH**	195
7	**LOKOMOTIV PLOVDIV**	196
8	**LOKOMOTIV SOFIA**	197
9	**METALURG PERNIK**	198
10	**MINIOR PERNIK**	199

11	**NEFTOCHIMIK BOURGAS**	200
12	**PIRIN BLAGOEVGRAD**	201
13	**SEPTEMVRI SOFIA**	202
14	**SHUMEN**	203
15	**SLAVIA SOFIA**	204
16	**SPARTAK VARNA**	205
Promoted clubs		
17	**CHERNOMORETS BOURGAS**	206
18	**BELASITSA PETRICH**	206
19	**OLIMPIK TETEVEN**	206

STOICHKOV BOWS OUT WITH 83 CAPS

Liteks hold off Levski to retain title

FEDERATION DIRECTORY

Bulgarski Futbolen Soius
ul. Karnigradska 19, 1000 Sofia

tel - (02) 877490/874725   Year of Formation - 1924
fax - (02) 9862538   President - Ivan Slavkov
     Secretary - Ivan Vutsov

Stadium - Vasil Levski, Sofia (70,000)

In retaining the Bulgarian championship, Liteks Lovech became the first provincial club to win back-to-back titles since Vladislav Varna in 1926. That was quite a coup for the generously-sponsored club from the Bulgarian hinterland who barely two years earlier had been celebrating promotion from the Second Division.

Liteks' first duty as champions was to represent the country in the Champions' League. Things started brightly enough when they came through a closely-fought preliminary-round tie with Swedish champions Halmstad, but against Spartak Moscow they were beaten to a pulp. A 0-5 humiliation at home was followed by a 6-2 hammering in Moscow. So, off into the UEFA Cup they went, to be eliminated in the first round by Grazer AK of Austria.

It was hardly an auspicious start to the season, and there was a further complication to their well-laid plans when, midway through that UEFA Cup tie, the club lost the services of their title-winning coach, Dimitar Dimitrov

- summoned to take charge of the Bulgarian national team. His replacement, Ferario Spasov, settled in quickly, however, and before long Liteks were making a concerted bid to catch early leaders Levski Sofia at the top of the table.

When the two clubs came head to head in Lovech in early November, the gap had been closed and they were level on points. A 1-1 draw maintained the status quo. But while Liteks went on to complete the first half of the season with four successive wins - including an amazing 8-0 victory at home to CSKA Sofia, the record champions' heaviest league defeat of all time - Levski twice slipped up away from home, drawing 2-2 against Minior Pernik and then dropping five points off the pace with a 0-1 defeat against Neftochimik Bourgas in the last match before the winter break.

Levski, celebrating their 85th anniversary, began the new year determined to make up the lost ground. They received some unexpected early encouragement when Liteks lost their first encounter away to Lokomotiv Sofia.

LEAGUE CHAMPIONSHIP RESULTS 98/99

		1	2	3	4	5	6	7	8	9	10	11	12	13	14	15	16
1	Botev Plovdiv		2-0	3-2	2-2	0-1	0-1	0-0	1-1	2-1	1-1	3-0	2-1	3-1	5-2	1-0	3-2
2	CSKA Sofia	5-0		3-0	3-2	2-3	2-3	6-0	2-0	0-2	2-0	1-1	3-0	3-1	3-2	1-1	2-1
3	Dobrudzha Dobrich	4-0	1-1		1-0	0-1	1-2	4-2	2-3	1-0	2-0	2-1	0-0	5-1	4-1	3-1	3-1
4	Levski Kiustendil	2-1	0-0	3-0		0-1	1-0	5-1	1-0	7-1	2-1	3-0	2-0	4-1	3-0	3-0	2-0
5	Levski Sofia	6-0	2-0	2-0	3-0		0-0	2-0	1-0	1-0	2-0	3-0	5-0	2-0	2-2	1-0	1-0
6	Liteks Lovech	2-0	8-0	5-0	2-0	1-1		5-1	3-1	2-1	3-1	3-1	8-1	4-1	2-0	3-1	3-2
7	Lokomotiv Plovdiv	2-1	0-0	3-1	1-2	1-2	1-4		1-3	2-0	0-1	2-4	0-0	2-0	1-3	0-0	1-3
8	Lokomotiv Sofia	2-0	0-2	5-2	1-0	0-1	1-0	4-1		1-0	1-0	1-0	4-1	0-0	2-1	0-2	3-1
9	Metalurg Pernik	3-1	1-0	1-0	1-2	0-3	1-2	1-0	2-1		1-2	0-0	2-0	4-2	2-1	1-1	2-0
10	Minior Pernik	1-0	2-0	4-2	0-0	2-2	2-3	2-0	1-5	3-4		1-0	2-1	2-2	2-0	1-1	5-0
11	Neftochimik Bourgas	3-1	2-0	2-0	3-1	1-0	1-4	4-1	0-0	2-0	2-1		6-1	1-3	6-1	2-0	4-1
12	Pirin Blagoevgrad	3-0	0-0	1-0	0-1	0-1	1-2	5-1	0-2	2-1	3-1	1-1		2-1	2-0	2-1	1-0
13	Septemvri Sofia	2-0	2-5	2-1	0-3	0-4	2-5	1-1	0-1	3-1	2-3	0-1	2-3		1-1	0-2	1-1
14	Shumen	1-1	2-5	0-0	3-3	0-1	0-0	1-0	2-0	1-0	1-1	1-0	4-1	3-2		2-1	1-1
15	Slavia Sofia	2-0	0-1	6-2	1-0	0-0	1-1	6-1	2-3	1-0	2-2	1-2	4-1	4-1	2-0		2-2
16	Spartak Varna	2-1	0-2	1-2	2-3	2-1	0-2	2-0	1-1	3-0	2-0	2-1	2-1	2-0	3-0	0-2	

LEAGUE CHAMPIONSHIP FINAL TABLE 98/99

			Home				Away				Total					
		P	W	D	L	F	A	W	D	L	F	A	W	D	L	F	A	P	GD
1	Liteks Lovech	30	14	1	0	54	11	10	3	2	29	14	24	4	2	83	25	76	+58
2	Levski Sofia	30	13	2	0	33	2	10	3	2	22	9	23	5	2	55	11	74	+44
3	Levski Kiustendil	30	13	1	1	38	6	5	3	7	19	23	18	4	8	57	29	58	+28
4	Lokomotiv Sofia	30	11	1	3	25	11	6	3	6	21	19	17	4	9	46	30	55	+16
5	CSKA Sofia	30	10	2	3	38	16	5	4	6	16	22	15	6	9	54	38	51	+16
6	Neftochimik Bourgas	30	12	1	2	39	14	3	3	9	12	24	15	4	11	51	38	49	+13
7	Slavia Sofia	30	8	4	3	34	16	3	4	8	13	20	11	8	11	47	36	41	+11
8	Minior Pernik	30	8	4	3	30	20	3	3	9	14	26	11	7	12	44	46	40	-2
9	Dobrudzha Dobrich	30	10	2	3	33	14	1	1	13	12	41	11	3	16	45	55	36	-10
10	Metalurg Pernik	30	9	2	4	22	15	2	0	13	11	31	11	2	17	33	46	35	-13
11	Pirin Blagoevgrad	30	9	2	4	24	12	1	2	12	11	46	10	4	16	35	58	34	-23
12	Spartak Varna	30	9	1	5	24	16	1	3	11	15	34	10	4	16	39	50	34	-11
13	Botev Plovdiv	30	9	4	2	28	15	0	1	14	6	40	9	5	16	34	55	32	-21
14	Shumen	30	7	6	2	22	16	1	2	12	14	40	8	8	14	36	56	32	-20
15	Lokomotiv Plovdiv	30	4	3	8	17	24	0	2	13	9	49	4	5	21	26	73	17	-47
16	Septemvri Sofia	30	3	3	9	18	32	1	2	12	16	41	4	5	21	34	73	17	-39

N.B. Where two or more teams are level on points, classification is determined by the results of the matches between them.

But thereafter there was nothing more they could do to close the two-point gap. They kept on winning, but so did Liteks. Everything appeared to hinge on the showdown between the two rivals in Levski's Georgi Asparuchov stadium on May 5.

40,000 Levski fans packed the arena in support of their team but the 11th straight win they sought just would not come. Liteks, who were on a hot winning streak of their own, gave as good as they got in 90 minutes of incessant rain, and the match, refereed by 'neutral' German official Bernd Heinemann, ended goalless. Advantage - still - to the defending champions.

Levski's only hope now seemed to rest with their bitter rivals CSKA, who played host to Liteks in the penultimate round. Levski fans hoped that CSKA would be desperate to reap revenge on Liteks for their eight-goal embarrassment in the autumn, but, sadly, there was more to the issue than that. As CSKA and Liteks had both reached the Cup final, to be played four days later, it was actually in CSKA's interests to lose the match and allow Liteks to win the title so that, even if they lost the Cup final, they would still qualify for the UEFA Cup. The risk for CSKA of beating Liteks in the league game was that Levski would then win the league, Liteks would win the Cup and they would miss out on Europe as a result of their insufficient placing in the league.

Given that scenario, there was a sense of dumbfounded disbelief when CSKA went 2-0 up. Perhaps it was a ploy, because at the final whistle Liteks had come back to win 3-2, with the CSKA players showing no sense of loss

or grievance. That they went on to defeat Liteks in the Cup final merely added to the suspicion that some sort of mutually beneficial deal had been struck between the two clubs - at the expense of innocent bystanders Levski.

The spectre of subterfuge had been hovering over the championship for much of the season, and there were many claims of fixed matches. Metalurg Pernik were eventually found guilty of 'selling' their two matches at home to title contenders Liteks and Levski and subjected to an enforced relegation - much to the pleasure of Shumen, who thus regained the place they thought they had lost.

Another scandal concerned the match between Levski Kiustendil and CSKA Sofia, which was abandoned when the team from the capital refused to play the second half after four of their players had allegedly been assaulted during the interval by local hooligans. Police found no proof, so the Federation disciplinary commission decided that the only just solution was to call the match a 0-0 draw without attributing any points to either side.

Liteks were also involved in an unsavoury incident when one of their key players, Albanian international Alban Bushi, was handed a six-match ban for allegedly spitting at a referee. After appeal, however, the suspension was reduced to just two games, which meant that Bushi was able to face Levski in the crunch title showdown.

The Albanian was also responsible for scoring the first of the two goals in the final home win over Botev Plovdiv that confirmed Levski's successful title defence. The other scorer was Dimcho Beliakov, whose 21st goal of the campaign secured his place as the league's leading marksman. His tally was especially impressive as it included no penalties. Runner-up Todor Pramatarov of Shumen netted as many as six of his 17 goals from the spot.

Aside from Bushi and Beliakov, Liteks had no truly outstanding individuals. The two Serbs, Zlatomir Zagorcic and Dragoljub Simonovic, both took out Bulgarian citizenship and played for the national team, where they joined the team's only other regular international, Radostin Kishishev. Romanian Laurentiu Reghecampf also played remarkably well for half a season given that he was in mourning following the tragic death of his two-year-old daughter.

Levski's disappointment in finishing second was particularly hard to take after their magnificent spring form, which had brought 14 wins and just that one crucial drawn match against Liteks. Perhaps even more impressive was their defensive record during that run - just two goals conceded (both in the same game, against CSKA) and none at all in their last 13 matches. Scotsman John Inglis, a surprise mid-season arrival from Aberdeen, could take much credit for that extraordinary statistic. So, too, could goalkeeper Dimitar Ivankov, who actually scored more goals than he conceded during the second half of the season, netting five penalty-kicks to bring

his total to six - a figure bettered by only two of Levski's outfield players, striker Georgi Ivanov (13 goals) and midfielder Aleksandar Aleksandrov (seven).

Levski announced the arrival of a new president, ex-player Nasko Sirakov, during the summer. This was perhaps a direct response to CSKA's decision to appoint Liuboslav Penev in the same role - a considerable surprise given that the big striker had just completed an excellent season in Spain with Celta, scoring goals galore in both league and UEFA Cup. It was one of Penev's old clubs, Atlético Madrid, who ended CSKA's eight-match UEFA Cup run - one of the best European performances by a Bulgarian club in recent years. Flying the flag in Europe and winning the Bulgarian Cup could not, however, disguise what had been a terrible season in the league for the Sofia 'Reds'.

INTERNATIONAL HONOURS

World Cup Finals appearances: 1962, 1966, 1970, 1974, 1986 (2nd round), 1994 (4th), 1998

European Championship appearances: 1968, 1996

DOMESTIC CUP 98/99

1/16 FINALS
Etar Veliko Tarnovo 0, CSKA Sofia 2
Spartak 94 Plovdiv 0, Lokomotiv Sofia 2
Kaliakra 1, Botev Plovdiv 1 (aet; 3-5 o pens.)
Strumska Slava Radomir 0, Spartak Varna 3
Neftochimik Bourgas 3, Kremikovtsi 1
Rodopa Smolian 1, Liteks Lovech 3
Planinez Aprilzi 1, Septemvri Sofia 1
(aet; 2-4 on pens.)
Vidima Rakovski Sevlievo 2, Lokomotiv Plovdiv 3
(aet)
Marek Dupnitsa 1, Minior Pernik 2
Loviko Suhindol 2, Dobrudzha Dobrich 3
Metalurg Pernik 1, Chardafon Gabrovo 0
Maritsa Plovdiv 0, Levski Kiustendil 3
Levski Sofia 4, Belasitsa Petrich 0
Botev Vratsa 1, Shumen 5
Dimitrovgrad 0, Slavia Sofia 2
Pirin Blagoevgrad 2, Akademik Sofia 1

1/8 FINALS
Lokomotiv Sofia v Botev Plovdiv 4-2; 2-1
(Lokomotiv Sofia 6-3)
Levski Sofia v Slavia Sofia 2-0; 0-3
(Slavia Sofia 3-2)
CSKA Sofia v Septemvri Sofia 2-0; 1-2
(CSKA Sofia 3-2)

Shumen v Spartak Varna 2-2; 0-6
(Spartak Varna 8-2)
Dobrudzha Dobrich v Levski Kiustendil 1-2; 0-2
(Levski Kiustendil 4-1)
Lokomotiv Plovdiv v Minior Pernik 3-3; 0-6
(Minior Pernik 9-3)
Pirin Blagoevgrad v Neftochimik Bourgas 3-0; 2-3
(Pirin Blagoevgrad 5-3)
Metalurg Pernik v Liteks Lovech 2-1; 1-3
(Liteks Lovech 4-3)

QUARTER-FINALS
Pirin Blagoevgrad 0, Lokomotiv Sofia 1 (Andonov 90)
Lokomotiv Sofia 2 (Doncic 8, Dafchev 30),
Pirin Blagoevgrad 2 (Topuzakov 71, Chipev 78)
(Lokomotiv Sofia 3-2)

Liteks Lovech 1 (Bushi 33), Slavia Sofia 0
Slavia Sofia 1 (Trenchev 11), Liteks Lovech 0
(1-1; Liteks Lovech 4-3 on pens.)

Spartak Varna 2 (Paskov 5, Velichkov 38p), Levski
Kiustendil 1 (Mikhailov M. 80p)
Levski Kiustendil 3 (Stoichev 52, Mikhailov V. 55,
Petrov P. 57), Spartak Varna 1 (Yordanov 46)
(Levski Kiustendil 4-3)

CSKA Sofia 2 (Zafirov 5p, Berbatov 74),
Minior Pernik 1 (Georgiev D. 26)

Minior Pernik 1 (Georgiev G. 86),
CSKA Sofia 4 (Stanchev 73, 81, Berbarov 75,
Hristov 90)
(CSKA Sofia 6-2)

SEMI-FINALS
CSKA Sofia 1 (Hristov 45), Levski Kiustendil 0
Levski Kiustendil 2 (Marashliev 4, Mikhailov M. 56p),
CSKA Sofia 2 (Berbatov 85, Petrov S. 90)
(CSKA Sofia 3-2)

Lokomotiv Sofia 0, Liteks Lovech 0
Liteks Lovech 1 (Haxhi 41), Lokomotiv Sofia 0
(Liteks Lovech 1-0)

FINAL
26/05/99, Sofia
CSKA SOFIA 1 Stanchev V. (82)
LITEKS LOVECH 0
referee - Ouzounov
CSKA SOFIA - Ivanov N.; Kremenliev, Lulchev,
Chomakov, Zafirov A., Petrov S., Bukarev
(Angelov 68), Berbatov (Nikolov M. 35),
Stanchev V., Deianov, Petkov M. (Slavchev I. 57).
LITEKS LOVECH - Stavrev; Reghecampf, Zhelev, Kolev,
Dimitrov N., Kishishev (Emilev 67), Todorov M.
(Petev 59), Stoilov (Kirov V. 46), Todorov S., Bushi,
Haxhi.

NATIONAL TEAM APPEARANCES 98/99

Coach - Hristo BONEV; Dimitar DIMITROV	POL	ENG	SWE	ALG	MAR	EGY	SVK	BEL	LUX	SVK	POL	ENG	Cps	Gls
Zdravko ZDRAVKOV (04/10/70) - Istanbulspor (TUR)	G	G	G					G	G	G	G		26	-
Gosho GINCHEV (02/02/69) - Antalyaspor (TUR)	D				D								19	-
Zlatomir ZAGORCIC (15/06/71) - Liteks Lovech	D50	D	D	D	D59	D	D			s7	D	D	10	-
Zakhari SIRAKOV (08/11/77) - Levski Sofia	D												1	-
Radostin KISHISHEV (30/07/74) - Liteks Lovech	M	D		M		M78	D74	D	D	D	D	D	33	-
Ivailo YORDANOV (22/04/68) - Sporting CP (POR)	M	D	D				D	M	D	s31			46	3
Daniel BORIMIROV (15/01/70) - TSV 1860 München (GER)	M46			M53			s46	s57				s60	45	4
Milen PETKOV (12/01/74) - CSKA Sofia	M46	M	M				M	M73	M	M41	M	M	11	-
Georgi BACHEV (18/04/77) - Slavia Sofia/Levski Sofia	A	s60	s60	A46	s53		s46			A75	s46	s73	13	1
Doncho DONEV (24/01/67) - Levski Sofia	A												1	-
Hristo STOICHKOV (08/02/66) - Kashiwa Reysol (JPN)	A	A60	A		A53	A		A28	A78		A63	A73	83	37
Mitko TRENDAFILOV (25/12/69) - Neftochimik Bourgas	s46												4	-
Ilia GRUEV (30/10/69) - Neftochimik Bourgas	s46	s63		A48	s68	s46	s66	s81		s41			11	1
Ivailo PETKOV (07/12/75) - Istanbulspor (TUR)	s50		D					s76	s46	s46	D80		18	-
Rosen KIRILOV (04/01/73) - Liteks Lovech/Adanaspor (TUR)		D	D18	s48	D		s66	D		D	D	D	9	-
Valentin NAIDENOV (27/07/72) - CSKA Sofia		D	D69		D	D46	s46						5	-
Zlatko YANKOV (07/06/66) - Adanaspor (TUR)/Neftochimik Bourgas		M	M	M46	M53	M	M			M	M31		77	4
Ilian ILIEV (02/07/68) - Bursaspor (TUR)/AEK (GRE)/Levski Sofia		M63	M60		M	M	M46	M57	M	M	s80	M60	28	2
Marian HRISTOV (29/07/73) - 1.FC Kaiserslautern (GER)		A90	A		A68								13	2
Georgi IVANOV (02/07/76) - Levski Sofia		s90	s69	A				s28	s77		s63		10	-
Velian PARUSHEV (20/03/68) - Neftochimik Bourgas			s18										1	-
Dimitar IVANKOV (30/10/75) - Levski Sofia			G	G63							G	G	4	-
Malin ORACHEV (03/12/72) - Neftochimik Bourgas			D48	s66	D46								3	-
Ilian STOIANOV (25/11/77) - Levski Kiustendil			D	D66	D	D46	D76	D46	D46				7	-
Vladimir YUNKOV (19/07/73) - Levski Sofia/Lokomotiv Sofia			D48	s59	s78								4	-
Stanimir DIMITROV (24/04/72) - Neftochimik Bourgas			A46										1	-
Dragoljub SIMONOVIC (30/10/72) - Liteks Lovech			s46										1	-
Aleksandar ALEKSANDROV (19/01/75) - Levski Sofia			s46										1	-
Dimcho BELIAKOV (26/10/71) - Liteks Lovech			s46										2	-
Milen RADUKANOV (12/12/72) - Levski Sofia			s48										1	-
Blagomir MITREV (28/05/72) - Neftochimik Bourgas			s48										1	-
Stilian PETROV (05/07/79) - CSKA Sofia				s53	s46	M66	M81	M	M	M	M	M	8	-
Hristo YOVOV (04/11/77) - TSV 1860 München (GER)/Lokomotiv Sofia				s53	A	A66	A69	A77	A	A46	A46		9	3
Gosho PETKOV (21/06/76) - Slavia Sofia				s63	G								2	-
Georgi ANTONOV (07/07/70) - Lokomotiv Sofia					M	s74							7	-
Svetoslav TODOROV (30/08/78) - Liteks Lovech						A46	s69	s78	s75				6	-
Georgi MARKOV (20/01/72) - Lokomotiv Sofia							D	D	D7	D	D	D	5	1
Asen NIKOLOV (05/08/76) - Levski Sofia							s73						1	-
Stanimir STOILOV (13/02/67) - Levski Sofia											M	D	8	2
Martin PETROV (15/01/79) - Servette FC Genève (SUI)												s46	1	-

Worse still was the season endured by the Bulgarian national team, who lost interest in the European Championship qualifying campaign very early on after a sobering 0-3 defeat at home to Poland. That proved to be a game too far for national coach Hristo Bonev, who, bizarrely, had resigned after the World Cup only to be immediately re-instated by the Bulgarian FA after a surprising vote of confidence. However, Bulgaria's first

home defeat for seven years changed all that, and out he went for good, with Liteks Lovech/Under-21 coach Dimitar Dimitrov taking over the reins.

A goalless draw at Wembley against England made for a promising beginning, but four days later Bulgaria lost another home game, 0-1 to Sweden. That was effectively that as far as qualification was concerned. But the team's rapid fall from grace hardly came as a surprise.

EUROPEAN CUPS 98/99

CHAMPIONS' CUP
● **LITEKS LOVECH**
Preliminary round HALMSTADS BK (SWE)
H 2-0   Bushi (8), Yurukov (90)
Stavrev; Kolev, Zagorcic, Kirilov, Haxhi, Todorov M., Kishishev, Simonovic, Beliakov (Motta 57; Yurukov 80), Stoilov, Bushi.
A 1-2   Yurukov (77)
Stavrev; Zagorcic, Kirilov, Kolev, Haxhi, Kishishev, Simonovic (Todorov M. 87), Stoilov, Dimitrov (Emilov 65), Bushi, Beliakov (Yurukov 69).

Qualifying round SPARTAK MOSKVA (RUS)
H 0-5
Stavrev; Dimitrov, Zagorcic, Balabanov (Yurukov 46), Kishishev, Emilov, Todorov M., Stoilov, Simonovic, Bushi, Motta (Sarbakov 55).
A 2-6   Beliakov (27), Bushi (70)
Vutov; Dimitrov, Karadaliev, Ignatov, Kolev, Haxhi, Emilov, Stoilov (Kirov 61), Todorov M., Bogdanovic (Bushi 46), Beliakov (Motta 85).

CUP WINNERS' CUP
● **LEVSKI SOFIA**
Qualifying round LOKOMOTIV-96 VITEBSK (BLS)
H 8-1   Ivanov (8, 32), Borisov (23, 44, 88), Donev (42), Radukanov (52), Todorov (85)
Ivankov; Sirakov, Nikolov (Aleksandrov 55), Dimitrov, Vasilev (Radukanov 46), Yonkov, Donev, Stoilov, Ivanov (Lazarov 75), Todorov, Borisov.
A 1-1   Lazarov (50)
Ivankov; Sirakov (Chipev 60), Gospodoinov, Radukanov, Harkovchenko (Vachev 59), Yonkov, Donev, Aleksandrov, Shopov, Todorov (Topuzakov 78), Lazarov.

1st round FC KØBENHAVN (DEN)
H 0-2
Ivankov; Sirakov, Gospodinov, Radukanov, Nikolov, Yonkov, Donev (Dimitrov 13), Stoilov, Ivanov, Todorov, Borisov (Aleksandrov 80).
A 1-4   Lazarov (85)
Ivankov; Dimitrov, Vachev (Goranov 72), Radukanov, Vasilev, Stoilov, Donev (Aleksandrov 68), Yakimenko, Ivanov, Todorov, Borisov (Lazarov 54).

UEFA CUP
● **CSKA SOFIA**
Preliminary round BELSHINA BOBRUISK (BLS)
A 0-0
Ivanov I.; Kremenliev, Chomakov, Naidenov, Yordanov, Radev, Genchev, Hristov (Andonov 59), Petkov (Petrov S. 60), Stanchev, Petrov M. (Bukarev 83).

H 3-1   Petrov M. (6), Naidenov (38), Stanchev (90)
Ivanov I.; Kremenliev, Chomakov, Naidenov, Radev, Yordanov (Petrov S. 61), Genchev, Petkov M., Stanchev, Hristov (Bukarev 64), Petrov M..

Qualifying round MOLDE FK (NOR)
A 0-0
Ivanov I.; Ivanov G., Chomakov, Naidenov, Lulchev, Radev, Petrov M. (Bukarev 90), Yordanov (Andonov 77), Stanchev, Genchev, Petrov S..
H 2-0   Petkov (39), Stanchev (60)
Ivanov I.; Ivanov G., Radev, Naidenov, Lulchev, Yordanov, Genchev, Petkov, Hristov (Andonov 63), Stanchev (Bukarev 74), Petrov M. (Petrov S. 67).

1st round SERVETTE FC GENEVE (SUI)
A 1-2   Stanchev (45)
Ivanov I.; Ivanov G. (Kremenliev 84), Radev, Naidenov, Lulchev, Chomakov (Slavchev 90), Petrov S., Yordanov, Stanchev, Genchev (Andonov 30), Petkov M..
H 1-0   Stanchev (9)
Ivanov I.; Kremenliev, Radev, Yordanov (Tomash 64), Chomakov, Petrov S., Hristov (Bukarev 79), Petkov, Stanchev, Genchev, Petrov M. (Slavchev 84).

2nd round ATLÉTICO MADRID (ESP)
H 2-4   Genchev (53), Naidenov (84)
Ivanov I.; Kremenliev, Radev, Naidenov, Lulchev, Petrov S. (Dimov 74), Yordanov, Petkov, Stanchev, Genchev, Petrov M. (Hristov 33).
A 0-1
Ivanov I.; Kremenliev, Radev, Naidenov, Chomakov, Lulchev (Yordanov 69), Petrov S., Petrov M., Petkov, Stanchev, Hristov (Bukarev 69).

● **LITEKS LOVECH**
1st round GRAZER AK (AUT)
H 1-1   Stoilov (60)
Stavrev; Dimitrov, Kishishev, Kolev, Karadaliev, Haxhi, Simonovic (Emilov 75), Stoilov, Yurukov, Bushi (Motta 88), Beliakov (Bogdanovic 58).
A 0-2
Vutov; Zagorcic, Kirilov (Yurukov 77), Kolev, Haxhi, Emilov (Dimitrov 46), Kishishev, Stoilov, Todorov M., Beliakov, Bushi.

TOP SCORERS

21	Dimcho BELIAKOV	(Liteks Lovech)
17	Todor PRAMATAROV	(Shumen)
16	Hristo MARASHLIEV	(Levski Kiustendil)
15	Georgi GEORGIEV	(Minior Pernik)
13	Georgi IVANOV	(Levski Sofia)
12	Dian BOZHILOV	(Dobrudzha Dobrich)
11	Ilia GRUEV	(Neftochimik Bourgas)
	Dimitar TELKIISKI	(Botev Plovdiv)
	Serge YOFFU	(Dobrudzha Dobrich)
10	Genadi SIMEONOV	(Metalurg Pernik)
	Boiko VELICHKOV	(Spartak Varna)
	Petar MIKHTARSKI	(Pirin Blagoevgrad)
	Alban BUSHI	(Liteks Lovech)
	Mikhail MIKHAILOV	(Levski Kiustendil)

NATIONAL TEAM RESULTS 98/99

06/09/98	Poland (ECQ)	H	Bourgas	0-3	
10/10/98	England (ECQ)	A	Wembley	0-0	
14/10/98	Sweden (ECQ)	H	Bourgas	0-1	
04/11/98	Algeria	H	Sofia	0-0	
23/12/98	Morocco	A	Agadir	1-4	Bachev (58)
12/02/99	Egypt	N	Hong Kong	1-3	Yovov (88)
03/03/99	Slovakia	H	Stara Zagora	2-0	Iliev (22), Yovov (41)
27/03/99	Belgium	A	Bruges	1-0	Yovov (11)
31/03/99	Luxembourg (ECQ)	A	Luxembourg	2-0	Stoichkov (17), Yordanov (38)
19/05/99	Slovakia	A	Dubnica	0-2	
04/06/99	Poland (ECQ)	A	Warsaw	0-2	
09/06/99	England (ECQ)	H	Sofia	1-1	Markov (18)

France '98 had been the swansong of Bulgaria's golden generation, with most of the team's prominent individuals calling time on their international careers after the 6-1 demolition by Spain in Lens.

One of the few stars who did stay on was Hristo Stoichkov. Despite playing his club football halfway across the world in Japan, he was happy to take the captain's armband and make regular trips back to Europe to lead the team in both competitive and friendly combat. His eagerness to please was seen by those of a cynical disposition as a blatant attempt to land the job of national coach for the next World Cup qualifying tournament.

The curtain came down on the international career of Bulgaria's greatest-ever footballer on June 9, 1999 when he played his 83rd and final game, in the Euro 2000 qualifier at home to England. He could not mark the occasion with a goal but he did earn himself a heap of mementoes prior to the match, with his ex-Barcelona boss Johan Cruijff having been flown in to present him with plaques, flowers and sundry other nick-nacks. There was also a noisy and emotional ovation from the crowd when the great man walked off the field 17 minutes from time. Amongst the applause and acknowledgement there was surely also a feeling of great sadness among the Bulgarian fans that they would never see their idol play again. For them, and for many other football-lovers the world over, Hristo Stoichkov is simply irreplaceable.

PLAYERS OF THE SEASON

MILEN PETKOV
If there is to be a resurgence from the Bulgarian national team in time for the 2002 World Cup qualifiers, Milen Petkov could be the man to provide the kick-start. The CSKA Sofia midfielder went to France '98 as a mere squad player and didn't play, but he was the best Bulgarian on view during the six European Championship qualifiers played by the team in 1998/99. The only player other than skipper Stoichkov to start all six games, he provided some classy touches and proved that he is a skilful as well as versatile midfielder who can take over the rôle of playmaker previously filled by Krasimir Balakov. A host of foreign clubs showed interest in him during the summer but, surprisingly, he opted to stay with CSKA.

GEORGI BACHEV
If Petkov is the natural replacement for Balakov, then 22-year-old Georgi Bachev looks ready-made to take over the wide-left attacking berth from Hristo Stoichkov. He it was who subbed the former European Footballer of the Year in the two European Championship qualifiers against England, and now he seems poised to become his permanent replacement. Formerly with Pirin Blagoevgrad, Bachev made his name with Slavia Sofia before moving across town to neighbours Levski midway through the 1998/99 campaign. He made a great start for his new club, featuring strongly in the remarkable winning run that came so close to giving Levski the championship.

BOTEV PLOVDIV

CLUB DIRECTORY

FC Botev Plovdiv
Bul. Istochen 10
4000 Plovdiv
tel - (032) 226375/225736
fax - (032) 226388
Year of Formation - 1912
President - Dimitar Hristolov
Coach - Petar Zekhtinski
Stadium - Hristo Botev (21,000)

MAJOR HONOURS
League Championship - (2) 1929, 1967.

APPEARANCES 98/99

	P	Ap	(s)	Gls
Armen AMBARTSUMIAN	G	15	(1)	
Kiril ANDONOV	D	15	(1)	
Decho ARIZANOV	A	6	(6)	1
Marin BAKALOV	M	27	(3)	4
Ilian BANEV	A	3	(3)	
Olgin CHOBAN	M		(1)	
Geno DOBREVSKI	A	20	(4)	5
Ivan DOBREVSKI	M	2	(10)	
Ivan DZHULEV	D	3	(4)	
Hristo FURDZHEV	A	16	(8)	2
Ivan GANEV	D	2		
Anastas GEORGIEV	M	3	(5)	
Zarko GOGOV	M		(3)	
Hristo HRISTOV	D	3	(4)	
Borislav IVANOV	A	10	(14)	1
Yosko IVANOV	M	4		
Martin KAMBUROV	A	4	(5)	1
Georgi KATREV	M	3	(1)	
Boris KHVOINEV	A	2		
Nikolai KIROV	G	15	(1)	
Georgi LIUBENOV	A	7		
Georgi MINKOV	D	1	(5)	
Veselin PALAZOV	M		(1)	
Petar PENCHEV	D	25		1
Zaprian RAKOV	D	29		1
RUSENOV	M		(1)	
Petar SHOPOV	D	25		
Ivan TANCHOVSKI	D	25	(4)	3
Dimitar TELKIISKI	M	26		11
Vladimir TILEV	D	15	(3)	
Stefan UCHIKOV	M	24		4

LEAGUE RESULTS 1998/99

08/08/98	Minior Pernik	A	0-1	
15/08/98	Neftochimik Bourgas	H	3-0	Furdzhev, Telkiiski 2
21/08/98	CSKA Sofia	A	0-5	
30/08/98	Levski Sofia	A	0-6	
12/09/98	Lokomotiv Sofia	H	1-1	Bakalov
19/09/98	Shumen	A	1-1	Tanchovski
26/09/98	Pirin Blagoevgrad	H	2-1	Telkiiski 2
03/10/98	Levski Kiustendil	A	1-2	Dobrevski G.
17/10/98	Metalurg Pernik	H	2-1	Bakalov, Penchev
24/10/98	Septemvri Sofia	A	0-2	
07/11/98	Lokomotiv Plovdiv	H	0-0	
14/11/98	Slavia Sofia	A	0-2	
21/11/98	Dobrudzha Dobrich	H	3-2	Uchikov 2, Ivanov B.
28/11/98	Spartak Varna	A	1-2	Dobrevski G.
05/12/98	Liteks Lovech	H	0-1	
27/02/99	Minior Pernik	H	1-1	Furdzhev
06/03/99	Neftochimik Bourgas	A	1-3	Kamburov
13/03/99	CSKA Sofia	H	2-0	Telkiiski 2 (1p)
20/03/99	Levski Sofia	H	0-1	
03/04/99	Lokomotiv Sofia	A	0-2	
07/04/99	Shumen	H	5-2	Dobrevski G. 2, Telkiiski 2 (1p), Tanchovski
10/04/99	Pirin Blagoevgrad	A	0-3	
17/04/99	Levski Kiustendil	H	2-2	Uchikov, Tanchovski
24/04/99	Metalurg Pernik	A	1-3	Rakov (p)
01/05/99	Septemvri Sofia	H	3-1	Telkiiski (p), Dobrevski G., Bakalov
05/05/99	Lokomotiv Plovdiv	A	1-2	Bakalov
08/05/99	Slavia Sofia	H	1-0	Uchikov
15/05/99	Dobrudzha Dobrich	A	0-4	
22/05/99	Spartak Varna	H	3-2	Telkiiski 2 (1p), Arizanov
29/05/99	Liteks Lovech	A	0-2	

CSKA SOFIA

FC CSKA Sofia
Stadion Bulgarska Armia
Bul. Dragan Tsankov 3, 1504 Sofia
tel - (02) 656037/658200/566859/659011
Year of Formation - 1948
President - Ilia Pavlov
Coach - Dimitar Penev
Stadium - Bulgarska Armia (30,000)

MAJOR HONOURS
League Championship - (28)
1948, 1951, 1952, 1954, 1955, 1956, 1957,
1958, 1959, 1960, 1961, 1962, 1966, 1969,
1971, 1972, 1973, 1975, 1976, 1980, 1981,
1982, 1983, 1987, 1989, 1990, 1992, 1997.
Domestic Cup - (9) 1981, 1983, 1985, 1987,
1988, 1989, 1993, 1997, 1999.

	P	Ap	(s)	Gls
Aleksandar ALEKSANDROV	M		(2)	
Vlado ANDONOV	D	2	(6)	1
Stanislav ANGELOV	M	3	(4)	
Dimitar BERBATOV	A	2	(9)	3
Asen BUKAREV	A	8	(11)	2
Krasimir CHOMAKOV	D	22	(4)	3
Metodi DEIANOV	M	2	(6)	1
Ivo DIMOV	M	11	(3)	4
Boncho GENCHEV	A	8		3
Stanimir GOSPODINOV	D	4		
Igor HARKOVCHENKO	D	2		
Rumen HRISTOV	A	18	(5)	9
Galin IVANOV	D	13	(4)	
Ivailo IVANOV	G	23		
Todor KIUCHUKOV	G	6	(2)	
Emil KREMENLIEV	D	22		
Stefan LULCHEV	D	12	(2)	
Vladimir MANCHEV	A	6	(2)	2
Valentin NAIDENOV	D	11		
Miroslav NIKOLOV	A		(2)	
Milen PETKOV	M	24		7
Martin PETROV	M	11	(1)	3
Stilian PETROV	M	28		3
Zdravko RADEV	D	14		
Ivo SLAVCHEV	M	5	(9)	2
Valentin STANCHEV	A	19	(1)	6
Vladimir STOIKOV	D	1		
Aleksandar TOMASH	D	5	(3)	
Mitko TRENDAFILOV	M	10	(1)	1
Veselin VELIKOV	D	9	(1)	
Georgi YORDANOV	M	9	(4)	3
Adalbert ZAFIROV	D	9		

09/08/98	Neftochimik Bourgas	A	0-2	
16/08/98	Levski Sofia	A	0-2	
21/08/98	Botev Plovdiv	H	5-0	Stanchev 2, Genchev 2, Hristov
29/08/98	Lokomotiv Sofia	A	2-0	Genchev, Petrov S.
11/09/98	Shumen	H	3-2	Petrov M., Yordanov, Andonov
19/09/98	Pirin Blagoevgrad	A	0-0	
25/09/98	Levski Kiustendil	H	3-2	Stanchev, Yordanov, Hristov
03/10/98	Metalurg Pernik	A	0-1	
16/10/98	Septemvri Sofia	H	3-1	Petrov M., Yordanov, Hristov
24/10/98	Lokomotiv Plovdiv	A	0-0	
07/11/98	Slavia Sofia	H	1-1	Petrov M.
14/11/98	Dobrudzha Dobrich	A	1-1	Petrov S.
21/11/98	Spartak Varna	H	2-1	Stanchev, Petkov (p)
29/11/98	Liteks Lovech	A	0-8	
05/12/98	Minior Pernik	H	2-0	Hristov, Slavchev
27/02/99	Neftochimik Bourgas	H	1-1	Petkov (p)
06/03/99	Levski Sofia	A	2-3	Petkov (p), Bukarev
13/03/99	Botev Plovdiv	A	0-2	
20/03/99	Lokomotiv Sofia	H	2-0	Chomakov 2
03/04/99	Shumen	A	5-2	Hristov, Trendafilov, Dimov,
				Chomakov, Slavchev
07/04/99	Pirin Blagoevgrad	H	3-0	Petkov 2 (1p), Stanchev
11/04/99	Levski Kiustendil	A	0-0	(forfeit; no points awarded)
17/04/99	Metalurg Pernik	H	0-2	
24/04/99	Septemvri Sofia	A	5-2	Dimov 3 (1p), Petkov (p),
				Manchev
01/05/99	Lokomotiv Plovdiv	H	6-0	Petkov, Hristov 2, Dimov,
				Berbatov 2
04/05/99	Slavia Sofia	A	1-0	Stanchev
08/05/99	Dobrudzha Dobrich	H	3-0	Petrov S., Berbatov, Hristov
15/05/99	Spartak Varna	A	2-0	Hristov, Bukarev
22/05/99	Liteks Lovech	H	2-3	Manchev, Deianov
29/05/99	Minior Pernik	A	0-2	

DOBRUDZHA DOBRICH

CLUB DIRECTORY

FC Dobrudzha
Bul 25 Septemvri 10
Dobrich
tel - (058) 22591/28283
Year of Formation - 1919
President - Stefan Kolev
Coach - Ivan Manolov; Dimitar Aleksiev
Stadium - Dobrudzha (20,000)

APPEARANCES 98/99

	P	Ap	(s)	Gls
Sasho ANGELOV	D	14		
Atanas BORNOSUZOV	M	5		
Dian BOZHILOV	M	24		12
Vladko DAVIDOV (MAC)	A	27	(2)	9
Sergei DIMITROV	D	5	(6)	
Georgi GEORGIEV	M	21	(6)	1
Svetoslav KRASTEV	D	28		
Zvetan KRASTEV	D	9		
Deian MINEV	D		(1)	
Valentin PENCHEV	D	1		
Milen PENCHEV	M	24		3
Svetoslav PETROV	M	19	(3)	
Venko POPOV	D	22	(2)	
Desislav RUSEV	M		(1)	
Ivan RUSEV	M	12	(2)	3
Svilen SIMEONOV	G	19	(4)	1
Rumen SLAVOV	D	27	(1)	1
Stefan SLAVOV	D	8	(6)	
Stanislav STOIANOV	D	7	(15)	
Metodi STOINEV	A	10	(2)	3
Hristo TERZIEV	A	1	(4)	1
Tikhomir TODOROV	G	11		
Mitko VASILEV	D	1	(6)	
Damian VELKOV	D		(1)	
Ogust YOFFU (CIV)	M		(3)	
Serge YOFFU (CIV)	A	23	(1)	11
Slavi ZHEKOV	M	6	(3)	
Stoian ZHELEV	D	6	(6)	
Ventsislav ZHELEV	D		(2)	

LEAGUE RESULTS 1998/99

08/08/98	Pirin Blagoevgrad	H	0-0	
15/08/98	Levski Kiustendil	A	0-3	
12/08/98	Metalurg Pernik	H	1-0	Yoffu S.
29/08/98	Septemvri Sofia	A	1-2	Yoffu S.
12/09/98	Lokomotiv Plovdiv	H	4-2	Davidkov 2, Bozhilov, Yoffu S.
18/09/98	Slavia Sofia	A	2-6	Yoffu S., Davidkov
26/09/98	Levski Sofia	H	0-1	
03/10/98	Spartak Varna	H	3-1	Penchev (p), Yoffu S. 2
17/10/98	Liteks Lovech	A	0-5	
24/10/98	Minior Pernik	H	2-0	Bozhilov, Yoffu S.
08/11/98	Neftochimik Bourgas	A	0-2	
14/11/98	CSKA Sofia	H	1-1	Davidkov
21/11/98	Botev Plovdiv	A	2-3	Bozhilov 2
28/11/98	Lokomotiv Sofia	H	2-3	Slavov R., Penchev
05/12/98	Shumen	A	0-0	
27/02/99	Pirin Blagoevgrad	A	0-1	
06/03/99	Levski Kiustendil	H	1-0	Davidkov
14/03/99	Metalurg Pernik	A	0-1	
20/03/99	Septemvri Sofia	H	5-1	Stoinev 2, Georgiev, Bozhilov, Rusev I.
03/04/99	Lokomotiv Plovdiv	A	1-3	Stoinev
07/04/99	Slavia Sofia	H	3-1	Bozhilov 2, Rusev I.
11/04/99	Levski Sofia	A	0-2	
17/04/99	Spartak Varna	A	2-1	Davidkov, Rusev I.
24/04/99	Liteks Lovech	H	1-2	Terziev
01/05/99	Minior Pernik	A	2-4	Davidkov, Penchev
05/05/99	Neftochimik Bourgas	H	2-1	Yoffu S. 2
08/05/99	CSKA Sofia	A	0-3	
15/05/99	Botev Plovdiv	H	4-0	Bozhilov, Davidkov 2, Yoffu S.
22/05/99	Lokomotiv Sofia	A	2-5	Bozhilov 2
29/05/99	Shumen	H	4-1	Yoffu S., Bozhilov 2, Simeonov (p)

LEVSKI KIUSTENDIL

CLUB DIRECTORY

FC Levski
Stadium Osogovo
2500 Kiustendil
tel - (078) 20498/24274
Year of Formation - 1920
President - Georgi Iliev
Coach - Asparuch Nikodimov
Stadium - Osogovo (11,000)

APPEARANCES 98/99

	P	Ap	(s)	Gls
Rumen ANGELOV	M	15	(5)	4
Krasimir BISLIMOV	D	13		1
Borislav GEORGIEV	D	10	(1)	
Stefan GOSHEV	D	25		2
GRANCHAROV	D		(1)	
Velko HRISTEV	M	13	(7)	2
Ivan IVANOV	D	9	(7)	1
KARAKASHKI	D		(1)	
Liudmil KIROV	D	1	(5)	
Petar KOLEV	D	22		3
Zorko MACHEV	D	2	(3)	1
Hristo MARASHLIEV	A	23	(2)	16
Mario METUSHEV	M		(7)	
Misho MIKHAILOV	A	17	(3)	10
Viktor MIKHAILOV	A	4	(8)	2
Nedko MILENOV	M	9	(5)	
Krasimir PETKOV	G	14		
Petko PETKOV	G	10	(1)	
Georgi PETROV	D	24	(1)	
Plamen PETROV	A	21	(3)	8
Rosen PETROV	D	16	(2)	1
Mikhail ROLEV	G	5		
Zdravko STANKOV	M	16	(4)	1
Ilian STOIANOV	D	22		1
Ivan STOICHEV	A	10		4
Nikolai VAZELOV	D	6	(4)	
Sasa VUKOJEVIC (YUG)	M	5		
Daniel YORDANOV	M	7	(12)	

LEAGUE RESULTS 1998/99

08/08/98	Slavia Sofia	A	0-1	
15/08/98	Dobrudzha Dobrich	H	3-0	Angelov 2, Goshev
22/08/98	Spartak Varna	A	3-2	Angelov, Machev, Hristev
29/08/98	Liteks Lovech	H	1-0	Petrov P.
12/09/98	Minior Pernik	A	0-0	
19/09/98	Neftochimik Bourgas	H	3-0	Mikhailov M., Marashliev 2
25/09/98	CSKA Sofia	A	2-3	Marashliev 2
03/10/98	Botev Plovdiv	H	2-1	Marashliev 2
17/10/98	Lokomotiv Sofia	A	0-1	
24/10/98	Shumen	H	3-0	Petrov R., Angelov, Kolev P.
07/11/98	Pirin Blagoevgrad	A	1-0	Kolev P.
14/11/98	Levski Sofia	A	0-3	
21/11/98	Metalurg Pernik	H	7-1	Mikhailov M., Kolev P., Stankov, Marashliev, Petrov Pl., Hristev, Mikhailov V.
29/11/98	Septemvri Sofia	A	3-0	Marashliev 2, Petrov P.
05/12/98	Lokomotiv Plovdiv	H	5-1	Goshev, Marashliev 3 (1p), Mikhailov M.
27/02/99	Slavia Sofia	H	3-0	Mikhailov M. 2, Petrov P.
06/03/99	Dobrudzha Dobrich	A	0-1	
13/03/99	Spartak Varna	H	2-0	Mikhailov M. 2 (2p)
21/03/99	Liteks Lovech	A	0-2	
03/04/99	Minior Pernik	H	2-1	Marashliev, Bislimov
07/04/99	Neftochimik Bourgas	A	1-3	Marashliev
11/04/99	CSKA Sofia	H	0-0	(forfeit; no points awarded)
17/04/99	Botev Plovdiv	A	2-2	Ivanov, Stoichev
24/04/99	Lokomotiv Sofia	H	1-0	Mikhailov M.
01/05/99	Shumen	A	3-3	Petrov P., Stoichev (p), Stoianov
05/05/99	Pirin Blagoevgrad	H	2-0	Mikhailov V., Petrov P.
09/05/99	Levski Sofia	H	0-1	
15/05/99	Metalurg Pernik	A	2-1	Stoichev 2
22/05/99	Septemvri Sofia	H	4-1	Mikhailov M., Marashliev 2, Petrov P.
29/05/99	Lokomotiv Plovdiv	A	2-1	Petrov P., Mikhailov M. (p)

LEVSKI SOFIA

CLUB DIRECTORY

FC Levski Sofia
ul. Todorini Kukli 47
Kv. Poduene
1517 Sofia
tel - (02) 457013/459121/476064
Year of Formation - 1914
President - Tomas Lavchis
Coach - Viacheslav Groznyi; Angel Stankov
Stadium - Georgi Asparuchov (45,000)

MAJOR HONOURS
League Championship - (20)
1933, 1937, 1942. 1946, 1947, 1949, 1950,
1953, 1965, 1968, 1970, 1974, 1977, 1979,
1984, 1985, 1988, 1993, 1994, 1995.
Domestic Cup - (8) 1942, 1982, 1984, 1986,
1991, 1992, 1994, 1998.

APPEARANCES 98/99

	P	Ap	(s)	Gls
Aleksandar ALEKSANDROV	M	16	(2)	7
Georgi BACHEV	A	12		4
Georgi BORISOV	A	7	(2)	
Zvetomir CHIPEV	M		(1)	
Krasimir DIMITROV	D	14	(7)	
Aleksei DIONISIEV	D	12		
Doncho DONEV	A	10	(1)	6
Stanislav GENCHEV	M	3	(1)	1
Martin GORANOV	D		(5)	
Stanimir GOSPODINOV	D	8	(3)	
Igor HARKOVCHENKO (UKR)	D	3		
Ilian ILIEV	M	11		
John INGLIS (SCO)	D	12		3
Dimitar IVANKOV	G	29		6
Georgi IVANOV	A	26		13
Zdravko LAZAROV	A	10	(13)	3
Yordan MARINOV	D	8	(3)	
Asen NIKOLOV	M	18	(2)	
Viktorio PAVLOV	M	2	(6)	
Milen RADUKANOV	D	28		2
Vesko SARBAKOV	M	1	(5)	
Georgi SHEITANOV	G	1		
Petar SHOPOV	A		(18)	4
Zakhari SIRAKOV	M	19		1
Martin STANKOV	D	12		
Stanimir STOILOV	M	26		1
Nikolai TODOROV	M	21	(4)	3
Elin TOPUZAKOV	A	4	(4)	
Veselin VACHEV	D	2	(3)	
Ivan VASILEV	D	1	(1)	
Aleksei YAKIMENKO (UKR)	M	3	(4)	
Vladimir YONKOV	M	11	(1)	1

LEAGUE RESULTS 1998/99

16/08/98	CSKA Sofia	H	2-0	Ivanov, Donev
19/08/98	Septemvri Sofia	A	4-0	Ivanov, Aleksandrov, Lazarov, Shopov
21/08/98	Lokomotiv Plovdiv	A	2-1	Ivanov, Shopov
30/08/98	Botev Plovdiv	H	6-0	Todorov, Donev 2, Aleksandrov 2, Shopov
12/09/98	Slavia Sofia	A	0-0	
21/09/98	Lokomotiv Sofia	H	1-0	Ivanov
26/09/98	Dobrudzha Dobrich	A	1-0	Todorov
03/10/98	Shumen	H	2-2	Aleksandrov, Ivanov
17/10/98	Spartak Varna	A	1-2	Sirakov
23/10/98	Pirin Blagoevgrad	H	5-0	Ivankov (p), Radukanov, Stoilov, Donev, Yonkov
08/11/98	Liteks Lovech	A	1-1	Aleksandrov
14/11/98	Levski Kiustendil	H	3-0	Ivanov, Donev 2
21/11/98	Minior Pernik	A	2-2	Ivanov, Lazarov
28/11/98	Metalurg Pernik	H	1-0	Ivanov
05/12/98	Neftochimik Bourgas	A	0-1	
27/02/99	Septemvri Sofia	H	2-0	Ivankov (p), Shopov
06/03/99	CSKA Sofia	A	3-2	Ivanov 2, Aleksandrov
12/03/99	Lokomotiv Plovdiv	H	2-0	Inglis, Aleksandrov
20/03/99	Botev Plovdiv	A	1-0	Ivanov
03/04/99	Slavia Sofia	H	1-0	Bachev
07/04/99	Lokomotiv Sofia	A	1-0	Inglis
11/04/99	Dobrudzha Dobrich	H	2-0	Lazarov, Ivankov (p)
17/04/99	Shumen	A	1-0	Todorov
25/04/99	Spartak Varna	H	1-0	Inglis
01/05/99	Pirin Blagoevgrad	A	1-0	Ivanov
05/05/99	Liteks Lovech	H	0-0	
09/05/99	Levski Kiustendil	A	1-0	Ivankov (p)
15/05/99	Minior Pernik	H	2-0	Bachev, Ivanov
22/05/99	Metalurg Pernik	A	3-0	Ivankov (p), Radukanov, Genchev
28/05/99	Neftochimik Bourgas	H	3-0	Ivankov (p), Bachev 2

LITEKS LOVECH

CLUB DIRECTORY

FC Liteks
Stadion Lovech
5500 Lovech
tel - (068) 29091/24420
fax - (068) 20012
Year of Formation - 1921
President - Christofer Iliev
Coach - Dimitar Dimitrov; Ferario Spasov
Stadium - Lovech (7,000)

MAJOR HONOURS
League Championship - (2) 1998, 1999.

APPEARANCES 98/99

	P	Ap	(s)	Gls
Dimitar BALABANOV	D		(1)	
Dimcho BELIAKOV	A	23	(2)	21
Georgi BOGDANOV	A	2	(1)	
Igor BOGDANOVIC (YUG)	A	4	(6)	5
Alban BUSHI (ALB)	A	19	(3)	10
Nikolai DIMITROV	D	18	(4)	
Rosen EMILOV	M	4	(11)	
Ivan GEMEDZHIEV	A		(2)	
Altin HAXHI (ALB)	M	20	(4)	6
Veselin IGNATOV	D	4	(1)	1
Dimitar KARADALIEV	D	11	(5)	1
Rosen KIRILOV	D	11		1
Vasil KIROV	D	7	(9)	1
Radostin KISHISHEV	M	26		2
Stefan KOLEV	D	26		
Svetlan KONDEV	M		(2)	
Luís MOTTA (BRA)	A	2	(9)	1
Ivailo PETEV	M	1	(4)	
Laurentiu REGHECAMPF (ROM)	D	13	(1)	4
Veselin SARBAKOV	M		(2)	
Dragoljub SIMONOVIC	A	22	(2)	8
Stoian STAVREV	G	11		
Stoicho STOILOV	M	24		9
Metodi STOINEV	A		(1)	
Marian TODOROV	M	16	(6)	2
Svetoslav TODOROV	A	7	(4)	2
Vitomir VUTOV	G	19		
Stefan YURUKOV	A	13	(6)	7
Zlatomir ZAGORCIC	D	19		1
Zhivko ZHELEV	D	8		1

LEAGUE RESULTS 1998/99

07/08/98	Lokomotiv Sofia	H	3-1	Haxhi, Yurukov, Simonovic
15/08/98	Shumen	A	0-0	
22/08/98	Pirin Blagoevgrad	H	8-1	Zagorcic, Bushi 2, Simonovic,
				Bogdanovic 3, Todorov M.
29/08/98	Levski Kiustendil	A	0-1	
11/09/98	Metalurg Pernik	H	2-1	Beliakov, Haxhi
19/09/98	Septemvri Sofia	A	5-2	Stoilov (p), Simonovic,
				Beliakov 2, Haxhi
25/09/98	Lokomotiv Plovdiv	H	5-1	Bogdanovic, Haxhi, Beliakov 2,
				Bushi
03/10/98	Slavia Sofia	A	1-1	Beliakov
17/10/98	Dobrudzha Dobrich	H	5-0	Beliakov, Yurukov, Ignatov, Bushi,
				Todorov M.
24/10/98	Spartak Varna	A	2-0	Motta, Kishishev
08/11/98	Levski Sofia	H	1-1	Bushi
14/11/98	Minior Pernik	H	3-1	Bogdanovic, Yurukov 2
21/11/98	Neftochimik Bourgas	A	4-1	Stoilov (p), Beliakov 2, Yurukov
29/11/98	CSKA Sofia	H	8-0	Kirilov, Beliakov 3, Yurukov,
				Simonovic, Stoilov 2
05/12/98	Botev Plovdiv	A	1-0	Beliakov
26/02/99	Lokomotiv Sofia	A	0-1	
06/03/99	Shumen	H	2-0	Bushi, Reghecampf
14/03/99	Pirin Blagoevgrad	A	2-1	Todorov S., Kishishev
21/03/99	Levski Kiustendil	H	2-0	Bushi, Beliakov
03/04/99	Metalurg Pernik	A	2-1	Kirov (p), Beliakov
07/04/99	Septemvri Sofia	H	4-1	Stoilov (p), Beliakov,
				Reghecampf 2 (1p)
10/04/99	Lokomotiv Plovdiv	A	4-1	Beliakov, Karadaliev, Bushi 2
18/04/99	Slavia Sofia	H	3-1	Stoilov 2 (1p), Haxhi
24/04/99	Dobrudzha Dobrich	A	2-1	Stoilov, Simonovic
01/05/99	Spartak Varna	H	3-2	Beliakov, Simonovic, Zhelev
05/05/99	Levski Sofia	A	0-0	
08/05/99	Minior Pernik	A	3-2	Todorov S., Simonovic 2
15/05/99	Neftochimik Bourgas	H	3-1	Beliakov, Yurukov, Haxhi
22/05/99	CSKA Sofia	A	3-2	Beliakov, Reghecampf, Stoilov
29/05/99	Botev Plovdiv	H	2-0	Bushi, Beliakov

LOKOMOTIV PLOVDIV

CLUB DIRECTORY

FC Lokomotiv
Sport komplex Lokomotiv
Kvartal Lauta
4000 Plovdiv
tel - (032) 262511
Year of Formation - 1936
President - Filcho Kolev
Coach - Ivan Gluchchev; Georgi Vasilev;
Dinko Dermendzhiev; Vladimir Fatov
Stadium - Lokomotiv (25,000)

APPEARANCES 98/99

	P	Ap	(s)	Gls
Angel ANGELOV	M	14	(2)	
Lilcho ARSOV	G	12		
Danail BACHKOV	D	17		1
Dian BAIRAKTAROV	M		(1)	
Rumen BOEV	D	12	(1)	
Grozdiu BOTEV	A	2	(6)	
Rumen DIMITROV	D	12	(3)	
Yulian DZHEVIZOV	A	20		4
Atanas GEORGIEV	M	26	(2)	
Marian GERMANOV	D	11	(1)	
Goran GORANOV	M	4	(10)	1
Yovko IVANOV	A	9	(1)	3
Krasimir KAMBUROV	A	2	(3)	
Angel KIOSEV	A	2		
Stoian KOLEV	G	8		
Vasil KOLEV	M	13	(1)	
Ivo KOSTADINOV	M	25	(3)	1
Vasko KRASTEV	M	12	(1)	3
Georgi LAZAROV	D	15	(1)	2
Yonko NEDELCHEV	D	2		
Yulian NEICHEV	A	4	(2)	
Dimitar PASHEV	A		(4)	
Ivailo PETROV	M	9	(9)	1
Milen RAIKOVSKI	G	10	(1)	
Petar STANEV	A	18		4
Chavdar STOICHEV	A	4	(4)	
Hristo TELKIISKI	A	6	(3)	
Valentin TODOROV	M	1	(2)	
Spas URUMOV	A	10	(4)	3
Kiril VASILEV	A	4		
Georgi VELICHKOV	M	2	(1)	
Sasha VUKOJEVIC (YUG)	M	13	(1)	1
Valeri YOCHEV	D	22		1
Georgi ZDRAVKOV	A	9	(11)	1

LEAGUE RESULTS 1998/99

08/08/98	Metalurg Pernik	H	2-0	Ivanov, Krastev
14/08/98	Septemvri Sofia	A	1-1	Ivanov
21/08/98	Levski Sofia	H	1-2	Dzhevizov
29/08/98	Slavia Sofia	H	0-0	
12/09/98	Dobrudzha Dobrich	A	2-4	Krastev, Ivanov
19/09/98	Spartak Varna	H	1-3	Krastev
25/09/98	Liteks Lovech	A	1-5	Stanev
03/10/98	Minior Pernik	H	0-1	
17/10/98	Neftochimik Bourgas	A	1-4	Stanev
24/10/98	CSKA Sofia	H	0-0	
07/11/98	Botev Plovdiv	A	0-0	
14/11/98	Lokomotiv Sofia	H	1-3	Zdravkov
21/11/98	Shumen	A	0-1	
28/11/98	Pirin Blagoevgrad	H	0-0	
05/12/98	Levski Kiustendil	A	1-5	Petrov
27/02/99	Metalurg Pernik	A	0-1	
06/03/99	Septemvri Sofia	H	2-0	Lazarov, Vukojevic
12/03/99	Levski Sofia	A	0-2	
20/03/99	Slavia Sofia	A	1-6	Urumov
03/04/99	Dobrudzha Dobrich	H	3-1	Dzhevizov 2, Kostadinov
07/04/99	Spartak Varna	A	0-2	
10/04/99	Liteks Lovech	H	1-4	Stanev
17/04/99	Minior Pernik	A	0-2	
24/04/99	Neftochimik Bourgas	H	2-4	Lazarov, Yochev
01/05/99	CSKA Sofia	A	0-6	
05/05/99	Botev Plovdiv	H	2-1	Bachkov, Dzhevizov
08/05/99	Lokomotiv Sofia	A	1-4	Goranov
15/05/99	Shumen	H	1-3	Stanev (p)
22/05/99	Pirin Blagoevgrad	A	1-6	Urumov
29/05/99	Levski Kiustendil	H	1-2	Urumov

LOKOMOTIV SOFIA

CLUB DIRECTORY

FC Lokomotiv
Bul. Rozhen 23, 1220 Sofia
tel - (02) 9360356
fax - (02) 9360341
Year of Formation - 1929
President - Nikolai Gigov
Coach - Georgi Vasilev
Stadium - Lokomotiv (25,000)

MAJOR HONOURS
League Championship - (4)
1940, 1945, 1964, 1978.
Domestic Cup - (1) 1995.

APPEARANCES 98/99

	P	Ap	(s)	Gls
Nikolai ALEKSANDROV	D	10	(4)	1
Ivailo ANDONOV	A	24		7
Georgi ANTONOV	M	18	(3)	
Georgi BORISOV	A	4	(8)	2
Simeon CHILIBONOV	M	10		3
Marcho DAFCHEV	A	19	(8)	5
Slaveiko DIMITROV	D	2		
Danilo DONCIC (YUG)	A	10	(11)	4
Dejan DZURIC (YUG)	D	12	(2)	
Anton EVTIMOV	A	1	(6)	1
Guncho EVTIMOV	D	16	(2)	3
Emil GARGOROV	A	1	(4)	
Deian GENCHEV	M	13	(5)	1
Hristi GEORGIEV	D	6	(4)	
Georgi MARKOV	D	21	(2)	
Dobri MITOV	D	11		
Valentin NAIDENOV	D	11		
Anatoli NANKOV	A	15	(1)	
Ivo PARGOV	A	11	(9)	8
Georgi PEEV	A	14	(5)	1
Yasen PETROV	M	11	(5)	
Dian POPOV	M		(2)	
Stefan SALAMANOV	D	1	(4)	
Radostin STANEV	G	22		
Yavor VALCHINOV	D	19	(3)	1
Dimitar VASEV	D	19		2
Ilian VASILEV	G	8		
Vladimir YONKOV	M	9	(1)	
Hristo YOVOV	A	12		6

LEAGUE RESULTS 1998/99

07/08/98	Liteks Lovech	A	1-3	Doncic
15/08/98	Minior Pernik	H	1-0	Pargov
22/08/98	Neftochimik Bourgas	A	0-0	
29/08/98	CSKA Sofia	H	0-2	
12/09/98	Botev Plovdiv	A	1-1	Andonov
21/09/98	Levski Sofia	A	0-1	
26/09/98	Shumen	H	2-1	Pargov, Andonov
03/10/98	Pirin Blagoevgrad	A	2-0	Andonov, Evtimov A.
17/10/98	Levski Kiustendil	H	1-0	Dafchev
24/10/98	Metalurg Pernik	A	1-2	Andonov
06/11/98	Septemvri Sofia	H	0-0	
14/11/98	Lokomotiv Plovdiv	A	3-1	Doncic, Andonov, Dafchev
21/11/98	Slavia Sofia	H	0-2	
28/11/98	Dobrudzha Dobrich	A	3-2	Evtimov G., Aleksandrov, Dafchev
05/12/98	Spartak Varna	H	3-1	Peev, Andonov, Doncic (p)
26/02/99	Liteks Lovech	A	1-0	Andonov
06/03/99	Minior Pernik	A	5-1	Yovov, Pargov, og (Karakanov), Evtimov G.
14/03/99	Neftochimik Bourgas	H	1-0	Valchinov (p)
20/03/99	CSKA Sofia	A	0-2	
03/04/99	Botev Plovdiv	H	2-0	Vasev (p), Pargov
07/04/99	Levski Sofia	H	0-1	
10/04/99	Shumen	A	0-2	
17/04/99	Pirin Blagoevgrad	H	4-1	Yovov 2, Evtimov G., Doncic
24/04/99	Levski Kiustendil	A	0-1	
01/05/99	Metalurg Pernik	H	1-0	Vasev (p)
05/05/99	Septemvri Sofia	A	1-0	Chilibonov
08/05/99	Lokomotiv Plovdiv	H	4-1	Pargov 2, Borisov 2
15/05/99	Slavia Sofia	A	3-2	Dafchev, Yovov, Pargov
22/05/99	Dobrudzha Dobrich	H	5-2	Yovov 2, Chilibonov 2, Genchev
29/05/99	Spartak Varna	A	1-1	Dafchev

METALURG PERNIK

CLUB DIRECTORY

FC Metalurg
Kvartal Iztok
2300 Pernik
tel - (076) 74491/22091
Year of Formation - 1957
President - Parvan Parvanov
Coach - Georgi Haralampiev
Stadium - Metalurg (12,000)

APPEARANCES 98/99

	P	Ap	(s)	Gls
Spas BOIANOV	M	15	(8)	3
Nikolai CHAVDAROV	G	3	(2)	
Borislav DAVIDKOV	M		(2)	
Nevil DEDE (ALB)	A		(1)	
Cristian DOBREV	M		(6)	
Stoicho DRAGOV	G	27		
Kiril DZHOROV	D	26	(1)	3
Airon GASHI (ALB)	A		(1)	
Veselin IGNATOV	D	11		
Filip ILKOV	D	24		2
Rumen ISTREVSKI	M		(3)	
David MUKA (ALB)	M		(1)	
Kiril NIKOLOV	A	25	(2)	1
Rosen OLEGOV	A		(1)	
Geno PAPAZOV	D	2	(2)	
Rumen PETROV	D	12	(5)	1
Krasimir PINGOV	D		(5)	
RAICHEV	M		(1)	
Radostin RUSEV	D	26		
Plamen RUSINOV	A	12	(1)	4
Kamen SHERBETOV	A	25	(1)	2
Shaban SHEVKED	D	23		1
Genadi SIMEONOV	A	27		10
Marin STOIANOV	M	2	(6)	1
Rumen STOITSOV	A	2	(12)	2
Krasimir SVILENOV	A	30		
Luis TABOKO (DRC)	M		(1)	
Georgi VARADEV	A	3	(7)	1
Valentin VARADINOV	M	8	(6)	
Ivailo YORDANOV	D	1	(3)	
Zdravko ZDRAVKOV	D	26		

LEAGUE RESULTS 1998/99

08/08/98	Lokomotiv Plovdiv	A	0-2	
18/08/98	Slavia Sofia	H	1-1	Simeonov
22/08/98	Dobrudzha Dobrich	A	0-1	
29/08/98	Spartak Varna	H	2-0	Shevked, Ilkov
11/09/98	Liteks Lovech	A	1-2	Simeonov
19/09/98	Minior Pernik	H	1-2	Rusinov
26/09/98	Neftochimik Bourgas	A	0-2	
03/10/98	CSKA Sofia	H	1-0	Rusinov
17/10/98	Botev Plovdiv	A	1-2	og (Rakov)
24/10/98	Lokomotiv Sofia	H	2-1	og (Markov), Boianov
07/11/98	Shumen	A	0-1	
14/11/98	Pirin Blagoevgrad	H	2-0	Rusinov 2 (1p)
21/11/98	Levski Kiustendil	A	1-7	Stoitsov
28/11/98	Levski Sofia	A	0-1	
05/12/98	Septemvri Sofia	H	4-2	Ilkov, Simeonov 2, Varadev
27/02/99	Lokomotiv Plovdiv	H	1-0	Sherbetov
05/03/99	Slavia Sofia	A	0-1	
14/03/99	Dobrudzha Dobrich	H	1-0	Nikolov
20/03/99	Spartak Varna	A	0-3	
03/04/99	Liteks Lovech	H	1-2	Simeonov
07/04/99	Minior Pernik	A	4-3	Dzhorov 2, Simeonov, Stoitsov
10/04/99	Neftochimik Bourgas	H	0-0	
17/04/99	CSKA Sofia	A	2-0	Simeonov 2
24/04/99	Botev Plovdiv	H	3-1	Sherbetov, Dzhorov, Simeonov
01/05/99	Lokomotiv Sofia	A	0-1	
05/05/99	Shumen	H	2-1	Boianov, Petrov
08/05/99	Pirin Blagoevgrad	A	1-2	Stoianov
15/05/99	Levski Kiustendil	H	1-2	Simeonov
22/05/99	Levski Sofia	H	0-3	
29/05/99	Septemvri Sofia	A	1-3	Boianov

MINIOR PERNIK

CLUB DIRECTORY

Minior Pernik
ul. Fizkulturna 1
2300 Pernik
tel - (076) 24963
Year of Formation - 1919
President - Krasimir Mikhailov
Coach - Ventsislav Arsov; Yanko Dinkov
Stadium - Minior (20,000)

APPEARANCES 98/99

	P	Ap	(s)	Gls
Petar ANESTIEV	D	9	(2)	
Nikolai ARNAUDOV	M	15		
Vladimir ARNAUDOV	D	11	(1)	
Ivo BANKIN	A	1	(1)	1
Daniel BELCHEV	M	1		
Georgi BOGDANOV	A	11	(2)	2
Ivailo BRANKOV	A	8	(8)	3
Slaveiko DIMITROV	D	4	(2)	1
Velizar DIMITROV	A	18	(5)	4
Liudmil EVGENIEV	D	26		1
Biser GEORGIEV	M	6	(1)	
Dimitar GEORGIEV	M	14	(6)	4
Georgi GEORGIEV	A	25		15
Viktor GEORGIEV	G	17	(1)	
Georgi KARAKANOV	M	25	(1)	1
Georgi KIOSEV	A	22		3
Angelo KIUCHUKOV	M	13	(9)	3
Yanek KIUCHUKOV	D	28		3
Metodi METODIEV	A	1	(7)	
Aleksandar NANOV	D	7	(6)	
Yakov PAPARKOV	D	18	(5)	
Slavcho PAVLOV	M	23		1
Krasimir STOEV	A		(5)	
Spas STOIMENOV	M	7	(7)	
Emil VARADINOV	G	13		
Vladislav VLADOV	M	1	(3)	1
Yulian YANAKIEV	M	6	(10)	

LEAGUE RESULTS 1998/99

08/08/98	Botev Plovdiv	H	1-0	Bankin
15/08/98	Lokomotiv Sofia	A	0-1	
22/08/98	Shumen	H	2-0	Kiosev, Georgiev G.
29/08/98	Pirin Blagoevgrad	A	1-3	Georgiev G.
12/09/98	Levski Kiustendil	H	0-0	
19/09/98	Metalurg Pernik	A	2-1	Karakanov, Kiosev
26/09/98	Septemvri Sofia	H	2-2	Georgiev G., Kiuchukov Y. (p)
03/10/98	Lokomotiv Plovdiv	A	1-0	Brankov
17/10/98	Slavia Sofia	H	1-1	Bogdanov
24/10/98	Dobrudzha Dobrich	A	0-2	
07/11/98	Spartak Varna	H	5-0	Evgeniev, Georgiev G. 2, Kiuchukov Y. (p), Brankov
14/11/98	Liteks Lovech	A	1-3	Dimitrov V.
21/11/98	Levski Sofia	H	2-2	Bogdanov, Dimitrov V.
28/11/98	Neftochimik Bourgas	H	1-0	Georgiev G.
05/12/98	CSKA Sofia	A	0-2	
27/02/99	Botev Plovdiv	A	1-1	Brankov
06/03/99	Lokomotiv Sofia	H	1-5	Kiosev
14/03/99	Shumen	A	1-1	Georgiev G.
20/03/99	Pirin Blagoevgrad	H	2-1	Georgiev G., Georgiev D.
03/04/99	Levski Kiustendil	A	1-2	Georgiev D.
07/04/99	Metalurg Pernik	H	3-4	Georgiev G. 2, Vladov
10/04/99	Septemvri Sofia	A	3-2	Georgiev G. 2, Georgiev D.
17/04/99	Lokomotiv Plovdiv	H	2-0	Georgiev G. 2 (1p)
24/04/99	Slavia Sofia	A	2-2	Georgiev G., og (Irenchev)
01/05/99	Dobrudzha Dobrich	H	4-2	Dimitrov S., Dimitrov V., Kiuchukov A., Georgiev D.
05/05/99	Spartak Varna	A	0-2	
08/05/99	Liteks Lovech	H	2-3	Dimitrov V., Kiuchukov A.
15/05/99	Levski Sofia	A	0-2	
22/05/99	Neftochimik Bourgas	A	1-2	Kiuchukov A.
29/05/99	CSKA Sofia	H	2-0	Pavlov, Kiuchukov Y.

NEFTOCHIMIK BOURGAS

CLUB DIRECTORY

FC Neftochimik
Stadium Neftochimik
8000 Bourgas
tel - (056) 800320/800325
fax - (056) 24898
Year of Formation - 1932
President - Hristo Portochanov
Coach - Dimitar Stoichev
Stadium - Neftochimik (22,000)

APPEARANCES 98/99

	P	Ap	(s)	Gls
Boian ANDONOV	G		(2)	
Veselin BRANIMIROV	D	26		
Georgi CHILIKOV	A	4	(5)	1
Krasimir DENEV	D	10	(4)	
Stanislav DIMITROV	A	28		5
Kristian DOBREV	M	1	(7)	
Milen GEORGIEV	A	1	(2)	
Yordan GOSPODINOV	G	29		
Ilia GRUEV	M	29		11
Daniel HRISTOV	D	7	(2)	
Milen HRISTOV	D	1	(1)	1
Said IBRAIMOV	D	24	(1)	3
Todor KISELICHKOV	M	12	(10)	2
Nikolai KRASTEV	D	2	(1)	
Marko MARKOV	M		(7)	1
Blagomir MITREV	M	19	(4)	1
Marian NIKOLOV	G	1		
Svetoslav NONCHEV	M		(5)	
Malin ORACHEV	D	27		
Velian PARUSHEV	D	25		4
Dian PETKOV	M	8	(5)	2
Vesko PETKOV	A	13	(1)	5
Rosen PETROV	D	2	(2)	
Plamen RUSINOV	A		(3)	1
Stoiko SAKALIEV	A	11	(12)	6
Anton SPASOV	A	6	(1)	
Mitko TRENDAFILOV	M	2	(1)	
Borislav VELICHKOV	M		(5)	
Todor YANCHEV	A	29		7
Zlatko YANCHEV	D	13		1

LEAGUE RESULTS 1998/99

09/08/98	CSKA Sofia	H	2-0	Gruev, Petkov V.
15/08/98	Botev Plovdiv	A	0-3	
22/08/98	Lokomotiv Sofia	H	0-0	
29/08/98	Shumen	A	0-1	
12/09/98	Pirin Blagoevgrad	H	6-1	Dimitrov, Petkov V. 2, Gruev (p), Parushev (p), Markov
19/09/98	Levski Kiustendil	A	0-3	
26/09/98	Metalurg Pernik	H	2-0	Petkov V., Parushev
02/10/98	Septemvri Sofia	A	1-0	Sakaliev
17/10/98	Lokomotiv Plovdiv	H	4-1	Petkov V., Gruev 2, Dimitrov
24/10/98	Slavia Sofia	A	2-1	Gruev (p), Petkov D.
08/11/98	Dobrudzha Dobrich	H	2-0	Gruev, Sakaliev
14/11/98	Spartak Varna	A	1-2	Dimitrov
21/11/98	Liteks Lovech	H	1-4	Parushev
28/11/98	Minior Pernik	A	0-1	
05/12/98	Levski Sofia	H	1-0	Ibraimov
27/02/99	CSKA Sofia	A	1-1	Yanchev Z.
06/03/99	Botev Plovdiv	H	3-1	Gruev (p), Yanchev T., Kiselichkov
14/03/99	Lokomotiv Sofia	A	0-1	
20/03/99	Shumen	H	6-1	Ibraimov, Gruev, Dimitrov, Rusinov, Parushev, Sakaliev
03/04/99	Pirin Blagoevgrad	A	1-1	Chilikov
07/04/99	Levski Kiustendil	H	3-1	Yanchev T. 3
10/04/99	Metalurg Pernik	A	0-0	
17/04/99	Septemvri Sofia	H	1-3	Sakaliev
24/04/99	Lokomotiv Plovdiv	A	4-2	Gruev, Kiselichkov, Yanchev T. 2
01/05/99	Slavia Sofia	H	2-0	Mitrev, Petkov D.
05/05/99	Dobrudzha Dobrich	A	1-2	Hristov M.
08/05/99	Spartak Varna	H	4-1	Gruev (p), Sakaliev, Yanchev T., Ibraimov
15/05/99	Liteks Lovech	A	1-3	Dimitrov
22/05/99	Minior Pernik	H	2-1	Gruev (p), Sakaliev
29/05/99	Levski Sofia	A	0-3	

PIRIN BLAGOEVGRAD

CLUB DIRECTORY

FC Pirin
ul Dabravka 1
Stadion Hristo Botev
2700 Blagoevgrad
tel - (073) 27052/23090
Year of Formation - 1922
President - Ognean Krastev
Coach - Yordan Samokovliiski; Boris Nikolov
Stadium - Hristo Botev (15,000)

APPEARANCES 98/99

	P	Ap	(s)	Gls
Kamuran AHMED	D	8		
Hristo ARANGELOV	D	17	(4)	
Stanislav BACHEV	D	29	(1)	
Krum BIBISHKOV	A	4	(2)	1
Georgi BIZHEV	A		(4)	1
Zvetomir CHIPEV	M	7	(5)	
Stoimen DONCHEV	M		(7)	
Nikolai GAVALIUGOV	D	7		
Svetoslav GEORGIEV	M	8	(2)	
Trifon GEORGIEV	D	25		
Konstantin GERGANCIIEV	M	21	(3)	7
Stoine ILIEV	D	24		1
Ivo IVANKOV	G	21	(1)	
Yuri IVANKOV	A	15	(11)	1
Zdravko IVANOV	M		(2)	
KOEMDZHIEV	M		(1)	
Petar MIKHTARSKI	A	22	(3)	10
Miroslav MITEV	G	9	(1)	
Nikolai NIKOLOV	M	7	(8)	
Mario PETKOV	A	5	(8)	
Asen SLANCHEV	D	2	(2)	
Lachezar SOTIROV	D		(1)	
Ivelin SPASOV	A	21	(3)	6
Ivan STOICHEV	A	15		3
Elin TOPUZAKOV	A	13	(1)	3
Konstantin TRENDAFILOV	D	13	(1)	
Hristo VOINOV	D	13		
Boris YANEV	A	10	(11)	2

LEAGUE RESULTS 1998/99

Date	Opponent	H/A	Score	Scorers
08/08/98	Dobrudzha Dobrich	A	0-0	
15/08/98	Spartak Varna	H	1-0	Ivankov Y.
22/08/98	Liteks Lovech	A	1-8	Spasov
29/08/98	Minior Pernik	H	3-1	Mikhtarski 2, Spasov
12/09/98	Neftochimik Bourgas	A	1-6	Spasov
19/09/98	CSKA Sofia	H	0-0	
26/09/98	Botev Plovdiv	A	1-2	Stoichev
03/10/98	Lokomotiv Sofia	H	0-2	
17/10/98	Shumen	A	1-4	Stoichev
23/10/98	Levski Sofia	A	0-5	
07/11/98	Levski Kiustendil	H	0-1	
14/11/98	Metalurg Pernik	A	0-2	
21/11/98	Septemvri Sofia	H	2-1	Stoichev (p), Gerganchev
28/11/98	Lokomotiv Plovdiv	A	0-0	
05/12/98	Slavia Sofia	H	2-1	Gerganchev, Bibishkov
27/02/99	Dobrudzha Dobrich	H	1-0	Mikhtarski
06/03/99	Spartak Varna	A	1-2	Yanev
14/03/99	Liteks Lovech	H	1-2	Iliev
20/03/99	Minior Pernik	A	1-2	Spasov
03/04/99	Neftochimik Bourgas	H	1-1	Mikhtarski (p)
07/04/99	CSKA Sofia	A	0-3	
10/04/99	Botev Plovdiv	H	3-0	Spasov, Yanev, Gerganchev
17/04/99	Lokomotiv Sofia	A	1-4	Spasov
24/04/99	Shumen	H	2-0	Mikhtarski (p), Gerganchev
01/05/99	Levski Sofia	H	0-1	
05/05/99	Levski Kiustendil	A	0-2	
08/05/99	Metalurg Pernik	H	2-1	Mikhtarski 2
14/05/99	Septemvri Sofia	A	3-2	Gerganchev 2, Topuzakov
22/05/99	Lokomotiv Plovdiv	H	6-1	Mikhtarski 3, Topuzakov 2, Bizhev
29/05/99	Slavia Sofia	A	1-4	Gerganchev (p)

SEPTEMVRI SOFIA

CLUB DIRECTORY

Septemvri Sofia
Stadion Septemvri
Kvartal Krasna Poliana
Sofia
tel - (02) 9200265
Year of Formation - 1944
President - Hristo Ambukeli
Coach - Pavel Panov
Stadium - Septemvri (20,000)

MAJOR HONOURS
Domestic Cup - (1) 1960.

APPEARANCES 98/99

	P	Ap	(s)	Gls
Alessandro ALESSANDRI (ITA)	M	2	(7)	2
Veselin ANGELOV	A	3	(4)	
Ilian ANTONOV	M	21	(3)	1
Chavdar ATANASOV	A	23		8
Veselin AVRAMOV	D	9	(1)	
Martin BECHEV	D	21	(1)	1
Biser GODINAICHKI	D	11		
Milen IGNATOV	M	11	(12)	
Ilia ILIEV	M	9	(14)	3
Liubomir IVANOV	M	11	(5)	
Nikolai KOLEV	D	19		
Borislav KOSTOV	D	3	(1)	
Petar MALINOV	A	6	(3)	1
Vlado MANOLKOV	G	9	(1)	
Miroslav MIKHAILOV	A			
Rosen MITKOV	D	5	(2)	
Miroslav NIKOLOV	A	14	(1)	3
Plamen NIKOLOV	G	9		
Yuri NIKOLOV	M	20	(1)	
Georgi PANTELEEV	M		(2)	
Nikolai POPOV	D	4	(7)	
Ivan RUSEV	M	27		2
SIMBA (SAF)	A	14	(1)	7
Valentin STANKOV	M	5	(2)	
Krasimir STOIANOV	M	14		
Anatoli TONOV	A	1		1
Ivan TOPALOV	A	1		
Slavcho TOSHEV	G	12	(1)	
Georgi VALCHEV	D	8	(3)	
Ilia VALCHEV	M	6	(10)	2
Ivan VALKOV	M		(1)	
Georgi YORDANOV	D	9		1
Ivo ZAHARIEV	M		(1)	
Antoni ZDRAVKOV	D	23		2

LEAGUE RESULTS 1998/99

14/08/98	Lokomotiv Plovdiv	H	1-1	Zdravkov A.
19/08/98	Levski Sofia	H	0-4	
22/08/98	Slavia Sofia	A	1-4	Atanasov
29/08/98	Dobrudzha Dobrich	H	2-1	Valchev I., Atanasov
12/09/98	Spartak Varna	A	0-2	
19/09/98	Liteks Lovech	H	2-5	Atanasov, Nikolov M.
26/09/98	Minior Pernik	A	2-2	Atanasov, Nikolov M.
02/10/98	Neftochimik Bourgas	H	0-1	
16/10/98	CSKA Sofia	A	1-3	Nikolov M.
24/10/98	Botev Plovdiv	H	2-0	Zdravkov A., Atanasov
06/11/98	Lokomotiv Sofia	A	0-0	
13/11/98	Shumen	H	1-1	Atanasov (p)
21/11/98	Pirin Blagoevgrad	A	1-2	Bechev
29/11/98	Levski Kiustendil	H	0-3	
05/12/98	Metalurg Pernik	A	2-4	Rusev, Tonov
27/02/99	Levski Sofia	A	0-2	
06/03/99	Lokomotiv Plovdiv	A	0-2	
14/03/99	Slavia Sofia	H	0-2	
20/03/99	Dobrudzha Dobrich	A	1-5	Simba
03/04/99	Spartak Varna	H	1-1	Atanasov
07/04/99	Liteks Lovech	A	1-4	Alessandri
10/04/99	Minior Pernik	H	2-3	Atanasov, Alessandri (p)
17/04/99	Neftochimik Bourgas	A	3-1	Yordanov, Simba 2
24/04/99	CSKA Sofia	H	2-5	Iliev, Simba
01/05/99	Botev Plovdiv	A	1-3	Iliev
05/05/99	Lokomotiv Sofia	H	0-1	
08/05/99	Shumen	A	2-3	Simba, Iliev
14/05/99	Pirin Blagoevgrad	H	2-3	Antonov, Simba
22/05/99	Levski Kiustendil	A	1-4	Valchev I.
29/05/99	Metalurg Pernik	H	3-1	Rusev, Simba, Malinov

SHUMEN

CLUB DIRECTORY

FC Shumen
Ul Preslav 6
Shumen
tel - (054) 69894
Year of Formation - 1919
President - Hristo Hristov
Coach - Todor Todorov
Stadium - Panaiot Volov (30,000)

APPEARANCES 98/99

	P	Ap	(s)	Gls
Georgi ANDONOV	D	26		
Rumen CHAKAROV	D	1	(7)	
Dimo DIMITROV	G	2		
Asen GAIDARDZHIEV	M	2	(5)	
Yordan GALABOV	D	1		
Georgi GEORGIEV	A	17	(10)	6
Marian GERASIMOV	M	12	(7)	
Stanislav ILIEV	M	8	(1)	
Kostadin KOLEV	A	18	(2)	2
Filip KRUMOV	D	8	(7)	
Ivan MILCHEV	G	8		
Miroslav MIROSLAVOV	A	16	(3)	5
Stoian NEDIALKOV	A		(2)	
Kiril PENEV	M	16	(2)	
Todor PRAMATAROV	A	29		17
Shaner RAMZI	M	22	(2)	3
Rumen RANGELOV	G	20		
Emil RAVNACHKI	D	6	(3)	
Dimitar SIRAKOV	M	3		
Stefan SLAVOV	D	1	(3)	
Zakhari VASILEV	M	12	(3)	2
Valeri VENKOV	A	25		
Milen YORDANOV	D	22	(3)	
Yuksel YUMEROV	D	26		
Dimitar ZAKHARIEV	M	2	(14)	
Nikolai ZHELIAZKOV	M	27		1

LEAGUE RESULTS 1998/99

08/08/98	Spartak Varna	A	0-3	
15/08/98	Liteks Lovech	H	0-0	
22/08/98	Minior Pernik	A	0-2	
29/08/98	Neftochimik Bourgas	H	1-0	Pramatarov (p)
11/09/98	CSKA Sofia	A	2-3	Kolev, Pramatarov
19/09/98	Botev Plovdiv	H	1-1	Kolev
26/09/98	Lokomotiv Sofia	A	1-2	Miroslavov
03/10/98	Levski Sofia	A	2-2	Vasilev, Pramatarov
17/10/98	Pirin Blagoevgrad	H	4-1	Ramzi, Georgiev, Pramatarov 2
24/10/98	Levski Kiustendil	A	0-3	
07/11/98	Metalurg Pernik	H	1-0	Georgiev
13/11/98	Septemvri Sofia	A	1-1	Miroslavov
21/11/98	Lokomotiv Plovdiv	H	1-0	Zheliazkov
28/11/98	Slavia Sofia	A	0-2	
05/12/98	Dobrudzha Dobrich	H	0-0	
27/02/99	Spartak Varna	H	1-1	Pramatarov
06/03/99	Liteks Lovech	A	0-2	
14/03/99	Minior Pernik	H	1-1	Pramatarov (p)
20/03/99	Neftochimik Bourgas	A	1-6	Pramatarov (p)
03/04/99	CSKA Sofia	H	2-5	Pramatarov 2
07/04/99	Botev Plovdiv	A	2-5	Pramatarov, Miroslavov
10/04/99	Lokomotiv Sofia	H	2-0	Georgiev, Ramzi
17/04/99	Levski Sofia	H	0-1	
24/04/99	Pirin Blagoevgrad	A	0-2	
01/05/99	Levski Kiustendil	H	3-3	Pramatarov (p), Miroslavov 2 (1p)
05/05/99	Metalurg Pernik	A	1-2	Georgiev (p)
08/05/99	Septemvri Sofia	H	3-2	Pramatarov 2 (1p), Georgiev
15/05/99	Lokomotiv Plovdiv	A	3-1	Pramatarov, Ramzi, Georgiev
22/05/99	Slavia Sofia	H	2-1	Pramatarov, Vasilev
29/05/99	Dobrudzha Dobrich	A	1-4	Pramatarov

SLAVIA SOFIA

CLUB DIRECTORY

FC Slavia
Bul. Koloman 1, 1618 Sofia
tel - (02) 551137/550075/569197
fax - (02) 555231/552137
Year of Formation - 1913
President - Ventseslav Stefanov
Coach - Stoian Kotsev
Stadium - Slavia (32,000)

MAJOR HONOURS
League Championship - (7)
1928, 1930, 1936, 1939, 1941, 1943, 1996.
Domestic Cup - (1) 1996.

APPEARANCES 98/99

		P	Ap	(s)	Gls
Petar ADZHOV		M	9	(3)	2
Vladimir ANDONOV		M	9	(2)	5
Stoian ATSAROV		D	14	(1)	3
Georgi BACHEV		A	15		4
Simeon CHILIBONOV		M	11		4
Marian GERMANOV		D	11		
Georgi IVANOV		A	23	(2)	1
Vladimir KOLEV		A	6	(12)	2
Stefan KOSTADINOV		A	2	(6)	1
Martin KUSHEV		A	20	(3)	7
Blagoi LATINOV		D	4		
Neno NENOV		D	16	(2)	
Zvetan NIKOLOV		A	8	(4)	2
Rumen PANAIOTOV		M	12	(6)	3
Georgi PETKOV		G	19		
Rusi PETKOV		G	11	(1)	
Traian RADULOV		M	3	(3)	
Ivan REDOVSKI		M		(2)	
Vlado SHALAMANOV		M	23	(1)	6
Martin STANKOV		D	11	(1)	
Ivan TONCHEV		A	4	(7)	
Martin TOPUZOV		D	18	(4)	1
Ivo TRENCHEV		D	25	(1)	2
Petar TSVETANOV		D	15	(2)	
Marius URUKOV		D	18	(1)	1
Aleksandar VALENTINOV		A	9	(5)	1
Bozhidar YANKOV		A	3	(7)	2
Mikhail ZAHARIEV		D	11	(5)	

LEAGUE RESULTS 1998/99

08/08/98	Levski Kiustendil	H	1-0	Chilibonov
15/08/98	Metalurg Pernik	A	1-1	Kolev
22/08/98	Septemvri Sofia	H	4-1	Valentinov, Chilibonov (p),
				Kushev, Bachev
29/08/98	Lokomotiv Plovdiv	A	0-0	
12/09/98	Levski Sofia	H	0-0	
18/09/98	Dobrudzha Dobrich	H	6-2	Shalamanov 3, Urukov, Bachev,
				Chilibonov
26/09/98	Spartak Varna	A	2-0	Trenchev, Chilibonov
03/09/98	Liteks Lovech	H	1-1	Yankov
17/10/98	Minior Pernik	A	1-1	Bachev
24/10/98	Neftochimik Bourgas	H	1-2	Shalamanov (p)
07/11/98	CSKA Sofia	A	1-1	Bachev
14/11/98	Botev Plovdiv	H	2-0	Yankov, Atsarov
21/11/98	Lokomotiv Sofia	A	2-0	Topuzov, Shalamanov
28/11/98	Shumen	H	2-0	Nikolov, Kushev
05/12/98	Pirin Blagoevgrad	A	1-2	Ivanov
27/02/99	Levski Kiustendil	A	0-3	
05/03/99	Metalurg Pernik	H	1-0	Kolev
14/03/99	Septemvri Sofia	A	2-0	Atsarov, Panaiotov
20/03/99	Lokomotiv Plovdiv	H	6-1	Kushev 4, Panaiotov, Atsarov
03/04/99	Levski Sofia	A	0-1	
07/04/99	Dobrudzha Dobrich	A	1-3	Adzhov
10/04/99	Spartak Varna	H	2-2	Andonov 2
18/04/99	Liteks Lovech	A	1-3	Andonov
24/04/99	Minior Pernik	H	2-2	Adzhov, Kushev
01/05/99	Neftochimik Bourgas	A	0-2	
04/05/99	CSKA Sofia	H	0-1	
08/05/99	Botev Plovdiv	A	0-1	
15/05/99	Lokomotiv Sofia	H	2-3	Shalamanov, Nikolov
22/05/99	Shumen	A	1-2	Andonov
29/05/99	Pirin Blagoevgrad	H	4-1	Panaiotov, Andonov, Kostadinov,
				Trenchev

SPARTAK VARNA

CLUB DIRECTORY

FC Spartak
Ul Seliolu 39
9000 Varna
tel - (052) 245020/225780/253090
fax - (052) 237541
Year of Formation - 1919
President - Nikolai Ishkov
Coach - Radi Zdravkov
Stadium - Spartak (12,000)

MAJOR HONOURS
League Championship - (1) 1932.

APPEARANCES 98/99

	P	Ap	(s)	Gls
Georgi ALEKSANDROV	D	1	(4)	
Georgi ARNAUDOV	G	12		
Kalin DENEV	D	1	(1)	
Traian DIANKOV	M	17	(9)	1
Dian DONCHEV	M	18	(4)	
Nikolai FILIPOV	A	17	(7)	5
Borislav GEORGIEV	D	11	(3)	
Emil GEORGIEV	D	2	(5)	
Kaloian GENCHEV	M		(2)	
Ivan ILIEV	A		(1)	
Ivelin KAZANDZHIEV	M		(2)	
Nasko KOSTADINOV	M	11	(5)	1
Ivo MIKHAILOV	M	1	(5)	1
Zlatin MIKHAILOV	D	23		3
Dimitar MITOV	D	11	(3)	
Ivailo NEGENTSOV	G	1	(1)	
Svetlin NONCHEV	M		(4)	
Ivan PASKOV	A	24		6
Anastas PETROV	A	27	(2)	3
Marin PETROV	A	14	(7)	2
Dimitar POPOV	G	17		
Zdravko RADEV	D	9		1
Nikolai STANCHEV	A	14		
Plamen TIMNEV	A	13		5
Radomir TODOROV	M		(2)	
Anton VALCHANOV	D	20	(6)	
Boiko VELICHKOV	A	26	(2)	10
Aleksandar VESELINOVIC (YUG)	D	18		
Krasimir VLAHOV	D	4	(4)	
Velislav VUTSOV	A		(1)	
Evgeni YORDANOV	M		(6)	
Martin ZAFIROV	A	18		1

LEAGUE RESULTS 1998/99

08/08/98	Shumen	H	3-0	Velichkov (p), Paskov, Timnev
15/08/98	Pirin Blagoevgrad	A	0-1	
22/08/98	Levski Kiustendil	H	2-3	Velichkov, Mikhailov I.
29/08/98	Metalurg Pernik	A	0-2	
12/09/98	Septemvri Sofia	H	2-0	Velichkov (p), Mikhailov Z.
19/09/98	Lokomotiv Plovdiv	A	3-1	Filipov 2, Timnev
26/09/98	Slavia Sofia	H	0-2	
03/10/98	Dobrudzha Dobrich	A	1-3	Kostadinov
17/10/98	Levski Sofia	H	2-1	Petrov A. 2
24/10/98	Liteks Lovech	H	0-2	
07/11/98	Minior Pernik	A	0-5	
14/11/98	Neftochimik Bourgas	H	2-1	Timnev 2
21/11/98	CSKA Sofia	A	1-2	Zafirov
28/11/98	Botev Plovdiv	H	2-1	Timnev, Mikhailov Z.
05/12/98	Lokomotiv Sofia	A	1-3	Mikhailov Z.
27/02/99	Shumen	A	1-1	Filipov
06/03/99	Pirin Blagoevgrad	H	2-1	Velichkov 2 (2p)
13/03/99	Levski Kiustendil	A	0-2	
20/03/99	Metalurg Pernik	H	3-0	Velichkov 2 (1p), Paskov
03/04/99	Septemvri Sofia	A	1-1	Paskov
07/04/99	Lokomotiv Plovdiv	H	2-0	Filipov, Diankov
10/04/99	Slavia Sofia	A	2-2	Petrov A., Radev
17/04/99	Dobrudzha Dobrich	H	1-2	Velichkov
25/04/99	Lovski Sofia	A	0-1	
01/05/99	Liteks Lovech	A	2-3	Filipov, Petrov M.
05/05/99	Minior Pernik	H	2-0	Paskov 2
08/05/99	Neftochimik Bourgas	A	1-4	Velichkov
15/05/99	CSKA Sofia	H	0-2	
22/05/99	Botev Plovdiv	A	2-3	Velichkov, Petrov M.
29/05/99	Lokomotiv Sofia	H	1-1	Paskov

PROMOTED CLUBS

SECOND DIVISION FINAL TABLE 98/99

		Pd	W	D	L	F	A	Pt	GD
1	**Chernomorets Bourgas**	**30**	**21**	**3**	**6**	**62**	**20**	**66**	**+42**
2	**Belasitsa Petrich**	**30**	**20**	**2**	**8**	**60**	**27**	**62**	**+33**
3	**Olimpik Teteven**	**30**	**20**	**2**	**8**	**46**	**21**	**62**	**+25**
4	Maritsa Plovdiv	30	19	4	7	64	25	61	+39
5	Kremikovtsi	30	17	1	12	48	41	52	+7
6	Antibiotik Razgrad	30	14	4	12	46	35	46	+11
7	Cherno More Varna	30	14	2	14	36	48	44	-12
8	Svetkavitsa Targoviste	30	12	4	14	40	45	40	-5
9	Khaskovo	30	13	1	16	45	49	40	-4
10	Spartak Pleven	30	12	4	14	41	42	40	-1
11	Botev Vratsa	30	12	4	14	50	42	40	+8
12	Etar Veliko Tarnovo	30	11	4	15	30	47	37	-17
13	Dimitrovgrad	30	11	1	18	36	56	34	-20
14	Chardafon Gabrovo	30	10	4	16	35	56	34	-21
15	Akademik Sofia	30	6	6	18	22	49	24	-27
16	Olimpik Sliven	30	4	2	24	36	94	14	-58

CLUB DIRECTORY

Chernomorets Bourgas
Year of Formation - 1919
President - Dimitar Terziev
Coach - Stoian Popov
Stadium - Chernomorets (22,000)

CLUB DIRECTORY

Belasitsa Petrich
Year of Formation - 1923
President - Kostadin Hadzhiivanov
Coach - Grigor Petkov
Stadium - Tsar Samuil (12,000)

CLUB DIRECTORY

Olimpik Teteven
Year of Formation - 1992
President - Strakhil Dimchev
Coach - Dimitar Aleksiev; Ivan Zafirov;
Stefan Parvanov
Stadium - Benkovski (10,000)

CROATIA

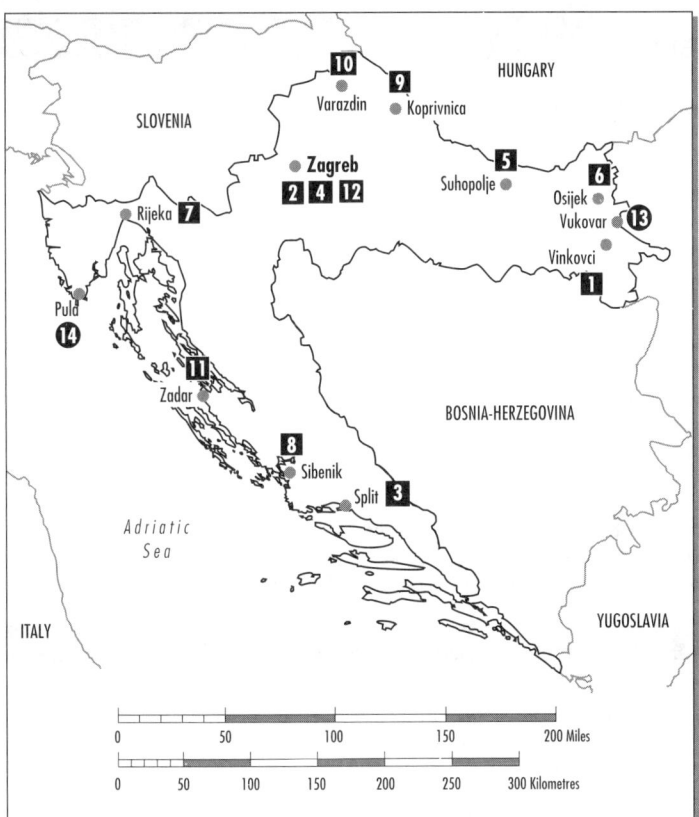

1	CIBALIA VINKOVCI	215
2	CROATIA ZAGREB	216
3	HAJDUK SPLIT	217
4	HRVATSKI DRAGOVOLJAC ZAGREB	218
5	MLADOST 127 SUHOPOLJE	219
6	OSIJEK	220
7	RIJEKA	221
8	SIBENIK	222

9	SLAVEN BELUPO KOPRIVNICA	223
10	VARTEKS VARAZDIN	224
11	ZADARKOMERC ZADAR	225
12	ZAGREB	226
Promoted clubs		
13	VUKOVAR '91	227
14	ISTRA PULA	227

REFEREEING CONTROVERSY FOILS RIJEKA

Hollow title triumph for Croatia Zagreb

FEDERATION DIRECTORY

Croatian Football Federation
Ilica 31/II, 10 000 Zagreb
tel - (01) 4554100
fax - (01) 424639

Year of Formation - 1991
President - Vlatko Markovic
Secretary - Zorislav Srebric

Stadium - Maksimir, Zagreb (45,000)

It has been whispered among Croatian fans for some time that the predominance of Croatia Zagreb, the country's most high-profile club, is not purely down to their actions on the field of play. There has long been a feeling that 'outside forces' have conspired to ensure regular success for the team from the capital. And in 1998/99 those suspicions of unfair play were aroused to new levels.

Croatia Zagreb won their fourth successive title in the most controversial circumstances imaginable. They went into their final fixture one point adrift of Rijeka, whose last

game was at home to Osijek. There had already been a number of odd refereeing decisions that had gone in Croatia's favour during the run-in to the title, but with just one minute of the season left came the most damning piece of evidence yet for the conspiracy theorists.

While there was no dispute about Croatia's 2-0 victory over Varteks Varazdin, a massive scandal erupted in Rijeka, where 25,000 fans could not believe their eyes as the referee ruled out an 89th-minute winning goal from Rijeka striker Admir Hasancic. At first the match official

LEAGUE CHAMPIONSHIP RESULTS 98/99

FIRST PHASE

		1	2	3	4	5	6	7	8	9	10	11	12
1	Cibalia Vinkovci		0-1	2-2	1-1	2-0	1-0	1-2	1-0	1-0	3-0	1-2	1-1
2	Croatia Zagreb	2-1		1-0	2-1	3-0	4-2	3-0	4-1	2-1	2-0	4-0	4-0
3	Hajduk Split	2-0	1-1		2-0	3-0	2-1	3-1	2-1	5-0	3-0	2-0	1-0
4	Hrvatski dragovoljac Zagreb	3-1	1-0	0-0		0-0	0-0	1-0	1-2	0-0	0-0	2-1	3-2
5	Mladost 127 Suhopolje	0-0	0-4	1-1	3-0		1-4	1-2	4-0	0-0	4-1	2-1	0-1
6	Osijek	3-1	0-1	0-1	2-1	1-3		1-0	4-0	3-0	1-0	2-0	3-0
7	Rijeka	2-0	1-0	2-1	3-0	1-0	1-0		3-1	1-1	3-2	4-1	1-0
8	Sibenik	2-1	1-2	1-0	0-2	4-1	2-1	0-1		3-1	0-0	4-2	2-2
9	Slaven Belupo Koprivnica	1-0	0-1	1-1	1-0	4-1	1-4	1-3	3-1		2-3	1-1	2-1
10	Varteks Varazdin	3-0	2-0	1-4	1-0	6-0	2-3	0-1	7-0	3-2		2-1	3-1
11	Zadarkomerc Zadar	0-2	1-1	1-1	2-1	2-0	1-1	0-1	0-0	2-1	5-3		1-1
12	Zagreb	2-2	1-2	3-1	0-0	2-1	1-1	1-2	3-2	1-1	1-1	4-3	

FINAL ROUND
CHAMPIONSHIP GROUP

		1	2	3	4	5	6
1	Croatia Zagreb		1-1	1-0	1-1	0-1	2-0
2	Hajduk Split	1-0		6-1	4-1	1-3	4-1
3	Hrvatski dragovoljac Zagreb	1-1	3-1		3-2	1-2	3-0
4	Osijek	0-1	1-1	2-1		5-2	0-2
5	Rijeka	0-2	3-3	3-0	1-1		2-1
6	Varteks Varazdin	1-2	1-2	3-2	0-1	1-1	

RELEGATION GROUP

		1	2	3	4	5	6
1	Cibalia Vinkovci		1-1	2-1	0-1	1-1	3-2
2	Mladost 127 Suhopolje	1-2		3-3	0-0	1-0	2-1
3	Sibenik	1-0	5-0		1-1	5-1	2-1
4	Slaven Belupo Koprivnica	0-1	4-0	3-0		1-0	2-2
5	Zadarkomerc Zadar	4-1	2-0	3-1	1-0		1-2
6	Zagreb	3-1	4-0	0-2	2-3	2-0	

LEAGUE CHAMPIONSHIP FINAL TABLES 98/99

FIRST PHASE

		Pd	Home W	D	L	F	A	Away W	D	L	F	A	Total W	D	L	F	A	Pt	GD
1	Croatia Zagreb	22	11	0	0	31	6	6	2	3	13	8	17	2	3	44	14	53	+30
2	Rijeka	22	10	1	0	22	6	7	0	4	13	12	17	1	4	35	18	52	+17
3	Hajduk Split	22	10	1	0	26	4	2	5	4	12	13	12	6	4	38	17	42	+21
4	Osijek	22	8	0	3	20	7	3	3	5	17	16	11	3	8	37	23	36	+14
5	Varteks Varazdin	22	8	0	3	30	12	1	3	7	10	24	9	3	10	40	36	30	+4
6	Hrvatski dragovoljac Zagreb	22	5	5	1	11	6	1	2	8	6	17	6	7	9	17	23	25	-6
7	Sibenik	22	6	2	3	19	13	1	1	9	8	32	7	3	12	27	45	24	-18
8	Cibalia Vinkovci	22	5	3	3	14	9	1	2	8	8	20	6	5	11	22	29	23	-7
9	Zagreb	22	4	5	2	19	16	1	3	7	9	21	5	8	9	28	37	23	-9
10	Zadarkomerc Zadar	22	4	5	2	15	12	1	1	9	12	28	5	6	11	27	40	21	-13
11	Slaven Belupo Koprivnica	22	5	2	4	17	16	0	4	7	7	21	5	6	11	24	37	21	-13
12	Mladost 127 Suhopolje	22	4	3	4	16	14	1	1	9	6	28	5	4	13	22	42	19	-20

FINAL ROUND

CHAMPIONSHIP GROUP

		Pd	Home W	D	L	F	A	Away W	D	L	F	A	Total W	D	L	F	A	Pt	GD	
1	Croatia Zagreb	10	2	2	1	5	3	3	1	1	6	3	5	3	2	11	6	45	+5	(27)
2	Rijeka	10	2	2	1	9	7	3	1	1	9	8	5	3	2	18	15	44	+3	(26)
3	Hajduk Split	10	4	0	1	16	6	1	3	1	8	9	5	3	2	24	15	39	+9	(21)
4	Osijek	10	2	1	2	8	7	1	2	2	6	9	3	3	4	14	16	30	-2	(18)
5	Hrvatski dragovoljac Zagreb	10	3	1	1	11	6	0	0	5	4	15	3	1	6	15	21	23	-6	(13)
6	Varteks Varazdin	10	1	1	3	6	8	1	0	4	4	11	2	1	7	10	19	22	-9	(15)

RELEGATION GROUP

		Pd	Home W	D	l	F	A	Away W	D	L	F	A	Total W	D	L	F	A	Pt	GD	
7	Slaven Belupo Koprivnica	10	3	1	1	10	3	2	2	1	5	4	5	3	2	15	7	29	+8	(11)
8	Sibenik	10	4	1	0	14	3	1	1	3	7	11	5	2	3	21	14	29	+7	(12)
9	Cibalia Vinkovci	10	2	2	1	7	6	2	0	3	5	9	4	2	4	12	15	26	-3	(12)
10	Zagreb	10	3	0	2	11	6	1	1	3	8	10	4	1	5	19	16	25	+3	(12)
11	Zadarkomerc Zadar	10	4	0	1	11	4	0	1	4	2	10	4	1	5	13	14	24	-1	(11)
12	Mladost 127 Suhopolje	10	2	2	1	7	6	0	1	4	1	16	2	3	5	8	22	19	-14	(10)

N.B. Where two or more teams are level on points, classification is determined by the results of the matches between them. After 22 matches the top six teams play off for the title. The other six teams play off to avoid relegation. Figures in brackets indicate points carried forward from First Phase.

consulted his linesman but between them they came to the conclusion that the goal would not stand. Their reasoning was that an offside offence had been committed, yet pictures relayed by a private Slovenian television station proved beyond doubt that there was no offside. Without that goal Rijeka could only draw 1-1 and thus missed out on the first championship triumph in their history.

Although Croatia Zagreb took the title, their celebrations were distinctly muted. Even the club's diehard fans, the so-called 'Bad Blue Boys', smelled a rat and sent messages of solidarity and condolence to their counterparts in Rijeka. In Rijeka itself the local fans paid tribute to their own team by proclaiming them as the 'moral champions' and celebrated accordingly.

TOP SCORERS

20	Josko POPOVIC (Sibenik)
14	Barnabás SZTIPÁNOVICS (Rijeka)
	Igor MUSA (Rijeka)
	Zvonimir DERANJA (Hajduk Split)
13	Nino BULE (Zagreb)
	Miljenko MUMLEK (Varteks Varazdin)
10	Jaksa KRSTULOVIC (Zadarkomerc Zadar)
	Veldin KARIC (Varteks Varazdin)
	Stanko BUBALO (Osijek)
	Mirza GOLUBICA (Mladost 127 Suhopolje)
	Edin MUJCIN (Croatia Zagreb)

NATIONAL TEAM RESULTS 98/99

Date	Opponent		Venue	Score	Scorers
05/09/98	Republic of Ireland (ECQ)	A	Dublin	0-2	
10/10/98	Malta (ECQ)	A	Ta' Qali	4-1	Simic D. (54), Vugrinec (67, 74), Suker (80)
14/10/98	Macedonia (ECQ)	H	Zagreb	3-2	Suker (16), Boban (45, 70)
10/02/99	Denmark	H	Split	0-1	
10/03/99	Greece	A	Athens	2-3	Vlaovic (67), Suker (80p)
28/04/99	Italy	H	Zagreb	0-0	
05/05/99	Spain	A	Seville	1-3	Suker (10)
05/06/99	Macedonia (ECQ)	A	Skopje	1-1	Suker (19)
13/06/99	Egypt	N	Seoul	2-2	Cvitanovic I. (45p), Vugrinec (78)
16/06/99	Mexico	N	Seoul	2-1	Biscan (45), Simic J. (64)
20/06/99	South Korea	A	Seoul	1-1	Tomas (88)

An escape from reality? Perhaps, but throughout the country there was almost unanimous support for Rijeka's cause. In fact, the issue became a major national talking-point, with politicians and the secret service being accused of corrupting the championship in order to serve their own interests. An official statement by the Croatian FA denied any wrongdoing by the referees, explaining away the favourable treatment of the perennial champions as merely a series of coincidences. Croatian national boss Miroslav Blazevic, a former coach of Croatia Zagreb, went even further, condemning the whole episode as "a concoction of lies" and making astonishing proposals as to what should be done with the perpetrators. If anything, however, his hang-'em-high approach merely confirmed the views of those who believed that there was something terribly wrong with the morality and integrity of the people responsible for the running of Croatian football.

Rijeka did gain the consolation prize of a place in the

DOMESTIC CUP 98/99

1/16 FINALS
Mosor Zrnovnica 0, Osijek 1
Bojovnik Novi Golubovec 2, Hajduk Split 3
TSK Topolovac 0, Varteks Varazdin 1
Halubjan Viskovo 1, Rijeka 2
Marsonia Slavonski Brod 0, Slaven Belupo Koprivnica 4
Cakovec 2, Dubrovnik 0
Moslavina Kutina 2, Segesta Sisak 3
Rastane 2, Inker Zapresic 0
Samobor 1, Hrvatski dragovoljac Zagreb 2
Istra Pula 1, Sibenik 1 (1-4 on pens.)
Slavonija Pozega 0, Belisce 3
Podravac Virje 1, Zadarkomerc Zadar 5
Pazinka Pazin 0, Cibalia Vinkovci 6
Dugo Selo 3, Croatia Zagreb 2
Amater Slavonski Brod 2, Zagreb 2 (4-2 on pens.)
Mladost 127 Suhopolje 4, Bjelovar 2

1/8 FINALS
Cibalia Vinkovci 1, Rijeka 0
Sibenik 0, Varteks Varazdin 1
Cakovec 0, Zadarkomerc Zadar 0 (5-4 on pens.)
Segesta Sisak 4, Rastane 0
Belisce 4, Amater Slavonski Brod 1

Osijek 3, Hrvatski dragovoljac Zagreb 1
Slaven Belupo Koprivnica 8, Dugo Selo 0
Hajduk Split 5, Mladost 127 Suhopolje 1

QUARTER-FINALS
Slaven Belupo Koprivnica 4
(Sliskovic 18, 28, Kulenovic 44, Vata 72),
Segesta Sisak 1 (Kvesic 50p)
Segesta Sisak 0,
Slaven Belupo Koprivnica 1 (Kremenovic 88)
(Slaven Belupo Koprivnica 5-1)

Belisce 0, Cibalia Vinkovci 4
(Mestrovic 37p, Bosnjak 46, Jurcec 58, Andricevic 78)
Cibalia Vinkovci 3 (Bosnjak 6, Bojko 75, Jurcec 90p),
Belisce 0
(Cibalia Vinkovci 7-0)

Cakovec 0, Hajduk Split 0
Hajduk Split 2 (Racunica 30p, Leko 76), Cakovec 0
(Hajduk Split 2-0)

Varteks Varazdin 2 (Karic 50, Sabolcki 56),
Osijek 1 (Prisc 20)
Osijek 3 (Mitu 50, Bubalo 80, 87),
Varteks Varazdin 0
(Osijek 4-2)

SEMI-FINALS
Cibalia Vinkovci 2 (Jurcec 53, Crncevic 58),
Hajduk Split 1 (Baturina 38)
Hajduk Split 2 (Ratkovic 73, Deranja 80),
Cibalia Vinkovci 1 (Jurcec 63)
(3-3; Cibalia Vinkovci 6-5 on pens.)

Osijek 1 (Besirevic 90p), Slaven Belupo Koprivnica 0
Slaven Belupo Koprivnica 0, Osijek 0
(Osijek 1-0)

FINAL
30/05/99, Zagreb
OSIJEK 2 Mitu (90), Lasic (97)
CIBALIA VINKOVCI 1 Juric (36)
(asd)
referee - Sinovcic
OSIJEK - Galinovic; Beljan, Vuica (Vranjes J. 46),
Vranjes S., Lasic, Besirevic, Ergovic, Gaspar, Perkovic,
Prisc (Surac 72), Bubalo (Mitu 66).
CIBALIA VINKOVCI - Ibrahimovic; Juric (Bisaku 62),
Bognar, Ravlic, Bogdan, Andricevic, Mestrovic
(Gusic 68), Raic-Sudar, Bosnjak, Maroslavac, Jurcec
(Bojko 37).

NATIONAL TEAM APPEARANCES 98/99

Coach - Miroslav BLAZEVIC

Player	IRL	MLT	MAC	DEN	GRE	ITA	ESP	MAC	EGY	MEX	KOR	Cps	Gls
Drazen LADIC (01/01/63) - Croatia Zagreb	G	G	G		G	G	G	G				55	-
Zvonimir SOLDO (02/11/67) - VfB Stuttgart (GER)	D77	D	M	M	D	M		D				39	1
Igor STIMAC (06/09/67) - Derby County (ENG)	D		D	D								39	2
Dari SIMIC (12/11/75) - Croatia Zagreb/Inter (ITA)	D	D81	D	D46		D	D	D				30	1
Igor TUDOR (16/04/78) - Juventus (ITA)	D65	D	D			s69	D					13	-
Krunoslav JURCIC (26/11/67) - Croatia Zagreb	M	s80				s77		M				16	-
Zvonimir BOBAN (08/10/68) - Milan (ITA)	M	M	M	M	M		M	M				48	12
Aljosa ASANOVIC (14/12/65) - Panathinaikos (GRE)	M	M	M62	M46	M61	M77		M				53	3
Robert JARNI (26/10/68) - Real Madrid (ESP)	M	M87	M	M78	M	M	M	M				53	1
Silvio MARIC (20/03/75) - Croatia Zagreb/Newcastle United (ENG)	A46	M	A			s46	s79					16	1
Mario STANIC (10/04/72) - Parma (ITA)	A		M80	M46		M69						27	4
Igor PAMIC (19/11/69) - FC Hansa Rostock (GER)	s46											5	1
Petar KRPAN (01/07/74) - Sporting CP (POR)	s65											3	-
Mario TOKIC (23/07/75) - Croatia Zagreb	s77	s81		s46	M							4	-
Danijel SARIC (04/08/72) - Croatia Zagreb		M	s62	s46	M			M	M	M	M	11	-
Davor SUKER (01/01/68) - Real Madrid (ESP)	A	A	A	A		A	A					49	41
Jurica VUCKO (10/08/76) - Hajduk Split	A16											1	-
Davor VUGRINEC (24/03/75) - Trabzonspor (TUR)	s16							M64	A	A79	A46	6	3
Mario CVITANOVIC (06/05/75) - Croatia Zagreb		s87	s78						D65	D	D	5	-
Marijan MRMIC (06/05/65) - Varteks Varazdin					G46							13	-
Damir MILINOVIC (15/10/72) - Rijeka				D	D	D46						4	-
Goran VLAOVIC (07/08/72) - Valencia CF (ESP)				A46	s46	M	A72	s64				39	13
Stipe PLETIKOSA (08/01/79) - Hajduk Split					s46					G	G	3	-
Milan RAPAIC (16/08/73) - Perugia (ITA)					s46	A69	A79	s19				7	-
Alen PETERNAC (16/01/72) - Real Valladolid (ESP)					s46	A46						2	-
Goran JURIC (05/02/63) - Croatia Zagreb					D61	D	D	D				15	-
Jasmin AGIC (26/12/74) - Rijeka					s61				M72	s62		3	-
Igor CVITANOVIC (01/11/70) - Real Sociedad (ESP)					s61	s69	s72		A	A	A	27	4
Alen BOKSIC (21/01/70) - Lazio (ITA)						A46		A19				26	6
Robert KOVAC (06/04/74) - Bayer 04 Leverkusen (GER)					s46	D						2	-
Mario GALINOVIC (15/11/76) - Osijek								G				1	-
Jurica VRANJES (01/01/80) - Osijek									D	D	D	3	-
Stjepan TOMAS (06/03/75) - Croatia Zagreb									D	D	D	4	1
Ante SERIC (15/01/75) - Hajduk Split									D	D	D	6	-
Igor BISCAN (04/05/78) - Croatia Zagreb									M	M	M	3	1
Josip SIMIC (16/09/77) - Croatia Zagreb									A88	A88	A	3	1
Ivan LEKO (07/02/78) - Hajduk Split									s65	s79	s46	3	-
Nino BULE (19/03/76) - Zagreb									s72			1	-
Mate BATURINA (01/08/73) - Hajduk Split									s88			1	-
Josip BULAT (18/03/72) - Hajduk Split										D65		1	-
Renato PILIPOVIC (14/01/77) - Rijeka										s65		1	-
Stanko BUBALO (26/04/73) - Osijek										s88		1	-
Darko MILADIN (04/04/79) - Hajduk Split										D62		1	-

EUROPEAN CUPS 98/99

CHAMPIONS' CUP
● CROATIA ZAGREB
Qualifying round CELTIC (SCO)
A 0-1
Ladic; Juric, Simic D., Tokic, Rukavina, Prosinecki, Jurcic,
Jelicic (Mujcin 75), Cvitanovic, Viduka, Maric (Simic J. 83)
H 3-0 Maric (23), Prosinecki (44p, 69)
Ladic; Juric, Simic D., Tokic, Rukavina, Jurcic, Prosinecki,
Jelicic (Mujcin 60), Cvitanovic, Viduka (Sokota 73), Maric (Saric 84).

Champions' League
1st match AJAX (HOL)
H 0-0
Ladic; Juric, Simic D., Tokic, Rukavina (Saric 58), Prosinecki,
Jelicic (Sokota 79), Mujcin, Cvitanovic, Maric, Viduka (Mikic 69).

2nd match OLYMPIAKOS (GRE)
A 0-2
Ladic; Juric, Simic D., Tokic, Rukavina, Jurcic, Jelicic (Sokota 75),
Mujcin (Sabic 46), Cvitanovic, Viduka (Simic J. 82), Maric.

3rd round FC PORTO (POR)
A 0-3
Ladic; Juric, Simic D., Tokic, Rukavina, Jelicic (Mujcin 46), Jurcic,
Saric (Sabic 46), Krznar, Maric (Viduka 58), Sokota.

4th round FC PORTO (POR)
H 3-1 Mikic (7), Rukavina (37), Mujcin (67)
Ladic; Juric, Saric (Cvitanovic 76), Simic D., Krznar (Biscan 46), Rukavina,
Tokic, Jelicic, Mujcin, Mikic, Maric (Simic J. 56).

5th match AJAX (HOL)
A 1-0 Simic J. (58)
Ladic; Juric, Tokic, Simic D., Cvitanovic, Rukavina (Sabic 81), Biscan,
Jelicic, Saric (Simic J. 53). Maric, Krznar (Jurcic 46).

6th match OLYMPIAKOS (GRE)
H 1-1 Jelicic (35)
Ladic; Juric, Saric, Mujcin, Biscan (Simic J. 69), Simic D., Tokic, Rukavina,
Jelicic (Jurcic 87), Mikic (Abramovic 72), Maric.

CUP WINNERS' CUP
● VARTEKS VARAZDIN
1st round RUDAR VELENJE (SLO)
A 1-0 Matas (90)
Solomun; Besek, Balajic (Hrman 74), Madunovic, Gregoric, Dalic, Muzek,
Karic (Matas 83), Sabolcki, Kamberovic, Posavec (Mumlek 63).
H 1-0 Kamberovic (7)
Solomun; Besek, Madunovic, Gregoric, Hrman, Dalic (Kastel 75),
Muzek (Posavec 70), Mumlek, Karic (Ivankovic 88), Kamberovic, Balajic.

2nd round SC HEERENVEEN (HOL)
A 1-2 Mumlek (63)
Solomun; Besek, Madunovic, Balajic, Sabolcki, Posavec, Muzek, Dalic,
Mumlek, Karic (Matas 90), Ivankovic (Kastel 71).
H 4-2 Mumlek (67, 117), Kamberovic (82, 98)
(aet) Solomun; Besek (Beli 42), Madunovic, Gregoric,
Sabolcki (Kamberovic 59), Muzek, Posavec, Mumlek, Balajic, Karic,
Ivankovic (Hrman 46).

Quarter-final RCD MALLORCA (ESP)
H 0-0
Mrmic; Kastel, Madunovic, Balajic, Gregoric, Dalic, Muzek,
Mumlek (Ivankovic 88), Hrman, Kamberovic (Posavec 70),
Karic (Matas 78).
A 1-3 Balajic (90)
Mrmic; Kastel, Madunovic (Sabolcki 46), Balajic, Gregoric,
Dalic (Posavec 65), Hrman, Muzek, Mumlek, Karic (Kamberovic 73),
Ivankovic.

UEFA CUP
● HAJDUK SPLIT
Qualifying round MALMÖ FF (SWE)
H 1-1 Brajkovic (44)
Gabric; Brajkovic, Sablic (Anic 56), Mrzlecki, Lalic (Miladin 63), Skoko,
Vulic, Leko (Seric 75), Mujdza, Vucko, Baturina.
A 2-1 Vucko (40, 55)
Gabric; Brajkovic, Sablic, Mrzlecki, Miladin, Skoko, Seric (Mujdza 78),
Racunica (Weiss 81), Baturina (Leko 64), Vucko, Deranja.

1st round FIORENTINA (ITA)
A 1-2 Vucko (45)
Gabric; Brajkovic, Sablic, Biliskov, Miladin, Skoko, Leko,
Mujdza (Seric 75), Racunica (Vulic 83), Vucko, Baturina (Deranja 68).
H 0-0
Gabric; Brajkovic, Sablic, Biliskov, Miladin (Lalic 81), Skoko, Leko,
Racunica (Deranja 66), Mujdza, Vucko, Baturina.

● OSIJEK
Qualifying round RSC ANDERLECHT (BEL)
H 3-1 Krpan (29), Prisc (53), Vranjes J. (81)
Susnjara; Beljan, Vranjes S., Vidovic, Vuica, Ergovic, Balatinac (Grnja 74),
Vranjes J. (Bubalo 82), Besirevic, Prisc (Gaspar 74), Krpan.
A 0-2
Susnjara; Beljan, Vranjes S., Vidovic, Vuica, Ergovic, Vranjes J., Balatinac,
Besirevic, Prisc, Krpan.

Champions' League qualifying round, but the history books
will show that the 1998/99 Croatian championship was
won by Croatia Zagreb, who finished one point ahead of
their challengers both at the end of the 'regular season'
and the play-offs.

Although those tables give the impression that the championship was a two-horse race, another team, Hajduk

Split, were also very much in the running until they lost their
last two matches, the first of them 1-3 at home to Rijeka
- their only home defeat all season. Hajduk, inspired by
the return of the prolific Tomislav Erceg from Italy, had a
storming run in the play-offs, but that shock defeat ended
their interest.

The unbeaten home records of Croatia Zagreb and

Rijeka had also ended during the play-offs, with the two title challengers each claiming a victory in the other's back-yard. When Rijeka won 1-0 in the Maksimir in their second play-off fixture, they became the clear favourites, but a 0-2 home defeat by Croatia Zagreb the following month put the defending champions right back in the contest. Under normal circumstances the climax to the campaign would have been riveting, but that final minute of the season ruined everything - and not just for Rijeka.

It was a turbulent season all round for Croatia Zagreb. They went through three different coaches and also lost the services of three of their best players when Dario Simic, Silvio Maric and Mark Viduka were all sold to foreign clubs during the winter break. Their first coach, Zlatko Kranjcar, was dismissed as the combined result of the team's failure to reach the quarter-finals of the Champions' League (they were always up against it after failing to score in their first three group games) and a handful of unexpected setbacks in domestic competition, first and foremost the extraordinary 2-3 defeat by amateur side Dugo Selo in the early stages of the Croatian Cup. Croatia Zagreb had won the competition for each of the previous three seasons, but their long reign came to an end in the most incredible fashion as they surrendered a 2-0 lead to the Fourth Division 'nobodies', who, almost inevitably, crashed back to earth in the next round, losing 8-0 to Slaven Belupo Koprivnica.

Velimir Zajec and Ilija Loncarevic were the men in charge during the spring, with the latter eventually seeing the team home to their fifth Croatian title. Loncarevic's style was pragmatic and unspectacular. Unloved by the fans, he, too, was dismissed in the summer to make way for the well-known former Argentinian World Cup-winner Ossie Ardiles. With little money to spend on new players, Ardiles effectively inherited the same team, which featured veterans such as goalkeeper Drazen Ladic, sweeper Goran Juric and playmaker Robert Prosinecki as well as impressive newcomers Mario Tokic and Igor Biscan.

With Croatia Zagreb slipping out of the Champions' League in December, the only Croatian club remaining in European competition after Christmas was Varteks Varazdin, who caused a major shock by reaching the last eight of the Cup-winners' Cup. The provincial side, who struggled in the domestic championship, finishing bottom of the play-off group, achieved a truly memorable extra-time victory over Heerenveen of Holland in the second round, and their captain and 'number ten', Miljenko Mumlek, proved to be a worthy match-winner when he struck his third goal of the tie three minutes from the end. Varteks were no match for Mallorca in the quarter-finals, but their honour was already secure.

Had there been a Cup-winners' Cup in 1999/2000,

the qualifiers would have been Osijek, who, assisted by the early exit of Croatia Zagreb, won the Croatian Cup - their first major trophy - after an incredible comeback in the final in Zagreb. 0-1 down in stoppage-time against Cibalia Vinkovci, Osijek snatched a dramatic late equaliser and won the game with a 'golden goal' seven minutes into extra-time.

It was the first Croatian Cup final played in a single match, and the excitement which it produced certainly justified the change from the old two-legged model. A modification to the league system has also been put into place for the 1999/2000 season, with the two-tiered play-off experiment now having been abandoned. Although 12 teams remain - with promoted Vukovar and Istra Pula having replaced relegated Zadarkomerc and Mladost 127 - the teams will now play each other three times over the course of the season, resulting in a total of 33 matches being played by each club, one more than in 1998/99.

Another change effected during the season was the appointment of a new Croatian FA president, the sixth of the decade, with Vlatko Markovic coming in for Branko Miksa. One of Miksa's last jobs before stepping down was to hand national coach Miroslav Blazevic a new four-year contract, taking him through to the 2002 World Cup finals.

The bronze medallists from the last World Cup, in France, made a poor start to Euro 2000 qualification. Hampered by the absence through injury of star strikers Davor Suker and Alen Boksic, Croatia lost their opening match, 2-0 in Dublin. They were also a goal down in their next two games, away to Malta and at home to Macedonia, before coming back to win. An away draw with the Macedonians in their only other qualifying match of the season (due to the conflict in nearby Kosovo) left Blazevic's team in a rather precarious position, with group leadership looking an unlikely possibility in a section comprising both Yugoslavia and the Republic of Ireland.

The team also performed poorly in a series of friendlies, and although Blazevic was back to his boasting ways after Croatia won the Korea Cup in Seoul in June, the tournament was a minor one, and success was achieved with a largely home-based experimental team which managed just one victory (against Mexico) in their three games. It was hardly the ideal warm-up for the big games coming up in the summer and early autumn.

INTERNATIONAL HONOURS

World Cup Finals appearances: 1998 (3rd)

European Championship appearances: 1996

European Club Competitions
Fairs' Cup - (1)   Dinamo Zagreb (1967)

PLAYERS OF THE SEASON

★ SUPERSTAR PROFILE
ZVONIMIR BOBAN

The passionate, deep-thinking captain of the Croatian national team, Zvonimir Boban has never played in the Croatian domestic league but he always gets a hero's reception when he returns home to play for his country. No one is more committed to the cause, and it was his magnificent double-strike against Macedonia in Zagreb - one brilliant volley, one spectacular free-kick - which enabled the team finally to get their Euro 2000 qualifying campaign into gear. The 31-year-old midfielder also had an excellent season in Italy with Milan, probably the best of the seven he has spent with the *Rossoneri*. Although he contributed to Milan's Serie A title wins in 1993, 1994 and 1996, he was a fairly marginal figure then. In 1999, though, he was the principal architect of the team's

remarkable end-of-season resurgence which saw them catch and then overtake Lazio to win yet another *scudetto*. Milan coach Alberto Zaccheroni's decision to change his formation and employ Boban in the playmaker rôle behind two, rather than three, strikers, reaped maximum dividends. The Croatian scored only two goals himself - both of them in the same game, a 5-1 win in Udine - but his influence on the rest of the team from that position was massive, as reflected by the consistently high marks awarded to him in the Italian press during the championship run-in.

MILAN RAPAIC

Another Croatian star of the Italian league, Milan Rapaic showed glittering form throughout the 1998/99 Serie A campaign. He played in all 34 matches for Perugia and scored nine goals - one fewer than Japanese import Hidetoshi Nakata, with whom he formed a fruitful and entertaining partnership. A tough and technically accomplished left-footer, he can play anywhere in attack but is at his most effective striking from deep. A former three-time Croatian championship-winner with Hajduk Split, his three-year association was Perugia was expected to end in the summer when Juventus and Inter showed an interest in signing him, but the deals fell through and he stayed on. Now 26, he is back as a regular in the Croatian national squad, having originally made his international début as a 20-year-old in 1994.

IGOR BISCAN

There is considerable debate as to which is Igor Biscan's best position. The tall, physically powerful 21-year-old spent much of the 1998/99 season - his first as a regular first-teamer - playing in Croatia Zagreb's defence but later moved into midfield and it was in that position that he won his first international caps, at the end-of-season Korea Cup. He demonstrated his goalscoring ability in that tournament, finding the net against Mexico, and there was a body of opinion back home that felt he could also be used in attack. He only scored two goals in the domestic campaign, but both of those were against title rivals Rijeka, with the second of them, in his team's all-important 2-0 away win, proving to be arguably the most significant goal in the entire championship.

CIBALIA VINKOVCI

CLUB DIRECTORY

HNK Cibalia
Ruzina 13
32100 Vinkovci
tel - (032) 332356
fax - (032) 332364
Year of Formation - 1919
President - Bozo Galic
Director - Djuro Curic
Coach - Krasnodar Rora; Mijo Rucevic; Srecko Lusic
Stadium - Mladost (15,000)

APPEARANCES 98/99

	P	Ap	(s)	Gls
Antun ANDRICEVIC	D	18	(4)	1
Mladen BARTOLOVIC	A	14	(5)	1
Dinko BESLIC	M	1	(6)	
Leonard BISAKU	M	16	(7)	
Danijel BOGDAN	D	27		3
Dalibor BOGNAR	M	10	(12)	
Miroslav BOJKO	A	11	(4)	3
Ivan BOSNJAK	A	20	(7)	7
Ante CRNCEVIC	M	15	(4)	1
Mario CUTURA	D	15	(7)	3
Oliver GUDELJ	D	5	(2)	
Radosav GUSIC	D	5	(3)	
Miralem IBRAHIMOVIC	G	32		
Renato JURCEC	A	23		5
Jure JURCIC	M	5		
Zvonimir KISELJAK	A	6	(8)	
Mario LUCIC	D	2	(1)	
Ivica MARINCIC	M	2		
Ivan MAROSLAVAC	M	28	(1)	2
Goran MESTROVIC	M	28		5
Darko RAIC-SUDAR	M	8	(5)	2
Ivan RAVLIC	D	19	(5)	
Nino SABLIC	D	19	(4)	
Ervin SMAJLAGIC (BOS)	D		(2)	
Igor TKALCEVIC	D	23		

LEAGUE RESULTS 1998/99

09/08/98	Rijeka	H	1-2	Mestrovic
16/08/98	Zagreb	A	2-2	Mestrovic 2 (1p)
21/08/98	Hajduk Split	H	2-2	Mestrovic (p), Cutura
30/08/98	Sibenik	A	1-2	Andricevic
13/09/98	Zadarkomerc Zadar	H	1-2	Mestrovic (p)
20/09/98	Croatia Zagreb	A	1-2	Jurcec
29/09/98	Hrvatski dragovoljac Zagreb	H	1-1	Bosnjak
04/10/98	Mladost 127 Suhopolje	A	0-0	
18/10/98	Osijek	H	1-0	Jurcec
25/10/98	Slaven Belupo Koprivnica	H	1-0	Cutura
31/10/98	Varteks Varazdin	A	0-3	
07/11/98	Rijeka	A	0-2	
15/11/98	Zagreb	H	1-1	Bogdan
22/11/98	Hajduk Split	A	0-2	
29/11/98	Sibenik	H	1-0	Bogdan
06/12/98	Zadarkomerc Zadar	A	2-0	Crncevic, Bojko
14/12/98	Croatia Zagreb	H	0-1	
21/02/99	Hrvatski dragovoljac Zagreb	A	1-3	Bosnjak
28/02/99	Mladost 127 Suhopolje	H	2-0	Jurcec, Bojko
07/03/99	Osijek	A	1-3	Cutura
14/03/99	Slaven Belupo Koprivnica	A	0-1	
21/03/99	Varteks Varazdin	H	3-0	Bartulovic, Bosnjak, og (Balajic)
18/04/99	Slaven Belupo Koprivnica	H	0-1	
21/04/99	Sibenik	A	0-1	
25/04/99	Mladost 127 Suhopolje	H	1-1	Bogdan
02/05/99	Zagreb	H	3-2	Jurcec 2 (1p), Bosnjak
09/05/99	Zadarkomerc Zadar	A	1-4	Bosnjak
12/05/99	Slaven Belupo Koprivnica	A	1-0	Maroslavac
16/05/99	Sibenik	H	2-1	Raic-Sudar, Bosnjak
19/05/99	Mladost 127 Suhopolje	A	2-1	Bosnjak, Maroslavac
23/05/99	Zagreb	A	1-3	Bojko
26/05/99	Zadarkomerc Zadar	H	1-1	Raic-Sudar

CROATIA ZAGREB

CLUB DIRECTORY

NK Croatia
Maksimirska 128, 10 000 Zagreb
tel - (01) 2334111
fax - (01) 212316
Year of Formation - 1945
President - Zlatko Canjuga
Director - Mirko Novosel
Coach - Zlatko Kranjcar; Velimir Zajec; Ilija
Loncarevic (99/00 - Osvaldo Ardiles)
Stadium - Maksimir (45,000)

MAJOR HONOURS
League Championship - (5)
1993, 1996, 1997, 1998, 1999.
Domestic Cup - (4) 1994, 1996, 1997, 1998.
League Championship (Yugoslavia) - (4)
1948, 1954, 1958, 1982.
Domestic Cup (Yugoslavia) - (8) 1951, 1960,
1963, 1965, 1969, 1973, 1980, 1983.
Fairs' Cup - (1) 1967.

APPEARANCES 98/99

	P	Ap	(s)	Gls
Branko BANOVIC	D		(1)	
Igor BISCAN	M	18	(1)	2
Mario CVITANOVIC	D	24	(4)	1
Josko JELICIC	M	15	(5)	6
Krunoslav JURCIC	M	16	(7)	3
Goran JURIC	D	25		
Ardijan KOZNIKU	A	7	(11)	3
Damir KRZNAR	D	12	(2)	1
Drazen LADIC	G	31		
Silvio MARIC	A	14		5
Mihael MIKIC	A	8	(7)	6
Grazvydas MIKULENAS (LIT)	A	9	(2)	3
Kazuyoshi MIURA (JPN)	A	4	(8)	
Srdjan MLADINIC	D		(1)	
Edin MUJCIN (BOS)	M	23	(4)	10
Robert PROSINECKI	M	15		4
Tomislav RUKAVINA	M	20	(3)	
Nermin SABIC (BOS)	M	7	(10)	
Danijel SARIC	M	18	(8)	1
Goce SEDLOSKI (MAC)	D	2	(1)	
Dario SIMIC	D	13		1
Josip SIMIC	A	10	(5)	3
Tomislav SOKOTA	A	11	(10)	4
Danijel STEFULJ	D	1	(3)	
Mario TOKIC	D	30		
Stjepan TOMAS	D	11		
Vladimir VASILJ	G	1		
Mark VIDUKA (AUS)	A	7		2

LEAGUE RESULTS 1998/99

07/08/98	Sibenik	H	4-1	Maric 2, Jelicic, Simic J.
16/08/98	Zadarkomerc Zadar	A	1-1	Jurcic
20/08/98	Osijek	H	4-2	Jelicic 2, Simic D., Sokota
30/08/98	Hrvatski dragovoljac Zagreb	H	2-1	Maric, Sokota
11/09/98	Mladost 127 Suhopolje	A	4-0	Mujcin 2, Viduka, Mikic
20/09/98	Cibalia Vinkovci	H	2-1	Mujcin (p), Saric
25/09/98	Slaven Belupo Koprivnica	A	1-0	Maric
04/10/98	Varteks Varazdin	H	2-0	Sokota, Krznar
25/10/98	Zagreb	H	4-0	Mujcin 3 (2p), Maric
30/10/98	Hajduk Split	A	1-1	Viduka
08/11/98	Sibenik	A	2-1	Mikic 2
11/11/98	Rijeka	A	0-1	
15/11/98	Zadarkomerc Zadar	H	4-0	Mujcin 2, Mikic, Jelicic
20/11/98	Osijek	A	1-0	Jelicic
29/11/98	Hrvatski dragovoljac Zagreb	A	0-1	
14/12/98	Cibalia Vinkovci	A	1-0	Kozniku
17/02/99	Mladost 127 Suhopolje	H	3-0	Jelicic, Mikulenas, Mikic
21/02/99	Slaven Belupo Koprivnica	H	2-1	Mikulenas, Jurcic
26/02/99	Varteks Varazdin	A	0-2	
07/03/99	Rijeka	H	3-0	Mujcin, Biscan, Prosinecki (p)
14/03/99	Zagreb	A	2-1	Prosinecki (p), Mikulenas
21/03/99	Hajduk Split	H	1-0	Cvitanovic
18/04/99	Hrvatski dragovoljac Zagreb	H	1-0	Mujcin
21/04/99	Rijeka	H	0-1	
25/04/99	Hajduk Split	A	0-1	
02/05/99	Osijek	H	1-1	Prosinecki (p)
09/05/99	Varteks Varazdin	A	2-1	Mikic, Jurcic
12/05/99	Hrvatski dragovoljac Zagreb	A	1-1	Prosinecki (p)
16/05/99	Rijeka	A	2-0	Biscan, Sokota
19/05/99	Hajduk Split	H	1-1	Simic J.
23/05/99	Osijek	A	1-0	Kozniku
26/05/99	Varteks Varazdin	H	2-0	Simic J., Kozniku

HAJDUK SPLIT

CLUB DIRECTORY

HNK Hajduk
Poljudsko setaliste bb, 21 000 Split
tel - (021) 341755/355444
fax - (021) 585630
Year of Formation - 1911
President - Zeljko Kovacevic
Director - Ivan Marsic
Coach - Ivan Katalinic
Stadium - Poljud (50,000)

MAJOR HONOURS
League Championship - (3) 1992, 1994, 1995.
Domestic Cup - (2) 1993, 1995.
League Championship (Yugoslavia) - (9)
1927, 1929, 1950, 1952, 1955, 1971, 1974,
1975, 1979.
Domestic Cup (Yugoslavia) - (9) 1967, 1972,
1973, 1974, 1976, 1977, 1984, 1987, 1991.

APPEARANCES 98/99

	P	Ap	(s)	Gls
Bosko ANIC	D		(1)	
Mate BATURINA	A	22	(6)	6
Mate BILIC	A		(1)	
Marino BILISKOV	D	25	(1)	2
Elvis BRAJKOVIC	D	9	(2)	
Josip BULAT	D	16	(3)	1
Niko CEKO	D		(1)	
Zvonimir DERANJA	A	10	(15)	14
Tomislav ERCEG	A	12		7
Tonci GABRIC	G	15		
Ivan JERKOVIC	M	1	(6)	
Vik LALIC	D	25	(4)	
Ivan LEKO	M	15	(7)	4
Stipe MATIC	D		(1)	
Darko MILADIN	D	14	(3)	2
Alen MRZLECKI	D	12	(3)	1
Jasmin MUJDZA (BOS)	D	21	(3)	1
Stipe PLETIKOSA	G	16	(3)	
Nenad PRALIJA	M	14		3
Dean RACUNICA	M	21	(3)	8
Zoran RATKOVIC	A	2	(10)	
Goran SABLIC	D	15	(4)	
Ante SERIC	D	12	(4)	
Josip SKOKO (AUS)	M	24		3
Hrvoje SUNARA	G	1		
Jurica VUCKO	A	29	(2)	8
Hrvoje VUKOVIC	D	4	(1)	2
Kazimir VULIC	M	12	(7)	
Miroslav WEISS (MAC)	D	5	(3)	

LEAGUE RESULTS 1998/99

07/08/98	Hrvatski dragovoljac Zagreb	A	0-0	
16/08/98	Mladost 127 Suhopolje	H	3-0	Deranja 3
21/08/98	Cibalia Vinkovci	A	2-2	Racunica, Vucko
30/08/98	Slaven Belupo Koprivnica	H	5-0	Racunica 3 (1p), Baturina, Vucko
11/09/98	Varteks Varazdin	A	4-1	Racunica, Leko, Baturina, Deranja
20/09/98	Rijeka	H	3-1	Racunica (p), Deranja 2
25/09/98	Zagreb	A	1-3	Leko
04/10/98	Osijek	A	1-0	Baturina
18/10/98	Sibenik	H	2-1	Baturina 2
25/10/98	Zadarkomerc Zadar	A	1-1	Skoko
30/10/98	Croatia Zagreb	H	1-1	Leko
07/11/98	Hrvatski dragovoljac Zagreb	H	2-0	Vucko, Deranja
15/11/98	Mladost 127 Suhopolje	A	1-1	Racunica
22/11/98	Cibalia Vinkovci	H	2-0	Deranja 2
29/11/98	Slaven Belupo Koprivnica	A	1-1	Deranja
06/12/98	Varteks Varazdin	H	3-0	Bulat, Deranja, Vucko
13/12/98	Rijeka	A	1-2	Deranja
21/02/99	Zagreb	H	1-0	Skoko
28/02/99	Osijek	H	2-1	Vucko, Biliskov
07/03/99	Sibenik	A	0-1	
14/03/99	Zadarkomerc Zadar	H	2-0	Pralija, Deranja (p)
21/03/99	Croatia Zagreb	A	0-1	
17/04/99	Osijek	H	4-1	Erceg 2 (1p), Vucko, Pralija
21/04/99	Varteks Varazdin	A	2-1	Erceg 2 (1p)
25/04/99	Croatia Zagreb	H	1-0	Erceg
02/05/99	Rijeka	A	3-3	Baturina, Vucko, Biliskov
09/05/99	Hrvatski dragovoljac Zagreb	H	6-1	Mujdza, Pralija, Leko, Erceg, Skoko, Mrzlecki
12/05/99	Osijek	A	1-1	Vucko
16/05/99	Varteks Varazdin	H	4-1	Vukovic, Miladin, Deranja, Racunica
19/05/99	Croatia Zagreb	A	1-1	Vukovic
23/05/99	Rijeka	H	1-3	Miladin
26/05/99	Hrvatski dragovoljac Zagreb	A	1-3	Erceg

HRVATSKI DRAGOVOLJAC ZAGREB

CLUB DIRECTORY

NK Hrvatski dragovoljac
Aleja pomoraca 25
10 000 Zagreb
tel - (01) 6554644/6555030
fax - (01) 6520341
Year of Formation - 1975
President - Stjepan Spajic
Director - Ivica Perkovic
Coach - Ilija Loncarevic; Branko Tucak
Stadium - Kranjceviceva (12,000);
Stanko Vlajinic Dida, Slavonski Brod (2,000)

APPEARANCES 98/99

	P	Ap	(s)	Gls
Mario ANDRACIC	A	10	(11)	3
Josip BABIC	D	2	(3)	
Mario BAZINA	A	26	(2)	7
Nevio BERDI	M	5	(10)	
Ivo BERKOVIC	M	1		
Spomenko BOSNJAK	D	23		3
Mislav BRADVIC	A	1	(8)	
Slaven DAMJANOVIC	A	3	(12)	1
Vlatko DJOLONGA	D	26	(1)	3
Bernard GULIC	M	3	(9)	
Branko HUCIKA	D	19	(3)	
Ante JAZIC	D	20	(5)	2
Predrag JURIC	M	26	(1)	3
Jaksa JURKOVIC	A	1	(3)	
Neno KATULIC	A	15		
Fabijan KOMLJENOVIC	A	13	(2)	3
Daniel KOVACEVIC	M	5	(7)	
Marin LALIC	M	12		2
Elvis MARGETA	D	18		
Ivan MILAS	M	8	(5)	1
Nikica MILETIC	M	25	(3)	1
Anto PETROVIC	D	18	(1)	
Kreso POLETI	D	12	(1)	
Zankarlo SIMUNIC	G	32		
Zeljko SKOPLJANAC	D	28	(1)	2

LEAGUE RESULTS 1998/99

Date	Opponent	H/A	Score	Scorers
07/08/98	Hajduk Split	H	0-0	
16/08/98	Sibenik	A	2-0	Bazina, Miletic
23/08/98	Zadarkomerc Zadar	H	2-1	Bazina, Damjanovic
30/08/98	Croatia Zagreb	A	1-2	Bosnjak
13/09/98	Osijek	H	0-0	
20/09/98	Mladost 127 Suhopolje	H	0-0	
29/09/98	Cibalia Vinkovci	A	1-1	Bazina
04/10/98	Slaven Belupo Koprivnica	H	0-0	
18/10/98	Varteks Varazdin	A	0-1	
24/10/98	Rijeka	H	1-0	Andracic
31/10/98	Zagreb	A	0-0	
07/11/98	Hajduk Split	A	0-2	
15/11/98	Sibenik	H	1-2	Andracic
22/11/98	Zadarkomerc Zadar	A	1-2	Bazina
29/11/98	Croatia Zagreb	H	1-0	Djolonga
06/12/98	Osijek	A	1-2	Juric (p)
13/12/98	Mladost 127 Suhopolje	A	0-3	
21/02/99	Cibalia Vinkovci	H	3-1	Juric, Katulic, Bosnjak
28/02/99	Slaven Belupo Koprivnica	A	0-1	
07/03/99	Varteks Varazdin	H	0-0	
14/03/99	Rijeka	A	0-3	
21/03/99	Zagreb	H	3-2	Jozic, Komljenovic, Skopljanac
18/04/99	Croatia Zagreb	A	0-1	
21/04/99	Osijek	H	3-2	Skopljanac, Juric (p), Bazina
25/04/99	Rijeka	A	0-3	
02/05/99	Varteks Varazdin	H	3-0	Lalic, Bazina 2
09/05/99	Hajduk Split	A	1-6	Bosnjak
12/05/99	Croatia Zagreb	H	1-1	Jazic
16/05/99	Osijek	A	1-2	Lalic
19/05/99	Rijeka	H	1-2	Komljenovic
23/05/99	Varteks Varazdin	A	2-3	Djolonga, Milas
26/05/99	Hajduk Split	H	3-1	Komljenovic, Andracic, Djolonga (p)

MLADOST 127 SUHOPOLJE

CLUB DIRECTORY

NK Mladost 127
Vukovarska ulica 6, 33 200 Suhopolje
tel - (033) 771727 / fax - (033) 771046
Year of Formation - 1945
President - Mijo Fett
Director - Zdravko Novoselac
Coach - Zlatko Tot; Zvonko Menegati;
Stanko Poklepovic; Zvonko Menegati,
Tonko Vukusic; Mato Saric
Stadium - Mladost (8,500)

APPEARANCES 98/99

		P	Ap	(s)	Gls
Nenad BACINA	D	28			1
Blazenko BEKAVAC	D	8	(6)		
Zeljko BOGADI	M	17	(4)		1
Petar BOSNJAK	A	4	(4)		1
Stipe BOSNJAK	D	15			
Mladen BUBEK	M	6	(4)		
Zvonimir DIVIC	D		(1)		
Antun DUNKOVIC	M	3	(5)		
Viktor DVIRNIK (UKR)	A	8			2
Asmir DZAFIC	A	14	(2)		6
Ivica FERENCEVIC	D	11			
Tomislav FILIPOVIC	A	2	(7)		
Ante FRANTAL	D	1	(3)		
Mirza GOLUBICA (BOS)	A	27			10
Branko GOMERCIC	A	1			
Jasmin GULIC	G	3	(1)		
Resum HADZIIIJ	A	6	(11)		
Igor ILECIC	D	11			
Ivan ILECIC	A	14			2
Branko JOVANOVIC	D		(2)		
Jure JURIC	M	21	(2)		
Marin LALIC	M	9	(1)		3
Vlatko LOKINGER	M	6	(1)		
Stjepan LONCAREVIC	M	7	(1)		1
Vedran MADZAR	A	10			1
Mario MATAJA	M	9	(2)		1
Goran MATOS	M	1	(2)		
Danijel NOVAK	D		(2)		
Hrvoje PIPINIC	D	25			
Lucian POPESCU (ROM)	M	11			1
Stipe REBIC	G	10	(3)		
Krunoslav SAFRAN	D	12	(1)		
Mato SARIC	M		(1)		
Zoran SLAVICA	G	19			
Dragan TOMAS	M	20	(5)		
Zdeslav TONKOVIC	D	1			
Jadranko TOPIC	A		(1)		
Damir VRANIC	M	4	(2)		
Lucano ZGRABLIC	D	8			

LEAGUE RESULTS 1998/99

09/08/98	Zagreb	H	0-1	
16/08/98	Hajduk Split	A	0-3	
23/08/98	Sibenik	H	4-0	Golubica 3 (1p), Mataja
30/08/98	Zadarkomerc Zadar	A	0-2	
11/09/98	Croatia Zagreb	H	0-4	
20/09/98	Hrvatski dragovoljac Zagreb	A	0-0	
27/09/98	Osijek	H	1-4	Popescu
04/10/98	Cibalia Vinkovci	H	0-0	
18/10/98	Slaven Belupo Koprivnica	A	1-4	Dzafic
27/10/98	Varteks Varazdin	H	4-1	Lalic 2, Dzafic 2
31/10/98	Rijeka	A	0-1	
08/11/98	Zagreb	A	1-2	Golubica
15/11/98	Hajduk Split	H	1-1	Lalic (p)
22/11/98	Sibenik	A	1-4	Dzafic
29/11/98	Zadarkomerc Zadar	H	2-1	Dvirnik, Loncarevic
13/12/98	Hrvatski dragovoljac Zagreb	H	3-0	Dzafic 2, Bosnjak P.
17/02/99	Croatia Zagreb	A	0-3	
21/02/99	Osijek	A	3-1	Ilecic Iv., Golubica, Dvirnik
28/02/99	Cibalia Vinkovci	A	0-2	
07/03/99	Slaven Belupo Koprivnica	H	0-0	
12/03/99	Varteks Varazdin	A	0-6	
21/03/99	Rijeka	H	1-2	Bacina
18/04/99	Sibenik	A	0-5	
21/04/99	Zadarkomerc Zadar	H	1-0	Golubica
25/04/99	Cibalia Vinkovci	A	1-1	Madzar
02/05/99	Slaven Belupo Koprivnica	H	0-0	
09/05/99	Zagreb	A	0-4	
12/05/99	Sibenik	H	3-3	Golubica 3 (1p)
16/05/99	Zadarkomerc Zadar	A	0-2	
19/05/99	Cibalia Vinkovci	H	1-2	Golubica
23/05/99	Slaven Belupo Koprivnica	A	0-4	
26/05/99	Zagreb	H	2-1	Ilecic Iv., Bogadi

OSIJEK

CLUB DIRECTORY

NK Osijek
Wilsonova bb
31 000 Osijek
tel - (031) 141300/141400
fax - (031) 141500
Year of Formation - 1947
President - Antun Novalic
Director - Milan Spanjic
Coach - Milan Djuricic; Stanko Poklepovic
Stadium - Gradski vrt (22,000)

MAJOR HONOURS
Domestic Cup - (1) 1999

APPEARANCES 98/99

	P	Ap	(s)	Gls
Marko BABIC	M	1	(1)	
Josip BALATINAC	M	15	(7)	4
Ivica BELJAN	D	29		
Bakir BESIREVIC	M	28		7
Stanko BUBALO	A	20	(10)	10
Ivo ERGOVIC	D	27		1
Mario GALINOVIC	G	10	(1)	
Josip GASPAR	M	15	(5)	
Ronald GRNJA	M	2	(12)	1
Petar KRPAN	A	2	(1)	1
Davor LASIC	D	19	(4)	
Dumitru MITU (ROM)	A	13	(10)	1
Borimir PERKOVIC	M	18	(4)	9
Mario PRISC	A	25	(2)	3
Darko RAIC-SUDAR	M	1	(2)	1
Jakov SURAC	M	8	(11)	
Filip SUSNJARA	G	21		
Mario TADIC	M	1	(3)	1
Drazen VIDOVIC	D	21	(2)	
Jurica VRANJES	M	20	(5)	5
Stjepan VRANJES	D	20	(2)	
Damir VUICA	D	25		3

LEAGUE RESULTS 1998/99

06/08/98	Zadarkomerc Zadar	A	1-1	Bubalo
16/08/98	Varteks Varazdin	H	1-0	Krpan
20/08/98	Croatia Zagreb	A	2-4	Perkovic, Tadic
30/08/98	Rijeka	H	1-0	Bubalo
13/09/98	Hrvatski dragovoljac Zagreb	A	0-0	
20/09/98	Zagreb	H	3-0	(w/o)
27/09/98	Mladost 127 Suhopolje	A	4-1	Bubalo, Perkovic, Vranjes J. 2
04/10/98	Hajduk Split	H	0-1	
18/10/98	Cibalia Vinkovci	A	0-1	
25/10/98	Sibenik	H	4-0	Vranjes J. 2, Raic-Sudar, Bubalo
31/10/98	Slaven Belupo Koprivnica	A	4-1	Balatinac, Vranjes J., Besirevic 2 (2p)
08/11/98	Zadarkomerc Zadar	H	2-0	Mitu, Prisc
15/11/98	Varteks Varazdin	A	3-2	Balatinac, og (Sabolcki), Besirevic (p)
20/11/98	Croatia Zagreb	H	0-1	
29/11/98	Rijeka	A	0-1	
06/12/98	Hrvatski dragovoljac Zagreb	H	2-1	Bubalo, Perkovic
13/12/98	Zagreb	A	1-1	Perkovic
21/02/99	Mladost 127 Suhopolje	H	1-3	Besirevic (p)
28/02/99	Hajduk Split	A	1-2	Bubalo
07/03/99	Cibalia Vinkovci	H	3-1	Prisc, Balatinac, Besirevic (p)
14/03/99	Sibenik	A	1-2	Grnja
21/03/99	Slaven Belupo Koprivnica	H	3-0	Vuica, Bubalo, Balatinac
17/04/99	Hajduk Split	A	1-4	Bubalo
21/04/99	Hrvatski dragovoljac Zagreb	A	2-3	Besirevic 2 (2p)
25/04/99	Varteks Varazdin	H	0-2	
02/05/99	Croatia Zagreb	A	1-1	Vuica
09/05/99	Rijeka	H	5-2	Perkovic 3, Bubalo, Prisc
12/05/99	Hajduk Split	H	1-1	Perkovic
16/05/99	Hrvatski dragovoljac Zagreb	H	2-1	Perkovic, Ergovic
19/05/99	Varteks Varazdin	A	1-0	Vuica
23/05/99	Croatia Zagreb	H	0-1	
26/05/99	Rijeka	A	1-1	Bubalo

RIJEKA

CLUB DIRECTORY

NK Rijeka
Partic 3
51 000 Rijeka
tel - (051) 261622/261626
fax - (051) 261174
Year of Formation - 1946
President - Zarko Tomljenovic
Director - Nikola Tomac
Coach - Nenad Gracan
Stadium - Kantrida (21,000)

MAJOR HONOURS
Domestic Cup (Yugoslavia) - (2) 1978, 1979.

APPEARANCES 98/99

	P	Ap	(s)	Gls
Jasmin AGIC	M	19	(5)	1
Bosko BALABAN	A	7	(16)	4
Drazen BOSKOVIC	D	1	(1)	
Goran BRAJKOVIC	M	16	(9)	
Igor BUDAN	A	16	(7)	1
Bozidar CACIC	M	22		4
Kristijan CAVAL	M	4	(2)	
Admir HASANCIC	A	23	(4)	9
Mladen IVANCIC	D	28		2
Ilija KLJAJIC	A	2	(5)	
Sladjenko MARIC	M		(2)	
Yoshika MATSUBARA (JPN)	A		(2)	
Andre MIJATOVIC	D	28		1
Damir MILINOVIC	D	30		1
Igor MUSA	M	30		14
Mico PERANOVIC	M		(2)	
Renato PILIPOVIC	M	27	(1)	2
Zdravko SIMIC	A		(2)	
Barnabás SZTIPÁNOVICS (HUN)	A	24	(2)	14
Dzoni TAFRA	G	32		
Mauro TOMISIC	D	15	(5)	
Dalibor VISKOVIC	M	28		

LEAGUE RESULTS 1998/99

09/08/98	Cibalia Vinkovci	A	2-1	Musa 2
16/08/98	Slaven Belupo Koprivnica	H	1-1	Musa
23/08/98	Varteks Varazdin	A	1-0	Budan
30/08/98	Osijek	A	0-1	
13/09/98	Zagreb	H	1-0	Cacic
20/09/98	Hajduk Split	A	1-3	Musa
27/09/98	Sibenik	H	3-1	Musa, Mijatovic, Ivancic
04/10/98	Zadarkomerc Zadar	A	1-0	Sztipánovics
24/10/98	Hrvatski dragovoljac Zagreb	A	0-1	
31/10/98	Mladost 127 Suhopolje	H	1-0	Musa
07/11/98	Cibalia Vinkovci	H	2-0	Sztipánovics, Musa (p)
11/11/98	Croatia Zagreb	H	1-0	Ivancic
15/11/98	Slaven Belupo Koprivnica	A	3-1	Musa, Cacic, Sztipánovics
22/11/98	Varteks Varazdin	H	3-2	Sztipánovics 2, Musa (p)
29/11/98	Osijek	H	1-0	Balaban
13/12/98	Hajduk Split	H	2-1	Hasancic 2
17/02/99	Zagreb	A	2-1	Sztipánovics 2
21/02/99	Sibenik	A	1-0	Milinovic
28/02/99	Zadarkomerc Zadar	H	4-1	Agic, Hasancic, Musa (p), Sztipánovics
07/03/99	Croatia Zagreb	A	0-3	
14/03/99	Hrvatski dragovoljac Zagreb	H	3-0	Musa (p), Hasancic, Sztipánovics
21/03/99	Mladost 127 Suhopolje	A	2-1	Hasancic, Musa
17/04/99	Varteks Varazdin	H	2-1	Pilipovic 2 (1p)
21/04/99	Croatia Zagreb	A	1-0	Balaban
25/04/99	Hrvatski dragovoljac Zagreb	H	3-0	Sztipánovics 2, Musa
02/05/99	Hajduk Split	H	3-3	Hasancic, Balaban, Sztipánovics
09/05/99	Osijek	A	2-5	Hasancic, Balaban
12/05/99	Varteks Varazdin	A	1-1	Hasancic
16/05/99	Croatia Zagreb	H	0-2	
19/05/99	Hrvatski dragovoljac Zagreb	A	2-1	Sztipánovics, Cacic
23/05/99	Hajduk Split	A	3-1	Cacic, Hasancic, Sztipánovics
26/05/99	Osijek	H	1-1	Musa (p)

SIBENIK

CLUB DIRECTORY

HNK Sibenik
Bana Jelacica bb
22 000 Sibenik
tel - (022) 218163
fax - (022) 218406
Year of Formation - 1932
President - Miho Mioc
Director - Zvonko Vidacak
Coach - Stipe Kezdo; Rajko Magic; Stanko Mrsic
Stadium - Subicevac (12,000)

APPEARANCES 98/99

	P	Ap	(s)	Gls
Ivica ANTOLIC	D	21		1
Marijan BAKULA	M	25	(1)	
Kresimir BRKLJACIC	A		(7)	1
Ivan BULAT	M	27		3
Tihomir BULAT	G	22		
Niko CEKO	D	8		1
Darko DRAZIC	D	25		2
Anton GRDIC	M	27		1
Ive GRGAS-GRANDO	D		(3)	
Mario HARMAT	A	2	(12)	1
Ante IVICA	D	24	(1)	
Bojan JURIC	M		(4)	
Anel KARABEG	M	29		1
Marko KARTELO	G	1	(2)	
Mladen KOVACIC	M	10	(14)	1
Ivo MARASOVIC	A	1	(9)	3
Armando MARENZI	M	7	(12)	1
Mario NOVAKOVIC	M	9	(2)	
Ante PESIC	D	9	(10)	
Sinisa PETROVIC	M		(3)	
Josko POPOVIC	A	26		20
Zvonko RADOS	G	9	(1)	
Krunoslav RENDULIC	M	27		3
Zoran STANIC	D	19	(2)	
Ivo SUPE	D	5		
Klaudio VUKOVIC	A	19	(4)	8

LEAGUE RESULTS 1998/99

07/08/98	Croatia Zagreb	A	1-4	Popovic
16/08/98	Hrvatski dragovoljac Zagreb	H	0-2	
23/08/98	Mladost 127 Suhopolje	A	0-4	
30/08/98	Cibalia Vinkovci	H	2-1	Vukovic, Popovic
13/09/98	Slaven Belupo Koprivnica	A	1-3	Vukovic
20/09/98	Varteks Varazdin	H	0-0	
27/09/98	Rijeka	A	1-3	Popovic (p)
04/10/98	Zagreb	H	2-2	Grdic, Drazic
18/10/98	Hajduk Split	A	1-2	Rendulic
25/10/98	Osijek	A	0-4	
31/10/98	Zadarkomerc Zadar	H	4-2	Rendulic, Popovic 2, Brkljacic
08/11/98	Croatia Zagreb	H	1-2	Bulat I.
15/11/98	Hrvatski dragovoljac Zagreb	A	2-1	Ceko, Rendulic
22/11/98	Mladost 127 Suhopolje	H	4-1	Popovic 3, Karabeg
29/11/98	Cibalia Vinkovci	A	0-1	
06/12/98	Slaven Belupo Koprivnica	H	3-1	Popovic 2 (1p), Vukovic (p)
13/12/98	Varteks Varazdin	A	0-7	
21/02/99	Rijeka	H	0-1	
28/02/99	Zagreb	A	2-3	Antolic, Vukovic
07/03/99	Hajduk Split	H	1-0	Kovacic
14/03/99	Osijek	H	2-1	Drazic, Popovic
21/03/99	Zadarkomerc Zadar	A	0-0	
18/04/99	Mladost 127 Suhopolje	H	5-0	Bulat I. 2 (1p), Harmat, Marasovic 2
21/04/99	Cibalia Vinkovci	H	1-0	Vukovic
25/04/99	Zagreb	A	2-0	Vukovic, Marenzi
02/05/99	Zadarkomerc Zadar	H	5-1	Popovic 3 (1p), Vukovic, og (Spanjic)
09/05/99	Slaven Belupo Koprivnica	A	0-3	
12/05/99	Mladost 127 Suhopolje	A	3-3	Popovic 3 (1p)
16/05/99	Cibalia Vinkovci	A	1-2	Vukovic
19/05/99	Zagreb	H	2-1	Popovic (p), Marasovic
23/05/99	Zadarkomerc Zadar	A	1-3	Popovic (p)
26/05/99	Slaven Belupo Koprivnica	H	1-1	Popovic (p)

SLAVEN BELUPO KOPRIVNICA

CLUB DIRECTORY

NK Slaven Belupo
Ante Starcevica 29
48 000 Koprivnica
tel - (048) 621203
fax - (048) 621203
Year of Formation - 1912
President - Nikola Felak
Director - Tomislav Brinc
Coach - Marijan Vlak; Davor Puljic; Luka Bonacic
Stadium - Gradski (6,000)

APPEARANCES 98/99

		P	Ap	(s)	Gls
Frane AMIZIC	D	16	(4)		
Petar BOSNJAK	A	3			
Stipe BOSNJAK	D	14			
Zoran BRLENIC	M	18	(3)		
Vedran CELISCAK	M		(3)		
Pavo CRNAC	D	18	(6)	2	
Marijo DODIK	A	10	(2)	6	
Oliver DRVOSEK	A	2	(10)	6	
Damir FERENCINA	D	9	(3)	1	
Roy FERENCINA	D	28	(1)	2	
Antun HAVAIC	M	20	(2)	1	
Mario JOZIC	G	9	(2)		
Hasan KACIC	M	14			
Abu KANU (SRL)	A	5	(1)		
Vladimir KOKOL (SLO)	D	18	(5)	1	
Grgica KOVAC	D	11			
Mario KOVACEVIC	D	12	(1)		
Ratko KREMENOVIC	M	4	(5)	1	
Almin KULENOVIC (BOS)	D	10			
Marijan LAMESIC	D		(1)		
Robert LISJAK	G	1			
Stjepan LONCAREVIC	M	4	(6)	1	
Josip MARKOVINOVIC	A	3	(6)	1	
Zdravko MEDJIMOREC	D	20			
Zemir MUJCIN (BOS)	M	11	(12)	5	
Darko NEKRET-KATIC	D	13			
Zoran OGRIZOVIC	A	1	(3)		
Zeljko PAKASIN	M	8	(1)	3	
Danijel RADICEK	D	2	(2)		
Davor SILIC	D	3	(2)		
Josip SIMUNOVIC	M		(1)		
Zoran SLISKOVIC	A	16	(4)	7	
Ivica SOLOMUN	G	11			
Dragan STOJKIC	G	11			
Slobodan SUDEC	D	11	(2)		
Robert TEZACKI	M	5		1	
Fatmir VATA (ALB)	A	11		1	

LEAGUE RESULTS 1998/99

09/08/98	Varteks Varazdin	H	2-3	Vata, Pakasin
16/08/98	Rijeka	A	1-1	Crnac
23/08/98	Zagreb	H	2-1	Markovinovic, Sliskovic
30/08/98	Hajduk Split	A	0-5	
13/09/98	Sibenik	H	3-1	Mujcin (p), Havaic, Ferencina D.
20/09/98	Zadarkomerc Zadar	A	1-2	Sliskovic
25/09/98	Croatia Zagreb	H	0-1	
04/10/98	Hrvatski dragovoljac Zagreb	A	0-0	
18/10/98	Mladost 127 Suhopolje	H	4-1	Pakasin 2 (2p), Sliskovic, Ferencina R.
25/10/98	Cibalia Vinkovci	A	0-1	
31/10/98	Osijek	H	1-4	Ferencina R.
08/11/98	Varteks Varazdin	A	2-3	Mujcin 2 (2p)
15/11/98	Rijeka	H	1-3	Kremenovic
22/11/98	Zagreb	A	1-1	Crnac
29/11/98	Hajduk Split	H	1-1	Drvosek
06/12/98	Sibenik	A	1-3	Drvosek
13/12/98	Zadarkomerc Zadar	H	1-1	Drvosek
21/02/99	Croatia Zagreb	A	1-2	Drvosek
28/02/99	Hrvatski dragovoljac Zagreb	H	1-0	Mujcin (p)
07/03/99	Mladost 127 Suhopolje	A	0-0	
14/03/99	Cibalia Vinkovci	H	1-0	Drvosek
21/03/99	Osijek	A	0-3	
18/04/99	Cibalia Vinkovci	A	1-0	Sliskovic
21/04/99	Zagreb	H	2-2	Dodik (p), Mujcin
25/04/99	Zadarkomerc Zadar	A	0-1	
02/05/99	Mladost 127 Suhopolje	A	0-0	
09/05/99	Sibenik	H	3-0	Drvosek, Dodik 2
12/05/99	Cibalia Vinkovci	H	0-1	
16/05/99	Zagreb	A	3-2	Dodik 2, Sliskovic
19/05/99	Zadarkomerc Zadar	H	1-0	Sliskovic
23/05/99	Mladost 127 Suhopolje	H	4-0	Loncarevic, Kokol, Tezacki, Sliskovic (p)
26/05/99	Sibenik	A	1-1	Dodik

VARTEKS VARAZDIN

CLUB DIRECTORY

NK Varteks
Zagrebacka 96
42 000 Varazdin
tel - (042) 241332/177529
fax - (042) 240250
Year of Formation - 1931
President - Andjelko Herjavec
Director - Nevenko Herjavec
Coach - Drazen Besek
Stadium - Gradski (12,000)

APPEARANCES 98/99

	P	Ap	(s)	Gls
Andrija BALAJIC	M	21	(4)	
Krunoslav BELI	D	8	(2)	
Drazen BESEK	D	11		
Tomo CIKOVIC	D		(1)	
Zlatko DALIC	M	19	(4)	2
Vjeran GRABANT	A		(3)	
Krunoslav GREGORIC	D	23	(3)	1
Mihail HLEBALIN (RUS)	A		(6)	
Drazen HORVAT	A	3	(4)	
Danijel HRMAN	M	18	(7)	1
Mario IVANKOVIC	A	16	(12)	1
Veldin KARIC	A	20	(1)	10
Zoran KASTEL	D	19	(4)	1
Faik KAMBEROVIC (BOS)	A	20	(4)	7
Rikard KLEMENCIC	D		(1)	
Matija KRISTIC	D	2	(1)	
Drazen MADUNOVIC	D	29		3
Paul MATAS	A	10	(10)	4
Marijan MRMIC	G	15		
Miljenko MUMLEK	M	23	(2)	13
Damir MUZEK	M	27		2
Zvonimir NORAC-KEVO	A		(3)	
Mladen POSAVEC	M	18	(6)	2
Silvester SABOLCKI	D	19	(6)	
Nikola SAFARIC	A	3		
Hrvoje SKLEPIC	M	2	(2)	
Ivica SOLOMUN	G	17		
Nikola SRPAK	A	2		1
Dalibor TUKSER	D	1	(3)	
Goran VITKOVIC	M	6	(1)	1

LEAGUE RESULTS 1998/99

09/08/98	Slaven Belupo Koprivnica	A	3-2	Matas, Mumlek, Dalic
16/08/98	Osijek	A	0-1	
23/08/98	Rijeka	H	0-1	
30/08/98	Zagreb	A	1-1	Matas
11/09/98	Hajduk Split	H	1-4	Hrman
20/09/98	Sibenik	A	0-0	
27/09/98	Zadarkomerc Zadar	H	2-1	Kamberovic, Matunovic
04/10/98	Croatia Zagreb	A	0-2	
18/10/98	Hrvatski dragovoljac Zagreb	H	1-0	Mumlek
27/10/98	Mladost 127 Suhopolje	A	1-4	Madunovic
31/10/98	Cibalia Vinkovci	H	3-0	Mumlek 2 (1p), Gregoric
08/11/98	Slaven Belupo Koprivnica	H	3-2	Kastel, Mumlek (p), Kamberovic
15/11/98	Osijek	H	2-3	Karic, Mumlek
22/11/98	Rijeka	A	2-3	Mumlek, Muzek (p)
29/11/98	Zagreb	H	3-1	Mumlek, Kamberovic, Posavec
06/12/98	Hajduk Split	A	0-3	
13/12/98	Sibenik	H	7-0	Mumlek 3, Karic 2, Kamberovic, og (Grdic)
21/02/99	Zadarkomerc Zadar	A	3-5	Mats, Mumlek, Madunovic
26/02/99	Croatia Zagreb	H	2-0	Posavec, Karic
07/03/99	Hrvatski dragovoljac Zagreb	A	0-0	
12/03/99	Mladost 127 Suhopolje	H	6-0	Kamberovic, Dalic, Karic 4
21/03/99	Cibalia Vinkovci	A	0-3	
17/04/99	Rijeka	A	1-2	Matas
21/04/99	Hajduk Split	H	1-2	Kamberovic
25/04/99	Osijek	A	2-0	Karic 2
02/05/99	Hrvatski dragovoljac Zagreb	A	0-3	
09/05/99	Croatia Zagreb	H	1-2	Kamberovic
12/05/99	Rijeka	H	1-1	Mumlek
16/05/99	Hajduk Split	A	1-4	Vitkovic
19/05/99	Osijek	H	0-1	
23/05/99	Hrvatski dragovoljac Zagreb	H	3-2	Ivankovic, Srpak, Muzek (p)
26/05/99	Croatia Zagreb	A	0-2	

ZADARKOMERC ZADAR

CLUB DIRECTORY

NK Zadarkomerc
Stadionska 2
23000 Zadar
tel - (023) 314677
fax - (023) 312124
Year of Formation - 1945
President - Ante Jurjevic
Director - Josko Basic
Coach - Boris Ticic; Josip Skoblar; Josip Bajlo
Stadium - Stanovi (10,000)

APPEARANCES 98/99

	P	Ap	(s)	Gls
Hrvoje ANCIC	A	1		
Damir BISKUP	M	20		1
Sasa BJELANOVIC	A	24	(7)	6
Niksa BOLJAT	D	3	(2)	
Marijan BULJAT	M		(2)	
Josip BUTIC	M	4	(10)	
Ives CAKARUN	M	1	(5)	
Ante GALESIC	A	4	(13)	3
Marin JERMEN (SLO)	A	7	(4)	1
Zvonimir JURIC	M	24	(2)	
Toni JURIEV	G	2	(1)	
Juksu KRSTULOVIC	M	27		10
Jerko MIKULIC	D	17	(1)	
Ferdo MILIN	M	3	(3)	
Josip MODRIC	M	2	(9)	
Sergei NEIMAN (RUS)	D	17	(1)	1
Elvis PINCIC	M	1	(2)	
Anton PRANJIC	A	6	(5)	1
Marin PRPIC	M	29	(2)	3
Hrvoje RODIN	M	11	(4)	
Tomislav ROGIC	G	1		
Fahrudin SEHIC	G	29		
Josko SPANJIC	D	17	(1)	2
Petre STOILOV (MAC)	M		(2)	
Mario STRILIC	M	3	(3)	
Almir TURKOVIC (BOS)	A	27		9
Ognjen UGRCIC	M	7	(3)	
Nikola VERSIC	D	16	(2)	
Dalibor ZEBIC	D	27	(1)	
Antonio ZUPAN	M	22	(3)	1

LEAGUE RESULTS 1998/99

06/08/98	Osijek	H	1-1	Turkovic
16/08/98	Croatia Zagreb	H	1-1	Zupan
23/08/98	Hrvatski dragovoljac Zagreb	A	1-2	Biskup
30/08/98	Mladost 127 Suhopolje	H	2-0	Pranjic, Turkovic
13/09/98	Cibalia Vinkovci	A	2-1	og (Sablic), Prpic
20/09/98	Slaven Belupo Koprivnica	H	2-1	Bjelanovic, Jermen
27/09/98	Varteks Varazdin	A	1-2	Krstulovic (p)
04/10/98	Rijeka	H	0-1	
18/10/98	Zagreb	A	3-4	Turkovic, Krstulovic, Bjelanovic
25/10/98	Hajduk Split	H	1-1	Krstulovic
31/10/98	Sibenik	A	2-4	Galesic, Turkovic
08/11/98	Osijek	A	0-2	
15/11/98	Croatia Zagreb	A	0-4	
22/11/98	Hrvatski dragovoljac Zagreb	H	2-1	Turkovic, Neiman (p)
29/11/98	Mladost 127 Suhopolje	A	1-2	Krstulovic
06/12/98	Cibalia Vinkovci	H	0-2	
13/12/98	Slaven Belupo Koprivnica	A	1-1	Turkovic
21/02/99	Varteks Varazdin	H	5-3	Bjelanovic 2, Prpic, Turkovic, Galesic
28/02/99	Rijeka	A	1-4	Krstulovic (p)
07/03/99	Zagreb	H	1-1	Krstulovic
14/03/99	Hajduk Split	A	0-2	
21/03/99	Sibenik	H	0-0	
17/04/99	Zagreb	A	0-2	
21/04/99	Mladost 127 Suhopolje	A	0-1	
25/04/99	Slaven Belupo Koprivnica	H	1-0	Spanjic (p)
02/05/99	Sibenik	A	1-5	Bjelanovic
09/05/99	Cibalia Vinkovci	H	4-1	Bjelanovic, Turkovic, og (Lucic), Krstulovic
12/05/99	Zagreb	H	1-2	Krstulovic
16/05/99	Mladost 127 Suhopolje	H	2-0	Spanjic (p), Turkovic
19/05/99	Slaven Belupo Koprivnica	A	0-1	
23/05/99	Sibenik	H	3-1	Krstulovic 2, Galesic
26/05/99	Cibalia Vinkovci	A	1-1	Prpic

ZAGREB

CLUB DIRECTORY

NK Zagreb
Kranjceviceva 4
10 000 Zagreb
tel - (01) 368111
fax - (01) 338156
Year of Formation - 1945
President - Ante Vrdoljak
Director - Zlatko Dracic
Coach - Josip Kuze (99/00 - Ivo Susak)
Stadium - Kranjceviceva (12,000)

APPEARANCES 98/99

	P	Ap	(s)	Gls
Valter ANDROSIC	D		(1)	
Ivica BANOVIC	M	15	(7)	1
Mirsad BEBER	A		(1)	
Drazen BISKUP	D	28		1
Erjon BOGDANI (ALB)	A	14		6
Nino BULE	A	29		13
Jozo CACIC	M		(1)	
Mario CIZMEK	M	27	(1)	3
Dario DABAC	D	4	(3)	
Goran DASOVIC	M	5	(1)	
Lovro IVEKOVIC	M	1		
Igor JOVICEVIC	M	4	(5)	
Sunaj KEQI	M	18	(1)	
Domagoj KOSIC	M	25		4
Paul LAPIC	G	8	(2)	
Kruno LOVREK	A	4	(15)	2
Ivo MILIC	D	7	(2)	
Marijo OSIBOV	D	23		2
Benedikt PANIC	M	2	(11)	
Darko PERIC	M	16	(5)	1
Robert REGVAR	A	9	(12)	5
Fuad SASIVAREVIC (BOS)	M	8	(2)	5
Vjekoslav SKRINJAR	M	16	(4)	2
Zeljko SOIC	M	2		
Goran STAVREVSKI (MAC)	D	26	(1)	
Sandro TOMIC	G	23		
Hrvoje VEJIC	M	19	(4)	2
Hari VUKAS	A	6	(4)	
Miroslav VUKIC	A	2	(3)	

LEAGUE RESULTS 1998/99

09/08/98	Mladost 127 Suhopolje	A	1-0	Osibov
16/08/98	Cibalia Vinkovci	H	2-2	Bule, Regvar
23/08/98	Slaven Belupo Koprivnica	A	1-2	Vejic
30/08/98	Varteks Varazdin	H	1-1	Bule
13/09/98	Rijeka	A	0-1	
20/09/98	Osijek	A	0-3	(w/o)
25/09/98	Hajduk Split	H	3-1	Sasivarevic 2, Vejic
04/10/98	Sibenik	A	2-2	Sasivarevic, Bule
18/10/98	Zadarkomerc Zadar	H	4-3	Sasivarevic, Osibov, Regvar, Peric
25/10/98	Croatia Zagreb	A	0-4	
31/10/98	Hrvatski dragovoljac Zagreb	H	0-0	
08/11/98	Mladost 127 Suhopolje	H	2-1	Sasivarevic, Regvar
15/11/98	Cibalia Vinkovci	A	1-1	Biskup
22/11/98	Slaven Belupo Koprivnica	H	1-1	Cizmek
29/11/98	Varteks Varazdin	A	1-3	Bogdani
13/12/98	Osijek	H	1-1	Bogdani
18/02/99	Rijeka	H	1-2	Bogdani
21/02/99	Hajduk Split	A	0-1	
28/02/99	Sibenik	H	3-2	Bule 2, Skrinjar
07/03/99	Zadarkomerc Zadar	A	1-1	Lovrek
14/03/99	Croatia Zagreb	H	1-2	Kosic (p)
21/03/99	Hrvatski dragovoljac Zagreb	A	2-3	Cizmek 2
17/04/99	Zadarkomerc Zadar	H	2-0	Bule, Regvar
21/04/99	Slaven Belupo Koprivnica	A	2-2	Bogdani, Bule
25/04/99	Sibenik	H	0-2	
02/05/99	Cibalia Vinkovci	A	2-3	Kosic, Bule
09/05/99	Mladost 127 Suhopolje	H	4-0	Skrinjar, Banovic, Bule, Lovrek
12/05/99	Zadarkomerc Zadar	A	2-1	Bule, Regvar
16/05/99	Slaven Belupo Koprivnica	H	2-3	Bule 2
19/05/99	Sibenik	A	1-2	Kosic
23/05/99	Cibalia Vinkovci	H	3-1	Bogdani 2, Kosic
26/05/99	Mladost 127 Suhopolje	A	1-2	Bule

PROMOTED CLUBS

SECOND DIVISION FINAL TABLE 98/99

		Pd	W	D	L	F	A	Pt	GD
1	Vukovar '91	36	22	8	6	69	29	74	+40
2	Istra Pula	36	21	9	6	71	27	72	+44
3	Segesta Sisak	36	22	4	10	84	34	70	+50
4	Cakovec	36	19	8	9	62	38	65	+24
5	Split	36	17	8	11	60	34	59	+26
6	Belisce	36	17	8	11	67	50	59	+17
7	Bjelovar	36	17	7	12	53	43	58	+10
8	Otok	36	16	7	13	56	49	55	+7
9	Zagorec Krapina	36	15	6	15	50	55	51	-5
10	Jadran Porec	36	13	9	14	58	45	48	+13
11	Solin Gradja	36	14	6	16	49	49	48	0
12	Croatia Sesvete	36	14	6	16	52	58	48	-6
13	Orijent Rijeka	36	13	9	14	39	48	48	-9
14	Imotska krajina Prolozac	36	13	8	15	49	54	47	-5
15	Croatia Djakovo	36	11	12	13	45	48	45	-3
16	Buducnost Hodosan	36	12	8	16	49	85	44	-36
17	Samobor	36	5	11	20	40	84	26	-44
18	Posavina Zagreb	36	5	7	24	29	76	22	-47
19	Inker Zapresic	36	3	5	28	25	103	14	-76

CLUB DIRECTORY

Vukovar '91
Borisa Kidrica bb
32000 Vukovar
tel - (032) 441284
fax - (032) 441283
President - Stipe Seremet
Director - Dragutin Guzovski
Coach - Davor Mladina
Stadium - Gradski (6,000)

CLUB DIRECTORY

NK Istra
Marsovo polje 8
52100 Pula
tel - (052) 210870
fax - (052) 223856
Year of Formation - 1961
President - Mladen Ivancic
Director - Branko Bubic
Coach - Dragan Simeunovic
Stadium - Gradski (7,000)

CYPRUS

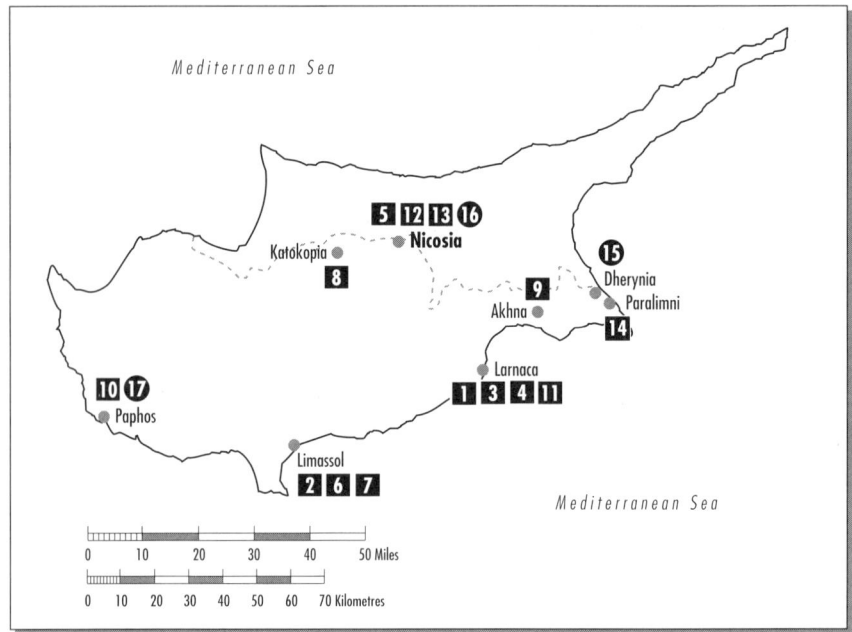

Mediterranean Sea

Katokopia ●   **5 12 13 16**   ● **Nicosia**   **15**
    8   Dherynia
                        9   ● Paralimni
              Akhna ●   **14**

                        ● Larnaca
10 17   **1 3 4 11**
● Paphos

            Limassol
            2 6 7
                        Mediterranean Sea

0   10   20   30   40   50 Miles

0   10   20   30   40   50   60   70 Kilometres

SPAIN VICTORY LEADS TO NOWHERE

Goal-crazy Anorthosis land title hat-trick

FEDERATION DIRECTORY

Cyprus Football Association
Stasinos Street 1, Engomi 2404, PO Box 5071, Nicosia

tel - (02) 352341   Year of Formation - 1934
fax - (02) 590544   President - Marios Lefkaritis
                      Secretary - Lambros Adamou

Goals win matches, and if scored in sufficient quantity over the duration of a season, they also win titles. That was certainly the secret of Anorthosis Famagusta's success as they lifted the Cypriot championship for the third year in a row, beating stubborn, resilient challengers Omonia Nicosia into second place...on goal difference.

Anorthosis and Omonia totalled a record 67 points each, but the decisive statistic that settled the championship in Anorthosis's favour was their 'goals for' column. From 26 games they plundered a staggering haul of 95 goals - the highest figure in the history of the Cypriot First Division, beating Omonia's 38-year record of 91. Furthermore, they found the net in each and every match, scoring in multiples on all but three occasions.

Anorthosis lost just one match - 3-4 away to APOEL after leading 3-1 - and the only team they failed to beat was Omonia, with whom they shared two draws. The second of those, played in the first fixture after the brief winter break, enabled Anorthosis to remain four points in front. But from then on Omonia did not drop any further points. The gap closed to two points when Anorthosis were held 3-3 by local rivals AEK in round 17, and and it was down to nothing except goal difference when, three games later, the defending champions slipped up again with a 1-1 home draw against APOEL.

There were still six games to go, and with APOEL themselves only two points behind the leading duo, anything was still possible. APOEL, however, dropped out of the race when they lost to an injury-time winner from Omonia in the Nicosia derby, but although Omonia had the league's most prolific marksman in German centre-forward Rainer Rauffmann, their goal difference was too inferior to that of the leaders, who clung defiantly to their slender advantage in the closing weeks of the campaign, eventually sealing the championship with a 4-0 victory over Evaghoras, who went into the match needing a big win themselves to have any hope of avoiding relegation.

Anorthosis's three straight titles had all been won with the same coach, Yugoslav Dusan Mitosevic, which was some achievement in a country where appointing new foreign coaches at least once a year is the established norm. Mitosevic had the on-field assistance of three of his fellow countrymen. Slobodan Krcmarevic was the undisputed star of the first half of the season before he left to join top Greek side PAOK, but Vesko Mihajlovic and Vladan Tomic stayed on, and the former became the team's key figure during the spring, rallying his team-mates in impressive fashion as the pressure from Omonia became ever more intense. By scoring in the last-day win against Evaghoras, Mihajlovic took his goalscoring tally for the season to 20 - one more than that of the departed Krcmarevic but 15 fewer

LEAGUE CHAMPIONSHIP RESULTS 98/99

		1	2	3	4	5	6	7	8	9	10	11	12	13	14
1	AEK Larnaca		1-1	5-1	3-3	3-1	3-5	5-1	7-0	2-5	2-0	4-1	4-2	0-1	3-0
2	AEL Limassol	3-2		2-2	2-3	2-1	2-1	4-1	4-3	2-3	4-0	8-3	4-2	3-3	0-1
3	Alki Larnaca	5-4	1-3		0-4	0-6	0-2	3-2	2-1	2-3	3-1	0-2	1-3	1-4	2-2
4	Anorthosis Famagusta	1-0	2-0	5-0		1-1	4-2	5-0	7-0	2-0	6-1	5-3	7-1	2-2	5-1
5	APOEL Nicosia	3-1	2-0	4-1	4-3		1-0	5-2	3-0	1-0	4-1	3-0	2-0	1-2	2-2
6	Apollon Limassol	5-0	3-2	4-1	1-3	2-1		2-1	5-2	1-2	2-0	1-2	1-0	1-5	1-0
7	Aris Limassol	1-2	0-4	1-4	1-4	1-4	0-5		2-1	1-3	2-4	3-1	0-2	0-4	2-4
8	Doxa Katokopia	1-5	0-1	3-1	0-4	0-4	1-2	5-1		0-0	0-0	0-3	1-4	2-3	4-5
9	Ethnikos Akhna	1-1	2-1	2-0	0-2	2-3	6-1	3-2	0-0		2-0	2-3	1-1	2-4	1-1
10	Evaghoras Paphos	2-0	0-0	0-2	0-4	2-3	2-1	5-2	4-0	1-2		0-0	1-0	1-8	1-1
11	Nea Salamina Famagusta	0-1	0-0	1-2	2-3	0-1	2-2	2-3	2-0	4-0	4-1		0-0	2-3	4-5
12	Olympiakos Nicosia	1-2	0-1	2-2	1-4	0-5	2-0	4-0	4-0	1-1	2-1	2-1		0-1	2-2
13	Omonia Nicosia	0-1	3-0	3-0	1-1	1-0	2-0	5-1	1-0	4-0	6-1	4-1	5-4		5-0
14	Paralimni	1-2	0-2	1-1	2-5	3-5	1-1	6-2	5-3	3-6	6-1	0-3	2-0	1-1	

LEAGUE CHAMPIONSHIP FINAL TABLE 98/99

		P	W	D	L	F	A	W	D	L	F	A	W	D	L	F	A	P	GD
				Home					Away					Total					
1	Anorthosis Famagusta	26	11	2	0	52	11	10	2	1	43	17	21	4	1	95	28	67	+67
2	Omonia Nicosia	26	11	1	1	40	9	10	3	0	41	16	21	4	1	81	25	67	+56
3	APOEL Nicosia	26	11	1	1	35	12	8	1	4	35	17	19	2	5	70	29	59	+41
4	AEK Larnaca	26	8	2	3	42	21	6	1	6	21	24	14	3	9	63	45	45	+18
5	AEL Limassol	26	8	2	3	40	25	5	3	5	15	14	13	5	8	55	39	44	+16
6	Ethnikos Akhna	26	5	4	4	24	19	7	2	4	25	24	12	6	8	49	43	42	+6
7	Apollon Limassol	26	9	0	4	29	19	4	2	7	22	26	13	2	11	51	45	41	+6
8	Paralimni	26	4	3	6	31	32	4	5	4	24	32	8	8	10	55	64	32	-9
9	Olympiakos Nicosia	26	5	3	5	21	20	3	2	8	19	29	8	5	13	40	49	29	-9
10	Nea Salamina Famagusta	26	3	3	7	23	21	5	1	7	23	32	8	4	14	46	53	28	-7
11	Alki Larnaca	26	4	1	8	20	37	3	3	7	17	33	7	4	15	37	70	25	-33
12	Evaghoras Paphos	26	5	3	5	19	23	1	1	11	11	43	6	4	16	30	66	22	-36
13	Doxa Katokopia	26	2	2	9	17	32	0	1	12	10	46	2	3	21	27	78	9	-51
14	Aris Limassol	26	2	0	11	14	42	1	0	12	18	54	3	0	23	32	96	9	-64

than Omonia's Rauffmann, who completed his second season on the island with an incredible aggregate total of 77 league goals.

Anorthosis were unable to register a second successive 'double'. They reached the Cup final but lost 2-0 to APOEL in a match full of incident, excitement and controversy, with referee Yiannakis Kyprianides making a number of disputed calls that ultimately affected the final result.

Cyprus's standing in European club competition continued to improve, with all three 1998/99 representatives

DOMESTIC CUP 98/99

FIRST ROUND
AEL Limassol 7, Akritas Hloraka 1
Ethnikos Akhna 5, Doxa Paliometohou 0
Anorthosis Famagusta 5, THOI Lakatamia 0
AEZ Zakaki 0, Paralimni 3
APOP Paphos 1, Olympiakos Nicosia 2
Omonia Aradippou 0, AEK Larnaca 6
Aris Limassol 3, AEK Kythrea 0
Apollon Limassol 9, Elia Lithronta 0
Ethnikos Ashia 2, Evaghoras Paphos 5
Anagennisis Dherynia 1, Apollon Lympia 3
Doxa Katokopia 2, ATE-PEK Ergaton 0
AEK Kakopetria 1, APOEL Nicosia 5
Omonia Nicosia 8, APEP Pelentriou 0
PAEEK Kerynia 0, Alki Larnaca 2
Nea Salamina Famagusta 6, Onisilios Sotiras 0
THOI Avghorou 2, Ayia Napa 0

SECOND ROUND
AEL Limassol v Ethnikos Akhna 4-2; 0-2
(4-4; Ethnikos Akhna on away goals)
Alki Larnaca v AEK Larnaca 0-4; 2-5
(AEK Larnaca 9-2)
Anorthosis Famagusta v Apollon Limassol 1-1; 2-1
(Anorthosis Famagusta 3-2)
APOEL Nicosia v Doxa Katokopia 1-0; 2-2
(APOEL Nicosia 3-2)
Aris Limassol v Evaghoras Paphos 2-3; 2-4
(Evaghoras Paphos 7-4)

Omonia Nicosia v Olympiakos Nicosia 4-0; 2-1
(Omonia Nicosia 6-1)
Paralimni v Apollon Lympia 9-0; 2-0
(Paralimni 11-0)
Nea Salamina Famagusta v THOI Avghorou 9-0; 4-0
(Nea Salamina Famagusta 13-0)

QUARTER-FINALS
AEK Larnaca 4 (Evair 19, Edvaldo 36, Paulinho 44, Theodotou 62), Nea Salamina Famagusta 3
(Nicolaou N.K. 15, Stoic 20, Mihic 23)
Nea Salamina Famagusta 4 (Mihic 9, 56, 89, Panayiotou 48), AEK Larnaca 1 (Xiourouppas 49)
(Nea Salamina Famagusta 7-5)

APOEL Nicosia 2 (Costa 23, Petkovic 77),
Omonia Nicosia 2 (Rauffmann 5, 52)
Omonia Nicosia 0, APOEL Nicosia 3 (Kocis 37, Marcelo 55, Hadjilucas 83)
(APOEL Nicosia 5-2)

Ethnikos Akhna 1 (Music 85), Paralimni 0
Paralimni 0, Ethnikos Akhna 0
(Ethnikos Akhna 1-0)

Evaghoras Paphos 0, Anorthosis Famagusta 3
(Sotiriou 25, Andreou 58, 79)
Anorthosis Famagusta 2 (Lambrou 20, 57),
Evaghoras Paphos 3 (Savva 35, Varnavides 54, Pahtalias 60)
(Anorthosis Famagusta 5-3)

SEMI-FINALS
Anorthosis Famagusta 2 (Okkas 3, 21),
Ethnikos Akhna 2 (Poyiatzis 45, Music 56)
Ethnikos Akhna 1 (Neocleous 16),
Anorthosis Famagusta 3 (Mihajlovic 29, 34, 56)
(Anorthosis Famagusta 5-3)

Nea Salamina Famagusta 2 (Nicolaou N.A. 2, Telaputin 68),
APOEL Nicosia 3 (Kocis 85, 89, Marcelo 59)
APOEL Nicosia 4 (Marcelo 49, 53, Christodoulou 46, Yiasemakis 61),
Nea Salamina Famagusta 1 (Telaputin 47)
(APOEL Nicosia 7-3)

FINAL
08/05/99, Limassol
APOEL NICOSIA 2 Marcelo (74, 81p)
ANORTHOSIS FAMAGUSTA 0
referee - Kyprianides
APOEL NICOSIA - Petrides; Satsias, Aristocleous, Christodoulou, Stavrou, Aloneftis, Aristotelous (Timotheou 44), Petkovic, Kocis (Yiasemakis 76), Ioannou, Marcelo (Hadjilucas 87).
ANORTHOSIS FAMAGUSTA - Panayiotou; Melanarkitis, Foukaris, Charalambous, Ioannou, Pounas, Andreou (Luca 79), Iosiphides (Engomitis 46), Okkas (Sotiriou 80), Mihajlovic, Tomic.

putting up a noble effort. Anorthosis once again came close to qualifying for the Champions' League group phase. They lost 1-2 away to Olympiakos and were 1-0 up at home in the return before eventually conceding four second-half goals. Apollon Limassol, whose domestic campaign was best forgotten, reached the second round of the Cup-winners' Cup before they, like Anorthosis, failed to get the home win they required against opponents from the Greek mainland. Omonia's UEFA Cup bid was halted in the qualifying round by Rapid Vienna, but only on the away-goals rule.

The big story of the season for Cypriot football came before the league campaign had even started when Panikos Georgiou's national team sensationally beat Spain 3-2 in Limassol. It was a truly magnificent performance, and the result constituted one of the biggest upsets in European Championship history. But, alas, it proved to be no more than a flash in the pan. A month later Cyprus were humbled 0-3 at home by Austria, and despite two victories over San Marino, the season ended in further disappointment with another 0-3 defeat, away to Israel.

NATIONAL TEAM APPEARANCES 98/99

Coach - Panikos GEORGIOU	ALB	ESP	AUT	SMR	BEL	FIN	SMR	EST	ISR	Cps	Gls
Nicos PANAYIOTOU (06/12/70) - Anorthosis Famagusta	G78	G	G	G	G		G	G67	G	35	-
Yiotis ENGOMITIS (26/05/72) - Anorthosis Famagusta	D73	D	D	D						24	5
Marios CHARALAMBOUS (18/06/69) - Apollon Limassol	D78	D	D	D	D		D		D	43	2
Dimitris IOANNOU (0812/68) - Anorthosis Famagusta	D	D85	D						D	44	3
Pambos PITTAS (26/07/66) - Apollon Limassol	D64	D	D67	D	D		D	D	D	77	7
Vassos MELANARKITIS (11/08/72) - Anorthosis Famagusta	M	M	M68	M	M77		M	M60	M	15	1
Milenko SPOLJARIC (24/01/67) - Apollon Limassol	M	M	M	M	M		M	M	M79	11	3
Marios CHRISTODOULOU (04/07/74) - Iraklis (GRE)	M	M	M		A		M	A	A	18	2
Costas MALEKKOS (09/04/71) - Omonia Nicosia	A66	A55		A72	A70		A89		M46	33	2
Sinisa GOGIC (20/10/63) - Olympiakos (GRE)	A64	A61	A	A85	A78		A80			33	7
Yiannakis OKKAS (11/02/77) - Anorthosis Famagusta	A65		s46	s85	s78	A	s80	A61	s66	18	2
Michalis CONSTANDINOU (19/02/78) - Iraklis (GRE)	s64		s68	s72	A		A80		A66	8	2
Charis CHARALAMBOUS (25/03/71) - Anorthosis Famagusta	s64									8	-
Marios AGATHOCLEOUS (08/09/74) - Aris (GRE)	s65	s61	A46	A72				A74	s79	19	6
Ioakim IOAKIM (16/09/75) - Omonia Nicosia	s66	s85			D		D			5	1
Stavros FOUKARIS (15/04/75) - Anorthosis Famagusta	s73					D				2	-
Alexandros MICHAEL (15/09/74) - Apollon Limassol	s78									1	-
Paris ELIA (06/01/72) - Nea Salamina Famagusta	s78									1	-
Costas COSTA (04/01/69) - APOEL Nicosia		M	M							31	1
Panikos POUNAS (14/08/69) - Anorthosis Famagusta		s55								7	-
Nicolas GEORGIOU (24/02/76) - Omonia Nicosia			s67							5	1
Andreas SOPHOCLEOUS (07/09/73) - AEL Limassol				D	s70	D46		D55	D	5	-
Yiotis PANAYIOTOU (01/02/75) - Omonia Nicosia				M		D				2	-
Yiannos IOANNOU (25/01/66) - APOEL Nicosia				s72		A	s80			45	6
George THEODOTOU (01/01/74) - AEK Larnaca					D77		D	M	D	19	-
Tomis CHRYSOSTOMOU (20/10/74) - Alki Larnaca					s77	M46		s60		3	-
Aristos ARISTOCLEOUS (28/02/74) - APOEL Nicosia					s77	D	s89			12	-
Michalis SHIMITRAS (05/09/74) - Ethnikos Akhna						G57		s67		2	-
Angelos MISOS (07/03/71) - AEK Larnaca						D				11	-
Charis NICOLAOU (31/03/74) - Omonia Nicosia						M77			s46	5	-
Andros SOTIRIOU (07/06/68) - Anorthosis Famagusta						A55				39	8
Nikodemos PAPAVASILIOU (31/08/70) - Apollon Limassol						s46				35	5
George IOSIPHIDES (08/01/69) - Anorthosis Famagusta						s46				4	-
Marios DIMITRIOU (01/08/73) - AEL Limassol						s55		s61		2	-
Savvas CONSTANDINOU (28/08/71) - AEK Larnaca						s57				1	-
Marios KYRIAKOU (13/01/74) - Apollon Limassol						s77				1	-
George CHRISTODOULOU (22/08/65) - APOEL Nicosia								D46		26	-
Marios PASHIALIS (30/10/70) - APOP Paphos								D67		7	-
Ermogenis CHRISTOPHI (21/09/74) - AEL Limassol								s46		1	-
Nicos K. NICOLAOU (05/08/73) - Nea Salamina Famagusta								s55		1	-
Xenios ARISTOTELOUS (24/04/68) - APOEL Nicosia								s67		1	-
Andonis NICOLAOU (29/10/74) - Aris Limassol								s74		1	-

NATIONAL TEAM RESULTS 98/99

19/08/98	Albania	H	Nicosia	3-2	Engomitis (63), Ioakim (84), Ioannou D. (90)
05/09/98	Spain (ECQ)	H	Limassol	3-2	Engomitis (44), Gogic (48), Spoljaric (77)
10/10/98	Austria (ECQ)	H	Nicosia	0-3	
18/11/98	San Marino (ECQ)	A	Serravalle	1-0	Spoljaric (40)
03/02/99	Belgium	H	Limassol	0-1	
05/02/99	Finland	H	Paralimni	2-1	Karjalainen (40og), Papavasiliou (100)
10/02/99	San Marino (ECQ)	H	Limassol	4-0	Melanarkitis (18), Constandinou M. (32, 45),
					Christodoulou M. (88)
16/03/99	Estonia	H	Larnaca	1-2	Christodoulou M. (81)
28/03/99	Israel (ECQ)	A	Tel-Aviv	0-3	

TOP SCORERS

35 Rainer RAUFFMANN (Omonia Nicosia)
20 Vesko MIHAJLOVIC (Anorthosis Famagusta)
    Marios NEOPHYTOU (AEL Limassol)
19 Slobodan KRCMAREVIC
    (Anorthosis Famagusta)
18 Panikos XIOUROUPPAS (AEK Larnaca)
    Mirko MIHIC (Nea Salamina Famagusta)
    Slavisa CULA (Paralimni)

INTERNATIONAL HONOURS

None

EUROPEAN CUPS 98/99

CHAMPIONS' CUP
● ANORTHOSIS FAMAGUSTA
Preliminary round VALLETTA (MLT)
A 2-0 Elia (50), Okkas (78)
Panayiotou; Foukaris (Elia 46), Melanarkitis, Ioannou, Tomic, Mihajlovic, Engomitis, Lambrou, Sotiriou (Okkas 66), Agathocleous, Krcmarevic (Ciric 46).
H 6-0 Ciric (16), Charalambous (18), Andreou (45p), Sotiriou (51, 90), Okkas (75)
Panayiotou; Elia, Charalambous (Lambrou 58), Foukaris, Tomic, Pounas, Melanarkitis, Andreou, Okkas, Ciric (Engomitis 40), Mihajlovic (Sotiriou 46).

Qualifying round OLYMPIAKOS (GRE)
A 1-2 Mihajlovic (68)
Panayiotou; Engomitis, Ioannou, Tomic, Luca (Foukaris 46), Charalambous (Lambrou 73), Melanarkitis, Pounas, Elia, Mihajlovic (Andreou 81), Krcmarevic.
H 2-4 Mihajlovic (36), Krcmarevic (80)
Panayiotou; Lambrou (Andreou 60), Charalambous (Luca 74), Foukaris, Tomic, Engomitis (Ciric 82), Melanarkitis, Pounas, Okkas, Mihajlovic, Krcmarevic.

CUP WINNERS' CUP
● APOLLON LIMASSOL
Qualifying round EKRANAS PANEVEZYS (LIT)
A 2-1 Cârstea (17), Pittas (89)
Michael; Kais (Papavasiliou 54), Pittas, Charalambous, Philippou, Sburlea, Kyriakou, Spoljaric, Cârstea (Kavazis 73), Mladenovic, Da Silva (Voskarides 58).
H 3-3 Spoljaric (51, 89), Kavazis (60)
Michael; Kavazis, Pittas, Philippou (Kais 35), Charalambous, Sburlea (Aresti 78), Themistocleous, Spoljaric, Cârstea (Juras 67), Mladenovic, Kyriakou.

1st round FK JABLONEC (CZE)
H 2-1 Kavazis (45), Cârstea (67)
Avgousti; Kyriakou, Germanos, Pittas, Juras, Charalambous, Philippou, Themistocleous (Voskarides 70), Kavazis, Mladenovic, Cârstea (Christophi 80).
A 1-2 Themistocleous (58)
(aet; 3-4 on pens.)
Avgousti; Juras, Philippou, Spoljaric, Themistocleous (Christophi 66), Aresti, Kyriakou, Voskarides (Papavasiliou 73), Kais, Mladenovic (Germanos 70), Kavazis.

2nd round PANIONIOS (GRE)
A 2-3 Spoljaric (14, 42)
Avgousti (Michael 46); Juras, Pittas, Philippou, Charalambous, Kyriakou (Kais 73), Themistocleous, Spoljaric, Kavazis, Mladenovic, Cârstea (Papavasiliou 64).
H 0-1
Michael; Juras (Christophi 78), Pittas, Kavazis, Charalambous, Germanos, Spoljaric, Cârstea, Papavasiliou, Themistocleous (Voskarides 57), Kais.

● OMONIA NICOSIA
Preliminary round LINFIELD (NIR)
H 5-1 Kitanov (40, 61), Rauffmann (43p), Panayiotou (64), Kotolefteros (88)
Christophi; Kaiafas, Georgiou, Ioakim, Panayiotou, Constandinides, Andreou, Marangos (Nicolaou C. 75), Rauffmann (Kocic 63), Malekkos, Kitanov (Kontolefteros 86).
A 3-5 Marangos (2), Kitanov (35, 43)
Christophi; Kaiafas, Nicolaou N., Ioakim, Panayiotou, Constandinides, Andreou, Marangos (Nicolaou C. 74), Rauffmann (Kocic 63), Malekkos, Kitanov (Kontolefteros 86).

Qualifying round SK RAPID WIEN (AUT)
H 3-1 Rauffmann (42, 58), Malekkos (46)
Charitou; Kaiafas, Nicolaou N., Andreou, Ioakim, Panayiotou, Nicolaou C., Marangos (Odyseos 88), Rauffmann (Kocic 80), Malekos, Kitanov (Kontolefteros 70).
A 0-2
Charitou; Nicolaou N., Georgiou, Konafis, Panayiotou, Andreou, Marangos (Kitanov 72), Kaiafas (Kontolefteros 72), Rauffmann (Kocic 76), Malekos, Nicolaou C..

UEFA CUP
● ANORTHOSIS FAMAGUSTA
1st round FC ZÜRICH (SUI)
A 0-4
Panayiotou; Melanarkitis (Andreou 75), Elia (Charalambous 58), Ioannou, Foukaris, Pounas, Engomitis, Tomic, Okkas, Luca, Krcmarevic (Sotiriou 68).
H 2-3 Fischer (45og), Krcmarevic (71)
Panayiotou; Melanarkitis, Foukaris, Ioannou, Tomic, Engomitis, Luca, Okkas (Agathocleous 59), Mihajlovic, Krcmarevic (Sotiriou 72), Pounas (Andreou 69).

AEK LARNACA

CLUB DIRECTORY

AEK FC
Kilkis str.
6015 Larnaca
tel - (04) 655999/652464
fax - (04) 657173
Year of Formation - 1994
President - Dinos Lefkaritis
Secretary - Photis Photiou
Coach - Stavros Papadopoulos (99/00 - Radmilo Ivanisevic)
Stadium - Zenon (14,000)

APPEARANCES 98/99

	P	Ap	(s)	Gls
Klimis ALEXANDROU	A	18	(1)	2
Christos BAKARIS	A	17	(4)	1
George CONSTANDINOU	D	9	(5)	
Savvas CONSTANDINOU	G	17	(1)	
Yiannakis DIMOSTHENOUS	M		(3)	
EDVALDO da Paola (BRA)	A	26		13
EVAIR dos Santos (BRA)	M	18	(1)	4
Eleftherios ELEFTHERIOU	D	10	(8)	6
Sergios KOUNIS	A	3	(4)	
George KOUNOUSHIS	M	1	(4)	
Panayiotis KOUZOUPPAS	M	3	(8)	
Paris KYRIAKOU	M		(1)	
Neophytos LARKOU	D	15	(4)	
Michalis MARKOU	D	15	(2)	
Pavlos MARKOU	M	18	(1)	5
Andreas MAVRIS	G	9		
Angelos MISOS	D	14	(1)	1
Dimitris PANAYIOTOU	M	12	(4)	1
Michalis PAPAIOANNOU	A	2	(6)	2
Paulo Almeira Crispin "PAULINHO"	A	20	(3)	4
Louis STEPHANI	M	10	(5)	
Stelios STYLIANIDES	A	9	(6)	3
George THEODOTOU	D	19	(1)	3
Panikos XIOUROUPPAS	A	21		18

LEAGUE RESULTS 1998/99

13/09/98	Olympiakos Nicosia	A	2-1	Stylianides (p), Misos
19/09/98	AEL Limassol	H	1-1	Alexandrou
27/09/98	Alki Larnaca	A	4-5	Xiuorouppas 3, Eleftheriou
04/10/98	Ethnikos Akhna	H	2-5	Eleftheriou, Markou P.
18/10/98	Anorthosis Famagusta	A	0-1	
24/10/98	Evaghoras Paphos	H	2-0	Markou P. 2
01/11/98	Omonia Nicosia	A	1-0	Xiourouppas
07/11/98	Doxa Katokopia	H	7-0	Xiourouppas 4, Markou P., Eleftheriou, Edvaldo
21/11/98	Apollon Limassol	A	0-5	
28/11/98	Nea Salamina Famagusta	A	1-0	Eleftheriou
06/12/98	Paralimni	H	3-0	Xiourouppas, Evair, Edvaldo
12/12/98	Aris Limassol	A	2-1	Evair, Xiourouppas
19/12/98	APOEL Nicosia	H	3-1	Edvaldo 2, Xiourouppas
09/01/99	AEL Limassol	A	2-3	Xiourouppas 2
17/01/99	Alki Larnaca	H	5-1	Theodotou 2, Edvaldo 2, Eleftheriou
23/01/99	Ethnikos Akhna	A	1-1	Paulinho
13/02/99	Anorthosis Famagusta	H	3-3	Stylianides, Xiourouppas, Edvaldo
20/02/99	Evaghoras Paphos	A	0-2	
28/02/99	Omonia Nicosia	H	0-1	
07/03/99	Doxa Katokopia	A	5-1	Edvaldo 2, Xiourouppas, Paulinho, Eleftheriou
14/03/99	Apollon Limassol	H	3-5	Edvaldo 2, Evair
21/03/99	Nea Salamina Famagusta	H	4-1	Paulinho, Bakaris, Alexandrou, Evair
03/04/99	Paralimni	A	2-1	Xiourouppas, Theodotou
17/04/99	Aris Limassol	H	5-1	Papaioannou 2, Stylianides, Panayiotou, Markou P.
25/04/99	APOEL Nicosia	A	1-3	Xiourouppas
02/05/99	Olympiakos Nicosia	H	4-2	Edvaldo 2, Paulinho, Xiourouppas

AEL LIMASSOL

CLUB DIRECTORY

AEL FC
P.O. Box 51606
Limassol
tel - (05) 362598
fax - (05) 373960
Year of Formation - 1930
President - Dimitris Solomonides
Secretary - Ayis Agapiou
Coach - Panikos Orphanides
Stadium - Tsirion (20,000)

MAJOR HONOURS
League Championship - (5)
1941, 1953, 1955, 1956, 1968.
Domestic Cup - (6)
1939, 1940, 1948, 1985, 1987, 1989.

APPEARANCES 98/99

	P	Ap	(s)	Gls
Andonis ANDONIOU	A	16	(5)	1
Sozos ANDREOU	D	22	(1)	1
George CONSTANDI	D	5	(4)	1
Panayiotis CONSTANDINIDES (GRE)	D	20	(1)	2
Christos CHRISTODOULOU	D	10	(8)	1
Erikos CHRISTOPHI	D	21	(2)	1
Andreas DIMITRIOU	M	5	(13)	7
Marios DIMITRIOU	A	20	(2)	
Alexandros GARPOZIS	A		(4)	2
Christos IOANNOU	D	4	(5)	
George IOANNOU	A	2	(4)	
Sasa JOVANOVIC (YUG)	A	6		3
Alvin KIE (LIB)	A	6	(6)	1
Kyriakos KYRIAKOU	M	18	(2)	
Dimitris LEONIS	G	26		
Chrysis MICHAEL	D	26		5
Marios NEOPHYTOU	A	26		20
Michalis PATOUNAS	A	2	(6)	
Pavlos SAVVA	M	19	(3)	1
Andreas SOPHOCLEOUS	D	24		5
Angelos TSOLAKIS	A	8	(9)	4

LEAGUE RESULTS 1998/99

12/09/98	Apollon Limassol	H	2-1	Neophytou (p), Jovanovic
19/09/98	AEK Larnaca	A	1-1	Neophytou
26/09/98	Paralimni	H	0-1	
03/10/98	Aris Limassol	A	4-0	Michael, Sophocleous, Constandinides, Jovanovic
17/10/98	APOEL Nicosia	H	2-1	Neophytou (p), Jovanovic
24/10/98	Olympiakos Nicosia	A	1-0	Neophytou
31/10/98	Nea Salamina Famagusta	H	8-3	Dimitriou 3, Neophytou 2, Sophocleous, Kie, Tsolakis
08/11/98	Alki Larnaca	H	2-2	Neophytou, Michael
21/11/98	Ethnikos Akhna	A	1-2	Christophi
29/11/98	Anorthosis Famagusta	H	2-3	Sophocleous, Neophytou
05/12/98	Evaghoras Paphos	A	0-0	
13/12/98	Omonia Nicosia	H	3-3	Neophytou, Constandinides, Sophocleous
20/12/98	Doxa Katokopia	A	1-0	Tsolakis
09/01/99	AEK Larnaca	H	3-2	Michael 2, Tsolakis
16/01/99	Paralimni	A	2-0	Neophytou 2
23/01/99	Aris Limassol	H	4-1	Neophytou (p), Savva, Dimitriou, Andreou
13/02/99	APOEL Nicosia	A	0-2	
20/02/99	Olympiakos Nicosia	H	4-2	Constandi, Christodoulou, Michael, Andoniou
27/02/99	Nea Salamina Famagusta	A	0-0	
07/03/99	Alki Larnaca	A	3-1	Neophytou, Sophocleous, Dimitriou
14/03/99	Ethnikos Akhna	H	2-3	Neophytou 2 (2p)
20/03/99	Anorthosis Famagusta	A	0-2	
03/04/99	Evaghoras Paphos	H	4-0	Neophytou 2, Tsolakis, Dimitriou
17/04/99	Omonia Nicosia	A	0-3	
25/04/99	Doxa Katokopia	H	4-3	Garpozis 2, Dimitriou, Noophytou
02/05/99	Apollon Limassol	A	2-3	Neophytou 2 (2p)

ALKI LARNACA

CLUB DIRECTORY

Alki FC
23 Loukis Akritas str.
6015 Larnaca
tel - (04) 654099
fax - (04) 652955
Year of Formation - 1948
President - Akis Stavrou
Secretary - George Adamou
Coach - Spas Jevisov; Loizos Mavroudis
Stadium - Zenon (14,000)

APPEARANCES 98/99

	P	Ap	(s)	Gls
Michalis ANDREOU	G	26		
Gustavo ARBELAIZ	M	2	(2)	
Justin BABKO (CMR)	M	23		4
Christos CHAILIS	A	6	(4)	
Nicos CHARALAMBOUS	D	20	(4)	2
Michalis CHRISTOU	M	3	(8)	
Tomis CHRYSOSTOMOU	A	2	(4)	3
Costas CONSTANDINOU	D	25		2
George CONSTANDINOU	M	10	(4)	
Savvas DAMIANOU	A		(5)	
Christos GEORGIOU	M	24	(1)	
Loizos HADJIANDONIS	A	22	(2)	3
Kyriakos HAPERIS	M	6	(8)	
Serge HONI (CMR)	A	26		17
Nicos KARAYIORGIS	M	5	(6)	1
Michael MICHAEL	M	9		
Andreas NICOLAOU	D	19	(2)	1
Nicos NICOLAOU	M	8	(6)	
George PAKOULAS	M	5	(9)	
Andreas PONTIKOS	A	3	(1)	
Andreas YIATROU	A	18	(2)	2
Nicolae ZAMFIR (ROM)	M	24		2

LEAGUE RESULTS 1998/99

13/09/98	Doxa Katokopia	H	2-1	Honi 2
20/09/98	Apollon Limassol	A	1-4	Babko
27/09/98	AEK Larnaca	H	5-4	Honi 2, Yiatrou, Babko, Hadjiandonis
03/10/98	Paralimni	A	1-1	Hadjiandonis
17/10/98	Aris Limassol	H	3-2	Yiatrou, Hadjiandonis, Honi
25/10/98	APOEL Nicosia	A	1-4	Charalambous
01/11/98	Olympiakos Nicosia	H	1-3	Honi (p)
08/11/98	AEL Limassol	A	2-2	Nicolaou A., Zamfir
22/11/98	Nea Salamina Famagusta	H	0-2	
29/11/98	Ethnikos Akhna	H	2-3	Honi (p), Constandinou C.
05/12/98	Anorthosis Famagusta	A	0-5	
12/12/98	Evaghoras Paphos	H	3-1	Honi (p), Chrysostomou 2
18/12/98	Omonia Nicosia	A	0-3	
10/01/99	Apollon Limassol	H	0-2	
17/01/99	AEK Larnaca	A	1-5	Honi (p)
23/01/99	Paralimni	H	2-2	Honi, Chrysostomou
14/02/99	Aris Limassol	A	4-1	Honi 2 (1p), Babko, Constandinou C.
25/02/99	APOEL Nicosia	H	0-6	
27/02/99	Olympiakos Nicosia	A	2-2	Honi (p), Charalambous
06/03/99	AEL Limassol	H	1-3	Babko
13/03/99	Nea Salamina Famagusta	A	2-1	Honi, Karayiorgis
20/03/99	Ethnikos Akhna	A	0-2	
03/04/99	Anorthosis Famagusta	H	0-4	
18/04/99	Evaghoras Paphos	A	2-0	Honi 2
24/04/99	Omonia Nicosia	H	1-4	Honi
02/05/99	Doxa Katokopia	A	1-3	Zamfir

ANORTHOSIS FAMAGUSTA

CLUB DIRECTORY

Anorthosis FC of Famagusta
Stadio Andonis Papadopoulos
6053 Larnaca
tel - (04) 635834
fax - (04) 635833
Year of Formation - 1911
President - Kikis Constandinou
Secretary - Christakis Pittas
Coach - Dusan Mitosevic
Stadium - Andonis Papadopoulos (11,000)

MAJOR HONOURS
League Championship - (10) 1950, 1957, 1958,
1960, 1962, 1963, 1995, 1997, 1998, 1999.
Domestic Cup - (6)
1949, 1962, 1963, 1971, 1975, 1998.

APPEARANCES 98/99

	P	Ap	(s)	Gls
Pambis ANDREOU	A	14	(10)	12
Zacharias CHARALAMBOUS	D	21		1
Panayiotis ENGOMITIS	M	17	(3)	3
Stavros FOUKARIS	D	19	(3)	
Kyriakos HAILIS	M		(3)	1
Dimitris IOANNOU	D	18	(4)	3
George IOSIPHIDES	A	16	(4)	
Tassos KARSERAS	M		(4)	
Slobodan KRCMAREVIC (YUG)	A	13	(1)	19
Lambros LAMBROU	M	10	(9)	
Lucas LUCA	D	11	(4)	2
Vassos MELANARKITIS	D	21	(2)	3
Vesko MIHAJLOVIC (YUG)	A	26		20
Yiannakis OKKAS	A	25		15
Nicos PANAYIOTOU	G	26		
Panikos POUNAS	M	13	(6)	
Andros SOTIRIOU	A	8	(12)	9
Panayiotis SPYROU	D	8	(10)	
Savavs THOUPOS	M		(3)	
Vladan TOMIC (YUG)	M	20		4

LEAGUE RESULTS 1998/99

11/09/98	Evaghoras Paphos	H	6-1	Krcmarevic (p), Luca, Engomitis, Ioannou, Okkas, Andreou
20/09/98	Omonia Nicosia	A	1-1	Okkas
25/09/98	Doxa Katokopia	H	7-0	Krcmarevic 2, Okkas, Mihajlovic, Tomic, Andreou, Sotiriou
04/10/98	Apollon Limassol	A	3-1	Krcmarevic 3
18/10/98	AEK Larnaca	H	1-0	Krcmarevic
24/10/98	Paralimni	A	5-2	Mihajlovic, Melanarkitis, Okkas, Krcmarevic, Andreou
31/10/98	Aris Limassol	H	5-0	og (Longras), Krcmarevic, Mihajlovic, Okkas, Melanarkitis
07/11/98	APOEL Nicosia	A	3-4	Engomitis, Mihajlovic 2 (1p)
22/11/98	Olympiakos Nicosia	H	7-1	Krcmarevic 4, Okkas 2, Mihajlovic
29/11/98	AEL Limassol	A	3-2	Okkas, Mihajlovic, Krcmarevic (p)
05/12/98	Alki Larnaca	H	5-0	Mihajlovic, Krcmarevic 3, Tomic
12/12/98	Ethnikos Akhna	A	2-0	Okkas 2
20/12/98	Nea Salamina Famagusta	H	5-3	Krcmarevic 2, Mihajlovic 2, og (Nicolaou)
09/01/99	Omonia Nicosia	H	2-2	Melanarkitis, Ioannou
16/01/99	Doxa Katokopia	A	4-0	Engomitis, Okkas, Luca, Sotiriou
23/01/99	Apollon Limassol	H	4-2	Andreou 2 (2p), Sotiriou 2
13/02/99	AEK Larnaca	A	3-3	Mihajlovic 2, Sotiriou
20/02/99	Paralimni	H	5-1	Mihajlovic, Okkas, Charalambous, Hailis, Tomic
28/02/99	Aris Limassol	A	4-1	Andreou 3 (1p), Mihajlovic
06/03/99	APOEL Nicosia	H	1-1	Mihajlovic
14/03/99	Olympiakos Nicosia	A	4-1	Andreou, Sotiriou, Okkas, Mihajlovic
20/03/99	AEL Limassol	H	2-0	Mihajlovic (p), Okkas
03/04/99	Alki Larnaca	A	4-0	og (Christou), Tomic, Andreou 2
17/04/99	Ethnikos Akhna	H	2-0	Mihajlovic, Sotiriou
24/04/99	Nea Salamina Famagusta	A	3-2	Okkas, Ioannou, Mihajlovic
02/05/99	Evaghoras Paphos	A	4-0	Andreou, Mihajlovic, Sotiriou 2

APOEL NICOSIA

CLUB DIRECTORY

APOEL Football Co.
12 Michalakopoulou
1075 Nicosia
tel - (02) 760424
fax - (02) 762497
Year of Formation - 1926
President - Chris Triantafilides
Secretary - Phivos Constandinides
Coach - George Parashos; Slobodan Vucekovic
(99/00 - Andreas Michaelides)
Stadium - Makarion (22,000)

MAJOR HONOURS
League Championship - (16) 1936, 1937, 1938,
1939, 1940, 1947, 1948, 1949, 1952, 1965,
1973, 1980, 1986, 1990, 1992, 1996.
Domestic Cup - (17) 1937, 1941, 1947, 1951,
1963, 1968, 1969, 1973, 1976, 1978, 1979,
1984, 1993, 1995, 1996, 1997, 1999.

APPEARANCES 98/99

	P	Ap	(s)	Gls
Alexis ALEXANDROU	A	4	(9)	2
George ALONEFTIS	A	9	(3)	4
Aristos ARISTOCLEOUS	M	20		2
Xenios ARISTOTELOUS	D	13	(3)	1
Costas COSTA	D	9	(2)	3
George CHRISTODOULOU	D	24		1
Marios ELIA	M		(2)	
Lucas HADJILUCAS	M	8	(11)	3
Yiannos IOANNOU	A	18	(3)	11
Robert KOCIS (SVK)	A	17	(1)	12
MARCELO Veridiano (BRA)	A	23		13
Michalis MORFIS	G	4		
Marios PANAYIOTOU	D	1	(5)	1
Miloje PETKOVIC (YUG)	M	23		4
Andros PETRIDES	G	22		
Petros PETROU	M	19	(3)	
Costas PHASOULIOTIS	M	2	(4)	1
Marinos SATSIAS	D	17	(2)	1
Costas STAVROU	D	20		
Andreas STEPHANOU	D	13	(8)	
Nicos TIMOTHEOU	D	8	(4)	
Yiosemis YIASEMAKIS	A	12	(8)	11

LEAGUE RESULTS 1998/99

12/09/98	Paralimni	H	2-2	Ioannou, Yiasemakis
19/09/98	Aris Limassol	A	4-1	Ioannou 3, Petkovic
27/09/98	Nea Salamina Famagusta	H	3-0	Costa, Ioannou, Aristotelous
03/10/98	Olympiakos Nicosia	H	2-0	Christodoulou, Yiasemakis
17/10/98	AEL Limassol	A	1-2	Kocis
25/10/98	Alki Larnaca	H	4-1	Marcelo 2, Kocis, Ioannou
31/10/98	Ethnikos Akhna	A	3-2	Kocis, Marcelo 2 (1p)
07/11/98	Anorthosis Famagusta	H	4-3	Marcelo 2 (2p), Kocis 2
22/11/98	Evaghoras Paphos	A	3-2	Marcelo (p), Petkovic, Kocis
28/11/98	Omonia Nicosia	H	1-2	Costa
05/12/98	Doxa Katokopia	A	4-0	Aristocleous, Ioannou, Phasouliotis, Kocis (p)
12/12/98	Apollon Limassol	H	1-0	Marcelo
19/12/98	AEK Larnaca	A	1-3	Costa
10/01/99	Aris Limassol	H	5-2	Ioannou, Aloneftis, Yiasemakis, Marcelo 2
16/01/99	Nea Salamina Famagusta	A	1-0	Kocis
24/01/99	Olympiakos Nicosia	A	5-0	Yiasemakis 2, Ioannou 2, Marcelo
14/02/99	AEL Limassol	H	2-0	Marcelo 2 (1p)
25/02/99	Alki Larnaca	A	6-0	Hadjilucas 2, Kocis 2, Yiasemakis, Aloneftis
28/02/99	Ethnikos Akhna	H	1-0	Yiasemakis
06/03/99	Anorthosis Famagusta	A	1-1	Yiasemakis
13/03/99	Evaghoras Paphos	H	4-1	Yiasemakis 2, Aloneftis, Petkovic
20/03/99	Omonia Nicosia	A	0-1	
04/04/99	Doxa Katokopia	H	3-0	Petkovic, Hadjilucas, Panayiotou
17/04/99	Apollon Limassol	A	1-2	Alexandrou
25/04/99	AEK Larnaca	H	3-1	Satsias, Alexandrou, Yiasemakis
02/05/99	Paralimni	A	5-3	Kocis 2, Aristocleous, Ioannou, Aloneftis

APOLLON LIMASSOL

CLUB DIRECTORY

Apollon FC
1 Mesolongiou Str.
PO Box 53206
Limassol
tel - (05) 363702/379082
fax - (05) 359116
Year of Formation - 1954
President - Frixos Savvides
Secretary - George Papas
Coach - Dumitru Dumitriu; Dieter Ferner
Stadium - Tsirion (20,000)

MAJOR HONOURS
League Championship - (2) 1991, 1994.
Domestic Cup - (4) 1966, 1967, 1986, 1992.

APPEARANCES 98/99

	P	Ap	(s)	Gls
Sofronis AVGOUSTI	G	8		
Florin CÂRSTEA (ROM)	M	19	(3)	4
Costas CONSTANDINOU	D	8	(3)	4
Marios CHARALAMBOUS	D	23		2
Christos GERMANOS	D	23		3
Chrysostomos JURAS	D	18		1
George KAIS	D	5	(10)	1
Loizos KAKOYIANNIS	M		(1)	
George KAVAZIS	M	16		3
Alexandros MICHAEL	G	18		
Nebojsa MLADENOVIC (YUG)	A	11	(8)	1
Andreas PANAYIOTOU	M	12	(2)	2
Marios PANAYIOTOU	D	3	(1)	
Nikodemos PAPAVASILIOU	M	13	(3)	6
Philippos PHILIPPOU	D	19	(2)	2
Pambos PITTAS	D	26		3
Costas SOLOMOU	A		(2)	
Milenko SPOLJARIC	M	21		12
Ion SBURLEA (ROM)	M	1		1
Marios THEMISTOCLEOUS	A	19	(6)	4
Christos THEOPHILOU	D	7	(2)	
Stephanos VOSKARIDES	A	16	(7)	1

LEAGUE RESULTS 1998/99

12/09/98	AEL Limassol	A	1-2	Sburlea
20/09/98	Alki Larnaca	H	4-1	og (Pontikos), Constandinou, Voskarides, Kavazis
26/09/98	Ethnikos Akhna	A	1-6	Kavazis
04/10/98	Anorthosis Famagusta	H	1-3	Spoljaric (p)
17/10/98	Evaghoras Paphos	A	1-2	Kavazis
25/10/98	Omonia Nicosia	H	1-5	Mladenovic
31/10/98	Doxa Katokopia	A	2-1	Philippou, Themistocleous
08/11/98	Nea Salamina Famagusta	A	2-2	Pittas, Papavasiliou (p)
21/11/98	AEK Larnaca	H	5-0	Spoljaric 3 (2p), Papavasiliou (p), Themistocleous
28/11/98	Paralimni	A	1-1	Spoljaric
05/12/98	Aris Limassol	H	2-1	Charalambous, Germanos
12/12/98	APOEL Nicosia	A	0-1	
19/12/98	Olympiakos Nicosia	H	1-0	Germanos
10/01/99	Alki Larnaca	A	2-0	Constandinou, Papavasiliou
16/01/99	Ethnikos Akhna	H	1-2	Germanos
23/01/99	Anorthosis Famagusta	A	2-4	Juras, Spoljaric (p)
13/02/99	Evaghoras Paphos	H	2-0	Spoljaric (p), Themistocleous
21/02/99	Omonia Nicosia	A	0-2	
27/02/99	Doxa Katokopia	H	5-2	Cârstea 2, Philippou, Panayiotou A., Constandinou
06/03/99	Nea Salamina Famagusta	H	1-2	Papavasiliou
14/03/99	AEK Larnaca	A	5-3	Pittas 2, Cârstea 2, Constandinou
20/03/99	Paralimni	H	1-0	Papavasiliou
04/04/99	Aris Limassol	A	5-0	Spoljaric, Charalambous, Papavasiliou, Themistocleous, Panayiotou A.
17/04/99	APOEL Nicosia	H	2-1	Kais, Spoljaric (p)
24/04/99	Olympiakos Nicosia	A	0-2	
02/05/99	AEL Limassol	H	3-2	Spoljaric 3 (1p)

ARIS LIMASSOL

CLUB DIRECTORY

Aris FC
1 A. Sikelianou str.
3085 Limassol
tel - (05) 382075/381076
fax - (05) 379689
Year of Formation - 1930
President - Doros Ieropoulos
Secretary - Charalambos Illambas
Coach - Dimos Kareklas (99/00 - Andreas
Kissonergis)
Stadium - Tsirion (22,000)

APPEARANCES 98/99

	P	Ap	(s)	Gls
Dimitris AGISILAOU	D	6	(8)	
Alekos ALEKOU	M		(1)	
Theophilos ATHANASIOU	G	17		
Panikos CHARALAMBOUS	D	2	(2)	
George DIMITRIADES	M	14	(1)	3
Marios DIMOSTHENOUS	M	10	(10)	
Christos HADJICONSTANDIS	D	19	(1)	
Kyriakos KAFKALIAS	M	17	(1)	
Lambros LAMBROU	M	13	(6)	3
Loyd LISLEVAND (NOR)	A	7		
Stelios LONGRAS	D	18	(1)	2
Dimitris MICHAELIDES	M		(2)	
Jovo MISELJIC (YUG)	M	14		3
Dimitris NEOPHYTOU	A	5	(3)	
Andonis NICOLAOU	A	19	(2)	8
Marios NICOLAOU	M	6	(1)	
Nana OWUSU (GHA)	A	10		
Panayiotis PANAYIOTOU	A	3	(2)	1
Kyriakos PAPAKYRIAKOU	M	15	(3)	3
George PETASIS	M	19	(2)	
Iosiph PIERI	A		(3)	
Marios STAVRINIDES	G	9		
Stavros STAVROU	D	10	(4)	
Stelios TRATTOS	A	5	(3)	4
Yiannis VASSILIOU	D	16		
Avgoustinos YENNARIS	D	12	(7)	4
Christos ZINONOS	D	20	(3)	1

LEAGUE RESULTS 1998/99

13/09/98	Nea Salamina Famagusta	H	3-1	Miseljic 2, Zinonos
19/09/98	APOEL Nicosia	H	1-4	Lambrou
26/09/98	Olympiakos Nicosia	A	0-4	
03/10/98	AEL Limassol	H	0-4	
17/10/98	Alki Larnaca	A	2-3	Nicolaou 2
24/10/98	Ethnikos Akhna	H	1-3	Yennaris
31/10/98	Anorthosis Famagusta	A	0-5	
07/11/98	Evaghoras Paphos	H	2-4	Nicolaou A., Miseljic (p)
22/11/98	Omonia Nicosia	A	1-5	Nicolaou A.
28/11/98	Doxa Katokopia	H	2-1	Lambrou, Papakyriakou
05/12/98	Apollon Limassol	A	1-2	Papakyriakou
12/12/98	AEK Larnaca	H	1-2	Dimitriades
19/12/98	Paralimni	A	2-6	Dimitriades 2
10/01/99	APOEL Nicosia	A	2-5	Nicolaou A., Lambrou
17/01/99	Olympiakos Nicosia	H	0-2	
23/01/99	AEL Limassol	A	1-4	Yennaris
14/02/99	Alki Larnaca	H	1-4	Papakyriakou (p)
20/02/99	Ethnikos Akhna	A	2-3	Nicolaou A., Panayiotou
28/02/99	Anorthosis Famagusta	H	1-4	Nicolaou A.
06/03/99	Evaghoras Paphos	A	2-5	Nicolaou A., Trattos
13/03/99	Omonia Nicosia	H	0-4	
21/03/99	Doxa Katokopia	A	1-5	Yennaris
04/04/99	Apollon Limassol	H	0-5	
17/04/99	AEK Larnaca	A	1-5	Yennaris
24/04/99	Paralimni	H	2-4	Trattos 2
02/05/99	Nea Salamina Famagusta	A	3-2	Longras 2, Trattos

DOXA KATOKOPIA

CLUB DIRECTORY

Doxa Katokopia FC
P.O. Box 28293
Nicosia
tel - (02) 821929
fax - (02) 368186
Year of Formation - 1954
President - Photis Yiannakas
Secretary - Stavros Loizou
Coach - Evaghoras Christophi; Akis Ayiomammitis
Stadium - Kykkos (3,000)

APPEARANCES 98/99

	P	Ap	(s)	Gls
Andonis ANDONIOU	M	25		2
Panikos ARGYROU	M	4	(18)	1
Pambos CHRISTODOULOU	A	17		2
Evaghoras CHRISTOPHI	M	18		
Marios CHRISTOPHI	D	20		
George CHRISTOPHOROU	G	16		
Robert CLARK (ENG)	A	7	(1)	
Dimitris DIMITRIOU	M	20	(3)	2
George GEORGIOU	D		(4)	
Sasa ILIC (YUG)	A	19	(1)	5
Irotodos IROTODOU	D	21	(1)	
Stavros KALLIS	A	5	(5)	1
Andreas KYRIAKOU	D	10	(1)	1
Stelios MAVROFTIS	A	21	(1)	6
Kyriakos MITSINGAS	A	13	(2)	
Andreas MYLONAS	D		(3)	
Neoclis NEOCLEOUS	G	9		
Neophytos NEOPHYTOU	D		(3)	
Ioannis NICOLAOU	G	1		
Stelios OKKARIDES	M	16	(6)	1
Nicos PANAYIOTIDES (GRE)	D	11		
Lucas PHILIPPOU	A		(1)	
Marios POHOUZOURIS	M	19	(2)	5
Loizos POLYVIOU	A	14	(2)	
Yianns VASSILIADES	M		(2)	
Danos YERLEMIDES	M		(1)	

LEAGUE RESULTS 1998/99

13/09/98	Alki Larnaca	A	1-2	Kallis
19/09/98	Ethnikos Akhna	H	0-0	
25/09/98	Anorthosis Famagusta	A	0-7	
04/10/98	Evaghoras Paphos	H	0-0	
17/10/98	Omonia Nicosia	A	0-1	
25/10/98	Nea Salamina Famagusta	A	0-2	
31/10/98	Apollon Limassol	H	1-2	Christodoulou
07/11/98	AEK Larnaca	A	0-7	
21/11/98	Paralimni	H	4-5	Pohouzouris, Mavroftis 2, Christodoulou (p)
28/11/98	Aris Limassol	A	1-2	Pohouzouris
05/12/98	APOEL Nicosia	H	0-4	
13/12/98	Olympiakos Nicosia	A	0-4	
20/12/98	AEL Limassol	H	0-1	
09/01/99	Ethnikos Akhna	A	0-0	
16/01/99	Anorthosis Famagusta	H	0-4	
23/01/99	Evaghoras Paphos	A	0-4	
14/02/99	Omonia Nicosia	H	2-3	Mavroftis, Pohouzouris
20/02/99	Nea Salamina Famagusta	H	0-2	
27/02/99	Apollon Limassol	A	2-5	Mavroftis, Pohouzouris
07/03/99	AEK Larnaca	H	1-5	Ilic
13/03/99	Paralimni	A	3-5	Pohouzouris, Ilic, Mavroftis
21/03/99	Aris Limassol	H	5-1	Ilic, Andoniou, Kyriakou, Dimitriou, og (Zinonos)
04/04/99	APOEL Nicosia	A	0-3	
18/04/99	Olympiakos Nicosia	H	1-4	Andoniou
25/04/99	AEL Limassol	A	3-4	Argyrou, Dimitriou, Ilic
02/05/99	Alki Larnaca	H	3-1	Okkarides, Ilic, Mavroftis

ETHNIKOS AKHNA

CLUB DIRECTORY

Ethnikos FC of Akhna
Dasaki Akhna
tel - (04) 721302
fax - (04) 722060
Year of Formation - 1968
President - Kikis Philippou
Secretary - Costas Constantinides
Coach - Andreas Kissonergis (99/00 - Moca Vukotic)
Stadium - Dasaki (8,000)

APPEARANCES 98/99

	P	Ap	(s)	Gls
Chrysaphis CHRYSAPHI	M		(13)	1
Kenny DYER (ENG)	M	14	(2)	
Dimitris DIMITRIOU	D	15	(2)	
Stavros GEORGIOU	A	22	(1)	3
Borce GJUREV (MAC)	A	13	(1)	7
Dimitris KARAPASHIS	D	7	(6)	
Spyros KASTANAS	D	15	(5)	
Andreas KATZIS	D	23		
Liasis LIASI	M	12	(7)	2
Dragan MUSIC (YUG)	A	24		16
Panikos NEOCLEOUS	A	23	(1)	11
Christos PASHIALIS	D	26		
Marios PASHIALIS	D	26		2
Christos PHOULIS	D	18		1
Christos POYIATZIS	M	17	(1)	4
Nicos SATSIAS	A	2	(9)	1
Dimitris SERGIOU	M	1	(8)	
Michalis SHIMITRAS	G	26		
Nicos SOPHOCLEOUS	A	2	(4)	

LEAGUE RESULTS 1998/99

12/09/98	Omonia Nicosia	H	2-4	Music (p), Pashialis M.
19/09/98	Doxa Katokopia	A	0-0	
26/09/98	Apollon Limassol	H	6-1	Neocleous 2, Gjurev, Georgiou, Poyiatzis, Music
04/10/98	AEK Larnaca	A	5-2	Gjurev 3, Poyiatzis, Music
17/10/98	Paralimni	H	1-1	Neocleous
24/10/98	Aris Limassol	A	3-1	Gjurev 2 (1p), Neocleous
31/10/98	APOEL Nicosia	H	2-3	Music, Gjurev (p)
08/11/98	Olympiakos Nicosia	A	1-1	Georgiou
21/11/98	AEL Limassol	H	2-1	Music, Neocleous
29/11/98	Alki Larnaca	A	3-2	Liasi (p), Music, Neocleous (p)
05/12/98	Nea Salamina Famagusta	H	2-3	Neocleous, Pashialis M.
12/12/98	Anorthosis Famagusta	H	0-2	
19/12/98	Evaghoras Paphos	A	2-1	Georgiou, Satsias
09/01/99	Doxa Katokopia	H	0-0	
16/01/99	Apollon Limassol	A	2-1	Neocleous, Music
23/01/99	AEK Larnaca	H	1-1	Phoulis
13/02/99	Paralimni	A	6-3	Music 2 (1p), Neocleous 2, Chrysaphi, og (Loizou)
20/02/99	Aris Limassol	H	3-2	Liasi, Music, Neocleous
28/02/99	APOEL Nicosia	A	0-1	
06/03/99	Olympiakos Nicosia	H	1-1	Music (p)
14/03/99	AEL Limassol	A	3-2	Poyiatzis 2, Music (p)
20/03/99	Alki Larnaca	H	2-0	Music 2
04/04/99	Nea Salamina Famagusta	A	0-4	
17/04/99	Anorthosis Famagusta	A	0-2	
24/04/99	Evaghoras Paphos	H	2-0	Music 2 (2p)
02/05/99	Omonia Nicosia	A	0-4	

EVAGHORAS PAPHOS

CLUB DIRECTORY

Evaghoras FC
36 E. Pallikarides str.
8010 Paphos
tel - (06) 232550
fax - (06) 246301
Year of Formation - 1961
President - George Hadjikyriakos
Secretary - Andreas Komodromos
Coach - Phytos Neophytou
Stadium - Paphiako (8,000)

APPEARANCES 98/99

		P	Ap	(s)	Gls
Sinisa BERTOVIC (YUG)	M	17	(2)		4
Dinos CONSTANDINOU	G	19			
Stevo DRAGISIC (YUG)	A	19			7
Marinos IACOVOU	M	10	(11)		2
Panayiotis HADJIANDONIS	A	8	(14)		2
Kyriakos IGNATIOU	D	13	(1)		
Yiannakis IOANNOU	D		(2)		
Dimitris IRODOTOU	D	8	(7)		
Branko KOKOL (YUG)	A	19	(1)		1
Kyriakos LYSANDROU	M	1			
Michael MICHAEL	D	6	(5)		
Dimos NEOPHYTOU	G	7			
Nicos NICOLAOU	G		(1)		
Yiannis PAHTALIAS	A	21	(1)		5
Panikos PAPADOPOULOS	M	20	(2)		1
Panikos PHILIOTIS	A	21	(1)		4
Andreas POLYDOROU	D	22			
Costas PRODROMOU	D		(2)		
George SAMPSON	A		(11)		
Savvas SAVVA	D	18	(3)		
Costas SOCRATOUS	M	11			
Lucas SOCRATOUS	M	10	(5)		
Yiannakis SYMEOU	D		(4)		
Marios TSIAKKAS	D	17	(2)		
Nicos VARNAVIDES	A	19	(5)		4

LEAGUE RESULTS 1998/99

11/09/98	Anorthosis Famagusta	A	1-6	Dragisic
20/09/98	Nea Salamina Famagusta	A	1-4	Philiotis
26/09/98	Omonia Nicosia	H	1-8	Dragisic
04/10/98	Doxa Katokopia	A	0-0	
17/10/98	Apollon Limassol	H	2-1	Papadopoulos, Varnavides
24/10/98	AEK Larnaca	A	0-2	
31/10/98	Paralimni	H	1-1	Pahtalias
07/11/98	Aris Limassol	A	4-2	Dragisic 3 (1p), Pahtalias
22/11/98	APOEL Nicosia	H	2-3	Philiotis, Dragisic (p)
29/11/98	Olympiakos Nicosia	A	1-2	Iacovou
05/12/98	AEL Limassol	H	0-0	
12/12/98	Alki Larnaca	A	1-3	Bertovic
19/12/98	Ethnikos Akhna	H	1-2	Bertovic
09/01/99	Nea Salamina Famagusta	H	0-0	
17/01/99	Omonia Nicosia	A	1-6	Kokol
23/01/99	Doxa Katokopia	H	4-0	Bertovic 2, Hadjiandonis 2
13/02/99	Apollon Limassol	A	0-2	
20/02/99	AEK Larnaca	H	2-0	Philiotis, Varnavides
27/02/99	Paralimni	A	1-6	Pahtalias
06/03/99	Aris Limassol	H	5-2	Iacovou, Pahtalias, Philiotis,
				Varnavides, Dragisic
13/03/99	APOEL Nicosia	A	1-4	Varnavides
21/03/99	Olympiakos Nicosia	H	1-0	Pahtalias (p)
03/04/99	AEL Limassol	A	0-4	
18/04/99	Alki Larnaca	H	0-2	
24/04/99	Ethnikos Akhna	A	0-2	
02/05/99	Anorthosis Famagusta	H	0-4	

NEA SALAMINA FAMAGUSTA

CLUB DIRECTORY

Nea Salamina FC of Famagusta
Stadio Ammohostos
4 Rangavi
6047 Larnaca
tel - (04) 652317/663090
fax - (04) 663228
Year of Formation - 1948
President - Christakis Poliviou
Secretary - Pambos Stylianou
Coach - Andreas Mouskalis
(99/00 - Slobodan Vucekovic)
Stadium - Ammohostos (8,000)

APPEARANCES 98/99

	P	Ap	(s)	Gls
Adamos ADAMOU	D	15	(2)	1
Andonis AFXENTIS	M	9	(3)	
Nicos ANDREOU	D	13		1
Andreas ANGELI	D	4	(15)	3
Pantelis DIMITRIOU	M	9	(7)	
George ELIA	A	12		3
Paris ELIA	M	20		2
Andreas IOANNIDES	D	19	(2)	2
Liasos LUCA	M	8	(8)	
Andreas LONGRIDES	G	6		
Andonis LYSANDROU	G	1	(1)	
Alkis MARKOU	G	19		
Michael MICHAEL	M	10	(1)	
Mirko MIHIC (YUG)	A	23		18
Floros NICOLAOU	D	13		
Nicos A. NICOLAOU	M	21	(2)	2
Nicos K. NICOLAOU	D	12	(12)	3
Andreas PANAYIOTOU	M	22		
Tasos PORPHYRIOU	D	4	(6)	
Elisseos PSARAS	D	8	(1)	
Dejan STOIC (YUG)	A	14	(11)	4
Nouro TELAPUTIN (MOZ)	A	24	(2)	7

LEAGUE RESULTS 1998/99

13/09/98	Aris Limassol	A	1-3	Mihic (p)
20/09/98	Evaghoras Paphos	H	4-1	Mihic 2, Telaputin, Stoic
27/09/98	APOEL Nicosia	A	0-3	
03/10/98	Omonia Nicosia	H	2-3	Mihic, Nicolaou N.K.
18/10/98	Olympiakos Nicosia	A	1-2	Nicolaou N.K.
25/10/98	Doxa Katokopia	H	2-0	Mihic (p), Telaputin
31/10/98	AEL Limassol	A	3-8	Mihic 2 (2p), Elia P.
08/11/98	Apollon Limassol	H	2-2	Elia P., Mihic
22/11/98	Alki Larnaca	A	2-0	Nicolaou N.A., Ioannides
28/11/98	AEK Larnaca	H	0-1	
05/12/98	Ethnikos Akhna	A	3-2	Stoic, Nicolaou N.K., Angeli
13/12/98	Paralimni	H	4-5	Mihic 2 (2p), Elia G., Andreou
20/12/98	Anorthosis Famagusta	A	3-5	Telaputin 2, Mihic
09/01/99	Evaghoras Paphos	A	0-0	
16/01/99	APOEL Nicosia	H	0-1	
23/01/99	Omonia Nicosia	A	1-4	Mihic (p)
14/02/99	Olympiakos Nicosia	H	0-0	
20/02/99	Doxa Katokopia	A	3-0	Telaputin 2, Nicolaou N.A.
27/02/99	AEL Limassol	H	0-0	
06/03/99	Apollon Limassol	A	2-1	Mihic 2
13/03/99	Alki Larnaca	H	1-2	Mihic
20/03/99	AEK Larnaca	A	1-4	Stoic
04/04/99	Ethnikos Akhna	H	4-0	Stoic, Adamou, Telaputin, Mihic
18/04/99	Paralimni	A	3-0	Eliu G. 2, Ioannides
24/04/99	Anorthosis Famagusta	H	2-3	Mihic, Angeli
02/05/99	Aris Limassol	H	2-3	Angeli, Mihic (p)

OLYMPIAKOS NICOSIA

CLUB DIRECTORY

Olympiakos FC
6A Athinas str.
1021 Nicosia
tel - (02) 430405/348337
fax - (02) 466292
Year of Formation - 1931
President - Christos Hadjitophis
Secretary - George Hadjisavvas
Coach - Slobodan Dogantic
(99/00 - Ronnie Whelan)
Stadium - Makarion (20,000)

MAJOR HONOURS
League Championship - (3) 1967, 1969, 1971.
Domestic Cup - (1) 1977.

APPEARANCES 98/99

	P	Ap	(s)	Gls
Akis APOSTOLOU	M	22	(2)	
Dimitris ASHIOTIS	M	22	(1)	3
Andreas AVLONITIS	A	20	(3)	3
Elias CHRYSOSTOMOU	D	9	(7)	2
Zoran CIRIC (YUG)	A	21	(1)	10
Costas CONSTANDINOU	D	2	(10)	
Renos DIMITRIADES	M	3	(7)	2
Thomas KAPSALIS	M		(9)	
Michalis KAVELIS	G	4	(1)	
Digran KAZATZIAN	M	13	(5)	2
Marios MARKOU	D	23		1
Andros MELANARKITIS	D	21		
Marios NICOLAOU	A		(3)	
Dragan NIKOLIC (YUG)	D	23		1
Miloje PETKOVSKI (YUG)	A	21		14
Philippos PHILIPPOU	M	6	(7)	
Petros SAVVA	G	22		
Nicos STAVROU	D	23		
Savvas TSIAKLIS	D	22		2
Michalis TZIAPOURAS	D	9	(6)	
Marios YIANNAS	M		(2)	

LEAGUE RESULTS 1998/99

13/09/98	AEK Larnaca	H	1-2	Ciric
19/09/98	Paralimni	A	0-2	
26/09/98	Aris Limassol	H	4-0	Ciric 3, Avlonitis
03/10/98	APOEL Nicosia	A	0-2	
18/10/98	Nea Salamina Famagusta	H	2-1	Petkovski 2
24/10/98	AEL Limassol	H	0-1	
01/11/98	Alki Larnaca	A	3-1	Avlonitis 2, Petkovski (p)
08/11/98	Ethnikos Akhna	H	1-1	Ciric
22/11/98	Anorthosis Famagusta	A	1-7	Petkovski (p)
29/11/98	Evaghoras Paphos	H	2-1	Ciric, Ashiotis
05/12/98	Omonia Nicosia	A	4-5	Petkovski 3, Dimitriades
13/12/98	Doxa Katokopia	H	4-0	Petkovski 2 (1p), Ashiotis, Dimitriades
19/12/98	Apollon Limassol	A	0-1	
09/01/99	Paralimni	H	2-2	Ciric, Petkovski (p)
17/01/99	Aris Limassol	A	2-0	Chrysostomou, Markou
24/01/99	APOEL Nicosia	H	0-5	
14/02/99	Nea Salamina Famagusta	A	0-0	
21/02/99	AEL Limassol	A	2-4	Chrysostomou, Ashiotis
27/02/99	Alki Larnaca	H	2-2	Tsiaklis, Ciric
06/03/99	Ethnikos Akhna	A	1-1	Nikolic
14/03/99	Anorthosis Famagusta	H	1-4	Tsiaklis
21/03/99	Evaghoras Paphos	A	0-1	
07/04/99	Omonia Nicosia	H	0-1	
18/04/99	Doxa Katokopia	A	4-1	Petkovski 3, Ciric
24/04/99	Apollon Limassol	H	2-0	Kazatzian 2
02/05/99	AEK Larnaca	A	2-4	Ciric, Petkovski

OMONIA NICOSIA

CLUB DIRECTORY

Omonia FC
5 Papanicoli Str.
PO Box 617
1077 Nicosia
tel - (02) 377377
fax - (02) 377496
Year of Formation - 1948
President - Lakis Polykarpou
Secretary - Savvas Nicolaou
Coach - Andreas Michaelides
(99/00 - Dusan Galis)
Stadium - Makarion (20,000)

MAJOR HONOURS
League Championship - (17) 1961, 1966, 1972,
1974, 1975, 1976, 1977, 1978, 1979, 1981,
1982, 1983, 1984, 1985, 1987, 1989, 1993.
Domestic Cup - (10) 1965, 1972, 1974, 1980,
1981, 1982, 1983, 1988, 1991, 1994.

APPEARANCES 98/99

	P	Ap	(s)	Gls
Sakis ANDREOU	M	6	(5)	
Andros CHRISTOPHI	G	11		
George CONSTANDINIDES	M	14	(2)	
Nicolas GEORGIOU	D	20	(2)	3
Ioakim IOAKIM	D	22	(1)	2
Costas KAIAΓAS	M	20	(1)	3
Costas KALOTHEOU	D	7	(2)	
Yiannos KALOTHEOU	D	10		
Boban KITANOV (YUG)	A	18	(2)	16
Petros KONAFIS	D	12	(4)	1
Lefteris KONTOLEFTEROS	M	8	(10)	6
Nicos LOIZIDES	D	3		
Costas MALEKKOS	A	23	(1)	8
Spyros MARANGOS (GRE)	M	17	(1)	2
Charis NICOLAOU	M	19	(2)	1
Nicos NICOLAOU	M	9	(3)	
Odyseas ODYSEOS	D	2	(5)	2
Christos PANAYIOTOU	M	4	(5)	
Yiotis PANAYIOTOU	D	14		
Yiannakis PONTIKOS	A	8	(13)	
Rainer RAUFFMANN (GER)	A	24		35
Tasos YIALLOURIS	G	15		

LEAGUE RESULTS 1998/99

12/09/98	Ethnikos Akhna	A	4-2	Rauffmann 4 (1p)
20/09/98	Anorthosis Famagusta	H	1-1	Rauffmann
26/09/98	Evaghoras Paphos	A	8-1	Kitanov 3, Rauffmann 2,
				Kontolefteros 2, Kaiafas
03/10/98	Nea Salamina Famagusta	A	3-2	Georgiou, Rauffmann (p), Kitanov
17/10/98	Doxa Katokopia	H	1-0	Kitanov
25/10/98	Apollon Limassol	A	5-1	Rauffmann 3, Malekkos, Kitanov
01/11/98	AEK Larnaca	H	0-1	
07/11/98	Paralimni	A	1-1	Malekkos
22/11/98	Aris Limassol	H	5-1	Rauffmann 2 (2p), Kitanov,
				Kaiafas, Kontolefteros
28/11/98	APOEL Nicosia	A	2-1	Malekkos, Rauffmann (p)
06/12/98	Olympiakos Nicosia	H	5-4	og (Stavrou), Kitanov 2,
				og (Petkovski), Rauffmann
13/12/98	AEL Limassol	A	3-3	Kitanov, Kaiafas, Malekkos
19/12/98	Alki Larnaca	H	3-0	Malekkos, Kitanov, Rauffmann
09/01/99	Anorthosis Famagusta	A	2-2	Malekkos, Rauffmann (p)
17/01/99	Evaghoras Paphos	H	6-1	Rauffmann 3, Marangos,
				Georgiou, Odyseos
23/01/99	Nea Salamina Famagusta	H	4-1	Rauffmann 2 (2p), Malekkos,
				Kitanov
14/02/99	Doxa Katokopia	A	3-2	Rauffmann 2, Konafis
21/02/99	Apollon Limassol	H	2-0	Ioakim, Rauffmann
28/02/99	AEK Larnaca	A	1-0	Kontolefteros
06/03/99	Paralimni	H	5-0	Rauffmann 2, Kitanov, Marangos,
				Odyseos
13/03/99	Aris Limassol	A	4-0	Rauffmann 3 (1p), Georgiou
20/03/99	APOEL Nicosia	H	1-0	Kontolefteros
07/04/99	Olympiakos Nicosia	A	1-0	Ioakim
17/04/99	AEL Limassol	H	3-0	Rauffmann 2, Kontolefteros
24/04/99	Alki Larnaca	A	4-1	Rauffmann 2, Nicolaou C.,
				Malekkos
02/05/99	Ethnikos Akhna	H	4-0	Kitanov 3, Rauffmann

PARALIMNI

CLUB DIRECTORY

Union of Paralimni FC
PO Box 20
Paralimni
tel - (03) 821352
fax - (03) 820514
Year of Formation - 1936
President - Michalis Michael
Secretary - Marios Makronisos
Coach - Angel Kolev (99/00 - Nenad Starovlach)
Stadium - Municipal (8,000)

APPEARANCES 98/99

	P	Ap	(s)	Gls
Epaminondas CHRISTINAKIS	G	16		
Miltos CHRISTINAKIS	D	1	(8)	
Slavisa CULA (YUG)	M	24		17
George GAVRIEL	M	20	(3)	1
Dimos GOUMENOS	M	19		2
Michalis ECONOMOU	A	18	(1)	4
Costas ELIA	M	8	(5)	2
George HADJIGEORGIOU	M	3	(1)	
Marios KARRAS	D	19		1
Stelios KITTOS	D	3	(6)	
George KOLANIS	M	3	(3)	
George KOSMA	D	4	(4)	
Christos KOTSONIS	D	20		
George KYZAS	M	6	(5)	
Kyriakos MASTROU	D	22		
George MERTAKAS	G	10	(1)	
McDonald MUKASI (SAF)	A	24		12
Andreas PITIRIS	A	4	(4)	1
Martinos SOLOMOU	A		(1)	
Andonis STYLIOTIS	M	2	(1)	
Marios THOMA	A	5	(10)	8
Dinos TSOUKKAS	M	8	(7)	
Arian XHUMBA (ALB)	D	24		2
Andonis ZEMBASHIS	M	23		4

LEAGUE RESULTS 1998/99

12/09/98	APOEL Nicosia	A	2-2	Cula, Mukasi
19/09/98	Olympiakos Nicosia	H	2-0	Mukasi, Cula
26/09/98	AEL Limassol	A	1-0	Zembashis
03/10/98	Alki Larnaca	H	1-1	Mukasi
17/10/98	Ethnikos Akhna	A	1-1	Cula
24/10/98	Anorthosis Famagusta	H	2-5	Gavriel, Cula (p)
31/10/98	Evaghoras Paphos	A	1-1	Karras
07/11/98	Omonia Nicosia	H	1-1	Mukasi
21/11/98	Doxa Katokopia	A	5-4	Thoma 2, Cula 2 (1p), Xhumba
28/11/98	Apollon Limassol	H	1-1	Mukasi
06/12/98	AEK Larnaca	A	0-3	
13/12/98	Nea Salamina Famagusta	A	5-4	Mukasi 2, Economou, Cula, Zembashis
19/12/98	Aris Limassol	H	6-2	Elia 2, Xhumba, Mukasi, Thoma 2 (1p)
09/01/99	Olympiakos Nicosia	A	2-2	Cula, og (Petkovski)
16/01/99	AEL Limassol	H	0-2	
23/01/99	Alki Larnaca	A	2-2	Thoma, Cula
13/02/99	Ethnikos Akhna	H	3-6	Cula 3
20/02/99	Anorthosis Famagusta	A	1-5	Cula
27/02/99	Evaghoras Paphos	H	6-1	Goumenos, Economou, Pitiris, Mukasi (p), Cula, Zembashis
06/03/99	Omonia Nicosia	A	0-5	
13/03/99	Doxa Katokopia	H	5-3	Cula 3 (1p), Thoma, Mukasi
20/03/99	Apollon Limassol	A	0-1	
03/04/99	AEK Larnaca	H	1-2	Zembashis
18/04/99	Nea Salamina Famagusta	H	0-3	
24/04/99	Aris Limassol	A	4-2	Mukasi 2, Goumenos, Economou
02/05/99	APOEL Nicosia	H	3-5	Thoma 2, Economou

PROMOTED CLUBS

SECOND DIVISION FINAL TABLE 98/99

		Pd	W	D	L	F	A	Pt	GD
1	**Anagennisis Dherynia**	26	16	6	4	48	23	54	+25
2	**Ethnikos Ashia**	26	15	6	5	48	26	51	+22
3	**APOP Paphos**	26	14	7	5	51	29	49	+22
4	AEK Achilleas	28	10	10	6	38	32	40	+6
5	AEK Zakakiou	26	11	7	8	35	36	40	-1
6	Ermis Aradippou	26	11	4	11	43	37	37	+6
7	Onisillos Sotiras	26	10	6	10	45	37	36	+8
8	Dighenis Akritas Morphou	26	8	11	7	41	34	35	+7
9	Anagennisis Germasoyia	26	10	4	12	36	37	34	-1
10	PAEEK Kyrenia	26	9	7	10	37	39	34	-2
11	Omonia Aradippou	26	9	7	10	35	39	34	-4
12	Rotsides Mammari	26	10	3	13	34	47	33	-13
13	Asil Lysi	26	4	5	17	22	60	17	-38
14	Akritas Hloraka	26	3	1	22	23	60	10	-37

CLUB DIRECTORY

Anagennisis FC
6 Ammohostou Street
Dherynia
tel - (03) 821436
fax - (03) 730089
Year of Formation - 1920
President - George Melekis
Secretary - Marios Pantelis
Coach - Adamos Adamou
Stadium - Municipal (6,000)

CLUB DIRECTORY

Ethnikos FC of Ashia
Kavaphi Street
2121 Aglatzia
Nicosia
tel - (09) 621389
fax - (02) 474073
President - Costas Leontiou
Secretary - Andonis Mavris
Coach - Nicos Andronicou
Stadium - Kykkos (3,000)

CLUB DIRECTORY

APOP FC
PO Box 60080
Paphos
tel - (06) 232004/235353
fax - (06) 237210
Year of Formation - 1953
President - Stathis Tourvas
Secretary - Panikos Facontis
Coach - Milovan Ristivojevic
Stadium - Paphiako (8,000)

CZECH REPUBLIC

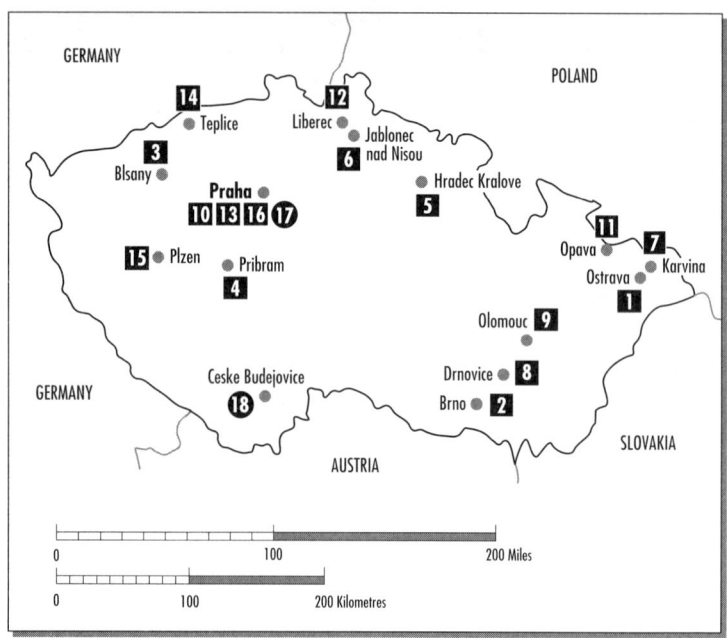

1	BANIK OSTRAVA	256	11	SLEZSKY OPAVA	266
2	BOBY BRNO	257	12	SLOVAN LIBEREC	267
3	CHMEL BLSANY	258	13	SPARTA PRAHA	268
4	DUKLA PRIBRAM	259	14	FK TEPLICE	269
5	SK HRADEC KRALOVE	260	15	VIKTORIA PLZEN	270
6	FK JABLONEC 97	261	16	VIKTORIA ZIZKOV	271
7	FC KARVINA	262	Promoted clubs		
8	PETRA DRNOVICE	263	17	BOHEMIANS PRAHA	272
9	SIGMA OLOMOUC	264	18	SK CESKE BUDEJOVICE	272
10	SLAVIA PRAHA	265			

SPARTA COMPLETE TITLE HAT-TRICK

Chovanec's charges book early for Euro 2000

FEDERATION DIRECTORY

Ceskomoravsky Fotbalovy Svaz
Diskarska 100, 169 00 Praha 6 - Strahov
tel - (02) 20513575/   Year of Formation - 1990
20511194-6   President - Ing. Frantisek Chvalovsky
fax - (02) 33353107   Secretary - JUDr. Ivan Hasek
Stadium - Strahov, Praha (20,000)

Perfection is virtually unattainable in football, but nothing more could possibly have been asked of the Czech Republic national team as they sealed their place at the Euro 2000 finals in Belgium and Holland by winning each of their first seven qualifying matches.

It was a magnificent achievement for a team that had failed to qualify for the 1998 World Cup and which was in the hands of a new, relatively inexperienced coach. No matter that the Czechs found themselves in by far the easiest of the nine qualifying groups. To win every one of their matches and become the first country other than the two host nations to reserve their place at the finals took some doing. The joyous adulation heaped on the team following the seventh of those victories, against Scotland in Prague in early June, was thoroughly deserved.

The man showered with most of the plaudits was coach Jozef Chovanec. After 15 months in the job his record was 12 wins, two draws and two defeats, with all of his competitive matches resulting in victory. The 39-year-old will probably be one of the youngest coaches on duty at Euro 2000 (he'll be 40 by then) and he will no doubt relish his return to Holland, where for several years he was a commanding sweeper with PSV.

Chovanec's team got their European Championship show on the road with a rather fortunate 1-0 win in the foggy Faroe Islands, but there were strong performances in the next two fixtures, away to Bosnia-Herzegovina (3-1) and at home to Estonia (4-1). The new coach's unbeaten record ended in a friendly against England at Wembley, but when the Czechs returned to the British Isles four and a half months later to face Scotland, they were back to their best, inflicting on the Scots their first home defeat in a competitive international for 12 years. That 2-1 victory at Celtic Park, coming four days after a 2-0

LEAGUE CHAMPIONSHIP RESULTS 98/99

		1	2	3	4	5	6	7	8	9	10	11	12	13	14	15	16
1	Banik Ostrava		1-0	2-2	1-2	0-0	4-1	0-0	2-1	1-1	5-0	1-1	2-0	2-0	0-0	0-1	2-1
2	Boby Brno	3-0		1-0	1-1	0-1	3-0	4-2	3-2	0-0	1-0	4-1	0-2	0-1	0-3	3-0	1-0
3	Chmel Blsany	1-2	3-1		1-0	3-0	3-0	3-2	3-1	3-2	2-2	2-0	2-2	1-1	3-2	1-1	2-0
4	Dukla Pribram	1-0	1-1	2-0		0-0	1-1	3-1	0-2	1-2	1-2	3-1	1-0	0-0	2-3	2-0	0-1
5	SK Hradec Kralove	0-2	1-0	0-4	3-0		2-2	3-0	3-1	1-3	0-2	1-0	2-2	2-1	0-3	3-0	0-1
6	FK Jablonec 97	2-2	1-1	1-0	3-0	1-2		1-1	1-2	3-2	5-2	1-0	1-0	0-3	1-2	2-0	0-1
7	FC Karvina	1-3	1-3	2-0	2-0	1-1	1-0		0-2	1-2	1-2	2-1	2-0	0-3	0-2	2-0	1-1
8	Petra Drnovice	0-0	0-0	2-0	1-2	0-2	1-1	1-1		0-0	1-1	3-2	1-1	4-4	0-2	1-0	4-2
9	Sigma Olomouc	3-2	1-1	2-1	0-0	1-0	3-1	2-0	0-1		1-1	3-1	3-0	1-1	2-0	1-1	2-1
10	Slavia Praha	0-0	1-1	5-2	2-0	1-0	1-1	1-0	4-0	4-0		3-0	1-0	1-0	2-1	1-1	4-1
11	Slezsky Opava	0-0	2-1	1-1	2-2	3-1	2-1	2-1	4-0	2-2	0-4		2-0	2-1	3-3	1-1	2-0
12	Slovan Liberec	2-2	0-0	2-0	4-0	1-1	1-0	3-1	1-1	1-1	1-1	1-0		1-1	0-1	1-0	2-2
13	Sparta Praha	1-1	4-1	3-0	3-0	3-1	2-0	5-0	1-0	2-2	0-0	4-2	1-0		2-0	2-0	5-0
14	FK Teplice	0-0	2-1	1-3	1-1	4-0	1-2	3-0	2-2	1-0	3-1	4-0	4-0	1-1		4-2	2-0
15	Viktoria Plzen	1-1	2-0	2-1	2-1	0-3	2-3	3-2	2-0	1-0	1-1	1-1	1-2	0-1	0-0		1-0
16	Viktoria Zizkov	1-1	0-2	2-1	1-1	1-0	1-1	1-0	0-1	2-0	2-1	3-2	0-3	1-6	2-0	3-0	

LEAGUE CHAMPIONSHIP FINAL TABLE 98/99

			Home				Away					Total						
		P	W	D	L	F	A	W	D	L	F	A	W	D	L	F	A	P	GD
1	Sparta Praha	30	12	3	0	38	7	5	6	4	24	16	17	9	4	62	23	60	+39
2	FK Teplice	30	9	4	2	33	13	7	3	5	22	17	16	7	7	55	30	55	+25
3	Slavia Praha	30	11	4	0	31	7	4	6	5	20	24	15	10	5	51	31	55	+20
4	Sigma Olomouc	30	9	5	1	25	11	3	6	6	17	23	12	11	7	42	34	47	+8
5	Banik Ostrava	30	7	6	2	23	10	3	9	3	16	16	10	15	5	39	26	45	+13
6	Chmel Blsany	30	10	4	1	33	16	2	2	11	15	28	12	6	12	48	44	42	+4
7	Boby Brno	30	9	2	4	24	13	2	6	7	13	20	11	8	11	37	33	41	+4
8	SK Hradec Kralove	30	7	2	6	21	21	4	4	7	12	19	11	6	13	33	40	39	-7
9	Slovan Liberec	30	6	8	1	21	11	3	3	9	12	23	9	11	10	33	34	38	-1
10	Viktoria Zizkov	30	8	3	4	20	19	3	2	10	11	28	11	5	14	31	47	38	-16
11	Petra Drnovice	30	4	8	3	19	18	5	2	8	16	26	9	10	11	35	44	37	-9
12	FK Jablonec 97	30	7	3	5	23	18	2	5	8	14	28	9	8	13	37	46	35	-9
13	Dukla Pribram	30	6	4	5	18	14	2	5	8	10	27	8	9	13	28	41	33	-13
14	Slezsky Opava	30	8	6	1	28	18	0	2	13	12	36	8	8	14	40	54	32	-14
15	Viktoria Plzen	30	7	4	4	19	16	1	4	10	7	27	8	8	14	26	43	32	-17
16	FC Karvina	30	6	2	7	17	20	0	3	12	11	35	6	5	19	28	55	23	-27

home win against Lithuania, completed a clean sweep for the Czechs against all of their group rivals.

Phase two began with another victory, 2-0 in Estonia, which meant that the return match with the Scots in Prague offered the prospect of guaranteed qualification with three matches still to play. It proved to be the Czechs' toughest ordeal by far, but even after going two goals down they never lost their resolve, and after defender Tomas Repka had swiftly put them back into the game with his first international goal, it was left to substitute strikers Pavel Kuka and Jan Koller to deliver the decisive strikes that broke Scottish hearts and clinched one of the Czech Republic's most memorable victories.

Chovanec's job has been made easier by the fact that when he took over from Dusan Uhrin he inherited a team that needed few alterations. Despite the disappointment of World Cup qualifying failure, the players in the side had proved their worth by finishing second at Euro '96. Many of that successful team are still around - defenders Jan Suchoparek, Karel Rada and Michal Hornak, midfielders

TOP SCORERS

18 Horst SIEGL (Sparta Praha)
13 Pavel VERBIR (FK Teplice)
12 Robert VAGNER (Slavia Praha)
11 Frantisek KOUBEK (SK Hradec Kralove)
Vratislav LOKVENC (Sparta Praha)
Vitezslav TUMA (Petra Drnovice)
10 Ludek ZELENKA (Viktoria Zizkov/
Slavia Praha)
9 Roman HOGEN (Chmel Blsany)
Radim HOLUB (FK Jablonec 97)
Radomir PRASEK (Slezsky Opava)
Tomas DOSEK (Viktoria Plzen)
Michal SEMAN (Dukla Pribram)
Leandro Hernán LAZZARO LIUNI
(Slovan Liberec)
Marek HEINZ (Sigma Olomouc)
Milan PACANDA (Boby Brno)

NATIONAL TEAM RESULTS 98/99

19/08/98	Denmark	H	Prague	1-0	Rada (8)
06/09/98	Faroe Islands (ECQ)	A	Toftir	1-0	Smicer (85)
10/10/98	Bosnia-Herzegovina (ECQ)	A	Sarajevo	3-1	Baranek (12), Smicer (59), Kuka (90)
14/10/98	Estonia (ECQ)	H	Teplice	4-1	Nedved (9), Berger (22, 42), Lokvenc (45)
18/11/98	England	A	Wembley	0-2	
09/02/99	Belgium	A	Brussels	1-0	Koller (73)
27/03/99	Lithuania (ECQ)	H	Teplice	2-0	Hornak (10), Berger (74p)
31/03/99	Scotland (ECQ)	A	Glasgow	2-1	Elliott (27og), Smicer (36)
28/04/99	Poland	A	Warsaw	1-2	Lokvenc (79)
05/06/99	Estonia (ECQ)	A	Tallinn	2-0	Berger (45), Koller (83)
09/06/99	Scotland (ECQ)	H	Prague	3-2	Repka (65), Kuka (75), Koller (87)

DOMESTIC CUP 98/99

SECOND ROUND
Podjestedsky Cesky Dub 2, FK Jablonec 97 5
TJ Klatovy 0, Sparta Praha 2
Mesto Albrechtice 1, Slezsky Opava 3
Spartak Chocen 1, Sigma Olomouc 3
Biocel Vratimov 1, FC Karvina 5
Slovan Pardubice 0, Slavia Praha 6
IZOS Libocany 1, FK Teplice 8
TJ Prestice 1, Viktoria Plzen 3
FK Ricany 0, Atlantic Lazne Bohdanec 3
TVD Slavicin 0, Sokol Myslocovice 3
SK Hranice 2, FC Vitkovice 4
Admira/Slavoj Praha 3, Viktoria Zizkov 2
CZU Praha 1, Spolana Neratovice 2
Sparta Brno 0, Boby Brno 9
VMG Kyjov 0, FC Zlin 2
VTJ Znojmo 0, LeRK Prostejov 6
Kaucuk Kralupy 1, FC Chomutov 1 (3-5 on pens.)
Sparta Krc 2, Bohemians Praha 2 (4-1 on pens.)
FC Kaunovice 1, Synot Stare Mesto 0
SK Kravare 1, Banik Ostrava 3
Banik Ratiskovice 3, Tatran Postorna 2
Tatran VTJ Prachatice 0, Dukla Pribram 0
(3-4 on pens.)
SK Chrudim 2, SK Ceske Budejovice 0 (2-4 on pens.)
Spartak Rychnov nad Kneznou 2, 1.FC Ceska Lipa 2
(3-5 on pens.)
FK Mlada Boleslav 3, SK Hradec Kralove 0
FK Krnov 0, Zelezarny Trinec 1
PSJ Jihlava 0, Petra Drnovice 3
FK Holice 1932 1, Hanacky FK Prerov 4

1.FC Plzen 0, Chmel Blsany 4
FK Tachov 0, MUS Most 3
Dropa CKD Kompresory Strizkov 5,
Olympia Hradec Kralove 0
Cesky lev TONASO Nestemice 2, Slovan Liberec 5

THIRD ROUND
LeRK Prostejov 0, Slezsky Opava 0 (4-5 on pens.)
SK Ceske Budejovice 2, Dukla Pribram 1
MUS Most 1, Chmel Blsany 1 (5-4 on pens.)
FC Zlin 1, Boby Brno 2
1.FC Ceska Lipa 0, Slovan Liberec 1
Banik Ratiskovice 2, Banik Ostrava 2 (5-6 on pens.)
Sparta Krc 1, Viktoria Plzen 1 (6-5 on pens.)
FC Vitkovice 3, FC Karvina 1
Admira/Slavoj Praha 1, Spolana Neratovice 1
(4-2 on pens.)
FK Mlada Boleslav 4, Zelezarny Trinec 0
Atlantic Lazne Bohdanec 0, FK Teplice 0
(3-4 on pens.)
FC Chomutov 1, FK Jablonec 97 3
FC Kunovice 0, Sigma Olomouc 1
Hanacky FK Prerov 1, Petra Drnovice 3
Sokol Myslocovice 0, Sparta Praha 8
Dropa CKD Kompresory Strizkov 0, Slavia Praha 2

FOURTH ROUND
Sparta Krc 0, Sigma Olomouc 4
Slezsky Opava 2, FK Jablonec 97 2 (4-3 on pens.)
FK Mlada Boleslav 1, Slovan Liberec 2
Petra Drnovice 2, FK Teplice 1

SK Ceske Budejovice 1, Banik Ostrava 2
Admira/Slavoj Praha 1, Boby Brno 3
MUS Most 0, Slavia Praha 2
FC Vitkovice 1, Sparta Praha 1 (3-4 on pens.)

QUARTER-FINALS
Sparta Praha 1 (Obajdin 73), Boby Brno 0
Petra Drnovice 1 (Nehoda 90), Sigma Olomouc 0
Slezsky Opava 0, Slovan Liberec 1 (Lazzaro Luini 29)
Slavia Praha 2 (Dostalek 35, Horvath 54p),
Banik Ostrava 2 (Bolf 2, Sionko 70)
(aet; 3-0 on pens.)

SEMI-FINALS
Sparta Praha 0, Slavia Praha 1 (Rada 19)
Petra Drnovice 1 (Tuma 4),
Slovan Liberec 4 (Lazzaro Liuni 21, Breda 33,
Klusacek 62, Janacek 90)

FINAL
25/05/99, Prague
SLAVIA PRAHA 1 Horvath (97)
SLOVAN LIBEREC 0
(aet)
SLAVIA PRAHA - Cerny; Vlcek, Rada, Petrous, Labant,
Lerch, Ulich, Horvath, Skala (Dostalek 77), Zelenka
(Malar 60), Vagner.
SLOVAN LIBEREC - Kinsky; Pilny, Novotny, Marek,
Lexa, Capek, Breda, Janu, Michalik (Cupr 96), Kincl
(Jarosik 46), Lazzaro Liuni.

Karel Poborsky, Jiri Nemec, Pavel Nedved and Patrik Berger, and forwards Vladimir Smicer and Pavel Kuka. And there are others, like Radoslav Latal, Radek Bejbl and Petr Kouba, who could, with improved form and fitness, still have a part to play as the team bids for further European Championship glory next summer.

Regular new additions to the squad include giant centre-forward Jan Koller plus the Sparta Prague contingent of Tomas Votava, Michal Baranek, Martin Jasek and Vratislav Lokvenc. Another Sparta player, goalkeeper Tomas Postulka, began the Euro 2000 qualifying campaign as first choice before he lost form at club level and was replaced by English-based Pavel Srnicek, a non-playing squad member at Euro '96.

The Czech Republic's outstanding results during Hovanec's reign have lifted the country into third place, behind Brazil and France, in FIFA's world ranking table. The position may be flattering, but the calculation methods flawed, but it still makes for good reading in a country of just 10 million inhabitants.

There were other reasons for the Czechs to be cheerful in 1998/99. Jan Koller topped the goalscoring charts in Belgium, Pavel Nedved scored the winning goal in the last-ever European Cup-winners' Cup final, Karel Poborsky was voted the most popular player in Portugal, and Vladimir Smicer became the country's most expensive player ever when he joined Patrik Berger at Liverpool in a £4.2m transfer from Lens. Furthermore, the Czech Republic climbed to ninth in the UEFA coefficient table, which enabled the country to present two teams in the new, expanded Champions' League, with the champions having the added bonus of being guaranteed a place in the lucrative group phase.

That honour went to Sparta Prague, who, amid general apathy, won the Czech championship for the third year in a row, for the fifth season out of six, and, with Czechoslovakian titles included, for the 28th time in all. It was just as everybody had expected. With their abundant collection of Czech internationals, Sparta had by far the strongest squad in the country. The only thing that could halt them in their tracks was the club's decaying financial status. But the mid-season sale of Martin Cizek to 1860 Munich was sufficiently profitable to prevent the departure of others, so the team was able to survive a brief mini-crisis and ultimately steer a steady course towards yet another title.

Sparta were unbeaten in the autumn - a stark contrast to their depressing results in Europe - but they went through a very sticky patch in the spring, taking just one point from four successive away games and only scraping a couple of home wins thanks to late goals. Durability and resilience were positive features of Zdenek Scesny's team,

NATIONAL TEAM APPEARANCES 98/99

Coach - Jozef CHOVANEC	DEN	FAR	BOS	EST	ENG	BEL	LIT	SCO	POL	EST	SCO	Cps	Gls
Tomas POSTULKA (02/02/74) - Sparta Praha	G	G	G	G								7	-
Tomas VOTAVA (21/02/74) - Sparta Praha	D	D	D	D53	D			D	D39			8	-
Karel RADA (02/03/72) - Trabzonspor (TUR)/Slavia Praha	D	D	s71	s53		D		s76	D63			26	4
Jan SUCHOPAREK (23/09/69) - RC Strasbourg (FRA)	D	D	D	D		D	D	D		D	D	57	4
Michal HORNAK (28/04/70) - Sparta Praha	M46				D70	D		D	s89	D	D	37	1
Martin CIZEK (09/06/74) - Sparta Praha/TSV 1860 München (GER)	M56	M55		s80					M76			16	-
Karel POBORSKY (30/03/72) - SL Benfica (POR)	M68	M81			M	M20	M63	M76	M58	M	M69	46	1
Jiri NEMEC (15/05/66) - FC Schalke 04 (GER)	M	M	M	M	M46	M70	M	D	M	M	M	71	1
Pavel NEDVED (30/08/72) - Lazio (ITA)	M74	M		M			M	M	M54	M85	M	35	5
Vratislav LOKVENC (27/09/73) - Sparta Praha	A	A	A79	A61	s46		A71	A70	s63	A70	A69	21	3
Vladimir SMICER (24/05/73) - RC Lens (FRA)	A78	A	A86	A	A46	A84	A80	M84		A65	A	38	16
Tomas GALASEK (15/01/73) - Willem II (HOL)	s46				s84				M	s85		10	-
Radoslav LATAL (06/01/70) - FC Schalke 04 (GER)	s56	s81	M	M	M46							50	3
Roman VONASEK (08/07/68) - KSC Lokeren (BEL)	s68			s46	s70							8	-
Radek SLONCIK (29/05/73) - Banik Ostrava	s74	s81	s86		s73							14	-
Martin LUKES (17/11/78) - Banik Ostrava	s78											2	2
Radek BEJBL (29/08/72) - Atlético Madrid (ESP)		M81	M	M80	M							38	3
Patrik BERGER (10/11/73) - Liverpool (ENG)		s55	M	M	M		M	M		M	M	34	16
Tomas REPKA (02/01/74) - Fiorentina (ITA)			D	D	D	D				D	D	29	1
Miroslav BARANEK (01/11/73) - Sparta Praha			M71		s46	M90	s80	s84			s61	7	1
Pavel KUKA (19/07/68) - 1.FC Nürnberg (GER)			s79	s61	A73		s63	s70	A	s65	s69	72	25
Petr KOUBA (28/01/69) - Viktoria Zizkov				G								40	-
Jiri NOVOTNY (07/04/70) - Sparta Praha				D46								23	2
Martin KOTULEK (11/09/69) - Sigma Olomouc				s46								8	-
Pavel SRNICEK (10/03/68) - Sheffield Wednesday (ENG)					G	G	G	G	G	G	G	25	-
Pavel HORVATH (22/04/75) - Slavia Praha					M			s54				2	-
Martin HASEK (11/10/69) - Sparta Praha					M	M	M		M	M61		10	-
Jan KOLLER (30/03/73) - KSC Lokeren (BEL)					A	s71		A89	s70	s69		5	3
Petr VLCEK (18/10/73) - Slavia Praha					s20			s39				13	-
Pavel NOVOTNY (14/09/73) - Sparta Praha					s70							2	-
Robert VAGNER (12/05/74) - Slavia Praha					s90							2	-
Marek NIKL (20/02/76) - 1.FC Nürnberg (GER)						D						1	-
Libor SIONKO (01/02/77) - Banik Ostrava								s58				1	-
Jan POLAK (14/03/81) - Boby Brno								s76				1	-

however, and in the closing weeks they put together a run of wins that proved sufficient to secure the championship with two rounds remaining. A 2-0 win at home to Jablonec sewed everything up, and it was appropriate that both of the goals were scored by veteran striker Horst Siegl, who for the third year running collected the Czech First Division top scorer crown. His excellent forward partnership with Vratislav Lokvenc (29 goals between them) ensured that Sparta finished the season with the best attack. They also had the best defence, for which sweeper Tomas Votava and his international colleague Michal Hornak took particular credit.

It was not all sweetness and light, though, for the new champions. The average gate at the Letna was down to just 4,939 - the lowest figure in the club's recent history - and a financial crisis was generated by the withdrawal of the club's chief sponsor, the Slovakian steel works VSZ Kosice, after Sparta became involved in a rather unsavoury political row. Salvation for the club seemed to arrive a few weeks after the season ended when a German publishing group decided to become Sparta's new owners. The major attraction, of course, was that Sparta were certain to play in the 1999/2000 Champions' League (they had missed out on the 1998/99 event in tortuous fashion after a penalty shoot-out defeat by eventual semi-finalists Dynamo Kiev). But the club's dwindling band of hard-core fans refused to get too excited when the new investors talked enthusiastically of a bright, lucrative new future. Their mistrust was understandable given the empty, unfulfilled promises of the previous régime.

EUROPEAN CUPS 98/99

CHAMPIONS' CUP
● SPARTA PRAHA
Qualifying round DYNAMO KYIV (UKR)
A 1-0   Baranek (5)
       Postulka; Hornak, Votava, Novotny J., Svoboda V., Baranek, Hasek, Cizek (Mlejnsky 77), Novotny P., Siegl, Lokvenc.
H 0-1
(aet; 1-3 on pens.)
       Postulka; Hornak, Votava, Novotny J., Mlejnsky (Straceny 93), Hasek, Cizek, Baranek, Novotny P. (Gabriel 87), Siegl, Lokvenc.

CUP WINNERS' CUP
● FK JABLONEC 97
1st round APOLLON LIMASSOL (CYP)
A 1-2   Fukal (39)
       Janos; Vejprava, Penicka, Skuhravy, Fukal, Barteska, Necas, Jirousek (Navratil 65), Neumann, Prochazka (Kohout 62), Holub (Vavra 75).
H 2-1   Prochazka (24, 45)
(aet; 3-4 on pens.)
       Janos; Jirousek, Sopko, Skuhravy, Barteska, Navratil (Cizek 81), Necas, Penicka, Just, Holub (Kohout 70; Fukal 106), Prochazka.

UEFA CUP
● SIGMA OLOMOUC
Qualifying round KILMARNOCK (SCO)
H 2-0   Krohmer (27), König (79)
       Skacel; Kovar, Machala, Kotulek, König, Barborik (Ryska 83), Mucha (Stefka 86), Ujfalusi, Krohmer, Drulak (Cupak 75), Heinz.
A 2-0   Heinz (13), Mucha (20)
       Skacel; Kovar, Machala, Kotulek, König, Barborik (Stefka 85), Mucha (Ryska 82), Ujfalusi, Kucera, Balcarek, Heinz (Vlcek 70).

1st round OLYMPIQUE MARSEILLE (FRA)
H 2-2   Heinz (35, 41)
       Skacel; Kovar, Machala, Kotulek, König, Mucha, Ujfalusi, Stefka (Ryska 61), Kucera, Vlcek (Krohmer 77), Heinz.
A 0-4
       Skacel; Kovar, Machala, Kotulek, König (Krohmer 64), Mucha, Ujfalusi, Stefka (Barborik 63), Kucera, Heinz (Balcarek 80), Vlcek.

● SLAVIA PRAHA
Qualifying round INTER BRATISLAVA (SVK)
H 4-0   Vagner (22, 90), Kozel (55), Skala (71)
       Stejskal; Lerch, Kozel, Petrous, Labant (Vacha 87), Kuchar, Ulich (Skala 46), Dostalek, Horvath, Vagner, Kucera (Adippe 68).
A 0-2
       Stejskal; Lerch, Kozel, Petrous, Skala, Kuchar (Hrubina 46), Krejcik, Dostalek, Horvath, Vagner (Adippe 76), Kucera.

1st round FC SCHALKE 04 (GER)
A 0-1
       Cerny; Lerch, Kozel, Petrous, Labant, Dostalek, Ulich (Kuchar 78), Horvath, Skala, Kucera (Adippe 75), Vagner.
H 1-0   Dostalek (18)
(aet; 5-4 on pens.)
       Cerny; Lerch, Kozel, Petrous, Labant, Kuchar, Dostalek, Horvath, Skala, Kucera (Adippe 115), Vagner

2nd round BOLOGNA (ITA)
A 1-2   Dostalek (68)
       Cerny; Lerch, Kozel, Petrous, Labant, Kucera, Kuchar, Ulich, Dostalek, Vagner, Adippe.
H 0-2
       Cerny; Lerch, Kozel, Petrous, Labant, Ulich, Horvath, Dostalek, Skala (Hrubina 90), Adippe (Kucera 46), Vagner.

● SPARTA PRAHA
1st round REAL SOCIEDAD (ESP)
H 2-4   Cizek (31), Lokvenc (40)
       Postulka; Hornak, Votava, Novotny J., Svoboda V. (Papousek 81), Straceny, Hasek, Cizek, Novotny P., Siegl, Lokvenc.
A 0-1
       Caloun; Mlejnsky, Novotny J., Gabriel, Svoboda V. (Straceny 67), Baranek, Hasek, Cizek, Obajdin, Siegl, Lokvenc.

PLAYERS OF THE SEASON

★ SUPERSTAR PROFILE
PATRIK BERGER

Patrik Berger's big ambition is to play in the finals of the World Cup - if for no other reason than that after 34 appearances for the Czech national team (and 16 goals) he had still to play his first match against non-European opposition. But while he waits

for Japan/Korea 2002 the gifted midfielder can look forward with eager anticipation to his second appearance at the finals of the European Championship. Although he played in the 1996 final, against Germany, and scored the goal from the penalty spot that gave the Czechs the lead, he was not a fixed member of Dusan Uhrin's team in England. In Belgium and Holland, however, he is sure to be one of the team's main attractions. An elegant schemer with a venomous left foot, he passes the ball with economy and accuracy and is extremely dangerous at free-kicks. His third season at Liverpool, in 1998/99, was far and away his best. The arrival of Frenchman Gérard Houllier as manager allowed Berger to break free of his chains and give the Anfield crowd what they had been promised when he first arrived from Borussia Dortmund at a cost of £3.25m in August 1996. He endeared himself to the Kop early on with a couple of thrilling goals in the Premiership, but it was his wonderful solo strike in the UEFA Cup away to Valencia that really had them purring - a highlight matched later on in the season when he scored the winner in the Merseyside derby against Everton. Even more spectacular were the two truly magnificent free-kicks he scored for the Czech Republic at home to Estonia - goals that will be forever lodged in the memories of those who witnessed them.

The drop in attendances at Sparta was reflected nationwide, with only a handful of clubs - Boby Brno, Dukla Pribram and FK Teplice - boasting larger crowds than in the previous season. There was a general disillusionment with the way the league was run. Czech fans could just about cope with the reduced quality brought about by the steady departure of the country's leading players, but they could not tolerate what they saw to be an increase in the number of 'manipulated' matches, where players appeared to have pre-ordained instructions as to how the games should end. But this widespread suspicion of malpractice was given no official credence by the authorities, which only served to alienate the fans even further.

Coach-changing was also rife, with only six of the 16 First Division clubs completing the season with the same man who had started the campaign. One of those lucky few, Slavia Prague's Jaroslav Hrebik, only survived until the summer. He was controversially ditched by Slavia's English owners, ENIC, despite enjoying popular support among the club's fans and 'football people'. He even had

a trophy to produce in his defence as Slavia had just won the Czech Cup.

But Hrebik's big failure, in the eyes of his peers, had been his inability to take Slavia into second place in the league. His fate was effectively sealed in the penultimate round of the championship when Slavia were sensationally beaten 3-1 by FK Teplice - a result which meant that Teplice, not Slavia, took the second Champions' League place on offer.

Another team disgruntled by the outcome of that match were Slavia's Cup final opponents Slovan Liberec. They had been banking on Slavia to claim the Champions'

INTERNATIONAL HONOURS

World Cup Finals appearances: 1934 (runners-up), 1938 (qtr-finals), 1954, 1958, 1962 (runners-up), 1970, 1982, 1990 (qtr-finals)

European Championship appearances (last 8): 1960 (3rd), 1976 (Winners), 1980 (3rd), 1996 (runners-up)

League spot in order to free a place in the UEFA Cup for them. But now the only way they could achieve their first-ever European qualification was by beating Slavia in the final. They tried their best, but an extra-time goal by Czech international midfielder Pavel Horvath ended Liberec's dream of double glory. It was a dull final but Slavia deserved to take the Cup - if for no other reason than that they had eliminated Sparta in the semi-finals. Karel Rada's goal enabled Slavia to beat their great rivals in the Cup for the very first time.

Slavia were joined in the UEFA Cup for the second successive year by Sigma Olomouc, who finished fourth in the league. Teplice, though, were the season's revelation. A mere seventh the previous season, Josef Pesice's unsung side shook off an opening home defeat by top-flight newcomers Chmel Blsany to become Sparta's main challengers during the first half of the season, and their strong finish, capped by that tremendous 3-1 victory over Slavia, booked them a place in the Champions' League qualifiers. Europe's most prestigious club competition had a fitting stage in Teplice's excellent stadium, the finest in the country, which twice during the season had been chosen by the Czech national team as the venue for Euro 2000 qualifiers in preference to Prague.

PLAYERS OF THE SEASON

PAVEL VERBIR
One of many Czech players with his sights trained on a transfer abroad is FK Teplice striker Pavel Verbir (below). He was the most prominent individual in Teplice's outstanding 1998/99 campaign, which resulted in a totally unexpected second-place finish behind champions Sparta Prague. He top-scored with 13 goals - a total bettered only by Sparta's Horst Siegl in the entire league - and was the man who crowned Teplice's remarkable qualification for the Champions' League with the decisive third goal in the all-important 3-1 league win over Slavia Prague. Surprisingly, his good form went unnoticed

by Czech coach Jozef Chovanec, so he was unable to add to his six previous international caps.

JAN KOLLER
He stands well over six feet tall and was the run-away top scorer in the Belgian First Division in 1998/99 despite playing for modest Lokeren. He also made quite an impression both in his homeland and his country of residence when he scored the winning goal for the Czech Republic against Belgium in Brussels on his international début. An even more important goal followed four months later when he headed home the late winner against Scotland that confirmed the Czechs' qualification for the Euro 2000 finals. Though lean and gangly, Jan Koller has an exceptional touch for a big man, and his shooting is on a par with his heading. After scoring 24 goals there was no way that Lokeren could afford to keep him, so he left in the summer for Anderlecht, who were willing to pay very good money for his services.

MIROSLAV BARANEK
25-year-old Miroslav Baranek was voted as the best midfielder in the Czech First Division during the 1998/99 season. His dynamic contributions provided many goals for Sparta Prague's twin spearhead of Horst Siegl and Vratislav Lokvenc, and he also got on the scoresheet eight times himself. There was an important goal, too, for the Czech Republic against Bosnia-Herzegovina in Sarajevo - 13 minutes into his first international for almost three years. He will be one of the Czech Republic's new faces at Euro 2000 and will hope to use that tournament as a springboard for a move to a foreign club, preferably one in Germany, his favoured destination.

BANIK OSTRAVA

CLUB DIRECTORY

FC Banik Ostrava
Stadion Bazaly
Bukovanskeho 4/1028
710 00 Ostrava
tel - (069) 6241687
fax - (069) 6241827
Year of Formation - 1922
President - Ing. Lumir Palyza
Secretary - Vladimir Janosko
Coach - Werner Licka
Stadium - Bazaly (19,048)

MAJOR HONOURS
League Championship - (3) 1976, 1980, 1981.
Domestic Cup - (3) 1973, 1978, 1991.

APPEARANCES 98/99

	P	Ap	(s)	Gls
Jan BARANEK	M	13		
Vit BARANEK	G	23		
Milan BAROS	A		(6)	
Rene BOLF	D	29		3
Robert CAHA	M	5	(10)	
Vladimir CAP	D	20		
Pavel HARAZIM	D	10	(1)	
Marek JANKULOVSKI	M	23	(3)	2
Marcel LICKA	M	28		6
Martin LUKES	A	16	(2)	7
Milan PALENIK	M		(2)	
Michal PANCIK (SVK)	M	8	(10)	
Milan POSTULKA	D	29		3
Petr RUMAN	A	13	(13)	4
Petr SAMEC	A	5	(7)	2
Ivo SCHMUCKER	G	1	(1)	
Libor SIONKO	A	23	(4)	8
Radomir SLONCIK	M	19	(3)	1
Pavel SRNICEK	G	6		
Tomas STASTKA	D	21	(3)	
Petr VESELY	D	14		
Dusan VRTO	D	10	(3)	1
Radim WOZNIAK	D	2		
Libor ZATEK (SVK)	M	12		
Libor ZUREK	A		(5)	

LEAGUE RESULTS 1998/99

02/08/98	Slovan Liberec	A	2-2	Sloncik, Vrto
08/08/98	Slavia Praha	H	5-0	Bolf 2, Ruman, Lukes, Licka
24/08/98	FK Teplice	A	0-0	
30/08/98	Chmel Blsany	H	2-2	Sionko, Lukes
13/09/98	Dukla Pribram	A	0-1	
20/09/98	Sigma Olomouc	A	2-3	Sionko 2
27/09/98	Boby Brno	H	1-0	Postulka
04/10/98	Viktoria Zizkov	A	1-1	Samec
18/10/98	FK Jablonec 97	H	4-1	Ruman 2, Sionko, Bolf
25/10/98	Sparta Praha	A	1-1	Jankulovski
01/11/98	SK Hradec Kralove	H	0-0	
08/11/98	Viktoria Plzen	A	1-1	Samec
14/11/98	FC Karvina	H	0-0	
22/11/98	Petra Drnovice	A	0-0	
29/11/98	Slezsky Opava	H	1-1	Postulka
21/02/99	Slovan Liberec	H	2-0	Jankulovski, Licka
01/03/99	Slavia Praha	A	0-0	
07/03/99	FK Teplice	H	0-0	
14/03/99	Chmel Blsany	A	2-1	Sionko 2
21/03/99	Dukla Pribram	H	1-2	Sionko
04/04/99	Sigma Olomouc	H	1-1	Ruman
11/04/99	Boby Brno	A	0-3	
19/04/99	Viktoria Zizkov	H	2-1	Licka (p), Sionko
24/04/99	FK Jablonec 97	A	2-2	og 2 (Skuhravy 2)
01/05/99	Sparta Praha	H	2-0	Licka, Lukes
09/05/99	SK Hradec Kralove	A	2-0	Licka 2 (2p)
12/05/99	Viktoria Plzen	H	0-1	
16/05/99	FC Karvina	A	3-1	Lukes 3
22/05/99	Petra Drnovice	H	2-1	Postulka, Lukes
30/05/99	Slezsky Opava	A	0-0	

BOBY BRNO

THE EUROPEAN FOOTBALL YEARBOOK 1999-2000

CLUB DIRECTORY

FC Boby Sport Brno
Drobneho 45
602 00 Brno
tel - (05) 7272483/4
fax - (05) 7272850
Year of Formation - 1913
President - PaeDr. Lubomir Hrstka
Secretary - Radek Belak
Coach - Karel Jarusek
Stadium - Za Luzankami (50,000)

MAJOR HONOURS
League Championship - (1) 1978.

APPEARANCES 98/99

		P	Ap	(s)	Gls
Tomas ABRAHAM	M			(5)	
Petr BASTAR	D	9		(6)	
Zdenek CIHLAR	D	23			1
Libor DOSEK	M			(2)	
Pavel HOLOMEK	A	26		(1)	6
Martin HYSKY	D	3			
Lukes JIRIKOVSKY	M			(1)	
Petr KOCMAN	M	4		(9)	
Michal KOLOMAZNIK	M	13		(12)	6
Premysl KOVAR	A			(1)	
Petr KRIVANEK	D	26			3
Jan MAROSI	M	24		(2)	1
Pavel MEZLIK	A			(1)	
Milan PACANDA	A	23			9
Jan PALINEK	D	25			2
Jan POLAK	M	20			
Lubos PRIBYL	G	28			
Patrik SIEGL	M	27		(2)	2
Petr SVANCARA	A	20		(6)	6
Zdenek VALNOHA	M	8		(3)	1
Karel VECERA	M			(1)	
Radim VLASAK	G	2		(1)	
Martin ZBONCAK	M	24		(4)	
Marek ZUBEK	M	25		(2)	

LEAGUE RESULTS 1998/99

Date	Opponent	H/A	Score	Scorers
02/08/98	Slezsky Opava	A	1-2	Pacanda
09/08/98	Slovan Liberec	H	0-2	
22/08/98	Slavia Praha	A	1-1	Kolomaznik
30/08/98	FK Teplice	H	0-3	
14/09/98	Chmel Blsany	A	1-3	Valnoha
20/09/98	Dukla Pribram	H	1-1	Svancara
27/09/98	Banik Ostrava	A	0-1	
05/10/98	Sigma Olomouc	A	1-1	Pacanda
18/10/98	Viktoria Zizkov	H	1-0	Krivanek
25/10/98	FK Jablonec 97	A	1-1	Svancara
02/11/98	Sparta Praha	H	0-1	
08/11/98	SK Hradec Kralove	A	0-1	
14/11/98	Viktoria Plzen	H	3-0	Pacanda 2, Holomek
22/11/98	FC Karvina	A	3-1	Cihlar, Marosi, Siegl
30/11/98	Petra Drnovice	H	3-2	Krivanek, Pacanda (p), Holomek
21/02/99	Slezsky Opava	H	4-1	Pacanda (p), Palinek, Siegl, Krivanek
28/02/99	Slovan Liberec	A	0-0	
08/03/99	Slavia Praha	H	1-0	Svancara
15/03/99	FK Teplice	A	1-2	Pacanda
21/03/99	Chmel Blsany	H	1-0	Holomek
04/04/99	Dukla Pribram	A	1-1	Pacanda
11/04/99	Banik Ostrava	H	3-0	Pacanda (p), Palinek, Holomek
18/04/99	Sigma Olomouc	H	0-0	
24/04/99	Viktorin Zizkov	A	2-0	Kolomaznik 2
02/05/99	FK Jablonec 97	H	3-0	Kolomaznik 2, Svancara
09/05/99	Sparta Praha	A	1-4	Kolomaznik
12/05/99	SK Hradec Kralove	H	0-1	
16/05/99	Viktoria Plzen	A	0-2	
22/05/99	FC Karvina	H	4-2	Svancara 2, Holomek 2
30/05/99	Petra Drnovice	A	0-0	

FK CHMEL BLSANY

CLUB DIRECTORY

FK Chmel Blsany
U stadionu 14
439 88 Blsany
tel - (0399) 214523
fax - (0399) 214592
Year of Formation - 1946
President - Jiri Hendrych
Secretary - Zdenek Kovar
Coach - Miroslav Beranek
Stadium - FK Chmel (4,600)

APPEARANCES 98/99

	P	Ap	(s)	Gls
Sergio José BASTIDA (ARG)	M		(1)	
Günter BITTENGEL	A	28	(1)	4
Tomas BULDRA	M		(1)	
Ales CHVALOVSKY	G	15		
Libor CIHAK	M	23	(2)	1
Jaroslav DIEPOLD	D	7	(1)	1
Libor DOSEK	M	9	(6)	2
Vaclav DROBNY	D	9		
Pavel DRSEK	D	28		6
Patrik GEDEON	M	26	(2)	2
Roman HOGEN	A	23	(4)	9
Ondrej HOUDA	M	1		
Ales JINDRA	D	19	(2)	2
Jindrich JIRASEK	D	2	(5)	
Jan KYKLHORN	M		(3)	
Jiri NEMECEK	G	2	(1)	
Pavel PERGL	D	8	(13)	1
Michal POSPISIL	A	11	(13)	3
Petr PRUCHA	A	3	(20)	2
Jan SIMAK	M	28	(2)	8
Jiri SYKORA	M	7	(3)	
Karel TICHOTA	D	28		
Jan VOREL	D	18	(2)	1
Michal VOREL	G	13		
Petr VRABEC	D	22	(5)	3

LEAGUE RESULTS 1998/99

02/08/98	FK Teplice	A	3-1	og (Rampacek), Bittengel, Pergl
08/08/98	Sigma Olomouc	A	1-2	Gedeon
23/08/98	Dukla Pribram	H	1-0	Prucha
30/08/98	Banik Ostrava	A	2-2	Vrabec, Jindra
14/09/98	Boby Brno	H	3-1	Hogen, Bittengel, Drsek
20/09/98	Viktoria Zizkov	A	1-2	Pospisil
27/09/98	FK Jablonec 97	H	3-0	Bittengel, Hogen, Prucha
04/10/98	Sparta Praha	A	0-3	
18/10/98	SK Hradec Kralove	H	3-0	Jindra, Gedeon, Simak
25/10/98	Viktoria Plzen	A	1-2	Vorel
01/11/98	FC Karvina	H	3-2	Drsek, Pospisil, Simak
08/11/98	Petra Drnovice	A	0-2	
14/11/98	Slezsky Opava	H	2-0	Drsek 2 (1p)
22/11/98	Slovan Liberec	A	0-2	
29/11/98	Slavia Praha	H	2-2	Diepold, Cihak
21/02/99	FK Teplice	H	3-2	Dosek, Hogen 2
28/02/99	Sigma Olomouc	H	3-2	Dosek, Drsek, Hogen
07/03/99	Dukla Pribram	A	0-2	
14/03/99	Banik Ostrava	H	1-2	Simak
21/03/99	Boby Brno	A	0-1	
04/04/99	Viktoria Zizkov	H	2-0	Pospisil, Simak
11/04/99	FK Jablonec 97	A	0-1	
19/04/99	Sparta Praha	H	1-1	Drsek
24/04/99	SK Hradec Kralove	A	4-0	Vrabec 2, Simak, Hogen
02/05/99	Viktoria Plzen	H	1-1	Simak
09/05/99	FC Karvina	A	0-2	
13/05/99	Petra Drnovice	H	3-1	Hogen 3
16/05/99	Slezsky Opava	A	1-1	og (Fencl)
22/05/99	Slovan Liberec	H	2-2	Bittengel, Simak
30/05/99	Slavia Praha	A	2-5	Simak, og (Labant)

DUKLA PRIBRAM

CLUB DIRECTORY

FC Dukla Pribram
Stadion Na Litavce
P.O. Box 65, 261 02 Pribram VII
tel - (0306) 20023
fax - (0306) 26173
Year of Formation - 1948
President - Ing. Bohumir Duricko
Secretary - Miloslav Jicha
Coach - Josef Csaplar; Jiri Kotrba
Stadium - Na Litavce (10,000)

MAJOR HONOURS
League Championship - (11)
1953, 1956, 1958, 1961, 1962, 1963, 1964,
1966, 1977, 1979, 1982.
Domestic Cup - (8) 1961, 1965, 1966, 1969,
1981, 1983, 1985, 1990.

APPEARANCES 98/99

	P	Ap	(s)	Gls
Jiri ANTOS	A	2	(3)	
Vaclav CERNY	A		(1)	
Radek CIZEK	M	21	(4)	1
Michal HOFFMANN	A	4	(12)	
Ales HYNEK	M	22		
Lukas JAROLIM	M	12	(2)	3
Josef JINOCH	M	4	(1)	
Michal KANIK	M	6	(1)	
Jan KLIMA	G	12	(1)	
Martin KOKSAL	M	1		
Radek KREJCIK	M	10	(3)	
Tomas KUKOL	M	14		
Michal MACEK	G	1	(1)	
Marcel MACHA	D	26		
Jaroslav MASEK	M	13	(8)	1
Lumir MISTR	M	1	(7)	
Radek MYNAR	D	29		1
David NEHODA	D	21	(1)	2
Frantisek ONDRUSEK	G	17		
Marcel PACOVSKY	M	3	(3)	
Petr PODZEMSKY	D	11	(4)	
Jan RIEGEL	M	1		
Jiri RYCHLIK	D	1	(6)	
Jan SAIDL	A	3	(15)	2
Michal SEMAN	A	27	(2)	9
Martin SPINAR	D	27		
Hynek TALPA	D	7	(4)	
Zdenek VALNOHA	A	15		1
Miroslav VAPENIK	D	4	(4)	1
Ludek VYSKOCIL	A	15		7

LEAGUE RESULTS 1998/99

02/08/98	Slavia Praha	A	0-2	
09/08/98	FK Teplice	H	2-3	Jarolim, Vapenik
23/08/98	Chmel Blsany	A	0-1	
30/08/98	Sigma Olomouc	A	0-0	
13/09/98	Banik Ostrava	H	1-0	Seman
20/09/98	Boby Brno	A	1-1	Seman
28/09/98	Viktoria Zizkov	H	0-1	
04/10/98	FK Jablonec 97	A	0-3	
18/10/98	Sparta Praha	H	0-0	
25/10/98	SK Hradec Kralove	A	0-3	
08/11/98	FC Karvina	A	0-2	
14/11/98	Petra Drnovice	H	0-2	
22/11/98	Slezsky Opava	A	2-2	Seman, Vyskocil
25/11/98	Viktoria Plzen	H	2-0	Mynar, Vyskocil
29/11/98	Slovan Liberec	H	1-0	Seman
21/02/99	Slavia Praha	H	1-2	Vyskocil
28/02/99	FK Teplice	A	1-1	Masek
07/03/99	Chmel Blsany	H	2-0	Seman, Vyskocil
14/03/99	Sigma Olomouc	H	1-2	Valnoha
21/03/99	Banik Ostrava	A	2-1	Saidl 2
04/04/99	Boby Brno	H	1-1	Seman (p)
11/04/99	Viktoria Zizkov	A	1-1	Seman
18/04/99	FK Jablonec 97	H	1-1	Nehoda
24/04/99	Sparta Praha	A	0-3	
30/04/99	SK Hradec Kralove	H	0-0	
09/05/99	Viktoria Plzen	A	1-2	Vyskocil
12/05/99	FC Karvina	H	3-1	Nehoda, Seman 2
16/05/99	Petra Drnovice	A	2-1	Cizek, Vyskocil
22/05/99	Slezsky Opava	H	3-1	Jarolim 2, Vyskocil
30/05/99	Slovan Liberec	A	0-4	

SK HRADEC KRALOVE

CLUB DIRECTORY

SK Hradec Kralove
Vsesportovni stadion
500 09 Hradec Kralove 9
tel - (049) 551552/3
fax - (049) 5511485
Year of Formation - 1905
President - Ing. Vladimir Voda
Secretary - Vaclav Kynos
Coach - Ladislav Skorpil; Stanislav Kocourek
Stadium - Vsesportovni stadion (25,000)

MAJOR HONOURS
League Championship - (1) 1960.
Domestic Cup - (1) 1995.

APPEARANCES 98/99

	P	Ap	(s)	Gls
Tomas BOUSKA	A	5	(10)	1
Pavel CERNY	M	4	(19)	1
Jaroslav DVORAK	M	25	(1)	8
Walter Rodrigo FLEITA (ARG)	A	1	(3)	
Karel HAVLICEK	D	16		
David HOMOLAC	M	9	(9)	
Richard JUKL	M	28		6
David KALOUSEK	D	24	(4)	1
Peter KAVKA (SVK)	A		(4)	
Frantisek KOUBEK	A	26		11
Michal LESAK	M	8	(2)	
Jaroslav MICHALICKA (SVK)	D	18	(4)	1
Karel NOVOTNY	G		(1)	
Bohuslav PILNY	D	11		
Jaroslav PLASIL	M		(1)	
Karel PODHAJSKY	G	30		
Petr POKORNY	D	26		3
Milan PTACEK	M		(2)	
Vlastimil RYSAVY	A	10	(3)	
Juan Manuel SARA (ARG)	A	5	(2)	
Michal SMID	A	2	(3)	
Martin SVOBODA	G		(1)	
Ondrej SZABO (SVK)	M	1	(6)	
Jiri ZALESKY	M	27		1
Miroslav ZEMANEK	M	29		
David ZOUBEK	A	25		

LEAGUE RESULTS 1998/99

02/08/98	Sigma Olomouc	H	1-3	Pokorny
09/08/98	Viktoria Plzen	H	3-0	Koubek, Michalicka, Jukl
23/08/98	FC Karvina	A	1-1	Koubek
30/08/98	Petra Drnovice	H	3-1	Dvorak 2, Jukl
13/09/98	Slezsky Opava	A	1-3	Dvorak
20/09/98	Slovan Liberec	H	2-2	Cerny, Koubek
25/09/98	Slavia Praha	A	0-1	
04/10/98	FK Teplice	H	0-3	
18/10/98	Chmel Blsany	A	0-3	
25/10/98	Dukla Pribram	H	3-0	Dvorak, Koubek, Jukl (p)
01/11/98	Banik Ostrava	A	0-0	
08/11/98	Boby Brno	H	1-0	Jukl
15/11/98	Viktoria Zizkov	A	0-1	
22/11/98	FK Jablonec 97	H	2-2	Jukl, Pokorny
29/11/98	Sparta Praha	A	1-3	Jukl
22/02/99	Sigma Olomouc	A	0-1	
28/02/99	Viktoria Plzen	A	3-0	Koubek 2, Dvorak
07/03/99	FC Karvina	H	3-0	Koubek 3
14/03/99	Petra Drnovice	A	2-0	Kalousek, Koubek
21/03/99	Slezsky Opava	H	1-0	Zalesky
04/04/99	Slovan Liberec	A	1-1	Bouska
12/04/99	Slavia Praha	H	0-2	
18/04/99	FK Teplice	A	0-4	
24/04/99	Chmel Blsany	A	0-4	
30/04/99	Dukla Pribram	A	0-0	
09/05/99	Banik Ostrava	H	0-2	
12/05/99	Boby Brno	A	1-0	Dvorak
16/05/99	Viktoria Zizkov	H	0-1	
22/05/99	FK Jablonec 97	A	2-1	Dvorak 2
30/05/99	Sparta Praha	H	2-1	Koubek, Pokorny

FK JABLONEC 97

CLUB DIRECTORY

FK Jablonec 97
U stadionu 5
466 01 Jablonec nad Nisou
tel - (0428) 21507/312139
fax - (0428) 22947
Year of Formation - 1945
President - Miroslav Pelta
Secretary - Lubos Srejma
Coach - Jiri Kotrba: Juilius Bielik
Stadium - Strelnice (14,730)

MAJOR HONOURS
Domestic Cup - (1) 1998.

APPEARANCES 98/99

	P	Ap	(s)	Gls
Milan BARTESKA	M	25	(1)	2
Vladimir CHALOUPKA	A	9	(10)	
Tomas CIZEK	M	15	(3)	
Petr DROBISZ	G	3		
Milan FUKAL	D	23	(1)	3
Martin HAPIAK	D	2	(7)	1
Radim HOLUB	A	29		9
Zdenek JANOS	G	27		
Pavel JIROUSEK	M	12	(7)	
Josef JUST	M	4	(8)	
Ales KOHOUT	A	2	(4)	
Miloslav KORDULE	D	13		1
Jiri MASEK	M	2	(5)	
Jaromir NAVRATIL	M	9	(1)	
Radim NECAS	M	26		5
Robert NEUMANN	M	14	(4)	1
Pavel PENICKA	M	21	(2)	1
Tomas POZAR	D	18	(1)	
Martin PROCHAZKA	A	13	(9)	7
Richard SITARCIK	M		(1)	
Roman SKUHRAVY	D	22	(1)	2
Dalibor SLEZAK	A	12		3
Jan SOPKO	D	7	(1)	
Jiri VAVRA	A	12	(10)	1
Martin VEJPRAVA	D	10	(2)	1

LEAGUE RESULTS 1998/99

02/08/98	FC Karvina	A	0-1	
10/08/98	Petra Drnovice	H	1-2	Holub
23/08/98	Slezsky Opava	A	1-2	Holub
30/08/98	Slovan Liberec	H	1-0	Vejprava
12/09/98	Slavia Praha	A	1-1	Prochazka
21/09/98	FK Teplice	H	1-2	Penicka (p)
27/09/98	Chmel Blsany	A	0-3	
04/10/98	Dukla Pribram	H	3-0	Prochazka 2, Necas
18/10/98	Banik Ostrava	A	1-4	Barteska
25/10/98	Boby Brno	H	1-1	Skuhravy
08/11/98	Sigma Olomouc	A	1-3	Holub
14/11/98	Sparta Praha	H	0-3	
22/11/98	SK Hradec Kralove	A	2-2	Neumann, Prochazka
25/11/98	Viktoria Zizkov	A	1-1	Fukal
29/11/98	Viktoria Plzen	H	2-0	Prochazka 2 (1p)
21/02/99	FC Karvina	H	1-1	Holub
28/02/99	Petra Drnovice	A	1-1	Kordule
07/03/99	Slezsky Opava	H	1-0	Hapiak
14/03/99	Slovan Liberec	A	0-1	
04/04/99	FK Teplice	A	2-1	Necas (p), Slezak
08/04/99	Slavia Praha	H	5-2	Holub 3, Necas, Slezak
11/04/99	Chmel Blsany	H	1-0	Prochazka
18/04/99	Dukla Pribram	A	1-1	Holub
24/04/99	Banik Ostrava	H	2-2	Skuhravy, Holub
02/05/99	Boby Brno	A	0-3	
09/05/99	Viktoria Zizkov	H	0-1	
12/05/99	Sigma Olomouc	H	3-2	Barteska, Fukal 2
16/05/99	Sparta Praha	A	0-2	
22/05/99	SK Hradec Kralove	H	1-2	Slezak
30/05/99	Viktoria Plzen	A	3-2	Vavra, Necas 2 (1p)

FC KARVINA

CLUB DIRECTORY

FC Karvina
Stadion Kovona Karvina
735 06 Karvina - Nove Mesto
tel - (069) 63113674/5
fax - (069) 6346627
Year of Formation - 1953
President - Mgr. Vladimir Kolder
Secretary - Vaclav Javorek
Coach - Jaroslav Netolicka
Stadium - Kovona Karvina (12,000)

APPEARANCES 98/99

	P	Ap	(s)	Gls
Pavel BARCUCH	G	22		
Rene BENEFI	M	19	(4)	
Pavel BERNATIK	D		(1)	
Marek BIELAN	M	1	(1)	
Vaclav CINCALA	A	17	(7)	3
Milan DUHAN	M	16	(7)	3
Robert KAFKA	M	11	(3)	1
David KOTRYS	M	8		
Radim KRUPNIK	A	3	(9)	1
Pavel KUBES	M	26	(1)	1
Petr MALER	D	13		
Petr MASLEJ	M	22		6
Milan MIKLAS	G	8		
Martin PLACHTA	D	20		
Marek POSTULKA	A	3	(2)	3
Roman PRIBYL	A	6	(7)	
Martin ROZHON	A	17	(8)	3
Ales RYSKA	M	8	(1)	
Michal SLACHTA	D	25	(1)	4
David SOURADA	A	11	(13)	
Martin SPICKA	M		(2)	
Kamil STEPANIK	M	5	(3)	
Ladislav SULAK	M	25	(3)	
Radomir SULAK	D	19	(1)	
Marian TIBENSKY (SVK)	D	12		
Gocha TRAPAIDZE (GEO)	A		(5)	
Roman ZELENAY (SVK)	D	13	(3)	2

LEAGUE RESULTS 1998/99

02/08/98	FK Jablonec 97	H	1-0	Kubes
08/08/98	Sparta Praha	A	0-5	
23/08/98	SK Hradec Kralove	H	1-1	Zelenay
30/08/98	Viktoria Plzen	A	2-3	Cincala (p), Krupnik
12/09/98	Sigma Olomouc	H	1-2	Cincala
20/09/98	Petra Drnovice	H	0-2	
27/09/98	Slezsky Opava	A	1-2	Slachta
04/10/98	Slovan Liberec	H	2-0	Rozhon, og (Klusacek)
16/10/98	Slavia Praha	A	0-1	
25/10/98	FK Teplice	H	0-2	
01/11/98	Chmel Blsany	A	2-3	Slachta 2
08/11/98	Dukla Pribram	H	2-0	Rozhon, Maslej
14/11/98	Banik Ostrava	A	0-0	
22/11/98	Boby Brno	H	1-3	Zelenay
29/11/98	Viktoria Zizkov	A	0-1	
21/02/99	FK Jablonec 97	A	1-1	Slachta
28/02/99	Sparta Praha	H	0-3	
07/03/99	SK Hradec Kralove	A	0-3	
14/03/99	Viktoria Plzen	H	2-0	Postulka (p), Duhan
21/03/99	Sigma Olomouc	A	0-2	
04/04/99	Petra Drnovice	A	1-1	Maslej
11/04/99	Slezsky Opava	H	2-1	Postulka, Maslej
18/04/99	Slovan Liberec	A	1-3	Rozhon
24/04/99	Slavia Praha	H	1-2	Cincala (p)
02/05/99	FK Teplice	A	0-3	
09/05/99	Chmel Blsany	H	2-0	Postulka, Maslej
12/05/99	Dukla Pribram	A	1-3	Maslej
16/05/99	Banik Ostrava	H	1-3	Duhan
22/05/99	Boby Brno	A	2-4	Duhan, Kafka (p)
30/05/99	Viktoria Zizkov	H	1-1	Maslej

PETRA DRNOVICE

CLUB DIRECTORY

FC Petra Drnovice
Sportovni areal
683 04 Drnovice 704
tel - (0507) 353265/353547
fax - (0507) 353265
Year of Formation - 1932
President - Ing. Vaclav Junek Csc.
Secretary - Vitezslav Zboril
Coach - Jindrich Dejmal (99/00 - Karel Vecera)
Stadium - Sportovni areal (9,500)

APPEARANCES 98/99

	P	Ap	(s)	Gls
Erich BRABEC	D	10	(1)	1
Bronislav CERVENKA	M	20	(4)	6
Vlastimil CHYTRY	A		(1)	
Rene FORMANEK	D	3	(1)	
Zdenek GRYGERA	D	22	(3)	
Miroslav HOLENAK	M	23	(1)	3
Miroslav KADLEC	D	26		2
Jiri KAUFMAN	A	4	(1)	1
Ivan KOPECKY	A	8	(3)	
Miloslav KUĽA	A	4	(4)	
Marek KULIC	A	10	(2)	1
Petr MALER	D	1	(1)	
Zdenek MIKOLAS	A		(5)	
Martin MÜLLER	D	28		
Emil NECAS	M	6	(7)	
Michal NEHODA	A	8	(16)	1
Rudolf OTEPKA	M	22	(5)	3
Martin PARIZEK	G	2	(1)	
Jiri POSPISIL	D	18	(6)	1
Vitezslav TUMA	A	26		11
Karel URBANEK	D		(5)	
Ivan VALACHOVIC (SVK)	D	22	(3)	
Martin VANIAK	G	28		
Petr VESELY	M	15		1
Josef WEBER	M	24	(3)	4

LEAGUE RESULTS 1998/99

02/08/98	Viktoria Zizkov	H	4-2	Tuma 2, Kadlec (p), Otepka
10/08/98	FK Jablonec 97	A	2-1	Holenak, Tuma
23/08/98	Sparta Praha	H	4-4	Tuma 3 (1p), Holenak
30/08/98	SK Hradec Kralove	A	1-3	Weber
13/09/98	Viktoria Plzen	H	1-0	Cervenka
20/09/98	FC Karvina	A	2-0	Cervenka, Weber
25/09/98	Sigma Olomouc	H	0-0	
04/10/98	Slezsky Opava	H	3-2	Weber, Tuma, Cervenka
18/10/98	Slovan Liberec	A	1-1	Kadlec (p)
26/10/98	Slavia Praha	H	1-1	Otepka
08/11/98	Chmel Blsany	H	2-0	Otepka, Tuma
14/11/98	Dukla Pribram	A	2-0	Nehoda, Vesely
22/11/98	Banik Ostrava	H	0-0	
25/11/98	FK Teplice	A	2-2	Tuma, Cervenka
30/11/98	Boby Brno	A	2-3	Tuma, Weber
21/02/99	Viktoria Zizkov	A	1-0	Kulic
28/02/99	FK Jablonec 97	H	1-1	Cervenka
07/03/99	Sparta Praha	A	0-1	
14/03/99	SK Hradec Kralove	H	0-2	
21/03/99	Viktoria Plzen	A	0-2	
04/04/99	FC Karvina	H	1-1	Tuma
11/04/99	Sigma Olomouc	A	1-0	Kaufman
18/04/99	Slezsky Opava	A	0-4	
24/04/99	Slovan Liborec	H	1-1	Brabec
01/05/99	Slavia Praha	A	0-4	
09/05/99	FK Teplice	H	0-2	
13/05/99	Chmel Blsany	A	1-3	Pospisil
16/05/99	Dukla Pribram	H	1-2	Cervenka
22/05/99	Banik Ostrava	A	1-2	Holenak
30/05/99	Boby Brno	H	0-0	

SIGMA OLOMOUC

CLUB DIRECTORY

SK Sigma Olomouc
Legionarska 12
771 00 Olomouc
tel - (068) 5222956
fax - (068) 5220953
Year of Formation - 1919
President - Ing. Jaromir Gajda
Secretary - Mgr. Dalibor Jarolim
Coach - Milan Boksa (99/00 - Dan Matuska)
Stadium - Andruv stadion (12,630)

APPEARANCES 98/99

	P	Ap	(s)	Gls
Jiri BALCAREK	A	10	(12)	3
Jiri BARBORIK	M	18	(2)	1
Marcel CUPAK	A		(2)	
Ales CHMELICEK	A		(1)	
Radek DRULAK	A		(2)	
Pavel HAPAL	M	11	(1)	8
Marek HEINZ	A	22	(6)	9
Radim KÖNIG	M	7	(1)	
Martin KOTULEK	D	29		2
Radoslav KOVAC	D	11	(9)	
Michal KOVAR	D	28		1
Jiri KROHMER	M	8	(17)	2
Radim KUCERA	M	26	(1)	3
Ales LISKA	M		(1)	
Oldrich MACHALA	D	30		
Josef MUCHA	M	28	(1)	4
Petr PIZANOWSKI	G	14	(2)	
Ales RYSKA	M	3	(3)	
Jindrich SKACEL	G	16		
Michal STEFKA	M	11	(11)	1
Tomas UJFALUSI	M	25	(3)	1
Ales URBANEK	M	9	(2)	1
Stanislav VLCEK	M	24	(1)	4
Pavel ZAVADIL	M		(2)	

LEAGUE RESULTS 1998/99

02/08/98	SK Hradec Kralove	A	3-1	Heinz, Kucera, Vlcek
08/08/98	Chmel Blsany	H	2-1	Heinz, Krohmer
22/08/98	Viktoria Plzen	A	0-1	
30/08/98	Dukla Pribram	H	0-0	
12/09/98	FC Karvina	A	2-1	Heinz, Mucha
20/09/98	Banik Ostrava	H	3-2	Heinz 2 (1p), Krohmer
25/09/98	Petra Drnovice	A	0-0	
05/10/98	Boby Brno	H	1-1	Kucera
18/10/98	Slezsky Opava	A	2-2	Heinz, Mucha
25/10/98	Viktoria Zizkov	H	2-1	og (Hunal), Barborik
01/11/98	Slovan Liberec	A	1-1	Vlcek
08/11/98	FK Jablonec 97	H	3-1	Balcarek 2 (1p), Kotulek
14/11/98	Slavia Praha	A	0-4	
23/11/98	Sparta Praha	H	1-1	Kucera
29/11/98	FK Teplice	A	0-1	
22/02/99	SK Hradec Kralove	H	1-0	Hapal
28/02/99	Chmel Blsany	A	2-3	Hapal, Kovar
07/03/99	Viktoria Plzen	H	1-1	Heinz
14/03/99	Dukla Pribram	A	2-1	Hapal, Heinz
21/03/99	FC Karvina	H	2-0	Stefka, Heinz
04/04/99	Banik Ostrava	A	1-1	Hapal (p)
11/04/99	Petra Drnovice	H	0-1	
18/04/99	Boby Brno	A	0-0	
24/04/99	Slezsky Opava	H	3-1	Mucha, Ujfalusi, Vlcek
02/05/99	Viktoria Zizkov	A	0-2	
09/05/99	Slovan Liberec	H	3-0	Mucha, Hapal, og (Lexa)
12/05/99	FK Jablonec 97	A	2-3	Kotulek, Hapal
16/05/99	Slavia Praha	H	1-1	Hapal
23/05/99	Sparta Praha	A	2-2	Hapal, Urbanek
30/05/99	FK Teplice	H	2-0	Balcarek, Vlcek

SLAVIA PRAHA

CLUB DIRECTORY

SK Slavia Praha
Vladivostocka 12
100 00 Praha 10
tel - (02) 67311102/67311070/749794
fax - (02) 71736889
Year of Formation - 1893
President - Ing. Vladimir Leska
Secretary - PaeDr. Zdenek Kudela
Coach - Jaroslav Hrebik (99/00 - Frantisek Cipro)
Stadium - Dr. Vacka "Eden" (16,258)

MAJOR HONOURS
League Championship - (10) 1925, 1929, 1930,
1931, 1933, 1934, 1935, 1937, 1947, 1996.
Domestic Cup - (2) 1997, 1999.

APPEARANCES 98/99

	P	Ap	(s)	Gls
Karim ADIPPE (URU)	A	3	(8)	1
Radek CERNY	G	25		
Tomas DIXA	M		(1)	
Richard DOSTALEK	M	27		5
Pavel HORVATH	M	28	(1)	7
Peter HRUBINA (SVK)	M	2	(8)	
Marek ISTENIK	A		(3)	
Lubos KOZEL	D	25		1
Radek KREJCIK	M	2	(1)	
Tomas KUCERA	A	10	(6)	3
Tomas KUCHAR	M	10	(11)	1
Vladimir LABANT (SVK)	M	26		1
Jiri LERCH	D	19	(7)	
Vladimir MALAR	A	9	(2)	4
Adam PETROUS	D	29		
Samir PINJO (BOS)	A		(1)	
Tomas POLACEK	M		(2)	
Karel RADA	D	14		1
Jiri SKALA	M	26	(2)	7
Jan STEJSKAL	G	4		
Ivo ULICH	M	25		5
Karel VACHA	A		(2)	
Michal VACLAVIK	G	1		
Robert VAGNER	A	24	(3)	12
Jaroslav VELTRUSKY	D	1	(2)	
Petr VLCEK	D	14		1
Ludek ZELENKA	A	6	(4)	1

LEAGUE RESULTS 1998/99

02/08/98	Dukla Pribram	H	2-0	Kucera 2
08/08/98	Banik Ostrava	A	0-5	
22/08/98	Boby Brno	H	1-1	Horvath
31/08/98	Viktoria Zizkov	A	1-2	Adippe
12/09/98	FK Jablonec 97	H	1-1	Ulich
21/09/98	Sparta Praha	A	0-0	
25/09/98	SK Hradec Kralove	H	1-0	Vagner
04/10/98	Viktoria Plzen	A	1-1	Kucera
16/10/98	FC Karvina	H	1-0	Vagner
26/10/98	Petra Drnovice	A	1-1	Horvath
30/10/98	Slezsky Opava	H	3-0	Horvath (p), Skala, Vagner
08/11/98	Slovan Liberec	A	1-1	Skala
14/11/98	Sigma Olomouc	H	4-0	Ulich 2, Petrous, Vagner
22/11/98	FK Teplice	H	2-1	Skala 2
29/11/98	Chmel Blsany	A	2-2	Horvath, Vagner
21/02/99	Dukla Pribram	A	2-1	Dostalek 2
01/03/99	Banik Ostrava	H	0-0	
08/03/99	Boby Brno	A	0-1	
14/03/99	Viktoria Zizkov	H	4-1	Ulich 2, Vagner, Skala
05/04/99	Sparta Praha	H	1-0	Horvath (p)
08/04/99	FK Jablonec 97	A	2-5	Dostalek, Malar
12/04/99	SK Hradec Kralove	A	2-0	Malar, Horvath
19/04/99	Viktoria Plzen	H	1-1	Kozel
24/04/99	FC Karvina	A	2-1	Rada, Vagner
01/05/99	Petra Drnovice	H	4-0	Skala, Vagner, Dostalek, Malar
10/05/99	Slezsky Opava	A	4-0	Malar, Vagner, Dostalek, Vlcek
13/05/99	Slovan Liberec	H	1-0	Vagner
16/05/99	Sigma Olomouc	A	1-1	Skala
22/05/99	FK Teplice	A	1-3	Vagner
30/05/99	Chmel Blsany	H	5-2	Labant, Zelenka, Horvath, Vagner, Kuchar

SLEZSKY OPAVA

CLUB DIRECTORY

Slezsky FC Opava
Stadion v Mestskych sadech
746 01 Opava
tel - (0653) 213745/211246
fax - (0653) 215125
Year of Formation - 1901
President - Alois Sommer
Secretary - Jiri Berousek
Coach - Jiri Bartl
Stadium - Stadion v Mestskych sadech (15,000)

APPEARANCES 98/99

	P	Ap	(s)	Gls
Jan BARANEK	M	15		6
Jiri BARBORIK	M	5		
Lukas CERNIN	D	14	(7)	
Jiri FENCL	D	19	(3)	1
Alois GRUSSMANN	M	25	(1)	6
Pavel HARAZIM	D	14		
Ales HELLEBRAND	D	2	(2)	
Roman HENDRYCH	A	28	(1)	3
Roman JANOUSEK	A		(7)	
Miroslav KAMAS	D	24	(3)	
Jaroslav KOLINEK	M	26	(3)	1
Frantisek METELKA	M	1	(4)	
Roman NOHAVICA	D	14		2
Jan PEJSA	D	13	(8)	2
Zdenek POSPECH	M	1	(2)	
Radomir PRASEK	A	23		9
Lubomir PUHAK (SVK)	M	2	(15)	1
Vladimir PUTRAS (BLS)	A	5	(4)	
Lumir SEDLACEK	M	25		5
Radek SPILACEK	M	6	(5)	
Jiri STUDENIK	M	9	(2)	
Rene TWARDZIK	G	28		
Michal VOREL	G	2	(1)	
Tomas VYCHODIL	D	29	(1)	2

LEAGUE RESULTS 1998/99

02/08/98	Boby Brno	H	2-1	Prasek 2
09/08/98	Viktoria Zizkov	A	2-3	Baranek 2
23/08/98	FK Jablonec 97	H	2-1	Prasek, Baranek
30/08/98	Sparta Praha	A	2-4	Baranek, Prasek
13/09/98	SK Hradec Kralove	H	3-1	Grussmann 2, Sedlacek
20/09/98	Viktoria Plzen	A	1-1	Pejsa
27/09/98	FC Karvina	H	2-1	Baranek, Hendrych
04/10/98	Petra Drnovice	A	2-3	Prasek 2
18/10/98	Sigma Olomouc	H	2-2	Baranek, og (Machala)
25/10/98	Slovan Liberec	H	2-0	Grussmann, Hendrych
30/10/98	Slavia Praha	A	0-3	
08/11/98	FK Teplice	H	3-3	Grussmann, Fencl, Sedlacek
14/11/98	Chmel Blsany	A	0-2	
22/11/98	Dukla Pribram	H	2-2	Pejsa, Sedlacek
29/11/98	Banik Ostrava	A	1-1	Prasek
21/02/99	Boby Brno	A	1-4	Vychodil
28/02/99	Viktoria Zizkov	H	2-0	Grussmann (p), Prasek
07/03/99	FK Jablonec 97	A	0-1	
14/03/99	Sparta Praha	H	2-1	Vychodil, Sedlacek
21/03/99	SK Hradec Kralove	A	0-1	
04/04/99	Viktoria Plzen	H	1-1	Puhak
11/04/99	FC Karvina	A	1-2	Nohavica
18/04/99	Petra Drnovice	H	4-0	Grussmann, Hendrych, og (Müller), Sedlacek (p)
24/04/99	Sigma Olomouc	A	1-3	Prasek
02/05/99	Slovan Liberec	A	0-1	
10/05/99	Slavia Praha	H	0-4	
13/05/99	FK Teplice	A	0-4	
16/05/99	Chmel Blsany	H	1-1	Nohavica
22/05/99	Dukla Pribram	A	1-3	Kolinek
30/05/99	Banik Ostrava	H	0-0	

SLOVAN LIBEREC

CLUB DIRECTORY

FC Slovan Liberec
Na Hradbach 1300
460 01 Liberec 1
tel - (048) 5103714
fax - (048) 5103715
Year of Formation - 1958
President - Ing. Zdenek Stiller
Secretary - Pavel Jirous
Coach - Josef Petrik; Ladislav Skorpil
Stadium - Mestsky stadion (6,809)

APPEARANCES 98/99

	P	Ap	(s)	Gls
Martin BARBARIC	A	7	(4)	3
Tomas BARTA	G	1		
Zdenek BENO	D	5	(1)	
David BREDA	M	20	(6)	2
Pavel CAPEK	M	27	(1)	2
Richard CULEK	M	11	(5)	1
Martin CUPR	M	11	(5)	
Pablo GOBERVILLE (ARG)	A		(1)	
Zbynek HAUZR	G	1		
Michal HRBEK	D	19		2
Libor JANACEK	M	23	(3)	
Tomas JANU	M	20		1
Jiri JAROSIK	M	7	(14)	2
Marek KINCL	A	20	(7)	5
Antonin KINSKY	G	28		
Ludek KLUSACEK	D	15		2
Leandro Hernán LAZZARO LIUNI (ARG)	A	17	(5)	9
Josef LEXA	D	22	(2)	1
Stanislav MAREK	D	24		
Rastislav MICHALIK (SVK)	M	22	(3)	
Pavel NEGRU	A	2	(1)	1
Pavel NEMCICKY	M	2	(2)	
Lukas NOVOTNY	A	9	(4)	
Bohuslav PILNY	D	11	(2)	
Lubos ZAKOSTELSKY	A	6	(15)	2

LEAGUE RESULTS 1998/99

02/08/98	Banik Ostrava	H	2-2	Lazzaro Liuni, Jarosik
09/08/98	Boby Brno	A	2-0	Breda, Jarosik
23/08/98	Viktoria Zizkov	H	2-2	Klusacek, Barbaric
30/08/98	FK Jablonec 97	A	0-1	
12/09/98	Sparta Praha	H	1-1	Lazzaro Luini
20/09/98	SK Hradec Kralove	A	2-2	Lazzaro Liuni, Culek
27/09/98	Viktoria Plzen	H	1-0	Hrbek
04/10/98	FC Karvina	A	0-2	
18/10/98	Petra Drnovice	H	1-1	Hrbek
25/10/98	Slezsky Opava	A	0-2	
01/11/98	Sigma Olomouc	H	1-1	Lexa
08/11/98	Slavia Praha	H	1-1	Zakostelsky
16/11/98	FK Teplice	A	0-4	
22/11/98	Chmel Blsany	H	2-0	Kincl, Negru
29/11/98	Dukla Pribram	A	0-1	
21/02/99	Banik Ostrava	A	0-2	
28/02/99	Boby Brno	H	0-0	
07/03/99	Viktoria Zizkov	A	3-0	Capek, Kincl, Zakostelsky
14/03/99	FK Jablonec 97	H	1-0	Lazzaro Liuni
22/03/99	Sparta Praha	A	0-1	
04/04/99	SK Hradec Kralove	H	1-1	Lazzaro Liuni
11/04/99	Viktoria Plzen	A	2-1	Barbaric, Lazzaro Liuni
18/04/99	FC Karvina	H	3-1	Lazzaro Liuni 2 (1p), Barbaric
24/04/99	Petra Drnovice	A	1-1	Klusacek
02/05/99	Slezsky Opava	H	1-0	Kincl
09/05/99	Sigma Olomouc	A	0-3	
13/05/99	Slavia Praha	A	0-1	
16/05/99	FK Teplice	H	0-1	
22/05/99	Chmel Blsany	A	2-2	Janu, Lazzaro Liuni
30/05/99	Dukla Pribram	H	4-0	Kincl 2, Breda, Capek

SPARTA PRAHA

CLUB DIRECTORY

AC Sparta Praha
Milady Horakove 98
170 00 Praha 7
tel - (02) 20570323
fax - (02) 20571665/6
Year of Formation - 1893
President - Vlastimil Kostal
Secretary - Magda Sebekova
Coach - Zdenek Scasny (99/00 - Ivan Hasek)
Stadium - AC Sparta Praha (20,893)

MAJOR HONOURS
League Championship - (24) 1926, 1927, 1932,
1936, 1938, 1946, 1948, 1952, 1954, 1965,
1967, 1984, 1985, 1987, 1988, 1989, 1990,
1991, 1993, 1994, 1995, 1997, 1998, 1999.
Domestic Cup - (9) 1964, 1972, 1976, 1980,
1984, 1988, 1989, 1992, 1996.

APPEARANCES 98/99

	P	Ap	(s)	Gls
Miroslav BARANEK	M	26	(1)	8
Michal CALOUN	G	18		
Martin CIZEK	M	13		
Petr GABRIEL	D	20		3
Martin HASEK	M	29		2
Michal HORNAK	D	24		1
Vratislav LOKVENC	A	29		11
Antonin MLEJNSKY	D	12	(6)	1
Jiri NOVOTNY	D	16	(1)	1
Pavel NOVOTNY	M	24	(3)	1
Josef OBAJDIN	A	24	(3)	6
Petr PAPOUSEK	M	2	(8)	
Tomas POSTULKA	G	12		
Martin PROHASZKA (SVK)	A	3	(9)	4
Tomas ROSICKY	M	2	(1)	
Horst SIEGL	A	30		18
Michal SMARDA	M	5	(8)	3
Miroslav SOVIC (SVK)	A	8	(2)	2
Ludek STRACENY	A	2	(11)	
Vlastimil SVOBODA	M	8	(5)	1
Zdenek SVOBODA	M	1	(3)	
Tomas VOTAVA	D	22		

LEAGUE RESULTS 1998/99

03/08/98	Viktoria Plzen	A	1-0	Baranek
08/08/98	FC Karvina	H	5-0	Siegl 2, Lokvenc, Novotny J.,
				Baranek
23/08/98	Petra Drnovice	A	4-4	Siegl 3, Lokvenc
30/08/98	Slezsky Opava	H	4-2	Lokvenc, Hasek, Siegl, Baranek
12/09/98	Slovan Liberec	A	1-1	Lokvenc
21/09/98	Slavia Praha	H	0-0	
25/09/98	FK Teplice	A	1-1	Obajdin
04/10/98	Chmel Blsany	H	3-0	Gabriel, Baranek, Lokvenc
18/10/98	Dukla Pribram	A	0-0	
25/10/98	Banik Ostrava	H	1-1	Lokvenc
02/11/98	Boby Brno	A	1-0	Obajdin
09/11/98	Viktoria Zizkov	H	5-0	Siegl 3 (1p), Smarda, Hasek
14/11/98	FK Jablonec 97	A	3-0	Siegl 2, Baranek
23/11/98	Sigma Olomouc	A	1-1	Lokvenc
29/11/98	SK Hradec Kralove	H	3-1	Novotny P., Baranek, Lokvenc
21/02/99	Viktoria Plzen	H	2-0	Gabriel, Prohaszka
28/02/99	FC Karvina	A	3-0	Lokvenc, Svoboda Z., Obajdin
07/03/99	Petra Drnovice	H	1-0	Obajdin
14/03/99	Slezsky Opava	A	1-2	Baranek
22/03/99	Slovan Liberec	H	1-0	Prohaszka
05/04/99	Slavia Praha	A	0-1	
11/04/99	FK Teplice	H	2-0	Prohaszka, Siegl (p)
19/04/99	Chmel Blsany	A	1-1	Siegl
24/04/99	Dukla Pribram	H	3-0	Mlejnsky, Sovic, Obajdin
01/05/99	Banik Ostrava	A	0-2	
09/05/99	Boby Brno	H	4-1	Gabriel, Obajdin, Sovic, Smarda
12/05/99	Viktoria Zizkov	A	6-1	Siegl 2, Baranek, Lokvenc,
				Prohaszka, Hornak
16/05/99	FK Jablonec 97	H	2-0	Siegl 2 (1p)
23/05/99	Sigma Olomouc	H	2-2	Siegl, Lokvenc
30/05/99	SK Hradec Kralove	A	1-2	Smarda

FK TEPLICE

CLUB DIRECTORY

FK Teplice
Na Stinadlech 2796
415 01 Teplice
tel - (0417) 27612/23224
fax - (0417) 29017
Year of Formation - 1945
President - Stepan Popovic
Secretary - Frantisek Snobr
Coach - Ing. Josef Pesice
Stadium - Stadion Na Stinadlach (18,464)

APPEARANCES 98/99

	P	Ap	(s)	Gls
Michal BILEK	M	24	(1)	3
Petr BRABEC	D	26	(2)	3
Radek DIVECKY	A	21	(6)	8
Michal DOLEZAL	M	1	(13)	
Petr FOUSEK	M	30		7
Zdeno FRTALA (SVK)	M	20	(6)	
Tomas HERMAN	A	2	(14)	1
Petr HRUSKA	M	7	(2)	
Jaromir JINDRACEK	M	22	(2)	8
David KÖSTL	D		(2)	
Libor MACHACEK	G	30		
Ales PIKL	D	12	(10)	
Miroslav RADA	D	26	(1)	
Zbynek RAMPACEK	D	23	(4)	2
Marian RIZEK	A	27		4
Petr STROUHAL	M		(1)	
Dusan TESARIK	M	29		5
Vit TURTENWALD	M		(3)	
Stepan VACHOUSEK	A	1	(9)	1
Pavel VERBIR	A	29		13
Petr VORISEK	M		(5)	

LEAGUE RESULTS 1998/99

02/08/98	Chmel Blsany	H	1-3	Brabec
09/08/98	Dukla Pribram	A	3-2	Verbir, Jindracek, Divecky
24/08/98	Banik Ostrava	H	0-0	
30/08/98	Boby Brno	A	3-0	Divecky 2, Rizek
13/09/98	Viktoria Zizkov	H	2-0	Verbir (p), Divecky
21/09/98	FK Jablonec 97	A	2-1	Verbir (p), Tesarik
25/09/98	Sparta Praha	H	1-1	Verbir
04/10/98	SK Hradec Kralove	A	3-0	Rampacek, Bilek, Jindracek
19/10/98	Viktoria Plzen	H	4-2	Tesarik 2, Verbir, Fousek
25/10/98	FC Karvina	A	2-0	Divecky, Herman
08/11/98	Slezsky Opava	A	3-3	Jindracek, Verbir, Rizek
16/11/98	Slovan Liberec	H	4-0	Verbir 2 (1p), Bilek, Fousek
22/11/98	Slavia Praha	A	1-2	Jindracek
25/11/98	Petra Drnovice	H	2-2	Tesarik, Jindracek
29/11/98	Sigma Olomouc	H	1-0	Verbir (p)
21/02/99	Chmel Blsany	A	2-3	Bilek, Divecky
28/02/99	Dukla Pribram	H	1-1	Verbir
07/03/99	Banik Ostrava	A	0-0	
15/03/99	Boby Brno	H	2-1	Fousek, Rizek
21/03/99	Viktoria Zizkov	A	0-2	
04/04/99	FK Jablonec 97	H	1-2	Divecky
11/04/99	Sparta Praha	A	0-2	
18/04/99	SK Hradec Kralove	H	4-0	Jindracek 2, Verbir, Vachousek
26/04/99	Viktoria Plzen	A	0-0	
02/05/99	FC Karvina	H	3-0	Fousek 2, Rampacek
09/05/99	Petra Drnovice	A	2-0	Brabec, Tesarik
13/05/99	Slezsky Opava	H	4-0	Fousek, Verbir, Jindracek, Brabec
16/05/99	Slovan Liberec	A	1-0	Divecky
22/05/99	Slavia Praha	H	3-1	Rizek, Fousek, Verbir
30/05/99	Sigma Olomouc	A	0-2	

VIKTORIA PLZEN

CLUB DIRECTORY

FC Viktoria Plzen
Struncovy sady 3
301 12 Plzen
tel - (019) 7235180
fax - (019) 7236520
Year of Formation - 1911
President - Ing. Jaroslav Penicka
Secretary - Vaclav Korinek
Coach - Petr Ulicny: Milan Sip
Stadium - Struncovy sady (28,218)

APPEARANCES 98/99

	P	Ap	(s)	Gls
Zdenek BECKA	D	14		
Jaroslav DIEPOLD	M	14		2
Pavel DOBRY	A	6	(3)	1
Lukas DOSEK	D	29		
Tomas DOSEK	A	29		9
Dejan DRENOVAC (CRO)	M	13	(4)	3
Radek HAVEL	G	30		
Petr HLAVSA	M	3	(3)	1
Miroslav JANOTA	D	11	(2)	1
Pavel MEJDR	D	3	(8)	
Miroslav MIKA	M	21	(2)	1
David NOVAK	D	11	(7)	
Lukas PLESKO	D	25	(1)	
Stanislav PURKART	M	21	(8)	2
Jaroslav SEDIVEC	A	8	(5)	
Milos SLABY	D	26		1
Libor SMETANA	A	8	(11)	
Petr SMISEK	A	2	(2)	
Jiri STUDENIK	M	14	(1)	
Marcel SVEJDIK	M	16	(7)	
Martin SVEJNOHA	D		(1)	
Jan VELKOBORSKY	D	24	(3)	4
Dejan VRAJIC (CRO)	A	2	(4)	
Ondrej ZAPOMNEL	M		(1)	

LEAGUE RESULTS 1998/99

03/08/98	Sparta Praha	H	0-1	
09/08/98	SK Hradec Kralove	A	0-3	
22/08/98	Sigma Olomouc	H	1-0	Dosek T.
30/08/98	FC Karvina	H	3-2	Dosek T. 2, Janota
13/09/98	Petra Drnovice	A	0-1	
20/09/98	Slezsky Opava	H	1-1	Dobry
27/09/98	Slovan Liberec	A	0-1	
04/10/98	Slavia Praha	H	1-1	Velkoborsky
19/10/98	FK Teplice	A	2-4	og (Brabec), Velkoborsky
25/10/98	Chmel Blsany	H	2-1	Dosek T. 2
08/11/98	Banik Ostrava	H	1-1	Purkart
14/11/98	Boby Brno	A	0-3	
22/11/98	Viktoria Zizkov	H	1-0	Drenovac (p)
25/11/98	Dukla Pribram	A	0-2	
29/11/98	FK Jablonec 97	A	0-2	
21/02/99	Sparta Praha	A	0-2	
28/02/99	SK Hradec Kralove	H	0-3	
07/03/99	Sigma Olomouc	A	1-1	Dosek T.
14/03/99	FC Karvina	A	0-2	
21/03/99	Petra Drnovice	H	2-0	Diepold, Dosek T.
04/04/99	Slezsky Opava	A	1-1	Drenovac
11/04/99	Slovan Liberec	H	1-2	Dosek T.
19/04/99	Slavia Praha	A	1-1	Velkoborsky
26/04/99	FK Teplice	H	0-0	
02/05/99	Chmel Blsany	A	1-1	Drenovac
09/05/99	Dukla Pribram	H	2-1	Diepold, Mika
12/05/99	Banik Ostrava	A	1-0	Purkart
16/05/99	Boby Brno	H	2-0	Dosek T., Velkoborsky
22/05/99	Viktoria Zizkov	A	0-3	
30/05/99	FK Jablonec 97	H	2-3	Hlavsa, Slaby

VIKTORIA ZIZKOV

CLUB DIRECTORY

FK Viktoria Zizkov
Seifertova trida
130 00 Praha 3
tel - (02) 22722045
fax - (02) 22716295
Year of Formation - 1903
President - Jiri Steinbroch
Secretary - Jiri Jechoutek
Coach - Julius Bielik; Petr Ulicny
Stadium - FK Viktoria (8,000)

MAJOR HONOURS
League Championship - (1) 1928.
Domestic Cup - (1) 1994.

APPEARANCES 98/99

	P	Ap	(s)	Gls
Karim ADIPPE (URU)	A	4	(1)	
Miroslav BACEK (SVK)	M		(1)	
Zdenek BECKA	D	11	(1)	1
Jan BURYAN	D	19	(8)	
Kennedy CHIHURI (ZIM)	M	13	(10)	3
Roman GIBALA	M	22	(6)	6
Rostislav HERTL	M	18	(5)	
Petr HOLOTA	M	20	(5)	
Tomas HUNAL	D	27		
Tomas KLINKA	A		(6)	
Jiri KOBR	G	15	(1)	
Miloslav KORDULE	D	13		2
Petr KOUBA	G	11		
Tomas KUCERA	A	2	(2)	1
Milan LINDENTHAL	M	1	(6)	
Jaromir NAVRATIL	M	10		
Pavol PAVLUS (SVK)	D	10	(1)	
Jaromir PLOCEK	M	23	(4)	
Jiri SABOU	M	1	(4)	
Miroslav SEBESTA	A	19		3
Jaroslav SILHAVY	D	20		1
Jan STEJSKAL	G	4		
Marek STRATIL	A	2	(2)	
Tomas URBAN	D	6	(1)	2
Karel VALKOUN	A	1	(8)	2
Jan ZAKOPAL	D	21	(4)	
Pavel ZBOZINEK	M	17	(5)	1
Ludek ZELENKA	A	20		9

LEAGUE RESULTS 1998/99

Date	Opponent		Score	Scorers
02/08/98	Petra Drnovice	A	2-4	Zelenka 2
09/08/98	Slezsky Opava	H	3-2	Zelenka, Sebesta, Silhavy
23/08/98	Slovan Liberec	A	2-2	Zelenka, Kordule
31/08/98	Slavia Praha	H	2-1	Gibala, Sebesta
13/09/98	FK Teplice	A	0-2	
20/09/98	Chmel Blsany	H	2-1	Kordule, Zelenka
28/09/98	Dukla Pribram	A	1-0	Zelenka
04/10/98	Banik Ostrava	H	1-1	Sebesta
18/10/98	Boby Brno	A	0-1	
25/10/98	Sigma Olomouc	A	1-2	Zelenka
09/11/98	Sparta Praha	A	0-5	
15/11/98	SK Hradec Kralove	H	1-0	Becka
22/11/98	Viktoria Plzen	A	0-1	
25/11/98	FK Jablonec 97	H	1-1	Zelenka
29/11/98	FC Karvina	H	1-0	Zelenka
21/02/99	Petra Drnovice	H	0-1	
28/02/99	Slezsky Opava	A	0-2	
07/03/99	Slovan Liberec	H	0-3	
14/03/99	Slavia Praha	A	1-4	Chihuri
21/03/99	FK Teplice	H	2-0	Gibala (p), Kucera
04/04/99	Chmel Blsany	A	0-2	
11/04/99	Dukla Pribram	H	1-1	Urban
19/04/99	Banik Ostrava	A	1-2	Urban
24/04/99	Boby Brno	H	0-2	
02/05/99	Sigma Olomouc	H	2-0	Chihuri, Valkoun
09/05/99	FK Jablonec 97	A	1-0	Chihuri
12/05/99	Sparta Praha	H	1-6	Gibala
16/05/99	SK Hradec Kralove	A	1-0	Gibala
22/05/99	Viktoria Plzen	H	3-0	Zbozinek, Gibala 2
30/05/99	FC Karvina	A	1-1	Valkoun

PROMOTED CLUBS

SECOND DIVISION FINAL TABLE 98/99

		Pd	W	D	L	F	A	Pt	GD
1	**FC Bohemians Praha**	**30**	**23**	**4**	**3**	**62**	**12**	**73**	**+50**
2	**SK Ceske Budejovice JCE**	**30**	**22**	**6**	**2**	**65**	**18**	**72**	**+47**
3	FC SYNOT Stare Mesto	30	20	7	3	64	26	67	+38
4	FC MUS Most	30	16	8	6	47	31	56	+16
5	FK Vitkovice	30	13	7	10	40	37	46	+3
6	FC Nova Hut Ostrava	30	10	10	10	28	28	40	0
7	1.AFK Atlantic Lazne Bohdanec	30	9	10	11	25	32	37	-7
8	FC Zlin	30	10	6	14	26	33	36	-7
9	FK Mlada Boleslav	30	9	7	14	33	40	34	-7
10	FK VP Frydek-Mistek	30	9	7	14	23	30	34	-7
11	FC Tatran Postorna	30	9	7	14	31	41	34	-10
12	SK Chrudim	30	10	4	16	30	48	34	-18
13	SK Zelezarny Trinec	30	8	6	16	32	52	30	-20
14	LeRK Prostejov	30	8	5	17	24	39	29	-15
15	FK Hanacka Kyselka Prerov	30	7	5	18	27	56	26	-29
16	1.FC Ceska Lipa	30	4	7	19	17	51	19	-34

CLUB DIRECTORY

FC Bohemians Praha (now - CU Bohemians Praha)
Vrsovicka 31
101 00 Praha 10
tel - (02) 71721459
fax - (02) 71721459
Year of Formation - 1905
President - Pavel Svarc
Secretary - Jan Sanytrnik
Coach - Vlastimil Petrzela
Stadium - FC Bohemians (13,716)

MAJOR HONOURS
League Championship - (1) 1983.

CLUB DIRECTORY

SK Ceske Budejovice
Strelecky ostrov 3
370 21 Ceske Budejovice
tel - (038) 7312502/7312504
fax - (038) 7312503
Year of Formation - 1905
President - Zdenek Cadek
Secretary - Milan Cadek
Coach - Pavel Tobias
Stadium - Strelecky ostrov (12,000)

DENMARK

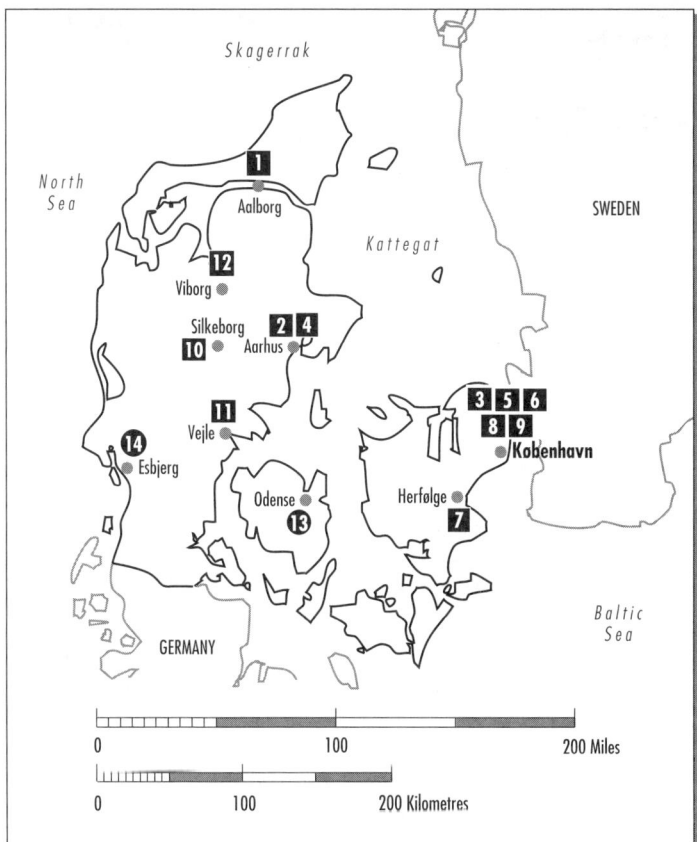

1	AAB	280	9	LYNGBY FC	288
2	AARHUS FREMAD	281	10	SILKEBORG IF	289
3	AB	282	11	VEJLE BK	290
4	AGF	283	12	VIBORG FF	291
5	B93	284		Promoted clubs	
6	BRØNDBY IF	285	13	OB	292
7	HERFØLGE BK	286	14	ESBJERG FB	292
8	FC KØBENHAVN	287			

LIFE AFTER LAUDRUPS PROVES DIFFICULT

Foreign influence gives AaB the edge

FEDERATION DIRECTORY

Dansk Boldspil Union
Idraettens Hus, Brøndby stadion 20, 2605 Brøndby

tel - (43) 262222 — Year of Formation - 1889
fax - (43) 262245 — President - Poul Hyldgaard
Secretary - Jim Stjerne Hansen

Stadium - Parken, København (41,641)

Brøndby's run of Danish championship successes came to an unexpected end in 1998/99 as they surrendered their title to unfancied AaB of Aalborg.

The outcome surprised everybody. After the winter break AaB sat rather uncomfortably in fourth place. They trailed leaders AB by six points, and with both Brøndby and the other favourites, FC Copenhagen, positioned ahead of them, it looked a very tall order for the Jutland side to come from behind and reclaim the title they had last won four years earlier. However, they succeeded - thanks largely to the misadventures of their rivals.

That AB should be out in front at the mid-season juncture was a major shock to everyone, but despite losing their coach Christian Andersen to FC Copenhagen during the winter break they appeared to be in safe hands after welcoming in Ole Mørch as their new coach. Mørch had been in charge of village club Herfølge for five years, leading them to the top of the table for the very first time three rounds into the campaign. Things initially went to plan for AB and their new leader, but the month of May was to prove catastrophic. Four successive defeats effectively erased them from contention, leaving the club's long-awaited tenth Danish title on hold for at least one more year.

Considerable compensation came in the Danish Cup as AB took the trophy for the first time in their 110-year history with a 2-1 victory over AaB in the final, having earlier eliminated both FC Copenhagen and Brøndby. Scorer of the winning goal, aptly enough, was the club's top marksman in the league, Chris Hermansen, who could count himself unlucky not to gain international recognition during the season. That honour did go to three other AB players - René Henriksen, Brian Steen Nielsen and Claus Thomsen - although the latter left for German club Wolfsburg in mid-season.

One man moving in the opposite direction was Brian Laudrup. The superstar's return to Denmark after several years away was the story of the season, and his arrival at FC

LEAGUE CHAMPIONSHIP RESULTS 98/99

	1	2	3	4	5	6	7	8	9	10	11	12
1 AaB		3-1	2-0	4-0	2-0	1-0	1-1	3-3	3-3	2-4	5-2	1-1
		3-2		2-1	0-0			4-3			4-2	
2 Aarhus Fremad	1-3		1-4	2-1	2-0	1-3	0-1	3-3	1-2	2-2	3-3	3-1
	1-3				2-0				2-4	0-1		3-2
3 AB	1-1	1-0		1-1	7-0	0-4	1-0	4-1	1-3	4-2	0-1	1-1
	0-1			1-0	1-3		2-1	0-0		2-0		
4 AGF	1-0	3-2	3-1		2-1	1-3	2-1	2-1	1-0	2-3	2-1	3-2
	1-1					3-3			1-1	2-3		0-0
5 B93	1-5	1-3	0-1	1-2		1-5	1-2	0-0	1-3	0-1	0-1	0-5
	0-3			4-2		1-0			1-2		0-2	
6 Brøndby IF	1-2	2-0	0-1	4-1	4-1		5-1	3-2	2-3	3-0	1-2	2-5
	1-1	3-0					1-0		6-0	3-0		2-1
7 Herfølge BK	0-0	3-1	0-1	1-1	3-1	1-2		2-3	0-2	1-1	2-2	4-1
	3-2	2-2		0-0	0-0					2-0		
8 FC København	2-2	2-2	1-0	0-2	1-0	1-0	0-3		5-1	2-2	0-1	3-2
	3-0		1-1		1-0	0-1	2-0					4-2
9 Lyngby FC	2-2	1-1	0-3	1-1	2-1	2-6	0-0	3-1		0-0	2-0	2-3
	1-1		3-2		1-0	1-3				2-2		3-1
10 Silkeborg IF	0-0	4-1	1-2	2-0	2-0	1-2	0-1	3-3	1-1		1-0	1-2
	0-0		1-1		2-2	1-1	2-2				4-3	
11 Vejle BK	0-1	4-2	0-2	3-0	2-0	1-2	1-1	1-3	1-2	4-1		4-0
	4-1		2-2		0-0			1-0	1-2			4-1
12 Viborg FF	1-2	2-4	0-1	3-1	5-0	2-0	0-3	1-0	5-2	2-1	0-1	
	0-0		1-0		5-1		1-0			3-3		

LEAGUE CHAMPIONSHIP FINAL TABLE 98/99

		Home					Away					Total						
		P	W	D	L	F	A	W	D	L	F	A	W	D	L	F	A	P	GD
1	AaB	33	10	5	1	40	23	7	8	2	25	14	17	13	3	65	37	64	+28
2	Brøndby IF	33	11	1	5	43	20	8	3	5	30	17	19	4	10	73	37	61	+36
3	AB	33	8	4	5	27	19	9	1	6	22	17	17	5	11	49	36	56	+13
4	Lyngby FC	33	6	7	4	26	27	8	3	5	29	33	14	10	9	55	60	52	-5
5	Herfølge BK	33	5	7	4	24	19	7	4	6	20	17	12	11	10	44	36	47	+8
6	Vejle BK	33	8	3	6	33	20	6	2	8	21	28	14	5	14	54	48	47	+6
7	FC København	33	9	4	4	28	19	3	6	7	27	33	12	10	11	55	52	46	+3
8	Viborg FF	33	9	2	5	31	19	4	3	10	30	40	13	5	15	61	59	44	+2
9	Silkeborg IF	33	5	8	4	26	21	5	6	5	26	32	10	14	9	52	53	44	-1
10	AGF	33	9	4	3	29	23	2	6	9	16	32	11	10	12	45	55	43	-10
11	Aarhus Fremad	33	5	3	8	27	33	2	5	10	24	40	7	8	18	51	73	29	-22
12	B93	33	2	1	13	12	37	1	2	14	10	43	3	3	27	22	80	12	-58

Copenhagen from Chelsea (a day after he had scored the winner for the Londoners to knock his club-to-be out of the European Cup-winners' Cup!) was expected to tip the title balance in their favour.

Almost from day one, though, the alliance looked fragile. It did not help that FC Copenhagen's new coach Christian Andersen was sacked after just one match when the players complained they could not work with him. Kim Brink, who had preceded Andersen as temporary coach, returned, but by then the damage had been done, morale was low, and with Laudrup having an awful time trying to readjust to the insatiable demands of the Danish press and public, FC Copenhagen floated slowly down the table, eventually settling in seventh place - a totally unacceptable conclusion to a season that had promised so much.

Laudrup's début came in the classic derby confrontation away to Brøndby on March 14. The majority of the 18,316 spectators - a new record for the Brøndby stadium - jeered his every touch. It was tough treatment from the supporters of his old club, and Laudrup was clearly disheartened by the reception. He felt even worse when FC Copenhagen lost the game 3-2 and then managed just two victories in the next 12 matches before they faced Brøndby again in round 31.

By then FC Copenhagen were out of the title race but they were still in a position to have a big say about its

INTERNATIONAL HONOURS

World Cup Finals appearances: 1986 (2nd round), 1998 (qtr-finals)
European Championship appearances: 1964 (4th), 1984 (semi-finals), 1988, 1992 (Winners), 1996

outcome. Watched by a huge crowd of 37,940 fans, far and away the largest crowd of the Superliga season, Laudrup and co. played their best game of the spring campaign, winning 1-0 and leaving Brøndby five points behind AaB with just two games left.

It was sweet revenge for Laudrup, but that match proved to be his last in Denmark. Quite simply, he could not take the pressure. He was particularly hurt by the incessant rumours about his private life that circulated in the Danish tabloid press. Having already burned his bridges with Chelsea, he decided to pursue his career in Holland with Ajax - the club where his elder brother Michael had ended his career a year earlier.

AaB made maximum capital out of their challengers' misery. In a 14-match unbeaten run during the spring they picked up 32 points, and after beating FC Copenhagen 4-3 in the game of the season on the last day of April they never left first place. The championship was secured in the penultimate round at home to Lyngby. Although they only managed a 3-3 draw, Brøndby, their sole remaining challengers, lost 1-2 at home to Vejle, so the crown was theirs.

Never before had a team won the Dansh title with such a strong foreign influence. Not only did AaB have a Swedish coach in Hans Backe. Four of their key players were from other Scandinavian countries - defender Jozo Matovac and midfielder Anders Andersson from Sweden, Ståle Solbakken and Frank Strandli from Norway. Solbakken was the best of the bunch, winning the title in his first full season at the club after failing to make the grade with Wimbledon in the English Premiership. He played in all but one of AaB's games and was never substituted, and it was his spectacular double-strike which gave the club the memorable 4-3 comeback victory over

TOP SCORERS

23	Heine FERNANDEZ (Viborg FF)	
19	Chris HERMANSEN (AB)	
	Ebbe SAND (Brøndby IF)	
18	Søren HERMANSEN (Lyngby FC)	
17	Søren FREDERIKSEN (AaB)	
16	Henrik PEDERSEN (Silkeborg IF)	
	Carsten FREDGAARD (Lyngby FC)	
15	David NIELSEN (FC København)	
13	Kaspar DALGAS (Vejle BK)	
12	Bo HANSEN (Brøndby IF)	
	Bo NIELSEN (AGF)	

NATIONAL TEAM RESULTS 98/99

19/08/98	Czech Republic	A	Prague	0-1	
05/09/98	Belarus (ECQ)	A	Minsk	0-0	
10/10/98	Wales (ECQ)	H	Copenhagen	1-2	Frederiksen (58)
14/10/98	Switzerland (ECQ)	A	Zürich	1-1	Tobiasen (90)
10/02/99	Croatia	A	Split	1-0	Sand (45)
27/03/99	Italy (ECQ)	H	Copenhagen	1-2	Sand (56)
28/04/99	South Africa	H	Copenhagen	1-1	Sand (40)
05/06/99	Belarus (ECQ)	H	Copenhagen	1-0	Heintze (23)
09/06/99	Wales (ENG)	A	Liverpool	2-0	Tomasson (84), Tøfting (90p)

FC Copenhagen that took them to the top of the table. Of the Danish players in the team, the one who caught the eye most was striker Søren Frederiksen, the team's top scorer with 17 goals.

The last round of the season was decidedly odd, with Lyngby going into their final game, against Brøndby, having to lose in order to qualify for the UEFA Cup! This perverse state of affairs was caused by UEFA's mangled qualification rules. An explanation:

Second place brought qualification for the Champions' League, while third and fourth merited UEFA Cup spots. AB had already qualified for the UEFA Cup as Cup-winners, but if they won their final game and Brøndby lost at Lyngby, they would finish second and thus swap their UEFA Cup place for the Champions' League berth,

with Brøndby doing vice-versa. Normally, in that instance, the Cup losers would have taken the vacant UEFA Cup spot, but as that team was AaB, the champions, that would have meant the two losing semi-finalists, Silkeborg and Brøndby, playing-off for the UEFA Cup place. And if Silkeborg had won that encounter, they and already-qualified Brøndby would have gone into the UEFA Cup, leaving Lyngby with nothing. Thus, bizarrely, it was in Lyngby's interests to lose to Brøndby to make their European participation safe.

As it happened, AB lost away to FC Copenhagen, so the theory was not called into practice. Lyngby did lose 6-2 to Brøndby - a suspicious result, to say the least - but observers from UEFA who watched the game reported that fair play had not been undermined. They could hardly

DOMESTIC CUP 98/99

FOURTH ROUND
B1913 0, OB 1
Frederikshavn BI 0, Herfølge BK 2
BK Frem 0, Aarhus Fremad 2
Haderslev FK 0, Viborg FF 4
Herning Fremad 5, Køge BK 0
HIK 0, AGF 7
AC Horsens 4, AaB 5
Ringsted IF 2, Naestved BK 4 (aet)
Svendborg FB 3, B93 2
Tårnby BK 1, Esbjerg FB 3
byes - AB, Brøndby IF, FC København, Lyngby FC, Silkeborg IF, Vejle BK

FIFTH ROUND
Esbjerg FB 1, AaB 3
Herning Fremad 1, Herfølge BK 2 (aet)
Lyngby FC 1, Vejle BK 0
Naestved BK 1, AB 7

OB 1, AGF 0
Silkeborg IF 5, Aarhus Fremad 1
Svendborg FB 0, FC København 3
Viborg FF 0, Brøndby IF 3

QUARTER-FINALS
AB 1 (Stokholm 103), FC København 0 (aet)
Lyngby FC 1 (Fredgaard 92),
AaB 1 (Frederiksen 116) (aet; 2-4 on pens.)
OB 1 (Wael 34),
Brøndby IF 3 (Sand 7, 75, 76p)
Silkeborg IF 2 (Pedersen 7, Lassen 46),
Herfølge BK 1 (Lykke 33)

SEMI-FINALS
Brøndby IF 1 (Sand 86), AB 1 (Larsen 90)
AB 2 (Michaelsen 16, Bjur 90), Brøndby IF 0
(AB 3-1)

Silkeborg IF 4 (Petersen 28, Zivkovic 36, Jokovic 47, 65),
AaB 4 (Strandli 5, Jessen 7, Frederiksen 63, 73)
AaB 2 (Solbakken 6, 59), Silkeborg IF 0
(AaB 6-4)

FINAL
13/05/99, Copenhagen
AB 2 Nielsen A. (42), Hermansen (73)
AAB 1 Frederiksen (43)
referee - Hald

AB - Hoffmann; Olesen, Henriksen, Larsen, Michaelsen, Bjur, Rasmussen, Nielsen B.S., Nielsen A. (Metin 72), Hermansen (Albrechtsen 88), Falck.

AAB - Nielsen; Priske, Baelum, Matovac, Jessen, Thomsen (Gaardsøe 78), Solbakken, Rasmussen (Gaarde 56), Andersson (Boye 65), Strandli, Frederiksen.

NATIONAL TEAM APPEARANCES 98/99

Coach - Bo JOHANSSON	CZE	BLS	WAL	SUI	CRO	ITA	SAF	BLS	WAL	Cps	Gls
Peter SCHMEICHEL (18/11/63) - Manchester United (ENG)	G	G			G	G	G	G	G	112	-
Søren COLDING (02/09/72) - Brøndby IF	D		s59	D	s83	D	D	D	16	-
Ole TOBIASEN (08/07/75) - Ajax (HOL)	D	D	D	D						6	1
René HENRIKSEN (27/08/69) - AB	D			D	D	D	D	D	8	-
Jan HEINTZE (17/08/63) - Bayer 04 Leverkusen (GER)	D	D	D	D	D	D	D	D	D	53	2
Thomas GRAVESEN (11/03/76) - Hamburger SV (GER)	M58	s66	s76		s56		M80			5	-
Thomas HELVEG (24/06/71) - Milan (ITA)	M78	M	M	M	M	D	D87			42	2
Allan NIELSEN (13/03/71) - Tottenham Hotspur (ENG)	M78	M			M	M77		M	M83	29	6
Jon Dahl TOMASSON (29/08/76) - Feyenoord (HOL)	A68	A80		A78			M61		s70	9	1
Ebbe SAND (19/07/72) - Brøndby IF	A58		s66	s61	A	A	A	A78	A	15	4
Peter MØLLER (23/03/72) - Real Oviedo (ESP)	A	A66								16	3
Claus THOMSEN (31/05/70) - AB/VfL Wolfsburg (GER)	s58	M			M32	M				20	-
Søren ANDERSEN (31/01/70) - Bristol City (ENG)	s58	s66								9	-
Niclas JENSEN (17/08/74) - FC København	s68									1	-
Bjarne GOLDBAEK (06/10/68) - FC København/Chelsea (ENG)	s78				M83	s61	M	M	16	-
Per FRANDSEN (06/02/70) - Bolton Wanderers (ENG)	s78		M76	M59					s90	18	-
Marc RIEPER (05/06/68) - Celtic (SCO)		D	D	D						61	2
Jes HØGH (07/05/66) - Fenerbahçe (TUR)		D	D	D	D			D	D	49	1
Martin JØRGENSEN (06/10/75) - Udinese (ITA)		M66	M	A	M56	A	M61	A	M90	17	1
Søren FREDERIKSEN (27/01/72) - AaB		s80	A	A61	s67		s87			6	1
Mogens KROGH (31/10/63) - Brøndby IF		G	G							10	-
Brian Steen NIELSEN (28/12/68) - AB			M	M	s32		M	s80	s67	44	-
Mikkel BECK (12/05/73) - Middlesbrough (ENG)			A66	s78						16	3
Miklos MOLNAR (10/04/70) - Sevilla FC (ESP)				A67	s53	s61	s78	A70	15	2
Jesper GRØNKJAER (18/02/77) - Ajax (HOL)					M53	A80	A	M	4	-
Stig TØFTING (14/08/69) - MSV Duisburg (GER)						s77	M	M67	s83	10	1
Michael SCHJØNBERG (19/01/67) - 1.FC Kaiserslautern (GER)							s80			33	3

have said otherwise given that the whole mess was of their own making!

Brøndby's big win included four goals from star striker Ebbe Sand, who thus signed off in style before leaving to join German club Schalke in a £2m transfer. It was also the end of a long road at Brøndby for coach Ebbe Skovdahl, who left to join Aberdeen, and for veteran Danish international midfielder John Jensen, who decided to take up the offer of becoming the new coach at Herfølge.

The trio's final season at Brøndby had seen the club rub shoulders with the might of Europe in the Champions' League. Having been drawn in a group that contained Manchester United, Barcelona and Bayern Munich, there was never any realistic hope that Brøndby would reach the latter stages, but they did make a phenomenal start, scoring twice late on to beat Bayern at home. Two heavy defeats by Manchester United soon put them in their place, though, and those three opening points were to remain the only ones they won in the entire six-match series.

There was little joy, either, for the Danish national team during that busy period in the early autumn. The World Cup quarter-finalists badly missed the absent Laudrup brothers - both retired from international football - as they began their Euro 2000 qualifying quest with a 0-0 draw away to Belarus, a 1-2 home defeat by Wales and a 1-1 draw in Switzerland, which was only achieved thanks to a last-gasp equaliser. With another home defeat, by Italy,

EUROPEAN CUPS 98/99

CHAMPIONS' CUP
● BRØNDBY IF
Qualifying round 1.FC KOSICE (SVK)
A 2-0 Daugaard (54), Thygesen (85)
Andersen; Colding, Rasmussen, Nielsen, Jensen B., Bjur (Thygesen 81), Jensen J., Daugaard, Lindrup (Bagger 69), Hansen (Jensen M. 86), Sand.
H 0-1
Andersen; Colding, Rasmussen, Nielsen, Bjerregaard, Bjur, Jensen J., Daugaard, Thygesen (Bagger 65; Lindrup 78), Hansen (Ravn 83), Sand.

Champions' League
1st match FC BAYERN MÜNCHEN (GER)
H 2-1 Helmer (87og), Ravn (89)
Krogh M.; Colding, Rasmussen, Nielsen, Jensen B., Bjur, Ravn, Jensen J., Daugaard (Jensen M. 73), Sand (Hansen 56), Lindrup (Krogh S. 76).

2nd match FC BARCELONA (ESP)
A 0-2
Krogh M.; Skarbalius, Rasmussen, Nielsen, Jensen B., Bjur (Krogh S. 77), Daugaard, Ravn (Jensen M. 12), Jensen J., Lindrup (Hansen 65), Sand.

3rd match MANCHESTER UNITED (ENG)
H 2-6 Daugaard (35), Sand (90)
Krogh M.; Colding, Rasmussen, Nielsen (Jensen M. 31), Jensen B. (Da Silva 27), Bjur, Ravn, Daugaard, Lindrup, Sand, Hansen (Bagger 67).

4th match MANCHESTER UNITED (ENG)
A 0-5
Andersen; Colding, Rasmussen, Nielsen, Skarbalius, Bjur (Krogh S. 74), Jensen J., Ravn, Daugaard, Bagger (Thygesen 68), Sand (Hansen 77).

5th match FC BAYERN MÜNCHEN (GER)
A 0-2
Andersen; Colding, Rasmussen, Nielsen (Da Silva 68), Skarbalius, Bjur, Jensen J., Sand, Daugaard, Bagger (Lindrup 65), Hansen (Christensen 70).

6th match FC BARCELONA (ESP)
H 0-2
Krogh M.; Colding, Rasmussen, Nielsen, Skarbalius, Bjur, Jensen J. (Thygesen 80), Daugaard (Christensen 70), Sand, Bagger (Lindrup 74), Hansen.

CUP WINNERS' CUP
● FC KØBENHAVN
Qualifying round KARABAKH AGDAM (AZB)
H 6-0 Nielsen Ma. (2). Thorninger (6), Nielsen P. (12, 40), Goldbaek (19), Falch (25)
Stensgaard; Haren, Nielsen Mio, Falch, Jensen N., Nielsen Ma. (Larsen 62), Goldbaek (Jensen K. 46), Hemmingsen, Nielsen P., Thorninger, Nielsen D. (Nielsen C. 74).
A 4-0 Jensen N. (64), Nielsen P. (68), Nielsen D. (75, 84)
Stensgaard; Haren, Nielsen Mio, Madsen, Jensen N., Nielsen Ma. (Dogan 71), Goldbaek (Nielsen D. 46), Hemmingsen, Nielsen P., Thorninger, Jonsson (Nielsen C. 56).

1st round LEVSKI SOFIA (BUL)
A 2-0 Goldbaek (34), Thorninger (76)
Stensgaard; Haren, Nielsen Mio, Madsen, Jensen N., Nielsen Ma., Falch, Nielsen P., Goldbaek, Nielsen D. (Jensen K. 83), Jonsson (Thorninger 64).
H 4-1 Nielsen Ma. (17), Nielsen L.H. (49), Thorninger (58, 76)
Stensgaard; Haren, Nielsen Mio, Falch, Jensen N., Nielsen Ma., Nielsen L.H. (Jensen C.V. 84), Goldbaek, Nielsen P. (Nielsen C. 76), Thorninger, Jonsson (Larsen 74).

2nd round CHELSEA (ENG)
A 1-1 Goldbaek (81)
Stensgaard; Haren, Nielsen Mio, Hemmingsen, Jensen N., Rytter (Madsen 73), Nielsen L.H. (Falch 86), Goldbaek, Nielsen P., Thorninger (Jonsson 80), Nielsen D..
H 0-1
Stensgaard; Rytter, Haren (Larsen M.B. 88), Nielsen Mio, Jensen N., Nielsen L.H., Goldbaek, Hemmingsen, Nielsen P., Nielsen D., Thorninger (Jonsson 56).

UEFA CUP
● SILKEBORG IF
Qualifying round MURA MURSKA SOBOTA (SLO)
A 0-0
Kjaer; Bruun, Hansen J., Zivkovic, Petersen, Brøgger (Hansen M. 81), Sørensen, Larsen T.R., Poulsen (Svenningsen 62) Jokovic, Pedersen (Nørholt 81).
H 2-0 Sørensen (63), Larsen T.R. (64)
Kjaer; Bruun, Hansen J., Zivkovic, Petersen, Hansen M., Sørensen, Larsen T.R., Poulsen, Jokovic, Pedersen.

1st round ROMA (ITA)
A 0-1
Kjaer; Petersen, Zivkovic, Larsen M., Hansen M., Lyhne (Brøgger 72), Sørensen, Bruun, Knudsen (Larsen T.R. 72), Poulsen, Pedersen (Nørholt 78).
H 0-2
Kjaer; Hansen M. (Brøgger 60), Hansen J., Zivkovic, Larsen M. (Petersen 65), Bruun, Sørensen, Larsen T.R., Poulsen, Jokovic, Pedersen (Lyhne 83).

● VEJLE BK
Qualifying round OTELUL GALATI (ROM)
H 3-0 Wael (31, 42), Søgaard (62)
Boye; Risom, Scholz, Sønksen, Facius, Søgaard, Wael (Dalgas 78), Christiansen (Eskildsen 70), Mikkelsen, Graulund (Nørlund 83), Jung.
A 3-0 Jung (22), Graulund (36), Wael (53)
Boye; Risom, Sørensen, Sønksen (Eskildsen 81), Facius, Søgaard, Wael (Mikkelsen 78), Christiansen, Nørlund, Graulund (Dalgas 37), Jung.

1st round REAL BETIS (ESP)
H 1-0 Graulund (86)
Boye; Risom, Scholz, Sønksen, Christiansen, Søgaard (Nørlund 78), Facius, Wael, Sørensen, Dalgas, Jung (Graulund 69).
A 0-5
Boye; Risom, Scholz, Sønksen, Sørensen, Harder (Dalgas 54), Søgaard, Facius, Jung (Mikkelsen 59), Fig (Wael 65), Graulund.

following in the spring, it looked all but certain that Denmark's fifth successive European Championship participation would not take place, but some hope of a play-off place was rekindled with a couple of victories against Belarus and Wales in early June.

Coach Bo Johansson decided that whatever the outcome of the qualifying campaign he would not be renewing his contract once it ended in the summer of 2000. He will be replaced by former international Morten Olsen, the captain of the famous Danish dynamite team of the mid-'80s.

The coach of that wonderful team, German-born Sepp Piontek, announced his decision to retire from the game at the end of the 1998/99 season. A heart-attack convinced him it was time to call it a day. He will forever be remembered with affection in Denmark for the way his team always tried to play attractive, spectator-friendly football. The magnificent 6-1 demolition of Uruguay at the 1986 World Cup remains arguably the greatest game ever played by Denmark. That was Piontek's team. Now his chief apprentice, Olsen, will attempt to revive those glory days in the new millennium.

PLAYERS OF THE SEASON

SØREN COLDING
Søren Colding (below) used the 1998/99 season to establish himself as the first-choice right-back in the Danish national team. The second long-term injury sustained by Ajax's Ole Tobiasen in as many seasons certainly helped his cause, but the Brøndby man proved to be a more than adequate replacement, reproducing the form that had made him a regular in Denmark's 1998 World Cup side. The 27-year-old has been Brøndby's right-back since 1994, when he joined from Frem. The club's failure to win a fourth successive title in 1999 was no fault of his as he played consistently well all season and was probably Brøndby's best player, offering a constant source of danger with his purposeful touchline gallops and pin-point crosses.

HEINE FERNANDEZ
The top scorer in the 1998/99 Superliga is no stranger to putting the ball in the net. In all but three seasons since he began senior-level football in Denmark in 1987 he has finished as his club's leading marksman. What's more, he has only played for two teams - Silkeborg, for whom he holds the club record of 74 league goals, and Viborg, where he returned for a second spell in 1998 and promptly notched 23 goals, the largest tally of his career, to keep the team away from the threat of relegation. Despite his fine record, he has played just once for Denmark - in 1991, against Iceland - but at 33 the chances of him becoming that long-awaited 'new Preben Elkjaer' appear to be about as remote as a comeback of the great man himself.

PETER SCHMEICHEL
When Peter Schmeichel announced in November 1998 that he would be leaving Manchester United at the end of the season, he could not possibly have imagined the dream-like scenario that would await him six months later. Not only did he play a prominent role in United's historic 'treble' triumph, but it was he, as the stand-in skipper for the suspended Roy Keane, who had the honour and privilege of being the man who lifted the European Champions' Cup in Barcelona - on his farewell appearance! Denmark's all-time record international will never be forgotten at Old Trafford, where he spent eight glorious years, but at 35 he still believes in himself and has a strong ambition to do well in Portugal with his new team Sporting - a club desperate to win the Portuguese title after an 18-year drought.

AAB

Aalborg Boldspilklub A/S
Hornevej 2
9220 Aalborg Øst
Year of Formation - 1885
tel - (98) 157222
fax - (98) 153334
Chairman - Jørgen Brix Steby
Secretary - Børge Bach
Coach - Hans Backe
Stadium - Aalborg Stadion (13,374)

MAJOR HONOURS
League Championship - (2) 1995, 1999.
Domestic Cup - (2) 1966, 1970.

APPEARANCES 98/99

	P	Ap	(s)	Gls
Anders ANDERSSON (SWE)	M	18	(3)	1
Thomas BAELUM	D	30		
Torben BOYE	D	17	(7)	
Søren FREDERIKSEN	A	30	(1)	17
Allan GAARDE	M	11	(20)	8
Thomas GAARDSØE	M	3	(14)	2
Steffen HØJER	A	14	(4)	2
Thomas JENSEN	M		(1)	
Jens JESSEN	D	32		4
Jacob KRÜGER	D	8	(2)	
Jozo MATOVAC (SWE)	D	32		1
Jimmy NIELSEN	G	33		
Jari PEDERSEN	A	4	(9)	4
Brian PRISKE	D	18		
Henrik RASMUSSEN	M	29	(4)	4
Dan SAHLIN (SWE)	A	5		2
Ståle SOLBAKKEN (NOR)	M	32		7
Frank STRANDLI (NOR)	A	17		9
Thomas THOMASBERG	M	4	(8)	1
Lars THOMSEN	M	24		3
Peter TRANBERG	M	2	(10)	

LEAGUE RESULTS 1998/99

26/07/98	AGF	H	4-0	Sahlin, Frederiksen 2, Jessen	
02/08/98	AB	A	1-1	Frederiksen	
07/08/98	Brøndby IF	H	1-0	Pedersen	
16/08/98	B93	A	5-1	Thomsen, Højer, Frederiksen 3	
21/08/98	Vejle BK	H	5-2	Thomsen, Jessen, Rasmussen 2, Frederiksen	
30/08/98	Lyngby FC	A	2-2	Frederiksen 2	
13/09/98	Herfølge BK	A	0-0		
20/09/98	Aarhus Fremad	H	3-1	Frederiksen, Pedersen 2	
27/09/98	Viborg FF	A	2-1	Thomasberg, Pedersen	
04/10/98	FC København	H	3-3	Solbakken, Sahlin, Frederiksen	
18/10/98	Silkeborg IF	A	0-0		
25/10/98	Vejle BK	H	4-2	Gaarde 3, Højer	
01/11/98	FC København	A	2-2	Solbakken, Gaardsøe	
08/11/98	Silkeborg IF	H	2-4	Gaarde 2	
29/11/98	Herfølge BK	H	1-1	Jessen	
07/03/99	AGF	A	0-1		
14/03/99	B93	A	3-0	Andersson, Frederiksen, Strandli	
21/03/99	Viborg FF	H	1-1	Strandli	
29/03/99	Lyngby FC	A	1-1	Gaarde	
01/04/99	AB	A	1-0	Strandli	
05/04/99	Aarhus Fremad	H	3-2	Frederiksen 2, Strandli	
12/04/99	Brøndby IF	A	2-1	Rasmussen, Frederiksen	
19/04/99	AGF	A	2-1	Solbakken, Frederiksen	
23/04/99	Silkeborg IF	A	0-0		
30/04/99	FC København	H	4-3	Jessen, Matovac, Solbakken 2	
05/05/99	Vejle BK	A	1-0	Strandli	
10/05/99	Brøndby IF	H	0-0		
16/05/99	Aarhus Fremad	A	3-1	Strandli 2, Thomsen	
20/05/99	AB	H	2-0	Gaarde, Solbakken	
24/05/99	Viborg FF	A	0-0		
30/05/99	B93	H	2-0	Gaarde, Rasmussen	
13/06/99	Lyngby FC	H	3-3	Strandli 2, Frederiksen	
16/06/99	Herfølge BK	A	2-3	Gaardsøe, Solbakken	

AARHUS FREMAD

CLUB DIRECTORY

Aarhus Fremad
Hans Egedesvej 21
8200 Aarhus N
tel - (86) 164100
fax - (86) 164166
Year of Formation - 1947
Chairman - Jan Nielsen
Secretary - Morten Nysom
Coach - Kim Poulsen; Peer Danefeld
Stadium - Aarhus Stadion (18,500)

APPEARANCES 98/99

		P	Ap	(s)	Gls
Ukrik BALLING	A	18	(3)		7
Wassim El BANNA	A	3	(6)		2
Jacob BERGER	M	12	(3)		
Henrik BRUND	M		(2)		
Henrik BUNDGAARD	G	6			
Jesper DUPONT	M	12			
Stig HAALAND (NOR)	D	19	(5)		3
Ove HANSEN	A	14	(9)		4
Peder HENRIKSEN	D	9	(2)		1
Søren HOLDGAARD	D	6	(1)		1
Chris IWELUMO (SCO)	A	18	(9)		4
Henrik JESPERSEN	M	11	(2)		3
Niels Christian JØRGENSEN	G	27			
Lars KLAUSEN	A	21	(2)		1
Frank KROGSDAL	A	1	(2)		
Lars LAMBAEK	M	2	(1)		
Frode LANGAGERGAARD	D	21			
Jan LARSEN	D	25			1
Klaus LILDHOLT	M		(1)		
Ken MARTIN	D	29			2
Rune METHLING	M	4	(1)		
Thomas NIELSEN	D	6	(5)		
Tommy NIELSEN	D	29			2
Brian PRISKE	M	17			3
Nikolaj RASMUSSEN	A	6	(3)		1
Lasse SALL	M		(3)		
Carsten SIERSBAEK	A	6	(10)		2
Jesper SOMMER	M	18	(7)		4
Gregers ULRICH	M	23	(10)		10

LEAGUE RESULTS 1998/99

26/07/98	AB	H	1-4	Martin
03/08/98	Brøndby IF	A	0-2	
09/08/98	B93	H	2-0	Nielsen To. (p), Klausen
16/08/98	Herfølge BK	A	1-3	Balling
23/08/98	Viborg FF	H	3-1	Ulrich, Balling 2
30/08/98	Vejle BK	A	2-4	Rasmussen, Iwelumo
13/09/98	Lyngby FC	H	1-2	Priske
20/09/98	AaB	A	1-3	Balling
27/09/98	FC København	A	2-2	Nielsen To., Balling
04/10/98	Silkeborg IF	H	2-2	Jespersen, Balling
18/10/98	AGF	A	2-3	Hansen, Ulrich
25/10/98	Viborg FF	A	4-2	Hansen, Ulrich, Priske 2
08/11/98	Lyngby FC	H	2-4	Jespersen 2 (2p)
15/11/98	Brøndby IF	A	1-1	Sommer
18/11/98	AB	A	0-1	
22/11/98	FC København	A	0-3	
29/11/98	Vejle BK	H	3-3	Siersbaek, Henriksen, Hansen
14/03/99	Silkeborg IF	H	0-1	
21/03/99	AGF	A	1-1	Ulrich
01/04/99	Herfølge BK	H	0-1	
05/04/99	AaB	A	2-3	Larsen, Martin
11/04/99	B93	H	2-0	Ulrich 2
18/04/99	Brøndby IF	H	1-3	Sommer
26/04/99	Lyngby FC	A	1-1	Sommer
30/04/99	AB	H	1-3	Balling
05/05/99	Viborg FF	H	3-2	Hansen, Iwelumo, Banna
09/05/99	B93	A	3-1	Ulrich 2, Iwelumo
16/05/99	AaB	H	1-3	Haaland
20/05/99	Herfølge BK	A	2-2	Haaland, Iwelumo
24/05/99	AGF	H	2-1	Haaland, Banna
30/05/99	Silkeborg IF	A	1-4	Sommer
13/06/99	FC København	H	3-3	Siersbaek, Holdgaard, Ulrich
16/06/99	Vejle BK	A	1-4	Ulrich

AB

CLUB DIRECTORY

Akademisk Boldklub
Skovdiget 1
2880 Bagsvaerd
tel - (44) 989842
fax - (44) 989733
Year of Formation - 1889
Chairman - Denis Holmark
Secretary - Henrik Mostrup
Coach - Christian Andersen; Peter Frandsen;
Ole Mørch
Stadium - Gladsaxe Idraetspark (13,800)

MAJOR HONOURS
League Championship - (9) 1919, 1921, 1937,
1943, 1945, 1947, 1951, 1952, 1967.
Domestic Cup - (1) 1999.

APPEARANCES 98/99

	P	Ap	(s)	Gls
Martin ALBRECHTSEN	D	5	(4)	1
Søren ANDERSEN	A		(3)	
Jan BJUR	D	24	(7)	4
Jesper FALCK	M	25	(2)	1
Brian FLIES	G	1		
Peter FRANK	D	4	(3)	
René HENRIKSEN	D	33		
Chris HERMANSEN	A	30	(3)	19
Jan HOFFMANN	G	32		
Peter KNUDSEN	M	7	(3)	1
Lars Bo LARSEN	D	27		1
Peter LØVENKRANDS	A	6	(12)	2
Tommy LØVENKRANDS	A	1	(9)	
Kaan METIN	A	2	(13)	1
Jan MICHAELSEN	M	31		2
Alex NIELSEN	A	25	(6)	5
Brian Steen NIELSEN	M	28		2
Allan OLESEN	D	16		
Jacques PIGNOT	M		(1)	
Peter RASMUSSEN	M	32		2
Thomas SCHØNNEMANN	D	9		
Mads SPUR-MORTENSEN	M	1	(3)	
Nicolai STOKHOLM	M	8	(14)	1
Abdul SPULE (NIG)	A	6		3
Jesper SØRENSEN	M	2	(3)	
Claus THOMSEN	M	8		1

LEAGUE RESULTS 1998/99

26/07/98	Aarhus Fremad	A	4-1	Hermansen 2, Løvenkrands P., Nielsen B.S.
02/08/98	AaB	H	1-1	Hermansen
09/08/98	Lyngby FC	A	3-0	Hermansen 2, Nielsen A.
16/08/98	Vejle BK	H	0-1	
23/08/98	AGF	H	1-1	Hermansen (p)
30/08/98	Silkeborg IF	A	2-1	Hermansen, og (Zivkovic)
13/09/98	FC København	H	4-1	og (Madsen), Bjur, Hermansen, Nielsen B.S.
20/09/98	Viborg FF	A	1-0	Thomsen
27/09/98	Herfølge BK	H	1-0	Hermansen
04/10/98	Brøndby IF	A	1-0	Bjur
18/10/98	B93	H	7-0	Hermansen 4 (1p), og (Fazal), Bjur, Larsen
04/11/98	Lyngby FC	A	2-3	Hermansen 2
08/11/98	Brøndby IF	H	0-4	
15/11/98	Vejle BK	A	2-0	Stokholm, Nielsen A.
18/11/98	Aarhus Fremad	H	1-0	Nielsen A.
22/11/98	Silkeborg IF	A	1-1	Metin
29/11/98	FC København	H	0-0	
15/03/99	AGF	H	1-0	Michaelsen
21/03/99	Herfølge BK	A	1-0	Albrechtsen
01/04/99	AaB	H	0-1	
05/04/99	B93	A	1-0	Sule
11/04/99	Viborg FF	H	1-1	Sule
18/04/99	Vejle BK	H	2-0	Rasmussen, Sule
25/04/99	Brøndby IF	A	0-3	
30/04/99	Aarhus Fremad	A	3-1	Nielsen A., Falck, Hermansen
05/05/99	Lyngby FC	H	1-3	Rasmussen
09/05/99	Viborg FF	A	0-1	
16/05/99	B93	H	1-3	Bjur
20/05/99	AaB	A	0-2	
24/05/99	Herfølge BK	H	2-1	Knudsen, Hermansen
31/05/99	AGF	A	1-3	Nielsen A.
13/06/99	Silkeborg IF	H	4-2	Michaelsen, Hermansen 2, Løvenkrands P.
16/06/99	FC København	A	0-1	

AGF

CLUB DIRECTORY

Aarhus Gymnastik Forening af 1880
Fredensvang
Terp Skovvej 16-18
8260 Viby J
tel - (86) 112733
fax - (86) 145779
Year of Formation - 1880
Chairman - Poul Viggo Bartels Petersen
Secretary - John Skovbjerg
Coach - Peter Rudbaek
Stadium - Aarhus Stadion (18,500)

MAJOR HONOURS
League Championship - (5)
1955, 1956, 1957, 1960, 1986.
Domestic Cup - (9) 1955, 1957, 1960, 1961,
1965, 1987, 1988, 1992, 1996.

APPEARANCES 98/99

	P	Ap	(s)	Gls
Anders BJERRE	D	32		7
Allan BORGVARDT	A	4	(7)	
Kenneth CHRISTIANSEN	M	8		2
Peter DEGN	M	13		3
Carsten HALLUM	A	5	(7)	1
Jes HØJEN	D	3	(1)	
Bjarne JENSEN	M	3	(5)	1
John JENSEN	D	26	(2)	1
Mads JØRGENSEN	M	27	(3)	4
Jakob KRAGH	G	4		
Ulrik KRISTENSEN	A	3	(2)	
Ólafur KRISTJÁNSSON (ISL)	D	13	(8)	
Eric LIND	A		(1)	
Gunner LIND	M	16	(9)	1
Henrik MORTENSEN	M		(4)	
Johnny MØLBY	M	22	(2)	3
Bo NIELSEN	A	24	(6)	12
Michael NONBO	M	29		2
Torben PIECHNIK	D	14	(1)	1
Allan REESE	A	7	(12)	
Mads RIEPER	D	16	(2)	
Dennis SIIM	D	30	(1)	1
Jesper SØRENSEN	M	13	(3)	
Kenny THORUP	A	9	(5)	2
Tómas Ingi TÓMASSON (ISL)	A	13	(4)	3
Lars WINDFELD	G	29		

LEAGUE RESULTS 1998/99

26/07/98	AaB	A	0-4	
02/08/98	Lyngby FC	H	1-0	Nielsen
07/08/98	Vejle BK	A	0-3	
16/08/98	Viborg FF	H	3-2	Degn 2, Nielsen
23/08/98	AB	A	1-1	Nielsen
30/08/98	Herfølge BK	A	1-1	Thorup
11/09/98	Silkeborg IF	H	2-3	Degn, Nielsen
20/09/98	FC København	A	2-0	Thorup, Nielsen
25/09/98	Brøndby IF	H	1-3	Mølby
04/10/98	B93	A	2-1	Siim, Bjerre
18/10/98	Aarhus Fremad	H	3-2	Nielsen, Jensen J., Lind G.
01/11/98	Lyngby FC	A	1-1	Nielsen
08/11/98	Herfølge BK	A	0-0	
25/11/98	Silkeborg IF	H	2-3	Bjerre 2 (1p)
29/11/98	B93	A	2-4	Tómasson, Thorup
07/03/99	AaB	H	1-0	Bjerre (p)
15/03/99	AB	A	0-1	
21/03/99	Aarhus Fremad	H	1-1	Hallum
01/04/99	Brøndby IF	A	1-4	Jensen B.
05/04/99	Vejle BK	H	2-1	Mølby (p), Nielsen
09/04/99	FC København	A	1-1	Nonbo
14/04/99	Viborg FF	H	0-0	
19/04/99	AaB	A	1-2	Tómasson
25/04/99	Herfølge BK	H	2-1	Christiansen, Nielsen
02/05/99	Lyngby FC	H	1-1	Nielsen
05/05/99	Silkeborg IF	A	0-2	
09/05/99	FC København	H	2-1	Bjerre, Nonbo
14/05/99	Vejle BK	A	2-2	Christiansen, Nielsen
20/05/99	Brøndby IF	H	3-3	Tómasson, Bjerre 2 (2p)
24/05/99	Aarhus Fremad	A	1-2	og (Dupont)
31/05/99	AB	H	3-1	Jørgensen 2, Nielsen
13/06/99	Viborg FF	A	1-3	Jørgensen
16/06/99	B93	H	2-1	Jørgensen, Piechnik (p)

B93

CLUB DIRECTORY

Boldklubben af 1893 (B93)
Ved Sporsløjfen 10
2100 København Ø
tel - (39) 271890
fax - (39) 273011
Year of Formation - 1893
Chairman - Paw Engsbye Rasmussen
Secretary - Henrik Engel
Coach - Erling Bøje Pedersen; Jan Jacobsen;
Peter Grahn (99/00 - Christian Andersen)
Stadium - Østerbro Stadion (7,000)

MAJOR HONOURS
League Championship - (9) 1916, 1927, 1929,
1930, 1934, 1935, 1939, 1942, 1946.
Domestic Cup - (1) 1982.

APPEARANCES 98/99

		P	Ap	(s)	Gls
Christian BANK	D	17	(3)	1	
Casper BØJE	M	1	(4)		
Kenneth CHRISTIANSEN	M	16	(3)	2	
Jan CHRISTOFFERSEN	D	20	(1)		
Ketil CLORIUS	M	3	(1)		
Asaf FAZAL	D	21	(2)		
Flemming FRANDSEN	M	29	(3)	2	
Riffi HADDAOUI	A	6	(6)	1	
Anders HØJLUND	A	14	(1)	3	
Thomas HØY	A	20	(5)	2	
Niels JOCHUMSEN	A	3	(1)	1	
Morten JØRGENSEN	M	3	(4)		
Morten KARLSEN	D	28	(1)		
Christian KRONHOLM	A	1	(6)		
Jonny LAURSEN	D	27		2	
Per LAURSEN	M		(1)		
Rajko LEKEC	A	1			
Thomas MAALE	A	21	(10)	3	
Thomas MADSEN	M	31	(1)		
Thomas Axel MADSEN	D	8	(4)		
Patrick MTILIGA	M	10	(3)		
Nicolas NIELSEN	G	19			
David RASMUSSEN	M	16	(3)	1	
Morten RUTKJAER	D	9	(6)		
Lasse SIGDAL	M	15	(3)	2	
Michael SZYMANSKI	M	1	(7)		
Christian TAYLOR (ENG)	M	2			
Jeppe TENGBJERG	A	7	(14)		
Kim TOXWAERD	G	14			

LEAGUE RESULTS 1998/99

26/07/98	Brøndby IF	H	1-5	Højlund
02/08/98	Herfølge BK	A	1-3	Laursen J.
09/08/98	Aarhus Fremad	A	0-2	
16/08/98	AaB	H	1-5	Bank
23/08/98	FC København	H	0-0	
30/08/98	Viborg FF	A	0-5	
11/09/98	Vejle BK	H	0-1	
20/09/98	Lyngby FC	A	1-2	Maale
25/09/98	Silkeborg IF	A	0-2	
04/10/98	AGF	H	1-2	Christiansen
18/10/98	AB	A	0-7	
25/10/98	Brøndby IF	H	1-0	og (Jensen B.)
01/11/98	Vejle BK	A	0-2	
08/11/98	FC København	H	1-2	Sigdal
15/11/98	Silkeborg IF	A	2-2	Jochumsen, Sigdal
29/11/98	AGF	H	4-2	Haddaoui, Høy 2, Maale
14/03/99	AaB	H	0-3	
17/03/99	Herfølge BK	A	0-0	
21/03/99	Lyngby FC	A	0-1	
01/04/99	Viborg FF	A	1-5	Christiansen (p)
05/04/99	AB	H	0-1	
11/04/99	Aarhus Fremad	A	0-2	
18/04/99	Silkeborg IF	H	0-1	
25/04/99	FC København	A	0-1	
02/05/99	Vejle BK	H	0-2	
05/05/99	Brøndby IF	A	1-4	Maale
09/05/99	Aarhus Fremad	H	1-3	Højlund
16/05/99	AB	A	3-1	Laursen J., Frandsen, Højlund
20/05/99	Viborg FF	H	0-5	
24/05/99	Lyngby FC	H	1-3	Rasmussen
30/05/99	AaB	A	0-2	
13/06/99	Herfølge BK	H	1-2	Frandsen
16/06/99	AGF	A	1-2	og (Højen)

BRØNDBY IF

CLUB DIRECTORY

Brøndbyernes Idraets Forening
Gildhøjcentret
Brøndbyvester Boulevard 8
2605 Brøndby
tel - (43) 630810
fax - (43) 432627
Year of Formation - 1964
Chairman - Ole Borch
Secretary - Per Bjerregaard
Coach - Ebbe Skovdahl (99/00 - Tom Køhlert)
Stadium - Brøndby Stadion (18,500)

MAJOR HONOURS
League Championship - (8) 1985, 1987, 1988,
1990, 1991, 1996, 1997, 1998.
Domestic Cup - (3) 1989, 1994, 1998.

APPEARANCES 98/99

	P	Ap	(s)	Gls
Emeka ANDERSEN	G	11		
Ruben BAGGER	A	18	(7)	8
Anders BJERREGAARD	D	4	(5)	
Ole BJUR	M	32		6
Bent CHRISTENSEN	A	3	(7)	4
Søren COLDING	D	32		2
Vragel DA SILVA (BRA)	D	18	(3)	3
Kim DAUGAARD	M	33		7
Peter GRAULUND	A	3	(6)	3
Bo HANSEN	A	12	(4)	12
Brian JENSEN	D	8		
John JENSEN	M	29		1
Mikkel JENSEN	M	3	(16)	
Dan Anton JOHANSEN	D	2	(3)	
Mogens KROGH	G	22		
Søren KROGH	M		(4)	
Thomas LINDRUP	M	12	(15)	2
Peter MADSEN	A	13	(5)	3
Per NIELSEN	D	29		
Mads OLSEN	M	7	(2)	
Allan RAVN	M	6	(5)	
Kenneth RASMUSSEN	D	16		
Ebbe SAND	A	31		19
Martin Ditlev SMITH	D	7	(1)	
Aurelius SKARBALIUS (LIT)	M	6		
Jesper THYGESEN	M	6	(7)	2

LEAGUE RESULTS 1998/99

26/07/98	B93	A	5-1	Bjur, Sand, Hansen, Daugaard 2
03/08/98	Aarhus Fremad	H	2-0	Colding, Sand
07/08/98	AaB	A	0-1	
16/08/98	Lyngby FC	H	2-3	Sand, Hansen
21/08/98	Silkeborg IF	H	3-0	Hansen 2, Sand
30/08/98	FC København	A	0-1	
11/09/98	Viborg FF	H	2-5	Da Silva, Hansen
20/09/98	Vejle BK	A	2-1	Jensen J., Hansen
25/09/98	AGF	A	3-1	Hansen, Sand, Lindrup
04/10/98	AB	H	0-1	
16/10/98	Herfølge BK	H	5-1	Sand 2, Hansen 2, Daugaard
25/10/98	B93	A	0-1	
30/10/98	Viborg FF	H	2-1	Sand, Bjur
08/11/98	AB	A	4-0	Bagger 2, Graulund, Hansen
15/11/98	Aarhus Fremad	H	1-1	Da Silva
29/11/98	Lyngby FC	H	6-0	Hansen 2, Sand 2, Christensen 2
07/03/99	Vejle BK	A	0-0	
14/03/99	FC København	H	3-2	Christensen, Bjur, Bagger
22/03/99	Silkeborg IF	A	2-1	Bjur, Sand
01/04/99	AGF	H	4-1	Thygesen, Madsen, Bagger, Daugaard
05/04/99	Herfølge BK	A	2-1	Thygesen, Daugaard (p)
12/04/99	AaB	H	1-2	Christensen
18/04/99	Aarhus Fremad	A	3-1	Sand, Daugaard, Madsen
25/04/99	AB	H	3-0	Sand 2, Bjur
02/05/99	Viborg FF	A	0-2	
05/05/99	B93	H	4-1	Sand, Daugaard (p), Madsen, Bagger
10/05/99	AaB	A	0-0	
17/05/99	Herfølge BK	H	1-0	Colding
20/05/99	AGF	A	3-3	Da Silva, Graulund, og (Piechnik)
24/05/99	Silkeborg IF	H	3-0	Bagger 2, Graulund
28/05/99	FC København	A	0-1	
13/06/99	Vejle BK	H	1-2	Lindrup
16/06/99	Lyngby FC	A	6-2	Sand 4, Bjur, Bagger

HERFØLGE BK

CLUB DIRECTORY

Herfølge Boldklub
Vordingborgvej 124
Postbox 57
4681 Herfølge
tel - (56) 274230
fax - (56) 276141
Year of Formation - 1921
Chairman - Martin Juul
Secretary - Kenneth Wegner
Coach - Ole Mørch; Jesper Pedersen
(99/00 - John Jensen)
Stadium - Herfølge Stadion (8,500)

APPEARANCES 98/99

		P	Ap	(s)	Gls
Thomas ABEL	M	8	(7)	2
Morten AVNSKJOLD	M		(1)	
Daniel BAERENHOLT	M		(4)	
Torben CHRISTIANSEN	D	21		1
Ulrik DROST	A	4	(8)	4
Bo HENRIKSEN	A	19	(4)	6
Jesper HEYDE	M	1		
Thomas HØYER	M	31		4
Jesper JACOBSEN	A	12	(7)	4
Lars JAKOBSEN	M	19	(5)	3
Kenneth JENSEN	A		(5)	
Jimmy KASTRUP	A	26	(6)	8
Kenneth KASTRUP	M	31	(2)	
Thomas KNUDSEN	A	4	(10)	2
Steven LUSTÜ	D	31		
Dan LÜBBERS	D	9	(9)	
Henrik LYKKE	D	29		1
Jens MADSEN	M	20	(5)	4
Jakup MIKKELSEN (FAR)	G	33		2
Morten B. NIELSEN	A	4	(2)	1
Gert NODIN	D	4	(2)	
Ole PUGGAARD	M	2	(7)	
Tommy SCHRAM	M	22	(6)	1
Michael THOMSEN	D	5	(1)	
Iørn ULDBJERG	M	13	(5)	
Jeppe VESTERGAARD	D	15		1

LEAGUE RESULTS 1998/99

26/07/98	Viborg FF	A	3-0	Jacobsen 2, Kastrup J.
02/08/98	B93	H	3-1	Jacobsen, Lykke, Knudsen
09/08/98	FC København	A	3-0	Mikkelsen (p), Schram, Jakobsen
16/08/98	Aarhus Fremad	H	3-1	Mikkelsen (p), Madsen, Kastrup J.
23/08/98	Lyngby FC	A	0-0	
30/08/98	AGF	H	1-1	Knudsen
13/09/98	AaB	H	0-0	
20/09/98	Silkeborg IF	A	1-0	Høyer
27/09/98	AB	A	0-1	
04/10/98	Vejle BK	H	2-2	Jakobsen, Kastrup J.
16/10/98	Brøndby IF	A	1-5	Høyer
25/10/98	FC København	H	2-3	Kastrup J., Henriksen
01/11/98	Silkeborg IF	A	1-1	Henriksen
08/11/98	AGF	H	0-0	
15/11/98	Lyngby FC	A	3-1	Høyer (p), Jacobsen, Henriksen
29/11/98	AaB	A	1-1	Vestergaard
14/03/99	Viborg FF	A	0-1	
17/03/99	B93	H	0-0	
21/03/99	AB	H	0-1	
01/04/99	Aarhus Fremad	A	1-0	Christiansen
05/04/99	Brøndby IF	H	1-2	Abel
11/04/99	Vejle BK	A	1-1	Nielsen
18/04/99	Lyngby FC	H	0-2	
25/04/99	AGF	A	1-2	Madsen
02/05/99	Silkeborg IF	H	1-1	Kastrup J.
05/05/99	FC København	A	1-0	Kastrup J.
09/05/99	Vejle BK	H	2-0	Kastrup J., Madsen
17/05/99	Brøndby IF	A	0-1	
20/05/99	Aarhus Fremad	H	2-2	Henriksen, Kastrup J.
24/05/99	AB	A	1-2	Abel
30/05/99	Viborg FF	H	4-1	Drost 3, Henriksen
13/06/99	B93	A	2-1	Drost, Henriksen
16/06/99	AaB	H	3-2	Jakobsen, Madsen, Høyer

FC KØBENHAVN

CLUB DIRECTORY

FC København
Øster Allé 50
2100 København Ø
tel - (35) 437400
fax - (35) 437422
Year of Formation - 1992
Chairman - Peter Norvig
Secretary - Charles Maskelyne
Coach - Kent Karlsson; Kim Brink; Christian
Andersen; Kim Brink
Stadium - Parken (41,641)

MAJOR HONOURS
League Championship - (1) 1993.
Domestic Cup - (2) 1995, 1997.

APPEARANCES 98/99

	P	Ap	(s)	Gls
Clement CLIFORD	A		(6)	
Kofi DAKINAH	M		(1)	
Morten FALCH	D	9	(9)	1
Thomas GILL (NOR)	G	5		
Bjarne GOLDBAEK	M	12		3
Piotr HAREN	D	19	(3)	
Carsten HEMMINGSEN	M	27	(2)	2
Carsten Vagn JENSEN	D		(4)	
Kenneth JENSEN	A		(4)	
Niclas JENSEN	M	31	(2)	4
Todi JONSSON (FAR)	A	21	(9)	8
Henrik LARSEN	M	2	(2)	
Martin Bill LARSEN	A	4	(5)	2
Brian LAUDRUP	A	12		2
Christian LØNSTRUP	D	11		
Kim MADSEN	D	10	(6)	
Claus NIELSEN	M	14	(8)	2
David NIELSEN	A	26	(4)	15
Lars Højer NIELSEN	M	18		5
Martin NIELSEN	D	10	(3)	1
Michael "Mio" NIELSEN	D	25		
Peter NIELSEN	M	27		3
Thomas RYTTER	M	21		1
Michael STENSGAARD	G	17		
Thomas THORNINGER	A	18	(12)	5
Diego TUR	D	13	(3)	
Karim ZAZA	G	11		

LEAGUE RESULTS 1998/99

26/07/98	Vejle BK	A	3-1	Jensen N., Jonsson 2
02/08/98	Viborg FF	H	3-2	Falch, Nielsen D., Jonsson
09/08/98	Herfølge BK	H	0-3	
16/08/98	Silkeborg IF	A	3-3	Jonsson, Nielsen P. 2
23/08/98	B93	A	0-0	
30/08/98	Brøndby IF	H	1-0	Goldbaek
13/09/98	AB	A	1-4	Nielsen C.
20/09/98	AGF	H	0-2	
27/09/98	Aarhus Fremad	H	2-2	Goldbaek (p), Nielsen D.
04/10/98	AaB	A	3-3	Nielsen P., Thorninger, Goldbaek
18/10/98	Lyngby FC	H	5-1	Nielsen L.H. 2, Nielsen D. 3
25/10/98	Herfølge BK	A	3-2	Thorninger, Nielsen D., Nielsen Ma.
01/11/98	AaB	H	2-2	Nielsen L.H., Thorninger
08/11/98	B93	A	2-1	Jonsson 2
15/11/98	Viborg FF	H	4-2	Nielsen D. 2, Nielsen L.H., Jonsson
22/11/98	Aarhus Fremad	A	3-0	Nielsen D., Thorninger, Jensen
29/11/98	AB	A	0-0	
14/03/99	Brøndby IF	A	2-3	Jensen N., Hemmingsen
19/03/99	Vejle BK	H	0-1	
01/04/99	Lyngby FC	H	2-0	Nielsen D., Larsen M.B.
05/04/99	Silkeborg IF	A	2-2	Laudrup, Larsen M.B.
09/04/99	AGF	H	1-1	Nielsen D.
18/04/99	Viborg FF	A	0-1	
25/04/99	B93	H	1-0	Thorninger
30/04/99	AaB	A	3-4	Nielsen L.H., Jensen N., Jonsson
05/05/99	Herfølge BK	H	0-1	
09/05/99	AGF	A	1-2	Nielsen D.
16/05/99	Silkeborg IF	H	2-2	Nielsen D., Laudrup
20/05/99	Lyngby FC	A	1-3	Nielsen C.
24/05/99	Vejle BK	A	0-1	
28/05/99	Brøndby IF	H	1-0	Nielsen D.
13/06/99	Aarhus Fremad	A	3-3	Nielsen D., og (Bundgaard), Hemmingsen
16/06/99	AB	H	1-0	Rytter

LYNGBY FC

CLUB DIRECTORY

Lyngby Fodbold Club
Lundtoftevej 61, 2800 Lyngby
tel - (45) 884060
fax - (45) 874445
Year of Formation - 1921
Chairman - Poul Hedegaard
Secretary - Peter Packness & René Dupont
Coach - Poul Hansen
Stadium - Lyngby Stadion (15,000)

MAJOR HONOURS
League Championship - (2) 1983, 1992.
Domestic Cup - (3) 1984, 1985, 1990.

APPEARANCES 98/99

		P	Ap	(s)	Gls
Bo ANDERSEN	G	16			
Thomas ANDIE	M	11	(3)	1	
Stefan BIDSTRUP	D	29		1	
Martin BIRN	D	27			
Ayeni BOSUN (NIG)	M	4	(1)	1	
Bent CHRISTENSEN	M	3			
Kim CHRISTENSEN	A		(6)	1	
Per FAHLSTRÖM (SWE)	G	17			
Carsten FREDGAARD	A	31		16	
Andreas HAVLYKKE	A	10	(12)	1	
Søren HERMANSEN	A	27		18	
Nichlas HINDSBERG	M	23	(7)	3	
Peter HOLM	M	1	(3)		
Mikkel Bo JENSEN	D	10	(7)	3	
Martin JOHANSEN	M	24	(1)	3	
Kim Bjørn JØRGENSEN	M	1			
Lars LARSEN	M	3	(2)		
Lennart Lynge LARSEN	D	24		2	
Michael LARSEN	M		(1)		
Thomas LORAN	D	1	(2)		
Jimmi LÜTHJE	M	22	(4)	2	
Christian MAGLEBY	M	19	(4)	1	
Rasmus MARVITS	M	7	(9)		
Henrik PEDERSEN	M	2	(7)		
Morten PEDERSEN	D	30			
Ronny B. PETERSEN	A	2	(21)	1	
Ulrich VINZENTS	D	19			

LEAGUE RESULTS 1998/99

26/07/98	Silkeborg IF	H	0-0	
02/08/98	AGF	A	0-1	
09/08/98	AB	H	0-3	
16/08/98	Brøndby IF	A	3-2	Fredgaard, Bidstrup, Jensen
23/08/98	Herfølge BK	H	0-0	
30/08/98	AaB	H	2-2	og (Matovac), Hermansen
13/09/98	Aarhus Fremad	A	2-1	Hermansen, Fredgaard
20/09/98	B93	H	2-1	Fredgaard 2
25/09/98	Vejle BK	A	2-1	Fredgaard, Hermansen
04/10/98	Viborg FF	H	2-3	Larsen L.L., Hermansen
18/10/98	FC København	A	1-5	Andie
01/11/98	AGF	H	1-1	Hermansen
04/11/98	AB	H	3-2	Fredgaard 2, Hermansen
08/11/98	Aarhus Fremad	A	4-2	Hermansen 2, Lüthje (p), Jensen
15/11/98	Herfølge BK	H	1-3	Hermansen
29/11/98	Brøndby IF	A	0-6	
14/03/99	Vejle BK	A	2-1	Johansen, Larsen L.L.
21/03/99	B93	H	1-0	Petersen R.B.
29/03/99	AaB	H	1-1	Hermansen
01/04/99	FC København	A	0-2	
05/04/99	Viborg FF	H	3-1	Lüthje, Hermansen (p), Fredgaard
11/04/99	Silkeborg IF	A	1-1	Havlykke
18/04/99	Herfølge BK	A	2-0	Hermansen, Fredgaard
26/04/99	Aarhus Fremad	H	1-1	Fredgaard
02/05/99	AGF	A	1-1	Fredgaard
05/05/99	AB	A	3-1	Hindsberg, Fredgaard, Hermansen
09/05/99	Silkeborg IF	H	2-2	Johansen, Hermansen
16/05/99	Viborg FF	A	2-5	Hermansen, Fredgaard
20/05/99	FC København	H	3-1	Jensen, Hindsberg, Christensen K.
24/05/99	B93	A	3-1	Fredgaard 2, Hermansen
30/05/99	Vejle BK	H	2-0	Hermansen, Magleby
13/06/99	AaB	A	3-3	Hermansen, Bosun, Hindsberg
16/06/99	Brøndby IF	H	2-6	Fredgaard, Johansen

SILKEBORG IF

Silkeborg Idraets Forening
Ansvej 110
8600 Silkeborg
tel - (86) 804477
fax - (86) 804647
Year of Formation - 1917
Chairman - Ole Hansen
Secretary - Orla Madsen
Coach - Sepp Piontek (99/00 Benny Johansen)
Stadium - Silkeborg Stadion (11,000)

MAJOR HONOURS
League Championship - (1) 1994.

	P	Ap	(s)	Gls
Morten BRUUN	M	28	(1)	
Lars BRØGGER	M	7	(8)	
Jukka HAKALA (FIN)	D	1		
Johnny HANSEN	D	26		7
Michael HANSEN	D	11	(5)	
Henrik IPSEN	G	4		
Nocko JOKOVIC	A	19	(4)	3
Peter KJAER	G	29		2
Peder KNUDSEN	M	18	(3)	1
Jan LARSEN	D		(2)	
Michael LARSEN	D	20	(1)	
Thomas Røll LARSEN	M	22	(6)	1
Peter LASSEN	A	19	(2)	11
Kern LYHNE	A	9	(13)	2
Kim NØRHOLT	A	5	(18)	6
Jens OVERGAARD	M	3		
Henrik PEDERSEN	A	33		16
Christian Duus PETERSEN	D	24	(4)	
Thomas POULSEN	M	32		1
Rasmus SVENNINGSEN	M	2	(7)	
Peter SØRENSEN	M	20	(4)	1
Bora ZIVKOVIC	D	31		1

26/07/98	Lyngby FC	A	0-0	
02/08/98	Vejle BK	H	1-0	Sørensen
07/08/98	Viborg FF	A	1-2	Hansen J. (p)
16/08/98	FC København	H	3-3	Pedersen 2, Zivkovic
21/08/98	Brøndby IF	A	0-3	
30/08/98	AB	H	1-2	Nørholt
11/09/98	AGF	A	3-2	Jokovic 2, Pedersen
20/09/98	Herfølge BK	H	0-1	
25/09/98	B93	H	2-0	Pedersen, Nørholt
04/10/98	Aarhus Fremad	A	2-2	Pedersen 2
18/10/98	AaB	H	0-0	
01/11/98	Herfølge BK	H	1-1	Lassen
08/11/98	AaB	A	4-2	Hansen J. (p), Lyhne, Lassen, Pedersen
15/11/98	B93	H	2-2	Larsen T.R., Hansen J. (p)
22/11/98	AB	H	1-1	Lyhne
25/11/98	AGF	A	3-2	Knudsen, Pedersen 2
29/11/98	Viborg FF	A	3-3	Pedersen, Nørholt 2
14/03/99	Aarhus Fremad	A	1-0	Jokovic
22/03/99	Brøndby IF	H	1-2	Hansen J. (p)
01/04/99	Vejle BK	A	1-4	Lassen
05/04/99	FC København	H	2-2	Pedersen, Hansen J. (p)
11/04/99	Lyngby FC	H	1-1	Pedersen
18/04/99	B93	A	1-0	Hansen I (p)
23/04/99	AaB	H	0-0	
02/05/99	Herfølge BK	A	1-1	Lassen
05/05/99	AGF	H	2-0	Lassen, Pedersen
09/05/99	Lyngby FC	A	2-2	Lassen, Pedersen
16/05/99	FC København	A	2-2	Lassen, Hansen J. (p)
20/05/99	Vejle BK	H	4-3	Lassen, Nørholt, Pedersen, Poulsen
24/05/99	Brøndby IF	A	0-3	
30/05/99	Aarhus Fremad	H	4-1	Lassen 2, Nørholt, Kjaer (p)
13/06/99	AB	A	2-4	Lassen, Kjaer (p)
16/06/99	Viborg FF	H	1-2	Pedersen

VEJLE BK

Vejle Boldklub
Helligkildevej 2
7100 Vejle
tel - (75) 727500
fax - (75) 833033
Year of Formation - 1891
Chairman - Ole Vedel
Secretary - Henrik Lund
Coach - Ole Fritsen
Stadium - Vejle Stadion (15,332)

MAJOR HONOURS
League Championship - (5)
1958, 1971, 1972, 1978, 1984.
Domestic Cup - (6)
1958, 1959, 1972, 1975, 1977, 1981.

	P	Ap	(s)	Gls
Erik BOYE	G	31		
Jerry BROWN	A	3	(1)	2
Peter CHRISTIANSEN	D	28	(1)	1
Kaspar DALGAS	A	25	(7)	13
Lars DAMSBO	D		(2)	
Allan DYRING	M		(2)	
Klaus ESKILDSEN	D	5	(4)	1
Calle FACIUS	M	30		
Henrik FIG	M	13	(1)	2
Claus FRANDSEN	A	4	(3)	1
Peter GRAULUND	A	10	(2)	4
Boye HABEKOST	G	2		
Bo HARDER	D		(2)	
Henrik HOLM	M		(1)	
Lars JENSEN	D		(2)	
Danny JUNG	A	17	(4)	3
Nicolai JØRGENSEN	M	1	(2)	
Christian KELLER	A	3	(8)	
Jesper LJUNG (SWE)	M	11	(5)	1
Jens MADSEN	M	13	(3)	
Jesper MIKKELSEN	M	16	(15)	7
Alex NØRLUND	M	22	(6)	6
Nikolaj RASMUSSEN	M		(2)	
Henrik RISOM	D	31		4
Kent SCHOLZ (GER)	D	26		
Jesper SØGAARD	M	15	(1)	3
Jan SØNKSEN	D	29		2
Dan SØRENSEN	D	18	(9)	
Nicolai WAEL	M	10		3

26/07/98	FC København	H	1-3	Mikkelsen
02/08/98	Silkeborg IF	A	0-1	
07/08/98	AGF	H	3-0	Søgaard, Nørlund (p), Mikkelsen
16/08/98	AB	A	1-0	Graulund
21/08/98	AaB	A	2-5	Risom (p), Graulund
30/08/98	Aarhus Fremad	H	4-2	Jung, Wael 3
11/09/98	B93	A	1-0	Dalgas
20/09/98	Brøndby IF	H	1-2	Sønksen
25/09/98	Lyngby FC	H	1-2	Fig
04/10/98	Herfølge BK	A	2-2	Dalgas, Graulund
18/10/98	Viborg FF	H	4-0	Graulund, Christiansen, Dalgas, Mikkelsen
25/10/98	AaB	A	2-4	Dalgas (p), Søgaard
01/11/98	B93	H	2-0	Dalgas (p), Risom
08/11/98	Viborg FF	A	1-0	Nørlund
15/11/98	AB	H	0-2	
29/11/98	Aarhus Fremad	A	3-3	Eskildsen, Risom (p), Søgaard
07/03/99	Brøndby IF	H	0-0	
14/03/99	Lyngby FC	H	1-2	Mikkelsen
19/03/99	FC København	A	1-0	Frandsen
01/04/99	Silkeborg IF	H	4-1	Mikkelsen 2, Risom, Nørlund
05/04/99	AGF	A	1-2	Fig
11/04/99	Herfølge BK	H	1-1	og (Lustü)
18/04/99	AB	A	0-2	
25/04/99	Viborg FF	H	4-1	Nørlund, Dalgas 2 (2p), Mikkelsen
02/05/99	B93	A	2-0	Dalgas (p), Nørlund
05/05/99	AaB	H	0-1	
09/05/99	Herfølge BK	A	0-2	
14/05/99	AGF	H	2-2	Dalgas, Jung
20/05/99	Silkeborg IF	A	3-4	Jung, Sønksen, Ljung
24/05/99	FC København	H	1-0	Nørlund
30/05/99	Lyngby FC	A	0-2	
13/06/99	Brøndby IF	A	2-1	Dalgas 2
16/06/99	Aarhus Fremad	H	4-1	Dalgas 2, Brown 2

VIBORG FF

CLUB DIRECTORY

Viborg Fodsports Forening
Kirkebækvej 94
Postbox 214
8800 Viborg
tel - (86) 601066
fax - (86) 601046
Year of Formation - 1896
Chairman - Bruno Jensen
Secretary - Bjarne Vestdam
Coach - Ove Christensen (99/00 - Kim Poulsen)
Stadium - Viborg Stadion (15,000)

APPEARANCES 98/99

	P	Ap	(s)	Gls
Carsten DETHLEFSEN	D	12	(10)	
Hans EKLUND (SWE)	A	16	(1)	6
Heine FERNANDEZ	A	31		23
Thomas FRANDSEN	D	13	(12)	2
Morten HAMM	D	26	(2)	1
Dennis HANSEN	D	20		2
Steffen HØJER	A	4		1
Casper JACOBSEN	G	5		
Klaus KAERGAARD	M	15	(10)	5
Henrik KASTBJERG	D	13		1
René KJAERSGAARD	D		(4)	
Jeppe Lynge LARSEN	M		(1)	
Claus NIELSEN	D	4	(3)	
Jakob Glerup NIELSEN	M	28		1
John NIELSEN	M	1	(7)	
Leif NIELSEN	M	5		1
Martin NIELSEN	D	10	(6)	
Arkadiusz ONYSZKO (POL)	G	28		
Ralf PEDERSEN	D	15	(3)	
Morten POULSEN	A	31	(1)	7
Peter RASMUSSEN	M	4	(1)	
Kenni SOMMER	A	2	(10)	5
Claus STRUCK	M	10	(7)	
Palle SØRENSEN	M	19	(2)	1
Thomas TENGSTEDT	D	21		1
Claus TROELSEN	A		(2)	
Johnny TVEEN	A	2	(8)	
Anders WINTHER	M	28	(1)	4

LEAGUE RESULTS 1998/99

26/07/98	Herfølge BK	H	0-3	
02/08/98	FC København	A	2-3	Nielsen L. (p), Fernandez
07/08/98	Silkeborg IF	H	2-1	Kaergaard, Poulsen
16/08/98	AGF	A	2-3	Poulsen, Kastbjerg
23/08/98	Aarhus Fremad	A	1-3	Sommer
30/08/98	B93	H	5-0	Nielsen J.G., Fernandez 2, Hamm, Sommer
11/09/98	Brøndby IF	A	5-2	Kaergaard 2, Fernandez 3
20/09/98	AB	H	0-1	
27/09/98	AaB	H	1-2	Fernandez
04/10/98	Lyngby FC	A	3-2	Poulsen 3
18/10/98	Vejle BK	A	0-4	
25/10/98	Aarhus Fremad	H	2-4	Kaergaard, Fernandez
30/10/98	Brøndby IF	A	1-2	Hansen
08/11/98	Vejle BK	H	0-1	
15/11/98	FC København	A	2-4	Winther 2
29/11/98	Silkeborg IF	H	3-3	Fernandez 2, Poulsen
14/03/99	Herfølge BK	H	1-0	Tengstedt
21/03/99	AaB	A	1-1	Sommer
01/04/99	B93	H	5-1	Fernandez 4, Winther
05/04/99	Lyngby FC	A	1-3	Winther
11/04/99	AB	A	1-1	Højer
14/04/99	AGF	A	0-0	
18/04/99	FC København	H	1-0	Fernandez
25/04/99	Vejle BK	A	1-4	Eklund
02/05/99	Brøndby IF	H	2-0	Fernandez 2
05/05/99	Aarhus Fremad	A	2-3	Poulsen, Fernandez
09/05/99	AB	H	1-0	Eklund
16/05/99	Lyngby FC	H	5-2	Eklund 2, Hansen, Fernandez 2
20/05/99	B93	A	5-0	Fernandez, Eklund, Frandsen, Sommer 2
24/05/99	AaB	H	0-0	
30/05/99	Herfølge BK	A	1-4	Sørensen
13/06/99	AGF	H	3-1	Eklund, Fernandez 2
16/06/99	Silkeborg IF	A	2-1	Frandsen, Kaergaard

PROMOTED CLUBS

SECOND DIVISION FINAL TABLE 98/99

		Pd	W	D	L	F	A	Pt	GD
1	OB	30	24	2	4	81	24	74	+57
2	Esbjerg FB	30	19	7	4	69	33	64	+36
3	Ikast FS	30	19	5	6	73	43	62	+30
4	Herning Fremad	30	15	4	11	61	41	49	+20
5	Haderslev FK	30	14	5	11	76	58	47	+18
6	AC Horsens	30	13	5	12	47	44	44	+3
7	BK Fremad Amager	30	12	6	12	48	48	42	0
8	Køge BK	30	12	6	12	49	56	42	-7
9	BK Frem	30	12	5	13	45	63	41	-18
10	Svendborg FB	30	10	8	12	39	43	38	-4
11	Hvidovre IF	30	10	7	13	36	53	37	-17
12	B1909	30	8	10	12	52	58	34	-6
13	Glostrup IF 32	30	8	9	13	48	60	33	-12
14	Holstebro BK	30	7	4	19	42	66	25	-24
15	Naestved BK	30	7	4	19	44	82	25	-38
16	Brønshøj BK	30	5	3	22	41	79	18	-38

CLUB DIRECTORY

Odense Boldklub
Box 344
Sdr. Boulevard 172
5100 Odense C
tel - (65) 119090
fax - (65) 119080
Year of Formation - 1887
Chairman - Fritz Bonde
Secretary - Jørgen Baekkelund
Coach - Jens Plambech
Stadium - Odense Stadion (15,633)

MAJOR HONOURS
League Championship - (3) 1977, 1982, 1989.
Domestic Cup - (3) 1983, 1991, 1993.

CLUB DIRECTORY

Esbjerg Forenede Boldklubber
Gl. Vardevej 88
6700 Esbjerg
tel - (75) 453355
fax - (75) 122833
Year of Formation - 1924
Chairman - Jørgen L. Jensen
Secretary - Niels Erik Søndergaard
Coach - Viggo Jensen
Stadium - Esbjerg Idraetspark (20,000)

MAJOR HONOURS
League Championship - (5)
1961, 1962, 1963, 1965, 1979.
Domestic Cup - (2) 1964, 1976.

ENGLAND

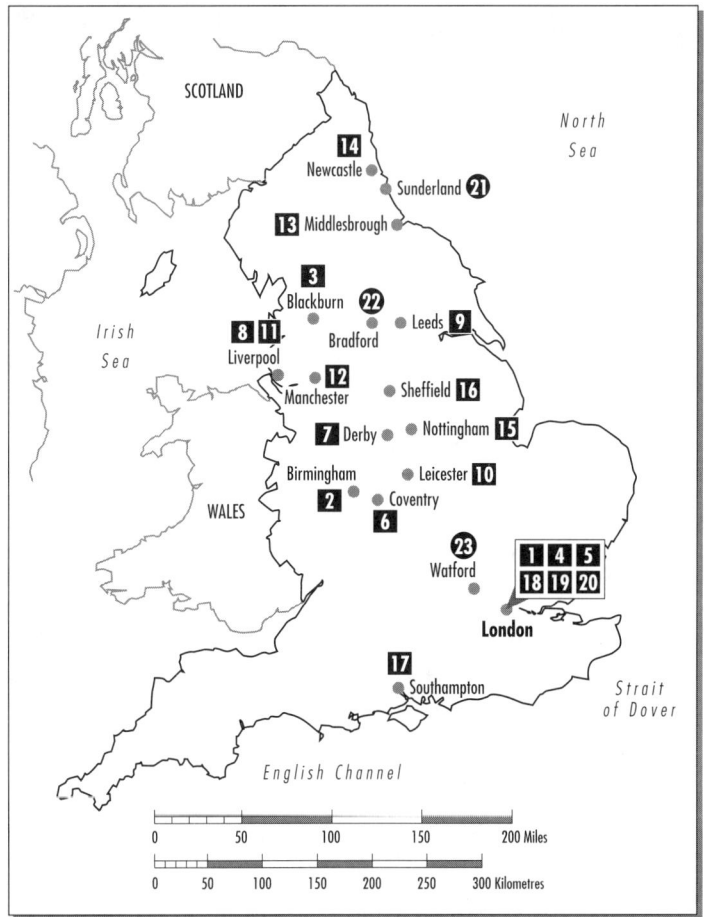

SCOTLAND

14 Newcastle ●

Sunderland **21**

13 Middlesbrough ●

North Sea

3

Blackburn ● **22**

● Leeds **9**

Irish Sea

8 11

Bradford ●

Liverpool ●

12

Manchester ●

● Sheffield **16**

7 Derby ● ● Nottingham **15**

Birmingham ● ● Leicester **10**

WALES

2 ● Coventry

6

23

Watford ●

1 4 5
18 19 20

London

17

Southampton ●

Strait of Dover

English Channel

| 0 | 50 | 100 | 150 | 200 Miles |

| 0 | 50 | 100 | 150 | 200 | 250 | 300 Kilometres |

1	ARSENAL	305	13	MIDDLESBROUGH	317
2	ASTON VILLA	306	14	NEWCASTLE UNITED	318
3	BLACKBURN ROVERS	307	15	NOTTINGHAM FOREST	319
4	CHARLTON ATHLETIC	308	16	SHEFFIELD WEDNESDAY	320
5	CHELSEA	309	17	SOUTHAMPTON	321
6	COVENTRY CITY	310	18	TOTTENHAM HOTSPUR	322
7	DERBY COUNTY	311	19	WEST HAM UNITED	323
8	EVERTON	312	20	WIMBLEDON	324
9	LEEDS UNITED	313	**Promoted clubs**		
10	LEICESTER CITY	314	21	SUNDERLAND	325
11	LIVERPOOL	315	22	BRADFORD CITY	325
12	MANCHESTER UNITED	316	23	WATFORD	325

HODDLE OUT, KEEGAN IN, ENGLAND OUT?

All-conquering United save their best till last

FEDERATION DIRECTORY

The Football Association
16 Lancaster Gate, London W2 3LW
tel - (0171) 2624542/4027151   Year of Formation - 1863
fax - (0171) 4020486   Chairman - Geoff Thompson
Stadium - Wembley, London (79,045)

Manchester United took their supporters into dreamland in 1998/99. They won a unique, unprecedented combination of Premiership, FA Cup and European Champions' Cup - an extraordinary achievement, a multiple conquest the like of which may never be equalled again. But if the United fans felt an inner glow of supreme satisfaction, it was partly because of the manner in which the 'treble' had been secured. Behind the bare facts lay a remarkable tale of heroism, adventure and implausible plot-twists that might have been borrowed from the world of fantasy fiction.

Alex Ferguson's team did not do things the easy way.

They played wonderful football and were an absolute joy to watch. But they liked to make their supporters sweat. So many times during the season, in all three competitions, they teased their followers into believing that the 'treble' dream was about to end...only to send them into a state of ecstasy with a glorious late fightback. Sensational, gripping, edge-of-the-seat entertainment was United's stock in trade - with a happy ending always guaranteed.

The ultimate example of United's incredible powers of resilience and recovery came in the match that mattered more than any other - the final of the Champions' Cup against Bayern Munich. With the domestic 'double' - the

LEAGUE CHAMPIONSHIP RESULTS 98/99

		1	2	3	4	5	6	7	8	9	10	11	12	13	14	15	16	17	18	19	20
1	Arsenal		1-0	1-0	0-0	1-0	2-0	1-0	1-0	3-1	5-0	0-0	3-0	1-1	3-0	2-1	3-0	1-1	0-0	1-0	5-1
2	Aston Villa	3-2		1-3	3-4	0-3	1-4	1-0	3-0	1-2	1-1	2-4	1-1	3-1	1-0	2-0	2-1	3-0	3-2	0-0	2-0
3	Blackburn Rovers	1-2	2-1		1-0	3-4	1-2	0-0	1-2	1-0	1-0	1-3	0-0	0-0	0-0	1-2	1-4	0-2	1-1	3-0	3-1
4	Charlton Athletic	0-1	0-1	0-0		0-1	1-1	1-2	1-2	1-1	0-0	1-0	0-1	1-1	2-2	0-0	0-1	5-0	1-4	4-2	2-0
5	Chelsea	0-0	2-1	1-1	2-1		2-1	2-1	3-1	1-0	2-2	2-1	0-0	2-0	1-1	2-1	1-1	1-0	2-0	0-1	3-0
6	Coventry City	0-1	1-2	1-1	2-1	2-1		1-1	3-0	2-2	1-1	2-1	0-1	1-2	1-5	4-0	1-0	1-0	1-1	0-0	2-1
7	Derby County	0-0	2-1	1-0	0-2	2-2	0-0		2-1	2-2	2-0	3-2	1-1	2-1	3-4	1-0	1-0	0-0	0-1	0-2	0-0
8	Everton	0-2	0-0	0-0	4-1	0-0	2-0	0-0		0-0	0-0	0-0	1-4	5-0	1-0	0-1	1-2	1-0	0-1	6-0	1-1
9	Leeds United	1-0	0-0	1-0	4-1	0-0	2-0	4-1	1-0		0-1	0-0	1-1	2-0	0-1	3-1	2-1	3-0	2-0	4-0	2-2
10	Leicester City	1-1	2-2	1-1	1-1	2-4	1-0	1-2	2-0	1-2		1-0	2-6	0-1	2-0	3-1	0-2	2-0	2-1	0-0	1-1
11	Liverpool	0-0	0-1	2-0	3-3	1-1	2-0	1-2	3-2	1-3	0-1		2-2	3-1	4-2	5-1	2-0	7-1	3-2	2-2	3-0
12	Manchester United	1-1	2-1	3-2	4-1	1-1	2-0	1-0	3-1	3-2	2-2	2-0		2-3	0-0	3-0	3-0	2-1	2-1	4-0	5-1
13	Middlesbrough	1-6	0-0	2-1	2-0	0-0	2-0	1-1	2-2	0-0	0-0	1-3	0-1		2-2	1-1	4-0	3-0	0-0	1-0	3-1
14	Newcastle United	1-1	2-1	1-1	0-0	0-1	4-1	2-1	1-3	0-3	1-0	1-4	1-2	1-1		2-0	1-1	4-0	1-1	0-3	3-1
15	Nottingham Forest	0-1	2-2	2-2	0-1	1-3	1-0	2-2	0-2	1-1	1-0	2-2	1-8	1-2	1-2		2-0	1-1	0-1	0-0	0-1
16	Sheffield Wednesday	1-0	0-1	3-0	3-0	0-0	1-2	0-1	0-0	0-2	0-1	1-0	3-1	3-1	1-1	3-2		0-0	0-0	0-1	1-2
17	Southampton	0-0	1-4	3-3	3-1	0-2	2-1	0-1	2-0	3-0	2-1	1-2	0-3	3-3	2-1	1-2	1-0		1-1	1-0	3-1
18	Tottenham Hotspur	1-3	1-0	2-1	2-2	2-2	0-0	1-1	4-1	3-3	1-2	2-1	2-2	0-3	2-0	2-0	0-3	3-0		1-2	0-0
19	West Ham United	0-4	0-0	2-0	0-1	1-1	2-0	5-1	2-1	1-5	3-2	2-1	0-0	4-0	2-0	2-1	0-4	1-0	2-1		3-4
20	Wimbledon	1-0	0-0	1-1	2-1	1-2	2-1	2-1	1-2	1-1	0-1	1-0	1-1	2-2	1-1	1-3	2-1	0-2	3-1	0-0	

LEAGUE CHAMPIONSHIP FINAL TABLE 98/99

		P	Home					Away					Total					P	GD
			W	D	L	F	A	W	D	L	F	A	W	D	L	F	A		
1	Manchester United	38	14	4	1	45	18	8	9	2	35	19	22	13	3	80	37	79	+43
2	Arsenal	38	14	5	0	34	5	8	7	4	25	12	22	12	4	59	17	78	+42
3	Chelsea	38	12	6	1	29	13	8	9	2	28	17	20	15	3	57	30	75	+27
4	Leeds United	38	12	5	2	32	9	6	8	5	30	25	18	13	7	62	34	67	+28
5	West Ham United	38	11	3	5	32	26	5	6	8	14	27	16	9	13	46	53	57	-7
6	Aston Villa	38	10	3	6	33	28	5	7	7	18	18	15	10	13	51	46	55	+5
7	Liverpool	38	10	5	4	44	24	5	4	10	24	25	15	9	14	68	49	54	+19
8	Derby County	38	8	7	4	22	19	5	6	8	18	26	13	13	12	40	45	52	-5
9	Middlesbrough	38	7	9	3	25	18	5	6	8	23	36	12	15	11	48	54	51	-6
10	Leicester City	38	7	6	6	25	25	5	7	7	15	21	12	13	13	40	46	49	-6
11	Tottenham Hotspur	38	7	7	5	28	26	4	7	8	19	24	11	14	13	47	50	47	-3
12	Sheffield Wednesday	38	7	5	7	20	15	6	2	11	21	27	13	7	18	41	42	46	-1
13	Newcastle United	38	7	6	6	26	25	4	7	8	22	29	11	13	14	48	54	46	-6
14	Everton	38	6	8	5	22	12	5	2	12	20	35	11	10	17	42	47	43	-5
15	Coventry City	38	8	6	5	26	21	3	3	13	13	30	11	9	18	39	51	42	-12
16	Wimbledon	38	7	7	5	22	21	3	5	11	18	42	10	12	16	40	63	42	-23
17	Southampton	38	9	4	6	29	26	2	4	13	8	38	11	8	19	37	64	41	-27
18	Charlton Athletic	38	4	7	8	20	20	4	5	10	21	36	8	12	18	41	56	36	-15
19	Blackburn Rovers	38	6	5	8	21	24	1	9	9	17	28	7	14	17	38	52	35	-14
20	Nottingham Forest	38	3	7	9	18	31	4	2	13	17	38	7	9	22	35	69	30	-34

club's third in five years - already in the bag, United faced their date with destiny in Barcelona. Victory in Europe was what the club craved most. The loss through suspension of midfielders Roy Keane and Paul Scholes forced Alex Ferguson to reshuffle his midfield, and for 90 minutes it appeared as if he had blundered in his team selection, with Bayern controlling the game almost from the moment they took the lead in the sixth minute. But even with the odds stacked against them, United refused to give in. The introduction of substitutes Teddy Sheringham and Ole Gunnar Solskjaer reinvigorated them, and the final moments...well, they had to be seen to be believed. A goal apiece for the two subs and then mayhem. Absolute mayhem. Not even the most committed optimist among United's red legion could have imagined such an outlandish and euphoric climax to the club's incredible season.

The victory in Barcelona was preceded by other great escapes. In the FA Cup the team staged a similar late fight-back to eliminate Liverpool at Old Trafford. They then came back from the dead against Arsenal in an epic semi-final replay (the last of its kind), with Peter Schmeichel saving a last-minute penalty and Ryan Giggs taking United to Wembley with a truly breathtaking extra-time winner.

United also shredded their supporters' nerves in the last match of the Premiership campaign. Needing to win at home to Spurs to secure the first instalment of the 'treble', they went a goal behind but came back to win 2-1. In Europe, too, the team's ability to sneer in the face of impending doom was illustrated perfectly by their semi-final triumph over Juventus. A last-minute equaliser at Old Trafford (Giggs again) was followed a fortnight later in Turin by the team's most accomplished performance of the season, when they responded to the setback of conceding two early goals by calmly and confidently taking the game to the Italians and beating them 3-2.

Allied to the team's great spirit and resolve was an abundance of footballing quality. Alex Ferguson reacted to the team's trophyless 1997/98 campaign by spending £27m on three new players. The two most expensive - Tobagan striker Dwight Yorke from Aston Villa and Dutch defender Jaap Stam from PSV - more than justified their large fees. Yorke scored consistently all season and was particularly impressive in Europe, where he peaked with two headed goals in the quarter-final against Inter. He also formed a dynamic alliance with Andy Cole, who responded to Yorke's presence by playing his best football in a United shirt. Stam started slowly but gradually became a colossus in the heart of the back-line, proving himself to be one of the world's best (as well as costliest) defenders.

United also benefitted enormously from the return of their captain, Irishman Roy Keane, who had missed virtually all of the previous season with a knee injury. He coaxed and cajoled his team-mates from the thick of the action in midfield and was a massive influence in several of United's big games, notably the away victory at Juventus and the Premiership-clinching win at home to Spurs. Peter Schmeichel, in his last season at the club, was as important (and eccentric) as ever in goal, and the band of young Englishmen - the so-called 'Fergie's fledglings' - also continued to improve and progress, none more so than the brilliant David Beckham, who responded to all the barracking he received from opposing fans after his *faux pas* for England at the World Cup in the best way possible - by silencing them with some fantastic football.

United, for all the talent of their playing staff, would probably have won nothing had it not been for the guiding hand of their manager. Alex Ferguson might have got lucky in the Champions' Cup showdown against Bayern but nobody could honestly say that he did not deserve his place in history. The United manager since 1986, he achieved his own lifetime's ambition by lifting the European Champions' Cup, and a few days later he joined former United greats Matt Busby and Bobby Charlton by being proclaimed as a knight of the realm. Arise, Sir Alex Ferguson!

Of course, United's clean sweep of all the trophies they cared about left many other clubs feeling decidedly second-rate and, consequently, more than a little envious. Although the Champions' Cup final victory was projected as a triumph for English football and was received with general delight up and down the country - the fact that the beaten opposition were Germans might have had a lot to do with that - United continue

to be loved and loathed in equal measure. Although instruments of torture would probably be necessary to get fans of rival clubs like Leeds, Liverpool or (remember them?) Manchester City to admit it, admiration for United's achievements during the 1990s - and especially in 1999 - is widespread. But will there be any team in England capable of rivalling "the world's richest club" in the first years of the New Millennium?

Arsenal have in recent years become United's most consistent rivals. They won the 'double' themselves, of course, in 1997/98, and but for the odd moment of misfortune and misbehaviour, they might even have repeated that feat in 1998/99. They took United to the wire in the Premiership, missing out by a solitary point, and really should have beaten them in the FA Cup semi-final replay, but Dennis Bergkamp's last-minute penalty miss and the team's failure to break down a stubborn ten-man United rearguard in extra-time was punished by Ryan Giggs' wonder goal.

In an earlier round of the FA Cup Arsenal had caused quite a stir when they scored an 'ungentlemanly' winning goal at home to Sheffield United (they failed to return the ball to their opponents who had kicked it into touch to allow treatment to be given to an injured player) and made the conciliatory gesture of having the match replayed, albeit at Highbury (a standard replay would have been staged on their opponents' ground; it was 1-1 at the time of the incident). The man at the centre of that controversy was Arsenal's Nigerian newcomer Nwankwo Kanu. It was an unsettling start for him in English football but he quickly got over it, and it was his elaborate skill and vision which re-generated Arsenal's title challenge. The Gunners went five months without a league defeat as they repeated their outstanding late surge of the previous season, but the run ended in their penultimate fixture, away at Leeds, and that 0-1 defeat handed the initative to Manchester United prior to the drama of the final Sunday.

TOP SCORERS

18	Jimmy Floyd HASSELBAINK (Leeds United)
	Michael OWEN (Liverpool)
	Dwight YORKE (Manchester United)
17	Nicolas ANELKA (Arsenal)
	Andy COLE (Manchester United)
15	Hamilton RICARD (Middlesbrough)
14	Robbie FOWLER (Liverpool)
	Julian JOACHIM (Aston Villa)
	Alan SHEARER (Newcastle United)
13	Dion DUBLIN (Coventry City/Aston Villa)
	Gianfranco ZOLA (Chelsea)
12	Ole Gunnar SOLSKJAER (Manchester United)

NATIONAL TEAM RESULTS 98/99

Date	Opponent	H/A	Venue	Score	Scorers
05/09/98	Sweden (ECQ)	A	Solna	1-2	Shearer (2)
10/10/98	Bulgaria (ECQ)	H	Wembley	0-0	
14/10/98	Luxembourg (ECQ)	A	Luxembourg	3-0	Owen (19), Shearer (39p), Southgate (89)
18/11/98	Czech Republic	H	Wembley	2-0	Anderton (22), Merson (39)
10/02/99	France	H	Wembley	0-2	
27/03/99	Poland (ECQ)	H	Wembley	3-1	Scholes (11, 21, 70)
28/04/99	Hungary	A	Budapest	1-1	Shearer (21p)
05/06/99	Sweden (ECQ)	H	Wembley	0-0	
09/06/99	Bulgaria (ECQ)	A	Sofia	1-1	Shearer (15)

DOMESTIC CUP 98/99

THIRD ROUND
Aston Villa 3, Hull City 0
Blackburn Rovers 2, Charlton Athletic 0
Bolton Wanderers 1, Wolverhampton Wanderers 2
Bournemouth 1, West Bromwich Albion 0
Bradford City 2, Grimsby Town 1
Bristol City 0, Everton 2
Bury 0, Stockport County 3
Cardiff City 1, Yeovil Town 1
(replay) Yeovil Town 1, Cardiff City 2
Coventry City 7, Macclesfield Town 0
Crewe Alexandra 1, Oxford United 3
Leicester City 4, Birmingham City 2
Lincoln City 0, Sunderland 1
Newcastle United 2, Crystal Palace 1
Nottingham Forest 0, Portsmouth 1
Oldham Athletic 0, Chelsea 2
Plymouth Argyle 0, Derby County 3
Queens Park Rangers 0, Huddersfield Town 1
Rotherham 0, Bristol Rovers 1
Rushden & Diamonds 0, Leeds United 0
(replay) Leeds United 3, Rushden & Diamonds 1
Sheffield United 1, Notts County 1
(replay) Notts County 3, Sheffield United 4 (aet)
Southampton 1, Fulham 1
(replay) Fulham 1, Southampton 0
Southport 0, Leyton Orient 2
Swindon Town 0, Barnsley 0
(replay) Barnsley 3, Swindon Town 1
Tottenham Hotspur 5, Watford 2
Tranmere Rovers 0, Ipswich Town 1
West Ham United 1, Swansea City 1
(replay) Swansea City 1, West Ham United 0
Wimbledon 1, Manchester City 0
Wrexham 4, Scunthorpe United 3

Manchester United 3, Middlesbrough 1
Port Vale 0, Liverpool 3
Sheffield Wednesday 4, Norwich City 1
Preston North End 2, Arsenal 4

FOURTH ROUND
Aston Villa 0, Fulham 2
Barnsley 3, Bournemouth 1
Blackburn Rovers 1, Sunderland 0
Bristol Rovers 3, Leyton Orient 0
Everton 1, Huddersfield Town 0
Leicester City 0, Coventry City 3
Newcastle United 3, Bradford City 0
Portsmouth 1, Leeds United 5
Sheffield Wednesday 2, Stockport County 0
Swansea City 0, Derby County 1
Wimbledon 1, Tottenham Hotspur 1
(replay) Tottenham Hotspur 3, Wimbledon 0
Wrexham 1, Huddersfield Town 1
(replay) Huddersfield Town 2, Wrexham 1
Manchester United 2, Liverpool 1
Wolverhampton Wanderers 1, Arsenal 2
Oxford United 1, Chelsea 1
(replay) Chelsea 4, Oxford United 2
Sheffield United 4, Cardiff City 1

FIFTH ROUND
Arsenal 2, Sheffield United 1
Barnsley 4, Bristol Rovers 1
Everton 2, Coventry City 1
Huddersfield Town 2, Derby County 2
(replay) Derby County 3, Huddersfield Town 1
Leeds United 1, Tottenham Hotspur 1
(replay) Tottenham Hotspur 2, Leeds United 0
Sheffield Wednesday 0, Chelsea 1

Manchester United 1, Fulham 0
Newcastle United 0, Blackburn Rovers 0
(replay) Blackburn Rovers 0, Newcastle United 1

QUARTER-FINALS
Arsenal 1 (Kanu 89), Derby County 0
Manchester United 0, Chelsea 0
(replay) Chelsea 0,
Manchester United 2 (Yorke 4, 59)
Newcastle United 4 (Ketsbaia 21, 73, Yeoryadis 62, Shearer 81), Everton 1 (Unsworth 57)
Barnsley 0, Tottenham Hotspur 1 (Ginola 68)

SEMI-FINALS
Newcastle United 2 (Shearer 108p, 119), Tottenham Hotspur 0 (aet)
Manchester United 0, Arsenal 0 (aet)
(replay)
Manchester United 2 (Beckham 17, Giggs 109), Arsenal 1 (Bergkamp 68) (aet)

FINAL
22/05/99, Wembley
MANCHESTER UNITED 2
Sheringham (11), Scholes (53)
NEWCASTLE UNITED 0
referee - Jones
MANCHESTER UNITED - Schmeichel; Neville G., May, Johnson, Neville P.; Beckham, Keane (Sheringham 9), Scholes (Stam 78), Giggs; Solskjaer, Cole (Yorke 60).
NEWCASTLE UNITED - Harper; Griffin, Charvet, Dabizas, Domi; Lee, Hamann (Ferguson 46), Speed, Solano (Maric 68); Shearer, Ketsbaia (Glass 79).

On reflection, Arsenal could look to a number of suspensions to key players as a factor in their failure to win a trophy. Frenchman Emmanuel Petit was outstanding when he played, but three red cards meant that he sat out too many important matches. And he was not the only offender. The pick of the Arsenal players was probably Nicolas Anelka, who began the season by running rings round Jaap Stam as Arsenal beat Manchester United 3-0 in the Charity Shield and took it on from there, eclipsing a rather disappointing Dennis Bergkamp as Arsenal's most potent forward threat and finishing up as the club's leading goalscorer. Unfortunately, the young Frenchman never seemed at peace with either himself or his environment and quit the club in the summer after a tiresome and dishonourable contract wrangle.

Arsenal boss Arsène Wenger continues to feed his club with imported rather than locally-nurtured talent, and

Gianluca Vialli, of Chelsea, is another who appears to suscribe to the view that "British is not best". The Italian added four big-name foreigners to his squad at the start of the campaign, but only two of them - Marcel Desailly, of France, and Albert Ferrer, of Spain - went on to prosper in the Premiership. Italian striker Pierluigi Casiraghi suffered a terrible injury to his right knee in the autumn and was ruled out for the rest of the season, while Brian Laudrup realised fairly early on that he had made the wrong move and sought asylum back in his native Denmark - though not before bowing out with a farewell goal against his new club-to-be FC Copenhagen that sent Chelsea into the quarter-finals of the European Cup-winners' Cup.

Like all Cup-winners' Cup holders before them, Chelsea were unable to defend their European crown - Mallorca put them out in the semi-finals - but the West Londoners

EUROPEAN CUPS 98/99

CHAMPIONS' CUP

● ARSENAL

Champions' League

1st match RC LENS (FRA)
A 1-1   Overmars (51)
Seaman; Dixon, Winterburn, Vieira, Keown, Adams, Petit (Hughes 73), Parlour, Anelka, Bergkamp (Garde 90), Overmars.

2nd match PANATHINAIKOS (GRE)
H 2-1   Adams (63), Keown (73)
Seaman; Dixon, Winterburn, Vieira, Adams, Anelka, Bergkamp, Overmars, Keown, Petit, Garde (Vivas 79).

3rd match DYNAMO KYIV (UKR)
H 1-1   Bergkamp (73)
Seaman; Dixon, Winterburn, Adams, Anelka (Vivas 84), Bergkamp, Overmars, Keown, Parlour, Hughes, Garde.

4th match DYNAMO KYIV (UKR)
A 1-3   Hughes (83)
Seaman; Dixon, Keown, Bould (Grimandi 44), Winterburn, Parlour, Vieira, Petit, Vivas (Garde 84), Wreh, Boa Morte (Hughes 67).

5th match RC LENS (FRA)
H 0-1
Seaman; Dixon, Winterburn, Adams (Bould 46), Anelka, Overmars, Wreh (Boa Morte 67), Keown, Parlour, Hughes, Garde (Vivas 67).

6th match PANATHINAIKOS (GRE)
A 3-1   Mendez (66), Anelka (78), Boa Morte (85)
Seaman; Vivas, Vernazza, Bould, Upson, Mendez (Black 78), Grondin, Grimandi, Boa Morte, Anelka, Wreh.

● MANCHESTER UNITED

Qualifying round LKS LODZ (POL)
H 2-0   Giggs (16), Cole (81)
Schmeichel; Neville G., Irwin, Johnsen, Stam, Keane, Beckham, Butt, Cole, Scholes (Solskjaer 82), Giggs.
A 0-0
Schmeichel; Irwin, Neville P., Johnsen, Stam, Keane, Beckham, Butt, Sheringham, Scholes, Giggs (Solskjaer 65).

Champions' League

1st match FC BARCELONA (ESP)
H 3-3   Giggs (17), Scholes (24), Beckham (64)
Schmeichel; Neville G., Irwin (Neville P. 79), Stam, Beckham, Giggs (Blomqvist 84), Keane, Scholes, Yorke, Solskjaer (Butt 55), Berg.

2nd match FC BAYERN MÜNCHEN (GER)
A 2-2   Yorke (29), Scholes (49)
Schmeichel; Irwin, Neville P., Neville G., Stam, Keane, Scholes, Beckham, Blomqvist (Cruijff 69), Sheringham, Yorke.

3rd match BRØNDBY IF (DEN)
A 6-2   Giggs (2, 21), Cole (28), Keane (55), Yorke (59), Solskjaer (62)
Schmeichel; Brown, Neville P., Neville G., Stam, Keane, Scholes, Blomqvist, Cole (Solskjaer 60), Yorke (Wilson 65), Giggs (Cruijff 60).

4th match BRØNDBY IF (DEN)
H 5-0   Beckham (7), Cole (13), Neville P. (16), Yorke (28), Scholes (62)
Schmeichel; Irwin, Neville G., Stam, Neville P. (Brown 32), Beckham, Scholes, Keane, Blomqvist (Cruijff 46), Yorke, Cole (Solskjaer 55).

5th match FC BARCELONA (ESP)
A 3-3   Yorke (25, 68), Cole (53)
Schmeichel; Neville G., Irwin, Stam, Beckham (Butt 81), Brown, Blomqvist, Keane, Cole, Yorke, Scholes.

6th match FC BAYERN MÜNCHEN (GER)
H 1-1   Keane (43)
Schmeichel; Neville G., Irwin (Johnsen 46), Stam, Beckham, Cole, Giggs, Keane, Scholes, Yorke (Butt 64), Brown.

Quarter-final INTER (ITA)
H 2-0   Yorke (6, 45)
Schmeichel; Neville G., Irwin, Johnsen (Berg 46), Stam, Beckham, Cole, Giggs, Keane, Scholes (Butt 69), Yorke.
A 1-1   Scholes (88)
Schmeichel; Berg, Irwin, Stam, Johnsen (Scholes 77), Keane, Beckham, Cole, Yorke, Neville G., Giggs (Neville P. 82).

Semi-final JUVENTUS (ITA)
H 1-1   Giggs (90)
Schmeichel; Neville G., Irwin, Stam, Beckham, Cole, Giggs, Keane, Scholes, Yorke (Sheringham 79), Berg (Johnsen 46).
A 3-2   Keane (24), Yorke (34), Cole (84)
Schmeichel; Neville G., Irwin, Johnsen, Stam, Beckham, Keane, Butt, Blomqvist (Scholes 68), Yorke, Cole.

Final FC BAYERN MÜNCHEN (GER)
Barcelona
2-1   Sheringham (90), Solskjaer (90)
Schmeichel; Neville G., Stam, Johnsen, Irwin, Giggs, Beckham, Butt, Blomqvist (Sheringham 66), Yorke, Cole (Solskjaer 80).

CUP WINNERS' CUP

● CHELSEA

1st round HELSINGBORGS IF (SWE)
H 1-0   Leboeuf (43)
Kharin; Ferrer, Le Saux, Leboeuf, Desailly, Wise, Laudrup, Di Matteo, Babayaro (Poyet 63), Vialli (Nicholls 84), Flo (Casiraghi 55).
A 0-0
De Goey; Babayaro, Leboeuf, Desailly, Poyet, Vialli (Casiraghi 90), Duberry, Le Saux, Di Matteo, Ferrer, Flo.

EUROPEAN CUPS 98/99 (CONTINUED)

2nd round FC KØBENHAVN (DEN)
H 1-1 Desailly (90)
De Goey; Leboeuf, Desailly, Laudrup, Poyet, Casiraghi (Flo 69), Wise, Le Saux, Di Matteo, Ferrer (Petrescu 69), Zola.
A 1-0 Laudrup (32)
De Goey; Ferrer, Leboeuf, Desailly, Le Saux, Laudrup (Petrescu 67), Di Matteo, Babayaro, Zola (Flo 76), Wise, Casiraghi (Poyet 90).

Quarter-final VÅLERENGA IF (NOR)
H 3-0 Babayaro (10), Zola (30), Wise (85)
De Goey; Petrescu, Babayaro, Desailly, Vialli, Wise, Le Saux, Di Matteo, Ferrer, Lambourde, Zola (Flo 46).
A 3-2 Vialli (12), Lambourde (15), Flo (33)
De Goey; Terry, Duberry, Lambourde, Le Saux, Petrescu, Di Matteo, Wise (Newton 46), Babayaro (Myers 46), Flo (Nicholls 46), Vialli.

Semi-final RCD MALLORCA (ESP)
H 1-1 Flo (50)
De Goey; Petrescu, Babayaro (Flo 46), Leboeuf, Desailly, Vialli, Wise, Le Saux, Ferrer (Lambourde 80), Zola (Poyet 60), Morris.
A 0-1
De Goey; Ferrer, Petrescu (Morris 78), Desailly, Leboeuf, Di Matteo, Poyet, Wise, Flo, Zola, Le Saux (Babayaro 46).

● NEWCASTLE UNITED
1st round PARTIZAN BEOGRAD (YUG)
H 2-1 Shearer (12), Dabizas (71)
Given; Watson, Pearce, Dabizas, Charvet, Andersson (Solano 46), Lee, Speed, Shearer, Ketsbaia, Glass.
A 0-1
Given; Griffin (Albert 73), Charvet, Dabizas, Pearce, Solano, Speed, Batty, Glass, Ketsbaia, Shearer.

UEFA CUP
● ASTON VILLA
1st round STRØMSGODSET IF (NOR)
H 3-2 Charles (83), Vassell (89, 90)
Bosnich; Charles, Southgate, Barry, Wright, Draper (Scimeca 66), Hendrie, Grayson (Taylor 37), Thompson, Joachim, Byfield (Vassell 80).
A 3-0 Collymore (11, 24, 64)
Bosnich; Charles (Scimeca 51), Wright, Southgate, Ehiogu, Taylor (Ferraresi 70), Draper, Collymore, Thompson, Joachim (Vassell 67), Grayson.

2nd round RC CELTA (ESP)
A 1-0 Joachim (14)
Oakes; Charles, Ehiogu, Southgate, Wright, Draper, Barry, Scimeca, Hendrie, Collymore, Joachim.
H 1-3 Collymore (27p)
Oakes; Charles (Draper 46), Ehiogu, Southgate, Barry (Vassell 65), Wright, Taylor, Hendrie, Thompson (Grayson 83), Joachim, Collymore.

● BLACKBURN ROVERS
1st round OLYMPIQUE LYONNAIS (FRA)
H 0-1
Flowers; Dailly, Henchoz, Peacock, Davidson, Perez (Dahlin 68), Sherwood, Flitcroft, Wilcox, Davies, Sutton.
A 2-2 Perez (26), Flitcroft (56)
Flowers; Kenna (Davidson 67), Peacock, Henchoz, Sherwood, Flitcroft, Wilcox, Duff, Perez (Johnson 46), McKinlay (Taylor 82), Dailly.

● LEEDS UNITED
1st round CS MARÍTIMO (POR)
H 1-0 Hasselbaink (84)
Martyn; Hiden, Radebe, Molenaar, Harte, Hopkin (Sharpe 76), Bowyer, Håland (Ribeiro 66), Kewell, Wijnhard (Lilley 62), Hasselbaink.
A 0-1
(aet; 1-4 on pens.)
Martyn; Håland, Radebe, Hopkin (Granville 120), Harte, Molenaar, Halle, Bowyer (Wijnhard 75), Hiden, Kewell (Sharpe 76), Hasselbaink.

2nd round ROMA (ITA)
A 0-1
Martyn; Halle, Hiden, Molenaar, Radebe, Ribeiro, Bowyer, Hopkin, Kewell (Håland 70), Hasselbaink (Wijnhard 80), McPhail.
H 0-0
Martyn; Hiden, Woodgate, Molenaar, Harte, Hopkin, Bowyer, Sharpe (Wijnhard 60), McPhail, Kewell, Hasselbaink.

● LIVERPOOL
1st round 1.FC KOSICE (SVK)
A 3-0 Berger (19), Riedle (23), Owen (59)
Friedel; Babb, Staunton, Carragher, Heggem, Harkness, McManaman (McAteer 78), Redknapp (Leonhardsen 83), Riedle (Fowler 50), Owen, Berger.
H 5-0 Redknapp (23, 55), Ince (52), Fowler (53, 90)
James; McAteer (Heggem 66), Babb (Matteo 63), Leonhardsen, Fowler, Owen, Redknapp, Berger, Ince (Staunton 71), Bjørnebye, Carragher.

2nd round VALENCIA CF (ESP)
H 0-0
James; McAteer, Staunton, McManaman, Fowler (Owen 73), Riedle, Heggem, Berger (Leonhardsen 75), Ince, Bjørnebye, Carragher.
A 2-2 McManaman (80), Berger (86)
James; Heggem (Dundee 79), Carragher, Staunton, Bjørnebye, McManaman, Ince, Redknapp, Berger (Harkness 90), Fowler (McAteer 84), Owen.

3rd round RC CELTA (ESP)
A 1-3 Owen (35)
James; Heggem, Kvarme, Staunton, Bjørnebye, McManaman, Ince, Redknapp, Berger (Harkness 90), Fowler (McAteer 84), Owen.
H 0-1
James (Friedel 63); McAteer, Staunton, Babb (Murphy 46), Fowler, Owen, Berger, Matteo, Carragher, Thompson (Riedle 58), Gerrard.

did put up a decent fight in the Premiership. Although they lost at Coventry on the opening day for the second year in succession, they were not beaten again in the league for another five and a half months. Vialli had sharpened up the team's competitiveness and they were less prone to conceding sloppy goals than they had been the season before. Desailly and Ferrer were the two main reasons for that, while at the other end Gianfranco Zola returned to his best form and was ably backed up in the goalscoring department by Tore André Flo and - before he sustained yet another injury - Gustavo Poyet. Vialli rarely selected himself and announced a halt to his playing career at the end of the season - even though he still looked very capable of performing at Premiership level for another year at least.

Chelsea's title hopes were extinguished by three successive draws in April, but third place did enable the Londoners to compete in the European Champions' Cup for the first time in their history, having been forbidden to participate in the very first competition by the Football League when they were the reigning English champions (for the one and only time) in the mid-1950s.

For a while it looked as if Chelsea would be pressed hard for that third place by Leeds United. The Yorkshire side had a run of seven successive victories in the spring and received rave notices for the style of their play under new manager David O'Leary, who was in the process of building an exciting new team based on a crop of hugely talented youngsters. Dutchman Jimmy Floyd Hasselbaink was the team's main goal-getter (he shared the Premership Golden Boot with Dwight Yorke and Liverpool wonderboy Michael Owen) but he had it made thanks to the excellent support of young colts Harry Kewell, Alan Smith and Lee Bowyer. 19-year-old central defender Jonathon Woodgate also had a wonderful first season and was a full England international by the summer.

O'Leary was appointed as the new Leeds manager in October following the shock departure of George Graham to Tottenham. Leeds had been keen to bring in the highly-rated Martin O'Neill from Leicester, but the East Midlands club stood firm and refused to allow Leeds to poach their greatest asset. So, O'Neill stayed at Leicester, Graham went to Spurs and O'Leary was promoted to the Leeds job.

All three clubs were to benefit from the moving and shaking. While Leeds blossomed in the spring, Tottenham and Leicester went on to reach the final of the League Cup. There was a UEFA Cup place at stake, and Tottenham took it thanks to a last-minute winner from Danish midfielder Allan Nielsen in a drab Wembley final. Leicester had another chance to join Leeds and Spurs in the 1999/2000 UEFA Cup when they won the Premiership Fair Play prize

and were put into a lucky-dip draw with teams from seven other European countries. But the wheel of fortune did not spin their way so they had to be content with a third successive season in the top half of the Premiership - quite an achievement for a club of such meagre resources.

Tottenham's trophy success was their first for eight years and proved that Graham had lost none of the managerial skills that had made him such a huge success at North London rivals Arsenal. The Scotsman received a mixed reception when he first arrived at White Hart Lane (many Spurs diehards saw him as an enemy in the camp) but by the end of the season, with a trophy won and a jaunt to Europe in the offing, the dissenters had all but disappeared.

Tottenham came close to reaching the final of the FA Cup final as well. Inspired by the individual class of David Ginola, voted Players' Player of the Year and (more contentiously) Footballer of the Year, Spurs got to the semi-finals, where they were beaten after extra-time by Newcastle as a result of two goals from England captain Alan Shearer. The Magpies thus went to Wembley for the second successive year, but they had a new manager this time, Ruud Gullit having replaced Kenny Dalglish right at the start of the campaign. But the club's quest to win a first trophy in 30 years was once again stymied in the final. Arsenal had easily overcome them 2-0 the year before and it was the same story against Manchester United, with Shearer looking especially grim-faced afterwards as he watched another set of opposing fans celebrate a 'double'. Still, Newcastle did earn themselves another shot at Europe, so there was some gold at the end of the black and white rainbow for the long-suffering Geordie fans.

Aston Villa and Liverpool would have quite happily traded places with Newcastle. They both failed to gain their accustomed European place. Villa were the dominant team during the first half of the season, leading the table until Christmas. But they went into freefall in the New Year and dropped all the way down to sixth place, two points behind worthy InterToto qualifiers West Ham. Liverpool never got their act together at all. The gamble of having two joint-managers, with Frenchman Gérard Houllier being brought in to work alongside Roy Evans, did not pay off. One of them had to go, and it was Evans who was handed the short straw. There was no discernible improvement during the remainder of the season, and although a few individuals stood out - notably Patrik Berger and Michael Owen - there were more bad tidings than good, with Robbie Fowler in particular disgracing himself for a couple of laddish pranks that went wrong. His warped sense of humour earned him a six-match ban at the end of the season - a time when Liverpool needed him most as Owen was out with a hamstring injury.

NATIONAL TEAM APPEARANCES 98/99

Coach - Glenn HODDLE; Howard WILKINSON; Kevin KEEGAN	SWE	BUL	LUX	CZE	FRA	POL	HUN	SWE	BUL	Cps	Gls
David SEAMAN (19/09/63) - Arsenal	G	G	G		G46	G	G	G	G	52	-
Gareth SOUTHGATE (03/09/70) - Aston Villa	D	D	D						D	31	1
Tony ADAMS (10/10/66) - Arsenal	D				D					57	4
Sol CAMPBELL (18/09/74) - Tottenham Hotspur	D75	D	D	D		D		D	D	27	-
Darren ANDERTON (03/03/72) - Tottenham Hotspur	M42	M67	M63	M	M					27	7
Paul INCE (21/10/67) - Liverpool	M				M					45	2
Jamie REDKNAPP (25/06/73) - Liverpool	M	M			M85		s85		M	13	-
Paul SCHOLES (16/11/74) - Manchester United	M86	M77	M76		s85	M		M		17	7
Graeme LE SAUX (17/10/68) - Chelsea	M	s34		M	D	D		D46		35	1
Michael OWEN (14/12/79) - Liverpool	A	A	A		A66					13	4
Alan SHEARER (13/08/70) - Newcastle United	A	A	A		A	A	A	A	A	51	24
Robert LEE (01/02/66) - Newcastle United	s42	M	s63							21	2
Paul MERSON (20/03/68) - Middlesbrough/Aston Villa	s75			M77						21	3
Teddy SHERINGHAM (02/04/66) - Manchester United	s86	s77							A	38	9
Gary NEVILLE (18/02/75) - Manchester United		D				D				32	-
Andy HINCHCLIFFE (05/02/69) - Sheffield Wednesday		M34								7	-
David BATTY (02/12/68) - Newcastle United		s67	M				M	M	M	40	-
Rio FERDINAND (07/11/78) - West Ham United			D	D	s72		D63	s34		8	-
David BECKHAM (02/05/75) - Manchester United			M	M	M	M78		M75		23	1
Philip NEVILLE (21/01/77) - Manchester United			M			s78	D	D	M	17	-
Ian WRIGHT (03/11/63) - West Ham United			s76	A71						33	9
Nigel MARTYN (11/08/66) - Leeds United				G	s46					9	-
Martin KEOWN (24/07/66) - Arsenal				D	D86	D		D	D34	23	1
Nicky BUTT (21/01/75) - Manchester United				M			M			8	-
Dion DUBLIN (22/04/69) - Aston Villa				A						4	-
Robbie FOWLER (09/04/75) - Liverpool					s71				A81	9	2
Lee HENDRIE (18/05/77) - Aston Villa					s77					1	-
Lee DIXON (17/03/64) - Arsenal					D72					22	1
Andy COLE (15/10/71) - Manchester United					s66	A		A		5	-
Jason WILCOX (15/07/71) - Blackburn Rovers					s86					2	-
Tim SHERWOOD (02/02/69) - Tottenham Hotspur						M	M	M		3	-
Steve McMANAMAN (11/02/72) - Liverpool						M70	M85			24	-
Ray PARLOUR (07/03/73) - Arsenal						s70		s75	s64	3	-
Wes BROWN (16/03/79) - Manchester United						D74				1	-
Kevin PHILLIPS (25/07/73) - Sunderland						A83				1	-
Jamie CARRAGHER (28/01/78) - Liverpool						s63				1	-
Michael GRAY (03/08/74) - Sunderland						s74	s46	M		3	-
Emile HESKEY (11/01/78) - Leicester City						s83			s81	2	-
Jonathon WOODGATE (22/01/80) - Leeds United									D64	1	-

PLAYERS OF THE SEASON

★ SUPERSTAR PROFILE
DAVID BECKHAM

Throughout the 1998/99 season David Beckham was never allowed to forget his misdemeanour at the World Cup. Mercilessly jeered and whistled by opposing fans at every English ground he visited bar Old Trafford, the young midfielder could have been forgiven for packing his bags and moving abroad to a league where his talents would be more widely appreciated. There would have been no shortage of takers, that's for sure. But instead he decided to stay at Manchester United and take the flak. It was a measure of his new-found maturity that he responded to the challenge so well. Showing absolute confidence in his own ability, he produced one outstanding performance after another to help United towards the fulfilment of their 'treble' dream. Perhps his best display of all came in the European Champions' Cup quarter-final first leg at home to Inter when he caused constant panic in the Italian defence with his consistently accurate crossing from the right touchline. Later that week he enjoyed his own personal highlight when his famous wife-to-be

Victoria "Posh Spice" Adams gave birth to his first child. If anything, fatherhood inspired him to even greater heights in the last two months of the season, and he was United's best player in the European Cup final against Bayern Munich - despite being switched to a central midfield rôle, which many observers (though not Alex Ferguson) believe to be his natural position. The great dilemma, of course, is that by fielding Beckham in the middle, the team misses out on his magnificent crosses. Wherever he plays, though, his natural footballing talent is there for all to see. With half of the year complete, there was no stronger candidate for the 1999 European Footballer of the Year award.

DWIGHT YORKE

When Manchester United signed Dwight Yorke from Aston Villa for £12.6m on Champions' League transfer deadline day, there were many United fans who believed that the Caribbean striker was no more than a panic buy. There had been strong talk of United signing a proven international striker like Gabriel Batistuta or Patrick Kluivert, but in the end it was Yorke who arrived at Old Trafford - for a club record fee. Nine months later nobody was left in any doubt that he had been worth the money. All season long he tore defences apart, both at home and in Europe. He was United's top scorer in each of the three competitions that they won, scoring 18 goals in the Premiership, three in the FA Cup and eight in the European Champions' Cup. He was the joint-leading marksman in both the Premiership and European listings and his presence also brought the best out of Andy Cole, who scored goals in similar abundance and was recalled to the England side as a result. If Yorke were English, he would be an automatic selection for the national side. But he comes from Tobago and is proud of his Caribbean roots, even though he knows that the only serious international football he will ever play is in European and World club competitions.

HARRY KEWELL

Another of the Premiership's non-European contingent who would walk into the England team if he were homegrown is Australian left-winger Harry Kewell. The Sydney-born youngster had an outstanding season for Leeds United and was one of the main reasons for the Yorkshire club's rise up the

PLAYERS OF THE SEASON

and new England coach Kevin Keegan demonstrated how highly he rates the red-booted defender by selecting him in each of his first three internationals. He would have been in the fourth, too, had he not been injured against Sweden at Wembley.

ROD WALLACE
After 12 years in English top-flight football with Southampton and Leeds, Rod Wallace decided to try his luck in Scotland with Rangers. He cost the Glasgow giants nothing and arrived almost unnoticed amidst a flurry of big-buck transfer activity at Ibrox during the summer of 1998. Initially he was thought to be a mere squad player, but new Rangers boss Dick Advocaat quickly took a shine to him and before long he had taken up permanent residence in the side, scoring goals in each of his first four Scottish Premier League outings and many more besides in the Cup competitions. He ended the season as the club's top scorer with 26 goals, including 18 in the league - a tally bettered only by Celtic's Henrik Larsson. The goal which gave him most pleasure was the winner against Celtic in the Scottish Cup final. It secured the completion of the Ibrox club's domestic 'treble' and earned the 30-year-old Londoner the undying affection of the Rangers support.

table in the second half of the campaign. Beautifully balanced and always in complete control when the ball is at his feet, he has a formidable left foot and poses a real danger whenever he comes within 30 yards of goal. He scored nine goals for Leeds in 1998/99, including six in the Premiership, and was responsible for the creation of many others with his tricky ball skills and pin-point passing. Only 21 years old, he could go on to become one of Australia's finest-ever footballers.

MARTIN KEOWN
At 33, Martin Keown is approaching the veteran stage of his career, but the truth is he has never played better. He started out at Arsenal during the mid-'80s and it is at Highbury that he is likely to play out his last few seasons. He rejoined the Gunners in early 1993 but it is only in the last couple of years that he has broken the tried and tested Tony Adams/Steve Bould partnership in central defence. A prominent 'double'-winner in 1997/98, he had an even greater influence in 1998/99, playing in 34 of Arsenal's 38 Premiership matches and doing more than anyone else to give the Gunners the best defensive record in the Premiership. Keown has lost none of his considerable pace through age

At the foot of the table there was no surprise in the relegation of Premiership new boys Nottingham Forest and Charlton Athletic, but Blackburn Rovers' demise was a major shock. The cash-rich Lancashire club, champions in 1994/95 and sixth in 1997/98, got off to an awful start, for which manager Roy Hodgson paid the inevitable price. The arrival of Brian Kidd, assistant manager to Alex Ferguson at Manchester United, looked to have steadied the ship but the team tumbled to another succession of defeats in the spring and could not fulfil all the predictions that said they were too good to go down. The beneficiaries of Blackburn's fall from grace were Southampton, who, true to tradition, rescued themselves *in extremis* with victories in each of their last three games. Everton, too, had been in trouble before the arrival of Kevin Campbell from Turkey suddenly heralded a glut of goals from the previously shot-shy Merseysiders.

Sunderland made up for their heartbreaking play-off defeat the previous season by storming to victory in the First Division. Peter Reid's outfit also reached the League Cup semi-finals and were massively superior to the other teams in the division. They were joined in promotion by two rank outsiders - from the North, Bradford City, who just pipped Ipswich Town for the runners-up spot; from the South, Watford, who used the play-off route to secure their second successive promotion under former England manager Graham Taylor.

There was another addition to the ranks of ex-England bosses when Glenn Hoddle was forced to resign from his post as head coach in early February after being foolish enough to talk publicly of his very personal views about reincarnation and, in particular, the plight of the disabled. It was a silly, idle way for him to lose his job, especially as he knew that the press were gunning for him anyway following England's less than promising start to the Euro 2000 campaign.

An opening 2-1 defeat in Sweden was followed by a ghastly goalless draw at home to Bulgaria and a stumbling 3-0 win in Luxembourg. England were not playing well, and there was a widely-held suspicion that the players had lost faith in Hoddle following his exposé of internal affairs in the ill-conceived 'World Cup Diary', to which Hoddle attached his name in unison with FA spin doctor David Davies.

By the time of Hoddle's departure, Davies was the main figure at the FA following the resignations of both Chief Executive Graham Kelly and Chairman Keith Wiseman over a scandal involving the payment of money to the Welsh FA in exchange for votes at forthcoming FIFA elections. The image of English football's governing body was in need of a quick makeover, so Davies, eager to adopt the populist approach so favoured by his chums in the

Labour government, decided to appoint Kevin Keegan as the new England coach.

It took a humiliating home defeat by France for the FA's Director of Football Howard Wilkinson to be ejected from consideration, but, in truth, he had more qualifications for the job than Keegan, who, despite his affable persona, had never won anything significant as a club manager and in any case had no great desire to give up his day job at Fulham. Initially Keegan took the job part-time, but when England beat Poland 3-1 in his first match as caretaker, his fancy was tickled, and by the end of the season, he was the full-time coach and had a nice three-year contract to prove it.

Unfortunately, Keegan's optimism for the future was not reciprocated by his team, who reverted to their very worst form with two dour displays against Sweden (0-0 at Wembley) and Bulgaria (1-1 in Sofia). All hope of topping their qualifying group had vanished, and there was a strong possibility that England would not even make it to the play-offs - a terrible indictment on the state of the national team in a country that had just spawned the best club side in Europe.

INTERNATIONAL HONOURS

World Cup Finals appearances: 1950, 1954 (qtr-finals), 1958, 1962 (qtr-finals), 1966 (Winners), 1970 (qtr-finals), 1982 (2nd phase), 1986 (qtr-finals), 1990 (4th), 1998 (2nd round)

European Championship appearances: 1968 (3rd), 1972, 1980, 1988, 1992, 1996 (semi-finals)

European Club Competitions	
Champions' Cup	Manchester United (1968, 1999)
	Liverpool (1977, 1978, 1981, 1984)
	Nottingham Forest (1979, 1980)
	Aston Villa (1982)
Cup-winners' Cup	Tottenham Hotspur (1963)
	West Ham United (1965)
	Manchester City (1970)
	Chelsea (1971, 1998)
	Everton (1985)
	Manchester United (1991)
	Arsenal (1994)
Fairs' Cup	Leeds United (1968, 1971)
	Newcastle United (1969)
	Arsenal (1970)
UEFA Cup	Tottenham Hotspur (1972, 1984)
	Liverpool (1973, 1976)
	Ipswich Town (1981)
Super Cup	Liverpool (1977)
	Nottingham Forest (1979)
	Aston Villa (1982)
	Chelsea (1998)

ARSENAL

CLUB DIRECTORY

Arsenal FC
Arsenal Stadium
Highbury, London N5 1BU
tel - (0171) 7044000
fax - (0171) 7044001
Year of Formation - 1886
Chairman - Peter Hill-Wood
Managing Director - Ken Friar
Manager - Arsène Wenger
Stadium - Highbury (38,500)

MAJOR HONOURS
League Championship - (11)
1931, 1933, 1934, 1935, 1938, 1948, 1953,
1971, 1989, 1991, 1998.
FA Cup - (7)
1930, 1936, 1950, 1971, 1979, 1993, 1998.
League Cup - (2) 1987, 1993.
European Cup-winners' Cup - (1) 1994.
Fairs' Cup - (1) 1970.

APPEARANCES 98/99

		P	Ap	(s)	Gls
Tony ADAMS		D	26		1
Nicolas ANELKA (FRA)		A	34	(1)	17
Dennis BERGKAMP (HOL)		A	28	(1)	12
Luís BOA MORTE (POR)		A	2	(6)	
Steve BOULD		D	14	(5)	
Fabian CABALLERO (ARG)		D		(1)	
Kaba DIAWARA (FRA)		A	2	(10)	
Lee DIXON		D	36		
Rémi GARDE (FRA)		M	6	(4)	
Gilles GRIMANDI (FRA)		D	3	(5)	
David GRONDIN (FRA)		D	1		
Stephen HUGHES		M	4	(9)	1
Nwankwo KANU (NIG)		A	5	(7)	6
Martin KEOWN		D	34		1
Fredrik LJUNGBERG (SWE)		M	10	(5)	1
Alex MANNINGER (AUT)		G	6		
Alberto MENDEZ		A		(1)	
Marc OVERMARS (HOL)		M	37		6
Ray PARLOUR		M	35		6
Emmanuel PETIT (FRA)		M	26	(1)	4
David SEAMAN		G	32		
Matthew UPSON		D		(5)	
Patrick VIEIRA (FRA)		M	34		3
Nélson VIVAS (ARG)		D	10	(13)	
Nigel WINTERBURN		D	30		
Christopher WREH (LIB)		A	3	(9)	

LEAGUE RESULTS 1998/99

17/08/98	Nottingham Forest	H	2-1	Petit, Overmars
22/08/98	Liverpool	A	0-0	
29/08/98	Charlton Athletic	H	0-0	
09/09/98	Chelsea	A	0-0	
12/09/98	Leicester City	A	1-1	Hughes
20/09/98	Manchester United	H	3-0	Adams, Anelka, Ljungberg
26/09/98	Sheffield Wednesday	A	0-1	
04/10/98	Newcastle United	H	3-0	Bergkamp 2 (1p), Anelka
17/10/98	Southampton	H	1-1	Anelka
25/10/98	Blackburn Rovers	A	2-1	Anelka, Petit
31/10/98	Coventry City	A	1-0	Anelka
08/11/98	Everton	H	1-0	Anelka
14/11/98	Tottenham Hotspur	H	0-0	
21/11/98	Wimbledon	A	0-1	
29/11/98	Middlesbrough	H	1-1	Anelka
05/12/98	Derby County	A	0-0	
13/12/98	Aston Villa	A	2-3	Bergkamp 2
20/12/98	Leeds United	H	3-1	Bergkamp, Vieira, Petit
26/12/98	West Ham United	H	1-0	Overmars
28/12/98	Charlton Athletic	A	1-0	Overmars (p)
09/01/99	Liverpool	H	0-0	
16/01/99	Nottingham Forest	A	1-0	Keown
31/01/99	Chelsea	H	1-0	Bergkamp
06/02/99	West Ham United	A	4-0	Bergkamp, Overmars, Anelka, Parlour
17/02/99	Manchester United	A	1-1	Anelka
20/02/99	Leicester City	H	5-0	Anelka 3, Parlour 2
28/02/99	Newcastle United	A	1-1	Anelka
09/03/99	Sheffield Wednesday	H	3-0	Bergkamp 2, Kanu
13/03/99	Everton	A	2-0	Parlour, Bergkamp (p)
20/03/99	Coventry City	H	2-0	Parlour, Overmars
03/04/99	Southampton	A	0-0	
06/04/99	Blackburn Rovers	H	1-0	Bergkamp
19/04/99	Wimbledon	H	5-1	Parlour, Vieira, og (Thatcher), Bergkamp, Kanu
24/04/99	Middlesbrough	A	6-1	Overmars (p), Anelka 2, Kanu 2, Vieira
02/05/99	Derby County	H	1-0	Anelka
05/05/99	Tottenham Hotspur	A	3-1	Petit, Anelka, Kanu
11/05/99	Leeds United	A	0-1	
16/05/99	Aston Villa	H	1-0	Kanu

ASTON VILLA

CLUB DIRECTORY

Aston Villa FC
Villa Park
Trinity Road, Birmingham B6 6HE
tel - (0121) 3272299
fax - (0121) 3222107
Year of Formation - 1874
Chairman - Doug Ellis
Secretary - Steven Stride
Manager - John Gregory
Stadium - Villa Park (39,217)

MAJOR HONOURS
League Championship - (7)
1894, 1896, 1897, 1899, 1900, 1910, 1981.
FA Cup - (7)
1887, 1895, 1897, 1905, 1913, 1920, 1957.
League Cup - (5)
1961, 1975, 1977, 1994, 1996.
European Champions' Cup - (1) 1982.
European Super Cup - (1) 1982.

APPEARANCES 98/99

		P	Ap	(s)	Gls
Gareth BARRY	D	27	(5)	2
Mark BOSNICH (AUS)	G	15		
Colin CALDERWOOD (SCO)	D	8		
Gary CHARLES	D	10	(1)	1
Stan COLLYMORE	A	11	(9)	1
Mark DELANEY (WAL)	M		(2)	
Mark DRAPER	M	13	(10)	2
Dion DUBLIN	A	24		11
Ugo EHIOGU	D	23	(2)	2
Simon GRAYSON	M	4	(11)	
Lee HENDRIE	M	31	(1)	3
Julian JOACHIM	A	29	(7)	14
Paul MERSON	M	21	(5)	5
Michael OAKES	G	23		
Adam RACHEL	G		(1)	
Riccardo SCIMECA	D	16	(2)	2
Gareth SOUTHGATE	D	38		1
Steve STONE	M	9	(1)	
Ian TAYLOR	M	31	(2)	4
Alan THOMPSON	M	20	(5)	2
Darius VASSELL	A		(6)	
Steve WATSON	D	26	(1)	
Alan WRIGHT	D	38		
Dwight YORKE (TRI)	A	1		

LEAGUE RESULTS 1998/99

15/08/98	Everton	A	0-0	
23/08/98	Middlesbrough	H	3-1	Joachim (p), Charles, Thompson
29/08/98	Sheffield Wednesday	A	1-0	Joachim
09/09/98	Newcastle United	H	1-0	Hendrie (p)
12/09/98	Wimbledon	H	2-0	Merson, Taylor
19/09/98	Leeds United	A	0-0	
26/09/98	Derby County	H	1-0	Merson
03/10/98	Coventry City	A	2-1	Taylor 2
17/10/98	West Ham United	A	0-0	
24/10/98	Leicester City	H	1-1	Ehiogu
07/11/98	Tottenham Hotspur	H	3-2	Dublin 2, Collymore
14/11/98	Southampton	A	4-1	Dublin 3, Merson
21/11/98	Liverpool	H	2-4	Dublin 2
28/11/98	Nottingham Forest	A	2-2	Joachim 2
05/12/98	Manchester United	H	1-1	Joachim
09/12/98	Chelsea	A	1-2	Hendrie
13/12/98	Arsenal	H	3-2	Joachim, Dublin 2
21/12/98	Charlton Athletic	A	1-0	og (Rufus)
26/12/98	Blackburn Rovers	A	1-2	Scimeca
28/12/98	Sheffield Wednesday	H	2-1	Southgate, Ehiogu
09/01/99	Middlesbrough	A	0-0	
18/01/99	Everton	H	3-0	Joachim 2, Merson
30/01/99	Newcastle United	A	1-2	Merson
06/02/99	Blackburn Rovers	H	1-3	Joachim
17/02/99	Leeds United	H	1-2	Scimeca
21/02/99	Wimbledon	A	0-0	
27/02/99	Coventry City	H	1-4	Dublin (p)
10/03/99	Derby County	A	1-2	Thompson
13/03/99	Tottenham Hotspur	A	0-1	
21/03/99	Chelsea	H	0-3	
02/04/99	West Ham United	H	0-0	
06/04/99	Leicester City	A	2-2	Hendrie, Joachim
10/04/99	Southampton	H	3-0	Draper, Joachim, Dublin
17/04/99	Liverpool	A	1-0	Taylor
24/04/99	Nottingham Forest	H	2-0	Draper, Barry
01/05/99	Manchester United	A	1-2	Joachim
08/05/99	Charlton Athletic	H	3-4	Barry, Joachim 2
16/05/99	Arsenal	A	0-1	

BLACKBURN ROVERS

CLUB DIRECTORY

Blackburn Rovers FC
Ewood Park
Blackburn BB2 4JF
tel - (01254) 698888
fax - (01254) 671042
Year of Formation - 1875
Chairman - R.D. Coar
Secretary - Tom Finn
Manager - Roy Hodgson; Brian Kidd
Stadium - Ewood Park (31,367)

MAJOR HONOURS
League Championship - (3) 1912, 1914, 1995.
FA Cup - (6)
1884, 1885, 1886, 1890, 1891, 1928.

APPEARANCES 98/99

	P	Ap	(s)	Gls
Nathan BLAKE (WAL)	A	9	(2)	3
Marlon BROOMES	D	8	(5)	
Lee CARSLEY (IRL)	M	7	(1)	
Gary CROFT	D	10	(2)	
Martin DAHLIN (SWE)	A	2	(3)	
Christian DAILLY (SCO)	D	14	(3)	
Callum DAVIDSON (SCO)	D	34		1
Kevin DAVIES	A	9	(12)	1
Damien DUFF (IRL)	M	18	(10)	1
David DUNN	M	10	(5)	1
Alan FETTIS (NIR)	G	2		
John FILAN (AUS)	G	26		
Garry FLITCROFT	M	8		2
Tim FLOWERS	G	10		
Kevin GALLACHER (SCO)	A	13	(3)	5
Keith GILLESPIE (NIR)	M	13	(3)	1
Stéphane HENCHOZ (SUI)	D	34		
Matt JANSEN	A	10	(1)	3
Damien JOHNSON (NIR)	M	14	(7)	1
Jeff KENNA (IRL)	D	22	(1)	
Jason McATEER (IRL)	M	13		1
Billy McKINLAY (SCO)	M	14	(2)	
Dario MARCOLIN (ITA)	M	5	(5)	1
Darren PEACOCK	D	27	(3)	1
Sébastien PEREZ (FRA)	M	4	(1)	1
Tim SHERWOOD	M	19		3
Chris SUTTON	A	17		3
Martin TAYLOR	M	1	(2)	
Ashley WARD	A	17		5
Jason WILCOX	M	28	(2)	3

LEAGUE RESULTS 1998/99

15/08/98	Derby County	H	0-0	
24/08/98	Leeds United	A	0-1	
29/08/98	Leicester City	H	1-0	Gallacher
09/09/98	Tottenham Hotspur	A	1-2	Gallacher
12/09/98	Sheffield Wednesday	A	0-3	
21/09/98	Chelsea	H	3-4	Sutton 2 (1p), Perez
26/09/98	Everton	A	0-0	
03/10/98	West Ham United	H	3-0	Flitcroft 2, Davidson
17/10/98	Middlesbrough	A	1-2	Sherwood
25/10/98	Arsenal	H	1-2	Johnson
31/10/98	Wimbledon	A	1-1	Sutton (p)
07/11/98	Coventry City	H	1-2	Sherwood
14/11/98	Manchester United	A	2-3	Marcolin, Blake
21/11/98	Southampton	H	0-2	
29/11/98	Liverpool	A	0-2	
05/12/98	Charlton Athletic	H	1-0	Davies
12/12/98	Newcastle United	H	0-0	
19/12/98	Nottingham Forest	A	2-2	Blake 2
26/12/98	Aston Villa	H	2-1	Gallacher, Sherwood
28/12/98	Leicester City	A	1-1	Gallacher
09/01/99	Leeds United	H	1-0	Gillespie
16/01/99	Derby County	A	0-1	
30/01/99	Tottenham Hotspur	H	1-1	Jansen
06/02/99	Aston Villa	A	3-1	og (Southgate), Ward, Dunn
17/02/99	Chelsea	A	1-1	Ward
20/02/99	Sheffield Wednesday	H	1-4	McAteer
27/02/99	West Ham United	A	0-2	
10/03/99	Everton	H	1-2	Ward
13/03/99	Coventry City	A	1-1	Wilcox
20/03/99	Wimbledon	H	3-1	Ward, Jansen 2
03/04/99	Middlesbrough	H	0-0	
06/04/99	Arsenal	A	0-1	
17/04/99	Southampton	A	3-3	Ward, Peacock, Wilcox
24/04/99	Liverpool	H	1-3	Duff
01/05/99	Charlton Athletic	A	0-0	
08/05/99	Nottingham Forest	H	1-2	Gallacher
12/05/99	Manchester United	H	0-0	
16/05/99	Newcastle United	A	1-1	Wilcox

CHARLTON ATHLETIC

CLUB DIRECTORY

Charlton Athletic FC
The Valley
Floyd Road, Charlton
London SE7 8BL
tel - (0181) 3334000
fax - (0181) 3334001
Year of Formation - 1905
Chairman - M.A. Simons
Manager - Alan Curbishley
Stadium - The Valley (20,043)

MAJOR HONOURS
FA Cup - (1) 1947.

APPEARANCES 98/99

	P	Ap	(s)	Gls
John BARNES	M	2	(11)	
Anthony BARNESS	D		(3)	
Mark BOWEN (WAL)	D	2	(4)	
Mark BRIGHT	A	1	(4)	1
Steve BROWN	D	13	(5)	
Andy HUNT	A	32	(2)	6
Sasa ILIC (YUG)	G	23		
Keith JONES	M	13	(9)	1
Steve JONES	A	7	(19)	1
Mark KINSELLA (IRL)	M	38		3
Paul KONCHESKY	A	1	(1)	
Kevin LISBIE	A		(1)	
Clive MENDONCA	A	19	(6)	8
Danny MILLS	D	36		2
Paul MORTIMER	M	10	(7)	1
Shaun NEWTON	M	13	(3)	
Scott PARKER	M		(4)	
Andy PETTERSON (AUS)	G	7	(3)	
Chris POWELL	D	38		
Martin PRINGLE (SWE)	A	15	(3)	3
Neil REDFEARN	M	29	(1)	3
John ROBINSON (WAL)	M	27	(3)	3
Simon ROYCE	G	8		
Richard RUFUS	D	27		
Graham STUART	M	9		3
Carl TILER	D	27		1
Eddie YOUDS	D	21	(1)	2

LEAGUE RESULTS 1998/99

15/08/98	Newcastle United	A	0-0	
22/08/98	Southampton	H	5-0	Robinson, Redfearn,
				Mendonca 3 (1p)
29/08/98	Arsenal	A	0-0	
09/09/98	Manchester United	A	1-4	Kinsella
12/09/98	Derby County	H	1-2	Mendonca (p)
19/09/98	Liverpool	A	3-3	Rufus, Mendonca, Jones S.
26/09/98	Coventry City	H	1-1	Hunt
03/10/98	Nottingham Forest	A	1-0	Youds
17/10/98	Chelsea	A	1-2	Youds
24/10/98	West Ham United	H	4-2	Tiler, Mills, Hunt, Redfearn (p)
02/11/98	Tottenham Hotspur	A	2-2	Hunt 2
07/11/98	Leicester City	H	0-0	
14/11/98	Middlesbrough	H	1-1	Mendonca (p)
21/11/98	Leeds United	A	1-4	Mortimer
28/11/98	Everton	H	1-2	Kinsella
05/12/98	Blackburn Rovers	A	0-1	
12/12/98	Sheffield Wednesday	A	0-3	
21/12/98	Aston Villa	H	0-1	
26/12/98	Wimbledon	A	1-2	Redfearn
28/12/98	Arsenal	H	0-1	
09/01/99	Southampton	A	1-3	Hunt
17/01/99	Newcastle United	H	2-2	Bright, Pringle
31/01/99	Manchester United	H	0-1	
08/02/99	Wimbledon	H	2-0	Pringle, og (Blackwell)
13/02/99	Liverpool	H	1-0	Jones K.
20/02/99	Derby County	A	2-0	Hunt, Pringle
27/02/99	Nottingham Forest	H	0-0	
06/03/99	Coventry City	A	1-2	Robinson
13/03/99	Leicester City	A	1-1	Mendonca
03/04/99	Chelsea	H	0-1	
05/04/99	West Ham United	A	1-0	Stuart
10/04/99	Middlesbrough	A	0-2	
17/04/99	Leeds United	H	1-1	Stuart
20/04/99	Tottenham Hotspur	H	1-4	Kinsella
24/04/99	Everton	A	1-4	Stuart (p)
01/05/99	Blackburn Rovers	H	0-0	
08/05/99	Aston Villa	A	4-3	og (Barry), Mendonca, Robinson,
				Mills
16/05/99	Sheffield Wednesday	H	0-1	

CHELSEA

CLUB DIRECTORY

Chelsea FC
Stamford Bridge
London SW6 1HS
tel - (0171) 3855545
fax - (0171) 3814831
Year of Formation - 1905
Chairman - Ken Bates
Managing Director - Colin Hutchinson
Manager - Gianluca Vialli
Stadium - Stamford Bridge (35,421)

MAJOR HONOURS
League Championship - (1) 1955.
FA Cup - (2) 1970, 1997.
League Cup - (2) 1965, 1998.
European Cup-winners' Cup - (2) 1971, 1998.

APPEARANCES 98/99

	P	Ap	(s)	Gls
Celestine BABAYARO (NIG)	D	26	(2)	3
Pierluigi CASIRAGHI (ITA)	A	10		1
Ed DE GOEY (HOL)	G	35		
Marcel DESAILLY (FRA)	D	30	(1)	
Roberto DI MATTEO (ITA)	M	26	(4)	2
Michael DUBERRY	D	18	(7)	
Albert FERRER (ESP)	D	30		
Tore André FLO (NOR)	A	18	(12)	10
Mikael FORSSELL (FIN)	A	4	(6)	1
Bjarne GOLDBAEK (DEN)	M	13	(10)	5
Kevin HITCHCOCK	G	2	(1)	
Dmitri KHARIN (RUS)	G	1		
Bernard LAMBOURDE (FRA)	D	12	(5)	
Brian LAUDRUP (DEN)	A	5	(2)	
Frank LEBOEUF (FRA)	D	33		4
Graeme LE SAUX	D	30	(1)	
Jody MORRIS	M	14	(4)	1
Andy MYERS	D	1		
Eddie NEWTON	M	1	(6)	
Mark NICHOLLS	A		(9)	
Dan PETRESCU (ROM)	M	23	(9)	4
Gustavo POYET (URU)	M	21	(7)	11
John TERRY	D		(2)	
Gianluca VIALLI (ITA)	A	9		1
Dennis WISE	M	21	(1)	
Gianfranco ZOLA	A	35	(2)	13

LEAGUE RESULTS 1998/99

15/08/98	Coventry City	A	1-2	Poyet
22/08/98	Newcastle United	H	1-1	Babayaro
09/09/98	Arsenal	H	0-0	
12/09/98	Nottingham Forest	H	2-1	Zola, Poyet
21/09/98	Blackburn Rovers	A	4-3	Zola, Leboeuf (p), Flo 2
26/09/98	Middlesbrough	H	2-0	og (Pallister), Zola
04/10/98	Liverpool	A	1-1	Casiraghi
17/10/98	Charlton Athletic	H	2-1	Leboeuf (p), Poyet
25/10/98	Leeds United	A	0-0	
08/11/98	West Ham United	A	1-1	Babayaro
14/11/98	Wimbledon	H	3-0	Zola, Poyet, Petrescu
21/11/98	Leicester City	A	4-2	Zola 2, Poyet, Flo
28/11/98	Sheffield Wednesday	H	1-1	Zola
05/12/98	Everton	A	0-0	
09/12/98	Aston Villa	H	2-1	Zola, Flo
12/12/98	Derby County	A	2-2	Flo, Poyet
16/12/98	Manchester United	A	1-1	Zola
19/12/98	Tottenham Hotspur	H	2-0	Poyet, Flo
26/12/98	Southampton	A	2-0	Flo, Poyet
29/12/98	Manchester United	H	0-0	
09/01/99	Newcastle United	A	1-0	Petrescu
16/01/99	Coventry City	H	2-1	Leboeuf, Di Matteo
31/01/99	Arsenal	A	0-1	
06/02/99	Southampton	H	1-0	Zola
17/02/99	Blackburn Rovers	H	1-1	Morris
20/02/99	Nottingham Forest	A	3-1	Forssell, Goldbaek 2
27/02/99	Liverpool	H	2-1	Leboeuf (p), Goldbaek
13/03/99	West Ham United	H	0-1	
21/03/99	Aston Villa	A	3-0	Flo 2, Goldbaek
03/04/99	Charlton Athletic	A	1-0	Di Matteo
11/04/99	Wimbledon	A	2-1	Flo, Poyet
14/04/99	Middlesbrough	A	0-0	
18/04/99	Leicester City	H	2-2	Zola, Petrescu
25/04/99	Sheffield Wednesday	A	0-0	
01/05/99	Everton	H	3-1	Zola 2, Petrescu
05/05/99	Leeds United	H	1-0	Poyet
10/05/99	Tottenham Hotspur	A	2-2	Poyet, Goldbaek
16/05/99	Derby County	H	2-1	Babayaro, Vialli

COVENTRY CITY

CLUB DIRECTORY

Coventry City FC
Highfield Road Stadium
King Richard Street, Coventry CV2 4FW
tel - (01203) 234000
fax - (01203) 234099
Year of Formation - 1883
Chairman - Bryan Richardson
Secretary - Graham Hover
Manager - Gordon Strachan
Stadium - Highfield Road (23,611)

MAJOR HONOURS
FA Cup - (1) 1987.

APPEARANCES 98/99

	P	Ap	(s)	Gls
John ALOISI (AUS)	A	7	(9)	5
George BOATENG (HOL)	M	29	(4)	4
Gary BREEN (IRL)	D	21	(4)	
David BURROWS	D	23		
Philippe CLEMENT (BEL)	M	6	(6)	
Dion DUBLIN	A	10		3
Marc EDWORTHY	D	16	(6)	
Steve FROGGATT	M	23		1
Stefano GIOACCHINI (ITA)	A		(3)	
Marcus HALL	D	2	(3)	
Paul HALL (JAM)	A	2	(7)	
Simon HAWORTH (WAL)	A	1		
Magnus HEDMAN (SWE)	G	36		
Darren HUCKERBY	A	31	(3)	9
Darren JACKSON (SCO)	A		(3)	
Muhamed KONJIC (BOS)	D	3	(1)	
Gary McALLISTER (SCO)	M	29		3
Gary McSHEFFREY	A		(1)	
Roland NILSSON (SWE)	D	28		
Steve OGRIZOVIC	G	2		
Barry QUINN	M	6	(1)	
Richard SHAW	D	36	(1)	
Sam SHILTON	M	1	(4)	
Trond Egil SOLTVEDT (NOR)	M	21	(6)	2
Paul TELFER (SCO)	M	30	(2)	2
Jean-Guy WALLEMME (FRA)	D	4	(2)	
Noel WHELAN	M	31		10
Paul WILLIAMS	D	20	(2)	

LEAGUE RESULTS 1998/99

15/08/98	Chelsea	H	2-1	Huckerby, Dublin
22/08/98	Nottingham Forest	A	0-1	
29/08/98	West Ham United	H	0-0	
09/09/98	Liverpool	A	0-2	
12/09/98	Manchester United	A	0-2	
19/09/98	Newcastle United	H	1-5	Whelan
26/09/98	Charlton Athletic	A	1-1	Whelan
03/10/98	Aston Villa	H	1-2	Soltvedt
18/10/98	Sheffield Wednesday	H	1-0	Dublin
24/10/98	Southampton	A	1-2	Dublin
31/10/98	Arsenal	H	0-1	
07/11/98	Blackburn Rovers	A	2-1	Huckerby, Whelan
15/11/98	Everton	H	3-0	Froggatt, Huckerby, Whelan
21/11/98	Middlesbrough	A	0-2	
28/11/98	Leicester City	H	1-1	Huckerby
05/12/98	Wimbledon	A	1-2	McAllister (p)
14/12/98	Leeds United	A	0-2	
19/12/98	Derby County	H	1-1	Whelan
26/12/98	Tottenham Hotspur	H	1-1	Aloisi
28/12/98	West Ham United	A	0-2	
09/01/99	Nottingham Forest	H	4-0	Huckerby 3, Telfer
16/01/99	Chelsea	A	1-2	Huckerby
30/01/99	Liverpool	H	2-1	Boateng, Whelan
06/02/99	Tottenham Hotspur	A	0-0	
17/02/99	Newcastle United	A	1-4	Whelan
20/02/99	Manchester United	H	0-1	
27/02/99	Aston Villa	A	4-1	Aloisi 2, Boateng 2
06/03/99	Charlton Athletic	H	2-1	Whelan, Soltvedt
13/03/99	Blackburn Rovers	H	1-1	Aloisi
20/03/99	Arsenal	A	0-2	
03/04/99	Sheffield Wednesday	A	2-1	McAllister (p), Whelan
05/04/99	Southampton	H	1-0	Boateng
11/04/99	Everton	A	0-2	
17/04/99	Middlesbrough	H	1-2	McAllister
24/04/99	Leicester City	A	0-1	
01/05/99	Wimbledon	H	2-1	Huckerby, Whelan
08/05/99	Derby County	A	0-0	
16/05/99	Leeds United	H	2-2	Aloisi, Telfer

DERBY COUNTY

CLUB DIRECTORY

Derby County FC
Pride Park Stadium, Derby DE24 8XL
tel - (01332) 202202
fax - (01332) 667519
Year of Formation - 1884
Chairman - Lionel Pickering
Secretary - Keith Pearson
Manager - Jim Smith
Stadium - Pride Park (33,258)

MAJOR HONOURS
League Championship - (2) 1972, 1975.
FA Cup - (1) 1946.

APPEARANCES 98/99

	P	Ap	(s)	Gls
Francesco BAIANO (ITA)	A	17	(5)	4
Mikkel BECK (DEN)	A	6	(1)	1
Paul BOERTIEN	D		(1)	
Lars BOHINEN (NOR)	M	29	(3)	
Vassilis BORBOKIS (GRE)	D	3	(1)	
Marc BRIDGE-WILKINSON	M		(2)	
Deon BURTON (JAM)	A	14	(7)	9
Horacio CARBONARI (ARG)	D	28	(1)	5
Lee CARSLEY (IRL)	M	20	(2)	1
Malcolm CHRISTIE	M		(2)	
Christian DAILLY (SCO)	D	1		
Rory DELAP (IRL)	M	21	(2)	
Tony DORIGO	D	17	(1)	1
Steve ELLIOT	M	7	(4)	
Stefano ERANIO (ITA)	M	18	(7)	
Kevin HARPER (SCO)	M	6	(21)	1
Russell HOULT	G	23		
Jonathan HUNT	M		(6)	1
Robert KOZLUK	M	3	(4)	
Brian LAUNDERS	M		(1)	
Jacob LAURSEN (DEN)	D	37		
Adam MURRAY	A		(4)	
Mart POOM (EST)	G	15	(2)	
Darryl POWELL (JAM)	M	30	(3)	
Spencer PRIOR	D	33	(1)	1
Marvin ROBINSON	M		(1)	
Stefan SCHNOOR (GER)	D	20	(3)	2
Igor STIMAC (CRO)	D	14		
Dean STURRIDGE	A	23	(6)	5
Paulo WANCHOPE (CRC)	A	33	(2)	9

LEAGUE RESULTS 1998/99

15/08/98	Blackburn Rovers	A	0-0	
22/08/98	Wimbledon	H	0-0	
29/08/98	Middlesbrough	A	1-1	Wanchope
09/09/98	Sheffield Wednesday	H	1-0	Sturridge
12/09/98	Charlton Athletic	A	2-1	Wanchope, Baiano
19/09/98	Leicester City	H	2-0	Schnoor, Wanchope
26/09/98	Aston Villa	A	0-1	
03/10/98	Tottenham Hotspur	H	0-1	
17/10/98	Newcastle United	A	1-2	Burton
24/10/98	Manchester United	H	1-1	Burton
31/10/98	Leeds United	H	2-2	Schnoor (p), Sturridge
07/11/98	Liverpool	A	2-1	Harper, Wanchope
16/11/98	Nottingham Forest	A	2-2	Dorigo (p), Carbonari
22/11/98	West Ham United	H	0-2	
28/11/98	Southampton	A	1-0	Carbonari
05/12/98	Arsenal	H	0-0	
12/12/98	Chelsea	H	2-2	Carbonari, Sturridge
19/12/98	Coventry City	A	1-1	Carsley
26/12/98	Everton	A	0-0	
28/12/98	Middlesbrough	H	2-1	Sturridge, Hunt
09/01/99	Wimbledon	A	1-2	Wanchope
16/01/99	Blackburn Rovers	H	1-0	Burton
30/01/99	Sheffield Wednesday	A	1-0	Prior
03/02/99	Manchester United	A	0-1	
07/02/99	Everton	H	2-1	Burton 2
20/02/99	Charlton Athletic	H	0-2	
27/02/99	Tottenham Hotspur	A	1-1	Burton
10/03/99	Aston Villa	H	2-1	Baiano, Burton
13/03/99	Liverpool	H	3-2	Burton, Wanchope 2
20/03/99	Leeds United	A	1-4	Baiano (p)
03/04/99	Newcastle United	H	3-4	Burton, Baiano (p), Wanchope
10/04/99	Nottingham Forest	A	1-0	Carbonari
17/04/99	West Ham United	A	1-5	Wanchope
24/04/99	Southampton	H	0-0	
02/05/99	Arsenal	A	0-1	
05/05/99	Leicester City	A	2-1	Sturridge, Beck
08/05/99	Coventry City	H	0-0	
16/05/99	Chelsea	A	1-2	Carbonari

EVERTON

CLUB DIRECTORY

Everton FC
Goodison Park, Liverpool L4 4EL
tel - (0151) 3302200 / fax - (0151) 2869112
Year of Formation - 1878
Chairman - Sir Philip Carter
Secretary - Michael Dunford
Manager - Walter Smith
Stadium - Goodison Park (40,200)

MAJOR HONOURS
League Championship - (9) 1891, 1915, 1928, 1932, 1939, 1963, 1970, 1985, 1987.
FA Cup - (5) 1906, 1933, 1966, 1984, 1995.
European Cup-winners' Cup - (1) 1985.

APPEARANCES 98/99

		P	Ap	(s)	Gls
Ibrahima BAKAYOKO (CIV)	A	17	(6)		4
Michael BALL	D	36	(1)		3
Nick BARMBY	A	20	(4)		3
Slaven BILIC (CRO)	D	4			
Michael BRANCH	A	1	(6)		
Danny CADAMARTERI	A	11	(19)		4
Kevin CAMPBELL	A	8			9
Alex CLELAND (SCO)	D	16	(2)		
John COLLINS (SCO)	M	19	(1)		1
Olivier DACOURT (FRA)	M	28	(2)		2
Peter DEGN (DEN)	M		(4)		
Richard DUNNE (IRL)	D	15	(1)		
Adam FARLEY	D		(1)		
Gareth FARRELLY (IRL)	M		(1)		
Duncan FERGUSON (SCO)	A	13			4
Scot GEMMILL (SCO)	M	7			1
Tony GRANT	M	13	(3)		
Don HUTCHISON (SCO)	M	29	(4)		3
Francis JEFFERS	A	11	(4)		6
Phil JEVONS	M		(1)		
Michaël MADAR (FRA)	A	2			
Marco MATERAZZI (ITA)	D	26	(1)		1
Jamie MILLIGAN	A		(3)		
Thomas MYHRE (NOR)	G	38			
John O'KANE	M	2			
John OSTER (WAL)	M	6	(3)		
Craig SHORT	D	22			
John SPENCER (SCO)	A	2	(1)		
Tony THOMAS	M		(1)		
Carl TILER	D	2			
David UNSWORTH	D	33	(1)		1
Mitch WARD	M	4	(2)		
Dave WATSON	D	22			
David WEIR (SCO)	D	11	(3)		

LEAGUE RESULTS 1998/99

15/08/98	Aston Villa	H	0-0	
22/08/98	Leicester City	A	0-2	
29/08/98	Tottenham Hotspur	H	0-1	
08/09/98	Nottingham Forest	A	2-0	Ferguson 2
12/09/98	Leeds United	H	0-0	
19/09/98	Middlesbrough	A	2-2	Ball (p), Collins
26/09/98	Blackburn Rovers	H	0-0	
03/10/98	Wimbledon	A	2-1	Cadamarteri, Ferguson
17/10/98	Liverpool	H	0-0	
24/10/98	Sheffield Wednesday	A	0-0	
31/10/98	Manchester United	H	1-4	Ferguson
08/11/98	Arsenal	A	0-1	
15/11/98	Coventry City	A	0-3	
23/11/98	Newcastle United	H	1-0	Ball (p)
28/11/98	Charlton Athletic	A	2-1	Cadamarteri 2
05/12/98	Chelsea	H	0-0	
12/12/98	Southampton	H	1-0	Bakayoko
19/12/98	West Ham United	A	1-2	Cadamarteri
26/12/98	Derby County	H	0-0	
28/12/98	Tottenham Hotspur	A	1-4	Bakayoko
09/01/99	Leicester City	H	0-0	
18/01/99	Aston Villa	A	0-3	
30/01/99	Nottingham Forest	H	0-1	
07/02/99	Derby County	A	1-2	Barmby
17/02/99	Middlesbrough	H	5-0	Barmby 2, Dacourt, Materazzi, Unsworth
20/02/99	Leeds United	A	0-1	
27/02/99	Wimbledon	H	1-1	Jeffers
10/03/99	Blackburn Rovers	A	2-1	Bakayoko 2
13/03/99	Arsenal	H	0-2	
21/03/99	Manchester United	A	1-3	Hutchison
03/04/99	Liverpool	A	2-3	Dacourt, Jeffers
05/04/99	Sheffield Wednesday	H	1-2	Jeffers
11/04/99	Coventry City	H	2-0	Campbell 2
17/04/99	Newcastle United	A	3-1	Campbell 2, Gemmill
24/04/99	Charlton Athletic	H	4-1	Hutchison, Campbell 2, Jeffers
01/05/99	Chelsea	A	1-3	Jeffers
08/05/99	West Ham United	H	6-0	Campbell 3, Ball (p), Hutchison, Jeffers
16/05/99	Southampton	A	0-2	

LEEDS UNITED

CLUB DIRECTORY

Leeds United FC
Elland Road, Leeds LS11 OES
tel - (0113) 2266000
fax - (0113) 2266050
Year of Formation - 1919
Chairman - Peter Ridsdale
Secretary - Ian Silvester
Manager - George Graham; David O'Leary
Stadium - Elland Road (40,000)

MAJOR HONOURS
League Championship - (3) 1969, 1974, 1992.
FA Cup - (1) 1972.
League Cup - (1) 1968.
Fairs' Cup - (2) 1968, 1971.

APPEARANCES 98/99

		P	Ap	(s)	Gls
David BATTY	M	10			
Lee BOWYER	M	35			9
Danny GRANVILLE	D	7	(2)		
Alf Inge HÅLAND (NOR)	M	24	(5)		1
Gunnar HALLE (NOR)	D	14	(3)		2
Ian HARTE (IRL)	D	34	(1)		4
Jimmy Floyd HASSELBAINK (HOL)	A	36			18
Martin HIDEN (AUT)	D	14			
David HOPKIN (SCO)	M	32	(2)		4
Matthew JONES (WAL)	M	3	(5)		
Harry KEWELL (AUS)	M	36	(2)		6
Willem KORSTEN (HOL)	M	4	(3)		2
Derek LILLEY (SCO)	A		(2)		
Stephen McPHAIL (IRL)	M	11	(6)		
Nigel MARTYN	G	34			
Robert MOLENAAR (HOL)	D	17			2
Lucas RADEBE (SAF)	D	29			
Bruno RIBEIRO (POR)	M	7	(6)		1
Paul ROBINSON	G	4	(1)		
Lee SHARPE	M	2	(2)		
Alan SMITH	A	15	(7)		7
David WETHERALL	D	14	(7)		
Clyde WIJNHARD (HOL)	A	11	(7)		3
Jonathon WOODGATE	D	25			2

LEAGUE RESULTS 1998/99

15/08/98	Middlesbrough	A	0-0	
24/08/98	Blackburn Rovers	H	1-0	Hasselbaink
29/08/98	Wimbledon	A	1-1	Bowyer
08/09/98	Southampton	H	3-0	og (Marshall), Harte, Wijnhard
12/09/98	Everton	A	0-0	
19/09/98	Aston Villa	H	0-0	
26/09/98	Tottenham Hotspur	A	3-3	Halle, Hasselbaink, Wijnhard
03/10/98	Leicester City	H	0-1	
17/10/98	Nottingham Forest	A	1-1	Halle
25/10/98	Chelsea	H	0-0	
31/10/98	Derby County	A	2-2	Molenaar, Kewell
08/11/98	Sheffield Wednesday	H	2-1	Hasselbaink, Woodgate
14/11/98	Liverpool	A	3-1	Smith, Hasselbaink 2
21/11/98	Charlton Athletic	H	4-1	Hasselbaink, Bowyer, Smith, Kewell
29/11/98	Manchester United	A	2-3	Hasselbaink, Kewell
05/12/98	West Ham United	H	4-0	Bowyer 2, Molenaar, Hasselbaink
14/12/98	Coventry City	H	2-0	Hopkin, Bowyer
20/12/98	Arsenal	A	1-3	Hasselbaink
26/12/98	Newcastle United	A	3-0	Kewell, Bowyer, Hasselbaink
29/12/98	Wimbledon	H	2-2	Ribeiro, Hopkin
09/01/99	Blackburn Rovers	A	0-1	
16/01/99	Middlesbrough	H	2-0	Smith, Bowyer
30/01/99	Southampton	A	0-3	
06/02/99	Newcastle United	H	0-1	
17/02/99	Aston Villa	A	2-1	Hasselbaink 2
20/02/99	Everton	H	1-0	Korsten
01/03/99	Leicester City	A	2-1	Kewell, Smith
10/03/99	Tottenham Hotspur	H	2-0	Smith, Kewell
13/03/99	Sheffield Wednesday	A	2-0	Hasselbaink, Hopkin
20/03/99	Derby County	H	4-1	Bowyer, Hasselbaink, Korsten, Harte
03/04/99	Nottingham Forest	H	3-1	Hasselbaink, Harte, Smith
12/04/99	Liverpool	H	0-0	
17/04/99	Charlton Athletic	A	1-1	Woodgate
25/04/99	Manchester United	H	1-1	Hasselbaink
01/05/99	West Ham United	A	5-1	Hasselbaink, Smith, Harte (p), Bowyer, Håland
05/05/99	Chelsea	A	0-1	
11/05/99	Arsenal	H	1-0	Hasselbaink
16/05/99	Coventry City	A	2-2	Wijnhard, Hopkin

LEICESTER CITY

CLUB DIRECTORY

Leicester City FC
City Stadium
Filbert Street, Leicester LE2 7FL
tel - (0116) 2915000
fax - (0116) 2470585
Year of Formation - 1884
Chairman - John Elsom
Chief Executive - Barrie Pierpoint
Manager - Martin O'Neill
Stadium - Filbert Street (22,000)

MAJOR HONOURS
League Cup - (2) 1964, 1997.

APPEARANCES 98/99

	P	Ap	(s)	Gls
Pegguy ARPHEXAD (FRA)	G	2	(2)	
Stuart CAMPBELL (SCO)	M	1	(11)	
Tony COTTEE	A	29	(2)	10
Matt ELLIOTT (SCO)	D	37		3
Graham FENTON	A	3	(6)	
Arnar GUNNLAUGSSON (ISL)	A	5	(4)	
Steve GUPPY	M	38		4
Emile HESKEY	A	29	(1)	6
Andrew IMPEY	M	17	(1)	
Muzzy IZZET	M	31		5
Pontus KÅMARK (SWE)	D	15	(4)	
Kasey KELLER (USA)	G	36		
Neil LENNON (NIR)	M	37		1
Ian MARSHALL	A	6	(4)	3
Charlie MILLER (SCO)	M	1	(3)	
Stefan OAKES	M	2	(1)	
Garry PARKER	M	2	(5)	
Robbie SAVAGE (WAL)	M	29	(5)	1
Frank SINCLAIR (JAM)	D	30	(1)	1
Gerry TAGGART (NIR)	D	9	(6)	
Rob ULLATHORNE	D	25		
Steve WALSH	D	17	(5)	3
Stuart WILSON	A	1	(8)	
Theo ZAGORAKIS (GRE)	M	16	(3)	1

LEAGUE RESULTS 1998/99

15/08/98	Manchester United	A	2-2	Heskey, Cottee
22/08/98	Everton	H	2-0	Cottee, Izzet
29/08/98	Blackburn Rovers	A	0-1	
09/09/98	Middlesbrough	H	0-1	
12/09/98	Arsenal	H	1-1	Heskey
19/09/98	Derby County	A	0-2	
27/09/98	Wimbledon	H	1-1	Elliott
03/10/98	Leeds United	A	1-0	Cottee
19/10/98	Tottenham Hotspur	H	2-1	Heskey, Izzet
24/10/98	Aston Villa	A	1-1	Cottee
31/10/98	Liverpool	H	1-0	Cottee
07/11/98	Charlton Athletic	A	0-0	
14/11/98	West Ham United	A	2-3	Izzet, og (Lampard)
21/11/98	Chelsea	H	2-4	Izzet, Guppy
28/11/98	Coventry City	A	1-1	Heskey
05/12/98	Southampton	H	2-0	Heskey, Walsh
12/12/98	Nottingham Forest	H	3-1	Heskey, Elliott (p), Guppy
19/12/98	Newcastle United	A	0-1	
26/12/98	Sheffield Wednesday	A	1-0	Cottee
28/12/98	Blackburn Rovers	H	1-1	Walsh
09/01/99	Everton	A	0-0	
16/01/99	Manchester United	H	2-6	Zagorakis, Walsh
30/01/99	Middlesbrough	A	0-0	
06/02/99	Sheffield Wednesday	H	0-2	
20/02/99	Arsenal	A	0-5	
01/03/99	Leeds United	H	1-2	Cottee
06/03/99	Wimbledon	A	1-0	Guppy
13/03/99	Charlton Athletic	H	1-1	Lennon
03/04/99	Tottenham Hotspur	A	2-0	Elliott, Cottee
06/04/99	Aston Villa	H	2-2	Savage, Cottee
10/04/99	West Ham United	H	0-0	
18/04/99	Chelsea	A	2-2	og (Duberry), Guppy
21/04/99	Liverpool	A	1-0	Marshall
24/04/99	Coventry City	H	1-0	Marshall
01/05/99	Southampton	A	1-2	Marshall
05/05/99	Derby County	H	1-2	Sinclair
08/05/99	Newcastle United	H	2-0	Izzet, Cottee
16/05/99	Nottingham Forest	A	0-1	

LIVERPOOL

CLUB DIRECTORY

Liverpool FC
Anfield Road, Liverpool L4 0TH
tel - (0151) 2632361 / fax - (0151) 2608813
Year of Formation - 1892
Chairman - David Moores
Chief Executive - Rick Parry
Manager - Roy Evans & Gérard Houllier;
Gérard Houllier
Stadium - Anfield (45,362)

MAJOR HONOURS
League Championship - (18)
1901, 1906, 1922, 1923, 1947, 1964, 1966,
1973, 1976, 1977, 1979, 1980, 1982, 1983,
1984, 1986, 1988, 1990.
FA Cup - (5) 1965, 1974, 1986, 1989, 1992.
League Cup - (5)
1981, 1982, 1983, 1984, 1995.
European Champions' Cup - (4)
1977, 1978, 1981, 1984.
UEFA Cup - (2) 1973, 1976.
European Super Cup - (1) 1977.

APPEARANCES 98/99

	P	Ap	(s)	Gls
Phil BABB (IRL)	D	24	(1)	
Patrik BERGER (CZE)	M	30	(2)	7
Stig Inge BJØRNEBYE (NOR)	D	20	(3)	
Jamie CARRAGHER	D	34		1
Sean DUNDEE (SAF)	A		(3)	
Jean-Michel FERRI (FRA)	M		(2)	
Robbie FOWLER	A	23	(2)	14
Brad FRIEDEL (USA)	G	12		
Steven GERRARD	M	4	(8)	
Steve HARKNESS	D	4	(2)	
Vegard HEGGEM (NOR)	D	27	(2)	2
Paul INCE	M	34		6
David JAMES	G	26		
Bjørn Tore KVARME (NOR)	D	2	(5)	
Øyvind LEONHARDSEN (NOR)	M	7	(2)	1
Jason McATEER (IRL)	M	6	(7)	
Steve McMANAMAN (ENG)	M	25	(3)	4
Dominic MATTEO	D	16	(4)	1
Danny MURPHY	M		(1)	
Michael OWEN	A	30		18
Jamie REDKNAPP	M	33	(1)	8
Karlheinz RIEDLE (GER)	A	16	(18)	5
Rigobert SONG (CMR)	D	10	(3)	
Steve STAUNTON (IRL)	D	31		
David THOMPSON	M	4	(10)	1

LEAGUE RESULTS 1998/99

16/08/98	Southampton	A	2-1	Riedle, Owen
22/08/98	Arsenal	H	0-0	
30/08/98	Newcastle United	A	4-1	Owen 3, Berger
09/09/98	Coventry City	H	2-0	Berger, Redknapp
12/09/98	West Ham United	A	1-2	Riedle
19/09/98	Charlton Athletic	H	3-3	Fowler 2 (1p), Berger
24/09/98	Manchester United	A	0-2	
04/10/98	Chelsea	H	1-1	Redknapp
17/10/98	Everton	A	0-0	
24/10/98	Nottingham Forest	H	5-1	Owen 4 (1p), McManaman
31/10/98	Leicester City	A	0-1	
07/11/98	Derby County	H	1-2	Redknapp
14/11/98	Leeds United	H	1-3	Fowler (p)
21/11/98	Aston Villa	A	4-2	Ince, Fowler 3
29/11/98	Blackburn Rovers	H	2-0	Ince, Owen
05/12/98	Tottenham Hotspur	A	1-2	Berger
13/12/98	Wimbledon	A	0-1	
19/12/98	Sheffield Wednesday	H	2-0	Berger, Owen
26/12/98	Middlesbrough	A	3-1	Owen, Redknapp, Heggem
28/12/98	Newcastle United	H	4-2	Owen 2, Riedle 2
09/01/99	Arsenal	A	0-0	
16/01/99	Southampton	H	7-1	Fowler 3, Matteo, Carragher, Owen, Thompson
30/01/99	Coventry City	A	1-2	McManaman
06/02/99	Middlesbrough	H	3-1	Owen, Heggem, Ince
13/02/99	Charlton Athletic	A	0-1	
20/02/99	West Ham United	H	2-2	Fowler, Owen
27/02/99	Chelsea	A	1-2	Owen
13/03/99	Derby County	A	2-3	Fowler 2 (1p)
03/04/99	Everton	H	3-2	Fowler 2 (1p), Berger
05/04/99	Nottingham Forest	A	2-2	Redknapp, Owen
12/04/99	Leeds United	A	0-0	
17/04/99	Aston Villa	H	0-1	
21/04/99	Leicester City	H	0-1	
24/04/99	Blackburn Rovers	A	3-1	McManaman, Redknapp, Leonhardsen
01/05/99	Tottenham Hotspur	H	3-2	Redknapp (p), Ince, McManaman
05/05/99	Manchester United	H	2-2	Redknapp (p), Ince
08/05/99	Sheffield Wednesday	A	0-1	
16/05/99	Wimbledon	H	3-0	Berger, Riedle, Ince

MANCHESTER UNITED

CLUB DIRECTORY

Manchester United FC
Sir Matt Busby Way, Old Trafford
Manchester M16 0RA
tel - (0161) 8721661/9301968
fax - (0161) 8765502
Year of Formation - 1878
Chairman - Martin Edwards
Secretary - Ken Merrett
Manager - Sir Alex Ferguson
Stadium - Old Trafford (56,387)

MAJOR HONOURS
League Championship - (12)
1908, 1911, 1952, 1956, 1957, 1965, 1967,
1993, 1994, 1996, 1997, 1999.
FA Cup - (10) 1909, 1948, 1963, 1977, 1983,
1985, 1990, 1994, 1996, 1999.
League Cup - (1) 1992.
European Champions' Cup - (2) 1968, 1999.
European Cup-winners' Cup - (1) 1991.
European Super Cup - (1) 1991.

APPEARANCES 98/99

		P	Ap	(s)	Gls
David BECKHAM	M	33	(1)	6
Henning BERG (NOR)	D	10	(6)	
Jesper BLOMQVIST (SWE)	M	20	(5)	1
Wes BROWN	D	11	(3)	
Nicky BUTT	M	22	(9)	2
Andy COLE	A	26	(6)	17
Jordi CRUIJFF (HOL)	A		(5)	2
John CURTIS	D	1	(3)	
Ryan GIGGS (WAL)	M	20	(4)	3
Jonathan GREENING	A		(3)	
Denis IRWIN (IRL)	D	26	(3)	2
Ronny JOHNSEN (NOR)	D	19	(3)	3
Roy KEANE (IRL)	M	33	(2)	2
David MAY	D	4	(2)	
Gary NEVILLE	D	34		1
Philip NEVILLE	D	19	(9)	
Peter SCHMEICHEL (DEN)	G	34		
Paul SCHOLES	M	24	(7)	6
Teddy SHERINGHAM	A	7	(10)	2
Ole Gunnar SOLSKJAER (NOR)	A	9	(10)	12
Jaap STAM (HOL)	D	30		1
Raimond VAN DER GOUW (HOL)	G	4	(1)	
Dwight YORKE (TRI)	A	32		18

LEAGUE RESULTS 1998/99

15/08/98	Leicester City	H	2-2	Sheringham, Beckham
22/08/98	West Ham United	A	0-0	
09/09/98	Charlton Athletic	H	4-1	Solskjaer 2, Yorke 2
12/09/98	Coventry City	H	2-0	Yorke, Johnsen
20/09/98	Arsenal	A	0-3	
24/09/98	Liverpool	H	2-0	Irwin (p), Scholes
03/10/98	Southampton	A	3-0	Yorke, Cole, Cruijff
17/10/98	Wimbledon	H	5-1	Cole 2, Giggs, Beckham, Yorke
24/10/98	Derby County	A	1-1	Cruijff
31/10/98	Everton	A	4-1	Yorke, og (Short), Cole, Blomqvist
08/11/98	Newcastle United	H	0-0	
14/11/98	Blackburn Rovers	H	3-2	Scholes 2, Yorke
21/11/98	Sheffield Wednesday	A	1-3	Cole
29/11/98	Leeds United	H	3-2	Solskjaer, Keane, Butt
05/12/98	Aston Villa	A	1-1	Scholes
12/12/98	Tottenham Hotspur	A	2-2	Solskjaer 2
16/12/98	Chelsea	H	1-1	Cole
19/12/98	Middlesbrough	H	2-3	Butt, Scholes
26/12/98	Nottingham Forest	H	3-0	Johnsen 2, Giggs
29/12/98	Chelsea	A	0-0	
10/01/99	West Ham United	H	4-1	Yorke, Cole 2, Solskjaer
16/01/99	Leicester City	A	6-2	Yorke 3, Cole 2, Stam
31/01/99	Charlton Athletic	A	1-0	Yorke
03/02/99	Derby County	H	1-0	Yorke
06/02/99	Nottingham Forest	A	8-1	Yorke 2, Cole 2, Solskjaer 4
17/02/99	Arsenal	H	1-1	Cole
20/02/99	Coventry City	A	1-0	Giggs
27/02/99	Southampton	H	2-1	Keane, Yorke
13/03/99	Newcastle United	A	2-1	Cole 2
21/03/99	Everton	H	3-1	Solskjaer, Neville G., Beckham
03/04/99	Wimbledon	A	1-1	Beckham
17/04/99	Sheffield Wednesday	H	3-0	Solskjaer, Sheringham, Scholes
25/04/99	Leeds United	A	1-1	Cole
01/05/99	Aston Villa	H	2-1	og (Watson), Beckham
05/05/99	Liverpool	A	2-2	Yorke, Irwin (p)
09/05/99	Middlesbrough	A	1-0	Yorke
12/05/99	Blackburn Rovers	A	0-0	
16/05/99	Tottenham Hotspur	H	2-1	Beckham, Cole

MIDDLESBROUGH

CLUB DIRECTORY

Middlesbrough FC
Cellnet Riverside Stadium
Middlesbrough
Cleveland
TS3 6RS
tel - (01642) 877700
fax - (01642) 877840
Year of Formation - 1876
Chairman - Steve Gibson
Chief Executive - Keith Lamb
Manager - Bryan Robson
Stadium - Cellnet Riverside (35,000)

APPEARANCES 98/99

	P	Ap	(s)	Gls
Alun ARMSTRONG	A		(6)	1
Steve BAKER	D	1	(1)	
Mikkel BECK (DEN)	A	13	(14)	5
Marlon BERESFORD	G	4		
Marco BRANCA (ITA)	A		(1)	
Andy CAMPBELL	A	1	(7)	
Colin COOPER	D	31	(1)	1
Michael CUMMINS (IRL)	M	1		
Brian DEANE	A	24	(2)	6
Gianluca FESTA (ITA)	D	25		2
Curtis FLEMING (IRL)	D	17	(2)	1
Paul GASCOIGNE	M	25	(1)	3
Jason GAVIN (IRL)	D	2		
Dean GORDON	D	38		3
Craig HARRISON	D	3	(1)	
Vladimir KINDER (SVK)	D		(5)	2
Neil MADDISON	M	10	(10)	
Paul MERSON	A	3		
Alan MOORE (IRL)	A	3	(1)	
Robbie MUSTOE	M	32	(1)	4
Keith O'NEILL (IRL)	A	4	(2)	
Gary PALLISTER	D	26		
Hamilton RICARD (COL)	A	32	(4)	15
Mark SCHWARZER (AUS)	G	34		
Phil STAMP	M	5	(11)	2
Robbie STOCKDALE	D	17	(2)	
Mark SUMMERBELL	M	7	(4)	
Andy TOWNSEND (IRL)	M	35		1
Steve VICKERS	D	30	(1)	1

LEAGUE RESULTS 1998/99

15/08/98	Leeds United	H	0-0	
23/08/98	Aston Villa	A	1-3	Beck
29/08/98	Derby County	H	1-1	Ricard
09/09/98	Leicester City	A	1-0	Gascoigne
13/09/98	Tottenham Hotspur	A	3-0	Ricard 2, Kinder
19/09/98	Everton	H	2-2	Ricard 2
26/09/98	Chelsea	A	0-2	
03/10/98	Sheffield Wednesday	H	4-0	Beck 2, Ricard, Gascoigne
17/10/98	Blackburn Rovers	H	2-1	Ricard, Fleming
24/10/98	Wimbledon	A	2-2	Mustoe, Ricard
01/11/98	Nottingham Forest	H	1-1	Deane
07/11/98	Southampton	A	3-3	Gascoigne, og (Lundekvam), Festa
14/11/98	Charlton Athletic	A	1-1	Stamp
21/11/98	Coventry City	H	2-0	Gordon, Ricard
29/11/98	Arsenal	A	1-1	Deane
06/12/98	Newcastle United	H	2-2	Townsend, Cooper
12/12/98	West Ham United	H	1-0	Deane
19/12/98	Manchester United	A	3-2	Ricard, Gordon, Deane
26/12/98	Liverpool	H	1-3	Deane
28/12/98	Derby County	A	1-2	Beck
09/01/99	Aston Villa	H	0-0	
16/01/99	Leeds United	A	0-2	
30/01/99	Leicester City	H	0-0	
06/02/99	Liverpool	A	1-3	Stamp
17/02/99	Everton	A	0-5	
20/02/99	Tottenham Hotspur	H	0-0	
27/02/99	Sheffield Wednesday	A	1-3	Mustoe
14/03/99	Southampton	H	3-0	Beck, Ricard, Vickers
20/03/99	Nottingham Forest	A	2-1	Ricard, Deane
03/04/99	Blackburn Rovers	A	0-0	
05/04/99	Wimbledon	H	3-1	Ricard 2, Festa
10/04/99	Charlton Athletic	H	2-0	Ricard, Mustoe
14/04/99	Chelsea	H	0-0	
17/04/99	Coventry City	A	2-1	Kinder, Gordon
24/04/99	Arsenal	H	1-6	Armstrong
01/05/99	Newcastle United	A	1-1	Mustoe
09/05/99	Manchester United	H	0-1	
16/05/99	West Ham United	A	0-4	

NEWCASTLE UNITED

CLUB DIRECTORY

Newcastle United FC
St. James' Park, Newcastle-upon-Tyne, NE1 4ST
tel - (0191) 2018400 / fax - (0191) 2018600
Year of Formation - 1881
Chairman - Freddy Shepherd
Secretary - Russell Cushing
Manager - Kenny Dalglish; Ruud Gullit
Stadium - St. James' Park (36,834)

MAJOR HONOURS
League Championship - (4)
1905, 1907, 1909, 1927.
FA Cup - (6)
1910, 1924, 1932, 1951, 1952, 1955.
Fairs' Cup - (1) 1969.

APPEARANCES 98/99

	P	Ap	(s)	Gls
Philippe ALBERT (BEL)	D	3	(3)	
Andreas ANDERSSON (SWE)	A	11	(4)	2
John BARNES	M		(1)	
Warren BARTON	D	17	(7)	
David BATTY	M	6	(2)	
David BEHARALL	D	4		
Garry BRADY (SCO)	M	3	(6)	
Laurent CHARVET (FRA)	D	30	(1)	1
Nikos DABIZAS (GRE)	D	25	(5)	3
Paul DALGLISH (SCO)	A	6	(5)	1
Didier DOMI (FRA)	D	14		
Duncan FERGUSON (SCO)	A	7		2
Keith GILLESPIE (NIR)	M	5	(2)	
Shay GIVEN (IRL)	G	31		
Stephen GLASS (SCO)	M	18	(4)	3
Andy GRIFFIN	D	14		
Stéphane GUIVARC'H (FRA)	A	2	(2)	1
Dietmar HAMANN (GER)	M	22	(1)	4
Steve HARPER	G	7	(1)	
Steve HOWEY	D	14		
Aaron HUGHES (NIR)	D	12	(2)	
Temuri KETSBAIA (GEO)	M	14	(12)	5
Robert LEE	M	20	(6)	
Jamie McCLEN	M	1		
Silvio MARIC (CRO)	M	9	(1)	
Stuart PEARCE	D	12		
Alessandro PISTONE (ITA)	D	2	(1)	
Louis SAHA (FRA)	A	5	(6)	1
Carl SERRANT	D	3	(1)	
Alan SHEARER	A	29	(1)	14
Nolberto SOLANO (PER)	M	24	(5)	6
Gary SPEED (WAL)	M	34	(4)	4
Steve WATSON	D	7		
Yeorgos YEORYADIS (GRE)	M	7	(3)	

LEAGUE RESULTS 1998/99

15/08/98	Charlton Athletic	H	0-0	
22/08/98	Chelsea	A	1-1	Andersson
30/08/98	Liverpool	H	1-4	Guivarc'h
09/09/98	Aston Villa	A	0-1	
12/09/98	Southampton	H	4-0	Shearer 2 (1p), og (Marshall), Ketsbaia
19/09/98	Coventry City	A	5-1	Dabizas, Shearer 2, Speed, Glass
26/09/98	Nottingham Forest	H	2-0	Shearer 2 (1p)
04/10/98	Arsenal	A	0-3	
17/10/98	Derby County	H	2-1	Dabizas, Glass
24/10/98	Tottenham Hotspur	A	0-2	
31/10/98	West Ham United	H	0-3	
08/11/98	Manchester United	A	0-0	
14/11/98	Sheffield Wednesday	H	1-1	Dalglish
23/11/98	Everton	A	0-1	
28/11/98	Wimbledon	H	3-1	Solano, Ferguson 2
06/12/98	Middlesbrough	A	2-2	Charvet, Dabizas
12/12/98	Blackburn Rovers	A	0-0	
19/12/98	Leicester City	H	1-0	Glass
26/12/98	Leeds United	H	0-3	
28/12/98	Liverpool	A	2-4	Solano, Andersson
09/01/99	Chelsea	H	0-1	
17/01/99	Charlton Athletic	A	2-2	Ketsbaia, Solano
30/01/99	Aston Villa	H	2-1	Shearer, Ketsbaia
06/02/99	Leeds United	A	1-0	Solano
17/02/99	Coventry City	H	4-1	Shearer 2, Speed, Saha
20/02/99	Southampton	A	1-2	Hamann
28/02/99	Arsenal	H	1-1	Hamann
10/03/99	Nottingham Forest	A	2-1	Shearer (p), Hamann
13/03/99	Manchester United	H	1-2	Solano
20/03/99	West Ham United	A	0-2	
03/04/99	Derby County	A	4-3	Speed 2, Ketsbaia, Solano
05/04/99	Tottenham Hotspur	H	1-1	Ketsbaia
17/04/99	Everton	H	1-3	Shearer (p)
21/04/99	Sheffield Wednesday	A	1-1	Shearer (p)
24/04/99	Wimbledon	A	1-1	Shearer
01/05/99	Middlesbrough	H	1-1	Shearer (p)
08/05/99	Leicester City	A	0-2	
16/05/99	Blackburn Rovers	H	1-1	Hamann

NOTTINGHAM FOREST

CLUB DIRECTORY

Nottingham Forest FC
City Ground, Nottingham, NG2 5FJ
tel - (0115) 9824444 / fax - (0115) 9824455
Year of Formation - 1865
Chief Executive - Phil Soar
Secretary - Paul White
Manager - Dave Bassett; Ron Atkinson
(99/00 - David Platt)
Stadium - City Ground (30,602)

MAJOR HONOURS
League Championship - (1) 1978.
FA Cup - (2) 1898, 1959.
League Cup - (4) 1978, 1979, 1989, 1990.
European Champions' Cup - (2) 1979, 1980.
European Super Cup - (1) 1979.

APPEARANCES 98/99

	P	Ap	(s)	Gls
Bernard ALLOU (FRA)	M		(2)	
Craig ARMSTRONG	D	20	(2)	
Chris BART-WILLIAMS	M	20	(4)	3
Dave BEASANT	G	26		
Thierry BONALAIR (FRA)	D	24	(4)	1
Steve CHETTLE	D	32	(2)	2
Mark CROSSLEY (WAL)	G	12		
Jean-Claude DARCHEVILLE (FRA)	A	14	(2)	2
Christopher DOIG (SCO)	D	1	(1)	
Christian EDWARDS (WAL)	D	7	(5)	
Dougie FREEDMAN (SCO)	A	20	(11)	9
Scot GEMMILL (SCO)	M	18	(2)	
Richard GOUGH (SCO)	D	7		
Andy GRAY (SCO)	M	3	(5)	
Marlon HAREWOOD	A	11	(12)	1
John HARKES (USA)	M	3		
Jan Olav HJELDE (NOR)	D	16	(1)	1
Glyn HODGES (WAL)	M	3	(2)	
Andy JOHNSON (WAL)	M	25	(3)	
Matthieu LOUIS-JEAN (FRA)	D	15	(1)	
Des LYTTLE	D	5	(5)	
Jesper MATTSSON (SWE)	D	5	(1)	
Stephen MELTON	M	1		
Carlton PALMER	M	13		
Hugo PORFÍRIO (POR)	M	3	(6)	1
Nigel QUASHIE	M	12	(4)	
Alan ROGERS	D	34		4
Neil SHIPPERLEY	A	12	(8)	1
Ståle STENSAAS (NOR)	D	6	(1)	
Steve STONE	M	26		3
Geoff THOMAS	M	5		1
Pierre VAN HOOIJDONK (HOL)	A	19	(2)	6
Ian WOAN	M		(2)	

LEAGUE RESULTS 1998/99

17/08/98	Arsenal	A	1-2	Thomas
22/08/98	Coventry City	H	1-0	Stone
29/08/98	Southampton	A	2-1	Darcheville, Stone
08/09/98	Everton	H	0-2	
12/09/98	Chelsea	A	1-2	Darcheville
19/09/98	West Ham United	H	0-0	
26/09/98	Newcastle United	A	0-2	
03/10/98	Charlton Athletic	H	0-1	
17/10/98	Leeds United	H	1-1	Stone
24/10/98	Liverpool	A	1-5	Freedman
01/11/98	Middlesbrough	A	1-1	Harewood
07/11/98	Wimbledon	H	0-1	
16/11/98	Derby County	H	2-2	Freedman, Van Hooijdonk
21/11/98	Tottenham Hotspur	A	0-2	
28/11/98	Aston Villa	H	2-2	Bart-Williams, Freedman
07/12/98	Sheffield Wednesday	A	2-3	Bonalair, Van Hooijdonk
12/12/98	Leicester City	A	1-3	Van Hooijdonk
19/12/98	Blackburn Rovers	H	2-2	Chettle (p), Freedman
26/12/98	Manchester United	A	0-3	
28/12/98	Southampton	H	1-1	Chettle (p)
09/01/99	Coventry City	A	0-4	
16/01/99	Arsenal	H	0-1	
30/01/99	Everton	A	1-0	Van Hooijdonk
06/02/99	Manchester United	H	1-8	Rogers
13/02/99	West Ham United	A	1-2	Hjelde
20/02/99	Chelsea	H	1-3	Van Hooijdonk
27/02/99	Charlton Athletic	A	0-0	
10/03/99	Newcastle United	H	1-2	Freedman
13/03/99	Wimbledon	A	3-1	Rogers, Freedman, Shipperley
20/03/99	Middlesbrough	H	1-2	Freedman
03/04/99	Leeds United	A	1-3	Rogers
05/04/99	Liverpool	H	2-2	Freedman, Van Hooijdonk
10/04/99	Derby County	A	0-1	
17/04/99	Tottenham Hotspur	H	0-1	
24/04/99	Aston Villa	A	0-2	
01/05/99	Sheffield Wednesday	H	2-0	Porfirio, Rogers
08/05/99	Blackburn Rovers	A	2-1	Freedman, Bart-Williams
16/05/99	Leicester City	H	1-0	Bart-Williams

SHEFFIELD WEDNESDAY

CLUB DIRECTORY

Sheffield Wednesday FC
Hillsborough, Sheffield S6 1SW
tel - (0114) 2212121
fax - (0114) 2212122
Year of Formation - 1867
Chairman - David Richards
Secretary - Alan Sykes
Manager - Danny Wilson
Stadium - Hillsborough (39,859)

MAJOR HONOURS
League Championship - (4)
1903, 1904, 1929, 1930.
FA Cup - (3) 1896, 1907, 1935.
League Cup - (1) 1991.

APPEARANCES 98/99

		P	Ap	(s)	Gls
Manuel AGOGO (GHA)	M			(1)	
Niclas ALEXANDERSSON (SWE)	M	31		(1)	3
Peter ATHERTON	D	38			2
Earl BARRETT	D			(5)	
Andy BOOTH	A	34			6
Lee BRISCOE	M	5		(11)	1
Benito CARBONE (ITA)	A	31			8
Juan COBIAN (ARG)	D	7		(2)	
Richard CRESSWELL	A	1		(6)	1
Paolo DI CANIO (ITA)	A	5		(1)	3
EMERSON Thome (BRA)	D	38			1
Steven HASLAM	M	2			
Andy HINCHCLIFFE	D	32			3
Ritchie HUMPHREYS	A	10		(9)	1
Graham HYDE	M			(1)	
Wim JONK (HOL)	M	38			2
Mark McKEEVER (NIR)	A	1		(2)	
Jim MAGILTON (MIR)	M	1		(5)	
Owen MORRISON	M			(1)	
Jon NEWSOME	D	2		(2)	
Scott OAKES	M			(1)	
Kevin PRESSMAN	G	14		(1)	
Alan QUINN (IRL)	A	1			
Petter RUDI (NOR)	M	33		(1)	6
Francesco SANETTI (ITA)	A			(3)	
Philip SCOTT (SCO)	M			(4)	1
Danny SONNER (NIR)	M	24		(2)	3
Pavel SRNICEK (CZE)	G	24			
Dejan STEFANOVIC (YUG)	D	8		(3)	
Des WALKER	D	37			
Guy WHITTINGHAM	M	1		(1)	

LEAGUE RESULTS 1998/99

15/08/98	West Ham United	H	0-1	
22/08/98	Tottenham Hotspur	A	3-0	Atherton, Di Canio, Hinchcliffe
29/08/98	Aston Villa	H	0-1	
09/09/98	Derby County	A	0-1	
12/09/98	Blackburn Rovers	H	3-0	Atherton, Hinchcliffe, Di Canio
19/09/98	Wimbledon	A	1-2	Di Canio
26/09/98	Arsenal	H	1-0	Briscoe
03/10/98	Middlesbrough	A	0-4	
18/10/98	Coventry City	A	0-1	
24/10/98	Everton	H	0-0	
31/10/98	Southampton	H	0-0	
08/11/98	Leeds United	A	1-2	Booth
14/11/98	Newcastle United	A	1-1	Rudi
21/11/98	Manchester United	H	3-1	Alexandersson 2, Jonk
28/11/98	Chelsea	A	1-1	Booth
07/12/98	Nottingham Forest	H	3-2	Alexandersson, Carbone 2
12/12/98	Charlton Athletic	H	3-0	Booth, Carbone, Rudi
19/12/98	Liverpool	A	0-2	
26/12/98	Leicester City	H	0-1	
28/12/98	Aston Villa	A	1-2	Carbone
09/01/99	Tottenham Hotspur	H	0-0	
16/01/99	West Ham United	A	4-0	Hinchcliffe, Rudi, Humphreys, Carbone (p)
30/01/99	Derby County	H	0-1	
06/02/99	Leicester City	A	2-0	Jonk, Carbone
20/02/99	Blackburn Rovers	A	4-1	Sonner, Rudi 2, Booth
27/02/99	Middlesbrough	H	3-1	Booth 2, Sonner
03/03/99	Wimbledon	H	1-2	Emerson
09/03/99	Arsenal	A	0-3	
13/03/99	Leeds United	H	0-2	
20/03/99	Southampton	A	0-1	
03/04/99	Coventry City	H	1-2	Rudi
05/04/99	Everton	A	2-1	Carbone 2
17/04/99	Manchester United	A	0-3	
21/04/99	Newcastle United	H	1-1	Scott
25/04/99	Chelsea	H	0-0	
01/05/99	Nottingham Forest	A	0-2	
08/05/99	Liverpool	H	1-0	Cresswell
16/05/99	Charlton Athletic	A	1-0	Sonner

SOUTHAMPTON

CLUB DIRECTORY

Southampton FC
The Dell
Milton Road, Southampton SO15 2XH
tel - (01703) 220505
fax - (01703) 330360
Year of Formation - 1885
Chairman - Rupert Lowe
Secretary - Brian Truscott
Manager - Dave Jones
Stadium - The Dell (15,000)

MAJOR HONOURS
FA Cup - (1) 1976.

APPEARANCES 98/99

	P	Ap	(s)	Gls
Steve BASHAM	M		(4)	1
James BEATTIE	A	22	(13)	5
Francis BENALI	D	19	(4)	
John BERESFORD	D	1	(3)	
Shayne BRADLEY	A		(3)	
Wayne BRIDGE	M	15	(8)	
Patrick COLLETER (FRA)	D	16		1
Jason DODD	D	27	(1)	1
Richard DRYDEN	D	4		
Kevin GIBBENS	A	2	(2)	
Scott HILEY	D	27	(2)	
David HIRST	A		(2)	
David HOWELLS	M	8	(1)	1
David HUGHES	M	6	(3)	
Mark HUGHES (WAL)	A	32		1
Paul JONES (WAL)	G	31		
Hassan KACHLOUL (MAR)	M	18	(4)	5
Matt LE TISSIER	M	20	(10)	7
Claus LUNDEKVAM (NOR)	D	30	(3)	
Chris MARSDEN	M	14		2
Scott MARSHALL (SCO)	D	2		
Gary MONK	D	4		
Ken MONKOU (HOL)	D	22		1
Neil MOSS	G	7		
Matthew OAKLEY	M	21	(1)	2
Egil ØSTENSTAD (NOR)	A	27	(7)	7
Marian PAHARS (LAT)	A	4	(2)	3
Carlton PALMER	M	18	(1)	
Stuart RIPLEY	M	16	(6)	
Phil WARNER	M	5		
Andy WILLIAMS (WAL)	M		(1)	

LEAGUE RESULTS 1998/99

16/08/98	Liverpool	H	1-2	Østenstad
22/08/98	Charlton Athletic	A	0-5	
29/08/98	Nottingham Forest	H	1-2	Le Tissier (p)
08/09/98	Leeds United	A	0-3	
12/09/98	Newcastle United	A	0-4	
19/09/98	Tottenham Hotspur	H	1-1	Le Tissier
28/09/98	West Ham United	A	0-1	
03/10/98	Manchester United	H	0-3	
17/10/98	Arsenal	A	1-1	Howells
24/10/98	Coventry City	H	2-1	Le Tissier, Østenstad
31/10/98	Sheffield Wednesday	A	0-0	
07/11/98	Middlesbrough	H	3-3	Monkou, Beattie, Østenstad
14/11/98	Aston Villa	H	1-4	Le Tissier
21/11/98	Blackburn Rovers	A	2-0	Oakley, Basham
28/11/98	Derby County	H	0-1	
05/12/98	Leicester City	A	0-2	
12/12/98	Everton	A	0-1	
19/12/98	Wimbledon	H	3-1	Østenstad 2, Kachloul
26/12/98	Chelsea	H	0-2	
28/12/98	Nottingham Forest	A	1-1	Kachloul
09/01/99	Charlton Athletic	H	3-1	Kachloul, Colleter, Beattie
16/01/99	Liverpool	A	1-7	Østenstad
30/01/99	Leeds United	H	3-0	Kachloul, Oakley, Østenstad
06/02/99	Chelsea	A	0-1	
20/02/99	Newcastle United	H	2-1	Beattie, Dodd (p)
27/02/99	Manchester United	A	1-2	Le Tissier
02/03/99	Tottenham Hotspur	A	0-3	
06/03/99	West Ham United	H	1-0	Kachloul
14/03/99	Middlesbrough	A	0-3	
20/03/99	Sheffield Wednesday	H	1-0	Le Tissier
03/04/99	Arsenal	H	0-0	
05/04/99	Coventry City	A	0-1	
10/04/99	Aston Villa	A	0-3	
17/04/99	Blackburn Rovers	H	3-3	Marsden, Hughes M., Pahars
24/04/99	Derby County	A	0-0	
01/05/99	Leicester City	H	2-1	Marsden, Beattie
08/05/99	Wimbledon	A	2-0	Beattie, Le Tissier
16/05/99	Everton	H	2-0	Pahars 2

TOTTENHAM HOTSPUR

CLUB DIRECTORY

Tottenham Hotspur FC
748 High Road
Tottenham, London N17 0AP
tel - (0181) 3655000
fax - (0181) 3655005
Year of Formation - 1882
Chairman - Alan Sugar
Secretary - Peter Barnes
Manager - Christian Gross; David Pleat;
George Graham
Stadium - White Hart Lane (33,083)

MAJOR HONOURS
League Championship - (2) 1951, 1961.
FA Cup - (8) 1901, 1921, 1961, 1962, 1967,
1981, 1982, 1991.
League Cup - (3) 1971, 1973, 1999.
European Cup-winners' Cup - (1) 1963.
UEFA Cup - (2) 1972, 1984.

APPEARANCES 98/99

	P	Ap	(s)	Gls
Rory ALLEN	A		(4)	
Darren ANDERTON	M	31	(1)	3
Chris ARMSTRONG	A	24	(10)	7
Espen BAARDSEN (NOR)	G	12		
Nicola BERTI (ITA)	M	4		
Colin CALDERWOOD (SCO)	D	11	(1)	
Sol CAMPBELL	D	37		6
Stephen CARR (IRL)	D	37		
Stephen CLEMENCE	M	9	(9)	
José DOMINGUEZ (POR)	M	2	(11)	2
Justin EDINBURGH	D	14	(2)	
Les FERDINAND	A	22	(2)	5
Ruel FOX	M	17	(3)	3
Steffen FREUND (GER)	M	17		
David GINOLA (FRA)	M	30		3
Steffen IVERSEN (NOR)	A	22	(5)	9
Allan NIELSEN (DEN)	M	24	(4)	3
Roger NILSEN (NOR)	D	3		
Moussa SAÏB (ALG)	M		(4)	
John SCALES	D	7		
Hans SEGERS (HOL)	G	1		
Tim SHERWOOD	M	12	(2)	2
Andy SINTON	M	12	(10)	
Mauricio TARICCO (ARG)	D	12	(1)	
Paolo TRAMEZZANI (ITA)	D	6		
Ramon VEGA (SUI)	D	13	(3)	2
Ian WALKER	G	25		
Luke YOUNG	D	14	(1)	

LEAGUE RESULTS 1998/99

15/08/98	Wimbledon	A	1-3	Fox
22/08/98	Sheffield Wednesday	H	0-3	
29/08/98	Everton	A	1-0	Ferdinand
09/09/98	Blackburn Rovers	H	2-1	Ferdinand, Nielsen
13/09/98	Middlesbrough	H	0-3	
19/09/98	Southampton	A	1-1	Fox
26/09/98	Leeds United	H	3-3	Vega, Iversen, Campbell
03/10/98	Derby County	A	1-0	Campbell
19/10/98	Leicester City	A	1-2	Ferdinand
24/10/98	Newcastle United	H	2-0	Iversen 2
02/11/98	Charlton Athletic	H	2-2	Nielsen, Armstrong
07/11/98	Aston Villa	A	2-3	Anderton (p), Vega
14/11/98	Arsenal	A	0-0	
21/11/98	Nottingham Forest	H	2-0	Armstrong, Nielsen
28/11/98	West Ham United	A	1-2	Armstrong
05/12/98	Liverpool	H	2-1	Fox, og (Carragher)
12/12/98	Manchester United	H	2-2	Campbell 2
19/12/98	Chelsea	A	0-2	
26/12/98	Coventry City	A	1-1	Campbell
28/12/98	Everton	H	4-1	Ferdinand, Armstrong 3
09/01/99	Sheffield Wednesday	A	0-0	
16/01/99	Wimbledon	H	0-0	
30/01/99	Blackburn Rovers	A	1-1	Iversen
06/02/99	Coventry City	H	0-0	
20/02/99	Middlesbrough	A	0-0	
27/02/99	Derby County	H	1-1	Sherwood
02/03/99	Southampton	H	3-0	Armstrong, Iversen, Dominguez
10/03/99	Leeds United	A	0-2	
13/03/99	Aston Villa	H	1-0	Sherwood
03/04/99	Leicester City	H	0-2	
05/04/99	Newcastle United	A	1-1	Anderton (p)
17/04/99	Nottingham Forest	A	1-0	Iversen
20/04/99	Charlton Athletic	A	4-1	Iversen, Campbell, Dominguez, Ginola
24/04/99	West Ham United	H	1-2	Ginola
01/05/99	Liverpool	A	2-3	og (Carragher), Iversen
05/05/99	Arsenal	H	1-3	Anderton
10/05/99	Chelsea	H	2-2	Iversen, Ginola
16/05/99	Manchester United	A	1-2	Ferdinand

WEST HAM UNITED

CLUB DIRECTORY

West Ham United FC
Boleyn Ground
Green Street
Upton Park, London E13 9AZ
tel - (0181) 5482748
fax - (0181) 5482758
Year of Formation - 1895
Chairman - Terence Brown
Secretary - Graham Mackrell
Manager - Harry Redknapp
Stadium - Upton Park (26,054)

MAJOR HONOURS
FA Cup - (3) 1964, 1975, 1980.
European Cup-winners' Cup - (1) 1965.

APPEARANCES 98/99

	P	Ap	(s)	Gls
Samassi ABOU (FRA)	A	2	(1)	
Eyal BERKOVIC (ISR)	M	28	(2)	3
Tim BREACKER	D	2	(1)	
Joe COLE	M	2	(6)	
Chris COYNE (AUS)	D		(1)	
Paolo DI CANIO (ITA)	A	12	(1)	4
Julian DICKS	D	9		
Rio FERDINAND	D	31		
Marc-Vivien FOE (CMR)	M	13		
Craig FORREST (CAN)	G	1	(1)	
John HARTSON (WAL)	A	16	(1)	4
Shaka HISLOP	G	37		
Lee HODGES	A		(1)	
Gavin HOLLIGAN	M		(1)	
Andrew IMPEY	M	6	(2)	
Marc KELLER (FRA)	M	17	(4)	5
Paul KITSON	A	13	(4)	3
Frank LAMPARD	M	38		5
Stan LAZARIDIS (AUS)	M	11	(4)	
Steve LOMAS (NIR)	M	30		1
Javier MARGAS (CHL)	D	3		
Scott MINTO	D	14	(1)	
John MONCUR	M	6	(8)	
Manny OMOYINMI (NIG)	M		(3)	
Ian PEARCE	D	33		2
Steve POTTS	D	11	(8)	
Neil RUDDOCK	D	27		2
Trevor SINCLAIR	M	36		7
Ian WRIGHT	A	20	(2)	9

LEAGUE RESULTS 1998/99

15/08/98	Sheffield Wednesday	A	1-0	Wright
22/08/98	Manchester United	H	0-0	
29/08/98	Coventry City	A	0-0	
09/09/98	Wimbledon	H	3-4	Hartson, Wright 2
12/09/98	Liverpool	H	2-1	Hartson, Berkovic
19/09/98	Nottingham Forest	A	0-0	
28/09/98	Southampton	H	1-0	Wright
03/10/98	Blackburn Rovers	A	0-3	
17/10/98	Aston Villa	H	0-0	
24/10/98	Charlton Athletic	A	2-4	og (Rufus), Berkovic
31/10/98	Newcastle United	A	3-0	Wright 2, Sinclair
08/11/98	Chelsea	H	1-1	Ruddock
14/11/98	Leicester City	H	3-2	Kitson, Lomas, Lampard
22/11/98	Derby County	A	2-0	Hartson, Keller
28/11/98	Tottenham Hotspur	H	2-1	Sinclair 2
05/12/98	Leeds United	A	0-4	
12/12/98	Middlesbrough	A	0-1	
19/12/98	Everton	H	2-1	Keller, Sinclair
26/12/98	Arsenal	A	0-1	
28/12/98	Coventry City	H	2-0	Wright, Hartson
10/01/99	Manchester United	A	1-4	Lampard
16/01/99	Sheffield Wednesday	H	0-4	
30/01/99	Wimbledon	A	0-0	
06/02/99	Arsenal	H	0-4	
13/02/99	Nottingham Forest	H	2-1	Pearce, Lampard
20/02/99	Liverpool	A	2-2	Lampard (p), Keller
27/02/99	Blackburn Rovers	H	2-0	Pearce, Di Canio
06/03/99	Southampton	A	0-1	
13/03/99	Chelsea	A	1-0	Kitson
20/03/99	Newcastle United	H	2-0	Di Canio, Kitson
02/04/99	Aston Villa	A	0-0	
05/04/99	Charlton Athletic	H	0-1	
10/04/99	Leicester City	A	0-0	
17/04/99	Derby County	H	5-1	Di Canio, Berkovic, Wright, Ruddock, Sinclair
24/04/99	Tottenham Hotspur	A	2-1	Wright, Keller
01/05/99	Leeds United	H	1-5	Di Canio
08/05/99	Everton	A	0-6	
16/05/99	Middlesbrough	H	4-0	Lampard, Keller, Sinclair 2

WIMBLEDON

CLUB DIRECTORY

Wimbledon FC
Selhurst Park
South Norwood
London SE25 6PY
tel - (0181) 7712233
fax - (0181) 7680641
Year of Formation - 1889
Chairman - S.G. Reed
Secretary - Steve Rooke
Manager - Joe Kinnear (99/00 - Egil Olsen)
Stadium - Selhurst Park (26,297)

MAJOR HONOURS
FA Cup - (1) 1988.

APPEARANCES 98/99

	P	Ap	(s)	Gls
Gareth AINSWORTH	M	5	(3)	
Neal ARDLEY	M	16	(7)	
Dean BLACKWELL	D	27	(1)	
Stewart CASTLEDINE	M	1		
Carl CORT	A	6	(10)	3
Kenny CUNNINGHAM (IRL)	D	35		
Robbie EARLE (JAM)	M	35		5
Efan EKOKU (NIG)	A	11	(11)	6
Jason EUELL	M	31	(2)	10
Peter FEAR	M		(2)	
Marcus GAYLE (JAM)	A	31	(4)	10
Jon GOODMAN (IRL)	A		(1)	
John HARTSON (WAL)	A	12	(2)	2
Ceri HUGHES (WAL)	M	8	(5)	
Michael HUGHES (NIR)	M	28	(3)	2
Duncan JUPP (SCO)	M	3	(3)	
Mark KENNEDY (IRL)	M	7	(10)	
Alan KIMBLE	D	22	(4)	
Carl LEABURN	A	14	(8)	
Chris PERRY	D	34		
Andy ROBERTS	M	23	(5)	2
Neil SULLIVAN (SCO)	G	38		
Ben THATCHER	D	31		

LEAGUE RESULTS 1998/99

15/08/98	Tottenham Hotspur	H	3-1	Earle, Ekoku 2
22/08/98	Derby County	A	0-0	
29/08/98	Leeds United	H	1-1	Hughes M.
09/09/98	West Ham United	A	4-3	Gayle 2, Euell, Ekoku
12/09/98	Aston Villa	A	0-2	
19/09/98	Sheffield Wednesday	H	2-1	Euell 2
27/09/98	Leicester City	A	1-1	Earle
03/10/98	Everton	H	1-2	Roberts
17/10/98	Manchester United	A	1-5	Euell
24/10/98	Middlesbrough	H	2-2	Gayle 2
31/10/98	Blackburn Rovers	H	1-1	Earle
07/11/98	Nottingham Forest	A	1-0	Gayle
14/11/98	Chelsea	A	0-3	
21/11/98	Arsenal	H	1-0	Ekoku
28/11/98	Newcastle United	A	1-3	Gayle
05/12/98	Coventry City	H	2-1	Euell 2
13/12/98	Liverpool	H	1-0	Earle
19/12/98	Southampton	A	1-3	Gayle
26/12/98	Charlton Athletic	H	2-1	Euell, Hughes M.
29/12/98	Leeds United	A	2-2	Earle, Cort
09/01/99	Derby County	H	2-1	Euell, Roberts
16/01/99	Tottenham Hotspur	A	0-0	
30/01/99	West Ham United	H	0-0	
08/02/99	Charlton Athletic	A	0-2	
21/02/99	Aston Villa	H	0-0	
27/02/99	Everton	A	1-1	Ekoku
03/03/99	Sheffield Wednesday	A	2-1	Ekoku, Gayle
06/03/99	Leicester City	H	0-1	
13/03/99	Nottingham Forest	H	1-3	Gayle
20/03/99	Blackburn Rovers	A	1-3	Euell
03/04/99	Manchester United	H	1-1	Euell
05/04/99	Middlesbrough	A	1-3	Cort
11/04/99	Chelsea	H	1-2	Gayle
19/04/99	Arsenal	A	1-5	Cort
24/04/99	Newcastle United	H	1-1	Hartson
01/05/99	Coventry City	A	1-2	Hartson
08/05/99	Southampton	H	0-2	
16/05/99	Liverpool	A	0-3	

PROMOTED CLUBS

SECOND DIVISION FINAL TABLE 98/99

		Pd	W	D	L	F	A	Pt	GD
1	**Sunderland**	**46**	**31**	**12**	**3**	**91**	**28**	**105**	**+63**
2	**Bradford City**	**46**	**26**	**9**	**11**	**82**	**47**	**87**	**+35**
3	Ipswich Town	46	26	8	12	69	32	86	+37
4	Birmingham City	46	23	12	11	66	37	81	+29
5	**Watford**	**46**	**21**	**14**	**11**	**65**	**56**	**77**	**+9**
6	Bolton Wanderers	46	20	16	10	78	59	76	+19
7	Wolverhampton Wanderers	46	19	16	11	64	43	73	+21
8	Sheffield United	46	18	13	15	71	66	67	+5
9	Norwich City	46	15	17	14	62	61	62	+1
10	Huddersfield Town	46	15	16	15	62	71	61	-9
11	Grimsby Town	46	17	10	19	40	52	61	-12
12	West Bromwich Albion	46	16	11	19	69	76	59	-7
13	Barnsley	46	14	17	15	59	56	59	+3
14	Crystal Palace	46	14	16	16	58	71	58	-13
15	Tranmere Rovers	46	12	20	14	63	61	56	+2
16	Stockport County	46	12	17	17	49	60	53	-11
17	Swindon Town	46	13	11	22	59	81	50	-22
18	Crewe Alexandra	46	12	12	22	54	78	48	-24
19	Portsmouth	46	11	14	21	57	73	47	-16
20	Queens Park Rangers	46	12	11	23	52	61	47	-9
21	Port Vale	46	13	8	25	45	75	47	-30
22	Bury	46	10	17	19	35	60	47	-25
23	Oxford United	46	10	14	22	48	71	44	-23
24	Bristol City	46	9	15	22	57	80	42	-23

N.B. Teams level on points are classified by the number of goals scored.

PROMOTION PLAY-OFFS

Bolton Wanderers 1, Ipswich Town 0
Ipswich Town 4, Bolton Wanderers 3 (aet)
(4-4; Bolton Wanderers on away goals)

Watford 1, Birmingham City 0
Birmingham City 1, Watford 0 (aet)
(1-1; Watford 7-6 on pens.)

Watford 2, Bolton Wanderers 0

CLUB DIRECTORY

Sunderland AFC
Sunderland Stadium of Light
Sunderland
Tyne and Wear
SR5 1SU
tel - (0191) 5515000
fax - (0191) 5515123
Year of Formation - 1879
Chairman - Bob Murray
Chief Executive - John Fickling
Manager - Peter Reid
Stadium - Stadium of Light (42,000)

MAJOR HONOURS
League Championship - (6)
1892, 1893, 1895, 1902, 1913, 1936.
FA Cup - (2) 1937, 1973.

CLUB DIRECTORY

Bradford City FC
Valley Parade
Bradford
BD8 7DY
tel - (01274) 773355
fax - (01274) 773356
Year of Formation - 1903
Chairman - Geoffrey Richmond
Secretary - Jon Pollard
Manager - Paul Jewell
Stadium - Valley Parade (18,018)

MAJOR HONOURS
FA Cup - (1) 1911.

CLUB DIRECTORY

Watford FC
Vicarage Road Stadium
Watford
WD1 8ER
tel - (01923) 496000
fax - (01923) 496001
Year of Formation - 1881
Chairman - Sir Elton John
Secretary - John Alexander
Manager - Graham Taylor
Stadium - Vicarage Road (22,000)

ESTONIA

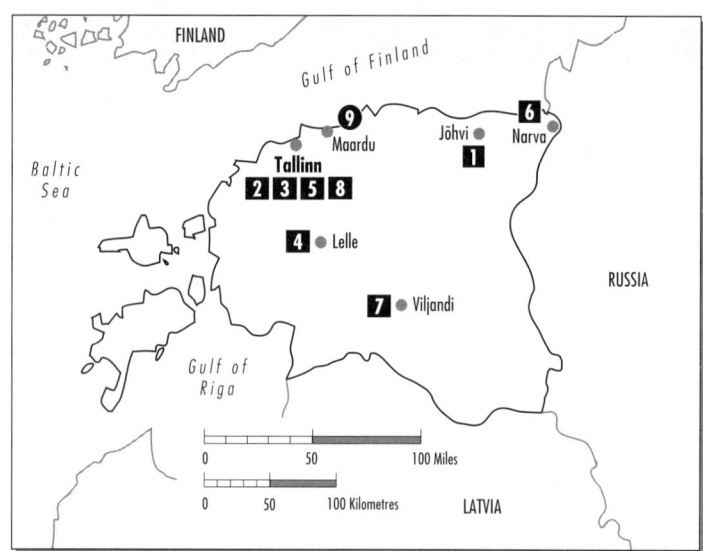

TWO TITLES IN FOUR MONTHS FOR FLORA

Thrilling climax to transitional championship

FEDERATION DIRECTORY

Eesti Jalgpalli Liit
Võidu 16, 11213 Tallinn

tel - (6) 542715/6/7   Year of Formation - 1921
fax - (6) 542719   President - Peeter Küttis
Secretary - Tõnu Sirel

Stadium - Kadriorg, Tallinn (6,000)

The decision to bring the Estonian championship into line with those of neighbouring countries Finland, Latvia and Russia and introduce a spring-autumn fixture schedule ed to the staging of a transitional mini-championship n the second half of 1998. It was the briefest of brief competitions, lasting a little over three months and ncorporating just 14 rounds. Effectively it was a repeat of he first phase of the previous championship, only without he spring attachment.

LEAGUE CHAMPIONSHIP RESULTS 1998

		1	2	3	4	5	6	7	8
1	EP Jõhvi		2-7	1-2	1-0	0-3	0-1	0-2	0-2
2	FC Flora Tallinn	6-0		3-0	6-1	0-3	3-3	1-0	3-0
3	FC Lantana Tallinn	4-1	3-3		1-1	0-1	3-3	3-0	0-0
4	Lelle SK	1-2	2-5	0-2		0-7	1-5	0-0	1-1
5	Tallinna Sadam	6-2	0-1	5-1	3-2		5-0	3-0	4-0
6	Trans Narva	5-1	0-1	1-3	1-0	0-0		4-1	2-2
7	Tulevik Viljandi	1-0	0-5	0-3	3-0	4-3	0-0		2-1
8	VMK Tallinn	4-0	0-2	1-2	2-1	0-5	0-3	2-2	

Not surprisingly, the leading contenders were the same ones that had challenged for the 1997/98 title. Champions FC Flora Tallinn sent a chilling early-warning signal to the rest by winning their first seven games and constructing a five-point lead. Their first major test, however, came in a delayed match against the previous season's runners-up (and their closest pursuers again), Tallinna Sadam. The outcome - a handsome 3-0 away win for Sadam - suddenly opened up the title race, and when Flora were held to a surprise 3-3 draw by Trans Narva in their next home fixture a fortnight later, it meant that, with Sadam hammering VMK Tallinn 4-0, the defending champions had surrendered the leadership of the table on goal difference.

There was all to play for, with the issue set to be determined one way or another when the two teams came face to face in the penultimate round on October 21. The days and weeks leading up to that showdown had been very taxing for the Flora players, who had been involved in two big European Championship qualifying matches in the Estonian national team. But against Sadam, Teitur Thórdarson's team dug deep and won the game 1-0 with a goal from their leading scorer Andres Oper.

LEAGUE CHAMPIONSHIP FINAL TABLE 1998

		Home					Away					Total						
		P	W	D	L	F	A	W	D	L	F	A	W	D	L	F	A	P	GD
1	FC Flora Tallinn	14	5	1	1	22	7	6	1	0	24	7	11	2	1	46	14	35	+32
2	Tallinna Sadam	14	6	0	1	26	6	5	1	1	22	4	11	1	2	48	10	34	+38
3	FC Lantana Tallinn	14	2	4	1	14	9	5	0	2	13	11	7	4	3	27	20	25	+7
4	Trans Narva	14	3	2	2	13	8	3	3	1	15	12	6	5	3	28	20	23	+8
5	Tulevik Viljandi	14	4	1	2	10	12	1	2	4	5	13	5	3	6	15	25	18	-10
6	VMK Tallinn	14	2	1	4	9	15	1	3	3	6	12	3	4	7	15	27	13	-12
7	EP Jõhvi	14	1	0	6	4	17	1	0	6	6	27	2	0	12	10	44	6	-34
8	Lelle SK	14	0	2	5	5	22	0	1	6	5	17	0	3	11	10	39	3	-29

N.B. After the end of the championship, Tallinna Sadam merged with promoted club Levadia Maardu. Lelle SK were therefore not relegated.

DOMESTIC CUP 98/99

1/8 FINALS
Baltika Narva 0, VMK Tallinn 1
Warrior-1 Valga 0, Trans Narva 25
MC Tallinn 0, Tallinna Sadam 2
FC Lootus Kohtla-Järve 1, Tulevik Viljandi 5
FC Valga 1, Lelle SK 3 (aet)
Levadia Maardu 3, EP Jõhvi 0
KSK Vigri Tallinn 1, FC Flora Tallinn 9
FC Kuressaare 1, FC Lantana Tallinn 1
(aet; 5-6 on pens.)

QUARTER-FINALS
VMK Tallinn 0, Trans Narva 0
Trans Narva 2 (Toshtshev 66, Marashov 78p),
VMK Tallinn 2 (Kisslejov 42, Embrich 71)
(2-2; VMK Tallinn on away goals)
FC Lantana Tallinn 0, FC Flora Tallinn 1 (Oper 85)
FC Flora Tallinn 6 (Terehhov 35, Oper 54, 79,
Zelinski 62, 68, Reim 64p),
FC Lantana Tallinn 1 (Krasnopjorov 34p)
(FC Flora Tallinn 7-1)

Tulevik Viljandi 0, Lelle SK 1 (Fossum 79)
Lelle SK 0, Tulevik Viljandi 6 (Ustritski 11, Dovydenas
50, 51, Mussaev 72p, Rooba 77, Õun 81)
(Tulevik Viljandi 6-1)

FC Maardu 0, Levadia Maardu 10 (Rõtshkov 5,
Krõlov 13, 29, 65, 68, 82, Staleliunas 34, Olumets
42, Kolbassenko 45, O'Konnel-Bronin 86)
Levadia Maardu 13 (Gussev 11, Rõtshkov 14, 45,
76, 89, Olumets 31, 43, 79, Afanasov 34, 35,
Kolbassenko 55, 67, Silkin 83),
FC Maardu 1 (Anissimov)
(Levadia Maardu 23-1)

SEMI-FINALS
Levadia Maardu 1 (O'Konnel-Bronin 75),
FC Flora Tallinn 1 (Terehhov 21)
FC Flora Tallinn 2 (Reim 22p, Oper 48),
Levadia Maardu 3 (Olumets 20, Krõlov 55, 61)
(Levadia Maardu 4-3)

Tulevik Viljandi 1 (Rooba 76), VMK Tallinn 0
VMK Tallinn 0, Tulevik Viljandi 0
(Tulevik Viljandi 1-0)

FINAL
25/05/99, Valga
LEVADIA MAARDU 3
O'Konnel-Bronin (17), Gussev (52), Krõlov (75)
TULEVIK VILJANDI 2 Ustritski (15), Allas (68)
referee - Saar
LEVADIA MAARDU - Martinsons; Leitan, Vinogradov,
Prins, Leetma, Kolbassenko, Svetogor (Bratshuk 89),
Gussev (Afanassov 88), O'Konnel-Bronin, Olumets
(Rõtshkov 90), Krõlov.
TULEVIK VILJANDI - Tammus; Allas, Nõmmik, Pari,
Olesk, Vahtramäe (Jürisson 85), Dovydenas, Lelov
(Rooba 63), Anis, Õun, Ustritski.

N.B. After the 1/8 finals Tallinna Sadam merged with
Levadia Maardu, thus permitting Levadia's reserve
team, FC Maardu, to compete in the quarter-finals.

Three points ahead and with just one game left, the hard work for Flora appeared to be over. But they were to undergo a real crisis of nerves in their final match, away to FC Lantana. 3-0 up and cruising, they let their guard drop and, incredibly, Lantana, a young side who were already sure of finishing third, raised their game sufficiently to pull all three goals back. Because of their inferior goal difference Flora could not afford a defeat but they just managed to hang on - despite two clear chances for Lantana to score the winner in the final minutes.

The 3-3 draw was enough for Flora to beat Sadam to the title by a solitary point and thus claim the championship trophy for the second time in four months. The team was more or less unaltered from the previous season, which meant more silverware for the team's vas

NATIONAL TEAM RESULTS 98/99

20/08/98	Moldova		H	Kohtla-Järve	0-1
05/09/98	Bosnia-Herzegovina (ECQ)	A		Sarajevo	1-1 Hibic (29og)
23/09/98	Egypt		H	Tallinn	2-2 Kirs (29), Zelinski (43)
10/10/98	Scotland (ECQ)	A		Edinburgh	2-3 Hohlov-Simson (35), Smirnov (76)
14/10/98	Czech Republic (ECQ)	A		Teplice	1-4 Arbeiter (90)
18/11/98	Georgia		A	Tbilisi	1-3 Arbeiter (90)
21/11/98	Armenia		A	Abovyan	1-2 Zelinski (55)
28/11/98	Azerbaijan		A	Ganca	1-2 Kirs (68)
18/01/99	Israel		A	Tel-Aviv	0-7
22/01/99	Norway		N	Umm el-Fahm	3-3 Reim (75p), Zelinski (82, 89)
03/03/99	Romania		A	Bucharest	0-2
06/03/99	Azerbaijan		N	Larnaca	2-2 Viikmäe (46), Saviauk (71)
16/03/99	Cyprus		A	Larnaca	2-1 Zelinski (59), Terehhov (85)
31/03/99	Lithuania (ECQ)	A		Vilnius	2-1 Terehhov (49, 78)
05/06/99	Czech Republic (ECQ)	H		Tallinn	0-2
09/06/99	Lithuania (ECQ)	H		Tallinn	1-2 Oper (10)

TOP SCORERS

13 Konstantin KOLBASSENKO (Tallinna Sadam)
10 Andres OPER (FC Flora Tallinn)
   Indrek ZELINSKI (FC Flora Tallinn)
   Andrei KRÕLOV (Tallinna Sadam)
7 Tomas RAZHANAUSKAS (FC Flora Tallinn)
   Dmitri LIPARTOV (Trans Narva)
6 Indro OLUMETS (Tallinna Sadam)
5 Sergei TEREHHOV (FC Flora Tallinn)
   Stanislav KITTO (Trans Narva)
   Mark SHVETS (Tallinna Sadam)
   Ilja GUSSEV (Tallinna Sadam)
   Sergei KULICHENKO (FC Lantana Tallinn)

contingent of Estonian internationals, including veterans such as Urmas Kirs, Marko Kristal, Martin Reim and Viktor Alonen plus the excellent strike-force of Oper and Indrek Zelinski.

As for Tallinna Sadam, their final-day victory over Tulevik Viljandi was to be the last of the club's short history. Shortly after the conclusion of the championship it was announced that Sadam would be merged into newly-promoted Levadia Maardu, a club with strong financial backing and the ambition to match.

Levadia did not have to wait long before the arrival of their first trophy. A side featuring many of the best Sadam players together with a number of new-comers who had returned from spells abroad won the 1999 Estonian Cup, beating FC Flora in an eventful and exciting two-legged semi-final and then Tulevik Viljandi 3-2 in the final itself.

Estonian clubs continue to struggle in European competition - only Flora put up a fight, against Steaua Bucharest, as all three teams exited in the first round once again - but the national team, coached by FC Flora boss Teitur Thórdarson, continue to make progress, albeit of a rather jerky, stop-start nature.

INTERNATIONAL HONOURS

None

NATIONAL TEAM APPEARANCES 98/99

Coach - Teitur THÓRDARSON	MOL	BOS	EGY	SCO	CZE	GEO	ARM	AZB	ISR	NOR	ROM	AZB	CYP	LIT	CZE	LIT	Cps	Gls
Toomas TOHVER (24/04/73) - FC Flora Tallinn	G	G					G	G	G	G	G	G					21	-
Urmas KIRS (05/11/66) - FC Flora Tallinn	D	D	D	D	D74	D	D	D78	D	D	D53	D	D	D	D		69	5
Sergei HOHLOV-SIMSON (22/04/72) - FC Flora Tallinn	D	D	D	D	D	D	D	D83	D41	D	D	D	D	D			44	2
Viktor ALONEN (23/03/69) - FC Flora Tallinn	D	M	M	M	M	M	M85	D	s46	M82	s75	s53	M86	s90	M65	D	56	-
Janek MEET (02/05/74) - FC Flora Tallinn	D88	s81		D		D	s70	D57	s46	s90							33	-
Marko KRISTAL (02/06/73)																		
- FC Flora Tallinn/IF Elfsborg (SWE)	M	M	M	M		M89	M	M71	M90	s66	s69	M	s68	M	M81		85	6
Martin REIM (14/05/71) - FC Flora Tallinn	M	D	D	D	D				M	M	M	M	M	M	M	M	78	9
Maksim SMIRNOV (28/12/79) - FC Flora Tallinn	M	M	M	M	M46	M	M36	M	M46	s82	M	M	s86	M90	s65		20	1
													/74					
Sergei TEREHHOV (18/04/75) - FC Flora Tallinn	M63	M	M	M	M63			M	M74	M75	M	M86	M	M80	M75		24	4
Andres OPER (07/11/77) - FC Flora Tallinn	A	A	A68	A	A	A85	A65	A28	A	A		A55	A66	A	A		41	5
Indrek ZELINSKI (13/11/74) - FC Flora Tallinn	A76	A81	A85	A88	A	A53	s28		A46	s74	A	A69	s55	s66		A	50	13
Kristen VIIKMÄE (10/02/79) - FC Flora Tallinn	s63	s81	s68	s88	M46	s80	s36	M	s46	A74	A	A	A	A		M	36	2
Ivan O'KONNEL-BRONIN (10/02/73)																		
- Tulevik Viljandi/Levadia Maardu	s76					s63	s85	s65	s28					s74	s75		15	-
Teet ALLAS (02/06/77) - Tulevik Viljandi	s88					s89	s74										5	-
Mart POOM (03/02/72) - Derby County (ENG)			G	G	G	G							G	G	G	G	67	-
Urmas ROOBA (08/07/78) - FC Flora Tallinn		D81	D	D	D	D	D	s57	D46	s41							19	1
Jan ÕUN (08/02/77) - Tulevik Viljandi				s85		s77											4	-
Argo ARBEITER (05/12/77) - KTP (FIN)						s46	s53	A74	A77								25	6
Raivo NÕMMIK (11/02/77) - Tulevik Viljandi						s46											16	-
Mark SHVETS (01/10/76) - FC Flora Tallinn					M80	M28	M	s71	s74	M66	M	s86	M68	s80	s81		11	1
Erko SAVIAUK (20/10/77) - FC Flora Tallinn						s74	D70	D	s78	D	D	D	D	D	D		16	1
Raio PIIROJA (11/07/79) - Lelle SK						s85		s83									2	-
Marek LEMSALU (24/11/72) - FC Flora Tallinn									D	D	D	D	D	D	D	D	62	1
Urmas KAAL (06/04/73) - FC Kuressaare																D	1	-

The brilliant beginning to Estonia's Euro 2000 qualifying campaign - a 5-0 home win against the Faroe Islands - continued with a 1-1 draw away to Bosnia-Herzegovina. A month later the team were on the brink of an even more sensational result when they led 2-1 away to Scotland with only 12 minutes left. But the controversial sending-off of Marko Kristal took its toll and the Scots scored twice late on to win the match 3-2. Four days later a visit to the Czech Republic brought another defeat, this time a far more clear-cut one, by four goals to one, with Estonia's consolation coming only in stoppage-time.

A November trip to Caucasia brought three rather disheartening defeats, and there was a disastrous start to

PLAYERS OF THE SEASON

SERGEI TEREHHOV
Sergei Terehhov is not generally renowned for his goalscoring, but in 1998/99 the left-sided midfielder of FC Flora Tallinn and the Estonian national team made a habit of finding the net at vital times. Buoyed by a brilliant goal in Estonia's Euro 2000 opener against the Faroe Islands, he struck again against Steaua Bucharest in the Champions' League and five times more during his club's successful title defence. His most important goals, however, were saved until the following spring when he scored twice in Estonia's stunning 2-1 win in Lithuania - a feat which turned him overnight into a national hero. A naturally quiet and reserved individual, he has a very professional attitude to the game and is unlikely to allow his new-found status to affect him in any adverse manner.

ANDRES OPER
A young striker full of pace and enthusiasm, Andres Oper has long courted the interest of foreign clubs, his future prospects having received regular and lavish attention in the Estonian media. The talk and speculation is now over, however, for in the summer the 21-year-old agreed to a transfer from FC Flora Tallinn to newly-crowned Danish champions AaB in a deal worth a million US dollars. That makes Oper Estonia's costliest footballer, but the price-tag should not unduly trouble him. His new club will hope to see him reproduce the form he showed for Flora in the 1998 mini-championship, which he effectively settled in his team's favour by scoring the only goal in the Tallinna Sadam-Flora title decider.

EUROPEAN CUPS 98/99

CHAMPIONS' CUP
● FC FLORA TALLINN
Preliminary round STEAUA BUCURESTI (ROM)

A 1-4   Terehhov (40)
Tohver; Alonen, Hohlov-Simson, Lemsalu (Oper 61), Meet, Kristal, Reim, Razhanauskas, Terehhov, Zelinski (Smirnov 85), Viikmäe (Alsaker 46).

H 3-1   Smirnov (42), Zelinski (46), Oper (81)
Tohver; Alonen, Reim, Hohlov-Simson, Kirs, Terehhov (Oper 64), Razhanauskas, Smirnov, Alsaker, Kristal, Zelinski (Viikmäe 80).

CUP WINNERS' CUP
● FC LANTANA TALLINN
Qualifying round HEART OF MIDLOTHIAN (SCO)

H 0-1
Ussoltsev; Krasnopjorov, Kalimullin, Kolotsei, Bahmatski, Mitjunov, Borissov, Leitan, Valuiski (Tshelnokov 80), Gorjatshov (Kulikov 78), Kulitchenko.

A 0-5
Ussoltsev; Krasnopjorov, Kolotsei, Bahmatski, Mitjunov, Kulikov, Tjunin, Leitan, Valuiski (Tshelnokov 80), Gorjatshov, Kulitchenko.

UEFA CUP
● TALLINNA SADAM
Preliminary round POLONIA WARSZAWA (POL)

H 0-2
Martinsons; Vinogradov, Staleliunas, Prins, Liivamaa, Shvets, Rötshkov, Linnumäe, Kolbassenko, Olumets, Semjonov (Gussev 78).

A 1-3   Krõlov (3)
Martinsons; Vinogradov, Staleliunas, Prins, Liivamaa, Shvets, Rötshkov (Svetogor 60), Linnumäe, Kolbassenko, Olumets, Krõlov (Gussev 83).

1999 when Estonia were hammered 7-0 in Israel. However, a reinvigorating training programme in Cyprus brought the desired results when, in the first of the team's three spring qualifiers, they beat their near neighbours and long-time superiors Lithuania, 2-1 in Vilnius. But just when it seemed as if the Estonians were forcing themselves back into contention for the runners-up spot in the group, they lost both of their home fixtures in June - the first, not unexpectedly, against runaway group leaders the Czech Republic; the second, rather more distressingly, against a vengeful Lithuania, who came from behind to reverse the scoreline of the earlier fixture and significantly reduce Estonia's qualifying chances.

Even so, the profile of Estonian football is steadily improving, and several of the country's leading internationals have now joined goalkeeper Mart Poom as foreign professionals. Summer activity was particularly frantic, with FC Flora offloading Indrek Zelinski to Blackpool, Marek Lemsalu to Norwegian club Strømsgodset, Urmas Kirs and Martin Reim to Finnish side KTP and, for a record Estonian fee, Andres Oper to Danish champions AaB.

EP JÕHVI

Jalgpalliklubi Eesti Põlevkivi Jõhvi
Jaama 10
Jõhvi EE 2045
tel - (33) 64427
fax - (33) 70054
Year of Formation - 1974
President - Väino Viilup
Secretary - Rudolf Varunov
Coach - Pavel Lukyanov
Stadium - Eesti Põlevkivi (2,000)

	P	Ap	(s)	Gls
Roman ABORNEV	M	10	(3)	
Oleg BOGDANOV	D	13		
Juri BRAIKO	A	13		3
Aleksei GALOTSHKIN	A	2	(3)	1
Sergei IVANOV	D	1	(1)	
Pjotr JANUSHKEVITSH	M	12		1
Alex LUIK	M		(5)	
Oleg LUKJANOV	A	1	(10)	
Sergei MELNIKOV	M	10		1
Dmitri PEREDKOV	D	5	(5)	
Levani PARTSHIDZE	G	7		
Konstantin RUBTSOV	G/D	9		
Eduard SARAJEV	D	14		
Andrei SHKALETA	D	14		
Nikolai SHISHELOV	M	14		3
Erik SHTEINBERG	A	6		1
Vladimir TIHHON	M	11	(1)	
Artur VARUNOV	A	2	(3)	
Dmitri VORONIN	D	10		

18/07/98	Tulevik Viljandi	A	0-1	
25/07/98	Trans Narva	H	0-1	
01/08/98	FC Flora Tallinn	A	0-6	
08/08/98	FC Lantana Tallinn	H	1-2	Shteinberg
15/08/98	Tallinna Sadam	A	2-6	Braiko, Melnikov
22/08/98	Lelle SK	H	1-0	Shishelov
29/08/98	VMK Tallinn	A	0-4	
09/09/98	Tulevik Viljandi	H	0-2	
13/09/98	Trans Narva	A	1-5	Janushkevitsh
19/09/98	FC Flora Tallinn	H	2-7	Shishelov, Galotshkin
26/09/98	FC Lantana Tallinn	A	1-4	Braiko
03/10/98	Tallinna Sadam	H	0-3	
17/10/98	Lelle SK	A	2-1	Braiko, Shishelov
25/10/98	VMK Tallinn	H	0-2	

FC FLORA TALLINN

CLUB DIRECTORY

Football Club Flora Tallinn
Toomkooli 21
10130 Tallinn
tel - (6) 311397/279940/279941
fax - (6) 418021
Year of Formation - 1990
President - Aivar Pohlak
Secretary - Ainar Leppänen
Coach - Teitur Thórdarson
Stadium - Kadriorg (6,000)

MAJOR HONOURS
League Championship - (4)
1994, 1995, 1998, 1998 (autumn).
Domestic Cup - (2) 1995, 1998.

APPEARANCES 1998

		P	Ap	(s)	Gls
Viktor ALONEN	D		12	(1)	
Pål Christian ALSAKER (NOR)	M		2		
Trond Inge HAUGLAND (NOR)	D		2	(2)	
Sergei HOHLOV-SIMSON	D		11		1
Rene KAAS	G			(1)	
Urmas KIRS	D		12	(1)	1
Marko KRISTAL	M		13	(1)	3
Marek LEMSALU	D		3	(2)	
Janek MEET	D		4	(6)	
Andres OPER	A		13		10
Tomas RAZHANAUSKAS (LIT)	M		13	(1)	7
Martin REIM	M		13		2
Urmas ROOBA	D		3	(5)	1
Maksim SMIRNOV	M		11	(1)	2
Sergei TEREHHOV	M		11		5
Toomas TOHVER	G		14		
Kristen VIIKMÄE	M		6	(8)	4
Indrek ZELINSKI	A		11	(1)	10

LEAGUE RESULTS 1998

17/07/98	VMK Tallinn	H	3-0	Zelinski 2, Viikmäe
01/08/98	EP Jõhvi	H	6-0	Terehhov 2, Hohlov-Simson, Oper, Razhanauskas, Zelinski
08/08/98	Trans Narva	A	1-0	Smirnov
16/08/98	Lelle SK	A	5-2	Zelinski 2, Oper, Razhanauskas, Viikmäe
24/08/98	Tulevik Viljandi	A	5-0	Oper 2, Razhanauskas 2, Zelinski
01/09/98	FC Lantana Tallinn	H	3-0	Razhanauskas 2, Terehhov
09/09/98	VMK Tallinn	A	2-0	Terehhov, Oper
13/09/98	Tallinna Sadam	H	0-3	
19/09/98	EP Jõhvi	A	7-2	Viikmäe 2, Smirnov, Kristal, Razhanauskas, Reim, Terehhov
27/09/98	Trans Narva	H	3-3	Rooba, Kirs, Zelinski
02/10/98	Lelle SK	H	6-1	Zelinski 2, Oper 2, Reim, Kristal
17/10/98	Tulevik Viljandi	H	1-0	Oper
21/10/98	Tallinna Sadam	A	1-0	Oper
25/10/98	FC Lantana Tallinn	A	3-3	Kristal, Oper, Zelinski

FC LANTANA TALLINN

CLUB DIRECTORY

Football Club Lantana Tallinn
Kaupmehe 4-28
Tallinn EE 0001
tel - (2) 445549
fax - (2) 443738
Year of Formation - 1995
President - Sergei Belov
Secretary - Juri Tshurilkin
Coach - Anatoli Belov; Sergei Belov
Stadium - Viimsi (3,000)

MAJOR HONOURS
League Championship - (2) 1996, 1997.
Domestic Cup - (1) 1993.

LEAGUE RESULTS 1998

18/07/98	Lelle SK	A	2-0	Gruznov, Kalimullin
25/07/98	Tulevik Viljandi	H	3-0	Valuiski, Gruznov, Gorjatshov
01/08/98	Trans Narva	A	3-1	Mitjunov, Gruznov (p), Leitan
08/08/98	EP Jõhvi	A	2-1	Kulikov, Kulichenko
17/08/98	VMK Tallinn	H	0-0	
21/08/98	Tallinna Sadam	H	0-1	
01/09/98	FC Flora Tallinn	A	0-3	
09/09/98	Lelle SK	H	1-1	Gorjatshov
13/09/98	Tulevik Viljandi	A	3-0	Kulichenko, Leitan, Dolinin
21/09/98	Trans Narva	H	3-3	Krasnopjorov, Kulikov, Dolinin
26/09/98	EP Jõhvi	H	4-1	Dolinin 2, Tjunin, Krasnopjorov
05/10/98	VMK Tallinn	A	2-1	Jershov, Kulichenko
16/10/98	Tallinna Sadam	A	1-5	Leitan
25/10/98	FC Flora Tallinn	H	3-3	Kulichenko 2, Kolotsei

APPEARANCES 1998

	P	Ap	(s)	Gls
Andrei AFANASSOV	M	4	(3)	
Igor BAHMATSKI	D	13		
Andrei BORISSOV	M	4		
Vadim DOLININ	M	8		4
Oleg GORJATSHOV	M	10		2
Maksim GRUZNOV	A	3		3
Denis JERSHOV	M	8	(3)	1
Andrei KALIMULLIN	D	6		1
Dmitri KIRILLOV	M		(2)	
Pavel KISSELJOV	G	5	(1)	
Oleg KOLOTSEI	D	12		1
Andrei KRASNOPJOROV	D	14		2
Dmitri KULIKOV	D	9	(3)	2
Sergei KULICHENKO (RUS)	M	10		5
Vitali LEITAN	A	14		3
Sergei LEVOTSHSKI	M	2	(2)	
Dmitri MARTSHENKO	M		(1)	
Andrei MITJUNOV	M	13	(1)	1
Andrei TJUNIN	D	5		1
Vladimir TSHELNOKOV	A		(7)	
Sergei USSOLTSEV	G	9		
Vitali VALUISKI	A	5	(1)	1

LELLE SK

Lelle SK
Pargi 3
Kehtna EE3505
tel - (48) 75297
fax - (48) 75536
Year of Formation - 1990
President - Janno Kaljuvee
Secretary - Anne Raudnagel
Coach - Zaur Tsilingarashvili
Stadium - Kehtna Football School (1,500)

APPEARANCES 1998

	P	Ap	(s)	Gls
Aivar ANNISTE	M	14		1
Simen FOSSUM (NOR)	A	6		3
Kert HAAVISTU	M	14		1
Jesper JOHANSSON (FIN)	M	4	(4)	
Jaanus JUHALU	A	4	(3)	1
Rene KAAS	G	2	(1)	
Marek KAHR	D	10		
Kuldar KALJUSTE	D	4	(3)	
Siksten KASIMIR	M		(1)	
Margus KORJU	A	4	(6)	
Martin LEPA	D	5		
Joel LINDPERE	A		(1)	
Raio PIIROJA	D	6		1
Meelis ROOBA	M	3		1
Kristjan SAAR	M		(1)	
Tomas SIREVICIUS (LIT)	M	14		1
Andrei STEPANOV	D	13		
Janek TAAN	M	9	(1)	
Siim TEKKEL	M	8	(5)	
Silver TIKS	M	2	(2)	
Toomas TREIEL	G	11		
Unnar VALGEIRSSON (ISL)	M	8		1
Rain VESSENBERG	G	1		
Vitali VINK	D	12	(1)	

LEAGUE RESULTS 1998

18/07/98	FC Lantana Tallinn	H	0-2	
25/07/98	VMK Tallinn	A	1-2	Rooba (p)
01/08/98	Tallinna Sadam	H	0-7	
11/08/98	Tulevik Viljandi	A	0-3	
16/08/98	FC Flora Tallinn	H	2-5	Anniste, Juhalu
22/08/98	EP Jõhvi	A	0-1	
29/08/98	Trans Narva	H	1-5	Haavistu
09/09/98	FC Lantana Tallinn	A	1-1	Fossum
13/09/98	VMK Tallinn	H	1-1	Sirevicius
19/09/98	Tallinna Sadam	A	2-3	Valgeirsson, Piiroja
27/09/98	Tulevik Viljandi	H	0-0	
02/10/98	FC Flora Tallinn	A	1-6	Fossum
17/10/98	EP Jõhvi	H	1-2	Fossum
25/10/98	Trans Narva	A	0-1	

TALLINNA SADAM

CLUB DIRECTORY

Tallinna Sadama Jalgpalliklubi
Sadama Str. 21
Tallinn EE 0100
tel - (6) 318374
fax - (6) 318101
Year of Formation - 1992
President - Joel Tammeka
Secretary - Ivo Laino
Coach - Sergei Ratnikov
Stadium - Kadriorg (6,000)

MAJOR HONOURS
Domestic Cup - (2) 1996, 1997

APPEARANCES 1998

	P	Ap	(s)	Gls
Ilja GUSSEV	A	1	(10)	5
Konstantin KOLBASSENKO	M	13		13
Andrei KRÕLOV	A	13		10
Sergei LEONTJEV	A	7	(7)	3
Karl LEPIST	M		(2)	
Urmas LIIVAMAA	D	11		
Tarmo LINNUMÄE	D	13		1
Ernest MARTINSONS	G	13		
Indro OLUMETS	M	13		6
Igor PRINS	D	14		
Sergei RATNIKOV	M		(1)	
Andrei RUSSAK	M		(2)	
Maksim RÕTSHKOV	M	8	(4)	2
Aleksei SEMJONOV (LAT)	A	10	(1)	1
Dalius STALELIUNAS (LIT)	D	13	(1)	
Mark SHVETS	M	13		5
Stanislav SVETOGOR	M	11		2
Vaiko TAMMEVÄLI	G	1	(1)	

LEAGUE RESULTS 1998

17/07/98	Trans Narva	A	0-0	
01/08/98	Lelle SK	A	7-0	Krõlov 2, Svetogor, Kolbassenko,
				Leontjev, Shvets, Rõtshkov
07/08/98	VMK Tallinn	A	5-0	Shvets 2, Kolbassenko, Krõlov,
				Gussev
15/08/98	EP Jõhvi	H	6-2	Olumets 2, Linnumäe,
				Kolbassenko (p), Krõlov, Gussev
21/08/98	FC Lantana Tallinn	A	1-0	Olumets
30/08/98	Tulevik Viljandi	A	3-4	Semjonov, Olumets, Krõlov
09/09/98	Trans Narva	H	5-0	Kolbassenko 3 (1p), Svetogor,
				Krõlov
13/09/98	FC Flora Tallinn	A	3-0	Kolbassenko 2 (1p), Leontjev
19/09/98	Lelle SK	H	3-2	Kolbassenko, Rõtshkov, Olumets
28/09/98	VMK Tallinn	H	4-0	Olumets, Gussev, Krõlov,
				Kolbassenko
03/10/98	EP Jõhvi	A	3-0	Krõlov, Kolbassenko 2 (1p)
16/10/98	FC Lantana Tallinn	H	5-1	Krõlov 2, Shvets 2, Gussev
21/10/98	FC Flora Tallinn	H	0-1	
25/10/98	Tulevik Viljandi	H	3-0	Leontjev, Gussev, Kolbassenko

TRANS NARVA

CLUB DIRECTORY

Jalgpalliklubi Trans Narva
Kangelaste 45-20
Narva EE 2000
tel - (35) 43696/43975
fax - (35) 44284
Year of Formation - 1979
President - Nikolai Burdakov
Coach - Sergei Zamorski
Stadium - Kreenholm (2,000)

APPEARANCES 1998

	P	Ap	(s)	Gls
Andrei FROLOV	M	10	(4)	2
Konstantin GOLITSÕN	M	5	(8)	
Andrei JELISSEJEV	D	11	(2)	
Konstantin KARIN	M	5	(1)	1
Stanislav KITTO	D	14		5
Oleg KUROTSHKIN	D	9		
Dmitri LIPARTOV (RUS)	A	13		7
Aleksandr MARASHOV	M	12	(1)	4
Aleksandr MOLEV (RUS)	D	13		
Boris NEJOLOV	A		(6)	2
Jevgeni NOVIKOV	M		(8)	
Aleksandr RJABTSHUN	G	14		
Aleksandr TARASSENKOV	M	9	(3)	2
Nikolai TOSHTSHEV	M	13		4
Vitali VASHTSHENKO	D		(2)	
Viktor VJALOV	D	13		
Sergei ZAMORSKI	M	13	(2)	1

LEAGUE RESULTS 1998

17/07/98	Tallinna Sadam	H	0-0	
25/07/98	EP Jõhvi	A	1-0	Toshtshev (p)
01/08/98	FC Lantana Tallinn	H	1-3	Zamorski
08/08/98	FC Flora Tallinn	H	0-1	
15/08/98	Tulevik Viljandi	H	4-1	Tarassenkov, Karin, Nejolov, Toshtshev
22/08/98	VMK Tallinn	H	2-2	Kitto, Lipartov
29/08/98	Lelle SK	A	5-1	Lipartov 2, Marashov, Toshtshev, Nejolov
09/09/98	Tallinna Sadam	A	0-5	
13/09/98	EP Jõhvi	H	5-1	Lipartov, Tarassenkov, Marashov, Frolov 2
21/09/98	FC Lantana Tallinn	A	3-3	Kitto (p), Toshtshev, Lipartov
27/09/98	FC Flora Tallinn	A	3-3	Lipartov, Kitto 2
03/10/98	Tulevik Viljandi	A	0-0	
17/10/98	VMK Tallinn	A	3-0	Lipartov, Marashov, Kitto
25/10/98	Lelle SK	H	1-0	Marashov (p)

TULEVIK VILJANDI

CLUB DIRECTORY

Jalgpalliklubi Tulevik Viljandi
Ranna pst 6
Viljandi EE2900
tel - (43) 48015
fax - (43) 48016
Year of Formation - 1990
President - Dzintar Klavan
Secretary - Pille Söstra
Coach - Tarmo Rüütli
Stadium - Kalev (1,000)

APPEARANCES 1998

	P	Ap	(s)	Gls
Teet ALLAS	M	14		4
Andre ANIS	D	12	(1)	1
Janno JÜRISSON	M	3	(6)	1
Alari LELL	D	14		
Marko LELOV	M	1		
Priit MURUMETS	A	5		
Roland MÄE	A	4	(2)	
Eigo MÄGI	M	1	(3)	
Raivo NÕMMIK	D	13		
Ivan O'KONNEL-BRONIN	M	14		2
Gert OLESK	M	9		
Mati PARI	M	10		
Tarmo SAKS	A	11	(1)	1
Mihkel SIIM	D	11		1
Jaanus SIREL	M	8	(5)	2
Ain TAMMUS	G	14		
Vahur VAHTRAMÄE	M	2	(1)	
Jan ÕUN	A	8	(2)	2

LEAGUE RESULTS 1998

18/07/98	EP Jõhvi	H	1-0	Allas
25/07/98	FC Lantana Tallinn	A	0-3	
01/08/98	VMK Tallinn	A	2-2	O'Konnel-Bronin, Sirel
11/08/98	Lelle SK	H	3-0	Saks, Allas 2
15/08/98	Trans Narva	A	1-4	O'Konnel-Bronin
24/08/98	FC Flora Tallinn	H	0-5	
30/08/98	Tallinna Sadam	H	4-3	Allas (p), Õun 2, Sirel
09/09/98	EP Jõhvi	A	2-0	og (Abornev), Anis
13/09/98	FC Lantana Tallinn	H	0-3	
19/09/98	VMK Tallinn	H	2-1	Siim, Jürisson
27/09/98	Lelle SK	A	0-0	
03/10/98	Trans Narva	H	0-0	
17/10/98	FC Flora Tallinn	A	0-1	
25/10/98	Tallinna Sadam	A	0-3	

VMK TALLINN

CLUB DIRECTORY

VMK Tallinn
Pärnu mnt 69
Tallinn EE 0001
tel - (6) 261616
fax - (6) 261622
Year of Formation - 1995
President - Vjatsheslav Smirnov
Coach - Vjatsheslav Smirnov
Stadium - Kalev (12,000)

APPEARANCES 1998

	P	Ap	(s)	Gls
Oleg ANDREJEV	G	14		
Aleksandr EMBRICH	A	3	(2)	
Ruslan JAGUDIN	M	1	(4)	
Vitali IVAHNENKO	D	3	(1)	
Aleksei KAPUSTIN	D	14		1
Maksim KISSELJOV	M	14		3
Andrei KOSTIN	M	13		1
Jevgeni KURJANOV	D	14		1
Juri LEBRET	M	14		1
Denis MALOV	D		(1)	
Anton MÕKOLENKO	M	11		1
Ivan NOVIKOV	M	1	(1)	
Anatoli NOVOZILOV	A	12		4
Viktor PASSIKUTA	M	2	(1)	
Anton PAITSEV	A	10	(2)	2
Anton SEREDA	M		(1)	
Dmitri SKIPERSKI	M	10	(1)	1
Andrei SHAPOVALOV	M	2		
Semjon TROJANOV	M	9	(3)	
Vladimir URJUPIN	D	7		

LEAGUE RESULTS 1998

17/07/98	FC Flora Tallinn	A	0-3	
25/07/98	Lelle SK	H	2-1	Novozilov, Kisseljov
01/08/98	Tulevik Viljandi	H	2-2	Novozilov, Mõkolenko
07/08/98	Tallinna Sadam	H	0-5	
17/08/98	FC Lantana Tallinn	A	0-0	
22/08/98	Trans Narva	A	2-2	Paitsev, Novozilov
29/08/98	EP Jõhvi	H	4-0	Kapustin, Lebret, Paitsev, Kisseljov
09/09/98	FC Flora Tallinn	H	0-2	
13/09/98	Lelle SK	A	1-1	Kurjanov
19/09/98	Tulevik Viljandi	A	1-2	Kostin
28/09/98	Tallinna Sadam	A	0-4	
05/10/98	FC Lantana Tallinn	H	1-2	Kisseljov
17/10/98	Trans Narva	H	0-3	
25/10/98	EP Jõhvi	A	2-0	Novozilov, Skiperski

PROMOTED CLUB

SECOND DIVISION FINAL TABLE 1998

		Pd	W	D	L	F	A	Pt	GD
1	**Levadia Maardu**	**14**	**9**	**5**	**0**	**29**	**7**	**32**	**+22**
2	KSK Vigri Tallinn	14	8	3	3	28	12	27	+16
3	Lootus Kohtla-Järve	14	6	4	4	21	19	22	+2
4	FC Valga	14	5	4	5	14	11	19	+3
5	Sillamäe JK	14	5	3	6	15	23	18	-8
6	FC Kuressare	14	4	5	5	20	19	17	+1
7	Merkuur Tartu	14	5	0	9	21	31	15	-10
8	Pärnu JK	14	1	2	11	14	40	5	-26

PROMOTION/RELEGATION PLAY-OFF

KSK Vigri Tallinn 0, EP Jõhvi 2
EP Jõhvi 0, KSK Vigri Tallinn 0
(EP Jõhvi 2-0)

CLUB DIRECTORY

Levadia Maardu
Karjääri 4
EE 0030 Maardu
tel - (6) 379147
fax - (6) 319846
Year of Formation - 1998
President - Victor Levada
Secretary - Vladimir Plesjakov
Coach - Vladimir Plesjakov (99 - Sergei Ratnikov)
Stadium - Maardu (2,000)

FAROE ISLANDS

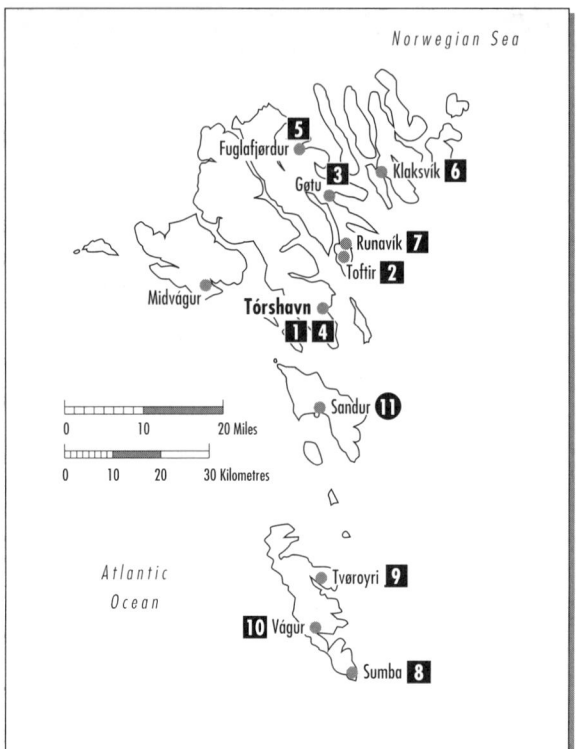

Norwegian Sea

Atlantic
Ocean

1	B36	344	7	NSÍ	350
2	B68	345	8	SUMBA	351
3	GÍ	346	9	TB	352
4	HB	347	10	VB	353
5	ÍF	348		Promoted clubs	
6	KÍ	349	11	B71	354

ROMANIAN BRINGS 'DOUBLE' TO HB

Simonsen's hard work starts to pay dividends

FEDERATION DIRECTORY

Fotboltssamband Føroya
Postboks 3028, Gundadalur, 110 Tórshavn

tel - 16707/57607	Year of Formation - 1979
fax - 19079	President - Torleif Sigurdsson
	Secretary - Isak Mikladal

Stadium - Svangaskard, Toftir (6,000)

After the humiliation of their opening 5-0 defeat away to Estonia, it went without saying that the Faroe Islands' Euro 2000 qualifying campaign could only get better. But not even national coach Allan Simonsen would have been bold enough to predict the extent of his team's improvement over the next 12 months.

There were no victories for the Faroes in their next six qualifiers, but with three draws and three narrow defeats, Simonsen and his players had every reason to feel proud and delighted with their progress. The local fans were nothing short of ecstatic as they watched their team draw with both Scotland and Bosnia-Herzegovina at the beginning of June.

In fact, the team should have been boasting an unbeaten home record. Their first game in Toftir, against the Czech Republic, was heading for a 0-0 draw when the visitors unsportingly failed to return the ball after it had been kicked out of play to enable assistance to be given to a

Czech player. In the ensuing move Vladimir Smicer scored the winning goal - to the understandable rage of the home players and fans.

It was another nine months before the islanders' next home qualifier, but it was certainly worth the wait as

LEAGUE CHAMPIONSHIP RESULTS 1998

		1	2	3	4	5	6	7	8	9	10
1	B36		2-1	1-1	0-1	7-2	3-2	2-0	6-2	7-0	8-2
2	B68	2-3		0-1	0-0	3-3	1-5	3-2	6-0	4-3	2-1
3	Gĺ	5-2	2-2		1-3	3-1	2-2	5-1	11-1	3-0	0-2
4	HB	2-3	3-1	3-0		3-2	4-0	2-1	4-1	4-3	5-1
5	ĺF	0-0	2-2	0-4	1-10		0-0	1-1	6-0	1-2	2-5
6	Kĺ	1-1	4-3	4-2	2-2	2-0		4-1	4-1	10-0	2-1
7	NSĺ	2-0	4-1	3-1	0-4	1-1	0-0		3-0	1-0	4-1
8	Sumba	0-10	1-2	1-1	1-2	1-0	2-5	1-6		3-2	1-1
9	TB	0-3	0-5	1-5	1-4	2-2	1-3	2-2	2-2		2-2
10	VR	1-1	3-1	3-1	1-1	1-1	0-4	0-5	7-0	0-0	

LEAGUE CHAMPIONSHIP FINAL TABLE 1998

			Home				Away				Total						
		P	W	D	L	F	A	W	D	L	F	A	W	D	L	F	A	P	GD
1	HB	18	8	0	1	30	12	6	3	0	27	7	14	3	1	57	19	45	+38
2	Kĺ	18	7	2	0	33	11	4	3	2	21	13	11	5	2	54	24	38	+30
3	B36	18	7	1	1	36	11	4	3	2	23	13	11	4	3	59	24	37	+35
4	Gĺ	18	5	2	2	32	14	3	2	4	16	16	8	4	6	48	30	28	+18
5	NSĺ	18	6	2	1	18	8	2	2	5	19	20	8	4	6	37	28	28	+9
6	B68	18	4	2	3	21	18	2	2	5	18	21	6	4	8	39	39	22	0
7	VB	18	3	4	2	11	14	2	2	5	16	26	5	6	7	27	40	21	-13
8	ĺF	18	1	4	4	13	24	0	4	5	12	23	1	8	9	25	47	11	-22
9	Sumba	18	2	5	2	11	29	0	1	8	7	44	2	3	13	18	73	9	-55
10	TB	18	0	4	5	11	28	1	1	7	10	33	1	5	12	21	61	8	-40

defender Hans Frodi Hansen, a relative newcomer to the team, headed in a last-gasp equaliser to earn an unexpected point against Scotland. Four days later Iceland-based striker Uni Arge struck twice to give the Faroes' fans further cause for celebration in a 2-2 draw with Bosnia.

As yet the club sides from the Faroe Islands still have some way to go to match the exploits of the national team in international competition. Once again, in 1998, all three European representatives fell at the first hurdle. The six matches produced five defeats and one victory.

Not surprisingly, that solitary win was achieved by HB of Torshavn - unquestionably the Islands' team of the year. With a 2-0 first-leg advantage over VPS of Finland, there was considerable optimism that HB would go through to the qualifying round of the UEFA Cup. But they suffered a collapse in the return, going down 4-0.

That was one of just three defeats incurred by HB in the 28 official matches they played in 1998 - as opposed to 22 victories. For the first time in eight years the club from the capital shook off their 'nearly men' tag and won the national title. The Cup came their way, too - for the 25th time in the club's history.

NATIONAL TEAM RESULTS 98/99

19/08/98	Bosnia-Herzegovina (ECQ)	A	Sarajevo	0-1	
06/09/98	Czech Republic (ECQ)	H	Toftir	0-1	
10/10/98	Lithuania (ECQ)	A	Vilnius	0-0	
14/10/98	Scotland (ECQ)	A	Aberdeen	1-2	Petersen (86p)
03/03/99	Andorra	A	San Fernando	0-0	
05/06/99	Scotland (ECQ)	H	Toftir	1-1	Hansen H.F. (90)
09/06/99	Bosnia-Herzegovina (ECQ)	H	Toftir	2-2	Arge (38, 47)

HB were revitalised by the arrival of Romanian coach Ion Geolgau, who was recruited by the club's president Gunnar Mohr on a monthly salary of US$2,000 plus board and expenses (quite a package by local standards) and who immediately brought a professional approach to training and tactics. His promise that HB would not lose a game under his command was not far short of coming true. The team ran away with the title, finishing up with a seven-point winning margin over runners-up KÍ after leading the way throughout.

Between them striker Suni Fridi Johannesen and national team veteran Allan Mørkøre scored 35 of the team's 57 goals, with each of them scoring at a rate of precisely one goal per game. Johannesen managed to outscore his team-mate by netting four goals in the final match - a 10-1 victory over ÍF. HB thus became the fourth different team to score ten goals or more in a single match during the season, the

NATIONAL TEAM APPEARANCES 98/99

Coach - Allan SIMONSEN	BOS	CZE	LIT	SCO	AND	SCO	BOS	Cps	Gls
Jakup MIKKELSEN (14/08/70) - Herfølge BK (DEN)	G	G	G	G		G	G	10	-
Hans Frodi HANSEN (25/08/75) - HB	D	D	D	D	D69	D	D	7	1
Jens Kristian HANSEN (03/09/71) - B36	D	D	D	D	D			27	2
Pol THORSTEINSSON (17/11/73) - B36	D	D	D	D	D	D	D	15	-
Oli JOHANNESEN (06/05/72) - TB	D	D	D	D	D	D	D	40	1
Henning JARNSKOR (15/11/72) - GÍ	D	D	D	D81	M		s65	28	2
Samal JOENSEN (15/01/75) - GÍ	M		M	M		M	M	9	-
Julian JOHNSSON (24/02/75) - Kongsvinger IL (NOR)	M	M	M	M	M	M	M	26	1
Allan MØRKØRE (22/11/71) - HB	M	M				M	M	D	47	1
Uni ARGE (21/01/71) - Leiftur (ISL)/Aarhus Fremad (DEN)	A78	A79	A87	A69	A	s82	A87	24	5
John PETERSEN (22/04/72) - B36	A	A	A	A		A82	A	21	2
Jakup a BORG (26/10/79) - B36	s78		s87	s69	A71	s70		5	-
Todi JONSSON (02/02/72) - FC København (DEN)		M	M	M		M	M	34	8
Magni JARNSKOR (16/11/68) - GÍ		s79						34	1
John HANSEN (16/03/74) - KÍ			s81		s85			3	-
Jens Martin KNUDSEN (11/06/67) - Leiftur (ISL)				G				56	-
Øssur HANSEN (07/01/71) - GÍ					M	M85	M65	33	1
Joannes JOENSEN (27/11/70) - HB					s69	D70	s87	3	-
Hedin a LAKJUNI (13/02/78) - KÍ					s71			1	-

INTERNATIONAL HONOURS

None

TOP SCORERS

20	Jakup a BORG (B36)
18	Suni Fridi JOHANNESEN (HB)
	Kurt MØRKØRE (KÍ)
17	John PETERSEN (B36)
	Allan MØRKØRE (HB)
13	Samal JOENSEN (GÍ)
11	Henning JARNSKOR (GÍ)
10	Røgvi JACOBSEN (KÍ)

EUROPEAN CUPS 98/99

CHAMPIONS' CUP
● B36
Preliminary round BEITAR JERUSALEM (ISR)
A 1-4 Petersen (73p)
Høgnesen E.; Borg (Guttesen 46), Hansen, Danielsen, Thorsteinsson, Milenkovic, Thomassen, Larsen (Mørk 78), Samuelsen, Sivic, Petersen.
H 0-1
Høgnesen E.; Thorsteinsson, Danielsen, Hansen, Guttesen, Thomassen (Joensen 82), Samuelsen (Mørk 74), Sivic (Larsen 87), Milenkovic, Borg, Petersen.

CUP WINNERS' CUP
● GÍ
Qualifying round MTK HUNGÁRIA FC (HUN)
H 1-3 Olsen Su. (8)
Joensen Su.; Justinussen R., Olsen Sv. (Nesa 83), Justinussen S.P., Ennigard, Jørgensen (Olsen J.P. 59), Jarnskor P. (Jacobsen 65), Olsen Su., Joensen Sa., Jarnskor M., Jarnskor H..
A 0-7
Joensen Su.; Justinussen R. (Hansen L. 85), Olsen J.P., Jørgensen, Olsen Sv., Olsen Su., Jarnskor P., Koensen Sa. (Tvorfoss 46), Jacobsen, Jarnskor M., Jarnskor H..

UEFA CUP
● HB
Preliminary round VPS (FIN)
H 2-0 Johannesen S.F. (28, 73)
Johannesen K.L.; Joensen, Hansen, Dam J., Lag, Mørkøre, Nolsø, Danielsen (Arting 63), Rasmussen J.E., Flotum (Dam J.H. 69), Johannesen S.F. (Mohr 78).
A 0-4
Johannesen K.L.; Joensen, Hansen, Dam J. (Lag 46), Mohr, Mørkøre, Rasmussen I., Nolsø, Rasmussen J.E., Flotum, Johannesen S.F..

others being GÍ (11-1 v Sumba), KÍ (10-0 v TB) and B36 10-0 v Sumba).

KÍ, coached by former national team sweeper Joannes Jakobsen, returned to the fore in 1998 but they had to

PLAYER OF THE SEASON

JAKUP A BORG
B36 had to concede the championship to their Tórshavn rivals HB but they had the undisputed player of the year in teenage striker Jakup a Borg. The youngster had only had a marginal influence on B36's title triumph the previous season, but the club's Yugoslav coach Tomislav Sivic placed great faith in him and that was repaid with a succession of goals, 20 in total, which made him the league's top scorer. A national team representative at youth level, his first senior cap came against Bosnia-Herzegovina in Sarajevo in August 1998 and he remained in the squad for all of the subsequent Euro 2000 qualifiers. Alerted by reports of his talent, Liverpool and Watford have already invited him over to England for trials.

settle for second place in both league and Cup. They had a nasty habit of conceding costly late goals - as in their 2-3 defeat by B36 and the 2-2 draw with HB - and that flaw was to condemn them in the Cup final, when three minutes of defensive madness allowed HB to score twice, through Hans a Lag and Andrew av Flotum, and secure the first leg of their 'double'.

B36 and GÍ, two of the pre-season favourites, both made wretched starts to the league campaign and only began to do themselves justice in the second half of the season. B36, the defending champions, were the only team to beat HB (3-2) and they also provided the league's top scorer in 20-goal Jakup a Borg. His strike-partner John Petersen was not far behind, and he also scored 13 goals in the Cup to become the country's top aggregate marksman with 30 goals over the two competitions.

DOMESTIC CUP 1998

1/8 FINALS
(Played in Groups)
Final Positions
Group A - 1 HB 13 pts; 2 KÍ 13 pts; 3 NSÍ 9 pts, 4 FS Vágar 0 pts
Group B - 1 B36 13 pts; 2 ÍF 10 pts; 3 TB 8 pts; 4 Sumba 3 pts
Group C - 1 GÍ 14 pts; 2 B68 10 pts; 3 VB 9 pts; 4 Royn 0 pts

QUARTER-FINALS
GÍ 4 (Jarnskor H. 15, 74p, Olsen J.P. 40, og 64), NSÍ 1 (Hansen O. 44)
KÍ 3 (Lakjuni 19, Wierzbicki 60, Danielsen 87), ÍF 1 (Eliasen B. 44)
B36 8 (Borg 5, 51, 58, Petersen 33, 60, 79, 87, Clementsen 83), VB 0
HB 2 (Johannesen S.F. 14, Mørkøre 88p), B68 0

SEMI-FINALS
KÍ 2 (Wierzbicki 28, Jacobsen 72),
GÍ 1 (Olsen Sv. 46)
GÍ 1 (Jørgensen 1), KÍ 1 (Wierzbicki 69)
(KÍ 3-2)

HB 4
(Flotum 47, 81, Danielsen 61, Lag 72),
B36 1 (Sivic 85)
B36 2 (Borg 3, Petersen 33),
HB 2 (Johannesen S.F. 26, 84)
(HB 6-3)

FINAL
17/06/98, Tórshavn
HB 2 Lag (70), Flotum (73)
KÍ 0
referee - Lidarenda
HB - Johannesen K.L.; Mohr (Joensen 67), Hansen, Dam J., Lag, Rasmussen J.E., Nolsøe, Danielsen (Arting 36), Mørkøre, Johannesen S.F. (Rasmussen I. 90), Flotum.
KÍ - Steig; Andreasen J., Mørkøre, Høgnesen, Hansen, Jacobsen, Wierzbicki, Joensen J., Joensen A., Bertholdsen (Joensen Ar. 65), Lakjuni (Danielsen 80).

B36

CLUB DIRECTORY

Boltfelagid 36 (B 36)
Postrum 1136
110 Tórshavn
tel - 311936
fax - 318036
Year of Formation - 1936
President - Sjurdur Horsdal
Secretary - Per Hansen
Coach - Tomislav Sivic
Stadium - Gundadalur (8,000)

MAJOR HONOURS
League Championship - (6)
1936, 1948, 1950, 1959, 1962, 1997.
Domestic Cup - (1) 1991.

APPEARANCES 1998

	P	Ap	(s)	Gls
Jakup a BORG	A	16	(1)	20
Sigfridur CLEMENTSEN	A	1	(1)	
Arnbjørn DANIELSEN	D	18		1
Jan GUTTESEN	M	17	(1)	
Jens Kristian HANSEN	M	16		5
Carl HØGNESEN	D	3	(3)	
Egin HØGNESEN	G	18		
Kenneth JACOBSEN	M		(1)	
Jakup Martin JOENSEN	D	1	(7)	
Herbert i Lon JACOBSEN	D	2	(4)	
Allan MANAI	M	6	(8)	1
Ninoslav MILANKOVIC (YUG)	M	12	(2)	3
Aki MØRK	D	1	(4)	
Gunnar NIELSEN	A		(4)	
John PETERSEN	A	16		17
Toralvur POULSEN	D	1		
Bjarni PRIOR	M	10	(3)	1
Røgvi ROIN	M	10	(6)	1
Ronnie SAMUELSEN	D	13	(3)	4
Tomislav SIVIC (YUG)	M	4	(3)	2
Sigmund av TEIGUM	G		(1)	
Mikkjal THOMASSEN	M	16	(1)	3
Pol THORSTEINSSON	D	17		

LEAGUE RESULTS 1998

03/05/98	HB	H	0-1	
10/05/98	KÍ	A	1-1	Petersen
17/05/98	Sumba	H	6-2	Borg 3 (1p), Petersen, Roin, og
24/05/98	ÍF	A	0-0	
01/06/98	B68	H	2-1	Petersen 2
07/06/98	TB	H	7-0	Borg 4, Petersen 2, Manai
13/06/98	NSÍ	A	0-2	
21/06/98	GÍ	H	1-1	Hansen
28/06/98	VB	A	1-1	Borg
02/08/98	HB	A	3-2	Danielsen, Borg, Petersen
08/08/98	KÍ	H	3-2	Borg, Thomassen, Milankovic
16/08/98	Sumba	A	10-0	Borg 5, Petersen 4, Milankovic
23/08/98	ÍF	H	7-2	Thomassen, Petersen 2, Borg,
				Samuelsen, Milankovic, Sivic
30/08/98	B68	A	3-2	Thomassen, Petersen 2
13/09/98	TB	A	3-0	Hansen 2, Sivic
20/09/98	NSÍ	H	2-0	Samuelsen 2
27/09/98	GÍ	A	2-5	Borg 2 (1p)
03/10/98	VB	H	8-2	Borg 2, Petersen 2, Hansen 2,
				Samuelsen, Prior

B68

CLUB DIRECTORY

Tofta Ítrottarfelag B 68
650 Toftir
tel - 448068
fax - 449050
Year of Formation - 1962
President - Niclas Davidsen
Secretary - Olavur Jensen
Coach - Petur Simonsen (99 - Bjørn Krogh)
Stadium - Svangaskard (6,000)

MAJOR HONOURS
League Championship - (3) 1984, 1985, 1992.

APPEARANCES 1998

	P	Ap	(s)	Gls
Frodi BENJAMINSEN	M	16	(1)	8
Johannus DANIELSEN	D	1		
Jakup DJURHUUS	D	17		1
Ingi HANSEN	M	8	(3)	6
Øssur HANSEN	M	17		6
Samal Erik HENTZE	D	14		
Aksel HØJGAARD	A	2	(1)	3
Olaf HØJGAARD	M	10	(2)	1
Edmund JACOBSEN	D	9		
Øssur JACOBSEN	M	8	(6)	3
Allan G. JOENSEN	G	3		
Oleif JOENSEN	D	4		
Sergei KREKSJIN (RUS)	M	3	(6)	
Mannbjørn NESA	D		(3)	
Arnfinn OLSEN	M	9	(3)	1
Jakup Eli OLSEN	M	13	(1)	
Bogi PETERSEN	A	1	(2)	1
Jan PETERSEN	D	17		3
Magnus POULSEN	G	15		
Niels S. POULSEN	D	13		
Andrei STAKHANOV (RUS)	A	9	(5)	6
Janus THOMSEN	D	9	(3)	

LEAGUE RESULTS 1998

03/05/98	Sumba	A	2-1	Petersen J. (p), Benjaminsen
10/05/98	GÍ	H	0-1	
17/05/98	ÍF	A	2-2	Stakhanov, Højgaard O.
24/05/98	VB	H	2-1	Stakhanov, Hansen Ø.
01/06/98	B36	A	1-2	Jacobsen Ø.
07/06/98	HB	H	0-0	
13/06/98	TB	A	5-0	Hansen Ø., Benjaminsen,
				Stakhanov, Hansen I. 2
21/06/98	KÍ	H	1-5	Djurhuus
28/06/98	NSÍ	A	1-4	Jacobsen Ø.
02/08/98	Sumba	H	6-0	Hansen Ø., Benjaminsen,
				Stakhanov, Hansen I. 3
08/08/98	GÍ	A	2-2	Stakhanov, Hansen I.
16/08/98	ÍF	H	3-3	Stakhanov (p), Hansen Ø.,
				Petersen J.
23/08/98	VB	A	1-3	Petersen J. (p)
30/08/98	B36	H	2-3	Benjaminsen, Jacobsen Ø.
13/09/98	HB	A	1-3	Petersen B.
20/09/98	TB	H	4-3	Benjaminsen 2, Olsen A.,
				Højgaard A.
27/09/98	KÍ	A	3-4	Hansen Ø. 2, Højgaard A.
03/10/98	NSÍ	H	3-2	Benjaminsen 2, Højgaard A.

GÍ

CLUB DIRECTORY

Gotu Ítrottarfelag (GÍ)
Postrum 4
510 Gotu
tel - 442024
fax - 442024
Year of Formation - 1926
President - Jøgvan Gregersen
Secretary - Sonja a Lidarenda
Coach - Johan Nielsen
Stadium - Gotu (3,000)

MAJOR HONOURS
League Championship - (6)
1983, 1986, 1993, 1994, 1995, 1996.
Domestic Cup - (4) 1983, 1985, 1996, 1997.

APPEARANCES 1998

	P	Ap	(s)	Gls
Poul ENNIGARD	D	17		1
Leivur HANSEN	M		(4)	
Ronni HANSEN	D		(1)	
Heini HEINASON	A	1		
Magni JACOBSEN	D	4	(8)	2
Henning JARNSKOR	A	18		11
Magni JARNSKOR	M	16		4
Pauli JARNSKOR	M	17		
Samal JOENSEN	M	16		13
Sunnvard JOENSEN	G	18		
Søren Skov JØRGENSEN (DEN)	A	15		3
Runi JUSTINUSSEN	D	9	(1)	2
Simun Petur JUSTINUSSEN	D	12		7
Samson NESA	D	6	(2)	
Joan Petur OLSEN	M	13	(2)	1
Suni OLSEN	M	12	(4)	3
Svenn OLSEN	D	15		1
Hans Pauli PETERSEN	A		(1)	
Johannes PETERSEN	D		(1)	
Janus RASMUSSEN	D	8		
Jan SKORADAL	M		(4)	
Erland TVORFOSS	A	1	(2)	

LEAGUE RESULTS 1998

03/05/98	NSÍ	A	1-3	Jørgensen
10/05/98	B68	A	1-0	Jarnskor M.
17/05/98	VB	H	0-2	
24/05/98	HB	A	0-3	
01/06/98	KÍ	H	2-2	Joensen Sa., Jacobsen
07/06/98	Sumba	A	1-1	Ennigard
13/06/98	ÍF	H	3-1	Joensen Sa. 2, Olsen Sv.
21/06/98	B36	A	1-1	Jarnskor H.
28/06/98	TB	H	3-0	Jarnskor H. 2, Olsen Su.
02/08/98	NSÍ	H	5-1	Jarnskor H., Joensen Sa. 3,
				Justinussen S.P.
08/08/98	B68	H	2-2	Joensen Sa., Jørgensen
16/08/98	VB	A	1-3	Jarnskor H.
23/08/98	HB	H	1-3	Jarnskor H. (p)
30/08/98	KÍ	A	2-4	Jarnskor H., Jacobsen
13/09/98	Sumba	H	11-1	Jarnskor H., Joensen Sa. 3,
				Jarnskor M., Olsen J.P.,
				Justinussen S.P. 4, Justinussen R.
20/09/98	ÍF	A	4-0	Jarnskor H., Joensen Sa. 2 (1p),
				Justinussen S.P.
27/09/98	B36	H	5-2	Jarnskor H. (p), Joensen Sa.,
				Jarnskor M., Olsen Su.,
				Justinussen S.P.
03/10/98	TB	A	5-1	Jarnskor H., Jarnskor M., Olsen Su.,
				Justinussen R., Jørgensen

HB

CLUB DIRECTORY

Havnar Boltfelag (HB)
Postrum 1333
110 Tórshavn
tel - 314046/283346
fax - 318502
Year of Formation - 1904
President - Gunnar Mohr
Secretary - Steinfinnur Mittelstein
Coach - Ion Geolgau
Stadium - Gundadalur (8,000)

MAJOR HONOURS
League Championship - (15) 1955, 1960, 1963,
1964, 1965, 1971, 1973, 1974, 1975, 1978,
1981, 1982, 1988, 1990, 1998.
Domestic Cup - (25) 1955, 1957, 1959, 1962,
1963, 1964, 1968, 1969, 1971, 1972, 1973,
1975, 1976, 1978, 1979, 1980, 1981, 1982,
1984, 1987, 1988, 1989, 1992, 1995, 1998.

APPEARANCES 1998

	P	Ap	(s)	Gls
Roi ARTING	M	4	(12)	1
Jan DAM	D	7	(2)	
John Heri DAM	M	4	(10)	2
Hallur DANIELSEN	D	11	(3)	1
Andrew av FLOTUM	A	8	(3)	3
Hans Frodi HANSEN	D	17		2
Eydun HØJGAARD	D		(1)	
Johannes JOENSEN	A	16		5
Bardur JOHANNESEN	G	2	(1)	
Kaj Leo JOHANNESEN	G	16		
Suni Fridi JOHANNESEN	A	18		18
Hans a LAG	D	17		
Magni a LAKJUNI	M	7		2
Bjarki MOHR	D	15	(3)	1
Allan MØRKØRE	M	17		17
Bardur MORTANSSON	M		(1)	
Runi NOLSØE	D	16		1
Ingi RASMUSSEN	M	6	(12)	
Jens Erik RASMUSSEN	M	17	(1)	4

LEAGUE RESULTS 1998

03/05/98	B36	A	1-0	Mørkøre (p)
10/05/98	TB	H	4-3	Johannesen S.F., Mørkøre, Nolsøe,
				Dam J.H.
17/05/98	NSÍ	A	4-0	Johannesen S.F., Mohr, Joensen,
				Flotum
24/05/98	GÍ	H	3-0	Johannesen S.F. 2, Mørkøre
01/06/98	VB	A	1-1	Flotum
07/06/98	B68	A	0-0	
13/06/98	KÍ	H	4-0	Rasmussen J.E., Mørkøre 2, Flotum
21/06/98	Sumba	A	2-1	Mørkøre 2
28/06/98	ÍF	H	3-2	Johannesen S.F., Hansen, Joensen
02/08/98	B36	H	2-3	Johannesen S.F., Rasmussen J.E.
08/08/98	TB	A	4-1	Mørkøre 2 (1p), Dam J.H., Lakjuni
16/08/98	NSÍ	H	2-1	Johannesen S.F. 2
23/08/98	GÍ	A	3-1	Johannesen S.F., Joensen, Mørkøre
30/08/98	VB	H	5-1	Arting, Mørkøre 2 (1p),
				Johannesen S.F. 2
13/09/98	B68	H	3-1	Mørkøre 2, Johannesen S.F.
20/09/98	KÍ	A	2-2	Rasmussen J.E., Mørkøre
27/09/98	Sumba	H	4-1	Joensen, Johannesen S.F. 2, Hansen
03/10/98	ÍF	A	10-1	Lakjuni, Johannesen S.F. 4,
				Rasmussen J.E., Mørkøre 2,
				Danielsen, Joensen

ÍF

CLUB DIRECTORY

Ítrottarfelag Fuglafjardar (ÍF)
Postrum 94
530 Fuglafjørdur
tel - 444636
fax - 444696/444225
Year of Formation - 1946
President - Unn E. Petersen
Secretary - Jon Niclasen
Coach - Piotr Krakowski
Stadium - Fuglafjordur (3,000)

MAJOR HONOURS
League Championship - (1) 1979.

APPEARANCES 1998

		P	Ap	(s)	Gls
Ken BAERENDSEN	G			(1)	
Ken BAERENDSEN	D			(2)	
Jakup BALDVINSSON	A			(2)	
Hergeir ELDEVIG	D	1		(3)	
Bartal ELIASEN	D	16			
Simun ELIASEN	A	2			
Høgni HANSEN	D	15		(1)	
Torkil HANSEN	D	15		(3)	
Jacek JARLACZYK (POL)	M	12			
Erling JOENSEN	G	17			
Torstein JOENSEN	D	11			
Viggo JOHANNESEN	M	4		(1)	1
Piotr KRAKOWSKI (POL)	M	4		(2)	
Bardur a LAKJUNI	A	15		(2)	6
Maciej MARINJAK (POL)	A	17			7
Bogi NON	D	1		(1)	
Alfred OLSEN	G	1			
Aslakkur R. PETERSEN	A	17		(1)	5
Eydalvur PETERSEN	D	17			2
Janus PETERSEN	D			(2)	
Runi PETERSEN	A			(1)	
Roy ROIN	D	15		(1)	
Mortan THOMSEN	M	1		(6)	
Egil ZACHARIASSEN	M	17			4

LEAGUE RESULTS 1998

03/05/98	KÍ	H	0-0	
10/05/98	Sumba	A	0-1	
17/05/98	B68	H	2-2	Marinjak 2
24/05/98	B36	H	0-0	
01/06/98	TB	A	2-2	Zachariassen, Lakjuni
07/06/98	NSÍ	H	1-1	Petersen A.R.
13/06/98	VB	H	2-5	Petersen E., Marinjak
21/06/98	GÍ	A	1-3	Marinjak
28/06/98	HB	A	2-3	Petersen A.R., Petersen E.
02/08/98	KÍ	A	0-2	
08/08/98	Sumba	H	6-0	Petersen A.R., Zachariassen 2,
				Marinjak 2, Lakjuni
16/08/98	B68	A	3-3	Marinjak, Lakjuni 2
23/08/98	B36	A	2-7	Zachariassen, Lakjuni
30/08/98	TB	H	1-2	Lakjuni
13/09/98	NSÍ	A	1-1	Petersen A.R.
20/09/98	GÍ	H	0-4	
27/09/98	VB	A	1-1	Johannesen
03/10/98	HB	H	1-10	Petersen A.R. (p)

KÍ

CLUB DIRECTORY

Klaksvíkar Ítróttarfelag (KÍ)
Postrum 204
700 Klaksvik
tel - 456184
fax - 456167
Year of Formation - 1904
President - Svend Jacobsen
Secretary - Heri Ellingsgaard
Coach - Joannes Jakobsen (99 - Petur Mohr)
Stadium - Klaksvik (4,000)

MAJOR HONOURS
League Championship - (16) 1942, 1945, 1952,
1953, 1954, 1956, 1957, 1958, 1961, 1966,
1967, 1968, 1969, 1970, 1972, 1991.
Domestic Cup - (4) 1966, 1967, 1990, 1994.

APPEARANCES 1998

	P	Ap	(s)	Gls
Jan ANDREASEN	D	18		
Kristian ANDREASEN	D		(2)	
Harley BERTHOLDSEN	D	16		3
Olgar DANIELSEN	A	3	(5)	2
John HANSEN	M	17		6
Simun Waag HØGNESEN	D	13	(4)	1
Røgvi JACOBSEN	A	16	(1)	10
Allan JOENSEN	M	8		
Arnold JOENSEN	M	18		4
Jan JOENSEN	D	12		
Hedin a LAKJUNI	M	16	(1)	4
Helmar LASSEN	D		(1)	
Johan LUTZEN	D	1	(4)	1
Zoran MANCIC (YUG)	M	6	(10)	1
Kurt MØRKØRE	A	12	(3)	18
Gunnar a STEIG	G	18		
Marek WIERZBICKI (POL)	M	18		2
Poul Juul WILHELMSEN	A	6	(2)	1
Fridin ZISKASON	D		(1)	

LEAGUE RESULTS 1998

03/05/98	ÍF	A	0-0	
10/05/98	B36	H	1-1	Jacobsen
17/05/98	TB	A	3-1	Danielsen, Jacobsen, Bertholdsen
24/05/98	NSÍ	H	4-1	Joensen Ar., Jacobsen 2, Lakjuni
01/06/98	GÍ	A	2-2	Hansen, Danielsen
07/06/98	VB	H	2-1	Jacobsen 2
13/06/98	HB	A	0-4	
21/06/98	B68	A	5-1	Joensen Ar. 2, Hansen, Jacobsen, og
28/06/98	Sumba	H	4-1	Wierzbicki, Hansen 2, Mørkøre
02/08/98	ÍF	H	2-0	Høgnesen (p), Mørkøre
08/08/98	B36	A	2-3	Hansen, Lakjuni
16/08/98	TB	H	10-0	Lakjuni (p), Joensen Ar., Wierzbicki,
				Mancic, Mørkøre 5, Wilhelmsen
23/08/98	NSÍ	A	0-0	
30/08/98	GÍ	H	4-2	Hansen, Mørkøre 2, Lutzen
13/09/98	VB	A	4-0	Lakjuni, Mørkøre 3
20/09/98	HB	H	2-2	Bertholdsen, Mørkøre
27/09/98	B68	H	4-3	Jacobsen, Bertholdsen, Mørkøre 2 (1p)
03/10/98	Sumba	A	5-2	Jacobsen 2, Mørkøre 3

NSÍ

CLUB DIRECTORY

Nes Soknar Íttrotarfelag (NSÍ)
Postrum 173
620 Runavik
tel - 448100
fax - 448566
Year of Formation - 1957
President - Jakup Mortensen
Secretary - Eydalvur Knudsen
Coach - Petur Mohr (99 - Milan Cimburovic)
Stadium - Runavik (2,000)

MAJOR HONOURS
Domestic Cup - (1) 1986.

APPEARANCES 1998

		P	Ap	(s)	Gls
Pall DIDRIKSEN	A			(1)	
Petur HAMMER	D		2	(6)	
Abraham HANSEN	G		1		
Bergur HANSEN	M			(1)	
Danjal HANSEN	D		17		
Kari HANSEN	M		12	(1)	6
Mortan HANSEN	G		1		
Mortan HANSEN	A		7	(5)	5
Oli HANSEN	A		11		7
Olavur HØJGAARD	G		1		
Christian Høgni JACOBSEN	M		12	(1)	3
Kasper L. JACOBSEN (DEN)	A		15	(1)	3
Jakup Martin JACOBSEN	D		1		
Petur Meinhardt JACOBSEN	A			(4)	
Sjurdur JACOBSEN	M		13	(3)	2
Dann KNUDSEN	A		5	(3)	
Arnfinn LANGAARD	D		17		3
Gert LANGAARD	A		4		
Eddie MIKKELSEN	M		12	(5)	1
Dejan MILANOVIC (YUG)	G		16		
Ken NONKLETT	M		2	(4)	1
Dagfinn OLSEN	D			(1)	
Helgi L. PETERSEN	D		2		
Jonstein PETERSEN	M		18		2
Sonni L. PETERSEN	A			(6)	1
Kari SIGVARDSEN	D		12	(1)	
Eydstein SKIPANES	M		17		

LEAGUE RESULTS 1998

03/05/98	GÍ	H	3-1	Petersen J., Jacobsen K.L., Hansen O.
10/05/98	VB	A	5-0	Langaard A., Jacobsen S., Hansen M.,
				Hansen O. 2
17/05/98	HB	H	0-4	
24/05/98	KÍ	A	1-4	Langaard A.
01/06/98	Sumba	H	3-0	Jacobsen K.L., Hansen K., Hansen M.
07/06/98	ÍF	A	1-1	Hansen O.
13/06/98	B36	H	2-0	Jacobsen C.H., Hansen O.
21/06/98	TB	A	2-2	Skipanes, Hansen K.
28/06/98	B68	H	4-1	Mikkelsen, Jacobsen C.H. 2, Hansen O.
02/08/98	GÍ	A	1-5	Hansen K. (p)
08/08/98	VB	H	4-1	Petersen J., Skipanes, Hansen K.,
				Hansen O.
16/08/98	HB	A	1-2	Hansen K.
23/08/98	KÍ	H	0-0	
30/08/98	Sumba	A	6-1	Skipanes, Jacobsen K.L., Jacobsen S.,
				Hansen K., Hansen M. 2
13/09/98	ÍF	H	1-1	Hansen M.
20/09/98	B36	A	0-2	
27/09/98	TB	H	1-0	Langaard A.
03/10/98	B68	A	2-3	Nonklett, Petersen S.L.

SUMBA

Sumbiar Itrottarfelag (Sumba)
970 - Sumba
tel - 370213
fax - 370111
Year of Formation - 1940
President - Jacob Poulsen
Secretary - Maibritt ur Horg
Coach - Spasoje Bibercic
Stadium - Sumba (7,000)

	P	Ap	(s)	Gls
Spasoje BIBERCIC (YUG)	D	17		3
Thomas BIRCH (DEN)	M	16	(1)	2
Mortan ur HORG	D	17	(1)	
Sammy JACOBSEN	A		(3)	
Danjal Joan JOENSEN	A	17		3
Eirikur JOENSEN	A	10	(2)	4
Hallur Dam JOENSEN	M	3	(7)	
Birgir JØRGENSEN	A	6	(2)	2
Leon KJAERBAEK	D		(2)	
Pall Magnar KJAERBAEK	M	17		
Georg KJAERBO	D	7	(4)	
Marlon KJAERBO	D	17		
Sonni KJAERBO	M	10	(1)	
Robert LARSEN	D		(1)	
Jon LISBERG	D	3	(1)	
Runi LISBERG	G	17		
Jøgvan Sofus MÜLLER	A		(1)	
Trygvi NIELSEN	D		(1)	
Kristian OLSEN	M	3	(5)	
Egil PETERSEN	A		(1)	
Jan POULSEN	M	15		2
Annfinn THOMSEN	G	1		
Eydbjørn THOMSEN	A	6	(1)	
René THOMSEN	M	16	(1)	2
Hjarnar VAGFJALL	M		(1)	

03/05/98	B68	H	1-2	Thomsen R.
10/05/98	ÍF	H	1-0	Joensen D.J.
17/05/98	B36	A	2-6	Bibercic 2
24/05/98	TB	H	3-2	Joensen D.J., Poulsen, Joensen E.
01/06/98	NSÍ	A	0-3	
07/06/98	GÍ	H	1-1	Poulsen
13/06/98	VB	A	0-2	
21/06/98	HB	H	1-2	Birch
28/06/98	KÍ	A	1-4	Joensen D.J.
02/08/98	B68	A	0-6	
08/08/98	ÍF	A	0-6	
16/08/98	B36	H	0-10	
23/08/98	TB	A	2-2	Bibercic, Thomsen R.
30/08/98	NSÍ	H	1-6	Birch
13/09/98	GÍ	A	1-11	Joensen E.
20/09/98	VB	H	1-1	Joensen E.
27/09/98	HB	A	1-4	Jørgensen
03/10/98	KÍ	H	2-5	Joensen E., Jørgensen

TB

CLUB DIRECTORY

Tvoroyrar Boltfelag (TB)
Postrum 35
800 Tvoroyri
tel - 371570
fax - 371570
Year of Formation - 1892
President - Finn Thomsen
Secretary - Jens Johannesen
Coach - Zoran Pavlovic; Egil Steintorsson
Stadium - Sevmyra (4,000)

APPEARANCES 1998

	P	Ap	(s)	Gls
Jan ALBINUS	M	4	(10)	1
Rolf CHRISTIANSEN	G	10		
André DALFOSS	D		(2)	
Hans HAMMER	D	16		
Magni HENTZE	G	7		
Jon Tordur HOLM	M	15	(2)	
Tordur HOLM	M	13	(1)	1
Petur Oluf JOENSEN	D	11	(3)	
Pol F. JOENSEN	G		(1)	
Pol F. JOENSEN	M	15		
Bogi JOHANNESEN	A	1		
Jon JOHANNESEN	D	2		
Jonas JOHANNESEN	G	1		
Just JOHANNESEN	D		(1)	
Oli JOHANNESEN	D	13		3
Bjarni MORTENSEN	D	6	(1)	
Dan MORTENSEN	A	16		2
Herman MORTENSEN	M		(2)	
Tordur MORTENSEN	M	9	(5)	
Andraas NOLSØE	D	8	(4)	
Vagnur NOLSØE	A	6	(7)	
Karl ØSTER	A	2	(1)	
Zoran PAVLOVIC (YUG)	M	9	(2)	1
Einar PETERSEN	A	13	(4)	4
Niels Gunnar PETERSEN	D		(1)	
Aleksandar RADOSAVLJEVIC (YUG)	A	14		5
Teitur RASMUSSEN	M	1	(1)	
Jens Roi SØRENSEN	D		(2)	
Steen SØRENSEN	M	2		
Eydun Gullok SVALBARD	A	4		4

LEAGUE RESULTS 1998

03/05/98	VB	H	2-2	Svalbard, Radosavljevic
10/05/98	HB	A	3-4	Petersen E., Svalbard 2
17/05/98	KÍ	H	1-3	Johannesen O. (p)
24/05/98	Sumba	A	2-3	Johannesen O., Svalbard
01/06/98	ÍF	H	2-2	Petersen E., Albinus
07/06/98	B36	A	0-7	
13/06/98	B68	H	0-5	
21/06/98	NSÍ	H	2-2	Mortensen D., Holm T.
28/06/98	GÍ	A	0-3	
02/08/98	VB	A	0-0	
08/08/98	HB	H	1-4	Pavlovic
16/08/98	KÍ	A	0-10	
23/08/98	Sumba	H	2-2	Radosavljevic, Johannesen O. (p)
30/08/98	ÍF	A	2-1	Petersen E. 2
13/09/98	B36	H	0-3	
20/09/98	B68	A	3-4	Mortensen D., Radosavljevic 2
27/09/98	NSÍ	A	0-1	
03/10/98	GÍ	H	1-5	Radosavljevic

VB

CLUB DIRECTORY

VB
Postrum 54
900 Vagur
tel - 373679
fax - 373679
Year of Formation - 1905
President - Petur Ludvig
Secretary - Karin Strøm
Coach - Milan Milanovic; Krzysztof Popczynski
Stadium - Vestri a Eidinum (3,000)

APPEARANCES 1998

	P	Ap	(s)	Gls
Palli AUGUSTINUSSEN	M		(4)	
Milan CULJIC (YUG)	A	15		7
Hans Pauli DAHL	D	6		
Dan DJURHUUS	M	8	(1)	1
John EYSTBERG	M	17		1
Jon GAERDBO	D	18		
Eydun JACOBSEN	D	18		
Magni JACOBSEN	M	16		
Bjarni JOHANSEN	G	18		
Birgir JØRGENSEN	A	3	(1)	1
Eydun KJAERBO	D	11	(2)	
Janus KJAERBO	D	3	(1)	
Mikael i LAGABO	M	11	(7)	1
Niclas LUDVIG	A	1	(2)	
Magni MAGNUSSEN	M	9		
Sigmund MIKKELSEN	A		(2)	
Milan MILANOVIC (YUG)	M	7		
Magni MOHR	A	4		2
Jon Pauli OLSEN	A	13		8
Krzysztof POPCZYNSKI (POL)	A	8		5
Marner RICHARDT	D	6	(5)	
Petur Oli SAMUELSEN	M	4	(3)	
Røgvi THORSTEINSSON	A	1	(2)	1
Bergur VINTHER	D	1	(4)	

LEAGUE RESULTS 1998

03/05/98	TB	A	2-2	Lagabo, Jørgensen
10/05/98	NSÍ	H	0-5	
17/05/98	GÍ	A	2-0	Eystberg, Culjic
24/05/98	B68	A	1-2	Olsen
01/06/98	HB	H	1-1	Djurhuus
07/06/98	KÍ	A	1-2	Culjic (p)
13/06/98	ÍF	A	5-2	Culjic 2 (1p), Olsen 3
21/06/98	Sumba	H	2-0	Olsen 2
28/06/98	B36	H	1-1	Olsen
02/08/98	TB	H	0-0	
08/08/98	NSÍ	A	1-4	Mohr
16/08/98	GÍ	H	3-1	Olsen, Popczynski 2
23/08/98	B68	H	3-1	Culjic 2, Mohr
30/08/98	HB	A	1-5	Thorsteinsson
13/09/98	KÍ	H	0-4	
20/09/98	Sumba	A	1-1	Popczynski
27/09/98	ÍF	H	1-1	Popczynski
03/10/98	B36	A	2-8	Culjic, Popczynski

PROMOTED CLUB

SECOND DIVISION FINAL TABLE 1998

		Pd	W	D	L	F	A	Pt	GD
1	B71	18	13	2	3	43	19	41	+24
2	LÍF	18	10	3	5	38	21	33	+17
3	FS Vágar	18	8	5	5	37	30	29	+7
4	Royn	18	9	2	7	33	34	29	-1
5	KÍ II	18	8	2	8	33	38	26	-5
6	GÍ II	18	8	1	9	36	28	25	+8
7	HB II	18	6	2	10	27	37	20	-10
8	NSÍ	18	6	2	10	23	33	20	-10
9	EB/Streymur	18	6	2	10	26	40	20	-14
10	B36 II	18	5	1	12	31	47	16	-16

PROMOTION/RELEGATION PLAY-OFF

LÍF 2, Sumba 1
Sumba 2, LÍF 0
(Sumba 3-2)

CLUB DIRECTORY

Sandoyar Ítrottarfelag B 71
210 Sandur
tel - 361655
fax - 361733/361835
Year of Formation - 1970
President - Joannes Johannesen
Secretary - Eli Hentze
Coach - Ivan Hristov
Stadium - Sandur (2,000)

MAJOR HONOURS
League Championship - (1) 1989.
Domestic Cup - (1) 1983.

FINLAND

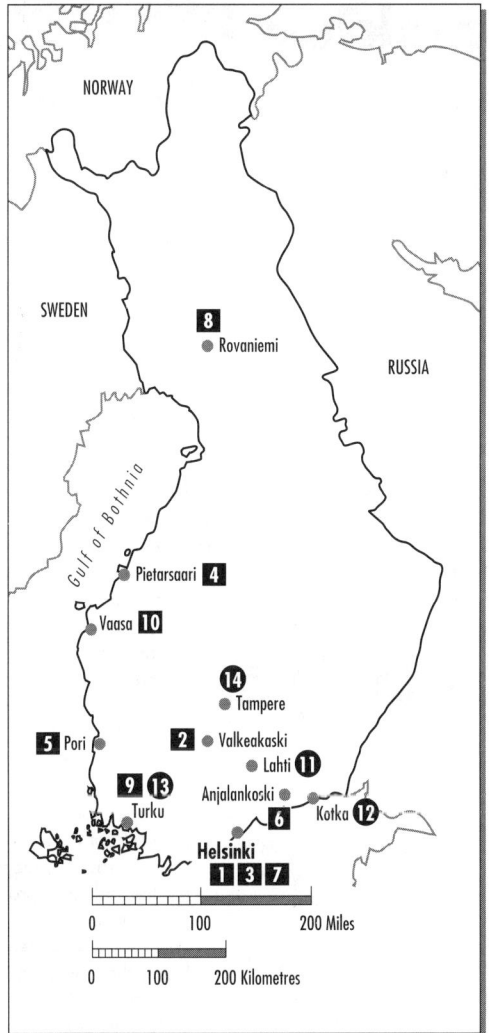

NORWAY

SWEDEN

8
● Rovaniemi

RUSSIA

Gulf of Bothnia

● Pietarsaari **4**

Vaasa **10**

14
● Tampere

5 Pori ●

2 ● Valkeakaski
● Lahti **11**

9 **13**
Turku   ● Anjalankoski ●
6   Kotka **12**

Helsinki
1 **3** **7**

```
0          100         200 Miles
```

```
0    100    200 Kilometres
```

1	FINNPA	361
2	FC HAKA	362
3	HJK	363
4	FF JARO	364
5	FC JAZZ	365
6	MYPA	366
7	PK-35	367
8	ROPS	368

9	TPS	369
10	VPS	370
Promoted clubs		
11	FC LAHTI	371
12	KTP	371
13	FC INTER	371
14	TPV	371

FC HAKA ROLLERCOAST TO TITLE

History-making HJK reach Champions' League

FEDERATION DIRECTORY

Suomen Palloliitto
Finlands Bollförbund, PO Box 179, Läntinen Brahenkatu 2
00510 Helsinki

tel - (09) 7010101   Year of Formation - 1907
fax - (09) 70101098   President - Pekka Hämäläinen
                               Secretary - Pertti Alaja

Stadium - Olympiastadion, Helsinki (40,000)

1998 was a memorable year for Finnish football. It ended with the national team leading their European Championship group and the country's leading club, HJK of Helsinki, flying the Finnish flag proudly for the first time in the UEFA Champions' League.

Alas, Finland's hopes of qualifying for the Euro 2000 finals were to take a steep nosedive the following spring when Richard Møller-Nielsen's team suffered an alarming home defeat by Turkey in Helsinki. Two goals to the good after 15 minutes, the Finns looked set to repeat their sensational 3-1 triumph in Istanbul, but they subsequently went to pieces and the Turks stole an improbable victory with two goals in the last five minutes. A goalless draw in Moldova four days later all but killed off the team's chances of qualification, which was a major disappointment not only for the Finnish fans but also for the likes of Jari Litmanen, Jonatan Johansson, Antti Niemi and Sami Hyypiä - players of international class who would certainly not be out of place competing in a major championship.

HJK's qualification for the group phase of the 1998/99 Champions' League bordered on the sensational. No Finnish team had come close to qualifying before, but Antti Muurinen's men managed to shake off their rather disappointing domestic form and knock out French side FC Metz, thus earning themselves the right to rub shoulders with European giants Benfica, PSV and Kaiserslautern.

Few dared to predict anything other than a total whitewash for the Finnish champions in such illustrious company, but the HJK players had not come so far simply to pose for the cameras. They prepared themselves carefully for the task and produced some extraordinary results.

Cruelly beaten by a last-minute winner in their opening match away to PSV (after leading at half-time), they took points from each of their next three games, including four from the two matches against Benfica. Remarkably, with two games remaining, they still had a chance of reaching the quarter-finals. Football fever had really gripped the nation, and a record Finnish crowd for a European club match of 34,000 visited the Olympic Stadium for the final home fixture against PSV. But it was there that the fairytale ended, with new Dutch superstar Ruud van Nistelrooy bagging himself a hat-trick in a 3-1 win. HJK eventually finished bottom of the group, but the memories of their

LEAGUE CHAMPIONSHIP RESULTS 1998

		1	2	3	4	5	6	7	8	9	10
1	FinnPa		1-3	1-2	6-2	4-2	2-2	0-0	1-2	1-1	2-2
			2-2	4-2						2-0	0-0
2	FC Haka	1-1		2-2	1-1	2-3	2-1	0-0	4-2	1-0	2-1
						3-2	4-0	3-1	0-0	0-1	
3	HJK	2-4	1-1		1-1	1-0	1-1	0-0	2-0	1-2	1-1
			0-1		4-2		0-0		0-2		3-1
4	FF Jaro	0-0	0-4	0-1		1-0	4-3	0-3	1-1	5-0	0-1
		2-2	1-2						0-0		1-1
5	FC Jazz	5-1	0-4	2-1	0-0		1-2	1-1	2-1	0-0	0-1
		1-0		2-1	5-1			4-1			
6	MyPa	3-0	0-0	1-1	2-0	1-0		0-2	2-2	0-1	0-3
		2-1			3-0	1-3			1-1		
7	PK-35	1-0	5-1	0-1	1-0	2-2	2-0		1-1	3-1	1-1
		1-0		1-1	2-1		1-0				1-1
8	RoPS	1-1	1-1	0-1	0-1	1-1	0-2	1-1		2-0	2-1
		0-0					0-0			2-1	3-3
9	TPS	1-0	1-2	1-1	3-0	1-1	2-2	1-1	0-0		1-2
			0-1	1-1	1-0	1-0	0-2				
10	VPS	3-1	3-0	1-1	3-0	4-0	3-2	2-1	0-2	0-2	
			1-0			0-0	2-4		4-0	0-0	

LEAGUE CHAMPIONSHIP FINAL TABLE 1998

				Home				Away					Total						
		P	W	D	L	F	A	W	D	L	F	A	W	D	L	F	A	P	GD
1	FC Haka	27	7	5	2	25	15	6	4	3	21	16	13	9	5	46	31	48	+15
2	VPS	27	8	3	3	26	13	4	6	3	16	14	12	9	6	42	27	45	+15
3	PK-35	27	8	5	1	22	10	3	6	4	14	14	11	11	5	36	24	44	+12
4	HJK	27	4	6	4	17	16	5	5	3	16	15	9	11	7	33	31	38	+2
5	FC Jazz	27	7	3	3	23	14	2	5	7	14	22	9	8	10	37	36	35	+1
6	TPS	27	4	6	4	14	13	4	4	5	11	18	8	10	9	25	31	34	-6
7	MyPa	27	5	4	4	16	14	3	4	7	19	25	8	8	11	35	39	32	-4
8	RoPS	27	3	7	3	13	13	3	7	4	14	18	6	14	7	27	31	32	-4
9	FinnPa	27	4	6	3	26	20	1	5	8	11	23	5	11	11	37	43	26	-6
10	FF Jaro	27	3	5	5	15	18	1	4	9	10	32	4	9	14	25	50	21	-25

participation in UEFA's flagship competition were destined to last and last...

In the midst of their European adventure HJK also found time to win the Finnish Cup. Their sixth victory in the competition arrived after an exciting final, which they won 3-2 in their home stadium against city rivals PK-35, with the winning goal, from defender Hannu Tihinen, coming three minutes from time. Victory was doubly important because it ensured HJK's European participation in 1999/2000. They had not qualified via the league, where, disappointingly in the season of their championship defence, they could finish no higher than fourth, ten points behind the winners, FC Haka.

Haka's winning tally of 48 points was ten fewer than HJK's a year earlier, but it was a deserved title all the same for the team from Valkeakoski. It is no easy achievement to win a championship the season after promotion, but that is what Haka managed thanks to a season-long consistency unmatched by any of their rivals. Their impressive feat had only been achieved twice before.

The late 1990s have been one long rollercoaster ride for Haka and their fans. After winning the title in 1995 they were relegated the following year. In 1997 they won both the Cup and promotion, and in 1998 they had another national title to celebrate.

Keith Armstrong may be a name unfamiliar to most football followers in his native England, but the FC Haka coach has earned himself an impressive reputation in Finland,

NATIONAL TEAM RESULTS 98/99

19/08/98	Slovakia	A	Kosice	0-0	
05/09/98	Moldova (ECQ)	H	Helsinki	3-2	Kolkka (8), Johansson (44),
					Paatelainen (63)
10/10/98	Northern Ireland (ECQ)	A	Belfast	0-1	
14/10/98	Turkey (ECQ)	A	Istanbul	3-1	Paatelainen (6), Johansson (52),
					Litmanen (90)
03/02/99	Greece	N	Larnaca	1-2	Kaijasilta (63)
05/02/99	Cyprus	A	Paralimni	1-2	Kaijasilta (7)
10/02/99	Poland	N	Ta' Qali	1-1	Johansson (20)
31/03/99	Germany (ECQ)	A	Nuremberg	0-2	
28/04/99	Slovenia	A	Ljubljana	1-1	Paatelainen (22p)
05/06/99	Turkey (ECQ)	H	Helsinki	2-4	Tihinen (10), Paatelainen (14)
09/06/99	Moldova (ECQ)	A	Chisinau	0-0	

TOP SCORERS

11	Matti HIUKKA (RoPS)
10	Oleg IVANOV (FC Haka)
	Valeri POPOVITS (FC Haka)
9	Kalle LEHTINEN (PK-35)
	Sükrü UZUNER (FinnPa)
8	Jukka RUHANEN (FC Haka)
	Kimmo TARKKIO (VPS)
7	Niclas GRÖNHOLM (FinnPa)
	Mika KOTTILA (HJK)
	Ville PRIHA (VPS)
	Sami VÄISÄNEN (MyPa)

where he has spent the past 20 years of his life, first as a player then as a coach. "Keke", as the Finns like to call him, takes particular credit for Haka's renaissance, although not far behind are the club's Russian imports Oleg Ivanov and Valeri Popovits, both of whom also won championship winner's medals with the club back in 1995.

The two Russians had identical records in 1998, each playing from the start in all 27 league games and scoring ten goals apiece - just one fewer than the league's

NATIONAL TEAM APPEARANCES 98/99

Coach - Richard MØLLER-NIELSEN	SVK	MOL	NIR	TUR	GRE	CYP	POL	GER	SLO	TUR	MOL	Cps	Gls
Antti NIEMI (31/05/72) - Rangers (SCO)	G46	G	G	G			G46	G	G46	G	G	36	-
Marko TUOMELA (03/03/72) - Tromsø IL (NOR)	D	D		D	D	D	D					16	-
Harri YLÖNEN (21/12/71) - FC Haka/SK Brann (NOR)	D	D	D	D	D	D	D	D	D	D	D	25	1
Sami HYYPIÄ (07/10/73) - Willem II (HOL)	D	D	D	D			D	D	D46	D	D	28	-
Tommi KAUTONEN (24/12/71) - MyPa/VPS	D	D	D	D				D70	D	s46		7	-
Aarno TURPEINEN (21/03/71) - HJK	D	D46										12	-
Sami MAHLIO (12/01/72) - MyPa	M	s72										21	-
Jari LITMANEN (20/02/71) - Ajax (HOL)	M57	M	s75	M				M		M		58	14
Jarkko WISS (17/04/72) - HJK	M	M										17	1
Jonatan JOHANSSON (16/08/75) - Rangers (SCO)	A75	A80	A	A90			A	A		A	A61	22	6
Antti SUMIALA (20/02/74) - FC Twente (HOL)	A57	s80										28	7
Jussi JÄÄSKELÄINEN (19/04/75) - Bolton Wanderers (ENG)	s46						s46		s46			4	-
Aki RIIHILAHTI (09/09/76) - HJK/Vålerenga IF (NOR)	s57		M75	M76			M	M	M	M	M	14	1
Joonas KOLKKA (28/09/74) - PSV (HOL)	s57	A72	A	s46			A	s70	A	A	A	23	4
Mika-Matti PAATELAINEN (03/02/67) - Wolverhampton Wanderers (ENG) /Hibernian (SCO)	s75	A	A	A46				A46	A	A	A	65	18
Juha REINI (19/03/75) - KRC Genk (BEL)		s46	D	D			D52	D88		D86		11	-
Jari ILOLA (24/11/78) - HJK			M	M	M46	M	M	M			M	7	-
Simo VALAKARI (28/04/73) - Motherwell (SCO)		M	s76					M	M	M	M	12	-
Jarmo SAASTAMOINEN (20/09/67) - HJK			s90	D	D				s46	s46		11	-
Jani VIANDER (18/08/72) - HJK					G	G						2	-
Ville NYLUND (14/08/72) - HJK					D	D						3	-
Jouni RÄSÄNEN (29/01/70) - FC Haka					D88	D77						2	-
Lasse KARJALAINEN (22/01/74) - FC Haka					M46	D59						11	-
Matti HIUKKA (05/05/75) - FC Jokerit					M	s76						2	-
Mika KOTTILA (22/09/74) - SK Brann (NOR)						A	A95	A				5	-
Ville PRIHA (19/09/75) - VPS						A69	s77					2	-
Tommi GRÖNLUND (09/12/69) - Trelleborgs FF (SWE)						s46	s59					17	1
Petteri KAIJASILTA (03/08/74) - TPS						s46	A76					3	2
Antti POHJA (11/01/77) - FC Jokerit						s69	M					3	-
Janne SALLI (14/12/77) - FC Haka						s88						1	-
Toni TERVONEN (14/03/77) - FK Haugesund (NOR)							s95					4	1
Mika LEHKOSUO (08/01/70) - Perugia (ITA)								s52	s88	M	s86	7	-
Tomi KINNUNEN (28/03/69) - KRC Genk (BEL)									D	D46		6	-
Ville VILJANEN (02/02/71) - Västra Frölunda IF (SWE)									A			1	-
Toni KUIVASTO (31/12/75) - HJK									s46	D		9	-
Hannu TIHINEN (01/07/76) - HJK										D	D46	2	1
Mikael FORSSELL (15/03/81) - Chelsea (ENG)											s61	1	-

EUROPEAN CUPS 98/99

CHAMPIONS' CUP
● HJK
Preliminary round FK YEREVAN (ARM)
H 2-0   Wiss (50), Kuqi (85)
   Koivistoinen; Lehkosuo, Kanerva, Nylund, Turpeinen; Lehtola (Kopteff 41),
   Wiss, Ilola, Vasara (Forssell 73); Jäväjä (Kuqi 70), Kottila.
A 3-0   Lehkosuo (1, 81p), Jäväjä (27)
   Koivistoinen; Kanerva, Nylund, Saastamoinen, Turpeinen; Lehkosuo,
   Riihilahti, Wiss, Vasara (Kopteff 72); Jäväjä (Manduca 77), Kottila
   (Kuqi 46).

Qualifying round FC METZ (FRA)
H 1-0   Riihilahti (72)
   Koivistoinen; Ilola, Nylund, Saastamoinen, Turpeinen; Wiss, Riihilahti,
   Lehkosuo, Piracaía (Jäväjä 86); Kuqi (Luiz António 66), Kottila
   (Tihinen 88).
A 1-1   Vasara (69)
   Koivistoinen; Ilola, Nylund, Saastamoinen, Turpeinen; Piracaía (Vasara 66),
   Wiss, Riihilahti, Lehkosuo; Kuqi (Tihinen 90), Kottila (Kanerva 76).

Champions' League
1st match PSV (HOL)
A 1-2   Kottila (32)
   Koivistoinen; Ilola, Saastamoinen, Nylund, Tihinen; Kuqi (Kanerva 85),
   Lehkosuo, Riihilahti, Vasara (Kopteff 68); Kottila (Jäväjä 68), Piracaía.

2nd match 1.FC KAISERSLAUTERN (GER)
H 0-0
   Viander; Tihinen, Kanerva, Saastamoinen, Nylund; Ilola (Lehtonen 83),
   Riihilahti, Wiss, Lehkosuo; Piracaía (Vasara 69), Kuqi (Luiz António 75).

3rd match SL BENFICA (POR)
H 2-0   Lehkosuo (20p), Kottila (70)
   Viander; Nylund, Kanerva, Saastamoinen, Tihinen; Lehkosuo, Ilola, Kuqi
   (Luiz António 63), Vasara (Riilahti 30); Piracaía, Kottila (Kopteff 79).

4th match SL BENFICA (POR)
A 2 2   Minto (3og), Luiz António (05)
   Koivistoinen; Nylund, Saastamoinen, Kanerva, Tihinen; Lehkosuo, Riihilahti,
   Ilola, Kuqi (Kopteff 88); Piracaía (Forssell 57), Kottila (Luiz António 81).

5th match PSV (HOL)
H 1-3   Lehkosuo (70p)
   Koivistoinen; Nylund, Saastamoinen, Kanerva (Luiz António 45),
   Turpeinen; Lehkosuo, Tihinen (Forssell 82), Riihilahti, Piracaía; Kottila,
   Kuqi (Kopteff 72).

6th match 1.FC KAISERSLAUTERN (GER)
A 2-5   Ilola (29), Luiz António (68)
   Viander; Tihinen, Saastamoinen, Nylund, Turpeinen; Lehkosuo, Riihilahti,
   Ilola, Piracaía (Kopteff 66); Kottila (Forssell 83), Kuqi (Luiz António 59).

CUP WINNERS' CUP
● FC HAKA
Qualifying round BANGOR CITY (WAL)
A 2-0   Niemi (40), Salli (59)
   Vilnrotter; Heikkinen, Ylönen, Salli, Räsänen; Karjalainen, Mäkelä, Niemi
   (Ruhanen 71), Ivanov (Okkonen 78); Harewood (Torkkeli 82), Popovits.
H 1-0   Ruhanen (28)
   Vilnrotter; Ylönen, Mäkelä, Salli, Heikkinen (Okkonen 78), Räsänen;
   Popovits, Karjalainen, Ivanov; Niemi (Rantala 84), Ruhanen (Torkkeli 66).

1st round PANIONIOS (GRE)
A 0-2
   Vilnrotter; Ylönen, Heikkinen, Salli, Räsänen (Hyökyvaara 69); Karjalainen,
   Mäkelä, Ivanov, Niemi (Torkkeli 80); Ruhanen (Rantala 72), Popovits.
H 1-3   Popovits (74)
   Vilnrotter; Ylönen, Mäkelä, Salli, Heikkinen (Hyökyvaara 77); Räsänen;
   Ivanov, Karjalainen (Okkonen 28), Niemi; Rantala (Torkkeli 61), Popovits.

UEFA CUP
● FINNPA
Preliminary round HAPOEL TEL-AVIV (ISR)
A 1-3   Hautala (45)
   Laukkanen; Laine, Räsänen, Tervonen, Pylkäs; Linna (Elomaa 78), Järvinen,
   Savolainen (Vanhala 70), Grönholm; Uzuner, Hautala (Pohja 59).
H 1-3   Geagea (88)
   Laukkanen; Tervonen, Da Silva, Räsänen, Pylkäs; Grönholm (Hautala 46),
   Linna (Geagea 38), Pohja, Järvinen; Vanhala (Elomaa 73), Uzuner.

● VPS
Preliminary round HB (FAR)
A 0-2
   Stringheim; Iivonen, Peltola, Lange, Suoste (Tarkkio 46); Huhtamäki,
   Karvinen, Kokko, Nygård 71), Lipponen; Kangaskorpi, Priha (Nyman 88).
H 4-0   Suoste (3, 17), Tarkkio (72), Nygård (90)
   Juhola; Peltola, Lange, Suoste (Nygård 79), Iivonen; Karvinen, Huhtamäki,
   Lipponen, Kokko; Iarkkio, Kangaskorpi (Suominen 88).

Qualifying round GRAZER AK (AUT)
H 0-0
   Stringheim; Huhtamäki (Tarkkio 40); Nygård 89), Peltola, Suoste
   (Iivonen 53), Lange; Kokko, Lipponen, Norebø, Karvinen; Kangaskorpi, Priha.
A 0-3
   Stringheim; Peltola, Lange, Suoste (Tarkkio 63), Iivonen; Karvinen, Kokko,
   Lipponen, Norebø; Kangaskorpi, Priha (Nygård 74).

---

op marksman, Matti Hiukka of RoPS. Haka had the best
ttack in the division - ex-Finland international striker
Jkka Ruhanen also chipped in with eight goals - but
nere was no shortage of quality in the defence, either,
vith centre-back Harri Ylönen enjoying a particularly
nemorable season - hence his permanent residence in
ne national side.

Haka won the title with a strong run in the final
third of the season but they also had the decline of
earlier front-runners VPS to thank for their triumph. VPS
led by three points after 18 matches but they suffered
severely from the mid-season sale of two of their
leading lights, Juha Reini and Tommi Kinnunen, to
Belgian club Genk - coach Hanni Touru threatened to quit

DOMESTIC CUP 1998

SIXTH ROUND
FC Lahti 6, HIK 0
Lahden TP 0, PK-35 3
Kings 1, JJK 3 (aet)
FC Inter 3, TP-Seinäjoki 0
IG Gnistan 0, FinnPa 4
FC Honka 1, KTP 3
Mypa 3, RoPS 3 (aet; 6-5 on pens.)
MuSa 3, Pyry Nokia 3 (aet; 7-8 on pens.)
VarTP 0, MP 1
KajHa 4, P-Iirot 2
KPT-85 1, VPS 0
FC Raahe 0, FC Haka 8

SEVENTH ROUND
JJK 2, FF Jaro 1
Pyry Nokia 2, FC Inter 1

KajHa 1, FinnPa 2
KTP 0, PK-35 2
MP 0, FC Jazz 3
KPT-85 0, MyPa 1
FC Lahti 0, FC Haka 3
TPS 0, HJK 5

QUARTER-FINALS
OK-35 3 (Lehtinen 2, Rantanen),
FC Jazz 2 (Marco, Ricky)
JJK 0, Pyry Nokia 2 (Heinänen, Aaltonen)
FinnPa 1 (Soto 90), FC Haka 1 (Popovits 90)
(aet; 5-4 on pens.)
HJK 3 (Kottila 53, 72, Lehkosuo 90),
MyPa 2 (Mahlio 8, 88)

SEMI-FINALS
FinnPa 0,
PK-35 3 (Pilvi 29, Suokonautio 34, Helin M. 77)
HJK 1 (Ilola 80), Pyry Nokia 0

FINAL
31/10/98, Helsinki
HJK 3 Riihilahti (17), Lehkosuo (54), Tihinen (87)
PK-35 2 Pihamaa (50), Suokonautio (57)
referee - Peltola
HJK - Koivistoinen; Tihinen, Nylund, Saastamoinen,
Turpeinen (Forssell); Ilola, Piracaia (Kopteff),
Kanerva, Lehkosuo, Riihilahti; Kottila (Luiz António).
PK-35 - Laaksonen; Helin M., Holmgren, Ylä-Jussila;
Paavola, Helin P., Suokonautio (Pilvi), Pihamaa,
Nenonen; Lehtinen (Viren), Paavola.

as a result - and they were visibly short of stamina in the run-in. They did, however, manage to beat the champions 1-0 in their final match, which not only gave them the runners-up spot for the second year in succession but also ensured their immediate return to the UEFA Cup - a competition they had just exited after a comprehensive defeat by Austrian side Grazer AK.

PK-35, the team which had accompanied FC Haka up into the National League the previous year, were the revelations of the season. Third place was no more than they deserved at the end of a year in which they played arguably the most attractive football in the league, the highlight being a stunning 5-1 victory over Haka at the end of July. Pasi Rautiainen's side also performed splendidly in the Cup and were unlucky losers in the final to HJK.

The Cup final was the last official game played by the club as PK-35. During the winter they were bought by Helsinki businessman Harri Harkimo and re-named FC Jokerit - a familiar name to European ice-hockey fans.

It was not all sweetness and light in the capital, however. FinnPa, a club jointly-sponsored by Finland's national airline and one of the country's biggest forestry companies, suffered the trauma of relegation, going down on away-goals after a two-legged play-off with TPV, one of four clubs promoted as the National League

returned once more to a 12-team complement in 1999, continuing its never-ending cycle of structural change.

The other three newcomers were FC Inter of Turku, the newly-formed FC Lahti (incorporating former clubs Reipas and FC Kuusysi) and KTP of Kotka, with FF Jaro travelling in the other direction in the company of a distraught FinnPa.

PLAYER OF THE SEASON

MIKAEL FORSSELL
Finnish football has been waiting for some time for a new wonderkid to come along and steal some of the thunder from superstar Jari Litmanen. There are high hopes that Mikael Forssell can be 'the one'. A former winner of Finland's football skills competition at the age of just 13, he was voted the country's best youth player three years running from 1996-98. He managed to break through into HJK's senior team in 1998 and also had a dabble in the Champions' League, but it was not until his transfer to English Premiership glamour club Chelsea that he really commanded attention. He scored twice in an FA Cup replay against Oxford and also notched his first Premiership goal away to Nottingham Forest - all while he was still only 17. His senior national team début came in June 1999 as a substitute appearance against Moldova. Assuming he can get a look-in at star-studded Chelsea, that first cap should be followed by many, many more...

INTERNATIONAL HONOURS

None

FINNPA

Finnairin Palloilijat
Vanha Talvitie 2-5 A 12
00580 Helsinki
tel - (09) 72310020
fax - (09) 72310021
Year of Formation - 1965
President - Claes Andersson
Secretary - Rauno Halme
Coach - Jari-Pekka Keurulainen; Jari Rantanen
Stadium - Olympiastadion (40,000)

APPEARANCES 98

	P	Ap	(s)	Gls
Ville ANDERSSON	D	9	(4)	
BIGU (BRA)	D	1		
Toni ELOMAA	A	10	(7)	5
Stuart GALLAGHER (SCO)	A	8		1
Oscar GEAGEA	M	12	(7)	1
Niclas GRÖNHOLM	A	19	(3)	7
Merka HAUTALA	A	8	(2)	2
Antti JOKINEN	G	1		
Petri JÄRVINEN	M	17	(2)	
Janne LAINE	D	22	(1)	
Kari LAUKKANEN	G	20		
Reijo LINNA	D	13		
Antti POHJA	M	8	(5)	1
Jani PYLKÄS	M	19	(3)	
Anders ROTH	M	4	(3)	
Janne RÄSÄNEN	D	26		1
Peter SAMPO	A	15	(8)	3
Janne SAVOLAINEN	M	14	(7)	1
Jari TAKATALO	M	6	(5)	1
Toni TERVONEN	D	20	(2)	2
Paul TISDALE (ENG)	A	6	(1)	1
Jani TUOMALA	G	6		
Sükrü UZUNER (TUR)	A	22	(2)	9
Jari VANHALA	A	10	(8)	1
John WECKSTRÖM	A	1	(4)	

LEAGUE RESULTS 1998

02/05/98	FC Haka	A	1-1	Elomaa
06/05/98	HJK	H	1-2	Grönholm
10/05/98	FC Jazz	H	4-2	Uzuner 2, Grönholm, Sampo
13/05/98	MyPa	A	0-3	
18/05/98	TPS	H	1-1	Räsänen
23/05/98	RoPS	H	1-2	Grönholm (p)
01/06/98	PK-35	A	0-1	
09/06/98	FF Jaro	H	6-2	Takatalo, og, Uzuner 3, Geagea
17/06/98	VPS	A	1-3	Uzuner
23/06/98	FC Haka	H	1-3	Uzuner
28/06/98	FC Jazz	A	1-5	Savolainen
01/07/98	MyPa	H	2-2	Grönholm, Vanhala
07/07/98	TPS	A	0-1	
12/07/98	HJK	A	4-2	Uzuner, Tervonen, Hautala 2
15/07/98	RoPS	A	1-1	Uzuner
25/07/98	FF Jaro	A	0-0	
01/08/98	VPS	H	2-2	Grönholm, Sampo
04/08/98	PK-35	H	0-0	
09/08/98	MyPa	A	1-2	Tervonen
14/08/98	VPS	H	0-0	
24/08/98	PK-35	A	0-1	
30/08/98	FC Haka	H	2-2	Grönholm 2
08/09/98	FC Jazz	A	0-1	
12/09/98	HJK	H	4-2	Elomaa 3, Gallagher
20/09/98	RoPS	A	0-0	
27/09/98	TPS	H	2-0	Sampo, Tisdale
04/10/98	FF Jaro	A	2-2	Pohja, Elomaa

FC HAKA

CLUB DIRECTORY

FC Haka
Kirjaskatu 1
37600 Valkeakoski
tel - (03) 5845364
fax - (02) 04163629
Year of Formation - 1934
President - Heikki Huoviala
Manager - Erkki Salo
Secretary - Jukka Malm
Coach - Keith Armstrong
Stadium - Tehtaankenttä (6,000)

MAJOR HONOURS
League Championship - (6)
1960, 1962, 1965, 1977, 1995, 1998.
Domestic Cup - (10) 1955, 1959, 1960, 1963,
1969, 1977, 1982, 1985, 1988, 1997.

APPEARANCES 98

	P	Ap	(s)	Gls
Marlon HAREWOOD (ENG)	A	7	(5)	3
Ari HEIKKINEN	D	12	(5)	
Janne HYÖKYVAARA	M	19	(5)	1
Oleg IVANOV (RUS)	M	27		10
Tibor KALINA (HUN)	A		(1)	
Lasse KARJALAINEN	D	19	(2)	3
Pekka KUNNOLA	A		(1)	
Janne MÄKELÄ	D	25		
Jari NIEMI	M	22	(4)	3
Jarkko OKKONEN	D	1	(9)	1
Jarkko PASANEN	D		(1)	
Jussi PELLIKKA	D	2	(14)	1
Valeri POPOVITS (RUS)	A	27		10
Jukka RANTALA	M	16	(5)	
Anders ROTH	M		(1)	
Jukka RUHANEN	A	17	(7)	8
Jouni RÄSÄNEN	D	18	(4)	2
Janne SALLI	D	21	(1)	3
Panu TOIVONEN	G	20		
Tommi TORKKELI	M	10	(16)	1
András VILNROTTER (HUN)	G	7		
Harri YLÖNEN	D	27		

LEAGUE RESULTS 1998

02/05/98	FinnPa	H	1-1	Ivanov
11/05/98	VPS	A	0-3	
13/05/98	FC Jazz	A	4-0	Niemi 3, Popovits
17/05/98	MyPa	H	2-1	Ivanov, Räsänen
20/05/98	TPS	A	2-1	Harewood, Pellikka
23/05/98	HJK	H	2-2	Ivanov, Harewood
30/05/98	RoPS	A	1-1	Popovits
02/06/98	HJK	A	1-1	Ivanov
09/06/98	PK-35	H	0-0	
17/06/98	FF Jaro	A	4-0	Ivanov 3 (1p), Popovits
23/06/98	FinnPa	A	3-1	Popovits 2 (1p), Salli
28/06/98	VPS	H	2-1	Popovits, Ivanov
01/07/98	FC Jazz	H	2-3	Ivanov, Hyökyvaara
05/07/98	MyPa	A	0-0	
18/07/98	RoPS	H	4-2	Harewood, Popovits 2, Ivanov
23/07/98	TPS	H	1-0	Ruhanen
27/07/98	PK-35	A	1-5	Karjalainen
04/08/98	FF Jaro	H	1-1	Karjalainen
09/08/98	RoPS	H	0-0	
16/08/98	FF Jaro	A	2-1	Ruhanen 2
22/08/98	MyPa	H	4-0	Popovits, Ruhanen, Salli 2
30/08/98	FinnPa	A	2-2	Ruhanen 2
09/09/98	TPS	H	0-1	
13/09/98	FC Jazz	H	3-2	Ruhanen, Karjalainen, Popovits
21/09/98	HJK	A	1-0	Räsänen
26/09/98	PK-35	H	3-1	Ruhanen, Torkkeli, Okkonen
04/10/98	VPS	A	0-1	

HJK

CLUB DIRECTORY

Helsingin Jalkapalloklubi
Mannerheimintie 29
00250 Helsinki
tel - (09) 4774550
fax - (09) 47745510
Year of Formation - 1907
President - Olli-Pekka Lyytikäinen
Manager - Erkki Alaja
Coach - Antti Muurinen
Stadium - Olympiastadion (40,000)

MAJOR HONOURS
League Championship - (19)
1911, 1912, 1917, 1918, 1919, 1923, 1925,
1936, 1938, 1964, 1973, 1978, 1981, 1985,
1987, 1988, 1990, 1992, 1997.
Domestic Cup - (6)
1966, 1981, 1984, 1993, 1996, 1998.

APPEARANCES 98

	P	Ap	(s)	Gls
Mikael FORSSELL	A	12	(4)	1
Jari ILOLA	M	18	(4)	2
Jari JÄVÄJÄ	A	9	(13)	3
Markku KANERVA	D	8	(6)	1
Mikko KAVEN	G	5		
Tommi KOIVISTOINEN	G	15		
Peter KOPTEГГ	A	4	(2)	
Mika KOTTILA	A	13	(13)	7
Shefki KUQI (ALB)	A	13	(9)	1
Mika LEHKOSUO	M	17	(5)	5
Erkka LEHTOLA	A	3	(4)	
LUIZ ANTÓNIO (BRA)	A	9	(7)	1
Gustavo MANDUCA (BRA)	M	1	(1)	
Timo NYBÄCK	D		(1)	
Ville NYLUND	D	21		
PIRACAÍA (BRA)	M	9	(1)	1
Aki RIIHILAHTI	M	27		4
Hannu TIHINEN	D	11	(2)	2
Jarmo SAASTAMOINEN	D	24	(2)	
Aarno TURPEINEN	D	25		
Vesa VASARA	M	22	(1)	2
Jani VIANDER	G	7	(1)	
Jarkko WISS	M	24	(2)	3

LEAGUE RESULTS 1998

02/05/98	VPS	H	1-1	Jäväjä
06/05/98	FinnPa	A	2-1	Wiss, Ilola
10/05/98	RoPS	A	1-0	Jäväjä
13/05/98	PK-35	H	0-0	
16/05/98	FF Jaro	A	1-0	Kuqi
23/05/98	FC Haka	A	2-2	Vasara, Luiz António
30/05/98	FC Jazz	H	1-0	Kanerva
02/06/98	FC Haka	H	1-1	Kottila
09/06/98	MyPa	A	1-1	Lehkosuo
17/06/98	TPS	H	1-2	Kottila
24/06/98	VPS	A	1-1	Lehkosuo
28/06/98	RoPS	H	2-0	Forssell, Kottila
02/07/98	PK-35	A	1-0	Ilola
05/07/98	FF Jaro	H	1-1	Lehkosuo (p)
12/07/98	FinnPa	H	2-4	Lehkosuo (p), Riihilahti
18/07/98	FC Jazz	A	1-2	Riihilahti
25/07/98	MyPa	H	1-1	Jäväjä
03/08/98	TPS	A	1-1	Lehkosuo
08/08/98	TPS	A	1-0	Kottila
15/08/98	MyPa	H	0-0	
22/08/98	FC Jazz	A	1-2	Wiss
31/08/98	RoPS	H	0-2	
09/09/98	FF Jaro	H	4-2	Kottila, Tihinen, Riihilahti, Wiss
12/09/98	FinnPa	A	7-4	Tihinen, Piracaía
21/09/98	FC Haka	H	0-1	
26/09/98	VPS	H	3-1	Kottila 2, Riihilahti
04/10/98	PK-35	A	1-1	Vasara

FF JARO

CLUB DIRECTORY

FF Jaro
Södermalmggatan 20
68600 Jakobstad
tel - (06) 7247936
fax - (06) 7230220
Year of Formation - 1965
President - Stig Nickull
Manager - Craig Ramsay
Coach - Jan Westerlund; Keijo Paananen
Stadium - Keskuskenttä (5,000)

APPEARANCES 98

	P	Ap	(s)	Gls
Örjan ENGSTRÖM (SWE)	M	17	(4)	2
Henrik FRIBERG	D	2		
Hans GILLHAUS (HOL)	A	6	(1)	2
Johan GRÖNROOS	G	1	(1)	
Tommi KAINULAINEN	G	19	(1)	
Toomas KALLASTE (EST)	M	20	(2)	
Timo KIVILOMPOLO	M	26		1
Toomas KRÖM (EST)	A	8	(9)	3
Ville LAAKKONEN	A	5	(6)	1
Paul LINDHOLM	M	27		4
Billy MacDONALD (SCO)	A	1	(1)	
Mladen MILINKOVIC (YUG)	D	25		2
Janusz PRUCHENSKI (POL)	A	3	(1)	
Daniel SNELLMAN	D	15	(6)	2
Pasi SOLEHMAINEN	D	16	(6)	
Niklas STORBACKA	D	17	(3)	
Fredrik SVANBÄCK	M	17	(4)	2
Tuomas TUOMILEHTO	G	1		
Tuomas UUSIMÄKI	M	17	(3)	
Vitaliy VARIVONCHIK (BLS)	G	6		
Niklas WIDJESKOG	M	20	(1)	2
Piotr ZAJACZKOWSKI (POL)	A	13	(1)	1
Ridvan ZENELI (YUG)	A	4	(5)	
Miodrag ZEZEVIC (YUG)	A	11	(7)	3

LEAGUE RESULTS 1998

03/05/98	FC Jazz	A	0-0	
09/05/98	MyPa	H	4-3	Lindholm (p), Milinkovic, Zezevic 2
13/05/98	TPS	A	0-3	
16/05/98	HJK	H	0-1	
20/05/98	RoPS	A	1-0	Laakkonen
24/05/98	PK-35	H	0-3	
31/05/98	VPS	A	0-3	
09/06/98	FinnPa	A	2-6	Lindholm (p), Kröm
17/06/98	FC Haka	H	0-4	
24/06/98	FC Jazz	H	1-0	Snellman
27/06/98	MyPa	A	0-2	
01/07/98	TPS	H	5-0	Snellman, Lindholm, Kivilompolo, Zezevic, Kröm
05/07/98	HJK	A	1-1	Svanbäck
13/07/98	RoPS	H	1-1	Engström
16/07/98	PK-35	A	0-1	
19/07/98	VPS	H	0-1	
25/07/98	FinnPa	H	0-0	
04/08/98	FC Haka	A	1-1	Engström
09/08/98	PK-35	A	1-2	Zajaczkowski
16/08/98	FC Haka	H	1-2	Milinkovic
24/08/98	TPS	A	1-1	Gillhaus
30/08/98	VPS	H	1-1	Gillhaus
09/09/98	HJK	A	2-4	Widjeskog, Kröm
13/09/98	RoPS	H	0-0	
20/09/98	MyPa	A	0-3	
27/09/98	FC Jazz	A	1-5	Lindholm (p)
04/10/98	FinnPa	H	2-2	Svanbäck, Widjeskog

FC JAZZ

CLUB DIRECTORY

FC Jazz
Isolinnankatu 2
28 100 Pori
tel - (02) 6331999
fax - (02) 6331244
Year of Formation - 1934
President - Arto Vitikka
Secretary - Pentti Joensuu
Coach - Tapio Raatikainen; Pertti Lundell
Stadium - Porin (10,000)

MAJOR HONOURS
League Championship - (2) 1993, 1996.

APPEARANCES 98

	P	Ap	(s)	Gls
EDUARDO (BRA)	M	15	(5)	1
Rami HAKANPÄÄ	D	24	(2)	
Jarno HEINIKANGAS	M	2	(7)	1
JOE (BRA)	M	7	(11)	1
Tero KOSKELA	M	25		4
Antti KUISMALA	G	14		
Saku LAAKSONEN	A	14	(8)	1
Vesa LAMMINEN	A	1	(3)	
Tomi LEIVO-JOKIMÄKI	M	2	(6)	
MARCO (BRA)	A	18		6
Rumi NIEMINEN	D	25		3
Janne PUPUTTI	M	10	(8)	
RAFAEL (BRA)	A	15		4
Vesa RANTANEN	D	26		1
RICKY (BRA)	A	8		6
Juha RIIPPA	D	25		3
RODRIGO (BRA)	M	20		6
Ari-Pekka ROIKO	D	22	(2)	
Jyrki ROVIO	G	13		
Mikko SALO	D	7	(6)	
Teemu VIHTILÄ	M	4	(8)	

LEAGUE RESULTS 1998

03/05/98	FF Jaro	H	0-0	
10/05/98	FinnPa	A	2-4	Marco 2
13/05/98	FC Haka	H	0-4	
16/05/98	VPS	H	0-1	
20/05/98	MyPa	A	0-1	
24/05/98	TPS	H	0-0	
30/05/98	HJK	A	0-1	
08/06/98	RoPS	H	2-1	Laaksonen, Rantanen
15/06/98	PK-35	A	2-2	Koskela, Rodrigo
24/06/98	FF Jaro	A	0-1	
28/06/98	FinnPa	H	5-1	Rafael, Rodrigo, Koskela 2, Nieminen (p)
01/07/98	FC Haka	A	3-2	Rafael 2, Eduardo
05/07/98	VPS	A	0-4	
11/07/98	MyPa	H	1-2	Nieminen
15/07/98	TPS	A	1-1	Rafael
18/07/98	HJK	H	2-1	Riippa, Nieminen (p)
26/07/98	RoPS	A	1-1	Koskela (p)
01/08/98	PK-35	H	1-1	Ricky
08/08/98	VPS	A	0-0	
15/08/98	PK-35	H	4-1	Ricky, Riippa, Rodrigo, Joe
22/08/98	HJK	H	2-1	Marco, Heinikangas
29/08/98	MyPa	A	3-1	Marco 2, Rodrigo
08/09/98	FinnPa	H	1-0	Marco
13/09/98	FC Haka	A	2-3	Ricky, Riippa
21/09/98	TPS	A	0-1	
27/09/98	FF Jaro	H	5-1	Ricky 3, Rodrigo 2
04/10/98	RoPS	A	0-0	

MYPA

CLUB DIRECTORY

Myllykosken Pallo-47
Koulutie 1
46800 Anjalankoski
tel - (05) 3656686
fax - (05) 3255292
Year of Formation - 1947
President - Matti Tiihonen
Manager - Seppo Mäkinen
Coach - Juha Malinen
Stadium - Anjalankosken stadion (8,000)

MAJOR HONOURS
Domestic Cup - (2) 1992, 1995.

APPEARANCES 98

	P	Ap	(s)	Gls
Neathan GIBSON (POR)	A	10		3
Markus HEIKKINEN	D	14		
Mika HERNESNIEMI	M	3	(1)	
Björn HOFVENDAHL (SWE)	A	17	(2)	6
Toni HUTTUNEN	D	26		2
Petri JAKONEN	G	27		
Tommi KAUTONEN	M	26		
Mauri KESKITALO	A	19	(5)	4
Mikko KORHONEN	A	4	(15)	3
Jarkko KOSKINEN	M	21	(2)	
Toni KUIVASTO	D	19		1
Arto LAUTAMATTI	A	4	(15)	1
Janne LINDBERG	M	15		
Jukka LINDSTRÖM	D	8	(4)	1
Ismo LIUS	A	3	(2)	
Sami MAHLIO	M	22	(1)	2
Miikka MULTAHARU	D	22	(2)	2
Reino NÖMMIK (EST)	A	2		
Antti POHJA	M	1	(5)	
Arto SIVONEN	D	5	(6)	2
Sampsa TIMOSKA	D		(1)	
Jani UOTINEN	M	6	(13)	1
Sami VÄISÄNEN	A	23	(2)	7

LEAGUE RESULTS 1998

04/05/98	PK-35	H	0-2	
09/05/98	FF Jaro	A	3-4	Korhonen, Mahlio, Kuivasto
13/05/98	FinnPa	H	3-0	Hofvendahl, Keskitalo 2
17/05/98	FC Haka	A	1-2	Korhonen
20/05/98	FC Jazz	H	1-0	Hofvendahl
23/05/98	VPS	H	0-3	
01/06/98	TPS	A	2-2	Huttunen, Lautamatti
09/06/98	HJK	H	1-1	Multaharju
17/06/98	RoPS	A	2-0	Hofvendahl, Mahlio
24/06/98	PK-35	A	0-2	
27/06/98	FF Jaro	H	2-0	Korhonen, Väisänen
01/07/98	FinnPa	A	2-2	Huttunen, Hofvendahl
05/07/98	FC Haka	H	0-0	
11/07/98	FC Jazz	A	2-1	Multaharju, Väisänen
15/07/98	VPS	A	2-3	Hofvendahl, Väisänen
20/07/98	TPS	H	0-1	
25/07/98	HJK	A	1-1	Sivonen
02/08/98	RoPS	H	2-2	Hofvendahl, Sivonen
09/08/98	FinnPa	H	2-1	Väisänen 2
15/08/98	HJK	A	0-0	
22/08/98	FC Haka	A	0-4	
29/08/98	FC Jazz	H	1-3	Gibson
09/09/98	VPS	A	4-2	Gibson, Keskitalo 2, Väisänen
13/09/98	PK-35	A	0-1	
20/09/98	FF Jaro	H	3-0	Gibson, Lindström, Uotinen
27/09/98	RoPS	H	1-1	Väisänen
04/10/98	TPS	A	0-1	

PK-35

CLUB DIRECTORY

Pallo-Kerho-35 (now - FC Jokerit)
Areenakuja 1
00240 Helsinki
tel - (09) 02041997
fax - (09) 02041994
Year of Formation - 1935
President - Harry Harkimo
Manager - Jarmo Koskinen
Coach - Pasi Rautiainen
Stadium - Olympiastadion (40,000)

APPEARANCES 98

	P	Ap	(s)	Gls
Michael BELFIELD (ENG)	A	7	(6)	4
Tuomas BRINCK	D		(1)	
Brandon FONSECA (USA)	A		(1)	
Riffi HADDAOUI (ALG)	A	1	(1)	
Juuso HEIKURAINEN	G	4		
Mika HELIN	M	1		
Petri HELIN	M	27		2
Erik HOLMGREN	D	25		4
Sauli KOUVA	M	1	(4)	
Pasi LAAKSONEN	G	23		
Kalle LEHTINEN	A	18	(5)	9
Jani MYLLYNIEMI	A	10	(10)	
Mika NENONEN	M	18	(4)	3
Tommi PAAVOLA	A	27		6
Pasi PIHAMAA	M	13	(5)	1
Tero PILVI	A	14	(7)	1
Jari RANTANEN	A		(3)	
Rami RANTANEN	M	25		2
Timo SALO	M		(2)	
Mikko SIMULA	M	14	(12)	1
Janne SUOKONAUTIO	M	7	(9)	
Jarmo TUUNAINEN	D	10	(2)	
Anssi VIREN	D	26		
Sami YLÄ-JUSSILA	M	26		3

LEAGUE RESULTS 1998

04/05/98	MyPa	A	2-0	Lehtinen, Paavola
09/05/98	TPS	H	3-1	Paavola, Pilvi, Holmgren
13/05/98	HJK	A	0-0	
17/05/98	RoPS	H	1-1	Lehtinen
20/05/98	VPS	A	1-2	Lehtinen
24/05/98	FF Jaro	A	3-0	Paavola 2, Lehtinen
29/05/98	TPS	A	1-1	Lehtinen
01/06/98	FinnPa	H	1-0	Nenonen
09/06/98	FC Haka	A	0-0	
15/06/98	FC Jazz	H	2-2	Helin P., Paavola
24/06/98	MyPa	H	2-0	Rantanen R., Paavola
02/07/98	HJK	H	0-1	
06/07/98	RoPS	A	1-1	Lehtinen
11/07/98	VPS	H	1-1	Holmgren
16/07/98	FF Jaro	H	1-0	Helin P.
27/07/98	FC Haka	H	5-1	Simula, Holmgren, Nenonen, Pihamaa, Belfield
01/08/98	FC Jazz	A	1-1	Ylä-Jussila (p)
04/08/98	FinnPa	A	0-0	
09/08/98	FF Jaro	H	2-1	Belfield, Ylä-Jussila
15/08/98	FC Jazz	A	1-4	Ylä-Jussila
24/08/98	FinnPa	H	1-0	Holmgren
31/08/98	TPS	A	2-0	Belfield, Nenonen
09/09/98	RoPS	A	1-2	Lehtinen
13/09/98	MyPa	H	1-0	Belfield
19/09/98	VPS	H	1-1	Lehtinen
26/09/98	FC Haka	A	1-3	Lehtinen
04/10/98	HJK	H	1-1	Rantanen R.

ROPS

CLUB DIRECTORY

Rovaniemen Palloseura
PL 2254
96201 Rovaniemi
tel - (016) 314977
fax - (016) 319837
Year of Formation - 1950
President - Matti Pelttari
Manager - Jouko Kiistala
Coach - Kari Virtanen
Stadium - Keskuskenttä (4,000)

MAJOR HONOURS
Domestic Cup - (1) 1986.

APPEARANCES 98

	P	Ap	(s)	Gls
John ALLEN (ENG)	A	21	(5)	4
Dabid CHILUFYA (ZAM)	D	8	(1)	
Matti HIUKKA	A	25	(2)	11
Mika HUIKARI	M	1	(1)	
Tero KEMPPAINEN	D	26		1
Matti KILPELÄ	A	1		
Marko KOIVURANTA	M	17	(5)	
Timo KORSUMÄKI	D	7	(4)	
Tuomo KÖNÖNEN	A	1	(6)	1
Joni LEHTONEN	M	11	(6)	
Mika LUMIJÄRVI	M	19	(5)	1
Mordon MALITOLI (ZAM)	D	21		1
Jani MERILÄINEN	G	27		
Silvester MOSANDA (ZAM)	A	3	(1)	
Ilkka MÄKELÄ	D	25		
Tomi PAKARINEN	D	26	(1)	1
Zeddy SAILETI (ZAM)	M	26		6
Tero TAIPALE	M	12	(8)	
Mikko TUOMAINEN	D	1	(1)	
Vesa WIMMER	D	18	(4)	
Samuli YLIASKA	M	1	(12)	

LEAGUE RESULTS 1998

02/05/98	TPS	A	0-0	
06/05/98	VPS	A	2-0	Hiukka 2
10/05/98	HJK	H	0-1	
17/05/98	PK-35	A	1-1	Saileti
20/05/98	FF Jaro	H	0-1	
23/05/98	FinnPa	A	2-1	Saileti, Allen
30/05/98	FC Haka	H	1-1	Saileti (p)
08/06/98	FC Jazz	A	1-2	Malitoli
14/06/98	TPS	H	2-0	Pakarinen, Hiukka
17/06/98	MyPa	H	0-2	
28/06/98	HJK	A	0-2	
01/07/98	VPS	H	2-1	Saileti, Lumijärvi
06/07/98	PK-35	H	1-1	Hiukka
13/07/98	FF Jaro	A	1-1	Hiukka
15/07/98	FinnPa	H	1-1	og
18/07/98	FC Haka	A	2-4	Hiukka 2
26/07/98	FC Jazz	H	1-1	Kemppainen
02/08/98	MyPa	A	2-2	Saileti, Hiukka
09/08/98	FC Haka	A	0-0	
15/08/98	TPS	H	3-3	Allen, Hiukka 2
22/08/98	VPS	A	0-4	
31/08/98	HJK	A	2-0	Hiukka, Allen
09/09/98	PK-35	H	2-1	Allen, Könönen
13/09/98	FF Jaro	A	0-0	
20/09/98	FinnPa	H	0-0	
27/09/98	MyPa	A	1-1	Saileti
04/10/98	FC Jazz	H	0-0	

TPS

Turun Palloseura
PL 653
20701 Turku
tel - (02) 2762760
fax - (02) 2762770
Year of Formation - 1922
President - Juhka Aarnivaara
Coach - Siegfried Melzig; Seppo Miettinen
Stadium - Kupittaa (10,000)

MAJOR HONOURS
League Championship - (8) 1928, 1939, 1941,
1949, 1968, 1971, 1972, 1975.
Domestic Cup - (2) 1991, 1994.

	P	Ap	(s)	Gls
Jukka BJÖRN	D	1		
Marco CASAGRANDE	M	23	(1)	3
Tom ENBERG	A	19	(3)	2
Peter ENCKELMAN	G	24		
Mikko HARJU	D	4	(1)	
Juha HERNE	M	14	(6)	
Petri IHONEN	D	21		
Petri JALAVA	D	12	(5)	
Toni JÄRVINEN	D	8	(5)	
Petteri KAIJASILTA	A	18	(5)	3
Juha LALLUKKA	D	1		
Kim LEHTONEN	M	25		
Joni MELTORANTA	A		(9)	2
Vesa NOPONEN	M	7	(13)	
Tommi PAATTAKAINEN	G	3		
Markus PAIJA	D	24		1
Saku PUHAKAINEN	A	23	(1)	5
Petro PUNNA	M	11	(2)	1
Tuukka SALONEN	A	9	(11)	3
Petri SULONEN	D	17	(1)	
Mika WALLDEN	M	12	(1)	1
Hans WIKBERG	M	19	(4)	4
Jussi VILJANEN	A	2	(3)	

02/05/98	RoPS	H	0-0	
09/05/98	PK-35	A	1-3	Kaijasilta
13/05/98	FF Jaro	H	3-0	Enberg, Kaijasilta, Puhakainen
18/05/98	FinnPa	A	1-1	Wikberg
20/05/98	FC Haka	H	1-2	Wikberg
24/05/98	FC Jazz	A	0-0	
29/05/98	PK-35	H	1-1	Casagrande
01/06/98	MyPa	H	2-2	Wallden, Paija
09/06/98	VPS	H	1-2	Casagrande
14/06/98	RoPS	A	0-2	
17/06/98	HJK	A	2-1	Salonen, Meltoranta
01/07/98	FF Jaro	A	0-5	
07/07/98	FinnPa	H	1-0	Casagrande
15/07/98	FC Jazz	H	1-1	Puhakainen
20/07/98	MyPa	A	1-0	Puhakainen
23/07/98	FC Haka	A	0-1	
26/07/98	VPS	A	2-0	Wikberg, Salonen
03/08/98	HJK	H	1-1	Puhakainen
08/08/98	HJK	H	0-1	
15/08/98	RoPS	A	3-3	Salonen, Wikberg, Meltoranta
24/08/98	FF Jaro	H	1-1	Kaijasilta
31/08/98	PK-35	H	0-2	
09/09/98	FC Haka	A	1-0	Puhakainen
12/09/98	VPS	A	0-0	
21/09/98	FC Jazz	H	1-0	Enberg
27/09/98	FinnPa	A	0-2	
04/10/98	MyPa	H	1-0	Punna

VPS

CLUB DIRECTORY

Vaasan Palloseura
Hartmanninkuja 4
65100 Vaasa
tel - (06) 3620705
fax - (06) 3620706
Year of Formation - 1924
President - Jukka Niemi
Manager - Kari Kujanpää
Coach - Hannu Touru (99 - Sören Cratz)
Stadium - Hietalahti (5,000)

MAJOR HONOURS
League Championship - (2) 1945, 1948.

APPEARANCES 98

		P	Ap	(s)	Gls
Roy ESSENDOH (SCO)		A	4		
Jyrki HUHTAMÄKI		M	21		4
Sasu IIVONEN		M	16	(3)	
Markus JUHOLA		D	1	(2)	
Miikka KAJANDER		M	16	(4)	3
Juuso KANGASKORPI		A	25	(1)	4
Juha KARVINEN		A	26	(1)	5
Tomi KINNUNEN		D	8		2
Petri KOKKO		M	20	(1)	
Timo LAHTIVUORI		A	6	(3)	
Roger LANGE (NOR)		D	11	(1)	
Kimmo LIPPONEN		M	25		2
Rami LOUKE		A		(1)	
Gunnar NOREBØ (NOR)		M	3	(5)	1
Tomas NYGÅRD		A	4	(9)	1
Björn NYMAN		D	1	(9)	2
Mike PELTOLA		D	24	(2)	1
Ville PRIHA		A	16	(8)	7
Juha REINI		D	7		
Henri SILLANPÄÄ		G	2	(1)	
Björn STRINGHEIM (SWE)		G	25		
Tero SUOMINEN		D	3	(5)	
Marko SUOSTE		D	22	(1)	2
Kimmo TARKKIO		A	11	(15)	8

LEAGUE RESULTS 1998

02/05/98	HJK	A	1-1	Kinnunen
06/05/98	RoPS	H	0-2	
11/05/98	FC Haka	H	3-0	Karvinen, Kajander, Priha
16/05/98	FC Jazz	A	1-0	Kinnunen
20/05/98	PK-35	H	2-1	Lipponen, Priha
23/05/98	MyPa	A	3-0	Kangaskorpi, Kajander, Nyman
31/05/98	FF Jaro	H	3-0	Priha, Tarkkio, Kajander
09/06/98	TPS	A	2-1	Priha, Tarkkio
17/06/98	FinnPa	H	3-1	Kangaskorpi 2, Karvinen
24/06/98	HJK	H	1-1	Suoste
28/06/98	FC Haka	A	1-2	Nyman
01/07/98	RoPS	A	1-2	Huhtamäki (p)
05/07/98	FC Jazz	H	4-0	Karvinen, Lipponen, Tarkkio 2
11/07/98	PK-35	A	1-1	Tarkkio
15/07/98	MyPa	H	3-2	Priha 2, Nygård
19/07/98	FF Jaro	A	1-0	Tarkkio
26/07/98	TPS	H	0-2	
01/08/98	FinnPa	A	2-2	Karvinen, Suoste
08/08/98	FC Jazz	H	0-0	
14/08/98	FinnPa	A	0-0	
22/08/98	RoPS	H	4-0	Karvinen, Norebø, Tarkkio, Kangaskorpi
30/08/98	FF Jaro	A	1-1	Huhtamäki
09/09/98	MyPa	H	2-4	Priha, Tarkkio
12/09/98	TPS	H	0-0	
19/09/98	PK-35	A	1-1	Peltola
26/09/98	HJK	A	1-3	Huhtamäki (p)
04/10/98	FC Haka	H	1-0	Huhtamäki (p)

PROMOTED CLUBS

SECOND DIVISION FINAL TABLES 1998

FIRST PHASE

NORTH

		Pd	W	D	L	F	A	Pt	GD
1	KPT-85	18	9	5	4	33	22	32	+11
2	FC Ilves	18	10	1	7	32	19	31	+13
3	Pyry Nokia	18	9	4	5	24	16	31	+8
4	TP-Seinäjoki	18	9	3	6	31	24	30	+7
5	TPV	18	8	5	5	28	28	29	0
6	MP	18	6	3	9	35	37	21	-2
7	KajHa	18	5	5	8	23	32	20	-9
8	JJK	18	6	2	10	15	32	20	-17
9	KPV-j	18	4	7	7	25	26	19	-1
10	VarTP	18	3	7	8	19	29	16	-10

SOUTH

		Pd	W	D	L	F	A	Pt	GD
1	FC Lahti	18	9	5	4	36	15	32	+21
2	FC Inter	18	9	5	4	32	16	32	+16
3	KTP	18	10	2	6	40	25	32	+15
4	HIK	18	9	4	5	31	21	31	+10
5	Atlantis	18	5	8	5	19	22	23	-3
6	FC Honka	18	5	5	8	16	23	23	-7
7	P-Iirot	18	5	6	7	21	29	21	-8
8	Kultsu	18	4	7	7	17	24	19	-7
9	Gnistan	18	4	5	9	24	41	17	-17
10	FC Hämeenlinna	18	2	6	10	12	32	12	-20

SECOND PHASE

		Pd	W	D	L	F	A	Pt	GD
1	**FC Lahti**	9	7	1	1	18	7	27	+11
2	**KTP**	9	7	1	1	18	4	24	ı14
3	**FC Inter**	9	4	2	3	9	10	17	-1
4	TPV	9	4	3	2	11	11	15	0
5	FC Ilves	9	3	3	3	14	16	15	-2
6	KPT-85	9	2	2	5	13	14	13	-1
7	TP-Seinäjoki	9	3	3	3	7	8	13	-1
8	HIK	9	1	4	4	10	15	8	-5
9	Pyry Nokia	9	1	2	6	10	20	7	-10
10	Atlantis	9	1	3	5	15	20	6	-5

N.B. The top five teams from the two First Phase Groups qualify for the Second Phase with the following bonus points: 1st place = 5 pts; 2nd = 3 pts; 3rd = 2 pts; 4th = 1 pts; 5th = 0 pts.

PROMOTION PLAY-OFFS

FC Ilves 1, TPV 4

TPV 1, FinnPa 1
FinnPa 2, TPV 2
(3-3; TPV on away goals)

CLUB DIRECTORY

FC Lahti
Rautatienkatu 19, 15110 Lahti
tel - (03) 880810
fax - (03) 8808131
Year of Formation - 1996
President - Erkki Puolakka
Manager - Jussi Lumio
Coach - Esa Pekonen
Stadium - Lahden Stadion (15,000)

CLUB DIRECTORY

Kotkan TP
Puistotie 9-11, 48100 Kotka
tel - (05) 2181600
fax - (05) 2181601
Year of Formation - 1927
President - Jaakko Kilpeläinen
Manager - Jukka Vakkila
Coach - Hannu Touru
Stadium - Kotkan Urheilukeskus (10,000)

CLUB DIRECTORY

FC International
Linnankatu 36 A1, 20100 Turku
tel - (02) 2312552
fax - (02) 2342500
Year of Formation - 1993
President - Stefan Håkans
Coach - Timo Askolin
Stadium - Kupittaa (10,000)

CLUB DIRECTORY

TPV
Teiskontie 1 A 7, 33540 Tampere
tel - (03) 2617214
fax - (03) 2617241
Year of Formation - 1995
President - Jukka Gustafsson
Manager - Miika Juntunen
Coach - Jan Mak; Ian Crawford (99 - Jan Mak)
Stadium - Tammelan Stadion (6,000)

MAJOR HONOURS
League Championship - (1) 1994.

FRANCE

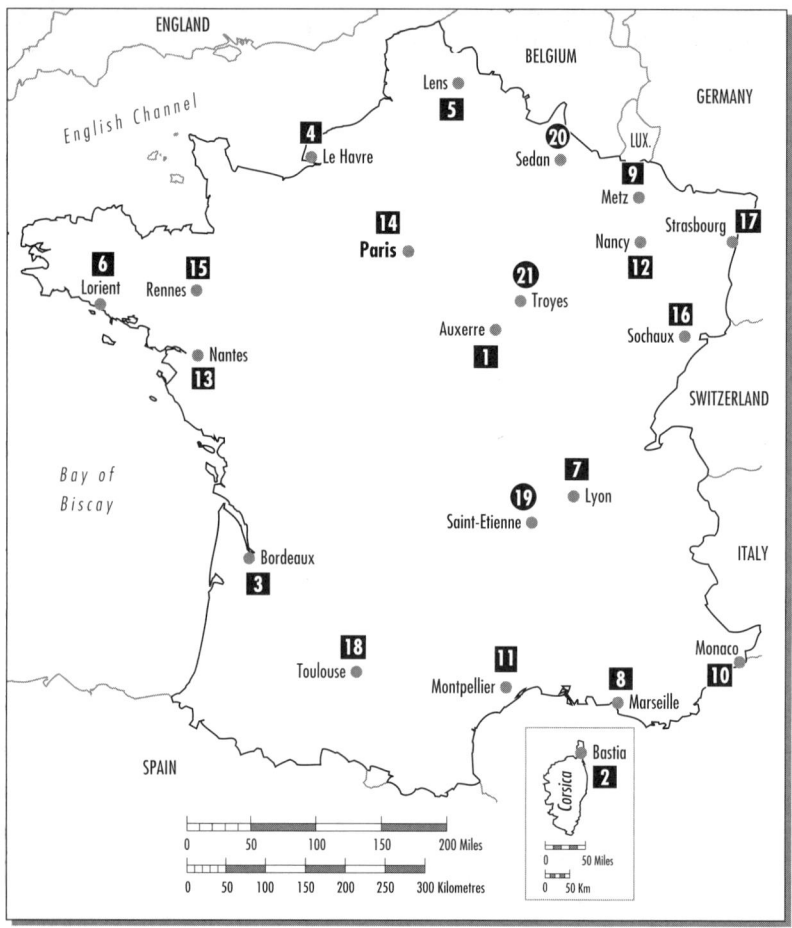

1	AJ AUXERRE	383	12	AS NANCY-LORRAINE	394
2	SC BASTIA	384	13	FC NANTES	395
3	GIRONDINS DE BORDEAUX	385	14	PARIS SAINT-GERMAIN	396
4	LE HAVRE AC	386	15	STADE RENNAIS FC	397
5	RC LENS	387	16	FC SOCHAUX	398
6	FC LORIENT	388	17	RC STRASBOURG	399
7	OLYMPIQUE LYONNAIS	389	18	TOULOUSE FC	400
8	OLYMPIQUE MARSEILLE	390	Promoted clubs		
9	FC METZ	391	19	AS SAINT-ETIENNE	401
10	AS MONACO	392	20	CS SEDAN ARDENNES	401
11	MONTPELLIER HSC	393	21	A TROYES AC	401

WORLD CHAMPIONS START TO WOBBLE

'Unknown' gives final twist to title thriller

FEDERATION DIRECTORY

Fédération Française de Football
60 bis Avenue d'Iena, 75783 Paris cedex 16
tel - (1 44) 317300   Year of Formation - 1919
fax - (1 47) 208296   President - Claude Simonet
                             Secretary - Gérard Ernault
Stadium - Stade de France, Saint-Denis (80,000)

The season after World Cup victory was a predictably positive one for French football. Although *Les Bleus* made rather a meal of their Euro 2000 qualification, the domestic game boomed like never before. First Division crowds rose sharply to a new average high of 19,807, there was a best-ever collective performance from French clubs in the UEFA Cup, and the title race remained undecided until the very last minute of the final game, with a different club being proclaimed champions of France for the sixth year in succession.

Intense, nerve-racking excitement was also evident in the race for European qualification, the battle to avoid relegation and the quest for promotion. But it was the season-long duel at the top of the table between Bordeaux and Marseille which captured the biggest headlines. For nine months the two clubs played cat-and-mouse with each other, swapping places incessantly and never allowing the other to stray out of reach. It was edge-of-the-seat entertainment for partisans and neutrals alike. Nobody dared predict how it would end, because the only certainty was that the outcome would be uncertain right through to the last kick of the season.

With three games left and both clubs beginning to feel the pressure, Marseille held a two-point lead. Both faced important away games - Bordeaux at defending champions Lens, Marseille at arch-rivals Paris Saint-Germain. For most of that Tuesday evening it looked as if Marseille were going to break clear. With ten minutes remaining

LEAGUE CHAMPIONSHIP RESULTS 98/99

		1	2	3	4	5	6	7	8	9	10	11	12	13	14	15	16	17	18
1	AJ Auxerre		1-0	3-1	0-0	1-2	5-0	1-0	1-1	1-0	0-3	2-2	3-2	1-1	0-1	2-0	3-1	3-1	1-2
2	SC Bastia	2-0		2-0	2-0	1-1	2-1	4-1	0-2	3-0	3-1	2-2	1-2	1-0	2-0	0-1	1-1	0-0	1-1
3	Girondins de Bordeaux	1-0	2-0		3-0	1-0	0-0	1-0	4-1	6-0	0-1	3-1	2-0	2-0	3-1	4-0	0-0	1-0	3-1
4	Le Havre AC	2-1	1-1	2-3		3-1	0-1	1-0	0-0	0-0	1-2	1-1	1-1	2-1	0-4	2-0	3-0	0-1	0-0
5	RC Lens	2-2	1-0	2-4	0-1		1-1	0-3	4-0	2-0	1-1	1-0	2-1	2-4	2-1	3-1	1-1	3-0	3-1
6	FC Lorient	1-1	3-1	0-2	0-0	1-1		0-1	1-3	1-1	1-2	1-1	0-1	1-1	2-0	1-1	4-1	0-1	1-0
7	Olympique Lyonnais	2-1	2-1	2-1	0-0	3-1	2-2		2-1	2-0	1-1	2-0	2-1	2-1	1-1	1-2	4-1	3-2	6-1
8	Olympique Marseille	1-0	3-1	2-2	2-0	1-0	4-1	0-0		3-0	1-0	5-4	4-0	2-0	0-0	1-1	4-0	1-0	2-0
9	FC Metz	2-0	4-0	0-2	1-0	0-1	3-0	3-2	0-1		1-0	3-1	2-3	1-0	1-1	0-0	1-1	1-0	0-0
10	AS Monaco	3-2	1-1	0-2	3-0	2-0	1-0	0-1	1-2	0-0		2-0	3-0	3-1	2-1	4-2	4-1	2-1	1-1
11	Montpellier HSC	3-0	3-0	1-1	2-0	1-0	5-1	1-3	0-1	1-1	2-3		1-1	1-2	2-1	3-1	0-0	1-1	3-0
12	AS Nancy-Lorraine	1-1	1-2	2-3	1-0	0-1	2-0	0-0	2-3	1-0	1-2	0-1		1-0	0-0	0-1	1-1	1-1	2-0
13	FC Nantes	2-2	2-0	0-0	1-1	2-0	1-1	2-0	0-1	0-0	0-1	1-1	2-0		0-0	2-1	2-0	1-0	2-0
14	Paris Saint-Germain	2-0	2-0	2-3	3-0	0-1	1-2	0-1	2-1	2-2	1-0	0-1	1-2	0-0		2-1	2-1	0-0	0-0
15	Stade Rennais FC	1-0	2-0	1-1	2-1	2-0	1-0	0-0	1-1	1-0	2-1	3-2	2-1	2-3	2-1		4-0	1-1	1-0
16	FC Sochaux	1-1	2-1	2-0	1-0	0-4	0-1	1-2	0-0	1-1	1-1	4-0	1-1	1-1	1-0	0-3		1-1	2-1
17	RC Strasbourg	2-1	1-1	3-2	0-1	1-1	2-0	0-0	0-2	0-0	1-1	2-1	1-2	2-2	0-1	1-1	1-1		2-0
18	Toulouse FC	0-0	2-1	0-3	0-0	3-2	1-4	0-0	1-0	1-0	0-0	2-5	1-1	2-3	2-1	0-1	1-1	0-1	

LEAGUE CHAMPIONSHIP FINAL TABLE 98/99

			Home				Away					Total						
		P	W	D	L	F	A	W	D	L	F	A	W	D	L	F	A	P	GD
1	Girondins de Bordeaux	34	14	2	1	36	5	8	4	5	30	24	22	6	6	66	29	72	+37
2	Olympique Marseille	34	13	4	0	36	9	8	4	5	20	19	21	8	5	56	28	71	+28
3	Olympique Lyonnais	34	12	4	1	37	17	6	5	6	14	14	18	9	7	51	31	63	+20
4	AS Monaco	34	11	3	3	32	15	7	5	5	20	17	18	8	8	52	32	62	+20
5	Stade Rennais FC	34	12	4	1	28	12	5	4	8	17	26	17	8	9	45	38	59	+7
6	RC Lens	34	9	4	4	30	21	5	3	9	16	22	14	7	13	46	43	49	+3
7	FC Nantes	34	8	7	2	20	8	4	5	8	20	26	12	12	10	40	34	48	+6
8	Montpellier HSC	34	8	5	4	30	16	3	5	9	23	34	11	10	13	53	50	43	+3
9	Paris Saint-Germain	34	7	4	6	20	15	3	5	9	14	20	10	9	15	34	35	39	-1
10	FC Metz	34	9	4	4	23	12	0	8	9	5	25	9	12	13	28	37	39	-9
11	AS Nancy-Lorraine	34	5	5	7	16	16	5	4	8	19	29	10	9	15	35	45	39	-10
12	RC Strasbourg	34	5	8	4	19	17	3	6	8	11	19	8	14	12	30	36	38	-6
13	SC Bastia	34	9	5	3	27	13	1	3	13	10	33	10	8	16	37	46	38	-9
14	AJ Auxerre	34	9	4	4	28	17	0	6	11	12	28	9	10	15	40	45	37	-5
15	Le Havre AC	34	6	6	5	19	17	2	5	10	4	21	8	11	15	23	38	35	-15
16	FC Lorient	34	4	7	6	18	18	4	4	9	15	31	8	11	15	33	49	35	-16
17	FC Sochaux	34	6	7	4	19	18	0	8	9	11	36	6	15	13	30	54	33	-24
18	Toulouse FC	34	5	6	6	16	23	1	5	11	8	30	6	11	17	24	53	29	-29

they led 1-0 in Paris while Bordeaux were being held 2-2 in Lens. A four-point lead with two games left looked imminent. But then the entire picture changed. Bordeaux scored twice to beat Lens 4-2, and, in a remarkable turnaround at the Parc des Princes, PSG came from behind to win the game 2-1, with Bruno Rodriguez scoring the winner in the 89th minute. Now, suddenly, it was Bordeaux who headed the table, by a single point.

There was a long 18-day gap before the two clubs resumed their duel. Both scraped narrow 1-0 home wins, against Lyon and Auxerre, respectively, which meant that everything hinged on the events of the final day. Marseille, a point behind and with a significantly inferior goal difference, simply had to win at Nantes. If they didn't, then, barring a freakishly heavy defeat in Paris, Bordeaux would be the champions. But if Marseille did take the three points, then Bordeaux had to do likewise.

There was a widely-held suspicion among Marseille fans that PSG, their arch-enemy, would simply hand the title to Bordeaux, but it did not pan out that way at all. While Marseille scored first in Nantes, through Robert Pires, and held onto their lead, Bordeaux went ahead twice, through the league's leading scorer Sylvain Wiltord, only for PSG to equalise on each occasion. The Girondins' dream looked to be over but with 89 minutes on the clock striker Lilian Laslandes fed a pass into the penalty area. The man on the end of it was an 18-year-old trialist from

Guinea who had only just come on as a substitute and was making only his third appearance for the club. His name was Pascal Feindouno. Few people in France had ever heard of him, but in the blink of an eye the youngster became a household name. That was all the time it took for him to slip the ball between the legs of PSG 'keeper Bernard Lama and give Bordeaux the 3-2 victory that made them the new champions of France.

It was an incredible finale to an extraordinary season. The symapthy for Marseille was widespread. To lose out in such a manner was cruel and unfortunate in the extreme. But, on the other hand, nobody could deny Bordeaux what had been a famous triumph, even if they had waited until the 3,059th minute of the season to secure it. The scenes of jubilation back in their home town were incredible. While the team flew back to Bordeaux from Paris straight after the game, 40,000 fans headed for the Parc Lescure, where they eventually greeted their conquering heroes for a mass celebration at three o'clock in the morning. While the rest of France slept, Bordeaux partied.

The neutral perspective was that the Girondins deserved to finish first. They spent 19 weeks on top of the table (compared to 13 for Marseille) and never fell below second place. Unfancied at the start of the season, they were the most consistent and attractive team in the land, scoring a league-best total of 66 goals - ten more than

INTERNATIONAL HONOURS

World Cup Finals appearances: 1930, 1938 (2nd round), 1954, 1958 (3rd), 1966, 1978, 1982 (4th), 1986 (3rd), 1998 (Winners)

European Championship appearances : 1960 (4th), 1964, 1968, 1984 (Winners), 1992, 1996 (semi-finals)

European Club Competitions

Champions' Cup	Olympique Marseille (1993)
Cup-winners' Cup	Paris Saint-Germain FC (1996)

of coach Elie Baup that Bordeaux would go for victory in every game, and he was able to put that into practice thanks to a superb attacking quartet of Ali Benarbia, Johan Micoud, Lilian Laslandes and Sylvain Wiltord. All four players enjoyed the best season of their careers, as did skipper Michel Pavon in the midfield engine-room and Ulrich Ramé in goal.

While Bordeaux savoured the plaudits, Marseille licked their wounds. They had been one minute from glory and that was hard to take, but on reflection they knew that they had made one mistake too many during the closing weeks. Losing in both Lens and Paris, the scenes of Bordeaux's two famous wins, proved fatal, and, going further back, they should have taken more than one point from successive vsits to relegation-bound Toulouse and Sochaux. Marseille found their best form in the autumn when they set a new club record by winning eight successive matches. Their average attendance at the enlarged Stade Vélodrome was 51,409 (almost twice that of Bordeaux),

Marseille - which was achieved without the assistance of a single penalty award in their favour. If the end-of-season wins in Lens and Paris ranked as their most telling victories, the 4-1 bludgeoning of Marseille in January, with all four goals coming in the first half, was their most enjoyable. They won 14 of their 17 home games but were equally ambitious on their travels. It was the philosophy

DOMESTIC CUP 98/99

1/32 FINALS
Olympique Marseille 2, AJ Auxerre 0
FC Metz 1, Girondins de Bordeaux 0
Chamois Niortais 1, RC Strasbourg 1
(aet; 2-3 on pens.)
FC Sochaux 3, AS Beauvais-Oise 1
SAOS Troyes 2, Montpellier HSC 1
Amiens SCF 1, AS Monaco 1 (aet; 5-4 on pens.)
Stade Lavallois 1, AS Nancy-Lorraine 0
LB Châteauroux 1, Olympique Lyonnais 0
Paris FC 1, FC Lorient 0
Armentiéres 2, RC Lens 5 (aet)
La Roche/Yon 0, FC Nantes 1
Dijon 2, SC Bastia 1
Coulaines 0, Stade Rennais FC 4
Jura-Sud 1, Toulouse FC 1 (aet; 8-7 on pens.)
Blagnac 0, Le Havre AC 2 (aet)
En Avant Guingamp 1, Red Star 93 0
FC Istres 1, Nîmes Olympique 3
GFCO Ajaccio 1, OGC Nice 1 (aet; 4-2 on pens.)
Le Mans UC 72 4, Louhans-Cuiseaux 71 1
Valenciennes FC 2, ES Wasquehal 3
Chaumont 0, CS Sedan Ardennes 3
Dives 0, Lille OSC 2
Saint-Denis-Saint-Leu 1, SCO Angers 0
Saint-Georges-Les-Ancizes 1, FC Martigues 1
(aet; 5-4 on pens.)
Mende 1, AS Angoulême 4
Rodez 0, Clermont Foot 1
Châtellerault 2, Fontenay 2 (aet; 6-5 on pens.)
Chasselay 0, Grenoble Foot 3
Vauban Strasbourg 1, Boulogne 2

Grand Rouen 1, Sarrebourg 0 (aet)
Mondeville 0, La Montagnarde 0 (aet 1-3 on pens.)
Thouars Foot 79 1, Paris Saint-Germain 2 (aet)

1/16 FINALS
RC Lens 3, Olympique Marseille 1
Paris Saint-Germain 1, FC Nantes 1
(aet; 4-5 on pens.)
ES Wasquehal 0, FC Metz 2
Le Mans UC 72 2, Stade Rennais FC 0
Amiens SCF 1, Le Havre AC 0
En Avant Guingamp 2, RC Strasbourg 1 (aet)
Saint-Georges-Les-Ancizes 1, FC Sochaux 0
LB Châteauroux 1, Stade Lavallois 2
GFCO Ajaccio 1, SAOS Troyes 1 (aet; 1-3 on pens.)
Dijon 0, CS Sedan Ardennes 4
Boulogne 1, Lille OSC 2
La Montagnarde 4, Paris FC 0
AS Angoulême 4, Châtellerault 0
Grand Rouen 2, Saint-Denis-Saint-Leu 0
Clermont Foot 4, Jura-Sud 1
Grenoble Foot 2, Nîmes Olympique 3 (aet)

1/8 FINALS
FC Metz 1, FC Nantes 3
RC Lens 1, Stade Lavallois 1 (aet; 2-4 on pens.)
En Avant Guingamp 1, Lille OSC 0
Amiens SCF 1, CS Sedan Ardennes 2
AS Angoulême 1, SAOS Troyes 0
Clermont Foot 0, Le Mans UC 72 2
Saint-Georges-Les-Ancizes 0, Nîmes Olympique 2
La Montagnarde 0, Grand Rouen 2 (aet)

QUARTER-FINALS
FC Nantes 2 (Monterrubio 30, Deroff 90),
En Avant Guingamp 0

Le Mans UC 72 3 (Revillet 28, Haddadou 65, 68),
Stade Lavallois 1 (Chaouch 39)

AS Angoulême 0,
Nîmes Olympique 2 (Ecker 49, Mendy 66p)

Grand Rouen 0,
CS Sedan Ardennes 2 (Di Rocco 21, Borbiconi 52)

SEMI-FINALS
FC Nantes 1 (Savinaud 77),
Nîmes Olympique 0

CS Sedan Ardennes 4
(Di Rocco 76, Quint 96, N'Diefi 108, 118),
Le Mans UC 72 3
(Bakari 41p, Chagnaud 114, Revillet 119) (aet)

FINAL
15/05/99, Saint-Denis
FC NANTES 1 Monterrubio (57p)
CS SEDAN ARDENNES 0
referee - Garibian

FC NANTES - Landreau; Chanelet, Decroix, Fabbri
(Gillet 67); Deroff, Carrière, Devineau (Savinaud 87),
Piocelle, Olembé; Monterrubio, Da Rocha (Suffo 90).

CS SEDAN ARDENNES - Sachy; Borbiconi (Crosnier
70), Oliveira (Dangbeto 70), Satorra, Elzéard;
Deblock, Pabois (N'Diefi 61), Faure, Quint; Di Rocco,
Mionnet.

NATIONAL TEAM APPEARANCES 98/99

Coach - Roger LEMERRE	AUT	ISL	RUS	AND	MAR	ENG	UKR	ARM	RUS	AND	Cps	Gls
Bernard LAMA (07/04/63) - Paris Saint-Germain	G		G	G							40	-
Christian KAREMBEU (03/12/70) - Real Madrid (ESP)	D	D						s79		D	40	1
Lilian THURAM (01/01/72) - Parma (ITA)	D	D	D		D	D	D	D79	D		47	2
Frank LEBOEUF (22/01/68) - Chelsea (ENG)	D79	D		D	s46	s46				D	22	3
Bixente LIZARAZU (09/12/69) - FC Bayern München (GER)	D46	D	D	D			D	D			45	2
Alain BOGHOSSIAN (27/10/70) - Parma (ITA)	M	s46	s83	M			s78	D	s90	M	19	2
Didier DESCHAMPS (15/10/68) - Juventus (ITA)	M46	M	M	M	M46	M90	M	M	M		85	4
Zinedine ZIDANE (23/06/72) - Juventus (ITA)	M46	M	M	M	M66	M					45	11
Tony VAIRELLES (10/04/73) - RC Lens	A		s88	A							3	-
Lilian LASLANDES (04/09/71) - Girondins de Bordeaux	A82	A									3	1
Thierry HENRY (17/08/77) - AS Monaco	A65	s67									11	3
Vincent CANDELA (24/10/73) - Roma (ITA)	s46			D	D	s90		D88	D		17	1
Frédéric DEHU (01/12/72) - RC Lens	s46										1	-
Youri DJORKAEFF (09/03/68) - Inter (ITA)	s46	M	A54	M83	M	M83	M	M69	M90		54	20
Robert PIRES (29/01/73) - Olympique Marseille	s65	A	M	s69	s46	M46	M84	s69	s88	s61	27	3
Alain GOMA (05/10/72) - Paris Saint-Germain	s79										2	-
Florian MAURICE (20/01/74) - Olympique Marseille	s82				A						5	-
Fabien BARTHEZ (28/06/71) - AS Monaco		G			G	G	G	G	G		26	-
Christophe DUGARRY (24/03/72) - Olympique Marseille		A67		A69	A46	s46	A68	A46	A59	A	35	5
Laurent BLANC (19/11/65) - Olympique Marseille			D	D	D46	D46	D	D	D	D	81	14
Marcel DESAILLY (07/09/68) - Chelsea (ENG)			D		D	D	D	D	D	D	56	2
Emmanuel PETIT (22/09/70) - Arsenal (ENG)			M46		s46	M	M78		M	M56	32	3
Nicolas ANELKA (14/03/79) - Arsenal (ENG)			A88	s69	s66	A83	A	A	A	A	9	3
Patrick VIEIRA (23/06/76) - Arsenal (ENG)			s54			s83		M	s59	s56	14	-
David TREZEGUET (15/10/77) - AS Monaco			A69					s46			13	2
Sylvain WILTORD (10/05/74) - Girondins de Bordeaux						s83	s68	A	A	A	5	2
Vikash DHORASOO (10/10/73) - Olympique Lyonnais							s84		M61		2	-
Ulrich RAME (19/09/72) - Girondins de Bordeaux									G		1	-

which certainly contributed towards their unbeaten home record. Coach Rolland Courbis operated a relatively successful 'turnover' policy, although occasionally he decided to throw caution to the wind and field all four of his attacking aces - Faustino Ravanelli, Florian Maurice, Christophe Dugarry and Robert Pires. Marseille's most consistent player was skipper Laurent Blanc, who formed an excellent central defensive alliance with Cyril Domoraud - one which was transported en bloc to the big-spending Italians of Inter during the summer.

Marseille also took the silver medals in the UEFA Cup. They were the standard-bearers of a strong four-piece French delegation in that competition, in which Monaco reached the third round (prior to elimination by Marseille) and both Bordeaux and Lyon got as far as the quarter-finals before falling to Italian opposition. Bordeaux were really shaken up by a 6-0 mauling from Parma (after winning the first leg 2-1 at home), and it was that Italian club which also extinguished Marseille's bid for glory, in the final. Marseille went into that Moscow showdown severely depleted, mostly through suspension, and they were no match at all for the Serie A side, who cruised to an easy 3-0 win. So, there was no second European trophy for OM, but at least their runners-up spot in the league allowed them to return at last to the Champions' Cup - six years after they had lfted it in triumph in Munich.

Lyon also earned themselves a stab at a higher grade of European competition by finishing third in the league. Bernard Lacombe's team maintained their position throughout the final third of the season, and with a new backer arriving with a fistful of cash, the club from France's third-largest city appear to have the base for a promising future. Their UEFA Cup run was full of unexpected exploits, with victories in Blackburn, Bucharest and Bruges embroidering an eventful journey to the last eight which was brought to a halt by a 0-3 defeat in Bologna.

Only one UEFA Cup place was up for grabs via league placings, and that went to Monaco, who came on strong at the end to deny surprise package Rennes, taking 16 points from their last six games, which included a 1-0 win at Bordeaux - the champions' only home defeat of the campaign. Monaco's late surge was masterminded by new coach Claude Puel, who stepped up to replace the increasingly despondent Jean Tigana in January. Another mid-season departure was that of Thierry Henry, who left for Juventus. He, along with fellow French international David Trezeguet, had been the target of harsh criticism from club president Jean-Louis Campora and was clearly delighted to get away...even if, by the summer, he would be on the move again, leaving Juve for Arsenal.

Marseille's Cyril Domoraud (right) and Enrico Chiesa in UEFA Cup final action.

Internal disharmony was a constant factor throughout the season at Paris Saint-Germain. The pre-season favourites went from one catastrophe to another until they became the laughing stock of the league. Newly-appointed coach Alain Giresse failed miserably to make a competitive team out of all the high-profile summer signings - Alain Goma, Christian Wörns, Nicolas Ouédec, Igor Yanovskiy and French transfer record-breaker Jay-Jay Okocha, among others - and when PSG were dumped unceremoniously out of the European Cup-winners' Cup first round by Maccabi Haifa of Israel, it was only a matter of time before he departed. The call went out for former championship-winning boss Artur Jorge to return, but the experienced Portuguese coach forgot to pack his magic formula and he, too, failed to see out the season. PSG president Charles Biétry, who had never seen eye to eye with Artur Jorge in the past and was a lone voice in opposition to his re-appointment, decided to throw in the towel, and it was his successor, Pierre Lescure, who rubber-stamped the nomination of Giresse's former assistant Philippe Bergeroo to become PSG's third coach of the season in mid-March.

For once, PSG did not make up for their poor league form with a victory or two in the Cups. The best they managed was a place in the quarter-finals of the League Cup. Their defence of the French Cup ended in a penalty shoot-out defeat by Nantes at the 1/16-finals stage. They were not the only big name to go out early in that competition. In fact, by the time the quarter-finals arrived, remarkably, Nantes were the only First Division team still in the hat. It was an incredible scenario, but order was eventually restored in the latter stages and Nantes went

Florian Maurice of Marseille (left), comes into close contact with Alain Boghossian of Parma in the UEFA Cup final.

EUROPEAN CUPS 98/99

CHAMPIONS' CUP
● RC LENS
Champions' League
1st match ARSENAL (ENG)
H 1-1 Keown (90og)
Warmuz; Sikora, Méride (Rool 76), Déhu, Etchi (Sankharé 82); Debève, Nyarko, Dalmat; Smicer, Nouma (Moreira 70), Vairelles.

2nd match DYNAMO KYIV (UKR)
A 1-1 Vairelles (62)
Warmuz; Etchi, Déhu, Magnier, Méride; Dalmat, Rool, Nyarko, Debève (Moreira 74); Smicer (Eloi 82), Vairelles (Nouma 67).

3rd match PANATHINAIKOS (GRE)
H 1-0 Eloi (81)
Warmuz; Sikora, Déhu, Méride; Debève, Dalmat (Eloi 65), Nyarko, Rool; Smicer (Moreira 72), Nouma, Vairelles.

4th match PANATHINAIKOS (GRE)
A 0-1
Warmuz; Sikora, Déhu, Magnier, Méride; Debève (Smicer 58), Nyarko, Rool, Dalmat; Vairelles, Nouma (Eloi 70).

5th match ARSENAL (ENG)
A 1-0 Debève (72)
Warmuz; Sikora, Magnier, Déhu, Lachor; Nyarko, Rool, Debève, Smicer (Moreira 81); Vairelles, Nouma (Eloi 60).

6th match DYNAMO KYIV (UKR)
H 1-3 Smicer (77)
Warmuz; Lachor, Magnier, Déhu, Méride (Brunel 81); Nyarko, Debève, Dalmat (Moreira 88), Smicer; Nouma, Eloi (Foé 64).

● FC METZ
Qualifying round HJK (FIN)
A 0-1
Letizi; Pierre, Strasser, Kastendeuch, Régis; Proment, Boffin (Diani 86), Rizzetto (Le Grix 73), Histilloles, Meyrieu; Lukic.
H 1-1 Meyrieu (79p)
Letizi; Pierre, Strasser, Kastendeuch, Régis (Asuar 69); Proment, Rizzetto, Boffin, Meyrieu; Lukic, Saha.

CUP WINNERS' CUP
● PARIS SAINT-GERMAIN
1st round MACCABI HAIFA (ISR)
H 1-1 Simone (83p)
Lama; Algerino, Goma, Wörns, Domi; Carotti, Yanovskiy (Lachuer 89), Adailton (Loko 46), Okocha; Ouédec, Simone.
A 2-3 Ouédec (72), Okocha (86)
Lama; Laspalles, Rabesandratana, Goma, Algerino; Ducrocq, Lachuer (Loko 84), Yanovskiy (Leroy J. 75), Okocha; Ouédec, Simone.

UEFA CUP
● AS MONACO
1st round LKS LODZ (POL)
A 3-1 Bendkowski (57og), Trezeguet (68p), Spehar (84)
Barthez; Sagnol, Konjic, Dumas, Pignol; Diao, Da Costa (Christanval 66), Gava; Giuly, Trezeguet (Spehar 73), Henry (Ikpeba 66).
H 0-0
Aubry; Martin, Konjic, Dumas (Pignol 68), Léonard; Da Costa (Christanval 46), Diao, Spehar; Giuly, Ikpeba (Trezeguet 68), Henry.

2nd round GRAZER AK (AUT)
A 3-3 Spehar (17, 60), Giuly (78)
Barthez; Sagnol, Irles, Dumas, Léonard; Da Costa (Giuly 46), Diao, Gava, Christanval (Diawara 60); Spehar, Ikpeba (Riise 83).
H 4-0 Gava (8, 67), Spehar (16), Diawara (55)
Barthez; Sagnol (Martin 46), Irles, Dumas, Konjic, Léonard; Diawara, Gava (Trezeguet 69); Giuly; Spehar, Ikpeba (Henry 69).

3rd round OLYMPIQUE MARSEILLE (FRA)
H 2-2 Trezeguet (17p), Giuly (56)
Barthez; Sagnol, Dumas, Djetou, Léonard; Giuly, Legwinski, Diawara (Lamouchi 68); Gava; Trezeguet, Ikpeba (Henry 68).
A 0-1 Barthez; Diawara, Konjic, Christanval, Pignol; Lamouchi (Irles 43); Legwinski, Djetou, Gava (Henry 71); Trezeguet, Ikpeba (Giuly 56).

● GIRONDINS DE BORDEAUX
1st round SK RAPID WIEN (AUT)
H 1-1 Hatz (23og)
Ramé; Jemmali (Diawara 70), Saveljic, Alicarte, Torres Mestre; Pavon, Diabaté, Micoud, Benarbia; Laslandes, Wiltord.
A 2-1 Alicarte (28), Diabaté (87)
Ramé; Jemmali (Diabaté 41), Saveljic, Alicarte, Torres Mestre; Pavon, Micoud (Vukomanovic 89), Musampa (Diawara 65), Benarbia; Laslandes, Wiltord.

2nd round VITESSE (HOL)
A 1-0 Wiltord (45)
Ramé; Afanou, Saveljic, Alicarte, Torres Mestre; Diabaté, Micoud, Musampa (Ferrier 83), Benarbia (Grenet 85); Laslandes, Wiltord (Diawara 90).
H 2-1 Micoud (9), Wiltord (63)
Ramé; Jemmali (Grenet 72), Saveljic, Alicarte, Torres Mestre; Diabaté, Micoud, Pavon, Benarbia; Laslandes (Diawara 80), Wiltord (Da Rocha 90).

3rd round GRASSHOPPER-CLUB ZÜRICH (SUI)
A 3-3 Wiltord (6, 74), Micoud (20)
Ramé; Afanou (Da Rocha 47), Saveljic, Alicarte; Diabaté, Pavon, Grenet, Micoud (Ferrier 88); Wiltord (Diawara 81).
H 0-0
Ramé; Jemmali (Musampa 60), Saveljic, Afanou, Torres Mestre; Pavon, Diabaté (Da Rocha 42), Grenet, Micoud; Laslandes (Diawara 89), Wiltord.

EUROPEAN CUPS 98/99 (CONTINUED)

Quarter-final PARMA (ITA)
H 2-1   Micoud (40), Wiltord (45)
Ramé; Grenet, Saveljic, Alicarte, Ferrier (Jemmali 74); Pavon, Diabaté, Micoud, Benarbia; Laslandes, Wiltord.
A 0-6
Ramé; Grenet, Saveljic, Alicarte, Torres Mestre; Pavon, Diabaté (Musampa 67), Micoud, Benarbia; Laslandes, Wiltord.

● **OLYMPIQUE LYONNAIS**
1st round BLACKBURN ROVERS (ENG)
A 1-0   Bak (85)
Coupet; Carteron, Fournier, Laville, Delmotte; Bak, Violeau, Bassila, Dhorasoo; Grassi, Caveglia (Linarès 70).
H 2-2   Caveglia (3), Grassi (36p)
Coupet; Carteron, Fournier, Laville, Delmotte; Violeau, Bak, Linarès, Dhorasoo; Grassi (Bassila 67), Caveglia (Cocard 27).

2nd round CRVENA ZVEZDA BEOGRAD (YUG)
A 2-1   Grassi (70), Kanouté (84)
Coupet; Uras, Laville, Bak, Carteron; Bassila, Violeau, Dhorasoo, Delmotte; Caveglia (Kanouté 68), Grassi (Linarès 86).
H 3-2   Caveglia (17, 44), Cocard (41)
Coupet; Uras, Fournier, Bak, Laville; Violeau, Bassila (Linarès 56), Delmotte, Dhorasoo; Caveglia (Malbranque 71), Cocard (Kanouté 81).

3rd round CLUB BRUGGE KV (BEL)
H 1-0   Bak (45)
Coupet; Carteron, Laville, Fournier, Delmotte; Malbranque (Cocard 76), Violeau, Bak, Dhorasoo (Uras 87); Caveglia, Grassi.
A 4-3   Caveglia (16, 55, 71), Dhorasoo (76)
Coupet; Carteron (Uras 63), Laville, Fournier, Delmotte; Bak, Violeau, Linarès; Malbranque (Bassila 72), Dhorasoo; Caveglia (Kanouté 77).

Quarter-final BOLOGNA (ITA)
A 0-3
Coupet; Carteron, Fournier, Laville, Bréchet; Bak, Violeau (Cocard 57), Linarès, Dhorasoo; Job, Caveglia.
H 2-0   Caveglia (16), Job (40)
Coupet; Carteron (Braizat 89), Fournier, Laville, Delmotte; Violeau (Bak 84), Malbranque (Linarès 60); Cocard, Dhorasoo, Job, Caveglia.

● **OLYMPIQUE MARSEILLE**
1st round SIGMA OLOMOUC (CZE)
A 2-2   Ravanelli (27), Roy (82)
Köpke; Issa, Blondeau, Domoraud; Brando (Gallas 72), Roy; Dugarry (Moses 78), Pires, Camara; Ravanelli, Maurice (Luccin 46).
H 4-0   Dugarry (18, 75), Pires (22, 83)
Köpke; Blondeau (Gallas 49), Blanc, Domoraud, Colleter; Roy, Pires, Luccin; Ravanelli, Maurice (Camara 78), Dugarry (Brando 76).

2nd round SV WERDER BREMEN (GER)
A 1-1   Maurice (67)
Köpke; Blondeau, Blanc, Domoraud, Luccin (Gallas 90); Brando, Roy, Pires; Ravanelli (Camara 84), Maurice, Dugarry (Bravo 72).
H 3-2   Maurice (35), Issa (52), Dugarry (78)
Köpke; Blondeau (Colleter 62); Blanc, Issa, Gallas; Domoraud, Luccin (Brando 77), Pires; Ravanelli (Dugarry 65), Maurice, Camara.

3rd round AS MONACO (FRA)
A 2-2   Pires (9), Camara (39)
Porato; Blondeau, Blanc, Issa, Colleter; Roy, Pires (Luccin 79), Brando; Camara (Moses 90), Maurice, Dugarry (Bravo 60).
H 1-0   Camara (71)
Porato; Blondeau, Blanc, Domoraud, Gallas; Brando, Roy, Luccin (Issa 87), Bravo (Gourvennec 61); Pires, Dugarry (Camara 46).

Quarter-final RC CELTA (ESP)
H 2-1   Maurice (33, 67)
Porato; Blondeau (Brando 78), Blanc, Domoraud, Gallas; Roy, Luccin, Pires, Dugarry; Maurice (Edson 86), Ravanelli (Camara 73).
A 0-0
Porato; Gallas, Blanc, Issa (Edson 80), Domoraud; Brando, Luccin, Bravo, Pires; Maurice (Guel 78), Dugarry (Camara 89).

Semi-final BOLOGNA (ITA)
H 0-0
Porato; Gallas, Issa, Blanc, Domoraud; Brando, Pires, Luccin (Bravo 78); Ravanelli, Maurice (Camara 78), Dugarry (Edson 67).
A 1-1   Blanc (86p)
Porato; Gallas, Blanc, Domoraud, Edson; Brando (Maurice 46), Luccin, Pires, Bravo (Gourvennec 77); Ravanelli, Dugarry (Camara 68)

Final PARMA (ITA)
Moscow
0-3
Porato; Blondeau, Domoraud, Blanc, Issa, Edson (Camara 46); Brando, Bravo, Gourvennec, Pires; Maurice.

● **FC METZ**
1st round CRVENA ZVEZDA BEOGRAD (YUG)
A 1-2   Rodriguez (89)
Letizi; Pierre, Toyes, Kastendeuch, Régis; Boffin, Proment (Strasser 23), Meyrieu; Jestrovic (Saha 70), Rodriguez, Lukic.
H 2-1   Kastendeuch (39), Meyrieu (68p)
(aet; 3-4 on pens.)
Letizi; Pierre (Rondelaere 90), Strasser (Proment 63), Kastendeuch, Régis; Boffin, Toyes, Meyrieu, Rizzetto; Jestrovic, Kraouche (Saha 63).

on to lift the trophy for only the second time, beating Second Division promotion-chasers Sedan 1-0 in the final in front of a packed house in the Stade de France - thanks to a scandalous penalty awarded in their favour and converted by man of the match Olivier Monterrubio.

A week before Nantes' controversial triumph Lens had also booked their place in Europe with a 1-0 win over Metz in the League Cup final - another game played to a capacity audience in French football's gleaming new national stadium. Midfielder Daniel Moreira scored an excellent winner to give Lens their second major title in two years following the 1997/98 championship win. Overall, it was no more than a fair-to-middling season for Daniel Leclercq's Blood and Gold army. Their title defence never got off the ground, and they failed to pass beyond the group stage of the Champions' League. The Clarets of Metz, runners-up to Lens the previous season, did not even make it to the Champions' League. They were bounced out in the qualifying round by HJK of Helsinki and then fell at the first hurdle of the UEFA Cup as well. On top of that they also went through their first six league games without scoring a goal. As with Lens, the story of Metz's downfall was that they simply sold off too many good players and failed to replace them.

Metz did eventually lift themselves clear of the relegation zone but not by much. A rare old struggle developed in the bottom half of the table, and although it looked for a while as if a big name might go down - Metz, PSG and Auxerre all went through spells of considerable unease - the final three to fall were all pretty much as expected. Toulouse were the first to go, followed by Sochaux and then, on the final day and only by the narrowest of goal difference margins, Lorient.

The bells rang out to welcome Saint-Etienne back to their rightful place in the top flight. *Les Verts* were the dominant force in the Second Division and sealed their promotion early, but the two teams who accompanied them up, Sedan and Troyes, both had to wait until the final game of the season before they finally saw off the challenge of Lille. Sedan's promotion was especially well received by the neutrals. The team from the Ardennes beat Saint-Etienne 3-0 at home in their last match to clinch second place and relieve some of the pain they had suffered through the injustice of their French Cup final defeat by Nantes.

Sedan were not the only team to go through hell in the Stade de France. The French national team, newly coached by Roger Lemerre, suffered a potentially decisive 2-3 defeat by Russia in their new citadel at the beginning of June. Had *Les Bleus* won that game, they would have been favourites to top a difficult group, but the defeat, which was a mirror-image of France's own 3-2 win in Moscow

★ SUPERSTAR PROFILE
DAVID GINOLA

Demeaned and disavowed in his native France, David Ginola is as big a star as they come in his adopted home of England. Ever since he arrived in the Premiership in 1995 to play for Newcastle United the English have been fascinated by him. That is not to say they all love him to bits. His footballing skills are mesmering, and he can cut defences to ribbons with his dazzling dribbles and power-packed shots, but while the admiration for his two-footed talent is universal, many are those who condemn and berate him for the ease in which he goes to ground under a challenge. In England, the home of fair play, 'diving' is considered to be football's ultimate sin, and Ginola, unfortunately, has a reputation of being a master of the 'art'. But what good is a genius who has no flaws? That was clearly the line taken by the professional footballers and football writers of England who each in turn voted for the Frenchman as their Footballer of the Year for 1999. In truth, Ginola took advantage of the Manchester United split vote and was therefore a controversial winner, but nobody could deny that he had a majestic season for Tottenham. It was said that he would be unable to co-exist with George Graham when he arrived as the new Spurs manager, but the dour Scotsman was just as enthralled by Ginola's skills as everybody else, and between them they took the North London club to their first trophy success in eight years with victory in the League Cup.

PLAYERS OF THE SEASON

NICOLAS ANELKA

His spoilt-brat behaviour during the summer, when he decided to walk out on his contract at Arsenal in favour of a big-money move to the Continent, offered a less than engaging view of Nicolas Anelka as a human being. But as a footballer, even those embittered Arsenal fans he left behind would acknowledge that the young French striker is in a class of his own - a fact backed up by the £21.5m transfer fee which Real Madrid ultimately agreed to pay for his services. Anelka's second season at Highbury, unlike the first, brought no club honours, but it certainly put the young Frenchman on the road to individual stardom. He replaced the legendary Ian Wright as Arsenal's chief goalgetter and scored 17 times in the Premiership - just one short of the league's best total. He also became the final piece in the French national team jigsaw, scoring against Russia in Moscow and then twice at Wembley to give France their first win on English soil.

SYLVAIN WILTORD

Bordeaux's first French championship victory in 12 years would not have been possible without the consistent goalscoring of Sylvain Wiltord. The league's top scorer with 22 goals, he found the net for the Girondins at key times. He was on target in each of

the first five matches of the season and struck important doubles in both the 4-1 home win over Marseille and the decisive last-day victory at Paris Saint-Germain. The 25-year-old jumped the queue ahead of his Bordeaux strike-partner Lilian Laslandes to partner Nicolas Anelka in the French national team and scored within two minutes of his first start, against Armenia, before netting one of the best goals of the entire Euro 2000 qualifying series in the shock 2-3 defeat at home to Russia.

ALAIN CAVEGLIA

Now well into his 32nd year, Alain Caveglia's chance of becoming an international footballer appears to have gone forever. But there have been few strikers in France over the past decade who can match the frequency and regularity of his goalscoring at the top domestic level. He has scored more goals in the French First Division than any other current player, reaching his century in April 1999 with a penalty against Montpellier - one of 17 goals he struck during the league campaign to help Lyon finish third and qualify for the Champions' League. He also struck seven goals in the UEFA Cup to become the second-highest scorer in that competition as well. Naturally right-footed, he has a strong shot and is also a handful in the air. His leadership and organisational qualities also make him an ideal captain.

OLIVIER MONTERRUBIO

Nantes have a reputation as a selling club but they are also one of the best clubs in Europe at nurturing their own local talent. Several big names have emanated from their ranks in recent years - Desailly, Deschamps, Loko etc. - and one current player who seems set for similar stardom is Olivier Monterrubio, a smart young schemer whose impish skills were much in evidence during the 1998/99 season. He is reminiscent of Reynald Pedros, a championship-winner with Nantes in 1995, both in his looks and the way he plays. He likes to dart around between midfield and attack, making things happen with quick passes and jinking runs into space. He had not scored a First Divison goal prior to the season but struck eight to become the club's leading marksman. And it was he who assumed the responsibility of converting the controversial penalty in the French Cup final that gave Nantes their first victory in the competition for 20 years.

France's Tony Vairelles (centre) surges between Andorra's Ramirez (left) and Antonio Lima in the Group Four Euro 2000 qualifier.

France's chief problem was the lack of an effective substitute for World and European Footballer of the Year Zinedine Zidane, who missed all four qualifiers in the spring through injury. When he was absent, the team could not cope. Conversely, when he did play, the whole side was full of verve and sparkle. Their best performance of the season was the 2-0 victory over England at Wembley in February - a match in which Nicolas Anelka, with his two fine goals (plus another wrongly ruled out), seemed to end France's search for a top-class goalscorer at a stroke. But just as the long-awaited 'number nine' had announced his arrival, the 'number ten' was heading for the operating theatre. For Aimé Jacquet one problem, for Roger Lemerre another.

at the start of the campaign, left them exposed to the elements, with qualification for the Euro 2000 finals anything but guaranteed.

The home defeat by Russia was not the only disappointing result of the World Cup winners' qualifying campaign. Drawing 1-1 away to Iceland in their opening match was a very sobering experience after the intoxicating triumph over Brazil. And there was little credit to be gained from the 0-0 home draw with Ukraine, which, had it not been for the excellence of goalkeeper Fabien Barthez, would have been a defeat. And who could have imagined that the French would have such a torrid time against little Andorra? The second of those encounters against the group minnows, in neutral Barcelona, almost resulted in one of international football's greatest upsets... until the Northern Irish referee took pity on the feeble French and gifted them a penalty four minutes from time.

1998 European Footballer of the Year – Zinedine Zidane.

TOP SCORERS

22 Sylvain WILTORD (Girondins de Bordeaux)
17 Alain CAVEGLIA (Olympique Lyonnais)
15 Lilian LASLANDES (Girondins de Bordeaux)
    Shabani NONDA (Stade Rennais FC)
14 Florian MAURICE (Olympique Marseille)
13 Fabrizio RAVANELLI (Olympique Marseille)
12 David TREZEGUET (AS Monaco)
    Tony CASCARINO (AS Nancy-Lorraine)
11 Frédéric NEE (SC Bastia)
    Victor IKPEBA (AS Monaco)
    Laurent ROBERT (Montpellier HSC)
    Bruno RODRIGUEZ (FC Metz/
    Paris Saint-Germain)
10 Bernard BOUGER (FC Sochaux)

NATIONAL TEAM RESULTS 98/99

19/08/98	Austria	A	Vienna	2-2	Laslandes (16), Boghossian (84)
05/09/98	Iceland (ECQ)	A	Reykjavik	1-1	Dugarry (36)
10/10/98	Russia (ECQ)	A	Moscow	3-2	Anelka (13), Pires (29), Boghossian (82)
14/10/98	Andorra (ECQ)	H	Saint-Denis	2-0	Candela (53), Djorkaeff (59)
20/01/99	Morocco	H	Marseille	1-0	Djorkaeff (48)
10/02/99	England	A	Wembley	2-0	Anelka (69, 76)
27/03/99	Ukraine (ECQ)	H	Saint-Denis	0-0	
31/03/99	Armenia (ECQ)	H	Saint-Denis	2-0	Wiltord (2), Dugarry (45)
05/06/99	Russia (ECQ)	H	Saint-Denis	2-3	Petit (48), Wiltord (54)
09/06/99	Andorra (ECQ)	A	Barcelona	1-0	Leboeuf (86p)

AJ AUXERRE

CLUB DIRECTORY

Association de la Jeunesse Auxerroise
Stade de l'Abbé-Deschamps
Route de Vaux
89000 Auxerre
tel - (0386) 723232
fax - (0386) 522087
Year of Formation - 1905
President - Jean-Claude Hamel
Secretary - Jean Edy
Coach - Guy Roux
Stadium - Abbé-Deschamps (21,000)

MAJOR HONOURS
League Championship - (1) 1996.
French Cup - (2) 1994, 1996.

APPEARANCES 98/99

	P	Ap	(s)	Gls
Kuami AGBOH	M	20	(4)	
Eric ASSATI	D	20		
Gérald BATICLE	M	34		4
Stéphane CARNOT	M	32		7
Laurent CIECHELSKI	D	9	(4)	
Djibril CISSE	A		(1)	
Fabien COOL	G	34		
Frédéric DANJOU	D	29	(1)	2
Thomas DENIAUD	A	18	(5)	6
Oumar DIENG	D	28		
Bernard DIOMEDE	A	27		5
Arnaud GONZALES	A		(1)	
Jean-Sébastien JAURES	M	6	(3)	
Frédéric JAY	D	10	(5)	
Cyril JEUNECHAMP	M	25		2
Narcisse KAPO	A		(1)	
Tomasz KLOS (POL)	D	30		4
Marcin KUZBA (POL)	A	3	(2)	
Guénaël LE MAUX	A	2		
Steve MARLET	A	32		7
Benjamin NIVET	M	1	(5)	
Pedro REYES (CHL)	D	9	(1)	1
Johan RADET	M	2	(2)	
Tarik SEKTIOUI	A	1	(1)	
Teemu TAINIO (FIN)	M	2	(11)	1

LEAGUE RESULTS 1998/99

08/08/98	Stade Rennais FC	A	0-1	
15/08/98	AS Nancy-Lorraine	H	3-2	Diomède 2, Klos
22/08/98	Girondins de Bordeaux	A	0-1	
30/08/98	SC Bastia	H	1-0	Baticle
10/09/98	FC Lorient	A	1-1	Baticle
19/09/98	FC Sochaux	H	3-1	Klos, Baticle, Marlet
24/09/98	Toulouse FC	A	0-0	
03/10/98	RC Strasbourg	H	3-1	Carnot (p), Danjou, Tainio
17/10/98	RC Lens	A	2-2	Carnot, Marlet
24/10/98	Olympique Lyonnais	H	1-0	Marlet
30/10/98	Paris Saint-Germain	A	0-2	
07/11/98	FC Nantes	H	1-1	Carnot
11/11/98	AS Monaco	A	2-3	Deniaud, Carnot
14/11/98	Montpellier HSC	A	0-3	
20/11/98	FC Metz	H	1-0	Klos
28/11/98	Le Havre AC	A	1-2	Deniaud
03/12/98	Olympique Marseille	H	1-1	Carnot (p)
12/12/98	AS Nancy-Lorraine	A	1-1	Jeunechamp
15/12/98	Girondins de Bordeaux	H	3-1	Marlet 2, Deniaud
19/12/98	SC Bastia	A	0-2	
16/01/99	FC Lorient	H	5-0	Diomède, Deniaud 2, Marlet 2
30/01/99	FC Sochaux	A	1-1	Carnot
07/02/99	Toulouse FC	H	1-2	Danjou
26/02/99	RC Lens	H	1-2	Klos
10/03/99	Olympique Lyonnais	A	1-2	Carnot (p)
14/03/99	RC Strasbourg	A	1-2	Diomède
20/03/99	Paris Saint-Germain	H	0-1	
03/04/99	FC Nantes	A	2-2	Deniaud, Jeunechamp
14/04/99	AS Monaco	H	0-3	
24/04/99	Montpellier HSC	H	2-2	og (Rodriguez), Baticle
01/05/99	FC Metz	A	0-2	
05/05/99	Le Havre AC	H	0-0	
22/05/99	Olympique Marseille	A	0-1	
29/05/99	Stade Rennais FC	H	2-0	Reyes, Diomède

SC BASTIA

Sporting Club de Bastia
Stade Armand-Cesari-Furiani
BP 640, 20601 Bastia Cedex
tel - (0495) 300080   fax - (0495) 336774
Year of Formation - 1905
President - François Nicolaï
Secretary - Christian Villanova
Coach - Henryk Kasperczak; Laurent Fournier
(99/00 - Frédéric Antonetti)
Stadium - Armand-Cesari-Furiani (13,000)

MAJOR HONOURS
French Cup - (1) 1981.

APPEARANCES 98/99

		P	Ap	(s)	Gls
Pierre-Yves ANDRE	A	22			9
Hervé ANZIANI	M		(2)	
Ali BOUMNIJEL	G	4	(1)	
Laurent CASANOVA	M	11	(1)	
CHRISTOFARI	M		(1)	
José CLAYTON (TUN)	D	20	(2)	1
Christophe DEGUERVILLE	D	20	(4)	
DUCOURTIOUX	M		(2)	
Eric DURAND	G	30		
Laurent FOURNIER	M	4	(1)	
Andrés GRANDE (ARG)	M		(1)	
Franck JURIETTI	D	25		2
Nebojsa KRUPNIKOVIC (YUG)	M	6	(4)	1
Pierre LAURENT	A	20	(7)	6
Franck MATINGOU	D	4	(9)	
David MAZZONCINI	M	17	(5)	
MENDIL	A		(1)	
Frédéric MENDY	M	18		
François MODESTO	D	12	(2)	
Patrick MOREAU	D	23		
Frédéric NEE	A	25	(2)	11
Stéphane ODET	M	8	(6)	
PAULO ALVES (POR)	A	10	(9)	3
Nicolas PENNETEAU	G		(1)	
Sébastien PEREZ	M	10	(1)	2
Mariusz PIEKARSKI (POL)	M	6	(7)	
PRINCE Daye (LIB)	A	5	(10)	1
Morlaye SOUMAH (GUI)	D	30		
Ousmane SOUMAH (GUI)	A		(1)	
Piotr SWIERCZEWSKI (POL)	M	18	(2)	1
Patrick VALERY	D	26		

LEAGUE RESULTS 1998/99

08/08/98	Montpellier HSC	H	2-2	André 2 (1p)
15/08/98	Paris Saint-Germain	A	0-2	
22/08/98	FC Metz	H	3-0	André, Née, Paulo Alves
30/08/98	AJ Auxerre	A	0-1	
11/09/98	Le Havre AC	H	2-0	Laurent 2
19/09/98	Stade Rennais FC	A	0-2	
24/09/98	Olympique Marseille	H	0-2	
03/10/98	Girondins de Bordeaux	H	2-0	Paulo Alves, André
18/10/98	Toulouse FC	A	1-2	Jurietti
24/10/98	RC Strasbourg	H	0-0	
30/10/98	AS Nancy-Lorraine	A	2-1	Née (p), André
06/11/98	FC Lorient	H	2-1	André (p), Née
11/11/98	FC Sochaux	A	1-2	Née
14/11/98	AS Monaco	H	3-1	Swierczewski, André, Née
20/11/98	RC Lens	A	0-1	
28/11/98	Olympique Lyonnais	H	4-1	Jurietti, Née, André 2 (1p)
04/12/98	FC Nantes	A	0-2	
12/12/98	Paris Saint-Germain	H	2-0	Née 2
15/12/98	FC Metz	A	0-4	
19/12/98	AJ Auxerre	H	2-0	Paulo Alves, Laurent
16/01/99	Le Havre AC	A	1-1	Née
29/01/99	Stade Rennais FC	H	0-1	
06/02/99	Olympique Marseille	A	1-3	Laurent
13/02/99	Girondins de Bordeaux	A	0-2	
26/02/99	Toulouse FC	H	1-1	Prince
10/03/99	RC Strasbourg	A	1-1	Clayton
19/03/99	AS Nancy-Lorraine	H	1-2	Krupnikovic
03/04/99	FC Lorient	A	1-3	Perez
13/04/99	FC Sochaux	H	1-1	Perez
24/04/99	AS Monaco	A	1-1	Née
01/05/99	RC Lens	H	1-1	Laurent
05/05/99	Olympique Lyonnais	A	1-2	Laurent
22/05/99	FC Nantes	H	1-0	Née
29/05/99	Montpellier HSC	A	0-3	

GIRONDINS DE BORDEAUX

CLUB DIRECTORY

Football Club des Girondins de Bordeaux
Rue Juliot-Curie
BP 33
33186 Le Haillan Cedex
tel - (0556) 161111
fax - (0556) 161135
Year of Formation - 1881
President - Jean-Louis Triaud
Secretary - Jean D'Arthuys
Coach - Elie Baup
Stadium - Parc Lescure (34,462)

MAJOR HONOURS
League Championship - (5)
1950, 1984, 1985, 1987, 1999.
French Cup - (3) 1941, 1986, 1987.

APPEARANCES 98/99

		P	Ap	(s)	Gls
Kodjo AFANOU	D	15	(4)		
Hervé ALICARTE	D	29		2	
Cédric ANSELIN	M		(1)		
Ali BENARBIA	M	25		3	
Bruno DA ROCHA	M	3	(16)		
Marc DELAROCHE	G	2			
Lassina DIABATE (CIV)	M	29	(1)	1	
Kaba DIAWARA	A	7	(10)	5	
Pascal FEINDOUNO (GUI)	A		(3)	1	
Romain FERRIER	D	12	(10)		
François GRENET	M	22	(1)		
IVAN Pérez (ESP)	A	2	(9)	3	
David JEMMALI	D	12	(1)	1	
Lilian LASLANDES	A	31	(2)	15	
Johan MICOUD	M	30	(1)	9	
Kiki MUSAMPA (HOL)	M	10	(7)	1	
Michel PAVON	M	29		2	
Pascal PHILIPPE	D		(1)		
Ulrich RAME	G	32			
Nisa SAVELJIC (YUG)	D	25			
Víctor TORRES MESTRE (ESP)	D	24			
Ivan VUKOMANOVIC (YUG)	M	5	(3)		
Sylvain WILTORD	A	30	(3)	22	

LEAGUE RESULTS 1998/99

08/08/98	Paris Saint-Germain	H	3-1	Laslandes, Wiltord, Benarbia
15/08/98	Le Havre AC	A	3-2	Wiltord 2, Laslandes
22/08/98	AJ Auxerre	H	1-0	Wiltord
30/08/98	FC Metz	A	2-0	og (Kastendeuch), Wiltord
11/09/98	Montpellier HSC	H	3-1	Alicarte, Diawara, Wiltord
20/09/98	Olympique Marseille	A	2-2	Diawara 2
25/09/98	Stade Rennais FC	H	4-0	Laslandes, Musampa, Jemmali, Wiltord
03/10/98	SC Bastia	A	0-2	
16/10/98	FC Nantes	H	2-0	Micoud, Diawara
25/10/98	AS Nancy-Lorraine	H	2-0	Laslandes 2
30/10/98	RC Strasbourg	A	2-3	Diawara, Micoud
07/11/98	Toulouse FC	H	3-1	Wiltord 2, Benarbia
11/11/98	FC Lorient	A	2-0	Pavon, Wiltord
14/11/98	FC Sochaux	H	0-0	
19/11/98	AS Monaco	A	2-0	Laslandes, Micoud
29/11/98	RC Lens	H	1-0	Micoud
03/12/98	Olympique Lyonnais	A	1-2	Wiltord
12/12/98	Le Havre AC	H	3-0	Laslandes 2, Benarbia
15/12/98	AJ Auxerre	A	1-3	Laslandes
19/12/98	FC Metz	H	6-0	Micoud 2, Wiltord, Laslandes 3
16/01/99	Montpellier HSC	A	1-1	Laslandes
29/01/99	Olympique Marseille	H	4-1	Wiltord 2, Micoud, Laslandes
06/02/99	Stade Rennais FC	A	1-1	Wiltord
13/02/99	SC Bastia	H	2-0	Wiltord 2
25/02/99	FC Nantes	A	0-0	
09/03/99	AS Nancy-Lorraine	A	3-2	Wiltord 2, Alicarte
20/03/99	RC Strasbourg	H	1-0	Pavon
03/04/99	Toulouse FC	A	3-0	Laslandes, Iván, Micoud
14/04/99	FC Lorient	H	0-0	
24/04/99	FC Sochaux	A	0-2	
30/04/99	AS Monaco	H	0-1	
04/05/99	RC Lens	A	4-2	Iván 2, Wiltord, Micoud
22/05/99	Olympique Lyonnais	H	1-0	Diabaté
29/05/99	Paris Saint-Germain	A	3-2	Wiltord 2, Feindouno

LE HAVRE AC

CLUB DIRECTORY

Le Havre Athletic Club Football Association
32 rue de la Cavée-Verte
76620 Le Havre
tel - (0235) 131415
fax - (0235) 131400
Year of Formation - 1872
President - Jean-Pierre Hureau
Secretary - Alain Belsoeur
Coach - Denis Troch; Joël Beaujouan
(99/00 - Francis Smerecki)
Stadium - Jules-Deschaseaux (18,000)

MAJOR HONOURS
French Cup - (1) 1959.

APPEARANCES 98/99

	P	Ap	(s)	Gls
Miladin BECANOVIC (YUG)	A	26	(2)	6
Jean-Alain BOUMSONG	D	16	(2)	1
Stéphane CASSARD	G	16		
William CORREIA	A	2	(7)	
Adnan CUSTOVIC (BOS)	A	7	(2)	
Jean-Pierre DELAUNAY	D	2		
Thierry DE NEEF	M	31	(1)	
Souleymane DIAWARA	D	2	(1)	
Sébastien HAMEL	G	18	(1)	
Jérémy HENIN	D	25	(3)	
Nicolas HUYSMAN	M	18	(4)	
Karim KERKAR	M		(4)	
Jean-Michel LESAGE	M	4	(1)	
Mamar MAMOUNI	D	10	(3)	2
Yazid MANSOURI	M	5	(12)	
Lilian NALIS	M	21	(6)	3
Dzoni NOVAK (SLO)	D	20	(1)	
Marinos OUZOUNIDIS (GRE)	D	23	(1)	
Milinko PANTIC (YUG)	M	17	(2)	2
Sébastien PARMENTIER	M	1		
Ludovic POLLET	D	20	(1)	
Cyrille POUGET	A	15		4
Lionel PRAT	A	6	(6)	1
Stéphane SAMSON	A	2	(3)	
Oumar SANE (SEN)	A	7	(8)	
Yann SOLOY	M	25	(5)	
Mohammed SYLLA	M	7	(3)	
Nicolas WEBER	D	28	(3)	1

LEAGUE RESULTS 1998/99

07/08/98	FC Metz	H	0-0	
15/08/98	Girondins de Bordeaux	H	2-3	Pouget, Becanovic
22/08/98	Stade Rennais FC	A	1-2	Becanovic (p)
29/08/98	Olympique Marseille	H	0-0	
11/09/98	SC Bastia	A	0-2	
19/09/98	RC Strasbourg	H	0-1	
25/09/98	AS Monaco	A	0-3	
03/10/98	FC Sochaux	H	3-0	Pantic, Becanovic, Prat
17/10/98	FC Lorient	A	0-0	
24/10/98	Toulouse FC	H	0-0	
29/10/98	Olympique Lyonnais	A	0-0	
07/11/98	RC Lens	H	3-1	Becanovic, og (Méride), Mamouni
10/11/98	FC Nantes	A	1-1	Nalis
15/11/98	Paris Saint-Germain	H	0-4	
20/11/98	AS Nancy-Lorraine	A	0-1	
28/11/98	AJ Auxerre	H	2-1	Mamouni, Becanovic
04/12/98	Montpellier HSC	A	0-2	
12/12/98	Girondins de Bordeaux	A	0-3	
16/12/98	Stade Rennais FC	H	2-0	og (Weiser), Nalis
19/12/98	Olympique Marseille	A	0-2	
16/01/99	SC Bastia	H	1-1	Pantic
30/01/99	RC Strasbourg	A	1-0	Becanovic
06/02/99	AS Monaco	H	1-2	og (Christanval)
26/02/99	FC Lorient	H	0-1	
10/03/99	Toulouse FC	A	0-0	
20/03/99	Olympique Lyonnais	H	1-0	Pouget
03/04/99	RC Lens	A	1-0	Pouget
14/04/99	FC Nantes	H	2-1	Weber, Boumsong
25/04/99	Paris Saint-Germain	A	0-3	
01/05/99	AS Nancy-Lorraine	H	1-1	Nalis
05/05/99	AJ Auxerre	A	0-0	
14/05/99	FC Sochaux	A	0-1	
22/05/99	Montpellier HSC	H	1-1	Pouget
29/05/99	FC Metz	A	0-1	

RC LENS

Racing Club de Lens
Stade Félix-Bollaert
Avenue A.-Maës
62300 Lens
tel - (0321) 692899
fax - (0321) 692884
Year of Formation - 1906
President - Gervais Martel
Secretary - Louis Plet
Coach - Daniel Leclercq
Stadium - Félix-Bollaert (42,300)

MAJOR HONOURS
League Championship - (1) 1998.
League Cup - (1) 1999.

	P	Ap	(s)	Gls
Philippe BRUNEL	A	10	(7)	2
Stéphane DALMAT	M	19	(6)	3
Michaël DEBEVE	M	24	(5)	3
Frédéric DEHU	D	31	(1)	
Ludovic DELPORTE	A		(2)	
P DIOP	A		(1)	
Wagneau ELOI	A	8	(9)	7
Ernest ETCHI OREN (CMR)	D	4	(1)	
Marc-Vivien FOE (CMR)	M	4	(1)	2
Valérien ISMAËL	D	20		
Yoan LACHOR	D	9	(4)	
Nicolas LASPALLES	D	8	(2)	1
Cyrille MAGNIER	D	28	(1)	
Xavier MERIDE	D	10	(4)	
Daniel MOREIRA	M	15	(16)	4
Pascal NOUMA	A	27		8
Alex NYARKO (GHA)	M	18	(6)	3
José PIERRE-FANFAN	D	2	(2)	
Cyril ROOL	M	23	(1)	
Aboubacar SANKHARE	D	1		
Eric SIKORA	D	28	(2)	
Vladimir SMICER (CZE)	A	25	(5)	4
Tony VAIRELLES	A	26	(4)	8
Guillaume WARMUZ	G	34		

Date	Opponent	H/A	Score	Scorers
08/08/98	Toulouse FC	A	2-3	Vairelles, Dalmat
14/08/98	FC Lorient	H	1-1	Dalmat
23/08/98	FC Sochaux	A	4-0	Smicer, Vairelles, Nouma 2
29/08/98	AS Nancy-Lorraine	H	2-1	Nouma 2
10/09/98	AS Monaco	A	0-2	
19/09/98	Olympique Lyonnais	A	1-3	Eloi
25/09/98	FC Nantes	H	2-4	Vairelles 2
04/10/98	Paris Saint-Germain	A	1-0	Eloi
17/10/98	AJ Auxerre	H	2-2	Eloi 2
25/10/98	Montpellier HSC	A	0-1	
30/10/98	FC Metz	H	2-0	Nouma, Debève
07/11/98	Le Havre AC	A	1-3	Eloi
11/11/98	Stade Rennais FC	H	3-1	Eloi, Debève, Vairelles
14/11/98	Olympique Marseille	A	0-1	
20/11/98	SC Bastia	H	1-0	Debève
29/11/98	Girondins de Bordeaux	A	0-1	
04/12/98	RC Strasbourg	H	3-0	Smicer, Nyarko, Eloi
12/12/98	FC Lorient	A	1-1	Foé
16/12/98	FC Sochaux	H	1-1	Nouma
19/12/98	AS Nancy-Lorraine	A	1-0	Foé
16/01/99	AS Monaco	H	1-1	Nouma
30/01/99	Olympique Lyonnais	H	0-3	
06/02/99	FC Nantes	A	0-2	
13/02/99	Paris Saint-Germain	H	2-1	Dalmat, Laspalles
26/02/99	AJ Auxerre	A	2-1	Nouma, Brunel
10/03/99	Montpellier HSC	H	1-0	Nyarko
20/03/99	FC Metz	A	1-0	Brunel
03/04/99	Le Havre AC	H	0-1	
13/04/99	Stade Rennais FC	A	0-2	
24/04/99	Olympique Marseille	H	4-0	Vairelles 2, Moreira 2
01/05/99	SC Bastia	A	1-1	Moreira
04/05/99	Girondins de Bordeaux	H	2-4	Moreira, Nyarko
22/05/99	RC Strasbourg	A	1-1	Smicer
29/05/99	Toulouse FC	H	3-1	Vairelles (p), Smicer, og (Diatta)

FC LORIENT

CLUB DIRECTORY

Football Club Lorient Bretagne Sud
Rue Jean-Le-Coutaller
BP 404
56104 Lorient Cedex
tel - (0297) 841220
fax - (0297) 645205
Year of Formation - 1926
President - Noël Couëdel
Secretary - Daniel Bouvier
Coach - Christian Gourcuff
Stadium - Le Moustoir-Yves-Allainmat (16,448)

APPEARANCES 98/99

	P	Ap	(s)	Gls
Ross ALOISI (AUS)	A		(1)	
Pascal BEDROSSIAN	A	12	(5)	1
Ali BOUAFIA (ALG)	A	21	(4)	8
Laurent BOURMAUD	M	7	(8)	
Pascal CAMADINI	M	32		5
Nicolas CLOAREC	M	20	(8)	
Loïc DRUON	D	23	(8)	1
Eben DUGBATHEY (GHA)	D	22		
EMERSON Otacílio (BRA)	A	7	(11)	
Yannick FISCHER	D	29	(1)	1
Angelo HUGUES	G	30		
Gilles KERHUIEL	D	22	(1)	
Pierrick LE BERT	M	8	(13)	
LEE SANG-YOON (KOR)	A	1	(3)	
Stéphane LE GARREC	G	4	(2)	
Christophe LE GRIX	M	14		1
Arnaud LE LAN	D	9	(1)	
Patrice LOKO	A	20		9
Jean-Louis MONTERO	D	15	(9)	1
Stéphane PEDRON	M	33		3
Sylvain RIPOLL	M	22		
Ousmane SOUMAH (GUI)	A	8	(5)	2
Ismaël TRIKI (MAR)	D	15	(2)	
Bülent UCUNCU (YUR)	M		(8)	

LEAGUE RESULTS 1998/99

07/08/98	AS Monaco	H	1-2	Bouafia
14/08/98	RC Lens	A	1-1	Bouafia
22/08/98	Olympique Lyonnais	H	0-1	
29/08/98	Paris Saint-Germain	A	2-1	Soumah, Pédron
10/09/98	AJ Auxerre	H	1-1	Camadini
19/09/98	FC Nantes	A	1-1	Bouafia
25/09/98	FC Metz	H	1-1	Bouafia (p)
03/10/98	Montpellier HSC	A	1-5	Bedrossian
17/10/98	Le Havre AC	H	0-0	
24/10/98	Stade Rennais FC	A	0-1	
29/10/98	Olympique Marseille	H	1-3	Bouafia
06/11/98	SC Bastia	A	1-2	Camadini
11/11/98	Girondins de Bordeaux	H	0-2	
15/11/98	RC Strasbourg	A	0-2	
20/11/98	Toulouse FC	H	1-0	Loko
28/11/98	AS Nancy-Lorraine	H	0-1	
04/12/98	FC Sochaux	A	1-0	Fischer
12/12/98	RC Lens	H	1-1	Loko
16/12/98	Olympique Lyonnais	A	2-2	Pédron, Loko
19/12/98	Paris Saint-Germain	H	2-0	Loko 2 (1p)
16/01/99	AJ Auxerre	A	0-5	
30/01/99	FC Nantes	H	1-1	Soumah
06/02/99	FC Metz	A	0-3	
13/02/99	Montpellier HSC	H	1-1	Druon
26/02/99	Le Havre AC	A	1-0	Loko
10/03/99	Stade Rennais FC	H	1-1	og (Sommeil)
20/03/99	Olympique Marseille	A	1-4	Camadini
03/04/99	SC Bastia	H	3-1	Loko, Pédron, Camadini
14/04/99	Girondins de Bordeaux	A	0-0	
24/04/99	RC Strasbourg	H	0-1	
30/04/99	Toulouse FC	A	4-1	Bouafia 2, Loko, Camadini
05/05/99	AS Nancy-Lorraine	A	0-2	
22/05/99	FC Sochaux	H	4-1	Le Grix, Bouafia, Loko, Montero
29/05/99	AS Monaco	A	0-1	

OLYMPIQUE LYONNAIS

CLUB DIRECTORY

Olympique Lyonnais
350 avenue Jean-Jaurès
69007 Lyon
tel - (0478) 767604
fax - (0478) 720399
Year of Formation - 1950
President - Jean-Michel Aulas
Secretary - Marino Faccioli
Coach - Bernard Lacombe
Stadium - Gerland (42,000)

MAJOR HONOURS
French Cup - (3) 1964, 1967, 1973.

APPEARANCES 98/99

	P	Ap	(s)	Gls
Jacek BAK (POL)	D	22	(3)	2
Christian BASSILA	D	15	(7)	1
Serge BLANC	D	5		
Jérémie BRECHET	D	11	(4)	
Patrice CARTERON	D	31		1
Alain CAVEGLIA	A	29		17
Christophe COCARD	A	11	(15)	4
Grégory COUPET	G	34		
Christophe DELMOTTE	M	23	(6)	1
Jean-Christophe DEVAUX	D	3	(2)	
Vikash DHORASOO	M	33	(1)	2
Hubert FOURNIER	D	27		
Marco GRASSI (SUI)	A	17	(7)	6
David HELLEBUYCK	A	1	(1)	
Joseph-Desiré JOB (CMR)	A	9	(10)	6
Frédéric KANOUTE	A	6	(3)	2
Florent LAVILLE	D	28	(1)	
David LINARES	M	16	(12)	3
Steed MALBRANQUE	M	16	(5)	
Patrice OVERDI	M		(1)	
Cédric URAS	D	7	(8)	
Philippe VIOLEAU	M	30		3

LEAGUE RESULTS 1998/99

08/08/98	RC Strasbourg	A	0-0	
14/08/98	Toulouse FC	H	6-1	Caveglia 2, Grassi, Kanouté, Bak, Dhorasoo
22/08/98	FC Lorient	A	1-0	Grassi
29/08/98	AS Monaco	H	1-1	Caveglia
11/09/98	FC Sochaux	A	2-1	Delmotte, Grassi
19/09/98	RC Lens	H	3-1	Grassi, Caveglia, Job
25/09/98	AS Nancy-Lorraine	A	0-0	
03/10/98	FC Nantes	A	0-2	
16/10/98	Paris Saint-Germain	H	1-1	Cocard
24/10/98	AJ Auxerre	A	0-1	
29/10/98	Le Havre AC	H	0-0	
07/11/98	FC Metz	A	2-3	Cocard, Kanouté
11/11/98	Montpellier HSC	H	2-0	Caveglia, Violeau
14/11/98	Stade Rennais FC	A	0-0	
19/11/98	Olympique Marseille	H	2-1	Linarès, Violeau
28/11/98	SC Bastia	A	1-4	Grassi
03/12/98	Girondins de Bordeaux	H	2-1	Caveglia, Dhorasoo
12/12/98	Toulouse FC	A	0-0	
16/12/98	FC Lorient	H	2-2	og (Fischer), Linarès
19/12/98	AS Monaco	A	1-0	Bak
30/01/99	RC Lens	A	3-0	Caveglia, Job 2
06/02/99	AS Nancy-Lorraine	H	2-1	Grassi, Job
13/02/99	FC Nantes	H	2-1	Caveglia 2 (1p)
25/02/99	Paris Saint-Germain	A	1-0	Caveglia (p)
10/03/99	AJ Auxerre	H	2-1	Caveglia (p), Carteron
20/03/99	Le Havre AC	A	0-1	
03/04/99	FC Metz	H	2-0	og (Toyes), Violeau (p)
08/04/99	FC Sochaux	H	4-1	Caveglia 2, Cocard, Linarès
14/04/99	Montpellier HSC	A	3-1	Caveglia 2 (1p), Bassila
25/04/99	Stade Rennais FC	H	1-2	Cocard
30/04/99	Olympique Marseille	A	0-0	
05/05/99	SC Bastia	H	2-1	Job, og (Casanova)
22/05/99	Girondins de Bordeaux	A	0-1	
29/05/99	RC Strasbourg	H	3-2	Caveglia 2, Job

OLYMPIQUE MARSEILLE

CLUB DIRECTORY

Olympique de Marseille
25 rue Negresko
BP 124
13267 Marseille Cedex 08
tel - (0491) 765609
fax - (0491) 760777
Year of Formation - 1899
President - Yves Marchand
Secretary - Louis Vassalucci
Coach - Rolland Courbis
Stadium - Vélodrome (60,000)

MAJOR HONOURS
League Championship - (8) 1937, 1948, 1971, 1972, 1989, 1990, 1991, 1992.
French Cup - (10) 1924, 1926, 1927, 1935, 1938, 1943, 1969, 1972, 1976, 1989.
European Champions' Cup - (1) 1993.

APPEARANCES 98/99

		P	Ap	(s)	Gls
Jacques ABARDONADO	M			(2)	
Laurent BLANC	D	32			2
Patrick BLONDEAU	D	22	(1)		
Frédéric BRANDO	M	20	(10)		
Daniel BRAVO	M	13	(7)		1
Aboubacar CAMARA (GUI)	A	14	(16)		6
Patrick COLLETER	D	9	(1)		
Cyril DOMORAUD	D	28			
Christophe DUGARRY	A	20	(8)		4
EDSON da Silva (BRA)	D	6	(2)		1
William GALLAS	D	28	(2)		
Jocelyn GOURVENNEC	M	13	(10)		5
Tchiressou GUEL (CIV)	N	1	(1)		
Pierre ISSA (SAF)	D	9	(7)		
Hamada JAMBAY	D		(3)		
Andreas KÖPKE (GER)	G	4			
Peter LUCCIN	M	21	(2)		1
Florian MAURICE	A	28	(4)		14
Arthur MOSES (GHA)	A	1	(2)		
Cédric MOURET	A	1	(3)		
Robert PIRES	M	27	(7)		6
Stéphane PORATO	G	30			
Fabrizio RAVANELLI (ITA)	A	27	(2)		13
Martial ROBIN	M		(2)		
Eric ROY	M	20	(4)		3

LEAGUE RESULTS 1998/99

08/08/98	FC Nantes	H	2-0	Ravanelli, Roy
15/08/98	FC Metz	A	1-0	Gourvennec
22/08/98	Montpellier HSC	H	5-4	Maurice, Dugarry 2, Roy, Blanc (p)
29/08/98	Le Havre AC	A	0-0	
11/09/98	Stade Rennais FC	H	1-1	Maurice
20/09/98	Girondins de Bordeaux	H	2-2	Ravanelli, Roy
24/09/98	SC Bastia	A	2-0	Pires, Camara
03/10/98	Toulouse FC	H	2-0	Maurice, Ravanelli
16/10/98	RC Strasbourg	A	2-0	Maurice 2
24/10/98	FC Sochaux	H	4-0	Ravanelli 2, Camara 2
29/10/98	FC Lorient	A	3-1	Ravanelli 2, Pires
06/11/98	AS Monaco	H	1-0	Maurice
10/11/98	AS Nancy-Lorraine	A	3-2	Maurice 2, Gourvennec
14/11/98	RC Lens	H	1-0	Dugarry
19/11/98	Olympique Lyonnais	A	1-2	Maurice
29/11/98	Paris Saint-Germain	H	0-0	
03/12/98	AJ Auxerre	A	1-1	Blanc
12/12/98	FC Metz	H	3-0	Camara, Maurice, Gourvennec
16/12/98	Montpellier HSC	A	1-0	Maurice
19/12/98	Le Havre AC	H	2-0	Pires 2
16/01/99	Stade Rennais FC	A	1-1	Camara
29/01/99	Girondins de Bordeaux	A	1-4	Dugarry
06/02/99	SC Bastia	H	3-1	Bravo, Ravanelli 2
14/02/99	Toulouse FC	A	0-1	
25/02/99	RC Strasbourg	H	1-0	Pires
09/03/99	FC Sochaux	A	0-0	
20/03/99	FC Lorient	H	4-1	Ravanelli 2, Maurice, Gourvennec (p)
02/04/99	AS Monaco	A	2-1	Camara, Ravanelli
15/04/99	AS Nancy-Lorraine	H	4-0	Edson, Gourvennec, Ravanelli, Maurice
24/04/99	RC Lens	A	0-4	
30/04/99	Olympique Lyonnais	H	0-0	
04/05/99	Paris Saint-Germain	A	1-2	Maurice
22/05/99	AJ Auxerre	H	1-0	Luccin
29/05/99	FC Nantes	A	1-0	Pires

FC METZ

CLUB DIRECTORY

Football Club de Metz
Stade Saint-Symphorien
Nouvelle Tribune
57050 Longeville-lès-Metz
tel - (0387) 667215
fax - (0387) 561429
Year of Formation - 1932
President - Charles Molinari
Secretary - Patrick Razurel
Coach - Joël Muller
Stadium - Saint-Symphorien (26,304)

MAJOR HONOURS
French Cup - (2) 1984, 1988.
League Cup - (1) 1996.

APPEARANCES 98/99

	P	Ap	(s)	Gls
Ludovic ASUAR	M	11	(4)	
Danny BOFFIN (BEL)	M	31		3
Philippe GAILLOT	D	21		
Franck HISTILLOLES	M	4	(6)	
Christophe HORLAVILLE	A	7	(2)	2
Jonathan JAGER	M	4	(3)	
Nenad JESTROVIC (YUG)	A	14	(10)	5
Sylvain KASTENDEUCH	D	34		
Nasredine KRAOUCHE	A	1	(8)	
Christophe LE GRIX	M	1		
Lionel LETIZI	G	34		
Vladan LUKIC (YUG)	A	17	(3)	4
Sylvain MARCHAL	D		(3)	
Frédéric MEYRIEU	M	29		3
Didier NEUMANN	M		(1)	
Djima OYAWOLE (TOG)	A	3	(4)	
Pascal PIERRE	D	23		
Grégory PROMENT	M	14	(7)	
David REGIS (USA)	D	20	(1)	
Franck RIZZETTO	M	17	(11)	1
Bruno RODRIGUEZ	A	11	(1)	6
Stéphane RONDELAERE	M	2		
Louis SAHA	A	1	(2)	
Sébastien SCHEMMEL	D	20		1
Jeff STRASSER (LUX)	D	19	(11)	
Mihály TÓTH (HUN)	A		(2)	
Geoffray TOYES	D	27	(2)	1
Gunter VAN HANDENHOVEN (BEL)	A	9	(3)	1

LEAGUE RESULTS 1998/99

07/08/98	Le Havre AC	A	0-0	
15/08/98	Olympique Marseille	H	0-1	
22/08/98	SC Bastia	A	0-3	
29/08/98	Girondins de Bordeaux	H	0-2	
11/09/98	RC Strasbourg	A	0-0	
19/09/98	Toulouse FC	H	0-0	
25/09/98	FC Lorient	A	1-1	Jestrovic
04/10/98	AS Nancy-Lorraine	H	2-3	Boffin, Meyrieu (p)
17/10/98	FC Sochaux	A	1-1	Lukic
24/10/98	AS Monaco	H	1-0	Rodriguez (p)
30/10/98	RC Lens	A	0-2	
07/11/98	Olympique Lyonnais	H	3-2	Rodriguez 2, Toyes
11/11/98	Paris Saint-Germain	A	2-2	Meyrieu, Rodriguez
14/11/98	FC Nantes	H	1-0	Rodriguez
20/11/98	AJ Auxerre	A	0-1	
28/11/98	Montpellier HSC	H	3-1	Rodriguez, Lukic 2
04/12/98	Stade Rennais FC	H	0-0	
12/12/98	Olympique Marseille	A	0-3	
15/12/98	SC Bastia	H	4-0	Jestrovic 3, Lukic (p)
19/12/98	Girondins de Bordeaux	A	0-6	
17/01/99	RC Strasbourg	H	1-0	Boffin
30/01/99	Toulouse FC	A	0-1	
06/02/99	FC Lorient	H	3-0	Meyrieu, Boffin, Horlaville
26/02/99	FC Sochaux	H	1-1	Schemmel
10/03/99	AS Monaco	A	0-0	
20/03/99	RC Lens	H	0-1	
03/04/99	Olympique Lyonnais	A	0-2	
09/04/99	AS Nancy-Lorraine	A	0-1	
14/04/99	Paris Saint-Germain	H	1-1	Jestrovic
24/04/99	FC Nantes	A	0-0	
01/05/99	AJ Auxerre	H	2-0	og (Danjou), Horlaville
04/05/99	Montpellier HSC	A	1-1	Van Handenhoven
22/05/99	Stade Rennais FC	A	0-1	
29/05/99	Le Havre AC	H	1-0	Rizzetto

AS MONACO

CLUB DIRECTORY

Association Sportive de Monaco
7 avenue des Castelans
98000 Monaco
tel - (37792) 057473
fax - (37792) 052454
Year of Formation - 1924
President - Jean-Louis Campora
Secretary - Emile Rossi
Coach - Jean Tigana; Claude Puel
Stadium - Louis II (20,000)

MAJOR HONOURS
League Championship - (6)
1961, 1963, 1978, 1982, 1988, 1997.
French Cup - (5)
1960, 1963, 1980, 1985, 1991.

APPEARANCES 98/99

		P	Ap	(s)	Gls
Jean-Marc AUBRY	G	2		(1)	
Fabien BARTHEZ	G	32			
Philippe CHRISTANVAL	D	18	(5)	1	
Ulliano COURVILLE	A		(3)		
Francisco DA COSTA (POR)	M	14	(7)	2	
Salif DIAO (SEN)	M	11	(3)		
Djibril DIAWARA	D	11	(2)		
Di TOMMASO	D	3	(1)		
Martin DJETOU	D	14	(1)		
Franck DUMAS	D	24	(1)		
Wagneau ELOI	A	4	(6)	1	
Pontus FARNERUD (SWE)	A		(4)		
Franck GAVA	M	25	(2)	2	
Ludovic GIULY	M	26	(6)	8	
Thierry HENRY	A	8	(5)	1	
Victor IKPEBA (NIG)	A	25	(1)	11	
Bruno IRLES	D	2	(5)		
Muhamed KONJIC (BOS)	D	16	(2)	2	
Sabri LAMOUCHI	M	20	(4)	2	
Fabien LEFEVRE	M	2	(4)		
Sylvain LEGWINSKI	M	13	(1)	1	
Philippe LEONARD (BEL)	D	16		1	
Lilian MARTIN	D	8	(2)		
Sylvain N'DIAYE	A	2	(9)	2	
Christophe PIGNOL	D	14	(3)		
John RIISE (NOR)	M	4	(3)		
Julien RODRIGUEZ	D	9	(1)		
Willy SAGNOL	D	19	(1)		
Robert SPEHAR (CRO)	A	8	(6)	3	
David TREZEGUET	A	24	(3)	12	

LEAGUE RESULTS 1998/99

07/08/98	FC Lorient	A	2-1	Gava, Giuly (p)
15/08/98	FC Sochaux	H	4-1	Da Costa, Ikpeba 2, Henry
22/08/98	Toulouse FC	A	0-0	
29/08/98	Olympique Lyonnais	A	1-1	Spehar
10/09/98	RC Lens	H	2-0	Trezeguet 2
20/09/98	Paris Saint-Germain	A	0-1	
25/09/98	Le Havre AC	H	3-0	Trezeguet 2 (1p), Ikpeba
03/10/98	Stade Rennais FC	A	1-2	og (Reveillère)
17/10/98	Montpellier HSC	H	2-0	Spehar 2
24/10/98	FC Metz	A	0-1	
29/10/98	FC Nantes	H	3-1	Gava, Léonard, og (Fabbri)
06/11/98	Olympique Marseille	A	0-1	
11/11/98	AJ Auxerre	H	3-2	Trezeguet 2, Konjic
14/11/98	SC Bastia	A	1-3	Giuly
19/11/98	Girondins de Bordeaux	H	0-2	
28/11/98	RC Strasbourg	A	1-1	Christanval
03/12/98	AS Nancy-Lorraine	H	3-0	Trezeguet 2, Ikpeba
16/12/98	Toulouse FC	H	1-1	Konjic
19/12/98	Olympique Lyonnais	H	0-1	
16/01/99	RC Lens	A	1-1	Trezeguet (p)
29/01/99	Paris Saint-Germain	H	2-1	Ikpeba, og (Cissé)
06/02/99	Le Havre AC	A	2-1	Ikpeba, N'Diaye
13/02/99	Stade Rennais FC	H	4-2	Ikpeba 2 (1p), N'Diaye, Giuly
25/02/99	Montpellier HSC	A	3-2	Giuly, Trezeguet, Eloi
10/03/99	FC Metz	H	0-0	
14/03/99	FC Sochaux	A	1-1	Trezeguet
19/03/99	FC Nantes	A	1-0	Lamouchi
02/04/99	Olympique Marseille	H	1-2	Ikpeba
14/04/99	AJ Auxerre	A	3-0	Giuly 2, Ikpeba
24/04/99	SC Bastia	H	1-1	Legwinski
30/04/99	Girondins de Bordeaux	A	1-0	Lamouchi
05/05/99	RC Strasbourg	H	2-1	Giuly, Trezeguet
22/05/99	AS Nancy-Lorraine	A	2-1	Giuly, Da Costa
29/05/99	FC Lorient	H	1-0	Ikpeba

MONTPELLIER HSC

CLUB DIRECTORY

Montpellier Hérault Sports Club
Avenue Albert-Einstein
Domaine de Grammont
34000 Montpellier-La Paillade
tel - (0467) 154600
fax - (0467) 221273/154615
Year of Formation - 1974
President - Louis Nicollin
Secretary - Philippe Peybernes
Coach - Jean-Louis Gasset
Stadium - La Mosson (35,500)

MAJOR HONOURS
French Cup - (1) 1990.

APPEARANCES 98/99

	P	Ap	(s)	Gls
Didier AGATHE	A		(2)	
Pascal BAILLS	D	21	(3)	
Ibrahima BAKAYOKO (CIV)	A	7		4
Cédric BARBOSA	M	7	(15)	1
S BERTRAND	M		(3)	
Stéphane CASSARD	G	14		
Philippe DELAYE	M	29	(2)	9
Manuel DOS SANTOS	D	31	(1)	
Nenad DZODIC (YUG)	D	13	(3)	1
Philippe FLUCKLINGER	G	11		
Pascal FUGIER	D	27	(1)	
Frédéric GARNY	A	1	(7)	1
Xavier GRAVELAINE	A	18		3
Eric GUEI (CIV)	A	1	(3)	
Marcel MAHOUVE (CMR)	M	15	(10)	
Toifilou MAOULIDA	A	9	(19)	2
Bruno MARTINI	G	9	(1)	
Nicolas OUEDEC	A	14		2
Laurent ROBERT	A	32		11
Michel RODRIGUEZ	D	17	(2)	1
Jean-Christophe ROUVIERE	M	32	(1)	
Franck SAUZEE	D	10		2
Cyril SERREDSZUM	M	9		
Franck SILVESTRE	D	33		6
Didier THIMOTHEE	A	14	(7)	9

LEAGUE RESULTS 1998/99

08/08/98	SC Bastia	A	2-2	Sauzée, Maoulida
15/08/98	Stade Rennais FC	H	3-1	Robert 2, Delaye
22/08/98	Olympique Marseille	A	4-5	Bakayoko 2, Robert, Sauzée
29/08/98	Toulouse FC	H	3-0	Bakayoko 2, Delaye
11/09/98	Girondins de Bordeaux	A	1-3	Delaye
19/09/98	AS Nancy-Lorraine	H	1-1	Gravelaine (p)
25/09/98	RC Strasbourg	A	1-2	Thimothée
03/10/98	FC Lorient	H	5-1	Gravelaine, Thimothée 2, Delaye, Barbosa
17/10/98	AS Monaco	A	0-2	
25/10/98	RC Lens	H	1-0	Maoulida
31/10/98	FC Sochaux	A	0-4	
07/11/98	Paris Saint-Germain	H	2-1	Delaye, Dzodic
11/11/98	Olympique Lyonnais	A	0-2	
14/11/98	AJ Auxerre	H	3-0	Thimothée 2, Gravelaine
20/11/98	FC Nantes	A	1-1	Silvestre
28/11/98	FC Metz	A	1-3	og (Pierre)
04/12/98	Le Havre AC	H	2-0	Silvestre 2
11/12/98	Stade Rennais FC	A	2-3	Thimothée, Delaye
16/12/98	Olympique Marseille	H	0-1	
19/12/98	Toulouse FC	A	5-2	Robert 3, Thimothée, Garny
16/01/99	Girondins de Bordeaux	H	1-1	Silvestre
30/01/99	AS Nancy-Lorraine	A	1-0	Robert
07/02/99	RC Strasbourg	H	1-1	Rodriguez
13/02/99	FC Lorient	A	1-1	Thimothee
25/02/99	AS Monaco	H	2-3	Robert 2 (1p)
10/03/99	RC Lens	A	0-1	
20/03/99	FC Sochaux	H	0-0	
03/04/99	Paris Saint-Germain	A	1-0	Ouédec
14/04/99	Olympique Lyonnais	H	1-3	Delaye
24/04/99	AJ Auxerre	A	2-2	Delaye, Robert
01/05/99	FC Nantes	H	1-2	Silvestre
04/05/99	FC Metz	H	1-1	Thimothée (p)
22/05/99	Le Havre AC	A	1-1	Ouédec
29/05/99	SC Bastia	H	3-0	Silvestre, Robert, Delaye

AS NANCY-LORRAINE

CLUB DIRECTORY

Association Sportive Nancy-Lorraine
BP 1117
54523 Laxou Cedex
tel - (0383) 232822
fax - (0383) 233037
Year of Formation - 1967
President - Jacques Rousselot
Secretary - Pascal Rivière
Coach - Laszlo Bölöni
Stadium - Marcel-Picot (16,708)

MAJOR HONOURS
Domestic Cup - (1) 1978.

APPEARANCES 98/99

	P	Ap	(s)	Gls
Christophe BASTIEN	M	28	(2)	3
Frédéric BIANCALANI	M	29	(2)	2
Tony CASCARINO (IRL)	A	31	(1)	12
Pablo CORREA (URU)	A	6	(8)	3
Demetrius FERREIRA LEITE (BRA)	D	22	(5)	
Paul FISCHER	D	19		
Youssouf HADJI	A		(1)	
Vincent HOGNON	D	20		
Soufiane KONE	A	26	(4)	6
Bertrand LAQUAIT	G	4	(1)	
Cédric LECLUSE	D	33		
Jinyn LI (CHN)	A	1	(5)	
Medhi MENIRI	D	28	(1)	2
Laurent MORACCHINI	M	28		
Youssef MOUSTAID	M	5	(13)	
Egutu OLISEH (NIG)	M	1	(3)	
Abdelnasser OUADAH	M	11	(8)	
Olivier RAMBO	D	25	(7)	
Mickoël RODRIGUES	D	3	(11)	
Frédéric ROUX	G	30		
Jessy SAVINE	M	1		
Samuel WIART	A	20	(11)	6
Marc ZANOTTI	M	3	(7)	

LEAGUE RESULTS 1998/99

08/08/98	FC Sochaux	H	1-1	Cascarino
15/08/98	AJ Auxerre	A	2-3	Koné, Bastien (p)
23/08/98	FC Nantes	H	1-0	Wiart
29/08/98	RC Lens	A	1-2	Cascarino
11/09/98	Paris Saint-Germain	H	0-0	
19/09/98	Montpellier HSC	A	1-1	Koné
25/09/98	Olympique Lyonnais	H	0-0	
04/10/98	FC Metz	A	3-2	Koné 2, Cascarino
17/10/98	Stade Rennais FC	H	0-1	
25/10/98	Girondins de Bordeaux	A	0-2	
30/10/98	SC Bastia	H	1-2	Wiart
07/11/98	RC Strasbourg	A	2-1	Cascarino 2
10/11/98	Olympique Marseille	H	2-3	Cascarino, Koné
14/11/98	Toulouse FC	A	1-1	Cascarino
20/11/98	Le Havre AC	H	1-0	Cascarino
28/11/98	FC Lorient	A	1-0	Wiart
03/12/98	AS Monaco	A	0-3	
12/12/98	AJ Auxerre	H	1-1	Meniri
16/12/98	FC Nantes	A	0-2	
19/12/98	RC Lens	H	0-1	
17/01/99	Paris Saint-Germain	A	2-1	Koné, Wiart
30/01/99	Montpellier HSC	H	0-1	
07/02/99	Olympique Lyonnais	A	1-2	Cascarino
26/02/99	Stade Rennais FC	A	1-2	Cascarino
09/03/99	Girondins de Bordeaux	H	2-3	Meniri, Cascarino
19/03/99	SC Bastia	A	2-1	Correa, Bastien (p)
03/04/99	RC Strasbourg	H	1-1	Correa
09/04/99	FC Metz	H	1-0	Wiart
15/04/99	Olympique Marseille	A	0-4	
24/04/99	Toulouse FC	H	2-0	og (Méride), Correa
01/05/99	Le Havre AC	A	1-1	Bastien
05/05/99	FC Lorient	H	2-0	Cascarino, Biancalani
22/05/99	AS Monaco	H	1-2	Biancalani
29/05/99	FC Sochaux	A	1-1	Wiart

FC NANTES

Football Club de Nantes Atlantique
Centre sportif José-Arribas-la Jonelière
44240 La Chappelle-sur-Erdre
tel - (0240) 372929
fax - (0240) 372921
Year of Formation - 1943
President - Kléber Bobin
Coach - Reynald Denoueix
Stadium - La Beaujoire-Louis-Fonteneau (38,285)

MAJOR HONOURS
League Championship - (7)
1965, 1966, 1973, 1977, 1980, 1983, 1995.
French Cup - (2) 1979, 1999.

		P	Ap	(s)	Gls
Diego BUSTOS (ARG)	A	3			
Eric CARRIERE	M	33		1	
Jean-Marc CHANELET	D	32		1	
COMBA (ARG)	A		(2)		
Frédéric DA ROCHA	A	30		7	
Eric DECROIX	D	25	(1)	1	
Pascal DELHOMMEAU	D	2	(1)		
Yves DEROFF	M	15	(7)		
Charles DEVINEAU	M	14	(8)	2	
Néstor FABBRI (ARG)	D	31		4	
Samuel FENILLAT	M		(1)		
Nicolas GILLET	D	11	(6)	1	
Michaël LANDREAU	G	31			
Christophe LE ROUX	M	15		3	
Medhi LEROY	M	4			
Eric LOUSSOUARN	G	3			
Sébastien MACE	M		(2)		
Olivier MONTERRUBIO	A	30		8	
Samba N'DIAYE (SEN)	A		(3)		
Salomon OLEMBE (CMR)	M	22	(7)	1	
Sébastien PIOCELLE	M	22	(2)		
Nicolas SAVINAUD	M	18	(3)	1	
Antoine SIBIERSKI	M	20	(2)	4	
Patrick SUFFO	A	6	(15)	4	
Alioune TOURE	A	7	(10)	2	
M VAHIRUA	M		(1)		

08/08/98	Olympique Marseille	A	0-2	
15/08/98	RC Strasbourg	H	1-0	Olembé
23/08/98	AS Nancy-Lorraine	A	0-1	
29/08/98	FC Sochaux	H	2-0	Sibierski (p), Carrière
11/09/98	Toulouse FC	A	3-2	Monterrubio 2, Touré
19/09/98	FC Lorient	H	1-1	Le Roux (p)
25/09/98	RC Lens	A	4-2	Le Roux (p), Gillet, Savinaud,
				Monterrubio
03/10/98	Olympique Lyonnais	H	2-0	Da Rocha, Monterrubio
16/10/98	Girondins de Bordeaux	A	0-2	
24/10/98	Paris Saint-Germain	H	0-0	
29/10/98	AS Monaco	A	1-3	Fabbri
07/11/98	AJ Auxerre	A	1-1	Sibierski
10/11/98	Le Havre AC	H	1-1	Suffo
14/11/98	FC Metz	A	0-1	
20/11/98	Montpellier HSC	H	1-1	Decroix
28/11/98	Stade Rennais FC	A	3-2	Sibierski, Suffo, Le Roux
04/12/98	SC Bastia	H	2-0	Da Rocha 2
11/12/98	RC Strasbourg	A	2-2	Fabbri, Monterrubio
16/12/98	AS Nancy-Lorraine	H	2-0	Fabbri, Da Rocha
19/12/98	FC Sochaux	A	1-1	Fabbri
16/01/99	Toulouse FC	H	2-0	Da Rocha, Monterrubio
30/01/99	FC Lorient	A	1-1	Sibierski
06/02/99	RC Lens	H	2-0	Monterrubio, Devineau
13/02/99	Olympique Lyonnais	A	1-2	Suffo
25/02/99	Girondins de Bordeaux	H	0-0	
10/03/99	Paris Saint-Germain	A	0-0	
19/03/99	AS Monaco	H	0-1	
03/04/99	AJ Auxerre	H	2-2	Da Rocha, Monterrubio
14/04/99	Le Havre AC	A	1-2	Da Rocha
24/04/99	FC Metz	H	0-0	
01/05/99	Montpellier HSC	A	2-1	Devineau, Suffo
05/05/99	Stade Rennais FC	H	2-1	Chanelet, Touré
22/05/99	SC Bastia	A	0-1	
29/05/99	Olympique Marseille	H	0-1	

PARIS SAINT-GERMAIN

CLUB DIRECTORY

Paris Saint-Germain Football Club
24 rue du Cdt-Guilbaud
75016 Paris
tel - (0141) 107171
fax - (0141) 107100
Year of Formation - 1970
President - Pierre Lescure
Coach - Alain Giresse; Artur Jorge;
Philippe Bergeroo
Stadium - Parc des Princes (48,527)

MAJOR HONOURS
League Championship - (2) 1986, 1994.
French Cup - (5)
1982, 1983, 1993, 1995, 1998.
League Cup - (2) 1995, 1998.
European Cup-winners' Cup - (1) 1996.

APPEARANCES 98/99

	P	Ap	(s)	Gls
ADAILTON Martins (BRA)	A	5	(14)	2
Jimmy ALGERINO	D	29	(1)	3
Bruno CAROTTI	M	9	(10)	
Dominique CASAGRANDE	G	2		
Aliou CISSE	M	8		
Didier DOMI	D	7	(1)	
Pierre DUCROCQ	M	26	(2)	
Alain GOMA	D	30		
Xavier GRAVELAINE	A	5	(2)	
HÉLDER (POR)	M	5		
Yann LACHUER	M	16	(4)	1
Bernard LAMA	G	32		
Nicolas LASPALLES	D	4	(1)	
Jérôme LEROY	M	4	(17)	1
Laurent LEROY	M		(5)	
Francis LLACER	M	12	(3)	
Patrice LOKO	A	6	(3)	
Michaël MADAR	A	8	(3)	3
Augustine "Jay-Jay" OKOCHA (NIG)	M	23	(2)	4
Nicolas OUEDEC	A	6	(6)	
Grégory PAISLEY	D	11	(1)	1
Eric RABESANDRATANA	M	27	(1)	1
Bruno RODRIGUEZ	A	12	(3)	5
Marco SIMONE (ITA)	A	30	(1)	9
Christian WÖRNS (GER)	D	28		2
Igor YANOVSKIY (RUS)	M	29	(2)	

LEAGUE RESULTS 1998/99

08/08/98	Girondins de Bordeaux	A	1-3	Okocha
15/08/98	SC Bastia	H	2-0	Wörns, Simone
22/08/98	RC Strasbourg	A	1-0	Simone
29/08/98	FC Lorient	H	1-2	Simone (p)
11/09/98	AS Nancy-Lorraine	A	0-0	
20/09/98	AS Monaco	H	1-0	Lachuer
25/09/98	FC Sochaux	A	0-1	
04/10/98	RC Lens	H	0-1	
16/10/98	Olympique Lyonnais	A	1-1	Simone
24/10/98	FC Nantes	A	0-0	
30/10/98	AJ Auxerre	H	2-0	Okocha 2
07/11/98	Montpellier HSC	A	1-2	Okocha
11/11/98	FC Metz	H	2-2	og (Kastendeuch), Simone (p)
15/11/98	Le Havre AC	A	4-0	Algerino, Simone 2, Paisley
20/11/98	Stade Rennais FC	H	2-1	Rabesandratana, Leroy J.
29/11/98	Olympique Marseille	A	0-0	
04/12/98	Toulouse FC	H	0-0	
12/12/98	SC Bastia	A	0-2	
16/12/98	RC Strasbourg	H	0-0	
19/12/98	FC Lorient	A	0-2	
17/01/99	AS Nancy-Lorraine	H	1-2	og (Fischer)
29/01/99	AS Monaco	A	1-2	Rodriguez
06/02/99	FC Sochaux	H	2-1	Madar, Rodriguez
13/02/99	RC Lens	A	1-2	Simone
25/02/99	Olympique Lyonnais	H	0-1	
10/03/99	FC Nantes	H	0-0	
20/03/99	AJ Auxerre	A	1-0	Rodriguez
03/04/99	Montpellier HSC	H	0-1	
14/04/99	FC Metz	A	1-1	Algerino
25/04/99	Le Havre AC	H	3-0	Madar 2, Wörns
01/05/99	Stade Rennais FC	A	1-2	Adailton
04/05/99	Olympique Marseille	H	2-1	Simone, Rodriguez
22/05/99	Toulouse FC	A	1-2	Algerino
29/05/99	Girondins de Bordeaux	H	2-3	Rodriguez, Adailton

STADE RENNAIS FC

Stade Rennais Football Club
111 route de Lorient
35000 Rennes
tel - (0299) 144151
fax - (0299) 143577
Year of Formation - 1901
President - Pierre Blayau
Coach - Paul Le Guen
Stadium - Route de Lorient (16,000)

MAJOR HONOURS
French Cup - (2) 1965, 1971.

	P	Ap	(s)	Gls
Dominique ARRIBAGE	D	25		2
Cédric BARDON	A	26	(5)	8
Yoann BIGNE	M	26	(3)	1
Philippe BRINQUIN	D	13	(5)	
Edouard CISSE	M	26	(2)	2
Jean-Luc DOGON	D	17	(3)	1
Fabrice FERNANDES	A	12	(3)	2
Nicolas GOUSSE	A	16	(18)	6
Stéphane GREGOIRE	M	33	(1)	2
Tony HEURTEBIS	G	5		
Laurent HUARD	M	8	(10)	1
Benoît LE BRIS	A		(5)	
Christophe LE ROUX	M	13		3
Shabani NONDA (BUR)	A	32		15
Christophe REVAULT	G	29		
Anthony REVEILLERE	D	31	(1)	
Youssef ROSSI (MAR)	D	19		
Ronan SALAÜN	M	1	(8)	
David SOMMEIL	D	33		
Laurent VIAUD	M	2	(4)	
Patrick WEISER (GER)	M	5	(7)	1
Cyril YAPI	A	2	(6)	

08/08/98	AJ Auxerre	H	1-0	Huard
15/08/98	Montpellier HSC	A	1-3	Fernandes
22/08/98	Le Havre AC	H	2-1	Nonda, og (Pollet)
30/08/98	RC Strasbourg	H	1-1	Goussé
11/09/98	Olympique Marseille	A	1-1	Dogon
19/09/98	SC Bastia	H	2-0	Fernandes, Nonda
25/09/98	Girondins de Bordeaux	A	0-4	
03/10/98	AS Monaco	H	2-1	Goussé, Nonda
17/10/98	AS Nancy-Lorraine	A	1-0	Cissé
24/10/98	FC Lorient	H	1-0	Nonda
30/10/98	Toulouse FC	A	1-0	Arribagé
07/11/98	FC Sochaux	H	4-0	Bardon 2 (1p), Nonda, Cissé
11/11/98	RC Lens	A	1-3	Nonda
14/11/98	Olympique Lyonnais	H	0-0	
20/11/98	Paris Saint-Germain	A	1-2	Nonda
28/11/98	FC Nantes	H	2-3	Nonda, Grégoire
04/12/98	FC Metz	A	0-0	
11/12/98	Montpellier HSC	H	3-2	Nonda, Bardon, Goussé
16/12/98	Le Havre AC	A	0-2	
19/12/98	RC Strasbourg	A	1-1	Bardon
16/01/99	Olympique Marseille	H	1-1	Arribagé
24/01/99	SC Bastia	A	1-0	Nonda
06/02/99	Girondins de Bordeaux	H	1-1	Weiser
13/02/99	AS Monaco	A	2-4	Le Roux, Bardon
26/02/99	AS Nancy-Lorraine	H	2-1	Le Roux, Gousse
10/03/99	FC Lorient	A	1-1	Nonda
20/03/99	Toulouse FC	H	1-0	Goussé
02/04/99	FC Sochaux	A	3-0	Bigné, Nonda, Le Roux (p)
13/04/99	RC Lens	H	2-0	Nonda, Goussé
25/04/99	Olympique Lyonnais	A	2-1	Bardon, Nonda (p)
01/05/99	Paris Saint-Germain	H	2-1	Grégoire, Bardon
05/05/99	FC Nantes	A	1-2	Bardon
22/05/99	FC Metz	H	1-0	Nonda (p)
29/05/99	AJ Auxerre	A	0-2	

FC SOCHAUX

CLUB DIRECTORY

Football Club Sochaux-Montbéliard
Bungalow du Stade Bonal
25200 Montbéliard
tel - (0381) 945346
fax - (0381) 954657
Year of Formation - 1928
President - Gilles Daget
Secretary - Jean-Claude Vienot
Coach - Faruk Hadzibegic; Philippe Anziani
Stadium - Auguste-Bonal (13,370)

APPEARANCES 98/99

	P	Ap	(s)	Gls
Olivier BAUDRY	M	10	(2)	1
Eric BONIFACE	D	6	(4)	
Bernard BOUGER	A	25	(4)	10
Yves BOUGER	D	20		
Christophe CHAINTREUIL	M	9		
Adel CHEDLI	M	11	(2)	
Oumar DAF	D	13		
Sébastien DALLET	A	14	(4)	5
Stéphane DEDEBANT	M	13	(11)	1
Elhadji DIOUF	M	11	(4)	
Vincent FAIVRE	M	1		
Vincent FERNANDEZ	G	34		
Koffi FIAWOO (TOG)	A	7	(10)	2
Maxence FLACHEZ	D	29		3
Pierre-Alain FRAU	A	4	(16)	1
Mickaël ISABEY	M	1	(3)	
László KLAUSZ (HUN)	A	5	(9)	
Didier LANG	D	19	(5)	
LICINA	M	1		
Daniel LJUBOJA	A	21	(5)	4
Erwan MANAC'H	M	21	(1)	
Bernard MARAVAL	D	25	(1)	2
Frédéric MARTIN	D	3		
Kamel MERIEM	M	15	(3)	1
Philippe RASCHKE	D	24	(1)	
Michaël RAVAUX	D	11	(5)	
Stéphane SANTINI	M	4	(1)	
Antony SIRUFO	M	3	(2)	
Franck VANDECASTEELE	A	1		
Jean-Guy WALLEMME	D	13		

LEAGUE RESULTS 1998/99

08/08/98	AS Nancy-Lorraine	A	1-1	Fiawoo
15/08/98	AS Monaco	A	1-4	Maraval
23/08/98	RC Lens	H	0-4	
29/08/98	FC Nantes	A	0-2	
11/09/98	Olympique Lyonnais	H	1-2	Dedebant (p)
19/09/98	AJ Auxerre	A	1-3	Dallet
25/09/98	Paris Saint-Germain	H	1-0	Dallet
03/10/98	Le Havre AC	A	0-3	
17/10/98	FC Metz	H	1-1	Baudry
24/10/98	Olympique Marseille	A	0-4	
31/10/98	Montpellier HSC	H	4-0	Bouger B., Maraval, Ljuboja 2
07/11/98	Stade Rennais FC	A	0-4	
11/11/98	SC Bastia	H	2-1	Bouger B. 2
14/11/98	Girondins de Bordeaux	A	0-0	
20/11/98	RC Strasbourg	H	1-1	Fiawoo
28/11/98	Toulouse FC	A	1-1	Bouger B.
04/12/98	FC Lorient	H	0-1	
16/12/98	RC Lens	A	1-1	Flachez
19/12/98	FC Nantes	H	1-1	Bouger B.
30/01/99	AJ Auxerre	H	1-1	Ljuboja
06/02/99	Paris Saint-Germain	A	1-2	Bouger B.
26/02/99	FC Metz	A	1-1	Bouger B.
09/03/99	Olympique Marseille	H	0-0	
14/03/99	AS Monaco	H	1-1	Flachez
20/03/99	Montpellier HSC	A	0-0	
02/04/99	Stade Rennais FC	H	0-3	
08/04/99	Olympique Lyonnais	A	1-4	Bouger B. (p)
13/04/99	SC Bastia	A	1-1	Dallet
24/04/99	Girondins de Bordeaux	H	2-0	Dallet, Bouger B.
01/05/99	RC Strasbourg	A	1-1	Flachez
05/05/99	Toulouse FC	H	2-1	Bouger B., Frau
14/05/99	Le Havre AC	H	1-0	Ljuboja
22/05/99	FC Lorient	A	1-4	Dallet
29/05/99	AS Nancy-Lorraine	H	1-1	Meriem

RC STRASBOURG

CLUB DIRECTORY

Racing Club de Strasbourg
Stade de la Meinau
12 rue d'Extenwoerth
67100 Strasbourg
tel - (0388) 445500
fax - (0388) 445501
Year of Formation - 1906
President - Patrick Proisy
Manager - Claude Le Roy
Coach - Pierre Mankowski
Stadium - Meinau (41,228)

MAJOR HONOURS
League Championship - (1) 1979.
French Cup - (2) 1951, 1966.
League Cup - (1) 1997.

APPEARANCES 98/99

	P	Ap	(s)	Gls
Gharib AMZINE (MAR)	M	18		
Frédéric ARPINON	M	10	(3)	1
Teddy BERTIN	D	34		8
Habib BEYE	D	18	(5)	
Stéphane COLLET	M	31	(2)	1
Denni CONTEH (DEN)	A	9	(10)	3
Thierry DEBES	G	4		
Olivier ECHOUAFNI	M	32		3
Fabrice EHRET	M	2	(8)	
Peter FRANK (DEN)	D	2		
Brahim HEMDANI	M	9	(3)	
Christophe KINET (BEL)	M	3	(7)	
Pegguy LUYINDULA	A	3	(15)	
Mickaël MARSIGLIA	M	9	(3)	1
Corentin MARTINS	M	33		4
Rafik MEZRICHE	M		(3)	
Raphaël MICELI (BEL)	A	10	(9)	
Morten NIELSEN (DEN)	D	5	(5)	
Godwin OKPARA (NIG)	D	32		
Per PEDERSEN (DEN)	A	7		
Lionel ROUXEL	A	23	(4)	5
SEO JUNG-WON (KOR)	A	1	(3)	
Jan SUCHOPAREK (CZE)	D	29		
Alexander VENCEL (SVK)	G	30		
Luciano ZAVAGNO (ARG)	D	7	(2)	1
David ZITELLI	A	13		3

LEAGUE RESULTS 1998/99

08/08/98	Olympique Lyonnais	H	0-0	
15/08/98	FC Nantes	A	0-1	
22/08/98	Paris Saint-Germain	H	0-1	
30/08/98	Stade Rennais FC	A	1-1	Echouafni
11/09/98	FC Metz	H	0-0	
19/09/98	Le Havre AC	A	1-0	Echouafni
25/09/98	Montpellier HSC	H	2-1	Bertin, Conteh
03/10/98	AJ Auxerre	A	1-3	Rouxel
16/10/98	Olympique Marseille	H	0-2	
24/10/98	SC Bastia	A	0-0	
30/10/98	Girondins de Bordeaux	H	3-2	Rouxel 2, Bertin
07/11/98	AS Nancy-Lorraine	H	1-2	Collet
11/11/98	Toulouse FC	A	1-0	Bertin
15/11/98	FC Lorient	H	2-0	Rouxel, Martins
20/11/98	FC Sochaux	A	1-1	Arpinon
28/11/98	AS Monaco	H	1-1	Martins
04/12/98	RC Lens	A	0-3	
11/12/98	FC Nantes	H	2-2	Conteh, Bertin (p)
16/12/98	Paris Saint-Germain	A	0-0	
19/12/98	Stade Rennais FC	H	1-1	Conteh
17/01/99	FC Metz	A	0-1	
30/01/99	Le Havre AC	H	0-1	
07/02/99	Montpellier HSC	A	1-1	Zitelli
25/02/99	Olympique Marseille	A	0-1	
10/03/99	SC Bastia	H	1-1	Zavagno
14/03/99	AJ Auxerre	H	2-1	Bertin (p), Rouxel
20/03/99	Girondins de Bordeaux	A	0-1	
03/04/99	AS Nancy-Lorraine	A	1-1	Echouafni
14/04/99	Toulouse FC	H	2-0	Bertin (p), Martins
24/04/99	FC Lorient	A	1-0	Zitelli
01/05/99	FC Sochaux	H	1-1	Zitelli
05/05/99	AS Monaco	A	1-2	Bertin
22/05/99	RC Lens	H	1-1	Marsiglia
29/05/99	Olympique Lyonnais	A	2-3	Martins, Bertin (p)

TOULOUSE FC

CLUB DIRECTORY

Toulouse Football Club
Stadium Municipal
Allée Gabriel-Biènes
31400 Toulouse
tel - (0561) 551111
fax - (0561) 535567
Year of Formation - 1937
President - Jacques Rubio
Coach - Guy Lacombe; Alain Giresse
Stadium - Stadium Municipal (37,000)

MAJOR HONOURS
French Cup - (1) 1957.

APPEARANCES 98/99

	P	Ap	(s)	Gls
Loïc ANDRAUD	A		(1)	
Christophe AVEZAC	A	1	(1)	
Laurent BATTLES	D	25	(5)	2
Jérôme BILLAC	M	1		
José COBOS	D	19	(2)	
Lamine DIATTA	D	25		
Joachim FERNANDEZ	D	1		
José Manuel GALDAMES (ESP)	D	23		
Alain GOUAMENE	G	8		
Stéphane GUIRAUD	M		(1)	
Laurent GUYOT	D	14	(1)	
Samuel IPOUA (CMR)	A	6	(3)	1
Fabrice JAU	M	23	(1)	
Christophe LAUWERS (BEL)	A	3	(4)	1
Ahmed MAHARZI	A	19	(10)	2
Robert MALM	A	13	(16)	2
Patrice MAUREL	M	3	(1)	1
Xavier MERIDE	D	9	(1)	
Thierry MOREAU	M	21		
Ernest MTAWALI (MWI)	M	1	(1)	
Medhi NAFTI	M	3	(8)	
OCEANO Cruz (POR)	M	30		6
Nicolas PAVIOT	D	19	(8)	
Vladimir PETROVIC (YUG)	A	26	(1)	6
Antoine PREGET	D	17	(5)	1
Teddy RICHERT	G	26		
Yannick ROTT	D	10	(9)	
Aboubacar SANKHARE	D	9	(1)	
Didier SANTINI	D	11	(1)	
Mickaël SERREAU	A	2	(4)	
Donald SIE (CIV)	M	6	(4)	1

LEAGUE RESULTS 1998/99

08/08/98	RC Lens	H	3-2	Malm, Maharzi, og (Méride)
14/08/98	Olympique Lyonnais	A	1-6	Petrovic
22/08/98	AS Monaco	H	0-0	
29/08/98	Montpellier HSC	A	0-3	
11/09/98	FC Nantes	H	2-3	Petrovic, Ipoua
19/09/98	FC Metz	A	0-0	
24/09/98	AJ Auxerre	H	0-0	
03/10/98	Olympique Marseille	A	0-2	
18/10/98	SC Bastia	H	2-1	Petrovic 2
24/10/98	Le Havre AC	A	0-0	
30/10/98	Stade Rennais FC	H	0-1	
07/11/98	Girondins de Bordeaux	A	1-3	Oceano
11/11/98	RC Strasbourg	H	0-1	
14/11/98	AS Nancy-Lorraine	H	1-1	Oceano
20/11/98	FC Lorient	A	0-1	
28/11/98	FC Sochaux	H	1-1	Petrovic
04/12/98	Paris Saint-Germain	A	0-0	
12/12/98	Olympique Lyonnais	H	0-0	
16/12/98	AS Monaco	A	1-1	Malm
19/12/98	Montpellier HSC	H	2-5	Préget, Oceano (p)
16/01/99	FC Nantes	A	0-2	
30/01/99	FC Metz	H	1-0	Battles
07/02/99	AJ Auxerre	A	2-1	Oceano (p), Petrovic
14/02/99	Olympique Marseille	H	1-0	Oceano (p)
26/02/99	SC Bastia	A	1-1	Oceano
10/03/99	Le Havre AC	H	0-0	
20/03/99	Stade Rennais FC	A	0-1	
03/04/99	Girondins de Bordeaux	H	0-3	
14/04/99	RC Strasbourg	A	0-2	
24/04/99	AS Nancy-Lorraine	A	0-2	
30/04/99	FC Lorient	H	1-4	Maharzi
05/05/99	FC Sochaux	A	1-2	Lauwers
22/05/99	Paris Saint-Germain	H	2-1	Sié, Battles
29/05/99	RC Lens	A	1-3	Maurel

PROMOTED CLUBS

SECOND DIVISION FINAL TABLE 98/99

		Pd	W	D	L	F	A	Pt	GD
1	AS Saint-Etienne	38	18	14	6	56	38	68	+18
2	CS Sedan Ardennes	38	18	12	8	59	31	66	+28
3	Troyes AC	38	17	13	8	48	31	64	+17
4	Lille OSC	38	19	7	12	45	35	64	+10
5	SM Caen	38	16	11	11	47	39	59	+8
6	FC Gueugnon	38	14	15	9	44	39	57	+5
7	En Avant Guingamp	38	14	11	13	36	38	53	-2
8	LB Châteauroux	38	12	15	11	38	38	51	0
9	AC Ajaccio	38	13	12	13	49	56	51	-7
10	Stade Lavallois	38	12	14	12	37	35	50	+2
11	Chamois Niortais	38	11	15	12	41	40	48	+1
12	AS Cannes	38	12	11	15	34	45	47	-11
13	Nîmes Olympique	38	11	13	14	49	46	46	+3
14	OGC Nice	38	11	13	14	31	34	46	-3
15	ES Wasquehal	38	11	12	15	35	41	45	-6
16	Amiens SCF	38	11	11	16	39	43	44	-4
17	Le Mans UC 72	38	9	15	14	41	41	42	0
18	ASOA Valence	38	10	10	18	41	56	40	-15
19	AS Red Star 93	38	9	12	17	52	72	39	-20
20	AS Beauvais-Oise	38	10	8	20	43	67	38	-24

CLUB DIRECTORY

Association Sportive de Saint-Etienne
Stade Geoffroy-Guichard
14 rue Paul-et-Pierre-Guichard
42028 Saint-Etienne Cedex 01
tel - (0477) 923170
fax - (0477) 923182
Year of Formation - 1933
President - Alain Bompard
Secretary - Didier Lacombe
Coach - Robert Nouzaret
Stadium - Geoffroy-Guichard (36,000)

MAJOR HONOURS
League Championship - (10) 1957, 1964, 1967,
1968, 1969, 1970, 1974, 1975, 1976, 1981.
Domestic Cup - (6)
1962, 1968, 1970, 1974, 1975, 1977.

CLUB DIRECTORY

Club Sportif Sedan Ardennes
Boulevard de Lattre-de-Tassigny
BP 1
08200 Sedan
tel - (0324) 270059
fax - (0324) 293110
Year of Formation - 1919
Presidents - Michel Bérard & Francis Roumy
Secretary - Francis Tissot
Coach - Patrick Rémy
Stadium - Emile-Albeau (17,000)

MAJOR HONOURS
Domestic Cup - (2) 1956, 1961

CLUB DIRECTORY

Association Troyes Aube Champagne
Stade de l'Aube
Avenue Robert-Schuman
BP 226
10000 Troyes
tel - (0325) 704830
fax - (0325) 704833
Year of Formation - 1986
President - Daniel Vacelet
Secretary - Jean-Marc Pellissier
Coach - Alain Perrin
Stadium - Stade de l'Aube (12,000)

GEORGIA

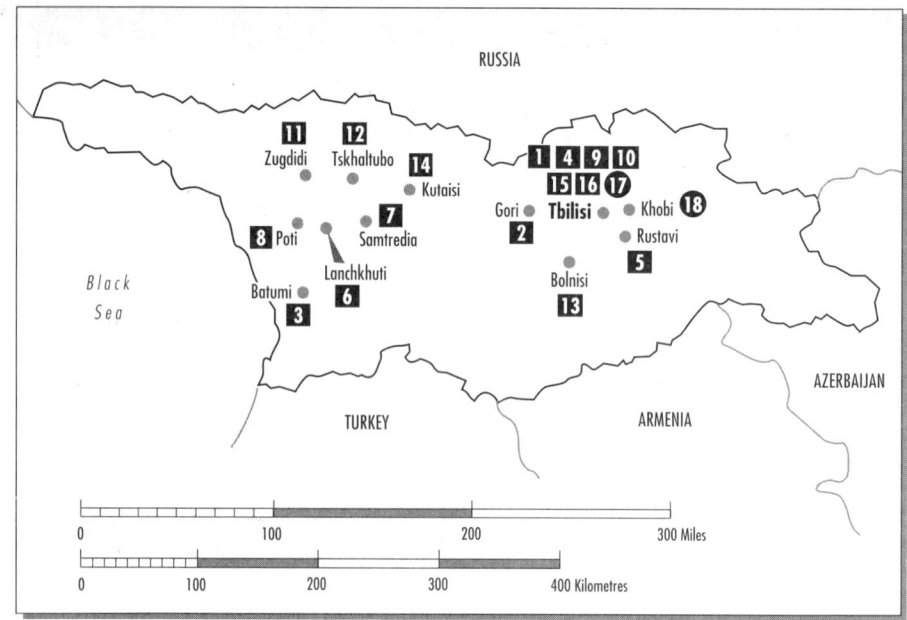

1	ARSENALI TBILISI	407
2	DILA GORI	408
3	DINAMO BATUMI	409
4	DINAMO TBILISI	410
5	GORDA RUSTAVI	411
6	GURIA LANCHKHUTI	412
7	IBERIA SAMTREDIA	413
8	KOLKHETI 1913 POTI	414
9	LOKOMOTIVI TBILISI	415
10	MERANI 91 TBILISI	416

11	ODISHI ZUGDIDI	417
12	SAMGURALI TSKHALTUBO	418
13	SIONI BOLNISI	419
14	TORPEDO KUTAISI	420
15	TSU TBILISI	421
16	VIT GEORGIA TBILISI	422
Promoted clubs		
17	FC TBILISI	423
18	KOLKHETI KHOBI	423

DUTCHMAN BOSKAMP HANDED TWO TOP JOBS

European record for Dinamo Tbilisi

FEDERATION DIRECTORY

Football Federation of Georgia
5 Shota Iamanidze Str., Tbilisi 380 012
tel - (32) 960750/960780   Year of Formation - 1990
fax - (32) 001128   President - Merab Jordania
                              Secretary - Valeri Cholaria
Stadium - Boris Paichadze, Tbilisi (75,000)

By winning their tenth straight Georgian title, Dinamo Tbilisi set a new European record. No club in any other European country has ever achieved ten straight national titles.

It might be argued that the first three of those championship wins, earned under the name Iberia Tbilisi, do not strictly count as they were won during a time when the Georgian league was not officially recognised by UEFA (the Soviet Union was still a going concern in those days). But, given the total dominance of Dinamo in their own land, it is surely only a matter of time before they extend their record to incorporate ten 'proper' consecutive titles.

Pedantic observations aside, the fact remains that Dinamo Tbilisi have won every national championship they

INTERNATIONAL HONOURS

EUROPEAN CLUB COMPETITIONS
Cup-winners' Cup   Dinamo Tbilisi (1981)

have entered in the 1990s. Despite once again undergoing a heavy turnover of players in 1998/99, they completed the clean sweep with the same degree of ease that had accompanied most of their previous triumphs. Challengers to their crown were few and distant, and the championship outcome was resolved long in advance, even if mathematical confirmation was delayed until the 7-1 thrashing of bottom club Guria Lanchkhuti three rounds from the end - a match in which the league's leading scorer, and Dinamo's player of the season, Mikheil Ashvetia, scored his only hat-trick of the campaign.

The only team to beat Dinamo in the league were Torpedo Kutaisi, who, appropriately, finished as runners-up - their best-ever placing. What's more, they also landed their first trophy by winning the Georgian Cup, defeating Samgurali Tskhaltubo on penalties in the final after the two hours of regular play had failed to produce a goal.

Dinamo Tbilisi had also been knocked out of the Cup on penalties after two goalless games with Lokomotivi Tbilisi. Their early exit - in the eighth-finals - was the shock of the season. It was the first time in eight years that they failed to reach the final. Their fate was shared in identical fashion by holders Dinamo Batumi, who also fell victim to Lokomotivi's outstanding defensive and penalty-taking skills in the quarter-finals.

The failure felt most keenly by Dinamo Tbilisi, however, was

LEAGUE CHAMPIONSHIP RESULTS 98/99

		1	2	3	4	5	6	7	8	9	10	11	12	13	14	15	16
1	Arsenali Tbilisi		2-2	0-1	1-7	1-0	5-1	2-5	0-0	0-0	1-1	3-0	1-1	2-1	0-2	0-0	0-0
2	Dila Gori	1-2		0-1	1-2	3-0	5-3	2-1	2-1	0-2	3-3	1-0	0-1	2-0	3-0	0-0	1-3
3	Dinamo Batumi	1-1	6-0		0-0	1-1	4-0	1-0	2-1	1-1	0-0	9-0	6-1	1-0	2-1	4-2	0-1
4	Dinamo Tbilisi	5-1	4-0	1-1		2-0	7-1	7-2	6-1	1-0	5-1	5-0	6-0	8-1	1-0	0-0	3-2
5	Gorda Rustavi	0-1	1-1	0-0	0-0		2-2	1-0	0-0	0-2	0-3	6-2	2-0	3-1	1-7	0-0	3-2
6	Guria Lanchkhuti	0-2	4-2	0-1	0-1	3-4		1-3	1-4	0-4	3-7	1-2	2-3	1-1	1-5	2-0	2-0
7	Iberia Samtredia	3-1	2-0	3-1	0-1	1-2	4-1		2-2	2-3	0-0	0-0	3-1	1-2	0-0	4-2	0-1
8	Kolkheti 1913 Poti	3-2	2-3	1-0	0-1	5-0	3-0	3-1		0-0	3-0	5-1	4-2	4-0	1-2	2-0	2-1
9	Lokmotivi Tbilisi	2-1	0-0	1-0	0-0	0-0	1-0	2-0	1-1		1-0	3-0	2-0	3-0	1-1	3-1	1-0
10	Merani 91 Tbilisi	0-0	4-0	1-0	0-2	1-1	3-0	0-2	1-0	0-0		0-1	0-0	2-0	2-1	1-0	0-0
11	Odishi Zugdidi	1-2	2-1	2-1	0-4	1-0	4-2	0-1	0-2	0-1	0-1		0-2	1-4	1-3	1-1	1-3
12	Samgurali Tskhaltubo	2-0	3-1	0-0	0-3	1-0	2-1	2-3	0-1	1-2	1-2	1-0		1-0	2-3	0-1	1-3
13	Sioni Bolnisi	0-1	1-0	1-1	1-3	0-0	2-2	1-0	1-1	0-0	1-4	1-0	4-0		1-2	1-1	2-1
14	Torpedo Kutaisi	1-1	3-0	3-3	3-1	4-0	3-0	4-0	5-1	3-1	2-0	2-0	3-1	4-0		1-0	0-1
15	TSU Tbilisi	4-1	0-1	0-1	1-3	0-0	0-0	1-1	2-4	1-4	1-0	4-1	1-3	1-0	1-3		2-5
16	Vit Georgia Tbilisi	0-0	1-2	0-0	0-2	2-1	3-0	4-1	0-0	1-2	1-0	1-0	3-0	2-0	1-2	0-1	

their miserable form in Europe. Lucky to survive their first Champions' League qualifier against Vllaznia Shkodër of Albania by default, they gave themselves a glimpse of the promised land by going 2-0 up at home in the next round against Athletic Bilbao before eventually going out on the away-goals rule. The less said about their subsequent visit to the UEFA Cup, the better, as Dutch club Willem II thrashed them 3-0 in both matches.

It was to a Dutchman that Dinamo sought salvation when, in the closing weeks of the season, they brought in

LEAGUE CHAMPIONSHIP FINAL TABLE 98/99

			Home					Away					Total					
		P	W	D	L	F	A	W	D	L	F	A	W	D	L	F	A	P	GD
1	Dinamo Tbilisi	30	13	2	0	61	10	11	3	1	30	7	24	5	1	91	17	77	+74
2	Torpedo Kutaisi	30	12	2	1	41	9	9	2	4	32	18	21	4	5	73	27	67	+46
3	Lokomotivi Tbilisi	30	10	5	0	21	4	8	5	2	22	10	18	10	2	43	14	64	+29
4	Kolkheti 1913 Poti	30	11	1	3	38	13	4	6	5	19	23	15	7	8	57	36	52	+21
5	Dinamo Batumi	30	9	5	1	38	9	4	6	5	11	13	13	11	6	49	22	50	+27
6	Merani 91 Tbilisi	30	7	5	3	15	7	5	4	6	22	22	12	9	9	37	29	45	+8
7	Vit Georgia Tbilisi	30	7	3	5	19	11	7	2	6	23	18	14	5	11	42	29	44	+13
8	Iberia Samtredia	30	6	4	5	25	17	5	1	9	20	31	11	5	14	45	48	38	-3
9	Arsenali Tbilisi	30	4	7	4	18	21	5	4	6	16	23	9	11	10	34	44	38	-10
10	Dila Gori	30	7	2	6	24	19	3	3	9	13	35	10	5	15	37	54	35	-17
11	Samgurali Tskhaltubo	30	6	1	8	17	20	4	2	9	15	37	10	3	17	32	57	33	-25
12	Gorda Rustavi	30	5	6	4	19	21	2	5	8	9	25	7	11	12	28	46	32	-18
13	Sioni Bolnisi	30	5	6	4	17	16	2	1	12	10	36	7	7	16	27	52	28	-25
14	TSU Tbilisi	30	4	3	8	19	27	2	6	7	9	19	6	9	15	28	46	27	-18
15	Odishi Zugdidi	30	4	1	10	14	28	2	1	12	7	42	6	2	22	21	70	20	-49
16	Guria Lanchkhuti	30	3	1	11	21	39	0	3	12	13	48	3	4	23	34	87	13	-53

N.B. Vit Georgia Tbilisi deducted 3pts.

EUROPEAN CUPS 98/99

CHAMPIONS' CUP
● DINAMO TBILISI
Preliminary round VLLAZNIA SHKODËR (ALB)
H 1-0   Khomeriki (53)
(awarded as 3-0)
Sogolashvili; Didava, Jeladze, Guchua, Kemoklidze (Sakhvadze 78), Kobiashvili, Kvaratskhelia, Aleksidze, Mujiri (Ashvetia 53), Tskitishvili, Khomeriki.
A 1-3   Ashvetia (89)
Sogolashvili; Didava, Tskitishvili, Guchua, Jeladze, Sakhvadze, Kvaratskhelia (Kemoklidze 83), Kobiashvili, Aleksidze, Mujiri (Melkadze 75), Khomeriki (Ashvetia 69).

Qualifying round ATHLETIC BILBAO (ESP)
H 2-1   Khomeriki (15), Tskitishvili (30)
Gvaramadze; Makharadze, Didava, Guchua, Jeladze, Mujiri (Melkadze 87), Kiknadze, Aleksidze, Ashvetia, Tskitishvili, Khomeriki (Shengelia G. 89).
A 0-1
Gvaramadze; Jeladze, Didava, Makharadze, Kobiashvili, Guchua, Tskitishvili, Kiknadze, Mujiri, Ashvetia (Melkadze 55), Khomeriki.

CUP WINNERS' CUP
● DINAMO BATUMI
Qualifying round PARTIZAN BEOGRAD (YUG)
A 0-2
Togonidze; Sichinava, Papidze, Makharadze M., Mindadze (Glonti 46), Veremchuk, Chichvelishvili, Kantidze (Gadelia 57), Tugushi, Rusia, Machutadze.

H 1-0   Sichinava (28)
Togonidze; Sichinava, Papidze, Makharadze M., Veremchuk, Glonti, Kulejishvili, Kantidze (Makatsaria 46), Tugushi, Gadelia (Apkhazava 85), Machutadze.

UEFA CUP
● KOLKHETI 1913 POTI
Preliminary round CRVENA ZVEZDA BEOGRAD (YUG)
H 0-4
Kvachakhia; Mikaberidze (Makharadze 46), Torchinava, Giorgadze, Giorgobiani, Kobuladze, Gaganidze, Inalishvili, Nozadze (Sukhiashvili 74), Gvasalia E., Tsivtsivadze (Kalandadze 37).
A 0-7
Kvachakhia; Kobuladze, Torchinava, Kutidze (Giorgadze 59), Kuntelia, Inalishvili, Gaganidze, Gvasalia E. (Shalamberidze 64), Nozadze (Tsivtsivadze 75), Kalandadze, Makharadze.

● DINAMO TBILISI
1st round WILLEM II (HOL)
A 0-3
Gvaramadze; Mikadze L., Didava, Archvadze, Jeladze, Makharadze, Kiknadze, Aleksidze, Ashvetia, Tskitishvili, Khomeriki.
H 0-3
Gvaramadze; Mikadze L., Didava, Jeladze, Guchua, Mujiri (Sakhvadze 76), Kiknadze (Melkadze 75), Aleksidze, Ashvetia (Kvaratskhelia 75), Tskitishvili, Khomeriki.

NATIONAL TEAM APPEARANCES 98/99

Coach - Vladimir GUTSAEV; Johan BOSKAMP	AZB	UKR	ALB	LAT	GRE	EST	UKR	SLO	NOR	NOR	GRE	Cps	Gls
Soso GRISHIKASHVILI (31/12/72) - FK Ventspils (LAT)/Alania Vladikavkaz (RUS)	G					G76	G	G				5	-
Zurab POPKHADZE (02/06/72) - Krylya Sovetov Samara (RUS)	D					s64			s46	s46		4	-
Giorgi CHANKOTADZE (04/10/77) - Vit Georgia Tblisi	D											1	-
Giorgi DAVITNIDZE (18/08/78) - Merani 91 Tbilisi	D46											1	-
Kakhaber CHKHETIANI (24/02/78) - Torpedo Kutaisi	M											1	-
Giorgi GUDUSHAURI (18/02/73) - Lokomotivi Tbilisi	M70						s62					8	-
Irakli GEMEZASHVILI (06/07/77) - Arsenali Tbilisi	M65											1	-
Gocha JAMARAULI (23/07/71) - Trabzonspor (TUR)/FC Zürich (SUI)	M	M	M	M	M			M82	M	M	M	37	5
Levan KOBIASHVILI (10/07/77) - Dinamo Tbilisi/SC Freiburg (GER)	M	M	M	D	M			M	M	M	M	20	-
Giorgi MEGRELADZE (21/07/78) - Torpedo Kutaisi	A46											1	-
Aleksandre KAIDARASHVILI (02/11/78) - Dila Gori	A											1	-
Irakli VASHAKIDZE (13/03/76) - Torpedo Kutaisi	s46											1	-
Lasha MONASELIDZE (02/01/77) - Torpedo Moskva (RUS)	s46											1	-
Giorgi KIPIANI (12/08/78) - Torpedo Kutaisi	s65											1	-
Kakhaber KVETENADZE (03/06/70) - Torpedo Kutaisi	s70					M56						2	-
Nikoloz TOGONIDZE (24/04/71) - Dinamo Batumi	G46		G						G			11	-
Kakhi KALADZE (27/02/78) - Dynamo Kyiv (UKR)	D	D	D	D				M	D	D	D	18	-
Gela SHEKILADZE (14/09/70) - K Lierse SK (BEL)	D		D	D					D46			13	-
Givi DIDAVA (21/03/76) - Dinamo Tbilisi	D73				D				D	D46	s10	8	-
Levan TSKITISHVILI (10/10/76) - Dinamo Tbilisi/SC Freiburg (GER)	D	D								D	D56	14	1
Giorgi NEMSADZE (10/05/72) - Grasshopper-Club Zürich (SUI)/Reggiana (ITA)	M46	M	D	M			M75	M	M	M	M	42	-
Temur KETSBAIA (18/03/68) - Newcastle United (ENG)		M	A54	M	M				A46	M	A	36	11
Giorgi KINKLADZE (06/07/73) - Ajax (HOL)		A	M	M	M			s46				34	6
Aleksandre IASHVILI (23/10/77) - SC Freiburg (GER)	A61	A62										7	2
David GVARAMADZE (08/11/75) - Dinamo Tbilisi	s46	G	G							G	G	8	-
Mamuka TSERETELI (17/01/79) - Alania Vladikavkaz (RUS)	s46	D						D	D	D	D	7	-
Giorgi DEMETRADZE (26/09/76) - Alania Vladikavkaz (RUS)	s61		s60					A	A74	s46	A78	9	-
Levan SILAGADZE (04/08/76) - Skonto Riga (LAT)	s73	D43										7	-
Giorgi KIKNADZE (26/04/76) - Dinamo Tbilisi			s43					s81				10	1
Zaza JANASHIA (10/02/76) - Lokomotiv Moskva (RUS)			s54					A	A			5	3
Archil ARVELADZE (22/02/73) - NAC (HOL)			s62									17	4
Giorgi GAKHOKIDZE (05/11/75) - PSV (HOL)				M60	s59		s75					12	-
Mikhail KAVELASHVILI (22/07/71) - Grasshopper-Club Zürich (SUI)			A	A59			s74				A	27	6
Shota ARVELADZE (22/02/73) - Ajax (HOL)			A	A								30	11
Murtaz SHELIA (25/03/69) - Manchester City (ENG)					D							29	-
Giorgi BALASHVILI (07/08/73) - Lokomotivi Tbilisi						D	D	D				3	-
Vaja TARKHNISHVILI (25/08/71) - Lokomotivi Tbilisi/Sheriff Tiraspol (MOL)						D64	D					2	-
Gia CHKHAIDZE (27/02/70) - Torpedo Kutaisi/Alania Vladikavkaz (RUS)						D72	D	D				3	-
Giorgi REVAZISHVILI (31/03/77) - Krylya Sovetov Samara (RUS)						M62						1	-
Rati ALEKSIDZE (03/08/78) - Dinamo Tbilisi						M	s30	M46			s56	4	-
David JANASHIA (07/08/72) - Torpedo Kutaisi						A	M30					9	3
Mikheil ASHVETIA (10/11/77) - Dinamo Tbilisi						A	s57			s78	A	5	2
David MUJIRI (02/01/78) - Dinamo Tbilisi						s56						1	-
Zviad JELADZE (16/12/73) - Dinamo Tbilisi						s72						3	-
Giorgi LOMAIA (08/08/79) - Merani 91 Tbilisi						s76						1	-
Mikhail POTSKHVERIA (12/08/75) - Dnipro Dnipropetrovsk (UKR)							A57					3	-
Giorgi DARASELIA (17/09/68) - Zafririm Holon (ISR)								s82				9	2
Aleksandre REKHVIASHVILI (06/08/74) - Skonto Riga (LAT)									M81			1	-
Valter GUCHUA (06/07/75) - Dinamo Tbilisi									M63			4	-
David CHICHVEISHVILI (23/01/75) - Dinamo Batumi										s63	D10	2	-
Otar KHIZANEISHVILI (26/06/81) - Dinamo Tbilisi											D	1	-
Badri AKHVLEDIANI (19/10/81) - Torpedo Kutaisi											M65	1	-
Zurab KHIZANISHVILI (06/10/81) - Dinamo Tbilisi											s65	1	-

ZAZA JANASHIA

Lokomotiv Moscow striker Zaza Janashia was a worthy winner of the 1998/99 Georgian Footballer of the Year award. The 23-year-old was well out in front in the voting, beating Dynamo Kiev defender Kakhi Kaladze into second place by almost 100 points. Janashia was the star of Lokomotiv's run to the semi-finals of the European Cup-winners' Cup and he finished as the last-ever top scorer of that competition with a handsome total of six goals. He also made his mark for the Georgian national team. In each of the two Euro 2000 qualifiers he started - at home to Slovenia and Norway - he found the net. But his indiscipline did not go down well with new coach Johan Boskamp, who ejected him from the squad after he failed to comply with the Dutchman's strict new training routine.

former Anderlecht boss Johan Boskamp to replace Murtaz Khurtsilava. His mission was to make Dinamo a force outside their own borders, but that was not his only brief. Newly-appointed federation president Merab Jordania also commissioned Boskamp to take charge of the Georgian national team.

On the face of it, it was the national team which needed him most. The European Championship qualifying campaign had gone badly awry, with a series of disappointing results and performances ending the 18-month reign of veteran coach Vladimir Gutsaev. Boskamp's first match was away to Norway in Oslo, followed a week later by a home game with Greece. Alas, both matches were lost - the second in suicidal fashion after Georgia had led with five minutes to go - providing ample proof, if any were needed, that there would be no quick fix for a team that had long since lost the plot.

TOP SCORERS

26	Mikheil ASHVETIA (Dinamo Tbilisi)
21	David MAKHARADZE (Guria Lanchkhuti)
18	Levan KHOMERIKI (Dinamo Tbilisi/ Dinamo Batumi)
16	Zurab IONANIDZE (Torpedo Kutaisi)
15	Gamlet TSIVTSIVADZE (Kolkheti 1913 Poti/ Lokomotivi Tbilisi)
14	Giorgi MEGRELADZE (Torpedo Kutaisi)
	David JANASHIA (Torpedo Kutaisi)
13	Rati ALEKSIDZE (Dinamo Tbilisi)
	Eldar GVASALIA (Kolkheti 1913 Poti)
12	Robert ZIRAKISHVILI (Arsenali Tbilisi)

NATIONAL TEAM RESULTS 98/99

12/08/98	Azerbaijan	A	Ganja	0-1	
19/08/98	Ukraine	A	Kiev	0-4	
05/09/98	Albania (ECQ)	H	Tbilisi	1-0	Arveladze A. (65)
10/10/98	Latvia	A	Riga	0-1	
14/10/98	Greece (ECQ)	A	Athens	0-3	
18/11/98	Estonia	H	Tbilisi	3-1	Ashvetia (65, 85), Janashia D. (72)
20/03/99	Ukraine	H	Tbilisi	0-1	
27/03/99	Slovenia (ECQ)	H	Tbilisi	1-1	Janashia Z. (42)
28/04/99	Norway (ECQ)	H	Tbilisi	1-4	Janashia Z. (58)
30/05/99	Norway (ECQ)	A	Oslo	0-1	
05/06/99	Greece (ECQ)	H	Tbilisi	1-2	Ketsbaia (55)

DOMESTIC CUP 98/99

QUARTER-FINALS

Lokomotivi Tblisi 0, Dinamo Batumi 0
Dinamo Batumi 0, Lokomotivi Tbilisi 0
(0-0; Lokomotivi Tbilisi 3-2 on pens.)

Vit Georgia Tbilisi 2 (Koridze 71, Eradze 81),
Samgurali Tskhaltubo 0
Samgurali Tskhaltubo 2 (Giorgobiani 30, Dzagnidze 33),
Vit Georgia Tbilisi 0
(2-2; Samgurali Tskhaltubo 4-2 on pens.)

Torpedo Kutaisi 8 (Khvadagiani 7, 27, Megreladze 32, 62, Janashia D. 40, Chkhetiani 32, 65, Ionanidze 80p),
Gorda Rustavi 0
Gorda Rustavi 0, Torpedo Kutaisi 1 (Ionanidze 26)
(Torpedo Kutaisi 9-0)

Arsenali Tbilisi 3 (Kolbaia 6, Maisuradze 20, Davitnidze 21og),
Merani 91 Tbilisi 0
Merani 91 Tbilisi 2 (Khutsishvili 63, 73),
Arsenali Tbilisi 1 (Maisuradze 59)
(Arsenali 4-2)

SEMI-FINALS

Lokomotiv Tbilisi 0, Samgurali Tskhaltubo 0
Samgurali Tskhaltubo 1 (Aptsiauri 67), Lokomotivi Tbilisi 0
(Samgurali Tskhaltubo 1-0)

Arsenali Tbilisi 1 (Zirakishvili 47),
Torpedo Kutaisi 2 (Chkhetiani 53, 59)
Torpedo Kutaisi 3
(Megreladze 7, Mazanishvili 26, Vachiberadze 63),
Arsenali Tbilisi 0
(Torpedo Kutaisi 5-1)

FINAL

26/05/99, Tbilisi
TORPEDO KUTAISI 0
SAMGURALI TSKHALTUBO 0
(aet; 4-2 on pens.)
referee - Kvaratskhelia
TORPEDO KUTAISI - Chanturia; Akhvlediani (Imedadze 59), Ionanidze, Khvadagiani, Maglakelidze, Shekriladze, Kvetenadze, Turmanidze, Janashia D., Megreladze, Chkhetiani (Mazanishvili 66).
SAMGURALI TSKHALTUBO - Aslanadze; Makhviladze, Burnadze, Voskanov, Janeldze (Darsadze 101), Kilasonia, Aptsiauri (Jincharadze 79), Jugeli, Petriashvili (Prangishvili 101), Sukhiashvili, Shengelia.

ARSENALI TBILISI

CLUB DIRECTORY

Arsenali Tbilisi
Bochormi street 19
Tbilisi
tel - (32) 942350
Year of Formation - 1940
President - Joni Pirtskhalaishvili
Coach - Otar Korgalidze; Mamuka Gegechkori;
David Chakhava
Stadium - ASC (2,000)

APPEARANCES 98/99

	P	Ap	(s)	Gls
Dimitri ABAZADZE	D	9	(1)	
Levan ABASHIDZE	G	3	(1)	
Vepkhia AMIRIDZE	M	10	(7)	
Gocha CHIKOVANI	D	13		
Temur CHLAIDZE	G	26		
Gela GABISONIA	A	2		
Vakhtang GAGUA	M	5		
Giorgi GAMZARDIA	M		(1)	
Irakli GEMEZASHVILI	D	4	(2)	
Vakhtang GVELESIANI	D	28		3
Akaki KAKASHVILI	A	24	(1)	6
Demur KAKUBAVA	M	4		
Dimitri KAPANADZE	M	7	(1)	
Guram KHOSROSHVILI	M	14	(9)	3
Zviad KIKAVA	M	2	(4)	
Lasha KOLBAIA	D	22	(2)	
Levan KORGALIDZE	M	12	(2)	
Irakli KOKHREIDZE	M	2	(4)	
Levan KUPARADZE	D	2	(11)	
Zviad KUPATADZE	G	1		
Temur KVIRKVELIA	M	3	(3)	
Shalva LATSABIDZE	D	18	(1)	
Giorgi LOMIDZE	M	11	(1)	
Mukhran MAISURADZE	M	25	(4)	1
Zurab METREVELI	M		(1)	
Giorgi PIRTSKHALAVA	D	12		
Giorgi SULADZE	M	1	(8)	
David TARIELASHVILI	A	28		9
Merab TEVZADZE	D	4	(1)	
Avtandil TSERTSVADZE	D	8		
Kakhaber TSOTADZE	D	12		
Giorgi TVALABEISHVILI	M		(5)	
Robert ZIRAKISHVILI	A	18	(2)	12

LEAGUE RESULTS 1998/99

06/08/98	Dinamo Tbilisi	A	1-5	Kakashvili
14/08/98	Vit Georgia Tbilisi	H	0-0	
21/08/98	Merani 91 Tbilisi	A	0-0	
28/08/98	Iberia Samtredia	H	2-5	Kakashvili 2 (1p)
08/09/98	Gorda Rustavi	A	1-0	Kakashvili
14/09/98	Lokomotivi Tbilisi	H	0-0	
19/09/98	Sioni Bolnisi	A	1-0	Maisuradze
27/09/98	Torpedo Kutaisi	H	0-2	
02/10/98	TSU Tbilisi	A	1-4	Zirakishvili
19/10/98	Guria Lanchkhuti	H	5-1	Khosroshvili, Tarielashvili,
				Zirakishvili 2, Gvelesiani
24/10/98	Kolkheti 1913 Poti	A	2-3	Kakashvili, Tarielashvili
03/11/98	Dila Gori	H	2-2	Tarielashvili, Zirakishvili
07/11/98	Odishi Zugdidi	A	2-1	Zirakishvili, Khosroshvili
14/11/98	Samgurali Tskhaltubo	H	1-1	Zirakishvili
22/11/98	Dinamo Batumi	A	1-1	Zirakishvili (p)
02/03/99	Dinamo Tbilisi	H	1-7	Kakashvili
06/03/99	Vit Georgia Tbilisi	A	0-0	
12/03/99	Merani 91 Tbilisi	H	1-1	Khosroshvili
17/03/99	Iberia Samtredia	A	1-3	Gvelesiani
29/03/99	Gorda Rustavi	H	1-0	Tarielashvili
03/04/99	Lokomotivi Tbilisi	A	1-2	Tarielashvili
10/04/99	Sioni Bolnisi	H	2-1	Zirakishvili, Gvelesiani
17/04/99	Torpedo Kutaisi	A	1-1	Zirakishvili
23/04/99	TSU Tbilisi	H	0-0	
01/05/99	Guria Lanchkhuti	A	2-0	Tarielashvili, Zirakishvili
05/05/99	Kolkheti 1913 Poti	H	0-0	
09/05/99	Dila Gori	A	2-1	Zirakishvili 2
15/05/99	Odishi Zugdidi	H	3-0	Tarielashvili 3
19/05/99	Samgurali Tskhaltubo	A	0-2	
23/05/99	Dinamo Batumi	H	0-1	

DILA GORI

CLUB DIRECTORY

Dila Gori
David Guramishvili street 5
Gori
tel - (270) 22107
Year of Formation - 1949
President - Zviad Shermadini
Coach - Ivane Takadze
Stadium - Central (8,230)

APPEARANCES 98/99

		P	Ap	(s)	Gls
Nikoloz AKHALKATSI	M	1	(1)		
Roman AKHALKATSI	A	17	(9)	5	
Vakhtang AKOPIAN	D	13	(2)	1	
Noe ARUTUNIAN	M	3	(3)		
Beka CHITAIA	M	4	(7)	1	
Giorgi CHITAIA	M	9	(1)		
Khvicha GAGNIDZE	D	27		1	
Levan GOCHASHVILI	M	21	(2)	1	
Kakhaber GUDURASHVILI	D	1	(4)		
Tamaz ILURIDZE	G	5			
Aleksandre KAIDARASHVILI	A	12		9	
Lasha KARELIDZE	M	1	(1)		
Revaz KHACHAPURIDZE	D	24			
Khvicha KHIKHALASHVILI	M	1	(5)		
Giorgi LOMIDZE	M	14		1	
David MAISURADZE	M	3	(3)		
Jimsher MAREKHASHVILI	M	29		6	
David MDIVANI	G	13			
Makhare MINDIASHVILI	A	6	(4)	3	
Giorgi MOSULISHVILI	M	7	(2)	1	
Paata PEZUASHVILI	D	28	(1)		
Albert SAKVARELIDZE	M		(2)		
Vladimer SAMKHARADZE	D	18	(1)		
Kristepore SHATAKISHVILI	M	26	(2)	1	
Ramaz SOGOLASHVILI	G	12			
Saba SULTANISHVILI	A	5	(7)	3	
Mikheil TAKADZE	M	12	(1)	2	
Tamaz TSITKISHVILI	M	18	(4)	2	

LEAGUE RESULTS 1998/99

08/08/98	Gorda Rustavi	A	1-1	Takadze	
15/08/98	Sioni Bolnisi	H	2-0	Kaidarashvili 2	
23/08/98	TSU Tbilisi	A	1-0	Tsitkishvili	
29/08/98	Kolkheti 1913 Poti	H	2-1	Kaidarashvili, Marekhashvili	
08/09/98	Odishi Zugdidi	A	1-2	Mosulishvili	
12/09/98	Dinamo Batumi	H	0-1		
19/09/98	Vit Georgia Tbilisi	A	2-1	Kaidarashvili 2	
26/09/98	Iberia Samtredia	H	2-1	Marekhashvili, Kaidarashvili	
04/10/98	Lokomotivi Tbilisi	A	0-0		
17/10/98	Torpedo Kutaisi	H	3-0	Marekhashvili 2, Takadze	
28/10/98	Guria Lanchkhuti	A	2-4	Kaidarashvili 2	
03/11/98	Arsenali Tbilisi	A	2-2	Chitaia B., Akhalkatsi R.	
07/11/98	Samgurali Tskhaltubo	H	0-1		
15/11/98	Dinamo Tbilisi	A	0-4		
22/11/98	Merani 91 Tbilisi	H	3-3	Kaidarashvili (p), Gochashvili, Tsitkishvili	
28/02/99	Gorda Rustavi	H	3-0	Akopian, Mindiashvili, Sultanishvili	
05/03/99	Sioni Bolnisi	A	0-1		
12/03/99	TSU Tbilisi	H	0-0		
17/03/99	Kolkheti 1913 Poti	A	3-2	Akhalkatsi R. 2, Mindiashvili (p)	
30/03/99	Odishi Zugdidi	H	1-0	Marekhashvili	
03/04/99	Dinamo Batumi	A	0-6		
10/04/99	Vit Georgia Tbilisi	H	1-3	Mindiashvili	
17/04/99	Iberia Samtredia	A	0-2		
23/04/99	Lokomotivi Tbilisi	H	0-2		
01/05/99	Torpedo Kutaisi	A	0-3		
05/05/99	Guria Lanchkhuti	H	5-3	Gagnidze, Lomidze, Akhalkatsi R., Sultanishvili, Shatakishvili	
09/05/99	Arsenali Tbilisi	H	1-2	Marekhashvili	
15/05/99	Samgurali Tskhaltubo	A	1-3	Akhalkatsi R.	
19/05/99	Dinamo Tbilisi	H	1-2	Sultanishvili	
23/05/99	Merani 91 Tbilisi	A	0-4		

DINAMO BATUMI

CLUB DIRECTORY

Dinamo Batumi
H. Barbusse street 32
Batumi
tel - (222) 72369
fax - (222) 72377
Year of Formation - 1923
President - Temur Bejanidze
Coach - Shota Cheishvili
Stadium - Central (18,000)

MAJOR HONOURS
Domestic Cup - (1) 1998.

APPEARANCES 98/99

		P	Ap	(s)	Gls
Shalva APKHAZAVA	A	8	(11)	3
David CHICHVEISHVILI	D	22		1
Temur GADELIA	M	23	(1)	5
Avtandil GLONTI	M	14	(3)	1
Pomeo GOGITADZE	D	2		
Gocha GUJABIDZE	D	15		
Aleksandre KANTIDZE	M	15	(5)	3
Levan KHOMERIKI	A	9		10
Gocha KULEJISHVILI	A	4	(1)	1
Ilo KUTIDZE	D	2	(2)	
Paata MACHUTADZE	A	20		11
David MAKATSARIA	M	8	(2)	1
Ivane MAKHARADZE	D	10		
Malkhaz MAKHARADZE	D	28		
Mirian MALAKMADZE	G	8		
Zurab MINDADZE	D	11		
Kakhaber MJAVANADZE	M	1	(4)	
Zviad PAPIDZE	D	25		
Badri PUTKARADZE	M		(4)	
Archil ROMANADZE	M	3	(6)	1
Mamuka RUSIA	A	20	(3)	3
Tengiz SICHINAVA	M	30		2
Nikoloz TOGONIDZE	G	22		1
Rostom TORGASHVILI	M	12	(3)	
Temur TUGUSHI	M	11		6
Uche UVAKVE (NIG)	A		(2)	
Dmitri VEREMCHUK	D	7	(4)	

LEAGUE RESULTS 1998/99

07/08/98	Vit Georgia Tbilisi	H	0-1	
16/08/98	Iberia Samtredia	A	1-3	Machutadze
22/08/98	Lokomotivi Tbilisi	H	1-1	Machutadze
30/08/98	Torpedo Kutaisi	A	3-3	Sichinava, Tugushi 2 (1p)
08/09/98	Guria Lanchkhuti	H	4-0	Sichinava, Gadelia 2, Rusia
12/09/98	Dila Gori	A	1-0	Kantidze
21/09/98	Samgurali Tskhaltubo	H	6-1	Tugushi 3 (1p), Machutadze 2,
				Kantidze
25/09/98	Dinamo Tbilisi	A	1-1	Tugushi (p)
03/10/98	Merani 91 Tbilisi	H	0-0	
17/10/98	Gorda Rustavi	A	0-0	
25/10/98	Sioni Bolnisi	H	1-0	Machutadze
01/11/98	TSU Tbilisi	A	1-0	Machutadze
07/11/98	Kolkheti 1913 Poti	H	2-1	Gadelia, Machutadze
16/11/98	Odishi Zugdidi	A	1-2	Apkhazava
22/11/98	Arsenali Tbilisi	H	1-1	Makatsaria
01/03/99	Vit Georgia Tbilisi	A	0-0	
05/03/99	Iberia Samtredia	H	1-0	Rusia
13/03/99	Lokomotivi Tbilisi	A	0-1	
17/03/99	Torpedo Kutaisi	H	2-1	Gadelia, Khomeriki
30/03/99	Guria Lanchkhuti	A	1-0	Khomeriki
03/04/99	Dila Gori	H	6-0	Khomeriki 4, Kantidze, Glonti
10/04/99	Samgurali Tskhaltubo	A	0-0	
17/04/99	Dinamo Tbilisi	H	0-0	
24/04/99	Merani 91 Tbilisi	A	0-1	
01/05/99	Gorda Rustavi	H	1-1	Rusia
05/05/99	Sioni Bolnisi	A	1-1	Machutadze
15/05/99	Kolkheti 1913 Poti	A	0-1	
18/05/99	Odishi Zugdidi	H	9-0	Khomeriki 4, Machutadze,
				Chichveishvili, Gadelia,
				Apkhazava, Romanadze
21/05/99	TSU Tbilisi	H	4-2	Machutadze 2, Togonidze (p),
				Apkhazava
23/05/99	Arsenali Tbilisi	A	1-0	Kulejishvili

DINAMO TBILISI

CLUB DIRECTORY

Dinamo Tbilisi
Digomi Township, 3rd Block, Tbilisi
tel - (32) 984017/237023 fax - (32) 237027
Year of Formation - 1925
President - Roman Shotadze
Coach - Murtaz Khurtsilava; Johan Boskamp
Stadium - Boris Paichadze (75,000)

MAJOR HONOURS
League Championship (USSR) - (2) 1964, 1978.
League Championship - (10) 1990, 1991, 1992,
1993, 1994, 1995, 1996, 1997, 1998, 1999.
Domestic Cup (USSR) - (2) 1976, 1979.
Domestic Cup - (6)
1992, 1993, 1994, 1995, 1996, 1997.
European Cup-winners' Cup - (1) 1981.

APPEARANCES 98/99

	P	Ap	(s)	Gls
Rati ALEKSIDZE	M	22	(1)	13
Zurab ARCHVADZE	D	8	(1)	
Mikheil ASHVETIA	A	28		26
Zurab BATIASHVILI	G	2		
Shota CHOMAKHIDZE	M	6	(7)	2
Givi DIDAVA	D	22		
Kakhi GOGICHAISHVILI	M	2	(4)	1
Valter GUCHUA	D	21	(1)	1
David GVARAMADZE	G	25		
Zviad JELADZE	D	15		
Paata JINCHARADZE	D	6	(3)	1
Levan KEBADZE	M	8	(5)	1
Revaz KEMOKLIDZE	D		(2)	
Otar KHIZANEISHVILI	D	6	(1)	
Zurab KHIZANISHVILI	D	2		1
Levan KHOMERIKI	A	5		8
Giorgi KIKNADZE	M	16	(3)	5
Levan KOBIASHVILI	M	1	(1)	
Givi KVARATSKHELIA	M	3	(8)	
Mamuka MACHAVARIANI	D	13	(1)	
Ivane MAKHARADZE	D	8	(1)	
Levan MELKADZE	M	1	(6)	2
Giorgi MIKADZE	A		(2)	
Levan MIKADZE	D	25		2
Amiran MUJIRI	M	7	(2)	1
David MUJIRI	M	14		4
Tornike RUKHADZE	D		(4)	
Edik SAJAIA	D		(1)	
Archil SAKHVADZE	D	17	(9)	2
Besik SHENGELIA	M		(1)	
Giorgi SHENGELIA	A	5	(7)	6
Ramaz SOGOLASHVILI	G	3		
Klimenti TSITAISHVILI	A	9	(2)	3
Levan TSKITISHVILI	M	12		8
Temur TUGUSHI	M	5	(4)	3
Irakli VASHKADZE	D	13	(1)	

LEAGUE RESULTS 1998/99

06/08/98	Arsenali Tbilisi	H	5-1	Ashvetia, Khomeriki 2, Kiknadze, Melkadze
15/08/98	Merani 91 Tbilisi	H	5-1	Ashvetia 2, Tskitishvili (p), Khomeriki 2
30/08/98	Sioni Bolnisi	H	8-1	Khomeriki 2, Aleksidze 2, Tskitishvili, Shengelia G. 2, Melkadze
08/09/98	TSU Tbilisi	A	3-1	Khomeriki, Tskitishvili (p), Ashvetia
20/09/98	Odishi Zugdidi	A	4-0	Ashvetia 2, Tskitishvili, Shengelia G.
25/09/98	Dinamo Batumi	H	1-1	Khomeriki
03/10/98	Vit Georgia Tbilisi	A	2-0	Tskitishvili, Shengelia G.
19/10/98	Iberia Samtredia	H	7-2	Kiknadze, Mujiri D., Ashvetia 2, Shengelia G. 2, og (Lursmanashvili)
24/10/98	Lokomotivi Tbilisi	A	0-0	
28/10/98	Gorda Rustavi	A	0-0	
31/10/98	Torpedo Kutaisi	H	1-0	Ashvetia
07/11/98	Guria Lanchkhuti	A	1-0	Ashvetia
15/11/98	Dila Gori	H	4-0	Mujiri D. 2, Aleksidze, Ashvetia
22/11/98	Samgurali Tskhaltubo	A	3-0	Ashvetia 2, Mujiri D.
30/11/98	Kolkheti 1913 Poti	H	6-1	Aleksidze 3, Tskitishvili 3
02/03/99	Arsenali Tbilisi	A	7-1	Tsitaishvili, Mikadze L., Ashvetia 2, Aleksidze 2, Guchua
05/03/99	Merani 91 Tbilisi	A	2-0	Chomakhidze, Tsitaishvili
13/03/99	Gorda Rustavi	H	2-0	Mikadze L., Ashvetia
17/03/99	Sioni Bolnisi	A	3-1	Ashvetia 2 (1p), Tugushi
31/03/99	TSU Tbilisi	H	0-0	
04/04/99	Kolkheti 1913 Poti	A	1-0	Ashvetia
10/04/99	Odishi Zugdidi	H	5-0	Ashvetia, Aleksidze, Tugushi, Kiknadze, Sakhvadze
17/04/99	Dinamo Batumi	A	0-0	
23/04/99	Vit Georgia Tbilisi	H	3-2	Aleksidze 2, Tsitaishvili
01/05/99	Iberia Samtredia	A	1-0	Sakhvadze
05/05/99	Lokomotivi Tbilisi	H	1-0	Tugushi
09/05/99	Torpedo Kutaisi	A	1-3	Ashvetia
15/05/99	Guria Lanchkhuti	H	7-1	Ashvetia 3, Jincharadze, Kiknadze, Aleksidze, Chomakhidze
19/05/99	Dila Gori	A	2-1	Kebadze, Gogichaishvili
23/05/99	Samgurali Tskhaltubo	H	6-0	Kiknadze, Ashvetia 2, Mujiri A., Aleksidze, Khizanishvili

GORDA RUSTAVI

CLUB DIRECTORY

Gorda Rustavi
Gagarini street 12
Rustavi
tel - (235) 192010
Year of Formation - 1948
President - Valeri Kokiashvili
Coach - Iason Aladashvili
Stadium - Poladi (10,700)

APPEARANCES 98/99

	P	Ap	(s)	Gls
Kakhaber ALADASHVILI	M	14		1
Lasha ALADASHVILI	A	19	(6)	5
Giga BABUNASHVILI	M		(1)	
Grigol BEDIASHVILI	G	12		
Pavle BEKAURI	D	19	(3)	
David BERIDZE	M		(2)	
Aleksandre BURNADZE	D	15		
Koba CHIGOSHVILI	M	9	(1)	
David CHOKHELI	D	2	(4)	
Jumber CHUKHUA	A	10	(2)	3
Mikheil GABELAIA	M	19		
David INASARIDZE	M	12	(2)	2
Mikheil KALMAKHELIDZE	M	1	(1)	
Shermadin KAPANADZE	A	2		
Amiran KEDELASHVILI	D	18		
Irakli KHUJADZE	D	6	(1)	
Varlam KILASONIA	A	12		2
Aleksandre KITEISHVILI	M	11	(3)	
Zurab KOIAVA	A	1	(2)	
Mamuka KORIDZE	G	17		
Zurab LABADZE	M	9	(9)	
Ruben MAKHARADZE	A	2		
Mamuka MELADZE	M	12		4
David MENTESHASHVILI	A	1	(5)	1
Paata MESHKI	M	1	(1)	
Khvicha MCHEDLIDZE	D	17	(3)	
Giorgi MISHVELIDZE	A	8	(1)	2
David NEBULISHVILI	G		(1)	
Zurab OKROPIDZE	G	1		
Zaza PATARIDZE	D	6		2
Mikheil SAKHVADZE	D	17	(6)	2
Kakha SIDAMONIDZE	D	14		1
Lasha SILAGADZE	M		(2)	1
Giorgi SIMONISHVILI	M		(3)	
Normen TARTARASHVILI	D	14	(4)	
Valeri ZIRAKADZE	A	29		2

LEAGUE RESULTS 1998/99

08/08/98	Dila Gori	H	1-1	Menteshashvili
15/08/98	Samgurali Tskhaltubo	A	0-1	
25/08/98	Merani 91 Tbilisi	A	1-1	Chukhua
08/09/98	Arsenali Tbilisi	H	0-1	
12/09/98	Sioni Bolnisi	H	3-1	Kilasonia, Chukhua 2
21/09/98	TSU Tbilisi	A	0-0	
26/09/98	Kolkheti 1913 Poti	H	0-0	
03/10/98	Odishi Zugdidi	A	0-1	
17/10/98	Dinamo Batumi	H	0-0	
25/10/98	Vit Georgia Tbilisi	A	1-2	Aladashvili L.
28/10/98	Dinamo Tbilisi	H	0-0	
31/10/98	Iberia Samtredia	H	1-0	Kilasonia
07/11/98	Lokomotivi Tbilisi	A	0-0	
15/11/98	Torpedo Kutaisi	H	1-7	Sakhvadze
22/11/98	Guria Lanchkhuti	A	4-3	Aladashvili L., Sakhvadze,
				Aladashvili K., Silagadze
28/02/99	Dila Gori	A	0-3	
05/03/99	Samgurali Tskhaltubo	H	2-0	Meladze, Mishvelidze
13/03/99	Dinamo Tbilisi	A	0-2	
17/03/99	Merani 91 Tbilisi	H	0-3	
29/03/99	Arsenali Tbilisi	A	0-1	
03/04/99	Sioni Bolnisi	A	0-0	
10/04/99	TSU Tbilisi	H	0-0	
18/04/99	Kolkheti 1913 Poti	A	0-5	
23/04/99	Odishi Zugdidi	H	6-2	Mishvelidze, Pataridze, Meladze,
				Sidamonidze (p), Zirakadze,
				Inasaridze
01/05/99	Dinamo Batumi	A	1-1	Aladashvili L.
05/05/99	Vit Georgia Tbilisi	H	3-2	Meladze 2, Zirakadze
09/05/99	Iberia Samtredia	A	2-1	Aladashvili L., Pataridze
15/05/99	Lokomotivi Tbilisi	H	0-2	
19/05/99	Torpedo Kutaisi	A	0-4	
23/05/99	Guria Lanchkhuti	H	2-2	Inasaridze, Aladashvili L.

GURIA LANCHKHUTI

CLUB DIRECTORY

Guria Lanchkhuti
Queen Tamar street 6, Lanchkhuti
tel - (32) 4455
Year of Formation - 1952
President - Amiran Tsilosani
Coach - Joni Janelidze; Avtandil Nariashvili
Stadium - Evgrapi Shevardnadze (22,000)

MAJOR HONOURS
Domestic Cup - (1) 1990.

APPEARANCES 98/99

	P	Ap	(s)	Gls
Giorgi BARDZENISHVILI	A	1	(1)	
David BOLKVADZE	A	10	(1)	
Ivane BUKHRIKIDZE	D	7		
Mamuka BULUKHIA	A	8	(2)	
Giorgi CHIABRISHVILI	M	8	(3)	
David CHIGOSHVILI	M	3	(2)	
Vasil CHIKVILADZE	D		(7)	
Lasha CHKHAIDZE	M	11	(4)	1
Ramaz CHKHAIDZE	G		(2)	
Temur CHKHAIDZE	D	10	(3)	1
Merab DZODZUASHVILI	A	7	(5)	
Tengiz ENUKIDZE	A	14		1
Aleksandre GANEV	M	7		2
Gia GIORGADZE	M	10		1
Gia GOGUA	G	15		
Imeda GONGADZE	M		(1)	
Elguja GULORDAVA	M	12	(2)	
Gocha IMNAISHVILI	M		(1)	
Zaza INIASHVILI	M	10		1
Rati IOBIDZE	M	3	(1)	
Baadur KAKACHIA	D	10		
Anzor KAVTELADZE	M	4	(3)	
Merab KUKULADZE	D	11		
Zaza KVEKVESKIRI	D	23	(2)	1
Temur LORIA	M	6	(5)	
Gela MACHITIDZE	D	6	(2)	
David MAKHARADZE	A	27		21
Shota MAKHARADZE	D	12		
Mamuka MELADZE	M	13		4
Giorgi NIKURADZE	G	10		
Tengiz PATARAIA	A	1	(5)	
Irakli PATSURIA	D	13	(1)	
Kakha PIRTSKHALAISHVILI	D	9	(2)	
Archil SHAVSHISHVILI	M	12	(2)	
David SULAKVELIDZE	D	1	(2)	
Kakhaber SVANIDZE	D	12	(2)	1
Otar TIBILIASHVILI	D	9	(2)	
Otar VARDANIDZE	G	4	(1)	

LEAGUE RESULTS 1998/99

08/08/98	Sioni Bolnisi	A	2-2	Meladze 2
15/08/98	TSU Tbilisi	H	2-0	Makharadze D. 2
22/08/98	Kolkheti 1913 Poti	A	0-3	
29/08/98	Odishi Zugdidi	H	1-2	Iniashvili
08/09/98	Dinamo Batumi	A	0-4	
13/09/98	Vit Georgia Tbilisi	H	2-0	Giorgadze, Meladze
19/09/98	Iberia Samtredia	A	1-4	Makharadze D. (p)
26/09/98	Lokomotivi Tbilisi	H	0-4	
03/10/98	Torpedo Kutaisi	A	0-3	
19/10/98	Arsenali Tbilisi	A	1-5	Makharadze D.
28/10/98	Dila Gori	H	4-2	Makharadze D. 2, Ganev 2
31/10/98	Samgurali Tskhaltubo	A	1-2	Meladze
07/11/98	Dinamo Tbilisi	H	0-1	
16/11/98	Merani 91 Tbilisi	A	0-3	(w/o)
22/11/98	Gorda Rustavi	H	3-4	Makharadze D. 3
28/02/99	Sioni Bolnisi	H	1-1	Kvekveskiri
04/03/99	TSU Tbilisi	A	0-0	
13/03/99	Kolkheti 1913 Poti	H	1-4	Makharadze D.
17/03/99	Odishi Zugdidi	A	2-4	Makharadze D. 2 (1p)
30/03/99	Dinamo Batumi	H	0-1	
03/04/99	Vit Georgia Tbilisi	A	0-3	
10/04/99	Iberia Samtredia	H	1-3	Makharadze D. (p)
17/04/99	Lokomotivi Tbilisi	A	0-1	
23/04/99	Torpedo Kutaisi	H	1-5	Makharadze D.
01/05/99	Arsenali Tbilisi	H	0-2	
05/05/99	Dila Gori	A	3-5	Chkhaidze L., Makharadze D., Chkhaidze T.
09/05/99	Samgurali Tskhaltubo	H	2-3	Makharadze D. 2 (1p)
15/05/99	Dinamo Tbilisi	A	1-7	Makharadze D.
19/05/99	Merani 91 Tbilisi	H	3-7	Makharadze D. 2 (2p), Enukidze
23/05/99	Gorda Rustavi	A	2-2	Makharadze D., Svanidze

IBERIA SAMTREDIA

CLUB DIRECTORY

Iberia Samtredia
Ketskhoveli street 87
Samtredia
tel - (211) 24988
Year of Formation - 1936
President - Nugzar Nikoleishvili
Coach - Gabriel Koridze; Anatoli Mesiarenko;
Soso Pruidze
Stadium - Erosi Manjgaladze (15,000)

APPEARANCES 98/99

	P	Ap	(s)	Gls
Besik AMASHUKELI	M	8	(1)	1
Koba BAKURADZE	A		(3)	
Cocha BREGVADZE	A	11		
Zaza CHACHUA	G	3	(2)	
Gia CHELIDZE	M	2	(5)	1
Aleksandre CHOMAKHIDZE	G		(1)	
Shota CHOMAKHIDZE	M	14		6
Giorgi DARASELIA	M	8		2
Gubaz DOLIDZE	G	19		
Mamuka GABRICHIDZE	D	2		
Valeri GEGESHIDZE	D	28	(1)	
Soso GIGIADZE	M	30		4
Vasil GIGIADZE	A	22	(1)	9
Nikoloz GIORGADZE	A		(5)	
Bidzina IVECHIANI	A	19	(10)	8
David KHUCHUA	A	24	(2)	7
Zaza KOBESASHVILI	D	7	(2)	
Givi KVELADZE	D	12		
Avtandil LABADZE	G	4	(1)	
David LORTKIPANIDZE	M	1	(1)	
Gela LURSMANASHVILI	D	19	(4)	2
Mamuka MESIACHENKO	M	3		
Zaza MIKELTADZE	D	17	(4)	
Shalva MUMLADZE	M	15	(5)	
Giga NIKOLEISHVILI	D	20	(4)	
Levan PILIPASHVILI	A	4	(5)	
Otar PKHADZE	M		(2)	
Zviad PKHAKADZE	M	1	(2)	
Koba SADILIANI	D	5	(1)	1
Sevasti TODUA	M	17		
Robert TSOMAIA	M	1	(3)	
Otar VARDANIDZE	G	4		
David VARDIASHVILI	A	10	(10)	2

LEAGUE RESULTS 1998/99

08/08/98	Odishi Zugdidi	A	1-0	Amashukeli (p)
16/08/98	Dinamo Batumi	H	3-1	Khuchua (p), Gigiadze V., Daraselia
24/08/98	Vit Georgia Tbilisi	A	1-4	Gigiadze V.
28/08/98	Arsenali Tbilisi	A	5-2	Sadiliani, Ivechiani, Chomakhidze 2, Khuchua
08/09/98	Lokomotivi Tbilisi	H	2-3	Gigiadze V., Chomakhidze
13/09/98	Torpedo Kutaisi	A	0-4	
19/09/98	Guria Lanchkhuti	H	4-1	Khuchua, Gigiadze V., Chomakhidze, Ivechiani
26/09/98	Dila Gori	A	1-2	Daraselia
03/10/98	Samgurali Tskhaltubo	H	3-1	Chomakhidze, Ivechiani, Gigiadze V.
19/10/98	Dinamo Tbilisi	A	2-7	Ivechiani, Chelidze (p)
24/10/98	Merani 91 Tbilisi	H	0-0	
31/10/98	Gorda Rustavi	A	0-1	
07/11/98	Sioni Bolnisi	H	1-2	Chomakhidze
15/11/98	TSU Tbilisi	A	1-1	Vardiashvili
22/11/98	Kolkheti 1913 Poti	H	2-2	Gigiadze V., Vardiashvili
28/02/99	Odishi Zugdidi	H	0-0	
05/03/99	Dinamo Batumi	A	0-1	
13/03/99	Vit Georgia Tbilisi	H	0-1	
17/03/99	Arsenali Tbilisi	H	3-1	Ivechiani, Lursmanashvili, Khuchua (p)
30/03/99	Lokomotivi Tbilisi	A	0-2	
03/04/99	Torpedo Kutaisi	H	0-0	
10/04/99	Guria Lanchkhuti	A	3-1	Ivechiani, Khuchua 2 (1p)
17/04/99	Dila Gori	H	2-0	Gigiadze S. (p), Ivechiani
23/04/99	Samgurali Tskhaltubo	A	3-2	Gigiadze S. 2 (1p), Khuchua
01/05/99	Dinamo Tbilisi	H	0-1	
05/05/99	Merani 91 Tbilisi	A	2-0	Ivechiani, Gigiadze V.
09/05/99	Gorda Rustavi	H	1-2	Lursmanashvili
15/05/99	Sioni Bolnisi	A	0-1	
18/05/99	TSU Tbilisi	H	4-2	Gigiadze V., Gigiadze S., og 2 (Japaridze 2)
23/05/99	Kolkheti 1913 Poti	A	1-3	Gigiadze V.

KOLKHETI 1913 POTI

CLUB DIRECTORY

Kolkheti 1913 Poti
Shevchenko street 17
Poti
tel - (293) 25814
fax - (293) 22688
Year of Formation - 1913
President - Jemal Inaishvili
Coach - Soso Pilia; Gia Tkebuchava
Stadium - Fazisi (6,000)

APPEARANCES 98/99

	P	Ap	(s)	Gls
Badri AKHVLEDIANI	D	13		
Besik AMASHUKELI	M	6	(4)	
Levan ANJAPARIDZE	M	11		
Spartak BACHILAVA	A		(3)	
Mamuka BULUKHIA	A	4	(5)	1
Zaza BUKVADZE	M		(3)	
Giorgi CHADUNELI	M	7	(3)	
Paata CHAGANAVA	M		(1)	
Bizina CHEMIA	G		(2)	
Kakhaber EBRALIDZE	D		(1)	
Gela GABISONIA	A	7		4
Zaveli GAGANIDZE	M	24	(3)	6
Gia GIORGADZE	M	15		1
Irakli GIORGOBIANI	M	7	(5)	
Kakhaber GOROZIA	D	16	(5)	
Eldar GVASALIA	A	28	(1)	13
Mamuka GVASALIA	G	15		
Jumber KALANDADZE	M	30		3
Mikheil KOBULADZE	D	28		5
Giorgi KRASOVSKI	A		(6)	1
Gogita KUNTELIA	D	5		
Ilo KUTIDZE	D	4	(2)	
Zurab KVACHAKHIA	G	15		
David NOZADZE	M	6	(1)	1
Elguja PAPAVA	D	5	(1)	
Joni SHALAMBERIDZE	D	14	(2)	1
Levan SHAVGULIDZE	A	7	(14)	5
Giorgi SUKHIASHVILI	M	9	(2)	3
Valeri TORCHINAVA	D	28		
Gocha TRAPAIDZE	A	12		1
Gamlet TSIVTSIVADZE	A	14		11

LEAGUE RESULTS 1998/99

06/08/98	Lokomotivi Tbilisi	H	0-0	
15/08/98	Torpedo Kutaisi	A	1-5	Tsivtsivadze
22/08/98	Guria Lanchkhuti	H	3-0	Nozadze, Gvasalia E., Tsivtsivadze
29/08/98	Dila Gori	A	1-2	Kalandadze
08/09/98	Samgurali Tskhaltubo	H	4-2	Sukhiashvili 3 (2p), Tsivtsivadze
19/09/98	Merani 91 Tbilisi	H	3-0	Gvasalia E., Tsivtsivadze 2
26/09/98	Gorda Rustavi	A	0-0	
03/10/98	Sioni Bolnisi	H	4-0	Tsivtsivadze 2, Gvasalia E. 2
17/10/98	TSU Tbilisi	A	4-2	Kobuladze, Tsivtsivadze 2, Gabisonia
24/10/98	Arsenali Tbilisi	H	3-2	Tsivtsivadze, Gabisonia, Kalandadze
31/10/98	Odishi Zugdidi	H	5-1	Gabisonia, Kobuladze, Gaganidze, Gvasalia E., Krasovski
07/11/98	Dinamo Batumi	A	1-2	Gvasalia E.
15/11/98	Vit Georgia Tbilisi	H	2-1	Tsivtsivadze, Shalamberidze
22/11/98	Iberia Samtredia	A	2-2	Gvasalia E. 2
30/11/98	Dinamo Tbilisi	A	1-6	Gabisonia
28/02/99	Lokomotivi Tbilisi	A	1-1	Kobuladze
05/03/99	Torpedo Kutaisi	H	1-2	Shavgulidze
13/03/99	Guria Lanchkhuti	A	4-1	Gvasalia E. 3, og (Machitidze)
17/03/99	Dila Gori	H	2-3	Gaganidze, Shavgulidze
30/03/99	Samgurali Tskhaltubo	A	1-0	Gaganidze
04/04/99	Dinamo Tbilisi	H	0-1	
10/04/99	Merani 91 Tbilisi	A	0-1	
18/04/99	Gorda Rustavi	H	5-0	Gaganidze, Gvasalia E., Shavgulidze 2, Kalandadze
23/04/99	Sioni Bolnisi	A	1-1	Shavgulidze
30/04/99	TSU Tbilisi	H	2-0	Kobuladze, Bulukhia
05/05/99	Arsenali Tbilisi	A	0-0	
09/05/99	Odishi Zugdidi	A	2-0	Gvasalia E., Giorgadze
15/05/99	Dinamo Batumi	H	1-0	Kobuladze
19/05/99	Vit Georgia Tbilisi	A	0-0	
23/05/99	Iberia Samtredia	H	3-1	Gaganidze 2, Trapaidze

LOKOMOTIVI TBILISI

Lokomotivi Tbilisi
Digomi Township
3rd Block
Tbilisi
tel - (32) 993668
Year of Formation - 1936
President - Akaki Chkhaidze
Coach - Temur Makhoradze
Stadium - Lokomotivi (16,000)

	P	Ap	(s)	Gls
Zurab ARCHVADZE	D	6		
Dimitri ARSOSHVILI	D	10		
David BAKRADZE	D	14	(11)	1
Nodar BAKRADZE	M		(1)	
Giorgi BALASHVILI	D	28		1
Paata BARNOV	D	25		
Giorgi CHIKHRADZE	D	9		
Kakhaber DAUSHVILI	A	11	(4)	
Levan DOLABERIDZE	G	9		
Merab DZODZUASHVILI	A		(1)	1
Isidore GILAURI	M		(4)	
David GODERDZISHVILI	A	21	(5)	9
Aleksandre GOGOBERISHVILI	M	13		7
Kakha GOGOLADZE	A	7	(1)	2
Giorgi GUDUSHAURI	M	12	(1)	4
David JANELIDZE	G	21		
Genadi KATSIASHVILI	M	23	(6)	
Zurab KHORGUASHVILI	A	10	(3)	1
Shalva KHUJADZE	D	10	(3)	1
Varlam KILASONIA	M	4	(2)	3
Zurab KOIAVA	M	1	(4)	1
Giorgi KORIDZE	A	2	(5)	
Valeri KOTORASHVILI	M	7	(8)	2
Mamuka KVARTSKHAVA	D	1	(3)	
Gela KVITATIANI	D	4	(1)	
Roin MARGISHVILI	M	12	(1)	2
Nodar MELADZE	M		(1)	
Konstantine MELKADZE	M	22	(7)	1
Makhare MINDIASHVILI	A		(3)	
Nikoloz MINDIASHVILI	M	12	(7)	1
David MUJIRI	M	11		
Vaja TARKHNISHVILI	D	14		
Gamlet TSIVTSIVADZE	A	11	(1)	4

06/08/98	Kolkheti 1913 Poti	A	0-0	
16/08/98	Odishi Zugdidi	H	3-0	Khorguashvili, Margishvili (p), Mindiashvili N.
22/08/98	Dinamo Batumi	A	1-1	Goderdzishvili
31/08/98	Vit Georgia Tbilisi	H	1-0	Margishvili (p)
08/09/98	Iberia Samtredia	A	3-2	Goderdzishvili 2, Balashvili
14/09/98	Arsenali Tbilisi	A	0-0	
20/09/98	Torpedo Kutaisi	H	1-1	Gudushauri
26/09/98	Guria Lanchkhuti	A	4-0	Bakradze D., Gudushauri 2, Dzodzuashvili
04/10/98	Dila Gori	H	0-0	
17/10/98	Samgurali Tskhaltubo	A	2-1	Goderdzishvili, Melkadze
24/10/98	Dinamo Tbilisi	H	0-0	
02/11/98	Merani 91 Tbilisi	A	0-0	
07/11/98	Gorda Rustavi	H	0-0	
15/11/98	Sioni Bolnisi	A	0-0	
22/11/98	TSU Tbilisi	H	3-1	Kotorashvili, Gogoladze, Goderdzishvili
28/02/99	Kolkheti 1913 Poti	H	1-1	Goderdzishvili (p)
05/03/99	Odishi Zugdidi	A	1-0	Goderdzishvili (p)
13/03/99	Dinamo Batumi	H	1-0	Gogoberishvili (p)
17/03/99	Vit Georgia Tbilisi	A	2-1	Khujadze, Kotorashvili
30/03/99	Iberia Samtredia	H	2-0	Kilasonia, Tsivtsivadze
03/04/99	Arsenali Tbilisi	H	2-1	Kilasonia 2
10/04/99	Torpedo Kutaisi	A	1-3	Gogoladze
17/04/99	Guria Lanchkhuti	H	1-0	Gogoberishvili (p)
23/04/99	Dila Gori	A	2-0	Goderdzishvili 2
01/05/99	Samgurali Tskhaltubo	H	2-0	Gogoberishvili, Tsivtsivadze
05/05/99	Dinamo Tbilisi	A	0-1	
09/05/99	Merani 91 Tbilisi	H	1-0	Gudushauri
15/05/99	Gorda Rustavi	A	2-0	Gogoberishvili 2
19/05/99	Sioni Bolnisi	H	3-0	Gogoberishvili (p), og (Japaridze E.), og (Svanidze)
23/05/99	TSU Tbilisi	A	4-1	Gogoberishvili (p), Tsivtsivadze 2, Koiava

MERANI 91 TBILISI

CLUB DIRECTORY

Merani 91 Tbilisi
Abastumani street 8
Tbilisi
tel - (32) 341703/341255
Year of Formation - 1991
President - Nugzar Navadze
Coach - Sergo Gabelaia
Stadium - Sinatle (2,000)

APPEARANCES 98/99

		P	Ap	(s)	Gls
Edisher ALADASHVILI	D	15	(1)		
Bakhva AMBIDZE	M	12		8	
Guram ASPINDZELASHVILI	D	26			
Levan BAJELIDZE	M	8	(12)		
Shalva BERAIA	M	1	(4)		
David CHELIDZE	D	2	(3)		
Malkhaz CHINCHARAULI	M	15	(2)		
Jumber CHUKHUA	A	9		3	
Shermadin DANELIA	D	15	(1)		
Suliko DAVITASHVILI	A	24	(1)	6	
Giorgi DAVITNIDZE	D	16	(1)	2	
Ioseb DEVIDZE	M	6	(10)	2	
Mirian GETSADZE	D	9			
Shalva IVANISHVILI	D	7			
David JISHKARIANI	D	17	(9)	1	
David KARIAULI	D	5	(2)		
Guram KHAREBAVA	M	5	(5)		
Mikheil KHUTSISHVILI	A	26		3	
Gela KORIDZE	M	25		5	
Andro KOROSHINADZE	G	1			
Giorgi KVETENADZE	M	12	(1)		
Giorgi LOMAIA	G	22			
Levan MELIKIA	M		(1)		
Mikheil MESKHI	M	9	(4)		
Revaz NACHKEPIA	G	6			
Levan TOLORDAVA	A	10	(2)	4	
Zaza TSKIPURISHVILI	D	16	(3)		

LEAGUE RESULTS 1998/99

07/08/98	Samgurali Tskhaltubo	H	0-0	
15/08/98	Dinamo Tbilisi	A	1-5	Davitnidze
21/08/98	Arsenali Tbilisi	H	0-0	
29/08/98	Gorda Rustavi	H	1-1	Koridze (p)
08/09/98	Sioni Bolnisi	A	4-1	Davitashvili 2, Koridze, Khutsishvili
13/09/98	TSU Tbilisi	H	1-0	Davitashvili
19/09/98	Kolkheti 1913 Poti	A	0-3	
26/09/98	Odishi Zugdidi	H	0-1	
03/10/98	Dinamo Batumi	A	0-0	
19/10/98	Vit Georgia Tbilisi	H	0-0	
24/10/98	Iberia Samtredia	A	0-0	
02/11/98	Lokomotivi Tbilisi	H	0-0	
07/11/98	Torpedo Kutaisi	A	0-2	
16/11/98	Guria Lanchkhuti	H	3-0	(w/o)
22/11/98	Dila Gori	A	3-3	Koridze, Devidze, Davitashvili (p)
28/02/99	Samgurali Tskhaltubo	A	2-1	Koridze, Davitnidze
05/03/99	Dinamo Tbilisi	H	0-2	
12/03/99	Arsenali Tbilisi	A	1-1	Chukhua
17/03/99	Gorda Rustavi	A	3-0	Ambidze, Chukhua 2
30/03/99	Sioni Bolnisi	H	2-0	Tolordava, Ambidze
04/04/99	TSU Tbilisi	A	0-1	
10/04/99	Kolkheti 1913 Poti	H	1-0	Tolordava
17/04/99	Odishi Zugdidi	A	1-0	Tolordava
24/04/99	Dinamo Batumi	H	1-0	Ambidze
30/04/99	Vit Georgia Tbilisi	A	0-1	
05/05/99	Iberia Samtredia	H	0-2	
09/05/99	Lokomotivi Tbilisi	A	0-1	
15/05/99	Torpedo Kutaisi	H	2-1	Ambidze 2
19/05/99	Guria Lanchkhuti	A	7-3	Khutsishvili, Koridze, Jishkariani, Tolordava, Ambidze 2, Davitashvili
23/05/99	Dila Gori	H	4-0	Davitashvili, Khutsishvili, Ambidze, Devidze

ODISHI ZUGDIDI

CLUB DIRECTORY

Odishi Zugdidi
David Agmashenebeli street 8
Zugdidi
tel - (215) 26157/26927
Year of Formation - 1918
President - Vakhtang Nanava
Coach - Soso Chedia
Stadium - Central (7,500)

APPEARANCES 98/99

	P	Ap	(s)	Gls
Levan AKOBIA	D	17	(1)	
Koba ALANIA	M	4	(2)	
Levan ANJAPARIDZE	M	4		
Zaza APAKIDZE	M	9		
Irakli BARKAIA	M	9		
Giorgi CHADUNELI	M	6		
Zviad CHEDIA	A		(1)	1
Koba CHEJIA	D	1		
Severiane CHIKOBAVA	A	1		
Giorgi CHURGULIA	M	2	(2)	
Zviad ENDELADZE	A	11		6
Roman GABISONIA	D	6		
Shota GOGIA	G	7		
Malkhaz GOGOKHIA	A	13	(2)	4
Temur GURTSKAIA	D	19		1
Zaza GVICHIA	A	12		1
David IOSAVA	M	14	(5)	
Lukhumi JABUA	D	8		
Devi JAVASHVILI	D	6		
Vladimer JOJUA	M	1	(1)	
Gia JURKHANDZE	D	1		
David KAKULIA	M	11	(2)	
Mikheil KIPAROIDZE	D	14		
Manuchar KUTALIA	M	24	(2)	1
Koba KVEKVESKIRI	D	18		2
Paata LURSMANASHVILI	D	12		
Jimsher MARKOZIA	A	16	(4)	1
Irakli MEBONIA	M	1	(4)	
Mamuka NAKOPIA	G	23		
Giga SHEDANIA	M	2	(3)	
Boris SHELIA	M	4	(3)	
Koba SHONIA	D	4		
Koba TABAGUA	M	17	(5)	
Badri TKEMALADZE	M	10		
Tengiz TODUA	M	4		
Grigol TOLORAIA	M	1	(11)	
Levan TOLORDAVA	M	10		2
Manucha TSATSUA	M	6	(2)	1
Giorgi VAKHANIA	M	1	(2)	1
Koba VAZGANAVA	M	1	(1)	

LEAGUE RESULTS 1998/99

08/08/98	Iberia Samtredia	H	0-1	
16/08/98	Lokomotivi Tbilisi	A	0-3	
29/08/98	Guria Lanchkhuti	A	2-1	Endeladze, Kutalia
08/09/98	Dila Gori	H	2-1	Kvekveskiri, Endeladze
12/09/98	Samgurali Tskhaltubo	A	0-1	
20/09/98	Dinamo Tbilisi	H	0-4	
26/09/98	Merani 91 Tbilisi	A	1-0	Endeladze (p)
03/10/98	Gorda Rustavi	H	1-0	Endeladze
17/10/98	Sioni Bolnisi	A	0-1	
24/10/98	TSU Tbilisi	H	1-1	Tolordava
28/10/98	Torpedo Kutaisi	H	1-3	Endeladze (p)
31/10/98	Kolkheti 1913 Poti	A	1-5	Gurtskaia
07/11/98	Arsenali Tbilisi	H	1-2	Endeladze (p)
16/11/98	Dinamo Batumi	H	2-1	Markozia, Tolordava
23/11/98	Vit Georgia Tbilisi	A	0-1	
28/02/99	Iberia Samtredia	A	0-0	
05/03/99	Lokomotivi Tbilisi	H	0-1	
13/03/99	Torpedo Kutaisi	A	0-2	
17/03/99	Guria Lanchkhuti	H	4-2	Gogokhia 3, Vakhania
30/03/99	Dila Gori	A	0-1	
03/04/99	Samgurali Tskhaltubo	H	0-2	
10/04/99	Dinamo Tbilisi	A	0-5	
17/04/99	Merani 91 Tbilisi	H	0-1	
23/04/99	Gorda Rustavi	A	2-6	Kvekveskiri, Gvichia
01/05/99	Sioni Bolnisi	H	1-4	Chedia
05/05/99	TSU Tbilisi	A	1-4	Tsatsua
09/05/99	Kolkheti 1913 Poti	H	0-2	
15/05/99	Arsenali Tbilisi	A	0-3	
18/05/99	Dinamo Batumi	A	0-9	
23/05/99	Vit Georgia Tbilisi	H	1-3	Gogokhia

SAMGURALI TSKHALTUBO

CLUB DIRECTORY

Samgurali Tskhaltubo
Chavchavadze street 1, Tskhaltubo
tel - (240) 24077/23615
Year of Formation - 1945
President - Grigol Katamadze
Coach - Gaioz Darsadze; David Gendzekhadze;
Revaz Burkadze
Stadium - 26 Maisi (12,000)

APPEARANCES 98/99

	P	Ap	(s)	Gls
Kakha AKHALADZE	D		(2)	
Mamuka APTSIAURI	M	8	(1)	
David ASLANADZE	G	10		
Otar BOBOKHIDZE	G	3	(1)	
Aleksandre BURNADZE	D	9		
David CHELIDZE	D	12	(1)	
Shota DARSADZE	M	9	(10)	1
Gela DZAGNIDZE	M	19	(4)	2
Arsena GABLAIA	M		(1)	
Irakli GIORGOBIANI	M	12		
Revaz GLUNCHADZE	A	3	(4)	1
Shalva GONGADZE	M	8	(4)	1
Kakhaber JANASHIA	A	12	(2)	1
Givi JANELIDZE	D	9	(1)	
Ilia JAVAKHADZE	M	14	(4)	
Malkhaz JINCHARADZE	M	17	(5)	4
Irakli KHACHAPURIDZE	M	9	(4)	
Zviad KHACHIRASHVILI	G	9		
Giorgi KILASONIA	M	10	(1)	4
Levan KOBULADZE	D	19	(1)	
Ramaz KOGUASHVILI	D	4		
Levan KOPALIANI	M		(1)	
Zviad KUTATELADZE	M	2	(15)	1
Mikheil MAKHVILADZE	D	25		2
David NAKANI	M	1		
Mamuka NEBIERIDZE	M		(1)	
Teimuraz PAIKIDZE	A	7	(6)	6
David PETRIASHVILI	A	5	(1)	2
Levan PILIPASHVILI	A	3	(1)	
Shalva PRANGISHVILI	D	18	(4)	
Giorgi SHENGELIA	A	12		5
Paata SHVANGIRADZE	M		(1)	
Zviad STURUA	G	8		
Giorgi SUKHIASHVILI	M	12		1
Malkhaz TEVDORADZE	A	13	(1)	1
Grigol TEVZADZE	D	13		
Temur UGULAVA	A	4	(5)	
Malkhaz VOSKANOV	M	11		

LEAGUE RESULTS 1998/99

07/08/98	Merani 91 Tbilisi	A	0-0	
15/08/98	Gorda Rustavi	H	1-0	Paikidze (p)
22/08/98	Sioni Bolnisi	A	0-4	
29/08/98	TSU Tbilisi	H	0-1	
08/09/98	Kolkheti 1913 Poti	A	2-4	Tevdoradze, Jincharadze
12/09/98	Odishi Zugdidi	H	1-0	Paikidze (p)
21/09/98	Dinamo Batumi	A	1-6	Paikidze
26/09/98	Vit Georgia Tbilisi	H	1-3	Paikidze (p)
03/10/98	Iberia Samtredia	A	1-3	Paikidze
17/10/98	Lokomotivi Tbilisi	H	1-2	Makhviladze
24/10/98	Torpedo Kutaisi	A	1-3	Jincharadze
31/10/98	Guria Lanchkhuti	H	2-1	Jincharadze, Paikidze
07/11/98	Dila Gori	A	1-0	Makhviladze
14/11/98	Arsenali Tbilisi	A	1-1	Janashia
22/11/98	Dinamo Tbilisi	H	0-3	
28/02/99	Merani 91 Tbilisi	H	1-2	Dzagnidze
05/03/99	Gorda Rustavi	A	0-2	
12/03/99	Sioni Bolnisi	H	1-0	Kilasonia (p)
16/03/99	TSU Tbilisi	A	3-1	Sukhiashvili, Shengelia, Jincharadze
30/03/99	Kolkheti 1913 Poti	H	0-1	
03/04/99	Odishi Zugdidi	A	2-0	Shengelia, Darsadze
10/04/99	Dinamo Batumi	H	0-0	
17/04/99	Vit Georgia Tbilisi	A	0-3	
23/04/99	Iberia Samtredia	H	2-3	Shengelia, Kutateladze
01/05/99	Lokomotivi Tbilisi	A	0-2	
05/05/99	Torpedo Kutaisi	H	2-3	Gongadze, Glunchadze
09/05/99	Guria Lanchkhuti	A	3-2	Dzagnidze, Shengelia, Kilasonia
15/05/99	Dila Gori	H	3-1	Petriashvili, Kilasonia, Shengelia
19/05/99	Arsenali Tbilisi	H	2-0	Petriashvili, Kilasonia
23/05/99	Dinamo Tbilisi	A	0-6	

SIONI BOLNISI

CLUB DIRECTORY

Sioni Bolnisi
Orbeliani street 106
Bolnisi
tel - (258) 22468/22372
Year of Formation - 1936
President - Shukri Devnozashvili
Coach - Boris Dudauri; Spartak Archvadze;
Piruz Rekhviashvili
Stadium - Temur Stepania (3,000)

APPEARANCES 98/99

	P	Ap	(s)	Gls
Lasha AMBIDZE	D	9	(1)	
Pridon ARCHVADZE	M	1	(4)	
Valeri ASATIANI	M		(1)	
David BERIDZE	D	3	(1)	
Lasha CHAGELISHVILI	M		(1)	
Giorgi CHALADZE	M	4	(8)	
Nikoloz CHALADZE	M		(2)	
Nugzar DALAKISHVILI	G	12	(1)	
Giorgi DZNELADZE	M	7		1
Valeri GAGUA	A	19	(9)	3
Kakhaber GODERDZISHVILI	D	24		
Murman GOGOLADZE	M	28	(1)	2
Konstantine GUGUNAVA	G	11		
Shalva ISIANI	A	7		
Joni JAGIDISI	A	10	(2)	4
David JAPARIDZE	M	1	(14)	
Elguja JAPARIDZE	M	20	(3)	
Kakha JAPARIDZE	D		(1)	
Giorgi KHAREBASHVILI	A	1	(2)	
Papuna KHIDASHELI	M	3	(3)	
Giorgi KIPSHIDZE	D	22		
Givi KOBELASHVILI	A		(8)	1
Giorgi MAZANISHVILI	M	9		
Zurab METREVELI	M		(1)	
Bakhva MOSESHVILI	A	25	(3)	8
Seiran POZOIAN	M	2	(2)	
Mirza SAMKHARADZE	M	29		3
Temur SAMKHARADZE	M	26		
Vakhtang SAMKHARADZE	M		(1)	
Archil SHAKIASHVILI	D	28		3
Dimitri SULTANOV	D	7		
David SVANIDZE	D	10	(5)	
Giorgi TKAVADZE	A	5		1
Teimuraz VOLKOV	G	7		

LEAGUE RESULTS 1998/99

08/08/98	Guria Lanchkhuti	H	2-2	Shakiashvili 2
15/08/98	Dila Gori	A	0-2	
22/08/98	Samgurali Tskhaltubo	H	4-0	Samkharadze M., Jagidisi 2, Kobelashvili
30/08/98	Dinamo Tbilisi	A	1-8	Moseshvili
08/09/98	Merani 91 Tbilisi	H	1-4	Jagidisi
12/09/98	Gorda Rustavi	A	1-3	Gogoladze
19/09/98	Arsenali Tbilisi	H	0-1	
26/09/98	TSU Tbilisi	H	1-1	Dzneladze
03/10/98	Kolkheti 1913 Poti	A	0-4	
17/10/98	Odishi Zugdidi	H	1-0	Samkharadze M.
25/10/98	Dinamo Batumi	A	0-1	
31/10/98	Vit Georgia Tbilisi	H	2-1	Jagidisi (p), Moseshvili
07/11/98	Iberia Samtredia	A	2-1	Samkharadze M., Shakiashvili (p)
15/11/98	Lokomotivi Tbilisi	H	0-0	
22/11/98	Torpedo Kutaisi	A	0-4	
28/02/99	Guria Lanchkhuti	A	1-1	og (Kvekveskiri)
05/03/99	Dila Gori	H	1-0	Moseshvili
12/03/99	Samgurali Tskhaltubo	A	0-1	
17/03/99	Dinamo Tbilisi	H	1-3	Gagua
30/03/99	Merani 91 Tbilisi	A	0-2	
03/04/99	Gorda Rustavi	H	0-0	
10/04/99	Arsenali Tbilisi	A	1-2	Moseshvili
16/04/99	TSU Tbilisi	A	0-1	
23/04/99	Kolkheti 1913 Potl	H	1-1	Gagua
01/05/99	Odishi Zugdidi	A	4-1	Moseshvili 2, Gogoladze, Gagua
05/05/99	Dinamo Batumi	H	1-1	Moseshvili
09/05/99	Vit Georgia Tbilisi	A	0-2	
15/05/99	Iberia Samtredia	H	1-0	Moseshvili
19/05/99	Lokomotivi Tbilisi	A	0-3	
23/05/99	Torpedo Kutaisi	H	1-2	Tkavadze

TORPEDO KUTAISI

CLUB DIRECTORY

Torpedo Kutaisi
Akhalgazrdobis street Mesame Shesakhvevi 2
Kutaisi
tel - (231) 78364
Year of Formation - 1949
President - Mikheil Korkia
Coach - Soso Pruidze; Jemal Kherkhadze
Stadium - Givi Kiladze (28,800)

MAJOR HONOURS
Domestic Cup - (1) 1999.

APPEARANCES 98/99

		P	Ap	(s)	Gls
Badri AKHVLEDIANI	D	13			1
David ASLANADZE	G	9			
Giorgi CHANTURIA	G	20			
Archil CHKHABERIDZE	D	17	(4)		
Gia CHKHAIDZE	D	10	(2)		
Kakhaber CHKHETIANI	M	25			3
Valeri GENEBASHVILI	A	1			
Goderdzi GOGOLADZE	D	1			
Grigol IMEDADZE	A	5	(8)		6
Zurab IONANIDZE	A	22	(2)		16
David JANASHIA	A	27			14
Kakha JANASHIA	M	1	(3)		
Paata JINCHARADZE	D	7			
Levan KEBADZE	M	6	(3)		4
Giorgi KIPIANI	M	1	(3)		
Vakhtang KHVADACIANI	D	12			
Revaz KVERNADZE	M	1			
Kakhaber KVETENADZE	M	24	(2)		5
Irakli MAGLAKELIDZE	D	26	(3)		
David MAMARDASHVILI	G		(4)		
Giorgi MAZANISHVILI	M	4	(5)		1
Giorgi MEGRELADZE	A	17	(5)		14
Konstantine METREVELI	A	4	(13)		2
Badri MUSHKUDIANI	M	1			
Aleksandre SHEKRILADZE	D	29			
Zviad STURUA	G	1	(1)		
Vakhtang TURMANIDZE	D	23	(3)		
Zaza VACHIBERADZE	M	15	(7)		4
Kakhaber VADACHKORIA	M	1			
Irakli VASHAKIDZE	D	7			3

LEAGUE RESULTS 1998/99

08/08/98	TSU Tbilisi	A	3-1	Janashia D., Vashakidze, Kvetenadze
15/08/98	Kolkheti 1913 Poti	H	5-1	Janashia D., Vashakidze,
				Ionanidze 2 (1p), Vachiberadze
30/08/98	Dinamo Batumi	H	3-3	Janashia D., Megreladze, Ionanidze
09/09/98	Vit Georgia Tbilisi	A	2-1	Vashakidze, Ionanidze
13/09/98	Iberia Samtredia	H	4-0	Ionanidze 2 (1p), Janashia D.,
				Megreladze
20/09/98	Lokomotivi Tbilisi	A	1-1	Kvetenadze
27/09/98	Arsenali Tbilisi	A	2-0	Ionanidze, Megreladze
03/10/98	Guria Lanchkhuti	H	3-0	Kebadze 2, Megreladze
17/10/98	Dila Gori	A	0-3	
24/10/98	Samgurali Tskhaltubo	H	3-1	Megreladze 2, Ionanidze
28/10/98	Odishi Zugdidi	A	3-1	Ionanidze, Kebadze, Janashia D.
31/10/98	Dinamo Tbilisi	A	0-1	
07/11/98	Merani 91 Tbilisi	H	2-0	Kvetenadze, Ionanidze (p)
15/11/98	Gorda Rustavi	A	7-1	Janashia D. 3, Ionanidze,
				Vachiberadze, Kebadze, Imedadze
22/11/98	Sioni Bolnisi	H	4-0	Kvetenadze, Ionanidze 2 (2p),
				Imedadze
28/02/99	TSU Tbilisi	H	1-0	Megreladze
05/03/99	Kolkheti 1913 Poti	A	2-1	Ionanidze, Megreladze
13/03/99	Odishi Zugdidi	H	2-0	Megreladze, Ionanidze
17/03/99	Dinamo Batumi	A	1-2	Akhvlediani
30/03/99	Vit Georgia Tbilisi	H	0-1	
03/04/99	Iberia Samtredia	A	0-0	
10/04/99	Lokomotivi Tbilisi	H	3-1	Kvetenadze, Chkhetiani, Janashia D.
17/04/99	Arsenali Tbilisi	H	1-1	Vachiberadze
23/04/99	Guria Lanchkhuti	A	5-1	Vachiberadze, Megreladze,
				Janashia D. 2, Imedadze
01/05/99	Dila Gori	H	3-0	Megreladze 2, Janashia D.
05/05/99	Samgurali Tskhaltubo	A	3-2	Janashia D., Chkhetiani, Metreveli
09/05/99	Dinamo Tbilisi	H	3-1	Megreladze, Chkhetiani, Janashia D.
15/05/99	Merani 91 Tbilisi	A	1-2	Mazanishvili
19/05/99	Gorda Rustavi	H	4-0	Imedadze 2, Megreladze, Ionanidze
23/05/99	Sioni Bolnisi	A	2-1	Imedadze, Metreveli

TSU TBILISI

CLUB DIRECTORY

TSU Tbilisi
Chavchavadze street 39a, Tbilisi
tel - (32) 222371   fax - (32) 922080
Year of Formation - 1906
President - Aleksandre Bukia
Coach - Otar Gabelia
Stadium - Central (Mtskheta) (3,000)

APPEARANCES 98/99

	P	Ap	(s)	Gls
Giorgi ADAMIA	A	3	(1)	2
Irakli BAKHTADZE	A	2	(5)	1
Levan BALIANI	G	1		
Zurab BATIASHVILI	G	9		
Aleksandre BUKIA	M	6	(3)	2
Dimitri CHELIDZE	M		(4)	
Giorgi CHIABRISHVILI	M		(2)	
Kakha CHUMBURIDZE	M	25		1
Giorgi DEKANOSIDZE	M	7	(1)	1
Kakhaber EBRALIDZE	D	4	(2)	1
Zurab EMRASHVILI	M		(1)	
Giorgi GABELIA	G	16		
David GOGOLADZE	A	7		4
Boris GONCHAROV	A	7	(4)	1
Vladimer GUDUSHAURI	D	11	(3)	
Nugzar GVALIA	D	4		
Giorgi ILURIDZE	D	21	(1)	
Aleksandre INTSKIRVELI	D	6	(2)	1
Temur JAPARIDZE	D	2		
Giorgi KADAGIDZE	M	1		
Demur KAKUBAVA	M	15		2
David KANTARIA	D	4		
Irakli KHUJADZE	D	10		
Tengiz KOBIASHVILI	D	23		4
Giorgi KVAKHADZE	M		(2)	
Levan MAGRADZE	A	25		1
Mirza MERLANI	G	3		
Mikheil MESKHI	M	1	(1)	
Giorgi NIKURADZE	G	1		
Koba NINUA	M	17	(7)	
Revaz PERTENAVA	M	3	(1)	
Otar ROSTIASHVILI	A	25		3
Giorgi SHASHIASHVILI	D	11		
Otar SULADZE	M		(2)	
David SULAVA	M		(1)	
Ramaz SVANADZE	M	4	(3)	
Kakhaber SVANIDZE	D	6	(5)	
Irakli TSINARIDZE	M		(2)	
Klimenti TSITAISHVILI	A	14		4
David TSOMAIA	D	15		
Zaza ZAMTARADZE	D	21	(1)	

LEAGUE RESULTS 1998/99

08/08/98	Torpedo Kutaisi	H	1-3	Bakhtadze
15/08/98	Guria Lanchkhuti	A	0-2	
23/08/98	Dila Gori	H	0-1	
29/08/98	Samgurali Tskhaltubo	A	1-0	Kobiashvili
08/09/98	Dinamo Tbilisi	H	1-3	Tsitaishvili
13/09/98	Merani 91 Tbilisi	A	0-1	
21/09/98	Gorda Rustavi	H	0-0	
26/09/98	Sioni Bolnisi	A	1-1	Rostiashvili
02/10/98	Arsenali Tbilisi	H	4-1	Rostiashvili, Kakubava, Tsitaishvili (p), Ebralidze
17/10/98	Kolkheti 1913 Poti	H	2-4	Kakubava, Tsitaishvili (p)
24/10/98	Odishi Zugdidi	A	1-1	Kobiashvili
01/11/98	Dinamo Batumi	H	0-1	
06/11/98	Vit Georgia Tbilisi	A	1-0	Rostiashvili
15/11/98	Iberia Samtredia	H	1-1	Dekanosidze
22/11/98	Lokomotivi Tbilisi	A	1-3	Tsitaishvili
28/02/99	Torpedo Kutaisi	A	0-1	
04/03/99	Guria Lanchkhuti	H	0-0	
12/03/99	Dila Gori	A	0-0	
16/03/99	Samgurali Tskhaltubo	H	1-3	Kobiashvili
31/03/99	Dinamo Tbilisi	A	0-0	
04/04/99	Merani 91 Tbilisi	H	1-0	Magradze
10/04/99	Gorda Rustavi	A	0-0	
16/04/99	Sioni Bolnisi	H	1-0	Kobiashvili
23/04/99	Arsenali Tbilisi	A	0-0	
30/04/99	Kolkheti 1913 Poti	A	0-2	
05/05/99	Odishi Zugdidi	H	4-1	Bukia, Gogoladze 2, Chumburidze
15/05/99	Vit Georgia Tbilisi	H	2-5	Bukia, Intskirveli
18/05/99	Iberia Samtredia	A	2-4	Adamia, Gogoladze
21/05/99	Dinamo Batumi	A	2-4	Adamia, Goncharov (p)
23/05/99	Lokomotivi Tbilisi	H	1-4	Gogoladze

VIT GEORGIA TBILISI

CLUB DIRECTORY

Vit Georgia Tbilisi
Leselidze street 18
Tbilisi
tel - (32) 982356
Year of Formation - 1998
President - Guram Rikhadze
Coach - Spartak Archvadze; Jemal Makharashvili;
Sergo Kotrikadze
Stadium - Central (Mtskheta) (3,000)

APPEARANCES 98/99

	P	Ap	(s)	Gls
Dimitri ABAZADZE	D	10	(2)	
Kakhaber ALADASHVILI	M	14		1
Irakli BARKAIA	D	6		
Archil BOKERIA	A	6	(10)	6
Tamaz BOKERIA	M	6	(3)	
Giorgi CHANKOTADZE	D	23		2
Igor CHOKHONELIDZE	D	6	(2)	
Sergo CHURADZE	G	28		
David DOLIDZE	M	12	(7)	1
Kakha DVALISHVILI	M	3	(1)	
Tengiz ENUKIDZE	A	1	(2)	
Malkhaz ERADZE	M	6	(3)	
Giorgi GAMBASHIDZE	M		(5)	
Vladimer GOCHASHVILI	A	22	(4)	6
Konstantine GUGUNAVA	G		(1)	
Grigol GVAZAVA	A	13	(5)	4
Zviad GVAZAVA	D	20	(6)	1
Paata GVIRJISHVI	M		(3)	
Irakli KAPANADZE	M	17	(3)	
Revaz KEMOKLIDZE	D	15		
Levan KHABULIANI	A		(1)	1
Giorgi KORIDZE	A	15		7
Vladimer KUTATELADZE	M	1	(2)	
Levan KVITSIANI	M		(5)	
Vasil MAISURADZE	D	29		2
David MAMARDASHVILI	G	2	(1)	
Mikheil MAZIASHVILI	M	16		5
Zurab MENTESHASHVILI	D	14		1
Jaba MUJIRI	D	22		
Lasha NOZADZE	M	20	(4)	5
David PETRIASHVILI	A	3	(3)	

LEAGUE RESULTS 1998/99

07/08/98	Dinamo Batumi	A	1-0	Gvazava G.
14/08/98	Arsenali Tbilisi	A	0-0	
24/08/98	Iberia Samtredia	H	4-1	Nozadze, Gochashvili 2 (1p),
				Gvazava G.
31/08/98	Lokomotivi Tbilisi	A	0-1	
09/09/98	Torpedo Kutaisi	H	1-2	Chankotadze
13/09/98	Guria Lanchkhuti	A	0-2	
19/09/98	Dila Gori	H	1-2	Gvazava G.
26/09/98	Samgurali Tskhaltubo	A	3-1	Nozadze 2, Chankotadze
03/10/98	Dinamo Tbilisi	H	0-2	
19/10/98	Merani 91 Tbilisi	A	0-0	
25/10/98	Gorda Rustavi	H	2-1	Gvazava G., Gvazava Z.
31/10/98	Sioni Bolnisi	A	1-2	Nozadze
06/11/98	TSU Tbilisi	H	0-1	
15/11/98	Kolkheti 1913 Poti	A	1-2	Menteshashvili
23/11/98	Odishi Zugdidi	H	1-0	Maziashvili
01/03/99	Dinamo Batumi	H	0-0	
06/03/99	Arsenali Tbilisi	H	0-0	
13/03/99	Iberia Samtredia	A	1-0	Koridze
17/03/99	Lokomotivi Tbilisi	H	1-2	Koridze
30/03/99	Torpedo Kutaisi	A	1-0	Nozadze
03/04/99	Guria Lanchkhuti	H	3-0	Gochashvili 2, Maisuradze
10/04/99	Dila Gori	A	3-1	Koridze 2, Bokeria A. (p)
17/04/99	Samgurali Tskhaltubo	H	3-0	Bokeria A. (p), Koridze,
				Aladashvili
23/04/99	Dinamo Tbilisi	A	2-3	Gochashvili 2
30/04/99	Merani 91 Tbilisi	H	1-0	Koridze (p)
05/05/99	Gorda Rustavi	A	2-3	Bokeria A., Maziashvili
09/05/99	Sioni Bolnisi	H	2-0	Koridze, Dolidze
15/05/99	TSU Tbilisi	A	5-2	Maziashvili 3, Maisuradze,
				Bokeria A.
19/05/99	Kolkheti 1913 Poti	H	0-0	
23/05/99	Odishi Zugdidi	A	3-1	Bokeria A. 2, Khabuliani

PROMOTED CLUBS

SECOND DIVISION FINAL TABLES 98/99

EAST GROUP B

		Pd	W	D	L	F	A	Pt	GD
1	**Dinamo 2 Tbilisi**	**26**	**24**	**0**	**2**	**79**	**17**	**72**	**+62**
2	Tskhinvali	26	21	2	3	73	15	62	+58
3	Lokomotivi 2 Tbilisi	26	17	3	6	66	38	54	+28
4	Iberia Kareli	26	15	4	7	49	25	49	+24
5	Iveria Khashuri	26	13	6	7	58	38	45	+20
6	Tskhumi Sokhumi	26	13	4	9	43	33	43	+16
7	SAU Tbilisi	26	10	5	11	50	44	35	+6
8	Gantiadi Kaspi	26	10	5	11	40	47	35	-7
9	Tori Borjomi	26	9	2	15	36	42	29	-6
10	Meskheti Akhaltsikhe	26	8	5	13	39	51	29	-12
11	SK Iberia Tbilisi	26	8	1	17	49	64	25	-15
12	Vardzia Aspindza	26	5	4	17	22	68	19	-46
13	Dila 2 Gori	26	5	3	18	28	62	18	-34
14	Jineri Jinvali	26	1	2	23	18	112	5	-94

N.B. Tskhinvali deducted 3 pts.

EAST GROUP A winners - Gartskali Dzveli Anaga

WEST GROUP B

		Pd	W	D	L	F	A	Pt	GD
1	**Kolkheti Khobi**	**24**	**18**	**2**	**4**	**71**	**21**	**56**	**+50**
2	Koleji Batumi	24	14	5	5	49	22	47	+27
3	Shukura Kobuleti	24	14	3	7	51	30	45	+21
4	Pazisi Poti	24	14	2	8	53	34	44	+19
5	Skuri Tsalenjikha	24	13	2	9	49	47	41	+2
6	Enguri Ganmukhuri	24	12	5	7	51	37	41	+14
7	Udishi 2 Zugdidi	24	10	6	8	39	30	36	+9
8	Mertskhali Ozurgeti	24	9	2	13	35	45	29	-10
9	Bakhmaro Chokhatauri	24	8	4	12	23	37	28	-14
10	Egrisi Senaki	24	7	5	12	27	47	26	-20
11	Kolkheti 2 Poti	24	7	4	13	22	48	25	-26
12	Samegrelo Chkhorotsku	24	5	4	15	28	47	19	-19
13	Salkhino Martvili	24	3	0	21	36	89	9	-53

WEST GROUP A winners - Sulori Vani

PROMOTION/RELEGATION PLAY-OFFS

Sioni Bolnisi 2, TSU Tbilisi 0

Dinamo 2 Tblisi 1, Gartskali Dzveli Anaga 1 (aet; 4-2 on pens.)
Kolkheti Khobi 1, Sulori Vani 0

Gartskali Dzveli Anaga 1, Sulori Vani 0

TSU Tbilisi 3, Gartskali Dzveli Anaga 0

CLUB DIRECTORY

Dinamo 2 Tbilisi (now - FC Tbilisi)
A. Tsereteli Avenue 2
Tbilisi
tel - (32) 940095
fax - (32) 940095
Year of Formation - 1999
General Director - Otar Shengelia
Coach - Otar Korgalidze
Stadium - Boris Paichadze (75,000)

CLUB DIRECTORY

Kolkheti Khobi
Tsotsne Dadiani street 105
Khobi
tel - (32) 3062/2327
Year of Formation - 1948
President - Joni Kachibaia
Coach - Pridon Gotsiridze
Stadium - Central (12,000)

GERMANY

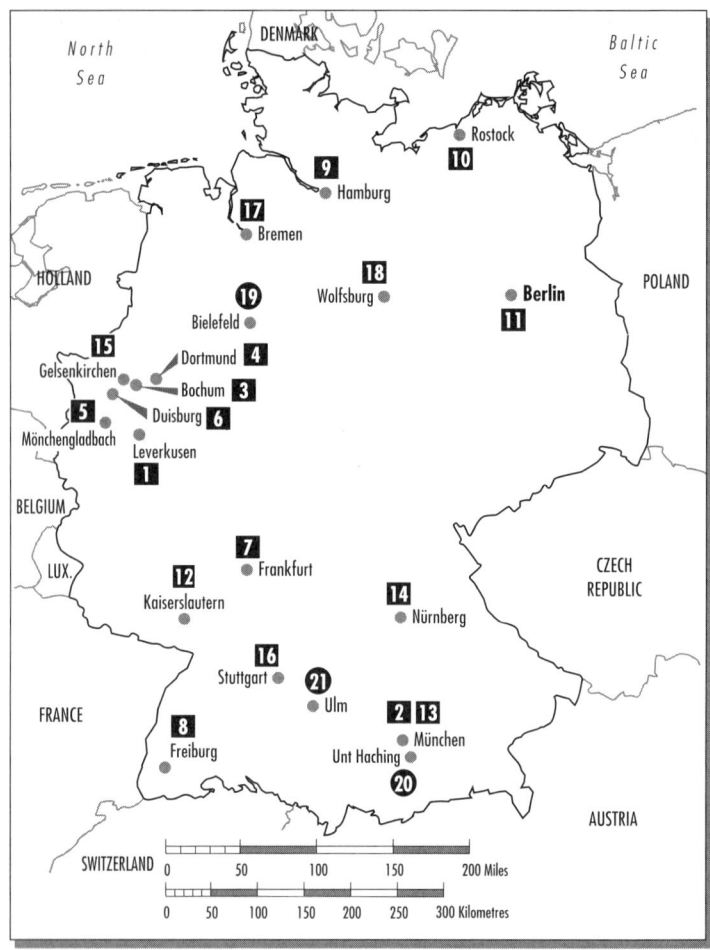

QUALITY SHORTAGE HITS NATIONAL TEAM

One out of three is bad for Bayern

FEDERATION DIRECTORY

Deutscher Fussball-Bund
Otto-Fleck-Schneise 6, Postfach 710405, 60528 Frankfurt am Main
tel - (069) 67880/1   Year of Formation - 1900
fax - (069) 6788266   President - Dr. Egidius Braun
Secretary - Horst R. Schmidt

Franz Beckenbauer maintained repeatedly during the 1998/99 season that Bayern Munich had never had a better team. That included the one which he personally had captained to three successive European Champions' Cup victories in the mid-'70s. His argument was that while the team he played in contained superstars and journeymen in equal measure, the latest version had no weaknesses; top-class players filled every position, there was harmony in the camp, the football was attractive, and crowds flocked regularly to sold-out venues to watch them.

But, to prove the *Kaiser's* theory beyond reasonable doubt, Bayern needed to fulfil their season's objective - which was to claim the unprecedented 'treble' of Bundesliga, DFB-Pokal and European Champions' Cup. They were to come extremely close to achieving it, but

in the end, amidst much torment and torture, only one of the three prizes, the German championship, came their way. The clean sweep could, probably should, have been theirs, but a double dose of the Cup final jitters, in Barcelona against Manchester United and in Berlin against Werder Bremen, left Bayern and their fans in a state of shock and disbelief. What had seemed likely to be the greatest season in the club's 99-year history ultimately turned out to be one of massive anti-climax.

Hard though it will always be for the Bayern fans to erase from their minds the 100-second horror-show that ended their hopes of European glory in Barcelona or the two missed penalties that brought about their downfall in Berlin, reflections on the 1998/99 season will otherwise be memorable.

LEAGUE CHAMPIONSHIP RESULTS 98/99

		1	2	3	4	5	6	7	8	9	10	11	12	13	14	15	16	17	18
1	Bayer 04 Leverkusen		1-2	2-0	3-1	4-1	2-0	2-1	1-1	1-2	3-1	2-2	2-2	1-1	3-0	1-1	0-0	2-0	3-0
2	FC Bayern München	2-0		4-2	2-2	4-2	3-1	3-1	2-0	5-3	6-1	1-1	4-0	3-1	2-0	1-1	2-0	1-0	3-0
3	VfL Bochum	1-5	2-2		0-1	2-1	0-2	0-0	1-2	2-0	2-3	2-0	1-2	2-0	0-3	1-2	3-3	2-0	0-2
4	Borussia Dortmund	1-0	2-2	0-1		1-1	2-0	3-1	2-1	2-1	2-0	3-0	1-0	3-1	3-0	3-0	3-0	2-1	2-1
5	Borussia Mönchengladbach	2-8	0-2	2-2	0-2		0-2	1-1	3-1	2-2	1-1	2-4	0-2	2-0	0-2	3-0	2-3	0-1	5-2
6	MSV Duisburg	0-0	0-3	2-0	3-2	2-2		2-1	1-0	2-3	4-1	0-0	3-1	1-1	1-1	1-2	2-0	2-0	6-1
7	Eintracht Frankfurt	2-3	1-0	1-0	2-0	0-0	0-0		3-1	2-2	2-2	1-1	5-1	2-3	3-2	1-2	1-1	0-2	0-1
8	SC Freiburg	1-1	0-2	1-1	2-2	2-1	2-2	2-0		0-0	3-0	0-2	0-1	1-2	1-0	0-2	2-0	0-2	0-0
9	Hamburger SV	0-0	0-2	1-0	0-0	3-0	4-1	0-1	2-1		1-0	0-4	2-0	3-0	2-0	2-2	3-1	1-1	1-1
10	FC Hansa Rostock	1-1	0-4	3-0	2-0	1-1	3-0	2-2	0-2	0-1		1-2	2-1	4-1	1-1	2-2	3-0	2-1	3-3
11	Hertha BSC Berlin	0-1	1-0	4-1	3-0	4-1	1-3	3-1	1-0	6-1	2-0		1-1	2-1	3-0	2-0	2-0	1-0	2-0
12	1.FC Kaiserslautern	0-1	2-1	2-3	1-0	2-1	3-0	2-1	0-2	1-0	3-2	4-3		1-1	2-0	4-1	1-1	4-0	1-1
13	TSV 1860 München	0-2	1-1	2-1	2-0	3-1	0-0	4-1	2-0	0-0	2-1	2-0	1-2		1-2	4-5	1-1	1-3	2-3
14	1.FC Nürnberg	2-2	2-0	2-2	0-0	2-0	0-2	0-2	1-2	1-1	1-2	0-0	1-1	1-5		3-0	2-2	1-1	1-1
15	FC Schalke 04	0-1	1-3	2-2	1-1	1-0	2-0	2-3	1-1	1-4	1-0	0-0	0-2	2-2	2-2		1-0	1-2	2-0
16	VfB Stuttgart	0-1	0-2	4-2	2-1	2-2	0-0	2-0	3-1	3-1	1-1	0-0	4-0	0-1	0-0	2-1		1-0	1-2
17	SV Werder Bremen	2-2	0-1	1-1	1-1	4-1	1-1	1-2	2-3	0-0	0-3	2-1	0-1	4-1	2-3	1-0	2-2		0-1
18	VfL Wolfsburg	1-0	0-1	4-1	0-0	7-1	4-2	2-0	1-1	4-1	1-1	2-1	2-1	1-0	1-1	0-0	3-2	2-4	

LEAGUE CHAMPIONSHIP FINAL TABLE 98/99

		P		Home					Away					Total				
			W	D	L	F	A	W	D	L	F	A	W	D	L	F	A	P	GD
1	FC Bayern München	34	14	3	0	48	15	10	3	4	28	13	24	6	4	76	28	78	+48
2	Bayer 04 Leverkusen	34	9	6	2	33	15	8	6	3	28	15	17	12	5	61	30	63	+31
3	Hertha BSC Berlin	34	14	1	2	38	10	4	7	6	21	22	18	8	8	59	32	62	+27
4	Borussia Dortmund	34	14	2	1	35	10	2	7	8	13	24	16	9	9	48	34	57	+14
5	1.FC Kaiserslautern	34	11	3	3	33	18	6	3	8	18	29	17	6	11	51	47	57	+4
6	VfL Wolfsburg	34	10	5	2	35	17	5	5	7	19	32	15	10	9	54	49	55	+5
7	Hamburger SV	34	9	5	3	25	14	4	6	7	22	32	13	11	10	47	46	50	+1
8	MSV Duisburg	34	9	5	3	32	18	4	5	8	16	27	13	10	11	48	45	49	+3
9	TSV 1860 München	34	7	4	6	28	23	4	4	9	21	33	11	8	15	49	56	41	-7
10	FC Schalke 04	34	5	6	6	20	23	5	5	7	21	31	10	11	13	41	54	41	-13
11	VfB Stuttgart	34	8	5	4	25	15	1	7	9	16	33	9	12	13	41	48	39	-7
12	SC Freiburg	34	5	6	6	17	18	5	3	9	19	26	10	9	15	36	44	39	-8
13	SV Werder Bremen	34	4	6	7	23	24	6	2	9	18	23	10	8	16	41	47	38	-6
14	FC Hansa Rostock	34	7	6	4	30	22	2	5	10	19	36	9	11	14	49	58	38	-9
15	Eintracht Frankfurt	34	6	6	5	26	21	3	4	10	18	33	9	10	15	44	54	37	-10
16	1.FC Nürnberg	34	3	11	3	23	23	4	5	8	17	27	7	16	11	40	50	37	-10
17	VfL Bochum	34	5	3	9	21	28	2	5	10	19	37	7	8	19	40	65	29	-25
18	Borussia Mönchengladbach	34	4	4	9	25	35	0	5	12	16	44	4	9	21	41	79	21	-38

It was a year in which Bayern at last discovered a coach capable of bringing internal order and discipline as well as fielding a team that could play wonderfully attractive

Bayern's Thomas Linke puts an end to a run by Andy Cole of Manchester United.

football. The recruitment of Ottmar Hitzfeld from Borussia Dortmund was a masterstroke. A personable, decent and refreshingly honest man, he immediately gained the respect of all the highly-paid internationals on Bayern's books. He was not afraid to wield the proverbial iron rod to impose his authority, but it was rarely required. He adopted a successful rotation policy which kept everybody happy and prevented the forming of mutinous cliques. For once, outspoken team members such as Lothar Matthäus, Mario Basler, Thomas Helmer and even the biggest blabbermouth of them all, new signing Stefan Effenberg, all kept their feelings to themselves rather than sharing them with the outside world via a TV camera or a newspaper column. Not that they had much to complain about. Bayern began the season by winning the inaugural pre-season League Cup and then threw down the gauntlet in the Bundesliga by winning each of their first six matches. It was obvious straight away that Hitzfeld's men meant business, but a couple of away defeats, against Eintracht Frankfurt and Hertha Berlin, proved that they were still vulnerable, and when they could only draw 2-2 with struggling Bochum in their next away game, they dropped from first place, albeit on goal difference and with a match in hand.

The team who had replaced them, Bayer Leverkusen were scheduled to travel to Munich the following week. I was a game of huge importance for both clubs, bu

NATIONAL TEAM APPEARANCES 98/99

Coach - Berti VOGTS; Erich RIBBECK	MLT	ROM	TUR	MOL	HOL	USA	COL	NIR	FIN	SCO	MOL	Cps	Gls
Oliver KAHN (15/06/69) - FC Bayern München	G	G	G	G	G	G	G46	G	G		G	20	-
Markus BABBEL (08/09/72) - FC Bayern München	D	D	D	D		D	D	D	D		s74	41	1
Jens NOWOTNY (11/01/74) - Bayer 04 Leverkusen	D	s46	D	D	D46			s46	s72	D	D	14	-
Thomas LINKE (26/12/69) - FC Bayern München	D46											3	-
Marko REHMER (29/04/72) - FC Hansa Rostock	D	D	D	D	s46	D	M					7	-
Mario BASLER (18/12/68) - FC Bayern München	M74	M			M72							30	2
Stefan EFFENBERG (02/08/68) - FC Bayern München	M	M										35	5
Stefan BEINLICH (13/01/72) - Bayer 04 Leverkusen	M		M	M83								3	-
Jörg HEINRICH (06/12/69) - Fiorentina (ITA)	M46		M76		M			M	M	M	M	27	2
Oliver BIERHOFF (01/05/68) - Milan (ITA)	A46	A72	A	A	A			A	A	A60	A	40	24
Olaf MARSCHALL (19/03/66) - 1.FC Kaiserslautern	A63				s21	A						11	3
Stephan PASSLACK (24/08/70) - Borussia Mönchengladbach	s46	D46										2	1
Michael TARNAT (27/10/69) - FC Bayern München	s46	s46		M								19	-
Ulf KIRSTEN (04/12/65) - Bayer 04 Leverkusen	s46	A	A	A74	A21				s65	s60	A54	44	17
Paulo Roberto RINK (21/02/73) - Bayer 04 Leverkusen	s63	s72										2	-
Oliver NEUVILLE (01/05/73) - FC Hansa Rostock	s74		s76	s53			A74	A68	A65	A	A	8	1
Christian NERLINGER (21/03/73) - Borussia Dortmund		M		M		s46	s46					4	1
Jens JEREMIES (05/03/74) - FC Bayern München		M	M		M	M	M46	M	M	M46	M46	17	-
Jörg ALBERTZ (29/01/71) - Rangers (SCO)		M46										3	-
Lars RICKEN (10/07/76) - Borussia Dortmund			M81	M53		M	s79					6	-
Carsten RAMELOW (20/03/74) - Bayer 04 Leverkusen			M	M	s70	M46				s46	s54	6	-
Marco BODE (23/07/69) - SV Werder Bremen			s81			s46	M	A78	A76		A	14	4
Carsten JANCKER (28/08/74) - FC Bayern München				s74				s68	s76	s88		4	-
Dariusz WOSZ (08/06/69) - Hertha BSC Berlin				s83								7	1
Lothar MATTHÄUS (21/03/61) - FC Bayern München					D70	D	D	D46	D	D	D74	136	22
Christian WÖRNS (10/05/72) - Paris Saint-Germain (FRA)					D		D	D	D	D		27	-
Thomas STRUNZ (25/04/68) - FC Bayern München					M86			M	M	M88	M	39	1
Andreas MÖLLER (02/09/67) - Borussia Dortmund					M	M	M					85	30
Alexander ZICKLER (28/02/74) - FC Bayern München					s72	M46	s74					3	-
Dietmar HAMANN (27/08/73) - Newcastle United (ENG)					s86			M	M72	M60	M	17	2
Michael PREETZ (17/08/67) - Hertha BSC Berlin						A	A	s78				3	2
Marco REICH (30/12/77) - 1.FC Kaiserslautern						M79						1	-
Jens LEHMANN (10/11/69) - Borussia Dortmund (GER)						s46			G			4	-
Horst HELDT (09/12/69) - TSV 1860 München									A			1	-
Michael BALLACK (26/09/76) - 1.FC Kaiserslautern										s60		1	-
Mehmet SCHOLL (16/10/70) - FC Bayern München											s46	16	2

Bayern, feeling confident after clinching their Champions' Cup quarter-final place with a 1-1 draw at Old Trafford, showed their opponents who was boss with a convincing 2-0 win. Two more victories followed in the next six days, enabling Bayern to go into the winter break with a huge eight-point lead.

Two months later they returned to action in the same all-conquering form, winning five matches in succession to stretch their lead to 14 points and effectively seal their 15th title. Their eight straight wins had all been achieved without conceding a goal, which enabled goalkeeper Oliver Kahn to set a new Bundesliga record of having his goal unbreached for 735 minutes. There was bad news for Bayern in the seventh of those eight victories when leading goalscorer Giovane Elber sustained a knee ligament injury that was to rule him out for the remainder of the season, but Hitzfeld's response was to switch to a new attacking formation, with the orthodox twin strike-force being replaced by a three-man spearhead of centre-forward Carsten Jancker and two wingers.

It was with this attacking strategy that Bayern went to battle in the latter stages of their European campaign. Having won their Champions' League group - thanks predominantly to home and away wins against Barcelona - they easily accounted for Kaiserslautern, the team they were about to overthrow in the Bundesliga, and then used all their traditional powers of resilience to come back from a 3-1 deficit to oust Dynamo Kiev in the semi-finals. That led to a final showdown with Manchester United, with whom they had already shared two draws in the autumn.

For 84 minutes in the Nou Camp, Bayern appeared to be masters of their own destiny. Following Basler's early free-kick they commanded the game and should have extended their lead in the second half when Jancker and Mehmet Scholl both struck the woodwork. But then came that climax to beat all climaxes

Carsten Jancker of Bayern Munich and Germany.

as United struck twice in stoppage-time to win the Cup and complete an historic 'treble' of their own.

Bayern were struck numb and dumb by what had happened to them. But although they were entitled to shake

TOP SCORERS

23	Michael PREETZ (Hertha BSC Berlin)
19	Ulf KIRSTEN (Bayer 04 Leverkusen)
14	Anthony YEBOAH (Hamburger SV)
	Oliver NEUVILLE (FC Hansa Rostock)
13	Markus BEIERLE (MSV Duisburg)
	Giovane ELBER (FC Bayern München)
	Carsten JANCKER (FC Bayern München)
	Sasa CIRIC (1.FC Nürnberg)
	Andrzej JUSKOWIAK (VfL Wolfsburg)
12	Olaf MARSCHALL (1.FC Kaiserslautern)
	Bernd HOBSCH (TSV 1860 München)

NATIONAL TEAM RESULTS 98/99

02/09/98	Malta	A	Ta' Qali	2-1	Debono (6og), Passlack (72)
05/09/98	Romania	N	Ta' Qali	1-1	Nerlinger (86)
10/10/98	Turkey (ECQ)	A	Bursa	0-1	
14/10/98	Moldova (ECQ)	A	Chisinau	3-1	Kirsten (19, 36), Bierhoff (38)
18/11/98	Holland	H	Gelsenkirchen	1-1	Marschall (52)
06/02/99	United States	A	Jacksonville	0-3	
09/02/99	Colombia	N	Miami	3-3	Preetz (33, 55), Bode (74)
27/03/99	Northern Ireland (ECQ)	A	Belfast	3-0	Bode (11, 43), Hamann (62)
31/03/99	Finland (ECQ)	H	Nuremberg	2-0	Jeremies (31), Neuville (36)
28/04/99	Scotland	H	Bremen	0-1	
04/06/99	Moldova (ECQ)	H	Leverkusen	6-1	Bierhoff (2, 56, 82), Kirsten (27),
					Bode (38), Scholl (71)

DOMESTIC CUP 98/99

FIRST ROUND
Karlsruher SC 3, VfL Wolfsburg 4
1.FC Köln 0, FC Hansa Rostock 1
Fortuna Köln 1, 1.FC Kaiserslautern 3
1.FC Saarbrücken 1, Borussia Dortmund 1
(aet; 1-3 on pens.)
FC St. Pauli (amat.) 0, Bayer 04 Leverkusen 5
FC Hansa Rostock (amat.) 0, MSV Duisburg 3
SV Waldhof Mannheim 1, Borussia Mönchengladbach 5
FC Denzlingen 0, Hamburger SV 3
Chemnitzer FC 1, SC Freiburg 2
Bayer 04 Leverkusen (amat.) 1, SV Werder Bremen 2
(aet)
VfB Lübeck 1, VfB Stuttgart 2
VfB Leipzig 2, TSV 1860 München 4 (aet)
VfB Lichterfelde 0, FC Schalke 04 6
VfL Osnabrück 0, 1.FC Nürnberg 2
Post Süd Regensburg 0, Hertha BSC Berlin 2
FSV Zwickau 2, VfL Bochum 5
Rot-Weiss Erfurt 0, Eintracht Frankfurt 5
LR Ahlen 0, FC Bayern München 5
Tennis Borussia Berlin 1, Hannover 96 0
SV Schalding-Heining 0, SpVgg Unterhaching 1
Sportfreunde Eisbachtal 1, FC Gütersloh 0 (aet)
Kickers Offenbach 0, SV Wattenscheid 09 1
FC Energie Cottbus (amat.) 0, SpVgg Greuter Fürth 1
SF Dorfnerkingen 0, Stuttgarter Kickers 3
SG Hoechst 1, FC Energie Cottbus 2
SV Straelen 4, Fortuna Düsseldorf 7
Sportfreunde Siegen 3, FSV Mainz 05 1 (aet)
FC Carl Zeiss Jena 1, SSV Ulm 46 0
SC 07 Idar-Oberstein 0, Arminia Bielefeld 1
1.FC Magdeburg 1, KFC Uerdingen 05 2
SV Werder Bremen (amat.) 0, Rot-Weiss Oberhausen 1
SV Meppen 0, FC St. Pauli 1

SECOND ROUND
Sportfreunde Eisbachtal 1, Rot-Weiss Oberhausen 4
Tennis Borussia Berlin 4, Stuttgarter Kickers 2
SV Werder Bremen 3, FC Hansa Rostock 2
VfB Stuttgart 3, Eintracht Frankfurt 2
Fortuna Düsseldorf 2, TSV 1860 München 1
Arminia Bielefeld 2, SG Wattenscheid 09 1
Sportfreunde Siegen 1, SC Freiburg 0
SpVgg Greuther Fürth 0, FC Bayern München 0
(aet; 3-4 on pens.)
Borussia Dortmund 1, FC Schalke 04 0 (aet)
VfL Wolfsburg 3, 1.FC Nürnberg 0
KFC Uerdingen 05 1, FC St. Pauli 1
(aet; 4-3 on pens.)
Bayer 04 Leverkusen 1, Hertha BSC Berlin 1
(aet; 2-3 on pens.)
1.FC Kaiserslautern 1, VfL Bochum 1
(aet; 3-4 on pens.)
FC Carl Zeiss Jena 1, MSV Duisburg 2
FC Energie Cottbus 2, Borussia Mönchengladbach 4
Hamburger SV 4, SpVgg Unterhaching 0

THIRD ROUND
MSV Duisburg 2, FC Bayern München 4
VfB Stuttgart 3, Borussia Dortmund 1
VfL Bochum 0, Borussia Mönchengladbach 1
VfL Wolfsburg 3, Arminia Bielefeld 1
Tennis Borussia Berlin 4, Hertha BSC Berlin 2
SV Werder Bremen 3, Fortuna Düsseldorf 2
Rot-Weiss Oberhausen 3, Hamburger SV 3
(aet; 4-3 on pens.)
Sportfreunde Siegen 1, KFC Uerdingen 05 0

QUARTER-FINALS
FC Bayern München 3
(Jancker 26, Basler 71, Zickler 79), VfB Stuttgart 0
Sportfreunde Siegen 1 (Cirba 22),
VfL Wolfsburg 3 (Juskowiak 6, 45, Reyna 63)
Rot-Weiss Oberhausen 2 (Toborg 71, Weber 83),
Borussia Mönchengladbach 0
SV Werder Bremen 2 (Flo 86, Wojtala 108),
Tennis Borussia Berlin 1 (Kovacec 10) (aet)

SEMI-FINALS
VfL Wolfsburg 0, SV Werder Bremen 1 (Bode 52)
Rot-Weiss Oberhausen 1 (Scheinhardt 85p),
FC Bayern München 3
(Jancker 25, Effenberg 42, Linke 79)

FINAL
12/06/99, Berlin
SV WERDER BREMEN 1 Maximov (3)
FC BAYERN MÜNCHEN 1 Jancker (45)
(aet; 5-4 on pens.)
referee - Aust
SV WERDER BREMEN - Rost; Trares, Todt, Wicky, Eilts,
Dabrowski (Bogdanovic 69), Maximov, Wiedener,
Herzog (Wojtala 45), Frings, Bode.
FC BAYERN MÜNCHEN - Kahn; Matthäus, Linke,
Kuffour (Daei 37), Babbel, Jeremies (Fink 57),
Effenberg, Tarnat, Basler, Jancker, Scholl
(Salihamidzic 84).

---

their fists at the heavens, it was not cursed fate alone that had condemned them to their suffering. Complacency, both in terms of Hitzfeld's substitutions (of key men Matthäus and Basler) and the team's lacklustre defending, had also contributed to the shattering of a dream. The look of combined anger and bewilderment on Lothar Matthäus's face as he sat transfixed at the end said it all.

Matthäus was to have a more direct part in the second unhappy ending of Bayern's season when he missed the last, decisive kick in the German Cup final penalty shoot-out against Werder Bremen ten days later. With Bremen keeper Frank Rost having put his team back in front following Stefan Effenberg's miss, Matthäus now needed to score to keep the match alive but his shot was kept out by Rost with a routine dive to his left. And so another trophy slipped out of Bayern's grasp.

For Werder, of course, joy was unrestrained. Their fourth German Cup win had come at the end of a turbulent season, during which they used three coaches and came close to being relegated. Former defender Thomas Schaaf had ultimately turned everything around, however, keeping Werder in the Bundesliga, winning the Cup and also taking them back into Europe.

Germany was allotted four places in the 1999/2000 Champions' Lerague - two of them gaining automatic access, another two requiring pre-qualification. Thus, despite Bayern's overwhelming superiority in the Bundesliga - they eventually won by a record 15-point margin with three games to spare - the subsidiary battle for European places kept interest alive at the top of the table.

Bayer Leverkusen were always the favourites to finish second, and they duly secured their second Champions' League participation in three seasons with a five-match

EUROPEAN CUPS 98/99

CHAMPIONS' CUP
● 1.FC KAISERSLAUTERN
Champions' League
1st match SL BENFICA (POR)
H 1-0   Wagner (41)
Reinke; Ramzy, Roos (Reich 72), Schjønberg, Buck, Ratinho (Riedl 88), Sforza, Wagner, Koch, Marschall, Hristov.

2nd match HJK (FIN)
A 0-0
Reinke; Ramzy, Ojigwe, Samir, Buck (Rische 65), Riedl (Koch 85), Sforza, Wagner, Reich (Rösler 70), Hristov, Marschall.

3rd match PSV (HOL)
A 2-1   Riedle (67), Rische (80)
Reinke; Ramzy, Samir, Koch, Roos, Ballack (Riedl 59), Sforza, Ojigwe, Reich (Hrutka 59), Rösler (Rische 75), Hristov.

4th match PSV (HOL)
H 3-1   Rische (68), Reich (77), Hristov (90)
Reinke; Sforza, Koch (Reich 34), Samir, Buck (Júnior 68), Riedle, Ballack, Roos, Hristov, Marschall, Rösler (Rische 46).

5th match SL BENFICA (POR)
A 1-2   Rische (90)
Reinke; Ramzy, Samir, Roos (Koch 46), Buck (Júnior 46), Riedl, Ballack, Ojigwe (Rische 56), Reich, Marschall, Hristov.

6th match HJK (FIN)
H 5-2   Rösler (43, 61, 80), Marschall (49), Rische (85)
Reinke; Sforza, Samir, Hrutka, Buck, Ramzy, Ballack (Rische 46), Koch (Rösler 38), Reich, Marschall, Hristov.

Quarter-final FC BAYERN MÜNCHEN (GER)
A 0-2
Reinke; Sforza, Ramzy, Hrutka (Koch 69), Buck, Riedl, Ballack, Wagner, Reich, Rische (Samir 73), Rösler.
H 0-4
Reinke; Sforza, Koch, Hrutka, Ratinho (Roos 46), Riedl (Júnior 60), Ballack, Reich, Wagner, Rösler (Ojigwe 77), Rische.

● FC BAYERN MÜNCHEN
Qualifying round OBILIC BEOGRAD (YUG)
H 4-0   Effenberg (59), Elber (63), Zickler (65), Fink (76)
Kahn; Babbel, Matthäus, Linke, Strunz, Effenberg (Lizarazu 77), Fink, Tarnat (Jancker 57), Basler (Zickler 57), Elber, Salihamidzic.
A 1-1   Matthäus (89)
Kahn; Matthäus, Linke, Helmer, Strunz, Jeremies, Effenberg (Fink 82), Tarnat, Salihamidzic, Elber (Daei 65), Jancker (Zickler 65).

Champions' League
1st match BRØNDBY IF (DEN)
A 1-2   Babbel (77)
Kahn; Matthäus, Babbel, Helmer, Strunz (Jeremies 74), Effenberg, Fink, Lizarazu, Basler (Zickler 74), Elber, Jancker (Salihamidzic 78).

2nd match MANCHESTER UNITED (ENG)
H 2-2   Elber (11, 90)
Kahn; Matthäus, Babbel, Linke, Strunz, Jeremies (Fink 62), Effenberg, Lizarazu, Salihamidzic (Göktan 63), Elber, Jancker (Daei 63).

3rd match FC BARCELONA (ESP)
H 1-0   Effenberg (45)
Kahn; Jeremies, Babbel (Linke 80), Kuffour, Lizarazu, Fink, Effenberg, Tarnat, Basler, Elber (Jancker 89), Salihamidzic (Zickler 80).

4th match FC BARCELONA (ESP)
A 2-1   Zickler (47), Salihamidzic (87)
Kahn; Babbel, Matthäus, Kuffour, Lizarazu, Fink, Effenberg, Tarnat (Strunz 74), Basler (Daei 64), Elber, Zickler (Salihamidzic 64).

5th match BRØNDBY IF (DEN)
H 2-0   Jancker (51), Basler (57)
Kahn; Matthäus, Babbel, Kuffour, Strunz, Jeremies (Fink 70), Tarnat, Lizarazu, Basler, Elber (Salihamidzic 84), Zickler (Jancker 46).

6th match MANCHESTER UNITED (ENG)
A 1-1   Salihamidzic (56)
Kahn; Babbel, Matthäus (Linke 61), Kuffour, Strunz, Jeremies, Effenberg, Lizarazu, Zickler (Basler 82), Elber (Jancker 81), Salihamidzic.

Quarter-final 1.FC KAISERSLAUTERN (GER)
H 2-0   Elber (31), Effenberg (35)
Kahn; Matthäus, Babbel, Linke, Strunz (Zickler 76), Jeremies, Lizarazu, Basler (Salihamidzic 83), Elber, Jancker.
A 4-0   Effenberg (9p), Jancker (22, 39), Basler (56)
Kahn; Matthäus, Kuffour, Linke, Babbel, Jeremies (Fink 46), Effenberg (Scholl 46), Lizarazu, Basler (Salihamidzic 73), Jancker, Zickler.

Semi-final DYNAMO KYIV (UKR)
A 3-3   Tarnat (45), Effenberg (78), Jancker (89)
Kahn; Babbel, Matthäus, Kuffour, Strunz, Effenberg, Jeremies, Tarnat, Salihamidzic, Jancker (Daei 90), Scholl (Zickler 71).
H 1-0   Basler (35)
Kahn; Matthäus, Kuffour, Linke, Babbel, Jeremies, Effenberg, Tarnat (Fink 84), Basler, Jancker (Daei 75), Zickler (Salihamidzic 84).

Final MANCHESTER UNITED (ENG)
Barcelona
1-2   Basler (6)
Kahn; Linke, Matthäus (Fink 80), Kuffour, Babbel, Jeremies, Effenberg, Tarnat, Basler (Salihamidzic 89), Jancker, Zickler (Scholl 71).

CUP WINNERS' CUP
● MSV DUISBURG
1st round KRC GENK (BEL)
H 1-1   Wedau (83)
Gill; Emmerling, Wohlert, Hajto, Hoersen (Wolters 45), Tøfting (Wedau 78), Moravcik, Komljenovic, Neun, Spies (Andersen 68), Beierle.
A 0-5
Gill; Emmerling, Wohlert, Hajto, Hoersen, Tøfting (Vana 60), Wedau, Komljenovic (Hirsch 75), Neun, Spies, Beierle.

EUROPEAN CUPS 98/99

UEFA CUP

● BAYER 04 LEVERKUSEN
1st round UDINESE (ITA)

A 1-1   Kirsten (12)
Matysek; Nowotny, Kovac R., Zivkovic, Ramelow, Emerson, Beinlich, Zé Roberto (Pashazadeh 66), Heintze, Kirsten (Kovac N. 90), Meijer (Rink 80).

H 1-0   Beinlich (77)
Matysek; Nowotny, Kovac R. (Kovac N. 56), Happe, Heintze, Zivkovic, Ramelow, Beinlich, Zé Roberto, Kirsten (Rink 82), Meijer (Mamic 85).

2nd round RANGERS (SCO)

H 1-2   Reichenberger (90)
Matysek; Nowotny, Kovac R., Happe (Reichenberger 77), Reeb, Emerson (Heintze 59), Ramelow (Kovac N. 59), Beinlich, Zé Roberto, Rink, Meijer.

A 1-1   Kirsten (79)
Matysek; Nowotny, Kovac R. (Emerson 39), Happe, Reeb, Ramelow, Heintze (Reichenberger 66), Zé Roberto, Beinlich, Kirsten, Meijer (Kovac N. 77).

● FC SCHALKE 04
1st round SLAVIA PRAHA (CZE)

H 1-0   Wilmots (40)
Schober; Müller, De Kock, Eigenrauch, Latal (Van Hoogdalem 70), Kmetsch, Nemec, Van Kerckhoven, Wilmots (Mulder 71), Max, Eijkelkamp (Büskens 81).

A 0-1
(aet; 5-4 on pens.)
Schober; Thon, Eigenrauch, Van Hoogdalem, Latal (Goossens 63), Nemec, Kmetsch (Wilmots 72; Anderbrügge 99), Van Kerckhoven, Büskens, Max, Eijkelkamp.

● SV WERDER BREMEN
1st round SK BRANN (NOR)

A 0-2
Rost; Trares, Flo, Benken (Kunz 46), Wicky (Seidel 83), Eilts, Todt, Maximov, Wiedener, Frings (Flock 65), Bode.

H 4-0   Wicky (33), Wiedener (70), Maximov (107), Flo (110)
(aet)   Rost; Trares, Todt, Wiedener, Roembiak, Wicky, Maximov, Herzog (Flo 102), Eilts, Frings (Kunz 59), Bode.

2nd round OLYMPIQUE MARSEILLE (FRA)

H 1-1   Herzog (69)
Rost; Trares, Todt, Wicky, Flock, Eilts, Roembiak, Herzog, Bode, Frings (Kunz 74), Flo (Maximov 60).

A 2-3   Eilts (47), Herzog (83)
Brasas; Trares (Wicky 60), Roembiak, Benken, Skrypnyk, Maximov, Eilts, Wiedener (Herzog 46), Bode, Seidel (Frings 46), Flo.

● VFB STUTTGART
1st round FEYENOORD (HOL)

H 1-3   Bobic (31)
Wohlfahrt; Thiam, Verlaat, Berthold, Djordjevic, Soldo (Spanring 46), Keller, Stojkovski (Zeyer 24), Balakov, Ristic, Bobic (Akpoborie 46).

A 3-0   Balakov (34), Djordjevic (69), Bobic (90)
Ziegler; Verlaat, Berthold, Soldo, Keller, Djordjevic, Lisztes, Zeyer (Blessin 77), Balakov, Stojkovski (Ristic 78), Bobic.

2nd round CLUB BRUGGE KV (BEL)

H 1-1   Akpoborie (8)
Ziegler; Keller, Verlaat, Berthold, Lisztes (Rost 46), Soldo, Thiam, Poschner (Zeyer 76), Balakov, Bobic, Akpoborie.

A 2-3   Verlaat (76), Bobic (109)
(aet)   Ziegler; Thiam, Verlaat, Berthold, Lisztes (Ristic 59), Schneider (Zeyer 32), Balakov, Keller, Djordjevic, Akpoborie (Spanring 79), Bobic.

---

winning run in April, during which veteran striker Ulf Kirsten showed a resounding return to form, brilliantly supported by the immensely skilful Brazilian midfielder Zé Roberto and his compatriot Emerson. Leverkusen boss Christoph Daum showed a touch too much arrogance when he predicted mid-season that his team would actually beat Bayern to the title, but there was no doubting his skill and wisdom as a coach. He, too, like Hitzfeld at Bayern, introduced an exciting new three-pronged attacking formation, and at times he also dispensed with the traditional libero. The results of his experiments spoke for themselves.

Hertha BSC took third place, enabling the city of Berlin to figure prominently on the footballing map of Europe for the first time in many years. Hertha's chief asset was centre-forward Michael Preetz, whose 23 goals earned him the Bundesliga top-scorer title. In a team of many

foreigners, eccentric Hungarian goalkeeper Gábor Király was the most impressive import. Coach Jürgen Röber, who had been close to the sack at the start of the previous season, showed the value of perseverance, and the Berliners came to the Olympic stadium in droves to watch his well-groomed, stylish team.

While Hertha drew the three biggest Bundesliga crowds of the season - 76,000 sell-outs for the matches against Bayern, Hansa Rostock and Hamburg - the club with the largest average gate was Borussia Dortmund, with 65,735. That was just over twice the league average and was made possible by the expansion of the Westfalenstadion - now even more intimidating than ever with its giant steeply-banked stands.

On the field Dortmund often flattered to deceive under their new, young homegrown coach Michael Skibbe. There was also a major problem with new signing Thomas

PLAYERS OF THE SEASON

★ SUPERSTAR PROFILE
STEFAN EFFENBERG

No sooner had Stefan Effenberg returned from his enforced four-year exile from the German national team than he decided that he didn't really want to be part of the scene again after all. It was probably a wise move. With the paucity of talent coming through at international level in Germany these days, the experienced midfielder would probably have had his hands full trying to make excuses for the relative inferiority of those around him. So, instead of relaunching his international career, the one-time 'bad boy' of German football decided to concentrate full-time on becoming the leader of an exciting new Bayern Munich side. It was second time around at Bayern for the blond schemer. An expensive arrival from Borussia Mönchengladbach (the club that had previously sold him to Bayern in 1990), he took no time at all to impose himself as the team's chief midfield orchestrator. A commanding presence in the heart of the action, his supply of quality passes was matched by the number of rasping shots he unleashed on goal. He scored eight goals in the Bundesliga and five more in the Champions' League, including a smartly-taken winner at home to Barcelona and an outrageously ambitious free-kick away to Dynamo Kiev. Despite the ill feeling he created with his 'middle finger'

gesture to German fans at the 1994 World Cup, Effenberg has always been considered a class act by his fellow countrymen. Never, however, have they held him in such high regard as now.

Hässler, and away from their fortress the yellow-and-blacks could only manage two victories. Even so, they had their moments, notably in halting Bayern's two long winning streaks and in taking maximum points from their last two matches to qualify as Germany's fourth representative in the Champions' League.

Defending champions Kaiserslautern, who had looked odds-on to return to Europe's blue riband event, were elbowed into a UEFA Cup spot on goal difference. They only had themselves to blame. Coach 'King Otto' Rehhagel blundered in the transfer market, failing adequately to replace Czechs Kadlec and Kuka, and he also made a costly error in a Bundesliga match at home to Bochum, when he mistakenly fielded four non-EC players. Kaiserslautern's greatest sin, however, was to lose their final match 5-1 in Frankfurt.

That was a game with huge significance not just for Europe but also for the battle against relegation. At the start of the final day no fewer than five clubs were still in danger of joining already relegated Borussia

Mönchengladbach (after 34 years in the top flight) and VfL Bochum. But, incredibly, the team that started out as the most likely to survive, Nuremberg, ended up by going down. Their 1-2 home defeat by Freiburg would not have been fatal but for Frankfurt's extraordinary second-half goal spree against Kaiserslautern. The match in the Waldstadion was goalless at half-time, but Frankfurt, who had seemed dead and buried a few weeks earlier, suddenly blitzed Kaiserslautern with a barrage of goals. And they needed every one of them, because in the final calculations they finished above Nuremberg only by having scored more goals (the goal difference of the two clubs was identical). The decisive strike which kept Frankfurt up came in the final minute, from Norwegian forward Jan Åge Fjørtoft. The contrast in the emotions of the Frankfurt and Nuremberg fans at the final whistle could hardly have been greater.

The loss of Nuremberg, Bochum and 'Gladbach means that the crowd figures in the 1999/2000 Bundesliga are almost certain to fall, because those three well-supported

PLAYERS OF THE SEASON

MICHAEL PREETZ

For most of his career Michael Preetz has been seen as an unexceptional centre-forward of little more than average ability and ambition. But since joining Hertha BSC in 1996 he has enjoyed a colossal rise to prominence. In his first season he helped Hertha to gain promotion to the Bundesliga. In his second he scored 14 goals to become the club's top scorer. And in his third he improved his tally to 23 goals to become the leading marksman in the entire Bundesliga. He also won his first international caps, at the age of 31, and scored twice on only his second appearance, in a 3-3 draw against Colombia. A deputy for skipper Oliver Bierhoff that day, he seems likely to fulfil that role for the foreseeable future. Tall and strapping, his great strength is his ability in the air, but he is also sharp on the ground and rarely misses a chance when through on goal on his favoured left foot.

OLIVER NEUVILLE

It might be seen by outsiders as an act of desperation when Germany start looking beyond their borders to find players for the national team. In his first post-World Cup squad Berti Vogts selected a Brazilian (Paulo Rink) and a Turk (Mustafa Dogan) as well as a Swiss. Only the latter, 26-year-old Oliver Neuville (below), managed to survive into the Erich Ribbeck régime, but although his eligibility was questionable - he is a French-speaker from Locarno - there were no quibbles about his ability. The elf-like winger

earned his place in the *Nationalmannschaft* with several stunning displays for Hansa Rostock. The north-easterners would not have extended their Bundesliga stay to a fifth successive season had it not been for their pocket dynamo, who contributed 14 goals, including one in the vital last-day win at Bochum, where his performance was truly heroic. It was to be his last appearance for Rostock as in the summer he transferred to Champions' League qualifiers Bayer Leverkusen.

CARSTEN JANCKER

Bayern Munich have always loved their big, battling centre-forwards. Their latest offering is Carsten Jancker, as strong and as courageous as they come. He says his role model is Marco van Basten but the styles are rather different. Whereas the Dutchman was all refined technique and spectacular goals, Jancker is raw power and blood and thunder. He likes to go in where it hurts and make things happen in the penalty box through his sheer physical presence. That was a common occurrence during the 1998/99 season, in which he scored 13 Bundesliga goals, among them the one which sealed the title against Hertha BSC, and three more in Europe, including the all-important late equaliser in Kiev. A native of East Germany, Jancker is one of many ex-GDR citizens regularly performing for the German national team. Kirsten, Marschall, Heinrich, Jeremies, Rehmer - the list is long, and growing...

HANS-JÖRG BUTT

Ghanaian striker Tony Yeboah was Hamburg's leading scorer in 1998/99 with 14 goals, but in joint-second place, with half of that total, was the team's...goalkeeper. 25-year-old Hans-Jörg Butt was nominated as the team's penalty-taker at the start of the season. By the end of it he had converted seven spot-kicks, including two in one game, at home to Stuttgart - a Bundesliga record. When asked to perform his regular duties at the other end the youngster also performed with supreme confidence, showing strong technical ability as well as a keen awareness to come out of his area and use his feet when necessary. With both Oliver Kahn and Jens Lehmann aged around the 30 mark, the opportunity is there for a young 'keeper to come in and impress national boss Erich Ribbeck. After his outstanding 1998/99 season, Butt heads the queue.

clubs were replaced by yo-yo club Arminia Bielefeld and two top-flight novices, Unterhaching and Ulm.

Ulm were the real surprise package, especially as they had to cede their coach Ralf Rangnick to big-city neighbours Stuttgart before the season was out. He was the fourth coach of the struggling Swabian side, who had rather hastily dismissed Jogi Löw at the end of the previous season. Rangnick did save Stuttgart from relegation, but only on the final day of a season they will want to forget in a hurry. Schalke and 1860 Munich were among the other underachievers of the season, with the latter picking up a mere ten points in the second half of the campaign having been up at the top of the table challenging ground-sharers Bayern during the autumn.

Wolfsburg and MSV Duisburg did things the other way round. Wolfsburg were bottom after seven matches but they jetted up the table in double-quick time and relied on outstanding home form during the spring to qualify for Europe for the first time. Duisburg were able only to join Hamburg in the InterToto, but the pre-season relegation candidates had the third-best record in the league during the second half of the season (after Bayern and Hertha).

There was also a spring revival of sorts for the German national team after a wretched autumn and winter, during which the fears of imminent doom and gloom expressed in the immediate wake of the World Cup came all too closely into focus. Initially, Berti Vogts stayed on to take charge of a completely remodelled team. But after two awful displays in a Malta mini-tournament, with only the return of long-time absentee Stefan Effenberg providing any spark, the man who had held the job of *Bundestrainer* for eight years decided to bow to press criticism and call it quits.

The DFB had to act quickly to find a replacement because the Euro 2000 qualifying campaign was just around the corner. Needing to find someone who was immediately available, they went for ex-Bayer Leverkusen and Bayern Munich boss 'Sir' Erich Ribbeck, with former international sweeper Uli Stielike as his second-in-command.

The pair could not have got off to a worse start. Although the team did not play badly against Turkey in the first match of their European Championship defence, they lost it, 1-0. A few days later they were also a goal down to lightweights Moldova, but, to much relief all round, they came back to win 3-1. Worse, much worse, was to follow when a rather ill-conceived winter-sun getaway to Florida began with a deeply embarrassing 3-0 defeat by the United States.

Ribbeck offered his resignation when the team returned but it was not accepted, so he stayed in place... and proceeded to take the team to three convincing victories in their next three Euro 2000 qualifiers against Northern

---

INTERNATIONAL HONOURS

World Cup Finals appearances: 1934 (3rd), 1938, 1954 (Winners), 1958 (4th), 1962 (qtr-finals), 1966 (runners-up), 1970 (3rd), 1974 (Winners), 1978 (2nd phase), 1982 (runners-up), 1986 (runners-up), 1990 (Winners), 1994 (qtr-finals), 1998 (qtr-finals)

European Championship appearances: 1972 (Winners), 1976 (runners-up), 1980 (Winners), 1984, 1988 (semi-finals), 1992 (runners-up), 1996 (Winners)

European Club Competitions

Champions' Cup	FC Bayern München (1974, 1975, 1976)
	Hamburger SV (1983)
	Borussia Dortmund (1997)
Cup-winners' Cup	Borussia Dortmund (1966)
	FC Bayern München (1967)
	Hamburger SV (1977)
	SV Werder Bremen (1992)
UEFA Cup	Borussia Mönchengladbach (1975, 1979)
	Eintracht Frankfurt (1980)
	Bayer 04 Leverkusen (1988)
	FC Bayern München (1996)
	FC Schalke 04 (1997)
World Club Cup	FC Bayern München (1976)
	Borussia Dortmund (1997)

Ireland (3-0), Finland (2-0) and Moldova (6-1). Granted, the opposition was weak, but the points were certainly welcome, and by the end of the season it looked as if, despite everything, Germany - the new, inferior Germany - would still be there in neighbouring Belgium and Holland to defend their European title in the summer of 2000. Whether they would be hanging around for long in the finals, however, was another matter entirely...

Oliver Bierhoff is tackled by Northern Ireland's Kevin Horlock during the Euro 2000 qualifier in Belfast.

BAYER 04 LEVERKUSEN

CLUB DIRECTORY

TSV Bayer 04 Leverkusen
Postfach 120140
51349 Leverkusen
tel - (0214) 86600
fax - (0214) 62709
Year of Formation - 1904
President - Werner Wenning
Manager - Reiner Calmund
Secretary - Kuno Wack
Coach - Christoph Daum
Stadium - BayArena (25,050)

MAJOR HONOURS
Domestic Cup - (1) 1993.
UEFA Cup - (1) 1988.

APPEARANCES 98/99

		P	Ap	(s)	Gls
Stefan BEINLICH	M	23			6
Francis da Rosa EMERSON (BRA)	M	26	(2)		5
Markus HAPPE	D	20	(4)		
Jan HEINTZE (DEN)	M	19	(7)		1
Frankie HEJDUK (USA)	M	10			1
Ulf KIRSTEN	A	31			19
Nico KOVAC (CRO)	M	11	(16)		4
Robert KOVAC (CRO)	D	31			
Adam LEDWON (POL)	M	2	(1)		
Hans-Peter LEHNHOFF	M	2	(14)		
Dirk LOTTNER	D	3			
Zoran MAMIC (CRO)	D	1	(7)		
Adam MATYSEK (POL)	G	34			
Erik MEIJER (HOL)	A	14	(12)		4
Jens NOWOTNY	D	33			1
Carsten RAMELOW	M	27			4
Jörg REEB	M	23	(1)		1
Thomas REICHENBERGER	A	2	(18)		3
Paulo Roberto RINK	A	12	(6)		5
ZÉ ROBERTO (BRA)	M	31	(1)		4
Boris ZIVKOVIC (CRO)	D	19	(3)		2

LEAGUE RESULTS 1998/99

15/08/98	FC Hansa Rostock	H	3-1	Beinlich 2, Reeb
22/08/98	SC Freiburg	A	1-1	Beinlich
09/09/98	Hamburger SV	H	1-2	Meijer
12/09/98	SV Werder Bremen	A	2-2	Kirsten (p), Rink
19/09/98	Borussia Dortmund	H	3-1	Kovac N., og (Feiersinger),
				Meijer
26/09/98	FC Schalke 04	A	1-0	Kirsten
03/10/98	1.FC Kaiserslautern	H	2-2	Zé Roberto, Rink
17/10/98	Eintracht Frankfurt	A	3-2	Kirsten, Kovac N., Reichenberger
25/10/98	TSV 1860 München	H	1-1	Kirsten (p)
30/10/98	Borussia Mönchengladbach	A	8-2	Kirsten 3 (1p), Zé Roberto,
				Nowotny, Reichenberger 2,
				Kovac N.
08/11/98	VfB Stuttgart	H	0-0	
11/11/98	Hertha BSC Berlin	A	1-0	Meijer
14/11/98	1.FC Nürnberg	H	3-0	Meijer, Emerson, Ramelow
21/11/98	VfL Bochum	A	5-1	Beinlich, Zivkovic, Rink, Heintze,
				Kovac N.
28/11/98	MSV Duisburg	H	2-0	Rink, Emerson
05/12/98	VfL Wolfsburg	H	3-0	Kirsten 2, Zé Roberto
13/12/98	FC Bayern München	A	0-2	
19/12/98	FC Hansa Rostock	A	1-1	Zivkovic
20/02/99	SC Freiburg	H	1-1	Rink
27/02/99	Hamburger SV	A	0-0	
07/03/99	SV Werder Bremen	H	2-0	Kirsten, Beinlich
12/03/99	Borussia Dortmund	A	0-1	
19/03/99	FC Schalke 04	H	1-1	Beinlich
04/04/99	1.FC Kaiserslautern	A	1-0	Kirsten
10/04/99	Eintracht Frankfurt	H	2-1	Kirsten 2
14/04/99	TSV 1860 München	A	2-0	Emerson, Zé Roberto
17/04/99	Borussia Mönchengladbach	H	4-1	Kirsten 3, Ramelow
23/04/99	VfB Stuttgart	A	1-0	Kirsten
01/05/99	Hertha BSC Berlin	H	2-2	Ramelow, Emerson
05/05/99	1.FC Nürnberg	A	2-2	Ramelow, Emerson
08/05/99	VfL Bochum	H	2-0	Kirsten, Hejduk
15/05/99	MSV Duisburg	A	0-0	
22/05/99	VfL Wolfsburg	A	0-1	
29/05/99	Bayer 04 Leverkusen	H	1-2	Kirsten

FC BAYERN MÜNCHEN

CLUB DIRECTORY

FC Bayern München
Postfach 90 04 51
81504 München
tel - (089) 699310
fax - (089) 644165
Year of Formation - 1900
President - Franz Beckenbauer
Manager - Uli Hoeness
Secretary - Karl Hopfner
Coach - Ottmar Hitzfeld
Stadium - Olympiastadion (69,000)

MAJOR HONOURS
League Championship - (15) 1932, 1969, 1972,
1973, 1974, 1980, 1981, 1985, 1986, 1987,
1989, 1990, 1994, 1997, 1999.
Domestic Cup - (9) 1957, 1966, 1967, 1969,
1971, 1982, 1984, 1986, 1998.
European Champions' Cup - (3) 1974, 1975, 1976.
European Cup-winners' Cup - (1) 1967.
UEFA Cup - (1) 1996.
World Club Cup - (1) 1976.

APPEARANCES 98/99

		P	Ap	(s)	Gls
Markus BABBEL	D		27		1
Mario BASLER	M		25	(2)	5
Alexander BUGERA	M			(2)	
Ali DAEI (IRN)	A		12	(11)	6
Bernd DREHER	G		2	(2)	
Stefan EFFENBERG	M		31		8
Giovane ELBER (BRA)	A		20	(1)	13
Thorsten FINK	M		18	(10)	
Berkant GÖKTAN (TUR)	A			(1)	
Thomas HELMER	D		17	(4)	2
Carsten JANCKER	A		19	(7)	13
David JAROLIM (CZE)	M			(1)	
Jens JEREMIES	M		25	(5)	1
Nils-Eric JOHANSSON (SWE)	M			(2)	
Oliver KAHN	G		30		
Samuel Osei KUFFOUR (GHA)	D		12	(3)	
Thomas LINKE	D		20	(7)	1
Bixente LIZARAZU (FRA)	M		18	(1)	2
Lothar MATTHÄUS	D		24	(1)	1
Hasan SALIHAMIDZIC (BOS)	M		16	(14)	3
Sven SCHEUER	G		2	(1)	
Mehmet SCHOLL	M		7	(6)	4
Thomas STRUNZ	M		22	(2)	4
Michael TARNAT	M		15	(5)	1
Alexander ZICKLER	A		12	(14)	7

LEAGUE RESULTS 1998/99

15/08/98	VfL Wolfsburg	A	1-0	Elber
22/08/98	MSV Duisburg	H	3-1	Jancker, Strunz, Effenberg (p)
09/09/98	FC Hansa Rostock	H	6-1	Effenberg (p), Helmer, Lizarazu, Zickler 2, Jancker
12/09/98	SC Freiburg	A	2-0	Elber, Strunz
20/09/98	Hamburger SV	H	5-3	Daei 2, Effenberg 2 (1p), Elber
26/09/98	SV Werder Bremen	A	1-0	Elber
05/10/98	Borussia Dortmund	H	2-2	Elber, Jancker
17/10/98	FC Schalke 04	A	3-1	og (Eigenrauch), Basler, Jancker
24/10/98	1.FC Kaiserslautern	H	4-0	Basler, Daei, Elber 2
01/11/98	Eintracht Frankfurt	A	0-1	
07/11/98	TSV 1860 München	H	3-1	Jeremies, Zickler, Linke
14/11/98	VfB Stuttgart	H	2-0	Effenberg, Daei
21/11/98	Hertha BSC Berlin	A	0-1	
28/11/98	1.FC Nürnberg	H	2-0	Elber, Lizarazu
04/12/98	VfL Bochum	A	2-2	Jancker, Strunz (p)
13/12/98	Bayer 04 Leverkusen	H	2-0	Tarnat, Elber
16/12/98	Borussia Mönchengladbach	A	2-0	Effenberg 2 (1p)
20/12/98	VfL Wolfsburg	H	3-0	Jancker, Elber, Salihamidzic (p)
20/02/99	MSV Duisburg	A	3-0	Jancker, Effenberg, Helmer
28/02/99	FC Hansa Rostock	A	4-0	Elber 2, Jancker, Matthäus
06/03/99	SC Freiburg	H	2-0	og (Schwinkendorf), Daei
13/03/99	Hamburger SV	A	2-0	og (Butt), Salihamidzic
20/03/99	SV Werder Bremen	H	1-0	Jancker
04/04/99	Borussia Dortmund	A	2-2	Zickler, Jancker
10/04/99	FC Schalke 04	H	1-1	Zickler
13/04/99	1.FC Kaiserslautern	A	1-2	Daei
16/04/99	Eintracht Frankfurt	H	3-1	Zickler, Strunz, og (Bindewald)
25/04/99	TSV 1860 München	A	1-1	Babbel
01/05/99	Borussia Mönchengladbach	H	4-2	Basler, Zickler 2, Scholl
04/05/99	VfB Stuttgart	A	2-0	Scholl, Jancker
09/05/99	Hertha BSC Berlin	H	1-1	Jancker
15/05/99	1.FC Nürnberg	A	0-2	
22/05/99	VfL Bochum	H	4-2	Basler, Jancker, Scholl, Salihamidzic
29/05/99	Bayer 04 Leverkusen	A	2-1	Basler, Scholl

VFL BOCHUM

CLUB DIRECTORY

VfL Bochum
Ruhrstadion
Castroper Strasse 145
44728 Bochum
tel - (0234) 951848
fax - (0234) 951895
Year of Formation - 1848
President - Werner Altegoer
Manager - Klaus Hilpert
Coach - Klaus Toppmöller
(99/00 - Ernst Middendorp)
Stadium - Ruhrstadion (36,344)

APPEARANCES 98/99

	P	Ap	(s)	Gls
Yildiray BASTÜRK (TUR)	M	20	(8)	1
Michael BEMBEN	D	4	(4)	
Delron BUCKLEY (SAF)	A	27	(6)	5
Mirko DICKHAUT	D	3		
Zdravko DRINCIC (CRO)	A	14	(2)	1
Emir DZAFIC (CRO)	A	1	(5)	1
Thomas ERNST	G	32		
Frank FAHRENHORST	D	16	(2)	1
Maurizio GAUDINO	M	14	(6)	2
Nesat GÜLÜNOGLU (TUR)	M		(12)	
Norbert HOFMANN	M	24	(3)	1
Viorel ION (ROM)	M	11	(1)	1
Björn JOPPE	M	2	(1)	
Maik KISCHKO	G	2		
Torsten KRACHT	D	26		1
Stefan KUNTZ	A	14	(6)	6
Mehdi MAHDAVIKIA (TUR)	M	7	(5)	3
Jan MAJEWSKI	M		(1)	
Kai MICHALKE	A	10	(2)	1
Peter PESCHEL	M	6	(10)	2
Alen PETROVIC (CRO)	D	3	(4)	
Thomas REIS	M	21	(4)	5
Sebastian SCHINDZIELORZ	M	26	(2)	3
Olaf SCHREIBER	M	8	(2)	
Thomas STICKROTH	M	1	(2)	
Axel SUNDERMANN	D	31		1
Samir TOPLAK (CRO)	D	14	(9)	1
Tomasz WALDOCH (POL)	D	27		
Andreas ZEYER	M	10	(1)	3

LEAGUE RESULTS 1998/99

Date	Opponent		Score	Scorers
15/08/98	SC Freiburg	H	1-2	Kuntz
21/08/98	Hamburger SV	A	0-1	
08/09/98	SV Werder Bremen	H	2-0	Fahrenhorst, Toplak
13/09/98	Borussia Dortmund	A	1-0	Buckley
19/09/98	FC Schalke 04	H	1-2	Kracht
26/09/98	1.FC Kaiserslautern	A	3-2	Reis, Buckley, Dzafic
03/10/98	Eintracht Frankfurt	H	0-0	
16/10/98	TSV 1860 München	A	1-2	Schindzielorz
24/10/98	Borussia Mönchengladbach	H	2-1	Reis, Schindzielorz
01/11/98	VfB Stuttgart	A	2-4	Gaudino, Reis
07/11/98	Hertha BSC Berlin	H	2-0	Sundermann, Drincic
11/11/98	1.FC Nürnberg	A	2-2	Kuntz 2 (2p)
14/11/98	MSV Duisburg	A	0-2	
21/11/98	Bayer 04 Leverkusen	H	1-5	Reis
28/11/98	VfL Wolfsburg	A	1-4	Ion
04/12/98	FC Bayern München	H	2-2	Hofmann, Kuntz (p)
12/12/98	FC Hansa Rostock	A	0-3	
18/12/98	SC Freiburg	A	1-1	Schindzielorz
26/02/99	SV Werder Bremen	A	1-1	Kuntz
06/03/99	Borussia Dortmund	H	0-1	
13/03/99	FC Schalke 04	A	2-2	Reis (p), Bastürk
16/03/99	Hamburger SV	H	2-0	og (Fischer), Mahdavikia
20/03/99	1.FC Kaiserslautern	H	1-2	Zeyer
04/04/99	Eintracht Frankfurt	A	0-1	
11/04/99	TSV 1860 München	H	2-0	Buckley, Zeyer
14/04/99	Borussia Mönchengladbach	A	2-2	Peschel, Mahdavikia
17/04/99	VfB Stuttgart	H	3-3	Mahdavikia (p), Michalke, Buckley
24/04/99	Hertha BSC Berlin	A	1-4	Buckley
30/04/99	1.FC Nürnberg	H	0-3	
05/05/99	MSV Duisburg	H	0-2	
08/05/99	Bayer 04 Leverkusen	A	0-2	
15/05/99	VfL Wolfsburg	H	0-2	
22/05/99	FC Bayern München	A	2-4	Gaudino, Zeyer
29/05/99	FC Hansa Rostock	H	2-3	Kuntz, Peschel

BORUSSIA DORTMUND

CLUB DIRECTORY

BV 09 Borussia Dortmund
Westfalenstadion
Strobelallee, Postfach 100509
44005 Dortmund
tel - (0231) 90200
fax - (0231) 9020105
Year of Formation - 1909
President - Dr. Gerd Niebaum
Manager - Michael Meier
Secretary - Josef Schneck
Coach - Michael Skibbe
Stadium - Westfalenstadion (68,600)

MAJOR HONOURS
League Championship - (5)
1956, 1957, 1963, 1995, 1996.
Domestic Cup - (2) 1965, 1989.
European Champions' Cup - (1) 1997.
European Cup-winners' Cup - (1) 1966.
World Club Cup - (1) 1997.

APPEARANCES 98/99

		P	Ap	(s)	Gls
Sergej BARBAREZ (BOS)	M	16	(6)	4
Karsten BAUMANN	D	20	(10)	
Manfred BINZ	D	1		
Vladimir BUT (RUS)	M	10	(13)	3
Stéphane CHAPUISAT (SUI)	A	18	(12)	8
Wolfgang DE BEER	G	3		
DEDÉ (BRA)	M	27	(2)	
Wolfgang FEIERSINGER (AUT)	D	9	(2)	
Steffen FREUND	M	12	(1)	
Thomas HÄSSLER	M	8	(10)	2
Thomas HENGEN	M	6	(7)	
Heiko HERRLICH	A	15	(6)	6
JÚLIO CÉSAR (BRA)	D	4	(1)	
Stefan KLOS	G	18		
Jürgen KOHLER	D	29		2
Jens LEHMANN	G	13		
Andreas MÖLLER	M	28	(2)	7
Christian NERLINGER	M	21	(2)	1
Alfred NIJHUIS (HOL)	D	23	(4)	4
Knut REINHARDT	M	4		
Stefan REUTER	M	25		
Lars RICKEN	M	26	(2)	5
Bachirou SALOU (TOG)	A	21	(4)	5
Miroslav STEVIC (YUG)	M	14		1
Ibrahim TANKO (GHA)	A	2	(5)	
Christian TIMM	M	1	(4)	

LEAGUE RESULTS 1998/99

14/08/98	VfB Stuttgart	A	1-2	Salou
22/08/98	Hertha BSC Berlin	H	3-0	Barbarez 2, Salou
09/09/98	1.FC Nürnberg	A	0-0	
13/09/98	VfL Bochum	H	0-1	
19/09/98	Bayer 04 Leverkusen	A	1-3	Möller
26/09/98	VfL Wolfsburg	H	2-1	Ricken, Hässler (p)
05/10/98	FC Bayern München	A	2-2	Chapuisat, Nerlinger
18/10/98	FC Hansa Rostock	H	2-0	Möller, Barbarez
23/10/98	SC Freiburg	A	2-2	Chapuisat, Nijhuis
06/11/98	SV Werder Bremen	A	1-1	Ricken
11/11/98	MSV Duisburg	H	2-0	Ricken, Chapuisat
14/11/98	FC Schalke 04	H	3-0	Nijhuis, Hässler (p), Möller
21/11/98	1.FC Kaiserslautern	A	0-1	
24/11/98	Hamburger SV	H	2-1	Salou, Kohler
27/11/98	Eintracht Frankfurt	H	3-1	Chapuisat, Salou, Möller
06/12/98	TSV 1860 München	A	0-2	
11/12/98	Borussia Mönchengladbach	H	1-1	But
18/12/98	VfB Stuttgart	H	3-0	Herrlich, But, Salou
21/02/99	Hertha BSC Berlin	A	0-3	
27/02/99	1.FC Nürnberg	H	3-0	Möller, Chapuisat, But
06/03/99	VfL Bochum	A	1-0	Ricken
12/03/99	Bayer 04 Leverkusen	H	1-0	Herrlich
19/03/99	VfL Wolfsburg	A	0-0	
04/04/99	FC Bayern München	H	2-2	Herrlich 2
10/04/99	FC Hansa Rostock	A	0-2	
14/04/99	SC Freiburg	H	2-1	Barbarez, Ricken
18/04/99	Hamburger SV	A	0-0	
23/04/99	SV Werder Bremen	H	2-1	Herrlich, Möller
02/05/99	MSV Duisburg	A	2-3	Stevic (p), Nijhuis
05/05/99	FC Schalke 04	A	1-1	Nijhuis
08/05/99	1.FC Kaiserslautern	H	1-0	Chapuisat
15/05/99	Eintracht Frankfurt	A	0-2	
22/05/99	TSV 1860 München	H	3-1	Möller, Kohler, Herrlich
29/05/99	Borussia Mönchengladbach	A	2-0	Chapuisat 2

BORUSSIA MÖNCHENGLADBACH

CLUB DIRECTORY

VfL 1900 Borussia Mönchengladbach
Bökelstrasse 165
41063 Mönchengladbach
tel - (02161) 92930
fax - (02161) 929319
Year of Formation - 1900
President - Wilfried Jacobs
Coach - Friedel Rausch; Rainer Bonhof
Stadium - Bökelberg (34,500)

MAJOR HONOURS
League Championship - (5)
1970, 1971, 1975, 1976, 1977.
Domestic Cup - (3) 1960, 1973, 1995.
UEFA Cup - (2) 1975, 1979.

APPEARANCES 98/99

		P	Ap	(s)	Gls
Thorsten ALBUSTIN	G	2			
Chrissoualantis ANAGNOSTOU (GRE)	M	1	(5)		
Patrik ANDERSSON (SWE)	D	28			
Sladjan ASANIN (CRO)	D	30	(1)	3	
Augusto da Silva CHIQUINHO (BRA)	M	1	(6)	1	
Sebastian DEISLER	M	15	(2)	1	
Max EBERL	D	15			
Thomas EICHIN	D	4			
Robert ENKE	G	32			
Markus FELDHOFF	A	7	(11)	1	
Michael FRONTZECK	M	15		1	
Berkant GÖKTAN (TUR)	A	2	(3)		
Matthias HAGNER	M	9	(9)	2	
Markus HAUSWEILER	M	14	(2)	2	
Marcel KETELAER	M	17	(9)	1	
Michael KLINKERT	D	22	(2)	3	
Stephan PASSLACK	D	10	(4)	1	
Jörgen PETTERSSON (SWE)	A	24	(3)	6	
Karlheinz PFLIPSEN	M	17	(4)	3	
Anton POLSTER (AUT)	A	24	(7)	11	
Markus REITER	D	2	(8)		
Martin SCHNEIDER	M	21	(4)		
Zeljko SOPIC (CRO)	M	21	(2)	2	
Marco VILLA	A	1	(6)	1	
Marcel WITECZEK	M	29	(2)	2	
Peter WYNHOFF	M	11	(1)		

LEAGUE RESULTS 1998/99

15/08/98	FC Schalke 04	H	3-0	Polster, Pettersson, Hagner
23/08/98	1.FC Kaiserslautern	A	1-2	Asanin
08/09/98	Eintracht Frankfurt	H	1-1	Pettersson
11/09/98	TSV 1860 München	A	1-3	Klinkert
20/09/98	MSV Duisburg	A	2-2	Polster (p), Villa
26/09/98	VfB Stuttgart	H	2-3	Polster 2 (1p)
02/10/98	Hertha BSC Berlin	A	1-4	Polster
17/10/98	1.FC Nürnberg	H	0-2	
24/10/98	VfL Bochum	A	1-2	Pflipsen
30/10/98	Bayer 04 Leverkusen	H	2-8	Polster, Chiquinho
07/11/98	VfL Wolfsburg	A	1-7	Polster
13/11/98	FC Hansa Rostock	A	1-1	Pflipsen
22/11/98	SC Freiburg	H	3-1	Klinkert, Hagner, Polster
28/11/98	Hamburger SV	A	0-3	
08/12/98	SV Werder Bremen	H	0-1	
11/12/98	Borussia Dortmund	A	1-1	Polster
16/12/98	FC Bayern München	H	0-2	
19/12/98	FC Schalke 04	A	0-1	
20/02/99	1.FC Kaiserslautern	H	0-2	
27/02/99	Eintracht Frankfurt	A	0-0	
06/03/99	TSV 1860 München	H	2-0	Klinkert, Deisler
13/03/99	MSV Duisburg	H	0-2	
20/03/99	VfB Stuttgart	A	2-2	Frontzeck, Ketelaer
04/04/99	Hertha BSC Berlin	H	2-4	Witeczek 2
10/04/99	1.FC Nürnberg	A	0-2	
14/04/99	VfL Bochum	H	2-2	Asanin, Passlack
17/04/99	Bayer 04 Leverkusen	A	1-4	Pettersson
24/04/99	VfL Wolfsburg	H	5-2	Sopic, Pettersson 2, Polster, Pflipsen
01/05/99	FC Bayern München	A	2-4	Polster (p), Pettersson
04/05/99	FC Hansa Rostock	H	1-1	Feldhoff
08/05/99	SC Freiburg	A	1-2	Hausweiler
14/05/99	Hamburger SV	H	2-2	Sopic, Hausweiler
22/05/99	SV Werder Bremen	A	1-4	Asanin
29/05/99	Borussia Dortmund	H	0-2	

MSV DUISBURG

CLUB DIRECTORY

MSV Duisburg
Postfach 120438
47124 Duisburg
tel - (0203) 429240
fax - (0203) 4292444
Year of Formation - 1902
President - Dr. Hans Spick
Secretary - Dirk Keiper
Coach - Friedhelm Funkel
Stadium - Wedaustadion (30,160)

APPEARANCES 98/99

	P	Ap	(s)	Gls
Erik Bo ANDERSEN (DEN)	A	11	(13)	2
Markus BEIERLE	A	24	(4)	13
Alexander BUGERA	M	9	(4)	1
Mamadou DIALLO (SEN)	A	1	(6)	
Markus EBBERS	M		(2)	
Stefan EMMERLING	D	18	(5)	1
Martin FRYDEK (CZE)	M	3	(2)	
Thomas GILL (NOR)	G	12		
Tomasz HAJTO (POL)	D	28	(1)	4
Dietmar HIRSCH	M	26	(3)	1
Thomas HOERSEN	D	12	(3)	3
Slobodan KOMLJENOVIC (YUG)	M	29	(2)	1
Andreas MENGER	G	2		
Lubomir MORAVCIK (SVK)	M	5		
Jörg NEUN	D	25		2
Markus OSTHOFF	M	21	(3)	2
Thorsten SCHRAMM	D		(10)	
Peter SCHYBRA	M		(1)	
Uwe SPIES	A	27	(5)	6
Gintaras STAUCE (LIT)	G	20		
Stig TØFTING (DEN)	M	23	(5)	2
Thomas VANA	M	11	(3)	1
Marcus WEDAU	M	16	(12)	3
Torsten WOHLERT	D	30		2
Carsten WOLTERS	M	21	(5)	1

LEAGUE RESULTS 1998/99

14/08/98	Eintracht Frankfurt	H	2-1	Spies, Hoersen
22/08/98	FC Bayern München	A	1-3	Wedau
08/09/98	TSV 1860 München	H	1-1	Beierle
12/09/98	FC Hansa Rostock	A	0-3	
20/09/98	Borussia Mönchengladbach	H	2-2	og (Schneider), Emmerling
26/09/98	SC Freiburg	A	2-2	Neun (p), Hoersen
05/10/98	VfB Stuttgart	H	2-0	Hoersen, Beierle
17/10/98	Hamburger SV	A	1-4	Beierle
25/10/98	Hertha BSC Berlin	H	0-0	
01/11/98	SV Werder Bremen	A	1-1	Neun
06/11/98	1.FC Nürnberg	H	1-1	Vana
11/11/98	Borussia Dortmund	A	0-2	
14/11/98	VfL Bochum	H	2-0	Wedau, Andersen
20/11/98	FC Schalke 04	A	0-2	
28/11/98	Bayer 04 Leverkusen	A	0-2	
12/12/98	VfL Wolfsburg	A	2-4	og (Nowak), Spies
16/12/98	1.FC Kaiserslautern	H	3-1	Beierle, Tøfting, Andersen
19/12/98	Eintracht Frankfurt	A	0-0	
20/02/99	FC Bayern München	H	0-3	
27/02/99	TSV 1860 München	A	0-0	
05/03/99	FC Hansa Rostock	H	4-1	Beierle 3, Bugera
13/03/99	Borussia Mönchengladbach	A	2-0	Spies, Tøfting
20/03/99	SC Freiburg	H	1-0	Beierle
03/04/99	VfB Stuttgart	A	0-0	
09/04/99	Hamburger SV	H	2-3	Osthoff, Hajto
14/04/99	Hertha BSC Berlin	A	3-1	Wolters, og (Van Burik), Wedau
17/04/99	SV Werder Bremen	H	2-0	Hajto (p), Osthoff
24/04/99	1.FC Nürnberg	A	2-0	Wohlert, Beierle
02/05/99	Borussia Dortmund	H	3-2	Spies, Hirsch, Beierle
05/05/99	VfL Bochum	A	2-0	Hajto, Wohlert
08/05/99	FC Schalke 04	H	1-2	Hajto
15/05/99	Bayer 04 Leverkusen	H	0-0	
22/05/99	1.FC Kaiserslautern	A	0-3	
29/05/99	VfL Wolfsburg	H	6-1	Beierle 3, Spies 2, Komljenovic

EINTRACHT FRANKFURT

CLUB DIRECTORY

Eintracht Frankfurt
Sportplatz am Riederwald
Am Erlenbruch 25
60386 Frankfurt-am-Main
tel - (01805) 7431899
fax - (069) 42097043
Year of Formation - 1899
President - Rolf Heller
Secretary - Klaus Lötzbeier
Coach - Horst Ehrmanntraut; Bernrad Lippert;
Reinhold Fanz; Jörg Berger
Stadium - Waldstadion (61,146)

MAJOR HONOURS
League Championship - (1) 1959
Domestic Cup - (4) 1974, 1975, 1981, 1988.
UEFA Cup - (1) 1980.

APPEARANCES 98/99

		P	Ap	(s)	Gls
Sascha AMSTÄTTER	M	2			
Uwe BINDEWALD	M	32			
Mourad BOUNOUA	M	4	(3)		
Ansgar BRINKMANN	A	22	(7)	1	
Thomas EPP	A	7	(2)	1	
Jan Åge FJØRTOFT (NOR)	A	15	(2)	6	
Thorsten FLICK	M		(1)		
Marco GEBHARDT	M	6	(11)	?	
Frank GERSTER	M	1			
Petar HUBCHEV (BUL)	D	23	(4)		
Olaf JANSSEN	M	15	(1)	1	
Burhabettin KAYMAK (TUR)	D	6	(2)		
Alexander KUTSCHERA	D	25	(4)		
Oka NIKOLOV (MAC)	G	34			
Henry NWOSU (NIG)	A		(4)		
Tore PEDERSEN (NOR)	D	19	(1)	1	
István PISONT (HUN)	A	6	(11)		
Alexander ROSEN	M		(1)		
Bernd SCHNEIDER	M	32	(1)	4	
Uwe SCHNEIDER	D	6	(3)		
Alexander SCHUR	M	30		4	
Thomas SOBOTZIK	A	28	(2)	7	
Damir STOJAK (YUG)	A	1	(8)	1	
Ralf WEBER	M	19	(1)	4	
Christoph WESTERTHALER (AUT)	A	4	(23)	3	
Chen YANG (CHN)	A	23		8	
Thomas ZAMPACH	M	14	(6)	1	
Stefan ZINNOW	A		(1)		

LEAGUE RESULTS 1998/99

14/08/98	MSV Duisburg	A	1-2	Sobotzik
22/08/98	TSV 1860 München	H	2-3	Schur, Weber
08/09/98	Borussia Mönchengladbach	A	1-1	Yang
11/09/98	VfB Stuttgart	H	1-1	Brinkmann (p)
18/09/98	Hertha BSC Berlin	A	1-3	Yang
27/09/98	1.FC Nürnberg	H	3-2	Weber 2, Westerthaler
03/10/98	VfL Bochum	A	0-0	
17/10/98	Bayer 04 Leverkusen	H	2-3	Yang, Schur
24/10/98	VfL Wolfsburg	A	0-2	
01/11/98	FC Bayern München	H	1-0	Sobotzik
07/11/98	FC Hansa Rostock	A	2-2	Pedersen, Schneider B.
11/11/98	SC Freiburg	H	3-1	Schneider B., Epp, Gebhardt
14/11/98	Hamburger SV	A	1-0	Sobotzik
20/11/98	SV Werder Bremen	H	0-2	
27/11/98	Borussia Dortmund	A	1-3	Weber
05/12/98	FC Schalke 04	H	1-2	Fjørtoft
12/12/98	1.FC Kaiserslautern	A	1-2	Stojak
19/12/98	MSV Duisburg	H	0-0	
20/02/99	TSV 1860 München	A	1-4	Westerthaler
27/02/99	Borussia Mönchengladbach	H	0-0	
06/03/99	VfB Stuttgart	A	0-2	
14/03/99	Hertha BSC Berlin	H	1-1	Yang
20/03/99	1.FC Nürnberg	A	2-2	Yang 2
04/04/99	VfL Bochum	H	1-0	Fjørtoft
10/04/99	Bayer 04 Leverkusen	A	1-2	Zampach
13/04/99	VfL Wolfsburg	H	0-1	
16/04/99	FC Bayern München	A	1-3	Fjørtoft
24/04/99	FC Hansa Rostock	H	2-2	Schneider B., Westerthaler
30/04/99	SC Freiburg	A	0-2	
04/05/99	Hamburger SV	H	2-2	Schur, Yang
07/05/99	SV Werder Bremen	A	2-1	Schur, Sobotzik
15/05/99	Borussia Dortmund	H	2-0	Fjørtoft, Sobotzik
22/05/99	FC Schalke 04	A	3-2	Fjørtoft, Sobotzik (p), Janssen
29/05/99	1.FC Kaiserslautern	H	5-1	Yang, Sobotzik, Gebhardt,
				Schneider B., Fjørtoft

SC FREIBURG

CLUB DIRECTORY

SC Freiburg
Schwarzwaldstrasse 193
79117 Freiburg
tel - (0761) 385510
fax - (0761) 3855150
Year of Formation - 1904
President - Achim Stocker
Manager - Andreas Rettig
Coach - Volker Finke
Stadium - Dreisamstadion (25,000)

APPEARANCES 98/99

	P	Ap	(s)	Gls
Zoubeir BAYA (TUN)	M	32		6
Mehdi BEN SLIMANE (TUN)	A	12	(10)	1
Damir BURIC (CRO)	D		(1)	
Boubacar DIARRA (MLI)	D	16		
Michael FRONTZECK	M	12	(5)	
Richard GOLZ	G	34		
Ali Mehmet GÜNES (TUR)	M	26	(6)	4
Stefan HAMPL	A	1	(3)	
Lars HERMEL	M	21	(3)	
Torben HOFFMANN	D	15	(5)	2
Alexander IASHVILI (GEO)	A	11		6
Levan KOBIASHVILI (GEO)	M	26		3
Ralf KOHL	M	27	(1)	2
Steffen KORELL	M	12	(4)	1
Stefan MÜLLER	D	21	(5)	1
Miran PAVLIN (SLO)	M	20	(9)	1
Thomas RADLSPECK	M		(1)	
Mike RIETPIETSCH	M	5	(8)	
Daniel SCHUMANN	D	16	(9)	
Jörn SCHWINKENDORF	D	1	(4)	
Adel SELLIMI (TUN)	A	19	(11)	1
Levan TSKITISHVILI (GEO)	M	11	(3)	
Uwe WASSMER	A	7	(10)	2
Marco WEISSHAUPT	M	27	(1)	6
Tobias WILLI	M	2		

LEAGUE RESULTS 1998/99

15/08/98	VfL Bochum	A	2-1	Weisshaupt (p), Iashvili
22/08/98	Bayer 04 Leverkusen	H	1-1	Iashvili
08/09/98	VfL Wolfsburg	A	1-1	Hoffmann
12/09/98	FC Bayern München	H	0-2	
18/09/98	FC Hansa Rostock	A	2-0	Sellimi, Iashvili
26/09/98	MSV Duisburg	H	2-2	Iashvili, Kohl
03/10/98	Hamburger SV	H	0-0	
17/10/98	SV Werder Bremen	A	3-2	Müller, Hoffmann, Weisshaupt
23/10/98	Borussia Dortmund	H	2-2	Baya 2
03/11/98	FC Schalke 04	A	1-1	Korell
07/11/98	1.FC Kaiserslautern	H	0-1	
11/11/98	Eintracht Frankfurt	A	1-3	Wassmer
15/11/98	TSV 1860 München	H	1-2	Kohl
22/11/98	Borussia Mönchengladbach	A	1-3	Wassmer
28/11/98	VfB Stuttgart	H	2-0	Iashvili 2
12/12/98	1.FC Nürnberg	H	1-0	Kobiashvili
15/12/98	Hertha BSC Berlin	A	0-1	
18/12/98	VfL Bochum	H	1-1	Baya
20/02/99	Bayer 04 Leverkusen	A	1-1	Weisshaupt (p)
27/02/99	VfL Wolfsburg	H	0-0	
06/03/99	FC Bayern München	A	0-2	
12/03/99	FC Hansa Rostock	H	3-0	Kobiashvili, Baya, Weisshaupt
20/03/99	MSV Duisburg	A	0-1	
04/04/99	Hamburger SV	A	1-2	Weisshaupt
09/04/99	SV Werder Bremen	H	0-2	
14/04/99	Borussia Dortmund	A	1-2	Günes
17/04/99	FC Schalke 04	H	0-2	
24/04/99	1.FC Kaiserslautern	A	2-0	Weisshaupt, Baya
30/04/99	Eintracht Frankfurt	H	2-0	Ben Slimane, Kobiashvili
05/05/99	TSV 1860 München	A	0-2	
08/05/99	Borussia Mönchengladbach	H	2-1	Baya, Pavlin
15/05/99	VfB Stuttgart	A	1-3	Günes
22/05/99	Hertha BSC Berlin	H	0-2	
29/05/99	1.FC Nürnberg	A	2-1	Günes 2

HAMBURGER SV

CLUB DIRECTORY

Hamburger Sport-Verein
Sylvesterallee 7
22525 Hamburg
tel - (040) 41550
fax - (040) 4155109
Year of Formation - 1897
President - Rolf Mares
Manager - Bernd Wehmayer
Coach - Frank Pagelsdorf
Stadium - Volksparkstadion (55,000)

MAJOR HONOURS
League Championship - (6)
1923, 1928, 1960, 1979, 1982, 1983.
Domestic Cup - (3) 1963, 1976, 1987.
European Champions' Cup - (1) 1983.
European Cup-winners' Cup - (1) 1977.

APPEARANCES 98/99

	P	Ap	(s)	Gls
Christoph BABATZ	M	7	(7)	
Stefan BÖGER	D	4	(4)	
Hans-Jörg BUTT	G	34		7
Alexander CURTIANU (MOL)	M	5	(3)	
Martin DAHLIN (SWE)	A	7	(1)	
Jacek DEMBINSKI (POL)	A	23	(8)	3
Thomas DOLL	M		(13)	
Fabian ERNST	D	24	(5)	
Andreas FISCHER	M	14	(5)	
Dimitrios GRAMMOZIS (GRE)	M	7	(8)	
Thomas GRAVESEN (DEN)	D	20	(2)	3
Martin GROTH	M	33		7
Vanja GRUBAC (YUG)	A		(7)	1
Ingo HERTZSCH	D	30		
Bernd HOLLERBACH	M	29		2
Nico-Jan HOOGMA (HOL)	D	30		1
Allan JEPSEN (DEN)	M	9	(5)	1
Sergei KIRYAKOV (RUS)	A	21	(8)	5
Andrej PANADIC (CRO)	M	26		2
Harald SPÖRL	M	7	(4)	
Oliver STRAUBE	M	1	(5)	
Marek TREJGIS (POL)	A		(1)	
Thomas VOGEL	D	9	(4)	
Dirk WEETENDORF	A		(1)	
Pawel WOJTALA (POL)	D		(1)	
Anthony YEBOAH (GHA)	A	34		14
Mahmut YILMAZ (TUR)	M		(1)	

LEAGUE RESULTS 1998/99

15/08/98	1.FC Nürnberg	A	1-1	Yeboah
21/08/98	VfL Bochum	H	1-0	Dembinski
09/09/98	Bayer 04 Leverkusen	A	2-1	Groth 2
12/09/98	VfL Wolfsburg	H	1-1	Butt (p)
20/09/98	FC Bayern München	A	3-5	Yeboah, Butt (p), Groth
25/09/98	FC Hansa Rostock	H	1-0	Panadic
03/10/98	SC Freiburg	A	0-0	
17/10/98	MSV Duisburg	H	4-1	Gravesen, Kiryakov 3 (1p)
23/10/98	SV Werder Bremen	H	1-1	Yeboah
07/11/98	FC Schalke 04	H	2-2	Hollerbach, Yeboah
10/11/98	1.FC Kaiserslautern	A	0-1	
14/11/98	Eintracht Frankfurt	H	0-1	
21/11/98	TSV 1860 München	A	0-0	
24/11/98	Borussia Dortmund	A	1-2	Jepsen
28/11/98	Borussia Mönchengladbach	H	3-0	Yeboah 3
05/12/98	VfB Stuttgart	A	1-3	Hollerbach
11/12/98	Hertha BSC Berlin	H	0-4	
19/12/98	1.FC Nürnberg	H	2-0	Gravesen (p), Grubac (p)
27/02/99	Bayer 04 Leverkusen	H	0-0	
06/03/99	VfL Wolfsburg	A	1-4	og (Ballwanz)
13/03/99	FC Bayern München	H	0-2	
16/03/99	VfL Bochum	A	0-2	
21/03/99	FC Hansa Rostock	A	1-0	Gravesen
04/04/99	SC Freiburg	H	2-1	Yeboah 2
09/04/99	MSV Duisburg	A	3-2	Groth, Dembinski 2
13/04/99	SV Werder Bremen	A	0-0	
18/04/99	Borussia Dortmund	H	0-0	
24/04/99	FC Schalke 04	A	4-1	Panadic, Groth, Butt (p), Yeboah
01/05/99	1.FC Kaiserslautern	H	2-0	Yeboah, Kiryakov
04/05/99	Eintracht Frankfurt	A	2-2	Yeboah, Hoogma
08/05/99	TSV 1860 München	H	3-0	Groth 2, Butt (p)
14/05/99	Borussia Mönchengladbach	A	2-2	Yeboah, Butt (p)
22/05/99	VfB Stuttgart	H	3-1	Kiryakov, Butt 2 (2p)
29/05/99	Hertha BSC Berlin	A	1-6	Yeboah

FC HANSA ROSTOCK

CLUB DIRECTORY

FC Hansa Rostock
Trotzenburger Weg 14
18057 Rostock
tel - (0381) 499990
fax - (0381) 4999970
Year of Formation - 1965
President - Eckhardt Rehberg
Manager - Herbert Maronn
Secretary - Helmut Hergesell
Coach - Ewald Lienen; Andreas Zachhuber
Stadium - Ostseestadion (24,500)

MAJOR HONOURS
League Championship (GDR) - (1) 1991.
Domestic Cup (GDR) - (1) 1991.

APPEARANCES 98/99

		P	Ap	(s)	Gls
Victor AGALI (NIG)	A		9	(13)	6
Miroslav BICANIC (CRO)	M		2	(2)	
Mattias BREITKREUTZ	M		18	(7)	3
Jens DOWE	M		13	(10)	1
Uwe EHLERS	D		18	(6)	2
Mohamed EMARA (NIG)	M		14		
Ralf EWEN	M			(2)	
Henri FUCHS	A		4	(17)	1
Thomas GANSAUGE	D		12	(5)	
Olaf HOLETSCHEK	D		11	(9)	
Björn LAARS	M			(1)	
Timo LANGE	M		29	(1)	2
Slawomir MAJAK (POL)	M		24	(9)	5
Zoran MILINKOVIC (YUG)	M		6		
Oliver NEUVILLE	A		33		14
Nikolche NOVESKI	D			(1)	
Igor PAMIC (CRO)	A		9	(1)	6
Martin PIECKENHAGEN	G		34		
Abder RAMDANE (EGY)	M		13	(6)	2
Marko REHMER	D		30		2
Hilmar WEILANDT	D		28		
Peter WIBRÅN	M		20		2
Radwan YASSER (EGY)	M		33		1
Marco ZALLMANN	D		14	(4)	1

LEAGUE RESULTS 1998/99

15/08/98	Bayer 04 Leverkusen	A	1-3	Pamic
21/08/98	VfL Wolfsburg	H	3-3	Pamic 2, og (Kovacevic)
09/09/98	FC Bayern München	A	1-6	Ramdane
12/09/98	MSV Duisburg	H	3-0	Zallmann, Neuville (p), Pamic
18/09/98	SC Freiburg	H	0-2	
25/09/98	Hamburger SV	A	0-1	
03/10/98	SV Werder Bremen	H	2-1	Neuville, Breitkreutz
18/10/98	Borussia Dortmund	A	0-2	
24/10/98	FC Schalke 04	H	2-2	Pamic, Dowe
30/10/98	1.FC Kaiserslautern	A	2-3	Pamic, Neuville
07/11/98	Eintracht Frankfurt	H	2-2	Ehlers, Lange
10/11/98	TSV 1860 München	A	1-2	Fuchs
13/11/98	Borussia Mönchengladbach	H	1-1	Majak
21/11/98	VfB Stuttgart	A	1-1	Breitkreutz
27/11/98	Hertha BSC Berlin	H	1-2	Radwan
04/12/98	1.FC Nürnberg	A	2-2	Ramdane, Agali
12/12/98	VfL Bochum	H	3-0	Neuville 2, Majak
19/12/98	Bayer 04 Leverkusen	H	1-1	Neuville
19/02/99	VfL Wolfsburg	A	1-1	Rehmer
27/02/99	FC Bayern München	H	0-4	
05/03/99	MSV Duisburg	A	1-4	Breitkreutz
12/03/99	SC Freiburg	A	0-3	
21/03/99	Hamburger SV	H	0-1	
04/04/99	SV Werder Bremen	A	3-0	Agali, Lange, Neuville
10/04/99	Borussia Dortmund	H	2-0	Neuville, Agali
13/04/99	FC Schalke 04	A	0-1	
16/04/99	1.FC Kaiserslautern	H	2-1	Neuville, Ehlers
24/04/99	Eintracht Frankfurt	A	2-2	Wibrån, Agali
01/05/99	TSV 1860 München	H	4-1	Neuville 3, Agali
04/05/99	Borussia Mönchengladbach	A	1-1	Wibrån
07/05/99	VfB Stuttgart	H	3-0	Rehmer, Majak 2
14/05/99	Hertha BSC Berlin	A	0-2	
22/05/99	1.FC Nürnberg	H	1-1	Neuville (p)
29/05/99	VfL Bochum	A	3-2	Neuville, Agali, Majak

HERTHA BSC BERLIN

CLUB DIRECTORY

Hertha BSC Berlin
Hans-Braun-Strasse
Friesenhaus 2
14053 Berlin
tel - (030) 3009280
fax - (030) 30092899
Year of Formation - 1892
President - Walter Müller
Manager - Dieter Hoeness
Secretary - Matthias Huber
Coach - Jürgen Röber
Stadium - Olympiastadion (76,243)

MAJOR HONOURS
League Championship - (2) 1930, 1931.

APPEARANCES 98/99

	P	Ap	(s)	Gls
Ilja ARACIC (CRO)	A	7	(6)	5
Ante COVIC (CRO)	A	7	(6)	
Pál DÁRDAI (HUN)	M	7	(14)	1
Michael HARTMANN	M	19	(8)	2
Hendrik HERZOG	D	26		2
Gábor KIRÁLY (HUN)	G	34		
Rob MAAS (HOL)	M	1	(5)	
Sergej MANDREKO (TAD)	M	12	(1)	1
Andreas NEUENDORF	M	7	(7)	3
Ivica OLIC (YUG)	M	1	(1)	
Michael PREETZ	A	34		23
Piotr REISS (POL)	A	9	(1)	1
Kjetil REKDAL (NOR)	D	23	(1)	1
Bryan ROY (HOL)	A	3	(4)	
Anthony SANNEH (USA)	D	2	(3)	
Andreas SCHMIDT	M	23	(4)	1
Eyjólfur SVERRISSON (ISL)	D	23	(4)	2
Alphonse TCHAMI (CMR)	A	6	(5)	2
Andreas THOM	A	26	(2)	3
René TRETSCHOK	M	32		4
Sixten VEIT	M	23	(2)	4
Dick VAN BURIK (HOL)	D	18	(6)	
Dariusz WOSZ	M	31		3

LEAGUE RESULTS 1998/99

16/08/98	SV Werder Bremen	H	1-0	Preetz
22/08/98	Borussia Dortmund	A	0-3	
09/09/98	FC Schalke 04	H	2-0	Rekdal (p), Tretschok
12/09/98	1.FC Kaiserslautern	A	3-4	Veit, Thom, Dárdai
18/09/98	Eintracht Frankfurt	H	3-1	Preetz 2, Tchami
25/09/98	TSV 1860 München	A	0-2	
02/10/98	Borussia Mönchengladbach	H	4-1	Veit, Preetz 3
17/10/98	VfB Stuttgart	A	0-0	
25/10/98	MSV Duisburg	A	0-0	
02/11/98	1.FC Nürnberg	H	3-0	Mandreko, Veit, Tchami
07/11/98	VfL Bochum	A	0-2	
11/11/98	Bayer 04 Leverkusen	H	0-1	
14/11/98	VfL Wolfsburg	A	1-2	Tretschok
21/11/98	FC Bayern München	H	1-0	Preetz
27/11/98	FC Hansa Rostock	A	2-1	Veit, Preetz
11/12/98	Hamburger SV	A	4-0	Reiss, Wosz, Tretschok, Preetz
15/12/98	SC Freiburg	H	1-0	Preetz
20/12/98	SV Werder Bremen	A	1-2	Preetz
21/02/99	Borussia Dortmund	H	3-0	Aracic 2, Preetz
28/02/99	FC Schalke 04	A	0-0	
06/03/99	1.FC Kaiserslautern	H	1-1	Preetz
14/03/99	Eintracht Frankfurt	A	1-1	Sverrisson
20/03/99	TSV 1860 München	H	2-1	Preetz (p), Tretschok
04/04/99	Borussia Mönchengladbach	A	4-2	Preetz 2 (1p), Thom, Sverrisson
10/04/99	VfB Stuttgart	H	2-0	Aracic, Neuendorf
14/04/99	MSV Duisburg	H	1-3	Preetz
17/04/99	1.FC Nürnberg	A	0-0	
24/04/99	VfL Bochum	H	4-1	Wosz 2, Herzog, Hartmann
01/05/99	Bayer 04 Leverkusen	A	2-2	og (Nowotny), Herzog
05/05/99	VfL Wolfsburg	H	2-0	Preetz 2
09/05/99	FC Bayern München	A	1-1	Schmidt
14/05/99	FC Hansa Rostock	H	2-0	Neuendorf, Hartmann
22/05/99	SC Freiburg	A	2-0	Preetz, Aracic
29/05/99	Hamburger SV	H	6-1	Preetz 3 (1p), Aracic, Neuendorf, Thom

1.FC KAISERSLAUTERN

CLUB DIRECTORY

1.FC Kaiserslautern
Fritz-Walter-Stadion
67653 Kaiserslautern
tel - (0631) 31880
fax - (0631) 3188290
Year of Formation - 1900
President - Robert Wieschemann
Manager - Jürgen Friedrich
Secretary - Gerhard Herzog
Coach - Otto Rehhagel
Stadium - Fritz-Walter-Stadion (41,582)

MAJOR HONOURS
League Championship - (4)
1951, 1953, 1991, 1998.
Domestic Cup - (2) 1990, 1996.

APPEARANCES 98/99

	P	Ap	(s)	Gls
Michael BALLACK	M	17	(13)	4
Andreas BUCK	M	22	(1)	2
Daniel GRAF	A		(2)	
Marian HRISTOV (BUL)	M	16	(3)	3
Janos HRUTKA (HUN)	D	4	(8)	1
José Carlos JESUS JÚNIOR (BRA)	A	2	(6)	
Harry KOCH	D	21	(3)	
Olaf MARSCHALL	A	28		12
Pascal OJIGWE (NIG)	M		(4)	
Hany RAMZY (EGY)	D	32		3
Rodrigues RATINHO (BRA)	M	19	(2)	2
Marco REICH	A	22	(5)	3
Andreas REINKE	G	34		
Thomas RIEDL	M	19	(10)	
Jürgen RISCHE	A	12	(17)	3
Axel ROOS	D	16	(7)	
Uwe RÖSLER	A	21	(7)	8
Ibrahim SAMIR (EGY)	M	18	(1)	1
Oliver SCHÄFER	D	3	(5)	
Michael SCHJØNBERG (DEN)	D	15		6
Ciriaco SFORZA (SUI)	M	32		
Martin WAGNER	M	21		1

LEAGUE RESULTS 1998/99

15/08/98	TSV 1860 München	A	2-1	Marschall, Samir
22/08/98	Borussia Mönchengladbach	H	2-1	Wagner, Marschall
08/09/98	VfB Stuttgart	A	0-4	
12/09/98	Hertha BSC Berlin	H	4-3	Marschall 2, Schjønberg 2 (1p)
19/09/98	1.FC Nürnberg	A	1-1	Marschall
26/09/98	VfL Bochum	H	2-3	Rische, Marschall
03/10/98	Bayer 04 Leverkusen	A	2-2	Marschall, Hristov
16/10/98	VfL Wolfsburg	H	1-1	Reich
24/10/98	FC Bayern München	A	0-4	
30/10/98	FC Hansa Rostock	H	3-2	Marschall (p), Ballack, Rösler
07/11/98	SC Freiburg	A	1-0	Hristov
10/11/98	Hamburger SV	H	1-0	Rösler
13/11/98	SV Werder Bremen	A	1-0	Ramzy
21/11/98	Borussia Dortmund	H	1-0	Reich
29/11/98	FC Schalke 04	H	4-1	Hristov, Rösler, Hrutka,
				Marschall (p)
12/12/98	Eintracht Frankfurt	H	2-1	Ballack, Ramzy
16/12/98	MSV Duisburg	A	1-3	Rösler
19/12/98	TSV 1860 München	H	1-1	Reich
20/02/99	Borussia Mönchengladbach	A	2-0	Marschall, og (Asanin)
26/02/99	VfB Stuttgart	H	1-1	Ramzy
06/03/99	Hertha BSC Berlin	A	1-1	Ballack
13/03/99	1.FC Nürnberg	H	2-0	Rösler, Ratinho
20/03/99	VfL Bochum	A	2-1	Ratinho, Rösler
04/04/99	Bayer 04 Leverkusen	H	0-1	
10/04/99	VfL Wolfsburg	A	1-2	Ballack (p)
13/04/99	FC Bayern München	H	2-1	Buck, Rische
16/04/99	FC Hansa Rostock	A	1-2	Rösler
24/04/99	SC Freiburg	H	0-2	
01/05/99	Hamburger SV	A	0-2	
04/05/99	SV Werder Bremen	H	4-0	Schjønberg 2 (1p), Rösler, Rische
08/05/99	Borussia Dortmund	A	0-1	
16/05/99	FC Schalke 04	A	2-0	Schjønberg (p), Rische
22/05/99	MSV Duisburg	H	3-0	Marschall 2, Buck
29/05/99	Eintracht Frankfurt	A	1-5	Schjønberg (p)

TSV 1860 MÜNCHEN

CLUB DIRECTORY

TSV 1860 München
Grünwalder Strasse 114
81547 München
tel - (089) 64278560
fax - (089) 64278580
Year of Formation - 1860
President - Karl-Heinz Wildmoser
Manager - Edgar Geenen
Secretary - Detlef Romeiko
Coach - Werner Lorant
Stadium - Olympiastadion (69,000)

MAJOR HONOURS
League Championship - (1) 1966.
Domestic Cup - (2) 1942, 1964.

APPEARANCES 98/99

	P	Ap	(s)	Gls
Paul AGOSTINO (AUS)	A		(7)	
Manfred BENDER	M	3	(3)	
Daniel BORIMIROV (BUL)	M	19	(4)	2
Harald CERNY (AUT)	M	29		3
Martin CIZEK	M	12	(2)	
Michel DINZEY (CON)	M	5	(9)	1
Guido GORGES	D	8	(3)	
Holger GREILICH	D	21	(1)	
Horst HELDT	M	19	(8)	1
Bernd HOBSCH	A	18	(7)	12
Michael HOFMANN	G	34		
Awudu ISSAKA (GHA)	M		(1)	
Jochen KIENTZ	D	3	(3)	1
Marco KURZ	D	26		4
Stefan MALZ	M	15	(7)	1
Abderrahim OUAKILI (MAR)	M	20	(7)	3
Thomas RICHTER	M	3	(2)	
Thomas SCHLÜTER	M		(1)	
Markus SCHROTH	A	23	(10)	6
Miroslav STEVIC (YUG)	M	15	(2)	
Martin STRANZL	M		(3)	
Roman TYCE (CZE)	M	17	(1)	
Gerald VANENBURG (HOL)	D	27		2
Bernhard WINKLER	A	24		11
Hristo YOVOV (BUL)	A		(4)	1
Ned ZELIC (AUS)	D	33		1

LEAGUE RESULTS 1998/99

15/08/98	1.FC Kaiserslautern	H	1-2	Winkler (p)
22/08/98	Eintracht Frankfurt	A	3-2	Borimirov, Ouakili, Winkler
08/09/98	MSV Duisburg	A	1-1	Winkler
11/09/98	Borussia Mönchengladbach	H	3-1	Winkler 2, Kurz
19/09/98	VfB Stuttgart	A	1-0	Vanenburg
25/09/98	Hertha BSC Berlin	H	2-0	Ouakili, Hobsch
03/10/98	1.FC Nürnberg	A	5-1	Schroth, Winkler, Cerny, Dinzey, Yovov
16/10/98	VfL Bochum	H	2-1	Winkler, Hobsch
25/10/98	Bayer 04 Leverkusen	A	1-1	Hobsch
01/11/98	VfL Wolfsburg	H	2-3	Schroth, Hobsch
07/11/98	FC Bayern München	A	1-3	Kientz
10/11/98	FC Hansa Rostock	H	2-1	Winkler 2
15/11/98	SC Freiburg	A	2-1	Malz, Hobsch
21/11/98	Hamburger SV	H	0-0	
28/11/98	SV Werder Bremen	A	1-4	Ouakili
06/12/98	Borussia Dortmund	H	2-0	Schroth 2
12/12/98	FC Schalke 04	A	2-2	Schroth, Cerny
19/12/98	1.FC Kaiserslautern	A	1-1	Winkler
20/02/99	Eintracht Frankfurt	H	4-1	Borimirov, Heldt, Kurz, Hobsch
27/02/99	MSV Duisburg	H	0-0	
06/03/99	Borussia Mönchengladbach	A	0-2	
13/03/99	VfB Stuttgart	H	1-1	Zelic
20/03/99	Hertha BSC Berlin	A	1-2	Winkler
03/04/99	1.FC Nürnberg	H	1-2	Hobsch
11/04/99	VfL Bochum	A	0-2	
14/04/99	Bayer 04 Leverkusen	H	0-2	
17/04/99	VfL Wolfsburg	A	0-1	
25/04/99	FC Bayern München	H	1-1	Kurz
01/05/99	FC Hansa Rostock	A	1-4	Hobsch
05/05/99	SC Freiburg	H	2-0	Vanenburg, Hobsch
08/05/99	Hamburger SV	A	0-3	
15/05/99	SV Werder Bremen	H	1-3	Hobsch
22/05/99	Borussia Dortmund	A	1-3	Schroth
29/05/99	FC Schalke 04	H	4-5	Hobsch 2, Cerny, Kurz

1.FC NÜRNBERG

CLUB DIRECTORY

1.FC Nürnberg
Valznerweiherstrasse 200, 90480 Nürnberg
tel - (0911) 940790
fax - (0911) 9407977
Year of Formation - 1900
President - Michael A. Roth
Manager - Ignaz Good
Coach - Felix Magath; Willi Reimann;
Thomas Brunner; Friedel Rausch
Stadium - Frankenstadion (44,600)

MAJOR HONOURS
League Championship - (9) 1920, 1921, 1924,
1925, 1927, 1936, 1948, 1961, 1968.
Domestic Cup - (3) 1932, 1935, 1962.

APPEARANCES 98/99

	P	Ap	(s)	Gls
Frank BAUMANN	D	30		1
Henning BÜRGER	M	13	(3)	
Sasa CIRIC (MAC)	A	28		13
Martin DRILLER	A	16	(3)	1
Heiko GERBER	M	19	(5)	2
Markus GRASSER	D	10	(2)	
Sven GÜNTHER	D	10	(9)	
Andreas HILFIKER	G	17		
Zivojin JUSKIC (YUG)	M	2	(1)	
Darius KAMPA	G	1		
Andreas KÖPKE	G	16		
Pavel KUKA (CZE)	A	28		10
Markus KURTH	A	6	(15)	2
Markus LÖSCH	D	21		
Ersen MARTIN	M		(1)	
Matthias MAUCKSCH	M	3	(2)	
Martin MOLZ	M		(1)	
Marek NIKL (CZE)	D	22		1
Marc OECHLER	M	10	(8)	1
Andriy POLUNIN (UKR)	M	12	(4)	2
Helmut RAHNER	D	9	(4)	
Knut REINHARDT	M	6	(3)	
Thomas RICHTER	D	11		
Niklas SKOOG (SWE)	A	3	(7)	1
Armin STÖRZENHOFECKER	M	24	(8)	1
Stephan TÄUBER	D	10		
René VAN ECK	D	16		
Jochen WEIGL	M	2	(9)	1
Michael WIESINGER	M	22		1
Tobias ZELLNER	M	1		
Thomas ZIEMER	M	6	(4)	1

LEAGUE RESULTS 1998/99

15/08/98	Hamburger SV	H	1-1	Polunin
22/08/98	SV Werder Bremen	A	3-2	Kuka 2, Ciric
09/09/98	Borussia Dortmund	H	0-0	
12/09/98	FC Schalke 04	A	2-2	Ciric, Kurth
19/09/98	1.FC Kaiserslautern	H	1-1	Kuka
27/09/98	Eintracht Frankfurt	A	2-3	Polunin, Ciric
03/10/98	TSV 1860 München	H	1-5	Richter
17/10/98	Borussia Mönchengladbach	A	2-0	Ciric 2 (1p)
24/10/98	VfB Stuttgart	H	2-2	Kuka, Täuber
02/11/98	Hertha BSC Berlin	A	0-3	
06/11/98	MSV Duisburg	A	1-1	Gerber
11/11/98	VfL Bochum	H	2-2	Wiesinger, Kuka
14/11/98	Bayer 04 Leverkusen	A	0-3	
21/11/98	VfL Wolfsburg	H	1-1	Skoog
28/11/98	FC Bayern München	A	0-2	
04/12/98	FC Hansa Rostock	H	2-2	Ciric 2
12/12/98	SC Freiburg	A	0-1	
19/12/98	Hamburger SV	A	0-2	
20/02/99	SV Werder Bremen	H	1-1	Kuka
27/02/99	Borussia Dortmund	A	0-3	
05/03/99	FC Schalke 04	H	3-0	Kuka 2, Ciric
13/03/99	1.FC Kaiserslautern	A	0-2	
20/03/99	Eintracht Frankfurt	H	2-2	Kuka, Ciric
03/04/99	TSV 1860 München	A	2-1	Kuka, Störzenhofecker
10/04/99	Borussia Mönchengladbach	H	2-0	Ziemer, Oechler
13/04/99	VfB Stuttgart	A	0-0	
17/04/99	Hertha BSC Berlin	H	0-0	
24/04/99	MSV Duisburg	H	0-2	
30/04/99	VfL Bochum	A	3-0	Ciric 2, Kurth
05/05/99	Bayer 04 Leverkusen	H	2-2	Ciric, Weigl
08/05/99	VfL Wolfsburg	A	1-1	Baumann
15/05/99	FC Bayern München	H	2-0	Ciric, Driller
22/05/99	FC Hansa Rostock	A	1-1	Gerber
29/05/99	SC Freiburg	H	1-2	Nikl

FC SCHALKE 04

CLUB DIRECTORY

FC Schalke 04
Postfach 20 08 61
45843 Gelsenkirchen
tel - (0209) 700870
fax - (0209) 7008750
Year of Formation - 1904
President - Gerd Rehberg
Manager - Rudi Assauer
Secretary - Peter Peters
Coach - Huub Stevens
Stadium - Parkstadion (62,004)

MAJOR HONOURS
League Championship - (7)
1934, 1935, 1937, 1939, 1940, 1942, 1958.
Domestic Cup - (2) 1937, 1972.
UEFA Cup - (1) 1997.

APPEARANCES 98/99

	P	Ap	(s)	Gls
Ingo ANDERBRÜGGE	M	3	(13)	
Michael BÜSKENS	M	26	(1)	2
Johan DE KOCK (HOL)	D	20		1
Yves EIGENRAUCH	D	21	(1)	
René EIJKELKAMP (HOL)	A	13	(2)	5
Michael GOOSSENS (BEL)	A	10	(2)	1
Frode GRODÅS (NOR)	G	2		
HAMI Mandirali (TUR)	A	13	(9)	3
Oliver HELD	M	19	(2)	2
Denis KLIOUEV (RUS)	M	1	(2)	
Sven KMETSCH	M	17	(1)	2
Radoslav LATAL (CZE)	M	7	(9)	
Martin MAX	A	22	(6)	6
Youri MULDER (HOL)	A	24	(2)	6
Andreas MÜLLER	M	22	(5)	1
Jiri NEMEC (CZE)	M	27		2
Miguel Francisco PEREIRA (ANG)	A	2	(3)	
Oliver RECK	G	18		
Mathias SCHOBER	G	14		
Filip TAPALOVIC (CRO)	M	12	(6)	
Olaf THON	D	15	(1)	2
ÜNAL Alpugan (TUR)	M	13	(2)	1
Marco VAN HOOGDALEM (HOL)	D	25		1
Nico VAN KERCKHOVEN (BEL)	M	19	(3)	1
Marc WILMOTS (BEL)	M	6	(6)	1
Sascha WOLF	A	3	(11)	3

LEAGUE RESULTS 1998/99

15/08/98	Borussia Mönchengladbach	A	0-3	
22/08/98	VfB Stuttgart	H	1-0	Max
09/09/98	Hertha BSC Berlin	A	0-2	
12/09/98	1.FC Nürnberg	H	2-2	Eijkelkamp, Max (p)
19/09/98	VfL Bochum	A	2-1	Eijkelkamp 2
26/09/98	Bayer 04 Leverkusen	H	0-1	
02/10/98	VfL Wolfsburg	A	0-0	
17/10/98	FC Bayern München	H	1-3	Eijkelkamp
24/10/98	FC Hansa Rostock	A	2-2	Max, Wolf
03/11/98	SC Freiburg	H	1-1	Nemec
07/11/98	Hamburger SV	A	2-2	Mulder, Max
14/11/98	Borussia Dortmund	A	0-3	
20/11/98	MSV Duisburg	H	2-0	Eijkelkamp, Goossens
24/11/98	SV Werder Bremen	H	1-2	Van Kerckhoven
29/11/98	1.FC Kaiserslautern	A	1-4	Max
05/12/98	Eintracht Frankfurt	A	2-1	Van Hoogdalem, Kmetsch
12/12/98	TSV 1860 München	H	2-2	Kmetsch, og (Kurz)
19/12/98	Borussia Mönchengladbach	H	1-0	Wilmots
19/02/99	VfB Stuttgart	A	1-2	Mulder
28/02/99	Hertha BSC Berlin	H	0-0	
05/03/99	1.FC Nürnberg	A	0-3	
13/03/99	VfL Bochum	H	2-2	Mulder (p), Büskens
19/03/99	Bayer 04 Leverkusen	A	1-1	Mulder
03/04/99	VfL Wolfsburg	H	2-0	Büskens, De Kock
10/04/99	FC Bayern München	A	1-1	Held
13/04/99	FC Hansa Rostock	H	1-0	Wolf
17/04/99	SC Freiburg	A	2-0	Ünal, Wolf
24/04/99	Hamburger SV	H	1-4	Thon
05/05/99	Borussia Dortmund	H	1-1	Mulder
08/05/99	MSV Duisburg	A	2-1	Müller, Mulder
11/05/99	SV Werder Bremen	A	0-1	
16/05/99	1.FC Kaiserslautern	H	0-2	
22/05/99	Eintracht Frankfurt	H	2-3	Held, Hami
29/05/99	TSV 1860 München	A	5-4	Hami 2 (1p), Nemec, Max, Thon

VFB STUTTGART

CLUB DIRECTORY

VfB Stuttgart
Mercedesstrasse 109
70372 Stuttgart
tel - (0711) 550070
fax - (0711) 5500733
Year of Formation - 1893
President - Gerhard Mayer-Vorfelder
Manager - Karl-Heinz Förster
Secretary - Ulrich Schäfer
Coach - Winfried Schäfer; Wolfgang Rolff;
Rainer Adrion; Ralf Rangnick
Stadium - Gottlieb-Daimler-Stadion (47,000)

MAJOR HONOURS
League Championship - (4)
1950, 1952, 1984, 1992.
Domestic Cup - (3) 1954, 1958, 1997.

APPEARANCES 98/99

		P	Ap	(s)	Gls
Jonathan AKPOBORIE (NIG)	A		26	(2)	11
Krasimir BALAKOV (BUL)	M		24		5
Thomas BERTHOLD	D		22		
Alexander BLESSIN	A			(7)	
Fredi BOBIC	A		28		8
Bradley CARNELL (SAF)	M		19	(1)	2
Kristijan DJORDJEVIC (YUG)	M		19	(4)	2
Jochen ENDRESS	D		6	(5)	
Nico FROMMER	A		1	(7)	
Ahmed Salah HOSNY (TUR)	M			(2)	
Jens KELLER	D		24		1
Thomas KIES	D		3		1
Thorsten LEGAT	D			(1)	
Krisztián LISZTES (HUN)	M		17	(14)	2
Sasa MARKOVIC (YUG)	A		1	(3)	1
Kai OSWALD	D		3		
Roberto PINTO	M		2	(4)	
Gerhard POSCHNER	M		8	(3)	
Sreto RISTIC (YUG)	A		8	(16)	3
Timo ROST	M		5	(11)	1
Thomas SCHNEIDER	D		10	(2)	1
Zvonimir SOLDO (CRO)	M		29		1
Martin SPANRING	D		9	(3)	
Mitko STOJKOVSKI (MAC)	M		3	(1)	
Pablo THIAM (GUI)	M		24	(3)	2
Eberhard TRAUTNER	G			(1)	
Frank VERLAAT (HOL)	D		29		
Franz WOHLFAHRT (AUT)	G		26		
Michael ZEYER	M		20	(6)	
Marc ZIEGLER	G		8	(1)	

LEAGUE RESULTS 1998/99

14/08/98	Borussia Dortmund	H	2-1	Keller, Djordjevic
22/08/98	FC Schalke 04	A	0-1	
08/09/98	1.FC Kaiserslautern	H	4-0	Ristic 2, Bobic, Balakov (p)
11/09/98	Eintracht Frankfurt	A	1-1	Balakov
19/09/98	TSV 1860 München	H	0-1	
26/09/98	Borussia Mönchengladbach	A	3-2	Akpoborie, Bobic, Soldo
05/10/98	MSV Duisburg	A	0-2	
17/10/98	Hertha BSC Berlin	H	0-0	
24/10/98	1.FC Nürnberg	A	2-2	Akpoborie, Bobic
01/11/98	VfL Bochum	H	4-2	Akpoborie 2, Carnell, Ristic
08/11/98	Bayer 04 Leverkusen	A	0-0	
11/11/98	VfL Wolfsburg	H	1-2	Akpoborie
14/11/98	FC Bayern München	A	0-2	
21/11/98	FC Hansa Rostock	H	1-1	Lisztes
28/11/98	SC Freiburg	A	0-2	
05/12/98	Hamburger SV	H	3-1	Akpoborie 3
12/12/98	SV Werder Bremen	A	2-2	Schneider, Bobic
18/12/98	Borussia Dortmund	A	0-3	
19/02/99	FC Schalke 04	H	2-1	Djordjevic, Markovic
26/02/99	1.FC Kaiserslautern	A	1-1	Bobic
06/03/99	Eintracht Frankfurt	H	2-0	Balakov, Carnell
13/03/99	TSV 1860 München	A	1-1	Balakov
20/03/99	Borussia Mönchengladbach	H	2-2	Lisztes, Balakov
03/04/99	MSV Duisburg	H	0-0	
10/04/99	Hertha BSC Berlin	A	0-2	
13/04/99	1.FC Nürnberg	H	0-0	
17/04/99	VfL Bochum	A	3-3	Akpoborie 3
23/04/99	Bayer 04 Leverkusen	H	0-1	
01/05/99	VfL Wolfsburg	A	2-3	Kies, Rost
04/05/99	FC Bayern München	H	0-2	
07/05/99	FC Hansa Rostock	A	0-3	
15/05/99	SC Freiburg	H	3-1	Thiam 2, Bobic
22/05/99	Hamburger SV	A	1-3	Bobic
29/05/99	SV Werder Bremen	H	1-0	Bobic

SV WERDER BREMEN

CLUB DIRECTORY

SV Werder Bremen
Am Weserstadion 7
28205 Bremen
tel - (0180) 5937337
fax - (0421) 493555
Year of Formation - 1899
President - Jürgen L. Born
Manager - Klaus Allofs
Secretary - Wolfgang Barkhausen
Coach - Wolfgang Sidka; Felix Magath;
Thomas Schaaf
Stadium - Weserstadion (35,282)

MAJOR HONOURS
League Championship - (3) 1965, 1988, 1993.
Domestic Cup - (4) 1961, 1991, 1994, 1999.
European Cup-winners' Cup - (1) 1992.

APPEARANCES 98/99

	P	Ap	(s)	Gls
Gustavo da Silva AILTON (BRA)	M	4	(8)	2
Mike BARTEN	D	1	(1)	
Sven BENKEN	D	19	(4)	
Marco BODE	M	29		8
Rade BOGDANOVIC (YUG)	A	20	(3)	8
Christian BRAND	M		(4)	
Stefan BRASAS	G	6		
Christoph DABROWSKI	M	0	(7)	1
Dieter EILTS	M	31	(1)	
Håvard FLO (NOR)	A	6	(10)	
Dirk FLOCK	M	5	(13)	
Dieter FREY	D	5		1
Torsten FRINGS	A	17	(6)	3
Danny FÜTTERER	M	1		
Andreas HERZOG (AUT)	M	26	(1)	3
Adrian KUNZ	A	1	(3)	
Yuriy MAXIMOV (UKR)	M	15	(5)	3
Lodewijk ROEMBIAK (HOL)	M	12	(4)	3
Frank ROST	G	28		
Björn SCHIERENBECK	M		(1)	
Sören SEIDEL	A		(5)	
Viktor SKRYPNYK (UKR)	D	16		
Jens TODT	D	19	(1)	3
Bernhard TRARES	D	31		3
Dirk WEETENDORF	M	1	(6)	
Raphaël WICKY (SUI)	D	30	(1)	1
André WIEDENER	D	26	(4)	
Pawel WOJTALA (POL)	D	17	(2)	1

LEAGUE RESULTS 1998/99

16/08/98	Hertha BSC Berlin	A	0-1	
22/08/98	1.FC Nürnberg	H	2-3	Roembiak (p), Todt
08/09/98	VfL Bochum	A	0-2	
12/09/98	Bayer 04 Leverkusen	H	2-2	Roembiak (p), Frings
19/09/98	VfL Wolfsburg	A	4-2	Frey, Bode 2, Bogdanovic
26/09/98	FC Bayern München	H	0-1	
03/10/98	FC Hansa Rostock	A	1-2	Trares
17/10/98	SC Freiburg	H	2-3	Ailton, Bogdanovic
23/10/98	Hamburger SV	A	1-1	Maximov
01/11/98	MSV Duisburg	H	1-1	Bogdanovic
06/11/98	Borussia Dortmund	H	1-1	Bogdanovic
13/11/98	1.FC Kaiserslautern	H	0-1	
20/11/98	Eintracht Frankfurt	A	2-0	Herzog, Bogdanovic
24/11/98	FC Schalke 04	A	2-1	Todt, Herzog
28/11/98	TSV 1860 München	H	4-1	Bode 2, Roembiak, Herzog (p)
08/12/98	Borussia Mönchengladbach	A	1-0	Bode
12/12/98	VfB Stuttgart	H	2-2	Trares, Bode
28/12/98	Hertha BSC Berlin	H	2-1	Bogdanovic 2
20/02/99	1.FC Nürnberg	A	1-1	Frings
26/02/99	VfL Bochum	H	1-1	Ailton
07/03/99	Bayer 04 Leverkusen	A	0-2	
13/03/99	VfL Wolfsburg	H	0-1	
20/03/99	FC Bayern München	A	0-1	
03/04/99	FC Hansa Rostock	H	0-3	
09/04/99	SC Freiburg	A	2-0	Frings, Bogdanovic
13/04/99	Hamburger SV	H	0-0	
17/04/99	MSV Duisburg	A	0-2	
23/04/99	Borussia Dortmund	A	1-2	Trares
04/05/99	1.FC Kaiserslautern	A	0-4	
07/05/99	Eintracht Frankfurt	H	1-2	Bode
11/05/99	FC Schalke 04	H	1-0	Dabrowski
15/05/99	TSV 1860 München	A	3-1	Wojtala, Bode, Maximov
22/05/99	Borussia Mönchengladbach	H	4-1	Todt, Wicky, Maximov, og (Albustin)
29/05/99	VfB Stuttgart	A	0-1	

VFL WOLFSBURG

CLUB DIRECTORY

VfL Wolfsburg
Elsterweg 5
38446 Wolfsburg
tel - (05361) 85170
fax - (05361) 851748
Year of Formation - 1945
President - Werner Schlimme
Manager - Peter Pander
Secretary - Bernd Sudholt
Coach - Wolfgang Wolf
Stadium - VfL-Stadion (21,600)

APPEARANCES 98/99

		P	Ap	(s)	Gls
Charles AKONNOR (GHA)	M	28	(4)		6
Holger BALLWANZ	M	22	(1)		1
Steffen BAUMGART	A	14	(17)		5
André BREITENREITER	A	1	(12)		1
Nico DÄBRITZ	M	2	(6)		
Detlef DAMMEIER	M	29	(2)		3
Frank GREINER	M	28	(3)		1
Andrzej JUSKOWIAK (POL)	A	28	(3)		13
Sead KAPETANOVIC (BOS)	M	24	(4)		1
Peter KLEESCHÄTZKY	D	2	(4)		
Marijan KOVACEVIC (CRO)	D	8	(5)		2
Waldemar KRYGER (POL)	D	25	(2)		
Marcel MALTRITZ	M	11	(4)		
Vitus NAGORNY	A		(4)		
Krzysztof NOWAK (POL)	M	30			4
Brian O'NEIL (SCO)	D	23	(3)		2
Roy PRÄGER	A	27	(2)		9
Claus REITMAIER	G	34			
Claudio REYNA (USA)	M	9	(11)		2
Jan SCHANDA	M		(2)		
Gerald SCHRÖDER	M		(2)		1
Mathias STAMMANN	M	3	(6)		
Claus THOMSEN (DEN)	D	26			2

LEAGUE RESULTS 1998/99

15/08/98	FC Bayern München	H	0-1	
21/08/98	FC Hansa Rostock	A	3-3	Kovacevic (p), Juskowiak, Breitenreiter
08/09/98	SC Freiburg	H	1-1	O'Neil
12/09/98	Hamburger SV	A	1-1	Baumgart
19/09/98	SV Werder Bremen	H	2-4	Baumgart, Akonnor
26/09/98	Borussia Dortmund	A	1-2	Kapetanovic
02/10/98	FC Schalke 04	H	0-0	
16/10/98	1.FC Kaiserslautern	A	1-1	Dammeier
24/10/98	Eintracht Frankfurt	H	2-0	Ballwanz, Juskowiak
01/11/98	TSV 1860 München	A	3-2	Dammeier, Baumgart, Kovacevic (p)
07/11/98	Borussia Mönchengladbach	H	7-1	Akonnor 2, Juskowiak 2, Präger 2, O'Neil
11/11/98	VfB Stuttgart	A	2-1	Präger, Juskowiak
14/11/98	Hertha BSC Berlin	H	2-1	Juskowiak, Nowak
21/11/98	1.FC Nürnberg	A	1-1	Juskowiak
28/11/98	VfL Bochum	H	4-1	Juskowiak 2, Präger, Greiner
05/12/98	Bayer 04 Leverkusen	A	0-3	
12/12/98	MSV Duisburg	H	4-2	Dammeier, Akonnor, Juskowiak 2
19/12/98	FC Bayern München	A	0-3	
19/02/99	FC Hansa Rostock	H	1-1	Nowak
27/02/99	SC Freiburg	A	0-0	
06/03/99	Hamburger SV	H	4-1	Thomsen, Reyna 2, Akonnor
13/03/99	SV Werder Bremen	A	1-0	Nowak
19/03/99	Borussia Dortmund	H	0-0	
03/04/99	FC Schalke 04	A	0-2	
10/04/99	1.FC Kaiserslautern	H	2-1	Präger 2
13/04/99	Eintracht Frankfurt	A	1-0	og (Schur)
17/04/99	TSV 1860 München	H	1-0	Nowak
24/04/99	Borussia Mönchengladbach	A	2-5	Präger, Akonnor
01/05/99	VfB Stuttgart	H	3-2	Schröder, Baumgart, Präger
05/05/99	Hertha BSC Berlin	A	0-2	
08/05/99	1.FC Nürnberg	H	1-1	Präger
15/05/99	VfL Bochum	A	2-0	Thomsen, Baumgart
22/05/99	Bayer 04 Leverkusen	H	1-0	Juskowiak
29/05/99	MSV Duisburg	A	1-6	Juskowiak

PROMOTED CLUBS

SECOND DIVISION FINAL TABLE 98/99

		Pd	W	D	L	F	A	Pt	GD
1	Arminia Bielefeld	34	20	7	7	62	32	67	+30
2	SpVgg Unterhaching	34	19	6	9	47	30	63	+17
3	SSV Ulm 1846	34	15	13	6	63	51	58	+12
4	Hannover 96	34	16	9	9	52	36	57	+16
5	Karlsruher SC	34	17	5	12	54	43	56	+11
6	Tennis Borussia Berlin	34	15	9	10	47	39	54	+8
7	1.FSV Mainz 05	34	14	8	12	48	44	50	+4
8	SpVgg Greuther Fürth	34	13	10	11	40	31	49	+9
9	FC St. Pauli	34	12	9	13	49	46	45	+3
10	1.FC Köln	34	12	9	13	46	53	45	-7
11	FC Energie Cottbus	34	10	11	13	48	42	41	+6
12	Rot-Weiss Oberhausen	34	9	14	11	40	47	41	-7
13	Stuttgarter Kickers	34	11	8	15	38	53	41	-15
14	Fortuna Köln	34	9	13	12	49	55	40	-6
15	FC Gütersloh	34	10	7	17	39	58	37	-19
16	KFC Uerdingen 05	34	7	10	17	34	57	31	-23
17	SG Wattenscheid 09	34	7	9	18	31	46	30	-15
18	Fortuna Düsseldorf	34	5	13	16	35	59	28	-24

CLUB DIRECTORY

Arminia Bielefeld
Melanchthonstrasse 2
33615 Bielefeld
tel - (0521) 966110
fax - (0521) 9661111
Year of Formation - 1905
President - Hans-Hermann Schwick
Secretary - Werner Vogt
Coach - Ernst Middendorp; Thomas von Heesen
(99/00 - Hermann Gerland)
Stadium - Alm (22,512)

CLUB DIRECTORY

Spielvereinigung Unterhaching
Am Sportpark 1
82008 Unterhaching
tel - (089) 61559160
fax - (089) 615591688
Year of Formation - 1925
President - Engelbert Kupka
Manager - Norbert Hartmann
Coach - Lorenz-Günther Köstner
Stadium - Sportpark (10,000)

CLUB DIRECTORY

SSV Ulm 1846
Stadionstrasse 17
89073 Ulm
tel - (0731) 18460
fax - (0731) 1846101
Year of Formation - 1970
President - Florian Ebner
Secretary - Hartmut Häussler
Coach - Ralf Rangnick; Martin Andermatt
Stadium - Donaustadion (19,500)

GREECE

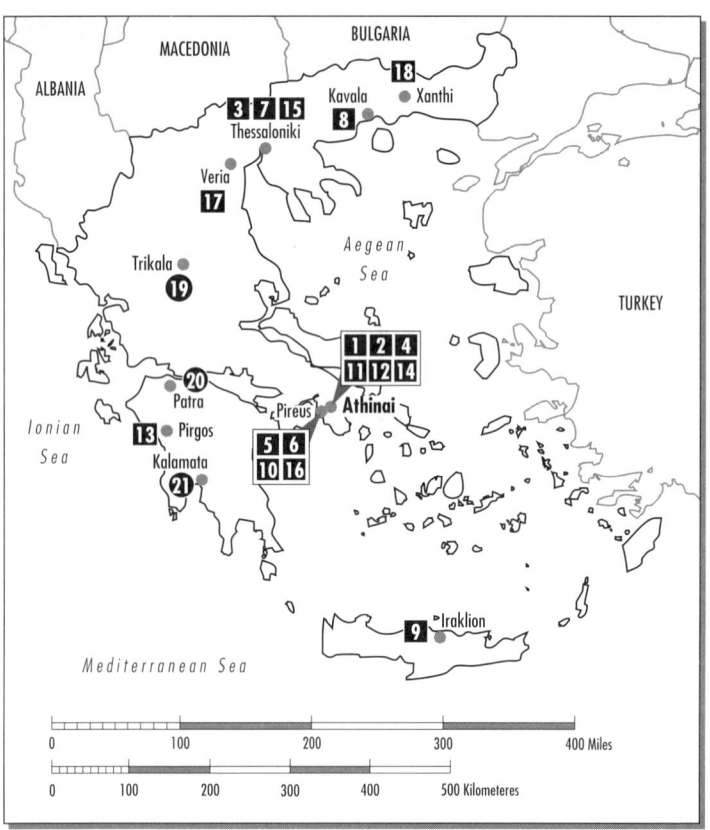

1	AEK	461
2	APOLLON	462
3	ARIS	463
4	ETHNIKOS ASTERAS	464
5	ETHNIKOS PIRAEUS	465
6	IONIKOS	466
7	IRAKLIS	467
8	KAVALA	468
9	OFI	469
10	OLYMPIAKOS	470
11	PANATHINAIKOS	471

12	PANELEFSINIAKOS	472
13	PANILIAKOS	473
14	PANIONIOS	474
15	PAOK	475
16	PROODEFTIKI	476
17	VERIA	477
18	XANTHI	478
Promoted clubs		
19	TRIKALA	479
20	PANAHAIKI	479
21	KALAMATA	479

IORDANESCU MAKES EARLY EXIT

Tenth 'double' for omnipotent Olympiakos

FEDERATION DIRECTORY

Elliniki Podosferiki Omospondia
Leoforos Singrou 137, Athinai 17121

tel - 9311500   Year of Formation - 1926
fax - 9359666   President - Kostas Trivelas

Stadium - OAKA 'Spiros Louis', Athinai (74,433)

Everything Olympiakos touched in 1998/99 seemed to turn to gold. Well, almost everything... The Piraeus giants could not quite add European glory to their undisputed domestic supremacy, but they weren't far away. Only an improbable error of judgment from goalkeeper Dimitris Eleftheropoulos five minutes from the end of an intriguing quarter-final clash with Juventus prevented the club from claiming a place in the last four of the Champions' League.

Who knows what might have happened had Antonio Conte not scored that decisive goal in Athens? Perhaps Olympiakos, not Manchester United, would have gone on to win an historic 'treble'...

Dusan Bajevic's side might not have been quite up to the mark in Europe - although reaching the quarter-finals constituted the club's best ever performance in continental competition - but at home they were a class above the rest.

For the third year running Olympiakos claimed the Greek championship, winning it by a full ten points from runners-up AEK. What's more, they added the Greek Cup, beating arch-rivals Panathinaikos 2-0 in the final despite having a one-man disadvantage for most of the match following defender Yeorgios Amanatis's first-half dismissal. Victories in both league and Cup gave Olympiakos the tenth 'double' in their history.

Such was Olympiakos's superiority in the league that they were able to celebrate their title hat-trick three rounds from the finish with a 3-2 home win over Iraklis. The team produced their best form in the second half of the campaign, when they collected 45 points from a possible 51. It was only after a 0-2 defeat by AEK at the end of January that they looked at all vulnerable, but a run of ten straight victories dispelled any doubts, leaving AEK and Panathinaikos to wage a private battle for second place.

LEAGUE CHAMPIONSHIP RESULTS 98/99

		1	2	3	4	5	6	7	8	9	10	11	12	13	14	15	16	17	18
1	AEK		3-1	6-0	3-1	2-0	2-1	2-2	4-0	2-0	2-0	2-0	6-2	3-1	3-0	2-0	1-0	2-0	2-1
2	Apollon	1-1		1-3	2-2	4-0	1-1	1-3	1-1	1-0	2-5	1-3	1-1	5-0	0-0	1-4	2-2	2-0	2-1
3	Aris	2-0	2-1		2-0	4-0	1-1	2-1	3-1	3-1	1-0	0-1	0-0	3-1	2-1	2-0	1-0	2-0	1-2
4	Ethnikos Asteras	2-3	5-1	0-1		1-0	1-1	1-0	3-2	1-0	1-3	0-1	0-0	1-0	2-2	1-0	2-2	4-0	0-1
5	Ethnikos Piraeus	1-4	2-3	1-1	1-2		1-2	1-2	0-2	1-3	0-3	0-0	2-2	1-1	0-4	1-1	0-2	0-2	1-1
6	Ionikos	2-1	3-0	3-0	5-0	5-0		0-2	4-2	2-0	1-3	4-4	3-0	1-1	4-3	1-0	2-0	1-0	0-1
7	Iraklis	2-3	2-0	2-1	1-1	4-0	2-1		2-2	3-0	0-2	3-3	2-3	3-1	2-0	1-0	0-1	2-0	2-2
8	Kavala	2-1	0-1	3-1	3-0	3-0	1-3	2-0		0-2	0-2	2-1	3-0	1-1	1-5	1-1	2-1	2-1	1-1
9	OFI	0-1	0-1	2-4	1-1	3-0	2-1	3-1	4-0		1-2	2-3	3-0	1-0	3-2	0-0	3-0	4-2	
10	Olympiakos	0-0	0-0	1-0	4-2	2-0	2-0	3-2	4-1	3-0		0-0	1-1	3-0	5-0	2-1	6-1	5-0	3-1
11	Panathinaikos	0-0	5-0	3-1	4-1	5-1	2-1	3-2	6-2	1-0	2-4		2-0	2-1	2-1	0-1	1-0	1-0	2-1
12	Panelefsiniakos	0-0	1-0	0-1	1-2	3-0	1-1	0-0	1-1	1-2	0-2	1-2		1-2	1-0	0-4	0-1	2-0	0-0
13	Paniliakos	0-1	3-1	3-1	1-0	2-0	1-4	2-1	2-0	1-2	1-0	1-2	2-0		2-0	1-2	1-2	0-0	0-0
14	Panionios	1-3	4-2	3-2	2-0	2-0	0-2	3-2	1-2	0-1	1-4	0-2	3-0	5-2		0-1	0-0	0-0	0-2
15	PAOK	2-1	3-1	1-4	5-1	0-0	0-0	2-1	1-0	3-1	1-2	2-0	3-1	2-0	3-0		1-0	2-0	0-0
16	Proodeftiki	1-1	0-1	2-1	3-0	0-0	0-0	1-0	1-0	0-1	0-1	1-2	0-1	2-0	0-0	2-1		1-0	1-2
17	Veria	0-3	1-1	0-1	3-1	4-3	0-2	0-2	0-2	0-0	0-3	0-1	0-1	0-0	3-1	1-2	3-1		2-0
18	Xanthi	2-1	1-0	2-0	0-1	2-0	2-2	0-0	4-1	3-1	0-2	1-0	0-0	2-1	1-0	0-1	4-1	2-0	

LEAGUE CHAMPIONSHIP FINAL TABLE 98/99

				Home				Away					Total						
		P	W	D	L	F	A	W	D	L	F	A	W	D	L	F	A	P	GD
1	Olympiakos	34	13	4	0	44	9	14	0	3	38	13	27	4	3	82	22	85	+60
2	AEK	34	16	1	0	47	9	7	5	5	24	18	23	6	5	71	27	75	+44
3	Panathinaikos	34	14	1	2	41	16	9	4	4	25	20	23	5	6	66	36	74	+30
4	PAOK	34	12	3	2	31	12	7	2	8	21	19	19	5	10	52	31	62	+21
5	Ionikos	34	12	2	3	41	17	5	7	5	23	19	17	9	8	64	36	60	+28
6	Aris	34	13	2	2	31	10	6	1	10	22	33	19	3	12	53	43	60	+10
7	Xanthi	34	11	3	3	26	11	5	5	7	18	22	16	8	10	44	33	56	+11
8	OFI	34	10	2	5	36	19	6	1	10	14	25	16	3	15	50	44	51	+6
9	Iraklis	34	9	4	4	33	20	4	4	9	21	25	13	8	13	54	45	47	+9
10	Kavala	34	9	3	5	27	21	3	3	11	19	41	12	6	16	46	62	42	-16
11	Ethnikos Asteras	34	8	4	5	25	17	3	3	11	15	41	11	7	16	40	58	40	-18
12	Proodeftiki	34	6	5	6	14	11	4	4	9	14	26	10	9	15	28	37	39	-9
13	Paniliakos	34	10	1	6	24	16	1	4	12	13	38	11	5	18	37	54	38	-17
14	Apollon	34	5	7	5	28	27	4	2	11	14	35	9	9	16	42	62	36	-20
15	Panionios	34	7	2	8	25	25	2	3	12	17	33	9	5	20	42	58	32	-16
16	Panelefsiniakos	34	4	5	8	13	18	3	6	8	12	31	7	11	16	25	49	32	-24
17	Veria	34	5	3	9	17	24	1	2	14	3	31	6	5	23	20	55	23	-35
18	Ethnikos Piraeus	34	0	6	11	13	35	0	2	15	4	46	0	8	26	17	81	8	-64

N.B. Where two or more teams are level on points, classification is determined by the results of the matches between them.

By the time the curtain came down on the season there were few people prepared to dispute Olympiakos's right to be proclaimed champions for the 28th time. However, in the first half of the season many accusations of favouritism from referees were hurled in their direction. The most controversial matches were the victories gained by Olympiakos away to PAOK (2-1) and Panathinaikos (4-2). Both produced disturbing crowd scenes generated by hotly disputed decisions made by the match officials in the visitors' favour. In Salonika an 82nd-minute pitch invasion led to the match being abandoned - and PAOK being punished with a five-game stadium ban - after Olympiakos had been handed a non-existent penalty.

Remarkably, Olympiakos were awarded a total of 11 penalties over the course of the season - the highest number in the division - but not one was given against them. The evidence for a conspiracy on their behalf was, of course, only circumstantial, but it was strengthened by another statistic - not a single red card shown to an Olympiakos player during the entire league campaign. Olympiakos argued that the reason for this flawless record was quite simply that the team played fair and were able to maintain their discipline despite constant pressure and provocation.

Olympiakos's Champions' League exploits did a lot to sway nationwide opinion in their favour. Few expected

them to top a group containing Ajax, FC Porto and Croatia Zagreb, but they did just that, thanks predominantly to a perfect home record. The main stars of the domestic and European campaigns were shaven-headed left-winger Grigorios Yeorgatos, defender Yeorgios Anatolakis, rejuvenated playmaker Vasilios Karapialis and Cypriot international striker Sinisa Gogic. First and foremost, however, Olympiakos succeeded through their collective endeavour, with Bajevic, the 'man from Mostar', re-affirming his unchallenged reputation as the outstanding coach in the country.

Like Olympiakos, Panathinaikos reached the group phase of the Champions' League. But despite the unexpected boost of a 2-1 win at home to Dynamo Kiev in their opening group fixture they could not raise their game sufficiently away from home and went out at the end of the group stage, bowing out meekly with a 1-3 defeat in Athens against a team of Arsenal reserves. The club were to suffer a third successive season without a trophy. They could win none of their big games in the

INTERNATIONAL HONOURS

World Cup Finals appearances: 1994
European Championship appearances (last 8): 1980

championship, and their Cup final defeat by Olympiakos completed an unwanted hat-trick of losses in that fixture. Coach Vasilios Daniil was sacked after a home defeat by PAOK and replaced by ex-boss Juan Ramón Rocha, but by the end of the season the club had decided to start afresh with another coach, former player Ioanis Kirastas.

Panathinaikos missed out on a return to the Champions' League after finishing a point behind Athens rivals AEK. The 'Yellow and Blacks' also went through a season of instability but were rescued by the goals of the league's top

scorer, 22-goal Themistoklis Nikolaidis. New coach Dragoslav Stepanovic was sacked after a sensational Cup defeat by a Third Division side and replaced by Oleg Blokhin. Although the Ukrainian steered AEK into second place, he, too, was dismissed at the season's end, with Ljubisa Tumbakovic, of Partizan Belgrade, being brought in to oversee the new campaign.

Four Greek clubs were granted UEFA Cup places in 1999/2000. Panathinaikos and PAOK took two of them, while the other berths went, rather surprisingly, to Ionikos (who had never qualified for Europe before) and Aris (just

NATIONAL TEAM APPEARANCES 98/99

Coach - Anghel IORDANESCU; Vasilios DANIIL	SLO	GEO	ALB	FIN	BEL	CRO	NOR	LAT	SUI	GEO	LAT	Cps	Gls
Ilias ATMATSIDIS (24/04/69) - AEK	G	G	G	G		G	G	G	G46	G	G	43	-
Vasilios BORBOKIS (10/02/69) - Sheffield United (ENG)	D83											2	-
Marinos OUZOUNIDIS (10/10/68) - Le Havre AC (FRA)	D	D	D			D	D	D	D	D	D	27	2
Ioanis KALITZAKIS (10/12/66) - AEK	D	D	D		D	D82						71	-
Nikolaos DABIZAS (03/08/73) - Newcastle United (ENG)	D	D	D89				D	D				28	-
Mihail KASAPIS (06/06/71) - AEK	D78							D	D	D	D	31	-
Theodoros ZAGORAKIS (17/10/71) - Leicester City (ENG)	M	M	M		M	M46	s74	s46	M79	M		43	-
Dimitrios MARKOS (31/01/71) - AEK	M	M	M	M62		M	M55				s73	15	1
Vasilios TSARTAS (12/11/72) - Sevilla FC (ESP)	M46	s74										26	3
Nikolaos MAHLAS (16/06/73) - Vitesse (HOL)	A	A84	A			s55	A80		A	A		44	14
Themistoklis NIKOLAIDIS (17/09/73) - AEK	A		A69	A	s67	A	A	A				27	10
Konstandinos FRANTZESKOS (04/01/69) - PAOK	s46	M74	M46			s76	s74	s46	s79	M60		32	7
Grigoris YEORGATOS (31/10/72) - Olympiakos	s78	M	M	M	s67	M59	M	M74	M	M61	M73	22	2
Nikolaos LIBEROPOULOS (04/08/75) - Panathinaikos	s83	A68	s46	A85	s83	A82	A76	A	A			12	1
Ilias POURSANIDIS (13/04/72) - Olympiakos		M	M	M	s71	M	M	M46	M			20	-
Stilianos YANAKOPOULOS (12/07/74) - Olympiakos		s68		s62	M	M59	M	M74	M80			10	3
Dimitrios MAVROYENIDIS (23/12/76) - Olympiakos		s84		D	s67		s46	D	D	D	D	8	-
Konstandinos KONSTANDINIDIS (31/08/72) - Panathinaikos			s69		M67	M71			s33	M46		21	1
Leonidas VOKOLOS (02/06/70) - Panathinaikos			s89									1	-
Panayotis FISAS (12/06/73) - Panathinaikos			D70									1	-
Yeorgos ANATOLAKIS (16/03/74) - Olympiakos				D		s82	D		D	D	D	10	-
Ioanis GOUMAS (24/05/75) - Panathinaikos				D		D						2	-
Andreas ZIKOS (01/06/74) - AEK				M	M67				s80		M	4	-
Pantelis KONSTANDINIDIS (16/08/75) - PAOK				s70	M83	s59						3	-
Sotirios KONSTANDINIDIS (16/08/75) - Iraklis				s85	A	s59						3	-
Dimitrios ELEFTHEROPOULOS (07/08/76) - Olympiakos				G					s46			2	-
Paraskevas ANTZAS (18/08/76) - Olympiakos				D								1	-
Anastasios KATSIABIS (30/07/73) - PAOK				M								1	-
Apostolos LIOLIDIS (13/08/77) - Aris				A67								1	-
Ioanis ANASTASIOU (05/03/73) - RSC Anderlecht (BEL)					s82		s80		s61	s60		4	-
Andreas NINIADIS (18/02/71) - Olympiakos									M46	M	M79	4	1
Thomas KIPARISIS (26/03/70) - Xanthi									A33			1	-
Nikolaos FROUSOS (29/04/74) - Ionikos									s46	s79		2	-

EUROPEAN CUPS 98/99

CHAMPIONS' CUP
● OLYMPIAKOS
Qualifying round ANORTHOSIS FAMAGUSTA (CYP)
H 2-1 Yanakopoulos (11), Luciano (32)
Eleftheropoulos; Karataidis, Yeorgatos (Sfakianakis 63), Ofori-Quaye, Luciano, Ivic (Aboague 68), Pasalis (Anatolakis 46), Poursanidis, Djordjevic, Yanakopoulos, Mavroyenidis.

A 4-2 Yeorgatos (47), Djordjevic (57, 85), Gogic (90)
Eleftheropoulos; Karataidis, Yeorgatos, Ofori-Quaye, Anatolakis (Karapialis 46), Luciano (Gogic 89), Ivic (Yanakopoulos 70), Poursanidis, Djordjevic, Mavroyenidis, Amanatidis.

Champions' League
1st match FC PORTO (POR)
A 2-2 Yanakopoulos (79), Gogic (90)
Eleftheropoulos; Karataidis, Yeorgatos, Ofori-Quaye, Anatolakis, Luciano (Gogic 89), Ivc (Yanakopoulos 78), Poursanidis, Djordjevic, Mavroyenidis, Amanatidis (Karapialis 83).

2nd match CROATIA ZAGREB (CRO)
H 2-0 Alexandris (21), Gogic (80)
Eleftheropoulos; Karataidis, Anatolakis, Poursanidis, Djordjevic, Yanakopoulos, Mavroyenidis, Amanatidis (Antzas 75), Gogic, Karapialis (Niniadis 72), Alexandris (Luciano 90).

3rd match AJAX (HOL)
H 1-0 Alexandris (38)
Eleftheropoulos; Karataidis, Yeorgatos, Anatolakis, Poursanidis, Djordjevic, Yanakopoulos, Amanatidis, Gogic (Ofori-Quaye 74), Karapialis (Niniadis 85), Alexandris (Pasalis 68).

4th match AJAX (HOL)
A 0-2
Eleftheropoulos; Karataidis, Yeorgatos, Anatolakis, Pasalis, Djordjevic (Niniadis 67), Yanakopoulos, Mavroyenidis, Gogic (Ivic 75), Karapialis, Alexandris (Ofori-Quaye 54).

5th match FC PORTO (POR)
H 2-1 Gogic (18), Djordjevic (54)
Eleftheropoulos; Karataidis, Yeorgatos (Luciano 82), Anatolakis, Poursanidis, Djordjevic, Yanakopoulos (Pasalis 54), Mavroyenidis, Gogic, Karapialis (Antzas 69), Alexandris.

6th match CROATIA ZAGREB (CRO)
A 1-1 Yanakopoulos (64)
Eleftheropoulos; Karataidis, Yeorgatos, Anatolakis, Poursanidis, Djordjevic (Luciano 61), Yanakopoulos (Alexandris 79), Mavroyenidis, Amanatidis, Gogic (Ofori-Quaye 84), Niniadis.

Quarter-final JUVENTUS (ITA)
A 1-2 Niniadis (90p)
Eleftheropoulos; Karataidis, Yeorgatos (Niniadis 90), Anatolakis, Poursanidis, Djordjevic, Yanakopoulos (Ivic 75), Mavroyenidis, Amanatidis, Gogic, Karapialis (Alexandris 75).
H 1-1 Gogic (12)
Eleftheropoulos; Karataidis, Yeorgatos (Luciano 86), Anatolakis, Poursanidis, Djordjevic, Yanakopoulos, Mavroyenidis, Amanatidis (Alexandris 86), Gogic, Karapialis (Abonsai 78).

● PANATHINAIKOS
Qualifying round STEAUA BUCURESTI (ROM)
A 2-2 Asanovic (5), Liberopoulos (68)
Wandzik; Alexopoulos, Apostolakis (Konstandinidis 82), Milojevic, Asanovic, Goumas, Lagonikakis, Liberopoulos (Kola 84), Mykland, Warzycha, Basinas.

H 6-3 Milojevic (8p), Licar (27og), Liberopoulos (34), Warzycha (59, 67), Asanovic (87)
Wandzik; Alexopoulos, Apostolakis, Milojevic, Asanovic, Goumas, Lagonikakis (Konstandinidis 57), Liberopoulos (Strandli 85), Mykland, Warzycha, Basinas (Kola 77).

Champions' League
1st match DYNAMO KYIV (UKR)
H 2-1 Mykland (57), Liberopoulos (69)
Wandzik; Konstandinidis, Apostolakis, Milojevic, Asanovic, Goumas, Liberopoulos (Alexopoulos 88), Mykland, Warzycha (Strandli 86), Vokolos (Kola 68), Kiasos.

2nd match ARSENAL (ENG)
A 1-2 Mauro (88)
Wandzik; Konstandinidis, Apostolakis, Milojevic, Asanovic, Goumas, Lagonikakis, Liberopoulos (Mauro 83), Mykland, Strandli (Sypniewski 83), Kiasos (Kola 71).

3rd match RC LENS (FRA)
A 0-1
Wandzik; Konstandinidis, Apostolakis, Asanovic, Goumas, Lagonikakis (Mykland 82), Liberopoulos, Kola, Vokolos, Kiasos (Basinas 46), Mauro (Alexoudis 58).

4th match RC LENS (FRA)
H 1-0 Vokolos (53)
Wandzik; Konstandinidis, Apostolakis, Milojevic, Asanovic (Kiasos 81), Goumas, Lagonikakis, Liberopoulos, Warzycha (Mauro 88), Basinas, Vokolos.

5th match DYNAMO KYIV (UKR)
A 1-2 Lagonikakis (36)
Wandzik; Konstandinidis, Alexopoulos, Apostolakis (Kola 77), Asanovic, Lagonikakis, Liberopoulos, Warzycha, Basinas, Vokolos, Kiasos (Mauro 85).

6th match ARSENAL (ENG)
H 1-3 Sypniewski (74)
Wandzik; Konstandinidis (Strandli 69), Apostolakis, Milojevic, Asanovic, Goumas, Lagonikakis, Liberopoulos, Kola (Sypniewski 56), Warzycha, Basinas (Vokolos 78).

CUP WINNERS' CUP
● PANIONIOS
1st round FC HAKA (FIN)
H 2-0 Haylock (36), Robins (53)
Strakosha; Kruse, Ioanidis, Bougas, Robins (Kouvalis 86), Haylock (Nalitzis 90), Sapountzis (Kafalis 64), Mitsiopoulos, Fisas, Zahopoulos, Karasavidis

A 3-1 Fisas (33), Kouvalis (45), Sapountzis (57)
Strakosha; Kruse (Kamitsis 73), Ioanidis, Bougas, Kouvalis, Haylock (Robins 58), Sapountzis, Mitsiopoulos, Fisas, Zahopoulos (Gazis 84), Karasavidis.

a year after their return to the First Division).

Panionios, who reached the quarter-finals of the last-ever Cup-winners' Cup before being torn apart by eventual winners Lazio, had a wretched season in the league and were lucky to avoid relegation. Only their superior head-to-head record with Panelefsiniakos kept

EUROPEAN CUPS 98/99 (CONT.)

2nd round APOLLON LIMASSOL (CYP)
H 3-2   Sapountzis (25), Haylock (40), Robins (57)
Strakosha; Kruse, Ioanidis, Robins, Kouvalis, Haylock, Sapountzis (Kafalis 46), Mitsiopoulos, Fisas, Zahopoulos (Nalitzis 82), Karasavidis (Bergersen 90).
A 1-0   Sapountzis (18)
Strakosha; Ioanidis, Bougas, Haylock (Nalitzis 65), Sapountzis, Mitsiopoulos, Fisas (Markesinis 90), Zahopoulos, Karasavidis, Kamitsis, Bergersen (Kafalis 85).

Quarter-final LAZIO (ITA)
H 0-4
Strakosha; Ioanidis, Bougas, Haylock, Sapountzis, Zahopoulos, Karasavidis (Robins 63), Gazis, Bakkerud, Roberts, Tisdale.
A 0-3
Strakosha; Robins (Haylock 60), Sapountzis, Mitsiopoulos, Zahopoulos (Ioanidis 46), Karasavidis, Kamitsis, Gazis, Bakkerud (Bougas 71), Roberts, Tisdale.

UEFA CUP
● **AEK**
Qualifying round FERENCVÁROS (HUN)
A 2-4   Nikolaidis (87), Sebwe (89)
Atmatsidis; Kalitzakis, Kasapis, Babunski, Lakis, Zikos, Markos (Savevski 56), Maladenis (Sebwe 70), Kopitsis (Donis 72), Nikolaidis, Kostenoglou.
H 4-0   Nikolaidis (8, 12p, 25), Donis (62)
Atmatsidis; Kalitzakis, Kasapis, Lakis (Babunski 45), Zikos, Markos, Maladenis (Donis 57), Suvevski, Kopitsis (Grétarsson 50), Nikolaidis, Kostenoglou.

1st round VITESSE (HOL)
A 0-3
Atmatsidis; Kalitzakis, Kasapis, Babunski, Lakis, Markos, Maladenis (Iliev 81), Savevski (Karayanis 70), Kopitsis (Grétarsson 72), Nikolaidis, Kostenoglou.
H 3-3   Nikolaidis (14, 76), Kopitsis (67)
Mihailidis; Babunski (Grétarsson 83), Zikos, Markos, Maladenis (Sebwe 75), Kopitsis, Nikolaidis, Kostenoglou, Iliev (Lakis 63), Karayanis, Kefalas.

● **PAOK**
Qualifying round RANGERS (SCO)
A 0-2
Mihopoulos; Olivares, Bandovic, Maheridis, Katsiabis, Vrizas (Cominges 65), Frantzeskos, Konstandinidis, Nagbe, Kapetanopoulos, Toursounidis (Zafiriou 46).
H 0-0
Mihopoulos; Olivares, Bandovic, Koulakiotis, Katsiabis, Vrizas (Cominges 52), Frantzeskos, Toursounidis (Mirafaliev 64), Kapetanopoulos, Nagbe, Zafiriou (Kafes 72).

PLAYERS OF THE SEASON

THEMISTOKLIS NIKOLAIDIS
Even to Greeks his first name is considered something of a mouthful, so Themistoklis Nikoliadis is regularly referred to as either "Demis" (the common abbreviation) or "Deminio" (the AEK fans like to think of him as having Brazilian-type skills). A regular member of the Greek national team, he is an elusive striker with a keen goalscorer's instinct. He topped the Greek First Division goal charts with 22 goals in 1998/99 to bring his all-time haul to 79 in 128 appearances. He also made quite an impression in Europe, netting six UEFA Cup goals in just four games. A big AEK fan since childhood, he joined the club from Apollon in 1996 and was quickly idolised by the AEK supporters, who consider him to be one of their own.

NIKOLAOS FROUSOS
Runner-up to Nikolaidis in the 1998/99 Greek goal charts was 25-year-old Ionikos forward Nikolaos "Nikos" Frousos. His 18 goals were the main reason behind the club's first ever European qualification. He failed to score at all during the first three months of the campaign, but once he got his eye in, he proved unstoppable, peaking with eight goals in the team's eight-match unbeaten run that concluded their successful drive for Europe. A first call-up to the Greek national team soon followed, and there was more for him to celebrate later in the summer when he ended his seven-year association with Ionikos by signing a lucrative contract with Aris of Salonika - another team qualified to compete in the 1999/2000 UEFA Cup.

them in the top flight. Panelefsiniakos were joined in relegation by Veria and Ethnikos Piraeus. The latter set a new record, becoming the first team ever to complete a First Division season without a single victory. Their meagre total of eight points constituted another 'worst-ever' tally, matching Kastoria's record underachievement of two years earlier.

There was much hype surrounding the appointment of Romanian Anghel Iordanescu as the new coach of the Greek national team, but his period in charge ended prematurely after just eight months. Never comfortable in his new surroundings, he threw in the towel after a crucial European Championship qualifying defeat at home to

DOMESTIC CUP 98/99

FIRST ROUND
Posidon 1, AEK 0
Anayenisi K. 4, Apollon K.V. 2
Paniliakos 6, Ayersani 1
Marko 6, Apollon Kalamaria 2
Athinaikos 2, Kastoria 1
Larisa 3, Proodeftiki 0
Ambelokipi 3, Doxa Drama 1
Iraklis 4, Nafpaktiakos 1
Panseraikos 2, Yanina 1
Aris 2, Naousa 0
Panetolikos 2, Edesaikos 1
Panargiakos 1, Trikala 0
Kavala 1, Atromitos 0
Panelefsiniakos 5, Preveza 0
Kozani 2, Apollon 1
Eolikos 2, Ethnikos Asteras 1
EAR 2, Kilkisiakos 1
PAOK 5, Aetos 0
Panahaiki 2, Veria 0
AO Karditsa 4, Levadiakos 0
Paneyalios 0, Ayos Nikolaos 0
(4-1 on pens.)
Liki 2, Ahaiki 0
Xanthi 2, Kalithea 0
Ethnikos Piraeus 2, Niki 1
Ialisos 1, Keratsini 0
Kalamata 1, Pierikos 0
Panathinaikos 2, Panionios 1
Olympiakos 4, Egaleo 2

Ionikos 1, Olympiakos Volos 1
(4-3 on pens.)
OFI 3, Doxa Virona 1

SECOND ROUND
Ionikos 3, OFI 2
Eolikos 0, Anayenisi K. 0 (5-4 on pens.)
Kalamata 2, Marko 0
Posidon 1, Panahaiki 1 (8-7 on pens.)
Paniliakos 3, Kavala 0
AO Karditsa 2, Panetolikos 1
PAOK 3, Paneyalios 1
Larissa 1, Ambelokipi 0
Liki 2, EAR 1
Panathinaikos 2, Panelefsiniakos 1
Athinaikos 2, Panargiakos 1
Olympiakos 3, Aris 1
Iraklis 2, Ialisos 2 (4-2 on pens.)
Xanthi 1, Ethnikos Piraeus 0

THIRD ROUND
Olympiakos 7, Ionikos 4
Xanthi 2, AO Karditsa 0
Iraklis 2, Posidon 1
Athinaikos 2, Lariss 0
Panseraikos 1, PAOK 0
Kalamata 3, Eolikos 0
Liki 5, Kozani 1
Panathinaikos 2, Paniliakos 0

QUARTER-FINALS
Liki 1 (Pandelis 12),
Iraklis 3 (Semos 18, Andersson 84,
Ignatiadis 90og)
Iraklis 1 (Xenidis 49),
Liki 2 (Klokidis 27, Katikaridis 90)
(Iraklis 4-3)

Athinaikos 0, Kalamata 0
Kalamata 1 (Troupkos 51),
Athinaikos 1 (Kozanidis 34)
(1-1; Athinaikos on away goal)

Panseraikos 0,
Panathinaikos 3 (Goumas 16,
Sypniewski 28, Vokolos 86)
Panathinaikos 2
(Milojevic 45, Sypniewski 85),
Panseraikos 0
(Panathinaikos 5-0)

Olympiakos 3 (Karapialis 1,
Yeorgatos 61, Alexandris 76),
Xanthi 1 (Mansourian 50)
Xanthi 1 (Kiparisis 52), Olympiakos 0
(Olympiakos 3-2)

SEMI-FINALS
Panathinaikos 6 (Warzycha 22, 41,
64, Luciano 4, 74, Karagounis 24),
Athinaikos 1 (Veletakos 17)

Athinaikos 2 (Miselic 78, Haristeas 82),
Panathinaikos 2
(Podaras 41, Alexoudis 86)
(Panathinaikos 8-3)

Olympiakos 4
(Anatolakis 23, Mavroyenidis 65,
Xenidis 69og, Gogic 86), Iraklis 0
Iraklis 1 (Tavlaridis 47),
Olympiakos 1 (Gogic 30)
(Olympiakos 5-1)

FINAL
05/05/99, Athens
OLYMPIAKOS 2 Mavroyenidis (54),
Ofori-Quaye (89)
PANATHINAIKOS 0
referee - Douros
OLYMPIAKOS - Eleftheropoulos;
Mavroyenidis, Amanatidis, Anatolakis,
Karataidis, Djordjevic, Yeorgatos,
Karapialis (Antzas 82), Gogic
(Miniadis 87), Poursanidis, Alexandris
(Ofori-Quaye 72).
PANATHINAIKOS - Nikopolidis; Kiasos
(Lagonikakis 66), Vokolos, Goumas,
Basinas, Konstandinidis, Asanovic
(Alexoudis 72), Mykland, Liberopoulos
(Kola 81), Karagounis, Warzycha.

Norway. Recently-dismissed Panathinaikos coach Vasilios Daniil stepped in to fill the vacancy, but after leading the team to positive results in Riga and Tbilisi, he could only look on in horror in as Greece's qualifying chances suffered a devastating blow with another crippling home defeat, 1-2 against Latvia, with the opposition's winner arriving from the penalty spot in the last minute.

With just four points collected from four home games, Greece's prospects of going to Belgium and Holland in the summer of 2000 looked decidedly slim...

TOP SCORERS

22	Themistoklis NIKOLAIDIS (AEK)
18	Nikolaos FROUSOS (Ionikos)
14	Leszek PISZ (Kavala)
	Ismail BA (Xanthi)
13	Krzysztof WARZYCHA (Panathinaikos)
	Nikolaos LIBEROPOULOS (Panathinaikos)
	Paulo ANDRIOLI (Ionikos/Aris)
	Hristos MALADENIS (AEK)
12	Grigoris YEORGATOS (Olympiakos)
11	Apostolos LIOLIDIS (Aris)
10	Davor JAKOVLJEVIC (Ethnikos Asteras)
	Yeorgios NASIOPOULOS (Kavala)
	Andonis SAPOUNTZIS (Panionios)
	Alexios ALEXANDRIS (Olympiakos)

NATIONAL TEAM RESULTS 98/99

Date	Opponent		Venue	Score	Scorers
06/09/98	Slovenia (ECQ)	H	Athens	2-2	Mahlas (54p), Frantzeskos (58)
14/10/98	Georgia (ECQ)	H	Athens	3-0	Mahlas (13), Liberopoulos (15), Ouzounidis (36)
18/11/98	Albania (ECQ)	A	Tirana	0-0	
03/02/99	Finland	N	Larnaca	2-1	Nikolaidis (66p), Yeorgatos (88)
05/02/99	Belgium	N	Nicosia	1-0	Yanakopoulos (90)
10/03/99	Croatia	H	Athens	3-2	Yanakopoulos (11, 54), Nikolaidis (85)
27/03/99	Norway (ECQ)	H	Athens	0-2	
31/03/99	Latvia (ECQ)	A	Riga	0-0	
28/04/99	Switzerland	H	Athens	1-1	Yeorgatos (58)
05/06/99	Georgia (ECQ)	A	Tbilisi	2-1	Frantzeskos (86), Mahlas (90)
09/06/99	Latvia (ECQ)	H	Athens	1-2	Niniadis (38p)

AEK

CLUB DIRECTORY

Athlitiki Enosi Konstantinoupoleos (AEK)
Tritis Septemvriou 144
11251 Athinai
tel - 8224666/8215645
fax - 8234454
Year of Formation - 1924
President - Lakis Nikolaou
Coach - Dragoslav Stepanovic; Oleg Blokhin
(99/00 - Ljubisa Tumbakovic)
Stadium - Nikos Goumas (33,494)

MAJOR HONOURS
League Championship - (11)
1939, 1940, 1963, 1968, 1971, 1978, 1979,
1989, 1992, 1993, 1994.
Domestic Cup - (10) 1932, 1939, 1949, 1950,
1956, 1966, 1978, 1983, 1996, 1997.

APPEARANCES 98/99

	P	Ap	(s)	Gls
Ilias ATMATSIDIS	G	28		1
Boban BABUNSKI (MAC)	D	8		
Alvin CECCOLI (ITA)	D	3	(1)	1
Yeorgios DONIS	A	11	(2)	
Arnar GRÉTARSSON (ISL)	M	15	(11)	
Ilian ILIEV (BUL)	M	2	(6)	
Ioanis KALITZAKIS	D	25		
Mihail KAPSIS	D	12	(3)	
Vaios KARAYANIS	D	5	(2)	
Vasilios KARAYANIS	G		(1)	
Mihail KASAPIS	D	24	(2)	1
Evripidis KATSAVOS	M	7	(3)	
Evangelos KEFALAS	D	2	(6)	
Harilaos KOPITSIS	M	21	(2)	1
Nikolaos KOSTENOGLOU	D	24	(1)	1
Vasilios LAKIS	M	15	(9)	2
Daniel Batista LIMA	A	6	(6)	4
Hristos MALADENIS	M	22	(3)	13
Dimitrios MARKOS	M	24	(6)	1
Alberto MENDEZ (ENG)	M	7	(4)	
Branko MILOVANOVIC (YUG)	M	9	(5)	2
Hrisostomos MIHAILIDIS	G	6		
Themistoklis NIKOLAIDIS	A	29		22
Yeorgios PASIOS	D		(3)	
Toni SAVEVSKI (MAC)	M	25		7
Kelvin SEBWE (LIB)	M	5	(8)	2
Christopher WREH (LIB)	A	8	(3)	4
Andreas ZIKOS	M	26		2
Parskevas ZOUBOULIS	A	5	(12)	6

LEAGUE RESULTS 1998/99

22/08/98	Panionios	A	3-1	Savevski, Nikolaidis, Kopitsis
30/08/98	Apollon	H	3-1	Maladenis, Nikolaidis 2
12/09/98	Panelefsiniakos	A	0-0	
20/09/98	Veria	H	2-0	Maladenis, Nikolaidis
26/09/98	OFI	A	1-0	Nikolaidis
04/10/98	Paniliakos	H	3-1	Zouboulis 2, Savevski
25/10/98	Proodeftiki	A	1-1	Nikolaidis
01/11/98	Ethnikos Asteras	H	3-1	Zouboulis, Nikolaidis 2 (1p)
07/11/98	PAOK	A	1-2	Nikolaidis
22/11/98	Ionikos	H	2-1	Maladenis, Kostenoglou
30/11/98	Aris	H	6-0	og (Katsiaros), Maladenis,
				Savevski, Nikolaidis 3
06/12/98	Kavala	A	1-2	Savevski
13/12/98	Panathinaikos	H	2-0	Lakis, Savevski
21/12/98	Ethnikos Piraeus	A	4-1	Kasapis, Lima 2, Zikos
17/01/99	Iraklis	H	2-2	Nikolaidis, Lakis
24/01/99	Xanthi	A	1-2	Savevski
31/01/99	Olympiakos	H	2-0	Lima, Nikolaidis
07/02/99	Panionios	H	3-0	Lima, Nikolaidis, Wreh
14/02/99	Apollon	A	1-1	Maladenis
21/02/99	Panelefsiniakos	H	6-2	Wreh, Nikolaidis, Ceccoli, Zikos,
				Markos, Sebwé
28/02/99	Veria	A	3-0	Milovanovic, Nikolaidis, Maladenis
07/03/99	OFI	H	2-0	Nikolaidis 2 (1p)
14/03/99	Paniliakos	A	1-0	Savevski
21/03/99	Proodeftiki	H	1-0	Maladenis
04/04/99	Ethnikos Asteras	A	3-2	Maladenis 2, Nikolaidis
18/04/99	PAOK	H	2-0	Nikolaidis (p), Wreh
25/04/99	Ionikos	A	1-2	Zouboulis
02/05/99	Aris	A	0-2	
09/05/99	Kavala	H	4-0	Maladenis, Milovanovic,
				Zouboulis, Wreh
12/05/99	Panathinaikos	A	0-0	
16/05/99	Ethnikos Piraeus	H	2-0	Sebwé, Zouboulis
19/05/99	Iraklis	A	3-2	Maladenis 3
23/05/99	Xanthi	H	2-1	Nikolaidis, Atmatsidis (p)
30/05/99	Olympiakos	A	0-0	

APOLLON

Apollon
Antheon 45
Rizopolis
11143 Athinai
tel - 2516632
fax - 2517632
Year of Formation - 1891
President - Andreas Alamanos
Coach - Dragan Kokotovic; Yeorgios Stilianopoulos;
Andreas Mihalopoulos
(99/00 - Hristos Arhondidis)
Stadium - Rizoupolis (15,000)

APPEARANCES 98/99

	P	Ap	(s)	Gls
Waldemar ADAMCZYK (POL)	A	5	(12)	
Theodoros ALEXIS	M	20	(7)	4
Ilias ANASTASAKOS	M	14	(5)	3
Rajco BANIAC (YUG)	M	1		
Dietmar BERCHTOLD (AUT)	A	12	(3)	3
Guy BUELE (CMR)	M	13	(4)	1
Yeorgios DIAMANDIS	D	8	(5)	
Edmond DALIPI (ALB)	M	13		2
Andonios DAMIGOS	M	20	(1)	7
Nicolas DIKOUME (CMR)	A	21	(3)	2
Indrit FORTUZI (ALB)	M	6	(6)	
Dragan GLOGOVAC (YUG)	M	7	(1)	
Konstandinos HALKIAS	G	16		
Mihail HATZIS	A	9	(9)	
Spiridon HATZIS	D	25	(4)	
Konstandinos IOANOU	D	27		
Athanasios KARANIKOLAS	M	7	(7)	1
Evangelos KOENDAS	G	6		
Athanasios KOLITSIDAKIS	D	14		
Nikolaos KOURKOUNAS	G	11		
Panayotis LAHANAS	D	20	(5)	1
Hristos LAIOS	M	13	(3)	1
Stavros LAMBRIAKOS	A	25	(3)	8
Fotios MATSANGOS	A	3	(4)	
Theodoros PAPADIMITRIOU	A	29	(2)	6
Dimitrios RAPTIS	G	1		
Nikolaos SAKELARIDIS	M	13	(1)	2
Konstandinos THEODORAKOS	M	11	(3)	
Yeorgios VUREXAKIS	M	3	(4)	
Konstandinos YANAKIS	M	1	(3)	

LEAGUE RESULTS 1998/99

22/08/98	Olympiakos	H	2-5	Dikoumé, Damigos
30/08/98	AEK	A	1-3	Laios
12/09/98	Panionios	A	2-4	Alexis 2
20/09/98	Panelefsiniakos	H	1-1	Damigos
27/09/98	Veria	A	1-1	Sakelaridis
04/10/98	OFI	H	1-0	Damigos
25/10/98	Paniliakos	A	1-3	Alexis
01/11/98	Proodeftiki	H	2-2	Papadimitriou, Alexis
07/11/98	Ethnikos Asteras	A	1-5	Dikoumé (p)
22/11/98	PAOK	H	1-4	Papadimitriou
30/11/98	Ionikos	A	0-3	
06/12/98	Aris	H	1-3	Lambriakos
13/12/98	Kavala	H	1-1	Sakelaridis
20/12/98	Panathinaikos	A	0-5	
17/01/99	Ethnikos Piraeus	H	4-0	Anastasakos, Buele, Berchtold 2
24/01/99	Iraklis	A	0-2	
31/01/99	Xanthi	H	2-1	Papadimitriou, Lambriakos
07/02/99	Olympiakos	A	0-0	
14/02/99	AEK	H	1-1	Lambriakos
21/02/99	Panionios	H	0-0	
28/02/99	Panelefsiniakos	A	0-1	
07/03/99	Veria	H	2-0	og (Huaman), Damigos
14/03/99	OFI	A	1-0	Damigos
21/03/99	Paniliakos	H	5-0	Papadimitriou 2, Damigos 2, Anastasakos
04/04/99	Proodeftiki	A	1-0	Lahanas
17/04/99	Ethnikos Asteras	H	2-2	Lambriakos, Dalipi (p)
25/04/99	PAOK	A	1-3	Lambriakos
02/05/99	Ionikos	H	1-1	Berchtold
09/05/99	Aris	A	1-2	Lambriakos
12/05/99	Kavala	A	1-0	Karanikolas
16/05/99	Panathinaikos	H	1-3	Papadimitriou
20/05/99	Ethnikos Piraeus	A	3-2	Dalipi, Lambriakos 2
23/05/99	Iraklis	H	1-3	Anastasakos
30/05/99	Xanthi	A	0-1	

ARIS

CLUB DIRECTORY

Aris
Vasilisis Olgas 126
Thessaloniki
tel - (031) 862700
fax - (031) 862632
Year of Formation - 1914
President - Lakis Ioannidis
Coach - Yeorgos Firos; Yeorgos Parashos;
Alketas Panagoulias (99/00 - Ilija Petkovic)
Stadium - Harilaou (28,000)

MAJOR HONOURS
League Championship - (3) 1928, 1932, 1946.
Domestic Cup - (1) 1970.

APPEARANCES 98/99

		P	Ap	(s)	Gls
Marios AGATHOKLEOUS (CYP)	M	10	(6)		3
Paulo ANDRIOLI (BRA)	M	19			2
Vasilios BAKOYANIS	A	3	(4)		
David CHEVEZ (PER)	A	4	(4)		
Theodoros DALKIDIS	M	11	(10)		
Alexandros DELIOS	G	8			
Predrag ERAK (CRO)	M	14	(4)		
Carlos FLORES (PER)	M	14	(7)		2
Angelos HARISTEAS	A	6	(6)		4
Theofanis KATERGIANAKIS	G	25			
Panayotis KATSIAROS	D	19			
KENNEDY Nagoli (SAF)	M	31	(2)		5
Nikolaos KIZERIDIS	M	17			4
Yeorgios KOLTSIDAS	D	19			1
Yeorgios KOUTSIS	M	16			2
Apostolos LIOLIDIS	A	25	(4)		11
Konstandinos LOUBOUTIS	M	20	(3)		2
Ioanis MALOUS	M	12	(2)		1
Apostolos MANTZIOS	D	25	(1)		2
Lumir MISTR (CZE)	A	1	(3)		
Emanuil MITSOPOULOS	D	24	(1)		2
Haralambos NIKOLAOU	D		(2)		
Mihail PANOPOULOS	A	13	(9)		3
Kristófer SIGURGEIRSSON (ISL)	M	5	(10)		
Zoran STOJNOVIC (YUG)	M	1	(6)		
Ilias TALIKRIADIS	G	1			
Yeorgios K. THEODORIDIS	D		(1)		
Yeorgios S. THEODORIDIS	M	7	(3)		
Konstandinis VAKIRTSIS	D	2	(2)		
Yeorgios VLAHOUDIS	M	10	(11)		1
Yeorgios YEORGIADIS	M	12			5

LEAGUE RESULTS 1998/99

22/08/98	Ethnikos Asteras	H	2-0	Mantzios, Liolidis
29/08/98	PAOK	A	4-1	Haristeas 2, og (Koulakiotis), Panopoulos
13/09/98	Ionikos	H	1-1	Mitsopoulos
20/09/98	Panionios	H	2-1	Mitsopoulos, Liolidis
27/09/98	Kavala	A	1-3	Haristeas
04/10/98	Panathinaikos	H	0-1	
24/10/98	Ethnikos Piraeus	A	1-1	Vlahoudis
01/11/98	Iraklis	H	2-1	Flores, Liolidis
08/11/98	Xanthi	A	0-2	
22/11/98	Olympiakos	H	1-0	Liolidis
30/11/98	AEK	A	0-6	
06/12/98	Apollon	A	3-1	Kennedy, Louboutis, Mantzios (p)
13/12/98	Panelefsiniakos	H	0-0	
20/12/98	Veria	A	1-0	Haristeas
17/01/99	OFI	H	3-1	Yeorgiadis (p), og (Adamou), Kizeridis
24/01/99	Paniliakos	A	1-3	Koltsidas
31/01/99	Proodeftiki	H	1-0	Kizeridis
07/02/99	Ethnikos Asteras	A	1-0	og (Jakovljevic)
14/02/99	PAOK	H	2-0	Yeorgiadis (p), Kennedy
21/02/99	Ionikos	A	0-3	
28/02/99	Panionios	A	2-3	Kizeridis, Yeorgiadis (p)
07/03/99	Kavala	H	3-1	Liolidis 2, Yeorgiadis
14/03/99	Panathinaikos	A	1-3	Malous
21/03/99	Ethnikos Piraeus	H	4-0	Andrioli, Agathokleous, Koutsis, Yeorgiadis
04/04/99	Iraklis	A	1-2	Agathokleous
18/04/99	Xanthi	H	1-2	Liolidis
25/04/99	Olympiakos	A	0-1	
02/05/99	AEK	H	2-0	Liolidis 2
09/05/99	Apollon	H	2-1	Panopoulos (p), Kennedy
12/05/99	Panelefsiniakos	A	1-0	Koutsis
16/05/99	Veria	H	2-0	Liolidis 2
19/05/99	OFI	A	4-2	Kizeridis, Agathokleous, Kennedy, Louboutis
23/05/99	Paniliakos	H	3-1	Kennedy, Flores, Andrioli
30/05/99	Proodeftiki	A	1-2	Panopoulos

ETHNIKOS ASTERAS

CLUB DIRECTORY

Ethnikos Asteras
Ethnikis Antistasis 118
Kesariani
Athens
tel - 7238652
Year of Formation - 1927
President - Nikos Papadopoulos
Coach - Spiros Livathinos
Stadium - Kaisariadis (4,200)

APPEARANCES 98/99

	P	Ap	(s)	Gls
Serafim ANGELINAS	D		(1)	
Stefanos BASINAS	D	28		4
Ilias BOTAITIS	M	6	(2)	
Apostolos DIMOPOULOS	D	4	(2)	
Zarko DRAGAC (YUG)	M	18	(6)	5
Filipos FRONTZOS	D	9	(1)	1
Evangelos HOSADAS	G	29		
Davor JAKOVLJEVIC (YUG)	A	19	(6)	10
Vladimir JOVANOVIC (YUG)	D	9	(5)	
Theodosios KIKIDAKIS	D	2		
Yeorgios KONDOPOULOS	M	26	(5)	3
Nikolaos KOSTAKIS	G	4	(1)	
Nikolaos KOUSANAS	M	1	(7)	
Yeorgios KOYOGLOU	M	9	(15)	1
Fotios LAGOS	D	27		
André LEONARDO (BRA)	A		(1)	
Yeorgios MASTROYANIS	M	1	(3)	
Tzanis MONOS	D	1	(1)	
Dimitrios NALITZIS	A	12	(1)	6
Dimitrios NIARHAKOS	G	1	(1)	
Slobodan NOVAKOVIC (YUG)	M	3		
Ribeiro ORSAI (BRA)	M	1	(1)	
Nikolaos PANAYOTARAS	M	6	(2)	1
Yeorgios PAPASTAMOU	A		(1)	
Dimosthenis PAPATHANASIOU	D	4	(1)	
Milan PAVLOVIC (YUG)	D	31		
Dusan RADOJEVIC (YUG)	M		(4)	
Hristos SAMARAS	D	5	(2)	1
Mohamed SAQIL (SYR)	M	4	(7)	
Spiridon STAMATOUKOS	M	21		
Ilias TRIANDAFILOU	D	12	(1)	
Konstandinos TSALIKIS	M	28		2
Zisis TSEKOS	M	21	(4)	
Nikolaos TSIANDAKIS	M	3	(3)	
Vasilios XANTHIS	M	24	(1)	2
Yeorgios ZAFIROPOULOS	D	2	(4)	
Yeorgios ZAHAROPOULOS	A	3	(13)	2

LEAGUE RESULTS 1998/99

23/08/98	Aris	A	0-2	
30/08/98	Kavala	H	3-2	Dragac, Jakovljevic 2 (1p)
12/09/98	Panathinaikos	A	1-4	Jakovljevic
20/09/98	Ethnikos Piraeus	H	1-0	Tsalikis
27/09/98	Iraklis	A	1-1	Kondopoulos
04/10/98	Xanthi	H	0-1	
25/10/98	Olympiakos	H	1-3	Xanthis
01/11/98	AEK	A	1-3	Dragac
08/11/98	Apollon	H	5-1	Basinas, Jakovljevic (p),
				Dragac 2, og (Ioanou)
22/11/98	Panelefsiniakos	A	2-1	Basinas, Zaharopoulos (p)
30/11/98	Veria	H	4-0	Jakovljevic 3 (1p), Dragac
06/12/98	OFI	A	1-1	og (Dermitzakis)
13/12/98	Paniliakos	H	1-0	Basinas
20/12/98	Proodeftiki	A	0-3	
17/01/99	Panionios	A	0-2	
24/01/99	PAOK	H	1-0	Koyoglou
31/01/99	Ionikos	A	0-5	
07/02/99	Aris	H	0-1	
14/02/99	Kavala	A	0-3	
21/02/99	Panathinaikos	H	0-1	
28/02/99	Ethnikos Piraeus	A	2-1	Nalitzis 2
07/03/99	Iraklis	H	1-0	Kondopoulos
14/03/99	Xanthi	A	1-0	Kondopoulos
21/03/99	Olympiakos	A	2-4	Panayotaras (p), Nalitzis
04/04/99	AEK	H	2-3	Frontzos, Tsalikis
17/04/99	Apollon	A	2-2	Nalitzis (p), Jakovljevic (p)
25/04/99	Panelefsiniakos	H	0-0	
02/05/99	Veria	A	1-3	Nalitzis
09/05/99	OFI	H	1-0	Xanthis
12/05/99	Paniliakos	A	0-1	
16/05/99	Proodeftiki	H	2-2	Samaras, Zaharopoulos
19/05/99	Panionios	H	2-2	Jakovljevic 2
23/05/99	PAOK	A	1-5	Basinas
30/05/99	Ionikos	H	1-1	Nalitzis

ETHNIKOS PIRAEUS

CLUB DIRECTORY

Ethnikos
2as Merarhias 11, Piraeus
tel - 4111447
fax - 4112385
Year of Formation - 1925
President - Vasilios Tsiamakis
Coach - Yorgos Ioakimidis; Vasilios Papahristou;
Lisandros Yeorgamlis; Howard Kendall;
Takis Alexopoulos
Stadium - Yorgos Karaiskakis (28,132)

APPEARANCES 98/99

	P	Ap	(s)	Gls
Joseph ADDO (GHA)	M	12	(1)	
Iraklis ANASTASAKIS	A	4	(5)	1
Paul BEAVERS (ENG)	M	9		2
Karl Lawton COLLINS (ENG)	A	1	(3)	
Konstandinos DAMIRIS	M	28	(1)	
Andreas DERTINIS	M	25	(1)	
Apostolos DIMOPOULOS	D	12		
Joël EBALE (CMR)	M	19	(3)	
Dominic FOLEY (IRL)	M	7		3
Armir GRIMA (ALB)	G	2		
Mihail HARALAMBOPOULOS	A	13	(6)	
Dimitrios HIOTIS	G	17		
Panayotis IKONOMOU	G	2	(4)	
Yeorgios KAIDATZIS	M		(6)	
Nikolaos KAKANOULIAS	A	1	(2)	
Mihail KAPSIS	D	13		
Stavros KOMIOTIS	M	18	(4)	1
Hristos KONDIS	M	24	(3)	1
Pandeleimon KOUMBIS	M	23	(5)	3
Panayotis MAHERAS	M	16	(5)	
Emanuil PAPADOPOULOS	D	14		
PAPOUTSIS	A		(1)	
Manthos PLATAKIS	A	8	(5)	2
John REED (ENG)	A	7		
Castro SANTOS (BRA)	M		(4)	
Stamatios SIRIGOS	M	16		
Carl SMITH (ENG)	A	5	(2)	1
Alessandro SOUSA (BRA)	M	9	(7)	1
Vasilios STAVRAKAKIS	M	3	(2)	
Petros TASIOULAS	M	8	(12)	1
Konstandinos TSANAS	M	15		
Nikolaos TSIAMAKIS	M	4	(2)	
Armato TSUGU (ALB)	M	5	(3)	
Ioanis VITEVIS	A	2	(3)	
Vasilios VOUZAS	M	5	(1)	
Nikolaos YALESAKIS	G	13		
Lisandros YEORGAMLIS	D	14		

LEAGUE RESULTS 1998/99

22/08/98	OFI	A	0-3	
29/08/98	Paniliakos	A	0-2	
13/09/98	Proodeftiki	H	0-2	
20/09/98	Ethnikos Asteras	A	0-1	
27/09/98	PAOK	H	1-1	Anastasakis
04/10/98	Ionikos	A	0-5	
24/10/98	Aris	H	1-1	Sousa
01/11/98	Kavala	A	0-3	
08/11/98	Panathinaikos	H	0-0	
22/11/98	Panionios	H	0-4	
30/11/98	Iraklis	A	0-4	
06/12/98	Xanthi	H	1-1	Koumbis
13/12/98	Olympiakos	A	0-2	
20/12/98	AEK	H	1-4	og (Grétarsson)
17/01/99	Apollon	A	0-4	
24/01/99	Panelefsiniakos	H	2-2	Beavers, Tasioulas
31/01/99	Veria	A	3-4	Foley 3
06/02/99	OFI	H	1-3	Smith
14/02/99	Paniliakos	H	1-1	Kondis
21/02/99	Proodeftiki	A	0-0	
28/02/99	Ethnikos Asteras	H	1-2	Beavers
07/03/99	PAOK	A	0-0	
14/03/99	Ionikos	H	1-2	Platakis
21/03/99	Aris	A	0-4	
04/04/99	Kavala	II	0-2	
18/04/99	Panathinaikos	A	1-5	Koumbis
26/04/99	Panionios	A	0-2	
02/05/99	Iraklis	H	1-2	Platakis
09/05/99	Xanthi	A	0-2	
12/05/99	Olympiakos	H	0-3	
16/05/99	AEK	A	0-2	
20/05/99	Apollon	H	2-3	Komiotis, Koumbis
23/05/99	Panelefsiniakos	A	0-3	
30/05/99	Veria	H	0-2	

IONIKOS

Ionikos
Petrou Ralli 248
18451 Nikea Piraeus
tel - (01) 4945000
fax - (01) 4964502
Year of Formation - 1965
President - Nikos Kanelakis
Coach - Sergio Markayan
(99/00 - Konstandinos Polihroniou)
Stadium - Neapolis (7,000)

APPEARANCES 98/99

	P	Ap	(s)	Gls
Mohamed AFASH (SYR)	M	31		3
Dimitrios AFENDOULIDIS	A	1	(6)	
Paulo ANDRIOLI (BRA)	M	13		11
Hrisostomos BENIAMIN	G	1	(1)	
Craig BREWSTER (SCO)	A	26	(2)	8
Yeorgios DARAKLITSAS	M	27	(1)	1
Dimitrios DELIYANIS	M	6	(19)	1
Vasilios FILIS	D	17	(1)	
Nikolaos FROUSOS	M	29	(3)	18
Ioanis GIRIHIDIS	M	1	(4)	
Miloje KLAEVIC (YUG)	D	31		1
Paulo KOBAJASI (ARG)	M	6	(8)	4
Konstandinos KONSTANDINOU	D	3	(2)	
Dario MUCHOTRIGO (PER)	M	24	(3)	7
Sokratis OFRIDOPOULOS	M	12	(5)	2
Athanasios PAGOURAS	D	9	(6)	
Theodoros PAHATOURIDIS	D	31		1
Evengelis POURLIOTOPOULOS	G	33		
Martin RODRIGUEZ (ARG)	M	27		
Yeorgios STAMBOULIS	M	3	(12)	2
Nikolaos TSIAVDARIS	M		(1)	
Apostolos TSOPTSIS	D		(1)	
Kornelius UTEBULUZOR (NIG)	M	1	(12)	3
Nikolaos VAVILIS	M	13	(6)	
Ioanis XANTHOPOULOS	D	29		1

LEAGUE RESULTS 1998/99

Date	Opponent	H/A	Score	Scorers
23/08/98	PAOK	H	1-0	Utebuluzor
30/08/98	Panionios	H	4-3	Andrioli 3, Deliyanis
13/09/98	Aris	A	1-1	Brewster
20/09/98	Kavala	H	4-2	Afash, Andrioli 3 (2p)
27/09/98	Panathinaikos	A	1-2	Brewster
04/10/98	Ethnikos Piraeus	H	5-0	Brewster, Stamboulis 2, Andrioli 2
25/10/98	Iraklis	A	1-2	Andrioli
01/11/98	Xanthi	H	0-1	
09/11/98	Olympiakos	A	0-2	
22/11/98	AEK	A	1-2	Andrioli (p)
30/11/98	Apollon	H	3-0	Brewster, og (Diamandis), Frousos
07/12/98	Panelefsiniakos	A	1-1	Daraklitsas
13/12/98	Veria	H	1-0	Andrioli
20/12/98	OFI	A	1-2	Muchotrigo
17/01/99	Paniliakos	H	1-1	Brewster
24/01/99	Proodeftiki	A	0-0	
31/01/99	Ethnikos Asteras	H	5-0	Frousos 3, Muchotrigo, Brewster (p)
07/02/99	PAOK	A	0-0	
14/02/99	Panionios	A	2-0	Klaevic, Frousos
21/02/99	Aris	H	3-0	Frousos, Afash, Muchotrigo
28/02/99	Kavala	A	3-1	Muchotrigo, Xanthopoulos, Kobajasi
07/03/99	Panathinaikos	H	4-4	Frousos 2, Utebuluzor 2
14/03/99	Ethnikos Piraeus	A	2-1	Ofridopoulos, Frousos
21/03/99	Iraklis	H	0-2	
04/04/99	Xanthi	A	2-2	Frousos, Afash
18/04/99	Olympiakos	H	1-3	Pahatouridis
25/04/99	AEK	H	2-1	Frousos, Brewster
02/05/99	Apollon	A	1-1	Brewster (p)
09/05/99	Panelefsiniakos	H	3-0	Frousos 2, Muchotrigo
12/05/99	Veria	A	2-0	Ofridopoulos, Frousos
16/05/99	OFI	H	2-0	Kobajasi, Muchotrigo
19/05/99	Paniliakos	A	4-1	Frousos 3, Kobajasi
23/05/99	Proodeftiki	H	2-0	Frousos (p), Muchotrigo
30/05/99	Ethnikos Asteras	A	1-1	Kobajasi

IRAKLIS

CLUB DIRECTORY

Iraklis
Vasileos Yeorgiou 33 A
54640 Thessaloniki
tel - (031) 834300/834534
fax - (031) 836262
Year of Formation - 1908
President - Petros Theodoridis
Coach - Ciril Dojcinovski; Mats Jingblad (99/00 -
Angelos Anastasiadis)
Stadium - Kaftantzoglio (45,000)

MAJOR HONOURS
Domestic Cup - (1) 1976.

APPEARANCES 98/99

		P	Ap	(s)	Gls
Robert ANDERSSON (SWE)	A	2	(5)		
Mihail BERNEANOU	D	8	(4)		
Panayotis DILBERIS	G	1			
Zafirios DIMITRIADIS	M		(1)		
Ebenezer HAGAN (GHA)	M	27	(4)	8	
Marios HRISTODOULOU (CYP)	M	22	(5)	6	
Ivan JOVANOVIC (YUG)	M	15	(6)	4	
Sasa KARATSOV (MAC)	D	16	(3)		
Hristos KARKAMANIS	G	15			
N'Keleda KASIMBA (DRC)	M	11	(1)		
N'Tsoukani KIDOTA (CON)	M	16	(1)		
Anastasios KIRIAZIS	D	20	(2)	4	
Savas KOFIDIS	M	31		1	
Sotirios KONSTANDINIDIS	M	10	(4)	1	
Mihail KONSTANDINOU (CYP)	A	29	(2)	9	
Yeorgios KOSTIS	M	7	(15)		
Loukense MOGOGO (CON)	M	5			
Athanasios MOUTSIOS	M		(1)		
Ilias SAPANIS	A	8	(14)	2	
Lazaros SEMOS	D	23	(1)	5	
Haralambos STEFANIDIS	A	1	(5)	1	
Ieroklis STOLTIDIS	M	30		6	
Ilias STOYANIS	G	18	(1)		
Efstathios TAVLARIDIS	M	8	(3)	1	
Stavros TZORTZOPOULOS	D	10	(1)	1	
Eleftherios VELENTZAS	M	20	(7)	4	
Yeorgios XENIDIS	M	21	(1)	1	

LEAGUE RESULTS 1998/99

23/08/98	Veria	A	2-0	Xenidis, Stoltidis (p)
30/08/98	OFI	H	3-0	Konstandinou, Jovanovic, Hagan
13/09/98	Paniliakos	A	1-2	Konstandinidis
20/09/98	Proodeftiki	A	0-0	
27/09/98	Ethnikos Asteras	H	1-1	Hagan
04/10/98	PAOK	A	1-2	Stoltidis (p)
25/10/98	Ionikos	H	2-1	Jovanovic, Konstandinou
01/11/98	Aris	A	1-2	Jovanovic
08/11/98	Kavala	H	2-2	Velentzas, Hagan
22/11/98	Panathinaikos	A	2-3	Jovanovic, Konstandinou
30/11/98	Ethnikos Piraeus	H	4-0	Kiriazis, Sapanis, Velentzas, Stoltidis
06/12/98	Panionios	H	2-0	Semos, Kofidis
12/12/98	Xanthi	A	0-0	
21/12/98	Olympiakos	H	0-2	
17/01/99	AEK	A	2-2	Semos, Hagan
24/01/99	Apollon	H	2-0	Hristodoulou, Konstandinou
31/01/99	Panelefsiniakos	A	0-0	
07/02/99	Veria	H	2-0	Hagan, Velentzas
14/02/99	OFI	A	1-3	Stoltidis
21/02/99	Paniliakos	H	3-1	Semos, Konstandinou 2 (2p)
28/02/99	Proodeftiki	H	0-1	
07/03/99	Ethnikos Asteras	A	0-1	
14/03/99	PAOK	H	1-0	Semos
21/03/99	Ionikos	A	2-0	Konstandinou 2
04/04/99	Aris	H	2-1	Stoltidis, Hristodoulou
18/04/99	Kavala	A	0-2	
25/04/99	Panathinaikos	H	3-3	Konstandinou, Hagan, Velentzas
02/05/99	Ethnikos Piraeus	A	2-1	Semos, Sapanis
08/05/99	Panionios	A	2-3	Hagan, Hristodoulou
12/05/99	Xanthi	H	2-2	Stoltidis, Kiriazis
16/05/99	Olympiakos	A	2-3	Kiriazis, Hristodoulou
19/05/99	AEK	H	2-3	Kiriazis, Hristodoulou
23/05/99	Apollon	A	3-1	Tavlaridis, Hagan, Hristodoulou
30/05/99	Panelefsiniakos	H	2-3	Tzortzopoulos, Stefanidis

KAVALA

CLUB DIRECTORY

Kavala
Filikis Eterias 7
65403 Kavala
tel - (051) 225094
fax - (051) 225094
Year of Formation - 1965
President - Yeorgios Karagianis
Coach - Nikolaos Goulis; Thomas Katsavakis
(99/00 - Evangelos Vlahos)
Stadium - Kavala (17,000)

APPEARANCES 98/99

	P	Ap	(s)	Gls
Anastasios ATHANASIADIS	M	17	(8)	4
Hristos ATHANASIADIS	M	4	(4)	1
Yeorgios BAKIRTZIDIS	G	1		
Angelos DIGOZIS	M	21	(4)	4
James ENUAGUANA (GHA)	M	17	(3)	1
Yeorgios HATZIZISIS	M	9	(11)	2
Kirilos KALIMANIS	D	24	(4)	
Lukas KARADIMOS	M	23	(4)	5
Yeorgios KARAISARIDIS	D	25	(2)	
Nikolaos KATSAVAKIS	M	3	(8)	
Timotheos KAVAKAS	M	21	(2)	1
Evangelos KEFALAS	D	8		1
Fotios KIPOUROS	G	9		
Yeorgios KOLTSIS	D	26	(4)	
Konstandinos KONSTANDINIDIS	M	2	(3)	
Panayotis LOGARAS	G	22		
Yeorgios MALIOS	M	21	(9)	1
Ivan MITEV (BUL)	D	19	(3)	1
Haralambos MOURATIDIS	M	5	(4)	
Dimitrios MOUTAS	M	2	(4)	1
Nima NAKISA (IRN)	G	2		
Yeorgios NASIOPOULOS	A	28		10
Ifani OUDESE (NIG)	M	12	(2)	
Petros PAVLIDIS	M	2		
Yeorgios PEGLIS	M	16	(5)	
Leszek PISZ (POL)	M	30	(1)	14
Nasko RADONIC (YUG)	A		(2)	
Yeorgios STRANTZALIS	M	1	(3)	
Haralambos TELIADIS	M	4	(7)	

LEAGUE RESULTS 1998/99

23/08/98	Proodeftiki	H	2-1	Nasiopoulos, Athanasiadis A.
30/08/98	Ethnikos Asteras	A	2-3	Pisz 2
13/09/98	PAOK	H	1-1	Pisz
20/09/98	Ionikos	A	2-4	Pisz 2
27/09/98	Aris	H	3-1	Nasiopoulos (p), Pisz, Digozis
05/10/98	Panionios	H	1-5	Digozis
26/10/98	Panathinaikos	A	2-6	Kavakas, Nasiopoulos
01/11/98	Ethnikos Piraeus	H	3-0	Enuaguana, Athanasiadis A., Moutas
08/11/98	Iraklis	A	2-2	Nasiopoulos, Karadimos
22/11/98	Xanthi	H	1-1	Digozis
30/11/98	Olympiakos	A	1-4	Nasiopoulos
06/12/98	AEK	H	2-1	Nasiopoulos, Pisz
13/12/98	Apollon	A	1-1	Digozis
20/12/98	Panelefsiniakos	A	1-1	Pisz
16/01/99	Veria	H	2-1	Nasiopoulos, Mitev
24/01/99	OFI	A	0-4	
31/01/99	Paniliakos	H	1-1	Pisz
07/02/99	Proodeftiki	A	0-1	
14/02/99	Ethnikos Asteras	H	3-0	Malios, Kefalas, Nasiopoulos
21/02/99	PAOK	A	0-1	
28/02/99	Ionikos	H	1-3	Nasiopoulos
07/03/99	Aris	A	1-3	Athanasiadis A.
14/03/99	Panionios	A	2-1	Nasiopoulos, Hatzizisis
21/03/99	Panathinaikos	H	2-1	Pisz 2 (1p)
04/04/99	Ethnikos Piraeus	A	2-0	Karadimos, Pisz
18/04/99	Iraklis	H	2-0	Karadimos, Hatzizisis
25/04/99	Xanthi	A	1-4	Pisz (p)
02/05/99	Olympiakos	H	0-2	
09/05/99	AEK	A	0-4	
12/05/99	Apollon	H	0-1	
16/05/99	Panelefsiniakos	H	3-0	Karadimos 2, Pisz
19/05/99	Veria	A	2-0	Athanasiadis H., Athanasiadis A.
23/05/99	OFI	H	0-2	
30/05/99	Paniliakos	A	0-2	

OFI

CLUB DIRECTORY

Omilos Filathlon Irakliou (OFI)
Ikostis Pemptis Avgoustou 18
71202 Iraklion
Kriti
tel - (081) 283920
fax - (081) 288341
Year of Formation - 1925
President - Ioanis Papamattheakis
Coach - Eugeniusz Gerard
Stadium - Irakliou (14,000)

MAJOR HONOURS
Domestic Cup - (1) 1987.

APPEARANCES 98/99

		P	Ap	(s)	Gls
Waldemar ADAMCZYK (POL)	A	9	(5)	2
Pavlos ADAMOS	D	15		
Ioanis ANASTASIOU	A	14		5
Arjan BEQAJ (ALB)	G	32		
Paúl COMINGES (PER)	A	3	(6)	
Einar Thór DANÍELSSON (ISL)	M	10	(3)	1
Alexandros DEDES	M	21	(7)	
Emanuil DERMITZAKIS	D	29	(1)	
Harouna DIARRA (MLI)	A	14	(8)	5
Mohamadou DIARRA (MLI)	M	15	(6)	2
Haralambos HARALAMBAKIS	D		(2)	
Nikolaos IORDANIDIS	A	13	(2)	8
Ilias KOTSIOS	D	2	(5)	1
Nikolaos KOUNENAKIS	D	3	(2)	
Yeorgios KOUTSOUPIAS	D	9	(5)	
Konstandinos MANGOS	D	5		
Petros MARINAKIS	M	29	(1)	9
Predrag MITIC (YUG)	M	17	(11)	2
Nikolaos NIOPLIAS	M	28	(1)	4
Nikolaos PAPADOPOULOS	D	28		4
Yeorgios PAPAYANAKIS	A	2	(8)	1
Konstandinos PAVLOPOULOS	D	21	(3)	1
Andreas SKENTZOS	D	24	(1)	1
Konstandinos STAVRAKAKIS	D	19	(6)	
Nikolaos TSIANDAKIS	M	1	(4)	
Nikolaos TZANETIS	A	4	(5)	2
Miguel VARGAS (CHL)	M	5	(8)	
Ioanis VOSKAKIS	G	1		
Nikolaos YALAMAS	G	1	(3)	

LEAGUE RESULTS 1998/99

23/08/98	Ethnikos Piraeus	H	3-0	Diarra H., Anastasiou, Diarra M.
30/08/98	Iraklis	A	0-3	
13/09/98	Xanthi	H	4-2	Papadopoulos (p), Anastasiou,
				Diarra H., Skentzos
20/09/98	Olympiakos	A	0-3	
27/09/98	AEK	H	0-1	
04/10/98	Apollon	A	0-1	
25/10/98	Panelefsiniakos	H	3-0	Papadopoulos (p), Marinakis,
				Mitic
01/11/98	Veria	A	0-0	
08/11/98	Panionios	A	1-0	Anastasiou
22/11/98	Paniliakos	H	3-1	Adamczyk, Anastasiou, Marinakis
30/11/98	Proodeftiki	A	1-0	Adamczyk
06/12/98	Ethnikos Asteras	H	1-1	Marinakis
13/12/98	PAOK	A	1-3	Papadopoulos (p)
20/12/98	Ionikos	H	2-1	Anastasiou, Nioplias
17/01/99	Aris	A	1-3	Papayanakis
24/01/99	Kavala	H	4-0	Iordanidis, Diarra M., Mitic,
				Nioplias
31/01/99	Panathinaikos	A	0-1	
06/02/99	Ethnikos Piraeus	A	3-1	Nioplias, Diarra H.,
				Papadopoulos (p)
14/02/99	Iraklis	H	3-1	Iordanidis, Marinakis 2
21/02/99	Xanthi	A	1-3	Iordanidis
28/02/99	Olympiakos	H	1-2	Marinakis
07/03/99	AEK	A	0-2	
14/03/99	Apollon	H	0-1	
21/03/99	Panelefsiniakos	A	2-1	Daníelsson, Marinakis
04/04/99	Veria	H	3-0	Iordanidis, Pavlopoulos, Marinakis
18/04/99	Panionios	H	2-0	Iordanidis, Marinakis
24/04/99	Paniliakos	A	2-1	Nioplias, Iordanidis
02/05/99	Proodeftiki	H	0-0	
09/05/99	Ethnikos Asteras	A	0-1	
12/05/99	PAOK	H	3-2	Koutsoupias, Iordanidis, Kotsios
16/05/99	Ionikos	A	0-2	
20/05/99	Aris	H	2-4	Diarra H., Tzanetis
23/05/99	Kavala	A	2-0	Tzanetis, Nioplias (p)
30/05/99	Panathinaikos	H	2-3	Diarra H., Iordanidis

OLYMPIAKOS

CLUB DIRECTORY

Olympiakos
Ipsilantou 170
18535 Piraeus
tel - 4297223-7
fax - 4297228
Year of Formation - 1925
President - Sokratis Kokalis
Coach - Dusan Bajevic
Stadium - OAKA, 'Spiros Louis' (74,433)

MAJOR HONOURS

League Championship - (28)
1931, 1933, 1934, 1936, 1937, 1938, 1947,
1948, 1951, 1954, 1955, 1956, 1957, 1958,
1959, 1966, 1967, 1973, 1974, 1975, 1980,
1981, 1982, 1983, 1987, 1997, 1998, 1999.
Domestic Cup - (20)
1947, 1951, 1952, 1953, 1954, 1957, 1958,
1959, 1960, 1961, 1963, 1965, 1968, 1971,
1973, 1975, 1981, 1990, 1992, 1999.

APPEARANCES 98/99

	P	Ap	(s)	Gls
Felix ABOAGUE (GUI)	M	2	(9)	1
Kofi ABONSAI (GHA)	D	5		
Alexios ALEXANDRIS	M	15	(9)	10
Yeorgios AMANATIDIS	M	21	(1)	3
Yeorgios ANATOLAKIS	D	27	(1)	2
Paraskevas ANTZAS	D	6	(12)	
Predrag DJORDJEVIC (YUG)	M	28	(2)	8
Dimitrios ELEFTHEROPOULOS	G	31		
Sinisa GOGIC (CYP)	A	17	(11)	5
Ilija IVIC (YUG)	A	13	(2)	8
Vasilios KARAPIALIS	M	22	(3)	9
Kiriakos KARATAIDIS	D	28	(1)	
LUCIANO de Souza (BRA)	M	11	(18)	6
Dimitrios MAVROYENIDIS	D	29	(2)	1
Andreas NINIADIS	M	23	(3)	2
Peter OFORI-QUAYE (GHA)	A	13	(2)	3
Petros PASALIS	M	6	(2)	
Savas POURSAITIDIS	A	3	(2)	2
Ilias POURSANIDIS	M	27	(1)	
Stilianos SFAKIANAKIS	M	3	(7)	2
Kiriakos THOUROGLOU	G	3		
Stilianos YANAKOPOULOS	M	16	(7)	7
Grigoris YEORGATOS	M	25	(1)	12

LEAGUE RESULTS 1998/99

22/08/98	Apollon	A	5-2	Djordjevic, Ofori-Quaye, Ivic 2 (1p), Karapialis
30/08/98	Panelefsiniakos	H	1-1	Yanakopoulos
12/09/98	Veria	A	3-0	Karapialis, Ofori-Quaye, Luciano
20/09/98	OFI	H	3-0	Alexandris, Karapialis, Gogic
26/09/98	Paniliakos	A	0-1	
04/10/98	Proodeftiki	H	6-1	Alexandris 2, Ivic 2, Yanakopoulos 2
25/10/98	Ethnikos Asteras	A	3-1	Yanakopoulos 2, Yeorgatos (p)
01/11/98	PAOK	A	2-1	Ofori-Quaye, Yeorgatos (p)
08/11/98	Ionikos	H	2-0	Ivic, Yeorgatos
21/11/98	Aris	A	0-1	
30/11/98	Kavala	H	4-1	Alexandris, Luciano 2, Djordjevic(p)
04/12/98	Panathinaikos	A	4-2	og (Alexopoulos), Karapialis 2, Anatolakis
13/12/98	Ethnikos Piraeus	H	2-0	Gogic (p), Djordjevic
21/12/98	Iraklis	A	2-0	Luciano, Yeorgatos
17/01/99	Xanthi	H	3-1	Luciano, Yeorgatos, Ivic
24/01/99	Panionios	H	5-0	Karapialis 2, Ivic 2, Djordjevic
31/01/99	AEK	A	0-2	
08/02/99	Apollon	H	0-0	
14/02/99	Panelefsiniakos	A	2-0	Amanatidis, Djordjevic
21/02/99	Veria	H	5-0	Yeorgatos 3 (1p), Amanatidis, Luciano
28/02/99	OFI	A	2-1	Yeorgatos (p), Karapialis
07/03/99	Paniliakos	H	3-0	Gogic, Alexandris, Djordjevic
14/03/99	Proodeftiki	A	1-0	Amanatidis
22/03/99	Ethnikos Asteras	H	4-2	Niniadis 2, Yeorgatos (p), Alexandris
04/04/99	PAOK	H	2-1	Djordjevic, Yeorgatos (p)
18/04/99	Ionikos	A	3-1	Anatolakis, Yanakopoulos, Alexandris
24/04/99	Aris	H	1-0	Yanakopoulos
02/05/99	Kavala	A	2-0	Alexandris, Karapialis
09/05/99	Panathinaikos	H	0-0	
12/05/99	Ethnikos Piraeus	A	3-0	Djordjevic (p), Alexandris, Aboague (p)
16/05/99	Iraklis	H	3-2	Gogic 2, Mavroyenidis
19/05/99	Xanthi	A	2-0	Poursaitidis 2
23/05/99	Panionios	A	4-1	Sfakianakis 2, Yeorgatos (p), Alexandris
30/05/99	AEK	H	0-0	

PANATHINAIKOS

CLUB DIRECTORY

Panathinaikos
Athlitikes Egatastasis "Peania"
Karela Peanias, 19002 Attiki
tel - 6647160
fax - 6029536
Year of Formation - 1908
President - Yeorgios Vardinoyanis
Coach - Vasilios Daniil; Juan Ramón Rocha
(99/00 - Ioanis Kirastas)
Stadium - OAKA 'Spiros Louis' (74,433)

MAJOR HONOURS
League Championship - (21)
1911, 1912, 1916, 1930, 1949, 1953, 1960,
1961, 1962, 1964, 1965, 1969, 1970, 1972,
1977, 1984, 1986, 1990, 1991, 1995, 1996.
Domestic Cup - (15) 1940, 1948, 1955, 1967,
1969, 1977, 1982, 1984, 1986, 1988, 1989,
1991, 1993, 1994, 1995.

APPEARANCES 98/99

	P	Ap	(s)	Gls
Yeorgios ALEXOPOULOS	D	8	(4)	
Alexandros ALEXOUDIS	A		(6)	
Efstratios APOSTOLAKIS	M	16	(4)	1
Aljosa ASANOVIC (CRO)	M	25		5
Angelos BASINAS	D	19	(1)	
Panayotis FISAS	D	18		3
Ioanis GOUMAS	D	24	(2)	1
JÚLIO CÉSAR Silva (BRA)	D	3		
Yeorgios KARAGOUNIS	M	15	(9)	6
Konstadinos KIASOS	D	17	(6)	
Bledar KOLA (ALB)	M	16	(9)	1
Konstandinos KONSTANDINIDIS	M	25	(1)	4
Stefanos KOTSOLIS	G	1		
Andreas LAGONIKAKIS	M	21	(2)	1
Nikolaos LIBEROPOULOS	M	30	(1)	13
MAURO da Silva (BRA)	A	8	(12)	4
Vladan MILOJEVIC (YUG)	D	19	(2)	4
Erik MYKLAND (NOR)	M	19	(2)	
Theofilaktos NIKOLAIDIS	D	3	(3)	
Andonis NIKOPOLIDIS	G	18		
Yeorgios PODARAS	M		(1)	
Yeorgios SIMOS	M	1	(1)	
Frank STRANDLI (NOR)	A	2	(7)	3
Igor SYPNIEWSKI (POL)	A	4	(14)	5
Andreas VLAHOS	A		(2)	
Leonidas VOKOLOS	D	22	(2)	
Jozef WANDZIK (POL)	G	15	(1)	
Krzysztof WARZYCHA (POL)	A	25		13

LEAGUE RESULTS 1998/99

22/08/98	Paniliakos	H	2-1	Strandli, Milojevic (p)
30/08/98	Proodeftiki	A	2-1	Warzycha, Gounas
13/09/98	Ethnikos Asteras	H	4-1	Warzycha 2, Strandli, og (Lagos)
20/09/98	PAOK	A	0-2	
27/09/98	Ionikos	H	2-1	Liberopoulos, Strandli
05/10/98	Aris	A	1-0	Liberopoulos
25/10/98	Kavala	H	6-2	Liberopoulos 2, Asanovic,
				Milojevic 2 (2p), Mauro
31/10/98	Panionios	H	2-1	Asanovic, Liberopoulos
08/11/98	Ethnikos Piraeus	A	0-0	
21/11/98	Iraklis	H	3-2	Asanovic, og (Konstandinou),
				Sypniewski
30/11/98	Xanthi	A	0-1	
04/12/98	Olympiakos	H	2-4	Konstandinidis, Warzycha
13/12/98	AEK	A	0-2	
20/12/98	Apollon	H	5-0	Warzycha 2, Sypniewski 3
18/01/99	Panelefsiniakos	A	2-1	Liberopoulos, Konstandinidis
24/01/99	Veria	A	1-0	Warzycha
31/01/99	OFI	H	1-0	Warzycha
07/02/99	Paniliakos	A	2-1	Konstandinidis, Fisos
15/02/99	Proodeftiki	H	1-0	Liberopoulos (p)
21/02/99	Ethnikos Asteras	A	1-0	Liberopoulos
28/02/99	PAOK	H	0-1	
07/03/99	Ionikos	A	4-4	Warzycha 2, Sypniewski, Mauro
14/03/99	Aris	H	3-1	Liberopoulos, Asanovic, Milojevic
21/03/99	Kavala	A	1-2	Fisas
04/04/99	Panionios	A	2-0	Warzycha, Lagonikakis
18/04/99	Ethnikos Piraeus	H	5-1	Karagounis 2, Warzycha, Kola,
				Liberopoulos
25/04/99	Iraklis	A	3-3	Liberopoulos, Konstandinidis,
				Karagounis
02/05/99	Xanthi	H	2-1	Warzycha, Karagounis (p)
09/05/99	Olympiakos	A	0-0	
12/05/99	AEK	H	0-0	
16/05/99	Apollon	A	3-1	Asanovic, Karagounis, Apostolakis
20/05/99	Panelefsiniakos	H	2-0	Fisas, Liberopoulos
23/05/99	Veria	H	1-0	Liberopoulos
30/05/99	OFI	A	3-2	Mauro 2, Karagounis

PANELEFSINIAKOS

CLUB DIRECTORY

Panelefsiniakos
Y. Pavlou 6
Elefsina
tel - 5546261
Year of Formation - 1931
President - Klearhos Tzaferis
Coach - Haralambos Tenes; Vasilios Alexiou &
Evangelos Filipsis; Yeorgios Firos; Efstathios
Stathopoulos
Stadium - Elefsinas (6,500)

APPEARANCES 98/99

	P	Ap	(s)	Gls
Kofi ABONSAI (GHA)	D	14	(1)	1
Alexandros ANASTOPOULOS	D	1	(2)	
Vasilios ANDREADIS	A	15	(12)	4
Dimitrios ARGIROPOULOS	D		(1)	
Athanasios BEKOS	M		(1)	
Silvian CRISTESCU (ROM)	M	7	(7)	
Ioanis DIMITRIADIS	M	28	(2)	3
Yeorgios GILEKAS	M	2	(4)	1
Anastasios HATZIDIMITRIOU	D	3	(3)	
Alexandros KAKLAMANOS	A	23	(2)	7
Dimitrios KALIKAS	M	21	(2)	1
Yeorgios KOUTSIS	M	14		1
Ioanis LAMBRIANDIS	A	1	(1)	
Anastasios MAVRIDIS	G	1		
Jean-Martin MULUGI (CMR)	A	1	(1)	
Dimitrios MOUTAS	M	16		1
Konstandinos NIKOLAIDIS	G	5		
Edin OYANGA (CMR)	M	16	(7)	
Ioanis PANOU	M		(2)	
Filipos PAPAS	G	1		
Yeorgios PODARAS	M	14	(1)	
Emanuil PSOMAS	M	11	(4)	
Alexandros RANDOS	G	27		
Dimitrios ROUSOS	D	28		
Zoran SARABA (YUG)	M	28		
Stavros STAMATIS	M	17	(6)	
Goran STEVANOVIC (YUG)	M		(4)	
Yeorgios THEODORIDIS	D	12	(1)	
Yeorgios TRIHIAS	A	2	(6)	3
Konstandinos TSIRONIS	D	27	(1)	2
Yeorgios TSOLAKIS	M	3	(2)	
Mihail TZIVELEKIS	M	22	(5)	
Yeorgios VASILIOU	M	4	(1)	
Haralambos ZELENITSAS	M	10	(12)	

LEAGUE RESULTS 1998/99

22/08/98	Xanthi	H	0-0	
30/08/98	Olympiakos	A	1-1	Koutsis
12/09/98	AEK	H	0-0	
20/09/98	Apollon	A	1-1	Dimitriadis
27/09/98	Panionios	A	0-3	
03/10/98	Veria	H	2-0	Andreadis, Kaklamanos
25/10/98	OFI	A	0-3	
01/11/98	Paniliakos	H	1-2	Tsironis
08/11/98	Proodeftiki	A	1-0	Kalikas
22/11/98	Ethnikos Asteras	H	1-2	Abonsai
30/11/98	PAOK	A	1-3	Kaklamanos
07/12/98	Ionikos	H	1-1	Kaklamanos
13/12/98	Aris	A	0-0	
20/12/98	Kavala	H	1-1	Kaklamanos
18/01/99	Panathinaikos	H	1-2	Dimitriadis
23/01/99	Ethnikos Piraeus	A	2-2	Kaklamanos, Tsironis
31/01/99	Iraklis	H	0-0	
07/02/99	Xanthi	A	0-0	
15/02/99	Olympiakos	H	0-2	
21/02/99	AEK	A	2-6	Andreadis, og (Zikos)
28/02/99	Apollon	H	1-0	Dimitriadis
08/03/99	Panionios	H	1-0	Moutas
14/03/99	Veria	A	1-0	Andreadis
21/03/99	OFI	H	1-2	Andreadis
04/04/99	Paniliakos	A	0-2	
18/04/99	Proodeftiki	H	0-1	
25/04/99	Ethnikos Asteras	A	0-0	
01/05/99	PAOK	H	0-4	
09/05/99	Ionikos	A	0-3	
12/05/99	Aris	H	0-1	
16/05/99	Kavala	A	0-3	
20/05/99	Panathinaikos	A	0-2	
23/05/99	Ethnikos Piraeus	H	3-0	Trihias 2, Kaklamanos
30/05/99	Iraklis	A	3-2	Trihias, Kaklamanos, Gilekas

PANILIAKOS

Paniliakos
Ahileos 4
Pirgos
tel - (0621) 25749
fax - (0621) 25749
Year of Formation - 1958
President - Sakis Stavropoulos
Coach - Ioannis Kirastas; Haralambos Tenes
Stadium - Pirgos (10,000)

		P	Ap	(s)	Gls
César CHARUN (PER)	M		20	(2)	2
Konstandinos DEMBEGLERAS	M		21	(4)	2
Ioanis EFTHIMIOU	M		3	(3)	
Anastasios FEREKIDIS	M		19	(7)	
Hristos IOANOU	M			(2)	
Radoslaw JASINSKI (POL)	M		7	(14)	
Yeorgios KOLTZOS	M		19	(6)	
Sokratis KOPSAHILIS	G		9		
Ioanis LIOURDIS	G		1	(1)	
Yeorgios MITKOS	M		3		
Xenofon MOSHOYANIS	M		16	(4)	1
Spiridon NOUSIAS	M		23	(3)	1
Nikolaos PAPADOPOULOS	D			(1)	
Yeorgios PAPANDREOU	A		31	(2)	8
Dionisios PAPAS	M		17	(7)	
Nieguy ROGER (GAB)	M		4	(1)	
César ROZALES (PER)	M		19	(12)	5
Miltiadis SAPANIS	M		16	(4)	2
Nebojsa SCEPANOVIC (YUG)	M		1	(4)	
Mohamed SYLLA (GUI)	M		6	(9)	1
Anastasios TASIOPOULOS	D		29		
Ioanis TATSIS	M		31		2
Evangelos TOYAS	D		26	(1)	3
Savas YANAKIDIS	A		4	(10)	
Angelos YEORGIOU	G		24		
Panayotis ZIAKAS	A		25	(1)	6

22/08/98	Panathinaikos	A	1-2	Tatsis
30/08/98	Ethnikos Piraeus	H	2-0	Tasiopoulos, Rozales
13/09/98	Iraklis	H	2-1	Papandreou, Toyas
20/09/98	Xanthi	A	1-2	Papandreou
27/09/98	Olympiakos	H	1-0	Toyas
04/10/98	AEK	A	1-3	Toyas
25/10/98	Apollon	H	3-1	Charun, Ziakas 2
01/11/98	Panelefsiniakos	A	2-1	Ziakas, Sylla
08/11/98	Veria	H	0-0	
22/11/98	OFI	A	1-3	Nousias
30/11/98	Panionios	A	2-5	Ziakas, Moshoyanis
06/12/98	Proodeftiki	H	1-2	Papandreou
13/12/98	Ethnikos Asteras	A	0-1	
20/12/98	PAOK	H	1-2	Sapanis
17/01/99	Ionikos	A	1-1	Papandreou (p)
24/01/99	Aris	H	3-1	Papandreou (p), Rozales, og (Malous)
31/01/99	Kavala	A	1-1	Tasiopoulos
07/02/99	Panathinaikos	H	1-2	Papandreou (p)
14/02/99	Ethnikos Piraeus	A	1-1	Rozales
21/02/99	Iraklis	A	1-3	Papandreou
28/02/99	Xanthi	H	1-0	og (Efendopoulos)
08/03/99	Olympiakos	A	0-3	
14/03/99	AEK	H	0-1	
21/03/99	Apollon	A	0-5	
04/04/99	Panelefsiniakos	H	2-0	Charun, Papandreou
18/04/99	Veria	A	0-0	
24/04/99	OFI	H	1-2	Rozales
02/05/99	Panionios	H	2-0	Sapanis, Ziakas
09/05/99	Proodeftiki	A	0-2	
12/05/99	Ethnikos Asteras	H	1-0	Rozales
16/05/99	PAOK	A	0-2	
20/05/99	Ionikos	H	1-4	Tatsis
23/05/99	Aris	A	1-3	Dembegleras
30/05/99	Kavala	H	2-0	Dembegleras, Ziakas

PANIONIOS

CLUB DIRECTORY

Panionios
25is Martiou
Nea Smirni
17122 Athens
tel - 9326707
fax - 9332036
Year of Formation - 1890
President - Ahileas Beos
Coach - Ronnie Whelan
Stadium - Neas Smirnis (15,000)

MAJOR HONOURS
Domestic Cup - (2) 1979, 1998.

APPEARANCES 98/99

	P	Ap	(s)	Gls
Lars BAKKERUD (NOR)	M	11	(1)	
Kent BERGERSEN (NOR)	D	7	(5)	1
Dimitrios BOUGAS	M	26		
Ioanis FAKIS	G	10		
Panayotis FISAS	D	11		3
Athanasios GAZIS	D	15	(2)	
Keith GUMPS (TRI)	D	5	(4)	
Garry HAYLOCK (ENG)	A	21	(6)	6
Vasilios IOANIDIS	D	26		6
Ilias IOANOU	M	6	(12)	1
Eduard IORDANESCU (ROM)	A	1	(1)	
Konstandinos KAFALIS	M	15	(10)	1
Ioanis KAMITSIS	D	11	(7)	
Theofilos KARASAVIDIS	M	25	(4)	6
Jan Erlend KRUSE (NOR)	D	16	(1)	1
Vasilios KOUVALIS	D	13	(2)	
Nikolaos MAKRIYANIS	D	4	(4)	1
Dimitrios MARKESINIS	D	4	(1)	
Yeorgios MITSIOPOULOS	D	22	(1)	
Dimitrios NALITZIS	A	4	(8)	3
Gareth ROBERTS (WAL)	M	13	(2)	
Mark ROBINS (ENG)	M	13	(1)	2
Andonis SAPOUNTZIS	A	20	(3)	10
Foto STRAKOSHA (ALB)	G	24		
Paul TISDALE (ENG)	M	17	(1)	1
Anastasios ZAHOPOULOS	D	25	(1)	
Spiridon ZARAS	D	9	(3)	

LEAGUE RESULTS 1998/99

22/08/98	AEK	H	1-3	Ioanidis
30/08/98	Ionikos	A	3-4	Sapountzis 3 (1p)
13/09/98	Apollon	H	4-2	Kruse, Ioanidis, Robins, Bergersen
20/09/98	Aris	A	1-2	Haylock
27/09/98	Panelefsiniakos	H	3-0	Sapountzis 2 (2p), Haylock
04/10/98	Kavala	A	5-1	Fisas, Haylock 3, Ioanidis
24/10/98	Veria	H	0-0	
31/10/98	Panathinaikos	A	1-2	Karasavidis
09/11/98	OFI	H	0-1	
22/11/98	Ethnikos Piraeus	A	4-0	Fisas 2, Sapountzis, Karasavidis
30/11/98	Paniliakos	H	5-2	Nalitzis 3, Sapountzis, Ioanou
06/12/98	Iraklis	A	0-2	
13/12/98	Proodeftiki	H	0-0	
21/12/98	Xanthi	A	0-1	
17/01/99	Ethnikos Asteras	H	2-0	Tisdale, Robins
24/01/99	Olympiakos	A	0-5	
30/01/99	PAOK	H	0-1	
08/02/99	AEK	A	0-3	
14/02/99	Ionikos	H	0-2	
21/02/99	Apollon	A	0-0	
28/02/99	Aris	H	3-2	Sapountzis (p), Karasavidis, Haylock
08/03/99	Panelefsiniakos	A	0-1	
14/03/99	Kavala	H	1-2	Ioanidis
22/03/99	Veria	A	1-3	Sapountzis
04/04/99	Panathinaikos	H	0-2	
18/04/99	OFI	A	0-2	
26/04/99	Ethnikos Piraeus	H	2-0	Karasavidis, Ioanidis
02/05/99	Paniliakos	A	0-2	
09/05/99	Iraklis	H	3-2	Karasavidis, Sapountzis (p), Ioanidis
12/05/99	Proodeftiki	A	0-0	
16/05/99	Xanthi	H	0-2	
20/05/99	Ethnikos Asteras	A	2-2	Makriyanis, Karasavidis
23/05/99	Olympiakos	H	1-4	Kafalis
30/05/99	PAOK	A	0-3	

PAOK

CLUB DIRECTORY

PAOK
Lora Margariti 13
54622 Thessaloniki
tel - (031) 238560/912362
fax - (031) 238557
Year of Formation - 1926
President - Petros Kalafatis
Coach - Oleg Blokhin; Angelos Anastasiadis; Arie
Haan
Stadium - Toumbas (40,000)

MAJOR HONOURS
League Championship - (2) 1976, 1985.
Domestic Cup - (2) 1972, 1974.

APPEARANCES 98/99

	P	Ap	(s)	Gls
Nikolaos ARGIRIOU	G	16	(1)	
Bozidar BANDOVIC (BOS)	D	22	(6)	6
Dietmar BERCHTOLD (AUT)	A		(1)	
Paúl COMINGES (PER)	A	5	(8)	2
Konstandinos FRANTZESKOS	M	29	(1)	8
Pandeleimon KAFES	M	22	(5)	7
Dimitrios KAPETANOPOULOS	D	17	(7)	
Anastasios KATSIABIS	D	30	(1)	4
Konstandinos KIRIAKIDIS	A	3	(3)	
Nikolaos KOLOMBOURDAS	D	2		
Pandeleimon KONSTANDINIDIS	M	19	(7)	4
Yeorgios KOULAKIOTIS	D	12	(2)	
Slobodan KRCMAREVIC (YUG)	A	10	(5)	3
Konstandinos LAGONIDIS	M		(1)	
Triandafilos MAHERIDIS	M	15	(7)	
Adnikohor MARAVALIEV (BUL)	A		(1)	
Nikolaos MIHOPOULOS	G	18	(1)	
Joe NAGBE (LIB)	M	26		1
Evangelos NASTOS	D	2	(3)	
Percy OLIVARES (PER)	D	25	(2)	2
Vasilios SAMARAS	D	6		
Mirko TACCOLA (ITA)	D	15	(3)	5
Yeorgios TOURSOUNIDIS	M	14	(8)	2
Adolfo VALENCIA (COL)	A	9	(4)	3
Hristos VELIS	M	11	(10)	
Zisis VRIZAS	A	25	(8)	4
Ahilleas ZAFIRIOU	M	21	(6)	

LEAGUE RESULTS 1998/99

22/08/98	Ionikos	A	0-1	
29/08/98	Aris	H	1-4	Kafes
13/09/98	Kavala	A	1-1	Kafes
20/09/98	Panathinaikos	H	2-0	Katsiabis, Frantzeskos
27/09/98	Ethnikos Piraeus	A	1-1	Cominges
04/10/98	Iraklis	H	2-1	Frantzeskos, Kafes
25/10/98	Xanthi	A	1-0	Vrizas
31/10/98	Olympiakos	H	1-2	Frantzeskos
07/11/98	AEK	H	2-1	Olivares 2 (1p)
22/11/98	Apollon	A	4-1	Taccola, Toursounidis, Katsiabis, Cominges
30/11/98	Panelefsiniakos	H	3-1	Konstandinidis, Taccola 2
06/12/98	Veria	A	2-1	Bandovic 2
13/12/98	OFI	H	3-1	Katsiabis, Konstandinidis, Taccola
20/12/98	Paniliakos	A	2-1	Bandovic, Taccola
17/01/99	Proodeftiki	H	1-0	Nagbé
24/01/99	Ethnikos Asteras	A	0-1	
30/01/99	Panionios	A	1-0	Krcmarevic
07/02/99	Ionikos	H	0-0	
15/02/99	Aris	A	0-2	
21/02/99	Kavala	H	1-0	Bandovic
28/02/99	Panathinaikos	A	1-0	Frantzeskos
07/03/99	Ethnikos Piraeus	H	0-0	
14/03/99	Iraklis	A	0-1	
21/03/99	Xanthi	H	0-0	
04/04/99	Olympiakos	A	1-2	Vrizas
18/04/99	AEK	A	0-2	
25/04/99	Apollon	H	3-1	Valencia, Krcmarevic, Konstandinidis
02/05/99	Panelefsiniakos	A	4-0	Frantzeskos 2, Krcmarevic (p), Toursounidis
09/05/99	Veria	H	2-0	Kafes 2
12/05/99	OFI	A	2-3	Vrizas, Konstandinidis
16/05/99	Paniliakos	H	2-0	Frantzeskos, Bandovic
20/05/99	Proodeftiki	A	1-2	Valencia
23/05/99	Ethnikos Asteras	H	5-1	og (Tsalikis), Kafes, Frantzeskos, Katsiabis, Bandovic
30/05/99	Panionios	H	3-0	Vrizas, Valencia, Kafes

PROODEFTIKI

CLUB DIRECTORY

Proodeftiki
Taxiarhon 49
18120 Piraeus
tel - 4952012/5398160
fax - 4976485
Year of Formation - 1927
President - Markos Takas
Coach - Martti Kuusela; Mario Bonic;
Stefanos Gaitanos; Andreas Mihalopoulos;
Nikolaos Alefandos
Stadium - Nikeas (5,500)

APPEARANCES 98/99

	P	Ap	(s)	Gls
Agapitos ABELAS	M	28	(1)	1
Halem AL JAHER (SYR)	M	28		2
Isaak ALMANIDIS	A	30		9
Vasilios ANASTASIADIS	D	8	(4)	
Paraskevas ANDRALAS	M	6	(9)	
Ioanis ANGELOPOULOS	M	28		
Ioanis ARHONDOULIS	A		(2)	
Stepan ATAJAN (SYR)	M		(3)	
Yeorgios BARIAMOGLOU	M	1	(4)	
William BARTOLOMEU	A		(3)	
Evangelos DANGAS	D	27		2
Markos DIMOS	M	17	(8)	2
Nikolaos FOUSKAS	M	7	(14)	1
Athanasios GOGAS	D	1	(1)	
Evangelos GOUTIS	D	8	(5)	
Ilias HOUZOURIS	M	25		
Evangelos KARASAVAS	G	31		
Yeorgios KAZANTZIS	A	2	(4)	
Efthimios KOULOUHERIS	M	1		
Hristos MAIMANIS	G	2		
Savas PANDELIDIS	D	18	(7)	
Anastasios PANDOS	D	16	(1)	
Anastasios PAPADOPOULOS	D	3	(5)	
Mihail POLITIS	D	14	(6)	
Oleg PROTASOV (UKR)	A	28		5
Petros ROUTZIERIS	D	6	(3)	
Vasilios SPERTOS	M		(1)	
Asterios THEMELIS	G	1		
Panayotis YANOPOULOS	D	23		2
Roland ZAJMI (ALB)	A	15	(5)	3

LEAGUE RESULTS 1998/99

22/08/98	Kavala	A	1-2	Protasov
30/08/98	Panathinaikos	H	1-2	Almanidis (p)
13/09/98	Ethnikos Piraeus	A	2-0	Protasov, Almanidis (p)
20/09/98	Iraklis	H	0-0	
27/09/98	Xanthi	H	1-2	Almanidis
04/10/98	Olympiakos	A	1-6	Zajmi
25/10/98	AEK	H	1-1	og (Zikos)
01/11/98	Apollon	A	2-2	Zajmi 2
08/11/98	Panelefsiniakos	H	0-1	
22/11/98	Veria	A	1-3	Almanidis
30/11/98	OFI	H	0-1	
06/12/98	Paniliakos	A	2-1	Dimos, Almanidis
13/12/98	Panionios	A	0-0	
20/12/98	Ethnikos Asteras	H	3-0	Yanopoulos, Protasov, Fouskas
17/01/99	PAOK	A	0-1	
24/01/99	Ionikos	H	0-0	
31/01/99	Aris	A	0-1	
07/02/99	Kavala	H	1-0	Almanidis (p)
15/02/99	Panathinaikos	A	0-1	
21/02/99	Ethnikos Piraeus	H	0-0	
28/02/99	Iraklis	A	1-0	Almanidis
07/03/99	Xanthi	A	1-4	Protasov
13/03/99	Olympiakos	H	0-1	
21/03/99	AEK	A	0-1	
04/04/99	Apollon	H	0-1	
18/04/99	Panelefsiniakos	A	1-0	Almanidis (p)
25/04/99	Veria	H	1-0	Abelas
02/05/99	OFI	A	0-0	
09/05/99	Paniliakos	H	2-0	Dangas, Almanidis
12/05/99	Panionios	H	0-0	
16/05/99	Ethnikos Asteras	A	2-2	Protasov (p), Al Jaher
20/05/99	PAOK	H	2-1	Dimos, Yanopoulos
23/05/99	Ionikos	A	0-2	
30/05/99	Aris	H	2-1	Dangas, Al Jaher

VERIA

CLUB DIRECTORY

Veria
Stadiou 34
Veria
tel - (0331) 29469
fax - (0331) 29469
Year of Formation - 1960
President - Vasilios Tsiamitros
Coach - Stefanos Gaitanos; Yeorgios Hantzaras;
Petros Ravousis
Stadium - Veria (10,000)

APPEARANCES 98/99

	P	Ap	(s)	Gls
Juan BALASAR (PER)	M	18	(1)	
Ormeno BASOBRIO (PER)	D	14	(1)	
Alexandros DELIOS	G	10		
Efstratios DELITSIKOS	A		(2)	
Athanasios DERMIZOGLOU	M	20	(5)	3
Roberto FARFAN (PER)	A	1	(4)	
Ioanis FASIDIS	M	21	(2)	
Minas HATZIDIS	M	20	(5)	2
Jorge HUAMAN (PER)	D	20		
Vasilios KASTANIOTIS	D	26	(2)	
Yeorgios KONDOGOULIDIS	A		(1)	
Lambros KOTSIOPOULOS	G	9		
Ioanis MALOUS	M	14		1
Pandeleimon MANOS	M		(3)	
Fotios MITSAKIS	A	2	(17)	
Srdjan MLADENOVIC (YUG)	M	9	(2)	
Alejandro MULIET (PER)	G	5		
Andonis NATSOURAS	M	6	(3)	
Vasilios NIRAS	M	4	(8)	
Theodoros PAKALTSIS	M	10	(3)	1
Ioanis PROVIDAS	M	13		3
Frank RUIZ (PER)	D	9	(1)	
Nikolaos SAKELARIDIS	M	13	(7)	1
Efthimios SIDIROPOULOS	D	15	(3)	1
Panayotis SIDIROPOULOS	D	4	(2)	
Goran STEVANOVIC (YUG)	M	8	(4)	
Stefan STOICA (ROM)	M	12	(7)	1
Ioanis THOMAIDIS	A	26	(6)	5
Athanasios TOLIOS	G	10	(2)	
Panayotis TSALOUHIDIS	M	26		
Ioanis TSIYANIS	D	23	(1)	1
Ljubomir VORKAPIC (YUG)	M	6	(4)	1

LEAGUE RESULTS 1998/99

23/08/98	Iraklis	H	0-2	
30/08/98	Xanthi	A	0-2	
12/09/98	Olympiakos	H	0-3	
20/09/98	AEK	A	0-2	
27/09/98	Apollon	H	1-1	Tsiyanis
03/10/98	Panelefsiniakos	A	0-2	
26/10/98	Panionios	A	0-0	
01/11/98	OFI	H	0-0	
08/11/98	Paniliakos	A	0-0	
22/11/98	Proodeftiki	H	3-1	Thomaidis, Vorkapic (p), Malous
28/11/98	Ethnikos Asteras	A	0-4	
04/12/98	PAOK	H	1-2	Thomaidis
13/12/98	Ionikos	A	0-1	
21/12/98	Aris	H	0-1	
16/01/99	Kavala	A	1-2	Dermizoglou
24/01/99	Panathinaikos	H	0-1	
31/01/99	Ethnikos Piraeus	H	4-3	Stoica (p), Providas, Sidiropoulos, Hatzidis (p)
07/02/99	Iraklis	A	0-2	
15/02/99	Xanthi	H	2-0	Thomaidis 2
21/02/99	Olympiakos	A	0-5	
01/03/99	AEK	H	0-3	
06/03/99	Apollon	A	0-2	
14/03/99	Panelefsiniakos	H	0-1	
22/03/99	Panionios	H	3-1	Dermizoglou 2, Providas
04/04/99	OFI	A	0-3	
18/04/99	Paniliakos	H	0-0	
25/04/99	Proodeftiki	A	0-1	
02/05/99	Ethnikos Asteras	H	3-1	Hatzidis (p), Pakaltsis, Sakelaridis
09/05/99	PAOK	A	0-2	
12/05/99	Ionikos	H	0-2	
16/05/99	Aris	A	0-2	
20/05/99	Kavala	H	0-2	
23/05/99	Panathinaikos	A	0-1	
30/05/99	Ethnikos Piraeus	A	2-0	Thomaidis, Providas

XANTHI

Xanthi Skoda
Vasilisis Sofias 3
67100 Xanthi
tel - (0541) 24466/22977
fax - (0541) 25852
Year of Formation - 1967
President - Aristidis Pialoglou
Coach - Ioanis Mantzourakis
Stadium - Xanthi (12,800)

APPEARANCES 98/99

	P	Ap	(s)	Gls
Sotirios ANDONIOU	M	23	(2)	1
Konstandinos ANGOS	M	2	(2)	
Dimitrios AVRAMIDIS	M		(1)	
Ismail BA (SEN)	A	31	(1)	14
Juraj BUCEK (SVK)	G	32		
Vasilios DAMIANOS	M	15	(9)	2
Yeorgios EFENDOPOULOS	M	2	(4)	
Ioakim HAVOS	M	29		1
Hristos ILIOPOULOS	M		(2)	
Nikolaos KARAYEORGIOU	D	21	(1)	
Prokopios KARTALIS	M	5	(14)	2
Nikolaos KEHAYAS	M	22		2
Thomas KIPARISIS	A	23	(5)	9
Nugzar LOBJANIDZE (GEO)	A	1		
Thomas MAKRIS	A	2	(5)	1
Cyril MANGAN (CMR)	M	3	(4)	
Alireza MANSOURIAN (IRN)	M	8	(9)	
Haralambos NIKOLAOU	D	5	(7)	
Ioanis PAPADIMITRIOU	M	25		
Hristos PATSANTZOGLOU	M	29	(1)	2
Hristos SAMARAS	D		(1)	
Mohamed SAQIL (SYR)	M	6	(3)	
Abdul Salem SOW (SYR)	A	2		
Petros TENGELIDIS	A	5	(13)	3
Ioanis TSAKONAKIS	G	2		
Nikolaos TSETINES	D		(1)	
Theofanis TSOUVALIDIS	D	1		
Stilianos VENETIDIS	D	31		1
Angelos VILANAKIS	M	19	(8)	4
Dimitrios YELADARIS	M	24	(5)	1
Nikolaos ZAPROPOULOS	M	4	(1)	
Dimitrios ZOGRAFAKIS	M	2	(2)	

LEAGUE RESULTS 1998/99

Date	Opponent	H/A	Score	Scorers
23/08/98	Panelefsiniakos	A	0-0	
30/08/98	Veria	H	2-0	Tengelidis, Damianos
13/08/98	OFI	A	2-4	Ba 2
20/09/98	Paniliakos	H	2-1	Yeladaris, Kiparisis
27/09/98	Proodeftiki	A	2-1	Kehayas, Ba
04/10/98	Ethnikos Asteras	A	1-0	Vilanakis
25/10/98	PAOK	H	0-1	
01/11/98	Ionikos	A	1-0	Andoniou
08/11/98	Aris	H	2-0	Ba 2
21/11/98	Kavala	A	1-1	Tengelidis
30/11/98	Panathinaikos	H	1-0	Kiparisis
06/12/98	Ethnikos Piraeus	A	1-1	Ba
12/12/98	Iraklis	H	0-0	
21/12/98	Panionios	H	1-0	Kiparisis
17/01/99	Olympiakos	A	1-3	Ba
24/01/99	AEK	H	2-1	Kiparisis, Ba
31/01/99	Apollon	A	1-2	Kehayas
07/02/99	Panelefsiniakos	H	0-0	
15/02/99	Veria	A	0-2	
21/02/99	OFI	H	3-1	Kiparisis, Ba (p), Kartalis
28/02/99	Paniliakos	A	0-1	
06/03/99	Proodeftiki	H	4-1	Vilanakis, Ba 2 (1p), Kiparisis
14/03/99	Ethnikos Asteras	H	0-1	
22/03/99	PAOK	A	0-0	
04/04/99	Ionikos	H	2-2	Tengelidis, Vilanakis
18/04/99	Aris	A	2-1	og (Yeorgiadis), Damianos
25/04/99	Kavala	H	4-1	Vilanakis, Kiparisis 2, Havos
02/05/99	Panathinaikos	A	1-2	Patsantzoglou
09/05/99	Ethnikos Piraeus	H	2-0	Venetidis, Ba (p)
12/05/99	Iraklis	A	2-2	Kartalis, Ba
16/05/99	Panionios	A	2-0	Ba, Patsantzoglou
20/05/99	Olympiakos	H	0-2	
23/05/99	AEK	A	1-2	Makris
30/05/99	Apollon	H	1-0	Kiparisis

PROMOTED CLUBS

SECOND DIVISION FINAL TABLE 98/99

		Pd	W	D	L	F	A	Pt	GD
1	Trikala	34	20	8	6	59	29	68	+30
2	Panahaiki	34	20	8	6	56	30	68	+26
3	Kalamata	34	19	8	7	47	25	65	+22
4	Yanina	34	19	8	7	51	22	65	+29
5	Kalithea	34	19	5	10	59	40	62	+19
6	Ayos Nikolaos	34	14	10	10	36	35	52	+1
7	Panseraikos	34	15	4	15	44	37	49	+7
8	Larisa	34	13	7	14	45	47	46	-2
9	Athinaikos	34	13	5	16	38	32	44	+6
10	Pierikos	34	11	10	13	39	38	43	+1
11	Apollon Kalamaria	34	11	9	14	42	45	42	-3
12	Karditsa	34	10	11	13	35	35	41	0
13	Ialisos	34	11	8	15	33	45	41	-12
14	Panetolikos	34	11	8	15	43	56	41	-13
15	Liki	34	11	4	19	28	51	37	-23
16	Doxa Virona	34	8	13	13	39	43	37	-4
17	Niki	34	8	4	22	35	63	28	-28
18	Edesaikos	34	4	8	22	17	73	20	-56

CLUB DIRECTORY

Trikala
Asklipiou 13
Trikala
tel - (0431) 28587
President - Sakis Karatzounis
Coach - Stefan Ostoic (99/00 - Mihail Filipou)
Stadium - Trikalon (8,000)

CLUB DIRECTORY

Panahaiki
Makariou & Kitiou
Patra
tel - (061) 434542
fax - (061) 434543
Year of Formation - 1924
President - Aris Loukopoulos
Coach - Takis Kiriakopoulos
(99/00 - Mojas Radonic)
Stadium - Panahaikis (19,200)

CLUB DIRECTORY

Kalamata
Andonakopoulou & Dagre 2
Kalamata
tel - (0721) 94000
fax - (0721) 24605
Year of Formation - 1967
President - Stavros Papadopoulos
Coach - Jacek Gmoch (99/00 - Eduardo Amorim)
Stadium - Mesiniakos (9,500)

HOLLAND

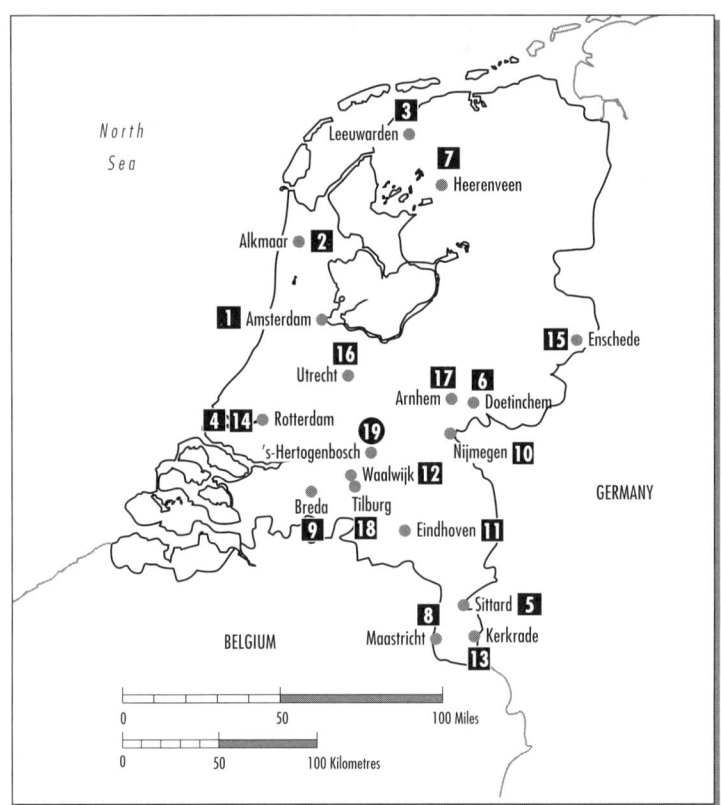

1	AJAX	489
2	AZ	490
3	SC CAMBUUR LEEUWARDEN	491
4	FEYENOORD	492
5	FORTUNA SITTARD	493
6	DE GRAAFSCHAP	494
7	SC HEERENVEEN	495
8	MVV	496
9	NAC	497
10	NEC	498

11	PSV	499
12	RKC WAALWIJK	500
13	RODA JC	501
14	SPARTA	502
15	FC TWENTE	503
16	FC UTRECHT	504
17	VITESSE	505
18	WILLEM II	506
Promoted club		
19	FC DEN BOSCH	507

RIJKAARD EXPERIMENTS BEFORE EURO 2000

Beenhakker fulfils his Feyenoord dream

FEDERATION DIRECTORY

Koninklijke Nederlandsche Voetbalbond
Woudenbergseweg 56-58, PO Box 515, 3700 AM Zeist

tel - (0343) 499211	Year of Formation - 1889
fax - (0343) 499189	President - Jeu Sprengers
	Secretary - Drs. Harry Been

Stadium - Feyenoord, Rotterdam (51,180)

Four years on, the Bosman verdict is still a hot topic of conversation in Holland. Its implications are many and far-reaching, but most Dutch football fans would agree that it has been responsible for a noticeable slump in standards of the domestic game.

Dutch football is renowned the world over for its high level of technical ability and the flair and fluency of its top players. But because Holland is a relatively small country, it does not have the financial infrastructure to compete with the larger European nations of England, Germany, Italy and Spain. Since Bosman, more and more Dutch players have been tempted abroad in order to further their careers, and there appears to be no imminent halt to the flow.

Consequently, Dutch clubs are finding it increasingly difficult to compete in international competition. In 1995 Ajax were the champions of Europe. Now, less than five years later, not one of the players who appeared in that final against Milan is still at the club. With the exception of Danny Blind, who has retired, and Frank Rijkaard, who is now the Dutch national team coach, all of the others are currently contracted to leading foreign clubs. It is hardly surprising, then, that in 1998/99 the Amsterdammers failed to overcome the hurdle of the Champions' League group phase. Nor that Holland's other five European representatives all failed to extend their European participation beyond December - something which had not happened since 1990/91 (the season when Ajax were serving a European ban).

LEAGUE CHAMPIONSHIP RESULTS 98/99

		1	2	3	4	5	6	7	8	9	10	11	12	13	14	15	16	17	18
1	Ajax		5-1	4-0	6-0	1-3	1-1	0-0	1-1	1-0	3-0	2-2	2-0	2-1	5-1	5-0	5-2	0-1	2-0
2	AZ	1-1		3-1	0-2	0-3	1-3	1-3	4-2	3-0	1-1	4-1	2-1	1-0	2-0	1-1	4-3	0-0	1-1
3	SC Cambuur Leeuwarden	4-1	0-0		1-5	3-1	2-0	0-0	1-0	3-1	2-2	1-1	1-1	1-1	2-4	0-2	1-1	2-2	0-2
4	Feyenoord	1-1	1-2	4-0		4-1	5-0	2-1	3-1	2-2	1-0	3-1	1-0	0-0	1-0	3-1	4-2	2-1	3-2
5	Fortuna Sittard	1-0	2-2	2-0	1-2		0-0	1-0	0-1	2-0	2-3	6-4	3-2	0-1	2-1	0-3	3-2	0-2	1-2
6	De Graafschap	1-3	1-1	2-2	3-4	0-0		1-1	3-1	0-1	2-1	1-0	2-2	2-3	0-3	0-2	0-0	0-0	2-2
7	SC Heerenveen	2-2	2-1	1-1	0-1	2-0	4-1		1-1	2-1	3-2	3-3	2-0	2-2	0-0	1-0	1-0	2-1	2-2
8	MVV	1-4	2-1	3-0	1-3	3-3	1-2	1-0		3-3	0-3	1-1	1-0	0-0	1-1	2-5	1-4	4-2	1-1
9	NAC	2-2	1-1	2-3	0-1	1-1	0-1	2-2	2-0		1-2	3-4	0-2	0-0	5-0	1-1	2-4	0-2	2-2
10	NEC	0-4	2-2	1-0	0-3	0-3	1-1	2-0	1-1	1-1		2-2	1-1	3-1	3-1	2-2	0-1	3-1	0-3
11	PSV	3-1	7-1	3-0	1-2	2-0	2-2	1-2	2-0	2-0	2-0		2-2	3-3	4-0	3-0	5-0	3-1	1-0
12	RKC Waalwijk	0-1	2-3	4-1	0-5	0-0	1-2	0-4	2-2	2-1	0-1	3-4		4-1	5-1	2-2	2-5	0-2	1-3
13	Roda JC	0-2	8-2	1-0	1-0	5-3	3-1	2-1	2-1	3-1	5-2	1-3	0-0		1-0	2-0	3-0	3-1	0-2
14	Sparta	2-0	0-0	1-2	1-2	5-0	2-3	3-1	0-0	0-2	1-0	0-5	0-1	1-1		4-2	0-1	1-3	0-4
15	FC Twente	2-1	0-3	0-0	1-1	2-2	2-1	1-2	2-1	2-2	2-0	2-2	1-0	0-0	1-0		1-1	0-0	5-1
16	FC Utrecht	2-2	2-2	3-0	2-3	1-1	2-1	2-2	0-2	2-0	2-3	2-3	1-1	0-3	4-1	0-3		1-2	2-0
17	Vitesse	3-2	0-1	4-2	1-1	1-2	2-1	1-2	2-1	3-1	1-0	3-3	2-0	1-0	5-1	1-1	2-0		3-2
18	Willem II	3-1	2-0	2-1	4-1	1-0	2-0	3-2	4-1	2-1	1-0	4-2	3-0	1-2	3-2	1-2	1-0	3-5	

LEAGUE CHAMPIONSHIP FINAL TABLE 98/99

			Home				Away					Total						
		P	W	D	L	F	A	W	D	L	F	A	W	D	L	F	A	P	GD
1	Feyenoord	34	13	3	1	40	15	12	2	3	36	23	25	5	4	76	38	80	+38
2	Willem II	34	14	0	3	40	20	6	5	6	29	26	20	5	9	69	46	65	+23
3	PSV	34	12	3	2	46	14	5	7	5	41	41	17	10	7	87	55	61	+32
4	Vitesse	34	11	3	3	35	20	7	4	6	26	24	18	7	9	61	44	61	+17
5	Roda JC	34	13	1	3	40	19	4	8	5	19	21	17	9	8	59	40	60	+19
6	Ajax	34	11	4	2	45	13	5	5	7	28	28	16	9	9	73	41	57	+32
7	SC Heerenveen	34	9	7	1	30	18	5	5	7	23	23	14	12	8	53	41	54	+12
8	FC Twente	34	7	8	2	24	17	6	5	6	27	28	13	13	8	51	45	52	+6
9	AZ	34	8	5	4	29	23	4	7	6	23	37	12	12	10	52	60	48	-8
10	Fortuna Sittard	34	8	2	7	26	25	4	6	7	23	31	12	8	14	49	56	44	-7
11	NEC	34	5	7	5	22	27	5	2	10	20	29	10	9	15	42	56	39	-14
12	FC Utrecht	34	5	5	7	28	29	5	3	9	26	35	10	8	16	54	64	38	-10
13	De Graafschap	34	3	8	6	20	26	5	4	8	20	31	8	12	14	40	57	36	-17
14	MVV	34	5	6	6	26	33	2	5	10	16	30	7	11	16	42	63	32	-21
15	SC Cambuur Leeuwarden	34	5	8	4	24	24	2	3	12	13	40	7	11	16	37	64	32	-27
16	RKC Waalwijk	34	4	3	10	28	38	2	6	9	13	24	6	9	19	41	62	27	-21
17	Sparta	34	5	3	9	21	27	2	2	13	16	44	7	5	22	37	71	26	-34
18	NAC	34	2	7	8	24	28	2	4	11	17	33	4	11	19	41	61	23	-20

The first of the Dutch fallers were Feyenoord, who, despite winning the first leg of their UEFA Cup first-round tie 3-1 away to VfB Stuttgart, somehow contrived to lose out to the Germans in the return, going down 0-3 in Rotterdam after conceding a last-minute goal. The defeat left everybody at the club speechless. It was particularly unexpected because Feyenoord were firing on all cylinders at the time in the league, having made a perfect start to the Eredivisie campaign with victories in each of their first six matches.

The Rotterdammers suffered another blow when they lost at home to an AZ side coached by their ex-boss Wim van Hanegem, but they recovered rapidly and went on to carve out a handsome lead at the top of the table. This was largely due to the inspired work of their coach, Leo Beenhakker.

Back in 1968, when he first started out as a coach in rural Veendam, Beenhakker had a dream that one day he would lead Feyenoord to the Dutch title. Born only a short distance from the Feyenoord stadium, he has had a lifelong affection for the club (which did not disappear even when he was in charge of arch-rivals Ajax). Thus, his appointment as Feyenoord's head coach in November 1997 was the first stage of the fulfilment of his dream. Completing stage two would take him just 18 months longer.

Beenhakker succeeded in transforming a bunch of individuals lacking a common purpose into a hardened, disciplined unit. The basis of the team's success was a solid defence, in which goalkeeper Jerzy Dudek, libero Bert Konterman and stopper Kees van Wonderen proved to be the best players in their respective positions in the whole country. First and foremost Feyenoord were difficult to beat, but they had other assets, notably an outstanding captain in midfielder Jean-Paul van Gastel, a dazzling winger in the 'born-again' Peter van Vossen and two reliable goalscorers in Argentinian centre-forward Julio Cruz and his nifty accomplice Jon Dahl Tomasson.

The latter's exhilarating form could hardly have been in greater contrast to his nightmare season in England with Newcastle, and it was fitting that he should score the first goal in the match that completed the formality of Feyenoord's 14th title. Beenhakker's dream finally came true on April 25, 1999 when the final whistle sounded on Feyenoord's 2-2 draw at home to NAC. It was not the most distinguished of results - NAC were the league's bottom club - but it didn't matter. With five matches still to play Feyenoord were too far out in front to be caught. The championship was theirs.

Alas, Feyenoord's celebrations were marred by an ugly outbreak of street violence later that evening in the Rotterdam city centre. The fighting lasted for hours and

TOP SCORERS

31	Ruud VAN NISTELROOY (PSV)
24	Luc NILIS (PSV)
21	Jan VENNEGOOR OF HESSELINK
	(FC Twente)
20	Michael MOLS (FC Utrecht)
18	Nikos MACHLAS (Vitesse)
17	Mariano BOMBARDA (Willem II)
	Peter VAN HOUDT (Roda JC)
15	Julio CRUZ (Feyenoord)
	Jack DE GIER (NEC)
14	Ronald HAMMING (Fortuna Sittard)

NATIONAL TEAM RESULTS 98/99

10/10/98	Peru	H	Eindhoven	2-0	Stam (67), Van Vossen (75)
13/10/98	Ghana	H	Arnhem	0-0	
18/11/98	Germany	A	Gelsenkirchen	1-1	Reiziger (22)
10/02/99	Portugal	N	Paris	0-0	
31/03/99	Argentina	H	Amsterdam	1-1	Davids (10)
28/04/99	Morocco	H	Arnhem	1-2	Van Nistelrooy (90)
05/06/99	Brazil	A	Salvador de Bahia	2-2	Kluivert (64), Van Vossen (67)
08/06/99	Brazil	A	Goiânia	1-3	Van Hooijdonk (78)

resulted in 80 arrests, causing terrible distress to local residents and, of course, to the genuine Feyenoord fans. It was not the first example of serious misbehaviour by hooligans attaching themselves to the club. A few months earlier a group of Feyenoord followers had gone on the rampage in Germany after a friendly with Bayer Leverkusen. UEFA subsequently issued a warning that the club would be kicked out of Europe if similar incidents took place again, so Feyenoord took the pre-emptive step of placing a total travel ban on their fans for the 1999/2000 Champions' League. How different from 1970 when tens of thousands of Feyenoord fans travelled peacefully to Milan to see their team lift the European Cup...

While Feyenoord were led by a Dutchman in 1998/99, rivals Ajax and PSV both began the season with foreign coaches. Ajax retained the services of their 'double'-winning Dane, Morten Olsen, whereas PSV were placed

under the command of Englishman Bobby Robson, the man who had led the club to back-to-back Dutch titles during his previous stint at the start of the decade. Robson's was the tougher task, especially as he knew that he was being employed as a mere stop-gap before the arrival of Eric Gerets from Bruges 12 months later. PSV were a club in transition. The simultaneous departure of five leading Dutch internationals had been counterbalanced by the arrival of almost twice as many newcomers, most of them from abroad.

An alchemist's touch was required from Robson, and although he found the formula in his first game, when PSV continued their fine run of form in Amsterdam, beating Ajax 2-0 to win the Johan Cruijff Shield (aka Dutch Super Cup), many important points were squandered in the league through a lack of cohesion in defence. Once the back four was sorted out and Belgian ace Luc Nilis

DOMESTIC CUP 98/99

SECOND ROUND
FC Groningen 2, TONEGIDO 0
Feyenoord 2, ADO Den Haag 1 (asd)
Ajax 9, UDI '19 Uden 0
Roda JC 2, SC Veendam 1 (asd)
FC Utrecht 2, NEC 2 (aet; 5-4 on pens.)
Excelsior 0, PSV 5
Sparta 1, SC Cambuur Leeuwarden 1
(aet; 3-4 on pens.)
Go Ahead Eagles 3, De Graafschap 2
Willem II 0, FC Zwolle 2
Fortuna Sittard 5, RKC Waalwijk 0
Eindhoven 3, FC Den Bosch 1
Emmen 3, SC Heerenveen 2
SC Heracles 0, NAC 0 (aet; 4-5 on pens.)
Vitesse 3, FC Volendam 0
FC Twente 2, VVV 1
AZ 3, MVV 1

THIRD ROUND
Vitesse 4, NAC 0
FC Twente 2, Fortuna Sittard 5
PSV 2, AZ 0
Emmen 2, SC Cambuur Leeuwarden 0
Eindhoven 2, FC Groningen 1
FC Zwolle 5, Go Ahead Eagles 2
FC Utrecht 1, Feyenoord 2
Roda JC 0, Ajax 3

QUARTER-FINALS
Eindhoven 0, PSV 5 (Nilis 33, Van Nistelrooy 36,
Khokhlov 61, De Bilde 79, 90)
Fortuna Sittard 3 (Jeffrey 37, Simons 69, 89),
Emmen 1 (Nurmela 36)
Feyenoord 2 (Van Gastel 48p, Korneev 98),
Vitesse 1 (Curovic 90) (asd)
FC Zwolle 1 (Zijm 51),
Ajax 2 (Litmanen 45, Sibon 61)

SEMI-FINALS
Ajax 2 (Wamberto 45, Melchiot 71),
Feyenoord 1 (Van Gastel 55)
PSV 1 (Van Nistelrooy 26), Fortuna Sittard 3
(Hamming 28, Roest 65, Bouma 83)

FINAL
13/05/99, Rotterdam
AJAX 2 Grønkjaer (11, 15)
FORTUNA SITTARD 0
referee - Uilenberg
AJAX - Van der Sar; Melchiot, Rudy, Oliseh, De Cler,
Witschge, Litmanen, Hoekstra, Wamberto
(McCarthy 25), Arveladze, Grønkjaer.
FORTUNA SITTARD - Van Zwam; Lee, Hofland, Roest,
Hermans, Paciorec, Gesthuizen (Hamming 62), Kool,
Jeffrey, Simons, Bouma (Heering 73).

EUROPEAN CUPS 98/99

CHAMPIONS' CUP
● AJAX
Champions' League
1st match CROATIA ZAGREB (CRO)
A 0-0
Van der Sar; Tobiasen, Blind, Oliseh, De Boer F., Dani (De Boer R. 63),
Litmanen, Witschge, Babangida (Kinkladze 77), McCarthy,
Hoekstra (Grønkjaer 71).

2nd match FC PORTO (POR)
H 2-1   Rudy (57), Litmanen (86p)
Van der Sar; Tobiasen, Rudy, Oliseh, De Boer F., De Boer R., Litmanen,
Witschge (Dani 65), Babangida (Grønkjaer 90), Arveladze (Sibon 79),
Hoekstra.

3rd match OLYMPIAKOS (GRE)
A 0-1
Van der Sar; Tobiasen, Rudy, Oliseh, De Boer F., De Boer R., Litmanen,
Witschge, Wamberto (Dani 46), Arveladze (McCarthy 79),
Grønkjaer (Kinkladze 46).

4th match OLYMPIAKOS (GRE)
H 2-0   Witschge (33), Gorré (88)
Van der Sar; Tobiasen (Dani 37), Oliseh, De Boer F., Sier, De Boer R.,
Litmanen (Gorré 40), Witschge, Wamberto, Arveladze (McCarthy 27),
Hoekstra.

5th match CROATIA ZAGREB (CRO)
H 0-1
Van der Sar; Mensah, Blind, De Boer F., Sier (Melchiot 41), De Boer R.,
Dani, Witschge, Wamberto (Babangida 72), Hose (McCarthy 64),
Hoekstra.

6th match FC PORTO (POR)
A 0-3
Van der Sar; Mensah, Blind, Oliseh, De Boer F., Rudy (McCarthy 74),
Gorré (Dani 46), Hoekstra, Wamberto, De Boer R.,
Grønkjaer (Babangida 76).

● PSV
Qualifying round MARIBOR TEATANIC (SLO)
A 1-2   Marcos (61)
Lodewijks; Abel Xavier, Marcos, Nikiforov, Oyen, Iwan (Rommedahl 72),
Ooijer (Van der Doelen 75), Khokhlov (Jorginho 81), Kolkka,
Van Nistelrooy, De Bilde.
H 4-1   Van Nistelrooy (8), Bruggink (70), Rommedahl (100), De Bilde (103)
(aet)   Lodewijks; Ooijer, Abel Xavier, Marcos (Rommedahl 70), Lucius,
Jorginho (Bruggink 46), Iwan, Khokhlov, Kolkka (Van der Doelen 111),
De Bilde, Van Nistelrooy.

Champions' League
1st match HJK (FIN)
H 2-1   Ooijer (57), Bruggink (90)
Waterreus; Lucius, Abel Xavier, Marcos, Oyen, Khokhlov, Nikiforov
(Bruggink 54), Iwan (Rommedahl 59), Ooijer, De Bilde (Claúdio 90),
Kolkka.

2nd match SL BENFICA (POR)
A 1-2   Rommedahl (71)
Waterreus; Lucius, Marcos, Faber, Abel Xavier, Iwan (Rommedahl 62),
Khokhlov, Van der Doelen (Bruggink 80), De Bilde (Nilis 62),
Van Nistelrooy, Kolkka.

3rd match 1.FC KAISERSLAUTERN (GER)
H 1-2   Khokhlov (78)
Waterreus; Lucius, Skerla, Nikiforov (Bruggink 73), Van der Weerden,
Rommedahl, Khokhlov, Van der Doelen (Iwan 80), Nilis, Van Nistelrooy,
Kolkka (De Bilde 73).

4th match 1.FC KAISERSLAUTERN (GER)
A 1-3   Van Nistelrooy (18)
Lodewijks; Abel Xavier, Skerla, Nikiforov, Oyen, Van der Weerden
(Marcos 60), Khokhlov, Van der Doelen (Rommedahl 75), Iwan,
Van Nistelrooy, Nilis (Need 26).

5th match HJK (FIN)
A 3-1   Van Nistelrooy (30, 67, 81p)
Waterreus; Van der Weerden, Abel Xavier, Nikiforov, Oyen, Iwan,
Van der Doelen, Khokhlov, Kolkka (Lucius 75), Nilis (Bruggink 85),
Van Nistelrooy.

6th match SL BENFICA (POR)
H 2-2   Khokhlov (41), Van Nistelrooy (89)
Waterreus; Lucius, Skerla, Abel Xavier, Van der Weerden,
Iwan (Rommedahl 72), Khokhlov, Van der Doelen (Bruggink 82),
Kolkka (Gakhokidze 72), Van Nistelrooy, Nilis.

CUP WINNERS' CUP
● SC HEERENVEEN
1st round AMICA WRONKI (POL)
H 3-1   Talan (38), Mitrita (45), Pahlplatz (66)
Vonk; Radomski, Klompe, Hansma, Mitrita, Pahlplatz,
De Nooijer G. (Pander 64), De Visser, Talan, De Nooijer D. (Gusatu 81),
Samardzic (Zvetkov 87).
A 1-0   De Nooijer D. (30)
Vonk; Radomski, Klompe, Hansma, Mitrita, Pahlplatz,
De Nooijer G. (Pander 84), De Visser, Talan, De Nooijer D.,
Samardzic (Ebiede 75).

2nd round VARTEKS VARAZDIN (CRO)
H 2-1   De Nooijer D. (56), Hansma (89)
Vonk; Radomski, Klompe, Hansma, Mitrita, Houttuin (Gusatu 71),
De Nooijer G., De Visser, Pahlplatz (El Khattabi 46), De Nooijer D.,
Samardzic.
A 2-4   Samardzic (18), De Visser (114)
(aet)   Vonk; Houttuin (El Khattabi 105), Klompe, Hansma, Pander, Radomski,
De Nooijer G., De Visser, Talan, De Nooijer D. (Gusatu 78),
Samardzic (Pahlplatz 91).

UEFA CUP
● FEYENOORD
1st round VFB STUTTGART (GER)
A 3-1   Van Gastel (19), Tomasson (22, 33)
Dudek; Van Gobbel, Van Wonderen, Konterman, Tininho, Bosvelt,
Van Gastel, Paauwe, Tomasson (Gyan 82), Cruz (Kalou 63),
Van Vossen.
H 0-3
Dudek; Van Gobbel, Van Wonderen, Konterman, Gyan, Bosvelt,
Van Gastel, Paauwe, Tomasson (De Haan 85), Cruz,
Van Vossen (Kalou 71).

EUROPEAN CUPS 98/99 (CONT.)

● VITESSE

1st round AEK (GRE)
H 3-0   Laros (48), Perovic (51), Mahlas (89)
         Westerveld; Jochemsen, Veldman (Kuiper 23), Goossen, Van Hintum,
         Trustfull, Perovic, Kreek, Laros (Shukov 71), Mahlas, Reuser.
A 3-3   Mahlas (13, 17), Reuser (54)
         Westerveld; Van der Hoeven (Van der Schaaf 38), Goossen,
         De Marchi, Van Hintum, Shukov (Haniotakis 44), Kreek, Jochemsen,
         Laros, Mahlas (Mamadou 82), Reuser.

2nd round GIRONDINS DE BORDEAUX (FRA)
H 0-1
         Haniotakis; Jochemsen, Goossen, Zeman, Van Hintum, Shukov
         (Trustfull 46), Curovic, Kreek, Laros, Mahlas,
         Reuser (Korsten 82).
A 1-2   Jochemsen (8)
         Haniotakis; Van der Schaaf (Zongo 67), Jochemsen, Goossen, Van
         Hintum, Kuiper, Trustfull, Kreek (Korsten 67), Mahlas, Reuser.

● WILLEM II

1st round DINAMO TBILISI (GEO)
H 3-0   Ramzi (73), Arts (79), Schenning (85)
         Van Fessem; Prommayon, Hyypiä, Schenning, Hill, Valk, Galasek,
         Arts, Ramzi (Schulp 73), Bombarda (Heering 61),
         Abdellaoui (Ceesay 88).
A 3-0   Valk (18), Ceesay (81), Ramzi (90)
         Van Fessem; Prommayon, Hyypiä, Schenning (Loeffen 77), Hill, Valk,
         Galasek, Arts, Heering (Ceesay 61), Ramzi, Abdellaoui.

2nd round REAL BETIS (ESP)
H 1-1   Bombarda (85)
         Van Fessem; Prommayon, Hyypiä (Bombarda 71), Schenning, Hill,
         Valk (Ceesay 81), Galasek, Arts, Heering, Ramzi, Abdellaoui.
A 0-3
         Van Fessem; Prommayon, Hendriks (Hill 60), Schenning, Hyypiä,
         Valk, Galasek, Arts (Bombarda 60), Ceesay, Ramzi,
         Loeffen (Abdellaoui 46).

INTERNATIONAL HONOURS

World Cup Finals appearances: 1934, 1938, 1974 (Runners-up),
1978 (Runners-up), 1990 (2nd round), 1994 (qtr-finals),
1998 (semi-finals)

European Championship appearances (last 8): 1976 (3rd), 1980,
1988 (Winners), 1992 (semi-finals), 1996

European Club Competitions

Champions' Cup	Feyenoord (1970)
	Ajax (1971, 1972, 1973, 1995)
	PSV (1988)
Cup-winners' Cup	Ajax (1987)
UEFA Cup	Feyenoord (1974)
	PSV (1978)
	Ajax (1992)
Super Cup	Ajax (1972, 1973, 1995)
World Club Cup	Feyenoord (1970)
	Ajax (1972, 1995)

returned from injury, PSV began an impressive run,
scoring goals in abundance, with record domestic
signing Ruud van Nistelrooy finding the target in almost
every game. But they had too much ground to make up
on Feyenoord, and their only realistic target was to try to
finish high enough to make an immediate return to the
Champions' League.

With one match remaining, PSV found themselves in
fifth place. They could not finish second, and third place
also looked an unlikely target, especially after they went
0-2 down away to Utrecht. But a truly astonishing
sequence of events, both in their match and in those involving rivals Vitesse and Roda JC, conspired to turn PSV's
misery into absolute joy. A lucky penalty, a scrambled
second goal and then, in the last minute of stoppage-time,
a misplaced winning header gave Bobby Robson's men
an improbable victory. With both Vitesse and Roda losing,
PSV were through to join Feyenoord and Willem II in the
Champions' League.

Willem II, led by the outspoken Co Adriaanse (a
member of the Ajax technical staff when Louis van Gaal
was the coach), surprised everybody with their sensational
charge up the table in the second half of the season. A
mere 11th at the winter break, the team from Tilburg
picked off all their opponents one by one, taking 37 points
from 13 games to book the second automatic Champions'
League place one round from the end.

Roda JC, with their large number of Belgian players,
also had a season to remember under affable coach Sef
Vergoossen. A UEFA Cup ticket was just reward for their
efforts, although, like Vitesse, their ultimate feeling was one
of disappointment that they had failed to grasp a place
in the Champions' League. Vitesse were just seconds away
from claiming that prize, but in truth their form had long
since deserted them. Unstoppable in their magnificent new
Gelredome stadium at the start of the season, they took
just two points from five successive home games in the
spring. As expected, the footloose Artur Jorge did not last
long in Arnhem - seven games, to be precise, before he
left for Paris Saint-Germain - and it was Vitesse's former
coach Herbert Neumann who returned to oversee the
team's subsequent rise and fall.

And what of Ajax? The good news was that they
retained the Dutch Cup, beating Fortuna Sittard 2-0 in a
final that was decided early on by two almost identical
goals from Danish youngster Jesper Grønkjaer. But, apart
from that, it was a thoroughly depressing season for the
Amsterdam club. Some fans even suggested it was the
worst since the club's all-time low of 1964/65.

Trouble brewed early on when the De Boer twins decided that they wanted to join Barcelona, even going to
a tribunal in an attempt to extricate themselves from their

long-binding contracts. They lost the case, but in the event that hardly mattered, because halfway through the season they left anyway. By then Ajax had just about given up on the season. They had a poor Champions' League, failing to score in any of their away matches, and their domestic form was not much better. Morten Olsen, who had enjoyed such an impressive first season, went from hero to zero within a few months and was sacked three days after the Champions' League exit.

One of the reasons for his dismissal was the constant criticism from the fans that he had abandoned the traditional 'Ajax style'. Expensive newcomer Giorgi Kinkladze was a total flop, and many other players failed to reproduce the form they had shown the previous season. The lack of youngsters breaking through into the first team was also a source of discomfort, but new coach Jan Wouters, an Ajax man through and through, attempted to address this soon after taking over, and in the summer he also brought back several Ajax old boys - Aron Winter, Frank Verlaat, Stanley Menzo - all of whom were familiar with the special wants and needs of the club's demanding fans. Although Wouters' team could not improve on sixth place in the league, they did achieve their minimum target of qualifying for Europe by virtue of the Cup win, the highlight of which was their 2-1 semi-final victory over Feyenoord.

While Ajax prolonged their lengthy unbroken record of European qualification, Sparta, Holland's oldest professional club, just managed to cling on to their long-held top-flight status after beating FC Groningen 3-0 in the final match of the relegation play-off series. Other than the 'big three' of Ajax, Feyenoord and PSV, Sparta are the only club ever-present in the Eredivisie since its inception in 1956. RKC Waalwijk also survived the play-off ordeal - for the third season running - which left NAC as the only relegated team, with Eerste Divisie champions FC Den Bosch coming up to replace them.

Holland's preparations for Euro 2000 are complete as far as the venues are concerned, with the stadiums in Amsterdam, Arnhem, Eindhoven and Rotterdam being confirmed alongside those in the Belgian cities of Bruges, Brussels, Charleroi and Liège to host the 31 matches of the first major international footballing event of the 21st century. As far as the Dutch team is concerned, however, much work still remains to be done if they are to go into the finals as genuine pre-tournament favourites.

Frank Rijkaard was appointed as the new *Bondscoach* in succession to Real Madrid-bound Guus Hiddink in August 1998. He was not the KNVB's first choice. They had initially wanted Johan Cruijff and, following his inevitable refusal, Wim Jansen, but it was Rijkaard, a man with no previous experience as a head coach, who got

PLAYERS OF THE SEASON

★ SUPERSTAR PROFILE
RUUD VAN NISTELROOY

He has the look and the talent of Marco van Basten, but can Ruud van Nistelrooy do for Holland on home soil at the 2000 European Championship what Van Basten did at the same tournament 12 years earlier in Germany? It's a tall order, but there is no doubt that the 23-year-old PSV striker is the most impressive of the newcomers tested by national team boss Frank Rijkaard in the countdown to Euro 2000. Van Nistelrooy exploded into contention with a phenomenal first season in Eindhoven following his expensive summer transfer from Heerenveen. He clicked into top gear straight away, and when the brilliant Belgian 'number ten' Luc Nilis moved alongside him after recovering from injury, the pair began to bang in the goals right, left and centre. The season's statistics showed them to be the

most prolific strike-partnership in the whole of Europe, with Van Nistelrooy's 31 Eredivisie goals earning him second place behind FC Porto's Mário Jardel in the European Golden Boot rankings. His fellow professionals in Holland voted him Dutch Player of the Year for 1998/99 - just a few weeks after he scored his first international goal, against

Morocco in Arnhem. Van Nistelrooy's contract with PSV runs until 2003 but it is highly unlikely that he will be in Eindhoven for the full term. One of Europe's superpowers will surely be in for him long before then. He is a forward who has just about everything. Quick, mobile and strong in the air, he also poses a threat at set-pieces and his shooting is violent and spectacular, especially when the ball is served to him on his favoured right side. There is definitely something to that 'new Van Basten' tag...

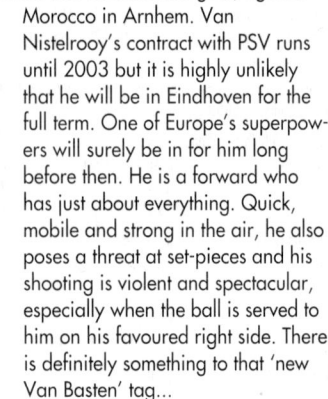

PLAYERS OF THE SEASON

JEAN-PAUL VAN GASTEL

Having been abandoned by his accomplice Giovanni van Bronckhorst (who left for Rangers), Jean-Paul van Gastel became the focal point of the Feyenoord midfield in 1998/99. Named club skipper by coach Leo Beenhakker, he proved to be a strong leader in every sense. With his hustling and harrying he provided an impeneterable protective screen in front of the back three, and he also contributed handsomely to the team's goal tally with a steady supply of penalties and free-kicks. The Dutch title was his first major honour, and nobody deserved it more. Roma were all set to whisk him away to Italy in the summer but negotiations broke down and he remained in Rotterdam to lead Feyenoord into the 1999/2000 Champions' League.

MICHAEL MOLS

March 22, 1999 was a grey day for the followers of FC Utrecht. It was the day that their favourite striker decided to sign a four-year contract with Scottish giants Rangers. 20,000 Utrecht fans had signed a petition pleading with Michael Mols to stay, but their efforts were in vain. In fairness, the 28-year-old was overdue a profitable move abroad. He had become a star at Utrecht following a five-year spell of steady progress at FC Twente. A forward of considerable skill, balance and finishing prowess, he achieved a season's-best total of 20 Eredivisie goals in 1998/99, which earned him not only a nomination for the Dutch PFA's player of the year award but also a recall to the Dutch national team. Whether his move

to Glasgow will assist in his chances of making the Euro 2000 squad, only time will tell, but he certainly has the talent to challenge the likes of Kluivert and Van Nistelrooy for a place in the Dutch team.

MARK VAN BOMMEL

It is not easy to make a strong and lasting impression in Holland without playing for one of the 'big three' clubs, but 22-year-old Mark van Bommel won many admirers with his consistent top-class performances for Fortuna Sittard in 1998/99. A versatile player who can operate as a libero, a midfield anchor-man or a wing-back, he was the instigator of a superb run from the Limburg club in the second half of the season that only ended in the Dutch Cup final, which they lost 2-0 to Ajax. Sittard's semi-final victims were PSV, and the Eindhoven club certainly took note of Van Bommel's qualities because at the end of the season they recruited the Dutch Under-21 international on a five-year contract, beating Ajax to his signature in the process. With his profile now suitably enhanced, a first full cap for Holland is surely just around the corner.

JULIO CRUZ

Every centre-forward who comes to Feyenoord is always compared with the legendary Swedish striker Ove Kindvall, the greatest 'number nine' in the club's history. Virtually all of his successors have been stifled by the comparison, and at first it looked as if Julio Cruz, Feyenoord's record signing from Argentina, would be yet another added to the casualty list. However, the arrival of Leo Beenhakker as coach in November 1997 turned things around for the former River Plate star. He scored 15 goals in 1997/98 and equalled that total a year later as Feyenoord romped home to win the Eredivisie title. He may not be ready to stand shoulder to shoulder with Kindvall just yet, but he has become hugely popular with the Feyenoord fans and has also done enough to be called up by Argentina - despite the long list of fellow-contenders for that position headed by the untouchable Gabriel Batistuta.

he nod, with another legendary former player, Johan Neeskens, acting as his assistant. Both men had served nder Hiddink during Holland's brilliant yet ultimately nfulfilling France '98 World Cup campaign, but straight

from the off the new régime made it clear that the 1998/99 season would be used for experimentation purposes only.
Rijkaard got off to a positive start with a 2-0 win over

Peru, but there were no more victories in the seven matches that followed. The results did not worry the former Ajax and Milan star. He claimed that his work could only be evaluated properly at the European finals - which, in general, the Dutch fans and media accepted. The results were not actually as bad as they looked, and of the ten previously uncapped players who were introduced, defender Konterman and striker Van Nistelrooy looked to have genuine international-class potential. Holland were the better side in the draws against Germany, Portugal, Argentina and Brazil, and although they lost twice, those defeats were easily explained.

Against Morocco, the Dutch were without their entire Barcelona contingent (which, nowadays, is effectively half the team) and in the second of the end-of-season clashes with Brazil the entire squad were suffering from a bout of Montezuma's revenge after an unpleasant experience with the local cuisine the night before. Three players were also sent off in that 3-1 defeat - a new Dutch record. It was far from the ideal way for the team to close phase one of their European Championship preparation, but, as Rijkaard stated, proper judgment on the new *Oranje* remains suspended until the Big Kick-Off, in the Amsterdam ArenA, on Sunday June 11, 2000.

NATIONAL TEAM APPEARANCES 98/99

Coach - Frank RIJKAARD	PER	GHA	GER	POR	ARG	MAR	BRA	BRA	Cps	Gls
Edwin VAN DER SAR (29/10/70) - Ajax	G	G46	G	G	G	G	G		39	-
Michael REIZIGER (03/05/73) - FC Barcelona (ESP)	D	D	D68		D		D46		35	1
Jaap STAM (17/07/72) - Manchester United (ENG)	D	D54	D	D46					25	2
Frank DE BOER (15/05/70) - Ajax/FC Barcelona (ESP)	D	D	D	D	D		D	D	69	6
Philip COCU (29/10/70) - FC Barcelona (ESP)	D	D	M75	D	M		M34	M	34	4
Jeffrey TALAN (29/09/71) - SC Heerenveen	M	M46	M73						3	-
Ronald DE BOER (15/05/70) - Ajax/FC Barcelona (ESP)	M71	M68		M46			M46	M70	52	12
Edgar DAVIDS (13/03/73) - Juventus (ITA)	M	M		M	M		M	M	24	2
Marc OVERMARS (29/03/73) - Arsenal (ENG)	M68	M68	M81		M57	M46			51	10
Dennis BERGKAMP (10/05/69) - Arsenal (ENG)	A	A		A76	A79				68	36
Patrick KLUIVERT (01/07/76) - FC Barcelona (ESP)	A	A	A46	A60	A		A	A67	31	14
Peter VAN VOSSEN (21/04/68) - Feyenoord	s68	s68	s81	M76	s57	s46	s34	M	26	9
Clarence SEEDORF (01/04/76) - Real Madrid (ESP)	s71	s68	M	s46	M	M80	M		42	7
Oscar MOENS (01/04/73) - AZ		s46							1	-
Martijn REUSER (01/02/75) - Vitesse		s46							1	-
Kees VAN WONDEREN (04/01/69) - Feyenoord		s54	s68	D	D46	D			5	-
Marc VAN HINTUM (22/06/67) - Vitesse			D	s86	s79	D		s70	5	-
Ruud VAN NISTELROOY (01/07/76) - PSV			A	s76	A	A	A		5	1
Michael MOLS (17/12/70) - FC Utrecht			s46	s60	A				6	-
Dries BOUSSATTA (23/12/72) - AZ			s73	M86		M66			3	-
Giovanni VAN BRONCKHORST (05/02/75) - Rangers (SCO)			s75			M	D		10	1
Jean-Paul VAN GASTEL (28/04/72) - Feyenoord				s46		D			4	2
Boudewijn ZENDEN (15/08/76) - FC Barcelona (ESP)				s76	M		s46	M	14	1
Bert KONTERMAN (14/01/71) - Feyenoord					s46	D	D	D	4	-
Aron WINTER (01/03/67) - Inter (ITA)						s66			77	6
Youri MULDER (23/03/69) - FC Schalke 04 (GER)						s80			9	3
André OOIJER (11/07/74) - PSV						s46	D		2	-
Sander WESTERVELD (23/10/74) - Vitesse							G		1	-
Pierre VAN HOOIJDONK (29/11/69) - Nottingham Forest (ENG)								s67	16	7

AJAX

Ajax
Postbus 12522, 1100 AM Amsterdam
tel - (020) 3111444   fax - (020) 3111480
Year of Formation - 1900
President - Michael van Praag
Coach - Morten Olsen; Jan Wouters
Stadium - Amsterdam ArenA (51,324)

MAJOR HONOURS
League Championship - (27)
1918, 1919, 1931, 1932, 1934, 1937, 1939,
1947, 1957, 1960, 1966, 1967, 1968, 1970,
1972, 1973, 1977, 1979, 1980, 1982, 1983,
1985, 1990, 1994, 1995, 1996, 1998.
Domestic Cup - (14)
1917, 1943, 1961, 1967, 1970, 1971, 1972,
1979, 1983, 1986, 1987, 1993, 1998, 1999.
European Champions' Cup - (4)
1971, 1972, 1973, 1995.
European Cup-winners' Cup - (1) 1987.
UEFA Cup - (1) 1992.
European Super Cup - (3) 1972, 1973, 1995.
World Club Cup - (2) 1972, 1995.

	P	Ap	(s)	Gls
Shota ARVELADZE (GEO)	A	12	(7)	7
Tijjani BABANGIDA (NIG)	A	7	(11)	2
Danny BLIND	D	19		3
Kevin BOBSON	A		(1)	
Frank DE BOER	D	15		3
Ronald DE BOER	M	15		2
Tim DE CLER	D	9	(3)	
DANI (POR)	M	11	(7)	1
Dean GORRÉ	M	7	(7)	1
Jesper GRØNKJAER (DEN)	A	19	(6)	8
Peter HOEKSTRA	A	14	(7)	6
Brutil HOSE	A	3	(2)	
Giorgi KINKLADZE (GEO)	M	9	(3)	
Richard KNOPPER	M	9	(2)	
Jari LITMANEN (FIN)	M	23		11
Benni McCARTHY (SAF)	A	14	(5)	11
Mario MELCHIOT	D	21	(3)	1
Kofi MENSAH	D	10	(5)	
Andy VAN DER MEYDE	A		(1)	
Sunday OLISEH (NIG)	D	24	(1)	3
Andrzej RUDY (POL)	M	11	(7)	1
Edwin VAN DER SAR	G	34		
Gerald SIBON	A	3	(8)	2
Tom SIER	D	7	(1)	
Arno SPLINTER	D	3	(2)	
Ole TOBIASEN (DEN)	D	11		
Ferdy VIERKLAU	D	8		
WAMBERTO (BRA)	A	24	(3)	8
Richard WITSCHGE	M	32		2

23/08/98	Willem II	H	2-0	Arveladze, Blind
28/08/98	Roda JC	A	2-0	Hoekstra, Babangida
09/09/98	AZ	H	5-1	Dani, McCarthy, Litmanen (p), Oliseh, Hoekstra
13/09/98	FC Utrecht	A	2-2	Litmanen, McCarthy
20/09/98	De Graafschap	H	1-1	Litmanen
23/09/98	Fortuna Sittard	A	0-1	
27/09/98	NAC	H	1-0	De Boer R.
04/10/98	Sparta	A	0-2	
18/10/98	FC Twente	H	5-0	Rudy, Witschge, Litmanen, De Boer F., Wamberto
25/10/98	SC Cambuur Leeuwarden	H	4-0	De Boer R., Wamberto, Arveladze, Hoekstra
01/11/98	NEC	A	4-0	Litmanen, Arveladze, Wamberto, Witschge
08/11/98	AZ	A	1-1	McCarthy
11/11/98	Roda JC	H	2-1	Wamberto, McCarthy
15/11/98	PSV	H	2-2	Wamberto, De Boer F.
22/11/98	RKC Waalwijk	A	1-0	Blind
29/11/98	Vitesse	A	2-3	Blind, De Boer F. (p)
06/12/98	MVV	H	1-1	Oliseh
13/12/98	SC Heerenveen	H	0-0	
20/12/98	Feyenoord	A	1-1	McCarthy
14/02/99	FC Twente	A	1-2	Grønkjaer
17/02/99	SC Heerenveen	A	2-2	Babangida, Oliseh
28/02/99	Sparta	H	5-1	Arveladze 2, Gorré, Hoekstra, Grønkjaer
07/03/99	FC Utrecht	H	5-2	og (Nwakire), McCarthy 3, Grønkjaer
16/03/99	MVV	A	4-1	Grønkjaer 3, Litmanen
21/03/99	Vitesse	H	0-1	
04/04/99	PSV	A	1-3	McCarthy
11/04/99	SC Cambuur Leeuwarden	A	1-4	Arveladze
18/04/99	Fortuna Sittard	H	1-3	Litmanen
21/04/99	NEC	H	3-0	Wamberto 2, Grønkjaer
25/04/99	Willem II	A	1-3	Hoekstra
02/05/99	Feyenoord	H	6-0	Grønkjaer, Wamberto, Sibon, Litmanen 2, Arveladze
09/05/99	De Graafschap	A	3-1	Sibon, Melchiot, Hoekstra
16/05/99	RKC Waalwijk	H	2-0	Litmanen 2
23/05/99	NAC	A	2-2	McCarthy 2

AZ

AZ
Postbus 1010
1801 KA Alkmaar
tel - (072) 5154744
fax - (072) 5158388
Year of Formation - 1967
President - Dirk Scheringa
Secretary - Bert Rozemond
Technical Director - Hans van der Zee
Coach - Wim van Hanegem
(99/00 - Gerard van der Lem)
Stadium - Alkmaarderhout (10,537)

MAJOR HONOURS
League Championship - (1) 1981.
Domestic Cup - (3) 1978, 1981, 1982.

APPEARANCES 98/99

	P	Ap	(s)	Gls
Fahad AL GHESHAYAN (SAU)	A	5	(4)	
Peter VAN DEN BERG	D	17	(1)	
Michael BUSKERMOLEN	M	34		5
Elbekay BOUCHIBA	D	12	(3)	
Dries BOUSSATTA	M	29	(1)	1
CANIGIA (BRA)	A	3	(5)	
Abdelkrim EL HADRIOUI (MAR)	D	27		
Youssef FERTOUT (MAR)	A	16	(9)	6
José FORTES RODRIGUEZ (ESP)	D	17	(1)	
Barry VAN GALEN	M	27		5
Ferdino HERNANDEZ	A	8	(3)	
Max HUIBERTS	A	24	(3)	10
Brian JENSEN (DEN)	G	1		
Rolf LANDERL (AUT)	A		(1)	
Michel LANGERAK	M	24	(5)	11
Oscar MOENS	G	33		
John MUTSAERS	A	7	(17)	7
Mike OBIKU (NIG)	A	9	(4)	2
Barry OPDAM	A	7	(15)	
Fernando RICKSEN	D	31		
Dennis DEN TURK	M	8	(2)	1
Robert VAN DER WEERT	A	3	(12)	2
Peter WIJKER	D	32		2

LEAGUE RESULTS 1998/99

22/08/98	Sparta	H	2-0	Langerak 2
29/08/98	Vitesse	H	0-0	
09/09/98	Ajax	A	1-5	Huiberts
12/09/98	Fortuna Sittard	A	2-2	Mutsaers, Van der Weert (p)
19/09/98	Willem II	H	1-1	Langerak
23/09/98	NAC	A	1-1	Langerak
27/09/98	PSV	H	4-1	Langerak 2, Fertout (p), Van der Weert
04/10/98	RKC Waalwijk	A	3-2	Fertout 2, Wijker
16/10/98	SC Heerenveen	H	1-3	Huiberts
23/10/98	NEC	A	2-2	Fertout, Langerak
31/10/98	Feyenoord	A	2-1	Buskermolen, Den Turk
08/11/98	Ajax	H	1-1	Mutsaers
11/11/98	SC Cambuur Leeuwarden	A	0-0	
14/11/98	MVV	A	1-2	Huiberts
22/11/98	Sparta	A	0-0	
02/12/98	Roda JC	H	1-0	Mutsaers
06/12/98	FC Twente	H	1-1	Van Galen
13/12/98	FC Utrecht	H	4-3	Huiberts 2, Van Galen 2
19/12/98	De Graafschap	A	1-1	Huiberts
06/02/99	FC Twente	A	3-0	Van Galen, Langerak, Huiberts
20/02/99	RKC Waalwijk	H	2-1	Buskermolen 2 (1p)
27/02/99	Roda JC	A	2-8	Boussatta, Wijker
06/03/99	SC Cambuur Leeuwarden	H	3-1	Huiberts 2, Mutsaers
14/03/99	FC Utrecht	A	2-2	Buskermolen (p), Van Galen
20/03/99	Fortuna Sittard	H	0-3	
02/04/99	Feyenoord	H	0-2	
10/04/99	Willem II	A	0-2	
13/04/99	NAC	H	3-0	Mutsaers 3
17/04/99	De Graafschap	H	1-3	Obiku
21/04/99	SC Heerenveen	A	1-2	Fertout
01/05/99	Vitesse	A	1-0	Huiberts
08/05/99	NEC	H	1-1	Langerak
16/05/99	PSV	A	1-7	Obiku
23/05/99	MVV	H	4-2	Fertout, Buskermolen, Langerak 2

SC CAMBUUR LEEUWARDEN

CLUB DIRECTORY

SC Cambuur Leeuwarden
Postbus 547
8901 BH Leeuwarden
tel - (058) 2963300
fax - (058) 2963399
Year of Formation - 1964
President - Chris Arlman
Executive Director - Wout de Jong
Coach - Gert Kruys
Stadium - Cambuur (10,000)

APPEARANCES 98/99

	P	Ap	(s)	Gls
Johan ABMA	D	32		2
Richard BEEKINK	A	4	(7)	
Frank BERGHUIS	A	1	(7)	
Gregg BERHALTER (USA)	D	27	(1)	2
Kenan DURMUSOGLU (TUR)	M	23	(4)	4
Marinus DIJKHUIZEN	A	30		7
Richard ELZINGA	M	33		
Maickel FERRIER	D	11	(2)	
Sandor VAN DER HEIDE	M	19	(7)	5
Roy HENDRIKSEN	D	26	(1)	1
Yevgeniy LEVCHENKO (RUS)	A	9	(7)	2
Robert LOONTJENS	D	5	(16)	
Danny MÜLLER	A		(5)	2
Jan ROELOFSEN	A		(1)	
Wim DE RON	G	34		1
Peter DE ROO	M	20	(3)	
René VAN RIJSWIJK	A	28	(3)	7
Twan SCHEEPERS	M	6	(6)	1
Fuat USTA	M	18	(3)	
Leonard VAN UTRECHT	A	26	(1)	2
Dominik VERGOOSSEN	D	6	(4)	
Gaart-Jelle DE VRIES	D	16	(4)	1
Richard VAN DER WAL	A		(6)	

LEAGUE RESULTS 1998/99

22/08/98	PSV	H	1-1	Scheepers
30/08/98	FC Utrecht	A	0-3	
09/09/98	NEC	H	2-2	Van der Heide, Abma
12/09/98	Vitesse	A	2-4	Dijkhuizen, Van der Heide
19/09/98	FC Twente	H	0-2	
23/09/98	Willem II	A	1-2	Dijkhuizen
26/09/98	De Graafschap	H	2-0	Van Rijswijk, Durmusoglu
03/10/98	MVV	A	0-3	
17/10/98	RKC Waalwijk	H	1-1	Dijkhuizen
25/10/98	Ajax	A	0-4	
31/10/98	NAC	H	3-1	Dijkhuizen 2, Van Rijswijk
07/11/98	Roda JC	A	0-1	
11/11/98	AZ	H	0-0	
21/11/98	Feyenoord	A	0-4	
24/11/98	SC Heerenveen	A	1-1	Van der Heide
27/11/98	Fortuna Sittard	H	3-1	Van Rijswijk, Müller 2
02/12/98	FC Utrecht	H	1-1	Dijkhuizen (p)
06/12/98	Sparta	A	2-1	De Vries, Van Rijswijk
16/12/98	NAC	A	3-2	Berhalter, Hendriksen, Van Rijswijk
20/02/99	Fortuna Sittard	A	0-2	
26/02/99	Vitesse	H	2-2	Van der Heide, Van Rijswijk
06/03/99	AZ	A	1-3	Durmusoglu
13/03/99	PSV	A	0-3	
17/03/99	Feyenoord	H	1-5	Van Utrecht
20/03/99	MVV	H	1-0	Van der Heide
02/04/99	NEC	A	0-1	
06/04/99	Roda JC	H	1-1	Berhalter
11/04/99	Ajax	H	4-1	Durmusoglu 2, Levchenko, Van Utrecht
17/04/99	FC Twente	A	0-0	
24/04/99	Sparta	H	2-4	Van Rijswijk, Dijkhuizen
01/05/99	SC Heerenveen	H	0-0	
09/05/99	RKC Waalwijk	A	1-4	De Ron (p)
16/05/99	Willem II	H	0-2	
22/05/99	De Graafschap	A	2-2	Levchenko, Abma

FEYENOORD

CLUB DIRECTORY

Feyenoord
Olympiaweg 50
3077 AL Rotterdam
tel - (010) 2926888
fax - (010) 4325819
Year of Formation - 1908
President - Jorien van den Herik
Manager - Hans Hagelstein
Coach - Leo Beenhakker
Stadium - Feyenoord (51,180)

MAJOR HONOURS
League Championship - (14)
1924, 1928, 1936, 1938, 1940, 1961, 1962,
1965, 1969, 1971, 1974, 1984, 1993, 1999.
Domestic Cup - (10) 1930, 1935, 1965, 1969,
1980, 1984, 1991, 1992, 1994, 1995.
European Champions' Cup - (1) 1970.
UEFA Cup - (1) 1974.
World Club Cup - (1) 1970.

APPEARANCES 98/99

	P	Ap	(s)	Gls
Patrick ALLOTEY (GHA)	D		(1)	
Paul BOSVELT	M	33		4
René BOT	D		(1)	
Ellery CAIRO	A	5	(4)	2
Julio Ricardo CRUZ (ARG)	A	29		15
René VAN DIEREN	D		(1)	
Jerzy DUDEK (POL)	G	34		
Jean-Paul VAN GASTEL	M	27		10
Ulrich VAN GOBBEL	D	27		1
Patricio GRAFF (ARG)	D	3	(1)	
Christian GYAN (GHA)	D	9	(3)	1
Ferry DE HAAN	D	6	(3)	
Bonaventure KALOU (CIV)	A	13	(15)	3
Igor KORNEEV (RUS)	M	4	(13)	5
Bert KONTERMAN	D	32		1
Robin NELISSE	A		(5)	1
Patrick PAAUWE	M	29	(1)	5
Fernando PASCALE	D	1		
Brian PINAS	A	1	(3)	
Bernard SCHUITEMAN	D		(1)	
TININHO (BRA)	A	25	(3)	1
Jon Dahl TOMASSON (DEN)	A	33		13
Kees VAN WONDEREN	D	33		1
Henk VOS	A	3	(8)	3
Peter VAN VOSSEN	A	27	(3)	6
Edwin ZOETEBIER	G		(1)	

LEAGUE RESULTS 1998/99

21/08/98	Fortuna Sittard	A	2-1	Korneev, Vos
30/08/98	MVV	H	3-1	Vos, Korneev, Van Vossen
08/09/98	De Graafschap	H	5-0	Van Vossen, og (Rzasa),
				Paauwe, Van Gastel (p), Nelisse
11/09/98	SC Heerenveen	A	1-0	Tininho
22/09/98	PSV	A	2-1	Van Vossen, Cruz
26/09/98	Willem II	H	3-2	Cruz 2, Korneev (p)
04/10/98	FC Twente	A	1-1	og (Ten Hag)
17/10/98	Roda JC	H	0-0	
25/10/98	FC Utrecht	A	3-2	Van Gastel 2, Kalou
31/10/98	AZ	H	1-2	Van Gastel
11/11/98	MVV	A	3-1	Konterman, Cruz, Van Gastel
15/11/98	Fortuna Sittard	H	4-1	Bosvelt, Paauwe, Tomasson,
				Van Vossen (p)
21/11/98	SC Cambuur Leeuwarden	H	4-0	og (Dijkhuizen), Cruz 2,
				Van Vossen
29/11/98	Sparta	A	2-1	Tomasson, Cruz
06/12/98	NEC	H	1-0	og (Maes)
10/12/98	RKC Waalwijk	A	5-0	Paauwe, Cruz, Tomasson, Kalou,
				Bosvelt
13/12/98	Vitesse	A	1-1	Van Gastel
20/12/98	Ajax	H	1-1	Van Wonderen
21/02/99	PSV	H	3-1	Van Gastel (p), Cruz 2 (1p)
24/02/99	RKC Waalwijk	H	1-0	Korneev
28/02/99	SC Heerenveen	H	2-1	Tomasson 2
07/03/99	De Graafschap	A	4-3	Van Gastel 2 (1p), Korneev,
				Cairo
17/03/99	SC Cambuur Leeuwarden	A	5-1	Kalou, Tomasson, Cruz 2,
				Van Gobbel
21/03/99	Willem II	A	1-4	Van Gastel (p)
02/04/99	AZ	A	2-0	Cruz 2
05/04/99	Sparta	H	1-0	Tomasson
11/04/99	FC Utrecht	H	4-2	Tomasson 2, Bosvelt 2
18/04/99	NAC	A	1-0	Tomasson
25/04/99	NAC	H	2-2	Tomasson, Cruz
02/05/99	Ajax	A	0-6	
09/05/99	FC Twente	H	3-1	Paauwe, Cairo, Tomasson
12/05/99	Roda JC	A	0-1	
16/05/99	NEC	A	3-0	Van Vossen, Vos, Gyan
23/05/99	Vitesse	H	2-1	Paauwe, Tomasson

FORTUNA SITTARD

CLUB DIRECTORY

Fortuna Sittard
Postbus 36
6130 AA Sittard
tel - (046) 4203600
fax - (046) 4580032
Year of Formation - 1968
President - Juul Coenen
Secretary - Wil Dols
Executive Director - Jacques Opgenoord
Coach - Bert van Marwijk
Stadium - De Baandert (14,000)

APPEARANCES 98/99

	P	Ap	(s)	Gls
Alin BANCEU (ROM)	M		(1)	
Mark VAN BOMMEL	M	31		5
Wilfred BOUMA	A	33		5
Mark BURKE (ENG)	M	5	(4)	
Jürgen DIRKX	D	12		
François GESTHUIZEN	M	25	(1)	
Ronald HAMMING	A	28	(1)	14
Marco HEERING	A	6	(3)	1
Edwin HERMANS	D	31		
Kevin HOFLAND	D	22	(7)	1
Michael JEFFREY (ENG)	A	28		5
Roger JUFFING	G	3	(1)	
Wim KIEKENS (BEL)	D	3	(4)	
Ruud KOOL	M	30		2
Urvin LEE	D	28	(1)	
Jaromir PACIOREC (CZE)	M	4	(5)	
Robert ROEST	D	30		2
Regilio SIMONS	A	16	(13)	12
Georges TYCHON	A		(6)	
Freek DE WINTER	M		(2)	
Dorel ZEGREAN (ROM)	D	8	(9)	
Arno VAN ZWAM	G	31		

LEAGUE RESULTS 1998/99

21/08/98	Feyenoord	H	1-2	Hamming
29/08/98	Willem II	A	0-1	
09/09/98	Vitesse	H	0-2	
12/09/98	AZ	H	2-2	Bouma, Hamming
20/09/98	FC Utrecht	A	1-1	Hofland
23/09/98	Ajax	H	1-0	Roest (p)
26/09/98	MVV	H	0-1	
03/10/98	PSV	A	0-2	
17/10/98	Sparta	H	2-1	og (Van der Linden), Van Bommel
23/10/98	Roda JC	A	3-5	Hamming, Van Bommel 2 (2p)
30/10/98	FC Twente	H	0-3	
08/11/98	SC Heerenveen	A	0-2	
11/11/98	De Graafschap	H	0-0	
15/11/98	Feyenoord	A	1-4	Simons
21/11/98	NAC	A	1-1	Hamming
27/11/98	SC Cambuur Leeuwarden	A	1-3	Simons
03/12/98	RKC Waalwijk	H	3-2	Bouma 2, Hamming
11/12/98	MVV	A	3-3	Heering, Hamming, Kool
20/12/98	NEC	A	3-0	Roest (p), Simons, Hamming
06/02/99	NAC	H	2-0	Hamming, Jeffrey
17/02/99	RKC Waalwijk	A	0-0	
20/02/99	SC Cambuur Leeuwarden	H	2-0	Bouma, Van Bommel
06/03/99	Vitesse	A	2-1	Hamming, Simons
17/03/99	FC Utrecht	H	3-2	Kool, Jeffrey, Hamming
20/03/99	AZ	A	3-0	Hamming 3
02/04/99	SC Heerenveen	H	1-0	Jeffrey
07/04/99	Willem II	H	1-2	Hamming
10/04/99	De Graafschap	A	0-0	
18/04/99	Ajax	A	3-1	Simons 2, Van Bommel
25/04/99	Roda JC	H	0-1	
01/05/99	FC Twente	A	2-2	Simons, Jeffrey
07/05/99	PSV	H	6-4	Simons 4, Bouma, og (Ooijer)
16/05/99	Sparta	A	0-5	
21/05/99	NEC	H	2-3	Simons, Jeffrey

DE GRAAFSCHAP

CLUB DIRECTORY

De Graafschap
Postbus 249
7000 AE Doetinchem
tel - (0314) 324380
fax - (0314) 362892
Year of Formation - 1954
President - Hylke Enzerink
Secretary - Cor Huntelaar
Coach - Fritz Korbach; Hans van Doorneveld;
Jurrie Koolhof (99/00 - Frans Thijssen)
Stadium - De Vijverberg (10,900)

APPEARANCES 98/99

	P	Ap	(s)	Gls
Martijn BESSELINK	G	2	(1)	
René BOT	D	8	(1)	
Dennis TE BRAAK	D	11	(7)	
Hazem EMAM (EGY)	A	10	(3)	2
Purrel FRANKEL	D	11	(5)	
Robert FUCHS	M	10		3
Dennis GERRITSEN	A	21	(9)	6
Edwin GODEE	M	26	(5)	4
Hans VAN DER HAAR	M		(3)	
Dave DE JONG	D	14	(1)	
Marcel KEIZER	M	9		
Olaf LINDENBERGH	D	23	(2)	1
Martijn MEERDINK	M	1	(4)	
Michel NOK	M	21	(2)	1
Ron OLYSLAGER	G	32		
Erik REDEKER	D	11	(4)	1
Richard ROELOFSEN	A	14	(6)	3
Tomasz RZASA (POL)	M	28		2
Sonny SILOOY	D	29		
Zico TUMBA (CON)	A	12	(5)	2
Dennis DEN TURK	M	13		2
Rody TURPIJN	A		(3)	
Ville VÄISÄNEN (FIN)	A		(4)	1
Eric VISCAAL	A	26	(6)	10
Jan VREMAN	D	23	(3)	
Fabian WILNIS	D	19		

LEAGUE RESULTS 1998/99

22/08/98	MVV	A	2-1	Viscaal, Fuchs
05/09/98	RKC Waalwijk	H	2-2	Roelofsen, Fuchs
08/09/98	Feyenoord	A	0-5	
13/09/98	NEC	H	2-1	Roelofsen (p), Gerritsen
20/09/98	Ajax	A	1-1	Fuchs
23/09/98	Sparta	H	0-3	
26/09/98	SC Cambuur Leeuwarden	A	0-2	
04/10/98	Vitesse	H	0-0	
18/10/98	FC Utrecht	H	0-0	
24/10/98	FC Twente	A	1-2	Gerritsen
01/11/98	RKC Waalwijk	A	2-1	Väisänen, og (Van Zundert)
07/11/98	Willem II	H	2-2	Tumba, Gerritsen
11/11/98	Fortuna Sittard	A	0-0	
14/11/98	Roda JC	H	2-3	Viscaal, Tumba
21/11/98	SC Heerenveen	H	1-1	og (Mitrita)
28/11/98	PSV	A	2-2	Viscaal 2
06/12/98	FC Utrecht	A	1-2	Gerritsen
13/12/98	NAC	H	0-1	
19/12/98	AZ	H	1-1	Lindenbergh
05/02/99	NEC	A	1-1	Viscaal
21/02/99	FC Twente	H	0-2	
24/02/99	NAC	A	1-0	Godee
07/03/99	Feyenoord	H	3-4	Roelofsen, Redeker, Rzasa
13/03/99	Willem II	A	0-2	
20/03/99	SC Heerenveen	A	1-4	Emam
27/03/99	MVV	H	3-1	Viscaal 2, Godee
02/04/99	Sparta	A	3-2	Den Turk, Gerritsen, Rzasa
10/04/99	Fortuna Sittard	H	0-0	
17/04/99	AZ	A	3-1	Gerritsen, Emam, Viscaal
23/04/99	PSV	H	1-0	Den Turk
01/05/99	Roda JC	A	1-3	Viscaal
09/05/99	Ajax	H	1-3	Godee (p)
16/05/99	Vitesse	A	1-2	Viscaal
22/05/99	SC Cambuur Leeuwarden	H	2-2	Godee (p), Nok

SC HEERENVEEN

CLUB DIRECTORY

SC Heerenveen
Postbus 513
8440 AM Heerenveen
tel - (0513) 612100
fax - (0513) 615061
Year of Formation - 1920
President - Riemer van der Velde
Manager - Tjisse Wallendal
Coach - Foppe de Haan
Stadium - Abe Lenstra (13,870)

APPEARANCES 98/99

	P	Ap	(s)	Gls
Florin CONSTANTINOVICI (ROM)	D	1	(3)	
Romano DENNEBOOM	A	5	(6)	2
Emanuel EBIEDE (NIG)	M	3	(8)	
Ali EL KHATTABI (MAR)	A		(8)	1
Marc VAN EIJK	A	3	(3)	
Radu Mugur GUSATU (ROM)	A	5	(12)	1
Johan HANSMA	D	31		1
Thomas HOLM (NOR)	M	1	(1)	
Max HOUTTUIN	M	21	(3)	1
Daniel JENSEN (DEN)	M		(1)	
Tieme KLOMPE	D	29		
Mile KRSTEV (MAC)	M		(1)	
Dumitru MITRITA (ROM)	D	26		2
Dennis DE NOOIJER	A	17		3
Gerard DE NOOIJER	D	33	(1)	9
Godfrey NWANKPA (NIG)	D	5	(1)	
Henry ONWUZURUIKE (NIG)	A	1	(5)	
Boudewijn PAHLPLATZ	A	18	(12)	7
Ronnie PANDER	M	8	(5)	
Arek RADOMSKI (POL)	M	26		
Radoslav SAMARDZIC (YUG)	A	28	(1)	12
Jeffrey TALAN	A	28	(3)	8
Brian TEVREDEN	D	15	(5)	
Ivan TZVETKOV (BUL)	M	2	(9)	2
Jan DE VISSER	M	34		1
Hans VONK (SAF)	G	34		

LEAGUE RESULTS 1998/99

20/08/98	FC Twente	H	1-0	Talan
29/08/98	PSV	A	2-1	De Nooijer D., Samardzic
08/09/98	Willem II	H	2-2	Mitrita, Pahlplatz
11/09/98	Feyenoord	H	0-1	
20/09/98	RKC Waalwijk	A	4-0	De Nooijer D., Pahlplatz, Talan 2
23/09/98	FC Utrecht	H	1-0	og (Van Mol)
26/09/98	NEC	A	0-2	
04/10/98	NAC	H	2-1	Samardzic 2 (1p)
16/10/98	AZ	A	3-1	Pahlplatz, Houttuin, Talan
25/10/98	Sparta	A	1-3	De Nooijer D.
31/10/98	Vitesse	H	2-1	Samardzic, De Nooijer G.
08/11/98	Fortuna Sittard	H	2-0	Talan, Samardzic
11/11/98	FC Twente	A	2-1	og (Ten Hag), Pahlplatz
21/11/98	De Graafschap	A	1-1	Mitrita
24/11/98	SC Cambuur Leeuwarden	H	1-1	Samardzic
01/12/98	PSV	H	3-3	De Visser, Talan, Samardzic
13/12/98	Ajax	A	0-0	
18/12/98	MVV	H	1-1	El Khattabi
06/02/99	Willem II	A	2-3	De Nooijer G., Samardzic
17/02/99	Ajax	H	2-2	og (Oliseh), Pahlplatz
21/02/99	FC Utrecht	A	2-2	Gusatu, Pahlplatz
28/02/99	Feyenoord	A	1-2	Samardzic
06/03/99	NAC	A	2-2	De Nooijer G., Denneboom
13/03/99	RKC Waalwijk	H	2-0	De Nooijer G. 2
20/03/99	De Graafschap	H	4-1	Pahlplatz, Samardzic, Denneboom, De Nooijer G.
23/03/99	Roda JC	A	1-2	Talan
02/04/99	Fortuna Sittard	A	0-1	
10/04/99	NEC	H	3-2	De Nooijer G., Talan, Tzvetkov
16/04/99	Vitesse	A	2-1	Hansma, De Nooijer G.
24/04/99	AZ	H	2-1	Samardzic, Tzvetkov
01/05/99	SC Cambuur Leeuwarden	A	0-0	
08/05/99	Roda JC	H	2-2	De Nooijer G., Samardzic
16/05/99	MVV	A	0-1	
23/05/99	Sparta	H	0-0	

MVV

MVV
Postbus 4444
6202 ZV Maastricht
tel - (043) 3525757
fax - (043) 3525758
Year of Formation - 1902
President - Alfons Cremers
Secretary - Sietze Fennema
Manager - Ron Weijzen
Coach - Wim Koevermans
Stadium - De Geusselt (10,000)

APPEARANCES 98/99

	P	Ap	(s)	Gls
Alami AHANNACH (MAR)	D		(4)	
Roel BUIKEMA	M	3	(9)	
Rein VAN DUIJNHOVEN	G	33		
EMERSON (BRA)	A	24		9
Rodney FALIX	D	12	(8)	
Jeroen HEUBACH	D	28		1
Roel JANSSEN	D	13	(5)	1
Jerry DE JONG	D	32		5
Yvo JOORDENS	M	30		3
Husseyin KARAPINAR (BEL)	A	15	(4)	
Edik KORTCHAGIN (RUS)	A	10		2
Danny LANDZAAT	M	34		4
Kenneth PEREZ (DEN)	A	20	(2)	8
Rick PLUM	D	29		
Hans SPILLMANN	G	1		
Jerry TAIHUTTU	A	12	(3)	2
Wasiu TAIWO (NIG)	A	25	(9)	3
Jack VAESSEN	A	3	(1)	
Arjan VERMEULEN	D		(2)	
Joost VOLMER	D	32		1
Michel VONK	D	4	(4)	
Anton VRIESDE	M	14	(13)	3

LEAGUE RESULTS 1998/99

22/08/98	De Graafschap	H	1-2	Taiwo
30/08/98	Feyenoord	A	1-3	Landzaat
09/09/98	FC Utrecht	H	1-4	Joordens
12/09/98	PSV	A	0-2	
19/09/98	Vitesse	H	4-2	Joordens, De Jong (p), Landzaat, Emerson
23/09/98	FC Twente	A	1-2	Emerson
26/09/98	Fortuna Sittard	A	1-0	Emerson
03/10/98	SC Cambuur Leeuwarden	H	3-0	Landzaat, Taiwo, Taihuttu
17/10/98	NAC	A	0-2	
24/10/98	RKC Waalwijk	H	1-0	Emerson
31/10/98	Willem II	H	1-1	De Jong (p)
08/11/98	Sparta	A	0-0	
11/11/98	Feyenoord	H	1-3	Perez
14/11/98	AZ	H	2-1	Perez, Taihuttu
20/11/98	NEC	H	0-3	
27/11/98	Roda JC	A	1-2	Joordens
06/12/98	Ajax	A	1-1	Perez
11/12/98	Fortuna Sittard	H	3-3	Heubach, Perez, Landzaat
18/12/98	SC Heerenveen	A	1-1	Emerson
07/02/99	RKC Waalwijk	A	2-2	Emerson, Perez
20/02/99	Vitesse	A	1-2	Emerson
27/02/99	NEC	A	1-1	Vriesde
06/03/99	FC Twente	H	2-5	Vriesde, Kortchagin
16/03/99	Ajax	H	1-4	Perez
20/03/99	SC Cambuur Leeuwarden	A	0-1	
27/03/99	De Graafschap	A	1-3	Taiwo
01/04/99	Roda JC	H	0-0	
09/04/99	PSV	H	1-1	Vriesde
17/04/99	Sparta	H	1-1	Volmer
25/04/99	FC Utrecht	A	2-0	Emerson, De Jong
30/04/99	NAC	H	3-3	De Jong, Perez, Janssen
08/05/99	Willem II	A	1-4	De Jong (p)
16/05/99	SC Heerenveen	H	1-0	Emerson
23/05/99	AZ	A	2-4	Perez, Kortchagin

NAC

NAC
Postbus 3356
4800 DJ Breda
tel - (076) 5214500
fax - (076) 5211975
Year of Formation - 1912
Executive Director - Roelant Oltmans
Coach - Herbert Neumann; Ron Spelbos
(99/00 - Kees Zwamborn)
Stadium - FujiFilm (16,522)

MAJOR HONOURS
League Championship - (1) 1921.
Domestic Cup - (1) 1973.

		P	Ap	(s)	Gls
Archil ARVELADZE (GEO)	A	28	(2)		10
Jeffrey VAN AS	D	26	(2)		1
Maarten ATMODIKORO	D	25			
Peter BOSZ	M	23	(3)		1
Frank BROERS	D	2	(1)		
CHRISTIANO (BRA)	A		(1)		
Paulo DA COSTA TAVARES	A		(1)		
John FESKENS	M	20	(3)		
Remco FRIJTERS	M		(1)		
Jan GAASBEEK	M		(1)		
Nebojsa GUDELJ (YUG)	M	31	(2)		
Michael HANSEN (DEN)	M	9	(6)		
Glenn HELDER	A		(3)		1
John KARELSE	G	28			
Ahmed KASMI	D		(1)		
Erwin VAN DE LOOI	D	15	(3)		
Ante MILICIC (AUS)	A	19	(8)		5
Stanley MacDONALD	D	5	(6)		1
NOH JUNG-YOON (KOR)	M	15	(1)		1
Alfred SCHREUDER	D	31			1
Dmitriy SHOUKOV (RUS)	M	21			6
Earnest STEWART (USA)	A	26	(2)		7
Peter THOMSON (ENG)	A	2	(1)		
Rick VERSTEEG	D	22	(3)		
Wilco DE VOGT	G	6	(1)		
Robert VAN DER WEERT	A	1	(9)		2
ZEFILINO (BRA)	A	4	(14)		3
Clemens ZWIJNENBERG	D	15	(2)		

23/08/98	FC Utrecht	H	2-4	Zefilino, Stewart (p)
30/08/98	NEC	A	1-1	Milicic
09/09/98	FC Twente	H	1-1	Zefilino
12/09/98	Roda JC	A	1-3	MacDonald
20/09/98	Sparta	A	2-0	og (Marilia), Zefilino
23/09/98	AZ	H	1-1	Noh
27/09/98	Ajax	A	0-1	
04/10/98	SC Heerenveen	A	1-2	Milicic
17/10/98	MVV	H	2-0	Stewart, og (De Jong)
31/10/98	SC Cambuur Leeuwarden	A	1-3	Milicic
11/11/98	NEC	H	1-2	Arveladze
15/11/98	Willem II	A	1-2	Helder
21/11/98	Fortuna Sittard	H	1-1	Stewart (p)
06/12/98	PSV	H	3-4	Arveladze, Shoukov, Bosz
09/12/98	Vitesse	H	0-2	
13/12/98	De Graafschap	A	1-0	Schreuder
16/12/98	SC Cambuur Leeuwarden	H	2-3	Arveladze (p), Milicic
20/12/98	RKC Waalwijk	A	1-2	Van As
06/02/99	Fortuna Sittard	A	0-2	
17/02/99	Vitesse	A	1-3	Shoukov
24/02/99	De Graafschap	H	0-1	
27/02/99	PSV	A	0-2	
06/03/99	SC Heerenveen	H	2-2	Stewart 2
17/03/99	RKC Waalwijk	H	0-2	
21/03/99	FC Utrecht	A	0-2	
04/04/99	Willem II	H	2-2	Milicic, Arveladze
10/04/99	Roda JC	H	0-0	
13/04/99	AZ	A	0-3	
18/04/99	Feyenoord	H	0-1	
25/04/99	Feyenoord	A	2-2	Shoukov, Arveladze
30/04/99	MVV	A	3-3	Shoukov, Arveladze, Van der Weert
08/05/99	Sparta	H	5-0	Arveladze 3, Stewart, Van der Weert
16/05/99	FC Twente	A	2-2	Shoukov 2
23/05/99	Ajax	H	2-2	Arveladze, Stewart

NEC

CLUB DIRECTORY

NEC
Stadionplein 1
Postbus 6562
6303 GB Nijmegen
tel - (024) 3590360
fax - (024) 3567475
Year of Formation - 1900
President - Hans van Delft
Secretary - Eric Oomen
Coach - Jimmy Calderwood
Stadium - De Goffert (12,500)

APPEARANCES 98/99

	P	Ap	(s)	Gls
Krzysztof BOCIEK (POL)	A	1	(3)	
Ulrich CRUDEN	M	3	(7)	1
Juul ELLERMAN	A	10	(11)	3
Dennis GENTENAAR	G	7		
Jack DE GIER	A	30	(1)	15
Roy GROOTAERT	D	5	(4)	
Peter HENDRIKS	D		(2)	
Michael HENDRIKS	M	1		
Danny HESP	D	21	(5)	
Anton JANSSEN	M	28		3
Benito KEMBLE	D		(3)	
Marcel KONING	M	19		1
Bart LATUHERU	A	31	(2)	2
Jeffrey LEIWAKABESSY	D	1	(1)	
Luuk MAES	D	28		3
Pavel MIKHALEVICH (BLS)	M	6	(1)	
Mark OOSTERHOF	D	8	(1)	
Patrick POTHUIZEN	M	27		1
Oleg PUTILO (BLS)	A		(1)	
Peter VAN PUTTEN	M	5	(4)	
Maikel RENFURM	A	25		8
Hennie DE ROMIJN	D	26	(3)	1
Bas ROORDA	G	27		
Dzevdet SAINOVSKI (MAC)	M	6	(9)	1
Marchanno SCHULTZ	M	30		
Ayhan TUMANI (TUR)	A	5	(19)	3
Mark VERHOEVEN	D	24		

LEAGUE RESULTS 1998/99

22/08/98	RKC Waalwijk	A	1-0	Ellerman
30/08/98	NAC	H	1-1	Maes (p)
09/09/98	SC Cambuur Leeuwarden	A	2-2	Ellerman, Tumani
13/09/98	De Graafschap	A	1-2	De Gier
18/09/98	Roda JC	H	3-1	Renfurm 2, De Gier
26/09/98	SC Heerenveen	H	2-0	Renfurm, Cruden
04/10/98	FC Utrecht	A	3-2	Renfurm, Latuheru, De Gier
18/10/98	PSV	H	2-2	Renfurm 2
23/10/98	AZ	H	2-2	De Gier 2
01/11/98	Ajax	H	0-4	
08/11/98	Vitesse	A	0-1	
11/11/98	NAC	A	2-1	De Gier, Janssen
14/11/98	FC Twente	H	2-2	Maes (p), De Gier
20/11/98	MVV	A	3-0	Koning, Ellerman, Tumani
02/12/98	Sparta	H	3-1	Renfurm, De Gier 2
06/12/98	Feyenoord	A	0-1	
12/12/98	Willem II	A	0-1	
16/12/98	RKC Waalwijk	H	1-1	Pothuizen
20/12/98	Fortuna Sittard	H	0-3	
05/02/99	De Graafschap	H	1-1	De Gier
09/02/99	Roda JC	A	2-5	Janssen, Sainovski
17/02/99	Willem II	H	0-3	
27/02/99	MVV	H	1-1	Renfurm
07/03/99	Sparta	A	0-1	
19/03/99	FC Twente	A	0-2	
02/04/99	SC Cambuur Leeuwarden	H	1-0	Maes (p)
10/04/99	SC Heerenveen	A	2-3	De Gier, De Romijn
17/04/99	PSV	A	0-2	
21/04/99	Ajax	A	0-3	
25/04/99	Vitesse	H	3-1	Latuheru, De Gier 2
02/05/99	FC Utrecht	H	0-1	
08/05/99	AZ	A	1-1	Janssen
16/05/99	Feyenoord	H	0-3	
21/05/99	Fortuna Sittard	A	3-2	De Gier 2, Tumani

PSV

PSV
Frederiklaan 10 A
5616 NH Eindhoven
tel - (040) 2505502
fax - (040) 2505696
Year of Formation - 1913
President - Harry van Raay
Manager - Frank Arnesen
Coach - Bobby Robson (99/00 - Eric Gerets)
Stadium - Philips (30,024)

MAJOR HONOURS
League Championship - (14)
1929, 1935, 1951, 1963, 1975, 1976, 1978,
1986, 1987, 1988, 1989, 1991, 1992, 1997.
Domestic Cup - (7)
1950, 1974, 1976, 1988, 1989, 1990, 1996.
European Champions' Cup - (1) 1988.
UEFA Cup - (1) 1978.

		P	Ap	(s)	Gls
ABEL XAVIER (POR)	D	15	(4)	2
Arnold BRUGGINK	A	10	(14)	5
Gilles DE BILDE (BEL)	A	8	(12)	4
Jürgen DIRKX	D	21		
Björn VAN DER DOELEN	A	21	(3)	1
Ernest FABER	D	7	(1)	
Robert FUCHS	M	19	(1)	1
Giorgi GAKHOKIDZE (GEO)	M		(4)	1
Tomasz IWAN (POL)	M	18	(3)	3
JORGINHO (BRA)	D	2		
Dmitriy KHOKHLOV (RUS)	M	29	(4)	5
Joonas KOLKKA (FIN)	A	9	(10)	1
Patrick LODEWIJKS	G	1	(3)	
Theo LUCIUS	D	13	(12)	1
MARCOS (BRA)	D	4	(2)	
Wilbert NEED	G	1		
Yuriy NIKIFOROV (RUS)	D	24	(1)	1
Luc NILIS (BEL)	A	27		24
Ruud VAN NISTELROOY	A	34		31
André OOIJER	M	20	(1)	2
Davy OYEN (BEL)	D	18	(1)	
Dennis ROMMEDAHL (DEN)	A	10	(9)	2
Andrius SKERLA (LIT)	D	11	(6)	
Stan VALCKX	D	2		
Ronald WATERREUS	G	32		
Chris VAN DER WEERDEN	D	23		3

22/08/98	SC Cambuur Leeuwarden	A	1-1	Ooijer
29/08/98	SC Heerenveen	H	1-2	Van Nistelrooy
08/09/98	RKC Waalwijk	A	4-3	Khokhlov, De Bilde 2 (1p),
				Van Nistelrooy
12/09/98	MVV	H	2-0	De Bilde, Nikiforov
22/09/98	Feyenoord	H	1-2	Ooijer
27/09/98	AZ	A	1-4	Van Nistelrooy
03/10/98	Fortuna Sittard	H	2-0	Nilis, Van Nistelrooy
18/10/98	NEC	A	2-2	Van Nistelrooy, Nilis
25/10/98	Willem II	A	2-4	Nilis, Van Nistelrooy
31/10/98	Sparta	H	4-0	Van Nistelrooy 3, Nilis
08/11/98	FC Twente	A	2-2	Iwan, Van Nistelrooy
12/11/98	Vitesse	H	3-1	Nilis 2, Van Nistelrooy
15/11/98	Ajax	A	2-2	Iwan, Nilis
22/11/98	FC Utrecht	H	5-0	Abel Xavier, Van Nistelrooy 2 (1p),
				Fuchs, De Bilde
28/11/98	De Graafschap	H	2-2	Nilis 2
01/12/98	SC Heerenveen	A	3-3	Nilis, Khokhlov, Iwan
06/12/98	NAC	A	4-3	Khokhlov, Nilis, Van Nistelrooy,
				Bruggink
12/12/98	Roda JC	H	3-3	Van Nistelrooy 2, Nilis
19/12/98	Willem II	H	1-0	Bruggink
18/02/99	FC Twente	H	3-0	Khokhlov, Van Nistelrooy 2
21/02/99	Feyenoord	A	1-3	Van Nistelrooy
27/02/99	NAC	H	2-0	Van Nistelrooy (p),
				Van der Weerden (p)
05/03/99	Roda JC	A	3-1	Nilis 2, Bruggink
13/03/99	SC Cambuur Leeuwarden	H	3-0	Nilis 2, Van Nistelrooy
21/03/99	Sparta	A	5-0	Bruggink, Van Nistelrooy,
				Van der Doelen, Kolkka, Khokhlov
04/04/99	Ajax	H	3-1	Nilis 2, Van Nistelrooy
09/04/99	MVV	A	1-1	Van Nistelrooy
17/04/99	NEC	H	2-0	Van Nistelrooy (p), Nilis
20/04/99	Vitesse	A	3-3	Van Nistelrooy, Nilis 2
23/04/99	De Graafschap	A	0-1	
01/05/99	RKC Waalwijk	H	2-2	Rommedahl, Van Nistelrooy
07/05/99	Fortuna Sittard	A	4-6	Van Nistelrooy 2 (1p), Nilis, Lucius
16/05/99	AZ	H	7-1	Van der Weerden 2, Nilis 2,
				Abel Xavier, Van Nistelrooy,
				Rommedahl
23/05/99	FC Utrecht	A	3-2	Van Nistelrooy (p), Gakhokidze,
				Bruggink

RKC WAALWIJK

CLUB DIRECTORY

RKC Waalwijk
Postbus 4
5140 AA Waalwijk
tel - (0416) 334356
fax - (0416) 342310
Year of Formation - 1940
President - Jan Snoeren
Secretary - Jan Gerrits
Manager - Henk van Delft
Coach - Peter Boeve; Martin Jol
Stadium - Mandemakers (6,100)

APPEARANCES 98/99

	P	Ap	(s)	Gls
Romeo VAN AERDE	M	6	(4)	
Hans VAN ARUM	A	3	(25)	2
Richard BEEKINK	A	3	(9)	1
Adrie BOGERS	D	14	(1)	
Charles CHIEMEZIE (NIG)	A		(1)	
Tim CORNELISSE	D	20	(3)	1
Garry DE GRAEF (BEL)	M	28		5
Adilson DOS SANTOS	A	14	(6)	
Bas DREEF	D		(1)	
Augustus DUMBAR (NIG)	A		(1)	
Rob VAN DIJK	G	34		
Leeroy ECHTELD	A	25	(2)	3
Dejan GOVEDARICA (YUG)	M	18		3
Ron HEESAKKERS	A		(3)	1
Rick HOOGENDORP	A	20		9
Darije KALEZIC (BOS)	D	17		
Roberto LANCKOHR	M	28	(3)	6
Tom VAN DER LEEGTE	M	12	(2)	3
Ad LEEMANS	D	1		
Santinho LOPES	A		(1)	
David NASCIMENTO (POR)	D	19		
Leon VAN NIEUWKERK	A	8	(1)	
Dennis VAN DER PENNEN	M	11	(8)	1
Yuriy PETROV (RUS)	A	21	(11)	4
Maarten SCHOPS (BEL)	D	30		2
Virgilio TEIXEIRA (POR)	D	18	(1)	
Ruud VAN DER VELDEN	D	1		
Carlos VAN WANROOY	M	21		
Michel VAN ZUNDERT	D	2	(6)	

LEAGUE RESULTS 1998/99

22/08/98	NEC	H	0-1	
05/09/98	De Graafschap	A	2-2	De Graef, Van der Leegte
08/09/98	PSV	H	3-4	Petrov, De Graef, Beekink
13/09/98	FC Twente	A	0-1	
20/09/98	SC Heerenveen	H	0-4	
23/09/98	Vitesse	A	0-2	
26/09/98	Roda JC	A	0-0	
04/10/98	AZ	H	2-3	Lanckohr, Petrov
17/10/98	SC Cambuur Leeuwarden	A	1-1	Lanckohr
24/10/98	MVV	A	0-1	
01/11/98	De Graafschap	H	1-2	Echteld
06/11/98	FC Utrecht	H	2-5	De Graef, Lanckohr
11/11/98	Willem II	A	0-3	
15/11/98	Sparta	H	5-1	Van der Pennen, Schops 2,
				Petrov, Hoogendorp
22/11/98	Ajax	H	0-1	
03/12/98	Fortuna Sittard	A	2-3	De Graef, Hoogendorp
10/12/98	Feyenoord	H	0-5	
16/12/98	NEC	A	1-1	De Graef
20/12/98	NAC	H	2-1	Lanckohr, Van Arum
07/02/99	MVV	H	2-2	Hoogendorp 2 (1p)
17/02/99	Fortuna Sittard	H	0-0	
20/02/99	AZ	A	1-2	Echteld
24/02/99	Feyenoord	A	0-1	
07/03/99	Willem II	H	1-3	Hoogendorp (p)
13/03/99	SC Heerenveen	A	0-2	
17/03/99	NAC	A	2-0	Hoogendorp, Echteld
03/04/99	Vitesse	H	0-2	
09/04/99	Sparta	A	1-0	Van Arum
18/04/99	FC Utrecht	A	1-1	Hoogendorp
25/04/99	FC Twente	H	2-2	Van der Leegte 2
01/05/99	PSV	A	2-2	Hoogendorp 2
09/05/99	SC Cambuur Leeuwarden	H	4-1	Govedarica, Cornelisse, Lanckohr,
				Petrov
16/05/99	Ajax	A	0-2	
23/05/99	Roda JC	H	4-1	Govedarica 2, Lanckohr (p),
				Heesakkers

RODA JC

Roda JC
Postbus 1156
6460 BD Kerkrade
tel - (045) 5411053
fax - (045) 5426606
Year of Formation - 1962
President - Theo Pickée
Secretary - Jo Ploum
Coach - Sef Vergoossen
Stadium - Gemeentelijk Sportpark Kaalheide
(25,000)

MAJOR HONOURS
Domestic Cup - (1) 1997.

APPEARANCES 98/99

	P	Ap	(s)	Gls
Gregory DELWARTE (BEL)	G	1		
Arno DOOMERNIK	M	13	(10)	
Ramon VAN HAAREN	D	31		
Stephan 'T HART	D	2		
Zeljko KALAC (AUS)	G	33		
Garba LAWAL (NIG)	A	13	(10)	2
Eric VAN DER LUER	M	33		4
Mark LUIJPERS	D	34		3
Marc NYGAARD (DEN)	A	28	(2)	10
Bob PEETERS (BEL)	A	31	(2)	13
Melvin PLET	M		(1)	
Humphrey RUDGE	D	7	(6)	
Ger SENDEN	D	22		
Samuel Bernard TCHOUTANG (CMR)	A	19	(4)	1
Igor TOMASIC (CRO)	D	7	(7)	
Gábor TORMA (HUN)	A	3	(15)	2
Stéphan VAN DER HEYDEN (BEL)	M	23	(2)	1
Joos VALGAEREN (BEL)	M	1	(5)	1
Peter VAN HOUDT (BEL)	A	32		17
Regilio VREDE	D	31		3
Davy ZAFARIN	A	10	(12)	2

22/08/98	Vitesse	A	0-1	
28/08/98	Ajax	H	0-2	
06/09/98	Sparta	A	1-1	Peeters
12/09/98	NAC	H	3-1	Peeters, Van Houdt 2
18/09/98	NEC	A	1-3	Peeters
26/09/98	RKC Waalwijk	H	0-0	
03/10/98	Willem II	A	2-1	Van Houdt 2
17/10/98	Feyenoord	A	0-0	
23/10/98	Fortuna Sittard	H	5-3	Peeters, Nygaard, Vrede (p), Van Houdt 2
01/11/98	FC Utrecht	A	3-0	Van Houdt, Luijpers, Peeters
07/11/98	SC Cambuur Leeuwarden	H	1-0	Van Houdt
11/11/98	Ajax	A	1-2	Van Houdt
14/11/98	De Graafschap	A	3-2	Zafarin, Luijpers, Van Houdt
21/11/98	Vitesse	H	3-1	Nygaard 2, Vrede (p)
27/11/98	MVV	H	2-1	Nygaard, Van der Luer
02/12/98	AZ	A	0-1	
12/12/98	PSV	A	3-3	Peeters, Lawal, Nygaard
16/12/98	FC Twente	H	2-0	Van Houdt, Nygaard
09/02/99	NEC	H	5-2	Van der Heyden, Van Houdt 2, Luijpers, Nygaard
20/02/99	Sparta	H	1-0	Torma
27/02/99	AZ	H	8-2	Peeters 2, Tchoutang, Nygaard 2, Van Houdt, Van der Luer, Vrede (p)
05/03/99	PSV	H	1-3	Peeters
14/03/99	FC Twente	A	0-0	
18/03/99	Willem II	H	0-2	
23/03/99	SC Heerenveen	H	2-1	Van der Luer, Van Houdt
01/04/99	MVV	A	0-0	
06/04/99	SC Cambuur Leeuwarden	A	1-1	Torma
10/04/99	NAC	A	0-0	
25/04/99	Fortuna Sittard	A	1-0	Peeters
01/05/99	De Graafschap	H	3-1	Nygaard, Valgaeren, Zafarin
08/05/99	SC Heerenveen	A	2-2	Peeters, Van der Luer
12/05/99	Feyenoord	H	1-0	Lawal
16/05/99	FC Utrecht	H	3-0	Van Houdt 2, Peeters
23/05/99	RKC Waalwijk	A	1-4	Peeters

SPARTA

CLUB DIRECTORY

Sparta
Postbus 1802
3000 BV Rotterdam
tel - (010) 4151087
fax - (010) 4154960
Year of Formation - 1888
President - Jan Bossink
Secretary - Peter Haubrich
Manager - Charles van der Steene
Coach - Hans van der Zee; Dolf Roks; Jan Everse
Stadium - ENECO (11,000)

MAJOR HONOURS
League Championship - (6)
1909, 1911, 1912, 1913, 1915, 1959.
Domestic Cup - (3) 1958, 1962, 1966.

APPEARANCES 98/99

	P	Ap	(s)	Gls
Gert AANDEWIEL	M	2	(2)	
Mourad AMGHIZRAT (MAR)	M	4	(8)	
Nixon DIAS	M		(1)	
John DEN DUNNEN	A	21	(8)	4
Alex VAN DUIJVENBODE	D	5	(11)	
Ali EL KHATTABI (MAR)	A	15		4
Darren FERGUSON (SCO)	M	14		1
Jochem VAN DER HOEVEN	M	20		1
Kew JALIENS	D	32		
Nico JALINK	M	22	(1)	2
Roland JANSEN	G	34		
Yurtcan KAYIS (TUR)	M	17	(3)	
Dennis KRIJGSMAN	A	18	(10)	7
Arjan VAN DER LAAN	A	31	(1)	4
Antoine VAN DER LINDEN	D	13	(2)	
MARILIA (BRA)	D	27	(2)	1
Dave VAN DER MEER	D	23	(2)	
Anders NIELSEN (DEN)	M	8	(5)	
John NIEUWENBURG	M	30		2
Mark NOORLANDER	D	5	(2)	
Erik TAMMER	A	25	(6)	9
Romeo WOUDEN	A	8	(23)	2

LEAGUE RESULTS 1998/99

22/08/98	AZ	A	0-2	
30/08/98	FC Twente	A	0-1	
06/09/98	Roda JC	H	1-1	Tammer
12/09/98	Willem II	A	2-3	Tammer, Krijgsman
20/09/98	NAC	H	0-2	
23/09/98	De Graafschap	A	3-0	Nieuwenberg, Tammer, Van der Laan (p)
26/09/98	Vitesse	A	1-5	Tammer
04/10/98	Ajax	H	2-0	Tammer, Krijgsman
17/10/98	Fortuna Sittard	A	1-2	Krijgsman
25/10/98	SC Heerenveen	H	3-1	Den Dunnen 2, Van der Laan
31/10/98	PSV	A	0-4	
08/11/98	MVV	H	0-0	
15/11/98	RKC Waalwijk	A	1-5	Jalink (p)
22/11/98	AZ	H	0-0	
29/11/98	Feyenoord	H	1-2	Tammer
02/12/98	NEC	A	1-3	Jalink
06/12/98	SC Cambuur Leeuwarden	H	1-2	Van der Laan (p)
13/12/98	FC Twente	H	4-2	Marilia, Tammer, Den Dunnen, Krijgsman
20/12/98	FC Utrecht	A	1-4	Van der Hoeven
14/02/99	FC Utrecht	H	0-1	
20/02/99	Roda JC	A	0-1	
28/02/99	Ajax	A	1-5	Nieuwenberg
07/03/99	NEC	H	1-0	El Khattabi
14/03/99	Vitesse	H	1-3	Krijgsman
21/03/99	PSV	H	0-5	
02/04/99	De Graafschap	H	2-3	Tammer, El Khattabi
05/04/99	Feyenoord	A	0-1	
09/04/99	RKC Waalwijk	H	0-1	
17/04/99	MVV	A	1-1	Wouden
24/04/99	SC Cambuur Leeuwarden	A	4-2	Den Dunnen, Tammer, Wouden, Van der Laan
02/05/99	Willem II	H	0-4	
08/05/99	NAC	A	0-5	
16/05/99	Fortuna Sittard	H	5-0	Ferguson, El Khattabi 2, Krijgsman 2
23/05/99	SC Heerenveen	A	0-0	

FC TWENTE

CLUB DIRECTORY

FC Twente
Colosseum 65
7521 PP Enschede
tel - (053) 8525525
fax - (053) 8525555
Year of Formation - 1965
President - Herman Wessels
Executive Manager - Ben van Dijk
Technical Manager - Theo Vonk
Coach - Hans Meyer
Stadium - Arke (13,500)

MAJOR HONOURS
Domestic Cup - (1) 1977.

APPEARANCES 98/99

	P	Ap	(s)	Gls
Ansar AYUPOV (RUS)	D	3	(12)	2
Berthil TER AVEST	M	33	(1)	4
Sander BOSCHKER	G	34		
John BOSMAN	A	25	(5)	8
Theo TEN CAAT	M	3	(12)	
Chris DE WITTE (BEL)	A	9	(19)	5
Spiro GRUJIC (YUG)	D	12	(2)	
Erik TEN HAG	D	27	(2)	
Jan VAN HALST	M	29		
Nico-Jan HOOGMA	D	4		1
Dennis HULSHOFF	D	24	(6)	
André KARNEBEEK	D	30		
Niels OUDE KAMPHUIS	M	31		3
Rahim OUEDRAOGO (BFA)	D		(4)	
Cees PAAUWE	G		(1)	
Rik PLATVOET	A		(7)	
Jörg SOBIECH (GER)	D	25	(4)	
Rico STEINMANN (GER)	M	19	(2)	3
Antti SUMIALA (FIN)	A		(4)	
Aldo SWAGER	G		(1)	
Kurt VAN DE PAAR (BEL)	M	32	(1)	3
Jan VENNEGOOR OF HESSELINK	A	34		21
Pascal DE VRIES	M		(2)	

LEAGUE RESULTS 1998/99

20/08/98	SC Heerenveen	A	0-1	
30/08/98	Sparta	H	1-0	Bosman
09/09/98	NAC	A	1-1	Hoogma
13/09/98	RKC Waalwijk	H	1-0	Vennegoor of Hesselink
19/09/98	SC Cambuur Leeuwarden	A	2-0	Steinmann, Vennegoor of Hesselink
23/09/98	MVV	H	2-1	Oude Kamphuis,
				Vennegoor of Hesselink
27/09/98	FC Utrecht	A	3-0	Bosman, Van de Paar 2
04/10/98	Feyenoord	H	1-1	Vennegoor of Hesselink
18/10/98	Ajax	A	0-5	
24/10/98	De Graafschap	H	2-1	Steinmann, De Witte
30/10/98	Fortuna Sittard	A	3-0	Vennegoor of Hesselink 3
08/11/98	PSV	H	2-2	Ter Avest, Bosman
11/11/98	SC Heerenveen	H	1-2	Steinmann
14/11/98	NEC	A	2-2	Vennegoor of Hesselink, Ter Avest
21/11/98	Willem II	H	5-1	Bosman 2, Ter Avest,
				Oude Kamphuis,
				Vennegoor of Hesselink
06/12/98	AZ	A	1-1	Ter Avest
13/12/98	Sparta	A	2-4	Vennegoor of Hesselink, Ayupov
16/12/98	Roda JC	A	0-2	
19/12/98	Vitesse	H	0-0	
06/02/99	AZ	H	0-3	
14/02/99	Ajax	H	2-1	Ayupov, Vennegoor of Hesselink
18/02/99	PSV	A	0-3	
21/02/99	De Graafschap	A	2-0	Bosman, Vennegoor of Hesselink
06/03/99	MVV	A	5-2	De Witte, Vennegoor of Hesselink 3,
				Van de Paar
14/03/99	Roda JC	H	0-0	
19/03/99	NEC	H	2-0	Vennegoor of Hesselink, Bosman
05/04/99	FC Utrecht	H	1-1	Oude Kamphuis
10/04/99	Vitesse	A	1-1	Vennegoor of Hesselink
17/04/99	SC Cambuur Leeuwarden	H	0-0	
25/04/99	RKC Waalwijk	A	2-2	Vennegoor of Hesselink 2
01/05/99	Fortuna Sittard	H	2-2	De Witte, og (Kiekens)
09/05/99	Feyenoord	A	1-3	De Witte
16/05/99	NAC	H	2-2	De Witte, Vennegoor of Hesselink
23/05/99	Willem II	A	2-1	Vennegoor of Hesselink, Bosman (p)

FC UTRECHT

CLUB DIRECTORY

FC Utrecht
Herculesplein 331
3584 AA Utrecht
tel - (030) 2512521
fax - (030) 2540374
Year of Formation - 1970
President - Hans Herremans
Secretary - Albert van Santbrink
Technical Director - Hans van Breukelen
Coach - Mark Wotte
Stadium - Nieuw Galgewaard (14,000)

MAJOR HONOURS
Domestic Cup - (1) 1985.

APPEARANCES 98/99

		P	Ap	(s)	Gls
Mourad AMGHIZRAT (MAR)	A		8	(4)	1
Hendrik VAN BEELEN	M		1	(1)	
Ruud BERGER	A			(2)	
Pascal BOSSCHAART	M		14	(14)	
Costas COSTA	D		7	(2)	
Emiel VAN EIJKEREN	A		18	(13)	3
Mitchell VAN DER GAAG	D		16		2
Alfons GROENENDIJK	M		16		2
Stefan HAAKSMAN	A			(1)	
Jean-Paul DE JONG	D		30		
John DE JONG	A		33		8
Leon KANTELBERG	M			(1)	
Frank KOOIMAN	G		33		
Dirk KUIJT	A		7	(21)	5
Didier MARTEL (FRA)	A		6	(7)	2
Tom VAN MOL (BEL)	D		31		
Michael MOLS	A		31		20
David NASCIMENTO (POR)	D		7	(2)	
Emmanuel NWAKIRE (NIG)	D		6	(1)	
John O'BRIEN (USA)	D		18	(1)	2
Stefan POSTMA	G		1		
Dennis VAN DER REE	D		7	(7)	
Reinier ROBBEMOND	M		31		6
Dennis SCHARRENBURG	M		5	(6)	
Henny VAN SCHOONHOVEN	D		10	(7)	1
Bernard SCHUITEMAN	D		12	(3)	
Etienne SHEW A TJON	D		14	(3)	1
Jordy ZUIDAM	M		3		
Patrick ZWAANSWIJK	D		9	(2)	1

LEAGUE RESULTS 1998/99

23/08/98	NAC	A	4-2	Mols, Robbemond, Groenendijk, De Jong J.
30/08/98	SC Cambuur Leeuwarden	H	3-0	Mols, Robbemond, O'Brien
09/09/98	MVV	A	4-1	De Jong J. 2, Shew A Tjon, Mols
13/09/98	Ajax	H	2-2	O'Brien, Mols
20/09/98	Fortuna Sittard	H	1-1	Kuijt
23/09/98	SC Heerenveen	A	0-1	
27/09/98	FC Twente	H	0-3	
04/10/98	NEC	H	2-3	Van Schoonhoven, Kuijt
18/10/98	De Graafschap	A	0-0	
25/10/98	Feyenoord	H	2-3	Van der Gaag, De Jong J.
01/11/98	Roda JC	H	0-3	
06/11/98	RKC Waalwijk	A	5-2	Mols 3, De Jong J., Robbemond (p)
15/11/98	Vitesse	A	0-2	
22/11/98	PSV	A	0-5	
29/11/98	Willem II	H	2-0	Van der Gaag, Kuijt
02/12/98	SC Cambuur Leeuwarden	A	1-1	Mols
06/12/98	De Graafschap	H	2-1	De Jong J., Mols
13/12/98	AZ	A	3-4	De Jong J., Mols, Groenendijk
20/12/98	Sparta	H	4-1	Robbemond 2, Kuijt, Martel
14/02/99	Sparta	A	1-0	Van Eijkeren
21/02/99	SC Heerenveen	H	2-2	Martel, Van Eijkeren
27/02/99	Willem II	A	0-1	
07/03/99	Ajax	A	2-5	Mols 2
14/03/99	AZ	H	2-2	Mols, Van Eijkeren
17/03/99	Fortuna Sittard	A	2-3	Robbemond (p), Mols
21/03/99	NAC	H	2-0	Zwaanswijk, Kuijt
05/04/99	FC Twente	A	1-1	Amghizrat
11/04/99	Feyenoord	A	2-4	Mols 2
18/04/99	RKC Waalwijk	H	1-1	Mols
25/04/99	MVV	H	0-2	
02/05/99	NEC	A	1-0	Mols
09/05/99	Vitesse	H	1-2	Mols
16/05/99	Roda JC	A	0-3	
23/05/99	PSV	H	2-3	Mols, De Jong J.

VITESSE

Vitesse
Postbus 366
6800 AJ Arnhem
tel - (026) 8807321
fax - (026) 8807009
Year of Formation - 1892
President - Karel Aalbers
Technical Director - Rein Papenburg
Coach - Artur Jorge; Herbert Neumann
Stadium - Gelredome (26,600)

APPEARANCES 98/99

	P	Ap	(s)	Gls
Matthew AMOAH (BFA)	A	1	(16)	2
Patrick AX	A		(1)	
Scott BOOTH (SCO)	A	14	(4)	4
John VAN DEN BROM	M	19	(7)	1
Darko BUTOROVIC (CRO)	D	3	(2)	
Dejan CUROVIC (YUG)	A	6	(5)	5
Carlos FORTES	A	7	(4)	
Steve GOOSSEN	D	22	(1)	
Kostas HANIOTAKIS (GRE)	G	1	(1)	
Marc VAN HINTUM	D	29		2
Jochem VAN DER HOEVEN	D	2	(1)	
Theo JANSSEN	M	3	(2)	
Arco JOCHEMSEN	M	31	(2)	5
Willem KORSTEN	M		(5)	
Michel KREEK	M	24		4
Martijn KUIPER	D	13	(7)	
Louis LAROS	A	30	(2)	1
Nikos MAHLAS (GRE)	A	31		18
Marco DE MARCHI (ITA)	D	7	(2)	
Rahamat MUSTAPHA	A		(1)	
Marko PEROVIC (YUG)	M	10	(2)	5
Martijn REUSER	A	28	(4)	8
Remco VAN DER SCHAAF	D	14	(8)	
Dmitriy SHOUKOV (RUS)	M	4	(1)	
Orlando TRUSTFULL	M	5		1
John VELDMAN	D	16	(1)	
Sander WESTERVELD	G	33		
Menno WILLEMS	D	1		
Marian ZEMAN (SVK)	D	9	(4)	
Mamadou ZONGO (BFA)	A	11	(5)	5

LEAGUE RESULTS 1998/99

22/08/98	Roda JC	H	1-0	Mahlas
29/08/98	AZ	A	0-0	
09/09/98	Fortuna Sittard	A	2-0	Mahlas 2
12/09/98	SC Cambuur Leeuwarden	H	4-2	Perovic 3, Mahlas
19/09/98	MVV	A	2-4	Trustfull, Reuser
23/09/98	RKC Waalwijk	H	2-0	Perovic, Curovic (p)
26/09/98	Sparta	H	5-1	Mahlas 2, Curovic, Van Hintum, Reuser
04/10/98	De Graafschap	A	0-0	
17/10/98	Willem II	H	3-2	Mahlas 3
31/10/98	SC Heerenveen	A	1-2	Kreek
08/11/98	NEC	H	1-0	Mahlas (p)
12/11/98	PSV	A	1-3	Jochemsen
15/11/98	FC Utrecht	H	2-0	Perovic, Reuser
21/11/98	Roda JC	A	1-3	Booth
29/11/98	Ajax	H	3-2	Mahlas, Jochemsen, Booth
04/12/98	Willem II	A	5-3	Mahlas, Zongo 2, Reuser, Laros
09/12/98	NAC	A	2-0	Zongo 2
13/12/98	Feyenoord	H	1-1	Amoah
19/12/98	FC Twente	A	0-0	
17/02/99	NAC	H	3-1	Mahlas, Van Hintum, Amoah
20/02/99	MVV	H	2-1	Mahlas (p), Booth
26/02/99	SC Cambuur Leeuwarden	A	2-2	Reuser, Curovic
06/03/99	Fortuna Sittard	H	1-2	Curovic
14/03/99	Sparta	A	3-1	Curovic, Jochemsen, Mahlas
21/03/99	Ajax	A	1-0	Mahlas
03/04/99	RKC Waalwijk	A	2-0	Kreek 2
10/04/99	FC Twente	H	1-1	Jochemsen
16/04/99	SC Heerenveen	H	1-2	Zongo
20/04/99	PSV	H	3-3	Kreek, Reuser 2
25/04/99	NEC	A	1-3	Van den Brom
01/05/99	AZ	H	0-1	
09/05/99	FC Utrecht	A	2-1	Jochemsen, Booth
16/05/99	De Graafschap	H	2-1	Mahlas 2
23/05/99	Feyenoord	A	1-2	Reuser

WILLEM II

CLUB DIRECTORY

Willem II
Postbus 235
5000 AE Tilburg
tel - (013) 5490590
fax - (013) 5490500
Year of Formation - 1896
President - Jan Vullings
Secretary - Mark Willems
Director of Football - Martin van Geel
Coach - Co Adriaanse
Stadium - Willem II (14,700)

MAJOR HONOURS
League Championship - (3) 1916, 1952, 1955.
Domestic Cup - (2) 1944, 1963.

APPEARANCES 98/99

		P	Ap	(s)	Gls
Yassine ABDELLAOUI (MAR)	A	21	(7)		4
Arno ARTS	M	34			5
Mariano BOMBARDA (ARG)	A	24	(3)		17
Jatto CEESAY (GAM)	A	20	(12)		6
Jim VAN FESSEM	G	34			
Tomas GALASEK (CZE)	M	32			5
Marco HEERING	A	11			2
Reinder HENDRIKS	D	8	(8)		
Erwin HERMES	A	8	(3)		1
Delano HILL	D	29	(1)		
Sami HYYPIÄ (FIN)	D	26			2
Jukka KOSKINEN (FIN)	D	3	(2)		
Frank VAN KOUWEN	D		(1)		
Huub LOEFFEN	M	3	(6)		1
Joris MATHIJSEN	D		(1)		
Jos VAN NIEUWSTADT	D		(1)		
Marino PROMES	A		(3)		
Geoffrey PROMMAYON (THA)	D	32			
Adil RAMZI (MAR)	A	29			11
Ousmane SANOU (BFA)	A	1	(9)		1
Mark SCHENNING	D	16	(8)		1
Dennis SCHULP	A	5	(15)		7
István SZEKÉR (HUN)	M	1			
Marcel VALK	M	22	(8)		3
Raymond VICTORIA	D	15			1

LEAGUE RESULTS 1998/99

23/08/98	Ajax	A	0-2	
29/08/98	Fortuna Sittard	H	1-0	Hyypiä
08/09/98	SC Heerenveen	A	2-2	Galasek, Bombarda
12/09/98	Sparta	H	3-2	Arts, Schulp, Ramzi
19/09/98	AZ	A	1-1	Abdellaoui
23/09/98	SC Cambuur Leeuwarden	H	2-1	Ramzi, Heering
26/09/98	Feyenoord	A	2-3	Ramzi, Loeffen
03/10/98	Roda JC	H	1-2	Heering
17/10/98	Vitesse	A	2-3	Schenning, Arts (p)
25/10/98	PSV	H	4-2	Valk, Ramzi 2, Ceesay
31/10/98	MVV	A	1-1	Abdellaoui
07/11/98	De Graafschap	A	2-2	Bombarda, Arts (p)
11/11/98	RKC Waalwijk	H	3-0	Bombarda 3
15/11/98	NAC	H	2-1	Bombarda, Schulp
21/11/98	FC Twente	A	1-5	Bombarda
29/11/98	FC Utrecht	A	0-2	
04/12/98	Vitesse	H	3-5	Bombarda, Galasek, Sanou
12/12/98	NEC	H	1-0	Ramzi
19/12/98	PSV	A	0-1	
06/02/99	SC Heerenveen	H	3-2	Ceesay, Galasek, Valk
17/02/99	NEC	A	3-0	Bombarda, og (Oosterhof), Ramzi
27/02/99	FC Utrecht	H	1-0	Bombarda
07/03/99	RKC Waalwijk	A	3-1	Bombarda, Victoria, Ramzi
13/03/99	De Graafschap	H	2-0	Ramzi, Schulp
18/03/99	Roda JC	A	2-0	Arts, Bombarda
21/03/99	Feyenoord	H	4-1	Arts (p), Hyypiä, Ceesay, Abdellaoui
04/04/99	NAC	A	2-2	Ceesay, Bombarda
07/04/99	Fortuna Sittard	A	2-1	Galasek, Abdellaoui
10/04/99	AZ	H	2-0	Bombarda, Schulp
25/04/99	Ajax	H	3-1	Bombarda, Schulp 2
02/05/99	Sparta	A	4-0	Bombarda, Ramzi, Ceesay, Schulp
08/05/99	MVV	H	4-1	Bombarda, og (Plum), Valk, Ramzi
16/05/99	SC Cambuur Leeuwarden	A	2-0	Gaalsek, Hermes
23/05/99	FC Twente	H	1-2	Ceesay

PROMOTED CLUB

SECOND DIVISION FINAL TABLE 98/99

		Pd	W	D	L	F	A	Pt	GD
1	**FC Den Bosch (*3)**	**34**	**23**	**8**	**3**	**80**	**35**	**77**	**+45**
2	FC Groningen	34	19	7	8	69	33	64	+36
3	Emmen (*2)	34	19	4	11	53	37	61	+16
4	Helmond Sport	34	16	7	11	55	52	55	+3
5	FC Zwolle	34	15	9	10	57	42	54	+15
6	Excelsior (*1)	34	16	6	12	74	63	54	+11
7	Go Ahead Eagles	34	14	8	12	59	57	50	+2
8	FC Volendam	34	14	7	13	63	66	49	-3
9	Eindhoven	34	14	6	14	64	73	48	-9
10	ADO Den Haag	34	12	9	13	52	52	45	0
11	VVV	34	12	6	16	59	66	42	-7
12	RBC	34	11	7	16	54	65	40	-11
13	SC Veendam	34	11	6	17	47	54	39	-7
14	Dordrecht '90 (*4)	34	11	5	18	51	66	38	-15
15	Haarlem	34	9	11	14	45	67	38	-22
16	TOP Oss	34	9	10	15	43	50	37	-7
17	SC Heracles	34	9	7	18	37	58	34	-21
18	SC Telstar	34	5	11	18	45	71	26	-26

N.B. (*) = period champion; period = eight matches.

PROMOTION/RELEGATION PLAY-OFFS

GROUP A FINAL TABLE

		Pd	W	D	L	F	A	Pt	GD
1	RKC	6	5	1	0	11	3	16	+8
2	FC Zwolle	6	2	2	2	8	10	8	-2
3	Dordrecht '90	6	2	1	3	12	13	7	-1
4	Emmen	6	1	0	5	10	15	3	-5

GROUP B FINAL TABLE

		Pd	W	D	L	F	A	Pt	GD
1	Sparta	6	5	0	1	19	6	15	+13
2	FC Groningen	6	4	1	1	16	8	13	+8
3	Excelsior	6	2	1	3	16	18	7	-2
4	Helmond Sport	6	0	0	6	5	24	0	-19

CLUB DIRECTORY

FC Den Bosch
Victorialaan 21
5213 JG's Hertogenbosch
tel - (073) 6464700
fax - (073) 6464709
Year of Formation - 1964
President - Jan Schouten
Secretary - Jos van de Wouw
Coach - Kees Zwamborn; Martin Koopman
Stadium - ECCO (4,500)

HUNGARY

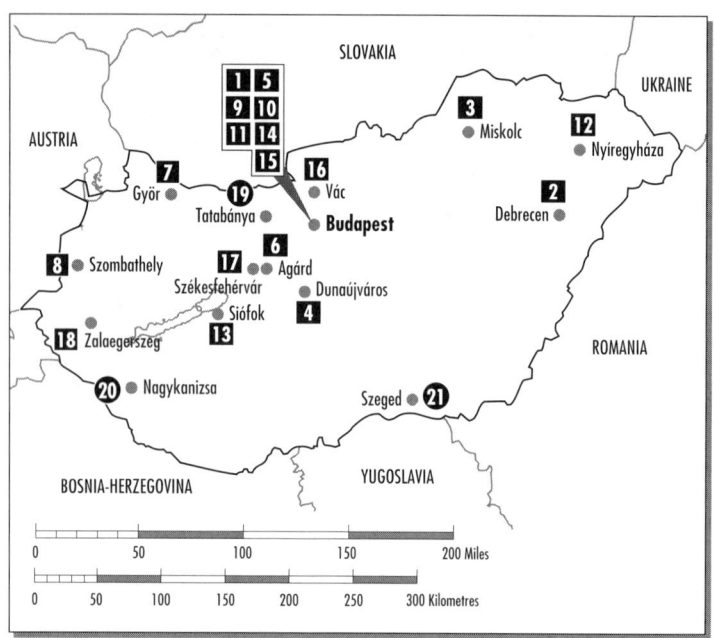

MTK COME OF AGE WITH TITLE NO. 21

Cash crisis envelops Hungarian game

FEDERATION DIRECTORY

Magyar Labdarúgó Szövetség
Népstadion Toronyépület, Istvánmezei út 1-3, 1146 Budapest

tel - (1) 2220343   Year of Formation - 1901
fax - (1) 2220324   President - Attila Kovács
                                   Secretary - Sándor Berzi

Stadium - Népstadion, Budapest (60,000)

1998/99 was yet another season of disappointment and underachievement for Hungarian football, both on and off the field. Financial problems spread through the game like a disease without a cure. Virtually all of the clubs were operating in debt, and many players had to make do with reduced salaries or, in some cases, no money at all.

The one club which stood apart from the rest like a beacon of prosperity was MTK-Hungária FC. Thanks predominantly to the funding of the club's rich owner, Gábor Várszegi, MTK were able to live a fairly comfortable existence, and they certainly let that show on the field of play, dominating the championship to such an extent that they were able to wrap up the 21st Hungarian title in their history with five matches still to play.

There was considerable dismay when MTK were eliminated from the first round of the European Cupwinners' Cup by Austrian provincials SV Ried, especially as they lost both matches without scoring a goal. But at home MTK reigned supreme. They made an almost perfect start, winning seven of their first eight games and drawing the other away to Budapest rivals Ferencváros. By the winter break they had a commanding six-point lead, and when they won each of their first eight matches after the resumption, it was simply a matter of when their triumph would be completed. That came on Saturday, May 8 with a 2-0 win at home to Gázszer FC - a result which gave them an insurmountable 16-point lead.

Despite their utter dominance, MTK did not always

LEAGUE CHAMPIONSHIP RESULTS 98/99

		1	2	3	4	5	6	7	8	9	10	11	12	13	14	15	16	17	18
1	BVSC-Zugló		0-1	1-3	3-2	0-1	1-2	2-1	0-3	3-0	3-0	0-2	0-0	0-1	0-3	1-2	2-1	0-1	1-1
2	DVSC-Epona	3-1		5-0	1-2	6-1	4-0	1-2	1-1	0-0	0-2	3-1	2-0	1-0	0-2	0-0	2-1	5-0	2-0
3	Diósgyöri FC	2-1	0-0		1-1	1-3	2-0	1-1	5-1	5-1	0-0	1-1	1-0	1-1	1-1	4-2	0-1	1-0	1-1
4	Dunaferr SE	1-1	2-0	2-3		2-1	2-1	0-0	2-0	3-0	2-1	0-3	6-1	2-1	2-0	2-1	1-1	3-1	2-0
5	Ferencváros	1-0	2-0	3-4	1-3		2-0	1-1	1-0	7-1	0-1	2-2	2-1	2-0	1-0	3-1	2-2	2-0	4-0
6	Gázszer FC	0-0	2-1	2-0	3-0	1-1		0-2	4-0	3-2	0-0	1-3	0-0	1-3	2-1	1-1	1-0	0-0	2-0
7	Györi ETO FC	1-1	3-1	5-4	2-1	1-2	0-0		2-0	3-0	2-2	1-0	0-1	1-1	3-1	3-3	1-0	3-0	1-0
8	Haladás-Milos	3-1	1-1	2-1	0-1	1-2	1-1	0-1		5-1	0-2	2-1	3-2	2-1	4-1	0-0	0 1	2 0	0-0
9	III. Kerület FC	0-0	1-5	1-2	3-1	1-2	2-1	3-3	3-1		1-1	1-5	2-2	2-3	2-3	1-4	2-3	1-2	0-2
10	Kispest-Honvéd FC	1-5	0-0	3-0	0-0	2-2	1-3	4-0	1-0	2-0		0-2	4-3	3-0	2-3	0-4	2-1	0-0	0-1
11	MTK Hungária FC	3-2	1-2	4-0	3-0	2-0	2-0	4-1	2-4	5-0	3-0		2-0	1-0	2-0	2-0	3-1	2-1	2-1
12	Nyírség-Spartacus	1-0	4-2	3-1	3-1	0-1	0-0	0-0	2-1	3-3	3-0	1-3		3-1	0-2	0-2	3-4	4-2	2-0
13	Siófok	0-1	0-1	2-1	0-1	0-2	2-2	1-2	1-0	2-1	1-1	0-1	1-1		0-2	2-3	2-4	0-0	0-2
14	Újpest FC	3-1	3-2	1-3	3-0	2-1	2-1	1-2	2-0	4-1	3-0	1-2	1-0	2-1		2-0	2-0	1-0	2-2
15	Vasas DH	3-2	2-0	0-0	3-2	2-1	2-0	1-4	5-0	0-3	2-1	0-4	1-1	0-0	1-0		0-0	2-1	1-0
16	Vác FC-Zollner	1-0	1-1	1-3	1-0	1-1	1-1	1-0	3-1	1-0	4-1	1-2	2-2	0-2	4-3	1-1		2-1	2-2
17	Videoton FC Fehérvár	4-1	1-0	2-3	4-4	1-3	0-2	0-0	0-0	5-0	0-1	0-1	1-0	1-1	0-0	2-2	3-2		1-2
18	Zalahús ZTE FC	2-0	3-0	2-1	0-1	1-1	2-0	2-1	3-1	2-1	2-0	0-1	1-0	2-2	0-1	1-0	2-2	4-2	

LEAGUE CHAMPIONSHIP FINAL TABLE 98/99

			Home				Away					Total						
		P	W	D	L	F	A	W	D	L	F	A	W	D	L	F	A	P	GD
1	MTK Hungária FC	34	15	0	2	43	12	12	2	3	34	14	27	2	5	77	26	83	+51
2	Ferencváros	34	11	3	3	36	16	8	4	5	25	24	19	7	8	61	40	64	+21
3	Újpest FC	34	13	1	3	35	16	7	2	8	23	24	20	3	11	58	40	63	+18
4	Györi ETO FC	34	10	5	2	32	17	6	6	5	21	22	16	11	7	53	39	59	+14
5	Vasas DH	34	10	4	3	25	19	5	6	6	26	25	15	10	9	51	44	55	+7
6	Zalahús ZTE FC	34	11	3	3	29	14	4	5	8	14	23	15	8	11	43	37	53	+6
7	Diósgyöri FC	34	7	8	2	27	15	7	1	9	29	39	14	9	11	56	54	51	+2
8	DVSC-Epona	34	10	3	4	36	13	4	4	9	17	26	14	7	13	53	39	49	+14
9	Vác FC-Zollner	34	8	6	3	27	21	5	4	8	24	28	13	10	11	51	49	49	+2
10	Gázszer FC	34	8	6	3	23	14	3	5	9	14	26	11	11	12	37	40	44	-3
11	Dunaferr SE	34	12	3	2	34	15	5	3	9	20	31	17	6	11	54	46	42	+8
12	Kispest-Honvéd FC	34	7	4	6	25	24	4	5	8	13	26	11	9	14	38	50	42	-12
13	Nyírség Spartacus	34	9	3	5	32	23	1	6	10	14	29	10	9	15	46	52	39	-6
14	Haladás-Milos	34	8	4	5	26	17	2	2	13	13	37	10	6	18	39	54	36	-15
15	Siófok	34	3	6	10	14	25	4	5	8	18	24	7	9	18	32	49	30	-17
16	Videoton FC Fehérvár	34	5	6	6	25	22	2	3	12	11	32	7	9	18	36	54	30	-18
17	BVSC-Zugló	34	5	2	10	17	24	2	4	11	17	29	7	6	21	34	53	26	-19
18	III. Kerület FC	34	3	6	10	26	40	1	2	14	14	53	4	6	24	40	93	18	-53

N.B. Dunaferr SE deducted 15pts; BVSC-Zugló deducted 1pt.

receive a favourable press. Indeed, sometimes the reaction to their style of play was downright hostile, with several articles criticising the team's functional, no-risk methods which made for a less than appealing spectacle. Várszegi evidently caught the drift himself, because at the end of the season he decided to terminate the contract of the club's successful coach, Sándor Egervári, substituting him for the new season with Dutchman Henk ten Cate - a former right-hand man of Louis van Gaal at Ajax.

Certainly, no other Hungarian club could have afforded the wages of a foreign coach, least of all Újpest FC, whose financial crisis was perhaps the most critical of the lot. The Lilacs, champions only a year earlier, ended the season in such a mess that there was even talk of a possible

TOP SCORERS

22	Béla ILLÉS (MTK Hungária FC)
18	Nicolae ILEA (DVSC-Epona)
17	Gábor EGRESSY (Diósgyöri FC)
13	Attila KORSÓS (Újpest FC)
12	Ferenc LENGYEL (Dunaferr SE)
	Gábor ZAVADSZKY (Dunaferr SE)
	Imre SZABICS (Ferencváros)
	István BORGULYA (Kispest-Honvéd FC)
	Krisztián KENESEI (MTK Hungária FC)
	Zoltán PÁL (Vasas DH)
	Róbert WALTNER (Videoton FC Fehérvár)

NATIONAL TEAM RESULTS 98/99

19/08/98	Slovenia	H	Zalaegerszeg	2-1	Dombi (69), Sebök V. (85p)
06/09/98	Portugal (ECQ)	H	Budapest	1-3	Horváth (32)
10/10/98	Azerbaijan (ECQ)	A	Baku	4-0	Dárdai (58), Illés (84p), Pisont (88), Fehér M. (90)
14/10/98	Romania (ECQ)	H	Budapest	1-1	Hrutka (83)
18/11/98	Switzerland	H	Budapest	2-0	Korsós G. (1), Sebök J. (7)
10/03/99	Bosnia-Herzegovina	H	Budapest	1-1	Illés (65p)
27/03/99	Liechtenstein (ECQ)	H	Budapest	5-0	Sebök J. (17), Sebök V. (33, 41, 86p), Illés (74)
31/03/99	Slovakia (ECQ)	A	Bratislava	0-0	
28/04/99	England	H	Budapest	1-1	Hrutka (77)
05/06/99	Romania (ECQ)	A	Bucharest	0-2	
09/06/99	Slovakia (ECQ)	H	Györ	0-1	

merger with old enemy MTK. The attraction for MTK supremo Várszegi was that he would buy into a club which was more popular than his own and thereby create a Budapest 'super club'. However, the idea was swiftly nipped in the bud when MTK's fans staged a vehement protest. They claimed that co-existence with the allegedly anti-semitic supporters of Újpest was impossible given the strong Jewish element among their own following.

In view of their pecuniary plight, Újpest achieved something of a minor miracle to finish in third place and thus book themselves a place in the UEFA Cup. Their European efforts in 1998/99 had been predictably woeful, with heavy defeats by Sturm Graz in the Champions' Cup and Club Bruges in the UEFA Cup cutting short their participation in two competitions. The valiant efforts of coach Péter Várhidi and his players in the league did give the Újpest fans some encouragement, but that was wiped out at the end of the campaign when the club was forced to sell seven of their international players.

Money problems did not escape Hungary's most popular club, Ferencváros, either. They too were obliged to let many of their leading players go in the summer,

NATIONAL TEAM APPEARANCES 98/99

Coach - Bertalan BICSKEI	SLO	POR	AZB	ROM	SUI	BOS	LIE	SVK	ENG	ROM	SVK	Cps	Gls
Gábor KIRÁLY (01/04/76) - Hertha BSC Berlin (GER)	G	G	G	G	G	G	G	G	G	G	G	12	-
Vilmos SEBÖK (13/06/73) - Újpest FC/Bristol City (ENG)	D		D65	D	D	D	D	D	D	D	D	26	5
Csaba FEHÉR (02/09/75) - Újpest FC	D	D78	D	D								7	-
János HRUTKA (26/10/74) - 1.FC Kaiserslautern (GER)	D89	D	D	D	D	D	D78	D	D	D	D	15	3
János MÁTYUS (20/12/74) - Ferencváros	D	D	D	D	D		D	D	D	D	D	14	-
Krisztián LISZTES (02/06/76) - VfB Stuttgart (GER)	M46	M46	M75	s78								11	-
Gábor HALMAI (07/01/72) - MTK Hungária FC	M86	M				M	M	M	M	M73		44	4
Béla ILLÉS (27/04/68) - MTK Hungária FC	M46	M	M	M		M	M	M	M	M83	M	50	12
József SEBÖK (18/06/75) - Zalahús ZTE FC	A60			A76		A71	A55		A76		A	8	2
Ferenc HORVÁTH (06/05/73) - KRC Genk (BEL)	A46	A	A6									13	2
István HAMAR (06/10/70) - Beitar Jerusalem (ISR)	A	A	A	A69		s76	s64					15	4
Pál DÁRDAI (16/03/76) - Hertha BSC Berlin (GER)	s46	s46	M	M	M	M46			M	M	M	9	1
Norbert TÓTH (11/08/76) - Újpest FC	s46			s69		s51	A76	A	s65			10	-
									/90				
Zoltán KOVÁCS (24/09/73) - Újpest FC	s46	s78			s85							12	2
Tibor DOMBI (11/11/73) - DVSC-Epona	s60	A78	s75			s57	s71	s55	A		s60	24	1
Tamás SZEKERES (18/09/72) - MTK Hungária FC/Újpest FC	s86				D							4	-
Ferenc SZILVESZTER (26/11/71) - Vasas DH	s89											4	-
Pál LAKOS (21/01/74) - Györi ETO FC		D										2	-
György KORSÓS (22/08/76) - Györi ETO FC	s78	s65		D	D	D	D	D	D	D		10	1
István PISONT (16/05/70) - Eintracht Frankfurt (GER)		M	M	M	s46	M	M	M46	s46	s73		29	1
Miklós FEHÉR (20/07/79) - FC Porto (POR)		s6	A75	A90	A57	A	A64		A46			7	1
Gábor EGRESSY (11/02/74) - Diósgyöri FC			A78	A	A51				A	A60		14	-
Ferenc HÁMORI (14/10/72) - Vasas DH			s75									9	1
József SOMOGYI (23/05/68) - Györi ETO FC				M	M	s78		s46		M78		6	-
Miklós HERCZEG (26/03/74) - Újpest FC				s76				s90	s76			7	-
Róbert WALTNER (20/09/77) - Videoton FC Fehérvár				s90								1	-
Barnabás SZIPÁNOVICS (02/07/74) - Rijeka (CRO)					A85							1	-
Attila KORSÓS (25/12/71) - Újpest FC								A65				5	1
Sándor PREISINGER (11/12/73) - MTK Hungária FC									s83	s78		2	-

DOMESTIC CUP 98/99

THIRD ROUND
Borsod Volán 2, Gázszer FC 1
Büki TK 2, Diósgyöri FC 2 (5-6 on pens.)
Haladás-Milos 2, Kispest-Honvéd FC 1
Royal Goldavis Zalaapáti 2, Nyírség-Spartacus 3
Kunszentmártoni TE 0, Györi ETO FC 2
III. Kerület FC 0, Ferencváros 1
Dunaferr SE 1, Újpest FC 2
Lébény-Földgép-Agro 1, DVSC-Epona 3
Hartai SE 2, Videoton FC Fehérvár 3
Dunakeszi 1, Tiszaújvaros 0
Edelény 1, MTK Hungária FC 3
Lombard FC Tatabánya 4, Hajduszoboszló 0
Sárvár FC 1, Vasas DH 3
Palotás 1, BVSC-Zugló 0
Zalahús ZTE FC 2, Soproni Dreher 2 (4-2 on pens.)
Vác FC-Zollner 3, Siófok 0

FOURTH ROUND
Videoton FC Fehérvár 3, Haladás-Milos 3 (3-4 on pens.)
Borsod Volán 0, Györi ETO FC 4
Nyírség-Spartacus 2, Zalahús ZTE FC 1
Dunakeszi 1, Vác FC-Zollner 2
Paloteas 0, Diósgyöri FC 4
Vasas DH 2, DVSC-Epona 3
MTK Hungária FC 1, Lombard FC Tatabánya 2
Újpest FC 3, Ferencváros 1

QUARTER-FINALS
DVSC-Epona 3 (Ilea 56, Sabo 84, Dombi 90),
Diósgyöri FC 1 (Domokos 69)
Lombard FC Tatabánya 3 (Kiprich 4, Kovács 48, 66p),
Újpest FC 1 (Urbán 88)
Györi ETO FC 1 (Baumgartner 72), Nyírség-Spartacus 0
Vác FC-Zollner 3 (Vitelki 10, Füle 76p, Sipeki 89),
Haladás-Milos 1 (Tóth P. 90)

SEMI-FINALS
DVSC-Epona 2 (Dombi 7, Sabo 24),
Györi ETO FC 1 (Korsós 18)
Lombard FC Tatabánya 3
(Nagy 12, Szekeres 27, Kovács 43),
Vác FC-Zollner 0

FINAL
20/05/99, Vác
DVSC-EPONA 2 Bagoly (22), Gelei (80og)
LOMBARD FC TATABÁNYA 1 Kiprich (50)
referee - Puhl
DVSC-EPONA - Téglási; Gojan; Bodnár (Szatmári 89),
Petö; Dombi, Sándor, Vadicska, Bagoly, Böör; Sabo
(Csehi 57), Ilea.
LOMBARD FC TATABÁNYA - Gelei; Bukva, Szabó,
Szalma, Virág (Van de Merwe 41); Süveges, Kovács
(Csernák 67), Tüske, Szekeres (Szoboszlai 39);
Kiprich, Nagy.

---

having run up debts high enough to warrant an independent investigation. On the field Ferencváros were delighted to finish second, especially after a pitiful first half of the campaign when they dropped into mid-table in the league, got hammered by Greek side AEK in the UEFA Cup and ultimately announced the parting of the ways with their legendary coach, Tibor Nyilasi.

In the spring 'Fradi' employed Croatian Marijan Vlak and suddenly began to string a few victories together, which saw them soar up the table into second place. Inevitably, given his results, Vlak proved popular with the fans, but not so with club president Jószef Torgyán (also the leader of the second biggest political party in Hungary, 'Független Kisgazdapárt'), who decided to sack him because in Ferencváros's centenary year, he said, the club needed a cocah with a "100 per cent Fradi-heart".

Another coach desperately unlucky to lose his job was Diósgyör's Barnabás Tornyi. Press reports revealed that he had been offered a significant financial award if the team finished the season in the top three places. So, when Diósgyör did actually make it up into third place halfway through the campaign, the reaction of the club directors was to give him the sack! But they certainly paid for that miserly attitude in the spring when the team plummeted down the table after a run of just one win in 13 games.

While Diósgyör were the surprise package in the autumn, newly-promoted Dunaferr were the unlikely lads of the spring. They would have finished fifth but for an extremely severe 15-point penalty imposed on them because they failed to pay the transfer fee due to Diósgyör for the purchase of Slovakian goalkeeper Julius Nota.

That was not the only Federation decision which affected the shape of the table. In the autumn Vasas beat III. Kerület 6-0, but the three points were subsequently attributed to the losers, the reason being that Vasas left-back Imre Aranyos had been sent off in a summer tournament in Spain and, under Hungarian league rules, should therefore have missed the match through suspension.

BVSC also had a victory turned into a defeat when it was ruled that ex-world-class Hungarian international Lajos Détári should not have been eligible to play in their home match with Haladás (he scored one goal and set up the other in BVSC's 2-1 win), having signed after the official transfer deadline from Austrian Second Division club VSE St. Pölten. BVSC also suffered further disciplinary action when they were deducted a point in the spring following the ineligibility of another player, Attila Forrai. The club ultimately paid for their administrative incompetence with relegation, finishing four points below the safety zone.

Videoton also went down, narrowly missing out in a dog-fight with Siófok, while bottom place was filled by III. Kerület, who managed just three proper wins all season in addition to that 3-0 'gift' from Vasas.

The Second Division was completely dominated by Tatabánya - or, to comply with their sponsor's demands, Lombard FC Tatabánya - who were almost as overwhelming as MTK in the top league, finishing 12 and 13 points, respectively, ahead of the two other promoted teams, Nagykanizsa and Szeged. Tatabánya, inspired by well-known veteran striker József Kiprich, also had great fun in the Hungarian Cup, knocking out both MTK and

Újpest en route to reaching the final, against DVSC-Epona (formerly Debrecen), which, sadly, they lost as a result of a bizarre own-goal from their goalkeeper Károly Gelei.

Victory in the final brought Debrecen the first major title in their 97-year history. It was their second significant feat of the season. A few weeks earlier they had thrashed

PLAYERS OF THE SEASON

BÉLA ILLÉS

Gifted 31-year-old attacking midfielder Béla Illés has never played for a foreign club, which makes

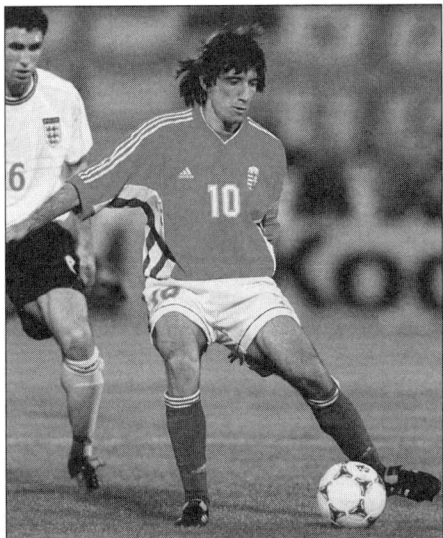

him something of an exception among the leading Hungarian internationals of his generation. Neverthless, he remains a permanent fixture in the national team, having collected his 50th cap in the Euro 2000 defeat at home to Slovakia in June 1999. Illés would have wished for a happier occasion to mark his half-century, but over the previous few months he had certainly enjoyed many more good days than bad, captaining MTK-Hungária FC to their runaway title triumph, top-scoring in the league with 22 goals and also collecting both Hungarian Player of the Year awards - one from sports daily Nemzeti Sport, the other from his fellow professionals.

JÓZSEF KIPRICH

The leading goalscorer of the Hungarian national team over the past decade, 36-year-old József Kiprich made a dramatic return to his hometown club Tatabánya in 1998/99, scoring the goals that

aided their return to the top flight for the first time in seven years. "Kipu" had only ever played for Tatabánya in Hungary before leaving for Dutch club Feyenoord in 1989, and now, a decade on, he is the club's new coach-cum-technical director, having proved himself to be an inspirational figure on the field of play as he guided the team not only towards promotion but also into the Hungarian Cup final, where he scored Tatabánya's consolation goal in their 2-1 defeat by DVSC-Epona.

GÁBOR KIRÁLY

In Hungarian his surname means 'king' - a title that befits Gábor Király's present status in Hungarian football. The Szombathely-born goalkeeper, whose father played some 400 senior games for Haladás, had a wonderful 1998/99 season for both his club, Hertha Berlin, and his country. According to official Bundesliga statistics, he was was the best goalkeeper in Germany, helping Hertha into the Champions' League with a string of classy performances. He also played from start to finish in all of Hungary's 11 internationals during the season, becoming a cult figure and strong favourite of the Hungarian fans. While many goalkeepers these days like to wear elaborate, fancy-coloured costumes, Király's trade-mark is a pair of scruffy grey tracksuit bottoms.

Ferencváros 6-1 - the Budapest club's heaviest league defeat for 23 years.

Th gloom gathering over Hungarian football was not lifted by the national team, who appeared to be making hesitant progress under coach Bertalan Bicskei until the month of June, when two defeats in four days - 0-2 in Romania, 0-1 at home to Slovakia - put the seal on their already slim chances of making it through to the Euro 2000 finals.

To Bicskei's credit, he did offer the Hungarian fans the most settled team they had seen for years, with players such as goalkeeper Gábor Király, defenders János Hrutka and Vilmos Sebök, and the ever-reliable MTK duo of Gábor Halmai and Béla Illés all meriting consistent selection. But the 0-1 defeat by Slovakia in Györ ended the season on a really sour note, and it was questionable whether the coach and his chosen ones would be able to ride out that particular storm without any lasting damage.

Meanwhile, at the Hungarian Federation HQ there were other problems for the nation's football-lovers to digest.

On February 4 the country's Minister for Youth and Sports, Tamás Deutsch, formally suspended FA president Attila Kovács and his entire board of directors from office. This prompted the intervention of FIFA, which in turn raised the possible threat of exclusion from international competition of Hungary's clubs and national team. By the summer the issue was still ongoing, with FIFA having commissioned an independent company of legal and financial experts to investigate and report back to them on the affair...

INTERNATIONAL HONOURS

World Cup Finals appearances: 1934 (2nd round), 1938 (Runners-up), 1954 (Runners-up), 1958, 1962 (qtr-finals), 1966 (qtr-finals), 1978, 1982, 1986

European Championship appearances (last 8): 1964 (3rd), 1968, 1972 (4th)

European Club Competitions
Fairs' Cup   Ferencváros (1965)

EUROPEAN CUPS 98/99

CHAMPIONS' CUP
● ÚJPEST FC
Preliminary round ZIMBRU CHISINAU (MOL)
A 0-1
    Bíró; Sebök; Tamási, Kiskapusi (Kopunovic); Petö, Kvasz, Miriuta, Fehér, Tóth; Kovács Z., Korsós.
H 3-1 Miriuta (17), Kovács Z. (72, 90)
    Bíró; Sebök; Fehér, Tamási; Jenei, Petö, Miriuta, Tóth (Kiskapusi 71); Herczeg, Kovács Z., Korsós (Kopunovic 57).

Qualifying round SK STURM GRAZ (AUT)
H 2-3 Kovács Z. (36), Jenei (72)
    Bíró; Sebök; Mogyorósi, Kiskapusi (Bérczy 60); Jenei, Fehér, Tóth, Szlezák; Herczeg (Eszenyi 80), Kovács Z., Korsós (Kvasz 64).
A 0-4
    Bíró; Fehér; Kiskapusi, Tamási; Kopunovic, Jenei, Korsós (Kvasz 89), Szlezák, Tóth (Bérczy 65); Herczeg, Kovács Z..

CUP WINNERS' CUP
● MTK HUNGÁRIA FC
Qualifying round GÍ (FAR)
A 3-1 Kenesei (18), Preisinger (19), Szekeres 90)
    Babos; Lörincz; Molnár, Komlósi, Szamosi; Erös, Halmai, Illés, Madar (Szekeres 46); Preisinger (Balaskó 74), Kenesei.
H 7-0 Kenesei (16, 71, 76), Preisinger (34), Halmai (37), Illés 63), Balaskó (72),
    Babos; Lörincz; Molnár, Szekeres, Szamosi; Erös, Halmai (Czvitkovics 65), Illés (Csordás 75), Madar; Preisinger (Balaskó 65), Kenesei.

1st round SV RIED (AUT)
A 0-2
    Babos; Molnár, Komlósi, Szekeres, Szamosi; Erös (Csordás 82), Halmai, Illés, Madar; Balaskó (Orosz 57), Kenesei (Preisinger 73).

H 0-1
    Babos; Molnár (Erös 46), Komlósi, Szekeres, Szamosi; Csordás, Halmai, Illés, Madar; Kenesei, Preisinger (Balaskó 46).

UEFA CUP
● FERENCVÁROS
Preliminary round CE PRINCIPAT (AND)
H 6-0 Fülöp (25), Selimi (42), Schultz (48, 75p), Vámosi (63), Mátyus (90)
    Udvarácz; Telek; Szücs (Vámosi 20), Mátyus; Kriston, Nyilas (Kovács 65), Lendvai, Schultz, Füzi (Jagodics 65); Fülöp, Selimi.
A 8-1 Selimi (18, 74), Kovács (23, 83), Kriston (51), Nagy (52), Jagodics (58), Schultz (84)
    Vámos; Telek; Simon, Szücs (Baranyai 66); Kriston, Jagodics, Vámosi (Schultz 60), Kovács, Nagy; Fülöp, Selimi.

Qualifying round AEK (GRE)
H 4-2 Selimi (9), Lendvai (28), Nyilas (55p), Vincze (83)
    Udvarácz; Telek; Szücs, Mátyus; Nyilas (Jagodics 84), Vámosi (Vincze 56), Lendvai, Kovács, Nagy, Bükszegi, Selimi (Fülöp 66).
A 0-4
    Udvarácz; Telek; Szücs (Füzi 23), Mátyus; Nyilas, Lendvai, Vámosi (Jagodics 66), Vincze (Kovács 46), Nagy; Bükszegi, Selimi.

● ÚJPEST FC
1st round CLUB BRUGGE KV (BEL)
H 0-5
    Bíró; Sebök (Kiskapusi 29); Mogyorósi, Tamási; Jenei, Petö, Szanyó (Eszenyi 56), Fehér, Szlezák; Kovács Z., Kopunovic (Kvasz 69).
A 2-2 Kopunovic (50), Szanyó (90p)
    Bíró; Fehér; Kiskapusi, Tamási; Jenei, Kvasz (Bérczy 78), Szanyó, Szlezák, Löw; Kopunovic (Pintér 81), Eszenyi (Thaly 90).

BVSC-ZUGLÓ

CLUB DIRECTORY

BVSC-Zugló
Szönyi út 2
1142 Budapest
tel - (1) 2513888
fax - (1) 2513698
Year of Formation - 1911
Chairman - József Ádám
Coach - István Sándor; József Tajti
Stadium - BVSC (10,000)

APPEARANCES 98/99

	P	Ap	(s)	Gls
Catalin ANGHEL (ROM)	A	8	(5)	1
Zsolt AUBEL	A	19	(7)	5
Djordje BAJIC (YUG)	A	7	(9)	2
Zoltán BALOG	D	11	(1)	
Balázs BÉRCZY	D	13		1
Alexandr BONDARENKO (UKR)	D	29		2
Levente BOZSIK	A	1	(11)	
Viktor BROVCHENKO (UKR)	M	13		1
Krisztián CSILLAG	M	22	(5)	
Lajos DÉTÁRI	M	17		7
Attila FORRAI	M	9	(1)	
Zsolt FÜZESI	D	2	(2)	
Krisztián FÜZI	M	15	(5)	1
Csaba GELBMANN	D	3		
János KERTÉSZ	M	1		
István KISS	A	15	(1)	4
János KOSZTA	G	22		
Csaba LÁSZLÓ	D	10		
Zoltán MOLNÁR	D	11		
Gábor NAGY	G	1		
Attila POLONKAI	M	14	(13)	
Tibor POMPER	D	23	(4)	1
Károly POTEMKIN	A	6		
Miroslav RESKO (UKR)	D	15		
Dénes RÓSA	M	10	(3)	4
Ferenc ROTT	G	11	(1)	
Csaba SZAKOS	D	11	(1)	
Ferenc SZASZOVSZKY	D	6	(4)	
Szabolcs SZEGLETES	M	1	(7)	
Gábor SZILÁGYI	A	4	(8)	
Daniel USVAT (ROM)	M	24	(2)	3
Zoltán VINCZE	D	20	(4)	1

LEAGUE RESULTS 1998/99

01/08/98	Újpest FC	H	0-3	
08/08/98	Györi ETO FC	A	1-1	Brovchenko
15/08/98	Zalahús ZTE FC	H	1-1	Bondarenko
22/08/98	Vác FC-Zollner	A	0-1	
29/08/98	Ferencváros	H	0-1	
01/09/98	III. Kerület FC	A	0-0	
08/09/98	DVSC-Epona	A	1-3	Kiss
12/09/98	Videoton FC Fehérvár	A	1-4	Kiss
19/09/98	Nyírség Spartacus	H	0-0	
26/09/98	Dunaferr SE	A	1-1	Bajic
03/10/98	Vasas DH	H	1-2	Bondarenko
17/10/98	Kispest-Honvéd FC	A	5-1	Kiss 2, Aubel 2, Füzi
24/10/98	Haladás-Milos	H	0-3	(w/o)
08/11/98	MTK Hungária FC	H	0-2	
14/11/98	Gázszer FC	A	0-0	
21/11/98	Siófok	H	0-1	
28/11/98	Diósgyöri FC	A	1-2	Bajic
28/02/99	DVSC-Epona	H	0-1	
06/03/99	Újpest FC	A	1-3	Rósa
13/03/99	BVSC-Zugló	H	2-1	Rósa, Détári
20/03/99	Zalahús ZTE FC	A	0-2	
02/04/99	Vác FC-Zollner	H	2-1	Rósa, Détári
07/04/99	Ferencváros	A	0-1	
10/04/99	Videoton FC Fehérvár	H	0-1	
17/04/99	Nyírség Spartacus	A	0-1	
24/04/99	Dunaferr SE	H	3-2	Rósa, Détári 2
01/05/99	Vasas DH	A	2-3	Détári, Anghel
05/05/99	Kispest-Honvéd FC	H	3-0	Détári, Usvat, Aubel
10/05/99	Haladás-Milos	A	1-3	Vincze
16/05/99	III. Kerület FC	H	3-0	Bérczy, Aubel 2
23/05/99	MTK Hungária FC	A	2-3	Pomper, Détári
29/05/99	Gázszer FC	H	1-2	Usvat
12/06/99	Siófok	A	1-0	Usvat
16/06/99	Diósgyöri FC	H	1-3	og (Kovács)

DVSC-EPONA

CLUB DIRECTORY

Debreceni VSC-Epona
Oláh Gábor u. 5
4028 Debrecen
tel - (52) 417655
fax - (52) 417595
Year of Formation - 1902
Chairman - Zoltán Erdei
Coach - András Herczeg; Lajos Garamvölgyi
Stadium - Nagyerdei (10,000)

MAJOR HONOURS
Domestic Cup - (1) 1999.

APPEARANCES 98/99

		P	Ap	(s)	Gls
Gábor BAGOLY	M	19	(7)		2
Péter BAJZÁT	A		(1)		
Zsolt BENCZIK	M	2	(2)		
Csaba BERNÁTH	D	5	(6)		
László BODNÁR	D	20	(3)		1
Zoltán BÖÖR	M	29	(4)		5
Cornel CONSTANTIN (ROM)	D	1	(2)		
Zoltán CSEHI	A	15	(9)		2
Tibor DOMBI	A	27			5
Miklós ERDÉLYI	G	1			
Róbert FEKETE	G	21			
Ferenc FRIDA	D	1	(1)		
Liviu GOJAN (ROM)	D	30			2
Nicolae ILEA (ROM)	A	23	(9)		18
Zoltán KISS	A	5	(2)		1
Norbert KOVÁCS	M	8	(4)		
Tamás MADAR	M		(13)		
Zoltán PETÖ	D	30			1
Radu SABO (ROM)	A	20	(3)		8
Csaba SÁNDOR	M	26	(2)		1
Csaba SIKLÓSI	M	8	(18)		2
Dan STUPAR (ROM)	D	9	(1)		
Csaba SZATMÁRI	M	32	(1)		1
Gábor TÉGLÁSI	G	12			
Zoltán ULVECZKI	M	1	(6)		1
Zsolt VADICSKA	M	29			2

LEAGUE RESULTS 1998/99

01/08/98	Diósgyöri FC	A	0-0	
08/08/98	Újpest FC	A	2-3	Dombi, Petö
15/08/98	Györi ETO FC	H	1-2	Dombi
22/08/98	Zalahús ZTE FC	A	0-3	
29/08/98	Vác FC-Zollner	H	2-1	Gojan, Böör
08/09/98	BVSC-Zugló	H	3-1	Kiss, Ilea, Böör
12/09/98	Ferencváros	A	0-2	
19/09/98	Videoton FC Fehérvár	H	5-0	Vadicska 2, Csehi, Böör, Dombi
26/09/98	Nyírség Spartacus	A	2-4	Siklósi, Gojan
03/10/98	Dunaferr SE	H	1-2	Dombi
17/10/98	Vasas DH	A	0-2	
24/10/98	Kispest-Honvéd FC	H	0-2	
31/10/98	Haladás-Milos	A	1-1	Ulveczki
07/11/98	III. Kerület FC	H	0-0	
14/11/98	MTK Hungária FC	A	2-1	Sabo, Ilea
21/11/98	Gázszer FC	H	4-0	Ilea 2, Sabo, Siklósi
28/11/98	Siófok	A	1-0	Böör
28/02/99	BVSC-Zugló	A	1-0	Ilea (p)
06/03/99	Diósgyöri FC	H	5-0	Sabo 2, Böör, Dombi, Szatmári
13/03/99	Újpest FC	H	0-2	
20/03/99	Györi ETO FC	A	1-3	Bagoly
03/04/99	Zalahús ZTE FC	H	2-0	Sándor, Ilea
07/04/99	Vác FC-Zollner	A	1-1	Ilea (p)
10/04/99	Ferencváros	H	6-1	Sabo 3, Ilea 2 (1p), Bodnár
17/04/99	Videoton FC Fehérvár	A	0-1	
24/04/99	Nyírség Spartacus	H	2-0	Ilea 2
01/05/99	Dunaferr SE	A	0-2	
05/05/99	Vasas DH	H	0-0	
10/05/99	Kispest-Honvéd FC	A	0-0	
15/05/99	Haladás-Milos	H	1-1	Sabo
24/05/99	III. Kerület FC	A	5-1	Ilea 3, Bagoly, Csehi
29/05/99	MTK Hungária FC	H	3-1	Ilea 3
12/06/99	Gázszer FC	A	1-2	og (Zimmermann)
16/06/99	Siófok	H	1-0	Ilea

DIÓSGYÖRI FC

Diósgyöri FC
Andrássy u. 61
3533 Miskolc
tel - (46) 379451
fax - (46) 379552
Year of Formation - 1910
Chairman - Zoltán Kövy
Coach - Barnabás Tornyi; Gábor Szapor; Miklós
Temesvári
Stadium - Diósgyöri (28,000)

MAJOR HONOURS
Domestic Cup - (2) 1977, 1980.

	P	Ap	(s)	Gls
Ádám BABOS	M	3	(9)	
Relu BULIGA (ROM)	M	3	(5)	
Attila BUZÁS	M	24	(7)	5
Béla DOMOKOS	A	14	(6)	2
Gábor EGRESSY	A	31		17
János FARKAS	D	4	(9)	
Tibor FÖLDVÁRI	D	24	(3)	
István KÁKÓCZKI	M	11	(6)	
László KISER	M	29		2
Tibor KOVÁCS	D	31	(1)	
Sándor KULCSÁR (ROM)	A	17		10
Attila KUTTOR	D	15		2
László LIPTÁK	M	3	(4)	1
Zoltán NAGY	G	4		
Julius NOTA (SVK)	G	17		
Róbert RÁCZ	G	13		
Mico SMILJANIC (YUG)	D	30		3
Attila SZABADOS (YUG)	A	6	(19)	4
Tibor SZABÓ (YUG)	M	26	(2)	2
Viktor TAKÁCS	D	2		
István TÉGER	D	33		4
Ferenc TERNOVÁN	M	7	(7)	2
Mihály TURÓCZI	M	27	(3)	
Endre VARGA	D		(13)	

25/07/98	Dunaferr SE	A	3-2	Kulcsár 2, Egressy
01/08/98	DVSC-Epona	H	0-0	
08/08/98	Vasas DH	H	4-2	Egressy 2, Buzás 2
15/08/98	Újpest FC	A	3-1	Téger, Kulcsár, Szabados
22/08/98	Kispest-Honvéd FC	H	0-0	
29/08/98	Györi ETO FC	A	4-5	Kiser, Téger, Kulcsár, Egressy
12/09/98	Haladás-Milos	H	5-1	Smiljanic, Szabó, Kuttor,
				Szabados, Egressy
19/09/98	Zalahús ZTE FC	A	1-2	Egressy
26/09/98	III. Kerület FC	H	5-1	Kulcsár 3, Buzás, Kiser
03/10/98	Vác FC-Zollner	A	3-1	Egressy 2, Szabados
17/10/98	MTK Hungária FC	H	1-1	Smiljanic
24/10/98	Ferencváros	A	4-3	Kulcsear 2, Egressy, Szabó
31/10/98	Gázszer FC	H	2-0	Buzás (p), Kuttor
07/11/98	Videoton FC Fehérvár	A	3-2	Smiljanic, Egressy 2
14/11/98	Siófok	H	1-1	Kulcsár
21/11/98	Nyírség Spartacus	A	1-3	Egressy
28/11/98	BVSC-Zugló	H	2-1	Egressy, Szabados
28/02/99	Dunaferr SE	H	1-1	og (Éger)
06/03/99	DVSC-Epona	A	0-5	
14/03/99	Vasas DH	A	0-0	
20/03/99	Újpest FC	H	1-1	Ternován
03/04/99	Kispest-Honvéd FC	A	0-3	
07/04/99	Györi ETO FC	H	1-1	og (Molnár)
10/04/99	Haladás-Milos	A	1-2	Egressy
19/04/99	Zalahús ZTE FC	H	1-1	Egressy
25/04/99	III. Kerület FC	A	2-1	Domokos 2
01/05/99	Vác FC-Zollner	H	0-1	
05/05/99	MTK Hungária FC	A	0-4	
08/05/99	Ferencváros	H	1-3	Egressy
15/05/99	Gázszer FC	A	0-2	
24/05/99	Videoton FC Fehérvár	H	1-0	Lipták
29/05/99	Siófok	A	1-2	Buzás (p)
12/06/99	Nyírség Spartacus	H	1-0	Egressy
16/06/99	BVSC-Zugló	A	3-1	Téger 2, Ternován

DUNAFERR SE

CLUB DIRECTORY

Dunaferr SE
Eszperantó út 4
2400 Dunaújváros
tel - (25) 311857
fax - (25) 83266
Year of Formation - 1951
Chairman - dr. József Szabó
Coach - Zoltán Varga; Ferenc Ebedli
(99/00 - Sándor Egervári)
Stadium - Dunaferr (12,000)

APPEARANCES 98/99

		P	Ap	(s)	Gls
Tamás BALOGH	G	2			
László BITA	G	9			
László CSEKE	M	1	(19)	2	
Péter DUDÁS	D	12	(11)	2	
László ÉGER	D	29	(2)		
Antal JÄKL	M	32	(1)		
Eguia JAVRAUJAN (RUS)	M		(5)		
Ferenc KÓCZIÁN	M	5	(5)		
Árpád KOVÁCSEVICS	G	15			
Ferenc LENGYEL	M	30	(2)	12	
Lajos MIKLER	M	13	(5)		
Dejan MILOVANOVIC (YUG)	D	23	(2)	1	
Tamás NAGY	M	11	(4)	1	
Igor NICHENKO (UKR)	A	30		10	
Julius NOTA (SVK)	G	8			
Lajos POPOVICS	M	17	(4)		
Henrik RÓSA	M	24	(7)	1	
Gábor RUPPERT	D		(1)		
Miklós SALAMON	D	33		1	
Róbert SZÁNTÓ	M		(1)		
Attila TÖKÖLI	A	22	(6)	7	
József VASKÓ	D		(3)		
Vyacheslav YEREMEEV (RUS)	M	24	(8)	4	
Gábor ZAVADSZKY	M	34		12	

LEAGUE RESULTS 1998/99

25/07/98	Diósgyöri FC	H	2-3	Salamon, Lengyel
01/08/98	Vasas DH	A	2-3	Zavadszky, Lengyel (p)
08/08/98	Kispest-Honvéd FC	H	2-1	Lengyel (p), Tököli
15/08/98	Haladás-Milos	A	1-0	Tököli
22/08/98	III. Kerület FC	H	3-0	Lengyel, Cseke, Zavadszky
30/08/98	MTK Hungária FC	A	0-3	
12/09/98	Gázszer FC	H	2-1	Nichenko, Dudás
19/09/98	Siófok	A	1-0	Zavadszky
26/09/98	BVSC-Zugló	H	1-1	Zavadszky
03/10/98	DVSC-Epona	A	2-1	Yeremeev, Nichenko
17/10/98	Újpest FC	H	2-0	Lengyel (p), Yeremeev
24/10/98	Györi ETO FC	A	1-2	Yeremeev
31/10/98	Zalahús ZTE FC	H	2-0	Yeremeev, Zavadszky
07/11/98	Vác FC-Zollner	A	0-1	
14/11/98	Ferencváros	H	2-1	Nichenko 2
21/11/98	Videoton FC Fehérvár	A	4-4	Nichenko 2, Tököli, Lengyel
28/11/98	Nyírség Spartacus	H	6-1	Tököli, Zavadszky 2, Rósa,
				Milovanovic, Nichenko
28/02/99	Diósgyöri FC	A	1-1	Lengyel
06/03/99	Vasas DH	H	2-1	Nichenko, Zavadszky
15/03/99	Kispest-Honvéd FC	A	0-0	
20/03/99	Haladás-Milos	H	2-0	Zavadszky, Cseke
03/04/99	III. Kerület FC	A	1-3	Zavadszky
07/04/99	MTK Hungária FC	H	0-3	
10/04/99	Gázszer FC	A	0-3	
17/04/99	Siófok	H	2-1	Lengyel, Nichenko
24/04/99	BVSC-Zugló	A	2-3	Dudás, Nagy
01/05/99	DVSC-Epona	H	2-0	Nichenko, Lengyel (p)
05/05/99	Újpest FC	A	0-3	
08/05/99	Györi ETO FC	H	0-0	
15/05/99	Zalahús ZTE FC	A	1-0	Tököli
22/05/99	Vác FC-Zollner	H	1-1	Lengyel (p)
29/05/99	Ferencváros	A	3-1	Lengyel 2, Tököli
12/06/99	Videoton FC Fehérvár	H	3-1	Zavadszky 2, og (Tóth)
16/06/99	Nyírség Spartacus	A	1-3	Tököli

FERENCVÁROS

Ferencvárosi Torna Club
Üllői út 129
1091 Budapest
tel - (1) 2156025
fax - (1) 2153698
Year of Formation - 1899
Chairman - dr. István Szívós
Coach - Tibor Nyilasi; Marijan Vlak
(99/00 - József Mucha)
Stadium - Üllői út (18,000)

MAJOR HONOURS
League Championship - (26)
1903, 1905, 1907, 1909, 1910, 1911, 1912,
1913, 1926, 1927, 1928, 1932, 1934, 1938,
1940, 1941, 1949, 1963, 1964, 1967, 1968,
1976, 1981, 1992, 1995, 1996.
Domestic Cup - (18) 1913, 1922, 1927, 1928,
1933, 1935, 1942, 1943, 1944, 1958, 1972,
1974, 1976, 1978, 1991, 1993, 1994, 1995.
Fairs' Cup - (1) 1965.

	P	Ap	(s)	Gls
Alen BJELIC (CRO)	M	1	(2)	
Tamás BÓCZ	M	2	(4)	1
Zoltán BÜKSZEGI	A	16	(3)	9
Dénes FSZFNYI	A	2	(7)	
Tibor FODOR	M	2	(1)	
Zoltán FÜLÖP	A	5	(3)	2
Ykos FÜZI	M	24	(4)	3
Zoltán JAGODICS	M	3	(13)	1
Béla KOVÁCS	M	13	(11)	2
Attila KRISTON	M	13	(3)	
Sándor KULCSÁR (ROM)	A	14	(3)	2
Miklós LENDVAI	M	29		1
Pál LILIK	D	3		
János MÁTYUS	D	28		6
Norbert NAGY	D	16	(1)	1
Elek NYILAS	M	29	(4)	3
Levente SCHULTZ	M	9	(10)	2
Zenun SELIMI (YUG)	A	13	(5)	5
Tibor SIMON	D	3	(1)	
Imre SZABICS	A	17	(7)	12
Mihály SZÜCS	D	21		
András TELEK	D	33		
Milán UDVARÁCZ	G	22		
János VÁMOS	G	12		
Csaba VÁMOSI	D	21	(6)	2
Ottó VINCZE	M	23	(5)	7

25/07/98	Haladás-Milos	H	1-0	Mátyus
01/08/98	III. Kerület FC	A	2-1	Selimi, Vámosi
07/08/98	MTK Hungária FC	H	2-2	Nyilas (p), Bükszegi
15/08/98	Gázszer FC	A	1-1	Bükszegi
22/08/98	Siófok	H	2-0	Vincze, Selimi
29/08/98	BVSC-Zugló	A	1-0	Bükszegi
12/09/98	DVSC-Epona	H	2-0	Bükszegi, Schultz
19/09/98	Újpest FC	A	1-2	Vincze
26/09/98	Györi ETO FC	H	1-1	Szabics
03/10/98	Zalahús ZTE FC	A	1-1	Kovács
17/10/98	Vác FC-Zollner	H	2-2	Mátyus, Szabics
24/10/98	Diósgyöri FC	H	3-4	Szabics 2, Bükszegi
31/10/98	Videoton FC Fehérvár	A	3-1	Fülöp 2, Füzi
07/11/98	Nyírség Spartacus	H	2-1	Szabics 2
14/11/98	Dunaferr SE	A	1-2	Mátyus
21/11/98	Vasas DH	H	3-1	Selimi 2, Vincze
28/11/98	Kispest-Honvéd FC	A	2-2	Vincze, Selimi
06/03/99	III. Kerület FC	H	7-1	Szabics 4, Nyilas (p), Vincze, Schultz
13/03/99	MTK Hungária FC	A	0-2	
20/03/99	Gázszer FC	H	2-0	Bócz, Szabics
03/04/99	Siófok	A	2-0	Nyilas (p), Füzi
07/04/99	BVSC-Zugló	H	1-0	Vámosi
10/04/99	DVSC-Epona	A	1-6	Nagy
17/04/99	Újpest FC	H	1-0	Mátyus
21/04/99	Haladás-Milos	A	2-1	Lendvai, og (Tóth P.)
24/04/99	Györi ETO FC	A	2-1	Bükszegi, Jagodics
01/05/99	Zalahús ZTE FC	H	4-0	Mátyus, Bükszegi, Vincze, Kulcsár
05/05/99	Vác FC-Zollner	A	1-1	Kulcsár
08/05/99	Diósgyöri FC	A	3-1	Bükszegi 2, Szabics
16/05/99	Videoton FC Fehérvár	H	2-0	Mátyus, Füzi
23/05/99	Nyírség Spartacus	A	1-0	Vincze
29/05/99	Dunaferr SE	H	1-3	og (Salamon)
12/06/99	Vasas DH	A	1-2	Kovács
16/06/99	Kispest-Honvéd FC	H	0-1	

GÁZSZER FC

Gázszer FC
Gesztenye sor 17/A
1484 Agárd
tel - (22) 370258
Year of Formation - 1994
Chairman - László Németh
Coach - Gábor Hartyáni
(99/00 - Ferenc Csongrádi)
Stadium - Stadler, Akasztó (18,000)

APPEARANCES 98/99

		P	Ap	(s)	Gls
Gábor	ÁRKI	M	12		
Balázs	BEKÖ	M	30		3
Josip	DULIC (YUG)	D	27	(3)	
Zsolt	DVÉRI	M	31		5
Gábor	FÖLDES	A	27	(4)	8
Attila	FORRAI	M	4	(2)	
Péter	KIRÁLY	A	6	(11)	1
Oleg	KOROL (BLS)	D	29	(1)	1
István	KÖVESFALVI	G	33		
Antal	LÖRINCZ	D		(1)	
Sándor	MATUS	G	1		
Vyacheslav	MEDVID (UKR)	M	27		2
Tamás	MEZÖ	D	1		
Lajos	NAGY	M	12		1
János	SALACZ	D	15	(6)	
Zoltán	SALACZ	D	20	(1)	
Péter	SIMEK	M	21	(7)	1
Csaba	SZALAI	D	29		4
Zsolt	SZEKERES	M	1	(10)	
Krisztián	TIBER	A	24	(8)	6
András	TULÁK	M	1	(2)	
Valdas	URBONAS (LIT)	D	11	(3)	1
Tamás	ZIMMERMANN	M	12	(4)	1

LEAGUE RESULTS 1998/99

26/07/98	Györi ETO FC	A	0-0	
01/08/98	Zalahús ZTE FC	H	2-0	Bekö, Dvéri
08/08/98	Vác FC-Zollner	A	1-1	Földes
15/08/98	Ferencváros	H	1-1	Szalai
23/08/98	Videoton FC Fehérvár	A	2-0	Nagy, Földes
29/08/98	Nyírség Spartacus	H	0-0	
12/09/98	Dunaferr SE	A	1-2	Szalai
19/09/98	Vasas DH	H	1-1	Tiber
25/09/98	Kispest-Honvéd FC	A	3-1	Szalai, Földes, Korol
09/10/98	Haladás-Milos	H	4-0	Dvéri, og (Zugor), Földes, Tiber
18/10/98	III. Kerület FC	A	1-2	Medvid
25/10/98	MTK Hungária FC	H	1-3	Tiber
31/10/98	Diósgyöri FC	A	0-2	
07/11/98	Siófok	A	2-2	Tiber, Bekö
14/11/98	BVSC-Zugló	H	0-0	
21/11/98	DVSC-Epona	A	0-4	
28/11/98	Újpest FC	H	2-1	og (Tamási), Tiber
22/02/99	Györi ETO FC	H	0-2	
06/03/99	Zalahús ZTE FC	A	0-2	
13/03/99	Vác FC-Zollner	H	1-0	Dvéri
20/03/99	Ferencváros	A	0-2	
03/04/99	Videoton FC Fehérvár	H	0-0	
07/04/99	Nyírség Spartacus	A	0-0	
10/04/99	Dunaferr SE	H	3-0	og (Milovanovic), Király, Földes
12/04/99	Vasas DH	A	0-2	
24/04/99	Kispest-Honvéd FC	H	0-0	
01/05/99	Haladás-Milos	A	1-1	Dvéri
05/05/99	III. Kerület FC	H	3-2	Medvid, Földes, Szalai
08/05/99	MTK Hungária FC	A	0-2	
15/05/99	Diósgyöri FC	H	2-0	Bekö, Dvéri
22/05/99	Siófok	H	1-3	Simek
29/05/99	BVSC-Zugló	A	2-1	Földes 2
12/06/99	DVSC-Epona	H	2-1	Tiber, Urbonas
16/06/99	Újpest FC	A	1-2	Zimmermann

GYÖRI ETO FC

Györi ETO FC
Nagysándor József u. 31
9027 Györ
tel - (96) 312433
fax - (96) 312457
Year of Formation - 1904
Chairman - János Borbényi
Coach - István Reszeli-Soós
(99/00 - Károly Gergely)
Stadium - Györi (26,000)

MAJOR HONOURS
League Championship - (3)
1963 (autumn), 1982, 1983.
Domestic Cup - (4) 1965, 1966, 1967, 1979.

	P	Ap	(s)	Gls
Tamás BAJI	G	3	(2)	
Mihály BALLA	A	21	(7)	7
Attila BAUMGARTNER	M	26	(1)	1
Zsolt BOGNÁR	D	12	(3)	
Attila BÖJTE	D	3	(8)	
Sándor CSATÓ	M	19	(2)	1
Ákos CSISZÁR	M	22	(4)	4
Gábor ERÖS	M	1	(3)	
Tibor FODOR	M	3	(2)	
György KORSÓS	D	29		11
Pál LAKOS	D	33		
Ilea LAZAR (ROM)	A	7	(16)	1
Levente MOLNÁR (ROM)	G	31		
Mihály MRACSKÓ	M	19		1
László NAGY	M	1	(1)	
Márton OROSS	A	3	(4)	
Dénes RÓSA	M		(6)	
Claudiu SALAGEAN (ROM)	M	31		5
József SOMOGYI	M	30		8
Péter STARK	D	33		1
Péter SÜTÖRI	A	2	(2)	
János SZARVAS	A	10	(24)	6
Gábor VAYER	A	32	(2)	7
Zoltán ZAHORÁN	D	3	(1)	

25/07/98	Gázszer FC	H	0-0	
01/08/98	Siófok	A	2-1	Korsós, Somogyi
08/08/98	BVSC-Zugló	H	1-1	Salagean
15/08/98	DVSC-Epona	A	2-1	Korsós, Vayer
22/08/98	Újpest FC	H	3-1	Balla 2, Salagean
29/08/98	Diósgyöri FC	H	5-4	Vayer, Somogyi, Korsós, Szarvas 2
12/09/98	Zalahús ZTE FC	A	1-2	Korsós
19/09/98	Vác FC-Zollner	H	1-0	Korsós
26/09/98	Ferencváros	A	1-1	Vayer
03/10/98	Videoton FC Fehérvár	H	3-0	Somogyi (p), Korsós, Csató
17/10/98	Nyírség Spartacus	A	0-0	
24/10/98	Dunaferr SE	H	2-1	Korsós, Szarvas
31/10/98	Vasas DH	A	4-1	Vayer, Szarvas, Mracskó, Csiszár
07/11/98	Kispest-Honvéd FC	H	2-2	Balla, Somogyi (p)
14/11/98	Haladás-Milos	A	1-0	Baumgartner
21/11/98	III. Kerület FC	H	3-0	Korsós, Vayer, Salagean
28/11/98	MTK Hungária FC	A	1-4	Lazar
27/02/99	Gázszer FC	A	2-0	Korsós, Somogyi
06/03/99	Siófok	H	1-1	Salagean
13/03/99	BVSC-Zugló	A	1-2	Balla
20/03/99	DVSC-Epona	H	3-1	Somogyi (p), Szarvas, Balla
03/04/99	Újpest FC	A	2-1	Balla, Csiszár
07/04/99	Diósgyöri FC	A	1-1	Stark
10/04/99	Zalahús ZTE FC	H	1-0	Korsós
18/04/99	Vác FC-Zollner	A	0-1	
24/04/99	Ferencváros	H	1-2	Somogyi
01/05/99	Videoton FC Fehérvár	A	0-0	
05/05/99	Nyírség Spartacus	H	0-1	
08/05/99	Dunaferr SE	A	0-0	
15/05/99	Vasas DH	H	3-3	Korsós, Vayer, Csiszár (p)
22/05/99	Györi ETO FC	A	0-4	
29/05/99	Haladás-Milos	H	2-0	Salagean, Balla
12/06/99	III. Kerület FC	A	3-3	Csiszár (p), Somogyi, Szarvas
16/06/99	MTK Hungária FC	H	1-0	Vayer

HALADÁS-MILOS

Haladás-Milos
Rohonczi út. 3
9700 Szombathely
tel - (94) 311494
fax - (94) 314966
Year of Formation - 1919
Chairman - Péter Török
Coach - László Dajka; István Mihalecz
(99/00 - Géza Vincze)
Stadium - Haladás (18,000)

APPEARANCES 98/99

	P	Ap	(s)	Gls
János ÁRGYELÁN	M		(5)	
Péter BALASSA	D	23	(3)	3
Csaba BALOG	M	32		1
István BODOR	A	11	(4)	3
Liviu BONCHIS (ROM)	M	30	(2)	3
Csaba FEHÉR	A	20	(4)	1
Péter HALMOSI	A		(2)	
András HORVÁTH	D	25	(1)	2
Stevan JAKOBA (YUG)	A	9	(2)	2
Dejan JAKSIMOVIC (YUG)	A		(1)	
Mirko JOVANOVIC (YUG)	A	8	(4)	2
György KECSKÉS	M		(1)	
Ernö KIRÁLY	A		(1)	
István KOCSIS	A	15	(11)	2
Ákos KOLLER	D	11	(1)	1
Srdjan KOSTIC (YUG)	A	1	(1)	
Sándor KOVÁCS	M	30		2
Csaba NAGY	M	10	(14)	3
Gábor NECZPÁL	M		(1)	
Gábor NÉMETH	G	20		
Mihály PLÓKAI	A	9	(7)	1
Barnabás SÁTORI	A		(4)	
Gábor SOMOGYI	A		(2)	
Suleyman SYLLA (GUI)	A	1	(2)	
András SZTRAPÁK	A	5	(3)	
Tamás TAKÁCS	G	14	(1)	
Miklós TÓTH	D	26		4
Péter TÓTH	M	18	(8)	2
Krisztián VARGA	D	15	(3)	
József VIDÓCZI	M	13	(11)	2
Péter ZUGOR	D	28	(1)	2

LEAGUE RESULTS 1998/99

25/07/98	Ferencváros	A	0-1	
01/08/98	Videoton FC Fehérvár	H	2-0	Kocsis, Kovács (p)
08/08/98	Nyírség Spartacus	A	1-2	Bodor
15/08/98	Dunaferr SE	H	0-1	
29/08/98	Kispest-Honvéd FC	H	0-2	
12/09/98	Diósgyöri FC	A	1-5	Vidóczi
16/09/98	Vasas DH	A	0-5	
20/09/98	III. Kerület FC	A	1-3	Vidóczi
26/09/98	MTK Hungária FC	H	2-1	Kocsis, Balog
03/10/98	Gázszer FC	A	0-4	
17/10/98	Siófok	H	2-1	Bodor, Plókai
24/10/98	BVSC-Zugló	A	3-0	(w/o)
31/10/98	DVSC-Epona	H	1-1	Koller
06/11/98	Újpest FC	A	0-2	
14/11/98	Györi ETO FC	H	0-1	
21/11/98	Zalahús ZTE FC	A	1-3	Nagy
28/11/98	Vác FC-Zollner	H	0-1	
07/03/99	Videoton FC Fehérvár	A	0-0	
13/03/99	Nyírség Spartacus	H	3-2	Fehér, Zugor, Bonchis
20/03/99	Dunaferr SE	A	0-2	
03/04/99	Vasas DH	H	0-0	
07/04/99	Kispest-Honvéd FC	A	0-1	
10/04/99	Diósgyöri FC	H	2-1	Balassa, Jakoba
17/04/99	III. Kerület FC	H	5-1	Balassa, Bonchis, Tóth M. 3 (1p)
21/04/99	Ferencváros	H	1-2	Jovanovic
24/04/99	MTK Hungária FC	A	4-2	Horváth, Kovács, Tóth P., Bonchis
01/05/99	Gázszer FC	H	1-1	Horváth
05/05/99	Siófok	A	0-1	
10/05/99	BVSC-Zugló	H	3-1	Jovanovic, Balassa, Tóth P.
15/05/99	DVSC-Epona	A	1-1	Nagy
22/05/99	Újpest FC	H	4-1	Zugor, Tóth M. (p), Bodor, Jakoba
29/05/99	Györi ETO FC	A	0-2	
12/06/99	Zalahús ZTE FC	H	0-0	
16/06/99	Vác FC-Zollner	A	1-3	Nagy

III. KERÜLET FC

CLUB DIRECTORY

III. Kerület FC
Kalap u. 1, 1037 Budapest
tel - (1) 3887662
fax - (1) 3887662
Year of Formation - 1951
Chairman - Konstantinos Mokalis
Coach - Ralf Wilhelms; Lajos Schróth
Stadium - Hévizi úti (10,500)

APPEARANCES 98/99

	P	Ap	(s)	Gls
Zsolt BENCZE	M	15		2
István BODOR	A	3	(3)	
Tamás BRANDHUBER	M		(3)	
Zoltán CRAVERÓ	M		(1)	
András DUNAI	A	1	(5)	1
Tamás FILÓ	D	13	(7)	
István GÁL	D	13		
Endre GÁSPÁR	D	29	(1)	3
László GUBÁN	A		(4)	
István GYURA	M	4	(7)	
Naeem JOHNSON (SAF)	M		(3)	
Péter JUHOS	A	13	(1)	3
Zoltán KECSKÉS	D	13		
Balázs KILIK	D	9	(2)	
Szabolcs KISS	G	8		
Norbert KOVÁCS	M	26	(6)	1
György KUN	M	14	(1)	2
Viktor KUTI	D	3	(4)	
Mátyás LÁZÁR	M	11	(3)	
Péter LENDVAI	A	27	(4)	8
József LIPPAI	G	13		
Tibor METZGER	D	12		
Tamás PÁLFI	D	15		
Attila SÁGI	A	3	(10)	
Ádám SCHLACHTOVSZKY	M		(1)	
László SCHULTZ	D	5	(6)	
László STRANYÓCZKY	M	4	(5)	3
Ntuthoko SYBAYA (SAF)	M	6	(1)	
András SZÖLÖSI	A		(1)	
Balázs TORDAI	M	33		3
Iván TÓTH	G	13		
Márk UGHY	M	1	(1)	
István URBÁNYI	D	2		
László VARGA	D	14		
Zoltán VÁRKONYI	M		(1)	
Gábor VINCZE	D	21	(3)	
Lafe VITTITOE (SAF)	A	1	(5)	
László WUKOVICS	A	29	(2)	10

LEAGUE RESULTS 1998/99

25/07/98	Vác FC-Zollner	A	0-1	
01/08/98	Ferencváros	H	1-2	Gáspár
07/08/98	Videoton FC Fehérvár	A	0-5	
16/08/98	Nyírség Spartacus	H	2-2	Kun, Lendvai
22/08/98	Dunaferr SE	A	0-3	
28/08/98	Vasas DH	A	3-0	(w/o; original result 0-6)
11/09/98	Kispest-Honvéd FC	A	0-2	
20/09/98	Haladás-Milos	H	3-1	Lendvai 2, Bencze
26/09/98	Diósgyöri FC	A	1-5	Wukovics
04/10/98	MTK Hungária FC	A	0-5	
18/10/98	Gázszer FC	H	2-1	Bencze, Kovács
24/10/98	Siófok	A	1-2	Kun
01/11/98	BVSC-Zugló	H	0-0	
07/11/98	DVSC-Epona	A	0-0	
14/11/98	Újpest FC	H	2-3	og (Filó), Tordai
21/11/98	Györi ETO FC	A	0-3	
29/11/98	Zalahús ZTE FC	H	0-2	
28/02/99	Vác FC-Zollner	H	2-3	Wukovics 2
06/03/99	Ferencváros	A	1-7	Lendvai
15/03/99	Videoton FC Fehérvár	H	1-2	Tordai
20/03/99	Nyírség Spartacus	A	3-3	Tordai, Wukovics, Juhos
03/04/99	Dunaferr SE	H	3-1	Wukovics 2 (1p), Juhos
07/04/99	Vasas DH	H	1-4	Lendvai
11/04/99	Kispest-Honvéd FC	H	1-1	Dunai
17/04/99	Haladás-Milos	A	1-5	Juhos
25/04/99	Diósgyöri FC	H	1-2	Wukovics
02/05/99	MTK Hungária FC	H	1-5	Lendvai
05/05/99	Gázszer FC	A	2-3	Gáspár, Wukovics
09/05/99	Siófok	H	2-3	Gáspár, Wukovics
16/05/99	BVSC-Zugló	A	0-3	
24/05/99	DVSC-Epona	H	1-5	Stranyóczky
29/05/99	Újpest FC	A	1-4	Lendvai
12/06/99	Györi ETO FC	H	3-3	Stranyóczky 2, Lendvai
16/06/99	Zalahús ZTE FC	A	1-2	Wukovics

KISPEST-HONVÉD FC

CLUB DIRECTORY

Kispest-Honvéd Fútball Club
Újtemetö u. 1-3
1194 Budapest
tel - (1) 2807240
fax - (1) 2829791
Year of Formation - 1909
Chairman - László Benkö
Coach - György Gálhidi (99/00 - Imre Komora)
Stadium - József Bozsik (15,000)

MAJOR HONOURS

League Championship - (13) 1950, 1950
(autumn), 1952, 1954, 1955, 1980, 1984,
1985, 1986, 1988, 1989, 1991, 1993.
Domestic Cup - (5)
1926, 1964, 1985, 1989, 1996.

APPEARANCES 98/99

		P	Ap	(s)	Gls
Catalin AZOITEI (ROM)	A	3	(5)	2
Zoltán BÁNFÖLDI	M	22	(3)	2
István BORGULYA	A	29		12
Zoltán CIPF	M	1		
József CSÁBI	D	18	(3)	
István CSEKE	M	3	(7)	1
Aurél CSERTÖI	A	12	(7)	1
János DUBECZ	M	30	(1)	2
András FARKAS	D	5	(2)	1
Krisztián GABALA	D	29	(1)	6
Zoltán HERCEGFALVI	M	4	(4)	1
Richárd HOLLÓ	A	1	(16)	
Gábor HUNGLER	D	21	(2)	
Péter KABÁT	A	26	(3)	6
Mansour KANE (SEN)	A	1	(4)	
Róbert LÓCZI	M	12	(4)	
László MEDGYESI	D	15		
Krisztián MÜLLER	D	10		
László NÉMETHY	M	6	(6)	
Zoltán PINTÉR	M	15	(5)	
Attila PLÓKAI	D	30		3
Ferenc ROTT	G	4	(2)	
László SCHULTZ	D	6	(4)	
Szilárd SIPOS	M	1	(2)	
Róbert SZÁNTÓ	M	10	(2)	1
Philip TARLUE (LIB)	M	11		
László TÖRÖK	A	4	(5)	
Meziane TOUATI (ALG)	A		(1)	
Ádám VEZÉR	G	30		
János ZOVÁTH	M	15		

LEAGUE RESULTS 1998/99

24/07/98	Videoton FC Fehérvár	A	1-0	Borgulya (p)
31/07/99	Nyírség Spartacus	H	4-3	Borgulya 2 (1p), Gabala, Cseke
08/08/98	Dunaferr SE	A	1-2	Plókai
14/08/98	Vasas DH	H	0-4	
22/08/98	Diósgyöri FC	A	0-0	
29/08/98	Haladás-Milos	A	2-0	Borgulya, Bánföldi
11/09/98	III. Kerület FC	H	2-0	Gabala, Kabát
21/09/98	MTK Hungária FC	A	0-3	
25/09/98	Gázszer FC	H	1-3	Kabát
03/10/98	Siófok	A	1-1	Szántó
17/10/98	BVSC-Zugló	H	1-5	Kabát
24/10/98	DVSC-Epona	A	2-0	Borgulya, Farkas
31/10/98	Újpest FC	H	2-3	Bánföldi, Csertöi
07/11/98	Györi ETO FC	A	2-2	Azoitei 2 (1p)
14/11/98	Zalahús ZTE FC	H	0-1	
21/11/98	Vác FC-Zollner	A	1-4	Plókai (p)
28/11/98	Ferencváros	H	2-2	Borgulya 2
01/03/99	Videoton FC Fehérvár	H	0-0	
06/03/99	Nyírség Spartacus	A	0-3	
15/03/99	Dunaferr SE	H	0-0	
21/03/99	Vasas DH	A	1-2	Gabala
03/04/99	Diósgyöri FC	H	3-0	Gabala, Dubecz 2
07/04/99	Haladás-Milos	H	1-0	Borgulya
11/04/99	III. Kerület FC	A	1-1	Gabala
17/04/99	MTK Hungária FC	H	0-2	
24/04/99	Gázszer FC	A	0-0	
30/04/99	Siófok	H	3-0	Borgulya, Gabala, Kabát
05/05/99	BVSC-Zugló	A	0-3	
10/05/99	DVSC-Epona	H	0-0	
17/05/99	Újpest FC	A	0-3	
22/05/99	Györi ETO FC	H	4-0	Plókai, Borgulya 2, Hercegfalvi
29/05/99	Zalahús ZTE FC	A	0-2	
12/06/99	Vác FC-Zollner	H	2-1	Kabát 2
16/06/99	Ferencváros	A	1-0	Borgulya

MTK HUNGÁRIA FC

CLUB DIRECTORY

MTK Hungária FC
Salgótarjáni út 12-14
1087 Budapest
tel - (1) 3030590
fax - (1) 3338368
Year of Formation - 1888
Chairman - Gábor Várszegi
Coach - Sándor Egervári (99/00 - Henk ten Cate)
Stadium - Hungária úti (12,000)

MAJOR HONOURS
League Championship - (21)
1904, 1908, 1914, 1917, 1918, 1919, 1920,
1921, 1922, 1923, 1924, 1925, 1929, 1936,
1937, 1951, 1953, 1958, 1987, 1997, 1999.
Domestic Cup - (11) 1910, 1911, 1912, 1914,
1923, 1925, 1932, 1952, 1968, 1997, 1998.

APPEARANCES 98/99

		P	Ap	(s)	Gls
Ádám BABOS	M	7	(8)		
Gábor BABOS	G	30			
Iván BALASKÓ	M	14	(17)	5	
Csaba CSORDÁS	A		(9)		
Péter CZVITKOVICS	M		(3)		
Norbert ELEK	D	7	(5)		
Károly ERÖS	M	29	(2)	3	
Viktor FARKAS	D	3	(4)	1	
Gilberto GIBA (BRA)	M		(2)		
Gábor HALMAI	M	30		3	
Béla ILLÉS	M	30		22	
Krisztián KENESEI	A	29	(2)	12	
Péter KINCSES	A	1	(2)		
Ádám KOMLÓSI	D	27	(1)		
Gábor KOROLOVSZKY	D		(4)		
Kearoly KOVACSICS	A	1	(1)		
József KOZMA	M	1	(2)		
Mihály LIPCSEI	A		(3)		
Emil LÖRINCZ	D	25		1	
Csaba MADAR	M	32		4	
Zoltán MOLNÁR	D	26			
Ferenc OROSZ	A	9	(6)	7	
Sándor PREISINGER	A	19	(8)	11	
Balázs RABÓCZKI	G	4			
Tamás SZAMOSI	D	29	(2)		
István SZEKÉR	D	10	(2)	1	
Tamás SZEKERES	D	11	(4)	3	

LEAGUE RESULTS 1998/99

25/07/98	Zalahús ZTE FC	A	1-0	Orosz
01/08/98	Vác FC-Zollner	H	3-1	Illés 3
07/08/98	Ferencváros	A	2-2	Kenesei, Halmai
16/08/98	Videoton FC Fehérvár	H	2-1	Preisinger, Illés
22/08/98	Nyírség Spartacus	A	3-1	Szekeres, Illés 2
30/08/98	Dunaferr SE	H	3-0	Illés, Kenesei 2
12/09/98	Vasas DH	A	4-0	Balaskó 2, Illés (p), Kenesei
21/09/98	Kispest-Honvéd FC	H	3-0	Szekeres, Orosz, Kenesei
26/09/98	Haladás-Milos	A	1-2	Illés
04/10/98	III. Kerület FC	H	5-0	Illés 2 (1p), Szekeres, Preisinger, og (Kecskés)
17/10/98	Diósgyöri FC	A	1-1	Madar
25/10/98	Gázszer FC	A	3-1	Illés, Madar, Kenesei
31/10/98	Siófok	H	1-0	Kenesei
08/11/98	BVSC-Zugló	A	2-0	Balaskó 2
14/11/98	DVSC-Epona	H	1-2	Balaskó
21/11/98	Újpest FC	A	2-1	Preisinger, Kenesei
28/11/98	Györi ETO FC	H	4-1	Erös, Preisinger, Kenesei, Illés
27/02/99	Zalahús ZTE FC	H	2-1	Illés, Kenesei
06/03/99	Vác FC-Zollner	A	2-1	Preisinger, og (Nagy)
13/03/99	Ferencváros	H	2-0	Kenesei, Madar
20/03/99	Videoton FC Fehérvár	A	1-0	og (Filipovic)
03/04/99	Nyírség Spartacus	H	2-0	Kenesei, Halmai
07/04/99	Dunaferr SF	A	3-0	Preisinger 2, Orosz
10/04/99	Vasas DH	H	2-0	Szekér, Halmai
17/04/99	Kispest-Honvéd FC	A	2-0	Illés 2
24/04/99	Haladás-Milos	H	2-4	Preisinger 2
02/05/99	III. Kerület FC	A	5-1	Orosz 3, Lörincz, Illés
05/05/99	Diósgyöri FC	H	4-0	Illés 2, Preisinger 2
08/05/99	Gázszer FC	H	2-0	Illés (p), Orosz
15/05/99	Siófok	A	1-0	Erös
23/05/99	BVSC-Zugló	H	3-2	Erös, Illés, Madar
29/05/99	DVSC-Epona	A	1-3	Illés
12/06/99	Újpest FC	H	2-0	og (Urbán), Farkas
16/06/99	Györi ETO FC	A	0-1	

NYÍRSÉG-SPARTACUS FC

CLUB DIRECTORY

Nyírség-Spartacus FC
Sóstói út 24/A
4400 Nyíregyháza
tel - (42) 402618
fax - (42) 402618
Year of Formation - 1928
Chairman - János Kulimár
Coach - Tibor Öze
Stadium - Sóstói (18,000)

APPEARANCES 98/99

	P	Ap	(s)	Gls
Gusztáv ÁCS	D	31	(1)	1
Catalin AZOITEI (ROM)	A	4	(11)	1
Zoltán BALÁZSY	G	1		
Miklós BARANYI	A	22	(5)	6
Miklós BARNA	D	3	(3)	
Gyula BESSENYEI	M	2	(10)	
Valeriy CAP (UKR)	D	9	(1)	
Valeri CAPATINA (MOL)	A		(2)	
Danco CELESKI (MAC)	G	29		
Máté GERLICZKI	D	2	(4)	1
Bertalan GÖNCZ	M	12	(4)	
Decebal GRADINARIU (ROM)	M	10	(2)	3
Milos JANIC (YUG)	A	5	(4)	1
Anasztáz KARKUSZ	M	29	(1)	2
Tibor KIRCHMAYER	M	22	(10)	9
György KISS	D	31	(1)	3
József KONDORA	M	28	(1)	2
Barnabás LÁSZLÓ	D	10	(13)	
Sasa MARKOVIC (YUG)	D	2	(1)	
Tibor MÁRKUS	A	1	(4)	
Sándor NAGY	D	22	(4)	3
János NOVÁK	A	26	(3)	2
István SIRA	A	9	(3)	
Attila SZABÓ	M	27	(6)	5
Zoltán SZATKE	D	33		7
Attila SZÉCSI	A		(1)	
Lajos VADON	G	4	(1)	

LEAGUE RESULTS 1998/99

Date	Opponent	H/A	Score	Scorers
25/07/98	Vasas DH	H	0-2	
31/07/98	Kispest-Honvéd FC	A	3-4	Szabó, Kirchmayer (p), Baranyi
08/08/98	Haladás-Milos	H	2-1	Kirchmayer (p), Kondora
16/08/98	III. Kerület FC	A	2-2	Szatke, Baranyi
22/08/98	MTK Hungária FC	H	1-3	Kirchmayer
29/08/98	Gázszer FC	A	0-0	
12/09/98	Siófok	H	3-1	Janics, Szatke, Kirchmayer (p)
19/09/98	BVSC-Zugló	A	0-0	
26/09/98	DVSC-Epona	H	4-2	Kiss, Kirchmayer (p), Novák, Kondora
03/10/98	Újpest FC	A	0-1	
17/10/98	Győri ETO FC	H	0-0	
24/10/98	Zalahús ZTE FC	A	0-1	
31/10/98	Vác FC-Zollner	H	3-4	Kirchmayer (p), Szatke, Novák
07/11/98	Ferencváros	A	1-2	Szatke
14/11/98	Videoton FC Fehérvár	H	4-2	Kirchmayer 2 (2p), Szatke, Gradinariu
21/11/98	Diósgyőri FC	H	3-1	Kiss, Szatke, Baranyi
28/11/98	Dunaferr SE	A	1-6	Nagy
27/02/99	Vasas DH	A	1-1	Karkusz
06/03/99	Kispest-Honvéd FC	H	3-0	Gradinariu 2, Szabó
13/03/99	Haladás-Milos	A	2-3	Szabó, Kirchmayer
20/03/99	III. Kerület FC	H	3-3	Azoitei, Szabó, Nagy
03/04/99	MTK Hungária FC	A	0-2	
07/04/99	Gázszer FC	H	0-0	
12/04/99	Siófok	A	1-1	Gerliczki
17/04/99	BVSC-Zugló	H	1-0	Szabó
24/04/99	DVSC-Epona	A	0-2	
01/05/99	Újpest FC	H	0-2	
05/05/99	Győri ETO FC	A	1-0	Ács
08/05/99	Zalahús ZTE FC	H	2-0	Baranyi 2
15/05/99	Vác FC-Zollner	A	2-2	Karkusz, Baranyi
23/05/99	Ferencváros	H	0-1	
29/05/99	Videoton FC Fehérvár	A	0-1	
12/06/99	Diósgyőri FC	A	0-1	
16/06/99	Dunaferr SE	H	3-1	Szatke, Nagy, Kiss

SIÓFOK

Siófoki Bányász SE
Révész Géza u. 1
8600 Siófok
tel - (84) 312443
fax - (84) 312443
Year of Formation - 1921
Chairman - János Illés
Coach - László Nagy; József Mészáros
(99/00 - László Borbély)
Stadium - Bányász (12,000)

MAJOR HONOURS
Domestic Cup - (1) 1984.

	P	Ap	(s)	Gls
Tamás BIMBÓ	D	31		
György BOZSÉR	M	12	(6)	
Tamás CSÁK	M		(2)	
Norbert CSOKNAY (SVK)	M	14	(2)	1
Csaba FELFÖLDI	M	1	(3)	
János GYÖRI	M	28		3
Viktor HANÁK	A		(2)	
Tameas JUHÁSZ	D	24	(2)	
Gábor KASZA	A	1	(5)	
Béla KOVÁCS	M	30	(1)	3
György KUN	M	5	(8)	
András LÁSZLÓ	D	32		
Zoltán LUKÁCS	A	14	(1)	6
Tibor MÁRKUS	A	5	(10)	
József ÖRDÖG	A	21	(6)	
András PERGER	D	22	(3)	1
Krisztián PEST	A	14	(7)	3
Roland PEST	A	8		2
Zsolt POSZA	G	34		
Tibor SALLAI	M	33		1
Krisztián SOÓS	M	7	(20)	1
Csaba SZABADI	D	14	(9)	
Sándor SZABÓ	A		(3)	
Zoltán SZABÓ	A	24	(1)	9

25/07/98	Újpest FC	A	1-2	Szabó Z.
01/08/98	Györi ETO FC	H	1-2	Szabó Z.
08/08/98	Zalahús ZTE FC	A	2-2	Szabó Z., Pest R.
15/08/98	Vác FC-Zollner	H	2-4	Kovács, Györi
22/08/98	Ferencváros	A	0-2	
29/08/98	Videoton FC Fehérvár	H	0-0	
12/09/98	Nyírség Spartacus	A	1-3	Györi
19/09/98	Dunaferr SE	H	0-1	
26/09/98	Vasas DH	A	0-0	
03/10/98	Kispest-Honvéd FC	H	1-1	Szabó Z.
17/10/98	Haladás-Milos	A	1-2	Pest R.
24/10/98	III. Kerület FC	H	2-1	Kovács, Györi
31/10/98	MTK Hungária FC	A	0-1	
07/11/98	Gázszer FC	H	2-2	Szabó Z. 2
14/11/98	Diósgyöri FC	A	1-1	Perger
21/11/98	BVSC-Zugló	A	1-0	Szabó Z.
28/11/98	DVSC-Epona	H	0-1	
27/02/99	Újpest FC	H	0-2	
06/03/99	Györi ETO FC	A	1-1	Lukács
13/03/99	Zalahús ZTE FC	H	0-2	
20/03/99	Vác FC-Zollner	A	2-0	og (Nagy), Kovács
03/04/99	Ferencváros	H	0-2	
07/04/99	Videoton FC Fehérvár	A	1-1	Szabó Z.
12/04/99	Nyírség Spartacus	H	1-1	Lukács
17/04/99	Dunaferr SE	A	1-2	Lukács
24/04/99	Vasas DH	H	2-3	Csoknay, Sallai
30/04/99	Kispest-Honvéd FC	A	0-3	
05/05/99	Haladás-Milos	H	1-0	Szabó Z.
09/05/99	III. Kerület FC	A	3-2	Lukács, Pest K. 2
15/05/99	MTK Hungária FC	H	0-1	
22/05/99	Gázszer FC	A	3-1	og (Simek), Pest K., Soós
29/05/99	Diósgyöri FC	H	2-1	Lukács
12/06/99	BVSC-Zugló	H	0-1	
16/06/99	DVSC-Epona	A	0-1	

ÚJPEST FC

CLUB DIRECTORY

Újpest FC
Megyeri út 13
1043 Budapest
tel - (1) 1687333
fax - (1) 1428432
Year of Formation - 1885
Chairman - Bence Szabó
Coach - Péter Várhidi
Stadium - Megyeri út (30,000)

MAJOR HONOURS
League Championship - (20)
1930, 1931, 1933, 1935, 1939, 1945, 1946,
1947, 1960, 1969, 1970, 1971, 1972, 1973,
1974, 1975, 1978, 1979, 1990, 1998.
Domestic Cup - (7) 1969, 1970, 1975, 1982,
1983, 1987, 1992.

APPEARANCES 98/99

	P	Ap	(s)	Gls
Balázs BÉRCZY	D		(5)	
Szabolcs BÍRÓ	G	34		
Dénes ESZENYI	A		(9)	2
Csaba FEHÉR	M	24		1
Miklós HERCZEG	A	30	(2)	4
Sándor JENEI	M	14	(5)	1
Norbert KERÉNYI	D	1	(2)	
Balázs KISKAPUSI	D	18	(6)	
Goran KOPUNOVIC (YUG)	A	7	(19)	5
Attila KORSÓS	A	25	(3)	13
Balázs KOVÁCS	M	12	(2)	
Zoltán KOVÁCS	A	26	(3)	10
István KOZMA	M	4		
Krisztián KVASZ	M	7	(8)	2
Zsolt LÖW	D	1	(1)	
József MOGYORÓSI	D	2		
Norbert NÉMEDI	D		(2)	
Tamás PETÖ	M	28		3
Vilmos SEBÖK	D	12		4
Levente SZÁNTAI	G		(1)	
Károly SZANYÓ	M	14	(10)	4
Tamás SZEKERES	D	15		3
Zoltán SZÉLESI	M	1	(2)	
Zoltán SZLEZÁK	D	29		
Zoltán TAMÁSI	D	23	(1)	1
Lajos TERJÉK	A	1	(1)	
Tibor TOKODY	M	1	(1)	
Norbert TÓTH	M	30	(1)	2
Flórián URBÁN	D	15		2

LEAGUE RESULTS 1998/99

25/07/98	Siófok	H	2-1	Sebök, Kovács Z.
01/08/98	BVSC-Zugló	A	3-0	Korsós 3
08/08/98	DVSC-Epona	H	3-2	Kovács Z. 2, Korsós
15/08/98	Diósgyöri FC	H	1-3	Kopunovic
22/08/98	Györi ETO FC	A	1-3	Szanyó
29/08/98	Zalahús ZTE FC	H	2-2	Kovács Z., Sebök
11/09/98	Vác FC-Zollner	A	3-4	Szanyó, Jenei, Kopunovic
19/09/98	Ferencváros	H	2-1	Tamási, Herczeg
26/09/98	Videoton FC Fehérvár	A	0-0	
03/10/98	Nyírség Spartacus	H	1-0	Tóth
17/10/98	Dunaferr SE	A	0-2	
24/10/98	Vasas DH	H	2-0	Kovács Z., Petö
31/10/98	Kispest-Honvéd FC	A	3-2	Petö, Herczeg, Korsós
06/11/98	Haladás-Milos	H	2-0	Sebök (p), Kvasz
14/11/98	III. Kerület FC	A	3-2	Eszenyi 2 (1p), og (Filó)
21/11/98	MTK Hungária FC	H	1-2	Sebök
28/11/98	Gázszer FC	A	1-2	Kopunovic
27/02/99	Siófok	A	2-0	Korsós, Kovács Z.
06/03/99	BVSC-Zugló	H	3-1	Korsós, Fehér, Kvasz
13/03/99	DVSC-Epona	A	2-0	Herczeg, Kovács Z.
20/03/99	Diósgyöri FC	A	1-1	Szekeres
03/04/99	Györi ETO FC	H	1-2	Urbán
07/04/99	Zalahús ZTE FC	A	1-0	Korsós
10/04/99	Vác FC-Zollner	H	2-0	Korsós 2
17/04/99	Ferencváros	A	0-1	
24/04/99	Videoton FC Fehérvár	H	1-0	Tóth
01/05/99	Nyírség Spartacus	A	2-0	Korsós, Kopunovic
05/05/99	Dunaferr SE	H	3-0	Kovács Z. 2, Korsós
09/05/99	Vasas DH	A	0-1	
17/05/99	Kispest-Honvéd FC	H	3-0	Szekeres, Korsós, Urbán (p)
22/05/99	Haladás-Milos	A	1-4	Petö
29/05/99	III. Kerület FC	H	4-1	Herczeg, Szekeres, Szanyó 2
12/06/99	MTK Hungária FC	A	0-2	
16/06/99	Gázszer FC	H	2-1	Kopunovic, Kovács Z.

VASAS DH

CLUB DIRECTORY

Vasas Danubius Hotels
Fáy u. 58
1139 Budapest
tel - (1) 1294074
fax - (1) 1296073
Year of Formation - 1944
Chairman - András Gyalog
Coach - Imre Gellei (99/00 - András Komjáti)
Stadium - Fáy útcai (18,000)

MAJOR HONOURS
League Championship - (6)
1957, 1961, 1962, 1965, 1966, 1977.
Domestic Cup - (4) 1955, 1973, 1981, 1986.

APPEARANCES 98/99

		P	Ap	(s)	Gls
Imre ARANYOS	D	22	(4)	1	
Gábor EIPL	D		(1)		
László FARKASHÁZY	M	26	(3)	3	
Péter GALASCHEK	M	31			
Zoltán GERESS	D	12	(1)		
Anatoliy GRITSAYUK (UKR)	M	7	(5)		
Attila GRÓF	G	1	(2)		
Ferenc HÁMORI	A	27	(2)	10	
Csaba HERCZEG	D	3	(4)		
Tamás JUHÁR	D	26	(1)	5	
Tamás KOLTAI	A	3	(12)	1	
Miklós MACZÓ	D	17	(8)		
Tamás MÓNOS	M	33		1	
Krisztián NYERGES	A		(14)		
Zoltán PÁL	A	29		12	
Balázs SALLAI	M		(2)		
Thomas SOWUNMI	A	8	(10)	7	
Ferenc SZILVESZTER	M	25	(4)	3	
András TÓTH	D	28	(1)		
Zoltán VÁCZI	M	22	(4)	7	
Zoltán VÉGH	G	33			
Zalán ZOMBORI	M	21	(5)	1	

LEAGUE RESULTS 1998/99

25/07/98	Nyírség Spartacus	A	2-0	Hámori, Pál
01/08/98	Dunaferr SE	H	3-2	Pál, Hámori 2
08/08/98	Diósgyöri FC	A	2-4	Pál, Aranyos
14/08/98	Kispest-Honvéd FC	A	4-0	Farkasházy, Váczi, Szilveszter, Hámori
29/08/98	III. Kerület FC	H	0-3	(w/o; original result 6-0 Váczi 2, Hámori, Pál, Farkasházy, Aranyos)
12/09/98	MTK Hungária FC	H	0-4	
16/09/98	Haladás-Milos	H	5-0	Pál 2, Szilveszter, Váczi, Hámori
19/09/98	Gázszer FC	A	1-1	Pál
26/09/98	Siófok	H	0-0	
03/10/98	BVSC-Zugló	A	2-1	Farkasházy, Hámori
17/10/98	DVSC-Epona	H	2-0	Váczi 2
24/10/98	Újpest FC	A	0-2	
31/10/98	Györi ETO FC	H	1-4	Hámori
07/11/98	Zalahús ZTE FC	A	0-1	
14/11/98	Vác FC-Zollner	H	0-0	
21/11/98	Ferencváros	A	1-3	Pál
28/11/98	Videoton FC Fehérvár	H	2-1	Juhár, Váczi
27/02/99	Nyírség Spartacus	H	1-1	Farkasházy
06/03/99	Dunaferr SE	A	1-2	Váczi
14/03/99	Diósgyöri FC	H	0-0	
21/03/99	Kispest-Honvéd FC	H	2-1	Hámori, Juhár
03/04/99	Haladás-Milos	A	0-0	
07/04/99	III. Kerület FC	A	4-1	Pál 2, Koltai, Hámori
10/04/99	MTK Hungária FC	A	0-2	
17/04/99	Gázszer FC	H	2-0	Zombori, Juhár
24/04/99	Siófok	A	3-2	Szilveszter, Juhár, Sowunmi
01/05/99	BVSC-Zugló	H	3-2	Juhár (p), Pál, Sowunmi
05/05/99	DVSC-Epona	A	0-0	
09/05/99	Újpest FC	H	1-0	Sowunmi
15/05/99	Györi ETO FC	A	3-3	Sowunmi, Pál 2
22/05/99	Zalahús ZTE FC	H	1-0	Sowunmi
29/05/99	Vác FC-Zollner	A	1-1	Váczi
12/06/99	Ferencváros	H	2-1	Mónos, Sowunmi
16/06/99	Videoton FC Fehérvár	A	2-2	Sowunmi, Hámori

VÁC FC-ZOLLNER

CLUB DIRECTORY

Vác FC-Zollner
Stadion u. 2
2600 Vác
tel - (27) 314795
fax - (27) 314324
Year of Formation - 1889
Chairman - István Lajtai
Coach - János Csank (99/00 - Károly Kis)
Stadium - Városi (12,000)

MAJOR HONOURS
League Championship - (1) 1994.

APPEARANCES 98/99

	P	Ap	(s)	Gls
Csaba ANDRÁSSY (ROM)	A	4	(16)	1
Tibor BÁBIK	M	1	(15)	1
József BODA	D	1	(5)	
Attila BURZI	A	3	(2)	
Antal FÜLE	A	25	(3)	5
Zsolt GREZSÁK	A	1	(5)	
Attila HADÁR	A		(1)	
Sándor HALÁSZ	G	10		
István HÁMORI	G	24		
Péter HORVÁTH	A	31		9
István KASZA	D	27	(2)	
Velibor KOPUNOVIC (YUG)	A	10	(5)	
Péter KOVÁCS	M	14	(3)	2
Gábor KRISKA	M	1	(4)	
András LÉVAI	D	30		3
Tibor NAGY	D	31		6
József NYIKOS	M	25		
Kornél ROB	A	7	(5)	5
János ROMANEK	M	23	(7)	1
Zoltán SCHWARCZ	M	20		5
István SIPEKI	M	11	(9)	2
Tamás UDVARI	D	4		
Gábor VÉN	M	25	(4)	2
Zoltán VITELKI	M	15	(13)	3
Csaba VOJTEJOVSZKI	M	31		4

LEAGUE RESULTS 1998/99

25/07/98	III. Kerület FC	H	1-0	Füle
01/08/99	MTK Hungária FC	A	1-3	Vojtekovszki
08/08/98	Gázszer FC	H	1-1	Vitelki
15/08/98	Siófok	A	4-2	Horváth 2, Nagy, Vén
22/08/98	BVSC-Zugló	H	1-0	Schwarcz
29/08/98	DVSC-Epona	A	1-2	Vojtekovszki (p)
11/09/98	Újpest FC	H	4-3	Vojtekovszki, Schwarcz, Füle, Lévai
19/09/98	Györi ETO FC	A	0-1	
26/09/98	Zalahús ZTE FC	H	2-2	Horváth, Schwarcz
03/10/98	Diósgyöri FC	H	1-3	Schwarcz
17/10/98	Ferencváros	A	2-2	Horváth, Nagy (p)
24/10/98	Videoton FC Fehérvár	H	2-1	Horváth, Nagy
31/10/98	Nyírség Spartacus	A	4-3	Lévai, Vojtekovszki, Horváth, Vitelki
07/11/98	Dunaferr SE	H	1-0	og (Lengyel)
14/11/98	Vasas DH	A	0-0	
21/11/98	Kispest-Honvéd FC	H	4-1	Horváth, Rob, Vitelki, Vén
28/11/98	Haladás-Milos	A	1-0	Füle (p)
28/02/99	III. Kerület FC	A	3-2	Horváth, Füle, Kovács
06/03/99	MTK Hungária FC	H	1-2	Romanek
13/03/99	Gázszer FC	A	0-1	
20/03/99	Siófok	H	0-2	
02/04/99	BVSC-Zugló	A	1-2	Kovács
07/04/99	DVSC-Epona	H	1-1	Füle
10/04/99	Újpest FC	A	0-2	
18/04/99	Györi ETO FC	H	1-0	Sipeki
24/04/99	Zalahús ZTE FC	A	2-2	Horváth, Nagy
01/05/99	Diósgyöri FC	A	1-0	Rob
05/05/99	Ferencváros	H	1-1	Schwarcz
08/05/99	Videoton FC Fehérvár	A	2-3	Rob, Bábik
15/05/99	Nyírség Spartacus	H	2-2	Rob, Lévai
22/05/99	Dunaferr SE	A	1-1	Rob
29/05/99	Vasas DH	H	1-1	og (Maczó)
12/06/99	Kispest-Honvéd FC	A	1-2	Nagy (p)
16/06/99	Haladás-Milos	H	3-1	Andrássy, Sipeki, Nagy

VIDEOTON FC FEHÉRVÁR

Videoton FC Fehérvár
Csíkvári u.10, 8000 Székesfehérvár
tel - (22) 319055
fax - (22) 319057
Year of Formation - 1941
Chairman - dr. László Bérces
Coach - Ferenc Csongrádi; József Verebes
(99/00 - János Csank)
Stadium - Sóstói (18,200)

	P	Ap	(s)	Gls
Ákos BARVA	A	3		
Balázs BOBORY	A	2	(4)	
Tamás CSORDÁS	D	11		1
Zoran DJURISIC (YUG)	A	4	(4)	1
Gábor FÉSŰ	D	2	(1)	
Vladan FILIPOVIC (YUG)	M	2	(5)	
Gergely FOGARASI	A	1	(5)	
Tamás GYÖRÖK	M	4	(16)	
Attila HORVÁTH	D	2	(5)	
Csaba HORVÁTH	M	14		
Zsolt KELLNER	D	2	(2)	
István KISS	A	10	(3)	1
István KOZMA	D	14		1
Zoran KUNTIC (YUG)	A	14	(2)	
Attila KUTTOR	D	13		4
Csaba LÁSZLÓ	D	2	(1)	
Mátyás LÁZÁR	M	5	(5)	1
Zoltán LUKÁCS	A	9	(2)	3
Viktor MAKRITSKIY (UKR)	D	14		
Zsolt MÁRIÁSI	M	10	(1)	1
Árpád MESTER	D	8	(7)	
Krisztián MIKÓCZI	A	4	(2)	
Árpád MILINTE	G	33		
István MITRING	G	1		
Lajos NAGY	M	16		2
Vladimir PETRIC (YUG)	M	6	(1)	
Dragan PUSKÁS (YUG)	M	12		
Ferenc RÓTH	A	12	(5)	
Szabolcs SCHINDLER	D	20	(6)	
Tamás SCHNEIDER	D	5	(3)	
Tamás SZALAI	M	15	(4)	
László SZILÁGYI	M		(5)	
Attila TÓTH	D	25	(1)	1
Valdas URBONAS (LAT)	D	10	(1)	
Miklós VANCSA	M	19	(1)	4
Róbert WALTNER	A	24	(8)	12
Gyula ZSIVÓCZKY	M	26		4

24/07/98	Kispest-Honvéd FC	H	0-1	
01/08/98	Haladás-Milos	A	0-2	
07/08/98	III. Kerület FC	H	5-0	Lukács 2, Tóth, Waltner 2
16/08/98	MTK Hungária FC	A	1-2	Lukács
23/08/98	Gázszer FC	H	0-2	
29/08/98	Siófok	A	0-0	
12/09/98	BVSC-Zugló	H	4-1	Zsivóczky, Vancsa, Máriási, Lázár
19/09/98	DVSC-Epona	A	0-5	
26/09/98	Újpest FC	H	0-0	
03/10/98	Györi ETO FC	A	0-3	
18/10/98	Zalahús ZTE FC	H	1-2	Csordás
24/10/98	Vác FC-Zollner	A	1-2	Waltner
31/10/98	Ferencváros	H	1-3	Djurisic
07/11/98	Diósgyöri FC	H	2-3	Waltner 2
14/11/98	Nyírség Spartacus	A	2-4	Waltner 2
21/11/98	Dunaferr SE	H	4-4	Vancsa 2, Waltner 2 (1p)
28/11/98	Vasas DH	A	1-2	Waltner
01/03/99	Kispest-Honvéd FC	A	0-0	
07/03/99	Haladás-Milos	H	0-0	
15/03/99	III. Kerület FC	A	2-1	Waltner, Nagy
20/03/99	MTK Hungária FC	H	0-1	
03/04/99	Gázszer FC	A	0-0	
07/04/99	Siófok	H	1-1	Vancsa
10/04/99	BVSC-Zugló	A	1-0	Zsivóczky
17/04/99	DVSC-Epona	H	1-0	Kuttor
24/04/99	Újpest FC	A	0-1	
01/05/99	Györi ETO FC	H	0-0	
05/05/99	Zalahús ZTE FC	A	2-4	Zsivóczky 2
08/05/99	Vác FC-Zollner	H	3-2	Waltner, Kiss, Nagy
16/05/99	Ferencváros	A	0-2	
24/05/99	Diósgyöri FC	A	0-1	
29/05/99	Nyírség Spartacus	H	1-0	Kuttor
12/06/99	Dunaferr SE	A	1-3	Kuttor
16/06/99	Vasas DH	H	2-2	Kuttor, Kozma (p)

ZALAHÚS ZTE FC

CLUB DIRECTORY

Zalahús ZTE FC
Október 6. tér 16
8900 Zalaegerszeg
tel - (92) 314090
Year of Formation - 1920
Chairman - László Zalatnai
Coach - László Strausz (99/00 - Barnabás Tornyi)
Stadium - Városi (20,000)

APPEARANCES 98/99

	P	Ap	(s)	Gls
László ARANY	M	17	(7)	5
Ferenc BABATI	A	23	(8)	
Cornel CASOLTAN (ROM)	A	19	(10)	6
Zsolt CSÓKA	D	23	(8)	1
István FERENCZI	A	23	(1)	8
Attila FILÓ	D	29		1
László GAÁL	M		(1)	
Attila KÁMÁN	A	5	(12)	5
Gergely KOCSÁRDI	D	24	(1)	
Attila MOLNÁR	M		(4)	
Balázs MOLNÁR	M	28	(2)	1
Attila NAGY	M		(1)	
Tamás NÉMETH	M	28	(4)	1
József SEBÖK	A	32		7
Csaba SOMFALVI	M	12	(7)	
László STRASSER	D	15	(5)	1
Zsolt SZABÓ I	D	20	(2)	1
Zsolt SZABÓ II	M	23	(6)	5
Péter SZÖKE	M	18	(8)	
Zoltán TÓTH	A		(10)	
Tamás VARGA	M	1	(4)	
Géza VLASZÁK	G	34		

LEAGUE RESULTS 1998/99

25/07/98	MTK Hungária FC	H	0-1	
01/08/98	Gázszer FC	A	0-2	
08/08/98	Siófok	H	2-2	Csóka, Kámán
15/08/98	BVSC-Zugló	A	1-1	Sebök
22/08/98	DVSC-Epona	H	3-0	Strasser, Németh, Sebök (p)
29/08/98	Újpest FC	A	2-2	Szabó II, Kámán
12/09/98	Györi ETO FC	H	2-1	Filó, Arany
19/09/98	Diósgyöri FC	H	2-1	Arany, Casoltan
26/09/98	Vác FC-Zollner	A	2-2	Szabó I, Kámán (p)
03/10/98	Ferencváros	H	1-1	Ferenczi
28/10/98	Videoton FC Fehérvár	A	2-1	Sebök, Ferenczi
24/10/98	Nyírség Spartacus	H	1-0	og (Cap)
31/10/98	Dunaferr SE	A	0-2	
07/11/98	Vasas DH	H	1-0	Szabó II
14/11/98	Kispest-Honvéd FC	A	1-0	Casoltan
21/11/98	Haladás-Milos	H	3-1	Ferenczi, Szabó II, Casoltan
28/11/98	III. Kerület FC	A	2-0	Casoltan, Arany
27/02/99	MTK Hungária FC	A	1-2	Casoltan
06/03/99	Gázszer FC	H	2-0	Sebök, Arany
13/03/99	Siófok	A	2-0	Molnár B., Sebök
20/03/99	BVSC-Zugló	H	2-0	Ferenczi, Szabó II
03/04/99	DVSC-Epona	A	0-2	
07/04/99	Újpest FC	H	0-1	
10/04/99	Györi ETO FC	A	0-1	
19/04/99	Diósgyöri FC	A	1-1	Kámán
24/04/99	Vác FC-Zollner	H	2-2	Casoltan, Kámán (p)
01/05/99	Ferencváros	A	0-4	
05/05/99	Videoton FC Fehérvár	H	4-2	Ferenczi 3, Arany
08/05/99	Nyírség Spartacus	A	0-2	
15/05/99	Dunaferr SE	H	0-1	
22/05/99	Vasas DH	A	0-1	
29/05/99	Kispest-Honvéd FC	H	2-0	Szabó II, Sebök
12/06/99	Haladás-Milos	A	0-0	
16/06/99	III. Kerület FC	H	2-1	Ferenczi, Sebök

PROMOTED CLUBS

SECOND DIVISION FINAL TABLE 98/99

		Pd	W	D	L	F	A	Pt	GD
1	Lombard FC Tatabánya	38	25	8	5	85	50	83	+35
2	Nagykanizsa	38	20	11	7	66	38	71	+28
3	Szeged LC	38	19	13	6	72	32	70	+40
4	Salgótarján	38	20	7	11	63	39	67	+24
5	Matáv Sopron	38	17	11	10	61	50	62	+11
6	Tiszaújvárosi FC	38	16	12	10	54	48	60	+6
7	Komáromi FC	38	17	6	15	59	50	57	+9
8	Érdi Sport	38	17	6	15	59	52	57	+7
9	Szolnoki MÁV	38	14	11	13	57	55	53	+2
10	Komlói Bányász	38	14	11	13	56	59	53	-3
11	Tiszakécskei FC	38	14	10	14	52	54	52	-2
12	ICN Tiszavasvári	38	12	14	12	46	40	50	+6
13	Békéscsaba	38	12	13	13	45	38	49	+7
14	Rákóczi FC	38	13	8	17	49	66	47	-17
15	Demecser FC	38	11	12	15	47	54	45	-7
16	Pécsi MFC	38	12	9	17	52	63	45	-11
17	Hajdúszoboszló	38	12	8	18	63	69	44	-6
18	Soroksári TE	38	9	8	21	48	84	35	-36
19	Kecskeméti FC	38	4	7	27	32	81	19	-49
20	Soproni Dreher	38	5	9	24	39	83	9	-44

N.B. Soproni Dreher deducted 15 pts.

CLUB DIRECTORY

Lombard FC Tatabánya
Ságvári Endre út 9
2800 Tatabánya
tel - (93) 312066
Year of Formation - 1910
Chairman - Péter Bíró
Coach - Bálint Tóth (99/00 - József Kiprich)
Stadium - Városi (17,000)

CLUB DIRECTORY

Nagykanizsai Olajbányász
Zárda u. 16
8800 Nagykanizsa
tel - (93) 312066
Year of Formation - 1945
Chairman - Gyula Sipos
Coach - Ferenc Keszei
Stadium - Városi (10,000)

CLUB DIRECTORY

Szeged Labdarúgó Club
Etelka sor 3
6723 Szeged
tel - (62) 420712
Year of Formation - 1929
Chairman - Kálmán Nagylaki
Coach - Károly Gergely (99/00 - Ferenc Ebedli)
Stadium - Városi (20,000)

ICELAND

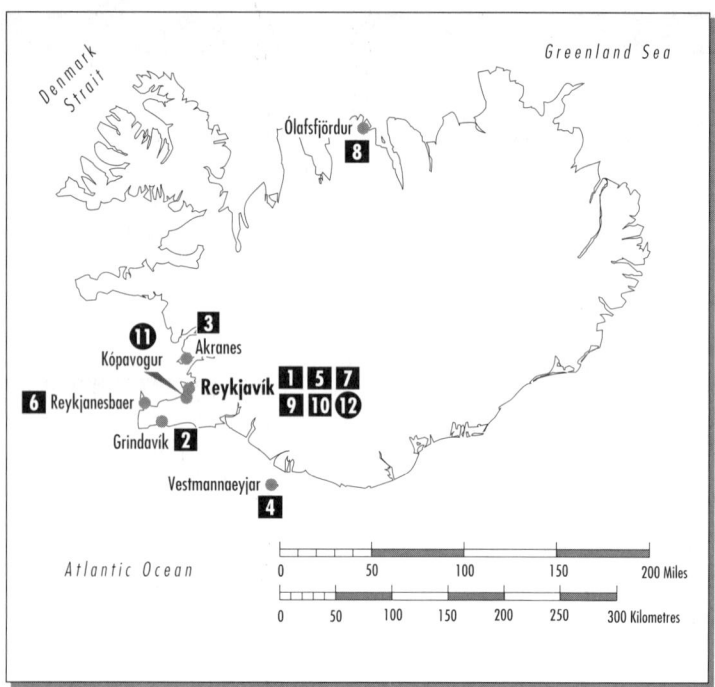

1	FRAM	539	8	LEIFTUR	546
2	GRINDAVÍK	540	9	THRÓTTUR	547
3	ÍA	541	10	VALUR	548
4	ÍBV	542	**Promoted clubs**		
5	ÍR	543	11	BREIDABLIK	549
6	KEFLAVÍK	544	12	VÍKINGUR	549
7	KR	545			

CLEAN SWEEP FOR ISLANDERS ÍBV

Thórdarson takes national team to new heights

FEDERATION DIRECTORY

The Football Association of Iceland
Laugardalur, PO Box 8511, 128 Reykjavík

tel - 510 2900   Year of Formation - 1947
fax - 568 9793   President - Eggert Magnússon
                        Secretary - Geir Thorsteinsson

Stadium - Laugardalsvöllur, Reykjavík (7,000)

That Iceland have never reached the finals of a major international football tournament is hardly a surprise. Expectations of sporting success in one of Europe's most sparsely populated countries are never high.

So, having been drawn in a European Championship qualifying group that included not only Eastern European heavyweights Russia and Ukraine but also reigning world champions France, it would have been reasonable for the Icelandic team to limit their ambitions simply to giving a creditable account of themselves and making sure that they finished no worse than fourth.

National coach Gudjón Thórdarson had other ideas. On taking over the job in 1997, he made it his mission to construct a new team, drawing on a rich blend of experience and youth. From day one he showed little tolerance for those who were unwilling to give their all for the cause - even if they included some of the country's most prominent players - and remained untroubled by

LEAGUE CHAMPIONSHIP RESULTS 1998

		1	2	3	4	5	6	7	8	9	10
1	Fram		0-0	1-1	0-2	0-0	2-3	0-2	0-0	4-2	3-1
2	Grindavík	4-2		0-3	1-0	1-1	2-1	0-4	3-1	0-1	2-2
3	ÍA	0-4	3-0		1-0	2-1	1-1	1-1	1-0	2-2	1-1
4	ÍBV	2-0	2-0	3-1		4-1	4-0	3-1	2-0	3-0	6-1
5	ÍR	0-3	4-2	1-1	1-0		1-2	0-1	1-1	2-2	3-2
6	Keflavík	1-0	3-0	0-1	0-3	1-0		1-0	1-0	1-5	2-2
7	KR	2-0	1-1	2-0	0-2	3-0	0-0		1-0	1-1	0-0
8	Leiftur	2-0	3-2	0-4	5-1	1-0	1-1	0-0		3-1	2-1
9	Thróttur	0-0	1-6	1-2	3-3	3-1	1-0	0-3	1-2		0-3
10	Valur	1-2	2-0	4-2	0-0	1-3	0-1	0-3	1-0	3-3	

INTERNATIONAL HONOURS

None

LEAGUE CHAMPIONSHIP FINAL TABLE 1998

			Home					Away					Total						
		P	W	D	L	F	A	W	D	L	F	A	W	D	L	F	A	P	GD
1	ÍBV	18	9	0	0	29	4	3	2	4	11	11	12	2	4	40	15	38	+25
2	KR	18	4	4	1	10	4	5	2	2	15	5	9	6	3	25	9	33	+16
3	ÍA	18	4	4	1	12	10	4	2	3	15	12	8	6	4	27	22	30	+5
4	Keflavík	18	5	1	3	10	11	3	3	3	9	12	8	4	6	19	23	28	-4
5	Leiftur	18	6	2	1	17	10	1	2	6	4	11	7	4	7	21	21	25	0
6	Fram	18	2	4	3	10	11	3	1	5	11	11	5	5	8	21	22	20	-1
7	Grindavík	18	4	2	3	13	15	1	2	6	11	19	5	4	9	24	34	19	-10
8	Valur	18	3	2	4	12	14	1	4	4	13	19	4	6	8	25	33	18	-8
9	Thróttur	18	2	2	5	10	20	2	4	3	17	19	4	6	8	27	39	18	-12
10	ÍR	18	3	3	3	13	14	1	2	6	7	16	4	5	9	20	30	17	-10

criticism, even after a relatively unsuccessful first year in charge. Soon, however, the results began to arrive. From February 1998 to June 1999 Iceland played 11 matches, six of them Euro 2000 qualifiers, and remarkably they were unbeaten in all of them. The country's previous record had been five matches without defeat. Now, at a stroke, they had more than doubled it.

When defeat finally came, it was a narrow 0-1 loss away to Russia in Moscow. In times gone by Icelandic players would have been proud of such a result. Not Thórdarson's troops. They were dejected.

Not only had their sequence been broken, but the impossible dream of reaching Euro 2000 had been dealt a potentially fatal blow.

It says something about the strategic abilities of Thórdarson and the new-found resilience of his players that throughout their 11-match unbeaten run, plus the defeat in Moscow, the team never conceded more than one goal in any game. The change of attitude is clear to see: the players hate to lose and are ready to run themselves into the ground for their coach and their country. Consequently, Icelandic fans have never been so smitten with their team. They cheered them to the rafters when they drew 1-1 against France (in their opponents' first competitive game since World Cup victory) and then beat the Russians at the the Laugardalsvöllur. Perhaps even more satisfying was the way Thórdarson's team fought back from a goal down to gain a potentially priceless point against Ukraine in hostile Kiev.

One undeniable factor in the national team's progress is the growing number of full-time professionals in the team. History was made in the August 1998 friendly against Latvia when for the first time ever the Icelandic team

NATIONAL TEAM RESULTS 98/99

19/08/98	Latvia	H	Reykjavík	4-1	Gudjónsson Th. (54, 77), Dadason (61), Helgason (90)
05/09/98	France (ECQ)	H	Reykjavík	1-1	Dadason (33)
10/10/98	Armenia (ECQ)	A	Yerevan	0-0	
14/10/98	Russia (ECQ)	H	Reykjavík	1-0	Kovtun (86og)
10/03/99	Luxembourg	A	Luxembourg	2-1	Gunnlaugsson A. (76), Sigurdsson H. (84)
27/03/99	Andorra (ECQ)	A	Andorra La Vella	2-0	Sverrisson E. (57), Adolfsson (66)
31/03/99	Ukraine (ECQ)	A	Kiev	1-1	Sigurdsson L. (66)
28/04/99	Malta	A	Ta' Qali	2-1	Gudjónsson Th. (36), Dadason (54)
05/06/99	Armenia (ECQ)	H	Reykjavík	2-0	Dadason (30), Kristinsson R. (46)
09/06/99	Russia (ECQ)	A	Moscow	0-1	

TOP SCORERS

16	Steingrímur JÓHANNESSON (ÍBV)
14	Tómas Ingi TÓMASSON (Thróttur)
8	Ásmundur ARNARSSON (Fram)
7	Arnór GUDJOHNSEN (Valur)
	Sigurdur Ragnar EYJÓLFSSON (ÍA)
	Gudmundur BENEDIKTSSON (KR)
6	Saevar Thór GÍSLASON (ÍR)

DOMESTIC CUP 1998

THIRD ROUND
Tindastóll 0, Leiftur 5
Dalvík 0, Grindavík 5
KR u-23 3, ÍA 1
Afturelding 0, ÍBV 1
Víkingur R. 5, Stjarnan 0
Bolungarvík 0, Valur 4
Haukar 1, Fram 5
Selfoss 0, ÍR 5
Leiknir F. 1, FH 3
KVA 1, Keflavík 0
ÍA u-23 1, Fylkir 2
Vidir 3, Skallagrímur 1
KA 1, KR 3
Leiknir R. 1, Thór 2
Stjarnan u-23 0, Breidablik 4
Valur u-23 0, Thróttur R. 2

FOURTH ROUND
KR 4, Valur 1
Breidablik 3, ÍR 0
Thór 1, ÍBV 2
Vidir 2, Víkingur R. 2 (aet; 1-3 on pens.)
KVA 2, Leiftur 4
Thróttur R. 5, Fram 2
Grindavík 2, KR u-23 0
Fylkir 3, FH 1

QUARTER-FINALS
Grindavík 2 (Kekic 13, Ásmundsson 38), Thróttur R. 0
Leiftur 2 (Kinnaird 35, Arge 79),
Víkingur R. 1 (Sigurdsson 77)
ÍBV 1 (Haflidason 100), KR 0 (aet)
Fylkir 1 (Gudjónsson 76),
Breidablik 3 (Jónsson 17, Kristjánsson 63, Pétursson 88)

SEMI-FINALS
ÍBV 2 (Bjarklind 61, 90), Breidablik 0
Grindavík 0, Leiftur 2 (Arge 83, Lazorik 86)

FINAL
30/08/98, Reykjavík
ÍBV 2 Jóhannesson S. (36), Jóhannesson H. (70)
LEIFTUR 0
referee - Jakobsson
ÍBV - Sigurdsson G.; Helgason, Stefánsson, Miljkovic, Jóhannesson H. (Georgsson 88); Gudgeirsson, Haflidason (Grétarsson 86), Ingimarsson; Sigurdsson I., Jóhannesson S. (Paeslack 85), Lárusson.
LEIFTUR - Knudsen; Reynisson, Marteinsson, Gunnarsson, Ogaba (Gíslason 76); Bragason, Kinnaird, Gudmundsson, Nielsen; Lazorik, Arge.

NATIONAL TEAM APPEARANCES 98/99

Coach -Gudjón THÓRDARSON	LAT	FRA	ARM	RUS	LUX	AND	UKR	MLT	ARM	RUS	Cps	Gls
Birkir KRISTINSSON (15/08/64)												
- IFK Norrköping (SWE)/Bolton Wanderers (ENG)/ÍBV	G80	G	G	G	G46	G	G	G55	G	G	61	-
Lárus Orri SIGURDSSON (04/06/73) - Stoke City (ENG)	D	D	D	D	D46		D			D	27	2
Eyjólfur SVERRISSON (30/08/68) - Hertha BSC Berlin (GER)	D	D			D	D60	M	D64	D	M	51	5
Pétur MARTEINSSON (14/07/73) - Hammarby IF (SWE)/Stabaek IF (NOR)	D	D						D	D	D	10	-
Audun HELGASON (18/06/74) - Viking FK (NOR)	M	D	D	D	D	D	D	D	D71	D	10	1
Helgi KOLVIDSSON (13/09/71) - 1.FSV Mainz 05 (GER)	M	M	M	M84	M46		s78	s64	s71	s46	15	-
Rúnar KRISTINSSON (05/09/69) - Lillestrøm SK (NOR)	M	M	M	M	M	M	M78	M	M	M	76	3
Hermann HREIDARSSON (11/07/74) - Crystal Palace (ENG)/Brentford (ENG)	M	D	D	D	D64	s71	D	D	D	D58	23	-
Thórdur GUDJÓNSSON (14/10/73) - KRC Genk (BEL)	A80	M	M	A4		M	M	M	M	M	31	7
Ríkhardur DADASON (26/04/72) - Viking FK (NOR)	A71	A	A	A	A			A55	A69	A	24	6
Tryggvi GUDMUNDSSON (30/07/74) - Tromsø IL (NOR)	A83			s46	s80						10	3
Stefán THÓRDARSON (27/03/75) - SK Brann (NOR)/Kongsvinger IL (NOR)	s71	s69		s84		A					5	1
Arni Gautur ARASON (07/05/75) - Rosenborg BK (NOR)	s80				s46			s55			3	-
Sverrir SVERRISSON (31/12/69) - Malmö FF (SWE)	s80				s46		s82				11	-
Ólafur Örn BJARNASON (15/05/75) - Malmö FF (SWE)	s83										2	-
Arnar GUNNLAUGSSON (06/03/73) - Bolton Wanderers (ENG)/Leicester City (ENG)		M69	M	A	A	A80		A69			30	3
Siggi JÓNSSON (27/09/66) - Dundee United (SCO)			D	D		D	D	D		D46	63	3
Steinar ADOLFSSON (25/01/70) - ÍA/Kongsvinger IL (NOR)			D	D	D	D	D			s58	13	1
Helgi SIGURDSSON (17/09/74) - Stabaek IF (NOR)				s4	A	A	A82	A	A80		27	4
Brynjar GUNNARSSON (16/10/75) - Örgryte IS (SWE)					s64	D71	M	M	M	M82	18	2
Arnar GRÉTARSSON (20/02/72) - AEK (GRE)						s60					44	2
Heidar HELGUSON (22/08/77) - Lillestrøm SK (NOR)								s55	s69	s82	3	-
Einar Thór DANÍELSSON (19/01/70) - OFI (GRE)/KR									s69	s80	16	1

was composed entirely of foreign-based players. Thórdarson has kept that trend going throughout the European Championship campaign, and with around 60 players from the country now earning their living in the leagues of Europe (mostly in Britain and Scandinavia), the national coach is certainly not short of potential candidates for selection.

The expatriation of Iceland's leading players has inevitably had a damaging effect on the national league. In 1998/99 all three of the country's European participants fell at the first hurdle in Europe - something which had not happened for years. ÍA and Keflavík both won their home ties against opposition from the Baltic states, but shock away defeats sent them spinning out of their respective competitions at the first attempt - a fate also suffered by ÍBV in the Champions' Cup.

The declining standard of the domestic league is something which the Icelandic clubs acknowledge and are

striving to arrest. Many of them have opted to pack their playing staff with imports, and there are always places kept open for ex-professionals wishing to end their career on the home front. Two Reykjavík clubs, KR and Fram, have even set up limited companies, and it is no longer the truth to label Icelandic clubs as 'part-timers'; a growing number of home-based players now earn their living exclusively from football.

The 1998 domestic season was dominated by ÍBV. The club from the Vestmann Islands won the Cup, successfully defended their league title and then secured the 'treble' by lifting the Super Cup.

ÍBV's defeated opponents in the Super Cup were Leiftur, also beaten into second place in the Icelandic Cup. However, the silver lining for the northerners from the tiny village of Ólafsfjördur (population 800) was qualification for Europe for the first time in their history - a handsome dividend for their policy of recruiting foreigners, including

Faroe Islands internationals Jens Martin Knudsen and Uni Arge, who were accompanied across the water by coach Páll Gudlaugsson, an Icelander who had previously been in charge of the Faroes national side.

ÍBV led the championship for each of the first 15 rounds, and at one stage it looked as if their title defence would be a mere formality. But a couple of shaky results near the end allowed KR to seize top spot after a magnificent run

of seven straight victories, during which they did not concede a single goal.

But with the long-cherished title in their sights, KR, coached by the legendary Atli Edvaldsson, suddenly buckled under the pressure. A 0-1 defeat away to Keflavík in the penultimate round meant that their residence at the top of the table lasted just one week, but they still held the key to their own fate because their final match was at home to ÍBV.

Everything was set for a grand finale to the season. KR, the country's oldest club, needed a win to take their first title in 30 years. ÍBV, who had won all nine home matches but whose away form had deserted them, required only a draw to retain their crown. A huge crowd of 5,400 packed the KR stadium (which raised the club's average attendance for the season to 1,809 - the best in the league), and the match was to be full of drama and suspense. ÍBV took the lead in the first half, but KR then missed a penalty and the visitors eventually sealed victory, the title and the 'double' with a second goal after the interval.

KR's long-suffering fans were understandably distraught. For the fifth time in eight years their team had finished runners-up. In contrast, ÍBV's second successive championship was celebrated with a ferry-ride back to the Vestmann Islands and a big outdoor party where all the local residents were invited to come and share in the success of their triumphant team.

PLAYER OF THE SEASON

THÓRDUR GUDJÓNSSON

Of all the many Icelandic players currently serving on the European mainland, none has attracted as much attention as attacking midfielder Thórdur Gudjónsson. For several years he struggled to make an impression in Germany with VfL Bochum, but since moving to Belgian club Genk, his fortunes have taken a dramatic rise. A Belgian Cup winner in his first season, he was a championship-winner in his second and even showed the Germans just how much he had improved by scoring a brace in Genk's 5-0 annihilation of MSV Duisburg in the Cup-winners' Cup. He has many fans, but the biggest of them all is his father, Gudjón Thórdarson. The national coach selected his son in each of Iceland's first seven Euro 2000 qualifiers, but accusations of nepotism were a non-starter; everybody knew he was in on merit.

EUROPEAN CUPS 98/99

CHAMPIONS' CUP
● ÍBV
Preliminary round OBILIC BEOGRAD (YUG)
A 0-2
    Sigurdsson G.; Bjarklind, Stefánsson, Miljkovic, Antonsson
    (Jóhannesson H. 75); Sigurdsson I., Haflidason (Paeslack 74),
    Ingimarsson, Helgason, Lárusson, Jóhannesson S. (Georgsson 82).
H 1-2 Haflidason (22)
    Sigurdsson G.; Bjarklind (Paeslack 74), Stefánsson, Miljkovic,
    Antonsson (Jóhannesson H. 77); Sigurdsson I., Haflidason, Ingimarsson,
    Helgason, Lárusson (Grétarsson 85); Jóhannesson S..

CUP WINNERS' CUP
● KEFLAVIK
Qualifying round METALURGS LIEPAYA (LAT)
A 2-4 Kristjánsson (60), Gylfason (90)
    Gudmundsson; Jónsson, Gudbrandsson, Gylfason, Finnbogason;
    Birgisson (Sigurdsson 70), Hauksson, Oddsson Gun. (Oddsson Gud. 59),
    Pavic, Kristjánsson (Sveinsson 75), Tanasic.

H 1-0 Hauksson (58)
    Gudmundsson: Jónsson, Gudbrandsson (Steinarsson 82), Gylfason
    Finnbogason; Birgisson (Sigurdsson 70), Oddsson Gun., Pavic,
    Hauksson (Ingólfsson 84), Tanasic; Kristjánsson.

UEFA CUP
● ÍA
Preliminary round ZALGIRIS VILNIUS (LIT)
H 3-2 Adolfsson (41), Eyjólfsson (61), Ivsic (86)
    Thórdarson; Haraldsson S., Leósson, Adolfsson, Haraldsson P.; Högnason,
    Gudjónsson H., Hardarson; Martin, Ivsic, Eyjólfsson.
A 0-1
    Thórdarson; Haraldsson S., Leósson (Milisic 60), Adolfsson, Haraldsson P.;
    Högnason (Gíslason S. 64), Gudjónsson H., Hardarson, Gudjónsson J.;
    Martin (Ivsic 75), Eyjólfsson.

FRAM

CLUB DIRECTORY

Knattspyrnufélagid Fram
Safamyri 28
105 Reykjavík
tel - 568 0342
fax - 568 1292
Year of Formation - 1908
President - Ólafur Helgi Árnason
Secretary - Ágúst Gudmundsson
Coach - Ásgeir Elíasson
Stadium - Laugardalsvöllur (7,000)

MAJOR HONOURS
League Championship - (18)
1913, 1914, 1915, 1916, 1917, 1918, 1921,
1922, 1923, 1925, 1939, 1946, 1947, 1962,
1972, 1986, 1988, 1990.
Domestic Cup - (7)
1970, 1973, 1979, 1980, 1985, 1987, 1989.

APPEARANCES 1998

	P	Ap	(s)	Gls
Hallsteinn ARNARSON	M	11	(1)	1
Ásmundur ARNARSSON	M	16	(1)	8
Thorvaldur ÁSGEIRSSON	M	16	(2)	
Thórir ÁSKELSSON	D	15	(2)	1
Baldur BJARNASON	A	18		3
Halldór BJÖRNSSON	G		(1)	
Arnljótur DAVÍDSSON	M	6	(2)	
Steindór ELÍSON	A		(5)	1
Saevar GUDJÓNSSON	D	17		
Vidar GUDJÓNSSON	D		(1)	
Dadi GUDMUNDSSON	M		(2)	
Ásgeir HALLDÓRSSON	D	4		
Haukur Snaer HAUKSSON	A	3	(5)	1
Halldór HILMISSON	M		(1)	
Freyr KARLSSON	M	9	(5)	
Anton Björn MARKÚSSON	M	10	(2)	
Ágúst ÓLAFSSON	D	13	(2)	
Ólafur PÉTURSSON	G	18		
Árni Ingi PJETURSSON	M	5	(3)	
Kristófer SIGURGEIRSSON	A	14	(4)	5
Eggert STEFÁNSSON	D		(2)	
Jón Thórir SVEINSSON	M	18		
Thorbjörn Atli SVEINSSON	A	5	(2)	1

LEAGUE RESULTS 1998

19/05/98	Leiftur	A	0-2	
24/05/98	KR	H	0-2	
28/05/98	Thróttur	A	0-0	
01/06/98	ÍA	H	1-1	Sveinsson T.
09/06/98	Keflavík	A	0-1	
13/06/98	ÍBV	H	0-2	
24/06/98	Valur	A	2-0	Bjarnason, Arnarsson Á.
05/07/98	ÍR	A	3-0	Arnarson H., Bjarnason, Hauksson
10/07/98	Grindavík	H	0-0	
18/07/98	Leiftur	H	0-0	
30/07/98	KR	A	0-2	
10/08/98	Thróttur	H	4-2	Sigurgeirsson 2, Arnarsson Á., Bjarnason (p)
16/08/98	ÍA	A	4-0	Sigurgeirsson (p), Arnarsson Á., Elíson, Áskelsson
23/08/98	Keflavík	H	2-3	Sigurgeirsson (p), Arnarsson Á.
08/09/98	ÍBV	A	0-2	
13/09/98	Valur	H	3-1	Arnarsson Á. 3
20/09/98	ÍR	H	0-0	
26/09/98	Grindavík	A	2-4	Arnarsson Á., Sigurgeirsson

GRINDAVÍK

CLUB DIRECTORY

Ungmennafélag Grindavíkur
Austurvegur 3
240 Grindavík
tel - 426 8605
fax - 426 7605
Year of Formation - 1963
President - Bjarni Andrésson
Secretary - Jónas Thórhallsson
Coach - Gudmundur Torfason
(99 - Milan Stefán Jankovic)
Stadium - Grindavíkurvöllur (1,000)

APPEARANCES 1998

	P	Ap	(s)	Gls
Gudjón ÁSMUNDSSON	D	17		
Árni Stefán BJÖRNSSON	A		(11)	1
Sigurbjörn DAGBJARTSSON	M	2	(2)	
Július B. DANÍELSSON	D	2	(4)	
Óli Stefán FLÓVENTSSON	M	14	(2)	4
Sveinn Ari GUDJÓNSSON	D	9	(2)	
Jón Fannar GUDMUNDSSON	D		(2)	
Gunnar Már GUNNASSON	D	4	(4)	
Hjálmar HALLGRÍMSSON	D	14	(2)	1
Ármann HARDARSON	G		(1)	
Vignir HELGASON	M	11	(3)	
Grétar HJARTARSON	A	8	(1)	5
Milan Stefán JANKOVIC	D	18		5
Sinisa KEKIC (YUG)	A	16	(1)	4
Zoran LJUBICIC (BOS)	M	16		
Paul McSHANE (SCO)	M	6	(1)	1
Thórarinn ÓLAFSSON	A	10	(5)	1
Scott RAMSEY (SCO)	M	17		2
Albert SAEVARSSON	G	18		
Björn SKÚLASON	D	16		

LEAGUE RESULTS 1998

19/05/98	ÍR	H	1-1	Kekic
24/05/98	Leiftur	H	3-1	Ramsey, Kekic, Flóventsson
27/05/98	KR	A	1-1	Kekic
01/06/98	Thróttur	H	0-1	
09/06/98	ÍA	A	0-3	
14/06/98	Keflavík	H	2-1	Flóventsson, Jankovic (p)
24/06/98	ÍBV	A	0-2	
05/07/98	Valur	H	2-2	Flóventsson, Jankovic (p)
10/07/98	Fram	A	0-0	
19/07/98	ÍR	A	2-4	Flóventsson, Hallgrímsson
30/07/98	Leiftur	A	2-3	Jankovic (p), Hjartarson
09/08/98	KR	H	0-4	
16/08/98	Thróttur	A	6-1	Hjartarson 2, Jankovic, McShane,
				Kekic, Björnsson
22/08/98	ÍA	H	0-3	
01/09/98	Keflavík	A	0-3	
12/09/98	ÍBV	H	1-0	Hjartarson
20/09/98	Valur	A	0-2	
26/09/98	Fram	H	4-2	Jankovic, Hjartarson, Ramsey (p)

ÍA

CLUB DIRECTORY

Knattspyrnufélag ÍA
Jadarsbakkar
300 Akranes
tel - 431 3311
fax - 431 3012
Year of Formation - 1946
President - Gylfi Thórdarson
Secretary - Örn Gunnarsson
Coach - Logi Ólafsson
Stadium - Akranesvöllur (3,000)

MAJOR HONOURS
League Championship - (17) 1951, 1953, 1954,
1957, 1958, 1960, 1970, 1974, 1975, 1977,
1983, 1984, 1992, 1993, 1994, 1995, 1996.
Domestic Cup - (7)
1978, 1982, 1983, 1984, 1986, 1993, 1996.

APPEARANCES 1998

	P	Ap	(s)	Gls
Steinar ADOLFSSON	D	18		
Mihajlo BIBERCIC (YUG)	A	1		
Freyr BJARNASON	D	2		
Sigurdur R. EYJÓLFSSON	A	11	(2)	7
Hálfdán GÍSLASON	A		(9)	
Sigursteinn GÍSLASON	D	8	(3)	
Heimir GUDJÓNSSON	M	16		1
Jóhannes GUDJÓNSSON	M	3	(5)	1
Pálmi HARALDSSON	D	18		3
Sturlaugur HARALDSSON	D	18		
Jóhannes HARDARSON	M	16		
Ragnar HAUKSSON	M	8	(4)	5
Alexander HÖGNASON	M	12		2
Zoran IVSIC (YUG)	A	11		4
Kristján JÓHANNSSON	D	4	(3)	1
Reynir LEÓSSON	D	15	(1)	
Dean MARTIN (ENG)	M	10		2
Slobodan MILISIC (YUG)	D	7	(5)	
Ruslan MOUSSAYEV (AZB)	D		(2)	
Zaur TAGIZADE (AZB)	A	1		
Thórdur THÓRDARSON	G	18		
Unnar Örn VALGEIRSSON	A	1	(3)	

LEAGUE RESULTS 1998

19/05/98	Keflavík	H	1-1	Eyjólfsson
24/05/98	ÍBV	A	1-3	Gudjónsson H.
28/05/98	Valur	H	1-1	Hauksson
01/06/98	Fram	A	1-1	Eyjólfsson
09/06/98	Grindavík	H	3-0	Högnason, Eyjólfsson, Haraldsson P.
14/06/98	Leiftur	A	4-0	Haraldsson P., Högnason, Eyjólfsson, Gudjónsson J.
24/06/98	KR	H	1-1	Jóhansson
28/06/98	ÍBV	H	1-0	Eyjólfsson
06/07/98	Thróttur	A	2-1	og (Jónsson), Martin
09/07/98	ÍR	H	2-1	Ivsic 2
18/07/98	Keflavík	A	1-0	Eyjólfsson
08/08/98	Valur	A	2-4	Ivsic (p), Eyjólfsson
16/08/98	Fram	H	0-4	
22/08/98	Grindavík	A	3-0	Hauksson, Ivsic, Haraldsson P.
08/09/98	Leiftur	H	1-0	Hauksson
12/09/98	KR	A	0-2	
20/09/98	Thróttur	H	2-2	Martin, Hauksson
26/09/98	ÍR	A	1-1	Hauksson

ÍBV

CLUB DIRECTORY

ÍBV - Íthróttafélag
Tysheimild v/Hásteinsvöll
900 Vestmannaeyjar
tel - 481 2060
fax - 481 1260
Year of Formation - 1945
President - Jóhannes Ólafsson
Secretary - Thorsteinn Gunnarsson
Coach - Bjarni Jóhansson
Stadium - Hásteinsvöllur (1,500)

MAJOR HONOURS
League Championship - (3) 1979, 1997, 1998.
Domestic Cup - (4) 1968, 1972, 1981, 1998.

APPEARANCES 1998

	P	Ap	(s)	Gls
Kjartan ANTONSSON	D	4	(4)	
Ívar BJARKLIND	D	10	(3)	2
Kristján GEORGSSON	D	1	(3)	
Jón Helgi GÍSLASON	D	1		
Sindri GRÉTARSSON	A	2	(10)	2
Steinar GUDGEIRSSON	M	18		
Kristinn HAFLIDASON	M	10	(3)	2
Gudni Rúnar HELGASON	D	5	(3)	2
Ívar INGIMARSSON	M	18		1
Hjalti JÓHANNESSON	D	15	(2)	
Steingrímur JÓHANNESSON	A	16	(1)	16
Hjalti JÓNSSON	D		(2)	
Kristinn LÁRUSSON	A	17		3
Zoran MILJKOVIC (YUG)	D	17		
Sigurvin ÓLAFSSON	M	4		1
Jens PAESLACK (GER)	A	9	(5)	4
Gunnar SIGURDSSON	G	18		
Ingi SIGURDSSON	A	15	(2)	4
Rútur SNORRASON	M		(4)	1
Hlynur STEFÁNSSON	D	18		2
Jóhann S. SVEINSSON	D		(1)	
Bjarni Geir VIDARSSON	A		(1)	
Sinisa ZBILJIC (YUG)	M		(2)	

LEAGUE RESULTS 1998

18/05/98	Thróttur	A	3-3	Jóhannesson S., Paeslack, Ólafsson
24/05/98	ÍA	H	3-1	Jóhannesson S. 2, Paeslack
28/05/98	Keflavík	A	3-0	Jóhannesson S. 2, Paeslack
01/06/98	ÍR	A	0-1	
09/06/98	Valur	H	6-1	Jóhannesson S. 3, Stefánsson, Grétarsson, Sigurdsson I.
13/06/98	Fram	A	2-0	Jóhannesson S., Lárusson
24/06/98	Grindavík	H	2-0	Paeslack, Snorrason
28/06/98	ÍA	A	0-1	
05/07/98	Leiftur	A	1-5	Bjarklind
09/07/98	KR	H	3-1	Jóhannesson S. 2, Haflidason
18/07/98	Thróttur	H	3-0	Jóhannesson S. 3
08/08/98	Keflavík	H	4-0	Helgason 2, Haflidason, Jóhannesson S.
16/08/98	ÍR	H	4-1	Sigurdsson I. 2, Jóhannesson, Lárusson
22/08/98	Valur	A	0-0	
08/09/98	Fram	H	2-0	Grétarsson, Bjarklind
12/09/98	Grindavík	A	0-1	
20/09/98	Leiftur	H	2-0	Ingimarsson, Stefánsson
26/09/98	KR	A	2-0	Sigurdsson I., Lárusson

ÍR

Íthróttafélag Reykjavíkur
ÍR-heimilid
Skógarsel 12
109 Reykjavík
tel - 557 5013
fax - 587 7081
Year of Formation - 1907
President - Stefán J. Stefánsson
Secretary - Sigurdur Arnthórsson
Coach - Njáll Eidsson
Stadium - ÍR-völlur (1,000)

APPEARANCES 1998

	P	Ap	(s)	Gls
Axel BENEDIKTSSON	M		(1)	
Brynjólfur BJARNASON	D	2	(5)	
Kristján Carnell BROOKS	A	17		3
Geir BRYNJÓLFSSON	M	16		3
Arnljótur DAVÍDSSON	M	6	(2)	1
Jón Thór EYJÓLFSSON	M	9	(1)	
Saevar Thór GÍSLASON	A	16	(1)	6
Gudmundur V. GUDMUNDSSON	D	4	(2)	
Ólafur Thór GUNNARSSON	G	18		
Bjarki Már HAFTHÓRSSON	A		(3)	1
Kristján HALLDÓRSSON	D	17		
Chris JACKSON (SCO)	M	7		
Ásbjörn JÓNSSON	M	5	(3)	
Kjartan KJARTANSSON	M	6	(5)	
Gardar NEWMAN	D	16		
Heidar ÓMARSSON	A		(3)	
Jón A. SIGURBERGSSON	A		(1)	
Bjarni Gaukur SIGURDSSON	M	16		2
Óli H. SIGURJÓNSSON	D	2	(2)	
Magni THÓRDARSON	D	15	(1)	1
Gudjón THORVARDARSON	M	7	(5)	3
Joe TORTOLANO (SCO)	D	16		
Arnar Thór VALSSON	M	3	(4)	

LEAGUE RESULTS 1998

19/05/98	Grindavík	A	1-1	Davídsson (p)
23/05/98	Keflavík	H	1-2	Brooks
28/05/98	Leiftur	A	0-1	
01/06/98	ÍBV	H	1-0	Gíslason
09/06/98	KR	A	0-3	
14/06/98	Valur	H	3-2	Thorvardarson, Thórdarson, Gíslason
24/06/98	Thróttur	A	1-3	Thorvardarson (p)
05/07/98	Fram	H	0-3	
09/07/98	ÍA	A	1-2	Brynjólfsson
19/07/98	Grindavík	H	4-2	Gíslason 2, Brooks, Sigurdsson
30/07/98	Keflavík	A	0-1	
09/08/98	Leiftur	H	1-1	Brynjólfsson
16/08/98	ÍBV	A	1-4	Thorvardarson (p)
23/08/98	KR	H	0-1	
01/09/98	Valur	A	3-1	Gíslason 2, Brynjólfsson
12/09/98	Thróttur	H	2-2	Sigurdsson, Brooks
20/09/98	Fram	A	0-0	
26/09/98	ÍA	H	1-1	Hafthórsson

KEFLAVÍK

CLUB DIRECTORY

Keflavík-Ungmenna-og Íþróttafélag
Hringbraut 108
230 Reykjanesbaer
tel - 421 5188
fax - 421 4137
Year of Formation - 1929
President - Rúnar Arnarson
Secretary - Ingvar Gudmundsson
Coaches - Gunnar Oddsson & Sigurdur Björgvinsson
Stadium - Keflavíkurvöllur (2,000)

MAJOR HONOURS
League Championship - (4)
1964, 1969, 1971, 1973.
Domestic Cup - (2) 1975, 1997.

APPEARANCES 1998

	P	Ap	(s)	Gls
Georg BIRGISSON	M	13	(5)	
Karl FINNBOGASON	D	12	(1)	
Kristinn GUDBRANDSSON	D	18		
Bjarki F. GUDMUNDSSON	G	18		
Gestur GYLFASON	D	17		
Eysteinn HAUKSSON	M	9		1
Ólafur INGÓLFSSON	A	11	(2)	2
Vilberg JÓNASSON	A	2	(12)	
Snorri Már JÓNSSON	D	18		1
Thórarinn KRISTJÁNSSON	A	8	(2)	5
Óli Thór MAGNÚSSON	A	2	(3)	
Gudmundur ODDSSON	D	11	(1)	
Gunnar ODDSSON	M	18		3
Sasa PAVIC (YUG)	A	8	(2)	3
Róbert SIGURDSSON	M	12	(5)	1
Gudmundur STEINARSSON	A	6	(6)	3
Ragnar STEINARSSON	M		(2)	
Adolf SVEINSSON	A	5	(2)	
Marko TANASIC (YUG)	M	10	(1)	

LEAGUE RESULTS 1998

19/05/98	ÍA	A	1-1	Steinarsson G.
23/05/98	ÍR	A	2-1	Ingólfsson, Oddsson Gun.
28/05/98	ÍBV	H	0-3	
01/06/98	Valur	A	1-0	Steinarsson G.
09/06/98	Fram	H	1-0	Kristjánsson
14/06/98	Grindavík	A	1-2	Steinarsson G.
23/06/98	Leiftur	H	1-0	Pavic
05/07/98	KR	A	0-0	
09/07/98	Thróttur	H	1-5	Pavic
18/07/98	ÍA	H	0-1	
30/07/98	ÍR	H	1-0	Ingólfsson
08/08/98	ÍBV	A	0-4	
17/08/98	Valur	H	2-2	Jónsson, Kristjánsson
23/08/98	Fram	A	3-2	Kristjánsson 2, Oddsson Gun.
01/09/98	Grindavík	H	3-0	Hauksson (p), Pavic, Kristjánsson
12/09/98	Leiftur	A	1-1	Oddsson Gun.
20/09/98	KR	H	1-0	Sigurdsson
26/09/98	Thróttur	A	0-1	

KR

CLUB DIRECTORY

Knattspyrnufélag Reykjavíkur
Frostaskjól 2
107 Reykjavík
tel - 511 5515
fax - 511 5517
Year of Formation - 1899
President - Björgúlfur Gudmundsson
Secretary - Jónas Kristinsson
Coach - Atli Edvaldsson
Stadium - KR-völlur (2,500)

MAJOR HONOURS
League Championship - (20)
1912, 1919, 1926, 1927, 1928, 1929, 1931,
1932, 1934, 1941, 1948, 1949, 1950, 1952,
1955, 1955, 1961, 1963, 1965, 1968.
Domestic Cup - (9) 1960, 1961, 1962, 1963,
1964, 1966, 1967, 1994, 1995.

LEAGUE RESULTS 1998

19/05/98	Valur	H	0-0	
24/05/98	Fram	A	2-0	Sigthórsson, Jónsson S.
27/05/98	Grindavík	H	1-1	Daníelsson
01/06/98	Leiftur	A	0-0	
09/06/98	ÍR	H	3-0	Júlíusson, Haxhiajdini, Benediktsson
14/06/98	Thróttur	H	1-1	Thorsteinsson B.
24/06/98	ÍA	A	1-1	Sigthórsson
05/07/98	Keflavík	H	0-0	
09/07/98	ÍBV	A	1-3	Benediktsson
20/07/98	Valur	A	3-0	Daníelsson, Benediktsson, Jakobsson
30/07/98	Fram	H	2-0	Benediktsson (p), Jónsson T.
09/08/98	Grindavík	A	4-0	Daníelsson, Haxhiajdini, Sigthórsson,
				Júlíusson
15/08/98	Leiftur	H	1-0	Jónsson S.
23/08/98	ÍR	A	1-0	Egilsson
01/09/98	Thróttur	A	3-0	Sigthórsson, Winnie, Benediktsson (p)
12/09/98	ÍA	H	2-0	Benediktsson 2 (1p)
20/09/98	Keflavík	A	0-1	
26/09/98	ÍBV	H	0-2	

APPEARANCES 1998

		P	Ap	(s)	Gls
Gudmundur BENEDIKTSSON	A	17	(1)	7
Einar Thór DANÍELSSON	M	18		3
Thormódur EGILSSON	D	18		1
Kristján FINNBOGASON	G	9		
Stefán GÍSLASON	M	3	(9)	
Eidur Smári GUDJOHNSEN	A	3	(3)	
Gunnleifur GUNNLEIFSSON	G	9	(1)	
Besim HAXHIAJDINI (YUG)	M	3	(8)	2
Thórhallur HINRIKSSON	M	9	(3)	
Edilon HREINSSON	D	2	(1)	
Björn JAKOBSSON	A	6	(5)	1
Sigurdur Örn JÓNSSON	M	16		2
Thorsteinn JÓNSSON	M	15		1
Sigthór JÚLÍUSSON	M	9	(5)	2
Birgir SIGFÚSSON	D	3		
Andri SIGTHÓRSSON	A	11	(2)	4
Indridi SIGURDSSON	D	9		
Arnar Jón SIGURGEIRSSON	M	3	(4)	
Bjarni THORSTEINSSON	D	18		1
Thorsteinn THORSTEINSSON	D	3	(1)	
Björgvin VILHJÁLMSSON	A	1		
David WINNIE (SCO)	D	13		1

LEIFTUR

CLUB DIRECTORY

Íthróttafélagid Leiftur
Aegisgata
625 Ólafsfjördur
tel - 466 2655
fax - 466 2665
Year of Formation - 1931
President - Thorsteinn Thorvaldsson
Secretary - Aegir Ólafsson
Coach - Páll Gudlaugsson
Stadium - Ólafsfjardarvöllur (1,000)

APPEARANCES 1998

	P	Ap	(s)	Gls
Uni ARGE (FAR)	A	8	(3)	5
Sindri BJARNASON	D	9	(1)	
Baldur BRAGASON	M	14		3
David GARDARSSON	M		(2)	
Páll V. GÍSLASON	D	11	(6)	
Thorvaldur GUDBJÖRNSSON	D	11	(2)	
Páll GUDMUNDSSON	M	13	(3)	4
Steinn V. GUNNARSSON	D	16		1
Heidar GUNNÓLFSSON	A	1	(3)	
Steinar INGIMUNDARSON	A	8	(7)	1
Bergur JACOBSEN (SWE)	M	1	(1)	1
Paul KINNAIRD (SCO)	M	10	(1)	
Jens Martin KNUDSEN (FAR)	G	18		
Rastislav LAZORIK (SVK)	A	13	(3)	3
Andri MARTEINSSON	D	14		
John NIELSEN (DEN)	M	14	(1)	
Peter OGABA (NIG)	D	13	(1)	
Kári Steinn REYNISSON	M	17	(1)	3
Hilmar Ingi RÚNARSSON	D	1		
Júlíus TRYGGVASON	D	6	(2)	

LEAGUE RESULTS 1998

19/05/98	Fram	H	2-0	Reynisson, Gunnarsson
24/05/98	Grindavík	A	1-3	Reynisson
28/05/98	ÍR	H	1-0	Reynisson
01/06/98	KR	H	0-0	
08/06/98	Thróttur	A	2-1	Bragason, Lazorik
14/06/98	ÍA	H	0-4	
23/06/98	Keflavík	A	0-1	
06/07/98	ÍBV	H	5-1	Arge 3, Gudmundsson, Lazorik (p)
09/07/98	Valur	A	0-1	
19/07/98	Fram	A	0-0	
30/07/98	Grindavík	H	3-2	Gudmundsson, Lazorik, Arge
09/08/98	ÍR	A	1-1	Ingimundarson
15/08/98	KR	A	0-1	
23/08/98	Thróttur	H	3-1	Bragason 2, Arge
08/09/98	ÍA	A	0-1	
12/09/98	Keflavík	H	1-1	Gudmundsson
20/09/98	ÍBV	A	0-2	
26/09/98	Valur	H	2-1	Jacobsen, Gudmundsson

THRÓTTUR

CLUB DIRECTORY

Knattspyrnufélagid Thróttur
Félagsheimilid v/Holtaveg
104 Reykjavík
tel - 581 1320
fax - 581 1339
Year of Formation - 1949
President - Ólafur Morthens
Secretary - Jón Gunnar Edvardsson
Coach - Willum Thór Thórsson
Stadium - Laugardalsvöllur (7,000),
Valbjarnarvöllur (2,000)

APPEARANCES 1998

	P	Ap	(s)	Gls
Claude CAUVY (FRA)	M	1		
Izudin Dadi DERVIC	D	17		
Páll EINARSSON	M	18		2
Gunnar GUNNARSSON	A		(7)	
Thorsteinn HALLDÓRSSON	D	17		
Sigurdur HALLVARDSSON	A		(2)	
Ásmundur HARALDSSON	A	11	(3)	3
Hreinn HRINGSSON	M	14	(2)	5
Kristján JÓNSSON	D	17		
Logi U. JÓNSSON	M	11	(3)	1
Arnaldur LOFTSSON	D	4	(2)	
Ingvar ÓLASON	M	16		1
Árni Sveinn PÁLSSON	D		(3)	
Gestur PÁLSSON	M	12	(4)	
Jens SAEVARSSON	D		(1)	
Andri SVEINSSON	D		(4)	
Vignir Thór SVERRISSON	M	6	(6)	1
Björgólfur TAKEFUSA	M		(2)	
Fjalar THORGEIRSSON	G	18		
Willum Thór THÓRSSON	M	1		
Tómas Ingi TÓMASSON	A	18		14
Vilhjálmur H. VILHJÁLMSSON	D	17		

LEAGUE RESULTS 1998

18/05/98	ÍBV	H	3-3	Hringsson 2, Tómasson
23/05/98	Valur	A	3-3	Hringsson, Tómasson, Einarsson
28/05/98	Fram	H	0-0	
01/06/98	Grindavík	A	1-0	Einarsson
08/06/98	Leiftur	H	1-2	Haraldsson
14/06/98	KR	A	1-1	Tómasson (p)
24/06/98	ÍR	H	3-1	Tómasson 2, Haraldsson
06/07/98	ÍA	H	1-2	Tómasson
09/07/98	Keflavík	A	5-1	Tómasson 3 (1p), Hringsson, Haraldsson
18/07/98	ÍBV	A	0-3	
29/07/98	Valur	H	0-3	
10/08/98	Fram	A	2-4	Tómasson 2
16/08/98	Grindavík	H	1-6	Tómasson (p)
23/08/98	Leiftur	A	1-3	Tómasson
01/09/98	KR	H	0-3	
12/09/98	ÍR	A	2-2	Sverrisson, Tómasson
20/09/98	ÍA	A	2-2	Hringsson, Jónsson L.
26/09/98	Keflavík	H	1-0	Ólason

VALUR

CLUB DIRECTORY

Knattspyrnufélagid Valur
Hlídarendi v/Laufásveg
105 Reykjavík
tel - 562 3730
fax - 562 3734
Year of Formation - 1911
President - Thorleifur Kr. Valdimarsson
Secretary - Lúdvík Bragason
Coach - Kristinn Björnsson
Stadium - Hlídarendi (2,000)

MAJOR HONOURS
League Championship - (19)
1930, 1933, 1935, 1936, 1937, 1938, 1940,
1942, 1943, 1944, 1945, 1956, 1966, 1967,
1976, 1978, 1980, 1985, 1987.
Domestic Cup - (8) 1965, 1974, 1976, 1977,
1988, 1990, 1991, 1992.

APPEARANCES 1998

	P	Ap	(s)	Gls
Dadi ÁRNASON	A	3	(3)	
Gudmundur BRYNJÓLFSSON	D	10	(5)	
Richard BURGESS (ENG)	A	1	(3)	
Grímur GARDARSSON	D	13	(3)	
Arnór GUDJOHNSEN	A	10		7
Ágúst GUDMUNDSSON	D	7		
Kristinn GUDMUNDSSON	G	1		
Arnór GUNNARSSON	A	4	(2)	
Jóhann H. HREIDARSSON	M		(1)	
Sigurbjörn HREIDARSSON	M	15		4
Ingólfur R. INGÓLFSSON	M	7	(6)	3
Páll S. JÓNASSON	D		(1)	
Ólafur V. JÚLÍUSSON	A		(6)	
Hördur Már MAGNÚSSON	M	16	(1)	3
Stefán M. ÓMARSSON	D	15		
Salih Heimir PORCA	M	12	(2)	1
Lárus SIGURDSSON	G	17		
Ólafur Páll SNORRASON	A		(2)	
Bjarki STEFÁNSSON	D	17		
Jón Th. STEFÁNSSON	A	11		5
Ólafur STÍGSSON	M	16		1
Brynjar SVERRISSON	M		(2)	
Sigurdur S. THORSTEINSSON	D	1		
Tryggvi VALSSON	A	3	(4)	
Vilhjálmur VILHJÁLMSSON	D	14	(1)	1
Mark WARD (ENG)	M	5		

LEAGUE RESULTS 1998

19/05/98	KR	A	0-0	
23/05/98	Thróttur	H	3-3	Hreidarsson S., Magnússon, Stefánsson J.
28/05/98	ÍA	A	1-1	Stefánsson J.
01/06/98	Keflavík	H	0-1	
09/06/98	ÍBV	A	1-6	Stefánsson J.
14/06/98	ÍR	A	2-3	Ingólfsson, Hreidarsson S.
24/06/98	Fram	H	1-2	Stefánsson J.
05/07/98	Grindavík	A	2-2	Hreidarsson S., Gudjohnsen
09/07/98	Leiftur	H	1-0	Gudjohnsen
20/07/98	KR	H	0-3	
29/07/98	Thróttur	A	3-0	Gudjohnsen 2, Hreidarsson S.
08/08/98	ÍA	H	4-2	Gudjohnsen 2, Vilhjálmsson (p), Magnússon
17/08/98	Keflavík	A	2-2	Ingólfsson, Stefánsson J.
22/08/98	ÍBV	H	0-0	
01/09/98	ÍR	H	1-3	Magnússon
13/09/98	Fram	A	1-3	Stígsson
20/09/98	Grindavík	H	2-0	Porca, Gudjohnsen
26/09/98	Leiftur	A	1-2	Ingólfsson

PROMOTED CLUBS

SECOND DIVISION FINAL TABLE 1998

		Pd	W	D	L	F	A	Pt	GD
1	**Breidablik**	**18**	**13**	**0**	**5**	**44**	**14**	**39**	**+30**
2	**Vikingur R.**	**18**	**10**	**4**	**4**	**30**	**18**	**34**	**+12**
3	FH	18	10	3	5	30	15	33	+15
4	Fylkir	18	9	5	4	31	23	32	+8
5	Skallagrímur	18	7	5	6	37	36	26	+1
6	Stjarnan	18	7	5	6	18	18	26	0
7	KA	18	7	4	7	24	28	25	-4
8	KVA	18	7	3	8	32	31	24	+1
9	Thór	18	2	2	14	19	43	8	-24
10	HK	18	2	1	15	19	58	7	-39

CLUB DIRECTORY

Ungmennafélagid Breidablik
Smárinn
Dalsmári 5
200 Kópavogur
tel - 564 2699
fax - 554 0050
Year of Formation - 1950
President - Gudmundur Oddsson
Secretary - Valgeir Ólafsson
Coach - Sigurdur Grétarsson
Stadium - Kópavogsvöllur (1,500)

CLUB DIRECTORY

Knattspyrnufélagid Víkingur
Víkin
Tradarland 1
108 Reykjavík
tel - 568 7755
fax - 588 7845
Year of Formation - 1908
President - Gudmundur H. Pétursson
Secretary - Björn Einarsson
Coach - Lúkas Kostic
Stadium - Víkin (1,000)

ISRAEL

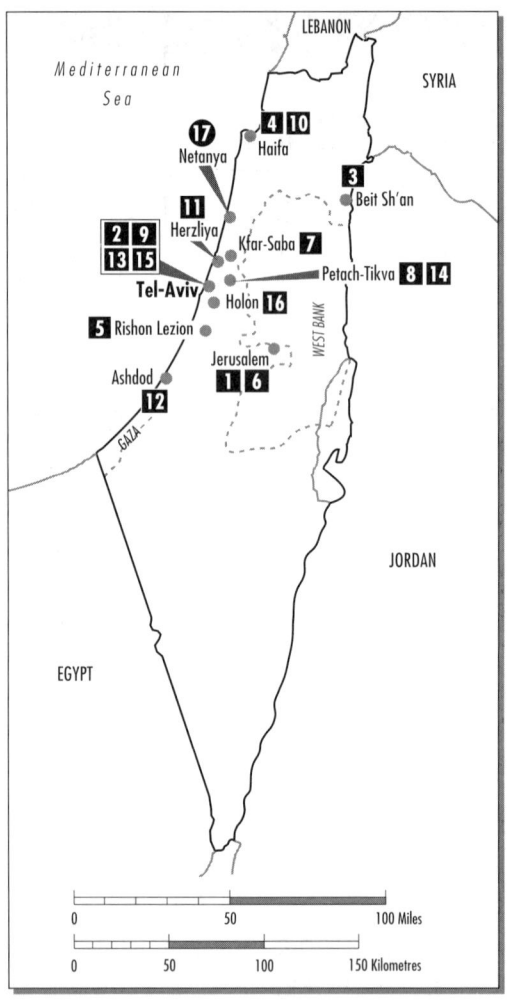

FIRST CHAMPIONSHIP FOR HAPOEL HAIFA

Five-goal blitz raises Euro 2000 hopes

FEDERATION DIRECTORY

Israel Football Association
Ramat-Gan Stadium, 299 Aba Hilell Street, Ramat-Gan, P.O. Box 3591

tel - (03) 5705999   Year of Formation - 1928
fax - (03) 5702044   President - Gavri Levi
                            Secretary - Jacob Erel

Stadium - Ramat-Gan, Tel-Aviv (46,000)

Never better. That was the unanimous verdict of the country's sports media after the Israeli national team's thumping 5-0 victory over Austria in the Ramat-Gan at the beginning of June. It was a performance without equal from Shlomo Sharf's side. They played spellbinding football from first minute to last, ripping ceaselessly and mercilessly through the Austrian defence until they had the five goals on the scoreboard that their superiority deserved.

It was the perfect finale to an excellent season for Israel. Although they had been beaten at the Ramat-Gan by Spain in the autumn - their first home defeat in tournament play for five years - they had posted convincing wins against each of the other teams in their qualifying group and, having also earned a 1-1 draw in Vienna, were well placed to reach the Euro 2000 play-offs and, perhaps, go on to reach their first major tournament since the 1970 World Cup.

Following the great win against the Austrians national euphoria was so widespread that football found its way onto the front pages (and beyond) of every daily newspaper. For once, Israel had something more exciting to talk about than the usual heavy-duty subjects of politics, finance and war.

Fêted above all others, even above two-goal hero Eyal Berkovic, who picked up a ten-out-of-ten rating for his performance, was coach Sharf. It was the 30th victory of his tenure and enabled him for the first time to present a positive balance-sheet (he had also led the side to 17 draws and 29 defeats). Those who had suggested that the start of the European Championship campaign would have been a good time for a new man to take over were silenced. The demolition of Austria was Israel's fifth win in a row, with the goal-ratio in that sequence being 14 for, one against. No wonder Israel had climbed up to 22nd in FIFA's official world rankings.

LEAGUE CHAMPIONSHIP RESULTS 98/99

		1	2	3	4	5	6	7	8	9	10	11	12	13	14	15	16
1	Beitar Jerusalem		1-1	6-0	1-1	2-2	3-1	4-1	2-0	0-1	1-1	1-0	4-2	7-1	2-0	1-0	1-2
2	Bnei Yehuda	0-3		3-2	0-3	1-1	2-0	3-0	1-2	1-0	2-0	0-1	1-0	6-1	0-2	0-6	5-1
3	Hapoel Beit Sh'an	1-4	2-1		0-1	4-2	0-5	0-2	2-3	1-3	2-1	0-1	1-1	2-1	0-3	0-5	1-1
4	Hapoel Haifa	2-1	3-1	4-0		4-0	1-0	6-0	1-0	1-0	0-0	2-0	2-2	3-0	4-0	3-2	3-1
5	Hapoel Irony Rishon Lezion	1-1	3-1	6-0	0-4		5-1	2-1	0-1	3-7	1-2	2-2	0-0	3-1	2-1	3-2	2-1
6	Hapoel Jerusalem	0-3	1-3	3-2	0-1	2-1		1-2	2-1	1-1	1-0	1-0	4-2	3-1	1-1	3-2	1-1
7	Hapoel Kfar-Saba	2-3	1-1	2-0	7-3	5-2	2-0		2-2	0-0	1-4	1-0	1-0	1-1	3-2	0-5	0-4
8	Hapoel Petach-Tikva	3-2	1-1	7-0	1-2	2-3	2-0	4-2		2-0	1-3	2-0	1-1	3-0	1-1	3-2	1-1
9	Hapoel Tel-Aviv	1-0	1-1	1-0	0-0	6-1	3-0	3-1	3-1		1-2	2-0	1-0	1-0	3-1	2-0	0-0
10	Maccabi Haifa	2-4	4-0	4-0	0-1	3-1	6-1	4-1	4-0	1-0		3-0	2-1	2-0	4-0	1-2	1-0
11	Maccabi Herzliya	1-4	3-2	3-1	2-1	3-2	0-0	0-1	2-2	1-1	0-1		3-1	3-0	0-2	0-1	0-0
12	Maccabi Irony Ashdod	2-1	3-0	2-1	3-2	0-3	0-1	1-1	4-1	3-1	0-0	2-1		2-0	2-7	3-3	2-2
13	Maccabi Jaffa	0-0	0-3	1-1	1-2	1-4	0-1	1-4	0-3	0-1	1-0	1-2	1-0		0-4	0-1	0-3
14	Maccabi Petach-Tikva	1-2	1-1	4-0	0-3	0-0	0-0	3-1	2-2	3-1	0-4	0-1	0-1	3-1		0-3	1-1
15	Maccabi Tel-Aviv	4-2	2-1	3-1	1-1	2-1	4-0	5-0	3-0	1-1	2-1	3-2	4-0	4-0	0-3		4-0
16	Zafririm Holon	0-1	3-1	0-1	0-2	1-2	3-1	2-2	1-2	1-0	0-2	3-0	0-0	1-1	2-0	0-1	

LEAGUE CHAMPIONSHIP FINAL TABLE 98/99

			Home					Away					Total						
		P	W	D	L	F	A	W	D	L	F	A	W	D	L	F	A	P	GD
1	Hapoel Haifa	30	13	2	0	39	7	9	3	3	27	16	22	5	3	66	23	71	+43
2	Maccabi Tel-Aviv	30	12	2	1	42	13	8	1	6	35	19	20	3	7	77	32	63	+45
3	Maccabi Haifa	30	12	0	3	41	11	7	3	5	21	13	19	3	8	62	24	60	+38
4	Beitar Jerusalem	30	9	4	2	36	13	8	2	5	31	20	17	6	7	67	33	57	+34
5	Hapoel Tel-Aviv	30	11	3	1	28	7	4	4	7	17	19	15	7	8	45	26	52	+19
6	Hapoel Petach-Tikva	30	8	4	3	34	18	5	3	7	20	29	13	7	10	54	47	46	+7
7	Hapoel Irony Rishon Lezion	30	8	3	4	33	25	4	3	8	25	36	12	6	12	58	61	42	-3
8	Hapoel Kfar-Saba	30	7	4	4	28	27	4	2	9	19	39	11	6	13	47	66	39	-19
9	Hapoel Jerusalem	30	8	3	4	24	21	3	2	10	11	31	11	5	14	35	52	38	-17
10	Maccabi Petach-Tikva	30	4	5	6	18	21	6	2	7	27	24	10	7	13	45	45	37	0
11	Bnei Yehuda	30	8	1	6	25	22	2	5	8	18	29	10	6	14	43	51	36	-8
12	Maccabi Irony Ashdod	30	8	4	3	29	24	1	5	9	11	25	9	9	12	40	49	36	-9
13	Maccabi Herzliya	30	6	4	5	21	19	4	1	10	10	23	10	5	15	31	42	35	-11
14	Zafririm Holon	30	5	3	7	17	16	3	7	5	18	22	8	10	12	35	38	34	-3
15	Hapoel Beit Sh'an	30	4	2	9	16	34	1	1	13	9	49	5	3	22	25	83	18	-58
16	Maccabi Jaffa	30	2	2	11	7	29	0	2	13	8	44	2	4	24	15	73	10	-58

Another major international success was Maccabi Haifa's qualification for the quarter-finals of the European Cup-winners' Cup. No Israeli side had ever previously reached that stage of a European competition, and although the team went no further, losing out comprehensively to Lokomotiv Moscow, 4-0 on aggregate, they could take enormous satisfaction from the way they had eliminated Glentoran, Paris Saint-Germain and SV Ried in earlier rounds. The victory over PSG was as enjoyable as it was dramatic, with late goals in both games contributing towards a memorable triumph.

There was no joy, however, in the other two European Cups. Beitar Jerusalem entertained their fans with a 4-2 victory over Benfica in the Champions' League qualifying round but it was all for nothing - they had been thrashed 6-0 in the first leg.

NATIONAL TEAM RESULTS 98/99

18/08/98	Poland	A	Krakow	0-2	
05/09/98	Austria (ECQ)	A	Vienna	1-1	Nimni (68p)
10/10/98	San Marino (ECQ)	A	Serravalle	5-0	Revivo (15), Nimni (17, 57), Mizrahi (31), Ghrayeb (82)
14/10/98	Spain (ECQ)	H	Tel-Aviv	1-2	Hazan (63)
18/11/98	Portugal	A	Setúbal	0-2	
23/12/98	Yugoslavia	H	Tel-Aviv	2-0	Tal (57), Abuksis (82)
18/01/99	Estonia	H	Tel-Aviv	7-0	Nimni (17p), Tikva (29), Harazi R. (31, 36), Mizrahi (43), Shitrit (81), Telasnikov (87)
20/01/99	Norway	H	Tel-Aviv	0-1	
09/02/99	Belarus	H	Haifa	2-1	Nimni (20, 51)
24/02/99	Latvia	H	Jerusalem	2-0	Revivo (23), Harazi R. (27)
10/03/99	Romania	A	Bucharest	2-0	Harazi R. (16), Badir (64)
28/03/99	Cyprus (ECQ)	H	Tel-Aviv	3-0	Banin (11), Mizrahi (47, 53)
06/06/99	Austria (ECQ)	H	Tel-Aviv	5-0	Berkovic (26, 47), Revivo (45), Mizrahi (54), Ghrayeb (75)

TOP SCORERS

21 Andrzej KUBICA (Maccabi Tel-Aviv)
20 Motti KAKUN (Hapoel Petach-Tikva)
19 Amir TURGEMAN (Maccabi Irony Ashdod)
17 Avi NIMNI (Maccabi Tel-Aviv)
   Nir SIVILIA (Beitar Jerusalem)
   Yaniv ABERGIL (Hapoel Kfar-Saba)
   Kobi REFUA (Bnei Yehuda)
16 Offer SHITRIT (Beitar Jerusalem)
   Yossi BENAYOUN (Maccabi Haifa)
14 Alon MIZRAHI (Maccabi Haifa)
   Nissan KAPETA (Hapoel Irony Rishon Lezion)

NATIONAL TEAM APPEARANCES 98/99

Coach - Shlomo SHARF	POL	AUT	SMR	ESP	POR	YUG	EST	NOR	BLS	LAT	ROM	CYP	AUT	Cps	Gls
Rafi COHEN (28/11/70) - Maccabi Tel-Aviv	G76	G	G	G										40	-
Alon HARAZI (13/02/71) - Maccabi Haifa	D	D	D	D	D	D46	D	D	D	D46	D82	D	D	58	1
Amir SHELACH (11/07/70) - Beitar Jerusalem	D	D46	s67		D	D	D46	D26	D	D	D	D	D	67	-
Arik BENADO (05/12/73) - Maccabi Haifa	D	D	D67	D	D	D	s46	D	D	s46	D	D	D	36	-
Ran BEN SHIMON (08/11/70) - Hapoel Haifa	D	D	D	D	D	D	D46	D	D46	D79	D			32	-
Yossi ABUKSIS (10/09/70) - Beitar Jerusalem	M46	M46			M63	s56			M67			M82		13	1
Walid BADIR (12/03/74) - Hapoel Petach-Tikva	M	M	M	M		M82	M46	M77	M	M46	M84	M46		16	1
Jan TELASNIKOV (11/02/72) - Beitar Jerusalem	M		M	M59	s63		s46		s86	s46	s87			13	4
Avi NIMNI (26/04/72) - Maccabi Tel-Aviv	M79	s46	M59	M	M77		M46	M	M70		M76		M	44	8
Haim REVIVO (22/02/72) - RC Celta (ESP)	A	A	A	A		A82		A88	M		M85		A	41	8
Alon MIZRAHI (22/11/71) - Maccabi Haifa/OGC Nice (FRA)	A46	s46	A	s59		s46	A46	s26			s46	A78		26	12
Avi TIKVA (28/06/76) - Grasshopper-Club Zürich (SUI)	s46					M56	M	M52			s36	s85	s78	7	1
Ronen HARAZI (30/03/70) - Bursaspor (TUR)/Maccabi Haifa	s46	A60			A74	A46	A46	A71	A46	A61	A72	A46		53	23
Nir DAVIDOVICH (17/12/76) - Maccabi Haifa	s76			G	G	G46	G	G56	G46	G	G	G		13	-
Idan TAL (13/09/75) - Maccabi Petach-Tikva/Hapoel Tel-Aviv	s79					s46	M	M	s46	s61	s76		s82	11	1
David AMSALEM (04/09/71) - Crystal Palace (ENG)		D												26	-
Eyal BERKOVIC (02/04/72) - West Ham United (ENG)		M	M71	M	M	M46			M86		M36	M	M77	54	6
Najwan GHRAYEB (30/01/74) - Hapoel Haifa		s60	D	D	D	D	D46	D	D83	D79	D87	D	D	15	4
Tal BANIN (07/03/71) - Brescia (ITA)			s59	s75	M				M	M	M	M		55	11
Offer SHITRIT (12/07/70) - Beitar Jerusalem			s71		s74		s46	s71	s88	s46				6	1
Alon HAZAN (11/09/67) - Watford (ENG)			D75										D	65	5
Yossi BENAYOUN (06/06/80) - Maccabi Haifa					s77	s82								2	-
Oren ZEYTOUNI (18/02/76) - Hapoel Haifa						s46	s46	s77	s70	s67	s84			6	-
Nir SIVILIA (26/05/73) - Beitar Jerusalem						s82	s46	s52	s46	A46	s72		s77	9	-
Sagie ELIMELECH (07/09/71) - Hapoel Tel-Aviv						s46								1	-
Shimon GERSHON (06/10/77) - Hapoel Tel-Aviv						s46			s79					2	-
Adoram KEISSY (17/06/72) - Maccabi Haifa						s46		s83	s79					5	-
Eran SHAIZINGER (03/12/76) - Maccabi Netanya								s56	s46					2	-
Offer TALKER (22/04/73) - Hapoel Haifa											s82	s46		3	-

There was to be no revival in the UEFA Cup, either, as the team from the holy city came out a distinct second best in their confrontation with Rangers.

Neither Maccabi Haifa nor Beitar Jerusalem were to feature significantly in the domestic championship. Indeed, neither managed even to win a return ticket to Europe, which was a major surprise. Maccabi appeared fatigued from their Cup-winners' Cup exploits. The hiring of Dusan Uhrin, the Czech Republic's successful boss at Euro '96, was seen as a coup at first but he did not last the season and was ushered out of office at the end of April following a heavy Cup defeat by Beitar. Nobody doubted that the start of Maccabi's demise was the mid-season sale of ace goal-poacher Alon Mizrahi, who demanded a move and

got it... but only to French Division Two side Nice. Not even the attraction of a European quarter-final could keep him. It seemed a bizarre move.

Beitar Jerusalem were unable to recapture the form that had brought them two successive titles. They made up for their disappointing league efforts by reaching the final of the Israeli Cup, but there they underperformed once again and ended up with only the silver medals after a penalty shoot-out defeat by Hapoel Tel-Aviv. It was a sweet victory indeed for Hapoel following the controversy of the championship climax the season before. It was the club's eighth Cup win and also enabled coach Eli Cohen to add another major honour to his already impressive haul before he left in the summer to take over at Maccabi Haifa.

EUROPEAN CUPS 98/99

CHAMPIONS' CUP
● **BEITAR JERUSALEM**
Preliminary round B36 (FAR)
H 4-1   Shitrit (2), Sallói (9, 45, 78)
       Korenfain; Bakhar, Domb, Tretyak, Deree; Mizrahi (Sivilia 46);
       Telasnikov, Abuksis, Hamar (Reichman 75); Sallói, Shitrit.
A 1-0   Hamar (68)
       Korenfain; Levi, Domb, Tretyak, Bakhar; Deree, Telasnikov, Abuksis,
       Hamar; Shitrit, Sivilia (Ohana 67).

Qualifying round SL BENFICA (POR)
A 0-6
       Korenfain; Bakhar, Tretyak, Domb, Shelach, Hamar; Levi, Abuksis,
       Telasnikov; Sallói, Shitrit (Ohana 65).
H 4-2   Hamar (24), Sallói (26), Shitrit (51), Abuksis (79)
       Korenfain; Bakhar, Shelach, Domb, Deree; Telasnikov, Abuksis, Hamar,
       Reichman (Mizrahi 83); Sallói, Shitrit (Ohana 68).

CUP WINNERS' CUP
● **MACCABI HAIFA**
Preliminary round GLENTORAN (NIR)
A 1-0   Mizrahi (22)
       Davidovich; Harazi A., Balanchuk, Benado, Elkayam, Keissy; Kopel, Jano,
       Duro (Silvas 84); Hromadko (Benayoun 64); Mizrahi (Vilner 90).
H 2-1   Mizrahi (16p, 79p)
       Davidovich; Harazi A., Balanchuk, Benado, Elkayam, Keissy; Duro
       (Benayoun 77), Kopel (Silvas 63), Jano; Hromadko, Mizrahi.

1st round PARIS SAINT-GERMAIN (FRA)
A 1-1   Benayoun (87)
       Davidovich; Harazi A., Balanchuk (Jano 24), Elkayam, Benado, Keissy;
       Silvas (Nagar 80), Kopel, Benayoun, Hromadko (Duro 88); Mizrahi.
H 3-2   Keissy (60), Mizrahi (78, 90)
       Davidovich; Jano, Harazi, Benado, Elkayam, Keissy; Kopel, Benayoun
       (Nagar 90), Duro (Katan 76), Hromadko; Mizrahi (Melamed 90).

2nd round SV RIED (AUT)
A 1-2   Mizrahi (14)
       Davidovich; Balanchuk, Harazi A., Melamed, Keissy; Nagar, Hromadko,
       Kopel, Duro (Kalman 46); Katan, Mizrahi.

H 4-1   Mizrahi (33), Keissy (62), Benayoun (74), Duro (90)
       Davidovich; Melamed, Harazi A., Benado, Keissy; Nagar, Kopel,
       Hromadko, Benayoun; Katan (Duro 83), Mizrahi.

Quarter-final LOKOMOTIV MOSKVA (RUS)
A 0-3
       Davidovich; Jano, Harazi A., Benado, Keissy; Melamed, Nagar, Hromadko
       (Duro 62), Benayoun (Silvas 86); Brzeczek; Harazi R. (Paço 77).
H 0-1
       Davidovich; Jano, Harazi A., Benado, Keissy; Kopel, Nagar (Duro 75),
       Brzeczek, Benayoun; Harazi R. (Katan 32), Paço (Hromadko 69).

UEFA CUP
● **HAPOEL TEL-AVIV**
Preliminary round FINNPA (FIN)
H 3-1   Cimerotic (31), Tubi (53), Tikva (63)
       Elimelech, Azoulay, Gershon, Ohaion, Cohen I. (Yaron 86); Ben Ami,
       Rupnik, Tikva (Udi 70), Tezacki (Balili 89); Tubi, Cimerotic.
A 3-1   Tikva (5, 18), Tubi (74)
       Elimelech; Azoulay (Cohen S. 81); Gershon, Ohaion, Cohen I.; Ben Ami,
       Rupnik (Yaron 76), Tikva, Tezacki; Tubi, Cimerotic (Tuaama 89).

Qualifying round STRØMSGODSET IF (NOR)
H 1-0   Tubi (75)
       Elimelech; Udi, Gershon, Cohen I., Ohaion, Ben Ami; Rupnik
       (Volnerman 70), Tikva, Tezacki; Tubi, Tuaama (Balili 56).
A 0-1
(aet; 4-2 on pens.)
       Elimelech; Udi, Gershon, Cohen I., Ohaion, Ben Ami; Yaron, Rupnik, Tikva,
       Tezacki; Tubi (Cimerotic 105).

● **BEITAR JERUSALEM**
1st round RANGERS (SCO)
H 1-1   Abuksis (17p)
       Korenfain; Levi, Domb, Shelach, Deree; Telasnikov, Abuksis, Hamar,
       Sándor; Yaacobi (Reichman 35), Shitrit.
A 2-4   Sallói (35), Ohana (80p)
       Korenfain; Levi (Ohana 66), Shelach, Deree, Mizrahi; Abuksis, Telasnikov,
       Sándor, Hamar; Sallói, Shitrit.

Hapoel replaced Cohen with Beitar's Dror Kashtan, who in turn made way for Eli Ohana, the man who had inspired Beitar to their 1996/97 championship title as a player.

One club with no need to take a ride on the managerial merry-go-round were Hapoel Haifa. They were 100 per cent delighted with their coach, Eli Gutman, whose

INTERNATIONAL HONOURS

World Cup Finals appearances: 1970

second season in charge had brought the club an historic first Israeli title. The 'Red and Blacks' led the way from as early as the third round and never looked back. Such was the quality and consistency of their play that by mid-season they had advanced into a nine-point lead.

Untouchable at home, they took maximum points in 13 successive matches in front of their own fans, and it was the last of those victories - 3-2 against Maccabi Tel-Aviv - that clinched the title with three matches still remaining. Maccabi had been the best side in the league since the turn of the year and possessed the league's top scorer in Polish striker Andrzej Kubica, but their terrible start - just

DOMESTIC CUP 98/99

1/16 FINALS
Maccabi Haifa 6, Hapoel Bat-Yam 1
Hapoel Kfar-Saba 2, Maccabi Aco 0
Maccabi Lazarus Holon 0, Hapoel Haifa 5
Beitar Jerusalem 7, Hapoel Kfar Shalem 0
Hapoel Raanana 1, Maccabi Tel-Aviv 3 (aet)
Hapoel Petach-Tikva 2, Beitar Beer Sheva 0
Maccabi Bnei Tira 0, Hapoel Tel Aviv 6
Hapoel Ashkelon 0, Hapoel Jerusalem 1
Maccabi Netanya 0, Zafririm Holon 1
Hapoel Migdal Ha'emek 0, Irony Ashdod 2
Maccabi Petach-Tkva 2, Maccabi Kfar Kana 1
Bnei Yehuda 1, Shimshon Tel-Aviv 0
Hapoel Irony Rishon Lezion 3, Hakoach Ramat-Gan 2
Hapoel Taibe 0, Maccabi Herzliya 8
Hapoel Bnei Lahish 1, Hapoel Beit Sh'an 1
(aet; 1-4 on pens.)
Maccabi Jaffa 1, Hapoel Beer Sheva 1
(aet; 1-3 on pens.)

1/8 FINALS
Japoel Haifa 2, Irony Ashdod 0
Maccabi Tel-Aviv 0, Hapoel Petach-Tikva 2
Maccabi Haifa 4, Zafririm Holon 1
Hapoel Irony Rishon Lezion 2, Beitar Jerusalem 3
Hapoel Beer Sheva 0, Hapoel Tel-Aviv 2
Hapoel Jerusalem 1, Hapoel Kfar-Saba 5
Bnei Yehuda 2, Maccabi Petach-Tikva 0
Maccabi Herzliya 5, Hapoel Beit Sh'an 1

QUARTER-FINALS
Bnei Yehuda 3 (Avihayil 63, Faygenbaum 75,
Meraro 83), Hapoel Haifa 2 (Bassis 37, 51)

Maccabi Haifa 1 (Zano 12),
Beitar Jerusalem 5 (Sivilia 68, Bakhar 102,
Shitrit 105, Hamar 109, Yaacobi 113) (aet)

Hapoel Kfar-Saba 0,
Hapoel Tel-Aviv 3 (Tubi 41, Udi 85, Tuaama 85)

Hapoel Petach-Tikva 1 (Makoveyev 68),
Maccabi Herzliya 0

SEMI-FINALS
Hapoel Tel-Aviv 2 (Ohaion 16, Tuaama 55),
Hapoel Petach-Tikva 0

Beitar Jerusalem 4 (Faygenbaum 7og, Shitrit 20,
Sándor 57, Bakhar 85);
Bnei Yehuda 2 (Shirazi 56, 75)

FINAL
19/05/99, Tel-Aviv
HAPOEL TEL-AVIV 1 Tikva (13)
BEITAR JERUSALEM 1 Sivilia (6)
(aet; 3-1 on pens.)
referee - Koren
HAPOEL TEL-AVIV - Elimelech; Halfon, Gershon, Cahila,
Ohaion, Ben Ami; Cohen S., Tal, Tikva (Márton 102);
Cimerotic, Tubi (Tuaama 72).
BEITAR JERUSALEM - Korenfain; Bakhar, Tretyak,
Domb, Telasnikov; Shelach (Deree 102), Abuksis,
Sándor, Hamar; Sivilia, Shitrit (Sallói 58).

---

five points after six games - had left them with too much to do. For them, finishing second, and thus qualifying for Europe, was a major bonus, and the concession of the title to Hapoel Haifa had been regarded as a foregone conclusion long before the defeat in the Kiriat Elezer.

Even so, the title decider ended in controversy when an

PLAYER OF THE SEASON

NAJWAN GHRAYEB
It was his Hapoel Haifa team-mate, extrovert Croatian playmaker Giovanni Rosso, who picked up Israel's official 1998/99 player of the season award (thus becoming its first foreign winner), but Najwan Ghrayeb was undoubtedly the best of the champions' homegrown players. An Israeli Arab, he cemented his place in the national team with a cluster of outstanding displays for both club and country. A former striker, he failed to make the grade at his previous clubs Maccabi Haifa and Maccabi Petech-Tikva but came into his own at Hapoel Haifa after coach Eli Gutman converted him into a left wing-back. The speedy 25-year-old was set to move to English Premiership side Tottenham Hotspur during the summer, but complications arose over a work permit and he eventually joined Aston Villa instead - at a cost of £1m.

estimated 17,000 fans took to the field to celebrate Hapoel Haifa's historic achievement... only for the referee, Dani Koren, to declare that there were still three minutes left to play. It took nearly half an hour for the pitch to be cleared, but the final moments were played in an unreal atmosphere, with fans packed densely against the touchline and the police powerless to avert any potential danger. No less a figure than Shlomo Sharf went on television to accuse the referee of an "act of stupidity", to which he received un equally strident response from the defendant.

Hapoel Haifa possessed no recognised stars, but as a team, evidently, they were second to none. Every player did his bit to make club president Robi Shapira's dream come true. Shapira had ploughed his personal fortune into the club in the hope of clinching a first-ever championship, and the players he brought in did not let him down. The three 'unknown' foreigners, Giovanni Rosso, Dmitriy Olianov and Goran Milenko, surpassed themselves, as did Israeli internationals Ran Ben Shimon (the captain) and Najwan Ghrayeb and the two exciting newcomers, Dudu Aouate (the goalkeeper) and Oren Zeytouni.

The 1998/99 championship was the last to be played under the 16-team system. With three clubs relegated and just one - Maccabi Netanya - promoted, the new Premier League contains just 14 clubs, and that will be further reduced to 12 for the 2000/01 campaign, when each top-flight club will be entitled to an enlarged quota of five foreign players and a considerable increase in television revenue. These truly are boom times for Israeli football.

BEITAR JERUSALEM

CLUB DIRECTORY

Beitar Jerusalem
Even Shmoel St. 13/3
Jerusalem 93715
tel - (02) 867771/385444
fax - (02) 323117
Year of Formation - 1939
Chairman - Moshe Dadash
Secretary - Avraham Levi
Coach - Dror Kashtan (99/00 - Eli Ohana)
Stadium - "Teddi", Malcha (13,000)

MAJOR HONOURS
League Championship - (4)
1987, 1993, 1997, 1998.
Domestic Cup - (5)
1976, 1979, 1985, 1986, 1989.

APPEARANCES 98/99

	P	Ap	(s)	Gls
Yossi ABUKSIS	M	27	(1)	2
Ilan BAKHAR	D	25	(4)	
Raanan DEREE	D	13	(9)	
Asi DOMB	D	21	(1)	3
Guy GRIF	G	1	(1)	
Matti HAJAJ	M	2	(1)	
István HAMAR (HUN)	M	27	(3)	4
Itzhak KORENFAIN	G	29		
Shmuel LEVI	D	11	(4)	2
Eitan MIZRAHI	D	14	(3)	
Eli OHANA	A		(5)	
Nir REICHMAN	M	2	(6)	
Yaacov REUVAN	M		(1)	
István SALLÓI (HUN)	M	18	(3)	7
Tamás SÁNDOR (HUN)	M	26		10
Amir SHELACH	D	29		1
Offer SHITRIT	A	26	(3)	16
Nir SIVILIA	A	17	(6)	17
Jan TELASNIKOV	M	24		2
Valentin THEODORIKA	M		(3)	
Serhiy TRETYAK (UKR)	D	18	(1)	1
Elad YAACOBI	A		(3)	

LEAGUE RESULTS 1998/99

22/08/98	Maccabi Petach-Tikva	A	2-1	Shitrit, Tretyak
29/08/98	Hapoel Irony Rishon Lezion	H	2-2	Shitrit, Abuksis
12/09/98	Maccabi Haifa	A	4-2	Domb, Sándor, Shitrit 2
19/09/98	Hapoel Jerusalem	H	3-1	Sallói 2 (1p), Sándor
17/10/98	Hapoel Tel-Aviv	A	0-1	
24/10/98	Zafririm Holon	H	1-2	Hamar
31/10/98	Maccabi Herzliya	A	4-1	Shitrit, Shelach, Abuksis, Sivilia
07/11/98	Maccabi Jaffa	H	7-1	Sallói 3, Sivilia, Shitrit 2, Hamar
14/11/98	Hapoel Petach-Tikva	A	2-3	Shitrit 2
21/11/98	Hapoel Beit Sh'an	H	6-0	Telasnikov, Sivilia, og (Elkaslasi), Levi 2, Hamar
05/12/98	Hapoel Haifa	A	1-2	Sivilia
12/12/98	Bnei Yehuda	A	3-0	Shitrit, Sivilia 2
19/12/98	Maccabi Tel-Aviv	H	1-0	Sándor
25/12/98	Hapoel Kfar-Saba	A	3-2	Shitrit 3 (1p)
02/01/99	Maccabi Irony Ashdod	H	4-2	Sándor, Sivilia 2, Shitrit
30/01/99	Maccabi Petach-Tikva	H	2-0	Domb, Shitrit
06/02/99	Hapoel Irony Rishon Lezion	A	1-1	Sivilia
13/02/99	Maccabi Haifa	H	1-1	Shitrit
20/02/99	Hapoel Jerusalem	A	3-0	Sallói, Domb, Sivilia
06/03/99	Hapoel Tel-Aviv	H	0-1	
13/03/99	Zafririm Holon	A	1-0	Sivilia
20/03/99	Maccabi Herzliya	H	1-0	Sándor
02/04/99	Maccabi Jaffa	A	0-0	
17/04/99	Hapoel Petach-Tikva	H	2-0	Sándor 2
23/04/99	Hapoel Beit Sh'an	A	4-1	Sándor, Sivilia, Hamar, Telasnikov
01/05/99	Hapoel Haifa	H	1-1	Sivilia
09/05/99	Bnei Yehuda	H	1-1	Sándor
15/05/99	Maccabi Tel-Aviv	A	2-4	Sivilia, og (Offir)
22/05/99	Hapoel Kfar-Saba	H	4-1	Sivilia 3, Sándor
29/05/99	Maccabi Irony Ashdod	A	1-2	Sallói (p)

BNEI YEHUDA

CLUB DIRECTORY

Bnei Yehuda
P.O. Box 19069
Tel-Aviv 61190
tel - (03) 395444
fax - (03) 5377877
Year of Formation - 1935
Chairman - Haim Barzilay
Secretary - David Tassa
Manager - Ya'acov Grondman
(99/00 - Giora Shpigel)
Coach - Rami Levi
Stadium - Shchonat Htikva (8,000)

MAJOR HONOURS
League Championship - (1) 1990.
Domestic Cup - (2) 1968, 1981.

APPEARANCES 98/99

	P	Ap	(s)	Gls
Shay ABUKSIS	M		(5)	
Yossi ABUKSIS	M	8	(5)	
Erez ALFIA	D	2	(3)	
Yossi ALFIA	D	10	(3)	1
Rotem ASRAF	M	2	(7)	1
Itzhak AVIHAIL	D	2		
Yaron AVIHAIL	D	29		
Yossi BALAS	D	15	(2)	
Assi BALDOT	M		(4)	
Dan BARKOLIN	M	6	(8)	
Ronen FAYGENBAUM	D	14	(1)	
Avi FLETCHER	D	14	(3)	1
Naor GALILI	A		(10)	
Yossi GORDANA	A	12	(2)	2
Alon KAPLAN	D	5		
Offer LEVI	D	14		3
Dudi LIBERMAN	M	23		1
Yossi MADAR	M	27		10
Hanoch MERARO	M	11	(4)	
Sahar MIZRAHI	M	7	(11)	
Roman PIVARNIK (SVK)	M	14	(3)	
Kobi REFUA	A	28		17
Roee SHARABI	M	1		
Hezi SHIRAZI	A	14		4
Ilan SHWAGER	M	14	(1)	
Shay SITON	M	24	(1)	
Shaul SMADGA	G	29		
Erez SMAMA	M	4	(2)	
Yaniv WHABA	G	1		

LEAGUE RESULTS 1998/99

21/08/98	Hapoel Kfar-Saba	A	1-1	og (Younay)
29/08/98	Maccabi Herzliya	H	0-1	
12/09/98	Maccabi Irony Ashdod	A	0-3	
19/09/98	Maccabi Jaffa	H	6-1	Alfia Y., Refua 2, Madar 3
03/10/98	Maccabi Petach-Tikva	A	1-1	Fletcher
24/10/98	Hapoel Petach-Tikva	H	1-2	Madar
31/10/98	Hapoel Irony Rishon Lezion	A	1-3	Gordana
07/11/98	Hapoel Beit Sh'an	H	3-2	Refua 2, Gordana
14/11/98	Maccabi Haifa	A	0-4	
21/11/98	Hapoel Haifa	H	0-3	
05/12/98	Hapoel Jerusalem	A	3-1	Refua, og (Gola), Liberman
12/12/98	Beitar Jerusalem	H	0-3	
19/12/98	Hapoel Tel-Aviv	A	1-1	Refua
26/12/98	Maccabi Tel-Aviv	H	0-6	
02/01/99	Zafririm Holon	A	1-3	Refua
29/01/99	Hapoel Kfar-Saba	H	3-0	Shirazi 2, Levi
06/02/99	Maccabi Herzliya	A	2-3	Refua, Madar (p)
13/02/99	Maccabi Irony Ashdod	H	1-0	Refua
19/02/99	Maccabi Jaffa	A	3-0	Refua 2, Madar (p)
06/03/99	Maccabi Petach-Tikva	H	0-2	
13/03/99	Hapoel Petach-Tikva	A	1-1	Madar
20/03/99	Hapoel Irony Rishon Lezion	H	1-1	Levi
02/04/99	Hapoel Beit Sh'an	A	1-2	Asraf
17/04/99	Maccabi Haifa	H	2-0	Madar (p), Refua
24/04/99	Hapoel Huifu	A	1-3	Levi
01/05/99	Hapoel Jerusalem	H	2-0	Shirazi, Refua
08/05/99	Beitar Jerusalem	A	1-1	Madar (p)
15/05/99	Hapoel Tel-Aviv	H	1-0	Refua
22/05/99	Maccabi Tel-Aviv	A	1-2	Levi
29/05/99	Zafririm Holon	H	5-1	Shirazi, Refua 3, Madar

HAPOEL BEIT SH'AN

CLUB DIRECTORY

Hapoel Beit Sh'an
PO Box 60
Beit Sh'an 10900
tel - (06) 581782
fax - (06) 581780
Year of Formation - 1958
Chairman - Zion Avidan
Coach - Avraham Aboukarat; Elias Levi
Stadium - Municipal (7,000)

APPEARANCES 98/99

	P	Ap	(s)	Gls
Yossi ARAMA	M	2	(3)	
Offir ASULIN	M	4	(2)	
Erez AZOULAY	A		(2)	
Motti BEN HAMO	M	5	(4)	
Yaniv BITON	M	11	(11)	1
Marius Gabriel CINCA (ROM)	M	13		2
Meir COHEN	G	26		1
Yehuda COHEN	M		(1)	
Srdjan CULKOVIC (YUG)	A	25		6
Dudu DAHAN	D	20		3
Avi DANAN	M	19		
Shimon DANAN	M	7	(2)	2
Roee ELBAZ	M		(1)	
Rafi ELGARISI	M	2	(3)	
Shlomi ELKASLASI	D	18		
Kobi GANON	D	10		
Jamil HADER	D	18	(4)	1
Almog HAZAN	M	16	(3)	
Haim IRMIAHO	A	3	(11)	1
Yossi ITAY	D	1		
Alon KAPLAN	D		(6)	
Valeriy KORLENCHUK (UKR)	A		(1)	1
Gili LEVI	M	4	(2)	
ODED	D		(1)	
Gela PANCHULIDZE (GEO)	M	18	(1)	2
Joso RADOSEVIC (CRO)	M	16		
Sahar RAHAMIM	G	4		
Roee SAGIE	A	9	(9)	
Nadav SANDROSI	A	6	(1)	
Gabi SAPIR	D	14	(1)	
Eitan TAYEB	D	22		2
Morris UZAN	A	20	(2)	3
Willy VINCENT (MAU)	M	3		
B ZOABI	D	3		
Eli ZOREF	A	11	(2)	

LEAGUE RESULTS 1998/99

22/08/98	Maccabi Haifa	A	0-4	
29/08/98	Hapoel Jerusalem	H	0-5	
12/09/98	Hapoel Tel-Aviv	A	0-1	
19/09/98	Zafririm Holon	H	1-1	Biton
03/10/98	Maccabi Herzliya	A	1-3	Korlenchuk
23/10/98	Maccabi Jaffa	H	2-1	Culkovic, Danan S.
31/10/98	Hapoel Petach-Tikva	A	0-7	
07/11/98	Bnei Yehuda	A	2-3	Dahan, Danan S.
13/11/98	Hapoel Haifa	H	0-1	
21/11/98	Beitar Jerusalem	A	0-6	
05/12/98	Maccabi Tel-Aviv	H	0-5	
12/12/98	Hapoel Kfar-Saba	A	0-2	
18/12/98	Maccabi Irony Ashdod	H	1-1	Panchulidze
26/12/98	Maccabi Petach-Tikva	A	0-4	
01/01/99	Hapoel Irony Rishon Lezion	H	4-2	Uzan 2, Culkovic 2
29/01/99	Maccabi Haifa	H	2-1	Cinca, Culkovic
05/02/99	Hapoel Jerusalem	A	2-3	Dahan 2 (1p)
12/02/99	Hapoel Tel-Aviv	H	1-3	Culkovic
20/02/99	Zafririm Holon	A	1-0	Tayeb (p)
05/03/99	Maccabi Herzliya	H	0-1	
13/03/99	Maccabi Jaffa	A	1-1	Panchulidze
20/03/99	Hapoel Petach-Tikva	H	2-3	Tayeb (p), Hader (p)
02/04/99	Bnei Yehuda	H	2-1	Cohen M. (p), Irmiaho
17/04/99	Hapoel Haifa	A	0-4	
23/04/99	Beitar Jerusalem	H	1-4	Uzan
01/05/99	Maccabi Tel-Aviv	A	1-3	Culkovic
07/05/99	Hapoel Kfar-Saba	H	0-2	
15/05/99	Maccabi Irony Ashdod	A	1-2	Cinca
21/05/99	Maccabi Petach-Tikva	H	0-3	
29/05/99	Hapoel Irony Rishon Lezion	A	0-6	

HAPOEL HAIFA

Hapoel Haifa
Hatzvi Blvd. 29
Haifa 32713
tel - (04) 361177/383408
fax - (04) 373881
Year of Formation - 1921
Chairman - Robi Shapira
Secretary - Avi Kaufman
Coach - Eli Gutman
Stadium - Kiriat Eliezer (17,000)

MAJOR HONOURS
League Championship - (1) 1999.
Domestic Cup - (3) 1963, 1966, 1974.

	P	Ap	(s)	Gls
Dudu AOUATE	G	27		
Rami AZIZ	A	3	(7)	
Ami AZOULAY	D	15	(10)	
Liron BASSIS	A	27	(1)	7
Meir BEN MARGI	D	6	(12)	
Ran BEN SHIMON	D	28	(1)	4
Kobi DANINO	D	1	(2)	
Najwan GHRAYEB	D	29		7
Haim HAJAJ	M	2	(14)	1
Alon HALFON	D	18		
Shay HOLTZMAN	A	5		1
Aleksandar JOVIC (YUG)	A	7	(4)	3
Levan KHOMERIKI (GEO)	A		(3)	
Kfir LEIBOVITZ	D	2	(3)	
Goran MILENKO (CRO)	M	26		4
Oren NISSIM	A	20	(4)	9
Dmitriy OLIANOV (RUS)	M	23		2
Avi PERETS	G	2		
Asanan PRO	G	1	(1)	
Giovanni ROSSO (CRO)	M	28		13
Ilan TAL	M	3	(17)	4
Offer TALKER	D	30		7
Eyal TARTASKY	M		(2)	
Eyal WOLF	M		(1)	
Oren ZEYTUNI	M	27		2

22/08/98	Hapoel Irony Rishon Lezion	A	4-0	Talker, Rosso, Ghrayeb, Bassis
09/09/98	Maccabi Haifa	H	0-0	
12/09/98	Hapoel Jerusalem	A	1-0	Rosso (p)
19/09/98	Hapoel Tel-Aviv	H	1-0	Holtzman (p)
03/10/98	Zafririm Holon	A	2-0	Milenko, Ben Shimon
24/10/98	Maccabi Herzliya	H	2-0	Olianov, Talker
31/10/98	Maccabi Jaffa	A	2-1	Bassis, Nissim
07/11/98	Hapoel Petach-Tikva	H	1-0	Nissim
14/11/98	Hapoel Beit Sh'an	A	1-0	Ghrayeb
21/11/98	Bnei Yehuda	A	3-0	Rosso 2 (1p), Talker
05/12/98	Beitar Jerusalem	H	2-1	Milenko, Rosso
12/12/98	Maccabi Tel-Aviv	A	1-1	Bassis
19/12/98	Hapoel Kfar-Saba	H	6-0	Nissim, Rosso 2, Ghrayeb 2, Jovic
26/12/98	Maccabi Irony Ashdod	A	2-3	Milenko, Rosso
02/01/99	Maccabi Petach-Tikva	H	4-0	og (Tal), Jovic, Rosso (p), Olianov
29/01/99	Hapoel Irony Rishon Lezion	H	4-0	Nissim 2, Milenko, Tal
06/02/99	Maccabi Haifa	A	1-0	Talker
13/02/99	Hapoel Jerusalem	H	1-0	Bassis
20/02/99	Hapoel Tel-Aviv	A	0-0	
06/03/99	Zafririm Holon	H	3-1	Rosso, Tal, Jovic
13/03/99	Maccabi Herzliya	A	1-2	Nissim
20/03/99	Maccabi Jaffa	H	3-0	Ghrayeb, Ben Shimon, Bassis
03/04/99	Hapoel Petach-Tikva	A	2-1	og (Bouron), Bassis
17/04/99	Hapoel Beit Sh'an	H	4-0	Bassis (p), Talker, Ghrayeb 2
24/04/99	Bnei Yehuda	H	3-1	Rosso 2 (2p), Talker
01/05/99	Beitar Jerusalem	A	1-1	Nissim
09/05/99	Maccabi Tel-Aviv	H	3-2	Zeytuni 2, Nissim
14/05/99	Hapoel Kfar-Saba	A	3-7	Ben Shimon, Nissim, Tal
22/05/99	Maccabi Irony Ashdod	H	2-2	Talker, Rosso
29/05/99	Maccabi Petach-Tikva	A	3-0	Tal, Ben Shimon, Hajaj

HAPOEL IRONY RISHON LEZION

CLUB DIRECTORY

Hapoel Irony Rishon Lezion
Hapardes H'rishon St.
Rishon-Lezion
tel - (03) 9641919
fax - (03) 9666760
Year of Formation - 1940
Chairman - Uri Izersky
Coach - Elisha Levi
Stadium - New Municipal (7,000)

APPEARANCES 98/99

	P	Ap	(s)	Gls
Shadi ABU DIB	M	2	(2)	
Kfir AGASI	D	8	(3)	
Dani ALBERT	D	28		2
Yehuda AMAR	D	11	(9)	
Shlomi BEN HAMO	G	1		
Alon BRUMER	M	12		
Eyal COHEN	M	4	(21)	1
Rafi COHEN	A	21	(4)	12
Golan DEREE	D	29		1
Tomer ELIAHO	M	27		1
Oren GABAY	M	1	(4)	
Kfir HAIM	D		(1)	
Udi KABUDI	M	30		12
Nissan KAPETA	A	28	(1)	14
Nenad MARKICEVIC (YUG)	M	14	(1)	
Yaniv MIZRAHI	G	29		
Nir NAHMANI	A		(1)	
Amir NUSBAUM	M	4	(1)	
Roni OHANA	M	1	(6)	
Avi PITUSI	M	30		2
Oren ROTEM	D	14		
Moshe SABAG	A	20	(4)	4
Assaf SHEMESH	D	1	(4)	
Nir SHIKVA	A	13	(9)	8
Marcin WLODARCZYK (POL)	D	2	(1)	
Yaniv YARON	M		(3)	

LEAGUE RESULTS 1998/99

22/08/98	Hapoel Haifa	H	0-4	
29/08/98	Beitar Jerusalem	A	2-2	Shikva, Pitusi
12/09/98	Maccabi Tel-Aviv	H	3-2	Kabudi, Shikva, Kapeta
18/09/98	Hapoel Kfar-Saba	A	2-5	Kabudi 2
17/10/98	Maccabi Irony Ashdod	H	0-0	
24/10/98	Maccabi Petach-Tikva	A	0-0	
31/10/98	Bnei Yehuda	H	3-1	Cohen R. 2, Kabudi
09/11/98	Maccabi Haifa	H	1-2	Cohen R.
14/11/98	Hapoel Jerusalem	A	1-2	Kapeta (p)
21/11/98	Hapoel Tel-Aviv	H	3-7	Cohen R. 2, Kapeta (p)
05/12/98	Zafririm Holon	A	2-1	Kabudi, Pitusi
12/12/98	Maccabi Herzliya	H	2-2	Kabudi, Kapeta
19/12/98	Maccabi Jaffa	A	4-1	Cohen R., Kapeta 2 (1p), Kabudi
26/12/98	Hapoel Petach-Tikva	H	0-1	
01/01/99	Hapoel Beit Sh'an	A	2-4	Cohen R., Shikva
28/01/99	Hapoel Haifa	A	0-4	
06/02/99	Beitar Jerusalem	H	1-1	Cohen R.
13/02/99	Maccabi Tel-Aviv	A	1-2	Eliaho
20/02/99	Hapoel Kfar-Saba	H	2-1	Shikva, og (Netzer)
06/03/99	Maccabi Irony Ashdod	A	3-0	Kabudi, Cohen R., Deree
13/03/99	Maccabi Petach-Tikva	H	2-1	Sabag 2
20/03/99	Bnei Yehuda	A	1-1	Kapeta
03/04/99	Maccabi Haifa	A	1-3	Shikva
17/04/99	Hapoel Jerusalem	H	5-1	Shikva 3, Kapeta, Cohen R.
24/04/99	Hapoel Tel-Aviv	A	1-6	Kapeta
01/05/99	Zafririm Holon	H	2-1	Kapeta, Sabag
07/05/99	Maccabi Herzliya	A	2-3	Kabudi, Cohen R.
15/05/99	Maccabi Jaffa	H	3-1	Kabudi, Cohen E., Kapeta
22/05/99	Hapoel Petach-Tikva	A	3-2	Kabudi 2, Sabag
29/05/99	Hapoel Beit Sh'an	H	6-0	Kapeta 3, Albert 2, Cohen R.

HAPOEL JERUSALEM

CLUB DIRECTORY

Hapoel Jerusalem
Stadium "Teddi"
Jerusalem
tel - (02) 611881
Year of Formation - 1953
Chairman - Victor Yona
Manager - (99/00 - Mishel Dayan)
Coach - Yossi Mizrahi (99/00 - Elias Levi)
Stadium - "Teddi", Malcha (13,000)

MAJOR HONOURS
Domestic Cup - (1) 1973.

APPEARANCES 98/99

		P	Ap	(s)	Gls
Shay AHARON	A	5	(8)	1
Salman AMAR	D	21	(2)	1
Yair ASIAG	A	1	(4)	
Eyal AVRAHAMI	M	17	(5)	
Yaniv AVRAHAMI	M	6	(4)	
Tommer AZOULAY	D	23		2
Dudu DAHAN	D	5	(3)	
Shlomi DANINO	D	27		7
Amir GOLA	M	15	(7)	
Golan HERMON	D	9	(3)	
Dudu HUDIDA	M	1	(1)	1
Jozef KOSTELNIK (CZE)	M	22	(6)	4
Gil LEVI	M	1	(7)	
LIANY	A	1	(4)	
Stefan MAHAJ (POL)	D	23		
Motti MENACHEM	A	21	(6)	1
Motti MIZRAHI	G	1		
Amiran MUJIRI (GEO)	M	9		1
Itzhak OKA	M	6	(1)	1
Victor PAÇO (ALB)	A	13		9
Mahmud SALMAN	M	16	(6)	3
Arik SASSON	D	15	(3)	
Ram SETTI	M	2	(8)	
Udi SHNORMAN	M	21	(2)	3
Liran SHTRAUBER	G	29		
Sandi VALENTINCIC (BOS)	A	5	(4)	
Shimon YOGEV	D	2	(3)	
Adnan ZILZEDOVIC (BOS)	M	13		

LEAGUE RESULTS 1998/99

22/08/98	Hapoel Petach-Tikva	H	2-1	og (Badir), Amar
29/08/98	Hapoel Beit Sh'an	A	5-0	Mujiri, Paço 2, Kostelnik 2 (1p)
12/09/99	Hapoel Haifa	H	0-1	
19/09/98	Beitar Jerusalem	A	1-3	Danino
03/10/98	Maccabi Tel-Aviv	H	3-2	Danino 2, Paço
23/10/98	Hapoel Kfar-Saba	A	0-2	
31/10/98	Maccabi Irony Ashdod	H	4-2	Paço 2, Azoulay, Kostelnik
07/11/98	Maccabi Petach-Tikva	A	0-0	
14/11/98	Hapoel Irony Rishon Lezion	H	2-1	Shnorman, Kostelnik
21/11/98	Maccabi Haifa	A	1-6	Paço
05/12/98	Bnei Yehuda	H	1-3	Paço
12/12/98	Hapoel Tel-Aviv	H	1-1	Paço
19/12/98	Zafririm Holon	A	1-3	Menachem
26/12/98	Maccabi Herzliya	H	1-0	Paço
01/01/99	Maccabi Jaffa	A	1-0	Shnorman
29/01/99	Hapoel Petach-Tikva	A	0-2	
05/02/99	Hapoel Beit Sh'an	H	3-2	Danino 2, Azoulay
13/02/99	Hapoel Haifa	A	0-1	
20/03/99	Beitar Jerusalem	H	0-3	
06/03/99	Maccabi Tel-Aviv	A	0-4	
13/03/99	Hapoel Kfar-Saba	H	1-2	Shnorman
20/03/99	Maccabi Irony Ashdod	A	1-0	Salman
03/04/99	Maccabi Petach-Tikva	H	1-1	Oka
17/04/99	Hapoel Irony Rishon Lezion	A	1-5	Danino
24/04/99	Maccabi Haifa	H	1-0	Salman
01/05/99	Bnei Yehuda	A	0-2	
08/05/99	Hapoel Tel-Aviv	A	0-3	
15/05/99	Zafririm Holon	H	1-1	Danino
22/05/99	Maccabi Herzliya	A	0-0	
29/05/99	Maccabi Jaffa	H	3-1	Hudida, Aharon, Salman

HAPOEL KFAR-SABA

CLUB DIRECTORY

Hapoel Kfar-Saba
P.O. Box 13
Kfar-Saba
tel - (09) 950588
fax - (09) 958116
Year of Formation - 1928
Chairman - Israel Neon
Secretary - Gabi Twilli
Coach - Shimon Shenhar; Moshe Sinai
(99/00 - Eyal Lahman)
Stadium - Kfar-Saba (7,500)

MAJOR HONOURS
League Championship - (1) 1982.
Domestic Cup - (3) 1975, 1980, 1990.

APPEARANCES 98/99

	P	Ap	(s)	Gls
Yaniv ABERGIL	A	27	(3)	17
Giorgi ANCHABADZE (GEO)	M	6	(3)	
Elad ARIE	M	1	(1)	
Tamir BEN HAIM	M	26	(3)	
Ehud CAHILA	D	11		1
Nicolae CATALIN (ROM)	D	20	(2)	
Yaniv CHICHIAN	M	3	(7)	
Alon COHEN	D	1	(1)	
Shimon DANAN	M	7	(10)	2
Yossi GANAH	A	1	(8)	
Kobi GANON	D	16	(1)	
Rami GLAM	D	2	(3)	
Avigdor ITZHAK	M	18	(3)	3
Alon KAPLAN	D	2		
Itay KOREN	D	27	(2)	
Ronny MAMAN	M	2		
Shalom MEIROVICH	D		(1)	
Avi MENASHE	M	1		
Mario MESTROVIC (CRO)	M	24	(1)	2
Tamir NETZER	D	17	(2)	
Ami ROZENBERG	G	4		
Avi SANDOR	D	3	(13)	
Tomer SHEM TOV	D	21	(5)	1
Sagie SHTRAUS	G	26		
Idan SHUM	D	17	(5)	
Niv TAL	M	21	(7)	10
Eli TZUR	M		(1)	
Adrian UNGUR (ROM)	A	25	(2)	11
Nir YOUNAY	M	1	(3)	

LEAGUE RESULTS 1998/99

21/08/98	Bnei Yehuda	H	1-1	Tal
28/08/98	Maccabi Irony Ashdod	H	1-0	Ungur
12/09/98	Maccabi Petach-Tikva	A	1-3	Abergil
18/09/98	Hapoel Irony Rishon Lezion	H	5-2	Abergil, Ungur 2, Tal, Cahila
17/10/98	Maccabi Haifa	A	1-4	Ungur
23/10/98	Hapoel Jerusalem	H	2-0	Ungur, Itzhak
30/10/98	Hapoel Tel-Aviv	A	1-3	Abergil
07/11/98	Zafririm Holon	H	0-4	
14/11/98	Maccabi Herzliya	A	1-0	Ungur
20/11/98	Maccabi Jaffa	H	1-1	Abergil (p)
05/12/98	Hapoel Petach-Tikva	A	2-4	Itzhak, Abergil (p)
12/12/98	Hapoel Beit Sh'an	H	2-0	Tal, Abergil (p)
19/12/98	Hapoel Haifa	A	0-6	
25/12/98	Beitar Jerusalem	H	2-3	Ungur, Abergil (p)
02/01/99	Maccabi Tel-Aviv	A	0-5	
29/01/99	Bnei Yehuda	A	0-3	
06/02/99	Maccabi Irony Ashdod	A	1-1	Danan
13/02/99	Maccabi Petach-Tikva	H	3-2	Ungur 2, Mestrovic
20/02/99	Hapoel Irony Rishon Lezion	A	1-2	Abergil (p)
01/03/99	Maccabi Haifa	H	1-4	Danan
13/03/99	Hapoel Jerusalem	A	2-1	Itzhak, Abergil
20/03/99	Hapoel Tel-Aviv	H	0-0	
03/04/99	Zafririm Holon	A	2-2	Shem Tov, Tal
17/04/99	Maccabi Herzliya	H	1-0	Ungur
24/04/99	Maccabi Jaffa	A	4-1	Tal 2, Abergil 2
30/04/99	Hapoel Petach-Tikva	H	2-2	Abergil 2
07/05/99	Hapoel Beit Sh'an	A	2-0	Ungur, Tal
14/05/99	Hapoel Haifa	H	7-3	Abergil 4, Tal 2, Mestrovic
22/05/99	Beitar Jerusalem	A	1-4	Tal
29/05/99	Maccabi Tel-Aviv	H	0-5	

HAPOEL PETACH-TIKVA

CLUB DIRECTORY

Hapoel Petach-Tikva
P.O. Box 2108
Volfson St. 39
Petach-Tikva
tel - (03) 9248353
fax - (03) 9218352
Year of Formation - 1930
Chairman - Lior Shahar
Manager - Giora Shpigel (99/00 - Nir Levin)
Coach - Eli Machpud
Stadium - Hapoel Petach-Tikva (7,500)

MAJOR HONOURS
League Championship - (6)
1955, 1959, 1960, 1961, 1962, 1963.
Domestic Cup - (2) 1957, 1992.

APPEARANCES 98/99

	P	Ap	(s)	Gls
Eli ABARBNEL	M	19	(8)	4
Daniel ABAS	M		(1)	
Eyal ABRAMOV	G	4	(1)	
Miodrag ANGELKOVIC (YUG)	A	1	(10)	
Rahamim AMAR	D	4		
Rehuven ATAR	M	25	(2)	5
Walib BADIR	M	26	(1)	8
Assif RFN YISHAI	M	9	(7)	1
Ilan BOURON	D	25	(1)	2
Manor HASSAN	M	17	(7)	4
Yaniv HERMESH	D	8	(2)	
Shay HESS	G	26		
Idan HILEL	A		(2)	
Motti KAKUN	A	29		20
Vitaliy KOMERANSKYI (UKR)	M	1	(1)	
Beni KOZOSHVILI	D	27		
Ivica KULESEVIC (CRO)	D	25		
LUZON	M		(1)	
Igor MAKOVEYEV (UKR)	M	8	(3)	2
Gábor MÁRTON (HUN)	M	13	(1)	2
Alon MAYA	D	15	(2)	2
Yossi ROZEN	M	3	(11)	1
Guy SHAMIR	M	7	(10)	1
Ilie STAN (ROM)	M	20	(2)	1
Avi YEHIEL	D	12	(1)	0
Michael ZANDBERG	M	6	(3)	1

LEAGUE RESULTS 1998/99

22/08/98	Hapoel Jerusalem	A	1-2	Kakun
29/08/98	Hapoel Tel-Aviv	H	2-0	Kakun 2
11/09/98	Zafririm Holon	A	2-1	Kakun, Abarbnel
19/09/98	Maccabi Herzliya	H	2-0	Stan, Márton
02/10/98	Maccabi Jaffa	A	3-0	Bouron, Kakun 2 (1p)
21/10/98	Bnei Yehuda	A	2-1	Maya, Kakun
31/10/98	Hapoel Beit Sh'an	H	7-0	Kakun 3, Hassan, Atar 2, Maya
07/11/98	Hapoel Haifa	A	0-1	
14/11/98	Beitar Jerusalem	H	3-2	Badir, Márton, Kakun
21/11/98	Maccabi Tel-Aviv	A	0-3	
05/12/98	Hapoel Kfar-Saba	H	4-2	Kakun, Badir 2, Atar
12/12/98	Maccabi Irony Ashdod	A	1-4	Kakun
19/12/98	Maccabi Petach-Tikva	H	1-1	Hassan
26/12/98	Hapoel Irony Rishon Lezion	A	1-0	Badir
02/01/99	Maccabi Haifa	H	1-3	Badir
29/01/99	Hapoel Jerusalem	H	2-0	Kakun, Atar
06/02/99	Hapoel Tel-Aviv	A	1-3	Hassan
12/02/99	Zafririm Holon	H	1-1	Badir
20/02/99	Maccabi Herzliya	A	2-2	Kakun, Ben Yishai
06/03/99	Maccabi Jaffa	H	3-0	Kakun, Makoveyev 2
13/03/99	Bnei Yehuda	H	1-1	Badir
20/03/99	Hapoel Beit Sh'an	A	3-2	Kakun (p), Bouron, Abarbnel
03/04/99	Hapoel Haifa	H	1-2	Kakun
17/04/99	Beitar Jerusalem	A	0-2	
24/04/99	Maccabi Tel-Aviv	H	3-2	Atar, Zandberg, Kakun (p)
30/04/99	Hapoel Kfar-Saba	A	2-2	Rozen, Abarbnel
08/05/99	Maccabi Irony Ashdod	H	1-1	Badir
15/05/99	Maccabi Petach-Tikva	A	2-2	Hassan, Shamir
22/05/99	Hapoel Irony Rishon Lezion	H	2-3	Abarbnel, Kakun
29/05/99	Maccabi Haifa	A	0-4	

HAPOEL TEL-AVIV

CLUB DIRECTORY

Hapoel Tel-Aviv
P.O. Box 8402
Tel-Aviv 61084
tel - (03) 6827711
fax - (03) 6827722
Year of Formation - 1927
Chairman - Moti Orenstein
Secretary - Arye Hershkovich
Coach - Eli Cohen (99/00 - Dror Kashtan)
Stadium - Bloomfield (20,800)

MAJOR HONOURS
League Championship - (12) 1934, 1935, 1936,
1938, 1940, 1943, 1957, 1966, 1969, 1981,
1986, 1988.
Domestic Cup - (8) 1928, 1934, 1937, 1938,
1940, 1960, 1972, 1999.

APPEARANCES 98/99

		P	Ap	(s)	Gls
Avi AZOULAY	D	9	(6)	1
Pini BALELI	A		(3)	
Eyal BEN AMI	D	21	(2)	2
Ehud CAHILA	D	11		
Sebastijan CIMEROTIC (SLO)	M	19	(7)	7
Israel COHEN	D	13	(3)	1
Shahar COHEN	D	9	(6)	
Sagie ELIMELECH	G	27	(1)	
Shimon GERSHON	D	30		2
Felix HALFON	D	21	(2)	
Yaacov HILEL	D	12	(1)	
Ziv KAVEDA	M	2	(10)	1
Gábor MÁRTON (HUN)	M	10	(2)	1
Ron NACHMAN	D	7	(7)	2
Motti OHAION	D	12	(3)	
Davor RUPNIK (CRO)	M	26		1
Kobi SHALO	G	3	(1)	
Idan TAL	M	13	(1)	2
Robert TEZACKI (CRO)	M	11		
Shalom TIKVA	M	20	(6)	6
Salim TUAAMA	A	9	(14)	6
Assi TUBI	A	24	(3)	10
Kfir UDI	A	14	(8)	2
Aviv VOLNERMAN	A	5	(1)	1
Yaniv YARON	D	2	(1)	

LEAGUE RESULTS 1998/99

Date	Opponent	H/A	Score	Scorers
22/08/98	Maccabi Jaffa	H	1-0	Volnerman
29/08/98	Hapoel Petach-Tikva	A	0-2	
12/09/98	Hapoel Beit Sh'an	H	1-0	Cohen I.
19/09/98	Hapoel Haifa	A	0-1	
17/10/98	Beitar Jerusalem	H	1-0	Cimerotic (p)
24/10/98	Maccabi Tel-Aviv	A	1-1	Nachman
30/10/98	Hapoel Kfar-Saba	H	3-1	Ben Ami, Tubi, Cimerotic
07/11/98	Maccabi Irony Ashdod	A	1-3	Gershon
14/11/98	Maccabi Petach-Tikva	H	3-1	Cimerotic 2 (1p), Azoulay
21/11/98	Hapoel Irony Rishon Lezion	A	7-3	Tuaama, Tubi 3, Ben Ami, Gershon, Tikva
05/12/98	Maccabi Haifa	H	1-2	Tubi
12/12/98	Hapoel Jerusalem	A	1-1	Tikva
19/12/98	Bnei Yehuda	H	1-1	Cimerotic (p)
26/12/98	Zafririm Holon	H	0-0	
02/01/99	Maccabi Herzliya	A	1-1	Kaveda
28/01/99	Maccabi Jaffa	A	1-0	Tubi
06/02/99	Hapoel Petach-Tikva	H	3-1	Tikva, Cimerotic 2 (1p)
12/02/99	Hapoel Beit Sh'an	A	3-1	Tubi, Tikva, Tuaama
20/02/99	Hapoel Haifa	H	0-0	
06/03/99	Beitar Jerusalem	A	1-0	Tal
13/03/99	Maccabi Tel-Aviv	H	2-0	Márton, Tubi
19/03/99	Hapoel Kfar-Saba	A	0-0	
03/04/99	Maccabi Irony Ashdod	H	1-0	Tikva
17/04/99	Maccabi Petach-Tikva	A	1-3	Tubi
24/04/99	Hapoel Irony Rishon Lezion	H	6-1	Udi, Rupnik, Tikva, Tal, Tuaama, Tubi (p)
01/05/99	Maccabi Haifa	A	0-1	
08/05/99	Hapoel Jerusalem	H	3-0	Nachman, Tuaama, Udi
15/05/99	Bnei Yehuda	A	0-1	
22/05/99	Zafririm Holon	A	0-1	
29/05/99	Maccabi Herzliya	H	2-0	Tuaama 2

MACCABI HAIFA

CLUB DIRECTORY

Maccabi Haifa
Heinrich Heine st. 14
Haifa
tel - (04) 8361177
fax - (04) 8373881
Year of Formation - 1910
Chairman - Ya'acov Shahar
Manager - Dusan Uhrin
Coach - Daniel Brailowski (99/00 - Eli Cohen)
Stadium - Kiriat Eliezer (18,000)

MAJOR HONOURS
League Championship - (5)
1984, 1985, 1989, 1991, 1994.
Domestic Cup - (5)
1962, 1991, 1993, 1995, 1998.

APPEARANCES 98/99

	P	Ap	(s)	Gls
Héctor ALMANDOS (ARG)	D	1		
Serhiy BALANCHUK (UKR)	D	5	(3)	
Arik BENADO	D	27		1
Shlomi BEN HAMO	M		(1)	1
Yossi BENAYOUN	M	29		16
Jerzy BRZECZEK (POL)	M	12	(1)	2
Shlomi DAHAN	M		(1)	
Nir DAVIDOVICH	G	26		
Ibrahim DURO (CRO)	M	13	(12)	2
Eliron ELKAYAM	D	3		
Alon HARAZI	D	26		3
Ronen HARAZI	A	6	(2)	2
Radovan HROMADKO (CZE)	A	17	(6)	5
Avishai JANO	D	24	(4)	2
Yaniv KATAN	A	16	(10)	1
Assi KELMAN	M	5	(4)	
Adoram KEISSY	D	28	(1)	3
Offir KOPEL	M	26		1
Guy MELAMED	D	8	(3)	
Alon MIZRAHI	A	15		14
Shuki NAGAR	D	22	(6)	2
Victor PAÇO (ALB)	A	8	(6)	4
Amos SASSI	D	6		
Haim SILVAS	M	3	(10)	2
Eyal VAKRAT	G	4		
Liron VILNER	A		(11)	

LEAGUE RESULTS 1998/99

22/08/98	Hapoel Beit Sh'an	H	4-0	Keissy, Hromadko, Silvas 2
09/09/98	Hapoel Haifa	A	0-0	
12/09/98	Beitar Jerusalem	H	2-4	og (Domb), Keissy
27/09/98	Maccabi Tel-Aviv	A	1-2	Mizrahi
17/10/98	Hapoel Kfar-Saba	H	4-1	Harazi A., Benayoun, Katan, Mizrahi
31/10/98	Maccabi Petach-Tikva	H	4-0	Mizrahi 2, Hromadko, Benayoun
09/11/98	Hapoel Irony Rishon Lezion	A	2-1	Mizrahi 2
14/11/98	Bnei Yehuda	H	4-0	Benayoun 3, Hromadko
21/11/98	Hapoel Jerusalem	H	6-1	Mizrahi 3 (1p), Hromadko, Benayoun, Jano
27/11/98	Maccabi Irony Ashdod	A	0-0	
05/12/98	Hapoel Tel-Aviv	A	2-1	Harazi A., Benayoun
12/12/98	Zafririm Holon	H	1-0	Mizrahi (p)
19/12/98	Maccabi Herzliya	A	1-0	Mizrahi
26/12/98	Maccabi Jaffa	H	2-0	Jano, Mizrahi
02/01/99	Hapoel Petach-Tikva	A	3-1	Mizrahi 2, Hromadko
29/01/99	Hapoel Beit Sh'an	A	1-2	Benayoun
06/02/99	Hapoel Haifa	H	0-1	
13/02/99	Beitar Jerusalem	A	1-1	Keissy (p)
20/02/99	Maccabi Tel-Aviv	H	1-2	Benayoun
26/02/99	Hapoel Kfar-Saba	A	4-1	Paço 2, Benayoun, Nagar
21/03/99	Maccabi Petach-Tikva	A	4-0	Benayoun 2, Paço, Duro
03/04/99	Hapoel Irony Rishon Lezion	H	3-1	Nagar, Duro, Harazi R.
07/04/99	Maccabi Irony Ashdod	H	2-1	Harazi R., Brzeczek
17/04/99	Bnei Yehuda	A	0-2	
24/04/99	Hapoel Jerusalem	A	0-1	
01/05/99	Hapoel Tel-Aviv	H	1-0	Benayoun
08/05/99	Zafririm Holon	A	2-0	Benayoun, Ben Hamo
15/05/99	Maccabi Herzliya	H	3-0	Benayoun, Paço, Harazi A.
22/05/99	Maccabi Jaffa	A	0-1	
29/05/99	Hapoel Petach-Tikva	H	4-0	Kopel, Benado, Brzeczek, Benayoun

MACCABI HERZLIYA

CLUB DIRECTORY

Maccabi Herzliya
Porzai Hadereech st. 2/10
Herzliya
tel - (09) 574774
fax - (09) 509865
Year of Formation - 1926
Chairman - Ariel Shaynman
Coach - Andrei Bal; Yehushua Faygenbaum
Stadium - Irony Herzliya (10,000)

APPEARANCES 98/99

	P	Ap	(s)	Gls
Igal ANTEBI	D	29		4
Eitan ARBEL	D	10	(3)	
Shay ASRAF	M	12		
Lior ASULIN	M	8	(17)	5
Alex BREMCHER	D	23	(2)	
Eliko COHEN	M	1	(4)	
Oren DANZIGER	A	6	(10)	2
Roman FILIPCHUK (BLS)	A	6	(7)	
Guy GAT	M	28		1
Shuli GILARDI	G	29		
Vasiliy IVANOV (RUS)	D	27		3
Yaacov KORATZKY	M	24	(1)	
Amit LEVI	D	22	(4)	
Meir LEVI	M		(1)	
Lior MALKA	M	1		
Erez MESIKA	A		(5)	1
Guy MISHAL	M	18	(2)	
Hamlet MKHITARYAN (ARM)	M	7	(6)	
Oleg NADUDA (RUS)	M	16		4
Vladimir NIDERGAUS (KAZ)	M	12	(2)	3
Guy PRIMOR	D	1		
Guy SALOMON	G	1		
Haim SHABU	M	6	(4)	1
Yair SIMHON	A	22	(7)	5
Tzahi ZANETI	M	12	(6)	
Liron VILNER	A	9	(2)	2

LEAGUE RESULTS 1998/99

22/08/98	Zafririm Holon	A	0-3	
29/08/98	Bnei Yehuda	A	1-0	Ivanov
12/09/98	Maccabi Jaffa	H	3-0	Danziger, Asulin, Mesika
19/09/98	Hapoel Petach-Tikva	A	0-2	
03/10/98	Hapoel Beit Sh'an	H	3-1	Asulin 2, Nidergaus
24/10/98	Hapoel Haifa	A	0-2	
31/10/98	Beitar Jerusalem	H	1-4	Danziger
07/11/98	Maccabi Tel-Aviv	A	2-3	Nidergaus, Antebi
14/11/98	Hapoel Kfar-Saba	H	0-1	
21/11/98	Maccabi Irony Ashdod	A	1-2	Simhon
05/12/98	Maccabi Petach-Tikva	H	0-2	
12/12/98	Hapoel Irony Rishon Lezion	A	2-2	Simhon 2
19/12/98	Hapoel Haifa	H	0-1	
26/12/98	Hapoel Jerusalem	A	0-1	
02/01/99	Hapoel Tel-Aviv	H	1-1	Nidergaus
28/01/99	Zafririm Holon	H	0-0	
06/02/99	Bnei Yehuda	H	3-2	Simhon, Antebi, Naduda
13/02/99	Maccabi Jaffa	A	2-1	Naduda, Asulin
20/02/99	Hapoel Petach-Tikva	H	2-2	Asulin, Ivanov
05/03/99	Hapoel Beit Sh'an	A	1-0	Naduda
13/03/99	Hapoel Haifa	H	2-1	Naduda, Vilner
20/03/99	Beitar Jerusalem	A	0-1	
03/04/99	Maccabi Tel-Aviv	H	0-1	
17/04/99	Hapoel Kfar-Saba	A	0-1	
24/04/99	Maccabi Irony Ashdod	H	3-1	Simhon, Vilner, Gat
01/05/99	Maccabi Petach-Tikva	A	1-0	Shabu
07/05/99	Hapoel Irony Rishon Lezion	H	3-2	Antebi 2, Ivanov
15/05/99	Maccabi Haifa	A	0-3	
22/05/99	Hapoel Jerusalem	H	0-0	
29/05/99	Hapoel Tel-Aviv	A	0-2	

MACCABI IRONY ASHDOD

CLUB DIRECTORY

Maccabi Irony Ashdod
Ashdod
tel - (08) 524761/555457
Year of Formation - 1983
Chairman - Rafi Asformas
Coach - Nir Levin; Nissim Bachar
Stadium - Municipal (8,500)

APPEARANCES 98/99

	P	Ap	(s)	Gls
Eyal ALMOSNINO	M	23		3
Yossi AIZENBERG	A	2		1
Yair AZOULAY	D		(2)	
Tibor BALOGH (HUN)	D	27	(1)	6
Shlomi BEN HAMO	M	9	(2)	
Baruch DAGO	M	21	(3)	3
Akaki DEVADZE (GEO)	G	26		
Hanan FADIDA	M	6	(11)	1
Gal FIBACH	D	14		
Naor GALILI	A	1	(10)	
Gadi HAZUT	D	21		1
Yossi MALKA	D	17	(3)	
Sharon MARZIANO	D	14	(7)	1
Géza MÉSZÖLY (HUN)	D	28		
Alberto NEVADA (ARG)	A	16	(2)	3
Yossi OFFIR	M	10	(9)	
Oren SHABTAY	M	1		
Adir SHARABI	M	20	(3)	
Eliezer SPAYER	D	22	(3)	
Lior SUDAMI	M		(1)	
Adir TUBUL	D	9	(10)	
Amir TURGEMAN	A	30		19
Shimon ZELIG	G	4	(3)	
Igal ZRIHAN	A	9	(11)	2

LEAGUE RESULTS 1998/99

22/08/98	Maccabi Tel-Aviv	H	3-3	Turgeman 2 (1p), Aizenberg
28/08/98	Hapoel Kfar-Saba	A	0-1	
12/09/98	Bnei Yehuda	H	3-0	Turgeman 2 (1p), Almosnino
19/09/98	Maccabi Petach-Tikva	H	2-7	Turgeman 2 (1p)
03/10/98	Hapoel Irony Rishon Lezion	A	0-0	
31/10/98	Hapoel Jerusalem	A	2-4	Turgeman, Nevada
07/11/98	Hapoel Tel-Aviv	H	3-1	Nevada, Almosnino, Turgeman
13/11/98	Zafririm Holon	A	0-0	
21/11/98	Maccabi Herzliya	H	2-1	Balogh, Turgeman
27/11/98	Maccabi Haifa	H	0-0	
05/12/98	Maccabi Jaffa	A	0-1	
12/12/98	Hapoel Petach-Tikva	H	4-1	Turgeman (p), Balogh 2, Zrihan
18/12/98	Hapoel Beit Sh'an	A	1-1	Dago
26/12/98	Hapoel Haifa	H	3-2	Nevada, Turgeman 2 (1p)
02/01/99	Beitar Jerusalem	A	2-4	Turgeman (p), Zrihan
29/01/99	Maccabi Tel-Aviv	A	0-4	
06/02/99	Hapoel Kfar-Saba	H	1-1	Turgeman
13/02/99	Bnei Yehuda	A	0-1	
20/02/99	Maccabi Petach-Tikva	A	1-0	Fadida
06/03/99	Hapoel Irony Rishon Lezion	H	0-3	
20/03/99	Hapoel Jerusalem	H	0-1	
03/04/99	Hapoel Tel-Aviv	A	0-1	
07/04/99	Maccabi Haifa	A	1-2	Balogh
17/04/99	Zafririm Holon	H	2-2	Hazut, Turgeman (p)
23/04/99	Maccabi Herzliya	A	1-3	Dugo
01/05/99	Maccabi Jaffa	H	2-0	Marziano, Balogh
08/05/99	Hapoel Petach-Tikva	A	1-1	Turgeman
15/05/99	Hapoel Beit Sh'an	H	2-1	Almosnino, Turgeman
22/05/99	Hapoel Haifa	A	2-2	Turgeman, Dago
29/05/99	Beitar Jerusalem	H	2-1	Balogh, Turgeman

MACCABI JAFFA

CLUB DIRECTORY

Maccabi Jaffa
Levi eshkol St. 64
Jaffa, Tel-Aviv
tel - (03) 6991246
fax - (03) 6822885
Year of Formation - 1949
Chairman - Itzhak Assa
Manager - Eli Cohen
Coach - Ben Hur Mizrahi; Boaz Sulami;
Moshe Onnana
Stadium - R.I. Gaon (5,000)

APPEARANCES 98/99

	P	Ap	(s)	Gls
Morad ABU KISHAK	D	15	(1)	
Michal ANTEL (POL)	M	3	(1)	
ASSIAG	D		(1)	
Sharon AVITAN	A	4		
Peter BINKOVSKI (SLO)	M	4		
David BELLA	G		(1)	
Imad BUCHRY	D	11	(6)	4
Ahmed CAHIL	M		(4)	
Orren COHAVI	A	6	(4)	
Nissim COHEN	M	12	(6)	1
Shmoel DALAWY	D	3		
Dudi DAVIDOV	G	8	(1)	
Rav DZILOVSKY	M	16	(2)	
Alon ELMEKAYES	D	17		1
Dudu HEFER	M	2	(1)	
Gal HERSHLIKOVIC	M	24		
Dan LEVI	D	17		
Zeev LUPO	D	8	(1)	
Offir MOIAL	D	14		
Guy NACHMAN	D	12	(2)	
Mahmid NIDAL	D	23	(1)	3
Omri OFEK	A	15	(2)	3
Yaniv OFFRI	A	3	(2)	
Ozzi OHAION	M	12	(2)	1
Raz RABINOVICH	D	22	(1)	
Ran RASHTI	M	8	(11)	1
Shlomo ROZOLIO	D	3	(2)	
Eyal SAIAG	D	4	(1)	
Motti SASON	M	9	(4)	
Eran SHAKROKA	M	3	(5)	
Dudi STOLPER	M	3		
Shlomi VAKNIN	D	6	(1)	
Sandi VALENTINCIC (BOS)	A	8	(1)	1
Adnan ZILZEDOVIC (BOS)	A	8	(2)	
Avivi ZOHAR	M	5		
Irakli ZOIDZE (GEO)	G	22		

LEAGUE RESULTS 1998/99

22/08/98	Hapoel Tel-Aviv	A	0-1	
28/08/98	Zafririm Holon	H	0-3	
12/09/98	Maccabi Herzliya	A	0-3	
19/09/98	Bnei Yehuda	A	1-6	Nidal
03/10/98	Hapoel Petach-Tikva	H	0-3	
23/10/98	Hapoel Beit Sh'an	A	1-2	Nidal
30/10/98	Hapoel Haifa	H	1-2	Cohen
07/11/98	Beitar Jerusalem	A	1-7	Valentincic
14/11/98	Maccabi Tel-Aviv	H	0-1	
20/11/98	Hapoel Kfar-Saba	A	1-1	Buchry
05/12/98	Maccabi Irony Ashdod	H	1-0	Ofek
12/12/98	Maccabi Petach-Tikva	A	1-3	Elmekayes
19/12/98	Hapoel Irony Rishon Lezion	H	1-4	Rashti
26/12/98	Maccabi Haifa	A	0-2	
01/01/99	Hapoel Jerusalem	H	0-1	
28/01/99	Hapoel Tel-Aviv	H	0-1	
06/02/99	Zafririm Holon	A	1-1	Ohaion
13/02/99	Maccabi Herzliya	H	1-2	Nidal
19/02/99	Bnei Yehuda	H	0-3	
06/03/99	Hapoel Petach-Tikva	A	0-3	
13/03/99	Hapoel Beit Sh'an	H	1-1	Ofek
20/03/99	Hapoel Haifa	A	0-3	
02/04/99	Beitar Jerusalem	H	0-0	
17/04/99	Maccabi Tel-Aviv	A	0-4	
24/04/99	Hapoel Kfar-Saba	H	1-4	Buchry
01/05/99	Maccabi Irony Ashdod	A	0-2	
07/05/99	Maccabi Petach-Tikva	H	0-4	
15/05/99	Hapoel Irony Rishon Lezion	A	1-3	Buchry
22/05/99	Maccabi Haifa	H	1-0	Buchry
29/05/99	Hapoel Jerusalem	A	1-3	Ofek

MACCABI PETACH-TIKVA

CLUB DIRECTORY

Maccabi Petach-Tikva
P.O. Box 67
Petach-Tikva
tel - (03) 9224484
fax - (09) 851383
Year of Formation - 1912
Chairman - Avraham Luzon
Secretary - Nahom Besser
Coach - Moshe Sinai; Eyal Lahman
(99/00 - Yossi Mizrahi)
Stadium - Hapoel Petach-Tikva (7,500)

MAJOR HONOURS
Domestic Cup - (2) 1935, 1952.

APPEARANCES 98/99

	P	Ap	(s)	Gls
Guy AGIV	D	12	(1)	
Ismael AMAR	D	26		5
M AMAR	M	1		
Fredi ASULIN	D		(2)	
Sharon AVITAN	A	16	(2)	6
Rajib BARANSI	M	16	(4)	10
Tomer BEN YOUSEF	D	21	(1)	
Erez BIALLA	M		(19)	2
Ohad COHEN	G	21		
Ehud GORESH	G	9		
Shay HABSHUSH	D	1		
Guy ITZHAK	D	20	(5)	9
Noam KEISSY	D		(1)	
Eran LEVI	D	12	(2)	
Jaroslav LOZEK (CZE)	D	26		1
Yetav LUZON	M		(1)	
Murat MAGOMEDOV (RUS)	D	27		
Idan MALIHI	M	14	(6)	1
Shabi MIRA	M		(5)	1
Sami MOSALEM	M	9	(2)	
Kfir PARTIELY	D	23		1
Artur PETROSYAN (ARM)	A	6	(8)	
Besnik PRENGA (ALB)	A	1	(1)	1
Haim SHABU	M	3	(3)	
Rave SHARABI	M	6	(7)	1
Tzahi SHMARIAHO	A	17	(6)	4
Idan TAL	M	14	(1)	3
Sharon TZOFIN	D	27	(2)	

LEAGUE RESULTS 1998/99

22/08/98	Beitar Jerusalem	H	1-2	Baransi (p)
29/08/98	Maccabi Tel-Aviv	A	3-0	Itzhak, Baransi 2 (1p)
12/09/98	Hapoel Kfar-Saba	H	3-1	Itzhak, Amar I., Prenga
19/09/98	Maccabi Irony Ashdod	A	7-2	Itzhak, Baransi 2, Amar I., Tal, Shmariaho, Bialla
03/10/98	Bnei Yehuda	H	1-1	Shmariaho
24/10/98	Hapoel Irony Rishon Lezion	H	0-0	
31/10/98	Maccabi Haifa	A	0-4	
07/11/98	Hapoel Jerusalem	H	0-0	
14/11/98	Hapoel Tel-Aviv	A	1-3	Amar I.
21/11/98	Zafririm Holon	H	1-1	Avitan
05/12/98	Maccabi Herzliya	A	2-0	Avitan, Baransi
12/12/98	Maccabi Jaffa	H	3-1	Tal 2 (1p), Avitan
19/12/98	Hapoel Petach-Tikva	A	1-1	Malihi
26/12/98	Hapoel Beit Sh'an	H	4-0	Shmariaho 2, Partiely, Baransi
02/01/99	Hapoel Haifa	A	0-4	
29/01/99	Beitar Jerusalem	A	0-2	
06/02/99	Maccabi Tel-Aviv	H	0-3	
13/02/99	Hapoel Kfar-Saba	A	2-3	Itzhak, Baransi
19/02/99	Maccabi Irony Ashdod	H	0-1	
06/03/99	Bnei Yehuda	A	2-0	Bialla, Amar I. (p)
21/03/99	Maccabi Haifa	H	0-4	
13/03/99	Hapoel Irony Rishon Lezion	A	1-2	Sharabi
03/04/99	Hapoel Jerusalem	A	1-1	Baransi (p)
17/04/99	Hapoel Tel-Aviv	H	3-1	Avitan 2, Itzhak
23/04/99	Zafririm Holon	A	0-2	
01/05/99	Maccabi Herzliya	H	0-1	
07/05/99	Maccabi Jaffa	A	4-0	Amar I., Avitan, Itzhak, Mira
15/05/99	Hapoel Petach-Tikva	H	2-2	Lozek, Itzhak
21/05/99	Hapoel Beit Sh'an	A	3-0	Itzhak 2, Baransi
29/05/99	Hapoel Haifa	H	0-3	

MACCABI TEL-AVIV

CLUB DIRECTORY

Maccabi Tel-Aviv
Maccabi St. 4
Tel-Aviv 63293
tel - (03) 5250712
fax - (03) 5288503
Year of Formation - 1906
Chairman - Loni Herzikovich
Secretary - Shimon Korek
Coach - Avraham Grant
Stadium - Ramat-Gan (46,000)

MAJOR HONOURS
League Championship - (18) 1937, 1939, 1941,
1947, 1949, 1950, 1951, 1952, 1954, 1956,
1968, 1970, 1972, 1977, 1979, 1992, 1995,
1996.
Domestic Cup - (19) 1929, 1930, 1933, 1941,
1946, 1947, 1954, 1955, 1958, 1959, 1964,
1965, 1967, 1970, 1977, 1987, 1988, 1994,
1996.

APPEARANCES 98/99

		P	Ap	(s)	Gls
Marco BALBUL	D	19	(1)		
Dedi BEN DAYAN	M	28	(1)	3	
Eli BITON	A	1		1	
Alon BRUMER	M	5	(1)		
Gadi BRUMER	D	17	(3)		
Rafi COHEN	G	5	(1)		
Eli DRIKS	A	2	(18)	3	
Kfir EDRY	D	23	(1)	6	
Michael EMENALO (NIG)	D	22			
Moshe GLAM	D	16	(7)	5	
Offir HAIM	M	7	(17)	1	
Haim HAJAJ	M	2			
Jefri ISHAY	D	5	(2)		
Aleksei KOSOLAPOV (RUS)	M	25		9	
Andrzej KUBICA (POL)	A	30		21	
Offer LEVI	D	2	(2)		
Ben LUZ	M	6	(9)		
Avi NIMNI	M	23	(1)	17	
Alon OFFIR	D	25		3	
David REVIVO	M	21	(4)	1	
Oren ROTEM	D	2			
Alin Marcel RUS (ROM)	D		(1)		
Avi STROL	M		(1)		
Guy TZARFATI	M	17	(6)	4	
Aleksander UVAROV	G	25			
Efi ZAFRIR	A		(1)		
Itzhak ZOHAR	M	2	(5)	2	

LEAGUE RESULTS 1998/99

22/08/98	Maccabi Irony Ashdod	A	3-3	Kosolapov, Kubica (p), Driks
29/08/98	Maccabi Petach-Tikva	H	0-3	
12/09/98	Hapoel Irony Rishon Lezion	A	2-3	Kubica, Ben Dayan
26/09/98	Maccabi Haifa	H	2-1	Revivo, Kubica (p)
03/10/98	Hapoel Jerusalem	A	2-3	Nimni, Kubica (p)
14/10/98	Hapoel Tel-Aviv	H	1-1	Kosolapov
31/10/98	Zafririm Holon	A	1-0	Offir
07/11/98	Maccabi Herzliya	H	3-2	Haim, Nimni, Kubica
14/11/98	Maccabi Jaffa	A	1-0	Nimni (p)
21/11/98	Hapoel Petach-Tikva	H	3-0	Kubica, Nimni 2
05/12/98	Hapoel Beit Sh'an	A	5-0	og (Hader), Glam, Kubica, Driks, Nimni (p)
12/12/98	Hapoel Haifa	H	1-1	Glam
19/12/98	Beitar Jerusalem	A	0-1	
26/12/98	Bnei Yehuda	A	6-0	Glam 2, Edry, Kosolapov, Kubica, Nimni
02/01/99	Hapoel Kfar-Saba	H	5-0	Nimni, Kubica 3, Edry
29/01/99	Maccabi Irony Ashdod	H	4-0	Edry, Kosolapov, Nimni, Kubica
06/02/99	Maccabi Petach-Tikva	A	3-0	Tzarfati, Nimni (p), Kosolapov
13/02/99	Hapoel Irony Rishon Lezion	H	2-1	Kubica, Nimni (p)
20/02/99	Maccabi Haifa	A	2-1	Nimni, Kubica
06/03/99	Hapoel Jerusalem	H	4-0	Kubica 2, Nimni 2
13/03/99	Hapoel Tel-Aviv	A	0-2	
20/03/99	Zafririm Holon	H	4-0	Edry 2, Kosolapov 2
02/04/99	Maccabi Herzliya	A	1-0	Tzarfati
17/04/99	Maccabi Jaffa	H	4-0	Glam, Kubica (p), Nimni 2
24/04/99	Hapoel Petach-Tikva	A	2-3	Nimni, Kosolapov (p)
01/05/99	Hapoel Beit Sh'an	H	3-1	Edry, Zohar, Ben Dayan
08/05/99	Hapoel Haifa	A	2-3	Kubica, Tzarfati
15/05/99	Beitar Jerusalem	H	4-2	Kubica, Offir, Ben Dayan, Zohar
22/05/99	Bnei Yehuda	H	2-1	Offir (p), Kosolapov
29/05/99	Hapoel Kfar-Saba	A	5-0	Tzarfati, Kubica 2 (1p), Driks, Biton

ZAFRIRIM HOLON

CLUB DIRECTORY

Zafririm Holon
Halochamim St. 1
P.O. Box 146
Holon 58101
tel - (03) 5059926
fax - (03) 5038666
Year of Formation - 1972
Chairman - Shtern Haluba
Secretary - Toby Malach
Coach - Guy Levi
Stadium - Zafririm (3,500)

APPEARANCES 98/99

	P	Ap	(s)	Gls
Amir AVIGDOR	D	18		2
Marco BEN BARUCH	M	10	(2)	
Ezra BUZAGLO	M	5	(12)	1
Tal CHEN	M	13	(8)	1
Shlomi DAHAN	M	26		
Giorgi DARASELIA (GEO)	M	26		7
Moshe DVIR	M		(2)	
Oren FLASH	M	28	(1)	3
Motti FLITER	D	22	(1)	
Reni HADAD	D	30		4
Avi IRMIAHO	A	1	(3)	
Alexander JIDKOV (AZB)	G	6		
David KAVEDA	M	3	(15)	1
Yaron MELIKA	G	5		
Oren NISSIM	A	3		
Martin PECKO (SVK)	G	19		
Rafi PUR	D	28		
Kobi PUSTAGI	A		(6)	
Samson SIASIA (NIG)	A	30		12
Nir SOHER	D	28		1
Efi ZAFRIR	M	6	(11)	2
Nezad ZARIC (BOS)	M	23	(7)	1

LEAGUE RESULTS 1998/99

22/08/98	Maccabi Herzliya	H	3-0	Siasia, Buzaglo, Kaveda
29/08/98	Bnei Yehuda	A	3-0	Flash 2, Hadad
01/09/98	Hapoel Petach-Tikva	H	1-2	Siasia
19/09/98	Hapoel Beit Sh'an	A	1-1	Zaric
03/10/98	Hapoel Haifa	H	0-2	
24/10/98	Beitar Jerusalem	A	2-1	Flash, Siasia
31/10/98	Maccabi Tel-Aviv	H	0-1	
07/11/98	Hapoel Kfar-Saba	A	4-0	Siasia, Chen, Avigdor, Daraselia
13/11/98	Maccabi Irony Ashdod	H	0-0	
21/11/98	Maccabi Petach-Tikva	A	1-1	Daraselia
05/12/98	Hapoel Irony Rishon Lezion	H	1-2	Siasia
12/12/98	Maccabi Haifa	A	0-1	
19/12/98	Hapoel Jerusalem	H	3-1	Daraselia, Hadad 2
26/12/98	Hapoel Tel-Aviv	A	0-0	
02/01/99	Bnei Yehuda	H	3-1	Siasia 2, Daraselia
28/01/99	Maccabi Herzliya	A	0-0	
06/02/99	Maccabi Jaffa	H	1-1	Siasia
12/02/99	Hapoel Petach-Tikva	A	1-1	Hadad
20/02/99	Hapoel Beit Sh'an	H	0-1	
06/03/99	Hapoel Haifa	A	1-3	Daraselia
13/03/99	Beitar Jerusalem	H	0-1	
20/03/99	Maccabi Tel-Aviv	A	0-4	
03/04/99	Hapoel Kfar-Saba	H	2-2	Siasia 2
17/04/99	Maccabi Irony Ashdod	A	2-2	Siasia, Daraselia
23/04/99	Maccabi Petach-Tikva	H	2-0	Siasia, Zafrir
01/05/99	Hapoel Irony Rishon Lezion	A	1-2	Zafrir
07/05/99	Maccabi Haifa	H	0-2	
15/05/99	Hapoel Jerusalem	A	1-1	Daraselia
22/05/99	Hapoel Tel-Aviv	H	1-0	Avigdor
29/05/99	Bnei Yehuda	A	1-5	Soher

PROMOTED CLUB

SECOND DIVISION FINAL TABLE 98/99

		Pd	W	D	L	F	A	Pt	GD
1	**Maccabi Netanya**	**30**	**18**	**9**	**1**	**54**	**20**	**63**	**+34**
2	Hapoel Ashkelon	30	19	5	6	62	34	62	+28
3	Hapoel Beer Sheva	30	17	9	4	54	16	60	+38
4	Beitar Beer Sheva	30	18	5	7	50	21	59	+29
5	Maccabi Ako	30	16	7	7	69	37	55	+32
6	Hakoah Ramat-Gan	30	15	10	5	62	31	55	+31
7	Maccabi Kiriat-Gat	30	14	9	7	52	37	49	+15
8	Maccabi Ahi Nazeret	30	12	9	9	44	36	45	+8
9	Bnei Sachnin	30	11	10	9	56	35	43	+21
10	Hapoel Ashdod	30	8	14	8	42	39	38	+3
11	Beitar Tel-Aviv	30	10	3	17	28	46	33	-18
12	Hapoel Bat-Yam	30	8	6	16	52	64	30	-12
13	Maccabi Kfar-Kana	30	6	5	19	34	54	23	-20
14	Hapoel Lod	30	6	5	19	32	69	23	-37
15	Seksiat Nes-Ziona	30	5	2	23	30	103	13	-73
16	Hapoel Taibe	30	2	0	28	27	106	6	-79

N.B. Seksiat Nes-Ziona deducted 4 pts; Maccabi Kiriat-Gat deducted 2 pts.

CLUB DIRECTORY

Maccabi Netanya
Zangvill st. 44
P.O. Box 2242
Netanya
tel - (09) 8620503
fax - (09) 8620503
Year of Formation - 1942
Chairman - Itzhak Tshuva
Secretary - Kobi Baladev
Coach - Uri Malmilian (99/00 - Motti Iwanir)
Stadium - Maccabi Netanya (14,000)

MAJOR HONOURS
League Championship - (5)
1971, 1974, 1978, 1980, 1983.
Domestic Cup - (1) 1978.

ITALY

1	**BARI**	585	13	**ROMA**	597
2	**BOLOGNA**	586	14	**SALERNITANA**	598
3	**CAGLIARI**	587	15	**SAMPDORIA**	599
4	**EMPOLI**	588	16	**UDINESE**	600
5	**FIORENTINA**	589	17	**VENEZIA**	601
6	**INTER**	590	18	**VICENZA**	602
7	**JUVENTUS**	591		**Promoted clubs**	
8	**LAZIO**	592	19	**VERONA**	603
9	**MILAN**	593	20	**TORINO**	603
10	**PARMA**	594	21	**REGGINA**	603
11	**PERUGIA**	595	22	**LECCE**	603
12	**PIACENZA**	596			

TWO CUPS FOR PARMA

Milan sneak up from behind to stun Lazio

FEDERATION DIRECTORY

Federazione Italiana Giuoco Calcio
Via Gregorio Allegri 14, CP 2450, 00198 Roma

tel - (06) 84911
fax - (06) 84912526

Year of Formation - 1898
President - Luciano Nizzola
Secretary - Guglielmo Petrosino

Italy's Serie A is still the number one league in the world. The competition from Spain and England is improving, but the game's top stars still prefer to flock to Italy, where money, it seems, is no object and the chances of international recognition and success are better than anywhere else.

In 1998/99, Italian clubs won two of the three European club competitions and provided no fewer than six quarter-finalists. The country's aggregate for the decade was three victories each in the Champions' Cup and Cup-winners' Cup and an incredible seven in the UEFA Cup (plus six beaten finalists). No other country comes even close to matching that level of consistency.

But although Serie A prides itself on being the richest, the most glamorous and most successful league in the business, for a long time it has consistently fallen short of being the most entertaining and exciting. Attitudes, however, appear to be changing. The caution and negativity of the past is gradually being replaced by a more hedonistic approach to the game. Whereas once, not so long ago, most Italian teams would go away from home with one attacker and try to get a 0-0 draw, they now send out three strikers and go for the win. Tactical warfare is still very much part of the deal, and there are some coaches to whom the old-dog/new-tricks proverb applies, but generally Italian football is a lot more enterprising and captivating than before.

The 1998/99 season was very much a case in point.

LEAGUE CHAMPIONSHIP RESULTS 98/99

		1	2	3	4	5	6	7	8	9	10	11	12	13	14	15	16	17	18
1	Bari		0-0	1-1	2-1	0-0	1-0	0-1	1-3	0-0	1-1	2-1	3-1	1-4	0-0	3-1	1-1	1-0	0-0
2	Bologna	3-1		1-3	2-0	3-0	2-0	3-0	0-1	2-3	0-0	1-1	3-1	1-1	1-1	2-2	1-3	2-1	4-2
3	Cagliari	3-3	0-1		5-1	1-1	2-2	1-0	0-0	1-0	1-0	2-2	3-2	4-3	3-1	5-0	1-2	0-1	1-0
4	Empoli	0-2	0-0	2-1		0-3	1-2	1-0	0-0	1-1	3-5	2-0	1-2	0-0	2-3	0-1	1-3	2-2	1-0
5	Fiorentina	2-2	1-0	4-2	2-0		3-1	1-0	1-1	0-0	2-1	5-1	2-1	0-0	4-0	1-0	1-0	4-1	3-0
6	Inter	2-3	3-1	5-1	5-1	2-0		0-0	3-5	2-2	1-3	2-0	1-0	4-1	2-1	3-0	1-3	6-2	1-1
7	Juventus	1-1	2-2	1-0	0-0	2-1	1-0		0-1	0-2	2-4	2-1	1-0	1-1	3-0	2-0	2-1	3-2	2-0
8	Lazio	0-0	2-0	2-0	4-1	2-0	1-0	1-3		0-0	2-1	3-0	4-1	3-3	6-1	5-2	3-1	2-0	1-1
9	Milan	2-2	3-0	1-0	4-0	1-3	2-2	1-1	1-0		2-1	2-1	1-0	3-2	3-2	3-2	3-0	2-1	1-0
10	Parma	2-1	1-1	1-1	1-0	2-0	1-0	1-0	1-3	4-0		3-1	0-1	1-1	2-0	1-1	4-1	2-2	0-0
11	Perugia	0-1	0-0	2-1	3-1	2-2	2-1	3-4	2-2	1-2	2-1		2-0	3-2	1-0	2-0	1-3	1-0	3-1
12	Piacenza	3-2	5-0	2-0	0-0	4-2	0-0	0-2	1-1	1-1	3-6	2-0		2-0	1-1	4-1	4-3	0-1	2-0
13	Roma	1-1	3-1	3-1	1-1	2-1	4-5	2-0	3-1	1-0	1-0	5-1	2-2		3-1	3-1	4-0	2-0	3-0
14	Salernitana	2-2	4-0	1-3	1-1	1-1	2-0	1-0	1-0	1-2	1-2	2-0	1-1	2-1		2-0	1-2	1-0	2-1
15	Sampdoria	1-0	1-1	0-0	3-0	3-2	4-0	1-2	0-1	2-2	0-2	1-1	3-2	2-1	1-0		1-1	2-1	0-0
16	Udinese	4-0	2-0	2-1	0-0	1-0	0-1	2-2	0-3	1-5	2-1	1-2	1-0	2-1	2-0	2-2		1-1	2-1
17	Venezia	2-1	0-2	1-0	3-2	4-1	3-1	1-1	2-0	0-2	0-0	2-1	0-0	3-1	0-0	0-0	1-0		1-2
18	Vicenza	1-0	0-4	2-1	2-0	1-2	1-1	1-1	1-2	0-2	0-0	3-0	1-0	1-4	1-0	1-0	2-3	0-0	

LEAGUE CHAMPIONSHIP FINAL TABLE 98/99

			Home				Away					Total						
		P	W	D	L	F	A	W	D	L	F	A	W	D	L	F	A	P	GD
1	Milan	34	13	3	1	35	17	7	7	3	24	17	20	10	4	59	34	70	+25
2	Lazio	34	12	4	1	41	14	8	5	4	24	17	20	9	5	65	31	69	+34
3	Fiorentina	34	13	4	0	36	10	3	4	10	19	31	16	8	10	55	41	56	+14
4	Parma	34	9	6	2	27	13	6	4	7	28	23	15	10	9	55	36	55	+19
5	Roma	34	13	3	1	43	16	2	6	9	26	33	15	9	10	69	49	54	+20
6	Juventus	34	10	4	3	25	16	5	5	7	17	20	15	9	10	42	36	54	+6
7	Udinese	34	9	4	4	25	20	7	2	8	27	32	16	6	12	52	52	54	0
8	Inter	34	10	3	4	43	24	3	4	10	16	30	13	7	14	59	54	46	+5
9	Bologna	34	8	5	4	31	20	3	6	8	13	27	11	11	12	44	47	44	-3
10	Bari	34	6	8	3	17	15	3	7	7	22	29	9	15	10	39	44	42	-5
11	Venezia	34	9	5	3	23	14	2	4	11	15	31	11	9	14	38	45	42	-7
12	Cagliari	34	9	5	3	33	19	2	3	12	16	31	11	8	15	49	50	41	-1
13	Piacenza	34	9	5	3	34	20	2	3	12	14	29	11	8	15	48	49	41	-1
14	Perugia	34	10	3	4	30	21	1	3	13	13	40	11	6	17	43	61	39	-18
15	Salernitana	34	9	4	4	26	16	1	4	12	11	35	10	8	16	37	51	38	-14
16	Sampdoria	34	8	6	3	25	16	1	4	12	13	39	9	10	15	38	55	37	-17
17	Vicenza	34	7	4	6	18	20	1	5	11	9	27	8	9	17	27	47	33	-20
18	Empoli	34	4	5	8	17	25	0	5	12	9	38	4	10	20	26	63	20	-37

N.B. Empoli deducted 2pts.

It offered the tightest and most enthralling championship race for years. Several teams were in contention for the *scudetto* at one stage or another, and although by the closing stages there were just two teams left in the race, it was not until the very last minute of the season that Lazio and Milan were finally separated.

That Milan came through to win was a minor sensation. Although they hovered near the top of the table all season, they were not generally considered to be championship material. In superstars like Paolo Maldini, George Weah, Leonardo and Oliver Bierhoff they certainly had the raw material, but their performance level rarely rose above moderate and there were problems of un-familiarity with the 3-4-3 formation favoured by new coach Alberto Zaccheroni. However, when push came to shove, Milan responded. It took a tweak in the system to get them to function properly, with Zaccheroni deciding to replace one of his forwards with a playmaker (Zvonimir Boban), but once they scented victory, Milan proved unstoppable.

After drawing 0-0 away to leaders Lazio on Easter Saturday, the comments emanating from the Milan camp were that the point was a large step towards their goal of Champions' League qualification. It seemed at that stage, with a seven-point gap distancing them from the

leaders, that Milan had given up on the championship. Yet two weeks later, after Lazio had lost two games in a row and Milan had simultaneously snatched six points, they were right back in the thick of it. Over the next few weeks Milan and Lazio matched each other victory for victory. Milan were extremely fortunate to win at home to Sampdoria, with the decisive goal, a wickedly deflected shot from Maurizio Ganz, coming five minutes into stoppage-time, but they were imperious in beating Juventus 2-0 in Turin.

When Lazio dropped two further points in their pen-ultimate fixture, away to Fiorentina, Milan returned to pôle position for the first time since September with an easy 4-0 home win against already-relegated Empoli. Now, suddenly, the pressure was on them. They went to their final match, away to relegation-threatened Perugia, needing a seventh successive win to secure their 16th Italian title…in the year of their Centenary. Two first-half goals from Andrés Guglielminpietro (known affectionately as plain 'Guly') and top scorer Oliver Bierhoff put them into the comfort zone, but a penalty just before half-time by Perugia's outstanding Japanese playmaker Hidetoshi Nakata re-opened the door to Lazio. Milan were a nervous bunch in the second half but thanks mainly to the brilliance of their young goalkeeper Christian Abbiati (the club's third choice earlier in the season) they held on for victory.

It was Milan's fifth championship win of the '90s and extended their joint-stranglehold on the *scudetto* with Juventus into an eighth successive year. For Zaccheroni, the thrill was particularly intense because it meant that he had emulated Arrigo Sacchi and Fabio Capello by winning Serie A in his first season as Milan coach.

Milan's timing had been immaculate and nobody could take that away from them, but the overriding feeling was that Lazio had handed the *scudetto* to them on a plate. The Rome club had gone a quarter of a century without a championship victory, and having built up a significant lead with just a handful of games remaining, it seemed inconceivable that they would allow the prize to slip from their grasp. But the two 1-3 defeats at the Stadio Olimpico in mid-April ultimately proved fatal.

Lazio had spent a fortune on new players the previous summer, bringing in players of world-class calibre like Marcelo Salas, Sinisa Mihajlovic and - for a record Italian fee of £20m - Christian Vieri. Their intentions were crystal clear - they wanted the championship. But they made a poor start and it was not until the return from injury of Vieri and club skipper Alessandro Nesta that the team finally settled into a rhythm. The kick-start came with a 1-0 win at Juventus in early December. Over the next two months they reeled off nine straight wins, and although they failed to match the Serie A record of ten, the 0-0 draw at Cagliari which brought that sequence to an end was enough to lift Lazio to the top of the table - a position they had not occupied for 24 years. Three further victories followed, and although they wasted a chance to extend their lead by drawing 0-0 at lowly Empoli, they were still six points clear of the pack after that goalless draw in the Olimpico with Milan.

It had been noted that Lazio faced a formidable run-in, and that they had fallen away alarmingly at a corresponding stage the previous season. But there was still a sense of disbelief at the way they allowed their advantage to unravel in those two consecutive 1-3 defeats - the first against, of all clubs, Roma, the second against fading Juventus. Although Swedish coach Sven Göran Eriksson revived his troops for their next three matches, the tough trip to Fiorentina, who had not lost at home all season, proved to be one big battle too many. Lazio came away from Florence with a point but it was not enough to keep them in front. The initiative had been handed to Milan, and even though a couple of Salas goals gave Lazio their 20th victory of the season on the final day, at home to Parma, Milan's 2-1 win in Perugia deprived them of the keys to paradise.

Four days before the title showdown Lazio gave themselves a considerable lift by winning their very first European trophy. They beat Mallorca 2-1 in Birmingham to become the last team ever to lift the Cup-winners' Cup. Lazio had been the pre-season favourites for the competition, and although their progress to Villa Park was not entirely convincing (they won only one of their four matches in Rome), they always had the look of potential winners. Goals by Vieri and Pavel Nedved against the Spaniards ensured that Eriksson's second season at the club, like his first, ended with a trophy - although the Swede, in common with everyone else associated with the club, would gratefully have pawned the Cup-winners' Cup for the *scudetto*.

Parma were Italy's other success story in Europe. Led by their gifted attacking triumvirate of Enrico Chiesa, Hernán Crespo and Juan Sebastián Verón, the richly-backed provincials won the UEFA Cup for the second time in five seasons, slamming three goals without reply past

TOP SCORERS

22	Márcio AMOROSO (Udinese)
21	Gabriel BATISTUTA (Fiorentina)
20	Oliver BIERHOFF (Milan)
18	Marco DELVECCHIO (Roma)
16	Roberto MUZZI (Cagliari)
	Hernán CRESPO (Parma)
15	Giuseppe SIGNORI (Bologna)
	Marcelo SALAS (Lazio)
	Simone INZAGHI (Piacenza)
14	RONALDO (Inter)

NATIONAL TEAM RESULTS 98/99

Date	Opponent		Venue	Score	Scorers
05/09/98	Wales (ECQ)	A	Liverpool	2-0	Fuser (19), Vieri (77)
10/10/98	Switzerland (ECQ)	H	Udine	2-0	Del Piero (19, 61)
18/11/98	Spain	H	Salerno	2-2	Inzaghi (14, 74)
16/12/98	Rest of the World	H	Rome	6-2	Inzaghi (9), Di Francesco (36), Fuser (43), Chiesa (57, 80, 86)
10/02/99	Norway	H	Pisa	0-0	
27/03/99	Denmark (ECQ)	A	Copenhagen	2-1	Inzaghi (1), Conte (68)
31/03/99	Belarus (ECQ)	H	Ancona	1-1	Inzaghi (31p)
28/04/99	Croatia	A	Zagreb	0-0	
05/06/99	Wales (ECQ)	H	Bologna	4-0	Vieri (7), Inzaghi (37), Maldini (40), Chiesa (89)
09/06/99	Switzerland (ECQ)	A	Lausanne	0-0	

COLOUR INDEX

Plate 2

NATIONAL FEDERATIONS

FIRST KIT	ALBANIA	SECOND KIT
FIRST KIT	ANDORRA	SECOND KIT
FIRST KIT	ARMENIA	SECOND KIT
FIRST KIT	AUSTRIA	SECOND KIT

Plate 3

NATIONAL FEDERATIONS

FIRST KIT   **AZERBAIJAN**   SECOND KIT

FIRST KIT   **BELARUS**   SECOND KIT

FIRST KIT   **BELGIUM**   SECOND KIT

FIRST KIT   **BOSNIA-HERZEGOVINA**   SECOND KIT

Plate 4

NATIONAL FEDERATIONS

FIRST KIT   **BULGARIA**   SECOND KIT

FIRST KIT   **CROATIA**   SECOND KIT

FIRST KIT   **CYPRUS**   SECOND KIT

FIRST KIT   **CZECH REPUBLIC**   SECOND KIT

Plate 5

NATIONAL FEDERATIONS

FIRST KIT   **DENMARK**   SECOND KIT

FIRST KIT   **ENGLAND**   SECOND KIT

FIRST KIT   **ESTONIA**   SECOND KIT

FIRST KIT   **FAROE ISLANDS**   SECOND KIT

Plate 6

NATIONAL FEDERATIONS

FIRST KIT   **FINLAND**   SECOND KIT

FIRST KIT   **FRANCE**   SECOND KIT

FIRST KIT   **GEORGIA**   SECOND KIT

FIRST KIT   **GERMANY**   SECOND KIT

Plate 7

NATIONAL FEDERATIONS

FIRST KIT   **GREECE**   SECOND KIT

FIRST KIT   **HOLLAND**   SECOND KIT

FIRST KIT   **HUNGARY**   SECOND KIT

FIRST KIT   **ICELAND**   SECOND KIT

Plate 8

NATIONAL FEDERATIONS

FIRST KIT   **ISRAEL**   SECOND KIT

FIRST KIT   **ITALY**   SECOND KIT

FIRST KIT   **LATVIA**   SECOND KIT

FIRST KIT   **LIECHTENSTEIN**   SECOND KIT

Plate 9

NATIONAL FEDERATIONS

FIRST KIT	LITHUANIA	SECOND KIT
FIRST KIT	LUXEMBOURG	SECOND KIT
FIRST KIT	MACEDONIA	SECOND KIT
FIRST KIT	MALTA	SECOND KIT

Plate 10

NATIONAL FEDERATIONS

FIRST KIT   **MOLDOVA**   SECOND KIT

FIRST KIT   **NORTHERN IRELAND**   SECOND KIT

FIRST KIT   **NORWAY**   SECOND KIT

FIRST KIT   **POLAND**   SECOND KIT

Plate 11

NATIONAL FEDERATIONS

FIRST KIT	**PORTUGAL**	SECOND KIT
FIRST KIT	**REPUBLIC OF IRELAND**	SECOND KIT
FIRST KIT	**ROMANIA**	SECOND KIT
FIRST KIT	**RUSSIA**	SECOND KIT

Plate 12

NATIONAL FEDERATIONS

FIRST KIT   **SAN MARINO**   SECOND KIT

FIRST KIT   **SCOTLAND**   SECOND KIT

FIRST KIT   **SLOVAKIA**   SECOND KIT

FIRST KIT   **SLOVENIA**   SECOND KIT

Plate 13

NATIONAL FEDERATIONS

FIRST KIT   **SPAIN**   SECOND KIT

FIRST KIT   **SWEDEN**   SECOND KIT

FIRST KIT   **SWITZERLAND**   SECOND KIT

FIRST KIT   **TURKEY**   SECOND KIT

Plate 14

NATIONAL FEDERATIONS

FIRST KIT	UKRAINE	SECOND KIT
FIRST KIT	WALES	SECOND KIT
FIRST KIT	YUGOSLAVIA	SECOND KIT

Plate 16

AUSTRIA

SC AUSTRIA LUSTENAU   FK AUSTRIA WIEN   GRAZER AK   LASK LINZ

SK RAPID WIEN   SV RIED   SV SALZBURG

SK VORWÄRTS STEYR   SK STURM GRAZ   FC TIROL INNSBRUCK

SW BREGENZ

Plate 17

AUSTRIA

SC AUSTRIA LUSTENAU

FK AUSTRIA WIEN

GRAZER AK

LASK LINZ

SK RAPID WIEN

SV RIED

SV SALZBURG

SK VORWÄRTS STEYR

SK STURM GRAZ

FC TIROL INNSBRUCK

SW BREGENZ

Plate 18

BELGIUM

RSC ANDERLECHT

KSK BEVEREN

CLUB BRUGGE KV

RSC CHARLEROI

KSC EENDRACHT AALST

R EXCELSIOR MOUSCRON

KRC GENK

KAA GENT

KFC GERMINAL EKEREN

KRC HARELBEKE

KV KORTRIJK

K LIERSE SK

KSC LOKEREN

KFC LOMMELSE SK

KV OOSTENDE

K ST.-TRUIDENSE VV

R STANDARD LIEGE

KVC WESTERLO

KV MECHELEN

FC VERBROEDERING GEEL

Plate 19

BELGIUM

RSC ANDERLECHT

KSK BEVEREN

CLUB BRUGGE KV

RSC CHARLEROI

KSC EENDRACHT AALST

R EXCELSIOR MOUSCRON

KRC GENK

KAA GENT

KFC GERMINAL EKEREN

KRC HARELBEKE

KV KORTRIJK

K LIERSE SK

KSC LOKEREN

KFC LOMMELSE SK

KV OOSTENDE

K ST.-TRUIDENSE VV

R STANDARD LIEGE

KVC WESTERLO

KV MECHELEN

FC VERBROEDERING GEEL

Plate 20

BULGARIA

BOTEV PLOVDIV

CSKA SOFIA

DOBRUDZHA DOBRICH

LEVSKI KIUSTENDIL

LEVSKI SOFIA

LITEKS LOVECH

LOKOMOTIV PLOVDIV

LOKOMOTIV SOFIA

METALURG PERNIK

MINIOR PERNIK

NEFTOCHIMIK BOURGAS

PIRIN BLAGOEVGRAD

SEPTEMVRI SOFIA

SHUMEN

SLAVIA SOFIA

SPARTAK VARNA

CHORNOMORETS BOURGAS

BELASITSA PETRICH

OLIMPIK TETEVEN

Plate 21

BULGARIA

BOTEV PLOVDIV

CSKA SOFIA

DOBRUDZHA DOBRICH

LEVSKI KIUSTENDIL

LEVSKI SOFIA

LITEKS LOVECH

LOKOMOTIV PLOVDIV

LOKOMOTIV SOFIA

METALURG PERNIK

MINIOR PERNIK

NEFTOCHIMIK BOURGAS

PIRIN BLAGOEVGRAD

SEPTEMVRI SOFIA

SHUMEN

SLAVIA SOFIA

SPARTAK VARNA

CHERNOMORETS BOURGAS

BELASITSA PETRICH

OLIMPIK TETEVEN

Plate 22

CROATIA

CIBALIA VINKOVCI

CROATIA ZAGREB

HAJDUK SPLIT

HRVATSKI DRAGOVOLJAC ZAGREB

MLADOST 127 SUHOPOLJE

OSIJEK

RIJEKA

SIBENIK

SLAVEN BELUPO KOPRIVNICA

VARTEKS VARAZDIN

ZADARKOMERC ZADAR

ZAGREB

VUKOVAR '91

ISTRA PULA

Plate 23

CROATIA

CIBALIA VINKOVCI

CROATIA ZAGREB

HAJDUK SPLIT

HRVATSKI DRAGOVOLJAC ZAGREB

MLADOST 127 SUHOPOLJE

OSIJEK

RIJEKA

SIBENIK

SLAVEN BELUPO KOPRIVNICA

VARTEKS VARAZDIN

ZADARKOMERC ZADAR

ZAGREB

VUKOVAR '91

ISTRA PULA

Plate 24

CYPRUS

AEK LARNACA

AEL LIMASSOL

ALKI LARNACA

ANORTHOSIS FAMAGUSTA

APOEL NICOSIA

APOLLON LIMASSOL

ARIS LIMASSOL

DOXA KATOKOPIA

ETHNIKOS AKHNA

EVAGHORAS PAPHOS

NEA SALAMINA FAMAGUSTA

OLYMPIAKOS NICOSIA

OMONIA NICOSIA

PARALIMNI

ANAGENNISIS DHERYNIA

ETHNIKOS ASHIA

APOP PAPHOS

Plate 25

CYPRUS

AEK LARNACA

AEL LIMASSOL

ALKI LARNACA

ANORTHOSIS FAMAGUSTA

APOEL NICOSIA

APOLLON LIMASSOL

ARIS LIMASSOL

DOXA KATOKOPIA

ETHNIKOS AKHNA

EVAGHORAS PAPHOS

NEA SALAMINA FAMAGUSTA

OLYMPIAKOS NICOSIA

OMONIA NICOSIA

PARALIMNI

ANAGENNISIS DHERYNIA

ETHNIKOS ASHIA

APOP PAPHOS

Plate 26

CZECH REPUBLIC

BANIK OSTRAVA

BOBY BRNO

FK CHMEL BLSANY

DUKLA PRIBRAM

SK HRADEC KRALOVE

FK JABLONEC 97

FC KARVINA

PETRA DRNOVICE

SIGMA OLOMOUC

SLAVIA PRAHA

SLEZSKY OPAVA

SLOVAN LIBEREC

SPARTA PRAHA

FK TEPLICE

VIKTORIA PLZEN

VIKTORIA ZIZKOV

BOHEMIANS PRAHA

SK CESKE BUDEJOVICE

Plate 27

CZECH REPUBLIC

BANIK OSTRAVA

BOBY BRNO

FK CHMEL BLSANY

FC DUKLA PRIBRAM

SK HRADEC KRALOVE

FK JABLONEC 97

FC KARVINA

PETRA DRNOVICE

SIGMA OLOMOUC

SLAVIA PRAHA

SLEZSKY OPAVA

SLOVAN LIBEREC

SPARTA PRAHA

FK TEPLICE

VIKTORIA PLZEN

VIKTORIA ZIZKOV

BOHEMIANS PRAHA

SK CESKE BUDEJOVICE

Plate 28

DENMARK

AAB	AARHUS FREMAD	AB	AGF
B93	BRØNDBY IF	HERFØLGE BK	FC KØBENHAVN
LYNGBY FC	SILKEBORG IF	VEJLE BK	VIBORG FF
OB	ESBJERG FB		

Plate 29

DENMARK

AAB

AARHUS FREMAD

AB

AGF

B93

BRØNDBY IF

HERFØLGE BK

FC KØBENHAVN

LYNGBY FC

SILKEBORG IF

VEJLE BK

VIBORG FF

OB

ESBJERG FB

Plate 30

ENGLAND

ARSENAL

ASTON VILLA

BLACKBURN ROVERS

CHARLTON ATHLETIC

CHELSEA

COVENTRY CITY

DERBY COUNTY

EVERTON

LEEDS UNITED

LEICESTER CITY

LIVERPOOL

MANCHESTER UNITED

MIDDLESBROUGH

NEWCASTLE UNITED

NOTTINGHAM FOREST

SHEFFIELD WEDNESDAY

SOUTHAMPTON

TOTTENHAM HOTSPUR

WEST HAM UNITED

WIMBLEDON

SUNDERLAND

BRADFORD CITY

WATFORD

Plate 31

ENGLAND

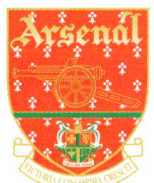
ARSENAL

ASTON VILLA

BLACKBURN ROVERS

CHARLTON ATHLETIC

CHELSEA

COVENTRY CITY

DERBY COUNTY

EVERTON

LEEDS UNITED

LEICESTER CITY

LIVERPOOL

MANCHESTER UNITED

MIDDLESBROUGH

NEWCASTLE UNITED

NOTTINGHAM FOREST

SHEFFIELD WEDNESDAY

SOUTHAMPTON

TOTTENHAM HOTSPUR

WEST HAM UNITED

WIMBLEDON

SUNDERLAND

BRADFORD CITY

WATFORD

Plate 32

FINLAND

FINNPA   FC HAKA   HJK   FF JARO

FC JAZZ   MYPA   PK-35   ROPS

TPS   VPS   FC LAHTI

KTP   FC INTER   TPV

Plate 33

FINLAND

FINNPA

FC HAKA

HJK

FF JARO

FC JAZZ

MYPA

PK-35

ROPS

TPS

VPS

FC LAHTI

KTP

FC INTER

TPV

Plate 34

FRANCE

AJ AUXERRE

SC BASTIA

GIRONDINS DE BORDEAUX

LE HAVRE AC

RC LENS

FC LORIENT

OLYMPIQUE LYONNAIS

OLYMPIQUE MARSEILLE

FC METZ

AS MONACO

MONTPELLIER HSC

AS NANCY-LORRAINE

FC NANTES

PARIS SAINT-GERMAIN

STADE RENNAIS FC

FC SOCHAUX

RC STRASBOURG

TOULOUSE FC

AS SAINT-ETIENNE

CS SEDAN ARDENNES

A TROYES AC

Plate 35

FRANCE

AJ AUXERRE

SC BASTIA

GIRONDINS DE BORDEAUX

LE HAVRE AC

RC LENS

FC LORIENT

OLYMPIQUE LYONNAIS

OLYMPIQUE MARSEILLE

FC METZ

AS MONACO

MONTPELLIER HSC

AS NANCY-LORRAINE

FC NANTES

PARIS SAINT-GERMAIN

STADE RENNAIS FC

FC SOCHAUX

RC STRASBOURG

TOULOUSE FC

AS SAINT-ETIENNE

CS SEDAN ARDENNES

A TROYES AC

Plate 36

GEORGIA

ARSENALI TBILISI

DILA GORI

DINAMO BATUMI

DINAMO TBILISI

GORDA RUSTAVI

GURIA LANCHKHUTI

IBERIA SAMTREDIA

KOLKHETI 1913 POTI

LOKOMOTIVI TBILISI

MERANI 91 TBILISI

ODISHI ZUGDIDI

SAMGURALI TSKHALTUBO

SIONI BOLNISI

TORPEDO KUTAISI

TSU TBILISI

VIT GEORGIA TBILISI

FC TBILISI

KOLKHETI KHOBI

Plate 37

GEORGIA

ARSENALI TBILISI

DILA GORI

DINAMO BATUMI

DINAMO TBILISI

GORDA RUSTAVI

GURIA LANCHKHUTI

IBERIA SAMTREDIA

KOLKHETI 1913 POTI

LOKOMOTIVI TBILISI

MERANI 91 TBILISI

ODISHI ZUGDIDI

SAMGURALI TSKHALTUBO

SIONI BOLNISI

TORPEDO KUTAISI

TSU TBILISI

VIT GEORGIA TBILISI

FC TBILISI

KOLKHETI KHOBI

Plate 38

GERMANY

BAYER 04 LEVERKUSEN

FC BAYERN MÜNCHEN

VFL BOCHUM

BORUSSIA DORTMUND

BORUSSIA MÖNCHENGLADBACH

MSV DUISBURG

EINTRACHT FRANKFURT

SC FREIBURG

HAMBURGER SV

FC HANSA ROSTOCK

HERTHA BSC BERLIN

1.FC KAISERSLAUTERN

TSV 1860 MÜNCHEN

1.FC NÜRNBERG

FC SCHALKE 04

VFB STUTTGART

SV WERDER BREMEN

VFL WOLFSBURG

ARMINIA BIELEFELD

SPVGG UNTERHACHING

SSV ULM

Plate 39

GERMANY

BAYER 04 LEVERKUSEN

FC BAYERN MÜNCHEN

VFL BOCHUM

BORUSSIA DORTMUND

BORUSSIA MÖNCHENGLADBACH

MSV DUISBURG

EINTRACHT FRANKFURT

SC FREIBURG

HAMBURGER SV

FC HANSA ROSTOCK

HERTHA BSC BERLIN

1.FC KAISERSLAUTERN

TSV 1860 MÜNCHEN

1.FC NÜRNBERG

FC SCHALKE 04

VFB STUTTGART

SV WERDER BREMEN

VFL WOLFSBURG

ARMINIA BIELEFELD

SPVGG UNTERHACHING

SSV ULM

Plate 40

GREECE

AEK

APOLLON

ARIS

ETHNIKOS ASTERAS

ETHNIKOS PIRAEUS

IONIKOS

IRAKLIS

KAVALA

OFI

OLYMPIAKOS

PANATHINAIKOS

PANELEFSINIAKOS

PANILIAKOS

PANIONIOS

PAOK

PROODEFTIKI

VERIA

XANTHI

TRIKALA

PANAHAIKI

KALAMATA

Plate 41

GREECE

AEK

APOLLON

ARIS

ETHNIKOS ASTERAS

ETHNIKOS PIRAEUS

IONIKOS

IRAKLIS

KAVALA

OFI

OLYMPIAKOS

PANATHINAIKOS

PANELEFSINIAKOS

PANILIAKOS

PANIONIOS

PAOK

PROODEFTIKI

VERIA

XANTHI

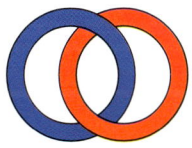

TRIKALA

PANAHAIKI

KALAMATA

Plate 42

HOLLAND

AJAX

AZ

SC CAMBUUR LEEUWARDEN

FEYENOORD

FORTUNA SITTARD

DE GRAAFSCHAP

SC HEERENVEEN

MVV

NAC

NEC

PSV

RKC WAALWIJK

RODA JC

SPARTA

FC TWENTE

FC UTRECHT

VITESSE

WILLEM II

FC DEN BOSCH

Plate 43

HOLLAND

AJAX

AZ

SC CAMBUUR LEEUWARDEN

FEYENOORD

FORTUNA SITTARD

DE GRAAFSCHAP

SC HEERENVEEN

MVV

NAC

NEC

PSV

RKC WAALWIJK

RODA JC

SPARTA

FC TWENTE

FC UTRECHT

VITESSE

WILLEM II

FC DEN BOSCH

Plate 44

HUNGARY

BVSC-ZUGLÓ

DVSC-EPONA

DIÓSGYÖRI FC

DUNAFERR SE

FERENCVÁROS

GÁZSZER FC

GYÖRI ETO FC

HALADÁS-MILOS

III. KERÜLET FC

KISPEST-HONVÉD FC

MTK HUNGÁRIA FC

NYÍRSÉG-SPARTACUS FC

SIÓFOK

ÚJPEST FC

VASAS DH

VÁC FC-ZOLLNER

VIDEOTON FC FEHÉRVÁR

ZALAHÚS ZTE FC

LOMBARD FC TATABÁNYA

NAGYKANIZSA

SZEGED LC

Plate 45

HUNGARY

BVSC-ZUGLÓ

DVSC-EPONA

DIÓSGYŐRI FC

DUNAFERR SE

FERENCVÁROS

GÁZSZER FC

GYŐRI ETO FC

HALADÁS-MILOS

III. KERÜLET FC

KISPEST-HONVÉD FC

MTK-HUNGÁRIA FC

NYÍRSÉG-SPARTACUS FC

SIÓFOK

ÚJPEST FC

VASAS DH

VÁC FC-ZOLLNER

VIDEOTON FC FEHÉRVÁR

ZALAHÚS ZTE FC

LOMBARD FC TATABÁNYA

NAGYKANIZSA

SZEGED LC

Plate 46

ICELAND

FRAM   GRINDAVÍK   ÍA   ÍBV

ÍR   KEFLAVÍK   KR

LEIFTUR   THRÓTTUR REYKJVÍK   VALUR

BREIDABLIK   VÍKINGUR

Plate 47

ICELAND

FRAM   GRINDAVÍK   ÍA   ÍBV

ÍR   KEFLAVÍK   KR

LEIFTUR   THRÓTTUR REYKJAVÍK   VALUR

BREIDABLIK   VÍKINGUR

Plate 48

ISRAEL

BEITAR JERUSALEM

BNEI YEHUDA

HAPOEL BEIT SH'AN

HAPOEL HAIFA

HAPOEL IRONY RISHON LEZION

HAPOEL JERUSALEM

HAPOEL KFAR-SABA

HAPOEL PETACH-TIKVA

HAPOEL TEL-AVIV

MACCABI HAIFA

MACCABI HERZLIYA

MACCABI IRONY ASHDOD

MACCABI JAFFA

MACCABI PETACH-TIKVA

MACCABI TEL-AVIV

ZAFRIRIM HOLON

MACCABI NETANYA

Plate 49

ISRAEL

BEITAR JERUSALEM

BNEI YEHUDA

HAPOEL BEIT SH'AN

HAPOEL HAIFA

HAPOEL IRONY RISHON LEZION

HAPOEL JERUSALEM

HAPOEL KFAR-SABA

HAPOEL PETACH-TIKVA

HAPOEL TEL-AVIV

MACCABI HAIFA

MACCABI HERZLIYA

MACCABI IRONY ASHDOD

MACCABI JAFFA

MACCABI PETACH-TIKVA

MACCABI TEL-AVIV

ZAFRIRIM HOLON

MACCABI NETANYA

Plate 50

ITALY

BARI

BOLOGNA

CAGLIARI

EMPOLI

FIORENTINA

INTER

JUVENTUS

LAZIO

MILAN

PARMA

PERUGIA

PIACENZA

ROMA

SALERNITANA

SAMPDORIA

UDINESE

VENEZIA

VICENZA

VERONA

TORINO

REGGINA

LECCE

Plate 51

ITALY

BARI

BOLOGNA

CAGLIARI

EMPOLI

FIORENTINA

INTER

JUVENTUS

LAZIO

MILAN

PARMA

PERUGIA

PIACENZA

ROMA

SALERNITANA

SAMPDORIA

UDINESE

VENEZIA

VICENZA

VERONA

TORINO

REGGINA

LECCE

Plate 52

LATVIA

DAUGAVA RIGA   DINABURG DAUGAVPILS   METALURGS LIEPAYA   RANTO/MKS RIGA

FK REZEKNE   SKONTO RIGA   FK VALMIERA

FK VENTSPILS   POLICE RIGA

Plate 53

LATVIA

DAUGAVA RIGA

DINABURG DAUGAVPILS

METALURGS LIEPAYA

RANTO/MKS RIGA

SKONTO RIGA

FK VALMIERA

FK VENTSPILS

POLICE RIGA

Plate 54

LUXEMBOURG

ARIS BONNEVOIE

AVENIR BEGGEN

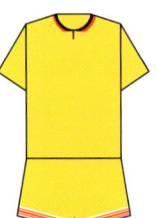

F91 DUDELANGE

CS GREVENMACHER

CS HOBSCHEID

JEUNESSE ESCH

FC MONDERCANGE

CS PETANGE

SPORA LUXEMBOURG

SPORTING MERTZIG

UNION LUXEMBOURG

FC WILTZ 71

US RUMELANGE

FC SCHIFFLANGE 95

Plate 55

LUXEMBOURG

ARIS BONNEVOIE

AVENIR BEGGEN

F91 DUDELANGE

CS GREVENMACHER

CS HOBSCHEID

JEUNESSE ESCH

FC MONDERCANGE

CS PETANGE

SPORA LUXEMBOURG

SPORTING MERTZIG

UNION LUXEMBOURG

FC WILTZ 71

US RUMELANGE

FC SCHIFFLANGE 95

Plate 56

MALTA

BIRKIRKARA

FLORIANA

HAMRUN SPARTANS

HIBERNIANS

NAXXAR LIONS

PIETA HOTSPURS

RABAT AJAX

ST. PATRICK

SLIEMA WANDERERS

VALLETTA

GOZO

ZURRIEQ

Plate 57

MALTA

BIRKIRKARA

FLORIANA

HAMRUN SPARTANS

HIBERNIANS

NAXXAR LIONS

PIETA HOTSPURS

RABAT AJAX

ST. PATRICK

SLIEMA WANDERERS

VALLETTA

GOZO

ZURRIEQ

Plate 58

NORTHERN IRELAND

BALLYMENA UNITED   CLIFTONVILLE   COLERAINE   CRUSADERS

GLENAVON   GLENTORAN   LINFIELD   NEWRY TOWN

OMAGH TOWN   PORTADOWN   LURGAN DISTILLERY

Plate 59

NORTHERN IRELAND

BALLYMENA UNITED

CLIFTONVILLE

COLERAINE

CRUSADERS

GLENAVON

GLENTORAN

LINFIELD

NEWRY TOWN

OMAGH TOWN

PORTADOWN

LURGAN DISTILLERY

Plate 60

NORWAY

FK BODØ/GLIMT   SK BRANN   FK HAUGESUND   KONGSVINGER IL   LILLESTRØM SK

MOLDE FK   MOSS FK   ROSENBORG BK   SOGNDAL IL   STABAEK IF

STRØMSGODSET IF   TROMSØ IL   VIKING FK   VÅLERENGA FOTBALL

ODD GRENLAND   SKEID

Plate 61

NORWAY

FK BODØ/GLIMT

SK BRANN

FK HAUGESUND

KONGSVINGER IL

LILLESTRØM SK

MOLDE FK

MOSS FK

ROSENBORG BK

SOGNDAL IL

STABAEK IF

STRØMSGODSET IF

TROMSØ IL

VIKING FK

VÅLERENGA FOTBALL

ODD GRENLAND

SKEID

Plate 62

POLAND

AMICA WRONKI

GKS BELCHATOW

GKS KATOWICE

GORNIK ZABRZE

LECH POZNAN

LEGIA WARSZAWA

LKS LODZ

ODRA WODZISLAW

POGON SZCZECIN

POLONIA WARSZAWA

RUCH CHORZOW

RUCH RADZIONKOW

STOMIL OLSZTYN

WIDZEW LODZ

WISLA KRAKOW

ZAGLEBIE LUBIN

PETROCHEMIA PLOCK

GROCLIN DYSKOBOLIA GRODZISK

Plate 63

POLAND

AMICA WRONKI

GKS BELCHATOW

GKS KATOWICE

GORNIK ZABRZE

LECH POZNAN

LEGIA WARSZAWA

LKS LODZ

ODRA WODZISLAW

POGON SZCZECIN

POLONIA WARSZAWA

RUCH CHORZOW

RUCH RADZIONKOW

STOMIL OLSZTYN

WIDZEW LODZ

WISLA KRAKOW

ZAGLEBIE LUBIN

PETROCHEMIA PLOCK

GROCLIN DYSKOBOLIA GRODZISK

Plate 64

PORTUGAL

ACADÉMICA COIMBRA   FC ALVERCA   SC BEIRA MAR   SL BENFICA   BOAVISTA FC

SC BRAGA   SC CAMPOMAIORENSE   GD CHAVES   CF ESTRELA AMADORA   SC FARENSE

CS MARÍTIMO   FC PORTO   RIO AVE FC   SC SALGUEIROS

SPORTING CP   UNIÃO LEIRIA   VITÓRIA GUIMARÃES   VITÓRIA SETÚBAL

GIL VICENTE FC   CF OS BELENENSES   CD SANTA CLARA

Plate 65

PORTUGAL

ACADÉMICA COIMBRA

FC ALVERCA

SC BEIRA MAR

SL BENFICA

BOAVISTA FC

SC BRAGA

SC CAMPOMAIORENSE

GD CHAVES

CF ESTRELA AMADORA

SC FARENSE

CS MARÍTIMO

FC PORTO

RIO AVE FC

SC SALGUEIROS

SPORTING CP

UNIÃO LEIRIA

VITÓRIA GUIMARÃES

VITÓRIA SETÚBAL

GIL VICENTE FC

CF OS BELENENSES

CD SANTA CLARA

Plate 66

REPUBLIC OF IRELAND

BOHEMIANS

BRAY WANDERERS

CORK CITY

DERRY CITY

DUNDALK

FINN HARPS

ST. PATRICK'S ATHLETIC

SHAMROCK ROVERS

SHELBOURNE

SLIGO ROVERS

UCD

WATERFORD UNITED

DROGHEDA UNITED

GALWAY UNITED

Plate 67

REPUBLIC OF IRELAND

BOHEMIANS

BRAY WANDERERS

CORK CITY

DERRY CITY

DUNDALK

FINN HARPS

ST. PATRICK'S ATHLETIC

SHAMROCK ROVERS

SHELBOURNE

SLIGO ROVERS

UCD

WATERFORD UNITED

DROGHEDA UNITED

GALWAY UNITED

Plate 68

ROMANIA

ASTRA PLOIESTI

FC ARGES DACIA PITESTI

FCM BACAU

CEAHLAUL PIATRA NEAMT

DINAMO BUCURESTI

FC FARUL CONSTANTA

FORESTA FALTICENI

GLORIA BISTRITA

FC NATIONAL BUCURESTI

OLIMPIA SATU MARE

FC ONESTI

OTELUL GALATI

PETROLUL PLOIESTI

RAPID BUCURESTI

CSM RESITA

STEAUA BUCURESTI

UNIVERSITATEA CLUJ

UNIVERSITATEA CRAIOVA

FC BRASOV

EXTENSIV CRAIOVA

ROCAR BUCURESTI

Plate 69

ROMANIA

ASTRA PLOIESTI

FC ARGES DACIA PITESTI

FCM BACAU

CEAHLAUL PIATRA NEAMT

DINAMO BUCURESTI

FC FARUL CONSTANTA

FORESTA FALTICENI

GLORIA BISTRITA

FC NATIONAL BUCURESTI

OLIMPIA SATU MARE

FC ONESTI

OTELUL GALATI

PETROLUL PLOIESTI

RAPID BUCURESTI

CSM RESITA

STEAUA BUCURESTI

UNIVERSITATEA CLUJ

UNIVERSITATEA CRAIOVA

FC BRASOV

EXTENSIV CRAIOVA

ROCAR BUCURESTI

Plate 70

RUSSIA

ALANIA VLADIKAVKAZ

BALTIKA KALININGRAD

CHERNOMORETS NOVOROSSIISK

CSKA MOSKVA

DINAMO MOSKVA

KRYLYA SOVETOV SAMARA

LOKOMOTIV MOSKVA

ROSTSELMASH ROSTOV-NA-DONU

ROTOR VOLGOGRAD

SHINNIK YAROSLAVL

SPARTAK MOSKVA

TORPEDO MOSKVA

FK TYUMEN

URALAN ELISTA

ZENIT SANKT-PETERBURG

ZHEMCHUZHINA SOCHI

SATURN RAMONSKOE

LOKOMOTIV NIZHNIY NOVGOROD

Plate 71

RUSSIA

ALANIA VLADIKAVKAZ

BALTIKA KALININGRAD

CHERNOMORETS NOVOROSSIISK

CSKA MOSKVA

DINAMO MOSKVA

KRYLYA SOVETOV SAMARA

LOKOMOTIV MOSKVA

ROSTSELMASH ROSTOV-NA-DONU

ROTOR VOLGOGRAD

SHINNIK YAROSLAVL

SPARTAK MOSKVA

TORPEDO MOSKVA

FK TYUMEN

URALAN ELISTA

ZENIT SANKT-PETERBURG

ZHEMCHUZHINA SOCHI

SATURN RAMONSKOE

LOKOMOTIV NIZHNIY NOVGOROD

Plate 72

SCOTLAND

ABERDEEN

CELTIC

DUNDEE

DUNDEE UNITED

DUNFERMLINE ATHLETIC

HEART OF MIDLOTHIAN

KILMARNOCK

MOTHERWELL

RANGERS

ST. JOHNSTONE

HIBERNIAN

Plate 73

SCOTLAND

ABERDEEN

CELTIC

DUNDEE

DUNDEE UNITED

DUNFERMLINE ATHLETIC

HEART OF MIDLOTHIAN

KILMARNOCK

MOTHERWELL

RANGERS

ST. JOHNSTONE

HIBERNIAN

Plate 74

SLOVAKIA

ARTMEDIA PETRZALKA   BANÍK PRIEVIDZA   BSC BARDEJOV   DUKLA BANSKA BYSTRICA   HFC HUMENNE

INTER BRATISLAVA   ZTS KERAMETAL DUBNICA   1.FC KOSICE   FC NITRA   OZETA DUKLA TRENCIN

SCP RUZOMBEROK   SLOVAN BRATISLAVA   SPARTAK TRNAVA   TATRAN PRESOV

TAURIS RIMAVSKA SOBOTA   MSK ZILINA   DAC DUNAJSKA STREDA   VTJ KOBA SENEC

Plate 75

SLOVAKIA

ARTMEDIA PETRZALKA

BANÍK PRIEVIDZA

BSC BARDEJOV

DUKLA BANSKA BYSTRICA

HFC HUMENNE

INTER BRATISLAVA

ZTS KERAMETAL DUBNICA

1.FC KOSICE

FC NITRA

OZETA DUKLA TRENCIN

SCP RUZOMBEROK

SLOVAN BRATISLAVA

SPARTAK TRNAVA

TATRAN PRESOV

TAURIS RIMAVSKA SOBOTA

MSK ZILINA

DAC DUNAJSKA STREDA

VTJ KOBA SENEC

Plate 76

SLOVENIA

BST DOMZALE

HIT GORICA

NK KOPER

KOROTAN PREVALJE

MARIBOR TEATANIC

MURA MURSKA SOBOTA

NK POTROSNIK BELTINCI

PRIMORJE AJDOVSCINA

PUBLIKUM CELJE

RUDAR VELENJE

SCT OLIMPIJA LJUBLJANA

ZIVILA TRIGLAV KRANJ

DRAVOGRAD

FEROTERM POHORJE

Plate 77

SLOVENIA

BST DOMZALE

HIT GORICA

NK KOPER

KOROTAN PREVALJE

MARIBOR TEATANIC

MURA MURSKA SOBOTA

NK POTROSNIK BELTINCI

PRIMORJE AJDOVSCINA

PUBLIKUM CELJE

RUDAR VELENJE

SCT OLIMPIJA LJUBLJANA

ZIVILA TRIGLAV KRANJ

DRAVOGRAD

FEROTERM POHORJE

Plate 78

SPAIN

CD ALAVÉS

ATHLETIC BILBAO

ATLETICO MADRID

FC BARCELONA

REAL BETIS

RC CELTA

RC DEPORTIVO

RCD ESPANYOL

CF EXTREMADURA

RCD MALLORCA

REAL OVIEDO

RACING SANTANDER

REAL MADRID

REAL SOCIEDAD

UD SALAMANCA

CD TENERIFE

VALENCIA CF

REAL VALLADOLID

VILLARREAL CF

REAL ZARAGOZA

MÁLAGA CF

CD NUMANCIA

SEVILLA FC

RAYO VALLECANO

Plate 79

SPAIN

CD ALVARÉS

ATHLETIC BILBAO

ATLETICO MADRID

FC BARCELONA

REAL BETIS

RC CELTA

RC DEPORTIVO

RCD ESPANYOL

CF EXTREMADURA

RCD MALLORCA

REAL OVIEDO

RACING SANTANDER

REAL MADRID

REAL SOCIEDAD

UD SALAMANCA

CD TENERIFE

VALENCIA CF

REAL VALLADOLID

VILLARREAL CF

REAL ZARAGOZA

MÁLAGA CF

CD NUMANCIA

SEVILLA FC

RAYO VALLECANO

Plate 80

SWEDEN

AIK

IF ELFSBORG

IFK GÖTEBORG

HALMSTADS BK

HAMMARBY IF

HELSINGBORGS IF

BK HÄCKEN

MALMÖ FF

IFK NORRKÖPING

TRELLEBORGS FF

VÄSTRA FRÖLUNDA IF

ÖREBRO SK

ÖRGRYTE IS

ÖSTERS IF

DJURGÅRDENS IF

KALMAR FF

Plate 81

SWEDEN

AIK

IF ELFSBORG

IFK GÖTEBORG

HALMSTADS BK

HAMMARBY IF

HELSINGBORGS IF

BK HÄCKEN

MALMÖ FF

IFK NORRKÖPING

TRELLEBORGS FF

VÄSTRA FRÖLUNDA IF

ÖREBRO SK

ÖRGRYTE IS

ÖSTERS IF

DJURGÅRDENS IF

KALMAR FF

Plate 82

SWITZERLAND

FC AARAU   FC BASEL   GRASSHOPPER-CLUB ZÜRICH   LAUSANNE-SPORTS

FC LUGANO   FC LUZERN   NEUCHATEL XAMAX FC   FC ST. GALLEN

SERVETTE FC GENEVE   FC SION   BSC YOUNG BOYS BERN   FC ZÜRICH

SR DELEMONT   YVERDON-SPORTS

Plate 83

SWITZERLAND

FC AARAU

FC BASEL

GRASSHOPPER-CLUB ZÜRICH

LAUSANNE-SPORTS

FC LUGANO

FC LUZERN

NEUCHATEL XAMAX FC

FC ST. GALLEN

SERVETTE FC GENEVE

FC SION

BSC YOUNG BOYS BERN

FC ZÜRICH

SR DELEMONT

YVERDON-SPORTS

Plate 84

TURKEY

ADANASPOR   ALTAY   ANKARAGÜCÜ   ANTALYASPOR   BESIKTAS

BURSASPOR   ÇANAKKALE DARDANELSPOR   ERZURUMSPOR   FENERBAHÇE   GALATASARAY

GAZIANTEPSPOR   GENÇLERBIRLIGI   ISTANBULSPOR   KARABÜKSPOR

KOCAELISPOR   SAKARYASPOR   SAMSUNSPOR   TRABZONSPOR

VANSPOR   DENZILISPOR   GÖZTEPE

Plate 85

TURKEY

ADANASPOR

ALTAY

ANKARAGÜCÜ

ANTALYASPOR

BESIKTAS

BURSASPOR

ÇANAKKALE DARDANELSPOR

ERZURUMSPOR

FENERBAHÇE

GALATASARAY

GAZIANTEPSPOR

GENÇLERBIRLIGI

ISTANBULSPOR

KARABÜKSPOR

KOCAELISPOR

SAKARYASPOR

SAMSUNSPOR

TRABZONSPOR

VANSPOR

DENIZLISPOR

GÖZTEPE

Plate 86

UKRAINE

CSKA KYIV   DNIPRO DNIPROPETROVSK   DYNAMO KYIV   KARPATY LVIV   KRYVBAS KRYVYI RIH

METALIST KHARKOV   METALURG DONETSK   METALURG MARIUPOL   METALURG ZAPORIZHZHYA   SK MYKOLAIV

NYVA TERNOPIL   PRYKARPATTYA IVANO-FRANKIVSK   SHAKHTAR DONETSK   TAVRIYA SIMFEROPOL

VORSKLA POLTAVA   ZIRKA KIROVOHRAD   CHORNOMORETS ODESA

Plate 87

UKRAINE

CSKA KYIV   DNIPRO DNIPROPETROVSK   DYNAMO KYIV   KARPATY LYIV

KRYVBAS KRYVYI RIH   METALIST KHARKOV   METALURG DONETSK   METALURG MARIUPOL

METALURG ZAPORIZHZHYA   SK MYKOLAIV   NYVA TERNOPIL   PRYKARPATTYA IVANO-FRANKIVSK

SHAKHTAR DONETSK   TAVRIYA SIMFEROPOL   VORSKLA POLTAVA   ZIRKA KIROVOHRAD

CHORNOMORETS ODESA

Plate 88

WALES

ABERYSTWYTH TOWN   AFAN LIDO   BANGOR CITY   BARRY TOWN   CAERNARFON TOWN

CAERSWS   CARMARTHEN TOWN   CONNAH'S QUAY NOMADS   CONWY UNITED   CWMBRAN TOWN

HAVERFORDWEST COUNTY   HOLYWELL TOWN   INTER CABLETEL   NEWTOWN

RHAYADER TOWN   RHYL   TOTAL NETWORK SOLUTIONS

LLANELLI AFC   FLEXSYS CEFN DRUIDS

Plate 89

WALES

ABERYSTWYTH TOWN

AFAN LIDO

BANGOR CITY

BARRY TOWN

CAERNARFON TOWN

CAERSWS

CARMARTHEN TOWN

CONNAH'S QUAY NOMADS

CONWY UNITED

CWMBRAN TOWN

HAVERFORDWEST COUNTY

HOLYWELL TOWN

INTER CABLETEL

NEWTOWN

RHAYADER TOWN

RHYL

TOTAL NETWORK SOLUTIONS FC

LLANELLI AFC

FLEXSYS CEFN DRUIDS

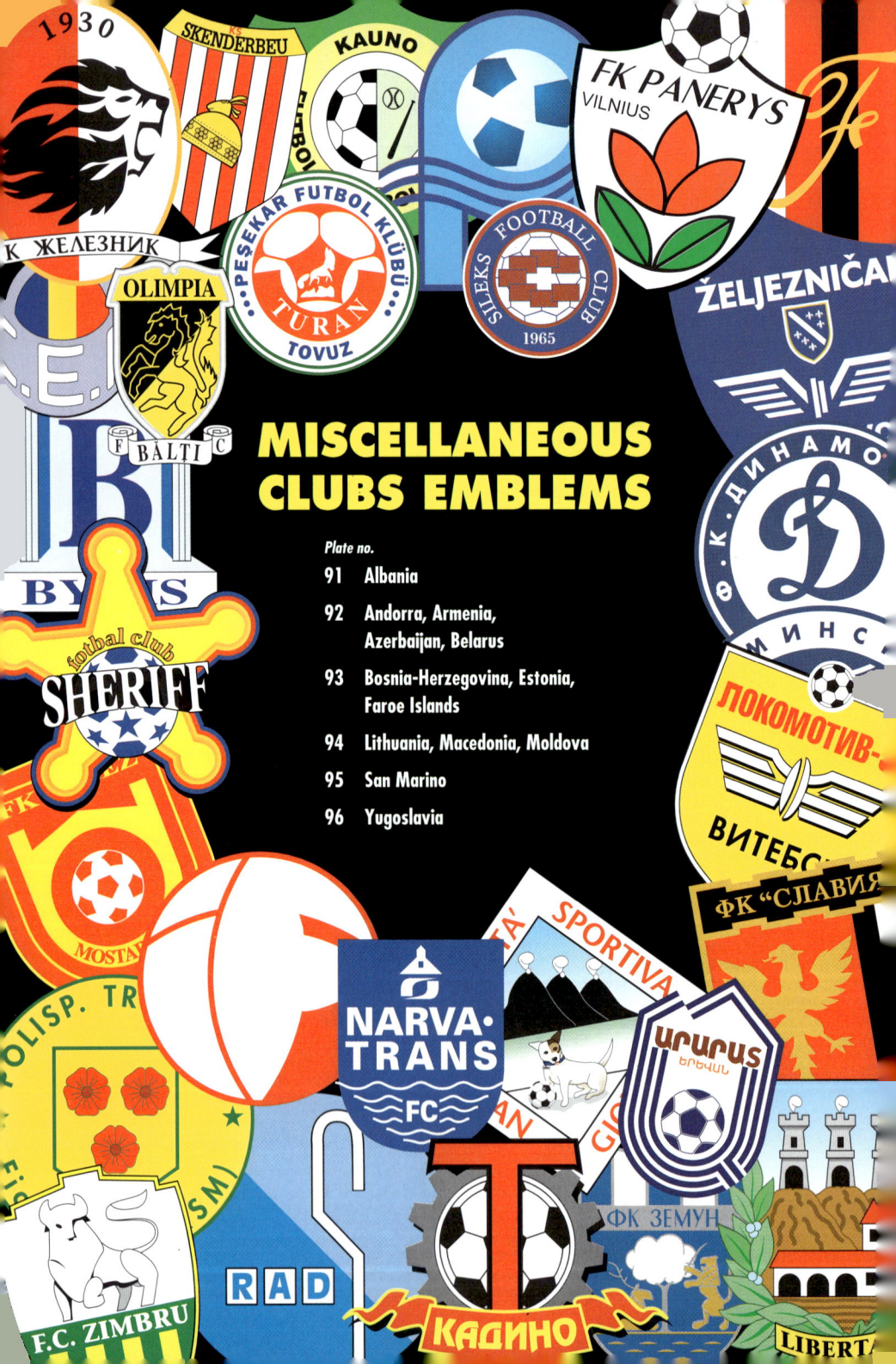

MISCELLANEOUS CLUBS EMBLEMS

Plate 91

MISCELLANEOUS

ALBANIA
APOLONIA FIER

ALBANIA
BESA KAVAJË

ALBANIA
BURRELI

ALBANIA
BYLIS BALLSH

ALBANIA
DINAMO TIRANË

ALBANIA
ELBASANI

ALBANIA
FLAMURTARI VLORË

ALBANIA
LAÇI

ALBANIA
LUSHNJA

ALBANIA
PARTIZANI TIRANË

ALBANIA
SHKUMBINI PEQIN

ALBANIA
SKËNDERBEU KORÇË

ALBANIA
TEUTA DURRËS

ALBANIA
SK TIRANA

ALBANIA
TOMORI BERAT

ALBANIA
VLLAZNIA SHKODËR

ALBANIA
SHQIPONJA GJIROKASTËR

Plate 92

MISCELLANEOUS

ANDORRA
PRINCIPAT

ARMENIA
ARARAT

ARMENIA
EREBUNI

AZERBAIJAN
TURAN TOVUZ

BELARUS
BATE BORISOV

BELARUS
BELSHINA BOBRUISK

BELARUS
DINAMO BREST

BELARUS
DINAMO MINSK

BELARUS
DNEPR-TRANSMASH MOGILEV

BELARUS
FC GOMEL

BELARUS
KOMMUNALNIK SLONIM

BELARUS
LOKOMOTIV-96 VITEBSK

BELARUS
FC MOLODECHNO

BELARUS
NAFTAN-DEVON NOVOPOLOTSK

BELARUS
NEMAN GRODNO

BELARUS
SHAKHTER SOLIGORSK

BELARUS
SLAVIYA MOZYR

BELARUS
TORPEDO MINSK

BELARUS
TORPEDO ATF-KADINO MOGILEV

Plate 93

MISCELLANEOUS

BOSNIA-HERZEGOVINA
SARAJEVO

BOSNIA-HERZEGOVINA
VELEZ MOSTAR

BOSNIA-HERZEGOVINA
ZELJEZNICAR SARAJEVO

ESTONIA
EP JÕHVI

ESTONIA
FC FLORA TALLINN

ESTONIA
FC LANTANA TALLINN

ESTONIA
TALLINNA SADAM

ESTONIA
TRANS NARVA

ESTONIA
JK TULEVIK VILJANDI

FAROE ISLANDS
B36

FAROE ISLANDS
B68

FAROE ISLANDS
GÍ

FAROE ISLANDS
HB

FAROE ISLANDS
ÍF

FAROE ISLANDS
KÍ

FAROE ISLANDS
NSÍ

FAROE ISLANDS
SUMBA

FAROE ISLANDS
TB

FAROE ISLANDS
VB

FAROE ISLANDS
B71

Plate 94

MISCELLANEOUS

LITHUANIA
ATLANTAS KLAIPEDA

LITHUANIA
FK EKRANAS PANEVEZYS

LITHUANIA
KAREDA SIAULIAI

LITHUANIA
FBK KAUNAS

LITHUANIA
PANERYS VILNIUS

LITHUANIA
ZALGIRIS VILNIUS

MACEDONIA
SILEKS KRATOVO

MACEDONIA
SLOGA JUGOMAGNAT SKOPJE

MOLDOVA
AGRO CHISINAU

MOLDOVA
CONSTRUCTORUL CHISINAU

MOLDOVA
OLIMPIA BALTI

MOLDOVA
SHERIFF TIRASPOL

MOLDOVA
TILIGUL TIRASPOL

MOLDOVA
ZIMBRU CHISINAU

Plate 95

MISCELLANEOUS

SAN MARINO
CAILUNGO

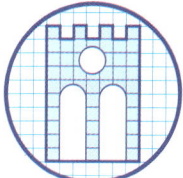

SAN MARINO
COSMOS

SAN MARINO
DOGANA

SAN MARINO
DOMAGNANO

SAN MARINO
FAETANO

SAN MARINO
FIORITA

SAN MARINO
FOLGORE

SAN MARINO
JUVENES

SAN MARINO
LIBERTAS

SAN MARINO
MONTEVITO

SAN MARINO
MURATA

SAN MARINO
PENNAROSSA

SAN MARINO
SAN GIOVANNI

SAN MARINO
TRE FIORI

SAN MARINO
TRE PENNE

SAN MARINO
VIRTUS

Plate 96

MISCELLANEOUS

YUGOSLAVIA
BUDUCNOST PODGORICA

YUGOSLAVIA
CRVENA ZVEZDA BEOGRAD

YUGOSLAVIA
HAJDUK KULA

YUGOSLAVIA
OBILIC BEOGRAD

YUGOSLAVIA
OFK BEOGRAD

YUGOSLAVIA
PARTIZAN BEOGRAD

YUGOSLAVIA
PROLETER ZRENJANIN

YUGOSLAVIA
RAD BEOGRAD

YUGOSLAVIA
RADNICKI NIS

YUGOSLAVIA
VOJVODINA NOVI SAD

YUGOSLAVIA
ZELEZNIK BEOGRAD

YUGOSLAVIA
FK ZEMUN

YUGOSLAVIA
FK BORAC CACAK

YUGOSLAVIA
FK SUTJESKA NIKSIC

YUGOSLAVIA
CUKARICKI BEOGRAD

DOMESTIC CUP 98/99

SECOND ROUND

Ravenna v Juventus 0-2; 0-4
(Juventus 6-0)
Cagliari v Venezia 0-0; 1-2
(Venezia 2-1)
Reggina v Bologna 1-1; 0-3
(Bologna 4-1)
Sampdoria v Verona 2-0; 0-1
(Sampdoria 2-1)
Lecce v Piacenza 1-2; 3-2 aet
(4-4; Lecce on away goals)
Padova v Fiorentina 0-1; 0-2
(Fiorentina 3-0)
Atalanta v Empoli 2-1; 0-0
(Atalanta 2-1)
Chievo v Roma 2-2; 1-2
(Roma 4-3)
Gualdo v Udinese 2-2; 0-4
(Udinese 6-2)
Brescia v Vicenza 3-2; 0-3
(Vicenza 5-3)
Parma v Genoa 3-0; 1-0
(Parma 4-0)
Lucchese v Bari 1-0; 0-2
(Bari 2-1)
Torino v Milan 2-0; 0-3
(Milan 3-2)
Lazio v Cosenza 2-1; 2-0
(Lazio 4-1)
Castel di Sangro v Salernitana 0-0; 2-0
(Castel di Sangro 2-0)
Inter v Cesena 1-0; 0-0
(Inter 1-0)

THIRD ROUND

Juventus v Venezia 1-1; 2-2 aet
(3-3; Juventus on away goals)
Sampdoria v Bologna 0-0; 1-2
(Bologna 2-1)
Fiorentina v Lecce 1-0; 4-0
(Fiorentina 5-0)
Atalanta v Roma 1-1; 1-1 aet
(2-2; Atalanta 6-5 on pens.)
Udinese v Vicenza 0-0; 1-0
(Udinese 1-0)
Bari v Parma 1-2; 0-0
(Parma 2-1)
Lazio v Milan 3-1; 1-1
(Lazio 4-2)
Inter v Castel di Sangro 1-0; 1-1
(Inter 2-1)

QUARTER-FINALS

Udinese 3 (Appiah 40, Amoroso 46, Navas 90),
Parma 2 (Balbo 42, Crespo 76)
Parma 4 (Verona 15, Crespo 18, 74, Balbo 90),
Udinese 0
(Parma 6-3)

Atalanta 3 (Torricelli 28og, Rossini 62, Carrera 83),
Fiorentina 2 (Rustico 7og, Edmundo 34)
Fiorentina 1 (Robbiati 10), Atalanta 0
(3-3; Fiorentina on away goals)

Lazio 2 (Salas 12p, 47), Inter 1 (Djorkaeff 31)
Inter 5 (Cauet 13, Djorkaeff 26, 69, Zé Elias 84,
Moriero 90), Lazio 2 (Vieri 10, Lombardo 34)
(Inter 6-4)

Juventus 1 (Perrotta 13),
Bologna 2 (Boselli 74, Ingesson 90p)
Bologna 0, Juventus 1 (Davids 33)
(2-2; Bologna on away goals)

SEMI-FINALS

Inter 0, Parma 2 (Verón 77, Balbo 86)
Parma 2 (Chiesa 4, Verón 36),
Inter 1 (Zamorano 10)
(Parma 4-2)

Bologna 0, Fiorentina 2 (Esposito 34, Rui Costa 67)
Fiorentina 2 (Cois 99, Rui Costa 118p),
Bologna 2 (Binotto 18, 65) (aet)
(Fiorentina 4-2)

FINAL

14/04/99, Parma
PARMA 1 Crespo (16)
FIORENTINA 1 Batistuta (81)
referee - Messina

PARMA - Buffon; Thuram, Sensini, Cannavaro; Stanic,
Fuser, Baggio, Vanoli; Verón; Chiesa (Mussi 69),
Crespo (Balbo 80).

FIORENTINA - Toldo; Padalino; Falcone, Repka,
Heinrich; Torricelli, Cois, Rui Costa, Amoroso;
Edmundo, Batistuta (Mareggini 85).

05/05/99, Florence
FIORENTINA 2 Repka (48), Cois (62)
PARMA 2 Crespo (44), Vanoli (71)
referee - Braschi

FIORENTINA - Toldo; Padalino; Falcone, Repka,
Heinrich; Torricelli, Cois (Oliveira 79), Rui Costa,
Amoroso; Batistuta, Edmundo.

PARMA - Buffon; Thuram, Sensini, Cannavaro; Stanic
(Fiore 69), Fuser, Boghossian, Vanoli; Verón (Mussi
79); Chiesa, Crespo (Balbo 85).

(3-3; Parma on away goals)

---

a depleted Marseille in a one-sided final. Parma were close to being eliminated on the away-goals rule by Fenerbahçe in the first round but thereafter they were unstoppable, moving their opponents into position in the first leg before finishing them off back on home soil in the return. The 6-0 destruction of French high-fliers Bordeaux in the quarter-finals was especially impressive, and had they not laid off a bit in the second half in Moscow, they might easily have inflicted a similar caning on Marseille in the final.

Parma preceded their UEFA Cup win by lifting the Italian Cup, also for the second time. An away-goals victory over Fiorentina in the final tasted especially sweet for Parma boss Alberto Malesani, who not only captured the first major honour of his career but did so at the expense of the club which had offloaded him the previous summer. To complete a happy first season for Malesani, Parma also finished fourth in Serie A to book a place in the qualifying round of the Champions' League.

Third place in Serie A went to Fiorentina, who for much of the season hoped for a lot better. The *Viola* set the pace in the autumn and were still out in front at halfway, claiming the spurious title of 'winter champions' in magnificent style with their ninth home win on the trot - a 4-2 victory over Cagliari, in which skipper Gabriel Batistuta scored a hat-trick to take his season's aggregate to 17 goals in as many games. 'BatiGol' had also struck three times earlier in the season away to Milan, thus becoming the first visting player to score a hat-trick against the *Rossoneri* in the San Siro for over 40 years, but in the

EUROPEAN CUPS 98/99

CHAMPIONS' CUP
● JUVENTUS
Champions' League
1st match GALATASARAY (TUR)
H 2-2   Inzaghi (16), Birindelli (67)
Peruzzi; Birindelli, Tudor, Tacchinardi, Pessotto (Blanchard 68); Di Livio, Deschamps, Davids; Fonseca (Rampulla 33), Inzaghi (Zidane 62), Del Piero.

2nd round ROSENBORG BK (NOR)
A 1-1   Inzaghi (27)
Rampulla; Birindelli, Tudor, Montero, Mirkovic (Pessotto 77); Tacchinardi, Deschamps, Davids; Zidane (Zalayeta 79); Inzaghi (Fonseca 61), Del Piero.

3rd match ATHLETIC BILBAO (ESP)
A 0-0
Peruzzi; Birindelli, Tudor, Montero; Di Livio, Deschamps, Davids (Tacchinardi 77), Pessotto (Iuliano 29); Zidane; Inzaghi, Del Piero (Fonseca 81).

4th match ATHLETIC BILBAO (ESP)
H 1-1   Lasa (69og)
Peruzzi; Tudor (Blanchard 46), Iuliano, Montero; Di Livio (Perrotta 84), Tacchinardi, Davids, Pessotto (Amoruso 55); Zidane; Inzaghi, Del Piero.

5th match GALATASARAY (TUR)
A 1-1   Amoruso (78)
Peruzzi (Rampulla 59); Birindelli, Ferrara, Montero, Iuliano; Blanchard, Conte, Deschamps, Pessotto (Amoruso 66); Inzaghi (Tudor 81), Zidane.

6th match ROSENBORG BK (NOR)
H 2-0   Inzaghi (16), Amoruso (36)
Peruzzi; Birindelli, Tudor, Montero, Pessotto (Davids 63); Conte (Di Livio 87), Deschamps, Tacchinardi; Zidane; Inzaghi, Amoruso (Iuliano 86).

Quarter-final OLYMPIAKOS (GRE)
H 2-1   Inzaghi (37), Conte (78)
Peruzzi; Mirkovic, Iuliano, Montero, Di Livio (Tacchinardi 90); Conte, Deschamps, Davids; Zidane; Inzaghi, Fonseca (Birindelli 82).
A 1-1   Conte (85)
Rampulla; Mirkovic (Birindelli 83), Iuliano, Montero, Di Livio; Conte, Deschamps, Davids; Zidane (Tacchinardi 89); Inzaghi, Esnáider (Amoruso 69).

Semi-final MANCHESTER UNITED (ENG)
A 1-1   Conte (24)
Peruzzi; Mirkovic, Iuliano, Montero (Ferrara 68), Pessotto; Conte, Deschamps, Davids, Di Livio (Tacchinardi 77); Zidane; Inzaghi (Esnáider 88).
H 2-3   Inzaghi (6, 10)
Peruzzi; Birindelli (Amoruso 46), Ferrara, Iuliano (Montero 46), Pessotto; Conte, Deschamps, Davids, Di Livio (Fonseca 80); Zidane; Inzaghi.

● INTER
Qualifying round SKONTO RIGA (LAT)
H 4-0   Zamorano (4), Simeone (10), Ventola (20), Baggio (59)
Pagliuca; Colonnese, Bergomi (Fresi 60), Galante; Cauet, Zé Elias (Zanetti J. 46), Simeone, Milanese; Baggio (Pirlo 66); Zamorano, Ventola.
A 3-1   Zamorano (8), Galante (54), Djorkaeff (70)
Pagliuca; Bergomi, Fresi, Galante; Zanetti J., Winter (Zanetti C. 74), Cauet, Milanese; Djorkaeff (Pirlo 71), Zamorano, Baggio (Recoba 71).

Champions' League
1st match REAL MADRID (ESP)
A 0-2
Pagliuca; Fresi; Bergomi, Galante, Milanese; Zanetti J., Cauet (Silvestre 46), Winter (Ventola 80), Simeone; Zamorano, Ronaldo (Pirlo 74).

2nd match SK STURM GRAZ (AUT)
H 1-0   Djorkaeff (90)
Pagliuca; Bergomi, Silvestre, Galante; Moriero (Pirlo 73), Cauet (Zamorano 65), Winter, Simeone, Zanetti J.; Djorkaeff, Ventola.

3rd match SPARTAK MOSKVA (RUS)
H 2-1   Ventola (32), Ronaldo (58)
Pagliuca; Simeone; West, Galante, Silvestre; Cauet, Paulo Sousa, Winter, Djorkaeff (Pirlo 34); Ronaldo (Zé Elias 73), Ventola (Zamorano 83).

4th match SPARTAK MOSKVA (RUS)
A 1-1   Simeone (90)
Pagliuca; Colonnese, Bergomi (Pirlo 76), Galante; Cauet, Paulo Sousa, Simeone, Zanetti J.; Moriero (Silvestre 90), Ronaldo (Ventola 68), Zamorano.

5th match REAL MADRID (ESP)
H 3-1   Zamorano (50), Baggio (86, 90)
Pagliuca; Bergomi; West, Galante, Colonnese; Moriero (Zanetti J. 57), Winter, Paulo Sousa (Cauet 75), Simeone; Zamorano (Baggio 68), Ronaldo.

6th match SK STURM GRAZ (AUT)
A 2-0   Zanetti J. (63), Baggio (80)
Pagliuca; Colonnese, Bergomi, Galante; Zanetti J., Winter, Zé Elias (Recoba 82), Simeone, Silvestre; Ronaldo (Zamorano 61), Djorkaeff (Baggio 70).

Quarter-final MANCHESTER UNITED (ENG)
A 0-2
Pagliuca; Colonnese, Bergomi, Galante; Zanetti J., Cauet, Simeone, Winter; Djorkaeff, Zamorano (Ventola 68), Baggio (Pirlo 78).
H 1-1   Ventola (63)
Pagliuca; Colonnese, Bergomi (Moriero 69), West; Zanetti, Cauet, Simeone (Zé Elias 77), Silvestre; Ronaldo (Ventola 60), Zamorano, Baggio.

CUP WINNERS' CUP
● LAZIO
1st round LAUSANNE-SPORTS (SUI)
H 1-1   Nedved (37)
Marchegiani; Fernando Couto, Lopez, Mihajlovic, Pancaro (Lombardi 60); Stankovic, Venturin, Nedved; De la Peña (Sérgio Conceição 23); Salas (Gottardi 81), Mancini.
A 2-2   Salas (7), Sérgio Conceição (25)
Marchegiani; Pancaro, Fernando Couto, Mihajlovic, Favalli (Lopez 88); Sérgio Conceição (Gottardi 84), Almeyda (Baronio 28), Venturin, Nedved; Salas, Mancini.

2nd round PARTIZAN BEOGRAD (YUG)
H 0-0
Marchegiani; Pancaro, Fernando Couto, Mihajlovic, Favalli; Sérgio Conceição, Almeyda, Venturin, Nedved, Gottardi (Marcolin 69); Mancini.

A 3-2 Salas (43p, 75), Stankovic (66)
Marchegiani; Pancaro, Fernando Couto, Mihajlovic, Favalli; Sérgio Conceição (Stankovic 53), Almeyda, Venturin, Nedved; Salas (Boksic 81), Mancini (Baronio 89).

Quarter-final PANIONIOS (GRE)
A 4-0 Stankovic (3, 60), Gazis (13og), Nedved (62)
Marchegiani; Negro (Lombardi 26), Nesta, Mihajlovic (Baronio 64), Pancaro; Lombardo, Fernando Couto, Stankovic, Nedved; Vieri (Gottardi 76), Salas.
H 3-0 Nedved (69), Stankovic (76), De la Peña (80)
Ballotta; Lombardo, Nesta, Mihajlovic (Crovari 71), Lombardi; Gottardi, Baronio, Fernando Couto, Nedved; Stankovic, De la Peña.

Semi-final LOKOMOTIV MOSKVA (RUS)
A 1-1 Boksic (77)
Marchegiani; Pancaro, Negro, Mihajlovic, Favalli; Stankovic, Almeyda, De la Peña, Lombardo; Vieri (Boksic 64), Salas (Mancini 73).
H 0-0
Marchegiani; Negro, Nesta, Mihajlovic, Pancaro; Lombardo, Stankovic, Fernando Couto (Almeyda 46), Nedved; Mancini (De la Peña 76), Vieri (Boksic 88).

Final RCD MALLORCA (ESP)
Birmingham
2-1 Vieri (7), Nedved (81)
Marchegiani; Pancaro, Nesta, Mihajlovic, Favalli; Stankovic (Sérgio Conceição 56), Mancini (Fernando Couto 90), Almeyda, Nedved (Lombardo 84); Vieri, Salas.

UEFA CUP
● FIORENTINA
1st round HAJDUK SPLIT (CRO)
H 2-1 Edmundo (51, 82)
Toldo; Tarozzi, Falcone, Torricelli, Repka, Heinrich; Cois (Amoroso 58), Morfeo (Esposito 27; Mirri 80), Amor; Batistuta, Edmundo.
A 0-0
Toldo; Tarozzi, Falcone, Padulano, Repka, Heinrich; Amor (Bigica 90), Cois, Amoroso; Edmundo (Esposito 76), Batistuta.

2nd round GRASSHOPPER-CLUB ZÜRICH (SUI)
A 2-0 Batistuta (20), Robbiati (47)
Toldo; Torricelli, Padalino, Repka; Tarozzi (Bettarini 60), Amoroso (Bigica 69), Amor (Mirri 81), Heinrich; Edmundo, Batistuta, Robbiati.
H 2-1 Oliveira (12, 38)
(match abandoned at half-time and awarded 0-3)
Toldo; Firicano; Falcone, Repka; Torricelli, Rui Costa, Amoroso, Heinrich; Edmundo, Batistuta, Oliveira.

● PARMA
1st round FENERBAHÇE (TUR)
A 0-1
Buffon; Stanic (Fuser 52), Sensini, Thuram, Cannavaro, Vanoli; Baggio, Fiore, Longo (Benarrivo 76); Balbo, Asprilla (Boghossian 65).
H 3-1 Saffet (14og), Crespo (45), Boghossian (73)
Buffon; Mussi, Sensini, Thuram; Fuser, Fiore, Boghossian, Benarrivo; Verón (Sartor 82); Crespo (Balbo 85), Asprilla (Orlandini 88).

2nd round WISLA KRAKOW (POL)
A 1-1 Chiesa (2)
Buffon; Thuram, Sensini, Cannavaro; Fuser, Baggio, Fiore, Vanoli; Verón (Mussi 90); Crespo (Balbo 46), Chiesa (Stanic 83).
H 2-1 Fiore (21), Zajac B. (47og)
Buffon; Thuram, Sensini, Cannavaro; Mussi, Boghossian, Fiore (Longo 75), Benarrivo; Verón; Balbo (Orlandini 87), Chiesa (Stanic 66).

3rd round RANGERS (SCO)
A 1-1 Balbo (51)
Buffon; Sartor, Thuram, Cannavaro; Stanic, Boghossian, Baggio, Benarrivo; Verón (Fiore 70); Balbo, Crespo (Orlandini 90).
H 3-1 Balbo (48), Fiore (63), Chiesa (68p)
Buffon; Thuram, Sensini, Cannavaro; Fuser (Mussi 85), Baggio, Boghossian (Fiore 57), Benarrivo; Verón; Balbo, Chiesa (Crespo 74).

Quarter-final GIRONDINS DE BORDEAUX (FRA)
A 1-2 Crespo (84)
Buffon; Thuram, Sensini, Cannavaro; Stanic (Vanoli 87), Fuser, Longo, Benarrivo; Verón; Balbo (Crespo 72), Asprilla (Chiesa 63).
H 6-0 Crespo (37, 67), Chiesa (43, 60), Sensini (49), Balbo (89p)
Buffon; Thuram, Sensini, Cannavaro; Fuser, Baggio, Boghossian (Asprilla 82), Vanoli; Verón; Crespo (Fiore 74), Chiesa (Balbo 70).

Semi-final ATLETICO MADRID (ESP)
A 3-1 Chiesa (14, 41), Crespo (62)
Buffon; Sartor, Sensini, Thuram; Fuser, Baggio, Fiore, Vanoli; Verón (Stanic 65); Crespo (Mussi 82), Chiesa (Balbo 68).
H 2-1 Balbo (35), Chiesa (84)
Buffon; Sartor (Mussi 40), Sensini, Thuram; Fuser, Baggio (Boghossian 54), Fiore, Benarrivo; Verón (Vanoli 85); Balbo, Chiesa.

Final OLYMPIQUE MARSEILLE (FRA)
H 3-0 Crespo (26), Vanoli (36), Chiesa (55)
Buffon; Thuram, Sensini, Cannavaro; Fuser, Baggio, Boghossian, Vanoli; Verón (Fiore 77); Chiesa (Balbo 72), Crespo (Asprilla 84).

● ROMA
1st round SILKEBORG (DEN)
H 1-0 Delvecchio (53)
Chimenti; Cafú, Zago, Wome, Candela; Tommasi, Tomic (Di Biagio 46), Alenichev (Di Francesco 71); Gautieri, Delvecchio (Bartelt 71), Totti.
A 2-0 Totti (62), Alenichev (70)
Chimenti; Cafú, Aldair, Wome, Candela; Tommasi (Di Francesco 70), Di Biagio, Tomic (Alenichev 46); Paulo Sérgio, Delvecchio (Bartelt 77), Totti.

2nd round LEEDS UNITED (ENG)
H 1-0 Delvecchio (18)
Chimenti; Cafú, Zago, Aldair, Candela; Tommasi, Di Biagio, Di Francesco (Alenichev 46); Frau (Bartelt 59), Delvecchio, Totti.
A 0-0
Chimenti; Aldair, Petruzzi, Zago, Wome; Tommasi, Tomic, Di Francesco; Paulo Sérgio (Candela 46), Delvecchio, Totti (Cafú 86).

3rd round FC ZÜRICH (SUI)
H 1-0 Totti (90p)
Chimenti; Tommasi, Zago, Aldair, Candela; Tomic, Di Biagio, Frau (Frau 30), Alenichev; Paulo Sérgio, Delvecchio (Dal Moro 68), Totti.

(Continued overleaf)

EUROPEAN CUPS 98/99 (CONTINUED)

A 2-2 Delvecchio (13), Totti (90)
Chimenti; Aldair, Petruzzi, Zago (Quadrini 90), Candela; Tommasi (Tomic 90), Di Biagio, Di Francesco; Paulo Sérgio, Delvecchio, Totti.

Quarter-final ATLETICO MADRID (ESP)
A 1-2 Di Biagio (75)
Chimenti; Cafú, Zago, Aldair, Candela (Wome 80); Tommasi (Alenichev 68), Di Biagio, Di Francesco; Paulo Sérgio, Delvecchio (Fábio Júnior 68), Totti.
H 1-2 Delvecchio (32)
Chimenti; Cafú, Zago, Aldair, Wome; Alenichev, Di Biagio, Di Francesco (Fábio Júnior 78); Paulo Sérgio (Candela 35; Tommasi 78), Delvecchio, Totti.

● **UDINESE**
1st round BAYER 04 LEVERKUSEN (GER)
H 1-1 Walem (81)
Turci; Bertotto, Calori, Pierini, Navas (Pineda 57), Giannichedda, Walem, Bachini; Poggi (Locatelli 51), Jørgensen (Sosa 63), Amoroso.
A 0-1
Turci; Gargo, Calori, Pierini (Navas 85); Bachini, Giannichedda, Walem, Pineda (Sosa 70); Poggi (Jørgensen 59), Locatelli, Amoroso.

● **BOLOGNA**
1st round SPORTING CP (POR)
A 2-0 Nervo (16), Eriberto (90)
Antonioli; Rinaldi, Paganin, Mangone; Nervo, Cappioli, Marocchi, Tarantino; Ingesson, Kolyvanov (Eriberto 72), Signori.
H 2-1 Nervo (78), Signori (90p)
Antonioli; Rinaldi, Boselli, Paganin (Gallicchio 28), Tarantino; Cappioli, Ingesson, Marocchi, Nervo; Kolyvanov (Eriberto 16), Signori.

2nd round SLAVIA PRAHA (CZE)
H 2-1 Signori (6), Ingesson (84)
Antonioli; Paramatti, Rinaldi, Mangone, Tarantino; Nervo, Ingesson, Marocchi, Cappioli (Eriberto 62); Andersson, Signori.
A 2-0 Signori (79), Cappioli (85)
Antonioli; Paramatti, Rinaldi, Mangone, Tarantino; Eriberto (Boselli 65), Ingesson, Marocchi, Fontolan (Cappioli 74); Andersson, Kolyvanov (Signori 73).

3rd round REAL BETIS (ESP)
H 4-1 Fontolan (25, 73), Kolyvanov (52), Eriberto (58)
Antonioli; Paramatti, Boselli, Rinaldi, Tarantino; Eriberto (Cappioli 76), Ingesson, Marocchi, Fontolan; Andersson (Pompei 90), Kolyvanov (Signori 74).
A 0-1
Antonioli; Rinaldi, Boselli, Mangone, Tarantino; Eriberto (Signori 84), Cappioli (Magoni 90); Ingesson, Marocchi, Fontolan; Andersson.

Quarter-final OLYMPIQUE LYONNAIS (FRA)
H 3-0 Signori (9, 49), Binotto (55)
Antonioli; Paramatti, Bia, Mangone, Tarantino; Binotto (Rinaldi 70), Ingesson, Marocchi, Fontolan (Cappioli 81); Andersson, Signori (Kolyvanov 87).
A 0-2
Antonioli; Rinaldi, Bia, Mangone (Paganin 25), Paramatti; Binotto (Cappioli 46), Ingesson, Marocchi, Nervo (Boselli 46); Andersson, Signori.

Semi-final OLYMPIQUE MARSEILLE (FRA)
A 0-0
Antonioli; Rinaldi, Bia, Mangone, Paramatti; Binotto (Cappioli 74), Ingesson, Marocchi, Fontolan (Nervo 67); Andersson, Signori (Maini 80).
H 1-1 Paramatti (18)
Antonioli; Rinaldi (Kolyvanov 89), Bia, Mangone, Paramatti; Binotto (Cappioli 76), Ingesson, Marocchi, Fontolan (Nervo 76); Andersson, Signori.

return game against Milan his and Fiorentina's title ambitions were to suffer irreparable damage. Not only did Fiorentina's 100 per cent home record come to an end (the match finished goalless), but they also lost their star striker for the next four games through injury. With Batistuta's strike-partner, the headstrong Edmundo, also controversially choosing this moment of the season to return to Brazil, for the Rio Carnival, the *Viola* were left barren up front and dropped from their perch, never to return. Still, they did make it to the Champions' League, which had been the original target set by coach Giovanni Trapattoni at the beginning of his first season in Florence.

Juventus and Inter, the top two teams in 1997/98, did not even make it into Europe. Both clubs went through nine months of torture and turmoil as they failed to match the standards they had set the previous season. They had a lot in common. They both got rid of their coach. They both lost their main striker through injury. They both went out of the Champions' League to eventual winners Manchester United. And they were both beaten in end-of-season play-offs to qualify for the UEFA Cup.

Everything looked fine for Juventus initially, but once Alessandro Del Piero suffered a serious knee injury away to Udinese in early November, their season went to pot. Without their brilliant 'number ten', sidelined for the remainder of the season, Juve failed to score in their next five Serie A matches - a run which killed off any chance they had of defending their championship crown. They also made desperately hard work of their bid to reach a fourth successive Champions' League final. How they managed to squeeze through to win their group remains a mystery, given that they drew each of their first five games, but the luck remained with them as they also sneaked past Olympiakos with a late goal from skipper Antonio Conte in the quarter-finals. They played their best football of the season away to Manchester United at Old Trafford in the first leg of the semi-final, but in Turin they surrendered an early two-goal lead and that was their season over.

Marcello Lippi, who had won six major titles during his first four seasons at the club, decided to abandon ship in February, thus becoming the first Juventus coach to leave the club in mid-season for 30 years. It was an open secret

NATIONAL TEAM APPEARANCES 98/99

Coach - Dino ZOFF	WAL	SUI	ESP	ROW	NOR	DEN	BLS	CRO	WAL	SUI	Cps	Gls
Angelo PERUZZI (16/02/70) - Juventus	G		G	G46	G						27	-
Christian PANUCCI (12/04/73) - Real Madrid (ESP)	D	D	D46	D	D46	D	D	D63	D	D69	17	1
Fabio CANNAVARO (13/09/73) - Parma	D	D	D	D46	D	D	D		D	D	28	-
Mark IULIANO (12/08/73) - Juventus	D										1	-
Gianluca PESSOTTO (11/08/70) - Juventus	D	s60	s65								10	-
Diego FUSER (11/11/68) - Parma	M	M	M46	M		M46		M46	M69	M69	22	2
Dino BAGGIO (24/07/71) - Parma	M	M	M46	M46	M46	M	M46				58	7
Demetrio ALBERTINI (23/08/71) - Milan	M66	M	M46	M46	M			M	M	M	63	2
Eusebio DI FRANCESCO (08/09/69) - Roma	M85	M61	M	M46	M	M	s46	M57	M	M	10	1
Alessandro DEL PIERO (09/11/74) - Juventus	A75	A70									25	9
Christian VIERI (12/07/73) - Lazio	A							A	A46	A60	17	9
Luigi DI BIAGIO (03/06/71) - Roma	s66		s46			M	M				12	1
Roberto BAGGIO (18/02/67) - Inter	s75				A81		s64				55	27
Michele SERENA (10/03/70) - Atlético Madrid (ESP)	s85										1	-
Gianluigi BUFFON (28/01/78) - Parma		G		s46		G	G	G	G	G	9	-
Paolo MALDINI (26/06/68) - Milan		D	D	D65	D	D	D	D	D	D	102	7
Moreno TORRICELLI (23/01/70) - Fiorentina		D	s46	s46	s46						9	-
Filippo INZAGHI (09/08/73) - Juventus		A	A	A46		A	A	A79	A80	A	14	6
Jonathan BACHINI (05/06/75) - Udinese		s61		s46							2	-
Francesco TOTTI (27/09/76) - Roma		s70	A	A55	s62	s63	M46	s79			7	-
Giuseppe FAVALLI (08/01/72) - Lazio			D60								2	-
Damiano TOMMASI (17/05/74) - Roma			s46	s46							2	-
Enrico CHIESA (29/12/70) - Parma			s46	s55	s81	A63	A64		s80	s60	16	7
Alessandro NESTA (19/03/76) - Lazio			D40	D	D	D	D				20	-
Paolo NEGRO (16/04/72) - Lazio			s40				D	D	D		7	-
Marco DELVECCHIO (07/04/73) - Roma			s46	A							2	-
Sandro COIS (09/06/72) - Fiorentina			s46	s46							3	-
Gian Luca ZAMBROTTA (19/02/77) - Bari				M62				s46			2	-
Antonio CONTE (31/07/69) - Juventus					s46	M	s57	M	M		13	1
Giuliano GIANNICHEDDA (21/09/74) - Udinese						s46	s46				2	-
Massimo AMBROSINI (29/05/77) - Milan							M46				1	-
Giuseppe PANCARO (26/08/71) - Lazio							s63			s69	2	-
Vincenzo MONTELLA (18/06/74) - Sampdoria									s46		1	-
Angelo DI LIVIO (26/07/66) - Juventus									s69	s69	27	-

that he would be joining Inter at the end of the season anyway, but he said that he had lost the confidence of the players and could not continue. It was also public knowledge that Carlo Ancelotti had been lined up as Lippi's successor. He was asked to step into the breach four months early and happily did so - despite considerable reservations from many Juve diehards that, as an ex-Milan player, he could not give his heart to the club. By the end of the season, however, all Ancelotti had achieved for Juve was a place in the InterToto Cup after they lost their UEFA Cup qualifier against Udinese. How the mighty had fallen!

PLAYERS OF THE SEASON

★ SUPERSTAR PROFILE
DEMETRIO ALBERTINI

The Italian national team has undergone a number of upheavals in recent years, but Milan midfielder Demetrio Albertini's presence in the side remains as rock-solid as ever. Since earning his first international cap midway through his début season in Serie A, Albertini has been an immovable object in the heart of Italy's central midfield. Some might argue that it is the lack of viable contenders that has kept him in situ for so long - and, indeed, Italy has not exactly been blessed with a surfeit of creative midfielders during the 1990s - but the truth is that the Milan *regista* has rarely had a bad game for the *Azzurri* and, at 28, he could yet stay on board long enough to match team-mate Paolo Maldini's century of caps. Successive Italian coaches have hesitated to omit him in the understandable apprehension that he might turn out to be one of those players whose importance to the team is only fully appreciated once he is not there. The same principle applies to his club career, and after picking up yet another championship winner's medal in 1998/99, his fifth in eight years at the San Siro, it is doubtful whether he will ever be ceded by Milan to another

club. Foreigners may come and go, but some local-born players remain forever loyal to the *Milanista* cause. Demetrio Albertini is one of them.

GIANLUIGI BUFFON

There can be no better judge of goalkeeping talent than Dino Zoff, so it is a considerable honour for Gianluigi Buffon to be chosen by the great man as the first-choice 'keeper for the Italian national team, especially as the competition for the position is intense and the Parma shot-stopper is still only 21. Buffon has extraordinary talent. He is lithe, flexible and supremely confident for one so young. His performances for Parma during the 1998/99 season were of a consistently high standard and he was every bit as important to the team's successes in the UEFA Cup and Coppa Italia as goal-grabbers Chiesa and Crespo or the two world-class defenders in front of him, Lilian Thuram and Fabio Cannavaro. Buffon also shone for Italy, conceding just two goals in six starts and making a brilliant and crucial one-handed save in the last minute to rescue the *Azzurri* from a potentially humiliating home defeat by Belarus.

MATIAS ALMEYDA

Of all the many highly-paid world-class stars in Sven Göran Eriksson's Lazio side, it was one of the least conspicuous who was arguably the team's best player during the 1998/99 campaign. Matias Almeyda, who played for Argentina at the 1998 World Cup in the 'Redondo rôle', i.e. sitting in front of the defence and dictating the tempo of the game, also operated in that position for Lazio and did it quite brilliantly. He saved his first (and last) goal of the season for round 32 of the 34-match campaign but played a major part in the build-up of many other goals which his team scored in domestic and European competition during the season. The Italian press rarely gave him a bad mark and a couple of publications even had him down as the most consistent player in the whole of Serie A.

FRANCESCO TOTTI

Roma were one of the most exciting teams to watch during the 1998/99 Serie A season. They scored at an average of over two goals per game and were the league's highest scorers, beating arch-rivals Lazio by four. The man chiefly responsible for that

PLAYERS OF THE SEASON

statistic was club captain Francesco Totti, who scored 12 goals himself and set up many others for team-mates Marco Delvecchio and Paulo Sérgio. Totti's set position was on the left side of a three-pronged attack but he had the licence to roam, which he exploited in some style. Some of his goals were wonderfully spectacular, and it was no surprise whatsoever that Dino Zoff called him up for national service during the European Championship qualifying campaign. He still awaits his big break-through for the *Azzurri* but he has the talent to succeed at the highest level and, at 23, time is very much on his side.

ENRICO CHIESA

It is fair to say that if Enrico Chiesa (right) had been born anywhere else but Italy, he would be playing regular international football. As it is, he rarely gets the chance to start a game for the *Azzurri* - despite a hugely impressive international strike-rate that was considerably boosted when he scored a hat-trick in the Italian Federation's Centenary match against the Rest of the World in Rome, a game which, though not strictly a bona fide international, was still officially recognised as such by the FIGC. Chiesa had a tremendous season for Parma, especially in the UEFA Cup. His magnificent net-busting goal in the final against Marseille was an appropriately

spectacular way for him to become the competition's outright top scorer. He netted eight goals in total, scoring in every round bar the first, with three of them coming in the semi-final against Atlético Madrid. Parma's loss was very much Fiorentina's gain when he chose to switch clubs during the summer.

AMOROSO

The man who has replaced Chiesa at Parma is Brazilian striker Márcio dos Santos Amoroso. He came at a cost of £20m and not without good reason, having won the 1998/99 Serie A top scorer prize with 22 goals for Udinese. That was some return from a player who had played second fiddle at the club to Oliver Bierhoff the previous season. His tally not only put him in front of the German (who tried hard to retain his crown, scoring 20 goals for new club Milan) but also ahead of Gabriel Batistuta, who had seemed certain to claim the prize halfway through the season. The Fiorentina man would probably have been a worthier winner given that none of his 21 goals came from penalties, but Amoroso's finishing burst of eight goals in six games proved conclusive and sent him off in good heart to the Copa América in Paraguay, where again he struck it rich, scoring four goals in Brazil's Cup-winning campaign after being selected as the new first-choice partner for Ronaldo.

It was an even sorrier scenario at Inter, who failed to reach Europe in any shape or form after losing both of their play-off matches with Bologna. They had only entered that last-chance saloon by virtue of reaching the Italian Cup semi-finals. In the league they could finish no higher than eighth - which was seven places lower than they had been tipped to finish by most pre-season pundits.

The big concern at Inter was the physical and mental state of their greatest asset, Ronaldo. The young Brazilian's traumatic experience before and during the World Cup final left a legacy of doubt and worry as to whether he could ever be the same player again. His second season at Inter was wrecked by persistent injury problems and he was never able to rediscover the form that had made him such a giant during his first year in blue and black stripes. That he eventually finished up as the team's top scorer with 14 goals (from just 19 appearances) was encouraging but also deceptive. Half of his goals were from penalties, and eight of them came in the final few games of the season when he at last began to look something like his normal self.

It was curious that Ronaldo should come alive at a time when Inter were onto their fourth coach of the season. Inter president Massimo Moratti was drowned in ridicule when he announced that the out-of-work Roy Hodgson was being brought back as caretaker for the closing games of the season. The Englishman had been preceded in the hot seat by two other stop-gap temps, Mircea Lucescu and Luciano Castellini, as Inter waited for Lippi. They would probably have done better to stick with Luigi Simoni, who was brutally shown the door in early December - just two hours after being officially voted Italy's Coach of the Year.

The other big casualties of the season were Sampdoria, who ended 17 largely glorious years in the top flight by dropping down into Serie B. They were also afflicted by the star-striker injury hoodoo, with Vincenzo Montella sitting out most of the first half of the campaign. His late burst of goals were not enough to save a team that had gone 13 games without a win in mid-season - a period in which Samp president Enrico Mantovani had engendered disbelief and anger by appointing the unqualified (and inexperienced) Englishman David Platt as the club's new coach. Platt lasted just six games before Luciano Spalletti, the man he had replaced, was asked to return.

Samp were accompanied down into Serie B by Empoli, Vicenza and, on the final day, Salernitana, whose misery was compounded by the death of four fans in a fire on the train bringing them back from the relegation-decider in Piacenza. Three familar names - Verona, Torino and Lecce - returned to Serie A, and they were joined by Reggina, who had never previously made it to the top division in their 85-year history.

Exciting times also appeared to lie ahead for the Italian national team, who had a productive first season under new coach Dino Zoff. The former World Cup-winning goalkeeper got off to the perfect start when Italy won their opening Euro 2000 qualifier against Wales in a fixture scheduled a week before the start of the new Serie A season. From that moment on the *Azzurri* were in complete control of their group and over the next nine months Zoff managed not only to keep an unbeaten record but to take the Italians to the brink of the European finals with four wins and two draws in their six qualifying matches.

Only in the return match against Wales did the Italians really cut loose, but Zoff's decision to revert to a 4-4-2 model from the stifling 3-5-2 system deployed by Cesare Maldini at the World Cup allowed the likes of Vieri, Albertini, Fuser and Inzaghi to express themselves more readily, bringing a broader and more appealing dimension to the team's style.

The national team has also, it would seem, been caught up in those winds of change that are refreshing the face of Italian football.

INTERNATIONAL HONOURS

World Cup Finals appearances: 1934 (Winners), 1938 (Winners), 1950, 1954, 1962, 1966, 1970 (Runners-up), 1974, 1978 (4th), 1982 (Winners), 1986 (2nd round), 1990 (3rd), 1994 (Runners-up), 1998 (qtr-finals)

European Championship appearances: 1968 (Winners),1972, 1980 (4th),1988 (semi-finals),1996

European Club Competitions

Champions' Cup	Milan (1963, 1969, 1989, 1990, 1994)
	Internazionale (1964, 1965)
	Juventus (1985, 1996)
Cup-winners' Cup	Fiorentina (1961)
	Milan (1968, 1973)
	Juventus (1984)
	Sampdoria (1990)
	Parma (1993)
	Lazio (1999)
Fairs' Cup	Roma (1961)
UEFA Cup	Juventus (1977, 1990, 1993)
	Napoli (1989)
	Internazionale (1991, 1994, 1998)
	Parma (1995, 1999)
Super Cup	Juventus (1985)
	Milan (1989, 1990, 1995)
	Parma (1994)
World Club Cup	Internazionale (1964, 1965)
	Milan (1969, 1989, 1990)
	Juventus (1985)

BARI

CLUB DIRECTORY

Associazione Sportiva Bari
Strada Torrebella
70124 Bari
tel - (080) 5055099
fax - (080) 5055164
Year of Formation - 1908
President - Vincenzo Matarrese
General Manager - Carlo Regalia
Secretary - Pietro Doronzo
Coach - Eugenio Fascetti
Stadium - San Nicola (58,270)

APPEARANCES 98/99

	P	Ap	(s)	Gls
Daniel ANDERSSON (SWE)	M	33		3
Mauro BRESSAN	M	29	(1)	
Grégory CAMPI (FRA)	M		(1)	
Diego DE ASCENTIS	M	28	(2)	2
Gaetano DE ROSA	D	29	(1)	1
Luigi GARZYA	D	32	(1)	
Rodolfo GIORGETTI	M		(10)	1
Attilio GREGORI	G	2		
Miguel GUERRERO (COL)	A	3	(8)	1
Giovanni INDIVERI	G	4		
Duccio INNOCENTI	D	21	(11)	3
Peter KNUDSEN (DEN)	M	10	(9)	3
Michael MADSEN (DEN)	D	12	(11)	
Francesco MANCINI	G	28		
Michele MARCOLINI	M	22	(4)	1
Phil MASINGA (SAF)	A	27		11
Rachid NEQROUZ (MAR)	D	27		1
Davide OLIVARES	M	5	(16)	1
Yksel OSMANOVSKI (SWE)	A	26	(5)	6
Rocco Roberto PARIS	D		(2)	
Hany SAID (SAU)	D		(1)	
Gionatha SPINESI	A	4	(8)	1
Michele TARALLO	A		(1)	
Gianluca ZAMBROTTA	M	32		4

LEAGUE RESULTS 1998/99

13/09/98	Venezia	H	1-0	Zambrotta
20/09/98	Lazio	A	0-0	
26/09/98	Bologna	H	0-0	
04/10/98	Vicenza	A	0-1	
18/10/98	Udinese	H	1-1	Spinesi
25/10/98	Cagliari	A	3-3	Andersson (p), Masinga, Zambrotta
01/11/98	Inter	A	3-2	Zambrotta, Masinga 2
08/11/98	Parma	H	1-1	Masinga
15/11/98	Milan	H	0-0	
21/11/98	Roma	A	1-1	Masinga
29/11/98	Fiorentina	H	0-0	
06/12/98	Salernitana	A	2-2	Osmanovski, Knudsen
13/12/98	Empoli	H	2-1	Innocenti, Zambrotta
20/12/98	Piacenza	A	2-3	Masinga, Innocenti
06/01/99	Perugia	H	2-1	Neqrouz, Innocenti
10/01/99	Juventus	A	1-1	Andersson (p)
17/01/99	Sampdoria	H	3-1	Masinga, De Rosa, Olivares
24/01/99	Venezia	A	1-2	De Ascentis
31/01/99	Lazio	H	1-3	Knudsen
07/02/99	Bologna	A	1-3	Knudsen
14/02/99	Vicenza	H	0-0	
21/02/99	Udinese	A	0-4	
28/02/99	Cagliari	H	1 1	Andersson (p)
07/03/99	Inter	H	1-0	Osmanovski
13/03/99	Parma	A	1-2	Masinga
21/03/99	Milan	A	2-2	Osmanovski 2
03/04/99	Roma	H	1-4	Masinga
11/04/99	Fiorentina	A	2-2	Osmanovski, Guerrero
18/04/99	Salernitana	H	0-0	
25/04/99	Empoli	A	2-0	Masinga, Marcolini
02/05/99	Piacenza	H	3-1	De Ascentis, Masinga, Giorgetti (p)
09/05/99	Perugia	A	1-0	Osmanovski
16/05/99	Juventus	H	0-1	
23/05/99	Sampdoria	A	0-1	

BOLOGNA

Bologna 1909 Football Club
Via Casteldebole 10
40132 Bologna
tel - (051) 6130420
fax - (051) 591442
Year of Formation - 1909
President - Giuseppe Gazzoni Frascara
General Manager - Gabriele Oriali
Secretary - Stefano Pedrelli
Coach - Carlo Mazzone (99/00 - Sergio Buso)
Stadium - Renato Dall'Ara (38,375)

MAJOR HONOURS
League Championship - (7)
1925, 1929, 1936, 1937, 1939, 1941, 1964.
Domestic Cup - (2) 1970, 1974.

APPEARANCES 98/99

	P	Ap	(s)	Gls
Kennet ANDERSSON (SWE)	A	25		6
Francesco ANTONIOLI	G	32		
Stefano BETTARINI	D	13	(1)	1
Giovanni BIA	D	19	(1)	
Jonatan BINOTTO	M	22	(7)	3
Nicola BOSELLI	D	6	(4)	
Alex BRUNNER	G	2	(1)	
Massimiliano CAPPIOLI	M	10	(12)	1
ERIBERTO da Silva (BRA)	M	6	(13)	1
Davide FONTOLAN	M	18	(6)	2
Klas INGESSON (SWE)	M	28	(2)	3
Igor KOLYVANOV (RUS)	A	10	(10)	6
Teddy LUCIC (SWE)	D	6	(2)	
Oscar MAGONI	M		(2)	
Giampiero MAINI	M	13	(6)	
Amedeo MANGONE	D	28		
Giancarlo MAROCCHI	M	24	(5)	
Carlo NERVO	M	13	(2)	2
Massimo PAGANIN	D	15	(2)	
Michele PARAMATTI	D	16		1
Alessandro RINALDI	D	18	(4)	
Christophe SANCHEZ (FRA)	A		(3)	
Giuseppe SIGNORI	A	27	(1)	15
Igor SIMUTENKOV (RUS)	A	3	(11)	3
Massimo TARANTINO	M	20		

12/09/98	Milan	A	0-3	
20/09/98	Udinese	H	1-3	Kolyvanov (p)
26/09/98	Bari	A	0-0	
04/10/98	Parma	H	0-0	
07/10/98	Empoli	A	0-0	
25/10/98	Piacenza	H	3-1	Nervo, Andersson 2
31/10/98	Venezia	A	2-0	Binotto, Eriberto
08/11/98	Roma	H	1-1	Signori
15/11/98	Vicenza	A	4-0	Signori 3 (1p), Kolyvanov
21/11/98	Perugia	H	1-1	Binotto
29/11/98	Juventus	H	3-0	Paramatti, Signori, Fontolan
05/12/98	Fiorentina	A	0-1	
13/12/98	Salernitana	H	1-1	Signori
20/12/98	Cagliari	A	1-0	Signori
06/01/99	Lazio	H	0-1	
10/01/99	Sampdoria	A	1-1	Signori
17/01/99	Inter	H	2-0	Signori (p), Fontolan
24/01/99	Milan	H	2-3	Signori 2
31/01/99	Udinese	A	0-2	
07/02/99	Bari	H	3-1	Signori, Andersson, Kolyvanov
14/02/99	Parma	A	1-1	Kolyvanov
21/02/99	Empoli	H	2-0	Binotto, Signori
27/02/99	Piacenza	A	0-5	
07/03/99	Venezia	H	2-1	Andersson, Signori
13/03/99	Roma	A	1-3	Andersson
21/03/99	Vicenza	H	4-2	Nervo, Simutenkov, Andersson, Ingesson (p)
03/04/99	Perugia	A	0-0	
11/04/99	Juventus	A	2-2	Kolyvanov, Cappioli
17/04/99	Fiorentina	H	3-0	Simutenkov, Bettarini, Kolyvanov
25/04/99	Salernitana	A	0-4	
02/05/99	Cagliari	H	1-3	Signori
09/05/99	Lazio	A	0-2	
16/05/99	Sampdoria	H	2-2	Ingesson 2 (1p)
23/05/99	Inter	A	1-3	Simutenkov

CAGLIARI

CLUB DIRECTORY

Cagliari Calcio
Via G. Battista Tuveri 128
09129 Cagliari
tel - (070) 454072
fax - (070) 454082
Year of Formation - 1920
President - Massimo Cellino
Secretary - Sergio Loviselli
Coach - Giampiero Ventura
(99/00 - Oscar Washington Tabarez)
Stadium - Sant'Elia (40,125)

MAJOR HONOURS
League Championship - (1) 1970.

APPEARANCES 98/99

	P	Ap	(s)	Gls
Nélson ABEIJON (URU)	M	2	(5)	
Daniele BERRETTA	M	31	(1)	6
Eupremio CARRUEZZO	A	1	(3)	
Gianni CAVEZZI	M	14	(13)	
Matteo CENTURIONI	D	3	(6)	
Tiziano DE PATRE	M	23	(3)	5
Vincenco ESPOSITO	D		(3)	
Maurizio FRANZONE	G	2		
Gianluca GRASSADONIA	D	29		
Mohamed KALLON (SRL)	A	15	(11)	6
Diego LOPEZ (URU)	D		(1)	
Fabio MACELLARI	D	30		2
Vincenzo MAZZEO	D	2	(14)	
Patrick MBOMA (CMR)	A	8	(5)	7
Roberto MUZZI	A	30	(2)	16
David NYATHI (SAF)	D	5	(1)	
Fabian O'NEILL (URU)	M	30	(1)	5
Andrea PISANU	A		(2)	
Alessio SCARPI	G	32		
Gaetano VASARI	A	32	(1)	1
Matteo VILLA	D	24		
Cristiano ZANETTI	M	15	(3)	
Francesco ZANONCELLI	D	29		
Jonathan ZEBINA (FRA)	D	17	(5)	

LEAGUE RESULTS 1998/99

13/09/98	Inter	H	2-2	Kallon, Muzzi
20/09/98	Juventus	A	0-1	
27/09/98	Sampdoria	H	5-0	Kallon 2, Muzzi, Vasari, Berretta
04/10/98	Lazio	A	0-2	
18/10/98	Milan	H	1-0	De Patre
25/10/98	Bari	H	3-3	Muzzi 2, De Patre
01/11/98	Vicenza	A	1-2	Berretta
08/11/98	Piacenza	H	3-2	Muzzi 2, Kallon
15/11/98	Empoli	A	1-2	Muzzi
21/11/98	Parma	H	1-0	Kallon
29/11/98	Udinese	A	1-2	De Patre
06/12/98	Venezia	H	0-1	
13/12/98	Perugia	A	1-2	Berretta
20/12/98	Bologna	H	0-1	
06/01/99	Salernitana	A	3-1	Macellari, Muzzi 2
10/01/99	Roma	H	4-3	Muzzi 2, O'Neill 2
17/01/99	Fiorentina	A	2-4	O'Neill, De Patre
24/01/99	Inter	A	1-5	Muzzi
31/01/99	Juventus	H	1-0	Berretta
07/02/99	Sampdoria	A	0-0	
14/02/99	Lazio	H	0-0	
21/02/99	Milan	A	0-1	
28/02/99	Bari	A	1-1	og (Neqrouz)
07/03/99	Vicenza	II	1-0	De Patre
14/03/99	Piacenza	A	0-2	
21/03/99	Empoli	H	5-1	Mboma 3, Muzzi 2 (1p)
03/04/99	Parma	A	1-1	Muzzi (p)
11/04/99	Udinese	H	1-2	Kallon
18/04/99	Venezia	A	0-1	
25/04/99	Perugia	H	2-2	Mboma, O'Neill
02/05/99	Bologna	A	3-1	O'Neill, Macellari, Mboma
09/05/99	Salernitana	H	3-1	Mboma, Berretta 2
16/05/99	Roma	A	1-3	Mboma
23/05/99	Fiorentina	H	1-1	Muzzi

EMPOLI

Empoli Football Club
Piazza Matteotti 29
50053 Empoli
tel - (0571) 72212
fax - (0571) 79606
Year of Formation - 1921
President - Fabrizio Corsi
General Manager - Fabrizio Lucchesi
Secretary - Nadia Corbinelli
Coach - Mauro Sandreani; Corrado Orrico
(99/00 - Elio Gustinetti)
Stadium - Carlo Castellani (19,800)

APPEARANCES 98/99

	P	Ap	(s)	Gls
Fabio ARTICO	A	1		
Daniele BALDINI	D	22		
Stefano BIANCONI	D	33		1
Pier Paolo BISOLI	M	18	(7)	
Claudio BONOMI	M	18	(12)	1
Zoumana CAMARA (FRA)	D	10	(2)	
Massimiliano CAPPELLINI	A	5	(3)	
Marco CARPARELLI	A	17	(5)	5
Raffaele CERBONE	A	4	(9)	2
Roberto CHIAPPARA	A	3	(10)	
Fábio Eduardo CRIBARI BINHO (BRA)	D	15	(8)	
Andrea CUPI	D	5	(3)	
David D'ANTONI	M		(1)	
Tomasso DEI	D		(1)	
Simone DEL NERI	A		(1)	
Arturo DI NAPOLI	A	18	(7)	11
Pietro FUSCO	D	30		1
Vincenzo GRELLA (AUS)	M	2	(3)	
Giorgio LUCENTI	D	23	(4)	1
Marco MARCHIONNI	A		(1)	
Giovanni MARTUSCIELLO	M	20	(7)	
Giacomo MAZZI	G	4		
Stefano MORRONE	M	24		
Vincenzo PALUMBO	A	1	(1)	
Alessandro PANE	M	29	(1)	1
Davide QUIRONI	G		(1)	
Ibrahiman SCANDROGLIO	D	1		
Matteo SERENI	G	30		
Max TONETTO	M	31		1
Marcelo ZALAYETA (URU)	A	10	(7)	2

LEAGUE RESULTS 1998/99

12/09/98	Fiorentina	A	0-2	
20/09/98	Roma	H	0-0	
27/09/98	Inter	H	1-2	Carparelli
04/10/98	Salernitana	A	1-1	Lucenti
17/10/98	Bologna	H	0-0	
25/10/98	Sampdoria	A	0-3	
01/11/98	Perugia	H	2-0	Di Napoli 2 (1p)
08/11/98	Lazio	A	1-4	Carparelli
15/11/98	Cagliari	H	2-1	Di Napoli 2 (1p)
22/11/98	Juventus	A	0-0	
29/11/98	Vicenza	H	1-0	Carparelli
06/12/98	Piacenza	A	0-0	
13/12/98	Bari	A	1-2	Carparelli
20/12/98	Parma	H	3-5	Pane, Di Napoli 2
10/01/99	Milan	H	1-1	Di Napoli
17/01/99	Udinese	A	0-0	
20/01/99	Venezia	A	2-3	Di Napoli 2 (1p)
24/01/99	Fiorentina	H	0-3	
31/01/99	Roma	A	1-1	Carbone
07/02/99	Inter	A	1-5	Carparelli
14/02/99	Salernitana	H	2-3	Carbone, Bonomi (p)
21/02/99	Bologna	A	0-2	
28/02/99	Sampdoria	H	0-1	
07/03/99	Perugia	A	1-3	Zalayeta
14/03/99	Lazio	H	0-0	
21/03/99	Cagliari	A	1-5	Di Napoli
03/04/99	Juventus	H	1-0	Bianconi
11/04/99	Vicenza	A	0-2	
18/04/99	Piacenza	H	1-2	Fusco
25/04/99	Bari	H	0-2	
02/05/99	Parma	A	0-1	
09/05/99	Venezia	H	2-2	Zalayeta, Tonetto
15/05/99	Milan	A	0-4	
23/05/99	Udinese	H	1-3	Di Napoli

FIORENTINA

CLUB DIRECTORY

Associazione Calcio Fiorentina
Piazza Girolamo Savonarola 6
50132 Firenze
tel - (055) 572625
fax - (055) 579556
Year of Formation - 1925
President - Vittorio Cecchi Gori
General Manager - Giancarlo Antognoni
Secretary - Raffaele Righetti
Coach - Giovanni Trapattoni
Stadium - Artemio Franchi (47,282)

MAJOR HONOURS
League Championship - (2) 1956, 1969.
Domestic Cup - (5) 1940,
1961, 1966, 1975, 1996.
European Cup-winners' Cup - (1) 1961.

APPEARANCES 98/99

	P	Ap	(s)	Gls
Guillermo AMOR (ESP)	M	3	(13)	
Christian AMOROSO	M	28		
Gabriel BATISTUTA (ARG)	A	28		21
Stefano BETTARINI	D		(2)	
Emiliano BIGICA	M	1	(6)	
Sandro COIS	M	22	(1)	
EDMUNDO Alves da Silva (BRA)	A	28		8
Carmine ESPOSITO	A	4	(11)	2
Giulio FALCONE	D	21	(5)	1
Fabrizio FICINI	M	5	(8)	
Aldo FIRICANO	D	8	(3)	
Jörg HEINRICH (GER)	D	33		3
Gian Matteo MAREGGINI	G	1		
Roberto MIRRI	D		(1)	
Domenico MORFEO	A		(2)	
Luís OLIVEIRA (BEL)	A	27	(3)	2
Pasquale PADALINO	D	28		3
Tomas REPKA (CZE)	D	31		
Anselmo ROBBIATI	A	3	(19)	1
RUI COSTA (POR)	M	31		10
Andrea TAROZZI	D	8	(7)	
Francesco TOLDO	G	33		
Moreno TORRICELLI	D	31		2

LEAGUE RESULTS 1998/99

12/09/98	Empoli	H	2-0	Rui Costa, Batistuta
20/09/98	Vicenza	A	2-1	Batistuta, Oliveira
26/09/98	Milan	A	3-1	Batistuta 3
04/10/98	Udinese	H	1-0	Edmundo
17/10/98	Roma	A	1-2	Batistuta
25/10/98	Salernitana	H	4-0	Edmundo 2, Batistuta 2
31/10/98	Parma	A	0-2	
08/11/98	Venezia	H	4-1	Padalino, Batistuta 2, Rui Costa (p)
15/11/98	Piacenza	A	2-4	Rui Costa (p), Edmundo (p)
22/11/98	Inter	H	3-1	Padalino, Batistuta, Heinrich
29/11/98	Bari	A	0-0	
05/12/98	Bologna	H	1-0	Batistuta
13/12/98	Juventus	H	1-0	Batistuta
20/12/98	Perugia	A	2-2	Robbiati, Batistuta
06/01/99	Sampdoria	H	1-0	Rui Costa
10/01/99	Lazio	A	0-2	
17/01/99	Cagliari	H	4-2	Batistuta 3, Edmundo
24/01/99	Empoli	A	3-0	Heinrich, Rui Costa, Edmundo
31/01/99	Vicenza	H	3-0	Falcone, Torricelli, Batistuta
07/02/99	Milan	H	0-0	
14/02/99	Udinese	A	0-1	
21/02/99	Roma	H	0-0	
28/02/99	Salernitana	A	1-1	Torricelli
07/03/99	Parma	H	2-1	Oliveira, Rui Costa (p)
14/03/99	Venezia	A	1-4	Esposito (p)
21/03/99	Piacenza	H	2-1	Batistuta, Esposito
03/04/99	Inter	A	0-2	
11/04/99	Bari	H	2-2	Rui Costa, Padalino
17/04/99	Bologna	A	0-3	
25/04/99	Juventus	A	1-2	og (Tacchinardi)
02/05/99	Perugia	H	5-1	Batistuta, Rui Costa 2, Edmundo 2 (1p)
09/05/99	Sampdoria	A	2-3	Rui Costa (p), Heinrich
15/05/99	Lazio	H	1-1	Batistuta
23/05/99	Cagliari	A	1-1	og (Zebina)

INTER

Internazionale Milano Football Club
Via Durini 24, 20122 Milano
tel - (02) 77151
fax - (02) 781514
Year of Formation - 1908
President - Massimo Moratti
General Manager - Luigi Predeval
Coach - Luigi Simoni; Mircea Lucescu; Luciano
Castellini; Roy Hodgson (99/00 - Marcello Lippi)
Stadium - Giuseppe Meazza (85,443)

MAJOR HONOURS
League Championship - (13)
1910, 1920, 1930, 1938, 1940, 1953, 1954,
1963, 1965, 1966, 1971, 1980, 1989.
Domestic Cup - (3) 1939, 1978, 1982.
European Champions' Cup - (2) 1964, 1965.
UEFA Cup - (3) 1991, 1994, 1998.
World Club Cup - (2) 1964, 1965.

APPEARANCES 98/99

		P	Ap	(s)	Gls
Roberto BAGGIO	A	17	(6)	5
Giuseppe BERGOMI	D	23		1
Benoît CAUET (FRA)	M	20	(8)	1
Francesco COLONNESE	D	28		1
Ousmane DABO (FRA)	M	4	(1)	
Youri DJORKAEFF (FRA)	M	17	(8)	8
Salvatore FRESI	D	1		
Sébastien FREY (FRA)	G	5	(2)	
Fabio GALANTE	D	16	(1)	
GILBERTO Mello da Silva (BRA)	D	2		
Nwankwo KANU (NIG)	A	1		
Mauro MILANESE	D	6	(1)	
Francesco MORIERO	M	6	(5)	1
Raffaele NUZZO	G		(1)	
Gianluca PAGLIUCA	G	29		
PAULO SOUSA (POR)	M	8	(2)	
Andrea PIRLO	M	4	(14)	
Alvaro RECOBA (URU)	A		(1)	
RONALDO Luiz Nazário (BRA)	A	17	(2)	14
Michaël SILVESTRE (FRA)	D	15	(3)	1
Diego SIMEONE (ARG)	M	27		5
Dario SIMIC (CRO)	D	16	(1)	2
Davide SINIGAGLIA	A		(1)	
Nicola VENTOLA	A	12	(9)	6
Taribo WEST (NIG)	D	18	(3)	
Aron WINTER (HOL)	M	24	(4)	1
Iván ZAMORANO (CHL)	A	21	(4)	9
Javier ZANETTI (ARG)	M	32	(2)	3
José Moedin ZÉ ELIAS (BRA)	M	5	(8)	

LEAGUE RESULTS 1998/99

13/09/98	Cagliari	A	2-2	Ventola 2
20/09/98	Piacenza	H	1-0	Ronaldo (p)
27/09/98	Empoli	A	2-1	Bergomi, Ventola
04/10/98	Perugia	H	2-0	Zamorano, Djorkaeff
18/10/98	Lazio	H	3-5	Winter, Ventola 2
25/10/98	Juventus	A	0-1	
31/10/98	Bari	H	2-3	Ronaldo (p), Colonnese
08/11/98	Milan	A	2-2	Ronaldo, Moriero
15/11/98	Sampdoria	H	3-0	Djorkaeff 2 (2p), Zamorano
22/11/98	Fiorentina	A	1-3	Djorkaeff (p)
29/11/98	Salernitana	H	2-1	Simeone, Zanetti
06/12/98	Vicenza	A	1-1	Silvestre
13/12/98	Udinese	A	1-0	Ronaldo
20/12/98	Roma	H	4-1	Cauet, Zamorano, Baggio, Zanetti
06/01/99	Parma	A	0-1	
10/01/99	Venezia	H	6-2	Ronaldo 2 (1p), Baggio, Zamorano 3
17/01/99	Bologna	A	0-2	
24/01/99	Cagliari	H	5-1	Baggio 2, Simic, Simeone 2
31/01/99	Piacenza	A	0-0	
07/02/99	Empoli	H	5-1	Baggio, Simeone, Djorkaeff 3 (1p)
14/02/99	Perugia	A	1-2	Djorkaeff (p)
21/02/99	Lazio	A	0-1	
27/02/99	Juventus	H	0-0	
07/03/99	Bari	A	0-1	
13/03/99	Milan	H	2-2	og (Ngotty), Zanetti
21/03/99	Sampdoria	A	0-4	
03/04/99	Fiorentina	H	2-0	Ronaldo 2 (2p)
11/04/99	Salernitana	A	0-2	
18/04/99	Vicenza	H	1-1	Ronaldo (p)
25/04/99	Udinese	H	1-3	Zamorano
03/05/99	Roma	A	5-4	Ronaldo 2, Zamorano 2, Simeone
08/05/99	Parma	H	1-3	Ronaldo
16/05/99	Venezia	A	1-3	Ronaldo (p)
23/05/99	Bologna	H	3-1	Ronaldo, Simic, Ventola

JUVENTUS

Juventus Football Club
Piazza Crimea 7, 10131 Torino
tel - (011) 65631 / fax - (011) 689657
Year of Formation - 1897
President - Vittorio Chiusano
General Manager - Luciano Moggi
Coach - Marcello Lippi; Carlo Ancelotti
Stadium - Delle Alpi (69,041)

MAJOR HONOURS
League Championship - (25)
1905, 1926, 1931, 1932, 1933, 1934, 1935,
1950, 1952, 1958, 1960, 1961, 1967, 1972,
1973, 1975, 1977, 1978, 1981, 1982, 1984,
1986, 1995, 1997, 1998.
Domestic Cup - (9) 1938, 1942, 1959, 1960,
1965, 1979, 1983, 1990, 1995.
European Champions' Cup - (2) 1985, 1996.
European Cup-winners' Cup - (1) 1984.
UEFA Cup - (3) 1977, 1990, 1993.
European Super Cup - (2) 1984, 1997.
World Club Cup - (2) 1985, 1996.

	P	Ap	(s)	Gls
Nicola AMORUSO	A	12	(8)	3
Alessandro BIRINDELLI	D	17	(7)	1
Jocelyn BLANCHARD (FRA)	M	2	(10)	
Antonio CONTE	M	23	(6)	4
Edgar DAVIDS (HOL)	M	27		2
Alessandro DEL PIERO	A	8		2
Morgan DE SANCTIS	G	2	(1)	
Didier DESCHAMPS (FRA)	M	26	(3)	
Angelo DI LIVIO	M	28	(5)	1
DIMAS Marques Teixeira (POR)	D		(1)	
Juan Eduardo ESNAIDER (ARG)	A	7	(3)	
Ciro FERRARA	D	17	(1)	
Daniel FONSECA (URU)	A	8	(17)	6
Thierry HENRY (FRA)	A	12	(4)	3
Filippo INZAGHI	A	25	(3)	13
Mark IULIANO	D	18	(2)	1
Zoran MIRKOVIC (YUG)	D	13	(6)	1
Paolo MONTERO (URU)	D	22		
Simone PERROTTA	M	1	(4)	
Angelo PERUZZI	G	25		
Gianluca PESSOTTO	D	15	(4)	1
Michelangelo RAMPULLA	G	7		
Marco RIGONI	M		(1)	
Alessio TACCHINARDI	M	17	(6)	1
Igor TUDOR (CRO)	D	18	(5)	1
Marcelo ZALAYETA (URU)	A		(1)	
Zinedine ZIDANE (FRA)	M	24	(1)	2

13/09/98	Perugia	A	4-3	Davids, Tudor, Pessotto, Fonseca
20/09/98	Cagliari	H	1-0	Inzaghi
26/09/98	Parma	A	0-1	
04/10/98	Piacenza	H	1-0	Inzaghi
18/10/98	Vicenza	A	1-1	Del Piero
25/10/98	Inter	H	1-0	Del Piero
01/11/98	Sampdoria	H	2-0	Inzaghi 2
08/11/98	Udinese	A	2-2	Zidane, Inzaghi
15/11/98	Roma	A	0-2	
22/11/98	Empoli	H	0-0	
29/11/98	Bologna	A	0-3	
06/12/98	Lazio	H	0-1	
13/12/98	Fiorentina	A	0-1	
20/12/98	Salernitana	H	3-0	Inzaghi 3
06/01/99	Milan	A	1-1	Fonseca
10/01/99	Bari	H	1-1	Davids
17/01/99	Venezia	A	1-1	Fonseca
24/01/99	Perugia	H	2-1	Fonseca, Zidane
31/01/99	Cagliari	A	0-1	
07/02/99	Parma	H	2-4	Tacchinardi, Fonseca
14/02/99	Piacenza	A	2-0	Mirkovic, Birindelli
21/02/99	Vicenza	H	2-0	Amoruso, Conte
27/02/99	Inter	A	0-0	
07/03/99	Sampdoria	A	2-1	Amoruso, Inzaghi
13/03/99	Udinese	H	2-1	Fonseca, Inzaghi
21/03/99	Roma	H	1-1	Iuliano
03/04/99	Empoli	A	0-1	
11/04/99	Bologna	H	2-2	Inzaghi, Di Livio
17/04/99	Lazio	A	3-1	Henry 2, Amoruso
25/04/99	Fiorentina	H	2-1	Inzaghi, Conte
02/05/99	Salernitana	A	0-1	
09/05/99	Milan	H	0-2	
16/05/99	Bari	A	1-0	Conte
23/05/99	Venezia	H	3-2	Conte, Inzaghi, Henry

LAZIO

CLUB DIRECTORY

Società Sportiva Lazio
Via di Santa Cornelia 14
00060 Formello (Roma)
tel - (06) 9040601
fax - (06) 90400022
Year of Formation - 1900
President - Sergio Cragnotti
General Manager - Nello Governato
Secretary - Gabriella Grassi
Coach - Sven Göran Eriksson
Stadium - Olimpico (83,000)

MAJOR HONOURS
League Championship - (1) 1974.
Domestic Cup - (2) 1958, 1998.
European Cup-winners' Cup - (1) 1999.

APPEARANCES 98/99

	P	Ap	(s)	Gls
Matias ALMEYDA (ARG)	M	25		1
Marco BALLOTTA	G		(3)	
Roberto BARONIO	M	2	(5)	
Alen BOKSIC (CRO)	A		(3)	
Iván DE LA PEÑA (ESP)	M	4	(11)	
Giuseppe FAVALLI	D	23	(2)	
FERNANDO COUTO (POR)	D	12	(10)	2
Guerino GOTTARDI (SUI)	M		(13)	
Alessandro IANNUZZI	A	1	(1)	
Stefano LOMBARDI	D	2	(2)	
Attilio LOMBARDO	M	7	(7)	1
Govanni LOPEZ	D	2	(2)	
Roberto MANCINI	A	30	(3)	10
Luca MARCHEGIANI	G	34		
Sinisa MIHAJLOVIC (YUG)	D	30		8
Pavel NEDVED (CZE)	M	18	(3)	1
Paolo NEGRO	D	20	(1)	3
Alessandro NESTA	D	20		1
Paul OKON (AUS)	M	3	(2)	
Giuseppe PANCARO	D	27	(3)	
Igor PROTTI	A		(2)	
Marcelo SALAS (CHL)	A	29	(1)	15
SÉRGIO CONCEIÇÃO (POR)	M	32	(1)	5
Dejan STANKOVIC (YUG)	M	22	(7)	4
Giorgio VENTURIN	M	10	(6)	
Christian VIERI	A	21	(1)	12

LEAGUE RESULTS 1998/99

13/09/98	Piacenza	A	1-1	Stankovic
20/09/98	Bari	H	0-0	
27/09/98	Perugia	A	2-2	Fernando Couto, Mihajlovic
04/10/98	Cagliari	H	2-0	Fernando Couto, Stankovic
18/10/98	Inter	A	5-3	Salas, Sérgio Conceição 2,
				Mancini, Nedved
25/10/98	Vicenza	H	1-1	Mancini
01/11/98	Salernitana	A	0-1	
08/11/98	Empoli	H	4-1	Negro 2, Salas, Mancini
15/11/98	Venezia	A	0-2	
22/11/98	Milan	A	0-1	
29/11/98	Roma	H	3-3	Mancini 2, Salas (p)
06/12/98	Juventus	A	1-0	Salas
13/12/98	Sampdoria	H	5-2	Mihajlovic 3, Stankovic, Salas
20/12/98	Udinese	H	3-1	Mancini, Salas 2
06/01/99	Bologna	A	1-0	Vieri
10/01/99	Fiorentina	H	2-0	Vieri, Mihajlovic
17/01/99	Parma	A	3-1	Salas (p), Mancini, Vieri
24/01/99	Piacenza	H	4-1	Mihajlovic, Salas, Stankovic,
				Mancini
31/01/99	Bari	A	3-1	Lombardo, Vieri 2
07/02/99	Perugia	H	3-0	Vieri, Salas 2
14/02/99	Cagliari	A	0-0	
21/02/99	Inter	H	1-0	Sérgio Conceição
28/02/99	Vicenza	A	2-1	Sérgio Conceição, og (Dicara)
07/03/99	Salernitana	H	6-1	Negro, Vieri, Salas 2, og (Fresi),
				Nesta
14/03/99	Empoli	A	0-0	
21/03/99	Venezia	H	2-0	Sérgio Conceição, Mihajlovic
03/04/99	Milan	H	0-0	
11/04/99	Roma	A	1-3	Vieri
17/04/99	Juventus	H	1-3	Mancini
25/04/99	Sampdoria	A	1-0	Vieri
02/05/99	Udinese	A	3-0	Mihajlovic (p), Vieri, Mancini
08/05/99	Bologna	H	2-0	Almeyda, Vieri
15/05/99	Fiorentina	A	1-1	Vieri
23/05/99	Parma	H	2-1	Salas 2

MILAN

CLUB DIRECTORY

Milan Associazione Calcio
Via Turati 3, 20121 Milano
tel - (02) 62281 / fax - (02) 6598876
Year of Formation - 1899
President - Silvio Berlusconi
General Manager - Adriano Galliani
Secretary - Rina Barbara Ercoli
Coach - Alberto Zaccheroni
Stadium - Giuseppe Meazza (85,443)

MAJOR HONOURS
League Championship - (16) 1901, 1906, 1907,
1951, 1955, 1957, 1959, 1962, 1968, 1979,
1988, 1992, 1993, 1994, 1996, 1999.
Domestic Cup - (4) 1967, 1972, 1973, 1977.
European Champions' Cup - (5)
1963, 1969, 1989, 1990, 1994.
European Cup-winners' Cup - (2) 1968, 1973.
European Super Cup - (3) 1989, 1990, 1995.
World Club Cup - (3) 1969, 1989, 1990.

APPEARANCES 98/99

	P	Ap	(s)	Gls
Christian ABBIATI	G	17	(1)	
Demetrio ALBERTINI	M	29		2
Mohammed ALIYU-DATI (NIG)	A		(1)	
Massimo AMBROSINI	M	23	(3)	1
Roberto AYALA (ARG)	D	6	(5)	
Ibrahim BA (FRA)	M	6	(9)	
Oliver BIERHOFF (GER)	A	34		20
Zvonimir BOBAN (CRO)	M	21	(6)	2
Francesco COCO	D		(6)	
Alessandro COSTACURTA	D	29		
André CRUZ (BRA)	D	1	(1)	
Roberto DONADONI	M		(9)	
Maurizio GANZ	A	11	(9)	4
Federico GIUNTI	M	2	(4)	
Andrés GUGLIELMINPIETRO (ARG)	M	20	(1)	4
Thomas HELVEG (DEN)	M	26	(1)	
Jens LEHMANN (GER)	G	5		
LEONARDO				
Nascimento de Araújo (BRA)	M	16	(11)	12
Giampiero MAINI	M		(1)	
Paolo MALDINI	D	31		1
Domenico MORFEO	A	6	(5)	
Bruno NGOTTY (FRA)	D	15	(10)	1
Sebastiano ROSSI	G	12	(1)	
Luigi SALA	D	24		
George WEAH (LIB)	A	26		8
Christian ZIEGE (GER)	M	14	(3)	2

LEAGUE RESULTS 1998/99

12/09/98	Bologna	H	3-0	Bierhoff 2 (1p), Leonardo
20/09/98	Salernitana	A	2-1	Bierhoff, Leonardo
26/09/98	Fiorentina	H	1-3	Bierhoff (p)
04/10/98	Venezia	A	2-0	Bierhoff, Leonardo
18/10/98	Cagliari	A	0-1	
25/10/98	Roma	H	3-2	Leonardo, Ziege, Weah
01/11/98	Piacenza	A	1-1	Ganz
08/11/98	Inter	H	2-2	Weah, Albertini (p)
15/11/198	Bari	A	0-0	
22/11/98	Lazio	H	1-0	Leonardo
29/11/98	Parma	A	0-4	
06/12/98	Udinese	H	3-0	Weah, Leonardo, Bierhoff
13/12/98	Vicenza	H	1-0	Weah
20/12/98	Sampdoria	A	2-2	Leonardo, Bierhoff
06/01/99	Juventus	H	1-1	Albertini (p)
10/01/99	Empoli	A	1-1	Ziege
17/01/99	Perugia	H	2-1	Guglielminpietro, Bierhoff
24/01/99	Bologna	A	3-2	Guglielminpietro, og (Magoni), Ngotty
31/01/99	Salernitana	H	3-2	Bierhoff 2, Weah
07/02/99	Fiorentina	A	0-0	
14/02/99	Venezia	H	2-1	Guglielminpietro, Ganz
21/02/99	Cagliari	H	1-0	Bierhoff
27/02/99	Roma	A	0-1	
07/03/99	Piacenza	H	1-0	Bierhoff
13/03/99	Inter	A	2-2	Leonardo 2
21/03/99	Bari	H	2-2	Bierhoff, Ganz (p)
03/04/99	Lazio	A	0-0	
11/04/99	Parma	H	2-1	Maldini, Ganz
18/04/99	Udinese	A	5-1	Boban 2 (1p), Bierhoff 2, Weah
25/04/99	Vicenza	A	2-0	Bierhoff, Leonardo
02/05/99	Sampdoria	H	3-2	Ambrosini, Leonardo, og (Castellini)
09/05/99	Juventus	A	2-0	Weah 2
15/05/99	Empoli	H	4-0	Bierhoff 3, Leonardo
23/05/99	Perugia	A	2-1	Guglielminpietro, Bierhoff

PARMA

CLUB DIRECTORY

Parma Associazione Calcio
Viale Partigiani 1
43100 Parma
tel - (0521) 505111
fax - (0521) 289924
Year of Formation - 1913
President - Stefano Tanzi
Secretary - Renzo Ongaro
Coach - Alberto Malesani
Stadium - Ennio Tardini (29,048)

MAJOR HONOURS
Domestic Cup - (2) 1992, 1999.
European Cup-winners' Cup - (1) 1993.
UEFA Cup - (2) 1995, 1999.
European Super Cup - (1) 1994.

APPEARANCES 98/99

	P	Ap	(s)	Gls
Luigi APOLLONI	D		(2)	
Faustino ASPRILLA (COL)	A	2	(6)	1
Dino BAGGIO	M	29		2
Abel BALBO (ARG)	A	10	(15)	4
Antonio BENARRIVO	D	25		
Alain BOGHOSSIAN (FRA)	M	23	(1)	3
Gianluigi BUFFON	G	34		
Fabio CANNAVARO	D	30		1
Enrico CHIESA	A	29	(1)	9
Hernán CRESPO (ARG)	A	29	(1)	16
Gianluca DE ANGELIS	A		(1)	
Stefano FIORE	M	16	(12)	1
Diego FUSER	M	31	(1)	7
Federico GIUNTI	M		(2)	
Saliou LASSISSI (FRA)	D		(1)	
Raffaele LONGO	M	1	(3)	
Roberto MUSSI	D	3	(14)	
Pierluigi ORLANDINI	M		(11)	
Luigi SARTOR	D	11	(2)	
Roberto Néstor SENSINI (ARG)	D	25	(1)	1
Mario STANIC (CRO)	M	7	(11)	7
Lilian THURAM (FRA)	D	34		
Paolo VANOLI	M	9	(5)	2
Juan Sebastián VERON (ARG)	M	26		1

LEAGUE RESULTS 1998/99

12/09/98	Vicenza	H	0-0	
20/09/98	Venezia	A	0-0	
26/09/98	Juventus	H	1-0	Baggio
04/10/98	Bologna	A	0-0	
17/10/98	Salernitana	H	2-0	Chiesa, Fuser
25/10/98	Perugia	A	1-2	Chiesa
31/10/98	Fiorentina	H	2-0	Crespo 2
08/11/98	Bari	A	1-1	Fuser
15/11/98	Udinese	H	4-1	Crespo 3 (1p), Stanic
21/11/98	Cagliari	A	0-1	
29/11/98	Milan	H	4-0	Chiesa, Crespo 2, Boghossian
05/12/98	Sampdoria	A	2-0	Chiesa 2
13/12/98	Roma	H	1-1	Crespo
20/12/98	Empoli	A	5-3	Crespo, Boghossian, Fuser 2, Fiore
06/01/99	Inter	H	1-0	Fuser
10/01/99	Piacenza	A	6-3	Boghossian, Balbo 3, Fuser, Crespo
17/01/99	Lazio	H	1-3	Crespo
24/01/99	Vicenza	A	0-0	
31/01/99	Venezia	H	2-2	Baggio, Chiesa
07/02/99	Juventus	A	4-2	Crespo 3, Chiesa
14/02/99	Bologna	H	1-1	Stanic
21/02/99	Salernitana	A	2-1	Cannavaro, Stanic
27/02/99	Perugia	H	3-1	Chiesa 2 (1p), Crespo
07/03/99	Fiorentina	A	1-2	Stanic
13/03/99	Bari	H	2-1	Verón, Crespo
21/03/99	Udinese	A	1-2	Vanoli
03/04/99	Cagliari	H	1-1	Stanic
11/04/99	Milan	A	1-2	Balbo
17/04/99	Sampdoria	H	1-1	Sensini
25/04/99	Roma	A	0-1	
02/05/99	Empoli	H	1-0	Stanic
08/05/99	Inter	A	3-1	Stanic, Asprilla, Fuser
16/05/99	Piacenza	H	0-1	
23/05/99	Lazio	A	1-2	Vanoli

PERUGIA

Perugia Calcio
Località Pian di Massiano
06125 Perugia
tel - (075) 5006641
fax - (075) 5051616
Year of Formation - 1905
President - Luciano Gaucci
Secretary - Ilvano Ercoli
Coach - Ilario Castagner; Vujadin Boskov
(99/00 - Carlo Mazzone)
Stadium - Renato Curi (27,900)

APPEARANCES 98/99

	P	Ap	(s)	Gls
Davide BAIOCCO	M		(1)	
Antonio BERNARDINI	M	1	(1)	1
Christian BUCCHI	A	12	(15)	5
Sergio CAMPOLO	M	10	(5)	
Gianluca COLONNELLO	D	27	(3)	
Juan Carlos DOCABO (ARG)	G	1		
EMERSON da Silva Pereira (BRA)	M	2		
Tomislav ERCEG (CRO)	A	2	(2)	
Gabriele GROSSI	D	1	(1)	
HILÁRIO Paulino Neves (POR)	D	10		
Jaime Juan KAVIEDES (ECU)	A	12	(2)	4
Mika LEHKOSUO (FIN)	M	4	(7)	
Antonio MANICONE	M	1		
Riccardo MASPERO	M	1	(9)	1
Salvatore MATRECANO	D	29		1
Andrea MAZZANTINI	G	17		
Alessandro MELLI	A	7	(6)	1
Luca MEZZANO	D	7	(1)	
Hidetoshi NAKATA (JPN)	M	33		10
Renato OLIVE	M	27		2
Angelo PAGOTTO	G	6		
Diego PELLEGRINI	D	3	(6)	
Gianluca PETRACHI	M	25	(3)	5
Milan RAPAIC (CRO)	A	34		9
Roberto RIPA	D	15	(6)	
Martin RIVAS (URU)	D	25	(1)	
Marco ROCCATI	G	10		
Pasquale ROCCO	M	1	(4)	
Sean SOGLIANO	D	15	(5)	
Pietro STRADA	M		(7)	
Andrea SUSSI	D	1		
Giovanni TEDESCO	M	21	(2)	4
Davide TENTONI	M	2	(7)	
Sandro TOVALIERI	A	1	(3)	
José Marcelo ZÉ MARIA (BRA)	D	11		

LEAGUE RESULTS 1998/99

13/09/98	Juventus	H	3-4	Nakata 2, Bernardini (p)
20/09/98	Sampdoria	A	1-1	Olive
27/09/98	Lazio	H	2-2	Bucchi, Nakata
04/10/98	Inter	A	0-2	
18/10/98	Venezia	H	1-0	Olive
25/10/98	Parma	H	2-1	Rapaic, Bucchi
01/11/98	Empoli	A	0-2	
08/11/98	Vicenza	H	3-1	Rapaic, Nakata (p), Melli
15/11/98	Salernitana	A	0-2	
21/11/98	Bologna	A	1-1	Rapaic
29/11/98	Piacenza	H	2-0	Nakata 2
06/12/98	Roma	A	1-5	Rapaic
13/12/98	Cagliari	H	2-1	Rapaic, Maspero
20/12/98	Fiorentina	H	2-2	Rapaic, Nakata (p)
06/01/99	Bari	A	1-2	Tedesco
10/01/99	Udinese	H	1-3	Nakata
17/01/99	Milan	A	1-2	Nakata (p)
24/01/99	Juventus	A	1-2	Kaviedes
31/01/99	Sampdoria	H	2-0	Kaviedes, Matrecano
07/02/99	Lazio	A	0-3	
14/02/99	Inter	H	2-1	Kaviedes, Rapaic
21/02/99	Venezia	A	1-2	Bucchi
27/02/99	Parma	A	1-3	Bucchi
07/03/99	Empoli	H	3-1	Tedesco, Petrachi, Bucchi
14/03/99	Vicenza	A	0-3	
21/03/99	Salernitana	H	1-0	Rapaic
03/04/99	Bologna	H	0-0	
11/04/99	Piacenza	A	0-2	
18/04/99	Roma	H	3-2	Tedesco, Petrachi, Rapaic
25/04/99	Cagliari	A	2-2	Tedesco, Petrachi
02/05/99	Fiorentina	A	1-5	Kaviedes
09/05/99	Bari	H	0-1	
16/05/99	Udinese	A	2-1	Petrachi 2
23/05/99	Milan	H	1-2	Nakata (p)

PIACENZA

CLUB DIRECTORY

Piacenza Football Club
Via Gorra 25
29100 Piacenza
tel - (0523) 757010
fax - (0523) 453405
Year of Formation - 1919
President - Stefano Garilli
General Manager - Gian Pietro Marchetti
Secretary - Paolo Armenia
Coach - Giuseppe Materazzi
(99/00 - Luigi Simoni)
Stadium - Leonardo Garilli (21,800)

APPEARANCES 98/99

	P	Ap	(s)	Gls
Renato BUSO	M	21	(8)	2
Giordano CAINI	D		(6)	
Paolo CRISTALLINI	M	21	(4)	3
Daniele DELLI CARRI	D	16	(4)	
Davide DIONIGI	A	5	(18)	5
Valerio FIORI	G	28		
Simone INZAGHI	A	28	(2)	15
Gianluca LAMACCHI	D	15	(9)	1
Alessandro LUCARELLI	D	15	(6)	
Giampaolo MANIGHETTI	D	32	(1)	1
Sergio MARCON	G	6	(2)	
Alessandro MAZZOLA	M	31		1
Giampiero PIOVANI	A	13	(14)	5
Cleto POLONIA	D	30		1
Massimo RASTELLI	A	29	(2)	5
Ruggiero RIZZITELLI	A	2	(10)	
Stefano SACCHETTI	D	18	(3)	
Adolfo SPERANZA	M		(2)	
Francesco STATUTO	M	11	(1)	1
Giovanni STROPPA	M	25	(5)	2
Pietro VIERCHOWOD	D	28		4

LEAGUE RESULTS 1998/99

13/09/98	Lazio	H	1-1	Inzaghi
20/09/98	Inter	A	0-1	
27/09/98	Vicenza	H	2-0	Polonia, Dionigi (p)
04/10/98	Juventus	A	0-1	
18/10/98	Sampdoria	H	4-1	Vierchowod, Inzaghi (p),
				Manighetti, Rastelli
25/10/98	Bologna	A	1-3	og (Mangone)
01/11/98	Milan	H	1-1	Inzaghi
08/11/98	Cagliari	A	2-3	Buso, Inzaghi
15/11/98	Fiorentina	H	4-2	Rastelli, Inzaghi (p), Cristallini,
				Piovani
22/11/98	Udinese	A	0-1	
29/11/98	Perugia	A	0-2	
06/12/98	Empoli	H	0-0	
13/12/98	Venezia	A	0-0	
20/12/98	Bari	H	3-2	Piovani, Stroppa, Rastelli
06/01/99	Roma	A	2-2	Stroppa, og (Dal Moro)
10/01/99	Parma	H	3-6	Inzaghi 2 (1p), Cristallini
17/01/99	Salernitana	A	1-1	Dionigi
24/01/99	Lazio	A	1-4	Buso
31/01/99	Inter	H	0-0	
07/02/99	Vicenza	A	0-1	
14/02/99	Juventus	H	0-2	
21/02/99	Sampdoria	A	2-3	Piovani, Dionigi (p)
27/02/99	Bologna	H	5-0	Inzaghi 3 (2p), Rastelli,
				Piovani (p)
07/03/99	Milan	A	0-1	
14/03/99	Cagliari	H	2-0	Inzaghi (p), Vierchowod
21/03/99	Fiorentina	A	1-2	Inzaghi (p)
03/04/99	Udinese	H	4-3	Piovani, Inzaghi (p), Vierchowod,
				Cristallini
11/04/99	Perugia	H	2-0	Lamacchi, Inzaghi
18/04/99	Empoli	A	2-1	Mazzola, Dionigi
25/04/99	Venezia	H	0-1	
02/05/99	Bari	A	1-3	Dionigi
09/05/99	Roma	H	2-0	Rastelli, Statuto
16/05/99	Parma	A	1-0	Inzaghi
23/05/99	Salernitana	H	1-1	Vierchowod

ROMA

Associazione Sportiva Roma
Via di Trigoria km. 3.600
00128 Roma
tel - (06) 5060200
fax - (06) 5061736
Year of Formation - 1927
President - Francesco Sensi
General Manager - Giorgio Perinetti
Coach - Zdenek Zeman (99/00 - Fabio Capello)
Stadium - Olimpico (83,000)

MAJOR HONOURS
League Championship - (2) 1942, 1983.
Domestic Cup - (7)
1964, 1969, 1980, 1981, 1984, 1986, 1991.
Fairs' Cup - (1) 1961.

	P	Ap	(s)	Gls
ALDAIR dos Santos (BRA)	D	27		
Dmitriy ALENICHEV (RUS)	M	11	(10)	1
Gustavo BARTELT (ARG)	A	1	(11)	
Marcos de Moraes CAFÚ (BRA)	D	20		1
Vincent CANDELA (FRA)	D	29	(1)	1
Antonio CHIMENTI	G	23	(1)	
Daniele CONTI	M	2	(2)	1
Filippo DAL MORO	D	5		
Marco DELVECCHIO	A	30	(1)	18
Daniele DE VEZZE	M		(1)	
Luigi DI BIAGIO	M	24	(3)	4
Eusebio DI FRANCESCO	M	32	(1)	8
FÁBIO JÚNIOR Pereira (BRA)	A	4	(3)	3
Luca FERRI	D		(2)	
Alessandro FRAU	A		(7)	
Carmine GAUTIERI	A	10	(14)	6
Michael KONSEL (AUT)	G	11		
Maurizio LANZARO	D	1		
PAULO SÉRGIO Silvestre (BRA)	A	27	(3)	12
Fabio PETRUZZI	D	13		
Marco QUADRONI	D	9	(3)	
Ivan TOMIC (YUG)	M	4	(5)	
Damiano TOMMASI	M	29	(4)	1
Francesco TOTTI	A	30	(1)	12
Pier Nlend WOME (CMR)	D	6	(2)	
António Carlos ZAGO (BRA)	D	26	(2)	

Date	Opponent	H/A	Score	Scorers
12/09/98	Salernitana	H	3-1	Paulo Sérgio 2, Totti
20/09/98	Empoli	A	0-0	
26/09/98	Venezia	H	2-0	Delvecchio 2
04/10/98	Sampdoria	A	1-2	Delvecchio
17/10/98	Fiorentina	H	2-1	Alenichev, Totti
25/10/98	Milan	A	2-3	Delvecchio 2
31/10/98	Udinese	H	4-0	Di Francesco, Totti 2, Paulo Sérgio
08/11/98	Bologna	A	1-1	Paulo Sérgio
15/11/98	Juventus	H	2-0	Paulo Sérgio, Candela
21/11/98	Bari	H	1-1	Totti (p)
29/11/98	Lazio	A	3-3	Delvecchio, Di Francesco, Totti
05/12/98	Perugia	H	5-1	Totti, Conti, Delvecchio 2, Gautieri
13/12/98	Parma	A	1-1	Gautieri
20/12/98	Inter	A	1-4	Paulo Sérgio
06/01/99	Piacenza	H	2-2	Di Francesco, Tommasi
10/01/99	Cagliari	A	3-4	Delvecchio 2, Gautieri
17/01/99	Vicenza	H	3-0	Di Francesco, Delvecchio, Gautieri
24/01/99	Salernitana	A	1-2	Di Biagio
31/01/99	Empoli	H	1-1	Paulo Sérgio
07/02/99	Venezia	A	1-3	Di Biagio
14/02/99	Sampdoria	H	3-1	Fábio Júnior, Paulo Sérgio 2
21/02/99	Fiorentina	A	0-0	
27/02/99	Milan	H	1-0	Paulo Sérgio
07/03/99	Udinese	A	1-2	Fábio Júnior
13/03/99	Bologna	H	3-1	Delvecchio 2, Gautieri
21/03/99	Juventus	A	1-1	Delvecchio
03/04/99	Bari	A	4-1	Di Biagio 2, Cafú, Di Francesco
11/04/99	Lazio	H	3-1	Delvecchio 2, Totti
18/04/99	Perugia	A	2-3	og (Matrecano), Di Francesco
25/04/99	Parma	H	1-0	Totti
03/05/99	Inter	H	4-5	Totti (p), Paulo Sérgio, Delvecchio, Di Francesco
09/05/99	Piacenza	A	0-2	
16/05/99	Cagliari	H	3-1	Totti 2, Di Francesco
23/05/99	Vicenza	A	4-1	Paulo Sérgio, Delvecchio, Gautieri, Fábio Júnior

SALERNITANA

CLUB DIRECTORY

Salernitana Sport
Lungomare Marconi 18
84127 Salerno
tel - (089) 750064
fax - (089) 750825
Year of Formation - 1919
President - Aniello Aliberti
Secretary - Diodato Abbagnara
Coach - Delio Rossi; Francesco Oddo
(99/00 - Adriano Cadregari)
Stadium - Arechi (37,894)

APPEARANCES 98/99

	P	Ap	(s)	Gls
Raffaele AMETRANO	M	2	(9)	
Daniele BALLI	G	31		
Emilio BELMONTE	A	9		1
Antonio BERNARDINI	M	18	(2)	1
Drazen BOLIC (YUG)	D	25	(6)	1
Roberto BREDA	M	25	(1)	2
Vincenzo CHIANESE	A	8	(10)	
Ciro DE CESARE	A	2		
Alessandro DEL GROSSO	D	31		1
David DI MICHELE	A	11	(15)	3
Marco DI VAIO	A	29	(2)	12
Ciro FERRARA	D	1	(1)	
Michele FINI	A		(1)	
Salvatore FRESI	D	25	(2)	3
Luca FUSCO	D	23	(1)	
Gennaro GATTUSO	M	24	(1)	
Federico GIAMPAOLO	A	17	(7)	3
Andrea IVAN	G	3	(1)	
Vaclav KOLOUSEK (CZE)	M	4	(4)	1
Aleksandar KRISTIC (YUG)	D		(2)	1
Salvatore MONACO	D	14	(4)	
Marco ROSSI	M	14	(4)	
Rigobert SONG (CMR)	D	4		1
Giacomo TEDESCO	M	12	(5)	1
Giovanni TEDESCO	M	5		
Vittorio TOSTO	D	19	(8)	
Ighli VANNUCCHI	M	18	(13)	3
Dragan VUKOJA (CRO)	A		(1)	

LEAGUE RESULTS 1998/99

12/09/98	Roma	A	1-3	Song
20/09/98	Milan	H	1-2	Breda
26/09/98	Udinese	A	0-2	
04/10/98	Empoli	H	1-1	Breda
17/10/98	Parma	A	0-2	
25/10/98	Fiorentina	A	0-4	
01/11/98	Lazio	H	1-0	Tedesco
08/11/98	Sampdoria	A	0-1	
15/11/98	Perugia	H	2-0	Di Vaio 2
22/11/98	Venezia	H	1-0	og (Bilica)
29/11/98	Inter	A	1-2	Di Michele
06/12/98	Bari	H	2-2	Vannucchi, Bolic
13/12/98	Bologna	A	1-1	og (Paramatti)
20/12/98	Juventus	A	0-3	
06/01/99	Cagliari	H	1-3	Belmonte
10/01/99	Vicenza	A	0-1	
17/01/99	Piacenza	H	1-1	Fresi
24/01/99	Roma	H	2-1	Bernardini (p), Giampaolo
31/01/99	Milan	A	2-3	Giampaolo, Del Grosso
07/02/99	Udinese	H	1-2	og (Pierini)
14/02/99	Empoli	A	3-2	Di Vaio 3
21/02/99	Parma	H	1-2	Di Vaio
28/02/99	Fiorentina	H	1-1	Di Vaio
07/03/99	Lazio	A	1-6	Vannucchi
14/03/99	Sampdoria	H	2-0	Kolousek, Fresi
21/03/99	Perugia	A	0-1	
03/04/99	Venezia	A	0-0	
11/04/99	Inter	H	2-0	Di Michele, Giampaolo
18/04/99	Bari	A	0-0	
25/04/99	Bologna	H	4-0	Di Vaio 3 (1p), Kristic
02/05/99	Juventus	H	1-0	Di Vaio
09/05/99	Cagliari	A	1-3	Di Vaio
16/05/99	Vicenza	H	2-1	Di Michele, Vannucchi
23/05/99	Piacenza	A	1-1	Fresi (p)

SAMPDORIA

Sampdoria Unione Calcio
Piazza Campetto 2
16123 Genova
tel - (010) 2549111
fax - (010) 2549160
Year of Formation - 1946
President - Enrico Mantovani
General Manager - Domenico Arnuzzo
Coach - Luciano Spalletti; David Platt;
Luciano Spalletti (99/00 - Gian Piero Ventura)
Stadium - Luigi Ferraris (40,117)

MAJOR HONOURS
League Championship - (1) 1991.
Domestic Cup - (4) 1985, 1988, 1989, 1994.
European Cup-winners' Cup - (1) 1990.

APPEARANCES 98/99

	P	Ap	(s)	Gls
Simone ALOE	A		(1)	
Marco AMBROSIO	G	3	(4)	
David BALLERI	D	29	(1)	
Marcello CASTELLINI	D	19	(8)	1
Marco António CATÉ (BRA)	A	1	(14)	1
Gaston CORDOBA (ARG)	M		(1)	
DORIVA Guidoni Júnior (BRA)	M	17		1
Fabrizio FERRON	G	31		
Fabrizio FICINI	M	6	(3)	
Marco FRANCESCHETTI	D	23		1
Alessandro GRANDONI	D	31		
HUGO Miguel Vieira (POR)	D	8	(7)	
Vincenzo IACOPINO	A	4	(13)	1
Pierre LAIGLE (FRA)	M	31		3
Saliou LASSISSI (FRA)	D	18	(1)	1
Moreno MANNINI	D	7	(3)	
Vincenzo MONTELLA	A	21	(1)	12
Stefano NAVA	D	6	(3)	
Ariel ORTEGA (ARG)	M	25	(2)	8
Francesco PALMIERI	A	33		8
Fabio PECCHIA	M	26		1
Giovanni PIREDDA	A		(1)	
Nenad SAKIC (YUG)	D	22	(3)	
Marco SGRÒ	M	4	(11)	
Lee SHARPE (ENG)	M	1	(2)	
Matteo SOLARI	M		(1)	
Simone VERGASSOLA	M	8	(11)	
Bratislav ZIVKOVIC (YUG)	M		(4)	

LEAGUE RESULTS 1998/99

12/09/98	Udinese	A	2-2	Castellini, Montella
20/09/98	Perugia	H	1-1	Laigle
27/09/98	Cagliari	A	0-5	
04/10/98	Roma	H	2-1	Palmieri, Iacopino
18/10/98	Piacenza	A	1-4	Ortega (p)
25/10/98	Empoli	H	3-0	Palmieri 2, Ortega
01/11/98	Juventus	A	0-2	
08/11/98	Salernitana	H	1-0	Ortega (p)
15/11/98	Inter	A	0-3	
22/11/98	Vicenza	H	0-0	
29/11/98	Venezia	A	0-0	
05/12/98	Parma	H	0-2	
13/12/98	Lazio	A	2-5	Palmieri 2 (2p)
20/12/98	Milan	H	2-2	Palmieri, Ortega
06/01/99	Fiorentina	A	0-1	
10/01/99	Bologna	H	1-1	Palmieri
17/01/99	Bari	A	1-3	Laigle
24/01/99	Udinese	H	1-1	Ortega
31/01/99	Perugia	A	0-2	
07/02/99	Cagliari	H	0-0	
14/02/99	Roma	A	1-3	Lassissi
21/02/99	Piacenza	H	3-2	Montella (p), Laigle, Ortega
28/02/99	Empoli	A	1-0	Pecchia
07/03/99	Juventus	H	1-2	Ortega
14/03/99	Salernitana	A	0-2	
21/03/99	Inter	H	4-0	Montella 3 (1p), Ortega
03/04/99	Vicenza	A	0-1	
11/04/99	Venezia	H	2-1	Montella (p), Caté
17/04/99	Parma	A	1-1	Montella (p)
25/04/99	Lazio	H	0-1	
02/05/99	Milan	A	2-3	Montella, Franceschetti
09/05/99	Fiorentina	H	3-2	Montella 2, Palmieri
16/05/99	Bologna	A	2-2	Montella 2
23/05/99	Bari	H	1-0	Doriva

UDINESE

CLUB DIRECTORY

Udinese Calcio
Via Candolini 2
33100 Udine
tel - (0432) 544911
fax - (0432) 482193
Year of Formation - 1896
President - Giovanni Caratozzolo
General Manager - Carlo Piazzolla
Secretary - Daniele Vidal
Coach - Francesco Guidolin
(99/00 - Luigi De Canio)
Stadium - Friuli (41,825)

APPEARANCES 98/99

	P	Ap	(s)	Gls
Márcio dos Santos AMOROSO (BRA)	A	31	(2)	22
Stephan APPIAH (GHA)	M	12	(9)	
Jonathan BACHINI	M	20	(6)	4
Valerio BERTOTTO	D	23	(4)	1
Morten BISGAARD (DEN)	M		(3)	
Alessandro CALORI	D	31		
Mohammed GARGO (GHA)	D	10	(1)	
Régis GENAUX (BEL)	D	16	(2)	
Giuliano GIANNICHEDDA	M	30		
Martin JØRGENSEN (DEN)	M	21	(5)	4
Tomas LOCATELLI	A	26	(4)	2
Mauro NAVAS (ARG)	D	10	(13)	
Alessandro PIERINI	D	32		3
Héctor Mauricio PINEDA (ARG)	D	5	(5)	
Paolo POGGI	A	16	(13)	2
Roberto Carlos SOSA (ARG)	A	19	(10)	11
Luigi TURCI	G	33		
Henry VAN DER VEGT (HOL)	M	2	(5)	
Johan WALEM (BEL)	M	27	(3)	3
Harold WAPENAAR (HOL)	G	1	(1)	
Marco ZANCHI	D	9	(3)	

LEAGUE RESULTS 1998/99

12/09/98	Sampdoria	H	2-2	Bachini, Amoroso
20/09/98	Bologna	A	3-1	Amoroso 2 (1p), Walem
26/09/98	Salernitana	H	2-0	Amoroso 2
04/10/98	Fiorentina	A	0-1	
18/10/98	Bari	A	1-1	Pierini
25/10/98	Venezia	H	1-1	Amoroso (p)
31/10/98	Roma	A	0-4	
08/11/98	Juventus	H	2-2	Bachini, Sosa
15/11/98	Parma	A	1-4	Amoroso
22/11/98	Piacenza	H	1-0	Poggi
29/11/98	Cagliari	H	2-1	Bachini, Amoroso
06/12/98	Milan	A	0-3	
13/12/98	Inter	H	0-1	
20/12/98	Lazio	A	1-3	Locatelli
06/01/99	Vicenza	H	2-1	Sosa, Amoroso
10/01/99	Perugia	A	3-1	Pierini, Amoroso, Sosa
17/01/99	Empoli	H	0-0	
24/01/99	Sampdoria	A	1-1	Sosa
31/01/99	Bologna	H	2-0	Sosa 2
07/02/99	Salernitana	A	2-1	Locatelli, Amoroso
14/02/99	Fiorentina	H	1-0	Sosa
21/02/99	Bari	H	4-0	Sosa 2, Amoroso, Bertotto
28/02/99	Venezia	A	0-1	
07/03/99	Roma	H	2-1	Jørgensen, Amoroso
13/03/99	Juventus	A	1-2	Sosa
21/03/99	Parma	H	2-1	Sosa, Amoroso
03/04/99	Piacenza	A	3-4	Jørgensen, Bachini, Pierini
11/04/99	Cagliari	A	2-1	Jørgensen, Walem
18/04/99	Milan	H	1-5	Amoroso
25/04/99	Inter	A	3-1	Amoroso 2 (1p), Poggi
02/05/99	Lazio	H	0-3	
09/05/99	Vicenza	A	3-2	Amoroso 2 (2p), Walem
16/05/99	Perugia	H	1-2	Amoroso (p)
23/05/99	Empoli	A	3-1	Jørgensen, Amoroso 2

VENEZIA

CLUB DIRECTORY

AC Venezia
Via Ceccherini 19
30174 Venezia - Mestre
tel - (041) 958100
fax - (041) 950104
Year of Formation - 1907
President - Maurizio Zamparini
Secretary - Stefano Bazzacco
Coach - Walter Novellino
(99/00 - Luciano Spalletti)
Stadium - Pierluigi Penzo (15,000)

APPEARANCES 98/99

	P	Ap	(s)	Gls
Augustine AHINFUL (GHA)	A	1	(2)	
Fabian BALLARIN	D	4	(9)	1
Alessio BANDIERI	G	1	(1)	
Fábio da Silva BILICA (BRA)	D	12		
Pierpaolo BRESCIANI	A	2	(3)	
Emanuele BRIOSCHI	D	23	(1)	
Enrico BUONOCORE	M		(6)	
Daniele CARNASCIALI	D	16		
Alessandro DAL CANTO	D	26	(1)	
Andrea DE CECCO	D		(1)	
Ivone DE FRANCESCHI	M	9	(8)	
Stefano GIOACCHINI	A	1	(2)	
Giuseppe IACHINI	M	15		
Gianluca LUPPI	D	30	(1)	
Filippo MANIERO	A	25	(2)	12
Nicola MARANGON	M	8	(13)	
Salvatore MICELI	M	25	(2)	1
Simone PAVAN	D	25	(1)	
Francesco PEDONE	M	31	(2)	3
Alessandro PISTONE	D	4	(6)	
Gerhard POSCHNER (GER)	M	1		
Alvaro RECOBA (URU)	A	19		11
Stefan SCHWOCH	A	11	(3)	2
Massimo TAIBI	G	33		
Moacir Bastos TUTA (BRA)	A	6	(12)	3
Fabian VALTOLINA	M	18	(11)	3
Sergio VOLPI	M	25	(2)	1
Kenneth ZEIGBO (NIG)	A		(2)	
Mauro ZIRONELLI	M	3	(3)	

LEAGUE RESULTS 1998/99

13/09/98	Bari	A	0-1	
20/09/98	Parma	H	0-0	
26/09/98	Roma	A	0-2	
04/10/98	Milan	H	0-2	.
18/10/98	Perugia	A	0-1	
25/10/98	Udinese	A	1-1	Schwoch
31/10/98	Bologna	H	0-2	
08/11/98	Fiorentina	A	1-4	Schwoch (p)
15/11/98	Lazio	H	2-0	Tuta, Pedone
22/11/98	Salernitana	A	0-1	
29/11/98	Sampdoria	H	0-0	
06/12/98	Cagliari	A	1-0	og (Zanoncelli)
13/12/98	Piacenza	H	0-0	
20/12/98	Vicenza	A	0-0	
10/01/99	Inter	A	2-6	Maniero 2
17/01/99	Juventus	H	1-1	Pedone
20/01/99	Empoli	H	3-2	Valtolina, Maniero 2
24/01/99	Bari	H	2-1	Maniero, Tuta
31/01/99	Parma	A	2-2	Maniero 2
07/02/99	Roma	H	3-1	Recoba, Maniero, Ballarin
14/02/99	Milan	A	1-2	Tuta
21/02/99	Perugia	H	2-1	Recoba, Maniero
28/02/99	Udinese	H	1-0	Recoba (p)
07/03/99	Bologna	A	1-2	Maniero (p)
14/03/99	Fiorentina	H	4-1	Recoba 3, Miceli
21/03/99	Lazio	A	0-2	
03/04/99	Salernitana	H	0-0	
11/04/99	Sampdoria	A	1-2	Valtolina
18/04/99	Cagliari	H	1-0	Recoba
25/04/99	Piacenza	A	1-0	Maniero
02/05/99	Vicenza	H	1-2	Valtolina
09/05/99	Empoli	A	2-2	Recoba 2 (1p)
16/05/99	Inter	H	3-1	Volpi, Recoba, Maniero
23/05/99	Juventus	A	2-3	Pedone, Recoba

VICENZA

CLUB DIRECTORY

Vicenza Calcio
Via Schio 21
36100 Vicenza
tel - (0444) 505044
fax - (0444) 544764
Year of Formation - 1902
President - Aronne Miola
General Manager - Sergio Gasparin
Secretary - Fabio Rizzitelli
Coach - Franco Colomba; Edoardo Reja
Stadium - Romeo Menti (20,920)

MAJOR HONOURS
Domestic Cup - (1) 1997.

APPEARANCES 98/99

	P	Ap	(s)	Gls
Gabriele AMBROSETTI	A	21	(3)	4
Massimo BEGHETTO	D	18	(4)	1
Davide BELOTTI	D	6	(2)	
Patrick BETTONI (SUI)	G	1	(1)	
Pierluigi BRIVIO	G	33		
Giuseppe CARDONE	D	12	(2)	1
Mirko CONTE	D	2	(8)	
Ousmane DABO (FRA)	M	11	(2)	
Giacomo DICARA	D	29	(2)	1
Domenico DI CARLO	M	18	(9)	
Nicola DILISO	D	16	(1)	
Arturo DI NAPOLI	A		(1)	
Pasquale LUISO	A	11	(2)	2
MARCO AURÉLIO (BRA)	D	13	(1)	
Stefano MAZZOCCO	M		(2)	
Giuliano MELOSI	M	3	(3)	
Gustavo MENDEZ (URU)	D	21	(3)	1
Davide MEZZANOTTI	D	2	(7)	
Giovanni MORABITO	D	11	(2)	
Marco NEGRI	A	8	(1)	1
Marcelo OTERO (URU)	A	25	(4)	10
Ottavio PALLADINI	M	4	(9)	
Gennaro SCARLATO	A	5	(6)	
Marco SCHENARDI	M	30	(2)	2
Lorenzo STOVINI	D	29	(2)	
Ivan TISCI	M		(6)	
Fabio VIVIANI	M	18	(9)	
Lamberto ZAULI	A	27	(2)	3

LEAGUE RESULTS 1998/99

12/09/98	Parma	A	0-0	
20/09/98	Fiorentina	H	1-2	og (Padalino)
27/09/98	Piacenza	A	0-2	
04/10/98	Bari	H	1-0	Otero
18/10/98	Juventus	H	1-1	Zauli
25/10/98	Lazio	A	1-1	Schenardi
01/11/98	Cagliari	H	2-1	Otero 2
08/11/98	Perugia	A	1-3	Ambrosetti
15/11/98	Bologna	H	0-4	
22/11/98	Sampdoria	A	0-0	
29/11/98	Empoli	A	0-1	
06/12/98	Inter	H	1-1	Luiso (p)
13/12/98	Milan	A	0-1	
20/12/98	Venezia	H	0-0	
06/01/99	Udinese	A	1-2	Ambrosetti
10/01/99	Salernitana	H	1-0	Luiso
17/01/99	Roma	A	0-3	
24/01/99	Parma	H	0-0	
31/01/99	Fiorentina	A	0-3	
07/02/99	Piacenza	H	1-0	Ambrosetti
14/02/99	Bari	A	0-0	
21/02/99	Juventus	A	0-2	
28/02/99	Lazio	H	1-2	Cardone
07/03/99	Cagliari	A	0-1	
13/03/99	Perugia	H	3-0	Zauli, Schenardi, Otero (p)
21/03/99	Bologna	A	2-4	Otero 2
03/04/99	Sampdoria	H	1-0	Otero
11/04/99	Empoli	H	2-0	Negri, Otero
18/04/99	Inter	A	1-1	Beghetto
25/04/99	Milan	H	0-2	
02/05/99	Venezia	A	2-1	Otero 2
09/05/99	Udinese	H	2-3	Zauli, Dicara
16/05/99	Salernitana	A	1-2	Méndez
23/05/99	Roma	H	1-4	Ambrosetti

PROMOTED CLUBS

SECOND DIVISION FINAL TABLE 98/99

		Pd	W	D	L	F	A	Pt	GD
1	**Verona**	38	18	12	8	60	38	66	+22
2	**Torino**	38	19	8	11	58	36	65	+22
3	**Reggina**	38	16	16	6	45	32	64	+13
4	**Lecce**	38	18	10	10	47	39	64	+8
5	Pescara	38	18	9	11	50	42	63	+8
6	Atalanta	38	14	19	5	44	27	61	+17
7	Brescia	38	14	14	10	44	33	56	+11
8	Treviso	38	14	14	10	52	42	56	+10
9	Napoli	38	12	15	11	41	38	51	+3
10	Ravenna	38	13	12	13	47	51	51	-4
11	Chievo	38	11	15	12	37	40	48	-3
12	Genoa	38	10	16	12	53	53	46	0
13	Cesena	38	10	15	13	37	41	45	-4
14	Monza	38	10	15	13	32	38	45	-6
15	Ternana	38	10	15	13	39	50	45	-11
16	Cosenza	38	11	10	17	41	53	43	-12
17	Reggiana	38	9	14	15	40	49	41	-9
18	Fidelis Andria	38	9	13	16	33	49	40	-16
19	Lucchese	38	8	13	17	35	45	37	-10
20	Cremonese	38	3	11	24	30	69	20	-39

CLUB DIRECTORY

Hellas Verona Football Club
Piazzale Olimpia-Cancello E
37138 Verona
tel - (045) 577555
fax - (045) 568665
Year of Formation - 1903
President - Giambattista Pastorello
Secretary - Enzo Bertolini
Coach - Claudio Cesare Prandelli
Stadium - Marc'Antonio Bentegodi (42,924)

MAJOR HONOURS
League Championship - (1) 1985.

CLUB DIRECTORY

Torino Calcio
Via Maria Vittoria 1
10123 Torino
tel - (011) 5623941
fax - (011) 5622018
Year of Formation - 1906
President - Massimo Vidulich
Secretary - Federico Bonetto
Coach - Emiliano Mondonico
Stadium - Delle Alpi (69,041)

MAJOR HONOURS
League Championship - (7)
1927, 1943, 1946, 1947, 1948, 1949, 1976.
Domestic Cup - (5)
1936, 1943, 1968, 1971, 1993.

CLUB DIRECTORY

Union Sportiva Lecce
Via Templari 11
73100 Lecce
tel - (0832) 240211
fax - (0832) 243171
Year of Formation - 1908
President - Mario Maroni
Secretary - Roberto Zanzi
Coach - Nedo Sonetti (99/00 - Alberto Cavasin)
Stadium - Via del Mare (38,900)

CLUB DIRECTORY

Reggina Calcio
Via Tommaso Gulli 1
89127 Reggio Calabria
tel - (0965) 811555
fax - (0965) 26343
Year of Formation - 1914
President - Pasquale Foti
Secretary - Francesco Iacopino
Coach - Elio Gustinetti; Bruno Bolchi
(99/00 - Franco Colomba)
Stadium - Oreste Granillo (28,000)

LATVIA

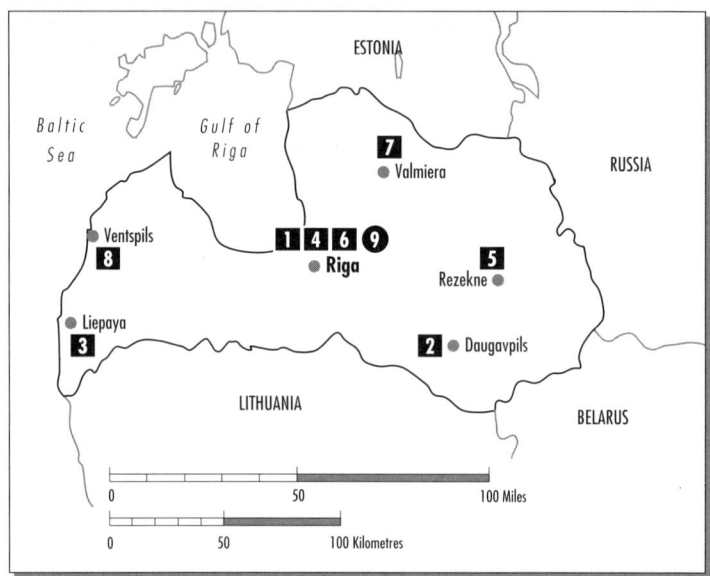

FIRST LATVIAN IN ENGLISH PREMIERSHIP

Skonto skate home after shaky start

FEDERATION DIRECTORY

Latvijas Futbola Federacija
1 Augsiela, LV-1009 Riga

tel - (2) 292988
fax - 7828331

Year of Formation - 1921
President - Guntis Indricksons
Secretary - Janis Mezhetsky

Stadium - Daugava, Riga (5,800)

The seventh independent Latvian championship brought a seventh consecutive title for Skonto Riga, but it was something of a scratched record for the country's ruling club.

The final table, which showed Skonto ten points out in front and with 98 goals to their credit - an amazing average of 3.5 per game - disguised the truth of a surprisingly difficult campaign by their standards.

All the trouble came early on. Skonto paid the price for the exodus of some of their leading players, including the Latvian international trio of Mikhail Zemlinsky, Yury Shevlyakov and Valery Ivanov, their 25-goal top scorer from the previous season, Georgian David Chaladze, and their experienced goalkeeper Raimonds Laizans. Coach Alexander Starkov had his work cut out to rebuild the team and put it back on a level footing. At first, however, he did not succeed.

Having opened their season with a 3-3 draw against Virsliga newcomers Ranto/Miks Riga, Skonto went on to lose three of their next six games. That was one defeat more than they had suffered in the previous five league campaigns put together. So, talk of a major crisis was not exaggerated, especially as Skonto found themselves down in the murky, uncharted waters of the bottom half of the table.

The catalyst for the team's revival was a 1-0 victory over Metalurgs Liepaya in the 1998 Latvian Cup final. Hot on the heels of that triumph Skonto won their next league game 9-0 and all of a sudden the team began to gel. Victory after victory followed, and before long Skonto had recovered sufficiently to reclaim their familiar perch at the top of the table.

A number of new arrivals had helped to trigger the improvement. Zemlinsky came back from Israel, Lithuanian international Andrius Tereskinas headed north from Vilnius, and two very experienced Latvian internationals - goalkeeper Oleg Karavayev and forward Vitas Rimkus - both arrived from Germany.

On October 4, Skonto hit peak form when they destroyed FK Valmiera 15-2. It was the biggest winning score in Latvian football's brief history and included five goals apiece for the team's two outstanding front men, Marian Pakhar and Mikhail Mikholap. In the five remaining matches neither Pakhar nor Mikholap could score enough goals to prevent Victor Dobretsov, of runners-up Metalurgs, from winning the league top-scorer prize, and there was a smidgen of disappointment, too, that Skonto as a team could not quite reach a century of goals.

But the big prize, that of the championship title, was safe and secure, enabling Skonto to prepare themselves for yet another

LEAGUE CHAMPIONSHIP RESULTS 1998

		1	2	3	4	5	6	7	8
1	Daugava Riga		2-2	0-0	3-0	8-2	3-5	4-2	1-1
			0-0	0-1	2-0	1-1	1-2	0-0	1-2
2	Dinaburg Daugavpils	0-0		0-1	6-1	0-0	0-1	6-1	1-1
		0-2		1-1	5-1	2-1	1-4	0-0	0-3
3	Metalurgs Liepaya	3-2	1-2		7-0	4-0	0-0	4-1	0-0
		2-1	3-0		5-1	7-0	1-1	2-1	1-0
4	Ranto/Miks Riga	2-1	0-6	3-4		1-3	3-3	0-0	0-1
		1-1	2-5	1-6		0-0	2-7	0-3	1-5
5	FK Rezekne	1-2	0-1	2-3	2-2		0-2	1-2	1-4
		2-1	2-4	1-2	1-2		1-6	0-5	0-3
6	Skonto Riga	2-3	0-2	1-0	9-0	7-0		4-0	1-0
		3-0	2-1	1-1	4-0	1-0		15-2	4-0
7	FK Valmiera	2-2	0-2	2-1	4-0	3-0	1-4		0-0
		2-1	1-1	2-1	1-0	0-0	1-5		0-3
8	FK Ventspils	1-0	0-0	0-1	9-0	4-1	2-1	0-3	
		3-0	1-1	2-0	3-2	3-0	2-3	3-0	

LEAGUE CHAMPIONSHIP FINAL TABLE 1998

				Home				Away				Total					
		P	W	D	L	F	A	W	D	L	F	A	W	D	L	F	A	P	GD
1	Skonto Riga	28	11	1	2	54	9	10	3	1	44	18	21	4	3	98	27	67	+71
2	Metalurgs Liepaya	28	10	3	1	40	9	7	3	4	22	16	17	6	5	62	25	57	+37
3	FK Ventspils	28	9	2	3	33	12	7	4	3	23	11	16	6	6	56	23	54	+33
4	Dinaburg Daugavpils	28	4	5	5	22	17	7	5	2	27	14	11	10	7	49	31	43	+18
5	FK Valmiera	28	6	4	4	19	20	4	3	7	20	39	10	7	11	39	59	37	-20
6	Daugava Riga	28	4	6	4	26	18	3	3	8	16	24	7	9	12	42	42	30	0
7	FK Rezekne	28	1	1	12	14	39	1	4	9	8	41	2	5	21	22	80	11	-58
8	Ranto/Miks Riga	28	1	4	10	16	54	1	1	11	9	52	2	5	21	25	106	11	-81

N.B. Where two or more teams are level on points, classification is determined by the results of the matches between them.

Champions' League qualifying campaign in 1999. Their European efforts in 1998 had been thwarted by Inter in the Champions' Cup and Dinamo Moscow in the UEFA Cup, the latter tie being lost on home soil despite three goals in the two games from Pakhar, who was to become the first Latvian to play in the English Premiership when he quit the club for Southampton the following February.

Just prior to his departure Pakhar played for Skonto in the 1999 CIS Cup in Moscow, helping his team to an impressive third place (behind Spartak Moscow and Dynamo Kiev) in the annual indoor competition for the champion clubs of the former Soviet republics. Skonto's star in Moscow was Mikhail Mikholap, who, with seven goals in five games, took the tournament's top-scorer crown - a notable achievement by the young striker from the Russian coastal enclave of Kaliningrad who had taken out Latvian citizenship just a few months earlier.

For the second year in a row the issue of relegation and promotion proved less than straightforward, although the ending was the same for FK Rezekne, who once more managed to cling onto their top-flight status by the skin of their teeth. The previous season they had been rescued from relegation following the withdrawal of two clubs due to financial problems. This time they escaped the drop thanks to a highly improbable and somewhat contentious last-day victory over Daugava Riga, which enabled them to finish ahead of Ranto/Miks by virtue of their superior head-to-head record.

In fact, it was the defeated Daugava Riga who would be making their last appearance in the Virsliga, as they were replaced for the 1999 season by newly-formed FK Riga, who obtained immediate success by winning

TOP SCORERS

23	Victor DOBRETSOV (Metalurgs Liepaya)
21	Roman GRIGORCHOUK (Dinaburg Daugavpils)
20	Mikhail MIKHOLAP (Skonto Riga)
19	Marian PAKHAR (Skonto Riga)
13	Rolands BOULDERS (Metalurgs Liepaya)
11	Vitas RIMKUS (Skonto Riga)
10	Vladimir BABICHEV (Skonto Riga)
9	Sabir KHAMZIN (FK Ventspils)
	Oleg RIDNY (Daugava Riga)
	Alexey SHARANDO (Daugava Riga)
	Vitaly VOSKANS (FK Rezekne)

NATIONAL TEAM RESULTS 98/99

19/08/98	Iceland	A	Reykjavik	1-4	Sharando (50)
06/09/98	Norway (ECQ)	A	Oslo	3-1	Pakhar (11), Shtolcers (53), Zemlinsky (65p)
10/10/98	Georgia (ECQ)	H	Riga	1-0	Shtolcers (2)
14/10/98	Slovenia (ECQ)	A	Maribor	0-1	
10/11/98	Tunisia	A	Tunis	0-3	
24/02/99	Israel	A	Jerusalem	0-2	
31/03/99	Greece (ECQ)	H	Riga	0-0	
28/04/99	Albania (ECQ)	H	Riga	0-0	
05/06/99	Slovenia (ECQ)	H	Riga	1-2	Pakhar (18)
09/06/99	Greece (ECQ)	A	Athens	2-1	Verpakovsky (25), Zemlinsky (90p)
26/06/99	Brazil	A	Curitiba	0-3	

NATIONAL TEAM APPEARANCES 98/99

Coach - Revaz DZODZUASHVILI	ISL	NOR	GEO	SLO	TUN	ISR	GRE	ALB	SLO	GRE	BRA	Cps	Gls
Oleg KARAVAYEV (13/02/61) - Skonto Riga/FK Riga	G	G	G	G			G	G				38	-
Igor N. STEPANOV (21/01/76) - Skonto Riga	D40				s46	D	s62	D84			s80	30	1
Igor TROITSKY (11/01/69) - Kristall Smolensk (RUS)	D											38	-
Mikhail ZEMLINSKY (21/12/69) - Skonto Riga	D	D	D	D	D	D	D		D	D	D	56	6
Valentin LOBANYOV (23/10/71) - Skonto Riga/Shinnik Yaroslavl (RUS)	D	D	D	D	M46	D68	D	D	D43	M		22	1
Yury LAIZANS (06/01/79) - Skonto Riga	M	D51	s51		M	s60		s60	D	D	D	16	-
Alexey SHARANDO (01/01/64) - Daugava Riga/FK Riga	M	M73	M	M	M46	s50	M62	s84	M59			23	2
Rolands BOULDERS (12/03/65) - Metalurgs Liepaya	M68	s73	s89	s79	s65		s46	A			s46	31	3
Vladimir BABICHEV (22/04/68) - Skonto Riga	M	M	M		A	M50			M	M		49	4
Marian PAKHAR (05/08/76) - Skonto Riga/Southampton (ENG)	A	A81	A89	A	A65	A	A		A	A		34	8
Vitas RIMKUS (21/06/73) - Skonto Riga	A52			s87								25	8
Andrey LAPSA (23/04/68) - FK Ventspils	s40											1	-
	/67												
Vladimir DRAGUN (13/12/72) - Metalurgs Liepaya	s52			s24								3	-
Ilya NOVIKOV (12/08/77) - Skonto Riga	s67											2	-
Andrey SHTOLCERS (07/07/74) - Shakhtar Donetsk (UKR)	s68	A	A	A		M	M	M60	M		s46	36	3
Artur ZAKRESHEVSKY (07/08/71) - Daugava Riga		D		D24								29	-
Valery IVANOV (23/02/70) - Uralan Elista (RUS)/Shinnik Yaroslavl (RUS)	M	D	D87		D80	D27	M					57	1
Imants BLEIDELIS (16/08/75) - Skonto Riga		M	M51	M51	s55			s59	s54	s46		37	4
Victor LUKASHEVICH (17/03/72) - FK Ventspils	s51	D	D			D	D	D	D			12	-
Alexander ISAKOV (16/09/73) - Dinaburg Daugavpils	s81	s75	M	D	s68	s27	D				D	13	-
Vitaly ASTAFYEV (03/04/71) - Skonto Riga			M75	M79	M55	M60	M		M41	M54	M46	61	7
Mikhail MIKHOLAP (24/08/74) - Skonto Riga			s51		A55	A46	A70	A	s46	A63		7	-
Raimonds LAIZANS (05/08/64) - Fakel Voronezh (RUS)					G46							31	-
Igor KORABLYOV (23/11/74) - Daugava Riga/FK Riga					D76			s43	D	D		4	-
Alexander KOLINKO (18/06/75) - Skonto Riga					s46	G			G	G	G87	6	-
Andrey RUBINS (26/11/78) - Skonto Riga					s46	s80		M	s41	M64	M80	6	-
Nickolay POLYAKOV (02/07/75) - FK Ventspils					s55							7	-
Dzintars ZIRNIS (25/04/77) - Metalurgs Liepaya					s76							2	-
Oleg BLAGONADEZHDIN (16/05/73) - Skonto Riga						M	M	M			M	31	1
Victor DOBRETSOV (09/01/77) - Metalurgs Liepaya							s70			A46		3	-
Maris VERPAKOVSKY (15/10/79) - Metalurgs Liepaya									A46	M46		2	1
Alexander ZHIZHMANOV (22/01/71) - FK Ventspils									s64			1	-
Vladimir KOLESNICHENKO (04/05/80) - Skonto Riga										s63		4	-
Andrey PIEDELS (17/09/70) - Skonto Riga										s87		2	-

EUROPEAN CUPS 98/99

CHAMPIONS' CUP
● SKONTO RIGA
Preliminary round DINAMO MINSK (BLS)
H 0-0
   Karavayev; Lobanyov, Silagadze, Stepanov, Tereshkinas (Novikov 73),
   Zemlinsky, Laizans (Bleidelis 46), Astafyev, Pakhar, Babichev,
   Mikholap (Rimkus 74).
A 2-1   Astafyev (45), Novikov 72)
   Karavayev; Laizans, Stepanov, Silagadze, Lobanyov, Zemlinsky,
   Astafyev, Pakhar, Babichev (Pindeyev 83), Rimkus (Novikov 50),
   Mikholap (Bleidelis 66).

Qualifying round INTER (ITA)
A 0-4
   Karavayev; Stepanov, Silagadze, Astafyev (Rimkus 6; Novikov 57),
   Rekhviashvili, Bleidelis, Pakhar, Babichev (Melnik 80), Mikholap, Lidaks,
   Laizans.
H 1-3   Mikholap (22)
   Karavayev; Stepanov, Silagadze, Zemlinsky, Lobanyov, Rekhviashvili,
   Bleidelis, Melnik (Novikov 46), Pakhar (Rubins 85), Babichev,
   Mikholap (Rimkus 85).

CUP WINNERS' CUP
● METALURGS LIEPAYA
Qualifying round KEFLAVIK (ISL)
H 4-2   Boulders (61, 85, 88), Magdishauskas (86)
   Bryaunis; Magdishauskas, Zirnis, Yuiko, Osichenko, Dragun,
   Atmanavichius, Rudenko, Vaineikis (Verpakovsky 75), Dobretsov
   (Chernyauskas 69), Boulders.
A 0-1
   Bryaunis; Magdishauskas, Zirnis, Lisyakov, Osichenko, Dragun
   (Yuiko 79), Vaineikis (Kudryashov 61), Dobretsov, Boulders, Rudenko,
   Atmanavichius.

1st round SC BRAGA (POR)
H 0-0
   Bryaunis; Magdishauskas, Atmanavichius, Zirnis, Osichenko, Yuiko,
   Vaineikis, Dragun, Rudenko (Rinkus 46), Dobretsov (Kudryashov 58),
   Boulders.
A 0-4
   Bryaunis; Magdishauskas, Rinkus, Zirnis, Lisyakov (Dobretsov 27),
   Yuiko, Osichenko, Vaineikis (Verpakovsky 72), Boulders, Rudenko
   (Kudryashov 51), Atmanavichius.

UEFA CUP
● DAUGAVA RIGA
Preliminary round MURA MURSKA SOBOTA (SLO)
A 1-6   Ridny (75)
   Grishikashvili; Sprogis, Zakreshevsky, Korablyov (Nalivaiko 77), Pumpa,
   Ridny, Sharando, Vutsans (Chernov 46), Pertiya (Molotkov 46),
   Stepanov, Teplov.
H 1-2   Sharando (69)
   Mikhailov; Sprogis, Zakreshevsky, Korablyov, Pumpa (Nesterenko 81),
   Chernov, Ridny (Bakanin 82), Molotkov, Sharando, Vutsans
   (Litovchenko 89), Teplov.

● SKONTO RIGA
1st round DINAMO MOSKVA (RUS)
A 2-2   Mikholap (39), Pakhar (49)
   Karavayev; Zemlinsky, Lobanyov, Rekhviashvili, Pakhar, Babichev,
   Mikholap (Rimkus 75), Melnik (Pindeyev 68), Rubins, Laizans,
   Tereshkinas (Lidaks 52).
H 2-3   Pakhar (75, 89)
   Karavayev; Zemlinsky, Lobanyov, Bleidelis, Pakhar, Babichev, Mikholap
   (Rimkus 63), Laizans, Lidaks (Rubins 63), Astafyev, Tereshkinas.

DOMESTIC CUP 98/99

FIRST ROUND
FK Lode 0, Metalurgs Liepaya 7
FK Mido Riga 0, FK Riga 4
Dinaburg Daugavpils 8, FK Stameriena 0
Skonto/metals-Rinar Riga 0, FK Valmiera 5
FK Saldus 0, Police FK Riga 2
FK Ventspils 8, FK Auda Riga 0
FK Tsesis 0, Skonto Riga 17

QUARTER-FINALS
FK Valmiera 1 (Kudryashov 51), Skonto Riga 4
(Savalnieks 4og, Mikholap 20, Kolesnichenko 37, 42)
Police FK Riga 0, FK Ventspils 4 (Rudakov 8,
Voronkov 41, Vdovenko 62, Bescastnikh 70p)

FK Riga 3 (Sharando 9, Sprogis 65, Aksyonov 80),
Dinaburg Daugavpils 1 (Dzhubanov 90)
Metalurgs Liepaya 4 (Boulders 37, Magdishauskas 40,
Verpakovsky 63, Dragun 73), FK Rezekne 0

SEMI-FINALS
FK Riga 2 (Molotkov 14, Aksyonov 15),
Metalurgs Liepaya 1 (Zakreshevsky 40)
Metalurgs Liepaya 0, FK Riga 1 (Aksyonov 88p)
(FK Riga 3-1)

FK Ventspils 0, Skonto Riga 1 (Babichev 11p)
Skonto Riga 3
(Zemlinsky 22p, Mikholap 34, Dzheladze 41),
FK Ventspils 3 (Polyakov 4, Rudakov 23, Voronkov 85)
(Skonto Riga 4-3)

FINAL
26/05/99, Riga
FK RIGA 1 Sharando (61)
SKONTO RIGA 1 Zemlinsky (44p)
(aet; 6-5 on pens.)
referee - Sipailo
FK RIGA - Grigyan; Kitto, Pumpa, Korablyov, Nesterenko,
Vasyukov, Sharando, Platonov (Kozlov 91),
Karashauskas, Molotkov (Balsyavichius 46), Aksyonov.
SKONTO RIGA - Kolinko; Zemlinsky, Silagadze,
Tereshkinas, Blagonadezhdin, Mentesashvili
(Kolesnichenko 65), Rekhviashvili, Rubin, Babichev,
Astafyev (Bleidelis 99), Mikholap.

MARIAN PAKHAR

When Marian Pakhar signed a four-year contract with English Premiership club Southampton in February 1999 he opened up a whole new avenue of publicity for Latvian football. While Latvian internationals had left their homeland before, none

had ever made such a high-profile, or expensive, move. Within no time the little striker was more than

justifying his £800,000 fee, scoring one crucial goal after another as Southampton escaped relegation on the final day of the season. The 23-year-old scored 51 goals in 118 matches in Latvia's top division and he has become an integral member of the Latvian national team, scoring and making goals from his favoured position as a deep-lying striker. Although he is now Latvia's most famous footballer, he was actually born in the Ukrainian town of Chernovol before moving to Riga a year later.

VICTOR DOBRETSOV

With 23 goals in 27 games, Metalurgs Liepaya striker Victor Dobretsov was the top scorer in the 1998 Latvian championship. His partnership with Rolands Boulders was every bit as effective as the Pakhar/Mikholap combo that took Skonto Riga to the title. His goals tended to come in chunks, with two doubles, three hat-tricks and one four-goal salvo contributing to his winning total. Still only 22, Dobretsov is precocious, gifted and ambitious. He remains on the fringes of the Latvian national team, having earned his first cap against Andorra in June 1998. He would also love to bring success to his hometown club Metalurgs, although a career-enhancing move away cannot be discounted if his

the 1999 Latvian Cup, beating champions Skonto on penalties in the final after a 1-1 draw, having earlier accounted for both Dinaburg Daugavpils and Metalurgs Liepaya. A new long-term challenger to Skonto appeared to have been born...

The Latvian national team made a sensational start to the 2000 European Championship qualifying series when they beat Norway 3-1 in Oslo in their opening fixture and then consolidated their position at the head of Group Two with a 1-0 home win against Georgia. The results were particularly remarkable because nobody had seen them coming. The team's new coach, Georgian Revaz Dzodzuashvili, had made a pretty awful start to his reign, and a heavy defeat in Iceland just a few weeks before the visit to Oslo left most Latvian fans fearing the worst.

No sooner had forlorn hope turned to rampant expectation, however, than Latvia lost away to Slovenia.

The following spring they would again go down to the Slovenians, losing 1-2 in Riga, but by way of compensation they took four points off Greece - firstly in a 0-0 draw in snow-bedecked Riga at the end of March, then with an extraordinary last-gasp win in Athens in June. Mikhail Zemlinsky's last-minute winner from the penalty spot, following a début goal from teenager Maris Verpakovsky, allowed Latvia to plan for their remaining three fixtures with renewed hope. First place had already gone out of the window, but for Dzodzuashvili and his players there was still a chance, albeit a fairly faint one, of reaching the play-offs...

DAUGAVA RIGA

CLUB DIRECTORY

Daugava Riga
Tallinas str. 49
1012 Riga
tel - (2) 270335
fax - (2) 310197
Year of Formation - 1995
President - Janis Melbardis
Secretary - Stanislav Androsov
Coach - Janis Skredelis; Sergey Semyonov
Stadium - LU (5,000)

APPEARANCES 1998

	P	Ap	(s)	Gls
Anton BAKANIN	M		(11)	
Roman BERSENEV	A	1	(5)	1
Andrey CHERNOV (UKR)	M	22	(3)	3
Alexander CHUMAKOV	G	2		
Igor KAPUSTIN	A		(3)	
Igor KORABLYOV	D	26		1
Sergey LITOVCHENKO (UKR)	M	10	(9)	
Mikhail MIKHAILOV	G	26		
Ruslan MIKHALCHOUK	M	3	(2)	
Yury MOLOTKOV	A	22	(3)	8
Alexander MUSAYEV	M		(3)	
Dmitry NALIVAIKO	M	12	(4)	1
Vladislav NESTERENKO	D	24	(1)	1
Sergey NIKIFOROV	M	2	(9)	1
Andrey OLEINIK	G		(1)	
Andrey PUMPA	D	20	(3)	
Victor REZYAPKIN	D		(1)	
Oleg RIDNY (RUS)	A	21		9
Alexey SHARANDO	M	25		9
Dzintars SPROGIS	D	22		2
Vitaly TEPLOV	A	22	(1)	1
Renars VUTSANS	M	24	(2)	1
Artur ZAKRESHEVSKY	D	24		2

LEAGUE RESULTS 1998

18/04/98	FK Ventspils	H	1-1	Vutsans
25/04/98	Skonto Riga	A	3-2	og (Stepanov), Sharando, Nikiforov
03/05/98	Metalurgs Liepaya	H	0-0	
12/05/98	Dinaburg Daugavpils	A	0-0	
20/05/98	Ranto/Miks Riga	H	3-0	Sprogis, Chernov, Zakreshevsky
24/05/98	FK Valmiera	A	2-2	Sharando 2
29/05/98	FK Rezekne	H	8-2	Ridny 3, Sprogis, Sharando, Korablyov, Nalivaiko, Molotkov
07/06/98	FK Ventspils	A	0-1	
11/06/98	Skonto Riga	H	3-5	Sharando, Molotkov, Ridny
17/06/98	Metalurgs Liepaya	A	2-3	Ridny, Molotkov
29/06/98	Ranto/Miks Riga	A	1-2	Molotkov
05/07/98	FK Valmiera	H	4-2	Ridny 2, Molotkov, Zakreshevsky
10/07/98	FK Ventspils	A	0-3	
16/07/98	FK Rezekne	A	2-1	og (Derbakov), Sharando
02/08/98	Skonto Riga	A	0-3	
06/08/98	Metalurgs Liepaya	H	0-1	
11/08/98	Dinaburg Daugavpils	H	2-2	Sharando 2
16/08/98	Dinaburg Daugavpils	A	2-0	Ridny, Sharando
24/08/98	Ranto/Miks Riga	H	2-0	Nesterenko, Bersenev
30/08/98	FK Valmiera	A	1-2	Chernov
12/09/98	FK Rezekne	H	1-1	Molotkov
19/09/98	FK Ventspils	H	1-2	Molotkov
25/09/98	Skonto Riga	H	1-2	Chernov
05/10/98	Metalurgs Liepaya	A	1-2	Teplov
18/10/98	Dinaburg Daugavpils	H	0-0	
24/10/98	Ranto/Miks Riga	A	1-1	Molotkov
31/10/98	FK Valmiera	H	0-0	
07/11/98	FK Rezekne	A	1-2	Ridny

DINABURG DAUGAVPILS

CLUB DIRECTORY

Dinaburg Daugavpils
Rigas str. 42-3
5400 Daugavpils
tel - (54) 39235
fax - (54) 39235
Year of Formation - 1996
President - Oleg Gavrilov
Secretary - Alexander Svirchkauskas
Coach - Victor Nesterenko; Roman Grigorchouk
Stadium - Tseltnieks (3,000)

APPEARANCES 1998

	P	Ap	(s)	Gls
Vitaly BARANOVSKY	M		(3)	
Edgar BURLAKOV	M	26	(1)	5
Vyacheslav DUSMANOV	G	1		
Alexander FEDOTOV	M	13	(2)	3
Roman GRIGORCHOUK (UKR)	A	27		21
Alexander ISAKOV	D	26		1
Yury KARASHAUSKAS	A	17	(3)	6
Kirill KURBATOV (RUS)	M	28		5
Dmitry LOGINOV	D	4		
Vitaly PINYASKIN (RUS)	M	14		
Sergey POGODIN	M	18	(1)	
Yury PUCHINSKY	M	13	(10)	2
Genady ROGOV	M	8	(5)	
Oleg SELIVANOV	D	7	(9)	
Georgy SHEBARSHIN (RUS)	D	25		
Nikita SHMIKOV (RUS)	D	24	(1)	
Victor SPOLE	G	27		
Alexey VOLOSANOV	M		(5)	
Vladimir ZHAVORONKOV	A	2	(15)	3
Mikhail ZIZILEV	M	28		2

LEAGUE RESULTS 1998

18/04/98	FK Valmiera	A	2-0	Karashauskas 2
25/04/98	FK Rezekne	H	0-0	
03/05/98	FK Ventspils	H	1-1	Zhavoronkov
12/05/98	Daugava Riga	H	0-0	
20/05/98	Metalurgs Liepaya	A	2-1	Grigorchouk, Fedotov
25/05/98	Skonto Riga	A	2-0	Burlakov 2
29/05/98	Ranto/Miks Riga	H	6-1	Zizilev, Fedotov, Kurbatov (p), Burlakov, Grigorchouk 2
07/06/98	FK Valmiera	H	6-1	Grigorchouk 4, Kurbatov, Fedotov
11/06/98	FK Rezekne	A	1-0	Burlakov
16/06/98	FK Ventspils	A	0-0	
01/07/98	Skonto Riga	H	0-1	
16/07/98	Ranto/Miks Riga	A	6-0	Grigorchouk 4, og (Klyuyev), Kurbatov
20/07/98	Metalurgs Liepaya	H	0-1	
23/07/98	FK Valmiera	A	1-1	Grigorchouk
02/08/98	FK Rezekne	H	2-1	Grigorchouk 2
06/08/98	FK Ventspils	A	1-1	Grigorchouk
11/08/98	Daugava Riga	A	2-2	Grigorchouk 2
16/08/98	Daugava Riga	H	0-2	
22/08/98	Metalurgs Liepaya	A	0-3	
30/08/98	Skonto Riga	A	1-2	Kurbatov
12/09/98	Ranto/Miks Riga	H	5-1	Karashauskas, Puchinsky 2, Grigorchouk 2
20/09/98	FK Valmiera	H	0-0	
26/09/98	FK Rezekne	A	4-2	Karashauskas, Zhavoronkov 2, Grigorchouk
04/10/98	FK Ventspils	H	0-3	
18/10/98	Daugava Riga	A	0-0	
25/10/98	Metalurgs Liepaya	H	1-1	Grigorchouk
31/10/98	Skonto Riga	H	1-4	Isakov
07/11/98	Ranto/Miks Riga	A	5-2	Karashauskas 2, Zizilev, Kurbatov, Burlakov

METALURGS LIEPAYA

CLUB DIRECTORY

Metalurgs Liepaya
Brivibas str. 93
3400 Liepaya
tel - (34) 22556
fax - (34) 22556
Year of Formation - 1996
President - Sergey Zakharyin
Secretary - Alexander Koroza
Coach - Yury Popkov
Stadium - Daugava Liepaya (6,000)

APPEARANCES 1998

	P	Ap	(s)	Gls
Saulyus ATMANAVICHIUS (LIT)	D	23		4
Rolands BOULDERS	A	28		13
Algis BRYAUNIS (LIT)	G	24	(1)	
Svayunas CHERNYAUSKAS (LIT)	A	3	(9)	1
Alexander DANILOV	D	5	(3)	
Victor DOBRETSOV	A	26	(1)	23
Vladimir DRAGUN	D	26	(1)	3
Girts KARLSONS	M		(1)	
Eduard KUDRYASHOV	A	1	(22)	2
Alexander LASHKO	M	1	(6)	
Mikhail LISYAKOV	D	18	(4)	
Daryus MAGDISHAUSKAS (LIT)	D	25		
Vladimir MALISHEV (BLS)	G	4		
Andrey OSICHENKO	M	21	(2)	
Vladlen OSIPOV	M		(2)	
Janis RINKUS	M	13	(2)	1
Oleg RUDENKO	M	16	(2)	1
Genady SOLONITSIN	A		(6)	
Rolandas VAINEIKIS (LIT)	M	23	(2)	6
Maris VERPAKOVSKY	A	3	(13)	2
Victor YUIKO (BLS)	M	23		4
Dzintars ZIRNIS	D	25		1

LEAGUE RESULTS 1998

18/04/98	FK Rezekne	A	3-2	Atmanavichius 2 (2p), Boulders
25/04/98	FK Ventspils	H	0-0	
03/05/98	Daugava Riga	A	0-0	
12/05/98	Skonto Riga	A	0-1	
20/05/98	Dinaburg Daugavpils	H	1-2	Dobretsov
24/05/98	Ranto/Miks Riga	A	4-3	Dobretsov 3, Boulders
29/05/98	FK Valmiera	H	4-1	Dobretsov 2, Vaineikis, Boulders
07/06/98	FK Rezekne	H	4-0	Dobretsov, Zirnis, Rinkus, Boulders
11/06/98	FK Ventspils	A	1-0	Dobretsov
17/06/98	Daugava Riga	H	3-2	Yuiko 2, Atmanavichius
21/06/98	Skonto Riga	H	0-0	
05/07/98	Ranto/Miks Riga	H	7-0	Dobretsov 3 (1p), Boulders, Yuiko, og (Parmalis), Chernyauskas
15/07/98	FK Valmiera	A	1-2	Boulders
20/07/98	Dinaburg Daugavpils	A	1-0	Kudryashov
25/07/98	FK Rezekne	A	2-1	Boulders, Vaineikis
02/08/98	FK Ventspils	H	1-0	Dragun
06/08/98	Daugava Riga	A	1-0	Vaineikis
22/08/98	Dinaburg Daugavpils	H	3-0	Dobretsov, Boulders, Kudryashov
31/08/98	Ranto/Miks Riga	A	6-1	Dragun, Dobretsov 2, Vaineikis, Boulders, Verpakovsky
12/09/98	FK Valmiera	H	2-1	Dobretsov 2
21/09/98	FK Rezekne	H	7-0	Dobretsov 4, Vaineikis, Boulders, Dragun
25/09/98	FK Ventspils	A	0-2	
05/10/98	Daugava Riga	H	2-1	Rudenko, Boulders
18/10/98	Skonto Riga	H	1-1	Atmanavichius (p)
25/10/98	Dinaburg Daugavpils	A	1-1	Boulders
28/10/98	Skonto Riga	A	1-1	Verpakovsky
31/10/98	Ranto/Miks Riga	H	5-1	Vaineikis, Dobretsov 3, Yuiko
07/11/98	FK Valmiera	A	1-2	Boulders

RANTO/MIKS RIGA

CLUB DIRECTORY

Ranto/Miks Riga
Kalpaka bulv. 10-26
1010 Riga
tel - (9) 554870
fax - 2585860
Year of Formation - 1994
President - Grant Asriyants
Secretary - Dmitry Karbovnichy
Coach - Grant Asriyants; Dmitry Karbovnichy
Stadium - Keizarmezhs (2,000)

APPEARANCES 1998

	P	Ap	(s)	Gls
Dainis ALKSNIS	M	8		
Artur ASRIYANTS	M		(4)	
Vladimir BOGDANOV	D	21		
Pavel DOROSHEV	G	11	(1)	
Valery FEOKTISTOV	D		(1)	
Vadim GORDEYEV	M		(8)	
Yevgeny GORYACHILOV	A	25		4
Dmitry KHOROLSKY	D	28		
Anatoly KLYUYEV	D	15	(5)	
Alexander KOZLOV	M	23		5
Andrey LEVCHENKO	A	7	(9)	
Genady LEVCHENKO	M	17	(4)	1
Vladimir LEVCHENKO	M	22		3
Alexander LOBANYOV	M	19	(1)	4
Alexander LOZBINYOV	G	16		
Vladimir LUKKONEN	G	1	(4)	
Andrey MAKSIMOV	A	12	(12)	5
Vitaly PARMALIS	M	21		3
Eduard POLYAKHOV	A	2	(2)	
Alexander RUDENKO	M		(1)	
Yurgis SAMSONOV	M	25		
Konstantin SUKHAREV	D	6		
Yevgeny VASYUKOV	D	28		
Alexey VLADIMIROV	M	1	(1)	

LEAGUE RESULTS 1998

18/04/98	Skonto Riga	H	3-3	Kozlov 2 (1p), Goryachilov
25/04/98	FK Valmiera	H	0-0	
03/05/98	FK Rezekne	A	2-2	Goryachilov, Maksimov
12/05/98	FK Ventspils	H	0-1	
20/05/98	Daugava Riga	A	0-3	
24/05/98	Metalurgs Liepaya	H	3-4	Levchenko V., Parmalis 2
29/05/98	Dinaburg Daugavpils	A	1-6	Maksimov
07/06/98	Skonto Riga	A	0-9	
11/06/98	FK Valmiera	A	0-4	
17/06/98	FK Rezekne	H	1-3	Lobanyov
21/06/98	FK Ventspils	H	0-9	
29/06/98	Daugava Riga	H	2-1	Goryachilov, Lobanyov
05/07/98	Metalurgs Liepaya	A	0-7	
16/07/98	Dinaburg Daugavpils	H	0-6	
25/07/98	Skonto Riga	H	2-7	Kozlov 2 (2p)
01/08/98	FK Valmiera	H	0-3	•
06/08/98	FK Rezekne	A	2-1	Maksimov 2
16/08/98	FK Ventspils	H	1-5	Lobanyov
24/08/98	Daugava Riga	A	0-2	
31/08/98	Metalurgs Liepaya	H	1-6	Kozlov (p)
12/09/98	Dinaburg Daugavpils	A	1-5	Maksimov
20/09/98	Skonto Riga	A	0-4	
26/09/98	FK Valmiera	A	0-1	
03/10/98	FK Rezekne	H	0-0	
18/10/98	FK Ventspils	A	2-3	Levchenko G. (p), Levchenko V.
24/10/98	Daugava Riga	H	1-1	Goryachilov
31/10/98	Metalurgs Liepaya	A	1-5	Levchenko V.
07/11/98	Dinaburg Daugavpils	H	2-5	Lobanyov (p), Parmalis

FK REZEKNE

CLUB DIRECTORY

FK Rezekne
18. Novembra str. 39
4600 Rezekne
tel - (46) 22055
fax - (46) 24052
Year of Formation - 1992
President - Vasily Alekseyev
Secretary - Peteris Tukishs
Coach - Alexander Dorofeyev
Stadium - Town Stadium (3,000)

APPEARANCES 1998

		P	Ap	(s)	Gls
Zhanis	ARMANIS	D	5	(2)	
Vadim	BEKERIS	M	8	(1)	
Vladislav	BELOV	M	9	(1)	
Aigars	BONDARS	M		(1)	
Yury	BOROVSKY	A	1	(2)	
Andrey	CHERNISHOV	D	17	(5)	
Igor	DERBAKOV	M	16	(8)	1
Vadim	FYODOROV	G	19	(1)	
Andris	GRUZDE	G	9		
Alexander	IVANOV	D	27		
Valery	KIRILLOV	M	26		1
Sergey	KRIKUNOV	D	10		
Alexander	KUCHEROV	D		(6)	
Dainis	LAIZANS	D	13	(7)	
Maris	LESCHINSKY	A		(3)	
Zhanis	LESCHINSKY	M	4	(3)	
Mark	LIVSHITS	A		(1)	
Ilmars	LOGINS	D	8	(3)	
Victor	MIVRINIEKS	M	19	(3)	1
Aivars	POZNYAK	A	26	(1)	4
Alexander	PUSHKASH	A		(4)	
Eduard	PUTRA	M	3	(5)	
Igor	RASTOPCHIN	M	5	(5)	
Alen	SHEIN	A	13	(10)	5
Andris	SHMAUKSTELIS	D	20	(3)	1
Alexey	SVIRIDENKOV	M	7		
Alexey	VISHNYAKOV	D		(1)	
Vitaly	VOSKANS	M	25		9
Alexey	YEGOROV	D	18	(1)	

LEAGUE RESULTS 1998

18/04/98	Metalurgs Liepaya	H	2-3	Voskans (p), Mivrinieks
25/04/98	Dinaburg Daugavpils	A	0-0	
03/05/98	Ranto/Miks Riga	H	2-2	Shein 2
12/05/98	FK Valmiera	A	0-3	
20/05/98	Skonto Riga	A	0-7	
24/05/98	FK Ventspils	H	1-4	Voskans (p)
29/05/98	Daugava Riga	A	2-8	Voskans 2 (1p)
07/06/98	Metalurgs Liepaya	A	0-4	
11/06/98	Dinaburg Daugavpils	H	0-1	
17/06/98	Ranto/Miks Riga	A	3-1	Shein, Voskans (p), Poznyak
21/06/98	FK Valmiera	H	1-2	Voskans (p)
28/06/98	Skonto Riga	H	0-2	
02/07/98	FK Ventspils	A	1-4	Poznyak
16/07/98	Daugava Riga	H	1-2	Shmaukstelis
25/07/98	Metalurgs Liepaya	H	1-2	Shein
02/08/98	Dinaburg Daugavpils	A	1-2	Kirillov
06/08/98	Ranto/Miks Riga	H	1-2	Poznyak
16/08/98	FK Valmiera	A	0-0	
22/08/98	Skonto Riga	A	0-1	
30/08/98	FK Ventspils	H	0-3	
12/09/98	Daugava Riga	A	1-1	Poznyak
21/09/98	Metalurgs Liepaya	A	0-7	
26/09/98	Dinaburg Daugavpils	H	2-4	Voskans, Derbakov
03/10/98	Ranto/Miks Riga	A	0-0	
18/10/98	FK Valmiera	H	0-5	
25/10/98	Skonto Riga	H	1-6	Voskans
31/10/98	FK Ventspils	A	0-3	
07/11/98	Daugava Riga	H	2-1	Shein, Voskans (p)

SKONTO RIGA

CLUB DIRECTORY

Skonto Riga
Elizabetes str. 75
1050 Riga
tel - 7282669
fax - 7284390
Year of Formation - 1991
President - Guntis Indricksons
Secretary - Genady Karavayev
Coach - Alexander Starkov
Stadium - Daugava (5,800)

MAJOR HONOURS
League Championship - (7)
1992, 1993, 1994, 1995, 1996, 1997, 1998.
Domestic Cup - (4) 1992, 1995, 1997, 1998.

APPEARANCES 1998

	P	Ap	(s)	Gls
Nickolay APILAT (UKR)	A		(2)	
Vitaly ASTAFYEV	M	23		7
Vladimir BABICHEV	M	18	(1)	10
Oleg BLAGONADEZHDIN	M		(2)	
Imants BLEIDELIS	M	24		8
David GVARAMADZE (GEO)	G	6		
Yevgeny ILOVAISKY	D		(2)	
Oleg KARAVAYEV	G	9		
Vladimir KOLESNICHENKO	A		(1)	
Alexander KOLINKO	G	5		
Yury LAIZANS	D	25	(1)	1
Vsevolod LIDAKS	D	6	(6)	1
Valentin LOBANYOV	D	22		1
Vladimir MELNIK (UKR)	M	5	(13)	1
Mikhail MIKHOLAP	A	24	(1)	20
Ilya NOVIKOV	M	3	(6)	3
Marian PAKHAR	A	24	(2)	19
Andrey PIEDELS	G	8		
Alexander PINDEYEV (UKR)	A	10	(5)	5
Alexander REKHVIASHVILI (GEO)	M	12	(5)	1
Vitas RIMKUS	A	8	(7)	11
Vitaly ROZGON (UKR)	D		(1)	
Andrey RUBINS	M	11	(8)	1
Levan SILAGADZE (GEO)	D	15		1
Sergey SOLOVYEV (RUS)	A	2	(7)	4
Igor N. STEPANOV	D	20	(4)	
Andreyus TERESHKINAS (LIT)	D	7		2
Mamuka TSERETELI (GEO)	D	8	(1)	1
Mikhail ZEMLINSKY	D	13		

LEAGUE RESULTS 1998

18/04/98	Ranto/Miks Riga	A	3-3	Mikholap 2, Pindeyev
25/04/98	Daugava Riga	H	2-3	Pindeyev, Mikholap
03/05/98	FK Valmiera	A	4-1	Mikholap, Pakhar, Solovyev 2
12/05/98	Metalurgs Liepaya	H	1-0	Bleidelis
20/05/98	FK Rezekne	H	7-0	Rubins, Mikholap 3, Pindeyev,
				Silagadze, Tsereteli
25/05/98	Dinaburg Daugavpils	H	0-2	
29/05/98	FK Ventspils	A	1-2	Babichev
07/06/98	Ranto/Miks Riga	H	9-0	Bleidelis 3, Pakhar 2, Astafyev,
				Babichev 2, Laizans
11/06/98	Daugava Riga	A	5-3	Babichev 2, Astafyev, Pakhar (p),
				Bleidelis
16/06/98	FK Valmiera	A	5-1	Bleidelis, Babichev, Mikholap,
				Pakhar 2
21/06/98	Metalurgs Liepaya	A	0-0	
28/06/98	FK Rezekne	A	2-0	Pindeyev 2
01/07/98	Dinaburg Daugavpils	A	1-0	Babichev
15/07/98	FK Ventspils	H	1-0	Astafyev
25/07/98	Ranto/Miks Riga	A	7-2	Mikholap 2 (1p), Rimkus 3,
				Pakhar, Novikov
02/08/98	Daugava Riga	H	3-0	Lobanyov, Rekhviashvili, Rimkus
06/08/98	FK Valmiera	H	4-0	Pakhar, Novikov 2, Babichev
22/08/98	FK Rezekne	H	1-0	Solovyev
30/08/98	Dinaburg Daugavpils	H	2-1	Babichev, Pakhar (p)
11/09/98	FK Ventspils	A	3-2	Mikholap, og (Stradinsh),
				Tereshkinas
20/09/98	Ranto/Miks Riga	H	4-0	Mikholap, Rimkus 2, Pakhar (p)
25/09/98	Daugava Riga	A	2-1	Astafyev, Tereshkinas
04/10/98	FK Valmiera	H	15-2	Pakhar 5 (1p), Mikholap 5,
				Babichev, Bleidelis, Solovyev,
				Astafyev, Rimkus
18/10/98	Metalurgs Liepaya	A	1-1	Bleidelis
25/10/98	FK Rezekne	A	6-1	Pakhar 2 (1p), Rimkus, Astafyev,
				Mikholap 2
28/10/98	Metalurgs Liepaya	H	1-1	Mikholap
31/10/98	Dinaburg Daugavpils	A	4-1	Rimkus, Melnik, Pakhar 2 (1p)
07/11/98	FK Ventspils	H	4-0	Rimkus 2, Astafyev, Lidaks

FK VALMIERA

CLUB DIRECTORY

FK Valmiera
Stacijas str. 22
4201 Valmiera
tel - (42) 21468/21577/28794/24528
fax - (7) 894216
Year of Formation - 1995
President - Imants Saulitis
Secretary - Valery Barkov
Coach - Vladimir Serbin
Stadium - J. Dalinsha Stadium (2,000)

APPEARANCES 1998

		P	Ap	(s)	Gls
Alexander ATAMAN	M	24	(3)	3	
Victor BASKAKOV	D	19			
Gatis ERGLIS	D	27		2	
Igor GARNIER	D	9	(5)	1	
Alexander GLAZOV	D	5			
Erik GRIGYAN	G	27	(1)		
Yury IDIONOV	M	1	(16)	2	
Boris KOROTKEVICH	A	22	(2)	6	
Rolands KRAGLIKS	D	25	(2)	1	
Andrey KRASOVSKY	M	1	(11)		
Leons MEDNIS	D		(1)		
Agnis MEZHGAILIS	M	7	(8)	2	
Maris MILLERS	D		(1)		
Alexey PASHIN	D	11	(2)		
Dzintars SAVALNIEKS	M	28		4	
Vitaly SHANDOV	G	1	(1)		
Roman SIDOROV	M	21	(1)	3	
Santis SILINSH	M		(1)		
Victor TERENTYEV	M	21	(3)	3	
Andrey TROITSKY	M	25		3	
Vyacheslav ZHEVNEROVICH	A	16	(1)	3	
Janis ZUYEV	A	1	(10)	1	
Modris ZUYEV	A	17	(4)	4	

LEAGUE RESULTS 1998

18/04/98	Dinaburg Daugavpils	H	0-2	
25/04/98	Ranto/Miks Riga	A	0-0	
03/05/98	Skonto Riga	H	1-4	Korotkevich
12/05/98	FK Rezekne	H	3-0	Korotkevich, Mezhgailis, Sidorov
20/05/98	FK Ventspils	A	3-0	Terentyev, Ataman, Sidorov
24/05/98	Daugava Riga	H	2-2	Korotkevich (p), Zhevnerovich
29/05/98	Metalurgs Liepaya	A	1-4	Ataman
07/06/98	Dinaburg Daugavpils	A	1-6	Ataman
11/06/98	Ranto/Miks Riga	H	4-0	Korotkevich (p), Kragliks, Savalnieks (p), Zhevnerovich
16/06/98	Skonto Riga	H	1-5	Zhevnerovich
21/06/98	FK Rezekne	A	2-1	Savalnieks, Idionov
28/06/98	FK Ventspils	H	0-0	
05/07/98	Daugava Riga	A	2-4	og (Sprogis), Sidorov
15/07/98	Metalurgs Liepaya	H	2-1	Erglis (p), Terentyev
23/07/98	Dinaburg Daugavpils	H	1-1	Savalnieks
01/08/98	Ranto/Miks Riga	A	3-0	Troitsky, Korotkevich, Idionov
06/08/98	Skonto Riga	A	0-4	
16/08/98	FK Rezekne	H	0-0	
23/08/98	FK Ventspils	A	0-3	
30/08/98	Daugava Riga	H	2-1	Erglis (p), Zuyev M.
12/09/98	Metalurgs Liepaya	A	1-2	Savalnieks
20/09/98	Dinaburg Daugavpils	A	0-0	
26/09/98	Ranto/Miks Riga	H	1-0	Garnier
04/10/98	Skonto Riga	A	2-15	Troitsky, Zuyev M.
18/10/98	FK Rezekne	A	5-0	Zuyev M. 2, Terentyev, Troitsky, Korotkevich
25/10/98	FK Ventspils	H	0-3	
31/10/98	Daugava Riga	A	0-0	
07/11/98	Metalurgs Liepaya	H	2-1	Mezhgailis, Zuyev J.

FK VENTSPILS

FK Ventspils
Kuldigas str. 25a
3602 Ventspils
tel - (36) 67079
fax - (36) 80380
Year of Formation - 1997
President - Oleg Stepanov
Secretary - Mikhail Kopcha
Coach - Sergey Borovsky; Saulius Tsekanavichius
Stadium - Daugava Ventspils (2,000)

	P	Ap	(s)	Gls
Mikhail BESCHASTNIKH (RUS)	A	12	(1)	2
Valery BOROVKOV	M	6	(5)	
Sergey DIGULYOV	G	16		
Armaz DZHELADZE (GEO)	A	16	(5)	8
Konstantin GENICH (RUS)	A	2	(12)	3
David GOGOLADZE (GEO)	A	8	(10)	5
Iosif GRISHIKASHVILI (GEO)	G	8		
Sergey IVANOV	M	11	(1)	1
Sabir KHAMZIN (RUS)	A	24	(2)	9
Edgar KVASHNIN	D	13	(2)	
Andrey LAPSA	D	22	(2)	1
Victor LUKASHEVICH	D	20		1
Tamaz PERTIYA (GEO)	A	11	(3)	3
Nickolay POLYAKOV	M	26	(1)	3
Gintaras RIMKUS (LIT)	M	21	(2)	6
Vitaly RYABININ	A	1	(9)	5
Dmitry SHKURATOV (BLS)	M	17	(3)	1
Igor V. STEPANOV	M	17	(5)	3
Alexander STRADINSH	D	27		
Andrey VANIN	G	4		
Victor VILMANIS	D	1	(6)	2
Victor VORONKOV (RUS)	M	14	(8)	3
Alexander ZHIZHMANOV	D	11	(1)	

18/04/98	Daugava Riga	A	1-1	Pertiya
25/04/98	Metalurgs Liepaya	A	0-0	
03/05/98	Dinaburg Daugavpils	A	1-1	Rimkus
12/05/98	Ranto/Miks Riga	A	1-0	Rimkus
20/05/98	FK Valmiera	H	0-3	
24/05/98	FK Rezekne	A	4-1	Khamzin (p), Pertiya (p), Gogoladze, Genich
29/05/98	Skonto Riga	H	2-1	Polyakov 2
07/06/98	Daugava Riga	H	1-0	Stepanov
11/06/98	Metalurgs Liepaya	H	0-1	
16/06/98	Dinaburg Daugavpils	H	0-0	
21/06/98	Ranto/Miks Riga	H	9-0	Khamzin 3, Rimkus, Gogoladze, Pertiya, Genich, Stepanov, Polyakov
28/06/98	FK Valmiera	A	0-0	
02/07/98	FK Rezekne	H	4-1	Khamzin, Genich, Gogoladze, Voronkov
10/07/98	Daugava Riga	H	3-0	Voronkov, Dzheladze 2
15/07/98	Skonto Riga	A	0-1	
02/08/98	Metalurgs Liepaya	A	0-1	
06/08/98	Dinaburg Daugavpils	H	1-1	Ryabinin
16/08/98	Ranto/Miks Riga	A	5-1	Lukashevich, Khamzin, Ryabinin, Gogoladze, Vilmanis
23/08/98	FK Valmiera	H	3-0	Gogoladze, Ryabinin, Dzheladze
30/08/98	FK Rezekne	A	3-0	Khamzin (p), Rimkus, Ryabinin
11/09/98	Skonto Riga	H	2-3	Khamzin 2
19/09/98	Daugava Riga	A	2-1	Rimkus, Dzheladze
25/09/98	Metalurgs Liepaya	H	2-0	Dzheladze, Ryabinin
04/10/98	Dinaburg Daugavpils	A	3-0	Beschastnikh 2, Dzheladze
18/10/98	Ranto/Miks Riga	H	3-2	Shkuratov, Ivanov, Lapsa
25/10/98	FK Valmiera	A	3-0	Rimkus, Dzheladze, Vilmanis
31/10/98	FK Rezekne	H	3-0	Dzheladze, Stepanov, Voronkov (p)
07/11/98	Skonto Riga	A	0-4	

PROMOTED CLUB

SECOND DIVISION FINAL TABLE 1998

		Pd	W	D	L	F	A	Pt	GD
1	**Police FK Riga**	**21**	**13**	**4**	**4**	**67**	**24**	**43**	**+43**
2	Yauniba Daugavpils	21	11	4	6	58	30	37	+28
3	Skonto/metals-Rinar Riga	21	10	4	7	32	26	34	+6
4	Tselinieks Ilukste	21	9	6	6	32	28	33	+4
5	Auda Riga	21	8	6	7	36	38	30	-2
6	Universitate Riga	21	7	4	10	43	47	25	-4
7	OFRISS Riga	21	5	8	8	26	43	17	-17
8	FK Saldus	21	1	4	16	24	82	7	-58

N.B. OFRISS Riga deducted 6pts.

CLUB DIRECTORY

Police FK Riga
Gauyas Str. 17/19
1026 Riga
tel - (9) 544809
fax - 7371763
Year of Formation - 1996
President - Roman Potanin
Coach - Vladimir Zhuk
Stadium - Daugava (5,800)

LIECHTENSTEIN

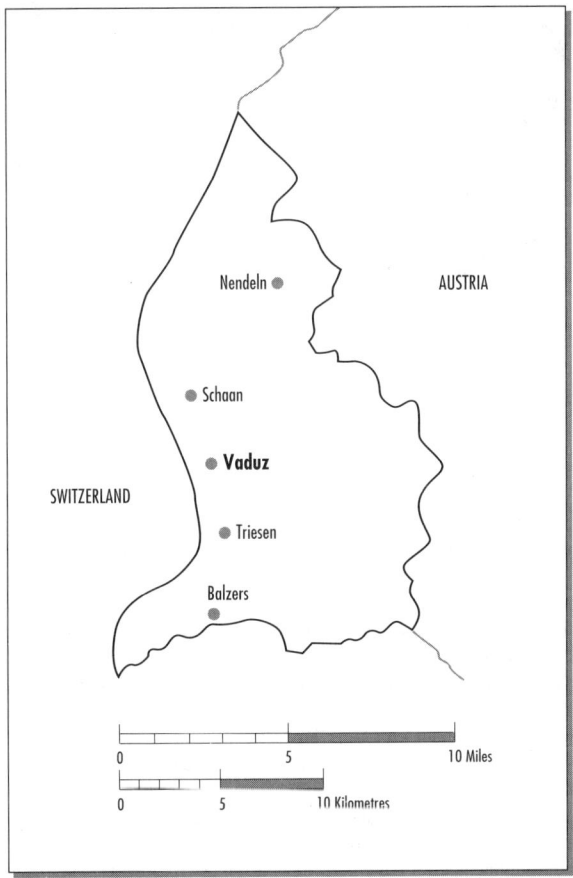

VADUZ TRIUMPH IN CUP FINAL THRILLER

History made as Liechtenstein record first win

FEDERATION DIRECTORY

Liechtensteiner Fussball-Verband
Malbuner Haus, Altenbach 11, Postfach 165, 9490 Vaduz

tel - 2374747   Year of Formation - 1933
fax - 2374748   President - Otto Biedermann
                              Secretary - Markus Schaper

Stadium - Rheinpark, Vaduz (3,548)

October 10, 1998 will go down in the annals of Liechteinstein football. It was the date of the national team's first-ever victory. And, what's more, it came in a competitive international - a Euro 2000 qualifier against Azerbaijan.

The champagne flowed as Liechtenstein's footballers celebrated a unique experience. Two goals in three minutes early in the second half - the first from the penalty spot by the country's only full-time professional footballer, FC Basel striker Mario Frick, the second from midfielder Martin Telser (three days before his 20th birthday), pointed Liechtenstein towards the promised land. Although the Azerbaijanis pulled a goal back soon afterwards, the home side held on for the win that gave them three very welcome European Championship points.

In two previous qualifying competitions - for Euro '96 and France '98 - the best that the team had been able to muster was one point from a goalless draw at home to the Republic of Ireland in June 1995. As the final whistle sounded and the players held their arms aloft in triumph, they were given a standing ovation from the crowd of 1,450.

It was a very different scene from four days earlier when Liechtenstein had trooped off the same field dejected after losing 4-0 against Slovakia. That game had been the first competitive international staged in the country's brand-new Rheinpark stadium - a small but modern and colourful arena which had taken a little over a year to construct and, unlike the national team's former home, the Sportpark in Eschen/Mauren, conformed fully with UEFA and FIFA requirements.

To baptise the new stadium with a victory was a dream come true, but although Ralf Loose and his players were able to dine out on that triumph for the best part of the next six months, it was unfortunately back to business as usual the following spring as the team went down to four heavy defeats in quick succession, conceding a total of 22 goals and scoring

none. It was then that youngster Peter Jehle, who had been promoted from the national Under-18 side and made his début in the home match with Azerbaijan, discovered what keeping goal for Liechtenstein was all about. He had a particularly torrid time in the last game of the season, away to Portugal, when he had to pick the ball out of his net no fewer than eight times. But despite all that the young 'keeper looked to be the pick of the new players introduced to the team by new coach Ralf Loose, with other teenagers such as Christof Ritter and Michael Stocklasa not far behind. All of Liechtenstein's youngsters have the handicap of going straight from junior to senior level because Liechtenstein does not have a national Under-21 team.

In addition to staging national team matches, the Rheinpark is also the new home of FC Vaduz, Liechtenstein's leading club side. And it is also the venue for the Liechtenstein Cup final, the only domestic match of any real significance that takes place in the Principality every year.

Consequently, FC Vaduz enjoyed home advantage when they faced FC Balzers in the 1999 Cup final. The two most decorated teams in the history of the competition were to produce a riveting spectacle which was lapped up by the 2,100 spectators, most of them supporting the trophy-holders Vaduz. The bonus prize for victory was, as ever, a place in Europe, although for the first time it was in the UEFA Cup rather than the now-defunct Cup-winners' Cup.

NATIONAL TEAM RESULTS 98/99

02/09/98	Romania (ECQ)	A	Bucharest	0-7	
10/10/98	Slovakia (ECQ)	H	Vaduz	0-4	
14/10/98	Azerbaijan (ECQ)	H	Vaduz	2-1	Frick M. (47p), Telser M. (49)
27/03/99	Hungary (ECQ)	A	Budapest	0-5	
31/03/99	Portugal (ECQ)	H	Vaduz	0-5	
05/06/99	Azerbaijan (ECQ)	A	Baku	0-4	
09/06/99	Portugal (ECQ)	A	Coimbra	0-8	

NATIONAL TEAM APPEARANCES 98/99

Coach - Ralf LOOSE	ROM	SVK	AZB	HUN	POR	AZB	POR	Cps	Gls
Martin OEHRY (11/10/64) - FC Rotweiss Rankweil (AUT)	G	G						8	-
Harry ZECH (25/02/69) - FC Balzers	D	D	D			D	D	22	1
Patrik HEFTI (19/11/69) - FC Vaduz	D	D76		s46				19	-
Thomas HANSELMANN (21/04/76) - FC Balzers	D	D		D46	D84			22	-
Christof RITTER (18/01/81) - FC Schaan	D	D	D	D	D	D	D	8	-
Hansjörg LINGG (01/11/71) - FC Schaan	M62	s76	M	M	M	M	s52	8	-
Michael STOCKLASA (02/12/80) - FC Vaduz	M	M	M	M	M65	M74	M66	8	-
Ralf OEHRI (26/10/76) - FC Rapperswil (SUI)	M	M46						10	-
Martin TELSER (16/10/78) - FC Balzers	M89	M	M	M	M	M	M75	14	1
Modesto HAAS (19/03/63) - FC Triesenberg	A63	A33						3	-
Thomas BECK (21/02/78) - FC Schaan	A		A74			s46	A	4	-
Marco BÜCHEL (30/08/79) - FC Balzers	s62		s74				s75	4	-
Martin STOCKLASA (29/05/79) - FC Vaduz	s63	s33	D	D	D	D		14	-
Marco ENDER (16/06/79) - FC USV Eschen-Mauren	s89							1	-
Daniel HASLER (18/05/74) - FC Vaduz		D	D	D	D	D	D	28	1
Mario FRICK (07/09/74) - FC Basel (SUI)		A	A	A	A			23	2
Jürgen OSPELT (16/01/74) - FC Vaduz		s46	s67	s78	s84		M	20	-
Peter JEHLE		G	G	G	G	G		5	-
Herbert BICKER (01/11/75) - FC Schaan		M67			M59	M		9	-
Albert WOHLWEND (06/11/79) - FC USV Eschen-Mauren				M	M82	s74	M	5	-
Matthias BECK				A78	s65	s59		3	-
Christoph FRICK (28/08/74) - FC Balzers					M	M		15	-
Patrick BURGMAIER					s82		s66	2	-
Harald BENZ (12/08/72) - FC Balzers						A46		1	-
Daniel TELSER (24/01/70) - FC Balzers							D52	23	-

Vaduz took a quick lead through international Martin Stocklasa but by half-time they were 2-1 down. But cometh the hour, cometh the man, and for the second year running Vaduz's specialist Cup goalscorer Daniele Polverino became their big-match hero. He had struck four times in the 1998 final and now he scored both the equaliser and the winner as Vaduz came from behind in the last 18 minutes to take the trophy for the 28th time (in 54 attempts).

EUROPEAN CUPS 98/99

CUP WINNERS' CUP
● FC VADUZ
Qualifying round HELSINGBORGS IF (SWE)
H 0-2
    Sieber; Keel, Bossi, Weber, Stocklasa, Stilz, Müller, Hasler D., Polverino (Hasler H. 89), Alge, Hafner (Schmid 80).
A 0-3
    Sieber; Weber (Ospelt 85), Bossi, Stocklasa, Keel, Erdogan, Müller, Stilz, Polverino, Alge, Hafner.

INTERNATIONAL HONOURS

None

Both coaches, Alfons Tobler of Vaduz and Manfred Frick of Balzers, were in agreement afterwards that it had been a classic final, but it was the former who was smiling as he anticipated taking the club into Europe for the second season in a row. His first visit, the previous summer, had seen Vaduz put up two reasonably satisfactory displays against Helsingborg of Sweden, but there was never any chance that Vaduz would repeat the exploit of their previous European campaign, when they actually won their qualifying tie and had the pleasure of inviting the mighty Paris Saint-Germain to the Liechtenstein capital.

DOMESTIC CUP 98/99

FINAL
13/05/99, Vaduz
FC VADUZ 3 Stocklasa (9), Polverino (72, 82)
FC BALZERS 2 Frick D. (20), Riederer (44)
referee - Stadler
FC VADUZ - Sieber; Bossi, Ospelt, Keel (Erdogan 88), Stocklasa, Kubli, Hasler, Alge, Stilz, Hafner (Heinzle 90), Schmid (Polverino 46).
FC BALZERS - Nüesch; Zech, Telser D., Stöber, Hanselmann (Risch 73), Büchel (Schädler 63), Frick C., Telser M., Benz, Riederer, Frick D.

LITHUANIA

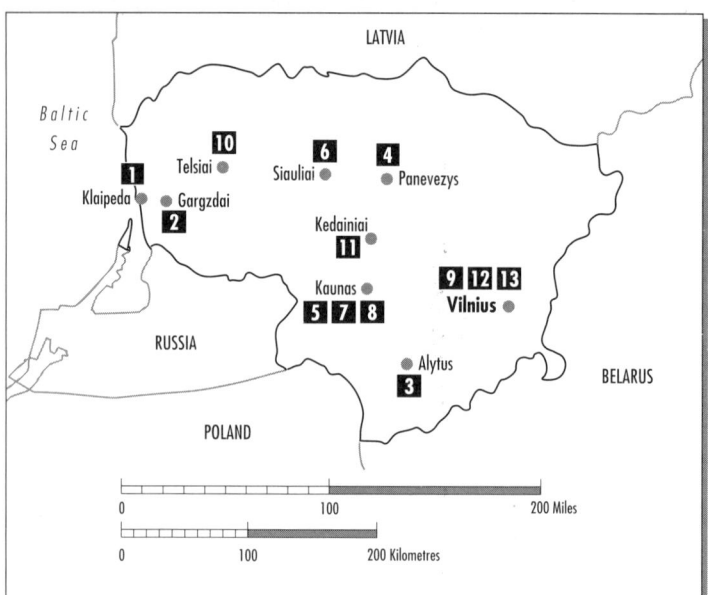

CHANGE OF CALENDAR FOR LEAGUE

Zalgiris ride luck to triumph at last

FEDERATION DIRECTORY

Lietuvos Futbolo Federacija
Seimyniskiu 15, 2051 Vilnius

tel - (2) 723654   Year of Formation - 1922
fax - (2) 723651   President - Vytautas Dirmeikis
                          Secretary - Robertas Mackevicius

Stadium - Zalgiris, Vilnius (13,000)

At last Zalgiris Vilnius can justifiably refer to themselves once again as the top club in Lithuania. After seven barren years the team from the capital finally recaptured the championship title. But it was a triumph stained with an indelible mark of controversy.

Zalgiris eventually finished on top of the final table after a season-long see-saw battle with two other clubs, Kareda Siauliai and FBK Kaunas. The neutrals agreed that they were worthy winners and had the most promising and talented squad of the three contenders, but the fact remained that they would not have been proclaimed champions but for a crucial administrative error made by their opponents Ekranas Panevezys in a decisive match three rounds from the end.

Until that game Zalgiris had been unbeaten, but they were showing distinct signs of fatigue. Two successive draws, followed by a narrow win against lowly Kauno Jegeriai, had seen them fall behind defending champions

Kareda in the title race. And when they went to Panevezys and lost, 0-1, it looked as if the club would end yet another season as also-rans. But it was then that they got lucky. Incredibly lucky. An eagle-eyed league administrator spotted that Ekranas had fielded an ineligible player. Young striker Deividas Cesnauskis should not have played because he had two yellow cards to his name. No matter that the first of them had been picked up eight months earlier in a Third Division match for Ekranas reserves. Rules were rules. He had played while under suspension, therefore Ekranas had to forfeit the match.

It was decided by the disciplinary commission that while Zalgiris would pocket the three points, there would be no imaginary goals added to their total. Even so, it was quite a reprieve, especially as their next match, just four days later, was now effectively a title-decider at home to Kareda. Zalgiris had been found wanting in these do-or-die matches before, but on this occasion, perhaps buoyed by their immense good fortune, they got the win they needed, courtesy of a single goal from striker Dainius Saulenas, who had not previously scored in eight games.

Having transformed a potential five-point deficit into a one-point lead within the space of a few days, Zalgiris now needed only to win their final game, at home to Dainava Alytus, to claim that long-awaited title. The task could not have been more straightforward. To the joy of their fans, they rattled in five goals without reply. Kareda and Kaunas both did what

LEAGUE CHAMPIONSHIP RESULTS 98/99

		1	2	3	4	5	6	7	8	9	10	11	12	13
1	Atlantas Klaipeda		0-1	1-3	1-1	3-1	0-3	1-2	7-1	3-1		0-1	1-2	2-0
2	Banga Gargzdai	0-0		2-0	0-2	0-0	1-2	2-1	1-2	2-0	3-1	2-1	1-3	1-1
3	Dainava Alytus	2-1	0-0		0-5	1-2	0-2	0-1	0-1	2-0		2-3	1-3	2-1
4	Ekranas Panevezys	0-0	4-0	3-1		2-0	2-2	1-2	1-0	2-1		2-2	+++	4-0
5	Inkaras Kaunas	2-1	2-0	2-1	0-3		1-3	0-2	0-0	2-0	5-1	3-0	0-2	3-0
6	Kareda Siauliai	6-0	5-1	3-0	1-1	2-1		2-0	4-0	7-0	9-0	2-0	0-0	3-1
7	FBK Kaunas	1-0	1-0	12-0	2-1	4-2	1-1		3-0	2-0		3-0	1-1	5-1
8	Kauno Jegeriai	1-3	0-0	2-3	1-2	0-4	1-2	0-5		3-1	3-0	2-1	0-1	0-2
9	Lokomotyvas Vilnius	1-5	0-1	0-2	0-1	0-1	0-1	1-2	1-0		1-0	0-1	0-1	0-3
10	Mastis Telsiai	0-1		0-1	0-8		0-1						0-6	2-1
11	Nevezis Kedainiai	0-2	1-0	0-1	1-0	0-0	0-3	0-2	2-1	1-2	1-0		1-1	0-0
12	Zalgiris Vilnius	2-0	3-0	5-0	3-0	1-1	1-0	1-1	3-0	5-1		6-0		8-0
13	Zalgiris II Vilnius	2-2	1-0	4-2	3-0	1-2	0-4	0-3	2-4	0-2		2-1	0-10	

+++ - match void; awarded as away win.

LEAGUE CHAMPIONSHIP FINAL TABLE 98/99

			Home				Away					Total						
		P	W	D	L	F	A	W	D	L	F	A	W	D	L	F	A	P	GD
1	Zalgiris Vilnius	23	9	2	0	38	3	9	3	0	30	5	18	5	0	68	8	59	+60
2	Kareda Siauliai	23	10	4	0	44	4	8	2	1	23	7	18	4	1	67	11	58	+56
3	FBK Kaunas	23	9	2	0	35	6	9	1	2	22	8	18	3	2	57	14	57	+43
4	Ekranas Panevezys	23	6	3	2	21	8	6	2	4	24	12	12	5	6	45	20	41	+25
5	Inkaras Kaunas	23	7	1	4	20	13	4	3	4	14	14	11	4	8	34	27	37	+7
6	Atlantas Klaipeda	23	4	1	6	19	16	4	3	5	15	17	8	4	11	34	33	28	+1
7	Banga Gargzdai	23	5	3	4	15	13	2	2	7	3	17	7	5	11	18	30	26	-12
8	Nevezis Kedainiai	23	4	3	5	7	12	3	1	7	10	24	7	4	12	17	36	25	-19
9	Dainava Alytus	23	3	1	7	10	19	5	0	7	14	34	8	1	14	24	53	25	-29
10	Zalgiris II Vilnius	23	4	1	6	15	30	2	2	8	10	30	6	3	14	25	60	21	-35
11	Kauno Jegeriai	23	3	1	8	13	24	3	1	7	9	24	6	2	15	22	48	20	-26
12	Lokomotyvas Vilnius	23	2	0	10	4	18	2	0	9	8	29	4	0	19	12	47	12	-35
13	Mastis Telsiai	12	1	0	5	2	18	0	0	6	2	22	1	0	11	4	40	3	-36

N.B. Panerys Vilnius withdrew after six matches - all of their matches annulled; Mastis Telsiai withdrew after 12 matches - all of their subsequent matches annulled.
Zalgiris II Vilnius and Kauno Jegeriai relegated as reserve teams of Zalgiris Vilnius and FBK Kaunas respectively.

they had to do by winning their games, but it was to no avail. A mere two points separated the top three, but up on top were Zalgiris. Seven years of pain and hurt were finally over.

Kareda and Kaunas both had the opportunity to bounce back from their disappointment four days later when they came face to face in the Cup final. Kareda had annihilated Zalgiris in the semi-finals, winning 3-0 at home and 4-0 away, and they had also beaten Kaunas 2-0 in the league, so they were the clear pre-match favourites. However, Kaunas, who had never won a major honour before, fought gamely for 90 minutes and took the match into extra-time before finally buckling under the pressure. Kareda scored three times in the extra half-hour to claim the Cup, thus ensuring that while Kaunas ended up as Cup-final losers for the second season running, they collected a major prize for the fourth year in a row.

In European terms, there was no advantage in winning the Cup, as both finalists were already entitled to a place in the qualifying round of the 1999/2000 UEFA Cup, with Zalgiris of course qualifying for the Champions' League. The situation at the bottom of the table, however, was much less clear-cut.

The 1998/99 campaign had begun with a 14-team top division - a reduction of two from the season before - but by halfway it was down to just 12. Panerys Vilnius withdrew after six matches, all of which were consequently annulled, and Mastis Telsiai stood down during the winter break, with the results from their matches being allowed to stand.

With the league deciding to switch to a new spring-autumn cycle in 2000, a transitionary championship was proposed for the autumn of 1999. This was to contain just ten teams, so in theory the club which finished in 12th and last place, Lokomotyvas Vilnius, should have been certainties for relegation. However, a new rule stated that reserve teams would no longer be permitted to compete in the top division, so Zalgiris II Vilnius and Kauno Jegeriai (the 'second' team of FBK Kaunas) - the sides placed, respectively, 10th and 11th

TOP SCORERS

14	Arturas FOMENKA (Kareda Siauliai)
13	Valdas TRAKYS (FBK Kaunas)
12	Igoris MORINAS (Zalgiris Vilnius)
11	Igoris STESKO (Zalgiris Vilnius)
10	Aivaras LAURISAS (FBK Kaunas)
9	Vidas KAUSPADAS (Inkaras Kaunas)
	Robertas POSKUS (Atlantas Klaipeda/ Kareda Siauliai)
	Darius MACIULEVICIUS (Kareda Siauliai)
8	Egidijus VARNAS (Ekranas Panevezys)
	Deimantas BICKA (Kareda Siauliai)
	Robertas ZALYS (Nevezis Kedainiai)
	Saulius LAIBINIS (Dainava Alytus)
	Andrius UPSTAS (Inkaras Kaunas)
	Dainius SAULENAS (Zalgiris Vilnius)
	Arturas STESKO (Zalgiris Vilnius)

INTERNATIONAL HONOURS

None

NATIONAL TEAM APPEARANCES 98/99

Coach - Kestutis LATOZA

	MOL	BLS	SCO	FAR	BOS	CZE	EST	BOS	EST	ARG	Cps	Gls
Arvydas SKRUPSKIS (07/09/72) - FBK Kaunas	G										6	-
Mantas SAMUSIOVAS (08/11/78) - FBK Kaunas	D									D84	5	-
Darius REGELSKIS (15/04/76) - FBK Kaunas	D										2	-
Martynas CIKAS (15/11/77) - FBK Kaunas	D										3	-
Naglis MIKNEVICIUS (22/12/67) - FBK Kaunas	D										12	-
Vadimas PETRENKA (26/05/74) - FBK Kaunas	M										1	-
Igoris KIRILOVAS (19/08/73) - FBK Kaunas	M										27	1
Audurius KSANAVICIUS (28/01/77) - FBK Kaunas	M68									s74	5	-
Marius BEZYKORNOVAS (22/08/76) - FBK Kaunas	M75										4	1
Aivaras LAURISAS (05/04/77) - FBK Kaunas	A46										1	-
Valdas TRAKYS (20/03/79) - FBK Kaunas	A80										1	-
Vytautas KARVELIS (01/04/72) - FBK Kaunas	s46										7	-
Gintaras JUODEIKIS (13/01/73) - Atlantas Klaipeda	s68										1	-
Arturas JAKELIUNAS (12/03/71) - FBK Kaunas	s75										1	-
Andrius VELICKA (05/04/79) - FBK Kaunas	s80										1	-
Audrius DILYS (20/03/74) - Zalgiris Vilnius		G									2	-
Virginijus BALTUSNIKAS (22/10/68) - Zalgiris Vilnius		D	D	D	s87						46	9
Darius ZUTAUTAS (30/09/78) - Zalgiris Vilnius/Alania Vladikavkaz (RUS)		D				D			D46		8	-
Rolandas DZIAUKSTAS (01/04/78) - Zalgiris Vilnius		D									1	-
Sergejus NOVIKOVAS (05/05/72) - Zalgiris Vilnius		D									4	-
Andrius JOSKAS (12/01/79) - Zalgiris Vilnius		D									2	-
Deividas SEMBERAS (02/08/78) - Dinamo Moskva (RUS)	M60	D		D	D	D	M64				12	-
Igoris STESKO (25/03/76) - Zalgiris Vilnius		M									6	-
Arturas STESKO (25/03/76) - Zalgiris Vilnius		M								s77	5	-
Tomas RAMELIS (28/05/71) - Zalgiris Vilnius		A46							A	A77	13	4
Igoris MORINAS (21/02/75) - Zalgiris Vilnius/Hannover 96 (GER)		A46								A74	11	2
Dainius SAULENAS (13/03/79) - Zalgiris Vilnius		s46									2	-
Giedrius BAREVICIUS (09/08/76) - Zalgiris Vilnius		s46 /77									2	-
Nerijus RADZIUS (27/08/75) - Zalgiris Vilnius		s60									3	-
Rolandas KARCEMARSKAS (07/09/80) - Zalgiris Vilnius		s77									1	-
Gintaras STAUCE (24/12/69) - MSV Duisburg (GER)			G	G	G	G	G				43	-
Andrius SKERLA (29/04/77) - PSV (HOL)			D	D	D	D	D	D	D		18	-
Raimondas ZUTAUTAS (04/09/72) - Alania Vladikavkaz (RUS)			D	M	M		M			D	23	-
Tomas ZVIRGZDAUSKAS (18/03/75) - Polonia Warszawa (POL)			D	D	D	D	D	D	D	D	10	-
Grazvydas MIKULENAS (16/12/73) - Polonia Warszawa (POL)/Croatia Zagreb (CRO)			M90	A46		s78	A46	s64			10	1
Gediminas SUGZDA (04/10/68) - FC Rot-Weiss Erfurt (GER)			M63								1	-
Aidas PREIKSAITIS (15/07/70) - Stomil Olsztyn (POL)			M	M	M	M	M	M	s87	M	33	3
Aurelijus SKARBALIUS (12/05/73) - Brøndby IF (DEN)			M	M	M62	M	D37		M		39	5
Edgaras JANKAUSKAS (12/03/75) - Club Brugge KV (BEL)			A	A	A79	A67					18	3
Orestas BUITKUS (11/04/75) - Baltika Kaliningrad (RUS)			s63	s46		s83	s56			s37	15	4
Vaidotas SLEKYS (02/11/72) - FC Wil (SUI)			s90								32	3
Saulius MIKALAJUNAS (06/09/72) - Rubin Kazan (RUS)/Uralan Elista (RUS)				M74	M87	M78	M	M	M		17	1
Valdas IVANAUSKAS (31/07/66) - SV Salzburg (AUT)/VSE St. Pölten (AUT)				A	A	M83		A	A87		25	8
Rimantas ZVINGILAS (03/09/73) - KRC Harelbeke (BEL)				s74	s62	s67					21	3
Dainius GLEVECKAS (05/03/77) - Ekranas Panevezys/Shakhtar Donetsk (UKR)				D		s37 /56					12	-
Tomas DANILEVICIUS (18/07/78) - Dinamo Moskva (RUS)				s79							1	-
Raimondas VAINORAS (16/07/65) - FBK Kaunas					D	D				s84	44	-
Darius MACIULEVICIUS (06/11/73) - Kareda Siauliai						M	M46	s46			22	7
Arturas FOMENKA (14/02/77) - Kareda Siauliai						s46	s46				4	1
Pavelas LEUSAS (15/09/78) - Zalgiris Vilnius						G	G	G			5	-
Marius SKINDERIS (13/10/74) - GKS Belchatow (POL)						D	D	D			8	-
Darius GVILDYS (26/12/70) - Lokomotiv Nizhniy Novgorod (RUS)						D					11	2
Tomas KANCELSKIS (19/08/75) - Kareda Siauliai						D					9	-
Tomas RAZANAUSKAS (07/01/76) - Servette FC Genève (SUI)							M				8	3
Andrejus SOROKINAS (10/08/70) - Zalgiris Vilnius								D			4	-
Andrius TERESKINAS (10/07/70) - Skonto Riga (LAT)								D			51	3
Zydrunas GRUDZINSKAS (08/07/75) - Zalgiris Vilnius								D			7	-
Giedrius ZUTAUTAS (15/08/74) - FBK Kaunas								M			12	-
Irmantas STUMBRYS (30/05/72) - Zenit Sankt-Peterburg (RUS)									M37		36	2

PLAYER OF THE SEASON

DARIUS MACIULEVICIUS

Seriously injured in 1997 while playing in Russia for Alania Vladikavkaz, Lithuanian international midfielder Darius Maciulevicius made a triumphant return to the domestic scene in 1998/99. Bought by defending champions Kareda Siauliai from Inkaras Kaunas, he became a key figure in the club's quest for honours and set Kareda up perfectly for their late league showdown with Zalgiris Vilnius by scoring a brilliant hat-trick against his old club. A couple of weeks later he also netted an important goal for the national team, coming on as a substitute to grab the winner away to Estonia that ended a disastrous run of results for Lithuania in the European Championship qualifiers.

GINTARAS STAUCE

Friendly internationals aside, the Lithuanian national team is made up of a wide selection of foreign-based players, most of whom have relatively marginal roles in some of the Continent's lesser leagues. An exception to that rule is goalkeeper and captain Gintaras Stauce, who, after spells in Russia and Turkey, made his mark in the German Bundesliga in 1998/99. Although not initially first choice for MSV Duisburg, he eventually replaced the Norwegian, Thomas Gill, and proved himself to be a class act during the second half of the season, keeping ten clean sheets in 20 Bundesliga matches before missing the last couple of games with an injury that also forced him to sit out Lithuania's end-of-season Euro 2000 qualifiers in Bosnia and Estonia.

- automatically dropped out, enabling Lokomotyvas to play off for their top-flight place with Second Division champions Lietava Jonava. They did so successfully, coming back in dramatic style to win 5-1 at home after a 0-3 first-leg defeat.

Lokomotyvas were one of four First Division teams to change their name during the course of the season. They originally started out as Lokomotyvas-Legela Vilnius. Others to follow their lead were Inkaras Kaunas (formerly Inkaras-Atletas Kaunas), Nevezis Kedainiai (from Nevezis-Lifosa Kedainiai) and Zalgiris II Vilnius, who reverted to their old name after a year and a half under the guise of Gelezinis Vilkas Vilnius.

Another team forced to undergo a series of different

EUROPEAN CUPS 98/99

CHAMPIONS' CUP
● **KAREDA SIAULIAI**
Preliminary round MARIBOR TEATANIC (SLO)
H 0-3
    Poskus M.; Graziunas, Zudys, Gelgota, Kancelskis (Barasa 46), Stukalinas, Zuta, Bicka, Rudzionis (Pocius 63), Fomenka (Dancenka 46), Razumov.
A 0-1
    Poskus M.; Graziunas, Zudys, Gelgota, Barasa, Maciulevicius (Fomenka 62), Stukalinas, Bicka, Juska, Dancenka, Razumov (Rudzionis 83).

CUP WINNERS' CUP
● **EKRANAS PANEVEZYS**
Qualifying round APOLLON LIMASSOL (CYP)
H 1-2 Stumbrys (38)
    Satas; Butkus, Gleveckas, Petrukaitis, Vileniskis (Cenys 69), Gardzijauskas, Danilicevas, Stumbrys, Staliunas, Luksys (Zeniauskas 58), Varnas.
A 3-3 Vileniskis (6, 9), Varnas (90)
    Satas; Butkus (Sarkis 60), Gleveckas, Petrukaitis, Vileniskis, Gardzijauskas, Danilicevas (Zeniauskas 72), Stumbrys, Staliunas, Luksys (Cerniauskis 65), Varnas.

UEFA CUP
● **ZALGIRIS VILNIUS**
Preliminary round ÍA (ISL)
A 2-3 Skinderis (11), Vasiliauskas (72)
    Dilys; Buzmakovas, Baltusnikas, Skinderis, Zutautas, Dziaukstas, Grudzinskas, Stesko I., Stesko A., Barevicius (Vasiliauskas 46), Morinas.
H 1-0 Stesko A. (15)
    Dilys; Skinderis (Dziaukstas 80), Baltusnikas, Zutautas, Radzius, Vasiliauskas, Grudzinskas, Stesko I. (Joksas 84), Stesko A., Poderis (Barevicius 75), Morinas.

Qualifying round SK BRANN (NOR)
A 0-1
    Dilys; Baltusnikas, Dziaukstas, Zutautas, Novikovas, Joksas, Stesko I., Stesko A., Buzmakovas (Radzius 33), Morinas, Ramelis (Saulenas 14).
H 0-0
    Dilys; Novikovas, Baltusnikas, Dziaukstas, Zutautas, Joksas (Barevicius 85), Stesko I., Stesko A., Vasiliauskas (Grudzinskas 64), Morinas, Ramelis (Saulenas 62).

DOMESTIC CUP 98/99

1/16 FINALS
Panerys Vilnius w/o Vakaru Zemaiciai Mazeikiai
Utenis Utena 0, Dainava Alytus 5
Anyksciai 0, Kareda Siauliai 12
JR Klaipeda 0, Inkaras-Atletas Kaunas 2 (aet)
Atletas II Kaunas 1, Lokomotyvas-Legela Vilnius 2
Visaginas 1, Nevezis-Lifosa Kedainiai 8
Klevas Siauliai 2, Kauno Jegeriai 2
(aet; 2-4 on pens.)
Laisve Silute 0, Gelezinis Vilkas Vilnius 4
Lietava Jonava 0, FBK Kaunas 4
Zerutis Radviliskis 2, Interas-AE Visaginas 1 (aet)
Babrungas Plunge 0, Zalgiris Vilnius 9
Vienybe Ukmerge 0, Tauras Taurage 1
Polonija Vilnius 0, Ekranas Panevezys 3
Atlantas Klaipeda w/o Panerys II Vilnius
Andas-Zalgiris II Vilnius 2, Mastis Telsiai 4
Suduva Marijampole 1, Banga Gargzdai 3

1/8 FINALS
Inkaras-Atletas Kaunas v Lokomotyvas-Legela Vilnius
2-0; 0-0
(Inkaras-Atletas Kaunas 2-0)
Zerutis Radviliskis v Banga Gargzdai 0-2; 0-1
(Banga Gargzdai 3-0)
Tauras Taurage v Panerys Vilnius 2-1; 8-3
(Tauras Taurage 10-4)
Andas-Zalgiris II Vilnius v Kareda Siauliai 0-2; 1-6
(Kareda Siauliai 8-1)
Dainava Alytus v Atlantas Klaipeda 1-2; 0-5
(Atlantas Klaipeda 7-1)

Gelezinis Vilkas Vilnius v Zalgiris Vilnius 1-4; 0-1
(Zalgiris Vilnius 5-1)
Nevezis-Lifosa Kedainiai v Kauno Jegeriai 3-1; 2-2
(Nevezis-Lifosa Kedainiai 5-3)
Ekranas Panevezys v FBK Kaunas 0-0; 0-3
(FBK Kaunas 3-0)

QUARTER-FINALS
Tauras Taurage 1 (Dapkus 70),
Kareda Siauliai 2 (Dancenka 36p, 50)
Kareda Siauliai 3 (Bicka 25, Pocius 35, 56),
Tauras Taurage 0
(Kareda Siauliai 5-1)

FBK Kaunas 3 (Karvelis 18, Bezykornovas 50,
Zelmikas 62og), Inkaras-Atletas Kaunas 0
Inkaras-Atletas Kaunas 1 (Upstas 25),
FBK Kaunas 1 (Laurisas 34)
(FBK Kaunas 4-1)

Atlantas Klaipeda 2 (Poskus R. 76, Zuta 90),
Nevezis-Lifosa Kedainiai 0
Nevezis-Lifosa Kedainiai 1 (Sakalys 34), Atlantas
Klaipeda 3 (Ringys 25, Raliukonis 32, Zuta 38)
(Atlantas Klaipeda 5-1)

Banga Gargzdai 0,
Zalgiris Vilnius 2 (Stesko I. 48, Saulenas 63)
Zalgiris Vilnius 6 (Saulenas 3, 8, Stesko A. 9,
Morinas 28, Joksas 39, Karcemarskas 66),
Banga Gargzdai 0
(Zalgiris Vilnius 8-0)

SEMI-FINALS
Atlantas Klaipeda 0, FBK Kaunas 0
FBK Kaunas 2 (Trakys 48, 57), Atlantas Klaipeda 0
(FBK Kaunas 2-0)

Kareda Siauliai 3 (Dancenka 11, 17, Bicka 41),
Zalgiris Vilnius 0
Zalgiris Vilnius 0, Kareda Siauliai 4 (Dancenka 62,
Fomenka 68, 82, Mazaliauskas 89)
(Kareda Siauliai 7-0)

FINAL
17/06/99, Panevezys
KAREDA SIAULIAI 3 Pocius (95, 115), Fomenka (98)
FBK KAUNAS 0
(aet)
referee - Rubys
KAREDA SIAULIAI - Martinkenas; Graziunas, Zudys,
Kancelskis, Barasa, Bicka, Stukalinas, Juodeikis,
Lunskis, Gedgaudas (Pocius 86), Fomenka.
FBK KAUNAS - Ramoska; Suliauskas, Vainoras,
Stradins, Samusiovas, Miknevicius, Petrenka, Slekys,
Papeckys (Velicka 100), Ksanavicius (Kirilovas 85),
Trakys (Laurisas 106).

---

identities were the Lithuanian national side. At the start of the season they were represented en bloc by local sides FBK Kaunas and Zalgiris Vilnius for the two friendlies against, respectively, Moldova and Belarus. The regulars returned (mostly from abroad) for the European Championship campaign, and they got off to a reasonable start with a home draw against Scotland and a resounding 4-2 victory over Bosnia-Herzegovina, in which veteran striker Valdas Ivanauskas grabbed a hat-trick - the first one ever scored by a Lithuanian international.

Hopes of sneaking a place in the play-offs took a serious turn for the worse when Kestutis Latoza's team lost three successive qualifiers in the spring, including, humiliatingly, the home tie with Balkan rivals Estonia. Fortunately, pride was restored when

Lithuania won the return fixture by the same 2-1 score-line in Tallinn, but by then their qualifying chances had already entered the realms of fantasy.

NATIONAL TEAM RESULTS 98/99

16/08/98	Moldova	H	Kaunas	1-1	Bezykornovas (24)
19/08/98	Belarus	H	Vilnius	0-3	
05/09/98	Scotland (ECQ)	H	Vilnius	0-0	
10/10/98	Faroe Islands (ECQ)	H	Vilnius	0-0	
14/10/98	Bosnia-Herzegovina (ECQ)	H	Vilnius	4-2	Ivanauskas (10, 67, 75), Baltusnikas (90)
27/03/99	Czech Republic (ECQ)	A	Teplice	0-2	
31/03/99	Estonia (ECQ)	H	Vilnius	1-2	Fomenka (83)
05/06/99	Bosnia-Herzegovina (ECQ)	A	Sarajevo	0-2	
09/06/99	Estonia (ECQ)	A	Tallinn	2-1	Ramelis (51), Maciulevicius (56)
20/06/99	Argentina	A	Buenos Aires	0-0	

ATLANTAS KLAIPEDA

CLUB DIRECTORY

FK Atlantas Klaipeda
Sportininku 46
5813 Klaipeda
tel - (6) 254862
fax - (6) 312449
Year of Formation - 1960
President - Aidas Rudys
Secretary - Arunas Suika
Coach - Fiodoras Finkelis; Vaclovas Lekevicius
Stadium - Zalgiris (10,000)

APPEARANCES 98/99

	P	Ap	(s)	Gls
Saulius ADOMAUSKAS	G	1	(1)	
Marius ANUZIS	M	5	(3)	
Andrius BALAIKA	D		(1)	
Rokas BLINSTRUBAS	M	2	(1)	
Rolandas BUBLIAUSKAS	A	5	(4)	1
Denisas BUDAJEVAS	M		(5)	
Mindaugas CEPAS	A	10		3
Mindaugas DELKUS	M	8		1
Kestutis DEVEIKA	M	13	(4)	
Saulius DRASUTIS	M	6	(6)	1
Edmundas GAIGALAS	D	22		5
Andrius GEDGAUDAS	M	10		1
Gintaras JUODEIKIS	M	1		1
Egidijus JUSKA	M	6		
Mindaugas KAIRYS	M	2	(3)	1
Gediminas KONTAUTAS	D	9	(1)	
Edvinas LUKOSEVICIUS	D	8	(6)	2
Deividas LUNSKIS	D	3		
Mindaugas MATULA	M	1		
Andrius MAZALIAUSKAS	M	10		1
Andrius PETREIKIS	M	7	(3)	2
Vadimas PETRENKA	M	2		
Marius POSKUS	G	16		
Robertas POSKUS	A	7		4
Julius RALIUKONIS	D	4	(1)	2
Robertas RINGYS	M	19	(1)	2
Romas STECKIS	D	6		
Einaras TARVYDAS	M	1		
Antanas TAUTVYDAS	A	5	(4)	2
Liudvikas VALIUS	G	6		
Aleksandras VESELJEVAS	A	7	(7)	1
Romas VOLUNGEVICIUS	D	12		
Dainius ZERNYS	D	21		1
Egidijus ZUKAUSKAS	D	9		
Algis ZUPERKA	M	3	(1)	
Audrius ZUTA	A	6		3

LEAGUE RESULTS 1998/99

10/07/98	Nevezis-Lifosa Kedainiai	H	0-1	
15/07/98	Mastis Telsiai	A	1-0	Drasutis
01/08/98	Gelezinas Vilkas Vilnius	H	2-0	Juodeikis, Bubliauskas
09/08/98	Banga Gargzdai	A	0-0	
23/08/98	Dainava Alytus	H	1-3	Lukosevicius
30/08/98	Kareda Siauliai	A	0-6	
12/09/98	Zalgiris Vilnius	H	1-2	Zuta
19/09/98	Ekranas Panevezys	A	0-0	
27/09/98	Inkaras-Atletas Kaunas	H	3-1	Gaigalas, Raliukonis 2
03/10/98	FBK Kaunas	A	0-1	
17/10/98	Kauno Jegeriai	H	7-1	Gedgaudas, Poskus R. 4, Zuta, Delkus
25/10/98	Lokomotyvas-Legela Vilnius	H	3-1	Zuta, Gaigalas, Lukosevicius
03/04/99	Kauno Jegeriai	A	3-1	Kairys, Mazaliauskas, Cepas
10/04/99	FBK Kaunas	H	1-2	Tautvydas
17/04/99	Inkaras Kaunas	A	1-2	Zernys
24/04/99	Ekranas Panevezys	H	1-1	Gaigalas
02/05/99	Zalgiris Vilnius	A	0-2	
08/05/99	Kareda Siauliai	H	0-3	
13/05/99	Dainava Alytus	A	1-2	Gaigalas
22/05/99	Zalgiris II Vilnius	A	2-2	Ringys, Gaigalas
26/05/99	Banga Gargzdai	H	0-1	
30/05/99	Nevezis Kedainiai	A	2-0	Ringys, Cepas
03/06/99	Lokomotyvas Vilnius	A	5-1	Tautvydas, Veseljevas, Cepas, Petreikis 2

BANGA GARGZDAI

CLUB DIRECTORY

Banga Gargzdai
Kranto 5
5840 Gargzdai
tel - (6) 452505
fax - (6) 452647
Year of Formation - 1957
President - Antanas Blinstrubas
Secretary - Antanas Blinstrubas
Coach - Vaidas Liutikas
Stadium - Gargzdai (2,000)

APPEARANCES 98/99

	P	Ap	(s)	Gls
Henrikas DAUBLYS	D	12		
Eduardas DOROFEJEVAS	M	1	(4)	
Saulius DRASUTIS	M	10		1
Egidijus GRUDYS	M	1	(3)	
Rimvydas GRUDYS	M		(1)	
Igoris GURJANOVAS	A	14	(5)	2
Saulius JOKUMAITIS	D	21		
Tadas KARINAUSKAS	A	14	(3)	1
Gintautas KNIUKSTA	M	5	(5)	
Romualdas MACIULEVICIUS	D	10	(13)	1
Andrius MIKALAUSKAS	D	3	(4)	
Kestutis NAZAROVAS	M	22	(1)	4
Romas PETKEVICIUS	M	21		
Retras RAUKTYS	M	18	(4)	1
Rimas RUDYS	D	22	(1)	
Genadijus SAMSONIKAS	M	8	(10)	5
Tomas TAMOSAUSKAS	M	4	(2)	
Raimondas VENSKUS	G	23		
Mindaugas VIJEIKIS	M	19	(2)	1
Romas VOLUNGEVICIUS	D	11		
Modestas ZVILAUSKAS	A	1	(2)	2

LEAGUE RESULTS 1998/99

10/07/98	Ekranas Panevezys	A	0-4	
01/08/98	FBK Kaunas	A	0-1	
09/08/98	Atlantas Klaipeda	H	0-0	
18/08/98	Lokomotyvas-Legela Vilnius	A	1-0	Samsonikas
22/08/98	Inkaras-Atletas Kaunas	H	0-0	
12/09/98	Nevezis-Lifosa Kedainiai	A	0-1	
19/09/98	Mastis Telsiai	H	3-1	Nazarovas (p), Gurjanovas, Rauktys (p)
27/09/98	Gelezinas Vilkas Vilnius	A	0-1	
04/10/98	Kauno Jegeriai	A	0-0	
20/10/98	Dainava Alytus	H	2-0	Zvilauskas 2
25/10/98	Kareda Siauliai	A	1-5	Nazarovas
07/11/98	Zalgiris Vilnius	H	1-3	Nazarovas (p)
03/04/99	Zalgiris Vilnius	A	0-3	
11/04/99	Kareda Siauliai	H	1-2	Karinauskas
17/04/99	Dainava Alytus	A	0-0	
24/04/99	Kauno Jegeriai	H	1-2	Gurjanovas
01/05/99	Zalgiris II Vilnius	H	1-1	Samsonikas
08/05/99	Nevezis Kedainiai	H	2-1	Maciulevicius, Samsonikas
13/05/99	Lokomotyvas Vilnius	H	2-0	Nazarovas, Vijeikis •
22/05/99	FBK Kaunas	H	2-1	Drasutis, Samsonikas
26/05/99	Atlantas Klaipeda	A	1-0	Samsonikas
30/05/99	Inkaras Kaunas	A	0-2	
13/06/99	Ekranas Panevezys	H	0-2	

DAINAVA ALYTUS

CLUB DIRECTORY

Dainava Alytus
Naujoji 94-17
4580 Alytus
tel - (35) 52953
fax - (35) 53990
Year of Formation - 1943
President - Anatolijus Kacalapas
Secretary - Rimas Pisaravicius
Coach - Rimas Kochanauskas
Stadium - Alytus (2,000)

APPEARANCES 98/99

	P	Ap	(s)	Gls
Eugenijus BALIONIS	D	8	(2)	
Kestas BALKEVICIUS	M	21		1
Arnas BALSEVICIUS	A	1	(1)	
Irmantas BARTKEVICIUS	M	3	(11)	
Dainius BARZDAITIS	G	12		
Martynas BIRZINIS	M	22		4
Saulius GRISKEVICIUS	M	4	(6)	
Ricardas JANKAUSKAS	D	21		
Aidas KALIMAVICIUS	M	6	(5)	
Andrius KAMANDAUSKAS	D		(1)	
Zydrunas KARCEMARSKAS	G	1	(1)	
Andrius KOCHANAUSKAS	A	1	(1)	
Saulius LAIBINIS	A	19	(4)	8
Sarunas LITVINAS	A	10	(3)	2
Zilvinas MARCIULIONIS	A	15	(2)	2
Ramunas MATEIKA	M	5		
Arturas MIKNEVICIUS	D	20	(2)	2
Virgis MIKNEVICIUS	M	22		2
Aurimas MINIAUSKAS	M	11		
Ricardas PADEGIMAS	M	22		3
Gintaras PAKETURAS	M	2		
Audrius PASKEVICIUS	G	10		
Vaidas POCEVICIUS	D	13	(5)	
Virgis SINKEVICIUS	M	4	(1)	

LEAGUE RESULTS 1998/99

14/07/98	Ekranas Panevezys	H	0-5	
02/08/98	Inkaras-Atletas Kaunas	A	1-2	Litvinas
09/08/98	FBK Kaunas	A	0-12	
23/08/98	Atlantas Klaipeda	A	3-1	Laibinis 2, Litvinas
29/08/98	Lokomotyvas-Legela Vilnius	H	2-0	Balkevicius, Padegimas
16/09/98	Zalgiris Vilnius	H	1-3	Birzinis
19/09/98	Nevezis-Lifosa Kedainiai	H	2-3	Padegimas, Birzinis
27/09/98	Mastis Telsiai	A	1-0	Birzinis
03/10/98	Gelezinas Vilkas Vilnius	H	2-1	Laibinis 2
20/10/98	Banga Gargzdai	A	0-2	
24/10/98	Kauno Jegeriai	H	0-1	
07/11/98	Kareda Siauliai	H	0-2	
03/04/99	Kareda Siauliai	A	0-3	
10/04/99	Kauno Jegeriai	A	3-2	Marciulionis 2, Miknevicius A.
17/04/99	Banga Gargzdai	H	0-0	
24/04/99	Zalgiris II Vilnius	A	2-4	Miknevicius V. 2
02/05/99	Nevezis Kedainiai	A	1-0	Laibinis
08/05/99	Lokomotyvas Vilnius	A	2-0	Laibinis, Birzinis
13/05/99	Atlantas Klaipeda	H	2-1	Laibinis, Padegimas (p)
22/05/99	Inkaras Kaunas	H	1-2	Miknevicius A. (p)
26/05/99	FBK Kaunas	H	0-1	
30/05/99	Ekranas Panevezys	A	1-3	Laibinis
13/06/99	Zalgiris Vilnius	A	0-5	

EKRANAS PANEVEZYS

CLUB DIRECTORY

FK Ekranas Panevezys
Elektronikos 1, 5319 Panevezys
tel - (5) 435515
fax - (5) 435515
Year of Formation - 1963
President - Valdemaras Steinas
Secretary - Valdemaras Steinas
Coach - Virginijus Liubsys
Stadium - Aukstaitija (10,000)

MAJOR HONOURS
League Championship - (1) 1993.
Domestic Cup - (1) 1998.

APPEARANCES 98/99

		P	Ap	(s)	Gls
Gerdas ALEKSA	M	1		(3)	
Audrius BANEVICIUS	A	15		(2)	5
Darius BUTKUS	D	7		(1)	
Zilvinas CENYS	M	7		(5)	
Deividas CESNAUSKIS	A	11		(5)	3
Vitalijus DANILICEVAS	M	22			6
Mindaugas GARDZIJAUSKAS	D	22		(1)	4
Dainius GLEVECKAS	D	12			1
Aurimas KUCYS	M	1		(3)	
Povilus LUKSYS	M	13		(8)	3
Raimondas PETRUKAITIS	D	20		(1)	
Dainius PETRUTIS	M	2		(3)	
Vaidotas SARKIS	D	4		(2)	
Irmantas SATAS	G	16			
Mantas SAVENAS	A			(1)	
Vidas SAVICKAS	D	9			
Simas SKINDERIS	G	7		(1)	
Andrius STALIUNAS	M	14		(4)	1
Marius STANKEVICIUS	D	8			
Romas STECKIS	D	10			
Irmantas STUMBRYS	M	12			4
Egidijus VARNAS	A	13		(7)	8
Raimondas VILENISKIS	M	21		(1)	5
Kestutis ZENIAUSKAS	M	6		(11)	3

LEAGUE RESULTS 1998/99

10/07/98	Banga Gargzdai	H	4-0	Varnas 3, og (Daublys)
14/07/98	Dainava Alytus	A	5-0	Vileniskis, Banevicius, og (Jankauskas), Zeniauskas, Stumbrys
02/08/98	Kareda Siauliai	H	2-2	Varnas, Gardzijauskas
08/08/98	Zalgiris Vilnius	A	0-3	
22/08/98	Kauno Jegeriai	H	1-0	Stumbrys
01/09/98	Inkaras-Atletas Kaunas	H	2-0	Varnas, Stumbrys
12/09/98	FBK Kaunas	H	1-2	Luksys
19/09/98	Atlantas Klaipeda	H	0-0	
26/09/98	Lokomotyvas-Legela Vilnius	A	1-0	Varnas
17/10/98	Nevezis-Lifosa Kedainiai	A	0-1	
25/10/98	Mastis Telsiai	A	8-0	Stumbrys, Danilicevas 2, Vileniskis 2, Gleveckas (p), Luksys, Varnas
06/11/98	Gelezinas Vilkas Vilnius	A	0-3	
03/04/99	Zalgiris II Vilnius	H	4-0	Cesnauskis 2, Danilicevas, Banevicius
10/04/99	Nevezis Kedainiai	H	2-2	Gardzijauskas 2 (1p)
18/04/99	Lokomotyvas Vilnius	H	2-1	Varnas, Zeniauskas
24/04/99	Atlantas Klaipeda	A	1-1	Danilicevas
02/05/99	FBK Kaunas	A	1-2	Danilicevas
08/05/99	Inkaras Kaunas	A	3-0	Vileniskis, Cesnauskis, Banevicius
13/05/99	Kauno Jegeriai	A	2-1	Staliunas, Banevicius
23/05/99	Kareda Siauliai	A	1-1	Gardzijauskas
26/05/99	Zalgiris Vilnius	H	-	(awarded as away win; original result 1-0 Luksys)
30/05/99	Dainava Alytus	H	3-1	Vileniskis, Banevicius, Luksys
13/06/99	Banga Gargzdai	A	2-0	Zeniauskas, Danilicevas

INKARAS KAUNAS

CLUB DIRECTORY

FK Inkaras Kaunas
Ausros 42
3005 Kaunas
tel - (7) 300153
fax - (7) 300153
Year of Formation - 1937
President - Kastytis Klimas
Secretary - Viaceslavas Novikovas
Coach - Stasys Stankus
(99/00 - Igoris Pankratjevas)
Stadium - Inkaras (4,000)

MAJOR HONOURS
League Championship - (2) 1995, 1996.
Domestic Cup - (1) 1995.

APPEARANCES 98/99

	P	Ap	(s)	Gls
Rimvydas BAKUS	D	23		1
Saulius BUTKUS	M	18	(4)	3
Vitoldas CEPAUSKAS	D	11	(8)	1
Nerijus DUNAUSKAS	M	6		
Gvidas GRIGAS	M	7	(1)	
Andrius JODEIKIS	M	3	(3)	
Egidijus KARCIAUSKAS	M	2	(4)	1
Vidas KAUSPADAS	M	23		9
Andrius KRASINSKAS	G	1	(1)	
Nerijus KUZMICKAS	M	17	(5)	
Vytautas LENKUTIS	G	8		
Paulius MALZINSKAS	M	2	(6)	
Raimondas MARKAUSKAS	D		(1)	
Arunas MIKA	D	14	(2)	
Remigijus MIKUCIONIS	G	14		
Alvydas NORVAISAS	M	1	(7)	
Eimantas PODERIS	A	2		1
Andrius PUOTKALIS	A	9	(1)	4
Kestutis RUDZIONIS	M	16		2
Arturas RUZEVSKIS	M	7	(4)	
Darius SANAJEVAS	D	11		3
Arturas SIRKA	D	20		
Andrius UPSTAS	M	20	(1)	8
Vytautas VASKUNAS	M	8	(5)	1
Irmantas ZELMIKAS	D	10		

LEAGUE RESULTS 1998/99

02/08/98	Dainava Alytus	H	2-1	Kauspadas 2
08/08/98	Kareda Siauliai	A	1-2	Upstas
22/08/98	Banga Gargzdai	A	0-0	
27/08/98	Gelezinas Vilkas Vilnius	H	3-0	Butkus 2 (1p), Poderis
01/09/98	Ekranas Panevezys	A	0-2	
12/09/98	Kauno Jegeriai	H	0-0	
19/09/98	FBK Kaunas	H	0-2	
27/09/98	Atlantas Klaipeda	A	1-3	Kauspadas (p)
03/10/98	Lokomotyvas-Legela Vilnius	A	1-0	Rudzionis
24/10/98	Nevezis-Lifosa Kedainiai	H	3-0	Butkus, Rudzionis, Kauspadas
28/10/98	Mastis Telsiai	H	5-1	Vaskunas, Upstas 3, Karciauskas
03/11/98	Zalgiris Vilnius	H	0-2	
03/04/99	Nevezis Kedainiai	A	0-0	
10/04/99	Lokomotyvas Vilnius	H	2-0	Puotkalis 2
17/04/99	Atlantas Klaipeda	H	2-1	Sanajevas, Kauspadas
25/04/99	FBK Kaunas	A	2-4	Kauspadas 2
01/05/99	Kauno Jegeriai	A	4-0	Sanajevas, Upstas 2 (2p),
				Cepauskas
08/05/99	Ekranas Panevezys	H	0-3	
13/05/99	Zalgiris Vilnius	A	1-1	Sanajevas
22/05/99	Dainava Alytus	A	2-1	Puotkalis, Bakus
26/05/99	Kareda Siauliai	H	1-3	Kauspadas
30/05/99	Banga Gargzdai	H	2-0	Kauspadas, Puotkalis
13/06/99	Zalgiris II Vilnius	A	2-1	Upstas 2

KAREDA SIAULIAI

CLUB DIRECTORY

FK Kareda Siauliai
Bielskio 30a
5419 Siauliai
tel - (1) 441279
fax - (1) 441982
Year of Formation - 1954
President - Egidijus Simkus
Secretary - Iveta Simkiene
Coach - Aleksandr Piskarev
(99/00 - Valdemaras Martinkenas)
Stadium - Siauliai (8,000)

MAJOR HONOURS
League Championship - (2) 1997, 1998.
Domestic Cup - (2) 1996, 1999.

APPEARANCES 98/99

	P	Ap	(s)	Gls
Nerijus BARASA	D	16	(2)	
Deimantas BICKA	A	23		8
Mindaugas CEPAS	A	1	(3)	
Vidas DANCENKA	M	8	(1)	6
Arturas FOMENKA	A	19	(2)	14
Andrius GEDGAUDAS	M	8	(2)	3
Gytis GELGOTA	D	11	(1)	
Tadas GRAZIUNAS	D	19		3
Gintaras JUODEIKIS	M	15	(1)	2
Egidijus JUSKA	M	3	(2)	
Tomas KANCELSKIS	D	20		4
Tomas KAVOLIS	M		(1)	
Eduardas KURSKIS	G	1		
Deividas LUNSKIS	D	4	(5)	
Darius MACIULEVICIUS	M	16	(2)	9
Valdemaras MARTINKENAS	G		(1)	
Andrius MAZALIAUSKAS	M	1	(2)	1
Remigijus POCIUS	A	12	(3)	4
Marius POSKUS	G	3		
Robertas POSKUS	A	7	(2)	5
Maksim RAZUMOV (RUS)	M	3	(2)	
Igoris STUKALINAS	M	17	(2)	7
Tomas ZIUKAS	D	3	(3)	
Zilvinas ZUDYS	D	22		
Audrius ZUTA	A	2	(2)	1
Vaidas ZUTAUTAS	G	19	(2)	

LEAGUE RESULTS 1998/99

10/07/98	Kauno Jegeriai	H	4-0	Fomenka, Zuta, Graziunas, Bicka
15/07/98	Zalgiris Vilnius	H	0-0	
02/08/98	Ekranas Panevezys	A	2-2	Fomenka, Stukalinas
08/08/98	Inkaras-Atletas Kaunas	H	2-1	Stukalinas 2 (1p)
23/08/98	FBK Kaunas	A	1-1	Maciulevicius
30/08/98	Atlantas Klaipeda	H	6-0	Kancelskis, Pocius, Fomenka 3, Bicka
12/09/98	Lokomotyvas-Legela Vilnius	A	1-0	Dancenka (p)
26/09/98	Nevezis-Lifosa Kedainiai	A	3-0	Pocius, Dancenka 2 (2p)
04/10/98	Mastis Telsiai	H	9-0	Pocius, Fomenka 3, Kancelskis, Maciulevicius, Mazaliauskas, Stukalinas, Bicka
17/10/98	Gelezinas Vilkas Vilnius	A	4-0	Fomenka, Kancelskis, Dancenka, Stukalinas
25/10/98	Banga Gargzdai	H	5-1	Bicka, Kancelskis, Dancenka, Fomenka 2
07/11/98	Dainava Alytus	A	2-0	Dancenka, Pocius
03/04/99	Dainava Alytus	H	3-0	Fomenka, Poskus R. 2
11/04/99	Banga Gargzdai	A	2-1	Poskus R., Bicka
17/04/99	Zalgiris II Vilnius	H	3-1	Maciulevicius 3
24/04/99	Nevezis Kedainiai	H	2-0	Juodeikis, Bicka
02/05/99	Lokomotyvas Vilnius	H	7-0	Bicka 2, Gedgaudas 2, Stukalinas 2 (1p), Juodeikis
00/05/99	Atlantas Klaipeda	A	3-0	Poskus R., Fomenka, Gedgaudas
13/05/99	FBK Kaunas	H	2-0	Fomenka, Graziunas
23/05/99	Ekranas Panevezys	H	1-1	Graziunas
26/05/99	Inkaras Kaunas	A	3-1	Maciulevicius 3 (1p)
30/05/99	Zalgiris Vilnius	A	0-1	
13/06/99	Kauno Jegeriai	A	2-1	Poskus R., Maciulevicius

FBK KAUNAS

CLUB DIRECTORY

FBK Kaunas
Donelaicio 60
3000 Kaunas
tel - (7) 221408
fax - (7) 202888
Year of Formation - 1960
President - Vidas Damalakas
Secretary - Romualdas Kontrimas
Coach - Senderis Girsovicius
Stadium - Dariaus ir Gireno (12,000)

APPEARANCES 98/99

	P	Ap	(s)	Gls
Vytautas APANAVICIUS	M	2	(1)	
Marius BEZYKORNOVAS	M	15	(3)	5
Martynas CIKAS	M	5	(2)	
Ignas DEDURA	D	12	(1)	2
Darius GVILDYS	D	11		
Arturas JAKELIUNAS	D	3	(2)	2
Gintaras JUODEIKIS	M		(1)	
Vytautas KARVELIS	A	8	(3)	
Igoris KIRILOVAS	M	18	(1)	3
Audrius KSANAVICIUS	A	20	(1)	5
Aivaras LAURISAS	A	14	(5)	9
Naglis MIKNEVICIUS	M	14	(4)	
Tadas PAPECKYS	M	8	(5)	1
Vadimas PETRENKA	M	20		2
Arturas RAMOSKA	G	4		
Darius REGELSKIS	D	4	(5)	
Vilmantas RUKAVICIUS	D	6	(9)	3
Mantas SAMUSIOVAS	D	20		6
Arvydas SKRUPSKIS	G	19		
Audrius SLEKYS	A	4	(4)	3
Aleksandrs STRADINS (LAT)	M	3	(3)	
Dainius SULIAUSKAS	D	9		1
Valdas TRAKYS	A	17	(6)	13
Raimondas VAINORAS	D	9		
Audrius VELICKA	A	1	(8)	1
Giedrius ZUTAUTAS	M	7	(1)	

LEAGUE RESULTS 1998/99

14/07/98	Gelezinas Vilkas Vilnius	A	3-0	Kirilovas, Laurisas, Jakeliunas
01/08/98	Banga Gargzdai	H	1-0	Bezykornovas (p)
09/08/98	Dainava Alytus	H	12-0	Laurisas 2, Trakys 5, Ksanavicius, Papeckys, Kirilovas, Bezykornovas 2 (1p)
23/08/98	Kareda Siauliai	H	1-1	Laurisas
27/08/98	Mastis Telsiai	A	1-0	Bezykornovas (p)
30/08/98	Zalgiris Vilnius	A	1-1	Rukavicius
12/09/98	Ekranas Panevezys	A	2-1	Samusiovas, og (Petrukaitis)
19/09/98	Inkaras-Atletas Kaunas	A	2-0	Samusiovas, Ksanavicius
26/09/98	Kauno Jegeriai	A	5-0	Laurisas, Ksanavicius, Velicka, Trakys, Jakeliunas
03/10/98	Atlantas Klaipeda	H	1-0	Bezykornovas
17/10/98	Lokomotyvas-Legela Vilnius	H	2-0	Samusiovas 2
07/11/98	Nevezis-Lifosa Kedainiai	A	2-0	Dedura, Trakys
03/04/99	Lokomotyvas Vilnius	A	2-1	Suliauskas, Samusiovas
10/04/99	Atlantas Klaipeda	A	2-1	Trakys 2
17/04/99	Kauno Jegeriai	H	3-0	Trakys 2 (1p), Petrenka
25/04/99	Inkaras Kaunas	H	4-2	Petrenka (p), Trakys, Dedura, Slekys
02/05/99	Ekranas Panevezys	H	2-1	Laurisas 2
09/05/99	Zalgiris Vilnius	H	1-1	Ksanavicius
13/05/99	Kareda Siauliai	A	0-2	
22/05/99	Banga Gargzdai	A	1-2	Rukavicius
26/05/99	Dainava Alytus	A	1-0	Slekys
29/05/99	Zalgiris II Vilnius	H	5-1	Slekys, Kirilovas, Laurisas, Trakys, Ksanavicius
13/06/99	Nevezis Kedainiai	H	3-0	Samusiovas, Laurisas, Rukavicius

KAUNO JEGERIAI

CLUB DIRECTORY

Kauno Jegeriai
Donelaicio 60
3000 Kaunas
tel - (7) 221408
fax - (7) 202888
Year of Formation - 1996
President - Vidas Damalakas
Secretary - Romualdas Kontrimas
Coach - Antanas Katavicius; Kazimieras Brickus
Stadium - Kariuomenes (1,000)

APPEARANCES 98/99

	P	Ap	(s)	Gls
Mindaugas BALVOCIUS	M	8		
Laimonas BYTAUTAS	A	6		3
Martynas CIKAS	M	10		1
Tadas DUMASIUS	M	2	(12)	
Ruslanas FIODOROVAS	M	11		2
Robertas GERKIS	D	9	(2)	
Genadijus GURJEVAS	A	14	(3)	2
Arturas JANUSKEVICIUS	D	19		
Darius JOKUBAITIS	A		(2)	
Mindaugas KARALIUS	M	16	(3)	2
Tomas KULBOKA	D	1	(4)	
Dainius KUNEVICIUS	D	20		2
Andrius LARCENKA	A	5	(3)	2
Laimonas MAJAUSKAS	D	12		1
Tomas MIKLINEVICIUS	M	17		1
Alvydas NORVAISAS	M	6	(1)	
Mindaugas PACEVICIUS	D	9	(1)	
Zydrunas RASINSKAS	D	4	(6)	
Darius REGELSKIS	D	2		
Arturas RUZEVSKIS	D	10		1
Nerijus SASNAUSKAS	D	11	(1)	
Linas STANKEVICIUS	M	21	(1)	1
Mindaugas STANKEVICIUS	G	1	(5)	
Modestas STONYS	G	22		
Laimonas TURSKIS	D	12	(4)	
Audrius VELICKA	A	5		4

LEAGUE RESULTS 1998/99

10/07/98	Kareda Siauliai	A	0-4	
02/08/98	Zalgiris Vilnius	A	0-3	
08/08/98	Nevezis-Lifosa Kedainiai	H	2-1	Gurjevas, Miklinevicius
22/08/98	Ekranas Panevezys	A	0-1	
29/08/98	Mastis Telsiai	H	3-0	Majauskas, Gurjevas, Stankevicius L.
12/09/98	Inkaras-Atletas Kaunas	A	0-0	
19/09/98	Gelezinas Vilkas Vilnius	H	0-2	
26/09/98	FBK Kaunas	H	0-5	
04/10/98	Banga Gargzdai	H	0-0	
17/10/98	Atlantas Klaipeda	A	1-7	Fiodorovas
24/10/98	Dainava Alytus	A	1-0	Fiodorovas
06/11/98	Lokomotyvas-Legela Vilnius	A	0-1	
03/04/99	Atlantas Klaipeda	H	1-3	Kunevicius (p)
10/04/99	Dainava Alytus	H	2-3	Larcenka (p), Cikas
17/04/99	FBK Kaunas	A	0-3	
24/04/99	Banga Gargzdai	A	2-1	Karalius, Larcenka
01/05/99	Inkaras Kaunas	H	0-4	
08/05/99	Zalgiris II Vilnius	A	4-2	Bytautas 2, Velicka, Kunevicius (p)
13/05/99	Ekranas Panevezys	H	1-2	Bytautas
22/05/99	Zalgiris Vilnius	H	0-1	
26/05/99	Nevezis Kedainiai	A	1-2	Ruzevskis
30/05/99	Lokomotyvas Vilnius	H	3-1	Velicka 2, Karalius
13/06/99	Kareda Siauliai	H	1-2	Velicka

LOKOMOTYVAS VILNIUS

CLUB DIRECTORY

Lokomotyvas Vilnius
Liepkalnio 5
2006 Vilnius
tel - (2) 695402
Year of Formation - 1951
President - Kamilis Manatovas
Secretary - Ivanas Svabovicius
Coach - Kestutis Latoza (99/00 - Saulius Sirmelis)
Stadium - Lokomotyvas (3,000)

APPEARANCES 98/99

	P	Ap	(s)	Gls
Ricardas ALISAUSKAS	M	13	(2)	
Miroslavas AVIZENIS	M	16	(3)	2
Vitalijus BAJUS	G	16		
Arunas BALSYS	M		(4)	
Tomas BEDALIS	D	5		
Aleksandras BILASTENIS	M	8	(5)	2
Albertas BOGDANAS	M	4	(5)	1
Vladimiras BUZMAKOVAS	D	11		
Remigijus CEPULIS	M	12		1
Audrius DANISAS	D	4		
Gintaras DARASKEVICIUS	M	3		
Konstantinas FREISDORFAS	A	2	(1)	1
Viktoras FRIZELIS	A		(1)	
Dainius GUDAITIS	D	5	(4)	
Piotras GUPTORIS	M	1	(1)	
Algirdas GUTAUSKAS	A	13	(1)	1
Jonas JAKIMAVICIUS	D	6		
Arturas JURGAITIS	M	1	(1)	
Aivaras KADZIAUSKAS	D	7	(1)	
Saulius KIJANSKAS	A	5	(2)	
Algirdas KONCEVICIUS	G	4		
Dmitrijus KOSTRIKOVAS	M		(1)	
Marekas KRUKOVSKIS	M		(2)	
Dainius KRUMINAS	M	9	(3)	1
Jurijus KURPIS	M	2		
Andrius KVASNEVAS	M	16	(2)	
Andzejus MAKSIMOVICIUS	A	9	(4)	
Paulius MALZINSKAS	M	8		1
Nikolajus MARCIULEVICIUS	M	2	(1)	
Nikolajus PASINSKIS	M		(1)	
Nikolajus PUPKINAS	M	15	(4)	1
Rimas SKIRMANTAS	D	8		
Vladimiras SOSTAKAS	M	1	(1)	
Vadimas SPAKAS	M	2		
Darius SPETYLA	G	3		
Andrius SRIUBAS	D	2		
Gzegozas STUPAKAS	M	18		
Aleksandras SUCHOJUS	M	1	(1)	
Robertas TAUTKUS	D	17		
Edvinas TRINKUNAS	A	4		

LEAGUE RESULTS 1998/99

15/07/98	Nevezis-Lifosa Kedainiai	A	2-1	Gutauskas, Kruminas
01/08/98	Mastis Telsiai	H	1-0	og (Kveinys)
09/08/98	Gelezinas Vilkas Vilnius	A	2-0	Avizenis 2
18/08/98	Banga Gargzdai	H	0-1	
29/08/98	Dainava Alytus	A	0-2	
12/08/98	Kareda Siauliai	H	0-1	
19/09/98	Zalgiris Vilnius	A	1-5	Bilastenis (p)
26/09/98	Ekranas Panevezys	H	0-1	
03/10/98	Inkaras-Atletas Kaunas	H	0-1	
17/10/98	FBK Kaunas	A	0-2	
25/10/98	Atlantas Klaipeda	A	1-3	Malzinskas
06/11/98	Kauno Jegeriai	H	1-0	Bilastenis (p)
03/04/99	FBK Kaunas	H	1-2	Cepulis
10/04/99	Inkaras Kaunas	A	0-2	
18/04/99	Ekranas Panevezys	A	1-2	Pupkinas
24/04/99	Zalgiris Vilnius	H	0-1	
02/05/99	Kareda Siauliai	A	0-7	
08/05/99	Dainava Alytus	H	0-2	
13/05/99	Banga Gargzdai	A	0-2	
22/05/99	Nevezis Kedainiai	H	0-1	
26/05/99	Zalgiris II Vilnius	H	0-3	
30/05/99	Kauno Jegeriai	A	1-3	Bogdanas
03/06/99	Atlantas Klaipeda	H	1-5	Freisdorfas

MASTIS TELSIAI

CLUB DIRECTORY

Mastis Telsiai
Birutes 60
2610 Telsiai
tel - (94) 53130
fax - (94) 51767
Year of Formation - 1956
President - Vygantas Garbaliauskas
Secretary - Ramunas Vaitiekaitis
Coach - Vygantas Garbaliauskas
Stadium - Centrinis (3,000)

APPEARANCES 98/99

	P	Ap	(s)	Gls
Audrius BAGUZIS	A	1	(5)	1
Rolandas BANYS	A	9	(1)	1
Arturas BUDGINAS	M	7	(3)	
Algis EINIKIS	D	7	(4)	
Mantas GARBALIAUSKAS	A	5	(1)	
Simas JUCINSKIS	D	5	(1)	
Raimondas KENSTAVICIUS	G	3	(1)	
Kastytis KVEDARAS	D	11		
Algis KVEINYS	D	11	(1)	
Domus NORKEVICIUS	M	2	(3)	
Vidas NORVAISAS	A	11		1
Dainius PETRUTIS	M	5		
Audrius REGELSKIS	D	7	(1)	
Ernestas REGELSKIS	G	9		
Zilvinas SAVICKIS	D	7	(2)	
Vaidas SEMETA	M	1		
Mindaugas SILGALIS	M	1		
Anatolijus VASILEVSKIS	M	9		
Vijunas VASILIAUSKAS	M	11		
Rimvaldas ZALYS	A	10		1

LEAGUE RESULTS 1998/99

15/07/98	Atlantas Klaipeda	H	0-1	
01/08/98	Lokomotyvas-Legela Vilnius	A	0-1	
23/08/98	Nevezis-Lifosa Kedainiai	A	0-1	
27/08/98	FBK Kaunas	H	0-1	
29/08/98	Kauno Jegeriai	A	0-3	
12/09/98	Gelezinas Vilkas Vilnius	H	2-1	Zalys, Norvaisas
19/09/98	Banga Gargzdai	A	1-3	Baguzis
27/09/98	Dainava Alytus	H	0-1	
04/10/98	Kareda Siauliai	A	0-9	
17/10/98	Zalgiris Vilnius	H	0-6	
25/10/98	Ekranas Panevezys	H	0-8	
28/10/98	Inkaras-Atletas Kaunas	A	1-5	Banys

NEVEZIS KEDAINIAI

CLUB DIRECTORY

Nevezis Kedainiai
Jaugelio-Telegos 2
5030 Kedainiai
tel - (57) 50669
fax - (57) 53537
Year of Formation - 1946
President - Juozas Baniota
Secretary - Vygantas Jodenis
Coach - Romas Juknevicius
Stadium - Kedainiai (3,000)

APPEARANCES 98/99

	P	Ap	(s)	Gls
Vidas ADOMAITIS	M	10		
Evaldas BABENSKAS	A	14	(3)	
Aidas BLAZYS	A	14	(4)	1
Darius BUTKUS	D	11		
Zygimantas CEPULIS	A	3	(9)	1
Laisvunas JONAVICIUS	M	17	(4)	1
Martynas JUKNEVICIUS	M	5	(1)	2
Vitalijus JUREVICIUS	D	11		
Romas KIULKIS	G	15		
Nerijus KRASAUSKAS	D	10		
Kestas MORDASAS	M	2	(1)	1
Gytis PADIMANSKAS	G	8		
Juozas PURONAS	M	8	(12)	
Edvinas SAKALYS	D	17	(1)	
Tomas SENDZIKAS	D	15	(3)	1
Robertas SILAJEVAS	M	17	(4)	1
Renaldas SKREBUTENAS	D	7	(4)	
Kestas SRUOGIS	M	22	(1)	1
Vaidas STRUMECKAS	D	20	(1)	
Ronaldas TUTORIUS	M	4	(9)	
Andrius URBSYS	D	3	(3)	
Robertas ZALYS	A	20		8

LEAGUE RESULTS 1998/99

10/07/98	Atlantas Klaipeda	A	1-0	Mordasas
15/07/98	Lokomotyvas-Legela Vilnius	H	1-2	Juknevicius
08/08/98	Kauno Jegeriai	A	1-2	Blazys
23/08/98	Mastis Telsiai	H	1-0	Zalys
29/08/98	Gelezinas Vilkas Vilnius	A	1-2	Zalys
12/09/98	Banga Gargzdai	H	1-0	Zalys
19/09/98	Dainava Alytus	A	3-2	Jonavicius, Zalys, Juknevicius
26/09/98	Kareda Siauliai	H	0-3	
04/10/98	Zalgiris Vilnius	A	0-6	
17/10/98	Ekranas Panevezys	H	1-0	Zalys
24/10/98	Inkaras-Atletas Kaunas	A	0-3	
07/11/98	FBK Kaunas	H	0-2	
03/04/99	Inkaras Kaunas	H	0-0	
10/04/99	Ekranas Panevezys	A	2-2	Zalys, Sendzikas (p)
17/04/99	Zalgiris Vilnius	H	1-1	Sruogis
24/04/99	Kareda Siauliai	A	0-2	
02/05/99	Dainava Alytus	H	0-1	
08/05/99	Banga Gargzdai	A	1-2	Zalys
13/05/99	Zalgiris II Vilnius	H	0-0	
22/05/99	Lokomotyvas Vilnius	A	1-0	Zalys
26/05/99	Kauno Jegeriai	H	2-1	Silajevas, Cepulis
30/05/99	Atlantas Klaipeda	H	0-2	
13/06/99	FBK Kaunas	A	0-3	

ZALGIRIS VILNIUS

CLUB DIRECTORY

FK Zalgiris Vilnius
Zolyno 29
2040 Vilnius
tel - (2) 341494
fax - (2) 344187
Year of Formation - 1947
President - Janusas Laputis
Secretary - Elena Leskovskaja
Coach - Eugenijus Riabovas; Kestutis Latoza
Stadium - Zalgiris (13,000)

MAJOR HONOURS
League Championship - (3) 1991, 1992, 1999.
Domestic Cup - (4) 1991, 1993, 1994, 1997.

APPEARANCES 98/99

		P	Ap	(s)	Gls
Virginijus BALTUSNIKAS	D	9			
Giedrius BAREVICIUS	M	10	(8)	1	
Aleksandr BOGAICHUK (BLS)	M	2	(5)		
Vladimiras BUZMAKOVAS	D	9			
Audrius DILYS	G	7			
Rolandas DZIAUKSTAS	D	11			
Gytis GELGOTA	D	5			
Zydrunas GRUDZINSKAS	D	17	(1)	1	
Andrius JOKSAS	D	15	(4)	4	
Egidijus JUSKA	M	5	(3)	4	
Rolandas KARCEMARSKAS	A	7	(7)	2	
Virmantas LEMEZIS	M		(1)		
Pavelas LEUSAS	G	16			
Mindaugas MAKSVYTIS	G		(1)		
Igoris MORINAS	A	12		12	
Sergejus NOVIKOVAS	D	11	(2)	1	
Eriks PELCIS (LAT)	A	5	(4)	7	
Nerijus RADZIUS	D	11	(4)	1	
Tomas RAMELIS	A	3		1	
Dainius SAULENAS	A	17	(4)	8	
Arunas SILALE	D		(3)		
Andzejus SIVINSKIS	M	1	(2)	1	
Arturas SOBOLIS	D	3	(1)		
Andrejus SOROKINAS	D	9		1	
Arturas STESKO	M	19	(2)	8	
Igoris STESKO	M	19	(1)	11	
Andrius TERESKINAS	D	1			
Narijus VASILIAUSKAS	A	12	(1)	4	
Audrius VEIKUTIS	D	6	(2)		
Darius ZUTAUTAS	D	11		1	

LEAGUE RESULTS 1998/99

15/07/98	Kareda Siauliai	A	0-0	
02/08/98	Kauno Jegeriai	H	3-0	Stesko I. (p), Joksas, Stesko A. (p)
08/08/98	Ekranas Panevezys	H	3-0	Stesko A., Vasiliauskas 2
30/08/98	FBK Kaunas	H	1-1	Ramelis
12/09/98	Atlantas Klaipeda	A	2-1	Saulenas, Stesko I. (p)
16/09/98	Dainava Alytus	A	3-1	Stesko I. (p), Pelcis, Morinas
19/09/98	Lokomotyvas-Legela Vilnius	H	5-1	Morinas 2, Stesko I., Stesko A. 2 (1p)
04/10/98	Nevezis-Lifosa Kedainiai	H	6-0	Stesko A., Morinas 3, Pelcis 2
17/10/98	Mastis Telsiai	A	6-0	Stesko I. 2 (1p), Stesko A., Pelcis, Zutautas
25/10/98	Gelezinas Vilkas Vilnius	H	8-0	Pelcis, Morinas 5, Saulenas, Karcemarskas
03/11/98	Inkaras-Atletas Kaunas	A	2-0	Joksas 2
07/11/98	Banga Gargzdai	A	3-1	Stesko I. (p), Pelcis, Morinas
03/04/99	Banga Gargzdai	H	3-0	Stesko I. (p), Vasiliauskas, Saulenas
10/04/99	Zalgiris II Vilnius	A	10-0	Grudzinskas, Juska 3, Stesko I. 2, Saulenas 3, Sivinskis
17/04/99	Nevezis Kedainiai	A	1-1	Joksas
24/04/99	Lokomotyvas Vilnius	A	1-0	Stesko I. (p)
02/05/99	Atlantas Klaipeda	H	2-0	Sorokinas, Stesko A.
09/05/99	FBK Kaunas	A	1-1	Radzius
13/05/99	Inkaras Kaunas	H	1-1	Novikovas
22/05/99	Kauno Jegeriai	A	1-0	Karcemarskas
26/05/99	Ekranas Panevezys	A	-	(awarded as away win; original result 0-1)
30/05/99	Kareda Siauliai	H	1-0	Saulenas
13/06/99	Dainava Alytus	H	5-0	Barevicius, Saulenas, Vasiliauskas, Stesko A., Juska

ZALGIRIS II VILNIUS

CLUB DIRECTORY

Zalgiris II Vilnius
Zolyno 29
2040 Vilnius
tel - (2) 341494
fax - (2) 344187
President - Janusas Laputis
Secretary - Elena Leskovskaja
Coach - Saulius Sirmelis
Stadium - Vingis (3,000)

APPEARANCES 98/99

		P	Ap	(s)	Gls
Vidas ALUNDERIS	D	16			
Darius ARTIOMOVAS	A	14	(2)		
Saulius BAREVICIUS	M	1			
maksimas BECHTEROVAS	G	1			
Aleksandr BOGAICHUK (BLS)	M		(3)		
Andrius BRAZAUSKAS	A	19		5	
Gediminas BUTRIMAVICIUS	M	12	(5)		
Vitoldas CEPAUSKAS	D		(1)		
Marijanas CHORUZIJUS	M	3	(7)	1	
Audrius DILYS	G	4			
Alius DOBROVOLSKIS	M	1			
Mindaugas GRIGALEVICIUS	A	9	(8)		
Mantas GRYBAUSKAS	D	3	(3)		
Algis JANKAUSKAS	M	2			
Karolis JASAITIS	M	3	(1)		
Andrius JODEIKIS	M	1	(1)		
Marius KIZYS	M	2	(1)		
Valerijus KOTUSEVAS	M	1			
Marekas KRUKOVSKIS	M	5	(1)		
Tomas LAURYNAS	D	1			
Virmantas LEMEZIS	M	18		4	
Mindaugas MAKSVYTIS	G		(1)		
Ramunas MERKELIS	G	9	(2)		
Mindaugas PUODZIUNAS	M	11	(3)	2	
Nerijus RADZIUS	D	3			
Audrius RAMONAS	G	9	(1)		
Arnas REDIKAS	A	2	(5)	2	
Andrejus SEMEROVAS	D	6	(2)		
Arunas SILALE	D	9		2	
Gintas SIRMELIS	M	14	(1)	3	
Andzejus SIVINSKIS	M	13	(2)	1	
Arturas SOBOLIS	D	8	(1)		
Gediminas STAKNEVICIUS	D	1			
Audrius TOLIS	D	17		1	
Audrius VEIKUTIS	D	11			
Anatoliy YAKUSHEV (RUS)	M	5	(1)	1.	
Mindaugas ZURZA	M	19	(1)	3	

LEAGUE RESULTS 1998/99

14/07/98	FBK Kaunas	H	0-3	
01/08/98	Atlantas Klaipeda	A	0-2	
09/08/98	Lokomotyvas-Legela Vilnius	H	0-2	
27/08/98	Inkaras-Atletas Kaunas	A	0-3	
29/08/98	Nevezis-Lifosa Kedainiai	H	2-1	Sirmelis, Redikas
12/09/98	Mastis Telsiai	A	1-2	Brazauskas
19/09/98	Kauno Jegeriai	A	2-0	Choruzijus, Lemezis
27/09/98	Banga Gargzdai	H	1-0	Zurza
03/10/98	Dainava Alytus	A	1-2	Sirmelis
17/10/98	Kareda Siauliai	H	0-4	
25/10/98	Zalgiris Vilnius	A	0-8	
06/11/98	Ekranas Panevezys	H	3-0	Brazauskas 2, Lemezis
03/04/99	Ekranas Panevezys	A	0-4	
10/04/99	Zalgiris Vilnius	H	0-10	
17/04/99	Kareda Siauliai	A	1-3	Sirmelis
24/04/99	Dainava Alytus	H	4-2	Brazauskas (p), Tolis, Puodziunas, Silale
01/05/99	Banga Gargzdai	A	1-1	Brazauskas
08/05/99	Kauno Jegeriai	H	2-4	Zurza (p), Yakushev
13/05/99	Nevezis Kedainiai	A	0-0	
22/05/99	Atlantas Klaipeda	H	2-2	Zurza, Lemezis
26/05/99	Lokomotyvas Vilnius	A	3-0	Puodziunas (p), Silale, Sivinskis (p)
29/05/99	FBK Kaunas	A	1-5	Redikas
13/06/99	Inkaras Kaunas	H	1-2	Lemezis

PROMOTED CLUBS

SECOND DIVISION FINAL TABLE 98/99

		Pd	W	D	L	F	A	Pt	GD
1	Lietava Jonava	27	20	4	3	58	18	64	+40
2	Atletas Kaunas	27	17	7	3	60	26	58	+34
3	Tauras Taurage	27	16	6	5	49	33	54	+16
4	Zalgiris III Vilnius	27	15	5	7	51	29	50	+22
5	Interas Visaginas	27	11	10	6	37	28	43	+9
6	Laisve Silute	27	11	7	9	45	33	40	+12
7	Vienybe Ukmerge	27	11	4	12	47	44	37	+3
8	Babrungas Plunge	27	10	7	10	31	41	37	-10
9	Klevas Siauliai	27	11	4	12	38	45	37	-7
10	Vakaru Zemaiciai Mazeikiai	27	9	4	14	45	60	31	-15
	Suduva Marijampole	14	7	1	6	23	17	22	+6
11	Visaginas	27	6	2	19	26	58	20	-32
12	Anyksciai	27	4	8	15	34	49	20	-15
13	Polonija Vilnius	27	6	2	19	38	64	20	-26
14	Utenis Utena	27	3	7	17	14	51	16	-37

N.B. Panerys II Vilnius withdrew after seven games, all of which were annulled; Suduva Marijampole withdrew during the winter break - all of their games in the second half of the season were annulled.

PROMOTION/RELEGATION PLAY-OFF

Lietava Jonava 3, Lokomotyvas Vilnius 0
Lokomotyvas Vilnius 5, Lietava Jonava 1
(Lokomotyvas Vilnius 5-4)

LUXEMBOURG

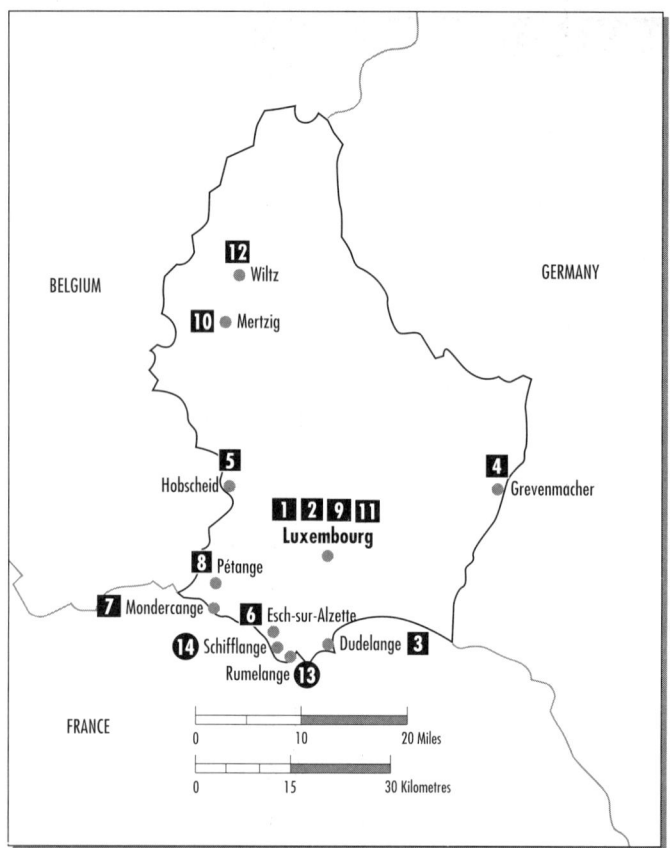

BELGIUM

GERMANY

12 ● Wiltz

10 ● Mertzig

5
Hobscheid ●

4
● Grevenmacher

1 2 9 11
Luxembourg
●

8 Pétange ●

7 Mondercange ●

6 Esch-sur-Alzette ●

14 Schifflange ● ● Dudelange 3

Rumelange ● 13

FRANCE

0   10   20 Miles

0   15   30 Kilometres

1	ARIS BONNEVOIE	647		9	SPORA LUXEMBOURG	655
2	AVENIR BEGGEN	648		10	SPORTING MERTZIG	656
3	F91 DUDELANGE	649		11	UNION LUXEMBOURG	657
4	CS GREVENMACHER	650		12	FC WILTZ 71	658
5	CS HOBSCHEID	651		**Promoted clubs**		
6	JEUNESSE ESCH	652		13	US RUMELANGE	659
7	FC MONDERCANGE	653		14	FC SCHIFFLANGE 95	659
8	CS PETANGE	654				

NO JOY FOR NEW-LOOK NATIONAL TEAM

Pecqueur's return peps all-conquering Jeunesse

FEDERATION DIRECTORY

Fédération Luxembourgeoise de Football
50 rue de Strasbourg, 2560 Luxembourg

tel - 488665-1   Year of Formation - 1908
fax - 400201   President - Henri Roemer
   Secretary - Joël Wolff

Stadium - Josy Barthel, Luxembourg (8,250)

1998/99 was yet another season of success for Jeunesse Esch. The 'Black and Whites' from the French border town won the Luxembourg championship for the fifth year in a row and a record 26th time in all. They also added an 11th Cup win, which, in turn, completed an eighth domestic 'double'. And they achieved all this under the guidance of a coach who had decided to quit the club the previous summer.

Alex Pecqueur, the Frenchman who had overseen Jeunesse's title wins in 1996, 1997 and 1998, stood down after the completion of his championship hat-trick and was replaced by Maurice Spitoni, a young and inexperienced coach who was the personal choice of Jeunesse president Jean-Pierre Borbiconi.

With a new coach came a new tactical system, and although Jeunesse began the season brightly enough against the lesser teams in the league, they were found wanting against the sides bidding to relieve them of their title, namely Union, F91 Dudelange, Grevenmacher and Avenir Beggen. In the last match before the winter break Jeunesse were beaten 1-0 at home by Dudelange, which

enabled their conquerors to leapfrog them into first place in the table. This constituted a crisis at Jeunesse, and their response was to dismiss Spitoni and recall Pecqueur as his replacement.

In the spring the Pecqueur-effect began to take hold and Jeunesse went from one victory to another to regain their familiar position at the top of the pile, overtaking Union and Dudelange along the way. For the second season running the title race was to go right to the wire. With one game left Jeunesse held a one-point advantage over Dudelange, whom they faced away from home in a final-day showdown. It should have been a thriller. After all, a crowd of almost 5,000 people (over five times the league average) had come to watch. But Dudelange, who had never won any major honour before and needed a victory and nothing less to change all that, could not handle the pressure and Jeunesse strolled to an easy 3-0 win with goals from Dany Theis, Patrick Morocutti and Paolo Amodio.

That was stage two of Jeunesse's 'double' and enabled coach Pecqueur to take a final bow with his reputation as

LEAGUE CHAMPIONSHIP RESULTS 98/99

		1	2	3	4	5	6	7	8	9	10	11	12
1	Aris Bonnevoie		0-2	0-1	1-4	2-1	0-5	1-1	1-4	0-1	0-3	1-1	1-0
2	Avenir Beggen	2-1		0-1	1-5	3-3	1-0	5-1	10-0	3-2	1-1	0-0	5-0
3	F91 Dudelange	4-1	1-0		2-1	7-3	0-3	0-1	0-0	3-0	2-1	0-1	3-0
4	CS Grevenmacher	2-3	0-5	0-1		3-1	2-0	4-1	7-1	2-0	0-2	0-0	3-1
5	CS Hobscheid	0-1	0-1	2-2	2-3		1-2	2-1	2-1	1-4	3-5	0-4	6-0
6	Jeunesse Esch	5-0	2-1	0-1	1-0	2-1		2-0	3-0	4-1	4-1	1-1	7-0
7	FC Mondercange	1-1	2-6	0-0	1-1	2-0	1-2		1-0	3-2	3-3	0-3	0-2
8	CS Pétange	0-6	0-8	0-3	0-5	0-4	0-5	0-1		3-0	3-0	2-2	1-2
9	Spora Luxembourg	0-3	0-5	1-3	0-2	1-2	0-5	1-1	0-1		1-3	0-5	0-2
10	Sporting Mertzig	5-0	1-4	2-2	2-3	5-1	0-0	3-1	4-0	5-0		3-1	1-2
11	Union Luxembourg	7-0	1-0	1-1	1-0	0-2	1-1	3-2	4-0	5-1	2-0		1-0
12	FC Wiltz 71	2-3	0-2	1-3	0-3	1-6	1-2	1-2	3-0	2-2	1-1	4-2	

TOP SCORERS

25 Frédéric CICCHIRILLO (Sporting Mertzig)
20 José LLAMAS (Avenir Beggen)
19 Marc DELAZZER (CS Hobscheid)
14 Luc HOLTZ (Avenir Beggen)
13 Sacha SCHNEIDER (CS Grevenmacher)
12 Patrick POSING (Avenir Beggen)
11 Benoît LAHERY (Union Luxembourg)
   Patrick GRETTNICH (Aris Bonnevoie)
   Stefano FANELLI (F91 Dudelange)
10 Marcel CHRISTOPHE (FC Mondercange)
   Gordon BRAUN (Jeunesse Esch)

LEAGUE CHAMPIONSHIP FINAL TABLE 98/99

			Home				Away					Total						
		P	W	D	L	F	A	W	D	L	F	A	W	D	L	F	A	P	GD
1	Jeunesse Esch	22	9	1	1	31	6	7	2	2	25	7	16	3	3	56	13	51	+43
2	F91 Dudelange	22	7	1	3	22	11	7	4	0	18	7	14	5	3	40	18	47	+22
3	Avenir Beggen	22	6	3	2	31	14	8	0	3	34	7	14	3	5	65	21	45	+44
4	Union Luxembourg	22	8	2	1	26	7	4	5	2	20	11	12	7	3	46	18	43	+28
5	CS Grevenmacher	22	6	1	4	23	15	7	1	3	27	11	13	2	7	50	26	41	+24
6	Sporting Mertzig	22	6	2	3	31	14	4	3	4	20	20	10	5	7	51	34	35	+17
7	FC Mondercange	22	3	4	4	14	20	3	2	6	12	22	6	6	10	26	42	24	-16
8	Aris Bonnevoie	22	2	2	7	7	23	5	1	5	19	28	7	3	12	26	51	24	-25
9	CS Hobscheid	22	3	1	7	19	24	4	1	6	24	26	7	2	13	43	50	23	-7
10	FC Wiltz 71	22	2	2	7	16	26	4	0	7	9	28	6	2	14	25	54	20	-29
11	CS Pétange	22	2	1	8	9	36	2	1	8	7	35	4	2	16	16	71	14	-55
12	Spora Luxembourg	22	0	1	10	4	32	2	1	8	13	31	2	2	18	17	63	8	-46

DOMESTIC CUP 98/99

SECOND ROUND
FC Bastendorf 0, Avenir Beggen 6
Old Boys Consdorf 1, Sporting Mertzig 5
Berdenia Berbourg 0, Koeppchen Wormeldange 10
Progrès Cessange 0, Union Luxembourg 7
Red Star Merl 0, F91 Dudelange 5
FC Mamer 4, Victoria Rosport 5 (after pens.)
Kischpelt Wilwerwiltz 0, FC Schifflange 7
Marisca Mersch 2, Etzella Ettelbruck 3
Etoile Sportive Clemency 1, UN Käerjéng 9
Racing Troisvierges 2, CS Pétange 1
Union Mertert/Wasserbillig 2, Progrès Niedercorn 1
Minerva Lintgen 0, FC Mondercange 7
US Rambrouch 0, CS Grevenmacher 4
Red Boys Aspelt 1, Spora Luxembourg 7
FC Munsbach 1, Aris Bonnevoie 6
Racing Heiderscheid/Eschdorf 1, Sporting Bertrange 2
FC Belvaux 0, CS Hobscheid 2
FC Noertzange 0, CS Hollerich 7
FC Medernach 0, FC Rodange 3
US Hostert 0, US Rumelange 5
FC Erpeldange 1, Fola Esch 6
Alisontia Steinsel 0, CS Sanem 7
FC Ehlerange 0, Tricolore Gasperich 1
FC Perlé 0, Sporting Beckerich 3
US Mondorf 1, Daring Echternach 3
US Reisdorf 4, AS Luxembourg 2
Young Boys Diekirch 2, Sport-Club Tétange 1 (aet)
Blue Boys Muhlenbach 1, Jeunesse Esch 3
FC Itzig 0, Swift Hesperange 2

FC Weiswampach 1, Jeunesse Koerich 6
Sport-Club Rodange 2, FC Wiltz 3
FC Kehlen 0, FC Hamm 2

1/16 FINALS
Daring Echternach 0, Union Mertert/Wasserbillig 2
CS Sanem 2, UN Kuaerjéng 4
Sporting Beckerich 0, US Rumelange 3
Spora Luxembourg 0, Union Luxembourg 1
F91 Dudelange 1, Sporting Mertzig 0
Racing Troisvierges 1, Jeunesse Esch 2
Tricolore Gasperich 1, Aris Bonnevoie 3 (aet)
Koeppchen Wormeldange 1, Avenir Beggen 2
CS Hollerich 1, CS Grevenmacher 3 (aet)
FC Hamm 0, CS Hobscheid 4
Fola Esch 1, FC Wiltz 0
FC Schifflange 1, Swift Hesperange 2 (aet)
Sporting Bertrange 0, FC Rodange 3
Young Boys Diekirch 2, Jeunesse Koerich 0
US Reisdorf 0, FC Mondercange 6
Victoria Rosport 1, Etzella Ettelbruck 2

1/8 FINALS
Jeunesse Esch 2, Swift Hesperange 1
Avenir Beggen 5, CS Hobscheid 0
Union Luxembourg 3, Young Boys Diekirch 0
Etzella Ettelbruck 5, Union Mertert/Wasserbillig 0
Aris Bonnevoie 2, US Rumelange 2
UN Käerjéng 8, FC Mondercange 9 (after pens.)
Fola Esch 6, F91 Dudelange 5 (after pens.)
CS Grevenmacher 2, FC Rodange 0

QUARTER-FINALS
Avenir Beggen 1 (Posing 3),
FC Mondercange 2 (Christophe 38, Leogrande 71)

Union Luxembourg 3 (Lauer 27, 55, Afrika 78),
US Rumelange 1 (Dillmann 37)

CS Grevenmacher 5 (Schneider 26, Heinz 49,
Alves Silva 83, 86, Alverdi 89),
Etzella Ettelbruck 0

Jeunesse Esch 6 (Meylender 32, Pace 39, 58,
Cardoni 56, Braun 65, Theis 73),
Fola Esch 0

SEMI-FINALS
Union Luxembourg 1 (Cognart 20),
FC Mondercange 2 (Braun 55, 108) (aet)

Jeunesse Esch 7 (Pace 2, Meylender 8, Braun 30,
53, Borbiconi 58, 76, 88)), CS Grevenmacher 0

FINAL
13/05/99, Luxembourg
JEUNESSE ESCH 3 Cardoni (22), Braun (53, 67p)
FC MONDERCANGE 0
referee - Hamer
JEUNESSE ESCH - Felgen; Schauls, Schaack
(Thill 76), Lamborelle, Divoy, Borbiconi, Scuto,
Amodio, Braun (Theis 70), Cardoni, Pace
(Morocutti 65).

FC MONDERCANGE - Schaber; Lohei, Sorcinelli,
Sannipoli, Minault, Fogel, Ferrassini, Romitelli
(Siegel 46), Christophe, Braun (Tenchini 85),
Leogrande (Joachim 73).

NATIONAL TEAM APPEARANCES 98/99

Coach - Paul PHILIPP	POL	ENG	BEL	ISL	SWE	BUL	POL	Cps	Gls
Paul KOCH (07/06/66) - F91 Dudelange	G	G	G					32	-
Ralph FERRON (13/05/72) - Avenir Beggen	D	D	s75	s69	D	D75		16	-
Nico FUNCK (17/10/72) - F91 Dudelange	D	D	D75	D81	D		D	8	-
Marc BIRSENS (17/09/66) - Union Luxembourg	D		M	D	M	M	M	50	1
Laurent DEVILLE (24/11/67) - Union Luxembourg	D	D	D	D	D	D		8	-
Jeff STRASSER (05/10/74) - FC Metz (FRA)	D	D	D		D	D	D	25	-
Jeff SAIBENE (13/09/68) - FC Locarno (SUI)	M	M	M	M	M88	M	M85	46	-
Dany THEIS (11/09/67) - Jeunesse Esch	M46	M61	s85	M	M69	M89	M46	25	-
Luc HOLTZ (14/06/69) - Avenir Beggen	M71	s61	M85	M49	s69	s75		32	1
Manuel CARDONI (22/09/72) - Jeunesse Esch	M	M	M88	M	M	M	M	33	2
Marcel CHRISTOPHE (19/08/74) - FC Mondercange	A65	A78	A46	A69	A80	A	A	7	1
Frank DEVILLE (12/08/70) - Avenir Beggen	s46	D84	s62	s49	s88	s89	M	24	-
Serge THILL (29/01/69) - CS Grevenmacher	s65							14	-
Eugène AFRIKA (14/04/71) - Union Luxembourg	s71			s81				2	-
Patrick POSING (09/09/71) - Avenir Beggen		M	M62			M46	s65	11	-
Paolo AMODIO (28/05/73) - Jeunesse Esch		s78	s46					10	1
Christian ALVERDI (05/11/73) - CS Grevenmacher		s84	s88				s85	4	-
Jean VANEK (19/01/69) - Avenir Beggen			D	D	D	D	D	25	1
Philippe FELGEN (08/10/75) - Jeunesse Esch				G	G	G	G	5	-
Mikhail ZARITSKI (03/10/73) - Fortuna Köln (GER)				A53	s80	s46	A65	4	-
Gordon BRAUN (25/05/77) - Jeunesse Esch				s53				3	-
Sacha SCHNEIDER (23/06/72) - CS Grevenmacher							s46	4	-

a winner still fully intact. A week earlier he had guided Jeunesse to another comfortable 3-0 victory against surprise package FC Mondercange (Monnerich in German) in the Cup final. Mondercange had sensationally knocked out Beggen and Union in the previous two rounds to reach the final and, ultimately, claim a UEFA Cup place. As for Jeunesse, the highlight of their path to the final was a 7-0 thrashing of holders Grevenmacher in the semis.

Grevenmacher could finish no higher than fifth in the league, 10 points off the pace. Above them were Beggen and Union, neither of whom could be happy with their season's balance-sheet. Union came a cropper in the title run-in for the second season running, losing three matches in row at a critical time, all to modest opposition, after remaining unbeaten for the first eight months of the campaign. As for Beggen, they suffered from deep-seated differences of opinion between the players and coach Carlo Weis and were never able to match the consistency of their co-challengers.

Sixth place went to Sporting Mertzig, who for the third

year in a row provided the league's leading scorer. Former goal-grabber Mikhail Zaritski had departed for German club Fortuna Cologne, but his replacement, Frenchman Frédéric Cicchirillo, went on to score at a similarly prolific rate, notching 25 goals in 21 games to finish five ahead of the competition.

As ever, the Luxembourg national team had a season full of defeats. The only one of their seven matches they did not lose was a friendly, at home to neighbours and Euro 2000 co-hosts Belgium. Credit could be taken from that 0-0 draw and there were also a couple of resilient defensive displays in the competitive matches, at home to England and away to Sweden. The only European Championship goals arrived in match number five, at home to Poland, but sadly Paul Philipp's side were 0-3 down before defenders Marc Birsens and Jean Vanek found the net with fine headers.

Birsens' goal was his first for Luxembourg and it came on the occasion of his 50th international. At 33, he is the oldest Luxembourg player still available for selection following the retirement of Carlo Weis, Roby Langers, Guy Hellers and - since December 1998 - Paul Koch. Another of the old guard, 32-year-old Dany Theis, had a great chance to break his duck at international level when, seven minutes into the first home European Championship qualifier, against England, Luxembourg were awarded a penalty. But the Jeunesse Esch midfielder fired his shot wildly over the bar - to the absolute agony of most of the spectators in the Josy Barthel stadium, who knew that they had just been denied a little piece of history. There would be no future tales of how they had been there when Luxembourg took the lead against England. Instead, the only memories they would take from the night would be of two poor teams struggling to cope with the lashing wind and rain and the visitors ultimately going home with a 3-0 win.

EUROPEAN CUPS 98/99

CHAMPIONS' CUP
● JEUNESSE ESCH
Preliminary round GRASSHOPPER-CLUB ZÜRICH (SUI)
A 0-6
   Felgen; Thill, Schaack, Meylender, Lamborelle, Ganser (Divoy 27), Scuto, Amodio, Morocutti (Schauls 46), Theis (Pace 71), Cardoni.
H 0-2
   Felgen; Thill (Borbiconi 73), Schaack, Meylender, Lamborelle, Scuto, Amodio, Morocutti (Ganser 89), Theis, Pace (Divoy 57), Cardoni.

CUP WINNERS' CUP
● CS GREVENMACHER
Qualifying round RAPID BUCURESTI (ROM)
H 2-6   Krahen (38, 70)
   Lohmer; Heinz, Schröder, Giesser (Alves Silva 56), Scholten, Mendoza, Thill, Schneider (Stocklosa 77), Alverdi, Krahen (Huss 85), Pauk.
A 0-2
   Köpke; Schröder (Birtz 56), Stocklosa, Giesser (Alves Silva 71), Scholten, Mendoza, Thill, Krahen (Huss 53), Dias, Dublin, Pauk.

UEFA CUP
● UNION LUXEMBOURG
Preliminary round IFK GÖTEBORG (SWE)
H 0-3
   Flick; Pellegrino, Deville, Crapa, Birsens, Afrika, Bernard (Lauer 62), Makoumbou (Cognart 79), Lahéry, Fernandes (Baum 88), Kunen.
A 0-4
   Besic; Pellegrino, Deville, Crapa, Birsens, Afrika (Fernandes 86), Makoumbou, Cognart (Chodakowski 55), Lahéry, Kunen (Lauer 68), Mestre.

INTERNATIONAL HONOURS

European Championship (last 8): 1964

NATIONAL TEAM RESULTS 98/99

10/10/98	Poland (ECQ)	A	Warsaw	0-3
14/10/98	England (ECQ)	H	Luxembourg	0-3
18/11/98	Belgium	H	Luxembourg	0-0
10/03/99	Iceland	H	Luxembourg	1-2 Christophe (23)
27/03/99	Sweden (ECQ)	A	Gothenburg	0-2
31/03/99	Bulgaria (ECQ)	H	Luxembourg	0-2
09/06/99	Poland (ECQ)	H	Luxembourg	2-3 Birsens (76), Vanek (83)

PLAYERS OF THE SEASON

MANUEL CARDONI
After two seasons as a professional in Germany, where he made the sum total of just one substitute appearance in the Bundesliga for Bayer Leverkusen, Luxembourg international midfielder Manuel Cardoni returned home to former club Jeunesse Esch. It was as if time had stood still during those two lost years because once he re-adjusted to life as an amateur, he became the key man in the Jeunesse team. His form particularly blossomed during the latter stages of the season when he imposed his extra class like never before, notably in the Cup final against Mondercange and the league showdown with F91 Dudelange. In recognition of his contribution to the club's 'double' success, Cardoni was voted Luxembourg's Player of the Year - for the third time in his career.

JEFF STRASSER
The Luxembourg national team still find scoring goals a major problem, but in recent years their defensive record has improved considerably. Heavy defeats are now few and far between, and one man who can take credit for that is 24-year-old left-back Jeff Strasser. After several years as a reserve with French club FC Metz, he at last broke through into the first team in 1998/99. However, it was to be his last for the club because in the summer he made the short journey across the German border to join Kaiserslautern, whose coach Otto Rehhagel had been sufficiently impressed after watching Strasser perform for Luxembourg against Belgium and Bulgaria to reward the youngster with a three-year contract. Very few Luxembourg players have made a name for themselves abroad, but Strasser has the talent to add his name to that list.

ARIS BONNEVOIE

CLUB DIRECTORY

FC Aris Bonnevoie
14 rue des Prés
2349 Luxembourg
tel - 485998
fax - 408922
Year of Formation - 1922
President - Laurent Mosar
Secretary - André Friedrich
Coach - Jean-Claude Wagener
Stadium - Camille Polfer (3,500)

MAJOR HONOURS
League Championshio - (3) 1964, 1966, 1972.
Domestic Cup - (1) 1967.

APPEARANCES 98/99

		P	Ap	(s)	Gls
Carlo ANTONICELLI	M			(2)	
Claude CONTER	M	17		(3)	2
Eric DE MARCHI	M			(2)	
Davide DI PASQUALE	M	1			
David EYSCHEN	D	9		(6)	
Patrick GRETTNICH	A	16		(1)	11
André HILGER	M			(1)	
Norbert HOOR	D	18			
Alain HOBSCHEID	A	21			
Wolf-Peter KLOHE	D	9			
Johny KRAUSE	D	1			
Patrick LEOGRANDE	D	14			
Frank LESSURE	D	21			1
Tomasz LIGENZA (POL)	M	14		(6)	
Luc MISCHO	A	21		(1)	9
Adis OMEROVIC	A	8		(3)	1
Franklin PEREIRA MONTEIRO	M	7		(5)	
Roby REILAND	M	11			
Marc REUTER	G	22			
Marc SCHODER	D	4		(11)	
Claude SCHUMACHER	D	10		(8)	
Haxhe SHALA (YUG)	M	18		(3)	2
Christian STEINMETZ	D			(1)	

LEAGUE RESULTS 1998/99

22/08/98	CS Grevenmacher	A	3-2	Mischo, Grettnich 2
29/08/98	CS Hobscheid	H	2-1	Grettnich 2
06/09/98	FC Mondercange	A	1-1	Grettnich
13/09/98	Jeunesse Esch	H	0-5	
19/09/98	Union Luxembourg	A	0-7	
04/10/98	FC Wiltz 71	A	3-2	Grettnich 3
20/10/98	F91 Dudelange	H	0-1	
24/10/98	Avenir Beggen	A	1-2	Mischo
15/11/98	CS Pétange	A	6-0	Shala, Lessure (p), Mischo 2, Grettnich, Omerovic
22/11/98	Sporting Mertzig	H	0-3	
31/01/99	Spora Luxembourg	H	0-1	
07/02/99	CS Grevenmacher	H	1-4	Mischo
28/02/99	FC Mondercange	H	1-1	Mischo
06/03/99	Jeunesse Esch	A	0-5	
14/03/99	Union Luxembourg	H	1-1	Mischo
21/03/99	CS Hobscheid	A	1-0	Mischo
11/04/99	FC Wiltz 71	H	1-0	Shala (p)
18/04/99	F91 Dudelange	A	1-4	Mischo
25/04/99	Avenir Beggen	H	0-2	
09/05/99	Spora Luxembourg	A	3-0	Grettnich 2, Conter
16/05/99	CS Pétange	H	1-4	Conter
21/05/99	Sporting Mertzig	A	0-5	

AVENIR BEGGEN

CLUB DIRECTORY

FC Avenir Beggen
BP 25
7201 Walferdange
tel - 787186
fax - 787060
Year of Formation - 1915
President - Théo Mersch
Secretary - Marc Peters
Coach - Carlo Weis
Stadium - Henri Dunant (5,500)

MAJOR HONOURS
League Championship - (6)
1969, 1982, 1984, 1986, 1993, 1994.
Domestic Cup - (6)
1983, 1984, 1987, 1992, 1993, 1994.

APPEARANCES 98/99

		P	Ap	(s)	Gls
Luc BIVER	A	12	(7)	3
Christophe BOULARD (FRA)	M	19	(1)	
Patrice CARASCOSA (FRA)	A	2		
Marc CHAUSSY	D	5	(6)	
Lionel DA SILVA	M	4	(3)	
Eric DELOBEL (FRA)	M	21		4
Frank DEVILLE	D	20		
Jean-Philippe FACQUES (FRA)	D	19	(1)	
Ralph FERRON	D	12		
Frank GOERGEN	D	5	(7)	2
Kevin HARTERT	G		(1)	
Luc HOLTZ	M	21	(1)	14
Nico KONSBRÜCK	G	21		
José LLAMAS	A	18	(4)	20
Gabriel LOPES (POR)	M	21		2
André MERGEN	M	11	(5)	5
Gregory MOLITOR	M		(2)	
Yves PICARD	M	1	(8)	
Albert POLO	G	1		
Patrick POSING	M	11	(7)	12
Mauro TEWES	A		(1)	
Jean VANEK	D	18		1

LEAGUE RESULTS 1998/99

22/08/98	Union Luxembourg	A	0-1	
29/08/98	F91 Dudelange	H	0-1	
05/09/98	Spora Luxembourg	A	5-0	Holtz, Vanek, Posing, Llamas, Goergen
13/09/98	Sporting Mertzig	H	1-1	Llamas
20/09/98	CS Hobscheid	A	1-0	Holtz
23/09/98	Jeunesse Esch	H	1-0	Llamas
24/10/98	Aris Bonnevoie	H	2-1	Lopes 2
12/11/98	CS Grevenmacher	A	5-0	Llamas 2, Posing 2, Holtz
27/01/99	FC Wiltz 71	A	2-0	Llamas, Holtz
31/01/99	CS Pétange	H	10-0	Holtz 2, Llamas 5, Delobel, Mergen 2
03/02/99	FC Mondercange	H	5-1	Holtz 3, og (Sannipoli), Delobel
07/02/99	Union Luxembourg	H	0-0	
12/02/99	F91 Dudelange	A	0-1	
28/02/99	Spora Luxembourg	H	3-2	Delobel, Llamas, Holtz
06/03/99	Sporting Mertzig	A	4-1	Mergen 2, Llamas, Holtz (p)
14/03/99	CS Hobscheid	H	3-3	Holtz, Biver 2
11/04/99	Jeunesse Esch	A	1-2	Llamas
18/04/99	FC Wiltz 71	H	5-0	Posing 3, Llamas, Mergen
25/04/99	Aris Bonnevoie	A	2-0	Goergen, Posing
09/05/99	CS Pétange	A	8-0	Llamas 4, Posing 2, Holtz 2
16/05/99	CS Grevenmacher	H	1-5	Posing
21/05/99	FC Mondercange ◂	A	6-2	Llamas, og (Ferrassini), Posing 2, Delobel, Biver

F91 DUDELANGE

F91 Dudelange
BP 287
3403 Dudelange
tel - 514267
fax - 516269
Year of Formation - 1991
President - Romain Schumacher
Secretary - Théo Fellerich
Coach - Angelo Fiorucci & Damon Damiani
Stadium - Jos Nosbaum (5,000)

APPEARANCES 98/99

	P	Ap	(s)	Gls
Florim ALIJAJ (YUG)	A	15	(2)	5
Cosimo BARNABO	A	19	(2)	9
Ludovic BIANCALANI (FRA)	M	1		
Ronny BONVINI	M	3	(8)	
Amar BOUCHEMLA (FRA)	M	19		2
Rico CARDONI	M	2	(12)	1
Philippe COHY (BEL)	D	6	(12)	1
Stefano FANELLI	A	13	(5)	11
Angelo FIORUCCI	M		(1)	
Nico FUNCK	D	22		1
Marco GALLI (FRA)	D	22		
Manuel GOMES (FRA)	D	19	(2)	
Joël GROFF	M	4		
Jerry HUTMACHER	M	4	(5)	
Paul KOCH	G	22		
Tommy LAMBERT	M	3	(1)	
Sauro MARINELLI	A	7	(9)	2
Marco MORGANTE (FRA)	M	22		7
Marc THOME	M	20	(2)	
Patrick UBALDINI (FRA)	M	19		1
Luc WEYLAND	M		(3)	

LEAGUE RESULTS 1998/99

23/08/98	FC Wiltz 71	H	3-0	Bouchemla, Alijaj, Barnabo
29/08/98	Avenir Beggen	A	1-0	Barnabo
06/09/98	CS Pétange	H	0-0	
12/09/98	CS Grevenmacher	A	1-0	Fanelli
20/09/98	FC Mondercange	H	0-1	
24/09/98	Union Luxembourg	A	1-1	Morgante
20/10/98	Aris Bonnevoie	A	1-0	Fanelli
12/11/98	CS Hobscheid	H	7-3	Funck, Fanelli 2, Barnabo 2, Ubaldini, Morgante
22/11/98	Jeunesse Esch	A	1-0	Morgante
24/01/99	Spora Luxembourg	H	3-0	Cardoni, Alijaj 2
31/01/99	Sporting Mertzig	A	2-2	Morgante 2 (2p)
13/02/99	Avenir Beggen	H	1-0	Morgante (p)
28/02/99	CS Pétange	A	3-0	Barnabo, Fanelli, Marinelli
06/03/99	CS Grevenmacher	H	2-1	Barnabo, Fanelli
13/03/99	FC Mondercange	A	0-0	
03/04/99	FC Wiltz 71	A	3-1	Barnabo, Fanelli 2
11/04/99	Union Luxembourg	H	0-1	
18/04/99	Aris Bonnevoie	H	4-1	Bouchemla, Alijaj, Morgante, Barnabo
24/04/99	Spora Luxembourg	A	3-1	Barnabo, Fanelli, Alijaj
09/05/99	Sporting Mertzig	H	2-1	Fanelli, Cohy
16/05/99	CS Hobscheid	A	2-2	Marinelli, Fanelli
21/05/99	Jeunesse Esch	H	0-3	

CS GREVENMACHER

CLUB DIRECTORY

Club Sportif Grevenmacher
3 rue de la Congrégation
1352 Grevenmacher
tel - 4782636
fax - 466212
Year of Formation - 1909
President - Jos Ronk
Secretary - Norry Stoltz
Coach - Harald Kohr; Michel Clement
Stadium - Op Flohr (4,500)

MAJOR HONOURS
Domestic Cup - (2) 1995, 1998.

APPEARANCES 98/99

	P	Ap	(s)	Gls
Christian ALVERDI	M	18	(2)	5
Lidio ALVES SILVA (POR)	A	12	(2)	5
Tom BAMBERG	M	2	(6)	
Steve BIRTZ	M	17	(3)	2
Adelino DIAS	A	2		1
Massimo DORMIO	M	1	(3)	
Claude DUBLIN	M	16		3
Laurent GIESSER	D	2		
Bernhard HEINZ (GER)	D	14	(2)	2
Daniel HUSS	A	11	(9)	6
Markus KRAHEN (GER)	A	6	(3)	2
Karl-Heinz LOHMER	G	4		
Paulo LOPES TANEIRO (POR)	M		(6)	
Mario MENDOZA (ARG)	M	20	(1)	2
Laurent OLINGER	G	18		
Thierry PAUK (FRA)	D	21	(1)	
Sacha SCHNEIDER	M	19	(1)	13
Théo SCHOLTEN	D	13		1
Erik SCHRÖDER (GER)	D	18	(2)	
Damian STOKLOSA	D	13	(8)	1
Serge THILL	A	15	(1)	7

LEAGUE RESULTS 1998/99

22/08/98	Aris Bonnevoie	H	2-3	Thill, Alverdi
01/09/98	FC Mondercange	H	4-1	Dublin 2, Dias, Alverdi
06/09/98	Union Luxembourg	A	0-1	
12/09/98	F91 Dudelange	H	0-1	
18/09/98	Spora Luxembourg	A	2-0	Thill, Krahen
23/09/98	Sporting Mertzig	H	0-2	
20/10/98	CS Hobscheid	A	3-2	Alves Silva 2 (2p), Schneider
12/11/98	Avenir Beggen	H	0-5	
24/11/98	CS Pétange	A	5-0	Schneider 2, Alves Silva 2, Huss
24/01/99	Jeunesse Esch	H	2-0	Schneider, Birtz
31/01/99	FC Wiltz 71	A	3-0	Thill 2, Dublin
07/02/99	Aris Bonnevoie	A	4-1	Mendoza, Huss, Thill 2
12/02/99	FC Mondercange	A	1-1	Alves Silva (p)
28/02/99	Union Luxembourg	H	0-0	
06/03/99	F91 Dudelange	A	1-2	Thill
14/03/99	Spora Luxembourg	H	2-0	Heinz, Huss
11/04/99	Sporting Mertzig	A	3-2	Stoklosa, Mendoza, Birtz
18/04/99	CS Hobscheid	H	3-1	Schneider 2, Huss
25/04/99	Jeunesse Esch	A	0-1	
09/05/99	FC Wiltz 71	H	3-1	Huss, Schneider 2
16/05/99	Avenir Beggen	A	5-1	Schneider 2, Heinz, Huss, Alverdi
21/05/99	CS Pétange	H	7-1	Schneider 3, Scholten, Alverdi 2, Krahen

CS HOBSCHEID

CLUB DIRECTORY

CS Hobscheid
4 op Eechelter
8366 Hagen
tel - 397540
fax - 390130
Year of Formation - 1932
President - Camille Stockreiser
Secretary - François Kalmes
Coach - John Van Rijswijck (99/00 - Nico Leider)
Stadium - Koericherberg (2,400)

APPEARANCES 98/99

	P	Ap	(s)	Gls
Claude BIVER	D	1	(3)	
Manuel CHANTRE (FRA)	A	13	(4)	2
Marc DELAZZER (FRA)	A	21		19
Werner DEPREZ	M	4	(2)	
José DIAS CAMPINHO	G	6		
Ahmed EL AOUAD (MAR)	A	19		8
Alain EVEN	D	20		1
Patrick GOMES	D	7	(1)	
Michael KABA (FRA)	D	18		
Enver KELMENDI (YUG)	D	22		2
Claude KOHL	M	14	(2)	1
Antoine KOSSOKO (FRA)	D	11		1
Claude KURTZ (FRA)	M	18	(1)	1
Pierre MANZANGALA (BUR)	D	18		1
Mario MUGE (POR)	M	13	(2)	
Carlos OLIVEIRA	M	1		
Baftijari PERPARIM (ALB)	M	2	(5)	
Serge ROHMANN	G	13	(1)	
Patrick SCHMIT	M	1		
Patrick THILL	G	1		
John VAN RIJSWIJCK	G	2		
Patrick WELTER	M	7	(6)	
Steve WELTER	A	10	(4)	7

LEAGUE RESULTS 1998/99

23/08/98	Sporting Mertzig	A	1-5	Delazzer
29/08/98	Aris Bonnevoie	A	1-2	Kurtz (p)
06/09/98	Jeunesse Esch	H	1-2	Delazzer
13/09/98	FC Wiltz 71	A	6-1	Delazzer 2, Welter S. 3, El Aouad
20/09/98	Avenir Beggen	H	0-1	
23/09/98	CS Pétange	A	4-0	Delazzer 2, Welter S., Chantre
20/10/98	CS Grevenmacher	H	2-3	Delazzer, Welter S.
12/11/98	F91 Dudelange	A	3-7	Delazzer 2, Manzangala
20/11/98	Spora Luxembourg	H	1-4	Kelmendi
24/01/99	FC Mondercange	A	0-2	
31/01/99	Union Luxembourg	H	0-4	
06/02/99	Sporting Mertzig	H	3-5	Delazzer 3 (1p)
28/02/99	Jeunesse Esch	A	1-2	El Aouad
07/03/99	FC Wiltz 71	H	6-0	Kossoko, Chantre, Delazzer 3, Kohl
14/03/99	Avenir Beggen	A	3-3	Even, El Aouad 2
21/03/99	Aris Bonnevoie	H	0-1	
11/04/99	CS Pétange	H	2-1	El Aouad, Kelmendi
18/04/99	CS Grevenmacher	A	1-3	El Aouad
25/04/99	FC Mondercange	H	2-1	Delazzer 2
09/05/99	Union Luxembourg	A	2-0	Welter S., El Aouad
16/05/99	F91 Dudelange	H	2-2	Delazzer 2
21/05/99	Spora Luxembourg	A	2-1	Welter S., El Aouad

JEUNESSE ESCH

CLUB DIRECTORY

AS La Jeunesse d'Esch
BP 45
4001 Esch-sur-Alzette
tel - 574130
fax - 543297
Year of Formation - 1907
President - Jean-Pierre Barboni
Secretary - John Fries
Coach - Maurice Spitoni; Alex Pecqueur
(99/00 - Eric Brusco)
Stadium - De la Frontière (7,000)

MAJOR HONOURS
League Championship - (26)
1921, 1937, 1951, 1954, 1958, 1959, 1960,
1963, 1967, 1968, 1970, 1973, 1974, 1975,
1976, 1977, 1980, 1983, 1985, 1987, 1988,
1995, 1996, 1997, 1998, 1999.
Domestic Cup - (11) 1935, 1937, 1946, 1954,
1973, 1974, 1976, 1981, 1988, 1997, 1999.

APPEARANCES 98/99

	P	Ap	(s)	Gls
Paolo AMODIO	A	21		6
David BORBICONI (FRA)	M	17	(5)	4
Gordon BRAUN	A	10	(3)	10
Manuel CARDONI	M	22		7
Yves DIVOY (BEL)	M	19	(3)	3
Philippe FELGEN	G	19		
Claude GANSER	M	3	(6)	
Marc LAMBORELLE	D	21		3
Claude MEYLENDER	M	11	(5)	
Laurent MOND	G	1		
Patrick MOROCUTTI	A	11	(9)	8
Carlo PACE	A	11	(11)	6
Ernad SABOTIC (YUG)	A	1	(3)	
Roland SCHAACK	D	14	(1)	
Manuel SCHAULS	D	18	(2)	
Denis SCUTO	M	22		
Dany THEIS	M	12	(3)	5
Johny THILL	D	3	(4)	
Jérôme TREDEMY	G	2		
Jean WAGNER	D	4		

LEAGUE RESULTS 1998/99

23/08/98	Spora Luxembourg	A	5-0	Morocutti, Theis, Braun 2, Pace
30/08/98	Sporting Mertzig	H	4-1	Theis, Pace, Morocutti, Divoy
06/09/98	CS Hobscheid	A	2-1	Borbiconi, Morocutti
13/09/98	Aris Bonnevoie	A	5-0	Cardoni 2, og (Klohe), Braun, Pace
19/09/98	FC Wiltz 71	H	7-0	Morocutti, og (Henri), Lamborelle, Cardoni 3, Pace
23/09/98	Avenir Beggen	A	0-1	
20/10/98	CS Pétange	H	3-0	Amodio 2, Lamborelle
12/11/98	Union Luxembourg	A	1-1	Amodio
22/11/98	F91 Dudelange	H	0-1	
24/01/99	CS Grevenmacher	A	0-2	
31/01/99	FC Mondercange	H	2-0	Amodio, og (Sorcinelli)
07/02/99	Spora Luxembourg	H	4-1	Morocutti 2, Cardoni, Theis
28/02/99	CS Hobscheid	H	2-1	Borbiconi, Braun (p)
06/03/99	Aris Bonnevoie	H	5-0	Braun 2, Pace, Morocutti, Lamborelle
14/03/99	FC Wiltz 71	A	2-1	Braun, Divoy
03/04/99	Sporting Mertzig	A	0-0	
11/04/99	Avenir Beggen	H	2-1	og (Boulard), Braun
18/04/99	CS Pétange	A	5-0	Borbiconi 2, Braun 2, Divoy
25/04/99	CS Grevenmacher	H	1-0	Amodio
09/05/99	FC Mondercange	A	2-1	Theis, Pace
16/05/99	Union Luxembourg	H	1-1	Cardoni
21/05/99	F91 Dudelange	A	3-0	Theis, Morocutti, Amodio

FC MONDERCANGE

CLUB DIRECTORY

FC Mondercange
110 Grand-rue
3927 Mondercange
tel - 551375
fax - 559010
Year of Formation - 1933
President - Jean Cazzaro
Secretary - Liane Galasso
Coach - Vinicio Monacelli
Stadium - Communal (2,200)

APPEARANCES 98/99

	P	Ap	(s)	Gls
Eric BRAUN	M	19	(3)	3
Claude CAZZARO	M		(1)	
Marcel CHRISTOPHE	A	21		10
Rocco CONSIGLIO	D		(1)	
Patrick DE BIASIO	G	1		
Dinis DE SOUSA	M	21	(1)	5
Marc ERBETTA	G	3		
Daniel FERRASSINI	D	21		1
Jean-Charles FOGEL	D	21		
Thierry GIACOMETTI	M		(1)	
André JOACHIM	M	1		
Luc KIEFFER	D	1	(4)	
Armin KRINGS	A		(5)	
Claude LEOGRANDE	M	14	(7)	2
David LOHEI	M	15	(2)	
Hervé MINAULT	D	21		3
Artur NEVES	A	19		1
Patrick ROMITELLI	M	10	(6)	1
Daniel SANNIPOLI	D	11	(3)	
Fernand SCHABER	G	18		
Christian SIEGEL	A	2	(1)	
Toni SORCINELLI	D	22		
Marco TENCHINI	A	1	(1)	
Médéric THILL	M		(7)	
Steve TOLLARDO	M		(6)	
Christian WEYER	M		(1)	

LEAGUE RESULTS 1998/99

23/08/98	CS Pétange	H	1-0	Christophe
01/09/98	CS Grevenmacher	A	1-4	Christophe
06/09/98	Aris Bonnevoie	H	1-1	Christophe
12/09/98	Union Luxembourg	H	0-3	
20/09/98	F91 Dudelange	A	1-0	De Sousa
23/09/98	Spora Luxembourg	H	3-2	Minault, Christophe 2 (1p)
18/10/98	Sporting Mertzig	A	1-3	Christophe
12/11/98	FC Wiltz 71	A	2-1	Christophe, Leogrande
24/01/99	CS Hobscheid	H	2-0	Minault, Braun
31/01/99	Jeunesse Esch	A	0-2	
03/02/99	Avenir Beggen	A	1-5	Braun
07/02/99	CS Pétange	A	1-0	Christophe (p)
12/02/99	CS Grevenmacher	H	1-1	De Sousa
28/02/99	Aris Bonnevoie	A	1-1	Romitelli
06/03/99	Union Luxembourg	A	2-3	Christophe, Neves
13/03/99	F91 Dudelange	H	0-0	
10/04/99	Spora Luxembourg	A	1-1	Leogrande
18/04/99	Sporting Mertzig	H	3-3	De Sousa, Minault, Christophe
25/04/99	CS Hobscheid	A	1-2	Braun
09/05/99	Jeunesse Esch	H	1-2	Ferrassini
16/05/99	FC Wiltz 71	H	0-2	
21/05/99	Avenir Beggen	H	2-6	De Sousa 2

CS PETANGE

CLUB DIRECTORY

CS Pétange
18 rue Charlotte
4719 Pétange
tel - 500375
fax - 650934
Year of Formation - 1909
President - Norbert Pierre
Secretary - Johny Majerus
Coach - Joé Hansen
Stadium - Municipal (3,300)

APPEARANCES 98/99

	P	Ap	(s)	Gls
Mustapha AFGOUR (FRA)	M	19		
Sébastien ALLIERI (FRA)	M	19	(3)	1
Steve BERTEMES	D	22		
Ahcene BOUCHAREB (FRA)	A	10	(3)	
Carl CARLIER (BEL)	M	19	(2)	2
Kristof CYLWIK (BEL)	M	12		1
Mariusz CYLWIK (BEL)	M	6	(1)	
Ernesto DA SILVA	D	12	(3)	
Adnan DERVISEVIC (YUG)	M	17	(1)	1
Jasmin DERVISEVIC (YUG)	M	15		4
José FERNANDES	M	1	(4)	
Bruno GASPAR	D		(1)	
Steve GLODY	G	5		
Toni IPPOLITO	D		(2)	
Franjo JAGODIN	M		(4)	
Stéphane LAFROGNE	M	9	(5)	
Marcelo MACHADO (POR)	A	13	(4)	3
Alberto RODRIGUES (POR)	A	13	(1)	2
Paul SCHANEN	G	17		
Yves SCHMIT	M		(1)	
Frédéric SCHROEDER	D	1		
Frédéric STEFANI (BEL)	A	17	(1)	1
Ramón TEIXEIRA	D		(1)	
Dany WABLE (FRA)	D	15	(3)	

LEAGUE RESULTS 1998/99

23/08/98	FC Mondercange	A	0-1	
30/08/98	Union Luxembourg	H	2-2	Dervisevic J., og (Birsens)
06/09/98	F91 Dudelange	A	0-0	
13/09/98	Spora Luxembourg	H	3-0	Dervisevic J. (p), Machado, Carlier
20/09/98	Sporting Mertzig	A	0-4	
23/09/98	CS Hobscheid	H	0-4	
20/10/98	Jeunesse Esch	A	0-3	
15/11/98	Aris Bonnevoie	H	0-6	
24/11/98	CS Grevenmacher	H	0-5	
24/01/99	FC Wiltz 71	H	1-2	Carlier
31/01/99	Avenir Beggen	A	0-10	
07/02/99	FC Mondercange	H	0-1	
12/02/99	Union Luxembourg	A	0-4	
28/02/99	F91 Dudelange	H	0-3	
06/03/99	Spora Luxembourg	A	1-0	Cylwik K.
14/03/99	Sporting Mertzig	H	3-0	Dervisevic A., Machado, Allieri
11/04/99	CS Hobscheid	A	1-2	Machado
18/04/99	Jeunesse Esch	H	0-5	
25/04/99	FC Wiltz 71	A	0-3	
09/05/99	Avenir Beggen	H	0-8	
16/05/99	Aris Bonnevoie	A	4-1	Rodrigues 2, Stefani, Dervisevic J.
21/05/99	CS Grevenmacher	A	1-7	Dervisevic J. (p)

SPORA LUXEMBOURG

CLUB DIRECTORY

CA Spora Luxembourg
15 rue du St. Esprit
1475 Luxembourg
tel - 332371
fax - 465569/332371
Year of Formation - 1923
President - Zénon Bernard
Secretary - Roger Lorang
Coach - Henri Hoffmann; Marcel Straus
Stadium - Josy Barthel (8,250)

MAJOR HONOURS
League Championship - (11)
1925, 1928, 1929, 1934, 1935, 1936, 1938,
1949, 1956, 1961, 1989.
Domestic Cup - (8) 1928, 1932, 1940, 1950,
1957, 1965, 1966, 1980.

APPEARANCES 98/99

	P	Ap	(s)	Gls
Jean-Pierre ALMEIDA	M	21	(1)	
Alain BARBIER (BEL)	A	3	(2)	
Danilo BEI	D	5	(7)	
Patrick BEI	D	3		
Rachid BENHELLA (ALG)	M	11	(6)	
Paul BIEVER	M	4	(1)	
Nicolas BUCK	G	1		
David CANGINI (FRA)	M	19		2
Luc CHARLIER	D	7		
Paulo DA COSTA	D	8	(2)	
Yvo DOS SANTOS PINTO (ESP)	A	10	(1)	3
Stéphane GILLET (BEL)	G	20		
Tomas GONZALEZ	M	9	(7)	
Xavier HELLENBRAND	M	19		
Georges HOFFMANN	M	1	(10)	1
Christian JOACHIM	A	13	(2)	1
Claude KOMES	M	3	(3)	
Franco LUISI	A	6	(4)	
Vincenzo LUISI	A	4	(2)	
Thierry MARX	D	2	(3)	
Dany SCHAMMEL	D	13	(2)	2
Eric SHIAVIO	D	3	(1)	2
Alain STRAUS	D	17	(2)	1
Christian STRAUS	D	19	(1)	
Pedro TAVARES	M	21	(1)	5

LEAGUE RESULTS 1998/99

23/08/98	Jeunesse Esch	H	0-5	
30/08/98	FC Wiltz 71	A	2-2	Schammel, Dos Santos Pinto
05/09/98	Avenir Beggen	H	0-5	
13/09/98	CS Pétange	A	0-3	
18/09/98	CS Grevenmacher	H	0-2	
23/09/98	FC Mondercange	A	2-3	Schiavio 2
20/10/98	Union Luxembourg	H	0-5	
15/11/98	Sporting Mertzig	H	1-3	Straus A.
20/11/98	CS Hobscheid	A	4-1	Tavares 3, Cangini
24/01/99	F91 Dudelange	A	0-3	
31/01/99	Aris Bonnevoie	A	1-0	Dos Santos Pinto
07/02/99	Jeunesse Esch	A	1-4	Tavares
12/02/99	FC Wiltz 71	H	0-2	
28/02/99	Avenir Beggen	A	2-3	Tavares, Schammel
06/03/99	CS Pétange	H	0-1	
14/03/99	CS Grevenmacher	A	0-2	
10/04/99	FC Mondercange	H	1-1	Joachim
18/04/99	Union Luxembourg	A	1-5	Dos Santos Pinto
24/04/99	F91 Dudelange	H	1-3	Cangini
09/05/99	Aris Bonnevoie	H	0-3	
16/05/99	Sporting Mertzig	A	0-5	
21/05/99	CS Hobscheid	H	1-2	Hoffmann

SPORTING MERTZIG

CLUB DIRECTORY

FC Sporting Mertzig
2 rue du Lavoir
9189 Vichten
tel - 889039
fax - 889176
Year of Formation - 1961
President - Norbert Gremling
Secretary - Claude Decker
Coach - Jean Fiedler
Stadium - An de Burwiesen (2,800)

APPEARANCES 98/99

	P	Ap	(s)	Gls
Walter ANTUNEZ (ARG)	A	16	(4)	3
Abdel BERRIH (FRA)	M	12		2
Yves BOSSERS	G	3	(2)	
Frédéric CICCHIRILLO (FRA)	A	21		25
Max CLEES	D	3	(5)	
Claude DIEDERICH	D		(2)	
Sydney FERREIRA	M	16	(3)	3
Armand GOLDSCHMIT	G	19		
Mario MACHADO	A	13	(2)	3
Jaba MOREIRA (POR)	D	13	(4)	
Kalambay MUTOMBO (DRC)	D	21		2
Sébastien REMY (FRA)	M	16		2
Laurent ROCHETTE (BEL)	M	17	(2)	
Christian SAVINO	D	1	(13)	1
Marc SCHEECK	D	3	(9)	1
Ralph STANGE (BRA)	D	13	(3)	
Laurent THILL (FRA)	D	22		
Georges TSAPANOS (BEL)	M	14	(5)	9
Philippe VALTELHAS TORRÃO (POR)	M	1	(1)	
Antoine WELLENREITER (BEL)	M	18		
Fernand WOSKO	A		(2)	

LEAGUE RESULTS 1998/99

23/08/98	CS Hobscheid	H	5-1	Berrih, Tsapanos 2, Ferreira, Cicchirillo
30/08/98	Jeunesse Esch	A	1-4	Cicchirillo
06/09/98	FC Wiltz 71	H	1-2	Cicchirillo
13/09/98	Avenir Beggen	A	1-1	Antunez
20/09/98	CS Pétange	H	4-0	Antunez, Remy, Ferreira, Cicchirillo
23/09/98	CS Grevenmacher	A	2-0	Cicchirillo 2
18/10/98	FC Mondercange	H	3-1	Cicchirillo (p), Machado, Savino
15/11/98	Spora Luxembourg	A	3-1	Mutombo, Cicchirillo, Machado
22/11/98	Aris Bonnevoie	A	3-0	Ferreira, Cicchirillo, Tsapanos
24/01/99	Union Luxembourg	A	0-2	
31/01/99	F91 Dudelange	H	2-2	Cicchirillo, Mutombo
06/02/99	CS Hobscheid	A	5-3	Cicchirillo 2, Machado, Scheeck, Tsapanos
28/02/99	FC Wiltz 71	A	1-1	Cicchirillo
06/03/99	Avenir Beggen	H	1-4	Cicchirillo
14/03/99	CS Pétange	A	0-3	
03/04/99	Jeunesse Esch	H	0-0	
11/04/99	CS Grevenmacher	H	2-3	Cicchirillo, Tsapanos
17/04/99	FC Mondercange	A	3-3	Antunez, Remy, Cicchirillo
25/04/99	Union Luxembourg	H	3-1	Cicchirillo 3 (1p)
09/05/99	F91 Dudelange	A	1-2	Tsapanos
16/05/99	Spora Luxembourg	H	5-0	Cicchirillo 3, Berrih, Tsapanos
21/05/99	Aris Bonnevoie	H	5-0	Cicchirillo 3, Tsapanos 2

UNION LUXEMBOURG

CLUB DIRECTORY

FC Union Sportive Luxembourg
BP 1614
1016 Luxembourg
tel - 308783
fax - 404747
Year of Formation - 1908
President - Rolphe Reding
Secretary - Daniel Melmer
Coach - Gilbert Neumann
Stadium - Achille Hammerel (6,500)

MAJOR HONOURS
League Championship - (11)
1912, 1914, 1915, 1916, 1917, 1927, 1962,
1971, 1990, 1991, 1992.
Domestic Cup - (10) 1947, 1959, 1963, 1964,
1969, 1970, 1986, 1989, 1991, 1996.

APPEARANCES 98/99

		P	Ap	(s)	Gls
Eugène AFRIKA	D	17	(4)	3
Marc BAUM	M		(1)	
Daniel BERNARD (FRA)	A	7	(13)	5
Alija BESIC (YUG)	G	22		
Marc BIRSENS	D	20		2
Pawel CHODAKOWSKI (POL)	M	2	(5)	1
Sébastien COGNART	M	15	(2)	5
Luciano CRAPA (BEL)	M	19		4
Laurent DEVILLE	D	21		
Georges FERNANDES	A	12	(3)	4
Steve KOENIG	M	3	(6)	
Marc KUNEN	M	10	(5)	2
Benoît LAHERY (FRA)	M	21		11
Jörg LAUER (GER)	M	16	(3)	6
Serge MAKOUMBOU (FRA)	M	18	(3)	2
Victor MESTRE	D	17	(3)	
Laurent PELLEGRINO (FRA)	D	20		
Paulino TAVARES	M		(6)	
Luc THIMMESCH	M	2	(3)	

LEAGUE RESULTS 1998/99

22/08/98	Avenir Beggen	H	1-0	Fernandes
30/08/98	CS Pétange	A	2-2	Afrika, Cognart
06/09/98	CS Grevenmacher	H	1-0	Cognart
12/09/98	FC Mondercange	A	3-0	Lauer, Birsens, Lahéry
19/09/98	Aris Bonnevoie	H	7-0	Lahéry (p), Birsens, Kunen,
				Cognart, og (Lessure), Afrika 2
24/09/98	F91 Dudelange	H	1-1	Cognart
20/10/98	Spora Luxembourg	A	5-0	Crapa, Cognart, Lahéry, Lauer 2
12/11/98	Jeunesse Esch	H	1-1	Lahéry (p)
24/01/99	Sporting Mertzig	H	2-0	Lahéry, Makoumbou
31/01/99	CS Hobscheid	A	4-0	Lauer, Crapa, Bernard, Fernandes
07/02/99	Avenir Beggen	A	0-0	
12/02/99	CS Pétange	H	4-0	Lahéry 2, Bernard, Chodakowski
28/02/99	CS Grevenmacher	A	0-0	
06/03/99	FC Mondercange	H	3-2	Fernandes, Crapa, Bernard
14/03/99	Aris Bonnevoie	A	1-1	Fernandes
11/04/99	F91 Dudelange	A	1-0	Lahéry (p)
18/04/99	Spora Luxembourg	H	5-1	Makoumbou, Lauer, Lahéry (p),
				Bernard, Kunen
25/04/99	Sporting Mertzig	A	1-3	Lahéry
28/04/99	FC Wiltz 71	A	2-4	Lahéry, Lauer
09/05/99	CS Hobscheid	H	0-2	
16/05/99	Jeunesse Esch	A	1-1	Crapa
21/05/99	FC Wiltz 71	H	1-0	Bernard

FC WILTZ 71

CLUB DIRECTORY

FC Wiltz 71
BP 47
9501 Wiltz
tel - 949343
fax - 957391
Year of Formation - 1971
President - John Shinn
Secretary - Jean-Claude Thines
Coach - Rachid Belhout; Charles Pauly
Stadium - Niederwiltz (3,200)

APPEARANCES 98/99

	P	Ap	(s)	Gls
Samuel BADIC	A	3	(12)	
Gaëtan BEAUDOT (BEL)	M	14	(2)	
Mike CZEKANOWICZ	D	1	(4)	
Patrick FLICK	M	12	(7)	
Frédéric FRANCIS (BEL)	A	11	(2)	7
Marc GIRA	A	18		
Pierre GRISIUS	D	20		3
Boris HENRY (BEL)	D	13	(2)	
Franco IOVINO (BEL)	A	21	(1)	6
Mustapha KHAROUBI (ALG)	A	8	(3)	3
David MALANNEE (BEL)	G	22		
Luc MELCHIOR	D	11	(1)	1
Dany MUNIKEN (BEL)	M	15		
Didier PANZOKOU (BEL)	D	22		3
Alain PAULY	D	9	(4)	
Jianni PETRIOLI (BEL)	D	6		1
Thierry ROUYR (BEL)	M	22		
Tom SCHAACK	M	3	(5)	
Chris SPOGEN	D	.	(5)	
Dan SPOGEN	M	11	(3)	

LEAGUE RESULTS 1998/99

23/08/98	F91 Dudelange	A	0-3	
30/08/98	Spora Luxembourg	H	2-2	Petrioli, Melchior (p)
06/09/98	Sporting Mertzig	A	2-1	og (Stange), Panzokou
13/09/98	CS Hobscheid	H	1-6	Iovino
19/09/98	Jeunesse Esch	A	0-7	
04/10/98	Aris Bonnevoie	H	2-3	Francis 2
12/11/98	FC Mondercange	H	1-2	Kharoubi
24/01/99	CS Pétange	A	2-1	Iovino 2
27/01/99	Avenir Beggen	H	0-2	
31/01/99	CS Grevenmacher	H	0-3	
12/02/99	Spora Luxembourg	A	2-0	Panzokou, Iovino
28/02/99	Sporting Mertzig	H	1-1	Grisius
07/03/99	CS Hobscheid	A	0-6	
14/03/99	Jeunesse Esch	H	1-2	Francis
03/04/99	F91 Dudelange	H	1-3	Grisius
11/04/99	Aris Bonnevoie	A	0-1	
18/04/99	Avenir Beggen	A	0-5	
25/04/99	CS Pétange	H	3-0	Iovino, Francis 2
28/04/99	Union Luxembourg	H	4-2	Iovino, Francis 2, Panzokou (p)
09/05/99	CS Grevenmacher	A	1-3	Grisius
16/05/99	FC Mondercange	A	2-0	Kharoubi 2
21/05/99	Union Luxembourg	A	0-1	

PROMOTED CLUBS

SECOND DIVISION FINAL TABLE 98/99

		Pd	W	D	L	F	A	Pt	GD
1	**US Rumelange**	**26**	**19**	**3**	**4**	**68**	**27**	**60**	**+41**
2	**FC Schifflange 95**	**26**	**16**	**7**	**3**	**59**	**26**	**55**	**+33**
3	FC Rodange	26	13	6	7	52	25	45	+27
4	Fola Esch	26	12	4	10	35	32	40	+3
5	Etzella Ettelbruck	26	11	5	10	45	41	38	+4
6	Koeppchen Wormeldange	26	11	4	11	42	37	37	+5
7	Progrès Niedercorn	26	10	6	10	43	36	36	+7
8	Swift Hesperange	26	9	7	10	34	36	34	-2
9	FC Hamm	26	8	10	8	33	39	34	-6
10	CS Hollerich	26	7	12	7	37	45	33	-8
11	UB Käerjéng	26	8	7	11	42	56	31	-14
12	Victoria Rosport	26	5	11	10	31	45	26	-14
13	Red Boys Differdange	26	5	4	17	33	60	19	-27
14	Sporting Bertrange	26	4	2	20	30	79	14	-49

CLUB DIRECTORY

US Rumelange
BP 3
3701 Rumelange
tel - 567382
fax - 567984
Year of Formation - 1908
President - René Minelli
Secretary - Fernand Oswald
Coach - Gérard Jeitz
Stadium - Municipal (4,000)

MAJOR HONOURS
Domestic Cup - (2) 1968, 1974.

CLUB DIRECTORY

FC Schifflange 95
72 Cité Paerchen
3870 Schifflange
tel - 545139
fax - 546814
Year of Formation - 1995
President - Oswaldo Costantini
Secretary - Nico Hansen
Coach - Augusto Dias Martins
Stadium - Am Emmeschbierchen (3,500)

MACEDONIA

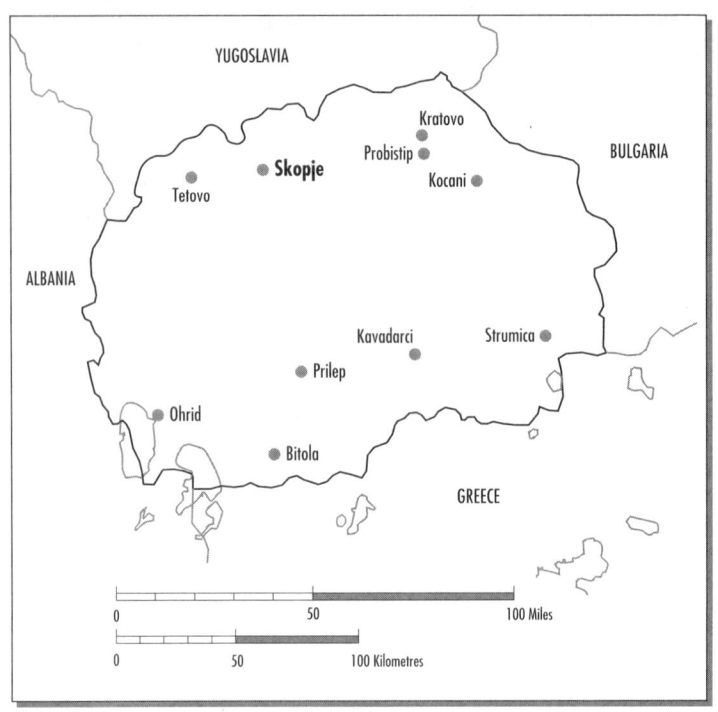

SLOGA OVERHAUL SILEKS IN LAST-DAY DRAMA

No surprises in Euro 2000 campaign

FEDERATION DIRECTORY

Football Union of Macedonia
8-ma Udarna Brigada 31a, 91000 Skopje

tel - (91) 229042 Year of Formation - 1992
fax - (91) 235448 President - Ljubisav Ivanov
Secretary - Ilija Atanasovski

Stadium - Gradski, Skopje (25,000)

Like every other team in European Championship Qualifying Group 8, the Former Yugoslav Republic of Macedonia had to cope with interruptions and postponements as the crisis in neighbouring Kosovo escalated into a full-scale international war. But when Djoko Hadzievski's team did get onto the field of play, they did no more and no less than was expected of them.

The Macedonians started the season with a record home victory - 4-0 against Malta - and ended it by losing 1-0 to the Republic of Ireland in Dublin. In between, they lost narrowly in Croatia, won by a single goal in Malta and then, in their best performance of all, came from behind to snatch a well-earned 1-1 draw in the return match against the Croatians. The big crowd in Skopje celebrated Georgi Hristov's late equaliser as if they had actually qualified for the European finals, but the delirious scenes were somewhat misplaced. In truth, the defeat in Dublin four days later probably ended Macedonia's last realistic hope of going to Holland and Belgium.

Hristov, of English club Barnsley, missed most of the season through injury. In his absence the two striking berths were shared around between Sasa Ciric, Risto Bozinov and Artim Sakiri. The latter two were among a surprisingly large contingent of home-based players called upon during the season. Midfielder Srdjan Zaharievski, who left defending Macedonian champions Sileks Kratovo for German club VfB Stuttgart midway through the season, was probably the best of the local players, while the most consistent of the exiles was goalkeeper Petar Milosevski, of Trabzonspor.

Milosevski's former club, Vardar Skopje, retained the Macedonian Cup. For the second year running Vardar took the trophy after defeating city rivals Sloga Jugomagnat 2-0 in the final. National team players Artim Sakiri and Vanco Trajcov scored the goals that allowed Vardar to book a place in Europe. They would not have made it through their league position.

A week later the two teams met again, on the final day of the league season, and this time Sloga emerged as the surprise victors. It was a crucial win because it meant that they took the league title from Sileks Kratovo, who, equally surprisingly, went down 2-0 to third placed Pobeda Prilep. The two challengers had begun the day level on points and Sileks, who had won the previous three championships, were clear favourites, but their first defeat since August condemned them to join Vardar in the UEFA Cup

LEAGUE CHAMPIONSHIP RESULTS 98/99

		1	2	3	4	5	6	7	8	9	10	11	12	13	14
1	Balkan BISI Skopje		1-1	2-1	1-1	0-0	0-1	0-1	2-6	0-4	0-3	2-1	0-1	1-0	1-0
2	Borec MHK Skopje	6-0		1-2	2-1	2-1	2-0	0-3	2-0	0-0	0-2	3-0	1-1	0-0	3-2
3	Cementarnica 55 Skopje	2-0	0-2		3-0	1-0	5-3	2-0	2-4	2-1	1-1	4-1	0-1	1-2	3-1
4	Makedonija Asiba Skopje	5-0	1-1	1-0		1-0	3-1	1-0	4-2	1-0	1-1	4-2	0-3	5-0	0-3
5	Osogovo Kocani	1-0	2-2	1-2	3-1		0-0	2-1	3-2	2-1	2-1	2-1	1-4	1-2	0-2
6	Pelister Bitola	0-0	3-1	2-1	4-2	1-0		2-2	1-1	3-2	0-2	1-1	0-5	3-3	1-2
7	Pobeda Prilep	2-0	3-0	4-1	2-1	5-1	5-0		2-1	5-0	2-0	6-0	2-0	2-1	1-0
8	Rabotnicki Kometal Skopje	2-0	0-0	2-4	2-2	3-2	3-1	1-0		2-1	0-2	3-2	0-1	1-1	0-1
9	Sasa Makedonska Kamenica	2-0	1-0	1-3	0-0	1-0	3-0	1-1	2-0		1-1	3-1	0-1	1-3	0-0
10	Sileks Kratovo	6-0	1-1	1-0	5-3	4-0	4-0	1-0	0-0	3-2		6-0	2-0	3-1	4-4
11	SK Skopje	2-0	2-0	1-3	1-3	1-1	0-1	1-0	1-2	2-0	1-3		0-1	2-0	1-2
12	Sloga Jugomagnat Skopje	3-0	1-0	1-2	1-0	6-1	1-1	1-0	1-0	1-0	0-1	2-0		2-1	1-0
13	Tikves Kavadarci	2-1	3-1	2-0	1-1	2-0	0-0	0-1	3-0	2-0	0-4	4-0	0-0		1-2
14	Vardar Skopje	7-2	4-0	2-2	2-2	2-1	2-1	1-2	6-1	5-1	2-1	3-2	0-1	6-0	

LEAGUE CHAMPIONSHIP FINAL TABLE 98/99

		Pd	W	Home D	L	F	A	W	Away D	L	F	A	W	Total D	L	F	A	Pt	GD
1	Sloga Jugomagnat Skopje	26	10	1	2	21	6	9	2	2	19	6	19	3	4	40	12	60	+28
2	Sileks Kratovo	26	10	3	0	40	11	7	3	3	22	10	17	6	3	62	21	57	+41
3	Pobeda Prilep	26	13	0	0	41	5	4	2	7	11	13	17	2	7	52	18	53	+34
4	Vardar Skopje	26	9	2	2	42	16	6	2	5	19	16	15	4	7	61	32	49	+29
5	Cementarnica 55 Skopje	26	8	1	4	26	16	6	1	6	21	21	14	2	10	47	37	44	+10
6	Makedonija Asiba Skopje	26	9	2	2	27	13	1	5	7	17	27	10	7	9	44	40	37	+4
7	Tikves Kavadarci	26	7	3	3	20	10	3	3	7	14	28	10	6	10	34	38	36	-4
8	Borec MHK Skopje	26	7	3	3	22	12	1	5	7	9	22	8	8	10	31	34	32	-3
9	Rabotnicki Kometal Skopje	26	6	3	4	19	17	3	2	8	19	29	9	5	12	38	46	32	-8
10	Pelister Bitola	26	5	5	3	21	22	2	3	8	9	28	7	8	11	30	50	29	-20
11	Sasa Makedonska Kamenica	26	6	4	3	16	10	1	1	11	12	28	7	5	14	28	38	26	-10
12	Osogovo Kocani	26	7	2	4	20	19	0	2	11	7	29	7	4	15	27	48	25	-21
13	SK Skopje	26	5	1	7	15	16	0	1	12	11	43	5	2	19	26	59	17	-33
14	Balkan BISI Skopje	26	4	3	6	10	20	0	1	12	3	40	4	4	18	13	60	16	-47

while Sloga, celebrating their first national title, marched into the Champions' League.

Claims by Sileks fans that Sloga and Vardar had conspired in a Cup-league trade-off were all very well, but had Sileks won their final game, the title would have been theirs. They only had themselves to blame.

DOMESTIC CUP 98/99

QUARTER-FINALS
Cementarnica Skopje v Vardar Skopje 2-2; 0-1 (Vardar Skopje 3-2)
Pobeda Prilep v Makedonija Skopje 2-0; 1-1 (Pobeda Prilep 3-1)
Osogovo Kocani v Sloga Jugomagnat Skopje 0-2; 0-3
(Sloga Jugomagnat Skopje 5-0)
Rabotnicki Kometal Skopje v Sileks Kratovo 1-0; 0-3 (Sileks Kratovo 3-1)

SEMI-FINALS
Pobeda Prilep v Vardar Skopje 4-2; 1-3
(5-5; Vardar Skopje on away goals)

Sloga Jugomagnat Skopje v Sileks Kratovo 0-0; 0-0
(0-0; Sloga Jugomagnat Skopje 3-1 on pens.)

FINAL
22/05/99, Skopje
VARDAR SKOPJE 2 Trajcov (66), Sakiri (89)
SLOGA JUGOMAGNAT SKOPJE 0
referee - Krstevski
VARDAR SKOPJE - Zekir; Jovanovski, Ljusev, Stojanov, Alomerovic, Karadzov, Eftimov (Nacevski 70), Djorgjioski, Trajcov, Sakiri, Avramovski.
SLOGA JUGOMAGNAT SKOPJE - Jovcev; Arif, Colakovic, Omeragic, Zdravevski, Abazi, Miserdovski, Memedi, Fetahi, Beganovic, Mustafi.

EUROPEAN CUPS 98/99

CHAMPIONS' CUP
● SILEKS KRATOVO
Preliminary round CLUB BRUGGE KV (BEL)
H 0-0
Trajcev; Tanusev, Veselinoski, Duzelov, Gosev (Konjanovski 89), Trajkovski (Kolev 67), Zaharievski, Novakov, Bozinov, Sinovski (Stojcevski 77), Stojanov.
A 1-2 Bozinov (76)
Trajcev; Tanusev (Petkovski 65), Veselinoski, Duzelov, Gosev (Georgiev 70), Trajkovski (Kolev 65), Zaharievski, Novakov, Bozinov, Sinovski, Stojanov.

CUP WINNERS' CUP
● VARDAR SKOPJE
Qualifying round SPARTAK TRNAVA (SVK)
H 0-1
Zekir; Jovanovski, Todorovski, Stojanov, Trajcev, Djorgjioski (Demjanski 71), Avramovski, Dimitkovski, Karadzov, Eftimov (Bajevski 76), Krstev (Nacevski 58).
A 0-2
Zekir; Jovanovski, Todorovski, Stojanov, Janev, Trajcev, Avramovski, Dimitkovski, Karadzov, Bajevski (Nacevski 65), Krstev.

UEFA CUP
● SLOGA JUGOMAGNAT SKOPJE
Preliminary round OTELUL GALATI (ROM)
A 0-3
Jovcev; Zdravevski, Colakovic, Omeragic, Beganovic H., Abazi, Memedi, Miserdovski (Stankovski 51), Beganovic F., Hodai (Presilski 47), Arif (Dimitrov 77).
H 1-1 Stankovski (42)
Kargov; Zdravevski, Colakovic, Beganovic H., Abazi, Stankovski, Memedi, Miserdovski (Mustafi 58), Beganovic F. (Bekirovski 78), Hodai, Presilski (Bajram 60).

TOP SCORERS

22 Roberto OLIVEIRA (Pobeda Prilep)
14 Vanco TRAJCOV (Vardar Skopje)

INTERNATIONAL HONOURS

None

NATIONAL TEAM RESULTS 98/99

06/09/98	Malta (ECQ)	H	Skopje	4-0	Bozinov (20, 48), Sakiri (75, 80)
29/09/98	Egypt	H	Kumanovo	2-2	
14/10/98	Croatia (ECQ)	A	Zagreb	2-3	Ciric (2), Sainovski (55)
18/11/98	Malta (ECQ)	A	Ta' Qali	2-1	Nikolovski (49), Zaharievski (62)
10/02/99	Albania	A	Tirana	0-2	
05/06/99	Croatia (ECQ)	H	Skopje	1-1	Hristov (80)
09/06/99	Republic of Ireland (ECQ)	A	Dublin	0-1	

NATIONAL TEAM APPEARANCES 98/99

Coach - Djoko HADZIEVSKI	MLT	EGY	CRO	MLT	ALB	CRO	IRL	Cps	Gls
Petar MILOSEVSKI (06/12/73) - Trabzonspor (TUR)	G		G	G	G80	G	G	12	-
Goce SEDLOSKI (10/04/74) - Croatia Zagreb (CRO)	D	D	D	D	D		s70	20	-
Goran STAVREVSKI (02/01/74) - Zagreb (CRO)	D	D74	D	D	D	D	D	7	-
Igor NIKOLOVSKI (16/07/73) - Sakaryaspor (TUR)	D78	D	D77	D	D80	D	D	26	1
Mitko STOJKOVSKI (18/12/72) - VfB Stuttgart (GER)	D80				D46			27	5
Srdjan ZAHARIEVSKI (12/09/73) - Sileks Kratovo/VfB Stuttgart (GER)	M	M	M	M		s75		18	2
Goran LAZAREVSKI (17/12/74) - Pobeda Prilep	M		M60		s46			9	-
Toni MICEVSKI (20/01/70) - Tennis Borussia Berlin (GER)	M	M63	M46	M		M	M	30	3
Milan STOJANOSKI (15/09/73) - Partizan Beograd (YUG)	M70		s77		M	D	D	7	1
Viktor TRENEVSKI (08/10/72) - Sileks Kratovo	M		M	s65	M46	M46	M77	15	-
Risto BOZINOV (10/04/69) - Sileks Kratovo	A	A70	s60	A65		s46		5	2
Artim SAKIRI (23/09/73) - Halmstads BK (SWE)/Vardar Skopje	s70	A	A	A	s46	A	A	22	3
Dzevdet SAINOVSKI (08/06/73) - NEC (HOL)	s78	M	M	M		M	M70	17	1
Vlatko GOSEV (10/09/74) - Sileks Kratovo	s80	M	s46		s46			20	-
Gogo JOVCEV (25/03/74) - Sloga Jugomagnat Skopje		G46			s80			2	-
Zlatko TODOROVSKI (30/04/72) - Vardar Skopje		M46						1	-
Oka NIKOLOV (25/05/74) - Eintracht Frankfurt (GER)		s46						1	-
Goran STANKOVSKI (20/11/76) - Sloga Jugomagnat Skopje		s46						1	-
Blagoja MILEVSKI (25/03/71)		s63						1	-
Vanco TRAJCOV (05/07/75) - Vardar Skopje		s70			M74	M75	M46	4	-
Vlatko NOVAKOV (28/09/78) - Sileks Kratovo		s74						1	-
Sasa CIRIC (11/01/68) - 1.FC Nürnberg (GER)			A		A	A	A	16	5
Boban BABUNSKI (05/05/68) - AEK (GRE)			D	D46	M75	D		16	1
Dragan VESELINOVSKI (11/08/68) - Sileks Kratovo			M	M				10	-
Miroslav DZOKIC (17/01/73) - Sileks Kratovo				s74				4	2
Marjan GERASIMOVSKI (12/03/74) - Partizan Beograd (YUG)				s80				1	-
Georgi HRISTOV (30/01/76) - Barnsley (ENG)						s75	s77	25	9
Nedzmedin MEMEDI (20/03/66) - Sloga Jugomagnat Skopje							s46	24	1

MALTA

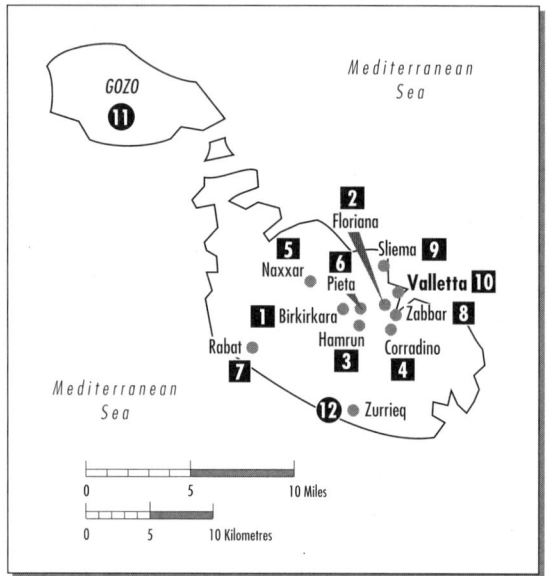

1	BIRKIRKARA	669	8	ST. PATRICK	676
2	FLORIANA	670	9	SLIEMA WANDERERS	677
3	HAMRUN SPARTANS	671	10	VALLETTA	678
4	HIBERNIANS	672	**Promoted clubs**		
5	NAXXAR LIONS	673	11	GOZO	679
6	PIETA HOTSPURS	674	12	ZURRIEQ	679
7	RABAT AJAX	675			

BIRKIRKARA LEFT EMPTY-HANDED AGAIN

Valletta lose battles but win the war

FEDERATION DIRECTORY

Malta Football Association
280 St. Paul Street, Valletta, VLT 07

tel - 222697/232581   Year of Formation - 1900
fax - 245136   President - Joseph Mifsud
                         Secretary - Joseph A. Sacco

Stadium - National, Ta' Qali (18,000)

There was a familiar outcome to the Maltese Premier Division in 1998/99. Valletta came first, with Birkirkara a brave and unfortunate second. That had been the way of it for the two previous seasons as well. Birkirkara must now be wondering what they have to do to wrest the title from their great rivals and win the championship for the first time.

Birkirkara threw the title away in 1997/98 when they lost to Valletta in the final game. A year on their fans were made to suffer again, but in different circumstances. On this occasion they did everything asked of them in the direct confrontations with Valletta, winning every one of the three matches. And yet it still wasn't enough. While Birkirkara lost only once in 27 games - an unexpected early reverse against Naxxar Lions - they drew five times, and that, sadly, proved to be once too many.

The only points Valletta dropped other than in those three defeats by Birkirkara were in a goalless draw with Rabat Ajax. That gave them a final, record tally of 70 points, two more than Birkirkara, whose own total would have been sufficient to win the league in each of the previous seasons since the adoption of the new, three-round formula.

Trailing Valletta at one stage by nine points, Birkirkara kept chipping away at the deficit with each victory over their rivals so that when they completed their remarkable hat-trick with a 2-1 win three rounds from the end, the gap was down to two points. Valletta were struggling badly with injuries and suspensions at the time, so Birkirkara felt that if they could win their last three matches and score a hatful of goals in the process, Valletta might drop a couple more points and the title would go to them on goal difference. But the Lilywhites did not slip up. They almost did, against Pieta Hostpurs and Sliema Wanderers, but on each occasion they showed enough grit and determination to sneak through by the odd goal. With

LEAGUE CHAMPIONSHIP RESULTS 98/99

		1	2	3	4	5	6	7	8	9	10
1	Birkirkara		4-0	3-0	1-1	5-1	2-0	5-3	1-0	3-2	1-0
			3-0	7-0	1-1	1-0	2-1	5-1	1-0	2-0	2-1
2	Floriana	2-2		2-0	0-2	2-1	2-1	5-1	5-1	1-1	1-4
				0-1	3-2	6-2	2-4	0-4	5-0	1-1	1-3
3	Hamrun Spartans	0-3	1-2		1-3	1-1	0-4	2-4	3-4	1-2	1-4
					1-2	2-1	1-4	1-2	1-2	2-1	1-2
4	Hibernians	0-3	3-2	5-0		0-0	1-1	2-1	3-1	0-0	1-3
					1-2	1-0	6-1	2-1	1-2	0-2	
5	Naxxar Lions	2-1	0-0	0-0	1-1		1-1	3-0	3-1	2-1	0-3
						1-4	0-2	1-1	0-3	0-2	
6	Pieta Hotspurs	0-2	1-2	3-0	0-2	3-5		4-0	0-0	0-2	0-1
							1-1	1-0	1-1	1-2	
7	Rabat Ajax	2-2	1-1	2-4	2-0	2-1	2-1		1-1	2-4	0-4
								1-2	0-3	0-0	
8	St. Patrick	2-3	2-2	1-1	0-6	2-2	1-1	1-1		0-5	3-4
									1-3	2-3	
9	Sliema Wanderers	0-0	1-0	3-0	3-1	0-2	4-2	2-0	7-0		1-3
										2-3	
10	Valletta	1-4	4-0	3-1	1-0	1-0	1-0	7-1	5-0	4-0	

LEAGUE CHAMPIONSHIP FINAL TABLE

		Pd	W	D	L	F	A	Pt	GD
1	Valletta	27	23	1	3	71	23	70	+48
2	Birkirkara	27	21	5	1	69	20	68	+49
3	Sliema Wanderers	27	14	5	8	54	32	47	+22
4	Hibernians	27	12	6	9	47	33	42	+14
5	Floriana	27	10	6	11	47	50	36	-3
6	Naxxar Lions	27	7	8	12	32	46	29	-14
7	Pieta Hotspurs	27	7	6	14	39	39	27	0
8	Rabat Ajax	27	7	6	14	37	67	27	-30
9	St. Patrick	27	3	8	16	29	71	17	-42
10	Hamrun Spartans	27	4	3	20	26	70	15	-44

THE EUROPEAN FOOTBALL YEARBOOK 1999-2000

NATIONAL TEAM RESULTS 98/99

02/09/98	Germany	H	Ta' Qali	1-2	Brincat (26)
06/09/98	Macedonia (ECQ)	A	Skopje	0-4	
10/10/98	Croatia (ECQ)	H	Ta' Qali	1-4	Suda (29p)
14/10/98	Republic of Ireland (ECQ)	A	Dublin	0-5	
18/11/98	Macedonia (ECQ)	H	Ta' Qali	1-2	Sixsmith (69)
27/01/99	Bosnia-Herzegovina	H	Ta' Qali	2-1	Carabott (45), Busuttil (84)
03/02/99	Poland	H	Ta' Qali	0-1	
10/02/99	Yugoslavia (ECQ)	H	Ta' Qali	0-3	
10/03/99	Moldova	H	Ta' Qali	0-2	
28/04/99	Iceland	H	Ta' Qali	1-2	Cutajar (45)
08/06/99	Yugoslavia (ECQ)	A	Salonika (Greece)	1-4	Saliba (6)

TOP SCORERS

20	Gilbert AGIUS (Valletta)
18	Joe BRINCAT (Birkirkara)
15	Paul ZAMMIT (Hamrun Spartans)
13	Richard BUHAGIAR (Floriana)
	Renis HYKA (St. Patrick)
	Dobrin RAGUIN (Pieta Hotspurs)
12	Stefan SULTANA (Hamrun Spartans/ Hibernians)
11	Carmel BUSUTTIL (Sliema Wanderers)
10	Michael CUTAJAR (Birkirkara)
	Roderick ASCIAK (Rabat Ajax)

Birkirkara hammering Hamrun Spartans 7-0 in their penultimate fixture, Valletta went into their final match knowing that a win would seal their third successive title. This time they got their victory with relative ease, beating Naxxar Lions 2-0 through goals from Stefan Giglio and Mark Galea. Birkirkara still had one fixture left to play but they were now five points in arrears. The race was over. Valletta had their 17th national title. Birkirkara would have to wait at least another year for their first. The battle of the 'big two' was still not finished, however. The next instalment of their rivalry arrived a few weeks later when they met in the final of the FA Trophy - the Maltese domestic Cup.. Neither team had been especially impressive in reaching the final, with penalty shoot-outs, extra-time and late goals all being required en route. It was as if the stressful league campaign had taken its toll on both of them.

The final was to be something of a let-down, too. Valletta were understandably cautious given the results they had had against Birkirkara in the league, whereas their opponents were nervous at the prospect of winning their first major honour. And so, with no goals in 90 minutes, the match went into extra-time. It was three minutes into the second extra period that the winning goal finally arrived, and it went to Valletta, with Yugoslav-born striker Nenad Veselji providing the crucial touch to complete his team's second 'double' in three seasons.

That 'double' became a 'treble' when Valletta brought further misery to the bridesmaids of Birkirkara by beating them 2-1 in the Super Cup. It was thus a clean sweep for Valletta's Bulgarian coach Krasimir Manolov in his first season at the helm, but Birkirkara's Vlado Pejovic, also in his first season, had to make do with three silver medals.

Birkirkara's frustration at missing out on a major prize was nothing compared to the absolute misery of Hamrun Spartans, who finished rock bottom of the table with just 15 points and were relegated. Hamrun, one of the best supported teams on the island, were doomed from the start, failing to win any of their first 15 matches. The one shaft of light illuminating their gloomy season was striker Paul Zammit, whose 15 goals amounted to

EUROPEAN CUPS 98/99

CHAMPIONS' CUP
● **VALLETTA**
Preliminary round ANORTHOSIS FAMAGUSTA (CYP)
H 0-2
Cini; Braunovic (Zarb 66), Chetcuti, Laferla, Debono, Camilleri, Agius G., Saliba, Ivanov (Veselji 74), Giglio, Bonnici.
A 0-6
Cini; Braunovic, Chetcuti, Laferla, Debono, Camilleri, Agius G., Zarb, Ivanov, Giglio (Veselji 46), Bonnici (Agius J. 34; Woods 78).

CUP WINNERS' CUP
● **HIBERNIANS**
Qualifying round AMICA WRONKI (POL)
A 0-4
Muscat; Attard L., Baldachino, Mbong, Walker, Spiteri, Kologbo, Mifsud, Carabott, Chukunyere, Mraz.
H 0-1
Muscat; Noteman, Borg (Baldachino 76), Mbong, Walker, Spiteri, Attard D. (Kologbo 61), Mifsud, Carabott, Chukunyere, Mraz.

UEFA CUP
● **BIRKIRKARA**
Preliminary round SHAKHTAR DONETSK (UKR)
A 1-2 Zammit (75)
Savic; Tellus, Matanovic, Antic, Magri Overand, Zammit (Bencini 85), Cutajar (Calascione 68), Brincat, Galea, Nwoko, Zahra.
H 0-4
Savic; Eminyan (Stefanovic 59), Matanovic, Antic, Magri Overand, Zammit, Cutajar (Calascione 68), Brincat, Galea, Nwoko, Zahra.

INTERNATIONAL HONOURS

None

DOMESTIC CUP 98/99

FIRST ROUND
St. Patrick 3, Xghajra Tornadoes 1
Rabat Ajax 4, Mellieha 2
Hamrun Spartans 4, Gozo 2
Marsa 0, Zurrieq 2
Pieta Hotspurs 3, Siggiewi 1
Floriana 4, St. Andrews 0
Lija Athletics 1, Naxxar Lions 3 (aet)
Mosta 1, Tarxien Rainbows 2

SECOND ROUND
Floriana 3, Rabat Ajax 1 (aet)
Pieta Hotspurs 1, Tarxien Rainbows 1
(aet; 2-3 on pens.)
Zurrieq 1, Naxxar Lions 2
Hamrun Spartans 2, St. Patrick 0

QUARTER-FINALS
Birkirkara 3 (Cutajar 10, Brincat 55p, Zahra 60),
Sliema Wanderers 3 (Mifsud 21, Grima 46,
Woods 75) (aet; 4-1 on pens.)

Floriana 6 (Mattocks 18, Zahra 34, Buhagiar 57, 60,
Zaitsev 67, Oba 87), Tarxien Rainbows 0

Hamrun Spartans 2 (Sylla 54p, 94), Valletta 4
(Veselji 67, Sacco 98, 120, Galea 105) (aet)

Hibernians 3 (Mbong 35, Abela 62, 75),
Naxxar Lions 2 (Oretan 20, 48)

SEMI-FINALS
Valletta 3 (Ivanov 23, Veselji 88, 90),
Floriana 1 (Buhagiar 75)

Birkirkara 2 (Galea 69, 97),
Hibernians 1 (Baldachino 88) (aet)

FINAL
27/05/99, Ta' Qali
VALLETTA 1 Veselji (108)
BIRKIRKARA 0
(aet)
referee - Sammut

VALLETTA - Cini; Braunovic, Forace, Giglio, Debono,
Camilleri (Trakosopoulos 112), Agius, Saliba, Bonnici,
Veselji (Sacco 114), Galea.

BIRKIRKARA - Savic; Tellus, Matanovic,
Eminyan (Sammut 37), Magri Overand, Suda,
Cutajar (Zammit 67), Brincat,
Galea (Calascione 109), Nwoko, Bencini.

the joint-third best total in the Premier Division. Top spot, with 20 goals, went to Valletta's Gilbert Agius.

The First Division was won by Gozo FC, who thus made history by reaching the top flight for the first time and bringing Premier Division football to Malta's sister island. They were joined in promotion by Zurrieq, with St. Patrick accompanying Hamrun Spartans in the opposite direction.

Malta's international record continues to go from bad to worse. In the 1998/99 European club competitions the three Maltese representatives were all beaten home and away in the first round, with only Birkirkara's Ivan Zammit getting his name on the scoresheet in the six matches. And

it was a similarly bleak and blank tale for the Maltese national team, who were unable to pick up any European Championship points in their first six qualifying matches.

The 1-4 defeat by Yugoslavia in neutral Greece at the end of the season brought Malta's losing sequence in competitive internationals to 20 in succession - a stretch lasting more than four years. In addition to their Euro 2000 games, Malta played five friendlies, all at Ta' Qali, and lost four of them. Their only success was a 2-1 victory over Bosnia-Herzegovina. It was their first win for a year and came as a result of a late winner from record cap-holder and goalscorer Carmel Busuttil, who marked

PLAYERS OF THE SEASON

NICKY SALIBA
Now 33 years of old, veteran midfielder once again showed his continued worth to Valletta in 1998/99, inspiring the Citizens to their third successive title and their second league and Cup 'double' in three years. His form was outstanding throughout the season but he particularly came to the fore in the closing stages when Valletta were missing a number of key players through injury and suspension. His cool authority was crucial during this period and had an important effect on those inexperienced youngsters who had been promoted into the first team. A long-serving Maltese international, Saliba was recalled by national team coach Josef Ilic in the second half of the season and scored his fourth international goal to give Malta a shock early lead against Yugoslavia in Salonika.

DAVID CARABOTT
Although Hibernians had a poor season in the league and failed to make a successful defence of the FA Trophy, their star player David Carabott was as influential and as consistent as ever. The 31-year-old was used by Hibs coach Mark Miller in a variety of positions - defence, midfield and attack - although it is common knowledge that he favours a position up front. 1998/99 was Carabott's 14th successive season with the Paola club. Birkirkara had wanted to sign him at the start of the campaign, but he turned down their substantial offer, saying that Hibernians were his first love and would also be his last.

his 89th appearance for Malta with his 22nd international goal.

There was a ray of hope for the future provided by the Maltese Under-21 side, whose 5-1 victory over their Macedonian equivalents was the biggest victory margin recorded by any Maltese representative team in history.

The Under-21s and other youth selections will now be playing their internationals in the new Centenary Stadium, which has been built on a site adjacent to the National Stadium in Ta' Qali. Its construction marks the 100th anniversary of the Malta Football Association, which was founded in 1900.

NATIONAL TEAM APPEARANCES 98/99

Coach - Josef ILIC	GER	MAC	CRO	IRL	MAC	BOS	POL	YUG	MOL	ISL	YUG	Cps	Gls
Mario MUSCAT (18/08/76) - Hibernians	G	G	G		G				s46	s66		16	-
Noel TURNER (09/12/74) - Sliema Wanderers	D86	M	s57	D	s68	D	D	D	D	s56		30	1
Jeffrey CHETCUTI (22/04/74) - Valletta	D	D	D	D		D	D83				D	33	-
Brian SAID (15/05/73) - Floriana	D	D			s47	D	D	D	D	D	D	14	-
Darren DEBONO (09/01/74) - Valletta	D	D	D	D	D						D	26	-
David CAMILLERI (21/08/74) - Hamrun Spartans	M	M	M	s77	M	s46	M	M72	M81	M84	M64	55	1
Carmel BUSUTTIL (29/02/64) - Sliema Wanderers	M52	M	M		M	M88	M46	M	s46		M	93	22
Joe BRINCAT (05/03/70) - Birkirkara	M	M	M	M	M	A46			M46		s64	78	5
Antoine ZAHRA (05/03/77) - Birkirkara	A61	A78	A77	A70						A85		24	1
Gilbert AGIUS (21/02/74) - Valletta	M68	A70	M54	s65	s60	A	A35	A58	A46			43	2
Hubert SUDA (29/09/69) - Birkirkara	A81	s70	A57	A65								65	8
Joe SANT FOURNIER (27/01/71) - Sliema Wanderers	s52											21	1
David CARABOTT (18/06/88) - Hibernians	s61	s78		D	s56	M	A	M	M	M	A	83	4
Jonathan MAGRI OVERAND (06/06/70) - Birkirkara	s68	D										5	1
Stefan SULTANA (18/07/68) - Hamrun Spartans/Hibernians	s81					s89			A46	A78	s83	32	4
Lino GALEA (26/03/76) - Sliema Wanderers	s86											2	-
Michael SPITERI (25/02/69) - Hibernians			D	D	D		D73	D	D			16	1
John BUTTIGIEG (05/10/63) - Floriana			D	D	D	D	D	D		D	D	85	-
Ivan ZAMMIT (17/03/72) - Birkirkara			s54	s70								21	-
Reggie CINI (22/10/70) - Valletta				G								26	-
Paul SIXSMITH (22/09/71) - Naxxar Lions			s77	D77	D		s78	s72	s81	s87		11	1
Nicky SALIBA (26/08/66) - Valletta					M68	M	M78	M	M		M	63	4
Chucks NWOKO (21/11/78) - Birkirkara					A56			A81	s46		A83	9	-
Michael CUTAJAR (14/02/71) - Birkirkara					A60	s46	s46	s81	s46	M63	s80	7	1
						/89							
Ernest BARRY (01/07/67) - Sliema Wanderers						G	G	G	G46	G66	G	8	-
Richard BUHAGIAR (17/03/72) - Floriana						D46	s83		D46	s78	D80	53	-
Silvio VELLA (08/02/67) - Hibernians						D47				D56		86	1
Graham BENCINI (25/07/76) - Birkirkara						s88	s73	s58				3	-
Adrian MIFSUD (11/12/74) - Rabat Ajax							s35		s46	s63		3	-
Massimo GRIMA (05/07/79) - Sliema Wanderers										D		1	-
Edward AZZOPARDI (13/12/77) - Rabat Ajax										D87		1	-
Jonathan HOLLAND (15/07/78) - Floriana										s84		1	-
Luke DIMECH (11/01/77) - Sliema Wanderers										s85		1	-

BIRKIRKARA

Birkirkara FC
Old Church Street
Birkirkara
tel - 447005
fax - 489214
Year of Formation - 1950
President - Victor Zammit
Secretary - Joe Brincat
Coach - Vlado Pejovic
Stadium - National, Ta' Qali (18,000)

APPEARANCES 98/99

	P	Ap	(s)	Gls
Zoran ANTIC (YUG)	M	24	(1)	
Graham BENCINI	D	20	(2)	
Patrick BRIFFA	D	1		
Joe BRINCAT	M	22	(1)	18
Jonathan BUHAGIAR	M		(4)	
Matthew CALASCIONE	D	5	(9)	
Reuben CINI	G	1	(1)	
Miguel CORBOLAN	A	1	(12)	
Michael CUTAJAR	M	21	(1)	10
Andy EMINYAN	D	15	(7)	1
Michael GALEA	A	24	(1)	9
Garreth MAGRI	D	1		
Jonathan MAGRI OVERAND	D	24		3
Velibor MATANOVIC (YUG)	D	21		
Clint MICALLEF	M		(1)	
Chuks NWOKO	A	21	(3)	9
Simon SAMMUT	A	11	(6)	1
Robert SAVIC (YUG)	G	26		
Gordon SPITERI	M		(3)	
Igor STEFANOVIC	A		(4)	
Hubert SUDA	A	5	(9)	3
Justin TELLUS	D	9	(3)	
Antoine ZAHRA	A	26	(1)	8
Stefan ZAHRA	A		(4)	
Ivan ZAMMIT	M	19	(3)	6

22/08/98	Hibernians	3-0	Galea 2, Cutajar
29/08/98	Pieta Hotspurs	2-0	Galea 2
12/09/98	Naxxar Lions	1-2	Magri Overand (p)
18/09/98	Floriana	2-2	Brincat 2 (1p)
23/09/98	Hamrun Spartans	3-0	Galea, Brincat, Zahra A.
26/09/98	Rabat Ajax	5-3	Brincat 2, Zammit, Nwoko 2
02/10/98	Valletta	4-1	Brincat, Zammit, Cutajar, Suda
18/10/98	Sliema Wanderers	0-0	
22/11/98	St. Patrick	1-0	Zahra A. (p)
13/12/98	Hibernians	1-1	Zammit
20/12/98	Pieta Hotspurs	2-0	Nwoko, Magri Overand (p)
27/12/98	Naxxar Lions	5-1	Brincat 2 (1p), Cutajar, Galea, Magri Overand
10/01/99	Floriana	4-0	Cutajar, Brincat (p), Zahra A., Galea
17/01/99	Rabat Ajax	2-2	Sammut, Zammit
24/01/99	Valletta	1-0	Suda
31/01/99	Sliema Wanderers	3-2	Nwoko, Eminyan, Zammit
14/02/99	Hamrun Spartans	3-0	Zammit, Nwoko, Zahra
20/02/99	St. Patrick	3-2	Zahra, Galea 2
28/02/99	Hibernians	1-1	Cutajar
07/03/99	Pieta Hotspurs	2-1	Brincat 2 (1p)
21/03/99	Naxxar Lions	1-0	Nwoko
05/04/99	Floriana	3-0	Brincat 2, Cutajar
11/04/99	Rabat Ajax	5-1	Cutajar 3, Brincat 2 (1p)
18/04/99	Valletta	2-1	Zahra A., Suda
24/04/99	Sliema Wanderers	2-0	Zahra A., Brincat
02/05/99	Hamrun Spartans	7-0	Nwoko 3, Cutajar, Brincat, Zahra A., og (Sylla)
09/05/99	St. Patrick	1-0	Brincat (p)

FLORIANA

CLUB DIRECTORY

Floriana FC
28 St. Anne Street
Floriana VLT 15
tel - 238664/236059
fax - 233498
Year of Formation - 1894
President - Anthony Grech Sant
Secretary - Mario Gauci
Coach - Traiko Sokolov; Eric Schembri
Stadium - National, Ta' Qali (18,000)

MAJOR HONOURS
League Championship - (25)
1910, 1912, 1913, 1921, 1922, 1925, 1927,
1928, 1929, 1931, 1935, 1937, 1950, 1951,
1952, 1953, 1955, 1958, 1962, 1968, 1970,
1973, 1975, 1977, 1993.
Domestic Cup - (18)
1938, 1945, 1947, 1949, 1950, 1953, 1954,
1955, 1957, 1958, 1961, 1966, 1967, 1972,
1976, 1981, 1993, 1994.

APPEARANCES 98/99

		P	Ap	(s)	Gls
Glenn BARRY	A	1		(1)	
Nicholas BILOCCA	A			(2)	
Richard BUHAGIAR	A	17			13
Albert BUSUTTIL	A	23		(4)	
John BUTTIGIEG	D	23			1
William CAMENZULI	M	19		(2)	1
Matthew CAMILLERI	G	2			
Mario CARUANA	M	14		(3)	2
Clinton CIANTAR	D	2		(3)	
Eudes DENGAKI (CON)	A	19		(3)	2
Stefan FARRUGIA	A	9		(7)	2
Kurt FORMOSA	A			(2)	
David GALEA	D	1			
Mark GALEA	A			(2)	
Justin HABER	G	1		(2)	
Jonathan HOLLAND	D	13		(4)	1
George MALLIA	A	17			3
Claude MATTOCKS	D	3		(7)	1
Alan MICALLEF	A			(2)	
James NAVARRO	D	17		(5)	
Rufin OBA (CON)	M	21			8
Mark PSAILA	M	1			
Brian SAID	M	24			2
Nicholas SCHEMBRI	M	2		(6)	
Charles SCIBERRAS	M	21		(2)	3
Sean SULLIVAN	G	24			
Antoine ZAHRA	A	6		(6)	1
Todor ZAITSEV (BUL)	M	17		(1)	4

LEAGUE RESULTS 1998/99

22/08/98	Naxxar Lions	0-0	
30/08/98	Valletta	0-4	
12/09/98	Rabat Ajax	5-1	Mallia, Oba, Buhagiar, Dengaki, og (Camilleri)
18/09/98	Birkirkara	2-2	Oba, og (Bencini)
27/09/98	Sliema Wanderers	1-1	Oba
04/10/98	Hamrun Spartans	2-1	Sciberras, Caruana
18/10/98	St. Patrick	5-1	Mallia 2, Said, Sciberras, Dengaki
08/11/98	Pieta Hotspurs	2-1	Sciberras, Zaitsev
24/11/98	Hibernians	2-3	Said, Caruana
29/11/98	Naxxar Lions	2-1	Oba (p), Camenzuli
13/12/98	Valletta	1-4	Oba
26/12/98	Rabat Ajax	1-1	Buhagiar
10/01/99	Birkirkara	0-4	
17/01/99	Sliema Wanderers	0-1	
24/01/99	Hamrun Spartans	2-0	Oba, Mattocks
30/01/99	St. Patrick	2-2	Zahra, Oba
14/02/99	Hibernians	0-2	
20/02/99	Pieta Hotspurs	2-1	Zaitsev, Holland
06/03/99	Naxxar Lions	6-2	Buhagiar 4, Farrugia, og (Degiorgio)
14/03/99	Valletta	1-3	Farrugia
20/03/99	Rabat Ajax	0-4	
05/04/99	Birkirkara	0-3	
14/04/99	Sliema Wanderers	1-1	Buttigieg
17/04/99	Hamrun Spartans	0-1	
25/04/99	St. Patrick	5-0	Buhagiar 3 (1p), Zaitsev, Oba
02/05/99	Hibernians	3-2	Buhagiar 2 (1p), Zaitsev
08/05/99	Pieta Hotspurs	2-4	Buhagiar 2

HAMRUN SPARTANS

CLUB DIRECTORY

Hamrun Spartans FC
42 Dun Nerik Cordina Perez str.
Hamrun
tel - 241682
fax - 251482
Year of Formation - 1907
President - Joseph Zammit
Secretary - A. Farrugia Sacco
Coach - Milisav Bogdanovic; Andy Weavill
Stadium - Victor Tedesco (6,000)

MAJOR HONOURS
League Championship - (7)
1914, 1918, 1947, 1983, 1987, 1988, 1991.
Domestic Cup - (6)
1983, 1984, 1987, 1988, 1989, 1992.

APPEARANCES 98/99

	P	Ap	(s)	Gls
Lawrence ATTARD	A	12	(7)	
Gaetano BARTOLO	A		(2)	
Ettienne BONNICI	A	12	(5)	
Jonathan BUTTIGIEG	D		(2)	
David CAMILLERI	M	23		
Edwin CAMILLERI	D	12	(3)	
Ivan CASHA	G	20	(1)	
James CUTAJAR	D		(1)	
David DAVIES (ENG)	A	1		
Jean Paul DESIRA	D	7	(8)	
Alan ELLUL	M	1	(4)	
Dado FARRUGIA	D	4	(4)	
Jeffrey FARRUGIA	D	4		
Nicky FASINELLI	D	19	(3)	
David GALEA	D	23		
Neville GALEA	A	2	(3)	
Mario GATT	D		(1)	
Waled LOVINI (TUN)	A	4	(4)	
Edmond LUFI	D	7		1
Charlo MAGRO	D	24		
Ramon MALLIA	M	2	(1)	
Claude MANGION	D	15	(1)	
Rupert MANGION	M	25		1
Peter OHAKA (NIG)	A	13	(3)	5
Kevin SAMMUT	A	17	(3)	
Charles SCIBERRAS	G	7		
Stefan SULTANA	A	3		2
Dybril SYLLA (GUI)	M	13	(2)	2
Paul ZAMMIT	A	27		15

LEAGUE RESULTS 1998/99

24/08/98	Valletta	1-3	Sultana
29/08/98	St. Patrick	3-4	Sultana (p), Zammit 2
13/09/98	Hibernians	0-5	
19/09/98	Pieta Hotspurs	0-4	
23/09/98	Birkirkara	0-3	
26/09/98	Naxxar Lions	1-1	Zammit
04/10/98	Floriana	1-2	Lufi
01/11/98	Rabat Ajax	2-4	Zammit 2
22/11/98	Sliema Wanderers	0-3	
29/11/98	Valletta	1-4	Ohaka
16/12/98	St. Patrick	1-1	Ohaka
27/12/98	Hibernians	1-3	Zammit
03/01/99	Pieta Hotspurs	0-3	
09/01/99	Naxxar Lions	0-0	
24/01/99	Floriana	0-2	
30/01/99	Rabat Ajax	4-2	Sylla, Zammit 3
14/02/99	Birkirkara	0-3	
28/02/99	Sliema Wanderers	1-2	Zammit
07/03/99	Valletta	1-2	Zammit
13/03/99	St. Patrick	1-2	Zammit
21/03/99	Hibernians	1-2	Ohaka (p)
04/04/99	Pieta Hotspurs	1-4	Zammit
11/04/99	Naxxar Lions	2-1	Ohaka, Zammit
17/04/99	Floriana	1-0	Zammit
25/04/99	Rabat Ajax	1-2	Sylla
02/05/99	Birkirkara	0-7	
08/05/99	Sliema Wanderers	2-1	Ohaka, Mangion R. (p)

HIBERNIANS

CLUB DIRECTORY

Hibernians FC
114 Paola square
Paola
tel - 677764
fax - 240887
Year of Formation - 1932
President - Anthony Bezzina
Secretary - Savior Cachia
Coach - Mark Miller
Stadium - Hibernians, Corradino (8,000)

MAJOR HONOURS
League Championship - (8) 1961, 1967, 1969,
1979, 1981, 1982, 1994, 1995.
Domestic Cup - (6)
1962, 1970, 1971, 1980, 1982, 1998.

APPEARANCES 98/99

	P	Ap	(s)	Gls
Kenneth ABELA	A	11	(6)	5
Darren ATTARD	A	5	(11)	4
Lawrence ATTARD	D	1		
Roderick BALDACHINO	D	10	(8)	3
Martin BORG	M	10	(8)	
David CARABOTT	A	25		5
Ndusi CHUKUNYERE (NIG)	A	16	(4)	3
Adrian CIANTAR	M	22	(2)	3
Ranier FARRUGIA	G	1	(2)	
Egiro KOLOGBO (NIG)	A	1		
Claude MANGION	M		(5)	
Essien MBONG (NIG)	M	20		2
Alan MIFSUD	D	23	(1)	
Mario MUSCAT	G	26		
Kevin NOTEMAN (ENG)	A	20		4
Charles SCERRI	M	10	(6)	3
Michael SPITERI	D	17		
Wilfred SPITERI	D	7	(3)	
Stefan SULTANA	A	18	(1)	10
Silvio VELLA	D	17	(2)	
Roger WALKER	D	20		3
Aaron XUEREB	D	11	(6)	1
Karl ZACCHAU (DEN)	A	6		1

LEAGUE RESULTS 1998/99

22/08/98	Birkirkara	0-3	
09/09/98	Sliema Wanderers	1-3	Walker
13/09/98	Hamrun Spartans	5-0	Abela 2, Zacchau, Ciantar, Attard D. (p)
20/09/98	St. Patrick	6-0	Abela, Attard D. 2, Chukunyere 2, Noteman
28/09/98	Valletta	0-1	
03/10/98	Pieta Hotspurs	1-1	Noteman (p)
17/10/98	Naxxar Lions	1-1	Ciantar
24/11/98	Floriana	3-2	Scerri, Walker, Sultana
06/12/98	Rabat Ajax	0-2	
13/12/98	Birkirkara	1-1	Sultana
20/12/98	Sliema Wanderers	0-0	
27/12/98	Hamrun Spartans	3-1	Sultana, Carabott, Abela
04/01/99	St. Patrick	3-1	Abela, Scerri, Attard D.
10/01/99	Valletta	1-3	Mbong
16/01/99	Pieta Hotspurs	2-0	Carabott, Chukunyere
23/01/99	Naxxar Lions	0-0	
14/02/99	Floriana	2-0	Sultana, Noteman
21/02/99	Rabat Ajax	2-1	Walker, Sultana
28/02/99	Birkirkara	1-1	Sultana
14/03/99	Sliema Wanderers	1-2	Sultana
21/03/99	Hamrun Spartans	2-1	Sultana, Carabott (p)
03/04/99	St. Patrick	2-1	Baldachino, Sultana
10/04/99	Valletta	0-2	
14/04/99	Pieta Hotspurs	1-0	Baldachino
24/04/99	Naxxar Lions	1-2	Sultana
02/05/99	Floriana	2-3	Xuereb, Noteman
09/05/99	Rabat Ajax	6-1	Carabott 2, Baldachino, Mbong, Scerri, Ciantar

NAXXAR LIONS

CLUB DIRECTORY

Naxxar Lions FC
29/30 Victory Square
Naxxar
tel - 411974
fax - 332004
Year of Formation - 1920
President - Michael Zammit Tabona
Secretary - Franco Vella Tabone
Coach - Sinisa Radak & Michael Degiorgio
Stadium - National, Ta' Qali (18,000)

APPEARANCES 98/99

	P	Ap	(s)	Gls
Alex AGIUS	M		(1)	
Oroseo ANONAM (NIG)	M	20	(1)	7
Victor BELLIA	A	13	(12)	2
Andrea BONNICI	D	10		
Gordon CAMENZULI	A		(4)	
CARBONARO	A		(2)	
Kevin CASSAR	D	1		
Marco CATANIA	D	20	(2)	1
Reuben DEBONO	G	26		
Michael DEGIORGIO	M	23	(1)	
Mark DEGUARA	D	1	(9)	
Jason GALEA	D	20	(1)	
Sandro GAMBIN	D	18		1
Charles MAGRI	D		(2)	
Mark MARLOW	M	15	(4)	2
Dennis MIZZI	M	1	(2)	
Franklin MUSCAT	M	2		
Simon MUSCAT	M	2	(4)	
Digger OKONKWO (NIG)	A	20	(1)	2
Chris ORETAN (NIG)	A	17	(4)	6
Sinisa RADAK (YUG)	M	25		6
Paul SIXSMITH	M	26		4
Igor STEFANOVIC	A	13	(4)	1
Michael WOODS	D	23		
Andrew XUEREB	G	1		

LEAGUE RESULTS 1998/99

22/08/98	Floriana	0-0	
30/08/98	Rabat Ajax	3-0	Sixsmith, Oretan, Catania
12/09/98	Birkirkara	2-1	Marlow 2
19/09/98	Sliema Wanderers	2-1	Anonam, Oretan
26/09/98	Hamrun Spartans	1-1	Oretan
03/10/98	St. Patrick	3-1	Radak, Anonam 2
17/10/98	Hibernians	1-1	Radak
01/11/98	Pieta Hotspurs	5-3	Bellia, Oretan 2, Anonam, Sixsmith (p)
24/11/98	Valletta	0-1	
29/11/98	Floriana	1-2	Radak
19/12/98	Rabat Ajax	1-2	Okonkwo
27/12/98	Birkirkara	1-5	Sixsmith (p)
04/01/99	Sliema Wanderers	2-0	Bellia, Anonam
09/01/99	Hamrun Spartans	0-0	
16/01/99	St. Patrick	2-2	Oretan, Sixsmith (p)
23/01/99	Hibernians	0-0	
13/02/99	Pieta Hotspurs	1-1	Anonam
27/02/99	Valletta	0-3	
06/03/99	Floriana	2-6	Gambin, Okonkwo
15/03/99	Rabat Ajax	0-2	
21/03/99	Birkirkara	0-1	
04/04/99	Sliema Wanderers	0-3	
11/04/99	Hamrun Spartans	1-2	Radak (p)
17/04/99	St. Patrick	1-1	Anonam
24/04/99	Hibernians	2-1	Radak (p), Stefanovic
01/05/99	Pieta Hotspurs	1-4	Radak
05/05/99	Valletta	0-2	

PIETA HOTSPURS

CLUB DIRECTORY

Pieta Hotspurs FC
Our Lady of Sorrows Street
Pieta
tel - 231336
fax - 234150
Year of Formation - 1932
President - Edward Schembri
Secretary - Mario Mallia
Coach - George Deanov
Stadium - National, Ta' Qali (18,000)

APPEARANCES 98/99

	P	Ap	(s)	Gls
Pierre AQUILINA	D	4	(3)	
Louis AZZOPARDI	D	17	(3)	
Marian BALAN (ROM)	D	8		
Kevin CHIRCOP	D	3	(1)	
Saviour DARMANIN	G	22		
Martin DEANOV (BUL)	A	18	(2)	4
Jesmond DELIA	D	18	(2)	
Kevin FARRUGIA	M	16	(4)	
Kurt FARRUGIA	D	3	(2)	
Carmel FORMOSA	A	16	(9)	4
Mark Anthony GALEA	A	4	(10)	
Malcolm LICARI	M	18	(4)	5
Edmond LUFI	M	8	(1)	1
Kevin MAMO	A	21	(4)	2
Ettiene MERCIECA	G	5	(1)	
Clive MIZZI	D	23	(2)	4
Kevin MONTANARO	M	3		
MONTEBELLO	A		(1)	
Dobrin RAGUIN (BUL)	A	23	(1)	13
Eric SALIBA	D	24		
Massimo SCHEMBRI	D	16	(2)	1
SPITERI	A		(2)	
Daniel THEWMA	A	13	(2)	5
Lazar TONOZLIEV (BUL)	M	14		

LEAGUE RESULTS 1998/99

23/08/98	Rabat Ajax	4-0	Licari, Deanov, Raguin 2 (1p)
29/08/98	Birkirkara	0-2	
13/09/98	Sliema Wanderers	0-2	
19/09/98	Hamrun Spartans	4-0	Raguin 2, Deanov, Formosa
27/09/98	St. Patrick	1-1	Licari
03/10/98	Hibernians	1-1	Formosa
17/10/98	Valletta	0-1	
01/11/98	Naxxar Lions	3-5	Lufi (p), Mamo, Raguin
08/11/98	Floriana	1-2	Mizzi (p)
16/12/98	Rabat Ajax	1-2	Mizzi (p)
20/12/98	Birkirkara	0-2	
26/12/98	Sliema Wanderers	2-4	Formosa, Raguin
03/01/99	Hamrun Spartans	3-0	Mizzi (p), Raguin 2
09/01/99	St. Patrick	0-0	
16/01/99	Hibernians	0-2	
31/01/99	Valletta	0-1	
13/02/99	Naxxar Lions	1-1	Thewma
20/02/99	Floriana	1-2	Mamo
27/02/99	Rabat Ajax	1-1	Licari
07/03/99	Birkirkara	1-2	Formosa
19/03/99	Sliema Wanderers	1-1	Raguin
04/04/99	Hamrun Spartans	4-1	Raguin 2, Deanov, Thewma (p)
10/04/99	St. Patrick	1-0	Licari
14/04/99	Hibernians	0-1	
23/04/99	Valletta	1-2	Schembri
01/05/99	Naxxar Lions	4-1	Thewma 2, Raguin, Deanov
08/05/99	Floriana	4-2	Thewma, Mizzi, Raguin, Licari

RABAT AJAX

CLUB DIRECTORY

Rabat Ajax FC
2nd Floor
Civic Centre
Parish Square
Rabat RBT 05
tel - 454244/455847
Year of Formation - 1930
President - vacant
Secretary - Mario Grima
Coach - Ziya Yildiz
Stadium - National, Ta' Qali (18,000)

MAJOR HONOURS
League Championship - (2) 1985, 1986.
Domestic Cup - (1) 1986.

APPEARANCES 98/99

	P	Ap	(s)	Gls
Roderick AGIUS	G	4		
Roderick ASCIAK	M	27		10
Alex AZZOPARDI	M		(2)	
Edward AZZOPARDI	D	24	(1)	4
Charles BORG	D	7	(7)	
Jason BORG	A	1	(3)	
Rodney CAMILLERI	D	24		
Cedric CARUANA	D	25		1
John CASSAR	A	3	(7)	
Dennis CAUCHI	D	20	(1)	
Franco DEGABRIELE	A	1		
Abu ERAMASH (LIB)	A	1	(2)	
Joseph FARRUGIA	M	13	(1)	
Michael FARRUGIA	D	9	(3)	
Keith FENECH	M	23		1
Donovan FRIGGIERI	M	5	(13)	
Jason GALEA	G	4		
Giles LANZON	A	2	(1)	
Kevin LOUGHBOROUGH	M	7	(10)	1
Keith MICALLEF	M	5	(5)	
Michael MICALLEF	M	13	(3)	7
Adrian MIFSUD	A	23		7
Vesko PETROVIC (YUG)	M	11	(1)	1
Stoian SIMEONOV (BUL)	G	19		
Ziya YILDIZ (YUG)	D	26		5

LEAGUE RESULTS 1998/99

Date	Opponent	Score	Scorers
23/08/98	Pieta Hotspurs	0-4	
30/08/98	Naxxar Lions	0-3	
12/09/98	Floriana	1-5	Yildiz
20/09/98	Valletta	1-7	Mifsud
26/09/98	Birkirkara	3-5	Caruana, Asciak 2
04/10/98	Sliema Wanderers	0-2	
01/11/98	Hamrun Spartans	4-2	Petrovic, Mifsud, Azzopardi E., Loughborough
08/11/98	St. Patrick	1-1	Mifsud
06/12/98	Hibernians	2-0	Asciak, Micallef M.
16/12/98	Pieta Hotspurs	2-1	Asciak 2
19/12/98	Naxxar Lions	2-1	Micallef M. 2
26/12/98	Floriana	1-1	Azzopardi E.
03/01/99	Valletta	0-4	
17/01/99	Birkirkara	2-2	Yildiz, Asciak
23/01/99	Sliema Wanderers	2-4	Micallef M. 2
30/01/99	Hamrun Spartans	2-4	Asciak, Azzopardi E.
16/02/99	St. Patrick	1-1	Asciak
21/02/99	Hibernians	1-2	Mifsud (p)
27/02/99	Pieta Hotspurs	1-1	Azzopardi E.
15/03/99	Naxxar Lions	2-0	Micallef M. 2
20/03/99	Floriana	4-0	Yildiz 2, Mifsud, Asciak
03/04/99	Valletta	0-0	
11/04/99	Birkirkara	1-5	Mifsud (p)
18/04/99	Sliema Wanderers	0-3	
25/04/99	Hamrun Spartans	2-1	Mifsud, Yildiz
05/05/99	St. Patrick	1-2	Asciak
09/05/99	Hibernians	1-6	Fenech (p)

ST. PATRICK

CLUB DIRECTORY

St. Patrick FC
217 Main Street
Zabbar
tel - 664889
Year of Formation - 1912
President - France Catania
Secretary - Manuel Gauci
Coach - Anatas Marinov
Stadium - National, Ta' Qali (18,000)

APPEARANCES 98/99

	P	Ap	(s)	Gls
Franklin AZZOPARDI	G		(1)	
AZZOPARDI	M	1		
BONNICI	M		(1)	
Alex CAMILLERI	G	27		
Robert CASSAR	D	26		
Fabio CAUCHI	D	21	(1)	1
Patrick CILIA	A	1	(3)	
Fatos DAJA (ALB)	D	21	(1)	
Gordon FAILLA	M		(3)	
Adrian FARRUGIA	A		(1)	
Alan GALEA	M	20	(2)	
Renis HYKA (ALB)	A	25		13
Patrick MIZZI	M		(5)	
Chris MUSCAT	A	7	(11)	
Adrian PULIS	D	10	(5)	1
Kenneth SCICLUNA	D	25		
Konrad SULTANA	A	25		8
Angel TERZIISKI (BUL)	D	24		2
Demmis TONNA	M	11	(13)	3
Darren VELLA	D	14	(1)	
Stefan ZAHRA	M	1	(9)	
Jeffrey ZAMMIT	M	20	(1)	1
Michael ZERAFA	D		(2)	
Simon ZERAFA	D	18	(7)	

LEAGUE RESULTS 1998/99

23/08/98	Sliema Wanderers	0-5	
29/08/98	Hamrun Spartans	4-3	Hyka 2 (1p), Sultana 2
09/09/98	Valletta	0-5	
20/09/98	Hibernians	0-6	
27/09/98	Pieta Hotspurs	1-1	Hyka
03/10/98	Naxxar Lions	1-3	Hyka (p)
18/10/98	Floriana	1-5	Sultana
08/11/98	Rabat Ajax	1-1	Sultana
22/11/98	Birkirkara	0-1	
06/12/98	Sliema Wanderers	0-7	
16/12/98	Hamrun Spartans	1-1	Cauchi
19/12/98	Valletta	3-4	Hyka 2, Terziiski (p)
04/01/99	Hibernians	1-3	Pulis
09/01/99	Pieta Hotspurs	0-0	
16/01/99	Naxxar Lions	2-2	Hyka (p), Sultana
30/01/99	Floriana	2-2	Sultana 2
16/02/99	Rabat Ajax	1-1	Tonna
20/02/99	Birkirkara	2-3	Tonna, Sultana
06/03/99	Sliema Wanderers	1-3	Tonna
13/03/99	Hamrun Spartans	2-1	Hyka, Terziiski
20/03/99	Valletta	2-3	Hyka 2 (1p)
03/04/99	Hibernians	1-2	Zammit
10/04/99	Pieta Hotspurs	0-1	
17/04/99	Naxxar Lions	1-1	Hyka
25/04/99	Floriana	0-5	
05/05/99	Rabat Ajax	2-1	Hyka 2 (1p)
09/05/99	Birkirkara	0-1	

SLIEMA WANDERERS

CLUB DIRECTORY

Sliema Wanderers FC
21 Tower Road
Sliema
tel - 332033
fax - 320219
Year of Formation - 1909
President - Robert Arrigo
Secretary - Alex Manfrè
Coach - Carmel Busuttil & Martin Gregory
Stadium - National, Ta' Qali (18,000)

MAJOR HONOURS
League Championship - (23) 1920, 1923, 1924, 1926, 1930, 1933, 1934, 1936, 1938, 1939, 1940, 1949, 1954, 1956, 1957, 1964, 1965, 1966, 1971, 1972, 1976, 1989, 1996.
Domestic Cup - (17) 1935, 1936, 1937, 1940, 1946, 1948, 1951, 1952, 1956, 1959, 1963, 1965, 1968, 1969, 1974, 1979, 1990.

APPEARANCES 98/99

	P	Ap	(s)	Gls
Wayne ATTARD	D	16	(7)	2
Ernest BARRY	G	26		
Mark Anthony BONNICI	A	5	(11)	
Fernando BRIFFA	A		(1)	
Paulo BUGEJA	G	1	(2)	
Carmel BUSUTTIL	M	21	(1)	11
Ian CIANTAR	D	24	(1)	
Ridha DARDOURI (TUN)	A	7	(3)	
Luke DIMECH	D	13	(2)	1
Mark DIMECH	D	1	(1)	
Joe FARRUGIA	M		(1)	
Davor FILIPOVIC (CRO)	A	6	(1)	
Lino GALEA	D	23	(2)	
Andrei GALEANO (ARG)	D		(3)	
Martin GREGORY	M	4	(6)	1
Massimo GRIMA	M	22	(1)	7
Michael MIFSUD	A	17	(5)	8
Uwa OGBODO (NIG)	A	14	(7)	5
Djordje PINTAC (YUG)	D	23		3
ROE	D		(1)	
Kevin SAMMUT	D	1		
Joe SANT FOURNIER	D	15	(4)	2
TEMPLEMAN	A		(1)	
Noel TURNER	M	23		5
Ivan WOODS	A	14	(6)	9
Brendan ZAMMIT	M		(2)	
Sandro ZAMMIT FAVA	D	21	(3)	

LEAGUE RESULTS 1998/99

23/08/98	St. Patrick	5-0	Busuttil, Woods, Mifsud 2, Turner
09/09/98	Hibernians	3-1	Busuttil 2, Mifsud
13/09/98	Pieta Hotspurs	2-0	Mifsud, Grima
19/09/98	Naxxar Lions	1-2	Ogbodo
23/09/98	Valletta	1-3	Woods
27/09/98	Floriana	1-1	Busuttil
04/10/98	Rabat Ajax	2-0	Grima, Pintac
18/10/98	Birkirkara	0-0	
22/11/98	Hamrun Spartans	3-0	Woods, Pintac, Attard
06/12/98	St. Patrick	7-0	Woods 4, Turner (p), Busuttil, Sant Fournier
20/12/98	Hibernians	0-0	
26/12/98	Pieta Hotspurs	4-2	Busuttil, Mifsud 2, Turner
04/01/99	Naxxar Lions	0-2	
17/01/99	Floriana	1-0	Busuttil
23/01/99	Rabat Ajax	4-2	Turner, Attard, Ogbodo 2
31/01/99	Birkirkara	2-3	Turner (p), Woods
21/02/99	Valletta	0-4	
28/02/99	Hamrun Spartans	2-1	Ogbodo, Grima
06/03/99	St. Patrick	3-1	Busuttil 2, Ogbodo
14/03/99	Hibernians	2-1	Sant Fournier, Busuttil
19/03/99	Pieta Hotspurs	1-1	Dimech L.
04/04/99	Naxxar Lions	3-0	Grima, Gregory, Pintac
14/04/99	Floriana	1-1	Busuttil
18/04/99	Rabat Ajax	3-0	Grima 2, Mifsud
24/04/99	Birkirkara	0-2	
01/05/99	Valletta	2-3	Mifsud, Grima (p)
08/05/99	Hamrun Spartans	1-2	Woods

VALLETTA

CLUB DIRECTORY

Valletta FC
126 St. Lucia Street
Valletta
tel - 224939
fax - 228083
Year of Formation - 1904
President - Joe Caruana Curran
Secretary - Benny Pace
Coach - Krasimir Manolov
Stadium - National, Ta' Qali (18,000)

MAJOR HONOURS
League Championship - (16) 1915, 1932, 1945,
1946, 1948, 1959, 1960, 1963, 1974, 1978,
1980, 1984, 1990, 1992, 1997, 1998.
Domestic Cup - (9) 1960, 1964, 1975, 1977,
1978, 1991, 1995, 1996, 1997.

APPEARANCES 98/99

	P	Ap	(s)	Gls
Gilbert AGIUS	A	24	(2)	20
Jonathan BONDIN	M		(1)	
Karl BONNICI	D	21	(5)	
Drasko BRAUNOVIC (YUG)	D	20	(3)	1
Chris CAMILLERI	D		(7)	
Joe CAMILLERI	D	19	(4)	2
Jeffrey CHETCUTI	D	19	(2)	3
Neville CIANTAR	G	2	(1)	
Jonathan CILIA	M		(1)	
Reggie CINI	G	25		
Darren DEBONO	D	19	(2)	
Mark ELLUL	M		(1)	
Rene FORACE	M	2	(9)	
Mark GALEA	A	6	(12)	5
Stefan GIGLIO	A	26		8
Boris HVOINEV (BUL)	A	7	(1)	4
Alexander IVANOV (BUL)	M	17	(3)	
Christian LAFERLA	D	13	(1)	9
E. LAPIRA	M		(1)	
Leonard MACKAY	M		(1)	
Pavel MRAZ (CZE)	A	14	(1)	3
Beppe PACE	M		(1)	
Nicky SALIBA	M	24		1
Dino TRAKOSOPOULOS	A		(3)	
Nenad VESELJI	A	15	(9)	9
Joe ZARB	M	24	(1)	6

LEAGUE RESULTS 1998/99

24/08/98	Hamrun Spartans	3-1	Braunovic, Zarb (p), Agius
30/08/98	Floriana	4-0	Hvoinev, Laferla 2, Agius
09/09/98	St. Patrick	5-0	Hvoinev, Laferla, Veselji, Camilleri J., Agius (p)
20/09/98	Rabat Ajax	7-1	Giglio 2, Agius 3, Hvoinev 2
23/09/98	Sliema Wanderers	3-1	Giglio, Veselji, Agius
28/09/98	Hibernians	1-0	Chetcuti
02/10/98	Birkirkara	1-4	Zarb (p)
17/10/98	Pieta Hotspurs	1-0	Agius
24/11/98	Naxxar Lions	1-0	Laferla
29/11/98	Hamrun Spartans	4-1	Agius 2 (1p), Giglio, Galea
13/12/98	Floriana	4-1	Chetcuti, Laferla, Mraz (p), Giglio
19/12/98	St. Patrick	4-3	Agius 3 (2p), Laferla
03/01/99	Rabat Ajax	4-0	Zarb, Giglio, Laferla, Veselji
10/01/99	Hibernians	3-1	Chetcuti, Laferla 2
24/01/99	Birkirkara	0-1	
31/01/99	Pieta Hotspurs	1-0	Agius (p)
21/02/99	Sliema Wanderers	4-0	Mraz 2, Veselji, Galea
27/02/99	Naxxar Lions	3-0	Agius 2 (2p), Veselji
07/03/99	Hamrun Spartans	2-1	Veselji 2
14/03/99	Floriana	3-1	Zarb 2, Agius
20/03/99	St. Patrick	3-2	Agius 2, Giglio
03/04/99	Rabat Ajax	0-0	
10/04/99	Hibernians	2-0	Camilleri J., Agius
18/04/99	Birkirkara	1-2	Veselji
23/04/99	Pieta Hotspurs	2-1	Galea, Zarb
01/05/99	Sliema Wanderers	3-2	Veselji, Saliba, Galea
05/05/99	Naxxar Lions	2-0	Giglio, Galea

PROMOTED CLUBS

SECOND DIVISION FINAL TABLE 98/99

		Pd	W	D	L	F	A	Pt	GD
1	**Gozo**	**18**	**10**	**5**	**3**	**42**	**22**	**35**	**+20**
2	**Zurrieq**	**18**	**10**	**3**	**5**	**39**	**32**	**33**	**+7**
3	Lija Athletics	18	9	5	4	30	25	32	+5
4	Tarxien Rainbows	18	8	4	6	34	27	28	+7
5	Marsa	18	7	4	7	30	28	25	+2
6	Xghajra Tornadoes	18	7	4	7	24	33	25	-9
7	St. Andrews	18	6	4	8	37	35	22	+2
8	Mosta	18	4	7	7	27	31	19	-4
9	Mellieha	18	5	1	12	30	44	16	-14
10	Siggiewi	18	3	5	10	21	37	14	-16

CLUB DIRECTORY

Gozo FC
Gozo Football Association
Gozo Stadium
Imgarr str. Xewija
Gozo
tel - 559448/558124
Year of Formation - 1936
President - Chris Said
Coach - Alfred Cardona
Stadium - Gozo Stadium (6,000)

CLUB DIRECTORY

Zurrieq FC
30 Main str.
Zurrieq
tel - 640642/640791
Year of Formation - 1949
President - Savior Farrugia
Secretary - Alfred Damato
Coach - Lawrence Borg
Stadium - National, Ta' Qali (18,000)

MAJOR HONOURS
Domestic Cup - (1) 1985.

MOLDOVA

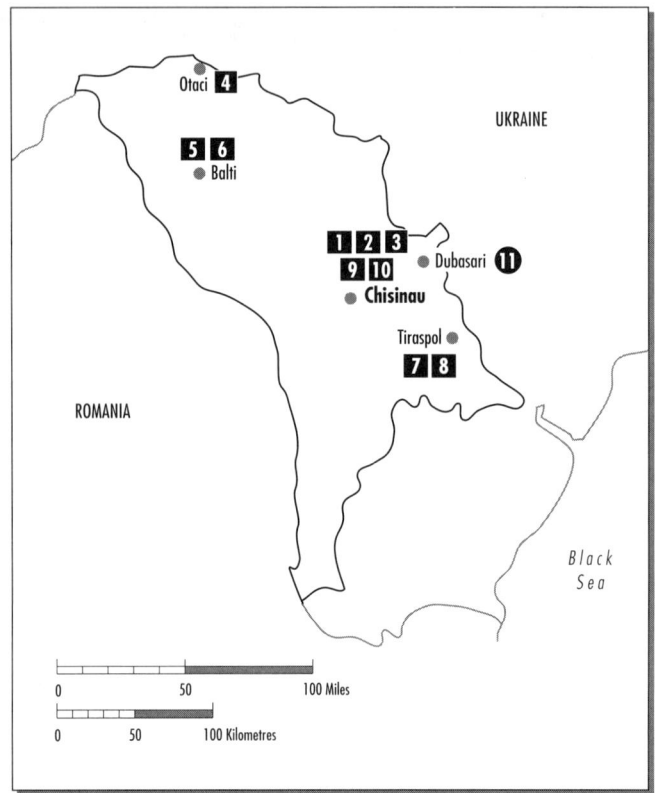

NEW TEN-TEAM LEAGUE DOMINATED BY ZIMBRU

Early leads fail to bring victories

FEDERATION DIRECTORY

Federatia Moloveneasca de Futbol
39 Tricolorului St. - MD, 2012 Chisinau

tel - (3732) 247878   Year of Formation - 1990
fax - (3732) 247890   President - Petru Comendant
                Secretary - Nicolae Cibotari

Stadium - Republican (22,500)

Moldova took just three points from their first seven Euro 2000 qualifying matches. They all came from draws - goalless stalemates at home to Northern Ireland and Finland and a 2-2 humdinger in Belfast, a match in which they twice held the lead.

In fact, Ivan Daniliant's team also went in front early on in their first two qualifiers, away to Finland and - remarkably - at home to Germany, but they ended up losers on both occasions. It was becoming rather a nasty habit. The only matches in which the Moldovans successfully defended a lead were friendly internationals, against Estonia and Malta.

A change of formula was introduced to the Moldovan national league in 1998/99, with just ten teams competing at the outset (instead of the previous 14), and two mini-leagues of five teams apiece being formed after the 18-match cut-off point. The purpose of this was to create extra excitement in a country where crowds of only a few hundred are the norm. However, the gamble did not pay off for the simple reason that perennial champions Zimbru Chisinau were once again a large cut above the rest.

11 points clear at the end of the regular season, Zimbru were able to maintain a similar distance between themselves and their pursuers right through the play-off section, remaining undefeated as they did so. The only team to beat them over the full league campaign were Olimpia Balti, who won 1-0 in the third match of the campaign. Olimpia, like the other four teams in the championship group, all ultimately retained the positions they had held at the 18-match cut-off.

There was even less interest in the relegation group - quite simply because there was no relegation place left to fill. Nistru Otaci, eighth in the regular season, withdrew from the league in the winter break after huge debts had rendered them inoperable. So they, and they alone, were relegated, with all of their subsequent matches being attributed as 'victories without goals' to their opponents.

LEAGUE CHAMPIONSHIP RESULTS 98/99

		1	2	3	4	5	6	7	8	9	10
1	Agro Chisinau		0-0	0-3	2-1	0-0	0-1	1-4	1-1	2-1	0-1
				1-3	xxx		0-0			1-1	
2	Constructorul Chisinau	0-0		5-0	xxx	2-1	1-0	1-1	2-0	1-0	1-2
						1-0		2-0	0-1		1-1
3	Moldova-Gaz Chisinau	1-2	0-1		xxx	0-0	1-0	2-1	2-3	1-2	1-2
			2-0			xxx		2-1			1-2
4	Nistru Otaci	0-0	3-0	0-0		2-1	1-0	1-1	+++	0-1	0-1
		+++		+++			+++			+++	
5	Olimpia Balti	0-0	0-1	2-0	1-0		0-2	1-1	0-0	2-0	1-0
			0-2					0-0	0-0		1-1
6	Roma Balti	1-0	xxx	2-3	0-1	0-1		1-1	0-1	1-3	0-2
		0-0		0-0	xxx					0-0	
7	Sheriff Tiraspol	2-1	1-0	2-1	3-4	0-1	6-1		2-0	5-1	0-0
		0-1				5-0			1-1		0-0
8	Tiligul Tiraspol	4-2	1-3	3-0	3-1	1-0	2-1	0-0		3-1	0-2
			1-2			1-0		0-1			0-2
9	Unisport Chisinau	0-2	0-2	0-0	2-2	1-2	0-1	0-0	0-0		0-3
		1-0		0-1	xxx	0-5					
10	Zimbru Chisinau	4-0	0-0	4-0	3-1	0-0	2-0	1-0	2-0	2-0	
			1-1			2-0		3-2	2-0		

+++ - match void; awarded as away win. xxx - match void; awarded as home win.

TOP SCORERS

21	Serghei ROGACIOV (Sheriff Tiraspol)
10	Vladislav GAVRILIUC (Zimbru Chisinau)
7	Vladimir PUSTOVIT (Moldova-Gaz Chisinau)
6	Vladimir DOVGHII (Constructorul Chisinau)
	Constantin KULIK (Zimbru Chisinau)
	Alexandru POPOVICI (Tiligul Tiraspol)
6	Gheorghe HAREA (Agro Chisinau)
	Vasile MALIUTA (Nistru Otaci)
	Alexandru GRAB (Olimpia Balti)

The one novelty of the season was the arrival of a new force from Tiraspol in the shape of newly-promoted Sheriff (they wish to be known as such rather than the original 'Serif'; it sounds more international). They could not, as originally planned, bring a first championship title to Moldova's second city (rivals Tiligul had repeatedly tried and failed in the past) but they did win the Cup, beating Zimbru in both legs of the quarter-finals and then

LEAGUE CHAMPIONSHIP FINAL TABLE 98/99

CHAMPIONSHIP GROUP			Home				Away				Total						
	Pd	W	D	L	F	A	W	D	L	F	A	W	D	L	F	A	Pt	GD
1 Zimbru Chisinau	26	10	3	0	26	4	8	4	1	17	5	18	7	1	43	9	61	+34
2 Constructorul Chisinau	26	8	3	2	17	6	7	3	3	13	7	15	6	5	30	13	51	+17
3 Tiligul Tiraspol	26	7	1	5	19	15	4	5	4	7	12	11	6	9	26	27	39	-1
4 Sheriff Tiraspol	26	7	3	3	27	11	2	7	4	12	13	9	10	7	39	24	37	+15
5 Olimpia Balti	26	4	6	3	8	7	3	3	7	6	15	7	9	10	14	22	30	-8

RELEGATION GROUP			Home				Away				Total						
	Pd	W	D	L	F	A	W	D	L	F	A	W	D	L	F	A	Pt	GD
6 Moldova-Gaz Chisinau	26	6	1	6	13	14	5	3	5	11	19	11	4	11	24	33	37	-9
7 Roma Balti	26	3	4	6	5	12	5	1	7	12	15	8	5	13	17	27	29	-10
8 Agro Chisinau	26	3	5	5	8	16	3	4	6	7	15	6	9	11	15	31	27	-16
9 Unisport Chisinau	26	2	4	7	4	18	5	2	6	12	19	7	6	13	16	37	27	-21
10 Nistru Otaci	26	3	3	7	7	4	2	1	10	10	14	5	4	17	17	18	18	-1

N.B. Nistru Otaci deducted 1 pt and withdrew after 15 matches - all subsequent matches were awarded as goalless victories to opponents.

NATIONAL TEAM APPEARANCES 98/99

Coach - Ivan DANILIANT	LIT	EST	FIN	GER	NIR	MLT	TUR	NIR	GER	FIN	Cps	Gls
Vasile COSELEV (17/02/72) - Zimbru Chisinau	G	G	G	G		s72					22	-
Oleg FISTICAN (02/02/75) - Zimbru Chisinau	D55	D	M76	D	D	D	D	D	D	D	22	-
Vladimir GAIDAMASCIUC (11/06/71) - Tiligul Tiraspol/Sheriff Tiraspol	D	M	M	M	M	M	M	M	M75	s79	33	1
Ion TESTIMITANU (27/04/74) - Zimbru Chisinau	D	D	D	D	D85						25	4
Alexandru GUZUN (29/09/66) - Agro Chisinau/Torpedo Zaporizhzhya (UKR)	D	D	D	D	D71	D	D	D	D	D	13	1
Serghei STROENCO (22/02/67) - Tiligul Tiraspol	M	M	M	M	M	D	M	M	D	D	32	-
Radu REBEJA (08/06/73) - Zimbru Chisinau	M	M46	D46	D	D	M64	D	M	M	M	31	1
Igor OPREA (05/10/69) - Zimbru Chisinau	M	M	M	M		M57		M90	M	M79	28	4
Gheorghe STRATULAT (13/12/76) - Nistru Otaci	M60	s75		M50			M	s90	s55	M	8	1
Sergiu EPUREANU (12/09/76) - Zimbru Chisinau	A46	M75	A71	A	A	A	A	A	A	M	21	1
Alexandru SUHAREV (03/07/70) - Dnipro Dnipropetrovsk (UKR)	A84	s46	s71	s52	s50	s57	s80	M		A89	15	1
Lilian POPESCU (15/11/73) - Nistru Otaci	s46	s77									3	-
Vitalie MAIEVICI (03/02/76) - Sheriff Tiraspol	s55			s85	D77			D55			4	-
Serghei CLESCENCO (20/05/72) - Zenit Sankt-Peterburg (RUS)/Zimbru Chisinau	s60	A89	A	A	A	A	A80	A	A81		35	6
Serghei CHIRILOV (05/06/73) - Nistru Otaci	s84	s89								s89	10	-
Alexandru CURTIANU (11/02/74) - Zenit Sankt-Peterburg (RUS)		M77	M	M52	M				M	M	28	2
Ghenadie PUSCA (22/04/75) - Constructorul Chisinau			s46		s71						3	-
Ivan TABANOV (07/08/66) - Constructorul Chisinau			s76			s77	D				4	1
Serghei DINOV (23/04/69) - Constructorul Chisinau					G	G72	G	G	G	G	8	-
Oleg SISCHIN (07/01/75) - Constructorul Chisinau						M81	M		s81	D75	15	-
Serghei BELOUS (21/11/71) - Tiligul Tiraspol						s64			s75	s75	24	1
Serghei ROGACIOV (20/05/77) - Sheriff Tiraspol						s81					9	-
Adrian SOSNOVSCHI (13/06/77) - Spartak Moskva (RUS)							D				1	-

Constructorul Chisinau 2-1 after extra-time in the final after scoring a sensational equaliser in the last minute of normal time. Sheriff also provided the league's top scorer in 21-goal Serghei Rogaciov. He won it by a street, with only one other player, Vladislav Gavriliuc of Zimbru, reaching double figures.

DOMESTIC CUP 98/99

1/8 FINALS
Olimpia Balti v Agro Chisinau 0-1; 4-2 (Olimpia Balti 4-3)
Venita Lipcani w/o Nistr Otaci
Roma Balti v Universul Popovca 5-0; 1-2 (Roma Balti 6-2)
Cimentul Râbnita v Constructorul Chisinau 1-4; 0-5 (Constructorul Chisinau 9-1)
Zimbru Chisinau w/o Locomotiva Basarabeasca
Maiak Chirsova v Sheriff Tiraspol 0-5; 0-2 (Sheriff Tiraspol 7-0)
Ulim Tebas Chisinau v Tiligul Tiraspol 0-2; 0-1 (Tiligul Tiraspol 3-0)
Moldova-Gaz Chisinau v Unisport Chisinau 2-1; 3-1 (Moldova-Gaz Chisinau 5-2)

QUARTER-FINALS
Zimbru Chisinau 0, Sheriff Tiraspol 1 (Tanurcov 49)
Sheriff Tiraspol 2 (Poroshin 28, 32), Zimbru Chisinau 0
(Sheriff Tiraspol 3-0)

Constructorul Chisinau 1 (Druta 51), Roma Balti 1 (Griner 27)
Roma Balti 0, Constructorul Chisinau 1 (Sischin 88)
(Constructorul Chisinau 2-1)

Moldova-Gaz Chisinau 1 (Pustovit 18), Tiligul Tiraspol 0
Tiligul Tiraspol 0, Moldova-Gaz Chisinau 1 (Cuciuc 87)
(Moldova-Gaz Chisinau 2-0)

Olimpia Balti 2 (Grab 48, Taralunga 65), Venita Lipcani 0
Venita Lipcani 1 (Karimov 69), Olimpia Balti 1 (Rusnac 49)
(Olimpia Balti 3-1)

SEMI-FINALS
Olimpia Balti 0,
Constructorul Chisinau 4 (Chirilov 15, 64, Comlionoc 25, Dovghii 87p)
Constructorul Chisinau 5 (Dovghii 30, 39, Ceres 44og, Chirilov 57, 74),
Olimpia Balti 0
(Constructorul Chisinau 9-0)

Moldova-Gaz Chisinau 0, Sheriff Tiraspol 2 (Rogaciov 38, 60p)
Sheriff Tiraspol 1 (Lacusta 108),
Moldova-Gaz Chisinau 2 (Martin 18, Badaluta 22) (aet)
(Sheriff Tiraspol 3-2)

FINAL
27/05/99, Chisinau
SHERIFF TIRASPOL 2 Pertia (90), Romaniuc (109)
CONSTRUCTORUL CHISINAU 1 Dovghii (57)
(asd)
referee - Iacovlev

SHERIFF TIRASPOL - Perhun; Arlet, Zenevich, Lacusta, Tarhnishvili; Gaidamasciuc, Ivanov S. (Barbaros 46), Tanurcov (Romaniuc 99), Poroshin; Mizenko (Perita 83), Rogaciov.

CONSTRUCTORUL CHISINAU - Dinov; Pogorelov, Mincev, Chirilov, Podgartchi; Zabolotnâi, Sischin, Osipenco (Tabanov 83), Comlionoc (Boicenco 71); Druta (Mârza 58), Dovghii.

EUROPEAN CUPS 98/99

CHAMPIONS' CUP
● ZIMBRU CHISINAU
Preliminary round ÚJPEST FC (HUN)
H 1-0   Kulik (11p)
        Coselev; Fistican, Kulik, Testimitanu, Telesnenco, Catansus, Rebeja (Zgura 69), Oprea, Miterev (Cebotari 69), Epureanu, Berco (Gavriliuc 72).
A 1-3   Kulik (18)
        Coselev; Kulik, Testimitanu, Telesnenko, Catansus, Rebeja, Oprea, Miterev, Epureanu (Robu 90), Cebotari, Berco (Gavriliuc 87).

CUP WINNERS' CUP
● CONSTRUCTORUL CHISINAU
Qualifying round RUDAR VELENJE (SLO)
A 0-2
        Dinov; Tricolici, Tabanov, Pusca, Apachitei, Caras (Ococo 46), Sischin (Comlionoc 46), Osipenco, Druta (Scrupschi 46), Filip, Dovghii.
H 0-0
        Bogdan; Tricolici, Tabanov, Apachitei, Pusca (Filip 46), Osipenco, Sischin, Caras (Druta 46), Ciorici (Comlionoc 46), Dovghii, Scrupschi.

UEFA CUP
● TILIGUL TIRASPOL
Preliminary round RSC ANDERLECHT (BEL)
H 0-1
        Hmaruc; Covalenco, Hodos (Golovcenko 60), Priganiuc (Chirilov V. 84), Gaidamasciuc (Gordienco 90), Stroenco S., Parhomenco, Belous, Kosse, Popovici, Stratulat.
A 0-5
        Hmaruc; Covalenco, Golovcenko, Priganiuc, Gaidamasciuc, Stroenco S., Parhomenco, Gordienco (Popov 43; Chirilov V. 75), Kosse, Popovici, Stratulat (Truhanov 83).

NATIONAL TEAM RESULTS 98/99

16/08/98	Lithuania	A	Kaunas	1-1	Miknevicius (44og)
20/08/98	Estonia	A	Kohtla-Järve	1-0	Clescenco (68)
05/09/98	Finland (ECQ)	A	Helsinki	2-3	Oprea (10, 12)
14/10/98	Germany (ECQ)	H	Chisinau	1-3	Guzun (6)
18/11/98	Northern Ireland (ECQ)	A	Belfast	2-2	Gaidamasciuc (23), Testimitanu (58)
10/03/99	Malta	A	Ta' Qali	2-0	Epureanu (74), Suharev (87)
27/03/99	Turkey (ECQ)	A	Istanbul	0-2	
31/03/99	Northern Ireland (ECQ)	H	Chisinau	0-0	
04/06/99	Germany (ECQ)	A	Leverkusen	1-6	Stratulat (76)
09/06/99	Finland (ECQ)	H	Chisinau	0-0	

INTERNATIONAL HONOURS

None

AGRO CHISINAU

CLUB DIRECTORY

FC Agro Chisinau
str. Miron Costin 7
camera 801
277001 Chisinau
tel - (2) 438130
President - Ion Taranu
Coach - Petru Efros
Stadium - Speia (12,000)

APPEARANCES 98/99

	P	Ap	(s)	Gls
Vasile ARLET	D	3		
Nicolae BALAN	G	3		
Serghei BARAN	A	11	(8)	1
Oleg BELAN	M	21	(1)	
Ghenadie BOLDURESCU	D	21		
Sergiu BOTNARI	D	8	(3)	
Daniel CANTEA (ROM)	M	2		
Valeriu CATANA	M	2	(4)	
Marcel COJOCARU (ROM)	A	12		4
FOTABE Atabong (CMR)	D	12	(1)	1
Viorel FRUNZA	A	7	(6)	1
Eugen GÂLCA	D	23		1
Vlad GOIAN	M	23		
Victor GRAUR	A	2		
Eduard GROSU	D	11		
Alexandru GUZUN	D	13		1
Gheorghe HAREA	A	22		5
Ion HOMITCHI	D	1	(2)	
Veaceslav JIGAILOV	G	21		
Ruslan KIRPIKOV (UKR)	M	2	(2)	
Mihail MANCOSI	M	2	(1)	
Vladimir MASLENNICOV	D	1	(2)	
Ghenadie MILCEV	D	4	(2)	
Nicolai NAGORNÂI	A	2		
Aivar PRIIDEL (EST)	M	4		
Svaiunas RAUCKIS (LIT)	A		(4)	1
Aurel REVENCO	M	16	(1)	
Iuri ROSSIP	M	2	(4)	
Alexandr SEVCIUC	M		(1)	
Oleg SOIMU	M	8		
Alexei VACARITA	M		(1)	
Serghei VACARIUC	D	5		

LEAGUE RESULTS 1998/99

11/07/98	Zimbru Chisinau	H	0-1	
17/07/98	Unisport Chisinau	A	2-0	Rauckis, Harea
25/07/98	Sheriff Tiraspol	H	1-4	Harea
02/08/98	Roma Balti	A	0-1	
06/08/98	Moldova-Gaz Chisinau	H	0-3	
29/08/98	Nistru Otaci	H	2-1	Harea, Baran
10/09/98	Constructorul Chisinau	A	0-0	
14/09/98	Tiligul Tiraspol	H	1-1	Cojocaru
27/09/98	Olimpia Balti	A	0-0	
03/10/98	Zimbru Chisinau	A	0-4	
07/10/98	Unisport Chisinau	H	2-1	Cojocaru 2 (1p)
18/10/98	Sheriff Tiraspol	A	1-2	Harea
21/10/98	Roma Balti	H	0-1	
24/10/98	Moldova-Gaz Chisinau	A	2-1	Guzun, Fotabe
28/10/98	Nistru Otaci	A	0-0	
01/11/98	Constructorul Chisinau	H	0-0	
07/11/98	Tiligul Tiraspol	A	2-4	Cojocaru (p), Frunza
11/11/98	Olimpia Balti	H	0-0	
17/04/99	Roma Balti	A	0-0	
23/04/99	Moldova-Gaz Chisinau	H	1-3	Harea
02/05/99	Unisport Chisinau	A	0-1	
08/05/99	Roma Balti	H	0-0	
16/05/99	Moldova-Gaz Chisinau	A	0-2	
22/05/99	Unisport Chisinau	H	1-1	Gâlca

CONSTRUCTORUL CHISINAU

CLUB DIRECTORY

FC Constructorul-93 Chisinau
str. Tudor Vladimirescu 18
277001 Chisinau
tel - (2) 439176
fax - (2) 439756
President - Valeriu Rotari
Coach - Valeri Rotar; Ion Caras
Stadium - Republican (18,500)

MAJOR HONOURS
League Championship - (1) 1997.
Domestic Cup - (1) 1996.

APPEARANCES 98/99

		P	Ap	(s)	Gls
Vasile APACHITEI (ROM)	D		15		2
Sevada ARZUMANYAN (ARM)	M		2	(2)	
Andrian BOGDAN	G		1		
Evhgheni BOICENCO	M		7	(8)	2
Iulian BURSUC	M		16		2
Emil CARAS	M		4		
Iurie CIORICI	D			(1)	
Sergiu CHIRILOV	A		6		3
Victor COMLIONOC	M		6	(9)	
Serghei DINOV	G		23		
Vladimir DOVGHII (UKR)	A		21		6
Aurel DRUTA	M		12	(9)	4
Igor FILIP	D		1	(4)	
Iuri GROSEV	M		1	(4)	
Iurie MÂRZA	M		6	(1)	
Nicolai MINCEV	D		2	(2)	
Rafael NAZARYAN (ARM)	M		5		
Ruslan NOVODARSKI	A		2	(1)	
Eric OCOCO	M		2	(4)	
Iurie OSIPENCO	M		19	(3)	1
Anatoli OSTAP	M		1	(1)	
Iurie PLATON	D		2	(3)	
Anatoli PODGAETCHI	D		6		
Valeri PGORELOV	D		6		
Sergei POGREBAN	M		2	(1)	
Ghenadie PUSCA	D		13		1
Alexandr SCRUPSCHI	A		1	(2)	
Alexei SKALA	M		1		
Denis SMAROVOZ (UKR)	A		5	(1)	
Igor STAHOV (UKR)	M		11	(1)	3
Oleg SISCHIN	M		20	(1)	4
Ivan TABANOV	D		18	(2)	
Dumitru TRICOLICI	D		18	(1)	
Vladimir VOLKOV (RUS)	M		1	(1)	
Ivan ZABOLOTNÂI	D		8	(1)	2

LEAGUE RESULTS 1998/99

11/07/98	Tiligul Tiraspol	H	2-0	Sischin (p), Pusca
17/07/98	Olimpia Balti	A	1-0	Dovghii
02/08/98	Unisport Chisinau	A	2-0	Sischin 2
06/08/98	Sheriff Tiraspol	H	1-1	Druta
31/08/98	Roma Balti	A	-	(w/o; home win)
10/09/98	Agro Chisinau	H	0-0	
14/09/98	Nistru Otaci	A	0-3	
18/09/98	Zimbru Chisinau	H	1-2	Dovghii
27/09/98	Moldova-Gaz Chisinau	H	5-0	Druta, Stahov, Osipenco,
				Boicenco, Apachitei
03/10/98	Tiligul Tiraspol	A	3-1	Bursuc, Stahov, Dovghii
07/10/98	Olimpia Balti	H	2-1	Stahov, Boicenco
18/10/98	Zimbru Chisinau	A	0-0	
21/10/98	Unisport Chisinau	H	1-0	Bursuc
24/10/98	Sheriff Tiraspol	A	0-1	
28/10/98	Roma Balti	H	1-0	Apachitei
01/11/98	Agro Chisinau	A	0-0	
11/11/98	Moldova-Gaz Chisinau	A	1-0	Dovghii (p)
10/04/99	Sheriff Tiraspol	A	1-0	Chirilov
20/04/99	Olimpia Balti	H	1-0	Doghii
24/04/99	Zimbru Chisinau	A	1-1	Druta
02/05/99	Tiligul Tiraspol	H	0-1	
16/05/99	Serif Tiraspol	H	2-0	Dovghii, Sischin
19/05/99	Olimpia Balti	A	2-0	Chirilov 2
22/05/99	Zimbru Chisinau	H	1-1	Zabolotnâi
13/06/99	Tiligul Tiraspol	A	2-1	Zabolotnâi, Druta

MOLDOVA-GAZ CHISINAU

CLUB DIRECTORY

FC Moldova-Gaz Chisinau
str. Albisoara 38
Chisinau
tel - (2) 578122
President - Mihai Lesnic
Coach - Vitalie Galat
Stadium - Dinamo (5,000)

APPEARANCES 98/99

	P	Ap	(s)	Gls
Cristinel BADALUTA (ROM)	A	17	(3)	2
Emil CARAS	D	9	(1)	
Alexandru CHIORU	D	2	(1)	
Alexandru CIUDAC	A	4	(1)	
Lilian CODA	M	2	(2)	
Vladimir COEV	G	3		
Vladimir COLBASIUC	D	17	(2)	
Sergiu CONDREA	D	23		
Ghenadie COSTIUC	D	1		
Igor CUCIUC	M	16	(3)	3
Vitalie CULIBABA	D	6	(2)	
Andrei DEMCHENKO (UKR)	D	14		
Oleg FLENTEA	M	16	(1)	3
Valentin GALUSHKA (UKR)	D	1		
Igor GHEORGHIES	A	11	(11)	3
Oleg IVANOV	G	10		
Alexei JMURCO	G	10		
Evgheni MAIOROV	M	3	(2)	
Andrei MARTIN	M	2	(9)	
Ghenadi MILCEV	M	6	(1)	
Roman ONICA	D	14		
Serghei PAVLENKO (UKR)	M	18	(4)	1
Serghei PROHOROV	M	8	(1)	
Vladimir PUSTOVIT	A	11	(12)	7
Marin SPÂNU	M	1		
Iaroslav SUBOTIN	M		(1)	
Alexandr SEVCIUC	D	1		
Vladimir SOHIREV	A	12	(6)	4
Anatol TÂMBUR	M	11	(4)	
Serghei VACARIUC	A	2		
Eduard VALUTA	D	2		

LEAGUE RESULTS 1998/99

11/07/98	Sheriff Tiraspol	A	1-2	Cuciuc
17/07/98	Tiligul Tiraspol	H	2-3	og (Covalenco), Pustovit
25/07/98	Roma Balti	A	3-2	Flentea 2, Cuciuc
02/08/98	Olimpia Balti	H	0-0	
06/08/98	Agro Chisinau	A	3-0	Flentea, Sohirev, Cuciuc
30/08/98	Zimbru Chisinau	H	1-2	Sohirev
10/09/98	Nistru Otaci	A	0-0	
14/09/98	Unisport Chisinau	H	1-2	Sohirev
27/09/98	Constructorul Chisinau	A	0-5	
03/10/98	Sheriff Tiraspol	H	2-1	Badaluta, Gheorghies
07/10/98	Tiligul Tiraspol	A	0-3	
18/10/98	Roma Balti	H	1-0	Pustovit
21/10/98	Olimpia Balti	A	0-2	
24/10/98	Agro Chisinau	H	1-2	Sohirev
28/10/98	Zimbru Chisinau	A	0-4	
07/11/98	Unisport Chisinau	A	0-0	
11/11/98	Constructorul Chisinau	H	0-1	
23/04/99	Agro Chisinau	A	3-1	Pustovit 2, Gheorghies
02/05/99	Roma Balti	H	2-1	Pustovit, Badaluta
08/05/99	Unisport Chisinau	A	1-0	Pustovit
16/05/99	FC Agro Chisinau	H	2-0	Pavlenko, Pustovit
19/05/99	Unisport Chisinau	H	1-2	Gheorghies
22/05/99	Roma Balti	A	0-0	

NISTRU OTACI

CLUB DIRECTORY

FC Nistru Otaci
str. S. Lazo 14
Otaci
tel - (271) 24965
fax - (271) 24965
President - Vasile Traghira
Coach - Nicolae Cuceruc; Alexandru Troskin
Stadium - Calaraseuca (1,000)

APPEARANCES 98/99

	P	Ap	(s)	Gls
Alexandr BLAJCO	A	10	(4)	2
Vladimir CAPATANA (UKR)	D		(5)	
Serghei CHIRILOV	A	7	(1)	1
Vitalie DÂNTU	G	15		
Iuri GROSHEV (UKR)	M	14		1
Alexandru GUZUN	D	2		
Nikolai KOPASTEANSKI (UKR)	M	15		2
Serghei LASHCHENKOV (UKR)	A	8	(2)	
Igor LOSAC	D	2	(3)	
Alexandr MALITSKI (UKR)	M	10	(3)	
Vasile MALIUTA	A	11	(4)	5
Anatol PODGAETCHI	D	14		
Lilian POPESCU	M	1		
Alexandru PRIHODKO	D	5		
Veaceslav REVENCO	A	13	(1)	3
Gheorghe STRATULAT	M	12		1
Anatol SABLEVSCHI	M	8	(3)	1
Igor SUMILO (UKR)	M	14		1
Vadim TABACIUC	M	1		
Alexandr TCACIUC (UKR)	D	3	(2)	

LEAGUE RESULTS 1998/99

11/07/98	Olimpia Balti	H	2-1	Kopasteanski, Maliuta
25/07/98	Unisport Chisinau	H	0-1	
02/08/98	Sheriff Tiraspol	A	4-3	Revenco 2, Maliuta, Stratulat
06/08/98	Roma Balti	H	1-0	Blajco
12/08/98	Zimbru Chisinau	A	1-3	Sumilo
29/08/98	Agro Chisinau	A	1-2	Groshev
10/09/98	Moldova-Gaz Chisinau	H	0-0	
14/09/98	Constructorul Chisinau	H	3-0	Maliuta 2, Sablevschi
27/09/98	Tiligul Tiraspol	A	1-3	Revenco
03/10/98	Olimpia Balti	A	0-1	
07/10/98	Zimbru Chisinau	H	0-1	
18/10/98	Unisport Chisinau	A	2-2	Blajco, Kopasteanski
21/10/98	Sheriff Tiraspol	H	1-1	Maliuta
24/10/98	Roma Balti	A	1-0	Chirilov
28/10/98	Agro Chisinau	H	0-0	

OLIMPIA BALTI

CLUB DIRECTORY

FC Olimpia Balti
str. Kiev 155
279200 Balti
tel - (231) 20314
fax - (231) 22378
President - Mihai Ciur
Coach - Vladimir Olianschi
Stadium - Municipal (7,000)

APPEARANCES 98/99

	P	Ap	(s)	Gls
Anatoli BALICA	D	4	(6)	
Oleg BOBU	D	15	(3)	
Grigori BODIU	D	2	(1)	
Dimitri BOGORAD	D	9	(1)	
Andrei BURCOVSCHI	M	11	(7)	
Valeriu CERES	D	26		2
Serghei DERENIOV	G	26		
Ion DOLINTA	D	19		
Iuri ERMOSHENKO (UKR)	A	13	(4)	2
Serghei FILIPCENCO	M	24		
Alexei GOLOVACIUC	M		(1)	
Alexandru GRAB	M	24	(1)	5
Nicolai LAHMAI	D	23		
Igor LAVROV	M	1	(3)	
Andrei LEVCO	M		(1)	
Alexandr PATROMAN	M	8	(12)	
Ruslan PERNAI	A	17	(7)	1
Nicolai REABOI	M		(1)	
Veaceslav RUSNAC	D	24	(1)	1
Mihail TCACIUC	A	11	(2)	1
Valeriu TOFAN	M	2	(8)	
Vladislav TARALUNGA	M	1	(2)	
Vadim TATURIN (UKR)	M	21	(2)	1
Vladimir TARANU	M	2	(5)	
Vitalie VARVARIUC	A	3		1

LEAGUE RESULTS 1998/99

11/07/98	Nistru Otaci	A	1-2	Varvariuc
17/07/98	Constructorul Chisinau	H	0-1	
25/07/98	Tiligul Tiraspol	A	0-1	
02/08/98	Moldova-Gaz Chisinau	A	0-0	
06/08/98	Zimbru Chisinau	H	1-0	Grab
29/08/98	Unisport Chisinau	A	2-1	Grab, Ermoshenko
10/09/98	Sheriff Tiraspol	H	1-1	Grab
14/09/98	Roma Balti	A	1-0	Ermoshenko
27/09/98	Agro Chisinau	H	0-0	
03/10/98	Nistru Otaci	H	1-0	Grab (p)
07/10/98	Constructorul Chisinau	A	1-2	Rusnac
18/10/98	Tiligul Tiraspol	H	0-0	
21/10/98	Moldova-Gaz Chisinau	H	2-0	Ceres 2 (1p)
24/10/98	Zimbru Chisinau	A	0-0	
28/10/98	Unisport Chisinau	H	2-0	Pernai, Tcaciuc
01/11/98	Sheriff Tiraspol	A	1-0	Grab
07/11/98	Roma Balti	H	0-2	
11/11/98	Agro Chisinau	A	0-0	
04/04/99	Zimbru Chisinau	A	0-2	
10/04/99	Tiligul Tiraspol	H	0-0	
20/04/99	Constructorul Chisinau	A	0-1	
24/04/99	Sheriff Tiraspol	H	0-0	
09/05/99	Zimbru Chisinau	H	1-1	Taturin
16/05/99	Tiligul Tiraspol	A	0-1	
19/05/99	Constructorul Chisinau	H	0-2	
22/05/99	Sheriff Tiraspol	A	0-5	

ROMA BALTI

FC Roma Balti
str. Moscovei 17
Balti
tel - (231) 25551
President - Nicolae Rotaru
Coach - Valeri Crohan; Serghei Cebotar;
Valeri Lebedev
Stadium - Municipal (7,000)

	P	Ap	(s)	Gls
Nicolae BOTNAR	M	1	(3)	
Nicolae BUNEA	G	6	(1)	
Vitaly CALESTIN (UKR)	M	15		1
Evgheny CARABULEA	M	5	(4)	3
Sergiu CEBOTAR	D	4		
Sergiu DARII	A	17	(2)	3
Iurie GAVRILIUC	A	1		
Vladimir GHENAITIS	M	15	(5)	1
Igor GLUSHOK (UKR)	D	11	(5)	
Oleg GREBENNICOV	D	18		
Andrei GRINER (UKR)	M	9	(1)	1
Igor ISTRATI	D	8	(6)	
Andronic KARAGIZIN (RUS)	G	11		
Maxim KIZILOV (RUS)	D	19		
Igor LAVROV	M	3		
Valeri LEBEDEV (RUS)	M	5		
Nikolai LIZUN (UKR)	M	19	(2)	
Igor MIHAESCU	A	16		3
Oleg OBOROC	D	22		1
Igor ONILOV	M	4	(2)	
Sergiu PLAMADEALA	M	5	(13)	
Alexandr REZNIC	G	6		
Serghei SAPOGOVSCHI	M	9	(4)	1
Andrei SCALETCHI	A		(3)	
Oleg STOEV (UKR)	M		(1)	
Andrei SUGAC (UKR)	A	11		1
Serghei TELESIN	M		(1)	
Oleg TVERDOHLEBOV	D	13	(2)	1
Alexandr USATÀI	D		(2)	
Alexandr ZUI	M		(1)	

11/07/98	Unisport Chisinau	A	1-0	og (Mârza)
17/07/98	Sheriff Tiraspol	A	1-6	Darii
25/07/98	Moldova-Gaz Chisinau	H	2-3	Tverdohlebov, Mihaescu
02/08/98	Agro Chisinau	H	1-0	Oboroc
06/08/98	Nistru Otaci	A	0-1	
31/08/98	Constructorul Chisinau	H	-	(w/o; home win)
10/09/98	Tiligul Tiraspol	A	1-2	Calesin
14/09/98	Olimpia Balti	H	0-1	
27/09/98	Zimbru Chisinau	A	0-2	
03/10/98	Unisport Chisinau	H	1-3	Sugac
07/10/98	Sheriff Tiraspol	H	1-1	Mihaescu (p)
18/10/98	Moldova-Gaz Chisinau	A	0-1	
21/10/98	Agro Chisinau	A	1-0	Sapogovschi
24/10/98	Nistru Otaci	H	0-1	
28/10/98	Constructorul Chisinau	A	0-1	
01/11/98	Tiligul Tiraspol	H	0-1	
07/11/98	Olimpia Balti	A	2-0	Darii, Mihaescu (p)
11/11/98	Zimbru Chisinau	H	0-2	
17/04/99	Agro Chisinau	H	0-0	
23/04/99	Unisport Chisinau	A	5-0	Carabulea 3, Griner, Ghenaitis
02/05/99	Moldova-Gaz Chisinau	A	1-2	Darii
08/05/99	Agro Chisinau	A	0-0	
16/05/99	Unisport Chisinau	H	0-0	
22/05/99	Moldova-Gaz Chisinau	H	0-0	

SHERIFF TIRASPOL

CLUB DIRECTORY

Sheriff Tiraspol
str. Sevcenko 81, Tiraspol
tel - (233) 32230/31312 / fax - (233) 32276
President - Victor Gusan
Coach - Ahmed Aleskerov; Vladimir Zemlianoi;
Serghei Borovski
Stadium - Municipal (9,000)

MAJOR HONOURS
Domestic Cup - (1) 1999.

APPEARANCES 98/99

	P	Ap	(s)	Gls
Marian ALIUTA (ROM)	M	5	(3)	2
Edward ANYAMKEGH (NIG)	A	11	(1)	2
Vasile ARLET	D	11	(1)	
Dimitri ARSOSHVILI (GEO)	D	5		
Victor BARÅSEV	M	1		
Ruslan BARBAROS	A	11	(6)	1
Veaceslav BUGNIAC	A	1	(11)	
Alexandru COVALCIUC	D	3	(5)	1
Vladimir GAIDAMASCIUC	M	6		
Gheorghi GOLOVATCHI	D	4	(3)	1
Cezar HURADZE (GEO)	A	1		
Evgheni IVANOV	G	2		
Stanislav IVANOV	M	6	(10)	1
Alexandr KIRILOV	G	3		
Alexandru LAPACI	M	2	(3)	
Dan LACUSTA (ROM)	D	20		2
Denis LOZINSCHI	M	4	(1)	
Vitalie MAIEVICI	D	13	(4)	
Alexandr MALEVANOV (UKR)	D	15	(1)	
Aleksandr MIZENKO (UKR)	M	7	(1)	1
Florin MOTROC (ROM)	D	8		1
Evgheni NEMODRUK (UKR)	G	15		
Serghei NUDNÅI	D	1	(2)	
Isak OKORONKVO (NIG)	M	6		
Emmanuel OLUKAYODE (NIG)	M	12	(4)	
Serghei PERHUN (UKR)	G	6		
Tamaz PERTIA (GEO)	M	9	(2)	
Lilian POPESCU	M	18	(2)	
Andrei POROSHIN (UKR)	A	5	(2)	1
Serghei ROGACIOV	A	24	(1)	21
Iuri ROMANIUC	M	1	(2)	
Gabriel ROTARU	M		(2)	
Vladislav SLIPAC	D		(1)	
Vadim SOLODKI (UKR)	M	11	(2)	1
Radu TALPA	D		(5)	
Vladimir TANURCOV	M	24		4
Vaja TARHNISHVILI (GEO)	D	7		
Serghei ZENEVICH (BLS)	M	8		

LEAGUE RESULTS 1998/99

11/07/98	Moldova-Gaz Chisinau	H	2-1	Tanurcov, Anyamkegh
17/07/98	Roma Balti	H	6-1	Solodki, Rogaciov 4 (1p),
				Tanurcov
25/07/98	Agro Chisinau	A	4-1	Motroc, Rogaciov 2, Anyamkegh
02/08/98	Nistru Otaci	H	3-4	Rogaciov, Aliuta 2
06/08/98	Constructorul Chisinau	A	1-1	Rogaciov
29/08/98	Tiligul Tiraspol	H	2-0	Lacusta, Rogaciov (p)
10/09/98	Olimpia Balti	A	1-1	Rogaciov
14/09/98	Zimbru Chisinau	H	0-0	
27/09/98	Unisport Chisinau	A	0-0	
03/10/98	Moldova-Gaz Chisinau	A	1-2	Covalciuc
07/10/98	Roma Balti	A	1-1	Rogaciov (p)
18/10/98	Agro Chisinau	H	2-1	Rogaciov 2 (1p)
21/10/98	Nistru Otaci	A	1-1	Rogaciov (p)
24/10/98	Constructorul Chisinau	H	1-0	Rogaciov
28/10/98	Tiligul Tiraspol	A	0-0	
01/11/98	Olimpia Balti	H	0-1	
07/11/98	Zimbru Chisinau	A	0-1	
11/11/98	Unisport Chisinau	H	5-1	Rogaciov 3, Barbaros, Tanurcov
04/04/99	Tiligul Tiraspol	A	1-0	Rogaciov (p)
10/04/99	Constructorul Chisinau	H	0-1	
24/04/99	Olimpia Balti	A	0-0	
02/05/99	Zimbru Chisinau	H	0-0	
10/05/99	Tiligul Tiraspol	H	1-1	Lacusta
16/05/99	Constructorul Chisinau	A	0-2	
22/05/99	Olimpia Balti	H	5-0	Golovatchi, Mizenko, Tanurcov,
				Rogaciov 2
13/06/99	Zimbru Chisinau	A	2-3	Poroshin, Ivanov S.

TILIGUL TIRASPOL

CLUB DIRECTORY

FC Tiligul Tiraspol
str. Sverdlov 46, ap.1
278000 Tiraspol
tel - (233) 61195
fax - (233) 51020
President - Grigori Corzun
Coach - Vladimir Kosse; Alexandru Spiridon
Stadium - Municipal (9,000)

MAJOR HONOURS
Domestic Cup - (3) 1993, 1994, 1995.

APPEARANCES 98/99

		P	Ap	(s)	Gls
Victor BARÂSEV	A	4	(1)		
Serghei BELOUS	M	13	(1)		
Boris CEBOTARI	M	5			
Valeri CHILIENKO	A	1	(7)	1	
Vadim CHIRILOV	A	1	(10)	1	
Vladimir CIUBCO	A		(3)		
Oleg CIUPAC	M	6			
Serghei COVALCIUC	M	3	(3)		
Alexandr COVALENCO	D	24			
Vitalie CULIBABA	D	5			
Vladimir GAIDAMASCIUC	M	13		3	
Vitalie GLAVCEV	M	16	(5)	1	
Serghei GOLOVCENCO	D	5	(1)		
Evgheni GORDIENCO	A	15	(4)	1	
Evgheni HMARUC	G	24			
Ruslan HODOS (UKR)	M	8	(9)		
Vladimir KOSSE	A	21	(3)	4	
Anatol LUCHIANCICOV	A	13	(4)	3	
Alexandr MURAHOVSKI	M		(7)		
Serghei PARHOMENCO	M	20			
Valeriu POGORELOV (UKR)	D	2			
Vitalie POPOV	D	7			
Alexandr POPOVICI	A	15	(1)	6	
Iuri PRIGANIUC	M	23		1	
Gheorghe STRATULAT	M		(1)		
Serghei STROENCO	D	20	(1)	1	
Veaceslav TRUHANOV	A	10	(7)	2	
Evgheni TUCANOV	G	1			

LEAGUE RESULTS 1998/99

11/07/98	Constructorul Chisinau	A	0-2	
17/07/98	Moldova-Gaz Chisinau	A	3-2	Gaidamasciuc, Kosse, Popovici
25/07/98	Olimpia Balti	H	1-0	Priganiuc
02/08/98	Zimbru Chisinau	A	0-2	
06/08/98	Unisport Chisinau	H	3-1	Kosse, Popovici, Gaidamasciuc
29/08/98	Sheriff Tiraspol	A	0-2	
10/09/98	Roma Balti	H	2-1	Popovici 2
14/09/98	Agro Chisinau	A	1-1	Chilienko
27/09/98	Nistru Otaci	H	3-1	Truhanov 2, Popovici
03/10/98	Constructorul Chisinau	H	1-3	og (Boicenco)
07/10/98	Moldova-Gaz Chisinau	H	3-0	Gaidamasciuc, Kosse, Popovici (p)
18/10/98	Olimpia Balti	A	0-0	
21/10/98	Zimbru Chisinau	H	0-2	
24/10/98	Unisport Chisinau	A	0-0	
28/10/98	Sheriff Tiraspol	H	0-0	
01/11/98	Roma Balti	A	1-0	Pogorelov
07/11/98	Agro Chisinau	H	4-2	Luchiancicov 2, Stroenco (p), Kosse
04/04/99	Sheriff Tiraspol	H	0-1	
10/04/99	Olimpia Balti	A	0-0	
20/04/99	Zimbru Chisinau	H	0-2	
02/05/99	Constructorul Chisinau	A	1-0	Gordienco
10/05/99	Sheriff Tiraspol	A	1-1	Glavcev
16/05/99	Olimpia Balti	II	1-0	Luchiancicov
19/05/99	Zimbru Chisinau	A	0-2	
13/06/99	Constructorul Chisinau	H	1-2	Chirilov

UNISPORT CHISINAU

FC Unisport Chisinau
str. Stefan Voda 3
or. Durlesti
Chisinau
tel - (2) 716474
fax - (2) 716484
President - Gheorghe Filip
Coach - Alexandru Spiridon; Valentin Garstea
Stadium - Codru (2,000)

APPEARANCES 98/99

	P	Ap	(s)	Gls
Ghenadie ANGHEL	M	22	(1)	1
Lucian Dumitru BOGHEAN (ROM)	A	1	(4)	
Anatoli BOROVICOV	G	8		
Ghenadie BOTGROS	M	6	(8)	
Oleg CIUPAC	M	11	(4)	1
Mihail COJUSEA	A	17	(6)	3
Igor CORJAN	A	5		1
Igor CRISTINOI	D	12		
Vladimir CRIVENCO	D	20	(1)	
Catalin Ionut CUSCA (ROM)	D	12	(4)	
Andrei DONICI	D	5	(1)	
Vladimir GENUNCHI	M	1	(4)	
Alin Ionut GEORGESCU (ROM)	A	13	(1)	1
Vitalie LUNGU	D	13	(5)	
Vitalie MASTALER	M		(2)	
Iurie MÂRZA	D	17		1
Andrei MIRON	A	20	(2)	
Vladimir MURA	G	16	(1)	
Aurel NELIPOVSCHI	A	11	(8)	3
Ivan PASECINIC	M	13	(5)	1
Aurel REVENCO	M	4	(2)	
Ruslan SCRELEA	D		(1)	
Vadim SOSNOVSKI	M	2	(1)	
Vasile TOLOCONNIKOV	D	16	(1)	4
Alexei TÂTIURA	D	18	(2)	
Alexandr ZUBAREV	D	1		

LEAGUE RESULTS 1998/99

11/07/98	Roma Balti	H	0-1	
17/07/98	Agro Chisinau	H	0-2	
25/07/98	Nistru Otaci	A	1-0	Nelipovschi
02/08/98	Constructorul Chisinau	H	0-2	
06/08/98	Tiligul Tiraspol	A	1-3	Toloconnikov
29/08/98	Olimpia Balti	H	1-2	Mârza
10/09/98	Zimbru Chisinau	A	0-2	
14/09/98	Moldova-Gaz Chisinau	A	2-1	Corjan, Cojusea
27/09/98	Sheriff Tiraspol	H	0-0	
03/10/98	Roma Balti	A	3-1	Anghel, Ciupac, Pasecinic
07/10/98	Agro Chisinau	A	1-2	Toloconnikov
18/10/98	Nistru Otaci	H	2-2	Toloconnikov 2
21/10/98	Constructorul Chisinau	A	0-1	
24/10/98	Tiligul Tiraspol	H	0-0	
28/10/98	Olimpia Balti	A	0-2	
01/11/98	Zimbru Chisinau	H	0-3	
07/11/98	Moldova-Gaz Chisinau	H	0-0	
11/11/98	Sheriff Tiraspol	A	1-5	Cojusea
23/04/99	Roma Balti	H	0-5	
02/05/99	Agro Chisinau	H	1-0	Nelipovschi
08/05/99	Moldova-Gaz Chisinau	H	0-1	
16/05/99	Roma Balti	A	0-0	
19/05/99	Moldova-Gaz Chisinau	A	2-1	Georgescu, Nelipovschi
22/05/99	Agro Chisinau	A	1-1	Cojusea

ZIMBRU CHISINAU

FC Zimbru Chisinau
str. Butuclui 1
277060 Chisinau
tel - (2) 766481
fax - (2) 762753
President - Nicolae Ciornâi
Coach - Semion Altman
Stadium - Speia (12,000)

MAJOR HONOURS
League Championship - (7)
1992, 1993, 1994, 1995, 1996, 1998, 1999.
Domestic Cup - (2) 1997, 1998.

APPEARANCES 98/99

	P	Ap	(s)	Gls
Victor BERCO	A	8	(3)	3
Vadim BORET	A	9	(8)	3
Sergiu BUTELSCHI	M	9	(5)	1
Valeriu CATANSUS	D	26		1
Boris CEBOTARI	M	3		1
Serghei CLESCENCO	A	8		
Lilian CODA	D		(2)	
Vasile COSELEV	G	4		
Sergiu DIACONU	G	5	(1)	
Sergiu EPUREANU	M	20	(1)	2
Oleg FISTICAN	D	21	(2)	
Vladislav GAVRILIUC	A	11	(8)	10
Ruslan GHILAZEV (UKR)	M	7		2
Dimitri GUSILA	A		(10)	4
Constantin KULIK (UKR)	M	25		6
Valeri LEBEDEV (RUS)	D	1	(4)	
Iurie MITEREV	A	13	(4)	2
Ghenadie OLEXICI	D		(2)	
Igor OPREA	M	22		4
Kiril RABAKOV (RUS)	M	4	(3)	2
Radu REBEJA	M	13	(2)	1
Vladislav ROBU	M	12	(7)	1
Denis ROMANENCO	G	17		
Andrei TELESNENKO (UKR)	D	24		
Ion TESTIMITANU	D	16		
Boris TROPANET	M	3	(2)	
Serghei ZGURA (UKR)	M	5	(5)	

LEAGUE RESULTS 1998/99

11/07/98	Agro Chisinau	A	1-0	Cebotari
02/08/98	Tiligul Tiraspol	H	2-0	Oprea, Berco
06/08/98	Olimpia Balti	A	0-1	
12/08/98	Nistru Otaci	H	3-1	Kulik (p), Gavriliuc, Oprea
30/08/98	Moldova-Gaz Chisinau	A	2-1	Berco, Gavriliuc
10/09/98	Unisport Chisinau	H	2-0	Berco, Gavriliuc
14/09/98	Sheriff Tiraspol	A	0-0	
18/09/98	Constructorul Chisinau	A	2-1	Kulik 2 (1p)
27/09/98	Roma Balti	H	2-0	Gusila, Rebeja
03/10/98	Agro Chisinau	H	4-0	Oprea, Gusila, Boret 2
07/10/98	Nistru Otaci	A	1-0	Epureanu
18/10/98	Constructorul Chisinau	H	0-0	
21/10/98	Tiligul Tiraspol	A	2-0	Butelschi, Kulik
24/10/98	Olimpia Balti	H	0-0	
28/10/98	Moldova-Gaz Chisinau	H	4-0	Miterev 2, Catansus, Gavriliuc
01/11/98	Unisport Chisinau	A	3-0	Robu, Gusila, Oprea (p)
07/11/98	Sheriff Tiraspol	H	1-0	Gavriliuc
11/11/98	Roma Balti	A	2-0	Gusila, Gavriliuc
04/04/99	Olimpia Balti	H	2-0	Gavriliuc, Epureanu
20/04/99	Tiligul Tiraspol	A	2-0	Gavriliuc 2
24/04/99	Constructorul Chisinau	H	1-1	Ghilazev
02/05/99	Sheriff Tiraspol	A	0-0	
09/05/99	Olimpia Balti	A	1-1	Boret
19/05/99	Tiligul Tiraspol	H	2 0	Rabakov, Kulik
22/05/99	Constructorul Chisinau	A	1-1	Kulik
13/06/99	Sheriff Tiraspol	H	3-2	Ghilazev, Gavriliuc, Rabakov

PROMOTED CLUB

SECOND DIVISION FINAL TABLE 98/99

		Pd	W	D	L	F	A	Pt	GD
1	Zimbru 2 Chisinau	30	23	4	3	84	20	73	+64
2	Sheriff 2 Tiraspol	30	21	5	4	77	26	68	+51
3	**Energhetic Dubasari**	**30**	**17**	**7**	**6**	**42**	**28**	**58**	**+14**
4	Migdal UA Carahasani	30	17	6	7	56	30	57	+26
5	Locomotiva Basarabeasca	30	17	3	10	41	38	54	+3
6	Ulim Tebas Chisinau	30	15	6	9	50	29	51	+21
7	Cimentul Râbnita	30	15	6	9	47	33	51	+14
8	Dumbrava Cojusna	30	13	9	8	41	32	48	+9
9	Venita Lipcani	30	13	6	11	36	34	45	+2
10	Petrocub Spicul Sarata Galbena	30	12	8	10	62	35	44	+27
11	Sporting USM Chisinau	30	10	7	13	45	42	37	+3
12	Victoria Chisinau	30	9	5	16	31	46	32	-15
13	Raut Orhei	30	8	3	19	29	79	27	-50
14	Codru Stimold Chisinau	30	5	4	21	19	74	19	-55
15	Speranta Nisporeni	30	1	4	25	13	99	7	-86
16	Dinamo Bender	30	1	3	26	12	40	6	-28

N.B. Zimbru 2 Chisinau and Sheriff 2 Tiraspol ineligible for promotion.

CLUB DIRECTORY

Energhetic Dubasari
str. Dzerjinschi 50
Dubasari 4500
tel - (245) 35077
fax - (245) 36999
President - Veaceslav Finagin
Coach - Anatoli Grigorenco
Stadium - Municipal (3,000)

NORTHERN IRELAND

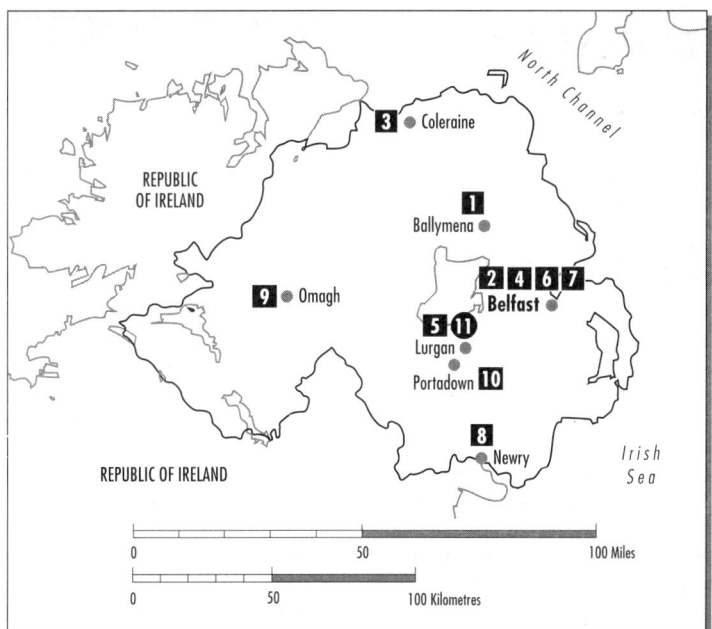

1	BALLYMENA UNITED	700	7	LINFIELD	706
2	CLIFTONVILLE	701	8	NEWRY TOWN	707
3	COLERAINE	702	9	OMAGH TOWN	708
4	CRUSADERS	703	10	PORTADOWN	709
5	GLENAVON	704		Promoted club	
6	GLENTORAN	705	11	LURGAN DISTILLERY	710

CUP FIASCO AFTER CLIFTONVILLE CLANGER

Goalscorer urgently required for McMenemy

FEDERATION DIRECTORY

The Irish Football Association
20 Windsor Avenue, Belfast BT9 6EE

tel - (01232) 669458/9   Year of Formation - 1880
fax - (01232) 667620   President - Jim Boyce
                              Secretary - David I. Bowen

Stadium - Windsor Park, Belfast (28,500)

They seek him here, they seek him there, but Northern Ireland don't seem able to find a decent striker anywhere.

The lack of a quality goalscorer has proved to be a real bugbear for the country's new management team of Lawrie McMenemy and Joe Jordan. The willing veteran Iain Dowie continues to wear the number nine shirt with pride, but he is in his mid-30s, is not a club regular, and cannot go on forever. Until and unless a worthy replacement is found, the chances are that Northern Ireland will continue to struggle in World Cup and European Championship qualifying tournaments.

The dearth of strikers meant that McMenemy felt obliged to push left-winger Michael Hughes up front for a couple of the team's Euro 2000 qualifiers. The Wimbledon star is one of an ever decreasing number of players currently available to the Northern Ireland boss who are weekly performers in the English Premiership. In fact, the whole of the midfield is well endowed, with both Neil Lennon (Leicester) and Steve Lomas (West Ham) offering genuine international class in the centre and talented wingers Keith Gillespie and Jon McCarthy battling for the berth on the right. But elsewhere, and especially up front, the quality simply isn't there.

Northern Irish fans still retain misty-eyed memories of their team's heyday under Billy Bingham in the '80s when they reached two World Cups, but there is no hint of a repeat nowadays. Negative vibrations underscored the Euro 2000 campaign at an early stage as McMenemy's first competitive fixture ended with a 0-3 defeat by Turkey in Istanbul. A 1-0 win at home to Finland quickly put the team back on track but a month later their old failing of not getting the three points at Windsor Park against minor opposition returned to haunt them in a 2-2 draw against Moldova.

In the two matches during the spring Northern Ireland's faint hopes of qualification were all but buried when they lost 0-3 at home to a fading Germany (a team they had done well against in the past) and then drew 0-0 against Moldova in Chisinau. Here, in particular, came evidence of the team's lack of forward penetration, with McMenemy choosing to play with just one striker (Dowie) against the Germans and then digging deep to select the inexperienced 24-year-old Bournemouth forward Steve Robinson for only his second cap in Moldova.

The participation of Northern Ireland's Under-21 team in the European Championship for the first time offers a glimmer of hope for the future, but there remains little likelihood of the country's goalscoring saviour emerging from the local Irish League - even though strikers Rory Hamill of Glentoran and Glenn Ferguson of Linfield did win

LEAGUE CHAMPIONSHIP RESULTS 98/99

		1	2	3	4	5	6	7	8	9	10
1	Ballymena United		1-2	1-0	2-0	1-0	1-1	1-0	1-1	0-0	1-0
			2-2	0-1	1-2	0-1	3-6	4-2	0-0	1-2	2-2
2	Cliftonville	0-1		1-1	2-3	2-2	2-4	1-1	1-4	2-1	0-2
		1-0		0-0	1-1	0-0	0-0	0-1	0-2	2-1	0-0
3	Coleraine	2-1	1-1		0-2	1-3	1-3	0-0	2-2	2-1	1-0
		0-1	3-1		0-2	0-0	0-1	2-1	3-0	1-0	0-2
4	Crusaders	2-0	2-1	0-1		1-0	0-0	1-4	2-0	5-0	1-1
		1-0	1-0	2-0		1-1	0-3	3-2	3-2	2-0	0-0
5	Glenavon	0-0	0-1	3-1	3-0		0-1	1-1	1-2	2-0	1-0
		1-0	0-0	3-1	2-0		0-1	2-2	1-1	6-1	2-2
6	Glentoran	2-1	0-1	5-4	1-4	5-2		0-1	1-3	2-0	1-0
		1-0	1-1	5-0	2-1	1-0		1-2	5-1	2-0	3-1
7	Linfield	1-0	1-0	2-1	2-1	2-0	1-1		2-2	2-0	2-2
		4-1	2-1	1-1	4-2	3-1	1-1		2-1	3-0	3-1
8	Newry Town	0-0	2-1	1-1	0-0	1-0	1-2	2-1		0-2	3-2
		1-0	1-0	1-0	3-0	0-2	1-0	2-1		1-1	1-2
9	Omagh Town	1-4	2-2	2-0	0-0	0-3	0-2	1-3	1-3		1-0
		0-5	1-1	1-1	1-2	0-3	1-4	1-5	2-3		1-0
10	Portadown	1-3	0-1	3-0	0-1	1-1	0-3	0-2	2-3	2-0	
		2-1	3-0	1-2	0-0	2-2	1-3	1-1	2-1	3-0	

LEAGUE CHAMPIONSHIP FINAL TABLE 98/99

		P	W	D	L	F	A	W	D	L	F	A	W	D	L	F	A	P	GD
				Home					Away					Total					
1	Glentoran	36	12	1	5	38	22	12	5	1	36	13	24	6	6	74	35	78	+39
2	Linfield	36	13	5	0	38	16	7	5	6	30	23	20	10	6	68	39	70	+29
3	Crusaders	36	11	4	3	27	15	7	4	7	21	24	18	8	10	48	39	62	+9
4	Newry Town	36	10	4	4	21	15	7	5	6	31	31	17	9	10	52	46	60	+6
5	Glenavon	36	8	6	4	28	14	5	6	7	21	21	13	12	11	49	35	51	+14
6	Ballymena United	36	6	6	6	22	22	5	2	11	18	20	11	8	17	40	42	41	-2
7	Coleraine	36	7	4	7	19	21	3	5	10	15	32	10	9	17	34	53	39	-19
8	Portadown	36	6	4	8	24	24	3	6	9	17	23	9	10	17	41	47	37	-6
9	Cliftonville	36	3	8	7	15	24	4	6	8	16	23	7	14	15	31	47	35	-16
10	Omagh Town	36	3	4	11	16	41	2	2	14	9	38	5	6	25	25	79	21	-54

their first senior caps after coming on as second-half substitutes in the friendly at home to Canada.

Both players earned their call-ups after impressing McMenemy and his locally-based observers with their consistent form in domestic competition. Glentoran and Linfield were the two outstanding teams of the season, with the former, led by ex-Linfield boss Roy Coyle, outpacing their crosstown rivals to win the championship for the 20th time.

It always looked to be a battle of the Belfast 'big two' after both teams set off with long, uninterrupted winning streaks at the start. Boosted by two respectable performances against Maccabi Haifa in the European Cup-winners' Cup, Glentoran won their first six matches, while Linfield, who had also performed with courage in Europe (winning a rousing UEFA Cup second leg 5-3 at home to Omonia Nicosia), recovered from a first-day defeat against ambitious newly-promoted Newry Town by going one better and winning seven on the trot. From then on the outcome of the championship was simply a question of which of the two teams would finish ahead of the other.

Linfield had the upper hand in the direct duels, winning both games at The Oval and drawing the two matches at Windsor Park. But it was Glentoran who collected points more regularly during the weeks in between. With three games remaining it was still very tight, with just three points separating the two. However, Glentoran were in no mood to surrender their lead and impressive back-to-back three-goal wins against Crusaders away and Portadown at home were enough to secure the club's first title for seven years.

Glentoran also added the Gold Cup and the Antrim Shield to their season's trophy haul, while Linfield's consolation at missing out on the big prize was a 2-1 victory over the champions in the final of the Coca-Cola Cup. As a sign of easing tensions in the province, Linfield also played a league fixture away to catholic club Cliftonville for the first time in 28 years.

Other than that moment of ground-breaking history, it was a desperately poor season for the defending champions. Thrashed out of sight by Kosice on their European

INTERNATIONAL HONOURS

World Cup Finals appearances: 1958 (qtr-finals), 1982 (2nd round), 1986

TOP SCORERS

19 Vinny ARKINS (Portadown)
17 Dessie GORMAN (Newry Town)
16 Stephen BAXTER (Glenavon)
15 Glenn FERGUSON (Linfield)
13 Rory HAMILL (Glentoran)
   David LARMOUR (Linfield)
12 Glenn HUNTER (Ballymena United)
   Crawford McRAE (Crusaders)
10 Dessie LOUGHERY (Ballymena United)
   Justin McBRIDE (Glentoran)
   Paul STOKES (Coleraine)

NATIONAL TEAM RESULTS 98/99

05/09/98	Turkey (ECQ)	A	Istanbul	0-3	
10/10/98	Finland (ECQ)	H	Belfast	1-0	Rowland (31)
18/11/98	Moldova (ECQ)	H	Belfast	2-2	Dowie (49), Lennon (63)
27/03/99	Germany (ECQ)	H	Belfast	0-3	
31/03/99	Moldova (ECQ)	A	Chisinau	0-0	
27/04/99	Canada	H	Belfast	1-1	Parker (90og)
29/05/99	Republic of Ireland	A	Dublin	1-0	Griffin (85)

Champions' Cup début, Cliftonville took just a single point from their first seven league games and would have been struggling to avoid automatic relegation had it not been for the woes of Omagh Town, who, in the season after the IRA bombing atrocity, could not get out of the starting-blocks and were long condemned to tenth place. Cliftonville finally saved themselves from the drop only by virtue of a play-off victory against Ards, the runners-up behind First Division champions Distillery - now to be known under their new name of Lurgan Distillery.

The ultimate indignity for Cliftonville, however, came right at the end of the season when, having qualified for the Irish Cup final at the expense of Glentoran and Linfield, among others, they were not permitted to contest it. It was discovered that for the semi-final replay against Linfield they had fielded a player, Simon Gribben, who was already Cup-tied having played for a junior team in an earlier round. The Irish FA had no alternative but to expel Cliftonville from the competition. More contentious was their reluctance to promote Linfield to the final instead, but competition rules, it was revealed, clearly stated that in such an eventuality a team already knocked out could not be reinstated. Thus, Portadown, who had beaten Ballymena United in the other semi-final, were declared

NATIONAL TEAM APPEARANCES 98/99

Manager - Lawrie McMENEMY	TUR	FIN	MOL	GER	MOL	CAN	IRL	Cps	Gls
Alan FETTIS (01/02/71) - Blackburn Rovers (ENG)	G	G	G					25	-
Aaron HUGHES (08/11/79) - Newcastle United (ENG)	D	D			s63	D	D	8	-
Keith ROWLAND (01/09/71) - Queens Park Rangers (ENG)	D46	M88	M77	M68		M	M74	19	1
Colin HILL (12/11/63) - Northampton Town (ENG)	D							27	1
Steve MORROW (02/07/70) - Queens Park Rangers (ENG)	D	D	D	D	D			37	1
Keith GILLESPIE (18/02/75) - Newcastle United (ENG)/Blackburn Rovers (ENG)	M73	M70	M88	M83	M			26	1
Neil LENNON (25/06/71) - Leicester City (ENG)	M	M	M	M68	M		M79	27	2
Philip MULRYNE (01/01/78) - Manchester United (ENG)/Norwich City (ENG)	M	M				M82		8	1
Kevin HORLOCK (01/11/72) - Manchester City (ENG)	M	D		D	D	D		17	-
Michael HUGHES (02/08/71) - Wimbledon (ENG)	M	A	A	M	M			47	3
Iain DOWIE (09/01/65) - Queens Park Rangers (ENG)	A	A79	A	A	A	A74	A46	56	12
James QUINN (15/12/74) - West Bromwich Albion (ENG)	s46	s88					A	15	1
Jim WHITLEY (14/04/75) - Manchester City (ENG)	s73							2	-
Darren PATTERSON (15/10/69) - Dundee United (ENG)			D	D	D	D63	D	17	1
Jon McCARTHY (18/08/70) - Birmingham City (ENG)		s70	s88	s83		M59	M	12	-
George O'BOYLE (14/12/67) - St. Johnstone (ENG)		s79						13	1
Peter KENNEDY (10/09/73) - Watford (ENG)			D	s68				2	-
Danny GRIFFIN (10/08/77) - St. Johnstone (SCO)			D				s79	9	1
Steve LOMAS (18/01/74) - West Ham United (ENG)			M	M	M	M		30	2
Phil GRAY (01/04/69) - Luton Town (ENG)			s77					21	5
Maik TAYLOR (04/09/71) - Fulham (ENG)				G	G	G46	G46	4	-
Mark WILLIAMS (28/09/70) - Chesterfield (ENG)				D	D	D	D	4	-
Danny SONNER (09/01/72) - Sheffield Wednesday (ENG)				s68		s82		3	-
Stephen ROBINSON (10/12/74) - Bournemouth (ENG)					A		A	3	-
Barry HUNTER (18/11/68) - Reading (ENG)						D	D	13	1
Adrian COOTE (03/09/78) - Norwich City (ENG)						A74	s46	2	-
Tommy WRIGHT (29/08/63) - Manchester City (ENG)						s46		30	-
Rory HAMILL (04/05/76) - Glentoran						s59		1	-
Glenn FERGUSON (10/07/69) - Linfield						s74		1	-
Paul McVEIGH (06/12/77) - Tottenham Hotspur (ENG)						s74		1	-
Roy CARROLL (30/09/77) - Wigan Athletic (ENG)							s46	2	-
Damien JOHNSON (18/11/78) - Blackburn Rovers (ENG)							s74	1	-

EUROPEAN CUPS 98/99

CHAMPIONS' CUP
● CLIFTONVILLE
Preliminary round 1.FC KOSICE (SVK)
H 1-5   Flynn (45)
        Reece; Small, Flynn (Kerr 51), Tabb, McCallion,
        Sliney (McMahon 75), McCann T., Collins (McDonagh 81), Tolan,
        McCann M., Donnelly.
A 0-8
        Reece; Small, Flynn, Tabb, McCallion, Sliney (Davey 72), McCann T.,
        Collins (McMahon 72), Tolan, McCann M. (McDonagh 72), Donnelly.

CUP WINNERS' CUP
● GLENTORAN
Preliminary round MACCABI HAIFA (ISR)
H 0-1
        Russell; Nixon, Kennedy, Walker, Devine, Leeman, Mitchell
        (Quigley 80), Hamill (Rainey 90), Kirk (McCallan 65), Batey, Elliott.
A 1-2   Batey (42)
        Russell; Nixon, Kennedy, Walker, Devine, Leeman, Mitchell, Hamill,
        Rainey (Elliott 77), Batey (Livingstone 83), McBride (Kirk 83).

UEFA CUP
● LINFIELD
Qualifying round OMONIA NICOSIA (CYP)
A 1-5   Ferguson (73)
        Geddes; McDonald (Collier 76), Easton, McCoosh (McShane 82),
        Murphy, Beatty, Marks, Gorman, Ferguson, Feeney (Larmour 66),
        Bailie.
H 5-3   Feeney (19), Gorman (35, 48), McDonald (45), Campbell (73)
        Geddes; McDonald (Marks 70), Easton, Semple (Campbell 60),
        Murphy, Beatty, Larmour (Cleland 80), Gorman, Ferguson, Feeney,
        Bailie.

Cup winners by default. It was the first time in 79 years that the Irish Cup final was not played, and naturally the issue provoked widespread criticism.

But one club not complaining were Portadown. They not only had the Cup in their hands for only the second time, but their generally miserable season (only eighth in the league despite Vinny Arkins winning the top scorer crown for the second season running) had been rendered largely irrelevant thanks to the added bonus of a place in the UEFA Cup.

PLAYER OF THE SEASON

JOHN DEVINE
The attribution of both Manager of the Year and Footballer of the Year were foregone conclusions in 1998/99. While Roy Coyle, of Glentoran, took the former award, his captain, John Devine, was a clear winner of the latter. The experienced centre-back was the only Glentoran player to feature in all 36 matches of the club's Championship-winning campaign. He also contributed a useful total of six goals and was the leading figure of a team in which other individuals such as Rory Hamill, Justin McBride, Scott Young and Andy Kirk also made a strong impression. There was bad news for the Glens at the end of the season, however, when Devine decided to quit the club after 13 years of service and move north to join Coleraine.

DOMESTIC CUP 98/99

FIFTH ROUND
Ards 1, Ards Rangers 0
Ballymena United 3, Larne 1
Bangor 0, Glenavon 3
Brantwood 3, Drummond United 1
Carrick Rangers 2, Dungannon Swifts 2
(replay) Dungannon Swifts 3, Carrick Rangers 4
Coleraine 1, Limavady United 1
(replay) Limavady United 0, Coleraine 1
Cliftonville 6, Crewe United 1
Crusaders 1, Newry Town 1
(replay) Newry Town 2, Crusaders 3 (aet)
Distillery 4, Harland & WW 0
Drumaness Mills 0, Lurgan Celtic Bhoys 2
Glentoran 3, Tobermore United 0
Institute 0, Chimney Corner 1
Linfield 6, Crumlin United 0
Loughgall 2, Dundela 1
Omagh Town 1, Ballyclare Comrades 2
Portadown 1, Ballymoney United 0

SIXTH ROUND
Ballymena United 3, Ballyclare Comrades 0
Carrick Rangers 2, Ards 0
Cliftonville 2, Glentoran 1
Coleraine 2, Loughgall 1
Distillery 5, Brantwood 0
Glenavon 3, Crusaders 0
Linfield 3, Chimney Corner 1
Lurgan Celtic Bhoys 0, Portadown 3

QUARTER-FINALS
Carrick Rangers 1 (Treanor 90),
Cliftonville 2 (McCallion 1, Donaghey 62)

Coleraine 1 (English 43),
Portadown 2 (Byrne 45, Arkins 47)

Distillery 1 (Kelly 65),
Ballymena United 1 (Hunter 12)
(replay) Ballymena United 2 (Knell 65, Patton 112),
Distillery 1 (McCloskey 26) (aet)

Linfield 0, Glenavon 0
(replay) Glenavon 1 (Arthur 90p),
Linfield 2 (Doherty 48og, Larmour 79)

SEMI-FINALS
Linfield 1 (Ferguson 25),
Cliftonville 1 (Tabb 29)
(replay) Linfield 0, Cliftonville 1 (Sliney 38p)

Ballymena United 0,
Portadown 2 (Strain 59, Clarke 78)

FINAL
The final was not played as Cliftonville fielded an ineligible player in the semi-final replay against Linfield. The IFA therefore expelled Cliftonville and declared Portadown winners of the Cup.

BALLYMENA UNITED

CLUB DIRECTORY

Ballymena United FC
The Showgrounds
Warden Street
Ballymena
tel - (01266) 652049
Year of Formation - 1928
Chairman - Edwin McLaughlin
Secretary - Don Stirling
Manager - Alan Fraser (99/00 - Nigel Best)
Stadium - The Showgrounds (8,000)

MAJOR HONOURS
Domestic Cup - (6)
1929, 1940, 1958, 1981, 1984, 1989.

APPEARANCES 98/99

		P	Ap	(s)	Gls
Jason ALLEN	D	31			
Robert BECK	G	22			
Nigel BOYD	D	20	(2)	1	
Ian BUSTARD	M	22	(6)	1	
David CALDERWOOD	M	11	(2)	1	
Neil CANDLISH (SCO)	A		(5)		
Mark CARLISLE	D	35		1	
Steven HANNA	M	1	(1)		
Glenn HUNTER	A	27	(7)	12	
Philip KNELL	M	32	(2)	4	
Des LOUGHERY	A	31	(4)	10	
John McCONNELL	D	24			
John McDOWELL	D	12	(2)		
Declan McGREEVY	M	2	(10)		
Richard McKINNEY	G	14	(1)		
Paul MUIR	M	26	(3)		
Peter MURRAY	M	5	(2)		
Patrick O'CONNELL (IRL)	A	16	(17)	2	
Kevin O'HAGEN	D	12	(1)		
Darren PARKER	M	25	(2)	2	
Barry PATTON (IRL)	A	13	(13)	2	
Keith PERCY	M	15	(3)	4	
Paul STOREY	A		(2)		
Terry TENNYSON	D		(2)		

LEAGUE RESULTS 1998/99

15/08/98	Glenavon	H	1-0	Hunter
22/08/98	Linfield	A	0-1	
28/08/98	Omagh Town	H	0-0	
01/09/98	Cliftonville	A	1-0	Loughery
05/09/98	Portadown	H	1-0	Bustard
12/09/98	Glentoran	A	1-2	Loughery
19/09/98	Newry Town	H	1-1	Hunter (p)
26/09/98	Coleraine	A	1-2	Loughery
03/10/98	Crusaders	A	0-2	
06/10/98	Linfield	H	1-0	Knell
17/10/98	Glenavon	A	0-0	
24/10/98	Omagh Town	A	4-1	Patton, Parker, Hunter 2
31/10/98	Cliftonville	H	1-2	Parker
07/11/98	Glentoran	H	1-1	Hunter
14/11/98	Portadown	A	3-1	Hunter, Loughery, Percy
21/11/98	Newry Town	A	0-0	
28/11/98	Coleraine	H	1-0	Percy
05/12/98	Crusaders	H	2-0	Knell 2
12/12/98	Linfield	A	1-4	Percy
19/12/98	Glenavon	H	0-1	
26/12/98	Coleraine	A	1-0	Loughery
30/12/98	Crusaders	H	1-2	Hunter
02/01/99	Cliftonville	A	0-1	
09/01/99	Portadown	H	2-2	Knell, Percy
30/01/99	Newry Town	H	0-0	
06/02/99	Glentoran	A	0-1	
13/02/99	Linfield	H	4-2	Loughery 2, O'Connell, Carlisle
27/02/99	Glenavon	A	0-1	
06/03/99	Coleraine	H	0-1	
20/03/99	Crusaders	A	0-1	
23/03/99	Cliftonville	H	2-2	Hunter, Boyd
30/03/99	Omagh Town	A	5-0	Calderwood, Hunter 2, O'Connell, Loughery
03/04/99	Portadown	A	1-2	Loughery
05/04/99	Omagh Town	H	1-2	Patton
17/04/99	Newry Town	A	0-1	
24/04/99	Glentoran	H	3-6	Hunter 2 (1p), Loughery

CLIFTONVILLE

CLUB DIRECTORY

Cliftonville FC
Solitude
Cliftonville Street
Belfast BT14 6LP
tel - (01232) 754628
fax - (01232) 729011
Year of Formation - 1879
Chairman - Hugh McCartan
Secretary - John Duffy
Manager - Marty Quinn
Stadium - Solitude (17,000)

MAJOR HONOURS
League Championship - (3) 1906, 1910, 1998.
Domestic Cup - (8) 1883, 1888, 1897, 1900,
1901, 1907, 1909, 1979.

APPEARANCES 98/99

		P	Ap	(s)	Gls
Tony AGANA (ENG)	A	6			
Stephen BOYD	D		(1)		
Michael COLLINS	M	28	(4)	2	
Damien DAVEY	D		(1)		
Brian DONAGHEY	M	13	(4)	1	
Michael DONNELLY	M	26		2	
Gerry FLYNN	D	21	(4)		
Simon GRIBBEN	M	1			
Michael INGHAM	G	18			
Barry JOHNSTON	M		(1)		
Gary KENNEDY	A		(1)		
Joe KERR	D	6			
Thomas McCALLION	D	35	(1)	3	
Marty McCANN	M	5	(5)	1	
Tim McCANN	M	14	(2)	4	
Michael McCLEAVE	A		(2)		
Fintan McCONVILLE	M	1	(1)		
Harry McCOURT	A	2	(3)	1	
Jim McDONAGH	A	1	(1)		
Ciaran McLAUGHLIN	G	3			
Larry McMAHON	M	21	(9)	2	
Shane MULHOLLAND	D	5	(5)		
Keith MULVENNA	D	24	(5)	1	
Peter MURRAY	M	14	(6)		
Sean MURRAY (IRL)	A	17	(1)	3	
Paul REECE (ENG)	G	15			
Chris SCANNELL	A	3	(6)		
Gary SLINEY (IRL)	M	29	(3)	5	
Stephen SMALL	D	21	(3)	1	
Martin TABB	D	33	(1)	1	
Jody TOLAN	A	24	(4)	3	
Peter WITHNELL	A	10	(1)	1	

LEAGUE RESULTS 1998/99

15/08/98	Portadown	H	0-2	
22/08/98	Glentoran	H	2-4	Sliney, McMahon
28/08/98	Newry Town	A	1-2	Collins
01/09/98	Ballymena United	H	0-1	
05/09/98	Crusaders	A	1-2	McCann M.
12/09/98	Glenavon	H	2-2	Sliney, Mulvenna
19/09/98	Linfield	A	0-1	
26/09/98	Omagh Town	H	2-1	Donnelly, McCallion
03/10/98	Coleraine	A	1-1	Collins
06/10/98	Glentoran	A	1-0	McCann T.
17/10/98	Portadown	H	0-0	
24/10/98	Newry Town	H	1-4	McCann T.
31/10/98	Ballymena United	A	2-1	McCallion (p), Tolan
07/11/98	Glenavon	A	1-0	Sliney (p)
14/11/98	Crusaders	H	2-3	Donnelly, Murray S.
21/11/98	Linfield	H	1-1	McCann T.
28/11/98	Omagh Town	A	2-2	Small, McCann T.
05/12/98	Coleraine	H	1-1	McCourt
12/12/98	Glenavon	A	0-0	
19/12/98	Coleraine	H	0-0	
26/12/98	Crusaders	A	0-1	
30/12/98	Omagh Town	A	1-1	McMahon
02/01/99	Ballymena United	H	1-0	Sliney (p)
09/01/99	Glentoran	H	0-0	
16/01/99	Portadown	A	1-0	Murray S.
30/01/99	Linfield	H	0-1	
06/02/99	Newry Town	A	0-1	
13/02/99	Glenavon	H	0-0	
27/02/99	Coleraine	A	1-3	Withnell
06/03/99	Crusaders	H	1-1	Tolan
20/03/99	Omagh Town	H	2-1	Tabb, Murray S.
23/03/99	Ballymena United	A	2-2	Donaghey, McCallion
03/04/99	Glentoran	A	1-1	Sliney
06/04/99	Portadown	A	0-3	
17/04/99	Linfield	A	1-2	Tolan
24/04/99	Newry Town	H	0-2	

COLERAINE

CLUB DIRECTORY

Coleraine FC
The Showgrounds
Ballycastle Road
Coleraine
tel - (01265) 53655
fax - (01265) 329188
Year of Formation - 1927
Chairman - Sammy Lyle
Secretary - Freddie Monahan
Manager - Kenny Shiels
Stadium - The Showgrounds (8,000)

MAJOR HONOURS
League Championship - (1) 1974.
Domestic Cup - (4) 1965, 1972, 1975, 1977.

APPEARANCES 98/99

		P	Ap	(s)	Gls
Brendan ASPINALL (ENG)	D	12		(4)	1
Stuart CLANACHAN	D	34			3
Kieran DUFFIN	A			(1)	
Mark ELDER	D	2		(1)	
Isaac ENGLISH (SCO)	A	29		(1)	8
Paul GASTON	D	29			2
Rory GINTY (IRL)	M	14		(3)	1
Barry GORMLEY	M			(1)	
Joe GRAY	A	23		(7)	3
John GREGG	M	9		(3)	1
Russell KERR	D			(1)	
Wesley LAMONT	G	31			
Aaron LYNCH (IRL)	A	18			
Conor LYNCH	D	1			
Patrick McALLISTER	M	12		(1)	
Oliver McAULEY	D	18		(1)	
Damien McDONALD	D	15		(5)	
Trevor McLERNON	M	6		(5)	
John McIVOR	A	3			
Shane McQUILLAN	A	15		(9)	2
Ross MURRAY	G	5			
Gavin NAYLOR (ENG)	M	4		(2)	1
John NEILL	D	1			
Mervyn NICHOLL	M			(1)	
Mark PICKING	M	8		(3)	
Damien REDDEN	M	1		(2)	
Michael ROGAN	M			(5)	
Barry ROONEY	A	2		(1)	1
Sammy SHIELS	A	3		(5)	
Michael SMYTH	D	24		(4)	
Alfie STEWART	D	31			
Paul STOKES (IRL)	A	23		(6)	10
Stephen YOUNG	M	23		(2)	

LEAGUE RESULTS 1998/99

Date	Opponent		Score	Scorers
15/08/98	Crusaders	A	1-0	English
22/08/98	Portadown	H	1-0	Rooney
28/08/98	Glenavon	A	1-3	English
01/09/98	Glentoran	H	1-3	og (Nixon)
05/09/98	Linfield	A	1-2	Stokes
12/09/98	Newry Town	H	2-2	Clanachan, Stokes
19/09/98	Omagh Town	A	0-2	
26/09/98	Ballymena United	H	2-1	Clanachan, Ginty
03/10/98	Cliftonville	H	1-1	Stokes (p)
06/10/98	Portadown	A	0-3	
17/10/98	Crusaders	H	0-2	
24/10/98	Glenavon	H	1-3	Stokes
31/10/98	Glentoran	A	4-5	Stokes 3 (2p), English
07/11/98	Newry Town	A	1-1	English
14/11/98	Linfield	H	0-0	
21/11/98	Omagh Town	H	2-1	Gaston, English
28/11/98	Ballymena United	A	0-1	
05/12/98	Cliftonville	A	1-1	Gray
12/12/98	Crusaders	H	0-2	
19/12/98	Cliftonville	A	0-0	
26/12/98	Ballymena United	H	0-1	
30/12/98	Portadown	A	2-1	Aspinall, Gregg
02/01/99	Glentoran	H	0-1	
09/01/99	Linfield	H	2-1	English 2
16/01/99	Newry Town	A	0-1	
29/01/99	Omagh Town	H	1-0	English
06/02/99	Glenavon	A	1-3	Gray
13/02/99	Crusaders	A	0-2	
27/02/99	Cliftonville	H	3-1	Naylor, Stokes 2
06/03/99	Ballymena United	A	1-0	McQuillan
20/03/99	Portadown	H	0-2	
23/03/99	Glentoran	A	0-5	
03/04/99	Linfield	A	1-1	Clanachan
05/04/99	Newry Town	H	3-0	Stokes (p), Gray, Gaston
17/04/99	Omagh Town	A	1-1	McQuillan
24/04/99	Glenavon	H	0-0	

CRUSADERS

CLUB DIRECTORY

Crusaders FC
Seaview
Shore Road, Belfast BT15 3PL
tel - (01232) 370777
Year of Formation - 1898
Chairman - Jim Semple
Secretary - Harry Davison
Manager - Aaron Callaghan
(99/00 - Martin Murray)
Stadium - Seaview (9,000)

MAJOR HONOURS
League Championship - (4)
1973, 1976, 1995, 1997.
Domestic Cup - (2) 1967, 1968.

APPEARANCES 98/99

	P	Ap	(s)	Gls
Gavin ARTHUR	A	15		5
Aaron CALLAGHAN (IRL)	D	31		3
Michael DEEGAN (IRL)	M	16	(9)	1
John DOUGLAS	A	1	(5)	
Stephen DOUGLAS	A	2		
Glenn DUNLOP	D	30		1
Liam DUNNE (IRL)	M	18	(1)	3
Paul DWYER	A	12	(9)	
Conor FRAWLEY (IRL)	D	13	(3)	2
Peter GILGUNN	D	1	(2)	
Ian HILL (IRL)	D	25	(1)	
Darren LOCKHART	M	23	(2)	6
Damian McAULEY	A		(1)	
Stephen McBRIDE	A	4	(5)	
John McIVOR	M	27	(4)	1
Trevor McMULLAN	M	34	(1)	5
Crawford McRAE	A	24	(1)	12
Stuart MELLON	D	20	(2)	
Damien MOONEY	M	2	(5)	
David O'HARE	G	36		
Pat O'TOOLE (IRL)	M	35		3
Brian RUSSELL	A	25	(6)	6
Ian YOUNG	D	2		

LEAGUE RESULTS 1998/99

15/08/98	Coleraine	H	0-1	
22/08/98	Glenavon	A	0-3	
29/08/98	Linfield	H	1-4	Lockhart
01/09/98	Omagh Town	A	0-0	
05/09/98	Cliftonville	H	2-1	McRae 2
12/09/98	Portadown	A	1-0	Dunne
19/09/98	Glentoran	H	0-0	
26/09/98	Newry Town	A	0-0	
03/10/98	Ballymena United	H	2-0	Callaghan 2
06/10/98	Glenavon	H	1-0	McRae
17/10/98	Coleraine	A	2-0	McRae, Arthur
24/10/98	Linfield	A	1-2	Deegan
31/10/98	Omagh Town	H	5-0	McIvor, Arthur 2 (1p), Russell, Lockhart
07/11/98	Portadown	H	1-1	McMullan
14/11/98	Cliftonville	A	3-2	Arthur 2, Frawley
21/11/98	Glentoran	A	4-1	Lockhart 3, O'Toole
28/11/98	Newry Town	H	2-0	McRae 2
05/12/98	Ballymena United	A	0-2	
12/12/98	Coleraine	A	2-0	Russell, McMullan (p)
19/12/98	Omagh Town	H	2-0	Russell, O'Toole
26/12/98	Cliftonville	H	1-0	McRae
30/12/98	Ballymena United	A	2-1	Dunne, McRae
02/01/99	Portadown	H	0-0	
09/01/99	Newry Town	H	3-2	Callaghan, McMullan, Russell
16/01/99	Glentoran	A	1-2	McRae
30/01/99	Glenavon	H	1-1	McMullan
06/02/99	Linfield	A	2-4	Russell 2
13/02/99	Coleraine	H	2-0	McRae 2
27/02/99	Omagh Town	A	2-1	O'Toole, McRae
06/03/99	Cliftonville	A	1-1	McMullan (p)
20/03/99	Ballymena United	H	1-0	Lockhart
23/03/99	Portadown	A	0-0	
03/04/99	Newry Town	A	0-3	
06/04/99	Glentoran	H	0-3	
17/04/99	Glenavon	A	0-2	
24/04/99	Linfield	H	3-2	Dunlop, Dunne, Frawley

GLENAVON

CLUB DIRECTORY

Glenavon FC
Mourneview Park
Lurgan BT66 8EW
tel - (01762) 322472
fax - (01762) 327694
Year of Formation - 1889
Chairman - Adrian Teer
Secretary - T.R. Kerr
Manager - Roy Walker
Stadium - Mourneview Park (15,000)

MAJOR HONOURS
League Championship - (3) 1952, 1957, 1960.
Domestic Cup - (5)
1957, 1959, 1961, 1992, 1997.

APPEARANCES 98/99

		P	Ap	(s)	Gls
Brian	ADAIR	A		(1)	
Stuart	ADDIS	G	5		
Gavin	ARTHUR	A	20		3
Stephen	BAXTER	A	26	(1)	16
Paul	BYRNE	D	6	(2)	
Paul Peter	BYRNE (IRL)	M	7	(2)	1
Stephen	CAFFREY (IRL)	D	23	(5)	
Michael	CASH	M	18		1
Lee	DOHERTY	M	30		1
Alan	DORNAN	D	35		
Ryan	EVANS	A	2		
Alan	EWING	M	21	(1)	2
Jim	GARDINER	A	4	(5)	1
Mark	GLENDINNING	D	25		5
Tony	GRANT (IRL)	A	24	(3)	7
John	GREGG	D	1	(1)	
Sam	HAUGHEY	A	1	(2)	
Kevin	KEEGAN	A	9	(9)	1
David	McCALLAN	A	5	(3)	2
Mark	McCANN	M	5	(5)	
James	McCARTAN	A	6	(4)	1
Donal	McCOURT	A	2		
Ray	McCOY	M	1	(4)	
Mark	McMENEMY	M	9	(2)	3
Paul	MILLIGAN	M		(2)	
Darren	MURPHY	M	11		
Patrick	O'CONNOR	M		(1)	
Dermot	O'NEILL (IRL)	G	31		
Darragh	PEDEN	D		(2)	
Nigel	QUIGLEY	D	1	(3)	
Colin	RUSSELL	D	7	(4)	
Gary	SMYTH	D	34		4
Jeff	SPIERS	D	27		
Vic	WELCH	A		(1)	

LEAGUE RESULTS 1998/99

15/08/98	Ballymena United	A	0-1	
22/08/98	Crusaders	H	3-0	Grant, Byrne P.P. (p), Baxter
28/08/98	Coleraine	H	3-1	Grant 2, Baxter
01/09/98	Linfield	A	0-2	
05/09/98	Omagh Town	H	2-0	Baxter, Glendinning
12/09/98	Cliftonville	A	2-2	Grant, Baxter
19/09/98	Portadown	H	1-0	Baxter
26/09/98	Glentoran	A	2-5	Baxter 2
03/10/98	Newry Town	H	1-2	Cash
06/10/98	Crusaders	A	0-1	
17/10/98	Ballymena United	H	0-0	
24/10/98	Coleraine	A	3-1	Baxter 3
31/10/98	Linfield	H	1-1	Grant
07/11/98	Cliftonville	H	0-1	
14/11/98	Omagh Town	A	3-0	Baxter, McCallan 2
21/11/98	Portadown	A	1-1	Smyth
28/11/98	Glentoran	H	0-1	
05/12/98	Newry Town	A	0-1	
12/12/98	Cliftonville	H	0-0	
19/12/98	Ballymena United	A	1-0	McCartan
01/01/99	Glentoran	A	0-1	
02/01/99	Newry Town	H	1-1	Arthur
09/01/99	Omagh Town	H	6-1	og (Crilly), Smyth, Keegan, Baxter, Arthur (p), Ewing
16/01/99	Linfield	A	1-3	Baxter
26/01/99	Portadown	H	2-2	McMenemy, Glendinning
30/01/99	Crusaders	A	1-1	Glendinning
06/02/99	Coleraine	H	3-1	Baxter 2, Arthur
13/02/99	Cliftonville	A	0-0	
27/02/99	Ballymena United	H	1-0	McMenemy
06/03/99	Portadown	A	2-2	Ewing, Doherty
20/03/99	Glentoran	H	0-1	
23/03/99	Newry Town	A	2-0	Gardiner, McMenemy
03/04/99	Omagh Town	A	3-0	Grant, Baxter, Glendinning
06/04/99	Linfield	H	2-2	Glendinning, Smyth
17/04/99	Crusaders	H	2-0	Smyth, Grant
24/04/99	Coleraine	A	0-0	

GLENTORAN

THE EUROPEAN FOOTBALL YEARBOOK 1999-2000

CLUB DIRECTORY

Glentoran FC
The Oval
Mersey Street, Belfast BT4 1FG
tel - (01232) 456137
fax - (01232) 732956
Year of Formation - 1882
Chairman - Ted Brownlee
Secretary - Jackie Warren
Manager - Roy Coyle
Stadium - The Oval (30,000)

MAJOR HONOURS
League Championship - (20)
1894, 1897, 1905, 1912, 1913, 1921, 1925,
1931, 1951, 1953, 1964, 1967, 1968, 1970,
1972, 1977, 1981, 1988, 1992, 1999.
Domestic Cup - (17) 1914, 1917, 1921, 1932,
1933, 1935, 1951, 1966, 1973, 1983, 1985,
1986, 1987, 1988, 1990, 1996, 1998.

APPEARANCES 98/99

	P	Ap	(s)	Gls
Neil ARMSTRONG	G	2		
Pete BATEY	M	19	(6)	2
John DEVINE	D	36		6
Stuart ELLIOTT	M	20	(11)	7
Michael FERGUSON	D	17	(1)	
Darren FINLAY	M	2	(5)	1
Rory HAMILL	A	35		13
John KENNEDY	D	13		
Andy KIRK	A	15	(9)	8
Paul LEEMAN	M	33	(2)	9
Rod LENNOX (SCO)	A	2		
Steven LIVINGSTONE	M		(1)	
Justin McBRIDE	A	26	(2)	10
David McCALLAN	A	2		1
Tim McCANN	M	12	(6)	4
Philip MITCHELL	M	10	(3)	3
Colin NIXON	D	32		2
James QUIGLEY	M	6	(3)	
David RAINEY	A	18	(8)	7
Wayne RUSSELL (WAL)	G	34		
Chris WALKER	D	35		
Scott YOUNG (SCO)	M	27	(3)	

LEAGUE RESULTS 1998/99

15/08/98	Omagh Town	H	2-0	Mitchell (p), Hamill
22/08/98	Cliftonville	A	4-2	Leeman 3 (1p), McCallan
01/09/98	Coleraine	A	3-1	Mitchell, Nixon, Elliott
05/09/98	Newry Town	A	2-1	og (Campbell), McBride (p)
12/09/98	Ballymena United	H	2-1	Elliott, McBride (p)
15/09/98	Portadown	H	1-0	Rainey
19/09/98	Crusaders	A	0-0	
26/09/98	Glenavon	H	5-2	Hamill, Rainey, McBride (p), Kirk, Elliott
03/10/98	Linfield	A	1-1	Batey
06/10/98	Cliftonville	H	0-1	
17/10/98	Omagh Town	A	2-0	Mitchell, McBride
24/10/98	Portadown	A	3-0	Hamill, McBride, Elliott
31/10/98	Coleraine	H	5-4	Rainey, Leeman, McBride (p), Elliott, Hamill
07/11/98	Ballymena United	A	1-1	Rainey
14/11/98	Newry Town	H	1-3	McBride
21/11/98	Crusaders	H	1-4	Rainey
28/11/98	Glenavon	A	1-0	Devine (p)
05/12/98	Linfield	H	0-1	
12/12/98	Omagh Town	A	4-1	Kirk 3, Leeman
19/12/98	Newry Town	H	5-1	Hamill 3, Kirk 2
26/12/98	Linfield	A	1-1	Kirk
01/01/99	Glenavon	H	1-0	Devine (p)
02/01/99	Coleraine	A	1-0	Devine
09/01/99	Cliftonville	A	0-0	
16/01/99	Crusaders	H	2-1	Rainey, Devine
30/01/99	Portadown	A	3-1	McBride, Hamill, Kirk
06/02/99	Ballymena United	H	1-0	McCann
13/02/99	Omagh Town	H	2-0	McCann, Elliott
06/03/99	Linfield	H	1-2	Finlay
11/03/99	Newry Town	A	0-1	
20/03/99	Glenavon	A	1-0	Leeman
23/03/99	Coleraine	H	5-0	Rainey, Leeman, Batey, Devine, Hamill
03/04/99	Cliftonville	H	1-1	Devine (p)
06/04/99	Crusaders	A	3-0	Hamill, McBride 2
17/04/99	Portadown	H	3-1	Nixon, Hamill, McCann
24/04/99	Ballymena United	A	6-3	Elliott, Hamill 2, McCann, Leeman 2

LINFIELD

Linfield FC
Windsor Park, Donegal Ave, Belfast BT12 6LW
tel - (01232) 244198   fax - (01232) 244691
Year of Formation - 1886
Chairman - Billy McCoubrey
Secretary - Derek Brooks
Manager - David Jeffrey
Stadium - Windsor Park (28,500)

MAJOR HONOURS
League Championship - (42)
1891, 1892, 1893, 1895, 1898, 1902, 1904,
1907, 1908, 1909, 1911, 1914, 1922, 1923,
1930, 1932, 1934, 1935, 1949, 1950, 1954,
1955, 1956, 1959, 1961, 1962, 1966, 1969,
1971, 1975, 1978, 1979, 1980, 1982, 1983,
1984, 1985, 1986, 1987, 1989, 1993, 1994.
Domestic Cup - (35)
1891, 1892, 1893, 1895, 1898, 1899, 1902,
1904, 1912, 1913, 1915, 1916, 1919, 1922,
1923, 1930, 1931, 1934, 1936, 1939, 1942,
1945, 1946, 1948, 1950, 1953, 1960, 1962,
1963, 1970, 1978, 1980, 1982, 1994, 1995.

APPEARANCES 98/99

	P	Ap	(s)	Gls
Noel BAILLIE	M	36		
Stephen BEATTY	M	35		8
Robert CAMPBELL	A	4	(7)	
Gary CHISHOLM	A	5	(8)	3
Thomas CLELAND	M	4	(7)	
Stephen COLLIER	D	10	(2)	
John EASTON	D	6		
Lee FEENEY	A	11	(5)	4
Glenn FERGUSON	A	27		15
Bobby GEDDES (SCO)	G	8		
Tony GORMAN (IRL)	M	34		7
David HENRY	G	2		
Neil INGLIS (SCO)	G	21		
David LARMOUR	A	28	(6)	13
Jamie MARKS	D	12	(5)	
Chris MORGAN	A	16	(3)	7
Ian McCOOSH	M	11	(5)	2
Thomas McDONALD	D	27		1
Ryan McLAUGHLIN	D	16		1
Pat McSHANE	D	20	(1)	
William MURPHY	D	27	(2)	2
Graeme PHILSON	D	5	(3)	1
Robert ROBINSON	G	5		
Philip ROGAN	M	1		
Ryan SEMPLE	M	6	(9)	
John SHAW	D	1	(2)	
Ian YOUNG	D	18	(2)	2

LEAGUE RESULTS 1998/99

14/08/98	Newry Town	A	1-2	Beatty (p)
22/08/98	Ballymena United	H	1-0	Larmour
29/08/98	Crusaders	A	4-1	Gorman, Ferguson, Larmour, McDonald
01/09/98	Glenavon	H	2-0	Ferguson, Beatty
05/09/98	Coleraine	H	2-1	og (Young), Larmour
12/09/98	Omagh Town	A	3-1	Ferguson, Larmour, Young
19/09/98	Cliftonville	H	1-0	Beatty
26/09/98	Portadown	A	2-0	Gorman, Feeney
03/10/98	Glentoran	H	1-1	Larmour
06/10/98	Ballymena United	A	0-1	
17/10/98	Newry Town	H	2-2	Beatty, Larmour
24/10/98	Crusaders	H	2-1	McCoosh, Feeney
31/10/98	Glenavon	A	1-1	Beatty (p)
07/11/98	Omagh Town	H	2-0	Larmour, Feeney
14/11/98	Coleraine	A	0-0	
21/11/98	Cliftonville	A	1-1	Murphy
28/11/98	Portadown	H	2-2	Feeney, Larmour
05/12/98	Glentoran	A	1-0	Beatty (p)
12/12/98	Ballymena United	H	4-1	Ferguson 2, Morgan, Larmour
18/12/98	Portadown	A	1-1	McLaughlin
26/12/98	Glentoran	H	1-1	Ferguson
01/01/99	Newry Town	A	1-2	Morgan
02/01/99	Omagh Town	H	3-0	Murphy, Beatty, Chisholm
09/01/99	Coleraine	A	1-2	Chisholm
16/01/99	Glenavon	H	3-1	McCoosh, Morgan, McLaughlin
30/01/99	Cliftonville	A	1-0	Young
06/02/99	Crusaders	H	4-2	Morgan 2, Ferguson, Gorman
13/02/99	Ballymena United	A	2-4	Ferguson, Gorman
27/02/99	Portadown	H	3-1	Morgan, Gorman 2
06/03/99	Glentoran	A	2-1	Chisholm, Morgan
20/03/99	Newry Town	H	2-1	Ferguson 2
23/03/99	Omagh Town	A	5-1	Philson, Ferguson, Gorman, Larmour 2
03/04/99	Coleraine	H	1-1	Larmour
06/04/99	Glenavon	A	2-2	Beatty (p), Ferguson
17/04/99	Cliftonville	H	2-1	Ferguson 2
24/04/99	Crusaders	A	2-3	Ferguson, Larmour

NEWRY TOWN

CLUB DIRECTORY

Newry Town FC
The Showgrounds
Newry
tel (01693) 252581
Year of Formation - 1923
Chairman - Joe Rice
Secretary - Eamon Cole
Managers - Ollie Ralph & Harry Fay
Stadium - The Showgrounds (5,000)

APPEARANCES 98/99

	P	Ap	(s)	Gls
Alan BYRNE (IRL)	M	24	(1)	3
David CAMPBELL (IRL)	D	5		
Chris COFFEY	M	13	(7)	1
John CONNOLLY (IRL)	G	1		
John DRAKE	D	29		
Paul EVANS	M	11	(2)	1
Dessie GORMAN (IRL)	A	28	(2)	17
Alan HALL	M	19	(5)	2
Michael HARTE (IRL)	M	1		
Seamus KANE	D	2	(2)	
John KENNY (IRL)	M	30		4
Adrian LARKIN	M	15	(12)	2
Aonghus MARTIN	M		(1)	
John McDONNELL (IRL)	D	17	(1)	
Kevin McKEOWN (SCO)	G	16		
Stuart McLEAN (SCO)	D	32		3
Tony MITCHELL (IRL)	D	27	(1)	1
Andy MYLER (IRL)	A	5	(8)	2
Garry PEEBLES (SCO)	M	17	(4)	2
Mark RUTHERFORD (ENG)	A	17		
Tony SCAPPATICCI	D	18	(4)	
Sammy SHIELS	A	20	(3)	6
John SLOAN	G	1		
Trevor SMITH (SCO)	A	15	(9)	5
Paul STRANEY	G	18	(1)	
Barry TUMILTY	M	10	(8)	2
John WHYTE (IRL)	D	5	(3)	

LEAGUE RESULTS 1998/99

14/08/98	Linfield	H	2-1	Gorman 2
28/08/98	Cliftonville	H	2-1	Smith, McLean
01/09/98	Portadown	A	3-2	Mitchell, Gorman, Myler
05/09/98	Glentoran	H	1-2	Peebles (p)
12/09/98	Coleraine	A	2-2	McLean, Tumilty
15/09/98	Omagh Town	A	3-1	Gorman 3 (2p)
19/09/98	Ballymena United	A	1-1	Myler
26/09/98	Crusaders	H	0-0	
03/10/98	Glenavon	A	2-1	Gorman 2 (1p)
07/10/98	Omagh Town	H	0-2	
17/10/98	Linfield	A	2-2	Kenny, Gorman
24/10/98	Cliftonville	A	4-1	Smith, Kenny 2, Shiels
31/10/98	Portadown	H	3-2	Gorman, Tumilty, Byrne
07/11/98	Coleraine	H	1-1	Gorman
14/11/98	Glentoran	A	3-1	Gorman 2, Kenny
21/11/98	Ballymena United	H	0-0	
28/11/98	Crusaders	A	0-2	
05/12/98	Glenavon	H	1-0	Evans
12/12/98	Portadown	H	1-2	Larkin
19/12/98	Glentoran	A	1-5	Smith
01/01/99	Linfield	H	2-1	Peebles, Shiels
02/01/99	Glenavon	A	1-1	Shiels
09/01/99	Crusaders	A	2-3	Hall, Shiels
16/01/99	Coleraine	II	1-0	Gorman
30/01/99	Ballymena United	A	0-0	
06/02/99	Cliftonville	H	1-0	Gorman
13/02/99	Portadown	A	1-2	Hall
20/02/99	Omagh Town	A	3-2	Shiels, Gorman (p), Larkin
11/03/99	Glentoran	H	1-0	Byrne
16/03/99	Omagh Town	H	1-1	Gorman
20/03/99	Linfield	A	1-2	Smith
23/03/99	Glenavon	H	0-2	
03/04/99	Crusaders	H	3-0	Shiels, Coffey, og (Mellon)
05/04/99	Coleraine	A	0-3	
17/04/99	Ballymena United	H	1-0	McLean
24/04/99	Cliftonville	A	2-0	Byrne, Smith (p)

OMAGH TOWN

CLUB DIRECTORY

Omagh Town FC
St. Julians Road, Mullaghmore, Omagh
tel - (01662) 242927   fax - (01662) 242927
Year of Formation - 1964
Chairman - N. Hunter
Secretary - Pat McGlinchey
Manager - Roy McCreadie
Stadium - St. Julians Road (8,000)

APPEARANCES 98/99

	P	Ap	(s)	Gls
John BARRETT	A	6	(7)	1
Dessie BEATTIE	A	2	(3)	
Emmett BOYLE	A		(1)	
Damien BRADLEY (IRL)	G	23		
Garrett CALLAGHAN (IRL)	A	14	(3)	1
Paul CARLYLE	M	2	(1)	
John CRILLY	M	21		
Patrick CUSACK	D	7	(1)	
Karl DEENEY	A	6	(4)	
Aidan DOHERTY	A	24	(2)	
George DOHERTY	A	3	(4)	
Brian DONAGHEY	M	13	(1)	
Mark DONNELLY	D	30		5
Dylan EARLY	G	13		
Colin ELLIOTT	M		(2)	
Danny GALLAGHER (IRL)	M	3	(4)	
Marty GALLAGHER	M	20		
Tony GRAY	D	2		
Stephen JOHNSTON	D	23		
Sean LIDDY	M		(2)	
Michael MAGILL	D	20	(1)	
Sean McCALLION	A		(3)	
Dermot McCAUL	D	2		
Harry McCOURT	A	9	(2)	4
Barry McCREADIE (ENG)	A	2	(2)	
Roy McCREADIE (ENG)	M		(1)	
John McELROY (IRL)	A	20	(1)	1
Martin McGINLEY (IRL)	M	4	(1)	
John McGLADE	G		(1)	
Raymond McGUINNESS	D	10		
Emmett McINTYRE	A	1	(6)	
Nigel MELLY	D	5	(3)	
Martin MOONEY	M		(2)	
Kevin MOORE	D	23	(3)	
Mark NIXON	M	15	(2)	
Emmett QUIGLEY	M	5	(1)	
Damien REDDEN	M	2	(3)	
Eamon SHERIDAN (IRL)	A	19		4
Kevin SLOAN	M		(5)	1
Damien SWEENEY	A		(4)	
Maurice TOLAND	D	5		1
Darren WALKER	D	11	(2)	
Frank WILSON	M	31		6

LEAGUE RESULTS 1998/99

15/08/98	Glentoran	A	0-2	
28/08/98	Ballymena United	A	0-0	
01/09/98	Crusaders	H	0-0	
05/09/98	Glenavon	A	0-2	
12/09/98	Linfield	H	1-3	Toland
15/09/98	Newry Town	H	1-3	Callaghan
19/09/98	Coleraine	H	2-0	Wilson 2
26/09/98	Cliftonville	A	1-2	Sheridan
03/10/98	Portadown	H	1-0	Donnelly
07/10/98	Newry Town	A	2-0	Donnelly, Sheridan
17/10/98	Glentoran	H	0-2	
24/10/98	Ballymena United	H	1-4	Sheridan
31/10/98	Crusaders	A	0-5	
07/11/98	Linfield	A	0-2	
14/11/98	Glenavon	H	0-3	
21/11/98	Coleraine	A	1-2	Wilson
28/11/98	Cliftonville	H	2-2	Sheridan, Wilson
05/12/98	Portadown	A	0-2	
12/12/98	Glentoran	H	1-4	og (Walker)
19/12/98	Crusaders	A	0-2	
30/12/98	Cliftonville	H	1-1	McCourt
02/01/99	Linfield	A	0-3	
09/01/99	Glenavon	A	1-6	Wilson (p)
29/01/99	Coleraine	A	0-1	
06/02/99	Portadown	H	1-0	McElroy
13/02/99	Glentoran	A	0-2	
20/02/99	Newry Town	H	2-3	Donnelly, Wilson (p)
27/02/99	Crusaders	H	1-2	Barrett
16/03/99	Newry Town	A	1-1	Donnelly
20/03/99	Cliftonville	A	1-2	McCourt
23/03/99	Linfield	H	1-5	McCourt
30/03/99	Ballymena United	H	0-5	
03/04/99	Glenavon	H	0-3	
05/04/99	Ballymena United	A	2-1	McCourt, Sloan
17/04/99	Coleraine	H	1-1	Donnelly
24/04/99	Portadown	A	0-3	

PORTADOWN

Portadown FC
Shamrock Park
Brownstown Road
Portadown
tel - (01762) 332726
fax - (01762) 334907
Year of Formation - 1924
Chairman - Roy McMahon
Secretary - Lewis Singleton
Manager - Ronnie McFall
Stadium - Shamrock Park (15,000)

MAJOR HONOURS
League Championship - (3) 1990, 1991, 1996.
Domestic Cup - (2) 1991, 1999.

APPEARANCES 98/99

		P	Ap	(s)	Gls
Vinny ARKINS (IRL)	A	36		19	
Gary BOWMAN (SCO)	A	8	(1)		
Raymond BYRNE	M	34	(1)	2	
Robert CASEY	M	29			
Neil CANDLISH (SCO)	A	12	(6)	2	
Richard CLARKE	M	31	(1)	3	
Chic CHARNLEY (SCO)	M	7	(6)		
Timothy DALTON (IRL)	G	35			
Gregg DAVIDSON	D	15	(4)		
Paul EVANS	A	2	(1)		
Gareth FULTON	D	30	(2)	1	
Rory GALLAGHER	D	6			
Dwyer HILL	A	3	(8)	1	
Peter HUTTON	M	7			
Stephen JOHNSTON	D	3			
Joe MAGUIRE	M		(1)		
Philip MAJOR	D	27	(1)	3	
Philip McKEOWN	D	19	(2)		
Jeff McNAMARA	D	10	(3)		
Barry MEEHAN	A	1	(3)		
Paul MILLAR	A	21	(6)	7	
Nigel QUIGLEY	M	17	(2)	2	
Steve PITTMAN (USA)	D	3			
Steve SCULLION	G	1			
Brian STRAIN	D	25	(3)	1	
John TOAL (IRL)	M	14	(5)		

LEAGUE RESULTS 1998/99

15/08/98	Cliftonville	A	2-0	Clarke, Arkins
22/08/98	Coleraine	A	0-1	
01/09/98	Newry Town	H	2-3	Arkins, Millar
05/09/98	Ballymena United	A	0-1	
12/09/98	Crusaders	H	0-1	
15/09/98	Glentoran	A	0-1	
19/09/98	Glenavon	A	0-1	
26/09/98	Linfield	H	0-2	
03/10/98	Omagh Town	A	0-1	
07/10/98	Coleraine	H	3-0	Quigley, Candlish, Arkins
17/10/98	Cliftonville	A	0-0	
24/10/98	Glentoran	H	0-3	
31/10/98	Newry Town	A	2-3	Arkins 2
07/11/98	Crusaders	A	1-1	Millar
14/11/98	Ballymena United	H	1-3	Major
21/11/98	Glenavon	H	1-1	Arkins
28/11/98	Linfield	A	2-2	Candlish, Major
05/12/98	Omagh Town	H	2-0	Fulton, Arkins
12/12/98	Newry Town	A	2-1	Millar, Arkins
18/12/98	Linfield	H	1-1	Arkins
30/12/98	Coleraine	H	1-2	Millar
02/01/99	Crusaders	A	0-0	
09/01/99	Ballymena United	A	2-2	Arkins 2 (1p)
16/01/99	Cliftonville	H	0-1	
26/01/99	Glenavon	A	2-2	Arkins (p), Strain
30/01/99	Glentoran	H	1-3	Arkins
06/02/99	Omagh Town	A	0-1	
13/02/99	Newry Town	H	2-1	Major, Hill
27/02/99	Linfield	A	1-3	Quigley
06/03/99	Glenavon	H	2-2	Arkins 2
20/03/99	Coleraine	A	2-0	Byrne 2
23/03/99	Crusaders	H	0-0	
03/04/99	Ballymena United	H	2-1	Millar, Arkins (p)
06/04/99	Cliftonville	H	3-0	Clarke, Millar, Arkins
17/04/99	Glentoran	A	1-3	Clarke
24/04/99	Omagh Town	H	3-0	Arkins 2 (1p), Millar

PROMOTED CLUB

SECOND DIVISION FINAL TABLE 98/99

		Pd	W	D	L	F	A	Pt	GD
1	**Distillery**	**28**	**17**	**4**	**7**	**44**	**30**	**55**	**+14**
2	Ards	28	16	1	11	47	34	49	+13
3	Bangor	28	15	3	10	37	35	48	+2
4	Ballyclare Comrades	28	11	5	12	55	44	38	+11
5	Dungannon Swifts	28	11	5	12	36	46	38	-10
6	Carrick Rangers	28	10	4	14	41	41	34	0
7	Larne	28	9	5	14	28	32	32	-4
8	Limavady United	28	6	7	15	37	63	25	-26

PROMOTION/RELEGATION PLAY-OFF

Ards 0, Cliftonville 1
Cliftonville 4, Ards 2
(Cliftonville 5-2)

CLUB DIRECTORY

Lisburn Distillery
New Grosvenor Stadium
Ballyskeagh
Lambeg
Lisburn
tel - (01232) 301148
Year of Formation - 1879
Chairman - Thomas Allen
Secretary - Fred Robinson
Manager - Paul Kirk
Stadium - New Grosvenor (14,000)

MAJOR HONOURS
League Championship - (6)
1896, 1899, 1901, 1903, 1906, 1963.
Domestic Cup - (12)
1884, 1885, 1886, 1889, 1894, 1896, 1903,
1905, 1910, 1925, 1956, 1971.

NORWAY

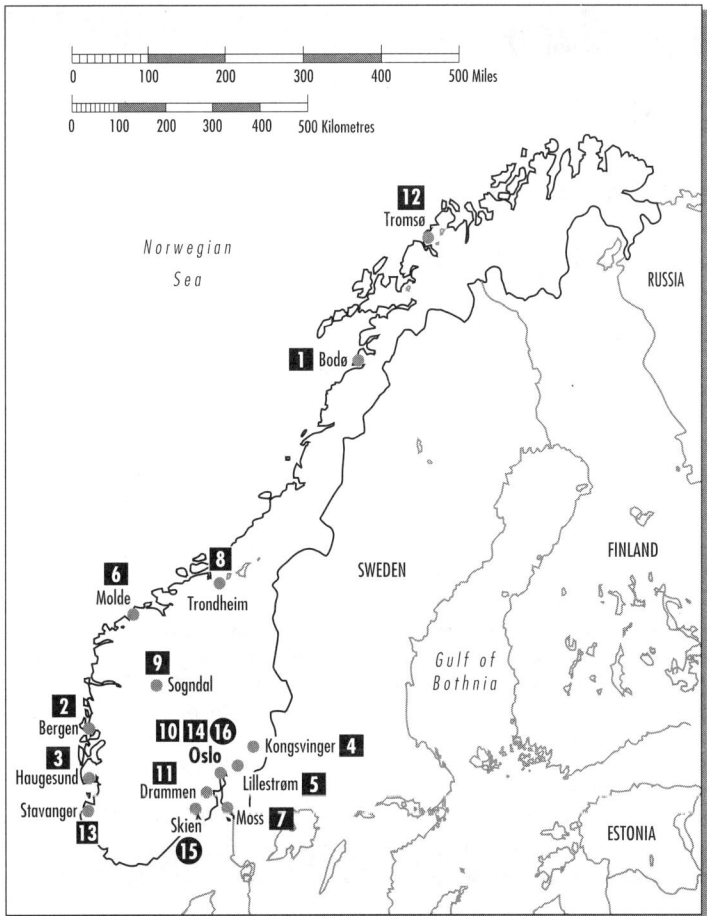

SEVEN UP FOR ROSENBORG

Away-day successes bring Euro début closer

FEDERATION DIRECTORY

Norges Fotballforbund
Boks 3823, Ullevaal Hageby, 0805 Oslo 8

tel - (22) 024500   Year of Formation - 1902
fax - (22) 951010   Chairman - Per Ravn Omdal
                           Secretary - Karen Espelund

Stadium - Ullevaal , Oslo (27,000)

Norway entered a new era in 1998. The retirement of Egil 'Drillo' Olsen as national coach after the World Cup finals in France provoked fears that the team would no longer be as effective or competitive without his unique style of command.

Initially there seemed just cause for concern as the first two home matches in the Euro 2000 qualifying campaign, against Latvia and Albania, yielded a solitary point - and that after a desperate late fightback against the Albanians. But Norway's bid to reach the finals of the European Championship for the first time recovered its momentum in dramatic style in the spring. Four wins out of four, including three away from home, put the Scandinavians firmly back in control of a group which, frankly, they were always clear favourites to win.

The goalscoring prowess of English-based strikers Ole Gunnar Solskjaer (Manchester United), Tore André Flo (Chelsea) and Steffen Iversen (Tottenham) ensured that Nils Johan Semb's first season as national team coach ended

on a high. Leading the group by five points with two home games to come in their remaining three fixtures, it was inconceivable that Norway would fail to clinch their Euro 2000 ticket, although many Norwegian fans were afraid to admit as much, remembering how Egil Olsen's team had thrown away qualification for the previous European Championship after apparently sitting pretty at a similar juncture of the campaign.

To nobody's surprise, Semb continued to employ the same formation and tactics as his illustrious predecessor. There were few modifications in personnel, either, with Olsen stalwarts such as Flo, Solbakken, Rekdal and Mykland continuing to add to their already significant haul of international caps. Only the defence had a fresh look to it, with centre-back Erik Hoftun and full-backs Vegard Heggem and André Bergdølmo all doing enough to hold down a regular place in the team.

Those three players were all members of the Rosenborg side that in 1998 won the Norwegian championship for the seventh successive season, enabling the club from Trondheim to register a winning sequence bettered in the history of European league football by only four clubs - Scottish giants Celtic and Rangers plus Eastern Europeans CSKA Sofia and MTK.

It was the first victory of the seven without coach Nils Arne Eggen, who had opted for a year's sabbatical before returning to duty in the late autumn. The man

		1	2	3	4	5	6	7	8	9	10	11	12	13	14
1	FK Bodø/Glimt		2-2	3-2	0-0	1-1	0-2	2-1	2-6	3-0	1-3	6-2	3-2	3-1	2-1
2	SK Brann	2-1		2-2	3-0	1-2	2-2	0-1	0-0	4-0	2-0	0-1	3-1	1-4	3-0
3	FK Haugesund	5-4	2-3		1-1	0-2	2-3	5-1	0-3	4-0	0-1	1-1	1-1	1-4	3-1
4	Kongsvinger IL	0-0	2-2	0-1		3-0	0-3	2-4	2-8	3-2	1-5	2-1	2-1	1-1	1-3
5	Lillestrøm SK	0-0	1-1	5-0	0-3		1-1	3-4	0-3	0-1	2-3	2-4	2-1	2-3	3-2
6	Molde FK	1-0	2-2	4-1	4-1	4-0		6-0	0-2	4-0	1-1	1-3	2-2	4-4	4-1
7	Moss FK	0-1	3-0	2-0	2-0	1-2	0-2		1-3	1-1	1-0	3-1	3-2	0-1	3-2
8	Rosenborg BK	3-0	4-2	1-0	4-0	6-1	1-2	6-0		4-0	2-2	7-1	1-1	3-1	1-0
9	Sogndal IL	1-2	2-1	0-4	2-5	2-2	1-4	4-3	2-1		0-9	2-2	0-0	1-2	1-3
10	Stabæk IF	3-2	1-1	1-1	2-1	1-1	1-4	4-0	2-0	5-1		4-0	1-0	4-3	2-0
11	Strømsgodset IF	2-2	0-2	4-1	1-0	2-3	1-2	2-0	0-2	2-1	2-1		3-2	1-5	0-5
12	Tromsø IL	4-4	1-0	2-1	3-0	1-0	2-6	0-0	3-4	3-1	0-4	2-2		1-2	2-1
13	Viking FK	1-1	2-3	3-1	4-2	0-1	3-1	5-2	1-2	5-1	1-3	4-1	1-2		3-0
14	Vålerenga IF	2-2	3-2	3-2	2-3	1-5	3-1	1-0	0-2	4-0	2-0	1-1	1-0	2-2	

LEAGUE CHAMPIONSHIP RESULTS 1998

LEAGUE CHAMPIONSHIP FINAL TABLE 1998

			Home					Away					Total						
		P	W	D	L	F	A	W	D	L	F	A	W	D	L	F	A	P	GD
1	Rosenborg BK	26	10	2	1	43	10	10	1	2	36	13	20	3	3	79	23	63	+56
2	Molde FK	26	7	4	2	37	17	9	2	2	33	17	16	6	4	70	34	54	+36
3	Stabæk IF	26	9	3	1	31	14	7	2	4	32	15	16	5	5	63	29	53	+34
4	Viking FK	26	7	1	5	33	20	7	3	3	33	24	14	4	8	66	44	46	+22
5	FK Bodø/Glimt	26	7	3	3	28	23	2	6	5	19	24	9	9	8	47	47	36	0
6	SK Brann	26	6	3	4	23	14	3	5	5	21	25	9	8	9	44	39	35	+5
7	Vålerenga IF	26	7	3	3	25	20	3	0	10	19	28	10	3	13	44	48	33	-4
8	Lillestrøm SK	26	3	3	7	21	26	6	3	4	20	23	9	6	11	41	49	33	-8
9	Moss FK	26	7	1	5	20	15	3	1	9	16	40	10	2	14	36	55	32	-19
10	Strømsgodset IF	26	6	1	6	20	26	3	4	6	20	35	9	5	12	40	61	32	-21
11	Tromsø IL	26	6	3	4	24	25	1	4	8	15	23	7	7	12	39	48	28	-9
12	Kongsvinger IL	26	4	3	6	19	31	3	2	8	16	28	7	5	14	35	59	26	-24
13	FK Haugesund	26	4	3	6	25	25	2	2	9	16	30	6	5	15	41	55	23	-14
14	Sogndal IL	26	3	3	7	18	38	1	1	11	8	42	4	4	18	26	80	16	-54

who filled in for him, Trond Sollied, achieved what he set out to, winning the title and taking Rosenborg into the Champions' League for the fourth successive year, but nobody in Trondheim was too upset when he left at the end of the season (for Belgian club Gent), paving the way for the old maestro to return.

Rosenborg's final victory margin was a clear-cut nine points, but for most of the season they had been challenged strongly by Molde FK. Led by new coach Erik Brakstad, Molde were an efficient and attractive amalgam of promising youngsters (Daniel Berg Hestad, Andreas Lund, Trond Andersen) and experienced veterans (Pål Lydersen, Odd Inge Olsen, Morten Bakke). Had they been able to sustain their impressive form through to the end of the campaign, they would surely have picked up their first Tippeligaen title. After 21 games they led Rosenborg by a point, but then the bubble burst. Unbeaten up until then, they proceeded to lose four of their last five matches, including the big one, at home to Rosenborg.

NATIONAL TEAM RESULTS 98/99

19/08/98	Romania	H	Oslo	0-0	
06/09/98	Latvia (ECQ)	H	Oslo	1-3	Solbakken (17)
10/10/98	Slovenia (ECQ)	A	Ljubljana	2-1	Flo T.A. (45), Rekdal (80)
14/10/98	Albania (ECQ)	H	Oslo	2-2	Rekdal (82p), Berg (88)
18/11/98	Egypt	A	Cairo	1-1	Flo T.A. (64)
20/01/99	Israel	A	Tel-Aviv	1-0	Skammelsrud (12p)
22/01/99	Estonia	N	Umm el-Fahm	3-3	Solbakken (22), Strand (56), Carew (72)
10/02/99	Italy	A	Pisa	0-0	
27/03/99	Greece (ECQ)	A	Athens	2-0	Solskjær (38, 87)
28/04/99	Georgia (ECQ)	A	Tbilisi	4-1	Shekiladze (16og), Flo T.A. (26, 38), Solskjær (35)
20/05/99	Jamaica	H	Oslo	6-0	Flo T.A. (5, 53), Iversen (71), Leonhardsen (75), Dahlum (82), Lund (90)
30/05/99	Georgia (ECQ)	H	Oslo	1-0	Iversen (4)
05/06/99	Albania (ECQ)	A	Tirana	2-1	Iversen (3), Flo T.A. (83)

TOP SCORERS

27 Sigurd RUSHFELDT (Rosenborg BK)
20 Rune LANGE (Tromsø IL)
19 Jostein FLO (Strømsgodset IF)
    Petter BELSVIK (Stabæk IF)
16 Andreas LUND (Molde FK)
    Rijhardur DADASON (Viking FK)
14 John Ivar JAKOBSEN (Rosenborg BK)
12 Kjetil LØVVIK (SK Brann)
    Roar STRAND (Rosenborg BK)
    Raymond KVISVIK (Moss FK/SK Brann)

NATIONAL TEAM APPEARANCES 98/99

Coach - Nils Johan SEMB	ROM	LAT	SLO	ALB	EGY	ISR	EST	ITA	GRE	GEO	JAM	GEO	ALB	Cps	Gls
Frode GRODÅS (24/10/64) - FC Schalke 04 (GER)	G		G	G	G46		G							48	-
Vegard HEGGEM (13/07/75) - Liverpool (ENG)	D	D61	M86		M	s46		D	D		D	D		10	1
Ronny JOHNSEN (10/06/69) - Manchester United (ENG)	D	D						D	D					41	2
Erik HOFTUN (03/03/69) - Rosenborg BK	D	D	D	D	D	D	D			D	D	D	D	15	-
Stig Inge BJØRNEBYE (11/12/69) - Liverpool (ENG)	D	D	D	D										70	1
Håvard FLO (04/04/70) -															
SV Werder Bremen (GER)/Wolverhampton Wanderers (ENG)	M46	s80						M75						16	3
Roar STRAND (02/02/70) - Rosenborg BK	M58		M78	M	M88	M24	M58	s67	M60	s46				16	3
Kjetil REKDAL (06/11/68) - Hertha BSC Berlin (GER)	M83	M	M	M	M			M		M68	s71	M		79	17
Ståle SOLBAKKEN (27/02/68) - AaB (DEN)	M	M	M	M90	M84		M	M67	M	M		M	M90	48	8
Ole Gunnar SOLSKJAER (26/02/73) - Manchester United (ENG)	M68	M63		s57				A90	A89	M46				22	11
Tore André FLO (15/06/73) - Chelsea (ENG)	A	A	A90	A	A90					A87	A77	A	A	38	20
Jostein FLO (03/10/64) - Strømsgodset IF	s46	s63	M	M57		s90	s46							21	11
Petter RUDI (17/09/73) - Sheffield Wednesday (ENG)	s58	M80			s90			M	M	M81	M46	s46	M79	26	3
Harald BRATTBAKK (01/02/71) - Celtic (SCO)	s68													9	3
Øyvind LEONHARDSEN (17/08/70) - Liverpool (ENG)	s83									M	M46			61	14
Espen BAARDSEN (07/12/77) - Tottenham Hotspur (ENG)		G			G46									2	-
Frank STRANDLI (16/05/72) - Panathinaikos (GRE)/AaB (DEN)		M			M90	M46								24	3
Henning BERG (01/09/69) - Manchester United (ENG)		s61	D	D	D			D						61	6
Alf Inge HÅLAND (23/11/72) - Leeds United (ENG)			D	D57	D46			D					D	33	-
Daniel BERG HESTAD (30/07/75) - Molde FK			s78		M46	s24	s56							5	-
Vidar RISETH (21/04/72) - Celtic (SCO)			s86		s88		s75		s81	M	M71	s90		17	2
Sigurd RUSHFELDT (11/12/72) - Rosenborg BK			s90	s90										9	-
Steffen IVERSEN (10/11/76) - Tottenham Hotspur (ENG)			s57	A				M		M	M79	M85	M	7	3
André BERGDØLMO (13/10/71) - Rosenborg BK					D	D	D77	D	D66	D	D79	D	D	12	-
Thomas MYHRE (16/10/73) - Everton (ENG)					s46			G	G	G	G83			6	-
John CAREW (05/09/79) - Vålerenga IF					s46	A	A	s90	s89	s87				6	1
Tommy SVINDAL LARSEN (11/08/73) - Stabaek IF					s84	M	M							5	-
Christer BASMA (01/08/72) - Rosenborg BK						D	s46							3	-
Bjørn Otto BRAGSTAD (05/01/71) - Rosenborg BK					D46	D	D			D			s63	5	-
Egil ØSTENSTAD (02/01/72) - Southampton (ENG)					M80	M56								17	6
Bent SKAMMELSRUD (18/05/66) - Rosenborg BK					M	s58								26	5
Frode OLSEN (12/10/67) - Stabaek IF					s46					s83	G	G		6	-
Claus LUNDEKVAM (22/02/73) - Southampton (ENG)					s46	D46								7	-
Eirik BAKKE (13/09/77) - Sogndal IL					s80					s68				2	-
Hai Ngoc TRAN (10/01/75) - Vålerenga IF					s77									1	-
Erik MYKLAND (21/07/71) - Panathinaikos (GRE)								M	M	M		M	M	62	2
Lars BOHINEN (08/09/69) - Derby County (ENG)								s60						49	10
Gunnar HALLE (11/08/65) - Leeds United (ENG)								s66		s79				63	5
Tore PEDERSEN (29/09/69) - Eintracht Frankfurt (GER)										D		D	D63	45	-
Tore André DAHLUM (21/06/68) - Rosenborg BK										s46	s85	s79		15	6
Andreas LUND (07/05/75) - Molde FK											s77			1	1
Trond ANDERSEN (06/01/75) - Molde FK											s79			1	-

DOMESTIC CUP 1998

THIRD ROUND
Fana IL 2, Molde FK 4
Harstad IL 1, FK Bodø/Glimt 4
Sarpsborg FK 0, Rosenborg BK 5
IK Start 1, Strømsgodset IF 3
Stryn TIL 0, SK Brann 1
Vålerenga IF 1, Skeid 3
Hamarkameratene 4, Sogndal IL (aet)
Kjelsås IL 0, FK Haugesund 2
Kongsvinger IL 2, Raufoss IL 1
Moss FK 2, Eik Tønsberg 0
Stabaek IF 1, Aalesund FK 0
Tromsdalen UIL 0, Tromsø IL 10
Strindheim IL 3, Lillestrøm SK 3 (aet; 4-3 on pens.)
Vidar FK 0, Viking FK 1
Byåsen IL 2, SFK Lyn 1
Odd Grenland 2, Bryne FK 1

FOURTH ROUND
Hamarkameratene 0, Moss FK 1 (aet)
Skeid 4, FK Haugesund 1 (aet)
FK Bodø/Glimt 1, Strindheim IL 0
Bryne FK 4, Tromsø IL 2
SK Brann 3, Byåsen IL 1
Kongsvinger IL 1, Stabaek IF 3 (aet)
Strømsgodset IF 1, Rosenborg BK 4
Molde FK 2, Viking FK 1

QUARTER-FINALS
Moss FK 2 (Enerly 2, Løvlien 3),
FK Bodø/Glimt 1 (Berg A. 76)
Rosenborg BK 5 (Strand 7, Jakobsen 21, Dahlum 75, 76, Johnsen B.I. 86), Bryne FK 0
Stabaek IF 3 (Belsvik 24, Olsen I.A. 43, Kolle 76), Skeid 1 (Halvorsen 84)
SK Brann 4 (Helstad 6, 75, Ludvigsen 70, Løvvik 87), Molde FK 0

SEMI-FINALS
SK Brann 2 (Løvvik 44p, Bergdølmo 74og),
Rosenborg BK 3 (Rushfeldt 37, 59, Skammelsrud 84)
Moss FK 0, Stabaek 0 (aet; 3-1 on pens.)

FINAL
01/11/98, Oslo
STABAEK IF 3 Sigurdsson (6, 106), Finstad (100)
ROSENBORG BK 1 Rushfeldt (65p)
(aet)
referee - Pedersen
STABAEK IF - Olsen F.; Olsen I.A. (Svensson 116), Skistad, Flem, Holter; Andresen, Jansson, Svindal Larsen (Hauger 119), Stenersen (Finstad 90); Belsvik, Sigurdsson.
ROSENBORG BK - Jamtfall; Basma, Bragstad, Hoftun, Bergdølmo; Strand (Winsnes 82), Skammelsrud, Berg; Hernes (Dahlum 60), Rushfeldt, Jakobsen (Sørensen 102).

A sell-out crowd of 13,308 in Molde's brand-new stadium came to witness the match billed as the 'championship final', but only the visiting fans went away happy thanks to two second-half goals which all but assured the outcome of the title in Rosenborg's favour.

Rosenborg captain Bent Skammelsrud duly made history by becoming the first player to scoop seven Norwegian championship-winning medals. The Player of the Year title went for the second year running to defender Erik Hoftun, who showed wonderful consistency all season long. Another player who matched his achievement of the previous year was striker Sigurd Rushfeldt, whose 27 league goals gave him the Tippeligaen Golden Boot for the second successive season. Veteran 'Mini' Jakobsen also excelled, while the fine form of Roar Strand, André Bergdølmo and Bjørn Otto Bragstad was reflected by their regular call-ups to the Norwegian national team.

Rosenborg did not have everything their own way, though. Stabaek IF caused the upset of the season when they defeated the champions 3-1 after extra-time in the Cup final. They had already beaten them 2-0 in the league, but with Rosenborg scenting a 'double', the odds on Stabaek adding to their best-ever league placing (third) by capturing a first major trophy were very long indeed. Yet their victory in the Ullevaal brooked no argument, with goalkeeper Frode Olsen playing the match of his life to keep the RBK forwards at bay and Icelandic international Helgi Sigurdsson rivalling him for the man of the match award with two goals. The

joy of victory was especially intense for Stabaek's veteran striker Petter Belsvik, whose long career with a number of Tippeligaen clubs had until that moment yielded many goals but no trophies.

1997 runners-up SK Brann were widely expected to challenge Rosenborg and Molde for the title in 1998 but they began the season disastrously, failing to win any of their first 11 matches. At once the club's objective turned from challenging at the top to avoiding relegation. To that end they signed four new players in mid-season and replaced coach Kjell Tennfjord with Harald Aabrekk. The result was a massive improvement, and with eight wins in their last dozen games, the boys from Bergen not only survived the drop but clambered their way up to sixth place.

Another remarkable end-of-season ascension was that of Vålerenga IF. After 17 matches the newly-promoted Oslo outfit looked doomed. But in stepped the messiah himself, Egil Olsen, and almost overnight the team's fortunes were transformed. Although the ex-national team boss was not officially appointed as coach, he was given responsibility for team affairs, and the effect of his introduction was remarkable. Playing in Olsen's favoured 4-5-1 formation, Vålerenga reeled off seven wins in their last nine games to shoot up the table into seventh place.

Even more impressive was the club's performance in Europe, where they eliminated Rapid Bucharest on away goals before producing an astonishing second-leg comeback in Istanbul to knock out Besiktas and become only the fourth Norwegian team to reach a European quarter-final. There were no further exploits the following spring as Cup-winners' Cup holders Chelsea put them in their place, but even in defeat Vålerenga left a positive impression, especially giant teenaged striker John Carew, who maintained his record of scoring in every round and confirmed his reputation as one of Norway's most exciting young talents.

VIF's passage into the last eight of the Cup-winners' Cup eclipsed another worthy Champions' League campaign by Rosenborg, who maintained their impressive home record in the competition, beating Bruges, Galatasaray and Athletic Bilbao in the Lerkendal as well as holding the mighty Juventus to a 1-1 draw. Sadly, however, their away form let them down, and a 0-2 defeat in Turin in their final game spelt elimination - despite the fact that they finished up with the same number of points as their Italian conquerors. How they were left to rue the

penalty missed by skipper Skammelsrud in the home game with Juve...

The good news for Rosenborg, however, was that their consistently good form in Europe over recent seasons meant that they were seeded automatically for the first group phase of the new-look 1999/2000 Champions' League - a privilege they shared with such illustrious names as Barcelona, Milan, Real Madrid and Manchester United.

Rosenborg, and Norwegian football in general, can be justly proud of the huge strides they have made in the last decade of the 20th century.

INTERNATIONAL HONOURS

World Cup Finals appearances: 1938, 1994, 1998 (2nd round)

PLAYERS OF THE SEASON

ERIK HOFTUN

It has become something of a ritual for fans of Rosenborg to bid farewell to their favourite players at the end of each domestic season. But one man who looks like staying around, perhaps for good, is 30-year-old defender Erik Hoftun. Despite being voted Tippeligaen Player of the Year in both 1997 and 1998, he rejected the approaches of overseas clubs in favour of a new five-year contract with the team from Trondheim. The reward for that loyalty was his appointment as club captain at the start of the 1999 campaign. A Rosenborg player since 1994 - he joined from Molde FK - Hoftun is a constructive centre-back whose strength in the air is matched by a fine sense of timing and anticipation. A lack of pace is his weakness, but that has not put off new Norway coach Nils Johan Semb, who has made him a fixture in the national team.

JOHN CAREW

Long, lanky and laden with talent, "Little" John Carew was the most exciting newcomer in Norway's Tippeligaen in 1998. Born of a Gambian father and Norwegian mother - hence his rather un-Scandinavian appearance - the big striker became a firm favourite of the 'Klan' (the Vålerenga IF fan club) in the club's Cup-winning/ promotion season of 1997 and fared even better in 1998 despite contracting an infection that laid him low for several weeks in the early part of the season. A Norwegian

international at every rung of the youth ladder, he won his first senior cap in November 1998 against Egypt, having bagged a hat-trick for the Under-21 side against Slovenia a month earlier. Fast, powerful and direct, the 20-year-old has a big future. A move abroad is inevitable, but for now he has decided to stay in Norway, leaving Vålerenga for Rosenborg midway through the 1999 season.

SIGURD RUSHFELDT

Sigurd Rushfeldt, now of Spanish club Racing Santander, became the most expensive player ever signed by a Norwegian club when he joined Rosenborg from Tromsø in early 1997. But with 52 goals in 51 Tippaligaen matches in his first two seasons in Trondheim he has more than justified the fee. Two Golden Boots and two championship medals now sit proudly alongside the Norwegian Cup winner's medal he earned in his final season with Tromsø. An eager front-runner, he is very sharp in the box and a cool finisher. He added to his impressive domestic goals tally by scoring six in Rosenborg's 1998/99 Champions' League campaign, the highlight being a 21-minute hat-trick against Galatasaray. Despite his evident goalscoring skills he remains an outcast from the Norwegian national team, with the likes of Flo, Solskjaer, Iversen and Carew all heading him in the queue to occupy the single striking berth in Norway's tried and trusted 4-5-1 formation.

EUROPEAN CUPS 98/99

CHAMPIONS' CUP
● ROSENBORG BK
Qualifying round CLUB BRUGGE KV (BEL)
H 2-0   Rushfeldt (61), Skammelsrud (81)
Jamtfall; Basma, Bragstad, Hoftun, Bergdølmo; Strand,
Skammelsrud, Berg; Hernes (Mayer 82), Rushfeldt, Sørensen
(Dahlum 68).
A 2-4   Rushfeldt (43, 71)
Jamtfall; Basma, Bragstad, Hoftun, Bergdølmo; Strand (Winsnes 90),
Skammelsrud, Berg (Mayer 82); Hernes, Rushfeldt, Jakobsen
(Sørensen 89).

Champions' League
1st match ATHLETIC BILBAO (ESP)
A 1-1   Strand (66)
Jamtfall; Basma, Bragstad, Hoftun, Bergdølmo; Strand,
Skammelsrud, Berg; Hernes (Sørensen 81), Rushfeldt, Jakobsen
(Dahlum 90).

2nd round JUVENTUS (ITA)
H 1-1   Skammelsrud (69p)
Jamtfall; Basma, Bragstad, Hoftun, Bergdølmo; Strand (Winsnes 85),
Skammelsrud, Berg; Sørensen (Hernes 56), Rushfeldt (Dahlum 61),
Jakobsen.

3rd match GALATASARAY (TUR)
H 3-0   Rushfeldt (69, 86, 90)
Arason; Basma, Bragstad, Hoftun, Bergdølmo; Strand,
Skammelsrud, Winsnes (Mayer 77); Sørensen (Dahlum 77), Rushfeldt,
Jakobsen (Hernes 56).

4th match GALATASARAY (TUR)
A 0-3
Arason; Basma, Johnsen B.I., Hoftun, Bergdølmo; Strand, Skammelsrud,
Berg; Dahlum (Hernes 67), Rushfeldt, Jakobsen (Sørensen 62).

5th match ATHLETIC BILBAO (ESP)
H 2-1   Sørensen (2, 50)
Jamtfall; Bergdølmo, Bragstad, Hottun, Pedersen; Strand (Winsnes 79),
Skammelsrud, Berg (Mayer 90); Sørensen (Dahlum 84), Rushfeldt,
Jakobsen.

6th match JUVENTUS (ITA)
A 0-2
Jamtfall; Bergdølmo, Bragstad, Hoftun, Pedersen (Hernes 66); Strand,
Johnsen B.I. (Winsnes 56), Berg, Jakobsen; Sørensen (Dahlum 46),
Rushfeldt.

CUP WINNERS' CUP
● VÅLERENGA IF
1st round RAPID BUCURESTI (ROM)
A 2-2   Carew (52, 88)
Krogstad; Walltin, Haraldsen, Kjølner, Tran; Kaasa (Kuvicek 46),
Viljugrein (Musaeus 68), Levernes, Hovi (Thorsen 85), Haug; Carew.
H 0-0
Krogstad; Walltin, Haraldsen, Kjølner, Tran; Ødegaard (Kaasa 87),
Viljugrein, Levernes, Haug (Thorsen 78), Hovi; Carew.

2nd round BESIKTAS (TUR)
H 1-0   Levernes (49)
Krogstad; Walltin, Haraldsen, Kjølner, Tran; Kaasa (Haug 59),
Viljugrein (Kuvicek 5), Levernes, Hovi, Riisnaes (Ødegaard 88); Carew.

A 3-3   Haraldsen (64), Kaasa (67), Carew (73)
Krogstad; Walltin, Haraldsen, Kjølner, Tran; Haug (Kuvicek 86), Viljugrein,
Levernes (Thorsen 89), Hovi, Riisnaes (Kaasa 46); Carew.

Quarter-final CHELSEA (ENG)
A 0-3
Kaven; Berntsen, Haraldsen, Kjølner, Tran; Haug (Kaasa 58), Walltin,
Levernes (Simpson 85), Hovi, Riisnaes; Carew.
H 2-3   Kjølner (27), Carew (41)
Kaven; Berntsen, Haraldsen, Kjølner, Tran; Walltin, Hovi (Haug 76),
Levernes, Riisnaes; Carew (Musaeus 85), Simpson (Thorsen 70).

UEFA CUP
● MOLDE FK
Qualifying round CSKA SOFIA (BUL)
H 0-0
Bakke; Dos Santos (Schiller 75), Andersen, Lydersen, Fostervold; Olsen,
Fjørtoft, Berg Hestad; Tessem, Lund (Televik 83), Hasselgård (Mork 79).
A 0-2
Bakke; Dos Santos, Andersen, Lydersen, Fostervold; Tessem (Mork 88),
Hasselgård (Singsaas 65), Fjørtoft, Berg Hestad, Lund (Televik 79); Olsen.

● SK BRANN
Qualifying round ZALGIRIS VILNIUS (LIT)
H 1-0   Kvisvik (75p)
Bahus; Brendsaether, Helland, Moen, Gylfason (Wassberg 46); Guntveit,
Paldan, Samuelsson; Kvisvik, Mjelde (Løvvik 43), Helstad (Ludvigsen 61).
A 0-0
Westad; Brendsaether, Helland, Moen, Wassberg; Guntveit,
Samuelsson, Paldan, Kvisvik (Hasund 90); Løvvik (Ludvigsen 55),
Helstad (Gunnlaugsson 65).

1st round SV WERDER BREMEN (GER)
H 2-0   Moen (29), Løvvik (56)
Westad; Brendsaether, Helland, Moen, Wassberg; Guntveit, Paldan,
Samuelsson, Kvisvik; Helstad (Gylfason 90), Løvvik (Ludvigsen 78).
A 0-4
(aet)
Bahus; Brendsaether, Helland (Gylfason 105), Moen, Wassberg;
Guntveit, Paldan, Samuelsson, Kvisvik; Løvvik (Gunnlaugsson 77), Helstad
(Ludvigsen 39).

● STRØMSGODSET IF
Qualifying round HAPOEL TEL-AVIV (ISR)
A 0-1
Hansen; Johnsen, Karlsen, Waehler; Lindqvist, Horsrud, Skistad, Kihle
(Ødegaard H.E. 74); Nyan, Michelsen (Olsen 60), Hagen R..
H 1-0   Michelsen (42)
(aet; 4-2 on pens.)
Hansen; Horsrud (Flo 63), Johnsen, Karlsen, Waehler, Granås
(Sannerholt 85); Nyan (Lindqvist 29), Kihle; Olsen, Michelsen, Hagen R..

1st round ASTON VILLA (ENG)
A 2-3   Michelsen (22), George (23)
Hansen; Granås, Waehler, Karlsen, Skistad; Nyan, Hagen R., Kihle,
Solberg, Ødegaard H.E. (George 10; Strøm 70); Michelsen (Olsen 87).
H 0-3
Hansen; Granås, Waehler, Johnsen, Skistad; George (Olsen 66), Nyan,
Solberg (Strøm 85), Hagen E. (Ødegaard H.E. 66), Hagen R.; Flo.

FK BODØ/GLIMT

CLUB DIRECTORY

Fotballklubben Bodø/Glimt
Boks 179
8001 Bodø
tel - (75) 545500
fax - (75) 545510
Year of Formation - 1916
Chairman - Harald Hansen
Coach - Øystein Gåre (99 - Dag Opjordsmoen)
Stadium - Aspmyra (13,000)

MAJOR HONOURS
Domestic Cup - (2) 1975, 1993.

APPEARANCES 1998

	P	Ap	(s)	Gls
Helge AUNE	D	13	(1)	2
Arild BERG	M	23	(1)	10
Christian BERG	M	10	(10)	
Ørjan BERG	M	7		
Tommy BERGERSEN	A	15	(7)	8
Aasmund BJØRKAN	A	26		9
Thomas BREIVIK	A		(2)	
Sturla EILERTSEN	A		(1)	
Terje ELLINGSEN	A	3	(4)	1
Andreas EVJEN	D	9	(1)	
Clas-André GUTTULSRØD	G	25		
Ola HALDORSEN	D	23	(1)	
Vebjørn HAGEN	D	6	(4)	
Cato HANSEN	D	15	(7)	
Trond Vidar HANSEN	A	12	(12)	2
Tor Egil HORN	G	1		
Bent Inge JOHNSEN	D	8		2
Thor MIKALSEN	M	25		
Jim PEDERSEN	M	1	(3)	
Lee ROBERTSON (SCO)	M	18		1
Odd Karl STANGNES	D	1		
Tom Kåre STAURVIK	M	2	(5)	2
Christian STEEN	D	17		
Bengt SAETERNES	A	26		9

LEAGUE RESULTS 1998

Date	Opponent		Score	
13/04/98	Stabaek IF	A	2-3	Bjørkan, Johnsen (p)
19/04/98	Sogndal IL	H	3-0	Saeternes 2, Bjørkan
26/04/98	Moss FK	H	2-1	Bjørkan, Berg A.
30/04/98	Kongsvinger IL	A	0-0	
03/05/98	Molde FK	H	0-2	
07/05/98	Vålerenga IF	A	2-2	Bjørkan, Johnsen
10/05/98	Rosenborg BK	H	2-6	Saeternes, Bjørkan (p)
16/05/98	Tromsø IL	A	4-4	Saeternes 2, Bjørkan, Ellingsen
01/07/98	Viking FK	A	1-1	og (Espevoll)
05/07/98	FK Haugesund	H	3-2	Berg A., Bergersen, Bjørkan
09/07/98	Lillestrøm SK	A	0-0	
12/07/98	SK Brann	H	2-2	Bergersen 2 (1p)
19/07/98	Stabaek IF	H	1-3	Berg A.
26/07/98	Sogndal IL	A	2-1	Berg A., Hansen T.V.
30/07/98	Strømsgodset IF	H	6-2	Berg A., Aune, Saeternes 3, Hansen T.V.
02/08/98	Moss FK	A	1-0	Berg A.
09/08/98	Kongsvinger IL	H	0-0	
16/08/98	Molde FK	A	0-1	
23/08/98	Vålerenga IF	H	2-1	Berg A., Bergersen (p)
30/08/98	Rosenborg BK	A	0-3	
13/09/98	Tromsø IL	H	3-2	Bergersen, Robertson, Staurvik
20/09/98	Strømsgodset IF	A	2-2	Bergersen, Staurvik
27/09/98	Viking FK	H	3-1	Bergersen (p), Berg A., Aune
04/10/98	FK Haugesund	A	4-5	Berg A. 2, Bergersen, Saeternes
17/10/98	Lillestrøm SK	H	1-1	Bjørkan
25/10/98	SK Brann	A	1-2	Bjørkan

SK BRANN

CLUB DIRECTORY

Sportsklubben Brann
Postboks 161
5032 Minde
tel - (55) 598500
fax - (55) 598525
Year of Formation - 1908
Chairman - Harald Schelderup
Manager - Kjell Tennfjord
Coach - Kjell Tennfjord; Harald Aabrekk
Stadium - Brann (19,000)

MAJOR HONOURS
League Championship - (2) 1962, 1963
Domestic Cup - (5)
1923, 1925, 1972, 1976, 1982.

APPEARANCES 1998

	P	Ap	(s)	Gls
Vidar BAHUS	G	9		
Lars BAKKERUD	M	11		
Geirmund BRENDESAETHER	D	16	(1)	1
Bjarki GUNNLAUGSSON (ISL)	A	2	(5)	1
Cato GUNTVEIT	M	21	(3)	3
Ágúst GYLFASON (ISL)	D	10	(6)	
Erlend HANSTVEIT	M	2	(2)	
Geir HASUND	M	2	(9)	1
Roger HELLAND	D	23		
Thorstein HELSTAD	A	19	(4)	6
Raymond KVISVIK	M	17		9
Per Ove LUDVIGSEN	D	6	(9)	2
Kjetil LØVVIK	A	18	(6)	12
Mons Ivar MJELDE	A	12	(4)	4
Arne Vidar MOEN	D	25		1
Gunnar NOREBØ	M		(1)	
Stefan PALDAN (SWE)	D	24		
Jan Ove PEDERSEN	M	11	(4)	
Morten PETTERSEN	M	1	(5)	
Svante SAMUELSSON (SWE)	M	16		2
Stefán THÓRDARSON (ISL)	A		(2)	
Egil ULFSTEIN	D	8	(3)	1
Alex VALENCIA	M		(3)	
Roy WASSBERG	D	16		
Rohnny WESTAD	G	17	(1)	

LEAGUE RESULTS 1998

13/04/98	Moss FK	H	0-1	
19/04/98	Kongsvinger IL	A	2-2	Løvvik, Mjelde (p)
26/04/98	Molde FK	H	2-2	Mjelde, Løvvik
30/04/98	Vålerenga IF	A	2-3	Mjelde, Helstad
04/05/98	Rosenborg BK	H	0-0	
07/05/98	Tromsø IL	A	0-1	
10/05/98	Strømsgodset IF	H	0-1	
16/05/98	Viking FK	H	1-4	Hasund
07/06/98	FK Haugesund	H	2-2	Ulfstein, Løvvik
01/07/98	Lillestrøm SK	A	1-1	Kvisvik
05/07/98	Sogndal IL	A	1-2	Kvisvik
09/07/98	Stabaek IF	H	2-0	og (Belsvik), Brendesaether
12/07/98	FK Bodø/Glimt	A	2-2	Kvisvik 2
19/07/98	Moss FK	A	0-3	
26/07/98	Kongsvinger IL	H	3-0	Guntveit, Helstad 2
01/08/98	Molde FK	A	2-2	Mjelde, Kvisvik (p)
08/08/98	Vålerenga IF	H	3-0	Helstad, Løvvik 2
15/08/98	Rosenborg BK	A	2-4	Løvvik, Gunnlaugsson
22/08/98	Tromsø IL	H	3-1	Helstad, Løvvik (p), Ludvigsen
30/08/98	Strømsgodset IF	A	2-0	Kvisvik, Samuelsson
12/09/98	Viking FK	A	3-2	Løvvik 3 (1p)
20/09/98	FK Haugesund	A	3-2	Guntveit, Løvvik, Kvisvik
26/09/98	Lillestrøm SK	H	1-2	Løvvik
04/10/98	Sogndal IL	H	4-0	Kvisvik (p), Ludvigsen, Samuelsson, Guntveit
18/10/98	Stabaek IF	A	1-1	Helstad
25/10/98	FK Bodø/Glimt	H	2-1	Moen, Kvisvik

FK HAUGESUND

CLUB DIRECTORY

Fotballklubben Haugesund
Postboks 406
5501 Haugesund
tel - (52) 714238
fax - (52) 717645
Year of Formation - 1993
Chairman - Pål Schiefloe
Coach - Conny Karlsson (99 - Åge Steen)
Stadium - Haugesund (12,000)

APPEARANCES 1998

		P	Ap	(s)	Gls
Vegard BERG JOHANSEN	A			(1)	
Morten BERRE	A		25		9
Trond BJØRNDAL	D		16		1
Bala Ahmed GARBA (NIG)	A		11	(10)	7
Jostein GRINDHAUG	M		6	(3)	
Per Andreas HAFTORSEN	G		26		
Jørgen HAMMERSLAND	D		9		
Sjur Jarle HAUGE	M		3	(3)	2
Asbjørn HELGELAND	M		23	(1)	7
Kjell Sture JENSEN	A			(10)	
Magnus JOHANSSON (SWE)	M		6	(5)	
Stig KALLESTAD	D		1	(1)	
Tor Åge LARSEN	D		26		1
Rune LOTHE	M		18	(1)	5
Håvard LUNDE	D		1	(3)	
Øyvind MELLEMSTRAND	D		25		
Tarje NORDSTRAND JACOBSEN	M		21	(3)	
Trygve NYGAARD	M		23		3
Thormod NESS	D		25		1
Eirik SKJAELAAEN	M			(3)	
Stian THOMASSEN	D		13	(2)	
Jarle WEE	A		8	(10)	3

LEAGUE RESULTS 1998

13/04/98	Molde FK	H	2-3	Helgeland, Garba
19/04/98	Vålerenga IF	A	2-3	Helgeland, Wee
26/04/98	Rosenborg BK	H	0-3	
30/04/98	Tromsø IL	A	1-2	Garba
03/05/98	Strømsgodset IF	H	1-1	Helgeland
07/05/98	Viking FK	A	1-3	Ness
10/05/98	Sogndal IL	A	4-0	Helgeland, Berre, Wee, Garba
16/05/98	Lillestrøm SK	H	0-2	
07/06/98	SK Brann	A	2-2	Lothe, Berre
01/07/98	Stabaek IF	H	0-1	
05/07/98	FK Bodø/Glimt	A	2-3	Nygaard, Helgeland
09/07/98	Moss FK	H	5-1	Berre 3, og (Sylte), Hauge
19/07/98	Molde FK	A	1-4	Berre
26/07/98	Vålerenga IF	H	3-1	Lothe 2, Berre
02/08/98	Rosenborg BK	A	0-1	
09/08/98	Tromsø IL	H	1-1	Helgeland
12/08/98	Kongsvinger IL	A	1-0	Nygaard
16/08/98	Strømsgodset IF	A	1-4	Garba
22/08/98	Viking FK	H	1-4	Berre
30/08/98	Sogndal IL	H	4-0	Lothe, Bjørndal, Larsen, Helgeland
13/09/98	Lillestrøm SK	A	0-5	
20/09/98	SK Brann	H	2-3	Garba, Berre
27/09/98	Stabaek IF	A	1-1	Lothe
04/10/98	FK Bodø/Glimt	H	5-4	og (Steen), Wee, Garba 2, Hauge
18/10/98	Moss FK	A	0-2	
25/10/98	Kongsvinger IL	H	1-1	Nygaard

KONGSVINGER IL

Kongsvinger Idrettslag Toppfotball
Postboks 629
2201 Kongsvinger
tel - (62) 888510
fax - (62) 888511
Year of Formation - 1892
Chairman - Elisabeth J. Holm
Coach - Per Anders Sjøvold; Per Brogeland
Stadium - Gjemselund (6,000)

APPEARANCES 1998

	P	Ap	(s)	Gls
Abdul-Karim AHMED (GHA)	M	3	(3)	
Andreas ALM (SWE)	M	22		6
Øyvind BERG	D	10	(3)	
Trym BERGMAN	M	24	(1)	8
Charles BERSTAD	D	22	(1)	
Eirik DYBENDAL	M	7	(12)	1
Ludwig ERNSTSSON (SWE)	A	13	(1)	4
Vidar EVENSEN	D	26		2
Marius GULLERUD	M	23	(2)	4
Vegard HANSEN	D	1	(4)	
Johan HAMMARSTROM (SWE)	M	5	(3)	
Jon Inge HØILAND	D	23		
Pål HÅPNES	A	16	(2)	1
Julian JOHNSSON (FAR)	M	21	(2)	1
Gunnlaugur JÓNSSON (ISL)	D	5		
Jørn KARLSRUD	M	2		
Johan Martin LIANES	G		(1)	
Ole Arvid PETTERSEN LANGNES	G	26		
Ståle RØNNINGEN	D	4		
André SCHEI LINDBAEK	A	5		1
Harald Martin SOLBERG	A	8	(16)	4
Harald STORMOEN	M		(3)	
Sven Erik SAETRE	M	12	(5)	3
Hai Ngoc TRAN	D	8		

13/04/98	Lillestrøm SK	A	3-0	Alm, Evensen, Saetre
19/04/98	SK Brann	H	2-2	Evensen, Gullerud
26/04/98	Stabaek IF	A	1-2	Alm
30/04/98	FK Bodø/Glimt	H	0-0	
03/05/98	Moss FK	A	0-2	
07/05/98	Sogndal IL	H	3-2	Solberg, Saetre (p), Bergman
10/05/98	Molde FK	H	0-3	
16/05/98	Vålerenga IF	A	3-2	Solberg 2, Alm
01/07/98	Tromsø IL	A	0-3	
09/07/98	Viking FK	A	2-4	Bergman, Ernstsson
19/07/98	Lillestrøm SK	H	3-0	Bergman 2, Ernstsson (p)
22/07/98	Strømsgodset IF	H	2-1	Saetre, Alm
26/07/98	SK Brann	A	0-3	.
02/08/98	Stabaek IF	H	1-5	Alm
09/08/98	FK Bodø/Glimt	A	0-0	
12/08/98	FK Haugesund	H	0-1	
16/08/98	Moss FK	H	2-4	Ernstsson, Bergman
23/08/98	Sogndal IL	A	5-2	Håpnes, Gullerud 2, Ernstsson, Solberg
30/08/98	Molde FK	A	1-4	Bergman
09/09/98	Rosenborg BK	H	2-8	Gullerud, Bergman (p)
13/09/98	Vålerenga IF	H	1-3	Schei Lindbaek
20/09/98	Rosenborg BK	A	0-4	
27/09/98	Tromsø IL	H	2-1	Johnsson, Dybendal
04/10/98	Strømsgodset IF	A	0-1	
18/10/98	Viking FK	H	1-1	Bergman (p)
25/10/98	FK Haugesund	A	1-1	Alm

LILLESTRØM SK

CLUB DIRECTORY

Lillestrøm Sportsklubb
Postboks 196
2001 Lillestrøm
tel - (63) 805660
fax - (63) 805670
Year of Formation - 1917
Chairman - Frank Grønlund
Coach - Arne Erlandsen
Stadium - Åråsen (15,000)

MAJOR HONOURS
League Championship (5)
1959, 1976, 1977, 1986, 1989.
Domestic Cup - (4) 1977, 1978, 1981, 1985.

APPEARANCES 1998

	P	Ap	(s)	Gls
Svein Are ANDREASSEN	D	5	(11)	4
Tommy BERNTSEN	D	20	(2)	5
Torgeir BJARMANN	D	11	(2)	2
Trond BJØRNSEN	M	4	(11)	3
Mamadou DIALLO (SEN)	A	12	(1)	9
Vegar GRISLINGÅS	M		(5)	
Jørn HEGGESTAD	D	2	(2)	
Tore HOLM	A		(10)	
Heidar HELGUSON (ISL)	A	16	(3)	2
Magnus KIHLBERG (SWE)	M	26		
Magnus KIHLSTEDT (SWE)	G	26		
Frode KIPPE	D	24		2
Rúnar KRISTINSSON (ISL)	M	17	(2)	2
Ole Einar MARTINSEN	D	24		
Kjetil NILSEN	M	11	(5)	1
Runar NORMANN	M	20	(3)	2
Kenneth NYSAETHER	A	2	(7)	1
Leif Gunnar SMERUD	M	25		2
Arild SUNDGOT	A	24	(1)	3
Arnar Thór VIDARSSON (ISL)	D	6		
Peter WERNI	D	11	(3)	1

LEAGUE RESULTS 1998

13/04/98	Kongsvinger IL	H	0-3	
18/04/98	Molde FK	A	0-4	
27/04/98	Vålerenga IF	H	3-2	Diallo, Normann, Nilsen
30/04/98	Rosenborg BK	A	1-6	Diallo
03/05/98	Tromsø IL	H	2-1	Sundgot, Andreassen
07/05/98	Strømsgodset IF	A	3-2	Sundgot, Diallo, Bjarmann
10/05/98	Viking FK	H	2-3	Werni, Bjarmann
16/05/98	FK Haugesund	A	2-0	Diallo (p), Kippe
07/06/98	Sogndal IL	A	2-2	Normann, Smerud
01/07/98	SK Brann	H	1-1	og (Moen)
04/07/98	Stabaek IF	A	1-1	Berntsen
09/07/98	FK Bodø/Glimt	H	0-0	
12/07/98	Moss FK	A	2-1	Helguson, Kristinsson
19/07/98	Kongsvinger IL	A	0-3	
26/07/98	Molde FK	H	1-1	Andreassen
02/08/98	Vålerenga IF	A	5-1	Andreassen, Diallo 4
09/08/98	Rosenborg BK	H	0-3	
16/08/98	Tromsø IL	A	0-1	
22/08/98	Strømsgodset IF	H	2-4	Berntsen 2
30/08/98	Viking FK	A	1-0	Nysaether
13/09/98	FK Haugesund	H	5-0	Kristinsson, og (Ness), Diallo, Bjørnsen 2
20/09/98	Sogndal IL	H	0-1	
26/09/98	SK Brann	A	2-1	Smerud, Sundgot
04/10/98	Stabaek IF	H	2-3	Helguson, Bjørnsen
17/10/98	FK Bodø/Glimt	A	1-1	Berntsen (p)
25/10/98	Moss FK	H	3-4	Andreassen, Kippe, Berntsen

MOLDE FK

CLUB DIRECTORY

Molde Fotballklubb
Julsundvegen 14
6400 Molde
tel - (71) 202500
fax - (71) 202501
Year of Formation - 1911
Chairman - Nils Olav Kringstad
Coach - Erik Brakstad
Stadium - Nye Molde (13,400)

MAJOR HONOURS
Domestic Cup - (1) 1994.

APPEARANCES 1998

		P	Ap	(s)	Gls
Trond ANDERSEN	D	24			2
Morten BAKKE	G	26			
Daniel BERG HESTAD	M	24			8
Karl Oskar FJØRTOFT	M	25			3
Knut Anders FOSTERVOLD	D	23			1
Bjarki GUNNLAUGSSON (ISL)	A	2	(6)		2
Anders HASSELGÅRD	A	10	(5)		3
Andreas LUND	A	23	(2)		16
Pål LYDERSEN	D	24			
Thomas MORK	A	8	(13)		3
Stian OHR	A	1	(1)		1
Odd Inge OLSEN	M	26			11
Sindre REKDAL	D	2	(2)		1
Ståle RØNNINGEN	D		(1)		
Freddy dos SANTOS	D	17	(5)		
Dennis SCHILLER (SWE)	D	11	(5)		2
Petter Christian SINGSAAS	D	3	(8)		
Trond STRANDE	D	1	(1)		
Ole Bjørn SUNDGOT	A	10	(9)		6
Geir TELEVIK	A		(12)		2
Jo TESSEM	A	26			8

LEAGUE RESULTS 1998

13/04/98	FK Haugesund	A	3-2	Lund, Andersen, Sundgot
18/04/98	Lillestrøm SK	H	4-0	og (Berntsen), Berg Hestad, Lund,
				Gunnlaugsson
26/04/98	SK Brann	A	2-2	Lund, Berg Hestad
30/04/98	Stabaek IF	H	1-1	Olsen
03/05/98	FK Bodø/Glimt	A	2-0	Sundgot, Berg Hestad
07/05/98	Moss FK	H	6-0	Olsen 2, Lund 2, Sundgot, Fjørtoft
10/05/98	Kongsvinger IL	A	3-0	Lund, Schiller, Sundgot
16/05/98	Sogndal IL	H	4-0	Lund, Sundgot, Tessem, Berg
				Hestad
07/06/98	Vålerenga IF	H	4-1	Tessem, Gunnlaugsson, Olsen,
				Rekdal
01/07/98	Rosenborg BK	A	2-1	Lund 2
05/07/98	Tromsø IL	H	2-2	Lund, Olsen
09/07/98	Strømsgodset IF	A	2-1	Berg Hestad, Olsen
13/07/98	Viking FK	H	4-4	Hasselgård 2, Mork, Olsen
19/07/98	FK Haugesund	H	4-1	Olsen, Mork, Berg Hestad, Televik
26/07/98	Lillestrøm SK	A	1-1	Berg Hestad
01/08/98	SK Brann	H	2-2	Olsen, Berg Hestad
08/08/98	Stabaek IF	A	4-1	Tessem 2, Hasselgård, Fostervold
16/08/98	FK Bodø/Glimt	H	1-0	Lund
22/08/98	Moss FK	A	2-0	Lund, Televik
30/08/98	Kongsvinger IL	H	4-1	Fjørtoft 2, Lund, Schiller
13/09/98	Sogndal IL	A	4-1	Lund, Olsen, Andersen, Mork
20/09/98	Vålerenga IF	A	1-3	Tessem
26/09/98	Rosenborg BK	H	0-2	
04/10/98	Tromsø IL	A	6-2	Tessem 3, Olsen, Lund, Sundgot
18/10/98	Strømsgodset IF	H	1-3	Lund (p)
25/10/98	Viking FK	A	1-3	Ohr

MOSS FK

CLUB DIRECTORY

Moss Fotballklubb
Postboks 47
1501 Moss
tel - (69) 243970
fax - (69) 256650
Year of Formation - 1906
Chairman - Per A. Bakke
Coach - Knut Thorbjørn Eggen
Stadium - Melløs (9,000)

MAJOR HONOURS
League Championship - (1) 1987.
Domestic Cup - (1) 1983.

APPEARANCES 1998

		P	Ap	(s)	Gls
Leif Erik ANDERSEN	D	12	(2)		
Dagfinn ENERLY	A	10	(1)	4	
Andreas GAARDER OLSEN	M	1	(1)		
Brynjar Björn GUNNARSSON (ISL)	D	3	(2)	2	
Rino André HANSEN	G	26			
Per Morten HAUGEN	M	2	(8)		
Pål HÅPNES	A	2	(1)		
Carsten JOHANSEN	D	21	(2)	2	
Geir JOHANSEN	D	15	(2)		
Christian JOHNSEN	A	15	(5)	3	
Anders JULIUSSEN	D	22			
Anders KIEL (SWE)	A	5	(13)	2	
Gard KRISTIANSEN	D	23	(3)		
Raymond KVISVIK	M	9		3	
Kenneth LØVLIEN	A	19	(4)	2	
Thomas MICHELSEN	M	2	(4)		
Jerry MÅNSSON (SWE)	A	18	(3)	7	
Jan Tore OPHAUG	M	15	(7)	4	
Hans PALMQVIST (SWE)	A	6	(6)	1	
Christian PETERSEN	A	1	(3)		
Hans Erik RAMBERG	M	20	(4)		
Tommy SYLTE	M	25		4	
Tor TRONDSEN	D	14		1	

LEAGUE RESULTS 1998

13/04/98	SK Brann	A	1-0	Johnsen
19/04/98	Stabaek IF	H	1-0	Sylte
26/04/98	FK Bodø/Glimt	A	1-2	Løvlien
30/04/98	Sogndal IL	H	1-1	Kvisvik
03/05/98	Kongsvinger IL	H	2-0	Løvlien, Sylte
07/05/98	Molde FK	A	0-6	
11/05/98	Vålerenga IF	H	3-2	Kvisvik (p), Kiel 2
16/05/98	Rosenborg BK	A	0-6	
07/06/98	Tromsø IL	H	3-2	Johansen C., Ophaug, Kvisvik
01/07/98	Strømsgodset IF	A	0-2	
05/07/98	Viking FK	H	0-1	
09/07/98	FK Haugesund	A	1-5	Månsson
12/07/98	Lillestrøm SK	H	1-2	Månsson
19/07/98	SK Brann	H	3-0	Ophaug, Trondsen, Johnsen
26/07/98	Stabaek IF	A	0-4	
02/08/98	FK Bodø/Glimt	H	0-1	
09/08/98	Sogndal IL	A	3-4	Palmqvist, Ophaug, og (Christiansen)
16/08/98	Kongsvinger IL	A	4-2	Månsson 2, Sylte, Johansen C.
22/08/98	Molde FK	H	0-2	
30/08/98	Vålerenga IF	A	0-1	
08/09/98	Strømsgodset IF	H	3-1	Månsson, Johnsen, Ophaug
13/09/98	Rosenborg BK	H	1-3	Enerly
20/09/98	Tromsø IL	A	0-0	
04/10/98	Viking FK	A	2-5	Gunnarsson, Enerly
18/10/98	FK Haugesund	H	2-0	Sylte (p), Enerly
25/10/98	Lillestrøm SK	A	4-3	Enerly, Månsson 2, Gunnarsson

ROSENBORG BK

Rosenborg Ballklubb
7005 Trondheim
tel - (73) 822100
fax - (73) 944070
Year of Formation - 1917
Chairman - Knut Skoglund
President - Rune Bratseth
General Manager - Nils Skutle
Coach- Trond Sollied (99 - Nils Arne Eggen)
Stadium - Lerkendal (25,000)

MAJOR HONOURS
League Championship - (13)
1967, 1969, 1971, 1985, 1988, 1990, 1992,
1993, 1994, 1995, 1996, 1997, 1998.
Domestic Cup - (7)
1960, 1964, 1971, 1988, 1990, 1992, 1995.

	P	Ap	(s)	Gls
Arni Gautur ARASON (ISL)	G	3		
Christer BASMA	D	11		
Runar BERG	M	26		4
André BERGDØLMO	D	24		1
Robert BOATENG (GHA)	A		(1)	
Bjørn Otto BRAGSTAD	D	25		4
Tore André DAHL IJM	A	1	(18)	5
Vegard HEGGEM	D	4	(1)	
Børge HERNES	A	4	(11)	1
Erik HOFTUN	D	23		2
John Ivar "Mini" JAKOBSEN	A	26		14
Jørn JAMTFALL	G	23		
Bent Inge JOHNSEN	D	4	(8)	1
Erland JOHNSEN	D	4	(2)	
Steinar LEIN	M		(6)	
Andreas MAYER (GER)	M	3	(3)	
Morten PEDERSEN	D	11	(1)	
Sigurd RUSHFELDT	A	26		27
Bent SKAMMELSRUD	M	20		2
Roar STRAND	M	23		12
Jan-Derek SØRENSEN	A	23	(2)	5
Kristian SØRLI	A		(2)	
Fredrik WINSNES	M	2	(12)	

13/04/98	Strømsgodset IF	A	2-0	Strand, Jakobsen
19/04/98	Viking FK	H	3-1	Rushfeldt, Strand 2
26/04/98	FK Haugesund	A	3-0	Jakobsen, Hoftun, Dahlum
30/04/98	Lillestrøm SK	H	6-1	Sørensen, Jakobsen 2,
				Rushfeldt 2 (1p), Bragstad
04/05/98	SK Brann	A	0-0	
07/05/98	Stabaek IF	H	2-2	Rushfeldt, Jakobsen
10/05/98	FK Bodø/Glimt	A	6-2	Rushfeldt 2, Hoftun, Bragstad,
				Jakobsen 2
16/05/98	Moss FK	H	6-0	Rushfeldt 4, Strand, Jakobsen
01/07/98	Molde FK	H	1-2	Jakobsen
05/07/98	Vålerenga IF	A	2-0	Rushfeldt (p), Sørensen
09/07/98	Sogndal IL	A	1-2	Johnsen B.I.
12/07/98	Tromsø IL	A	4-3	Rushfeldt (p), Bragstad,
				Sørensen, Berg
19/07/98	Strømsgodset IF	H	7-1	og (Thorvaldsson), Jakobsen 2,
				Rushfeldt 2, Strand, Berg
25/07/98	Viking FK	A	2-1	Rushfeldt (p), Jakobsen
02/08/98	FK Haugesund	H	1-0	Jakobsen
09/08/98	Lillestrøm SK	A	3-0	Hernes, Dahlum 2
15/08/98	SK Brann	H	4-2	Rushfeldt 2, Berg, Jakobsen
23/08/98	Stabaek IF	A	0-2	
30/08/98	FK Bodø/Glimt	H	3-0	Strand, Rushfeldt, Skammelsrud
09/09/98	Kongsvinger IL	A	8-2	Strand 2, Rushfeldt 4,
				Skammelsrud, Bergdølmo
13/09/98	Moss FK	A	3-1	Strand 2, Rushfeldt
20/09/98	Kongsvinger IL	H	4-0	Rushfeldt, Strand, Berg, Dahlum
26/09/98	Molde FK	A	2-0	Strand, Dahlum
04/10/98	Vålerenga IF	H	1-0	Rushfeldt (p)
18/10/98	Sogndal IL	H	4-0	Sørensen 2, Rushfeldt 2
25/10/98	Tromsø IL	H	1-1	Bragstad

SOGNDAL IL

CLUB DIRECTORY

Sogndal Idrettslag Fotball
Postboks 164
5801 Sogndal
tel - (57) 672050
fax - (57) 672005
Year of Formation - 1926
Chairman - Arild Hopen
Coach - Trond Fylling (99 - Mike Speight)
Stadium - Fosshaugane (6,000)

APPEARANCES 1998

	P	Ap	(s)	Gls
Arild ANDERSEN	M	20		1
Bent APNESETH	M	17	(2)	1
Eirik BAKKE	M	19		2
Petter BAKKE	D	19	(5)	
Ståle BOKALRUD	D	14	(4)	
Rune BUER JOHANSEN	M	10	(1)	3
Ørjan CHRISTIANSEN	M	10	(9)	2
Jarle FLO	D	16	(3)	1
Bjørn Tore HANSEN	A	8	(3)	3
Tommy HANSEN	D	3	(1)	
Håvard HEGG LUNDE	D	20	(1)	1
Trond HEGGESTAD	D		(2)	
André HERFINDAL	D	5		
Asle HILLESTAD	D	23		5
Eirik HILLESTAD	D	5	(8)	
Ole HJELMHAUG	D	15	(1)	1
Tommy HOVLAND	M		(2)	
Eivind KARLSBAKK	A	6	(6)	
Kai Erik MOEN	M	9	(9)	
Trevor MORLEY (ENG)	A	5		
Stian NESET	A		(1)	
Geir-Erik RØYSI	M		(1)	
Terje SKJELDESTAD	G	26		
Kjetil SØNNESYN	M	9	(4)	
Fredrik THORSEN	A	4	(4)	1
Torbjørn YLVESÅKER	M		(1)	
Tommy ØREN	A	23	(1)	4

LEAGUE RESULTS 1998

13/04/98	Tromsø IL	H	0-0	
19/04/98	FK Bodø/Glimt	A	0-3	
26/04/98	Strømsgodset IF	H	2-2	Hegg Lunde, Thorsen
30/04/98	Moss FK	A	1-1	Christiansen
03/05/98	Viking FK	H	1-2	Bakke E.
07/05/98	Kongsvinger IL	A	2-3	Øren, Hillestad A. (p)
10/05/98	FK Haugesund	H	0-4	
16/05/98	Molde FK	A	0-4	
07/06/98	Lillestrøm SK	H	2-2	Bakke E., Hillestad A. (p)
01/07/98	Vålerenga IF	A	0-4	
05/07/98	SK Brann	H	2-1	Andersen, Christiansen
09/07/98	Rosenborg BK	H	2-1	Apneseth, Hillestad A. (p)
12/07/98	Stabaek IF	A	1-5	Flo
19/07/98	Tromsø IL	A	1-3	Hillestad A. (p)
26/07/98	FK Bodø/Glimt	H	1-2	Hillestad A. (p)
02/08/98	Strømsgodset IF	A	1-2	Buer Johansen
09/08/98	Moss FK	H	4-3	Buer Johansen, Hansen B.T., Øren 2
16/08/98	Viking FK	A	1-5	og (Bjønsaas)
23/08/98	Kongsvinger IL	H	2-5	Hjelmhaug, Øren
30/08/98	FK Haugesund	A	0-4	
13/09/98	Molde FK	H	1-4	Buer Johansen
20/09/98	Lillestrøm SK	A	1-0	Hansen B.T.
27/09/98	Vålerenga IF	H	1-3	Hansen B.T.
04/10/98	SK Brann	A	0-4	
18/10/98	Rosenborg BK	A	0-4	
25/10/98	Stabaek IF	H	0-9	

STABAEK IF

Stabaek Idrettsforening Fotball
Postboks 103
1341 Bekkestua
tel - (67) 121212
fax - (67) 582610
Year of Formation - 1912
Chairman - vacant
Coach - Anders Linderoth
Stadium - Nadderud (10,000)

MAJOR HONOURS
Domestic Cup - (1) 1998.

		P	Ap	(s)	Gls
Richard ACKON (GHA)	M		10	(9)	
Martin ANDRESEN	M		25		8
Christer BASMA	D		9		
Petter BELSVIK	A		25	(1)	19
Thomas FINSTAD	A		13	(10)	10
André FLEM	D		19	(1)	3
David HANSSEN	M		4	(8)	
Andreas HAUGER	M			(2)	
Christian HOLTER	D		6	(3)	
Jesper JANSSON (SWE)	M		25		6
Axel KOLLE	M		14	(3)	1
Karl-Petter LØKEN	D		1	(1)	
Frode OLSEN	G		26		
Inge André OLSEN	D		23		2
Helgi SIGURDSSON (ISL)	A		14	(5)	7
John Arvid SKISTAD	D		19	(2)	
Tommy STENERSEN	D		19	(2)	1
Tom STENVOLL	D			(3)	
Niclas SVENSSON (SWE)	D		9	(3)	
Tommy SVINDAL LARSEN	M		25		5

Date	Opponent	H/A	Score	Scorers
13/04/98	FK Bodø/Glimt	H	3-2	Andresen, Belsvik (p), Svindal Larsen
19/04/98	Moss FK	A	0-1	
26/04/98	Kongsvinger IL	H	2-1	Belsvik, Finstad
30/04/98	Molde FK	A	1-1	Flem
03/05/98	Vålerenga IF	H	2-0	Jansson, Finstad
07/05/98	Rosenborg BK	A	2-2	Andresen, Finstad
10/05/98	Tromsø IL	H	1-0	Belsvik
16/05/98	Strømsgodset IF	A	1-2	Svindal Larsen
07/06/98	Viking FK	A	3-1	Sigurdsson, Jansson, Svindal Larsen
01/07/98	FK Haugesund	A	1-0	Andresen
04/07/98	Lillestrøm SK	H	1-1	Belsvik
09/07/98	SK Brann	A	0-2	
12/07/98	Sogndal IL	H	5-1	Finstad 2, Flem, Olsen I.A., og (Bakke E.)
19/07/98	FK Bodø/Glimt	A	3-1	Belsvik, Svindal Larsen 2
26/07/98	Moss FK	H	4-0	Andresen, Finstad 2, Sigurdsson
02/08/98	Kongsvinger IL	A	5-1	Belsvik 3, Jansson, Andresen
08/08/98	Molde FK	H	1-4	Belsvik
16/08/98	Vålerenga IF	A	0-2	
23/08/98	Rosenborg BK	H	2-0	Belsvik 2
30/08/98	Tromsø IL	A	4-0	Kolle, Belsvik 2, Finstad
12/09/98	Strømsgodset IF	H	4-0	Stenersen, Sigurdsson 2, Belsvik
19/09/98	Viking FK	H	4-3	Belsvik 2 (1p), Jansson, Finstad
27/09/98	FK Haugesund	H	1-1	Jansson
04/10/98	Lillestrøm SK	A	3-2	Sigurdsson 2, Jansson
18/10/98	SK Brann	H	1-1	Flem
25/10/98	Sogndal IL	A	9-0	Olsen I.A., Belsvik 3, Andresen 3, Sigurdsson, Finstad

STRØMSGODSET IF

CLUB DIRECTORY

Strømsgodset Idrettsforening
Fotballgruppa
Postboks 4140
3002 Drammen
tel - (32) 265770
fax - (32) 830175
Year of Formation - 1907
Chairman - Runar Hannevold
Coach - Dag Vidar Kristoffersen; Jens Martin Støten
Stadium - Marienlyst (12,000)

MAJOR HONOURS
League Championship - (1) 1970.
Domestic Cup - (4) 1969, 1970, 1973, 1991.

APPEARANCES 1998

	P	Ap	(s)	Gls
Lars-Gunnar CARLSTRAND	A	2	(7)	1
Kenneth DOKKEN	A		(4)	
Jostein FLO	A	19		19
Christer GEORGE	A	4	(14)	3
Valur GÍSLASON (ISL)	M	1	(2)	
Lars GRANÅS	M	6	(3)	
Erik HAGEN	D	7	(1)	
Rune HAGEN	A	26		3
Glenn Arne HANSEN	G	18		
Espen HORSRUD	D	13		2
Erland JOHNSEN	D	5	(2)	
Kenneth KARLSEN	D	16	(1)	3
Morten KIHLE	M	13	(1)	
Stefan LINDQVIST (SWE)	M	7		1
Anders MICHELSEN	M	16	(2)	3
Ousman NYAN	M	23		1
Lasse OLSEN	A	19	(7)	1
Christer PEDERSEN	M		(1)	
Tor Arne SANNERHOLT	M	4	(10)	1
Pål SKISTAD	D	21	(3)	
Sander SOLBERG	M	12	(3)	
Vegard STRØM	D	12	(2)	
Óskar Hravn THORVALDSSON (ISL)	D	6	(1)	
Thomas WAEHLER	D	20		1
Hans Erik ØDEGAARD	M	8	(8)	1
Thomas André ØDEGAARD	G	8	(2)	

LEAGUE RESULTS 1998

13/04/98	Rosenborg BK	H	0-2	
19/04/98	Tromsø IL	A	2-2	Waehler, Sannerholt
26/04/98	Sogndal IL	A	2-2	Hagen R., George
30/04/98	Viking FK	H	1-5	Flo
03/05/98	FK Haugesund	A	1-1	Flo
07/05/98	Lillestrøm SK	H	2-3	Michelsen, Carlstrand
10/05/98	SK Brann	A	1-0	Flo
16/05/98	Stabaek IF	H	2-1	Flo 2 (1p)
01/07/98	Moss FK	H	2-0	Hagen R., Flo
09/07/98	Molde FK	H	1-2	Flo
13/07/98	Vålerenga IF	A	1-1	Flo
19/07/98	Rosenborg BK	A	1-7	Ødegaard H.E.
23/07/98	Kongsvinger IL	A	1-2	Karlsen
26/07/98	Tromsø IL	H	3-2	Horsrud, Flo 2 (1p)
30/07/98	FK Bodø/Glimt	A	2-6	Lindqvist, Flo (p)
02/08/98	Sogndal IL	H	2-1	Flo, Horsrud
08/08/98	Viking FK	A	1-4	Flo
16/08/98	FK Haugesund	H	4-1	Flo 4
22/08/98	Lillestrøm SK	A	4-2	Hagen R., Michelsen 2, Nyan
29/08/98	SK Brann	H	0-2	
08/09/98	Moss FK	A	1-3	Olsen
12/09/98	Stabaek IF	A	0-4	
20/09/98	FK Bodø/Glimt	H	2-2	Flo, George
04/10/98	Kongsvinger IL	H	1-0	George
18/10/98	Molde FK	A	3-1	Flo, Karlsen 2
25/10/98	Vålerenga IF	H	0-5	

TROMSØ IL

Tromsø Idrettslag
Postboks 5
9001 Tromsø
tel - (77) 602600
fax - (77) 602601
Year of Formation - 1920
Chairman - Gunnar Wilhelmsen
Coach - Håkan Sandberg; Bård Flovik
(99 - Terje Skarsfjord)
Stadium - Alfheim (11,000)

MAJOR HONOURS
Domestic Cup - (2) 1986, 1996.

APPEARANCES 1998

	P	Ap	(s)	Gls
Stein BERG JOHANSEN	A	1	(6)	1
Robin BERNTSEN	D	23	(1)	
Jan Egil BREKKE	D	9	(5)	
Leif Arne BREKKE	A		(14)	
Roar CHRISTENSEN	M	23	(1)	2
Frode FERMANN	A	8	(5)	1
Tryggvi GUDMUNDSSON (ISL)	A	24	(1)	8
Thomas HAFSTAD	M	22	(2)	3
Henrik HANNU (SWE)	D		(1)	
Bjørn JOHANSEN	M	24		2
Svein Morten JOHANSEN	D	22		
Tor Inge KRISTIANSEN	G	1		
Morten KRAEMER	D	15		
Rune LANGE	A	26		20
Stian LARSEN	D	3	(4)	
Ole Andreas NILSEN	D	8	(3)	
Marko TUOMELA (FIN)	D	26		1
Thomas TØLLEFSEN	G	25		
Gaute UGELSTAD HELSTRUP	M	1	(5)	
Aleksei YEREMENKO (RUS)	M	25	(1)	

LEAGUE RESULTS 1998

13/04/98	Sogndal IL	A	0-0	
19/04/98	Strømsgodset IF	H	2-2	Gudmundsson, Lange
26/04/98	Viking FK	A	2-1	Lange, Gudmundsson
30/04/98	FK Haugesund	H	2-1	Johansen B., Lange
03/05/98	Lillestrøm SK	A	1-2	Lange
07/05/98	SK Brann	H	1-0	Lange (p)
10/05/98	Stabaek IF	A	0-1	
16/05/98	FK Bodø/Glimt	H	4-4	Berg Johansen, Christensen, Lange (p), Tuomela
07/06/98	Moss FK	A	2-3	Lange, og (Johansen G.)
01/07/98	Kongsvinger IL	H	3-0	Gudmundsson, Johansen B., Lange
05/07/98	Molde FK	A	2-2	Lange, Hafstad
09/07/98	Vålerenga IF	H	2-1	Gudmundsson, Lange
12/07/98	Rosenborg BK	H	3-4	Gudmundsson, Christensen, Lange
19/07/98	Sogndal IL	H	3-1	Hafstad 2, Lange
26/07/98	Strømsgodset IF	A	2-3	Gudmundsson 2
02/08/98	Viking FK	H	1-2	Lange
09/08/98	FK Haugesund	A	1-1	Fermann
16/08/98	Lillestrøm SK	H	1-0	Lange
22/08/98	SK Brann	A	1-3	Gudmundsson
30/08/98	Stabaek IF	H	0-4	
13/09/98	FK Bodø/Glimt	A	2-3	Lange 2
20/09/98	Moss FK	H	0-0	
27/09/98	Kongsvinger IL	A	1-2	Lange
04/10/98	Molde FK	H	2-6	Lange 2
18/10/98	Vålerenga IF	A	0-1	
25/10/98	Rosenborg BK	A	1-1	Lange

VIKING FK

CLUB DIRECTORY

Viking Fotballklubb
Postboks 4051
Tasta
4004 Stavanger
tel - (51) 840080
fax - (51) 840081
Year of Formation - 1899
Chairman - Geir Solstad
Coach - Poul Erik Andreassen
Stadium - Stavanger (17,000)

MAJOR HONOURS
League Championship - (8) 1958, 1972, 1973, 1974, 1975, 1979, 1982, 1991.
Domestic Cup - (4) 1953, 1959, 1979, 1989.

APPEARANCES 1998

		P	Ap	(s)	Gls
Gunnar AASE	A	18	(1)	5
Bjørn BERLAND	A	16	(1)	7
Helge BJØNSAAS	D	21	(1)	2
Per BLOHM (SWE)	M	1	(4)	
Lars Gaute BØ	G	17		
Rikhardur DADASON (ISL)	A	24	(1)	16
Bjørn DAHL	D	14	(6)	
Frode EIKE HANSEN	D	3	(6)	
Odd Arne ESPEVOLL	D	18	(3)	1
Christian FLINDT BJERG (DEN)	M	20	(5)	11
Jan Børge FRØLAND	A		(2)	
Jans Jørgen HAUGLAND	A		(1)	
Audun HELGASON (ISL)	D	23		2
Martin KNUDSEN	D	24	(2)	
Ronny KRISTENSEN	A	7	(8)	4
Bjarte LUNDE AARSHEIM	M	25		3
Idar MATHIASSEN	A	5	(4)	2
Erik NEVLAND	A	4	(4)	3
Vegard SKOGHEIM	A	11	(8)	5
Thomas SOLBERG	D		(6)	
Tore SNØRTELAND	G	9		
Magnus SVENSSON (SWE)	M	26		4
Arild SVAEREN	A		(5)	
Jørgen TENGESDAL	A		(2)	

LEAGUE RESULTS 1998

13/04/98	Vålerenga IF	H	3-0	Aase 2, Dadason
19/04/98	Rosenborg BK	A	1-3	Aase
26/04/98	Tromsø IL	H	1-2	Dadason
30/04/98	Strømsgodset IF	A	5-1	Berland 2, Lunde Aarsheim, Flindt Bjerg, Nevland
03/05/98	Sogndal IL	A	2-1	Berland, Flindt Bjerg
07/05/98	FK Haugesund	H	3-1	Dadason 2, Aase
10/05/98	Lillestrøm SK	A	3-2	Aase, Dadason 2
16/05/98	SK Brann	A	4-1	Dadason, Nevland 2, Skogheim
07/06/98	Stabaek IF	H	1-3	Svensson
01/07/98	FK Bodø/Glimt	H	1-1	Svensson
05/07/98	Moss FK	A	1-0	Berland
09/07/98	Kongsvinger IL	H	4-2	Flindt Bjerg (p), Dadason, Helgason, Berland
13/07/98	Molde FK	A	4-4	Flindt Bjerg 2, Dadason, Lunde Aarsheim
19/07/98	Vålerenga IF	A	2-2	Helgason, Berland
25/07/98	Rosenborg BK	H	1-2	Flindt Bjerg
02/08/98	Tromsø IL	A	2-1	Flindt Bjerg, Kristensen
08/08/98	Strømsgodset IF	H	4-1	Dadason, Berland, Flindt Bjerg, Skogheim
16/08/98	Sogndal IL	H	5-1	Kristensen, Dadason 2, Flindt Bjerg, Svensson
22/08/98	FK Haugesund	A	4-1	Kristensen, Flindt Bjerg, Dadason, Mathiassen
30/08/98	Lillestrøm SK	H	0-1	
12/09/98	SK Brann	H	2-3	Skogheim, Dadason
19/09/98	FK Haugesund	A	3-4	Bjønsaas, Skogheim, Mathiassen
27/09/98	FK Bodø/Glimt	A	1-3	Skogheim
04/10/98	Moss FK	H	5-2	Dadason, Svensson, Bjønsaas, Espevoll (p), Lunde Aarsheim
18/10/98	Kongsvinger IL	A	1-1	Dadason
25/10/98	Molde FK	H	3-1	og (Andersen), Kristensen, Flindt Bjerg

VÅLERENGA IF

CLUB DIRECTORY

Vålerenga Idrettsforening Fotball
Postboks 6064
Etterstad
0601 Oslo
tel - (22) 880480
fax - (22) 880491
Year of Formation - 1913
Chairman - Jon Harald Nordbrekken
Coach - Lars Tjaernås; Egil Olsen & Lars Tjaernås
Stadium - Bislett (20,000)

MAJOR HONOURS
League Championship - (4)
1965, 1981, 1983, 1984.
Domestic Cup - (2) 1980, 1997.

APPEARANCES 1998

		P	Ap	(s)	Gls
Thomas BERNTSEN	D	11	(1)	
John CAREW	A	15	(3)	7
Christer ELLEFSEN	D	1		
Fredrik GÄRDEMAN (SWE)	A		(3)	
Brynjar Björn GUNNARSSON (ISL)	D	1	(3)	
Knut Henry HARALDSEN	D	25		1
Espen HAUG	M	22	(3)	5
Tom Henning HOVI	M	19	(3)	1
Kjell Koar KAASA	A	15	(6)	7
Kent KARLSEN	D	5	(1)	
Fredrik KJØLNER	D	25		
Tore KROGSTAD	G	25		
Juro KUVICEK	A	9	(10)	3
Bjørn Arild LEVERNES	M	17	(7)	2
Håvard LUNDE	D		(2)	
Milos MIRKOVIC (YUG)	D	1		
Espen MUSAEUS	A	10	(6)	4
Dag RIISNAES	M	8		1
Ivar RØNNINGEN	G	1		
Kamal SALITI	A		(1)	
Pascal SIMPSON (SWE)	A	6	(9)	1
Viggo STRØMME	D	4	(1)	
Fredrik THORSEN	M	3	(1)	
Hai Ngoc TRAN	D	15		
Bjørn VILJUGREIN	M	23		6
Joachim WALLTIN	D	24		1
Jon Eirik ØDEGAARD	M	1	(9)	3

LEAGUE RESULTS 1998

13/04/98	Viking FK	A	0-3	
19/04/98	FK Haugesund	H	3-2	Kuvicek, Kaasa 2
27/04/98	Lillestrøm SK	A	2-3	Kaasa, Viljugrein
30/04/98	SK Brann	H	3-2	Simpson, og (Guntveit), Musaeus
03/05/98	Stabaek IF	A	0-2	
07/05/98	FK Bodø/Glimt	H	2-2	Viljugrein, Kuvicek
11/05/98	Moss FK	A	2-3	Kuvicek, Musaeus
16/05/98	Kongsvinger IL	H	2-3	Ødegaard, og (Evensen)
07/06/98	Molde FK	A	1-4	Kaasa
01/07/98	Sogndal IL	H	4-0	Kaasa, Viljugrein 3
05/07/98	Rosenborg BK	H	0-2	
09/07/98	Tromsø IL	A	1-2	Kaasa
13/07/98	Strømsgodset IF	H	1-1	Carew
19/07/98	Viking FK	H	2-2	Musaeus 2
26/07/98	FK Haugesund	A	1-3	Haug
02/08/98	Lillestrøm SK	H	1-5	Carew
08/08/98	SK Brann	A	0-3	
16/08/98	Stabaek IF	H	2-0	Haug, Carew
23/08/98	FK Bodø/Glimt	A	1-2	Carew
30/08/98	Moss FK	H	1-0	Haraldsen
13/09/98	Kongsvinger IL	A	3-1	Walltin, Levernes, Hovi
20/09/98	Molde FK	H	3-1	Carew, Viljugrein (p), Ødegaard
27/09/98	Sogndal IL	A	3-1	Haug, Ødegaard, Kaasa
04/10/98	Rosenborg BK	A	0-1	
18/10/98	Tromsø IL	H	1-0	Riisnaes
25/10/98	Strømsgodset IF	A	5-0	Carew 2, Haug 2, Levernes

PROMOTED CLUBS

SECOND DIVISION FINAL TABLE 1998

		Pd	W	D	L	F	A	Pt	GD
1	**Odd Grenland**	**26**	**16**	**7**	**3**	**55**	**18**	**55**	**+37**
2	**Skeid**	**26**	**13**	**5**	**8**	**40**	**37**	**44**	**+3**
3	Kjelsås IL	26	11	8	7	43	34	41	+9
4	Byåsen IL	26	12	4	10	38	30	40	+8
5	IK Start	26	11	6	9	37	29	39	+8
6	Bryne FK	26	12	3	11	46	42	39	+4
7	IL Hødd	25	12	2	12	40	45	38	-5
8	Raufoss IL	26	11	4	11	35	43	37	-8
9	SFK Lyn	26	9	9	8	44	26	36	+18
10	Eik-Tønsberg	26	9	8	9	39	35	35	+4
11	Aalesund FK	26	10	4	12	26	41	34	-15
12	Strindheim IL	26	8	8	10	37	37	32	0
13	Ullern IF	26	6	3	17	26	55	21	-29
14	Hamarkameratene	26	6	1	19	30	64	19	-34

PROMOTION/RELEGATION PLAY-OFF

Kongsvinger IL 2, Kjelsås IL 2
Kjelsås IL 0, Kongsvinger IL 5
(Kongsvinger IL 7-2)

CLUB DIRECTORY

Odd Grenland
Postboks 343
3701 Skien
tel - (35) 900150
fax - (35) 900159
Year of Formation - 1894
Chairman - Erik Holmberg
Coach - Tom Nordlie
Stadium - Odd (10,000)

MAJOR HONOURS
Domestic Cup - (11) 1903, 1904, 1905, 1906,
1913, 1915, 1919, 1922, 1924, 1926, 1931.

CLUB DIRECTORY

Skeid
Postboks 5
Grefsen
0409 Oslo
tel - (22) 222882
fax - (22) 222963
Year of Formation - 1915
Chairman - Anders Hornslien
Coach - Bengt Eriksen
Stadium - Voldsløkka (4,000)

MAJOR HONOURS
League Championship - (1) 1966.
Domestic Cup - (8) 1947, 1954, 1955, 1956,
1958, 1963, 1965, 1974.

POLAND

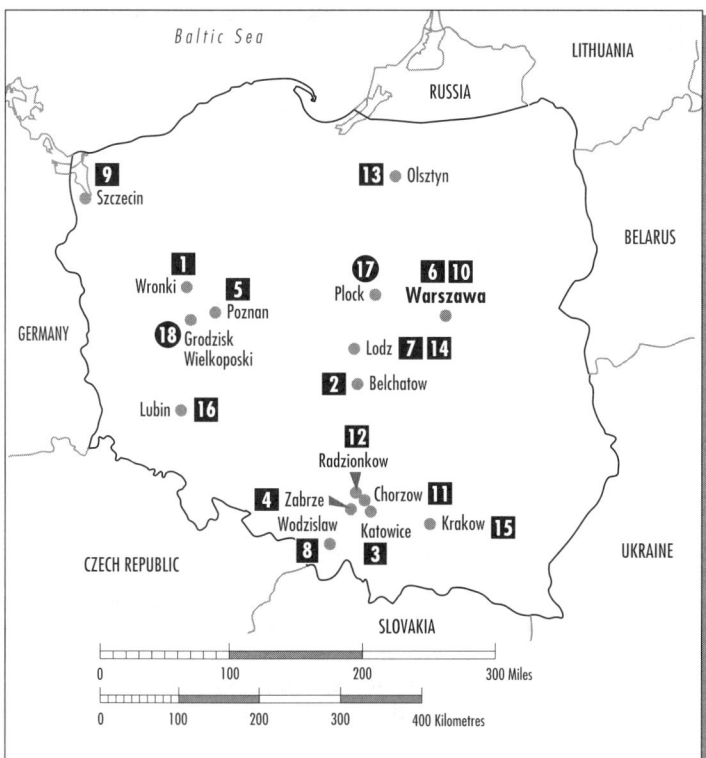

1	AMICA WRONKI	740
2	GKS BELCHATOW	741
3	GKS KATOWICE	742
4	GORNIK ZABRZE	743
5	LECH POZNAN	744
6	LEGIA WARSZAWA	745
7	LKS LODZ	746
8	ODRA WODZISLAW	747
9	POGON SZCZECIN	748
10	POLONIA WARSZAWA	749

11	RUCH CHORZOW	750
12	RUCH RADZIONKOW	751
13	STOMIL OLSZTYN	752
14	WIDZEW LODZ	753
15	WISLA KRAKOW	754
16	ZAGLEBIE LUBIN	755
Promoted clubs		
17	PETROCHEMIA PLOCK	756
18	GROCLIN DYSKOBOLIA GRODZISK	756

DZIUROWICZ DEPOSED IN PZPN POWER STRUGGLE

Knife-thrower punctures Wisla title celebrations

FEDERATION DIRECTORY

Polski Zwiazek Pilki Noznej
Miodowa 1, 00-080 Warszawa

tel - (022) 8271211   Year of Formation - 1919
fax - (022) 8270704   President - Michal Listkiewicz
   Secretary - Ludek Macela

Stadium - Slaski, Chorzow (35,000)

Just as many had predicted, Wisla Krakow won the 1998/99 Polish championship at a stroll. In a country as strapped for cash as Poland, money talks, and the millions of American dollars pumped into the famous Silesian club by sponsors Tele-Fonika were always likely to reap rich dividends.

The extent of Wisla's domination in the league table was an accurate reflection of the financial superiority they had over their rivals. The team dubbed 'White Star' had an 81 per cent success rate, taking the title by a huge 17-point margin and scoring a highly impressive total of 75 goals - an average of 2.5 per match. Wisla won 23 of their 30 games, which, given that the club paid out a total win bonus of $50,000 per victory, earned their players vast sums of money by Polish standards. It was hardly surprising that every footballer in the country wanted to join Wisla.

The championship was as good as over by the winter break. Although Wisla lost their final game of the autumn

campaign - 0-1 v Zaglebie Lubin - they had won 13 of their previous 14 and drawn the other. That commanding form continued in the spring as they reeled off another eight-match winning sequence, the last of those wins - 4-0 v GKS Belchatow - making the title mathematically secure with five matches still to play. It was Wisla's first Polish championship in 21 years, but for coach Franciszek Smuda it was the third title in four seasons. The ex-Widzew Lodz boss repaid all the faith placed in him by the club's owners and he proved once more that he was the top man-manager and coaching counsellor in the country, bringing the best out of several players such as Marek Zajac, Kazimierz Wegrzyn, Ryszard Czerwiec, Tomasz Kulawik and, especially, the league's top goalscorer Tomasz Frankowski.

Wisla's outstanding domestic form was carried into European competition where they passed three rounds of the UEFA Cup before bowing out to eventual winners Parma. More distressing than elimination, however, was

LEAGUE CHAMPIONSHIP RESULTS 98/99

		1	2	3	4	5	6	7	8	9	10	11	12	13	14	15	16
1	Amica Wronki		2-0	4-0	0-0	2-1	0-2	1-2	3-1	2-0	1-0	2-0	1-0	0-0	2-3	1-3	2-1
2	GKS Belchatow	1-1		1-2	1-1	1-3	1-2	2-3	1-1	2-0	0-1	0-2	2-1	1-0	3-2	0-3	0-1
3	GKS Katowice	0-0	1-1		1-1	1-2	1-3	1-1	1-1	1-0	1-3	0-1	1-0	1-0	0-2	1-2	2-2
4	Gornik Zabrze	0-0	1-3	2-1		1-2	1-0	0-0	0-1	4-0	2-0	2-0	1-1	1-1	0-1	2-2	2-2
5	Lech Poznan	2-0	3-0	3-1	3-1		0-0	3-1	3-0	2-2	0-1	5-0	1-2	1-1	2-0	1-3	4-0
6	Legia Warszawa	3-1	3-0	0-0	0-1	1-0		3-2	0-0	2-0	3-0	2-0	1-1	1-0	1-0	1-2	1-1
7	LKS Lodz	2-0	2-0	3-2	2-2	1-2	1-1		2-1	1-1	0-0	0-1	2-0	0-1	0-3	0-2	
8	Odra Wodzislaw	1-0	0-0	0-2	0-1	2-0	1-2	2-1		3-0	2-2	2-2	3-1	1-1	2-0	0-2	0-1
9	Pogon Szczecin	3-2	1-0	1-0	0-1	2-3	3-1	1-1	1-0		1-0	1-0	3-2	2-2	1-2	0-4	3-2
10	Polonia Warszawa	4-2	4-0	2-0	1-0	1-2	0-0	2-1	2-1	2-2		3-0	0-0	0-1	2-1	1-3	3-1
11	Ruch Chorzow	0-0	1-1	2-1	2-1	2-1	0-1	1-2	0-2	1-1	0-0		1-0	1-0	2-1	1-1	0-0
12	Ruch Radzionkow	1-1	1-1	1-1	0-0	4-1	1-2	4-0	2-0	3-2	0-0	1-0		1-0	5-0	1-1	3-3
13	Stomil Olsztyn	4-1	0-2	2-1	2-1	0-2	1-2	1-0	3-1	3-1	1-0	1-0	0-0		2-1	1-2	1-1
14	Widzew Lodz	3-0	1-0	1-0	0-1	3-0	3-2	5-0	2-0	2-1	4-1	1-1	2-1	5-0		1-0	1-1
15	Wisla Krakow	1-0	4-0	4-1	2-1	2-1	4-1	1-1	2-1	4-0	1-3	4-1	6-0	3-0	3-1		0-1
16	Zaglebie Lubin	1-0	1-2	4-0	3-3	1-2	0-0	2-2	4-4	2-0	1-0	0-2	1-2	3-1	0-1	0-3	

LEAGUE CHAMPIONSHIP FINAL TABLE 98/99

			Home				Away					Total						
		P	W	D	L	F	A	W	D	L	F	A	W	D	L	F	A	P	GD
1	Wisla Krakow	30	12	1	2	41	12	11	3	1	34	11	23	4	3	75	23	73	+52
2	Widzew Lodz	30	12	2	1	34	8	6	0	9	16	25	18	2	10	50	33	56	+17
3	Legia Warszawa	30	9	4	2	22	8	7	4	4	19	17	16	8	6	41	25	56	+16
4	Lech Poznan	30	9	3	3	33	12	8	0	7	22	24	17	3	10	55	36	54	+19
5	Polonia Warszawa	30	9	3	3	27	14	4	4	7	11	17	13	7	10·	38	31	46	+7
6	Ruch Radzionkow	30	7	7	1	28	12	3	4	8	12	23	10	11	9	40	35	41	+5
7	Gornik Zabrze	30	5	6	4	19	14	4	6	5	15	17	9	12	9	34	31	39	+3
8	Zaglebie Lubin	30	5	4	6	23	22	4	7	4	19	22	9	11	10	42	44	38	-2
9	Stomil Olsztyn	30	9	2	4	22	15	1	5	9	7	23	10	7	13	29	38	37	-9
10	Ruch Chorzow	30	6	6	3	14	12	3	3	9	9	24	9	9	12	23	36	36	-13
11	Amica Wronki	30	9	2	4	23	13	0	5	10	8	26	9	7	14	31	39	34	-8
12	LKS Lodz	30	5	5	5	16	16	3	5	7	17	29	8	10	12	33	45	34	-12
13	Pogon Szczecin	30	9	2	4	23	20	0	4	11	10	34	9	6	15	33	54	33	-21
14	Odra Wodzislaw	30	6	4	5	19	15	2	4	9	14	26	8	8	14	33	41	32	-8
15	GKS Belchatow	30	4	3	8	16	23	3	4	8	10	25	7	7	16	26	48	28	-22
16	GKS Katowice	30	3	6	6	13	19	2	2	11	12	30	5	8	17	25	49	23	-24

the one-year ban handed to the club by UEFA for a ghastly incident at the home leg of the Parma tie when Italian international Dino Baggio was struck on the head by a flick-knife thrown from the crowd. Wisla made strenuous efforts over the following weeks and months to improve security at their ground and show UEFA that they could not be held responsible for one deranged supporter, but, inevitably, the appeals fell on deaf ears and the club was deprived of a place in the 1999/2000 Champions' League. There were considerable concerns that Tele-Fonika would withdraw their backing as a consequence of this but, unlike UEFA, they showed mercy and decided to stand by the club.

The banning of Wisla, however, did not mean that Poland as a whole would be denied a place in the Champions' League. UEFA decreed that the club finishing second in the league would be permitted to take Wisla's place, and this effectively revived interest in the closing weeks of the championship.

With one game to go there were three teams still in

TOP SCORERS

21	Tomasz FRANKOWSKI (Wisla Krakow)
20	Artur WICHNIAREK (Widzew Lodz)
14	Mariusz NOSAL (Odra Wodzislaw)
12	Marian JANOSZKA (Ruch Radzionkow)
	Bartosz KARWAN (Legia Warszawa)
	Piotr REISS (Lech Poznan)
11	Maciej ZURAWSKI (Lech Poznan)
	Mariusz SRUTWA (Ruch Chorzow/ Legia Warszawa)

NATIONAL TEAM RESULTS 98/99

15/07/98	Ukraine	A	Kiev	2-1	Trzeciak (8), Czereszewski (55)
18/08/98	Israel	H	Krakow	2-0	Trzeciak (24), Siadaczka (71)
06/09/98	Bulgaria (ECQ)	A	Bourgas	3-0	Czereszewski (19, 45), Iwan (48)
10/10/98	Luxembourg (ECQ)	H	Warsaw	3-0	Brzeczek (18), Juskowiak (33), Trzeciak (63)
10/11/98	Slovakia	A	Bratislava	3-1	Reiss (56), Kowalczyk (66, 75)
03/02/99	Malta	A	Ta' Qali	1-0	Klos (90)
10/02/99	Finland	N	Ta' Qali	1-1	Kowalczyk (1)
03/03/99	Armenia	H	Warsaw	1-0	Trzeciak (4)
27/03/99	England (ECQ)	A	Wembley	1-3	Brzeczek (28)
31/03/99	Sweden (ECQ)	H	Chorzow	0-1	
28/04/99	Czech Republic	H	Warsaw	2-1	Trzeciak (16), Wichniarek (49)
04/06/99	Bulgaria (ECQ)	H	Warsaw	2-0	Hajto (16), Iwan (62)
09/06/99	Luxembourg (ECQ)	A	Luxembourg	3-2	Siadaczka (21), Wichniarek (45), Iwan (68)
16/06/99	Brazil	N	Bangkok	0-2	
19/06/99	New Zealand	N	Bangkok	0-0	

NATIONAL TEAM APPEARANCES 98/99

Coach - Janusz WOJCIK	UKR	ISR	BUL	LUX	SVK	MLT	FIN	ARM	ENG	SWE	CZE	BUL	LUX	BRA	NZL	Cps	Gls
Kazimierz SIDORCZUK (04/03/67) - SK Sturm Graz (AUT)	G34	G46	G			s46	G46	s46		G						14	-
Jacek BAK (24/03/73) - Olympique Lyonnais (FRA)	D	D	D	s75		D46	M		M	s88	s70					23	1
Tomasz LAPINSKI (01/08/69) - Widzew Lodz	D		D	D	D	D	D	D	D	D	D	D	D			36	-
Jacek ZIELINSKI (10/10/67) - Legia Warszawa	D	D	D	D	D	D46	D	D	D	D87	D					33	1
Rafal SIADACZKA (21/02/72) - Widzew Lodz/FK Austria Wien (AUT)	D	s46	D	s70	D89	D	M59	D	M68	D81	M84	M	M			14	2
Piotr SWIERCZEWSKI (08/04/72) - SC Bastia (FRA)/Gamba Osaka (JPN)	M77	M61	M68	M		s46	s59		M46							41	1
Tomasz KLOS (07/03/73) - AJ Auxerre (FRA)	M	M72	s67			D	s70	D69	s46		s62		D			12	1
Jerzy BRZECZEK (18/03/71) - LASK Linz (AUT)/Maccabi Haifa (ISR)	M87	M	M	M		M81	M		M	M	s74	s66				42	4
Sylwester CZERESZEWSKI (04/10/71) - Legia Warszawa	M81	M67	M	M75	M75	s46	s90	s66								22	4
Miroslaw TRZECIAK (11/04/68) - LKS Lodz/CA Osasuna (ESP)	A64	A	A80	A		A82	A90	A46	A83	A	A65	A	A			19	8
Marcin KUZBA (15/04/77) - AJ Auxerre (FRA)	A46															2	-
Boguslaw WYPARLO (29/11/74) - LKS Lodz	s34				G		s46									3	-
Radoslaw MICHALSKI (21/09/69) - Widzew Lodz	s46		s68			M	M46	s46	M66		M88	M	M	M	M	25	-
Grzegorz KALICIAK (10/03/75) - Wisla Krakow	s64										s84					3	-
Andrzej JASKOT (26/01/71) - Aluminium Konin	s77															1	-
Marcin ZAJAC (19/05/75) - Widzew Lodz	s81															3	-
Grzegorz WEDZYNSKI (04/06/70) - Polonia Warszawa	s87										s87					2	-
Tomasz HAJTO (16/10/72) - MSV Duisburg (GER)		D55	M67	M62		M46	D70	M46		D	M62	M80	M66			24	3
Krzysztof RATAJCZYK (09/11/73) - SK Rapid Wien (AUT)		D46			D70					D						12	2
Jacek DEMBINSKI (20/12/69) - Hamburger SV (GER)		A46														10	-
Adam MATYSEK (19/07/68) - Bayer 04 Leverkusen (GER)	s46		G			G46		G46		G		G	G	G		25	-
Mariusz SRUTWA (15/07/71) - Ruch Chorzow	s46															5	-
Tomasz IWAN (12/06/71) - PSV (HOL)	s55	A	M			M	M	A	M	M	M					23	4
Tomasz KULAWIK (04/05/69) - Wisla Krakow	s61															2	-
Maciej MURAWSKI (20/02/74) - Legia Warszawa	s67															1	-
Tomasz WALDOCH (10/05/71) - VfL Bochum (GER)	s72						s69		D	D	D	D	D			52	2
Andrzej JUSKOWIAK (03/11/70) - VfL Wolfsburg (GER)		s80	A						A62	s83	A					32	13
Slawomir MAJAK (12/01/69) - FC Hansa Rostock (GER)					s62	M46			s46	M69		s80	s87			21	-
Kazimierz WEGRZYN (13/04/67) - Wisla Krakow						D	s46	D								20	-
Ryszard CZERWIEC (28/02/68) - Wisla Krakow						M	s81		s46							26	-
Marek KOZMINSKI (07/02/71) - Brescia (ITA)					M61											24	1
Piotr REISS (20/06/72) - Lech Poznan/Hertha BSC Berlin (GER)					A69		s72									2	1
Wojciech KOWALCZYK (14/04/72) - UD Las Palmas (ESP)					A82	A72	A			s68	s69					39	11
Bogdan ZAJAC (16/11/72) - Wisla Krakow					s61											1	-
Maciej ZURAWSKI (12/09/76) - Lech Poznan					s69	s82				s71				M	M	5	-
Miroslaw SZYMKOWIAK (12/11/76) - Widzew Lodz					s75											3	-
Bartosz KARWAN (13/01/76) - Legia Warszawa					s82											1	-
Jacek KRZYNOWEK (15/05/76) - GKS Belchatow					s89											1	-
Krzysztof NOWAK (29/09/75) - VfL Wolfsburg (GER)									s46		M70	M74	M			7	1
Dariusz ADAMCZUK (21/10/69) - Dundee (SCO)									s46	s81						10	1
Artur WICHNIAREK (28/02/77) - Widzew Lodz									s62		A71	A59	A87	A66	A	6	2
Tomasz FRANKOWSKI (16/08/74) - Wisla Krakow											s65	s59				2	-
Grzegorz TOMALA (06/09/74) - Odra Wodzislaw														G	G	2	-
Przemyslaw URBANIAK (09/03/75) - Lech Poznan														D		1	-
Maciej STOLARCZYK (15/01/72) - Pogon Szczecin														D	D	3	-
Dariusz GESIOR (09/10/69) - Widzew Lodz														M	M	23	1
Maciej TERLECKI (09/03/77) - Widzew Lodz														M	D	2	-
Michal ZEWLAKOW (22/04/76) - KSK Beveren (BEL)														M85	D74	2	-
Mariusz NOSAL (13/10/74) - Odra Wodzislaw														A46	A68	2	-
Jacek CHANKO (25/01/74) - Stomil Olsztyn														s46	M	2	-
Igor SYPNIEWSKI (10/11/75) - Panathinaikos (GRE)														s66	s68	2	-
Ariel JAKUBOWSKI (07/09/77) - LKS Lodz														s85	s57	2	-
Krzysztof PISKULA (19/08/73) - Lech Poznan														M57		1	-
Rafal SZWED (18/07/73) - Stomil Olsztyn															s74	1	-

contention to finish as runners-up - Lech Poznan, Legia Warsaw and Widzew Lodz. Lech held a one-point lead over their rivals, but when they fell to a shock 1-4 defeat away to Ruch Radzionkow, the fight became a private affair between Legia and Widzew. Both clubs faced local rivals and they knew that they would have to score as many goals as possible in order to outdo the other on

goal difference. Legia, who began with a one-goal advantage, won 3-0 against Polonia, but Widzew did even better, destroying lacklustre LKS 5-0 to take the prize.

Rumours were rife that LKS had done a deal with Widzew to allow them to score as many goals as they required. Nothing was proved, but the 1997/98 champions certainly left a sour taste in the mouth at the end

EUROPEAN CUPS 98/99

CHAMPIONS' CUP
● LKS LODZ
Preliminary round KAPAZ GANJA (AZB)
H 4-1   Cebula (12), Trzeciak (50p, 76p), Wieszczycki (73)
Wyparlo; Pawlak, Bendkowski, Lenart, Darlington (Jakubowski 46), Kos (Pluciennik 58), Wyciszkiewicz, Niznik, Cebula (Paszulewicz 72), Wieszczycki, Trzeciak.
A 3-1   Trzeciak (44, 49), Wieszczycki (81)
Wyparlo; Pawlak (Paszulewicz 70), Bendkowski, Lenart (Jakubowski 33), Darlington (Pluciennik 72), Kos, Niznik, Wyciszkiewicz, Cebula, Trzeciak, Wieszczycki.

Qualifying round MANCHESTER UNITED (ENG)
A 0-2
Wyparlo; Krysiak, Bendkowski, Pawlak, Darlington (Jakubowski 79), Cebula, Kos, Wyciszkiewicz, Zuberek (Paszulewicz 68), Niznik (Rodrigo Carbone 53), Wieszczycki.
H 0-0
Wyparlo; Pawlak, Bendkowski, Krysiak, Jakubowski (Bugaj 84), Kos, Wyciszkiewicz, Niznik, Lenart (Pluciennik 81), Zuberek (Matys 51), Wieszczycki.

CUP WINNERS' CUP
● AMICA WRONKI
Qualifying round HIBERNIANS (MLT)
H 4-0   Kryszalowicz (36), Prerada (56), Sobocinski (63, 75)
Strozynski; Bosacki (Siara 69), Malachowski, Bajor, Przerada, Motyka, Sokolowski (Kasperski 85), Jackiewicz, Matlak, Krol (Sobocinski 61), Kryszalowicz.
A 1-0   Kryszalowicz (70)
Strozynski; Koscielniak (Motyka 22), Malachowski, Bajor, Bosacki, Przerada (Kalita 80), Sokolowski, Jackiewicz, Dawidowski, Kryszalowicz, Sobocinski (Krol 70).

1st round SC HEERENVEEN (HOL)
A 1-3   Krol (64)
Strozynski; Koscielniak, Malachowski, Bosacki, Bajor, Przerada, Jackiewicz, Sokolowski (Motyka 80), Matlak (Dawidowski 62), Krol (Sobocinski 64), Kryszalowicz.
H 0-1
Strozynski; Koscielniak, Malachowski, Bajor, Przerada (Kalita 84), Bosacki, Jackiewicz (Siara 64), Sokolwski (Sobocinski 73), Dawidowski, Krol, Kryszalowicz.

UEFA CUP
● POLONIA WARSZAWA
Preliminary round TALLINNA SADAM (EST)
A 2-0   Olisadebe (34), Bak (80)
Szczesny; Zvirzdauskas, Galuszka, Kaliszan, Bartczak (Vencevicius 84), Jalocha, Wedzynski, Bak, Dabrowski, Mikulenas (Moskal 75), Olisadebe (Sadzawicki 64).
H 3-1   Moskal (8), Wedzynski (16), Bak (21)
Szczesny; Zvirgzdauskas (Zewlakow Mi. 81), Galuszka, Kaliszan, Jalocha, Bartczak, Wedzynski (Vencevicius 73), Bak, Dabrowski (Mazurkiewicz 65), Mikulenas, Moskal.

Qualifying round DINAMO MOSKVA (RUS)
H 0-1
Szczesny; Sadzawicki, Galuszka, Zvirgzdauskas, Jalocha, Wdowczyk (Zewlakow Ma. 85), Wedzynski, Vencevicius (Bak 76), Dabrowski, Moskal (Mikulenas 58), Olisadebe.
A 0-1
Szczesny; Zvirgzdauskas, Galuszka, Zewlakow Mi., Bartczak, Sadzawicki, Wedzynski, Wdowczyk (Jalocha 66), Dabrowski, Olisadebe (Bak 69), Mikulenas (Moskal 81).

● WISLA KRAKOW
Preliminary round NEWTOWN (WAL)
A 0-0
Sarnat; Kaluzny, Zajac B., Wegrzyn, Zajac M., Pater (Nowak 85), Czerwiec, Sunday, Kulawik, Nicinski (Dubicki 46), Kaliciak.
H 7-0   Kulawik (28, 47, 51), Sunday (35), Dubicki (54), Pater (61, 66)
Sarnat; Matyja, Zajac B., Wegrzyn, Pater, Czerwiec (Nowak 54), Sunday, Kulawik (Piszczek 70), Kaliciak, Dubicki, Nicinski (Skrzynski 46).

Qualifying round TRABZONSPOR (TUR)
H 5-1   Dubicki (3), Kulawik (33, 71, 80), Zajac B. (89)
Sarnat; Matyja, Zajac B., Wegrzyn, Pater, Sunday, Czerwiec, Kulawik, Kaliciak (Bukalski 82), Dubicki (Frankowski 30), Nicinski.
A 2-1   Sunday (54), Kulawik (63)
Sarnat; Matyja, Zajac B., Zajac M., Wegrzyn, Pater (Dubicki 62), Sunday, Czerwiec (Bukalski 81), Kaliciak, Kulawik, Nicinski (Frankowski 77).

1st round MARIBOR TEATANIC (SLO)
A 2-0   Frankowski (22), Pater (45)
Sarnat; Zajac M., Zajac B., Wegrzyn, Pater, Czerwiec, Bukalski, Sunday (Dubicki 67), Kaliciak, Frankowski, Nicinski.
H 3-0   Zajac M. (85, 89), Kulawik (90)
Sarnat; Zajac M., Zajac B., Matyja, Wegrzyn, Pater (Zurek 90), Bukalski, Czerwiec, Kulawik, Nicinski, Frankowski (Nowak 82).

2nd round PARMA (ITA)
H 1-1   Kulawik (68)
Sarnat; Zajac M., Zajac B., Wegrzyn, Pater, Bukalski, Czerwiec, Kulawik, Kaliciak (Matyja 89), Frankowski, Dubicki.
A 1-2   Zajac B. (90)
Sarnat; Zajac M., Zajac B., Wegrzyn, Matyja (Nowak 61), Pater, Bukalski, Kulawik, Frankowski, Kaliciak, Dubicki.

● LKS LODZ
1st round AS MONACO (FRA)
H 1-3   Matys (10)
Wyparlo; Krysiak, Kos, Bendkowski, Pawlak, Lenart, Cebula, Wieszczycki (Niznik 65), Jakubowski (Zuberek 68), Matys, Darlington.
A 0-0
Wyparlo; Krysiak, Kos, Lenart, Pawlak, Wieszczycki, Jakubowski, Niznik, Darlington, Cebula, Matys (Zuberek 77).

of a season which had seen them struggling to avoid relegation for a long period, with owner Antoni Ptak even taking the desperate measure of allowing spectators in free to the club's home games in order to drum up support. LKS eventually finished safe in 12th place but the pre-season departure of their two best players, defender Tomasz Klos (to Auxerre) and 1998 Polish Player of the Year Miroslaw Trzeciak (to Osasuna), was a double handicap they had seriously failed to overcome.

City rivals Widzew, on the other hand, were elated to finish second and reach the Champions' League after missing out altogether on Europe in 1998/99. A very rocky road seemed to lie ahead when they lost their opening game of the season 5-0 - a result which brought new coach Andrzej Pyrdol the sack after just one match in charge - but the consistent efforts of the team's top players, such as libero Tomasz Lapinski, midfielders Radoslaw Michalski and Dariusz Gesior and young striker Artur Wichniarek, got the team back on track. Further encouragement came with the welcome return from long-term injury of one of Polish football's most promising players, Marek Citko.

Legia Warsaw were considered as the only potential challengers to Wisla Krakow at the start of the season. That was the theory, but the practice was rather different. The

club were beset by internal feuds all season long. Players openly criticised the actions of the club directors, and there was a mutiny against coach Jerzy Kopa. Stefan Bialas replaced him, but although Legia at times played some attractive football, they could find no consistency. Third place, which brought with it a UEFA Cup spot, was probably about as much as they deserved.

Against all odds the Polish Cup was retained by Amica Wronki. The little-known club from the west of Poland encountered major difficulties in the league during the spring, scoring just seven goals in their 15 matches. But the Cup brought the best out of them, especially the semi-final against Widzew Lodz, where they prevailed after a tense, long drawn-out penalty shoot-out following two 1-1 draws. The final, in nearby Poznan, proved slightly less taxing, and they were deserving 1-0 winners against GKS Belchatow, the all-important goal coming early in the second half from right-back Miroslaw Siara, one of just five survivors from Amica's Cup final win over Aluminium Konin at the same venue a year earlier.

Amica's triumph was achieved with their fourth different coach of the season, Stefan Majewski. Hiring and firing coaches was also a common occurence elsewhere, with just four clubs in the new 16-team First Division electing to hold on to their original choice for the duration

---

DOMESTIC CUP 98/99

1/16 FINALS
RKS Radomsko 1, Gornik Zabrze 0
Wawel Krakow 1, Grunwald Ruda Slaska 0
KemBud (Karkonosze) Jelenia Gora 1, Wisla Krakow 3
Aluminium Konin 6, Pogon Szczecin 0
Chemik Police 0, Amica Wronki 2
Cracovia Krakow 2, GKS Katowice 3
Groclin Dyskobolia Grodzisk 2, Zaglebie Lubin 2
(aet; 4-3 on pens.)
Hetman Zamosc 0, GKS Belchatow 4
Korona Kielce 2, Polonia Warszawa 0
KSZO Ostrowiec 0, LKS Lodz 1
Lechia/Polonia Gdansk 2, Stomil Olsztyn 3
Rakow Czestochowa 0, Widzew Lodz 0
(aet; 2-4 on pens.)
Naprzod Rydultpwy 1, Ruch Chorzow 1
(aet; 3-4 on pens.)
Petrochemia Plock 2, Lech Poznan 1 (aet)
Swit Nowy Dwor Mazowiecki 1, Legia Warszawa 3
Varta Namyslow (Odra/Varta Opole) 1,
Odra Wodzislaw 1 (aet; 2-4 on pens.)

1/8 FINALS
RKS Radomsko 3, Wisla Krakow 1
Aluminium Konin 1, Odra Wodzislaw 0
Amica Wronki 2, LKS Lodz 1
Petrochemia Plock 0, Stomil Olsztyn 1

GKS Belchatow 0, Legia Warszawa 0
(aet; 3-2 on pens.)
Groclin Dyskobolia Grodzisk 0, Widzew Lodz 4
Korona Kielce 1, GKS Katowice 0
Wawel Krakow 0, Ruch Chorzow 3

QUARTER-FINALS
Korona Kielce 2 (Pacon 87, Pastuszka 89),
GKS Belchatow 1 (Patalan 43)
GKS Belchatow 1 (Nocon A. 17), Korona Kielce 0
(2-2; GKS Belchatow on away goal)

Ruch Chorzow 2 (Wlodarczyk 2, Bizacki 71), RKS
Radomsko 1 (Lamch 10)
RKS Radomsko 0,
Ruch Chorzow 2 (Jamroz 31, Jordan 90)
(Ruch Chorzow 4-1)

Widzew Lodz 3 (Gesior 4, Czajkowski 13, 53),
Aluminium Konin 0
Aluminium Konin 1 (Lisewski 56), Widzew Lodz 0
(Widzew Lodz 3-1)

Amica Wronki 3 (Kryszalowicz 56, Dubiela 73, 90),
Stomil Olsztyn 0
Stomil Olsztyn 1 (Ramelis 38),
Amica Wronki 1 (Kalu 90)
(Amica Wronki 4-1)

SEMI-FINALS
GKS Belchatow 0, Ruch Chorzow 0
Ruch Chorzow 0, GKS Belchatow 1 (Krzynowek 64)
(GKS Belchatow 1-0)

Amica Wronki 1 (Bosacki 58),
Widzew Lodz 1 (Gesior 62)
Widzew Lodz 1 (Gesior 72), Amica Wronki 1 (Kalu 24)
(aet)
(2-2; Amica Wronki 8-7 on pens.)

FINAL
13/06/99, Poznan
AMICA WRONKI 1 Siara (47)
GKS BELCHATOW 0
referee - Granat
AMICA WRONKI - Strozynski; Siara, Kukielka, Bajor,
Bosacki, Wodkiewicz, Sokolowski (Bieniuk 73), Kalita
(Kasperski 57), Dubiela (Dawidowski 81),
Kryszalowicz, Kalu.
GKS BELCHATOW - Krupski; Wilczok (Nocon 78),
Wagner, Kaczmarek (Nowicki 66), Hinc, Szarpak,
Skinderis, Berensztajn, Krzynowek, Rezzniczek
(Bykowski 55), Patalan.

PLAYERS OF THE SEASON

TOMASZ FRANKOWSKI

Although no spring chicken at 24, Tomasz Frankowski was voted Polish football's 'Discovery of the Year' at the end of 1998. The award was not inappropriate because the Wisla Krakow striker had become something of a forgotten figure in Polish football since quitting his homeland for France as a teenager after a highly promising youth career. Spells with Strasbourg, Poitiers and Martigues plus a brief stint in Japan with Nagoya Grampus 8 kept him out of the limelight, but his return to Poland in the summer of 1998 met with immediate success as his goals and electric pace inspired Wisla into an unassailable lead in the Polish title race. He finished the season as the league's top marksman, with 21 goals, and was rewarded with his first senior caps for the Polish national team.

JACEK ZIELINSKI

He has been one of Poland's leading international figures for a number of years, but in 1998/99 Jacek Zieleinski had arguably his best season yet, both for his club, Legia Warsaw, and for his country, where his fine understanding with central defensive partner Tomasz Lapinski reached an impressive new stage of development. The 32-year-old has pace, great strength in the tackle and is very cool under pressure. He also distributes the ball intelligently from the back and is dominant in the air. The chance to prove his worth abroad has probably now passed him by, but he knows he is among friends and admirers at Legia, where he has been the team's key defender since arriving from Zaglebie Lubin in 1992.

of the campaign. Apart from championship-winning Wisla coach Smuda, the other men with the staying power were Lech Poznan's Adam Topolski, Gornik Zabrze's Jan Zurek and GKS Katowice's Marek Koniarek.

That Koniarek remained in place was quite astonishing given that Katowice finished rock-bottom of the league with just five wins from their 30 games. They were accompanied down into Division Two by defeated Cup finalists GKS Belchatow, with their places being taken by two teams relegated just 12 months earlier - Petrochemia Plock and Groclin Dyskobolia Grodzisk.

Another Polish coach who remained in place during 1998/99 was national team boss Janusz Wojcik. Indeed, he was voted as the country's Coach of the Year following Poland's excellent start to the Euro 2000 qualifying campaign, which brought back-to-back 3-0 victories over Bulgaria and Luxembourg. Those wins helped to contribute towards a remarkable seven-match winning sequence that lasted nine months and was only brought to an end in February 1999 with a 1-1 draw against Finland in Cyprus - a match in which striker Wojciech Kowalczyk scored the 1,000th goal in the history of the Polish national team.

Wojcik's men failed their two big tests away to England (1-3) and at home to Sweden (0-1) but another pair of victories at the beginning of June over Bulgaria and Luxembourg put the Poles right back in contention for a play-off place, with the decisive match being the September 8 head-to-head with old rivals England - a match switched from Chorzow to Warsaw in a bid to generate a more hostile atmosphere.

While Wojcik and his players were doing their best to win back popular support for the national team, a highly-publicised year-long power struggle between the autocratic president of the Polish Federation (PZPN), Marian Dziurowicz, and the Minister for Sport, Jacek Debski, threatened to undermine everything. When FIFA intervened to settle the dispute, there was a serious risk that all Polish teams, the national side included, might be expelled from international competition.

Fortunately, that did not arise, but the dispute dragged on interminably, with almost everyone in the country demanding that Dziurowicz resign, only for the PZPN boss to dig his heels in ever deeper at every renewed request for him to go. A dozen First Division clubs went on strike for two rounds of the championship in a bid to depose him, but to no avail. Finally, at the end of the season, elections were called at FIFA's behest and Dziurowicz was at last voted out of office, to be replaced by former international referee Michal Listkiewicz.

The new man's appointment was warmly welcomed by everyone concerned with the future of Polish football. His reformist manifesto had widespread appeal, especially to the clubs, who were promised a greater degree of administrative autonomy as well as a larger share of income from broadcasting and sponsorship fees.

INTERNATIONAL HONOURS

World Cup Finals appearances: 1938, 1974 (3rd), 1978 (2nd phase), 1982 (3rd), 1986 (2nd round)

AMICA WRONKI

Klub Sportowy Amica Wronki
ul. Lesna 15a, 64-510 Wronki
tel - (067) 2540724
fax - (067) 2540724
Year of Formation - 1992
President - Wojciech Kaszynski
Secretary - Ryszard Forbich
Coach - Wojciech Wasikiewicz; Marian Kurowski;
Mieczyslaw Broniszewski; Stefan Majewski
Stadium - Amica (6,000)

MAJOR HONOURS
Domestic Cup - (2) 1998, 1999.

APPEARANCES 98/99

		P	Ap	(s)	Gls
Marek BAJOR	D	27			1
Jaroslaw BIENIUK	M		(1)		
Radoslaw BILINSKI	M	17	(1)		
Bartosz BOSACKI	D	22			1
Tomasz DAWIDOWSKI	M	15	(13)		1
Piotr DUBIELA	M	11	(8)		1
Dariusz JACKIEWICZ	M	13	(1)		5
Miroslaw KALITA	M	9	(9)		1
Maxwell KANU (NIG)	A	7	(3)		2
Piotr KASPERSKI	M	1	(3)		
Ireneusz KOSCIELNIAK	D	11	(1)		
Grzegorz KROL	A	13	(3)		9
Pawel KRYSZALOWICZ	A	26	(1)		8
Mariusz KUKIELKA	M	14			1
Tomasz LEWANDOWSKI	M	1	(2)		
Slawomir MACIUSZEK	M	1	(3)		
Zbigniew MALACHOWSKI	D	20	(2)		
Grzegorz MATLAK	M	11	(3)		
Czeslaw MICHNIEWICZ	G	4			
Grzegorz MOTYKA	M	7	(4)		
Pawel PECZAK	D	6	(1)		
Andrzej PRZERADA	D	21	(1)		1
Miroslaw SIARA	D	9	(4)		
Andrei SINITSYN (BLS)	M	4	(1)		
Remigiusz SOBOCINSKI	A	7	(12)		
Tomasz SOKOLOWSKI	M	23	(1)		
Jaroslaw STROZUNSKI	G	26			
Tomasz SUWARY	A		(5)		
Grzegorz WODKIEWICZ	D	4	(4)		

25/07/98	Lech Poznan	H	2-1	Kryszalowicz, Jackiewicz
01/08/98	Ruch Radzionkow	A	1-1	Jackiewicz
22/08/98	Legia Warszawa	A	1-3	Kryszalowicz
30/08/98	GKS Belchatow	H	2-0	Kryszalowicz, Krol
09/09/98	Wisla Krakow	A	0-1	
12/09/98	Ruch Chorzow	H	2-0	Krol 2
20/09/98	LKS Lodz	A	0-2	
23/09/98	GKS Katowice	H	4-0	Kryszalowicz 2, Krol, Jackiewicz
26/09/98	Gornik Zabrze	H	0-0	
04/10/98	Pogon Szczecin	A	2-3	Jackiewicz, Kalita
17/10/98	Odra Wodzislaw	H	3-1	Bosacki, Krol (p), Dubiela
24/10/98	Polonia Warszawa	A	2-4	Krol (p), Kryszalowicz (p)
31/10/98	Zaglebie Lubin	H	2-1	Jackiewicz, Krol
14/11/98	Stomil Olsztyn	A	1-4	Bajor
18/11/98	Widzew Lodz	H	2-3	Krol 2
26/02/99	Lech Poznan	A	0-2	
06/03/99	Ruch Radzionkow	H	1-0	Kryszalowicz
14/03/99	Widzew Lodz	A	0-3	
20/03/99	GKS Katowice	A	0-0	
03/04/99	Legia Warszawa	H	0-2	
10/04/99	GKS Belchatow	A	1-1	Dawidowski
18/04/99	Wisla Krakow	H	1-3	Kalu
24/04/99	Ruch Chorzow	A	0-0	
01/05/99	LKS Lodz	H	1-2	Kukielka
08/05/99	Gornik Zabrze	A	0-0	
12/05/99	Pogon Szczecin	H	2-0	Kalu, Kryszalowicz
15/05/99	Odra Wodzislaw	A	0-1	
22/05/99	Polonia Warszawa	H	1-0	Przerada
26/05/99	Zaglebie Lubin	A	0-1	
29/05/99	Stomil Olsztyn	H	0-0	

GKS BELCHATOW

CLUB DIRECTORY

GKS Belchatow
Ul. Sportowa 3
97-400 Belchatow
tel - (044) 6322078/6325569
fax - (044) 6324572
Year of Formation - 1977
President - Zdzislaw Drobniewski
Secretary - Jozef Swider
Coach - Krzysztof Pawlak; Marek Pochopien
Stadium - GKS (7,000)

APPEARANCES 98/99

	P	Ap	(s)	Gls
Jacek BERENSZTAJN	M	18	(1)	2
Maciej BYKOWSKI	M	22	(1)	4
Grzegorz CHEDA	M	12	(8)	1
Andriy DANAYEV (UKR)	D		(1)	
Bartosz HINC	M	23	(3)	2
Marek JAKOBCZAK	A	6	(21)	4
Marcin KACZMAREK	D	12		
Maciej KALKOWSKI	M	12	(8)	
Slawomir KONKIEWICZ	M	13		
Andrzej KRETEK	G	1		
Juroslaw KRUPSKI	G	26		
Jacek KRZYNOWEK	M	27		6
Adam NOCON	D	10	(1)	
Marek NOWICKI	M	1	(1)	
Dariusz PATALAN	A	25	(4)	5
Pawel PRANAGAL	M		(1)	
Piotr PRZERYWACZ	D	22		
Aleksander PTAK	G	3	(1)	
Grzegorz RASIAK	M	1	(5)	1
Dariusz RZEZNICZEK	M	14	(4)	
Marius SKINDERIS (LIT)	M	13	(4)	
Adrian SOBCZYNSKI	A	4	(2)	
Dainius SULIAUSKAS (LIT)	M		(1)	
Piotr SZARPAK	M	18		1
Sylwester SZKUDLAREK	D	17	(7)	
Grzegorz WAGNER	D	10		
Dariusz WALECIAK	M	1		
Grzegorz WILCZOK	D	19	(3)	

LEAGUE RESULTS 1998/99

25/07/98	Polonia Warszawa	H	0-1	
01/08/98	Zaglebie Lubin	A	2-1	Patalan, Cheda
23/08/98	Ruch Radzionkow	H	2-1	Patalan 2
30/08/98	Amica Wronki	A	0-2	
09/09/98	GKS Katowice	H	1-2	Krzynowek (p)
12/09/98	Legia Warszawa	A	0-3	
18/09/98	Widzew Lodz	H	3-2	Bykowski, Krzynowek 2 (2p)
23/09/98	Lech Poznan	A	0-3	
26/09/98	Wisla Krakow	H	0-3	
03/10/98	Ruch Chorzow	A	1-1	Krzynowek
17/10/98	LKS Lodz	H	2-3	Jakobczak, Hinc
24/10/98	Gornik Zabrze	A	3-1	Patalan, Bykowski 2
31/10/98	Pogon Szczecin	H	2-0	Patalan, Jakobczak
14/11/98	Odra Wodzislaw	A	0-0	
18/11/98	Stomil Olsztyn	H	1-0	Jakobczak
27/02/99	Polonia Warszawa	A	0-4	
06/03/99	Zaglebie Lubin	H	0-1	
14/03/99	Stomil Olsztyn	A	2-0	Bykowski, Szarpak
20/03/99	Lech Poznan	H	1-3	Jakobczak
03/04/99	Ruch Radzionkow	A	1-1	Krzynowek
10/04/99	Amica Wronki	H	1-1	Krzynowek
17/04/99	GKS Katowice	A	1-1	Hinc
24/04/99	Legia Warszawa	H	1-2	Berensztajn (p)
01/05/99	Widzew Lodz	A	0-1	
08/05/99	Wisla Krakow	A	0-4	
12/05/99	Ruch Chorzow	H	0-2	
15/05/99	LKS Lodz	A	0-2	
22/05/99	Gornik Zabrze	H	1-1	Berensztajn
26/05/99	Pogon Szczecin	A	0-1	
29/05/99	Odra Wodzislaw	H	1-1	Rasiak

GKS KATOWICE

CLUB DIRECTORY

Gorniczy Klub Sportowy Katowice
ul. Bukowa 1
40-145 Katowice
tel - (032) 2500041/2501857
fax - (032) 2501825
Year of Formation - 1964
President - Stanislaw Wilk
Secretary - Dariusz Wolny
Coach - Marek Koniarek
Stadium - GKS (10,000)

MAJOR HONOURS
Domestic Cup - (3) 1986, 1991, 1993.

APPEARANCES 98/99

		P	Ap	(s)	Gls
Artur ADAMUS	D	20	(3)	1
Artur ANDRUSZCZAK	M	19	(4)	3
Adam BALA	M	24	(3)	1
Adam BOSOWSKI	D	8	(4)	
Dariusz DUDEK	M	13		1
Dariusz DZWIGALA	M	9		
Marcin FLOREK	A	1	(9)	2
Piotr JACYNA	D	6	(13)	
Pawel JERMAKOWICZ	D	3	(4)	
Ireneusz KOSCIELNIAK	D	8	(2)	
Marek KUBISZ	A	24	(5)	5
Adam KUCZ	M	14	(4)	2
Michal LORENS	M		(2)	
Mariusz LUNCIK	G	14	(1)	
Zbigniew MANDZIEJEWICZ	D	21		1
Pawel MIASZKIEWICZ	M	12		3
Mariusz MUSZALIK	A	23	(6)	2
Grzegorz OBERAJ	A	1	(9)	1
Adam OLCZAK	D	1	(2)	
Tomasz OWCZAREK	M	6	(8)	1
Pawel PECZAK	M	12		
Piotr PLEWNIA	A		(1)	
Marcin POLARZ	A	2	(2)	
Slawomir RYDEL	G	5		
Wojciech SZALA	D	23	(2)	1
Artur SZYMCZYK	M	21	(5)	
Jaroslaw TKOCZ	G	11		
Miroslaw WIDUCH	M	29		

LEAGUE RESULTS 1998/99

25/07/98	Stomil Olsztyn	H	1-0	Florek
01/08/98	Lech Poznan	A	1-3	Muszalik
08/08/98	Ruch Radzionkow	H	1-0	Andruszczak
22/08/98	Widzew Lodz	H	0-2	
29/08/98	Legia Warszawa	H	1-3	Bala
09/09/98	GKS Belchatow	A	2-1	Andruszczak, Kucz
12/09/98	Wisla Krakow	H	1-2	Florek
20/09/98	Ruch Chorzow	A	1-2	Kubisz
23/09/98	Amica Wronki	A	0-4	
26/09/98	LKS Lodz	H	1-1	Miaszkiewicz
02/10/98	Gornik Zabrze	A	1-2	Miaszkiewicz
17/10/98	Pogon Szczecin	H	1-0	Kubisz
24/10/98	Odra Wodzislaw	A	2-0	Szala, Miaszkiewicz
31/10/98	Polonia Warszawa	H	1-3	Oberaj
15/11/98	Zaglebie Lubin	A	0-4	
27/02/99	Stomil Olsztyn	A	1-2	og (Holc)
07/03/99	Lech Poznan	H	1-2	Muszalik
13/03/99	Ruch Radzionkow	A	1-1	Mandziejewicz
20/03/99	Amica Wronki	H	0-0	
02/04/99	Widzew Lodz	A	0-1	
10/04/99	Legia Warszawa	A	0-0	
17/04/99	GKS Belchatow	H	1-1	Kubisz
23/04/99	Wisla Krakow	A	1-4	Owczarek
30/04/99	Ruch Chorzow	H	0-1	
08/05/99	LKS Lodz	A	2-3	Kubisz, Kucz
12/05/99	Gornik Zabrze	H	1-1	Kubisz
16/05/99	Pogon Szczecin	A	0-1	
22/05/99	Odra Wodzislaw	H	1-1	Andruszczak
26/05/99	Polonia Warszawa	A	0-2	
29/05/99	Zaglebie Lubin	H	2-2	Dudek, Adamus

GORNIK ZABRZE

CLUB DIRECTORY

SSA Gornik Zabrze
Ul. Roosevelta 81
41-800 Zabrze
tel - (032) 2714926/2710941
fax - (032) 2710530
Year of Formation - 1948
President - Stanislaw Ploskon
Secretary - Stanislaw Oslizlo
Coach - Jan Zurek
Stadium - Gornik (20,000)

MAJOR HONOURS
League Championship - (14)
1957, 1959, 1961, 1963, 1964, 1965, 1966,
1967, 1971, 1972, 1985, 1986, 1987, 1988.
Domestic Cup - (6)
1965, 1968, 1969, 1970, 1971, 1972.

APPEARANCES 98/99

	P	Ap	(s)	Gls
Mieczyslaw AGAFON	M	23		1
Andrzej BLEDZEWSKI	G	30		
Marcin BROSZ	M	12	(11)	
Marcin CEBULA	M	4	(3)	
Tomasz DRAGAN	M		(3)	
Dariusz DZWIGALA	M	13		1
Daniel GACEK	A	13	(10)	5
Piotr GIERCZAK	A	27	(2)	9
Arkadiusz KAMPKA	A	11	(1)	2
Rafal KOCYBA	D	3	(1)	
Robert KOLASA	D	25	(1)	1
Adam KOMPALA	M	27		1
Marcin KONDZIELNIK	M	1	(4)	
Kamil KOSOWSKI	D	29		
Maciej KRZETOWSKI	D	7	(2)	
Grzegorz LEKKI	D	29		3
Arkadiusz MATEJKO	M	10	(7)	
Tomasz PRASNAL	A	4	(6)	1
Miroslaw PRASZELIK	A	1	(3)	
Michal PROBIERZ	M	26	(1)	3
Patryk RACHWAL	M		(1)	
Piotr ROCKI	M	8	(11)	4
Janusz SLATINSCHEK	M		(2)	
Tomasz SOBCZAK	A	2	(15)	2
Jacek WISNIEWSKI	D	25	(1)	1
Mariusz WLOKA	D		(2)	

LEAGUE RESULTS 1998/99

25/07/98	LKS Lodz	A	2-2	Kampka, Probierz (p)
01/08/98	Widzew Lodz	A	1-0	Kampka
22/08/98	Polonia Warszawa	H	2-0	Lekki, Gierczak
29/08/98	Zaglebie Lubin	A	3-3	Lekki, Gierczak, Dzwigala
09/09/98	Stomil Olsztyn	H	1-1	Gacek
12/09/98	Lech Poznan	A	1-3	Gacek
19/09/98	Ruch Radzionkow	H	1-1	Gacek
23/09/98	Odra Wodzislaw	A	1-0	Gierczak
26/09/98	Amica Wronki	A	0-0	
02/10/98	GKS Katowice	H	2-1	Kolasa, Probierz (p)
18/10/98	Legia Warszawa	A	1-0	Sobczak
24/10/98	GKS Belchatow	H	1-3	Gierczak
30/10/98	Wisla Krakow	A	1-2	Agafon
14/11/98	Ruch Chorzow	H	2-0	Gierczak, Rocki
18/11/98	Pogon Szczecin	H	4-0	Probierz (p), Gierczak, Rocki 2
27/02/99	LKS Lodz	H	0-0	
06/03/99	Widzew Lodz	H	0-1	
13/03/99	Pogon Szczecin	A	1-0	Gierczak
20/03/99	Odra Wodzislaw	H	0-1	
03/04/99	Polonia Warszawa	A	0-1	
10/04/99	Zaglebie Lubin	H	2-2	Gacek, Gierczak
18/04/99	Stomil Olsztyn	A	1-2	Lekki
23/04/99	Lech Poznan	H	1-2	Gacek
01/05/99	Ruch Radzionkow	A	0-0	
08/05/99	Amica Wronki	H	0-0	
12/05/99	GKS Katowice	A	1-1	Kompala
15/05/99	Legia Warszawa	H	1-0	Wisniewski
22/05/99	GKS Belchatow	A	1-1	Sobczak
26/05/99	Wisla Krakow	H	2-2	Rocki, Prasnal
29/05/99	Ruch Chorzow	A	1-2	Gierczak

LECH POZNAN

CLUB DIRECTORY

Wielkopolski Klub Pilkarski Lech Poznan
Ul. Bulgarska 5/7
60-320 Poznan
tel - (061) 8673061
fax - (061) 8672661
Year of Formation - 1922
President - Ryszard Dolata
Secretary - Roman Jakobczak
Coach - Adam Topolski
Stadium - Lech (15,000)

MAJOR HONOURS
League Championship - (5)
1983, 1984, 1990, 1992, 1993.
Domestic Cup - (3) 1982, 1984, 1988.

APPEARANCES 98/99

		P	Ap	(s)	Gls
Jaroslaw ARASZKIEWICZ	A	14	(1)	6	
Tomasz AUGUSTYNIAK	D	30			
Tadeusz BARTNIK	D		(2)		
Maciej BYKOWSKI	M	1	(1)		
Marcin DRAJER	D	7	(5)		
Sekou DRAME (GUI)	D		(7)		
Arkadiusz GLOWACKI	D	30		1	
Michal GOLINSKI	M	1	(8)		
Bleriot HEUYOT TOBIT (CMR)	M		(1)		
JUSTIN Chidi Nnoram (NIG)	A	4	(11)	1	
Krzysztof JUTRZENKA	M	1			
Michal KOKOSZANEK	G	17			
Robert KOLENDOWICZ	A		(3)		
Jaroslaw MACKIEWICZ	A	15		9	
Adam MAJEWSKI	M	26		2	
Maciej MALINOWSKI	M		(2)		
Tomasz NAJEWSKI	M		(6)		
Benedykt NOCON	D	1	(7)		
Krzysztof PISKULA	M	30		9	
Piotr REISS	A	15		12	
Maciej SCHERFCHEN	M	27			
Piotr SOLTYSIAK	M		(9)		
Marek SZEMONSKI	A		(2)		
Przemyslaw URBANIAK	D	30			
Robert WILK	M	28		3	
Andrzej WOZNIAK	G	13			
Leszek ZAWADZKI	D	10	(17)	1	
Damian ZIENIUK	D		(1)		
Maciej ZURAWSKI	A	30		11	

LEAGUE RESULTS 1998/99

25/07/98	Amica Wronki	A	1-2	Piskula
01/08/98	GKS Katowice	H	3-1	Reiss, Wilk 2
21/08/98	Wisla Krakow	A	1-2	Araszkiewicz
29/08/98	Ruch Chorzow	H	5-0	Reiss, Majewski, Zurawski 2, Araszkiewicz
09/09/98	LKS Lodz	A	2-1	Araszkiewicz, Reiss
12/09/98	Gornik Zabrze	H	3-1	Reiss (p), Glowacki, Araszkiewicz
19/09/98	Pogon Szczecin	A	3-2	Wilk, Piskula, Araszkiewicz
23/09/98	GKS Belchatow	H	3-0	Reiss 2, Piskula
26/09/98	Odra Wodzislaw	H	3-0	Reiss 3 (2p)
03/10/98	Polonia Warszawa	A	2-1	Zurawski, Reiss
17/10/98	Zaglebie Lubin	H	4-0	Araszkiewicz, Reiss 2 (1p), Piskula
24/10/98	Stomil Olsztyn	A	2-0	Piskula, Zurawski
30/10/98	Widzew Lodz	A	0-3	
14/11/98	Ruch Radzionkow	H	1-2	Zurawski
18/11/98	Legia Warszawa	A	0-1	
26/02/99	Amica Wronki	H	2-0	Mackiewicz, Zurawski
07/03/99	GKS Katowice	A	2-1	Zurawski, Mackiewicz
13/03/99	Legia Warszawa	H	0-0	
20/03/99	GKS Belchatow	A	3-1	Mackiewicz 2, Zurawski
03/04/99	Wisla Krakow	H	1-3	Piskula
10/04/99	Ruch Chorzow	A	1-2	Piskula
17/04/99	LKS Lodz	H	3-1	Piskula, Zawadzki, Zurawski
23/04/99	Gornik Zabrze	A	2-1	Mackiewicz, Zurawski
30/04/99	Pogon Szczecin	H	2-2	Mackiewicz, Zurawski
08/05/99	Odra Wodzislaw	A	0-2	
12/05/99	Polonia Warszawa	H	0-1	
15/05/99	Zaglebie Lubin	A	2-1	Mackiewicz, Piskula
22/05/99	Stomil Olsztyn	H	1-1	Mackiewicz
26/05/99	Widzew Lodz	H	2-0	Justin, Mackiewicz
29/05/99	Ruch Radzionkow	A	1-4	Majewski

LEGIA WARSZAWA

ASPN Legia Daewoo Warszawa
Ul. Lazienkowska 3
00-449 Warszawa
tel - (022) 6210896/6281360
fax - (022) 6218261
Year of Formation - 1916
President - Marek Pietruszka
Secretary - Wladyslaw Stachurski
Coach - Jerzy Kopa; Stefan Bialas
Stadium - Wojska Polskiego (15,000)

MAJOR HONOURS
League Championship - (6)
1955, 1956, 1969, 1970, 1994, 1995.
Domestic Cup - (12)
1955, 1956, 1964, 1966, 1973, 1980, 1981,
1989, 1990, 1994, 1995, 1997.

APPEARANCES 98/99

		P	Ap	(s)	Gls
Jacek BEDNARZ	M		16	(8)	
Sylwester CZERESZEWSKI	M		19		7
Dariusz CZYKIER	M		4	(7)	
Maciej JANIAK	M		9	(3)	
Bartosz KARWAN	A		26	(2)	12
Cezary KUCHARSKI	A		10	(1)	1
Jacok MAGIERA	M		24	(1)	3
Marcin MIECIEL	A		22	(3)	8
Piotr MOSOR	D		29		1
Frankline Njiwah MUDOH (CMR)	M			(4)	
Maciej MURAWSKI	D		27	(1)	1
Sebastian NOWAK	D		11	(2)	
Slawomir RUTKA	M		1	(4)	
Maciej SAWICKI	A			(7)	1
Pawel SKRZYPEK	M		17	(3)	1
Tomasz SOKOLOWSKI	M		7	(8)	
Dariusz SOLNICA	A		4	(7)	
Grzegorz SZAMOTULSKI	G		30		
Mariusz SRUTWA	A		12	(2)	4
Sergiusz WIECHOWSKI	M		24	(4)	
Piotr WLODARCZYK	A		3	(12)	
Jerzy WOJNECKI	D		1	(1)	
Radoslaw WROBLEWSKI	A		7	(2)	1
Jacek ZIELINSKI	D		27		

LEAGUE RESULTS 1998/99

25/07/98	Zaglebie Lubin	H	1-1	Mieciel
31/07/98	Stomil Olsztyn	A	2-1	Czereszewski, Mieciel
22/08/98	Amica Wronki	H	3-1	Czereszewski 2, Magiera
29/08/98	GKS Katowice	A	3-1	Karwan 2, og (Luncik)
09/09/98	Widzew Lodz	H	1-0	Karwan
13/09/98	GKS Belchatow	H	3-0	Karwan, Magiera, Czereszewski (p)
19/09/98	Wisia Krakow	A	1-4	Karwan
23/09/98	Ruch Radzionkow	A	2-1	Mosor, Karwan
27/09/98	Ruch Chorzow	H	2-0	Karwan, Czereszewski
03/10/98	LKS Lodz	A	1-1	Karwan
18/10/98	Gornik Zabrze	H	0-1	
25/10/98	Pogon Szczecin	A	1-3	Czereszewski
31/10/98	Odra Wodzislaw	H	0-0	
14/11/98	Polonia Warszawa	A	0-0	
18/11/98	Lech Poznan	H	1-0	Skrzypek
28/02/99	Zaglebie Lubin	A	0-0	
06/03/99	Stomil Olsztyn	H	1-0	Czereszewski
13/03/99	Lech Poznan	A	0-0	
20/03/99	Ruch Radzionkow	H	1-1	Srutwa
03/04/99	Amica Wronki	A	2-0	Mieciel 2
10/04/99	GKS Katowice	H	0-0	
18/04/99	Widzew Lodz	A	2-3	Kucharski, Mieciel
24/04/99	GKS Belchatow	A	2-1	Srutwa 2
30/04/99	Wisla Krakow	H	1-2	Wroblowski
08/05/99	Ruch Chorzow	A	1-0	Karwan
12/05/99	LKS Lodz	H	3-2	Mieciel, Srutwa, Karwan
15/05/99	Gornik Zabrze	A	0-1	
23/05/99	Pogon Szczecin	H	2-0	Mieciel 2
26/05/99	Odra Wodzislaw	A	2-1	Murawski, Magiera
29/05/99	Polonia Warszawa	H	3-0	Karwan 2, Sawicki

LKS LODZ

CLUB DIRECTORY

LKS-Ptak Lodz
Ul. Unii 2
94-020 Lodz
tel - (042) 6860668/6863745
fax - (042) 6881313
Year of Formation - 1908
President - Antoni Ptak
Secretary - Marek Lopinski
Coach - Marek Dziuba; Boguslaw Pietrzak;
Ryszard Polak
Stadium - LKS (30,000)

MAJOR HONOURS
League Championship - (2) 1958, 1998.
Domestic Cup - (1) 1957.

APPEARANCES 98/99

		P	Ap	(s)	Gls
Leandro Sérgio Santos BATATA (BRA)	D	19	(1)		
Witold BENDKOWSKI	D	14	(2)		
Artur BUGAJ	A	2	(2)	1	
Tomasz CEBULA	M	9	(3)	1	
Marcin DANIELEWICZ	M	5	(7)		
Omondiagbe DARLINGTON (NIG)	M	8	(1)		
Lord Eddy DOMBRAYE (NIG)	A	9	(2)	1	
Janusz DZIEDZIC	A	2	(11)		
FERNANDO Maía Batista (BRA)	M	3			
Robert GORSKI	A	13		3	
Rafal GRZELAK	D		(2)		
Austin HAMLET (NIG)	A	2			
Ariel JAKUBOWSKI	M	24	(1)		
JULCIMAR Conceição de Sousa (BRA)	M	13			
Tomasz KOS	M	14			
Artur KOSCIUK	M	19			
Grzegorz KRYSIAK	M	10	(2)		
Tomasz LENART	M	24			
Lukasz MADEJ	M		(3)		
Piotr MATYS	A	1	(4)		
Rafal NIZNIK	M	13	(2)	6	
Michal OSINSKI	M	12	(6)	1	
Jacek PASZULEWICZ	D	8	(6)		
Rafal PAWLAK	D	21	(3)	7	
Jacek PLUCIENNIK	A		(2)		
Krzysztof RUTKOWSKI	A		(1)		
Marek SAGANOWSKI	A	11	(4)	1	
Michal SLAWUTA	G		(1)		
Miroslaw TRZECIAK	A	1			
Tomasz WIESZCZYCKI	M	25	(3)	7	
Zbigniew WYCISZKIEWICZ	M	15	(3)	1	
Boguslaw WYPARLO	G	30			
Dzidoslaw ZUBEREK	A	3	(10)	2	

LEAGUE RESULTS 1998/99

25/07/98	Gornik Zabrze	H	2-2	Niznik, Wieszczycki
02/08/98	Pogon Szczecin	A	1-1	Zuberek
22/08/98	Zaglebie Lubin	H	0-2	
30/08/98	Stomil Olsztyn	A	0-1	
09/09/98	Lech Poznan	H	1-2	Bugaj
12/09/98	Ruch Radzionkow	A	0-4	
20/09/98	Amica Wronki	H	2-0	Pawlak 2
23/09/98	Polonia Warszawa	A	1-2	Wieszczycki
26/09/98	GKS Katowice	A	1-1	Niznik
03/10/98	Legia Warszawa	H	1-1	Niznik (p)
17/10/98	GKS Belchatow	A	3-2	Cebula, Zuberek, Niznik
24/10/98	Wisla Krakow	H	0-3	
30/10/98	Ruch Chorzow	A	2-1	Pawlak, Niznik
14/11/98	Widzew Lodz	H	0-1	
18/11/98	Odra Wodzislaw	H	2-1	Dombraye, Niznik
27/02/99	Gornik Zabrze	A	0-0	
06/03/99	Pogon Szczecin	H	1-1	Gorski
13/03/99	Odra Wodzislaw	A	1-2	Gorski (p)
20/03/99	Polonia Warszawa	H	0-0	
02/04/99	Zaglebie Lubin	A	2-2	Wieszczycki, Saganowski
10/04/99	Stomil Olsztyn	H	2-0	og (Holc), Gorski
17/04/99	Lech Poznan	A	1-3	Wieszczycki
24/04/99	Ruch Radzionkow	H	0-1	
01/05/99	Amica Wronki	A	2-1	Osinski, Pawlak
08/05/99	GKS Katowice	H	3-2	Pawlak, Wieszczycki, og (Luncik)
12/05/99	Legia Warszawa	A	2-3	Wieszczycki 2
15/05/99	GKS Belchatow	H	2-0	Pawlak 2 (1p)
22/05/99	Wisla Krakow	A	1-1	Wyciszkiewicz
26/05/99	Ruch Chorzow	H	0-0	
29/05/99	Widzew Lodz	A	0-5	

ODRA WODZISLAW

Miejski Klub Sportowy Odra Wodzislaw
Ul. Baguminska 8
44-300 Wodzislaw Slaski
tel - (036) 4551394
fax - (036) 4554435
Year of Formation - 1922
President - Ireneusz Serwotka
Secretary - Jerzy Knopek
Coach - Albin Mikulski; Marek Beben & Ryszard
Wieczorek; Jerzy Wyrobek
Stadium - Odra (8,000)

APPEARANCES 98/99

		P	Ap	(s)	Gls
Pawel ADAMCZYK	M	15			
Arkadiusz BALUSZYNSKI	A	1	(12)		
Marek BEBEN	G	4			
Adam JACHIMOWICZ	M	1	(2)		
Dariusz JACKIEWICZ	M	11	(1)	1	
Piotr JEGOR	D	27	(3)	3	
Arkadiusz KAMPKA	A	9	(3)	1	
Marek KOLEK	D	1	(1)		
Adam KRYGER	M	9	(2)		
Piotr KUS	M		(1)		
Marcin MALINOWSKI	D	20	(8)		
Jacek MATYIA	D	14			
Mariusz NOSAL	A	25	(4)	14	
Janusz NYLEC	M	4	(5)		
Slawomir PALUCH	A	11	(1)		
Marcin PAWLOWSKI	A		(4)		
Przemyslaw PLUTA	A	13	(6)	2	
Maciej POLAK	G	3			
Rafal POLICHT	A	15	(10)	4	
Pawel SIBIK	M	24	(5)	2	
Roman SKORUPA	M	8	(4)		
Piotr SOWISZ	D	24	(2)		
Krzysztof SMOLINSKI	D	6	(1)		
Miroslaw STANIEK	D	8	(2)	1	
Ryszard STANIEK	M	14	(4)	4	
Miroslaw SZWARGA	M	9	(4)		
Grzegorz TOMALA	G	23			
Daniel TUMAS	D	1			
Grzegorz WISELKA	M	1	(1)		
Jan WOS	M	29	(1)	1	

26/07/98	Wisla Krakow	A	1-2	Staniek M.
01/08/98	Ruch Chorzow	H	2-2	Jegor (p), Nosal
22/08/98	Pogon Szczecin	A	0-1	
29/08/98	Widzew Lodz	A	0-2	
09/09/98	Polonia Warszawa	H	2-2	Staniek R. 2
12/09/98	Zaglebie Lubin	A	4-4	Nosal 2, Staniek R. 2
19/09/98	Stomil Olsztyn	H	1-1	Nosal
23/09/98	Gornik Zabrze	H	0-1	
26/09/98	Lech Poznan	A	0-3	
03/10/98	Ruch Radzionkow	H	3-1	Nosal, Policht 2
17/10/98	Amica Wronki	A	1-3	Pluta
24/10/98	GKS Katowice	H	0-2	
31/10/98	Legia Warszawa	A	0-0	
14/11/98	GKS Belchatow	H	0-0	
18/11/98	LKS Lodz	A	1-2	Nosal
27/02/99	Wisla Krakow	H	0-2	
06/03/99	Ruch Chorzow	A	2-0	Nosal 2
13/03/99	LKS Lodz	H	2-1	Kampka, Nosal
20/03/99	Gornik Zabrze	A	1-0	Nosal
03/04/99	Pogon Szczecin	H	3-0	Pluta, Nosal, Policht
10/04/99	Widzew Lodz	H	2-0	Jegor (p), Sibik (p)
17/04/99	Polonia Warszawa	A	1-2	Jackiewicz
24/04/99	Zaglebie Lubin	H	0-1	
01/05/99	Stomil Olsztyn	A	1-3	Jegor (p)
08/05/99	Lech Poznan	H	2-0	Policht, Nosal
12/05/99	Ruch Radzionkow	A	0-2	
15/05/99	Amica Wronki	H	1-0	Nosal
22/05/99	GKS Katowice	A	1-1	Sibik
26/05/99	Legia Warszawa	H	1-2	Nosal
29/05/99	GKS Belchatow	A	1-1	Wos

POGON SZCZECIN

Morski Klub Sportowy Pogon Szczecin
Ul. Karlowicza 28
71-102 Szczecin
tel - (091) 4878658
fax - (091) 4878658
Year of Formation - 1948
President - Waldemar Folbrycht
Secretary - Andrzej Obst
Coach - Boguslaw Baniak; Leszek Jezierski
Stadium - Pogon (17,500)

		P	Ap	(s)	Gls
Rafal	ANDRUSZKO	A		(1)	
Piotr	BLASIUS	M		(3)	
Piotr	BURLIKOWSKI	A	11	(9)	
Jaroslaw	CHWASTEK	D	18	(1)	
Pawel	DRUMLAK	M	24	(2)	2
Robert	DYMKOWSKI	A	22	(5)	6
Maciej	FALTYNSKI	M	3		
Dariusz	FORNALAK	D	13		
Marcin	KACZMAREK	D	11		
Piotr	KLUZEK	A	3	(6)	
Mariusz	KURAS	M	14	(2)	
Marcin	LENCZEWSKI	D		(1)	
Zdzislaw	LESZCZYNSKI	M	4	(1)	
Dariusz	LEWANDOWSKI	D	16	(1)	1
Bartosz	LAWA	M	1	(2)	
Radoslaw	MAJDAN	G	24		
Piotr	MANDRYSZ	M	18		7
Damir	MARETIC (CRO)	M	6	(5)	1
Olgierd	MOSKALEWICZ	A	13	(1)	6
Andrzej	NOGA	M		(2)	
Mariusz	OSIECKI	M	1	(2)	
Rafal	PIOTROWSKI	M	19	(3)	2
Leszek	POKLADOWSKI	M	19	(6)	
Andrzej	RYCAK	M	22	(4)	1
Robert	SIKORSKI	A	9	(20)	2
Nicola	SIMIC (CRO)	A		(2)	
Dariusz	SOLNICA	M	13		2
Maciej	STOLARCZYK	D	26		2
Wojciech	TOMASZIEWICZ	G	6		
Marek	WALBURG	M	14	(2)	
Serhiy	ZAITSEV (UKR)	M		(1)	

02/08/98	LKS Lodz	H	1-1	Sikorski
22/08/98	Odra Wodzislaw	H	1-0	Mandrysz
29/08/98	Polonia Warszawa	A	2-2	Moskalewicz, Mandrysz (p)
09/09/98	Zaglebie Lubin	H	3-2	Mandrysz, Moskalewicz 2
13/09/98	Stomil Olsztyn	A	1-3	Piotrowski
16/09/98	Ruch Chorzow	A	1-1	Lewandowski
19/09/98	Lech Poznan	H	2-3	Moskalewicz, Mandrysz
23/09/98	Widzew Lodz	A	1-2	Mandrysz (p)
26/09/98	Ruch Radzionkow	A	2-3	Moskalewicz, Piotrowski
04/10/98	Amica Wronki	H	3-2	Dymkowski 2, Moskalewicz
17/10/98	GKS Katowice	A	0-1	
25/10/98	Legia Warszawa	H	3-1	Sikorski, og (Kucharski), Dymkowski
31/10/98	GKS Belchatow	A	0-2	
14/11/98	Wisla Krakow	H	0-4	
18/11/98	Gornik Zabrze	A	0-4	
27/02/99	Ruch Chorzow	H	1-0	Solnica
06/03/99	LKS Lodz	A	1-1	Maretic
13/03/99	Gornik Zabrze	H	0-1	
20/03/99	Widzew Lodz	H	1-2	Stolarczyk
03/04/99	Odra Wodzislaw	A	0-3	
10/04/99	Polonia Warszawa	H	1-0	Rycak
17/04/99	Zaglebie Lubin	A	0-2	
24/04/99	Stomil Olsztyn	H	2-2	Drumlak 2
30/04/99	Lech Poznan	A	2-2	Dymkowski 2
08/05/99	Ruch Radzionkow	H	3-2	Mandrysz, Dymkowski, Solnica
12/05/99	Amica Wronki	A	0-2	
16/05/99	GKS Katowice	H	1-0	Stolarczyk
23/05/99	Legia Warszawa	A	0-2	
26/05/99	GKS Belchatow	H	1-0	Mandrysz
29/05/99	Wisla Krakow	A	0-4	

POLONIA WARSZAWA

CLUB DIRECTORY

Klub Pilkarski Polonia Warszawa SSA
Ul. Konwiktorska 6
00-206 Warszawa
tel - (022) 6357204
fax - (022) 6351637
Year of Formation - 1911
President - Krzysztof Mencel
Secretary - Jerzy Engel
Coach - Zdzislaw Podedworny; Dariusz Wdowczyk
Stadium - Polonia (10,000)

MAJOR HONOURS
League Championship - (1) 1946.

APPEARANCES 98/99

	P	Ap	(s)	Gls
Mateusz BARTCZAK	M	16	(9)	
Arkadiusz BAK	M	25	(3)	7
Jacek DABROWSKI	M	26	(1)	2
Janusz GALUSZKA	D	6		
Igor GOLASZEWSKI	M	10	(6)	
Marcin JALOCHA	M	25	(1)	
Arkadiusz KALISZAN	D	20	(1)	2
Sebastian KESKA	A		(2)	
Piotr KOSIOROWSKI	A	1	(1)	
Mariusz LIBERDA	G	1		
Mariusz MALINOWSKI	D	18	(3)	
Jaroslaw MAZURKIEWICZ	M	6	(7)	
Grazvydas MIKULENAS (LIT)	A	10	(3)	5
Tomasz MOSKAL	A	13	(11)	6
Emmanuel OLISADEBE (NIG)	A	11	(5)	4
Mariusz PAWLAK	M	14	(4)	3
Rafal RUTA	M	3	(5)	
Krzysztof SADZAWICKI	D	19	(3)	
Maciej SZCZESNY	G	29		
Bartosz TARACHULSKI	A	15	(10)	4
Donatas VENCEVICIUS (LIT)	M	3	(3)	1
Dariusz WDOWCZYK	D	4	(1)	
Grzegorz WEDZYNSKI	M	23	(4)	3
Marcin ZEWLAKOW	A		(2)	
Michal ZEWLAKOW	D	6		
Tomas ZVIRGZDAUSKAS (LIT)	D	26		

LEAGUE RESULTS 1998/99

25/07/98	GKS Belchatow	A	1-0	Moskal
02/08/98	Wisla Krakow	H	1-3	Vencevicius
22/08/98	Gornik Zabrze	A	0-2	
29/08/98	Pogon Szczecin	H	2-2	og (Faltynski), Olisadebe
09/09/98	Odra Wodzislaw	A	2-2	Mikulenas, Bak
12/09/98	Widzew Lodz	A	1-4	Tarachulski
19/09/98	Zaglebie Lubin	H	3-1	Tarachulski, Bak 2
23/09/98	LKS Lodz	H	2-1	Dabrowski, Tarachulski
27/09/98	Stomil Olsztyn	A	0-1	
03/10/98	Lech Poznan	H	1-2	Moskal
17/10/98	Ruch Radzionkow	A	0-0	
24/10/98	Amica Wronki	H	4-2	Wedzynski (p), Mikulenas 3
31/10/98	GKS Katowice	A	3-1	Kaliszan, Bak, Mikulenas
14/11/98	Legia Warszawa	H	0-0	
18/11/98	Ruch Chorzow	A	0-0	
27/02/99	GKS Belchatow	H	4-0	Moskal, Olisadebe, Wedzynski, Pawlak
06/03/99	Wisla Krakow	A	3-1	Olisadebe 2, Bak
13/03/99	Ruch Chorzow	H	3-0	Moskal, Dabrowski, Tarachulski
20/03/99	LKS Lodz	A	0-0	
03/04/99	Gornik Zabrze	H	1-0	Pawlak
10/04/99	Pogon Szczecin	A	0-1	
17/04/99	Odra Wodzislaw	H	2-1	Moskal, Bak
24/04/99	Widzew Lodz	H	2 1	Bak, Kaliszan
01/05/99	Zaglebie Lubin	A	0-1	
08/05/99	Stomil Olsztyn	H	0-1	
12/05/99	Lech Poznan	A	1-0	Pawlak
15/05/99	Ruch Radzionkow	H	0-0	
22/05/99	Amica Wronki	A	0-1	
26/05/99	GKS Katowice	H	2-0	Moskal, Wedzynski
29/05/99	Legia Warszawa	A	0-3	

RUCH CHORZOW

CLUB DIRECTORY

Klub Sportowy Ruch Chorzow
Ul. Cicha 6
41-500 Chorzow
tel - (032) 2462012/2461040
fax - (032) 2461714
Year of Formation - 1920
President - Krystian Rogala
Secretary - Jan Rudnow
Coach - Orest Lenczyk; Edward Lorens
Stadium - Ruch (20,000)

MAJOR HONOURS
League Championship - (14)
1933, 1934, 1935, 1936, 1938, 1951, 1952,
1953, 1960, 1968, 1974, 1975, 1979, 1989.
Domestic Cup - (3) 1951, 1974, 1996.

APPEARANCES 98/99

	P	Ap	(s)	Gls
Dawid BARTOS	M		(4)	
Marcin BASZCZYNSKI	D	27	(1)	
Krzysztof BIZACKI	A	29	(1)	7
Mamia DZIKIJA (GEO)	M	19	(4)	
Marcin FOLGA	A	1	(3)	
Jerzy GASIOR	D	4	(3)	
Damian GORAWSKI	A	1	(3)	
Waldemar GRZANKA	G	1		
Bartlomiej JAMROZ	M	24	(1)	2
Miroslaw JAWORSKI	D	1	(3)	
Grzegorz JORDAN	A	1	(1)	
Rafal KWIECINSKI	M	21	(3)	
Piotr LECH	G	29		
Mariusz MASTERNAK	D	12		
Maciej MIZIA	D	28		1
Marcin MOLEK	M	15	(11)	
Janusz NAWROCKI	D	12	(2)	
Rafal OZIMINA	A	1	(7)	
Robert PIETRUSZKA	M	3	(1)	
Jaroslaw POTOK	M	2	(5)	
Seweryn SIEMIANOWSKI	M	3	(13)	
Lukasz SURMA	M	22	(8)	
Tomasz SZUFLITA	D	13		
Mariusz SRUTWA	A	15		7
Marek WLECIALOWSKI	M	26	(2)	
Piotr WLODARCZYK	A	15		6
Piotr ZABA	A	5	(5)	

LEAGUE RESULTS 1998/99

01/08/98	Odra Wodzislaw	A	2-2	Srutwa 2
21/08/98	Stomil Olsztyn	H	1-0	Jamroz
29/08/98	Lech Poznan	A	0-5	
09/09/98	Ruch Radzionkow	H	1-0	Srutwa
12/09/98	Amica Wronki	A	0-2	
16/09/98	Pogon Szczecin	H	1-1	Bizacki
20/09/98	GKS Katowice	H	2-1	Bizacki, Srutwa
23/09/98	Zaglebie Lubin	A	2-0	Bizacki, Srutwa
27/09/98	Legia Warszawa	A	0-2	
03/10/98	GKS Belchatow	H	1-1	Srutwa
17/10/98	Wisla Krakow	A	1-4	Bizacki
23/10/98	Widzew Lodz	H	2-1	Srutwa, Bizacki
30/10/98	LKS Lodz	H	1-2	Jamroz
14/11/98	Gornik Zabrze	A	0-2	
18/11/98	Polonia Warszawa	H	0-0	
27/02/99	Pogon Szczecin	A	0-1	
06/03/99	Odra Wodzislaw	H	0-2	
13/03/99	Polonia Warszawa	A	0-3	
20/03/99	Zaglebie Lubin	H	0-0	
02/04/99	Stomil Olsztyn	A	0-1	
10/04/99	Lech Poznan	H	2-1	Bizacki, Wlodarczyk
17/04/99	Ruch Radzionkow	A	0-1	
24/04/99	Amica Wronki	H	0-0	
30/04/99	GKS Katowice	A	1-0	Wlodarczyk (p)
08/05/99	Legia Warszawa	H	0-1	
12/05/99	GKS Belchatow	A	2-0	Wlodarczyk, Bizacki
15/05/99	Wisla Krakow	H	1-1	Wlodarczyk
22/05/99	Widzew Lodz	A	1-1	Wlodarczyk (p)
26/05/99	LKS Lodz	A	0-0	
29/05/99	Gornik Zabrze	H	2-1	Wlodarczyk, Mizia

RUCH RADZIONKOW

CLUB DIRECTORY

GKS Ruch Radzionkow
Ul. Narutowicza 11
41-933 Bytom
tel - (032) 2890011 ext.5140
fax - (032) 2893261/2890242
Year of Formation - 1919
President - Pawel Bomba
Secretary - Konrad Holewa
Coach - Andrzej Platek; Gothard Kokott
Stadium - Ruch (10,000)

APPEARANCES 98/99

	P	Ap	(s)	Gls
Grzegorz BONK	M	24	(1)	4
Roman CEGIELKA	M	3	(19)	2
Tomasz FORNALIK	M	30		2
Damian GALEJA	M	5	(10)	
Tomasz GROSMANI	M		(1)	
Wojciech GRZYB	M	4	(12)	1
Marian JANOSZKA	M	29		12
Rafal JAROSZ	A	30		6
Dariusz KLYTTA	G	29		
Krzysztof KOKOSZKA	M		(2)	
Dariusz KOSELA	M		(10)	
Andrzej MARKUSIK	M	4	(1)	
Wojciech MYSZOR	M	29		
Rafal OPRZONDEK	D	18	(5)	
Tomasz RUDEK	M	1	(1)	
Robert SIERKA	M	24		4
Marcin SUCHANSKI	G	1		
Marek SZYMINSKI	D	30		
Jacek TRZECIAK	M	1	(11)	
Andrzej URBANCZYK	G		(1)	
Ireneusz WALUS	M		(3)	
Andrzej WROBLEWSKI	D	24		
Czeslaw WRZESNIEWSKI	D	20		
Jozef ZYMANCZYK	A	24	(2)	9

LEAGUE RESULTS 1998/99

24/07/98	Widzew Lodz	H	5-0	Jarosz, Zymanczyk, Janoszka 2 (1p), Fornalik
01/08/98	Amica Wronki	H	1-1	Fornalik
08/08/98	GKS Katowice	A	0-1	
23/08/98	GKS Belchatow	A	1-2	Janoszka
29/08/98	Wisla Krakow	H	1-1	Sierka
09/09/98	Ruch Chorzow	A	0-1	
12/09/98	LKS Lodz	H	4-0	Janoszka (p), Bonk, Sierka 2
19/09/98	Gornik Zabrze	A	1-1	Bonk
23/09/98	Legia Warszawa	H	1-2	Zymanczyk
26/09/98	Pogon Szczecin	H	3-2	Janoszka 2, Cegielka
03/10/98	Odra Wodzislaw	A	1-3	Jarosz
18/10/98	Polonia Warszawa	H	0-0	
25/10/98	Zaglebie Lubin	A	2-1	Zymanczyk, Jarosz
31/10/98	Stomil Olsztyn	H	1-0	Bonk
14/11/98	Lech Poznan	A	2-1	Zymanczyk, Janoszka (p)
27/02/99	Widzew Lodz	A	1-2	Zymanczyk
06/03/99	Amica Wronki	A	0-1	
13/03/99	GKS Katowice	H	1-1	Jarosz
20/03/99	Legia Warszawa	A	1-1	Jarosz
03/04/99	GKS Belchatow	H	1-1	Janoszka
11/04/99	Wisla Krakow	A	0-6	
17/04/99	Ruch Chorzow	H	1-0	Janoszka (p)
24/04/99	LKS Lodz	A	1-0	Sierka
01/05/99	Gornik Zabrze	H	0-0	
08/05/99	Pogon Szczecin	A	2-3	Janoszka, Zymanczyk
12/05/99	Odra Wodzislaw	H	2-0	Jarosz, Janoszka (p)
15/05/99	Polonia Warszawa	A	0-0	
22/05/99	Zaglebie Lubin	H	3-3	Janoszka (p), Grzyb, Cegielka
26/05/99	Stomil Olsztyn	A	0-0	
29/05/99	Lech Poznan	H	4-1	Zymanczyk 3, Bonk

STOMIL OLSZTYN

CLUB DIRECTORY

Miejski Olsztynski Klub Sportowy Stomil Olsztyn
Ul. Pilsudskiego 69a
10-596 Olsztyn
tel - (089) 5333160
fax - (089) 5336133
Year of Formation - 1945
President - Roman Niemyjski
Secretary - Mariusz Koczkodon
Coach - Mieczyslaw Broniszewski;
Romuald Szukielowicz; Mieczyslaw Broniszewski
Stadium - Stomil (18,000)

APPEARANCES 98/99

		P	Ap	(s)	Gls
Jaroslaw BAKO	G	26			
Andrzej BIEDRZYCKI	M	24	(2)		
Jacek CHANKO	M	29		4	
Maciej DOLEGA	A	2	(5)		
Marcin FLOREK	A	4	(10)	2	
Pawel HOLC	D	23			
Artur JANUSZEWSKI	D	26	(2)		
Bartosz JURKOWSKI	D	30		2	
Vladimir KLIMOVICH (BLS)	M	2	(1)		
Krzysztof KOWALCZYK	A	2	(7)	1	
Marek KWIATKOWSKI	M	14	(10)	2	
Nuruddeen LAWAL (NIG)	A	1	(1)		
Krzysztof MACIEJCZUK	D	3			
Krzysztof MASNIK	A	2	(2)		
Piotr MATYS	A	8	(5)	4	
Piotr ORLINSKI	M	8	(6)	1	
Aidas PREIKSAITIS (LIT)	M	29		4	
Dariusz PREIS	M	19	(4)		
Tomasz RADZIWON	M	5	(1)		
Tomas RAMELIS (LIT)	A	21		5	
Robert RZECZYCKI	D	7	(7)		
Andrzej STRETOWICZ	M		(3)		
Marcin SZULIK	M	26		3	
Rafal SZWED	M	15	(9)	1	
Sylwester WYLUPSKI	G	4			

LEAGUE RESULTS 1998/99

25/07/98	GKS Katowice	A	0-1	
31/07/98	Legia Warszawa	H	1-2	Chanko
21/08/98	Ruch Chorzow	A	0-1	
30/08/98	LKS Lodz	H	1-0	Kwiatkowski
09/09/98	Gornik Zabrze	A	1-1	Jurkowski
13/09/98	Pogon Szczecin	H	3-1	Orlinski, Jurkowski, Szulik
19/09/98	Odra Wodzislaw	A	1-1	Szulik
23/09/98	Wisla Krakow	H	1-2	Ramelis
27/09/98	Polonia Warszawa	H	1-0	Szulik
03/10/98	Zaglebie Lubin	A	1-3	Chanko
17/10/98	Widzew Lodz	A	0-5	
24/10/98	Lech Poznan	H	0-2	
31/10/98	Ruch Radzionkow	A	0-1	
14/11/98	Amica Wronki	H	4-1	Kwiatkowski, Ramelis, Preiksaitis, Chanko
18/11/98	GKS Belchatow	A	0-1	
27/02/99	GKS Katowice	H	2-1	Florek, Chanko
06/03/99	Legia Warszawa	A	0-1	
14/03/99	GKS Belchatow	H	0-2	
20/03/99	Wisla Krakow	A	0-3	
02/04/99	Ruch Chorzow	H	1-0	Matys
10/04/99	LKS Lodz	A	0-2	
18/04/99	Gornik Zabrze	H	2-1	Preiksaitis, Kowalczyk
24/04/99	Pogon Szczecin	A	2-2	Ramelis, Florek
01/05/99	Odra Wodzislaw	H	3-1	Szwed, Ramelis, Matys
08/05/99	Polonia Warszawa	A	1-0	Matys
12/05/99	Zaglebie Lubin	H	1-1	Matys
16/05/99	Widzew Lodz	H	2-1	Ramelis, Preiksaitis
22/05/99	Lech Poznan	A	1-1	Preiksaitis
26/05/99	Ruch Radzionkow	H	0-0	
29/05/99	Amica Wronki	A	0-0	

WIDZEW LODZ

CLUB DIRECTORY

Sekcja Pilki Noznej Widzew Lodz
Ul. Pilsudskiego 138
92-230 Lodz
tel - (042) 6747218
fax - (042) 6740175
Year of Formation - 1910
President - Andrzej Pawelec
Secretary - Andrzej Wojciechowski
Coach - Andrzej Pydrol; Wojciech Lazarek;
Marek Dziuba
Stadium - Widzew (20,000)

MAJOR HONOURS
League Championship - (4)
1981, 1982, 1996, 1997.
Domestic Cup - (1) 1985.

APPEARANCES 98/99

	P	Ap	(s)	Gls
Piotr BAZLER	D		(1)	
Daniel BOGUSZ	D	26	(1)	3
Andrzej BOROWSKI	A	2	(13)	
Adrian BUDKA	A	1	(6)	
Slawomir CHALASKIEWICZ	M	2	(1)	
Chioma CHIEMEZE (NIG)	A		(2)	
Marek CITKO	A	16	(4)	2
Zbigniew CZAJKOWSKI	M	8	(2)	1
Dariusz GESIOR	M	28	(2)	5
Lukasz GORSZKOW	D	18	(6)	
Slawomir GULA	D	11	(7)	1
Rafal KACZMARCZYK	M	23	(1)	1
Tomasz LECH	G	1		
Marcin LUDWIKOWSKI	G	1		
Tomasz LAPINSKI	D	30		
Krzysztof MACIEJCZUK	D		(1)	
Lukasz MASLOWSKI	A		(4)	
Miroslaw MATEJKO	M	1	(1)	
Radoslaw MICHALSKI	M	29	(1)	9
Andriy MIKHALCHUK (UKR)	M	16	(3)	1
Slawomir OLSZEWSKI	G	28		
Michal PIETRZAK	A		(1)	
Rafal SIADACZKA	D	14		
Michal STASIAK	D	2	(3)	
Piotr SZARPAK	M		(5)	
Marek SZEMONSKI	A	1	(2)	
Miroslaw SZYMKOWIAK	M	11		4
Arkadiusz SWIETOSLAWSKI	M	4	(5)	1
Maciej TERLECKI	M	27		2
Artur WICHNIAREK	A	25		20
Marcin ZAJAC	M	5		

LEAGUE RESULTS 1998/99

24/07/98	Ruch Radzionkow	A	0-5	
01/08/98	Gornik Zabrze	H	0-1	
22/08/98	GKS Katowice	A	2-0	Wichniarek 2
29/08/98	Odra Wodzislaw	H	2-0	Michalski, Wichniarek
09/09/98	Legia Warszawa	A	0-1	
13/09/98	Polonia Warszawa	H	4-1	Szymkowiak, Wichniarek 2, Michalski
18/09/98	GKS Belchatow	A	2-3	Bogusz, Wichniarek
23/09/98	Pogon Szczecin	H	2-1	Michalski, Gesior
26/09/98	Zaglebie Lubin	H	1-1	Wichniarek
04/10/98	Wisla Krakow	A	1-3	Michalski (p)
17/10/98	Stomil Olsztyn	H	5-0	Wichniarek, Szymkowiak 2, Michalski 2 (1p)
23/10/98	Ruch Chorzow	A	1-2	Wichniarek
30/10/98	Lech Poznan	H	3-0	Bogusz, Wichniarek 2
14/11/98	LKS Lodz	A	1-0	Szymkowiak
18/11/98	Amica Wronki	A	3-2	Citko, Michalski, Gesior
27/02/99	Ruch Radzionkow	H	2-1	Wichniarek 2
06/03/99	Gornik Zabrze	A	1-0	Wichniarek
14/03/99	Amica Wronki	H	3-0	Wichniarek 2, Czajkowski
20/03/99	Pogon Szczecin	A	2-1	Bogusz, Michalski
02/04/99	GKS Katowice	H	1-0	Gesior
10/04/99	Odra Wodzislaw	A	0-2	
18/04/99	Legia Warszawa	H	3-2	Wichniarek, Gula, Michalski
24/04/99	Polonia Warszawa	A	1-2	Kaczmarczyk
01/05/99	GKS Belchatow	H	1-0	Terlecki
08/05/99	Zaglebie Lubin	A	1-0	Gesior
12/05/99	Wisla Krakow	H	1-0	Mikhalchuk (p)
16/05/99	Stomil Olsztyn	A	1-2	Terlecki
22/05/99	Ruch Chorzow	H	1-1	Citko
26/05/99	Lech Poznan	A	0-2	
29/05/99	LKS Lodz	H	5-0	Gesior, Swietoslawski, Wichniarek 3 (1p)

WISLA KRAKOW

ASPN Wisla Krakow
Ul. Reymonta 22
30-059 Krakow
tel - (012) 6373760/6377120/6101509
fax - (012) 6373760/6101551/6377120
Year of Formation - 1906
President - Ludwik Mietta-Mikolajewicz
Secretary - Zdzislaw Kapka
Coach - Franciszek Smuda
Stadium - Wisla (15,000)

MAJOR HONOURS
League Championship - (6)
1927, 1928, 1949, 1950, 1978, 1999.
Domestic Cup - (2) 1926, 1967.

APPEARANCES 98/99

	P	Ap	(s)	Gls
Pawel ADAMCZYK	M		(6)	
Krzysztof BUKALSKI	M	16	(11)	2
Ryszard CZERWIEC	M	27		7
Daniel DUBICKI	A	13	(12)	3
Tomasz FRANKOWSKI	A	28	(1)	21
Grzegorz KALICIAK	M	18		2
Radoslaw KALUZNY	D	15		4
Tomasz KULAWIK	M	27	(1)	9
Jacek MATYJA	D	6	(5)	
Olgierd MOSKALEWICZ	A	11	(3)	4
Grzegorz NICINSKI	A	17	(8)	6
Pawel NOWAK	M		(11)	
Slawomir PALUCH	A	4	(9)	
Grzegorz PATER	M	27	(3)	8
Artur SARNAT	G	27		
Krzysztof SMOLINSKI	D		(1)	
Ibrahim SUNDAY (NIG)	M	9	(4)	
Kazimierz WEGRZYN	D	26		3
Jakub WIERZCHOWSKI	G	3		
Bogdan ZAJAC	D	28	(1)	
Marek ZAJAC	D	28		4
Jakub ZUREK	M		(1)	

LEAGUE RESULTS 1998/99

26/07/98	Odra Wodzislaw	H	2-1	Pater, Kulawik
02/08/98	Polonia Warszawa	A	3-1	og (Jalocha), Nicinski, Frankowski
21/08/98	Lech Poznan	H	2-1	Nicinski, Frankowski
29/08/98	Ruch Radzionkow	A	1-1	Nicinski
09/09/98	Amica Wronki	H	1-0	Kulawik
12/09/98	GKS Katowice	A	2-1	Czerwiec, Pater
19/09/98	Legia Warszawa	H	4-1	Frankowski, Nicinski, Kaliciak, Dubicki
23/09/98	Stomil Olsztyn	A	2-1	Kulawik, Bukalski
26/09/98	GKS Belchatow	A	3-0	Bukalski, Czerwiec, Frankowski
04/10/98	Widzew Lodz	H	3-1	Pater, Frankowski 2 (1p)
17/10/98	Ruch Chorzow	H	4-1	Wegrzyn 2, Frankowski 2
23/10/98	LKS Lodz	A	3-0	Pater, Frankowski 2 (1p)
30/10/98	Gornik Zabrze	H	2-1	Kulawik, Czerwiec
14/11/98	Pogon Szczecin	A	4-0	Pater, Dubicki, Kulawik, Frankowski
18/11/98	Zaglebie Lubin	H	0-1	
27/02/99	Odra Wodzislaw	A	2-0	Wegrzyn, Kulawik
06/03/99	Polonia Warszawa	H	1-3	Frankowski
14/03/99	Zaglebie Lubin	A	3-0	Kaluzny, Frankowski 2
20/03/99	Stomil Olsztyn	H	3-0	Pater, Czerwiec, Zajac M.
03/04/99	Lech Poznan	A	3-1	Frankowski, Kaliciak, Czerwiec
11/04/99	Ruch Radzionkow	H	6-0	Zajac M., Pater, Kulawik 2, Czerwiec 2
18/04/99	Amica Wronki	A	3-1	Moskalewicz, Zajac M., Frankowski
23/04/99	GKS Katowice	H	4-1	Kaluzny, Nicinski, Frankowski, Zajac M.
30/04/99	Legia Warszawa	A	2-1	Kaluzny 2
08/05/99	GKS Belchatow	H	4-0	og (Szarpak), Frankowski 2, Dubicki
12/05/99	Widzew Lodz	A	0-1	
15/05/99	Ruch Chorzow	A	1-1	Pater
22/05/99	LKS Lodz	H	1-1	Moskalewicz
26/05/99	Gornik Zabrze	A	2-2	Nicinski, Frankowski
29/05/99	Pogon Szczecin	H	4-0	Moskalewicz 2, Frankowski, Kulawik

ZAGLEBIE LUBIN

CLUB DIRECTORY

Miedzyzakladowy Klub Sportowy Zaglebie Lubin
Ul. Marii Sklodowskiej-Curie 98
59-301 Lubin
tel - (076) 8478510
fax - (076) 8478565
Year of Formation - 1946
President - Jacek Kordela
Secretary - Tadeusz Wisniewski
Coach - Andrzej Szarmach; Bogdan Pisz;
Miroslaw Jablonski
Stadium - Zaglebie (32,000)

MAJOR HONOURS
League Championship - (1) 1991.

APPEARANCES 98/99

	P	Ap	(s)	Gls
Marcin ADAMSKI	M	12		
Jacek BANASZYNSKI	G	4		
Robert BUBNOWICZ	D	7	(3)	
Henryk CACKOWSKI	M	2	(3)	1
Edward CECOT	D	7	(7)	
Dariusz CZYKIER	M	4		
Dariusz DZIARMAGA	M	8	(3)	
Wojciech GORSKI	M	20		7
Zbigniew GRZYBOWSKI	M	29		
Austine IGBINOSA (NIG)	M		(2)	
Jedrzej KEDZIORA	G	2		
Arkadiusz KLIMEK	A	21	(4)	7
Igor KOZIOL	D	18		
Jaroslaw KRZYZANOWSKI	M	4	(1)	
Mariusz LEWANDOWSKI	M	7	(14)	
Boguslaw LIZAK	M	11	(5)	4
Jacek MANUSZEWSKI	M	15	(6)	
Robert MIODUSZEWSKI	G	22		
Moses MOLONGO (CMR)	A	21	(6)	9
Andrzej NIEDZIELAN	A		(8)	3
Przemyslaw NORKO	G	2		
Emil NOWAKOWSKI	M	11		
Maciej NUCKOWSKI	M	7	(4)	2
Pawel PIOTROWSKI	M	29	(1)	2
Tomasz SZEWCZUK	A		(4)	
Andrzej SZCZYPKOWSKI	M	25	(1)	3
Daniel TRESCINSKI	D	5		
Jerzy WOJNECKI	D	2		
Zbigniew WOJCIK	D	6	(2)	1
Dariusz ZURAW	D	29		1

LEAGUE RESULTS 1998/99

25/07/98	Legia Warszawa	A	1-1	Zuraw
01/08/98	GKS Belchatow	H	1-2	Molongo
22/08/98	LKS Lodz	A	2-0	Gorski (p), Lizak
29/08/98	Gornik Zabrze	H	3-3	Wojcik, og (Lekki), Gorski (p)
09/09/98	Pogon Szczecin	A	2-3	Szczypkowski, Gorski
12/09/98	Odra Wodzislaw	H	4-4	Molongo, Szczypkowski, Gorski, Klimek
19/09/98	Polonia Warszawa	A	1-3	Molongo
23/09/98	Ruch Chorzow	H	0-2	
26/09/98	Widzew Lodz	A	1-1	Lizak
03/10/98	Stomil Olsztyn	H	3-1	Gorski (p), Niedzielan 2
17/10/98	Lech Poznan	A	0-4	
25/10/98	Ruch Radzionkow	H	1-2	Molongo
31/10/98	Amica Wronki	A	1-2	Piotrowski
15/11/98	GKS Katowice	H	4-0	Klimek 2, Gorski, Niedzielan
18/11/98	Wisla Krakow	A	1-0	og (Zajac M.)
28/02/99	Legia Warszawa	H	0-0	
06/03/99	GKS Belchatow	A	1-0	Szczypkowski
14/03/99	Wisla Krakow	H	0-3	
20/03/99	Ruch Chorzow	A	0-0	
02/04/99	LKS Lodz	H	2-2	Molongo, Klimek
10/04/99	Gornik Zabrze	A	2-2	Lizak 2
17/04/99	Pogon Szczecin	H	2-0	Nuckowski, Gorski
24/04/99	Odra Wodzislaw	A	1-0	Molongo
01/05/99	Polonia Warszawa	H	1-0	Molongo
08/05/99	Widzew Lodz	H	0-1	
12/05/99	Stomil Olsztyn	A	1-1	Klimek
15/05/99	Lech Poznan	H	1-2	Molongo
22/05/99	Ruch Radzionkow	A	3-3	Klimek, Piotrowski, Molongo
26/05/99	Amica Wronki	H	1-0	Klimek
29/05/99	GKS Katowice	A	2-2	Cackowski, Nuckowski

PROMOTED CLUBS

SECOND DIVISION FINAL TABLES 98/99

GROUP ONE

		Pd	W	D	L	F	A	Pt	GD
1	**Groclin Dyskobolia Grodzisk**	**26**	**14**	**8**	**4**	**52**	**37**	**50**	**+15**
2	Rakow Czestochowa	26	14	5	7	44	20	47	+24
3	Slask Wroclaw	26	14	5	7	47	21	47	+26
4	Odra/Varta Opole	26	12	4	10	37	31	40	+6
5	Aluminium Konin	26	11	6	9	37	31	39	+6
6	Polonia Bytom	26	9	11	6	23	21	38	+2
7	Lechia/Polonia Gdansk	26	11	4	11	32	33	37	-1
8	Grunwald Ruda Slaska	26	11	4	11	40	44	37	-4
9	KS Myszkow	26	11	3	12	29	38	36	-9
10	Odra Szczecin	26	8	9	9	24	28	33	-4
11	Elana Torun	26	8	8	10	32	36	32	-4
12	Karkonosze Jelenia Gora	26	8	7	11	23	31	31	-8
13	Naprzod Rydultowy	26	7	4	15	21	35	25	-14
14	Lechia Zielona Gora	26	2	6	18	17	52	12	-35

GROUP TWO

		Pd	W	D	L	F	A	Pt	GD
1	**Petrochemia Plock**	**28**	**19**	**4**	**5**	**54**	**24**	**61**	**+30**
2	Ceramika Opoczno	28	16	9	3	46	20	57	+26
3	Gornik Leczna	28	16	7	5	47	20	55	+27
4	KSZO Ostrowiec	28	16	6	6	45	23	54	+22
5	RKS Radomsko	28	13	8	7	49	33	47	+16
6	Korona Kielce	28	12	7	9	32	27	43	+5
7	Hetman Zamosz	28	12	5	11	32	31	41	+1
8	Stal Stalowa Wola	28	11	7	10	35	34	40	+1
9	Jeziorak Ilawa	28	11	7	10	40	34	40	+6
10	Hutnik Krakow	28	11	7	10	44	39	40	+5
11	Unia Tarnow	28	11	6	11	41	32	39	+9
12	Piotrcovia Piotrkow Trybunalski	28	7	4	17	23	37	25	-14
13	Wawel Krakow	28	6	1	21	23	58	19	-35
14	Avia Swidnik	28	5	2	21	22	62	17	-40
15	Stal Sanok	28	2	4	22	15	74	10	-59

CLUB DIRECTORY

Klub Sportowy Groclin Dyskobolia Grodzisk Wielkopolski
Ul. Powstancow Chocieszynskich 52
64-340 Grodzisk Wielopolski
tel - (061) 4445343
fax - (061) 4446020
Year of Formation - 1922
President - Ryszard Kaczmarek
Secretary - Stanislaw Bamber
Coach - Marcin Bochynek
Stadium - Dyskobolia (6,000)

CLUB DIRECTORY

Sportowa Spolka Akcyjna Petrochemia Plock
Ul. Lukasiewicza 34
09-400 Plock
tel - (024) 2622555/2624638
fax - (024) 3655220
Year of Formation - 1947
President - Krzysztof Gawlowski
Secretary - Jan Franke
Coach - Jerzy Masztaler; Jerzy Kasalik
Stadium - Petrochemia (15,000)

PORTUGAL

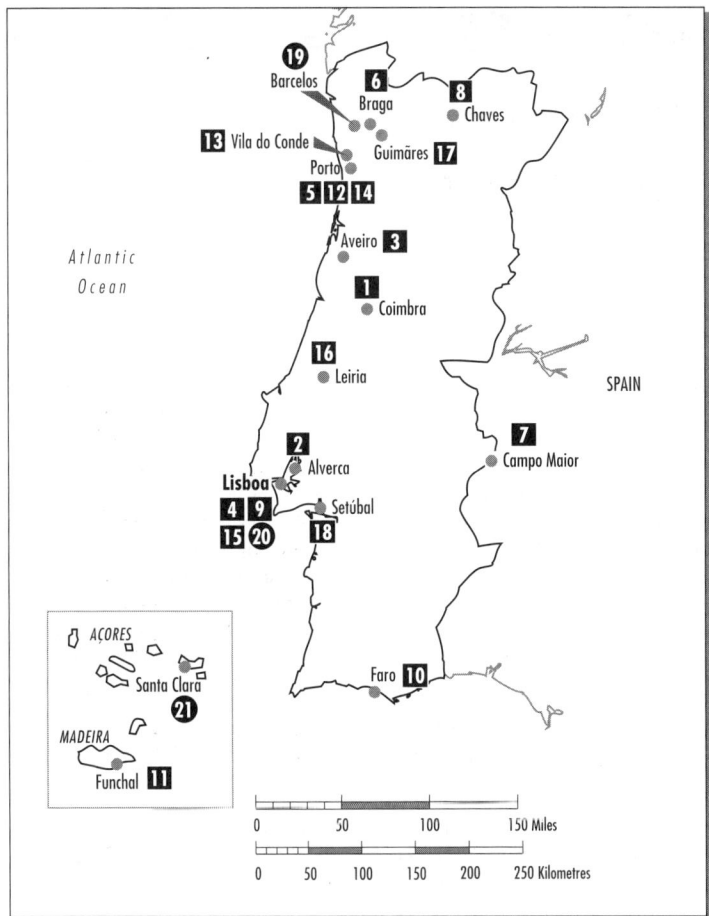

1	ACADÉMICA COIMBRA	766
2	FC ALVERCA	767
3	SC BEIRA MAR	768
4	SL BENFICA	769
5	BOAVISTA FC	770
6	SC BRAGA	771
7	SC CAMPOMAIORENSE	772
8	GD CHAVES	773
9	CF ESTRELA AMADORA	774
10	SC FARENSE	775
11	CS MARÍTIMO	776

12	FC PORTO	777
13	RIO AVE FC	778
14	SC SALGUEIROS	779
15	SPORTING CP	780
16	UNIÃO LEIRIA	781
17	VITÓRIA GUIMARÃES	782
18	VITÓRIA SETÚBAL	783
Promoted clubs		
19	GIL VICENTE FC	784
20	CF OS BELENENSES	784
21	CD SANTA CLARA	784

GOALS GALORE FOR NATIONAL TEAM

Five-star FC Porto break new ground

FEDERATION DIRECTORY

Federação Portuguesa de Futebol
Praça de Alegria 25, Caixa postal 21 100, 1128 Lisboa Codex

tel - (01) 3475932   Year of Formation - 1914
fax - (01) 3467231   President - Gilberto Madail
                            Secretary - António Sequeira

Stadium - National, Lisboa (51,000)

FC Porto have grown accustomed to winning the Portuguese championship, but their 1998/99 triumph was something special. It was the club's fifth title in successive years. No Portuguese club had ever accomplished that feat before, which made coach Fernando Santos and his class of '99 a team of history-makers and record-breakers.

The excessive celebrations that greeted the triumph emphasised the importance which Porto's fans attached to their club's unique achivement, although they were the first to admit that the so-called *penta* had never really been in any doubt. Yet again, Porto's march to victory had been straightforward and uncomplicated - partly through their own quality and consistency, partly through the trials and tribulations of their rivals.

But although Porto continued to rule the domestic roost, they had another forgettable season in Europe. Their Champions' League campaign looked cursed from the start when they conceded two late goals at home to Olympiakos in their opening match. It was an uphill battle from there on in, and although they managed to rediscover their home form, winning 3-0 at home to both Croatia Zagreb and Ajax, that was counterbalanced by defeats in all three of their away games. Naïve tactics and a spate of unforced defensive errors were the main reasons for their demise. No matter that Slovenian import Zlatko Zahovic scored more goals in those six group games than any other player in the competition. Porto's European adventure was over before Christmas - just as it had been 12 months earlier.

LEAGUE CHAMPIONSHIP RESULTS 98/99

		1	2	3	4	5	6	7	8	9	10	11	12	13	14	15	16	17	18
1	Académica Coimbra		0-5	1-0	0-3	2-3	1-1	1-5	1-2	2-2	2-1	1-3	0-2	1-1	0-1	2-2	0-1	1-1	2-0
2	FC Alverca	2-1		1-1	0-2	0-0	0-0	2-1	3-1	0-1	1-3	3-0	1-5	0-1	1-1	3-2	0-2	2-1	1-0
3	SC Beira Mar	0-2	2-1		1-1	1-1	4-2	2-1	1-1	0-0	0-1	1-1	2-1	1-2	4-1	2-2	1-1	0-0	1-1
4	SL Benfica	3-0	2-2	3-0		0-3	4-1	1-1	4-1	2-0	5-0	3-1	1-1	3-1	5-0	3-3	0-0	3-1	2-0
5	Boavista FC	3-1	3-0	2-1	2-1		1-0	2-1	4-1	2-1	3-0	1-2	0-0	1-0	2-1	2-2	1-0	2-0	1-1
6	SC Braga	2-2	0-0	2-1	2-1	1-2		0-2	1-0	1-1	0-0	1-1	3-3	2-0	1-1	2-0	2-4	2-1	3-0
7	SC Campomaiorense	2-1	2-2	4-1	0-5	1-1	2-0		4-1	3-0	3-1	0-2	0-2	0-0	0-0	0-0	0-3	1-0	1-2
8	GD Chaves	1-0	1-1	1-0	0-4	1-1	1-2	3-2		4-1	4-4	1-1	0-4	0-0	1-1	2-2	1-2	2-3	1-2
9	CF Estrela Amadora	2-1	1-0	1-2	0-1	2-1	0-0	1-0	2-1		2-1	1-0	1-1	1-0	1-1	0-1	1-1	1-1	5-0
10	SC Farense	2-0	1-0	2-1	1-0	2-2	0-2	2-1	2-1	1-1		0-0	0-3	0-1	2-1	1-3	1-1	1-2	1-1
11	CS Marítimo	4-1	3-3	1-1	1-0	3-0	3-0	0-1	2-2	1-1	1-3		0-1	2-0	2-2	1-3	3-2	1-0	0-1
12	FC Porto	7-1	3-1	7-0	3-1	0-2	1-0	2-0	1-0	2-0	2-0	1-0		4-0	4-1	3-2	3-1	2-0	6-0
13	Rio Ave FC	1-1	0-0	1-1	0-2	1-2	1-2	3-1	1-1	1-1	2-2	2-1	1-1		2-1	0-1	1-0	0-1	1-1
14	SC Salgueiros	1-1	1-0	4-4	1-1	0-0	1-1	1-1	2-0	1-1	4-2	2-2	1-3	5-1		2-1	0-0	3-2	1-0
15	Sporting CP	5-0	2-0	0-0	1-2	1-1	4-1	3-0	2-1	3-0	1-0	2-0	1-1	2-0	3-1		2-0	3-0	0-0
16	União Leiria	1-0	1-0	1-0	1-1	0-0	0-0	3-1	3-1	0-1	2-1	1-0	2-2	2-0	1-0	0-3		0-1	0-1
17	Vitória Guimarães	1-1	3-1	3-0	0-2	2-3	5-1	2-0	6-1	3-0	1-0	1-1	3-2	3-0	3-3	1-1	0-0		2-0
18	Vitória Setúbal	1-0	4-0	0-0	1-0	1-3	3-0	2-0	1-0	2-0	1-1	3-1	1-2	1-2	3-0	1-1	1-0	1-0	

LEAGUE CHAMPIONSHIP FINAL TABLE 98/99

			Home				Away					Total						
		P	W	D	L	F	A	W	D	L	F	A	W	D	L	F	A	P	GD
1	FC Porto	34	16	0	1	51	9	8	7	2	34	17	24	7	3	85	26	79	+59
2	Boavista FC	34	13	3	1	32	12	7	8	2	25	17	20	11	3	57	29	71	+28
3	SL Benfica	34	11	5	1	44	15	8	3	6	27	14	19	8	7	71	29	65	+42
4	Sporting CP	34	12	4	1	35	7	5	8	4	29	25	17	12	5	64	32	63	+32
5	Vitória Setúbal	34	11	3	3	27	10	4	5	8	10	28	15	8	11	37	38	53	-1
6	União Leiria	34	9	4	4	18	12	5	6	6	18	17	14	10	10	36	29	52	+7
7	Vitória Guimarães	34	10	5	2	39	16	4	3	10	14	25	14	8	12	53	41	50	+12
8	CF Estrela Amadora	34	9	5	3	22	12	2	7	8	11	28	11	12	11	33	40	45	-7
9	SC Braga	34	7	7	3	25	19	3	5	9	13	31	10	12	12	38	50	42	-12
10	CS Marítimo	34	7	5	5	28	21	3	6	8	16	24	10	11	13	44	45	41	-1
11	SC Farense	34	7	5	5	19	20	3	4	10	20	34	10	9	15	39	54	39	-15
12	SC Salgueiros	34	6	10	1	29	20	1	7	9	16	35	7	17	10	45	55	38	-10
13	SC Campomaiorense	34	7	5	5	23	21	3	2	12	18	30	10	7	17	41	51	37	-10
14	Rio Ave FC	34	4	8	5	17	19	4	3	10	9	28	8	11	15	26	47	35	-21
15	FC Alverca	34	7	4	6	20	22	1	7	9	16	28	8	11	15	36	50	35	-14
16	SC Beira Mar	34	5	9	3	23	19	1	6	10	13	34	6	15	13	36	53	33	-17
17	GD Chaves	34	4	7	6	24	30	1	3	13	15	40	5	10	19	39	70	25	-31
18	Académica Coimbra	34	3	5	9	17	33	1	4	12	13	38	4	9	21	30	71	21	-41

N.B. Where two or more teams are level on points, classification is determined by the results of the matches between them.

The championship script was equally familiar. Once Porto hit the front, they stayed put. Seemingly resistant to pressure, they just kept chalking up the points in their usual way until their pursuers lost hope and gave up. As in the previous two seasons, Porto had the formidable attacking presence of Jardel to rely on whenever they found themselves in trouble. The Brazilian, ably assisted by Zahovic, scored 36 goals in the league - ten more than his top-scoring tally of the previous season - and was by far the most influential player in the entire championship. Again.

Coach Fernando Santos, newly arrived from Estrela Amadora, where he had spent four years taking the Lisbon club slowly but surely up the table, proved a more than capable replacement for the departed António Oliveira, although, like his predecessor, he received heavy criticism for his lack of tactical versatility in Europe. The 44-year-old coach arrived at the same time as a number of new players, but almost without exception it was the old hands who played the key rôles in the club's historic triumph.

Aside from the goal-grabbing duo of Jardel and Zahovic up front, the dominant individuals were Yugoslav winger Ljubinko Drulovic, midfielder Capucho, centre-backs Jorge Costa and Aloísio and - after he had returned from Barcelona to replace disappointing Yugoslav international Ivica Kralj - goalkeeper Vítor Baía. Porto lost Brazilian midfielder Doriva to Sampdoria in mid-season and then Paulinho Santos to serious injury, but there was sufficient cover to see them safely through.

Porto managed to score in all but two of their 34 league games. Both of the blanks were against Boavista, their city rivals, who confounded all the pre-season predictions by not only taking four points off the champions but stalking them all the way to the penultimate round of the season and taking a well-deserved runners-up spot, which brought with it a place in the qualifying round of the Champions' League.

Boavista almost matched the consistency of their neighbours. They remained unbeaten during the second half of the season until the

TOP SCORERS

36 JARDEL (FC Porto)
24 NUNO GOMES (SL Benfica)
16 DEMÉTRIOS (SC Campomaiorense)
    SILVA (SC Braga)
15 AYEW Kwame (Boavista FC)
    Alex BUNBURY (CS Marítimo)
    Ion TIMOFTE (Boavista FC)
14 Zlatko ZAHOVIC (FC Porto)
    CHIQUINHO CONDE (Vitória Setúbal)
13 EDMILSON (Vitória Guimarães)
    Ivailo YORDANOV (Sporting CP)

very last game, by which time they knew they could finish no higher or lower than second. The match which secured the championship for Porto was Boavista's penultimate fixture in Faro. Leading 2-0 with a minute to go, Jaime Pacheco's team suffered a collective black-out. When they saw the light again, the score was 2-2, and their admittedly slim hopes of a first title were dead and buried. It meant that Porto could go into their match with Sporting later that evening relaxed in the knowledge that the title was already under wraps.

Disappintment was rare for Boavista during a season in which they lost only three matches and were unbeaten in all six games against the 'big three' of Porto, Benfica and Sporting. Their attacking triumvirate of Ion Timofte, Jorge Couto and Ayew produced a steady stream of goals, while at the back goalkeeper William Andem and left-back Quevedo were models of consistency.

Third place went to Benfica, which, of course, was seen as a disaster by the fans of Portugal's most famous club. It was another season of slash and burn at the Stadium of Light, with coach Graeme Souness invariably at the heart of all the commotion. The Scot had generally been well treated during his first season at the club, which ended with a second-place finish and qualification for the Champions' League, but in 1998/99 relations between Souness and the fans went from bad to worse.

Like Porto, Benfica flattered to deceive in the Champions' League. Losing to Finnish side HJK in Helsinki and then being held at home in the return was plainly unacceptable. There was no way back after that, even if a theoretical chance of finishing as one of the best runners-up did still remain as they began their final match in Eindhoven. In the Portuguese league the team began reasonably well but successive defeats in Oporto, against

DOMESTIC CUP 98/99

FOURTH ROUND
Juventude Évora 1, Boavista FC 3
Gil Vicente FC 3, Sporting CP 2
FC Porto 4, FC Famalicão 2 (aet)
SL Benfica 4, Académica Coimbra 1
Leça FC 3, Amora FC 0
GS Loures 2, AD Esposende 1
CF Estrela Amadora 0, SC Farense 0 (aet)
(replay) SC Farense 3, CF Estrela Amadora 2 (aet)
SC Covilhã 2, SC Salgueiros 4
SC Campomaiorense 3, SC Braga 2
AD Fafe 1, Vitória Setúbal 2
União Leiria 2, Rio Ave FC 1
SCU Torreense 2, GD Chaves 0
EFC Vendas Novas 1, CS Marítimo 3
Caçadores Taipas 1, FC Felgueiras 0
Vilanovense FC 3, CD Santa Clara 3 (aet)
(replay) CD Santa Clara 3, Vilanovense FC 1
FC Penafiel 0, Imortal DC 0 (aet)
(replay) Imortal DC 0, FC Penafiel 1
Vitória Guimarães 2, Moreirense FC 3
Naval 1. de Maio 3, Caldas SC 0
FC Paços Ferreira 3, AD San Joanense 0
Gondomar SC 2, SC Olhanense 0
FC Alverca 2, CS Câmara de Lobos 1
SC São João Ver 2, Oriental Lisboa 1
FC Maia 3, Seixal FC 0
UD Vilafranquense 2, GD Pevidém 3
CD Nacional 3, SC Rio Tinto 4 (aet)
Portimonense SC 4, RD Águeda 1
CD Feirense 3, Oliveira do Bairro SC 1
SC Beira Mar 4, Futebol Benfica 2
AD Portomosense 1, GD Sesimbra 0

FIFTH ROUND
Vitória Setúbal 2, SL Benfica 0
FC Penafiel 0, SC Sampomaiorense 1
Leça FC 0, União Leiria 1
CS Marítimo 3, SC Salgueiros 2 (aet)
Boavista FC 2, SC Farense 1
Gil Vicente FC 4, CD Santa Clara 1
AD Esposende 2, Naval 1. de Maio 0
Gondomar SC 3, FC Paços Ferreira 4
Portimonense SC 1, Moreirense FC 2
FC Maia 5, SC São João Ver 0
SC Rio Tinto 0, Caçadores Taipas 1 (aet)
FC Porto 2, SCU Torreense 1
CD Feirense 0, GD Pevidém 1
SC Beira Mar 7, AD Portomosense 0
bye - FC Alverca

1/8 FINALS
Boavista FC 3, Gil Vicente FC 2
FC Alverca 0, SC Campomaiorense 3
Caçadores Taipas 1, AD Esposende 2
SC Beira Mar 1, União Leiria 1 (aet)
(replay) União Leiria 1, SC Beira Mar 2
Vitória Setúbal 4, FC Paços Ferreira 0
Moreirense FC 3, FC Maia 2
CS Marítimo 5, GD Pevidém 1
bye - SCU Torreense

QUARTER-FINALS
AD Esposende 1 (Nuno Sousa 23), Boavista FC 0

CS Marítimo 2 (Roméu 49, 83),
SC Campomaiorense 2 (René Rivas 4, 34) (aet)
(replay) SC Campomaiorense 0, CS Marítimo 0
(aet; 6-5 on pens.)

SCU Torreense 0, Vitória Setúbal 0
(replay) Vitória Setúbal 3, SCU Torreense 0

Moreirense FC 1 (Gomes 33),

SC Beira Mar 1 (Simic 55p)
(replay) SC Beira Mar 1 (Gila 69), Moreirense FC 0

SEMI-FINALS
AD Esposende 0,
SC Campomaiorense 2 (Isaías 37, Demétrios 69)

SC Beira Mar 1 (Ricardo Sousa 32), Vitória Setúbal 0

FINAL
19/06/99, Lisbon
SC BEIRA MAR 1 Ricardo Sousa (68)
SC CAMPOMAIORENSE 0
referee - Lucílio Baptista

SC BEIRA MAR - Palatsi; Jorge Neves, Lobão, Gila, Caetano; Eusébio, Fusco, Paulo Sérgio (Quintas 82), Ricardo Sousa (André 77); Fernando, Fary Faye (Simic 65).

SC CAMPOMAIORENSE - Poleksic; Quim Machado, Marco Almeida, René Rivas, Basílio Marques; Mauro Soares, Rogério Matias, Nuno Campos; Isaías, Laelson, Demétrios.

NATIONAL TEAM APPEARANCES 98/99

Coach - HUMBERTO COELHO	MOZ	HUN	ROM	SVK	ISR	HOL	AZB	LIE	SVK	LIE	Cps	Gls
VÍTOR BAÍA (15/10/69) - FC Barcelona (ESP)/FC Porto	G	G	G	G	G46	G	G77	G	G	G	65	-
SECRETÁRIO (12/05/70) - FC Porto	D	D				D	D	D		D14	25	1
FERNANDO COUTO (02/08/69) - Lazio (ITA)	D		D	D	D	D63	D	D	D	D	57	6
PAULO MADEIRA (06/09/70) - SL Benfica	D	D			D	D	D	D	D	D	20	3
NÉLSON (05/11/71) - FC Porto	D46										7	-
CALADO (01/03/76) - SL Benfica	M										4	-
ABEL XAVIER (30/11/72) - PSV (HOL)	M		D85	D	D				D31		10	1
FIGO (04/11/72) - FC Barcelona (ESP)	M	M	M	M90	M46	M76	M73	M	M90	M	53	9
RUI COSTA (29/03/72) - Fiorentina (ITA)	M85	M	M	M67	M	M65	M83	M	M	M	44	15
NUNO GOMES (05/07/76) - SL Benfica	A73		s78		s76		s75				7	-
DOMINGOS (02/01/69) - CD Tenerife (ESP)	A46										34	9
LUÍS CARLOS (21/08/72) - SL Benfica	s46										1	-
JOÃO PINTO (19/08/71) - SL Benfica	s46	A	A78	A46		A65	A	A75	A61	A	50	16
EDGAR (07/08/77) - Real Madrid (ESP)	s73										1	-
PAIVA (07/02/73) - Vitória Guimarães	s85										1	-
JORGE COSTA (04/10/71) - FC Porto		D	D	D							22	-
DIMAS (16/02/69) - Juventus (ITA)/Fenerbahçe (TUR)		D	D	D		D	D	D	D	D	27	-
PAULO BENTO (20/06/69) - Real Oviedo (ESP)		M	M69	M	M	M			M		15	-
PAULINHO SANTOS (21/11/70) - FC Porto		M	M	M	D77	M88					30	2
SÁ PINTO (10/10/72) - Real Sociedad (ESP)		A	A	A	A65	A89	A	A61	A	A	29	7
SÉRGIO CONCEIÇÃO (15/11/74) - Lazio (ITA)			s69	s46	M	s65	M	M87	s31	M	16	2
DANI (02/11/76) - Ajax (HOL)			s85		s77						7	-
DA COSTA (01/12/74) - AS Monaco (FRA)				s67							1	-
CAPUCHO (21/02/72) - FC Porto				s90				s87	s61	s14	10	1
PAULO SOUSA (30/08/70) - Inter (ITA)					M46		M	M	M	M64	39	-
PEDRO ESPINHA (20/09/65) - Vitória Guimarães					s46		s77				2	-
PAULETA (28/04/73) - RC Deportivo (ESP)					s46	s89	s73	s61			6	2
SIMÃO SABROSA (31/10/79) - Sporting CP					s46						1	1
JORGE COUTO (01/07/70) - Boavista FC					s65						6	-
BETO (03/05/76) - Sporting CP						s63					3	-
HUGO LEAL (21/05/80) - SL Benfica						s65					1	-
LITOS (25/02/74) - Boavista FC						s88					1	-
PEDRO BARBOSA (06/08/70) - Sporting CP							s83		s90	s64	17	3

Boavista and FC Porto, served to temper the team's title ambitions.

It was the 0-3 home defeat by Boavista in mid-March that stopped Benfica dead in their tracks and signalled the beginning of the end of Souness's reign. He was already living on borrowed time in any case, having traded insults with a group of Benfica fans and persisted in fielding second-rate British players who, in general, had only come to Portugal because they could not get a game in the English Premiership. In fairness to Souness, he was not provided with money to go out and buy better-quality players. But his prickly, arrogant persona was always liable to condemn him if the team did not come up with the desired results. And that is precisely what happened. Behind his

EUROPEAN CUPS 98/99

CHAMPIONS' CUP
● **FC PORTO**
Champions' League
1st match OLYMPIAKOS (GRE)
H 2-2 Zahovic (64), Jardel (81)
Kralj; Jorge Costa, Aloísio, Fernando Mendes, Secretário,
Drulovic (Artur 58), Jardel (Panduru 89), Doriva, Paulinho Santos,
Capucho, Zahovic (Chippo 69).

2nd match AJAX (HOL)
A 1-2 Zahovic (69)
Rui Correia; Secretário, Jorge Costa, Aloísio, Fernando
Mendes (Chippo 46), Doriva, Zahovic, Paulinho Santos,
Capucho (Artur 66), Jardel, Drulovic (Rui Barros 82).

3rd round CROATIA ZAGREB (CRO)
H 3-0 Drulovic (33), Zahovic (43, 76)
Kralj; Secretário, Jorge Costa, Aloísio, Fernando Mendes, Paulinho Santos,
Doriva, Zahovic (Chippo 90), Capucho (Rui Barros 81),
Drulovic (Artur 64), Jardel.

4th round CROATIA ZAGREB (CRO)
A 1-3 Jardel (38)
Kralj; Secretário, João M. Pinto, Aloísio (Mielcarski 74),
Fernando Mendes (Chippo 74), Paulinho Santos, Doriva, Zahovic, Drulovic,
Capucho, Rui Barros (Jardel 26).

5th match OLYMPIAKOS (GRE)
A 1-2 Zahovic (80)
Rui Correia; Secretário, Jorge Costa, Aloísio, Fernando Mendes
(João M. Pinto 90), Doriva, Chainho (Rui Barros 56), Zahovic,
Capucho (Fehér 66), Drulovic, Jardel.

6th match AJAX (HOL)
H 3-0 Zahovic (53, 71), Drulovic (79)
Rui Correia; João M. Pinto, Jorge Costa, Aloísio, Paulinho Santos, Doriva,
Chainho, Panduru (Chippo 50), Zahovic (Rui Barros 82),
Drulovic (Mielcarski 87), Jardel.

● **SL BENFICA**
Qualifying round BEITAR JERUSALEM (ISR)
H 6-0 Pembridge (24, 82), Deane (29), Calado (63p), Shelach (80og),
Nuno Gomes (86p)
Preud'homme; Sousa, Paulo Madeira, Ronaldo, Minto, Thomas,
Poborsky (Porfírio 69), Calado, Pembridge, Deane (Nuno Gomes 77),
Pringle (João Pinto 57).
A 2-4 Nuno Gomes (17p), João Pinto (89)
Preud'homme; Sousa, Paulo Madeira, Ronaldo, Minto, Thomas,
Kandaurov (Poborsky 54), Calado (Tahar 74), Pembridge, João Pinto,
Nuno Gomes (Pringle 55).

Champions' League
1st match 1.FC KAISERSLAUTERN (GER)
A 0-1
Preud'homme; Tahar, Paulo Madeira, Ronaldo, Bruno Basto, Thomas,
Calado, João Pinto (Poborsky 65), Pembridge, Pringle,
Deane (Hugo Leal 75; Sousa 88).

2nd match PSV (HOL)
H 2-1 Nuno Gomes (46), João Pinto (76)
Preud'homme; Sousa, Andrade, Ronaldo, Bruno Basto,
Thomas (Kandaurov 58), Poborsky (Pringle 76), Hugo Leal, Pembridge,
João Pinto, Nuno Gomes (Deane 76).

3rd match HJK (FIN)
A 0-2
Preud'homme; Sousa, Paulo Madeira, Ronaldo, Minto, Hugo Leal, Thomas,
Kandaurov (Calado 79), Pembridge, Pringle (Porfírio 74),
Nuno Gomes (Poborsky 60).

4th match HJK (FIN)
H 2-2 Nuno Gomes (78), Calado (80)
Preud'homme; Andrade (Porfírio 46), Paulo Madeira, Ronaldo, Minto,
Poborsky (Pringle 81), Calado, Hugo Leal, Pembridge, João Pinto,
Nuno Gomes.

5th match 1.FC KAISERSLAUTERN (GER)
H 2-1 Nuno Gomes (39), João Pinto (69)
Ovchinnikov; Tahar, Paulo Madeira, Ronaldo, Minto, Poborsky, Calado,
Pembridge, Hugo Leal, João Pinto, Nuno Gomes.

6th match PSV (HOL)
A 2-2 Nuno Gomes (47p, 63)
Ovchinnikov; Andrade, Ronaldo, Tahar, Minto, Thomas (Calado 69),
Poborsky (Pringle 82), Pembridge (Bruno Basto 88), Hugo Leal,
João Pinto, Nuno Gomes.

CUP WINNERS' CUP
● **SC BRAGA**
1st round METALURGS LIEPAYA (LAT)
A 0-0
Paulo Morais; José Nuno Azevedo, Idalécio, Odair, Lino, Mozer,
Jordão (Formoso 81), Castanheira, Gamboa (Toni 72), Silva,
Karoglan (Luís Miguel 65).
H 4-0 Bruno (13p, 61), Karoglan (35), Silva (86)
Paulo Morais; José Nuno Azevedo, Odair, Idalécio, Lino,
Jordão (Castanheira 55), Mozer, Bruno, Luís Miguel (Silva 21), Toni,
Karoglan (Dé 79).

2nd round LOKOMOTIV MOSKVA (RUS)
A 1-3 Odair (47)
Paulo Morais; Odair, José Nuno Azevedo, Sérgio Abreu, Lino, Mozer,
Jordão, Artur Jorge, Bruno, Karoglan (Toni 74), Silva (Quim 90).
H 1-0 Karoglan (11)
Quim; José Nuno Azevedo, Artur Jorge (Sérgio Abreu 80), Odair,
Lino (Formoso 67), Mozer, Bruno, Jordão, Gamboa (Toni 59), Silva,
Karoglan.

EUROPEAN CUPS 98/99 (CONTINUED)

UEFA CUP

● **CS MARITIMO**
1st round LEEDS UNITED (ENG)
A 0-1
    Van der Straeten; Carlos Jorge, Jorge Soares, Zeca, Bunbury,
    Rui Óscar, Paulo Sérgio, Eusébio, Márcio António (Lino 87),
    Duveau (Herivelto 55), Toni (Tulipa 66).
H 1-0   Jorge Soares (45)
(aet; 1-4 on pens.)
    Van der Straeten; Carlos Jorge, Zeca, Bunbury,
    Jokanovic (Paulo Sérgio 61), Jorge Soares, Lino (Tulipa 62), Eusébio,
    Rui Óscar, Toni (Pedro Paulo 85), Márcio António.

● **SPORTING CP**
1st round BOLOGNA (ITA)
H 0-2
    Tiago; Saber, Beto, Marco Aurélio (Vidigal 55), Quiroga, Delfim,
    Duscher, Bino, Simão Sabrosa (Yordanov 46), Edmilson,
    Leandro (Giménez 66).
A 1-2   Leandro (64)
    Tiago; Saber, Beto, Quiroga (Ramírez 84), Patacas, Delfim, Duscher,
    Bino, Vinicius (Yordanov 46), Simão Sabrosa, Leandro.

● **VITORIA GUIMARÃES**
1st round CELTIC (SCO)
H 1-2   Geraldo (86)
    Pedro Espinha; José Carlos, Alexandre, Auri, Quim Berto,
    Vitor Paneira, Costa (Riva 37), Paiva, Geraldo,
    Edmilson (Milovanovic 79), Gilmar.
A 1-2   Söderström (86)
    Pedro Espinha; Quim Berto, Alexandre, Arley Alvarez, Kasongo, Costa,
    Riva, Söderström, Geraldo, Milovanovic (Edmilson 57),
    Gilmar (Edmilson 75).

NATIONAL TEAM RESULTS 98/99

19/08/98	Mozambique	H	Ponta Delgada	2-1	Rui Costa (56, 58)
06/09/98	Hungary (ECQ)	A	Budapest	3-1	Sá Pinto (56, 76), Rui Costa (84)
10/10/98	Romania (ECQ)	H	Oporto	0-1	
14/10/98	Slovakia (ECQ)	A	Bratislava	3-0	João Pinto (16, 33), Abel Xavier (69)
18/11/98	Israel	H	Setúbal	2-0	Fernando Couto (5), Simão Sabrosa (89)
10/02/99	Holland	N	Paris	0-0	
26/03/99	Azerbaijan (ECQ)	H	Guimarães	7-0	Sá Pinto (28), João Pinto (36, 71), Paulo Madeira (68), Sérgio Conceição (75), Pauleta (82, 83)
31/03/99	Liechtenstein (ECQ)	A	Vaduz	5-0	Rui Costa (15p, 79), Figo (49), Paulo Madeira (54, 60)
05/06/99	Slovakia (ECQ)	H	Lisbon	1-0	Capucho (62)
09/06/99	Liechtenstein (ECQ)	H	Coimbra	8-0	Sá Pinto (28, 44, 51), João Pinto (40, 59, 68), Rui Costa (80, 90p)

back Benfica president Vale e Azevedo negotiated a contract with ex-Bayern Munich and Real Madrid coach Jupp Heynckes in which the German agreed to take over at the start of the 1999/2000 season. This soon became public knowledge, and Souness, choosing to show his feelings with a display of carefree petulance on the bench during the home game with Campomaiorense, was subsequently suspended from his duties.

Sporting, coached by Mirko Jozic, a Croatian making his début in Portugal, played some fine football during the season but once again it won them nothing. It was the contention of everyone associated with the club that they were unfairly treated by referees and that, in consequence, the quality of their football was not accurately reflected by their position in the league table. Official statistics showed that Sporting had more corners and shots at goals than any other team over the course of the season. Less official were the calculations produced by the club's fans that Sporting had been denied a total of nine points by referees through disallowed goals and unrecognised penalty claims.

Even with those points added to their total, however, Sporting would still have fallen well short of first place, so it was hardly a surprise when, in the summer, the club decided to appoint yet another new coach - Italian Giuseppe Materazzi, a man with a reputation for discipline but, like Jozic before him, with no experience of the vagaries and idiosyncracies of Portuguese football.

Sporting's Cup form in 1998/99 was lamentable. Eliminated in the first round of the UEFA Cup by Italian InterToto qualifiers Bologna, they also fell at the first hurdle in the domestic Cup, losing 3-2 to Second Division Gil Vicente, who would later go on to acquire promotion in the company of Belenenses and Santa Clara - a team from the Azores. With Porto and Benfica also joining Sporting on the scrap heap in the next round - the former after a humbling 0-1 home defeat by Third Division outfit Torreense - it meant that for the first time ever none of the 'big three' were present in the last 16 of the competition.

Clearly, this paved the way for an 'unknown' to take the trophy and, sure enough, the final brought together two of the First Division's strugglers, Campomaiorense and Beira Mar. When the final came around, in mid-June, Beira Mar had already been relegated, but it was their intention to go down in style. With two men sent off in the second half, they didn't quite achieve that, but what they did manage was a dramatic victory, with the winning goal coming from Ricardo Sousa, the son of coach António Sousa. No team had ever previously won the Cup in the season that they had been relegated, and no Beira Mar team had ever previously won a major trophy. If ever there was a consolation prize for going down, this was surely it.

While Beira Mar's relegation had not been confirmed until the final seconds of the final match of the season, Académica Coimbra and Chaves had long been condemned to the drop. There was no escape this time for Chaves, who a year earlier had been rescued when Leça were relegated in their place following a Federation investigation into a bribery scandal that had taken place five years earlier.

Another victim of FPF discipline, national team striker Sá Pinto, returned triumphantly from his enforced one-year ban for punching ex-national team coach Artur Jorge. He started all of the seven Euro 2000 qualifiers played by Portugal during the season and had a dramatic impact in his first game back, scoring twice as Humberto Coelho's side grabbed a potentially crucial 3-1 win in Hungary. Four more goals were subsequently added to his account as the team suddenly went goal-crazy in the spring to lift themselves to the head of European Championship Group Seven.

Sá Pinto's return was clearly a major factor in revitalising an attack that had become renowned for its profligacy. But there were other players who got in on the act too, with Rui Costa, João Pinto and even defender Paulo Madeira all letting rip like never before. Of course, most of the goals were scored at the expense of cannon-fodder opponents Liechtenstein and Azerbaijan, but three goals apiece away to Hungary and Slovakia also painted a positive picture. It was just a shame that in the match that mattered more than any other, the home fixture against Romania, Portugal's old weakness came back to haunt them. They attacked throughout the match but couldn't score, and in the last minute the Romanians won the match with a soft free-kick.

INTERNATIONAL HONOURS

World Cup Finals appearances: 1966 (3rd), 1986

European Championship appearances: 1960, 1984 (semi-finals), 1996

European Club Competitions

Champions' Cup	SL Benfica (1961, 1962)
	FC Porto (1987)
Cup-winners' Cup	Sporting CP (1964)
Super Cup	FC Porto (1987)
World Club Cup	FC Porto (1987)

PLAYERS OF THE SEASON

★ SUPERSTAR PROFILE
JARDEL

Top-class Brazilian strikers are everywhere in Europe these days, but none of them have produced the astonishing goalscoring consistency of 26-year-old FC Porto marksman Mário Jardel Almeida Ribeiro. His continued absence from the Brazilian national team remains an unsolved mystery, as does the fact that he has not been bought by a top club in one of Europe's major leagues. The big centre-forward has had three seasons in the Portuguese First Division and has topped the scoring charts each time, putting the ball in the net on average once a game. In 1998/99 he managed his highest winning total yet, scoring 36 goals - a figure that enabled him to claim the Adidas Golden Shoe as Europe's number one

goalscorer. With three Portuguese championship-winning medals also in his possession, it seemed inevitable that the Brazilian would leave in the summer and take his talents elsewhere, but after links with Juventus and Bayern Munich, no concrete deal materialised so he decided to stay in Oporto. It has been mentioned as a criticism against him that most of his goals are scored against weak defences, but by the end of 1998/99 he had nine Champions' League goals to his credit, with two of them having come on his European début in a 3-2 win away to Milan. Jardel may not have the subtle skills of a Ronaldo or a Rivaldo, but the feeling persists that this giant of a player would stand out in any company. But will we ever know for sure?

As the qualifying campaign progressed, it became more and more obvious that first place in the group would be settled by the return match with the Romanians in Bucharest in early September, with a draw in that game likely to be of some benefit to Portugal - a team who, were they to qualify, would probably rank as one of the dark horses for the finals in Holland and Belgium, just as they did at Euro '96.

The team that shone in England is still virtually intact, with Figo, João Pinto, Fernando Couto and Vítor Baía all now having collected more than 50 caps and Rui Costa and Paulo Sousa close to joining them. With exciting newcomers like Nuno Gomes, Hugo Leal and Simão Sabrosa coming through, Portugal certainly have the makings of an outstanding team for the new millennium. The question, as ever, though, is can this talented pool of players go out and fully do themselves justice?

PLAYERS OF THE SEASON

SIMÃO SABROSA

Barcelona are a wealthy club, but they do not pay out 15 million US dollars for any old teenager. They know talent when they see it, and that was the price they were prepared to pay in order to secure the services of a player many in Portugal are already tagging as the 'new Figo'. Simão Sabrosa took the Portuguese league by storm in 1998/99, scoring ten league goals for Sporting and scooping more official 'man of the match' awards (seven in total) than any other player in the league. A winger of supreme natural ability, he has probably done the right thing by leaving his homeland, because towards the end of the season he increasingly became the victim of aggressive tackling as defenders ran out of ways to stop him.

SÉRGIO CONCEICÃO

When Sérgio Conceição left FC Porto to join Lazio in the summer of 1998, it was generally assumed that he would be only a bit-part player in Sven Göran Eriksson's multi-talented squad. But he impressed the Swedish coach straight away with his vitality and versatility and went on to become a fixture in the team, missing only one match all season as Lazio challenged strongly for the Serie A title. He scored his first two goals in an amazing 5-3 away win at

Inter and became a reliable service-provider for Christian Vieri and Marcelo Salas with his superb crosses from the flanks. Portuguese national team boss Humberto Coelho is another who has been won over by the 24-year-old's skill and enthusiasm and he has made him a regular cast-member of an illustrious midfield quartet that also features Figo, Paulo Sousa and Rui Costa.

NUNO GOMES

23-year-old Nuno Gomes was one of the few redeeming features of Benfica's season. He scored 24 goals in the league - 18 more than any of his team-mates - and another seven in the Champions' League, yet he was never fully appreciated by coach Graeme Souness, who frequently put him on the bench or brought him off during the course of a game. He actually played from start to finish in just 18 of his 34 league appearances. It was a similar story for the Portuguese national team, with just a couple of intro ductions as a sub coming his way during the Euro 2000 qualifying campaign. The former Boavista player has more than proved his worth in two seasons at the Stadium of Light. Another good showing in 1999/2000 will almost certainly see him sold abroad for a big fee.

ACADÉMICA COIMBRA

CLUB DIRECTORY

Associação Académica de Coimbra
Rua Infanta D. Maria
3000 Coimbra
tel - (039) 793890
Year of Formation - 1876
President - José Campos Coroa
Coach - Raul Águas; Vítor Manuel; Vítor Gervásio
(99/00 - Carlos Garcia)
Stadium - Municipal de Coimbra (25,000)

APPEARANCES 98/99

	P	Ap	(s)	Gls
Eduard ABAZI (ALB)	D	20	(3)	1
ABDUL	D		(1)	
ANDERSON (BRA)	D	1		
BARROSO	M	24	(2)	1
CAMILO	D	9	(1)	
CATTANEO	M	7	(7)	
DÁRIO (MOZ)	A	21	(4)	7
FEBRAS	A		(1)	
GAÚCHO (BRA)	M	29	(1)	1
JOÃO CAMPOS	M	10	(4)	
JOÃO PIRES	A		(7)	
JOÃO TOMÁS	A	9	(12)	1
LIM	M	6	(13)	3
LUÍS FILIPE	M	8	(10)	3
MADUREIRA	M		(1)	
MAURÍCIO (BRA)	A	28	(3)	7
MICKEY	M	26	(7)	2
Ched MOUNIR (MAR)	D	21		1
NUNO ROCHA	M		(3)	
PAULO ADRIANO	M	3	(7)	
PEDRO LAVOURA (VEN)	M	21	(3)	
PEDRO ROMA	G	26		
PERES	G	8		
ROCHA	M	18	(6)	1
RUI CAMPOS	M	1		
SÉRGIO CRUZ	D	7		
TÓ SÁ	D	28	(3)	1
VERÍSSIMO	D	30		
VÍTOR ALVES	G		(1)	
ZÉ NANDO	D	13		

LEAGUE RESULTS 1998/99

23/08/98	GD Chaves	A	0-1	
30/08/98	SC Campomaiorense	H	1-5	João Tomás
06/09/98	Sporting CP	H	2-2	Maurício 2
20/09/98	CF Estrela Amadora	A	1-2	Barroso
27/09/98	Rio Ave FC	H	1-1	Mounir
04/10/98	SC Beira Mar	A	2-0	Maurício, og (Gila)
11/10/98	SC Farense	H	2-1	Dário, Maurício
25/10/98	CS Marítimo	A	1-4	Dário
01/11/98	Vitória Guimarães	H	1-1	Dário
08/11/98	FC Alverca	A	1-2	Abazi
15/11/98	Boavista FC	H	2-3	Mickey, Gaúcho
22/11/98	União Leiria	A	0-1	
29/11/98	SC Salgueiros	H	0-1	
06/12/98	SC Braga	A	2-2	Maurício, Dário
13/12/98	FC Porto	H	0-2	
20/12/98	SL Benfica	A	0-3	
03/01/99	Vitória Setúbal	H	2-0	Lim 2
17/01/99	GD Chaves	H	1-2	Luís Filipe
23/01/99	SC Campomaiorense	A	1-2	Maurício (p)
30/01/99	Sporting CP	A	0-5	
06/02/99	CF Estrela Amadora	H	2-2	Maurício, Mickey
13/02/99	Rio Ave FC	A	1-1	Luís Filipe
20/02/99	SC Beira Mar	H	1-0	Luís Filipe
27/02/99	SC Farense	A	0-2	
14/03/99	CS Marítimo	H	1-3	Dário
21/03/99	Vitória Guimarães	A	1-1	Lim
03/04/99	FC Alverca	H	0-5	
16/04/99	Boavista FC	A	1-3	Rocha
25/04/99	União Leiria	H	0-1	
01/05/99	SC Salgueiros	A	1-1	Dário
08/05/99	SC Braga	H	1-1	Dário
15/05/99	FC Porto	A	1-7	Tó Sá
22/05/99	SL Benfica	H	0-3	
29/05/99	Vitória Setúbal	A	0-1	

FC ALVERCA

CLUB DIRECTORY

Futebol Clube de Alverca
Rua Coronel Henrique Nova
2615 Alverca do Ribatejo
tel - (01) 9580956/9570858
Year of Formation - 1939
President - Luís Filipe Ferreira Vieira
Coach - Mário Wilson; José Romão
Stadium - Complexo Desportivo (20,000)

APPEARANCES 98/99

	P	Ap	(s)	Gls
ABEL SILVA	D	30		
BETINHO	M		(1)	
BIRA (BRA)	M	1	(2)	
CAJU (BRA)	A	26	(3)	8
CAPUCHO	D	9	(6)	
DIAGO	M	14	(1)	1
FABINHO	M	1	(7)	
Ilshat FAIZULIN (RUS)	A	8	(2)	
FILIPE AZEVEDO	M	16	(11)	8
HUGO COSTA	D	29		
JAMIR	M	5	(1)	
JOÃO PIRES	A	3	(6)	
JOSÉ SOARES	D	30		1
JUBA	M	14		
LIMA	M	5	(1)	
MANICHE	A	13	(13)	3
MARCO FREITAS	M	29	(1)	3
Nikola MILINKOVIC (YUG)	M	8		3
NANDINHA	A	17		5
NÉLSON MORAIS	D	4	(1)	
PAULO SANTOS	G	30		
RAMIREZ	M	20	(7)	3
RUI BORGES	A	16	(14)	1
TÓ ZÉ	M	10	(6)	
VALENTE	D	23	(1)	
VALIDA	D	9	(5)	
VÍTOR VALENTE	G	4		

LEAGUE RESULTS 1998/99

23/08/98	SC Campomaiorense	A	2-2	Diogo, Filipe Azevedo
30/08/98	Boavista FC	H	0-0	
06/09/98	União Leiria	A	0-1	
20/09/98	SC Salgueiros	H	1-1	Marco Freitas
27/09/98	SC Braga	A	0-0	
04/10/98	FC Porto	H	1-5	Ramirez
11/10/98	SL Benfica	A	2-2	Marco Freitas, Maniche
25/10/98	Vitória Setúbal	H	1-0	Filipe Azevedo
01/11/98	GD Chaves	A	1-1	Filipe Azevedo
08/11/98	Académica Coimbra	H	2-1	Marco Freitas, Filipe Azevedo
15/11/98	Sporting CP	A	0-2	
22/11/98	CF Estrela Amadora	H	0-1	
29/11/98	Rio Ave FC	A	0-0	
06/12/98	SC Beira Mar	H	1-1	José Soares
13/12/98	SC Farense	A	0-1	
20/12/98	CS Marítimo	H	3-0	Filipe Azevedo, Caju 2
03/01/99	Vitória Guimarães	A	1-3	Caju
17/01/99	SC Campomaiorense	H	2-1	Filipe Azevedo (p), Nandinho
24/01/99	Boavista FC	A	0-3	
30/01/99	União Leiria	H	0-2	
06/02/99	SC Salgueiros	A	0-0	
13/02/99	SC Braga	H	0-0	
20/02/99	FC Porto	A	1-3	Maniche
27/02/99	SL Benfica	H	0-2	
14/03/99	Vitória Setúbal	A	0-4	
21/03/99	GD Chaves	H	3-1	Caju 2, Ramirez
03/04/99	Académica Coimbra	A	5-0	Nandinho, Caju 2, Maniche (p), Rui Borges
17/04/99	Sporting CP	H	3-2	Nandinho 3
24/04/99	CF Estrela Amadora	A	0-1	
01/05/99	Rio Ave FC	H	0-1	
08/05/99	SC Beira Mar	A	1-2	Filipe Azevedo (p)
15/05/99	SC Farense	H	1-3	Filipe Azevedo (p)
22/05/99	CS Marítimo	A	3-3	Caju, Milinkovic 2
29/05/99	Vitória Guimarães	H	2-1	Milinkovic, Ramirez (p)

SC BEIRA MAR

CLUB DIRECTORY

Sport Clube Beira-Mar
Avenida Lourenço Peixinho 12
3810 Aveiro
tel - (034) 422282
Year of Formation - 1922
President - Mano Nunes
Coach - António Sousa
Stadium - Mário Duarte (12,000)

MAJOR HONOURS
Domestic Cup - (1) 1999.

APPEARANCES 98/99

	P	Ap	(s)	Gls
ANDRÉ	M	27	(2)	1
CAETANO	D	31		
CÉSAR SANTOS (BRA)	A	3	(12)	
CRISTIANO	D	13		2
ELÍSIO	G	9		
EUSÉBIO	M	19	(2)	
Faye FARY (SEN)	A	23	(11)	10
FERNANDO	A	11	(7)	1
FUSCO	M	28	(3)	
GILA	D	34		5
JACKSON (BRA)	M	1	(4)	
JORGE NEVES	D	33		
JORGE SIVA	M	5	(3)	1
LOBÃO (BRA)	D	22	(2)	
MARCO CANEIRA	D	11	(1)	
MIGUEL ÂNGELO	M	14	(3)	
Jérôme PALATSI (FRA)	G	24		
PAULO SÉRGIO	A	12	(7)	2
QUINTAS	M	10	(13)	
Ermin RAKOVIC (SLO)	M		(4)	
RICARDO SOUSA	M	11	(3)	5
Sasa SIMIC (YUG)	A	26	(5)	8
TIBI	G	1	(2)	
WÉLDER (BRA)	A	6	(17)	1

LEAGUE RESULTS 1998/99

23/08/98	SC Braga	A	1-2	Jorge Silva
30/08/98	FC Porto	H	2-1	Gila, Fary
06/09/98	SL Benfica	A	0-3	
20/09/98	Vitória Setúbal	H	1-1	Gila
27/09/98	GD Chaves	A	0-1	
04/10/98	Académica Coimbra	H	0-2	
11/10/98	Sporting CP	A	0-0	
25/10/98	CF Estrela Amadora	H	0-0	
01/11/98	Rio Ave FC	A	1-1	Simic
08/11/98	SC Campomaiorense	H	2-1	Simic 2
15/11/98	SC Farense	H	0-1	
22/11/98	CS Marítimo	A	1-1	Cristiano
29/11/98	Vitória Guimarães	H	0-0	
06/12/98	FC Alverca	A	1-1	André
13/12/98	Boavista FC	H	1-1	Fary
20/12/98	União Leiria	A	0-1	
03/01/99	SC Salgueiros	H	4-1	Gila, Fary, Simic 2
17/01/99	SC Braga	H	4-2	Paulo Sérgio 2, Fary, Wélder
24/01/99	FC Porto	A	0-7	
31/01/99	SL Benfica	H	1-1	Gila
06/02/99	Vitória Setúbal	A	0-0	
13/02/99	GD Chaves	H	1-1	Simic
20/02/99	Académica Coimbra	A	0-1	
27/02/99	Sporting CP	H	2-2	Fary, Ricardo Sousa
14/03/99	CF Estrela Amadora	A	2-1	Fary, Cristiano
21/03/99	Rio Ave FC	H	1-2	Gila
03/04/99	SC Campomaiorense	A	1-4	Fary
17/04/99	SC Farense	A	1-2	Fary
25/04/99	CS Marítimo	H	1-1	Simic
01/05/99	Vitória Guimarães	A	0-3	
08/05/99	FC Alverca	H	2-1	Ricardo Sousa, Fary
15/05/99	Boavista FC	A	1-2	Simic
22/05/99	União Leiria	H	1-1	Ricardo Sousa
29/05/99	SC Salgueiros	A	4-4	Ricardo Sousa 2, Fernando, Fary

SL BENFICA

CLUB DIRECTORY

Sport Lisboa e Benfica
Avenida General Norton de Matos
1500 Lisboa
tel - (01) 7266129
fax - (01) 7264761
Year of Formation - 1904
President - João Vale e Azevedo
Coach - Graeme Souness; Sheu Han
(99/00 - Jupp Heynckes)
Stadium - Luz (77,844)

MAJOR HONOURS
League Championship - (30) 1936, 1937, 1938,
1942, 1943, 1945, 1950, 1955, 1957, 1960,
1961, 1963, 1964, 1965, 1967, 1968, 1969,
1971, 1972, 1973, 1975, 1976, 1977, 1981,
1983, 1984, 1987, 1989, 1991, 1994.
Domestic Cup - (26)
1930, 1931, 1935, 1940, 1943, 1944, 1949,
1951, 1952, 1953, 1955, 1957, 1959, 1962,
1964, 1969, 1970, 1972, 1980, 1981, 1983,
1985, 1986, 1987, 1993, 1996.
European Champions' Cup - (2) 1961, 1962.

APPEARANCES 98/99

	P	Ap	(s)	Gls
ANDRADE	D	9	(3)	
BRUNO BASTO	D	16	(2)	1
CADETE	A	5	(11)	3
CALADO	M	21	(3)	
Gary CHARLES (ENG)	D	4		1
Brian DEANE (ENG)	A	2	(2)	
Steve HARKNESS (ENG)	D	9		
HUGO LEAL	M	22	(5)	3
JOÃO PINTO	A	27	(1)	4
Sergei KANDAUROV (UKR)	M	10	(12)	5
LUÍS CARLOS	A	12	(7)	1
Scott MINTO (ENG)	D	9	(1)	
NANDINHO	M	2	(2)	1
NUNO GOMES	A	26	(8)	24
Sergei OVCHINNIKOV (RUS)	G	13	(1)	
PAULO MADEIRA	D	28		2
Mark PEMBRIDGE (WAL)	M	19		1
PEPA	A	1	(1)	1
Karel POBORSKY (CZE)	M	22	(5)	6
PORFÍRIO	A		(3)	
Michel PREUD'HOMME (BEL)	G	21		
Martin PRINGLE (SWE)	A	6	(6)	1
RONALDO (BRA)	D	30		2
Dean SAUNDERS (WAL)	A	12	(5)	5
SOUSA	D	9	(1)	
TAHAR El Khalej (MAR)	D	22		4
Michael THOMAS (ENG)	M	17	(1)	1

LEAGUE RESULTS 1998/99

23/08/98	CF Estrela Amadora	H	2-0	Poborsky, Tahar
30/08/98	Rio Ave FC	A	2-0	Nuno Gomes 2 (1p)
06/09/98	SC Beira Mar	H	3-0	Pringle, Luís Carlos, Ronaldo
20/09/98	SC Farense	A	0-1	
27/09/98	CS Marítimo	H	3-1	Nuno Gomes 3 (2p)
04/10/98	Vitória Guimarães	A	2-0	og (Alexandre), Kandaurov
11/10/98	FC Alverca	H	2-2	Poborsky, Nandinho
25/10/98	Boavista FC	A	1-2	Nuno Gomes
01/11/98	União Leiria	H	0-0	
08/11/98	SC Salgueiros	A	1-1	João Pinto
15/11/98	SC Braga	H	4-1	Kandaurov, Poborsky, João Pinto,
				Nuno Gomes
22/11/98	FC Porto	A	1-3	Kandaurov
29/11/98	SC Campomaiorense	A	5-0	Nuno Gomes 2 (1p), Hugo Leal 2,
				Kandaurov
06/12/98	Vitória Setúbal	H	2-0	Pembridge, Nuno Gomes
13/12/98	GD Chaves	A	4-0	Nuno Gomes 3, Tahar
20/12/98	Académica Coimbra	H	3-0	Poborsky, Nuno Gomes 2 (1p)
03/01/99	Sporting CP	A	2-1	og 2 (Beto 2)
17/01/99	CF Estrela Amadora	A	1-0	Saunders
23/01/99	Rio Ave FC	H	3-1	Nuno Gomes, Cadete, Pepa
30/01/99	SC Beira Mar	A	1-1	Tahar
06/02/99	SC Farense	H	5-0	Saunders 2, Nuno Gomes 2, og (King)
13/02/99	CS Marítimo	A	0-1	
20/02/99	Vitória Guimarães	H	3-1	João Pinto, Thomas, Nuno Gomes
27/02/99	FC Alverca	A	2-0	Saunders, Paulo Madeira
14/03/99	Boavista FC	H	0-3	
21/03/99	União Leiria	A	1-1	João Pinto
03/04/99	SC Salgueiros	H	5-0	Charles, Saunders, Ronaldo,
				Nuno Gomes 2 (1p)
17/04/99	SC Braga	A	1-2	Paulo Madeira
24/04/99	FC Porto	H	1-1	Bruno Basto
01/05/99	SC Campomaiorense	H	1-1	Cadete
08/05/99	Vitória Setúbal	A	0-1	
15/05/99	GD Chaves	H	4-1	Tahar, Cadete, Poborsky, Nuno Gomes
22/05/99	Académica Coimbra	A	3-0	Nuno Gomes, og (Mounir), Hugo Leal
29/05/99	Sporting CP	H	3-3	Kandaurov, Poborsky, Nuno Gomes

BOAVISTA FC

CLUB DIRECTORY

Boavista Futebol Clube
Rua O Primeiro de Janeiro
4100 Porto
tel - (02) 6071000/6071023/6071041
fax - (02) 6003743
Year of Formation - 1903
President - João Loureiro
Coach - Jaime Pacheco
Stadium - Bessa (23,000)

MAJOR HONOURS
Domestic Cup - (5)
1975, 1976, 1979, 1992, 1997.

APPEARANCES 98/99

	P	Ap	(s)	Gls
ALEXANDRE	D	4		
ARTUR JORGE VICENTE	A	1	(2)	
Serhiy ATELKIN (UKR)	A		(10)	3
AYEW Kwame (GHA)	A	26	(1)	15
CAVACA	A		(1)	
M'bela DOUALA (CMR)	A	17	(9)	5
HÉLDER	M	10		
ISAÍAS (BRA)	D	32		3
JORGE COUTO	M	34		5
JORGE SILVA	M	2	(5)	
LITOS	D	32		
LUÍS CARLOS (BRA)	M	1	(1)	
LUÍS MANUEL	M	19	(3)	1
MÁRIO SILVA	D	19	(2)	1
MARTELINHO	M		(8)	2
PAULO SOUSA	D	26		
PEDRO EMANUEL	D	6	(9)	
PEDRO MARTINS	M	4	(2)	
QUEVEDO	D	29	(2)	3
RENATO (BRA)	M	2	(3)	
RICARDO PEREIRA	G	4	(1)	
ROGERINHA (BRA)	A	4	(8)	
ROGÉRIO (BRA)	A	4	(11)	3
RUI BENTO	M	32		1
Erwin SANCHEZ (BOL)	M	4	(19)	
Ion TIMOFTE (ROM)	M	32		15
WILLIAM Andem (CMR)	G	30		

LEAGUE RESULTS 1998/99

23/08/98	Vitória Guimarães	H	2-0	Douala 2
30/08/98	FC Alverca	A	0-0	
06/09/98	SC Campomaiorense	A	1-1	Douala
20/09/98	União Leiria	H	1-0	Ayew
27/09/98	SC Salgueiros	A	0-0	
04/10/98	SC Braga	H	1-0	Timofte (p)
11/10/98	FC Porto	A	2-0	Timofte, Rogério
25/10/98	SL Benfica	H	2-1	Timofte (p), Martelinho
01/11/98	Vitória Setúbal	A	3-1	Douala, Jorge Couto, Martelinho
08/11/98	GD Chaves	H	4-1	Jorge Couto, Timofte 2 (2p), Ayew
15/11/98	Académica Coimbra	A	3-2	Timofte, Ayew, Rogério
22/11/98	Sporting CP	H	2-2	Timofte, Jorge Couto
29/11/98	CF Estrela Amadora	A	1-2	Quevedo
06/12/98	Rio Ave FC	H	1-0	Timofte
13/12/98	SC Beira Mar	A	1-1	Isaías
20/12/98	SC Farense	H	3-0	Timofte, Ayew 2
03/01/99	CS Marítimo	A	0-3	
17/01/99	Vitória Guimarães	A	3-2	Isaías, Timofte, Quevedo
23/01/99	FC Alverca	H	3-0	Douala, Timofte, Quevedo
30/01/99	SC Campomaiorense	H	2-1	Ayew, Timofte
06/02/99	União Leiria	A	0-0	
12/02/99	SC Salgueiros	H	2-1	Rogério, Ayew
20/02/99	SC Braga	A	2-1	Ayew, Timofte
27/02/99	FC Porto	H	0-0	
14/03/99	SL Benfica	A	3-0	Ayew 2, Luís Manuel
21/03/99	Vitória Setúbal	H	1-1	Ayew
03/04/99	GD Chaves	A	1-1	Mário Silva
16/04/99	Académica Coimbra	H	3-1	Jorge Couto, Atelkin 2
25/04/99	Sporting CP	A	1-1	Timofte
01/05/99	CF Estrela Amadora	H	2-1	Rui Bento, Ayew
08/05/99	Rio Ave FC	A	2-0	Ayew, Timofte
15/05/99	SC Beira Mar	H	2-1	Jorge Couto, Ayew
22/05/99	SC Farense	A	2-2	Isaías, Atelkin
29/05/99	CS Marítimo	H	1-2	Ayew

SC BRAGA

CLUB DIRECTORY

Sporting Clube de Braga
Parque da Ponte
4710 Braga
tel - (053) 610591
fax - (053) 611686
Year of Formation - 1921
President - João Gomes de Oliveira
Coach - Vítor Oliveira; Carlos Manuel
(99/00 - Manuel Cajuda)
Stadium - 1o de Maio (40,000)

MAJOR HONOURS
Domestic Cup - (2) 1966, 1992.

APPEARANCES 98/99

	P	Ap	(s)	Gls
ARTUR JORGE	D	17	(4)	1
BRUNO	M	23	(8)	
CABRAL	D	6		
CASTANHEIRA	M	15	(8)	
DÉ (BRA)	A		(3)	
FORMOSO	M	10	(11)	
GAMBOA	A	9	(14)	3
IDALÉCIO	D	20	(2)	2
JORDÃO	M	27	(2)	1
JOSÉ NUNO AZEVEDO	D	26		
Mladen KAROGLAN (CRO)	A	23	(3)	3
LINO	D	28		
LUÍS CARLOS	M	5	(6)	2
LUÍS MIGUEL	M	23	(5)	1
MOZER	M	28	(1)	
ODAIR (BRA)	D	21	(4)	2
PAULO DINIS	A		(2)	
PAULO MORAIS	G	6		
QUIM	G	28	(1)	
RUI GUERREIRO	D	6		
SÉRGIO ABREU	D	12	(3)	1
SILVA (BRA)	A	30	(2)	16
TONI	A	10	(18)	4
VÍTOR PEREIRA	D	1		

LEAGUE RESULTS 1998/99

23/08/98	SC Beira Mar	H	2-1	Karoglan (p), Silva
30/08/98	SC Farense	A	2-0	Silva 2
06/09/98	CS Marítimo	H	1-1	Silva
20/09/98	Vitória Guimarães	A	1-5	og (Alexandre)
27/09/98	FC Alverca	H	0-0	
04/10/98	Boavista FC	A	0-1	
11/10/98	União Leiria	H	2-4	Toni, Silva
25/10/98	SC Salgueiros	A	1-1	Artur Jorge
01/11/98	SC Campomaiorense	A	0-2	
08/11/98	FC Porto	H	3-3	Silva, Jordão, Toni
15/11/98	SL Benfica	A	1-4	Odair
22/11/98	Vitória Setúbal	H	3-0	Silva 3
29/11/98	GD Chaves	A	2-1	Silva, Luís Miguel
06/12/98	Académica Coimbra	H	2-2	Gamboa 2
13/12/98	Sporting CP	A	1-4	Idalécio
20/12/98	CF Estrela Amadora	H	1-1	Silva
03/01/99	Rio Ave FC	A	2-1	Sérgio Abreu, Karoglan
17/01/99	SC Beira Mar	A	2-4	og (Gila), Silva (p)
24/01/99	SC Farense	H	0-0	
31/01/99	CS Marítimo	A	0-3	
06/02/99	Vitória Guimarães	H	2-1	Toni, Gamboa
13/02/99	FC Alverca	A	0-0	
20/02/99	Boavista FC	H	1-2	Silva
27/02/99	União Leiria	A	0-0	
14/03/99	SC Salgueiros	H	1-1	Luís Carlos
21/03/99	SC Campomaiorense	H	0-2	
08/04/99	FC Porto	A	0-1	
17/04/99	SL Benfica	H	2-1	Toni, Odair
23/04/99	Vitória Setúbal	A	0-3	
01/05/99	GD Chaves	H	1-0	Idalécio
08/05/99	Académica Coimbra	A	1-1	Luís Carlos
15/05/99	Sporting CP	H	2-0	Silva, Karoglan
22/05/99	CF Estrela Amadora	A	0-0	
29/05/99	Rio Ave FC	H	2-0	Silva 2

SC CAMPOMAIORENSE

CLUB DIRECTORY

Sporting Clube Campomaiorense
Rua Francisco Marchã 1
7370 Campo Maior
tel - (068) 686385/699310
Year of Formation - 1926
President - João Nabeiro
Coach - João Alves; Fernando Pires
(99/00 - Carlos Manuel)
Stadium - Capitão César Correia (10,000)

APPEARANCES 98/99

	P	Ap	(s)	Gls
BASÍLIO MARQUES	M	11	(3)	
CARLOS FERNANDES	M	9	(3)	
DEMÉTRIOS (BRA)	A	22	(7)	16
ISAÍAS (BRA)	A	26	(5)	4
JORGE FERREIRA	D	21	(1)	
JORGINHO	A	7		1
LAELSON (BRA)	A	28	(4)	6
LUÍS MIGUEL	D	13	(4)	
MARCO ALMEIDA	D	20	(1)	2
MAURO SOARES (BRA)	M	23	(4)	2
MENDES	M	8	(3)	
MIRANDA (MOZ)	A		(1)	
NÉLSON MORAIS	D		(1)	
NUNO CAMPOS	D	24	(4)	1
PAULO SÉRGIO	G	15		
Dragoslav POLEKSIC (YUG)	G	19	(1)	
QUIM MACHADO	D	28	(4)	
RENÉ RIVAS (BRA)	D	22	(3)	3
ROGÉRIO MATIAS	D	22	(2)	
SABUGO	M	14	(8)	
SOUSA	M	15	(6)	
István VINCZE (HUN)	M		(8)	
VÍTOR MANUEL	M	16	(6)	3
WALDO	A	1		
WELLINGTON (BRA)	A	10	(19)	3

LEAGUE RESULTS 1998/99

23/08/98	FC Alverca	H	2-2	Demétrios, Laelson
30/08/98	Académica Coimbra	A	5-1	Demétrios 3 (1p), Vítor Manuel,
				Wellington
06/09/98	Boavista FC	H	1-1	Vítor Manuel
20/09/98	Sporting CP	A	0-3	
27/09/98	União Leiria	H	0-3	
04/10/98	CF Estrela Amadora	A	0-1	
11/10/98	SC Salgueiros	H	0-0	
25/10/98	Rio Ave FC	A	1-3	Wellington
01/11/98	SC Braga	H	2-0	René Rivas, Demétrios
08/11/98	SC Beira Mar	A	1-2	Demétrios
15/11/98	FC Porto	H	0-2	
22/11/98	SC Farense	A	1-2	Demétrios
29/11/98	SL Benfica	H	0-5	
06/12/98	CS Marítimo	A	1-0	René Rivas
13/12/98	Vitória Setúbal	H	1-2	Isaías
20/12/98	Vitória Guimarães	H	1-0	Isaías
03/01/99	GD Chaves	A	2-3	Marco Almeida, René Rivas
17/01/99	FC Alverca	A	1-2	Jorginho
23/01/99	Académica Coimbra	H	2-1	Laelson, Isaías
30/01/99	Boavista FC	A	1-2	Marco Almeida
06/02/99	Sporting CP	H	0-0	
13/02/99	União Leiria	A	1-3	Laelson
20/02/99	CF Estrela Amadora	H	3-0	Mauro Soares (p), Laelson,
				Demétrios
27/02/99	SC Salgueiros	A	1-1	Laelson
14/03/99	Rio Ave FC	H	0-0	
21/03/99	SC Braga	A	2-0	Nuno Campos, Mauro Soares
03/04/99	SC Beira Mar	H	4-1	Demétrios 2, Vítor Manuel, Isaías
17/04/99	FC Porto	A	0-2	
25/04/99	SC Farense	H	3-1	Demétrios 3
01/05/99	SL Benfica	A	1-1	Wellington
08/05/99	CS Marítimo	H	0-2	
15/05/99	Vitória Setúbal	A	0-2	
22/05/99	Vitória Guimarães	A	0-2	
29/05/99	GD Chaves	H	4-1	Demétrios 3 (1p), Laelson

GD CHAVES

CLUB DIRECTORY

Grupo Desportivo de Chaves
Rua de Santo António 24, 1.-F
5400 Chaves
tel - (075) 333269
fax - (075) 341846
Year of Formation - 1949
President - Luís Mário Carneiro
Coach - Horácio Gonçalves; Augusto; Inácio
Stadium - Municipal (25,000)

APPEARANCES 98/99

		P	Ap	(s)	Gls
ANDRÉ (BRA)	D	12	(2)	1	
Iñigo ARTEAGA (ESP)	G	25			
BARBOSA	D	23	(4)	1	
CARLOS Alvarez (ESP)	M	27		4	
Ovidiu CUC (ROM)	A	1	(3)		
FILIPE RAMOS	M	18	(2)	1	
HILÁRIO	D	17	(1)		
JOÃO	M	3	(7)		
JOEL	M		(8)	1	
JORGE RAMOS	A	3	(5)		
JORGINHO	M	1	(3)		
LARANJO	M		(3)		
LENILTON (BRA)	A		(8)	1	
LUISÃO (BRA)	D	29		4	
Ivan MATIC (CRO)	M	3	(10)		
MICHEL (ESP)	A	15	(1)		
MORGADO	D	21	(3)		
NEVES	D	19			
ORLANDO	G	9	(1)		
PAULO ALEXANDRE	D	28	(2)		
PAULO TORRES	D	10		1	
RICARDO	D	1	(1)		
RICARDO LOPES	A	16	(4)	2	
Jesús SEBA (ESP)	A	30	(1)	10	
Nikolai STANCHEV (BUL)	A	7			
Plamen TIMNEV (BUL)	M	2	(6)	1	
TÓ ZÉ	D	1			
TONIÑO (ESP)	M	16	(9)		
VINAGRE	M	19	(2)	1	
WANDERLEY (BRA)	A	18	(9)	10	

LEAGUE RESULTS 1998/99

23/08/98	Académica Coimbra	H	1-0	Seba
30/08/98	Sporting CP	A	1-2	Luisão
06/09/98	CF Estrela Amadora	H	4-1	Ricardo Lopes 2, Carlos, Luisão
20/09/98	Rio Ave FC	A	1-1	Seba (p)
27/09/98	SC Beira Mar	H	1-0	Seba
04/10/98	SC Farense	A	1-2	Seba
11/10/98	CS Marítimo	H	1-1	Jorge Ramos
25/10/98	Vitória Guimarães	A	1-6	Wanderley
01/11/98	FC Alverca	H	1-1	Filipe
08/11/98	Boavista FC	A	1-4	Seba
15/11/98	União Leiria	H	1-2	Seba
22/11/98	SC Salgueiros	A	0-2	
29/11/98	SC Braga	H	1-2	Lenilton
06/12/98	FC Porto	A	0-1	
13/12/98	SL Benfica	H	0-4	
20/12/98	Vitória Setúbal	A	0-1	
03/01/99	SC Campomaiorense	H	3-2	Carlos, Barbosa, Wanderley
17/01/99	Académica Coimbra	A	2-1	Luisão, Wanderley
23/01/99	Sporting CP	H	2-2	Wanderley 2
30/01/99	CF Estrela Amadora	A	1-2	Wanderley
06/02/99	Rio Ave FC	H	0-0	
13/02/99	SC Beira Mar	A	1-1	Wanderley
20/02/99	SC Farense	H	4-4	Wanderley, Paulo Torres, Luisão, Joel
27/02/99	CS Marítimo	A	2-2	André, Seba
13/03/99	Vitória Guimarães	H	2-3	Timnev, Seba
21/03/99	FC Alverca	A	1-3	Wanderley
03/04/99	Boavista FC	H	1-1	Seba (p)
18/04/99	União Leiria	A	1-3	Seba
26/04/99	SC Salgueiros	H	1-1	Wanderley
01/05/99	SC Braga	A	0-1	
08/05/99	FC Porto	H	0-4	
15/05/99	SL Benfica	A	1-4	Carlos
22/05/99	Vitória Setúbal	H	1-2	Vinagre
29/05/99	SC Campomaiorense	A	1-4	Carlos

CF ESTRELA AMADORA

CLUB DIRECTORY

Clube de Futebol Estrela da Amadora
Rua Gomes Freire 27
2700 Amadora
tel - (01) 4951309/4952395
fax - (01) 4952866
Year of Formation - 1932
President - José Maria Salvado
Coach - Jorge Jesus
Stadium - José Gomes (25,000)

MAJOR HONOURS
Domestic Cup - (1) 1990.

APPEARANCES 98/99

	P	Ap	(s)	Gls
ASSIS (BRA)	M	4	(8)	4
ASTÉNIO	M	3	(8)	
CAPITÃO (BRA)	A	4	(12)	2
CARLITOS (ESP)	A	4	(7)	
FONSECA	D	2	(2)	
GAÚCHO (BRA)	A	6	(4)	
GILBERTO (BRA)	A	26	(5)	8
HÉLDER QUENTAL	A	4	(4)	
HILÁRIO	G	27		
JORGE ANDRADE	M	11	(6)	2
JOSÉ CARLOS	D	31	(1)	
JÚLIO	A		(4)	
KENEDY	M	7	(1)	1
LÁZARO	M	32	(1)	2
LEAL	D	27		4
Leo LEWIS (TRI)	A	25	(4)	4
LUÍS VASCO	G	7		
MARINHO	D	1		
MIGUEL	M	1	(3)	
PAULO FERREIRA	A	5	(11)	1
PEDRO SIMÕES	M	9	(7)	
PAÚL OLIVEIRA	D	32		
REBELO	D	34		
RODOLFO	M	21		1
RUI NEVES	M	19	(5)	1
SÉRGIO MARQUÊS	M	7	(8)	
VÍTOR VIEIRA	A	25	(1)	2

LEAGUE RESULTS 1998/99

23/08/98	SL Benfica	A	0-2	
30/08/98	Vitória Setúbal	H	5-0	Leal (p), Lewis, Rui Neves,
				Lázaro, Gilberto
06/09/98	GD Chaves	A	1-4	Leal
20/09/98	Académica Coimbra	H	2-1	Vítor Vieira, Leal
27/09/98	Sporting CP	A	0-3	
04/10/98	SC Campomaiorense	H	1-0	Lewis
11/10/98	Rio Ave FC	H	1-0	Rodolfo
25/10/98	SC Beira Mar	A	0-0	
01/11/98	SC Farense	H	2-1	Assis 2
08/11/98	CS Marítimo	A	1-1	Gilberto (p)
15/11/98	Vitória Guimarães	H	1-1	Gilberto
22/11/98	FC Alverca	A	1-0	Gilberto
29/11/98	Boavista FC	H	2-1	Gilberto (p), Vítor Vieira
06/12/98	União Leiria	A	1-0	Gilberto
13/12/98	SC Salgueiros	H	1-1	Gilberto (p)
20/12/98	SC Braga	A	1-1	Assis
03/01/99	FC Porto	H	1-1	Assis
17/01/99	SL Benfica	H	0-1	
23/01/99	Vitória Setúbal	A	0-2	
30/01/99	GD Chaves	H	2-1	Gilberto, Lewis
06/02/99	Académica Coimbra	A	2-2	Paulo Ferreira, Jorge Andrade
14/02/99	Sporting CP	H	0-1	
20/02/99	SC Campomaiorense	A	0-3	
27/02/99	Rio Ave FC	A	1-1	Leal
14/03/99	SC Beira Mar	H	1-2	Capitão
21/03/99	SC Farense	A	1-1	Capitão
02/04/99	CS Marítimo	H	1-0	Kenedy
17/04/99	Vitória Guimarães	A	0-3	
24/04/99	FC Alverca	H	1-0	Lázaro
01/05/99	Boavista FC	A	1-2	og (Luís Manuel)
08/05/99	União Leiria	H	1-1	Jorge Andrade
15/05/99	SC Salgueiros	A	1-1	Lewis
22/05/99	SC Braga	H	0-0	
29/05/99	FC Porto	A	0-2	

SC FARENSE

CLUB DIRECTORY

Sporting Clube Farense
Estádio de São Luís
Praça de Tânger
8000 Faro
tel - (089) 803666
fax - (089) 802754
Year of Formation - 1910
President - David dos Santos
Coach - Paco Fortes; João Alves
Stadium - São Luís (15,000)

APPEARANCES 98/99

	P	Ap	(s)	Gls
Nail BESIROVIC (YUG)	M	32		2
CANDEIAS	G	21		
CARLOS COSTA	M	33		8
DA SILVA (BRA)	A	1	(4)	
DUARTE ROSA	D	1	(2)	
EUGÉNIO	M	29	(2)	
GOUVEIA	M	28	(2)	3
GRANOV	A	6	(9)	1
Radouane HAJRI (MAR)	M	13	(7)	2
HASSAN Nader (MAR)	A	24		4
IVO	G	2		
JEAN PAULISTA	A	16	(11)	3
JOÃO PINTO	M	18	(11)	2
KING (BRA)	D	25	(2)	5
LUÍS LOPES	D	4	(3)	
MARCO NUNO	M	16	(11)	3
MIGUEL ROSA	G	1		
MIGUEL SERÔDIO	D	16	(2)	
Zoran MIJANOVIC (YUG)	G	10		
MUTAPA	A	1	(1)	
PAIXÃO	D	17	(3)	1
PAULO SÉRGIO (BRA)	D	32	(1)	1
PAULO SERRÃO	D	9		
PEDRO MIGUEL	D	7		
PINTASSILGO	A	5	(9)	1
RAMOS	M	7	(15)	2

LEAGUE RESULTS 1998/99

23/08/98	SC Salgueiros	A	2-4	João Pinto, Ramos
30/08/98	SC Braga	H	0-2	
06/09/98	FC Porto	A	0-2	
20/09/98	SL Benfica	H	1-0	Hassan
27/09/98	Vitória Setúbal	A	1-1	Besirovic
04/10/98	GD Chaves	H	2-1	Gouveia, Carlos Costa
11/10/98	Académica Coimbra	A	1-2	Besirovic
25/10/98	Sporting CP	H	1-3	Granov
01/11/98	CF Estrela Amadora	A	1-2	Hassan
08/11/98	Rio Ave FC	H	0-1	
15/11/98	SC Beira Mar	A	1-0	Pintassilgo
22/11/98	SC Campomaiorense	H	2-1	King, Hassan
29/11/98	CS Marítimo	H	0-0	
06/12/98	Vitória Guimarães	A	0-1	
13/12/98	FC Alverca	H	1-0	Carlos Costa
20/12/98	Boavista FC	A	0-3	
03/01/99	União Leiria	H	1-1	Carlos Costa
17/01/99	SC Salgueiros	H	2-1	Hassan, Carlos Costa
24/01/99	SC Braga	A	0-0	
31/01/99	FC Porto	H	0-3	
06/02/99	SL Benfica	A	0-5	
13/02/99	Vitória Setúbal	H	1-1	King
20/02/99	GD Chaves	A	4-4	Paulo Sérgio, King 2, Marco Nuno
27/02/99	Académica Coimbra	H	2 0	Carlos Costa 2
13/03/99	Sporting CP	A	0-1	
21/03/99	CF Estrela Amadora	H	1-1	King (p)
03/04/99	Rio Ave FC	A	2-2	Hajri, Gouveia
17/04/99	SC Beira Mar	H	2-1	Carlos Costa, João Pinto
25/04/99	SC Campomaiorense	A	1-3	og (Mauro Soares)
01/05/99	CS Marítimo	A	3-1	Carlos Costa, Jean Paulista 2
08/05/99	Vitória Guimarães	H	1-2	Hajri (p)
15/05/99	FC Alverca	A	3-1	Jean Paulista, Marco Nuno, Ramos
22/05/99	Boavista FC	H	2-2	Marco Nuno, Gouveia
29/05/99	União Leiria	A	1-2	Paixão (p)

CS MARÍTIMO

CLUB DIRECTORY

Clube Sport Marítimo
Rua D. Carlos I 17
9050 Funchal
tel - (091) 205000
fax - (091) 222939
Year of Formation - 1910
President - José Carlos Rodrigues Pereira
Coach - Augusto Inácio; Nelo Vingada
Stadium - Dos Barreiros (33,000)

MAJOR HONOURS
Domestic Cup - (1) 1926.

APPEARANCES 98/99

		P	Ap	(s)	Gls
ALBERTINO	M	12	(7)	2	
ALEX BACH (BRA)	D	3	(3)		
Patrick ASSELMAN (BEL)	M	3	(1)	1	
BRUNO	M	20		2	
Alex BUNBURY (CAN)	A	28	(2)	15	
CARLOS JORGE	D	29		1	
DANI DIAZ (ESP)	M	9	(13)	3	
DUVEAU	M	3	(5)		
EUSÉBIO	M	32		3	
FERNANDO GOMES	M		(1)		
HERIVELTO (BRA)	A	13	(8)	5	
Predrag JOKANOVIC (YUG)	D	12	(10)		
JORGE SOARES	D	32		1	
LINA	M	7	(6)	1	
MÁRCIO ANTÓNIO (BRA)	D	30			
MARIANO	D	5		1	
NÉLSON	G	1			
NUNO AFONSO	D	5	(1)		
PAULO SÉRGIO (BRA)	D	8	(4)		
PEDRO PAULO	A	2	(5)		
ROMÉU	A	17		4	
RONALDO	M		(3)		
RUI ÓSCAR	D	29			
Tarik SEKTIOUI (FRA)	M	1	(1)		
TONI	A	5	(9)	3	
TULIPA	A	14	(9)	2	
Yves VAN DER STRAETEN (BEL)	G	33			
ZAKARIAS (MLI)	M		(2)		
ZECA	M	21	(2)		

LEAGUE RESULTS 1998/99

23/08/98	União Leiria	A	0-1	
30/08/98	SC Salgueiros	H	2-2	Toni, Bunbury
06/09/98	SC Braga	A	1-1	Herivelto
20/09/98	FC Porto	H	0-1	
27/09/98	SL Benfica	A	1-3	Herivelto
04/10/98	Vitória Setúbal	H	0-1	
11/10/98	GD Chaves	A	1-1	Bunbury
25/10/98	Académica Coimbra	H	4-1	Lino, Dani Díaz, Bunbury, Carlos Jorge
01/11/98	Sporting CP	A	0-2	
08/11/98	CF Estrela Amadora	H	1-1	Bunbury
15/11/98	Rio Ave FC	A	1-2	Herivelto
22/11/98	SC Beira Mar	H	1-1	Bunbury (p)
29/11/98	SC Farense	A	0-0	
06/12/98	SC Campomaiorense	H	0-1	
13/12/98	Vitória Guimarães	H	1-0	Dani Díaz
20/12/98	FC Alverca	A	0-3	
03/01/99	Boavista FC	H	3-0	Roméu 2, Toni
17/01/99	União Leiria	H	3-2	Toni, Tulipa, Bunbury
26/01/99	SC Salgueiros	A	2-2	Jorge Soares, Dani Díaz
30/01/99	SC Braga	H	3-0	Bunbury (p), Bruno, Eusébio
06/02/99	FC Porto	A	0-1	
13/02/99	SL Benfica	H	1-0	Tulipa
20/02/99	Vitória Setúbal	A	1-3	Bunbury
27/02/99	GD Chaves	H	2-2	Bunbury, Herivelto
14/03/99	Académica Coimbra	A	3-1	Herivelto, Roméu, Bunbury
21/03/99	Sporting CP	H	1-3	Albertino
02/04/99	CF Estrela Amadora	A	0-1	
18/04/99	Rio Ave FC	H	2-0	Eusébio, Bunbury (p)
25/04/99	SC Beira Mar	A	1-1	Bunbury (p)
01/05/99	SC Farense	H	1-3	Bunbury
08/05/99	SC Campomaiorense	A	2-0	Eusébio, Mariano
15/05/99	Vitória Guimarães	A	1-1	Bunbury (p)
22/05/99	FC Alverca	H	3-3	Albertino, Bunbury (p), Bruno
29/05/99	Boavista FC	A	2-1	Asselman, Roméu

FC PORTO

CLUB DIRECTORY

Futebol Clube do Porto
Estádio das Antas
Avenida Fernão de Magalhães, 4300 Porto
tel - (02) 5500186/5070500
fax - (02) 5570498
Year of Formation - 1893
President - Jorge Nuno Pinto da Costa
Coach - Fernando Santos
Stadium - Antas (76,000)

MAJOR HONOURS
League Championship - (18)
1935, 1939, 1940, 1956, 1959, 1978, 1979,
1985, 1986, 1988, 1990, 1992, 1993, 1995,
1996, 1997, 1998, 1999.
Domestic Cup - (13)
1922, 1925, 1932, 1937, 1956, 1958, 1968,
1977, 1984, 1988, 1991, 1994, 1998.
European Champions' Cup - (1) 1987.
European Super Cup - (1) 1987.
World Club Cup - (1) 1987.

APPEARANCES 98/99

	P	Ap	(s)	Gls
ALOÍSIO (BRA)	D	31	(2)	4
ARTUR (BRA)	A		(5)	
CAPUCHO	M	31	(2)	6
CARLOS MANUEL	M		(1)	
CHAINHO	M	15	(11)	2
Youssef CHIPPO (MAR)	M	1	(11)	
COSTINHA	G		(1)	
DECO	M	5	(1)	
DORIVA (BRA)	M	17		4
Ljubinko DRULOVIC (YUG)	A	31	(1)	3
ESQUERDINHA (BRA)	D	11	(1)	1
Miklós FEHÉR (HUN)	A		(5)	
FERNANDO MENDES	D	17	(2)	1
FOLHA	A		(1)	
Mário JARDEL (BRA)	A	31	(1)	36
JOÃO MANUEL PINTO	D	4	(12)	2
JORGE COSTA	D	33		2
Ivica KRALJ (YUG)	G	7		
Grzegorz MIELCARSKI (POL)	A	2	(10)	2
NÉLSON	D	2		
Basarab PANDURU (ROM)	M	3	(3)	
PAULINHO SANTOS	D	21		1
PEIXE	M	10	(1)	1
QUINZINHO	A	3	(9)	4
RICARDO CARVALHO	D	1		
RUI BARROS	M	11	(13)	2
RUI CORREIA	G	11		
SECRETÁRIO	D	31		
VÍTOR BAÍA	G	16		
Zlatko ZAHOVIC (SLO)	M	29	(2)	14

LEAGUE RESULTS 1998/99

23/08/98	Rio Ave FC	H	4-0	Doriva, Capucho, Mielcarski 2
30/08/98	SC Beira Mar	A	1-2	Zahovic
06/09/98	SC Farense	H	2-0	Capucho, Doriva
20/09/98	CS Marítimo	A	1-0	Jardel
27/09/98	Vitória Guimarães	H	2-0	Paulinho Santos, Jardel
04/10/98	FC Alverca	A	5-1	Zahovic, Jardel 2, Capucho,
				João Manuel Pinto
11/10/98	Boavista FC	H	0-2	
25/10/98	União Leiria	A	2-2	Capucho, Jardel
01/11/98	SC Salgueiros	H	4-1	Jardel 2, Drulovic (p), Quinzinho
08/11/98	SC Braga	A	3-3	Jardel 2, Zahovic
15/11/98	SC Campomaiorense	A	2-0	Jardel 2
22/11/98	SL Benfica	H	3-1	Chainho, Jardel 2
29/11/98	Vitória Setúbal	A	2-1	Jardel 2
06/12/98	GD Chaves	H	1-0	Jardel
13/12/98	Académica Coimbra	A	2-0	Zahovic (p), Rui Barros
20/12/98	Sporting CP	H	3-2	Doriva 2, Jardel
03/01/99	CF Estrela Amadora	A	1-1	Jardel
17/01/99	Rio Ave FC	A	1-1	Zahovic
23/01/99	SC Beira Mar	H	7-0	Capucho, Jardel 4,
				João Manuel Pinto, Zahovic
30/01/99	SC Farense	A	3-0	Rui Barros, Fernando Mendes,
				Zahovic
06/02/99	CS Marítimo	H	1-0	Drulovic
13/02/99	Vitória Guimarães	A	2-3	Jardel 2
20/02/99	FC Alverca	H	3-1	Jorge Costa, Jardel 2 (2p)
27/02/99	Boavista FC	A	0-0	
13/03/99	União Leiria	H	3-1	Aloísio, Jardel, Peixe
21/03/99	SC Salgueiros	A	3-1	Zahovic, Jardel 2
08/04/99	SC Braga	H	1-0	Zahovic
17/04/99	SC Campomaiorense	H	2-0	Quinzinho 2
24/04/99	SL Benfica	A	1-1	Zahovic
01/05/99	Vitória Setúbal	H	6-0	Capucho, Zahovic, Jardel, Aloísio 2,
				Quinzinho
08/05/99	GD Chaves	A	4-0	Zahovic, Jardel 2, Aloísio
15/05/99	Académica Coimbra	H	7-1	Jardel 3, Esquerdinha, Chainho,
				Zahovic, Jorge Costa
22/05/99	Sporting CP	A	1-1	Zahovic
29/05/99	CF Estrela Amadora	H	2-0	Drulovic, Jardel

RIO AVE FC

CLUB DIRECTORY

Rio Ave Futebol Clube
Praça da República 35
4480 Vila do Conde
tel - (052) 640590
Year of Formation - 1939
President - Paulo Carvalho
Coach - Carlos Brito
Stadium - Rio Ave (46,000)

APPEARANCES 98/99

	P	Ap	(s)	Gls
ALÉRCIO (BRA)	A	18	(6)	2
ANDRÉ JACARÉ (BRA)	A	15	(12)	6
ANDRÉ LUÍS (BRA)	A	1	(3)	1
ARMANDO (MOZ)	D	19		
BAÍCA (BRA)	A	15	(4)	1
BOLINHAS	M	9	(9)	
CAMBERRA	M	2	(6)	
CHIKBALLA	A	4	(5)	
Nenad DIVAC (YUG)	D	15	(2)	
DUDA	A	8		1
EMANUEL	M	30	(2)	1
FÁBIO	M	2	(1)	
GAMA	A	28	(6)	5
HELINHO (BRA)	M	1		
JORGE LARANJEIRA	M	1	(3)	
LUÍS COENTRÃO	M	9	(11)	1
MARTINS	D	28		
NELO	D	5		
NIQUINHA (BRA)	M	27	(2)	2
NITO	D	26		1
PAULO LIMA PEREIRA	M	9	(3)	1
PEU (BRA)	D	18	(2)	
SANDRO (BRA)	D	24		
SERGINHO	M		(8)	
SÉRGIO CHINA (BRA)	M	26	(7)	4
TIAGO	G	1		
TÓ LUÍS	G	33		

LEAGUE RESULTS 1998/99

23/08/98	FC Porto	A	0-4	
30/08/98	SL Benfica	H	0-2	
06/09/98	Vitória Setúbal	A	2-1	Paulo Lima Pereira, Gama
20/09/98	GD Chaves	H	1-1	Niquinha
27/09/98	Académica Coimbra	A	1-1	Gama
04/10/98	Sporting CP	H	0-1	
11/10/98	CF Estrela Amadora	A	0-1	
25/10/98	SC Campomaiorense	H	3-1	Gama, Niquinha, Baíca
01/11/98	SC Beira Mar	H	1-1	Alércio
08/11/98	SC Farense	A	1-0	Emanuel
15/11/98	CS Marítimo	H	2-1	Sérgio China (p), André Jacaré
22/11/98	Vitória Guimarães	A	0-3	
29/11/98	FC Alverca	H	0-0	
06/12/98	Boavista FC	A	0-1	
13/12/98	União Leiria	H	1-0	Gama
20/12/98	SC Salgueiros	A	1-5	Sérgio China
03/01/99	SC Braga	H	1-2	Sérgio China (p)
17/01/99	FC Porto	H	1-1	Sérgio China
23/01/99	SL Benfica	A	1-3	André Jacaré
30/01/99	Vitória Setúbal	H	1-1	André Luís
06/02/99	GD Chaves	A	0-0	
13/02/99	Académica Coimbra	H	1-1	André Jacaré (p)
19/02/99	Sporting CP	A	0-2	
27/02/99	CF Estrela Amadora	H	1-1	Nito
14/03/99	SC Campomaiorense	A	0-0	
21/03/99	SC Beira Mar	A	2-1	Alércio, Duda
03/04/99	SC Farense	H	2-2	André Jacaré 2
18/04/99	CS Marítimo	A	0-2	
26/04/99	Vitória Guimarães	H	0-1	
01/05/99	FC Alverca	A	1-0	André Jacaré
08/05/99	Boavista FC	H	0-2	
15/05/99	União Leiria	A	0-2	
22/05/99	SC Salgueiros	H	2-1	Gama, Luís Coentrão
29/05/99	SC Braga	A	0-2	

SC SALGUEIROS

CLUB DIRECTORY

Sport Comércio e Salgueiros
Rua Álvares Cabral 366
4050 Porto
tel - (02) 2000004
fax - (02) 2008397
Year of Formation - 1911
President - José António Linhares
Coach - Dito
Stadium - Vidal Pinheiro (11,000)

APPEARANCES 98/99

	P	Ap	(s)	Gls
ABÍLIO	M	34		4
ADEMIR (BRA)	D	24	(1)	3
CAO	M	31		1
CARLOS FERREIRA	M	18	(5)	2
CELSO (BRA)	A	22	(7)	10
CHICO FONSECA	D	29		1
DECO	M	9	(3)	2
EDU	M	6	(1)	1
FERNANDO ALMEIDA	A	23	(10)	5
FILIPE CÂNDIDO	A	2	(7)	2
GAMA	A		(16)	2
JOÃO PEDRO	A	17	(5)	7
JORGE PINTO	D	4	(3)	
JORGE SILVA	G	34		
JOSÉ LUÍS	M		(5)	1
MIGUEL	M	6	(5)	
NÉLSON	D	31		
PAULINHO	D	19	(7)	1
PEDRO REIS	D	28		2
SCHUSTER	M	15	(3)	
SEMEDO	M	4	(6)	
TONINHO (BRA)	A	4	(7)	
TONINHO CRUZ	M	14	(6)	1

LEAGUE RESULTS 1998/99

23/08/98	SC Farense	H	4-2	Celso 2, Abílio, Fernando Almeida
30/08/98	CS Marítimo	A	2-2	Celso, Ademir
06/09/98	Vitória Guimarães	H	3-2	Celso, José Luís, Chico Fonseca
20/09/98	FC Alverca	A	1-1	Gama
27/09/98	Boavista FC	H	0-0	
04/10/98	União Leiria	A	0-1	
11/10/98	SC Campomaiorense	A	0-0	
25/10/98	SC Braga	H	1-1	Toninho Cruz
01/11/98	FC Porto	A	1-4	Celso
08/11/98	SL Benfica	H	1-1	Pedro Reis
15/11/98	Vitória Setúbal	A	0-3	
22/11/98	GD Chaves	H	2-0	Deco, Cao
29/11/98	Académica Coimbra	A	1-0	Celso
06/12/98	Sporting CP	H	2-1	Fernando Almeida, João Pedro
13/12/98	CF Estrela Amadora	A	1-1	Fernando Almeida
20/12/98	Rio Ave FC	H	5-1	Carlos Ferreira 2, Deco,
				João Pedro, Abílio (p)
03/01/99	SC Beira Mar	A	1-4	João Pedro
17/01/99	SC Farense	A	1-2	Pedro Reis
24/01/99	CS Marítimo	H	2-2	Celso, Abílio (p)
31/01/99	Vitória Guimarães	A	3-3	Fernando Almeida 2, Celso
06/02/99	FC Alverca	H	0-0	
12/02/99	Boavista FC	A	1-2	Filipe Candido
20/02/99	União Leiria	H	0-0	
27/02/99	SC Campomaiorense	H	1-1	João Pedro
14/03/99	SC Braga	A	1-1	João Pedro
21/03/99	FC Porto	H	1-3	Filipe Candido
03/04/99	SL Benfica	A	0-5	
18/04/99	Vitória Setúbal	H	1-0	Gama
26/04/99	GD Chaves	A	1-1	Celso
01/05/99	Académica Coimbra	H	1-1	Celso
08/05/99	Sporting CP	A	1-3	Ademir
15/05/99	CF Estrela Amadora	H	1-1	João Pedro
22/05/99	Rio Ave FC	A	1-2	Edu
29/05/99	SC Beira Mar	H	4-4	Ademir, João Pedro, Abílio (p),
				Paulinho

SPORTING CP

CLUB DIRECTORY

Sporting Clube de Portugal
Rua Francisco Stromp
1600 Lisboa
tel - (01) 7514000
fax - (01) 7590087
Year of Formation - 1906
President - José Alfredo Roquette
Coach - Mirko Jozic (99/00 - Giuseppe Materazzi)
Stadium - José Alvalade (52,411)

MAJOR HONOURS
League Championship - (16) 1941, 1944, 1947,
1948, 1949, 1951, 1952, 1953, 1954, 1958,
1962, 1966, 1970, 1974, 1980, 1982.
Domestic Cup - (16) 1923, 1934, 1936, 1938,
1941, 1945, 1946, 1948, 1954, 1963, 1971,
1973, 1974, 1978, 1982, 1995.
European Cup-winners' Cup - (1) 1964.

APPEARANCES 98/99

		P	Ap	(s)	Gls
Alberto ACOSTA (ARG)	A	10	(3)	3
BETO	D	28		3
BINO	M	15	(1)	1
DELFIM	D	32		3
Aldo DUSCHER (ARG)	M	26	(1)	3
EDMILSON (BRA)	M	22	(2)	10
Bruno GIMENEZ (ARG)	A		(1)	
Gabriel HEINZE (ARG)	D	3	(2)	1
Julián KMET (ARG)	M		(1)	
Petar KRPAN (CRO)	A	14	(13)	3
LEANDRO (BRA)	A	5	(3)	2
MARCO AURÉLIO (BRA)	D	14		
MARCOS (BRA)	D	16		1
NÉLSON	G	6		
NUNO VALENTE	D	7	(5)	1
PATACAS	D	3	(1)	
PEDRO BARBOSA	M	15	(3)	2
QUIM BERTO	D	5	(4)	3
QUIROGA	D	4	(1)	
César RAMIREZ (PAR)	A	1	(3)	
RENATO	D	1	(1)	
RUI JORGE	M	13	(13)	2
Abdelilah SABER (MAR)	D	28		
SANTA MARIA	D		(2)	
SIMÃO SABROSA	A	30		10
TIAGO	G	28		
VIDIGAL	M	12	(7)	
VINICIUS (BRA)	D	19	(2)	1
Ivailo YORDANOV (BUL)	A	17	(12)	13

LEAGUE RESULTS 1998/99

23/08/98	Vitória Setúbal	A	1-1	Bino
30/08/98	GD Chaves	H	2-1	Leandro, Yordanov
06/09/98	Académica Coimbra	A	2-2	Simão Sabrosa, Edmilson
20/09/98	SC Campomaiorense	H	3-0	og (Quim Machado), Beto, Yordanov
27/09/98	CF Estrela Amadora	H	3-0	Edmilson, Yordanov, Leandro
04/10/98	Rio Ave FC	A	1-0	Simão Sabrosa
11/10/98	SC Beira Mar	H	0-0	
25/10/98	SC Farense	A	3-1	Simão Sabrosa, Delfim, Krpan
01/11/98	CS Marítimo	H	2-0	Nuno Valente, Yordanov
08/11/98	Vitória Guimarães	A	1-1	Yordanov
15/11/98	FC Alverca	H	2-0	Krpan, Yordanov
22/11/98	Boavista FC	A	2-2	Simão Sabrosa, Yordanov
29/11/98	União Leiria	H	2-0	Krpan, Simão Sabrosa (p)
06/12/98	SC Salgueiros	A	1-2	og (Cao)
13/12/98	SC Braga	H	4-1	Duscher 2, Yordanov, Rui Jorge
20/12/98	FC Porto	A	2-3	Edmilson, Heinze
03/01/99	SL Benfica	H	1-2	Delfim
17/01/99	Vitória Setúbal	H	0-0	
23/01/99	GD Chaves	A	2-2	Simão Sabrosa, Beto
30/01/99	Académica Coimbra	H	5-0	Beto, Edmilson, Simão Sabrosa, Acosta 2
06/02/99	SC Campomaiorense	A	0-0	
14/02/99	CF Estrela Amadora	A	1-0	Yordanov
19/02/99	Rio Ave FC	H	2-0	Pedro Barbosa, Edmilson
27/02/99	SC Beira Mar	A	2-2	Marcos, Edmilson
13/03/99	SC Farense	H	1-0	Edmilson
21/03/99	CS Marítimo	A	3-1	Edmilson 2, Quim Berto
03/04/99	Vitória Guimarães	H	3-0	Vinicius, Delfim, Acosta
17/04/99	FC Alverca	A	2-3	Edmilson (p), Quim Berto
24/04/99	Boavista FC	H	1-1	Quim Berto
01/05/99	União Leiria	A	3-0	Simão Sabrosa, Duscher, Yordanov
08/05/99	SC Salgueiros	H	3-1	Simão Sabrosa 2, Yordanov
15/05/99	SC Braga	A	0-2	
22/05/99	FC Porto	H	1-1	Pedro Barbosa
29/05/99	SL Benfica	A	3-3	Yordanov 2, Rui Jorge

UNIÃO LEIRIA

União Desportiva de Leiria
Arrabalde D'Aquem
Edifício Bingo
2400 Leiria
tel - (044) 823532/826701
Year of Formation - 1966
President - João Bartolomeu
Coach - Mário Reis
Stadium - Municipal Magalhães Pessoa (25,000)

APPEARANCES 98/99

	P	Ap	(s)	Gls
Augustine AHINFUL (GHA)	A	15		6
ARTUR JORGE VICENTE	A	6	(3)	1
BAKERO	M	30	(3)	2
BAPTISTA	G	2	(1)	
BILRO	D	31		2
DINDA (BRA)	M	29	(3)	3
Emmanuel DUAH (GHA)	A	15	(9)	5
HUGO	M	7	(17)	
IDO	M	6	(1)	
JOÃO MANUEL	M	23		1
Maxwell KONADU (GHA)	M	2	(10)	2
Nii LAMPTEY (GHA)	M	2	(5)	
LEÃO	M	31		
LUÍS VOUZELA	M	31	(1)	1
MÁRIO ARTUR (MOZ)	M	3	(4)	
MORGADO	D	14	(2)	
PAULO DUARTE	D	10	(7)	
REINALDO	A	12	(14)	7
RICARDO SILVA	D	28		1
SÉRGIO NUNES	D	29		1
SISOKO	M		(1)	
TAVARES	M	2		
ZEZINHO	A	14	(12)	2
Miroslav ZITNJAK (CRO)	G	32		

Date	Opponent	H/A	Score	Scorers
23/08/98	CS Marítimo	H	1-0	Duah
30/08/98	Vitória Guimarães	A	0-0	
06/09/98	FC Alverca	H	1-0	Konadu
20/09/98	Boavista FC	A	0-1	
27/09/98	SC Campomaiorense	A	3-0	Ahinful 3
04/10/98	SC Salgueiros	H	1-0	Reinaldo
11/10/98	SC Braga	A	4-2	Ahinful 2, Reinaldo, Dinda
25/10/98	FC Porto	H	2-2	Ahinful, Zezinho
01/11/98	SL Benfica	A	0-0	
08/11/98	Vitória Setúbal	H	0-1	
15/11/98	GD Chaves	A	2-1	Duah 2
22/11/98	Académica Coimbra	H	1-0	Bakero
29/11/98	Sporting CP	A	0-2	
06/12/98	CF Estrela Amadora	H	0-1	
13/12/98	Rio Ave FC	A	0-1	
20/12/98	SC Beira Mar	H	1-0	Reinaldo
03/01/99	SC Farense	A	1-1	Luís Vouzela
17/01/99	CS Marítimo	A	2-3	Dinda, Reinaldo
24/01/99	Vitória Guimarães	H	0-1	
31/01/99	FC Alverca	A	2-0	Dinda, Bakero
06/02/99	Boavista FC	H	0-0	
13/02/99	SC Campomaiorense	H	3-1	Artur Jorge Vicente, Reinaldo 2
20/02/99	SC Salgueiros	A	0-0	
27/02/99	SC Braga	H	0-0	
13/03/99	FC Porto	A	1-3	og (Jorge Costa)
21/03/99	SL Benfica	H	1-1	Sérgio Nunes
03/04/99	Vitória Setúbal	A	0-1	
18/04/99	GD Chaves	H	3-1	Zezinho, Reinaldo, Duah
25/04/99	Académica Coimbra	A	1-0	Konadu
01/05/99	Sporting CP	H	0-3	
08/05/99	CF Estrela Amadora	A	1-1	Bilro
15/05/99	Rio Ave FC	H	2-0	João Manuel, Ricardo Silva
22/05/99	SC Beira Mar	A	1-1	og (Fusco)
29/05/99	SC Farense	H	2-1	Bilro (p), Duah

VITÓRIA GUIMARÃES

CLUB DIRECTORY

Vitória Sport Clube
C.D.Dr. António Pimenta Machado
Apartado 505
7802 Guimarães
tel - (053) 432570
fax - (053) 432570
Year of Formation - 1922
President - António Pimenta Machado
Coach - Zoran Filipovic; Quinito
Stadium - D. Afonso Henriques (33,000)

APPEARANCES 98/99

	P	Ap	(s)	Gls
ALEXANDRE (BRA)	D	21	(1)	2
ARLEY ALVAREZ (BRA)	D	25	(2)	1
AURI (BRA)	D	1	(2)	
BASÍLIO ALMEIDA	M	1	(4)	
COSTA	M	2	(7)	1
Bozidar DJURKOVIC (YUG)	M	3	(6)	
EDMILSON (BRA)	A	20	(5)	13
EVALDO	D	7	(2)	
EVANDO	A	12	(18)	7
FONSECA (MOZ)	D	3	(1)	
GERALDO (BRA)	A	9	(13)	1
GILMAR (BRA)	A	31	(2)	10
JOSÉ CARLOS	D	12		
KASONGO Kabue (DRC)	D	13		
MÁRCIO THEODORO (BRA)	D	26	(1)	3
Branko MILOVANOVIC (YUG)	M	2	(3)	
MIRANDINHA	A		(2)	
Etienne N'TSUNDA (DRC)	A		(4)	
NENO	G	3		
David PAAS (BEL)	A	1	(1)	
PAIVA	M	26		1
PAULO GOMES	M	19	(2)	
PEDRO ESPINHA	G	31		
QUIM BERTO	D	15		2
RIVA (BRA)	A	21	(9)	5
Fredrik SÖDERSTRÖM (SWE)	M	25	(4)	4
TITO	D	16		2
VÍTOR PANEIRA	M	29	(3)	1

LEAGUE RESULTS 1998/99

23/08/98	Boavista FC	A	0-2	
30/08/98	União Leiria	H	0-0	
06/09/98	SC Salgueiros	A	2-3	Edmilson, Alexandre
20/09/98	SC Braga	H	5-1	Gilmar 3 (1p), Vítor Paneira, Söderström
27/09/98	FC Porto	A	0-2	
04/10/98	SL Benfica	H	0-2	
11/10/98	Vitória Setúbal	A	0-1	
25/10/98	GD Chaves	H	6-1	Alexandre, Evando 2, Riva, Quim Berto (p), Gilmar
01/11/98	Académica Coimbra	A	1-1	Evando
08/11/98	Sporting CP	H	1-1	Paiva
15/11/98	CF Estrela Amadora	A	1-1	Costa
22/11/98	Rio Ave FC	H	3-0	Márcio Theodoro, Gilmar, Evando
29/11/98	SC Beira Mar	A	0-0	
06/12/98	SC Farense	H	1-0	Márcio Theodoro
13/12/98	CS Marítimo	A	0-1	
20/12/98	SC Campomaiorense	A	0-1	
03/01/99	FC Alverca	H	3-1	Tito, Arley Alvarez, Quim Berto
17/01/99	Boavista FC	H	2-3	Gilmar, Edmilson
23/01/99	União Leiria	A	1-0	Gilmar
30/01/99	SC Salgueiros	H	3-3	Edmilson, Gilmar, Riva
06/02/99	SC Braga	A	1-2	Edmilson
13/02/99	FC Porto	H	3-2	Riva, Edmilson, Söderström
20/02/99	SL Benfica	A	1-3	Edmilson
27/02/99	Vitória Setúbal	H	2-0	Edmilson 2
13/03/99	GD Chaves	A	3-2	Söderström 2, Edmilson
21/03/99	Académica Coimbra	H	1-1	Gilmar
03/04/99	Sporting CP	A	0-3	
17/04/99	CF Estrela Amadora	H	3-0	Edmilson, Geraldo, Márcio Theodoro
26/04/99	Rio Ave FC	A	1-0	Evando
01/05/99	SC Beira Mar	H	3-0	Edmilson, Gilmar, Tito
08/05/99	SC Farense	A	2-1	Riva, Evando
15/05/99	CS Marítimo	H	1-1	Riva (p)
22/05/99	SC Campomaiorense	H	2-0	Edmilson 2
29/05/99	FC Alverca	A	1-2	Evando

VITÓRIA SETÚBAL

Vitória Futebol Clube
Rua do Bocage 4
2901 Setúbal
tel - (065) 526959
Year of Formation - 1910
President - José Sousa Silva
Coach - Carlos Cardoso
Stadium - Bonfim (35,000)

MAJOR HONOURS
Domestic Cup - (2) 1965, 1967.

	P	Ap	(s)	Gls
AMARAL (MOZ)	M	14		
BRASSARD	G	3	(1)	
CARLOS GOMES	G	3		
Raul CHIPENDA (TAN)	M	3	(18)	
CHIQUINHO CONDE (MOZ)	A	28		14
FIGUEIREDO	D	6	(4)	
FRECHAUT	A	26	(1)	1
HÉLIO	M	33		3
JOSÉ RUI	D	16		
Velli KASUMOV (AZB)	A	12	(5)	4
MAKI	A	2	(18)	1
MAMEDE	M	16		1
MANUEL CARMA	M	4	(9)	
MARCO TÁBUAS	G	28		
MÁRIO LOJA	D	24		
NANDO	A	17	(1)	6
PAULO FILIPE	D	25	(2)	1
PEDRO HENRIQUES	M	24	(3)	1
PEDRO MENDES	M		(7)	
QUIM	D	34		
RENATO	D	1		
RESENDE	M		(2)	
RIBEIRO	M	1	(4)	
RUI CARLOS	A	28		1
RUI GOMES	A		(1)	
SEMEDO	D	6	(1)	
TOÑITO (ESP)	A	20	(1)	4

Date	Opponent	H/A	Score	Scorers
23/08/98	Sporting CP	H	1-1	Chiquinho Conde
30/08/98	CF Estrela Amadora	A	0-5	
06/09/98	Rio Ave FC	H	1-2	Chiquinho Conde
20/09/98	SC Beira Mar	A	1-1	Chiquinho Conde
27/09/98	SC Farense	H	1-1	Nando
04/10/98	CS Marítimo	A	1-0	Frechaut
11/10/98	Vitória Guimarães	H	1-0	Hélio
25/10/98	FC Alverca	A	0-1	
01/11/98	Boavista FC	H	1-3	Paulo Filipe
08/11/98	União Leiria	A	1-0	Kasumov
15/11/98	SC Salgueiros	H	3-0	Nando 3
22/11/98	SC Braga	A	0-3	
29/11/98	FC Porto	H	1-2	Hélio
06/12/98	SL Benfica	A	0-2	
13/12/98	SC Campomaiorense	A	2-1	Chiquinho Conde, Hélio (p)
20/12/98	GD Chaves	H	1-0	Chiquinho Conde
03/01/99	Académica Coimbra	A	0-2	
17/01/99	Sporting CP	A	0-0	
23/01/99	CF Estrela Amadora	H	2-0	Toñito, Nando
30/01/99	Rio Ave FC	A	1-1	Nando
06/02/99	SC Beira Mar	H	0-0	
13/02/99	SC Farense	A	1-1	Rui Carlos
20/02/99	CS Marítimo	H	3-1	Kasumov (p), Chiquinho Conde 2
27/02/99	Vitória Guimarães	A	0-2	
14/03/99	FC Alverca	H	4-0	Kasumov, Toñito, Maki, Chiquinho Conde
21/03/99	Boavista FC	A	1-1	Kasumov
03/04/99	União Leiria	H	1-0	Chiquinho Conde
18/04/99	SC Salgueiros	A	0-1	
23/04/99	SC Braga	H	3-0	Chiquinho Conde 2, Mamede
01/05/99	FC Porto	A	0-6	
08/05/99	SL Benfica	H	1-0	Toñito
15/05/99	SC Campomaiorense	H	2-0	Chiquinho Conde 2
22/05/99	GD Chaves	A	2-1	Toñito, Chiquinho Conde
29/05/99	Académica Coimbra	H	1-0	Pedro Henriques

PROMOTED CLUBS

SECOND DIVISION FINAL TABLE 98/99

		Pd	W	D	L	F	A	Pt	GD
1	**Gil Vicente FC**	34	20	8	6	58	24	68	+34
2	**CF Os Belenenses**	34	17	10	7	55	28	61	+27
3	**CD Santa Clara**	34	14	13	7	53	37	55	+16
4	Desportivo Aves	34	14	9	11	46	43	51	+3
5	FC Felgueiras	34	12	14	8	60	40	50	+20
6	Leça FC	34	14	8	12	51	49	50	+2
7	SC Espinho	34	13	11	10	45	37	50	+8
8	Varzim SC	34	13	9	12	51	46	48	+5
9	FC Penafiel	34	11	14	9	56	49	47	+7
10	FC Maia	34	12	10	12	53	50	46	+3
11	FC Paços Ferreira	34	10	14	10	38	35	44	+3
12	Moreirense FC	34	11	8	15	40	56	41	-16
13	Naval 1. de Maio	34	9	11	14	34	54	38	-20
14	AD Esposende	34	8	14	12	24	34	38	-10
15	União Lamas	34	9	10	15	28	48	37	-20
16	CD Feirense	34	9	10	15	34	53	37	-19
17	União Madeira	34	8	9	17	34	50	33	-16
18	GD Estoril-Praia	34	6	10	18	23	50	28	-27

CLUB DIRECTORY

Gil Vicente Futebol Clube
Rua D. Diogo Pinheiro 25
4750 Barcelos
tel - (053) 811523/812090
fax - (053) 823102
Year of Formation - 1924
President - João Magalhães
Coach - Álvaro Magalhães
Stadium - Adelino Ribeiro Novo (12,200)

CLUB DIRECTORY

Clube de Futebol "Os Belenenses"
Avenida do Restelo
1400 Lisboa
tel - (01) 3010461/3011143
fax - (01) 3016525
Year of Formation - 1919
President - Ramos Lopes
Coach - Manuel Cajuda (99/00 Vítor Oliveira)
Stadium - Restelo (40,000)

MAJOR HONOURS
League Championship - (1) 1946.
Domestic Cup - (6)
1927, 1929, 1933, 1942, 1960, 1989.

CLUB DIRECTORY

Clube Desportivo Santa Clara
Rua Comandante Jaime de Sousa no. 21
9500 Ponta Delgada
tel - (096) 283191
fax - (096) 629044
Year of Formation - 1921
President - Paulino de Jesus Pavão
Coach - Manuel Fernandes
Stadium - São Miguel (20.000)

REPUBLIC OF IRELAND

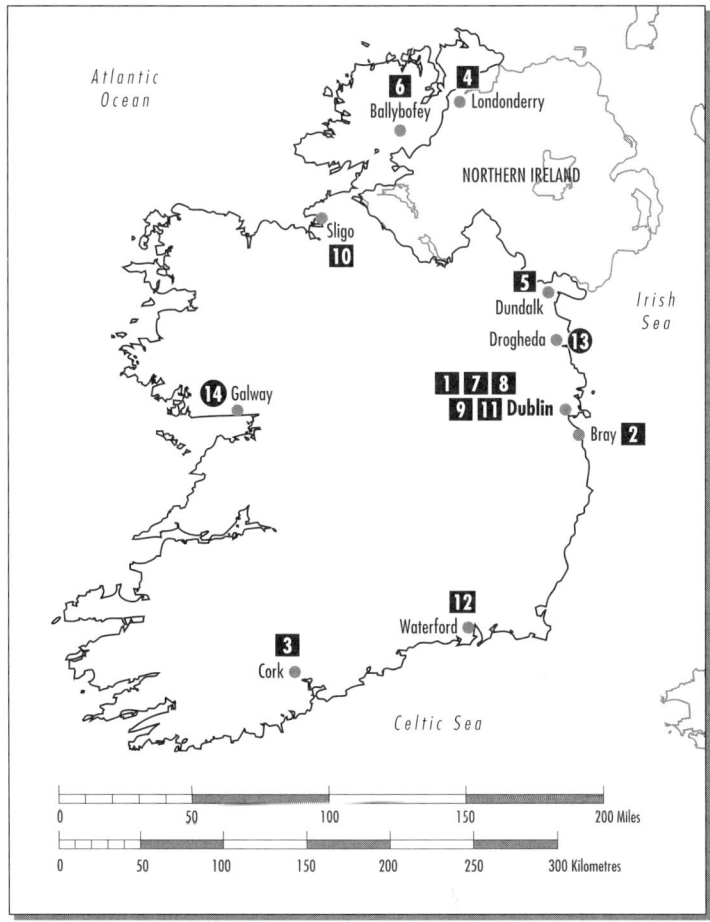

1	BOHEMIANS	792	9	SHELBOURNE	800
2	BRAY WANDERERS	793	10	SLIGO ROVERS	801
3	CORK CITY	794	11	UCD	802
4	DERRY CITY	795	12	WATERFORD UNITED	803
5	DUNDALK	796	**Promoted clubs**		
6	FINN HARPS	797	13	DROGHEDA UNITED	804
7	ST. PATRICK'S ATHLETIC	798	14	GALWAY UNITED	804
8	SHAMROCK ROVERS	799			

ST. PAT'S PIP CORK IN TITLE THRILLER

McCarthy plan beginning to bear fruit

FEDERATION DIRECTORY

The Football Association of Ireland
80 Merrion Square, Dublin 2

tel - (01) 6766864
fax - (01) 6610931

Year of Formation - 1921
Chairman - Michael Hyland
Secretary - Donal Crowther

Stadium - Lonsdowne Road, Dublin (48,000)

The road to Euro 2000 always looked to be pitted with traps and hazards for the Republic of Ireland once they found themselves thrown into the Balkan powderkeg of Group Eight. Finishing above Yugoslavia, Croatia and Macedonia looked a formidable enough task in itself for Mick McCarthy's transitional team without all the additional problems brought on by the conflict in Kosovo.

The Irish were scheduled to play five European Championship qualifying matches during the 1998/99 season. In the end they got round to playing four, with only the first two not being affected by cancellation and postponement. The clash with Yugoslavia in Belgrade was played a month after its original date. The away match with Macedonia was called off and replaced two and a half months later by a home tie against the same opponents. As for the return with the Yugoslavs at Lansdowne Road, that became something of a political hot potato as the Irish FA defied UEFA orders by unilaterally forcing the postponement of the fixture thanks to the assistance of the Irish government, who refused to issue entry visas to the Yugoslav delegation.

The disruption was particularly upsetting and unsettling because the Irish had made a splendid start to their qualifying campaign and were eager to establish themselves as the team to chase in the group. McCarthy's men exploited Croatian fatigue to beat the World Cup bronze medallists 2-0 in Dublin in their opening fixture, and they made mincemeat of Malta at the same venue a month later, with teenager Robbie Keane scoring the first two goals in a 5-0 win to become the Republic's youngest goalscorer in a senior international, beating the old record set by Johnny Giles. There was a big setback to

LEAGUE CHAMPIONSHIP RESULTS 98/99

		1	2	3	4	5	6	7	8	9	10	11	12
1	Bohemians		1-2	0-2	0-1	1-0	2-3	1-1	1-1	2-0	0-1	3-0	0-1
			0-0	0-2		2-1	0-1						0-1
2	Bray Wanderers	0-1		0-1	0-1	0-0	0-0	1-4	3-4	1-0	1-1	0-0	6-0
				1-3		1-0					0-1	1-2	0-1
3	Cork City	0-0	3-0		2-1	4-1	2-0	1-2	3-1	2-1	1-0	1-2	5-0
					0-1	2-0	2-1		3-0	2-1			0-4
4	Derry City	0-2	5-1	1-1		0-1	2-1	0-1	1-1	0-1	2-0	2-0	1-0
		0-1	1-1				1-0	0-0		1-0			
5	Dundalk	0-1	0-1	1-1	2-2		0-0	2-0	1-1	1-2	0-2	2-0	2-0
					0-1				1-1	1-2	3-2	0-2	
6	Finn Harps	1-0	6-2	1-1	2-2	0-0		2-1	2-1	3-2	1-1	0-0	1-2
			0-3			1-0		0-3	4-1			1-0	2-0
7	St. Patrick's Athletic	3-0	3-0	2-0	1-0	3-1	2-2		3-0	2-1	4-1	1-0	2-0
			1-3	1-0	1-0	1-0					4-0	0-0	
8	Shamrock Rovers	3-0	0-1	0-3	0-0	1-1	2-0	2-1		2-1	1-1	2-0	0-0
		1-1	0-0		1-0		0-1					0-0	
9	Shelbourne	2-1	1-0	3-3	2-0	1-2	0-0	0-1	2-2		1-1	1-1	1-0
		1-2					2-0	1-1	1-0		1-0		0-2
10	Sligo Rovers	2-2	0-0	0-2	3-3	2-0	1-1	1-4	2-3	1-3		0-1	1-1
		2-1		2-5	2-0		2-0		1-0				2-1
11	UCD	2-0	3-1	0-1	2-2	0-0	3-0	2-2	0-2	1-1	2-0		1-1
		2-0	1-3	2-2	2-1					0-1	0-0		
12	Waterford United	0-0	1-0	0-2	1-2	1-0	0-3	0-2	1-1	0-0	1-1	1-0	
				1-0	2-0		0-0		1-0			1-2	

LEAGUE CHAMPIONSHIP FINAL TABLE 98/99

				Home					Away					Total					
		P	W	D	L	F	A	W	D	L	F	A	W	D	L	F	A	P	GD
1	St. Patrick's Athletic	33	14	2	1	34	8	8	5	3	24	13	22	7	4	58	21	73	+37
2	Cork City	33	12	2	3	33	11	9	5	2	29	14	21	7	5	62	25	70	+37
3	Shelbourne	33	7	6	4	20	16	6	2	8	17	19	13	8	12	37	35	47	+2
4	Finn Harps	33	9	5	3	27	19	3	5	8	12	21	12	10	11	39	40	46	-1
5	Derry City	33	7	4	5	17	11	5	5	7	17	21	12	9	12	34	32	45	+2
6	UCD	33	6	7	4	23	17	4	5	7	8	15	10	12	11	31	32	42	-1
7	Waterford United	33	6	5	5	11	13	5	4	8	10	24	11	9	13	21	37	42	-16
8	Shamrock Rovers	33	6	7	3	15	10	3	6	8	19	30	9	13	11	34	40	40	-6
9	Sligo Rovers	33	6	5	6	24	27	3	6	7	13	23	9	11	13	37	50	38	-13
10	Bohemians	33	4	3	9	13	17	6	4	7	15	20	10	7	16	28	37	37	-9
11	Bray Wanderers	33	3	4	9	15	19	5	4	8	15	26	8	8	17	30	45	32	-15
12	Dundalk	33	4	5	7	16	18	2	4	11	7	22	6	9	18	23	40	27	-17

DOMESTIC CUP 98/99

FIRST ROUND
Ashtown Villa 0, Cherry Orchard 2
Athlone Town 0, Sligo Rovers 1
Bray Wanderers 5, St. Francis 0
Cobh Ramblers 2, Garda 2
(replay) Garda 1, Cobh Ramblers 6
Drogheda United 0, Galway United 0
(replay) Galway United 1, Drogheda United 0
Finn Harps 0, Belgrove 0
(replay) Belgrove 0, Finn Harps 6
Glenmore Celtic 0, St. Patrick's Athletic 3
Kilkenny City 3, Swilly Rovers 2
Limerick 0, Dundalk 0
(replay) Dundalk 2, Limerick 2
(2nd replay) Limerick 0, Dundalk 1
Longford Town 0, Derry City 1
Monaghan United 0, Cork City 2
Rockmount 1, UCD 1
(replay) UCD 2, Rockmount 0
St. Mary's 1, Bangor Celtic 0
Shamrock Rovers 0, Shelbourne 3
Waterford United 0, Bohemians 4
Workmans Dunleary 1, Home Farm Everton 3

SECOND ROUND
Bohemians 0, Shelbourne 1
Bray Wanderers 3, Cherry Orchard 0
Cork City 0, Finn Harps 0
(replay) Finn Harps 1, Cork City 0
Derry City 2, Dundalk 0
Galway United 1, Home Farm Everton 0
St. Mary's 0, Kilkenny City 3
St. Patrick's Athletic 1, UCD 0
Sligo Rovers 2, Cobh Ramblers 1

QUARTER-FINALS
Derry City 0, Shelbourne 2 (Geoghegan S. 28, 49)
Galway United 1 (Lavine 69), St. Patrick's Athletic 0
Kilkenny City 2 (Walsh 49, Rea 86),
Finn Harps 2 (Mulligan 33, Speak 68)
(replay) Finn Harps w/o Kilkenny City
Sligo Rovers 1 (Hallows 82),
Bray Wanderers 1 (Lynch 68)
(replay) Bray Wanderers 0, Sligo Rovers 0
(2nd replay) Bray Wanderers 1 (Tresson 51p),
Sligo Rovers 0

SEMI-FINALS
Galway United 1 (Keane 45),
Finn Harps 2 (O'Brien 3, Speak 59)

Shelbourne 1 (Scully 90),
Bray Wanderers 2 (Doohan 44, Tresson 51)

FINAL
10/05/99, Dublin (Tolka Park)
BRAY WANDERERS 0
FINN HARPS 0
referee - McDermott

BRAY WANDERERS - Walsh; Doohan, Tresson, Lynch,
Kenny, Tierney, Smyth, Farrell, Ryan (Brien 28), Fox,
Keogh.

FINN HARPS - McKenna; Scanlon, Boyle D., Dykes,
Minnock, Mohan, Harkin, O'Brien, Kavanagh, Speak,
Mulligan.

(replay)
16/05/99, Dublin (Tolka Park)
BRAY WANDERERS 2 O'Connor (87), O'Brien (120)
FINN HARPS 2 Speak (60), Mohan (103)
(aet)
referee - McDermott

BRAY WANDERERS - Walsh; Lynch, Tresson, Doohan,
Kenny, Tierney (Brien 27), Smyth (Byrne 68),
Keogh, Farrell (O'Connor 40), Fox, O'Brien.

FINN HARPS - McKenna; Scanlon, Boyle D., Dykes,
Minnock, Mohan (McGettigan 115), O'Brien,
Harkin (Bradley 108), McGrenaghan,
Speak (Sheridan 112), Mulligan.

(2nd replay)
20/05/99, Dublin (Tolka Park)
BRAY WANDERERS 2 Byrne (38, 73)
FINN HARPS 1 Speak (12)
referee - McDermott

BRAY WANDERERS - Walsh; Kenny, Doohan, Lynch,
Farrell (Smyth 87), O'Connor, Tresson, Fox, Keogh,
Byrne, O'Brien.

FINN HARPS - McKenna; Scanlon (Boyle R. 65),
Boyle D., Dykes, Minnock, Mohan (Bradley 83),
O'Brien, Harkin, McGrenaghan (Sheridan 77),
Mulligan, Speak.

qualifying hopes when the Irish lost somewhat unluckily to Yugoslavia in Belgrade after a rare defensive howler gifted their opponents the only goal of the game. Then came the long pause - all of seven months - before the victory trail was rediscovered with an important 1-0 win at Lansdowne Road against Macedonia. With maximum points from their first three home games, the Irish had placed themselves in a strong position to challenge both Yugoslavia and Croatia for first or second place. Their fate would be determined in all probability during a three-game stretch over the first eight days of September...

Irrespective of what was to follow, 1998/99 was undeniably a season of progress for Mick McCarthy's team. The blooding of new talent such as Robbie Keane, Damien Duff, Stephen Carr and Kevin Kilbane was an important and necessary step towards team-rebuilding following the gradual falling-away of the old guard from the Jack Charlton era. Not all of those stalwarts have gone, though. Roy Keane, of course, is still in his prime and has proved to be an inspirational captain, while Denis Irwin, Steve Staunton and Niall Quinn continue to serve dutifully despite all being the 'wrong' side of 30.

There is even still room, albeit on the substitutes' bench, for 37-year-old Tony Cascarino, who, on entering the field with 22 minutes left of the Euro 2000 qualifier at home to Macedonia, equalled Paul McGrath's all-time Irish appearance record of 83 caps. The big striker could not, however, find the net during the season, which left him still one goal short of Frank Stapleton's record total of 20. It is remarkable that more than half of Cascarino's caps have been earned as a substitute, including all seven that he collected during the 1998/99 season.

NATIONAL TEAM APPEARANCES 98/99

Manager - Mick McCARTHY	CRO	MLT	YUG	PAR	SWE	NIR	MAC	Cps	Gls
Shay GIVEN (20/04/76) - Newcastle United (ENG)	G	G	G	G68	G	G		23	-
Denis IRWIN (31/10/65) - Manchester United (ENG)	D		D	D			D	52	4
Ken CUNNINGHAM (28/06/71) - Wimbledon (ENG)	D	D	D	D	D	D	D	23	-
Phil BABB (30/11/70) - Liverpool (ENG)	D			s73	s46	D		29	-
Steve STAUNTON (19/01/69) - Liverpool (ENG)	D	D	D		D			78	5
Jason McATEER (18/06/71) - Liverpool (ENG)/Blackburn Rovers (ENG)	M	M84	M82	M83	M46			30	1
Mark KINSELLA (12/08/72) - Charlton Athletic (ENG)	M	M	M	M68	M46	M80	M	9	-
Roy KEANE (10/08/71) - Manchester United (ENG)	M	M	M	M				42	5
Damien DUFF (02/03/79) - Blackburn Rovers (ENG)	M46	M	M	M	s79	M56	M63	9	-
Robbie KEANE (08/07/80) - Wolverhampton Wanderers (ENG)	A61	A83		A68	s80	A56	A68	9	2
Keith O'NEILL (16/02/76) - Norwich City (ENG)/Middlesbrough (ENG)	A5		s82			s56		12	4
Tony CASCARINO (01/09/62) - AS Nancy-Lorraine (FRA)	s5	s74	s73	s70	s71	s72	s68	83	19
Jeff KENNA (27/08/70) - Blackburn Rovers (ENG)	s46	D						26	-
Lee CARSLEY (28/02/74) - Derby County (ENG)/Blackburn Rovers (ENG)	s61	s84		s68		M46	M	11	-
Gary BREEN (12/12/73) - Coventry City (ENG)		D	D	D	D46		D	20	3
Niall QUINN (06/10/66) - Sunderland (ENG)		A74	A73	A70	A80	A72	A81	69	18
Mark KENNEDY (15/05/76) - Wimbledon (ENG)		s83			M79	M	M	22	2
Alan McLOUGHLIN (20/04/67) - Portsmouth (ENG)			M73	s83	M	s46		38	2
David CONNOLLY (06/06/77) - Wolverhampton Wanderers (ENG)			s73	s68	A71	s56	s81	18	7
Ian HARTE (31/08/77) - Leeds United (ENG)				D73				19	2
Alan KELLY (11/08/68) - Sheffield United (ENG)				s68			G	22	-
Stephen CARR (29/08/76) - Tottenham Hotspur (ENG)					D	D	D	3	-
Kevin KILBANE (01/02/77) - West Bromwich Albion (ENG)					s46		s63	5	-
Graham KAVANAGH (02/12/73) - Stoke City (ENG)					s46	s80		3	1
Alan MAYBURY (08/08/78) - Leeds United (ENG)						D		2	-

EUROPEAN CUPS 98/99

CHAMPIONS' CUP
● **ST. PATRICK'S ATHLETIC**
Preliminary round CELTIC (SCO)
A 0-0
Wood; Clarke, Campbell, Lynch, Hawkins, Osam, Gormley, Russell, Malloy (Reilly 73), Braithwaite (Crolly 82), Gilzean.

H 0-2
Wood; Clarke, Campbell (Doyle 46), Lynch, Hawkins, Osam, Gormley, Morgan (Russell 46), Braithwaite, Gilzean (Reilly 74), Malloy.

CUP WINNERS' CUP
● **CORK CITY**
Qualifying round CSKA KYIV (UKR)
H 2-1 Flanagan (20p), Coughlan (31)
Mooney; Daly, Cronin, Hill, Coughlan, Freyne, Cahill, Flanagan, Hartigan (Kabia 72), Barry-Murphy (Dobbs 75), O'Halloran (Caulfield 81).

A 0-2
Mooney; Daly, Cronin, Hill, Coughlan, Freyne, Cahill, Flanagan (Caulfield 80), Hartigan (Kabia 55), Barry-Murphy (Dobbs 55), O'Halloran.

UEFA CUP
● **SHELBOURNE**
Preliminary round RANGERS (SCO)
H 3-5 Porrini (7og), Rutherford (41), Morley (58)
Gough; Geoghegan D., McCartney, Scully, Baker, Rutherford, Smith, Fenton, Fitzgerald, Morley, Kelly.

A 0-2
Gough; Geoghegan S., McCartney, Scully, Baker, Rutherford, Smith, Fenton, Fitzgerald, Morley (Sheridan 67), Kelly.

In advance of the national team's Euro 2000 campaign the country received quite a boost with the performances of the League of Ireland's three representatives in European club competition. As ever, all three failed to get through their opening ties, but this time they at least gave their fans something to shout about. Shelbourne were on course to make the biggest headlines of all when they sen-

TOP SCORERS

15 Trevor MOLLOY (St. Patrick's Athletic)
12 Ian GILZEAN (St. Patrick's Athletic)
11 Kelvin FLANAGAN (Cork City)
   Marcus HALLOWS (Sligo Rovers)
   Derek SWAN (Bohemians)
10 James MULLIGAN (Finn Harps)
   Tony SHERIDAN (Shelbourne)
9 Pat MORLEY (Cork City)
   Jonathan SPEAK (Finn Harps)
8 Ollie CAHILL (Cork City)
   Liam COYLE (Derry City)
   Michael McHUGH (Derry City)
   Jason SHERLOCK (Shamrock Rovers)
   Glen SHANNON (Sligo Rovers)

sationally went 3-0 up against Scottish heavyweights Rangers in a match played on English soil at Tranmere. But reality rapidly returned and they eventually lost the match 3-5 and the tie 3-7. Those other Glaswegian giants, Celtic, also struggled initially against opponents from Dublin when they were held 0-0 at Parkhead by Irish champions St. Patrick's Athletic. In the second leg, though, St. Pat's could not make home advantage count and were fortunate to lose by only two goals to nil. The solitary victory went to Cork City, who beat Ukrainian side CSKA Kiev 2-1 at home in the first leg but were made to pay for conceding a goal in the last minute of that game and eventually fell to a 2-3 aggregate defeat.

But if Cork felt frustrated by their European exit, they certainly didn't show it. In the League of Ireland, Dave Barry's men made the perfect start, winning every one of their first eight games to storm to the top of the table. Their winning run was eventually ended by defending champions St. Pat's, who beat them 2-0 at Richmond Park to maintain a thoroughly impressive start of their own. With both Cork and St. Pat's on 24 points from nine games, it was obvious even at this relatively advanced juncture of the season that the championship was set to become a two-horse race.

Over the course of the next five months the two clubs kept probing away, trying to string a run of results together that would force the other to abandon their chase. But it didn't happen. There were good and bad spells for both teams, and although St. Pat's were victorious in the second direct confrontation of the season at Turners Cross, when the third and final head-to-head arrived, three rounds from the end, both title contenders were exactly level in the table - both on points and on goal difference. The Dubliners had the home advantage, and they made it count, with midfielder and double Player of the Year Paul 'Ozo' Osam scoring the goal that won the match and, in consequence, brought St. Pat's to the brink of their third League of Ireland title in four years.

NATIONAL TEAM RESULTS 98/99

05/09/98	Croatia (ECQ)	H	Dublin	2-0	Irwin (2p), Keane Roy (15)
14/10/98	Malta (ECQ)	H	Dublin	5-0	Keane Rob. (16, 18), Keane Roy (54),
					Quinn (63), Breen (82)
18/11/98	Yugoslavia (ECQ)	A	Belgrade	0-1	
10/02/99	Paraguay	H	Dublin	2-0	Irwin (38p), Connolly (73)
28/04/99	Sweden	H	Dublin	2-0	Kavanagh (75), Kennedy (76)
29/05/99	Northern Ireland	H	Dublin	0-1	
09/06/99	Macedonia (ECQ)	H	Dublin	1-0	Quinn (67)

The pressure was now firmly on the defending champions, and, led skilfully by manager Liam Buckley (who had replaced Paul Dolan the previous summer), St. Pat's did what they had to in their final two matches, beating Shamrock Rovers and Bray Wanderers, 1-0 each time, to clinch the championship.

Although there was symaphty for Cork, who had posted two points more than the title-winning total from the previous season, there could be no doubt that St. Pat's were worthy champions. Their three wins out of three against Cork bore testimony to that. The consolation for the runners-up was a return ticket to Europe, in the UEFA Cup, and they also had some silverware to show for their season of enterprise after beating Shamrock Rovers 2-1 to win the final of the League Cup.

The FAI Cup brought surprisingly early exits for both Cork and St. Pat's, and with Cup specialists Shelbourne (a very distant third in the championship) also bowing out in the semis, there was a very unfamiliar look to the final, which featured Donegal's finest, Finn Harps, and the Wanderers from the County Wicklow seaside town of Bray.

Bray went into the final having just lost their place in the Premier Division. They had dropped down to the First Division alongside financially-stricken Dundalk (relegated for the very first time) and were determined to go out with a bang by winning the Cup. Finn Harps were similarly eager to win a trophy which had not belonged to them for a quarter of a century. The battle lines were drawn but, incredibly, it was to take five hours of football before a winner emerged.

The first game, at Tolka Park, ended goalless. Six days later Finn Harps were twice on the verge of victory when Bray scored late goals to deny them in both normal time and extra-time. The organisers of the FAI Cup clearly do not believe in the penalty shoot-out, because the two finalists were instructed to meet again, four days later, and resume their conflict. This time, though, the match at last produced a winner... and a match-winning hero as Bray striker Jason Byrne struck twice to enable his team to come from behind (again) and triumph 2-1. Thus, Bray ended the 1990s as they had begun it - with the FAI Cup in their possession - and also made history by becoming the first team to win that trophy and suffer relegation in the same season.

PLAYERS OF THE SEASON

★ SUPERSTAR PROFILE
ROY KEANE

Consigned to the treatment table for most of the 1997/98 season while recovering from a serious knee ligament injury, Roy Keane came roaring

back to top form in 1998/99. He was one of many heroes as Manchester United made history by securing the unprecedented 'treble' of Premiership, FA Cup and European Champions' Cup. Some might say that he was the most influential member of that fabulous team. His absence was certainly conspicuous when United had to do without their leader in the Champions' Cup final against Bayern Munich. Keane had played the game of his life in the semi-final away to Juventus but the yellow card he picked up in that 3-2 victory (after scoring the goal that sparked the comeback from 0-2 down) meant that he was suspended for the final. Thus, after United's dramatic triumph in Barcelona, their captain was not permitted to climb onto the podium and lift the Cup. Ironically, the Irishman had been injured in the FA Cup final five days earlier and would not

PLAYERS OF THE SEASON

have been fit to play anyway, but that was no consolation for missing out on the crowning moment of his career. Keane is now also the captain of the Republic of Ireland, and he marked his appointment by scoring in each of the team's first two Euro 2000 qualifiers, against Croatia and Malta. His club future remains uncertain after a summer of long drawn-out contract negotiations at Old Trafford, but whether he stays with United or moves on to Italy, he seems certain to remain the Irish national team's most prized asset for some years yet.

DENIS IRWIN
Controversially banned from the 1999 FA Cup final, Denis Irwin did not collect a winner's medal from that competition, but the veteran full-back has still amassed more silverware than any other Manchester United player during the club's amazing decade of success during the 1990s. Once again he was a key member of Alex Ferguson's team during their 'treble'-winning season, providing his usual mixture of composure and competitiveness in the left-back rôle (despite his stronger right foot). He also earned his 50th cap for the Republic of Ireland in their European Championship qualifier away to

Yugoslavia. In days gone by that would have earned him a testimonial, but now that the cap limit for such an honour has been raised to 75, it is doubtful whether, at 34, even he has enough fuel left in his tank to go on and reach that milestone.

IAN HARTE
Perhaps a touch of Irish logic is needed to explain the whys and wherefores of Ian Harte's international career. The naturally talented left-footer is still only 22 and has his whole career ahead of him, so perhaps things might change, but so far the scenario has been puzzling, to say the least. During the first two years of Mick McCarthy's managerial reign, Harte was consistently selected to the Irish team - despite failing to claim a regular place in his club side, Leeds United. Yet in 1998/99, when he finally became an indispensable in the Leeds side, missing just three Premiership matches all season, he lost his international place. One Irishman who was certainly singing his praises was new Leeds boss David O'Leary, under whose management Harte showed genuine class, both in his defensive resilience and his capacity to strike glorious long-range shots at goal, both from set-pieces and in open play.

BOHEMIANS

CLUB DIRECTORY

Bohemian FC
Dalymount Park, Phibsborough, Dublin 7
tel - (01) 8680923/8681022/8682880
fax - (01) 8681022
Year of Formation - 1890
Chairman - Tony O'Connell
Secretary - Donal Crowther
Manager - Joe McGrath; Roddy Collins
Stadium - Dalymount Park (14,700)

MAJOR HONOURS
League Championship - (7)
1924, 1928, 1930, 1934, 1936, 1975, 1978.
Domestic Cup - (5)
1928, 1935, 1970, 1976, 1992.

APPEARANCES 98/99

		P	Ap	(s)	Gls
Jason BATTY	G	4			
Robbie BEST	D	1			
Donal BROUGHAN	D	11	(1)		
Robbie BRUNTON	D	24	(1)		
Paul BYRNE	A	12	(3)		1
Tommy BYRNE	D	26	(3)		1
Graham CONWAY	M	1	(1)		
Robert COOMBES	M		(2)		
Raffaele DE GREGORIO (NZL)	M	5	(2)		
Michael DEMPSEY	G	27			
Dean DODDS (NZL)	M	3			
Paul DOOLIN	M		(1)		
Graham DOYLE	M	6	(2)		
David FAIRCLOUGH	D	3	(2)		
David GALLAGHER	G		(1)		
Peter HANRAHAN	A	9	(3)		2
Fergal HARKIN	M	11			
Kevin HUNT (ENG)	M	14	(1)		1
Ray KELLY	D	8	(4)		1
Graham LAWLOR	A	18	(9)		5
Derek McGRATH	M	6	(2)		1
Shaun MAHER	D	24	(1)		1
Dean MARTIN (ENG)	M	3			
Brian MOONEY	M	22	(5)		1
Eoin MULLEN	D	28	(1)		
Harry NGATA (NZL)	A	3	(1)		1
Tony O'CONNOR	D	28			2
Maurice O'DRISCOLL	D	8	(1)		
Graham O'HANLON	D	24	(2)		
Brian O'SHEA	G	2			
Brendan PLACE	D	2	(1)		
Derek SWAN	A	28	(1)		11
Glen WADE	M	2	(2)		

LEAGUE RESULTS 1998/99

25/08/98	Finn Harps	H	2-3	Swan 2 (1p)
05/09/98	Sligo Rovers	A	2-2	Ngata, Swan
11/09/98	Cork City	H	0-2	
18/09/98	St. Patrick's Athletic	A	0-3	
25/09/98	Bray Wanderers	H	1-2	Mooney
02/10/98	Shamrock Rovers	A	0-3	
11/10/98	Dundalk	H	1-0	Lawlor
18/10/98	Derry City	A	2-0	Lawlor, McGrath
26/10/98	Shelbourne	A	1-2	Swan
01/11/98	Waterford United	H	0-1	
08/11/98	UCD	A	0-2	
15/11/98	UCD	H	3-0	Hanrahan 2, Lawlor
21/11/98	Finn Harps	A	0-1	
27/11/98	Sligo Rovers	H	0-1	
06/12/98	Cork City	A	0-0	
11/12/98	St. Patrick's Athletic	H	1-1	Byrne T.
20/12/98	Bray Wanderers	A	1-0	Swan
27/12/98	Shamrock Rovers	H	1-1	Swan
03/01/99	Dundalk	A	1-0	Swan
22/01/99	Shelbourne	H	2-0	O'Connor, Swan
29/01/99	Waterford United	A	0-0	
12/02/99	Finn Harps	H	0-1	
20/02/99	Sligo Rovers	A	1-2	Swan
26/02/99	Cork City	H	0-2	
12/03/99	St. Patrick's Athletic	A	3-1	Lawlor 2, Hunt
21/03/99	Bray Wanderers	H	0-0	
26/03/99	Shamrock Rovers	A	1-1	O'Connor
04/04/99	Dundalk	H	2-1	Swan 2 (1p)
10/04/99	Derry City	A	1-0	Maher
15/04/99	Shelbourne	A	2-1	Kelly, Byrne P.
23/04/99	Waterford United	H	0-1	
27/04/99	Derry City	H	0-1	
02/05/99	UCD	A	0-2	

BRAY WANDERERS

CLUB DIRECTORY

Bray Wanderers FC
Carlisle Grounds
Bray
Co. Wicklow
tel - (01) 2828214
fax - (01) 2861685
Year of Formation - 1942
Chairman - Philip Hannigan
Secretary - John O'Brien
Manager - Pat Devlin
Stadium - Carlisle Grounds (6,500)

MAJOR HONOURS
Domestic Cup - (2) 1990, 1999.

APPEARANCES 98/99

	P	Ap	(s)	Gls
Glen BRIEN	M	3	(6)	
Jason BYRNE	A	15	(2)	5
Graham CASSIN	M	1	(1)	
Stuart CONNOLLY	M	14	(4)	1
Robbie COYLE	M	7		1
Alan DODD	M	8	(6)	
Mick DOOHAN	D	19		3
Justin DUTTON	M		(1)	
Maurice FARRELL	D	4	(1)	
Stephen FOX	A	20	(6)	2
Stephen GIFFORD	D	6		
Tommy GILL	D	9	(1)	
Steve HORAN	M		(3)	
Steve JONES (NIR)	M	3		
Alan KANE	G	11		
Ray KENNY	M		(4)	
Philip KEOGH	D	26	(1)	
Frankie LARKIN	M		(2)	
Aaron LYNCH	D		(1)	
Jody LYNCH	D	33		1
Anthony McKEEVER	D	14		
Kieran O'BRIEN	A	10	(10)	
Pat O'BRIEN	M	13	(5)	1
Barry O'CONNOR	A	22	(3)	5
Richie PARSONS	A	5	(15)	3
Darren POWER	M		(2)	
John RYAN	A	21	(2)	2
Alan SMYTH	A	22	(3)	2
Dom TIERNEY	M	22	(3)	1
Colm TRESSON	D	33		3
John WALSH	G	22		

LEAGUE RESULTS 1998/99

30/08/98	Cork City	H	0-1	
04/09/98	Shamrock Rovers	A	1-0	Byrne
13/09/98	Derry City	A	1-5	Smyth
19/09/98	Shelbourne	H	1-0	Byrne
25/09/98	Bohemians	A	2-1	Lynch J., Byrne
03/10/98	Dundalk	H	0-0	
11/10/98	UCD	A	1-3	Parsons
17/10/98	Waterford United	H	6-0	Byrne 2, Tresson, Tierney, Smyth, Parsons
30/10/98	Sligo Rovers	H	1-1	Tresson
06/11/98	St. Patrick's Athletic	A	0-3	
13/11/98	St. Patrick's Athletic	H	1-4	O'Connor
15/11/98	Finn Harps	A	2-6	O'Brien P., O'Connor
22/11/98	Cork City	A	0-3	
29/11/98	Shamrock Rovers	H	3-4	Ryan 2 (1p), Parsons
04/12/98	Derry City	H	0-1	
13/12/98	Shelbourne	A	0-1	
20/12/98	Bohemians	H	0-1	
27/12/98	Dundalk	A	1-0	Doohan
03/01/99	UCD	H	0-0	
22/01/99	Finn Harps	H	0-0	
30/01/99	Sligo Rovers	A	0-0	
12/02/99	Cork City	H	1-3	O'Connor
19/02/99	Shamrock Rovers	A	0-0	
28/02/99	Derry City	A	1-1	Connolly
13/03/99	Shelbourne	H	0-1	
21/03/99	Bohemians	A	0-0	
26/03/99	Dundalk	H	1-0	Coyle
05/04/99	UCD	A	3-1	Doohan, O'Connor, Fox
09/04/99	Waterford United	H	0-1	
17/04/99	Finn Harps	A	3-0	O'Connor, Tresson, Fox
23/04/99	Sligo Rovers	H	1-2	Doohan
25/04/99	Waterford United	A	0-1	
02/05/99	St. Patrick's Athletic	A	0-1	

CORK CITY

CLUB DIRECTORY

Cork City FC
Turner's Cross Stadium
Curragh Road
Turner's Cross, Cork
tel - (021) 543774
fax - (021) 342824
Year of Formation - 1984
Chairman - Terry Dunne
Secretary - Jim Murphy
Manager - Dave Barry
Stadium - Turner's Cross (10,850)

MAJOR HONOURS
League Championship - (1) 1993.
Domestic Cup - (1) 1998.

APPEARANCES 98/99

	P	Ap	(s)	Gls
Brian BARRY-MURPHY	M	22	(5)	1
Ollie CAHILL	M	33		8
John CAULFIELD	A	16	(12)	7
John COTTER	M		(7)	
Derek COUGHLAN	D	25		4
Gareth CRONIN	D	25	(2)	1
Declan DALY	D	28		
Gerald DOBBS (ENG)	A	23	(4)	5
Kelvin FLANAGAN	M	27	(1)	11
Patsy FREYNE	M	25	(1)	
Johnny GLYNN	A		(5)	
Phil HARRINGTON (WAL)	G		(1)	
Noel HARTIGAN	A	6	(10)	2
Mark HERRICK	M	31	(1)	4
Dave HILL (ENG)	D	27		
Jason KABIA (ENG)	A	9		1
Noel MOONEY	G	33		
Pat MORLEY	A	12	(8)	9
Colin O'BRIEN	M	6	(5)	3
Fergus O'DONOGHUE	D	6	(2)	
Greg O'HALLORAN	D	9	(4)	2

LEAGUE RESULTS 1998/99

30/08/98	Bray Wanderers	A	1-0	Flanagan (p)
06/09/98	Derry City	H	2-1	Dobbs, Coughlan
11/09/98	Bohemians	A	2-0	Kabia, Dobbs
19/09/98	Dundalk	H	4-1	Cahill 2, Herrick, Barry-Murphy
27/09/98	UCD	A	1-0	Flanagan (p)
04/10/98	Waterford United	H	5-0	Dobbs, Cahill 3, Coughlan
10/10/98	Sligo Rovers	A	2-0	Herrick, Caulfield
18/10/98	Finn Harps	H	2-0	Flanagan, Caulfield
23/10/98	St. Patrick's Athletic	A	0-2	
01/11/98	Shelbourne	H	2-1	Caulfield, Hartigan
08/11/98	Shamrock Rovers	H	3-1	Flanagan (p), Cahill, Coughlan
15/11/98	Shamrock Rovers	A	3-0	Coughlan, Caulfield, Dobbs
22/11/98	Bray Wanderers	H	3-0	Flanagan, Caulfield, O'Halloran
29/11/98	Derry City	A	1-1	Dobbs
06/12/98	Bohemians	H	0-0	
13/12/98	Dundalk	A	1-1	Hartigan
20/12/98	UCD	H	1-2	og (Lynch)
27/12/98	Waterford United	A	2-0	Herrick, Flanagan
03/01/99	Sligo Rovers	H	1-0	og (Hare)
16/01/99	Finn Harps	A	1-1	Morley
23/01/99	St. Patrick's Athletic	H	1-2	Morley
31/01/99	Shelbourne	A	3-3	O'Brien, Flanagan (p), Morley
12/02/99	Bray Wanderers	A	3-1	Morley 2, O'Halloran
21/02/99	Derry City	H	0-1	
26/02/99	Bohemians	A	2-0	Cronin, Caulfield
14/03/99	Dundalk	H	2-0	og (Gallogley), Cahill
21/03/99	UCD	A	2-2	Flanagan, og (Mahon)
28/03/99	Waterford United	H	0-0	
03/04/99	Sligo Rovers	A	5-2	Flanagan 3, Morley, Cahill (p)
10/04/99	Finn Harps	H	2-1	Herrick, Caulfield
16/04/99	St. Patrick's Athletic	A	0-1	
25/04/99	Shelbourne	H	2-1	O'Brien, Morley
02/05/99	Shamrock Rovers	H	3-0	Morley 2, O'Brien

DERRY CITY

CLUB DIRECTORY

Derry City FC
12 Queen Street
Londonderry BT48 7EF
Northern Ireland
tel - (01504) 374542
fax - (01504) 373677
Year of Formation - 1928
Chairman - Kevin Friel
Secretary - Desmond Doherty
Manager - Kevin Mahon
Stadium - Brandywell (7,500)

MAJOR HONOURS
League Championship - (2) 1989, 1997.
Domestic Cup - (2) 1989, 1995.

APPEARANCES 98/99

		P	Ap	(s)	Gls
Gary BECKETT (NIR)	M	21		3
James BOYLE	A	1		
Liam COYLE (NIR)	A	28	(2)	8
Ryan COYLE (NIR)	M		(4)	
Paul CURRAN (NIR)	D	30	(1)	2
Eamon DOHERTY (NIR)	D	26	(2)	3
Gerard DOHERTY (NIR)	G		(1)	
Eddie GALLAGHER (NIR)	M		(1)	
Shaun GALLAGHER (NIR)	D	4	(2)	1
Stuart GAULD (SCO)	D	16	(6)	
Floyd GILMOUR (NIR)	A	5	(9)	1
Sean HARGAN (NIR)	M	22		3
Paul HEGARTY	M	28		
Peter HUTTON (NIR)	D	29		
Darren KELLY (NIR)	D	20	(3)	
Michael KELLY (NIR)	D	16	(9)	
Eddie McCALLION (NIR)	D	24	(2)	1
Marty McCANN (NIR)	M	16	(4)	
Darren McCAUL (NIR)	A	8	(16)	3
Darren McCREADIE (NIR)	M	5	(1)	
Michael McHUGH	A	29		8
Paddy McLAUGHLIN (NIR)	M		(3)	
Greg O'DOWD	M	2		
Tony O'DOWD	G	3		
David PLATT (NIR)	G	30		

LEAGUE RESULTS 1998/99

30/08/98	St. Patrick's Athletic	H	0-1	
06/09/98	Cork City	A	1-2	Beckett
13/09/98	Bray Wanderers	H	5-1	McCallion, McHugh, Hargan,
				Gilmour, Coyle L.
20/09/98	Shamrock Rovers	A	0-0	
25/09/98	Dundalk	A	2-2	Coyle L., McHugh
04/10/98	Shelbourne	H	0-1	
10/10/98	Waterford United	A	2-1	McHugh, Coyle L.
18/10/98	Bohemians	H	0-2	
25/10/98	UCD	A	2-2	Doherty E., Hargan
01/11/98	Finn Harps	H	2-1	Curran, Hargan
07/11/98	Sligo Rovers	A	3-3	Coyle L., Doherty E., Beckett
15/11/98	Sligo Rovers	H	2-0	Beckett, McHugh
20/11/98	St. Patrick's Athletic	A	0-1	
29/11/98	Cork City	H	1-1	og (Herrick)
04/12/98	Bray Wanderers	A	1-0	Coyle L.
13/12/98	Shamrock Rovers	H	1-1	Coyle L.
19/12/98	Dundalk	H	0-1	
26/12/98	Shelbourne	A	0-2	
03/01/99	Waterford United	H	1-0	Doherty E.
24/01/99	UCD	H	2-0	Coyle L. (p), McCaul
30/01/99	Finn Harps	A	2-2	Curran, McHugh
14/02/99	St. Patrick's Athletic	H	0-0	
21/02/99	Cork City	A	1-0	McCaul
28/02/99	Bray Wanderers	H	1-1	Coyle L.
14/03/99	Shamrock Rovers	A	0-1	
18/03/99	Dundalk	A	1-0	McCaul
28/03/99	Shelbourne	H	1-0	Gallagher S.
02/04/99	Waterford United	A	0-1	
10/04/99	Bohemians	H	0-1	
18/04/99	UCD	A	1-2	McHugh
25/04/99	Finn Harps	H	1-0	McHugh
27/04/99	Bohemians	A	1-0	McHugh
02/05/99	Sligo Rovers	A	0-2	

DUNDALK

CLUB DIRECTORY

Dundalk FC
Oriel Park
Carrick Road
Dundalk, Co. Louth
tel - (042) 35894/35398
fax - (042) 30003
Year of Formation - 1926
Chairman - Phil Flynn
Secretary - Elizabeth Duffy
Manager - Jim McLaughlin (99/00 - Terry Eviston)
Stadium - Oriel Park (12,200)

MAJOR HONOURS
League Championship - (9) 1933, 1963, 1967,
1976, 1979, 1982, 1988, 1991, 1995.
Domestic Cup - (8) 1942, 1949, 1952, 1958,
1977, 1979, 1981, 1988.

APPEARANCES 98/99

	P	Ap	(s)	Gls
Kevin BRADY	D	27		
John BRENNAN	A	11	(2)	
Brian BYRNE	A	3	(2)	1
Raymond CAMPBELL (NIR)	M	29		1
David CAPPER (ENG)	D	10		
David CRAWLEY	D	30		1
Mick DOOHAN	D	11	(1)	
Paul DOOLIN	M	12		
Ciaran DUNNE	M	4	(10)	
Colin FORTUNE	M	9	(2)	1
Padraig GALLOGLEY	D	9	(2)	
Chris HAMMON (ENG)	A		(1)	
Michael HARTE	M	4	(8)	
Stephen HENDERSON	G	1		
David HOEY	M	13	(1)	1
Peter McGINNITY	M	2	(3)	
Tom McNULTY (SCO)	M	32		2
David MARTIN	A	6	(6)	2
Noel MELVIN	D	22	(1)	
Sean MURPHY	D		(2)	
Shane REDDISH (ENG)	D	25	(4)	2
John SHARKEY	A		(2)	1
Richard SINDEN (ENG)	A	2		
Lee THEW (ENG)	M	25	(1)	3
David WARD	A	29	(4)	4
Steve WILLIAMS (WAL)	G	32		
Peter WITHNELL (NIR)	A	15		4

LEAGUE RESULTS 1998/99

27/08/98	Sligo Rovers	H	0-2	
04/09/98	St. Patrick's Athletic	A	1-3	Withnell
10/09/98	Shamrock Rovers	H	1-1	Ward
19/09/98	Cork City	A	1-4	Withnell
25/09/98	Derry City	H	2-2	Withnell, Hoey
03/10/98	Bray Wanderers	A	0-0	
11/10/98	Bohemians	A	0-1	
15/10/98	Shelbourne	H	1-2	Campbell
23/10/98	Waterford United	A	0-1	
29/10/98	UCD	H	2-0	Thew, Reddish
07/11/98	Finn Harps	A	0-0	
12/11/98	Finn Harps	H	0-0	
21/11/98	Sligo Rovers	A	0-2	
26/11/98	St. Patrick's Athletic	H	2-0	Withnell, McNulty
04/12/98	Shamrock Rovers	A	1-1	Reddish
13/12/98	Cork City	H	1-1	Ward
19/12/98	Derry City	A	1-0	McNulty
27/12/98	Bray Wanderers	H	0-1	
03/01/99	Bohemians	H	0-1	
24/01/99	Waterford United	H	2-0	Thew, Ward
27/01/99	Shelbourne	A	2-1	Martin, Sharkey
31/01/99	UCD	A	0-0	
11/02/99	Sligo Rovers	H	3-2	Fortune, Ward, Byrne
19/02/99	St. Patrick's Athletic	A	0-1	
25/02/99	Shamrock Rovers	H	1-1	Thew
14/03/99	Cork City	A	0-2	
18/03/99	Derry City	H	0-1	
26/03/99	Bray Wanderers	A	0-1	
04/04/99	Bohemians	A	1-2	Crawley
08/04/99	Shelbourne	H	1-2	Martin
16/04/99	Waterford United	A	0-2	
22/04/99	UCD	H	0-2	
02/05/99	Finn Harps	A	0-1	

FINN HARPS

CLUB DIRECTORY

Finn Harps FC
Finn Park
Ballybofey
Co. Donegal
tel - (074) 32635/30070
fax - (074) 30075
Year of Formation 1954
Chairman - Conor Boyle
Secretary - Martin Hannigan
Manager - Charlie McGeever
Stadium - Finn Park (8,400)

MAJOR HONOURS
Domestic Cup - (1) 1974.

APPEARANCES 98/99

	P	Ap	(s)	Gls
Declan BOYLE	D	32		
Ruairi BOYLE (NIR)	D	2	(3)	
Damien BRADLEY	G	3		
Shane BRADLEY	D	3	(12)	
Davy DOWLING	A	5	(5)	2
Gavin DYKES	D	32		
Brian FLOOD	M	10		
John Paul GALLAGHER	M		(1)	
Fergal HARKIN	M	15	(3)	2
Stephen HENDERSON	G	2		
Eamon KAVANAGH (NIR)	M	23	(6)	4
Stephen KELLY	M	9	(5)	1
John Gerard McGETTIGAN	M	12	(10)	
Paddy McGRENAGHAN	M	11	(12)	1
Kevin McHUGH	A	3	(11)	
Brian McKENNA	G	28		
Jonathan MINNOCK	D	32	(1)	2
Tom MOHAN (NIR)	M	31		4
Hames MULLIGAN	A	32		10
Paul NASH	M		(4)	
Donal O'BRIEN	M	20	(5)	
Trevor SCANLON	D	3	(3)	
Eamonn SHERIDAN	A	3	(3)	1
Jonathan SPEAK (NIR)	A	26	(4)	9
Pascal VAUDEQUIN (FRA)	D	26		1

LEAGUE RESULTS 1998/99

28/08/98	Bohemians	A	3-2	og (Best), Mulligan 2
05/09/98	Waterford United	H	1-2	Dowling
11/09/98	Shelbourne	A	0-0	
19/09/98	UCD	H	0-0	
26/09/98	St. Patrick's Athletic	H	2-1	Minnock, Mulligan
03/10/98	Sligo Rovers	A	1-1	Speak
10/10/98	Shamrock Rovers	H	2-1	Mulligan, Dowling
18/10/98	Cork City	A	0-2	
01/11/98	Derry City	A	1-2	Mulligan
07/11/98	Dundalk	H	0-0	
13/11/98	Dundalk	A	0-0	
15/11/98	Bray Wanderers	H	6-2	Mulligan, Mohan 2, Speak 2, Minnock
21/11/98	Bohemians	H	1-0	Kavanagh
28/11/98	Waterford United	A	3-0	Mulligan, Speak, Kelly
05/12/98	Shelbourne	H	3-2	Kavanagh, Speak, Mulligan
13/12/98	UCD	A	0-3	
18/12/98	St. Patrick's Athletic	A	2-2	Vaudequin, Kavanagh
03/01/99	Shamrock Rovers	A	0-2	
16/01/99	Cork City	H	1-1	Mohan
22/01/99	Bray Wanderers	A	0-0	
30/01/99	Derry City	H	2-2	Speak, Mohan
12/02/99	Bohemians	A	1-0	Speak
20/02/99	Waterford United	H	2-0	Harkin, Speak
26/02/99	Shelbourne	A	0-2	
13/03/99	UCD	H	1-0	McGrenaghan
20/03/99	St. Patrick's Athletic	H	0-3	
26/03/99	Sligo Rovers	A	0-2	
10/04/99	Cork City	A	1-2	Speak
13/04/99	Shamrock Rovers	H	4-1	Kavanagh, Mulligan 2, og (Murray)
17/04/99	Bray Wanderers	H	0-3	
25/04/99	Derry City	A	0-1	
27/04/99	Sligo Rovers	H	1-1	Sheridan
02/05/99	Dundalk	H	1-0	Harkin

ST. PATRICK'S ATHLETIC

CLUB DIRECTORY

St. Patrick's Athletic FC
Stadium of Light
Richmond Park
125 Emmett Road
Inchicore, Dublin 8
tel - (01) 4546332/4546211
fax - (01) 4546211
Year of Formation - 1929
Chairman - Tim O'Flaherty
Secretary - Phil Mooney
Manager - Liam Buckley
Stadium - Richmond Park (5,800)

MAJOR HONOURS
League Championship - (7)
1952, 1955, 1956, 1990, 1996, 1998, 1999.
Domestic Cup - (2) 1959, 1961.

APPEARANCES 98/99

	P	Ap	(s)	Gls
Leon BRAITHWAITE (ENG)	A	3	(11)	2
Willie BURKE	D	7	(7)	1
Paul CAMPBELL	D	2	(7)	
Jeff CLARKE (CAN)	D	5		1
Trevor CROLY	D	32		
Robbie DEVEREUX (ENG)	M	3	(5)	
Keith DOYLE	D	25		
Ian GILZEAN (SCO)	A	27	(2)	12
Eddie GORMLEY	M	23	(1)	5
Colin HAWKINS	D	26		7
Keith LONG	D	1	(7)	
Packie LYNCH	D	30		1
Stephen McGUINNESS	D	31		3
Trevor MOLLOY	A	32		15
Mick MOODY	D	4	(2)	
Thomas MORGAN	M	6	(3)	
Paul OSAM	M	32		3
Warren PARKES	A		(1)	
Martin REILLY	A	8	(19)	4
Martin RUSSELL	M	33		2
Trevor WOOD (NIR)	G	33		

LEAGUE RESULTS 1998/99

30/08/98	Derry City	A	1-0	Gilzean
04/09/98	Dundalk	H	3-1	Gormley, Molloy, Gilzean
11/09/98	Waterford United	A	2-0	Gormley (p), Gilzean
18/09/98	Bohemians	H	3-0	og (Brunton), Gilzean, Osam
26/09/98	Finn Harps	A	1-2	Molloy
02/10/98	UCD	H	1-0	Molloy
11/10/98	Shelbourne	A	1-0	Molloy
16/10/98	Sligo Rovers	H	4-1	Gilzean, Hawkins, Gormley, Reilly
23/10/98	Cork City	H	2-0	Molloy 2
30/10/98	Shamrock Rovers	A	1-2	Molloy
06/11/98	Bray Wanderers	H	3-0	Gormley, McGuinness, Lynch
13/11/98	Bray Wanderers	A	4-1	Gilzean 2, Molloy 2
20/11/98	Derry City	H	1-0	Gilzean
26/11/98	Dundalk	A	0-2	
04/12/98	Waterford United	H	2-0	Gilzean 2 (1p)
11/12/98	Bohemians	A	1-1	Hawkins
18/12/98	Finn Harps	H	2-2	Hawkins, og (Minnock)
27/12/98	UCD	A	2-2	Molloy, Hawkins
01/01/99	Shelbourne	H	2-1	Molloy, Osam
17/01/99	Sligo Rovers	A	4-1	Gilzean 2, Reilly, Hawkins
23/01/99	Cork City	A	2-1	Braithwaite, McGuinness
29/01/99	Shamrock Rovers	H	3-0	Russell, Hawkins, Gormley
14/02/99	Derry City	A	0-0	
19/02/99	Dundalk	H	1-0	Russell
26/02/99	Waterford United	A	0-0	
12/03/99	Bohemians	H	1-3	Molloy
20/03/99	Finn Harps	A	3-0	Molloy, Burke, Braithwaite
28/03/99	UCD	H	0-0	
05/04/99	Shelbourne	A	1-1	Reilly
09/04/99	Sligo Rovers	H	4-0	Molloy 2, Reilly, McGuinness
16/04/99	Cork City	H	1-0	Osam
23/04/99	Shamrock Rovers	A	1-0	Hawkins
02/05/99	Bray Wanderers	H	1-0	Clarke

SHAMROCK ROVERS

CLUB DIRECTORY

Shamrock Rovers FC
Unit 29, Rowan Avenue
Stillorgan Industrial Park, Stillorgan, Co. Dublin
tel - (01) 2952619 / fax - (01) 2953623
Year of Formation - 1901
Chairman - Joe Colwell
Secretary - Joe Colwell
Manager - Mick Byrne
(99/00 - Damien Richardson)
Stadium - Morton Stadium (10,000)

MAJOR HONOURS
League Championship - (15) 1923, 1925, 1927,
1932, 1938, 1939, 1954, 1957, 1959, 1964,
1984, 1985, 1986, 1987, 1994.
Domestic Cup - (24) 1925, 1929, 1930, 1931,
1932, 1933, 1936, 1940, 1944, 1945, 1948,
1955, 1956, 1962, 1964, 1965, 1966, 1967,
1968, 1969, 1978, 1985, 1986, 1987.

APPEARANCES 98/99

	P	Ap	(s)	Gls
Gino BRAZIL	D	30	(1)	
Matt BRITTON	D	29		
Jason COLWELL	M	30	(1)	1
Tony COUSINS	A	26		6
Tommy DUNNE	D	17	(4)	
Robert FORDE	G	3	(1)	
Robbie HORGAN	G	3		
Marc KENNY	M	17	(8)	7
Anthony MANNERING	M		(1)	
Brendan MARKEY	A	4	(9)	1
Brian MORRISROE	M	15	(9)	3
Peter MURRAY	M	4	(2)	
Sean MURRAY	A	2	(3)	1
Gareth O'CONNOR	A	6	(2)	
Tony O'DOWD	G	27		
Eoghan O'MEARA	A		(6)	
Mark O'NEILL	M	11	(6)	1
Terry PALMER	D	19	(1)	
Richie PURDY	D	17	(1)	
Jason SHERLOCK	A	28	(3)	8
Derek TRACEY	M	31	(1)	1
Paul WHELAN	D	27		
Billy WOODS	M	17	(14)	1

LEAGUE RESULTS 1998/99

28/08/98	Shelbourne	A	2-2	Sherlock, Murray S.
04/09/98	Bray Wanderers	H	0-1	
10/09/98	Dundalk	A	1-1	Kenny
20/09/98	Derry City	H	0-0	
25/09/98	Waterford United	A	1-1	Cousins
02/10/98	Bohemians	H	3-0	Morrisroe, Sherlock, Cousins
10/10/98	Finn Harps	A	1-2	Tracey
16/10/98	UCD	H	2-0	Cousins, Morrisroe
30/10/98	St. Patrick's Athletic	H	2-1	O'Neill, og (Burke)
08/11/98	Cork City	A	1-3	Cousins
15/11/98	Cork City	H	0-3	
20/11/98	Shelbourne	H	2-1	Sherlock, og (Campbell)
24/11/98	Sligo Rovers	A	3-2	og (Callaghan), Kenny (p), Cousins
29/11/98	Bray Wanderers	A	4-3	Sherlock, Kenny 2 (1p), og (Smyth)
04/12/98	Dundalk	H	1-1	Sherlock
13/12/98	Derry City	A	1-1	Kenny (p)
27/12/98	Bohemians	A	1-1	Kenny (p)
03/01/99	Finn Harps	H	2-0	Kenny (p), Sherlock
17/01/99	UCD	A	2-0	Morrisroe, Woods
24/01/99	Sligo Rovers	H	1-1	Cousins
29/01/99	St. Patrick's Athletic	A	0-3	
07/02/99	Waterford United	H	0-0	
12/02/99	Shelbourne	A	0-1	
19/02/99	Bray Wanderers	H	0-0	
25/02/99	Dundalk	A	1-1	Markey
14/03/99	Derry City	H	1-0	Sherlock
19/03/99	Waterford United	A	0-1	
26/03/99	Bohemians	H	1-1	Sherlock
09/04/99	UCD	H	0-0	
13/04/99	Finn Harps	A	1-4	Colwell
17/04/99	Sligo Rovers	A	0-1	
23/04/99	St. Patrick's Athletic	H	0-1	
02/05/99	Cork City	A	0-3	

SHELBOURNE

CLUB DIRECTORY

Shelbourne FC
Tolka Park, Richmond Road, Dublin 3
tel - (01) 8375536/8375754/8368781
fax - (01) 8375588
Year of Formation - 1895
Chairman - Finbarr Flood
Secretary - Ollie Byrne
Manager - Dermot Keely
Stadium - Tolka Park (10,000)

MAJOR HONOURS
League Championship - (8) 1926, 1929, 1931,
1944, 1947, 1953, 1962, 1992.
Domestic Cup - (6)
1939, 1960, 1963, 1993, 1996, 1997.

APPEARANCES 98/99

		P	Ap	(s)	Gls
Dessie BAKER	M		24	(5)	3
Richie BAKER	M		11	(5)	2
Gareth BENSON	M			(1)	
Davy BYRNE	M		5	(2)	1
Paul BYRNE	A		1	(1)	
Dave CAMPBELL	M		8	(2)	
Shane CAREW	D			(1)	
Greg COSTELLO	D		13	(1)	1
Paul DOOLIN	M		17		
Graham DOYLE	D		3	(4)	
Pat FENLON	M		23		7
Dean FITZGERALD	M		14	(9)	
Declan GEOGHEGAN	D		29		
Stephen GEOGHEGAN	A		24	(2)	5
Stephen GIFFORD	D		4	(3)	
Rory GINTY	M		2		
Terry GLEESON	D		1		
Alan GOUGH	G		30		
Owen HEARY	D		28	(1)	2
James KEDDY	M		7		
Ben KELLY	A			(2)	
Liam KELLY	A		11	(4)	
John LUBY	D		2		
Tony McCARTHY	D		31	(1)	1
Damien MAHER	D		2		
Pat MORLEY	A		4	(3)	
Mick NEVILLE	D		4	(1)	
Keith O'BRIEN	D		1	(3)	
Ricky O'FLAHERTY	A			(2)	
Danny O'LEARY	G		3	(1)	
Mark RUTHERFORD (ENG)	M		1		
Pat SCULLY	D		27		4
Tony SHERIDAN	M		29	(1)	10
Neil TREBBLE (ENG)	A		4		1

LEAGUE RESULTS 1998/99

28/08/98	Shamrock Rovers	H	2-2	Sheridan, McCarthy
06/09/98	UCD	A	1-1	Fenlon
11/09/98	Finn Harps	H	0-0	
19/09/98	Bray Wanderers	A	0-1	
25/09/98	Sligo Rovers	H	1-1	Sheridan
04/10/98	Derry City	A	1-0	Heary
11/10/98	St. Patrick's Athletic	H	0-1	
15/10/98	Dundalk	A	2-1	Sheridan, Fenlon
26/10/98	Bohemians	H	2-1	Fenlon, Baker D. (p)
01/11/98	Cork City	A	1-2	Trebble
06/11/98	Waterford United	H	1-0	Costello
13/11/98	Waterford United	A	0-0	
20/11/98	Shamrock Rovers	A	1-2	Baker D.
27/11/98	UCD	H	1-1	Geoghegan S.
05/12/98	Finn Harps	A	2-3	Sheridan 2
13/12/98	Bray Wanderers	H	1-0	Fenlon
19/12/98	Sligo Rovers	A	3-1	Geoghegan S., Sheridan, Fenlon
26/12/98	Derry City	H	2-0	Fenlon, Sheridan
01/01/99	St. Patrick's Athletic	A	1-2	Sheridan
22/01/99	Bohemians	A	0-2	
27/01/99	Dundalk	H	1-2	Geoghegan S. (p)
31/01/99	Cork City	H	3-3	Sheridan, Fenlon, Scully
12/02/99	Shamrock Rovers	H	1-0	Baker R.
21/02/99	UCD	A	1-0	Sheridan
26/02/99	Finn Harps	H	2-0	Baker R., Scully
13/03/99	Bray Wanderers	A	1-0	Scully
19/03/99	Sligo Rovers	H	1-0	Heary
28/03/99	Derry City	A	0-1	
05/04/99	St. Patrick's Athletic	H	1-1	Geoghegan S.
08/04/99	Dundalk	A	2-1	Byrne D., Baker D.
15/04/99	Bohemians	H	1-2	Geoghegan S.
25/04/99	Cork City	A	1-2	Scully
02/05/99	Waterford United	H	0-2	

SLIGO ROVERS

Sligo Rovers FC
P.O. Box 275
Showgrounds
Sligo
tel - (071) 71212
fax - (071) 71331
Year of Formation - 1928
Chairman - Ray Gallagher
Secretary - Mary McGowan
Manager - Nicky Reid (99/00 - Jim McInally)
Stadium - The Showgrounds (7,000)

MAJOR HONOURS
League Championship - (2) 1937, 1977
Domestic Cup - (2) 1983, 1994.

APPEARANCES 98/99

	P	Ap	(s)	Gls
Steve BIRKS (ENG)	D	17	(1)	
Matt BOSWELL (ENG)	G	23		
Nick BROUJOS (USA)	G	10		
Packie CALLAGHAN	M	1		
Tony CALLAGHAN (ENG)	D	20	(1)	
Wesley CHARLES (STV)	D	22		
Sean FLANNERY	A	14	(6)	3
Phil GALLAGHER	M	1	(1)	
Marcus HALLOWS (ENG)	A	26	(4)	11
Matt HARE (ENG)	D	7	(4)	
Brian HETHERSTON (SCO)	M	8	(1)	
Johnny HOEKS (BEL)	A	13	(1)	3
Mark HUTCHISON (SCO)	D	32	(1)	2
Steve JONES (NIR)	M	16		1
Damien KENNEDY	A	6	(2)	1
Ian LYNCH	D	14	(1)	1
Ross McGLYNN	M	13		
Lee MARSHALL (ENG)	M	1	(3)	
Padraig MORAN	A	1		
Donagh OATES	A	5	(10)	1
Neil OGDEN (ENG)	D	19	(1)	1
Conor O'GRADY	M	18	(5)	1
Nicky REID (ENG)	D	18	(1)	1
Aled ROWLANDS (WAL)	M	21	(1)	1
Glen SHANNON	A	12	(16)	8
Jim SHERIDAN	D	25		2
Marco TORINO (ENG)	A		(1)	

LEAGUE RESULTS 1998/99

27/08/98	Dundalk	A	2-0	Hallows, O'Grady
05/09/98	Bohemians	H	2-2	Shannon, Hallows
13/09/98	UCD	A	0-2	
19/09/98	Waterford United	H	1-1	Shannon
25/09/98	Shelbourne	A	1-1	Shannon
03/10/98	Finn Harps	H	1-1	Sheridan
10/10/98	Cork City	H	0-2	
16/10/98	St. Patrick's Athletic	A	1-4	Flannery
30/10/98	Bray Wanderers	A	1-1	Shannon
07/11/98	Derry City	H	3-3	Hallows, Shannon, Ogden
15/11/98	Derry City	A	0-2	
21/11/98	Dundalk	H	2-0	Jones, Hallows
24/11/98	Shamrock Rovers	H	2-3	Shannon, Hallows
27/11/98	Bohemians	A	1-0	Hallows
05/12/98	UCD	H	0-1	
11/12/98	Waterford United	A	1-1	Flannery
19/12/98	Shelbourne	H	1-3	Hallows
03/01/99	Cork City	A	0-1	
17/01/99	St. Patrick's Athletic	H	1-4	Hutchison
24/01/99	Shamrock Rovers	A	1-1	Flannery
30/01/99	Bray Wanderers	H	0-0	
11/02/99	Dundalk	A	2-3	Oates, Rowlands
20/02/99	Bohemians	H	2-1	Reid, Lynch
28/02/99	UCD	A	0-0	
13/03/99	Waterford United	H	2-1	Hoeks, Kennedy
19/03/99	Shelbourne	A	0-1	
26/03/99	Finn Harps	H	2-0	Hutchison, Hallows
03/04/99	Cork City	H	2-5	Hoeks, Shannon
09/04/99	St. Patrick's Athletic	A	0-4	
17/04/99	Shamrock Rovers	H	1-0	Shannon
23/04/99	Bray Wanderers	A	2-1	Sheridan, Hoeks
27/04/99	Finn Harps	A	1-1	Hallows (p)
01/05/99	Derry City	H	2-0	Hallows 2

UCD

CLUB DIRECTORY

University College Dublin AFC
Room 202
Sports Centre UCD
Belfield, Stillorgan, Co. Dublin
tel - (01) 7062183
fax - (01) 2698099
Year of Formation - 1895
Chairman - Gerry Horkan
Secretary - Brendan Dillon
Manager - Theo Dunne
Stadium - Belfield Park (4,500)

MAJOR HONOURS
Domestic Cup - (1) 1984.

APPEARANCES 98/99

	P	Ap	(s)	Gls
Eoin BENNIS	A	24	(7)	5
Graham BRETT	D	16	(1)	
Clive DELANEY	D	31		2
Robbie DUNNE	M	23	(3)	3
Glen FITZPATRICK	A	14	(3)	3
Ciaran KAVANAGH	M	33		3
Ken KILMURRAY	A	3	(12)	
Aidan LYNCH	D	33		2
Robbie McAULEY	D	10		
Vincent McCARTHY	M		(1)	
Tony McDONNELL	D	20	(1)	4
Eamon McLOUGHLIN	D	31	(1)	
Alan MAHON	D	33		
John MARTIN	M	1	(2)	
Ciaran MARTYN	A	19	(5)	2
Darren O'BRIEN	M		(1)	
Michael O'BYRNE	A	31		7
Mick O'DONNELL	M	8	(3)	
Colin O'TOOLE	M		(1)	
Barry RYAN	G	33		
Ciaran TIGHE	A		(1)	

LEAGUE RESULTS 1998/99

28/08/98	Waterford United	A	0-1	
06/09/98	Shelbourne	H	1-1	Bennis
13/09/98	Sligo Rovers	H	2-0	Lynch, Dunne
19/09/98	Finn Harps	A	0-0	
27/09/98	Cork City	H	0-1	
02/10/98	St. Patrick's Athletic	A	0-1	
11/10/98	Bray Wanderers	H	3-1	Bennis, O'Byrne, Kavanagh
16/10/98	Shamrock Rovers	A	0-2	
25/10/98	Derry City	H	2-2	O'Byrne, Bennis
29/10/98	Dundalk	A	0-2	
08/11/98	Bohemians	H	2-0	Bennis, Martyn
15/11/98	Bohemians	A	0-3	
22/11/98	Waterford United	H	1-1	O'Byrne
27/11/98	Shelbourne	A	1-1	Kavanagh
05/12/98	Sligo Rovers	A	1-0	McDonnell
13/12/98	Finn Harps	H	3-0	O'Byrne, Dunne, Fitzpatrick
20/12/98	Cork City	A	2-1	Fitzpatrick 2
27/12/98	St. Patrick's Athletic	H	2-2	McDonnell, O'Byrne
03/01/99	Bray Wanderers	A	0-0	
17/01/99	Shamrock Rovers	H	0-2	
24/01/99	Derry City	A	0-2	
31/01/99	Dundalk	H	0-0	
12/02/99	Waterford United	A	2-1	McDonnell, O'Byrne
21/02/99	Shelbourne	H	0-1	
28/02/99	Sligo Rovers	H	0-0	
13/03/99	Finn Harps	A	0-1	
21/03/99	Cork City	H	2-2	Lynch, Martyn
29/03/99	St. Patrick's Athletic	A	0-0	
05/04/99	Bray Wanderers	H	1-3	Kavanagh
09/04/99	Shamrock Rovers	A	0-0	
18/04/99	Derry City	H	2-1	Delaney 2
22/04/99	Dundalk	A	2-0	O'Byrne, Bennis
02/05/99	Bohemians	H	2-0	Dunne, McDonnell

WATERFORD UNITED

CLUB DIRECTORY

Waterford United FC
15 Parnell Street
Waterford
Year of Formation - 1982
Chairman - Michael Finnegan
Secretary - John Delaney
Manager - Mike Flanagan
Stadium - Regional Sports Centre (8,250)

APPEARANCES 98/99

	P	Ap	(s)	Gls
Alan BARRY	D	1		
Steve BROWN (ENG)	A	7		
Jody BYRNE	G	6	(1)	
Paul CARR	D		(1)	
Michael DEVINE	G	27		
Padraig DULLY	A	10	(4)	2
Brian FLOOD	M	9	(2)	
John FROST	D	25	(1)	
Karl GANNON	M	23	(7)	4
Donal GOLDEN	M	1		
Robert GRIFFIN	A	22	(4)	2
Joe HARKIN	D	25	(1)	1
Dominic IORFA (NIG)	A	13		3
Jason KABIA (ENG)	A	10	(4)	
Joe KEITH (FNG)	A	4		
Dave KELLEHER	M	7		
Alan KELLY	M	1	(1)	
Alan KIRBY	M	14		2
John LACEY	M	5	(3)	
Tommy LYNCH	D	8		
Derek McGRATH	M	13		2
Tim McGRATH	D	30		
Liam MAHER	D	1		
John POWER	D	11	(1)	1
Alan QUINLAN	M		(1)	
Mark REID	A	6	(7)	1
Alan REYNOLDS	M	14	(2)	
Sean RIORDAN	D	32		1
Paul SCULLY	M	2	(7)	
Pat SINNOTT	M		(4)	
Dave SMITH	D	26		
Barry WOOD (SCO)	A	10	(15)	2

LEAGUE RESULTS 1998/99

28/08/98	UCD	H	1-0	Dully
05/09/98	Finn Harps	A	2-1	Power (p), Griffin
11/09/98	St. Patrick's Athletic	H	0-2	
19/09/98	Sligo Rovers	A	1-1	Harkin
25/09/98	Shamrock Rovers	H	1-1	Dully
04/10/98	Cork City	A	0-5	
10/10/98	Derry City	H	1-2	Wood
17/10/98	Bray Wanderers	A	0-6	
23/10/98	Dundalk	H	1-0	Gannon
01/11/98	Bohemians	A	1-0	Wood
06/11/98	Shelbourne	A	0-1	
13/11/98	Shelbourne	H	0-0	
22/11/98	UCD	A	1-1	Gannon
28/11/98	Finn Harps	H	0-3	
04/12/98	St. Patrick's Athletic	A	0-2	
11/12/98	Sligo Rovers	H	1-1	Reid
27/12/98	Cork City	H	0-2	
03/01/99	Derry City	A	0-1	
24/01/99	Dundalk	A	0-2	
29/01/99	Bohemians	H	0-0	
07/02/99	Shamrock Rovers	A	0-0	
12/02/99	UCD	H	1-2	Gannon
20/02/99	Finn Harps	A	0-2	
26/02/99	St. Patrick's Athletic	H	0-0	
13/03/99	Sligo Rovers	A	1-2	McGrath D. (p)
19/03/99	Shamrock Rovers	H	1-0	Gannon
28/03/99	Cork City	A	0-0	
02/04/99	Derry City	H	1-0	Iorfa
09/04/99	Bray Wanderers	A	1-0	Iorfa
16/04/99	Dundalk	H	2-0	Kirby, Iorfa
23/04/99	Bohemians	A	1-0	Griffin
25/04/99	Bray Wanderers	H	1-0	Kirby
02/05/99	Shelbourne	A	2-0	McGrath D., Riordan

PROMOTED CLUBS

SECOND DIVISION FINAL TABLE 98/99

		Pd	W	D	L	F	A	Pt	GD
1	**Drogheda United**	36	17	13	6	57	32	64	+25
2	**Galway United**	36	16	16	4	53	34	64	+19
3	Cobh Ramblers	36	17	7	12	55	43	58	+12
4	Longford Town	36	15	9	12	41	33	54	+8
5	Kilkenny City	36	14	11	11	49	46	53	+3
6	Limerick	36	13	13	10	39	35	52	+4
7	Monaghan United	36	10	14	12	44	44	44	0
8	Athlone Town	36	10	10	16	45	61	40	-16
9	Home Farm Everton	36	11	5	20	42	54	38	-12
10	St. Francis	36	2	12	22	25	68	18	-43

PROMOTION/RELEGATION PLAY-OFF

Cobh Ramblers 0, Bohemians 5
Bohemians 2, Cobh Ramblers 0
(Bohemians 7-0)

CLUB DIRECTORY

Drogheda United FC
United Park
Windmill Road
Drogheda
Co. Louth
tel - (041) 30190
fax - (041) 30195
Year of Formation - 1919
Chairman - John Little
Secretary - Gerald Kelly
Manager - Martin Lawlor
Stadium - United Park (6,000)

CLUB DIRECTORY

Galway United FC
Terryland Park
Dyke Road
Galway
tel - (091) 561000
fax - (091) 568866
Year of Formation - 1937
Chairman - Gerry Gray
Secretary - John Byrne
Manager - Don O'Riordan
Stadium - Terryland Park (6,580)

MAJOR HONOURS
Domestic Cup - (1) 1991.

ROMANIA

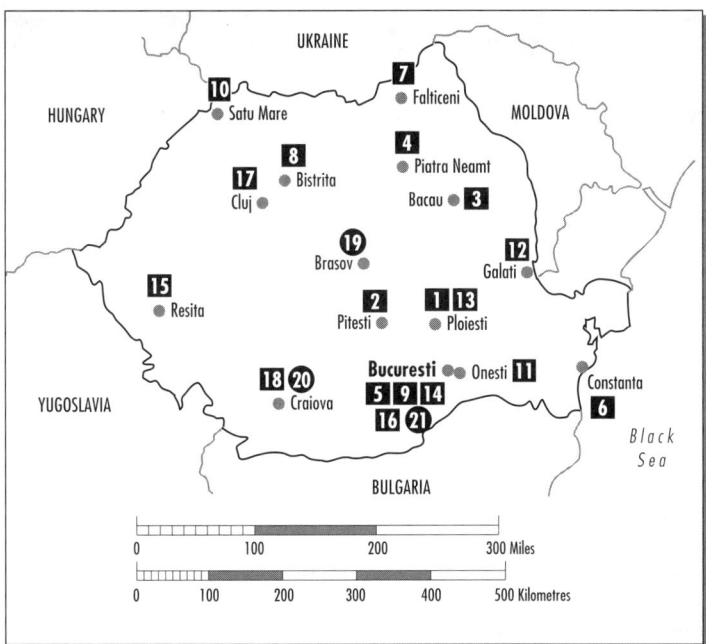

1	ASTRA PLOIESTI	812
2	FC ARGES DACIA PITESTI	813
3	FCM BACAU	814
4	CEAHLAUL PIATRA NEAMT	815
5	DINAMO BUCURESTI	816
6	FC FARUL CONSTANTA	817
7	FORESTA FALTICENI	818
8	GLORIA BISTRITA	819
9	FC NATIONAL BUCURESTI	820
10	OLIMPIA SATU MARE	821
11	FC ONESTI	822

12	OTELUL GALATI	823
13	PETROLUL PLOIESTI	824
14	RAPID BUCURESTI	825
15	CSM RESITA	826
16	STEAUA BUCURESTI	827
17	UNIVERSITATEA CLUJ	828
18	UNIVERSITATEA CRAIOVA	829
Promoted clubs		
19	FC BRASOV	830
20	EXTENSIV CRAIOVA	830
21	ROCAR BUCURESTI	830

HAGI STAGES EPIC COMEBACK

Rapid release Steaua's title stranglehold

FEDERATION DIRECTORY

Federatia Româna de Fotbal
Bdul Poligrafiei Nr.3, Sector 1, Bucuresti

tel - (01) 2229993
fax - (01) 3126337

Year of Formation - 1909
President - Mircea Sandu
Secretary - Adalbert Kassai

Stadium - Lia Manoliu, Bucuresti (70,000)

Steaua Bucharest's bid to win the Romanian championship for a record seventh year in succession never got going. Instead, the race for the title became a two-way tussle between their city rivals Rapid and Dinamo, with the former producing the stronger finish to come through and claim their first championship victory for 32 years and only the second in their entire history.

The two challengers were neck and neck from the beginning, each winning their opening five matches and each playing the sort of free-flowing, entertaining football that had become increasingly rare in the Romanian league since the systematic departure of all of the country's best players for foreign fields. Both clubs had made moves to reverse that trend during the summer, with Rapid bringing back veteran Romanian international Ioan Ovidiu

Sabau from Italy and Dinamo re-recruiting Ionut Lupescu and Ion Vladoiu from Germany.

Steaua also caught the bug, sending for two of their former favourites, Miodrag Belodedici and Ilie Dumitrescu. Before the season was out, however, Dumitrescu, the 1994 World Cup star, had decided to retire from football completely, preferring to become a players' agent despite still having much to offer at 30 years of age.

The Rapid/Dinamo duel was billed by the press as a battle of the two clubs' respective coaches, Mircea Lucescu and Cornel Dinu, former friends and team-mates with both Dinamo and the Romanian national team. But that story ended prematurely in December when Lucescu was summoned to Italy by Inter, who wanted him to see out the remainder of the Serie A season as their caretaker coach.

LEAGUE CHAMPIONSHIP RESULTS 98/99

		1	2	3	4	5	6	7	8	9	10	11	12	13	14	15	16	17	18
1	FC Arges Pitesti		1-2	0-3	1-0	2-1	6-0	1-1	2-1	1-0	3-1	2-0	2-1	3-1	0-1	1-0	3-2	3-0	2-0
2	Astra Ploiesti	0-1		1-1	0-0	0-1	4-0	1-0	3-1	1-2	3-1	3-1	3-1	1-1	1-5	3-0	1-1	2-1	2-2
3	FCM Bacau	3-2	2-0		0-0	0-2	1-0	4-1	3-1	4-1	2-1	2-1	1-0	3-1	1-1	2-0	0-0	0-0	2-0
4	Ceahlaul Piatra Neamt	1-2	3-1	4-1		1-0	2-0	2-1	3-2	1-0	4-0	3-1	1-1	1-3	0-2	4-0	0-3	5-1	2-1
5	Dinamo Bucuresti	1-0	2-0	1-0	6-1		2-1	4-1	3-0	5-0	5-0	3-1	2-1	3-1	0-1	7-0	0-0	8-0	2-1
6	FC Farul Constanta	0-2	1-0	2-0	2-1	1-3		3-2	3-1	0-1	3-1	2-0	0-1	1-0	0-0	0-0	0-3	3-1	2-1
7	Foresta Falticeni	2-2	0-1	0-1	0-2	2-3	2-0		0-0	1-0	2-0	3-1	1-2	1-2	0-1	0-0	1-2	1-0	1-2
8	Gloria Bistrita	3-1	1-0	2-0	4-2	2-3	4-2	5-0		2-4	3-1	3-1	2-1	2-0	2-4	2-2	2-1	4-0	1-1
9	FC National Bucuresti	2-3	1-0	5-0	4-2	1-2	0-0	4-1	5-1		2-1	3-0	0-1	2-0	1-3	3-0	0-1	3-1	1-0
10	Olimpia Satu Mare	0-3	1-2	0-2	0-1	0-4	0-3	0-1	1-0	3-1		1-6	0-1	3-0	1-1	1-3	0-3	0-1	1-1
11	FC Onesti	0-3	2-0	2-2	3-1	1-4	2-2	3-1	1-1	2-3	1-0		1-0	2-0	1-2	5-0	2-3	6-0	3-2
12	Otelul Galati	1-1	1-1	0-1	1-2	2-1	2-1	1-0	0-0	3-2	2-0	3-0		0-1	0-1	4-0	2-0	5-0	4-0
13	Petrolul Ploiesti	3-1	2-1	1-1	1-0	2-3	3-0	2-1	3-1	1-3	0-0	1-0	2-0		2-2	2-0	2-1	3-0	4-1
14	Rapid Bucuresti	2-0	1-0	3-0	4-0	1-4	3-0	2-0	5-0	5-0	1-0	6-0	3-0	2-1		2-1	3-0	3-0	1-0
15	CSM Resita	0-0	0-1	0-0	2-2	1-1	3-2	1-1	2-0	4-1	1-1	0-2	2-3	2-1	1-2		2-2	3-0	3-2
16	Steaua Bucuresti	1-2	1-0	2-1	3-2	1-1	1-0	6-1	0-0	1-0	3-2	4-1	2-0	2-2	1-1	2-0		4-0	2-0
17	Universitatea Cluj	2-1	0-2	1-2	1-0	0-6	1-3	2-2	1-1	1-4	1-0	0-2	0-2	1-2	1-4	0-0	0-2		1-2
18	Universitatea Craiova	2-0	0-0	0-1	2-1	2-2	1-0	1-0	2-1	0-2	5-1	4-2	0-1	2-0	0-1	0-1	2-2	4-1	

LEAGUE CHAMPIONSHIP FINAL TABLE 98/99

				Home					Away					Total					
		P	W	D	L	F	A	W	D	L	F	A	W	D	L	F	A	P	GD
1	Rapid Bucuresti	34	16	0	1	47	6	12	5	0	32	12	28	5	1	79	18	89	+61
2	Dinamo Bucuresti	34	15	1	1	54	8	11	3	3	41	19	26	4	4	95	27	82	+68
3	Steaua Bucuresti	34	12	4	1	36	13	7	5	5	26	20	19	9	6	62	33	66	+29
4	FC Arges Dacia Pitesti	34	13	1	3	33	14	7	3	7	24	23	20	4	10	57	37	64	+20
5	FCM Bacau	34	12	4	1	30	11	6	4	7	16	24	18	8	8	46	35	62	+11
6	Otelul Galati	34	10	3	4	31	11	7	1	9	16	22	17	4	13	47	33	55	+14
7	FC National Bucuresti	34	11	1	5	37	16	7	0	10	24	35	18	1	15	61	51	55	+10
8	Petrolul Ploiesti	34	12	3	2	34	15	4	2	11	16	31	16	5	13	50	46	53	+4
9	Ceahlaul Piatra Neamt	34	12	1	4	37	19	3	3	11	17	34	15	4	15	54	53	49	+1
10	Astra Ploiesti	34	8	5	4	29	19	5	2	10	11	19	13	7	14	40	38	46	+2
11	Gloria Bistrita	34	12	2	3	44	23	0	5	12	11	37	12	7	15	55	60	43	-5
12	FC Farul Constanta	34	10	2	5	23	17	2	2	13	14	37	12	4	18	37	54	40	-17
13	Universitatea Craiova	34	9	3	5	27	16	2	3	12	16	34	11	6	17	43	50	39	-7
14	FC Onesti	34	9	3	5	37	24	3	0	14	19	43	12	3	19	56	67	39	-11
15	CSM Resita	34	6	7	4	27	21	2	4	11	7	38	8	11	15	34	59	35	-25
16	Foresta Falticeni	34	5	3	9	17	19	1	3	13	14	42	6	6	22	31	61	24	-30
17	Universitatea Cluj	34	3	3	11	13	35	1	1	15	6	57	4	4	26	19	92	16	-73
18	Olimpia Satu Mare	34	3	2	12	12	33	0	2	15	10	41	3	4	27	22	74	13	-52

It was an offer the Rapid boss could not refuse, but naturally his departure was to have a disconcerting effect on the team he left.

Rapid appointed veteran defender Mircea Rednic as an intermediary before bringing in ex-Steaua coach Dumitru Dumitriu at the start of the spring campaign. He lasted just four matches, though, and was swiftly replaced by a fourth incumbent, Nicolae Manea, who, in turn, was only in charge for five games before...Lucescu arrived back from Milan.

He could hardly have timed his return better, because it came just days before the biggest game of the season, the head-to-head encounter with Dinamo. At that stage Rapid trailed their rivals by three points, so it was imperative for them to win the game even though they were playing away from home. They had been savaged

4-1 by Dinamo in the home fixture back in October, so prospects were far from good, but, with Lucescu back to lead them and a foreign referee having been drafted in by the league authorities to ensure fair play, Rapid performed superbly and won the game 1-0 to move level on points with their defeated rivals at the top of the table.

That was the match which decided the destiny of the championship, for while Dinamo went on to draw their next two games, the second of them against Steaua, a team they had failed to beat for eight years, Rapid slipped into overdrive and won not only their next two games but all of their last six through to the end of the season.

The title was theirs, and while the Rapid fans hailed Lucescu in particular, they also saluted the efforts of their players, who had thoroughly deserved their success. In the veterans' corner there were Sabau, Rednic and midfield playmaker Danut Lupu. Of the new faces the plaudits went mainly to goalkeeper Bogdan Lobont, left-back Stefan Nanu and goal-grabbing strikers Marius Sumudica and Ioan Ganea, the latter having arrived in mid-season from Gloria Bisitrita and earning himself the additional individual prize of the league's top scorer.

Although they ended the campaign empty-handed and desperately short of form, Dinamo took great credit for having made a fight of it. They, too, had individuals with much to be proud of, and it was a measure of the progress made by the club that no fewer than nine of their number

INTERNATIONAL HONOURS

World Cup Finals appearances: 1930, 1934, 1938, 1970, 1990 (2nd round), 1994 (qtr-finals), 1998 (2nd round)

European Championship appearances: 1960, 1972, 1984, 1996

European Club Competitions
Champions' Cup   Steaua Bucuresti (1986)

Super Cup   Steaua Bucuresti (1986)

EUROPEAN CUPS 98/99

CHAMPIONS' CUP
● STEAUA BUCURESTI
Preliminary round FC FLORA TALLINN (EST)

H 4-1   Ciocoiu (12, 40), Serban (77p), Danciulescu (89)
      Ritli; Matei, Rachita, Belodedici; Reghecampf (Baciu 84), Militaru,
      Serban, Rosu; Lacatus (Luca 74), Ciocoiu (Hrib 78), Danciulescu.

A 1-3   Danciulescu (71)
      Ritli; Belodedici, Rachita, Matei; Reghecampf, Serban, Lincar, Miu;
      Lacatus (Luca 80), Ciocoiu (Rosu 76), Danciulescu.

Qualifying round PANATHINAIKOS (GRE)

H 2-2   Serban (9), Szekely (75)
      Rotaru; Belodedici, Rachita, Matei; Miu (Luca 71), Serban (Hrib 89),
      Lincar, Szekely, Rosu; Lacatus, Danciulescu.

A 3-6   Rachita (13, 17), Belodedici (61)
      Rotaru; Reghecampf, Matei, Rachita, Belodedici; Miu, Serban, Lincar,
      Rosu (Militaru 72); Lacatus (Luca 83), Danciulescu.

CUP WINNERS' CUP
● RAPID BUCURESTI
Qualifying round CS GREVENMACHER (LUX)

A 6-2   Sabau (13), Pancu (62), Dulca (65), Stanciu (70), Lupu (76), Mutica (82)
      Lobont; Andone (Mutica 55), Dulca, Popa, Stanciu, Bolohan;
      Maldarasanu (Pancu 58), Lupu, Sabau; Maier, Sumudica (Radu 46).

H 2-0   Pancu (54, 88)
      Bratu; Mutica, Popa, Iencsi; Andone, Bundea, Bugeanu (Lupu 53),
      Maldarasanu (Maier 58), Zamfir (Bolohan 61); Pancu, Radu.

1st round VÅLERENGA IF (NOR)

H 2-2   Sumudica (52), Bundea (76)
      Lobont; Stanciu (Bolohan 67), Mutica, Rednic, Dulca, Nanu; Bundea,
      Lupu, Maier (Maldarasanu 60); Sumudica (Radu 75), Pancu.

A 0-0
      Lobont; Iencsi (Bolohan 85), Stanciu, Rednic, Mutica, Nanu; Bundea,
      Lupu, Maier (Maldarasanu 60); Sumudica (Radu 75), Pancu.

UEFA CUP
● FC ARGES DACIA PITESTI
Preliminary round DINAMO BAKU (AZB)

H 5-1   Emirbekov (7og), Barbu (9, 78p), Bârdes (27), Jilaveanu (88)
      Vintila; Mogosanu, Gâlmencea, Bogoi, Nastase, Crivac (Lacusta 82);
      Bârdes, Mutu (Neaga 84), Balasa; Bratu (Jilaveanu 65), Barbu.

A 2-0   Mutu (52), Jilaveanu (90)
      Vintila; Nastase, Gâlmencea, Bogoi, Mogosanu, Balasa, Mutu, Crivac
      (Lacusta 75); Bratu (Schumacher 61), Bârdes, Barbu (Jilaveanu 46).

Qualifying round ISTANBULSPOR (TUR)

H 2-0   Mutu (31), Barbu (45)
      Vintila; Mogosanu, Gâlmencea, Nastase, Cristescu; Bârdes (Jilaveanu 85),
      Balasa (Dita 73), Mutu, Crivac; Barbu, Bratu (Neaga 76).

A 2-4   Mutu (52), Barbu (73)
      Vintila; Mogosanu, Nastase, Gâlmencea (Dita 37), Cristescu; Balasa,
      Mutu, Crivac; Bârdes (Negru 46), Barbu, Bratu (Radu 64).

1st round RC CELTA (ESP)

H 0-1
      Vintila; Mogosanu, Balasa, Dita, Gâlmencea, Radu (Bratu 30);
      Schumacher (Neaga 70), Mutu, Crivac; Barbu, Negru (Bârdes 46).

A 0-7
      Vintila; Mogosanu (Radu 85), Dita, Gâlmencea, Nastase, Crivac; Balasa,
      Schumacher (Bratu 75), Mutu; Barbu, Bârdes (Negru 57).

● OTELUL GALATI
Preliminary round SLOGA JUGOMAGNAT SKOPJE (MAC)

H 3-0   Stefan (30), Mihalache (41), Males (90p)
      Bordeianu; Nemtanu, Haraga, Balint; Spirea, Stefan (Pelin 80), Tanase,
      Arhire (Gurita 71); Tofan; Mihalache (Males 64), Ion V..

A 1-1   Mihalache (59)
      Bordeianu; Balint, Nemtanu, Haraga, Pelin, Tofan; Spirea, Stefan,
      Tanase (Males 71); Ion V. (Gurita 88); Arhire (Mihalache 57).

Qualifying round VEJLE BK (DEN)

A 0-3
      Bordeianu; Balint, Nemtanu, Haraga, Pelin (Gurita 65), Tofan (Males 80);
      Spirea, Stefan, Tanase; Ion V., Mihalache.

H 0-3
      Bordeianu; Pelin (Arhire 56), Ion G., Balint; Gurita, Spirea (Cernat 84),
      Stefan, Tanase, Tofan; Ion V., Mihalache (Nemtanu 38).

● STEAUA BUCURESTI
1st round VALENCIA CF (ESP)

H 3-4   Lincar (29), Rosu (60), Dumitrescu (85)
      Tene; Reghecampf (Danciulescu 46), Belodedici, Baciu, Miu; Serban
      (Luca 73), Militaru, Lincar, Dumitrescu; Rosu, Lacatus.

A 0-3
      Tene (Ritli 63); Miu, Matei, Belodedici (Reghecampf 78), Rachita; Rosu,
      Serban, Baciu, Militaru (Lincar 46); Dumitrescu, Lacatus.

---

were selected for the Romanian national team during the course of the season - compared with just one solitary call-up in 1997/98. Lupescu and Vladoiu both did extremely well in their first year back, while defender Cosmin Contra, winger Florin Petre and striker Adrian Mihalcea were the most consistently impressive of the younger breed.

As for Steaua, theirs was a year of transition, and the 23-point gap that separated them from the champions told a rather revealing and depressing story. However, they did make up for a poor league campaign by winning the

Romanian Cup for the third time in four years, and the 21st time in all.

There was talk of Dinamo 'selling' their semi-final to Steaua in an alleged trade-off for a league win ten days later, but those rumours ceased when the league game finished goalless. In the final against Rapid, another match refereed by a foreigner, Frenchman Marc Batta, Steaua equalised through Belodedici in the 89th minute and went on to win the penalty shoot-out, with midfielder Erik Lincar converting the decisive kick after Bundea and Pancu had missed for the newly-crowned champions.

DOMESTIC CUP 98/99

1/16 FINALS
Crisul Alesd 0, Otelul Galati 5
Unirea Botosani 1, Gloria Bistrita 2
Rocar Bucuresti 2, CSM Resita 2 (aet; 2-3 on pens.)
Sportul Studentesc Bucuresti 2, Olimpia Satu Mare 0
Universitatea Cluj 3, Forest Falticeni 2
Farul Constanta 1, Petrolul Ploiesti 4
Unirea Dej 2, Universitatea Craiova 3
Nitramonia Fagaras 0, FC Onesti 3
Cimentul Fieni 1, FC Arges Dacia Pitesti 0
Diplomatic Vrancea Focsani 1, Rapid Bucuresti 4
Flacara Horezu 0, Ceahlaul Piatra Neamt 1
AS Midia Navodari 0, Steaua Bucuresti 3
UM Timisoara 2, Astra Ploiesti 0
ASA Tirgu Mures 0, Dinamo Bucuresti 1
FC Drobeta Turnu-Severin 1, FCM Bacau 2
Minaur Zlatna 0, FC National Bucuresti 3

1/8 FINALS
CSM Resita 0, Gloria Bistrita 2
Steaua Bucuresti 3, Universitatea Cluj 0
Otelul Galati 1, Sportul Studentesc Bucuresti 0
Rapid Bucuresti 3, Cimentul Fieni 0
Dinamo Bucuresti 3, Ceahlaul Piatra Neamt 0

Petrolul Ploiesti 3, Universitatea Craiova 2
FCM Bacau 4, FC Onesti 3
FC National Bucuresti 0, UM Timisoara 2

QUARTER-FINALS
FCM Bacau 2 (Ardeleanu 28, Pavel 74), Otelul Galati 0
Otelul Galati 1 (Tofan 5), FCM Bacau 0
(FCM Bacau 2-1)

Gloria Bistrita 1 (Turcu 66),
Rapid Bucuresti 1 (Radu 84)
Rapid Bucuresti 2 (Lupu 13, Sumudica 51),
Gloria Bistrita 1 (Ganea 39)
(Rapid Bucuresti 3-2)

Steaua Bucuresti 5
(Rosu 21, Trica 38, 77, Lincar 53, Danciulescu 90),
Petrolul Ploiesti 1 (Falemi 80)
Petrolul Ploiesti 1 (Vlad 40),
Steaua Bucuresti 1 (Trica 61)
(Steaua Bucuresti 6-2)

UM Timisoara 0, Dinamo Bucuresti 1 (Niculae 59)
Dinamo Bucuresti 2 (Niculae 10, 44), UM Timisoara 0
(Dinamo Bucuresti 3-0)

SEMI-FINALS
Rapid Bucuresti 1 (Barbu 77) , FCM Bacau 0
FCM Bacau 2 (Petcu 57, Ganea 73),
Rapid Bucuresti 1 (Iencsi 7)
(2-2; Rapid Bucuresti on away goal)

Dinamo Bucuresti 1 (Lupescu 25p),
Steaua Bucuresti 2 (Rosu 63, Danciulescu 71)
Steaua Bucuresti 3 (Danciulescu 8, Lutu 56, 60),
Dinamo Bucuresti 1 (Vladoiu 87)
(Steaua Bucuresti 5-2)

FINAL
16/06/99, Bucharest
STEAUA BUCURESTI 2 Ciocoiu (67), Belodedici (89)
RAPID BUCURESTI 2 Barbu (71, 81)
(aet; 4-2 on pens.)
referee - Batta (FRA)
STEAUA BUCURESTI - Ritli; Baciu, Matei, Belodedici,
Duro (Trica 84), Szekely, Lincar, Rosu, Ciocoiu
(Militaru 91), Lacatus, Danciulescu (Lutu 51).
RAPID BUCURESTI - Lobont; Bolohan, Rednic, Stanciu,
Nanu, Maldarasanu, Lupu (Pancu 72), Iencsi, Sabau,
Barbu (Bundea 88), Ganea (Sumudica 80).

It was certainly a better end to the season for Steaua than the beginning, when they failed to win any of their first four away fixtures in the league and were also knocked out of two European competitions within the space of a few weeks. The Steaua defence went AWOL as the team conceded eight goals in two games against

Panathinaikos to exit the Champions' Cup and then another seven against Valencia to drop out of the UEFA Cup. Some even suggested they were lucky to make it that far after they were gifted a penalty in their opening

TOP SCORERS

28	Ioan GANEA (Gloria Bistrita/ Rapid Bucuresti)
21	Constantin BARBU (FC Arges Dacia Pitesti/ Rapid Bucuresti)
19	Marian SAVU (FC National Bucuresti)
18	Adrian MIHALCEA (Dinamo Bucuresti)
17	Marius SUMUDICA (Rapid Bucuresti)
15	Ion DANCIULESCU (Steaua Bucuresti)
	Florin PETCU (FCM Bacau)
14	Ion VLADOIU (Dinamo Bucuresti)
	Laurentiu ROSU (Steaua Bucuresti)
13	Constantin BÂRSAN (FC Onesti)
	Ionel IRIZA (FC Onesti)
12	Velentin BERARU (Astra Ploiesti)
	Bogdan ONUT (Petrolul Ploiesti)

NATIONAL TEAM RESULTS 98/99

19/08/98	Norway	A	Oslo	0-0	
02/09/98	Liechtenstein (ECQ)	H	Bucharest	7-0	Popescu Gh. (17), Munteanu C. (29),
					Ilie (31, 44, 51), Moldovan (54),
					Haas (59og)
05/09/98	Germany	N	Ta' Qali	1-1	Moldovan (35p)
10/10/98	Portugal (ECQ)	A	Oporto	1-0	Munteanu D. (90)
14/10/98	Hungary (ECQ)	A	Budapest	1-1	Moldovan (50)
03/03/99	Estonia	H	Bucharest	2-0	Ganea (16, 81)
10/03/99	Israel	H	Bucharest	0-2	
27/03/99	Slovakia (ECQ)	H	Bucharest	0-0	
31/03/99	Azerbaijan (ECQ)	A	Baku	1-0	Petre (49)
28/04/99	Belgium	H	Bucharest	1-0	Ganea (48)
05/06/99	Hungary (ECQ)	H	Bucharest	2-0	Ilie (3), Munteanu D. (15)
09/06/99	Azerbaijan (ECQ)	H	Bucharest	4-0	Ganea (35), Munteanu D. (44p),
					Vladoiu (48), Rosu (90)

Champions' League qualifier against Flora Tallinn, who won the return leg 3-1 in Estonia. Not surprisingly, coach Mihai Stoichita did not last long after that and was subsequently replaced by a famous name from Steaua's past - Emerich Jenei, the man who led the club to European glory in 1986.

One of Jenei's former pupils in that golden team, Victor Piturca, was appointed as the new Romanian national team coach following Anghel Iordanescu's defection to Greece. Piturca, who had impressed as the Under-21 boss, brought a few faces from that side with him into the Euro 2000 qualifying campaign, but essentially he retained faith

NATIONAL TEAM APPEARANCES 98/99

Coach - Victor PITURCA	NOR	LIE	GER	POR	HUN	EST	ISR	SVK	AZB	BEL	HUN	AZB	Cps	Gls
Bogdan STELEA (05/12/67) - UD Salamanca (ESP)	G	G82	G	G	G		G	G		G			59	-
Gheorghe POPESCU (09/10/67) - Galatasaray (TUR)	D	D	D	D	D	M85	D				D	D	91	15
Dan PETRESCU (22/12/67) - Chelsea (ENG)	D	D	D	D85	D		M	D			D	D	82	12
Florin BATRÂNU (19/03/71) - Dinamo Bucuresti	D	D	D			s88	D						6	-
Iulian FILIPESCU (29/03/74) - Galatasaray (TUR)/Real Betis (ESP)	D		D	D					D	D	D	D	27	-
Constantin GÂLCA (08/03/72) - RCD Espanyol (ESP)	M48	M	M	M	M		M	M	M	M62	M	M	49	4
Catalin MUNTEANU (26/10/79) - UD Salamanca (ESP)	M76	M71	M	M62	s75		s60	M68					8	1
Dorinel MUNTEANU (25/06/68) - 1.FC Köln (GER)	M	M	M	M	M	M	M	M	M	M88	M	M	79	10
Florentin PETRE (15/01/76) - Dinamo Bucuresti	M49	M	M84	M	M69				M	M	M	M66	10	1
Viorel MOLDOVAN (08/08/72) - Fenerbahçe (TUR)	A	A	A72	A90	A80		A68	A72	A	A46	A60	s66	40	17
Adrian ILIE (20/04/74) - Valencia CF (ESP)	A	A68	A90				A	A		A87			30	9
Ionut LUPESCU (09/12/68) - Dinamo Bucuresti	s48		s72	s62	M	M	D	s68	M	M75	s46	M	64	5
Ioan Ovidiu SABAU (12/02/68) - Rapid Bucuresti	s49	s71											49	8
Denis SERBAN (05/10/76) - Steaua Bucuresti/Valencia CF (ESP)	s76		s84		s69	M74							10	-
Cosmin CONTRA (15/12/75) - Dinamo Bucuresti		D	s85			D	D			D	D		9	-
Adrian MIHALCEA (24/05/76) - Dinamo Bucuresti		s68	s90	s90	s80	s53		s89					6	-
Bogdan LOBONT (18/01/78) - Rapid Bucuresti		s82				G89			G		G	G	5	-
Liviu CIOBOTARIU (26/03/71) - Dinamo Bucuresti			D	D	D	D88	D			D	s88		15	-
Laurentiu ROSU (26/10/75) - Steaua Bucuresti						M	M61	s71	M	M74	s70	s77	7	1
Gheorghe CRAIOVEANU (14/02/68) - Villarreal CF (ESP)					A75		A60	s72	A89		s87	s60	25	4
Dumitru MITRITA (23/06/71) - SC Heerenveen (HOL)						D88							1	-
Ioan GANEA (10/08/73) - Rapid Bucuresti						A	s68			s46	s60	A60	5	4
Ion DANCIULESCU (06/12/76) - Steaua Bucuresti						A53							1	-
Ion LUTU (03/08/75) - Steaua Bucuresti						s61							1	-
Eugen TRICA (05/08/76) - Steaua Bucuresti						s74							1	-
Catalin HÂLDAN (03/02/76) - Dinamo Bucuresti						s85		s75					2	-
Daniel FLOREA (18/12/75) - Dinamo Bucuresti						s88		s74					2	-
Tiberiu LUNG (24/12/78) - Universitatea Craiova						s89							1	-
Tibor SELYMES (14/05/70) - RSC Anderlecht (BEL)							D71						46	-
Stefan NANU (08/09/68) - Rapid Bucuresti										D	D	D	3	-
Valentin NASTASE (04/10/74) - FC Arges Dacia Pitesti										D			1	-
Ion VLADOIU (05/11/68) - Dinamo Bucuresti										A70		A77	26	2
Erik LINCAR (16/10/78) - Steaua Bucuresti										s62			1	-
Gheorghe HAGI (05/02/65) - Galatasaray (TUR)											M46		116	33

in most of the players who had featured at the World Cup in France. The one notable exception was Gheorghe Hagi, who, despite his continued good form in Turkey with Galatasaray, had decided to end his international career after France '98.

Piturca and co. got off to the perfect start in a tricky qualifying group when they hammered Liechtenstein 7-0 in their opening game and, more importantly, won 1-0 away to chief group rivals Portugal in Oporto. It was a classic smash-and-grab victory. Portugal made the play and attacked throughout, but the Romanian defence held firm, Bogdan Stelea saved a penalty, débutant Laurentiu Rosu was sent off and then, with just a few minutes left, Dorinel Munteanu scored the winning goal after a rare breakaway.

But the Romanians could not build on that vital win. Their next two matches both ended in disappointing draws - away to Hungary and at home to Slovakia - and when the following encounter away to Azerbaijan produced a narrow, barely-deserved 1-0 win, FA President Mircea Sandu began to voice publc concern over Piturca's handling of the team.

Drastic action was needed, and Piturca travelled to Turkey to make a special plea to Hagi to make a comeback. At first the great man refused, but eventually, after some hard bargaining, he agreed to reappear... for one match only.

The game in question was at home to Hungary - a country Romania had not defeated for 63 years. Under normal circumstances the Romanians might have begun nervously, but the return of Hagi, for his 116th cap, triggered great excitement in the stands and that enthusiasm was transferred back to the pitch where the team, inspired by their stand-in skipper, produced the best 45 minutes of football seen in the country for years. Incessant Romanian pressure brought two quick goals from Adrian Ilie and Viorel Moldovan, plus another one (from Ilie) wrongly disallowed and a barrage of other chances, most of them set up by the ageless little general in the number ten shirt. The match ended 2-0. It was quite a comeback. Hagi did not reappear for the second half. Nor did he return for the 4-0 victory against Azerbaijan four days later. His job, apparently, was done. Romania were back in business. But the fans begged for more...

PLAYERS OF THE SEASON

IOAN VIOREL GANEA

It has become a recent ritual for the player who tops the Romanian First Division goal charts to take his leave immediately and move abroad. Ioan Ganea, the leading marksman in 1998/99, became the latest slave to the fashion when he decided to leave Rapid Bucharest for VfB Stuttgart in the summer. It meant that he had spent less than half a year with Rapid. He did not arrive until halfway through the season, having shot to the top of the scoring charts with 17 goals in 16 games for Gloria Bistrita. His strike-rate decreased slightly with Rapid, but he still found the net on 11 occasions to play a major part in the club's championship victory. Furthermore, he cut quite a dash in the yellow shirt of Romania, scoring twice on his début against Estonia and then again in a friendly against Belgium and a European Championship qualifier against Azerbaijan.

ADRIAN MIHALCEA

The return to Dinamo Bucharest of veteran international striker Ion Vladoiu did not at first appear to be good news for Adrian Mihalcea. The young striker had good reason to fear for his place, but instead he rolled up his sleeves and simply forced coach Cornel Dinu to keep him in the side by

scoring goal after goal to ignite Dinamo's championship challenge. By the end of the campaign he had chalked up 18 goals - four more than Vladoiu - to maintain a constant improvement in his ratio since arriving at the club in 1996. His fine club form was acknowledged with a regular place in the Romanian national squad, although by the end of the season the 23-year-old had still to start his first international.

ION TIMOFTE

He is the forgotten man of Romanian football, but in Portugal Ion Timofte continues to make waves with his bulldozing midfield play and his ferocious left-foot shots. In 1998/99 he scored 15 league goals for a Boavista side that shocked all and sundry by finishing above both Benfica and Sporting to finish runners-up behind local rivals FC Porto. It was Timofte's best tally in eight seasons of Portuguese league football, the first three of them with Porto, the other five with Boavista. Romanian fans remember him from his early days with Politehnica Timisoara as a kind of 'poor man's Hagi', but oddly, despite his undoubted talent, the 31-year-old has only ever won ten international caps, and none at all in the last four years.

ASTRA PLOIESTI

CLUB DIRECTORY

Astra Ploiesti
B-ul. Petrolului nr. 59
2000 Ploiesti
tel - (044) 147421
fax - (044) 144842
Year of Formation - 1934
President - Marian Manea
Coach - Gabriel Stan; Valentin Sinescu
(99/00 - Vasile Simionas)
Stadium - Astra (8,000)

APPEARANCES 98/99

	P	Ap	(s)	Gls
Valentin BERARU	M	29		12
Petrut BUTARU	M	3	(4)	
Costin CARAMAN	A	18	(6)	7
Mircea CIOREA	M	27	(6)	1
Ionel CIRES	D	3	(3)	
Mircea CRISTESCU	M	2	(1)	
Daniel DASCALESCU	M	2	(11)	
Mihai DASCALESCU	A	18	(9)	6
Daniel DUMITRACHE	D	10		
Florentin DUMITRU	D	30	(2)	
Daniel DUNAREANU	D	22	(1)	2
Ionel FULGA	M	10	(4)	
Eugen IACOB	G		(1)	
Robert ILYES	A	13	(3)	2
Daniel MOVILA	M	10	(14)	2
Catalin MULTESCU	G	33		
Eugen Gheorghe NAE	G	1		
Ioan Daniel PETROIESC	D	30		1
Silviu POPESCU	M	3	(3)	
Alin Gheorghe PUFU	M	17	(3)	
Gheorghe ROHAT	D	19	(5)	2
Marian ROHAT	M	1	(1)	
Ioan SAVU	A	11	(4)	2
Marius SCAIETEANU	A	1	(5)	
Pompiliu STOICA	M	30		1
Narcis VOICILA	M	4	(9)	2
Vasile VOINEA	D	27	(2)	

LEAGUE RESULTS 1998/99

01/08/98	FCM Bacau	H	1-1	Caraman
08/08/98	Petrolul Ploiesti	A	1-2	Beraru
15/08/98	Ceahlaul Piatra Neamt	H	0-0	
21/08/98	Otelul Galati	A	1-1	Beraru
29/08/98	Gloria Bistrita	H	3-1	Dascalescu M., Stoica, Voicila
12/09/98	Dinamo Bucuresti	A	0-2	
19/09/98	Foresta Falticeni	H	1-0	Dunareanu
26/09/98	FC National Bucuresti	A	0-1	
03/10/98	Olimpia Satu Mare	H	3-1	Dascalescu M. 2, Caraman
17/10/98	FC Farul Constanta	A	0-1	
24/10/98	Universitatea Craiova	A	0-0	
31/10/98	Universitatea Cluj	H	2-1	Caraman, Beraru
07/11/98	FC Arges Dacia Pitesti	A	2-1	Movila 2
14/11/98	FC Onesti	H	3-1	Beraru 2, Caraman
21/11/98	Rapid Bucuresti	A	0-1	
28/11/98	CSM Resita	H	3-0	Caraman 2, Beraru
05/12/98	Steaua Bucuresti	A	0-1	
06/03/99	FCM Bacau	A	0-2	
13/03/99	Petrolul Ploiesti	H	1-1	Beraru (p)
17/03/99	Ceahlaul Piatra Neamt	A	1-3	Voicila
20/03/99	Otelul Galati	H	3-1	Dascalescu M. 2, Dunareanu
03/04/99	Gloria Bistrita	A	0-1	
10/04/99	Dinamo Bucuresti	H	0-1	
17/04/99	Foresta Falticeni	A	1-0	Savu
21/04/99	FC National Bucuresti	H	1-2	Ilyes
24/04/99	Olimpia Satu Mare	A	2-1	Beraru (p), Petroiesc
30/04/99	FC Farul Constanta	H	4-0	Beraru 2 (1p), Ilyes, Dascalescu M.
08/05/99	Universitatea Craiova	H	2-2	Savu, Beraru (p)
12/05/99	Universitatea Cluj	A	2-0	Ciorea, Beraru (p)
15/05/99	FC Arges Dacia Pitesti	H	0-1	
22/05/99	FC Onesti	A	0-2	
26/05/99	Rapid Bucuresti	H	1-5	Rohat G.
29/05/99	CSM Resita	A	1-0	Caraman
06/06/99	Steaua Bucuresti	H	1-1	Rohat G.

FC ARGES DACIA PITESTI

CLUB DIRECTORY

FC Arges Dacia Pitesti
str. Armand Calinescu 15
0300 Pitesti
tel - (048) 632842
Year of Formation - 1953
President - Gabriel Sicoe
Coach - Silviu Dumitrescu; Nicolae Dobrin;
Mihai Zamfir
Stadium - Trivale (18,000)

MAJOR HONOURS
League Championship - (2) 1972, 1979.

APPEARANCES 98/99

	P	Ap	(s)	Gls
Constantin BARBU	A	16		13
Cristian BALASA	M	29	(2)	2
Vasile BÂRDES	A	27	(4)	7
Marius BILASCO	A	1	(5)	
Laurentiu Adrian BOGOI	D	28	(2)	
Cristian Nicolae BRATU	A	15	(11)	8
Augustin Eduard CHIRITA	M	8	(9)	1
Danut Dumitru COMAN	G		(2)	
Cornel CRISTESCU	M	17	(2)	
Iulian CRIVAC	M	32		1
Nicolae DITA	D	30	(1)	2
Mihai DRAGUS	A	3	(6)	1
Remus Ion GÂLMENCEA	D	6	(2)	
Marian JILAVEANU	M	1	(7)	
Adrian MALUSANU	M		(1)	
Daniel Emil MOGOSANU	D	27	(3)	
Adrian MUTU	M	14	(1)	7
Adrian Constantin NEAGA	M		(2)	
Cristian Eugen NEGRU	A	2	(4)	
Valentin Vasile NASTASE	D	30		1
Marius RADU	D	5	(2)	
Sorin Cristian RADU	M	7	(9)	1
Daniel Eugen REDNIC	M	17	(4)	3
Constantin SCHUMACHER	M	25	(5)	10
Daniel Eduard STANCIU	G	4	(1)	
Bogdan Arges VINTILA	G	30	(1)	

LEAGUE RESULTS 1998/99

02/08/98	Rapid Bucuresti	H	0-1	
07/08/98	CSM Resita	A	0-0	
16/08/98	Steaua Bucuresti	H	3-2	Barbu, Crivac, Bratu
22/08/98	FCM Bacau	A	2-3	Bratu, Nastase
30/08/98	Petrolul Ploiesti	H	3-1	Barbu 2 (1p), Schumacher
11/09/98	Ceahlaul Piatra Neamt	A	2-1	Barbu, Mutu
19/09/98	Otelul Galati	H	2-1	Barbu 2
25/09/98	Gloria Bistrita	A	1-3	Bârdes
03/10/98	Dinamo Bucuresti	H	2-1	Bârdes, Mutu
17/10/98	Foresta Falticeni	A	2-2	Barbu 2
24/10/98	FC National Bucuresti	H	1-0	Barbu
31/10/98	Olimpia Satu Mare	A	3-0	Bârdes 2, Schumacher
07/11/98	Astra Ploiesti	H	1-2	Barbu (p)
15/11/98	Universitatea Craiova	A	0-2	
21/11/98	Universitatea Cluj	H	3-0	Balasa, Mutu, Barbu
28/11/98	FC Farul Constanta	H	6-0	Barbu 2 (1p), Radu, Dita,
				Schumacher, Mutu
05/12/98	FC Onesti	A	3-0	Mutu 3
07/03/99	Rapid Bucuresti	A	0-2	
13/03/99	CSM Resita	H	1-0	Rednic
17/03/99	Steaua Bucuresti	A	2-1	Bârdes 2
20/03/99	FCM Bacau	H	0-3	
03/04/99	Petrolul Ploiesti	A	1-3	Schumacher
10/04/99	Ceahlaul Piatra Neamt	H	1-0	Dragus
17/04/99	Otelul Galati	A	1-1	Bratu
20/04/99	Gloria Bistrita	H	2-1	Bratu, Dita
24/04/99	Dinamo Bucuresti	A	0-1	
01/05/99	Foresta Falticeni	H	1-1	Schumacher
08/05/99	FC National Bucuresti	A	3-2	Rednic, Bârdes, Schumacher (p)
12/05/99	Olimpia Satu Mare	H	3-1	Bratu 2, Balasa
15/05/99	Astra Ploiesti	A	1-0	Chirita
22/05/99	Universitatea Craiova	H	2-0	Bratu, Schumacher
26/05/99	Universitatea Cluj	A	1-2	Bratu
29/05/99	FC Farul Constanta	A	2-0	Schumacher 2
02/06/99	FC Onesti	H	2-0	Schumacher, Rednic

FCM BACAU

FCM Bacau
str. Pictor Aman 94
5500 Bacau
tel (034) 141922
Year of Formation - 1950
President - Gheorghe Chivorchian
Coach - Florin Halagian; Gheorghe Poenaru
Stadium - Nicolae Paduraru (25,000)

APPEARANCES 98/99

	P	Ap	(s)	Gls
Florin ANTON	G	1		
Vasile Maricel ARDELEANU	D	19	(1)	2
Alexandru Cristian AXINTE	M	17	(8)	2
Daniel Jean BOGDAN	G	33		
Dan Vasile BOLFA	M	12	(5)	2
Ionel Giani CAPUSA	A	3	(9)	2
Radu Eduard CIOBANU	D	18		
Ciprian CIURLEA	D	3	(2)	
Sorin CONDURACHE	D	17	(2)	3
Florin GANEA	D	9	(11)	
Marius GIREADA	D	19	(3)	2
Danut MUNTEANU	M	27		
Vlad MUNTEANU	M	11	(4)	3
Florin PAVEL	M	22	(8)	2
Florin Lucian PETCU	A	32	(2)	15
Cristian Daniel POPOVICI	D	26		1
Narcis Claudiu RADUCAN	M	29	(1)	4
Vasile Ovidiu ROTARIU	M	30	(1)	1
Daniel SCÂNTEIE	A	13		1
Ionica SEREA	A	15	(15)	4
Ion Ovidiu STRATULAT	D	5	(3)	
Ionel Sorin TROFIN	M	7	(8)	1
Ionel VETREA	M	1	(1)	
VOICU	D	1		
ZAMFIRACHE	M		(2)	
Aurelian Ionel ZLATI	A	4	(12)	1

LEAGUE RESULTS 1998/99

01/08/98	Astra Ploiesti	A	1-1	Petcu
08/08/98	Universitatea Craiova	H	2-0	Axinte, Petcu (p)
15/08/98	Universitatea Cluj	A	2-1	Condurache 2
22/08/98	FC Arges Dacia Pitesti	H	3-2	Scânteie, Raducan, Petcu
29/08/98	FC Onesti	A	2-2	Ardeleanu, Rotariu
13/09/98	Rapid Bucuresti	H	1-1	Petcu (p)
19/09/98	CSM Resita	A	0-0	
25/09/98	Steaua Bucuresti	H	0-0	
03/10/98	FC Farul Constanta	H	1-0	Serea
17/10/98	Petrolul Ploiesti	A	1-1	Condurache
24/10/98	Ceahlaul Piatra Neamt	H	0-0	
31/10/98	Otelul Galati	A	1-0	Petcu
07/11/98	Gloria Bistrita	H	3-1	Capusa, Popovici, Petcu
14/11/98	Dinamo Bucuresti	A	0-1	
21/11/98	Foresta Falticeni	H	4-1	Serea, Petcu, Capusa, Raducanu
28/11/98	FC National Bucuresti	A	0-5	
05/12/98	Olimpia Satu Mare	H	2-1	Ardeleanu, Axinte
06/03/99	Astra Ploiesti	H	2-0	Petcu (p), Gireada
13/03/99	Universitatea Craiova	A	1-0	Munteanu
17/03/99	Universitatea Cluj	H	0-0	
20/03/99	FC Arges Dacia Pitesti	A	3-0	Petcu, Pavel, Zlati
03/04/99	FC Onesti	H	2-1	Munteanu, Petcu
10/04/99	Rapid Bucuresti	A	0-3	
17/04/99	CSM Resita	H	2-0	Munteanu, Raducan
20/04/99	Steaua Bucuresti	A	1-2	Petcu
24/04/99	FC Farul Constanta	A	0-2	
01/05/99	Petrolul Ploiesti	H	3-1	Serea 2, Bolfa
08/05/99	Ceahlaul Piatra Neamt	A	1-4	Trofin
12/05/99	Otelul Galati	H	1-0	Bolfa
15/05/99	Gloria Bistrita	A	0-2	
22/05/99	Dinamo Bucuresti	H	0-2	
26/05/99	Foresta Falticeni	A	1-0	Petcu
29/05/99	FC National Bucuresti	H	4-1	Raducan, Petcu 2, Pavel
12/06/99	Olimpia Satu Mare	A	2-0	Petcu, Gireada

CEAHLAUL PIATRA NEAMT

CLUB DIRECTORY

Ceahlaul Piatra Neamt
Str. Eroilor 18
5600 Piatra Neamt
tel - (033) 212702/119203
Year of Formation - 1919
President - Gheorghe Stefan
Coach - Nicolae Manea; Viorel Hizo
Stadium - Ceahlaul (15,000)

APPEARANCES 98/99

	P	Ap	(s)	Gls
ANICAI	D		(1)	
Angelo Dumitru ALISTAR	D	21	(2)	2
Cristinel ATOMULESEI	D	31		2
Vasile Florin AXINIA	A	23	(3)	7
Adrian BALDOVIN	D	24	(6)	
Eugen Daniel BASTON	A	3		2
Dumitru BOTEZ	M	24	(7)	2
Ioan Lucian COVRIG	G	10		
Codrut Stefan DOMSA	M	6	(3)	
Constantin ENACHE	A	14	(4)	4
Leo Florian GROZAVU	D	17	(2)	7
Constantin Ionut ILIE	M	27	(3)	5
Mihai Dan IONESCU	M	26	(6)	4
Radu Gabriel LEFTER	G	15	(1)	
Ovidiu MARC	M	25	(4)	7
Mihai Marian MATEI	D	14		1
Ioan Sebastian MOGA	M	4	(6)	1
Remus MUNTEANU	G	1		
Mihai NEMTANU	M		(2)	
Gheorghe NITU	G	2		
NOHAI	D	1		
Gheorghe PANTAZI	M	17	(9)	
Danut PERKA	D	27		3
SCUTARIU	D		(1)	
Adrian Constantin SOLOMON	M	20	(13)	4
Tiberiu SERBAN	M	2	(13)	2
Tudorel Cristian SOIMARU	M	13	(2)	
Paul STEFANESCU	G	6	(1)	
Eugen VOICA	M	1	(5)	1

LEAGUE RESULTS 1998/99

01/08/98	FC National Bucuresti	A	2-4	Moga, Baston
08/08/98	Olimpia Satu Mare	H	4-0	Enache (p), Solomon 2, Baston
15/08/98	Astra Ploiesti	A	0-0	
22/08/98	Universitatea Craiova	H	2-1	Perja, Voica
29/08/98	Universitatea Cluj	A	0-1	
11/09/98	FC Arges Dacia Pitesti	H	1-2	Ilie (p)
19/09/98	FC Onesti	A	1-3	Ilie (p)
26/09/98	Rapid Bucuresti	H	0-2	
03/10/98	CSM Resita	A	2-2	Axinia, Ilie
17/10/98	Steaua Bucuresti	H	0-3	
24/10/98	FCM Bacau	A	0-0	
31/10/98	Petrolul Ploiesti	H	1-3	Marc
07/11/98	FC Farul Constanta	H	2-0	Ilie, Ionescu
14/11/98	Otelul Galati	A	2-1	Matei, Alistar
21/11/98	Gloria Bistrita	H	3-2	Marc (p), Ionescu (p), Botez
28/11/98	Dinamo Bucuresti	A	1-6	Atomulesei
05/12/98	Foresta Falticeni	H	2-1	Axinia, Marc
06/03/99	FC National Bucuresti	H	1-0	Ionescu
13/03/99	Olimpia Satu Mare	A	1-0	Axinia
17/03/99	Astra Ploiesti	H	3-1	Solomon 2, Perja
20/03/99	Universitatea Craiova	A	1-2	Axinia
03/04/99	Universitatea Cluj	H	5-1	Grozavu (p), Marc 2, Axinia, Enache
10/04/99	FC Arges Dacia Pitesti	A	0-1	
17/04/99	FC Onesti	H	3-1	Axinia, Perja, Marc
21/04/99	Rapid Bucuresti	A	0-4	
24/04/99	CSM Resita	H	4-0	Enache, Axinia, Grozavu, Ilie
01/05/99	Steaua Bucuresti	A	2-3	Grozavu 2 (2p)
08/05/99	FCM Bacau	H	4-1	Botez, Ionescu, Marc, Serban
12/05/99	Petrolul Ploiesti	A	0-1	
15/05/99	FC Farul Constanta	A	1-2	Serban
22/05/99	Otelul Galati	H	1-1	Atomulesei
26/05/99	Gloria Bistrita	A	2-4	Alistar, Enache (p)
29/05/99	Dinamo Bucuresti	H	1-0	Grozavu (p)
12/06/99	Foresta Falticeni	A	2-0	Grozavu 2 (1p)

DINAMO BUCURESTI

CLUB DIRECTORY

FC Dinamo Bucuresti
Sos. Stefan cel Mare 9
71401 Bucuresti
tel - (01) 2110994/2113072
fax - (01) 2103519
Year of Formation - 1948
President - Mircea Stoenescu
Coach - Cornel Dinu
Stadium - Dinamo (18,000)

MAJOR HONOURS
League Championship - (14)
1955, 1962, 1963, 1964, 1965, 1971, 1973,
1975, 1977, 1982, 1983, 1984, 1990, 1992.
Domestic Cup - (7)
1959, 1964, 1968, 1982, 1984, 1986, 1990.

APPEARANCES 98/99

	P	Ap	(s)	Gls
ALDEA	M	1		
ANITA	G	1		
Florin Ionel BATRÂNU	M	27		6
Cosmin BODEA	D		(4)	
Aurel Augustin CALIN	A	1	(1)	
Razvan CHIRITA	A		(1)	
Liviu CIOBOTARIU	D	30		3
Cosmin Marius CONTRA	D	27	(2)	2
Cornel DOBRE	D	9	(10)	1
R DUMITRESCU	M		(1)	
Alexandru ENE	M		(1)	
Daniel FLOREA	D	26		1
Khalid FOUHAMI (MAR)	G	24		1
Ionel Tersinio GANE	A	5	(10)	7
Catalin HÂLDAN	M	29		1
Daniel IFTODI	M	27	(3)	9
Giani Stelian KIRITA	M	8	(15)	1
Ioan Angelo LUPESCU	M	32		8
Bogdan MARA	A		(2)	1
Adrian Dumitru MIHALCEA	A	32		18
Gheorghe MIHALI	D	8	(2)	
MILITARU	D	1		
Adrian MUTU	M	11	(4)	4
Marius NICOLAE	A	8	(20)	7
ONICA	D	1		
Florentin PETRE	M	28	(1)	8
Stefan Gabriel PREDA	G	9	(1)	
Daniel Eugen REDNIC	M	1	(7)	2
Marius Cristian STANCIU	M		(1)	
STIRBU	M	1		
Iulian TAMES	A	1		
Iosif Ovidiu TÂLVAN	D	2	(1)	
Ion VLADOIU	A	24		14

LEAGUE RESULTS 1998/99

01/08/98	Gloria Bistrita	H	3-0	Batrânu, Vladoiu, Lupescu (p)
09/08/98	FC Farul Constanta	A	3-1	Batrânu (p), Vladoiu, Ciobotariu
15/08/98	Foresta Falticeni	A	3-2	Iftodi, Petre 2
23/08/98	FC National Bucuresti	H	5-0	Vladoiu 2, Petre, Mihalcea, Rednic
29/08/98	Olimpia Satu Mare	A	4-0	Mihalcea 2, Batrânu (p), Iftodi
12/09/98	Astra Ploiesti	H	2-0	Vladoiu, Mihalcea
20/09/98	Universitatea Craiova	A	2-2	Mihalcea 2
26/09/98	Universitatea Cluj	H	8-0	Ciobotariu, Vladoiu, Batrânu (p), Iftodi 2, Mihalcea, Niculae, Rednic
03/10/98	FC Arges Dacia Pitesti	A	1-2	Batrânu (p)
17/10/98	FC Onesti	H	3-1	Gane 2, Petre
25/10/98	Rapid Bucuresti	A	4-1	Batrânu, Ciobotariu, Iftodi, Gane
31/10/98	CSM Resita	H	7-0	Iftodi, Petre, Vladoiu 2 (1p), Mihalcea, Gane, Fouhami (p)
08/11/98	Steaua Bucuresti	A	1-1	Contra
14/11/98	FCM Bacau	H	1-0	Lupescu (p)
21/11/98	Petrolul Ploiesti	A	3-2	Niculae, Lupescu, Mihalcea
28/11/98	Ceahlaul Piatra Neamt	H	6-1	Niculae 2, Mihalcea 2, Mara, Petre
06/12/98	Otelul Galati	A	1-2	Lupescu
06/03/99	Gloria Bistrita	A	3-2	Vladoiu, Lupescu (p), Mihalcea
13/03/99	FC Farul Constanta	H	2-1	Iftodi, Vladoiu
17/03/99	Foresta Falticeni	H	4-1	Mihalcea 3, Iftodi
21/03/99	FC National Bucuresti	A	2-1	Florea, Mutu
03/04/99	Olimpia Satu Mare	H	5-0	Vladoiu 2, Lupescu (p), Niculae, Hâldan
10/04/99	Astra Ploiesti	A	1-0	Mihalcea
18/04/99	Universitatea Craiova	H	2-1	Lupescu (p), Gane
21/04/99	Universitatea Cluj	A	6-0	Mutu 2, og (Matei), Vladoiu, Gane, Niculae
24/04/99	FC Arges Dacia Pitesti	H	1-0	Lupescu
01/05/99	FC Onesti	A	4-1	Petre 2, Contra, Vladoiu
09/05/99	Rapid Bucuresti	H	0-1	
12/05/99	CSM Resita	A	1-1	Mihalcea
15/05/99	Steaua Bucuresti	H	0-0	
22/05/99	FCM Bacau	A	2-0	Iftodi, Mihalcea
26/05/99	Petrolul Ploiesti	H	3-1	Mutu (p), Dobre, Niculae
29/05/99	Ceahlaul Piatra Neamt	A	0-1	
12/06/99	Otelul Galati	H	2-1	Gane, Kirita

FC FARUL CONSTANTA

CLUB DIRECTORY

FC Farul Constanta
str. Primaverii 2
8700 Constanta
tel - (041) 616142
fax - (041) 644827
Year of Formation - 1949
President - Jean Garabet
Coach - Ioan Andonie; Florin Marin
(99/00 - Gabriel Zahiu)
Stadium - Farul (20,000)

APPEARANCES 98/99

	P	Ap	(s)	Gls
Marcel Cristian ABALUTA	M	31		3
Marius AXINCIUC	D	24	(5)	
Ionut BADESCU	M	23	(9)	6
Vasile BRATIANU	D	11		1
Stefan CIOBANU	M		(3)	
Mugurel Florin CORNATEANU	A	6	(10)	2
Cosmin DRAGULIN	A	11	(4)	1
Petre GRIGORAS	A	26	(2)	4
HASOTI	M		(1)	
Alexandru ILIUCIUC	G	16	(1)	
Florin LUNGU	A		(7)	
Florin MACAVEI	D	6	(1)	1
MITRUT	D	1	(3)	
Bogdan MARA	A	10	(2)	3
Dan Marius MITU	M	29	(1)	
Robert MIU	D	1	(3)	
Victor NAICU	D	13	(2)	
Fanel Daniel NIIA	D	19	(2)	
Norbert Sorin NITA	D	21	(4)	3
Ionel Cristian PETCU	D	14	(1)	1
Ionel PÂRVU	M	3	(1)	
Mircea Valerica STAN	D	26	(4)	5
Adrian Eusebiu STATE	A	3	(2)	
Mihai STERE	M	13	(13)	2
Paul STEFANESCU	G	3		
Gabriel TOMA	M	2	(9)	
Grigorie TUDOR	M	30	(2)	4
Robert Emil TUFIS	G	15	(1)	
Gabriel VOCHIN	D	16		1
ZAMARIA	A	1	(1)	

LEAGUE RESULTS 1998/99

01/08/98	FC Onesti	A	2-2	Badescu, Nita
09/08/98	Dinamo Bucuresti	H	1-3	Tudor
16/08/98	Rapid Bucuresti	A	0-3	
22/08/98	Foresta Falticeni	H	3-2	Macavei, Tudor (p), Stan
29/08/98	CSM Resita	A	2-3	Petcu, Tudor (p)
12/09/98	FC National Bucuresti	H	0-1	
19/09/98	Steaua Bucuresti	A	0-1	
26/09/98	Olimpia Satu Mare	H	3-1	Grigoras, Stere, Stan
03/10/98	FCM Bacau	A	0-1	
17/10/98	Astra Ploiesti	H	1-0	Bratianu
24/10/98	Petrolul Ploiesti	A	0-3	
31/10/98	Universitatea Craiova	H	2-1	Grigoras (p), Abaluta
07/11/98	Ceahlaul Piatra Neamt	A	0-2	
14/11/98	Universitatea Cluj	A	3-1	Stan, Badescu, Cornateanu
21/11/98	Otelul Galati	H	0-1	
28/11/98	FC Arges Dacia Pitesti	A	0-6	
05/12/98	Gloria Bistrita	H	3-1	Dragulin, Cornateanu, Stan
06/03/99	FC Onesti	H	2-0	Vochin, Grigoras
13/03/99	Dinamo Bucuresti	A	1-2	Badescu
16/03/99	Rapid Bucuresti	H	0-0	
20/03/99	Foresta Falticeni	A	0-2	
03/04/99	CSM Resita	H	0-0	
10/04/99	FC National Bucuresti	A	0-0	
17/04/99	Steaua Bucuresti	H	0-3	
21/04/99	Olimpia Satu Mare	A	3-0	Stan, Mara, Abaluta
24/04/99	FCM Bacau	H	2-0	Tudor (p), Nita
30/04/99	Astra Ploiesti	A	0-4	
08/05/99	Petrolul Ploiesti	H	1-0	Grigoras
12/05/99	Universitatea Craiova	A	0-1	
15/05/99	Ceahlaul Piatra Neamt	H	2-1	Nita, Badescu
22/05/99	Universitatea Cluj	H	3-1	Mara, Stere, Badescu
26/05/99	Otelul Galati	A	1-2	Mara
29/05/99	FC Arges Dacia Pitesti	H	0-2	
02/06/99	Gloria Bistrita	A	2-4	Abaluta, Badescu

FORESTA FALTICENI

CLUB DIRECTORY

FC Foresta Falticeni
B-dul 1 Decembrie 1918 nr.7
Suceava
tel - (030) 216145
Year of Formation - 1954
President - Eugen Hutu
Coach - Mircea Crainiciuc; Petre Gigiu;
Marian Bucurescu
Stadium - Areni, Suceava (12,000)

APPEARANCES 98/99

	P	Ap	(s)	Gls
Mihai BAICU	A	25		5
Daniel BALAN	M	5		1
Valentin BALAN	D	17	(2)	
BEJINARU	M		(1)	
Adrian BELDIMAN	M	28	(1)	3
Dorel BERNARD	D	23	(3)	
Adrian BONTEA	G	9		
Silviu BUZEA	D	3	(3)	
Ionel Giani CAPUSA	A	12		2
Aristica CIOABA	D	15		
Ovidiu CIOBANU	D	31	(1)	2
Alexandru CIOLOCA	A	2	(1)	
Adrian DOBREA	A	3	(3)	
Vicentiu DRAGOMIR	G	3		
Viorel DUMITRESCU	G	8		
Dumitru ENE	M	24	(2)	3
Andre FANNIS (CAN)	A		(9)	
Dumitru GAVRILESCU	A	4	(8)	1
Alexandru GHEORGHE	A	18	(11)	6
Gheorghe Daniel GOIAN	D	16	(5)	
Robert ILYES	M	16	(1)	2
Remus Cezar MARTA	M	17	(5)	
Ioan Daniel MIHAILA	A	5	(6)	
Mircea MINESCU	D	25		
Eugen Gheorghe NAE	G	14		
Sergiu SAVA	D	4	(5)	
Constantin Dorin SEMEGHIN	M	21	(9)	1
Cristian SCHIOPU	M	26	(2)	4

LEAGUE RESULTS 1998/99

01/08/98	Otelul Galati	H	1-2	Gheorghe (p)
08/08/98	Gloria Bistrita	A	0-5	
15/08/98	Dinamo Bucuresti	H	2-3	Gheorghe, Gavrilescu
22/08/98	FC Farul Constanta	A	2-3	Ilyes, Baicu
29/08/98	FC National Bucuresti	A	1-4	Baicu
12/09/98	Olimpia Satu Mare	H	2-0	Baicu, Semeghin
19/09/98	Astra Ploiesti	A	0-1	
26/09/98	Universitatea Craiova	H	1-2	Gheorghe (p)
03/10/98	Universitatea Cluj	A	2-2	Ciobanu, Baicu
17/10/98	FC Arges Dacia Pitesti	H	2-2	Gheorghe, Beldiman
24/10/98	FC Onesti	A	1-3	Gheorghe (p)
31/10/98	Rapid Bucuresti	H	0-1	
07/11/98	CSM Resita	A	1-1	Ene
14/11/98	Steaua Bucuresti	H	1-2	Ilyes (p)
21/11/98	FCM Bacau	A	1-4	Gheorghe
28/11/98	Petrolul Ploiesti	H	1-2	Schiopu
05/12/98	Ceahlaul Piatra Neamt	A	1-2	Baicu
06/03/99	Otelul Galati	A	0-1	
13/03/99	Gloria Bistrita	H	0-0	
17/03/99	Dinamo Bucuresti	A	1-4	Schiopu
20/03/99	FC Farul Constanta	H	2-0	Ene, Balan D.
03/04/99	FC National Bucuresti	H	1-0	Capusa
10/04/99	Olimpia Satu Mare	A	1-0	Ciobanu (p)
17/04/99	Astra Ploiesti	H	0-1	
21/04/99	Universitatea Craiova	A	0-1	
24/04/99	Universitatea Cluj	H	1-0	Ene
01/05/99	FC Arges Dacia Pitesti	A	1-1	Beldiman
08/05/99	FC Onesti	H	3-1	og (Chiriac), Beldiman, Capusa
12/05/99	Rapid Bucuresti	A	0-2	
15/05/99	CSM Resita	H	0-0	
22/05/99	Steaua Bucuresti	A	1-6	Schiopu
26/05/99	FCM Bacau	H	0-1	
29/05/99	Petrolul Ploiesti	A	1-2	Schiopu
12/06/99	Ceahlaul Piatra Neamt	H	0-2	

GLORIA BISTRITA

Gloria Bistrita
str. Parcului 3
4400 Bistrita
tel - (063) 212998
fax - (063) 217437
Year of Formation - 1926
President - Jean Padureanu
Coach - Constantin Cârstea
Stadium - Gloria (12,000)

APPEARANCES 98/99

	P	Ap	(s)	Gls
Mihai Virgil ANTAL	M		(1)	
Narcis Mario BUGEANU	M	1	(1)	
Marius Gabriel CINCA	M	3	(2)	
Costel CÂMPEANU	G	31		
Ambrozie Cristian COROIAN	D	16	(7)	
Gabriel CRISTEA	D	11	(1)	
Florin Cristian DAN	M	2		
Emil Gavril DANCUS	M	31		2
Emilian DOLHA	G	1	(1)	
Pavel Adrian DULCEA	D	2	(4)	
Adrian FALUB	M	11		3
Ioan Viorel GANEA	A	16		17
Gheorghe Aurelian LEAHU	M	11	(7)	
Danut MATEI	A	19	(11)	4
Sergiu Sebastian MANDREAN	M	4		
Dan MIF	M	26	(3)	8
Alin MINTEUAN	M	15		2
Ioan MISZTI	D	27	(5)	2
NALATI	M		(1)	
Iulian NECULAI	D		(2)	
Bogdan Gheorghe NICOLAE	M	28	(1)	1
Vasile Nicolae POPA	D	23		
Marius POPESCU	M	10	(4)	1
David Stefan RADU	D		(1)	
Romeo RAILEANU	M		(1)	
Alin Valter RUS	M	10	(3)	
SÂNMARTEAN	M		(1)	
Valer SASARMAN	D	33		1
Dumitru TÂRTAU	A	9	(6)	5
Cristian Dorin TUDOR	A		(1)	1
Petru TURCAS	G	2	(2)	
Cristian TURCU	A	16	(14)	6
Cezar Iulius ZAMFIR	M	16	(4)	

LEAGUE RESULTS 1998/99

01/08/98	Dinamo Bucuresti	A	0-3	
08/08/98	Foresta Falticeni	H	5-0	Turcu, Falub, Ganea 2, Cinca
15/08/98	FC National Bucuresti	A	1-5	Nicolae
22/08/98	Olimpia Satu Mare	H	3-1	Ganea, og (Nan), Falub
29/08/98	Astra Ploiesti	A	1-3	Turcu
12/09/98	Universitatea Craiova	H	1-1	Ganea (p)
19/09/98	Universitatea Cluj	A	1-1	Popescu
25/09/98	FC Arges Dacia Pitesti	H	3-1	Ganea 3
03/10/98	FC Onesti	A	1-1	Ganea
17/10/98	Rapid Bucuresti	H	2-4	Ganea 2
24/10/98	CSM Resita	A	0-2	
01/11/98	Steaua Bucuresti	H	2-1	Ganea, Falub (p)
07/11/98	FCM Bacau	A	1-3	Turcu
14/11/98	Petrolul Ploiesti	H	2-0	Ganea 2
21/11/98	Ceahlaul Piatra Neamt	A	2-3	Ganea, Mif (p)
28/11/98	Otelul Galati	H	2-1	Ganea 2 (2p)
05/12/98	FC Farul Constanta	A	1-3	Ganea
06/03/99	Dinamo Bucuresti	H	2-3	Mif, Dancus
13/03/99	Foresta Falticeni	A	0-0	
17/03/99	FC National Bucuresti	H	2-4	Mif 2 (1p)
20/03/99	Olimpia Satu Mare	A	0-1	
03/04/99	Astra Ploiesti	H	1-0	Târtau
10/04/99	Universitatea Craiova	A	1-2	Mif (p)
16/04/99	Universitatea Cluj	H	4-0	Mintouan 2, Târtau 2
20/04/99	FC Arges Dacia Pitesti	A	1-2	Târtau
24/04/99	FC Onesti	H	3-1	Sasarman, Târtau, Miszti
01/05/99	Rapid Bucuresti	A	0-5	
08/05/99	CSM Resita	H	2-2	Mif (p), Turcu
12/05/99	Steaua Bucuresti	A	0-0	
15/05/99	FCM Bacau	H	2-0	Matei, Miszti
22/05/99	Petrolul Ploiesti	A	1-3	Dancus
26/05/99	Ceahlaul Piatra Neamt	H	4-2	Matei 2, Turcu 2
29/05/99	Otelul Galati	A	0-0	
02/06/99	FC Farul Constanta	H	4-2	Matei, Mif 2 (1p), Tudor

FC NATIONAL BUCURESTI

CLUB DIRECTORY

FC National Bucuresti
Str. Dr. Lister 37
76202 Bucuresti
tel - (01) 4106606
Year of Formation - 1934
President - Gino Iorgulescu
Coach - Florin Marin; Gabriel Zahiu;
José Ramón Alexanko; Gino Iorgulescu
(99/00 - Mihai Stoichita)
Stadium - Cotroceni (16,000)

MAJOR HONOURS
Domestic Cup - (1) 1960.

APPEARANCES 98/99

		P	Ap	(s)	Gls
Vasile Florin AXINIA	A	1		(1)	
Gheorghe BARBU	M	18	(2)		1
Gheorghe BUTOIU	M	25	(6)		4
Stelian CARABAS	M	22	(1)		4
Gabriel Gheorghe CARAMARIN	M	6	(15)		3
Vasile Sanshiro CIOCOI	D	11	(1)		1
CÎNU	M		(1)		
Gigel COMAN	M	22	(5)		1
Tiberiu Cristian CURT	D	31			
Marin DUNA	A	22	(3)		4
Constantin ENACHE	A	4	(6)		1
Adrian FALUB	M	18			1
Remus Traian GANEA	M	1			
Catalin Nicolae LITA	M	21	(3)		5
Razvan LUCESCU	G	14			
Cristian LUPUT	M		(1)		
Petre MARIN	D	28	(1)		1
Danut MOISESCU	M	3	(3)		
Cristian Marian MUNTEANU	G	20	(1)		
Radu Horia NICULESCU	A	14	(1)		7
OLAH	M		(1)		
Constantin PAUNESCU	D	6	(3)		
Mihai PÂRLOG	M	15	(11)		
Adrian Ion PIGULEA	M	23	(4)		6
Florin Flavius POGACEAN	M	1	(9)		1
Iulian Vasile ROSOAGA	M	2	(6)		
Marian SAVU	A	25	(5)		19
Ion SBURLEA	D	8			
Daniel Ionel STANA	M	1			
Gabriel VOCHIN	D	12			
Dorin Bogdan ZOTINCA	M		(2)		

LEAGUE RESULTS 1998/99

01/08/98	Ceahlaul Piatra Neamt	H	4-2	Lita, Savu 2, Butoiu
07/08/98	Otelul Galati	A	2-3	Pigulea, Butoiu
15/08/98	Gloria Bistrita	H	5-1	Barbu, Savu, Lita (p),
				og (Sasarman), Carabas
23/08/98	Dinamo Bucuresti	A	0-5	
29/08/98	Foresta Falticeni	H	4-1	Savu 2, Niculescu 2
12/09/98	FC Farul Constanta	A	1-0	Enache
19/09/98	Olimpia Satu Mare	A	1-3	Pogacean
26/09/98	Astra Ploiesti	H	1-0	og (Rohat)
03/10/98	Universitatea Craiova	A	2-0	Lita, Coman
17/10/98	Universitatea Cluj	H	3-1	Pigulea 2, Savu
24/10/98	FC Arges Dacia Pitesti	A	0-1	
31/10/98	FC Onesti	H	3-0	Savu 2, Pigulea
07/11/98	Rapid Bucuresti	A	0-5	
14/11/98	CSM Resita	H	3-0	Duna, Savu 2
22/11/98	Steaua Bucuresti	A	0-1	
28/11/98	FCM Bacau	H	5-0	Savu 4 (1p), Pigulea
05/12/98	Petrolul Ploiesti	A	3-1	Duna (p), Butoiu, Caramarin
06/03/99	Ceahlaul Piatra Neamt	A	0-1	
14/03/99	Otelul Galati	H	0-1	
17/03/99	Gloria Bistrita	A	4-2	Caramarin, Duna, Lita 2
21/03/99	Dinamo Bucuresti	H	1-2	Falub
03/04/99	Foresta Falticeni	A	0-1	
10/04/99	FC Farul Constanta	H	0-0	
17/04/99	Olimpia Satu Mare	H	2-1	Carabas, Niculescu
21/04/99	Astra Ploiesti	A	2-1	Niculescu, Pigulea
24/04/99	Universitatea Craiova	H	1-0	Duna
02/05/99	Universitatea Cluj	A	4-1	Savu 3 (2p), Butoiu
09/05/99	FC Arges Dacia Pitesti	H	2-3	Savu, Caramarin
12/05/99	FC Onesti	A	3-2	Niculescu 2, Carabas
15/05/99	Rapid Bucuresti	H	1-3	Carabas
22/05/99	CSM Resita	A	1-4	Niculescu
26/05/99	Steaua Bucuresti	H	0-1	
29/05/99	FCM Bacau	A	1-4	Savu
02/06/99	Petrolul Ploiesti	H	2-0	Ciocoi, Marin

OLIMPIA SATU MARE

CLUB DIRECTORY

Olimpia Satu Mare
str. Eliberarii nr. 6
Satu Mare
Year of Formation - 1921
President - Mircea Govor
Coach - Gavril Both; Gheorghe Staicu; Gavril Both
Stadium - Olimpia (18,000)

APPEARANCES 98/99

	P	Ap	(s)	Gls
Marian ALEXANDRU	A	25	(5)	4
Radu CHIOREANU	D	19	(4)	1
Petru CHIRATCU	A	24	(2)	5
Gheorghe CIOCAN	A	2	(10)	
Remus CIOLOBOC	M	8	(13)	
Igor CORJAN (MOL)	A	7	(2)	2
Claudiu Mircea CORNACI	D	28		1
COROIU	D		(2)	
Gabriel DANI	M		(8)	
Ioan DRAGOMIR	M	26	(2)	2
David Stelian FARCAU	A	1	(3)	
GOJA	M	4	(3)	
Adrian Ioan GONGOLEA	D	2		
Sorin IODI	D	22	(8)	2
Cristian IVAN	M	11	(3)	1
Emil Vidor KEMENES	D	1	(1)	
Cristian LUPUT	D	17	(3)	1
MIMOVIC	M		(1)	
Costel Ciprian MOZACU	M	6	(4)	1
Lucian NAN	D	34		
Petru Rodin NEGREA	M	15		1
PANTEA	M		(4)	
Mihai Iacob PAUL	M	27		
Nicolae POP	M	5		
Ciprian PRODAN	A	2	(7)	
REBEGEA	D	1		
Iulian Vasile ROSOAGA	M	10	(6)	
Florin SIMION	A		(1)	
Mircea STANCIU	A	10	(1)	1
Ovidiu Gheorghe SUCIU	G	8		
Zoltan SZABO	D	23	(3)	
Martin Gheorghe TUDOR	G	26		
Cristian TIPLEA	M	1		
Tudorel ZAMFIRESCU	D	10		

LEAGUE RESULTS 1998/99

01/08/98	Petrolul Ploiesti	H	3-0	Chiratcu 2, Alexandru
08/08/98	Ceahlaul Piatra Neamt	A	0-4	
15/08/98	Otelul Galati	H	0-1	
22/08/98	Gloria Bistrita	A	1-3	Dragomir
29/08/98	Dinamo Bucuresti	H	0-4	
12/09/98	Foresta Falticeni	A	0-2	
19/09/98	FC National Bucuresti	H	3-1	Ivan, Chiratcu, Mozacu
26/09/98	FC Farul Constanta	A	1-3	Chiratcu
03/10/98	Astra Ploiesti	A	1-3	Iodi
18/10/98	Universitatea Craiova	H	1-1	Cornaci
24/10/98	Universitatea Cluj	A	0-1	
31/10/98	FC Arges Dacia Pitesti	H	0-3	
07/11/98	FC Onesti	A	0-1	
14/11/98	Rapid Bucuresti	H	1-1	Corjan
21/11/98	CSM Resita	A	1-1	Corjan
28/11/98	Steaua Bucuresti	H	0-3	
05/12/98	FCM Bacau	A	1-2	Luput
06/03/99	Petrolul Ploiesti	A	0-0	
13/03/99	Ceahlaul Piatra Neamt	H	0-1	
17/03/99	Otelul Galati	A	0-2	
20/03/99	Gloria Bistrita	H	1-0	Negrea
03/04/99	Dinamo Bucuresti	A	0-5	
10/04/99	Foresta Falticeni	H	0-1	
17/04/99	FC National Bucuresti	A	1-2	Chiratcu
21/04/99	FC Farul Constanta	H	0-3	
24/04/99	Astra Ploiesti	H	1-2	Chioreanu
01/05/99	Universitatea Craiova	A	1-5	Stanciu
07/05/99	Universitatea Cluj	H	0-1	
12/05/99	FC Arges Dacia Pitesti	A	1-3	Alexandru
15/05/99	FC Onesti	H	1-6	Dragomir
22/05/99	Rapid Bucuresti	A	0-1	
26/05/99	CSM Resita	H	1-3	Alexandru
29/05/99	Steaua Bucuresti	A	2-3	Iodi, Alexandru
12/06/99	FCM Bacau	H	0-2	

FC ONESTI

CLUB DIRECTORY

FC Onesti
Onesti
Year of Formation - 1974
President - Nicolae Puiu
Coach - Toader Stet
Stadium - FC Onesti (10,000)

APPEARANCES 98/99

	P	Ap	(s)	Gls
Liviu ACHIM	D	3	(1)	
Danut Alin ARTIMON	D	10	(4)	1
AVADANEI	M		(1)	
Costel BÂRSAN	A	25	(6)	13
Constantin Adrian BLID	G	22	(1)	
Dumitru CHIRIAC	D	15		
Constantin Calin CONSTANTIN	D	7	(4)	
Ionut DRAGOMIRESCU	D	1	(2)	
Danut DUMITRIU	D	2	(4)	
Mihai FLORIA	G	11	(1)	
Gigi Claudiu GOICEANU	M	1		
Giani Marius GORGA	M	29	(2)	5
Ionel IRIZA	A	26	(8)	13
Vasile JERCALAU	D	31		3
Victor Claudiu LEPADATU	M			
Bogdan MANDRIC	G	1		
Altin MASATI (ALB)	D	16	(3)	1
Victor MEDELEANU	M	1	(7)	
Adrian MOLDOVEANU	M	9	(1)	
Constantin Stelian MUNTEANU	D	20	(2)	
Florin MUNTEANU	M	29	(2)	3
Petru Rodin NEGREA	M	10	(1)	1
Marian Nicu NICULITA	D	16	(6)	
Danut Stelian OPREA	A	16	(1)	5
Ionel Antonel PÂRVU	M	7	(1)	2
Nicolae PRISTOLIAN	M	2	(5)	
Valeriu RACHITA	D	10		
Remus Daniel SAFTA	A	5	(5)	
Daniel SCÂNTEIE	A	8	(3)	6
SITARU	M	1	(2)	
Anghel Cristian TANASE	M	2	(4)	
Leontin Alexandru TANASE	M		(2)	
Laurentiu URÂTU	M	16	(4)	1
Nicolae Adrian VELICIOIU	M	1	(11)	
Gheorghe Gelu VOICA	M	10		

LEAGUE RESULTS 1998/99

01/08/98	FC Farul Constanta	H	2-2	Oprea, Pârvu
08/08/98	Rapid Bucuresti	A	0-6	
15/08/98	CSM Resita	H	5-0	Bârsan 2, Pârvu, Gorga, Iriza (p)
21/08/98	Steaua Bucuresti	A	1-4	Bârsan
29/08/98	FCM Bacau	H	2-2	Gorga, og (Ardeleanu)
12/09/98	Petrolul Ploiesti	A	0-1	
19/09/98	Ceahlaul Piatra Neamt	H	3-1	Masati, Iriza, Oprea
26/09/98	Otelul Galati	A	0-3	
03/10/98	Gloria Bistrita	H	1-1	Negrea
17/10/98	Dinamo Bucuresti	A	1-3	Jercalau
24/10/98	Foresta Falticeni	H	3-1	Iriza (p), Munteanu, Oprea
31/10/98	FC National Bucuresti	A	0-3	
07/11/98	Olimpia Satu Mare	H	1-0	Iriza
14/11/98	Astra Ploiesti	A	1-3	Oprea
21/11/98	Universitatea Craiova	H	3-2	Munteanu, Artimon, Gorga
28/11/98	Universitatea Cluj	A	2-0	Bârsan, Oprea
05/12/98	FC Arges Dacia Pitesti	H	0-3	
06/03/99	FC Farul Constanta	A	0-2	
13/03/99	Rapid Bucuresti	H	1-2	Gorga
17/03/99	CSM Resita	A	2-0	Iriza, Munteanu
20/03/99	Steaua Bucuresti	H	2-3	Bârsan, Jercalau
03/04/99	FCM Bacau	A	1-2	Bârsan
10/04/99	Petrolul Ploiesti	H	2-0	Iriza, Scânteie
17/04/99	Ceahlaul Piatra Neamt	A	1-3	Iriza
21/04/99	Otelul Galati	H	1-0	Scânteie
24/04/99	Gloria Bistrita	A	1-3	Jercalau (p)
01/05/99	Dinamo Bucuresti	H	1-4	Scânteie
08/05/99	Foresta Falticeni	A	1-3	Bârsan
12/05/99	FC National Bucuresti	H	2-3	Iriza, Scânteie
15/05/99	Olimpia Satu Mare	A	6-1	Bârsan 3, Iriza 2, Lepadatu
22/05/99	Astra Ploiesti	H	2-0	Urâtu, Iriza
26/05/99	Universitatea Craiova	A	2-4	Bârsan 2
29/05/99	Universitatea Cluj	H	6-0	Scânteie 2, Iriza 2, Bârsan, Gorga
02/06/99	FC Arges Dacia Pitesti	A	0-2	

OTELUL GALATI

Otelul Galati
Regimentul nr. 11 Siret
Clubul SIDEX
6200 Galati
tel - (036) 463898/464677
fax (036) 462150
Year of Formation - 1964
President - Mihai Stoica
Coach - Vasile Simionas; Constantin Ploiesteanu
(99/00 - Dumitru Dumitriu)
Stadaium - Otelul (15,000)

APPEARANCES 98/99

	P	Ap	(s)	Gls
Mihai ALEXA	D		(1)	
Dorin ARCANU	G	28		
Iulian ARHIRE	M	8	(7)	
Adrian ARITON	D	1		
Marin Dorel BALINT	D	30	(1)	3
Ion BASALÂC	M		(1)	
Daniel Eugen BASTINA	M	16		1
Constantin BADAN	G		(1)	
Stelian BORDEIANU	G	6		
Romeo BUTESEACA	D	3	(3)	
Florin CERNAT	M	9	(9)	2
Sorin GHIONEA	D	6	(8)	
GUGOASA	M		(1)	
Mihai GURITA	D	19	(5)	3
Sorin Florin HARAGA	D	8	(2)	
Gigi ION	D	17	(8)	3
Viorel ION	A	10		3
Marian JIGLAU	M	1		
Costin MALES	M	21	(9)	2
Dragos Mihail MIHALACHE	A	20	(1)	3
MILOIU	D	1		
Costel Ciprian MOZACU	M	4	(2)	
Claudiu MUHA	M	1		
Adrian NEGRARU	M		(1)	
Leonard Ion NEMTANU	D	25	(2)	3
Robert NITA	A	7	(1)	1
Ion Vasile OANA	A		(7)	
Danut Stelian OPREA	A	12	(1)	3
Tudorel PELIN	D	14	(14)	2
SILIAN	A	1		1
Emil SPIREA	M	30	(1)	3
C STAN	M	1	(1)	
Valentin STEFAN	M	15	(3)	2
Viorel TANASE	M	30	(1)	10
Catalin TOFAN	D	30		2

LEAGUE RESULTS 1998/99

01/08/98	Foresta Falticeni	A	2-1	Gurita, Stefan (p)
07/08/98	FC National Bucuresti	H	3-2	Mihalache, Pelin, Ion V.
15/08/98	Olimpia Satu Mare	A	1-0	Gurita
21/08/98	Astra Ploiesti	H	1-1	Ion G.
29/08/98	Universitatea Craiova	A	1-0	Nemtanu
12/09/98	Universitatea Cluj	H	5-0	Tanase 3 (1p), Ion.V. 2
19/09/98	FC Arges Dacia Pitesti	A	1-2	Pelin
26/09/98	FC Onesti	H	3-0	Stefan (p), Nemtanu, Males
04/10/98	Rapid Bucuresti	A	0-3	
17/10/98	CSM Resita	H	4-0	Ion G., Spirea 2, Balint
24/10/98	Steaua Bucuresti	A	0-2	
31/10/98	FCM Bacau	H	0-1	
07/11/98	Petrolul Ploiesti	A	0-2	
14/11/98	Ceahlaul Piatra Neamt	H	1-2	Balint
21/11/98	FC Farul Constanta	A	1-0	Tanase
28/11/98	Gloria Bistrita	A	1-2	Tanase
06/12/98	Dinamo Bucuresti	H	2-1	Ion G., Tanase
06/03/99	Foresta Falticeni	H	1-0	Balint
14/03/99	FC National Bucuresti	A	1-0	Males
17/03/99	Olimpia Satu Mare	H	2-0	Oprea 2
20/03/99	Astra Ploiesti	A	1-3	Tanase
03/04/99	Universitatea Craiova	H	4-0	Mihalache, Spirea, Tanase, Bastina
10/04/99	Universitatea Cluj	A	2-0	Tofan ?
17/04/99	FC Arges Dacia Pitesti	H	1-1	Nemtanu
21/04/99	FC Onesti	A	0-1	
25/04/99	Rapid Bucuresti	H	0-1	
01/05/99	CSM Resita	A	3-2	Cernat 2, Tanase
08/05/99	Steaua Bucuresti	H	2-0	Mihalache, Oprea (p)
12/05/99	FCM Bacau	A	0-1	
15/05/99	Petrolul Ploiesti	H	0-1	
22/05/99	Ceahlaul Piatra Neamt	A	1-1	Tanase
26/05/99	FC Farul Constanta	H	2-1	Gurita, Nita (p)
29/05/99	Gloria Bistrita	H	0-0	
12/06/99	Dinamo Bucuresti	A	1-2	Silian

PETROLUL PLOIESTI

CLUB DIRECTORY

Petrolul Ploiesti
str. Stadionului 26
2000 Ploiesti
tel - (044) 122258
Year of Formation - 1924
Director - Eugeniu Goicea
Coach - Ion Marin (99/00 - Virgil Dridea)
Stadium - Ilie Oana (20,000)

MAJOR HONOURS
League Championship - (3) 1958, 1959, 1966.
Domestic Cup - (2) 1963, 1995.

APPEARANCES 98/99

	P	Ap	(s)	Gls
Daniel Eugen BASTINA	M	16		2
Vasile BOLMANDÂR	M	1	(7)	
Nicolae CONSTANTIN	A	30		2
Laurentiu Dumitru COSTACHE	M	6	(13)	2
Daniel COSTESCU	A	25	(7)	7
Cristian CRACIUN	M	29	(1)	5
Marian GRAMA	M	9	(2)	1
Octavian GRIGORE	D	32		1
Mihai Iulian ILIE	G	1		
Marius Ionut IRIMESCU	M	16		4
Gheorghe MATEI	D	19	(5)	
Giani Liviu NEGOITA	M	17	(3)	1
Falemi N'GASSAN	D	25	(3)	2
Victor Mihai OANCEA	M	1	(5)	
Bogdan Mihai ONUT	D	33		12
Florin PANCOVICI	A	14	(16)	4
Florin Cristian PÂRVU	M	16		3
Florentin RADULESCU	G	33		
Marin ROSU	D	24	(6)	
Romeo Constantin STAN	M		(4)	
Dinu Marius TODORAN	M	9	(20)	2
Georgel Ciprian TOPORAN	M	1	(2)	
Cristian Nicolae VLAD	M	17	(5)	1

LEAGUE RESULTS 1998/99

01/08/98	Olimpia Satu Mare	A	0-3	
08/08/98	Astra Ploiesti	H	2-1	Bolmandâr, Bastina
15/08/98	Universitatea Craiova	A	0-2	
22/08/98	Universitatea Cluj	H	3-0	Onut 2, Costescu
30/08/98	FC Arges Dacia Pitesti	A	1-3	Costescu
12/09/98	FC Onesti	H	1-0	Costescu
20/09/98	Rapid Bucuresti	A	1-2	Todoran
27/09/98	CSM Resita	H	2-0	Negoita, Costache
03/10/98	Steaua Bucuresti	A	2-2	N'Gassan, Pancovici
17/10/98	FCM Bacau	H	1-1	Grama (p)
24/10/98	FC Farul Constanta	H	3-0	Costescu, Constantin, Onut (p)
31/10/98	Ceahlaul Piatra Neamt	A	3-1	Pancovici, Craciun, Bastina
07/11/98	Otelul Galati	H	2-0	Onut 2 (2p)
14/11/98	Gloria Bistrita	A	0-2	
21/11/98	Dinamo Bucuresti	H	2-3	Craciun, N'Gassan
28/11/98	Foresta Falticeni	A	2-1	Onut, Craciun
05/12/98	FC National Bucuresti	H	1-3	Todoran
06/03/99	Olimpia Satu Mare	H	0-0	
13/03/99	Astra Ploiesti	A	1-1	Costache
16/03/99	Universitatea Craiova	H	4-1	Pârvu 3, Irimescu
20/03/99	Universitatea Cluj	A	2-1	Onut 2 (1p)
03/04/99	FC Arges Dacia Pitesti	H	3-1	Irimescu, Onut, Craciun
10/04/99	FC Onesti	A	0-2	
17/04/99	Rapid Bucuresti	H	2-2	Constantin, Onut
21/04/99	CSM Resita	A	1-2	Craciun
24/04/99	Steaua Bucuresti	H	2-1	Costescu, Grigore
01/05/99	FCM Bacau	A	1-3	Vlad
08/05/99	FC Farul Constanta	A	0-1	
12/05/99	Ceahlaul Piatra Neamt	H	1-0	Irimescu
15/05/99	Otelul Galati	A	1-0	Onut
22/05/99	Gloria Bistrita	H	3-1	Pancovici, Onut, Costescu
26/05/99	Dinamo Bucuresti	A	1-3	Pancovici
29/05/99	Foresta Falticeni	H	2-1	Irimescu, Costescu
02/06/99	FC National Bucuresti	A	0-2	

RAPID BUCURESTI

CLUB DIRECTORY

Rapid Bucuresti
Calea Giulesti 18
78254 Bucuresti
tel - (01) 2200447/2202080
fax - (01) 2203215
Year of Formation - 1923
President - Dinu Gheorghe
Coach - Mircea Lucescu; Mircea Rednic;
Dumitru Dumitriu; Nicolae Manea; Mircea Lucescu
Stadium - Rapid (18,000)

MAJOR HONOURS
League Championship - (2) 1967, 1999.
Domestic Cup - (10) 1935, 1937, 1938, 1939,
1940, 1941, 1942, 1972, 1975, 1998.

APPEARANCES 98/99

		P	Ap	(s)	Gls
Bogdan Ioan ANDONE	D	9		(5)	
Constantin BARBU	A	11			8
Mugur Cristian BOLOHAN	D	21		(1)	1
Marius BRATU	G	3		(1)	
Narcis Mario BUGEANU	M	2			
Zeno Marius BUNDEA	M	15		(10)	6
Daniel CHIRITA	D			(3)	1
Cristian Alexandru DULCA	D	14			3
Ioan Viorel GANEA	A	15		(1)	11
Mihai Adrian IENCSI	D	24		(2)	3
Bogdan Ionut LOBONT	G	31			
Danut LUPU	M	28			5
Ovidiu MAIER	M	4		(18)	1
Marius MALDARASANU	M	27		(6)	4
Alin MINTEUAN	M			(4)	
Dorel MUTICA	M	15		(7)	4
Stefan Dumitru NANU	D	22		(1)	1
Radu Horia NICULESCU	A	8			2
Daniel Gabriel PANCU	M	26		(1)	6
Vasile Nicolae POPA	D	1			
Sergiu Marian RADU	A	3		(12)	2
RAT	M			(3)	
Mircea REDNIC	D	32			1
Ioan Ovidiu SABAU	M	21		(1)	1
Nicolae STANCIU	D	26		(2)	1
Marius Ninel SUMUDICA	A	12		(18)	17
Ionut VOICU	D	4		(1)	

LEAGUE RESULTS 1998/99

02/08/98	FC Arges Dacia Pitesti	A	1-0	Lupu
08/08/98	FC Onesti	H	6-0	Maldarasanu, Maier, Dulca,
				Sumudica 3
16/08/98	FC Farul Constanta	H	3-0	Pancu, Lupu (p), Maldarasanu
22/08/98	CSM Resita	A	2-1	Pancu 2
30/08/98	Steaua Bucuresti	H	3-0	Sumudica, Dulca, Radu
13/09/98	FCM Bacau	A	1-1	Sumudica
20/09/98	Petrolul Ploiesti	H	2-1	Pancu, Sumudica
26/09/98	Ceahlaul Piatra Neamt	A	2-0	Mutica, Bundea
04/10/98	Otelul Galati	H	3-0	Niculescu 2 (1p), og (Tofan)
17/10/98	Gloria Bistrita	A	4-2	Iencsi, Bundea, Mutica,
				Maldarasanu
25/10/98	Dinamo Bucuresti	H	1-4	Sumudica
31/10/98	Foresta Falticeni	A	1-0	Sumudica
07/11/98	FC National Bucuresti	H	5-0	Sumudica (p), Lupu 2 (1p),
				Dulca, Maldarasanu
14/11/98	Olimpia Satu Mare	A	1-1	Sumudica
21/11/98	Astra Ploiesti	H	1-0	Sumudica
29/11/98	Universitatea Craiova	A	1-0	Sumudica (p)
05/12/98	Universitatea Cluj	H	3-0	Sumudica (p), Nanu, Pancu
07/03/99	FC Arges Dacia Pitesti	H	2-0	Rednic, Barbu
13/03/99	FC Onesti	A	2-1	Barbu, Bundea
16/03/99	FC Farul Constanta	A	0-0	
20/03/99	CSM Resita	H	2-1	Ganea, Bundea
04/04/99	Steaua Bucuresti	A	1-1	Ganea
10/04/99	FCM Bacau	H	3-0	Barbu (p), Ganea, Sumudica
17/04/99	Petrolul Ploiesti	A	2-2	Stanciu, Ganea
21/04/99	Ceahlaul Piatra Neamt	H	4-0	Ganea 2, Bundea, Barbu
25/04/99	Otelul Galati	A	1-0	Mutica
01/05/99	Gloria Bistrita	H	5-0	Barbu 2, Ganea, Bolohan, Bundea
09/05/99	Dinamo Bucuresti	H	1-0	Pancu
12/05/99	Foresta Falticeni	H	2-0	Ganea, Mutica
15/05/99	FC National Bucuresti	A	3-1	Ganea, Iencsi, Lupu (p)
22/05/99	Olimpia Satu Mare	H	1-0	Ganea
26/05/99	Astra Ploiesti	A	5-1	Sumudica 3 (1p), Sabau, Radu
29/05/99	Universitatea Craiova	H	1-0	Iencsi
11/06/99	Universitatea Cluj	A	4-1	Ganea, Chirita, Barbu 2

CSM RESITA

CSM Resita
str. Valea Domanului 1
Resita
tel - (055) 210052
Year of Formation - 1926
President - Marius Popescu
Coach - Silviu Stanescu; Ioan Sdrobis; Aurel Sunda;
Victor Rosca (99/00 - Gabriel Stan)
Stadium - Valea Domanului (12,000)

APPEARANCES 98/99

	P	Ap	(s)	Gls
Claudiu BALACI	A	14	(8)	2
Mircea Liviu Ben BATRÂNU	D	22	(4)	
BENGA	M		(1)	
Vasile Valentin BOSCA	G	14		
Ovidiu BREHUI	M	14	(6)	
Florin Daniel CAPRARIU	D	19		
Vasile Sanshiro CIOCOI	M	16		4
Ion Valentin CIUCUR	M	15	(7)	1
Ciprian Virgil DIANU	M	15	(4)	1
Florin Felix DINCA	D	1		
Leontin DOANA	M	23	(1)	2
Lucian Mihail DOBRE	D	3	(3)	
Danut Eugen FRUNZA	A	9	(10)	1
Daniel Petru HUZA	M	1		
Ion IBRIC	D	24	(4)	
Daniel Florin JILAVU	A	11	(9)	3
Alexandru Stefan KOVACS	D	11	(9)	1
Nicu NASTASIE	D	6		
Constantin Doru NICA	M	18	(2)	1
Adrian Alexandru PAUNA	M		(1)	
Alexandru PELICI	D	13		
Gabriel PERSA	A	14	(4)	3
Lucian PITURNEA	M		(2)	
Florin Flavius POGACEAN	A	12	(2)	2
Gheorghe POPA	G	3	(1)	
Marius Nicolae PRISECEANU	M	7	(4)	1
David Stefan RADU	D	11	(4)	
Roco Rafael SANDU	D	6	(1)	
Alin Mircea SAVU	M	15	(6)	3
Iosif SZIJJ	A	23	(3)	5
Valentin STEFAN	M	11		1
Andrei URAI	G	17		
Dorin Bogdan ZOTINCA	D	6	(3)	1

LEAGUE RESULTS 1998/99

01/08/98	Universitatea Cluj	A	0-0	
07/08/98	FC Arges Dacia Pitesti	H	0-0	
15/08/98	FC Onesti	A	0-5	
22/08/98	Rapid Bucuresti	H	1-2	Ciocoi (p)
29/08/98	FC Farul Constanta	H	3-2	og (Macavei), Ciocoi, Balaci
12/09/98	Steaua Bucuresti	A	0-2	
19/09/98	FCM Bacau	H	0-0	
27/09/98	Petrolul Ploiesti	A	0-2	
03/10/98	Ceahlaul Piatra Neamt	H	2-2	og (Nitu), Jilavu
17/10/98	Otelul Galati	A	0-4	
24/10/98	Gloria Bistrita	H	2-0	Frunza, Nica
31/10/98	Dinamo Bucuresti	A	0-7	
07/11/98	Foresta Falticeni	H	1-1	Ciocoi
14/11/98	FC National Bucuresti	A	0-3	
21/11/98	Olimpia Satu Mare	H	1-1	Ciocoi
28/11/98	Astra Ploiesti	A	0-3	
05/12/98	Universitatea Craiova	H	3-2	Savu, Doana, Szijj
06/03/99	Universitatea Cluj	H	3-0	Szijj, Balaci, Pogacean
13/03/99	FC Arges Dacia Pitesti	A	0-1	
17/03/99	FC Onesti	H	0-2	
20/03/99	Rapid Bucuresti	A	1-2	Doana
03/04/99	FC Farul Constanta	A	0-0	
09/04/99	Steaua Bucuresti	H	2-2	Zotinca, Stefan
17/04/99	FCM Bacau	A	0-2	
21/04/99	Petrolul Ploiesti	H	2-1	Szijj, Persa
24/04/99	Ceahlaul Piatra Neamt	A	0-4	
01/05/99	Otelul Galati	H	2-3	Szijj (p), Pogacean
08/05/99	Gloria Bistrita	A	2-2	Jilavu, Persa
12/05/99	Dinamo Bucuresti	H	1-1	Szijj
15/05/99	Foresta Falticeni	A	0-0	
22/05/99	FC National Bucuresti	H	4-1	Savu, Priseceanu, Ciucur, Dianu
26/05/99	Olimpia Satu Mare	A	3-1	Persa, Savu, Kovacs
29/05/99	Astra Ploiesti	H	0-1	
02/06/99	Universitatea Craiova	A	1-0	Jilavu

STEAUA BUCURESTI

CLUB DIRECTORY

Steaua Bucuresti
bd. Ghencea 35, 76803 Bucuresti
tel - (01) 4103075/4102182
fax - (01) 4100179
Year of Formation - 1947
President - Constantin Danilescu
Coach - Mihai Stoichita; Emerich Jenei
Stadium - Steaua (30,000)

MAJOR HONOURS
League Championship - (20)
1951, 1952, 1953, 1956, 1960, 1961, 1968,
1976, 1978, 1985, 1986, 1987, 1988, 1989,
1993, 1994, 1995, 1996, 1997, 1998.
Domestic Cup - (21)
1949, 1950, 1951, 1952, 1955, 1962, 1966,
1967, 1969, 1970, 1971, 1976, 1979, 1985,
1987, 1988, 1989, 1992, 1996, 1997, 1999.
European Champions' Cup - (1) 1986.
European Super Cup - (1) 1986.

APPEARANCES 98/99

	P	Ap	(s)	Gls
Marius Achim BACIU	D	23	(2)	3
Miodrag BELODEDICI	D	27		2
Elton CENO (ALB)	A		(1)	
Cristian CIOCOIU	A	16	(3)	2
Marius Mihai COPORAN	M	2	(8)	
Tiberiu CSIK	D	3	(1)	
Ion Daniel DANCIULESCU	A	29	(4)	15
Ilie DUMITRESCU	M	7		3
Albert DURO (ALB)	D	9	(1)	
Ion Lavi HRIB	M		(3)	
Marius Mihai LAVATUS	A	25		4
Virgil LASCARACHE	A		(1)	
Erik Augustin LINCAR	M	29		4
Marius Sebastian LUCA	A	1	(23)	3
Ion Ionut LUTU	M	11	(6)	
Adrian MATEI	D	26		
Damian MILITARU	M	9	(13)	1
Ilie Iulian MIU	D	33		2
George OGARARU	D	4	(1)	
Valeriu RACHITA	D	10	(2)	1
Laurentiu Aurelian REGHECAMPF	D	8	(1)	1
Zoltan RITLI	G	18		
Laurentiu Dumitru ROSU	M	31	(1)	14
Gabriel ROTARU	G	3		
Mihaita Gabriel SZEKELY	M	12	(10)	2
Denis Georgian SERBAN	M	9		3
Alexandru Florin TENE	G	13		
Eugen TRICA	M	15	(6)	2
Alexandru ZOTINCA	D	1	(2)	

LEAGUE RESULTS 1998/99

02/08/98	Universitatea Craiova	A	2-2	Lacatus, Luca
07/08/98	Universitatea Cluj	H	4-0	Rosu, Rachita, Danciulescu, Serban
16/08/98	FC Arges Dacia Pitesti	A	2-3	Lacatus, Serban (p)
21/08/98	FC Onesti	H	4-1	Danciulescu 2, Serban, Rosu
30/08/98	Rapid Bucuresti	A	0-3	
12/09/98	CSM Resita	H	2-0	Reghecampf, Militaru
19/09/98	FC Farul Constanta	H	1-0	Belodedici
25/09/98	FCM Bacau	A	0-0	
03/10/98	Petrolul Ploiesti	H	2-2	Dumitrescu 2
17/10/98	Ceahlaul Piatra Neamt	A	3-0	Danciulescu 3
24/10/98	Otelul Galati	H	2-0	Danciulescu, Lacatus
01/11/98	Gloria Bistrita	A	1-2	Dumitrescu (p)
08/11/98	Dinamo Bucuresti	H	1-1	Danciulescu
14/11/98	Foresta Falticeni	A	2-1	Rosu, Lincar
22/11/98	FC National Bucuresti	H	1-0	Danciulescu (p)
28/11/98	Olimpia Satu Mare	A	3-0	Danciulescu, Trica, Szekely
05/12/98	Astra Ploiesti	H	1-0	Trica
06/03/99	Universitatea Craiova	H	2-0	Lincar, Rosu
13/03/99	Universitatea Cluj	A	2-0	Baciu, Rosu (p)
17/03/99	FC Arges Dacia Pitesti	H	1-2	Rosu
20/03/99	FC Onesti	A	3-2	Miu, Rosu 2 (1p)
04/04/99	Rapid Bucuresti	H	1-1	Lincar
09/04/99	CSM Resita	A	2-2	Rosu, Danciulescu
17/04/99	FC Farul Constanta	A	3-0	Lacatus, Danciulescu, Ciocoiu
20/04/99	FCM Bacau	H	2-1	Belodedici, Rosu
24/04/99	Petrolul Ploiesti	A	1-2	Rosu
01/05/99	Ceahlaul Piatra Neamt	H	3-2	Baciu, Rosu (p), Ciocoiu
08/05/99	Otelul Galati	A	0-2	
12/05/99	Gloria Bistrita	H	0-0	
15/05/99	Dinamo Bucuresti	A	0-0	
22/05/99	Foresta Falticeni	H	6-1	Miu, Danciulescu, Lincar, Luca 2, Rosu
26/05/99	FC National Bucuresti	A	1-0	Danciulescu
29/05/99	Olimpia Satu Mare	H	3-2	Rosu, Danciulescu, Baciu
06/06/99	Astra Ploiesti	A	1-1	Szekely

UNIVERSITATEA CLUJ

CLUB DIRECTORY

Universitatea Cluj
str. Pacii 1-3, 3400 Cluj
tel - (064) 195590   fax - (064) 191692
Year of Formation - 1919   President - Ion Maja
Coach - Tiberiu Poraczky; Dan Anca
Stadium - Ion Moina (28,000)

MAJOR HONOURS
Domestic Cup - (1) 1965.

APPEARANCES 98/99

	P	Ap	(s)	Gls
Laurean ASTILEAN	M	12	(3)	2
Catalin Ion BABA	A	1	(2)	
Claudiu BALAN	M		(2)	
Tiberiu Gabriel BALAN	A	4	(5)	
Dragos CARAMISIN	A		(2)	
Horatiu Daniel CIOLOBOC	M	22	(3)	3
Andrei CIUBOTARIU	M	1	(3)	
Mugurel Mircea DAN	D	9	(6)	1
Francisc DICAN	M	13		1
Cristian Teodor FEDOR	D	5	(2)	
Paul Horatiu GHENTI	M	10	(6)	
Zoltan Martin IASKO	G	5	(1)	
IGNAT	A	6	(2)	1
Vasile Ilie JULA	D	8		
Emil Gabriel JULA	M		(2)	
Robert Marius KILIN	M	2	(1)	
Andrei Vasile LAZAR	D	13		1
Florin LAZAREANU	G	1	(2)	
LONGA	M		(1)	
LUPSA	M	1		
Dan MATEI	D	7	(4)	
Laurentiu MÂNDRU	D	5	(6)	
Marius Ioan MÂRNE	G	12		
Liviu MIHAI	A	26		
Ioan Sebastian MOGA	M	3	(1)	
MONEA	D	3		
Calin NAGY	A		(2)	
Stefan Sorin ONCICA	M	24	(2)	1
Ioan PAP-DEAC	G	8	(1)	
Nicolae Sorin PETRE	G	8		
Daniel Catalin PETRESCU	A	3	(9)	
Marius PREDATU	A	13	(1)	5
Sever Claudiu SALAGEAN	M		(3)	
Claudiu Ovidiu SARMASAN	D	25	(4)	2
Florin SOCACIU	D	13	(2)	1
Dragos STROE	D	21	(1)	
SZILAGHI	M		(1)	
Valentin SANDRU	D	27	(1)	
Dacian TÂRNOVEAN	M	9	(1)	
Adrian Calin TRUSCA	D	27		
Catalin Tiberiu TIPLEA	M		(1)	
Liviu VELTAN	D	12	(2)	
Eugen VOICA	M	4	(1)	
Andrei Calin ZANC	M	11	(1)	1

LEAGUE RESULTS 1998/99

Date	Opponent	H/A	Score	Scorers
01/08/98	CSM Resita	H	0-0	
07/08/98	Steaua Bucuresti	A	0-4	
15/08/98	FCM Bacau	H	1-2	Sarmasan
22/08/98	Petrolul Ploiesti	A	0-3	
29/08/98	Ceahlaul Piatra Neamt	H	1-0	Zanc
12/09/98	Otelul Galati	A	0-5	
19/09/98	Gloria Bistrita	H	1-1	Cioloboc
26/09/98	Dinamo Bucuresti	A	0-8	
03/10/98	Foresta Falticeni	H	2-2	Predatu 2
17/10/98	FC National Bucuresti	A	1-3	Predatu (p)
24/10/98	Olimpia Satu Mare	H	1-0	Oncica
31/10/98	Astra Ploiesti	A	1-2	Cioloboc
07/11/98	Universitatea Craiova	H	1-2	Predatu (p)
14/11/98	FC Farul Constanta	H	1-3	Predatu
21/11/98	FC Arges Dacia Pitesti	A	0-3	
28/11/98	FC Onesti	H	0-2	
05/12/98	Rapid Bucuresti	A	0-3	
06/03/99	CSM Resita	A	0-3	
13/03/99	Steaua Bucuresti	H	0-2	
17/03/99	FCM Bacau	A	0-0	
20/03/99	Petrolul Ploiesti	H	1-2	Dican (p)
03/04/99	Ceahlaul Piatra Neamt	A	1-5	Dan M.
10/04/99	Otelul Galati	H	0-2	
16/04/99	Gloria Bistrita	A	0-4	
21/04/99	Dinamo Bucuresti	H	0-6	
24/04/99	Foresta Falticeni	A	0-1	
02/05/99	FC National Bucuresti	H	1-4	Sarmasan
07/05/99	Olimpia Satu Mare	A	1-0	Ignat
12/05/99	Astra Ploiesti	H	0-2	
15/05/99	Universitatea Craiova	A	1-4	Astilean
22/05/99	FC Farul Constanta	A	1-3	Socaciu
26/05/99	FC Arges Dacia Pitesti	H	2-1	Cioloboc, Lazar
29/05/99	FC Onesti	A	0-6	
11/06/99	Rapid Bucuresti	H	1-4	Astilean

UNIVERSITATEA CRAIOVA

CLUB DIRECTORY

Universitatea Craiova
str. Libertatii 9, 1100 Craiova
tel - (051) 132480   fax - (051) 115067
Year of Formation - 1948
President - George Ilinca
Coach - Ilie Balaci; Silviu Lung; Marian Bondrea
Stadium - Ion Oblemenco (35,000)

MAJOR HONOURS
League Championship - (4)
1974, 1980, 1981, 1991.
Domestic Cup - (7)
1977, 1978, 1981, 1983, 1991, 1993, 1994.

APPEARANCES 98/99

	P	Ap	(s)	Gls
Cosmin BARCAUAN	A	8	(4)	3
Augustin Eduard CHIRITA	M	6	(7)	
Daniel CHIRITA	D	14	(1)	
Cristian Eugen CHIVU	M	26		3
Ion Valentin CIUCUR	M	2	(1)	
Catalin Petre CRACIUNESCU	D	17	(5)	
Valentin Ion DAVID	G	2	(1)	
Robert Barna DANI	M	16	(4)	1
Viorel DOMOKOS	A	8		1
Gabriel DUMITRU	M	9	(5)	
Florin FABIAN	A	2	(6)	
FILIP	M	1		
Danut Cornel FRASINEANU	M	25	(1)	
GRIGORIE	M		(1)	
Ion Lavi HRIB	A	5	(6)	2
Florin Paul IONESCU	D	9	(2)	
Marius Sandu IORDACHE	D	12		
Tiberiu LUNG	G	31	(1)	
Ion Ionut LUTU	A	14	(3)	6
Dorian MICLAUS	D	8		
Narcis Lucian MOHORA	D	10	(7)	
NEAMTU	G	1		
Cristian Eugen NEGRU	A	7	(6)	1
Alin Gabriel NICOLA	M	1	(3)	
Claudiu Iulian NICULESCU	A	20	(8)	9
Corneliu PAPURA	M	14		1
ROTARU	M	1		
Marius SAVA	M	21	(6)	6
Emil SANDOI	D	28		2
SERBAN	D	1	(1)	
Flavius Vladimir STOICAN	D	10	(5)	
Valentin Octavian SUCIU	M	3	(8)	
Adrian Orlin TOADER	A	5	(6)	3
Eugen TRICA	M	10		2
Robert Dumitru VANCEA	M	27	(1)	

LEAGUE RESULTS 1998/99

02/08/98	Steaua Bucuresti	H	2-2	Lutu, Toader
08/08/98	FCM Bacau	A	0-2	
15/08/98	Petrolul Ploiesti	H	2-0	Trica, Niculescu
22/08/98	Ceahlaul Piatra Neamt	A	1-2	Chivu
29/08/98	Otelul Galati	H	0-1	
12/09/98	Gloria Bistrita	A	1-1	Lutu
20/09/98	Dinamo Bucuresti	H	2-2	Lutu, Chivu
26/09/98	Foresta Falticeni	A	2-1	Trica, Lutu
03/10/98	FC National Bucuresti	H	0-2	
18/10/98	Olimpia Satu Mare	A	1-1	Sandoi
24/10/98	Astra Ploiesti	H	0-0	
31/10/98	FC Farul Constanta	A	1-2	Niculescu
07/11/98	Universitatea Cluj	A	2-1	Toader, Lutu
15/11/98	FC Arges Dacia Pitesti	H	2-0	Lutu, og (Nastase)
21/11/98	FC Onesti	A	2-3	Toader, Niculescu
29/11/98	Rapid Bucuresti	H	0-1	
05/12/98	CSM Resita	A	2-3	Dani, Sava
06/03/99	Steaua Bucuresti	A	0-2	
13/03/99	FCM Bacau	H	0-1	
16/03/99	Petrolul Ploiesti	A	1-4	og (Matei)
20/03/99	Ceahlaul Piatra Neamt	H	2-1	Sandoi, Hrib
03/04/99	Otelul Galati	A	0-4	
10/04/99	Gloria Bistrita	H	2-1	Sava, Chivu
18/04/99	Dinamo Bucuresti	A	1-2	Negru
21/04/99	Foresta Falticeni	H	1-0	Niculescu
24/04/99	FC National Bucuresti	A	0-1	
01/05/99	Olimpia Satu Mare	H	5-1	og (Szabo), Sava, Barcauan 2, Papura
08/05/99	Astra Ploiesti	A	2-2	Sava (p), Niculescu
12/05/99	FC Farul Constanta	H	1-0	Sava (p)
15/05/99	Universitatea Cluj	H	4-1	Niculescu 2, Domokos, Barcauan
22/05/99	FC Arges Dacia Pitesti	A	0-2	
26/05/99	FC Onesti	H	4-2	Niculescu 2, Hrib, Sava
29/05/99	Rapid Bucuresti	A	0-1	
02/06/99	CSM Resita	H	0-1	

PROMOTED CLUBS

SECOND DIVISION FINAL TABLES 98/99

SERIA I

		Pd	W	D	L	F	A	Pt	GD
1	**FC Brasov**	34	21	8	5	64	22	71	+42
2	**Rocar Bucuresti**	34	22	3	9	69	35	69	+34
3	Cimentuk Fieni	34	17	7	10	53	33	58	+20
4	Politehnica Iasi	34	15	7	12	49	45	52	+4
5	Laminorul Roman	34	16	4	14	43	33	52	+10
6	AS Midia Navadari	34	14	8	12	53	34	50	+19
7	Poiana Câmpina	34	14	8	12	42	47	50	-5
8	Precizia Sacele	34	15	4	15	45	40	49	+5
9	Metrom Brasov	34	14	6	14	48	37	48	+11
10	Gloria Buzau	34	15	3	16	40	42	48	-2
11	Dunarea Galati	34	14	5	15	44	45	47	-1
12	Chindia Târgoviste	34	14	5	15	43	46	47	-3
13	Sportul Studentesc Bucuresti	34	13	8	13	38	33	47	+5
14	Tractorul Brasov	34	15	2	17	47	54	47	-7
15	Petrolul Moinesti	34	14	5	15	45	41	47	+4
16	Rulmentul Alexandria	34	13	5	16	39	30	44	+9
17	Nitramonia Fagaras	34	9	6	19	30	62	33	-32
18	Dacia Unirea Braila	34	2	4	28	12	125	10	-113

SERIA a II-a

		Pd	W	D	L	F	A	Pt	GD
1	**Extensiv Craiova**	34	22	5	7	83	32	71	+51
2	UT Arad	34	20	6	8	73	41	66	+32
3	ARO Câmpulung	34	18	4	12	64	49	58	+15
4	Gaz Metian Medias	34	16	5	13	58	51	53	+7
5	Politehnica Timisoara	34	16	4	14	60	41	52	+19
6	FC Bihor Oradea	34	15	6	13	43	46	51	-3
7	ASA Tirgu Mures	34	16	2	16	47	48	50	-1
8	Chimica Târnaveni	34	14	5	15	39	51	47	-12
9	Minerul Motru	34	14	4	16	47	55	46	-8
10	Corvinul Hunedoara	34	14	4	16	52	59	46	-7
11	Inter Sibiu	34	14	3	17	50	49	45	+1
12	FC Drobeta Turnu-Severin	34	13	6	15	48	52	45	-4
13	Dacia Pitesti	34	13	5	16	50	56	44	-6
14	Apulum Alba Iulia	34	13	4	17	42	55	43	-13
15	Jiul Petrosani	34	13	4	17	38	55	43	-17
16	Vega Deva	34	12	5	17	35	66	41	-31
17	FC Baia Mare	34	11	6	17	45	53	39	-8
18	Unirea Dej	34	11	4	19	46	61	37	-15

PROMOTION PLAY-OFF
Rocar Bucuresti 2, UT Arad 0

CLUB DIRECTORY

Fotbal Club Brasov
str. Mihai Viteazul 168
2200 Brasov
Year of Formation - 1939
Coach - Cornel Talnar (99/00 - Ioan Andonie)
Stadium - Tineretului (15,000)

CLUB DIRECTORY

FC Extensiv Craiova
str. Stadionului nr.1
1100 Craiova
Year of Formation - 1949
Coach - Marian Bondrea; Grigore Sichitu
(99/00 - Sorin Cirtu)
Stadium - Electroputere (10,000)

CLUB DIRECTORY

Rocar Bucuresti
str. Drumul Gazarului-Ostrov nr.3
Year of Formation - 1953
President - Gheorghe Netoiu
Coach - Ion Dumitru; Silviu Dumitrescu
Stadium - Rocar (10,000)

RUSSIA

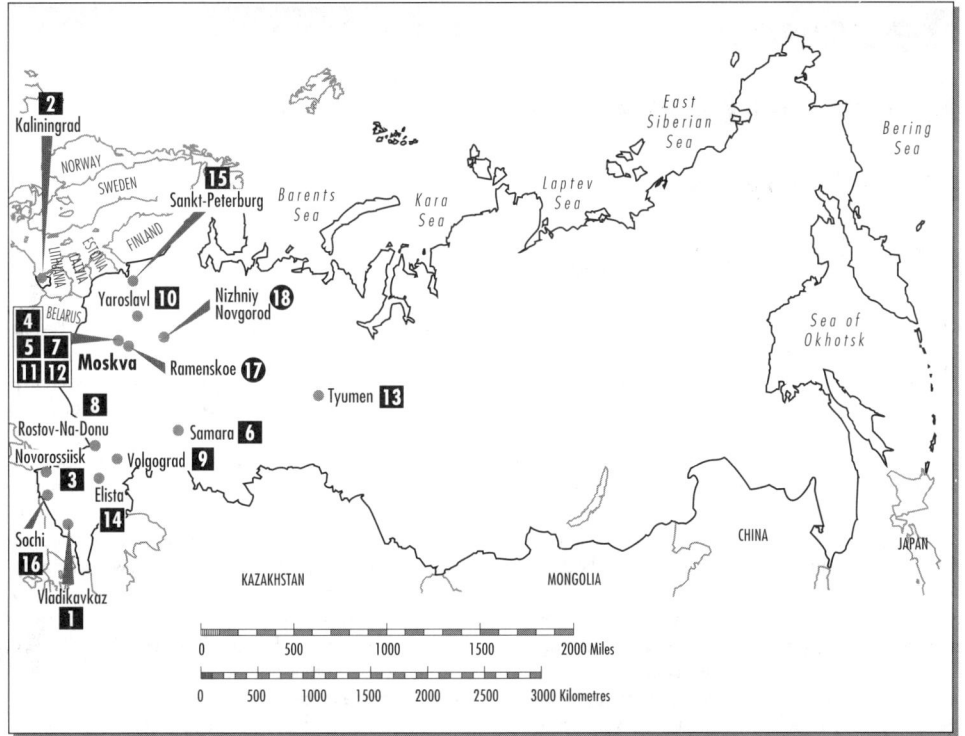

1	ALANIA VLADIKAVKAZ	838	11	SPARTAK MOSKVA	848
2	BALTIKA KALININGRAD	839	12	TORPEDO MOSKVA	849
3	CHERNOMORETS NOVOROSSIISK	840	13	FK TYUMEN	850
4	CSKA MOSKVA	841	14	URALAN ELISTA	851
5	DINAMO MOSKVA	842	15	ZENIT SANKT-PETERBURG	852
6	KRYLYA SOVETOV SAMARA	843	16	ZHEMCHUZHINA SOCHI	853
7	LOKOMOTIV MOSKVA	844	**Promoted clubs**	
8	ROSTSELMASH ROSTOV-NA-DONU	845	17	SATURN RAMENSKOE	854
9	ROTOR VOLGOGRAD	846	18	LOKOMOTIV NIZHNIY NOVGOROD	854
10	SHINNIK YAROSLAVL	847		

PARIS WIN REVIVES EURO 2000 HOPES

Rescuer Romantsev returns to centre stage

FEDERATION DIRECTORY

Russian Football Union
Luzhnetskaja Naberezhnaja 8, 119 270 Moskva

tel - (095) 2010834
fax - (095) 2011303

Year of Formation - 1991
President - Dr. Viacheslav Koloskov
Secretary - Vladimir Radionov

Stadium - Luzhniki, Moskva (96,000)

Where would Russian football be without Oleg Romantsev? The Spartak Moscow supremo returned in January 1999 to a national team in deep crisis. His mission impossible - and, surprisingly, he did choose to accept it - was to rescue a European Championship qualifying campaign that had begun with three straight defeats - away to Ukraine, at home to France, and away to Iceland - and was apparently going nowhere.

The appointment of Anatoliy Byshovets as the replacement national team coach for Boris Ignatyev had clearly been a disaster. With Byshovets in charge Russia not only suffered those three Euro 2000 setbacks but also ended up losers in three additional friendly internationals, against Sweden, Spain and Brazil. With six defeats in as many matches - an all-time low for Russia (and the USSR before them) - Byshovets could not hope to survive. In fact, the only surprise was that the push preceded the inevitable jump, with Russian Federation president Vyacheslav Koloskov, newly re-elected for a further five-year term,

putting him out of his misery a couple of days before Christmas and appointing Romantsev in his place.

To many, Romantsev was seen as a safe, conservative choice. He had done the job before (at Euro '96) and was widely respected by the players, especially those - and there were many - who had passed through his hands at one time or another at Spartak. Past differences meant that he ditched some of the Byshovets loyalists like Kanchelskis, Kharin and Kiryakov. But few questioned his selection policy after Russia got their Euro 2000 show back on the road with big wins against Armenia and Andorra. And there were no dissenters at all when the team went on to shock world champions France with a sensational 3-2 win in Paris, followed four days later by yet another crucial victory at home to Iceland.

What Romantsev had done was extraordinary. He had totally transformed the team's fortunes, reversing the earlier scorelines against France and Iceland and putting the team firmly back in the frame for at least a play-off

LEAGUE CHAMPIONSHIP RESULTS 1998

		1	2	3	4	5	6	7	8	9	10	11	12	13	14	15	16
1	Alania Vladikavkaz		2-0	3-1	0-1	2-2	5-0	1-2	0-1	3-1	1-2	2-1	0-2	6-0	1-0	0-0	3-0
2	Baltika Kaliningrad	1-3		1-0	1-1	0-2	1-1	0-3	3-0	2-2	3-1	1-1	0-0	2-0	1-1	3-2	2-1
3	Chernomorets Novorossiisk	1-2	2-1		1-1	1-1	4-0	1-1	1-1	2-1	3-1	1-1	4-1	2-0	0-0	0-0	
4	CSKA Moskva	0-0	2-0	4-1		1-1	3-0	0-1	1-0	2-0	0-1	4-1	1-3	3-1	3-0	1-2	3-0
5	Dinamo Moskva	4-1	1-1	0-0	0-3		1-1	2-1	1-2	2-2	1-1	0-0	0-0	1-0	0-3	0-0	4-1
6	Krylya Sovetov Samara	2-2	0-0	3-0	0-2	1-0		1-3	1-0	0-0	1-0	0-2	2-0	1-0	2-0	1-2	0-0
7	Lokomotiv Moskva	0-0	2-0	1-1	2-1	1-0	1-0		1-1	0-0	0-2	2-0	4-0	3-1	3-1	4-3	
8	Rostselmash Rostov-na-Donu	1-0	0-1	3-2	1-0	0-0	3-0	2-2		2-2	3-2	3-3	2-3	4-0	0-0	1-1	2-0
9	Rotor Volgograd	1-1	1-1	3-0	0-0	0-0	2-1	3-2	5-1		6-2	1-2	1-0	5-1	3-1	2-1	0-0
10	Shinnik Yaroslavl	3-2	3-1	0-0	1-2	0-2	0-0	0-1	0-0	2-0		0-1	1-0	3-2	0-0	0-0	1-2
11	Spartak Moskva	3-1	3-0	1-0	2-1	2-0	2-2	2-0	1-1	3-1	3-1		1-0	7-0	1-0	0-0	1-1
12	Torpedo Moskva	2-0	0-0	2-3	0-2	2-2	1-0	0-0	3-1	2-2	0-1	1-1		5-1	1-1	1-3	0-1
13	FK Tyumen	0-2	3-2	0-3	0-4	2-0	0-3	0-2	1-4	2-4	0-1	0-6	1-2		1-3	0-5	0-1
14	Uralan Elista	3-3	2-1	1-1	1-2	0-1	1-0	1-0	1-3	2-1	2-1	1-0	3-2	2-1		0-3	2-0
15	Zenit Sankt-Peterburg	2-0	2-2	0-1	0-1	1-1	2-0	2-2	3-0	0-1	3-0	2-1	1-1	0-0	2-1		1-0
16	Zhemchuzhina Sochi	3-0	2-1	3-1	2-1	1-2	0-2	2-0	0-0	1-1	2-2	1-4	0-4	0-0	2-6	2-1	

LEAGUE CHAMPIONSHIP FINAL TABLE 1998

			Home				Away					Total						
		P	W	D	L	F	A	W	D	L	F	A	W	D	L	F	A	P	GD
1	Spartak Moskva	30	11	4	0	32	8	6	4	5	26	19	17	8	5	58	27	59	+31
2	CSKA Moskva	30	9	2	4	28	11	8	3	4	22	11	17	5	8	50	22	56	+28
3	Lokomotiv Moskva	30	9	4	2	24	11	7	3	5	21	17	16	7	7	45	28	55	+17
4	Rotor Volgograd	30	9	5	1	33	13	3	7	5	19	24	12	12	6	52	37	48	+15
5	Zenit Sankt-Peterburg	30	7	5	3	21	11	5	6	4	21	14	12	11	7	42	25	47	+17
6	Rostselmash Rostov-na-Donu	30	7	6	2	27	16	4	5	6	15	22	11	11	8	42	38	44	+4
7	Uralan Elista	30	9	2	4	22	19	3	4	8	17	22	12	6	12	39	41	42	-2
8	Alania Vladikavkaz	30	8	2	5	29	13	3	5	7	17	26	11	7	12	46	39	40	+7
9	Dinamo Moskva	30	4	8	3	17	16	4	7	4	14	14	8	15	7	31	30	39	+1
10	Chernomorets Novorossiisk	30	6	7	2	24	13	3	4	8	14	25	9	11	10	38	38	38	0
11	Torpedo Moskva	30	4	6	5	20	18	5	4	6	18	16	9	10	11	38	34	37	+4
12	Krylya Sovetov Samara	30	7	4	4	15	11	2	4	9	10	26	9	8	13	25	37	35	-12
13	Zhemchuzhina Sochi	30	6	4	5	21	25	3	4	8	10	23	9	8	13	31	48	35	-17
14	Shinnik Yaroslavl	30	5	5	5	14	13	4	3	8	16	27	9	8	13	30	40	35	-10
15	Baltika Kaliningrad	30	6	5	3	20	17	1	6	9	12	26	7	11	12	32	43	32	-11
16	FK Tyumen	30	2	0	13	10	42	0	2	13	7	47	2	2	26	17	89	8	-72

N.B. Where two or more teams are level on points, classification is determined by the number of victories, then by the results of the matches between them.

place when they had previously seemed dead and buried. The Russians now had the summer to brace themselves for a dramatic date with destiny at home to Ukraine in early-October...

Of course, the players deserved credit for the revival, too, especially Valeriy Karpin, who scored the winning goals against both France and Iceland, and striker Aleksandr Panov, who bagged a brilliant brace in the Stade de France just a week or so after another of his double-strikes had helped Zenit St. Petersburg to victory in the Russian Cup final against Dinamo Moscow.

Zenit's Cup triumph brought the club their first major honour since the 1984 Soviet championship and it led to long and loud celebrations in Russia's second city. A return to European competition, in the UEFA Cup, was an additional reward for the club which had finished a respectable fifth in the 1998 Russian championship.

As expected, the title was won, for the sixth time in seven years, by Spartak Moscow. Oleg Romantsev's team were once again just that little bit too strong for the opposition. In 1996 and 1997 they had been taken all the way, first by Alania Vladikavkaz, then by Rotor Vologrod, but in 1998 they were able to celebrate victory comparatively early, thanks to a 3-1 victory over Shinnik Yaroslavl in the penultimate round.

The league had been reduced in size from 18 teams to 16, and with Russia having failed to qualify for the World Cup finals in France, Spartak had a fairly relaxed

schedule. But in the early weeks of the campaign they appeared to take things far too easy. A succession of sloppy displays away from home left them stuck in mid-table after the first few rounds. But the advent of summer sparked them into life, and with a run of ten victories and two draws in 12 matches from late June to early August, they managed to put themselves firmly in command at the top of the table before the priority bookings of the Champions' League came around.

Having missed out on the group phase of the Champions' League a year earlier (but gone on to reach the semi-finals of the UEFA Cup by way of consolation), Spartak were determined not to make the same mistake again. Their strong domestic form evidently fuelled the players with confidence as they absolutely annihilated Bulgarian champions Liteks Lovech, winning 5-0 away and 6-2 at home, to earn themselves a re-entry ticket to European football's promised land.

The hard bit was to come, however, as Spartak found themselves drawn in a group which contained not only holders Real Madrid but also Italian giants Inter, who

INTERNATIONAL HONOURS

World Cup Finals appearances: 1994
European Championship appearances: 1996

TOP SCORERS

22	Oleg VERETENNIKOV (Rotor Volgograd)
14	Giorgi DEMETRADZE (Alania Vladikavkaz)
	Yuriy ATVEYEV
	(Rostselmash Rostov-na-Donu)
	Vladimir KULIK (CSKA Moskva)
12	Oleg TERYOKHIN (Dinamo Moskva)
11	Valeriy YESIPOV (Rotor Volgograd)
10	Ilya TSYMBALAR (Spartak Moskva)
9	Viktor BULATOV (Torpedo Moskva)
	Yevgeniy DURNEV (Uralan Elista)
	Vyacheslav GERASCHENKO
	(Chornomorets Novorossiisk)
	Sergei SEMAK (CSKA Moskva)

NATIONAL TEAM RESULTS 98/99

Date	Opponent		Venue	Score	Scorers
19/08/98	Sweden	A	Örebro	0-1	
05/09/98	Ukraine (ECQ)	A	Kiev	2-3	Varlamov (66), Onopko (87)
23/09/98	Spain	A	Granada	0-1	
10/10/98	France (ECQ)	H	Moscow	2-3	Yanovskiy (45), Mostovoi (55)
14/10/98	Iceland (ECQ)	A	Reykjavik	0-1	
18/11/98	Brazil	A	Fortaleza	1-5	Kornaukhov (66p)
27/03/99	Armenia (ECQ)	A	Yerevan	3-0	Karpin (7, 63p), Beschastnykh (89)
31/03/99	Andorra (ECQ)	H	Moscow	6-1	Titov (8), Beschastnykh (12, 62), Onopko (43),
					Tsymbalar (50), Alenichev (90)
19/05/99	Belarus	H	Tula	1-1	Mostovoi (31)
05/06/99	France (ECQ)	A	Saint-Denis	3-2	Panov (38, 75), Karpin (86)
09/06/99	Iceland (ECQ)	H	Moscow	1-0	Karpin (44)

earlier in the year had eliminated them from the UEFA Cup. Reaching the quarter-finals seemed an unlikely target for Romantsev and his players, but they made a wonderful start, winning away to Sturm Graz and then memorably coming from behind to beat Real 2-1 at home. The team's goalscorers in both of those matches were midfielders Yegor Titov and Ilya Tsymbalar, the two outstanding individuals in the Spartak side over the course of the season.

Defeated by Inter in the San Siro, Spartak were within a minute of gaining their revenge with a crucial 1-0 win in the Luzhniki when Argentinian midfielder Diego

Simeone headed in a last-gasp equaliser. That goal marked the beginning of the end of Spartak's challenge, with a goalless draw at home to Sturm and a 1-2 defeat away to Real ending their campaign in a rather untidy and dispirited fashion.

In the midst of all the Champions' League excitement Spartak duly collected their domestic crown, but they were certainly not the strongest team in Russia over the closing weeks of the season. That honour went emphatically to city rivals CSKA, who were totally transformed by the

DOMESTIC CUP 98/99

1/16 FINALS
Torpedo-ZIL Moskva 0, Dinamo Moskva 7
Avtodor Vladikavkaz 2, Krylya Sovetov Samara 1
Druzhba Maikop 1, Rotor Volgograd 3
Arsenal Tula 1, Torpedo Moskva 0
Metallurg Lipetsk 2, Lokomotiv Moskva 2
(aet; 4-3 on pens.)
Dinamo Sankt-Peterburg 0, Alania Vladikavkaz 1
Saturn Ramenskoe 1, Chernomorets Novorossiisk 0
Spartak-Orekhovo Orekhovo-Zuevo 3, FK Tyumen 0
Energetic Uren 1, Zhemchuzhina Sochi 2
Sokol Saratov 2, Zenit Sankt-Peterburg 2
(aet; 1-4 on pens.)
Lada-Grad Dimitrovgrad 0, Rostselmash Rostov-na-Donu 1
Amkar Perm 1, Spartak Moskva 0
Amur-Energia Blagoveschensk 0, CSKA Moskva 2
Tom Tomsk 1, Uralan Elista 0
Chkalovets Novosibirsk 0, Shinnik Yaroslavl 0
(aet; 2-4 on pens.)
Nosta Novotroitsk 2, Baltika Kaliningrad 1

1/8 FINALS
Rotor Volgograd 3, Avtodor Vladikavkaz 3
(aet; 4-2 on pens.)
Arsenal Tula 4, Metallurg Lipetsk 1
Dinamo Moskva 1, Alania Vladikavkaz 0
Spartak-Orekhovo Orekhovo-Zuevo 0, Saturn
Ramenskoe 0 (aet; 2-4 on pens.)
CSKA Moskva 2, Tom Tomsk 1
Shinnik Yaroslavl 2, Nosta Novotroitsk 1 (aet)
Zhemchuzhina Sochi 1, Zenit Sankt-Peterburg 4
Rostselmash Rostov-na-Donu 1, Amkar Perm 0

QUARTER-FINALS
Rotor Volgograd 4
(Yesipov 5, Zubko 67, 89, Veretennikov 75),
Arsenal Tula 1 (Prizetko 86)
Dinamo Moskva 1 (Romaschenko 100),
Saturn Ramenskoe 0 (aet)
Zenit Sankt-Peterburg 2 (Zazulin 36, Popovich 43),
Rostselmash Rostov-na-Donu 0
CSKA Moskva 1 (Varlamov), Shinnik Yaroslavl 0

SEMI-FINALS
Rotor Volgograd 2 (Zernov 15, Zubko 56),
Dinamo Moskva 2 (Gusev 29, Klyuev 50)
(aet; 6-7 on pens.)
Zenit Sankt-Peterburg 1 (Popovich 77), CSKA Moskva 0

FINAL
26/05/99, Moscow
ZENIT SANKT-PETERBURG 3 Panov (57, 59),
Maximyuk (65)
DINAMO MOSKVA 1 Pisarev (26)
referee - Frolov
ZENIT SANKT-PETERBURG - Berezovskiy; Babiy,
Kondrashov, Ovsepyan, Igonin, Vernidub, Lepyokhin,
Gorshkov, Popovich (Zazulin 69), Maximyuk
(Kobelev 76), Panov.
DINAMO MOSKVA - Plotnikov; Klyuev, Ostrovskiy,
Tochilin, Golovskoi, Radimov, Grishin (Izibor 63),
Gusev, Pisarev (Kulchiy 53), Romaschenko, Teryokhin.

NATIONAL TEAM APPEARANCES 98/99

Coach - Anatoliy BYSHOVETS; Oleg ROMANTSEV	SWE	UKR	ESP	FRA	ISL	BRA	ARM	AND	BLS	FRA	ISL	Cps	Gls
Aleksandr FILIMONOV (15/10/73) - Spartak Moskva	G46						G	G		G	G	8	-
Igor DOBROVOLSKIY (27/08/67) - Fortuna Düsseldorf (GER)	D											18	2
Dmitriy KHLESTOV (21/01/71) - Spartak Moskva	D71		D	D			D	D	D	D	D	35	-
Yuriy KOVTUN (05/01/70) - Dinamo Moskva	D	D			D							31	1
Viktor ONOPKO (14/10/69) - Real Oviedo (ESP)	M	M	M	D	D		D	D	D	D	D	68	4
Igor YANOVSKIY (03/08/74) - Paris Saint-Germain (FRA)	M46	M		D	D		D		D65		s56	22	1
Andrei KANCHELSKIS (23/01/69) - Rangers (SCO)	M65	M70										36	5
Valeriy KARPIN (02/02/69) - RC Celta (ESP)	M46	s70	M	M	M59		M	M	M	M	M	47	13
Igor SHALIMOV (02/02/69) - Napoli (ITA)	M52					M						24	3
Aleksandr MOSTOVOI (22/08/68) - RC Celta (ESP)	M	s64	M	M	M				M75	M26		29	8
Sergei YURAN (11/06/69) - VfL Bochum (GER)/Spartak Moskva	A46						A84		s46			25	5
Dmitriy KHARIN (16/08/68) - Chelsea (ENG)	s46	G										23	-
Aleksandr SHMARKO (12/03/69) - Rotor Volgograd	s46		s46									2	-
Sergei SEMAK (27/02/75) - CSKA Moskva	s46	M74	M73	s70		M				M60	M46	12	-
Dmitriy ALENICHEV (20/10/72) - Roma (ITA)	s46	M64		M70			M65	M				22	4
Dmitriy KHOKHLOV (22/12/75) - PSV (HOL)	s52				s59			s84	s75	s26	M	14	-
Sergei KIRYAKOV (10/01/70) - Hamburger SV (GER)	s65		A80									28	10
Yuriy NIKIFOROV (16/09/70) - PSV (HOL)	s71											40	6
Igor CHUGAINOV (06/04/70) - Lokomotiv Moskva		D										15	-
Valeriy MINKO (08/08/71) - CSKA Moskva		D	D46									4	-
Yevgeniy VARLAMOV (25/07/75) - CSKA Moskva		D	D56	D	D	D			s65	D	D56	35	1
Igor KOLYVANOV (06/03/68) - Bologna (ITA)		A										35	12
Stanislav CHERCHESOV (02/09/63) - FC Tirol Innsbruck (AUT)		s74							G46			38	-
Sergei OVCHINNIKOV (11/10/70) - SL Benfica (POR)			G	G					s46			18	-
Valeriy YESIPOV (04/10/71) - Rotor Volgograd			M			M52						4	-
Vladimir BESCHASTNYKH (01/04/74) - Racing Santander (ESP)			A60	A60			s46	A	A46	s60	A72	38	12
Artyom YENIN (06/08/76) - Shinnik Yaroslavl		s56										1	-
Oleg TERYOKHIN (12/08/70) - Dinamo Moskva		s60										1	-
Vladislav RADIMOV (26/11/75) - Real Zaragoza (ESP)		s73										24	2
Dmitriy CHERYSHEV (11/05/69) - Sporting Gijón (ESP)		s80										9	1
Yegor TITOV (29/05/76) - Spartak Moskva					M	M	M	M	M	M		6	1
Andrei TIKHONOV (16/10/70) - Spartak Moskva					M	M13	s65	s46	M	M72	M	21	1
Aleksei GERASIMENKO (17/12/70) - Dynamo Kyiv (UKR)							s60					7	1
Aleksei SMERTIN (01/05/75) - Uralan Elista/Lokomotiv Moskva						M	M50	M	D80	M	M	6	-
Aleksei IGONIN (18/03/76) - Zenit Sankt-Peterburg					s13	D						2	-
Andrei NOVOSADOV (27/03/72) - CSKA Moskva						G60						1	-
Ramiz MAMEDOV (21/08/72) - Arsenal Tula						D						10	-
Sergei NEKRASOV (29/01/73) - Dinamo Moskva						D						1	-
Andrei SOLOMATIN (09/09/75) - Lokomotiv Moskva						M32						1	-
Sergei KORMILTSEV (22/01/74) - Uralan Elista						M38						1	-
Sergei FILIPPENKOV (02/08/71) - CSKA Moskva						A46						1	-
Oleg KORNAUKHOV (14/01/75) - CSKA Moskva						s32						1	1
Aleksei BAKHAREV (12/10/76) - Rotor Volgograd						s38						1	-
Viktor BULATOV (22/01/72) - Torpedo Moskva						s46			s80		s46	3	-
Andrei KONDRASHOV (07/08/72) - Zenit Sankt-Peterburg						s50						1	-
Aleksandr PANOV (21/09/75) - Zenit Sankt-Peterburg						s52	A46		A46	A	A	5	2
Andrei CHICHKIN (12/10/71) - Rotor Volgograd						s60						1	-
Yuriy DROZDOV (16/01/72) - Lokomotiv Moskva									D			1	-
Ilya TSYMBALAR (17/06/69) - Spartak Moskva							M	M	s46	s72	s72	28	4
Vadim YEVSEYEV (08/01/76) - Spartak Moskva							D46					1	-
Aleksandr SHIRKO (24/11/76) - Spartak Moskva							A					1	-

EUROPEAN CUPS 98/99

CHAMPIONS' CUP
● SPARTAK MOSKVA
Qualifying round LITEKS LOVECH (BUL)
A 5-0 Pisarev (55, 86), Titov (67), Samarone (77), Tsymbalar (90)
Filimonov; Parfyonov, Khlestov, Ananko, Bushmanov, Baranov, Titov,
Tsymbalar, Shirko (Samarone 62), Pisarev, Tikhonov.
H 6-2 Tikhonov (8, 32), Titov (37), Tsymbalar (49), Robson (56, 90)
Filimonov; Gorlukovich, Parfyonov, Tsymbalar, Bushmanov, Ananko,
Pisarev (Samarone 58), Baranov, Titov, Shirko (Robson 54), Tikhonov.

Champions' League
1st match SK STURM GRAZ (AUT)
A 2-0 Titov (60), Tsymbalar (63)
Filimonov; Parfyonov, Khlestov, Tsymbalar, Bushmanov, Ananko, Baranov,
Pisarev (Samarone 77), Titov, Shirko (Kanischev 46), Tikhonov.

2nd match REAL MADRID (ESP)
H 2-1 Tsymbalar (72), Titov (77)
Filimonov; Parfyonov, Khlestov, Tsymbalar, Bushmanov, Ananko, Baranov,
Pisarev (Kanischev 67), Titov, Robson (Buznikin 90), Tikhonov.

3rd match INTER (ITA)
A 1-2 Tsymbalar (65)
Filimonov; Parfyonov, Khlestov, Tsymbalar, Bushmanov, Ananko, Baranov
(Melyoshin 80), Romaschenko, Robson, Pisarev (Kanischev 66), Tikhonov.

4th match INTER (ITA)
H 1-1 Tikhonov (68)
Filimonov; Parfyonov, Romaschenko, Tsymbalar, Bushmanov, Ananko,
Baranov (Melyoshin 63), Buznikin (Pisarev 46), Titov, Robson, Tikhonov.

5th match SK STURM GRAZ (AUT)
H 0-0
Filimonov; Gorlukovich, Khlestov, Tsymbalar, Bushmanov, Ananko, Baranov,
Tikhonov, Titov, Shirko (Buznikin 70), Robson (Kanischev 57).

6th match REAL MADRID (ESP)
A 1-2 Khlestov (89)
Filimonov; Parfyonov, Khlestov, Tsymbalar, Bushmanov, Ananko, Baranov,
Robson (Kanischev 75), Titov, Shirko, Tikhonov.

CUP WINNERS' CUP
● LOKOMOTIV MOSKVA
1st round CSKA KYIV (UKR)
A 2-0 Kharlachyov (24), Janashia (51)
Nigmatullin; Pashinin, Drozdov, Kharlachyov, Lavrik, Chugainov, Solomatin,
Gurenko, Janashia (Bulykin 90), Borodyuk (Garas 80), Arifullin.
H 3-1 Bulykin (19, 51), Janashia (69)
Nigmatullin; Arifullin (Cherevchenko 74), Drozdov (Loskov 57),
Kharlachyov, Lavrik, Chugainov, Solomatin, Gurenko, Janashia, Borodyuk,
Bulykin (Pashinin).

2nd round SC BRAGA (POR)
H 3-1 Bulykin (22, 35), Chugainov (60p)
Nigmatullin; Cherevchenko, Drozdov, Kharlachyov (Sarkisyan 81),
Solomatin, Chugainov, Borodyuk, Gurenko, Janashia, Loskov (Lavrik 90),
Bulykin.
A 0-1
Nigmatullin; Cherevchenko, Drozdov (Lavrik 32), Kharlachyov
(Sarkisyan 64), Solomatin, Chugainov, Borodyuk, Gurenko, Janashia
(Arifullin 89), Loskov, Bulykin.

Quarter-final MACCABI HAIFA (ISR)
H 3-0 Janashia (44, 77, 89)
Nigmatullin; Arifullin (Cherevchenko 35), Chugainov, Drozdov, Sarkisyan
(Kharlachyov 60), Solomatin (Lavrik 43), Smertin, Gurenko, Janashia,
Loskov, Bulykin.
A 1-0 Chugainov (72p)
Nigmatullin; Arifullin, Chugainov, Drozdov, Maminov (Sarkisyan 81), Lavrik,
Smertin, Gurenko, Janashia, Loskov (Kharlachyov 46), Bulykin (Borodyuk 68).

Semi-final LAZIO (ITA)
H 1-1 Janashia (60)
Nigmatullin; Arifullin, Drozdov, Kharlachyov (Maminov 83), Cherevchenko,
Chugainov, Smertin (Loskov 46), Gurenko, Janashia, Lavrik, Bulykin
(Borodyuk 83).
A 0-0
Nigmatullin; Arifullin, Cherevchenko, Lavrik, Chugainov, Kharlachyov
(Maminov 66; Borodyuk 83), Smertin, Gurenko, Janashia, Loskov, Bulykin.

UEFA CUP
● DINAMO MOSKVA
Qualifying round POLONIA WARSZAWA (POL)
A 1-0 Gusev (54)
Kramarenko; Yakhimovich, Korablyov (Semberas 86), Ostrovskiy,
Shtanyuk, Kobelev (Golovskoi 59), Gusev, Romaschenko, Nekrasov, Isibor,
Danilevicius.
H 1-0 Teryokhin (90)
Tyapushkin; Yakhimovich, Korablyov (Golovskoi 46), Ostrovskiy, Shtanyuk,
Kobelev (Skokov 90), Gusev, Romaschenko, Nekrasov, Danilevicius
(Kulchiy 60), Teryokhin.

1st round SKONTO RIGA (LAT)
H 2-2 Golovskoi (2), Ostrovskiy (69)
Tyapushkin; Yakhimovich, Kovtun (Ostrovskiy 46), Golovskoi, Shtanyuk,
Kobelev, Gusev, Romaschenko (Skokov 35; Danilevicius 76), Nekrasov,
Isibor, Teryokhin.
A 3-2 Gusev (17), Golovskoi (51), Teryokhin (76)
Tyapushkin; Golovskoi (Semberas 82), Kovtun, Ostrovskiy, Shtanyuk,
Kobelev, Grishin (Tochilin 75), Gusev, Nekrasov, Danilevicius
(Romaschenko 64), Teryokhin.

2nd round REAL SOCIEDAD (ESP)
H 2-3 Nekrasov (72, 73)
Tyapushkin (Kramarenko 16); Yakhimovich, Kovtun, Semberas
(Romaschenko 79), Shtanyuk, Kobelev, Grishin, Gusev, Nekrasov,
Danilevicius (Isibor 46), Teryokhin.
A 0-3
Tyapushkin; Yakhimovich (Tochilin 46), Kovtun, Ostrovskiy, Golovskoi
(Semberas 84), Kobelev, Romaschenko, Gusev, Nekrasov, Isibor
(Kulchiy 54), Teryokhin.

● ROTOR VOLGOGRAD
Qualifying round CRVENA ZVEZDA BEOGRAD (YUG)
A 1-2 Abramov (66)
Chichkin; Shmarko (Geraschenko 74), Krivov, Berketov, Borzenkov, Zubko
(Borodin 78), Tischenko, Veretennikov, Yesipov, Abramov, Smirnov
(Olenikov 46).
H 1-2 Zernov (59)
Chichkin; Shmarko (Tischenko 82), Olenikov, Krivov, Berketov, Borzenkov,
Veretennikov, Yesipov, Abramov, Geraschenko, Bakharev

mid-season arrival of new coach Oleg Dolmatsov from Chernomorets Novorossiisk and completed their campaign with 12 straight victories - including a 4-1 destruction of Spartak (albeit a few days before the distracting visit to Moscow of Real Madrid), their first victory in that fixture for eight years. CSKA's phenomenal form hoisted them to second place, which came gift-wrapped with a passport to the qualifying phase of the Champions' League.

Third spot went to another club from the capital, Lokomotiv, who also came in with a strong finish, winning their last five matches to guarantee themselves a 1999/2000 UEFA Cup spot. First of all, however, Yuriy Syomin's accomplished side had their 1998/99 European Cup-winners' Cup campaign to think about, and for the second season running they were to reach the semi-finals, eliminating CSKA Kiev of Ukraine, Sporting Braga of Portugal and Maccabi Haifa of Israel before going down somewhat unluckily to Lazio on the away-goals rule. It was an outstanding team effort that

took Lokomotiv to the brink of the final, but worthy of special mention was the contribution made by Georgian striker Zaza Janashia, who scored six goals - some of them exquisite, all of them important - to become the competition's top scorer.

One man who has become accustomed to finishing at the head of goalscoring lists is Rotor Volgograd captain Oleg Veretennikov. The burly left-footed midfielder scored 22 goals for the second season running in the 1998 championship to win the Russian Golden Boot for the third time in four years. Once again, however, his goalscoring feats inexplicably failed to earn him recognition at international level and, perhaps in consequence, there was no major approach to sign him from a big foreign club. In fact, Veretennikov was lucky to be able to pursue his footballing career at all after being the victim of a terrifying incident when an unknown assailant threw acid at both him and his two-year-old daughter. Mercifully, both father and baby girl survived with only minor burns.

PLAYERS OF THE SEASON

YEGOR TITOV

The 1998 Russian Footballer of the Year award - as elected by the country's First Division players and coaches - went to young Spartak Moscow midfielder Yegor Titov. It was well deserved, with only his Spartak team-mates Ilya Tsymbalar and Andrei Tikhonov posing any serious threat. The mid-season sale of the 1997 winner, Dmitriy Alenichev, to Roma enabled Titov to come into his own as Spartak's central playmaker. He seized the opportunity brilliantly, becoming a dynamic, creative force with the ability to set up chance after chance for the forwards and also get on the score-sheet himself - as he did, notably, in four successive Champions' League matches, saving his best till last with a spectacular winner against Real Madrid. Ten days later he was given his first international cap, against France, and he has remained in the team ever since.

VALERIY KARPIN

Born in the Estonian capital of Tallinn, Valeriy Karpin opted to play international football for Russia. After his two crucial winning goals against France and Iceland in the June 1999 European Championship qualifiers, Russian fans are extremely grateful that he did. The blond midfielder has long

been one of Russia's most gifted and effective players but in 1998/99 he enjoyed the very best season of his career to date, both for club and country. The Spartak Moscow old boy was already a big hit in Spain following successful spells with Real Sociedad and Valencia, but he did even better at his third Primera Division club, Celta Vigo, his energetic attacking bursts down the right helping the unsung Galicians into the quarter finals of the UEFA Cup and the upper reaches of the Spanish table.

YEVGENIY VARLAMOV

Relegated with KamAZ Naberezhnye Chelny in 1997 through no fault of his own, Yevgeniy Varlamov left to join CSKA Moscow in 1998. It proved to be a very wise wove, both for the player and his new club. The young defender produced a string of classy performances as CSKA went from strength to strength, eventually finishing as championship runners-up to Spartak Moscow after a storming run in the second half of the season. Varlamov's excellent club form won him a place in the Russian national team and he quickly adjusted to the demands of international football, earning high praise for his tenacious ball-winning and his fearless enterprise in breaking forward to set up attacks.

ALANIA VLADIKAVKAZ

CLUB DIRECTORY

Alania Vladikavkaz
Shmulevicha Str. 6
362 007 Vladikavkaz
tel - (8672) 538548/530340
fax - (8672) 748806
Year of Formation - 1921
President - Soslan Andiev
General Manager - Batraz Bitarov
Secretary - Aleksandr Stelmakh
Coach - Valeriy Gazzayev
Stadium - Spartak (38,000)

MAJOR HONOURS
League Championship - (1) 1995.

APPEARANCES 1998

	P	Ap	(s)	Gls
Yuriy AFANASENKO (BLS)	G	6	(1)	
Alan AGAYEV	D	5	(1)	
Jambulat BAZAYEV	M	14	(10)	
Robert BITAROV	M	5	(8)	
Georgiy BOTSIYEV	A	1	(8)	1
Aleksandr CHAIKA (BLS)	M	30		4
David CHALADZE (GEO)	A	15	(1)	5
Aslan DATDEYEV	D	7	(6)	
Giorgi DEMETRADZE (GEO)	A	13	(2)	14
Anzor DZAMIKHOV	A	6	(13)	1
EMÍLIO Paulo Rocha Borges (BRA)	M	15		3
Andrei FYODOROV (UZB)	D	27	(1)	
Giorgi GAKHOKIDZE (GEO)	M	14		1
Zaur KHAPOV	G	24		
Yuriy KOKOYEV	M		(1)	
Oleg KORNIENKO	D	14	(8)	1
Veniyamin MANDRYKIN	G		(1)	
Roman MONARYOV (UKR)	A		(4)	
Araújo Eduardo MOREIRA (BRA)	A	14		5
Yuriy MOROZ (UKR)	D	26	(1)	
Artur PAGAYEV	D	22	(1)	
Alan SAKIEV	A		(1)	
Daryus SANAYEVAS (LIT)	D	4	(2)	
Andrius SHLYAKIS (LIT)	A		(3)	
Tamerlan SIKOYEV	A	1	(7)	
Igor TARLOVSKIY (BLS)	M	12	(1)	1
Mamuka TSERETELI (GEO)	D	13	(1)	
Igor YANOVSKIY	M	16		8
Aleksandr ZARUTSKIY	M		(1)	
Raimondas ZUTAUTAS (LIT)	D	26	(3)	1

LEAGUE RESULTS 1998

28/03/98	Uralan Elista	H	1-0	Chaladze
04/04/98	Krylya Sovetov Samara	A	2-2	Zutautas, Chaladze
11/04/98	Baltika Kaliningrad	H	2-0	Yanovskiy (p), Botsiyev
18/04/98	FK Tyumen	A	2-0	Yanovskiy 2 (1p)
25/04/98	Spartak Moskva	H	2-1	Chaika, Chaladze
02/05/98	CSKA Moskva	A	0-0	
09/05/98	Torpedo-Luzhniki Moskva	H	0-2	
13/05/98	Rotor Volgograd	A	1-1	Dzamikhov
23/05/98	Shinnik Yaroslavl	H	1-2	Gakhokidze
03/06/98	Chernomorets Novorossiisk	A	2-1	Chaladze 2
11/06/98	Zenit Sankt-Peterburg	H	0-0	
17/06/98	Lokomotiv Moskva	A	0-0	
21/06/98	Dinamo Moskva	H	2-2	Yanovskiy 2 (1p)
24/06/98	Zhemchuzhina Sochi	A	0-3	
01/07/98	Rostselmash Rostov-na-Donu	H	0-1	
15/07/98	Uralan Elista	A	3-3	Chaika, Demetradze 2 (1p)
22/07/98	Krylya Sovetov Samara	H	5-0	Moreira, Demetradze 3,
				og (Mazur)
29/07/98	Baltika Kaliningrad	A	3-1	Moreira, Yanovskiy, Emílio
01/08/98	FK Tyumen	H	6-0	Chaika, Demetradze 2,
				Yanovskiy 2, Moreira
08/08/98	Spartak Moskva	A	1-3	Moreira
15/08/98	CSKA Moskva	H	0-1	
22/08/98	Torpedo-Luzhniki Moskva	A	0-2	
30/08/98	Rotor Volgograd	H	3-1	Tarlovskiy, Demetradze (p),
				Emílio
09/09/98	Shinnik Yaroslavl	A	2-3	Demetradze, Moreira
20/09/98	Chernomorets Novorossiisk	H	3-1	Demetradze 3 (1p)
26/09/98	Zenit Sankt-Peterburg	A	0-2	
04/10/98	Lokomotiv Moskva	H	1-2	Chaika
17/10/98	Dinamo Moskva	A	1-4	Demetradze
25/10/98	Zhemchuzhina Sochi	H	3-0	Demetradze, Emílio, Kornienko
30/10/98	Rostselmash Rostov-na-Donu	A	0-1	

BALTIKA KALININGRAD

CLUB DIRECTORY

Baltika Kaliningrad
Dm. Donskogo Str. 2
236 000 Kaliningrad
tel - (0112) 211920/216501
fax - (0112) 216501
Year of Formation - 1955
President - Leonid Tkachenko
Secretary - Viktor Zibarovskiy
Coach - Leonid Tkachenko
Stadium - Baltika (18,000)

APPEARANCES 1998

	P	Ap	(s)	Gls
Beslan ADZHINDZHAL	M	24	(1)	
Ruslan ADZHINDZHAL	M	25	(2)	1
Vasiliy BARANOV (BLS)	M	15		1
Orestas BUITKUS (LIT)	A	11	(3)	1
Sergei BULATOV	A	5	(4)	3
Vyacheslav DAYEV	D	26	(1)	3
Andrei FEDKOV (UKR)	A	23	(5)	6
Aleksandr GORBACHYOV	D	8	(2)	
Oleg KASTORNYI (UKR)	D	6	(4)	
Igor KOROI (UKR)	D	2	(3)	
Dmitriy MARTSUN	D	7	(9)	
Viktor NAVOCHENKO	M	27	(2)	2
Maxim NIZOVTSEV	M	20	(1)	5
Aleksandr OVSYANNIKOV	A	1	(3)	
Aleksandr POMAZUN	G	21		
Zurab SANAYA	G	9		
Aleksandr SEDNYOV	D	25		3
Sergei SHISCHENKO (UKR)	M	5	(3)	
Dmitriy SILIN	A	26	(1)	6
Aleksandr STYOPIN	M	8	(6)	
Konstantin VIZENOK (UKR)	A	7	(9)	1
Viktor YABLONSKIY	M	29		

LEAGUE RESULTS 1998

28/03/98	Dinamo Moskva	A	1-1	Navochenko
04/04/98	Zhemchuzhina Sochi	H	2-1	Nizovtsev 2 (1p)
11/04/98	Alania Vladikavkaz	A	0-2	
18/04/98	Uralan Elista	H	1-1	Silin
25/04/98	Krylya Sovetov Samara	A	0-0	
02/05/98	Rostselmash Rostov-na-Donu	A	1-0	Silin
09/05/98	FK Tyumen	H	2-0	Baranov, Dayev
23/05/98	CSKA Moskva	A	1-1	Buitkus
03/06/98	Torpedo-Luzhniki Moskva	A	0-0	
07/06/98	Chernomorets Novorossiisk	H	1-0	Silin (p)
11/06/98	Rotor Volgograd	H	2-2	Fedkov 2
17/06/98	Shinnik Yaroslavl	A	1-3	Fedkov
24/06/98	Zenit Sankt-Peterburg	A	2-2	Adzhindzhal R., Dayev
01/07/98	Lokomotiv Moskva	H	0-3	
08/07/98	Spartak Moskva	A	0-3	
15/07/98	Dinamo Moskva	H	0-2	
22/07/98	Zhemchuzhina Sochi	A	1-2	Navochenko
29/07/98	Alania Vladikavkaz	H	1-3	Sednyov
01/08/98	Uralan Elista	A	1-2	Sednyov
08/08/98	Krylya Sovetov Samara	H	1-1	Bulatov S. (p)
15/08/98	Rostselmash Rostov-na-Donu	H	3-0	Vizenok, Sednyov, Fedkov
22/08/98	FK Tyumen	A	2-3	Bulatov 2
30/08/98	Spartak Moskva	H	1-1	Silin
09/09/98	CSKA Moskva	A	0-2	
20/09/98	Torpedo-Luzhniki Moskva	H	0-0	
26/09/98	Rotor Volgograd	A	1-1	Fedkov
03/10/98	Shinnik Yaroslavl	H	3-1	Nizovtsev 2 (1p), Fedkov
17/10/98	Chernomorets Novorossiisk	A	1-2	Silin
25/10/98	Zenit Sankt-Peterburg	H	3-2	Silin, Dayev, Nizovtsev
30/10/98	Lokomotiv Moskva	A	0-2	

CHERNOMORETS NOVOROSSIISK

CLUB DIRECTORY

Chernomorets Novorossiisk
Sovetov Str. 55
353 900 Novorossiisk
tel - (86172) 59801/54329
fax - (86172) 52191
Year of Formation - 1960
President - Valeriy Prokhorenko
General Manager - Viktor Ivasyev
Secretary - Avalu Shamkhanov
Coach - Oleg Dolmatov; Sergei Butenko
Stadium - Centralnyi (12,000)

APPEARANCES 1998

		P	Ap	(s)	Gls
Konstantin BELKOV	M			(2)	
Besik BERADZE (GEO)	M		13	(3)	
Lev BEREZNER	M		17	(5)	2
Sergei BURDIN	A		13	(6)	5
Albert DOGUZOV	M		25	(1)	5
Eduard DYOMIN	D		24	(1)	4
Erik EKUNGA (CMR)	M		7		3
Vyacheslav GERASCHENKO (BLS)	D		28		9
Konstantin GORDIYUK (BLS)	D		2		
Aleksandr GUMENYUK (UKR)	G		1		
Zhafar IRISMETOV (UZB)	A		5	(2)	1
Konstantin KAMNEV (UKR)	A		20	(5)	1
Tokam KOAGUE (CMR)	M		1	(2)	
Andrei KURDYUMOV (KAZ)	M		3	(14)	3
Oleg LEPIK	D		3	(6)	
Sergei LUTSEVICH	M			(1)	
Lev MAYOROV	M		24	(1)	1
Eduard MOMOTOV (UZB)	M		14	(3)	
Anatoliy MOROZOV	M		7	(11)	
Denis POPOV	A		4	(10)	1
Stanislav RUDENKO	G		12		
Roman RUSANOVSKIY (UKR)	D		5	(1)	
Andrei SHKURIN	D		22		
Yevgeniy SKACHKOV	M		1		
Badri SPANDERASHVILI	M		13	(7)	1
Gennadiy STYOPUSHKIN	D		23		1
Jerry TCHUISE (CMR)	D		15	(1)	
Igor USMINSKIY	G		8	(1)	
Mikhail VOLODIN	G		9		
Andre ZHIROV	D		11		

LEAGUE RESULTS 1998

28/03/98	CSKA Moskva	H	1-1	Burdin (p)
04/04/98	Torpedo-Luzhniki Moskva	A	3-2	Geraschenko, Popov, Burdin (p)
11/04/98	Rotor Volgograd	H	1-1	Mayorov
18/04/98	Shinnik Yaroslavl	A	0-0	
25/04/98	Rostselmash Rostov-na-Donu	H	1-1	Burdin (p)
02/05/98	Zenit Sankt-Peterburg	H	0-0	
09/05/98	Lokomotiv Moskva	A	1-1	Dyomin
16/05/98	Dinamo Moskva	H	1-1	Geraschenko
23/05/98	Zhemchuzhina Sochi	A	1-3	Geraschenko
03/06/98	Alania Vladikavkaz	H	1-2	Dyomin
07/06/98	Baltika Kaliningrad	A	0-1	
11/06/98	Uralan Elista	A	1-1	Burdin
17/06/98	Krylya Sovetov Samara	H	4-0	Doguzov 2 (2p), Geraschenko, Kurdyumov
24/06/98	FK Tyumen	H	4-1	Doguzov (p), Burdin, Geraschenko, Kurdyumov
01/07/98	Spartak Moskva	A	0-1	
15/07/98	CSKA Moskva	A	1-4	og (Borodkin)
22/07/98	Torpedo-Luzhniki Moskva	H	1-1	Doguzov (p)
29/07/98	Rotor Volgograd	A	0-3	
01/08/98	Shinnik Yaroslavl	H	2-1	Dyomin, Spanderashvili
08/08/98	Rostselmash Rostov-na-Donu	A	2-3	Berezner, Irismetov
15/08/98	Zenit Sankt-Peterburg	A	1-0	Kurdyumov
22/08/98	Lokomotiv Moskva	H	1-2	Geraschenko
30/08/98	Dinamo Moskva	A	0-0	
09/09/98	Zhemchuzhina Sochi	H	0-0	
20/09/98	Alania Vladikavkaz	A	1-3	Kurdyumov
26/09/98	Uralan Elista	H	2-0	Doguzov, Ekunga
03/10/98	Krylya Sovetov Samara	A	0-3	
17/10/98	Baltika Kaliningrad	H	2-1	Berezner, Dyomin
25/10/98	FK Tyumen	A	3-0	Geraschenko 3 (1p)
30/10/98	Spartak Moskva	H	3-1	Ekunga 2, Kamnev

CSKA MOSKVA

CLUB DIRECTORY

Centralnyi Sportivnyi Klub Armyi (CSKA) Moskva
Leningradskiy prospekt 39 A
125 167 Moskva
tel - (095) 2137329/2132538
fax - (095) 2132809
Year of Formation - 1923
President - Nikolai Stepanov
General Manager - Tengiz Verdzadze
Secretary - Anatoliy Korobochka
Coach - Pavel Sadyrin; Oleg Dolmatov
Stadium - Peschanoe (CSKA) (10,500)

MAJOR HONOURS
League Championship (USSR) - (7)
1946, 1947, 1948, 1950, 1951, 1970, 1991.
Domestic Cup (USSR) - (5)
1945, 1948, 1951, 1955, 1991.

APPEARANCES 1998

	P	Ap	(s)	Gls
Aleksei BABENKO	A	4	(7)	
Maxim BOKOV	D	26	(1)	1
Aleksandr BORODKIN	M	12	(2)	2
Aleksandr GERASIMOV	M	12	(12)	1
Aleksandr GRISHIN	D	21	(6)	
Sergei FILIPPENKOV	M	21	(6)	5
Vladimir ISAKOV	D		(1)	
Dmitriy KHOMUKHA (UKR)	M	29	(1)	8
Oleg KORNAUKHOV	D	27	(1)	3
Sergei KOROVUSHKIN	A		(4)	
Vladimir KULIK	A	28	(2)	14
Igor KUTEPOV (UKR)	G	10		
Dmitriy KUZNETSOV	D	5	(7)	
Valeriy MINKO	D	22	(3)	1
Andrei NOVOSADOV	G	20		
Aleksei SAVELIYEV	M	4	(16)	2
Aleksandr SCHYOGOLEV	D	9		
Sergei SEMAK	M	29		9
Dmitriy SENNIKOV	D	1	(6)	
Sergei SHUSTIKOV	M	4	(2)	
Aleksandr SHUTOV	M	1	(8)	1
Andrei TSAPLIN	M	16		1
Sergei VARLAMOV	M	29		1

LEAGUE RESULTS 1998

Date	Opponent		Score	Scorers
28/03/98	Chernomorets Novorossiisk	A	1-1	Gerasimov
04/04/98	Zenit Sankt-Peterburg	H	1-2	Semak
18/04/98	Dinamo Moskva	H	1-1	Semak
25/04/98	Zhemchuzhina Sochi	A	1-2	Khomukha
02/05/98	Alania Vladikavkaz	H	0-0	
09/05/98	Uralan Elista	A	2-1	Semak, Khomukha
13/05/98	Lokomotiv Moskva	A	1-2	Kulik
16/05/98	Krylya Sovetov Samara	H	3-0	Kulik 2, Bokov
23/05/98	Baltika Kaliningrad	A	1-1	Kulik
03/06/98	FK Tyumen	H	3-1	Semak, Kornaukhov (p), Kulik
11/06/98	Spartak Moskva	A	1-2	Varlamov
17/06/98	Rostselmash Rostov-na-Donu	A	0-1	
21/06/98	Torpedo-Luzhniki Moskva	H	1-3	Kulik
24/06/98	Rotor Volgograd	A	0-0	
01/07/98	Shinnik Yaroslavl	H	0-1	
15/07/98	Chernomorets Novorossiisk	H	4-1	Khomukha, Semak, Kornaukhov (p), Shutov
22/07/98	Zenit Sankt-Peterburg	A	1-0	Minko
29/07/98	Lokomotiv Moskva	H	0-1	
01/08/98	Dinamo Moskva	A	3-0	Saveliyev 2, Filippenkov
08/08/98	Zhemchuzhina Sochi	H	3-0	Kulik 2, Filippenkov
15/08/98	Alania Vladikavkaz	A	1-0	Semak
22/08/98	Uralan Elista	H	3-0	og (Tsaryov), Filippenkov, Khomukha
30/08/98	Krylya Sovetov Samara	A	2-0	Semak, Tsaplin (p)
09/09/98	Baltika Kaliningrad	H	2-0	Kornaukhov, Kulik
20/09/98	FK Tyumen	A	4-0	Khomukha (p), Borodkin, Kulik 2
26/09/98	Spartak Moskva	H	4-1	Khomukha 2, Filippenkov, Borodkin
03/10/98	Rostselmash Rostov-na-Donu	H	1-0	Kulik
17/10/98	Torpedo-Luzhniki Moskva	A	2-0	Kulik, Semak
25/10/98	Rotor Volgograd	H	2-0	Filippenkov, Kulik
30/10/98	Shinnik Yaroslavl	A	2-1	Semak, Khomukha

DINAMO MOSKVA

CLUB DIRECTORY

Dinamo Moskva
Leningradskiy prospekt 36
125 167 Moskva
tel - (095) 2128432
fax - (095) 2138305
Year of Formation - 1923
General Manager - Nikolai Tolstykh
Secretary - Sergei Nikulin
Coach - Adamas Golodets; Georgiy Yartsev
Stadium - Dinamo (36,880)

MAJOR HONOURS
League Championship (USSR) - (11)
1936, 1937, 1940, 1945, 1949, 1954, 1955,
1957, 1959, 1963, 1976.
Domestic Cup - (1) 1995.
Domestic Cup (USSR) - (6)
1937, 1953, 1967, 1970, 1977, 1984.

APPEARANCES 1998

	P	Ap	(s)	Gls
Sergei ARTYOMOV	A		(1)	
Tomas DANILEVICIUS (LIT)	M	7	(4)	
Konstantin GOLOVSKOI	M	8	(2)	3
Andrei GORDEYEV	A	1	(1)	
Sergei GRISHIN	M	16		2
Rolan GUSEV	M	15	(2)	1
Laki ISIBOR (NIG)	A	21	(6)	4
Andrei KOBELEV	M	20		
Yevgeniy KORABLYOV	D	4	(2)	
Eduard KOSOLAPOV	A		(2)	
Yuriy KOVTUN	D	26	(2)	1
Aleksei KOZLOV	D	2	(2)	
Dmitriy KRAMARENKO (AZB)	G	1	(1)	
Aleksandr KULCHIY (BLS)	M	12	(8)	1
Vitaliy KULEV	M		(5)	
Yuriy KUZNETSOV	M	1		
Aleksandr MAKAROV	A		(1)	
Sergei NEKRASOV	D	24		2
Andrei OSTROVSKIY (BLS)	D	26	(2)	2
Aleksandr PROKHORENKOV (UKR)	A		(5)	
Maxim ROMASCHENKO (BLS)	A	16	(9)	
Deyvidas SEMBERAS (LIT)	M	11	(3)	
Sergei SHTANYUK (BLS)	D	27		2
Vladimir SKOKOV	M	15	(5)	
Oleg TERYOKHIN	A	27		12
Aleksandr TOCHILIN	D	7	(3)	
Dmitriy TYAPUSHKIN	G	29		
Erik YAKHIMOVICH (BLS)	D	14		

LEAGUE RESULTS 1998

28/03/98	Baltika Kaliningrad	H	1-1	og (Dayev)
04/04/98	FK Tyumen	A	0-2	
18/04/98	CSKA Moskva	A	1-1	Isibor
25/04/98	Torpedo-Luzhniki Moskva	H	0-0	
02/05/98	Rotor Volgograd	A	0-0	
09/05/98	Shinnik Yaroslavl	H	1-1	Teryokhin (p)
13/05/98	Spartak Moskva	H	0-0	
16/05/98	Chernomorets Novorossiisk	A	1-1	Teryokhin (p)
23/05/98	Zenit Sankt-Peterburg	H	0-0	
03/06/98	Lokomotiv Moskva	A	0-1	
11/06/98	Rostselmash Rostov-na-Donu	H	1-2	Shtanyuk
17/06/98	Zhemchuzhina Sochi	H	4-1	Isibor, Kulchiy, Grishin 2
21/06/98	Alania Vladikavkaz	A	2-2	Kovtun, Teryokhin (p)
24/06/98	Uralan Elista	H	0-3	
01/07/98	Krylya Sovetov Samara	A	0-1	
15/07/98	Baltika Kaliningrad	A	2-0	Nekrasov, Teryokhin
22/07/98	FK Tyumen	H	1-0	Isibor
29/07/98	Spartak Moskva	A	0-2	
01/08/98	CSKA Moskva	H	0-3	
07/08/98	Torpedo-Luzhniki Moskva	A	2-2	Teryokhin, Nekrasov
15/08/98	Rotor Volgograd	H	2-2	Teryokhin 2
22/08/98	Shinnik Yaroslavl	A	2-0	Golovskoi, Gusev
30/08/98	Chernomorets Novorossiisk	H	0-0	
09/09/98	Zenit Sankt-Peterburg	A	1-1	Shtanyuk
20/09/98	Lokomotiv Moskva	H	2-1	Teryokhin 2
26/09/98	Rostselmash Rostov-na-Donu	A	0-0	
03/10/98	Zhemchuzhina Sochi	A	2-1	Isibor, Golovskoi
17/10/98	Alania Vladikavkaz	H	4-1	Teryokhin 3, Golovskoi
25/10/98	Uralan Elista	A	1-0	Ostrovskiy
30/10/98	Krylya Sovetov Samara	H	1-1	Ostrovskiy

KRYLYA SOVETOV SAMARA

CLUB DIRECTORY

Krylya Sovetov Samara
Shushenskaya Str. 50A
443 011 Samara
tel - (8462) 351635/355441
fax - (8462) 351633
Year of Formation - 1943
President - Boris Valkov
Secretary - Anatoliy Bytkin
Coach - Aleksandr Averyanov
Stadium - Metallurg (38,800)

APPEARANCES 1998

	P	Ap	(s)	Gls
Sergei ANDREYEV (UZB)	A		(3)	
Garnik AVALYAN (ARM)	A	24	(4)	3
Aleksandr AVERIYANOV	M	28		2
Yuriy BAVYKIN	M	14		1
Sergei BULATOV	A	6	(7)	1
Maxim DEMENKO	D	11	(2)	1
Yuriy GETIKOV	M	1	(7)	
Andrei GUZENKO	M	3		
Sergei KORCHAGIN	M	2	(3)	
Sergei LAPSHIN	M	5	(6)	
Sergei LUSCHAN (UKR)	D	18	(3)	1
Sergei MAKEYEV	M	2	(1)	
Mukhamed Anas MAKHLUF (SYR)	A	2	(9)	1
Vasiliy MAZUR	D	26		
Mamuka MINASHVILI (GEO)	A	6	(6)	
Aleksandr NIKULIN	M	1	(7)	
Aleksandr ORESHNIKOV (BLS)	M	14	(6)	
Zurab POPKHADZE (GEO)	D	23	(1)	1
Giorgi REVAZISHVILI (GEO)	M		(3)	
Andrei REZANTSEV	D	23		1
Vitaliy SAFRONOV	A	24	(4)	5
Sergei SHISHKIN	D	25		
Yuriy SHISHKIN	G	16		
Vasiliy SLOBODKO	G	14		
Zurab TSIKLAURI	A	22	(7)	6
Aleksandr TSYGANKOV	M	20	(4)	1

LEAGUE RESULTS 1998

28/03/98	Zhemchuzhina Sochi	A	2-0	Makhluf, Tsiklauri
04/04/98	Alania Vladikavkaz	H	2-2	Tsiklauri, og (Zutautas)
11/04/98	Uralan Elista	A	0-1	
18/04/98	Rostselmash Rostov-na-Donu	A	0-3	
25/04/98	Baltika Kaliningrad	H	0-0	
02/05/98	FK Tyumen	A	3-0	Avalyan, Bulatov (p), Tsiklauri
09/05/98	Spartak Moskva	H	0-2	
16/05/98	CSKA Moskva	A	0-3	
23/05/98	Torpedo-Luzhniki Moskva	H	2-0	Rezantsev, Safronov (p)
03/06/98	Rotor Volgograd	A	1-2	Avalyan
11/06/98	Shinnik Yaroslavl	H	1-0	Tsiklauri
17/06/98	Chernomorets Novorossiisk	A	0-4	
21/06/98	Zenit Sankt-Peterburg	H	1-2	Tsygankov
24/06/98	Lokomotiv Moskva	A	0-1	
01/07/98	Dinamo Moskva	H	1-0	Tsiklauri
15/07/98	Zhemchuzhina Sochi	H	0-0	
22/07/98	Alania Vladikavkaz	A	0-5	
29/07/98	Uralan Elista	H	2-0	Bavykin, Luschan
01/08/98	Rostselmash Rostov-na-Donu	H	1-0	Averiyanov
08/08/98	Baltika Kaliningrad	A	1-1	Avalyan
15/08/98	FK Tyumen	H	1-0	Safronov
22/08/98	Spartak Moskva	A	2-2	Demenko, Safronov
30/08/98	CSKA Moskva	H	0-2	
09/09/98	Torpedo-Luzhniki Moskva	A	0-1	
20/09/98	Rotor Volgograd	H	0-0	
26/09/98	Shinnik Yaroslavl	A	0-0	
03/10/98	Chernomorets Novorossiisk	H	3-0	Tsiklauri, Safronov 2 (1p)
17/10/98	Zenit Sankt-Peterburg	A	0-2	
25/10/98	Lokomotiv Moskva	H	1-3	Popkhadze (p)
30/10/98	Dinamo Moskva	A	1-1	Averiyanov

LOKOMOTIV MOSKVA

CLUB DIRECTORY

Lokomotiv Moskva
B. Cherkizovskaya Str. 125A
107 553 Moskva
tel - (095) 1619704/1614283
fax - (095) 1619977
Year of Formation - 1923
President - Valeriy Filatov
Secretary - Vladimir Korotkov
Coach - Yuriy Syomin
Stadium - Lokomotiv (29,300)

MAJOR HONOURS
Domestic Cup - (2) 1996, 1997.
Domestic Cup (USSR) - (2) 1936, 1957.

APPEARANCES 1998

		P	Ap	(s)	Gls
Aleksei ARIFULLIN	D	11	(2)		
Khasanbi BIDZHIEV	G	1			
Aleksandr BORODYUK	A	12	(3)		8
Dmitriy BULYKIN	A	7	(7)		3
Igor CHEREVCHENKO (TAD)	D	21			1
Igor CHUGAINOV	D	30			4
Yuriy DROZDOV	D	26			1
Oleg GARAS	A	11	(5)		2
Sergei GURENKO (BLS)	M	29			
Zaza JANASHIA (GEO)	A	28			8
Yevgeniy KHARLACHYOV	M	25	(2)		1
Aleksei KOSOLAPOV	M	6	(4)		2
Andrei LAVRIK (BLS)	D	18	(6)		1
Dmitriy LOSKOV	M	13	(5)		4
Vladimir MAMINOV	M	9	(10)		3
Ruslan NIGMATULIN	G	29	(1)		
Sarkis HOVHANNISYAN (ARM)	D	10	(2)		1
Oleg PASHININ	M	7	(3)		
Nikolai RYNDYUK (BLS)	A		(8)		
Albert SARKISYAN (ARM)	M	4	(5)		3
Oleg SERGEYEV	A	1			
Aleksandr SMIRNOV	M	2	(1)		
Andrei SOLOMATIN	D	20	(3)		
Bakhva TEDEYEV	M	9	(6)		1
Vitaliy VESELOV	A	1	(4)		1

LEAGUE RESULTS 1998

28/03/98	FK Tyumen	H	4-0	Maminov, Janashia, Kosolapov, Garas
05/04/98	Spartak Moskva	A	0-2	
19/04/98	Torpedo-Luzhniki Moskva	A	0-0	
25/04/98	Rotor Volgograd	H	0-1	
02/05/98	Shinnik Yaroslavl	A	1-0	Kosolapov
09/05/98	Chernomorets Novorossiisk	H	1-1	Janashia
13/05/98	CSKA Moskva	H	2-1	Lavrik, Janashia
16/05/98	Zenit Sankt-Peterburg	A	2-2	Loskov, Kharlachyov
23/05/98	Rostselmash Rostov-na-Donu	H	1-1	Hovhannisyan
03/06/98	Dinamo Moskva	H	1-0	Veselov
11/06/98	Zhemchuzhina Sochi	A	0-2	
17/06/98	Alania Vladikavkaz	H	0-0	
21/06/98	Uralan Elista	A	0-1	
24/06/98	Krylya Sovetov Samara	H	1-0	Cherevchenko
01/07/98	Baltika Kaliningrad	A	3-0	Maminov 2, Bulykin
15/07/98	FK Tyumen	A	2-0	og (Zhuravlyov), Janashia
22/07/98	Spartak Moskva	H	0-2	
29/07/98	CSKA Moskva	A	1-0	Garas
01/08/98	Torpedo-Luzhniki Moskva	H	2-0	Janashia, Chugainov (p)
07/08/98	Rotor Volgograd	A	2-3	Tedeyev, Loskov
15/08/98	Shinnik Yaroslavl	H	0-0	
22/08/98	Chernomorets Novorossiisk	A	2-1	Sarkisyan 2
30/08/98	Zenit Sankt-Peterburg	H	3-1	Sarkisyan, Borodyuk, Chugainov (p)
09/09/98	Rostselmash Rostov-na-Donu	A	2-2	Janashia, Bulykin
20/09/98	Dinamo Moskva	A	1-2	Borodyuk
26/09/98	Zhemchuzhina Sochi	H	4-3	Chugainov (p), Bulykin, Drozdov, Loskov
04/10/98	Alania Vladikavkaz	A	2-1	Chugainov (p), Borodyuk
17/10/98	Uralan Elista	H	3-1	Borodyuk 2, Janashia
25/10/98	Krylya Sovetov Samara	A	3-1	Loskov, Janashia, Borodyuk
30/10/98	Baltika Kaliningrad	H	2-0	Borodyuk 2

ROSTSELMASH ROSTOV-NA-DONU

THE EUROPEAN FOOTBALL YEARBOOK 1999-2000

CLUB DIRECTORY

Rostselmash Rostov-na-Donu
Pervoi Konnoi Armii Str. 6A
344 077 Rostov-na-Donu
tel - (8632) 527947/528367
fax - (8632) 519539
Year of Formation - 1930
President - Viktor Usachyov
General Manager - Vasiliy Maznev
Coach - Sergei Andreyev
Stadium - Rostselmash (15,600)

APPEARANCES 1998

		P	Ap	(s)	Gls
Yuriy ANTONOVICH (BLS)	M	11	(10)		
Anatoliy BESSMERTNYI (UKR)	M	28			2
Yuriy DUDIK (UKR)	M	3	(8)		1
Vladislav DUYUN (UKR)	M	9	(8)		1
Yuriy DYADYUK	M	28			1
Dmitriy GRADILENKO	D	14			3
Aleksei GUSCHIN	D	24	(1)		
Dmitriy KIRICHENKO	A	13	(10)		5
Igor KHANKEYEV	M	25	(2)		4
Sergei KOLOTOVKIN	D	20	(7)		
Andrei KOVALENKO	M	1	(6)		
Mikhail KUPRIYANOV	M	27	(1)		1
Yevgeniy LANDYREV	M		(2)		
Sergei MASLOV	A		(15)		
Vladimir MATSYGURA (UKR)	D	5	(4)		
Yuriy MATVEYEV	A	30			14
Sergei NECHAI	D		(1)		
Oleg PESTRYAKOV (UKR)	M	25	(5)		7
Vladislav PRUDIUS (UKR)	M	24	(5)		2
Oleg SANKO	M	13	(5)		1
Vladimir SAVCHENKO (UKR)	G	29			
Vladislav TERNAVSKIY	D		(1)		
Aleksandr VLADIMIROV	G	1			

LEAGUE RESULTS 1998

28/03/98	Rotor Volgograd	H	2-2	Pestryakov 2
04/04/98	Uralan Elista	A	3-1	Matveyev 2, Pestryakov
11/04/98	Shinnik Yaroslavl	A	0-0	
17/04/98	Krylya Sovetov Samara	H	3-0	Kupriyanov, Gradilenko, Matveyev (p)
25/04/98	Chernomorets Novorossiisk	A	1-1	Khankeyev (p)
02/05/98	Baltika Kaliningrad	H	0-1	
09/05/98	Zenit Sankt-Peterburg	A	0-3	
16/05/98	FK Tyumen	H	4-0	Matveyev 3, Kirichenko
23/05/98	Lokomotiv Moskva	A	1-1	Kirichenko
03/06/98	Spartak Moskva	H	3-3	Dyadyuk, Khankeyev 2
11/06/98	Dinamo Moskva	A	2-1	Kirichenko 2
17/06/98	CSKA Moskva	H	1-0	Bessmertnyi
21/06/98	Zhemchuzhina Sochi	A	0-0	
24/06/98	Torpedo-Luzhniki Moskva	H	2-3	Gradilenko 2
01/07/98	Alania Vladikavkaz	A	1-0	Matveyev
15/07/98	Rotor Volgograd	A	1-5	Pestryakov
22/07/98	Uralan Elista	H	0-0	
29/07/98	Shinnik Yaroslavl	H	3-2	Duyun, Sanko, Matveyev
01/08/98	Krylya Sovetov Samara	A	0-1	
08/08/98	Chernomorets Novorossiisk	H	3-2	Matveyev 2 (1p), Pestryakov
15/08/98	Baltika Kaliningrad	A	0-3	
22/08/98	Zenit Sankt-Peterburg	H	1-1	Matveyev
30/08/98	FK Tyumen	A	4-1	Pestryakov, Matveyev, Prudius, Dudnik
09/09/98	Lokomotiv Moskva	H	2-2	Kirichenko, Prudius
20/09/98	Spartak Moskva	A	1-1	Pestryakov
26/09/98	Dinamo Moskva	H	0-0	
03/10/98	CSKA Moskva	A	0-1	
17/10/98	Zhemchuzhina Sochi	H	2-0	Bessmertnyi, Matveyev
25/10/98	Torpedo-Luzhniki Moskva	A	1-3	Khankeyev
30/10/98	Alania Vladikavkaz	H	1-0	Matveyev (p)

ROTOR VOLGOGRAD

CLUB DIRECTORY

Rotor Volgograd
Prospekt Lenina 76
400 005 Volgograd
tel - (8442) 340053/341507
fax - (8442) 341507
Year of Formation - 1933
President - Vladimir Goryunov
Secretary - Rokhus Shokh
Coach - Viktor Prokopenko; Benjaminas Zelkevicius
Stadium - Centralnyi (40,000)

APPEARANCES 1998

	P	Ap	(s)	Gls
Vitaliy ABRAMOV	D	21	(5)	
Aleksei BAKHAREV	M	11	(4)	
Aleksandr BERKETOV	M	30		3
Iliya BORODIN	A	1	(5)	1
Albert BORZENKOV	D	29		
Valeriy BURLACHENKO	D	2	(6)	
Andrei CHICHKIN	G	14	(1)	
Andrei DUROV	D	3	(1)	
Vladimir GERASCHENKO	D	6	(3)	
Airat KARIMOV	G	4		
Sergei KOPNIN	D	1	(1)	
Andrei KRIVOV	M	18	(9)	3
Nikolai OLENIKOV	D	21	(5)	3
Mikhail OSINOV	M	15	(7)	
Dmitriy PARMUZIN	M		(1)	
Aleksandr SHMARKO	D	25		
Vladimir SMIRNOV	M	11	(7)	
Maxim TISCHENKO (UKR)	M	11	(6)	1
Oleg VERETENNIKOV	M	29	(1)	22
Valeriy YESIPOV	A	28		11
Platon ZAKHARCHUK (UKR)	G	12		
Aleksandr ZERNOV	A	12	(9)	3
Denis ZUBKO	A	26	(4)	5

LEAGUE RESULTS 1998

28/03/98	Rostselmash Rostov-na-Donu	A	2-2	Zernov, Veretennikov (p)
04/04/98	Shinnik Yaroslavl	H	6-2	Veretennikov 5 (1p), Zubko
11/04/98	Chernomorets Novorossiisk	A	1-1	Zubko
18/04/98	Zenit Sankt-Peterburg	H	2-1	Krivov, Olenikov
25/04/98	Lokomotiv Moskva	A	1-0	Zubko
02/05/98	Dinamo Moskva	H	0-0	
09/05/98	Zhemchuzhina Sochi	A	1-1	Veretennikov
13/05/98	Alania Vladikavkaz	H	1-1	Veretennikov
03/06/98	Krylya Sovetov Samara	H	2-1	Yesipov 2
07/06/98	Uralan Elista	A	1-2	Veretennikov
11/06/98	Baltika Kaliningrad	A	2-2	Veretennikov, Yesipov
17/06/98	FK Tyumen	H	5-1	Veretennikov, Yesipov 2, Krivov, Zubko
21/06/98	Spartak Moskva	A	1-3	Yesipov
24/06/98	CSKA Moskva	H	0-0	
01/07/98	Torpedo-Luzhniki Moskva	A	2-2	Yesipov, Zubko
15/07/98	Rostselmash Rostov-na-Donu	H	5-1	Veretennikov 2 (1p), Yesipov, Berketov 2
22/07/98	Shinnik Yaroslavl	A	0-2	
29/07/98	Chernomorets Novorossiisk	H	3-0	Veretennikov 2, Yesipov
01/08/98	Zenit Sankt-Peterburg	A	1-0	Borodin
07/08/98	Lokomotiv Moskva	H	3-2	Krivov, Veretennikov, Olenikov
15/08/98	Dinamo Moskva	A	2-2	Veretennikov, Olenikov
21/08/98	Zhemchuzhina Sochi	H	0-0	
30/08/98	Alania Vladikavkaz	A	1-3	Berketov
09/09/98	Uralan Elista	H	3-1	Zernov, Veretennikov 2 (1p)
20/09/98	Krylya Sovetov Samara	A	0-0	
26/09/98	Baltika Kaliningrad	H	1-1	Yesipov
03/10/98	FK Tyumen	A	4-2	Zernov, Veretennikov 2 (1p), Yesipov
17/10/98	Spartak Moskva	H	1-2	Veretennikov (p)
25/10/98	CSKA Moskva	A	0-2	
30/10/98	Torpedo-Luzhniki Moskva	H	1-0	Tischenko

SHINNIK YAROSLAVL

CLUB DIRECTORY

Shinnik Yaroslavl
Ploschad Truda
Stadion Shinnik
150 040 Yaroslavl
tel - (0852) 2720576/720566
fax - (0852) 720626
Year of Formation - 1957
President - Valeriy Frolov
Coach - Pyotr Shubin; David Kipiani
Stadium - Shinnik (24,000)

APPEARANCES 1998

	P	Ap	(s)	Gls
Sergei BULAVIN	M		(3)	
Aleksei BYCHKOV	A	10	(10)	1
Andrei GALIYANOV	M	7	(8)	1
Gennadiy GRISHIN	M	11	(1)	
Aleksandr GUTEYEV	G	2		
Vladimir KAZAKOV	M	20	(1)	1
Aleksei KAZALOV	M	17	(1)	2
Yevgeniy KORNYUKHIN	G	28		
Vladimir LEONCHENKO	M	30		6
Marat MAKHMUTOV	D	28		
Andrei NOVGORODOV	D	15	(3)	1
Vasiliy POTEKHIN	D	9	(1)	1
Maxim PUTILIN	D	24	(5)	1
Albert SCHERBAKOV	D	4	(1)	
Dmitriy SENNIKOV	D	7	(2)	
Sergei SEREBRENNIKOV	A	22	(2)	6
Nikolai SIDOROV	A		(12)	1
Yevgeniy SMERTIN	M	10	(1)	
Sergei SNYTKO	M	11	(13)	3
Andrei SOLOVTSOV	D	19	(2)	
Dmitriy VYAZMIKIN	A	13	(9)	2
Artyom YENIN	A	26	(3)	1
Sergei YUMINOV	A	17	(5)	3

LEAGUE RESULTS 1998

28/03/98	Torpedo-Luzhniki Moskva	H	1-0	Bychkov
04/04/98	Rotor Volgograd	A	2-6	Putilin, Leonchenko (p)
11/04/98	Rostselmash Rostov-na-Donu	H	0-0	
18/04/98	Chernomorets Novorossiisk	H	0-0	
25/04/98	Zenit Sankt-Peterburg	A	0-3	
02/05/98	Lokomotiv Moskva	H	0-1	
09/05/98	Dinamo Moskva	A	1-1	Sidorov
16/05/98	Zhemchuzhina Sochi	H	1-2	Serebrennikov
23/05/98	Alania Vladikavkaz	A	2-1	Kazakov, Serebrennikov
03/06/98	Uralan Elista	H	0-0	
11/06/98	Krylya Sovetov Samara	A	0-1	
17/06/98	Baltika Kaliningrad	H	3-1	Snytko, Vyazmikin, Novgorodov (p)
21/06/98	FK Tyumen	A	1-0	Leonchenko
24/06/98	Spartak Moskva	H	0-1	
01/07/98	CSKA Moskva	A	1-0	Snytko
15/07/98	Torpedo-Luzhniki Moskva	A	1-0	Snytko
22/07/98	Rotor Volgograd	H	2-0	Leonchenko, Galiyanov
29/07/98	Rostselmash Rostov-na-Donu	A	2-3	Serebrennikov, Vyazmikin
01/08/98	Chernomorets Novorossiisk	A	1-2	Serebrennikov
08/08/98	Zenit Sankt-Peterburg	H	0-0	
15/08/98	Lokomotiv Moskva	A	0-0	
22/08/98	Dinamo Moskva	H	0-2	
30/08/98	Zhemchuzhina Sochi	A	2-2	Serebrennikov, Yuminov
09/09/98	Alania Vladikavkaz	H	3-2	Yuminov, Yenin, Leonchenko (p)
20/09/98	Uralan Elista	A	1-2	Kazalov
26/09/98	Krylya Sovetov Samara	H	0-0	
03/10/98	Baltika Kaliningrad	A	1-3	Potekhin
17/10/98	FK Tyumen	H	3-2	Serebrennikov, Yuminov, Leonchenko (p)
25/10/98	Spartak Moskva	A	1-3	Leonchenko (p)
30/10/98	CSKA Moskva	H	1-2	Kazalov

SPARTAK MOSKVA

CLUB DIRECTORY

Spartak Moskva
1-st Koptelskiy per. 18 bild. 2
129 010 Moskva
tel - (095) 2088736/2088749
fax - (095) 9752385
Year of Formation - 1922
President - Oleg Romantsev
General Manager - Yuriy Zavarzin
Secretary - Valeriy Zilyayev
Coach - Oleg Romantsev
Stadium - Dinamo (36,880), Lokomotiv (29,300)

MAJOR HONOURS
League Championship - (6)
1992, 1993, 1994, 1996, 1997, 1998.
League Championship (USSR) - (12)
1936, 1938, 1939, 1952, 1953, 1956, 1958,
1962, 1969, 1979, 1987, 1989.
Domestic Cup - (2) 1994, 1998.
Domestic Cup (USSR) - (10) 1938, 1939, 1946,
1947, 1950, 1958, 1963, 1965, 1971, 1992.

APPEARANCES 1998

	P	Ap	(s)	Gls
Dmitriy ALENICHEV	M	13		2
Dmitriy ANANKO	D	19		
Vasiliy BARANOV (BLS)	M	14		3
Yevgeniy BUSHMANOV	D	14		1
Maxim BUZNIKIN	A	5	(9)	3
Aleksandr FILIMONOV	G	29		
Konstantin GOLOVSKOI	M		(1)	
Sergei GORLUKOVICH	D	19	(2)	1
Anatoliy KANISCHEV	A	12	(12)	6
Dmitriy KHLESTOV	D	23		1
Aleksei MELYOSHIN	M	6	(10)	1
Dmitriy PARFYONOV (UKR)	D	29		1
Nikolai PISAREV	A	14	(3)	7
Luis ROBSON				
Pereira da Silva (BRA)	M	10	(9)	3
Miroslav ROMASCHENKO (BLS)	D	17	(1)	3
Leandro SAMARONE				
da Rosa Fernandes (BRA)	M	4	(6)	
Aleksandr SHIRKO	A	11	(2)	5
Andrei SMETANIN	G	1	(1)	
Andrei TIKHONOV	M	30		4
Yegor TITOV	M	29		6
Ilya TSYMBALAR	M	29		10
Vadim YEVSEYEV	D	2	(4)	

LEAGUE RESULTS 1998

28/03/98	Zenit Sankt-Peterburg	A	1-2	Tsymbalar
04/04/98	Lokomotiv Moskva	H	2-0	Buznikin, Robson
18/04/98	Zhemchuzhina Sochi	H	1-1	Tikhonov
25/04/98	Alania Vladikavkaz	A	1-2	Khlestov
02/05/98	Uralan Elista	H	1-0	Tsymbalar
09/05/98	Krylya Sovetov Samara	A	2-0	Romaschenko, Melyoshin
13/05/98	Dinamo Moskva	A	0-0	
03/06/98	Rostselmash Rostov-na-Donu	A	3-3	Buznikin 2, Romaschenko
11/06/98	CSKA Moskva	H	2-1	Tikhonov, Tsymbalar
17/06/98	Torpedo-Luzhniki Moskva	A	1-1	Alenichev (p)
21/06/98	Rotor Volgograd	H	3-1	Kanischev 2, Romaschenko
24/06/98	Shinnik Yaroslavl	A	1-0	Alenichev
01/07/98	Chernomorets Novorossiisk	H	1-0	Robson
05/07/98	FK Tyumen	A	6-0	Kanischev 3, Pisarev, Tsymbalar, Titov
08/07/98	Baltika Kaliningrad	H	3-0	Gorlukovich, Tsymbalar 2
15/07/98	Zenit Sankt-Peterburg	H	0-0	
22/07/98	Lokomotiv Moskva	A	2-0	Baranov, Shirko
29/07/98	Dinamo Moskva	H	2-0	Bushmanov, Titov
01/08/98	Zhemchuzhina Sochi	A	4-1	Pisarev, og (Yeschenko), Tsymbalar 2
08/08/98	Alania Vladikavkaz	H	3-1	Tsymbalar, Titov (p), Kanischev
16/08/98	Uralan Elista	A	0-1	
22/08/98	Krylya Sovetov Samara	H	2-2	Pisarev 2
30/08/98	Baltika Kaliningrad	A	1-1	Titov
09/09/98	FK Tyumen	H	7-0	Shirko 4, Pisarev, Baranov, Tikhonov (p)
20/09/98	Rostselmash Rostov-na-Donu	H	1-1	Titov
26/09/98	CSKA Moskva	A	1-4	Robson
04/10/98	Torpedo-Luzhniki Moskva	H	1-0	Pisarev
17/10/98	Rotor Volgograd	A	2-1	Titov, Pisarev
25/10/98	Shinnik Yaroslavl	H	3-1	Parfyonov, Tikhonov, Baranov
30/10/98	Chernomorets Novorossiisk	A	1-3	Tsymbalar

TORPEDO MOSKVA

CLUB DIRECTORY

Torpedo Moskva
Luzhnetskaya Naberezhnaya 24
119 048 Moskva
tel - (095) 2010916/2011238
fax - (095) 2460105
Year of Formation - 1924
President - Pavel Borodin
General Manager - Nazar Petrosyan
Secretary - Mariyan Plakhetko
Coach - Aleksandr Tarkhonov; Valentin Ivanov
Stadium - Luzhniki (82,380), Torpedo (16,500)

MAJOR HONOURS
League Championship (USSR) - (3)
1960, 1965, 1976.
Domestic Cup - (1) 1993.
Domestic Cup (USSR) - (6)
1949, 1952, 1960, 1968, 1972, 1986.

APPEARANCES 1998

		P	Ap	(s)	Gls
Nikolai AREFIYEV	M	1	(1)		
Arsen AVAKOV (TAD)	A	12	(11)	5	
Viktor BULATOV	M	30		9	
Sergei BURCHENKOV	M	24	(3)	1	
Yevgeniy BUSHMANOV	D	14		1	
Andrei CHERNYSHOV	D	1	(1)		
Augustine EGUAVON (NIG)	D	6	(1)		
Andrei GASHKIN	M	25		3	
Dmitriy GRADILENKO	D	14			
Giorgi GUDUSHAURI (GEO)	M	6	(1)	2	
Vyacheslav KAMOLTSEV	A	8	(12)	2	
Sergei KRUKOVETS (UKR)	D	10	(5)		
Andrei MALAI	D	14	(1)		
Denis MASHKARIN	D	15	(1)		
Artur MKRCHYAN (ARM)	D	7			
Lasha MONASELIDZE (GEO)	M	1	(1)		
Mukhsin MUKHAMADIYEV (TAD)	A	8	(6)	2	
Rodislav ORLOVSKIY (BLS)	D	19	(5)	1	
Andrei PANFYOROV	M		(1)		
Aleksandr PRIZETKO (UKR)	M	7	(6)		
Leandro SAMARONE					
da Rocha Fernandes (BRA)	M	10	(2)		
Andrei SAPUGA (UKR)	M	6	(5)		
Aleksandr SAYUN (UZB)	D	10	(1)		
Igor SEMSHOV	M	18	(7)	6	
Valeriy SHANTALOSOV (BLS)	G	2			
Sergei SKACHENKO (UKR)	A	24	(5)	6	
Valeriy VOROBYOV (UKR)	G	28	(1)		
Vadim YEVSEYEV	D	10			

LEAGUE RESULTS 1998

28/03/98	Shinnik Yaroslavl	A	0-1	
04/04/98	Chernomorets Novorossiisk	H	2-3	Gashkin 2
11/04/98	Zenit Sankt-Peterburg	A	1-1	Gudushauri
19/04/98	Lokomotiv Moskva	H	0-0	
25/04/98	Dinamo Moskva	A	0-0	
02/05/98	Zhemchuzhina Sochi	H	0-1	
09/05/98	Alania Vladikavkaz	A	2-0	Avakov, Skachenko
16/05/98	Uralan Elista	H	1-1	Gudushauri
23/05/98	Krylya Sovetov Samara	A	0-2	
03/06/98	Baltika Kaliningrad	H	0-0	
11/06/98	FK Tyumen	A	2-1	Bulatov 2
17/06/98	Spartak Moskva	H	1-1	Semshov
21/06/98	CSKA Moskva	A	3-1	Skachenko, Avakov, Bulatov
24/06/98	Rostselmash Rostov-na-Donu	A	3-2	Avakov, Semshov, Burchenkov
01/07/98	Rotor Volgograd	H	2-2	Gashkin (p), Bushmanov
15/07/98	Shinnik Yaroslavl	H	0-1	
22/07/98	Chernomorets Novorossiisk	A	1-1	Skachenko
29/07/98	Zenit Sankt-Peterburg	H	1-3	Avakov
01/08/98	Lokomotiv Moskva	A	0-2	
07/08/98	Dinamo Moskva	H	2-2	Semshov, Bulatov
15/08/98	Zhemchuzhina Sochi	A	4-0	Mukhamadiyev, Bulatov 2, Semshov
22/08/98	Alania Vladikavkaz	H	2-0	Mukhamadiyev, Skachenko
30/08/98	Uralan Elista	A	2-3	Semshov, Kamoltsov
09/09/98	Krylya Sovetov Samara	H	1-0	Bulatov
20/09/98	Baltika Kaliningrad	A	0-0	
26/09/98	FK Tyumen	H	5-1	Bulatov 2 (1p), Orlovskiy, Kamoltsev, Avakov
04/10/98	Spartak Moskva	A	0-1	
17/10/98	CSKA Moskva	H	0-2	
25/10/98	Rostselmash Rostov-na-Donu	H	3-1	Skachenko 2, Semshov
30/10/98	Rotor Volgograd	A	0-1	

FK TYUMEN

CLUB DIRECTORY

FK Tyumen
Kommuny Str. 22
625 003 Tyumen
tel - (3452) 368792/291318
fax - (3452) 368792
Year of Formation - 1961
General Manager - Aleksandr Purtov
Secretary - Vladimir N. Dolbonosov
Coach - Aleksandr Ignatenko
Stadium - Tyumen (8,000)

APPEARANCES 1998

	P	Ap	(s)	Gls
Vyacheslav AFONIN	A	2	(7)	
Arif ASADOV (AZB)	D	25		
Vladimir BABANOV	G		(2)	
Roman BARANOV	M	7	(5)	
Aleksandr BORODKIN	M	11		1
Dmitriy BUSHMANOV	M	6	(4)	
Vladimir DOLBONOSOV	M	14		
Konstantin DYMARCHUK (UKR)	D	12		
Konstantin FISHMAN	M	20	(1)	
Yevgeniy GLUKHOV	D	12	(1)	1
Viktor GONCHAROV	A	30		1
Aleksandr GREKHOV	M	2	(4)	
Igor KACHMAZOV	M	3	(2)	
Aleksei KLESTOV	M	10	(1)	
Valeriy LEBEDEV	M	3	(5)	
Vyacheslav LYCHKIN (AZB)	A	11		4
Oleg MASLENNIKOV	G	15		
Yevgeniy MASLOV	D	16	(4)	
Aleksei NAUMOV	D	12		
Sergei PODPALYI	M	10		1
Mikhail POTYLCHAK	A	5	(5)	
Dmitriy RAZMAZIN	M	1	(3)	
Aleksei SCHEPIKOV	M		(1)	
Yevgeniy SKACHKOV	M	7	(3)	
Grigoriy SOKOLOVSKIY	G	15		
Aleksandr TSARENKO	M	8		1
Andrei TSUKANOV	M	5	(3)	
Igor VARLAMOV	D	14		1
Valentin YEGUNOV	A	27	(1)	7
Eduard ZAGUMENNYI	D	11		
Andrei ZHIROV	D	8	(1)	
Sergei ZHURAVLYOV	M	8	(6)	

LEAGUE RESULTS 1998

28/03/98	Lokomotiv Moskva	A	0-4	
04/04/98	Dinamo Moskva	H	2-0	Borodkin, Varlamov
11/04/98	Zhemchuzhina Sochi	A	0-0	
18/04/98	Alania Vladikavkaz	H	0-2	
25/04/98	Uralan Elista	A	1-2	Podpalyi (p)
02/05/98	Krylya Sovetov Samara	H	0-3	
09/05/98	Baltika Kaliningrad	A	0-2	
16/05/98	Rostselmash Rostov-na-Donu	A	0-4	
03/06/98	CSKA Moskva	A	1-3	Goncharov
11/06/98	Torpedo-Luzhniki Moskva	H	1-2	Yegunov
17/06/98	Rotor Volgograd	A	1-5	Tsarenko (p)
21/06/98	Shinnik Yaroslavl	H	0-1	
24/06/98	Chernomorets Novorossiisk	A	1-4	Yegunov
01/07/98	Zenit Sankt-Peterburg	H	0-5	
05/07/98	Spartak Moskva	H	0-6	
15/07/98	Lokomotiv Moskva	H	0-2	
22/07/98	Dinamo Moskva	A	0-1	
29/07/98	Zhemchuzhina Sochi	H	0-1	
01/08/98	Alania Vladikavkaz	A	0-6	
08/08/98	Uralan Elista	H	1-3	Yegunov
15/08/98	Krylya Sovetov Samara	A	0-1	
22/08/98	Baltika Kaliningrad	H	3-2	Glukhov, Lychkin 2
30/08/98	Rostselmash Rostov-na-Donu	H	1-4	Yegunov
09/09/98	Spartak Moskva	A	0-7	
20/09/98	CSKA Moskva	H	0-4	
26/09/98	Torpedo-Luzhniki Moskva	A	1-5	Yegunov
03/10/98	Rotor Volgograd	H	2-4	Lychkin 2 (1p)
17/10/98	Shinnik Yaroslavl	A	2-3	Yegunov 2
25/10/98	Chernomorets Novorossiisk	H	0-3	
30/10/98	Zenit Sankt-Peterburg	A	0-0	

URALAN ELISTA

CLUB DIRECTORY

Uralan Elista
Lenina str. 218
358004 Elista
tel - (84722) 20946/21907
fax - (84722) 20920
Year of Formation - 1958
President - Nikolai Shovgurov
General Manager - Anatoliy Koval
Secretary - Batr Maximov
Coach - Vitaliy Shevchenko
Stadium - Spartak (12,000)

APPEARANCES 1998

	P	Ap	(s)	Gls
Yuriy AKSYONOV	M	28	(2)	4
Dmitriy ALEKSEYEV	G	1	(1)	
Sergei ARMISHEV	G	4		
Igor BAKHTIN	M	19	(10)	1
Yevgeniy DURNEV	M	27	(1)	9
Aleksandr IGNATIYEV	M	29		5
Dmitriy IVANOV	A	23	(6)	3
Valery IVANOV (LAT)	D	29		
Sergei KORMILTSEV	D	20	(4)	2
Nikolai KOVARDAYEV	A		(1)	
Vitaliy LITVINOV	D	14	(1)	2
Aleksandr LUKHVICH	D	29		1
Albert OSKOLKOV	D	1		
Tigran PETROSYAN (ARM)	M		(16)	1
Andrei SAMORUKOV	G	25		
Aleksei SCHIGOLEV	D		(4)	
Makar SHEVTSOV	M		(3)	
Yuriy SHUKANOV (BLS)	M	10	(13)	4
Aleksie SMERTIN	M	26		3
Oleg TERESCHENKO (UKR)	D	6	(3)	
Vyacheslav TSARYOV	D	30		2
Artyom YASHKIN	M	6	(16)	2
Aleksandr YELISEYEV (LAT)	A	3	(1)	

LEAGUE RESULTS 1998

28/03/98	Alania Vladikavkaz	A	0-1	
04/04/98	Rostselmash Rostov-na-Donu	H	1-3	Litvinov
11/04/98	Krylya Sovetov Samara	H	1-0	Smertin
18/04/98	Baltika Kaliningrad	A	1-1	Durnev
25/04/98	FK Tyumen	H	2-1	Shukanov 2
02/05/98	Spartak Moskva	A	0-1	
09/05/98	CSKA Moskva	H	1-2	Petrosyan
16/05/98	Torpedo-Luzhniki Moskva	A	1-1	Litvinov
03/06/98	Shinnik Yaroslavl	A	0-0	
07/06/98	Rotor Volgograd	H	2-1	Ignatiyev, Yashkin
11/06/98	Chernomorets Novorossiisk	H	1-1	Shukanov
17/06/98	Zenit Sankt-Peterburg	A	1-2	Shukanov
21/06/98	Lokomotiv Moskva	H	1-0	Durnev
24/06/98	Dinamo Moskva	A	3-0	Durnev, Aksyonov, Ignatiyev
01/07/98	Zhemchuzhina Sochi	H	2-0	Yashkin, Durnev
15/07/98	Alania Vladikavkaz	H	3-3	Smertin, Kormiltsev, Durnev
22/07/98	Rostselmash Rostov-na-Donu	A	0-0	
29/07/98	Krylya Sovetov Samara	A	0-2	
01/08/98	Baltika Kaliningrad	H	2-1	Lukhvich, Bakhtin
08/08/98	FK Tyumen	A	3-1	Kormiltsev, Tsaryov (p), Ignatiyev
16/08/98	Spartak Moskva	H	1-0	Ignatiyev
22/08/98	CSKA Moskva	A	0-3	
30/08/98	Torpedo-Luzhniki Moskva	H	3-2	Smertin, Tsaryov (p), Durnev
09/09/98	Rotor Volgograd	A	1-3	Aksyonov
20/09/98	Shinnik Yaroslavl	H	2-1	Aksyonov, Durnev
26/09/98	Chernomorets Novorossiisk	A	0-2	
03/10/98	Zenit Sankt-Peterburg	H	0-3	
17/10/98	Lokomotiv Moskva	A	1-3	Aksyonov
25/10/98	Dinamo Moskva	H	0-1	
30/10/98	Zhemchuzhina Sochi	A	6-2	Ivanov 3, Durnev 2 (1p), Ignatiyev

ZENIT SANKT-PETERBURG

CLUB DIRECTORY

Zenit Sankt-Peterburg
Nekrasova Str. 3/5
191 104 Sankt Peterburg
tel - (812) 2750330
fax - (812) 2750333
Year of Formation - 1931
President - Vitaliy Mutko
General manager - Pyotr Treskov
Coach - Anatoliy Byshovets
Stadium - Petrovskiy (23,000)

MAJOR HONOURS
League Championship (USSR) - (1) 1984.
Domestic Cup (USSR) - (1) 1944.

APPEARANCES 1998

		P	Ap	(s)	Gls
Aleksandr BABIY (UKR)	D	22			
Roman BEREZOVSKI (ARM)	G	30			
Aleksandr CURTIANU (MOL)	M	26			2
Dmitriy DAVYDOV	D	27			1
Oleg DMITRIEV	M		(4)		
Sergei GERASIMETS (BLS)	M	21	(5)	7	
Aleksandr GORSHKOV	M	14	(11)	4	
Aleksei IGONIN	D	28			2
Sergei KLESCHENKO (MOL)	A	2	(4)		
Andrei KONDRASHOV	D	28			2
Vasiliy KULKOV	M	29	(1)		
Konstantin LEPYOKHIN	D	4	(8)	1	
Roman MAKSIMYUK (UKR)	M	26			8
Sergei OSIPOV	M	1	(15)	1	
Sarkis HOVSEPYAN (ARM)	D	30			
Aleksandr PANOV	A	10	(13)	8	
Gennadiy POPOVICH (UKR)	A	11	(8)	3	
Yuriy VERNIDUB (UKR)	D	21	(1)	1	
Igor ZAZULIN	M		(12)	1	

LEAGUE RESULTS 1998

28/03/98	Spartak Moskva	H	2-1	Gerasimets, Curtianu
04/04/98	CSKA Moskva	A	2-1	Maksimyuk, Gerasimets
11/04/98	Torpedo-Luzhniki Moskva	H	1-1	Maksimyuk
18/04/98	Rotor Volgograd	A	1-2	Gerasimets
25/04/98	Shinnik Yaroslavl	H	3-0	Kondrashov, Popovich, Maksimyuk
02/05/98	Chernomorets Novorossiisk	A	0-0	
09/05/98	Rostselmash Rostov-na-Donu	H	3-0	Popovich, Gorshkov, Panov
16/05/98	Lokomotiv Moskva	H	2-2	Maksimyuk, Lepyokhin
23/05/98	Dinamo Moskva	A	0-0	
03/06/98	Zhemchuzhina Sochi	H	1-0	Kondrashov
11/06/98	Alania Vladikavkaz	A	0-0	
17/06/98	Uralan Elista	H	2-1	Maksimyuk, Panov
21/06/98	Krylya Sovetov Samara	A	2-1	Maksimyuk, Gorshkov
24/06/98	Baltika Kaliningrad	H	2-2	Maksimyuk, og (Navochenko)
01/07/98	FK Tyumen	A	5-0	Gerasimets 3, Igonin, Vernidub
15/07/98	Spartak Moskva	A	0-0	
22/07/98	CSKA Moskva	H	0-1	
29/07/98	Torpedo-Luzhniki Moskva	A	3-1	Popovich, Gerasimets, Davydov
01/08/98	Rotor Volgograd	H	0-1	
08/08/98	Shinnik Yaroslavl	A	0-0	
15/08/98	Chernomorets Novorossiisk	H	0-1	
22/08/98	Rostselmash Rostov-na-Donu	A	1-1	Zazulin
30/08/98	Lokomotiv Moskva	A	1-3	Panov
09/09/98	Dinamo Moskva	H	1-1	Panov
20/09/98	Zhemchuzhina Sochi	A	1-2	Osipov
26/09/98	Alania Vladikavkaz	H	2-0	Maksimyuk, Panov
03/10/98	Uralan Elista	A	3-0	Panov, Igonin, Gorshkov
17/10/98	Krylya Sovetov Samara	H	2-0	Panov, Gorshkov
25/10/98	Baltika Kaliningrad	A	2-3	Curtianu, Panov
30/10/98	FK Tyumen	H	0-0	

ZHEMCHUZHINA SOCHI

CLUB DIRECTORY

Zhemchuzhina Sochi
Vinogradnaya Str. 43
354 008 Sochi
tel - (8622) 933650/933392
fax - (8622) 933398
Year of Formation - 1990
President - Nikolai Karpov
General Manager - Karp Nachariyan
Secretary - Vram Kakosiyan
Coach - Anatoliy Baidachnyi
Stadium - Centralnyi (12,500)

APPEARANCES 1998

	P	Ap	(s)	Gls
Assaf AL-KHALIFA (SYR)	A		(1)	
Timur BOGATYRYOV	A	2	(6)	
Stanislav BONDAREV	D	27	(1)	2
Gennadiy BONDARUK	D	19	(2)	
Dmitriy BUSHMANOV	M	2		
Sergei GALMAKOV	D	10		2
Aleksandr GELADZE (GEO)	D	1	(2)	
Giorgi GOGIASHVILI (GEO)	M	20	(4)	1
Gocha GOGRICHIANI (GEO)	A	14	(2)	4
Mamuk KAKOSYAN (ARM)	A	26	(1)	1
Artashes KALAIDZIIYAN (ARM)	M	26	(1)	3
Konstantin KOVALENKO	M	12	(1)	3
Yevgeniy KRYUKOV	G	16	(1)	
German KUTARBA	D	14	(4)	4
Artur KUZNETSOV	M	12	(7)	2
Nilton MENDES Pereira (BRA)	A	8	(17)	2
Vladislav MAYOROV	M		(2)	
Maxim SHVETSOV	M	3	(6)	
Vadim SOKOLOV	M	29		1
Nazim SULEYMANOV (AZB)	A	2	(8)	1
Gennadiy SUSHKO (UKR)	D	1	(5)	
Gennadiy TUMILOVICH (BLS)	G	14		
Aleksandr YESCHENKO	D	30		2
Eduard ZATSEPIN	A	15	(2)	3
Vladimir ZHURAVEL (BLS)	M	27		

LEAGUE RESULTS 1998

28/03/98	Krylya Sovetov Samara	H	0-2	
04/04/98	Baltika Kaliningrad	A	1-2	Mendes
11/04/98	FK Tyumen	H	0-0	
18/04/98	Spartak Moskva	A	1-1	Zatsepin
25/04/98	CSKA Moskva	H	2-1	Zatsepin (p), Gogrichiani
02/05/98	Torpedo-Luzhniki Moskva	A	1-0	Zatsepin (p)
09/05/98	Rotor Volgograd	H	1-1	Galmakov
16/05/98	Shinnik Yaroslavl	A	2-1	Gogrichiani, Yeschenko
23/05/98	Chernomorets Novorossiisk	H	3-1	Gogiashvili, Kuznetsov, Galmakov
03/06/98	Zenit Sankt-Peterburg	A	0-1	
11/06/98	Lokomotiv Moskva	H	2-0	Kuznetsov, Bondarev
17/06/98	Dinamo Moskva	A	1-4	Kalaidzhyan
21/06/98	Rostselmash Rostov-na-Donu	H	0-0	
24/06/98	Alania Vladikavkaz	H	3-0	Kakosyan, Kutarba 2
01/07/98	Uralan Elista	A	0-2	
15/07/98	Krylya Sovetov Samara	A	0-0	
22/07/98	Baltika Kaliningrad	H	2-1	Bondarev, Kovalenko
29/07/98	FK Tyumen	A	1-0	Sokolov
01/08/98	Spartak Moskva	H	1-4	Kutarba
08/08/98	CSKA Moskva	A	0-3	
15/08/98	Torpedo-Luzhniki Moskva	H	0-4	
21/08/98	Rotor Volgograd	A	0-0	
30/08/98	Shinnik Yaroslavl	H	2-2	Gogrichiani, Suleymanov
09/09/98	Chernomorets Novorossiisk	A	0-0	
20/09/98	Zenit Sankt-Peterburg	H	2-1	Kalaidzhyan, Kutarba
26/09/98	Lokomotiv Moskva	A	3-4	Kalaidzhyan, Mendes, Kovalenko
03/10/98	Dinamo Moskva	H	1-2	Kovalenko
17/10/98	Rostselmash Rostov-na-Donu	A	0-2	
25/10/98	Alania Vladikavkaz	A	0-3	
30/10/98	Uralan Elista	H	2-6	Gogrichiani, Yeschenko

PROMOTED CLUBS

SECOND DIVISION FINAL TABLE 1998

		Pd	W	D	L	F	A	Pt	GD
1	**Saturn Ramenskoe**	**42**	**24**	**12**	**6**	**74**	**34**	**84**	**+40**
2	**Lokomotiv Nizhniy Novgorod**	**42**	**23**	**8**	**11**	**65**	**34**	**77**	**+31**
3	Sokol Saratov	42	21	13	8	58	32	76	+26
4	CSK VVS-Kristall Saratov	42	23	3	16	59	47	72	+12
5	Arsenal Tula	42	18	11	13	65	53	65	+12
6	Lada-Grad Dimitrovgrad	42	19	7	16	65	63	64	+2
7	Rubin Kazan	42	19	6	17	56	50	63	+6
8	Dinamo Stavropol	42	16	15	11	51	40	63	+11
9	Gazovik-Gazprom Izhevsk	42	18	6	18	53	58	60	-5
10	Fakel Voronezh	42	17	9	16	54	45	60	+9
11	Lokomotiv Chita	42	17	8	17	60	50	59	+10
12	Anzhi Makhachkala	42	17	6	19	47	56	57	-9
13	Metallurg Lipetsk	42	16	8	18	41	50	56	-9
14	Tomy Tomsk	42	15	11	16	54	45	56	+9
15	Spartak Nalchik	42	15	11	16	49	52	56	-3
16	Lokomotiv Sankt-Peterburg	42	14	11	17	38	41	53	-3
17	Neftekhimik Nizhnekamsk	42	15	7	20	44	56	52	-12
18	Druzhba Maikop	42	13	11	18	45	55	50	-11
19	Lada-Toliatti-Vaz Toliatti	42	15	9	18	52	70	48	-18
20	Kuban Krasnodar	42	10	13	19	42	68	43	-26
21	Irtysh Omsk	42	11	8	23	36	58	41	-22
22	KamAZ-Chally Naberezhnye Chelny	42	7	5	30	32	82	20	-50

N.B. Lada-Toliatti-Vaz Toliatti and KamAZ-Chally Naberezhnye Chelny deducted 6 pts.

CLUB DIRECTORY

Saturn Ramenskoe
Gorodskoi park
Moskovskaya ob1
140103 Ramenskoe,
tel - (8246) 34474/31216
fax - (8246) 34474
Year of Formation - 1958
President - Nikolai Burlinov
Secretary - Sergei Tryapkin
Coach - Sergei Pavlov
Stadium - Saturn (9,000)

CLUB DIRECTORY

Lokomotiv Nizhniy Novgorod
Balaklavskiy per. 1
603 010 Nizhniy Novgorod
tel - (8312) 422929/429346
fax - (8312) 429346
Year of Formation - 1987
President - Valeriy Ovchinnikov
Secretary - Nikolai Kozin
Coach - Valeriy Ovchinnikov
Stadium - Lokomotiv (20,400)

SAN MARINO

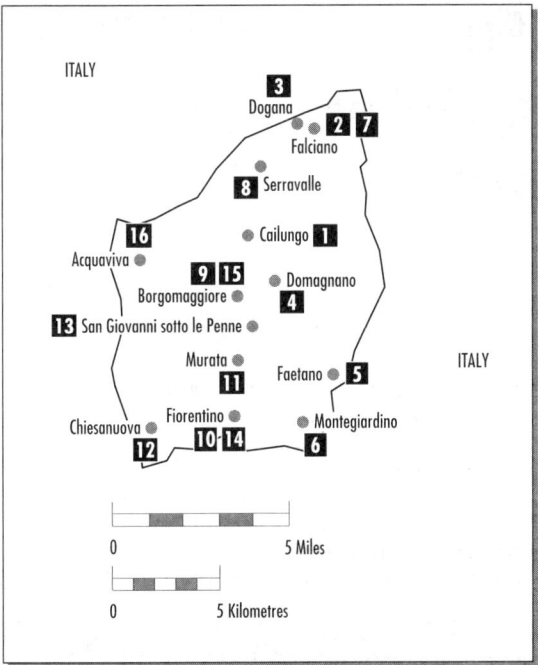

1	CAILUNGO	860	9	LIBERTAS	868
2	COSMOS	861	10	MONTEVITO	869
3	DOGANA	862	11	MURATA	870
4	DOMAGNANO	863	12	PENNAROSSA	871
5	FAETANO	864	13	SAN GIOVANNI	872
6	FIORITA	865	14	TRE FIORI	873
7	FOLGORE	866	15	TRE PENNE	874
8	JUVENES	867	16	VIRTUS	875

FOLGORE TITLE HAT-TRICK DENIED BY FAETANO

Lambs to the slaughter yet again

FEDERATION DIRECTORY

Federazione Sammarinese Giuoco Calcio
Via Campo dei Giudei 14, 47031 Rep. San Marino

tel - 990515
fax - 992348

Year of Formation - 1931
President - Giorgio Crescentini
Secretary - Luciano Casadei

Stadium - Olimpico, Serravalle (5,000)

San Marino changed their coach for the Euro 2000 qualifying campaign, with Gian Paolo Mazza replacing Massimo Bonini. But everything else stayed pretty much the same. The team played seven qualifying matches and lost every one. They managed just one goal themselves - a penalty - while conceding 37.

Honourable defeats have always been the height of San Marino's ambition but after restricting Cyprus to just one goal in their third fixture, results got progressively worse. They lost the return in Limassol 4-0, went down 5-0 at home to Spain, lost 7-0 in Austria, and finally, to cap another grim year, they were destroyed 9-0 by Spain in Villarreal.

That was not the heaviest defeat in San Marino's history - they lost their first World Cup match 10-0 against Norway in 1992 - but it was another confidence-shatterer for a team which had now lost 30 competitive internationals on the trot. The time when nations such as San Marino are placed in pre-qualifying competitions

LEAGUE CHAMPIONSHIP RESULTS 98/99

GROUP A

	1	2	3	4	5	6	7	8	9	10	11	12	13	14	15	16
1 Cosmos		1-1	0-0	0-1	1-1	3-2	2-1	1-0		2-1		1-0	5-1	0-1		
2 Domagnano	2-1		3-1	0-0	2-1	2-0	4-0	2-2	3-0	3-0					0-0	2-1
3 Fiorita	3-5	0-2		2-3	0-0	2-3	1-0	2-1	1-0	1-0			3-1			1-0
4 Folgore	3-0	1-0	1-2		3-4	2-1	3-1	3-3			1-1	0-0		3-0	3-3	
5 Montevito	0-3	4-0	2-2	1-4		1-1	2-1	1-2	1-1		0-1	2-0	1-1			
6 Pennarossa	0-1	2-6	1-1	1-4	2-2		0-3	1-2	1-0		2-1				7-3	2-2
7 San Giovanni	0-4	2-2	1-0	1-4	0-1	2-2		0-0		0-3	2-1		1-4			0-2
8 Tre Fiori	2-3	3-1	2-3	1-1	3-2	2-2	3-0					3-0	2-0	0-1	3-3	

GROUP B

	9	10	11	12	13	14	15	16	1	2	3	4	5	6	7	8
9 Cailungo		0-0	1-0	2-4	4-0	1-3	2-3	0-4	0-3		2-4				1-1	2-3
10 Dogana	1-0		0-1	0-0	0-0	2-4	1-3	0-0				1-2	1-2	3-0	1-3	
11 Faetano	2-0	1-1		0-0	3-1	4-0	0-1	3-1	1-1	1-2	2-0					1-0
12 Juvenes	2-1	0-3	1-2		0-0	0-1	0-1	2-1	1-1	1-2	3-1		2-4			
13 Libertas	1-1	0-1	2-1	2-2		1-3	3-6	1-3		2-3		1-4		2-3	2-2	
14 Murata	3-2	4-1	2-2	3-0	6-1		3-2	2-6	5-3	3-0		1-0	7-3			
15 Tre Penne	2-1	3-0	1-0	4-0	3-1	2-2		3-2	1-1		1-2		2-3		3-3	
16 Virtus	1-1	1-3	0-1	3-1	1-2	0-2	4-1		1-0				3-3	7-1		4-5

can surely not be far away. The agony can only go on for so long.

The San Marino national championship remains one of the most awkwardly structured in Europe. In 1998/99 the previous year's experiment of two eight-team leagues plus crossover fixtures and play-offs was retained.

The 'regular' season produced a couple of shocks when both Tre Fiori and Virtus, the two group winners a year earlier, failed to qualify for the play-offs. Group A was well-contested, with Folgore, Domagnano and Cosmos all packed tightly together within a couple of points at the top, but Group B belonged entirely

LEAGUE CHAMPIONSHIP FINAL TABLE 98/99

GROUP A

		Pd	Home W	D	L	F	A	Away W	D	L	F	A	Total W	D	L	F	A	Pt	GD
1	Folgore	22	5	4	2	23	15	7	3	1	29	15	12	7	3	52	30	43	+22
2	Domagnano	22	8	3	0	23	6	4	3	4	21	22	12	6	4	44	28	42	+16
3	Cosmos	22	6	3	2	16	9	6	2	3	22	13	12	5	5	38	22	41	+16
4	Tre Fiori	22	5	3	3	24	16	5	3	3	21	18	10	6	6	45	34	36	+11
5	Fiorita	22	6	1	4	16	15	4	3	4	13	17	10	4	8	29	32	34	-3
6	Montevito	22	3	4	4	15	16	4	3	4	17	22	7	7	8	32	38	28	-6
7	Pennarossa	22	3	3	5	19	25	4	3	4	23	26	7	6	9	42	51	27	-9
8	San Giovanni	22	2	3	6	9	23	1	3	7	12	24	3	6	13	21	47	15	-26

GROUP B

		Pd	Home W	D	L	F	A	Away W	D	L	F	A	Total W	D	L	F	A	Pt	GD
1	Murata	22	9	1	1	39	20	8	1	2	21	14	17	2	3	60	34	53	+26
2	Tre Penne	22	6	3	2	25	15	5	3	3	26	26	11	6	5	51	41	39	+10
3	Faetano	22	6	3	2	18	7	5	2	4	12	9	11	5	6	30	16	38	+14
4	Virtus	22	4	2	5	25	20	4	2	5	22	16	8	4	10	47	36	28	11
5	Doganu	22	2	3	6	10	15	3	3	5	11	16	5	6	11	21	31	21	-10
6	Juvenes	22	3	2	6	12	17	1	3	7	8	22	4	5	13	20	39	17	-19
7	Libertas	22	1	3	7	17	29	1	3	7	8	28	2	6	14	25	57	12	-32
8	Cailungo	22	2	2	7	15	25	0	3	8	7	18	2	5	15	22	43	11	-21

N.B. The top three teams in each group play off for the title.

CHAMPIONSHIP PLAY-OFFS

FIRST ROUND
Domagnano 1, Faetano 0
Cosmos 3, Tre Penne 1

SECOND ROUND
Folgore 2, Cosmos 1
Domagnano 3, Murata 2

THIRD ROUND
Tre Penne 3, Murata 2
Faetano 2, Cosmos 1
(Murata and Cosmos eliminated)

FOURTH ROUND
Folgore 3, Domagnano 3 (aet; 4-3 on pens.)
Faetano 2, Tre Penne 1 (aet)
(Tre Penne eliminated)

SEMI-FINAL
Faetano 1, Domagnao 1 (aet; 4-1 on pens.)
(Domagnano eliminated)

FINAL
11/05/99, Serravalle
FAETANO 1 Arcangeli (84)
FOLGORE 0
referee - Tura
FAETANO - Muccioli; Valentini (Gasperoni Ma. 90), Moroni, Donati, Dall'Olmo, Conti, Gennari, Della Valle P.D., Gianni (Arcangeli 58), Rinaldi (Cassadei 63), Mularoni D..
FOLGORE - Gasperoni Fed.; Pelliccioni Fed., Bianchi F., Corbelli C., Saccani, Pelliccioni Fa., Bartoli, Censoni (Bernardini 88), Mazza, Bianchi S., Ugolini.

NATIONAL TEAM APPEARANCES 98/99

Coach - Gian Paolo MAZZA	ISR	AUT	CYP	CYP	ESP	AUT	ESP	Cps	Gls
Federico GASPERONI (10/09/76) - CBR Pietracurta (ITA)	G	G	G	G	G	G	G	13	-
Mirco GENNARI (29/03/66) - Almas Ponte Rimini (ITA)	D	D	D	D	D	D46	D84	32	-
William GUERRA (24/02/68) - Juvenes (ITA)	D	D	D	D		D	D	40	-
Mauro VALENTINI (27/07/73) - Domagnano	D	D79	D		D			23	1
Simone BACCIOCCHI (22/01/77) - Torre Pedrera (ITA)	D59	D			s46			4	-
Mauro MARANI (09/03/75) - Juvenes (ITA)	D	D	D	D84	D		D	6	-
Riccardo MUCCIOLI (27/08/74) - Russi (ITA)	M	M	M83		s75	M		10	-
Pier Domenico DELLA VALLE (04/05/70) - Rivazzurra (ITA)	M68	s79		M69			M	18	1
Ivan MATTEONI (21/08/70) - Tre Fiori	M	M	M75					28	-
Paolo MONTAGNA (28/05/76) - Juvenes (ITA)	A76	s61	A67		A59	A84	A59	18	-
Andy SELVA (23/05/76) - Catanzaro (ITA)	A	A		A	A	A		5	1
Vittorio VALENTINI (09/10/73) - Juvenes (ITA)	s59	s61	D	D	D		s74	13	-
Fabio FRANCINI (06/03/69) - Juvenes (ITA)	s68	M61	s75					34	-
Davide GUALTIERI (27/04/71) - Almas Ponte Rimini (ITA)	s76			s59				10	1
Andrea UGOLINI (23/07/74) - Tropical Ospedaletto (ITA)		A61	A	A46			s59	6	-
Bryan GASPERONI (26/09/74) - CBR Pietracuta (ITA)			M		M75	M15		12	-
Nicola BACCIOCCHI (16/12/71) - Juvenes (ITA)			s67	s46			A	30	1
Luciano MULARONI (30/08/71) - Sammaurese (ITA)			s83	M				4	-
Luca GOBBI (12/06/71) - Juvenes (ITAO				D	D51	D	D	33	-
Ermanno ZONZINI (01/04/74) - San Giovanni Marignanese (ITA)				D	D	D	D	4	-
Pier Angelo MANZAROLI (25/03/69) - Cosmos/Olympia Secchiano (ITA)				s69	M	s15	M74	31	-
Damiano VANNUCCI (30/07/77) - CBR Pietracuta (ITA)				s84		D	s84	8	-
Simone DELLA BALDA (02/12/72) - Tre Penne					s51	M	M	3	-
Roberto SELVA (02/01/81) - Fiorita					s84			1	-

DOMESTIC CUP 98/99

FIRST ROUND
GROUP A
Juvenes 1, Tre Penne 0
Fiorita 2, Murata 1
Tre Penne 2, Murata 1
Fiorita 1, Juvenes 0
Fiorita 3, Tre Penne 3
Murata 6, Juvenes 2
(Fiorita and Tre Penne qualify)

GROUP B
Domagnano 4, Cailungo 1
Cosmos 5, San Giovanni 0
Domagnano 7, San Giovanni 0

Cailungo 0, Cosmos 0
Domagnano 3, Cosmos 1
San Giovanni 2, Cailungo 1
(Domagnano and Cosmos qualify)

GROUP C
Folgore 4, Faetano 1
Libertas 2, Montevito 1
Folgore 3, Libertas 2
Faetano 4, Montevito 0
Faetano 1, Libertas 1
Montevito 2, Folgore 0
(Folgore and Faetano qualify)

GROUP D
Pennarossa 5, Virtus 2
Tre Fiori 5, Dogana 1
Pennarossa 2, Dogana 2
Tre Fiori 3, Virtus 2
Virtus 2, Dogana 0
Pennarossa 3, Tre Fiori 1
(Pennarossa and Tre Fiori qualify)

QUARTER-FINALS
Domagnano 3, Faetano 2
Pennarossa 3, Tre Penne 1
Cosmos 1, Fiorita 0
Folgore 3, Tre Fiori 2

SEMI-FINALS
Domagnano 2, Pennarossa 2
(aet; 4-1 on pens.)
Folgore 1, Cosmos 2

FINAL
COSMOS 5
Albani F. (18), Selva (23p, 83),
Manzaroli (36), De Luigi (58)
DOMAGNANO 1 Baciocchi (45)

to Murata, who, inspired by goalgrabbing forwards Diego Gasparoni, Oriano Lazzaretti and, especially, Stefano De Luigi, set a new points record (53) to finish well ahead of fellow qualifiers Tre Penne and Faetano.

However, Murata could not carry their first-phase form into the play-offs. They were eliminated at stage three, having been beaten 3-2 in both of their matches, by Domagnano and Tre Penne. The other group winners, defending champions Folgore, did much better, beating Cosmos and Domagnano to reach the final, where they were joined by a Faetano side who, armed with a quartet of San Marino internationals (Stefano Muccioli, Mirco Gennari, Pier Domenico Della Valle and Denis Mularoni), recovered from a first-match defeat to win three games in a row, including a penalty shoot-out victory over their earlier conquerors Domagnano in the semi-final.

In fact, Faetano made it four wins in succession as they overcame Folgore 1-0 in the final to take their third national title. Folgore's bid for a hat-trick of championship wins was wrecked by a solitary Faetano strike, from substitute Arcangeli, six minutes from time. Around 900 spectators watched the match, taking the aggregate attendance figure for the ten play-off games to 3,000.

The Coppa Titano was won by Cosmos, who thus made up for the disappointment of being runners-up a year earlier. They qualified for the latter stages as the second-placed team in their group behind Domagnano,

PLAYER OF THE SEASON

ANDY SELVA
Although he was born in the Italian capital of Rome, Andy Selva qualifies to play for San Marino because his father is a native of the tiny Principality. The 23-year-old striker was called up by new San Marino boss Gian Paolo Mazza for the Euro 2000 qualifying campaign, and although he suffered along with the rest of the team as they prolonged their sorry sequence of defeats, he did have the pleasure of joining the select band of San Marino internationals to score a goal when he converted a penalty on only his second appearance - in the 1-4 home defeat by Austria. Selva played for Italian Serie C2 side Catanazro in 1998/99, having previously played for two years in the same division for Fano. That makes him the only true full-time professional in the San Marino squad.

who beat them 3-1, but when the two teams met again, in the final, it was Cosmos who prevailed. They put on a sumptuous display to win 5-1 and take the trophy for the second time.

Neither champions Faetano nor Cup-winners Cosmos gained European entry as a result of their triumphs, but that will change in 2000, when San Marino is set to join every other UEFA member by entering teams into the European club competitions for the very first time.

INTERNATIONAL HONOURS

None

TOP SCORERS

22	Paride RENZI (Tre Penne)
21	Gian Luca GUALTIERI (Pennarossa)
19	BETTONI (Tre Fiori)
17	Marco BENEDETTINI (Virtus)
15	Enea ZUCCHI (Domagnano)
14	Diego GASPERONI (Murata)
	Denis MULARONI (Faetano)
	Oriano LAZZARETTI (Murata)
12	Stefano DE LUIGI (Murata)
	Andrea DURELLI (Folgore)
	Andrea TOSI (Fiorita)

NATIONAL TEAM RESULTS 98/99

Date	Opponent	H/A	Venue	Score	Scorer
10/10/98	Israel (ECQ)	H	Serravalle	0-5	
14/10/98	Austria (ECQ)	H	Serravalle	1-4	Selva (80p)
18/11/98	Cyprus (ECQ)	H	Serravalle	0-1	
10/02/99	Cyprus (ECQ)	A	Limassol	0-4	
31/03/99	Spain (ECQ)	H	Serravalle	0-6	
28/04/99	Austria (ECQ)	A	Graz	0-7	
05/06/99	Spain (ECQ)	A	Villarreal	0-9	

CAILUNGO

CLUB DIRECTORY

Società Polisportiva Cailungo
Via cà del Lunghi 11
47031 Cailungo
tel - 902413
Year of Formation - 1974
President - Flavio Gasperoni
Secretary - Daniele Forcellini
Coach - Danilo Grassi
Stadium - Fonte dell' Ovo (500)

APPEARANCES 98/99

	P	Ap	(s)	Gls
Matteo ANDREINI	M	2	(5)	
Massimo BOLLINI	A	5		3
CAMPAGNA	A	3		1
CANDUCCI	G	14		
Mirko CANTI	M	8		
Roberto CASADEI	M	8		1
Fabrizio CENNI	D	2	(4)	
Mirko CONTI	M	17	(3)	1
Enrico ERCOLANI	M	13	(2)	
Daniele FORCELLINI	D	5		
Marino GASPERONI	G	5		
Paolo GASPERONI	M	1	(7)	
Gianluca GERLONI (ITA)	M	8	(2)	1
Paolo GIACOBBI	D	14		
LOMBARDI	A	7	(6)	
Riccardo MAESTRINI	M	6		
MERLONI	D	6	(3)	
Marco MORRI	M	6		1
David MUCCIOLI	A	1	(4)	
Angelo MURACCINI	D		(1)	
Claudio RENZETTI	M	8	(5)	2
Thomas ROMANI (ITA)	A	15		4
Davide RONDELLI	D	15	(2)	
Daniele ROSSI	D	19	(2)	
SANTUCCI (ITA)	G	3		
SCHIARATURA	M	12	(3)	3
Giovanni STEFANELLI	D	11	(2)	
Adriano TOSI (ITA)	D	15		2
Luciano VOLPINARI	A	8	(5)	1
Mauro VOLPINARI	D	5	(4)	1

LEAGUE RESULTS 1998/99

12/09/98	Libertas	A	1-1	Casadei
19/09/98	Dogana	A	0-1	
26/09/98	Virtus	A	1-1	Romani (p)
03/10/98	Murata	H	1-3	Volpinari M.
17/10/98	Juvenes	H	2-4	Campagna, Tosi
24/10/98	Tre Penne	H	2-3	Morri, Volpinari L.
31/10/98	Faetano	A	0-2	
07/11/98	Cosmos	H	0-3	
14/11/98	Tre Fiori	H	2-3	Gerloni, Schiaratura
28/11/98	Montevito	A	1-1	Schiaratura
05/12/98	San Giovanni	H	1-1	og (Gatti)
12/12/98	Pennarossa	A	0-1	
19/12/98	Domagnano	A	0-3	
30/01/99	Folgore	H	2-4	Tosi (p), Renzetti
06/02/99	Fiorita	A	0-1	
20/02/99	Libertas	H	4-0	Romani 3, Schiaratura
27/02/99	Dogana	H	0-0	
06/03/99	Virtus	H	0-4	
13/03/99	Murata	A	2-3	Conti, Bollini
20/03/99	Juvenes	A	1-2	Bollini
27/03/99	Tre Penne	A	1-2	Renzetti
10/04/99	Faetano	H	1-0	Bollini

COSMOS

Società Polisportiva Cosmos
Strada del Bargello 36
47031 Falciano
tel - 996392
Year of Formation - 1979
President - Adelmiro Bartolini
Secretary - Stefano Bevitori
Coach - Bruno Albani
Stadium - Falciano (500)

MAJOR HONOURS
League Championship - (2) 1980, 1981.
Domestic Cup - (2) 1995, 1999.

APPEARANCES 98/99

	P	Ap	(s)	Gls
Fabrizio ALBANI	M	20		11
Matteo ALBANI	D	15		1
Alessandro BEVITORI	M	9	(3)	
Dario BICCHIARELLI	D	13		1
Stefano BORGHINI (ITA)	M	5	(4)	3
Agostino BUCCI	M	1	(6)	
Maurizio CECCOLI	D	14		
CECCONI	A	3	(4)	
Emanuel CELLI	M	16		1
Cristian COLONNA	M	5	(7)	
William DEL BENE	D	7	(3)	3
DONATI	G	2		
Adriano FORCELLINI	A	5	(4)	
Roberto FORCELLINI	A	3	(6)	
Luigi GASPERONI	M	4	(3)	
Claudio GUERRA	G	16		
Alessandro LEARDINI	M	16		
MONGIUSTI	A	3	(6)	
Pier Angelo MANZAROLI	M	11		4
Luca NANNI	A		(4)	
Gian Piero PASQUALI	D	1	(3)	
Giovanni PODAVINI (ITA)	D	4	(2)	
Marco PROTTI	A	6	(4)	1
RICCI	G	4		
Jonny ROSSI	M	14	(1)	2
Emanuele SANTI	D	8	(3)	1
Cristian SELVA	M	21		8
Cristian SENSOLI	D	4	(1)	
Silvano ZONZINI	M	12		

Date	Opponent	H/A	Score	Scorers
12/09/98	Pennarossa	A	1-0	og (Boschi)
19/09/98	San Giovanni	H	2-1	Selva, Albania F.
26/09/98	Fiorita	A	5-3	Selva 2, Protti, Manzaroli, og (Mezzanotte)
03/10/98	Montevito	H	1-1	Selva
17/10/98	Folgore	A	0-3	
24/10/98	Domagnano	A	1-2	Manzaroli
31/10/98	Tre Fiori	H	1-0	Albani F.
07/11/98	Cailungo	A	3-0	Rossi, Manzaroli, Santi
14/11/98	Murata	H	0-1	
28/11/98	Faetano	A	1-1	Albani F.
05/12/98	Juvenes	H	1-0	Manzaroli
12/12/98	Dogana	H	2-1	Selva, Del Bene
19/12/98	Virtus	A	0-1	
30/01/99	Tre Penne	A	1-1	Bicchiarelli (p)
06/02/99	Libertas	H	5-1	Albani F. 2, Celli, Selva, Del Bene
20/02/99	Pennarossa	H	3-2	Albani F., Selva, Borghini
27/02/99	San Giovanni	A	4-0	Albani F. 3, Del Bene
06/03/99	Fiorita	H	0-0	
13/03/99	Montevito	A	3-0	Albani F. 2, Selva
20/03/99	Folgore	H	0-1	
27/03/99	Domagnano	H	1-1	Rossi
10/04/99	Tre Fiori	A	3-2	Borghini 2 (1p), Albani M.

DOGANA

CLUB DIRECTORY

Gruppo Sportiva Dogana
CP 21
47031 Dogana
tel - 905156
Year of Formation - 1970
President - Massimo Morri
Secretary - Raul Bianchi
Coach - Varchetta
Stadium - Dogana (500)

MAJOR HONOURS
League Championship - (2) 1977, 1979.

APPEARANCES 98/99

		P	Ap	(s)	Gls
Angelo BABBONI	A	14		
Roberto BORASCO	D	17		1
Emanuel CAPICCHIONI	M	4	(3)	
Gian Luca CELLI	A	12	(4)	5
Bruno DE MARINI	D	3	(4)	
Giancarlo FALCONE	A	15		2
FOSCHI	G	20		1
Ivan FRISONI	D	15		
Luciano FRISONI	D	19		
Giovanni GASPARELLI	M	6	(4)	
Leonardo GASPERONI	D	5	(6)	1
Rolando GASPERONI	D	12		1
Cristian GIARDI	M	13	(3)	2
Giorgio GUIDI	D	5	(2)	
Roberto GUIDI	G		(1)	
MARINI	A	1	(1)	
Stefano MORRI	D	16		
Federico NANNI	M	6	(3)	
PAMANTINI	A	5		
PARI	G	2		
Luigi PROTTI	M	7	(3)	1
Alessandro ROSSI	M	14		
Fulvio TAMAGNINI	D	9	(6)	
Massimo VAGNETTI	D	9	(1)	
VARCHETTA	M	13		5

LEAGUE RESULTS 1998/99

12/09/98	Faetano	A	1-1	Falcone
19/09/98	Cailungo	H	1-0	Falcone
26/09/98	Murata	A	1-4	Varchetta
03/10/98	Virtus	H	0-0	
17/10/98	Libertas	H	0-0	
24/10/98	Juvenes	A	3-0	Celli 3
31/10/98	Tre Penne	H	1-3	og (Santi W.)
07/11/98	Domagnano	A	0-3	
14/11/98	Montevito	H	1-2	Gasperoni R.
28/11/98	Tre Fiori	H	1-3	Protti
05/12/98	Fiorita	A	0-1	
12/12/98	Cosmos	A	1-2	Varchetta
19/12/98	Pennarossa	H	1-2	Gasperoni L.
30/01/99	San Giovanni	H	3-0	Celli, Borasco, Pamantini
06/02/99	Folgore	A	1-1	Varchetta
20/02/99	Faetano	H	0-1	
27/02/99	Cailungo	A	0-0	
06/03/99	Murata	H	2-4	Varchetta, Giardi
13/03/99	Virtus	A	3-1	Celli, Foschi (p), Giardi (p)
20/03/99	Libertas	A	1-0	Varchetta
27/03/99	Juvenes	H	0-0	
10/04/99	Tre Penne	A	0-3	

DOMAGNANO

CLUB DIRECTORY

Società Polisportiva Domagnano
Via Cà Giannino 1
47031 Domagnano
tel - 902059
Year of Formation - 1966
President - Marino Moretti
Secretary - Nazareno Marani
Coach - Marco Pazzini
Stadium - Domagnano (500)

MAJOR HONOURS
League Championship - (2) 1972, 1989.
Domestic Cup - (4) 1988, 1990, 1992, 1996.

APPEARANCES 98/99

		P	Ap	(s)	Gls
Fabio BACIOCCHI	D	15			1
BIANCONI	M	1	(4)		1
Enrico BOLLINI	M	1	(6)		
Silvano BOLLINI	D	6	(3)		
Samuele BUGLI	G	12			
Stefano CAPICCHIONI	D	21			1
Larry CAPICCHIONI	D		(5)		
Daniele DONATI	M	9			2
Federico DONATI	M	7	(3)		
Fabio FELICI	M	13			1
GASPERI	A	14			6
GENTILINI (ITA)	G	10			
Paolo GIACOBBI	D	4	(1)		
PAGNETTI	D	13	(4)		2
Loris PALMIERI	D	13			1
Alessandro PASOLINI	M	3	(7)		1
Oscar PASOLINI	M	21			
Marco PAZZINI	A	19			2
Andrea PIERINI	D	2	(6)		1
Roberto RASCHI	M	4	(5)		1
Massimo ROSSI	A	12	(4)		
William SANTI	D	3	(2)		5
SAPIGNI	D	4			3
Mauro VALENTINI	D	14			1
Enea ZUCCHI	A	21			15

LEAGUE RESULTS 1998/99

12/09/98	Tre Fiori	H	2-2	Zucchi 2
19/09/98	Montevito	A	0-4	
26/09/98	San Giovanni	A	2-2	Zucchi (p), Bianconi
03/10/98	Pennarossa	H	2-0	Pierini, Zucchi
17/10/98	Fiorita	A	2-0	Gasperi, Pasolini A.
24/10/98	Cosmos	H	2-1	Zucchi, Pagnetti
31/10/98	Folgore	A	0-1	
07/11/98	Dogana	H	3-0	Zucchi 2, Felici
14/11/98	Libertas	A	3-2	Zucchi 2, Sapigni
28/11/98	Murata	A	3-5	Pazzini, Zucchi, Sapigni
05/12/98	Virtus	H	2-1	Donati D., Sapigni
12/12/98	Faetano	A	2-1	Donati D., Zucchi
19/12/98	Cailungo	H	3-0	Zucchi, Baciocchi, Santi
30/01/99	Juvenes	A	1-1	Gasperi
06/02/99	Tre Penne	H	0-0	
20/02/99	Tre Fiori	A	1-3	Zucchi
27/02/99	Montevito	H	2-1	Capicchioni S., Santi
06/03/99	San Giovanni	H	4-0	Raschi, Valentini, Gasperi, Palmieri
13/03/99	Pennarossa	A	6-2	Pagnetti, Gasperi 2, Zucchi, Pazzini, Santi
20/03/99	Fiorita	H	3-1	Santi 2, Zucchi (p)
27/03/99	Cosmos	A	1-1	Gasperi
10/04/99	Folgore	H	0-0	

FAETANO

CLUB DIRECTORY

Società Calcio Faetano
Piazza del Massaro 2
47031 Faetano
tel - 996057
Year of Formation - 1962
President - Fabio Gasperoni
Secretary - Riccardo Gasperoni
Coach - Berto Carlino
Stadium - Faetano (500)

MAJOR HONOURS
League Championship - (3) 1986, 1991, 1999.
Domestic Cup - (3) 1993, 1994, 1998.

APPEARANCES 98/99

	P	Ap	(s)	Gls
Ettore BEDETTI	G	2		
Massimo BRANDOLINI	A	3	(2)	
Alessandro CASADEI	D	1	(3)	
Fulvio CASADEI	D	5	(3)	2
Marco CONTI	D	20		1
DALL'OLIO	M	1	(4)	
Agostino DALL'OLMO	D	19		
Pier Domenico DELLA VALLE	M	2	(4)	
Pier Marino DELLA VALLE	D	17	(1)	1
Paolo DONATI	D	13		
Maurizio GASPERONI	M	8	(4)	
Mirko GASPERONI	A	3	(2)	
Riccardo GASPERONI	D	14		
Massimiliano GIANNI	A	18		4
LANGELLA	D	11		
LIONETTI	M	2	(6)	
Federico MORONI	D	12		2
Michele MORONI	M	1	(5)	
Paolo MORONI	A	8	(3)	1
Stefano MUCCIOLI	G	20		
Denis MULARONI	M	13	(4)	14
Manuel MULARONI	M	6	(4)	
Denis RICCARDI	M	15	(3)	
Michele RICCARDI	D	2	(5)	
Silvio RINALDI	M	22		4
Gloriano ZONZINI	D	4	(3)	

LEAGUE RESULTS 1998/99

12/09/98	Dogana	H	1-1	og (Gasperoni R.)
19/09/98	Tre Penne	A	0-1	
26/09/98	Juvenes	H	0-0	
03/10/98	Libertas	A	1-2	Mularoni D.
17/10/98	Murata	H	4-0	Gianni 2, Mularoni D. 2
24/10/98	Virtus	A	1-0	Casadei F.
31/10/98	Cailungo	H	2-0	Rinaldi (p), Mularoni D.
07/11/98	Pennarossa	A	1-2	Della Valle P.M.
14/11/98	Fiorita	H	2-0	Mularoni D., Casadei F.
28/11/98	Cosmos	H	1-1	Mularoni D.
05/11/98	Folgore	A	0-0	
12/12/98	Domagnano	H	1-2	Mularoni D.
19/12/98	San Giovanni	A	3-0	Gianni, Mularoni D. 2
30/01/99	Montevito	A	1-0	Gianni
06/02/99	Tre Fiori	H	1-0	Rinaldi (p)
20/02/99	Dogana	A	1-0	Moroni F. (p)
27/02/99	Tre Penne	H	0-1	
06/03/99	Juvenes	A	2-1	Rinaldi 2
13/03/99	Libertas	H	3-1	Mularoni D. 2, Moroni P.
20/03/99	Murata	A	2-2	Mularoni D. 2
27/03/99	Virtus	H	3-1	Conti (p), Moroni F., Mularoni D.
10/04/99	Cailungo	A	0-1	

FIORITA

Società Polisportiva La Fiorita
Via del Dragone 17
47031 Montegiardino
tel - 996202
Year of Formation - 1967
President - Luciano Zanotti
Secretary - Paolo Crescentini
Coach - Luciano Zanotti
Stadium - Montegiardino (200)

MAJOR HONOURS
League Championship - (2) 1987, 1990.
Domestic Cup - (1) 1986.

	P	Ap	(s)	Gls
Julian ALYAJ (TUR)	M	16	(4)	1
Loris BALDACCI	D	12		1
Ivan BALZI	M	6	(6)	1
Cristian BERARDI	A	2	(5)	
BIORDI	M	9	(3)	
CANAREZZA	M	3	(6)	
Marcello FABBRI	G	1	(1)	
Federico FRANCINI	M	10	(3)	1
Giuseppe FRANCIONI	D	3	(4)	
GABRIELLI (ITA)	G	7	(1)	
Domenico GORGORONI (ITA)	M	4	(5)	
MANCINI	D	4	(2)	
Michele MASSARI	D	4	(3)	
MEZZANOTTE	M	18		1
MONTALI	D	16	(2)	2
Riccardo MULARONI	A	3	(2)	
Carlo MURACCINI	D	17		
Paolo RASCHI	A	4	(4)	2
Luca RICCARDI	A	13	(3)	
Claudio RIGHI	D	17	(1)	
Massimo TOCCACELI	D	1	(3)	
Silvano TOCCACELI	M	2	(2)	
Marco TOMASSONI	D	1		
Andrea TOSI	A	20		12
Michele ZAFFERANI	A	4	(2)	
Thomas ZAFFERANI	M	4		
Alessandro ZANOTTI	G	14		
Manuel ZANOTTI	A	3		2
Marco ZANOTTI	A	5		4
Paolo ZANOTTI	D	19		

12/09/98	Folgore	A	2-1	Tosi 2
19/09/98	Pennarossa	H	2-3	Tosi, Zanotti Man.
26/09/98	Cosmos	H	3-5	Baldacci, Tosi, og (Celli)
03/10/98	Tre Fiori	A	3-2	Zanotti Mar. 2, Tosi
17/10/98	Domagnano	H	0-2	
24/10/98	Montevito	H	0-0	
31/10/98	San Giovanni	A	0-1	
07/11/98	Libertas	H	3-1	Raschi 2, Tosi
14/11/98	Faetano	A	0-2	
28/11/98	Tre Penne	A	2-1	og (Santi W.), Tosi
05/12/98	Dogana	H	1-0	Tosi
12/12/98	Virtus	H	1-0	Tosi
19/12/98	Juvenes	A	2-1	Zanotti Mar., Tosi
30/01/99	Murata	A	0-3	
06/02/99	Cailungo	H	1-0	Zanotti Man.
20/02/99	Folgore	H	2-3	Mezzanotte, Balzi (p)
27/02/99	Pennarossa	A	1-1	Zanotti Mar.
06/03/99	Cosmos	A	0-0	
13/03/99	Tre Fiori	H	2-1	Montali 2 (2p)
20/03/99	Domagnano	A	1-3	Alyaj
27/03/99	Montevito	A	2-2	Tosi 2
10/04/99	San Giovanni	H	1-0	Francini

FOLGORE

CLUB DIRECTORY

Società Sportiva Folgore
Strada La Zanetta 10
47031 Falciano
tel - 908088
Year of Formation - 1972
President - Svenio Piastra
Secretary - Amato Bernardini
Coach - Sereno Uraldi
Stadium - Falciano (500)

MAJOR HONOURS
League Championship - (2) 1997, 1998.

APPEARANCES 98/99

		P	Ap	(s)	Gls
Gabriele BARTOLETTI	D	13		(2)	1
Andrea BARTOLI (ITA)	D	1		(4)	
Cristian BERNARDINI	M			(4)	1
Augusto BIANCHI	D	10		(3)	
Federico BIANCHI	A	1		(3)	
Simone BIANCHI	A	21			7
David BOLOGNA	M	7		(5)	2
Maurizio CENSONI	M	7		(1)	1
Claudio CORBELLI	M	22			
Giuliano CORBELLI	D			(8)	
Andrea DURELLI	A	18			12
Luigi FERRANTE (ITA)	D			(1)	
Federico GASPERONI	G	2			
Ferdinando GASPERONI	D	12		(2)	2
Graziano GIOVAGNOLI	M	14			
Simone GUIDI	A	2		(3)	
Matteo MAZZA	A	19			8
Fabrizio PELLICCIONI	D	18			2
Federico PELLICCIONI	M	16			3
Enrico PROSPERINI	D	1		(4)	
Matteo QUADRONI (ITA)	G	16			
Leonardo ROSSI	D	12		(1)	1
SACCANI	M	1		(3)	
Anselmo SENSOLI	G	4			
SOPRANZI	M	5		(1)	
Francesco UGOLINI	M	12		(2)	2
Alessandro ZANOTTI	A	11		(4)	8
Loris ZANOTTI	A	2		(3)	

LEAGUE RESULTS 1998/99

12/09/98	Fiorita	H	1-2	Pelliccioni Fa.
19/09/98	Tre Fiori	A	1-1	Bianchi S.
26/09/98	Montevito	H	3-4	Pelliccioni Fe., Zanotti A.,
				Gasperoni Fer.
03/10/98	San Giovanni	A	4-1	Bologna, Durelli, Bianchi S.,
				Mazza
17/10/98	Cosmos	H	3-0	Durelli 2, Pelliccioni Fe.
24/10/98	Pennarossa	A	4-1	Censoni, Durelli, Mazza, Bartoletti
31/10/98	Domagnano	H	1-0	Bologna
07/11/98	Virtus	A	3-3	Bianchi S., Mazza, Durelli
14/11/98	Tre Penne	H	3-3	Bianchi S. 2 (1p), Zanotti A.
28/11/98	Juvenes	A	1-3	Zanotti A.
05/12/98	Faetano	H	0-0	
12/12/98	Libertas	A	4-1	Ugolini, Zanotti A. 2, Durelli
19/12/98	Murata	H	3-0	Zanotti A., Durelli, Mazza
30/01/99	Cailungo	A	4-2	Mazza 2, Durelli, Rossi
06/02/99	Dogana	H	1-1	Gasperoni Fer.
20/02/99	Fiorita	A	3-2	Pelliccioni Fa., Ugolini, Mazza
27/02/99	Tre Fiori	H	3-3	Durelli 2 (1p), Pelliccioni Fe.
06/03/99	Montevito	A	4-1	Bianchi S., og (Casali),
				Zanotti A. 2
13/03/99	San Giovanni	H	3-1	Sopranzi, Durelli, Bernardini
20/03/99	Cosmos	A	1-0	Mazza
27/03/99	Pennarossa	H	2-1	Bianchi S., Durelli
10/04/99	Domagnano	A	0-0	

JUVENES

Società Sportiva Juvenes
Via Balducci
47031 Serravalle
tel - 900336
Year of Formation - 1953
President - Bruno Passerini
Secretary - Luigi Zafferani
Coach - Danilo Forcellini
Stadium - Domagnano (500)

MAJOR HONOURS
League Championship - (5)
1965, 1968, 1976, 1978, 1984.

APPEARANCES 98/99

	P	Ap	(s)	Gls
Pier Angelo AMATI	D	6	(3)	1
Gian Luigi BALDUCCI	M	3	(6)	
Luigi BELISARDI	D	2	(1)	
Fabrizio BERNARDI	M	3	(2)	
Daniele BERTI	M	9	(3)	5
Thomas BERTI	D	13	(2)	4
Alessandro BETTI	A	6	(2)	
Simone BIZZOCCHI	A	2	(2)	
Claudio CANTI	D	19		
Andrea CASADEI	A	14	(2)	
Carlo CASADEI	G	11	(1)	
Daniele CASADEI	G	10		
Roberto CASADEI	A	1	(2)	
Maurizio CECCOLI	D	4		
COLA	M	13		1
Thomas FORCELLINI	M	7	(1)	1
Federico FRANCINI	M	7	(1)	
Athos GASPERONI	M	13	(1)	4
Maurizio GASPERONI	D	2	(2)	
Raoul GHERARDI	D	4	(1)	
Michele GIACOBBI	M	6	(2)	
Gianluca GOTTI	A	1	(3)	
William GUERRA	D	15		
Paolo GUIDI	M	2	(3)	
LOLLI	A	1	(3)	
Gabriele LOTTI	A	19		
Federico MAZZA	M	1	(2)	
Paolo MONTAGNA	A	2		1
MURATORI	D	7	(3)	1
PANDOLFI	D	8	(3)	1
Paolo RASCHI	M	10	(2)	
Fabio ROSSI	M	1	(5)	
Roberto SARTI	A	7		
Daniele ZAFFERANI	D	2	(5)	

LEAGUE RESULTS 1998/99

12/09/98	Virtus	A	1-3	Montagna
19/09/98	Libertas	H	0-0	
26/09/98	Faetano	A	0-0	
03/10/98	Tre Penne	H	0-1	
17/10/98	Cailungo	A	4-2	Gasperoni A. 2, Forcellini, Muratori
24/10/98	Dogana	H	0-3	
31/10/98	Murata	H	0-1	
07/11/98	Tre Fiori	A	0-3	
14/11/98	Pennarossa	H	2-4	Amati, Berti D.
28/11/98	Folgore	H	3-1	Cola, Pandolfi, Berti T.
05/12/98	Cosmos	A	0-1	
12/12/98	Montevito	A	0-2	
19/12/98	Fiorita	H	1-2	Berti D.
30/01/99	Domagnano	H	1-1	Berti T.
06/02/99	San Giovanni	A	1-2	Gasperoni A.
20/02/99	Virtus	H	2-1	Berti T., Berti D.
27/02/99	Libertas	A	2-2	Berti D. (p), Gasperoni A.
06/03/99	Faetano	H	1-2	og (Gasperoni M.)
13/03/99	Tre Penne	A	0-4	
20/03/99	Cailungo	H	2-1	Berti D. (p)
27/03/99	Dogana	A	0-0	Berti T.
10/04/99	Murata	A	0-3	(w/o)

LIBERTAS

CLUB DIRECTORY

Società Polisportiva Libertas
Via 28 Luglio 1/B
47031 Borgomaggiore
tel - 906472
Year of Formation - 1928
President - Paride Andreoli
Secretary - Primo Toccaceli
Coach - Pier Luigi Parenti
Stadium - Fonte dell'Ovo (500)

MAJOR HONOURS
League Championship - (7)
1937, 1950, 1954, 1958, 1959, 1961, 1996.
Domestic Cup - (3) 1987, 1989, 1991.

APPEARANCES 98/99

	P	Ap	(s)	Gls
Franco AGARICI	M	20		7
Sandro AGARICI	D	15	(1)	
Nicola ALBANI	M	6	(3)	3
Agostino BIORDI	G	1		
Agostino BIORDI	A	12	(2)	
Stefano BIORDI	F	7	(3)	
Federico CAVALLI	M	7	(1)	1
Michele CECCOLI	G	2		
Federico FOSCOLI	G	4	(1)	
Franco FRANCIOSI	A	6	(2)	
Massimo GHIOTTI	M	15		5
Ivan GRASSI	D	2	(2)	
Giorgio MARANI	D	2	(6)	
Roberto MARCUCCI	D	1	(4)	
Fabio MINI	M	10	(2)	
Luca MORONI	D	14	(1)	
Matteo RIGHI	G	14	(1)	
Federico ROSSI	D	9	(7)	
Floriano SPERINDIO	A	15		2
Gianluca STEFANELLI	M	4	(3)	
Daniele TOCCACELI	M	8	(2)	1
Ivan TOCCACELI	M	18		1
Valerio TOCCACELI	M	17		
Andrea VANNUCCI	G	1		
Andrea VANNUCCI	A	17		3
Mario ZANOTTI	A		(6)	

L'EAGUE RESULTS 1998/99

12/09/98	Cailungo	H	1-1	Agarici F.
19/09/98	Juvenes	A	0-0	
26/09/98	Tre Penne	H	3-6	Ghiotti 2, Vannucci
03/10/98	Faetano	H	2-1	Albani 2
17/10/98	Dogana	A	0-0	
24/10/98	Murata	A	1-6	Albani
31/10/98	Virtus	H	1-3	Agarici F.
07/11/98	Fiorita	A	1-3	Agarici F.
14/11/98	Domagnano	H	2-3	Ghiotti, Cavalli
28/11/98	San Giovanni	H	2-2	Ghiotti, Agarici F.
05/12/98	Montevito	A	1-1	Toccaceli I.
12/12/98	Folgore	H	1-4	Ghiotti
19/12/98	Tre Fiori	A	0-2	
30/01/99	Pennarossa	H	2-3	Sperindio, Agarici F. (p)
06/02/99	Cosmos	A	1-5	Sperindio
20/02/99	Cailungo	A	0-4	
27/02/99	Juvenes	H	2-2	Vannucci
06/03/99	Tre Penne	A	1-3	Agarici F. (p)
13/03/99	Faetano	A	1-3	Vannucci
20/03/99	Dogana	H	0-1	
27/03/99	Murata	H	1-3	Toccaceli D.
10/04/99	Virtus	A	2-1	Agarici F. (p), Bonifazi

MONTEVITO

Società Sportiva Montevito
Via La Rena 19
47031 Fiorentino
tel - 888208
Year of Formation - 1974
President - Silvio Fabbri
Secretary - Mimmo Protti
Coach - Antonio Chiari
Stadium - Fiorentino (2,000)

MAJOR HONOURS
League Championship - (1) 1992.

APPEARANCES 98/99

	P	Ap	(s)	Gls
Denis AMICI	M	13	(1)	
Davide ANGELINI (ITA)	D	9	(2)	
Andrea ARLOTTI (ITA)	M	2	(5)	
Diego BALDACCI	M	13	(3)	3
Ettore BEDETTI	G	2		
Daniele BONCI (ITA)	M	16	(2)	4
Giacomo CASADEI	M	21		3
Maurizio CASALI	D	8	(3)	
Gian Luca CECCHETTI	M		(5)	
Andrea CHIARELLI	D		(4)	
Mauro COMANDUCCI (ITA)	M	20		5
Roberto CONTADINI	D	6	(4)	
Denis FABBRI	M	2	(4)	
Daniel FRANCESCONI	G	1		
Leo Marino FRANCIONI	D	6	(1)	
Fabio GIARDI	M	8	(1)	2
Roberto GIARDI	M	20		
Ivan GUERRA	A	6	(2)	
Roberto GUERRA	G	1	(1)	
Roberto GUERRA	A	3	(4)	
Loris MARANI	G	6	(1)	
Federico MARZI	D	3	(2)	
Fabrizio MINI	D	18		1
Cristian MONALDI	D	1	(1)	
Werther MONTANARI	G	12		
Mimmo PROTTI	M		(1)	
Stefano RIDOLFI	A	4	(1)	
Gustavo ROSSINI (ARG)	A	19		11
Armando SCHIANO	A	4	(2)	
Filippo ZAVOLI	M	13	(2)	3
Paolo ZONZINI	D	5	(3)	

LEAGUE RESULTS 1998/99

12/09/98	San Giovanni	A	1-0	Bonci
19/09/98	Domagnano	H	4-0	Baldacci, Bonci, Rossini 2
26/09/98	Folgore	A	4-3	Baldacci 2, Rossini, Zavoli
03/10/98	Cosmos	A	1-1	Comanducci (p)
17/10/98	Tre Fiori	H	1-2	Comanducci (p)
24/10/98	Fiorita	A	0-0	
31/10/98	Pennarossa	H	1-1	Casadei
07/11/98	Murata	A	0-1	
14/11/98	Dogana	A	2-1	Bonci 2
28/11/98	Cailungo	H	1-1	Rossini
05/12/98	Libertas	H	1-1	Comanducci (p)
12/12/98	Juvenes	H	2-0	Zavoli, Rossini
19/12/98	Tre Penne	A	3-2	Comanducci (p), Giardi F., Rossini
30/01/99	Faetano	H	0-1	
06/02/99	Virtus	A	1-7	Mini
20/02/99	San Giovanni	H	2-1	Rossini, Giardi F.
27/02/99	Domagnano	A	1-2	Rossini
06/03/99	Folgore	H	1-4	Comanducci (p)
13/03/99	Cosmos	H	0-3	
20/03/99	Tre Fiori	A	2-3	Rossini 2
27/03/99	Fiorita	H	2-2	Casadei, Rossini
10/04/99	Pennarossa	A	2-2	Casadei, Zavoli

MURATA

CLUB DIRECTORY

Società Sportiva Murata
Via del Serrone
47031 Murata
tel - 997440
Year of Formation - 1966
President - Libero Casadei
Secretary - Giancarlo Simoncini
Coach - Duilio Felici
Stadium - Acquaviva (1,000)

MAJOR HONOURS
Domestic Cup - (1) 1997.

APPEARANCES 98/99

	P	Ap	(s)	Gls
Alberto ALBERTINI (ITA)	M	18		
Michele BACCHIOCCHI	D	16		
Carlo BALSIMELLI	M	19		3
Manuel BERARDI	A		(4)	
Davide CHIARUZZI	G	5		
Agostino CORBELLI	D	13	(1)	1
Stefano DE LUIGI	A	16		12
Andrea GASPERONI	D	1	(6)	3
Diego GASPERONI	A	20		14
Giove GIANNINI	D	19		
Oriano LAZZARETTI	A	19		14
Lorenzo MANCHISI (ITA)	M	16		2
Giorgio MIGANI	M	8	(3)	
Alan MULARONI	M	17		1
Denis OTTAVIANI	M	1	(4)	
Nicola PELLICCIONI	D	1	(4)	
Stefano PENSERINI	D	8	(1)	2
PETRETI (ROM)	M	1	(1)	
Raffaele RICCI	M	1	(2)	
Alessandro SARTINI	M	4	(5)	2
Michele SERRA	D	1	(7)	
Serafino TERENZI	D	9	(4)	1
Jader VAGNINI	M	2	(7)	
Denis VENERUCCI	G	16		

LEAGUE RESULTS 1998/99

12/09/98	Tre Penne	H	3-2	Gasperoni D. (p), De Luigi, Mazzaretti
19/09/98	Virtus	H	2-6	Gasperoni D. 2
26/09/98	Dogana	H	4-1	Gasperoni D. 3 (2p), Lazzaretti
03/10/98	Cailungo	A	3-1	Balsimelli, Gasperoni D., og (Giacobbi)
17/10/98	Faetano	A	0-4	
24/10/98	Libertas	H	6-1	De Luigi 4, Lazzaretti, Gasperoni D.
31/10/98	Juvenes	A	1-0	Manchisi
07/11/98	Montevito	H	1-0	De Luigi
14/11/98	Cosmos	A	1-0	Lazzaretti
28/11/98	Domagnano	H	5-3	Lazzaretti 2, Gasperoni D. 2 (1p), Sartini
05/12/98	Tre Fiori	A	1-0	Manchisi
12/12/98	San Giovanni	A	4-1	Corbelli, Balsimelli, De Luigi, Terenzi
19/12/98	Folgore	A	0-3	
30/01/99	Fiorita	H	3-0	Lazzaretti, Balsimelli, Mularoni
06/02/99	Pennarossa	H	7-3	Gasperoni D., Lazzaretti 4, Penserini, og (Guerra)
20/02/99	Tre Penne	A	2-2	De Luigi, Gasperoni D. (p)
27/02/99	Virtus	A	2-0	Penserini, De Luigi
06/03/99	Dogana	A	4-2	Lazzaretti 2, De Luigi, Gasperoni D.
13/03/99	Cailungo	H	3-2	Gasperoni A. 3
20/03/99	Faetano	H	2-2	De Luigi 2
27/03/99	Libertas	A	3-1	Lazzaretti, Sartini, Gasperoni D.
10/04/99	Juvenes	H	3-0	(w/o)

PENNAROSSA

CLUB DIRECTORY

Società Sportiva Pennarossa
Via C. Forti 97
47031 Chiesanuova
tel - 924130
Year of Formation - 1968
President - Massimo Barbieri
Secretary - Ezio Zavoli
Coach - Riccardo Pancotti
Stadium - Chiesanuova (500)

APPEARANCES 98/99

	P	Ap	(s)	Gls
Nicola ALBERTINI	M	15	(1)	
Stefano BENEDETTINI	A	4	(3)	
Simone BERGANTINI	D	2	(1)	
Ivan BONCI	A	3	(2)	1
Vincenzo BOSCHI	M	14	(2)	
Marco BROCCOLI	A	2	(2)	
Gian Luca CESARINI	G	7	(1)	
Giovanni CHIARUZZI	D	1	(3)	
Danilo CIACCI	A	3	(2)	1
Nicola CIACCI	M	5	(2)	2
Ligor COBO (ALB)	M	12	(1)	8
Enrico ESPOSITO	D	3		
Angelo FAMIGLIETTI	M	8	(3)	
Gilberto FELICI	M	21		
Gabriele FRISONI	G	15		
Gian Luca GUALTIERI	A	20		21
Andrea GUERRA	D	18		
Paolo MARIOTTI	M	18		
Alessandro PANCOTTI	A	19		9
Paolo RAGANINI	A	1	(2)	
Nicola SATALINO (ITA)	D	20		
Davide SELVA	D	5	(1)	
Tiziano SELVA	M	3	(4)	
Emanuele SEMPRINI (ITA)	D	12		
Andrea TOSI (ITA)	M	11		

LEAGUE RESULTS 1998/99

12/09/98	Cosmos	H	0-1	
19/09/98	Fiorita	A	3-2	Gualtieri, Pancotti 2
26/09/98	Tre Fiori	H	1-2	Gualtieri
03/10/98	Domagnano	A	0-2	
17/10/98	San Giovanni	H	0-3	
24/10/98	Folgore	H	1-4	Ciacci D. (p)
31/10/98	Montevito	A	1-1	Gualtieri
07/11/98	Faetano	H	2-1	Gualtieri, Pancotti
14/11/98	Juvenes	A	4-2	Gualtieri 3, Cobo
28/11/98	Virtus	H	2-2	Gualtieri, Pancotti
05/12/98	Tre Penne	H	7-3	Cobo 3, Gualtieri 2, Ciacci N.
12/12/98	Cailungo	H	1-0	Gualtieri
19/12/98	Dogana	A	2-1	Pancotti, Gualtieri
30/01/99	Libertas	A	3-2	Cobo, Gualtieri 2
06/02/99	Murata	A	3-7	Gualtieri 3
20/02/99	Cosmos	A	2-3	Cobo, Bonci
27/02/99	Fiorita	H	1-1	Pancotti
06/03/99	Tre Fiori	A	2-2	Cobo, Gualtieri (p)
13/03/99	Domagnano	H	2-6	Cobo, Gualtieri
20/03/99	San Giovanni	A	2-2	Gualtieri 2
27/03/99	Folgore	A	1-2	Pancotti
10/04/99	Montevito	H	2-2	Pancotti 2

SAN GIOVANNI

CLUB DIRECTORY

Società Sportiva San Giovanni
Strada San Gianno
47031 San Giovanni
tel - 906715
Year of Formation - 1948
President - Valerio Zanotti
Secretary - Walter Santi
Coach - Marinelli
Stadium - Chiesanuova (500)

APPEARANCES 98/99

	P	Ap	(s)	Gls
Luca ALBANI	M	1	(5)	
Fabrizio BINDI	D	10	(4)	
Mario BECCARI	M	4	(6)	
Michele CAPICCHIONI	M	2	(5)	
Stefano CIACCI (ITA)	G	17		
Nicola CONTI	D	2	(6)	
Fabrizio COSTANTINI	M	9	(4)	
Alessandro FAITANINI	D	12	(3)	3
Daniele FRANCIONI	M	11	(3)	
Gianluca GATTI	A	12	(1)	4
Massimo GAZZI	M	22		2
MANNI	D	14		
Denis MANZI	M	4	(3)	
MARINELLI	M	18		1
Davide MASACCI	A	12	(3)	3
MIANI	D	2	(3)	
Diego PELLANDRA	D	3	(3)	
Cornell PETRE (ARG)	M	19		
Davide RASTELLI	M	10	(3)	
Luigi RASTELLI	G	5		
SERRA	M	4	(3)	
Loris VALENTINI	D	9	(1)	
VINCENZI	M	6	(4)	2
Yasar YAZICI (TUR)	A	19		6
Luca ZANOTTI	M	15	(2)	

LEAGUE RESULTS 1998/99

12/09/98	Montevito	H	0-1	
19/09/98	Cosmos	A	1-2	Masacci
26/09/98	Domagnano	H	2-2	Gatti 2
03/10/98	Folgore	H	1-4	Gazzi
17/10/98	Pennarossa	A	3-0	Gazzi, Tazici, Faitanini
24/10/98	Tre Fiori	H	0-0	
31/10/98	Fiorita	H	1-0	Faitanini
07/11/98	Tre Penne	A	3-3	Gatti, Marinelli, Masacci
14/11/98	Virtus	H	0-2	
28/11/98	Libertas	A	2-2	Masacci, Yazici (p)
05/12/98	Cailungo	A	1-1	Gatti
12/12/98	Murata	H	1-4	Yazici
19/12/98	Faetano	H	0-3	
30/01/99	Dogana	A	0-3	
06/02/99	Juvenes	H	2-1	Yazici 2
20/02/99	Montevito	A	1-2	Faitanini
27/02/99	Cosmos	H	0-4	
06/03/99	Domagnano	A	0-4	
13/03/99	Folgore	A	1-3	Yazici
20/03/99	Pennarossa	H	2-2	Vincenzi 2
27/03/99	Tre Fiori	A	0-3	
10/04/99	Fiorita	A	0-1	

TRE FIORI

CLUB DIRECTORY

Società Polisportiva Tre Fiori
Via 21 Settembre 93
47031 Fiorentino
tel - 878026
Year of Formation - 1949
President - Marino Casadei
Secretary - Mauro Mancini
Coach - Giorgio Leoni
Stadium - Fiorentino (2,000)

MAJOR HONOURS
League Championship - (9) 1966, 1971, 1974,
1975, 1985, 1988, 1993, 1994, 1995.

APPEARANCES 98/99

		P	Ap	(s)	Gls
Federico AMICI	D	1	(3)		
Roberto BENEDETTINI	G	2			
Roberto BENEDETTINI	M	17		5	
BETTONI	A	17		19	
Gabriele CAPICCHIONI	M	17			
Alfredo CECCHETTI	M	9	(4)		
Davide CECCHETTI	D	12	(3)	1	
Luca CONTI	M	10	(5)		
Massimo DOLCINI	M	8	(4)		
Fabio FERRARINI	D	8	(6)		
Nicola MANZARI	G	2	(1)		
Massimo MARIOTTI	D	14	(3)		
Ivan MATTEONI	D	16		3	
Jader MATTEONI	M	15	(1)	1	
Manuel MATTEONI	M	12	(2)		
Oscar MUSCIONI	M	9	(5)		
Nicola PARENTI	G	13			
Marco PELLICCIONI	G	5			
Dario SARTORI (ARG)	A	18		9	
Vasile TUDOSE (ROM)	A	5		2	
Khalid ZABOUL (MAR)	M	11	(4)	5	
Matteo ZAVOLI	D	21			

LEAGUE RESULTS 1998/99

Date	Opponent	H/A	Score	Scorers
12/09/98	Domagnano	A	2-2	Bettoni, Sartori
19/09/98	Folgore	H	1-1	Sartori
26/09/98	Pennarossa	A	2-1	Tudose, Sartori (p)
03/10/98	Fiorita	H	2-3	Tudose, Matteoni J.
17/10/98	Montevito	A	2-1	Bettoni, Zaboul
24/10/98	San Giovanni	A	0-0	
31/10/98	Cosmos	A	0-1	
07/11/98	Juvenes	H	3-0	Matteoni I., Bettoni 2
14/11/98	Cailungo	A	3-2	Matteoni I. 2, Bettoni
28/11/98	Dogana	A	3-1	Zaboul, Bettoni, Benedettini
05/12/98	Murata	H	0-1	
12/12/98	Tre Penne	H	3-3	Bettoni 2 (1p), Sartori
19/12/98	Libertas	H	2-0	Sartori, Zaboul
30/01/99	Virtus	A	5-4	Sartori 2, Benedettini 2, Bettoni (p)
06/02/99	Faetano	A	0-1	
20/02/99	Domagnano	H	3-1	Bettoni 3
27/02/99	Folgore	A	3-3	Bettoni 2 (1p), Zaboul
06/03/99	Pennarossa	H	2-2	Benedettini, Sartori
13/03/99	Fiorita	A	1-2	Bettoni (p)
20/03/99	Montevito	H	3-2	Cecchetti D., Benedettini, Bettoni
27/03/99	San Giovanni	H	3-0	Sartori, Bettoni 2 (1p)
10/04/99	Cosmos	H	2-3	Bettoni (p), Zaboul

TRE PENNE

Società Polisportiva Tre Penne
Via Ugo Bassi 13
47031 Borgo Maggiore
tel - 906699
fax - 903758
Year of Formation - 1956
President - Andrea Della Balda
Secretary - Franco Santi
Coach - Alessandro Giaquinto
Stadium - Fonte Dell'Ovo (500)

MAJOR HONOURS
League Championship - (4)
1967, 1970, 1982, 1983.

APPEARANCES 98/99

	P	Ap	(s)	Gls
Luca ANTONELLI	G	3	(1)	
Stefano BOLLINI	D	8	(3)	1
Aldo CAPICCHIONI	M	16		3
Marco CAPICCHIONI	D	3	(4)	2
DE ANGELI	G	15		
DE ANGELI	A	1		
Danilo DE BIAGI	D	3	(4)	
Sergio DEL BIANCO (ITA)	M	6	(4)	
Andrea DELLA BALDA	A	2	(5)	
Franco DELLA BALDA	M	8	(4)	
Simone DELLA BALDA	D	19		2
Daniele FANTINI	M	5	(3)	1
Alessandro GIAQUINTO	M	17		6
Loris GOBBI	A	1	(3)	
Paolo GOBBI	G	1		
Paolo GOBBI	D	6	(2)	
Andrea GUALTIERI	D	7	(3)	1
Davide GUALTIERI	M	15		2
MAZZA	G	2		
Paolo NANNI	G	1		
Paolo NANNI	M	8	(3)	
Carlo PIVA	A	2	(2)	
Paride RENZI	A	21		22
Reves SALVATORI	M	15		1
Emiliano SANTI	D	5	(4)	1
Franco SANTI	A	18		7
William SANTI	M	6	(3)	
Stefano ZANOTTI	D	10	(1)	

LEAGUE RESULTS 1998/99

12/09/98	Murata	A	2-3	Santi F. (p), Renzi
19/09/98	Faetano	H	1-0	Capicchioni A.
26/09/98	Libertas	A	6-3	Renzi 4, Santi F. 2 (1p)
03/10/98	Juvenes	A	1-0	Santi F.
17/10/98	Virtus	H	3-2	Giaquinto, Renzi 2
24/10/98	Cailungo	A	3-2	Renzi, Bollini, Giaquinto
31/10/98	Dogana	A	3-1	Renzi 2, Della Balda S.
07/11/98	San Giovanni	H	3-3	Renzi 3
14/11/98	Folgore	A	3-3	Renzi, Giaquinto, Santi F. (p)
28/11/98	Fiorita	H	1-2	Della Balda S.
05/12/98	Pennarossa	A	3-7	Santi F., Capicchioni A., Gualtieri A.
12/12/98	Tre Fiori	A	3-3	Santi F., Renzi 2
19/12/98	Montevito	H	2-3	Renzi, Fantini
30/01/99	Cosmos	H	1-1	Renzi
06/02/99	Domagnano	A	0-0	
20/02/99	Murata	H	2-2	Capicchioni A., Renzi
27/02/99	Faetano	A	1-0	Capicchioni M.
06/03/99	Libertas	H	3-1	Capicchioni M., Renzi, Giaquinto
13/03/99	Juvenes	H	4-0	Salvatori, Gualtieri D. 2, og (Balducci)
20/03/99	Virtus	A	1-4	Renzi (p)
27/03/99	Cailungo	H	2-1	Giaquinto 2
10/04/99	Dogana	H	3-0	Santi E., Renzi, og (Rossi)

VIRTUS

Società Sportiva Virtus
Via Il Gualdaria
47031 Acquaviva
tel - 999249
Year of Formation - 1960
President - Maurizo Ghiotti
Secretary - Pier Domenico Giulianelli
Coach - Tiziano Giacobbi
Stadium - Acquaviva (1,000)

APPEARANCES 98/99

		P	Ap	(s)	Gls
Fabio BASCHETTI (ITA)	M	11	(4)	1
Marco BENEDETTINI	A	18		17
Federico BRIZI	D	5	(3)	
Mirko BUCCI	M	1	(2)	
Corrado CASADEI	D	4	(3)	
Gian Luca COLA	G	1	(1)	
Irish DE BIAGI	M	5	(2)	4
Orazio DELLA VALLE	D	10	(2)	
Enrico FAZZARDI	M	13	(1)	
Giuseppe FELICITÀ	G	1	(1)	
Daniele FIACCONI	D	9		1
Giuseppe FRANCIONI	M	4	(2)	
Paolo GATTI	A	9	(2)	
Flavio GUIDI (ITA)	D	12		1
Fabrizio MUCCIOLI	A	1	(3)	
Andrea MULARONI	G	16		
Enrico NICOLINI	G	4		
Luigi NICOLINI	M	8	(3)	
Walter PAESINI (ITA)	M	14	(3)	4
Stefano PIATTELLI	G		(1)	
Andrea RAFFELLI	A	19		9
Paolo RASCHI	D	20		
SAMMARITANI	M	6	(1)	
Francesco SELVA	D	6	(1)	
Wladimiro SELVA	M	13		
Moris VALENTINI	A	2	(3)	1
Davide VANNUCCI	A	14		7
Evert ZAVOLI	M	16	(1)	1

LEAGUE RESULTS 1998/99

12/09/98	Juvenes	H	3-1	Benedettini (p), Raffelli 2
19/09/98	Murata	A	6-2	Benedettini 3, Vannucci, Raffelli, De Biagi
26/09/98	Cailungo	H	1-1	Zavoli
03/10/98	Dogana	A	0-0	
17/10/98	Tre Penne	A	2-3	Benedettini, Vannucci
24/10/98	Faetano	H	0-1	
31/10/98	Libertas	A	3-1	Benedettini, Raffelli, Fiacconi
07/11/98	Folgore	H	3-3	De Biagi, Benedettini, Raffelli
14/11/98	San Giovanni	A	2-0	Benedettini, Paesini
28/11/98	Pennarossa	A	2-2	Paesini, Benedettini
05/12/98	Domagnano	A	1-2	Benedettini
12/12/98	Fiorita	A	0-1	
19/12/98	Cosmos	H	1-0	Benedettini
30/01/99	Tre Fiori	H	4-5	Raffelli, Vannucci, Paesini, Benedettini (p)
06/02/99	Montevito	H	7-1	og (Casadei G.), Benedettini 2, Guidi, Baschetti, De Biagi, Paesini
20/02/99	Juvenes	A	1-2	De Biagi
27/02/99	Murata	H	0-2	
06/03/99	Cailungo	A	4-0	Benedettini (p), Raffelli, Vannucci 2
13/03/99	Dogana	H	1-3	Benedettini (p)
20/03/99	Tre Penne	H	4-1	Vannucci 2, Raffelli 2
27/03/99	Faetano	A	1-3	Bonadottini
10/04/99	Libertas	H	1-2	Valentini

SCOTLAND

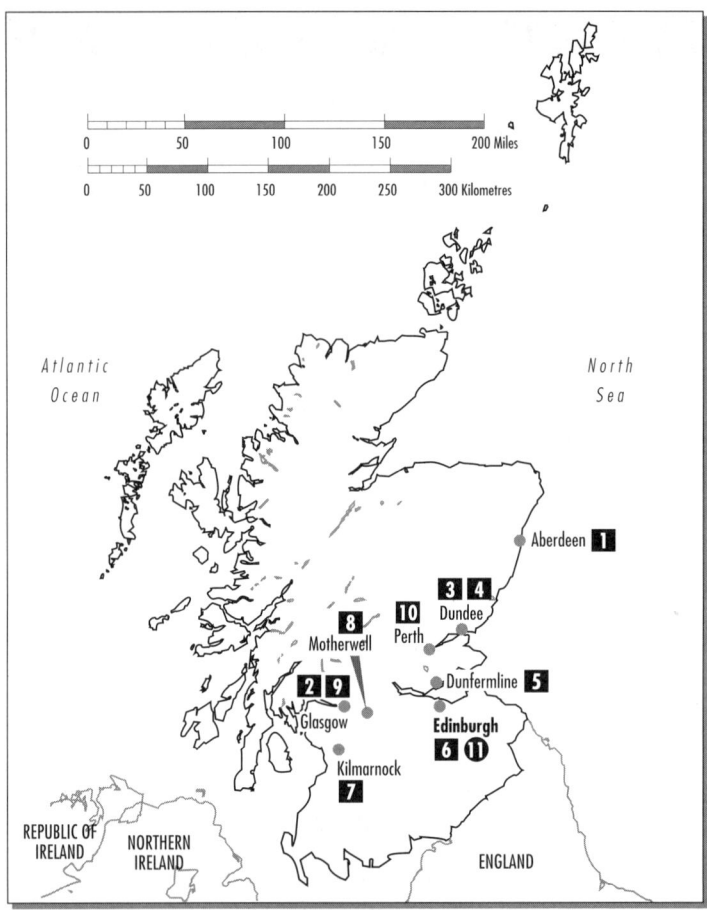

1	ABERDEEN	883	7	KILMARNOCK	889
2	CELTIC	884	8	MOTHERWELL	890
3	DUNDEE	885	9	RANGERS	891
4	DUNDEE UNITED	886	10	ST. JOHNSTONE	892
5	DUNFERMLINE ATHLETIC	887	**Promoted club**		
6	HEART OF MIDLOTHIAN	888	11	HIBERNIAN	893

TROUBLES MOUNT IN EURO 2000 QUEST

New-look Rangers back in charge

After the numbing pain of the previous season, during which they surrendered the title they wanted most to arch-foes Celtic and ended up with nothing, Rangers returned to happy days and winning ways in 1998/99. They became the first winners of the new Scottish Premier League and they also added additional layers to their stack of victories in the two domestic Cups to complete the sixth clean sweep in their history.

The 'treble' would not have been possible without the mini-revolution that took place at Ibrox in the summer of 1998. Recognising that a season without a trophy represented a time for change, Rangers chairman David Murray authorised a major clear-out of the old guard together with a £20m outlay on new players. So, while former favourites McCoist, McCall, Goram, Gough, Durrant, Cleland and Laudrup all moved out, a large consignment of newcomers arrived in their place. The recruitment net was cast wide, with Arthur Numan and Giovanni van Bronckhorst arriving from Holland, Gabriel Amato from Spain, Andrei Kanchelskis from Italy, Lionel Charbonnier from France and Rod Wallace and Colin Hendry from England. Clearly, the Europeanisation of Rangers had advanced to a new level, with only one Scot (Hendry) appearing among the new intake.

The major criticism hurled at Rangers during their shopping spree was that very few of their new signings were regular internationals. Only Numan, for example, had played at the World Cup. What the Gers did have, however, was a manager with an international pedigree to rival the best. Dick Advocaat had been in charge of the Dutch national team at the 1994 World Cup and had also enjoyed success in the Dutch league and Europe with PSV. His appointment as the replacement for Walter Smith epitomised the new direction Rangers were taking.

The results achieved by the Dutchman in his first season were to earn him a lucrative new contract extension. That offered a major contrast to the situation at Celtic, where Jozef Venglos, who had been appointed head coach the previous summer, was ushered into the obscure position of 'European talent scout' following his failure to win a single trophy. A turbulent season at Parkhead, both on and off the pitch, ended with a new 'dream team' of Kenny Dalglish (director of football) and John

LEAGUE CHAMPIONSHIP RESULTS 98/99

		1	2	3	4	5	6	7	8	9	10
1	Aberdeen		3-2	2-2	0-3	2-1	2-0	0-1	1-1	1-1	0-1
			1-5	1-2	0-4	3-1	2-5	2-1	1-1	2-4	1-0
2	Celtic	2-0		6-1	5-0	1-1	1-1	2-0	5-1	0-1	
		3-2		5-0	2-1	5-0	3-0	1-0	1-0	0-3	5-0
3	Dundee	0-2	1-1		2-2	1-0	1-0	1-1	1-0	0-4	0-1
		1-2	0-3		1-3	3-1	2-0	2-1	1-0	1-1	0-1
4	Dundee United	1-0	1-1	0-1		1-1	0-0	0-2	2-2	0-0	1-1
		3-0	1-2	0-2		1-1	1-3	0-0	0-3	1-2	0-1
5	Dunfermline Athletic	1-1	2-2	2-0	2-1		1-1	0-3	1-1	0-2	1-1
		1-2	1-2	2-0	2-2		0-0	0-6	1-2	0-2	1-0
6	Heart of Midlothian	2-0	2-1	0-2	0-1	2-1		2-1	3-0	2-1	1-1
		0-2	2-4	1-2	4-1	2-0		2-2	0-2	2-3	0-2
7	Kilmarnock	4-0	2-0	2-1	2-0	0-0	3-0		0-0	1-3	2-2
		4-2	0-0	0-0	2-0	0-0	1-0		0-1	0-5	1-1
8	Motherwell	2-2	1-2	2-1	1-0	0-0	3-2	0-0		1-0	1-0
		1-1	1-7	1-2	2-0	1-1	0-4	1-2		1-5	1-2
9	Rangers	2-1	0-0	1-0	2-1	1-1	3-0	1-0	2-1		4-0
		3-1	2-2	6-1	0-1	1-0	0-0	1-1	2-1		1-0
10	St. Johnstone	2-0	2-1	1-1	1-3	1-1	1-1	0-0	5-0	0-7	
		4-1	1-0	1-0	1-0	1-1	0-0	0-1	0-0	3-1	

LEAGUE CHAMPIONSHIP FINAL TABLE 98/99

				Home				Away					Total					
		P	W	D	L	F	A	W	D	L	F	A	W	D	L	F	A	P	GD
1	Rangers	36	12	5	1	32	11	11	3	4	46	20	23	8	5	78	31	77	+47
2	Celtic	36	14	2	2	49	12	7	6	5	35	23	21	8	7	84	35	71	+49
3	St. Johnstone	36	8	7	3	24	18	7	5	6	15	20	15	12	9	39	38	57	+1
4	Kilmarnock	36	8	7	3	24	15	6	7	5	23	14	14	14	8	47	29	56	+18
5	Dundee	36	7	4	7	18	23	6	3	9	18	33	13	7	16	36	56	46	-20
6	Heart of Midlothian	36	8	2	8	27	26	3	7	8	17	24	11	9	16	44	50	42	-6
7	Motherwell	36	6	5	7	20	31	4	6	8	15	23	10	11	15	35	54	41	-19
8	Aberdeen	36	6	4	8	24	35	4	3	11	19	36	10	7	19	43	71	37	-28
9	Dundee United	36	2	8	8	13	22	6	2	10	24	26	8	10	18	37	48	34	-11
10	Dunfermline Athletic	36	4	7	7	18	29	0	9	9	10	30	4	16	16	28	59	28	-31

Barnes (head coach) being brought in to take Celtic forward into the new millennium.

It had been Celtic's failure to mobilise their resources with sufficient speed and conviction 12 months earlier that was widely cited as the prime reason for their concession of the title to Rangers. The messy departure of championship-winning coach Wim Jansen and the relatively late appointment of Venglos meant that the summer came and went without new signings. Once the season began, the new faces did begin to arrive - Vidar Riseth, Lubomir Moravcik, Johan Mjällby and eventually, after a tedious will-he-won't-he soap opera, Mark Viduka - but after a terrible start (just ten points from their first eight games), Celtic were always trying to make up lost ground on Rangers, who also continued to add to their squad, bringing in Stéphane Guivarc'h, Neil McCann, Stefan Klos and Claudio Reyna.

The glorious 5-1 destruction of the enemy at Parkhead in November - Celtic's biggest win over Rangers for 30 years - offered hope, but although the Bhoys found consistent form at last after the turn of the year, with Swedish striker Henrik Larsson proving particularly lethal in front of goal, Rangers matched them pretty much stride for stride.

Celtic had only one card left to play when the two teams reconvened at Parkhead on Sunday, May 2. They simply had to win. A draw would merely prolong their misery, whereas a defeat was unthinkable as it would allow Rangers to win the championship in the home of their bitter rivals for the very first time.

Not surprisingly, the occasion proved too much for some of the Celtic diehards. Vexed by the officiating of referee Hugh Dallas, a couple of idiots ran on to the pitch to attack him and another managed to find his target after flinging a coin from the stands. It hit the referee on the forehead, producing a trickle of blood and an image that inevitably found its way onto large, front-page photographs in the following day's papers. As for the football, Celtic's worst nightmare came true as Rangers ran them ragged, scoring three goals without reply, to retrieve their championship crown in a manner that proved beyond doubt that they were the finest team in the land.

A few weeks later Rangers provided further confirmation when they beat Celtic once again to win the Scottish Cup final at a newly refurbished Hampden. One goal was all it took, with Englishman Rod Wallace, the most successful (and, ironically, the cheapest) of all the club's new signings, grabbing the winning goal that completed a nigh-on perfect season for the Ibrox club. The League Cup had been seized several months earlier thanks to a 2-1 victory in the final against St. Johnstone.

The only competition which Rangers entered and failed to win was the

NATIONAL TEAM RESULTS 98/99

05/09/98	Lithuania (ECQ)	A	Vilnius	0-0	
10/10/98	Estonia (ECQ)	H	Edinburgh	3-2	Dodds (70, 85), Hohlov-Simson (78og)
14/10/98	Faroe Islands (ECQ)	H	Aberdeen	2-1	Burley (22), Dodds (45)
31/03/99	Czech Republic (ECQ)	H	Glasgow	1-2	Jess (68)
28/04/99	Germany	A	Bremen	1-0	Hutchison (65)
05/06/99	Faroe Islands (ECQ)	A	Toftir	1-1	Johnston (38)
09/06/99	Czech Republic (ECQ)	A	Prague	2-3	Ritchie (30), Johnston (62)

NATIONAL TEAM APPEARANCES 98/99

Coach - Craig BROWN	LIT	EST	FAR	CZE	GER	FAR	CZE	Cps	Gls
Jim LEIGHTON (24/07/58) - Aberdeen	G	G						91	-
Matt ELLIOTT (01/11/68) - Leicester City (ENG)	D		D	D		D		7	-
Colin HENDRY (07/12/65) - Rangers	D	D	D		D			39	1
Tom BOYD (24/11/65) - Celtic	D	D	D	D	D	D	D	65	1
Colin CALDERWOOD (20/01/65) - Tottenham Hotspur (ENG)/Aston Villa (ENG)	M71	D57				D	M	34	1
Paul LAMBERT (07/08/69) - Celtic	M			M	M85	M	M	20	-
Darren JACKSON (25/07/66) - Celtic	M57	s18						28	4
John COLLINS (31/01/68) - Everton (ENG)	M							53	11
Christian DAILLY (23/10/73) - Blackburn Rovers (ENG)	M							14	1
Kevin GALLACHER (23/11/66) - Blackburn Rovers (ENG)	A	A18				A89	A	43	8
Ally McCOIST (24/09/62) - Kilmarnock	A83	A69						60	19
Barry FERGUSON (02/02/78) - Rangers	s57							1	-
Callum DAVIDSON (25/06/76) - Blackburn Rovers (ENG)	s71	M	M	M52	M79	M	M	7	-
Neil McCANN (11/08/74) - Heart of Midlothian/Rangers	s83			A				2	-
David WEIR (10/05/70) - Heart of Midlothian/Everton (ENG)		M	M	D	D	M	D	13	-
Billy McKINLAY (22/04/69) - Blackburn Rovers (ENG)		M	M46					29	4
Allan JOHNSTON (14/12/73) - Sunderland (ENG)		M	M79	s52	M	M86	M	6	2
Ian DURRANT (29/10/66) - Kilmarnock		M	s46		M73	M46	M71	16	-
Simon DONNELLY (01/12/74) - Celtic		s57	A					9	-
Billy DODDS (05/02/69) - Dundee United		s69	A		A	A	A	9	3
Neil SULLIVAN (24/02/70) - Wimbledon (ENG)			G	G	G	G	G	8	-
Craig BURLEY (24/09/71) - Celtic			M	M				30	3
Stephen GLASS (25/15/76) - Newcastle United (ENG)			s79					1	-
David HOPKIN (21/08/70) - Leeds United (ENG)				M				5	2
Gary McALLISTER (25/12/64) - Coventry City (ENG)				M64				57	5
Eoin JESS (13/12/70) - Aberdeen				A	s61	s89	s71	18	2
Don HUTCHISON (09/05/71) - Everton (ENG)				s64	A			2	1
Scot GEMMILL (02/01/71) - Everton (ENG)					M61	s86		15	-
Robbie WINTERS (04/11/74) - Aberdeen					s73			1	-
Derek WHYTE (31/08/88) - Aberdeen					s79			12	-
Colin CAMERON (23/10/72) - Heart of Midlothian					s85	s46		2	-
Paul RITCHIE (21/08/75) - Heart of Midlothian							D	1	1

UEFA Cup, but even there they had their moments, notably in winning 2-1 away to high-flying German club Bayer Leverkusen and subsequently knocking them out. They even gave themselves a half-decent chance of eliminating Parma when Jörg Albertz gave them the lead in the Ennio Tardini stadium after a 1-1 draw at Ibrox, but two calamitous errors by their Italian defenders Sergio Porrini (who was sent off) and Lorenzo Amoruso (who should have joined him after a deliberate hand-ball which gave away a penalty) led the last remaining Scottish club to the European exit door.

One round earlier Celtic had seen their UEFA Cup challenge halted by FC Zürich. It was their second elimination from a European Cup - in August they had been denied a place in the Champions' League by Croatia Zagreb, who tore them apart in the second leg after Celtic had travelled to the Croatian capital with a 1-0 lead. Of the other Scottish teams in action, Hearts went out in somewhat controversial fashion to Mallorca in the Cup-winners' Cup, while Kilmarnock had only themselves to blame after losing home and away to Sigma Olomouc in the UEFA Cup qualifying round.

"Killie" were to make up for their European misadventure with an impressive Premier League campaign. Bobby Williamson's team of Old Firm 'has-beens' (Durrant, McCoist, goalkeeper Gordon Marshall) were in the upper reaches of the table all season. They nearly paid the price for a poor finish but salvaged a return to Europe thanks to Scotland's first place in the UEFA Fair Play rankings. Kilmarnock were pipped at the post for third place by Sandy Clark's St. Johnstone, who thus capped a fine season in which they also reached the League Cup final and won three of their four Premier League encounters with Celtic. Theirs was very much a team success - not one of their players managed an individual total of more than four goals.

If anything, the new Premier League accentuated the great divide between the Old Firm and the rest. Hearts, who had threatened for a time to loosen the Glaswegian stranglehold in 1997/98, had a miserable season, even flirting

with relegation for a few weeks before the arrival of several reinforcements propelled them up into sixth place. The other traditional East coast challengers, Dundee United and Aberdeen, also had a season to forget. They were saved from the drop thanks to the consistent goalscoring of their leading strikers, Billy Dodds and Robbie Winters, who, curiously, had swapped clubs in the early weeks of the season.

The sole relegation place went to Dunfermline Athletic, who could not manage an away win all season and took just one point from their last eight games, while Hibernian made a swift return to the top flight, destroying all-comers in the First Division to finish up with a huge 23-point victory margin.

Part of the blueprint of the Scottish Premier League was to boost the quality of the national team. With so many foreigners now being lured to the country, it is difficult to see how that will take effect. Rangers and Celtic present fewer and fewer candidates for selection each season, and other Scottish clubs are increasingly following their lead. Quite where the next generation of Scottish international foot-

TOP SCORERS

29	Henrik LARSSON (Celtic)
18	Rod WALLACE (Rangers)
17	Billy DODDS (Dundee United)
14	Eoin JESS (Aberdeen)
13	Robbie WINTERS (Dundee United/ Aberdeen)
11	Jörg ALBERTZ (Rangers)
10	Gary McSWEGAN (Dundee United/Heart of Midlothian)
	Stéphane ADAM (Heart of Midlothian)
9	Craig BURLEY (Celtic)
	Eddie ANNAND (Dundee)
	Mark BURCHILL (Celtic)

DOMESTIC CUP 98/99

THIRD ROUND
Aberdeen 0, Livingston 1
Ayr United 3, Kilmarnock 0
Brechin City 1, Albion Rovers 1
(replay) Albion Rovers 3, Brechin City 1
Celtic 3, Airdrieonians 1
Falkirk 3, Huntly 0
Greenock Morton 2, Dundee 1
Hibernian 1, Stirling Albion 1
(replay) Stirling Albion 2, Hibernian 1
Partick Thistle 1, Dunfermline Athletic 2
Raith Rovers 0, Clyde 4
Rangers 2, Stenhousemuir 0
St. Johnstone 1, Forfar Athletic 0
St. Mirren 1, Hamilton Academical 1
(replay) Hamilton Academical 1, St. Mirren 0
Stranraer 1, East Stirling 0
Motherwell 3, Heart of Midlothian 1
Queens Park 0, Dundee United 0
(replay) Dundee United 1, Queens Park 0
Clydebank 1, Ross County 1
(replay) Ross County 2, Clydebank 3 (aet)

FOURTH ROUND
Ayr United 1, Albion Rovers 0
Celtic 4, Dunfermline Athletic 0
Greenock Morton 6, Clyde 1
Livingston 1, St. Johnstone 3
Motherwell 2, Stirling Albion 0
Stranraer 1, Falkirk 2
Hamilton Academical 0, Rangers 6
Clydebank 2, Dundee United 2
(replay) Dundee United 3, Clydebank 0

QUARTER-FINALS
Motherwell 0, St. Johnstone 2 (Dods 72, Simão 81)

Rangers 2 (McCann 52, Amoruso 76),
Falkirk 1 (Moss 59)

Greenock Morton 0,
Celtic 3 (Viduka 9, 83, Larsson 58)

Ayr United 0, Dundee United 0
(replay) Dundee United 2 (Murray 42,
Sköldmark 52),
Ayr United 1 (Walker 47)

SEMI-FINALS
Celtic 2 (Blinker 29, Viduka 39),
Dundee United 0

St. Johnstone 0,
Rangers 4 (Wallace 14, Van Bronckhorst 33,
Johansson 61, McCann 69)

FINAL
29/05/99, Glasgow
RANGERS 1 Wallace (48)
CELTIC 0
referee - Dallas
RANGERS - Klos; Porrini (Kanchelskis 77), Amoruso,
Hendry, Vidmar, McCann (Ferguson I. 67), McInnes,
Van Bronckhorst, Wallace, Amato (Wilson 90),
Albertz.
CELTIC - Gould; Boyd, Mahé (O'Donnell 78), Stubbs,
Larsson, Wieghorst, Lambert, Annoni (Johnson 60),
Blinker, Moravcik, Mjällby.

EUROPEAN CUPS 98/99

CHAMPIONS' CUP
● CELTIC
Preliminary round ST. PATRICK'S ATHLETIC (IRL)
H 0-0
    Gould; Boyd, Mahé, McNamara (Donnelly 55), Rieper (Annoni 84),
    Stubbs, Larsson, Burley, Brattbakk (Jackson 46), Lambert, Blinker.
A 2-0   Brattbakk (12), Larsson (72)
    Gould; Boyd, McNamara, Stubbs, Larsson, Burley, Brattbakk, Lambert,
    Jackson (Donnelly 67), Mackay, Blinker (McKinlay 74).

Qualifying round CROATIA ZAGREB (CRO)
H 1-0   Jackson (51)
    Gould; Boyd, McNamara, Rieper, Stubbs, Larsson, Burley,
    Brattback (Jackson 46), Donnelly, Lambert, Blinker.
A 0-3
    Gould; Boyd, Mahé, McNamara, Rieper, Stubbs, Larsson, Burley,
    Jackson (Donnelly 75), Lambert, Blinker (Brattbakk 62).

CUP WINNERS' CUP
● HEART OF MIDLOTHIAN
Qualifying round FC LANTANA TALLINN (EST)
A 1-0   Makel (20)
    Rousset; Naysmith, Weir, Salvatori, Ritchie, McCann, Adam (Murray 86),
    Hamilton (Quitongo 86), Locke, Flögel, Makel.
H 5-0   Hamilton (18), Fulton (29), McCann (41), Flögel (75), Holmes (90)
    Rousset; Weir, Ritchie, McCann, Fulton, Adam (Quitongo 60),
    Hamilton (Flögel 60), Locke, Makel (Holmes 76), McKinnon, Pressley.

1st round RCD MALLORCA (ESP)
H 0-1
    Rousset; McPherson, Naysmith, Weir, Salvatori, Ritchie, McCann, Adam,
    Hamilton (Holmes 82), Locke, Pressley.
A 1-1   Hamilton (75)
    Rousset; Naysmith, Weir, Salvatori, Ritchie, McCann (Holmes 52), Adam,
    Hamilton, Locke, Makel (McPherson 78), Pressley.

UEFA CUP
● KILMARNOCK
Preliminary round ZELJEZNICAR SARAJEVO (BOS)
A 1-1   McGowne (55)
    Marshall; MacPherson, Baker, Lauchlan, McGowne, Montgomerie,
    Mitchell, Holt, Wright (Roberts 80), Durrant, Mahood.
H 1-0   Mahood (31)
    Marshall; MacPherson, McGowne, Holt, Wright, Durrant, Mitchell,
    Mahood (Henry 89), Baker, Lauchlan, Burke (Nevin 74).

Qualifying round SIGMA OLOMOUC (CZE)
A 0-2
    Marshall; MacPherson, Baker, Lauchlan, Montgomerie, McGowne,
    Mitchell, Mahood (Burke 74), Wright (Vareille 63), Durrant, Holt.
H 0-2
    Marshall; MacPherson, Kerr D., McGowne, Nevin (McCutcheon 64), Holt
    (Mahood 46), Wright (Roberts 76), Durrant, Vareille, Lauchlan, Burke.

● RANGERS
Preliminary round SHELBOURNE (IRL)
A 5-3   Albertz (59p, 85p), Amato (72, 81), Van Bronckhorst (74)
    Niemi; Porrini, Amoruso, Petric, Van Bronckhorst, Thern (Ferguson I. 63),
    Albertz, Ferguson B., Durie, Gattuso (Johansson 46), Graham (Amato 46).

H 2-0   Johansson (4, 89)
    Niemi; Porrini, Moore, Amoruso, Numan, Kanchelskis (Amato 46),
    Ferguson B., Van Bronckhorst (Ferguson I. 74), Albertz,
    Durie (Gattuso 62), Johansson.

Qualifying round PAOK (GRE)
H 2-0   Kanchelskis (55), Wallace (68)
    Niemi; Porrini, Moore, Amoruso, Numan, Kanchelskis,
    Ferguson B. (Albertz 67), Ferguson I., Van Bronckhorst (Gattuso 78),
    Wallace, Durie (Amato 6).
A 0-0
    Charbonnier; Porrini, Moore, Amoruso (Petric 77), Numan, Ferguson I.,
    Ferguson B., Van Bronckhorst, Kanchelskis (Gattuso 81), Wallace,
    Albertz (Amato 60).

1st round BEITAR JERUSALEM (ISR)
A 1-1   Albertz (82)
    Charbonnier; Porrini, Amoruso, Ferguson B., Kanchelskis, Van Bronckhorst,
    Ferguson I., Wallace (Graham 89), Moore, Johansson (Albertz 78),
    Vidmar (Stensaas 46).
H 4-2   Gattuso (1), Porrini (25), Johansson (59), Wallace (63)
    Charbonnier; Porrini, Moore (Hendry 89), Amoruso, Vidmar, Gattuso,
    Ferguson B., Van Bronckhorst, Albertz, Wallace, Johansson (Miller 80).

2nd round BAYER 04 LEVERKUSEN (GER)
A 2-1   Van Bronckhorst (45), Johansson (64)
    Charbonnier; Porrini, Wilson, Hendry, Vidmar, Kanchelskis, Ferguson B.,
    Van Bronckhorst, Albertz, Wallace (Durie 86), Johansson (Ferguson I. 78).
H 1-1   Johansson (56)
    Charbonnier (Niemi 67); Porrini, Hendry, Amoruso, Numan,
    Kanchelskis (Ferguson I. 67), Ferguson B. (Wilson 90), Van Bronckhorst,
    Albertz, Wallace, Johansson.

3rd round PARMA (ITA)
H 1-1   Wallace (68)
    Niemi; Porrini (Durie 58), Amoruso, Hendry, Numan, Ferguson B.,
    Kanchelskis, Albertz, Ferguson I., Wallace, Johansson (Amato 46).
A 1-3   Albertz (28)
    Niemi; Porrini, Hendry, Amoruso, Numan, Albertz,
    Ferguson B. (Miller 76), Ferguson I., Van Bronckhorst,
    Wallace (Amato 72), Durie (Vidmar 53).

● CELTIC
1st round VITORIA GUIMARÃES (POR)
A 2-1   Larsson (1), Donnelly (69)
    Gould; Boyd (Annoni 21), Mahé, Rieper, Stubbs, Larsson, Burley,
    O'Donnell, Donnelly, Lambert, Jackson (Hannah 90).
H 2-1   Stubbs (39), Larsson (90)
    Gould; Mahé, Rieper, Stubbs, Larsson, Burley, Brattbakk (Jackson 85),
    Donnelly, Lambert, Hannah, McKinlay.

2nd round FC ZÜRICH (SUI)
H 1-1   Brattbakk (22)
    Gould; Boyd, Mahé, McNamara, Larsson, Burley, Brattbakk (Jackson 75),
    O'Donnell, Donnelly, Lambert, McKinlay.
A 2-4   O'Donnell (57), Larsson (72)
    Gould (Kerr 63); Mahé, McNamara, Larsson, Brattbakk, O'Donnell,
    Donnelly, Lambert, Jackson, Hannah, McKinlay.

ballers will come from remains a mystery. Even the English leagues are no longer a fertile breeding ground, and it is almost the case now that if a player with Scottish eligibility strings together a dozen games in the Premiership, he gets an immediate call-up.

The Euro 2000 qualifying campaign, following quickly on the heels of yet another World Cup let-down, saw Craig Brown keep faith with the majority of the players who performed in France. For want of better, he began the qualifying campaign with a host of veterans, which even included 40-year-old Jim Leighton and Rangers 'rejects' Ally McCoist and Ian Durrant. As the tournament progressed, the average age did go down - significantly so after Leighton announced his international retirement following criticism of his performance in the home game with Estonia - but of the newcomers to the team, only Callum Davidson and Paul Ritchie, aged 22 and 23, respectively, were recent graduates of the Under-21 side.

Scotland started off by banking seven points from their first three matches, but they were won in unconvincing style and, in any case, represented the minimum acceptable from fixtures against Lithuania, Estonia and the Faroe Islands, the latter two at home. In the spring, however, another three matches yielded just a single point - and that in a largely forgettable 1-1 draw away to the Faroes, a

game in which English-born central defender Matt Elliott effectively ended his international career by striking an opponent and earning himself not just a red card but a five-match ban and a volley of criticism from his manager.

Two defeats by the Czech Republic - including their first dropped points in a home qualifier for 11 matches and their first competitive defeat on home soil for 12 years - left the Scots with much to do in the early autumn if they were to reach their third successive European Championship finals. The automatic place had already been booked by the Czechs. For Craig Brown and his ageing team, it was the play-offs or bust...

INTERNATIONAL HONOURS

World Cup Finals appearances: 1954, 1958, 1974, 1978, 1982, 1986, 1990, 1998

European Championship appearances: 1992, 1996

European Club Competitions

Champions' Cup	Celtic (1967)
Cup-winners' Cup	Rangers (1972)
	Aberdeen (1983)
Super Cup	Aberdeen (1983)

PLAYERS OF THE SEASON

NEIL McCANN

Rangers' mid-season signing of Neil McCann from Hearts represented something of a departure from the Ibrox club's new purchase policy. Not only was he bought from another Premier League club; he was also a Scot! The young winger had had a tremendous season for Hearts in 1997/98 but had gone off the boil at the start of the new campaign. Once he donned the blue shirt of his new team, however, he began to produce the dazzling footwork, speed and enterprise that had marked him out as such an outstanding prospect the previous term. His day of

glory came at Celtic Park on Sunday, May 2 as he scored two of the three goals that clinched the title for Rangers. A few weeks earlier he had made his first start for Scotland on the same ground, appearing as a makeshift striker in the 1-2 defeat by the Czech Republic.

PAUL RITCHIE

Another newcomer to the Scotland side, Hearts defender Paul Ritchie seemed set for a dream début when he headed his team in front half an hour into the final Euro 2000 qualifier of the season, away to the Czechs in Prague. But it was not to be; the home side came back to win 3-2. The youngster could not escape the general criticism levelled at the Scottish defence for the concession of two headed goals but he certainly has the confidence and the ability to win many more caps in the future. He earned his first call-up after a superb finish to the season with Hearts, during which he played a vital part in steering the Edinburgh side away from the relegation zone and into mid-table safety.

ABERDEEN

CLUB DIRECTORY

Aberdeen FC
Pittodrie Stadium, Pittodrie Street
Aberdeen AB24 5QH
tel - (01224) 650400 / fax - (01224) 644173
Year of Formation - 1903
Chairman - Stewart Milne
Secretary - Richard A.M. Ramsay
Manager - Alex Miller; Paul Hegarty
(99/00 - Ebbe Skovdahl)
Stadium - Pittodrie Stadium (22,199)

MAJOR HONOURS
League Championship - (4)
1955, 1980, 1984, 1985.
Scottish Cup - (7)
1947, 1970, 1982, 1983, 1984, 1986, 1990.
League Cup - (5)
1956, 1977, 1986, 1990, 1996.
European Cup-winners' Cup - (1) 1983
European Super Cup - (1) 1983.

APPEARANCES 98/99

	P	Ap	(s)	Gls
Russell ANDERSON	D	13	(3)	
Paul BERNARD	M	8	(1)	1
Baldur BETT (ISL)	M	1		
Jamie BUCHAN	D	19	(4)	2
Billy DODDS	A	6		
Andy DOW	M	22	(3)	
Ricky GILLIES	M	4	(7)	
Iain GOOD	D		(1)	
Jim HAMILTON	A	6	(1)	1
Michael HART	A	5	(9)	
Craig HIGNETT (ENG)	M	13		2
John INGLIS	D	16	(1)	1
Eoin JESS	A	36		14
Ilian KIRIAKOV (BUL)	M	17	(5)	
Jim LEIGHTON	G	22		
Andreas MAYER (GER)	D	13		2
Mike NEWELL (ENG)	A	14	(9)	2
Alex NOTMAN	M		(2)	
Nigel PEPPER (ENG)	M	7	(3)	
Mark PERRY	D	32		4
David ROWSON	D	18	(4)	
Gary SMITH	D	30		
Derek STILLIE	G	8		
Tony WARNER	G	6		
Derek WHYTE	D	35		
Robbie WINTERS	A	28		12
Dennis WYNESS	M	6	(8)	1
Darren YOUNG	A	11		
Derek YOUNG	A		(4)	

LEAGUE RESULTS 1998/99

01/08/98	Dundee	A	2-0	Jess, Hignett
16/08/98	Celtic	H	3-2	Perry, og (Blinker), Hignett
22/08/98	Heart of Midlothian	A	0-2	
29/08/98	Dunfermline Athletic	A	1-1	Perry
12/09/98	Motherwell	H	1-1	Jess
19/09/98	St. Johnstone	A	0-2	
23/09/98	Rangers	H	1-1	Jess
27/09/98	Kilmarnock	H	0-1	
04/10/98	Dundee United	A	0-1	
17/10/98	Dundee	H	2-2	Jess 2
24/10/98	Celtic	A	0-2	
31/10/98	Motherwell	A	2-2	Newell, Winters
07/11/98	Dunfermline Athletic	H	2-1	Jess 2
14/11/98	Rangers	A	1-2	Jess
21/11/98	St. Johnstone	H	0-1	
28/11/98	Dundee United	H	0-3	
05/12/98	Kilmarnock	A	0-4	
12/12/98	Heart of Midlothian	H	2-0	Winters, Jess
19/12/98	Dundee	A	2-1	Winters 2
26/12/98	Dunfermline Athletic	A	2-1	Inglis, Jess
29/12/98	Motherwell	H	1-1	Jess
02/01/99	St. Johnstone	A	1-4	Buchan
30/01/99	Rangers	H	2-4	Newell, Jess
06/02/99	Kilmarnock	H	2-1	Jess, Mayer
20/02/99	Dundee United	A	0-3	
27/02/99	Heart of Midlothian	A	2-0	Bernard, Wyness
14/03/99	Celtic	H	1-5	Winters
20/03/99	Motherwell	A	1-1	Winters
03/04/99	Dunfermline Athletic	H	3-1	Winters 3
10/04/99	Kilmarnock	A	2-4	Winters, Hamilton
17/04/99	Dundee United	H	0-4	
25/04/99	Rangers	A	1-3	Perry
01/05/99	St. Johnstone	H	1-0	Winters
08/05/99	Dundee	H	1-2	Winters
15/05/99	Celtic	A	2-3	Mayer, Perry
23/05/99	Heart of Midlothian	H	2-5	Buchan, Jess

CELTIC

CLUB DIRECTORY

Celtic FC
Celtic Park, Glasgow G40 3RE
tel - (0141) 5562611 / fax - (0141) 5518106
Year of Formation - 1887
Chairman - Frank O'Callaghan
Chief Executive - Allan McDonald
(99/00 - Director of Football - Kenny Dalglish)
Head Coach - Dr. Jozef Venglos
(99/00 - John Barnes)
Stadium - Celtic Park (60,294)

MAJOR HONOURS
League Championship - (36) 1893, 1894, 1896,
1898, 1905, 1906, 1907, 1908, 1909, 1910,
1914, 1915, 1916, 1917, 1919, 1922, 1926,
1936, 1938, 1954, 1966, 1967, 1968, 1969,
1970, 1971, 1972, 1973, 1974, 1977, 1979,
1981, 1982, 1986, 1988, 1998.
Scottish Cup - (30) 1892, 1899, 1900, 1904,
1907, 1908, 1911, 1912, 1914, 1923, 1925,
1927, 1931, 1933, 1937, 1951, 1954, 1965,
1967, 1969, 1971, 1972, 1974, 1975, 1977,
1980, 1985, 1988, 1989, 1995.
League Cup - (10) 1957, 1958, 1966, 1967,
1968, 1969, 1970, 1975, 1983, 1997.
European Champions' Cup - (1) 1967.

APPEARANCES 98/99

		P	Ap	(s)	Gls
Enrico ANNONI (ITA)	D	9	(5)	
Regi BLINKER (HOL)	A	13	(2)	4
Tom BOYD	D	31		
Harold BRATTBAKK (NOR)	A	16	(8)	5
Mark BURCHILL	A	5	(16)	9
Craig BURLEY	M	20	(1)	9
Barry John CORR	G		(1)	
Simon DONNELLY	A	20	(3)	5
Jonathan GOULD	G	28		
David HANNAH	M	5	(4)	
Colin HEALY (IRL)	M	2	(1)	
Darren JACKSON	A	4	(2)	
Tommy JOHNSON (ENG)	A	3		3
Stewart KERR	G	4		
Paul LAMBERT	M	33		1
Henrik LARSSON (SWE)	A	35		29
John Paul McBRIDE	M		(1)	
Andrew McCONDICHIE	G	1		
Malky MACKAY	D	1		1
Tosh McKINLAY	D	11	(7)	
Jackie McNAMARA	M	15	(1)	
Stéphane MAHE (FRA)	D	24		
Scott MARSHALL	D	1	(1)	
Johan MJÄLLBY (SWE)	M	17		1
Lubomir MORAVCIK (SVK)	M	14		6
Phil O'DONNELL	M	13	(2)	2
Marc RIEPER (DEN)	D	7		
Vidar RISETH (NOR)	M	26	(1)	3
Alan STUBBS (ENG)	D	22	(1)	1
Mark VIDUKA (AUS)	A	8	(1)	5
Tony WARNER (ENG)	G	3		
Morten WIEGHORST (DEN)	M	5	(2)	

LEAGUE RESULTS 1998/99

01/08/98	Dunfermline Athletic	H	5-0	Burley 3, Donnelly, Mackay
16/08/98	Aberdeen	A	2-3	Larsson 2 (1p)
22/08/98	Dundee United	H	2-1	Burley, Burchill
29/08/98	Dundee	A	1-1	Burley
12/09/98	Kilmarnock	H	1-1	Blinker
20/09/98	Rangers	A	0-0	
23/09/98	St. Johnstone	H	0-1	
26/09/98	Heart of Midlothian	H	1-1	Donnelly
03/10/98	Motherwell	A	2-1	Brattbakk, Lambert
17/10/98	Dunfermline Athletic	A	2-2	Larsson, Brattbakk
24/10/98	Aberdeen	H	2-0	Donnelly 2
31/10/98	Kilmarnock	A	0-2	
07/11/98	Dundee	H	6-1	Larsson 3 (2p), Burchill 2, Donnelly
14/11/98	St. Johnstone	A	1-2	Larsson
21/11/98	Rangers	H	5-1	Moravcik 2, Larsson 2, Burchill
28/11/98	Motherwell	H	2-0	Larsson, O'Donnell
06/12/98	Heart of Midlothian	A	1-2	O'Donnell
12/12/98	Dundee United	A	1-1	Larsson
19/12/98	Dunfermline Athletic	H	5-0	Larsson 2 (1p), Mjällby, Moravcik 2
27/12/98	Dundee	A	3-0	Burchill, Riseth, Larsson
03/01/99	Rangers	A	2-2	Stubbs, Larsson
31/01/99	St. Johnstone	H	5-0	Brattbakk 3, Moravcik, Larsson
06/02/99	Heart of Midlothian	H	3-0	Larsson 3 (1p)
17/02/99	Kilmarnock	H	1-0	Riseth
21/02/99	Motherwell	A	7-1	Larsson 4 (1p), Moravcik, Burley, Larsson
27/02/99	Dundee United	H	2-1	Burley, Larsson
14/03/99	Aberdeen	A	5-1	Viduka 2, Larsson 2, Burley
21/03/99	Kilmarnock	A	0-0	
03/04/99	Dundee	H	5-0	Larsson 2 (1p), Burley, Viduka, Blinker
14/04/99	Heart of Midlothian	A	4-2	Riseth, Blinker, Viduka 2
17/04/99	Motherwell	H	1-0	Larsson (p)
24/04/99	St. Johnstone	A	0-1	
02/05/99	Rangers	H	0-3	
08/05/99	Dunfermline Athletic	A	2-1	Johnson 2
15/05/99	Aberdeen	H	3-2	Blinker, Johnson, Burchill
23/05/99	Dundee United	A	2-1	Burchill 2

DUNDEE

Dundee FC
Dens Park Stadium
Sandeman Street, Dundee, DD3 7JY
tel - (01382) 889966
fax - (01382) 832284
Year of Formation - 1893
Chairman - Jim Marr
Chief Executive - Peter Marr
Manager - Jocky Scott
Stadium - Dens Park (10,531)

MAJOR HONOURS
League Championship - (1) 1962
Scottish Cup - (1) 1910.
League Cup - (3) 1952, 1953, 1974.

APPEARANCES 98/99

	P	Ap	(s)	Gls
Dariusz ADAMCZUK (POL)	M	24	(2)	6
Iain ANDERSON	A	17	(11)	3
Eddie ANNAND	A	19	(10)	9
Graham BAYNE	A		(2)	
Stephen BOYACK	A	8		2
Tommy COYNE (IRL)	A	8	(8)	
Robert DOUGLAS	G	35		
Willie FALCONER	A	31	(2)	4
Derek FLEMING	D	1		
Eric GARCIN (FRA)	M	2	(1)	
Jim GRADY	A	20	(6)	3
Brian GRANT	M		(4)	
Gordon HUNTER	D	3		
Brian IRVINE	D	33		3
James LANGFIELD	G	1	(1)	
Steve McCORMICK	A		(1)	
Jim McINALLY	M	14	(1)	
Shaun McSKIMMING	M	25	(4)	2
Lee MADDISON	D	21		
Darren MAGEE	M	1	(1)	
Willie MILLER	D	26		
Jerry O'DRISCOLL	A		(1)	
Stéphane POUNEWATCHY (FRA)	D	2	(1)	
Gavin RAE	D	23	(7)	1
Robert RAESIDE	D	19	(2)	
Hugh ROBERTSON	D	9	(1)	
David ROGERS (ENG)	D	7	(4)	
Lee SHARP	D	4	(2)	1
Barry SMITH	D	29	(4)	
Gavin STRACHAN	M	4	(2)	
Steven TWEED	D	10		1

LEAGUE RESULTS 1998/99

01/08/98	Aberdeen	H	0-2	
15/08/98	Dunfermline Athletic	A	0-2	
23/08/98	St. Johnstone	H	0-1	
29/08/98	Celtic	H	1-1	Annand (p)
12/09/98	Heart of Midlothian	A	2-0	Adamczuk 2
19/09/98	Dundee United	H	2-2	Annand, Adamczuk
23/09/98	Kilmarnock	A	1-2	Annand
26/09/98	Motherwell	H	1-0	Irvine
04/10/98	Rangers	A	0-1	
17/10/98	Aberdeen	A	2-2	Annand 2
28/10/98	Dunfermline Athletic	H	1-0	Falconer
31/10/98	Heart of Midlothian	H	1-0	og (Weir)
07/11/98	Celtic	A	1-6	Annand
14/11/98	Kilmarnock	H	1-1	Annand
22/11/98	Dundee United	A	1-0	Grady
12/12/98	St. Johnstone	A	1-1	Adamczuk
16/12/98	Motherwell	A	1-2	Adamczuk
19/12/98	Aberdeen	H	1-2	Rae
27/12/98	Celtic	H	0-3	
30/12/98	Heart of Midlothian	A	2-1	Sharp (p), Falconer
02/01/99	Dundee United	H	1-3	McSkimming
27/01/99	Rangers	H	0-4	
30/01/99	Kilmarnock	A	0-0	
06/02/99	Motherwell	H	1-0	Tweed
20/02/99	Rangers	A	1-6	Adamczuk
27/02/99	St. Johnstone	H	0-1	
13/03/99	Dunfermline Athletic	A	0-2	
20/03/99	Heart of Midlothian	H	2-0	Annand 2
03/04/99	Celtic	A	0-5	
10/04/99	Motherwell	A	2-1	Falconer, Grady
18/04/99	Rangers	H	1-1	Anderson
24/04/99	Kilmarnock	H	2-1	Anderson, McSkimming
01/05/99	Dundee United	A	2-0	Irvine, Grady
08/05/99	Aberdeen	A	2-1	Boyack, Anderson
15/05/99	Dunfermline Athletic	H	3-1	Irvine, Boyack, Falconer
23/05/99	St. Johnstone	A	0-1	

DUNDEE UNITED

CLUB DIRECTORY

Dundee United FC
Tannadice Park, Tannadice Street
Dundee DD3 7JW
tel - (01382) 833166 / fax - (01382) 889398
Year of Formation - 1909
Chairman - Jim McLean
Secretary - Miss Priti Trivedi
Manager - Tommy McLean; Paul Stuurock
Stadium - Tannadice Park (14,209)

MAJOR HONOURS
League Championship - (1) 1983.
Scottish Cup - (1) 1994.
League Cup - (2) 1980, 1981.

APPEARANCES 98/99

		P	Ap	(s)	Gls
Roger BOLI (FRA)	A	3			
Alan COMBE	G	10			
Jason DE VOS (CAN)	D	23	(2)		
Sieb DIJKSTRA (HOL)	G	26	(1)		
Billy DODDS	A	29	(1)		17
Jamie DOLAN	M	4	(1)		
Neil DUFFY	M	12	(3)		
Craig EASTON	M	28	(2)		1
John EUSTACE (ENG)	M	8	(3)		1
David HANNAH	M	13			1
Ian JENKINS	D	5	(1)		
Sigurdur JÓNSSON (ISL)	M	12	(2)		1
Stephen McCONALOGUE	M		(1)		
Scott McCULLOCH	M	9			
Andy McLAREN	A	3	(5)		
Brian McLAUGHLIN	M	1	(2)		
Mark McNALLY	D	4	(1)		
Gary McSWEGAN	A	5			3
Maurice MALPAS	D	31			
Alex MATHIE	A	13	(9)		1
Joe MILLER	M	14	(10)		2
Tonny MOLS (BEL)	M	11			
Neil MURRAY	M	2	(1)		
Kjell OLOFSSON (SWE)	A	32	(2)		7
David PARTRIDGE	M		(1)		
Bernard PASCUAL (FRA)	D	16			
James PATERSON	M	8	(7)		
Darren PATTERSON (NIR)	D	17	(2)		
Erik PEDERSEN (NOR)	D	6			
Magnus SKÖLDMARK (SWE)	D	22	(3)		
Steven THOMPSON	A	5	(10)		1
José VALERIANI (PER)	M		(1)		
Robbie WINTERS	A	1	(2)		1
David WORRELL	M	3	(1)		
Lars ZETTERLUND (SWE)	M	20	(1)		1

LEAGUE RESULTS 1998/99

01/08/98	Kilmarnock	A	0-2	
16/08/98	Heart of Midlothian	H	0-0	
22/08/98	Celtic	A	1-2	Winters
30/08/98	Motherwell	A	0-1	
12/09/98	Rangers	H	0-0	
19/09/98	Dundee	A	2-2	McSwegan, Olofsson
23/09/98	Dunfermline Athletic	H	1-1	McSwegan
26/09/98	St. Johnstone	A	3-1	Dodds 3 (1p)
04/10/98	Aberdeen	H	1-0	McSwegan
17/10/98	Kilmarnock	H	0-2	
24/10/98	Heart of Midlothian	A	1-0	Dodds
31/10/98	Rangers	A	1-2	Dodds
07/11/98	Motherwell	H	2-2	Dodds, Jónsson
15/11/98	Dunfermline Athletic	A	1-2	Mathie
22/11/98	Dundee	H	0-1	
28/11/98	Aberdeen	A	3-0	Olofsson, Miller, Easton
05/12/98	St. Johnstone	H	1-1	Dodds
12/12/98	Celtic	H	1-1	Zetterlund
20/12/98	Kilmarnock	A	0-2	
26/12/98	Motherwell	A	0-2	
30/12/98	Rangers	H	1-2	Dodds
02/01/99	Dundee	A	3-1	Dodds, Thompson, Olofsson
30/01/99	Dunfermline Athletic	H	1-1	Olofsson
06/02/99	St. Johnstone	A	0-1	
20/02/99	Aberdeen	H	3-0	Olofsson, Dodds, Hannah
27/02/99	Celtic	A	1-2	Dodds
20/03/99	Rangers	A	1-0	Olofsson
03/04/99	Motherwell	H	0-3	
06/04/99	Heart of Midlothian	H	1-3	Dodds
17/04/99	Aberdeen	A	4-0	Dodds 2, Miller, Olofsson
20/04/99	St. Johnstone	H	0-1	
24/04/99	Dunfermline Athletic	A	2-2	Dodds 2 (1p)
01/05/99	Dundee	H	0-2	
08/05/99	Kilmarnock	H	0-0	
15/05/99	Heart of Midlothian	A	1-4	Eustace
23/05/99	Celtic	H	1-2	Dodds (p)

DUNFERMLINE ATHLETIC

CLUB DIRECTORY

Dunfermline Athletic FC
East End Park
Halbeath Road, Dunfermline
Fife, KY12 7RB
tel - (01383) 724295
fax - (01383) 723468
Year of Formation - 1885
Chairman - John Yorkston
Secretary - Paul A.M. D'Mello
Manager - Bert Paton; Dick Campbell
Stadium - East End Park (12,500)

MAJOR HONOURS
Scottish Cup - (2) 1961, 1968.

APPEARANCES 98/99

	P	Ap	(s)	Gls
Stephen BOYLE	A	1		1
Gerry BRITTON	A	13	(8)	2
Lee BUTLER	G	35		
Owen COYLE	A	11		1
Jason DAIR	M	9	(1)	
Ivo DEN BIEMAN (HOL)	M		(2)	
Jamie DOLAN	M	10		
EDINHO (BRA)	A	5	(4)	1
Craig FAULCONBRIDGE	M	1	(5)	
Derek FERGUSON	M	18	(3)	
John FRASER	M	2	(4)	
Hamish FRENCH	M	15	(6)	2
David GRAHAM	A	14	(7)	2
Richard HUXFORD (ENG)	M	22	(3)	
Craig IRELAND	D	21	(2)	
Gavin JOHNSON (ENG)	D	18		
David LINIGHAN (ENG)	D	1		
Scott McCULLOCH	D	19		1
Paul McDONALD	A		(1)	
Christopher McGROARTY	M	3	(1)	
Craig MARTIN	D	2	(1)	
Marc MILLAR	D	13	(8)	1
Colin NISH	A		(2)	
Stewart PETRIE	A	19	(11)	2
George SHAW	M	10	(8)	2
Greg SHIELDS	D	36		
Andy SMITH	A	29	(6)	8
Jamie SQUIRES (ENG)	M	19	(2)	2
Chris TEMPLEMAN	A	5	(7)	
Scott THOMSON	M	20	(1)	2
Andy TOD	D	24	(1)	1
Ian WESTWATER	G	1		

LEAGUE RESULTS 1998/99

01/08/98	Celtic	A	0-5	
15/08/98	Dundee	H	2-0	Smith, Shaw
22/08/98	Motherwell	A	0-0	
29/08/98	Aberdeen	H	1-1	French
12/09/98	St. Johnstone	A	1-1	Smith
19/09/98	Heart of Midlothian	H	1-1	Smith
23/09/98	Dundee United	A	1-1	Squires
26/09/98	Rangers	H	0-2	
03/10/98	Kilmarnock	A	0-0	
17/10/98	Celtic	H	2-2	Britton (p), French
28/10/98	Dundee	A	0-1	
31/10/98	St. Johnstone	H	1-1	Smith
07/11/98	Aberdeen	A	1-2	Squires
15/11/98	Dundee United	H	2-1	Tod, McCulloch
21/11/98	Heart of Midlothian	A	1-2	Edinho
28/11/98	Kilmarnock	H	0-3	
05/12/98	Rangers	A	1-1	Petrie
12/12/98	Motherwell	H	1-1	Smith
19/12/98	Celtic	A	0-5	
26/12/98	Aberdeen	H	1-2	Shaw
29/12/98	St. Johnstone	A	1-1	Smith (p)
02/01/99	Heart of Midlothian	H	0-0	
30/01/99	Dundee United	A	1-1	Smith
07/02/99	Rangers	H	0-3	
27/02/99	Motherwell	A	1-1	Britton
06/03/99	Kilmarnock	A	0-0	
13/03/99	Dundee	H	2-0	Thomson, Graham
20/03/99	St. Johnstone	H	1-0	Petrie
03/04/99	Aberdeen	A	1-3	Graham
14/04/99	Rangers	A	0-1	
17/04/99	Kilmarnock	H	0-6	
24/04/99	Dundee United	H	2-2	Millar (p), Smith
03/05/99	Heart of Midlothian	A	0-2	
08/05/99	Celtic	H	1-2	Coyle
15/05/99	Dundee	A	1-3	Thomson
23/05/99	Motherwell	H	1-2	Boyle

HEART OF MIDLOTHIAN

CLUB DIRECTORY

Heart of Midlothian FC
Tynecastle Park, Gorgie Road
Edinburgh EH11 2NL
tel - (0131) 2007200 / fax - (0131) 3460699
Year of Formation - 1874
Chairman - Douglas Smith
Chief Executive - Christopher P. Robinson
Manager - Jim Jefferies
Stadium - Tynecastle Park (18,000)

MAJOR HONOURS
League Championship - (4)
1895, 1897, 1958, 1960.
Scottish Cup - (6)
1891, 1896, 1901, 1906, 1956, 1998.
League Cup - (4) 1955, 1959, 1960, 1963.

APPEARANCES 98/99

		P	Ap	(s)	Gls
Stéphane ADAM (FRA)	A	28	(1)	10
Mohamed BERTHE (GUY)	M	1		
Stuart CALLAGHAN	A	2		
Colin CAMERON	M	10	(1)	6
Thomas FLÖGEL (AUT)	M	18	(2)	2
Steve FULTON	M	27		2
Vincent GUERIN (FRA)	M	9	(10)	1
Jim HAMILTON	A	20	(5)	6
Derek HOLMES	A	1	(5)	
Darren JACKSON	A	9		1
Kevin JAMES	D	1	(3)	
JUANJO Carricondo Pérez (ESP)	A	1	(10)	
Leigh JENKINSON (ENG)	A	3	(2)	
Andrew KIRK	M		(5)	
Derek LILLEY	A	3	(1)	1
Gary LOCKE	D	22	(3)	1
Neil McCANN	M	8		3
Roddy McKENZIE	G	10		
Rob McKINNON	D	14	(2)	
David McPHERSON	D	17	(1)	
Gary McSWEGAN	A	17	(4)	7
Lee MAKEL (ENG)	M	6	(8)	1
David MURIE	D		(4)	
Grant MURRAY	M	18	(3)	
Gary NAYSMITH	D	23	(3)	
Kris O'NEILL	M		(3)	
Steven PRESSLEY	D	29	(1)	1
José QUITONGO (ANG)	A	5	(7)	
Paul RITCHIE	D	29		1
Gilles ROUSSET (FRA)	G	26		
Stefano SALVATORI (ITA)	M	11	(1)	
Scott SEVERIN	M	5	(2)	
David WEIR	D	23		1

LEAGUE RESULTS 1998/99

01/08/98	Rangers	H	2-1	Adam, Hamilton
16/08/98	Dundee United	A	0-0	
22/08/98	Aberdeen	H	2-0	Fulton, Pressley
29/08/98	Kilmarnock	A	0-3	
12/09/98	Dundee	H	0-2	
19/09/98	Dunfermline Athletic	A	1-1	Hamilton
23/09/98	Motherwell	H	3-0	Weir, McCann 2 (1p)
26/09/98	Celtic	A	1-1	Hamilton
04/10/98	St. Johnstone	H	1-1	Makel
17/10/98	Rangers	A	0-3	
24/10/98	Dundee United	H	0-1	
31/10/98	Dundee	A	0-1	
07/11/98	Kilmarnock	H	2-1	Adam, Fulton
14/11/98	Motherwell	A	2-3	Hamilton (p), Guérin
21/11/98	Dunfermline Athletic	H	2-1	Flögel, McCann
06/12/98	Celtic	H	2-1	Adam 2
09/12/98	St. Johnstone	A	1-1	Hamilton
12/12/98	Aberdeen	A	0-2	
19/12/98	Rangers	H	2-3	Locke, Hamilton
26/12/98	Kilmarnock	A	0-1	
30/12/98	Dundee	H	1-2	Lilley
02/01/99	Dunfermline Athletic	A	0-0	
30/01/99	Motherwell	H	0-2	
06/02/99	Celtic	A	0-3	
20/02/99	St. Johnstone	H	0-2	
27/02/99	Aberdeen	H	0-2	
20/03/99	Dundee	A	0-2	
03/04/99	Kilmarnock	H	2-2	McSwegan 2
06/04/99	Dundee United	A	3-1	McSwegan, Adam, Cameron
14/04/99	Celtic	H	2-4	Adam 2
17/04/99	St. Johnstone	A	0-0	
24/04/99	Motherwell	A	4-0	Jackson, Adam 2, Cameron
03/05/99	Dunfermline Athletic	A	2-0	Cameron 2
09/05/99	Rangers	A	0-0	
15/05/99	Dundee United	H	4-1	Ritchie, McSwegan, Adam, Cameron
23/05/99	Aberdeen	A	5-2	McSwegan 3, Cameron (p), Flögel

KILMARNOCK

Kilmarnock FC
Rugby Park
Rugby Road
Kilmarnock
KA1 2DP
tel - (01563) 525184
fax - (01563) 522181
Year of Formation - 1869
Chairman - William Costley
Secretary - Kevin D. Collins
Manager - Bobby Wiliamson
Stadium - Rugby Park (18,128)

MAJOR HONOURS
League Championship - (1) 1965.
Scottish Cup - (3) 1920, 1929, 1997.

		P	Ap	(s)	Gls
David BAGAN	M	1	(4)		
Martin BAKER	A	23			
Alex BURKE	A	2	(17)		
Ian DURRANT	M	36			4
Steven HAMILTON	D	5			
John HENRY	A	7	(4)		3
Gary HOLT	M	33			3
Chris INNES	D	4			1
Dylan KERR	D	16			
Jim LAUCHLAN	D	14			
Ally McCOIST	A	16	(10)		7
Gary McCUTCHEON	A	2	(11)		2
Kevin McGOWNE	D	32			4
Gus MacPHERSON	D	31			1
Alan MAHOOD	M	16	(12)		2
Gordon MARSHALL	G	36			
Ally MITCHELL	M	27	(5)		4
Ray MONTGOMERIE	D	22			
Pat NEVIN	M	2	(1)		1
Mark REILLY	M	17	(1)		
Mark ROBERTS	A	9	(13)		3
Jérôme VAREILLE (FRA)	M	20	(3)		5
Paul WRIGHT	A	25	(8)		6

01/08/98	Dundee United	H	2-0	Wright, Nevin
15/08/98	St. Johnstone	A	0-0	
22/08/98	Rangers	H	1-3	Wright
29/08/98	Heart of Midlothian	H	3-0	McCoist 3
12/09/98	Celtic	A	1-1	Vareille
19/09/98	Motherwell	A	0-0	
23/09/98	Dundee	H	2-1	McCoist, McGowne
27/09/98	Aberdeen	A	1-0	Wright (p)
03/10/98	Dunfermline Athletic	H	0-0	
17/10/98	Dundee United	A	2-0	McGowne, Vareille
24/10/98	St. Johnstone	H	2-2	Roberts, og (Kernaghan)
31/10/98	Celtic	H	2-0	Roberts, Mitchell
07/11/98	Heart of Midlothian	A	1-2	Wright
14/11/98	Dundee	A	1-1	Vareille
21/11/98	Motherwell	H	0-0	
28/11/98	Dunfermline Athletic	A	3-0	Durrant 2, Holt
05/12/98	Aberdeen	H	4-0	Mitchell 2, Vareille, Wright (p)
12/12/98	Rangers	A	0-1	
20/12/98	Dundee United	H	2-0	Wright, Durrant
26/12/98	Heart of Midlothian	H	1-0	Holt
01/01/99	Motherwell	A	2-1	McCoist, McGowne
30/01/99	Dundee	H	0-0	
06/02/99	Aberdeen	A	1-2	Mahood
17/02/99	Celtic	A	0-1	
28/02/99	Rangers	H	0-5	
06/03/99	Dunfermline Athletic	H	0-0	
13/03/99	St. Johnstone	A	1-0	Holt
21/03/99	Celtic	H	0-0	
03/04/99	Heart of Midlothian	A	2-2	Henry, McCoist
10/04/99	Aberdeen	H	4-2	Mahood, MacPherson, McCutcheon 2
17/04/99	Dunfermline Athletic	A	6-0	Henry 2, Mitchell, Durrant, Vareille, McCoist
24/04/99	Dundee	A	1-2	Innes
01/05/99	Motherwell	H	0-1	
08/05/99	Dundee United	A	0-0	
15/05/99	St. Johnstone	H	1-1	Roberts
23/05/99	Rangers	A	1-1	McGowne

MOTHERWELL

CLUB DIRECTORY

Motherwell FC
Fir Park Stadium, Motherwell ML1 2QN
tel - (01698) 333333 / fax - (01698) 338001
Year of Formation - 1886
Chairman - John Boyle
Secretary - Alisdair Barron
Manager - Harri Kampman; Billy Davies
Stadium - Fir Park (13,742)

MAJOR HONOURS
League Championship - (1) 1932.
Scottish Cup - (2) 1952, 1991.
League Cup - (1) 1951.

APPEARANCES 98/99

	P	Ap	(s)	Gls
Derek ADAMS	A	11	(15)	3
Hervé BACQUE (FRA)	M		(1)	
Ged BRANNAN (ENG)	D	25		5
Kevin CHRISTIE	D	4	(1)	
Owen COYLE (IRL)	A	26		7
Stephen CRAIGAN	D	6	(4)	
Greig DENHAM	D		(1)	
Michel DOESBURG (HOL)	D	29	(1)	
Don GOODMAN (ENG)	A	8		1
Andy GORAM	G	13		
Mark GOWER (ENG)	M	8	(1)	1
Stephen HALLIDAY (ENG)	A	2	(2)	
Mikko KAVEN (FIN)	G	16		
Brian McCLAIR	M	8	(3)	
Lee McCULLOCH	M	14	(12)	3
Jamie McGOWAN	D	32		1
Stephen McMILLAN	D	30		2
Rob MATTHAEI (HOL)	M	14	(3)	
Eddie MAY	D	10	(4)	
Jan MICHELS (HOL)	M	7	(3)	
Greg MILLER	A	1	(3)	
Pat NEVIN	M	14	(16)	
Stephen NICHOLAS	M	1	(6)	1
Kai NYYSSÖNEN (FIN)	A	3		1
Douglas RAMSAY	M		(4)	1
Ian ROSS	M	8	(4)	
Eliphas SHIVUTE (NAM)	M		(1)	
John SPENCER	A	21		7
Jered STIRLING	D	4	(1)	1
Shaun TEALE (ENG)	D	29		1
Tony THOMAS (ENG)	D	10		
Simo VALAKARI (FIN)	M	35		
Stevie WOODS	G	7		

LEAGUE RESULTS 1998/99

Date	Opponent	H/A	Score	Scorers
01/08/98	St. Johnstone	H	1-0	Stirling
15/08/98	Rangers	A	1-2	Coyle
22/08/98	Dunfermline Athletic	H	0-0	
30/08/98	Dundee United	H	1-0	Nyyssönen
12/09/98	Aberdeen	A	1-1	Coyle
19/09/98	Kilmarnock	H	0-0	
23/09/98	Heart of Midlothian	A	0-3	
26/09/98	Dundee	A	0-1	
03/10/98	Celtic	H	1-2	Adams
17/10/98	St. Johnstone	A	0-5	
28/10/98	Rangers	H	1-0	Spencer
31/10/98	Aberdeen	H	2-2	Spencer, McGowan
07/11/98	Dundee United	A	2-2	Coyle 2
14/11/98	Heart of Midlothian	H	3-2	Spencer, Coyle 2
21/11/98	Kilmarnock	A	0-0	
28/11/98	Celtic	A	0-2	
12/12/98	Dunfermline Athletic	A	1-1	Spencer
16/12/98	Dundee	H	2-1	Coyle, McMillan
19/12/98	St. Johnstone	H	1-2	Adams
26/12/98	Dundee United	H	2-0	McMillan, Brannan
29/12/98	Aberdeen	A	1-1	McCulloch
01/01/99	Kilmarnock	H	1-2	Brannan
30/01/99	Heart of Midlothian	A	2-0	McCullouch, Adams
06/02/99	Dundee	A	0-1	
21/02/99	Celtic	H	1-7	Brannan
27/02/99	Dunfermline Athletic	H	1-1	McCulloch
13/03/99	Rangers	A	1-2	Gower
20/03/99	Aberdeen	H	1-1	Teale (p)
03/04/99	Dundee United	A	3-0	Brannan, Spencer 2
10/04/99	Dundee	H	1-2	Spencer
17/04/99	Celtic	A	0-1	
24/04/99	Heart of Midlothian	H	0-4	
01/05/99	Kilmarnock	A	1-0	Brannan (p)
08/05/99	St. Johnstone	A	0-0	
15/05/99	Rangers	H	1-5	Nicholas
23/05/99	Dunfermline Athletic	A	2-1	Goodman, Ramsay

RANGERS

Rangers FC
Ibrox Stadium, 150 Edmiston Drive
Glasgow G51 2XD
tel - (0141) 4278500 / fax - (0141) 4190600
Year of Formation - 1872
Chairman - David E. Murray
Secretary - R. Campbell Ogilvie
Manager - Dick Advocaat
Stadium - Ibrox Stadium (50,403)

MAJOR HONOURS
League Championship - (48)
1891, 1899, 1900, 1901, 1902, 1911, 1912,
1913, 1918, 1920, 1921, 1923, 1924, 1925,
1927, 1928, 1929, 1930, 1931, 1933, 1934,
1935, 1937, 1939, 1947, 1949, 1950, 1953,
1956, 1957, 1959, 1961, 1963, 1964, 1975,
1976, 1978, 1987, 1989, 1990, 1991, 1992,
1993, 1994, 1995, 1996, 1997, 1999.
Scottish Cup - (28)
1894, 1897, 1898, 1903, 1928, 1930, 1932,
1934, 1935, 1936, 1948, 1949, 1950, 1953,
1960, 1962, 1963, 1964, 1966, 1973, 1976,
1978, 1979, 1981, 1992, 1993, 1996, 1999.
League Cup - (21)
1947, 1949, 1961, 1962, 1964, 1965, 1971,
1976, 1978, 1979, 1982, 1984, 1985, 1987,
1988, 1989, 1991, 1993, 1994, 1997, 1999.
European Cup-winners' Cup - (1) 1972.

	P	Ap	(s)	Gls
Jörg ALBERTZ (GER)	M	33	(1)	11
Gabriel AMATO (ARG)	A	13	(7)	6
Lorenzo AMORUSO (ITA)	D	33		1
Lionel CHARBONNIER (FRA)	G	11		
Gordon DURIE	A	1	(4)	
Lee FEENEY	M		(1)	
Barry FERGUSON	M	23		1
Ian FERGUSON	M	4	(9)	
Gennaro GATTUSO (ITA)	M	3	(2)	
David GRAHAM	A		(3)	
Stéphane GUIVARC'H (FRA)	A	11	(3)	5
Colin HENDRY	D	16	(3)	
Jonatan JOHANSSON (FIN)	A	13	(12)	8
Andrei KANCHELSKIS (RUS)	M	29	(1)	8
Stefan KLOS (GER)	G	18		
Neil McCANN	M	15	(4)	5
Derek McINNES	M		(7)	
Charlie MILLER	M	2	(14)	3
Craig MOORE (AUS)	D	8		1
Barry NICHOLSON	M	3	(3)	
Antti NIEMI (FIN)	G	7		
Arthur NUMAN (HOL)	D	8	(2)	
Sergio PORRINI (ITA)	D	35		2
Claudio REYNA (USA)	M	6		
Luigi RICCIO (ITA)	D		(1)	
Sebastian ROZENTAL (CHL)	A		(3)	
Ståle STENSAAS (NOR)	D	1		
Jonas THERN (SWE)	M	1		
Giovanni VAN BRONCKHORST (HOL)	M	35		7
Tony VIDMAR (AUS)	D	26	(2)	1
Rod WALLACE (ENG)	A	34		18
Scott WILSON	D	7	(5)	1

01/08/98	Heart of Midlothian	A	1-2	Wallace
15/08/98	Motherwell	H	2-1	Wallace, Albertz (p)
22/08/98	Kilmarnock	A	3-1	Wallace, Albertz (p), Miller
29/08/98	St. Johnstone	H	4-0	Kanchelskis, Van Bronckhorst,
				Wallace, Albertz (p)
12/09/98	Dundee United	A	0-0	
20/09/98	Celtic	H	0-0	
23/09/98	Aberdeen	A	1-1	Wallace
26/09/98	Dunfermline Athletic	A	2-0	Johansson, Ferguson B.
04/10/98	Dundee	H	1-0	Albertz
17/10/98	Heart of Midlothian	H	3-0	Johansson, Wallace 2
28/10/98	Motherwell	A	0-1	
31/10/98	Dundee United	H	2-1	Wallace, Amoruso
08/11/98	St. Johnstone	A	7-0	Wallace, Johansson, Albertz 2 (2p),
				Kanchelskis, Guivarc'h 2
14/11/98	Aberdeen	H	2-1	Van Bronckhorst, Kanchelskis
21/11/98	Celtic	A	1-5	Van Bronckhorst
05/12/98	Dunfermline Athletic	H	1-1	Van Bronckhorst
12/12/98	Kilmarnock	H	1-0	Wallace
19/12/98	Heart of Midlothian	A	3-2	Guivarc'h 2, Kanchelskis
26/12/98	St. Johnstone	H	1-0	Porrini
30/12/98	Dundee United	A	2-1	Wilson, Wallace
03/01/99	Celtic	H	2-2	Amato, Wallace
27/01/99	Dundee	A	4-0	Miller 2, Guivarc'h, Johansson
30/01/99	Aberdeen	A	4-7	Porrini, Wallace, Albertz (p),
				Kanchelskis
07/02/99	Dunfermline Athletic	A	3-0	Kanchelskis, Johansson 2
20/02/98	Dundee	H	6-1	Albertz 3 (1p), McCann 2,
				Van Bronckhorst
28/02/99	Kilmarnock	A	5-0	McCann, Wallace 3, Johansson
13/03/99	Motherwell	H	2-1	Wallace, Johansson
20/03/99	Dundee United	H	0-1	
04/04/99	St. Johnstone	A	1-3	Moore
14/04/99	Dunfermline Athletic	H	1-0	Van Bronckhorst
18/04/99	Dundee	A	1-1	Vidmar
25/04/99	Aberdeen	H	3-1	Amato (p), Kanchelskis, Wallace
02/05/99	Celtic	A	3-0	McCann 2, Albertz (p)
09/05/99	Heart of Midlothian	H	0-0	
15/05/99	Motherwell	A	5-1	Amato 3 (1p), Van Bronckhorst,
				Kanchelskis
23/05/99	Kilmarnock	H	1-1	Amato

ST. JOHNSTONE

CLUB DIRECTORY

St. Johnstone FC
McDiarmid Park
Crieff Road
Perth
PH1 2SJ
tel - (01738) 459090
fax - (01738) 625771
Year of Formation - 1884
Chairman - Geoffrey S. Brown
Secretary - Stewart Duff
Manager - Paul Sturrock; Sandy Clark
Stadium - McDiarmid Park (10,673)

APPEARANCES 98/99

		P	Ap	(s)	Gls
Gary BOLLAN	M	32	(1)		4
Paddy CONNOLLY	A	6	(3)		1
Nick DASOVIC (CAN)	M	31			1
Darren DODS	D	34			2
Allan FERGUSON	G	2	(1)		
Roddy GRANT	A	14	(11)		4
Danny GRIFFIN (NIR)	D	14	(5)		1
Paul KANE	M	33	(1)		3
Alan KERNAGHAN (IRL)	D	26			3
Nathan LOWNDES (ENG)	A	12	(17)		2
Kieran McANESPIE	M	8	(10)		2
John Paul McBRIDE	M	2	(1)		
Stuart McCLUSKEY	D	5	(2)		
Gerry McMAHON (NIR)	M	13	(6)		1
John McQUILLAN	D	27	(1)		1
Alan MAIN	G	34			
George O'BOYLE (NIR)	A	12	(1)		2
Keith O'HALLORAN	M	10	(6)		1
John O'NEIL	M	33			2
Keigan PARKER	M		(2)		
Allan PRESTON	D	8	(7)		1
Philip SCOTT	M	14	(2)		2
Miguel SIMÃO (POR)	M	20	(6)		4
Jim WEIR	D	6	(1)		1
Andrew WHITEFORD	M		(1)		

LEAGUE RESULTS 1998/99

01/08/98	Motherwell	A	0-1	
15/08/98	Kilmarnock	H	0-0	
23/08/98	Dundee	A	1-0	Scott
29/08/98	Rangers	A	0-4	
12/09/98	Dunfermline Athletic	H	1-1	og (Squires)
19/09/98	Aberdeen	H	2-0	Lowndes, McMahon
23/09/98	Celtic	A	1-0	Dasovic
26/09/98	Dundee United	H	1-3	Grant
04/10/98	Heart of Midlothian	A	1-1	Preston
17/10/98	Motherwell	H	5-0	O'Boyle 2, Kernaghan, Simão, Dods
24/10/98	Kilmarnock	A	2-2	Dods, Lowndes
31/10/98	Dunfermline Athletic	A	1-1	McQuillan
08/11/98	Rangers	H	0-7	
14/11/98	Celtic	H	2-1	Simão, McAnespie
21/11/98	Aberdeen	A	1-0	Simão
05/12/98	Dundee United	A	1-1	Grant (p)
09/12/98	Heart of Midlothian	H	1-1	Kernaghan
12/12/98	Dundee	H	1-1	Bollan
19/12/98	Motherwell	A	2-1	Connolly, Grant
26/12/98	Rangers	A	0-1	
29/12/98	Dunfermline Athletic	H	1-1	Kane
02/01/99	Aberdeen	H	4-1	Bollan (p), Kernaghan, O'Neil 2
31/01/99	Celtic	A	0-5	
06/02/99	Dundee United	H	1-0	Bollan
20/02/99	Heart of Midlothian	A	2-0	Scott, Kane
27/02/99	Dundee	A	1-0	Grant
13/03/99	Kilmarnock	H	0-1	
20/03/99	Dunfermline Athletic	A	0-1	
04/04/99	Rangers	H	3-1	Weir, Simão, McAnespie
17/04/99	Heart of Midlothian	H	0-0	
20/04/99	Dundee United	A	1-0	Griffin
24/04/99	Celtic	H	1-0	O'Halloran
01/05/99	Aberdeen	A	0-1	
08/05/99	Motherwell	H	0-0	
15/05/99	Kilmarnock	A	1-1	Bollan
23/05/99	Dundee	H	1-0	Kane

PROMOTED CLUB

SECOND DIVISION FINAL TABLE 98/99

		Pd	W	D	L	F	A	Pt	GD
1	**Hibernian**	**36**	**28**	**5**	**3**	**84**	**33**	**89**	**+51**
2	Falkirk	36	20	6	10	60	38	66	+22
3	Ayr United	36	19	5	12	66	42	62	+24
4	Airdrieonians	36	18	5	13	42	43	59	-1
5	St. Mirren	36	14	10	12	42	43	52	-1
6	Greenock Morton	36	14	7	15	45	41	49	+4
7	Clydebank	36	11	13	12	36	38	46	-2
8	Raith Rovers	36	8	11	17	37	57	35	-20
9	Hamilton Academical	36	6	10	20	30	62	28	-32
10	Stranraer	36	5	2	29	29	74	17	-45

CLUB DIRECTORY

Hibernian FC
Easter Road Stadium
Albion Road
Edinburgh EH7 5QG
tel - (0131) 6612159
fax - (0131) 6596488
Year of Formation - 1875
Chairman - Malcolm McPherson
Secretary - Mary Anne McAdam
Manager - Alex McLeish
Stadium - Easter Road (16,032)

MAJOR HONOURS
League Championship - (4)
1903, 1948, 1951, 1952.
Scottish Cup - (2) 1887, 1902.
League Cup - (2) 1973, 1992.

SLOVAKIA

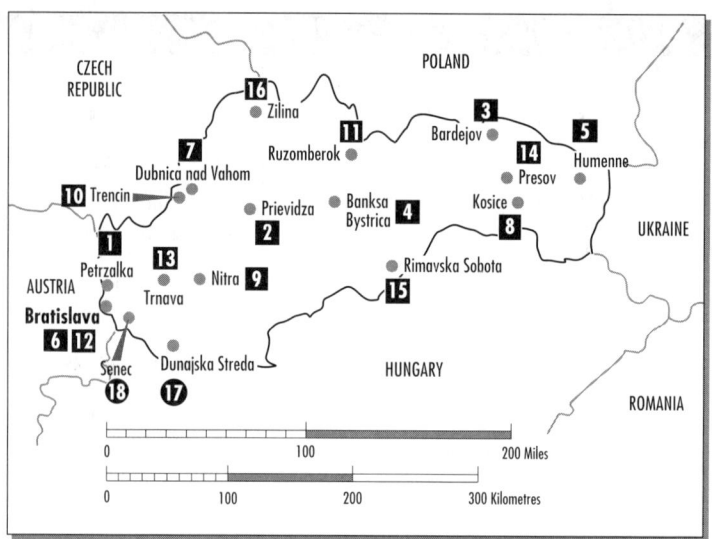

1	ARTMEDIA PETRZALKA	900
2	BANIK PRIEVIDZA	901
3	BSC BARDEJOV	902
4	DUKLA BANSKA BYSTRICA	903
5	HFC HUMENNE	904
6	INTER BRATISLAVA	905
7	ZTS KERAMETAL DUBNICA	906
8	1.FC KOSICE	907
9	FC NITRA	908
10	OZETA DUKLA TRENCIN	909

11	SCP RUZOMBEROK	910
12	SLOVAN BRATISLAVA	911
13	SPARTAK TRNAVA	912
14	TATRAN PRESOV	913
15	TAURIS RIMAVSKA SOBOTA	914
16	MSK ZILINA	915
Promoted clubs		
17	DAC DUNAJSKA STREDA	916
18	VTJ KOBA SENEC	916

GOAL SHORTAGE HITS EURO 2000 HOPES

Slovan Bratislava back where they belong

FEDERATION DIRECTORY

Slovensky Futbalovy Zvaz
Junácka 6, 835 80 Bratislava

tel - (07) 49249151
fax - (07) 49249554

Year of Formation - 1990
President - Frantisek Laurinec
Secretary - Ladislaw Veselsky

Stadium - Tehelne pole, Bratislava (33,000)

A new-look, remodelled Slovan Bratislava returned to familiar territory in 1998/99. Slovakia's most internationally renowned club regained the title they had last won three years previously and also added the domestic Cup to claim their second 'double' since Slovakian independence.

New coach Stanislav Griga - a former Czechoslovakian international striker who played at the 1990 World Cup - confirmed the potential he had shown the previous year in taking unfancied Ozeta Trencin to fourth place. His popularity with the Slovan fans was immense. Right from the start the team from the capital had the look of potential champions, and it was to Griga's enormous credit that he formed a winning team so quickly out of a group of players who were still getting to know each other.

Powered by their new sponsor, Slovak Gas, Slovan were able to make considerable reinforcements to the squad that had limped home in fifth place in 1997/98. There were no fewer than six major new signings - strikers Jozef Majoros (Petra Drnovice) and Tibor Jancula (Fortuna Düsseldorf), midfielders Marek Fabula (Tatran Presov) and Norbert Hrncar (MSK Zilina), and defenders Stanislav Varga (Tatran Presov) and Milan Timko (Banik Ostrava). Together with some of the more durable members of the old guard, such as goalkeeper Miroslav König, full-backs Ladislav Pecko and Zsolt Hornyak, and central midfield duo Robert Tomaschek and Pavol Sedlak, the new arrivals merged into a team of formidable all-round strength.

During the first half of the season Slovan lost only once - away to Griga's old club Trencin - but they still found themselves placed only third in what had become a four-horse race with Spartak Trnava, Kosice and local rivals Inter. In the spring, however, they were almost

LEAGUE CHAMPIONSHIP RESULTS 98/99

		1	2	3	4	5	6	7	8	9	10	11	12	13	14	15	16
1	Artmedia Petrzalka		0-0	2-0	1-1	2-0	0-0	2-1	3-1	2-1	1-3	1-1	0-2	2-3	1-0	5-2	2-0
2	Banik Prievidza	2-1		5-0	0-0	0-1	0-3	1-2	1-1	1-1	0-4	0-2	0-2	0-2	1-1	2-0	2-1
3	BSC Bardejov	3-0	1-2		1-0	0-1	0-3	0-2	1-2	1-4	0-2	1-3	0-2	0-0	0-3	0-1	0-1
4	Dukla Banska Bystrica	1-0	3-2	3-2		1-0	0-1	7-0	0-0	1-0	0-4	0-0	2-2	0-2	2-2	0-1	0-1
5	HFC Humenne	1-2	6-2	1-0	0-0		0-1	1-0	0-2	1-3	0-4	0-0	0-0	1-0	0-0	1-0	3-1
6	Inter Bratislava	4-1	1-0	10-0	1-1	1-2		1-0	2-1	3-1	2-1	2-0	0-1	3-1	2-1	5-3	5-0
7	ZTS Kerametal Dubnica	2-2	3-2	2-1	0-2	2-1	0-6		2-3	0-2	0-2	3-0	0-1	0-0	0-0	3-0	0-3
8	1.FC Kosice	3-1	1-3	2-1	6-0	1-0	1-0	3-1		2-0	5-1	1-0	0-2	0-1	1-2	2-0	3-0
9	FC Nitra	0-3	2-1	3-1	4-1	0-2	0-2	0-1	0-0		1-1	3-0	0-4	0-3	2-2	0-0	0-1
10	Ozeta Dukla Trencin	2-0	3-0	2-0	2-2	1-0	0-0	3-0	0-1	3-0		1-1	1-0	0-0	0-1	3-0	6-1
11	SCP Ruzomberok	0-2	2-1	2-1	2-0	3-0	0-0	2-0	1-3	0-0	1-0		0-0	2-0	0-0	2-1	1-1
12	Slovan Bratislava	3-0	4-2	3-0	3-0	3-1	1-0	2-0	3-0	2-0	1-1	2-1		0-1	3-0	3-0	3-0
13	Spartak Trnava	2-0	3-0	1-0	5-2	4-1	0-0	4-1	0-0	6-0	1-0	5-0	1-1		4-1	3-1	3-1
14	Tatran Presov	2-0	2-1	1-0	2-1	3-0	0-2	5-1	0-3	2-0	2-2	1-1	0-0	0-0		3-0	0-2
15	Tauris Rimavska Sobota	1-0	1-1	2-0	0-2	0-0	0-2	2-2	1-2	1-1	1-1	2-3	1-1	2-4	4-1		1-2
16	MSK Zilina	1-1	3-2	1-0	2-2	1-0	0-2	2-0	0-1	1-0	4-0	0-1	0-2	2-0	2-1	2-1	

LEAGUE CHAMPIONSHIP FINAL TABLE 98/99

			Home				Away					Total						
		P	W	D	L	F	A	W	D	L	F	A	W	D	L	F	A	P	GD
1	Slovan Bratislava	30	13	1	1	36	6	8	6	1	20	5	21	7	2	56	11	70	+45
2	Inter Bratislava	30	12	1	2	42	13	9	4	2	22	2	21	5	4	64	15	68	+49
3	Spartak Trnava	30	12	3	0	42	8	7	4	4	17	12	19	7	4	59	20	64	+39
4	1.FC Kosice	30	11	0	4	31	12	8	4	3	20	14	19	4	7	51	26	61	+25
5	Ozeta Dukla Trencin	30	9	4	2	27	6	6	4	5	26	19	15	8	7	53	25	53	+28
6	MSK Zilina	30	9	2	4	21	13	6	1	8	15	29	15	3	12	36	42	48	-6
7	SCP Ruzomberok	30	8	5	2	18	9	4	5	6	13	22	12	10	8	31	31	46	0
8	Tatran Presov	30	8	4	3	23	13	3	6	6	15	22	11	10	9	38	35	43	+3
9	Artmedia Petrzalka	30	8	4	3	24	15	3	2	10	13	27	11	6	13	37	42	39	-5
10	HFC Humenne	30	6	4	5	15	15	4	1	10	9	22	10	5	15	24	37	35	-13
11	Dukla Banska Bystrica	30	6	4	5	20	17	2	6	7	14	29	8	10	12	34	46	34	-12
12	FC Nitra	30	4	4	7	15	22	3	3	9	13	26	7	7	16	28	48	28	-20
13	ZTS Kerametal Dubnica	30	5	3	7	17	25	3	1	11	11	35	8	4	18	28	60	28	-32
14	Banik Prievidza	30	4	4	7	15	21	2	2	11	19	35	6	6	18	34	56	24	-22
15	Tauris Rimavska Sobota	30	3	6	6	19	22	2	1	12	10	34	5	7	18	29	56	22	-27
16	BSC Bardejov	30	2	1	12	8	26	0	0	15	6	40	2	1	27	14	66	7	-52

unstoppable. They were certainly impenetrable. For 12 matches running goalkeeper König kept his goal intact, and with Slovan finding a way through at the other end in all but two of those fixtures, the pace they set proved too tough for all of their challengers. It was bogey side Trencin who ended yet another run when they drew 1-1 with Slovan in round 28, but with Inter and Trnava also dropping points on the same day, Slovan were virtually home and dry. A week later they wrapped up their fourth Slovakian title with a 2-0 win away to Banik Prievidza.

The league triumph completed the 'double' as two weeks earlier Slovan had cruised to a one-sided Cup final victory over Dukla Banska Bystrica, with the team's regular substitutes, Miroslav Kriss and Lubomir Meszaros (2), supplying the goals. Bankla Bystrica were cheered by Slovan's subsequent championship win as it enabled them to book a place in the following season's UEFA Cup.

The other two UEFA Cup berths were filled by Inter and Trnava, with Kosice, the champions of the previous two seasons, missing out on Europe altogether after they shirked the opportunity to compete in the InterToto, citing

INTERNATIONAL HONOURS

European Club Competitions
Cup-winners' Cup   Slovan Bratislava (1969)

DOMESTIC CUP 98/99

1/8 FINALS
Tauris Rimavska Sobota 2, 1.FC Kosice 0
Slovan Bratislava 3, HFC Humenne 0
Dukla Banska Bystrica 5, FC Nitra 1
MSK Zilina 1, Inter Bratislava 2
BSC Bardejov 4, Tatran Presov 3
ZTS Kerametal Dubnica 4, DAC Dunajska Streda 1
SKP Devin 2, SCP Ruzomberok 2 (4-5 on pens.)
Spartak Trnava 4, Banik Prievidza 0

QUARTER-FINALS
Inter Bratislava 0, Spartak Trnava 0 (3-4 on pens.)
Slovan Bratislava 1, Tauris Rimavska Sobota 0
Dukla Banska Bystrica 1, SCP Ruzomberok 0
BSC Bardejov 0, ZTS Kerametal Dubnica 1

SEMI-FINALS
Slovan Bratislava v Spartak Trnava 1-1; 2-1
(Slovan Bratislava 3-2)
Dukla Banska Bystrica v ZTS Kerametal Dubnica 2-1; 2-3
(4-4; Dukla Banska Bystrica on away goals)

FINAL
08/05/99, Ziar nad Hronom
SLOVAN BRATISLAVA 3 Meszaros (63, 67), Kriss (43)
DUKLA BANSKA BYSTRICA 0
referee - Michel
SLOVAN BRATISLAVA - König; Pecko, Varga, Timko, Sobona; Meszaros, Hrncar, Tomaschek, Fabula; Borisenko (Kriss 37), Majoros.
DUKLA BANSKA BYSTRICA - Juracka (Seman 69); Karasek; Strelec, Kentos, Prazenica; Bazik, Libic, Helbich (Jelencik 80), Bohacik; Faktor, Rusnak.

major cash-flow problems. Kosice went into their final match level on points with Trnava, but a shock home defeat by Prievidza ended their UEFA Cup hopes, providing an appropriate ending to what had been a largely forgettable season for the 'Tigers'. It had opened with a glut of goals in the Champions' League against Northern Irish side Cliftonville, but bad times were soon to follow. They missed out on a second successive season in the Champions' League proper after losing to Brøndby in the qualifying round, but given what followed in the UEFA Cup, an 8-0 aggregate thrashing from Liverpool, it was probably better for team morale (if not their bank balance) that they

NATIONAL TEAM APPEARANCES 98/99

Coach - Jozef JANKECH; Jozef ADAMEC	FIN	AZB	LIE	POR	POL	BUL	ROM	HUN	BUL	POR	HUN	Cps	Gls
Alexander VENCEL (02/03/67) - RC Strasbourg (FRA)	G	G	G	G								19	-
Dusan TITTEL (27/12/66) - Spartak Trnava	D	D	D	D								45	7
Stanislav VARGA (08/10/72) - Slovan Bratislava	D	D	D65	D	D	D	D	D		D	D	16	-
Marek SPILAR (11/02/75) - 1.FC Kosice	D85	D	D	D	s20	D						24	-
Vladimir KINDER (04/03/69) - Middlesbrough (ENG)	M80	M	M30	M46								38	1
Miroslav SOVIC (09/03/70) - 1.FC Kosice	M	M	M	M83								12	1
Robert TOMASCHEK (25/08/72) - Slovan Bratislava	M80	M	M	M	M	M53	M	M	M	M		42	3
Peter DUBOVSKY (07/05/72) - Real Oviedo (ESP)	M57	M62	M	M		M	A87	A		M		30	12
Lubomir MORAVCIK (22/06/65) - MSV Duisburg (GER)	M	M	M	M								32	6
Jozef MAJOROS (19/03/70) - Slovan Bratislava	A	A82	A	A	A90	A	A71	A	A72	A85		22	5
Martin FABUS (11/11/76) - Ozeta Dukla Trencin	A57	A62	A61	A57	s90	A46			A79		A	10	2
Marek UJLAKY (26/03/74) - Spartak Trnava	s57	s82			M59	s46						22	2
Szilard NEMETH (08/08/78) - 1.FC Kosice	s57			s57								13	2
Tibor JANCULA (16/06/69) - Slovan Bratislava	s80	s62	s61		A76							24	9
Igor BALIS (05/01/70) - Spartak Trnava	s80				s59		M	M				28	-
Milan TIMKO (28/11/72) - Slovan Bratislava	s85		s65		s67				D	D	D	9	1
Vladislav ZVARA (11/12/71) - 1.FC Kosice		s62							M69	M31	M81	27	-
Ivan KOZAK (18/06/70) - 1.FC Kosice		s30	s46	D								32	-
Attila PINTE (06/06/71) - Inter Bratislava			s83	s76	s53		M83	M	M66	M		10	-
Miroslav KÖNIG (01/06/72) - Slovan Bratislava				G	G46	G	G	G90	G	G		14	-
Miroslav KARHAN (21/06/76) - Spartak Trnava				D20	D	D	D	D	D	D		30	-
Vladimir LEITNER (28/06/74) - Spartak Trnava				M67								1	-
Norbert HRNCAR (09/06/70) - Slovan Bratislava				M		s79						2	-
Peter DZURIK (29/12/68) - 1.FC Kosice				M	M	s77	s14	D		s81		11	-
Marian ZEMAN (07/07/74) - Vitesse (HOL)				D46	D	D14						22	2
Tibor ZATEK (14/06/71) - 1.FC Kosice				M	M77	M79						7	-
Kamil SUSKO (06/11/74) - Spartak Trnava				s46		s90						2	-
Roman KRATOCHVIL (24/06/74) - Inter Bratislava				s46	D	D	D	D	D	D		6	-
Vladimir LABANT (08/06/74) - Slavia Praha (CZE)				M		M69	M	M				4	-
Peter SLICHO (31/01/74) - 1.FC Kosice				s71	s83	s69	s66					4	-
Marian SUCHANCOK (13/07/71) - Inter Bratislava				s87								1	-
Peter NEMETH (14/09/72) - Inter Bratislava				s69		M						2	-
Vladimir KOZUCH (15/10/75) - Tatran Presov				s72	s85							2	-
Jozef VALACHOVIC (12/07/75) - Ozeta Dukla Trencin				s79	s31	M						3	-

PLAYERS OF THE SEASON

MIROSLAV KÖNIG

27-year-old Slovan Bratislava goalkeeper Miroslav König set a new Slovakian league record in the spring of 1999 by keeping 12 successive clean sheets and going 1,129 minutes without conceding a goal. Pretty impressive stuff, although official statistics rather took the gloss off his achievement when they revealed that over the course of that splendid run there had been a mere 11 shots on target for him to save. One man who was suitably impressed, however, was new national team boss Jozef Adamec, who made the Slovan 'keeper his first choice ahead of Alexander Vencel and was rewarded when König conceded just one goal in four Euro 2000 qualifiers - and that in a match in Lisbon where he performed miracles to keep the Portuguese attack at bay, making two world-class saves to deny Figo and Rui Costa.

ROBERT TOMASCHEK

Robert Tomaschek is on course to become the first Slovakian international to reach 50 caps. The 27-year-old central midfielder has been a key member of the team since earning his first national team cap against the United Arab Emirates in February 1994 - Slovakia's first official international as an independent state. Jozef Venglos and Jozef Jankech both had tremendous faith in him, and now Jozef Adamec looks set to follow suit. Tomaschek was picked out by Slovan Bratislava coach Stanislav Griga as the team's most important player during their 1998/99 'double'-winning campaign. An energetic, multi-purpose schemer, he has the class necessary to prosper in Western Europe but has so far resisted the temptation to leave the club of his youth.

did. An opening-day home defeat in the league to Trnava did not bode well, and although they recovered swiftly from that setback with a run of six straight victories, they were to come badly unstuck in the direct confrontations with the other title hopefuls.

Spartak Trnava ended the season by winning 1-0 away to champions Slovan, but it was too late to matter. Another championship challenge had ended in failure for the country's best-supported club (although with a decline in their average crowds from 11,557 to 8,662, even that reputation was looking a bit shaky). Leaders at halfway,

they lost important ground in April with a disastrous run of results that ended with coach Dusan Galis being given the sack. Galis had only just returned full-time to the club after an aborted attempt to carry out his functions in conjunction with running the Slovakian national team, but successive defeats in Humenne and Ruzomberok plus a costly home draw with Inter forced the ex-Slovan boss into total unemployment.

Inter were the surprise team of the season. They were delighted to finish second, although they would have gone one better had they not been beaten in both of the Bratislava derbies. Theirs was the best attack in the division, with their figures being considerably boosted late on in

NATIONAL TEAM RESULTS 98/99

19/08/98	Finland	H	Kosice	0-0	
05/09/98	Azerbaijan (ECQ)	H	Bratislava	3-0	Fabus (17), Dubovsky (26p), Moravcik (39)
10/10/98	Liechtenstein (ECQ)	A	Vaduz	4-0	Sovic (3), Dubovsky (13), Tomaschek (36, 61)
14/10/98	Portugal (ECQ)	H	Bratislava	0-3	
10/11/98	Poland	H	Bratislava	1-3	Jancula (57)
03/03/99	Bulgaria	A	Stara Zagora	0-2	
27/03/99	Romania (ECQ)	A	Bucharest	0-0	
31/03/99	Hungary (ECQ)	H	Bratislava	0-0	
19/05/99	Bulgaria	H	Dubnica	2-0	Timko (26), Tomaschek (89)
05/06/99	Portugal (ECQ)	A	Lisbon	0-1	
09/06/99	Hungary (ECQ)	A	Györ	1-0	Fabus (53)

TOP SCORERS

19	Martin FABUS (Ozeta Dukla Trencin)
13	Vladimir SYKORA (Tauris Rimavska Sobota)
	Peter BABNIC (Inter Bratislava)
	Lubos PERNIS (Banik Prievidza)
12	Ruslan LYUBARSKYI (1.FC Kosice)
11	Lubomir FAKTOR (Dukla Banska Bystrica)
	Attila PINTE (Inter Bratislava)
	Stefan RUSNAK (Dukla Banska Bystrica)
	Marek MINTAL (MSK Zilina)
10	Fábio Luís GOMES (Spartak Trnava)
	Vladislav ZVARA (1.FC Kosice)

the campaign by a 10-0 annihilation of bottom club Bardejov. They could have done with storing some of those goals for their next home game, because it was to result in a 1-2 defeat by Humenne that allowed Slovan to overtake them at the top of the table for the last time.

While Inter scored more goals as a team, the best individual marksman was Trencin's Martin Fabus, whose 19-goal total was six better than anybody else's. Fabus carried on where he had left off the previous season and confirmed that, at 22, he is one of the brightest hopes for the future of Slovakian football.

His winning goal away to Hungary at the end of the season provided the Slovakian national team with a very satisfying European Championship win just across the border in Györ, but, alas, the team's failure to find the net in any of their previous four qualifiers appeared to have ended their faint hopes of qualifying for the finals from a group that also included Romania and Portugal.

It was after the 0-3 home defeat by the Portuguese in the autumn that coach Jozef Jankech's three-year stint in charge was brought to an end. Dusan Galis, his appointed successor, was handed a contract that allowed him to continue as Spartak Trnava coach until the end of the season, but after 55 days in the job - a period that included no matches - Galis resigned, stating that he could not work under newly-elected FA president Frantisek Laurinec.

Next to take over was 57-year-old Tatran Presov coach Jozef Adamec, but although he made a positive start with a 0-0 draw away to group leaders Romania, another stalemate four days later at home to Hungary was less beneficial. Slovakia did reasonably well to restrict Portugal to a single goal in Lisbon in their next game, but their own goal-drought continued and that defeat effectively consigned them to the ranks of Euro 2000 also-rans.

EUROPEAN CUPS 98/99

CHAMPIONS' CUP
● **1.FC KOSICE**
Preliminary round CLIFTONVILLE (NIR)
A 5-1 Zvara (22, 28), Nemeth (35), Lyubarskyi (65), Prohaszka (78)
Seman; Semenik; Kozak I., Toth (Jambor 69); Sovic, Zvara (Kozak J. 53), Spilar, Dzurik (Kral 78); Lyubarskyi; Nemeth, Prohaszka.
H 8-0 Kozak J. (4), Janocko (14, 54), Nemeth (32), Prohaszka (59, 72), Lyubarskyi (67), Kozlej (84)
Seman; Semenik; Kozak I. (Toth 46), Gerich; Sovic (Lyubarskyi 59), Kozak J., Jambor, Kral, Janocko; Nemeth (Prochaszka 46); Kozlej.

Qualifying round BRØNDBY IF (DEN)
H 0-2
Molnar; Semenik; Kozak I., Dzurik, Spilar; Sovic, Zvara, Lyubarskyi (Kozlej 68), Toth; Nemeth (Janocko 68), Prohaszka.
A 1-0 Lapsansky (39)
Molnar; Semenik; Kral, Dzurik, Toth; Lapsansky (Janocko 66), Sovic, Zvara, Lyubarskyi; Kozlej, Prohaszka (Nemeth 55).

CUP WINNERS' CUP
● **SPARTAK TRNAVA**
Qualifying round VARDAR SKOPJE (MAC)
A 1-0 Ujlaky (76)
Susko; Tittel; Hrabal, Karhan, Leitner; Balis, Kristofik, Ujlaky, Macak (Formanko 46); Timko, Gomes.
H 2-0 Tittel (82), Gomes (86)
Susko; Tittel; Jakirovic (Horky 83), Karhan, Leitner; Balis, Kristofik, Ujlaky, Talda (Macak 70); Timko, Gomes.

1st round BESIKTAS (TUR)
A 0-3
Susko; Tittel; Hrabal, Karhan, Jakirovic, Leitner; Balis (Macak 70), Kristofik (Bugar 60), Gomes, Ujlaky; Timko.

H 2-1 Formanko (50), Timko (71)
Susko; Tittel; Hrabal, Karhan (Jakirovic 74), Leitner; Balis (Talda 64), Horky, Gomes, Ujlaky; Macak (Tomovcik 82), Formanko.

UEFA CUP
● **INTER BRATISLAVA**
Preliminary round SK TIRANA (ALB)
H 2-0 Suchancok (14), Miklos (58)
Hyll; Ovad; Cmilansky, Suchancok, Kratochvil; Pinte (Danko 68), Nemeth, Czinege, Gresko; Slezak (Miklos 46), Babnic (Majsniar 82).
A 2-0 Babnic (54), Miklos (80)
Hyll; Ovad (Futej 70), Cmilansky, Suchancok, Kratochvil; Czinege, Nemeth, Danko (Miklos 67), Gresko; Pinte, Babnic.

Qualifying round SLAVIA PRAHA (CZE)
A 0-4
Hyll; Suchancok; Ovad, Cmilansky, Kratochvil; Czinege, Kusalik, Nemeth, Pinte; Babnic, Miklos (Gresko 46).
H 2-0 Babnic (12), Ovad (52)
Hyll; Ovad; Cmilansky, Suchancok, Kratochvil; Czinege, Pinte (Kusalik 69), Danko, Gresko; Babnic, Miklos.

● **1.FC KOSICE**
1st round LIVERPOOL (ENG)
H 0-3
Molnar; Semenik; Kozak I., Spilar, Toth (Lyubarskyi 67); Sovic, Kral (Kozak J. 46), Dzurik, Zvara; Kozlej (Prohaszka 67), Nemeth.
A 0-5
Molnar; Semenik; Kozak I., Spilar, Kral (Jambor 57); Sovic (Lapsansky 61), Dzurik, Zvara, Kozak J.; Nemeth, Kozlej.

ARTMEDIA PETRZALKA

CLUB DIRECTORY

FC Artmedia Petrzalka
Krasovskeho 1
851 01 Bratislava
tel - (07) 850043
fax - (07) 850043
Year of Formation - 1898
President - Juraj Vysoky
Secretary - Vladimir Weiss
Coach - Peter Pavlovic
Stadium - Petrzalka (12,000)

APPEARANCES 98/99

	P	Ap	(s)	Gls
Martin BALIAK	M	24	(4)	1
Miroslav CHVILA	D	10	(3)	
Kornel CSICSAY	M		(1)	
Juraj COBEJ	G	15		
Ondrej DEBNAR	D	15	(2)	
Juraj ERÖS	M	2	(8)	
Miroslav FILIPKO	G	7	(1)	
Martin HEJTMANEK	G	6	(1)	
Jozef JURIGA	M	16	(7)	
Martin KARNAS	D	21	(2)	
Martin KUNA	D	20		
Stefan MAIXNER	A	17	(5)	5
Jozef MAJOROS	M	15	(11)	3
Tomas MEDVED	A	20	(2)	6
Martin MINAROVIC	M		(3)	
Rastislav MORES	M	5	(10)	
Jozef OLEJNIK	D		(1)	
Lubomir ORABINEC	M	26	(1)	
Roland PRAJ	G	2		
Milan STRELEC	A	14	(12)	6
Milos TOMAS	D	21		6
Radovan VASIK	A	16	(3)	4
Alexander VEGH	M	3	(3)	
Vladimir WEISS	M	9		4
Tomas ZARECKY	M	26		
Ivan ZIGA	M	20	(5)	2

LEAGUE RESULTS 1998/99

Date	Opponent	H/A	Score	Scorers
02/08/98	Inter Bratislava	H	0-0	
08/08/98	SCP Ruzomberok	A	2-0	Weiss, Ziga
16/08/98	Tauris Rimavska Sobota	H	5-2	Tomas 2, Ziga, Baliak, Maixner
22/08/98	FC Nitra	A	3-0	Weiss 2, Strelec
30/08/98	ZTS Kerametal Dubnica	H	2-1	Tomas, Weiss
13/09/98	MSK Zilina	H	2-0	Tomas, Strelec
19/09/98	Tatran Presov	A	0-2	
27/09/98	Slovan Bratislava	H	0-2	
03/10/98	1.FC Kosice	A	1-3	Strelec
18/10/98	Ozeta Dukla Trencin	H	1-3	Strelec
23/10/98	Banik Prievidza	A	1-2	Majoros
01/11/98	Spartak Trnava	H	2-3	Majoros, Maixner
07/11/98	BSC Bardejov	A	0-3	
15/11/98	Dukla Banska Bystrica	H	1-1	Strelec
21/11/98	HFC Humenne	A	2-1	Tomas, Maixner
27/02/99	Inter Bratislava	A	1-4	Vasik
07/03/99	SCP Ruzomberok	H	1-1	Maixner
13/03/99	Tauris Rimavska Sobota	A	0-1	
21/03/99	FC Nitra	H	2-1	Majoros (p), Vasik
03/04/99	ZTS Kerametal Dubnica	A	2-2	Medved, Vasik
10/04/99	MSK Zilina	A	1-1	Medved
13/04/99	Tatran Presov	H	1-0	Medved
17/04/99	Slovan Bratislava	A	0-3	
24/04/99	1.FC Kosice	H	3-1	Vasik, Strelec, Maixner
27/04/99	Ozeta Dukla Trencin	A	0-2	
01/05/99	Banik Prievidza	H	0-0	
04/05/99	Spartak Trnava	A	0-2	
15/05/99	BSC Bardejov	H	2-0	Tomas, Medved
22/05/99	Dukla Banska Bystrica	A	0-1	
29/05/99	HFC Humenne	H	2-0	Medved 2

BANIK PRIEVIDZA

FK Banik Prievidza
Sportova 37
971 01 Prievidza
tel - (0862) 422858/425692
fax - (0862) 425692
Year of Formation - 1919
President - Ctibor Stacha
Secretary - Jaroslav Vido
Coach - Viliam Ilko; Oldrich Briza
Stadium - Prievidza (6,500)

	P	Ap	(s)	Gls
Branislav BARTA	M		(5)	
Branislav BENKO	G	22		
Jozef BILIK	M	4	(11)	1
Dominik GASPAROVIC	M		(1)	
Marek GOGA	M	1	(6)	
Peter GREGOR	G	1	(1)	
Miroslav HAJDUCKO	A	25	(1)	1
Juraj HALASKA	D	14		
Norbert HOKSA	D	21	(1)	2
Marek HOLMIK	M	26	(3)	3
Stanislav HORNAK	D	25	(2)	1
Miroslav HRDINA	G	4		
Martin JELSIC	A		(2)	
Milos KRSKO	D	19	(1)	
Pavol KUBOVICH	D		(1)	
Ronald MODER	M	10	(14)	
Stefan ONDRAS	D	23	(1)	
Miroslav ORSULA	M	21	(5)	2
Miroslav PAPRANEC	M	16	(8)	2
Milan PASTVA	M		(1)	
Lubos PERNIS	A	18	(5)	13
Martin PETRAS	M	9	(5)	
Marian PUCHNER	D	3	(2)	
Milan RIMANOVSKY	M	23	(1)	6
Igor SUKENNIK	M	2	(2)	
Robert STOFAN	M	19	(3)	
Martin TRANCIK	G	3		
Jozef URBLIK	A	21	(1)	3

01/08/98	Ozeta Dukla Trencin	A	0-3	
08/08/98	ZTS Kerametal Dubnica	A	2-3	Rimanovsky, Pernis
16/08/98	Spartak Trnava	H	0-2	
22/08/98	BSC Bardejov	A	2-1	Orsula, Hoksa
29/08/98	Dukla Banska Bystrica	H	0-0	
12/09/98	HFC Humenne	A	2-6	Rimanovsky, Holmik
19/09/98	Inter Bratislava	H	0-3	
26/09/98	SCP Ruzomberok	A	1-2	Rimanovsky
03/10/98	Tauris Rimavska Sobota	H	2-0	Holmik, Bilik
17/10/98	FC Nitra	A	1-2	Urblik
23/10/98	Artmedia Petrzalka	H	2-1	Hornak, Rimanovsky
31/10/98	MSK Zilina	A	2-3	Hoksa, Orsula
07/11/98	Tatran Presov	H	1-1	Rimanovsky
14/11/98	Slovan Bratislava	A	2-4	Papranec, Pernis
21/11/98	1.FC Kosice	H	1-1	Pernis
06/03/99	ZTS Kerametal Dubnica	H	1-2	Pernis
13/03/99	Spartak Trnava	A	0-3	
16/03/99	Ozeta Dukla Trencin	H	0-4	
20/03/99	BSC Bardejov	H	5-0	Pernis 3, Rimanovsky (p), Holmik
03/04/99	Dukla Banska Bystrica	A	2-3	Urblik, Pernis
10/04/99	HFC Humenne	H	0-1	
13/04/99	Inter Bratislava	A	0-1	
17/04/99	SCP Ruzomberok	H	0-2	
24/04/99	Tauris Rimavska Sobota	A	1-1	Hajducko
27/04/99	FC Nitra	H	1-1	Papranec
01/05/99	Artmedia Petrzalka	A	0-0	
04/05/99	MSK Zilina	H	2-1	Urblik, Pernis
15/05/99	Tatran Presov	A	1-2	Pernis (p)
22/05/99	Slovan Bratislava	H	0-2	
29/05/99	1.FC Kosice	A	3-1	Pernis 3

BSC BARDEJOV

CLUB DIRECTORY

BSC Bardejov
Druzstevná 1
085 55 Bardejov
tel - (0935) 724264/722840
fax - (0935) 722840
Year of Formation - 1923
President - Milan Polca
Secretary - Milan Varganin
Coach - Mikulas Komanicky: Igor Novak
Stadium - Bardejov (12,000)

APPEARANCES 98/99

	P	Ap	(s)	Gls
Slavomir BABCAK	A		(3)	
Jozef BELAK	M	4	(2)	
Peter BILCIK	A	5	(5)	
Juraj COBEJ	G	15		
Ondrej DESIATNIK	M	14	(3)	3
Patrik DURKAC	M	3	(3)	
Marian FEDOR	G	2		
Jozef FRIGA	D	8	(5)	1
Martin GAJDOS	D	8	(3)	
Jan HEREDOS	G	3	(1)	
Lubomir HOROCHONIC	D	23	(1)	2
Jozef HRIVNAK	A	14	(2)	
Daniel JACECKO	M		(1)	
Lubomir JACKO	A	8	(4)	
Stefan JACKO	M	28		
Jozef JURCISIN	M	2	(4)	
Rastislav KASCAK	M	12	(3)	
Jan KMECIK	D	10	(2)	
Marian KOCIS	D	17	(4)	
Frantisek KUNDRA	M	5	(5)	
Jozef LUKAC	D	2		
Martin LUKAC	D	8		
Marian LALIK	A	9		4
Frantisek MYSLIK	M	9	(3)	
Jan NOVAK	M		(1)	
Martin NOVAK	M	3	(4)	
Vladislav PALSA	M	2		
Lubos PETRUSKA	M		(1)	
Pavol PILLAR	G	10	(2)	
Marian SKALKA	M	9	(1)	
Radovan STOJAK	A	9	(3)	
Anton SPISAK	D	27		
Zoltan SZORAD	M	10		
Anton SOLTIS	M	14		2
Alexander TYC	A	1	(2)	
Patrik VARGA	M	9		
Robert VOJVODA	D	12		1
Alexander VRHOVAC	A	15	(4)	1

LEAGUE RESULTS 1998/99

01/08/98	Slovan Bratislava	A	0-3	
08/08/98	1.FC Kosice	H	1-2	Soltis
15/08/98	Ozeta Dukla Trencin	A	0-2	
22/08/98	Banik Prievidza	H	1-2	Vrhovac
30/08/98	Spartak Trnava	A	0-1	
12/09/98	ZTS Kerametal Dubnica	A	1-2	Lalik
19/09/98	Dukla Banska Bystrica	H	1-0	Lalik
26/09/98	HFC Humenne	A	0-1	
03/10/98	Inter Bratislava	H	0-3	
17/10/98	SCP Ruzomberok	A	1-2	Friga
24/10/98	Tauris Rimavska Sobota	H	0-1	
31/10/98	FC Nitra	A	1-3	Lalik (p)
07/11/98	Artmedia Petrzalka	H	3-0	Soltis, Lalik, Vojvoda
14/11/98	MSK Zilina	A	0-1	
21/11/98	Tatran Presov	H	0-3	
06/03/99	1.FC Kosice	A	1-2	Desiatnik
10/03/99	Slovan Bratislava	H	0-2	
13/03/99	Ozeta Dukla Trencin	H	0-2	
20/03/99	Banik Prievidza	A	0-5	
03/04/99	Spartak Trnava	H	0-0	
10/04/99	ZTS Kerametal Dubnica	H	0-2	
13/04/99	Dukla Banska Bystrica	A	2-3	Horochonic (p), Desiatnik
17/04/99	HFC Humenne	H	0-1	
23/04/99	Inter Bratislava	A	0-10	
27/04/99	SCP Ruzomberok	H	1-3	Horochonic (p)
01/05/99	Tauris Rimavska Sobota	A	0-2	
04/05/99	FC Nitra	H	1-4	Desiatnik
15/05/99	Artmedia Petrzalka	A	0-2	
22/05/99	MSK Zilina	H	0-1	
29/05/99	Tatran Presov	A	0-1	

DUKLA BANSKA BYSTRICA

CLUB DIRECTORY

FK Dukla Banska Bystrica
Stiavnicky
Stadion SNP
974 01 Banska Bystrica
tel - (088) 32593/35251
fax - (088) 32593
Year of Formation - 1965
President - Jaroslav Cupka
Secretary - Tomas Geist
Coach - Stanislav Jarabek
Stadium - SNP na Stiavnickach (11,500)

APPEARANCES 98/99

	P	Ap	(s)	Gls
Stanislav BALAZ	M	3	(1)	
Marek BAZIK	M	19	(11)	
Tomas BOHACIK	D	7	(7)	
Lubomir FAKTOR	M	24	(2)	11
Vladimir HELBICH	M	24	(2)	1
Marcel JELENCIK	D	3	(14)	
Norbert JURACKA	G	27		
Stefan KARASEK	D	28		
Patrik KARASY	D	6	(2)	
Jaroslav KENTOS	D	11		
Maros KLIMPL	D	3	(4)	
Milan KMET	D	2	(1)	
Ondrej KOSTUR	A	26	(1)	3
Marian KOVAC	A	2	(4)	1
Martin LAURINC	D	3		
Tomas LIBIC	M	20	(8)	3
Milan MALATINSKY	M	27		4
Martin MINAROVIC	M	2	(3)	
Milan ONDRIK	D	10	(2)	
Roman PACKO	G	1		
Martin POLJOVKA	D	23		
Karol PRAZENICA	D	10		
Stefan RUSNAK	A	26		11
Stanislav SEMAN	G	2		
Marian STRELEC	M	21	(2)	
Richard ZAJAC	G		(1)	

LEAGUE RESULTS 1998/99

01/08/98	Tatran Presov	A	1-2	Rusnak
07/08/98	Slovan Bratislava	H	2-2	Kovac, Faktor
15/08/98	1.FC Kosice	A	0-6	
22/08/98	Ozeta Dukla Trencin	H	0-4	
29/08/98	Banik Prievidza	A	0-0	
12/09/98	Spartak Trnava	H	0-2	
19/09/98	BSC Bardejov	A	0-1	
26/09/98	ZTS Kerametal Dubnica	A	2-0	Rusnak 2 (1p)
03/10/98	HFC Humenne	H	1-0	Faktor
17/10/98	Inter Bratislava	A	1-1	Faktor
24/10/98	SCP Ruzomberok	H	0-0	
31/10/98	Tauris Rimavska Sobota	A	2-0	Rusnak, Faktor
07/11/98	FC Nitra	H	1-0	Kostur
15/11/98	Artmedia Petrzalka	A	1-1	Rusnak
21/11/98	MSK Zilina	H	0-1	
07/03/99	Slovan Bratislava	A	0-3	
13/03/99	1.FC Kosice	H	0-0	
20/03/99	Ozeta Dukla Trencin	A	2-2	Libic, Faktor
23/03/99	Tatran Presov	H	2-2	Kostur, Rusnak
03/04/99	Banik Prievidza	H	3-2	Libic, Faktor 2
10/04/99	Spartak Trnava	A	2-5	Kostur, Helbich
13/04/99	BSC Bardejov	H	3-2	Rusnak, Malatinsky 2
17/04/99	ZTS Kerametal Dubnica	H	7-0	Faktor 3, Malatinsky 2, Rusnak 2
24/04/99	HFC Humenne	A	0-0	
27/04/99	Inter Bratislava	H	0-1	
01/05/99	SCP Ruzomberok	A	0-2	
04/05/99	Tauris Rimavska Sobota	H	0-1	
15/05/99	FC Nitra	A	1-4	Libic
22/05/99	Artmedia Petrzalka	H	1-0	Rusnak
29/05/99	MSK Zilina	A	2-2	Faktor (p), Rusnak

HFC HUMENNE

CLUB DIRECTORY

HFC Humenne
Chemlonska 1
066 01 Humenne
tel - (0933) 62696/64643
fax - (0933) 64643
Year of Formation - 1903
President - Dusan Kapral
Secretary - Jozef Matta
Coach - Vladimir Gombar
Stadium - Chemlon (18,000)

MAJOR HONOURS
Domestic Cup - (1) 1996.

APPEARANCES 98/99

	P	Ap	(s)	Gls
Jozef ALUSIK	M		(3)	
Norbert BELAN	G	21	(1)	
Michal CERNEGA	A	8	(7)	2
Marian CISOVSKY	D	23	(2)	
Peter DURICA	M	4	(2)	
Lubomir FAJKUS	D	17	(1)	
Jozef GLIGANIC	M		(2)	
Frantisek HANC	D	25	(3)	1
Miroslav JANTEK	M	27		3
Dusan KAPRAL	A		(1)	1
Igor KASANA	M	29		
Jozef KNAPIK	M	9	(3)	1
Jan KOHUT	M	1	(3)	
Marek LUKAC	A	2	(6)	
Lubomir MATI	A	14	(1)	6
Gabriel MELNIK	A		(5)	
Lubomir MICAK	M	28		2
Peter MURINCAK	A	24	(5)	3
Martin OBSITNIK	M	13	(8)	1
Ivo PILIP	G	9		
Dusan SNINSKY	M	15	(6)	2
Miroslav SECEN	D	19		
Jaroslav SOVIC	M	14	(2)	1
Mikulas SOVIC	A		(1)	
Peter SUKOVSKY	D	21		1
Ivailo YONCHEV (BUL)	M	3	(5)	
Emil ZIGA	M	4	(3)	

LEAGUE RESULTS 1998/99

01/08/98	MSK Zilina	A	0-1	
08/08/98	Tatran Presov	H	0-0	
15/08/98	Slovan Bratislava	A	1-3	Micak
22/08/98	1.FC Kosice	H	0-2	
29/08/98	Ozeta Dukla Trencin	A	0-1	
12/09/98	Banik Prievidza	H	6-2	Sovic J., Micak, Murincak, Mati, Obsitnik, Jantek (p)
20/09/98	Spartak Trnava	A	1-4	Mati
26/09/98	BSC Bardejov	H	1-0	Mati
03/10/98	Dukla Banska Bystrica	A	0-1	
17/10/98	ZTS Kerametal Dubnica	A	1-2	Hanc
24/10/98	Inter Bratislava	H	0-1	
31/10/98	SCP Ruzomberok	A	0-3	
07/11/98	Tauris Rimavska Sobota	H	1-0	Mati
14/11/98	FC Nitra	A	2-0	Mati 2
21/11/98	Artmedia Petrzalka	H	1-2	Sukovsky
06/03/99	Tatran Presov	A	0-3	
13/03/99	Slovan Bratislava	H	0-0	
16/03/99	MSK Zilina	H	3-1	Sninsky, Knapik, Jantek (p)
20/03/99	1.FC Kosice	A	0-1	
03/04/99	Ozeta Dukla Trencin	H	0-4	
10/04/99	Banik Prievidza	A	1-0	Sninsky
13/04/99	Spartak Trnava	H	1-0	Cernega
17/04/99	BSC Bardejov	A	1-0	Murincak
24/04/99	Dukla Banska Bystrica	H	0-0	
27/04/99	ZTS Kerametal Dubnica	H	1-0	Murincak
01/05/99	Inter Bratislava	A	2-1	Cernega, Kapral
04/05/99	SCP Ruzomberok	H	0-0	
15/05/99	Tauris Rimavska Sobota	A	0-0	
22/05/99	FC Nitra	H	1-3	Jantek (p)
29/05/99	Artmedia Petrzalka	A	0-2	

INTER BRATISLAVA

ASK Inter Slovnaft Bratislava
Vajnorska 100
832 04 Bratislava
tel - (07) 271007
fax - (07) 5251341
Year of Formation - 1940
President - Juraj Oblozinsky
Secretary - Rudolf Jancek
Coach - Jozef Bubenko
Stadium - Inter (15,000)

MAJOR HONOURS
League Championship (Czechoslovakia) - (1) 1959.
Domestic Cup - (1) 1995.

	P	Ap	(s)	Gls
Peter BABNIC	A	25	(3)	13
Andrej BURZA	M		(1)	
Jan CHRENKO	M	5	(2)	
Juraj CZINEGE	M	29	(1)	6
Petr CMILANSKY	D	29		
Jozef DANKO	M	13	(8)	
Peter FUTEJ	D	3	(3)	
Vratislav GRESKO	M	29		5
Miroslav HYLL	G	30		
Roman KRATOCHVIL	D	29		7
Marek KREJCI	M	4	(6)	2
Milan KUSALIK	M	13	(9)	3
Vladimir MAJSNIAR	A	1	(9)	
Imrich MIKLOS	A	5	(10)	3
Peter NEMETH	M	27		7
Robert OVAD	D	26		
Attila PINTE	A	24	(5)	11
Andrej PORAZIK	A	6	(12)	3
Richard SLEZAK	A		(1)	
Martin SEVELA	D	2	(8)	
Marian SUCHANCOK	D	30		3

02/08/98	Artmedia Petrzalka	A	0-0	
07/08/98	MSK Zilina	H	5-0	Babnic, og (Ondras), Miklos 2, Pinte
15/08/98	Tatran Presov	A	2-0	Pinte, Czinege
22/08/98	Slovan Bratislava	H	0-1	
29/08/98	1.FC Kosice	A	0-1	
13/09/98	Ozeta Dukla Trencin	H	2-1	Kratochvil, Porazik
19/09/98	Banik Prievidza	A	3-0	Pinte, Gresko, Nemeth
27/09/98	Spartak Trnava	H	3-1	Pinte, Babnic, Kusalik
03/10/98	BSC Bardejov	A	3-0	Babnic, Porazik, Pinte
17/10/98	Dukla Banska Bystrica	H	1-1	Nemeth
24/10/98	HFC Humenne	A	1-0	Babnic
31/10/98	ZTS Kerametal Dubnica	A	6-0	Babnic 2, Pinte 2, Nemeth, Gresko
07/11/98	SCP Ruzomberok	H	2-0	Babnic, Nemeth
14/11/98	Tauris Rimavska Sobota	A	2-0	Gresko (p), Miklos
21/11/98	FC Nitra	H	3-1	Suchancok, Babnic, Nemeth
27/02/99	Artmedia Petrzalka	H	4-1	Pinte, Nemeth, Kratochvil, Kusalik
06/03/99	MSK Zilina	A	2-0	Suchancok, Kratochvil
13/03/99	Tatran Presov	H	2-1	Czinege, Kratochvil (p)
21/03/99	Slovan Bratislava	A	0-1	
03/04/99	1.FC Kosice	H	2-1	Pinte, Krejci
09/04/99	Ozeta Dukla Trencin	A	0-0	
13/04/99	Banik Prievidza	H	1-0	Kratochvil
16/04/99	Spartak Trnava	A	0-0	
23/04/99	BSC Bardejov	H	10-0	Nemeth, Pinte 2, Kratochvil (p), Czinege 2, Krejci, Gresko, Suchancok, Porazik
27/04/99	Dukla Banska Bystrica	A	1-0	Babnic
01/05/99	HFC Humenne	H	1-2	Babnic
04/05/99	ZTS Kerametal Dubnica	H	1-0	Czinege
15/05/99	SCP Ruzomberok	A	0-0	
22/05/99	Tauris Rimavska Sobota	H	5-3	Babnic 3, Kusalik, Gresko
29/05/99	FC Nitra	A	2-0	Czinege, Kratochvil (p)

ZTS KERAMETAL DUBNICA

CLUB DIRECTORY

ZTS Kerametal Dubnica nad Vahom
ul. Sportovcov 655
018 41 Dubnica nad Vahom
tel - (0827) 21906/269081
fax - (0827) 26982
Year of Formation - 1926
President - Ivan Nemeckay
Manager - Viliam Simko
Coach - Anton Dragun
Stadium - Spartak (8,000)

APPEARANCES 98/99

		P	Ap	(s)	Gls
Marian BAGIN	D	7	(3)		
Ivan BALCIR	A	1	(1)		
Eugen BARI	A	24	(2)	8	
Marian BOCHNOVIC	M	10	(1)	2	
Dragan GVOZDENOVIC (CRO)	A	10	(4)	1	
Michal HANEK	D	7	(1)		
Rastislav HEVESSY	D	24		1	
Alexander HOMER	D	27			
Erik JENES	A	2	(7)		
Pavel KOVAC	G	11	(1)		
Lubomir KRAJCOVIC	M	7	(6)	1	
Peter MASAROVIC	A	3	(7)	1	
Kan MISAK	A	3	(2)	1	
Peter NEMECKAY	A	16	(11)	5	
Lubomir NOSICKY	M	25		3	
Svetozar OKRUCKY	G	17	(1)		
Tomas POLACH (CZE)	M	27		3	
Frantisek SMAK	G	2			
Pavol STRAKA	A	2	(6)		
Anton SUCHY	M	21	(1)	1	
Peter SUCHY	A	12	(15)		
Jan SVIKRUHA	M	13	(9)		
Andrej SUPKA	D	28		1	
Stanislav TURZA	D	26	(2)		
Dezider VARGA	D	5	(2)		

LEAGUE RESULTS 1998/99

01/08/98	Tauris Rimavska Sobota	A	2-2	Suchy A., Polach
08/08/98	Banik Prievidza	H	3-2	Nosicky 2, Nemeckay
15/08/98	FC Nitra	A	1-0	Misak
22/08/98	Spartak Trnava	H	0-0	
30/08/98	Artmedia Petrzalka	A	1-2	Nosicky
12/09/98	BSC Bardejov	H	2-1	Bari 2 (1p)
18/09/98	MSK Zilina	A	0-2	
26/09/98	Dukla Banska Bystrica	H	0-2	
03/10/98	Tatran Presov	A	1-5	Bari (p)
17/10/98	HFC Humenne	H	2-1	Nemeckay, Masarovic
24/10/98	Slovan Bratislava	A	0-2	
31/10/98	Inter Bratislava	H	0-6	
07/11/98	1.FC Kosice	A	1-3	Hevessy
14/11/98	SCP Ruzomberok	H	3-0	Bari, Gvozdenovic, Krajcovic
21/11/98	Ozeta Dukla Trencin	A	0-3	
27/02/99	Tauris Rimavska Sobota	H	3-0	Bochnovic, Polach, Supka
06/03/99	Banik Prievidza	A	2-1	Bari, Bochnovic
13/03/99	FC Nitra	H	0-2	
20/03/99	Spartak Trnava	A	1-4	Bari
03/04/99	Artmedia Petrzalka	H	2-2	Nemeckay, Bari (p)
10/04/99	BSC Bardejov	A	2-0	Nemeckay 2
13/04/99	MSK Zilina	H	0-3	
17/04/99	Dukla Banska Bystrica	A	0-7	
24/04/99	Tatran Presov	H	0-0	
27/04/99	HFC Humenne	A	0-1	
01/05/99	Slovan Bratislava	H	0-1	
04/05/99	Inter Bratislava	A	0-1	
15/05/99	1.FC Kosice	H	2-3	Bari, Polach
22/05/99	SCP Ruzomberok	A	0-2	
29/05/99	Ozeta Dukla Trencin	H	0-2	

1.FC KOSICE

1.FC Kosice
Alejova 2
040 11 Kosice
tel - (095) 6424871/6224253/436956
fax - (095) 6444871/436956
Year of Formation - 1992
President - Julius Rezes
Secretary - Vladimir Varga
Coach - Jan Kozak; Jan Zachar
Stadium - Vsesportovy areal (30,300)

MAJOR HONOURS
League Championship - (2) 1997, 1998.
Domestic Cup (Czechoslovakia) - (1) 1993.

	P	Ap	(s)	Gls
Kamil CONTOFALSKY	G	3	(1)	
Peter DZURIK	M	29		3
Tomas GERICH	D	17	(1)	
Erik HRNCAR	D	1		
Milan JAMBOR	D		(7)	
Vladimir JANOCKO	M	5	(8)	1
Ivan KOZAK	D	13	(1)	
Jan KOZAK	M	1	(4)	
Jozef KOZLEJ	A	10	(4)	7
Radovan KRAL	D	14	(8)	1
Ivan LAPSANSKY	A	4	(10)	
Ruslan LYUBARSKYI (UKR)	A	22	(5)	12
Ladislav MOLNAR	G	11		
Miroslav NEMEC	A	7	(3)	1
Szilard NEMETH	A	15	(4)	8
Robert NOVAK	M	14		1
Ladislav ONOFREJ	M		(1)	
Tomas ORAVEC	M	3	(4)	1
Peter PIROSKO	A		(6)	
Jozef PISAR	A		(1)	
Martin PROHASZKA	A	6	(7)	3
Miroslav SEMAN	G	16		
Robert SEMENIK	D	15		
Peter SLICHO	A	15		1
Miroslav SOVIC	M	13		
Marek SPILAR	D	24	(1)	
Dusan TOTH	D	21	(1)	1
Rudolf URBAN	A	7	(2)	1
Radoslav ZABAVNIK	M		(1)	
Tibor ZATEK	M	15		
Vladislav ZVARA	M	29		10

01/08/98	Spartak Trnava	H	0-1	
08/08/98	BSC Bardejov	A	2-1	Prohaszka, Nemeth
15/08/98	Dukla Banska Bystrica	H	6-0	Zvara 3, Prohaszka, Lyubarskyi, Kozlej
22/08/98	HFC Humenne	A	2-0	Zvara, Kozlej
29/08/98	Inter Bratislava	H	1-0	Nemeth
12/09/98	SCP Ruzomberok	A	3-1	Zvara, Nemeth, Prohaszka
19/09/98	Tauris Rimavska Sobota	H	2-0	Dzurik, Zvara
26/09/98	FC Nitra	A	0-0	
03/10/98	Artmedia Petrzalka	H	3-1	Dzurik, Kozlej, Zvara (p)
17/10/98	MSK Zilina	A	1-0	Nemeth
24/10/98	Tatran Presov	H	1-2	Dzurik
30/10/98	Slovan Bratislava	A	0-3	
07/11/98	ZTS Kerametal Dubnica	H	3-1	Kozlej 2, Nemeth
14/11/98	Ozeta Dukla Trencin	H	5-1	Nemeth 2, Kozlej 2, Kral
21/11/98	Banik Prievidza	A	1-1	Nemeth
26/02/99	Spartak Trnava	A	0-0	
06/03/99	BSC Bardejov	H	2-1	Lyubarskyi, Slicho
13/03/99	Dukla Banska Bystrica	A	0-0	
20/03/99	HFC Humenne	H	1-0	Novak
03/04/99	Inter Bratislava	A	1-2	Lyubarskyi
10/04/99	SCP Ruzomberok	H	1-0	Janocko
13/04/99	Tauris Rimavska Sobota	A	2-1	Lyubarskyi, Toth
17/04/99	FC Nitra	H	2-0	Lyubarskyi 2
24/04/99	Artmedia Petrzalka	A	1-3	Lyubarskyi
27/04/99	MSK Zilina	H	3-0	Urban, Zvara, Nemec
30/04/99	Tatran Presov	A	3-0	Lyubarskyi 2 (1p), Zvara
04/05/99	Slovan Bratislava	H	0-2	
15/05/99	ZTS Kerametal Dubnica	A	3-2	Lyubarskyi 2, Oravec
22/05/99	Ozeta Dukla Trencin	A	1-0	Lyubarskyi
29/05/99	Banik Prievidza	H	1-3	Zvara

FC NITRA

CLUB DIRECTORY

FC Nitra
Jeseskeho 4
949 01 Nitra
tel - (087) 513255/414958
fax - (087) 414958
Year of Formation - 1919
President - Jan Kovarcik
Secretary - Branislav Varga
Coach - Jozef Prochotsky
Stadium - FC Nitra (11,000)

APPEARANCES 98/99

	P	Ap	(s)	Gls
Lubomir BAJTOS	D	10		
Miroslav BEDI	D	18	(2)	1
Henrich BENCIK	M	11	(7)	1
Peter BURAK	D	14	(2)	
Lamine DIAGNE (SEN)	A		(2)	
Marian DIRNBACH	A	10	(2)	2
Peter DOBIAS	D	1	(2)	
Jozef DOJCAN	D	13	(1)	1
Juraj DOVICOVIC	M	1	(2)	
Marian DATKO	D	14		
Richard HASA	D	29		5
Ivan HODUR	M	18	(8)	1
Peter HODUR	A		(8)	
Stefan HOK	M	4	(9)	
Eduard HRNCAR	D	21	(1)	1
Robert JEZ	M	1	(1)	1
Marian KLAGO	A	18	(4)	8
Jozef KOTULA	D	21	(3)	
Miroslav LORINC	A	9	(9)	
Jan MISAK	A	6	(2)	
Jan MUCHA	G	30		
Ondrej ONDROVIC	M	28	(1)	3
Peter OREMUS	M	20	(4)	
Stefan SENECKY	G		(1)	
Igor SUKENNIK	M	9	(2)	1
Martin SEVCIK	M	9	(6)	
Andrej STEFANKA	D	1	(4)	
Robert VOJVODA	D	14		3

LEAGUE RESULTS 1998/99

01/08/98	SCP Ruzomberok	H	3-0	Ondrovic 2, Hasa
08/08/98	Tauris Rimavska Sobota	A	1-1	Dirnbach
15/08/98	ZTS Kerametal Dubnica	H	0-1	
22/08/98	Artmedia Petrzalka	H	0-3	
29/08/98	MSK Zilina	A	0-1	
12/09/98	Tatran Presov	H	2-2	Jez, Dojcan
19/09/98	Slovan Bratislava	A	0-2	
26/09/98	1.FC Kosice	H	0-0	
02/10/98	Ozeta Dukla Trencin	A	0-3	
17/10/98	Banik Prievidza	H	2-1	Klago, Hasa
24/10/98	Spartak Trnava	A	0-6	
31/10/98	BSC Bardejov	H	3-1	Hasa, Klago 2
07/11/98	Dukla Banska Bystrica	A	0-1	
14/11/98	HFC Humenne	H	0-2	
21/11/98	Inter Bratislava	A	1-3	Dirnbach
06/03/99	Tauris Rimavska Sobota	H	0-0	
13/03/99	ZTS Kerametal Dubnica	A	2-0	Hasa, Hodur I.
16/03/99	SCP Ruzomberok	A	0-0	
21/03/99	Artmedia Petrzalka	A	1-2	Hrncar
03/04/99	MSK Zilina	H	0-1	
10/04/99	Tatran Presov	A	0-2	
13/04/99	Slovan Bratislava	H	0-4	
17/04/99	1.FC Kosice	A	0-2	
23/04/99	Ozeta Dukla Trencin	H	1-1	Vojvoda (p)
27/04/99	Banik Prievidza	A	1-1	Hasa
01/05/99	Spartak Trnava	H	0-3	
04/05/99	BSC Bardejov	A	4-1	Ondrovic, Vojvoda (p), Sukennik, Klago
15/05/99	Dukla Banska Bystrica	H	4-1	Bedi, Klago 2, Vojvoda (p)
22/05/99	HFC Humenne	A	3-1	Klago 2, Bencik
29/05/99	Inter Bratislava	H	0-2	

OZETA DUKLA TRENCIN

CLUB DIRECTORY

FK Ozeta Dukla Trencin
Mladeznicka 1
911 01 Trencin
tel - (0831) 441137
fax - (0831) 441137
Year of Formation - 1992
President - Pavol Hozlar
Secretary - Miroslav Karas
Coach - Robert Paldan
Stadium - Na Sihoti (12,000)

APPEARANCES 98/99

	P	Ap	(s)	Gls
Martin BARBARIC	M	8		2
Henrich BENCIK	A	2		
Vladimir CIFRANIC	D	13	(7)	1
Marian DIRNBACH	A	6	(4)	1
Martin FABUS	A	30		19
Robert HANKO	M	28	(2)	2
Miroslav HORVATOVIC	M	24		2
Roman HRNCAR	D	22	(5)	3
Jozef HUDEK	M		(4)	
Karol KISEL	M	16	(6)	2
Martin KONECNY	D	20	(1)	
Alojz KULLA	M	20	(7)	5
Martin LIPCAK	G	30		
Marek LUKAC	A	2	(8)	
Andrej MASAROVIC	A	2	(5)	1
Lubomir MATI	A	8	(5)	3
Vladimir ROZNIK	A		(7)	
Jozef RYBNIKAR	M	13	(14)	1
Karol SCHULZ	D	27		4
Martin SEVELA	M	9	(3)	3
Ondrej SMELKO	D	24	(3)	
Jozef VALACHOVIC	D	25	(1)	4
Robert ZELEZNIK	A	1	(5)	

LEAGUE RESULTS 1998/99

01/08/98	Banik Prievidza	H	3-0	Fabus 2, Kulla
08/08/98	Spartak Trnava	A	0-1	
15/08/98	BSC Bardejov	H	2-0	Fabus 2
22/08/98	Dukla Banska Bystrica	A	4-0	Schulz, Masarovic, Hanko,
				Valachovic
29/08/98	HFC Humenne	H	1-0	Hrncar
13/09/98	Inter Bratislava	A	1-2	Horvatovic
19/09/98	SCP Ruzomberok	H	1-1	Fabus (p)
26/09/98	Tauris Rimavska Sobota	A	1-1	Fabus (p)
02/10/98	FC Nitra	H	3-0	Fabus, Hrncar 2
18/10/98	Artmedia Petrzalka	A	3-1	Barbaric, Schulz, Fabus
24/10/98	MSK Zilina	H	6-1	Fabus, Horvatovic, Rybnikar, Kisel,
				Sevela, Schulz
31/10/98	Tatran Presov	A	2-2	Fabus, Sevela
07/11/98	Slovan Bratislava	H	1-0	Schulz
14/11/98	1.FC Kosice	A	1-5	Cifranic
21/11/98	ZTS Kerametal Dubnica	H	3-0	Sevela, Kisel, Barbaric
06/03/99	Spartak Trnava	H	0-0	
13/03/99	BSC Bardejov	A	2-0	Kulla, Fabus
16/03/99	Banik Prievidza	A	4-0	Fabus 2, Mati 2
20/03/99	Dukla Banska Bystrica	H	2-2	Kulla, Fabus
03/04/99	HFC Humenne	A	4-0	Mati, Dirnbach, Kulla, Fabus
09/04/99	Inter Bratislava	H	0-0	
13/04/99	SCP Ruzomberok	A	0-1	
17/04/99	Tauris Rimavska Sobota	H	3-0	Hanko, Valachovic, Fabus
23/04/99	FC Nitra	A	1-1	Valachovic
27/04/99	Artmedia Petrzalka	H	2-0	Valachovic, Fabus
01/05/99	MSK Zilina	A	0-4	
04/05/99	Tatran Presov	H	0-1	
15/05/99	Slovan Bratislava	A	1-1	Kulla
22/05/99	1.FC Kosice	H	0-1	
29/05/99	ZTS Kerametal Dubnica	A	2-0	Fabus 2

SCP RUZOMBEROK

CLUB DIRECTORY

FK SCP Ruzomberok
Zilinska cesta 21
034 01 Ruzomberok
tel - (0848) 323589/322506
fax - (0848) 323589
Year of Formation - 1906
President - Igor Bobula
Secretary - Vendelin Kniha
Coach - Ladislav Jurkemik
Stadium - Ruzomberok (8,600)

APPEARANCES 98/99

	P	Ap	(s)	Gls
Mario ADAMCIK	A	7	(5)	2
Juraj BAKOS	M		(8)	
Daniel BEZAK	M	3	(6)	
Peter BUGAR	M	5		
Jan GAJDOSCIK	M	1	(3)	
Robert HAZUCHA	A	10	(12)	1
Vladimir HUTKA	M	22		1
Viliam HYRAVY	M	26		5
Peter JAKUBECH	G	15		
Vladimir JANTEK	M		(1)	
Maros KLIMPL	D	4	(2)	
Martin LAURINC	M	14	(1)	1
Stefan MACKO	M		(7)	
Gabriel MAJOROS	M	9	(8)	
Jan MELICHERCIK	M	22	(2)	2
Milan MICENEC	M	20	(3)	
Frantisek MIKULAS	M	22	(2)	
Juraj MINTAL	D	21		
Eduard MYDLIAR	A	17	(1)	7
Rastislav PETREK	M		(2)	
Slavomir PRUCNY	D	15	(2)	
Peter RATAJ	D	26	(2)	2
Jan SAFRANKO	A	21	(5)	4
Ivan TRABALIK	G	13		
Vladimir VITEK	M	11	(8)	
Miroslav VRABEL	G	2	(1)	
Martin VYSKOC	A	24	(4)	5

LEAGUE RESULTS 1998/99

01/08/98	FC Nitra	A	0-3	
08/08/98	Artmedia Petrzalka	H	0-2	
14/08/98	MSK Zilina	A	1-0	Hyravy
22/08/98	Tatran Presov	H	0-0	
29/08/98	Slovan Bratislava	A	1-2	Hazucha
12/09/98	1.FC Kosice	H	1-3	Mydliar
19/09/98	Ozeta Dukla Trencin	A	1-1	og (Hrncar)
26/09/98	Banik Prievidza	H	2-1	Adamcik, Hyravy
04/10/98	Spartak Trnava	A	0-5	
17/10/98	BSC Bardejov	H	2-1	Vyskoc, Mydliar
24/10/98	Dukla Banska Bystrica	A	0-0	
31/10/98	HFC Humenne	H	3-0	Mydliar, Vyskoc, Adamcik
07/11/98	Inter Bratislava	A	0-2	
14/11/98	ZTS Kerametal Dubnica	A	0-3	
21/11/98	Tauris Rimavska Sobota	H	2-1	Mydliar 2
07/03/99	Artmedia Petrzalka	A	1-1	Safranko
13/03/99	MSK Zilina	H	1-1	Mydliar
16/03/99	FC Nitra	H	0-0	
20/03/99	Tatran Presov	A	1-1	Safranko
03/04/99	Slovan Bratislava	H	0-0	
10/04/99	1.FC Kosice	A	0-1	
13/04/99	Ozeta Dukla Trencin	H	1-0	Hyravy
17/04/99	Banik Prievidza	A	2-0	Hyravy, Melichercik (p)
24/04/99	Spartak Trnava	H	2-0	Hutka, Safranko
27/04/99	BSC Bardejov	A	3-1	Safranko, Hyravy, Vyskoc
01/05/99	Dukla Banska Bystrica	H	2-0	Rataj, Vyskoc
04/05/99	HFC Humenne	A	0-0	
15/05/99	Inter Bratislava	H	0-0	
22/05/99	ZTS Kerametal Dubnica	H	2-0	Laurinc, Vyskoc
29/05/99	Tauris Rimavska Sobota	A	3-2	Melichercik, Rataj, Mydliar

SLOVAN BRATISLAVA

CLUB DIRECTORY

SK Slovan Bratislava
Junacka 2
831 04 Bratislava
tel - (07) 272777
fax - (07) 273014/271493
Year of Formation - 1919
President - Ludovit Zlocha
Secretary - Mikulas Tarci
Coach - Stanislav Griga
Stadium - Tehelne pole (33,000)

MAJOR HONOURS
League Championship (Czechoslovakia) - (8) 1949,
1950, 1951, 1955, 1970, 1974, 1975, 1992.
League Championship - (4)
1994, 1995, 1996, 1999.
Domestic Cup (Czechoslovakia) - (5)
1962, 1963, 1968, 1974, 1982.
Domestic Cup - (3) 1994, 1997, 1999.
European Cup-winners' Cup - (1) 1969.

APPEARANCES 98/99

		P	Ap	(s)	Gls
Jozef ANTALOVIC	D			(2)	
Tomas BERNADY	G			(1)	
Serhiy BORISENKO (UKR)	A	3		(7)	1
Marek FABULA	M	15			
Marek HOLLY	M	1		(1)	
Zsolt HORNYAK	D	29			1
Norbert HRNCAR	M	29			9
Richard HÖGER	M	6		(2)	1
Martin JANCULA	A	3		(4)	1
Tibor JANCULA	A	12		(5)	9
András KERESZTÚRI (HUN)	M			(3)	
Miroslav KÖNIG	G	30			
Miroslav KRISS	A	8		(17)	2
Jozef MAJOROS	A	30			9
Tomas MEDVED	A			(3)	
Lubomir MESZAROS	M	6		(14)	6
Jozef MUZLAY	A	3			1
Robert NOVAK	M	5			
Ladislav PECKO	D	30			1
Pavol SEDLAK	M	23		(1)	2
Nilos SOBONA	D	5		(7)	
Roman SKRTEL	M	7		(2)	2
Milan TIMKO	D	29			3
Robert TOMASCHEK	M	28			3
Stanislav VARGA	D	28			3

LEAGUE RESULTS 1998/99

01/08/98	BSC Bardejov	H	3-0	Hrncar, Skrtel, Timko
07/08/98	Dukla Banska Bystrica	A	2-2	Hrncar, Jancula T.
15/08/98	HFC Humenne	H	3-1	Majoros, Hrncar 2 (1p)
22/08/98	Inter Bratislava	A	1-0	Jancula T.
29/08/98	SCP Ruzomberok	H	2-1	Kriss, Hrncar (p)
12/09/98	Tauris Rimavska Sobota	A	1-1	Tomaschek
19/09/98	FC Nitra	H	2-0	Jancula T., Majoros
27/09/98	Artmedia Petrzalka	A	2-0	Hrncar, Timko
03/10/98	MSK Zilina	H	3-0	Höger, Hrncar, Majoros
17/10/98	Tatran Presov	A	0-0	
24/10/98	ZTS Kerametal Dubnica	H	2-0	Kriss, Jancula M.
30/10/98	1.FC Kosice	H	3-0	Tomaschek, Majoros, Skrtel
07/11/98	Ozeta Dukla Trencin	A	0-1	
14/11/98	Banik Prievidza	H	4-2	Hrncar, Jancula T. 3
20/11/98	Spartak Trnava	A	1-1	Jancula T.
06/03/99	Dukla Banska Bystrica	H	3-0	Muzlay, Majoros, Pecko
10/03/99	BSC Bardejov	A	2-0	Timko, Tomaschek
13/03/99	HFC Humenne	A	0-0	
21/03/99	Inter Bratislava	H	1-0	Varga (p)
03/04/99	SCP Ruzomberok	A	0-0	
10/04/99	Tauris Rimavska Sobota	H	3-0	Varga (p), Majoros, Hornyak
13/04/99	FC Nitra	A	4-0	Jancula T., Meszaros, Majoros, Borisenko
17/04/99	Artmedia Petrzalka	H	3-0	Jancula T., og (Daliak), Majoros
24/04/99	MSK Zilina	A	2-0	Varga, Hrncar
27/04/99	Tatran Presov	H	3-0	Majoros, Meszaros 2
01/05/99	ZTS Kerametal Dubnica	A	1-0	Meszaros
04/05/99	1.FC Kosice	A	2-0	Sedlak, Meszaros
15/05/99	Ozeta Dukla Trencin	H	1-1	Meszaros
22/05/99	Banik Prievidza	A	2-0	Sedlak, og (Hajducko)
29/05/99	Spartak Trnava	H	0-1	

SPARTAK TRNAVA

CLUB DIRECTORY

FC Spartak Trnava
Sportova 1
917 60 Trnava
tel - (0805) 24210/26089
fax - (0805) 24976
Year of Formation - 1923
President - Jozef Bachraty
Secretary - Stefan Batalik
Coach - Dusan Galis; Peter Zelensky
Stadium - FC Spartak (24,500)

MAJOR HONOURS
League Championship (Czechoslovakia) - (5)
1968, 1969, 1971, 1972, 1973.
Domestic Cup (Czechoslovakia) - (4)
1967, 1971, 1975, 1986.
Domestic Cup - (1) 1998.

APPEARANCES 98/99

	P	Ap	(s)	Gls
Igor BALIS	M	26		1
Dusan BESTVINA	D		(2)	
Peter BUGAR	M	7	(9)	1
Martin CERNACEK	M		(1)	
Michal DIAN	A		(1)	
Robert FORMANKO	A	19	(7)	5
Fábio Luís GOMES (BRA)	A	27		10
Juraj HERIBAN	A		(1)	
Marcel HORKY	M	16	(7)	
Jaroslav HRABAL	D	20		2
Sergej JAKIROVIC (CRO)	M	16	(4)	2
Miroslav KARHAN	D	28		5
Rastislav KOSTKA	M	7	(9)	3
Ondrej KRISTOFIK	M	13	(5)	2
Vladimir LEITNER	D	26		
Jaroslav MACAK	A	9	(11)	4
Branislav RZESZOTO	G		(3)	
Kamil SUSKO	G	30		
Lubomir TALDA	M	7	(11)	4
Jaroslav TIMKO	A	24	(1)	7
Dusan TITTEL	D	23		3
Rastislav TOMOVCIK	A	6	(11)	2
Marek UJLAKY	M	26		8

LEAGUE RESULTS 1998/99

01/08/98	1.FC Kosice	A	1-0	Hrabal
08/08/98	Ozeta Dukla Trencin	H	1-0	Jakirovic
16/08/98	Banik Prievidza	A	2-0	Gomes, Timko
22/08/98	ZTS Kerametal Dubnica	A	0-0	
30/08/98	BSC Bardejov	H	1-0	Macak
12/09/98	Dukla Banska Bystrica	A	2-0	Balis, Karhan
20/09/98	HFC Humenne	H	4-1	Ujlaky, Gomes, Timko, Talda
27/09/98	Inter Bratislava	A	1-3	Ujlaky
04/10/98	SCP Ruzomberok	H	5-0	Formanko, Kostka, Tittel, Ujlaky, Macak
17/10/98	Tauris Rimavska Sobota	A	4-2	Kristofik, Tittel, Timko, Tomovcik
24/10/98	FC Nitra	H	6-0	Ujlaky, Karhan 2, Kristofik, Kostka, Jakirovic
01/11/98	Artmedia Petrzalka	A	3-2	Kostka, Karhan, Macak
07/11/98	MSK Zilina	H	3-1	Tomovcik, Gomes, Ujlaky
14/11/98	Tatran Presov	A	0-0	
20/11/98	Slovan Bratislava	H	1-1	Gomes
26/02/99	1.FC Kosice	H	0-0	
06/03/99	Ozeta Dukla Trencin	A	0-0	
13/03/99	Banik Prievidza	H	3-0	Timko, Ujlaky (p), Formanko
20/03/99	ZTS Kerametal Dubnica	H	4-1	Gomes 2, Formanko, Timko
03/04/99	BSC Bardejov	A	0-0	
10/04/99	Dukla Banska Bystrica	H	5-2	Timko, Gomes, Ujlaky, Talda, Bugar
13/04/99	HFC Humenne	A	0-1	
16/04/99	Inter Bratislava	H	0-0	
24/04/99	SCP Ruzomberok	A	0-2	
27/04/99	Tauris Rimavska Sobota	H	3-1	Formanko, Gomes, Ujlaky
01/05/99	FC Nitra	A	3-0	Formanko, Tittel, Gomes
04/05/99	Artmedia Petrzalka	H	2-0	Gomes, Macak
15/05/99	MSK Zilina	A	0-2	
22/05/99	Tatran Presov	H	4-1	Talda, Karhan, Timko, Hrabal
29/05/99	Slovan Bratislava	A	1-0	Talda

TATRAN PRESOV

CLUB DIRECTORY

FC Tatran Presov
Capajevova 47
080 01 Presov
tel - (091) 711464/718703
fax - (091) 713005
Year of Formation - 1898
President - Vladislav Sabol
Secretary - Jozef Matuscin
Coach - Jozef Adamec
Stadium - Tatran (14,000)

APPEARANCES 98/99

	P	Ap	(s)	Gls
Marian BOCHNOVIC	M	8	(5)	
Marek BUBENKO	A	1	(4)	
Miroslav DROBNAK	M	2	(5)	
Rastislav DORD	D	20	(2)	
Marek FABULA	M	15		1
Andrej FILIP	M	26	(3)	1
Frantisek HADVIGER	D	10	(2)	
Peter HLINKA	D	25		
Lubomir JACKO	A	3	(3)	
Patrik KAMINSKY	D		(3)	
Zsolt KIANEK	M	22	(3)	3
Anton KOCIS	A		(5)	
Radovan KOCUREK	M		(1)	
Vladimir KOZUCH	A	23		7
Milos LENGYEL	M	9	(12)	
Tomas MARTAUS	M	5	(2)	
Miroslav NEMEC	A	9	(5)	6
Pavol PIATKA	M	2	(15)	1
Lubomir REITER	A		(2)	
Marek SEMAN	D	16	(2)	1
Peter SLICHO	A	12	(2)	4
Vladimir STAS	M	2		
Anton SOLTIS	A	15		7
Richard TRUTZ	D	20	(1)	1
Martin URBAN	D	27		2
Jozef VALKUCAK	M	26		3
Viliam VIDUMSKY	D	2		
Daniel ZITKA	G	30		

LEAGUE RESULTS 1998/99

01/08/98	Dukla Banska Bystrica	H	2-1	Kozuch, Nemec
08/08/98	HFC Humenne	A	0-0	
15/08/98	Inter Bratislava	H	0-2	
22/08/98	SCP Ruzomberok	A	0-0	
28/08/98	Tauris Rimavska Sobota	H	3-0	Kozuch, Slicho, Trutz
12/09/98	FC Nitra	A	2-2	Kozuch 2
19/09/98	Artmedia Petrzalka	H	2-0	Urban, Valkucak
26/09/98	MSK Zilina	A	1-2	Kozuch
03/10/98	ZTS Kerametal Dubnica	H	5-1	Nemec, Fabula (p), Valkucak, og (Bagin), Piatka
17/10/98	Slovan Bratislava	H	0-0	
24/10/98	1.FC Kosice	A	2-1	Nemec, Valkucak
31/10/98	Ozeta Dukla Trencin	H	2-2	Nemec, Slicho
07/11/98	Banik Prievidza	A	1-1	Slicho
14/11/98	Spartak Trnava	H	0-0	
21/11/98	BSC Bardejov	A	3-0	Nemec 2, Slicho
06/03/99	HFC Humenne	H	3-0	Soltis 2 (1p), Kozuch
13/03/99	Inter Bratislava	A	1-2	Soltis
20/03/99	SCP Ruzomberok	H	1-1	Soltis (p)
23/03/99	Dukla Banska Bystrica	A	2-2	Soltis, Kozuch
03/04/99	Tauris Rimavska Sobota	A	1-4	Soltis
10/04/99	FC Nitra	H	2-0	Seman, Kianek
13/04/99	Artmedia Petrzalka	A	0-1	
17/04/99	MSK Zilina	H	0-2	
24/04/99	ZTS Kerametal Dubnica	A	0-0	
27/04/99	Slovan Bratislava	A	0-3	
30/04/99	1.FC Kosice	H	0-3	
04/05/99	Ozeta Dukla Trencin	A	1-0	Kianek
15/05/99	Banik Prievidza	H	2-1	Kianek, Urban (p)
22/05/99	Spartak Trnava	A	1-4	Soltis
29/05/99	BSC Bardejov	H	1-0	Filip

TAURIS RIMAVSKA SOBOTA

CLUB DIRECTORY

FC Tauris Rimavska Sobota
Sportova 2
979 01 Rimavska Sobota
tel - (866) 631208
fax - (866) 631344
Year of Formation - 1913
President - Stefan Szanto
Secretary - Peter Blasko
Coach - Frantisek Vas; Karol Kisel; Ondrej Danko
Stadium - Rimavska Sobota (8,000)

APPEARANCES 98/99

	P	Ap	(s)	Gls
Mario ADAMCIK	A	7	(3)	2
Csaba CSANYI	D	12	(2)	
Vaclav DVORAK (CZE)	M	12	(1)	2
Jozef DZUBARA	M	24	(1)	1
Gergely GERI	D	3	(1)	
Stefan GRENDEL	M	11		2
Juraj KAKAS	G	20		
Roman KALICIAK	D	11	(1)	
Richard KOSCO	D	12	(3)	1
Radoslav KOZINKA	M	5	(5)	
Stefan KYSELA	A	8	(6)	
Branislav LABANT	M		(3)	
Lubos LUKAC	G	10	(1)	
Ladislav MESZAROS	A	5	(6)	4
Jozef OLEJNIK	D	17	(1)	
Jozef PALO	M	13	(1)	
Joze PAVIC (CRO)	D	24	(1)	
Teo PIRIJA (CRO)	D	7	(1)	
Jozef PISAR	A	14		2
Roman PRIBYL (CZE)	A	7	(1)	
Robert RAK	D	1	(9)	
Vladimir SIAGO	M	12		1
Rastislav STEHLO	M	8	(4)	
Igor SUKENNIK	M	8	(2)	
Martin SVINTEK	A		(1)	
Vladimir SYKORA	A	28	(1)	13
Marian TIMKO	D	18		
Gabriel UNGVÖLGYI	M	15	(5)	1
Jozef URBLIK	A	5		
Ivan VACLAVIK	A		(2)	
Frantisek VILIM	D	4	(2)	
Marian WALLNER	M	9	(16)	

LEAGUE RESULTS 1998/99

01/08/98	ZTS Kerametal Dubnica	H	2-2	Sykora, Siago
08/08/98	FC Nitra	H	1-1	Sykora
16/08/98	Artmedia Petrzalka	A	2-5	Sykora 2
22/08/98	MSK Zilina	H	1-2	Sykora (p)
28/08/98	Tatran Presov	A	0-3	
12/09/98	Slovan Bratislava	H	1-1	Sykora
19/09/98	1.FC Kosice	A	0-2	
26/09/98	Ozeta Dukla Trencin	H	1-1	Dzubara
03/10/98	Banik Prievidza	A	0-2	
17/10/98	Spartak Trnava	H	2-4	Ungvölgyi, Sykora (p)
24/10/98	BSC Bardejov	A	1-0	Dvorak
31/10/98	Dukla Banska Bystrica	H	0-2	
07/11/98	HFC Humenne	A	0-1	
14/11/98	Inter Bratislava	H	0-2	
21/11/98	SCP Ruzomberok	A	1-2	Dvorak
27/02/99	ZTS Kerametal Dubnica	A	0-3	
06/03/99	FC Nitra	A	0-0	
13/03/99	Artmedia Petrzalka	H	1-0	Grendel
20/03/99	MSK Zilina	A	1-2	Pisar (p)
03/04/99	Tatran Presov	H	4-1	Adamcik, Sykora 3
10/04/99	Slovan Bratislava	A	0-3	
13/04/99	1.FC Kosice	H	1-2	Adamcik
17/04/99	Ozeta Dukla Trencin	A	0-3	
24/04/99	Banik Prievidza	H	1-1	Sykora
27/04/99	Spartak Trnava	A	1-3	Grendel
01/05/99	BSC Bardejov	H	2-0	Sykora, Kosco
04/05/99	Dukla Banska Bystrica	A	1-0	Pisar (p)
15/05/99	HFC Humenne	H	0-0	
22/05/99	Inter Bratislava	A	3-5	Meszaros 3
29/05/99	SCP Ruzomberok	H	2-3	Meszaros, Sykora (p)

MSK ZILINA

CLUB DIRECTORY

MSK Zilina
Uholna 3
010 01 Zilina
tel - (89) 622280/626955
fax - (89) 626955
Year of Formation - 1908
President - Jozef Antosik
Secretary - Karol Belanik
Coach - Anton Janos
Stadium - Pod Dubnom (15,000)

APPEARANCES 98/99

	P	Ap	(s)	Gls
Miroslav BARCIK	M	27	(3)	2
Lubos BOHUNSKY	G	5		
Michal DRAHNO	D	17	(6)	
Petr DROZD	D	26		1
Tomas DURICA	M	18	(5)	
Tibor GOLJAN	A	2	(3)	
Stefan HLOZNY	D	1		
Peter HLUSKO	D	24		
Peter HOLEC	G	25		
Ivan JURIK	M	9	(4)	
Marian KEKELI	M	1	(2)	
Viliam KOPECKY	M	18	(7)	1
Lubomir KOSTOLANSKY	M	5	(7)	1
Igor KUREK	A	14	(10)	4
Martin LACENA	M		(2)	
Ladislav MESZAROS	A	3		
Martin MIKULA	M	17	(1)	1
Marek MINTAL	M	26	(2)	11
Vladimir ONDRAS	D	18	(3)	
Miroslav PIKUS	A	4	(7)	3
Lubomir REITER	A	22	(4)	7
Jaroslav TRHANCIK	M	12	(7)	2
Jozef TRNOVEC	D	2	(1)	
Vladimir VESELY	D	6	(4)	
Slavomir ZATEK	D	22		
Jan ZEMLIK (CZE)	A	6	(4)	3

LEAGUE RESULTS 1998/99

01/08/98	HFC Humenne	H	1-0	Mintal
07/08/98	Inter Bratislava	A	0-5	
14/08/98	SCP Ruzomberok	H	0-1	
22/08/98	Tauris Rimavska Sobota	A	2-1	Mintal, Reiter (p)
29/08/98	FC Nitra	H	1-0	Reiter (p)
13/09/98	Artmedia Petrzalka	A	0-2	
18/09/98	ZTS Kerametal Dubnica	H	2-0	Zemlik, Mikula
26/09/98	Tatran Presov	H	2-1	Zemlik 2
03/10/98	Slovan Bratislava	A	0-3	
17/10/98	1.FC Kosice	H	0-1	
24/10/98	Ozeta Dukla Trencin	A	1-6	Kurek
31/10/98	Banik Prievidza	H	3-2	Kurek, Mintal, Reiter
07/11/98	Spartak Trnava	A	1-3	Reiter
14/11/98	BSC Bardejov	H	1-0	Reiter
21/11/98	Dukla Banska Bystrica	A	1-0	Barcik
06/03/99	Inter Bratislava	H	0-2	
13/03/99	SCP Ruzomberok	A	1-1	Trhancik
16/03/99	HFC Humenne	A	1-3	Barcik
20/03/99	Tauris Rimavska Sobota	H	2-1	Kurek, Kostolansky
03/04/99	FC Nitra	A	1-0	Mintal
10/04/99	Artmedia Petrzalka	H	1-1	Mintal
13/04/99	ZTS Kerametal Dubnica	A	3-0	Trhancik, Kurek, Pikus
17/04/99	Tatran Presov	A	2-0	Reiter (p), Mintal
24/04/99	Slovan Bratislava	H	0-2	
27/04/99	1.FC Kosice	A	0-3	
01/05/99	Ozeta Dukla Trencin	H	4-0	Reiter, Mintal 2, Drozd
04/05/99	Banik Prievidza	A	1-2	Pikus
15/05/99	Spartak Trnava	H	2-0	Mintal, Pikus
22/05/99	BSC Bardejov	A	1-0	Mintal
29/05/99	Dukla Banska Bystrica	H	2-2	Mintal, Kopecky

PROMOTED CLUBS

SECOND DIVISION FINAL TABLE 98/99

		Pd	W	D	L	F	A	Pt	GD
1	**DAC Dunajska Streda**	34	21	6	7	62	29	69	+33
2	**VTJ Koba Senec**	34	19	11	4	44	23	68	+21
3	SKP Devin	34	20	7	7	65	36	67	+29
4	Matador Puchov	34	18	11	5	51	21	65	+30
5	Slovan B Bratislava	34	16	8	10	49	40	56	+9
6	PFK Piestany	34	15	5	14	43	42	50	+1
7	Zeleziarne Podbrezova	34	14	7	13	37	36	49	+1
8	Steel Trans Licartovce	34	13	9	12	38	38	48	0
9	NCHZ Novaky	34	14	5	15	51	41	47	+10
10	Tesla Stropkov	34	14	4	16	36	40	46	-4
11	Slovan Levice	34	13	6	15	43	40	45	+3
12	Lokomotiva Kosice	34	12	9	13	38	37	45	+1
13	Slovan Dusla Sala	34	12	8	14	48	49	44	-1
14	FMK Nove Zamky	34	12	7	15	41	48	43	-7
15	Slovmag Jelsava	34	9	9	16	29	48	36	-19
16	Slavoj Trebisov	34	9	3	22	30	58	30	-28
17	Zemplin VTJ Michalovce	34	7	8	19	33	60	29	-27
18	Bukoza Vranov nad Toplou	34	4	5	25	23	75	17	-52

CLUB DIRECTORY

DAC Dunajska Streda
Sportova 18
929 01 Dunajska Streda
tel - (0709) 526874
fax - (0709) 524643
Year of Formation - 1904
President - Imrich Santa
Secretary - Zoltan Csoka
Coach - Vladimir Rusnak
Stadium - DAC (12,410)

MAJOR HONOURS
Domestic Cup (Czechoslovakia) - (1) 1987.

CLUB DIRECTORY

FK VTJ Koba Senec
Vodna ul.
903 01 Senec
tel - (07) 45925241
fax - (07) 45927242
Year of Formation - 1991
President - Daniel Bartko
Secretary - Stefan Mrva
Coach - Dusan Abraham; Stefan Mrva
Stadium - Koba Senec (5,000)

SLOVENIA

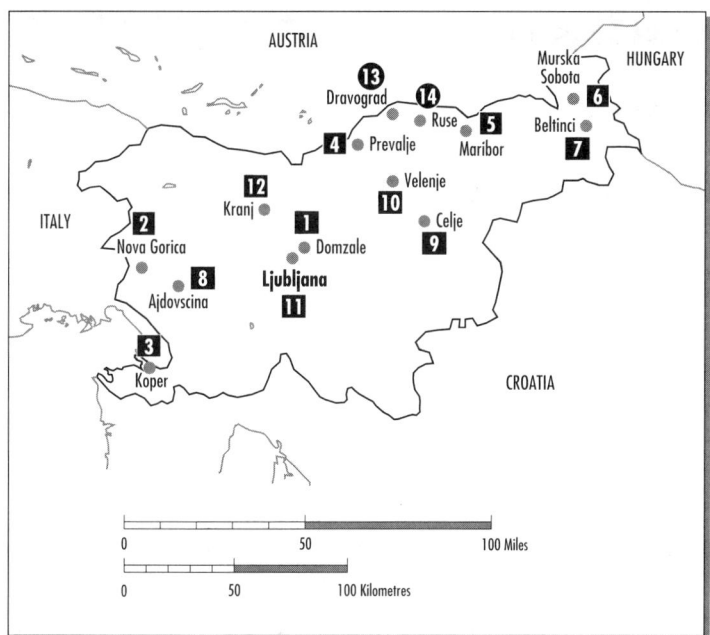

#		
1	BST DOMZALE	923
2	HIT GORICA	924
3	NK KOPER	925
4	KOROTAN PREVALJE	926
5	MARIBOR TEATANIC	927
6	MURA MURSKA SOBOTA	928
7	POTROSNIK BELTINCI	929
8	PRIMORJE AJDOVSCINA	930

#		
9	PUBLIKUM CELJE	931
10	RUDAR VELENJE	932
11	SCT OLIMPIJA LJUBLJANA	933
12	ZIVILA TRIGLAV KRANJ	934
Promoted clubs		
13	DRAVOGRAD	935
14	FEROTERM POHORJE	935

KATANEC - A CATALYST FOR SUCCESS

Marvellous Maribor march to the 'double'

FEDERATION DIRECTORY

Nogometna Zveza Slovenije
Cerinova 4, P.P.33986, 1101 Ljubljana

tel - (061) 1611500   Year of Formation - 1920
fax - (061) 1612220   President - Rudolf Zavrl
   Secretary - Dane Jost

Stadium - Bezigrad, Ljubljana (18,000)

The Slovenian championship adopted a different system in 1998/99, with 12 clubs playing a three-way series - as opposed to the ten-club, four-round format of the previous season. It was to produce one of the most exciting title races yet but there was little else of novelty value. Crowds were still low and money still tight, and when all the dust had settled, the champions were the same team who had taken the title in each of the previous two seasons - Maribor Teatanic.

This time Maribor were taken to the wire. With one game left they had a one-point lead over HIT Gorica - their last-day opponents. A crowd of around 10,000, the highest of the entire season, gathered at Maribor's Ljudski vrt stadium to witness the event. Though troubled at times, Maribor did not let their fans down, winning the match 2-0 with a goal apiece from their leading scorers, Croatian Dalibor Filipovic and Albanian Kliton Bozgo.

Just three days later Maribor sealed their second 'double' in three years when they won another vital home match 2-0 to complete a 5-2 aggregate win over SCT Olimpija Ljubljana in the final of the Slovenian Cup. Maribor had been 0-2 behind at one stage during the first leg in Ljubljana but second half strikes from Dejan Djuranovic and Bozgo (two) - both Olimpija old boys - ensured that they held a healthy advantage going into the return. Further goals from Filipovic and Goran Jolic put the seal on a comprehensive victory.

Maribor's claim on both trophies was beyond dispute. In the Cup they won all but one of their matches (a 2-2 draw away to holders Rudar Velenje in the quarter-finals being the exception). In the league they led all the ranking lists - not just most points, but also best attack, best defence, best home record, best away record and biggest crowds. They also had far and away the best coach, in ex-Olimpija and national team boss Bojan Prasnikar, who, in addition to winning the third Slovenian 'double' of his career, stood out as the only one of the First Division coaches who held on to his job for the duration of the season. Maribor also had four players in the official 'team of the

LEAGUE CHAMPIONSHIP RESULTS 98/99

		1	2	3	4	5	6	7	8	9	10	11	12
1	BST Domzale		1-1	4-0	1-3	2-2	0-1	3-0	3-1	2-2	0-1	0-3	0-0
			0-0						4-1	2-1	0-1	2-2	
2	HIT Gorica	3-0		3-1	1-0	2-5	3-1	3-1	2-1	3-0	2-1	4-1	3-1
					3-0		4-1	3-0	1-1	0-1			0-0
3	NK Koper	3-1	2-3		0-1	2-1	0-3	0-1	0-2	1-1	1-0	1-1	0-2
		0-4	0-0						0-1		0-2	3-3	
4	Korotan Prevalje	0-1	0-0	3-0		1-4	1-1	5-0	2-1	1-1	1-1	2-1	1-0
		0-0		1-2		1-0	1-2	2-0				0-3	
5	Maribor Teatanic	4-0	1-0	2-2	3-0		4-1	5-1	1-1	2-2	1-0	3-1	3-2
		1-1	2-0	5-0				1-1			3-0	5-0	
6	Mura Murska Sobota	6-0	0-1	6-2	4-0	1-0		3-0	2-1	0-1	0-0	0-0	4-0
		1-2		1-0		0-2		1-2			4-0	2-0	
7	Potrosnik Beltinci	2-0	2-2	2-2	2-1	1-2	2-0		1-1	4-1	0-2	2-0	4-1
		3-3		2-2					0-2	0-1			5-1
8	Primorje Ajdovscina	0-0	0-2	0-1	3-2	0-1	2-1	2-1		0-0	2-0	3-0	5-1
					1-4	1-0	0-1			2-1			1-1
9	Publikum Celje	0-0	2-1	0-1	1-1	0-0	0-1	0-1	3-0		0-0	0-2	1-0
				1-0	1-0	0-0	3-1						2-2
10	Rudar Velenje	1-3	3-0	2-1	2-0	2-0	2-2	2-0	4-1	0-0		1-2	1-0
			1-1		1-2			2-1	4-3	2-1			3-1
11	SCT Olimpija Ljubljana	5-0	2-1	2-3	3-4	1-4	0-1	1-0	1-0	3-0	0-0		1-1
			0-1					6-0	1-0	2-3	1-1		4-1
12	Zivila Triglav Kranj	1-0	0-2	1-1	1-2	2-2	0-0	2-0	0-0	1-0	0-1	2-2	
		0-1		0-3	1-2	1-3	2-1						

LEAGUE CHAMPIONSHIP FINAL TABLE 98/99

			Home					Away					Total						
		P	W	D	L	F	A	W	D	L	F	A	W	D	L	F	A	P	GD
1	Maribor Teatanic	33	12	5	0	46	12	7	4	5	26	17	19	9	5	72	29	66	+43
2	HIT Gorica	33	13	2	2	40	15	5	6	5	15	16	18	8	7	55	31	62	+24
3	Rudar Velenje	33	11	3	3	33	18	5	5	6	10	15	16	8	9	43	33	56	+10
4	Mura Murska Sobota	33	10	2	5	35	11	6	3	7	18	24	16	5	12	53	35	53	+18
5	Korotan Prevalje	33	7	5	5	22	17	7	1	8	22	28	14	6	13	44	45	48	-1
6	SCT Olimpija Ljubljana	33	8	3	6	33	20	4	5	7	21	30	12	8	13	54	50	44	+4
7	Publikum Celje	33	6	6	4	14	10	4	6	7	16	25	10	12	11	30	35	42	-5
8	BST Domzale	33	5	6	5	24	19	5	5	7	16	30	10	11	12	40	49	41	-9
9	Primorje Ajdovscina	33	8	3	5	22	16	3	4	10	17	29	11	7	15	39	45	40	-6
10	Potrosnik Beltinci	33	7	5	4	32	21	3	1	13	9	41	10	6	17	41	62	36	-21
11	NK Koper	33	3	4	9	13	26	5	4	8	21	35	8	8	17	34	61	32	-27
12	Zivila Triglav Kranj	33	4	5	7	14	20	1	5	11	14	38	5	10	18	28	58	25	-30

DOMESTIC CUP 98/99

FIRST ROUND
Izakovci 0, Nafta 6
Esotech Smartno 2, Korotan Prevalje 0
Zarica 1, Goriske Opekarne 3
Aluminij 2, Brda 0
Goricanka 3, Dornava 0
HIT Gorica 2, Mura Murska Sobota 3
Beltrans Verzej 5, Sostanj 3
Montavar Rogoza 2, Potrosnik Beltinci 4
Drava 0, Paloma Sega 1
Tabor Sezana 6, Turnisce 0
Publikum Celje 1, BST Domzale 0
Ivancna gorica 0, Zivila Triglav Kranj 2
Kolpa 3, Rudar Velenje 4
Pobrezje 0, Primorje Ajdovscina 4
Jadran Sepic 0, Maribor Teatanic 3
Set Vevce 0, SCT OLimpija Ljubljana 1

SECOND ROUND
Goricanka 0, SCT Olimpija Ljubljana 6
Esotech Smartno 4, Primorje Ajdovscina 2
Tabor Sezana 1, Maribor Teatanic 2
Zivila Triglav Kranj 1, Rudar Velenje 2
Beltrans Verzej 0, Paloma Sega 7
Mura Murska Sobota 5, Potrosnik Beltinci 2
Goriske Opekarne 1, Publikum Celje 0
Aluminij 0, Nafta 2

QUARTER-FINALS
Maribor Teatanic 1 (Bozgo 69), Rudar Velenje 0
Rudar Velenje 2 (Vidojevic 60, Pavlovic 66), Maribor
Teatanic 2 (Gajser 14, Bozgo 80)
(Maribor Teatanic 3-2)

Mura Murska Sobota 3 (Skaper 45, 55, Cipot 87),
Nafta 0
Nafta 1 (Sabjan 78), Mura Murska Sobota 1 (Gutalj 10)
(Mura Murska Sobota 4-1)

Goriske Opekarne 1 (Rescic 86),
SCT Olimpija Ljubljana 2 (Jukic 21, Grizold 32)
SCT Olimpija Ljubljana 6 (Ekmecic 31, 58, 74,
Pejkovic 37p, Filekovic 73, Deisinger 83)
Goriske Opekarne 0
(SCT Olimpija Ljubljana 8-1)

Esotech Smartno 3 (Javornik S. 68p, 75,
Smajlovic 75), Paloma Sega 0
Paloma Sega 1 (Cabota 28), Esotech Smartno 2
(Znuderl 32, Pokleka 38) (Esotech Smartno 5-1)

SEMI-FINALS
SCT Olimpija Ljubljana 1 (Ceh 55),
Esotech Smartno 1 (Mujanovic 7)
Esotech Smartno 0, SCT Olimpija Ljubljana 1 (Kosic 83)
(SCT Olimpija Ljubljana 2-1)

Maribor Teatanic 3 (Bozgo 46, 54, Djuranovic 76),
Mura Murska Sobota 1 (Skaper 51)
Mura Murska Sobota 1 (Cener 45), Maribor Teatanic 2
(Bozgo 10, Jolic 25) (Maribor Teatanic 5-2)

FINAL
26/05/99, Ljubljana
SCT OLIMPIJA LJUBLJANA 2
Pejkovic (47p), Causevic (52)
MARIBOR TEATANIC 3
Djuranovic (63), Bozgo (68, 88)
referee - Kos
SCT OLIMPIJA LJUBLJANA - Pejkovic; Trgo, Mirtic,
Boskovic, Ceh (Kmetec), Kosic, Agic, Causevic (Kebe),
Miskic (Grizold), Kujovic, Zezelj.
MARIBOR TEATANIC - Gresak; Vugdalic (Kek), Sarkezi,
Zidan, Karic, Filipovic, Cipi (Jolic), Balajic, Djuranovic,
Galic, Bozgo.

16/06/99, Maribor
MARIBOR TEATANIC 2 Filipovic (38), Jolic (82)
SCT OLIMPIJA LJUBLJANA 0
referee - Bohinc
MARIBOR TEATANIC - Gresak; Kek (Turk), Zidan, Karic
(Sterbal), Simundza, Filipovic (Jolic), Cipi, Balajic,
Djuranovic, Galic, Bozgo.
SCT OLIMPIJA LJUBLJANA - Pejkovic; Trgo, Mirtic, Jukic,
Boskovic, Ceh, Kosic, Agic (Ekmecic), Kebe (Ipavec),
Miskic (Kmetec), Kujovic.

(Maribor Teatanic 5-2)

season' - defensive pillar Marinko Galic, Croatian midfielder Stipe Balajic, plus the aforementioned Djuranovic (with 30 appearances, the club's most frequently selected player) and Bozgo (with 15 goals, the top scorer).

There were no fewer then seven ex-Olimpija players on Maribor's books, which goes some way to explaining the shift of power in Slovenian football over the last few seasons. Without a championship win since 1995, Olimpija did at least return to European competition after a three-year absence thanks to their appearance in the Cup final. In the league, however, they were a dissatisfying sixth, having lost more games than they won.

NATIONAL TEAM APPEARANCES 98/99

Coach - Srecko KATANEC	HUN	GRE	NOR	LAT	SUI	OMN	GEO	FIN	LAT	ALB	Cps	Gls
Marko SIMEUNOVIC (06/12/67) - Sekerspor (TUR)	G46	G	G	G	G		G		G	G	20	-
Robert ENGLARO (25/08/69) - Atalanta (ITA)	D46	s46	s46	D							37	-
Darko MILANIC (18/12/67) - SK Sturm Graz (AUT)	D	D	D	D	D	D77	D				33	-
Marinko GALIC (22/04/70) - Mura Murska Sobota/Maribor Teatanic	D	D	D	D	D68	s46		D	D	D	42	-
Aleksander KNAVS (05/12/75) - FC Tirol Innsbruck (AUT)	D69	D	D	D46	D	D46	D		D	D	14	1
Miran PAVLIN (08/10/71) - SC Freiburg (GER)	M58	D	D	M	M	s46	M78		M80	M	15	-
Ales CEH (07/04/68) - Grazer AK (AUT)	M	M	M		M74	M46	M		M	M	41	1
Zlatko ZAHOVIC (01/02/71) - FC Porto (POR)	M77	M	M	M	M	M	M	M	M	M	37	17
Dzoni NOVAK (04/09/69) - Le Havre AC (FRA)	M	M46	M	M					M	M	38	2
Milan OSTERC (04/07/75) - Hércules CF (ESP)	A46	A60	A46		A	A		s46	s86	A	10	4
Saso UDOVIC (13/12/68)												
- Lausanne-Sports (SUI)/BSC Young Boys Bern (SUI)	A52	A	A46	A87	A46	A	A60		A66	A63	27	12
Mladen DABANOVIC (13/09/71) - Rudar Velenje	s46					G		G			4	-
Marjan DOMINKO (03/09/69) - Mura Murska Sobota	s46			D46	s64		s77				4	-
Mladen RUDONJA (26/07/71) - K St.-Truidense VV (BEL)	s46	M	M	A	A63	A	A90		A86		27	-
Milenko ACIMOVIC (15/02/77) - Crvena zvezda Beograd (YUG)	s52	s62	s46	s65	s46	M46	s60	M46	s66	s63	10	1
Zeljko MITRAKOVIC (30/12/72) - HIT Gorica	s58			s63	s46	s90	M46				5	-
Zeljko MILINOVIC (12/01/76) - LASK Linz (AUT)	s69		s87			D	D	D	D		7	-
Zoran PAVLOVIC (27/06/76) - Rudar Velenje	s77						s46				2	-
Ermin SILJAK (11/05/73) - Servette FC Genève (SUI)		s60									18	4
		/62										
Rudi ISTENIC (10/01/71) - Fortuna Düsseldorf (GER)			M65			s78		s80			11	-
Primoz GLIHA (08/10/67)												
- SCT Olimpija Ljubljana/Hapoel Tel-Aviv (ISR)			s46								29	10
Saso GAJSER (11/02/74) - Rudar Velenje					s46	M64		M			3	1
Spasoje BULAJIC (24/11/75) - 1.FC Köln (GER)					s68	D	D	D77			6	1
Fabijan CIPOT (25/08/76) - Mura Murska Sobota					s74	s77					2	-
Amir KARIC (31/12/73) - Maribor Teatanic							M	M	M	M	15	1
Matjaz FLORJANCIC (18/10/67) - Fidelis Andria (ITA)								A46			20	1
Sebastjan CIMEROTIC (14/09/74) - Hapoel Tel-Aviv (ISR)								A			2	-
Elvis RIBARIC (21/05/72) - HIT Gorica								s46			1	-

Olimpija used three different coaches during the season. The second of those, Marin Kovacic, had a very busy, if rather unfulfilling, campaign. He started off with newly promoted Koper (who were eventually relegated, along with another newcomer, Zivila Triglav), then had his stint with Olimpija before leaving to join HIT Gorica, who, having led the league at the winter break, sacked the man who had taken them there, Rado Radmanovic, following two successive defeats (against Olimpija and Maribor) at the start of the spring campaign. Kovacic turned things round fairly swiftly but a run of four games without a goal in late April/early May was ultimately to prove costly for

Gorica, whose only sources of consolation at the season's end were a place in the UEFA Cup and the top scorer crown for their 17-goal striker, Novica Nikcevic.

Slovenian football is yet to distinguish itself internationally, but massive strides were made to rectify that during the 1998/99 season. Maribor came tantalisingly close to qualifying for the Champions' League - they led Dutch giants PSV for two and a half hours of their qualifying tie before going under in extra-time in Eindhoven - but it was the national team, led by new coach Srecko Katanec, that generated the most impressive shockwaves.

Katanec had had just half a season in club coaching,

PLAYERS OF THE SEASON

★ SUPERSTAR PROFILE
ZLATKO ZAHOVIC

It did not take a genius to predict that Zlatko Zahovic would win Slovenia's 1998/99 Player of the Year award by a landslide. The 27-year-old midfielder was not just the undisputed king of his homeland. He was also one of the best players in the whole of Europe. He performed brilliantly throughout the season both for the Slovenian national team and his club, FC Porto. With six European Championship goals to his credit, he was the inspiration behind his country's remarkable bid to qualify for the Euro 2000 finals. He was also the leading goalscorer in the Champions' League after the group stage,

having scored at an even more impressive rate (seven goals in six games) for Porto, who, despite his best efforts, failed to reach the quarter finals. His excellent understanding with Brazilian striker Jardel accounted for many more goals in the Portuguese championship, which Porto went to win for a record fifth time in succession. The curly-haired Slovenian did not hang around to see if he could make it six, however. In the summer he left for Greek champions Olympiakos - a team against whom he had scored home and away in the Champions' League. Interestingly, Zahovic has never played in the Slovenian domestic league. A native of Maribor, he packed his bags for Partizan Belgrade at the age of just 16. The way he has performed in recent seasons, it is unlikely that the local fans will ever get to see him on a regular basis.

NASTJA CEH

21-year-old Nastja Ceh could be a Zahovic of the future. He was certainly the most impressive youngster in the 1998/99 Slovenian championship. He started the season with Maribor but did not stay on to collect his third successive title. In the winter break he transferred to SCT Olimpija Ljubljana, and, if anything, played even better for his new club, adding power, technique and an all-round boost to what had previously been a rather malfunctioning midfield. A member of the Slovenian Under-21 team (but no relation to senior-side stalwart Ales Ceh), his chief assset is a formidable long-range shot. Almost all of the goals he has scored for Maribor and Olimpija have been nethusting drives from 25-30 yards out.

TOP SCORERS

17	Novica NIKCEVIC (HIT Gorica)
15	Kliton BOZGO (Maribor Teatanic)
	Issah MORO (Potrosnik Beltinci)
13	Dalibor FILIPOVIC (Maribor Teatanic)
12	Zivojin VIDOJEVIC (Rudar Velenje)
10	Dejan BARANJA (Mura Murska Sobota)
	Ivica VULIC (Primorje Ajdovscina)
9	Alfred JERMANIS (Korotan Prevalje)
	Saso JAKOMIN (NK Koper)
	Marko KMETEC (Maribor Teatanic/ SCT Olimpija Ljubljana)
	Janez MRAK (BST Domzale)
	Goran GUTALJ (Mura Murska Sobota)

NATIONAL TEAM RESULTS 98/99

19/08/98	Hungary	A	Zalaegerszeg	1-2	Acimovic (90)
06/09/98	Greece (ECQ)	A	Athens	2-2	Zahovic (19, 73)
10/10/98	Norway (ECQ)	H	Ljubljana	1-2	Zahovic (24)
14/10/98	Latvia (ECQ)	H	Maribor	1-0	Udovic (85)
06/02/99	Switzerland	N	Muscat	0-2	
08/02/99	Oman	A	Muscat	7-0	Osterc (8, 72, 82, 89), Gajser (26), Zahovic (87), Udovic (90)
27/03/99	Georgia (ECQ)	A	Tbilisi	1-1	Knavs (52)
28/04/99	Finland	H	Ljubljana	1-1	Zahovic (62p)
05/06/99	Latvia (ECQ)	A	Riga	2-1	Zahovic (27, 42p)
09/06/99	Albania (ECQ)	A	Tirana	1-0	Zahovic (25p)

with HIT Gorica, before he was commandeered by the Slovenian federation to take charge for the Euro 2000 qualifying campaign. This was a man who needed no references. He had been Slovenia's outstanding player of the previous decade, a lanky, workaholic midfielder who played for top European clubs VfB Stuttgart and Sampdoria as well as winning 31 international caps for the former Yugoslavia. At once he introduced a new work ethic to the team. The previous World Cup qualifying campaign had been a sorry tale of unending under-achievement, and Katanec immediately made it his business to get the best out of a group of players who, he believed, had the talent but were not always inclined to use it to maximum effect. Katanec also had a formidable on-field accomplice in captain Zlatko Zahovic, Slovenia's most successful export, whose knowledge and experience, gained at Portuguese champions FC Porto, also rubbed off on the other members of the team.

Having been drawn in one of the easier groups, Slovenia's task of qualifying for the European Championship finals had gone from impossible to improbable at the outset, but by the end of Katanec's first year in charge, astonishingly, the Slovenians were in with more than an even chance of at least reaching the play-offs.

The key to the transformation was the team's away form. After starting well with a 2-2 draw in Greece, they also shared the points in Tbilisi with Georgia. Then, in the space of four days in June, they collected a maximum six points from visits to Riga and Tirana, and all of a sudden they were casting a shadow over Norway's seemingly impenetrable lead at the top of the table. Of the eight goals scored by Slovenia in their first six matches, six of them, remarkably, had gone to Zahovic - and there was even a question mark over whether he should have been attributed another, the equaliser in Georgia, which was officially credited to defender Aleksander Knavs.

With their captain providing the goals and their coach adding the motivation and the self-belief, Slovenia went into the closing stages of the qualifying campaign bursting with confidence and bristling with excitement. Could a major sensation really be about to happen?

INTERNATIONAL HONOURS

None

EUROPEAN CUPS 98/99

CHAMPIONS' CUP
● **MARIBOR TEATANIC**
Preliminary round KAREDA SIAULIAI (LIT)
A 3-0 Gajser (42, 87), Filipovic (70)
Murko; Sterbal, Balajic, Vugdalic (Fridl 59), Kek, Sarkezi, Gajser, Djuranovic, Filipovic (Breznik 78), Ceh, Kmetec (Zidan 70).
H 1-0 Balajic (78)
Murko; Zidan (Breznik 68), Balajic, Vugdalic, Kek, Sarkezi, Gajser (Kollari 55), Djuranovic, Filipovic, Ceh, Kmetec (Pekic 84)

Qualifying round PSV (HOL)
H 2-1 Filipovic (14), Breznik (85)
Gresak, Zidan, Balajic, Vugdalic, Kek, Sarkezi, Gajser (Sterbal 61), Djuranovic, Filipovic, Ceh (Kollari 72), Kmetec (Breznik 82).
A 1-4 Filipovic (4)
(aet) Stankovic; Zidan, Balajic, Vugdalic, Kek, Sarkezi, Gajser (Sterbal 67), Djuranovic, Filipovic, Ceh (Breznik 80), Kmetec (Fridl 37).

CUP WINNERS' CUP
● **RUDAR VELENJE**
Qualifying round CONSTRUCTORUL CHISINAU (MOL)
H 2-0 Vidojevic (32), Sumnik (90)
Dabanovic; Granic, Sulejmanovic, Balagic, Caushllari, Brezic (Pirc 61), Gajser, Podvinski, Javornik (Sumnik 78), Pavlovic, Vidojevic.
A 0-0 Dabanovic; Granic, Sulejmanovic, Balagic, Pirc, Caushllari, Brezic, Gajser, Podvinski, Javornik, Pavlovic.

1st round VARTEKS VARAZDIN (CRO)
H 0-1 Dabanovic; Granic, Sulejmanovic, Balagic, Caushllari, Brezic, Gajser, Podvinski (Sumnik 80), Javornik, Pavlovic, Vidojevic.

A 0-1 Dabanovic; Granic, Balagic, Sulejmanovic, Javornik, Podvinski, Brezic (Sumnik 81), Caushllari, Purg (Lavric 58), Pavlovic, Vidojevic.

UEFA CUP
● **MURA MURSKA SOBOTA**
Preliminary round DAUGAVA RIGA (LAT)
H 6-1 Cifer (5, 31), Lukic (16, 88), Cipot (30), Galic (39)
Nemec; Dominko, Alihodzic, Ilic, Cifer, Lukic, Galic, Cipot (Baranja D. 47), Vogrincic, Gutalj, Skaper (Ristic 12).
A 2-1 Vogrincic (58), Ristic (66)
Nemec; Dominko, Alihodzic, Ilic, Cifer, Lukic, Galic (Baranja D. 72), Vogrincic (Oslaj 77), Baranja A., Ristic (Fras 85), Dvorsak.

Qualifying round SILKEBORG (DEN)
H 0-0 Nemec; Dominko, Alihodzic, Ilic, Cifer, Lukic, Galic, Dvorsak (Oslaj 75), Vogrincic (Cipot 46), Gutalj, Skaper (Ristic 46).
A 0-2 Nemec; Dominko, Alihodzic, Ilic, Cifer (Oslaj 44), Lukic, Galic, Cipot, Ristic (Baranja A. 66), Vogrincic (Baranja D. 66), Gutalj.

● **MARIBOR TEATANIC**
1st round WISLA KRAKOW (POL)
H 0-2 Gresak; Fridl (Ceh 46), Balajic, Vugdalic, Kek, Sarkezi, Djuranovic, Zidan, Filipovic, Gajser (Kollari 67), Kmetec (Bozgo 46).
A 0-3 Gresak; Kollari, Sterbal, Vugdalic, Kek, Sarkezi, Gajser (Breznik 46), Djuranovic, Bozgo (Sivko 46), Ceh (Fridl 82), Kmetec.

BST DOMZALE

BS Tehnik Domzale (now NK Domzale)
Kopaliska 4
1230 Domzale
tel - (061) 710373
fax - (061) 722031
President - Stane Orazem
Secretary - Vinko Capuder
Coach - Ivan Ledenko; Boris Bunc; Mihajlo Petrovic
Stadium - Domzale (2,000)

		P	Ap	(s)	Gls
Bostjan AVGUSTIN	D	15			
Darko BIRJUKOV (BOS)	M	24	(1)		3
Sinisa BRKIC	D	23	(2)		1
Marjan CVIJANOVIC	M	24	(2)		
Mesud DURAKOVIC (CRO)	D	14			
Safet HADZIC	D	11	(3)		
Janez HRIBAR	M	27	(1)		1
Predrag JOVANOVIC	M		(2)		
Vlado KARADZIC	G	11	(3)		
Martin KLESNIK	G	22			
Murko KUNSTELJ	D		(1)		
Danilo KUSAR	D	18	(4)		1
Branko LADZEVIC (CRO)	M	8	(3)		1
Robert LAH	M		(1)		
Emil LEDENKO	M	4			
Tomaz MARINSEK	M	5	(1)		
Asmir MEMIC	M	5	(4)		
Janez MRAK	A	27	(1)		9
Damjan PIPAN	M	1	(3)		
Nenad PROTEGA	M	30	(1)		7
Dejan STEFANOVIC	M	13			1
Alen SULEJMANI	M	10	(2)		2
Agron SALJA	M	17	(4)		3
Blaz SKOF	D	14	(10)		3
Tomaz URSIC	D		(1)		
Anton USNIK	M	21	(3)		3
Matej VIDOVIC	M	3			
Samo VIDOVIC	A	6	(1)		1
Marko ZAVRSAN	D	4	(4)		
Igor ZINIC	A	6	(19)		4

02/08/98	HIT Gorica	A	0-3	
09/08/98	SCT Olimpija Ljubljana	H	0-3	
16/08/98	Maribor Teatanic	A	0-4	
22/08/98	Mura Murska Sobota	H	0-1	
30/08/98	Korotan Prevalje	A	1-0	Vidovic S.
13/09/98	Zivila Triglav Kranj	H	0-0	
20/09/98	Primorje Ajdovscina	A	0-0	
25/09/98	Potrosnik Beltinci	A	0-2	
04/10/98	Publikum Celje	H	2-2	Mrak, Salja
18/10/98	Rudar Velenje	A	3-1	Mrak 2, Zinic
25/10/98	NK Koper	H	4-0	Skof, Mrak, Birjukov, Protega
31/10/98	HIT Gorica	H	1-1	Birjukov (p)
08/11/98	SCT Olimpija Ljubljana	A	0-5	
15/11/98	Maribor Teatanic	H	2-2	Mrak, Hribar
22/11/98	Mura Murska Sobota	A	0-6	
29/11/98	Korotan Prevalje	H	1-3	Birjukov
28/02/99	Zivila Triglav Kranj	A	0-1	
07/03/99	Primorje Ajdovscina	H	3-1	Usnik, Mrak, Zinic
14/03/99	Potrosnik Beltinci	H	3-0	Protega 2, Mrak
21/03/99	Publikum Celje	A	0-0	
04/04/99	Rudar Velenje	H	0-1	
11/04/99	NK Koper	A	1-3	Zinic
18/04/99	Korotan Prevalje	A	0-0	
25/04/99	Rudar Velenje	H	0-1	
28/04/99	Mura Murska Sobota	A	2-1	Salja, Mrak
02/05/99	HIT Gorica	H	0-0	
05/05/99	Maribor Teatanic	A	1-1	Skof
09/05/99	Primorje Ajdovscina	H	4-1	Salja, Stefanovic, Skof, Zinic
16/05/99	NK Koper	A	4-0	Protega 2, Mrak, Sulejmani
19/05/99	Publikum Celje	H	2-1	Usnik, Protega
23/05/99	Potrosnik Beltinci	A	3-3	Protega, Kusar, Brkic
30/05/99	Zivila Triglav Kranj	A	1-0	Usnik
13/06/99	SCT Olimpija Ljubljana	H	2-2	Ladzevic, Sulejmani

HIT GORICA

CLUB DIRECTORY

NK HIT Gorica
Cesta IX. Korpusa 35
5250 Solkan
tel - (065) 134086
fax - (065) 134087
Year of Formation - 1938
President - Branko Tomazic
Secretary - Vojko Konjedic
Coach - Rado Radmanovic; Marin Kovacic (99/00 -
Nedzad Verlasevic)
Stadium - Nova Gorica (4,200)

MAJOR HONOURS
League Championship - (1) 1996.

APPEARANCES 98/99

	P	Ap	(s)	Gls
Edo BAJREKTAREVIC	D	27	(2)	3
Vili BECAJ	M	30		4
Husein BEGANOVIC (MAC)	D	22		1
Erik CIRKVENCIC	M	20	(9)	3
Florijan DEBENJAK	A	13	(4)	
Edmond GUNJAC	D	16	(11)	2
Mahir HALILI (ALB)	A	14		1
Ales KOKOT	M	1	(8)	
Borut MAVRIC	G	30		
Zeljko MITRAKOVIC	D	28	(2)	6
Toshiyuki MORIYAMA (JPN)	M	5	(5)	1
Novica NIKCEVIC	A	30	(1)	17
Dragoljub NIKOLIC	A	17	(7)	3
Ivica PESIC	M	1	(3)	
Mitja PIRIH	G	3	(1)	
Elvis RIBARIC	M	30		
Miran SREBRNIC	M	30		1
Komi Massamesso TCHENGAI (TOG)	D	8	(2)	1
Marko VOGRIC	M	8	(15)	3
Tonci ZLOGAR	M	29	(2)	7
Tomaz ZNIDERCIC	A	1	(7)	1

LEAGUE RESULTS 1998/99

02/08/98	BST Domzale	H	3-0	Mitrakovic, Nikcevic, Slogar
09/08/98	Publikum Celje	A	1-2	Nikcevic
16/08/98	Rudar Velenje	H	2-1	Nikcevic 2
22/08/98	NK Koper	A	3-2	Becaj, Gunjac, Srebrnic
30/08/98	Potrosnik Beltinci	H	3-1	Cirkvencic, Zlogar, Nikcevic
13/09/98	SCT Olimpija Ljubljana	H	4-1	Becaj, Nikolic, Mitrakovic, Nikcevic
20/09/98	Maribor Teatanic	A	0-1	
25/09/98	Mura Murska Sobota	H	3-1	Zlogar, Nikcevic, Vogric
04/10/98	Korotan Prevalje	A	0-0	
18/10/98	Zivila Triglav Kranj	H	3-1	Beganovic, Znidercic, Moriyama
25/10/98	Primorje Ajdovscina	A	2-0	Cirkvencic 2
31/10/98	BST Domzale	A	1-1	Nikolic
08/11/98	Publikum Celje	H	3-0	Vogric, Zlogar, Nikcevic
15/11/98	Rudar Velenje	A	0-3	
22/11/98	NK Koper	H	3-1	Nikolic, Zlogar, Nikcevic
29/11/98	Potrosnik Beltinci	A	2-2	Nikcevic 2
28/02/99	SCT Olimpija Ljubljana	A	1-2	Nikcevic
07/03/99	Maribor Teatanic	H	2-5	Zlogar, og (Sterbal)
14/03/99	Mura Murska Sobota	A	1-0	Vogric
21/03/99	Korotan Prevalje	H	1-0	Bajrektarevic
04/04/99	Zivila Triglav Kranj	A	2-0	Nikcevic, Mitrakovic
11/04/99	Primorje Ajdovscina	H	2-1	Becaj (p), Nikcevic
18/04/99	Primorje Ajdovscina	H	1-1	Halimi
25/04/99	NK Koper	A	0-0	
28/04/99	Publikum Celje	H	0-1	
02/05/99	BST Domzale	A	0-0	
05/05/99	Zivila Triglav Kranj	H	0-0	
09/05/99	SCT Olimpija Ljubljana	A	1-0	Gunjac
16/05/99	Korotan Prevalje	H	3-0	Tchengai, Mitrakovic, Becaj
19/05/99	Rudar Velenje	A	1-1	Mitrakovic
23/05/99	Mura Murska Sobota	H	4-1	Nikcevic 2, Zlogar, Mitrakovic
30/05/99	Potrosnik Beltinci	H	3-0	Bajrektarevic 2, Nikcevic
13/06/99	Maribor Teatanic	A	0-2	

NK KOPER

NK Koper
Ljubljanska 2
pp 189
6000 Koper
tel - (066) 32222
fax - (066) 33033
Year of Formation - 1920
President - Bogomir Baraga
Secretary - Valter Valencic
Coach - Marin Kovacic; Vlado Badzim; Edi Pobega;
Salih Softic (99/00 - Branko Zupan)
Stadium - Bonifika (8,500)

MAJOR HONOURS
League Championship - (2) 1985, 1988.
Domestic Cup - (1) 1991.

APPEARANCES 98/99

	P	Ap	(s)	Gls
Andrej APOLLONIO	M		(3)	
Damir BAN	D	2	(3)	
Damir BASIC	M	4	(4)	
Admir BEGIC	M	6	(5)	
Abdoulaya CAMARA (MLI)	A	5		
Marjan CENDAK	M	8	(3)	
Ales FRANJKOVIC	M	5		
Ermin HASIC	G	4		
Damir HODAK	D	1	(3)	
Saso JAKOMIN	D	31	(1)	9
Amer JUKAN (BOS)	A	27	(4)	2
Marko JURATOVEC	M	1		
Ilija KITIC	A	18	(6)	2
Peter KOZELJ	G	19		
Davor LOKAS	A	10	(10)	4
Zeljko MAKSIC	G	10	(1)	
Zoran MALESEVIC	M	6	(13)	2
Manuel PERSIC	M	27		2
Franko POHLEN	D	5	(3)	
Martin PREGELJ	M	22	(2)	3
Dzevad RASTODER (YUG)	M	24	(3)	
Goran RELJIC	M	23	(6)	1
Valter SABADIN	M	12		
Zoran STOLCIC	M	1	(2)	
Samir SUHONJIC	G		(1)	
Andrej SANTIC	D	10	(3)	2
Dean SCULAC	D	17	(7)	
Miroslav STAMPFER	M	21	(2)	3
Goran SUKALO	A	1	(3)	
Peter TOSIC	D	14		
Samir ZULIC	D	29		4

LEAGUE RESULTS 1998/99

02/08/98	Publikum Celje	H	1-1	Malesevic
09/08/98	Rudar Velenje	A	1-2	Stampfer
16/08/98	Potrosnik Beltinci	H	0-1	
22/08/98	HIT Gorica	H	2-3	Lokas, Stampfer
30/08/98	SCT Olimpija Ljubljana	A	3-2	Lokas, Persic, Jakomin
13/09/98	Maribor Teatanic	H	2-1	Kitic, Jakomin
20/09/98	Mura Murska Sobota	A	2-6	Pregelj, Jakomin
25/09/98	Korotan Prevalje	H	0-1	
04/10/98	Zivila Triglav Kranj	A	1-1	Santic
18/10/98	Primorje Ajdovscina	H	0-2	
25/10/98	BST Domzale	A	0-4	
31/10/98	Publikum Celje	A	1-0	Jakomin
08/11/98	Rudar Velenje	H	1-0	Zulic (p)
15/11/98	Potrosnik Beltinci	A	2-2	Santic, Reljic
22/11/98	HIT Gorica	A	1-3	Pregelj
29/11/98	SCT Olimpija Ljubljana	H	1-1	Jakomin
28/02/99	Maribor Teatanic	A	2-2	Lokas 2
07/03/99	Mura Murska Sobota	H	0-3	
14/03/99	Korotan Prevalje	A	0-3	
21/03/99	Zivila Triglav Kranj	H	0-2	
04/04/99	Primorje Ajdovscina	A	1-0	Zulic
11/04/99	BST Domzale	H	3-1	Jakomin 2, Persic (p)
18/04/99	Mura Murska Sobota	A	0-1	
25/04/99	HIT Gorica	H	0 0	
28/04/99	Maribor Teatanic	A	0-5	
02/05/99	Primorje Ajdovscina	H	0-1	
05/05/99	Potrosnik Beltinci	A	2-2	Malesevic, Kitic
09/05/99	Publikum Celje	A	0-1	
16/05/99	BST Domzale	H	0-4	
19/05/99	Zivila Triglav Kranj	A	3-0	Jukan 2, Stampfer
23/05/99	SCT Olimpija Ljubljana	H	3-3	Zulic 2, Jakomin
30/05/99	Korotan Prevalje	A	2-1	Jakomin, Pregelj
13/06/99	Rudar Velenje	H	0-2	

KOROTAN PREVALJE

CLUB DIRECTORY

NK Korotan
Ugasle peci 1
2391 Prevalje
tel - (0602) 287620
fax - (0602) 287621
Year of Formation - 1933
President - Niko Kolar
Secretary - Damjan Hojnik
Coach - Albert Pobor; Toni Tomazic
Stadium - Korotan (5,000)

APPEARANCES 98/99

	P	Ap	(s)	Gls
Marko BARUN	M	14	(4)	1
Osman BEGIC	A	3	(8)	
Igor BENEDEJCIC	M	15		
Peter BINKOVSKI	M	1		
Peter BREZNIK	D	13	(2)	4
Stojan CEKLIC	D	1		
Bostjan DAMIS	M	8	(2)	
Alfred DELALIC (BOS)	D	4		
Alfred JERMANIS	M	30		9
Goran JOLIC	M	9	(2)	4
Dusan KORDEZ	G	1		
Matjaz LAKOVNIK	M		(3)	
Patrik OKOVIC (CRO)	M	4		
Bojan ONIC	M	16	(6)	
Ivica PESIC	M	1	(11)	1
Roman PLESEC	M	30		2
Bostjan RATKOVIC	D	17	(4)	
Vukasin RISTIC (YUG)	A	12	(4)	5
Dragan RUTESKI (MAC)	A	6	(4)	1
Ilir SILO (ALB)	D	30		5
Robert SRAGA	G	32		
Dejan STEFANOVIC	M	9	(1)	
Kristjan SVAB	D	24	(1)	
Andrej TASIC	D	13	(1)	
Senad TIGANJ	A	8	(2)	8
Nenad ULAGA	D	4	(4)	
Sandi VALENTINCIC	A	9		2
Luka VIDMAR	M	24	(3)	
Robert ZEC	M	2	(19)	2
Zoran ZETIC (CRO)	A	14		
Adnan ZILDZEVIC (BOS)	M	5		
Iztok ZOFIC	M	4	(3)	

LEAGUE RESULTS 1998/99

02/08/98	Mura Murska Sobota	A	0-4	
09/08/98	Potrosnik Beltinci	A	1-2	Barun
16/08/98	Zivila Triglav Kranj	H	1-0	Zec
22/08/98	Primorje Ajdovscina	A	2-3	Jermanis, Silo
30/08/98	BST Domzale	H	0-1	
13/09/98	Publikum Celje	A	1-1	Silo
20/09/98	Rudar Velenje	H	1-1	Valentincic
25/09/98	NK Koper	A	1-0	Valentincic
04/10/98	HIT Gorica	H	0-0	
18/10/98	SCT Olimpija Ljubljana	A	4-3	Jolic 2, Jermanis, Silo
25/10/98	Maribor Teatanic	H	1-4	Tiganj
31/10/98	Mura Murska Sobota	H	1-1	Tiganj
08/11/98	Potrosnik Beltinci	H	5-0	Tiganj 4, Jolic
15/11/98	Zivila Triglav Kranj	A	2-1	Tiganj 2
22/11/98	Primorje Ajdovscina	H	2-1	Silo, Jermanis
29/11/98	BST Domzale	A	3-1	Jermanis 2, Jolic
28/02/99	Publikum Celje	H	1-1	Ristic
07/03/99	Rudar Velenje	A	0-2	
14/03/99	NK Koper	H	3-0	Ristic 2, Plesec
21/03/99	HIT Gorica	A	0-1	
04/04/99	SCT Olimpija Ljubljana	H	2-1	Jermanis, Breznik
11/04/99	Maribor Teatanic	A	0-3	
18/04/99	BST Domzale	H	0-0	
25/04/99	Zivila Triglav Kranj	A	2-1	Pesic, Jermanis
28/04/99	SCT Olimpija Ljubljana	H	0-3	
02/05/99	Potrosnik Beltinci	H	2-0	Ruteski, Jermanis
05/05/99	Rudar Velenje	A	2-1	Plesec, Silo
09/05/99	Mura Murska Sobota	H	1-2	Jermanis
16/05/99	HIT Gorica	A	0-3	
19/05/99	Maribor Teatanic	H	1-0	Ristic
23/05/99	Primorje Ajdovscina	A	4-1	Breznik 3, Ristic
30/05/99	NK Koper	H	1-2	Zec
13/06/99	Publikum Celje	A	0-1	

MARIBOR TEATANIC

CLUB DIRECTORY

NK Maribor Teatanic
Mladinska 29
2000 Maribor
tel - (062) 228470
fax - (062) 226864
Year of Formation - 1958
President - Joze Jagodnik
Secretary - Zeljko Fundak
Coach - Bojan Prasnikar
Stadium - Ljudski vrt (7,311)

MAJOR HONOURS
League Championship - (8) 1961, 1976, 1982, 1984, 1986, 1997, 1998, 1999.
Domestic Cup - (17) 1965, 1966, 1968, 1973, 1974, 1978, 1980, 1982, 1984, 1986, 1987, 1989, 1990, 1992, 1994, 1997, 1999.

APPEARANCES 98/99

	P	Ap	(s)	Gls
Stipe BALAJIC (CRO)	M	26	(1)	7
Peter BINKOVSKI	M		(2)	
Ingemar BLOUDEK	M		(1)	
Kliton BOZGO (ALB)	A	28	(1)	15
Peter BREZNIK	D		(7)	1
Geri ÇIPI (ALB)	D	16	(1)	1
Nastja CEH	M	14	(1)	1
Dejan DJURANOVIC	M	30		1
Mehmet DRAGUSHA (YUG)	M		(3)	
Dalibor FILIPOVIC (CRO)	A	22	(2)	13
Franc FRIDL	M	3	(4)	
Damjan GAJSER	M	16	(7)	7
Marinko GALIC	D	12	(2)	2
Luka GRESA	G	26	(1)	
Goran JOLIC	M	9	(7)	3
Amir KARIC	M	15		3
Matjaz KEK	D	24		
Marko KMETEC	A	12	(3)	7
Besnik KOLLARI (YUG)	M	8	(6)	1
Tomaz MURKO	G	4		
Damir PEKIC	A	1	(1)	
Aljosa SIVKO	A		(5)	
Goran STANKOVIC	G	3		
Marinko SARKEZI	D	24	(3)	3
Ante SIMUNDZA	A	6	(8)	2
Milan STERBAL	D	14	(10)	
Ales TURK	D	3	(6)	
Muamer VUGDALIC	D	22	(4)	1
Zikica VUKSANOVIC	M		(1)	
Gregor ZIDAN	M	25	(8)	4

LEAGUE RESULTS 1998/99

02/08/98	Zivila Triglav Kranj	H	3-2	Balajic, Kmetec, Filipovic (p)
09/08/98	Primorje Ajdovscina	A	1-0	Filipovic
16/08/98	BST Domzale	H	4-0	Filipovic 3 (1p), Kmetec
22/08/98	Publikum Celje	A	0-0	
30/08/98	Rudar Velenje	H	1-0	Balajic
13/09/98	NK Koper	A	1-2	Zidan
20/09/98	HIT Gorica	H	1-0	Sarkezi
25/09/98	SCT Olimpija Ljubljana	A	4-1	Kollari, Ceh, Gajser, Kmetec
04/10/98	Potrosnik Beltinci	H	5-1	Bozgo 2, Kmetec 2, Vugdalic
18/10/98	Mura Murska Sobota	H	4-1	Bozgo 2, Gajser, Filipovic
25/10/98	Korotan Prevalje	A	4-1	Gajser, Filipovic, Bozgo, Breznik
31/10/98	Zivila Triglav Kranj	A	2-2	Bozgo, Filipovic
08/11/98	Primorje Ajdovscina	H	1-1	Sarkezi
15/11/98	BST Domzale	A	2-2	Kmetec, Gajser
22/11/98	Publikum Celje	H	2-2	Kmetec, Bozgo
29/11/98	Rudar Velenje	A	0-2	
28/02/99	NK Koper	H	2-2	Balajic, Gajser
07/03/99	HIT Gorica	A	5-2	Jolic, Galic, Filipovic, Zidan, Balajic
14/03/99	SCT Olimpija Ljubljana	H	3-1	Bozgo, Galic, Gajser
21/03/99	Potrosnik Beltinci	A	2-1	Balajic, Jolic
04/04/99	Mura Murska Sobota	A	0-1	
11/04/99	Korotan Prevalje	H	3-0	Bozgo, Jolic, Simundza
18/04/99	Potrosnik Beltinci	H	1-1	Zidan
25/04/99	Primorje Ajdovscina	A	0-1	
28/04/99	NK Koper	H	5-0	Karic 2, Balajic, Çipi, Bozgo
02/05/99	Publikum Celje	A	0-0	
05/05/99	BST Domzale	H	1-1	Gajser
09/05/99	Zivila Triglav Kranj	A	3-1	Bozgo 3
16/05/99	SCT Olimpija Ljubljana	H	5-0	Filipovic 2 (1p), Bozgo, Sarkezi, Zidan
19/05/99	Korotan Prevalje	A	0-1	
23/05/99	Rudar Velenje	H	3-0	Djuranovic, Balajic, Filipovic
30/05/99	Mura Murska Sobota	A	2-0	Karic, Simundza
13/06/99	HIT Gorica	H	2-0	Filipovic, Bozgo (p)

MURA MURSKA SOBOTA

CLUB DIRECTORY

NK Mura
Kopaliska ulica 45
9001 Murska Sobota
tel - (069) 32701
fax - (069) 32701
Year of Formation - 1924
President - Milan Moerec
Secretary - Vlado Banko
Coach - Milan Koblencer; Joze Karoli;
Milovan Tarbuk
Stadium - Fazanerija (5,400)

MAJOR HONOURS
League Championship - (1) 1970.
Domestic Cup - (1) 1995.

APPEARANCES 98/99

	P	Ap	(s)	Gls
Mesud AHMETAGIC (BOS)	M		(2)	
Haris ALIHODZIC (BOS)	D	23		
Adamo BARANJA	M	20	(3)	
Dejan BARANJA	M	25	(5)	10
Ivan BENKO	D		(1)	
Kristijan CENER	M	4	(2)	1
Franc CIFER	D	28	(1)	2
Fabijan CIPOT	M	24	(4)	8
Marjan DOMINKO	A	23		1
Simon DVORSAK	M	27	(1)	3
Roman FAJDIGA	D		(2)	
Matej FRAS	M	1	(10)	
Ales GABOR	M	10	(1)	
Marinko GALIC	D	10	(2)	1
Goran GUTALJ (YUG)	A	22	(7)	9
Srecko ILIC (YUG)	D	14	(2)	
Saso LUKIC	D	30	(2)	4
Alan MESARIC	M		(6)	
Dejan NEMEC	G	33		
Damjan OSLAJ	D	17	(2)	
Robert PETROVIC	A	1	(6)	
Goran RISTIC	M	10	(18)	6
Stefan SKAPER	A	26		8
Sebastjan VOGRINCIC	M	14	(9)	
Sebastjan ZILAVEC	M	1	(8)	

LEAGUE RESULTS 1998/99

02/08/98	Korotan Prevalje	H	4-0	Cifer, Gutalj, Ristic, Dvorsak
09/08/98	Zivila Triglav Kranj	A	0-0	
16/08/98	Primorje Ajdovscina	H	2-1	Baranja D. 2 (1p)
22/08/98	BST Domzale	A	1-0	Gutalj
30/08/98	Publikum Celje	H	0-1	
13/09/98	Rudar Velenje	A	2-2	Cipot 2
20/09/98	NK Koper	H	6-2	Gutalj 3, Skaper 2, Baranja D.
25/09/98	HIT Gorica	A	1-3	Cipot
04/10/98	SCT Olimpija Ljubljana	H	0-0	
18/10/98	Maribor Teatanic	A	1-4	Baranja D.
25/10/98	Potrosnik Beltinci	H	3-0	Baranja D. 3 (1p)
31/10/98	Korotan Prevalje	A	1-1	Lukic
08/11/98	Zivila Triglav Kranj	H	4-0	Skaper 2, Lukic, Gutalj
15/11/98	Primorje Ajdovscina	A	1-2	Cipot
22/11/98	BST Domzale	H	6-0	Cipot 3, Ristic, Baranja D. (p), Gutalj
29/11/98	Publikum Celje	A	1-0	Galic (p)
28/02/99	Rudar Velenje	H	0-0	
07/03/99	NK Koper	A	3-0	Skaper, Cener, Ristic
14/03/99	HIT Gorica	H	0-1	
21/03/99	SCT Olimpija Ljubljana	A	1-0	Lukic
04/04/99	Maribor Teatanic	H	1-0	Dvorsak
11/04/99	Potrosnik Beltinci	A	0-2	
18/04/99	NK Koper	H	1-0	Cifer
25/04/99	Publikum Celje	A	1-3	Dvorsak
28/04/99	BST Domzale	H	1-2	Dominko
02/05/99	Zivila Triglav Kranj	A	1-2	Gutalj
05/05/99	SCT Olimpija Ljubljana	H	2-0	Cipot, Ristic
09/05/99	Korotan Prevalje	A	2-1	Lukic, Baranja D.
16/05/99	Rudar Velenje	H	4-0	Baranja D., Gutalj, Skaper, Ristic
19/05/99	Potrosnik Beltinci	H	1-2	Ristic
23/05/99	HIT Gorica	A	1-4	Skaper
30/05/99	Maribor Teatanic	H	0-2	
13/06/99	Primorje Ajdovscina	A	1-0	Skaper

POTROSNIK BELTINCI

CLUB DIRECTORY

NK Potrosnik
Sportni park Beltinci
9231 Beltinci
tel - (069) 411444
fax - (069) 411444
Year of Formation - 1949
President - Vladimir Erjavec
Secretary - Janez Breznik
Coach - Drago Posavec; Joze Seckar; Borut Jarc;
Jedinko Perica (99/00 - Nikola Skrbic)
Stadium - Beltinci (5,500)

APPEARANCES 98/99

	P	Ap	(s)	Gls
David ADJEJI (GHA)	A	12		2
Cveto ANTOLIN	M	3	(5)	
Simon BARANJA	D	21	(5)	5
Igor BEDO	A	5	(1)	
Mihael BUKOVEC	D	3	(6)	
Zdravko CENER	M	6	(4)	
Gjergji DEMA (ALB)	M	9		
Enkeleid DOBI (ALB)	M	9		2
Mitja ERNISA	D	15	(3)	
Franc FRIDL	M	16		1
Tomislav GODINA	D	10	(4)	
Ilamij HALIMI (MAC)	D	6	(1)	1
Kasim HALKIC	M	2	(2)	
Jaksa JURKOVIC (CRO)	M	10	(3)	2
Edin KENDIC	M	6	(3)	1
Joze KOKAS	M	13	(3)	
Renato KOTNIK	M	3	(2)	
Ratko KREMENOVIC (CRO)	A	12		2
Dejan KRSLIN	A		(1)	
Stanko KUZMA	G	16		
LEAL (BRA)	A	5	(1)	1
Gregor MIRTIC	D	12		
Issah MORO (GHA)	A	20		15
Saso NOVAK	D	28	(1)	3
David ROPOSA	M		(5)	
Andrej STRUNA	A	11		
Borut SIFTAR	G	17	(1)	
Matej SKAFAR	M	5	(22)	3
Bostjan TRATNJEK	D	30	(1)	
Simon ULEN	D	24	(2)	
Dario UTROSA	A	5	(6)	2
Bostjan ZEMLJIC	D	26		
Mario ZVER	A	3	(4)	1

LEAGUE RESULTS 1998/99

02/08/98	Rudar Velenje	A	0-2	
09/08/98	Korotan Prevalje	H	2-1	Baranja, Dobi
16/08/98	NK Koper	A	1-0	Adjeji
22/08/98	Zivila Triglav Kranj	H	4-1	Moro 3, Adjeji
30/08/98	HIT Gorica	A	1-3	Moro (p)
13/09/98	Primorje Ajdovscina	H	1-1	Skafar
20/09/98	SCT Olimpija Ljubljana	A	0-1	
25/09/98	BST Domzale	H	2-0	Halimi, Leal
04/10/98	Maribor Teatanic	A	1-5	Dobi
18/10/98	Publikum Celje	H	4-1	Novak 2, Moro, Baranja
25/10/98	Mura Murska Sobota	A	0-3	
31/10/98	Rudar Velenje	H	0-2	
08/11/98	Korotan Prevalje	A	0-5	
15/11/98	NK Koper	H	2-2	Moro 2
22/11/98	Zivila Triglav Kranj	A	0-2	
29/11/98	HIT Gorica	H	2-2	Zver, Moro
28/02/99	Primorje Ajdovscina	A	1-2	Baranja (p)
07/03/99	SCT Olimpija Ljubljana	H	2-0	Kremenovic 2
14/03/99	BST Domzale	A	0-3	
21/03/99	Maribor Teatanic	H	1-2	Novak
04/04/99	Publikum Celje	A	1-0	Moro
11/04/99	Mura Murska Sobota	H	2-0	Utrosa, Skafar
18/04/99	Maribor Teatanic	A	1-1	Moro
25/04/99	SCT Olimpija Ljubljana	A	0-6	
28/04/99	Primorje Ajdovscina	H	0-2	
02/05/99	Korotan Prevalje	A	0-2	
05/05/99	NK Koper	H	2-2	Jurkovic, Fridl
09/05/99	Rudar Velenje	A	1-2	Moro
16/05/99	Publikum Celje	H	0-1	
19/05/99	Mura Murska Sobota	A	2-1	Baranja, Moro
23/05/99	BST Domzale	H	3-3	Kendic, Moro, Skafar
30/05/99	HIT Gorica	A	0-3	
13/06/99	Zivila Triglav Kranj	H	5-1	Moro 2, Baranja, Jurkovic, Utrosa

PRIMORJE AJDOVSCINA

CLUB DIRECTORY

NK Primorje
Goriska 44
p.p. 3, 5270 Ajdovscina
tel - (065) 61042
fax - (065) 61042
Year of Formation - 1924
President - Dusan Crnigoj
Secretary - Miran Lulik
Coach - Mihajlo Petrovic; Ivan Marjon
Stadium - Primorje (3,000)

MAJOR HONOURS
Domestic Cup - (1) 1976.

APPEARANCES 98/99

	P	Ap	(s)	Gls
ALVES (BRA)	M	5		1
FERNANDES (BRA)	M		(2)	
Elis FILIPIC	M		(1)	
Ehad GOGA (YUG)	M	27	(2)	
Simon GREGORIC	M	8	(3)	1
Dejan KECAN	M	12	(11)	4
Ales KODELJA	M	13	(9)	
Branislav KOJICIC (YUG)	M	10	(1)	3
Andrej KOMAC	D	2	(9)	
Erik KRZISNIK	D	11	(1)	
Dino LALIC	G	1		
Borivoje LUCIC (BOS)	A	26	(3)	5
Andi MAMIC	D	8	(5)	
Robert MARUSIC	A	23	(5)	6
Matej MAVRIC	D	13	(6)	1
Sefik MULAHMETOVIC (YUG)	M	29		3
Alen NADAL	M	2	(10)	1
Igor PANDZA	A	4	(4)	
Janez PATE	M	15		1
Andrej POLISAK	D	21		
Uros RUTAR	G	1		
Valter SABADIN	M		(3)	
Janez STRAJNAR	G	31		
Alen SCULAC	D	27		
Almir TANJIC	D	19	(10)	
Ivica VULIC	A	32		10
Andrej ZELKO	A	23		3

LEAGUE RESULTS 1998/99

02/08/98	SCT Olimpija Ljubljana	A	0-1	
09/08/98	Maribor Teatanic	H	0-1	
16/08/98	Mura Murska Sobota	A	1-2	Marusic
22/08/98	Korotan Prevalje	H	3-2	Vulic, Nadal, Alves
30/08/98	Zivila Triglav Kranj	A	0-0	
13/09/98	Potrosnik Beltinci	A	1-1	Vulic
20/09/98	BST Domzale	H	0-0	
25/09/98	Publikum Celje	A	0-3	
04/10/98	Rudar Velenje	H	2-0	Kecan, Marusic
18/10/98	NK Koper	A	2-0	Vulic, Kojicic
25/10/98	HIT Gorica	H	0-2	
31/10/98	SCT Olimpija Ljubljana	H	3-0	Marusic, Kecan, Lucic
08/11/98	Maribor Teatanic	A	1-1	Vulic
15/11/98	Mura Murska Sobota	H	2-1	Vulic, Mulahmetovic (p)
22/11/98	Korotan Prevalje	A	1-2	Kojicic
29/11/98	Zivila Triglav Kranj	H	5-1	Vulic 2, Mulahmetovic (p),
				Marusic, Lucic
28/02/99	Potrosnik Beltinci	H	2-1	Marusic, Kojicic
07/03/99	BST Domzale	A	1-3	Kecan
14/03/99	Publikum Celje	H	0-0	
21/03/99	Rudar Velenje	A	1-4	Marusic
04/04/99	NK Koper	H	0-1	
11/04/99	HIT Gorica	A	1-2	Pate
18/04/99	HIT Gorica	A	1-1	Gregoric
25/04/99	Maribor Teatanic	H	1-0	Zelko
28/04/99	Potrosnik Beltinci	A	2-0	Zelko, Mulahmetovic (p)
02/05/99	NK Koper	A	1-0	Zelko
05/05/99	Publikum Celje	H	2-1	Lucic, Vulic
09/05/99	BST Domzale	A	1-4	Mavric
16/05/99	Zivila Triglav Kranj	H	1-1	Vulic
19/05/99	SCT Olimpija Ljubljana	A	0-1	
23/05/99	Korotan Prevalje	H	1-4	Lucic
30/05/99	Rudar Velenje	A	3-4	Vulic, Kecan, Lucic
13/06/99	Mura Murska Sobota	H	0-1	

PUBLIKUM CELJE

CLUB DIRECTORY

NK Publikum
Cesta na grad 12
3000 Celje
tel - (063) 482250/482252
fax - (063) 482251
Year of Formation - 1946
President - Marjan Vengust
Secretary - Darko Zickar
Coach - Edin Osmanovic; Nikola Ilijevski
Stadium - Skalna klet (2,130)

MAJOR HONOURS
League Championship - (1) 1964.
Domestic Cup - (1) 1964.

APPEARANCES 98/99

		P	Ap	(s)	Gls
Dragan ANGELOVSKI (MAC)	M	12	(3)	3
Dominik BERSNJAK	M	4	(3)	
Gregor BLATNIK	D	27		
Stani BLATNIK	M	20	(3)	
Dragan BOSKOVSKI (MAC)	A	3	(2)	
Ivica BOZOVIC (CRO)	D	1		
Robert CUGMAS	M	4	(7)	
Sebastjan GOBEC	M	28		2
Uros GORENEK	M		(2)	
Andrej GORSEK	A	15	(1)	4
Bostjan HODZAR	M	15	(16)	5
Ales KACICNIK	M	30	(1)	1
Mladen KOLJIC	A	4	(5)	1
Marko KRIZNIK	D	14	(2)	
Marko MITIC	M	24	(1)	1
Amel MUJCINOVIC (BOS)	G	32		
Saso NOVAK	D	2	(4)	
Marko OPLOTNIK	M	2	(3)	
PAULINHO de Oliveira (BRA)	M	11		
Damjan ROMIH	M	27	(2)	3
Goran SANKOVIC	D	27	(1)	
Omar SISE (GAM)	A		(1)	
Aleksander SELIGA	G	1		
Danijel SIREC	A	18	(14)	6
Matjaz STANCAR	M	26	(2)	2
TAHARZADEH (IRN)	A	6		1
Zlatan TRNJANIN	A		(3)	
Nenad ULAGA	D	5	(2)	1
Brane VODOPIVEC	M	5	(10)	

LEAGUE RESULTS 1998/99

02/08/98	NK Koper	A	1-1	Ulaga
09/08/98	HIT Gorica	H	2-1	Gobec, Romih
16/08/98	SCT Olimpija Ljubljana	A	0-3	
22/08/98	Maribor Teatanic	H	0-0	
30/08/98	Mura Murska Sobota	A	1-0	Koljic
13/09/98	Korotan Prevalje	H	1-1	Romih
20/09/98	Zivila Triglav Kranj	A	0-1	
25/09/98	Primorje Ajdovscina	H	3-0	Mitic, Sirec, Hodzar
04/10/98	BST Domzale	A	2-2	Hodzar, Taharzadeh
18/10/98	Potrosnik Beltinci	A	1-4	Hodzar
25/10/98	Rudar Velenje	H	0-0	
31/10/98	NK Koper	H	0-1	
08/11/98	HIT Gorica	A	0-3	
15/11/98	SCT Olimpija Ljubljana	H	0-2	
22/11/98	Maribor Teatanic	A	2-2	Sirec 2
29/11/98	Mura Murska Sobota	H	0-1	
28/02/99	Korotan Prevalje	A	1-1	Sirec
07/03/99	Zivila Triglav Kranj	H	1-0	Kacicnik
14/03/99	Primorje Ajdovscina	A	0-0	
21/03/99	BST Domzale	H	0-0	
04/04/99	Potrosnik Beltinci	H	0-1	
11/04/99	Rudar Velenje	A	0-0	
18/04/99	Rudar Velenje	A	1-2	Gorsek
25/04/99	Mura Murska Sobota	H	3-1	Angelovski, Stancar (p), Gorsek
28/04/99	HIT Gorica	A	1-0	Hodzar
02/05/99	Maribor Teatanic	H	0-0	
05/05/99	Primorje Ajdovscina	A	1-2	Hodzar
09/05/99	NK Koper	H	1-0	Romih
16/05/99	Potrosnik Beltinci	A	1-0	Gorsek
19/05/99	BST Domzale	A	1-2	Sirec
23/05/99	Zivila Triglav Kranj	H	2-2	Gorsek, Angelovski
30/05/99	SCT Olimpija Ljubljana	A	3-2	Angelovski, Stancar (p), Gobec
13/06/99	Korotan Prevalje	H	1-0	Sirec

RUDAR VELENJE

CLUB DIRECTORY

NK Rudar
Cesta na jezero 7
p.p.54
3320 Velenje
tel - (063) 866181
fax - (063) 866181
Year of Formation - 1948
President - Janko Lukner
Secretary - Bojan Ograjensek
Coach - Drago Jostanjsek; Branko Oblak
Stadium - Ob jezeru (3,300)

MAJOR HONOURS
League Championship - (2) 1977, 1991.
Domestic Cup - (1) 1998.

APPEARANCES 98/99

	P	Ap	(s)	Gls
Samir BALAGIC	D	29		2
Danijel BREZIC	M	27	(2)	1
Ilir CAUSHLLARI (ALB)	M	21		
Zlatko CERIMOVIC	D	18	(5)	
Mladen DABANOVIC	G	33		
Goran DRAGIC	D		(1)	
Saso GAJSER	M	31		4
Miha GOLOB	M	1	(5)	
Goran GRANIC (CRO)	D	31		2
Anton GROBELSEK	M	5	(9)	1
Mitja HOJNIK	M		(2)	
Jernej JAVORNIK	M	24	(4)	5
Damjan JESENICNIK	M	2	(10)	1
Klemen LAVRIC	A	6	(7)	1
Darko MILANOVIC	A		(1)	
Zoran PAVLOVIC	M	31		8
Simon PIRC	M	4	(1)	
Niko PODVINSKI	M	32		5
Ales PURG	M	5	(4)	
Aljosa SIVKO	A	1	(5)	
Almir SULEJMANOVIC	M	26	(2)	1
Peter SUMNIK	A	8	(11)	
Zivojin VIDOJEVIC (YUG)	A	28	(4)	12

LEAGUE RESULTS 1998/99

02/08/98	Potrosnik Beltinci	H	2-0	Javornik, Vidojevic
09/08/98	NK Koper	H	2-1	Vidojevic, Pavlovic
16/08/98	HIT Gorica	A	1-2	Pavlovic (p)
22/08/98	SCT Olimpija Ljubljana	H	1-2	Pavlovic
30/08/98	Maribor Teatanic	A	0-1	
13/09/98	Mura Murska Sobota	H	2-2	Vidojevic, Brezic
20/09/98	Korotan Prevalje	A	1-1	Pavlovic
25/09/98	Zivila Triglav Kranj	H	1-0	Javornik
04/10/98	Primorje Ajdovscina	A	0-2	
18/10/98	BST Domzale	H	1-3	Podvinski
25/10/98	Publikum Celje	A	0-0	
31/10/98	Potrosnik Beltinci	A	2-0	Gajser, Balagic
08/11/98	NK Koper	A	0-1	
15/11/98	HIT Gorica	H	3-0	Gajser, Pavlovic, Grobelsek
22/11/98	SCT Olimpija Ljubljana	A	0-0	
29/11/98	Maribor Teatanic	H	2-0	Gajser, Pavlovic
28/02/99	Mura Murska Sobota	A	0-0	
07/03/99	Korotan Prevalje	H	2-0	Lavric, Granic (p)
14/03/99	Zivila Triglav Kranj	A	1-0	Javornik
21/03/99	Primorje Ajdovscina	H	4-1	Podvinski 2, Granic (p), Jesenicnik
04/04/99	BST Domzale	A	1-0	Vidojevic
11/04/99	Publikum Celje	H	0-0	
18/04/99	Publikum Celje	H	2-1	Vidojevic, Javornik
25/04/99	BST Domzale	A	1-0	Vidojevic
28/04/99	Zivila Triglav Kranj	H	3-1	Vidojevic, Balagic, Podvinski
02/05/99	SCT Olimpija Ljubljana	A	1-1	Pavlovic
05/05/99	Korotan Prevalje	H	1-2	Sulejmanovic
09/05/99	Potrosnik Beltinci	H	2-1	Javornik, Pavlovic
16/05/99	Mura Murska Sobota	A	0-4	
19/05/99	HIT Gorica	H	1-1	Gajser
23/05/99	Maribor Teatanic	A	0-3	
30/05/99	Primorje Ajdovscina	H	4-3	Vidojevic 3, Podvinski
13/06/99	NK Koper	A	2-0	Vidojevic 2

SCT OLIMPIJA LJUBLJANA

CLUB DIRECTORY

NK SCT Olimpija
Vodovodna 20, p.p.2620, 1000 Ljubljana
tel - (061) 348397   fax - (061) 341847
Year of Formation - 1911
President - Ivan Zidar
General Manager - Joze Prostor
Secretary - Emil Kajdiz
Coach - Jedinko Perica; Marin Kovacic;
Janez Zupancic (99/00 - Jedinko Perica)
Stadium - Bezigrad (12,000)

MAJOR HONOURS
League Championship - (8) 1947, 1952, 1962,
1987, 1992, 1993, 1994, 1995.
Domestic Cup - (17) 1953, 1954, 1955, 1956,
1958, 1962, 1963, 1969, 1970, 1971, 1972,
1976, 1977, 1981, 1988, 1993, 1996.

APPEARANCES 98/99

	P	Ap	(s)	Gls
Amir AGIC	M	21	(6)	2
Dean BAUMAN	M		(2)	
Klemen BINGO	D	3	(1)	
Milan BOSKOVIC (YUG)	M	31		3
Edin BUDIMLIC	A		(1)	
Rok CIRAR	D	3	(1)	
Edis CAUSEVIC	M	6	(16)	6
Nastja CEH	M	14		4
Bogomir DEISINGER	D	9	(4)	
Dejan DONCIC	D	12	(2)	1
Ismet EKMECIC (BOS)	A	17	(1)	6
Suad FILEKOVIC	D	15	(5)	
Primoz GLIHA	A	7		2
Bostjan GRIZOLD	A	19	(8)	3
Jasmin HANDANOVIC	G	5	(1)	
Patrik IPAVEC	A	3	(5)	
Sinisa JUKIC (CRO)	M	27	(1)	3
Miha KEBE	M	7	(7)	
Ilija KITIC	A	2	(2)	2
Marko KMETEC	A	12	(1)	2
Dusan KOSIC	D	32		2
Milos KOSTIC	D	4	(1)	
Selvad KUJOVIC	M	25	(3)	7
Gregor MIRTIC	D	10		1
Goran MISKIC	M	15	(9)	
Nihad PEJKOVIC	G	28		2
Bostjan PUS	A	1	(3)	1
Miha SPORAR	D	16		2
Sani TRGO	M	11	(1)	2
Drazen ZEZELJ	A	8	(9)	3

LEAGUE RESULTS 1998/99

02/08/98	Primorje Ajdovscina	H	1-0	Jukic
09/08/98	BST Domzale	A	3-0	Sporar, Grizold, Ekmecic
16/08/98	Publikum Celje	H	3-0	Causevic, Kitic, Ekmecic
22/08/98	Rudar Velenje	A	2-1	Kitic, Kujovic
30/08/98	NK Koper	H	2-3	Causevic, Agic
13/09/98	HIT Gorica	A	1-4	Ekmecic (p)
20/09/98	Potrosnik Beltinci	H	1-0	Causevic
25/09/98	Maribor Teatanic	H	1-4	Gliha
04/10/98	Mura Murska Sobota	A	0-0	
18/10/98	Korotan Prevalje	H	3-4	Jukic, Ekmecic, Causevic
25/10/98	Zivila Triglav Kranj	A	2-2	Gliha, Kujovic
31/10/98	Primorje Ajdovscina	A	0-3	
08/11/98	BST Domzale	H	5-0	Ekmecic 2, Pejkovic 2 (2p), Zezelj
15/11/98	Publikum Celje	A	2-0	Jukic, Zezelj
22/11/98	Rudar Velenje	H	0-0	
29/11/98	NK Koper	A	1-1	Doncic
28/02/99	HIT Gorica	H	2-1	Grizold, Sporar
07/03/99	Potrosnik Beltinci	A	0-2	
14/03/99	Maribor Teatanic	A	1-3	Kmetec
21/03/99	Mura Murska Sobota	H	0-1	
04/04/99	Korotan Prevalje	A	1-2	Mirtic
11/04/99	Zivila Triglav Kranj	H	1-1	Grizold
18/04/99	Zivila Triglav Kranj	H	4-1	Boskovic 2, Ceh 2
25/04/99	Potrosnik Beltinci	H	6-0	Kujovic 3, Ceh 2, Trgo
28/04/99	Korotan Prevalje	A	3-0	Kmetec, Pus, Kujovic
02/05/99	Rudar Velenje	H	1-1	Kujovic
05/05/99	Mura Murska Sobota	A	0-2	
09/05/99	HIT Gorica	H	0-1	
16/05/99	Maribor Teatanic	A	0-5	
19/05/99	Primorje Ajdovscina	H	1-0	Agic
23/05/99	NK Koper	A	3-3	Causevic, Zezelj, Trgo
30/05/99	Publikum Celje	H	2-3	Kosic, Causevic
13/06/99	BST Domzale	A	2-2	Boskovic, Kosic

ZIVILA TRIGLAV KRANJ

CLUB DIRECTORY

NK Zivila Triglav
Partizanska 39
4000 Kranj
tel - (064) 222639/241326
fax - (064) 241326
Year of Formation - 1920
President - Joze Likozar
Director - Miran Subic
Coach - Janez Zupancic; Rajko Korent;
Branko Zupan (99/00 - Rajko Korent)
Stadium - Mestne (4,600)

APPEARANCES 98/99

	P	Ap	(s)	Gls
David ADJEJI (GHA)	M	11	(3)	2
Nedzad ALIBABIC	D	22	(6)	2
Anze BERRA	M	1	(1)	
Oliver BOGATINOV	A	15	(3)	4
Branko BOZIC	D	5	(2)	
Adnan CUSTOVIC (BOS)	A	16		5
Denis DJURKOVIC	D	17	(2)	2
Matjaz DOLINAR	M	1	(4)	
Elvis DURAKOVIC	D		(3)	
Primoz EGART	D	22	(4)	
Gregor FEIGEL	D	11	(1)	3
Gregor GRASIC	M	5	(2)	
Andrej JOZEF	M	23	(3)	1
Miha KALCIC	G	5		
Besnik KOLLARI (YUG)	M	3		
Marjan KONC	A	4	(4)	1
Peter KOZELJ	G	9		
Alen KRUPIC	D	17	(5)	
Dino LALIC	G	16		
Dejan MARKELJ	M	16	(7)	
Denis MARKELJ	D	4	(9)	
Sebastjan PECAR	G	3	(1)	
Miha PITAMIC	A	7	(3)	
Gorazd PLEVNIK	A	7	(3)	2
Jalen POKORN	M	14	(2)	
Aleksander RADOSAVLJEVIC	M	28	(3)	1
Andrej RAZDRH	D	23	(2)	1
Alan SIRC	M	5	(2)	
Boris SIRK	D	26	(1)	
Vanja STARCEVIC	A	14	(1)	4
Dusko VICKOVIC (CRO)	A	4	(3)	
Davor ZUPANCIC	M	9	(5)	
Jure ZEGAR	A		(1)	
Matej ZNIDARSIC	D		(2)	

LEAGUE RESULTS 1998/99

02/08/98	Maribor Teatanic	A	2-3	Plevnik (p), Custovic
09/08/98	Mura Murska Sobota	H	0-0	
16/08/98	Korotan Prevalje	A	0-1	
22/08/98	Potrosnik Beltinci	A	1-4	Plevnik
30/08/98	Primorje Ajdovscina	H	0-0	
13/09/98	BST Domzale	A	0-0	
20/09/98	Publikum Celje	H	1-0	Bogatinov
25/09/98	Rudar Velenje	A	0-1	
04/10/98	NK Koper	H	1-1	Djurkovic
18/10/98	HIT Gorica	A	1-3	Custovic
25/10/98	SCT Olimpija Ljubljana	H	2-2	Bogatinov, Djurkovic
31/10/98	Maribor Teatanic	H	2-2	Custovic 2
08/11/98	Mura Murska Sobota	A	0-4	
15/11/98	Korotan Prevalje	H	1-2	Jozef
22/11/98	Potrosnik Beltinci	H	2-0	Custovic, Bogatinov
29/11/98	Primorje Ajdovscina	A	1-5	Radosavljevic
28/02/99	BST Domzale	H	1-0	Bogatinov
07/03/99	Publikum Celje	A	0-1	
14/03/99	Rudar Velenje	H	0-1	
21/03/99	NK Koper	A	2-0	Starcevic, Adjeji
04/04/99	HIT Gorica	H	0-2	
11/04/99	SCT Olimpija Ljubljana	A	1-1	Starcevic
18/04/99	SCT Olimpija Ljubljana	A	1-4	Adjeji
25/04/99	Korotan Prevalje	H	1-2	Alibabic (p)
28/04/99	Rudar Velenje	A	1-3	Feigel
02/05/99	Mura Murska Sobota	H	2-1	Feigel 2
05/05/99	HIT Gorica	A	0-0	
09/05/99	Maribor Teatanic	H	1-3	Konc
16/05/99	Primorje Ajdovscina	A	1-1	Starcevic
19/05/99	NK Koper	H	0-3	
23/05/99	Publikum Celje	A	2-2	Razdrh, Alibabic
30/05/99	BST Domzale	H	0-1	
13/06/99	Potrosnik Beltinci	A	1-5	Starcevic

PROMOTED CLUBS

SECOND DIVISION FINAL TABLE 98/99

		Pd	W	D	L	F	A	Pt	GD
1	Dravograd	30	18	7	5	69	31	61	+38
2	Feroterm Pohorje	30	16	6	8	56	35	54	+21
3	Zeleznicar	30	15	9	6	58	30	54	+28
4	Esotech Smartno	30	15	8	7	49	28	53	+21
5	Tabor Sezana	30	15	7	8	59	35	52	+24
6	Aluminij	30	14	9	7	57	42	51	+15
7	Drava	30	13	9	8	48	36	48	+12
8	Zagorje	30	12	7	11	45	43	43	+2
9	Sentjur	30	11	7	12	38	44	40	-6
10	Elan	30	11	6	13	45	61	39	-16
11	Nafta	30	10	6	14	35	47	36	-12
12	Jadran Sepic	30	10	5	15	36	42	35	-6
13	Goriske opekarne	30	9	7	14	37	53	34	-16
14	Factor Jezica	30	6	11	13	30	44	29	-14
15	Slovan Slavija	30	4	6	20	29	75	18	-46
16	Rudar Trbovlje	30	3	6	21	17	62	15	-45

CLUB DIRECTORY

NK Dravograd
Trg 4. julija 7
2370 Dravograd
tel - (0602) 84436
fax - (0602) 84431
Year of Formation - 1948
President - Rihard Versovnik
Coach - Marijan Pusnik
Stadium - NK Dravograd (1,000)

CLUB DIRECTORY

NK Feroterm Pohorje
Stadionska 15
2342 Ruse
tel - (062) 6688040
fax - (062) 6688041
Year of Formation - 1956
President - Peter Lamut
Secretary - Marjan Viher
Coach - Joze Hadler
Stadium - Ruse (3,000)

SPAIN

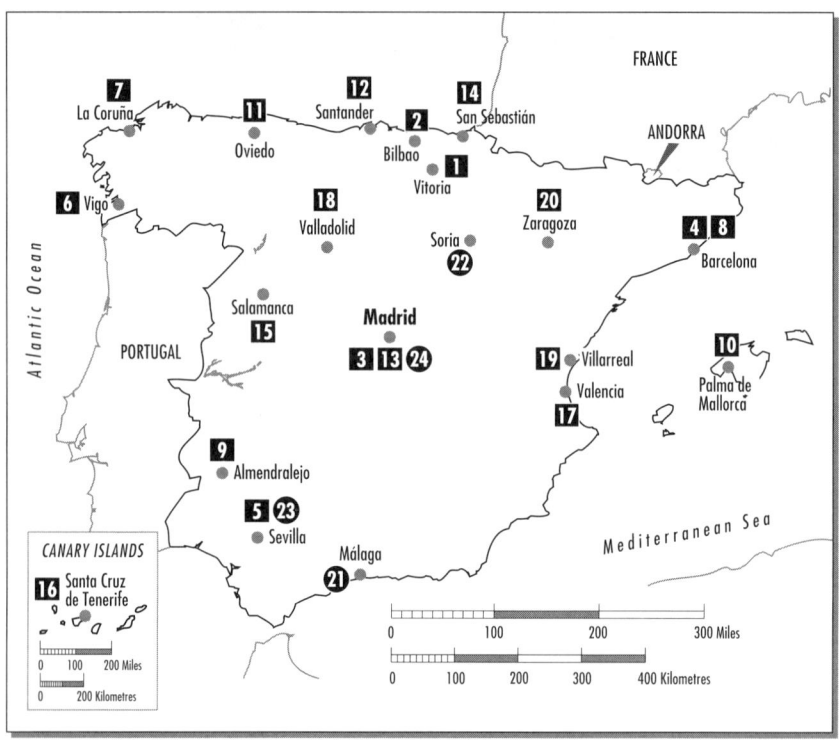

1	CD ALAVES	947
2	ATHLETIC BILBAO	948
3	ATLETICO MADRID	949
4	FC BARCELONA	950
5	REAL BETIS	951
6	RC CELTA	952
7	RC DEPORTIVO	953
8	RCD ESPANYOL	954
9	CF EXTREMADURA	955
10	RCD MALLORCA	956
11	REAL OVIEDO	957
12	RACING SANTANDER	958
13	REAL MADRID	959

14	REAL SOCIEDAD	960
15	UD SALAMANCA	961
16	CD TENERIFE	962
17	VALENCIA CF	963
18	REAL VALLADOLID	964
19	VILLARREAL CF	965
20	REAL ZARAGOZA	966
Promoted clubs		
21	MALAGA CF	967
22	CD NUMANCIA	967
23	SEVILLA FC	967
24	RAYO VALLECANO	967

CAMACHO LIBERATES NATIONAL TEAM

Centenary brings best out of Barcelona

FEDERATION DIRECTORY

Real Federación Española de Fútbol
Calle Alberto Bosch 13, 28014 Madrid

tel - (914) 201362/203321   Year of Formation - 1913
fax - (914) 204294/203304   President - Angel María Villar
                             Manager - Gerardo González Otero

In December 1998 there was just one wish at the top of every Barcelona fan's Christmas list. It read: "Bring me the head of Louis van Gaal!"

The Dutchman was about as popular in the Catalan city as a Real Madrid megastore. Under his brash, authoritarian leadership, Barcelona appeared to be irretrievably on the slide. They had been knocked out of the Champions' League and had just lost four Spanish league matches on the trot, the last of them, humiliatingly, at home to Primera Division débutants Villarreal. It was crisis time at the Nou Camp, no mistake about it, and the socios and scribes were united in their clamour for Van Gaal to pack his bags and leave.

And yet...he stayed. A narrow 1-0 win away to Valladolid allowed the Dutchman to survive into the festive break, and after that...came the miraculous transformation. 1999 was Barcelona's centenary year and they started it with a bang, hammering Alavés 7-1 in the Nou Camp. Four and a half months later, when those two teams met for the return match in northern Spain, Barça's fans would be rejoicing again, this time as the champions of Spain.

The metamorphosis of Barcelona was remarkable. And although it would be overstating the case to say that Van Gaal went from villain to hero during the team's barnstorming title-winning run of 16 wins in 20 matches from

LEAGUE CHAMPIONSHIP RESULTS 98/99

		1	2	3	4	5	6	7	8	9	10	11	12	13	14	15	16	17	18	19	20
1	CD Alavés		1-2	2-0	1-4	0-0	2-0	2-1	1-1	0-1	2-0	2-2	0-1	1-1	2-1	1-0	3-1	0-1	2-0	2-1	1-0
2	Athletic Bilbao	5-0		1-2	1-3	0-0	0-0	2-1	2-2	0-0	1-0	3-5	2-0	2-3	0-0	1-0	2-0	2-0	2-1	2-0	2-0
3	Atlético Madrid	3-0	0-0		1-1	2-3	2-1	1-1	1-2	5-0	1-2	0-0	1-1	3-1	4-1	2-0	2-0	1-2	6-1	2-2	0-0
4	FC Barcelona	7-1	4-2	0-1		4-1	2-2	4-0	3-0	1-0	2-1	3-1	3-2	3-0	4-1	1-1	4-1	2-4	1-1	1-3	3-1
5	Real Betis	1-0	1-4	0-0	0-3		0-3	0-3	0-1	1-1	1-3	5-0	1-1	3-2	1-0	1-0	1-0	0-1	2-0	4-1	1-3
6	RC Celta	1-1	3-2	0-1	0-0	4-0		0-0	2-0	5-1	4-2	6-2	3-0	5-1	2-2	1-0	2-0	2-2	0-0	4-1	2-0
7	RC Deportivo	2-2	1-1	1-1	2-1	2-2	2-1		1-0	1-1	1-1	4-0	1-2	4-0	0-1	1-0	2-0	1-0	3-0	2-1	2-1
8	RCD Espanyol	3-0	1-1	1-1	1-2	1-0	3-0	2-2		0-0	1-0	2-1	1-1	0-0	0-0	4-0	2-1	2-1	0-2	1-1	2-1
9	CF Extremadura	1-0	0-1	2-1	1-2	2-1	1-1	1-2	1-0		1-0	0-1	0-3	1-5	1-0	1-1	1-0	1-0	0-0	2-2	0-2
10	RCD Mallorca	2-1	6-1	4-0	1-0	1-0	2-0	1-2	2-0	2-0		0-0	1-1	2-1	1-0	1-0	1-1	0-1	1-0	1-0	1-0
11	Real Oviedo	1-0	0-0	3-1	2-1	0-1	1-3	1-2	1-1	1-0	1-3		1-0	1-0	2-1	3-2	0-1	2-2	0-0	0-0	1-2
12	Racing Santander	2-0	2-0	2-3	0-0	1-0	2-2	1-1	0-2	3-1	1-0	0-0		1-3	0-1	4-1	0-0	0-1	0-2	1-2	2-4
13	Real Madrid	3-2	0-1	4-2	2-2	0-1	1-2	3-1	2-0	2-0	2-1	2-1	2-2		3-2	3-1	4-0	3-1	3-2	4-1	3-2
14	Real Sociedad	2-1	3-1	3-2	0-2	1-0	2-0	2-0	1-2	2-0	0-1	3-3	2-0	3-2		4-0	1-1	1-1	1-0	1-1	0-0
15	UD Salamanca	1-0	2-1	2-1	1-4	1-3	1-1	3-1	2-3	2-1	0-0	1-1	1-2	1-1	0-1		1-2	0-1	1-0	1-0	1-2
16	CD Tenerife	1-2	0-1	1-0	2-3	3-2	0-2	1-1	0-0	1-1	1-1	0-2	2-2	2-3	2-2	1-0		3-2	2-2	2-2	1-1
17	Valencia CF	5-0	4-1	1-0	1-3	5-1	2-2	0-0	1-2	1-1	3-0	3-0	3-0	3-1	2-0	1-0	1-1		0-1	1-0	1-1
18	Real Valladolid	3-0	0-3	1-0	0-1	0-3	2-1	0-1	2-1	0-0	1-0	2-1	0-0	0-1	0-0	4-1	2-1	3-1		1-0	1-1
19	Villarreal CF	2-0	0-1	2-1	2-3	3-4	1-1	1-2	2-2	1-1	0-2	0-0	3-0	0-2	1-1	5-0	2-5	1-0	2-1		1-1
20	Real Zaragoza	1-1	2-0	2-0	2-0	2-2	0-1	3-1	0-3	3-1	0-1	1-0	3-1	3-4	1-1	2-0	3-1	1-4	2-0	4-0	

LEAGUE CHAMPIONSHIP FINAL TABLE 98/99

			Home					Away					Total					
		P	W	D	L	F	A	W	D	L	F	A	W	D	L	F	A	P	GD
1	FC Barcelona	38	13	3	3	52	23	11	4	4	35	20	24	7	7	87	43	79	+44
2	Real Madrid	38	14	2	3	46	24	7	3	9	31	38	21	5	12	77	62	68	+15
3	RCD Mallorca	38	14	3	2	30	8	6	3	10	18	23	20	6	12	48	31	66	+17
4	Valencia CF	38	11	5	3	38	14	8	3	8	25	25	19	8	11	63	39	65	+24
5	RC Celta	38	12	6	1	46	15	5	7	7	23	26	17	13	8	69	41	64	+28
6	RC Deportivo	38	11	6	2	33	15	6	6	7	22	28	17	12	9	55	43	63	+12
7	RCD Espanyol	38	9	8	2	27	14	7	5	7	22	24	16	13	9	49	38	61	+11
8	Athletic Bilbao	38	10	5	4	30	17	7	4	8	23	30	17	9	12	53	47	60	+6
9	Real Zaragoza	38	11	3	5	35	21	5	6	8	22	25	16	9	13	57	46	57	+11
10	Real Sociedad	38	11	5	3	32	17	3	7	9	15	26	14	12	12	47	43	54	+4
11	Real Betis	38	8	3	8	23	26	6	4	9	24	32	14	7	17	47	58	49	-11
12	Real Valladolid	38	10	4	5	22	16	3	5	11	13	28	13	9	16	35	44	48	-9
13	Atlético Madrid	38	8	7	4	37	18	4	3	12	17	32	12	10	16	54	50	46	+4
14	Real Oviedo	38	8	5	6	21	20	3	7	9	20	37	11	12	15	41	57	45	-16
15	Racing Santander	38	6	5	8	22	23	4	7	8	19	30	10	12	16	41	53	42	-12
16	CD Alavés	38	10	4	5	25	17	1	3	15	11	46	11	7	20	36	63	40	-27
17	CF Extremadura	38	8	4	7	17	22	1	8	10	10	31	9	12	17	27	53	39	-26
18	Villarreal CF	38	6	6	7	29	27	2	6	11	18	36	8	12	18	47	63	36	-16
19	CD Tenerife	38	4	9	6	25	29	3	4	12	16	34	7	13	18	41	63	34	-22
20	UD Salamanca	38	7	4	8	22	25	0	2	17	7	41	7	6	25	29	66	27	-37

early January to late May, there was barely a word of criticism hurled in his direction by the end of the season. After all, the facts were plain. He had been the Barcelona coach for two seasons and the team had won the championship - by some distance - on both occasions.

Some Catalan diehards still muttered under their breath that Barcelona were no longer a true representation of their region. The too-many-foreigners argument was irrefutable, especially as Van Gaal had gradually set up his own little Ajax old-boys colony at the club. The mid-season arrival of the De Boer twins, Frank and Ronald, raised the number of Dutch players on the Barça payroll to eight, meaning that more often than not Dutchmen outnumbered Spaniards, let alone Catalans, in Van Gaal's chosen starting line-up.

It would be unfair to say the De Boers' arrival merely coincided with Barcelona's resurgence in form because they did add something to the side, especially Frank, in defence. But much more influential to the team's dash up the table was the return from long-term injury of local hero Josep 'Pep' Guardiola. While his replacement as the team's midfield organiser, the youngster Xavi, had done his best (and it was he who saved Van Gaal with the winning goal in Valladolid), it was only after the return of Guardiola that Barça really began to function in a

manner commensurate with the sum of their parts. With Guardiola as the on-field governor of operations, Barcelona became a team. And a very good team, too. In December they had been down in ninth place but in Centenary Year they piled the victories one on top of the other and steadily increased their lead over the chasing pack until they were safely out of range, finally securing the title with three fixtures still to complete. Among the victories came special performances, like the ritual slaying of Real Madrid at the Nou Camp (3-0, two goals for Real old boy Luis Enrique) and a near-perfect display against Deportivo (4-0, four different scorers). Barça also won away in places where they usually struggle - San Sebastián, Tenerife - and they showed character as well as great skill and entertainment in lifting their 16th Spanish title.

Joy for Barcelona inevitably means pain for Real Madrid, and that was certainly the case in 1998/99. Real ultimately achieved their minimum objective, which was to finish as runners-up and claim the second automatic Champions' League berth, but the journey that took them there was long, winding and littered with obstacles. It was a season of great stress at the Bernabeu, with the bad news far outweighing the good and hardly a week going by without some internal crisis or another filling the newspapers.

The scene was set by Real president Lorenzo Sanz's decision to sack European Cup-winning coach Jupp Heynckes. Ex-Real defender José Antonio Camacho was hired as a replacement but he lasted a mere 22 days in the hot seat before deciding that it was not the place for him. So, in came Guus Hiddink, the man who had steered Holland to the World Cup semi-finals in France. He inherited the bulk of Heynckes' team, which meant that he was also left with a rather shambolic defence and a mutinous dressing-room. Real got off to a reasonable start, both in the league and in Europe, but troubles lurked around the corner, and with the defeats beginning to stack up and the white handkerchiefs being waved, Hiddink's position became perilous.

The nadir of Real's season came in January when they were destroyed 4-0 by Deportivo in La Coruña. Spanish television relayed post-match pictures of a broken team.

The players were almost queueing up to bad-mouth each other, with Seedorf, Mijatovic, Iván Campo and Hierro all voicing their opinions in no uncertain terms. A few weeks later Real were thrashed again, in Barcelona, and when that was followed by a 0-1 defeat in the Bernabeu against Athletic Bilbao, Hiddink's time had come.

At first Real wanted to recall their 1996/97 championship-winning coach, Fabio Capello, but he refused to take charge until the end of the season. That was no good to president Sanz, who then made a move for another ex-Real coach, Welshman John Toshack, at the time under contract to Turkish club Besiktas. Unlike Capello, Toshack was happy to make a swift return to the Bernabeu, but although he said all the right words to the attendant (and sceptical) media on his arrival, he was unable to provide the quick fix the team needed. The club's Champions' League defence ended ignominiously at the hands of

DOMESTIC CUP 98/99

THIRD ROUND
Levante UD v CF Extremadura 0-0; 0-0
(0-0; Levante UD on pens.)
Sporting Gijón v Real Zaragoza 1-1; 2-2
(3-3; Sporting Gijón on away goals)
Sevilla FC v UD Salamanca 0-0; 2-0
(Sevilla FC 2-0)
Málaga CF v Real Valladolid 1-2; 2-3
(Real Valladolid 5-3)
UE Lleida v CA Osasuna 1-1; 0-2
(CA Osasuna 3-1)
Jerez CF v RC Deportivo 1-3; 1-3
(RC Deportivo 6-2)
CD Numancia v Racing Santander 0-1; 1-1
(Racing Santander 2-1)
CD Badajoz v Real Oviedo 3-1; 1-0
(CD Badajoz 4-1)
Talavera CF v Villarreal CF 0-1; 0-3
(Villarreal CF 4-0)
SD Beasáin v Benidorm CD 0-0; 0-1
(Benidorm CD 1-0)
UD Las Palmas v CD Alavés 0-0; 2-2
(2-2; UD Las Palmas on away goals)
UD San Sebastián Reyes v CD Tenerife 2-0; 0-4
(CD Tenerife 4-2)

FOURTH ROUND
Villarreal CF v Sevilla FC 2-2; 3-1
(Villarreal CF 5-3)
UD Las Palmas v Levante UD 0-1; 0-0
(Levante UD 1-0)
CD Tenerife v Benidorm CD 2-2; 0-0
(2-2; Benidorm CD on away goals)
RC Deportivo v Sporting Gijón 1-1; 1-0
(RC Deportivo 2-1)

Racing Santander v CA Osasuna 2-0; 0-1
(Racing Santander 2-1)
Real Valladolid v CD Badajoz 1-1; 1-1
(2-2; Real Valladolid on pens.)

1/8 FINALS
RCD Espanyol v Real Valladolid 4-2; 2-2
(RCD Espanyol 6-4)
RC Celta v RC Deportivo 0-1; 1-1
(RC Deportivo 2-1)
Athletic Bilbao v Racing Santander 2-2; 0-1
(Racing Santander 3-2)
Benidorm CD v FC Barcelona 0-1; 0-3
(FC Barcelona 4-0)
Real Sociedad v Atlético Madrid 1-2; 1-0
(2-2; Atlético Madrid on away goals)
Real Betis v RCD Mallorca 0-1; 0-1
(RCD Mallorca 2-0)
Levante UD v Valencia CF 0-3; 0-1
(Valencia CF 4-0)
Real Madrid v Villarreal CF 2-0; 2-0
(Real Madrid 4-0)

QUARTER-FINALS
Racing Santander 2 (Victor 10, Munitis 14),
Real Madrid 6 (Guti 6, 45, Hierro 32p, Seedorf 36,
Sávio 40, Morientes 90)
Real Madrid 1 (Mijatovic 75), Racing Santander 0
(Real Madrid 7-2)

Atlético Madrid 2 (Correa 58, Juninho 84),
RCD Espanyol 1 (Posse 32)
RCD Espanyol 1 (Pochettino 5),
Atlético Madrid 4 (José Mari 7, 24, 51p, Roberto 64)
(Atlético Madrid 6-2)

RCD Mallorca 1 (Dani 71),
RC Deportivo 1 (Djalminha 55)
RC Deportivo 1 (Turu Flores 12), RCD Mallorca 0
(RC Deportivo 2-1)

FC Barcelona 2 (Kluivert 47, Rivaldo 59),
Valencia CF 3 (López 51, 57, Mendieta 80)
Valencia CF 4 (López 23, 34, Angulo 42,
Mendieta 70p),
FC Barcelona 3 (Rivaldo 58, Oscar 64, De Boer F. 80)
(Valencia CF 7-5)

SEMI-FINALS
Atlético Madrid 0, RC Deportivo 0
RC Deportivo 0, Atlético Madrid 1 (Serena 59)
(Atlético Madrid 1-0)

Valencia CF 6 (López 19, Roche 31, 42, Vlaovic 34,
Angulo 54, Mendieta 71), Real Madrid 0
Real Madrid 2 (Morientes 7, Mijatovic 65p),
Valencia CF 1 (López 87)
(Valencia CF 7-2)

FINAL
26/06/99, Seville
VALENCIA CF 3 López (22, 81), Mendieta (33)
ATLETICO MADRID 0
referee - Díaz Vega

VALENCIA CF - Cañizares; Angloma, Roche, Djukic,
Carboni (Juanfran 89); Farinós, Milla, Vlaovic (Angulo
62), Mendieta; Ilie, López (Björklund 87).

ATLETICO MADRID - Molina; Geli (Roberto 64),
Chamot, Santi, Serena; Aguilera, Valerón, Bejbl (Mena
82); Lardin (Solari 46); Juninho, José Mari.

Dynamo Kiev (or, more precisely, at the feet of Andriy Shevchenko) and, with Barcelona conquering all before them in the championship, Real were left with just the Copa del Rey and the runners-spot in the league to for.

Slowly but surely Toshack did bring his influence to bear and morale was restored. But although the results began to arrive, they were largely down to the individual scoring prowess of the reunited all-Spanish front pairing

NATIONAL TEAM APPEARANCES 98/99

Coach - Javier CLEMENTE; José Antonio CAMACHO	CYP	RUS	ISR	ITA	AUT	SMR	CRO	SMR	Cps	Gls
Santiago CAÑIZARES (18/12/69) - Valencia CF	G	G	G	G84	G	G	G	G	18	-
MICHEL SALGADO (22/10/75) - RC Celta	D		D	D	D	D	D67		7	-
Miguel Angel NADAL (28/07/66) - FC Barcelona	D65								46	2
Rafael ALKORTA (16/09/68) - Athletic Bilbao	D	D	D						54	-
Sergio Barjuán "SERGI" (28/12/71) - FC Barcelona	D	D		D	D	D			41	1
Fernando Ruiz HIERRO (23/03/68) - Real Madrid	M	D	D		D		D85	D	64	21
LUIS ENRIQUE Martínez (08/05/70) - FC Barcelona	M	M86	M			M52		M	43	11
RAUL González (27/06/77) - Real Madrid	M	A88	A90	A	A	A		A67	23	13
Joseba ETXEBERRIA (05/09/77) - Athletic Bilbao	M60	s76	s72	M46	M83	M	M	M	15	6
ALFONSO Pérez (26/09/72) - Real Betis	M39								29	8
Fernando MORIENTES (05/04/76) - Real Madrid	A	s66						A	7	7
Francisco Narváez "KIKO" (26/04/72) - Atlético Madrid	s39	A66	A88						26	5
Santiago EZQUERRO (14/12/76) - Athletic Bilbao	s60								1	-
Guillermo AMOR (04/12/67) - Fiorentina (ITA)	s65								37	4
Carlos AGUILERA (22/05/69) - Atlético Madrid		D76							7	-
Vicente ENGONGA (20/10/65) - RCD Mallorca		M	M	M46		s69	M46		5	1
Bittor ALKIZA (26/10/70) - Athletic Bilbao		M	M	M46					3	1
Francisco Javier DE PEDRO (04/08/73) - Real Sociedad		A30	M72	A64					3	1
Francisco Jémez "PACO" (18/04/70) - Real Zaragoza		s30		D		D	s85		4	-
Jordi LARDIN (04/05/73) - Atlético Madrid		s86							3	-
Antonio Alvarez "ITO" (21/01/75) - Real Betis		s88							1	-
Agustín ARANZABAL (15/03/73) - Real Sociedad		D	s64			D	D		10	-
Ismael URZAIZ (07/10/71) - Athletic Bilbao			s88	A78	A60	A62	A46	s67	8	3
Marcos VALES (05/04/75) - Real Zaragoza			s90						1	-
MARCELINO Elena (26/09/71) - RCD Mallorca				D	D	D	D	D	5	-
Daniel García "DANI" (22/12/74) - RCD Mallorca				s46	s83	s62	A		4	1
Iván HELGUERA (28/03/75) - RCD Espanyol				s46		s76	s68		3	-
Juan Carlos VALERON (17/06/75) - Atlético Madrid				s46	M70	M76			3	-
Juan Ginés SANCHEZ (15/05/72) - RC Celta				s78					1	-
Antonio Jiménez "TONI" (12/10/70) - RCD Espanyol				s84					1	-
Francisco Javier González "FRAN" (14/07/69) - RC Deportivo					M	M			10	2
Josep GUARDIOLA (18/01/71) - FC Barcelona					M	M69	M68	M	27	4
Pedro Manuel MUNITIS (19/06/75) - Racing Santander					s60		s46	s67	3	-
Gaizka MENDIETA (27/03/74) - Valencia CF					s70		s52	s80	3	1
José María Gutiérrez "GUTI" (31/10/76) - Real Madrid							s46		1	-
Julen GUERRERO (07/01/74) - Athletic Bilbao								M80	33	10

of Raúl and Morientes. The defence still remained a big problem, and it was to the club's considerable embarrassment that only a handful of teams at the bottom of the table had a worse goals-against record than theirs. There was another calamity in Galicia when Real were pulverised 5-1 in the league by Celta. Even worse was the 6-0 annihilation by Valencia in the first leg of the Cup semi-final - Real's heaviest defeat since 1953. But a 3-1 win over Deportivo on the final day saved Real's blushes. They had scrambled into second place. What's more, two-goal Raúl had pipped Barça's brilliant Brazilian Rivaldo to become the winner of the *Pichichi* award as the league's top scorer.

Third place went to Mallorca. The islanders were the revelation of the season. They began the campaign by lifting the Spanish Super Cup at the expense of Barcelona and went on to become the most difficult team to beat in the entire championship. Under the astute guidance of their Argentinian coach, Héctor Cúper, Mallorca became a genuine force. Their defence, with goalkeeper Carlos Roa and centre-back Marcelino at its hub, was almost unbreachable. In their first 17 games they conceded a mere eight goals - never more than one in any game - and led the table for an extended period. To go top, of course, required more than just a solid back-line, and Mallorca were blessed with two excellent counter-attacking raiders in Yugoslav winger Jovan Stankovic and former Real Madrid 'reject' striker Dani. Before the season Mallorca had never provided any players to the Spanish national team, but in 1998/99 no fewer than three of them made their international débuts - Dani, Marcelino and, beating them to the punch, 33-year-old midfielder Engonga.

Mallorca also made a big splash in their first season of European competition, reaching the final of the Cup-winners' Cup after knocking out Hearts, Genk, Varteks Varazdin and

holders Chelsea. Lazio were just that little bit too good for them in the final, however.

Spain had a thriving presence in the UEFA Cup, with five teams entered, including InterToto qualifiers Valencia. Atlético Madrid went the furthest, reaching the semi-finals for the second year running, while Celta dropped out in the quarter-finals and both Betis and Real Sociedad exited in round three. Valencia were the last to enter and the first to go out, after a thrilling second-round second-leg encounter with Liverpool. But that was to be a rare blemish for Claudio Ranieri's team during a season in which at last, after many years of unfulfilled promise, they lived up to their potential.

Valencia had a long season and occasionally allowed fatigue to get the better of them. But in the big games they were invariably at their best, with blond skipper Gaizka Mendieta and Argentinian striker Claudio López functioning brilliantly together and supplying a succession of glorious goals. Valencia were the one team that were able to stop Barcelona. They beat them three times in a ten-day period, twice in the Cup and once in the league, and their mauling of Real Madrid in the Cup semi-finals was a night which the spectators in the Mestalla stadium will never forget. Valencia also hit the heights in the final of the Copa del Rey, beating Atlético Madrid 3-0 to win their first trophy in 19 years.

It was ironic that Atlético should be Valencia's victims in that final because it had long been common knowledge that coach Ranieri would be leaving Valencia for Atlético during the summer. Fortunately for the Italian, Valencia's win had no adverse knock-on effect for him because Atlético had already clinched their 1999/2000 UEFA Cup spot the week before. By winning their final league game, 1-0 away at Celta, Atlético paved the way for Valencia

TOP SCORERS

25	RAUL González (Real Madrid)
24	RIVALDO (FC Barcelona)
21	Claudio LOPEZ (Valencia CF)
19	Fernando MORIENTES (Real Madrid)
	Julio César DELY VALDES (Real Oviedo)
17	Savo MILOSEVIC (Real Zaragoza)
	Ismael URZAIZ (Athletic Bilbao)
16	Darko KOVACEVIC (Real Sociedad)
14	TURU FLORES (RC Deportivo)
	Patrick KLUIVERT (FC Barcelona)
	Roy MAKAAY (CD Tenerife)
	Liuboslav PENEV (RC Celta)

NATIONAL TEAM RESULTS 98/99

Date	Opponent		Venue	Score	Scorers
05/09/98	Cyprus (ECQ)	A	Limassol	2-3	Raúl (71), Morientes (85)
23/09/98	Russia	H	Granada	1-0	Alkiza (39)
14/10/98	Israel (ECQ)	A	Tel-Aviv	2-1	Hierro (65), Etxeberria (77)
18/11/98	Italy	A	Salerno	2-2	De Pedro (22), Raúl (81p)
27/03/99	Austria (ECQ)	H	Valencia	9-0	Raúl (5, 16, 47, 73), Urzaiz (29, 45), Hierro (34p), Wetl (76og), Fran (83)
31/03/99	San Marino (ECQ)	A	Serravalle	6-0	Fran (20), Raúl (45, 59, 67), Urzaiz (49), Etxeberria (72)
05/05/99	Croatia	H	Seville	3-1	Engonga (34), Hierro (50p), Dani (84)
05/06/99	San Marino (ECQ)	H	Villarreal	9-0	Hierro (8p), Luis Enrique (22, 71, 75), Etxeberria (24, 45), Raúl (61), Gennari (89og), Mendieta (90)

EUROPEAN CUPS 98/99

CHAMPIONS' CUP
● REAL MADRID
Champions' League
1st match INTER (ITA)
H 2-0 Hierro (79p), Seedorf (90)
Illgner; Panucci, Hierro, Sanchis, Roberto Carlos; Raúl, Redondo, Seedorf, Sávio (Karembeu 89); Mijatovic, Morientes (Jarni 85).

2nd match SPARTAK MOSKVA (RUS)
A 1-2 Raúl (63)
Illgner; Panucci, Hierro, Sanchis, Roberto Carlos; Karembeu (Morientes 80), Seedorf, Redondo; Mijatovic, Raúl, Sávio.

3rd match SK STURM GRAZ (AUT)
H 6-1 Sávio (13, 90), Raúl (22), Jarni (61, 78), Popovic (67og)
Illgner; Panucci, Sanchis, Hierro, Roberto Carlos; Seedorf, Karembeu (Jaime 46), Jarni, Sávio; Raúl (Guti 80), Mijatovic (Suker 74).

4th match SK STURM GRAZ (AUT)
A 5-1 Panucci (8, 61), Mijatovic (34), Seedorf (57), Suker (74)
Illgner; Panucci (Karembeu 77), Hierro, Sanchis, Roberto Carlos; Seedorf (Guti 70), Redondo, Jarni; Raúl, Mijatovic, Sávio (Suker 62).

5th match INTER (ITA)
A 1-3 Seedorf (58)
Illgner; Campo, Sanchis (Suker 88), Sanz, Jaime; Seedorf, Redondo, Roberto Carlos (Jarni 80); Raúl, Sávio; Mijatovic.

6th match SPARTAK MOSKVA (RUS)
H 2-1 Raúl (34), Sávio (66)
Illgner; Campo, Hierro, Sanz; Panucci (Jaime 59), Seedorf, Redondo, Roberto Carlos; Raúl, Mijatovic, Sávio.

Quarter-final DYNAMO KYIV (UKR)
H 1-1 Mijatovic (66)
Illgner; Panucci, Hierro, Sanchis (Campo 57), Roberto Carlos; Guti, Redondo, Seedorf (Sávio 57); Raúl, Mijatovic, Morientes (Suker 76).
A 0-2
Illgner; Panucci, Hierro, Campo, Roberto Carlos; Sanchis (Guti 70), Redondo, Seedorf (Suker 65); Raúl, Jarni (Karembeu 80); Morientes.

● FC BARCELONA
1st match MANCHESTER UNITED (ENG)
A 3-3 Anderson (47), Giovanni (60p), Luis Enrique (71p)
Hesp; Luis Enrique, Reiziger, Abelardo, Sergi; Giovanni (Xavi 68), Cocu, Figo, Rivaldo; Zenden, Anderson.

2nd match BRØNDBY IF (DEN)
H 2-0 Anderson (43, 84)
Hesp; Okunowo (Zenden 74), Abelardo, Cocu (Reiziger 67), Sergi; Giovanni (Xavi 46), Roger, Figo, Luis Enrique; Rivaldo, Anderson.

3rd match FC BAYERN MÜNCHEN (GER)
A 0-1
Hesp; Okunowo, Abelardo, Reiziger, Cocu, Xavi (Oscar 87), Luis Enrique (Zenden 77), Giovanni; Figo, Anderson, Rivaldo.

4th match FC BAYERN MÜNCHEN (GER)
H 1-2 Giovanni (28p)
Hesp; Okunowo, Celades, Abelardo, Sergi; Xavi, Giovanni, Cocu; Figo, Anderson, Rivaldo.

5th match MANCHESTER UNITED (ENG)
H 3-3 Anderson (1), Rivaldo (56, 72)
Hesp; Celades, Okunowo, Reiziger, Sergi; Xavi, Giovanni, Figo, Rivaldo; Zenden, Anderson.

6th match BRØNDBY IF (DEN)
A 2-0 Figo (5), Rivaldo (35)
Hesp; Reiziger, Celades, Okunowo; Xavi, Guardiola, Rivaldo (Roger 64), Sergi; Figo, Anderson (Giovanni 46); Cocu (Cuadrado 88).

● ATHLETIC BILBAO
Qualifying round DINAMO TBILISI (GEO)
A 1-2 Imaz (47)
Etxeberria I.; César, Ferreira, García, Larrazábal; Imaz, Urrutia (Nagore 68), Alkiza, Ezquerro; González (Guerrero 82), Urzaiz (Etxeberria J. 64).
H 1-0 Etxeberria J. (51)
Etxeberria I.; Lacruz, García, Alkorta, Larrazábal; Imaz, Alkiza (José Mari 87), Etxeberria J. (González 82), Guerrero; Urzaiz (Pérez 86).

Champions' League
1st match ROSENBORG BK (NOR)
H 1-1 Etxeberria J. (5)
Etxeberria I.; Imaz, Ríos (Lacruz 46), Alkorta, Larrazábal; García, José Mari (Urrutia 73), González; Guerrero (Urzaiz 67), Etxeberria J., Ezquerro.

2nd match GALATASARAY (TUR)
A 1-2 Urzaiz (17)
Etxeberria I.; Ríos, García, Alkorta, Imaz; Urrutia (Guerrero 85), Alkiza, Larrazábal, Etxeberria J. (González 70); Urzaiz (Lacruz 79), Ezquerro.

3rd match JUVENTUS (ITA)
H 0-0
Etxeberria I.; Lacruz, Alkorta (Ríos 4), García, Larrazábal; Imaz, Urrutia (Pérez 85), Alkiza, Guerrero (Ezquerro 57); Etxeberria J., Urzaiz.

4th match JUVENTUS (ITA)
A 1-1 Guerrero (45)
Etxeberria I.; Ferreira, García, Larrazábal, Lasa (Pérez 71); Imaz (Lacruz 57), Ríos, Alkiza, Guerrero; Etxeberria J., Ezquerro (Urzaiz 66).

5th match ROSENBORG BK (NOR)
A 1-2 Pérez (90)
Etxeberria I.; Felipe, Ríos, Ferreira, Larrazábal (García 46); Imaz, Urrutia (Urzaiz 46), Alkiza, Guerrero (Pérez 61); Etxeberria J., Ezquerro.

6th match GALATASARAY (TUR)
H 1-0 Guerrero (43)
Etxeberria I.; Larraínzar, García, Ferreira, Larrazábal; Felipe, Nagore (César 83), González (Etxeberria J. 76), Guerrero; Pérez (Lasa 74), Ezquerro.

CUP WINNERS' CUP
● RCD MALLORCA
1st round HEART OF MIDLOTHIAN (SCO)
A 1-0 Marcelino (17)
Roa; Olaizola, Marcelino, Siviero, Soler M.; Lauren, Arpón (Niño 87), Engonga, Stankovic (Carreras 84); Dani, López (Carlos 69).
H 1-1 López (48)
Gálvez; Olaizola, Marcelino, Siviero, Soler M.; Lauren, Soler F. (Carreras 86), Stankovic, Arpón (Niño 80); Dani, López (Biagini 82).

EUROPEAN CUPS 98/99 (CONTINUED)

2nd round KRC GENK (BEL)
A 1-1   Dani (55)
         Roa; Olaizola, Marcelino, Siviero, Soler M.; Engonga, Lauren, Stankovic,
         Paunovic (Niño 79); Biagini (Carlos 80), Dani (Carreras 85).
H 0-0   Roa; Olaizola, Marcelino, Siviero, Soler M.; Engonga (Niño 60), Lauren,
         Carreras, Ibagaza (Arpón 78); Biagini (López 90), Dani.

Quarter-final VARTEKS VARAZDIN (CRO)
A 0-0   Roa; Olaizola, Marcelino, Siviero, Soler M.; Lauren, Soler F., Carreras,
         Paunovic; Biagini (López 80), Dani.
H 3-1   Ibagaza (53), Paunovic (56), Dani (75)
         Roa; Olaizola, Marcelino, Siviero, Soler M.; Lauren, Engonga,
         Ibagaza (Soler F. 72), Paunovic; Biagini (Luque 64), Dani (Carlos 83).

Semi-final CHELSEA (ENG)
A 1-1   Dani (32)
         Roa; Olaizola, Siviero, Marcelino, Soler M.; Lauren, Engonga,
         Ibagaza (Carreras 61), Paunovic; Dani, Biagini (Soler F. 84).
H 1-0   Biagini (14)
         Roa; Olaizola, Siviero (Carreras 46), Marcelino, Soler M.; Lauren,
         Engonga, Stankovic (Arpón 79), Paunovic; Dani, Biagini (Soler F. 67).

Final LAZIO (ITA)
A 1-2   Dani (11)
         Roa; Olaizola, Siviero, Marcelino, Soler M.; Lauren, Engonga, Ibagaza,
         Stankovic; Dani, Biagini (Paunovic 72).

UEFA CUP
● ATLÉTICO MADRID
1st round OBILIC BEOGRAD (YUG)
H 2-0   Juninho (15), José Mari (53)
         Molina; Aguilera, Torrisi, Santi, Serena; Mena, Roberto,
         Jugovic (Bejbl 36); Kiko (Correa 88), Juninho (José Mari 46), Lardín.
A 1-0   Kiko (54)
         Molina; Aguilera, Santi, Chamot, Serena (Toni 7); Roberto, Mena,
         Valerón, Lardín (Njegus 75); Kiko, José Mari (Jaro 56).

2nd round CSKA SOFIA (BUL)
A 4-2   Torrisi (40), Kiko (42, 87), Roberto (73)
         Jaro; Chamot, Torrisi, Santi, Serena; Roberto, Jugovic (Toni 76),
         Valerón (Bejbl 71), Lardín; Juninho (Njegus 86), Kiko.
H 1-0   Juninho (45p)
         Jaro; Serena (Ramón 59), Torrisi, Chamot, Toni; Njegus,
         Bejbl (Mena 78), Jugovic, Roberto; Juninho (Correa 65), José Mari.

3rd round REAL SOCIEDAD (ESP)
A 1-2   Juninho (3)
         Molina; Serena, Torrisi, Chamot (Ramón 27), Toni; Njegus (Aguilera 54),
         Mena, Valerón, Jugovic; Juninho (Roberto 66), Kiko.
H 4-1   Jugovic (17, 46p), Santi (94), José Mari (100)
(aet)   Molina; Serena, Santi, Chamot, Toni; Njegus, Jugovic (Bejbl 46), Mena,
         Lardín (Correa 80); Juninho (Roberto 103), José Mari.

Quarter-final ROMA (ITA)
H 2-1   José Mari (13), Roberto (46)
         Molina; Aguilera, Santi, Chamot, Toni (Geli 88); Roberto, Jugovic, Baraja,
         Serena; José Mari (Lardín 71), Juninho.
A 2-1   Aguilera (57), Roberto (89)
         Molina; Aguilera, Santi, Chamot (Ramón 64), Toni; Mena (Njegus 56),
         Baraja (Roberto 56), Jugovic, Serena; Juninho, José Mari.

Semi-final PARMA (ITA)
H 1-3   Juninho (21p)
         Molina; Aguilera, Santi, Chamot, Serena; Roberto (Tevenet 65), Jugovic,
         Juninho, Valerón; Solari, José Mari.
A 1-2   Roberto (62)
         Molina; Geli (Aguilera 54), Santi, Chamot, Toni; Valerón, Mena, Juninho,
         Roberto; Tevenet (Torrisi 66), Lardín (Serena 46).

● RC CELTA
1st round FC ARGES DACIA PITESTI (ROM)
A 1-0   Sánchez (25)
         Dutruel; Míchel Salgado, Cáceres, Djorovic, Josema; Mazinho, Makelele;
         Sánchez, Karpin; Revivo (Tomás 65), Penev (Cadete 76).
H 7-0   Penev (5, 13, 26), Mazinho (16), Sánchez (69), Tomás (78, 89)
         Dutruel; Míchel Salgado, Cáceres, Eggen, Josema; Mazinho (Cadete 46),
         Makelele, Sánchez, Mosotovoi (Bruno Caires 30); Tomás, Penev (Cainzos 55).

2nd round ASTON VILLA (ENG)
H 0-1   Dutruel; Míchel Salgado, Cáceres, Djorovic, Josema (Tomás 62);
         Mazinho, Makelele, Karpin (Cadete 82), Mostovoi; Revivo (Sánchez 46),
         Penev.
A 3-1   Sánchez (26), Mostovoi (33), Penev (48)
         Dutruel; Míchel Salgado, Cáceres, Djorovic, Berges; Makelele, Mazinho,
         Karpin (Tomás 70), Mostovoi; Sánchez (Eggen 58), Penev (Cadete 77).

3rd round LIVERPOOL (ENG)
H 3-1   Mostovoi (49), Karpin (55), Gudelj (90)
         Dutruel; Vales, Cáceres, Djorovic, Tomás; Mazinho, Karpin (Bruno
         Caires 82), Makelele, Mostovoi (Josema 88); Sánchez, Penev (Gudelj 83).
A 1-0   Revivo (56)
         Dutruel; Míchel Salgado, Cáceres, Djorovic, Berges; Mazinho
         (Bruno Caires 85), Makelele, Karpin; Mostovoi, Revivo (Tomás 70),
         Sánchez (Gudelj 76).

Quarter-final OLYMPIQUE MARSEILLE (FRA)
A 1-2   Mostovoi (63)
         Dutruel; Míchel Salgado, Cáceres, Djorovic, Josema (Eggen 67); Vales,
         Mazinho, Karpin, Mostovoi (Tomás 86); Revivo, Penev (Sánchez 62).
H 0-0   Dutruel; Míchel Salgado, Cáceres, Vales (Tomás 74), Djorovic; Makelele,
         Mazinho, Karpin (Sánchez 65), Mostovoi; Revivo, Penev (Gudelj 61).

● REAL BETIS
1st round VEJLE BK (DEN)
A 0-1   Prats; Jaime, Solozábal, Olías; Fernando, Ito, Alexis (Merino 89);
         Finidi, Denílson, Cuéllar, Oli (Gálvez 70).
H 5-0   Iván (1, 20, 87), Finidi (70), Gálvez (71)
         Prats; Jaime, Ureña, Solozábal, Luis; Finidi, Ito, Alexis (Merino 78),
         Denílson (Fernando 85); Oli (Gálvez 60), Iván.

2nd round WILLEM II (HOL)
A 1-1   Alexis (84)
         Prats; Ureña, Solozábal, Olías, Otero; Fernando, Merino, Alexis,
         Ito (Benjamín 60); Finidi, Iván.
H 3-0   Finidi (30), Benjamín (55), Fernando (90)
         Prats; Otero, Ureña, Solozábal, Luis; Finidi, Alexis (Cañas 21), Ito,
         Denílson (Fernando 82); Benjamín, Oli (Cuéllar 60).

(Continued overleaf.)

EUROPEAN CUPS 98/99 (CONTINUED)

3rd round BOLOGNA (ITA)
A 1-4 Benjamín (63)
Prats; Otero, Ureña, Solozábal, Luis; Finidi, Merino, Cañas (Ito 55), Benjamín, Denílson (Alexis 55); Gálvez (Oli 46).
H 1-0 Oli (4)
Prats; Merino, Solozábal (Benjamín 58), Olías, Luis; Finidi, Alexis (Cañas 68), Ito, Cuéllar (Gálvez 62); Oli, Iván.

● **REAL SOCIEDAD**
1st round SPARTA PRAHA (CZE)
A 4-2 Kovacevic (7, 57), Aldeondo (47), De Pedro (80)
Alberto; Fuentes, Loren, Pikabea, Aranzábal; Gómez, Kühbauer, De Pedro, Sá Pinto; Aldeondo (Mutiu 78), Kovacevic (De Paula 89).
H 1-0 Kovacevic (50)
Alberto; Fuentes, Gómez, Loren, Antía; López Rekarte, Jáuregui (Guerrero 46), Sá Pinto (Kühbauer 73), Aranzábal; De Paula (Aldeondo 63), Kovacevic.

2nd round DINAMO MOSKVA (RUS)
A 3-2 Kovacevic (3, 10), De Pedro (35p)
Alberto; López Rekarte, Loren, Antía, Aranzábal; Gómez, Kühbauer, Sá Pinto (Adepoju 46); De Pedro (Gracia 68), Aldeondo (De Paula 83), Kovacevic.
H 3-0 Kovacevic (57, 75), De Paula (69)
Alberto; López Rekarte, Loren, Antía, Aranzábal; Gómez, Kühbauer (Jáuregui 83), Sá Pinto; De Pedro, De Paula (Cvitanovic 72), Kovacevic (Idiákez 79).

3rd round ATLÉTICO MADRID (ESP)
H 2-1 Kovacevic (45), Roberto (85og)
Alberto; López Rekarte, Loren, Antía (Aldeondo 68), Aranzábal (Cvitanovic 76); Jáuregui (Kühbauer 46), Gómez, Sá Pinto, Gracia; De Paula, Kovacevic.
A 1-4 Gracia (50)
(aet) Alberto; López Rekarte, Picabea, Antín, Aranzábal; Guerrero (Adepoju 22), Gómez, Idiákez (Cvitanovic 46), Gracia; Kovacevic, De Paula (Aldeondo 91).

● **VALENCIA CF**
1st round STEAUA BUCURESTI (ROM)
A 4-3 Ilie (11, 24), Angulo (74, 85)
Cañizares; Angulo, Björklund, Roche, Djukic, Carboni; Mendieta, Milla (Farinós 87), Schwarz; López, Ilie (Popescu 68).
H 3-0 Roche (52), López (56), Lucarelli (86)
Cañizares; Angulo, Björklund (Angloma 46), Roche, Djukic, Carboni (Juanfran 79); Mendieta, Milla, Popescu; López, Ilie (Lucarelli 30).

2nd round LIVERPOOL (ENG)
A 0-0
Cañizares; Carboni, Björklund, Djukic, Roche (Soria 84); Angulo, Popescu, Milla (Farinós 81), Mendieta; Ilie (Lucarelli 82), López.
H 2-2 López (45, 90)
Cañizares; Björklund (Farinós 87), Soria, Djukic, Angulo; Mendieta, Schwarz, Popescu, Carboni; López, Ilie (Lucarelli 74).

PLAYERS OF THE SEASON

★ SUPERSTAR PROFILE
RAUL
The teenage prodigy has become a major international star. All the wonderful things that were predicted of Raúl González Blanco when he first came into the Real Madrid side as a scrawny 17-year-old have come true - and then some. He is without question the most talented Spanish footballer since Emilio Butragueño. He combines subtle technique with explosive shooting, but the quality which makes him great is his utter unpredictability. Although his left foot is stronger than his right, he can turn defenders both ways, and he is brilliant at disguising his intentions, chipping the ball over the 'keeper when it looks as if he is about to blast it, or curling a 25-yarder into the top corner when all around him are expecting a simple sideways lay-off. And on top of all this Raúl is a real charmer. While his team-mates go sounding off to the newspapers, he always keeps his mouth shut. He is not interested in controversy. Football is his means of communication, and in 1998/99 he played better than ever, both for Real and Spain. He became the first Spaniard for seven years to win the Primera Division top-scorer trophy and he also scored ten goals for his country, seven of them within the space of four days. As he grows older, his responsibilities will increase and the pressure of being a superstar will become more burdensome to him, but for now, in Spain, Raúl is simply the best.

PLAYERS OF THE SEASON (CONTINUED)

RIVALDO

Barcelona coach Louis van Gaal is not a man who readily accepts disobedeince from his players. Those who seek to stray from his rigidly constructed game-plan usually end up on the bench or the transfer-list. But with Rivaldo the Dutchman has been forced to admit that different rules apply. Cramping the Brazilian's style is simply not an option. He is a foot-balling free spirit, a ball-player, a match-winner. Shackling him to a set rôle would be foolhardy. And so it came to pass that, for the second season in a row, Rivaldo's raw individual brilliance propelled Barcelona to another Spanish title triumph. He scored 24 goals - just one fewer than Raúl - and dazzled spectators with his mind-blowing skills everywhere he went. In the summer he was the top marksman at the Copa América, scoring twice in the final to help Brazil retain the trophy and, in the eyes of many, eclipsing team-mate Ronaldo as the world's greatest player.

CARLOS ROA

"There is more to life than football" is a phrase often employed by coaches and managers to try to soften the impact of a disastrous defeat. However, when Carlos Roa, Argentina's 1998 World Cup goal-keeper, said it, he meant it. The 1998/99 season was the last of his professional career. He decided that football was incompatible with his religious beliefs and chose to return to Argentina to become a preacher. He certainly bowed out in style, performing heroics for Mallorca as the island club strode from one success to another in the Spanish league and the European Cup-winners' Cup. Defence was Mallorca's strong point, and Roa was the outstanding component, making key saves in almost every match. He conceded just 29 goals in 35 league games and six in eight in the Cup-winners' Cup. All 'keepers make mistakes, though, and unfortunately Roa made his biggest of all to allow Christian Vieri to open the scoring for Lazio at Villa Park. Perhaps his mind was on other things...

CLAUDIO LOPEZ

Claudio López did not play in the 1999 Copa América, and for good reason. He had no holiday the previous summer, going straight from the World Cup to help Valencia battle their way successfully through the InterToto competition and then going on to display wonderful stamina throughout a season in which he scored a total of 36 goals in all competitions. The Argentinian was courted by just about every top European club, with Barcelona not surprisingly leading the race for his signature after he hit three doubles against the Catalans in ten days in the early spring. He also struck twice in the final of the Copa del Rey to bring Valencia their first trophy in almost two decades. Many anticipated that would be his final game for Valencia but after looking set for a move to Lazio he decided to stay on and help Valencia in the Champions' League. His main assets are speed and a ferocious left-foot shot. When the two work in combination, the sight is invariably spectacular.

FERNANDO MORIENTES

Although his friend and team-mate Raúl was Real Madrid's top scorer in 1998/99, it was the consistent marksmanship of Fernando Morientes in the final weeks of the season that enabled Real to finish second to Barcelona and qualify automatically for a third successive season in the UEFA Champions' League. Morientes barely got a look-in during Guus Hiddink's six months in charge (foreigners Mijatovic, Sávio and Suker were all in competition with him), but under John Toshack he seized his opportunity brilliantly, scoring 15 goals in 15 games, most of them in doubles. That form also earned him a recall to the Spanish national team, where, given his impressive goal-a-game record, he is surely entitled to an extended run from new Spanish coach José Antonio Camacho.

to take the fourth Champions' League place, and that, in turn, secured for them the 'Cup-winners' place in the UEFA Cup, irrespective of the outcome in the final.

The Cup final defeat was the last stand for Radomir Antic, who had been asked to return to Atlético following the mid-season sacking of Arrigo Sacchi. The ex-Milan and Italy boss had become so disillusioned with his lack of success that he decided to retire from football altogether. Atlético were even worse off without him and were heading for relegation until they finally bucked their ideas up and won their last two games. The first of those was particularly welcome as it came against city rivals Real (3-1) and brought Atlético their first 'derby' victory since 1992.

The shuffling of places at the top of the table during the closing weeks of the season made for an interesting dénouement. In the final countdown most teams were happy with what they got, but the obvious exception were Celta, who, had they not lost their final match at home to Atlético, would have taken one of the Champions' League places. It was particularly sad because not only had the team from Vigo been unbeaten in all their previous home games, they had also proved one of the league's main attractions, playing scintillating pass-and-move football that earned them several astonishing victories, both in domestic and European competition. Celta's leading players - Mazinho, Karpin, Mostovoi and Míchel Salgado - all earned fulsome praise, as did their young coach, Víctor Fernández.

One team which failed miserably to live up to pre-season expectations was Betis. They spent more money than any other Spanish club in their summer recruitment drive, with most of that going on one player, Brazilian trick-merchant Denílson, who was signed from FC São Paulo for a world-record fee. He turned out to be a massive flop, failing to score for six months and losing his place in the Brazilian national team in the process. It was not his fault, however, that Betis went through four different coaches in his first few weeks at the club before they eventually settled down in mid-table under the last of that quartet, Javier Clemente.

Clemente arrived at Betis 47 days after being forced to resign his position as the coach of the national team. 99 Spaniards out of 100 had wanted him to depart after the fiasco of the World Cup in France, but miraculously he hung on in there, only to stoop to a new embarrassing low when his team lost their opening Euro 2000 qualifier 3-2 in...Cyprus. Even Clemente could not withstand the hail of criticism that rained down on him after that catastrophe, so he decided to jump before he was pushed, leaving behind a record of 36 wins, 19 draws and just six defeats in his six-year tenure - the second-longest in the history of the Spanish national team.

The Spanish federation approached veteran Luis Aragonés initially but he turned them down so they headed to the other end of the age scale and appointed José Antonio Camacho, the man who had been a success with Espanyol but who had barely lasted five minutes at Real Madrid.

Camacho was to be a breath of fresh air for Spain. The stifling tactics of the Clemente régime were gone, and with the old guard being supplemented by a steady stream of promising newcomers, not all of them in the first flush of youth, Spain began not only to rescue their European Championship qualifying campaign but also to play the sort of free-flowing, swashbuckling football that had not been seen from them for years.

Four Euro 2000 fixtures yielded 12 points and an amazing 26 goals, with just one conceded. The obvious highlight was the 9-0 destruction of Austria in Valencia - a night when the Spaniards in general, and Raúl in particular, ran riot against startled, disbelieving opponents. San Marino also came in for the same treatment, not once but twice, and by the end of the season the misadventure in Cyprus had been well and truly forgotten. Spain, seemed, were on a direct line towards the Euro 2000 finals, and with hopes rising that the senior team might even go on to emulate the country's successful junior sides - European Under-21 and World Youth champions - and lift a major international trophy.

INTERNATIONAL HONOURS

World Cup Finals appearances: 1934, 1950 (4th), 1962, 1966, 1978, 1982 (2nd phase), 1986 (qtr-finals), 1990 (2nd round), 1994 (qtr-finals), 1998

European Championship appearances: 1964 (Winners), 1968, 1976, 1980, 1984 (runners-up), 1988, 1996

European Club Competitions

Champions' Cup	Real Madrid (1956, 1957, 1958, 1959, 1960, 1966, 1998)
	FC Barcelona (1992)
Cup-winners' Cup	Atlético Madrid (1962)
	FC Barcelona (1979, 1982, 1989, 1997)
	Valencia CF (1980)
	Real Zaragoza (1995)
Fairs' Cup	FC Barcelona (1958, 1960, 1966)
	Valencia CF (1962, 1963)
	Real Zaragoza (1964)
UEFA Cup	Real Madrid (1985, 1986)
Super Cup	Valencia CF (1981)
	FC Barcelona (1992, 1998)
World Club Cup	Real Madrid (1960, 1998)
	Atlético Madrid (1974)

CD ALAVES

CLUB DIRECTORY

Club Deportivo Alavés
Paseo Cervantes s/n
01007 Vitoria
tel - (945) 131018
fax - (945) 232532
Year of Formation - 1921
President - Gonzalo Antón Sanjuán
Manager - Miguel Angel Pascual
Coach - José Manuel Esnal "Mané"
Stadium - Mendizorroza (19,900)

APPEARANCES 98/99

	P	Ap	(s)	Gls
Alberto ALBISTEGUI	D	14	(5)	
Alejandro Fernández "ALEX"	M		(4)	
ALFONSO Vera	M	11	(5)	
Jorge AZKOITIA	M	8	(16)	1
Ibón BEGOÑA	M	30		1
Alberto BELSUE	D	22		
José Ignacio BERRUET	D	31		
Nicola BERTI (ITA)	M		(8)	1
Manuel CANABAL	A	23	(7)	5
Hermes Aldo DESIO (ARG)	M	36		3
Ruúl GAÑAN	D	4	(3)	
GERARD López	M	26	(3)	7
ISMAEL López	A		(2)	
José Tomás "JOSETE"	D	9	(6)	
Antonio KARMONA	D	38		
Enrique Burgos "KIKE"	G	20		
MAGNO Mocelin (BRA)	A	16	(13)	3
Angel MORALES	M	4	(2)	
PABLO Gómez	M	34		5
Santiago REVILLA	A		(7)	
Iván ROCHA (BRA)	D	17	(7)	
Julio SALINAS	A	17	(5)	4
Pedro Andrés SANCHEZ (ARG)	A	15	(3)	1
Arturo Igoroín "SIVORI"	A	25	(11)	5
Alfonso SUBERO	G	18		

LEAGUE RESULTS 1998/99

29/08/98	Real Betis	H	0-0	
13/09/98	Real Oviedo	A	0-1	
20/09/98	Real Zaragoza	H	1-0	Canabal
27/09/98	CD Tenerife	A	2-1	Canabal, Begoña
04/10/98	Racing Santander	H	0-1	
18/10/98	RCD Mallorca	A	1-2	Desio (p)
25/10/98	CF Extremadura	H	0-1	
31/10/98	Atlético Madrid	A	0-3	
08/11/98	Real Madrid	H	1-1	Canabal
15/11/98	RC Deportivo	A	2-2	Canabal, Pablo (p)
21/11/98	RC Celta	H	2-0	Gerard, Sivori
29/11/98	Villarreal CF	A	0-2	
06/12/98	Valencia CF	H	0-1	
13/12/98	Real Valladolid	A	0-3	
20/12/98	UD Salamanca	H	1-0	Azkoitia
03/01/99	FC Barcelona	A	1-7	Pablo (p)
10/01/99	RCD Espanyol	H	1-1	Pablo (p)
17/01/99	Athletic Bilbao	H	1-2	Canabal
24/01/99	Real Sociedad	A	1-2	Sivori
30/01/99	Real Betis	A	0-1	
07/02/99	Real Oviedo	H	2-2	Gerard, Desio
14/02/99	Real Zaragoza	A	1-1	Gerard
21/02/99	CD Tenerife	H	3-1	Magno, Pablo (p), Berti
28/02/99	Racing Santander	A	0-2	
07/03/99	RCD Mallorca	H	2-0	Salinas 2
14/03/99	CF Extremadura	A	0-1	
21/03/99	Atlético Madrid	H	2-0	Desio, Gerard
04/04/99	Real Madrid	A	2-3	Pablo (p), Sivori
11/04/99	RC Deportivo	H	2-1	Sivori, Magno
18/04/99	RC Celta	A	1-1	Sánchez
25/04/99	Villarreal CF	H	2-1	Gerard, Sivori
01/05/99	Valencia CF	A	0-5	
09/05/99	Real Valladolid	H	2-0	Gerard 2
16/05/99	UD Salamanca	A	0-1	
22/05/99	FC Barcelona	H	1-4	Salinas
30/05/99	RCD Espanyol	A	0-3	
13/06/99	Athletic Bilbao	A	0-5	
20/06/99	Real Sociedad	H	2-1	Salinas, Magno

ATHLETIC BILBAO

CLUB DIRECTORY

Athletic Club
Alameda Mazarredo 23
48009 Bilbao
tel - (944) 240877
fax - (944) 233324
Year of Formation - 1898
President - José María Arrate
Manager - Fernando Lamikiz
Coach - Luis Fernandez
Stadium - San Mamés (46,223)

MAJOR HONOURS
League Championship - (8) 1930, 1931, 1934, 1936, 1943, 1956, 1983, 1984.
Domestic Cup - (23) 1903, 1904, 1910, 1911, 1914, 1915, 1916, 1921, 1923, 1930, 1931, 1932, 1933, 1943, 1944, 1945, 1950, 1955, 1956, 1958, 1969, 1973, 1984.

APPEARANCES 98/99

		P	Ap	(s)	Gls
Bittor ALKIZA	M	32	(5)		
Rafael ALKORTA	D	15		1	
Juan Antonio Pérez "BOLO"	A		(1)		
CESAR Fernández	M		(1)		
Imanol ETXEBERRIA	G	37			
Joseba ETXEBERRIA	A	29	(7)	6	
Santiago EZQUERRO	A	28	(10)	6	
FELIPE Guréndez	M	23	(4)	1	
Francisco FERREIRA	D	26		2	
Carlos GARCIA	M	25	(3)	1	
Javier GONZALEZ	M	12	(18)	1	
Julen GUERRERO	M	28	(8)	8	
Andoni IMAZ	M	11	(2)	1	
JOSE MARI García	M	7	(3)	2	
Jesús LACRUZ	D	23	(6)	1	
Iñigo LARRAINZAR	D	14			
Aitor LARRAZABAL	D	24	(5)	2	
Mikel LASA	D	4	(11)		
Domingo NAGORE	M	7	(2)		
Jorge PEREZ	M	1	(8)		
Roberto RIOS	D	15	(4)	1	
Josu URRUTIA	M	26		1	
Ismael URZAIZ	A	28	(8)	17	
Juan José VALENCIA	G	1			
Francisco Javier YESTE	A	2	(6)		

LEAGUE RESULTS 1998/99

30/08/98	Real Zaragoza	A	0-2	
12/09/98	Racing Santander	H	2-0	Imaz, Urzaiz
20/09/98	CF Extremadura	A	1-0	Urzaiz
26/09/98	Real Madrid	H	2-3	Urzaiz 2
04/10/98	RC Celta	A	2-3	Etxeberria J., Urzaiz
17/10/98	Valencia CF	H	2-0	Urzaiz, Guerrero
25/10/98	UD Salamanca	A	1-2	Urzaiz
31/10/98	RCD Espanyol	H	2-2	Etxeberria J., García
08/11/98	Real Sociedad	A	1-3	Larrazábal (p)
15/11/98	Real Oviedo	H	3-5	Urzaiz, Lacruz, Ezquerro
20/11/98	CD Tenerife	A	1-0	og (Alexis)
29/11/98	RCD Mallorca	H	1-0	Urzaiz
05/12/98	Atlético Madrid	A	0-0	
13/12/98	RC Deportivo	H	2-1	Etxeberria J., Urzaiz
20/12/98	Villarreal CF	A	1-0	Urzaiz
03/01/99	Real Valladolid	H	2-1	Ferreira, Urzaiz
09/01/99	FC Barcelona	A	2-4	Urzaiz, Guerrero
17/01/99	CD Alavés	A	2-1	Alkorta, Ezquerro
23/01/99	Real Betis	H	0-0	
30/01/99	Real Zaragoza	H	2-0	Etxeberria J., Guerrero
07/02/99	Racing Santander	A	0-2	
14/02/99	CF Extremadura	H	0-0	
20/02/99	Real Madrid	A	1-0	Ezquerro
27/02/99	RC Celta	H	0-0	
07/03/99	Valencia CF	A	1-4	Urzaiz
14/03/99	UD Salamanca	H	1-0	Ríos
20/03/99	RCD Espanyol	A	1-1	Urzaiz
04/04/99	Real Sociedad	H	0-0	
11/04/99	Real Oviedo	A	0-0	
18/04/99	CD Tenerife	H	2-0	Ezquerro, Urzaiz (p)
25/04/99	RCD Mallorca	A	1-6	Larrazábal (p)
02/05/99	Atlético Madrid	H	1-2	Guerrero
09/05/99	RC Deportivo	A	1-1	Guerrero
16/05/99	Villarreal CF	H	2-0	Guerrero, Ezquerro
23/05/99	Real Valladolid	A	3-0	Guerrero, Felipe, José Mari (p)
29/05/99	FC Barcelona	H	1-3	Ferreira
13/06/99	CD Alavés	H	5-0	José Mari, Etxeberria J., González, Urzaiz, og (Josete)
20/06/99	Real Betis	A	4-1	Ezquerro, Etxeberria J., Guerrero, Urzaiz (p)

ATLETICO MADRID

CLUB DIRECTORY

Club Atlético de Madrid
Paseo Virgen del Puerto 67, 28005 Madrid
tel - (913) 664707   fax - (913) 669811
Year of Formation - 1903
President - Jesús Gil y Gil
Manager - Miguel Angel Gil Marín
Coach - Arrigo Sacchi; Carlos Aguiar; Radomir Antic
(99/00 - Claudio Ranieri)
Stadium - Vicente Calderón (57,500)

MAJOR HONOURS
League Championship - (9) 1940, 1941, 1950,
1951, 1966, 1970, 1973, 1977, 1996.
Domestic Cup - (9) 1960, 1961, 1965, 1972,
1976, 1985, 1991, 1992, 1996.
European Cup-winners' Cup - (1) 1962.
World Club Cup - (1) 1974.

APPEARANCES 98/99

		P	Ap	(s)	Gls
Carlos AGUILERA	D	27	(1)		1
Rubén BARAJA	M	7	(1)		1
Radek BEJBL (CZE)	M	10	(4)		
José Antonio CHAMOT (ARG)	D	33			1
Fernando Edgardo CORREA (URU)	A	11	(10)		8
Quinton FORTUNE (SAF)	A	2			
GASPAR Gálvez	D		(2)		
Delfín GELI	D	4	(2)		
Juan Antonio GONZALEZ (URU)	A	7	(1)		2
Pedro Luis JARO	G		(2)		
JOSE MARI Romero	A	33	(4)		9
Vladimir JUGOVIC (YUG)	M	15	(2)		3
Oswaldo Giroldo Júnior					
"JUNINHO" (BRA)	M	20	(12)		8
Francisco Narváez "KIKO"	A	10	(1)		4
Jordi LARDIN	A	18	(3)		2
Lorenzo del Pino "LOREN"	A	1			
Oscar Alcides MENA (ARG)	M	19	(10)		2
José Francisco MOLINA	G	38			
Zoran NJEGUS (YUG)	M	8	(7)		1
RAMON González	D	3	(3)		
ROBERTO Fresnedoso	M	19	(11)		4
Santiago Denia "SANTI"	D	29	(1)		
Michele SERENA (ITA)	D	35			3
Santiago Hernán SOLARI (ARG)	M	5	(7)		1
Luis García TEVENET	A		(5)		
Antonio Muñoz "TONI"	D	16	(6)		
Stefano TORRISI (ITA)	D	15	(2)		1
Juan Carlos VALERON	M	26	(4)		3
Giorgio VENTURIN (ITA)	M	7	(4)		

LEAGUE RESULTS 1998/99

29/08/98	Valencia CF	A	0-1	
12/09/98	UD Salamanca	H	2-0	Jugovic (p), Kiko
20/09/98	RCD Espanyol	A	1-1	Kiko
26/09/98	Real Sociedad	H	4-1	Roberto, Kiko, Lardín (p), Correa
04/10/98	Real Oviedo	A	1-3	Juninho
17/10/98	CD Tenerife	H	2-0	Juninho (p), Roberto
25/10/98	RCD Mallorca	A	0-4	
31/10/98	CD Alavés	H	3-0	José Mari, Torrisi, Correa
08/11/98	RC Deportivo	H	1-1	José Mari
15/11/98	Villarreal CF	A	1-2	Juninho (p)
21/11/98	Real Valladolid	H	6-1	Mena, Jugovic, Njegus, Correa, Kiko, José Mari
28/11/98	FC Barcelona	A	1-0	Jugovic (p)
05/12/98	Athletic Bilbao	H	0-0	
12/12/98	Real Betis	A	0-0	
20/12/98	Real Zaragoza	H	0-0	
03/01/99	Racing Santander	A	3-2	Correa, José Mari, Chamot
10/01/99	CF Extremadura	H	5-0	Correa, Serena, Aguilera, Roberto, Valerón
17/01/99	Real Madrid	A	2-4	Juninho, Correa
24/01/99	RC Celta	H	2-1	Serena, Correa
30/01/99	Valencia CF	H	1-2	José Mari
07/02/99	UD Salamanca	A	1-2	Correa (p)
13/02/99	RCD Espanyol	H	1-2	José Mari
21/02/99	Real Sociedad	A	2-3	Juninho, Serena
27/02/99	Real Oviedo	H	0-0	
07/03/99	CD Tenerife	A	0-1	
13/03/99	RCD Mallorca	H	1-2	José Mari
21/03/99	CD Alavés	A	0-2	
03/04/99	RC Deportivo	A	1-1	Valerón
11/04/99	Villarreal CF	H	2-2	Roberto, Juninho
17/04/99	Real Valladolid	A	0-1	
25/04/99	FC Barcelona	H	1-1	Valerón
02/05/99	Athletic Bilbao	A	2-1	Juninho, Mena
09/05/99	Real Betis	H	2-3	González, Baraja
16/05/99	Real Zaragoza	A	0-2	
23/05/99	Racing Santander	H	1-1	González
30/05/99	CF Extremadura	A	1-2	José Mari
12/06/99	Real Madrid	H	3-1	José Mari, Lardín, Juninho
20/06/99	RC Celta	A	1-0	Solari

FC BARCELONA

CLUB DIRECTORY

Fútbol Club Barcelona
Arístides Maillol s/n, 08028 Barcelona
tel - (934) 963600   fax - (934) 112219
Year of Formation - 1899
President - Josep Lluís Núñez Clemente
Manager - Jaume Parés
Coach - Louis van Gaal
Stadium - Camp Nou (112,000)

MAJOR HONOURS
League Championship - (16) 1929, 1945, 1948,
1949, 1952, 1953, 1959, 1960, 1974, 1985,
1991, 1992, 1993, 1994, 1998, 1999.
Domestic Cup - (24) 1910, 1912, 1913, 1920,
1922, 1925, 1926, 1928, 1942, 1951, 1952,
1953, 1957, 1959, 1963, 1968, 1971, 1978,
1981, 1983, 1988, 1990, 1997, 1998.
European Champions' Cup - (1) 1992.
European Cup-winners' Cup - (4)
1979, 1982, 1989, 1997.
Fairs' Cup - (3) 1958, 1960, 1966.
European Super Cup - (2) 1992, 1998.

APPEARANCES 98/99

	P	Ap	(s)	Gls
ABELARDO Fernández	D	28	(2)	1
ANDERSON da Silva (BRA)	A	4	(20)	6
Francesc ARNAU	G	1		
Winston BOGARDE (HOL)	D		(1)	
Albert CELADES	M	11	(5)	2
Dragan CIRIC (YUG)	M		(5)	
Philip COCU (HOL)	M	36		12
Frank DE BOER (HOL)	D	19		2
Ronald DE BOER (HOL)	M	11	(2)	
Luís Filipe Madeira FIGO (POR)	M	34		7
GIOVANNI Silva (BRA)	M	9	(5)	2
Josep GUARDIOLA	M	21	(1)	1
Ruud HESP (HOL)	G	37		
Patrick KLUIVERT (HOL)	A	35		14
LUIS ENRIQUE Martínez	M	26		11
Miguel Angel NADAL	D	1	(1)	
Gbenga Samuel OKUNOWO (NIG)	D	8	(6)	
OSCAR García	M	1	(5)	2
Mauricio PELLEGRINO (ARG)	D	16	(7)	
Michael REIZIGER (HOL)	D	24	(2)	
RIVALDO Vítor Barbosa Ferreira (BRA)	M	37		24
ROGER García	M	1	(5)	
Sergio Barjuán "SERGI"	D	34	(1)	
Xavier Hernández "XAVI"	M	16	(1)	1
Boudewijn ZENDEN (HOL)	M	8	(17)	

LEAGUE RESULTS 1998/99

30/08/98	Racing Santander	A	0-0	
12/09/98	CF Extremadura	H	1-0	Figo
19/09/98	Real Madrid	A	2-2	Kluivert, Anderson
26/09/98	RC Celta	H	2-2	Kluivert 2
03/10/98	Valencia CF	A	3-1	og (Schwarz), Rivaldo, Anderson
17/10/98	UD Salamanca	H	1-1	Cocu
25/10/98	RCD Espanyol	A	2-1	Kluivert, Giovanni (p)
31/10/98	Real Sociedad	H	4-1	Rivaldo 2, Anderson 2
08/11/98	Real Oviedo	A	1-2	Rivaldo
15/11/98	CD Tenerife	H	4-1	Cocu 2, Rivaldo, Anderson
21/11/98	RCD Mallorca	A	0-1	
28/11/98	Atlético Madrid	H	0-1	
05/12/98	RC Deportivo	A	1-2	Rivaldo (p)
13/12/98	Villarreal CF	H	1-3	Giovanni
20/12/98	Real Valladolid	A	1-0	Xavi
03/01/99	CD Alavés	H	7-1	Figo, Luis Enrique 2, Rivaldo 2, Oscar 2
09/01/99	Athletic Bilbao	H	4-2	Luis Enrique, Cocu, Rivaldo 2
17/01/99	Real Betis	A	3-0	Figo, Luis Enrique, Guardiola
24/01/99	Real Zaragoza	H	3-1	Cocu, Rivaldo 2
31/01/99	Racing Santander	H	3-2	og (Merino), De Boer F., Cocu
07/02/99	CF Extremadura	A	2-1	Luis Enrique, Kluivert
14/02/99	Real Madrid	H	3-0	Luis Enrique 2, Rivaldo
21/02/99	RC Celta	A	0-0	
27/02/99	Valencia CF	H	2-4	Kluivert 2
07/03/99	UD Salamanca	A	4-1	Figo, Luis Enrique, Kluivert, Anderson
14/03/99	RCD Espanyol	H	3-0	Rivaldo 2 (1p), Kluivert
21/03/99	Real Sociedad	A	2-0	Cocu 2
04/04/99	Real Oviedo	H	3-1	Rivaldo 3 (2p)
10/04/99	CD Tenerife	A	3-2	Cocu, Rivaldo, Celades
17/04/99	RCD Mallorca	H	2-1	De Boer F., Kluivert
25/04/99	Atlético Madrid	A	1-1	Abelardo
02/05/99	RC Deportivo	H	4-0	Kluivert, Figo, Luis Enrique, Rivaldo
09/05/99	Villarreal CF	A	3-2	Kluivert, Cocu, Rivaldo
15/05/99	Real Valladolid	H	1-1	Luis Enrique
22/05/99	CD Alavés	A	4-1	Cocu, Kluivert, Figo, Luis Enrique
29/05/99	Athletic Bilbao	A	3-1	Kluivert, Rivaldo 2 (1p)
13/06/99	Real Betis	H	4-1	Cocu, Rivaldo (p), Figo, Celades
20/06/99	Real Zaragoza	A	0-2	

REAL BETIS

Real Betis Balompié
Avenida de Heliópolis s/n
41012 Sevilla
tel - (954) 610340
fax - (954) 614774
Year of Formation - 1907
President - Manuel Ruiz de Lopera
Manager - José Antonio González Flores
Coach - Vicente Cantatore; Javier Clemente
(99/00 - Carlos Timoteo Griguol)
Stadium - Benito Villamarín (47,500)

MAJOR HONOURS
League Championship - (1) 1935.
Domestic Cup - (1) 1977.

APPEARANCES 98/99

		P	Ap	(s)	Gls
Humberto ALEXIS Trujillo	M	17	(10)	3	
ALFONSO Pérez	A	8	(3)	3	
Celso Rafael AYALA (PAR)	D	16	(1)	1	
BENJAMIN Zarandona	M	20	(8)	1	
Juan José CAÑAS	M	12	(12)	1	
Angel Manuel CUELLAR	A	3		1	
DENÍLSON de Oliveira (BRA)	M	29	(6)	2	
FERNANDO Sánchez	M	23	(6)	2	
Iulian FILIPESCU (ROM)	D	10		3	
FINIDI George (NIG)	A	36		10	
José GALVEZ	A	9	(10)	5	
Antonio Alvarez "ITO"	M	24	(10)	1	
IVAN Pérez	A	4	(6)	1	
JAIME Quesada	D	8	(4)		
Rafael JAQUES (BRA)	A	2	(2)	1	
JUAN JESUS Cabrera	D	2	(1)	1	
LUIS Fernández	D	33	(3)		
Luis MARQUEZ	M		(3)		
Juan MERINO	D	25	(2)		
Oliverio Jesús Alvarez "OLI"	A	20	(12)	9	
Tomás OLIAS	D	24	(2)		
Jorge OTERO	D	19	(1)		
Antonio PRATS	G	31	(1)		
Roberto SOLAZABAL	D	15			
Juan Antonio González UREÑA	D	13	(3)		
Joaquín Enrique VALERIO	G	7	(1)		

LEAGUE RESULTS 1998/99

29/08/98	CD Alavés	A	0-0	
12/09/98	Real Zaragoza	H	1-3	Oli
20/09/98	Racing Santander	A	0-1	
26/09/98	CF Extremadura	H	1-1	Iván
04/10/98	Real Madrid	A	1-0	Finidi
17/10/98	RC Celta	H	0-3	
25/10/98	Valencia CF	A	1-5	Alexis
31/10/98	UD Salamanca	H	1-0	Oli
07/11/98	RCD Espanyol	A	0-1	
15/11/98	Real Sociedad	H	1-0	Fernando
21/11/98	Real Oviedo	A	1-0	Oli
29/11/98	CD Tenerife	H	1-0	Finidi
05/12/98	RCD Mallorca	A	0-1	
12/12/98	Atlético Madrid	H	0-0	
19/12/98	RC Deportivo	A	2-2	Benjamín, Cuéllar
03/01/99	Villarreal CF	H	4-1	Finidi 2 (2p), Alfonso, Jaques
10/01/99	Real Valladolid	A	3-0	(forfeit; original result 1-2 Oli)
17/01/99	FC Barcelona	H	0-3	
23/01/99	Athletic Bilbao	A	0-0	
30/01/99	CD Alavés	H	1-0	Filipescu
07/02/99	Real Zaragoza	A	2-2	Alfonso 2
14/02/99	Racing Santander	H	1-1	Denílson
20/02/99	CF Extremadura	A	1-2	Gálvez
27/02/99	Real Madrid	H	3-2	Fernando, Canas, Ito
07/03/99	RC Celta	A	0-4	
13/03/99	Valencia CF	H	0-1	
21/03/99	UD Salamanca	A	3-1	Gálvez, Ayala, Alexis (p)
04/04/99	RCD Espanyol	H	0-1	
11/04/99	Real Sociedad	A	0-1	
18/04/99	Real Oviedo	H	5-0	Finidi 2, Filipescu, Denílson, Oli
25/04/99	CD Tenerife	A	2-3	Filipescu, Alexis
02/05/99	RCD Mallorca	H	1-3	Oli
09/05/99	Atlético Madrid	A	3-2	Oli, Finidi 2 (1p)
16/05/99	RC Deportivo	H	0-3	
23/05/99	Villarreal CF	A	4-3	Juan Jesús, Gálvez 2, Finidi
30/05/99	Real Valladolid	H	2-0	Gálvez, Finidi (p)
13/06/99	FC Barcelona	A	1-4	Oli
20/06/99	Athletic Bilbao	H	1-4	Oli

RC CELTA

CLUB DIRECTORY

Real Club Celta de Vigo
Avenida de Balaídos s/n
36210 Vigo (Pontevedra)
tel - (986) 213230
fax - (986) 292040
Year of Formation - 1923
President - Horacio Gómez Araújo
Manager - Alfredo Rodríguez Millares
Coach - Víctor Fernández
Stadium - Balaídos (31,800)

APPEARANCES 98/99

	P	Ap	(s)	Gls
ADRIANO Félix (BRA)	D		(1)	
Rafael BERGES	D	16	(2)	1
BRUNO Ricardo CAIRES (POR)	M	1	(10)	
Fernando Gabriel CACERES (ARG)	D	36		1
Jorge CADETE (POR)	A		(7)	1
Francisco Manuel CAINZOS	D		(2)	
Jordi CRUIJFF (HOL)	A	1	(7)	2
Goran DJOROVIC (YUG)	D	31		1
Richard DUTRUEL (FRA)	G	37		
Dan EGGEN (NOR)	D	7	(9)	
Vladimir GUDELJ (BOS)	A	3	(11)	2
José María López "JOSEMA"	D	14	(4)	
Valeriy KARPIN (RUS)	M	34		7
Claude MAKELELE (FRA)	M	34	(2)	2
Iomar do Nascimento "MAZINHO" (BRA)	M	31		4
MICHEL SALGADO	D	35		4
Aleksandr MOSTOVOI (RUS)	M	30	(3)	6
Liuboslav PENEV (BUL)	A	30	(2)	14
José Manuel PINTO	G	1		
Haim REVIVO (ISR)	A	20	(6)	9
Juan Ginés SANCHEZ	A	24	(12)	13
TOMAS Alberto Hervás	M	17	(18)	2
Oscar VALES	D	16	(8)	

LEAGUE RESULTS 1998/99

30/08/98	RC Deportivo	H	0-0	
12/09/98	Villarreal CF	A	1-1	Penev
20/09/98	Real Valladolid	H	0-0	
26/09/98	FC Barcelona	A	2-2	Míchel Salgado, Mostovoi
04/10/98	Athletic Bilbao	H	3-2	Cáceres, Penev 2 (1p)
17/10/98	Real Betis	A	3-0	Makelele, Sánchez, Cadete
24/10/98	Real Zaragoza	H	2-0	Sánchez 2
31/10/98	Racing Santander	A	2-2	Sánchez, Berges
08/11/98	CF Extremadura	H	5-1	Mostovoi 2, Sánchez, Míchel Salgado, Karpin
14/11/98	Real Madrid	A	2-1	Penev (p), Makelele
21/11/98	CD Alavés	A	0-2	
29/11/98	Valencia CF	H	2-2	Mostovoi, Sánchez
05/12/98	UD Salamanca	A	1-1	Mazinho
13/12/98	RCD Espanyol	H	2-0	Penev, Míchel Salgado
20/12/98	Real Sociedad	A	0-2	
03/01/99	Real Oviedo	H	6-2	Revivo 2, Karpin, Penev 2, Sánchez
10/01/99	CD Tenerife	A	2-0	Karpin, Mazinho
16/01/99	RCD Mallorca	H	4-2	Karpin 2, Djorovic, Revivo
24/01/99	Atlético Madrid	A	1-2	Penev (p)
31/01/99	RC Deportivo	A	1-2	Sánchez
07/02/99	Villarreal CF	H	4-1	Sánchez, Míchel Salgado, Penev (p), Revivo
14/02/99	Real Valladolid	A	1-2	Revivo
21/02/99	FC Barcelona	H	0-0	
27/02/99	Athletic Bilbao	A	0-0	
07/03/99	Real Betis	H	4-0	Gudelj 2, Tomás, Revivo
13/03/99	Real Zaragoza	A	1-0	Revivo
21/03/99	Racing Santander	H	3-0	Mazinho, Sánchez, Mostovoi
04/04/99	CF Extremadura	A	1-1	Sánchez (p)
11/04/99	Real Madrid	H	5-1	Penev 3, Mazinho, Mostovoi
18/04/99	CD Alavés	H	1-1	Sánchez
24/04/99	Valencia CF	A	2-2	Sánchez, Karpin
02/05/99	UD Salamanca	H	1-0	Revivo
09/05/99	RCD Espanyol	A	0-3	
16/05/99	Real Sociedad	H	2-2	Karpin, Tomás
23/05/99	Real Oviedo	A	3-1	Penev 2 (1p), Cruijff
30/05/99	CD Tenerife	H	2-0	Revivo, Cruijff
13/06/99	RCD Mallorca	A	0-2	
20/06/99	Atlético Madrid	H	0-1	

RC DEPORTIVO

Real Club Deportivo de la Coruña
Plaza de Pontevedra 19
15003 La Coruña
tel - (981) 259500
fax - (981) 265919
Year of Formation - 1906
President - Augusto Joaquín César Lendoiro
Manager - Manuel Montiel Duque
Coach - Javier Iruretagoyena
Stadium - Riazor (30,000)

MAJOR HONOURS
Domestic Cup - (1) 1995.

	P	Ap	(s)	Gls
ARMANDO Alvarez	D	22	(5)	
Salaheddine BASSIR (MAR)	A	1	(14)	
Jérôme BONNISSEL (FRA)	D	5	(11)	
Djalma Feitoza "DJALMINHA" (BRA)	M	26	(4)	8
DONATO Gama da Silva	M	17	(14)	1
FLÁVIO da CONCEIÇÃO (BRA)	M	31		1
Francisco Javier González "FRAN"	M	32		6
Mustapha HADJI (MAR)	M	11	(10)	2
JOSE RAMON González	M	1		
Javier LOPEZ	D		(1)	
Javier MANJARIN	A		(10)	
MANUEL PABLO García	D	10	(4)	
MAURO da SILVA (BRA)	M	36		
Noureddine NAYBET (MAR)	D	29	(1)	1
Pedro Miguel Carreiro "PAULETA" (POR)	A	22	(6)	10
Luis Miguel RAMIS	D	9	(1)	
Enrique Fernández ROMERO	D	32	(2)	
Peter RUFAI (NIG)	G	1		
Lionel Sebastián SCALONI (ARG)	M	8	(13)	
Gabriel Francisco SCHURRER (ARG)	D	25	(3)	3
Jacques SONGO'O (CMR)	G	37		
José Oscar "TURU" FLORES (ARG)	A	30	(6)	14
Stéphane ZIANI (FRA)	A	33	(3)	6

30/08/98	RC Celta	A	0-0	
12/09/98	Valencia CF	H	1-0	Schurrer
20/09/98	UD Salamanca	A	1-3	og (Corino)
27/09/98	RCD Espanyol	H	1-0	Turu Flores
04/10/98	Real Sociedad	A	0-2	
18/10/98	Real Oviedo	H	4-0	og (Paulo Bento), Ziani 2, Fran
25/10/98	CD Tenerife	A	1-1	Turu Flores
01/11/98	RCD Mallorca	H	1-1	Djalminha (p)
08/11/98	Atlético Madrid	A	1-1	Djalminha
15/11/98	CD Alavés	H	2-2	Pauleta 2
22/11/98	Villarreal CF	H	2-1	Naybet, Turu Flores
29/11/98	Real Valladolid	A	1-0	Pauleta
05/12/98	FC Barcelona	H	2-1	Hadji, Fran
13/12/98	Athletic Bilbao	A	1-2	Pauleta
19/12/98	Real Betis	H	2-2	Djalminha (p), Schurrer
03/01/99	Real Zaragoza	A	1-3	Ziani
10/01/99	Racing Santander	H	1-2	Pauleta
17/01/99	CF Extremadura	A	2-1	Turu Flores, Fran
24/01/99	Real Madrid	H	4-0	Fran, Tutu Flores 2, Pauleta
31/01/99	RC Celta	H	2-1	Pauleta, Turu Flores
06/02/99	Valencia CF	A	0-0	
13/02/99	UD Salamanca	H	1-0	Turu Flores
21/02/99	RCD Espanyol	A	2-2	Fran, Turu Flores
28/02/99	Real Sociedad	H	0-1	
06/03/99	Real Oviedo	A	2-1	Djalminha, Fran
14/03/99	CD Tenerife	H	2-0	Turu Flores, Djalminha (p)
21/03/99	RCD Mallorca	A	2-1	og (Marcelino), Ziani
03/04/99	Atlético Madrid	H	1-1	Pauleta
11/04/99	CD Alavés	A	1-2	Turu Flores
18/04/99	Villarreal CF	A	2-1	Schurrer, Djalminha
25/04/99	Real Valladolid	H	3-0	Ziani 2, Turu Flores
02/05/99	FC Barcelona	A	0-4	
09/05/99	Athletic Bilbao	H	1-1	Donato
16/05/99	Real Betis	A	3-0	Pauleta 2, Flávio Conceição
23/05/99	Real Zaragoza	H	2-1	Djalminha, Hadji
30/05/99	Racing Santander	A	1-1	Djalminha (p)
12/06/99	CF Extremadura	H	1-1	Turu Flores
20/06/99	Real Madrid	A	1-3	Turu Flores

RCD ESPANYOL

CLUB DIRECTORY

Reial Club Deportiu Espanyol de Barcelona
Paseo Olímpico 17-19
08038 Barcelona
tel - (934) 248800
fax - (934) 254552
Year of Formation - 1900
President - Daniel Sánchez Llibre
Manager - Enric Mas
Coach - Marcelo Bielsa; Miguel Angel Brindisi
Stadium - Montjuïc (54,000)

MAJOR HONOURS
Domestic Cup - (2) 1929, 1940.

APPEARANCES 98/99

		P	Ap	(s)	Gls
Moisés García "ARTEAGA"	M		25	(3)	2
Miguel Angel BENITEZ (PAR)	A		23	(9)	7
Branko BRNOVIC (YUG)	M		5	(6)	
Juan CAPDEVILA	D		27	(2)	4
CRISTOBAL Parralo	D		35		1
Enrique DE LUCAS	M		5	(15)	5
Federico Hernán DOMINGUEZ (ARG)	M		5		
Juan Eduardo ESNAIDER (ARG)	A		13		2
Constantin GÂLCA (ROM)	D		21	(6)	4
Sergio GONZALEZ	M		23	(11)	
Iván HELGUERA	M		37		2
Alberto LOPO	A			(2)	
MANOLO Pérez	D			(1)	
Enrique "Quique" MARTIN	A		13	(7)	2
Goran MILOSEVIC (YUG)	D			(1)	
Fernando Muñoz "NANDO"	D		31	(3)	1
José Rojo "PACHETA"	M		13	(8)	
Mauricio Roberto POCHETTINO (ARG)	D		26		
Martín Andrés POSSE (ARG)	A		23	(9)	4
Nenad PRALIJA (CRO)	M			(1)	
Joan "Nan" RIBERA	M		16	(10)	2
Manuel SERRANO	A		1	(3)	1
Debray Dario SILVA (URU)	A		11	(4)	3
Raúl TAMUDO	A		15	(4)	9
Antonio Jiménez "TONI"	G		38		
Germán VILLA (MEX)	M		12		

LEAGUE RESULTS 1998/99

30/08/98	CD Tenerife	H	2-1	Esnáider, Benítez
13/09/98	RCD Mallorca	A	0-2	
20/09/98	Atlético Madrid	H	1-1	Benítez
27/09/98	RC Deportivo	A	0-1	
04/10/98	Villarreal CF	H	1-1	Martín
18/10/98	Real Valladolid	A	1-2	Martín
25/10/98	FC Barcelona	H	1-2	De Lucas
31/10/98	Athletic Bilbao	A	2-2	Benítez 2
07/11/98	Real Betis	H	1-0	Serrano
15/11/98	Real Zaragoza	A	3-0	Capdevila, Nando, Esnáider (p)
22/11/98	Racing Santander	H	1-1	Ribera
29/11/98	CF Extremadura	A	0-1	
05/12/98	Real Madrid	H	0-0	
13/12/98	RC Celta	A	0-2	
20/12/98	Valencia CF	H	2-1	Capdevila, Cristóbal
03/01/99	UD Salamanca	A	3-2	Ribera, Posse, De Lucas (p)
10/01/99	CD Alavés	A	1-1	Capdevila
17/01/99	Real Sociedad	H	0-0	
24/01/99	Real Oviedo	A	1-1	Posse
31/01/99	CD Tenerife	A	0-0	
07/02/99	RCD Mallorca	H	1-0	Benítez
13/02/99	Atlético Madrid	A	2-1	Arteaga, Silva
21/02/99	RC Deportivo	H	2-2	Helguera, Posse
28/02/99	Villarreal CF	A	2-2	De Lucas, Helguera
07/03/99	Real Valladolid	H	0-2	
14/03/99	FC Barcelona	A	0-3	
20/03/99	Athletic Bilbao	H	1-1	Tamudo
04/04/99	Real Betis	A	1-0	Tamudo
11/04/99	Real Zaragoza	H	2-1	Tamudo, Benítez
18/04/99	Racing Santander	A	2-0	Arteaga, Silva
25/04/99	CF Extremadura	H	0-0	
01/05/99	Real Madrid	A	0-2	
09/05/99	RC Celta	H	3-0	De Lucas, Gâlca (p), Tamudo
16/05/99	Valencia CF	A	2-1	Tamudo, Posse
23/05/99	UD Salamanca	H	4-0	Tamudo 3, Benítez
30/05/99	CD Alavés	H	3-0	Tamudo, De Lucas, Capdevila
13/06/99	Real Sociedad	A	2-1	Gâlca 2 (2p)
20/06/99	Real Oviedo	H	2-1	Silva, Gâlca (p)

CF EXTREMADURA

CLUB DIRECTORY

Club de Fútbol Extremadura
c/ Colombia s/n
06200 Almendralejo (Badajoz)
tel - (924) 670921
fax - (924) 670530
Year of Formation - 1928
President - Pedro Nieto Cortés
Manager - Pedro Sánchez Moreno
Coach - Rafael Benítez
Stadium - Francisco de la Hera (13,000)

APPEARANCES 98/99

	P	Ap	(s)	Gls
Francisco Rodríguez AMADOR	G	6	(1)	
David BELENGUER	D	34	(2)	
Goran BOGDANOVIC (YUG)	M	3	(4)	
DAVID Castedo	M	26	(6)	
DIEGO Torres	D		(1)	
Carlos Alejandro DURE (ARG)	A	25	(8)	6
Ignacio ERAÑA	M	4	(1)	
Antonio ESPOSITO (SUI)	M	16	(4)	2
FELIX Carballo	D	33	(2)	2
Jean Franco FERRARI (PER)	A		(1)	1
Iván César GABRICH (ARG)	M	16	(12)	2
Ronald GASPERCIC (BEL)	G	32		
Juan Rodríguez "JUANITO"	D	15	(5)	
Raymond KALLA (CMR)	D	34		
MANUEL Alfredo Mosquera	A	24	(13)	1
OSCAR Montiel	D	35	(2)	
Ahmed OUATTARA (CIV)	A	5	(2)	1
PEDRO JOSE Lorenzo	M	15	(15)	
Hipólito Fernández "POLI"	D	17	(9)	
Luis Enrique RUEDA (ARG)	A	6	(1)	
José Luis SOTO	M	19	(8)	2
Antonio "Toni" VELAMAZAN	M	27	(6)	6
José Alberto TORIL	M	8	(8)	2
Laurent VIAUD (FRA)	M	18	(1)	1

LEAGUE RESULTS 1998/99

30/08/98	Real Valladolid	H	0-0	
12/09/98	FC Barcelona	A	0-1	
20/09/98	Athletic Bilbao	H	0-1	
26/09/98	Real Betis	A	1-1	Ferrari
04/10/98	Real Zaragoza	H	0-2	
18/10/98	Racing Santander	A	1-3	Duré
25/10/98	CD Alavés	A	1-0	Soto
31/10/98	Real Madrid	H	1-5	Duré
08/11/98	RC Celta	A	1-5	Manuel
15/11/98	Valencia CF	H	1-0	Toril
22/11/98	UD Salamanca	A	1-2	Félix
29/11/98	RCD Espanyol	H	1-0	og (Helguera)
05/12/98	Real Sociedad	A	0-2	
13/12/98	Real Oviedo	H	0-1	
20/12/98	CD Tenerife	A	1-1	Velamazán
03/01/99	RCD Mallorca	H	1-0	Velamazán
10/01/99	Atlético Madrid	A	0-5	
17/01/99	RC Deportivo	H	1-2	Esposito
24/01/99	Villarreal CF	A	1-1	Velamazán
31/01/99	Real Valladolid	A	0-0	
07/02/99	FC Barcelona	H	1-2	Duré
14/02/99	Athletic Bilbao	A	0-0	
20/02/99	Real Betis	H	2-1	Toril (p), Duré
28/02/99	Real Zaragoza	A	1-3	Velamazán (p)
07/03/99	Racing Santander	H	0-3	
14/03/99	CD Alavés	H	1-0	Duré
21/03/99	Real Madrid	A	0-2	
04/04/99	RC Celta	H	1-1	Velamazán
11/04/99	Valencia CF	A	1-1	Esposito
18/04/99	UD Salamanca	H	1-1	Ouattara
25/04/99	RCD Espanyol	A	0-0	
02/05/99	Real Sociedad	H	1-0	Velamazán
09/05/99	Real Oviedo	A	0-1	
16/05/99	CD Tenerife	H	1-0	Viaud
23/05/99	RCD Mallorca	A	0-2	
30/05/99	Atlético Madrid	H	2-1	Félix, Duré
12/06/99	RC Deportivo	A	1-1	Soto
20/06/99	Villarreal CF	H	2-2	Gabrich 2

RCD MALLORCA

CLUB DIRECTORY

Real Club Deportivo Mallorca
Plaza de Barcelona 15
07011 Palma de Mallorca
tel - (971) 220020
fax - (971) 452351
Year of Formation - 1916
President - Guillermo Reynés
Manager - Ramón Servalls Batle
Coach - Héctor Raúl Cúper (99/00 - Mario Gómez)
Stadium - San Moix (22,500)

APPEARANCES 98/99

	P	Ap	(s)	Gls
Oscar ARPON	M	4	(9)	
Leonardo Angel BIAGINI (ARG)	A	26	(6)	11
CARLOS Domínguez	A	2	(11)	
Luis CARRERAS	D	7	(11)	
Daniel García "DANI"	A	34	(2)	12
Vicente ENGONGA	D	33		
César Augusto GALVEZ	G	3		
Ariel Miguel Santiago IBAGAZA (ARG)	M	23	(3)	5
LAUREN Bisan Etamé Mayer (CMR)	M	33		1
Ariel Maximiliano LOPEZ (ARG)	A	12	(11)	4
Alberto LUQUE	A	2	(3)	
MARCELINO Elena	D	34		3
Fernando NIÑO	D	6	(10)	
Javier OLAIZOLA	D	36		
Veljko PAUNOVIC (YUG)	M	8	(16)	5
Héctor Mauricio PINEDA (ARG)	A	3	(1)	
Carlos Angel ROA (ARG)	G	35		
Gustavo Lionel SIVIERO (ARG)	D	33		
Francisco SOLER	M	16	(12)	1
Miguel SOLER	D	33	(1)	
Jovan STANKOVIC (YUG)	M	35	(1)	4

LEAGUE RESULTS 1998/99

Date	Opponent	H/A	Score	Scorers
30/08/98	UD Salamanca	A	0-0	
13/09/98	RCD Espanyol	H	2-0	Dani, López
20/09/98	Real Sociedad	A	1-0	Marcelino
27/09/98	Real Oviedo	H	0-0	
04/10/98	CD Tenerife	A	1-1	Biagini
18/10/98	CD Alavés	H	2-1	Paunovic, Biagini
25/10/98	Atlético Madrid	H	4-0	Paunovic, Lauren, Stankovic (p), Soler F.
01/11/98	RC Deportivo	A	1-1	Biagini
08/11/98	Villarreal CF	H	1-0	Dani (p)
15/11/98	Real Valladolid	A	0-1	
21/11/98	FC Barcelona	H	1-0	og (Sergi)
29/11/98	Athletic Bilbao	A	0-1	
05/12/98	Real Betis	H	1-0	Dani
13/12/98	Real Zaragoza	A	1-0	Marcelino
20/12/98	Racing Santander	H	1-1	Dani
03/01/99	CF Extremadura	A	0-1	
10/01/99	Real Madrid	H	2-1	Ibagaza, López
16/01/99	RC Celta	A	2-4	López, Biagini (p)
24/01/99	Valencia CF	H	0-1	
30/01/99	UD Salamanca	H	1-0	Dani
07/02/99	RCD Espanyol	A	0-1	
13/02/99	Real Sociedad	H	1-0	Biagini (p)
21/02/99	Real Oviedo	A	3-1	Dani 2, Paunovic
28/02/99	CD Tenerife	H	1-1	Dani
07/03/99	CD Alavés	A	0-2	
13/03/99	Atlético Madrid	A	2-1	og (Chamot), Paunovic
21/03/99	RC Deportivo	H	1-2	Ibagaza
04/04/99	Villarreal CF	A	2-0	Biagini, Dani
11/04/99	Real Valladolid	H	1-0	Dani
17/04/99	FC Barcelona	A	1-2	Biagini (p)
25/04/99	Athletic Bilbao	H	6-1	Biagini 3, Ibagaza, Marcelino, Dani
02/05/99	Real Betis	A	3-1	Stankovic, Ibagaza, Paunovic
09/05/99	Real Zaragoza	H	1-0	Biagini (p)
14/05/99	Racing Santander	A	0-1	
23/05/99	CF Extremadura	H	2-0	López, Stankovic
30/05/99	Real Madrid	A	1-2	Dani
13/06/99	RC Celta	H	2-0	Ibagaza, Stankovic
20/06/99	Valencia CF	A	0-3	

REAL OVIEDO

CLUB DIRECTORY

Real Oviedo Club de Fútbol
Marqués de Santacruz 9
33007 Oviedo (Asturias)
tel - (985) 212897
fax - (985) 224058
Year of Formation - 1926
President - Eugenio Prieto Alvarez
Manager - Félix Ortega
Coach - Fernando Vázquez
(99/00 - Luis Aragonés)
Stadium - Carlos Tartiere (23,500)

APPEARANCES 98/99

	P	Ap	(s)	Gls
Daniel AMIEVA	M	4	(4)	
Ricardo González BANGO	D	11	(4)	
Alberto Martínez "BERTO"	M	2	(1)	
Sergio BORIS	D		(1)	
CESAR Martín	D	31		4
Julio César DELY VALDES (PAN)	A	36	(1)	19
Peter DUBOVSKY (SVK)	A	25	(7)	3
Xabier ESKURZA	M	21	(3)	
ESTEBAN Andrés	G	37		
FÁBIO PINTO (BRA)	A	2	(15)	1
Eugenio Suárez "GENI"	M		(1)	
Juan Antonio GONZALEZ (URU)	A		(2)	
IVAN Ania	M	17	(16)	2
IVAN Iglesias	M	15	(1)	3
JAIME Fernández	M	18	(8)	1
KEITA Idrissa (CIV)	A	5	(2)	
José Manuel Menéndez "MANEL"	D	34		1
Peter MØLLER (DEN)	D	8	(18)	2
Juan Luis MORA	G	1		
Joyce Renato MORENO	D	11	(8)	
Albert NADJ (YUG)	M	26	(1)	1
Viktor ONOPKO (RUS)	D	33		
PAULO Jorge Gomes BENTO (POR)	M	34		
Roberto Fabián POMPEI (ARG)	M	24	(3)	3
Franck RABARIVONY (FRA)	D	22	(8)	
Antonio RIVAS	D		(1)	
José Jorge SAAVEDRA	M	1		

LEAGUE RESULTS 1998/99

30/08/98	Real Sociedad	A	3-3	Dubovsky, Dely Valdés, Manel
13/09/98	CD Alavés	H	1-0	César
20/09/98	CD Tenerife	H	0-1	
27/09/98	RCD Mallorca	A	0-0	
04/10/98	Atlético Madrid	H	3-1	Iván Iglesias 2, Dely Valdés
18/10/98	RC Deportivo	A	0-4	
25/10/98	Villarreal CF	H	0-0	
01/11/98	Real Valladolid	A	1-2	Dely Valdés
08/11/98	FC Barcelona	H	2-1	Fábio Pinto, Møller
15/11/98	Athletic Bilbao	A	5-3	César, og (Lasa), Iván Iglesias,
				Dely Valdés, Iván Ania
21/11/98	Real Betis	H	0-1	
29/11/98	Real Zaragoza	A	0-1	
06/12/98	Racing Santander	H	1-0	Dely Valdés
13/12/98	CF Extremadura	A	1-0	Dely Valdés
20/12/98	Real Madrid	H	1-0	Dely Valdés
03/01/99	RC Celta	A	2-6	Pompei, Møller
10/01/99	Valencia CF	H	2-2	Dely Valdés 2
17/01/99	UD Salamanca	A	1-1	Nadj
24/01/99	RCD Espanyol	H	1-1	Dely Valdés
30/01/99	Real Sociedad	H	2-1	Iván Ania, Dely Valdés (p)
07/02/99	CD Alavés	A	2-2	César 2
14/02/99	CD Tenerife	A	2-0	Pompei, Dely Valdés (p)
21/02/99	RCD Mallorca	H	1-3	Pompei
27/02/99	Atlético Madrid	A	0-0	
06/03/99	RC Deportivo	H	1-2	Dely Valdés
14/03/99	Villarreal CF	A	0-0	
21/03/99	Real Valladolid	H	0-0	
04/04/99	FC Barcelona	A	1-3	Dely Valdés
11/04/99	Athletic Bilbao	H	0-0	
18/04/99	Real Betis	A	0-5	
25/04/99	Real Zaragoza	H	1-2	Dely Valdés
02/05/99	Racing Santander	A	0-0	
09/05/99	CF Extremadura	H	1-0	Dubovsky
16/05/99	Real Madrid	A	1-2	Dely Valdés
23/05/99	RC Celta	H	1-3	Dubovsky
29/05/99	Valencia CF	A	0-3	
13/06/99	UD Salamanca	H	3-2	Dely Valdés 3 (1p)
20/06/99	RCD Espanyol	A	1-2	Jaime

RACING SANTANDER

CLUB DIRECTORY

Real Racing Club de Santander
Avenida del Estadio s/n
39012 Santander
tel - (942) 282828
fax - (942) 283008
Year of Formation - 1913
President - Miguel Angel Díaz Díaz
Manager - Antonio Diestro Santamaría
Coach - Fernando Trío "Yosu"; Miguel Sánchez;
Gustavo Benítez
Stadium - El Sardinero (25,000)

APPEARANCES 98/99

		P	Ap	(s)	Gls
José Emilio AMAVISCA	M	13	(2)	1
Claudio David ARZENO	D	32	(2)	2
Vladimir BESCHASTNYKH (RUS)	A	22	(12)	6
Pablo CASAR	M		(1)	
José María CEBALLOS	G	27		
José María Alonso "CHEMA"	D	21	(4)	
Gonzalo COLSA	M		(1)	
Angel de Juana "GELI"	D	6	(14)	
Frode GRODÅS (NOR)	G	6		
ISMAEL Ruiz	M	34		4
Gerardo Federico MAGALLANES (URU)	M	12	(5)	1
Fernando MARCOS	G	5	(1)	
Olof MELLBERG (SWE)	D	25		
Jesús María MERINO	D	20	(1)	1
José Moratón "MORA"	D		(1)	
Pedro Manuel MUNITIS	A	37		8
Francisco de Borja Enrique "NERU"	D	21	(2)	
Leider PRECIADO (COL)	A	2	(14)	2
Salvador Ballesta "SALVA"	A	6	(10)	2
Francisco Javier SANCHEZ JARA	D	3	(2)	
Sergei SHUSTIKOV (RUS)	M	21	(6)	1
José María Suárez "SIETES"	M	20	(4)	
Washington TAIS (URU)	D	32	(3)	1
Domingo Arrotegui "TXOMIN"	D		(1)	
VICTOR Sánchez	A	34	(1)	12
David VILLABONA	M	3	(1)	
Angel VIVAR DORADO	M	16	(11)	

LEAGUE RESULTS 1998/99

30/08/98	FC Barcelona	H	0-0	
12/09/98	Athletic Bilbao	A	0-2	
20/09/98	Real Betis	H	1-0	Preciado
27/09/98	Real Zaragoza	A	1-3	Tais
04/10/98	CD Alavés	A	1-0	Munitis
18/10/98	CF Extremadura	H	3-1	Munitis, Beschastnykh, Víctor
25/10/98	Real Madrid	A	2-2	Merino, Beschastnykh
31/10/98	RC Celta	H	2-2	Víctor 2 (1p)
08/11/98	Valencia CF	A	0-3	
15/11/98	UD Salamanca	H	4-1	Shustikov, Víctor 3 (1p)
22/11/98	RCD Espanyol	A	1-1	Víctor
29/11/98	Real Sociedad	H	0-1	
06/12/98	Real Oviedo	A	0-1	
13/12/98	CD Tenerife	H	0-0	
20/12/98	RCD Mallorca	A	1-1	Víctor
03/01/99	Atlético Madrid	H	2-3	Ismael, Beschastnykh (p)
10/01/99	RC Deportivo	A	2-1	Víctor, Beschastnykh
17/01/99	Villarreal CF	H	1-2	Arzeno
24/01/99	Real Valladolid	A	0-0	
31/01/99	FC Barcelona	A	2-3	Víctor, Munitis
07/02/99	Athletic Bilbao	H	2-0	Preciado, Munitis
14/02/99	Real Betis	A	1-1	Munitis
20/02/99	Real Zaragoza	H	2-4	Arzeno, Ismael
28/02/99	CD Alavés	H	2-0	Munitis, Víctor (p)
07/03/99	CF Extremadura	A	3-0	Munitis, Beschastnykh, Víctor
13/03/99	Real Madrid	H	1-3	Ismael
21/03/99	RC Celta	A	0-3	
03/04/99	Valencia CF	H	0-1	
11/04/99	UD Salamanca	A	2-1	Magallanes, Salva
18/04/99	RCD Espanyol	H	0-2	
25/04/99	Real Sociedad	A	0-2	
02/05/99	Real Oviedo	H	0-0	
09/05/99	CD Tenerife	A	2-2	Salva, Amavisca
14/05/99	RCD Mallorca	H	1-0	Ismael
23/05/99	Atlético Madrid	A	1-1	Beschastnykh
30/05/99	RC Deportivo	H	1-1	Munitis
13/06/99	Villarreal CF	A	0-3	
19/06/99	Real Valladolid	H	0-2	

REAL MADRID

CLUB DIRECTORY

Real Madrid Club de Fútbol
Concha Espina 1, 28036 Madrid
tel - (913) 440052   fax - (913) 440695
Year of Formation - 1902
President - Lorenzo Sanz Mancebo
Manager - Manuel Fernández Trigo
Coach - Guus Hiddink; John Toshack
Stadium - Santiago Bernabéu (106,500)

MAJOR HONOURS
League Championship - (27)
1932, 1933, 1954, 1955, 1957, 1958, 1961,
1962, 1963, 1964, 1965, 1967, 1968, 1969,
1972, 1975, 1976, 1978, 1979, 1980, 1986,
1987, 1988, 1989, 1990, 1995, 1997.
Domestic Cup - (17) 1905, 1906, 1907, 1908,
1917, 1934, 1936, 1946, 1947, 1962, 1970,
1974, 1975, 1980, 1982, 1989, 1993.
European Champions' Cup - (7) 1956, 1957,
1958, 1959, 1960, 1966, 1998.
UEFA Cup - (2) 1985, 1986.
World Club Cup - (2) 1960, 1998.

APPEARANCES 98/99

		P	Ap	(s)	Gls
Iván CAMPO	D	24	(3)	1
Pedro CONTRERAS	G	4		
Samuel ETO'O (CMR)	A		(1)	
José María Gutiérrez "GUTI"	M	11	(17)	1
Fernando Ruiz HIERRO	D	28		6
Bodo ILLGNER (GER)	G	34		
JAIME Sánchez	M	5	(9)	
Robert JARNI (CRO)	M	19	(8)	1
Aitor KARANKA	D	3	(1)	
Christian KAREMBEU (FRA)	M	12	(8)	
Predrag MIJATOVIC (YUG)	A	26	(2)	5
Fernando MORIENTES	A	24	(9)	19
Perica OGNJENOVIC (YUG)	A		(1)	
Christian PANUCCI (ITA)	D	31		
RAUL González	A	37		25
Fernando Carlos REDONDO (ARG)	M	23		
ROBERTO CARLOS da Silva (BRA)	D	35		5
Roberto ROJAS	D	1	(4)	
Manuel SANCHIS	D	27	(6)	
Fernando SANZ	D	6	(3)	
SÁVIO Bortolini (BRA)	A	24	(10)	6
Clarence SEEDORF (HOL)	M	35	(2)	3
Davor SUKER (CRO)	A	9	(10)	4
Manuel TENA	D		(1)	
Jorge López "TOTE"	D		(1)	

LEAGUE RESULTS 1998/99

31/08/98	Villarreal CF	H	4-1	Raúl 2, Mijatovic, Sávio
12/09/98	Real Valladolid	A	1-0	Mijatovic
19/09/98	FC Barcelona	H	2-2	Raúl 2
26/09/98	Athletic Bilbao	A	3-2	Raúl, Mijatovic, Sávio
04/10/98	Real Betis	H	0-1	
17/10/98	Real Zaragoza	A	4-3	Hierro (p), Roberto Carlos, Raúl, Mijatovic
25/10/98	Racing Santander	H	2-2	Hierro 2 (1p)
31/10/98	CF Extremadura	A	5-1	Jarni, Sávio, Hierro (p), Suker, Seedorf
08/11/98	CD Alavés	A	1-1	Roberto Carlos
14/11/98	RC Celta	H	1-2	Roberto Carlos
21/11/98	Valencia CF	A	1-3	Sávio
05/12/98	RCD Espanyol	A	0-0	
13/12/98	Real Sociedad	H	3-2	Roberto Carlos, Raúl, Seedorf
20/12/98	Real Oviedo	A	0-1	
03/01/99	CD Tenerife	H	4-0	Raúl 2, Hierro (p), Sávio
06/01/99	UD Salamanca	H	3-1	Raúl, Suker 2
10/01/99	RCD Mallorca	A	1-2	Seedorf
17/01/99	Atlético Madrid	H	4-2	Mijatovic, Morientes 2, Campo
24/01/99	RC Deportivo	A	0-4	
30/01/99	Villarreal CF	A	2-0	Morientes 2
07/02/99	Real Valladolid	H	3-2	Raúl 3 (2p)
14/02/99	FC Barcelona	A	0-3	
20/02/99	Athletic Bilbao	H	0-1	
27/02/99	Real Betis	A	2-3	Raúl, Morientes
07/03/99	Real Zaragoza	H	3-2	Raúl 2 (1p), Morientes
13/03/99	Racing Santander	A	3-1	Raúl, Roberto Carlos, Suker
21/03/99	CF Extremadura	H	2-0	Raúl, og (Juanito)
04/04/99	CD Alavés	H	3-2	Hierro, Morientes, Raúl
11/04/99	RC Celta	A	1-5	Morientes
18/04/99	Valencia CF	H	3-1	Morientes, Raúl 2
25/04/99	UD Salamanca	A	1-1	Raúl
01/05/99	RCD Espanyol	H	2-0	Morientes 2
08/05/99	Real Sociedad	A	2-3	Guti, Sávio (p)
16/05/99	Real Oviedo	H	2-1	Morientes 2
23/05/99	CD Tenerife	A	3-2	Morientes 2, Raúl (p)
30/05/99	RCD Mallorca	H	2-1	Morientes 2
12/06/99	Atlético Madrid	A	1-3	Morientes
20/06/99	RC Deportivo	H	3-1	Raúl 2, Morientes

REAL SOCIEDAD

CLUB DIRECTORY

Real Sociedad de Fútbol
Paseo de Anoeta 1
20014 San Sebastián
tel - (943) 462833
fax - (943) 458941
Year of Formation - 1909
President - Luis Uranga Otaegui
Manager - Iñaki Otegi Arbelaiz
Coach - Bernd Krauss
Stadium - Anoeta (29,350)

MAJOR HONOURS
League Championship - (2) 1981, 1982.
Domestic Cup - (2) 1909, 1987.

APPEARANCES 98/99

		P	Ap	(s)	Gls
Mutiu ADEPOJU (NIG)	M	8	(10)		
ALBERTO López	G	37			
Aitor ALDEONDO	A	2	(16)	1	
Mikel ANTIA	D	15	(7)		
Mikel ARANBURU	M	13	(1)	1	
Agustín ARANZABAL	D	37		1	
José Javier BARKERO	M	1			
Igor CVITANOVIC (CRO)	A	3	(9)		
Oscar DE PAULA	A	19	(10)	6	
Francisco Javier DE PEDRO	M	25	(2)	6	
Miguel Angel FUENTES	D	14	(4)		
Juan Andrés GOMEZ (ARG)	D	32			
Javier GRACIA	M	9	(6)	1	
José Félix GUERRERO	D	7	(8)		
Iñigo IDIAQUEZ	M	19	(10)	7	
Igor JAUREGUI	M	15	(7)	2	
Darko KOVACEVIC (YUG)	A	30		16	
Dietmar KÜHBAUER (AUT)	M	14	(2)		
Aitor LOPEZ REKARTE	D	23	(3)		
Lorenzo Juarros "LOREN"	D	27			
Roberto OLABE	G	1			
José Antonio PIKABEA	D	32	(3)	1	
Ricardo SÁ PINTO (POR)	A	35	(1)	4	

LEAGUE RESULTS 1998/99

30/08/98	Real Oviedo	H	3-3	Sá Pinto, Pikabea, Aldeondo
12/09/98	CD Tenerife	A	2-2	Jáuregi, og (Vierklau)
20/09/98	RCD Mallorca	H	0-1	
26/09/98	Atlético Madrid	A	1-4	Aranzábal (p)
04/10/98	RC Deportivo	H	2-0	De Paula, De Pedro (p)
17/10/98	Villarreal CF	A	1-1	De Pedro
25/10/98	Real Valladolid	H	1-0	De Paula
31/10/98	FC Barcelona	A	1-4	Kovacevic
08/11/98	Athletic Bilbao	H	3-1	De Paula, Sá Pinto, Kovacevic
15/11/98	Real Betis	A	0-1	
21/11/98	Real Zaragoza	H	0-0	
29/11/98	Racing Santander	H	1-0	Kovacevic
05/12/98	CF Extremadura	H	2-0	De Paula, Idiákez
13/12/98	Real Madrid	A	2-3	Kovacevic 2
20/12/98	RC Celta	H	2-0	Kovacevic 2
02/01/99	Valencia CF	A	0-2	
10/01/99	UD Salamanca	H	4-0	Sá Pinto, Kovacevic 2, Gracia
17/01/99	RCD Espanyol	A	0-0	
24/01/99	CD Alavés	H	2-1	Kovacevic 2
30/01/99	Real Oviedo	A	1-2	Idiákez
07/02/99	CD Tenerife	H	1-1	De Pedro (p)
13/02/99	RCD Mallorca	A	0-1	
21/02/99	Atlético Madrid	H	3-2	Jáuregi, Aranburu, De Paula
28/02/99	RC Deportivo	A	1-0	Idiákez
07/03/99	Villarreal CF	H	1-1	De Paula
14/03/99	Real Valladolid	A	0-0	
21/03/99	FC Barcelona	H	0-2	
04/04/99	Athletic Bilbao	A	0-0	
11/04/99	Real Betis	H	1-0	Sá Pinto
18/04/99	Real Zaragoza	A	1-1	Idiákez
25/04/99	Racing Santander	H	2-0	Kovacevic 2
02/05/99	CF Extremadura	A	0-1	
08/05/99	Real Madrid	H	3-2	Idiákez, De Pedro (p), Kovacevic
16/05/99	RC Celta	A	2-2	Kovacevic (p), Idiákez
23/05/99	Valencia CF	H	1-1	Kovacevic
30/05/99	UD Salamanca	A	1-0	Idiákez
13/06/99	RCD Espanyol	H	1-2	De Pedro
20/06/99	CD Alavés	A	1-2	De Pedro

UD SALAMANCA

Unión Deportiva Salamanca
Carretera de Zamora s/n
37184 Villares de la Reina (Salamanca)
tel - (923) 222090
fax - (923) 247658
Year of Formation - 1923
President - Juan José Hidalgo Acera
Manager - Enrique Miguel
Coach - Miguel Angel Russo; Baltasar Sánchez;
Yosu Ortuondo; Carlos Martinez Diarte
Stadium - Helmántico (20,000)

APPEARANCES 98/99

		P	Ap	(s)	Gls
José Ignacio AIZPURUA	G	5	(1)	
Eduardo ALONSO	M	36		3
Joan BARBARA	A	9	(9)	1
Martin Alejandro CARDETTI (ARG)	A	20	(4)	4
Carlos David CASARTELLI (ARG)	A	15	(15)	2
Sergio CORINO	D	31	(2)	3
Jorge DINO Gonçalo (POR)	D	1		
Everton GIOVANELLA (BRA)	M	33		1
Marco LANNA (ITA)	D	34		1
Lorenzo Morón "LOREN"	D	19	(2)	2
Ricardo Gabriel LUNARI (ARG)	M	4	(10)	
Cristián Omar LUPIDIO (ARG)	D	6	(4)	
Lucian Cristian MARINESCU (ROM)	M	7	(3)	
Angel Pedro MEDINA	M		(1)	
Catalin MUNTEANU (ROM)	M	13	(14)	3
NUNO José Gonçalves LUÍS (POR)	D	9		
Dubravko PAVLICIC (CRO)	D	18		1
Leonardo RAMOS (URU)	D	15		2
Marcos REDERO	D	1		
ROGÉRIO Paulo Felisberto (POR)	M	19	(6)	
Walter Gustavo SILVANI (ARG)	A	25	(6)	3
Bogdan STELEA (ROM)	G	33		
José Américo TAIRA (POR)	M	19	(6)	
TOMAS Jiménez	M	5	(5)	
Martín VELLISCA	D	38		1
Paulo César ZEGARRA (PER)	A	3	(2)	1

LEAGUE RESULTS 1998/99

30/08/98	RCD Mallorca	H	0-0	
12/09/98	Atlético Madrid	A	0-2	
20/09/98	RC Deportivo	H	3-1	Silvani 2, Ramos
27/09/98	Villarreal CF	A	0-5	
04/10/98	Real Valladolid	H	1-0	Cardetti
17/10/98	FC Barcelona	A	1-1	Alonso
25/10/98	Athletic Bilbao	H	2-1	Alonso, Corino
31/10/98	Real Betis	A	0-1	
08/11/98	Real Zaragoza	H	1-2	Munteanu
15/11/98	Racing Santander	A	1-4	Loren
22/11/98	CF Extremadura	H	2-1	Cardetti, Munteanu
05/12/98	RC Celta	H	1-1	Casartelli
13/12/98	Valencia CF	A	0-1	
20/12/98	CD Alavés	A	0-1	
03/01/99	RCD Espanyol	H	2-3	Ramos (p), Munteanu
06/01/99	Real Madrid	A	1-3	Casartelli
10/01/99	Real Sociedad	A	0-4	
17/01/99	Real Oviedo	H	1-1	Pavlicic
24/01/99	CD Tenerife	A	0-1	
30/01/99	RCD Mallorca	A	0-1	
07/02/99	Atlético Madrid	H	2-1	Lanna, Alonso
13/02/99	RC Deportivo	A	0-1	
21/02/99	Villarreal CF	H	1-0	og (Téllez)
28/02/99	Real Valladolid	A	1-4	Giovanella
07/03/99	FC Barcelona	H	1-4	Cardetti
14/03/99	Athletic Bilbao	A	0-1	
21/03/99	Real Betis	H	1-3	Loren
04/04/99	Real Zaragoza	A	0-2	
11/04/99	Racing Santander	H	1-2	Corino (p)
18/04/99	CF Extremadura	A	1-1	Cardetti
25/04/99	Real Madrid	H	1-1	Corino
02/05/99	RC Celta	A	0-1	
09/05/99	Valencia CF	H	0-1	
16/05/99	CD Alavés	H	1-0	Silvani
23/05/99	RCD Espanyol	A	0-4	
30/05/99	Real Sociedad	H	0-1	
13/06/99	Real Oviedo	A	2-3	Barbará, Zegarra
19/06/99	CD Tenerife	H	1-2	Vellisca

CD TENERIFE

CLUB DIRECTORY

Club Deportivo Tenerife
Callejón del Combate 1
38002 Santa Cruz de Tenerife
tel - (922) 298100
fax - (922) 298329
Year of Formation - 1922
President - José Javier Pérez Pérez
Manager - Roberto Sicilia de Paz
Coach - Juan Manuel Lillo; Carlos Aimar;
Valentín Jorge "Robi"
Stadium - Heliodoro Rodríguez López (21,763)

APPEARANCES 98/99

	P	Ap	(s)	Gls
José ALEXIS Suárez	D	31		3
ANDRÉ LUIZ Moreira (BRA)	D	12		2
ANTONIO Mata	D	8	(3)	
Sergio Martínez BALLESTEROS	D	8		1
Federico BASAVILBASO (ARG)	M	12	(5)	
Sebastián Cruzado "CHANO"	M	16	(3)	
Daniel Ginzález "DANI"	M	29		
DOMINGOS de Oliveira (POR)	A	5	(14)	1
EMERSON Moisés Costa (BRA)	M	34		2
FELIPE Miñambres	M	14	(6)	
GUSTAVO García	M		(1)	
José IVAN González	D		(1)	
Juan JACOB González	D	1		
Slavisa JOKANOVIC (YUG)	M	25	(4)	2
JONAY Miguel Hernández	D	2	(4)	
Juan Castaño "JUANELE"	A	31	(2)	5
Meho KODRO (BOS)	A	1	(17)	
LEANDRO Machado (BRA)	A		(3)	
Julio LLORENTE	D	20	(1)	1
Javier LOPEZ	D	5	(6)	
Federico Guillermo LUSSENHOF (ARG)	D	13		
Roy MAKAAY (HOL)	A	32	(4)	14
MARCELINO Díaz	A		(4)	
Miguel Angeñ Ferrer "MISTA"	M	9	(4)	3
Carlos NAVARRO MONTOYA (ARG)	G	15		
Pablo PAZ (ARG)	D	17		
Pedro Luis Cherubino "PIER"	A	9	(3)	4
Antonio PINILLA	A	14	(5)	1
Antonio Segura ROBAINA	A	9	(6)	
Samuel SLOVAK (SVK)	M	15	(3)	1
Juan Carlos UNZUE	G	23		
Ferdy VIERKLAU (HOL)	D	8		

LEAGUE RESULTS 1998/99

30/08/98	RCD Espanyol	A	1-2	Jokanovic (p)
12/09/98	Real Sociedad	H	2-2	Juanele, Makaay
20/09/98	Real Oviedo	A	1-0	Alexis
27/09/98	CD Alavés	H	1-2	Domingos
04/10/98	RCD Mallorca	H	1-1	André Luiz
17/10/98	Atlético Madrid	A	0-2	
25/10/98	RC Deportivo	H	1-1	Makaay
01/11/98	Villarreal CF	A	5-2	Makaay 2, Emerson, André Luiz, Slovak
08/11/98	Real Valladolid	H	2-2	Makaay, Juanele
15/11/98	FC Barcelona	A	1-4	Makaay
20/11/98	Athletic Bilbao	H	0-1	
29/11/98	Real Betis	A	0-1	
06/12/98	Real Zaragoza	H	1-1	Makaay
13/12/98	Racing Santander	A	0-0	
20/12/98	CF Extremadura	H	1-1	Makaay
03/01/99	Real Madrid	A	0-4	
10/01/99	RC Celta	H	0-2	
17/01/99	Valencia CF	A	1-1	Juanele (p)
24/01/99	UD Salamanca	H	1-0	Juanele (p)
31/01/99	RCD Espanyol	H	0-0	
07/02/99	Real Sociedad	A	1-1	og (De Paula)
14/02/99	Real Oviedo	H	0-2	
21/02/99	CD Alavés	A	1-3	Juanele
28/02/99	RCD Mallorca	A	1-1	Alexis
07/03/99	Atlético Madrid	H	1-0	Makaay
14/03/99	RC Deportivo	A	0-2	
21/03/99	Villarreal CF	H	2-2	Makaay, Llorente
04/04/99	Real Valladolid	A	1-2	Makaay
10/04/99	FC Barcelona	H	2-3	Pinilla, Makaay
18/04/99	Athletic Bilbao	A	0-2	
25/04/99	Real Betis	H	3-2	Jokanovic (p), Mista, Makaay
02/05/99	Real Zaragoza	A	1-3	Ballesteros
09/05/99	Racing Santander	H	2-2	Mista, Pier
16/05/99	CF Extremadura	A	0-1	
23/05/99	Real Madrid	H	2-3	Pier, Alexis
30/05/99	RC Celta	A	0-2	
13/06/99	Valencia CF	H	3-2	Pier 2, Makaay
19/06/99	UD Salamanca	A	2-1	Mista, Emerson

VALENCIA CF

Valencia Club de Fútbol
Avda de Aragón 33
46010 Valencia
tel - (963) 372626
fax - (963) 611235
Year of Formation - 1919
President - Pedro Cortés
Manager - Manuel Llorente Martín
Coach - Claudio Ranieri (99/00 - Héctor Raúl Cúper)
Stadium - Mestalla (55,000)

MAJOR HONOURS
League Championship - (4)
1942, 1944, 1947, 1971.
Domestic Cup - (6)
1941, 1949, 1954, 1967, 1979, 1999.
European Cup-winners' Cup - (1) 1980.
Fairs' Cup - (2) 1962, 1963.
European Super Cup - (1) 1980.

	P	Ap	(s)	Gls
Jocelyn ANGLOMA (FRA)	D	22	(7)	1
Miguel Angel ANGULO	A	31	(5)	8
Joachim BJÖRKLUND (SWE)	D	23	(1)	1
Francisco José CAMARASA	D	2	(1)	
José Santiago CAÑIZARES	G	38		
Amedeo CARBONI (ITA)	D	36		
Miroslav DJUKIC (YUG)	D	32		1
Francisco Javier FARINOS	M	28	(4)	2
Bucurel Adrian ILIE (ROM)	A	22	(2)	10
Alejandro Castro "JANDRO"	A		(2)	
JUANFRAN García	D	15	(6)	
Claudio LOPEZ (ARG)	A	31	(1)	21
Cristiano LUCARELLI (ITA)	A	4	(8)	1
Gaizka MENDIETA	M	36	(1)	7
Luis MILLA	M	28	(3)	1
Rubén NAVARRO	M		(4)	
Gabriel POPESCU (ROM)	M	5	(20)	1
Alain ROCHE (FRA)	D	25	(4)	
Stefan SCHWARZ (SWE)	M	22	(8)	4
Denis SERBAN (ROM)	M		(10)	1
Miguel Angel SORIA	D	6	(4)	
Oscar TELLEZ	D	1		
Goran VLAOVIC (CRO)	A	11	(9)	2

29/08/98	Atlético Madrid	H	1-0	Angulo
12/09/98	RC Deportivo	A	0-1	
20/09/98	Villarreal CF	H	1-0	Angulo
26/09/98	Real Valladolid	A	1-3	Angulo
03/10/98	FC Barcelona	H	1-3	López
17/10/98	Athletic Bilbao	A	0-2	
25/10/98	Real Betis	H	5-1	López 2, Ilie 2, Schwarz
31/10/98	Real Zaragoza	A	4-1	Ilie, Lucarelli, Schwarz, Mendieta
08/11/98	Racing Santander	H	3-0	Djukic, Schwarz, López
15/11/98	CF Extremadura	A	0-1	
21/11/98	Real Madrid	H	3-1	Angulo, López 2
29/11/98	RC Celta	A	2-2	Popescu, Ilie
06/12/98	CD Alavés	A	1-0	López
13/12/98	UD Salamanca	H	1-0	Angulo
20/12/98	RCD Espanyol	A	1-2	Farinós
02/01/99	Real Sociedad	H	2-0	Schwarz, López
10/01/99	Real Oviedo	A	2-2	og (Morena), Milla
17/01/99	CD Tenerife	H	1-1	López (p)
24/01/99	RCD Mallorca	A	1-0	López
30/01/99	Atlético Madrid	A	2-1	López, Angulo
06/02/99	RC Deportivo	H	0-0	
14/02/99	Villarreal CF	A	0-1	
21/02/99	Real Valladolid	H	0-1	
27/02/99	FC Barcelona	A	4-2	Ilie, López 2, Angulo
07/03/99	Athletic Bilbao	H	4-1	Ilie 2 (1p), Angloma, López
13/03/99	Real Betis	A	1-0	Mendieta
21/03/99	Real Zaragoza	H	1-1	Ilie
03/04/99	Racing Santander	A	1-0	Björklund
11/04/99	CF Extremadura	H	1-1	Serban
17/04/99	Real Madrid	A	1-3	Mendieta
24/04/99	RC Celta	H	2-2	Vlaovic, Farinós
01/05/99	CD Alavés	H	5-0	López 3, Mendieta 2
09/05/99	UD Salamanca	A	1-0	Vlaovic
16/05/99	RCD Espanyol	H	1-2	López
23/05/99	Real Sociedad	A	1-1	Ilie
29/05/99	Real Oviedo	H	3-0	Mendieta (p), López 2 (1p)
13/06/99	CD Tenerife	A	2-3	Angulo, López (p)
20/06/99	RCD Mallorca	H	3-0	og (Marcelino), Mendieta, Ilie

REAL VALLADOLID

CLUB DIRECTORY

Real Valladolid
Avenida Mundial 82, s/n
47014 Valladolid
tel - (983) 360342
fax - (983) 372164
Year of Formation - 1928
President - Marcos Fernández Fermosell
Manager - Carlos Palacios Aparicio
Coach - Sergei Kresic (99/00 - Gregorio Manzano)
Stadium - José Zorrilla (31,000)

APPEARANCES 98/99

	P	Ap	(s)	Gls
ALBERTO López	A	4	(27)	4
José Luis Pérez CAMINERO	M	19	(8)	4
José Manuel Jiménez "CHEMA"	M	35	(2)	
Daniel DUTUEL (FRA)	D	2	(8)	
EMILIO José López	M	2	(12)	
EUSEBIO Sacristán	M	11	(10)	
José Antonio GARCIA CALVO	D	27	(1)	
Alvaro GUTIERREZ (URU)	M		(1)	
Dragan ISAILOVIC (YUG)	A	4	(2)	
JÚLIO CÉSAR Santos (BRA)	D	17	(2)	2
Diego Fernando KLIMOWICZ (ARG)	A	9	(12)	1
Harold LOZANO (COL)	M	16	(3)	1
Alberto MARCOS	D	36		
ORLANDO Gutiérrez	M	3		
Juan Manuel PEÑA (BOL)	D	33		
Alen PETERNAC (CRO)	A	32	(3)	13
César SANCHEZ	G	38		
José Luis SANTAMARIA	D	24	(1)	
Javier TORRES GOMEZ	D	31	(1)	2
Jesús Angel TURIEL	M	20	(9)	4
VICTOR Manuel Fernández	A	24	(4)	4
Juan VIZCAINO	M	31		1

LEAGUE RESULTS 1998/99

30/08/98	CF Extremadura	A	0-0	
12/09/98	Real Madrid	H	0-1	
20/09/98	RC Celta	A	0-0	
26/09/98	Valencia CF	H	3-1	Peternac, Torres Gómez, Alberto
04/10/98	UD Salamanca	A	0-1	
18/10/98	RCD Espanyol	H	2-1	Júlio César, og (Cristóbal)
25/10/98	Real Sociedad	A	0-1	
01/11/98	Real Oviedo	H	2-1	Caminero, Peternac
08/11/98	CD Tenerife	A	2-2	Torres Gómez, Peternac (p)
15/11/98	RCD Mallorca	H	1-0	Peternac
21/11/98	Atlético Madrid	A	1-6	Júlio César
29/11/98	RC Deportivo	H	0-1	
06/12/98	Villarreal CF	A	1-2	Peternac
13/12/98	CD Alavés	H	3-0	Turiel, Peternac 2
20/12/98	FC Barcelona	H	0-1	
03/01/99	Athletic Bilbao	A	1-2	Turiel
10/01/99	Real Betis	H	0-3	(forfeit; original result 2-1 Peternac 2 (1p))
17/01/99	Real Zaragoza	A	0-2	
24/01/99	Racing Santander	H	0-0	
31/01/99	CF Extremadura	H	0-0	
07/02/99	Real Madrid	A	2-3	Vizcaíno, Klimowicz
14/02/99	RC Celta	H	2-1	Caminero, Alberto
21/02/99	Valencia CF	A	1-0	Peternac
28/02/99	UD Salamanca	H	4-1	Peternac (p), Turiel, Alberto 2
07/03/99	RCD Espanyol	A	2-0	Peternac (p), Víctor (p)
14/03/99	Real Sociedad	H	0-0	
21/03/99	Real Oviedo	A	0-0	
04/04/99	CD Tenerife	H	2-1	Peternac, Víctor
11/04/99	RCD Mallorca	A	0-1	
17/04/99	Atlético Madrid	H	1-0	Víctor
25/04/99	RC Deportivo	A	0-3	
02/05/99	Villarreal CF	H	1-0	Víctor
09/05/99	CD Alavés	A	0-2	
15/05/99	FC Barcelona	A	1-1	Lozano
23/05/99	Athletic Bilbao	H	0-3	
30/05/99	Real Betis	A	0-2	
12/06/99	Real Zaragoza	H	1-1	Caminero
19/06/99	Racing Santander	A	2-0	Caminero, Turiel

VILLARREAL CF

Villarreal Club de Fútbol
Plaza Mayor 2
12540 Villarreal (Castellón)
tel - (964) 522714
fax - (964) 520337
Year of Formation - 1923
President - Fernando Roig Alfonso
Manager - Manuel Llorca Maset
Coach - José Antonio Irulegui;
Francisco García "Paquito"
Stadium - El Madrigal (12,000)

APPEARANCES 98/99

	P	Ap	(s)	Gls
David ALBELDA	M	35		2
ALBERTO Saavedra	M	24	(10)	3
Manuel ALFARO	A	22	(13)	12
ANGEL LUIS Fernández	M		(2)	
Aitor ARREGUI	D	30	(2)	
Thomas CHRISTIANSEN	A	6	(13)	1
Gheorghe CRAIOVEANU (ROM)	A	34	(1)	13
Antonio DIAZ	M	27	(8)	3
Walter Nicolás GAITAN (ARG)	M	5	(7)	
José Luis GARCIA SANTIJAN	M	11	(11)	
GERARDO García	M	31	(3)	2
IMANOL Alguacil	D	7	(1)	1
Marius IORDACHE (ROM)	A	1		
César LAINEZ	G	3		
Enrique MEDINA	D		(1)	
MOISES García	A	28	(5)	7
Andrés PALOP	G	35		
PASCUAL Donat	D	27	(4)	
Javier PRATS	D		(4)	
ROBERTO Fernández	M	35	(2)	2
Francisco Javier García "SALILLAS"	A		(2)	
Francisco Javier SANCHIS	M	2	(9)	
SANDRO Miguel Laranjeira (POR)	M	1	(1)	
José Pérez SERER	D	6	(2)	
Igor TASEVSKI (YUG)	D	28	(1)	
Oscar TELLEZ	D	20		

31/08/98	Real Madrid	A	1-4	Craioveanu
12/09/98	RC Celta	H	1-1	Craioveanu
20/09/98	Valencia CF	A	0-1	
27/09/98	UD Salamanca	H	5-0	Craioveanu 2, Díaz, Alfaro 2
04/10/98	RCD Espanyol	A	1-1	Díaz
17/10/98	Real Sociedad	H	1-1	Díaz
25/10/98	Real Oviedo	A	0-0	
01/11/98	CD Tenerife	H	2-5	Moisés (p), Imanol
08/11/98	RCD Mallorca	A	0-1	
15/11/98	Atlético Madrid	H	2-1	Craioveanu, Moisés
22/11/98	RC Deportivo	A	1-2	Moisés
29/11/98	CD Alavés	H	2-0	Alberto, Gerardo
06/12/98	Real Valladolid	H	2-1	Moisés 2
13/12/98	FC Barcelona	A	3-1	Craioveanu 2, Gerardo
20/12/98	Athletic Bilbao	H	0-1	
03/01/99	Real Betis	A	1-4	Alfaro (p)
10/01/99	Real Zaragoza	H	1-1	Alfaro (p)
17/01/99	Racing Santander	A	2-1	Christiansen, Alfaro
24/01/99	CF Extremadura	H	1-1	Roberto
30/01/99	Real Madrid	H	0-2	
07/02/99	RC Celta	A	1-4	Moisés
14/02/99	Valencia CF	H	1-0	Craioveanu
21/02/99	UD Salamanca	A	0-1	
28/02/99	RCD Espanyol	H	2-2	Alfaro, Alberto
07/03/99	Real Sociedad	A	1-1	Craioveanu
14/03/99	Real Oviedo	H	0-0	
21/03/99	CD Tenerife	A	2-2	Roberto, Alfaro (p)
03/04/99	RCD Mallorca	H	0-2	
11/04/99	Atlético Madrid	A	2-2	Craioveanu, Alberto
18/04/99	RC Deportivo	H	1-2	Alfaro (p)
25/04/99	CD Alavés	A	1-2	Albelda
02/05/99	Real Valladolid	A	0-1	
09/05/99	FC Barcelona	H	2-3	Alfaro, Moisés
16/05/99	Athletic Bilbao	A	0-2	
23/05/99	Real Betis	H	3-4	Alfaro (p), Craioveanu, og (Luis)
30/05/99	Real Zaragoza	A	0-4	
13/06/99	Racing Santander	H	3-0	Craioveanu, Alfaro 2 (1p)
20/06/99	CF Extremadura	A	2-2	Craioveanu, Albelda

REAL ZARAGOZA

CLUB DIRECTORY

Real Zaragoza
Luis Bermejo 3
50009 Zaragoza
tel - (976) 567777
fax - (976) 568863
Year of Formation - 1932
President - Alfonso Solans Solans
Manager - Jerónimo Suárez
Coach - José António Rojo
Stadium - La Romareda (34,741)

MAJOR HONOURS
Domestic Cup - (4)
1964, 1966, 1986, 1994.
European Cup-winners' Cup - (1) 1995.
Fairs' Cup - (1) 1964.

APPEARANCES 98/99

		P	Ap	(s)	Gls
Roberto Miguel ACUÑA (PAR)	M	29	(2)	2
Xavier AGUADO	D	36		4
Santiago ARAGON	M	22	(10)	3
Alberto BELSUE	D		(1)	
Luis Carlos CUARTERO	D	11	(2)	
Ander GARITANO	M	15	(4)	1
GILMAR Jorge dos Santos (BRA)	D		(1)	
Luis HELGUERA	M	2	(1)	
Paulo Roberto JAMELLI (BRA)	A	15	(8)	4
JOSE IGNACIO Sáenz	M	22	(9)	1
JUANMI García	G	25		
Cristián Alberto "KILY" GONZALEZ (ARG)	M	29		6
Gustavo Adrián LOPEZ (ARG)	A	18	(14)	5
Savo MILOSEVIC (YUG)	A	35		17
Farid MONDRAGON (COL)	G	13		
PABLO Javier Díaz	D	29	(3)	1
Francisco Jémez "PACO"	D	37		
Javier González PEÑA	A		(2)	
Vladislav RADIMOV (RUS)	M		(4)	
Jesús Angel SOLANA	D	15	(4)	
Gary SUNDGREN (SWE)	D	25		
Marcos VALES	M	29	(5)	6
Nordin WOOTER (HOL)	A	2	(16)	
Jorge González "YORDI"	A	9	(7)	5

LEAGUE RESULTS 1998/99

30/08/98	Athletic Bilbao	H	2-0	Vales, López
12/09/98	Real Betis	A	3-1	Vales, Jamelli, Milosevic
20/09/98	CD Alavés	A	0-1	
27/09/98	Racing Santander	H	3-1	Jamelli, Aragón, og (Villabona)
04/10/98	CF Extremadura	A	2-0	Kily González, Milosevic
17/10/98	Real Madrid	H	3-4	Milosevic, López, Kily González
24/10/98	RC Celta	A	0-2	
31/10/98	Valencia CF	H	1-4	Kily González
08/11/98	UD Salamanca	A	2-1	López, Jamelli
15/11/98	RCD Espanyol	H	0-3	
21/11/98	Real Sociedad	A	0-0	
29/11/98	Real Oviedo	H	1-0	Milosevic
06/12/98	CD Tenerife	A	1-1	Yordi
13/12/98	RCD Mallorca	H	0-1	
20/12/98	Atlético Madrid	A	0-0	
03/01/99	RC Deportivo	H	3-1	Yordi, Aragón, Milosevic
10/01/99	Villarreal CF	A	1-1	Milosevic
17/01/99	Real Valladolid	H	2-0	Aguado, Milosevic
24/01/99	FC Barcelona	A	1-3	Milosevic
30/01/99	Athletic Bilbao	A	0-2	
07/02/99	Real Betis	H	2-2	Aragón (p), Kily González
14/02/99	CD Alavés	H	1-1	José Ignacio
20/02/99	Racing Santander	A	4-2	Acuña, Pablo, Milosevic, Vales
28/02/99	CF Extremadura	H	3-1	Milosevic, Garitano, Vales
07/03/99	Real Madrid	A	2-3	Kily González 2
13/03/99	RC Celta	H	0-1	
21/03/99	Valencia CF	A	1-1	López
04/04/99	UD Salamanca	H	2-0	Aguado, Vales
11/04/99	RCD Espanyol	A	1-2	Vales
18/04/99	Real Sociedad	H	1-1	Milosevic
25/04/99	Real Oviedo	A	2-1	og (Bango), Milosevic
02/05/99	CD Tenerife	H	3-1	Aguado, Yordi, Milosevic
09/05/99	RCD Mallorca	A	0-1	
16/05/99	Atlético Madrid	H	2-0	López, Yordi
23/05/99	RC Deportivo	A	1-2	Acuña
30/05/99	Villarreal CF	H	4-0	Milosevic 2, Yordi, Aguado
12/06/99	Real Valladolid	A	1-1	Jamelli
20/06/99	FC Barcelona	H	2-0	Milosevic 2

PROMOTED CLUBS

SECOND DIVISION FINAL TABLE 98/99

		Pd	W	D	L	F	A	Pt	GD
1	**Málaga CF**	42	22	13	7	72	47	79	+25
2	Atlético Madrid B	42	21	11	10	73	51	74	+22
3	**CD Numancia**	42	21	10	11	68	40	73	+28
4	**Sevilla FC**	42	20	11	11	66	50	71	+16
5	**Rayo Vallecano**	42	19	14	9	64	49	71	+15
6	UD Las Palmas	42	17	17	8	57	38	68	+19
7	CD Toledo	42	18	11	13	54	49	65	+5
8	SD Compostela	42	16	13	13	60	53	61	+7
9	Sporting Gijón	42	16	11	15	47	47	59	0
10	CP Mérida	42	15	14	13	48	41	59	+7
11	UE Lleida	42	15	14	13	52	50	59	+2
12	RC Recreativo	42	14	16	12	40	35	58	+5
13	CA Osasuna	42	15	12	15	44	51	57	-7
14	CD Badajoz	42	12	15	15	35	39	51	-4
15	Albacete Balompié	42	12	14	16	38	43	50	-5
16	CD Logroñés	42	12	12	18	48	57	48	-9
17	CD Leganés	42	10	17	15	36	44	47	-8
18	SD Eibar	42	13	8	21	42	56	47	-14
19	RCD Mallorca B	42	12	10	20	52	64	46	-12
20	FC Barcelona B	42	13	5	24	51	68	44	-17
21	Hércules CF	42	10	10	22	38	66	40	-28
22	CD Ourense	42	7	6	29	35	82	27	-47

N.B. Atlético Madrid B ineligible for promotion.

PROMOTION/RELEGATION PLAY-OFFS

CF Extremadura 0, Rayo Vallecano 2
Rayo Vallecano 2, CF Extremadura 0
(Rayo Vallecano 4-0)

Villarreal CF 0, Sevilla FC 2
Sevilla FC 1, Villarreal CF 0
(Sevilla FC 3-0)

CLUB DIRECTORY

Málaga Club de Fútbol
Paseo de Martiricos s/n, 29011 Málaga
tel - (952) 614210 / fax - (952) 613737
Year of Formation - 1994
President - Fernando Puche
Coach - Joaquín Peiró
Stadium - La Rosaleda (37,000)

CLUB DIRECTORY

Club Deportivo Numancia
Av. Mariano Vicent 16, 42003 Soria
tel - (975) 227303 / fax - (975) 224081
Year of Formation - 1945
President - Francisco Rubio Garcés
Manager - Felipe Martínez Lago
Coach - Miguel Angel Lotina
(99/00 - Andoni Goikoetxea)
Stadium - Los Pajaritos (10,000)

CLUB DIRECTORY

Sevilla Fútbol Club
Estadio Sánchez Pizjuán, Avda Eduardo Dato s/n
41005 Sevilla
tel - (954) 535353 / fax - (954) 536061
Year of Formation - 1905
President - Rafael Carrión
Manager - Carmelo Gómez
Coach - Fernando Castro Santos; Marcos Alonso
Stadium - Sánchez Pizjuán (55,000)

MAJOR HONOURS
League Championship - (1) 1946.
Domestic Cup - (3) 1935, 1939, 1948.

CLUB DIRECTORY

Rayo Vallecano de Madrid
Avda Payaso Fofó s/n, 28018 Madrid
tel - (914) 782253 / fax - (914) 771754
Year of Formation - 1924
President - María Teresa Rivero Snchez
Manager - Félix Uceda
Coach - Juan de la Cruz Ramos
Stadium - Vallecas (15,500)

SWEDEN

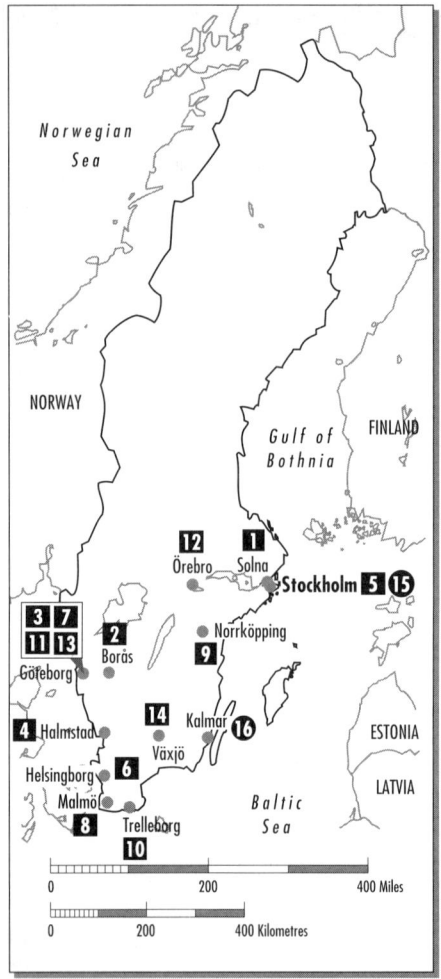

1	AIK	975	10	TRELLEBORGS FF	984
2	IF ELFSBORG	976	11	VÄSTRA FRÖLUNDA IF	985
3	IFK GÖTEBORG	977	12	ÖREBRO SK	986
4	HALMSTADS BK	978	13	ÖRGRYTE IS	987
5	HAMMARBY IF	979	14	ÖSTERS IF	988
6	HELSINGBORGS IF	980	Promoted clubs		
7	BK HÄCKEN	981	15	DJURGÅRDENS IF	989
8	MALMÖ FF	982	16	KALMAR FF	989
9	IFK NORRKÖPING	983			

TEAM WITH WORST ATTACK WINS TITLE

High-flying Swedes set for Low Countries swoop

FEDERATION DIRECTORY

Svenska Fotbollförbundet
P.O. Box 1216, 171 23 Solna

tel - (08) 7350900   Year of Formation - 1904
fax - (08) 275147   President - Lars-Åke Lagrell
                        Secretary - Lars-Christer Olsson

Stadium - Råsunda Stadion, Solna (36,000)

Having been frustrated onlookers at both Euro '96 and France '98, Sweden did just about everything possible during their first five Euro 2000 qualifying matches to ensure that they would be back on the big stage for the first major international tournament of the 21st century.

The Swedes closed the first stage of their European Championship qualifying campaign with a goalless draw against England at Wembley. The celebrations that broke out at the final whistle might have seemed incongruous to some given that the team had just dropped their first points of the competition against a team reduced to ten men for almost the entire second half. But Sweden had come for the draw and they had got what they wanted, which in essence was the security of taking first place in the group and qualifying automatically for the finals in Belgium and Holland. No matter that, with a touch more ambition, they could have beaten England for the second time in the competition.

Their first victory over the English had been achieved precisely nine months earlier when, in their opening qualifier, Sweden came from behind to win 2-1 in the Råsunda stadium - almost a replica of the triumph six years earlier during the finals of Euro '92. From that day forward Tommy Söderberg's side did everything asked of them. They won in Bulgaria, courtesy of in-form striker Henrik Larsson's only goal, and they also won in Poland, 1-0 again, with another British-based player, Arsenal's Fredrik Ljungberg, capturing the headlines thanks to a brilliant solo strike. With a routine home win against Luxembourg thrown into the mix, it seemed inconceivable that Sweden would fail to qualify for the finals - their first since the 1994 World Cup, when, of course, they finished third.

Söderberg, who replaced USA '94 boss Tommy Svensson after the team's failure to qualify for France '98, has made few significant changes to the side either tactically or in terms of personnel. 4-4-2 remains the tried-and-trusted norm, with a large proportion of the class of '94 still around to slot into the positions they have made their own. Thus, the back-four continues to feature Roland Nilsson (the third centurion in Swedish football history) at right-back, Patrik Andersson and Joachim Björklund in the centre, and right-footed Pontus Kåmark on the left. Stefan Schwarz still pulls the strings in midfield, while up front the towering Kennet Andersson remains a goal-scoring figurehead, with the ever-improving Henrik Larsson as his nifty accomplice.

LEAGUE CHAMPIONSHIP RESULTS 1998

		1	2	3	4	5	6	7	8	9	10	11	12	13	14
1	AIK		1-1	1-0	1-0	0-1	1-1	2-1	1-0	1-1	1-1	0-0	2-0	1-0	1-1
2	IF Elfsborg	1-1		1-0	3-4	0-1	0-1	2-0	2-1	1-1	1-1	0-2	0-1	2-2	2-1
3	IFK Göteborg	0-1	1-0		1-2	2-2	0-1	1-1	1-0	0-0	1-0	1-2	2-0	2-5	1-1
4	Halmstads BK	1-1	0-3	1-1		1-3	1-0	0-1	2-1	3-1	3-0	1-0	2-0	2-1	1-2
5	Hammarby IF	0-2	1-0	1-1	1-1		3-3	3-3	1-3	3-2	1-0	0-1	3-1	1-0	0-1
6	Helsingborgs IF	0-1	2-0	0-1	1-0	2-2		0-0	1-2	1-1	3-0	6-2	0-0	2-1	3-1
7	BK Häcken	1-1	0-2	1-1	3-2	4-3	2-1		2-1	0-1	0-5	0-1	2-4	0-2	0-1
8	Malmö FF	0-0	0-4	3-1	5-0	2-2	1-1	4-0		1-0	0-1	0-0	1-3	3-1	2-0
9	IFK Norrköping	2-0	1-1	0-1	4-6	1-2	3-4	5-1	2-1		3-0	1-3	4-0	1-1	1-0
10	Trelleborgs FF	0-0	2-2	0-2	1-3	1-1	4-2	0-1	0-0	0-0		3-0	1-0	2-1	2-0
11	Västra Frölunda IF	1-1	1-1	0-3	0-1	2-1	0-0	1-1	1-3	3-2	3-1		1-1	1-0	3-0
12	Örebro SK	1-1	4-2	4-0	3-2	0-1	1-3	1-0	0-0	1-3	4-2	1-1		1-1	2-1
13	Örgryte IS	0-1	2-2	1-2	2-2	0-1	0-2	2-1	2-0	1-1	1-2	2-0	2-0		4-4
14	Östers IF	1-2	2-3	1-1	1-1	1-1	1-3	0-2	2-1	0-2	2-2	1-0	1-2	0-1	

LEAGUE CHAMPIONSHIP FINAL TABLE 1998

		Home					Away					Total						
		P	W	D	L	F	A	W	D	L	F	A	W	D	L	F	A	P	GD
1	AIK	26	6	6	1	13	7	5	7	1	12	8	11	13	2	25	15	46	+10
2	Helsingborgs IF	26	6	4	3	21	11	6	4	3	22	17	12	8	6	43	28	44	+15
3	Hammarby IF	26	5	4	4	18	18	6	5	2	21	16	11	9	6	39	34	42	+5
4	Halmstads BK	26	7	2	4	18	14	5	3	5	24	26	12	5	9	42	40	41	+2
5	Västra Frölunda IF	26	5	5	3	17	15	5	3	5	12	16	10	8	8	29	31	38	-2
6	Örebro SK	26	6	4	3	23	17	4	2	7	12	21	10	6	10	35	38	36	-3
7	IFK Norrköping	26	6	2	5	28	20	3	6	4	15	15	9	8	9	43	35	35	+8
8	IFK Göteborg	26	4	4	5	13	15	5	4	4	14	14	9	8	9	27	29	35	-2
9	Malmö FF	26	6	4	3	22	13	3	2	8	13	17	9	6	11	35	30	33	+5
10	IF Elfsborg	26	4	4	5	15	16	4	5	4	21	17	8	9	9	36	33	33	+3
11	Trelleborgs FF	26	5	5	3	16	12	3	3	7	15	23	8	8	10	31	35	32	-4
12	Örgryte IS	26	4	4	5	19	18	3	3	7	16	18	7	7	12	35	36	28	-1
13	BK Häcken	26	4	2	7	15	25	3	4	6	12	21	7	6	13	27	46	27	-19
14	Östers IF	26	2	4	7	13	21	3	3	7	13	22	5	7	14	26	43	22	-17

The absence of other USA '94 veterans has largely been forced on Söderberg, with four key members of that contingent - Thomas Ravelli, Jonas Thern, Tomas Brolin and Martin Dahlin - all deciding, through age or injury, to quit football altogether in 1999.

Of the new intake, the most promising are Ravelli-replacement Magnus Hedman, striker Jörgen Pettersson and the two highly-talented young midfielders, Ljungberg and Daniel Andersson. Sweden have the team and the squad to give a good account of themselves in the European finals. Whether they can match their 1994 exploits, however, remains doubtful. To do so, they would probably need one of their leading individuals - Larsson, Ljungberg, etc. - to raise his game to unprecedented new heights; just as, for example, Dahlin and Kennet Andersson did in America.

That Söderberg's team is made up almost entirely of foreign-based professionals probably goes some way to explaining the contrast in recent fortunes of the national team and Sweden's clubs. In 1998/99 the four Allsvenskan representatives in the European club competitions combined to produce the most dismal collective performance in living memory. The only defeated opposition came from Liechtenstein, Luxembourg and Armenia, and the only Swedish team still involved after the preliminary rounds had been completed were Cup-winners' Cup participants Helsingborg, who lasted just one round longer.

TOP SCORERS

18 Arild STAVRUM (Helsingborgs IF)
13 Hans BERGGREN (Hammarby IF)
12 Christer MATTIASSON (IF Elfsborg)
11 Mats LILIENBERG (Halmstads BK)
10 Henrik BERTILSSON (Örgryte IS)
   Dejan PAVLOVIC (Malmö FF)
   Dan SAHLIN (Örebro SK)
8 Andreas HERMANSSON (IFK Göteborg)
   Andreas OTTOSSON (Östers IF)
   Tomas ROSENKVIST (Västra Frölunda IF)

NATIONAL TEAM RESULTS 98/99

19/08/98	Russia	H	Örebro	1-0	Pettersson (3)
05/09/98	England (ECQ)	H	Solna	2-1	Andersson A. (30), Mjällby (33)
14/10/98	Bulgaria (ECQ)	A	Bourgas	1-0	Larsson (62)
10/02/99	Tunisia	A	Tunis	1-0	Alexandersson (77)
27/03/99	Luxembourg (ECQ)	H	Gothenburg	2-0	Mjällby (34), Larsson (86)
31/03/99	Poland (ECQ)	A	Chorzow	1-0	Ljungberg (36)
28/04/99	Republic of Ireland	A	Dublin	0-2	
27/05/99	Jamaica	H	Solna	2-1	Osmanovski (18, 29)
05/06/99	England (ECQ)	A	Wembley	0-0	

In fairness, all four teams departed after narrow aggregate defeats, but Halmstad should have been able to beat Liteks Lovech of Bulgaria in the Champions' Cup while IFK Gothenburg and Malmö FF both surrendered advantageous first-leg situations in the UEFA Cup. With both Gothenburg and Malmö going out at the second qualifying round stage, it meant that for the first time in 20 years neither of Sweden's traditional top two were involved in European competition in September.

The ills of Gothenburg and Malmö were not confined to external affairs. Both clubs suffered a nightmare season in the domestic league, with respective coaches Mats Jingblad and Frans Thijssen both failing to last the duration. Gothenburg, who after heavy pre-season investment had been seen as clear favourites to regain the Allsvenskan crown, plunged headlong into crisis right at the start, suffering the double embarrassment of losing to supposedly inferior city rivals Västra Frölunda and Örgryte and never remotely looking like a team capable of winning the title. They eventually finished eighth, one place above Malmö, whose long-standing chairman, Hans Cavalli-Björkman,

NATIONAL TEAM APPEARANCES 98/99

Coach - Tommy SÖDERBERG	RUS	ENG	BUL	TUN	LUX	POL	IRL	JAM	ENG	Cps	Gls
Magnus HEDMAN (19/03/73) - Coventry City (ENG)	G	G	G	G46	G	G		G	G	16	-
Roland NILSSON (27/11/63) - Coventry City (ENG)	D46	D	D	D				D46	D	102	1
Patrik ANDERSSON (18/08/71) - Borussia Mönchengladbach (GER)	D	D	D	D	D	D	D	D67	D	70	2
Joachim BJÖRKLUND (15/03/71) - Valencia CF (ESP)	D46	D	D	D	D	D	D46		D	67	-
Pontus KÅMARK (05/04/69) - Leicester City (ENG)	D	D82		s65	D68	D	D	D	D	45	-
Stefan SCHWARZ (18/04/69) - Valencia CF (ESP)	M	M	M		M	M	M		M	62	6
Pär ZETTERBERG (14/10/70) - RSC Anderlecht (BEL)	M81									29	6
Henrik LARSSON (20/09/71) - Celtic (SCO)	M	A	A88	A46	A	A89	A		A69	42	9
Fredrik LJUNGBERG (16/04/77) - Halmstads BK/Arsenal (ENG)	M	M	M		M78	M		M46	M	10	2
Andreas ANDERSSON (10/04/74) - Newcastle United (ENG)	A69	M89	M84							23	5
Jörgen PETTERSSON (29/05/75) - Borussia Mönchengladbach (GER)	A	A		s46		s89	A80	A46		19	5
Teddy LUCIC (15/04/73) - IFK Göteborg/Bologna (ITA)	s46	s82	D76	D65	s68	D	D			24	-
Johan MJÄLLBY (09/02/71) - AIK/Celtic (SCO)	s46	M	M		M	M			M82	11	2
Daniel ANDERSSON (28/08/77) - Bari (ITA)	s69	s89		M	s78		M	M	s82	13	-
Magnus SVENSSON (10/03/69) - Viking FK (NOR)	s81							M	s69	5	-
Håkan MILD (14/06/71) - IFK Göteborg		M				M73	M46		M6	51	6
Martin ÅSLUND (10/11/76) - IFK Norrköping		A71								1	-
Jesper BLOMQVIST (05/02/74) - Manchester United (ENG)		s71	M				M			29	-
Gary SUNDGREN (25/10/67) - Real Zaragoza (ESP)		s76		D						25	1
Magnus ERLINGMARK (08/07/68) - IFK Göteborg		s88								37	1
Niclas ALEXANDERSSON (29/12/71) - Sheffield Wednesday (ENG)			M	M	s73	s46	M	s6		35	3
Kennet ANDERSSON (06/10/67) - Bologna (ITA)			A	A	A				A	69	30
Magnus KIHLSTEDT (29/02/72) - SK Brann (NOR)			s46			G				3	-
Mattias JONSSON (16/01/74) - Helsingborgs IF			s84			s80	s46			10	1
Andreas JACOBSSON (06/10/72) - Helsingborgs IF						s46				9	-
Mikael HELLSTRÖM (11/03/72) - Hammarby IF							D			1	-
Yksel OSMANOVSKI (24/02/77) - Bari (ITA)							A			4	2
Mikael GUSTAVSSON (15/08/74) - Halmstads BK							s46			2	-
Fredrik SÖDERSTRÖM (20/01/73) - Vitória Guimarães (POR)							s46			2	-
Johan ANEGRUND (01/03/73) - IFK Göteborg							s67			1	-

EUROPEAN CUPS 98/99

CHAMPIONS' CUP
● **HALMSTADS BK**
Preliminary round LITEKS LOVECH (BUL)
A 0-2
    Nordberg; Gustavsson, Svensson M., Jönsson, Andersson, Carlsson,
    Mattsson, Ljungberg, Sakiri (Aubynn 73), Lilienberg, Vougt.
H 2-1   Sakiri (39), Arvidsson (43)
    Nordberg; Gustavsson, Mattsson, Jönsson (Svensson M. 85),
    Andersson (Rolfsson 71), Carlsson (Selakovic 87), Arvidsson, Ljungberg,
    Sakiri, Lilienberg, Vougt.

CUP WINNERS' CUP
● **HELSINGBORGS IF**
Qualifying round FC VADUZ (LIE)
A 2-0   Stavrum (9), Wibrån (70)
    Andersson S.; Ljung P-O. (Nilsson 46), Jacobsson, Jovanovski, Edman,
    Wibrån, Lantz, Storvik, Stavrum (Jansson 72), Powell (Wahlstedt 36),
    Andersson C..
H 3-0   Wibrån (44), Edman (58), Powell (68)
    Andersson S.; Ljung P-O., Jacobsson, Jovanovski, Edman (Nilsson 72),
    Wibrån, Jansson, Lantz, Stavrum, Wahlstedt (Andersson C. 78), Storvik
    (Powell 46).

1st round CHELSEA (ENG)
A 0-1
    Andersson S.; Nilsson, Jacobsson, Jovanovski, Edman, Wibrån,
    Lantz, Storvik (Ljung P-O. 90), Stavrum (Wahlstedt 66), Johansen
    (Jonsson 75), Powell.
H 0-0
    Andersson S.; Nilsson, Jacobsson, Jovanovski, Edman (Andersson C. 82),
    Wibrån, Lantz, Storvik, Stavrum (Johansen 64), Powell, Jonsson
    (Wahlstedt 72).

UEFA CUP
● **IFK GÖTEBORG**
Preliminary round UNION LUXEMBOURG (LUX)
A 3-0   Ekström (58), Nilsson (63p), Hermansson (86)
    Last; Lucic, Karlsson C., Erlingmark, Nilsson, Pehrsson, Persson
    (Henriksson 73), Mild (Karlsson P. 80), Landberg, Tetteh (Ekström 55),
    Hermansson.

H 4-0   Ekström (17, 50, 79), Henriksson (71)
    Last; Lucic, Karlsson C., Erlingmark, Nilsson (Bärlin 68), Pehrsson,
    Persson, Mild (Henriksson 70), Landberg, Ekström, Hermansson
    (Andersson C. 65).

Qualifying round FENERBAHÇE (TUR)
H 2-1   Hermansson (37), Persson (74)
    Andersson B.; Lucic, Karlsson C., Erlingmark, Johansson (Magnusson 73),
    Bärlin, Persson, Mild (Ekström 64), Karlsson P., Landberg (Pehrsson 83),
    Hermansson.
A 0-1
    Andersson B.; Magnusson (Bärlin 75), Lucic, Erlingmark, Karlsson C.,
    Johansson, Pettersson (Henriksson 64), Persson, Karlsson P., Ekström,
    Hermansson.

● **MALMÖ FF**
Preliminary round SHIRAK GYUMRI (ARM)
A 2-0   Pavlovic (55), Ohlsson (68)
    Fedel; Thylander, Ohlsson, Persson, Roth, Tavell, Bjarnason (Kindvall 43),
    Sverrisson, Enqvist, Pavlovic (Waldh 85), Trpevski.
H 5-0   Thylander (19), Kindvall (33, 45, 77), Gudmundsson (68)
    Tidman; Thylander, Ohlsson, Wirmola, Roth (Mattisson 46), Tavell,
    Persson, Sverrisson, Enqvist (Trpevski 67), Pavlovic (Gudmundsson 46),
    Kindvall.

Qualifying round HAJDUK SPLIT (CRO)
A 1-1   Bjarnason (72)
    Simeunovic; Thylander, Ohlsson, Wirmola (Bjarnason 22), Persson,
    Tavell, Mattisson, Sverrisson, Gudmundsson, Pavlovic, Kindvall
    (Trpevski 83).
H 1-2   Ohlsson (90)
    Simeunovic; Thylander, Ohlsson, Wirmola, Persson, Tavell, Mattisson,
    Sverrisson, Gudmundsson, Pavlovic (Kindvall 75), Trpevski.

---

decided that enough was enough and stood down after
25 years.

Defending champions Halmstad also made a wretched
start, losing their opening home game and then all but
throwing in the towel after three successive defeats in May.
They somehow managed to climb their way up to fourth
place, but never at any stage was another title realistically
in their sights.

There were just three championship contenders -
Stockholm duo AIK and Hammarby plus Cup-winners
Helsingborg. Between them they were to deliver a battle
that was tense, absorbing and unpredictable but for the
most part sorely lacking in quality and entertainment. That
the most consistent but least spectacular of the three teams
should ultimately emerge triumphant was quite fitting, but
it is fair to say that, other than among their own fans, AIK's

tenth Swedish title was not exactly greeted with rapturous
acclaim.

AIK's statistics were truly extraordinary. They won the
championship despite scoring fewer goals than any
other team in the division - an incredible feat. In total they
managed just 25 goals - less than one a game. In normal
circumstances that would have been relegation form,
but so strong and reliable was the team's defence that
they rarely needed more than one goal for victory. In fact,
only on four occasions did they score a second. 1-0
was AIK's preferred victory margin. They settled for
that scoreline in seven matches, including the last of the
campaign, at home to Örgryte. That result proved good
enough to bring them their first title since 1992.

Tommy Söderberg had been the AIK coach then. Now
the man in charge was Stuart Baxter, a bearded Scotsman

virtually unknown in his homeland but with a proven track-record both in Scandinavia and the Far East. He constructed an efficient, highly consistent team, in which goalkeeper Mattias Asper, centre-back Patrick Englund and midfield colossus Johan Mjällby all made outstanding individual contributions, but not even he could have masterminded the dénouement of the title race, which effectively saw AIK handed the championship on a plate.

The big favourites with one match remaining were Helsingborg. They went into their final fixture, away to already relegated BK Häcken, on a roll. With four wins in succession, including a crucial 1-0 victory away to IFK Gothenburg, in which the league's top scorer, Norwegian Arild Stavrum, fired home the winning goal, Helsingborg were just one victory away from landing their first post-war championship - and also completing a calendar-year 'double', having already picked up the Swedish Cup

several months earlier. But the moment of truth found them wanting. Two goals from Häcken striker Matthias Larsson left them defeated 2-1, while over in the capital AIK were overtaking them with yet another 1-0 victory, courtesy of Alexander Östlund's all-important 50th-minute strike.

AIK's city rivals Hammarby were another team guilty of caving in and conceding the title, although not in quite such dramatic circumstances as Helsingborg. The newly-promoted team were on course for their first-ever championship until they hit the final straight. Then, suddenly, they began to throw away points at an alarming rate, failing to win any more matches until the title was mathematically beyond them. Hammarby could also look back with regret at the mid-season 0-2 defeat by AIK - an encounter switched to the Råsunda in order to fulfil the demand for tickets and which eventually drew a huge crowd of 33,094 - far and away the biggest of the season.

DOMESTIC CUP 98/99

THIRD ROUND
Kulladals FF 3, Malmö FF 4 (asd)
Mjällby AIF 1, Trelleborgs FF 4
Ängelholms FF 0, Halmstads BK 1
Landskrona BoIS 0, Helsingborgs IF 2
Lindome GIF 1, IK Oddevold 5
IS Halmia 0, Västra Frölunda IF 1 (asd)
Nässjö FF 5, Kalmar FF 1
Holmalunds IF 0, Stenungsunds IF 3
Hertzöga BK 1, Örebro SK 2
Forshaga IF 1, Motala AIK FK 5
Torslanda IK 1, IFK Göteborg 3
Köping FF 1, Spårvagens FF 2
IF Sylvia 1, IF Elfsborg 3
Bellevue IK 2, Assyriska Föreningen 4
Huddinge IF 1, Värtans IK 2
IFK Nyköping 0, IFK Eskilstuna 5
Qviding FIF 4, BK Häcken 2
Syrianska Föreningen 1, Enköpings SK FK 4
KB Karlskoga 1, IFK Norrköping 2 (asd)
Hamrånge GIF 0, IK Brage 5
IK Kongahälla 1, Panos Ljungskile SK 5
Bollnäs GolF FF 0, Ludvika FK 2
IK Huge 1, IK Sirius FK 7
Degerfors IF 2, Hammarby IF 3 (asd)
IFK Timrå 0, GIF Sundsvall 4
Alnö IF 0, Gefle IF 6
Tyresö FF 1, AIK 2
Domsjö IF 0, Gimonäs 1
Falkenbergs FF 0, Örgryte IS 4
Umedalens IF 5, Assi IF 3
Täfteå IK 0, Umeå FC 4
Kiruna FF 2, Piteå IF 1

FOURTH ROUND
IK Brage 0, Örebro SK 2
IK Oddevold 0, Malmö FF 5
IFK Eskilstuna 0, Örgryte IS 3
Nässjö FF 1, IF Elfsborg 4
Qviding FIF 2, Västra Frölunda IF 4
Stenungsunds IF 2, Trelleborgs FF 3
Assyriska 0, IFK Norrköping 1
Panos Ljungskile SK 0, IFK Göteborg 2
Enköpings SK FK 0, Helsingborgs IF 5
Motala AIF FK 0, Halmstads BK 3
Värtans IK 2, Ludvika FK 4
Gimonäs CK 1, Spårvagens FF 3
IK Sirius FK 1, Hammarby IF 3
Umedalens IF 1, GIF Sundsvall 3
Gefle IF 0, AIK 3
Kiruna FF 1, Umeå FC 2

FIFTH ROUND
IFK Göteborg 2, IF Elfsborg 1 (asd)
Örgryte IS 4, Umeå FC 0
Ludvika FK 2, Spårvägens FF 2 (aet; 4-2 on pens.)
Halmstads BK 0, AIK 1
Malmö FF 0, Örebro SK 0 (aet; 5-4 on pens.)
GIF Sundsvall 1, IFK Norrköping 2
Helsingborgs IF 1, Hammarby IF 0
Västra Frölunda IF 0, Trelleborgs FF 2

QUARTER-FINALS
Ludvika FK 0,
Malmö FF 5 (Lilienberg 28, Ohlsson 48, Pavlovic 52, Mattisson 56, Tavell 84)
Helsingborgs IF 2 (Jonsson 26, Stavrum 41),
Örgryte IS 1 (Allbäck 29)

AIK 1 (Englund 102), Trelleborgs FF 0 (asd)
IFK Norrköping 0, IFK Göteborg 3
(Hermansson 18, Erlingmark 31, Lundén 78)

SEMI-FINALS
AIK 2 (Novakovic 10p, Tjernström 12),
Helsingborgs IF 1 (Storvik 5)
Malmö FF 1 (Pavlovic 24),
IFK Göteborg 2 (Karlsson P. 85, Lundén 113) (asd)

FINAL
14/05/99, Solna
AIK 1 Englund (84)
IFK GÖTEBORG 0
AIK - Asper; Nordin, Corneliusson, Brundin, Gustafsson, Novakovic, Tjernström (Ishikazi 83), Mattiasson (Rahmberg 59), Lagerlöf; Englund, Johansson.
IFK GÖTEBORG - Andersson B.; Hoiland, Pedersen, Karlsson C., Nilsson; Persson (Bärlin 34), Erlingmark, Mild, Karlsson P.; Hermansson (Lundén 65), Andersson P..

20/05/99, Gothenburg
IFK GÖTEBORG 0
AIK 0
IFK GÖTEBORG - Andersson B.; Hoiland, Pedersen, Anegrund, Landberg; Persson (Bärlin 34), Erlingmark, Mild, Karlsson P.; Hermansson (Lundén 60), Andersson P. (Nevland 60).
AIK - Asper; Nordin, Englund, Brundin, Kjølø; Bergh (Rahmberg 29), Tjernström, Gustafsson, Lagerlöf; Mattiasson (Andersson 83); Johansson (Corneliusson 60).
(AIK 1-0)

PLAYERS OF THE SEASON

HENRIK LARSSON

Dreadlocked striker Henrik Larsson had few rivals for Sweden's 1998 Footballer of the Year prize. At the end of a year in which he had helped Scottish club Celtic to a long-awaited championship win and spearheaded Sweden's challenge for the Euro 2000 finals, the *Guldbollen* deservedly ended up in his hands for the first time. There was no let-up in his

form during 1999, either. Although Celtic failed to retain their Scottish title, Larsson topped the Premier League goal charts by a street, scoring 29 goals, to which he added five more in the Scottish Cup and another four in Europe. Not surprisingly, his considerable efforts earned him both Scottish Player of the Year awards. Big in Sweden. Big in Scotland. Now the smiling 28-year-old aims to be Big in Europe. It could happen for him in Belgium and Holland next summer.

DANIEL ANDERSSON

When Daniel Andersson left for Italy in mid-1998, his hometown club Malmö FF were going through a decidedly rough patch. Although they could ill afford to lose their best player, Malmö were undeniably proud to see their young midfielder head for a new career in Serie A with Bari. What they could not foresee, however, was that he would go on to be such a roaring success in the world's toughest, most glamorous league. He missed just one match all season for Bari and proved himself to be one of the most watchable playmakers in Italy, setting up a succession of goals for his ex-Malmö team-mate Yksel Osmanovski and South African striker Phil Masinga. Regular call-ups to the Swedish national squad ensued (at the expense of Anderlecht schemer Pär Zetterberg), but by the end of the season, surprisingly, he had still to start his first competitive international.

AIK and Hammarby had the best average attendances of the season (11,077 and 10,967, respectively), and there was a promise of more to come in 1999 with the promotion of a third Stockholm team, Djurgården, who came up as winners of the First Division North. Kalmar FF took the other automatic promotion place, thereby ending a 13-year absence from Allsvenskan, but Umeå and Landskrona, the two regional runners-up, failed to add to the count after both being comprehensively beaten in their play-off matches.

Djurgården and Kalmar were both sampling the high life by the time the latter stages of the 1998/99 Swedish Cup came around. The semi-finals offered either Gothenburg or Malmö a last chance of qualifying for Europe, and it was the former who seized the opportunity, reaching the final, against champions AIK, after a sudden-death 2-1 triumph. But there was no trophy for

Gothenburg to add to their UEFA Cup place. In keeping with the way they had won the championship six months earlier, AIK triumphed in the final by keeping their goal intact and scoring just the one goal. That was how the first leg finished, and the score remained unaltered after the return in Gothenburg. 1-0 to the AIK - an increasingly familiar refrain.

INTERNATIONAL HONOURS

World Cup Finals appearances: 1934 (2nd round), 1938 (4th), 1950 (3rd), 1958 (runners-up), 1970, 1974 (2nd phase), 1978, 1990, 1994 (3rd)

European Championship appearances (last 8): 1964, 1992 (semi-finals)

European Club Competitions
UEFA Cup   IFK Göteborg (1982, 1987)

AIK

Allmänna Idrottsklubben
Box 1408
171 27 Solna
tel - (08) 7359600
fax - (08) 7359696
Year of Formation - 1891
President - Sune Hellströmer
Secretary - Lars Pettersson
Coach - Stuart Baxter
Stadium - Råsunda Stadion (36,000)

MAJOR HONOURS
League Championship - (10) 1900, 1901, 1911,
1914, 1916, 1923, 1932, 1937, 1992, 1998.
Domestic Cup - (7) 1949, 1950, 1976, 1985,
1996, 1997, 1999.

APPEARANCES 1998

	P	Ap	(s)	Gls
Ola ANDERSSON	M	3	(2)	
Mattias ASPER	G	19		
Lee BAXTER (ENG)	G	7		
Hans BERGH	M	8	(3)	1
Michael BRUNDIN	D	23	(1)	
Patrick ENGLUND	D	18	(2)	1
Patrik FREDHOLM	A	10	(11)	1
Tomas GUSTAFSON	D	25		
Daniel HOCH	A	1	(1)	
Mike KJØLØ (NOR)	D	25		
Thomas LAGERLÖF	D	19	(5)	3
Anders LIMPAR	M	16	(2)	2
David LJUNG	D		(2)	
Olof MELLBERG	D	17		
Pär MILLQVIST	D	2	(8)	
Johan MJÄLLBY	M	24		2
Krister NORDIN	M	24		3
Nebojsa NOVAKOVIC (YUG)	A	24	(1)	5
PIRACAÍA (BRA)	M	1	(1)	
Marino RAHMBERG	A	7	(12)	3
Andreas YNGVESSON	M		(1)	
Alexander ÖSTLUND	A	13	(11)	1

LEAGUE RESULTS 1998

13/04/98	Trelleborgs FF	H	1-1	Limpar
18/04/98	Halmstads BK	H	1-0	Nordin
26/04/98	BK Häcken	A	1-1	Novakovic
05/05/98	IF Elfsborg	H	1-1	og (Alexandersson)
10/05/98	Örebro SK	A	1-1	Rahmberg
19/05/98	Hammarby IF	H	0-1	
04/06/98	IFK Norrköping	A	0-2	
08/06/98	Östers IF	H	1-1	Fredholm
11/06/98	Örgryte IS	A	1-0	Mjällby
15/06/98	Västra Frölunda IF	A	1-1	Rahmberg
24/06/98	Malmö FF	H	1-0	Mjällby
29/06/98	IFK Göteborg	A	1-0	Englund
20/07/98	Helsingborgs IF	A	1-0	Limpar
03/08/98	IFK Norrköping	H	1-1	og (Wallerstedt)
10/08/98	Hammarby IF	A	2-0	Lagerlöf, Novakovic
16/08/98	Västra Frölunda IF	H	0-0	
24/08/98	Östers IF	A	2-1	Novakovic, og (Thórdarson)
31/08/98	Helsingborgs IF	H	1-1	Lagerlöf
10/09/98	IFK Göteborg	H	1-0	Lagerlöf
21/09/98	Malmö FF	A	0-0	
28/09/98	BK Häcken	H	2-1	Bergh, Nordin
04/10/98	Halmstads BK	A	1-1	Novakovic (p)
19/10/98	Örebro SK	H	2-0	Nordin, Novakovic
26/10/98	IF Elfsborg	A	1-1	Rahmberg
31/10/98	Trelleborgs FF	A	0-0	
08/11/98	Örgryte IS	H	1-0	Östlund

IF ELFSBORG

CLUB DIRECTORY

Idrottsföreningen Elfsborg
Skaraborgsvägen 55
506 30 Borås
tel - (033) 139191
fax - (033) 129191
Year of Formation - 1904
President - Kjell Hallén
Secretary - Sture Svensson
Coach - Karl-Gunnar Björklund
Stadium - Ryavallen (19,400)

MAJOR HONOURS
League Championship - (4)
1936, 1939, 1940, 1961.

APPEARANCES 1998

		P	Ap	(s)	Gls
Joakim ALEXANDERSSON	D	23			2
Stefan ANDREASSON	M	12	(2)		4
Kristoffer ARVHAGE	D	11	(4)		
Gbassay BANGURA (SRL)	D	7			
Jesper BENGTSSON	M	19	(2)		1
Fredrik BERGLUND	A	7	(14)		4
Anders BOGSJÖ	G	26			
Haraldur INGÓLFSSON (ISL)	M	1	(3)		
Ulf JOHANSSON	D	4	(3)		
Andreas KLARSTRÖM	M		(1)		
Tobias LINDEROTH	M	14	(8)		3
Mikael MARTINSSON	A	11			1
Christer MATTIASSON	A	22	(3)		12
Joacim MODIGH	D	16	(1)		
Stefan MOGREN	D	26			
Andreas NICKLASSON	M	1	(3)		
Kjetil Ruthford PEDERSEN (NOR)	D	22	(1)		2
Niclas PETERSMO	M		(6)		
Anders SVENSSON	M	24	(2)		5
Daniel UNG	M	25			
Johan WAHLQVIST	D		(2)		
Jörgen WAHLQVIST	D		(2)		
Jörgen WÅLEMARK	A	15	(8)		2
Tomas ÖRN	M		(1)		

LEAGUE RESULTS 1998

13/04/98	Helsingborgs IF	H	0-1	
19/04/98	Örgryte IS	A	2-2	Svensson, Alexandersson
27/04/98	Trelleborgs FF	H	1-1	Mattiasson
03/05/98	AIK	A	1-1	Linderoth
07/05/98	IFK Norrköping	A	1-1	Mattiasson
11/05/98	BK Häcken	H	2-0	Wålemark, Berglund
18/05/98	Östers IF	H	2-1	Mattiasson 2
03/06/98	Västra Frölunda IF	A	1-1	Alexandersson
09/06/98	Malmö FF	H	2-1	Wålemark, Berglund
14/06/98	IFK Göteborg	A	0-1	
23/06/98	Halmstads BK	H	3-4	Mattiasson 2, Linderoth
29/06/98	Örebro SK	A	2-4	Bengtsson, Linderoth
20/07/98	Hammarby IF	A	0-1	
03/08/98	Västra Frölunda IF	H	0-2	
09/08/98	Östers IF	A	3-2	Andreasson, Mattiasson, Svensson
16/08/98	IFK Göteborg	H	1-0	Mattiasson
22/08/98	Malmö FF	A	4-0	Mattiasson 2, Andreasson, Martinsson
31/08/98	Hammarby IF	H	0-1	
14/09/98	Örebro SK	H	0-1	
21/09/98	Halmstads BK	A	3-0	Mattiasson, Andreasson, Pedersen
28/09/98	Trelleborgs FF	A	2-2	Mattiasson, Pedersen
05/10/98	Örgryte IS	H	2-2	Svensson 2
22/10/98	BK Häcken	A	2-0	Berglund, Andreasson (p)
26/10/98	AIK	H	1-1	Svensson
31/10/98	Helsingborgs IF	A	0-2	
08/11/98	IFK Norrköping	H	1-1	Berglund

IFK GÖTEBORG

CLUB DIRECTORY

Idrottsföreningen Kamraterna Göteborg
Alfreds Gärdes Väg
416 55 Göteborg
tel - (031) 7037300
fax - (031) 404121
Year of Formation - 1904
President - Gunnar Larsson
Secretary - Ronny Sjölund
Coach - Mats Jingblad; Reine Almqvist
Stadium - Gamla Ullevi (18,000)

MAJOR HONOURS
League Championship - (17) 1908, 1910, 1918,
1935, 1942, 1958, 1969, 1982, 1983, 1984,
1987, 1990, 1991, 1993, 1994, 1995, 1996.
Domestic Cup - (4) 1979, 1982, 1983, 1991.
UEFA Cup - (2) 1982, 1987.

APPEARANCES 1998

		P	(s)	Gls
Bengt ANDERSSON	G	12		
Patric ANDERSSON	A		(8)	
Robert ANDERSSON	A	3	(6)	
Magnus BRUNBÄCK	D	1		
Stefan BÄRLIN	M	21	(4)	3
Johnny EKSTRÖM	A	7	(4)	2
Peter ERIKSSON	M	4	(4)	
Magnus ERLINGMARK	M	23		3
Sebastian HENRIKSSON	M	7	(7)	
Andreas HERMANSSON	A	20	(5)	8
Magnus JOHANSSON	D	10	(2)	
Sören JÄRELÖV	G	1		
Christian KARLSSON	D	20	(1)	
Pär KARLSSON	M	12	(1)	
Stefan LANDBERG	D	12		
Dick LAST	G	13		
Teddy LUCIC	D	23		
Olof MAGNUSSON	D	7		
Mikael MARTINSSON	A	6	(2)	
Håkan MILD	M	10		1
Mikael NILSSON	D	20	(2)	1
Jonas OLSSON	D	2	(1)	
Magnus PEHRSSON	M	8	(4)	1
Joakim PERSSON	M	23		2
Stefan PETTERSSON	A	12		3
Jimmy SVENSSON	M		(1)	
Emmanuel TETTEH (GHA)	A	9	(3)	3

LEAGUE RESULTS 1998

14/04/98	Västra Frölunda IF	H	1-2	Ekström
19/04/98	Hammarby IF	A	1-1	Hermansson
27/04/98	IFK Norrköping	H	0-0	
04/05/98	Helsingborgs IF	A	1-0	Erlingmark
11/05/98	Örgryte IS	H	2-5	Tetteh, Hermansson
14/05/98	Östers IF	A	1-1	Hermansson
17/05/98	Örebro SK	A	0-4	
04/06/98	Malmö FF	H	1-0	Pehrsson
08/06/98	BK Häcken	A	1-1	Erlingmark
14/06/98	IF Elfsborg	H	1-0	Tetteh
21/06/98	Trelleborgs FF	A	2-0	Erlingmark, Tetteh
29/06/98	AIK	H	0-1	
18/07/98	Halmstads BK	H	1-2	Nilsson
01/08/98	Malmö FF	A	1-3	Persson
08/08/98	Örebro SK	H	2-0	Hermansson 2
16/08/98	IF Elfsborg	A	0-1	
22/08/98	BK Häcken	H	1-1	Ekström
30/08/98	Halmstads BK	A	1-1	Pettersson
10/09/98	AIK	A	0-1	
20/09/98	Trelleborgs FF	H	1-0	Pettersson (p)
24/09/98	IFK Norrköping	A	1-0	Hermansson
05/10/98	Hammarby IF	H	2-2	Bärlin, Hermansson
20/10/98	Örgryte IS	A	2-1	Mild, Bärlin
27/10/98	Helsingborgs IF	H	0-1	
31/10/98	Västra Frölunda IF	A	3-0	Hermansson, Bärlin, Pettersson
08/11/98	Östers IF	H	1-1	Persson

HALMSTADS BK

CLUB DIRECTORY

Halmstads Bollklubb
Box 223
301 06 Halmstad
tel - (035) 171880
fax - (035) 103436
Year of Formation - 1914
President - Stig Nilsson
Director - Mikael Kaller
Coach - Tom Prahl
Stadium - Örjans Vall (17,000)

MAJOR HONOURS
League Championship - (3) 1976, 1979, 1997.
Domestic Cup - (1) 1995.

APPEARANCES 1998

	P	Ap	(s)	Gls
Daniel ALEXANDERSSON	A		(3)	
Fredrik ANDERSSON	D	21		3
Torbjörn ARVIDSSON	M	20		2
Jeffrey AUBYNN	A	2	(5)	
Björn CARLSSON	M	10	(2)	2
Mikael GUSTAVSSON	D	26		
Petter HANSSON	D	2	(2)	
Mattais JOHANSSON	M	6	(7)	
Tommy JÖNSSON	D	23		3
Mattias KARLSSON	M	8	(2)	
Peter LENNARTSSON	M	2	(3)	
Mats LILIENBERG	A	26		11
Fredrik LJUNGBERG	M	18		2
Jesper MATTSSON	D	26		3
Björn NORDBERG	G	3	(1)	
Niclas NYLÉN	M	7	(2)	2
Henrik ROLFSSON	D	1	(1)	
Artim SAKIRI (MAC)	M	24		4
Stefan SELAKOVIC (BOS)	A	6	(11)	1
Håkan SVENSSON	G	23		
Michael SVENSSON	D	10	(4)	2
Peter VOUGT	A	22	(4)	7

LEAGUE RESULTS 1998

05/04/98	Trelleborgs FF	A	3-1	Lilienberg 2, Nylén
13/04/98	Östers IF	H	1-2	Andersson (p)
18/04/98	AIK	A	0-1	
26/04/98	Västra Frölunda IF	H	1-0	Andersson (p)
03/05/98	BK Häcken	A	2-3	Nylén, Lilienberg
11/05/98	Hammarby IF	H	1-3	Lilienberg
18/05/98	Malmö FF	A	0-5	
04/06/98	Örgryte IS	H	2-1	Mattsson, Carlsson
07/06/98	Örebro SK	A	2-3	Lilienberg, Vougt
15/06/98	Helsingborgs IF	H	1-0	Jönsson
23/06/98	IF Elfsborg	A	4-3	Sakiri, Carlsson, Vougt, Ljungberg
28/06/98	IFK Norrköping	H	3-1	Arvidsson, Vougt, Sakiri
18/07/98	IFK Göteborg	A	2-1	Lilienberg, Vougt
03/08/98	Örgryte IS	A	2-2	Sakiri, Mattsson
06/08/98	Malmö FF	H	2-1	Vougt, Jönsson
16/08/98	Helsingborgs IF	A	0-1	
22/08/98	Örebro SK	H	2-0	Andersson, Svensson M.
30/08/98	IFK Göteborg	H	1-1	Ljungberg
10/09/98	IFK Norrköping	A	6-4	Lilienberg 4, Jönsson, Vougt
21/09/98	IF Elfsborg	H	0-3	
26/09/98	Västra Frölunda IF	A	1-0	Arvidsson
04/10/98	AIK	H	1-1	Lilienberg
21/10/98	Hammarby IF	A	1-1	Vougt
26/10/98	BK Häcken	H	0-1	
31/10/98	Östers IF	A	1-1	Selakovic
08/11/98	Trelleborgs FF	H	3-0	Svensson M., Sakiri, Mattsson

HAMMARBY IF

CLUB DIRECTORY

Hammarby Idrottsförening
Box 200 56
104 60 Stockholm
tel - (08) 6413592
fax - (08) 4629320
Year of Formation - 1897
President - Göran Paulsson
Secretary - Tomas Eriksson
Coach - Rolf Zetterlund
Stadium - Söderstadion (10,200)

APPEARANCES 1998

	P	Ap	(s)	Gls
Johan ANDERSSON	D	22		2
Mikael ANDERSSON	A	19	(2)	3
Patrik ANDERSSON	A	18	(2)	8
Hans BERGGREN	A	24	(2)	13
Peter BERGGREN	M	20	(5)	1
Filip BERGMAN	D	14	(9)	
Kim BERGSTRAND	A	19	(5)	2
Kaj ESKELINEN	M	22	(2)	4
Hans ESKILSSON	D	23		1
Per FAHLSTRÖM	G	26		
Christer FURSTH	M	8	(3)	1
Jens GUSTAFSON	M	17	(8)	
Mikael HELLSTRÖM	M	23		1
Rickard ISAKSSON	M	1	(1)	
Pétur Björn JÓNSSON (ISL)	M	3	(5)	
Pétur MARTEINSSON (ISL)	D	24		2
Cesar PACHA	A	1	(2)	
Benyam SEYOUM	M		(1)	
Suleyman VARLI	D	2	(6)	
Christian ZEILOTH	A		(9)	

LEAGUE RESULTS 1998

04/04/98	Örebro SK	H	3-1	Berggren H. 2, Bergstrand
13/04/98	Malmö FF	A	2-2	Berggren H., Eskelinen
19/04/98	IFK Göteborg	H	1-1	Marteinsson
26/04/98	Östers IF	A	1-1	Bergstrand
04/05/98	Västra Frölunda IF	H	0-1	
11/05/98	Halmstads BK	A	3-1	og (Mattsson), Andersson J., Berggren H.
19/05/98	AIK	A	1-0	Eskelinen
03/06/98	BK Häcken	H	3-3	Andersson P. 2, Andersson J.
07/06/98	Örgryte IS	A	1-0	Andersson P.
14/06/98	Trelleborgs FF	H	1-0	Eskilsson
22/06/98	IFK Norrköping	A	2-1	Andersson P., Hellström
29/06/98	Helsingborgs IF	H	3-3	Berggren H., Berggren P., Andersson P.
20/07/98	IF Elfsborg	H	1-0	Andersson P.
02/08/98	BK Häcken	A	3-4	Berggren H. 2, Andersson M.
10/08/98	AIK	H	0-2	
16/08/98	Trelleborgs FF	A	1-1	Andersson P.
24/08/98	Örgryte IS	H	1-0	Berggren H.
31/08/98	IF Elfsborg	A	1-0	Marteinsson (p)
13/09/98	Helsingborgs IF	A	2-2	Berggren H. 2
20/09/98	IFK Norrköping	H	3-2	Andersson M., Berggren H. 2
29/09/98	Östers IF	H	0-1	
05/10/98	IFK Göteborg	A	2-2	Fursth, Berggren H.
21/10/98	Halmstads BK	H	1-1	Eskelinen
25/10/98	Västra Frölunda IF	A	1-2	Eskelinen
31/10/98	Malmö FF	H	1-3	Andersson P.
08/11/98	Örebro SK	A	1-0	Andersson M.

HELSINGBORGS IF

CLUB DIRECTORY

Helsingborgs Idrottsförening
Box 2074
250 02 Helsingborg
tel - (042) 199400
fax - (042) 180606
Year of Formation - 1907
President - Ingvar Wenehed
Secretary - Claes Johansson
Coach - Åge Hareide
Stadium - Olympia (17,000)

MAJOR HONOURS
League Championship - (5)
1929, 1930, 1933, 1934, 1941.
Domestic Cup - (2) 1941, 1998.

APPEARANCES 1998

	P	Ap	(s)	Gls
Christoffer ANDERSSON	M	7	(16)	1
Sven ANDERSSON	G	26		
Hans BERGH	M	4	(5)	
Hilmar BJÖRNSSON (ISL)	A		(1)	
Erik EDMAN	D	25		
Andreas JACOBSSON	D	26		1
Ulrik JANSSON	M	7	(4)	
Stig JOHANSEN (NOR)	A	4	(5)	2
Jakob JÓNHARDSSON (ISL)	D	1		
Mattias JONSSON	A	18	(2)	4
Zoran JOVANOVSKI (MAC)	D	19	(1)	
Marcus LANTZ	M	10	(5)	
Jesper LJUNG	M		(3)	
Per-Ola LJUNG	D	19	(3)	
Ola NILSSON	D	21	(3)	
Magnus POWELL	A	17	(5)	4
Rade PRICA	M		(1)	
Arild STAVRUM (NOR)	A	25	(1)	18
Kenneth STORVIK (NOR)	M	24		5
Erik WAHLSTEDT	A	8	(17)	2
Peter WIBRÅN	M	25		6

LEAGUE RESULTS 1998

04/04/98	BK Häcken	H	0-0	
13/04/98	IF Elfsborg	A	1-0	Stavrum
19/04/98	Örebro SK	H	0-0	
28/04/98	Malmö FF	A	1-1	Wibrån
04/05/98	IFK Göteborg	H	0-1	
10/05/98	Östers IF	A	3-1	Powell, Stavrum 2
17/05/98	Örgryte IS	A	2-0	Wibrån, Stavrum
04/06/98	Trelleborgs FF	H	3-0	Stavrum 3
08/06/98	IFK Norrköping	H	1-1	Storvik
15/06/98	Halmstads BK	A	0-1	
21/06/98	Västra Frölunda IF	H	6-2	Stavrum 3, Storvik 2, Powell
29/06/98	Hammarby IF	A	3-3	Andersson, Storvik, Stavrum
20/07/98	AIK	H	0-1	
04/08/98	Trelleborgs FF	A	2-4	Wibrån 2
09/08/98	Örgryte IS	H	2-1	Jonsson, Jacobsson
16/08/98	Halmstads BK	H	1-0	Stavrum
23/08/98	IFK Norrköping	A	4-3	Powell 2, Stavrum, Wahlstedt
31/08/98	AIK	A	1-1	Wibrån
13/09/98	Hammarby IF	H	2-2	Storvik, Stavrum
20/09/98	Västra Frölunda IF	A	0-0	
24/09/98	Malmö FF	H	1-2	Wibrån
06/10/98	Örebro SK	A	3-1	Wahlstedt, Stavrum, Johansen
18/10/98	Östers IF	H	3-1	Jonsson, Johansen, Stavrum
27/10/99	IFK Göteborg	A	1-0	Stavrum
31/10/98	IF Elfsborg	H	2-0	Jonsson, Stavrum
08/11/98	BK Häcken	A	1-2	Jonsson

BK HÄCKEN

CLUB DIRECTORY

Bollklubben Häcken
Box 22051
400 72 Göteborg
tel - (031) 859225
fax - (031) 543182
Year of Formation - 1940
President - Åke Nilsson
Secretary - Inge Niklasson
Coach - Kjell Pettersson
Stadium - Rambergsvallen (7,000)

APPEARANCES 1998

		P	Ap	(s)	Gls
Fredrik BRYNGELSSON	D	1	(1)		
Henrik DAHL	D	23			1
Per-Anders ELIASSON	M	2	(7)		
Peter ERIKSSON	M	12			2
Henrik HANSSON	M	2	(6)		1
Mikael HARALDSSON	D		(1)		
Jonas HENRIKSSON	A	11	(4)		
Ulf HOLLSTEN	D	22			1
Martin KARLSSON	M	22	(1)		3
Ola KARLSSON	M	5	(9)		
Patrik KARLSSON	A	24	(2)		6
Matthias LARSSON	A	22	(4)		7
Johan LIND	D	23	(1)		
Joakim OLSSON	G	26			
Peter PALMQVIST	D	23			
Ivica SKILJO (CRO)	M		(1)		
Joakim SÖNDERGAARD	M	24			1
Anders THORSTENSSON	M	22	(1)		2
Ville VILJANEN	M	22	(4)		3

LEAGUE RESULTS 1998

04/04/98	Helsingborgs IF	A	0-0	
13/04/98	Örgryte IS	H	0-2	
19/04/98	Trelleborgs FF	A	1-0	Karlsson P.
26/04/98	AIK	H	1-1	Karlsson P.
05/05/98	Halmstads BK	H	3-2	Larsson Ma. 2, Karlsson P.
11/05/98	IF Elfsborg	A	0-2	
18/05/98	Västra Frölunda IF	H	0-1	
03/06/98	Hammarby IF	A	3-3	Hansson, Karlsson M., Larsson Ma.
08/06/98	IFK Göteborg	H	1-1	Viljanen
14/06/98	Östers IF	A	2-0	Karlsson P., Karlsson M.
24/06/98	Örebro SK	H	2-4	Viljanen, Larsson Ma.
28/06/98	Malmö FF	A	0-4	
20/07/98	IFK Norrköping	A	1-5	Karlsson P.
02/08/98	Hammarby IF	H	4-3	Karlsson P., Larsson Ma., Dahl, Thorstensson
10/08/98	Västra Frölunda IF	A	1-1	Eriksson
16/08/98	Östers IF	H	0-1	
22/08/98	IFK Göteborg	A	1-1	Viljanen
30/08/98	IFK Norrköping	H	0-1	
10/09/98	Malmö FF	H	2-1	Karlsson M., Eriksson
21/09/98	Örebro SK	A	0-1	
28/09/98	AIK	A	1-2	Thorstensson
04/10/98	Trelleborgs FF	H	0-5	
22/10/98	IF Elfsborg	H	0-2	
26/10/98	Halmstads BK	A	1-0	Söndergaard
31/10/98	Örgryte IS	A	1-2	Hollsten
08/11/98	Helsingborgs IF	H	2-1	Larsson Ma. 2

MALMÖ FF

CLUB DIRECTORY

Malmö Fotbollförening
Box 19067
200 73 Malmö
tel - (040) 194245
fax - (040) 191707
Year of Formation - 1910
President - Hans Cavalli-Björkman
Secretary - Einar Malmborg
Coach - Frans Thijssen; Roland Andersson
Stadium - Malmö Stadion (32,000)

MAJOR HONOURS
League Championship - (14)
1944, 1949, 1950, 1951, 1953, 1965, 1967,
1970, 1971, 1974, 1975, 1977, 1986, 1988.
Domestic Cup - (14)
1944, 1946, 1947, 1951, 1953, 1967, 1973,
1974, 1975, 1977, 1980, 1984, 1986, 1989.

APPEARANCES 1998

		P	Ap	(s)	Gls
Daniel ANDERSSON		M	12		3
Ólafur Örn BJARNASSON (ISL)		M	4	(5)	1
Björn ENQVIST		M	9	(7)	1
Jonnie FEDEL		G	13		
Niklas GUDMUNDSSON		A	20		1
Niklas KINDVALL		A	18	(4)	6
Hans MATTISSON		M	23		3
Jörgen OHLSSON		D	26		1
Yksel OSMANOVSKI		A	9	(2)	1
Mike OWUSU		D	8	(1)	1
Dejan PAVLOVIC (YUG)		A	18	(7)	10
Olof PERSSON		D	14		
Mikael ROTH		D	18	(1)	
Milan SIMEUNOVIC (SLO)		G	12		
Ante SIMUNDZA (SLO)		A		(3)	
Sverrir SVERRISSON (ISL)		M	25		6
Brune TAVELL		M	24		1
Mattias THYLANDER		D	20		
Ola TIDMAN		G	1		
Goran TRPEVSKI		M	1	(5)	
Mattias WALDH		A	1		
Jonas WIRMOLA		D	10	(1)	

LEAGUE RESULTS 1998

13/04/98	Hammarby IF	H	2-2	Sverrisson, Andersson
19/04/98	IFK Norrköping	A	1-2	Sverrisson
28/04/98	Helsingborgs IF	H	1-1	Kindvall
04/05/98	Örgryte IS	A	0-2	
07/05/98	Västra Frölunda IF	A	3-1	Bjarnasson, Sverrisson, Osmanovski
11/05/98	Trelleborgs FF	H	0-1	
18/05/98	Halmstads BK	H	5-0	Andersson (p), Gudmundsson, Mattisson 2, Ohlsson
04/06/98	IFK Göteborg	A	0-1	
09/06/98	IF Elfsborg	A	1-2	Sverrisson
15/06/98	Örebro SK	H	1-3	Andersson
24/06/98	AIK	A	0-1	
28/06/98	BK Häcken	H	4-0	Pavlovic 3, Owusu
18/07/98	Östers IF	A	1-2	Tavell
01/08/98	IFK Göteborg	H	3-1	Sverrisson, Enqvist, Pavlovic
06/08/98	Halmstads BK	A	1-2	Pavlovic
16/08/98	Örebro SK	A	0-0	
22/08/98	IF Elfsborg	H	0-4	
31/08/98	Östers IF	H	2-0	Kindvall, Pavlovic
10/09/98	BK Häcken	A	1-2	Kindvall
21/09/98	AIK	H	0-0	
24/09/98	Helsingborgs IF	A	2-1	Pavlovic (p), Kindvall
05/10/98	IFK Norrköping	H	1-0	Pavlovic
17/10/98	Trelleborgs FF	A	0-0	
26/10/98	Örgryte IS	H	3-1	Pavlovic, Mattisson, Kindvall
31/10/98	Hammarby IF	A	3-1	Kindvall, Sverrisson, Pavlovic
08/11/98	Västra Frölunda IF	H	0-0	

IFK NORRKÖPING

Idrottsföreningen Kamraterna Norrköping
Box 12067
600 12 Norrköping
tel - (011) 215500
fax - (011) 215515
Year of Formation - 1897
President - Björn Ahlberg
Secretary - Tommy Wisell
Coach - Olle Nordin
Stadium - Norrköpings Idrottspark (21,000)

MAJOR HONOURS
League Championship - (12)
1943, 1945, 1946, 1947, 1948, 1952, 1956,
1957, 1960, 1962, 1963, 1989.
Domestic Cup - (6)
1943, 1945, 1969, 1988, 1992, 1994.

Date	Opponent		Score	Scorers
13/04/98	Örebro SK	A	3-1	Fyhr 2, Bergström
19/04/98	Malmö FF	H	2-1	Wallerstedt, Thomas
27/04/98	IFK Göteborg	A	0-0	
03/05/98	Östers IF	H	1-0	Hansson
07/05/98	IF Elfsborg	H	1-1	Wallerstedt
12/05/98	Västra Frölunda IF	A	2-3	Fyhr, Gravem
17/05/98	Trelleborgs FF	A	0-0	
04/06/98	AIK	H	2-0	Apelstav, Cetinkaya
08/06/98	Helsingborgs IF	A	1-1	Åslund
14/06/98	Örgryte IS	H	1-1	Cetinkaya
22/06/98	Hammarby IF	H	1-2	Fyhr (p)
28/06/98	Halmstads BK	A	1-3	Bergström
20/07/98	BK Häcken	H	5-1	Gravem, Wallerstedt 2,
				Andersson, Bjurström
03/08/98	AIK	A	1-1	Andersson
10/08/98	Trelleborgs FF	H	3-0	Gravem, Samuelsson, Wallerstedt
16/08/98	Örgryte IS	A	1-1	Andersson
24/08/98	Helsingborgs IF	H	3-4	Bergström 2, Fyhr
30/08/98	BK Häcken	A	1-0	Saarenpää
10/09/98	Halmstads BK	H	4-6	Hansson, Andersson, Wallerstedt,
				Åslund
20/09/98	Hammarby IF	A	2-3	Åslund, Wallerstedt
24/09/98	IFK Göteborg	H	0-1	
05/10/98	Malmö FF	A	0-1	
19/10/98	Västra Frölunda IF	H	1-3	Apelstav
25/10/98	Östers IF	A	2-0	Bergström, Andersson
31/10/98	Örebro SK	H	4-0	Hansson, Gravem, Andersson,
				Åslund
08/11/98	IF Elfsborg	A	1-1	Andersson

	P	Ap	(s)	Gls
Pär ANDERSSON	A	8	(11)	7
Filip APELSTAV	D	24		2
Kristian BERGSTRÖM	M	26		5
Jonas BJURSTRÖM	M	5	(14)	1
Mikael BLOMBERG	D	6	(4)	
Hasan CETINKAYA	M	11		2
Mathias FLORÉN	M	26		
Peter FYHR	A	15	(4)	5
Mathias GRAVEM (NOR)	A	22	(4)	4
Eddie GUSTAFSSON	G	23		
Mikael HANSSON	D	25		3
Janne HIETANEN (FIN)	D	2		
Birkir KRISTINSSON (ISL)	G	3		
Thomas OLSSON	M	2	(6)	
Klebér SAARENPÄÄ	D	23		1
Magnus SAMUELSSON	M	10	(5)	1
Mikael STRÖM	D	3	(6)	
Andreas THOMAS	A	2	(12)	1
Jonas WALLERSTEDT	M	26		7
Martin ÅSLUND	M	24		4

TRELLEBORGS FF

CLUB DIRECTORY

Trelleborgs Fotbollsförening
Hejderidaregatan 2
231 44 Trelleborg
tel - (0410) 13190
fax - (0410) 13125
Year of Formation - 1926
President - Gunnar Persson
Secretary - Bengt Cederberg
Coach - Sören Cratz
Stadium - Vångavallen (10,000)

APPEARANCES 1998

	P	Ap	(s)	Gls
Daniel ANDERSSON	G	26		
Patrick ANDERSSON	M	1		
Peter ANDERSSON	M	7	(11)	4
Magnus ARVIDSSON	A	20	(5)	7
Mikael DANIELSSON	D	14		1
Jörgen ERIKSSON	D	13	(3)	
Anders FRIBERG	D	25		3
Tommi GRÖNLUND (FIN)	M	24		
Michael HANSSON	M	25		5
Matias KRONVALL	D	23	(1)	
Patrik LARSSON	D	8	(1)	1
Ivica MOMCILOVIC (YUG)	M		(4)	
Håkan NILSSON	D	11		
Patrik OLSSON	A	22	(3)	5
Markus PERSSON	M		(2)	
Fredrik SANDELL	A	17	(1)	2
Petter SOLLI (NOR)	D	18	(4)	1
Vujadin STANOJKOVIC (MAC)	D	5	(4)	
Jörgen SVENSSON	A	2	(9)	
Amir TELJIGOVIC (BOS)	M	19	(3)	1
Stefaan VAN RIEL (BEL)	M	6	(1)	1

LEAGUE RESULTS 1998

05/04/98	Halmstads BK	H	1-3	Olsson
13/04/98	AIK	A	1-1	Olsson
19/04/98	BK Häcken	H	0-1	
27/04/98	IF Elfsborg	A	1-1	Solli
03/05/98	Örebro SK	H	1-0	Hansson
11/05/98	Malmö FF	A	1-0	Olsson
17/05/98	IFK Norrköping	H	0-0	
04/06/98	Helsingborgs IF	A	0-3	
07/06/98	Västra Frölunda IF	H	3-0	Sandell, Arvidsson, Teljigovic
14/06/98	Hammarby IF	A	0-1	
21/06/98	IFK Göteborg	H	0-2	
28/06/98	Östers IF	A	2-2	Larsson, Arvidsson
19/07/98	Örgryte IS	H	2-1	Hansson 2
04/08/98	Helsingborgs IF	H	4-2	Sandell, Friberg (p), Olsson, Danielsson
10/08/98	IFK Norrköping	A	0-3	
16/08/98	Hammarby IF	H	1-1	Arvidsson
24/08/98	Västra Frölunda IF	A	1-3	Friberg
31/08/98	Örgryte IS	A	2-1	Van Riel, Hansson
14/09/98	Östers IF	H	2-0	Olsson, Andersson Pe.
20/09/98	IFK Göteborg	A	0-1	
28/09/98	IF Elfsborg	H	2-2	Arvidsson, Andersson Pe.
04/10/98	BK Häcken	A	5-0	Arvidsson 3, Friberg (p), Andersson Pe.
18/10/98	Malmö FF	H	0-0	
25/10/98	Örebro SK	A	2-4	Andersson Pe., Hansson
31/10/98	AIK	H	0-0	
08/11/98	Halmstads BK	A	0-3	

VÄSTRA FRÖLUNDA IF

CLUB DIRECTORY

Västra Frölunda Idrettsförening
Box 213
421 23 Västra Frölunda
tel - (031) 452660/454939
fax - (031) 492080
Year of Formation - 1930
President - Mats Persson
Secretary - Rolf Nilsson
Coach - Torbjörn Nilsson
Stadium - Ruddalens Idrottsplats (5,500)

APPEARANCES 1998

	P	Ap	(s)	Gls
Gustaf ANDERSSON	A	16	(8)	2
Johan ANEGRUND	D	22	(1)	
Robert BENGTSSON	D	24	(1)	
Karl BERGDAHL	D	9	(1)	
Mikael BJÖRKQVIST	D	24		4
Hans BLOMQVIST	M	13	(4)	3
Claudio COVARRUBIAS	A		(4)	
Mikael GÖRANSSON	M	24		1
Mats HEDÉN	D	18	(1)	
Dime JANKULOVSKI	G	14		
Niclas JOHANSSON	M	2	(6)	
Ola JOHANSSON	M	22		1
Tinos LAPPAS	D	5		
Magnus LARSSON	A		(2)	
Christian LUNDSTRÖM	A	14	(9)	6
Anders MAGNUSSON	M	25		
Tomas ROSENKVIST	A	23	(2)	8
Mikael SANDKLEF	M	17	(4)	3
Anildo SPENCER	D	2	(4)	
Robert TRANBERG	G	12	(1)	

LEAGUE RESULTS 1998

14/04/98	IFK Göteborg	A	2-1	Johansson O., Göransson
18/04/98	Östers IF	H	3-0	Rosenkvist, Sandklef 2
26/04/98	Halmstads BK	A	0-1	
04/05/98	Hammarby IF	A	1-0	Andersson
07/05/98	Malmö FF	H	1-3	Björkqvist
11/05/98	IFK Norrköping	H	3-2	Björkqvist 2, Rosenkvist (p)
18/05/98	BK Häcken	A	1-0	Sandklef
03/06/98	IF Elfsborg	H	1-1	Rosenkvist
07/06/98	Trelleborgs FF	A	0-3	
15/06/98	AIK	H	1-1	Lundström
21/06/98	Helsingborgs IF	A	2-6	Lundström, Björkqvist
01/07/98	Örgryte IS	H	1-0	Lundström
22/07/98	Örebro SK	H	1-1	Lundström
03/08/98	IF Elfsborg	A	2-0	Lundström, Rosenkvist
10/08/98	BK Häcken	H	1-1	Rosenkvist (p)
16/08/98	AIK	A	0-0	
24/08/98	Trelleborgs FF	H	3-1	Lundström, og (Eriksson), Blomqvist
30/08/98	Örebro SK	A	1-1	Rosenkvist
14/09/98	Örgryte IS	A	0-2	
20/09/98	Helsingborgs IF	H	0-0	
26/09/98	Halmstads BK	H	0-1	
04/10/98	Östers IF	A	0-1	
19/10/98	IFK Norrköping	A	3-1	Andersson, Rosenkvist 2
25/10/98	Hammarby IF	II	2-1	Blomqvist 2
31/10/98	IFK Göteborg	H	0-3	
08/11/98	Malmö FF	A	0-0	

ÖREBRO SK

CLUB DIRECTORY

Örebro Sportklubb
Eyragatan 1
702 25 Örebro
tel - (019) 167300
fax - (019) 167319
Year of Formation - 1908
President - Kenneth Karlsson
Secretary - Kjell Gustafsson
Coach - Sven Dahlkvist
Stadium - Eyravallen (13,000)

APPEARANCES 1998

	P	Ap	(s)	Gls
Mikael ANDERSSON	M	24		3
Thomas ANDERSSON	D	26		3
Hlynur BIRGISSON (ISL)	D	7	(2)	
Dragan DJUKANOVIC (YUG)	A	2	(1)	1
Pär EKSTRÖM	M	11		1
Per GAWELIN	M		(1)	
Arnor GUDJOHNSEN (ISL)	M	10		2
Niklas GUSTAFSON	D	25		1
Christer GUSTAVSSON	D	1	(1)	
Fredrik JANSSON	D	6	(6)	
Gunnlaugur JÓNSSON (ISL)	D		(1)	
Anders KARLSSON	G	26		
Erik KARLSSON	A	5	(14)	
Peter KARLSSON	M	26		
Fredrik NORDBACK (FIN)	M	3	(6)	
Jonas PELGANDER	M	23		
Mathias PERSSON	A	1	(5)	
Niklas RASCK	M	25		1
Mats RUBARTH	M	3	(14)	1
Dan SAHLIN	A	12		10
Daniel TJERNSTRÖM	M	25	(1)	5
Johan WALLINDER	M	25		7

LEAGUE RESULTS 1998

Date	Opponent		Score	Scorers
04/04/98	Hammarby IF	A	1-3	Sahlin
13/04/98	IFK Norrköping	H	1-3	Sahlin
19/04/98	Helsingborgs IF	A	0-0	
27/04/98	Örgryte IS	H	1-1	Tjernström
03/05/98	Trelleborgs FF	A	0-1	
10/05/98	AIK	H	1-1	Gudjohnsen
17/05/98	IFK Göteborg	H	4-0	Gudjohnsen, Sahlin 2, Andersson M.
04/06/98	Östers IF	A	2-1	Sahlin 2
07/06/98	Halmstads BK	H	3-2	Sahlin, Andersson T., Rubarth
15/06/98	Malmö FF	A	3-1	Wallinder, Andersson M., Tjernström
24/06/98	BK Häcken	A	4-2	Tjernström, Sahlin 2, Wallinder
29/06/98	IF Elfsborg	H	4-2	Tjernström, Djukanovic, Andersson T. (p), Sahlin
22/07/98	Västra Frölunda IF	A	1-1	Wallinder
02/08/98	Östers IF	H	2-1	Gustafson, Tjernström
08/08/98	IFK Göteborg	A	0-2	
16/08/98	Malmö FF	H	0-0	
22/08/98	Halmstads BK	A	0-2	
30/08/98	Västra Frölunda IF	H	1-1	Ekström
14/09/98	IF Elfsborg	A	1-0	Wallinder
21/09/98	BK Häcken	H	1-0	Wallinder
28/09/98	Örgryte IS	A	0-2	
06/10/98	Helsingborgs IF	H	1-3	Wallinder
19/10/98	AIK	A	0-2	
25/10/98	Trelleborgs FF	H	4-2	Rasck, Wallinder, Andersson M., Andersson T. (p)
31/10/98	IFK Norrköping	A	0-4	
08/11/98	Hammarby IF	H	0-1	

ÖRGRYTE IS

CLUB DIRECTORY

Örgryte Idrottssällskap
Box 52025
400 25 Göteborg
tel - (031) 879310
fax - (031) 879547
Year of Formation - 1887
President - Benny Rosén
Secretary - Jan Björklund
Coach - Bo Backman; Erik Hamrén
Stadium - Gamla Ullevi (18,000)

MAJOR HONOURS
League Championship - (14)
1896, 1897, 1898, 1899, 1902, 1904, 1905,
1906, 1907, 1909, 1913, 1926, 1928, 1985.

APPEARANCES 1998

	P	Ap	(s)	Gls
Marcus ALLBÄCK	A	9	(3)	3
Ståle ANDERSEN (NOR)	M	6	(10)	
Henrik BERTILSSON	A	26		10
Karl CORNELIUSSON	M	22	(1)	1
Anders HOLMBERG	G	4		
Markus JOHANNESSON	D	19	(1)	
Erik JOHANSSON	A	9	(12)	1
Joachim KARLSSON	A	7	(11)	5
Allan KUHN (DEN)	M	11	(9)	4
Magnus KÄLLANDER	M	24		
Roger LINDQVIST	D	8	(6)	
Jozo MATOVAC	D	8		
Morgan NILSSON	M	23		1
Anders PRYTZ	D	11	(3)	
Freddie ROTH	G	22		
Svante SAMUELSSON	M	11		3
Niclas SJÖSTEDT	D	26		5
Walter TOMAZ Júnior (BRA)	D	2	(4)	
Martin ULANDER	M	21	(2)	
Stefan VENNBERG	M	17	(5)	1

LEAGUE RESULTS 1998

13/04/98	BK Häcken	A	2-0	Bertilsson, Karlsson
19/04/98	IF Elfsborg	H	2-2	og (Mogren), Bertilsson
27/04/98	Örebro SK	A	1-1	Bertilsson
04/05/98	Malmö FF	H	2-0	Bertilsson, Corneliusson
11/05/98	IFK Göteborg	A	5-2	Samuelsson 3, Bertilsson, Vennberg
17/05/98	Helsingborgs IF	H	0-2	
04/06/98	Halmstads BK	A	1-2	Karlsson
07/06/98	Hammarby IF	H	0-1	
11/06/98	AIK	H	0-1	
14/06/98	IFK Norrköping	A	1-1	Karlsson
17/06/98	Östers IF	H	4-4	Bertilsson, Karlsson, Sjöstedt (p), Johansson
01/07/98	Västra Frölunda IF	A	0-1	
19/07/98	Trelleborgs FF	A	1-2	Bertilsson
03/08/98	Halmstads BK	H	2-2	Sjöstedt (p), Nilsson
09/08/98	Helsingborgs IF	A	1-2	Kuhn
16/08/98	IFK Norrköping	H	1-1	Allbäck
24/08/98	Hammarby IF	A	0-1	
31/08/98	Trelleborgs FF	H	1-2	Bertilsson
14/09/98	Västra Frölunda IF	H	2-0	Karlsson, Kuhn
20/09/98	Östers IF	A	1-0	Sjöstedt (p)
28/09/98	Örebro SK	H	2-0	Bertilsson, Allbäck
05/10/98	IF Elfsborg	A	2-2	Kuhn, Bertilsson
20/10/98	IFK Göteborg	H	1-2	Kuhn
26/10/98	Malmö FF	A	1-3	Sjöstedt
31/10/98	BK Häcken	H	2-1	Allbäck, Sjöstedt (p)
08/11/98	AIK	A	0-1	

ÖSTERS IF

CLUB DIRECTORY

Östers Idrottsförening
Tipshallen
Värendsvallen
Hejaregatan
352 46 Växjö
tel - (0470) 19020/19021
fax - (0470) 16845
Year of Formation - 1930
President - Mats Gusting
Secretary - Tomas Hedevik
Coach - Bo Axberg; Jan Mattsson
Stadium - Värendsvallen (15,062)

MAJOR HONOURS
League Championship - (4)
1968, 1978, 1980, 1981.
Domestic Cup - (1) 1977.

APPEARANCES 1998

		P	Ap	(s)	Gls
Marcus ANDREASSON	D	3		(1)	
Rickard AXBERG	A	6	(10)		1
Andreas BILD	M	14	(2)		1
Fredrik BILD	D	25			3
Anders BLOMQVIST	A	5	(10)		
Peter FRIBERG	D	2			
Claes GREEN	G	11			
Fredrik GUSTAFSON	M	17	(2)		1
Lasse JOHANSSON	M	17	(4)		1
Mathias JOHANSSON	M	16	(4)		1
Joakim KARLSSON	D		(1)		
Patrik KARLSSON	M	2	(1)		
Christoffer KLOO (FIN)	D	10	(2)		
Pål LUNDIN	G	15			
Christoffer OLOFSSON	M	8	(4)		
Andreas OTTOSSON	M	24			8
Nicklas PERSSON	D	25			1
Daniel PETTERSSON	D	2	(13)		
Magnus SAMUELSSON	D	25			
Thorvaldur Makan SIGBJÖRNSSON (ISL)	A	4	(1)		1
Jens SVENSSON	M	16	(4)		5
Christer THOR	D	4	(3)		
Stefán THÓRDARSON (ISL)	A	16	(1)		3
Mark WATSON (CAN)	D	19	(1)		

LEAGUE RESULTS 1998

13/04/98	Halmstads BK	A	2-1	Ottosson, Persson (p)
18/04/98	Västra Frölunda IF	A	0-3	
26/04/98	Hammarby IF	H	1-1	Axberg
03/05/98	IFK Norrköping	A	0-1	
10/05/98	Helsingborgs IF	H	1-3	Bild F.
14/05/98	IFK Göteborg	H	1-1	Thórdarson
18/05/98	IF Elfsborg	A	1-2	Johansson M.
04/06/98	Örebro SK	H	1-2	Ottosson
08/06/98	AIK	A	1-1	Bild F.
14/06/98	BK Häcken	H	0-2	
17/06/98	Örgryte IS	A	4-4	Ottosson 2, Svensson 2
28/06/98	Trelleborgs FF	H	2-2	Thórdarson, Ottosson
18/07/98	Malmö FF	H	2-1	Bild A., Thórdarson
02/08/98	Örebro SK	A	1-2	Svensson
09/08/98	IF Elfsborg	H	2-3	Ottosson, Gustafson
16/08/98	BK Häcken	A	1-0	Ottosson
24/08/98	AIK	H	1-2	Bild F.
30/08/98	Malmö FF	A	0-2	
14/09/98	Trelleborgs FF	A	0-2	
20/09/98	Örgryte IS	H	0-1	
29/09/98	Hammarby IF	A	1-0	Svensson
04/10/98	Västra Frölunda IF	H	1-0	Sigbjörnsson
18/10/98	Helsingborgs IF	A	1-3	Ottosson
25/10/98	IFK Norrköping	H	0-2	
31/10/98	Halmstads BK	H	1-1	Johansson L.
08/11/98	IFK Göteborg	A	1-1	Svensson

PROMOTED CLUBS

SECOND DIVISION FINAL TABLES 1998

NORTH

		Pd	W	D	L	F	A	Pt	GD
1	Djurgårdens IF	26	17	3	6	53	30	54	+23
2	Umeå FC	26	14	7	5	59	40	49	+19
3	Västerås SK FK	26	14	5	7	48	32	47	+16
4	GIF Sundsvall	26	13	3	10	44	37	42	+7
5	Assyriska Föreningen	26	12	5	9	41	37	41	+4
6	IK Brage	26	10	8	8	37	41	38	-4
7	IK Sirius FK	26	10	6	10	29	27	36	+2
8	Degerfors IF	26	9	9	8	45	44	36	+1
9	Nacka FF	26	9	9	8	34	45	36	-11
10	Spårvägens FF	26	7	7	12	30	37	28	-7
11	Gefle IF	26	7	6	13	27	32	27	-5
12	Piteå IF	26	5	10	11	28	38	25	-10
13	Ludvika FK	26	7	4	15	35	46	25	-11
14	IFK Luleå	26	5	4	17	17	41	19	-24

SOUTH

		Pd	W	D	L	F	A	Pt	GD
1	Kalmar FF	26	15	6	5	49	23	51	+26
2	Landskrona BoIS	26	15	5	6	64	37	50	+27
3	IF Sylvia	26	14	5	7	37	26	47	+11
4	Åtvidabergs FF	26	14	4	8	49	38	46	+11
5	Stenungsunds IF	26	13	6	7	40	34	45	+6
6	Panos Ljungskile SK	26	12	4	10	37	34	40	+3
7	Falkenbergs FF	26	12	2	12	35	47	38	-12
8	Gunnilse IS	26	11	3	12	41	42	36	-1
9	Mjällby AIF	26	10	4	12	45	52	34	-7
10	Motala AIK FK	25	8	9	9	31	29	33	+2
11	Norrby IF	26	9	4	13	34	46	31	-12
12	IFK Hässleholm	26	7	5	14	34	42	26	-8
13	Lundby IF	26	5	4	17	25	47	19	-22
14	IS Halmia	26	5	3	18	24	48	18	-24

PROMOTION/RELEGATION PLAY-OFFS

Umeå FC 2, Örgryte IS 3

Örgryte IS 3, Umeå FC 0

(Örgryte IS 6-2)

Landskrona BoIS 2, Trelleborgs FF 3

Trelleborgs FF 4, Landskrona BoIS 1

(Trelleborgs FF 7-3)

CLUB DIRECTORY

Djurgårdens Idrettsförening

Klocktornet

Olympiastadion

114 33 Stockholm

tel - (08) 4115711

fax - (08) 211583

Year of Formation - 1891

President - Bo Lundqvist

Secretary - Dan Svanell

Coach - Michael Andersson

Stadium - Olympiastadion (17,500)

MAJOR HONOURS

League Championship - (8) 1912, 1915, 1917, 1920, 1955, 1959, 1964, 1966.

Domestic Cup - (1) 1990.

CLUB DIRECTORY

Kalmar FF

Box 169

391 22 Kalmar

tel - (0480) 411477

fax - (0480) 88720

Year of Formation - 1910

President - Ronny Nilsson

Coach - Nanne Bergstrand

Stadium - Fredriksskans (13,400)

MAJOR HONOURS

Domestic Cup - (2) 1981, 1987.

SWITZERLAND

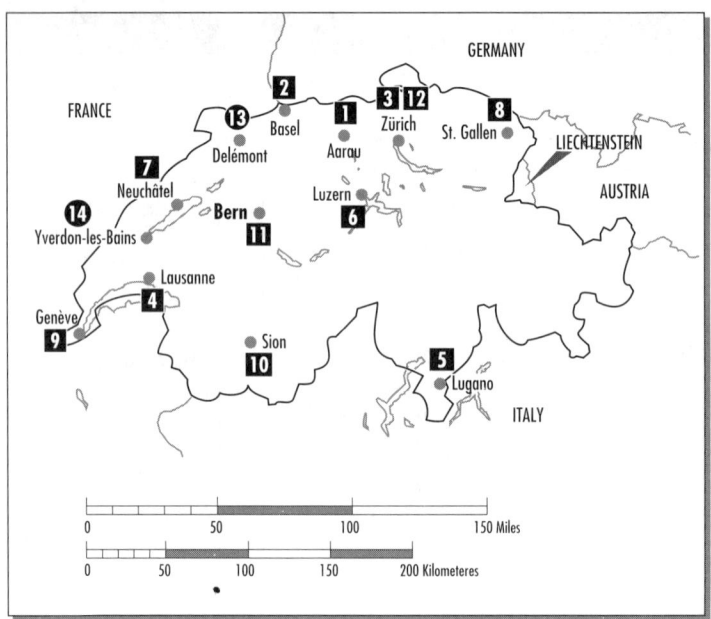

1	FC AARAU	997
2	FC BASEL	998
3	GRASSHOPPER-CLUB ZÜRICH	999
4	LAUSANNE-SPORTS	1000
5	FC LUGANO	1001
6	FC LUZERN	1002
7	NEUCHATEL XAMAX FC	1003
8	FC ST. GALLEN	1004

9	SERVETTE FC GENEVE	1005
10	FC SION	1006
11	BSC YOUNG BOYS BERN	1007
12	FC ZÜRICH	1008
Promoted clubs		
13	SR DELEMONT	1009
14	YVERDON-SPORTS	1009

ZÜRICH DUO MAKE TRACKS IN EUROPE

Servette hit the jackpot in last-day drama

FEDERATION DIRECTORY

Schweizerischer Fussballverband
Haus des Fussballs, Postfach, 3000 Bern 15

tel - (031) 9508111	Year of Formation - 1895
fax - (031) 9508181	President - Marcel Mathier
	Secretary - Peter Gilliéron

Stadium - Wankdorf, Bern (28,000)

It was a season of disharmony and unrest in Switzerland, with several clubs encountering financial difficulties, many coaches getting the chop, and attendance figures dropping through the roof. But on the field of play there was no lack of tension and excitement.

The NLA championship produced one of its most unpredictable and eventful title races in years; there were some strong performances by Swiss clubs in European competition; and the national team belatedly came good to offer the promise of a second successive appearance in the European Championship finals.

The closing stages of the championship produced an extraordinary collage of results. With no team having the strength and consistency to mount an irresistible challenge, the dénouement was open to endless permutations. With two games left, four teams were still in the hunt - defending champions Grasshopper, first-round leaders Servette and the two most entertaining sides in the division, Lausanne and FC Zürich.

The latter dropped out of the race in the penultimate round when their run of six successive wins came to an abrupt end at home to Lausanne. That 1-0 triumph, courtesy of Swedish veteran Stefan Rehn's all-important 84th-minute winner, put Lausanne two points ahead of both Grasshopper and Servette with one match remaining.

As luck would have it, Lausanne's final match was at home to Servette, while Grasshopper had a home fixture against Neuchâtel Xamax. Because of the Swiss league's indigenous rule whereby teams finishing level on points at the end of the season have their placings determined by the positions they held at the end of the first phase, the situation was clear-cut. If the Lausanne-Servette clash produced a winner, then that team would be crowned champions. But if the game ended in a draw,

LEAGUE CHAMPIONSHIP RESULTS 98/99

AUTUMN (FIRST PHASE)

		1	2	3	4	5	6	7	8	9	10	11	12
1	FC Aarau		5-0	0-3	2-2	2-0	0-0	0-2	2-6	1-4	2-2	1-1	0-2
2	FC Basel	1-0		1-1	1-1	1-3	1-0	2-0	1-0	0-2	0-0	1-1	2-1
3	Grasshopper-Club Zürich	2-0	2-1		2-2	3-2	2-0	1-1	4-1	3-0	4-1	2-1	1-2
4	Lausanne-Sports	2-1	0-2	3-1		3-2	2-2	1-0	1-0	0-0	2-1	1-0	1-1
5	FC Lugano	0-2	5-1	1-1	1-2		0-3	4-3	2-2	3-3	2-2	2-2	0-0
6	FC Luzern	2-2	4-1	1-0	1-0	1-2		1-1	1-1	0-0	1-2	0-0	3-7
7	Neuchâtel Xamax FC	0-0	3-1	0-2	4-1	1-0	1-1		2-0	1-1	3-1	1-1	1-1
8	FC St. Gallen	4-3	0-1	3-1	0-1	4-4	2-1	0-0		0-0	2-0	3-1	0-0
9	Servette FC Genève	3-2	3-1	2-0	2-2	1-0	3-2	1-1	1-0		2-1	0-1	3-1
10	FC Sion	3-2	1-0	0-1	0-4	2-0	0-0	1-1	2-1	2-2		1-1	0-0
11	BSC Young Boys Bern	1-1	1-2	3-1	7-2	0-1	1-2	2-3	0-1	3-4	3-0		1-2
12	FC Zürich	1-0	1-0	0-0	3-3	4-1	2-0	1-1	3-1	0-1	3-0	3-2	

SPRING (FINAL ROUND)

		1	2	3	4	5	6	7	8
1	FC Basel		2-0	1-2	1-1	1-0	3-3	0-0	1-0
2	Grasshopper-Club Zürich	4-2		5-0	4-0	5-0	4-0	0-1	0-2
3	Lausanne-Sports	3-0	2-3		5-1	4-0	4-1	2-5	3-1
4	FC Luzern	0-2	1-4	0-1		2-0	2-1	2-1	1-3
5	Neuchâtel Xamax FC	1-1	1-1	1-1	1-1		3-2	0-3	1-3
6	FC St. Gallen	1-2	0-0	0-0	0-2	0-0		2-0	1-3
7	Servette FC Genève	2-1	0-0	2-0	1-0	1-2	2-0		1-1
8	FC Zürich	2-1	0-1	0-1	3-0	2-2	0-2	4-0	

LEAGUE CHAMPIONSHIP FINAL TABLE 98/99

AUTUMN (FIRST PHASE)

			Home				Away				Total					
		Pd	W	D	L	F	A	W	D	L	F	A	W	D	L	F	A	Pt	GD
1	Servette FC Genève	22	8	2	1	21	11	4	6	1	17	13	12	8	2	38	24	44	+14
2	Grasshopper-Club Zürich	22	8	2	1	26	11	3	3	5	11	14	11	5	6	37	25	38	+12
3	FC Zürich	22	7	3	1	21	9	3	5	3	12	12	10	8	4	33	21	38	+12
4	Lausanne-Sports	22	7	3	1	16	10	3	5	3	20	23	10	8	4	36	33	38	+3
5	Neuchâtel Xamax FC	22	5	5	1	17	9	2	6	3	13	14	7	11	4	30	23	32	+7
6	FC Basel	22	5	4	2	11	9	3	0	8	10	25	8	4	10	21	34	28	-13
7	FC Luzern	22	4	5	2	15	11	2	4	5	11	14	6	9	7	26	25	27	+1
8	FC St. Gallen	22	5	4	2	18	12	2	2	7	13	19	7	6	9	31	31	27	0
9	FC Sion	22	4	5	2	12	12	1	3	7	10	24	5	8	9	22	36	23	-14
10	FC Lugano	22	2	6	3	20	21	3	1	7	15	22	5	7	10	35	43	22	-8
11	BSC Young Boys Bern	22	3	1	7	22	19	1	6	4	11	15	4	7	11	33	34	19	-1
12	FC Aarau	22	2	4	5	15	22	1	3	7	13	19	3	7	12	28	41	16	-13

SPRING (FINAL ROUND)

			Home				Away				Total					
		Pd	W	D	L	F	A	W	D	L	F	A	W	D	L	F	A	Pt	GD
1	Servette FC Genève	14	4	2	1	9	4	3	1	3	10	10	7	3	4	19	14	46	+5
2	Grasshopper-Club Zürich	14	5	0	2	22	5	3	3	1	9	6	8	3	3	31	11	46	+20
3	Lausanne-Sports	14	5	0	2	23	11	3	2	2	5	9	8	2	4	28	20	45	+8
4	FC Zürich	14	3	1	3	11	7	4	1	2	13	8	7	2	5	24	15	42	+9
5	FC Basel	14	3	3	1	9	6	2	1	4	9	13	5	4	5	18	19	33	-1
6	Neuchâtel Xamax FC	14	1	4	2	8	12	1	2	4	4	15	2	6	6	12	27	28	-15
7	FC Luzern	14	3	0	4	8	12	1	2	4	5	15	4	2	8	13	27	28	-14
8	FC St. Gallen	14	1	3	3	4	7	1	1	5	9	18	2	4	8	13	25	24	-12

N.B. After 22 matches the top eight play off for the title, taking half their points total. The bottom four enter a promotion/relegation play-off group with the top two from the Second Division. In the Final Round, when teams are level on points, classification is determined by the position of the teams at the end of the First Phase.

then the title would be retained by Grasshopper - assuming they won their game with Xamax. If they didn't, the title would be Lausanne's.

Given the circumstances, the odds did not seem to favour Servette. Their 2-0 win at home to St. Gallen three days earlier had brought their first three points, and their first goals, for four matches. But the victory had come at a cost, with the league's leading scorer Alexandre Rey, picking up a suspension for the showdown in Lausanne. However, Gérard Castella's team decided to go for broke. They knew a draw would be no use to them, so they opted for all-out attack. 0-1 down early on, they hit back straightaway with two goals from Dutchman Edwin Vurens, and by half-time they were 3-2 up. Vurens completed his hat-trick after the interval and with two minutes left Bulgarian youngster Martin

Petrov bagged his second goal of the game to confirm an amazing 5-2 triumph for the Geneva club.

Level on points with Grasshopper, Servette thus had their superior first-phase record to thank for their 17th Swiss title triumph. Until that dramatic final day their spring form had been fairly unimpressive, but back in the autumn they had been the clear front-runners, finishing up with a six-point lead over their traditional arch-rivals from Zürich. The departure of their star player Patrick Müller (to Grasshopper via Juventus) was one obvious reason for Servette's slide in form, but they managed to keep going, and with Alexandre Rey continuing to pilfer important goals (including the winner away to Grasshopper), they were able to put themselves in position for that final, decisive strike.

Thanks to the generous backing of French TV company

NATIONAL TEAM APPEARANCES 98/99

Coach - Gilbert GRESS	YUG	ITA	DEN	HUN	SLO	OMN	AUT	BLS	WAL	GRE	ITA	Cps	Gls
Andreas HILFIKER (11/02/69) - 1.FC Nürnberg (GER)	G	G	G	G46	G		G					7	-
Murat YAKIN (15/09/74) - Fenerbahçe (TUR)	D				D	D38						19	3
Stéphane HENCHOZ (07/09/74) - Blackburn Rovers (ENG)	D	D	D	D85	D			D	D			37	-
Stefan WOLF (31/01/71) - Servette FC Genève	D72	D65				s38			D	D		12	-
Régis ROTHENBÜHLER (11/10/70) - Neuchâtel Xamax FC	M	D	s76							M		17	-
Johann VOGEL (08/03/77) - Grasshopper-Club Zürich	M	D	M	D	M	M	M	M	M	M	M	28	1
Raphaël WICKY (26/04/77) - SV Werder Bremen (GER)	M64	M86	M	M	M	M57		M66	D		D70	24	-
Patrick MÜLLER (17/12/76) - Servette FC Genève/													
Grasshopper-Club Zürich	M	M	A77		A		s79	s66	A	D	D	11	1
David SESA (10/07/73) - Lecce (ITA)	A	M	M90	M		M65	A79	A74		A85	A	20	1
Stéphane CHAPUISAT (28/06/69) - Borussia Dortmund (GER)	A	A	A	A	A72	A83	A60	A	A	A79	A	74	17
Marco GRASSI (08/08/68) - Olympique Lyonnais (FRA)	A46											31	3
Fabio CELESTINI (31/10/75) - Lausanne-Sports	s46	s86	A							s56		5	-
Bernt HAAS (08/04/78) - Grasshopper-Club Zürich	s64		s90						M	s70		6	1
Ramon VEGA (14/06/71) - Tottenham Hotspur (ENG)	s72	D										21	2
Ciriaco SFORZA (02/03/70) - 1.FC Kaiserslautern (GER)		M	D	D46	M56	M	M	M	M	M	M	63	6
Frédéric CHASSOT (31/03/69) - FC Zürich		s65		A58	s90	s83						17	2
Sébastien JEANNERET (12/12/73) - Neuchâtel Xamax FC			D76	D		s57	D	D	D		M78	11	-
Sébastien FOURNIER (27/06/71) - Servette FC Genève			M			s46	D	D	M	M75		24	2
Franco DI JORIO (22/09/73) - FC Zürich			s77	s85	M	M46				s75	s78	6	-
Marc HODEL (06/11/70) - FC Zürich				M	D	D	D	D		D	D	7	1
Patrick BÜHLMANN (16/08/71) - Servette FC Genève				A	s56	s46	s65		s68			5	-
Marco PASCOLO (09/05/66) - FC Zürich/Nottingham Forest (ENG)				s46		G						45	-
Johan LONFAT (11/09/73) - Servette FC Genève				s46			D					6	-
Alexandre REY (22/09/72) - Servette FC Genève				s50	s72	s65	s60			s79		5	-
Marco ZWYSSIG (24/10/71) - FC St. Gallen					D	D						4	-
Alexandre COMISETTI (21/07/73) - Grasshopper-Club Zürich					A90	A46	A65	A	A68	A	A56	15	3
Martin BRUNNER (23/04/63) - Lausanne-Sports								G	G	G46		36	-
Patrick DE NAPOLI (17/11/75) - Grasshopper-Club Zürich							s74					4	-
Stefan HUBER (14/06/66) - FC Basel										s46	G	13	-
Thomas WYSS (29/08/66) - FC Luzern										s85		7	-

Canal Plus, Servette were one of the few NLA teams without money problems. They were also one of only three clubs in the division which ended the campaign with the same coach who had been in from the start, the others being FC Zürich and Xamax.

Lausanne got rid of their coach, Georges Bregy, as early as mid-autumn. His in-house replacement, Pierre-André Schurmann, did much better than was originally expected, and although Lausanne missed out on the title, with home and away defeats against both Grasshopper and Servette

in the spring proving fatal, the lakesiders did give their supporters something to treasure from a fine season when they retained the Swiss Cup - after revenge victories over Servette in the semi-final and then Grasshopper in the final. There was sadness, however, for the team's veteran goalkeeper Martin Brunner, who badly injured his knee on the eve of the Cup final and thus missed out on the victory over his old club. Worse still, the club doctors advised the 36-year-old, who had just made a sensational comeback to the Swiss national team, to hang up his gloves for good.

DOMESTIC CUP 98/99

1/16 FINALS
FC Bulle 1, Lausanne-Sports 5
FC Winterthur 1, Grasshopper-Club Zürich 2
FC Naters 1, Servette FC Genève 3
Red Star Zürich 3, FC Chiasso 0
SR Delémont 3, Neuchâtel Xamax FC 1
FC Schaffhausen 0, FC Luzern 1 (aet)
FC Solothurn 0, FC Sion 1
FC Lugano 2, FC Gossau 0
Stade Nyonnais 2, FC Basel 2 (aet; 4-2 on pens.)
FC Wil 3, FC Aarau 0
SC Buochs 1, FC St. Gallen 0
Yverdon-Sports 3, BSC Young Boys Bern 1
FC Wangen bei Olten 0, FC Thun 5 (aet)
AC Bellinzona 3, SC Kriens 0
FC Grenchen 2, Etoile-Carouge FC 0
FC Locarno 0, FC Zürich 0 (aet; 3-5 on pens.)

1/8 FINALS
FC Wil 1, Lausanne-Sports 4
Stade Nyonnais 1, Grasshopper-Club Zürich 1
(aet; 2-4 on pens.)
SC Buochs 0, Servette FC Genève 1
Red Star Zürich 2, Yverdon-Sports 1
FC Thun 1, SR Delémont 3
AC Bellinzona 2, FC Luzern 3
FC Grenchen 0, FC Sion 2
FC Zürich 0, FC Lugano 1

QUARTER-FINALS
SR Delémont 1 (Jinani 13),
Lausanne-Sports 2 (Pantelic 15, Gerber 38)

FC Luzern 1 (Scepanovic 49), Grasshopper-Club
Zürich 2 (Yakin 20, Cabanas 67)

FC Sion 1 (Biaggi 5), Servette FC Genève 2
(Bühlmann 72, Vurens 81)

Red Star Zürich 2 (Firat 29, Ronca 55),
FC Lugano 1 (Giallanza 68)

SEMI-FINALS
Servette FC Genève 0,
Lausanne-Sports 1 (Pantelic 19)

Red Star Zürich 0,
Grasshopper-Club Zürich 7 (Tikva 22, 48, 63, 87,
De Napoli 33, Gren 35, Yakin 82)

FINAL
13/06/99, Berne
LAUSANNE-SPORTS 2 Diogo (36), Mazzoni (90)
GRASSHOPPER-CLUB ZÜRICH 0
referee - Beck
LAUSANNE-SPORTS - Rapo; Ohrel, Puce, Londono,
Hänzi, Gerber (Shahgeldyan 76), Rehn, Celestini,
Diogo (Douglas 83), Thurre (Piffaretti 69), Mazzoni.
GRASSHOPPER-CLUB ZÜRICH - Zuberbühler; Cabanas,
Müller, Smiljanic, Berner, Vogel, Tararache
(Zanni 68), Yakin (Comisetti 59), De Napoli, Tikva,
Kavelashvili.

Consequently, he will not be able to reach his target of 500 LNA matches (he was on 487). But he will not be lost to Swiss football entirely, having been appointed the goal-keeping coach of the national team.

Grasshopper, who replaced Rolf Fringer with St. Gallen's Roger Hegi in mid-season, had a season full of controversy, both on the bench and in the boardroom. One of Hegi's first acts was to sack crowd favourite Kubilay Türkyilmaz. He might have got away with it had he gone on to win a trophy, but despite the team having the best record in the play-offs, the end result was second place in both league and Cup - not the ideal scenario for a club with the strongest pool of players in the country.

Grasshopper had a very active season in Europe. Eliminated from the Champions' League at the qualifying-round stage by Galatasaray, they went on to reach the third round of the UEFA Cup before losing narrowly (on the away-goals rule) to French champions-to-be Bordeaux. They would almost certainly have been eliminated by Fiorentina in round two but for the intervention of an idiot with a home-made bomb at half-time in the second leg, but they deserved great credit for knocking out Anderlecht in round one, having won 2-0 in Brussels.

FC Zürich emulated their city rivals by reaching the UEFA Cup third round before they, like Lausanne before them in the Cup-winners' Cup, lost to a team from the Italian

NATIONAL TEAM RESULTS 98/99

Date	Opponent		Venue	Score	Scorers
02/09/98	Yugoslavia	A	Nis	1-1	Sesa (58)
10/10/98	Italy (ECQ)	A	Udine	0-2	
14/10/98	Denmark (ECQ)	H	Zürich	1-1	Chapuisat (58)
18/11/98	Hungary	A	Budapest	0-2	
06/02/99	Slovenia	N	Muscat	2-0	Hodel (8), Comisetti (17)
10/02/99	Oman	A	Muscat	2-1	Comisetti (9, 34)
10/03/99	Austria	H	St. Gallen	2-4	Vogel (23p), Feiersinger (50og)
27/03/99	Belarus (ECQ)	A	Minsk	1-0	Fournier (72)
31/03/99	Wales (ECQ)	H	Zürich	2-0	Chapuisat (4, 70)
28/04/99	Greece	A	Athens	1-1	Haas (20)
09/06/99	Italy (ECQ)	H	Lausanne	0-0	

TOP SCORERS

19	Alexandre REY (Servette FC Genève)
13	Shaun BARTLETT (FC Zürich)
	Patrick DE NAPOLI (Grasshopper-Club Zürich)
12	Edwin VURENS (FC St. Gallen/ Servette FC Genève)
11	Mikheil KAVELASHVILI (Grasshopper-Club Zürich)
	Avi TIKVA (Grasshopper-Club Zürich)
	Léonard THURRE (Lausanne-Sports)
10	Mario FRICK (FC Basel)
	Patrick ISABELLA (Neuchâtel Xamax FC)
	Didier THOLOT (FC Sion)
	Rumen IVANOV (FC Aarau)

EUROPEAN CUPS 98/99

CHAMPIONS' CUP
● GRASSHOPPER-CLUB ZÜRICH
Preliminary round JEUNESSE ESCH (LUX)

H 6-0 N'Kufo (6, 51), Kavelashvili (29), Cabanas (41), Tikva (65p), Tararache (90)
Walker; Haas, Mazzarelli, Smiljanic, Christ; Tikva (Zanni 68), Tararache, Cabanas, Kavelashvili (Magro 65); Magnin, N'Kufo (Berner 71).

A 2-0 Esposito (37p), Türkyilmaz (44)
Walker; Haas, Mazzarelli, Smiljanic, Berner; Magnin (Zanni 46), Esposito, Cabanas, Savic (Magro 72); Türkyilmaz, N'Kufo (Kavelashvili 46).

Qualifying round GALATASARAY (TUR)

A 1-2 Vogel (87)
Zuberbühler; Haas, Smiljanic, Gren, Christ; Magnin, Esposito (Tikva 79), Vogel, Cabanas (Tararache 69); N'Kufo (Kavelashvili 69), Türkyilmaz.

H 2-3 Türkyilmaz (45), Vogel (71p)
Zuberbühler; Haas, Smiljanic, Gren, Christ; Tikva, Esposito (De Napoli 75), Vogel, Cabanas (Magnin 66); Kavelashvili (N'Kufo 46), Türkyilmaz.

CUP WINNERS' CUP
● LAUSANNE-SPORTS
Qualifying round TSEMENT ARARAT (ARM)

H 5-1 Celestini (28p, 47, 58, 71), Cavin (87)
Brunner; Hottiger, Puce, Londono (Hänzi 80); Ohrel (Gogoua 78), Piffaretti, Celestini (Cavin 85), Douglas; Udovic, Shahgeldyan (Thurre 65).

A 2-1 Douglas (66), Hottiger (89)
Brunner; Hottiger, Londono, Puce, Hänzi; Ohrel, Rehn, Celestini (Cavin 72), Diogo (Douglas 62); Thurre, Shahgeldyan (Minasyan 78).

1st round LAZIO (ITA)

A 1-1 Douglas (55)
Brunner; Hottiger, Puce, Londono (Hänzi Iglesias 80); Celestini, Rehn, Piffaretti, Douglas; Udovic (Thurre 59), Shahgeldyan (Gerber 66).

H 2-2 Douglas (10), Rehn (84)
Brunner; Hottiger, Iglesias (Puce 46), Londono, Hänzi; Celestini (Gerber 65), Piffaretti, Rehn, Douglas; Udovic, Thurre.

UEFA CUP
● FC ZÜRICH
Qualifying round SHAKHTAR DONETSK (UKR)

H 4-0 Sant'Anna (1), Djordjevic (61), Chassot (71), Tarone (88)
Pascolo; Hodel, Djordjevic, Fischer, Di Jorio; Sant'Anna (Castillo 85), Del Signore, Wiederkehr (Tarone 70); Chassot (Iodice 75), Bartlett, Nixon.

A 2-3 Bartlett (19, 28)
Pascolo; Del Signore, Djordjevic, Fischer, Hodel; Di Jorio, Iodice (Beyaz 72), Sant'Anna, Tarone (Albrecht 86); Bartlett, Nixon (Castillo 72).

1st round ANORTHOSIS FAMAGUSTA (CYP)

H 4-0 Nixon (35), Hodel (58), Bartlett (69), Chassot (81)
Pascolo; Huber (Opango 46), Hodel, Fischer (Tarone 74), Di Jorio; Sant'Anna, Del Signore, Lima, Nixon; Bartlett (Iodice 80), Chassot.

A 3-2 Sant'Anna (12), Bartlett (38, 62)
Pascolo; Tarone, Djordjevic, Fischer, Hodel (Huber 67); Sant'Anna, Opango, Lima; Chassot (Wiederkehr 46), Bartlett (Beyaz 74), Nixon.

2nd round CELTIC (SCO)

A 1-1 Fischer (76)
Pascolo; Tarone, Hodel, Fischer, Di Jorio; Sant'Anna (Castillo 84), Lima, Del Signore, Nixon (Wiederkehr 46); Chassot, Bartlett.

H 4-2 Del Signore (52), Chassot (56), Bartlett (61), Sant'Anna (75)
Pascolo; Tarone, Hodel, Fischer, Di Jorio; Del Signore, Sant'Anna (Castillo 78), Lima, Wiederkehr (Opango 66); Bartlett, Chassot (Nixon 78).

3rd round ROMA (ITA)

A 0-1
Shorunmu; Castillo, Djordjevic, Hodel, Di Jorio; Tarone (Iodice 81), Lima, Del Signore, Nixon (Huber 63); Chassot (Beyaz 83), Bartlett.

H 2-2 Bartlett (60, 81)
Shorunmu; Castillo (Huber 46), Fischer, Hodel, Di Jorio; Tarone (Iodice 56), Lima, Sant'Anna (Djordjevic 89), Nixon; Bartlett, Chassot.

● SERVETTE FC GENEVE
Qualifying round KFC GERMINAL EKEREN (BEL)

A 4-1 Rey (20p, 51), Wolf (35), Durix (78)
Pédat; Wolf, Barea, Juarez; Durix, Lonfat (Potocianu 82), Fournier, Müller, Bühlmann (Ouadja 75); Varela, Rey (Karlen 70).

H 1-2 Rey (83p)
Pédat; Barea (Tato 70), Karlen, Juarez; Durix (Pizzinat 74), Lonfat, Fournier, Müller, Bühlmann; Rey (Ouadja 89), Varela.

1st round CSKA SOFIA (BUL)

H 2-1 Pizzinat (85), Melunovic (89)
Pédat; Potocianu (Melunovic 78), Wolf, Juarez; Barea (Ouadja 68), Fournier, Lonfat, Durix, Bühlmann; Rey (Pizzinat 50), Varela.

A 0-1
Pédat; Potocianu (Melunovic 78), Wolf, Juarez; Müller, Lonfat, Müller, Durix (Pizzinat 70), Bühlmann; Rey, Varela (Ouadja 87).

● GRASSHOPPER-CLUB ZÜRICH
1st round RSC ANDERLECHT (BEL)

A 2-0 Comisetti (51), Tikva (84)
Zuberbühler; Haas, Smiljanic, Gren, Christ (Berner 25); Cabanas, Esposito, Vogel, Comisetti; Kavelashvili (N'Kufo 75), De Napoli (Tikva 85).

H 0 0
Zuberbühler; Haas, Smiljanic, Gren, Christ; Vogel, Magnin (Mazzarelli 70), Esposito, Kavelashvili (Tararache 62); De Napoli (Türkyilmaz 46), N'Kufo.

2nd round FIORENTINA (ITA)

H 0-2
Zuberbühler; Haas, Smiljanic, Gren, Christ; Magnin (Tikva 60), Cabanas (N'Kufo 69), Esposito, Comisetti; De Napoli (Kavelashvili 69), Türkyilmaz.

A 1-2 Gren (29)
(match abandoned at half-time and awarded 0-3)
Zuberbühler; Haas, Gren, Mazzarelli; Cabanas, Vogel, Tikva, Tararache, Comisetti; De Napoli, Kavelashvili

3rd round GIRONDINS DE BORDEAUX (FRA)

H 3-3 Kavelashvili (21), Türkyilmaz (33), Comisetti (53)
Zuberbühler; Cabanas (Smiljanic 77), Mazzarelli, Gren, Berner; Vogel, Tararache, Tikva (Magnin 77); Türkyilmaz, Kavelashvili (De Napoli 73), Comisetti.

A 0-0
Zuberbühler; Mazzarelli, Smiljanic (Berner 75), Gren, Christ; Tikva, Tararache, Vogel, Comisetti; Kavelashvili, Magnin (De Napoli 75).

PLAYERS OF THE SEASON

PATRICK MÜLLER

Servette eventually won the title without him, but Patrick Müller had every justification for believing that he was the 'real' champion. He had led Servette to a six-point lead at the end of the first phase in the autumn, and his new club, Grasshopper, had the best record during the spring. Throughout the season, however, he was actually the property of another club, Juventus. The Italian giants had bought him during the summer of 1998 and returned him on loan to Servette, but on seeing that he was being used as a right-sided midfielder at the Geneva club, they intervened and offered him to Grasshopper...on the condition that he played libero. Müller also flitted from one role to another during his season with the Swiss national team, even appearing at times as a right-winger, but it was as a sweeper in the 0-0 draw at home to Italy that he really excelled - which begged the question why Juventus decided the following month to make his stay at Grasshopper permanent, selling him back to Switzerland at a 25 per cent mark-up on their original purchase price.

STEPHANE HENCHOZ

Rated as Switzerland's best defender by some distance, Stéphane Henchoz was not exactly at ease when Gilbert Gress was appointed as Swiss national team coach. Although the two were together during the player's early days at Neuchâtel Xamax, they have different conceptions of what constitutes an effective defence. While Gress favours the German sweeper model, Henchoz is a staunch advocate of the British-style zonal back-four. He also plays it to perfection - witness his world-class display in the 1-0 victory away to Belarus - and could not be blamed for his club Blackburn Rovers' shock relegation from the Premiership. Bayern Munich were keen to sign the 25-year-old during the summer, but he preferred to stay in England, joining a new-look Liverpool in a £3.5m move.

---

capital following a 2-2 draw at home in the second leg. Raimondo Ponte's team had been in sensational scoring form on their Letzigrund turf in the earlier rounds, scoring four goals on each occasion to see off Shakhtar Donetsk, Anorthosis Famagusta and - most impressively of all - Celtic. South African World Cup striker Shaun Bartlett seemed particularly inspired by European competition, scoring eight goals, including at least one in every round and both at home to Roma. He was also the club's top scorer in the league, his 13-goal tally playing a major part in helping FCZ to finish fourth and earn a return ticket to Europe. Another African in form was Zürich's Nigerian goalkeeper Ike Shorunmu, who was voted the best foreigner in NLA - despite his relatively late introduction as a replacement for on-loan Swiss veteran Marco Pascolo.

Of the clubs struggling to keep afloat financially, FC Sion were undoubtedly the hardest hit, and their precarious position was certainly not helped when they dropped out of the top division for the first time in 29 years. Young Boys

Berne also ceded their place, which allowed Delémont and Yverdon, two clubs from the Jura region in the west of the country, to take out NLA membership in 1999/2000.

Delémont reacted positively to their promotion by taking on Swiss record-cap holder Heinz Hermann as their new coach, while Yverdon retained their faith in another former star of Swiss football, the ex-Servette midfield player Lucien Favre.

It took new Swiss national team boss Gilbert Gress almost a year before he registered his first victory. The professorial Frenchman came close to being deposed after his first seven matches in charge brought four draws and three defeats. And even when the team finally won, twice on the trot, the matches were no more than insignificant friendlies played in the Middle East.

Gress's insistence on playing with three forwards and a sweeper-style defence did not appear to be working, but after a mini-mutiny led by the team's best defender, Stéphane Henchoz, Switzerland got their first victory in the Euro 2000 campaign, 1-0 away to Belarus, and immediately followed that with a 2-0 triumph at home to Wales, in which Stéphane Chapuisat, enjoying arguably his best season with the national team, scored both goals. A 0-0 draw - and another clean sheet - at home to runaway group leaders Italy enabled the Swiss to end the season in a reasonably strong position, with their prospects of reaching a play-off place very much alive.

INTERNATIONAL HONOURS

World Cup Finals appearances: 1934, 1938 (2nd round), 1950, 1954 (qtr-finals), 1962, 1966, 1994 (2nd round)

European Championship appearances: 1996

FC AARAU

FC Aarau
Postfach 2738
5001 Aarau
tel - (062) 8232922
fax - (062) 8232924
Year of Formation - 1902
President - Ernst Lämmli
Secretaries - Rolf Suter & Fredy Strasser
Coach - Martin Trümpler; Freddy Strasser;
Jochen Dries
Stadium - Brügglifeld (13,200)

MAJOR HONOURS
League Championship - (3) 1912, 1914, 1993.
Domestic Cup - (1) 1985.

	P	Ap	(s)	Gls
Petar ALEKSANDROV (BUL)	A	17	(2)	4
Ross ALOISI (AUS)	D		(2)	
David BADER	D	16	(4)	1
Roberto BALDASSARI	A	17	(1)	2
Ivan BENITO	G	21		
Jan BERGER (CZE)	A	14	(5)	2
Gerardo DONATIELLO	M		(2)	
Mario EGGIMANN	D	?		
Lucio ESPOSITO (IIA)	A	3	(14)	1
Marcel HELDMANN	M	22		5
Rumen IVANOV (BUL)	A	20	(2)	10
Eric MANGIA	D	2	(3)	
Dejan MARKOVIC	M	15		
Frédéric PAGE	D	11	(2)	
Mirko PAVLICEVIC (CRO)	D	21		1
Ivan PREVITALI	M	17	(1)	
Dino ROSELLI	G	1		
Dariusz SKRZYPCZAK (POL)	M	21		1
Beat STUDER	D	14		
Remo TOVAGLIARO	A		(1)	
Carmine VICECONTE	A		(3)	
Slawomir WOJCIECHOWSKI (POL)	M	7	(7)	
Davide ZITOLA	A	1	(8)	

18/07/98	Servette FC Genève	A	2-3	Berger, Ivanov (p)
21/07/98	FC Basel	H	5-0	Aleksandrov 3, Ivanov, Heldmann
25/07/98	Neuchâtel Xamax FC	A	0-0	
31/07/98	FC St. Gallen	H	2-6	Ivanov (p), Skrzypczak
05/08/98	Grasshopper-Club Zürich	A	0-2	
16/08/98	Lausanne-Sports	H	2-2	Ivanov (p), Heldmann
22/08/98	BSC Young Boys Bern	A	1-1	Ivanov
29/08/98	FC Lugano	H	2-0	Berger, Esposito
08/09/98	FC Sion	A	2-3	Heldmann 2
13/09/98	FC Luzern	A	2-2	Ivanov 2
20/09/98	FC Zürich	H	0-2	
25/09/98	Servette FC Genève	H	1-4	Ivanov
04/10/98	FC Basel	A	0-1	
18/10/98	Neuchâtel Xamax FC	H	0-2	
25/10/98	FC St. Gallen	A	3-4	Heldmann, Baldassari 2
04/11/98	Grasshopper-Club Zürich	H	0-3	
08/11/98	Lausanne-Sports	A	1-2	Aleksandrov
15/11/98	BSC Young Boys Bern	H	1-1	Bader
22/11/98	FC Lugano	A	2-0	Pavlicevic, og (Giannini)
29/11/98	FC Sion	H	2-2	Ivanov 2 (2p)
06/12/98	FC Luzern	H	0-0	
13/12/98	FC Zürich	A	0-1	

FC BASEL

CLUB DIRECTORY

FC Basel 1893
Postfach 260
4028 Basel
tel - (061) 3133666
fax - (061) 3133633
Year of Formation - 1893
President - René C. Jäggi
Coach - Guy Mathez; Marco Schällibaum
(99/00 - Christian Gross)
Stadium - Schützenmatte (11,400)

MAJOR HONOURS
League Championship - (8) 1953, 1967, 1969,
1970, 1972, 1973, 1977, 1980.
Domestic Cup - (5)
1933, 1947, 1963, 1967, 1975.

APPEARANCES 98/99

	P	Ap	(s)	Gls
Robson Vicente Gonçalves				
"ABEDI" (BRA)	M	18	(7)	3
Sébastien BARBERIS	M	24	(3)	
Olivier BOUMELAHA	A		(1)	
Luis CALAPES	D	15	(3)	
Mario CANTALUPPI	M	6	(1)	2
Massimo CECCARONI	D	28	(1)	
Josip COLINA (ITA)	D		(2)	
Philippe CRAVERO	D	27		
Theodoros DISSERIS	D		(2)	
Fábio dos Santos "FABINHO" (BRA)	A	8	(8)	3
Mario FRICK (LIE)	M	24	(2)	10
Urs GÜNTENSPERGER	A		(1)	
Fabrice HENRY (FRA)	M	5	(1)	
Stefan HUBER	G	36		
Benjamin HUGGEL	A	1	(2)	
Oumar KONDE	M	10	(1)	
Oliver KREUZER (GER)	D	32		1
Slaven MATAN	G		(1)	
Deniz MENDI	M	2	(8)	
Ahmed OUATTARA (CIV)	A	14	(3)	3
Vaclav PECHOUCEK (CZE)	M	4	(3)	
Marco PEREZ (LIE)	A	17	(16)	4
Dan POTOCIANU (ROM)	D	10		
Ivan REIMANN	M	16	(2)	
Aleksandr RYCHKOV (RUS)	M	24		6
Attila SAHIN	A	22	(7)	1
Marco TSCHOPP	A	14	(13)	5
Carlos VARELA (ESP)	A	12		1
Argemiro VEIGA (BRA)	M	27		

LEAGUE RESULTS 1998/99

18/07/98	FC Sion	H	0-0	
21/07/98	FC Aarau	A	0-5	
25/07/98	FC Zürich	H	2-1	Rychkov, Sahin
31/07/98	Servette FC Genève	A	1-3	Abedi
05/08/98	FC Luzern	H	1-0	Tschopp
16/08/98	Neuchâtel Xamax FC	H	2-0	Ouattara (p), Perez
22/08/98	FC St. Gallen	A	1-0	Rychkov
29/08/98	Grasshopper-Club Zürich	H	1-1	Ouattara
08/09/98	Lausanne-Sports	A	2-0	Rychkov 2
12/09/98	BSC Young Boys Bern	H	1-1	Frick
19/09/98	FC Lugano	A	1-5	Rychkov
27/09/98	FC Sion	A	0-1	
04/10/98	FC Aarau	H	1-0	Ouattara
16/10/98	FC Zürich	A	0-1	
25/10/98	Servette FC Genève	H	0-2	
31/10/98	FC Luzern	A	1-4	Frick
07/11/98	Neuchâtel Xamax FC	A	1-3	Frick
15/11/98	FC St. Gallen	H	1-0	Tschopp
21/11/98	Grasshopper-Club Zürich	A	1-2	Perez
29/11/98	Lausanne-Sports	H	1-1	Frick
06/12/98	BSC Young Boys Bern	A	2-1	Rychkov, Tschopp
13/12/98	FC Lugano	H	1-3	Tschopp (p)
28/02/99	FC Luzern	A	2-0	Abedi, Frick
07/03/99	Neuchâtel Xamax FC	H	1-0	Abedi
13/03/99	Servette FC Genève	A	1-2	Fabinho
21/03/99	FC Zürich	H	1-0	Perez (p)
05/04/99	Grasshopper-Club Zürich	A	2-4	Varela, Frick
10/04/99	Lausanne-Sports	H	1-2	Frick
18/04/99	FC St. Gallen	H	3-3	Frick, Cantaluppi (p), Kreuzer
25/04/99	FC St. Gallen	A	2-1	Frick, Perez
01/05/99	Lausanne-Sports	A	0-3	
08/05/99	Grasshopper-Club Zürich	H	2-0	Fabinho, Tschopp
16/05/99	FC Zürich	A	1-2	Frick
22/05/99	Servette FC Genève	H	0-0	
30/05/99	Neuchâtel Xamax FC	A	1-1	Fabinho
02/06/99	FC Luzern	H	1-1	Cantaluppi

GRASSHOPPER-CLUB ZÜRICH

CLUB DIRECTORY

Grasshopper-Club Zürich
Fussball-Sektion
Postfach 217
8037 Zürich
tel - (01) 4474646
fax - (01) 4474690
Year of Formation - 1886
President - Dr. Peter Widmer
Coach - Rolf Fringer; Roger Hegi
Stadium - Hardturm (20,079)

MAJOR HONOURS
League Championship - (25)
1898, 1900, 1901, 1905, 1921, 1927, 1928,
1931, 1937, 1939, 1942, 1943, 1945, 1952,
1956, 1971, 1978, 1982, 1983, 1984, 1990,
1991, 1995, 1996, 1998.
Domestic Cup - (18) 1926, 1927, 1932, 1934,
1937, 1938, 1940, 1941, 1942, 1943, 1946,
1952, 1956, 1983, 1988, 1989. 1990, 1994.

APPEARANCES 98/99

		P	Ap	(s)	Gls
Bruno BERNER	D	12	(9)	
Ricardo CABANAS	M	15	(9)	
Sven CHRIST	D	19		
Alexandre COMISETTI	M	17	(6)	6
Patrick DE NAPOLI	A	22	(6)	13
Antonio ESPOSITO	M	10	(1)	1
Mats GREN (SWE)	D	32		2
Bernt HAAS	D	26	(2)	1
Mikheil KAVELSAHVILI (GEO)	A	25	(6)	11
Joël MAGNIN	A	17	(14)	3
Felix MAGRO	A	4	(10)	
Giuseppe MAZZARELLI	M	13	(5)	
Patrick MÜLLER	D	11	(1)	
Giorgi NEMSADZE (GEO)	A		(3)	
Blaise N'KUFO	A	9	(4)	2
James OBIORAH (NIG)	A		(2)	
Nenad SAVIC (BOS)	M		(2)	
Gürkan SERMETER (TUR)	A	1	(9)	1
Boris SMILJANIC	D	29	(2)	3
Mihai TARARACHE (ROM)	M	25	(1)	
Avi TIKVA (ISR)	M	29	(4)	11
Kubilay TÜRKYILMAZ	A	11	(1)	6
Johann VOGEL	M	27		5
Hakan YAKIN	M	5	(1)	2
Reto ZANNI	D	1	(7)	
Pascal ZUBERBÜHLER	G	36		

LEAGUE RESULTS 1998/99

15/07/98	BSC Young Boys Bern	A	1-3	N'Kufo
18/07/98	Lausanne-Sports	H	2-2	Gren, Tikva
25/07/98	FC Lugano	H	3-2	Vogel (p), N'Kufo, Tikva
02/08/98	FC Sion	A	1-0	Tikva
05/08/98	FC Aarau	H	2-0	Türkyilmaz, Vogel (p)
16/08/98	FC Zürich	A	0-0	
21/08/98	Servette FC Genève	H	3-0	Kavelashvili, Esposito, Türkyilmaz
29/08/98	FC Basel	A	1-1	De Napoli
05/09/98	Neuchâtel Xamax FC	H	1-1	Kavelashvili
11/09/98	FC St. Gallen	A	1-3	og (Sène)
19/09/98	FC Luzern	H	2-0	Vogel (p), Tikva
25/09/98	Lausanne-Sports	A	1-3	Kavelashvili
03/10/98	BSC Young Boys Bern	H	2-1	Magnin, Vogel (p)
16/10/98	FC Lugano	A	1-1	De Napoli
27/10/98	FC Sion	H	4-1	De Napoli, Comisetti, Türkyilmaz, Tikva
30/10/98	FC Aarau	A	3-0	Türkyilmaz, Haas, Smiljanic
08/11/98	FC Zürich	H	1-2	De Napoli
13/11/98	Servette FC Genève	A	0-2	
21/11/98	FC Basel	H	2-1	Tikva, Türkyilmaz
29/11/98	Neuchâtel Xamax FC	A	2-0	Kavelashvili, Tikva
05/12/98	FC St. Gallen	H	4-1	Türkyilmaz, Comisetti 2, Kavelashvili
13/12/98	FC Luzern	A	0-1	
03/03/99	Neuchâtel Xamax FC	A	1-1	De Napoli
07/03/99	FC Luzern	H	4-0	De Napoli 2, Smiljanic, Magnin
13/03/99	FC Zürich	A	1-0	Comisetti
21/03/99	Servette FC Genève	H	0-1	
05/04/99	FC Basel	H	4-2	De Napoli 3, Tikva
10/04/99	FC St. Gallen	A	0-0	
16/04/99	Lausanne-Sports	A	3-2	Gren, Kavelashvili, Yakin
23/04/99	Lausanne-Sports	H	5-0	Magnin, Kavelashvili, Tikva, Comisetti, Vogel
02/05/99	FC St. Gallen	H	4-0	Kavelashvili 2, Smiljanic, Tikva (p)
08/05/99	FC Basel	A	0-2	
14/05/99	Servette FC Genève	A	0-0	
24/05/99	FC Zürich	H	0-2	
30/05/99	FC Luzern	A	4-1	Yakin, De Napoli, Tikva, Comisetti
02/06/99	Neuchâtel Xamax FC	H	5-0	Kavelashvili 2, De Napoli 2, Sermeter

LAUSANNE-SPORTS

CLUB DIRECTORY

Lausanne-Sports
Case postale 175
1018 Lausanne 18
tel - (021) 6461341
fax - (021) 6461359
Year of Formation - 1896
President - Waldemar Kita
Coach - Georges Bregy; Pierre-André Schurmann
Stadium - Stade Olympique La Pontaise (16,000)

MAJOR HONOURS
League Championship - (7)
1913, 1932, 1935, 1936, 1944, 1951, 1965.
Domestic Cup - (9) 1935, 1939, 1944, 1950,
1962, 1964, 1981, 1998, 1999.

APPEARANCES 98/99

	P	Ap	(s)	Gls
Martin BRUNNER	G	35		
Vincent CAVIN	D		(5)	
Fabio CELESTINI	M	31	(1)	9
Paolo DIOGO	M	24	(6)	2
Philippe DOUGLAS	A	25	(8)	3
Andres GERBER	A	11	(16)	4
Serge GOGOUA (CIV)	D		(5)	
Vagner GOMES (POR)	M		(2)	
Urs GÜNTENSPERGER	A		(2)	
Erich HÄNZI	D	35		1
Marc HOTTIGER	D	15	(1)	1
Ricardo IGLESIAS	D	9	(2)	
Oscar LONDONO (FRA)	M	33		
Badile LUBAMBA	D	1		
Javier MAZZONI (ARG)	A	5	(7)	6
Artur MINASYAN (ARM)	A		(2)	
Christophe OHREL	M	27	(4)	
Marko PANTELIC (YUG)	A	19	(2)	8
Blaise PIFFARETTI	M	17	(12)	
Daniel PUCE (ITA)	D	29		2
Eric RAPO	G	1	(1)	
Stefan REHN (SWE)	M	30	(2)	4
Armen SHAHGELDYAN (ARM)	A	7	(10)	4
Léonard THURRE	A	27	(7)	11
Saso UDOVIC (SLO)	A	12	(6)	7
Goran ZARIC (YUG)	D	3	(2)	

LEAGUE RESULTS 1998/99

18/07/98	Grasshopper-Club Zürich	A	2-2	Udovic, Celestini
21/07/98	FC Luzern	H	2-2	Celestini (p), Udovic
25/07/98	BSC Young Boys Bern	H	1-0	Gerber
31/07/98	FC Lugano	A	2-1	Udovic, Thurre
05/08/98	FC Sion	H	2-1	Shahgeldyan, Udovic
16/08/98	FC Aarau	A	2-2	Celestini (p), Thurre
21/08/98	FC Zürich	H	1-1	Puce
29/08/98	Servette FC Genève	A	2-2	Udovic, Douglas
08/09/98	FC Basel	H	0-2	
12/09/98	Neuchâtel Xamax FC	A	1-4	Udovic
20/09/98	FC St. Gallen	H	1-0	Thurre
25/09/98	Grasshopper-Club Zürich	H	3-1	Hottiger, Rehn 2
04/10/98	FC Luzern	A	0-1	
16/10/98	BSC Young Boys Bern	A	2-7	Thurre, Shahgeldyan
27/10/98	FC Lugano	H	3-2	Celestini, Pantelic 2
30/10/98	FC Sion	A	4-0	Douglas 2, Thurre 2
08/11/98	FC Aarau	H	2-1	Thurre, Gerber
13/11/98	FC Zürich	A	3-3	Pantelic 2, Udovic
21/11/98	Servette FC Genève	H	0-0	
29/11/98	FC Basel	A	1-1	Pantelic
05/12/98	Neuchâtel Xamax FC	H	1-0	Shahgeldyan
13/12/98	FC St. Gallen	A	1-0	Shahgeldyan
28/02/99	Servette FC Genève	A	0-2	
07/03/99	FC Zürich	H	3-1	Thurre, Mazzoni 2
14/03/99	FC Luzern	A	1-0	Thurre
21/03/99	Neuchâtel Xamax FC	H	4-0	Pantelic, Celestini, Mazzoni, Diogo
03/04/99	FC St. Gallen	H	4-1	Celestini (p), Mazzoni 2, Hänzi
10/04/99	FC Basel	A	2-1	Gerber, og (Kreuzer)
16/04/99	Grasshopper-Club Zürich	H	2-3	Thurre, Rehn
23/04/99	Grasshopper-Club Zürich	A	0-5	
01/05/99	FC Basel	H	3-0	Puce, og (Barberis), Gerber
08/05/99	FC St. Gallen	A	0-0	
14/05/99	Neuchâtel Xamax FC	A	1-1	Thurre
24/05/99	FC Luzern	H	5-1	Diogo, Pantelic, Celestini 2 (1p), Mazzoni
30/05/99	FC Zürich	A	1-0	Rehn
02/06/99	Servette FC Genève	H	2-5	Celestini, Pantelic

FC LUGANO

CLUB DIRECTORY

FC Lugano
CP 4136
6904 Lugano
tel - (091) 9409040
fax - (091) 9409055
Year of Formation - 1908
President - Helios Jermini
Secretary - Angelo Maina
Coach - Karl Engel; Enzo Trossero
(99/00 - Giuliano Sonzogni)
Stadium - Cornaredo (15,000)

MAJOR HONOURS
League Championship - (3) 1938, 1941, 1949.
Domestic Cup - (3) 1931, 1968, 1993.

APPEARANCES 98/99

	P	Ap	(s)	Gls
Patrick ABATANGELO (ITA)	G	10		
Jørn ANDERSEN (NOR)	D	12	(1)	
Christian ANDREOLI	D	12	(1)	
Fabrizio BULLO	D	16	(3)	
Mirko DI NICOLANTONIO	D		(3)	
Marc EMMERS (BEL)	M	19	(3)	1
Walter FERNANDEZ	D	22		1
Alain GASPOZ	D	13		2
Gaetano GIALLANZA (ITA)	A	18	(3)	8
Mauro GIANNINI (ITA)	M	10	(6)	1
Christian GIMENEZ (ARG)	A	13		9
Erich HÜRZELER	G	12		
Massimo LOMBARDO	M	5	(1)	1
René MORF	D	4	(1)	
Nqobizitha NCUBE (CIV)	A	1	(7)	
David ORLANDO	M	3	(7)	1
Julio Hernán ROSSI (ARG)	A	10		8
Dario ROTA	D	20	(1)	
Eric TABORDA (FRA)	M	8	(2)	1
Julio TEJEDA (ESP)	M	9	(1)	
Romano THOMA	M	10	(4)	
Uwe WEGMANN (GER)	A	15	(2)	3

LEAGUE RESULTS 1998/99

18/07/98	Neuchâtel Xamax FC	A	0-1	
21/07/98	FC St. Gallen	H	2-2	Giallanza 2 (1p)
25/07/98	Grasshopper-Club Zürich	A	2-3	Gaspoz, Giménez
31/07/98	Lausanne-Sports	H	1-2	Giménez
08/08/98	BSC Young Boys Bern	A	1-0	Giménez
15/08/98	FC Luzern	A	2-1	Giménez 2
22/08/98	FC Sion	H	2-2	Emmers, Giménez (p)
29/08/98	FC Aarau	A	0-2	
07/09/98	FC Zürich	H	0-0	
11/09/98	Servette FC Genève	A	0-1	
19/09/98	FC Basel	H	5-1	Gaspoz, Orlando, Giménez 2, Giallanza (p)
26/09/98	Neuchâtel Xamax FC	H	4-3	Giménez, Rossi 3
03/10/98	FC St. Gallen	A	4-4	Rossi 3, Fernandez
16/10/98	Grasshopper-Club Zürich	H	1-1	Giallanza
25/10/98	Lausanne-Sports	A	2-3	Rossi 2
01/11/98	BSC Young Boys Bern	H	2-2	Giallanza, Taborda
08/11/98	FC Luzern	H	0-3	(w/o; original result 1-1 Giannini)
15/11/98	FC Sion	A	0-2	
22/11/98	FC Aarau	H	0-2	
29/11/98	FC Zürich	A	1-4	Wegmann
06/12/98	Servette FC Genève	H	3-3	Giallanza 3 (1p)
13/12/98	FC Basel	A	3-1	Wegmann 2, Lombardo

FC LUZERN

CLUB DIRECTORY

FC Luzern
Kauffmannweg 7
Postfach 2918
6002 Luzern
tel - (041) 2102041
fax - (041) 2102141
Year of Formation - 1901
President - Paul-André Cornu
Secretary - Roger Wehrli
Coach - Kudi Müller; Egon Coordes; Bigi Meier; Andy Egli
Stadium - Allmend (25,300)

MAJOR HONOURS
League Championship - (1) 1989.
Domestic Cup - (2) 1960, 1992.

APPEARANCES 98/99

	P	Ap	(s)	Gls
Melchior ARNOLD (USA)	M	8	(3)	
Stojan BELAIC (YUG)	D	4		
Markus BRUNNER	D	26	(1)	1
Oliver CAMENZIND	A	9		
Romain CREVOISIER	G	23		
Raffaele IZZO (ITA)	M	8	(5)	
Daniel JOLLER	M	13	(9)	2
Manfred JOLLER	D	16	(5)	
Ivan KNEZ	D	22		2
Patrick KOCH	M	18	(12)	3
Ludwig KÖGL	M	30	(1)	2
Hristo KOILOV (BUL)	M	17	(6)	2
George KOUMANTARAKIS (SAF)	A	19	(8)	9
Stephan LEHMANN	G	11		
Badile LUBAMBA	D	11	(2)	
Remo MEYER	D	3	(5)	
Heinz MOSER	M	20	(3)	3
Michel RENGGLI	A		(3)	
Pascal ROJKO	G	1		
Slobodan SCEPANOVIC (YUG)	A	17	(8)	9
Patrick SCHNARWILER	D	27	(3)	
Andy THALMANN	G	1	(1)	
Igor TRNINIC	D	25	(8)	
René VAN ECK (HOL)	D	20		
Miloje VUKIC (YUG)	M	28	(1)	3
Thomas WYSS	M	19	(10)	1

LEAGUE RESULTS 1998/99

18/07/98	FC Zürich	H	3-2	Scepanovic 3 (1p)
21/07/98	Lausanne-Sports	A	2-2	Scepanovic, Koumantarakis
25/07/98	Servette FC Genève	A	2-3	Koumantarakis, Koilov
31/07/98	BSC Young Boys Bern	H	0-0	
09/08/98	FC Basel	A	0-1	
15/08/98	FC Lugano	H	1-2	Scepanovic
22/08/98	Neuchâtel Xamax FC	A	1-1	Koumantarakis
28/08/98	FC Sion	H	1-2	Kögl
06/09/98	FC St. Gallen	A	1-2	Koumantarakis
13/09/98	FC Aarau	H	2-2	Moser, Koch
19/09/98	Grasshopper-Club Zürich	A	0-2	
25/09/98	FC Zürich	A	0-2	
04/10/98	Lausanne-Sports	H	1-0	Koilov
18/10/98	Servette FC Genève	H	0-0	
25/10/98	BSC Young Boys Bern	A	2-1	Vukic 2
31/10/98	FC Basel	H	4-1	Koch 2, Brunner, Moser
08/11/98	FC Lugano	A	3-0	(w/o; original result 1-1 Knez)
15/11/98	Neuchâtel Xamax FC	H	1-1	Scepanovic
22/11/98	FC Sion	A	0-0	
29/11/98	FC St. Gallen	H	1-1	Scepanovic
06/12/98	FC Aarau	A	0-0	
13/12/98	Grasshopper-Club Zürich	H	1-0	Moser
28/02/99	FC Basel	H	0-2	
07/03/99	Grasshopper-Club Zürich	A	0-4	
14/03/99	Lausanne-Sports	H	0-1	
20/03/99	FC St. Gallen	A	2-0	Vukic, Knez
05/04/99	Neuchâtel Xamax FC	A	1-1	Koumantarakis
11/04/99	Servette FC Genève	H	2-1	Koumantarakis 2
17/04/99	FC Zürich	A	0-3	
24/04/99	FC Zürich	H	1-3	Koumantarakis
01/05/99	Servette FC Genève	A	0-1	
08/05/99	Neuchâtel Xamax FC	H	2-0	Wyss, Kögl (p)
15/05/99	FC St. Gallen	H	2-1	Koumantarakis, Joller D.
24/05/99	Lausanne-Sports	A	1-5	Joller D.
30/05/99	Grasshopper-Club Zürich	H	1-4	Scepanovic
02/06/99	FC Basel	A	1-1	Scepanovic

NEUCHATEL XAMAX FC

CLUB DIRECTORY

Neuchâtel Xamax FC
Boîte postale 78
2000 Neuchâtel 8 Monruz
tel - (038) 7254428
fax - (038) 7242128
Year of Formation - 1970
President - Gilbert Facchinetti
Secretary - Michel Favre
Coach - Alain Geiger
Stadium - La Maladière (20,000)

MAJOR HONOURS
League Championship - (2) 1987, 1988.

APPEARANCES 98/99

	P	Ap	(s)	Gls
Bruno ALICARTE (FRA)	D	3	(12)	
Johan BERISHA (ALB)	A		(8)	
Rainer BIELI	A	6	(5)	1
Samir BOUGHANEM (FRA)	M	13	(6)	2
Joël CORMINBOEUF	G	21		
Florent DELAY	G	12		
Maxime DROZ-PORTNER	D	1	(1)	
Harald GÄMPERLE	D	17		
Edin GAZIC (BOS)	A	1	(5)	
Didier GIGON	M	4	(3)	
Patrick ISABELLA	A	28	(5)	10
Sébastien JEANNERET	D	18		1
Aimé KOUDOU (FRA)	A		(12)	1
Vladimir MARTINOVIC (YUG)	D	11	(4)	3
Moreno MERENDA	A		(1)	
Javier MOLIST (ESP)	A	35		7
Seyni N'DIAYE (SEN)	A	21	(10)	8
Joseph Cyrille NDO (CMR)	M	27	(1)	4
Pierre NJANKA (CMR)	D	22	(2)	
Pascal OPPLIGER	D		(2)	
Ivan QUENTIN	D	13		
Régis ROTHENBÜHLER	D	34		1
Martin RUEDA	D	35		1
Nenad SAVIC (YUG)	M	8	(1)	
Augustine SIMO (CMR)	M	8	(2)	
Julien STAUFFER	D		(4)	
Charles WITTL (GHA)	M	21		
Sébastien ZAMBAZ	M	34		2
Pascal ZETZMANN	G	3	(1)	

LEAGUE RESULTS 1998/99

18/07/98	FC Lugano	H	1-0	Martinovic
21/07/98	FC Sion	A	1-1	Molist
25/07/98	FC Aarau	H	0-0	
31/07/98	FC Zürich	A	1-1	Ndo
07/08/98	Servette FC Genève	H	1-1	Molist
15/08/98	FC Basel	A	0-2	
22/08/98	FC Luzern	H	1-1	Zambaz
29/08/98	FC St. Gallen	H	2-0	Molist, Martinovic (p)
05/09/98	Grasshopper-Club Zürich	A	1-1	N'Diaye
11/09/98	Lausanne-Sports	H	4-1	og (Puce), Isabella, Rueda, Ndo
19/09/98	BSC Young Boys Bern	A	3-2	Molist, Rothenbühler, N'Diaye
26/09/98	FC Lugano	A	3-4	Molist, Martinovic, Boughanem
03/10/98	FC Sion	H	3-1	Jeanneret, Isabella (p), Koudou
18/10/98	FC Aarau	A	2-0	Isabella, Zambaz
24/10/98	FC Zürich	H	1-1	N'Diaye
01/11/98	Servette FC Genève	A	1-1	N'Diaye
07/11/98	FC Basel	H	3-1	N'Diaye, Isabella, Ndo
15/11/98	FC Luzern	A	1-1	Ndo
22/11/98	FC St. Gallen	A	0-0	
29/11/98	Grasshopper-Club Zürich	H	0-2	
06/12/98	Lausanne-Sports	A	0-1	
12/12/98	BSC Young Boys Bern	H	1-1	Isabella
28/02/99	Grasshopper-Club Zürich	H	1-1	Isabella
07/03/99	FC Basel	A	0-1	
14/03/99	FC St. Gallen	H	3-2	Isabella, Molist, N'Diaye
20/03/99	Lausanne-Sports	A	0-4	
05/04/99	FC Luzern	H	1-1	Molist
10/04/99	FC Zürich	A	2-2	Isabella, N'Diaye
17/04/99	Servette FC Genève	H	0-3	
24/04/99	Servette FC Genève	A	2-1	Boughanem, Isabella
01/05/99	FC Zürich	H	1-3	Bieli
08/05/99	FC Luzern	A	0-2	
15/05/99	Lausanne-Sports	H	1-1	N'Diaye
24/05/99	FC St. Gallen	A	0-0	
30/05/99	FC Basel	H	1-1	Isabella
02/06/99	Grasshopper-Club Zürich	A	0-5	

FC ST. GALLEN

CLUB DIRECTORY

FC St. Gallen
Postfach 14
9009 St. Gallen
tel - (071) 2456765
fax - (071) 2454671
Year of Formation - 1879
President - Thomas Müller
Secretary - Patrick Caillet
Coach - Roger Hegi; Marcel Koller
Stadium - Espenmoos (13,700)

MAJOR HONOURS
League Championship - (1) 1904.
Domestic Cup - (1) 1969.

APPEARANCES 98/99

	P	Ap	(s)	Gls
Thomas ALDER	G	6		
Sergio COLACINO (ITA)	A	4	(2)	
Giorgio CONTINI	M	22	(10)	9
Ivan DAL SANTO (ITA)	D	21	(2)	2
Valdir DAMÁSIO (BRA)	M	10	(4)	1
Adrian EUGSTER	D	17	(2)	
Ribeiro GIL (BRA)	A	25	(7)	5
Wilco HELLINGA (HOL)	M	22		1
Luiz Filho JAIRO (BRA)	M	12		2
Philipp MEYER	D	7	(7)	
Mohammed "Simo" MOUIDI (MAR)	D		(2)	
Sascha MÜLLER	M	33	(2)	4
Francisco Souza Valmeirino NERI (BRA)	A	3	(6)	1
Dino PINELLI (ITA)	D	5	(2)	1
Anastasios SALONIDIS (GRE)	M	2	(6)	
David SENE (FRA)	D	30	(1)	1
Georgi SLAVCHEV (BUL)	M	17	(5)	2
Jörg STIEL	G	30		
Damiano TAMANTI	A		(3)	
Pascal THÜLER	D	9		
Dorjee TSAWA	D	30	(3)	1
Edwin VURENS (HOL)	A	20		5
Hakan YAKIN	A	16	(4)	7
Marc ZELLWEGER	D	31		
Vincenzo ZINNA	M	3	(9)	
Marco ZWYSSIG	M	21		1

LEAGUE RESULTS 1998/99

18/07/98	BSC Young Boys Bern	H	3-1	Dal Santo, Vurens, Yakin
21/07/98	FC Lugano	A	2-2	Zwyssig, Hellinga (p)
25/07/98	FC Sion	H	2-0	Müller, Contini
31/07/98	FC Aarau	A	6-2	Gil 2, Yakin, Vurens, Slavchev, Contini
05/08/98	FC Zürich	H	0-0	
15/08/98	Servette FC Genève	A	0-1	
23/08/98	FC Basel	H	0-1	
29/08/98	Neuchâtel Xamax FC	A	0-2	
05/09/98	FC Luzern	H	2-1	Vurens, Contini
11/09/98	Grasshopper-Club Zürich	H	3-1	Contini, Yakin, Gil
20/09/98	Lausanne-Sports	A	0-1	
26/09/98	BSC Young Boys Bern	A	1-0	Yakin
03/10/98	FC Lugano	H	4-4	Vurens, Yakin 2, Müller
18/10/98	FC Sion	A	1-2	Yakin
25/10/98	FC Aarau	H	4-3	Sène, Tsawa, og (Skrzypczak), Gil
29/10/98	FC Zürich	A	1-3	Slavchev
08/11/98	Servette FC Genève	H	0-0	
15/11/98	FC Basel	A	0-1	
22/11/98	Neuchâtel Xamax FC	H	0-0	
29/11/98	FC Luzern	A	1-1	Dal Santo
05/12/98	Grasshopper-Club Zürich	A	1-4	Vurens
13/12/98	Lausanne-Sports	H	0-1	
28/02/99	FC Zürich	A	2-0	Contini, Jairo
06/03/99	Servette FC Genève	H	2-0	Contini 2
14/03/99	Neuchâtel Xamax FC	A	2-3	Contini, Pinelli
20/03/99	FC Luzern	H	0-2	
03/04/99	Lausanne-Sports	A	1-4	Müller
10/04/99	Grasshopper-Club Zürich	H	0-0	
18/04/99	FC Basel	A	3-3	Contini, Müller, Jairo
25/04/99	FC Basel	H	1-2	Damásio
02/05/99	Grasshopper-Club Zürich	A	0-4	
08/05/99	Lausanne-Sports	H	0-0	
15/05/99	FC Luzern	A	1-2	Neri
24/05/99	Neuchâtel Xamax FC	H	0-0	
30/05/99	Servette FC Genève	A	0-2	
02/06/99	FC Zürich	H	1-3	Gil

SERVETTE FC GENEVE

CLUB DIRECTORY

Servette FC Genève
Case postale 431
1219 Châtelaine (Genève)
tel - (022) 9495949
fax - (022) 9495939
Year of Formation - 1890
President - Christian Hervé
Secretary - Patrick Trotignon
Coach - Gilbert Castella
Stadium - Les Charmilles (11,078)

MAJOR HONOURS
League Championship - (17) 1907, 1918, 1922,
1925, 1926, 1930, 1933, 1934, 1940, 1946,
1950, 1961, 1962, 1979, 1985, 1994, 1999.
Domestic Cup - (6)
1928, 1949, 1971, 1978, 1979, 1984.

APPEARANCES 98/99

		P	Ap	(s)	Gls
Eddy BAREA	D	22	(5)		
Patrick BÜHLMANN	M	33	(2)	6	
Emanuele DI ZENZO	M		(1)		
Franck DURIX (FRA)	M	33	(1)	4	
Patrick ESEOSA (NIG)	D		(4)		
Sébastien FOURNIER	M	27		1	
Sébastien JEANNERET	D	4	(3)		
Teixeira de Souza JUAREZ (BRA)	D	32			
Jean-Philippe KARLEN	D	12	(17)	1	
Laurent LEROY (FRA)	A		(2)		
Johan LONFAT	M	29		2	
Elvir MELUNOVIC	M	5	(7)		
Patrick MÜLLER	M	22		3	
Lanjame OUAJDA (TOG)	A	13	(8)		
Eric PEDAT	G	36			
Vitor PEREIRA	A		(1)		
Martin PETROV (BUL)	A	10	(2)	2	
Lionel PIZZINAT	M	15	(18)	2	
Dan POTOCIANU (ROM)	D	6	(6)		
Tomas RAZANAUSKAS (LIT)	M	2	(10)		
Alexandre REY	A	32	(1)	19	
Tadjou SALOU (TOG)	D		(3)		
Ermin SILJAK (SLO)	A		(1)		
Oscar TATO (ESP)	D	2	(5)		
Carlos VARELA (ESP)	A	17	(1)	6	
Edwin VURENS (HOL)	A	9	(5)	7	
Roger WAGNER	A		(1)		
Stefan WOLF	D	35		3	

LEAGUE RESULTS 1998/99

18/07/98	FC Aarau	H	3-2	Durix, og (Roselli), Wolf
21/07/98	FC Zürich	A	1-0	Rey
25/07/98	FC Luzern	H	3-2	Müller, Rey, Lonfat
01/08/98	FC Basel	H	3-1	Rey 3 (1p)
07/08/98	Neuchâtel Xamax FC	A	1-1	Fournier
15/08/98	FC St. Gallen	H	1-0	Rey (p)
21/08/98	Grasshopper-Club Zürich	A	0-3	
29/08/98	Lausanne-Sports	H	2-2	Rey, Wolf
06/09/98	BSC Young Boys Bern	A	4-3	Varela, Lonfat, Rey 2
11/09/98	FC Lugano	H	1-0	Müller
19/09/98	FC Sion	A	2-2	Varela, Müller
25/09/98	FC Aarau	A	4-1	Pizzinat, Bühlmann, Varela 2
03/10/98	FC Zürich	H	3-1	Varela, Rey, Bühlmann
18/10/98	FC Luzern	A	0-0	
25/10/98	FC Basel	A	2-0	Durix 2
01/11/98	Neuchâtel Xamax FC	H	1-1	Bühlmann
08/11/98	FC St. Gallen	A	0-0	
13/11/98	Grasshopper-Club Zürich	H	2-0	Rey, Bühlmann
22/11/98	Lausanne-Sports	A	0-0	
28/11/98	BSC Young Boys Bern	H	0-1	
06/12/98	FC Lugano	A	3-3	Bühlmann, Karlen, Varela
13/12/98	FC Sion	H	2-1	Pizzinat, Rey (p)
28/02/99	Lausanne-Sports	H	2-0	Vurens, Durix
06/03/99	FC St. Gallen	A	0-2	
14/03/99	FC Basel	H	2-1	Wolf, Rey
21/03/99	Grasshopper-Club Zürich	A	1-0	Rey
03/04/99	FC Zürich	H	1-1	Rey
11/04/99	FC Luzern	A	1-2	Rey
17/04/99	Neuchâtel Xamax FC	A	3-0	Vurens, Rey, Bühlmann
24/04/99	Neuchâtel Xamax FC	H	1-2	Vurens
01/05/99	FC Luzern	H	1-0	Rey
09/05/99	FC Zürich	A	0-4	
14/05/99	Grasshopper-Club Zürich	H	0-0	
22/05/99	FC Basel	A	0-0	
30/05/99	FC St. Gallen	H	2-0	Rey, Vurens
02/06/99	Lausanne-Sports	A	5-2	Vurens 3, Petrov 2 (1p)

FC SION

CLUB DIRECTORY

FC Sion
Rue des Echutes
1950 Sion
tel - (027) 2037172
fax - (027) 2037174
Year of Formation - 1909
President - Max Urscheler
Secretary - Paul-André Dubosson
Coach - Jochen Dries; Charly In Albon; Olivier Rouyer
Stadium - Tourbillon (19,526)

MAJOR HONOURS
League Championship - (2) 1992, 1997.
Domestic Cup - (9) 1965, 1974, 1980, 1982, 1986, 1991, 1995, 1996, 1997.

APPEARANCES 98/99

		P	Ap	(s)	Gls
Adrian ALLENSPACH	A	6	(9)	3
Daniel ANÇAY	G	14		
Yao AZIAWONOU (TOG)	A		(1)	
Owusu BENSON (GHA)	A	20		3
Dominique BERTONE (FRA)	A	7	(3)	
Olivier BIAGGI	D	6	(3)	
Fabrice BORER	G	8	(1)	
Alex BROWN (LIB)	M	14		
Yane BUGNARD	D	17	(2)	1
Hoang-Doc BUI	M	5	(2)	1
Javier DELGADO	A	2	(4)	
James DERIVAZ	A		(6)	
Grégory DURUZ	A	15		
Jean-Jacques EYDELIE (FRA)	M	19		1
Stéphane GRICHTING	D	20		
Servais GUESSAND (CIV)	A	3	(4)	
Jean-Pierre LA PLACA	A	15	(5)	1
Sébastien LIPAWSKY	A	3	(4)	
Nicolas MARAZZI	M		(2)	
Marco NICHETTI (ITA)	M	3	(3)	
Antonio PASCALE	A	6	(7)	
Alexandre QUENNOZ	A	19	(1)	
Stéphane SARNI	M		(2)	
Didier THOLOT (FRA)	A	21		10
Matteo VANETTA	D	19		1

LEAGUE RESULTS 1998/99

18/07/98	FC Basel	A	0-0	
21/07/98	Neuchâtel Xamax FC	H	1-1	Vanetta
25/07/98	FC St. Gallen	A	0-2	
02/08/98	Grasshopper-Club Zürich	H	0-1	
08/08/98	Lausanne-Sports	A	1-2	Bui
15/08/98	BSC Young Boys Bern	H	1-1	Benson
22/08/98	FC Lugano	A	2-2	Benson 2
28/08/98	FC Luzern	A	2-1	og (Van Eck), Bugnard
08/09/98	FC Aarau	H	3-2	Eydelie, Tholot 2
11/09/98	FC Zürich	A	0-3	
19/09/98	Servette FC Genève	H	2-2	La Placa, Allenspach
27/09/98	FC Basel	H	1-0	Tholot
03/10/98	Neuchâtel Xamax FC	A	1-3	Allenspach
18/10/98	FC St. Gallen	H	2-1	Allenspach, Tholot
27/10/98	Grasshopper-Club Zürich	A	1-4	Tholot
31/10/98	Lausanne-Sports	H	0-4	
08/11/98	BSC Young Boys Bern	A	0-3	
15/11/98	FC Lugano	H	2-0	Tholot 2 (1p)
22/11/98	FC Luzern	H	0-0	
29/11/98	FC Aarau	A	2-2	Tholot 2 (1p)
04/12/98	FC Zürich	H	0-0	
13/12/98	Servette FC Genève	A	1-2	Tholot

BSC YOUNG BOYS BERN

CLUB DIRECTORY

BSC Young Boys Bern
Postfach 61
3000 Bern 22
tel - (031) 3318484
fax - (031) 3330555
Year of Formation - 1898
President - Peter Siegerist
Secretary - Jürg Wittwer
Coach - Claude Ryf; Martin Weber
(99/00 - Roger Läubli)
Stadium - Wankdorf (37,551)

MAJOR HONOURS
League Championship - (11)
1903, 1909, 1910, 1911, 1920, 1929, 1957,
1958, 1959, 1960, 1986.
Domestic Cup - (6)
1930, 1945, 1953, 1958, 1977, 1987.

APPEARANCES 98/99

		P	Ap	(s)	Gls
André ALLENBACH	D			(1)	
Alain BAUMANN	D	21			1
Erol BEKIROVSKI (SWE)	M	20		(1)	3
Reto DURRI	A	4		(7)	1
Mario CASAMENTO (ITA)	M	9		(1)	
Massimo DEL DEGAN (ITA)	D			(2)	
Samuel DRAKOPOULOS (GRE)	A	11		(3)	3
Philipp EICH	M	4		(7)	
Martin FRYAND	M	12		(6)	2
Andres GERBER	A			(2)	2
Carlos GOMES (POR)	M			(5)	1
Raphael KEHRLI	A	17		(4)	4
Stefan KNUTTI	G	22			
Roger KÜFFER	M	16			
Martin LENGEN	D	21			2
Diango MALACARNE	D	10			
Dominik MOSER	M	1		(4)	1
André NIEDERHÄUSER	D			(1)	
Sanin PINTUL (BOS)	D	17		(2)	
Agent SAWU (ZIM)	A	18			8
Admir SMAJIC (BOS)	D	16		(3)	3
Hugo STREUN	D	3		(1)	
Jürg STUDER	M	20		(1)	2

LEAGUE RESULTS 1998/99

15/07/98	Grasshopper-Club Zürich	H	3-1	Burri, Drakopoulos, Gerber
18/07/98	FC St. Gallen	A	1-3	Gerber
29/07/98	Lausanne-Sports	A	0-1	
31/07/98	FC Luzern	A	0-0	
08/08/98	FC Lugano	H	0-1	
15/08/98	FC Sion	A	1-1	Drakopoulos
22/08/98	FC Aarau	H	1-1	Bekirovski
29/08/98	FC Zürich	A	2-3	Studer, Sawu
06/09/98	Servette FC Genève	H	3-4	Sawu, Bekirovski, Gomes
12/09/98	FC Basel	A	1-1	Bekirovski
19/09/98	Neuchâtel Xamax FC	H	2-3	Smajic, Drakopoulos (p)
27/09/98	FC St. Gallen	H	0-1	
03/10/98	Grasshopper-Club Zürich	A	1-2	Lengen
18/10/98	Lausanne-Sports	H	7-2	Fryand 2, Lengen, Sawu 2, Studer, Baumann
25/10/98	FC Luzern	H	1-2	Sawu
01/11/98	FC Lugano	A	2-2	Kehrli, Sawu
08/11/98	FC Sion	H	3-0	Kehrli, Moser, Smajic
15/11/98	FC Aarau	A	1-1	Kehrli
20/11/98	FC Zürich	H	1-2	Kehrli
28/11/98	Servette FC Genève	A	1-0	Smajic
06/12/98	FC Basel	H	1-2	Sawu
12/12/98	Neuchâtel Xamax FC	A	1-1	Sawu

FC ZÜRICH

CLUB DIRECTORY

FC Zürich
Postfach
8021 Zürich
tel - (01) 4927474
fax - (01) 4910759
Year of Formation - 1896
President - Sven Hotz
Secretary - Erich Schmid
Coach - Raimondo Ponte
Stadium - Letzigrund (23,500)

MAJOR HONOURS
League Championship - (9) 1902, 1924, 1963,
1966, 1968, 1974, 1975, 1976, 1981.
Domestic Cup - (5)
1966, 1970, 1972, 1973, 1976.

APPEARANCES 98/99

		P	Ap	(s)	Gls
Samir ALBRECHT	A	3	(6)		
Yolouba BAMBA (CIV)	M		(2)	1	
Shaun BARTLETT (SAF)	A	27		13	
Selcuk BEYAZ	D	1	(1)		
Pascal CASTILLO	A	18	(8)	3	
Frédéric CHASSOT	A	27	(5)	9	
Giorgio DEL SIGNORE (ITA)	D	19	(3)		
Franco DI JORIO	M	31	(1)		
Aleksandar DJORDJEVIC (YUG)	D	8	(2)		
Urs FISCHER	D	31		2	
Daniel GYGAX	D		(2)		
Marc HODEL	D	32		3	
Robert HUBER	M	12	(11)		
Gocha JAMARAULI (GEO)	M	10	(1)	1	
Luca JODICE	M	12	(13)		
Adrian KUNZ	A	10		3	
Francisco LIMA (BRA)	M	30		6	
Borislav MIKHAILOV (BUL)	G	1			
Jerren NIXON (TRI)	A	21	(12)	9	
David OPANGO (BUR)	D	7	(5)	1	
David PALLAS	M	1	(3)		
Marco PASCOLO	G	12			
César SANT'ANNA (BRA)	M	25	(4)	6	
Ike SHORUNMU (NIG)	G	19			
Daniel TARONE	M	26	(6)		
Christian TROMBINI (ITA)	G	4	(5)		
André WIEDERKEHR	M	9	(11)		

LEAGUE RESULTS 1998/99

18/07/98	FC Luzern	A	2-3	Chassot 2
21/07/98	Servette FC Genève	H	0-1	
25/07/98	FC Basel	A	1-2	Sant'Anna (p)
31/07/98	Neuchâtel Xamax FC	H	1-1	Nixon
05/08/98	FC St. Gallen	A	0-0	
16/08/98	Grasshopper-Club Zürich	H	0-0	
22/08/98	Lausanne-Sports	A	1-1	Nixon
29/08/98	BSC Young Boys Bern	H	3-2	Chassot, Bartlett, Sant'Anna (p)
05/09/98	FC Lugano	A	0-0	
11/09/98	FC Sion	H	3-0	Bartlett, Sant'Anna (p), Chassot
20/09/98	FC Aarau	A	2-0	Bartlett (p), Sant'Anna
25/09/98	FC Luzern	H	2-0	Lima, Chassot
03/10/98	Servette FC Genève	A	1-3	Sant'Anna
16/10/98	FC Basel	H	1-0	Chassot
24/10/98	Neuchâtel Xamax FC	A	1-1	Castillo
29/10/98	FC St. Gallen	H	3-1	Bartlett 2 (1p), Lima
08/11/98	Grasshopper-Club Zürich	A	2-1	Chassot, Opango
14/11/98	Lausanne-Sports	H	3-3	Chassot, Nixon 2
20/11/98	BSC Young Boys Bern	A	2-1	Nixon 2
29/11/98	FC Lugano	H	4-1	Fischer 2, Lima, Hodel
04/12/98	FC Sion	A	0-0	
13/12/98	FC Aarau	H	1-0	Bamba
28/02/99	FC St. Gallen	H	0-2	
06/03/99	Lausanne-Sports	A	1-3	Sant'Anna
13/03/99	Grasshopper-Club Zürich	H	0-1	
21/03/99	FC Basel	A	0-1	
03/04/99	Servette FC Genève	A	1-1	Kunz
10/04/99	Neuchâtel Xamax FC	H	2-2	Hodel, Kunz
17/04/99	FC Luzern	H	3-0	Jamarauli, Lima, Bartlett
24/04/99	FC Luzern	A	3-1	Bartlett, Kunz, Lima
01/05/99	Neuchâtel Xamax FC	A	3-1	Bartlett 3 (1p)
09/05/99	Servette FC Genève	H	4-0	Nixon, Hodel, Lima, Chassot
16/05/99	FC Basel	H	2-1	Castillo, Bartlett
24/05/99	Grasshopper-Club Zürich	A	2-0	Bartlett 2
30/05/99	Lausanne-Sports	H	0-1	
02/06/99	FC St. Gallen	A	3-1	Castillo, Nixon 2

PROMOTED CLUBS

		Pd	W	D	L	F	A	Pt	GD
1	FC Wil	22	12	7	3	45	27	43	+18
2	SR Delémont	22	12	4	6	43	27	40	+16
3	Etoile-Carouge FC	22	11	7	4	29	19	40	+10
4	Yverdon-Sports	22	11	4	7	33	28	37	+5
5	SC Kriens	22	9	7	6	30	29	34	+1
6	FC Schaffhausen	22	9	6	7	35	33	33	+2
7	FC Locarno	22	8	4	10	21	26	28	-5
8	FC Thun	22	6	7	9	28	33	25	-5
9	Stade Nyonnais	22	4	10	8	33	36	22	-3
10	FC Baden	22	6	4	12	31	36	22	-5
11	FC Solothurn	22	4	7	11	29	39	19	-10
12	FC Chiasso	22	2	9	11	14	38	15	-24

PROMOTION/RELEGATION PLAY-OFFS FINAL TABLE 97/98

		Pd	W	D	L	F	A	Pt	GD
1	FC Lugano	14	9	2	3	19	10	29	+9
2	**SR Delémont**	**14**	**7**	**2**	**5**	**23**	**20**	**23**	**+3**
3	**Yverdon-Sports**	**14**	**6**	**3**	**5**	**22**	**17**	**21**	**+5**
4	FC Aarau	14	6	2	6	24	24	20	0
5	FC Sion	14	6	1	7	16	17	19	-1
6	BSC Young Boys Bern	14	5	2	7	25	31	17	-6
7	FC Wil	14	5	1	8	26	30	16	-4
8	Etoile-Carouge FC	14	4	3	7	18	24	15	-6

CLUB DIRECTORY

Sports Réunis Delémont
Case postale 951
2800 Delémont 1
tel - (032) 4220633
fax - (032) 4231851
Year of Formation - 1909
President - Pierre Willemin
Secretary - Pierre-Alain Maeder
Coach - Michel Decastel (99/00 - Heinz Hermann)
Stadium - La Blancherie (6,000)

CLUB DIRECTORY

FC Yverdon-Sports
Case postale 564
1401 Yverdon-les-Bains
tel - (024) 4252610
fax - (024) 4361243
Year of Formation - 1897
President - Paul-André Cornu
Secretary - Patrick Caillet
Coach - Lucien Favre
Stadium - Stade Municipal (7,900)

TURKEY

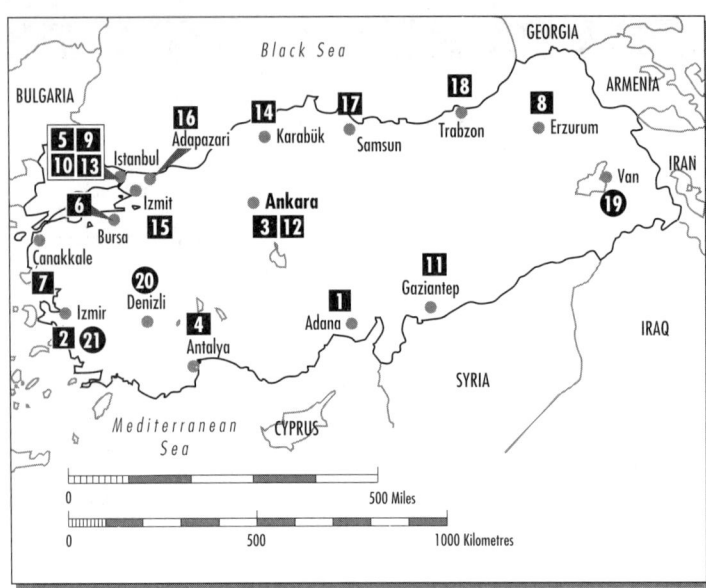

1	ADANASPOR	1016	12	GENÇLERBIRLIGI	1027
2	ALTAY	1017	13	ISTANBULSPOR	1028
3	ANKARAGÜCÜ	1018	14	KARABÜKSPOR	1029
4	ANTALYASPOR	1019	15	KOCAELISPOR	1030
5	BESIKTAS	1020	16	SAKARYASPOR	1031
6	BURSASPOR	1021	17	SAMSUNSPOR	1032
7	ÇANAKKALE DARDANELSPOR	1022	18	TRABZONSPOR	1033
8	ERZURUMSPOR	1023	**Promoted clubs**		
9	FENERBAHÇE	1024	19	VANSPOR	1034
10	GALATASARAY	1025	20	DENIZLISPOR	1034
11	GAZIANTEPSPOR	1026	21	GÖZTEPE	1034

HISTORIC VICTORY OVER GERMANY

Hat-tricks all the rage at Galatasaray

FEDERATION DIRECTORY

Türkiye Futbol Federasyonu
Konaklar Mahallesi Ihlamurlu Sokak 9, 80620, 4.Levent, Istanbul

tel - (212) 2827020   Year of Formation - 1923
fax - (212) 2827015   President - Haluk Ulusoy
                     Secretary - Ufuk Özerten

The Turkish championship was won for the third season running by Galatasaray - a feat achieved only once previously by the club, in the early 1970s. Gala coach Fatih Terim thus completed a hat-trick of title triumphs since joining the club from the Turkish national team in 1996. And there was also a hat-trick to celebrate for the team's prolific centre-forward Hakan Sükür, who, despite registering a modest total by his standards of 19 goals, captured the Turkish First Division top goalscorer crown for the third successive season - and the fifth time in all.

To add to Galatasaray's joy, they also won the Cup, gaining revenge in the final over Istanbul rivals Besiktas, who had defeated them on penalties in the same fixture a year earlier. Gala's decisive 2-0 victory in Besiktas's Inönü stadium in the second leg of the final came four days before the two teams met again in the league at the same venue. It was effectively the championship decider. Besiktas, trailing their rivals by five points, simply had to win, but as early as four minutes in they fell behind, to an opportunist strike from Gala midfielder Okan Buruk, and in the end they were grateful simply for a draw thanks to skipper Mehmet Özdilek's late equaliser.

That result meant that Galatasaray had completed the season with an unbeaten record against both Besiktas and their other great rivals Fenerbahçe. Therein lay the key to their success, because in the final table the margin that separated them from Besiktas was a mere point.

Winning the title enabled Galatasaray to match Fenerbahçe's all-time record of 13 championship wins. More importantly, it entitled them to have another crack at the Champions' League. Money was tight, and when Hakan's proposed transfer to Juventus fell through in

LEAGUE CHAMPIONSHIP RESULTS 98/99

		1	2	3	4	5	6	7	8	9	10	11	12	13	14	15	16	17	18
1	Adanaspor		2-0	1-0	4-2	0-1	4-1	3-0	2-0	0-3	2-2	3-1	1-1	0-1	2-0	1-1	2-1	0-0	0-2
2	Altay	3-2		5-1	2-4	0-1	4-1	1-1	3-1	0-4	0-2	0-0	0-0	2-1	1-0	3-1	2-0	2-0	2-5
3	Ankaragücü	2-2	2-1		0-0	0-1	2-2	3-0	3-0	2-4	2-2	1-1	0-1	5-0	1-1	0-2	1-0	3-4	1-0
4	Antalyaspor	2-0	4-2	1-4		0-3	0-0	2-0	1-0	1-0	1-1	3-1	1-1	2-3	3-1	2-1	2-2	1-2	0-1
5	Besiktas	2-0	1-1	4-1	2-1		3-3	0-0	2-1	3-2	1-1	1-1	2-0	2-1	1-1	0-3	3-0	0-0	2-0
6	Bursaspor	1-1	2-0	4-0	1-0	1-2		2-0	6-1	1-3	0-5	2-1	1-1	2-0	1-2	2-1	2-1	2-3	0-1
7	Çanakkale Dardanelspor	0-1	4-1	3-0	2-0	1-3	3-1		0-0	0-0	0-5	0-1	1-2	5-1	0-0	3-1	1-0	0-0	2-3
8	Erzurumspor	1-0	2-1	2-2	0-1	2-2	2-1	1-0		0-2	0-1	2-1	2-2	2-4	2-1	0-0	4-2	1-0	2-2
9	Fenerbahçe	6-0	5-0	2-1	3-1	1-2	4-1	3-1	4-1		2-2	4-0	3-0	2-0	4-1	1-1	3-0	6-2	1-0
10	Galatasaray	1-1	3-1	2-1	3-1	2-0	5-0	5-2	5-0	2-0		0-0	0-2	3-3	2-0	3-1	3-0	3-1	3-5
11	Gaziantepspor	3-1	1-1	1-0	1-1	2-0	5-2	1-0	3-0	2-2	1-2		2-2	2-1	4-2	1-2	2-0	1-1	1-1
12	Gençlerbirliği	2-1	1-1	3-1	1-2	0-1	1-4	0-0	5-1	0-3	1-2	3-0		2-3	2-1	1-1	1-0	3-0	0-1
13	Istanbulspor	6-0	3-0	1-4	0-1	0-2	2-3	1-1	0-2	1-2	1-4	0-0	0-0		3-0	2-1	4-0	2-1	0-0
14	Karabükspor	2-0	1-1	0-1	2-1	1-2	1-0	1-0	1-1	0-0	0-3	2-6	1-6	2-2		0-1	1-2	0-3	0-0
15	Kocaelispor	2-1	2-1	0-1	2-1	0-2	4-0	2-0	1-1	0-3	1-2	1-1	2-0	0-1	2-0		0-1	1-0	1-1
16	Sakaryaspor	0-0	1-2	4-0	0-0	0-2	4-1	1-3	1-1	2-1	0-0	6-2	3-1	3-0	4-0	2-2		0-1	1-1
17	Samsunspor	2-0	1-0	0-0	0-1	0-3	1-1	2-1	2-4	1-1	0-3	2-1	2-4	0-1	2-1	0-1	2-2		2-1
18	Trabzonspor	2-0	0-3	1-0	2-3	1-2	2-0	2-1	3-1	1-0	0-3	0-1	4-0	0-0	1-0	0-3	2-1	3-1	

LEAGUE CHAMPIONSHIP FINAL TABLE 98/99

				Home				Away					Total					
		P	W	D	L	F	A	W	D	L	F	A	W	D	L	F	A	P	GD
1	Galatasaray	34	12	3	2	45	18	11	6	0	40	12	23	9	2	85	30	78	+55
2	Besiktas	34	9	7	1	29	16	14	1	2	29	11	23	8	3	58	27	77	+31
3	Fenerbahçe	34	14	2	1	54	13	8	4	5	30	16	22	6	6	84	29	72	+55
4	Trabzonspor	34	10	1	6	24	19	7	6	4	24	18	17	7	10	48	37	58	+11
5	Kocaelispor	34	8	3	6	21	16	6	5	6	23	21	14	8	12	44	37	50	+7
6	Antalyaspor	34	8	4	5	26	22	6	3	8	20	25	14	7	13	46	47	49	-1
7	Gaziantepspor	34	9	6	2	33	18	3	6	8	18	30	12	12	10	51	48	48	+3
8	Gençlerbirligi	34	7	3	7	26	22	5	7	5	23	25	12	10	12	49	47	46	+2
9	Istanbulspor	34	6	4	7	26	21	6	3	8	22	34	12	7	15	48	55	43	-7
10	Samsunspor	34	6	4	7	19	25	5	4	8	19	28	11	8	15	38	53	41	-15
11	Altay	34	9	3	5	30	24	2	4	11	16	35	11	7	16	46	59	40	-13
12	Bursaspor	34	9	2	6	30	22	2	4	11	21	47	11	6	17	51	69	39	-18
13	Erzurumspor	34	8	5	4	25	22	2	4	11	15	42	10	9	15	40	64	39	-24
14	Ankaragücü	34	6	6	5	28	21	4	2	11	17	34	10	8	16	45	55	38	-10
15	Adanaspor	34	9	4	4	27	16	1	4	12	10	37	10	8	16	37	53	38	-16
16	Sakaryaspor	34	7	6	4	32	17	2	2	13	12	35	9	8	17	44	52	35	-8
17	Çanakkale Dardanelspor	34	7	4	6	25	19	1	4	12	10	30	8	8	18	35	49	32	-14
18	Karabükspor	34	4	5	8	15	29	1	3	13	11	35	5	8	21	26	64	23	-38

mid-season, the club was virtually forced to sell Romanian defender Iulian Filipescu to Spanish club Betis in order to keep the wolf from the door.

By then Gala's 1998/99 Champions' League campaign was already over. They had put up a worthy fight to try and reach the quarter-finals, but having muscled their way into a promising position thanks to home wins over Athletic Bilbao and Rosenborg and a couple of impressive draws against Juventus (the latter, in Istanbul, delayed for a week due to a political crisis), they blew their chance in the final game, losing to Bilbao 1-0 when a draw would have been enough to see them through.

Besiktas had also thrown away an excellent chance of reaching the quarter-finals of the Cup-winners' Cup a few weeks earlier

INTERNATIONAL HONOURS

World Cup Finals appearances: 1954

European Championship appearances: 1996

when, incredibly, they surrendered a 3-0 lead at home to Norwegian club Vålerenga IF. In domestic competition, however, Besiktas continued to plug away and remained in contention in both league and Cup despite the unexpected departure of coach John Toshack to Real Madrid in February. The appointment of ex-Galatasaray boss Karlheinz Feldkamp as his replacement received a mixed reaction from the Besiktas fans, and the 64-year-old German's popularity was not enhanced when the team ended the season as runners-up to Galatasaray in both competitions.

Fenerbahçe also had a German coach in ex-Stuttgart

TOP SCORERS

- 19 HAKAN Sükür (Galatasaray)
- 18 Elvir BALJIC (Fenerbahçe)
- 15 Viorel MOLDOVAN (Fenerbahçe)
- 14 Gheorghe HAGI (Galatasaray)
  - ARIF Erdem (Galatasaray)
  - ÜMIT Karan (Gençlerbirligi)
  - COSKUN Birdal (Erzurumspor)
- 13 MEHMET Özdilek (Besiktas)
- 12 Davor VUGRINEC (Trabzonspor)
- 11 MURAT Sözkesen (Bursaspor)
  - OKAN Buruk (Galatasaray)
  - MITHAT Yavas (Istanbulspor)
  - SERKAN Aykut (Samsunspor)

NATIONAL TEAM RESULTS 98/99

05/09/98	Northern Ireland (ECQ)	H	Istanbul	3-0	Oktay (19, 59), Tayfur (50p)
10/10/98	Germany (ECQ)	H	Bursa	1-0	Hakan Sükür (70)
14/10/98	Finland (ECQ)	H	Istanbul	1-3	Ogün (74)
27/03/99	Moldova (ECQ)	H	Istanbul	2-0	Hakan Sükür (35), Sergen (90)
05/06/99	Finland (ECQ)	A	Helsinki	4-2	Tayfur (26, 85), Hakan Sükür (35, 87)

boss Joachim Löw. When he arrived at the start of the season, he was one of many newcomers. Incoming president Aziz Yildirim had splashed out a fortune on foreign stars Elvir Baljic, Viorel Moldovan and Murat Yakin, although much of that money was recuperated by the sale of Jay-Jay Okocha to Paris Saint-Germain for a Turkish (and French) record £11.2m.

When Fenerbahçe were narrowly eliminated from the UEFA Cup in round one by Parma, it meant that they had only the league to go for. A controversial walk-off against Trabzonspor the previous season had earned them a ban from the Turkish Cup, so it was the title or bust for Löw and his expensively-assembled troops.

Early on, however, they began to encounter problems, drawing at home to Galatasaray and then losing three successive away games, one of them at Besiktas.

A storming run of nine successive wins in the middle of the campaign took them back to the top of the table but it was to prove a false dawn. When the big matches came around they were again found wanting, losing 0-2 at Galatasaray and then going down 1-2 at home to Besiktas in a comedy of errors that turned out to be the low point of Fenerbahçe's season, with injuries, bookings and red cards all adding to the misery of defeat.

It was no surprise when Löw was relieved of his duties at the end of the season, nor that the man to replace him was Ridvan Dilmen, the club's former international striker, who had just won promotion to the First Division as the coach of Vanspor. Ridvan, nicknamed the 'Little Devil', managed to take the eastern club straight back up to the top flight after just one season away and was elaborately fêted on his return to Istanbul by the Fenerbahçe fans.

The two clubs promoted alongside Vanspor were Denizlispor and Göztepe, the latter requiring three play-off victories before deservedly taking their place in the élite.

Relegation befell Karabükspor, Çanakkale Dardanelspor and Sakaryaspor. The latter had an unexpected chance to qualify for

Europe when they faced Ankaragücü in a play-off to determine Turkey's 'Cup-winning' representative in the UEFA Cup (finalists Galatasaray and Besiktas had both qualified for the Champions' League, so the place went on offer to the two losing semi-finalists). But Ankaragücu were far too strong, winning 5-0 to enter Europe for the first time in 18 years.

Trabzonspor thus had to make do with an InterToto place. Theirs had been a miserable season right from day one when Polish side Wisla Krakow thrashed them in the UEFA Cup. English coach Gordon Milne did not see out the season, nor did his fellow countryman Kevin Campbell, who went home in disgust after controversial club president Mehmet Ali Yen had showered him with a torrent of racial abuse. Campbell did not set the league alight, but he did endear himself to the Trabzonspor fans by scoring the winner against Fenerbahçe and a hat-trick away to Galatasaray.

While Turkish football continues to import expensive

NATIONAL TEAM APPEARANCES 98/99

Coach - MUSTAFA Denizli	NIR	GER	FIN	MOL	FIN	Cps	Gls
RÜSTU Reçber (10/05/73) - Fenerbahçe	G	G	G	G	G	37	-
MERT Korkmaz (16/08/71) - Kocaelispor	D	D	D46			4	-
SAFFET Akbas (13/04/68) - Fenerbahçe/Ankaragücü	D	s81			D	6	-
ALPAY Özalan (29/05/73) - Besiktas	D	D	D	D	D	40	1
OKAN Buruk (19/10/73) - Galatasaray	M88		s46	M		5	-
TAYFUR Havutçu (23/04/70) - Besiktas	M	M	M	M	M	16	3
TUGAY Kerimoglu (24/08/70) - Galatasaray	M75	M61	M46	M86	s75	52	2
ABDULLAH Ercan (08/12/71) - Trabzonspor	M	M	M	M	M89	47	-
SERGEN Yalçin (05/10/72) - Istanbulspor/Fenerbahçe	M	M81	M84	M	M89	23	5
HAKAN Sükür (01/09/71) - Galatasaray	A	A	A	A	A	46	26
OKTAY Derelioglu (17/12/75) - Besiktas	A80	s61	A	A25		12	8
OGUZ Çetin (15/02/63) - Adanaspor	s75					70	3
HAMI Mandirali (20/07/68) - FC Schalke 04 (GER)	s80		s46	s25		49	8
				/75			
ARIF Erdem (02/01/72) - Galatasaray	s88			s75		28	3
FATIH Akyel (26/12/77) - Galatasaray		D	D	D	D	10	-
OGÜN Temizkanoglu (06/10/69) - Trabzonspor		D89	D		D	54	5
TAYFUN Korkut (02/04/74) - Fenerbahçe		M			M	18	-
HAKAN Ünsal (14/05/73) - Galatasaray		s89			s89	10	-
HASAN Sas (01/08/76) - Galatasaray			s84			2	-
AYHAN Akman (23/02/77) - Besiktas				s86	A75	4	-
ALI EREN Beserler (25/10/75) - Besiktas					D	1	-
ÜMIT Davala (30/07/73) - Galatasaray					s89	2	-

DOMESTIC CUP 98/99

FIFTH ROUND
Adanaspor 3, Adanademirspor 1
Corluspor 2, Kirikkalespor 1
Kayserispor 2, Ankaragücü 3
Gençlerbirligi 2, A.Hopa 1
Kocaelispor 3, Antalyaspor 2
Usakspor 0, Sakaryaspor 2
Çanakkale Dardanelspor 0, Erzurumspor 2
Yeni Salihlispor 0, Gaziantepspor 2

SIXTH ROUND
Altay v Sakaryaspor 1-4; 3-0
(4-4; Sakaryaspor on away goals)
Samsunspor v Erzurumspor 3-2; 1-2
(4-4; Erzurumspor on away goals)
Istanbulspor v Gençlerbirligi 3-0; 2-2
(Istanbulspor 5-2)
Kocaelispor v Karabükspor 1-1; 4-1
(Kocaelispor 5-2)
Ankaragücü v Bursaspor 3-1; 0-0
(Ankaragücü 3-1)
Corluspor v Besiktas 1-4; 0-10
(Besiktas 14-1)
Trabzonspor v Gaziantepspor 5-4; 1-3
(Gaziantepspor 7-6)
Adanaspor v Galatasaray 0-2; 1-4
(Galatasaray 6-1)

QUARTER-FINALS
Gaziantepspor 1 (Ramazan 80), Ankaragücü 0
Ankaragücü 2 (Hakan Keles 53, 64), Gaziantepspor 0
(Ankaragücü 2-1)

Kocaelispor 1 (Engin 75),
Besiktas 2 (Ertugurul 41, Ayhan 47)
Besiktas 0, Kocaelispor 0
(Besiktas 2-1)

Erzurumspor 2 (Coskun 13, Muzaffer 46p),
Sakaryaspor 1 (Ömer 80og)
Sakaryaspor 2 (Aygün 44, Hüseyin 68), Erzurumsppor 0
(Sakaryaspor 3-2)

Istanbulspor 0, Galatasaray 0
Galatasaray 3 (Arif 40, Hagi 62, Hasan 79),
Istanbulspor 2 (Mithat 5, Mehmet 82)
(Galatasaray 3-2)

SEMI-FINALS
Sakaryaspor 2 (Hüseyin 10, Mehmet Ali 84),
Galatasaray 1 (Emre 71)
Galatasaray 2 (Arif 24, Ümit 64), Sakaryaspor 0
(Galatasaray 3-2)

Ankaragücü 0, Besiktas 1 (Oktay 70)
Besiktas 2 (Yasin 47, Ertugrul 63), Ankaragücü 0
(Besiktas 3-0)

FINAL
14/04/99, Istanbul (Ali Sami Yen)
GALATASARAY 0
BESIKTAS 0
referee - Muhittin Bosat
GALATASARAY - Taffarel; Bülent, Fatih, Ümit, Hakan
Ünsal, Emre (Ergün 75), Suat, Hagi, Okan, Arif
(Tugay 85), Hakan Sükür.
BESIKTAS - Fevzi; Ali Eren, Ertugrul, Sellami, Savas,
Mutlu, Yasin, Ayhan (Del Solar 69), Mehmet,
Amokachi (Serdar 89), Oktay (Nihat 77).

05/05/99, Istanbul (Inönü)
BESIKTAS 0
GALATASARAY 2 Ümit (51, 68)
referee - Ogus Sarvan
BESIKTAS - Fevzi; Alpay, Tayfur, Sellami (Erkan 84),
Savas, Mutlu, Yasin, Ayhan (Ohen 76), Mehmet,
Ertugrul (Nihat 65), Amokachi.
GALATASARAY - Taffarel; Popescu, Fatih, Bülent,
Hakan Ünsal, Emre, Suat, Okan (Vedat 86), Ergün
(Tugay 84), Hakan Sükür, Ümit (Ufuk 90).

(GALATASARAY 2-0)

foreign players, it remains very uncommon for a Turkish player to seek fame and fortune outside his home frontiers. Hami Mandirali left Trabzonspor to join German club Schalke 04 in 1998 but he was back within a year having failed to adapt. And rumours that talented left wing-back Abdullah Ercan would be moving to English club Newcastle were silenced when he plumped instead for the safe option, moving from Trabzonspor to Fenerbahçe in tandem with his team-mate Ogün Temizkanoglu.

Turkish national coach Mustafa Denizli is one man who has no qualms about the country's top players staying at home. It makes his job much easier when virtually all of

PLAYERS OF THE SEASON

ÜMIT DAVALA

There were a few players in Galatasaray's 'double'-winning team who caught the eye more often than versatility man Ümit Davala - star striker Hakan, midfield maestro Gheorghe Hagi, Brazilian 'keeper Taffarel, to name but a few - but nobody worked with more diligence or commitment to bring the club success. Coach Fatih Terim, a long-time admirer, selected him in every position bar goalkeeper, but he always gave his utmost, providing the team with pace and energy in every game and even sampling some rare personal glory with a superb goal against Juventus in the Champions' League and the two winning strikes against Besiktas that brought Galatasaray victory in the Turkish Cup final.

SERGEN YALÇIN

Sergen Yalçin is a true phenomenon of Turkish football. Apart from being the most skilful, creative midfielder in the country, he also attracts considerable publicity for his lifestyle outside football, which generally revolves around horseracing and nightclubbing. He began the 1998/99 season with Istanbulspor but when rich president Cem Uzan became disillusioned with the club's lack of success and withdrew his support, Sergen was bought by an independent company, Jet-Pa, who then loaned him to Fenerbahçe, where he scored just a few seconds into his début and went on to produce some of the best displays of his career. He also had a very productive year for Turkey, highlighted by a brilliant goal in the 2-0 victory at home to Moldova.

his charges are congregated on his doorstep in Istanbul. Indeed, that might explain why Turkey made such a promising start to their European Championship qualifying campaign.

After five matches, albeit four at home, Turkey seemed assured of reaching at least the play-offs. They had beaten all of the other teams in their group, including, remarkably, Germany, 1-0 in Bursa, thanks to a headed goal from the ever-reliable Hakan Sükür. Somewhat fortunate to win that game, the Turks were downright unlucky to lose 1-3 at home to Finland in Istanbul four days later, but they neutralised that setback by winning the return fixture 4-2 in Helsinki, with Hakan yet again coming to the fore as the Turks turned an early 0-2 deficit into a magnificent 4-2 victory - a result which kept alive the possibility that a mere draw in the final showdown with Germany in Munich on October 9 would be sufficient to take Turkey to the European finals for the second tournament in succession...

EUROPEAN CUPS 98/99

CHAMPIONS' CUP
● GALATASARAY
Qualifying round GRASSHOPPER-CLUB ZÜRICH (SUI)
H 2-1   Hagi (59p), Hakan Sükür (67)
        Taffarel; Filipescu, Popescu, Vedat (Fatih 84), Suat, Tugay,
        Emre (Okan 46), Hasan, Ergün, Hagi, Hakan Sükür.
A 3-2   Hakan Sükür (18, 45), Hagi (64p)
        Taffarel; Filipescu, Popescu, Vedat, Hakan Ünsal (Tolunay 83), Okan,
        Tugay (Ergün 46), Suat, Hasan, Hakan Sükür, Hagi (Bülent 82).

Champions' League
1st match JUVENTUS (ITA)
A 2-2   Hakan Sükür (44), Ümit (63)
        Taffarel; Filipescu, Popescu, Vedat, Okan, Ümit, Tugay (Arif 79),
        Hakan Ünsal, Hagi, Hasan (Ergün 81), Hakan Sükür.

2nd match ATHLETIC BILBAO (ESP)
H 2-1   Okan (16), Hagi (90)
        Taffarel; Filipescu (Fatih 33), Popescu, Vedat (Bülent 75), Okan,
        Ümit (Arif 70), Tugay, Hakan Ünsal, Hagi, Hasan, Hakan Sükür.

3rd match ROSENBORG BK (NOR)
A 0-3
        Taffarel; Fatih, Popescu, Vedat, Okan (Emre 87), Ümit (Tolunay 76),
        Ergün, Hakan Ünsal, Hagi, Hasan (Arif 87), Hakan Sükür.

4th match ROSENBORG BK (NOR)
H 3-0   Hakan Sükür (55, 74), Arif (66)
        Taffarel; Filipescu, Popescu, Fatih, Hakan Ünsal, Okan (Ufuk 84), Tugay,
        Ergün (Arif 46), Hasan, Hakan Sükür, Hagi (Ümit 79).

5th match JUVENTUS (ITA)
H 1-1   Suat (90)
        Taffarel; Fatih, Popescu, Filipescu, Hakan Ünsal (Vedat 90), Okan, Ümit,
        Tolunay (Suat 77), Hasan (Arif 77), Hakan Sükür, Hagi.

6th match ATHLETIC BILBAO (ESP)
A 0-1
        Taffarel; Popescu, Filipescu, Fatih, Okan, Hagi, Ümit, Tolunay (Burak 65),
        Suat (Vedat 65), Arif, Hasan (Emre 88).

CUP WINNERS' CUP
● BESIKTAS
1st round SPARTAK TRNAVA (SVK)
H 3-0   Mehmet (10), Oktay (21), Ohen (49)
        Hakan; Erkan, Ali Eren, Alpay, Tayfur, Hikmet (Sellami 71),
        Mehmet (Ertugrul 85), Del Solar, Serdar, Oktay, Ohen (Ayhan 80).
A 1-2   Oktay (45)
        Fevzi; Ali Eren, Rahim, Alpay, Erkan (Ertugrul 84), Sellami, Del Solar,
        Tayfur, Serdar (Yasin 46), Oktay, Mehmet (Amokachi 66).

2nd round VÅLERENGA IF (NOR)
A 0-1
        Fevzi; Erkan, Ali Eren, Sellami, Alpay, Hikmet (Ayhan 83), Del Solar,
        Mehmet (Ertugrul 75), Tayfur, Oktay, Ohen (Amokachi 70).
H 3-3   Oktay (8, 43), Tayfur (40)
        Fevzi; Ali Eren, Sellami, Alpay (Nihat 76), Tayfur, Ertugrul, Del Solar,
        Mehmet, Aydin (Erkan 28), Oktay, Ohen (Serdar 62).

UEFA CUP
● FENERBAHÇE
Qualifying round IFK GÖTEBORG (SWE)
A 1-2   Kemalettin (49)
        Rüstü; Saffet (Høgh 72), Uche, Mustafa, Kemalettin, Metin, Murat,
        Tayfun, Moshoeu (Erol 89), Baljic, Moldovan.
H 1-0   Baljic (64)
        Rüstü; Saffet, Uche, Mustafa, Tayfun, Moshoeu, Murat,
        Metin (Kemalettin 76), Erol, Moldovan (Høgh 86), Baljic (Sérgio 86).

1st round PARMA (ITA)
H 1-0   Moldovan (23)
        Rüstü; Saffet, Uche, Mustafa, Tayfun, Moshoeu, Metin (Kemalettin 85),
        Erol, Murat, Moldovan, Baljic.
A 1-3   Baljic (59)
        Rüstü; Saffet (Bolic 78), Uche, Høgh, Tayfun, Mustafa, Moshoeu, Murat,
        Erol, Moldovan (Metin 72), Baljic.

● ISTANBULSPOR
Qualifying round FC ARGES DACIA PITESTI (ROM)
A 0-2
        Zdravkov; Timur, Gralak (Güven 58), Petkov, Nesim, Ferri, Fuat, Ahmet,
        Oguz, Sergen (Mithat 46), Saffet (Hamza 46).
H 4-2   Saffet (14), Sergen (20), Mehmet (79), Aykut (86)
        Zdravkov; Halilagic, Gökhan (Mehmet 59), Petkov (Aykut 80), Hamza,
        Nesim, Oguz, Ferri, Ahmet (Güven 55), Sergen, Saffet.

● TRABZONSPOR
Qualifying round WISLA KRAKOW (POL)
A 1-5   Vugrinec (66)
        Milosevski; Rada, Ogün, Iskender, Recep, Abdullah, Erdal (Hasan 88),
        Okan, Orhan, Selahattin (Osman 54; Hüseyin 56), Vugrinec.
H 1-2   Hüseyin (67)
        Milosevski; Recep, Okan, Rada, Iskender (Dilaver 50), Mehmet Zengin,
        Erdal (Hüseyin 64), Ogün, Orhan, Vugrinec, Çetin (Selahattin 64).

ADANASPOR

CLUB DIRECTORY

Adanaspor Kulübü
Kenan Evren Bulvari 1873
Sokak No:2
Adana
tel - (322) 2340486
fax - (322) 2340486
Year of Formation - 1954
President - Hakan Uzan
Coach - Fuad Muzurovic; Gheorghe Multescu; Ziya
Dogan (99/00 - Nejat Biyedic)
Stadium - 5 Ocak (30,000)

APPEARANCES 98/99

		P	Ap	(s)	Gls
ALI Güncar	D	12			
ALI ASIM Balkaya	A	15	(12)	5	
ALTAN Aksoy	A	30	(3)	6	
ATAKAN Sancarbarlaz	M	23	(1)	6	
Ekrem BRADARIC (BOS)	D	14	(7)		
BÜLENT Selvü	M	11	(2)		
CANDAN Sayin	M		(1)		
CENK Isler	A	13	(2)	4	
Enes DEMIROVIC (BOS)	M	8	(2)	1	
EMRAH Eren	M	29	(1)	1	
ENDER Tras	M		(4)		
ENGIN Özdemir	M	2			
FUAT Buruk	M	25	(2)		
HAMDI Aslan	D	9	(12)	2	
HAMDI Demirtas	A	12	(7)	4	
HASAN Gültang	G	8			
HAYATI Köse	M	23	(4)		
IBRAHIM Köseoglu	M	7	(2)		
Suad KATANA (BOS)	D	12			
KORHAN Ataasik	M	12	(8)	2	
Ivan KIRILOV (BUL)	D	14	(1)		
MESUT Üretir	M	1			
OGUZ Çetin	M	16	(1)	3	
SERKAN	M		(2)		
SENOL Yavas	D	31	(2)	2	
UCHE Agbo	A	3	(7)		
VOLKAN Bekiroglu	M	13	(11)		
Zlatko YANKOV (BUL)	M	5	(2)		
YAVUZ	G	26	(1)		

LEAGUE RESULTS 1998/99

08/08/98	Istanbulspor	H	0-1	
16/08/98	Erzurumspor	A	0-1	
21/08/98	Fenerbahçe	H	0-3	
30/08/98	Gençlerbirligi	A	1-2	Demirovic
13/09/98	Çanakkale Dardanelspor	A	1-0	Hamdi Aslan
20/09/98	Samsunspor	H	0-0	
27/09/98	Karabükspor	A	0-2	
17/10/98	Galatasaray	H	2-2	Atakan 2
23/10/98	Trabzonspor	A	0-2	
01/11/98	Sakaryaspor	H	2-1	Atakan, Emrah
08/11/98	Besiktas	A	0-2	
15/11/98	Ankaragücü	H	1-0	Senol
22/11/98	Antalyaspor	A	0-2	
27/11/98	Gaziantepspor	H	3-1	Ali Asim, Hamdi Demirtas, Altan
06/12/98	Altay	A	2-3	og (Kenan), Hamdi Demirtas (p)
13/12/98	Bursaspor	H	4-1	Ali Asim 2, Hamdi Demirtas, Hamdi Aslan
20/12/98	Kocaelispor	A	1-2	Ali Asim
31/01/99	Istanbulspor	A	0-6	
07/02/99	Erzurumspor	H	2-0	Cenk 2
14/02/99	Fenerbahçe	A	0-6	
21/02/99	Gençlerbirligi	H	1-1	Atakan
28/02/99	Çanakkale Dardanelspor	H	3-0	Atakan, Oguz 2
07/03/99	Samsunspor	A	0-2	
14/03/99	Karabükspor	H	2-0	Altan, Cenk
19/03/99	Galatasaray	A	1-1	Altan
02/04/99	Trabzonspor	H	0-2	
11/04/99	Sakaryaspor	A	0-0	
17/04/99	Besiktas	H	0-1	
25/04/99	Ankaragücü	A	2-2	Hamdi Demirtas, Cenk (p)
02/05/99	Antalyaspor	H	4-2	Atakan, Korhan, Altan 2
09/05/99	Gaziantepspor	A	1-3	Senol
16/05/99	Altay	H	2-0	Ali Asim, Altan
23/05/99	Bursaspor	A	1-1	Oguz
29/05/99	Kocaelispor	H	1-1	Korhan

ALTAY

CLUB DIRECTORY

Altay Spor Kulübü
Sehitlar Caddesi
Alsancak Stadi C Blok
Alsancak
Izmir
tel - (232) 4210626
fax - (232) 4215668
Year of Formation - 1914
President - Nafiz Zorlu
Secretary - Iskender Odabasoglu
Coach - Sakip Özberk; Zinnur Sari; Ümit Kayihan
Stadium - Alsancak (20,000)

MAJOR HONOURS
Domestic Cup - (2) 1967, 1980.

APPEARANCES 98/99

	P	Ap	(s)	Gls
ALI KEMAL Alatas	M	1	(3)	
AYDIN Dagdelen	G	6	(1)	
BAYRAM Bektas	M	17	(2)	3
Senad BRKIC (BOS)	A	9	(4)	3
Ibrahim BUHARI (CAF)	A	8	(6)	2
CÜNEYT Yis	A	7	(17)	4
EMRE Güsar	D	13	(8)	
FERHAT Bölükbaso	M	6	(3)	
FERHAT Dogruel	A		(7)	
HASAN Özer	A	22	(2)	10
ILHAN Akgül	M	20	(1)	1
KADRI Sancak	D	9	(1)	
KENAN Arayici	M	31		
MURAT Alaçayir	M	28		3
NECATI	M		(3)	
NIHAT Tümkaya	G	26		
ORHAN Üstündag	D	25		
ÖZCAN Koçtürk	M	9	(1)	4
Patrick PASCAL (NIG)	A	16	(11)	6
SERDAR Meriç	M		(1)	
SERKAN Dökme	M	27	(6)	
SERKAN Karababa	D	19	(1)	1
Olivier SURAY (BEL)	M	22	(1)	2
SANVER Göymen	G	2		
SENOL Ibisi	D		(1)	
TAHIR Karapinar	M	26	(2)	2
TALAT Özden	M	4	(6)	2
Emmanuel TEBEREN (NIG)	D	19		
YAKUP Sertkaya	M	2	(5)	

LEAGUE RESULTS 1998/99

08/08/98	Galatasaray	A	1-3	Cüneyt (p)
16/08/98	Trabzonspor	H	2-5	Murat, Buhari
23/08/98	Sakaryaspor	A	2-1	Buhari, Talat
28/08/98	Besiktas	H	0-1	
13/09/98	Ankaragücü	A	1-2	Pascal
20/09/98	Antalyaspor	H	2-4	Pascal 2
27/09/98	Gaziantepspor	A	1-1	Özkan
18/10/98	Çanakkale Dardanelspor	H	1-1	Murat
25/10/98	Bursaspor	H	4-1	Hasan 3, Tahir
01/11/98	Kocaelispor	A	1-2	Hasan
08/11/98	Istanbulspor	H	2-1	Özkan, og (Hakan Aslanagiz)
14/11/98	Erzurumspor	A	1-2	Suray
20/11/98	Fenerbahçe	H	0-4	
29/11/98	Gençlerbirligi	A	1-1	Pascal
06/12/98	Adanaspor	H	3-2	Pascal, Özkan, Cüneyt (p)
13/12/98	Samsunspor	A	0-1	
20/12/98	Karabükspor	H	1-0	Özkan
31/01/99	Galatasaray	H	0-2	
07/02/99	Trabzonspor	A	3-0	Hasan 2, Bayram
13/02/99	Sakaryaspor	H	2-0	Brkic, Hasan
20/02/99	Besiktas	A	1-1	Murat
28/02/99	Ankaragücü	H	5-1	og (Gökmen), Hasan 2, og (Faruk), Cüneyt
07/03/99	Antalyaspor	A	2-4	Cüneyt, Serkan Karababa
14/03/99	Gaziantepspor	H	0-0	
21/03/99	Çanakkale Dardanelspor	A	1-4	Pascal
04/04/99	Bursaspor	A	0-2	
11/04/99	Kocaelispor	H	3-1	Bayram, Hasan, Brkic
17/04/99	Istanbulspor	A	0-3	
25/04/99	Erzurumspor	H	3-1	Suray, Ilhan, Tahir
02/05/99	Fenerbahçe	A	0-5	
09/05/99	Gençlerbirligi	H	0-0	
16/05/99	Adanaspor	A	0-2	
23/05/99	Samsunspor	H	2-0	Talat, Bayram
29/05/99	Karabükspor	A	1-1	Brkic

ANKARAGÜCÜ

CLUB DIRECTORY

Makina Kimya Endüstrisi Ankaragücü Kulübü
Sosyal Tesisleri
GMK Bulvari
Tandogan
Ankara
tel - (312) 2220175
fax - (312) 2312772
Year of Formation - 1910
President - Cemal Aydin
Secretary - Zülküf Aker
Coach - Samet Aybaba; Milorad Mitrovic;
Zlatko Krmpotic (99/00 - Tinaz Tirpan)
Stadium - 19 Mayis (24,000)

MAJOR HONOURS
Domestic Cup - (2) 1972, 1981.

APPEARANCES 98/99

		P	Ap	(s)	Gls
ABDI Güleryuz	M	1	(3)	
ADNAN Erkan	G	25	(2)	
Stephan BAIDOO (DRC)	M	30		5
BIROL Alsancak	A		(9)	
CENGIZHAN Hincal	M	10	(3)	1
Fernand COULIBALY (MLI)	A	3	(6)	2
James DEBBAH (LIB)	A	1	(1)	
DENIZ Kolgu	M	8	(3)	3
FARUK Sarman	D	13	(3)	
FATIH Sezer	M	25	(5)	1
GÖKMEN Baris	D	25	(3)	
GÖKMEN Yildiran	M	1	(4)	
HAKAN Keles	A	22	(9)	7
HAKAN Kutlu	D	31	(1)	
HAYATI Soydas	D	5	(1)	1
KEMALETTIN Sentürk	M	10	(4)	3
Ohene KENNEDY (GHA)	A	15		9
MAHIR Nergiz	M	2	(1)	
MEHMET Deliorman	M		(6)	1
Helman MKHALELE (SAF)	M	29	(2)	1
ÖZKAN Karsli	G	9		
RAMAZAN	M	11	(6)	
SAFFET Akbas	D	9	(2)	
SAMI EMRE Kötken	M		(1)	
SERKAN Bensol	M	26	(2)	
TARIK Dasgün	A	20	(4)	9
ÜMIT Hatipoglu	M	14	(7)	
Ion VASILE (ROM)	A	5	(2)	
YILMAZ Özen	D	24		2

LEAGUE RESULTS 1998/99

Date	Opponent		Score	Scorers
09/08/98	Besiktas	A	1-4	Cengizhan (p)
16/08/98	Çanakkale Dardanelspor	H	3-0	Kennedy 2, Hakan Keles
23/08/98	Antalyaspor	H	0-0	
30/08/98	Gaziantepspor	A	0-1	
13/09/98	Altay	H	2-1	Baidoo, Yilmaz
18/09/98	Bursaspor	A	0-4	
27/09/98	Kocaelispor	H	0-2	
17/10/98	Istanbulspor	A	4-1	Baidoo 2, Kennedy, Mehmet
25/10/98	Erzurumspor	H	3-0	Kennedy, Tarik 2
31/10/98	Fenerbahçe	A	1-2	Kennedy (p)
08/11/98	Gençlerbirligi	H	0-1	
15/11/98	Adanaspor	A	0-1	
22/11/98	Samsunspor	H	3-4	Kennedy 3
28/11/98	Karabükspor	A	1-0	Kennedy
13/12/98	Trabzonspor	A	0-1	
20/12/98	Sakaryaspor	H	1-0	Tarik
23/12/98	Galatasaray	H	2-2	Tarik (p), Hakan Keles
29/01/99	Besiktas	H	0-1	
07/02/99	Çanakkale Dardanelspor	A	0-3	
13/02/99	Antalyaspor	A	4-1	Tarik 2, Hakan Keles, Kemalettin
21/02/99	Gaziantepspor	H	1-1	Deniz
28/02/99	Altay	A	1-5	Fatih
06/03/99	Bursaspor	H	2-2	Tarik 2 (1p)
14/03/99	Kocaelispor	A	1-0	Hakan Keles
20/03/99	Istanbulspor	H	5-0	Baidoo 2, Coulibaly (p), Tarik, Hayati
04/04/99	Erzurumspor	A	2-2	Kemalettin, Hakan Keles
11/04/99	Fenerbahçe	H	2-4	Deniz 2
17/04/99	Gençlerbirligi	A	1-3	Coulibaly
25/04/99	Adanaspor	H	2-2	Kemalettin, Mkhalele
02/05/99	Samsunspor	A	0-0	
09/05/99	Karabükspor	H	1-1	Yilmaz
14/05/99	Galatasaray	A	1-2	Hakan Keles
23/05/99	Trabzonspor	H	1-0	Hakan Keles
29/05/99	Sakaryaspor	A	0-4	

ANTALYASPOR

CLUB DIRECTORY

Antalyaspor Kulübü
Kiliçarslan Mahallesi Park Sokak No:12
Antalya
tel - (242) 2478062
fax - (242) 2474760
Year of Formation - 1966
President - Ünal Öger
Secretary - Gültekin Çeki
Coach - Jozef Jarabinsky
Stadium - Atatürk (12,000)

APPEARANCES 98/99

		P	Ap	(s)	Gls
ADNAN Karahan	G	31			
AHMET Sönmez	D	27	(5)	3	
BAYRAM Bektas	M	8	(1)		
BURHAN Saatçioglu	D	34			
BÜLENT Selvü	M		(1)		
CÜNEYT Aydogan	G	1			
DURSUN Karaman	D	20	(4)		
EMRE Atil	M	2	(1)		
FAZLI Ulusal	A	33		9	
Gocho GINCHEV (BUL)	D	31	(1)	4	
KAMIL Çakor	M	28	(3)	3	
André KONA (DRC)	A	27	(3)	7	
MAHMUT Kariklar	M		(4)		
MEHMET ZEKI	G	2			
MUHAMMED	M	1	(3)		
Vedin MUSIC (BOS)	M	3	(20)	1	
MUSTAFA Gürsel	M	31		4	
NURI Kamburoglu	D	33		9	
OLGUN Karamanoglu	M	3	(22)	1	
ORHAN Atik	D	24	(2)	2	
ROGÉRIO (BRA)	M	29	(1)	1	
UGUR Yasan	M	1	(3)		
ZAFER	M	5	(8)		

LEAGUE RESULTS 1998/99

09/08/98	Sakaryaspor	A	0-0	
14/08/98	Besiktas	H	0-3	
23/08/98	Ankaragücü	A	0-0	
30/08/98	Çanakkale Dardanelspor	H	2-0	Ahmet, Nuri (p)
13/09/98	Gaziantepspor	H	3-1	Fazli, Nuri, Mustafa
20/09/98	Altay	A	4-2	Kona 2, Fazli, Nuri (p)
27/09/98	Bursaspor	H	0-0	
16/10/98	Kocaelispor	A	1-2	Nuri (p)
24/10/98	Istanbulspor	H	2-3	Nuri (p), Ginchev
01/11/98	Erzurumspor	A	1-0	Fazli
06/11/98	Fenerbahçe	H	1-0	og (Uche)
15/11/98	Gençlerbirligi	A	2-1	Kamil, Music
22/11/98	Adanaspor	H	2-0	Kona, Kamil
29/11/98	Samsunspor	A	1-0	Kona
06/12/98	Karabükspor	H	3-1	Orhan, Fazli, Ginchev
12/12/98	Galatasaray	A	1-3	Ginchev
19/12/98	Trabzonspor	H	0-1	
31/01/99	Sakaryaspor	H	2-2	Kona, Mustafa
05/02/99	Besiktas	A	1-2	Nuri (p)
13/02/99	Ankaragücü	H	1-4	Orhan
21/02/99	Çanakkale Dardanelspor	A	0-2	
28/02/99	Gaziantepspor	A	1-1	Nuri
07/03/99	Altay	H	4-2	og (Serkan Karababa), Mustafa, Fazli, Nuri (p)
12/03/99	Bursaspor	A	0-1	
21/03/99	Kocaelispor	H	2-1	Kona, Fazli
03/04/99	Istanbulspor	A	1-0	Kona
11/04/99	Erzurumspor	H	1-0	Rogério
16/04/99	Fenerbahçe	A	1-3	Olgun
25/04/99	Gençlerbirligi	H	1-1	Ahmet
02/05/99	Adanaspor	A	2-4	Mustafa, Ginchev
07/05/99	Samsunspor	H	1-2	Ahmet
16/05/99	Karabükspor	A	1-2	Nuri
23/05/99	Galatasaray	H	1-1	Fazli
30/05/99	Trabzonspor	A	3-2	Fazli 2, Kamil

BESIKTAS

CLUB DIRECTORY

Besiktas Jimnastik Kulübü
Akaretler Spor Caddesi No: 92
Besiktas
Istanbul
tel - (212) 2278790
fax - (212) 2588194
Year of Formation - 1903
President - Süleyman Seba
Secretary - Fahrettin Curoglu
Coach - John Toshack; Karlheinz Feldkamp
Stadium - Inönü (45,000)

MAJOR HONOURS
League Championship - (9) 1960, 1966, 1967,
1982, 1986, 1990, 1991, 1992, 1995.
Domestic Cup - (5)
1975, 1989, 1990, 1994, 1998.

APPEARANCES 98/99

	P	Ap	(s)	Gls
ALI EREN Beserler	D	23	(1)	
ALPAY Özalan	D	27		
Daniel AMOKACHI (NIG)	A	15	(5)	4
AYDIN Tuna	M	3	(4)	
AYHAN Akman	M	22	(4)	7
Alvarez DEL SOLAR (PER)	M	20	(1)	
EKREM Köse	G		(1)	
ERKAN Avseren	M	16	(8)	1
ERTUGRUL Saglam	A	20	(5)	4
FEVZI Tuncay	G	33		
HAKAN Caliskan	G	1	(1)	
HIKMET Çapanoglu	M	8	(5)	1
MEHMET Özdilek	M	24	(3)	13
MUTLU Topçu	M	16	(5)	
NIHAT Kahveci	A	4	(24)	7
Christopher OHEN (NIG)	A	16	(1)	10
OKTAY Derelioglu	A	22	(3)	8
RAHIM Zafer	D	16	(5)	
SAVAS Kaya	M	7	(4)	1
Jamal SELLAMI (MAR)	D	23	(2)	
SERDAR Topraktepe	M	13	(3)	1
TAYFUR Havutçu	M	33		1
TUNÇ Kip	D		(1)	
YASIN Sülün	M	11	(11)	

LEAGUE RESULTS 1998/99

Date	Opponent	H/A	Score	Scorers
09/08/98	Ankaragücü	H	4-1	Oktay 2, Hikmet, Ohen
14/08/98	Antalyaspor	A	3-0	Ohen, Mehmet, Oktay
23/08/98	Gaziantepspor	H	1-1	Mehmet
28/08/98	Altay	A	1-0	Ohen
13/09/98	Bursaspor	H	3-3	Tayfur (p), Oktay, Nihat
20/09/98	Kocaelispor	A	2-0	Nihat 2
26/09/98	Istanbulspor	H	2-1	Amokachi, Ohen
18/10/98	Erzurumspor	A	2-2	Mehmet, Ohen
25/10/98	Fenerbahçe	H	3-2	Amokachi 2 (1p), Mehmet
01/11/98	Gençlerbirligi	A	1-0	Oktay
08/11/98	Adanaspor	H	2-0	Ayhan, Ohen
15/11/98	Samsunspor	A	3-0	Ertugrul, Ayhan, Ohen
22/11/98	Karabükspor	H	1-1	Ohen
06/12/98	Trabzonspor	H	2-0	Ayhan, Oktay (p)
12/12/98	Sakaryaspor	A	2-0	Nihat, Ertugrul
16/12/98	Galatasaray	A	0-2	
20/12/98	Çanakkale Dardanelspor	H	0-0	
29/01/99	Ankaragücü	A	1-0	Ertugrul
05/02/99	Antalyaspor	H	2-1	Ayhan, Ertugrul
13/02/99	Gaziantepspor	A	0-2	
20/02/99	Altay	H	1-1	Oktay
27/02/99	Bursaspor	A	2-1	Erkan, Ayhan
06/03/99	Kocaelispor	H	0-3	
14/03/99	Istanbulspor	A	2-0	Amokachi, Ayhan
21/03/99	Erzurumspor	H	2-1	Oktay, Mehmet
04/04/99	Fenerbahçe	A	2-1	Mehmet (p), Ayhan
09/04/99	Gençlerbirligi	H	2-0	Mehmet 2 (1p)
17/04/99	Adanaspor	A	1-0	Mehmet
23/04/99	Samsunspor	H	0-0	
01/05/99	Karabükspor	A	2-1	Mehmet 2 (1p)
09/05/99	Galatasaray	H	1-1	Mehmet
16/05/99	Trabzonspor	A	2-1	Ohen 2
23/05/99	Sakaryaspor	H	3-0	Nihat 2, Serdar
28/05/99	Çanakkale Dardanelspor	A	3-1	Savas, Nihat, Mehmet

BURSASPOR

Bursaspor Kulübü
Vakifköy Tesisleri
Vakifköy
Bursa
tel - (224) 3664883
fax - (224) 3664995
Year of Formation - 1963
President - Kani Sen
Secretary - Osman Yilmaz
Coach - Nejat Biyedic; Ahmet Akcan; Sakip Özberk
(99/00 - Kemal Batmaz)
Stadium - Atatürk (24,000)

MAJOR HONOURS
Domestic Cup - (1) 1986.

APPEARANCES 98/99

	P	Ap	(s)	Gls
ADNAN Ilgin	D	10		1
AYDIN	M	1	(2)	
DENIZ Kolgu	M	14		2
ENDER Alkan	M	19	(11)	4
ENGIN Sertel	M		(2)	
ERKAN Özbey	D	23	(2)	
FUAT	D	2	(1)	
Ivko GANCHEV (BUL)	G	14		
Ronen HARAZI (ISR)	A	10	(3)	5
Rubenilson MONTEIRO (BEL)	A	10	(3)	2
MURAT Sözkesen	A	29	(1)	11
MUSTAFA Er	M	1	(3)	1
MUSTAFA Gönden	M	15	(11)	2
OKAN Yilmaz	A	16	(7)	3
OSMAN Coskan	M	6	(3)	1
ÖMER Kiliç	D	24		
Senad REPUH (BOS)	A	5	(11)	2
SELIM Özer	D	13		1
SINAN Yesil	M	27	(6)	8
SABAN Yilidirim	M		(1)	
SENOL Karagöl	G	20		
TANER Gülleri	M	3	(7)	
TAYFUN Seven	M		(4)	
TUNAHAN Akdogan	M	9	(6)	
TURAN Sen	D	23	(1)	
ÜNAL Sari	M	25	(3)	2
Mirza VARESANOVIC (BOS)	D	29	(1)	3
Konstantin VIDOLOV (BUL)	M	26	(4)	2

LEAGUE RESULTS 1998/99

09/08/98	Karabükspor	H	1-2	Harazi
16/08/98	Galatasaray	H	0-5	
22/08/98	Trabzonspor	A	0-2	
30/08/98	Sakaryaspor	H	2-1	Murat, Harazi (p)
13/09/98	Besiktas	A	3-3	Okan 2, Sinan
18/09/98	Ankaragücü	H	4-0	Murat 2, Osman, Mustafa Gönden
27/09/98	Antalyaspor	A	0-0	
18/10/98	Gaziantepspor	H	2-1	Vidolov, Selim
25/10/98	Altay	A	1-4	Repuh
01/11/98	Çanakkale Dardanelspor	H	2-0	Murat, Okan
08/11/98	Kocaelispor	H	2-1	Harazi, Sinan
15/11/98	Istanbulspor	A	3-2	Murat 2, Deniz (p)
22/11/98	Erzurumspor	H	6-1	Harazi 2, Murat, Deniz (p), Vidolov, Varesanovic
29/11/98	Fenerbahçe	A	1-4	Sinan (p)
06/12/98	Gençlerbirligi	H	1-1	Sinan
13/12/98	Adanaspor	A	1-4	Murat
18/12/98	Samsunspor	H	2-3	Sinan (p), Murat
31/01/99	Karabükspor	A	0-1	
07/02/99	Galatasaray	A	0-5	
14/02/99	Trabzonspor	H	0-1	
21/02/99	Sakaryaspor	A	1-4	Murat
27/02/99	Besiktas	H	1-2	Sinan (p)
06/03/99	Ankaragücü	A	2-2	Varesanovic, Repuh
12/03/99	Antalyaspor	H	1-0	Monteiro
20/03/99	Gaziantepspor	A	2-5	Sinan, Monteiro
04/04/99	Altay	H	2-0	Sinan (p), Mustafa Gönden
11/04/99	Çanakkale Dardanelspor	A	1-3	Varesanovic
17/04/99	Kocaelispor	A	0-4	
25/04/99	Istanbulspor	H	2-0	Murat, Adnan
02/05/99	Erzurumspor	A	1-2	Ünal
08/05/99	Fenerbahçe	H	1-3	og (Murat Yakin)
16/05/99	Gençlerbirligi	A	4-1	Ender 3, Ünal
23/05/99	Adanaspor	H	1-1	Mustafa Er
29/05/99	Samsunspor	A	1-1	Ender

ÇANAKKALE DARDANELSPOR

CLUB DIRECTORY

Çanakkale Dardanelspor Kulübü
Kordon Boyu Dardanel Ishani 2/3
Çanakkale
tel - (286) 2175699
fax - (286) 2175699
Year of Formation - 1966
President - Niyazi Önen
Secretary - Ismet Güneshan
Coach - Erol Tok; Milorad Mitrovic; Rasim Kara;
Yilmaz Vural
Stadium - 18 Mart (15,000)

APPEARANCES 98/99

	P	Ap	(s)	Gls
AYKIN Aydemr	D	1		
AYTEKIN Vidiplioglu	M		(7)	
BEKIR Gür	D	24		
BIRKAN Budak	M	1	(3)	
BÜLENT Uygun	M	20	(6)	4
Doncho DONEV (BUL)	A	21		10
DURSUN Albayrak	D	19	(3)	
ENGIN Çaliskan	M		(1)	
ENGIN Ipekoglu	G	33		
ENGIN Sentürk	M	9	(7)	
ERMAN Özgür	M	18	(7)	2
GÉRSON (BRA)	A	20	(3)	1
HÜSEYIN Sari	D	4	(3)	
ILKER Daspudak	M	24	(5)	
Norman MAPEZA (ZIM)	D	31		
MURAT Aslan	M		(2)	
Majid MUSISI (UGA)	A	30		9
OLCAY Çetinkaya	G	1	(1)	
SANTOS (BRA)	M	2	(2)	
SERKAN Kiliç	M	15	(7)	
SERKAN Rençber	M	26	(1)	1
Vladimir SUBERT (YUG)	M	3		1
SABAN Yilidirim	M	9	(9)	2
TAMER Tuna	M	30	(2)	3
TOLGA Seyhan	M	16	(2)	
TURAN Uzun	D	11		
UFUK Ates	A	6	(20)	2

LEAGUE RESULTS 1998/99

07/08/98	Fenerbahçe	H	0-0	
16/08/98	Ankaragücü	A	0-3	
23/08/98	Gençlerbirligi	H	1-2	Subert
30/08/98	Antalyaspor	A	0-2	
13/09/98	Adanaspor	H	0-1	
20/09/98	Gaziantepspor	A	0-1	
26/09/98	Samsunspor	H	0-0	
18/10/98	Altay	A	1-1	Ufuk
25/10/98	Karabükspor	H	0-0	
01/11/98	Bursaspor	A	0-2	
08/11/98	Galatasaray	H	0-5	
13/11/98	Kocaelispor	A	0-2	
21/11/98	Trabzonspor	H	2-3	Musisi 2
28/11/98	Istanbulspor	A	1-1	Musisi
06/12/98	Sakaryaspor	A	3-1	Tamer, Musisi, Donev
13/12/98	Erzurumspor	H	0-0	
20/12/98	Besiktas	A	0-0	
30/01/99	Fenerbahçe	A	1-3	Donev (p)
07/02/99	Ankaragücü	H	3-0	Musisi, Donev, Gérson
14/02/99	Gençlerbirligi	A	0-0	
21/02/99	Antalyaspor	H	2-0	Donev, Musisi
28/02/99	Adanaspor	A	0-3	
06/03/99	Gaziantepspor	H	0-1	
14/03/99	Samsunspor	A	1-2	Donev (p)
21/03/99	Altay	H	4-1	Donev (p), Musisi, Erman, Tamer
04/04/99	Karabükspor	A	0-1	
11/04/99	Bursaspor	H	3-1	Donev, Erman, Musisi
17/04/99	Galatasaray	A	2-5	Tamer, Bülent
25/04/99	Kocaelispor	H	3-1	Donev 2 (1p), Saban
02/05/99	Trabzonspor	A	1-2	Ufuk
09/05/99	Istanbulspor	H	5-1	Bülent 2, Serkan, Saban, Musisi
16/05/99	Sakaryaspor	H	1-0	Donev
23/05/99	Erzurumspor	A	0-1	
28/05/99	Besiktas	H	1-3	Bülent

ERZURUMSPOR

CLUB DIRECTORY

Erzurumspor
Havaalani Yolu Üzeri
Tesisleri
Erzurum
tel - (0442) 2183464
fax - (0442) 2349690
Year of Formation - 1968
President - Cemal Polat
Coach - Hikmet Karaman; Ümit Kayihan;
Sadi Tekelioglu
Stadium - Cemal Gürsel (17,500)

APPEARANCES 98/99

	P	Ap	(s)	Gls
ABDÜLKADIR Saksak	M	16	(4)	
ALI Yilmaz	M	9	(10)	2
ALPASLAN Tice	D	29		2
ALTAY Can	M	28		
ALTAY Dagdelen	G	23		
ATAY Efe	A	1	(12)	
Elvedin BEGANOVIC (BOS)	D	22	(1)	
BURAK Gök	M	2	(7)	
CENGIZ Yilmaz	G		(1)	
CEVAT	D	4	(1)	
COSKUN Birdal	A	29	(1)	14
ERKAN Güney	M		(2)	
FAYSAL (ALG)	M	6	(3)	1
FURKAN Sükürcü	D	20	(1)	
HÜSEYIN Topkaya	M	12	(4)	
KÜRSAT Karakas	M	27	(2)	1
MUHAMMED (MAR)	A	12	(1)	5
MUTLU Dervisoglu	A	14	(8)	7
MUZAFFER Bilazer	M	18	(6)	3
ÖMER Erdogan	D	18	(11)	1
Florian PRUNEA (ROM)	G	11		
SALIH	M	4	(6)	
SERKAN	M		(1)	
SONER Neliker	M	17	(8)	2
TANER Aykut	M	5	(3)	
ZAFER Demir	M	24		2

LEAGUE RESULTS 1998/99

09/08/98	Gençlerbirligi	A	1-5	Coskun
16/08/98	Adanaspor	H	1-0	Coskun
22/08/98	Samsunspor	A	4-2	Coskun, Kürpat, Soner, Zafer
30/08/98	Karabükspor	H	2-1	Ömer, Coskun
12/09/98	Galatasaray	A	0-5	
20/09/98	Trabzonspor	H	2-2	Coskun, Muhammed
27/09/98	Sakaryaspor	A	1-1	Coskun
18/10/98	Besiktas	H	2-2	Mutlu, Coskun (p)
25/10/98	Ankaragücü	A	0-3	
01/11/98	Antalyaspor	H	0-1	
08/11/98	Gaziantepspor	A	0-3	
14/11/98	Altay	H	2-1	Mutlu, Muhammed (p)
22/11/98	Bursaspor	A	1-6	Muhammed
28/11/98	Kocaelispor	H	0-0	
05/12/98	Istanbulspor	H	2-4	Alpaslan, Faysal
13/12/98	Çanakkale Dardanelspor	A	0-0	
20/12/98	Fenerbahçe	H	0-2	
31/01/99	Gençlerbirligi	H	2-2	Alpaslan, Soner
07/02/99	Adanaspor	A	0-2	
13/02/99	Samsunspor	H	1-0	Muhammed
21/02/99	Karabükspor	A	1-1	Muhammed
28/02/99	Galatasaray	H	0-1	
05/03/99	Trabzonspor	A	1-3	Coskun (p)
14/03/99	Sakaryaspor	H	4-2	Coskun 2 (2p), Ali, Zafer
21/03/99	Besiktas	A	1-2	Coskun
04/04/99	Ankaragücü	H	2-2	Mutlu 2 (1p)
11/04/99	Antalyaspor	A	0-1	
17/04/99	Gaziantepspor	H	2-1	Ali, Mutlu
25/04/99	Altay	A	1-3	Coskun
02/05/99	Bursaspor	H	2-1	Mutlu, Coskun
09/05/99	Kocaelispor	A	1-1	Muzaffer
16/05/99	Istanbulspor	A	2-0	Coskun, Muzaffer
23/05/99	Çanakkale Dardanelspor	H	1-0	Muzaffer
29/05/99	Fenerbahçe	A	1-4	Mutlu

FENERBAHÇE

CLUB DIRECTORY

Fenerbahçe Spor Kulübü
Dereagzi Tesisleri
Kadiköy
Istanbul
tel - (216) 3450940
fax - (216) 3483060
Year of Formation - 1907
President - Aziz Yildirim
Secretary - Köksal Özbek
Coach - Joachim Löw (99/00 - Ridvan Dilmen)
Stadium - Fenerbahçe Sükrü Saracoglu (30,000)

MAJOR HONOURS
League Championship - (13)
1959, 1961, 1964, 1965, 1968, 1970, 1974,
1975, 1978, 1983, 1985, 1989, 1996.
Domestic Cup - (4) 1968, 1974, 1979, 1983.

APPEARANCES 98/99

	P	Ap	(s)	Gls
ALI Turan	D		(1)	
Elvir BALJIC (BOS)	A	30		18
Elvir BOLIC (BOS)	A	7	(23)	6
Manuel DIMAS (POR)	M	22	(1)	4
ERKAN Sözeri	M	1	(2)	
EROL Bulut	M	19	(8)	1
FARUK Yigit	A	4	(12)	3
GÜVENÇ	M		(2)	
HALIL IBRAHIM Kara	M	4	(3)	
Jes HØGH (DEN)	D	24	(2)	2
ILKER Yagcioglu	M	11	(3)	
KEMALETTIN Sentürk	M	6	(3)	2
METIN Diyadin	M	15	(5)	4
Viorel MOLDOVAN (ROM)	A	27		15
John MOSHOEU (SAF)	M	34		8
MURAT Bölükbasi	A	2		3
MURAT Sahin	G	4		
MURAT Yakin (SUI)	M	22	(1)	3
MUSTAFA Dogan (GER)	D	28	(1)	
ÖMER Karabacak	M		(2)	
RÜSTÜ Reçber	G	30		
SAFFET Akbas	D	7		
SERGEN Yalçin	M	9	(6)	7
SÉRGIO Neves (BRA)	A		(3)	2
SERKAN Özsoy	D	10	(7)	
TANER Savut	M	1	(6)	
TAYFUN Korkut	M	33		2
UCHE Okechukwu (NIG)	D	24		1

LEAGUE RESULTS 1998/99

07/08/98	Çanakkale Dardanelspor	A	0-0	
15/08/98	Gençlerbirligi	H	3-0	Moldovan 2, Metin
21/08/98	Adanaspor	A	3-0	Baljic, Kemalettin, Sérgio
29/08/98	Samsunspor	H	6-2	Baljic 3, Moshoeu, Bolic, Sérgio
12/09/98	Karabükspor	H	4-1	Uche, Baljic, Murat Yakin, Metin
20/09/98	Galatasaray	H	2-2	Moldovan, Baljic
25/09/98	Trabzonspor	A	0-1	
18/10/98	Sakaryaspor	H	3-0	Faruk 2, Høgh
25/10/98	Besiktas	A	2-3	Moshoeu, Dimas
31/10/98	Ankaragücü	H	2-1	Kemalettin, Baljic
06/11/98	Antalyaspor	A	0-1	
14/11/98	Gaziantepspor	H	4-0	Baljic, Metin, Moldovan, Faruk
20/11/98	Altay	A	4-0	Moshoeu, Baljic, Bolic 2
29/11/98	Bursaspor	H	4-1	Baljic 2, Høgh, Bolic (p)
04/12/98	Kocaelispor	A	3-0	Moshoeu, Baljic, Metin
13/12/98	Istanbulspor	H	2-0	Dimas, Moshoeu
20/12/98	Erzurumspor	A	2-0	og (Burak), Moldovan
30/01/99	Çanakkale Dardanelspor	H	3-1	Moldovan, Baljic (p), Murat Yakin
06/02/99	Gençlerbirligi	A	3-0	Baljic, Moldovan 2
14/02/99	Adanaspor	H	6-0	Moldovan 3, Moshoeu, Dimas, Sergen
19/02/99	Samsunspor	A	1-1	Moldovan
28/02/99	Karabükspor	A	0-0	
07/03/99	Galatasaray	A	0-2	
13/03/99	Trabzonspor	H	1-0	Baljic
20/03/99	Sakaryaspor	A	1-2	Moshoeu
04/04/99	Besiktas	H	1-2	Erol
11/04/99	Ankaragücü	A	4-2	Moldovan 2, Murat Yakin, Sergen
16/04/99	Antalyaspor	H	3-1	Tayfun, og (Ginchev), Baljic (p)
24/04/99	Gaziantepspor	A	2-2	Moldovan, Bolic
02/05/99	Altay	H	5-0	Dimas, Bolic, Baljic 2, Sergen
08/05/99	Bursaspor	A	3-1	og (Varesanovic), Sergen 2
15/05/99	Kocaelispor	H	1-1	Moshoeu
23/05/99	Istanbulspor	A	2-1	Tayfun, Murat Bölükbasi
29/05/99	Erzurumspor	H	4-1	Murat Bölükbasi 2, Sergen 2 (1p)

GALATASARAY

CLUB DIRECTORY

Galatasaray Spor Kulübü
Metin Oktay Tesisleri
Florya
Istanbul
tel - (212) 6630090
fax - (212) 5740424/2511212
Year of Formation - 1905
President - Faruk Süren
Secretary - Ales Ünal Erzen
Coach - Fatih Terim
Stadium - Ali Sami Yen (40,000)

MAJOR HONOURS
League Championship - (13)
1962, 1963, 1969, 1971, 1972, 1973, 1987,
1988, 1993, 1994, 1997, 1998, 1999.
Domestic Cup - (12)
1963, 1964, 1965, 1966, 1973, 1976, 1982,
1985, 1991, 1993, 1996, 1999.

APPEARANCES 98/99

	P	Ap	(s)	Gls
ALPER Tezcan	A		(3)	
ARIF Erdem	A	22	(5)	14
BURAK Akdis	A	4	(13)	4
BÜLENT Korkmaz	D	14	(7)	1
FMRF Belözoglu	M	20	(7)	2
ERGÜN Penbe	M	5	(19)	1
Iulian FILIPESCU (ROM)	D	12		
FATIH Akyel	D	28	(2)	3
Gheorghe HAGI (ROM)	M	27	(1)	14
HAKAN Ünsal	M	30	(1)	3
HAKAN Sükür	A	33		19
HASAN Sas	A	21	(3)	4
MEHMET Bölükbasi	G	2		
OKAN Buruk	M	26	(2)	11
Gheorghe POPESCU (ROM)	D	29		1
SUAT Kaya	M	16	(7)	2
Claudio TAFFAREL (BRA)	G	32		
TOLUNAY Kafkas	M	4	(10)	1
TUGAY Kerimoglu	M	16	(6)	2
UFUK Talay (AUS)	M	3	(5)	
ÜMIT Davala	M	22	(3)	2
VEDAT Inceefe	D	8	(5)	

LEAGUE RESULTS 1998/99

08/08/98	Altay	H	3-1	Hagi 2, Suat
16/08/98	Bursaspor	A	5-0	Hakan Sükür 3, Hagi, Arif
22/08/98	Kocaelispor	H	3-1	Hagi (p), Hakan Ünsal, Hasan
30/08/98	Istanbulspor	A	4-1	Hasan 2, Tugay, Hakan Sükür
12/09/98	Erzurumspor	H	5-0	Hakan Sükür 2 (1p), Fatih, Ümit, Hakan Ünsal
20/09/98	Fenerbahçe	A	2-2	Hagi (p), Hakan Sükür
27/09/98	Gençlerbirligi	H	0-2	
17/10/98	Adanaspor	A	2-2	Tugay (p), Hasan
24/10/98	Samsunspor	H	3-1	Hakan Sükür 2, Hakan Ünsal
31/10/98	Karabükspor	A	3-0	Hagi 2, Arif
08/11/98	Çanakkale Dardanelspor	A	5-0	Hagi (p), Arif, Hakan Sükür, Okan, Tolunay
15/11/98	Trabzonspor	H	3-5	og (Ogün), Bülent, Burak
21/11/98	Sakaryaspor	A	0-0	
12/12/98	Antalyaspor	H	3-1	Emre, Okan, Arif
16/12/98	Besiktas	H	2-0	Fatih, Emre
20/12/98	Gaziantepspor	A	2-1	Hakan Sükür, Suat
23/12/98	Ankaragücü	A	2-2	Hakan Sükür, Okan
31/01/99	Altay	A	2-0	Hagi, Arif
07/02/99	Bursaspor	H	5-0	Hagi 3, Arif 2
12/02/99	Kocaelispor	A	2-1	Hakan Sükür 2
21/02/99	Istanbulspor	H	3-3	Okan, Arif, Fatih
28/02/99	Erzurumspor	A	1-0	Burak
07/03/99	Fenerbahçe	H	2-0	Okan, Hakan Sükür
14/03/99	Gençlerbirligi	A	2-1	Hagi, Okan
19/03/99	Adanaspor	H	1-1	Hakan Sükür
03/04/99	Samsunspor	A	3-0	Arif, Popescu, Ergün
10/04/99	Karabükspor	H	2-0	Arif, Okan
17/04/99	Çanakkale Dardanelspor	H	5-2	Arif 3, Ümit, Okan
25/04/99	Trabzonspor	A	3-0	Okan, Arif, Hakan Sükür (p)
30/04/99	Sakaryaspor	H	3-0	Okan, Hagi, Hakan Sükür (p)
09/05/99	Besiktas	A	1-1	Okan
14/05/99	Ankaragücü	H	2-1	Burak, Hakan Sükür
23/05/99	Antalyaspor	A	1-1	Burak
30/05/99	Gaziantepspor	H	0-0	

GAZIANTEPSPOR

<table>
<tr><td colspan="2">

CLUB DIRECTORY

Gaziantepspor Kulübü
Subarcu Caddesi No:2
Gaziantep
tel - (342) 2311259
fax - (342) 2308420
Year of Formation - 1969
President - Celal Dogan
Secretary - Naci Topcuoglu
Coach - Hüseyin Kalpar
Stadium - Kamil Ocak (20,000)

</td></tr>
</table>

APPEARANCES 98/99

	P	Ap	(s)	Gls
ABDÜLKADIR Demirci	M	23	(5)	
AHMET	M		(2)	
ALI IBRAHIM (GHA)	A	16		7
CEM Beceren	D	30	(1)	2
Fernand COULIBALY (MLI)	A	5		2
ENGIN Hossoy	D	12	(1)	
ERHAN Albayrak	A	16	(1)	7
ERHAN Namli	M	12	(17)	
EROL Kapusuz	M	7	(9)	1
HAKAN	M	10	(5)	1
HALIT Köprülü	M	1	(13)	1
HASAN Yigit	M	28		
IBRAHIM Üzülmez	M	13	(2)	
ILYAS Kahraman	M	25	(7)	6
Samuel JOHNSON (GHA)	M	33		2
Desire M'BONABUCYA (RWA)	A	29	(2)	10
MUHARREM Kasa	G	5	(2)	
MUSTAFA Sahintürk	A		(9)	1
NIYAZI Güney	M		(7)	
ORAL Küçükoral	M	2	(6)	
ÖMER Çatkiç	G	29		
Yaw PREKO (GHA)	A	25		7
RAMAZAN Tunç	D	30		3
ZIYA Sahin	D	23	(3)	1

LEAGUE RESULTS 1998/99

08/08/98	Trabzonspor	A	1-0	Coulibaly
16/08/98	Sakaryaspor	H	2-0	Erol, Halit
23/08/98	Besiktas	A	1-1	Preko
30/08/98	Ankaragücü	H	1-0	Cem
13/09/98	Antalyaspor	A	1-3	Johnson
20/09/98	Çanakkale Dardanelspor	H	1-0	M'Bonabucya
27/09/98	Altay	H	1-1	M'Bonabucya
18/10/98	Bursaspor	A	1-2	Johnson
25/10/98	Kocaelispor	H	1-2	M'Bonabucya
31/10/98	Istanbulspor	A	0-0	
08/11/98	Erzurumspor	H	3-0	M'Bonabucya, Preko, Coulibaly
14/11/98	Fenerbahçe	A	0-4	
22/11/98	Gençlerbirligi	H	2-2	Preko, M'Bonabucya
27/11/98	Adanaspor	A	1-3	Mustafa
06/12/98	Samsunspor	H	1-1	Ramazan
13/12/98	Karabükspor	A	6-2	Preko 3 (1p), Ilyas, M'Bonabucya, Ziya
20/12/98	Galatasaray	H	1-2	Cem
31/01/99	Trabzonspor	H	1-1	Erhan Albayrak
07/02/99	Sakaryaspor	A	2-6	Ali Ibrahim, Erhan Albayrak (p)
13/02/99	Besiktas	H	2-0	Ali Ibrahim, M'Bonabucya
21/02/99	Ankaragücü	A	1-1	Erhan Albayrak (p)
28/02/99	Antalyaspor	H	1-1	Ali Ibrahim
06/03/99	Çanakkale Dardanelspor	A	1-0	Erhan Albayrak
14/03/99	Altay	A	0-0	
20/03/99	Bursaspor	H	5-2	Ali Ibrahim 2, Ilyas 2, Preko
04/04/99	Kocaelispor	A	1-1	Ali Ibrahim
11/04/99	Istanbulspor	H	2-1	Ramazan, M'Bonabucya
17/04/99	Erzurumspor	A	1-2	Ilyas
24/04/99	Fenerbahçe	H	2-2	Erhan Albayrak 2
02/05/99	Gençlerbirligi	A	0-3	
09/05/99	Adanaspor	H	3-1	M'Bonabucya, Ali Ibrahim, Ilyas
16/05/99	Samsunspor	A	1-2	M'Bonabucya
22/05/99	Karabükspor	H	4-2	Erhan Albayrak, Ramazan, Ilyas, Hakan
30/05/99	Galatasaray	A	0-0	

GENÇLERBIRLIGI

Gençlerbirligi Spor Kulübü
Gazi Mustafa Kemal Bulvari 75/B
06570 Maltepe
Ankara
tel - (312) 2295852
fax - (312) 2212280
Year of Formation - 1923
President - Ilhan Cavcav
Secretary - Gültekin Aktan
Coach - Karol Pecze
Stadium - 19 Mayis (25,000)

MAJOR HONOURS
Domestic Cup - (1) 1987.

	P	Ap	(s)	Gls
Lahcen ABRAMI (MAR)	M	22	(5)	3
BERKAY	A		(3)	
ENGIN Sayan	D	1	(2)	
GEREMI Njitap (CMR)	M	29		5
HAKAN Biçici	M	18	(12)	3
HAKAN Demir	M	22	(10)	
HASAN Binici	M		(2)	
HASAN Sönmez	G	3	(1)	
IDRIS Gümüsdere	A	1	(8)	
ILKER Dalçiçek	A	9	(13)	
ISMAIL Dogan	D	18	(6)	
ISMAIL Güldüren	D	19	(2)	
MEHMET Simsek	M	24	(4)	4
Hamid MERAKSHI (ALG)	A	19	(3)	7
METIN Akçevre	G	30		
NIHAT Bastürk	M	22	(7)	1
Alfred PHIRI (SAF)	M	28	(2)	2
Robert SEMENIK (SVK)	A	13	(3)	6
SERDAR Malatyali	M	1	(15)	
TANER Taskin	D	1	(1)	
TOLGA Dogantez	D	31		
ÜMIT Karan	A	31		14
ÜMIT Özat	D	31		1
ZIYA	G	1		

09/08/98	Erzurumspor	H	5-1	Ümit Karan 2, Abrami,
				Hakan Biçici, Geremi
15/08/98	Fenerbahçe	A	0-3	
23/08/98	Çanakkale Dardanelspor	A	2-1	Mehmet, Ümit Karan
30/08/98	Adanaspor	H	2-1	Ümit Özat (p), Merakshi
12/09/98	Samsunspor	A	4-2	Ümit Karan 3, Geremi
19/09/98	Karabükspor	H	2-1	Mehmet, Merakshi
27/09/98	Galatasaray	A	2-0	Ümit Karan, Abrami
17/10/98	Trabzonspor	H	0-1	
25/10/98	Sakaryaspor	A	1-3	Ümit Karan
01/11/98	Besiktas	H	0-1	
08/11/98	Ankaragücü	A	1-0	Merakshi
15/11/98	Antalyaspor	H	1-2	Ümit Karan
22/11/98	Gaziantepspor	A	2-2	Abrami, Hakan Biçici
29/11/98	Altay	H	1-1	Merakshi
06/12/98	Bursaspor	A	1-1	Ümit Karan
11/12/98	Kocaelispor	H	1-1	Ümit Karan
20/12/98	Istanbulspor	A	0-0	
31/01/99	Erzurumspor	A	2-2	Mehmet 2
06/02/99	Fenerbahçe	H	0-3	
14/02/99	Çanakkale Dardanelspor	H	0-0	
21/02/99	Adanaspor	A	1-1	og (Kirilov)
28/02/99	Samsunspor	H	3-0	Ümit Karan, Merakshi, og (Sabri)
07/03/99	Karabükspor	A	6-1	og (Abdül), Merakshi, Phiri,
				Geremi, Semenik 2
14/03/99	Galatasaray	H	1-2	Merakshi
20/03/99	Trabzonspor	A	0-4	
04/04/99	Sakaryaspor	H	1-0	Ümit Karan
09/04/99	Besiktas	A	0-2	
17/04/99	Ankaragücü	H	3-1	Geremi 2, Nihat
25/04/99	Antalyaspor	A	1-1	Phiri
02/05/99	Gaziantepspor	H	3-0	Ümit Karan, Semenik 2
09/05/99	Altay	A	0-0	
16/05/99	Bursaspor	H	1-4	Semenik
21/05/99	Kocaelispor	A	0-2	
29/05/99	Istanbulspor	H	2-3	Hakan Biçici, Semenik

ISTANBULSPOR

CLUB DIRECTORY

Istanbulspor Kulübü
Basin Ekspres Yolu Star Sokak No:2
Ikitelli
Istanbul
tel - (212) 6979840
fax - (212) 6979840
Year of Formation - 1926
President - Tayfun Gündogar
Secretary - Adnan Sezgin
Coach - Safet Susic (99/00 - Ziya Dogan)
Stadium - Bayrampasa (15,000)

APPEARANCES 98/99

	P	Ap	(s)	Gls
AHMET Yildirim	M	25		1
AMIR Alibaz	M	3	(11)	
ATAKAN Sancarbarlaz	M		(1)	
AYDIN	M	3	(7)	1
AYKUT Kocaman	A	10	(6)	7
CENK	M	1	(1)	
Enes DEMIROVIC (BOS)	M	14	(1)	2
EMRE Asik	D	25		
ENGIN Özdemir	M	3	(3)	
ESER Öztürk	M	8	(6)	
Jean-Michel FERRI (FRA)	M	8		1
FUAT Buruk	M	1		
GÖKHAN Keskin	D	10	(2)	
Sérgio GRALAK (BRA)	D	3		
GÜVEN Kocabal	M	7	(5)	
HAKAN Aslanagiz	D	10	(5)	
HAKAN Dursun	M		(4)	
Sead HALILAGIC (BOS)	D	31		
HALUK Güngör	G	14	(1)	
HAMZA Hamzaoglu	M	26	(2)	4
MEHMET Yozgatli	A	11	(15)	4
MITHAT Yavas	A	23	(2)	11
NESIM Özgür	M	27	(1)	1
OGUZ Çetin	M	6		1
ORHAN	A	1		
Ivailo PETKOV (BUL)	M	30	(1)	2
SADULLAH			(2)	1
SAFFET Akyüz	A	26	(1)	4
SERGEN Yalçin	M	7	(1)	4
SUAT Türker	A		(8)	1
TIMUR Yanyali	D	21	(4)	1
Zdravko ZDRAVKOV (BUL)	G	20		

LEAGUE RESULTS 1998/99

08/08/98	Adanaspor	A	1-0	Sergen
16/08/98	Samsunspor	H	2-1	Sergen, Hamza
22/08/98	Karabükspor	H	3-0	Saffet, Sergen, Oguz
30/08/98	Galatasaray	H	1-4	Sergen
11/09/98	Trabzonspor	A	0-0	
19/09/98	Sakaryaspor	H	4-0	Aykut 3, og (Nikolovski)
26/09/98	Besiktas	A	1-2	Aykut
17/10/98	Ankaragücü	H	1-4	Saffet
24/10/98	Antalyaspor	A	3-2	Ferri, Mithat, Petkov
31/10/98	Gaziantepspor	H	0-0	
08/11/98	Altay	A	1-2	Mithat
15/11/98	Bursaspor	H	2-3	Hamza 2 (1p)
21/11/98	Kocaelispor	A	1-0	Nesim
28/11/98	Çanakkale Dardanelspor	H	1-1	Mehmet
05/12/98	Erzurumspor	A	4-2	Petkov, Saffet, Mithat, Mehmet
13/12/98	Fenerbahçe	A	0-2	
20/12/98	Gençlerbirligi	H	0-0	
31/01/99	Adanaspor	H	6-0	Mehmet 2, Mithat, Demirovic, Suat, Sadullah
07/02/99	Samsunspor	A	1-0	Ahmet
13/02/99	Karabükspor	A	2-2	Aykut 2
21/02/99	Galatasaray	A	3-3	og (Ümit), Demirovic (p), Mithat
27/02/99	Trabzonspor	H	0-0	
06/03/99	Sakaryaspor	A	0-3	
14/03/99	Besiktas	H	0-2	
20/03/99	Ankaragücü	A	0-5	
03/04/99	Antalyaspor	H	0-1	
11/04/99	Gaziantepspor	A	1-2	Mithat
17/04/99	Altay	H	3-0	Mithat 2, Saffet
25/04/99	Bursaspor	A	0-2	
02/05/99	Kocaelispor	H	2-1	Mithat, Aydin
09/05/99	Çanakkale Dardanelspor	A	1-5	Hamza (p)
16/05/99	Erzurumspor	H	0-2	
23/05/99	Fenerbahçe	H	1-2	Aykut
29/05/99	Gençlerbirligi	A	3-2	Mithat 2, Timur

KARABÜKSPOR

CLUB DIRECTORY

Kardemir Karabükspor Kulübü
Ergenekon Caddesi No:11
Yenisehir Kulübü Üstü
Yenisehi
Karabük
tel - (372) 4185050
fax - (372) 4125422
Year of Formation - 1969
President - Taner Canyurt
Coach - Ahmet Akcan; Orhan Yüce; Cihat Erbil;
Neset Muharrem
Stadium - Yenisehirz (15,000)

APPEARANCES 98/99

	P	Ap	(s)	Gls
ABDUL (CMR)	D	14		
DOGAN	D		(1)	
ENVER Sen	M	22	(5)	1
ERDOGAN Yilmaz	A	28	(3)	9
ERKAN	M		(1)	
FADIL	M	3	(1)	
GÜRKAN Zora	A	8	(12)	2
Sead HALILOVIC (BOS)	M	29	(1)	3
HALIM Karaköse	A	9	(7)	
HAYATI Sen	M	19	(6)	
IBRAHIM Üzülmez	M	16		
IHSAN	M	1	(4)	
ILKAN Aksoy	M	21	(4)	
IZZET Kaya	M	2	(3)	
Fanfan KALENGA (DRC)	A	8	(2)	2
KIM Doo-Young (KOR)	A	4	(1)	
Petrus MAREK (SVK)	D	1		
MEHMET	D	19		
MURAT Senvardar	A	1	(6)	1
NIYAZI Güney	M	11	(5)	
ÖZGÜR Yildirim	M	1	(8)	1
SEDAT Kalayci	M	31		1
SERKAN Damla	M	18	(5)	2
SEYIT Icgül	D	20	(7)	
SEVKI Eksi	G	16		
TAHIR Alagöz	D	30		4
TAYFUN Hut	M	21	(3)	
VEYSEL	G	8		
YAHYA (EGY)	D	2		
YASIN	M		(4)	
ZAFER Özgültekin	G	10	(1)	
Hadis ZUBONOVIC (BOS)	A	1	(4)	

LEAGUE RESULTS 1998/99

09/08/98	Bursaspor	A	2-1	Erdogan, Gürkan
16/08/98	Kocaelispor	A	0-2	
22/08/98	Istanbulspor	A	0-3	
30/08/98	Erzurumspor	A	1-2	Erdogan (p)
12/09/98	Fenerbahçe	A	1-4	Sedat
19/09/98	Gençlerbirligi	A	1-2	Erdogan
27/09/98	Adanaspor	H	2-0	Serkan, Erdogan (p)
17/10/98	Samsunspor	A	1-2	Erdogan
25/10/98	Çanakkale Dardanelspor	A	0-0	
31/10/98	Galatasaray	H	0-3	
07/11/98	Trabzonspor	A	0-1	
14/11/98	Sakaryaspor	H	1-2	Erdogan
22/11/98	Besiktas	A	1-1	Halilovic
28/11/98	Ankaragücü	H	0-1	
06/12/98	Antalyaspor	A	1-3	Halilovic
13/12/98	Gaziantepspor	H	2-6	Kalenga, Gürkan (p)
20/12/98	Altay	A	0-1	
31/01/99	Bursaspor	H	1-0	Kalenga
07/02/99	Kocaelispor	H	0-1	
13/02/99	Istanbulspor	H	2-2	Murat, Serkan
21/02/99	Erzurumspor	H	1-1	Erdogan
28/02/99	Fenerbahçe	H	0-0	
07/03/99	Gençlerbirligi	H	1-6	Halilovic
14/03/99	Adanaspor	A	0-2	
20/03/99	Samsunspor	H	0-3	
04/04/99	Çanakkale Dardanelspor	H	1-0	Tahir
10/04/99	Galatasaray	A	0-2	
15/04/99	Trabzonspor	H	0-0	
25/04/99	Sakaryaspor	A	0-4	
01/05/99	Besiktas	H	1-2	Erdogan (p)
09/05/99	Ankaragücü	A	1-1	Özgür
16/05/99	Antalyaspor	H	2-1	Enver, Tahir
22/05/99	Gaziantepspor	A	2-4	Tahir, Erdogan
29/05/99	Altay	H	1-1	Tahir

KOCAELISPOR

CLUB DIRECTORY

Kocaelispor Kulübü
Ankara Caddesi 396
Dostluk Ishani No:53 Kat 7
Izmit
tel - (262) 3215969
fax - (262) 3246467
Year of Formation - 1966
President - Sefa Sirmen
Secretary - Suat Temaçin
Coach - Güvenç Kurtar
Stadium - Ismetpasa (20,000)

MAJOR HONOURS
Domestic Cup - (1) 1997.

APPEARANCES 98/99

	P	Ap	(s)	Gls
AHMED HASSAN (EGY)	M	28		1
AHMET Dursun	A	21	(8)	7
BÜLENT Uygun	M		(1)	
CEM SINAN	M	1	(7)	
CIHAN	A	9	(17)	1
Roman DABROWSKI (POL)	A	29		7
ENGIN Öztonga	M	21	(9)	5
ERHAN Albayrak	A	8	(4)	
EVREN Turhan	M	27	(6)	3
MERT Korkmaz	D	34		1
METHAD Abdelhady (EGY)	D	21	(2)	
METIN Mert	G	5		
Misko MIRKOVIC (YUG)	D	23	(1)	1
MUSTAFA Özkan	A	2	(7)	2
NURI Çolak	M	23		2
ORHAN Kaynak	A	24	(2)	9
OSMAN Çakor	D	16	(3)	
ÖNER	M		(1)	
SAWIEH (LIB)	A	10	(4)	1
SELAHATTIN Özbir	M	1	(1)	
SONER Boz	M	22	(7)	2
Dumitru STÎNGACIU (ROM)	G	29	(1)	
SABAN	M		(1)	
TARIK Dasgün	A		(3)	
YALÇIN Kilidiran	D		(3)	
ZEKI Önatli	D	20	(2)	

LEAGUE RESULTS 1998/99

08/08/98	Samsunspor	A	1-0	Orhan
16/08/98	Karabükspor	H	2-0	Nuri, Orhan
22/08/98	Galatasaray	A	1-3	Nuri
30/08/98	Trabzonspor	H	1-1	Orhan
13/09/98	Sakaryaspor	A	2-2	Engin, Dabrowski
20/09/98	Besiktas	H	0-2	
27/09/98	Ankaragücü	A	2-0	Orhan, Cihan
16/10/98	Antalyaspor	H	2-1	Orhan, Ahmet
25/10/98	Gaziantepspor	A	2-1	Ahmet, og (Johnson)
01/11/98	Altay	H	2-1	Evren, Dabrowski (p)
08/11/98	Bursaspor	A	1-2	Engin
13/11/98	Çanakkale Dardanelspor	H	2-0	Evren, Dabrowski (p)
21/11/98	Istanbulspor	H	0-1	
28/11/98	Erzurumspor	A	0-0	
04/12/98	Fenerbahçe	H	0-3	
11/12/98	Gençlerbirligi	A	1-1	Soner
20/12/98	Adanaspor	H	2-1	Ahmed Hassan, Ahmet
30/01/99	Samsunspor	H	1-0	Engin
07/02/99	Karabükspor	A	1-0	Soner
12/02/99	Galatasaray	H	1-2	Dabrowski (p)
21/02/99	Trabzonspor	A	3-0	Dabrowski, Orhan, Mert
26/02/99	Sakaryaspor	H	0-1	
06/03/99	Besiktas	A	3-0	Dabrowski, Mirkovic, Ahmet
14/03/99	Ankaragücü	H	0-1	
21/03/99	Antalyaspor	A	1-2	Orhan
04/04/99	Gaziantepspor	H	1-1	Orhan
11/04/99	Altay	A	1-3	Ahmet
17/04/99	Bursaspor	H	4-0	Engin 2, Evren, Dabrowski
25/04/99	Çanakkale Dardanelspor	A	1-3	Orhan
02/05/99	Istanbulspor	A	1-2	Sawieh
09/05/99	Erzurumspor	H	1-1	Ahmet
15/05/99	Fenerbahçe	A	1-1	og (Dimas)
21/05/99	Gençlerbirligi	H	2-0	Mustafa, Ahmet
29/05/99	Adanaspor	A	1-1	Mustafa

SAKARYASPOR

CLUB DIRECTORY

Sakaryaspor Kulübü
Rüstemler Tesisleri
Adapazari
tel - (264) 2712900
fax - (264) 2712900
Year of Formation - 1965
President - Irfan Çelik
Coach - Radmilo Ivancevic; Senol Günes;
Giray Bulak
Stadium - Atatürk (17,000)

MAJOR HONOURS
Domestic Cup - (1) 1988.

APPEARANCES 98/99

	P	Ap	(s)	Gls
Alen AVDIC (YUG)	A	1	(1)	
AYGÜN Taskiran	A	29		7
BODEA (ROM)	D	10	(1)	
Marejo DODIK (YUG)	A	2		
HASAN Özdemir	D	19	(2)	
HASAN Tunçel	A		(2)	
HÜSEYIN	D	27	(1)	3
ISA Turan	M	5	(7)	
KADIR Kures	D	25	(3)	
Richard KINGSTON (GHA)	G	21		
MEHMET Gonulaçar	A	9	(8)	3
MEHMET ALI Honca	D	30	(1)	4
MESUT Ünal	D	10		1
MUHAMMET ALI Kurtulus	M	11	(8)	1
MURAT Kepez	A		(1)	
MURAT Yavasgül	M	8	(16)	3
MUSTAFA Sert	M	3	(5)	
Igor NIKOLOVSKI (MAC)	D	28	(1)	3
SEFER Yilmaz	M	6	(14)	1
SELIM Çatalbas	A	2	(4)	
SÉRGIO Neves (BRA)	A	8		5
SINAN Kahraman	M	16	(6)	
Mario STRIZU (ROM)	A	13	(1)	6
TIMUÇIN Beyazit	M	32	(1)	4
ÜNAL Odabas	G	11	(1)	
VEYSEL Besik	G	2	(1)	
YASIN Çelik	M	21	(7)	
YUSUF Tokuç	M	25	(3)	3

LEAGUE RESULTS 1998/99

09/08/98	Antalyaspor	H	0-0	
16/08/98	Gaziantepspor	A	0-2	
23/08/98	Altay	H	1-2	Nikolovski
30/08/98	Bursaspor	A	1-2	Mehmet
13/09/98	Kocaelispor	H	2-2	Mesut, Aygün
19/09/98	Istanbulspor	A	0-4	
27/09/98	Erzurumspor	H	1-1	Sérgio
18/10/98	Fenerbahçe	A	0-3	
25/10/98	Gençlerbirligi	H	3-1	Yusuf, Aygün, Sérgio
01/11/98	Adanaspor	A	1-2	Mehmet (p)
08/11/98	Samsunspor	H	0-1	
14/11/98	Karabükspor	A	2-1	Sérgio 2
21/11/98	Galatasaray	H	0-0	
28/11/98	Trabzonspor	A	1-2	Sefer
06/12/98	Çanakkale Dardanelspor	H	1-3	Sérgio
12/12/98	Besiktas	H	0-2	
20/12/98	Ankaragücü	A	0-1	
31/01/99	Antalyaspor	A	2-2	Timuçin, Strizu
07/02/99	Gaziantepspor	H	6-2	Mehmet Ali, Hüseyin, Strizu, Yusuf, Aygün, Timuçin
13/02/99	Altay	A	0-2	
21/02/99	Bursaspor	H	4-1	Murat, Aygün 2, Timuçin
26/02/99	Kocaelispor	A	1-0	Nikolovski
06/03/99	Istanbulspor	H	3-0	Timuçin, Strizu, Muhammet Ali
14/03/99	Erzurumspor	A	2-4	Mehmet Ali (p), Murat
20/03/99	Fenerbahçe	H	2-1	Yusuf, Strizu
04/04/99	Gençlerbirligi	A	0-1	
11/04/99	Adanaspor	H	0-0	
17/04/99	Samsunspor	A	2-2	Aygün, Mehmet Ali (p)
25/04/99	Karabükspor	H	4-0	Mehmet Ali (p), Strizu 2, Mehmet
30/04/99	Galatasaray	A	0-3	
09/05/99	Trabzonspor	H	1-1	Aygün
16/05/99	Çanakkale Dardanelspor	A	0-1	
23/05/99	Besiktas	A	0-3	
29/05/99	Ankaragücü	H	4-0	Nikolovski (p), Hüseyin 2, Murat

SAMSUNSPOR

CLUB DIRECTORY

Samsunspor Kulübü
Nuri Asar Tesisleri
Garajlar Karsisi
Samsun
tel - (362) 2383696
fax - (362) 2383788
Year of Formation - 1965
President - Ismail Uyanik
Secretary - Tarik Kaptan
Coach - Mehmet Ali Çinar; Metin Türel
(99/00 - Erdogan Arica)
Stadium - 19 Mayis (20,000)

APPEARANCES 98/99

	P	Ap	(s)	Gls
ALI Akdeniz	M	18	(8)	1
AZAD Akin	M	1		
Allium BOUKAR (CMR)	G	31		
CELIL Sagir	M	30		3
CENGIZ Alp	M	4	(1)	
CENK Isler	A	12	(1)	4
ERCAN Kologlu	D	23		1
ERMAN Güracar	D	18	(6)	1
GÖKSEL Gencer	G	2	(1)	
GÜNGÖR Öztürk	D	27	(2)	
HAKKI Hocaoglu	D	3	(1)	
ILHAN Mansiz	M	17	(10)	4
IMDAT Arslan	D	31	(1)	
ISMET Tasdemir	M	23	(6)	3
KÜRSAT Demir	G	1		
LEVENT Yilmaz	M	6	(15)	
MEHMET Nas	A	4	(7)	
MURAT	A		(1)	
Wilson ORUMA (NIG)	M	20	(1)	4
Andre OZZOY	M	1	(1)	
SABRI Sirinsoylu	D	8	(1)	
SERKAN Aykut	A	31		11
Daniel TIMOFTE (ROM)	M	9	(6)	1
TÜMER Metin	M	13	(7)	1
UGUR Dagdelen	A	14	(14)	3
VURAL Korkmaz	M	27		

LEAGUE RESULTS 1998/99

08/08/98	Kocaelispor	H	0-1	
16/08/98	Istanbulspor	A	1-2	Serkan
22/08/98	Erzurumspor	H	2-4	Ugur, Erman
29/08/98	Fenerbahçe	A	2-6	Timofte (p), Ilhan
12/09/98	Gençlerbirligi	H	2-4	Ugur, Serkan
20/09/98	Adanaspor	A	0-0	
26/09/98	Çanakkale Dardanelspor	A	0-0	
17/10/98	Karabükspor	H	2-1	Cenk (p), Oruma
24/10/98	Galatasaray	A	1-3	Cenk
30/10/98	Trabzonspor	H	2-1	Cenk 2
08/11/98	Sakaryaspor	A	1-0	Oruma
15/11/98	Besiktas	H	0-3	
22/11/98	Ankaragücü	A	4-3	Ilhan, Celil 2, Ali
29/11/98	Antalyaspor	H	0-1	
06/12/98	Gaziantepspor	A	1-1	Oruma
13/12/98	Altay	H	1-0	Serkan
18/12/98	Bursaspor	A	3-2	Ilhan, Serkan 2
30/01/99	Kocaelispor	A	0-1	
07/02/99	Istanbulspor	H	0-1	
13/02/99	Erzurumspor	A	0-1	
19/02/99	Fenerbahçe	H	1-1	Oruma (p)
28/02/99	Gençlerbirligi	A	0-3	
07/03/99	Adanaspor	H	2-0	Ismet (p), Ilhan
14/03/99	Çanakkale Dardanelspor	H	2-1	Serkan 2
20/03/99	Karabükspor	A	3-0	Serkan 2, Celil
03/04/99	Galatasaray	H	0-3	
11/04/99	Trabzonspor	A	1-3	Serkan
17/04/99	Sakaryaspor	H	2-2	Ercan, Ugur
23/04/99	Besiktas	A	0-0	
02/05/99	Ankaragücü	H	0-0	
07/05/99	Antalyaspor	A	2-1	Tümer, Serkan
16/05/99	Gaziantepspor	H	2-1	og (Cem), Ismet
23/05/99	Altay	A	0-2	
29/05/99	Bursaspor	H	1-1	Ismet (p)

TRABZONSPOR

CLUB DIRECTORY

Trabzonspor Kulübü
Mehmet Ali Yilmaz Tesisleri
Trabzon
tel - (462) 3266796
fax - (462) 3265767
Year of Formation - 1967
President - Mehmet Ali Yilmaz
Secretary - Hikmet Onur
Coach - Gordon Milne
(99/00 - Ahmet Suat Özyazici)
Stadium - Avni Aker (30,000)

MAJOR HONOURS
League Championship - (6)
1976, 1977, 1979, 1980, 1981, 1984.
Domestic Cup - (5)
1977, 1978, 1984, 1992, 1995.

APPEARANCES 98/99

	P	Ap	(s)	Gls
ABDULLAH Ercan	M	28	(2)	
Kevin CAMPBELL (ENG)	A	17	(1)	5
ÇETIN Güner	A	1	(2)	2
DILAVER Satilmis	M	3	(3)	
ERDAL Eraslan	M	3	(1)	
FATIII Tekke	A	15	(1)	4
FETI Okuroglu	D	6	(1)	1
HASAN Özer	A		(1)	
HÜSEYIN	D	1		
ISKENDER Eroglu	D	3		
Yuriy KALITVINTSEV (UKR)	M	12	(2)	1
MEHMET Ipek	M	17	(4)	1
MEHMET Zengin	M	24	(5)	5
METIN Aktas	G	4	(1)	
Petar MILOSEVSKI (MAC)	G	30		
MURAT Deniz	A	2	(2)	
OGÜN Temizkanoglu	D	22		5
OKAN Özke	D	21	(3)	
ORHAN Cikrikçi	M	13	(9)	1
OSMAN Özköylü	D	13	(1)	1
Karel RADA (CZE)	D	7		
RECEP Çetin	D	29		
SELAHATTIN Kinali	A	18	(6)	4
SELIM Özer	D	16		1
SEYIT CEM	A	1	(8)	
TANSEL	M	15	(1)	
ÜNAL Karaman	M	21	(1)	2
ÜNSAL	M	7	(10)	
Davor VUGRINEC (CRO)	A	25	(3)	12

LEAGUE RESULTS 1998/99

08/08/98	Gaziantepspor	H	0-1	
16/08/98	Altay	A	5-2	Vugrinec, Mehmet Zengin,
				Çetin 2, Ogün
22/08/98	Bursaspor	H	2-0	Ogün, Mehmet Zengin
30/08/98	Kocaelispor	A	1-1	Vugrinec
11/09/98	Istanbulspor	H	0-0	
20/09/98	Erzurumspor	A	2-2	Feti, Ogün
25/09/98	Fenerbahçe	H	1-0	Campbell
17/10/98	Gençlerbirligi	A	1-0	Vugrinec
23/10/98	Adanaspor	H	2-0	Vugrinec, Campbell
30/10/98	Samsunspor	A	1-2	Selahattin
07/11/98	Karabükspor	H	1-0	Mehmet Zengin
15/11/98	Galatasaray	A	5-3	Campbell 3, Selahattin, Orhan
21/11/98	Çanakkale Dardanelspor	A	3-2	Mehmet Zengin, Vugrinec 2 (1p)
28/11/98	Sakaryaspor	H	2-1	Mehmet Ipek, og (Timuçin)
06/12/98	Besiktas	A	0-2	
13/12/98	Ankaragücü	H	1-0	Vugrinec
19/12/98	Antalyaspor	A	1-0	og (Burhan)
31/01/99	Gaziantepspor	A	1-1	Fatih
07/02/99	Altay	H	0-3	
14/02/99	Bursaspor	A	1-0	Ünal
21/02/99	Kocaelispor	H	0-3	
27/02/99	Istanbulspor	A	0-0	
05/03/99	Erzurumspor	H	3-1	Vugrinec 3 (1p)
13/03/99	Fenerbahçe	A	0-1	
20/03/99	Gençlerbirligi	H	4-0	Ogün 2 (1p), Mehmet Zengin,
				Vugrinec
02/04/99	Adanaspor	A	2-0	Fatih 2
11/04/99	Samsunspor	H	3-1	Ünal, Selahattin, Vugrinec
15/04/99	Karabükspor	A	0-0	
23/04/99	Galatasaray	H	0-3	
02/05/99	Çanakkale Dardanelspor	H	2-1	Kalitvintsev, Selahattin
09/05/99	Sakaryaspor	A	1-1	og (Sinan)
16/05/99	Besiktas	H	1-2	Fatih
23/05/99	Ankaragücü	A	0-1	
30/05/99	Antalyaspor	H	2-3	Osman (p), Selim

PROMOTED CLUBS

SECOND DIVISION FINAL TABLE 98/99

PROMOTION GROUP

		Pd	W	D	L	F	A	Pt	GD
1	**Vanspor**	**18**	**9**	**5**	**4**	**32**	**15**	**32**	**+17**
2	**Denizlispor**	**18**	**9**	**5**	**4**	**40**	**30**	**32**	**+10**
3	**Göztepe**	**18**	**10**	**2**	**6**	**31**	**29**	**32**	**+2**
4	Kayserispor	18	9	4	5	40	28	31	+12
5	Çaykur Rizespor	18	8	5	5	27	24	29	+3
6	Elazigspor	18	7	6	5	29	27	27	+2
7	Istanbul Büyüksehirspor BLD	18	5	5	8	24	28	20	-4
8	Sariyer	18	4	6	8	32	36	18	-4
9	Aydinspor	18	4	2	12	21	40	14	-19
10	Sekerspor	18	3	4	11	25	44	13	-19

PROMOTION PLAY-OFFS

N.B. Teams 3-5 in Promotion Group join the five Second Division group winners after the second phase.

QUARTER-FINALS

Batman Petrolofisi 2, Marmarisspor 1
Göztepe 1, BSK Ankara 0
Yeni Yozgatspor 1, Kayserispor 0
Çaykur Rizespor 2, Mersin Idmanyurdu 0

SEMI-FINALS

Çaykur Rizespor 5, Yeni Yozgatspor 2
Göztepe 2, Batman Petrolofisi 1

FINAL

Göztepe 1, Çaykur Rizespor 0

CLUB DIRECTORY

Vanspor Kulübü
Iskele Caddesi
Çevik Kuvvet Arkasi
Van
tel - (432) 2231474
fax - (432) 2233495
Year of Formation - 1974
President - Feridun Irak
Secretary - Abdurrahman Çamas
Coach - Ridvan Dilmen (99/00 - Same Aybaba)
Stadium - Vali Mahmut Yilbas (10,000)

CLUB DIRECTORY

Denizlispor Kulübü
Lise Caddesi
Subay Gazinosu Karpisi
Denizli
tel - (258) 2620721
fax - (258) 2620721
Year of Formation - 1966
President - Ali Marim
Coach - Ersun Yanal
Stadium - Denizli Sehir (15,000)

CLUB DIRECTORY

Göztepe Kulübü
Ankara Asfalti Sirgeli Kavsagi No:3
Yeni Asir Gazetesi Bornova
Izmir
tel - (232) 4418814
fax - (232) 2477370
Year of Formation - 1925
President - Aydin Bilgin
Coach - Erdogan Arica; Oktay Çevik
(99/00 - Jozef Jarabinsky)
Stadium - Atatürk (80,000)

UKRAINE

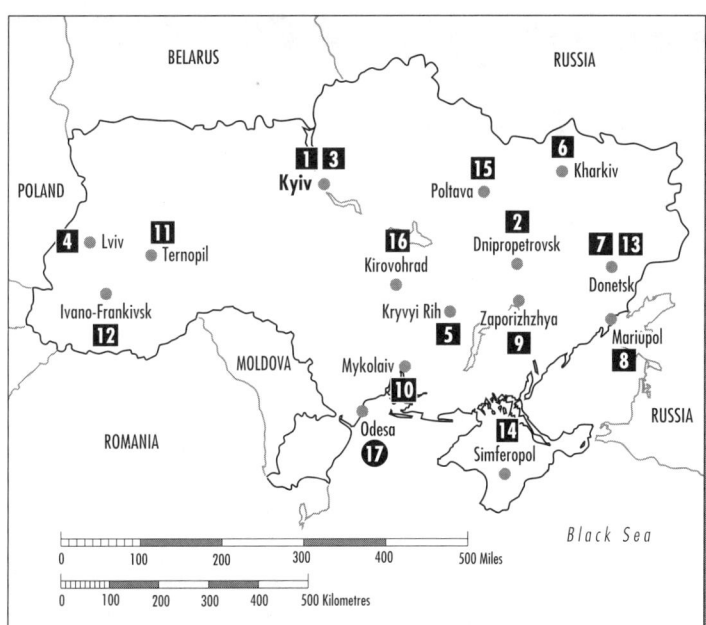

1	CSKA KYIV	1043
2	DNIPRO DNIPROPETROVSK	1044
3	DYNAMO KYIV	1045
4	KARPATY LVIV	1046
5	KRYVBAS KRYVYI RIH	1047
6	METALIST KHARKIV	1048
7	METALURG DONETSK	1049
8	METALURG MARIUPOL	1050
9	METALURG ZAPORIZHZHYA	1051

10	SK MYKOLAIV	1052
11	NYVA TERNOPIL	1053
12	PRYKARPATTYA IVANO-FRANKIVSK	1054
13	SHAKHTAR DONETSK	1055
14	TAVRIYA SIMFEROPOL	1056
15	VORSKLA POLTAVA	1057
16	ZIRKA KIROVOHRAD	1058
Promoted club		
17	CHORNOMORETS ODESA	1059

SUPERSTAR SHEVCHENKO OFF TO MILAN

Lobanovskyi's boys so close to Euro glory

FEDERATION DIRECTORY

Football Federation of Ukraine
vul. Ulyanovykh 1, 252 023 Kyiv

tel - (044) 2528474/2528457/ 2528700/2528935

fax - (044) 2528404/2529493

Year of Formation - 1991
President - Valeriy Pustovoitenko
Secretary - Anatoliy Popov

Stadium - National Sport Komplex Olimpiyskyi , Kyiv (83,160)

It goes almost without saying that Dynamo Kiev won the 1998/99 Ukrainian championship. It was the club's seventh straight title. For good measure they added the Ukrainian Cup to complete their fourth 'double' over the same period.

But, for Kiev, hogging the domestic silverware amounts to a mere fulfilment of duty. Were the title to go anywhere else, their fans would be aghast. But when they do complete their annual triumph, there is no great sense of achievement. In short, they are on a hiding to nothing.

What really counts for Dynamo is Europe. It is the only arena where they can match themselves against genuine opposition and accurately measure their progress. In 1998/99 the readings were extremely positive as Valeriy Lobanovskyi and his troops went all the way to the Champions' Cup semi-finals - and almost to the brink of the final itself.

The team's fans were kept enthralled for nine long months as Kiev entered Europe's premier club competition at the first qualifying stage in July and exited in April the following year, having played a grand total of 14 matches - more than any other club in the three major European competitions during the 98/99 season.

Kiev had good fortune in the early stages of their quest for glory, reaching the group phase only after a late own-goal and a penalty shoot-out in Prague. They also lost their first group game, away to Panathinaikos, and were still seeking their first victory three games in. But when push came to shove they responded, beating Arsenal and Panathinaikos at home and then cruising to a hugely

LEAGUE CHAMPIONSHIP RESULTS 98/99

		1	2	3	4	5	6	7	8	9	10	11	12	13	14	15	16
1	CSKA Kyiv		1-0	0-4	3-3	1-2	2-1	2-1	1-1	1-0	2-0	0-0	1-2	0-1	3-0	2-1	0-0
2	Dnipro Dnipropetrovsk	0-1		0-1	0-2	2-1	0-0	5-1	1-0	1-4	2-1	4-0	0-0	1-2	1-0	2-0	1-1
3	Dynamo Kyiv	2-0	2-3		0-0	1-0	1-0	3-0	2-0	6-2	2-1	1-0	7-0	2-1	0-0	4-0	1-0
4	Karpaty Lviv	3-3	4-1	2-1		2-1	0-1	2-0	3-1	1-1	5-1	1-0	3-0	1-0	2-1	2-1	2-1
5	Kryvbas Kryvyi Rih	0-0	2-1	0-0	0-0		1-0	2-0	3-1	4-0	0-0	2-1	2-0	1-0	1-1	3-1	1-0
6	Metalist Kharkiv	1-0	2-0	1-6	3-1	0-0		1-0	0-1	1-0	0-0	2-1	1-0	1-1	1-0	2-4	3-0
7	Metalurg Donetsk	2-2	2-0	1-4	4-3	0-2	0-0		1-1	0-2	0-0	2-1	1-0	0-4	2-0	0-0	1-0
8	Metalurg Mariupol	1-1	0-1	1-2	4-2	0-0	2-0	0-0		4-2	3-0	1-0	2-1	0-1	2-0	1-0	0-0
9	Metalurg Zaporizhzhya	1-0	2-2	1-3	3-1	1-1	3-2	0-0	3-0		4-1	2-1	1-1	2-3	3-0	0-1	1-0
10	SK Mykolaiv	2-3	2-0	0-4	0-3	0-4	0-2	0-1	1-2	0-4		0-1	1-1	0-3	1-2	1-0	2-2
11	Nyva Ternopil	1-2	0-0	1-5	0-0	1-2	2-0	3-2	1-0	1-0	3-1		3-1	0-3	0-0	2-2	3-2
12	Prykarpattya Ivano-Frankivsk	2-4	3-0	0-1	0-2	2-2	1-2	2-1	0-3	0-0	2-1	1-1		1-3	0-2	1-0	1-0
13	Shakhtar Donetsk	1-0	6-0	0-0	1-1	1-1	3-1	4-2	1-0	2-1	7-0	1-1	6-1		2-0	7-3	1-2
14	Tavriya Simferopol	1-1	3-0	3-3	1-1	0-2	0-1	3-2	0-2	2-3	2-0	1-0	3-0	2-1		2-0	1-0
15	Vorskla Poltava	1-0	1-0	0-2	0-0	0-0	1-2	2-0	0-1	3-0	2-1	2-1	4-0	1-2	2-2		4-2
16	Zirka Kirovohrad	1-1	2-0	0-5	2-2	2-3	2-0	3-1	0-1	1-0	1-1	1-0	2-1	0-2	3-1	1-0	

LEAGUE CHAMPIONSHIP FINAL TABLE 98/99

				Home				Away					Total						
		P	W	D	L	F	A	W	D	L	F	A	W	D	L	F	A	P	GD
1	Dynamo Kyiv	30	12	2	1	34	7	11	3	1	41	10	23	5	2	75	17	74	+58
2	Shakhtar Donetsk	30	10	4	1	43	13	10	1	4	27	12	20	5	5	70	25	65	+45
3	Kryvbas Kryvyi Rih	30	10	5	0	22	5	6	6	3	21	13	16	11	3	43	18	59	+25
4	Karpaty Lviv	30	12	2	1	33	13	3	8	4	21	21	15	10	5	54	34	55	+20
5	Metalurg Mariupol	30	8	4	3	21	10	6	2	7	14	17	14	6	10	35	27	48	+8
6	Metalist Kharkiv	30	9	3	3	19	14	5	2	8	12	18	14	5	11	31	32	47	-1
7	CSKA Kyiv	30	7	4	4	19	16	4	6	5	18	19	11	10	9	37	35	43	+2
8	Metalurg Zaporizhzhya	30	8	4	3	27	16	4	2	9	19	27	12	6	12	46	43	42	+3
9	Tavriya Simferopol	30	8	3	4	24	16	2	4	9	9	23	10	7	13	33	39	37	-6
10	Vorskla Poltava	30	8	3	4	23	13	2	2	11	13	30	10	5	15	36	43	35	-7
11	Zirka Kirovohrad	30	8	3	4	21	18	1	4	10	10	22	9	7	14	31	40	34	-9
12	Dnipro Dnipropetrovsk	30	7	3	5	20	14	2	2	11	8	32	9	5	16	28	46	32	-18
13	Nyva Ternopil	30	7	4	4	21	20	1	3	11	8	21	8	7	15	29	41	31	-12
14	Metalurg Donetsk	30	6	5	4	16	19	1	2	12	11	32	7	7	16	27	51	28	-24
15	Prykarpattya Ivano-Frankivsk	30	5	3	7	16	22	1	3	11	8	37	6	6	18	24	59	24	-35
16	SK Mykolaiv	30	2	2	11	10	32	0	4	11	8	35	2	6	22	18	67	12	-49

impressive 3-1 victory away to Lens in the match that settled the issue of group leadership.

The quarter-finals offered them holders Real Madrid. A year earlier Kiev had been humbled at the same stage by Juventus, but Lobanovskyi improved the team's preparation over the winter months and when the time of reckoning arrived, Kiev were ready, willing and able, especially star striker Andriy Shevchenko, who boosted his already awesome reputation by scoring all three goals as the Ukrainians power-blasted their way into the last four.

Against Bayern Munich, in the home leg, Dynamo played probably their finest football of the tournament. They were leading deservedly 3-1 midway through the second half when midfielder Vitaliy Kosovskyi missed a marvellous chance to score his second goal of the evening and put the tie beyond the Germans. After that Kiev fatally sat back, lost concentration and Bayern came back to draw 3-3. The initiative had passed and a single goal from Mario Basler in Munich was sufficient to send Kiev spinning out of a competition they might easily have won.

Still, there was no shame in going out at the semi-final stage. For the second

season in a row the standard-bearers of Ukrainian football had done their country proud, and players such as Shevchenko, Kosovskyi, Serhiy Rebrov, Oleh Luzhnyi and Vladyslav Vashchuk had proved themselves to be footballers of the highest calibre, winning legions of new admirers wherever they played.

After their European curtain call Dynamo had to attend to the annual ritual of sewing up the Ukrainian title in order to put themselves in the shake-up for the following

Real Madrid's Fernando Morientes slides in to dispossess Vitaliy Kosovskyi of Dynamo Kiev during the Champions' League quarter-final first leg in Madrid, which ended in a 1-1 draw.

DOMESTIC CUP 98/99

FOURTH ROUND
FC Lviv v Metalist Khrakiv 2-1; w/o
(Metalist Kharkiv w/o)
Zirka Kirovohrad v Kremin Kremenchuk 5-1; 3-0
(Zirka Kirovohrad 8-1)
CSKA Kyiv v Volyn Lutsk 0-0; 2-2
(2-2; CSKA Kyiv on away goals)
FC Cherkasy v Tavriya Simferopol 1-1; 2-3
(Tavriya Simferopol 4-3)
Metalurg Mariupol v Stal Alchevsk 2-0; 3-3
(Metalurg Mariupol 5-3)
Desna Chernihiv v Prykarpattya Ivano-Frankivsk 1-1; 0-1
(Prykarpattya Ivano-Frankivsk 2-1)
Metalurg Nikopol v SK Mykolaiv 1-1; 1-2
(SK Mykolaiv 3-2)
Metalurg Zaporizhzhya v SK Odesa 3-2; 1-3
(SK Odesa 5-4)

1/8 FINALS
Karpaty Lviv v Metalurg Mariupol 2-0; 2-3
(Karpaty Lviv 4-3)
Shakhtar Donetsk v Prykarpattya Ivano-Frankivsk 4-0; 3-4
(Shakhtar Donetsk 7-4)
SK Odesa v Dynamo Kyiv 2-4; 0-4
(Dynamo Kyiv 8-2)
Metalurg Donetsk v Metalist Kharkiv 0-1; 2-3
(Metalist Kharkiv 4-2)
Nyva Ternopil v Tavriya Simferopol 0-2; 0-2
(Tavriya Simferopol 4-0)

CSKA Kyiv v Vorskla Poltava 0-0; 0-1
(Vorskla Poltava 1-0)
SK Mykolaiv v Kryvbas Kryvyi Rih 1-2; 0-3
(Kryvbas Kryvyi Rih 5-1)
Zirka Kirovohrad v Dnipro Dnipropetrovsk 0-0; 1-0
(Zirka Kirovohrad 1-0)

QUARTER-FINALS
Metalist Kharkiv 1 (Pets 41),
Dynamo Kyiv 2 (Kosovskyi 16, Gusin 65)
Dynamo Kyiv 3 (Rebrov 64, 88, Pets 83og),
Metalist Kharkiv 0
(Dynamo Kyiv 5-1)

Shakhtar Donetsk 2 (Matveyev 75, 88p),
Kryvbas Kryvyi Rih 1 (Rymshin 5)
Kryvbas Kryvyi Rih 0, Shakhtar Donetsk 0
(Shakhtar Donetsk 2-1)

Vorskla Poltava 2 (Melashchenko 53, 82),
Karpaty Lviv 3 (Hetsko 22, 50, Mizin 85)
Karpaty Lviv 3 (Palyanytsya 22, 37, Hetsko 77),
Vorskla Poltava 0
(Karpaty Lviv 6-2)

Tavriya Simferopol 2 (Osipov 35, 79),
Zirka Kirovohrad 1 (Kouba 82)
Zirka Kirovohrad 1 (Martynov 35),
Tavriya Simferopol 0
(2-2; Zirka Kirovohrad on away goal)

SEMI-FINALS
Zirka Kirovohrad 1 (Gusev 57), Dynamo Kyiv 5
(Rebrov 23, 40, Shevchenko 26, Khatskevich 67, 86)
Dynamo Kiev 1 (Kormiltsev 86), Zirka Kirovohrad 0
(Dynamo Kyiv 6-1)

Karpaty Lviv 1 (Palyanytsya 65p), Shakhtar Donetsk 0
Shakhtar Donetsk 2 (Matveyev 54, 101p),
Karpaty Lviv 1 (Mizin 111) (aet)
(2-2; Karpaty Lviv on away goal)

FINAL
30/05/99, Kiev
DYNAMO KYIV 3 Shevchenko (18, 67), Belkevich (19)
KARPATY LVIV 0
referee - Melnychuk
DYNAMO KYIV - Shovkovskyi; Luzhnyi, Khatskevich
(Kormiltsev 80), Holovko, Vashchuk, Dmitrulin,
Gerasimenko, Belkevich, Gusin, Shevchenko, Rebrov
(Serebryannikov 78).
KARPATY LVIV - Strontsitskyi; Yevtushok, Chyzhevskyi
(Vilchynskyi 20), Mizin, Benio, Zakotyuk, Vovchuk
(Lutsyshyn 46), Nazarov (Kovalets 61), Palyanytsya,
Hetsko, Tolochko.

---

season's Champions' League. They still had 11 games (out of 30) left to play, but by winning nine of the first ten and drawing the other, away to their only challengers Shakhtar Donetsk, they made a thoroughly convincing job of re-affirming their status as the country's number one club. A 3-0 victory over Karpaty Lviv in the Cup final, including two goals from Shevchenko on his farewell appearance before moving to Italian champions Milan, provided some particularly sweet icing on the cake.

While it would be incorrect to suggest that Dynamo

TOP SCORERS

18 Andriy SHEVCHENKO (Dynamo Kyiv)
16 Ivan HETSKO (Karpaty Lviv)
   Olexandr PALYANYTSYA (Karpaty Lviv)
13 Valentyn POLTAVETS
   (Metalurg Zaporizhzhya)
11 Olexiy OSIPOV (Tavriya Simferopol)
   Andriy VOROBEI (Shakhtar Donetsk)
10 Avtandil KAPANADZE (Nyva Ternopil)
   Alexandr KHATSKEVICH (Dynamo Kyiv)
9 Serhiy REBROV (Dynamo Kyiv)
   Olexandr GAIDASH (Tavriya Simferopol)
   Ihor KOSTYUK (Vorskla Poltava)
   Ihor KISLOV (Zirka Kirovohrad)

NATIONAL TEAM RESULTS 98/99

15/07/98	Poland	H	Kiev	1-2	Shevchenko (87)
19/08/98	Georgia	H	Kiev	4-0	Rebrov (1, 42), Skachenko (57), Kovalev (75)
05/09/98	Russia (ECQ)	H	Kiev	3-2	Popov (14), Skachenko (25), Rebrov (74p)
10/10/98	Andorra (ECQ)	A	Andorra La Vella	2-0	Kosovskyi (31), Rebrov (44)
14/10/98	Armenia (ECQ)	H	Kiev	2-0	Skachenko (32), Gusin (80)
20/03/99	Georgia	A	Tbilisi	1-0	Konovalov (78)
27/03/99	France (ECQ)	A	Saint-Denis	0-0	
31/03/99	Iceland (ECQ)	H	Kiev	1-1	Vashchuk (59)
05/06/99	Andorra (ECQ)	H	Kiev	4-0	Popov (36), Rebrov (41), Dmitrulin (56), Gusin (90)
09/06/99	Armenia (ECQ)	A	Yerevan	0-0	

NATIONAL TEAM APPEARANCES 98/99

Coach - Jozsef SZABO	POL	GEO	RUS	AND	ARM	GEO	FRA	ISL	AND	ARM	Cps	Gls
Olexandr SHOVKOVSKYI (02/01/75) - Dynamo Kyiv	G	G46	G	G	G	s46	G	G			19	-
Mykhailo STAROSTYAK (13/10/73) - Shakhtar Donetsk	D	s70									5	-
Volodymyr YEZERSKYI (15/11/76) - Karpaty Lviv	D46										1	-
Olexandr CHYZHEVSKYI (27/05/71) - Karpaty Lviv	D46										1	-
Volodymyr MYKYTYN (28/04/70) - Karpaty Lviv/Shakhtar Donetsk	M46	M	M	M46		M	M	M	M69	M	9	-
Serhiy POPOV (22/04/71) - Shakhtar Donetsk	M46		M	M	M75	M	M	M76	M	M37	26	4
Yuriy KALITVINTSEV (05/05/68) - Dynamo Kyiv/Trabzonspor (TUR)	M77	M46	s46			M46		s76			22	1
Hennadiy ZUBOV (12/09/77) - Shakhtar Donetsk	M46										7	-
Valeriy KRIVENTSOV (30/07/73) - Shakhtar Donetsk	M46		s87	s53	s78						15	-
Eduard TSYKHMEISTRUK (24/06/73) - CSKA Kyiv	M46					s75			M	M	4	-
Serhiy SKACHENKO (18/11/72) - Torpedo Moskva (RUS)	A46	s46	A46		A59	A80	A68	A46	s74	s71	13	3
Yuriy DMITRULIN (10/02/75) - Dynamo Kyiv	s46		D		D				D80	D	15	1
Olexandr HOLOVKO (06/01/72) - Dynamo Kyiv	s46	D	D	D	D	D46	D	D	D	D	28	-
Andriy GUSIN (11/12/72) - Dynamo Kyiv	s46	M	M	M	M	s46	M85	M	M	M	18	4
Vladyslav VASHCHUK (02/01/75) - Dynamo Kyiv	s46	D	D	D	D	s46	D	D	D	D	20	1
Andriy SHEVCHENKO (29/09/76) - Dynamo Kyiv	s46	A	A	A69	A78		A	A	A74	A82	22	6
Vitaliy KOSOVSKYI (11/08/73) - Dynamo Kyiv	s46	M41		M	M		s54	M			19	2
Dmytro MYKHAILENKO (13/07/73) - Dynamo Kyiv	s46		s69								21	2
Serhiy REBROV (03/06/74) - Dynamo Kyiv	s46	A78	A	A	A		A	A	A	A71	28	9
Oleh VENHLYNSKYI (21/03/78) - Dynamo Kyiv	s77										1	-
Oleh LUZHNYI (06/08/68) - Dynamo Kyiv		D70		D	D		D	D	D	D	29	-
Olexandr YEVTUSHOK (11/01/70) - Karpaty Lviv		D46									7	-
Roman MAXYMYUK (14/06/74) - Zenit Sankt-Peterburg (RUS)		s41						s80			2	-
Valeriy VOROBIOV (14/01/70) - Torpedo Moskva (RUS)		s46				G46			G	G	5	-
Serhiy KOVALEV (22/11/71) - Shakhtar Donetsk		s46	M87	s46	s59	M	M54				6	1
Serhiy KONOVALOV (01/03/72) - Dynamo Kyiv		s78				s46				s37	15	3
Yuriy MAXIMOV (08/12/68) - SV Werder Bremen (GER)			M53	s75			s68	s46			19	5
Olexandr KIRYUKHIN (01/10/74) - Dynamo Kyiv						D					1	-
Olexandr KOVAL (30/06/74) - Shakhtar Donetsk						D					4	-
Vasyl KARDASH (14/01/73) - Dynamo Kyiv						M46				s82	8	-
Serhiy NAHORNYAK (05/09/71) - Shakhtar Donetsk						M75					11	-
Serhiy MIZIN (25/09/72) - Karpaty Lviv						s80			s69		4	-
Viktor SKRYPNYK (19/11/69) - SV Werder Bremen (GER)							s85				16	2

★ SUPERSTAR PROFILE
ANDRIY SHEVCHENKO

For the second season running Andriy Shevchenko was the star of the UEFA Champions' League. He had battered Barcelona into submission in 1997/98. Now it was the turn of Real Madrid (among others) to feel the full force of the young striker's devastating talent. It is no exaggeration to claim that the 23-year-old sharpshooter is among the top three strikers in the world. That is evidently the belief of Italian champions Milan, who have invested heavily in the young Ukrainian, bringing him to the San Siro during the summer at a cost of £15.7m and fastening him to a lucrative five-year contract which, if seen through to its conclusion, will see Shevchenko spend the peak years of his career in red and black stripes. Dynamo Kiev were evidently sorry to see him go, but he certainly left them with a clutch of abiding memories, top-scoring

not only in the Champions' League but also, for the first time, in the Ukrainian championship (with 18 goals). He also grabbed a brace in the Cup final for the second year in a row. With his extraordinary skill, pace and eye for a goal, he surely cannot fail. Or can he? On the very day of his signature for Milan - July 1, 1999 - the Italian press brashly predicted that he would become the 'new Van Basten'. Praise or pressure? In Italy, Shevchenko will have to handle both with equal magnanimity. It goes with the territory.

YURIY DMITRULIN

It was with great regret that Dynamo Kiev left-back Yuriy Dmitrulin missed his team's Champions' Cup quarter-final and semi-final matches against Real Madrid and Bayern Munich. He had played superbly in all of the group games and before that had struck the decisive penalty-kick that took Dynamo into the Champions' League at the expense of Sparta Prague. But injury struck at just the wrong time for both him and his club. Dynamo certainly missed his steely competitiveness in the latter stages of the home game with Bayern. He has long been considered one of the most consistent and intelligent players both for Dynamo and the Ukrainian national team, and when he played in 1998/99, he seemed to raise his game to a new level, defending and attacking down the left flank like a man possessed.

IVAN HETSKO

One of Ukraine's more widely-travelled footballers, 31-year-old striker Ivan Hetsko had a season to remember in 1998/99, reviving former glories with 16 league goals for Karpaty Lviv, the club he also helped into the Ukrainian Cup final. Hetsko's main claim to fame previously had been as the first man to score a goal for the national team of Ukraine - a feat he achieved against Hungary in April 1992. With the likes of Shevchenko, Rebrov and Skachenko around, his international abitions now appear to be over, but he remains a fine goal-scorer, a classic centre-forward of the old school, one who can find the net from any distance, with both head and feet. His speciality is a whiplash shooting technique, reminiscent, so his fans claim, of the great Eusébio.

EUROPEAN CUPS 98/99

CHAMPIONS' CUP
● DYNAMO KYIV
Preliminary round BARRY TOWN (WAL)
H 8-0 Rebrov (9, 16, 37, 82), Shevchenko (34, 60), Gerasimenko (48),
Belkevich (65)
Shovkovskyi; Khatskevich, Kaladze, Holovko, Vashchuk, Dmitrulin,
Gusin (Belkevich 55), Kalitvintsev (Gerasimenko 46), Kosovskyi
(Venhlynskyi 68), Shevchenko, Rebrov.
A 2-1 Mykhailenko (11), Venhlynskyi (50)
Kernozenko; Luzhnyi, Fedorov, Kaladze, Vashchuk, Khatskevich,
Mykhailenko, Belkevich (Kosovskyi 75), Konovalov (Rebrov 46),
Shevchenko (Gerasimenko 71), Venhlynskyi.

Qualifying round SPARTA PRAHA (CZE)
H 0-1
Shovkovskyi; Luzhnyi, Kaladze (Belkevich 78), Holovko, Vashchuk, Gusin,
Khatskevich, Kalitvintsev (Gerasimenko 46), Kosovskyi (Konovalov 56),
Shevchenko, Rebrov.
A 1-0 Votava (89og)
(aet; 1-3 on pens.)
Shovkovskyi; Luzhnyi, Gerasimenko (Makovskiy V. 84), Holovko,
Vashchuk (Konovalov 67), Dmitrulin, Kaladze, Gusin, Kosovskyi
(Belkevich 70), Shevchenko, Rebrov.

Champions' League
1st match PANATHINAIKOS (GRE)
A 1-2 Rebrov (31)
Shovkovskyi; Luzhnyi, Gerasimenko (Kalitvintsev 77), Holovko, Vashchuk,
Dmitrulin, Kaladze, Gusin, Belkevich (Konovalov 74), Shevchenko, Rebrov.

2nd match RC LENS (FRA)
H 1-1 Shevchenko (61)
Shovkovskyi; Luzhnyi, Gerasimenko (Kalitvintsev 78), Holovko, Vashchuk,
Dmitrulin (Kiryukhin 84), Kaladze, Gusin, Kosovskyi, Shevchenko, Rebrov.

3rd match ARSENAL (ENG)
A 1-1 Rebrov (90)
Shovkovskyi; Luzhnyi, Kaladze, Holovko, Vashchuk, Dmitrulin,
Gusin (Kardash 82), Belkevich, Kosovskyi, Shevchenko, Rebrov.

4th match ARSENAL (ENG)
H 3-1 Rebrov (27p), Holovko (62), Shevchenko (72)
Shovkovskyi; Luzhnyi, Kardash, Holovko, Vashchuk, Dmitrulin, Gusin,
Belkevich (Kalitvintsev 90), Kosovskyi, Shevchenko, Rebrov.

5th match PANATHINAIKOS (GRE)
H 2-1 Rebrov (72), Basinas (80og)
Shovkovskyi; Luzhnyi, Fedorov, Holovko, Khatskevich, Dmitrulin, Gusin,
Kardash (Mykhailenko 88), Kosovskyi (Belkevich 46), Shevchenko,
Rebrov.

6th match RC LENS (FRA)
A 3-1 Kaladze (60), Vashchuk (76), Shevchenko (85)
Shovkovskyi; Luzhnyi, Khatskevich, Holovko, Vashchuk, Dmitrulin
(Kosovskyi 46), Kaladze (Kiryukhin 67), Gusin, Kardash (Belkevich 51),
Shevchenko, Rebrov.

Quarter-final REAL MADRID (ESP)
A 1-1 Shevchenko (54)
Shovkovskyi; Luzhnyi (Kiryukhin 89), Khatskevich, Holovko, Vashchuk,
Gusin, Kaladze, Belkevich (Kardash 80), Kosovskyi (Kormiltsev 83),
Shevchenko, Rebrov.

H 2-0 Shevchenko (63, 80)
Shovkovskyi; Luzhnyi, Khatskevich, Holovko, Vashchuk, Gusin, Kaladze,
Kardash (Belkevich 46), Shevchenko, Rebrov, Kosovskyi (Yashkin 87).

Semi-final FC BAYERN MÜNCHEN (GER)
H 3-3 Shevchenko (15, 43), Kosovskyi (49)
Shovkovskyi; Luzhnyi, Khatskevich (Kiryukhin 80), Holovko, Vashchuk,
Gusin, Kaladze, Belkevich, Kosovskyi, Shevchenko, Rebrov.
A 0-1
Shovkovskyi; Luzhnyi, Khatskevich, Holovko, Vashchuk, Gusin
(Kardash 82), Kaladze, Belkevich, Kosovskyi, Shevchenko, Rebrov.

CUP WINNERS' CUP
● CSKA KYIV
Qualifying round CORK CITY (IRL)
A 1-2 Revut (90)
Reva; Levchenko, Revut, Bezhenar, Semchuk, Daraselia (Korenev 57),
Oliynyk, Shkapenko, Zakarlyuka (Olexiyenko 33), Leonenko
(Karyaka 74), Tsykhmeistruk.
H 2-0 Tsykhmeistruk (41), Leonenko (56)
Reva; Gregul, Revut, Bezhenar, Semchuk, Ulyanytskyi, Karyaka
(Korenev 33), Shkapenko, Zakarlyuka, Leonenko (Daraselia 64),
Tsykhmeistruk.

1st round LOKOMOTIV MOSKVA (RUS)
H 0-2
Reva; Levchenko, Balytskyi, Bezhenar, Gregul, Ulyanytskyi, Oliynuk
(Novokhatskyi 78), Kostyshyn (Olexiyenko 25), Zakarlyuka
(Daraselia 53), Leonenko, Tsykhmeistruk.
A 1-3 Bezhenar (13)
Reva; Levchenko, Balytskyi, Bezhenar, Gregul, Novokhatskyi (Revut 46),
Karyaka (Daraselia 75), Shkapenko, Zakarlyuka, Leonenko (Korneev 46),
Tsykhmeistruk.

UEFA CUP
● SHAKHTAR DONETSK
Preliminary round BIRKIRKARA (MLT)
H 2-1 Seleznev (62), Kriventsov (69p)
Nikitin; Leonov, Starostyak, Kotov (Popov 40), Yaksmanytskyi
(Seleznev 60), Potskhveria, Orbu, Kovalev, Zubov, Kriventsov, Shtolcers.
A 4-0 Seleznev (39), Kriventsov (49p), Kovalev (82, 90)
Nikitin; Leonov, Starostyak, Kotov, Yaksmanytskyi (Yaskovich 76),
Seleznev (Tymoshchuk 78), Orbu, Kovalev, Zubov (Potskhveria 65),
Kriventsov, Vorobei.

Qualifying round FC ZÜRICH (SUI)
A 0-4
Nikitin; Kovalenko (Yaskovich 54), Starostyak, Koval, Matveyev, Seleznev
(Shelayev 58), Orbu, Kovalev, Zubov (Potskhveria 62), Yaksmarytskyi,
Vorobei.
H 3-2 Orbu (24, 69), Shtolcers (90)
Nikitin; Leonov, Starostyak, Kotov, Kovalenko, Seleznev, Orbu,
Tymoshchuk, Zubov (Shtolcers 46), Yaksmarytskyi (Popov 75), Vorobei
(Shelayev 75).

Kiev are the only footballing institution of any stature in Ukraine, it is certainly true that they live beyond the means of any other club in the country. Their training base in Pushcha Vodytsya is one of the finest in the world, their stadium is big and beautiful, and they possess all the other trappings associated with the mega-clubs of Western Europe - the luxury Mercedes bus, the movie-star security, the souvenir outlets, the wide network of official fan-clubs etc. etc. Plus, of course, they demand and obtain the best young players in the country and have even ventured in recent seasons into the business of importing talent from abroad, albeit - for now - from the restricted catchment zone of the former USSR.

Kiev's pearly kingdom, however, is not ever-glistening. As with every big club, resentment resides in the followers of other teams, and it is not driven purely by jealousy. In Ukraine it is generally understood that Dynamo are 'protected' by the state. That can be interpreted in different ways, but there have been many incidences in recent years when the country's biggest club has seemed to be favoured by referees.

Not that they need the assistance. In 1998/99 only Shakhtar gave Kiev a run for their money. The club from Donetsk actually led the way for a significant portion of the autumn campaign but they were not helped when coach Valeriy Yaremchenko had to step down through ill health in the early spring. His replacement, recently sacked Russian national team coach Anatoliy Byshovets, kept things ticking over, but even with the mid-season additions of Ukrainian internationals Volodymyr Mykytyn and Serhiy Nahornyak, Shakhtar found the going too tough as they sought to keep pace with the perennial champions. Their failure to win the home fixture against Kiev four rounds from the end ensured a premature conclusion to the title race.

Third place went, rather surprisingly, to Kryvbas Kryvyi Rih, who managed to secure a berth in the UEFA Cup alongside Shakhtar and defeated Cup finalists Karpaty. The latter also finished fourth in the league thanks largely to their excellent forward partnership of Ivan Hetsko and Olexandr Palyanytsya, who scored 16 goals each to finish joint-second behind Shevchenko in the top-scorer charts.

Karpaty's stadium was one of many in the country in desperate need of a facelift. Others, notably in Kirovohrad, Ternopil and Zaporizhzhya, all looked as if they had been hit by a bomb, but the finance was not forthcoming for the owners to do anything about it. With average First Division crowds in Ukraine of 7,470, football is not the money-churning exercise that it is in other countries. Indeed, it was almost a relief for SK Mykolaiv to be relegated, so desperate was their financial plight.

The promotion issue was also coloured by money. Dynamo Kiev's reserve team actually won the Second Division, but clearly they could not be promoted, so the two First Division places went to second-placed Chornomorets Odesa (back after just one year away) and Torpedo Zaporizhzhya. Torpedo, however, pleaded poverty and refused to accept their promotion. As a result, the league organisers ordered a play-off between fourth-placed FC Cherkasy and the team that finished 15th in the First Division, Prykarpattya Ivano-Frankivsk - which the latter won 3-1 to retain their top-flight status.

The Ukrainian national team's bid to reach their first major competition began well when they opened their Euro 2000 qualifying campaign with a hat-trick of victories, the most important of them all being the first, when they came from behind to beat arch-rivals Russia 3-2 in Kiev. A 0-0 draw in the Stade de France against the world champions offered further encouragement, but it was then that things began to slip.

Four days after the trip to Paris they were held 1-1 at home by Iceland. And if that concession of two 'easy' points was not punishing enough, they went and did it again at the end of the season, drawing 0-0 in Armenia, to leave themselves undefeated and on top of the Group Four table but extremely vulnerable to both France and Russia with three tough matches still to play.

INTERNATIONAL HONOURS

European Club Competitions

Cup-winners' Cup	Dynamo Kyiv (1975, 1986)
Super Cup	Dynamo Kyiv (1975)

CSKA KYIV

CLUB DIRECTORY

CSKA Kyiv
Av. Povitryanoflotskyi 10
252049 Kyiv
tel - (044) 2464869/2454319/2253262
fax - (044) 2454337
Year of Formation - 1996
President - Viktor Topolov
Secretary - Anatoliy Linnyk
Coach - Volodymyr Bessonov
Stadium - CSK ZSU (12,000)

APPEARANCES 98/99

	P	Ap	(s)	Gls
Roman BAIRASHEVSKYI	G	1		
Anatoliy BALYTSKYI	D	14		1
Vitaliy BALYTSKYI	D	21	(5)	2
Serhiy BEZHENAR	D	23		1
Pavlo BLAZHAYEV	G	2		
Vitaliy DARASELIA (GEO)	M	1	(9)	1
Olexiy GORODOV	M	3	(2)	1
Valentyn GREGUL	D	12		
Ihor HOHIL	M	1	(2)	
Serhiy ILCHENKO	D	1		
Andriy KARYAKA	M	7	(14)	1
Dmytro KORENEV	M	3	(16)	
Ruslan KOSTYSHYN	A	15	(2)	
Yakiv KRIPAK	A	12		5
Viktor LEONENKO	A	12		5
Vitaliy LEVCHENKO (TAD)	D	20	(3)	
Ivan MALYMON	A		(1)	
Viktor MOROZ	M	4	(5)	
Vasyl NOVOKHATSKYI	A	1	(2)	
Olexandr OLEXIYENKO	A	9	(7)	2
Olexiy OLIYNYK	M	19	(5)	4
Oleh POLYARUSH	M		(1)	
Vitaliy REVA	G	27		
Serhiy REVUT	D	24	(1)	
Dmytro SEMCHUK	D	15	(1)	
Pavlo SHKAPENKO	M	14		2
Eduard TSYKHMEISTRUK	M	28		4
Viktor ULYANYTSKYI	D	15	(4)	1
Serhiy ZAKARLYUKA	M	26	(2)	7

LEAGUE RESULTS 1998/99

07/07/98	Metalurg Zaporizhzhya	A	0-1	
11/07/98	Karpaty Lviv	H	3-3	Leonenko 2, Shkapenko
18/07/98	Prykarpattya Ivano-Frankivsk	A	4-2	Shkapenko, Olexiyenko 2, Leonenko
26/07/98	Metalist Kharkiv	H	2-1	Daraselia, Tsykhmeistruk
02/08/98	Kryvbas Kryvyi Rih	A	0-0	
08/08/98	Nyva Ternopil	H	0-0	
17/08/98	Metalurg Donetsk	A	2-2	Ulyanytskyi, Zakarlyuka
31/08/98	Tavriya Simferopol	A	1-1	Leonenko
12/09/98	Dnipro Dnipropetrovsk	H	1-0	Leonenko
21/09/98	SK Mykolaiv	A	3-2	Tsykhmeistruk 2, Balytskyi A.
26/09/98	Zirka Kirovohrad	H	0-0	
05/10/98	Metalurg Mariupol	A	1-1	Karyaka
20/10/98	Shakhtar Donetsk	H	0-1	
26/10/98	Vorskla Poltava	H	2-1	Zakarlyuka, Gorodov
30/10/98	Dynamo Kyiv	A	0-2	
13/03/99	Vorskla Poltava	A	0-1	
03/04/99	Zirka Kirovohrad	A	1-1	Zakarlyuka
10/04/99	SK Mykolaiv	H	2-0	Balytskyi V., Kripak
17/04/99	Dnipro Dnipropetrovsk	A	1-0	Zakarlyuka (p)
24/04/99	Tavriya Simferopol	H	3-0	Kripak 2, Oliynyk
02/05/99	Shakhtar Donetsk	A	0-1	
09/05/99	Metalurg Donetsk	H	2-1	Zakarlyuka (p), Kripak
14/05/99	Nyva Ternopil	A	2-1	Oliynyk, Balytskyi V.
18/05/99	Kryvbas Kryvyi Rih	H	1-2	Kripak
22/05/99	Metalist Kharkiv	A	0-1	
27/05/99	Dynamo Kyiv	H	0-4	
31/05/99	Prykarpattya Ivano-Frankivsk	H	1-2	Zakarlyuka (p)
13/06/99	Metalurg Mariupol	H	1-1	Zakarlyuka (p)
17/06/99	Karpaty Lviv	A	3-3	Oliynyk, Tsykhmeistruk, Bezhenar
25/06/99	Metalurg Zaporizhzhya	H	1-0	Oliynyk

DNIPRO DNIPROPETROVSK

CLUB DIRECTORY

Dnipro Dnipropetrovsk
vul. Bilshovytska 1, 320 070 Dnipropetrovsk
tel - (0562) 283381/342990/423795/929796
fax - (0562) 342990
Year of Formation - 1936
President - Andriy Stetsenko
Secretary - Volodymyr Prach
Coach - Vadym Tyshchenko; Volodymyr Kobzarev;
Leonid Kolyun
Stadium - Meteor (30,352)

MAJOR HONOURS
League Championship (USSR) - (2) 1983, 1988.
Domestic Cup (USSR) - (1) 1989.

APPEARANCES 98/99

	P	Ap	(s)	Gls
Olexandr BABYCH	A	4	(2)	
Serhiy BESPALYKH	A	6	(8)	2
Ihor BEZDOLNYI	A		(1)	
Illya BLYZNYUK	G	1		
Borys BUTKHANOV	D	12		1
Serhiy DRANOV	A	5	(1)	1
Denys FILIMONOV	M	18	(6)	4
Maxym KALYNYCHENKO	M	24	(2)	6
Ihor KHOMENKO	D	10		
Ivan KORPONAJ	A	8	(3)	1
Serhiy KOSILOV	M	4		1
Hennadiy KOZAR	D	23		
Serhiy LAMTYUGIN	D	2	(2)	
Serhiy MATYUKHIN	M	4		
Andriy MATVEYEV	A		(11)	1
Serhiy MAXYMYCH	M		(1)	
Mykola MEDIN	G	21		
Yevhem MYKULA	D		(2)	
Serhiy NAHORNYAK	A	1		1
Ivan PAVLYUKH	D	16	(1)	
Serhiy PERKHUN	G	8	(1)	
Olexandr PERSHIN	D	13		
Olexandr PINENKO	D	1		
Andriy PISNYI	D		(1)	
Olexandr POKLONSKYI	D	24		1
Mikhail POTSKHVERIA (GEO)	A	9	(1)	3
Olexiy RACHYBA	M		(3)	
Olexandr RYKUN	M	10		
Olexandr SAVENCHUK	M	7	(5)	
Oleh SHELAYEV	M	12		2
Bohdan SHERSHUN	D	17	(4)	
Andriy SIDELNIKOV	D	12		
Gheorghe STRATULAT (MOL)	M	9	(3)	
Alexandru SUHAREV (MOL)	A	15	(6)	3
Olexiy TELYATNIKOV	A	4	(5)	
Vyacheslav TKACHOV	M	2		
Dmytro TUTYCHENKO	M	14		
Serhiy VALYAYEV	A	13	(4)	1
Olexandr ZAKHAROV	M	1	(3)	

LEAGUE RESULTS 1998/99

07/07/98	Metalurg Donetsk	A	0-2	
11/07/98	Tavriya Simferopol	H	1-0	Butkhanov
18/07/98	SK Mykolaiv	A	0-2	
26/07/98	Metalurg Mariupol	H	1-0	Filimonov
02/08/98	Dynamo Kyiv	A	3-2	Filimonov, Kalynychenko, Suharev
08/08/98	Karpaty Lviv	H	0-2	
22/08/98	Nyva Ternopil	H	4-0	Poklonskyi, Suharev 2, Bespalykh
30/08/98	Shakhtar Donetsk	A	0-6	
12/09/98	CSKA Kyiv	A	0-1	
20/09/98	Zirka Kirovohrad	H	1-1	Kalynychenko
26/09/98	Vorskla Poltava	A	0-1	
30/09/98	Metalist Kharkiv	A	0-2	
04/10/98	Metalurg Zaporizhzhya	H	1-4	Bespalykh
25/10/98	Prykarpattya Ivano-Frankivsk	A	0-3	
31/10/98	Kryvbas Kryvyi Rih	H	2-1	Nahornyak, Filimonov
07/03/99	Kryvbas Kryvyi Rih	A	1-2	Korponai
11/03/99	Prykarpattya Ivano-Frankivsk	H	0-0	
03/04/99	Vorskla Poltava	H	2-0	Valyayev, Dranov
10/04/99	Zirka Kirovohrad	A	0-2	
17/04/99	CSKA Kyiv	H	0-1	
24/04/99	Shakhtar Donetsk	H	1-2	Filimonov
02/05/99	Nyva Ternopil	A	0-0	
09/05/99	Metalist Kharkiv	H	0-0	
18/05/99	Dynamo Kyiv	H	0-1	
22/05/99	Metalurg Mariupol	A	1-0	Shelayev (p)
31/05/99	SK Mykolaiv	H	2-1	Kalynychenko, Shelayev (p)
13/06/99	Karpaty Lviv	A	1-4	Kalynychenko
17/06/99	Tavriya Simferopol	A	0-3	
21/06/99	Metalurg Zaporizhzhya	A	2-2	Kalynychenko, Potskhveria
25/06/99	Metalurg Donetsk	H	5-1	Kosilov, Potskhveria 2, Kalynychenko, Matveyev

DYNAMO KYIV

CLUB DIRECTORY

Dynamo Kyiv
vul. Hrushevskoho 3, 252 001 Kyiv
tel - (044) 2280209/2284533/2282573
fax - (044) 2284135/2284407
Year of Formation - 1927
President - Grigory Surkis
Secretary - Olexiy Semenenko
Coach - Valeriy Lobanovskyi
Stadium - National Sport Komplex Olimpiyskyi
(83,160)

MAJOR HONOURS
League Championship (USSR) - (13)
1961, 1966, 1967, 1968, 1971, 1974, 1975,
1977, 1980, 1981, 1985, 1986, 1990.
Domestic Cup (USSR) - (9) 1954, 1964, 1966,
1974, 1978, 1982, 1985, 1987, 1990.
League Championship - (7)
1993, 1994, 1995, 1996, 1997, 1998, 1999.
Domestic Cup - (4) 1993, 1996, 1998, 1999.
European Cup-winners' Cup - (2) 1975, 1986.
European Super Cup - (1) 1975.

APPEARANCES 98/99

	P	Ap	(s)	Gls
Valentin BELKEVICH (BLS)	M	13	(8)	5
Serhiy CHERNYAK	D		(2)	
Yuriy DMITRULIN	D	17		
Serhiy FEDOROV	D	4	(1)	
Alexei GERASIMENKO (RUS)	M	10	(8)	2
Andriy GUSIN	M	19	(7)	5
Olexandr B. HOLOVKO	D	24		2
Kakhi KALADZE (GEO)	D	26		3
Yuriy KALITVINTSEV	M	8	(2)	1
Vasyl KARDASH	M	10	(2)	1
Vyacheslav KERNOZENKO	G	6		
Alexandr KHATSKEVICH (BLS)	M	23		10
Olexandr KIRYUKHIN	D	6	(3)	
Serhiy KONOVALOV	M	5	(2)	1
Sergei KORMILTSEV (RUS)	M	5	(4)	1
Vitaliy KOSOVSKYI	M	14	(5)	3
Oleh LUZHNYI	D	21		
Vladimir MAKOVSKIY (BLS)	A	2	(1)	1
Dmytro MYKHAILENKO	M	6	(6)	1
Denys ONYSHCHENKO	M		(2)	
Olexandr RADCHENKO	D	3	(1)	
Serhiy REBROV	A	20	(2)	9
Sergei SEREBRYANNIKOV (RUS)	A	5	(4)	6
Andriy SHEVCHENKO	A	22	(4)	18
Olexandr SHOVKOVSKYI	G	24		
Vladyslav VASHCHUK	D	25		1
Oleh VENHLYNSKYI	A	3	(5)	4
Artem YASHKIN (RUS)	M	5	(8)	
Volodymyr YEZERSKYI	D	4	(1)	

LEAGUE RESULTS 1998/99

07/07/98	Karpaty Lviv	H	0-0	
11/07/98	Metalist Kharkiv	A	6-1	Shevchenko, Gusin, Rebrov,
				Gerasimenko, Venhlynskyi,
				Vashchuk
18/07/98	Nyva Ternopil	H	1-0	Khatskevich
02/08/98	Dnipro Dnipropetrovsk	H	2-3	Gusin, Khatskevich
06/08/98	Zirka Kirovohrad	A	5-0	Khatskevich 2, Kalitvintsev,
				Holovko, Gerasimenko
16/08/98	Vorskla Poltava	H	4-0	Kaladze, Rebrov, Kosovskyi,
				Shevchenko
30/08/98	Prykarpattya Ivano-Frankivsk	H	7-0	Makovskiy, Belkevich,
				Khatskevich, Rebrov (p),
				Shevchenko 2, Mykhailenko
10/09/98	Kryvbas Kryvyi Rih	A	0-0	
20/09/98	Metalurg Donetsk	H	3-0	Kaladze, Gusin, Rebrov
24/09/98	Tavriya Simferopol	A	3-3	Kosovskyi, Shevchenko, Rebrov
04/10/98	SK Mykolaiv	H	2-1	Rebrov, Belkevich
25/10/98	Metalurg Mariupol	A	2-1	Shevchenko 2
30/10/98	CSKA Kyiv	H	2-0	Kardash, Belkevich
29/11/98	Shakhtar Donetsk	H	2-1	Rebrov, Shevchenko
03/12/98	Metalurg Zaporizhzhya	H	6-2	Shevchenko 2, Khatskevich,
				Belkevich 2, Rebrov (p)
11/03/99	Metalurg Mariupol	H	2-0	Shevchenko, Serebryannikov
03/04/99	Tavriya Simferopol	H	0-0	
12/04/99	Metalurg Donetsk	A	4-1	Khatskevich 2, Kosovskyi,
				Shevchenko
16/04/99	Kryvbas Kryvyi Rih	H	1-0	Shevchenko
25/04/99	Prykarpattya Ivano-Frankivsk	A	1-0	Shevchenko
02/05/99	Metalurg Zaporizhzhya	A	3-1	Khatskevich 2, Gusin
10/05/99	Vorskla Poltava	A	2-0	Shevchenko 2
14/05/99	Zirka Kirovohrad	H	1-0	Holovko
18/05/99	Dnipro Dnipropetrovsk	A	1-0	og (Khomenko)
22/05/99	Shakhtar Donetsk	A	0-0	
27/05/99	CSKA Kyiv	A	4-0	Gusin, Shevchenko 2 (1p),
				Kormiltsev
13/06/99	SK Mykolaiv	A	4-0	Kaladze, Venhlynskyi,
				Serebryannikov 2
17/06/99	Metalist Kharkiv	H	1-0	Serebryannikov
21/06/99	Nyva Ternopil	A	5-1	Venhlynskyi 2, Serebryannikov,
				Konovalov, Rebrov
25/06/99	Karpaty Lviv	A	1-2	Serebryannikov (p)

KARPATY LVIV

CLUB DIRECTORY

Karpaty Lviv
Av. Adam Mickewicz 6/7
290 005 Lviv
tel - (0322) 271461/727744/421527
fax - (0322) 724072/724972
Year of Formation - 1963
President - Yaroslav Hrytsyuk
Secretary - Yuriy Nazarkevych
Coach - Myron Markevych; Stepan Yurchyshyn
Stadium - Ukraina (40,600)

MAJOR HONOURS
Domestic Cup (USSR) - (1) 1969.

APPEARANCES 98/99

	P	Ap	(s)	Gls
Yuriy BENIO	D	21	(5)	
Oleh BERESKYI	G	1		
Olexandr CHYZHEVSKYI	D	26		
Ivan HETSKO	A	26	(1)	16
Serhiy KOVALETS	M	18	(8)	4
Vasyl LESKIV	D	1		
Ihor LUCHKEVYCH	M	7		1
Mykhailo LUTSYSHYN	M	2	(7)	
Serhiy MIZIN	M	27		7
Volodymyr MYKYTYN	M	14		
Yevhen NAZAROV	M	23	(1)	1
Pavlo ONYSKO	A		(4)	
Olexandr PALYANYTSYA	A	29	(1)	16
Volodymyr RIZNYK	M	2		
Dmytro SEMOCHKO	A	1	(6)	
Volodymyr SHARAN	M	5	(8)	3
Hennadiy SKYDAN	A		(1)	
Alkaly SOUMAH (GUI)	M		(3)	
Bohdan STRONTSYTSKYI	G	29		
Roman TOLOCHKO	A	9	(12)	1
Oleh TYMCHYSHYN	D	4	(7)	
Volodymyr VILCHYNSKYI	D	9	(1)	
Lyubomyr VOVCHUK	M	22	(1)	
Serhiy YEVHLEVSKYI	M	4	(11)	1
Olexandr YEVTUSHOK	D	24		3
Volodymyr YEZERSKYI	D	15		
Mykola ZAKOTYUK	M	11	(11)	

LEAGUE RESULTS 1998/99

Date	Opponent		Score	Scorers
07/07/98	Dynamo Kyiv	A	0-0	
11/07/98	CSKA Kyiv	A	3-3	Sharan 2, Kovalets
18/07/98	Metalist Kharkiv	H	0-1	
26/07/98	Nyva Ternopil	A	0-0	
02/08/98	Shakhtar Donetsk	H	1-0	Palyanytsya
08/08/98	Dnipro Dnipropetrovsk	A	2-0	Palyanytsya, Mizin
16/08/98	Zirka Kirovohrad	H	2-1	Palyanytsya, Hetsko
22/08/98	Vorskla Poltava	A	0-0	
30/08/98	Metalurg Zaporizhzhya	H	1-1	Hetsko
12/09/98	Prykarpattya Ivano-Frankivsk	A	2-0	Luchkevych, Hetsko
20/09/98	Kryvbas Kryvyi Rih	H	2-1	Mizin, Kovalets
26/09/98	Metalurg Donetsk	A	3-4	Hetsko, Palyanytsya (p), Mizin
04/10/98	Tavriya Simferopol	H	2-1	Palyanytsya (p), Mizin
25/10/98	SK Mykolaiv	A	3-0	Kovalets, Hetsko 2
31/10/98	Metalurg Mariupol	H	3-1	Palyanytsya, Hetsko, Mizin
07/03/99	Metalurg Mariupol	A	2-4	Palyanytsya (p), Tolochko
13/03/99	SK Mykolaiv	H	5-1	Hetsko, Sharan, Nazarov, Yevhlevskyi, og (Storchak)
21/03/99	Tavriya Simferopol	A	1-1	Palyanytsya (p)
03/04/99	Metalurg Donetsk	H	2-0	Yevtushok, Hetsko
10/04/99	Kryvbas Kryvyi Rih	A	0-0	
17/04/99	Prykarpattya Ivano-Frankivsk	H	3-0	Palyanytsya 3
24/04/99	Metalurg Zaporizhzhya	A	1-3	Mizin
02/05/99	Vorskla Poltava	H	2-1	Hetsko 2
10/05/99	Zirka Kirovohrad	A	2-2	Palyanytsya (p), Kovalets
18/05/99	Shakhtar Donetsk	A	1-1	Mizin
22/05/99	Nyva Ternopil	H	1-0	Hetsko
13/06/99	Dnipro Dnipropetrovsk	H	4-1	Yevtushok, Hetsko, Palyanytsya 2
17/06/99	CSKA Kyiv	H	3-3	Hetsko, Palyanytsya, Yevtushok
21/06/99	Metalist Kharkiv	A	1-3	Hetsko
25/06/99	Dynamo Kyiv	H	2-1	Hetsko, Palyanytsya

KRYVBAS KRYVYI RIH

CLUB DIRECTORY

Kryvbas Kryvyi Rih
Av. Metalurgiv 5
320 070 Kryvyi Rih
tel - (0564)
232152/283019/716488/236161
fax - (0564) 235054/715045
Year of Formation - 1966
President - Serhiy Polishchuk
Secretary - Svyatoslav Azarkin
Coach - Oleh Taran
Stadium - Metalurg (38,000)

APPEARANCES 98/99

	P	Ap	(s)	Gls
Andriy ANISHCHENKO	D	27		
Andriy ANNENKOV	D	2	(1)	
Orest ATAMANCHUK	A	5	(7)	3
Serhiy BUHAI	M	20		1
Serhiy DATSENKO	D	16	(1)	1
Ihor DOROSHENKO	D	15	(2)	1
Volodymyr GASHCHIN	A	8	(2)	3
Olexandr GRANOVSKYI	M	23	(2)	
Denys KOLCHIN	D	11		
Stanislav KRIULIN	M	1	(1)	
Olexandr LAVRENTSOV	G	30		
Vladyslav MAYOROV	A	6	(4)	2
Roman MONAREV	A	4	(4)	4
Hennadiy MOROZ	A	26		5
Andriy OKSYMETS	D	10		
Valentyn PLATONOV	M	7	(12)	3
Volodymyr PONOMARENKO	M	27		6
Yevhen RYMSHIN	A	10	(10)	4
Oleh SIMAKOV	M	22	(7)	4
Serhiy STOROZHEVTSEV	M		(1)	
Andriy STROYENKO	M		(3)	
Serhiy SUKHORUCHENKO	D	1	(5)	
Olexandr TOLKACH	D	3		
Olexandr VOSKOBOINIK	A	7	(14)	3
Olexiy YAKYMENKO	M	14		
Yuriy YASKOV	A	2	(6)	
Olexandr YEVSYUKOV	M		(1)	
Ruslan ZABRANSKYI	A	11	(1)	2
Olexandr ZOTOV	M	22	(1)	1

LEAGUE RESULTS 1998/99

07/07/98	Zirka Kirovohrad	H	1-0	Buhai
15/07/98	Vorskla Poltava	A	0-0	
18/07/98	Metalurg Zaporizhzhya	H	4-0	Ponomarenko 2, Zabranskyi,
				Gashchin
26/07/98	Prykarpattya Ivano-Frankivsk	A	2-2	Datsenko, Atamanchuk
02/08/98	CSKA Kyiv	H	0-0	
08/08/98	Metalurg Donetsk	H	2-0	Atamanchuk, Simakov
16/08/98	Tavriya Simferopol	A	2-0	Gashchin, Zabranskyi
22/08/98	SK Mykolaiv	H	0-0	
30/08/98	Metalurg Mariupol	A	0-0	
10/09/98	Dynamo Kyiv	H	0-0	
20/09/98	Karpaty Lviv	A	1-2	Zotov
26/09/98	Metalist Kharkiv	H	1-0	Gashchin
04/10/98	Nyva Ternopil	A	2-1	Voskoboinik 2
25/10/98	Shakhtar Donetsk	H	1-0	Platonov
31/10/98	Dnipro Dnipropetrovsk	A	1-2	Atamanchuk
07/03/99	Dnipro Dnipropetrovsk	H	2-1	Ponomarenko (p), Voskoboinik
11/03/99	Shakhtar Donetsk	A	1-1	Moroz
21/03/99	Nyva Ternopil	H	2-1	Simakov, Ponomarenko
03/04/99	Metalist Kharkiv	A	0-0	
10/04/99	Karpaty Lviv	H	0-0	
16/04/99	Dynamo Kyiv	A	0-1	
24/04/99	Metalurg Mariupol	H	3-1	Mayorov, Rymshin, Moroz (p)
02/05/99	SK Mykolaiv	A	4-0	Rymshin, Mayorov, Platonov,
				Doroshenko
09/05/99	Tavriya Simferopol	H	1-1	Rymshin
14/05/99	Metalurg Donetsk	A	2-0	Simakov 2
18/05/99	CSKA Kyiv	A	2-1	Rymshin, Ponomarenko
22/05/99	Prykarpattya Ivano-Frankivsk	H	2-0	Moroz 2 (1p)
29/05/99	Metalurg Zaporizhzhya	A	1-1	Ponomarenko
17/06/99	Vorskla Poltava	H	3-1	Moroz, Monarev 2
21/06/99	Zirka Kirovohrad	A	3-2	Monarev 2, Platonov

METALIST KHARKIV

CLUB DIRECTORY

Metalist Kharkiv
vul. Plekhanivska 65
310 001 Kharkiv
tel - (0572) 277646/278807/272874
fax - (0572) 277936
Year of Formation - 1944
President - Volodymyr Buhai
Secretary - Yuriy Lander
Coach - Mykhailo Fomenko
Stadium - Metalist (25,000)

MAJOR HONOURS
Domestic Cup (USSR) - (1) 1988.

APPEARANCES 98/99

	P	Ap	(s)	Gls
Dmytro CHUPRYN	M		(1)	
Vadym GOLDIN	D	20	(5)	2
Olexandr GORYAINOV	G	26		
Viktor IVANENKO	D	29		4
Olexandr KARABUTA	M	11		2
Oleh KOLESOV	G	4	(1)	
Ruslan KOLOKOLOV	D	11	(2)	
Serhiy KOSTYUKOV	A	14	(4)	3
Oleh KUCHER	M	28	(1)	
Andriy KYRLYK	M	21	(2)	7
Vitaliy LOTS	D	2	(10)	
Oleh LUKASH	A	2		
Roman PETS	D	21	(1)	3
Ihor PLAKHOTIN	M	6	(5)	
Volodymyr PYATENKO	D	28	(1)	1
Dmytro RUDNYAK	A	25	(1)	3
Serhiy RYZHYKH	A	1	(4)	
Volodymyr SERIKOV	M	3		
Oleh SHEVCHENKO	A	3	(6)	
Yevhem SHKOLNIKOV	M	29		4
Ihor SHOPIN	M	16	(5)	
Vitaliy SKYSH	D	3	(7)	
Olexiy TARHONSKYI	D	2		
Vasyl TOFAN	D	21	(5)	1
Vacheslav ZAPOYASKO	D		(1)	
Oleh ZHILIN	D	4	(2)	

LEAGUE RESULTS 1998/99

07/07/98	Metalurg Mariupol	A	0-2	
11/07/98	Dynamo Kyiv	H	1-6	Ivanenko
18/07/98	Karpaty Lviv	A	1-0	Kyrlyk
26/07/98	CSKA Kyiv	A	1-2	Goldin
02/08/98	Nyva Ternopil	H	2-1	Shkolnikov, Kyrlyk
06/08/98	Shakhtar Donetsk	A	1-3	og (Shtolcers)
22/08/98	Zirka Kirovohrad	A	0-2	
30/08/98	Vorskla Poltava	H	2-4	Rudnyak, Kostyukov
12/09/98	Metalurg Zaporizhzhya	A	2-3	Kyrlyk 2
20/09/98	Prykarpattya Ivano-Frankivsk	H	1-0	Karabuta
26/09/98	Kryvbas Kryvyi Rih	A	0-1	
30/09/98	Dnipro Dnipropetrovsk	H	2-0	Ivanenko (p), Rudnyak
04/10/98	Metalurg Donetsk	H	1-0	Shkolnikov
25/10/98	Tavriya Simferopol	A	1-0	Kyrlyk
31/10/98	SK Mykolaiv	H	0-0	
07/03/99	SK Mykolaiv	A	2-0	Kyrlyk, Karabuta
13/03/99	Tavriya Simferopol	H	1-0	Pyatenko
21/03/99	Metalurg Donetsk	A	0-0	
03/04/99	Kryvbas Kryvyi Rih	H	0-0	
10/04/99	Prykarpattya Ivano-Frankivsk	A	2-1	Tofan, Shkolnikov
17/04/99	Metalurg Zaporizhzhya	H	1-0	Kostyukov
24/04/99	Vorskla Poltava	A	2-1	Goldin, Rudnyak
02/05/99	Zirka Kirovohrad	H	3-0	Ivanenko, Kostyukov, Shkolnikov
09/05/99	Dnipro Dnipropetrovsk	A	0-0	
14/05/99	Shakhtar Donetsk	H	1-1	Ivanenko
18/05/99	Nyva Ternopil	A	0-2	
22/05/99	CSKA Kyiv	H	1-0	Pets
17/06/99	Dynamo Kyiv	A	0-1	
21/06/99	Karpaty Lviv	H	3-1	Kyrlyk, Pets 2
25/06/99	Metalurg Mariupol	H	0-1	

METALURG DONETSK

CLUB DIRECTORY

Metalurg Donetsk
vul. Kuibysheva
Stadion im 125 richchya DMK
340 062 Donetsk
tel - (0622) 3613432/3613243/3613041
fax - (0622) 3612208
Year of Formation - 1995
President - Olexandr Kosevych
Secretary - Oleh Kerichok
Coach - Volodymyr Onyshchenko;
Volodymyr Gavrilov; Ihor Yavorskyi;
Mykhailo Sokolovskyi
Stadium - im 125 richchya DMK (10,000)

APPEARANCES 98/99

		P	Ap	(s)	Gls
Yuriy BELICHENKO	M	8			
Vyacheslav BOGODELOV	G	8	(1)		
Serhiy BOHORODYCHENKO	M	5	(2)		
Olexiy BULGAKOV	D	17	(5)	4	
Olexandr DOROKHOV	D	27	(1)		
Viktor DYAK	M		(4)		
Yuriy FOKIN	M	12			
Olexandr HURALSKYI	M		(1)		
Andriy KLYMENKO	M	5	(4)		
Alhert KOVALEV	D	28			
Vadym KROKHAN	D	3	(5)		
Vitaliy MINTENKO	A	13	(2)	3	
Yevhen MYKHAILIV	D	9			
Olexandr MYZENKO	A	11	(4)	2	
Andriy NIKITIN	G	7			
Roman OLIYNYK	D	15			
Andriy POKLADOK	A	18	(3)	5	
Yevhen POKOTYLO	A		(1)		
Serhiy POTAPOV	M	1	(1)		
Olexandr SEVIDOV	A	22	(4)	4	
Valentyn SLYUSAR	A	13		1	
Denys SOKOLOVSKYI	M	6	(11)	2	
Vadym SOLODKYI	D	11			
Yuriy SOLOVIYENKO	D	27	(1)		
Andriy SPIVAK	M	10		1	
Ihor STASYUK	A	1	(9)		
Yuriy VIRT	G	15			
Mykola VOLOSHYN	D	15	(8)	2	
Ihor ZHABCHENKO	M	5	(1)	1	
Andriy ZAVYALOV	M	18	(2)	2	

LEAGUE RESULTS 1998/99

07/07/98	Dnipro Dnipropetrovsk	H	2-0	Mintenko (p), Bulgakov
11/07/98	Zirka Kirovohrad	A	1-3	Bulgakov
26/07/98	Metalurg Zaporizhzhya	A	0-0	
02/08/98	Prykarpattya Ivano-Frankivsk	H	1-0	Pokladok
08/08/98	Kryvbas Kryvyi Rih	A	0-2	
17/08/98	CSKA Kyiv	H	2-2	Zavyalov, Myzenko
22/08/98	Tavriya Simferopol	H	2-0	Slyusar, Voloshyn
30/08/98	SK Mykolaiv	A	1-0	Bulgakov
03/09/98	Vorskla Poltava	H	0-0	
12/09/98	Metalurg Mariupol	H	1-1	Sevidov
20/09/98	Dynamo Kyiv	A	0-3	
26/09/98	Karpaty Lviv	H	4-3	Sevidov 2, Myzenko, Spivak
04/10/98	Metalist Kharkiv	A	0-1	
25/10/98	Nyva Ternopil	H	2-1	Mintenko, Zavyalov
30/10/98	Shakhtar Donetsk	A	2-4	Mintenko (p), Voloshyn
07/03/99	Shakhtar Donetsk	H	0-4	
13/03/99	Nyva Ternopil	A	2-3	Bulgakov, Pokladok
21/03/99	Metalist Kharkiv	H	0-0	
03/04/99	Karpaty Lviv	A	0-2	
12/04/99	Dynamo Kyiv	H	1-4	Zhabchenko
17/04/99	Metalurg Mariupol	A	0-0	
24/04/99	SK Mykolaiv	H	0-0	
02/05/99	Tavriya Simferopol	A	2-3	Pokladok 2 (1p)
09/05/99	CSKA Kyiv	A	1-2	Sokolovskyi
14/05/99	Kryvbas Kryvyi Rih	H	0-2	
18/05/99	Prykarpattya Ivano-Frankivsk	A	1-2	Pokladok
22/05/99	Metalurg Zaporizhzhya	H	0-2	
29/05/99	Vorskla Poltava	A	0-2	
17/06/99	Zirka Kirovohrad	H	1-0	Sevidov
25/06/99	Dnipro Dnipropetrovsk	A	1-5	Sokolovskyi

METALURG MARIUPOL

CLUB DIRECTORY

FC Metalurg Mariupol
vul. Yevpatoriiska 45A
341 015 Mariupol
tel - (0629)
381322/331240/371264/221437
fax - (0629) 333363/336124
Year of Formation - 1994
President - Pavlo Razumnyi
Secretary - Sarhiy Katrych
Coach - Mykola Pavlov
Stadium - Azovstal (9,000)

APPEARANCES 98/99

	P	Ap	(s)	Gls
Volodymyr ANIKEYEV	D	26		
Kostyantyn BABYCH	A	26	(2)	7
Volodymyr BRAILA	M	5	(16)	2
Yuriy BUKEL	D	1	(2)	
Serhiy DIRYAVKA	D	25		1
Ihor DUKHNOVSKYI	A	3	(3)	
Serhiy DUMENKO	A	2		
Yuriy FENIM	D	2		
Serhiy HONCHARENKO	M	5	(5)	1
Serhiy KOLESNYK	M	1	(10)	1
Vadym KOLESNYK	A	6	(5)	
Andriy KOTYUK	M	10	(5)	1
Olexiy LEVCHENKO	M		(4)	
Stepan MALOKUTSKO	A	15		1
Olexandr MEKHANOSKYN	M	1	(6)	1
Serhiy MITIN	D	1	(1)	
Vitaliy PANTILOV	M	27		8
Ivan PAPAZOV	M		(1)	
Ihor PLOTKO	M	30		5
Volodymyr POLISHCHUK	D	10		
Vitaliy PUSHKUTSA	A	23	(2)	3
Olexandr RYKUN	M	13		1
Yuriy SAK	D	2	(3)	
Kostyantyn SAKHAROV	M	29		
Ihor SHUKHOVTSEV	G	30		
Olexandr SOBKOVYCH	M	2	(4)	
Oleh SYZON	D	2	(1)	
Mykola VOLOSYANKO	D	30		2
Vitaliy ZALIZNYAK	D	3	(1)	

LEAGUE RESULTS 1998/99

07/07/98	Metalist Kharkiv	H	2-0	Babych, Braila
11/07/98	Nyva Ternopil	A	0-1	
18/07/98	Shakhtar Donetsk	H	0-1	
26/07/98	Dnipro Dnipropetrovsk	A	0-1	
02/08/98	Zirka Kirovohrad	H	0-0	
08/08/98	Vorskla Poltava	A	1-0	Babych
16/08/98	Metalurg Zaporizhzhya	H	4-2	Plotko 2, Kotyuk, Volosyanko
22/08/98	Prykarpattya Ivano-Frankivsk	A	3-0	Pantilov 2, Babych
30/08/98	Kryvbas Kryvyi Rih	H	0-0	
12/09/98	Metalurg Donetsk	A	1-1	Pantilov
19/09/98	Tavriya Simferopol	H	2-0	Honcharenko, Kolesnyk S.
26/09/98	SK Mykolaiv	A	2-1	Pushkutsa, Plotko
05/10/98	CSKA Kyiv	H	1-1	Plotko (p)
25/10/98	Dynamo Kyiv	H	1-2	Braila
31/10/98	Karpaty Lviv	A	1-3	Pushkutsa
07/03/99	Karpaty Lviv	H	4-2	Babych 3, Rykun
11/03/99	Dynamo Kyiv	A	0-2	
03/04/99	SK Mykolaiv	H	3-0	Pantilov 2 (2p), Volosyanko
10/04/99	Tavriya Simferopol	A	2-0	Malokutsko, Mekhanoskyn
17/04/99	Metalurg Donetsk	H	0-0	
24/04/99	Kryvbas Kryvyi Rih	A	1-3	Pantilov
02/05/99	Prykarpattya Ivano-Frankivsk	H	2-1	Babych, Dukhnovskyi
09/05/99	Metalurg Zaporizhzhya	A	0-3	
14/05/99	Vorskla Poltava	H	1-0	Plotko
18/05/99	Zirka Kirovohrad	A	1-0	Pantilov
22/05/99	Dnipro Dnipropetrovsk	H	0-1	
29/05/99	Shakhtar Donetsk	A	0-1	
13/06/99	CSKA Kyiv	A	1-1	Pantilov (p)
17/06/99	Nyva Ternopil	H	1-0	Pushkutsa
25/06/99	Metalist Kharkiv	A	1-0	Pantilov

METALURG ZAPORIZHZHYA

CLUB DIRECTORY

Metalurg Zaporizhzhya
vul. 12 April 2
330 037 Zaporizhzhya
tel - (0612) 322316/226281/571433
fax - (0612) 326672/326887
Year of Formation - 1949
President - Viktor Mezheiko
Secretary - Arkadiy Kopeliovych
Coach - Olexandr Shtelin; Myron Markevych
Stadium - Metalurg (25,000)

APPEARANCES 98/99

	P	Ap	(s)	Gls
Armen AKOPYAN	M	29		1
Olexandr BATRACHENKO	D	6	(5)	
Ivan BOHATYR	D	24	(1)	
Olexandr CHORNYAVSKYI	D	25	(1)	1
Andriy DEMCHENKO	A	12	(8)	6
Viktor GROMOV	A	17	(3)	6
Taras HREBENYUK	G	27		
Olexandr IVANOV	A		(1)	
Valeriy IVASHCHENKO	A		(2)	
Serhiy KLYUCHYK	M	14	(2)	1
Dmytro KOLODIN	M		(8)	
Volodymyr KONOVALCHUK	M	5	(6)	
Andriy KONYUSHENKO	D	24		1
Serhiy KOVALENKO	A	9	(5)	1
Valeriy KOVALENKO	D	4		
Leonid KOVALKOV	D		(1)	
Volodymyr KOZLENKO	M	3	(1)	
Viktor KRAVCHENKO	M	10	(2)	1
Oleh LYPSKYI	A		(1)	
Yuriy MARKIN	D	29		3
Anatoliy MATKEVYCH	M		(2)	
Olexiy MORGUNOV	M	6	(5)	3
Vitaliy OLIYNYK	G	3		
Olexandr OSTASHOV	A	16	(9)	4
Valentyn POLTAVETS	M	26	(2)	13
Oleh RATIY	D	14	(4)	
Vyacheslav SHEVCHUK	D	3	(2)	
Serhiy SKYSHCHENKO	M	3	(7)	1
Denys SMIRNOV	M	9	(5)	
Dmytro TOPCHIYEV	M	12	(1)	4

LEAGUE RESULTS 1998/99

07/07/98	CSKA Kyiv	H	1-0	Poltavets
11/07/98	Prykarpattya Ivano-Frankivsk	H	1-1	Gromov
18/07/98	Kryvbas Kryvyi Rih	A	0-4	
26/07/98	Metalurg Donetsk	H	0-0	
02/08/98	Tavriya Simferopol	A	3-2	Gromov 2, Poltavets
08/08/98	SK Mykolaiv	H	4-1	Markin, Poltavets, Kravchenko, Ostashov
16/08/98	Metalurg Mariupol	A	2-4	Akopyan, Gromov
30/08/98	Karpaty Lviv	A	1-1	Kovalenko S.
12/09/98	Metalist Kharkiv	H	3-2	Klyuchyk, Poltavets 2 (1p)
20/09/98	Nyva Ternopil	A	0-1	
24/09/98	Shakhtar Donetsk	H	2-3	Demchenko, Ostashov
04/10/98	Dnipro Dnipropetrovsk	A	4-1	Poltavets 2, Markin, Demchenko
25/10/98	Zirka Kirovohrad	H	1-0	Poltavets
31/10/98	Vorskla Poltava	A	0-3	
03/12/98	Dynamo Kyiv	A	2-6	Poltavets (p), Ostashov
07/03/99	Vorskla Poltava	H	0-1	
13/03/99	Zirka Kirovohrad	A	0-1	
03/04/99	Shakhtar Donetsk	A	1-2	Gromov
10/04/99	Nyva Ternopil	H	2-1	Demchenko, Morgunov
17/04/99	Metalist Kharkiv	A	0-1	
24/04/99	Karpaty Lviv	H	3-1	Morgunov, Topchiyev, Poltavets
02/05/99	Dynamo Kyiv	H	1-3	Poltavets (p)
09/05/99	Metalurg Mariupol	H	3-0	Ostashov, Demchenko, Topchiyev
14/05/99	SK Mykolaiv	A	4-0	Markin, Topchiyev, Poltavets, Morgunov
18/05/99	Tavriya Simferopol	H	3-0	Chornyavskyi, Topchiyev, Skyshchenko (p)
22/05/99	Metalurg Donetsk	A	2-0	Demchenko, Gromov
29/05/99	Kryvbas Kryvyi Rih	H	1-1	Demchenko
17/06/99	Prykarpattya Ivano-Frankivsk	A	0-0	
21/06/99	Dnipro Dnipropetrovsk	H	2-2	Konyushenko, Poltavets
25/06/99	CSKA Kyiv	A	0-1	

SK MYKOLAIV

CLUB DIRECTORY

SK Mykolaiv
vul. Sportyvna 1, 327 015 Mykolaiv
tel - (0512) 342072/340156/377243
fax - (0512) 349543/377837
Year of Formation - 1994
President - Viktor Vovchenko
Secretary - Olexandr Dvoinysyuk
Coach - Anatoliy Konkov; Leonid Nikolayenko; Ivan Krasnetskyi; Leonid Nikolayenko; Mykhailo Kalyta
Secretary - Volodymyr Stoyanov
Stadium - Central (25,175)

APPEARANCES 98/99

	P	Ap	(s)	Gls
Eldar ALLAKHVERDIYEV	M	2	(1)	
Ihor BAKHMETIYEV	M	13		
Serhiy BELIKOV	A	3	(1)	
Andriy BEREKULYA	D	1		
Andriy BEROZOVCHUK	D	5	(11)	1
Ihor BEZDOLNYI	A	6	(5)	
Olexandr BILYI	A		(7)	
Dmytro BOROVSKYI	M		(7)	
Serhiy BURYMENKO	M	16		
Olexiy CHYRVA	D	10		
Dmytro DOBROVOLSKYI	D	13	(2)	
Viktor DOTSENKO	D	12		1
Serhiy DRANOV	A	9	(1)	2
Ivan Mamuka DZHUGELI (GEO)	A	3	(2)	
Ovik GALSTYAN	A	9	(8)	
Dmytro HOROBETS	A	1	(1)	
Olexandr KLYMENKO	M		(1)	
Serhiy KOCHVAR	D	13		
Serhiy KOZLOV	A	11	(9)	
Ihor KRAPIVKIN	G	6		
Oleh LUKASH	M	8		2
Timur MARGUSHIA (GEO)	M	1	(1)	
Denys MYSHKO	D	3		
Vyacheslav NUZHNYI	M	7	(3)	2
Serhiy ONOPKO	M	13		4
Olexandr PALISHEV	M	4	(2)	
Kostyantyn POLISHCHUK	D	4		
Andriy RASPOPOV	D		(1)	
Andriy SHKURUPIY	A	10	(1)	
Artem SHTANKO	G	9		
Serhiy SOBESHCHAKOV	G	15		
Serhiy SOLOVIOV	D	10		
Vadym SOROKIN	M	7	(1)	2
Ihor STAKHIV	M	5	(2)	
Vasyl STORCHAK	D	15	(1)	
Serhiy SYLETSKYI	D	11		
Olexiy TELYATNIKOV	A	11	(1)	
Yuriy TEPCHUK	A	5		
Denys VAKAR	A	1	(2)	
Denys VASIN	M	8	(1)	
Dmytro YURCHENKO	A	5	(6)	1
Vladyslav ZAVHORODNIY	M	1		
Ihor ZELENYUK	D	14		
Vyacheslav ZHENYLENKO	D	28		2
Andriy ZHOVZHERENKO	M	2	(1)	

LEAGUE RESULTS 1998/99

07/07/98	Nyva Ternopil	H	0-1	
11/07/98	Shakhtar Donetsk	A	0-7	
18/07/98	Dnipro Dnipropetrovsk	H	2-0	Sorokin, Onopko
26/07/98	Zirka Kirovohrad	A	1-1	og (Bilozerskyi)
02/08/98	Vorskla Poltava	H	1-0	Sorokin (p)
08/08/98	Metalurg Zaporizhzhya	A	1-4	Dranov
16/08/98	Prykarpattya Ivano-Frankivsk	H	1-1	Onopko
22/08/98	Kryvbas Kryvyi Rih	A	0-0	
30/08/98	Metalurg Donetsk	H	0-1	
12/09/98	Tavriya Simferopol	A	0-2	
21/09/98	CSKA Kyiv	H	2-3	Onopko 2
26/09/98	Metalurg Mariupol	H	1-2	Dranov
04/10/98	Dynamo Kyiv	A	1-2	Dotsenko
25/10/98	Karpaty Lviv	H	0-3	
31/10/98	Metalist Kharkiv	A	0-0	
07/03/99	Metalist Kharkiv	H	0-2	
13/03/99	Karpaty Lviv	A	1-5	Zhenylenko (p)
03/04/99	Metalurg Mariupol	A	0-3	
10/04/99	CSKA Kyiv	A	0-2	
17/04/99	Tavriya Simferopol	H	1-2	Lukash (p)
24/04/99	Metalurg Donetsk	A	0-0	
02/05/99	Kryvbas Kryvyi Rih	H	0-4	
09/05/99	Prykarpattya Ivano-Frankivsk	A	1-2	Berezovchuk
14/05/99	Metalurg Zaporizhzhya	H	0-4	
18/05/99	Vorskla Poltava	A	1-2	Yurchenko (p)
22/05/99	Zirka Kirovohrad	H	2-2	Zhenylenko, Nuzhnyi
31/05/99	Dnipro Dnipropetrovsk	A	1-2	Lukash
13/06/99	Dynamo Kyiv	H	0-4	
17/06/99	Shakhtar Donetsk	H	0-3	
25/06/99	Nyva Ternopil	A	1-3	Nuzhnyi

NYVA TERNOPIL

CLUB DIRECTORY

Nyva Ternopil
pr. Stepan Bandera 5
282 002 Ternopil
tel - (0352) 220752/251837/334064
fax - (0352) 254742/335302
Year of Formation - 1983
President - Olexandr Kryvyi
Secretary - Ivan Hetsko
Coach - Ihor Yurchenko
Stadium - Central (17,000)

APPEARANCES 98/99

	P	Ap	(s)	Gls
Ihor BISKUP	D	24	(1)	
Serhiy BOHORODYCHENKO	D	11	(1)	
Yuriy CHUMAK	G	23		
Giorgi DAVITNIDZE (GEO)	M	5	(1)	
Mykhailo DEMYANCHUK	M	2	(11)	3
Kakhaber DGEBUADZE (GEO)	M	7	(5)	
Pavlo FILIPENKO	D	8	(4)	
Yuriy FOKIN	M	15		1
Avtandil GVIANIDZE (GEO)	A	6	(9)	1
Petro HOLUBKO	A	5	(6)	
Serhiy HONCHARENKO	M	14		1
Alexandr KAIDARASHVILI	M	8	(3)	2
Avtandil KAPANADZE (GEO)	A	28	(1)	10
Tariel KAPANADZE (GEO)	M	28		4
Serhiy KHOMENKO	A		(6)	1
Shalva KHUDZHADZE (GEO)	M	5	(1)	
Serhiy KRYVYI	M	20	(2)	1
Vitaliy KUT	D	5		
Mykola LAPA	D	4	(1)	
Hennadiy LOSEV	G	5		
Vladyslav MALTSEV	D		(1)	
Dmytro MAZUR	M	23	(2)	
Oleh MISHENIN	D	8	(4)	
Yuriy NIKITENKO	G	2	(1)	
Vitaliy PERVAK	D	29		2
Bohdan SAMARDAK	M	1	(10)	
Andriy SHPAK	A	14	(5)	3
Serhiy SKYMANSKYI	D	7		
Avtandil SIKHARULIDZE (GEO)	A	3	(2)	
Ihor SUSHKO	M	20	(2)	

LEAGUE RESULTS 1998/99

07/07/98	SK Mykolaiv	A	1-0	Kapanadze T.
11/07/98	Metalurg Mariupol	H	1-0	Demyanchuk
18/07/98	Dynamo Kyiv	A	0-1	
26/07/98	Karpaty Lviv	H	0-0	
02/08/98	Metalist Kharkiv	A	1-2	Kryvyi
08/08/98	CSKA Kyiv	A	0-0	
22/08/98	Dnipro Dnipropetrovsk	A	0-4	
30/08/98	Zirka Kirovohrad	H	3-2	Kapanadze A., Pervak, Fokin
12/09/98	Vorskla Poltava	A	1-2	Shpak
16/09/98	Shakhtar Donetsk	H	0-3	
20/09/98	Metalurg Zaporizhzhya	H	1-0	Pervak
26/09/98	Prykarpattya Ivano-Frankivsk	A	1-1	Shpak
04/10/98	Kryvbas Kryvyi Rih	H	1-2	Kapanadze A.
25/10/98	Metalurg Donetsk	A	1-2	Kapanadze A.
31/10/98	Tavriya Simferopol	H	0-0	
07/03/99	Tavriya Simferopol	A	0-1	
13/03/99	Metalurg Donetsk	H	3-2	Khomenko, Kapanadze T., Honcharenko
21/03/99	Kryvbas Kryvyi Rih	A	1-2	Kaidarashvili
03/04/99	Prykarpattya Ivano-Frankivsk	H	3-1	Kapanadze A. 2, Kaidarashvili
10/04/99	Metalurg Zaporizhzhya	A	1-2	Kapanadze A.
17/04/99	Vorskla Poltava	H	2-2	Kapanadze A., Demyanchuk
24/04/99	Zirka Kirovohrad	A	0-1	
02/05/99	Dnipro Dnipropetrovsk	H	0-0	
10/05/99	Shakhtar Donetsk	A	1-1	Gvianidze
14/05/99	CSKA Kyiv	H	1-2	Demyanchuk
18/05/99	Metalist Kharkiv	H	2-0	Kapanadze A. 2
22/05/99	Karpaty Lviv	A	0-1	
17/06/99	Metalurg Mariupol	A	0-1	
21/06/99	Dynamo Kyiv	H	1-5	Kapanadze A.
25/06/99	SK Mykolaiv	H	3-1	Kapanadze T. 2, Shpak

PRYKARPATTYA IVANO-FRANKIVSK

CLUB DIRECTORY

Prykarpattya Ivano-Frankivsk
vul. Taras Shevchenko 47
284 001 Ivano-Frankivsk
tel - (03422) 25222/25303/52432
fax - (03422) 52432
Year of Formation - 1981
President - Anatoliy Revutskyi
Secretary - Orest Babiy
Coach - Bohdan Blavatskyi; Anatoliy Boiko;
Anatoliy Zayayev; Ihor Yavorskyi
Stadium - Rukh (15,000)

APPEARANCES 98/99

	P	Ap	(s)	Gls
Andriy BUDNYK	M	8	(5)	1
Ivan Mamuka DZHUGELI (GEO)	A		(4)	
Vladyslav FRANKO	M	1		
Eldar IBRAGIMOV	A	1	(7)	
Ihor KARAS	D	9	(1)	
Mykola KHOMYN	G		(1)	
Olexiy KHRAMTSOV	D	14		
Anatoliy KOLOMIYETS	M		(2)	
Taras KOVALCHUK	M	20	(3)	1
Volodymyr KOVALYUK	M	13		1
Yuriy KOSTYSHYN	M	6	(2)	
Ihor KRIL	M	26	(1)	
Volodymyr KRYZHANIVSKYI	M	3	(1)	
Volodymyr LARIN	A	23	(1)	1
Vladyslav LYUTYI	M	10	(3)	
Vladyslav MALTSEV	A	1	(1)	
Volodymyr MARTYNOV	A	10	(1)	1
Olexandr MEKHANOSHYN	M	7	(1)	
Yuriy MOKRYTSKYI	D	2		
Ruslan MOSTOVYI	D	13		
Olexandr MYKULYAK	A	1	(1)	
Petro NOVIKOV	M		(1)	
Serhiy POLISHCHUK	G	14		
Anatoliy REDUSHKO	A	13	(10)	4
Petro RUSAK	A	16	(1)	1
Eduard SARKISOV	M	12	(1)	
Vitaliy SHUMSKYI	M	15	(1)	5
Anatoliy SIDENKO	A	1	(3)	
Pavlo SIROTIN	G	15		
Hennadiy SKYDAN	M	15		4
Olexandr SOBKIV	A	1	(7)	
Andriy SOKOLENKO	D		(1)	
Roman SVYSHCH	D		(2)	
Olexandr TSYSAR	D	7	(1)	
Volodymyr TSYTKIN	G	1	(2)	
Yaroslav VATAMANYUK	D	6	(2)	
Artur YAKUSHEV	D	11		
Ivan YAREMCHUK	M	2		
Ruslan ZABRANSKYI	A	10		3
Mykola ZUYENKO	D	23	(1)	1

LEAGUE RESULTS 1998/99

08/07/98	Vorskla Poltava	H	1-0	Larin
11/07/98	Metalurg Zaporizhzhya	A	1-1	Redushko
18/07/98	CSKA Kyiv	H	2-4	Shumskyi (p), Redushko
26/07/99	Kryvbas Kryvyi Rih	H	2-2	Shumskyi (p), Budnyk
02/08/98	Metalurg Donetsk	A	0-1	
08/08/98	Tavriya Simferopol	H	0-2	
16/08/98	SK Mykolaiv	A	1-1	og (Kochvar)
22/08/98	Metalurg Mariupol	H	0-3	
30/08/98	Dynamo Kyiv	A	0-7	
12/09/98	Karpaty Lviv	H	0-2	
20/09/98	Metalist Kharkiv	A	0-1	
26/09/98	Nyva Ternopil	H	1-1	Shumskyi (p)
04/10/98	Shakhtar Donetsk	A	1-6	Redushko
25/10/98	Dnipro Dnipropetrovsk	H	3-0	Redushko, Shumskyi (p), Zuyenko
31/10/98	Zirka Kirovohrad	A	1-2	Shumskyi (p)
07/03/99	Zirka Kirovohrad	H	1-0	Zabranskyi
11/03/99	Dnipro Dnipropetrovsk	A	0-0	
15/03/99	Shakhtar Donetsk	H	1-3	Kovalchuk
03/04/99	Nyva Ternopil	A	1-3	Kovalyuk
10/04/99	Metalist Kharkiv	H	1-2	Zabranskyi
17/04/99	Karpaty Lviv	A	0-3	
25/04/99	Dynamo Kyiv	H	0-1	
02/05/99	Metalurg Mariupol	A	1-2	Skydan
09/05/99	SK Mykolaiv	H	2-1	Rusak, Zabranskyi
14/05/99	Tavriya Simferopol	A	0-3	
18/05/99	Metalurg Donetsk	H	2-1	Martynov, Skydan (p)
22/05/99	Kryvbas Kryvyi Rih	A	0-2	
31/05/99	CSKA Kyiv	A	2-1	Skydan 2 (1p)
17/06/99	Metalurg Zaporizhzhya	H	0-0	
25/06/99	Vorskla Poltava	A	0-4	

SHAKHTAR DONETSK

CLUB DIRECTORY

Shakhtar Donetsk
vul. Artema 86a
340 050 Donetsk
tel - (062) 3354694/3353592/3662060
fax - (062) 3353193
Year of Formation - 1946
President - Rinat Akhmetov
Secretary - Vyacheslav Sharafutdinov
Coach - Valeriy Yaremchenko; Anatoliy Byshovets
Stadium - Shakhtar (40,483)

MAJOR HONOURS
Domestic Cup (USSR) - (4)
1961, 1962, 1980, 1983.
Domestic Cup - (2) 1995. 1997.

APPEARANCES 98/99

	P	Ap	(s)	Gls
Kostyantyn AKININ	A		(1)	
Alexei BAKHAREV (RUS)	M	11		1
Yuriy DANCHENKO	A		(4)	
Dainius GLEVECKAS (LIT)	D	5	(2)	
Yevhen KOTOV	D	14	(5)	
Olexandr KOVAL	D	16	(4)	
Olexandr KOVALENKO	M	3	(1)	
Serhiy KOVALEV	M	25		3
Volodymyr KOVAI YIIK	M		(6)	1
Valerly KRIVENTSOV	A	21	(7)	6
Andriy KURAYEV	G	10		
Ihor LEONOV	D	22	(1)	
Oleh MATVEYEV	M	7	(10)	7
Volodymyr MYKYTYN	M	14		
Serhiy NAHORNYAK	A	8	(1)	2
Andriy NIKITIN	G	6		
Hennadiy ORBU	M	18	(2)	5
Serhiy POPOV	D	24		7
Mikheil POTSKHVERIA (GEO)	A	3		1
Yuriy SELEZNEV	M	12	(7)	8
Oleh SHELAYEV	A		(2)	2
Andrey SHTOLCERS (LAT)	A	13	(8)	6
Dmytro SHUTKOV	G	14		
Mykhailo STAROSTYAK	D	23		
Anatoliy TYMOSHCHUK	A	14	(4)	2
Andriy VOROBEI	A	16	(2)	11
Volodymyr YAKSMANYTSKYI	D	5	(4)	2
Sergei ZHUNENKO (RUS)	D	5		
Hennadiy ZUBOV	M	21	(6)	4

LEAGUE RESULTS 1998/99

07/07/98	Tavriya Simferopol	A	1-2	Vorobei
11/07/98	SK Mykolaiv	H	7-0	Shtolcers 2, Potskhveria, Orbu 2,
				Seleznev 2
18/07/98	Metalurg Mariupol	A	1-0	og (Diryavka)
02/08/98	Karpaty Lviv	A	0-1	
06/08/98	Metalist Kharkiv	H	3-1	Vorobei, Kriventsov, Zubov
30/08/98	Dnipro Dnipropetrovsk	H	6-0	Popov 3, Vorobei 3
10/09/98	Zirka Kirovohrad	A	2-0	Popov, Vorobei
16/09/98	Nyva Ternopil	A	3-0	Yaksmanytskyi, Kriventsov,
				Shelayev
20/09/98	Vorskla Poltava	H	7-3	Yaksmanytskyi, Vorobei 3,
				Shelayev, Kovalev, Matveyev
24/09/98	Metalurg Zaporizhzhya	A	3-2	Kovalyuk, Matveyev, Seleznev
04/10/98	Prykarpattya Ivano-Frankivsk	H	6-1	Zubov 2, Matveyev,
				Kriventsov 2, og (Zuyenko)
20/10/98	CSKA Kyiv	A	1-0	Seleznev
25/10/98	Kryvbas Kryvyi Rih	A	0-1	
30/10/98	Metalurg Donetsk	H	4-2	Kovalev 2, Matveyev, Popov
29/11/98	Dynamo Kyiv	A	1-2	Matveyev
07/03/99	Metalurg Donetsk	A	4-0	Popov, Zubov, Tymoshchuk,
				Vorobei
11/03/99	Kryvbas Kryvyi Rih	H	1-1	Nahornyak
15/03/99	Prykarpattya Ivano-Frankivsk	A	3-1	Popov, Shtolcers, Nahornyak
03/04/99	Metalurg Zaporizhzhya	H	2-1	Orbu, Shtolcers
10/04/99	Vorskla Poltava	A	2-1	Kriventsov, Orbu
17/04/99	Zirka Kirovohrad	H	1-2	Kriventsov
24/04/99	Dnipro Dnipropetrovsk	A	2-1	Matveyev, Shtolcers
02/05/99	CSKA Kyiv	H	1-0	Shtolcers
10/05/99	Nyva Ternopil	H	1-1	Seleznev
14/05/99	Metalist Kharkiv	A	1-1	Matveyev (p)
18/05/99	Karpaty Lviv	H	1-1	Orbu
22/05/99	Dynamo Kyiv	H	0-0	
29/05/99	Metalurg Mariupol	H	1-0	Seleznev
17/06/99	SK Mykolaiv	A	3-0	Seleznev, Vorobei, Tymoshchuk
21/06/99	Tavriya Simferopol	H	2-0	Bakharev, Seleznev

TAVRIYA SIMFEROPOL

CLUB DIRECTORY

Tavriya Simferopol
vul. A. Pushkin 46
333 011 Simferopol
tel - (0652) 255383/276083/525057/252332
fax - (0652) 270147
Year of Formation - 1963
President - Roman Aronov
Secretary - Borys Levin
Coach - Viktor Grachov; Valeriy Petrov;
Anatoliy Korobochka
Stadium - Lokomotyv (23,612)

MAJOR HONOURS
League Championship - (1) 1992.

APPEARANCES 98/99

	P	Ap	(s)	Gls
Volodymyr ALEXEYEV	D	15		
Denys ANDRIYENKO	D	10	(6)	
Olexiy ANTYUKHIN	A	13	(1)	3
Olexiy BORODAI	M	1		
Vyacheslav BURMISTROV	A		(1)	
Dmytro DEMYANENKO	D	11		
Yuriy DONYUSHKIN	D	28	(1)	1
Olexandr GAIDASH	A	29		9
Valeriy GITYA-PETRYNSKYI	M	1		
Dmytro KOLTSOV	M		(1)	
Kostyantyn KOROL	M	1	(2)	
Sergei KUKALEVICH (BLS)	M	2	(3)	
Hennadiy KUNDENOK	M	6		2
Olexandr KUNDENOK	M	13		
Oleh KURATOV	M		(3)	
Maxym LEVYTSKYI	G	19	(1)	
Serhiy LEZHENTSEV	D	5		1
Gennadiy MARDAS (BLS)	M	11		
Olexandr MATVIYCHUK	D		(2)	
Olexandr MITROFANOV	D	22		1
Dmytro NAZAROV	D	5	(3)	
Andriy OPARIN	M	27		1
Olexiy OSIPOV	M	28		11
Anton ROMANENKO	A		(1)	
Vasyl SACHKO	A	4	(1)	
Anatoliy SKVORTSOV	M	1	(3)	
Viktor SMIGUNOV	D	18	(4)	1
Serhiy VELYCHKO	G	11		
Serhiy VETRENNIKOV	M	21		1
Roman VOINAROVSKYI	M	5	(14)	
Denys VOLK-KARACHEVSKYI	D	1	(3)	
Ihor VOPLYUSHKIN	M	1	(2)	
Serhiy YESIN	D	21	(5)	2

LEAGUE RESULTS 1998/99

07/07/98	Shakhtar Donetsk	H	2-1	Osipov 2
11/07/98	Dnipro Dnipropetrovsk	A	0-1	
18/07/98	Zirka Kirovohrad	H	1-0	Gaidash
02/08/98	Metalurg Zaporizhzhya	H	2-3	Gaidash, Kundenok H.
08/08/98	Prykarpattya Ivano-Frankivsk	A	2-0	Smigunov, Gaidash
16/08/98	Kryvbas Kryvyi Rih	H	0-2	
22/08/98	Metalurg Donetsk	A	0-2	
31/08/98	CSKA Kyiv	H	1-1	Gaidash
07/09/98	Vorskla Poltava	A	2-2	Osipov, Kundenok H.
12/09/98	SK Mykolaiv	H	2-0	Yesin, Osipov
19/09/98	Metalurg Mariupol	A	0-2	
24/09/98	Dynamo Kyiv	H	3-3	Osipov 3
04/10/98	Karpaty Lviv	A	1-2	Yesin (p)
25/10/98	Metalist Kharkiv	H	0-1	
31/10/98	Nyva Ternopil	A	0-0	
07/03/99	Nyva Ternopil	H	1-0	Gaidash
13/03/99	Metalist Kharkiv	A	0-1	
21/03/99	Karpaty Lviv	H	1-1	Gaidash
03/04/99	Dynamo Kyiv	A	0-0	
10/04/99	Metalurg Mariupol	H	0-2	
17/04/99	SK Mykolaiv	A	2-1	Gaidash, Vetrennikov
24/04/99	CSKA Kyiv	A	0-3	
02/05/99	Metalurg Donetsk	H	3-2	Gaidash, Osipov, Antyukhin
09/05/99	Kryvbas Kryvyi Rih	A	1-1	Antyukhin
14/05/99	Prykarpattya Ivano-Frankivsk	H	3-0	Osipov 2 (1p), Antyukhin
18/05/99	Metalurg Zaporizhzhya	A	0-3	
22/05/99	Vorskla Poltava	H	2-0	Donyushkin, Mitrofanov
29/05/99	Zirka Kirovohrad	A	1-3	Osipov
17/06/99	Dnipro Dnipropetrovsk	H	3-0	Lezhentsev, Oparin, Gaidash
21/06/99	Shakhtar Donetsk	A	0-2	

VORSKLA POLTAVA

CLUB DIRECTORY

Vorskla Poltava
Nezalezhnosti square 16
314 000 Poltava
tel - (05322) 22668/29598/21486
fax - (05322) 21670
Year of Formation - 1987
President - Volodymyr Artemov
Secretary - Stanislav Maizus
Coach - Olexandr Dovbiy; Serhiy Sobetskyi;
Anatoliy Konkov
Stadium - Vorskla (28,000)

APPEARANCES 98/99

		P	Ap	(s)	Gls
Olexiy ANTYUKHIN	A	8		(2)	3
Serhiy BEZHENAR	D	1			
Vyacheslav BOGODELOV	G	1			
Viktor BOHATYR	M	2			
Serhiy CHUICHENKO	A	2		(4)	
Viktor DOTSENKO	D	15			1
Volodymyr DYCHKO	D	7		(4)	
Andriy HOLOVKO	A	7		(7)	4
Olexandr M. HOLOVKO	D	18		(2)	
Mykhailo HURKA	M	4		(3)	
Andriy HUZENKO	M	24		(1)	2
Andriy KHOMYN	D	21		(3)	3
Vitaliy KOBZAR	M	21		(2)	1
Ihor KOSTYUK	M	21		(1)	9
Andriy KOVTUN	G	28			
Olexiy KUTS	G	1			
Serhiy LEZHENTSEV	D	5			
Vladislav LUNGU (MOL)	M			(1)	
Ihor MACHOHAN	D	26		(3)	
Hennadiy MEDVEDEV	A	5		(7)	
Olexandr MELASHCHENKO	M	4		(12)	2
Yuriy MOKRYTSKYI	D	7		(1)	
Volodymyr MUSOLITIN	A	19		(8)	4
Pavlo NESTERCHUK	A	1		(2)	
Daniel N'JOKU	M			(2)	
Olexandr OMELCHUK	M	21		(3)	1
Serhiy ONOPKO	M	14		(1)	3
Olexandr PERSHIN	D	9		(1)	
Yordan PETKOV (BUL)	D	24			1
Vitaliy SAMOILOV	M	14		(1)	1
Ivan SHARIY	A			(9)	1

LEAGUE RESULTS 1998/99

08/07/98	Prykarpattya Ivano-Frankivsk	A	0-1	
15/07/98	Kryvbas Kryvyi Rih	H	0-0	
02/08/98	SK Mykolaiv	A	0-1	
08/08/98	Metalurg Mariupol	H	0-1	
16/08/98	Dynamo Kyiv	A	0-4	
22/08/98	Karpaty Lviv	H	0-0	
30/08/98	Metalist Kharkiv	A	4-2	Kobzar, Musolitin 2, Kostyuk
03/09/98	Metalurg Donetsk	A	0-0	
04/09/98	Tavriya Simferopol	H	2-2	Antyukhin, Shariy (p)
17/09/98	Nyva Ternopil	H	2-1	Khomyn (p), Antyukhin
20/09/98	Shakhtar Donetsk	A	3-7	Samoilov, Antyukhin, Kostyuk
26/09/98	Dnipro Dnipropetrovsk	H	1-0	Kostyuk (p)
04/10/98	Zirka Kirovohrad	A	0-1	
26/10/98	CSKA Kyiv	A	1-2	Omelchuk
31/10/98	Metalurg Zaporizhzhya	H	3-0	Petkov, Khomyn 2
07/03/99	Metalurg Zaporizhzhya	A	1-0	Huzenko
13/03/99	CSKA Kyiv	H	1-0	Huzenko
03/04/99	Dnipro Dnipropetrovsk	A	0-2	
10/04/99	Shakhtar Donetsk	H	1-2	Kostyuk
17/04/99	Nyva Ternopil	A	2-2	Kostyuk, Musolitin (p)
24/04/99	Metalist Kharkiv	H	1-2	Onopko
02/05/99	Karpaty Lviv	A	1-2	Dotsenko
10/05/99	Dynamo Kyiv	H	0-2	
14/05/99	Metalurg Mariupol	A	0-1	
18/05/99	SK Mykolaiv	H	2-1	Onopko, Holovko A
22/05/99	Tavriya Simferopol	A	0-2	
29/05/99	Metalurg Donetsk	H	2-0	Holovko A., Kostyuk
13/06/99	Zirka Kirovohrad	H	4-2	Onopko, Kostyuk 2 (1p), Musolitin
17/06/99	Kryvbas Kryvyi Rih	A	1-3	Holovko A.
25/06/99	Prykarpattya Ivano-Frankivsk	H	4-0	Kostyuk, Melashchenko 2, Holovko A.

ZIRKA KIROVOHRAD

CLUB DIRECTORY

Zirka Kirovohrad
vul. Yuriy Gagarin 1A
P.O. Box 342
316 050 Kirovohrad
tel - (0522) 223430/240824/246906/241392
fax - (0522) 222457
Year of Formation - 1922
President - Olexandr Nikulin
Secretary - Andriy Perevoznyk
Coach - Olexandr Ishchenko
Stadium - Zirka (18,000)

APPEARANCES 98/99

	P	Ap	(s)	Gls
Borys BILOSHAPKA	G	24		
Olexandr BILOZERSKYI	D	26	(2)	1
Yuriy BOGDANOV	A		(6)	1
Volodymyr CHALYI	M	6	(12)	
Olexiy CHERVONOIVAN	A		(2)	
Leonid FEDOROV	M	22	(2)	
Serhiy GUSEV	A	10		1
Andriy HLUSHCHENKO	G	6		
Andriy HORBAN	D		(1)	
Stanislav KAZAKOV	M	2	(9)	
Ihor KHOMENKO	D	4	(7)	1
Ihor KISLOV	M	29		9
Denys KOVBA	A	5	(5)	2
Serhiy LAVRYNENKO	D	11	(2)	
Ihor MAKOHON	D	22		
Yuriy MARTYNOV	M	24	(5)	5
Ihor MOSHEVYCH	D	14		
Valeriy MYKHAILENKO	M		(3)	
Matviy NYKOLAICHUK	M	3		
Andriy POROSHIN	A	3	(8)	
Ivan RUSNAK	D	5	(6)	
Andriy RUSSOL	M		(1)	
Artem SAUTIN	M		(1)	
Valeriy SHAPOVALOV	D	25	(3)	2
Serhiy SHASHKEVYCH	D	1	(1)	
Vitaliy SKYSH	D	6		2
Olexandr SOBOL	D	29	(1)	1
Olexandr SPIVAK	M	21		3
Kostyantyn TUPCHIYENKO	M	1	(3)	
Bohdan YESYP	A	9	(3)	1
Vadym ZAYETS	M	9		1
Oleh ZHILIN	D	13		1

LEAGUE RESULTS 1998/99

07/07/98	Kryvbas Kryvyi Rih	A	0-1	
11/07/98	Metalurg Donetsk	H	3-1	Khomenko, Sobol, Kislov
18/07/98	Tavriya Simferopol	A	0-1	
26/07/98	SK Mykolaiv	H	1-1	Kislov
02/08/98	Metalurg Mariupol	A	0-0	
06/08/98	Dynamo Kyiv	H	0-5	
16/08/98	Karpaty Lviv	A	1-2	Spivak
22/08/98	Metalist Kharkiv	H	2-0	Martynov (p), Kislov
30/08/98	Nyva Ternopil	A	2-3	Yesyp, Kislov
10/09/98	Shakhtar Donetsk	H	0-2	
20/09/98	Dnipro Dnipropetrovsk	A	1-1	Martynov
26/09/98	CSKA Kyiv	A	0-0	
04/10/98	Vorskla Poltava	H	1-0	Bilozerskyi
25/10/98	Metalurg Zaporizhzhya	A	0-1	
31/10/98	Prykarpattya Ivano-Frankivsk	H	2-1	Martynov, Kislov
07/03/99	Prykarpattya Ivano-Frankivsk	A	0-1	
13/03/99	Metalurg Zaporizhzhya	H	1-0	Kislov
03/04/99	CSKA Kyiv	H	1-1	Shapovalov
10/04/99	Dnipro Dnipropetrovsk	H	2-0	Skysh, Gusev
17/04/99	Shakhtar Donetsk	A	2-1	Skysh, Bogdanov
24/04/99	Nyva Ternopil	H	1-0	Martynov (p)
02/05/99	Metalist Kharkiv	A	0-3	
10/05/99	Karpaty Lviv	H	2-2	Spivak 2
14/05/99	Dynamo Kyiv	A	0-1	
18/05/99	Metalurg Mariupol	H	0-1	
22/05/99	SK Mykolaiv	A	2-2	Kovba, Zayets
29/05/99	Tavriya Simferopol	H	3-1	Shapovalov, Kislov, Zhilin
13/06/99	Vorskla Poltava	A	2-4	Kovba, Kislov
17/06/99	Metalurg Donetsk	A	0-1	
21/06/99	Kryvbas Kryvyi Rih	H	2-3	Kislov, Martynov (p)

PROMOTED CLUB

SECOND DIVISION FINAL TABLE 98/99

		Pd	W	D	L	F	A	Pt	GD
1	Dynamo-2 Kyiv	38	27	7	4	78	28	88	+50
2	**Chornomorets Odesa**	**38**	**25**	**4**	**9**	**77**	**38**	**79**	**+39**
3	Torpedo Zaporizhzhya	38	24	5	9	55	29	77	+26
4	FC Cherkasy	38	24	4	10	68	42	76	+26
5	Poligraftekhnika Olexandriya	38	15	13	10	48	51	58	-3
6	FC Vynnytsya	38	16	9	13	45	39	57	+6
7	FC Lviv	38	15	12	11	58	43	57	+15
8	Naftovyk Okhtyrka	38	16	9	13	45	40	57	+5
9	Stal Alchevsk	38	16	7	15	55	52	55	+3
10	Shakhtar-2 Donetsk	38	15	7	16	51	44	52	+7
11	CSKA-2 Kyiv	38	14	10	14	45	48	52	-3
12	Polissya Zhytomyr	38	15	7	16	40	55	52	-15
13	Yavir-Sumy Sumy	38	15	7	16	36	42	52	-6
14	Volyn Lutsk	38	16	3	19	36	43	51	-7
15	Metalurg Nikopol	38	16	3	19	46	63	51	-17
16	Podillya Khmelnytskyi	38	13	12	13	39	42	51	-3
17	Kremin Kremenchuk	38	11	7	20	34	63	40	-29
18	Bukovyna Chernivtsi	38	6	9	23	26	68	27	-42
19	Desna Chernihiv	38	7	6	25	28	60	27	-32
20	Shakhtar Makiyvka	38	3	1	34	20	40	4	-20

N.B. Dynamo-2 Kyiv ineligible for promotion. Shakhtar Makiyvka deducted 6pts.

CLUB DIRECTORY

Chornomorets Odesa
Central Stadium
Shevchenko Park
270 014 Odesa
tel - (0482) 223367/226580/684894
fax - (0482) 637332
Year of Formation - 1959
President - Petro Naida
Secretary - Oleh Taradai
Coach - Volodymyr Kozerenko;
Olexandr Golokolosov
Stadium - ChMP (42,256)

MAJOR HONOURS
Domestic Cup - (2) 1992, 1994.

WALES

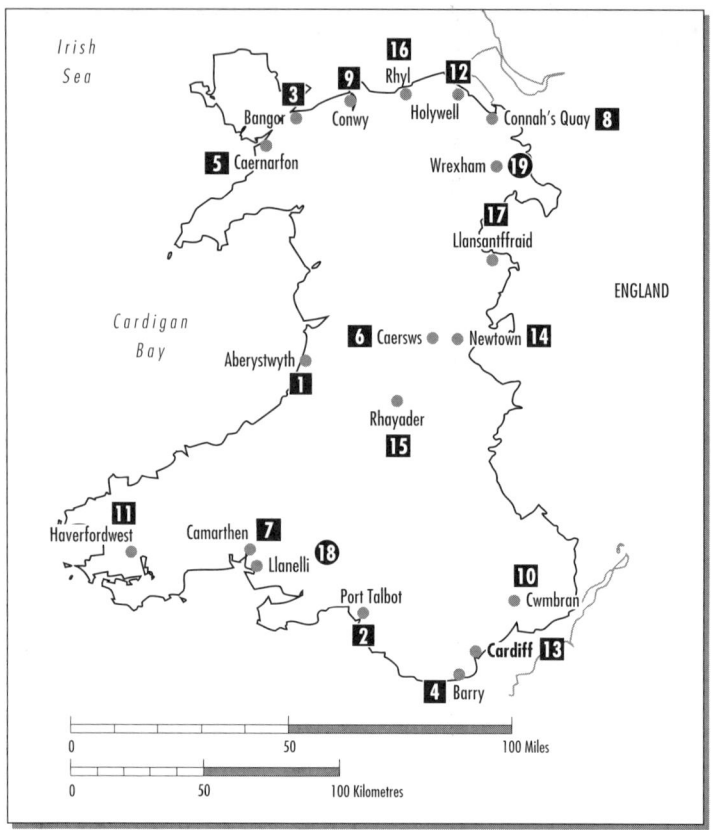

1	ABERYSTWYTH TOWN	1066
2	AFAN LIDO	1067
3	BANGOR CITY	1068
4	BARRY TOWN	1069
5	CAERNARFON TOWN	1070
6	CAERSWS	1071
7	CARMARTHEN TOWN	1072
8	CONNAH'S QUAY NOMADS	1073
9	CONWY UNITED	1074
10	CWMBRAN TOWN	1075

11	HAVERFORDWEST COUNTY	1076
12	HOLYWELL TOWN	1077
13	INTER CABLETEL	1078
14	NEWTOWN	1079
15	RHAYADER TOWN	1080
16	RHYL	1081
17	TOTAL NETWORK SOLUTIONS	1082
Promoted clubs		
18	LLANELLI	1083
19	FLEXSYS CEFN DRUIDS	1083

BARRY TOWN STILL ONE STEP BEYOND

Gould goes after battering in Bologna

FEDERATION DIRECTORY

The Football Association of Wales
Plymouth Chambers, 3 Westgate Street, Cardiff CF1 1DD

tel - (0222) 372325   Year of Formation - 1876
fax - (0222) 343961   Chairman - Brian Fear
   Secretary - David Collins

Stadium - The National Stadium, Cardiff Arms Park, Cardiff (40,240)

In the end Bobby Gould decided to do the honourable thing and resign. He, like everyone else with the interests of Welsh football at heart, decided that the nightmare could not continue. Wales had just been put to the sword for 90 minutes by Italy in Bologna, so it was only right that Gould should share in the collective torture.

The Englishman's decision was widely welcomed by Welsh fans, most of whom had never really wanted him appointed in the first place. Throughout his four-year reign Gould was subjected to continuous flak from the Welsh press and public. It was not simply that he failed to bring the desired results, but that his management methods were so contentious and his public relations so inept. He hit too many false notes, and the Welsh fans never truly accepted him as a genuine defender of their faith.

Gould would surely have gone earlier had the Welsh FA (FAW) been in a financial position to cut short his contract. But they weren't. They were seriously short-funded. That much became evident when they accepted a large 'loan' from the English FA in what became known as the 'cash for votes' scandal that effectively cleaned out the reigning politburo at Lancaster Gate.

The poverty of the FAW also hampered their choice of a successor for Gould. Many candidates were put forward in the newspapers, including jobless luminaries such as Roy Evans, Joe Kinnear, Roy Hodgson and - the biggest name of them all - Terry Venables. But it was

LEAGUE CHAMPIONSHIP RESULTS 98/99

		1	2	3	4	5	6	7	8	9	10	11	12	13	14	15	16	17
1	Aberystwyth Town		2-1	3-0	1-1	1-1	0-5	3-2	2-1	3-1	1-3	2-1	0-0	1-1	5-0	2-1	2-1	0-1
2	Afan Lido	2-2		0-2	0-0	1-3	0-1	1-1	1-3	0-1	0-4	0-2	2-0	0-2	0-2	2-0	2-1	3-3
3	Bangor City	1-2	0-1		0-3	1-1	0-1	4-0	0-2	1-3	2-2	3-0	5-2	1-0	2-3	0-1	4-1	2-1
4	Barry Town	5-1	0-2	4-2		3-0	5-2	6-2	1-0	1-1	2-1	2-0	4-0	1-1	1-0	7-1	2-0	2-0
5	Caernarfon Town	2-0	2-0	1-0	0-4		2-2	3-2	1-1	1-1	2-4	2-0	2-2	1-1	3-1	2-0	3-0	2-1
6	Caersws	2-3	2-1	2-0	2-4	3-2		1-2	2-0	0-3	1-3	4-4	3-2	0-2	1-1	0-0	3-1	3-1
7	Carmarthen Town	2-5	1-1	1-2	2-1	0-0	0-1		6-2	2-1	1-1	3-1	3-0	0-1	1-0	1-1	1-2	1-0
8	Connah's Quay Nomads	0-0	0-0	1-1	0-3	2-2	0-0	0-2		1-2	1-0	3-1	4-2	1-2	3-2	4-1	6-2	2-3
9	Conwy United	1-1	2-0	3-1	1-3	1-1	2-1	1-2	1-3		2-4	0-2	2-1	3-0	1-0	1-1	2-1	3-3
10	Cwmbran Town	0-1	1-4	2-4	0-4	6-0	2-1	2-0	2-1	3-0		4-0	4-0	0-0	3-0	3-6	6-1	0-4
11	Haverfordwest County	2-6	1-1	0-0	0-0	0-2	1-1	1-2	1-0	1-3	2-1		7-2	0-1	2-0	1-0	5-2	1-3
12	Holywell Town	3-6	0-0	1-1	2-3	1-2	0-0	1-1	0-0	4-3	0-4	4-0		1-2	0-3	2-2	0-3	3-3
13	Inter CableTel	6-1	0-1	3-0	1-2	3-0	6-0	1-2	1-1	3-0	0-1	1-0	5-1		0-2	1-0	3-2	1-1
14	Newtown	1-1	4-0	3-1	0-0	1-1	4-0	0-0	1-0	2-1	0-0	1-1	4-0	1-3		1-0	2-1	0-0
15	Rhayader Town	0-2	1-1	0-0	0-0	2-0	1-3	1-0	2-0	2-2	1-1	2-2	1-3	0-5	0-2		1-2	0-0
16	Rhyl	1-0	2-0	1-2	0-6	0-1	1-1	1-2	1-2	0-3	1-4	1-2	5-1	1-2	3-3	3-1		0-3
17	Total Network Solutions	0-0	1-1	1-2	1-2	2-0	2-1	1-1	2-0	1-4	2-2	4-2	2-0	1-3	1-1	1-0	6-0	

LEAGUE CHAMPIONSHIP FINAL TABLE 98/99

			Home				Away				Total						
		P	W	D	L	F	A	W	D	L	F	A	W	D	L	F	A	P	GD
1	Barry Town	32	13	2	1	46	13	10	5	1	36	10	23	7	2	82	23	76	+59
2	Inter CableTel	32	9	2	5	35	14	10	4	2	26	12	19	6	7	61	26	63	+35
3	Cwmbran Town	32	9	1	6	38	26	8	5	3	35	18	17	6	9	73	44	57	+29
4	Aberystwyth Town	32	9	4	3	28	20	7	5	4	31	28	16	9	7	59	48	57	+11
5	Caernarfon Town	32	9	5	2	29	19	4	6	6	16	27	13	11	8	45	46	50	-1
6	Newtown	32	8	7	1	25	9	5	3	8	20	26	13	10	9	45	35	49	+10
7	Conwy United	32	7	4	5	26	24	7	3	6	29	25	14	7	11	55	49	49	+6
8	Total Network Solutions	32	7	5	4	28	19	5	6	5	27	23	12	11	9	55	42	47	+13
9	Carmarthen Town	32	7	4	5	25	19	6	4	6	21	27	13	8	11	46	46	47	0
10	Caersws	32	7	3	6	29	29	5	5	6	20	26	12	8	12	49	55	44	-6
11	Bangor City	32	6	2	8	26	23	5	4	7	18	26	11	6	15	44	49	39	-5
12	Connah's Quay Nomads	32	6	5	5	28	23	4	3	9	16	24	10	8	14	44	47	38	-3
13	Haverfordwest County	32	6	4	6	25	24	3	3	10	18	36	9	7	16	43	60	34	-17
14	Afan Lido	32	3	4	9	14	27	4	6	6	14	19	7	10	15	28	46	31	-18
15	Rhayader Town	32	3	7	6	14	23	2	4	10	15	31	5	11	16	29	54	26	-25
16	Rhyl	32	4	2	10	21	33	3	0	13	20	48	7	2	23	41	81	23	-40
17	Holywell Town	32	2	7	7	22	33	1	2	13	16	53	3	9	20	38	86	18	-48

always on the cards that remuneration would prove to be a stumbling-block, especially in the case of the former England boss. So, ultimately, after much dilly-dallying, the job was given, on an extended temporary basis, to the team's veteran striker (or, latterly, midfielder), Mark Hughes.

Hughes had been in joint-charge with another golden oldie, Neville Southall, for the crucial home tie with Denmark that took place just four days after Gould's final stand in Bologna. Although there was an appreciable improvement in team spirit and application for that match, the final result, a 0-2 defeat, was even more serious than the mauling in Italy. It effectively ended Welsh hopes of reaching the European Championship finals - a feat that had not looked totally beyond them after their two wins in four days the previous October, away to Denmark (2-1) and at home to Belarus (3-2).

The return match with the Danes took place at Anfield in Liverpool. The Welsh players were in

agreement with their fans that it should have been switched to Cardiff (the venue for the win over Belarus), but Denmark, acting within their rights, objected, claiming that as Italy had been allowed to play their game at Anfield, it would be disadvantageous to them to have to play on Welsh rather than English soil. The squabbling over venues was all the result of the major construction work being carried out at the National Stadium, and the choice of Anfield was purely a consequence of the FAW's keenness to generate maximum revenue - irrespective of the effect that it had on the team's qualifying chances.

Whether Mark Hughes is confirmed in his position for the next World Cup qualifying series remains to be seen, but it is difficult to imagine that either he or anyone else will acquire by then the raw material necessary to end the team's abysmal qualifying record. On the evidence of the 1999/2000 season Wales are not sufficiently well-equipped to become an international force. The only areas

TOP SCORERS

28	Eifion WILLIAMS (Barry Town)
21	Chris SUMMERS (Cwmbran Town)
20	Mattie DAVIES (Cwmbran Town)
	John TONER (Conwy United)
16	Richard GAY (Haverfordwest County)
	Jamie HUGHES (Connah's Quay Nomads)
14	Richard JONES (Barry Town)
13	Sean JEHU (Caersws)
	Nicky WARD (Newtown)
12	Paul EVANS (Inter CableTel)
	Ken McKENNA (Total Network Solutions)
	Kevin MORRISON (Newtown/Aberystwyth Town)

on the field where they offer genuine quality are in goal (where Paul Jones played one blinder after another until cruelly making the mistake that led to the Danes' first goal at Anfield) and in whatever position Ryan Giggs chooses to deploy his unique talents. Other players with a future in the side include John Hartson, Robbie Savage and Craig Bellamy, but with Hughes himself close to burn-out and Dean Saunders not far behind, it is fair to say that one of the finest ever generations of Welsh players has now come to an end with nothing to show for their efforts except for a multitude of caps and a treasure trove of trophies won with their clubs.

Hughes will continue to look to the English leagues for fresh talent. The League of Wales, though gradually improving in standard, still occupies a place several rungs lower on the quality ladder. The LoW's perpetual champions, Barry Town, would probably struggle to hold their own in England's non-league

Conference, but in the Principality they continue to reign supreme.

Gary Barnett's side romped to their fourth successive Welsh title in 1998/99. Their victory margin in the final table was halved from 26 points to 13 in comparison with the previous season, but that was only in part down to the improvement made by the rest of the field. More significant was the fact that six games fewer were played as a result of the league being reduced in number from 20 participants to 17.

There should have been 18 teams in at the start, but Ebbw Vale were expelled pre-season for financial reasons. Having an odd number of participants provides fixture problems at the best of times, but in Wales, where the postponement and rescheduling of matches is a regular practice, it merely added to the chaos, which meant that for most weeks of the season, with the clubs having played a varying number of games, the league table provided a distorted snapshot of the reality. Clubs

NATIONAL TEAM APPEARANCES 98/99

Manager - Bobby GOULD/Neville SOUTHALL & Mark HUGHES	ITA	DEN	BLS	SUI	ITA	DEN	Cps	Gls
Paul JONES (18/04/67) - Southampton (ENG)	G	G	G	G26	G	G	11	-
John ROBINSON (29/08/71) - Charlton Athletic (ENG)	D	s80	D	D	D78	D87	16	2
Kit SYMONS (08/03/71) - Fulham (ENG)	D	D	D	D			31	1
Adrian WILLIAMS (16/08/71) - Wolverhampton Wanderers (ENG)	D	D			D		12	1
Chris COLEMAN (10/06/70) - Fulham (ENG)	D	D	D	D		D	24	4
Darren BARNARD (30/11/71) - Barnsley (ENG)	D	D	D		D	D90	6	-
Andy JOHNSON (02/05/74) - Nottingham Forest (ENG)	M	M54	M	M			4	-
Gary SPEED (08/09/69) - Newcastle United (ENG)	M	M		M	M	M	52	3
Mark HUGHES (01/11/63) - Southampton (ENG)	M80	M	M	M75	M	M	72	16
Nathan BLAKE (27/01/72) - Bolton Wanderers (ENG)/Blackburn Rovers (ENG)	A65	A69	A	A64			11	2
Ryan GIGGS (29/11/73) - Manchester United (ENG)	A				A	M	24	5
Dean SAUNDERS (21/06/64) - Sheffield United (ENG)/SL Benfica (POR)	s65	A80	A	A	A46	A	69	21
Robbie SAVAGE (18/10/74) - Leicester City (ENG)	s80	D	D	D			13	1
Mark PEMBRIDGE (29/11/70) - SL Benfica (POR)		s54	M	M	s78	s87	33	5
Craig BELLAMY (13/07/79) - Norwich City (ENG)		s69		s75	M78	s89	7	2
Mark CROSSLEY (16/06/69) - Nottingham Forest (ENG)				s26			2	-
John HARTSON (05/04/75) - Wimbledon (ENG)				s64	s46	A89	17	2
Robert PAGE (03/09/74) - Watford (ENG)				D			7	-
Andy MELVILLE (29/11/68) - Sunderland (ENG)					D	D	34	3
Steve JENKINS (16/07/72) - Huddersfield Town (ENG)				s78	D		12	-
Andy LEGG (28/07/66) - Cardiff City				s90			5	-

INTERNATIONAL HONOURS

World Cup Finals appearances: 1958 (qtr-finals)
European Championship appearances: 1976

PLAYERS OF THE SEASON

RICHARD JONES

When Richard Jones became Barry Town's first professional player in 1994, he could hardly have expected that he would go on to win four successive League of Wales championship medals, but the 30-year-old, who had previous spells with Newport County, Wimbledon, Hereford and Swansea City, has played a pivotal rôle in all of Barry's recent successes. Having been made the assistant coach of the side in 1998/99, he also swapped positions, abandoning his defensive midfield duties to act as a foil for Eifion Williams up front. The outcome was his best season yet, with an impressive 14 goals in the league and another four in the League Cup, including all three in the final against Caernarfon Town.

RYAN GIGGS

Richard Jones may be an unknown outside Wales. Not so his fellow countryman Ryan Giggs, who is among the most celebrated players in the whole of planet football. The Manchester United superstar's allegiance to Wales has been questioned many times, and in 1998/99 he was again mysteriously unavailable for three of the team's Euro 2000 qualifying matches, but there is no doubt that he, and possibly he alone, carries the nation's hopes into the new millennium. Still in his mid-20s, Giggs has already amassed a huge collection of club honours with Manchester United. Three of those came in 1998/99 as he helped United to win their illustrious 'treble'. His contributions in all three competitions were notable, but nothing could surpass the wonder of his extra-time winner against Arsenal in the FA Cup semi-final replay - an exploit of individual genius that the media in England were eager to categorise as one of the greatest goals ever scored.

like Connah's Quay Nomads and Aberystwyth Town led the table early on, but it was only when Barry Town reached the top that a proper sense of order prevailed.

Barry were clearly the best team in the league, but they were made to fight for every point and even lost a couple of games. Their 51-match unbeaten run was ended by a shock 0-2 home win by Afan Lido early on, and then, nine wins later, they also came a cropper away to Carmarthen Town.

In addition, Barry were knocked out of the Welsh Cup by Connah's Quay Nomads for the second year running. They did, however, ensure a hat-trick of League Cup triumphs, beating Caernarfon Town 3-0 in the final, played in Aberystwyth. And there was another Golden Boot for Barry's penalty-box predator Eifion Williams, who struck 28 league goals to add to the five he netted in the League Cup.

The Welsh Cup was won by Inter CableTel, who took the trophy for the first time after a dull final, against Carmarthen Town, which only came to life in extra-time.

EUROPEAN CUPS 98/99

CHAMPIONS' CUP
● **BARRY TOWN**
Preliminary round DYNAMO KYIV (UKR)
A 0-8
    Nurse; Lloyd, Jones, York, Barrow, Barnett, Carter, Williams (Evans C. 59), Dempsey, Thorpe, Evans T..
H 1-2 Williams (30)
    Mountain; Evans T., Lloyd, Jones, York, Barrow, Barnett, Carter, Evans C., Williams, Dempsey.

CUP WINNERS' CUP
● **BANGOR CITY**
Qualifying round FC HAKA (FIN)
H 0-2
    Williams L.; Williams G., Fox, Allen, McLoughlan, Horner, Hilditch, Taylor, Ayorinde, Sharratt, McGoona.
A 0-1
    Williams L.; Mooney (Gibney 90), Fox, Allen, Lloyd, Horner, Hilditch, Taylor, Ayorinde, Sharratt, Langley.

UEFA CUP
● **NEWTOWN**
Preliminary round WISLA KRAKOW (POL)
H 0-0
    Barton; Thomas M. (Line 82), Evans G., Reynolds, Thomas A., Roberts, Evans M., Wickham, Williams, Yates, Ruscoe.
A 0-7
    Barton; Line, Evans G., Reynolds, Thomas A., Roberts, Wickham (Clifford 59), Williams, Yates (Commerford 76), Evans M., Ruscoe (Davies 79).

A goal apiece in the second extra period sent the match into penalties, and Inter 'keeper Gary Wager proved to be the hero as his team won the shoot-out 4-2.

Inter were already through to the UEFA Cup by virtue of their second-place finish in the league, but Carmarthen's defeat ended their own hopes of a European spot. The second UEFA Cup place berth went, instead, to third-placed Cwmbran Town, while fourth-placed Aberystwyth took the consolation prize of a place in the InterToto Cup, which offered the club their first crack at international competition in 105 years.

Welsh clubs' annual summer fling in Europe was restricted once again to the bare minimum of games as Barry Town, Newtown and Bangor City all went tumbling at the first fence. On the positive side, all three were dismissed by clubs who went on to win their respective domestic championships, but, against that, there was only one goal to cheer - provided by the ever-prolific Eifion Williams in Barry's home game against Dynamo Kiev. Unfortunately, his team were already 9-0 down on aggregate at the time.

NATIONAL TEAM RESULTS 98/99

05/09/98	Italy (ECQ)	H	Liverpool	0-2	
10/10/98	Denmark (ECQ)	A	Copenhagen	2-1	Williams (59), Bellamy (86)
14/10/98	Belarus (ECQ)	H	Cardiff	3-2	Robinson (14), Coleman (53), Symons (84)
31/03/99	Switzerland (ECQ)	A	Zürich	0-2	
05/06/99	Italy (ECQ)	A	Bologna	0-4	
09/06/99	Denmark (ECQ)	H	Liverpool	0-2	

DOMESTIC CUP 98/99

SECOND ROUND
Total Network Solutions 2, Aberystwyth Town 2
(replay) Aberystwyth Town 2, Total Network Solutions 3 (aet)
Afan Lido 5, Caerleon 1
Caernarfon Town 3, Llangefni Town 0
Carmarthen Town 2, Hoover Sports 1
Cwmbran Town 2, Goytre United 0
Haverfordwest County 6, Bridgend Town 0
Guilsfield 0, Caersws 5
CPD Porthmadog 0, Holywell Town 2
Rhayader Town 3, Welshpool Town 1
Rhydymwyn 2, Conwy United 2
(replay) Conwy United 2, Rhydymwyn 1
Rhyl 5, Denbigh Town 4
Aberaman Athletic 2, Llanelli 3
Rhondda 1, Ammanford 1 (aet; 2-3 on pens.)
British Aerospace 5, Brymbo Broughton 1
Chepstow Town 4, Morriston Town 0
Flexsys Cefn Druids 2, Cemaes Bay 1
Fflint Town United 6, Castell Alun Colts 2
Gwynfi United 0, BP Llandarcy 2
Owens Corning 1, Holyhead Hotspur 4
CPD Penrhyncoch 3, Oswestry Town 2
Pontlottyn Blast Furnace 0, Tredegar Town 3
Porth Tywyn Suburbs 2, Ton Pentre 1
Port Talbot Athletic 2, Grange Harlequins 1
Ruthin Town 0, Colwyn Bay YMCA 1
Treowen Stars 5, Ely Rangers 0
UWIC Cardiff 1, Pontardawe Town 1
(replay) Pontardawe Town 4, UWIC Cardiff 3

THIRD ROUND
Barry Town 2, Haverfordwest County 0
British Aerospace 2, BP Llandarcy 2
(replay) BP Llandarcy 3, British Aerospace 2
Caersws 3, Cwmbran Town 4
Carmarthen Town 2, Chepstow Town 2
(replay) Chepstow Town 2, Carmarthen Town 5
Connah's Quay Nomads 2, Newtown 2
(replay) Newtown 0, Connah's Quay Nomads 1
CPD Penrhyncoch 2, Colwyn Bay YMCA 4
Flexsys Cefn Druids 1, Caernarfon Town 5
Holyhead Hotspur 1, Conwy United 3
Inter CableTel 1, Holywell Town 0
Llanelli 2, Tredegar Town 1
Porth Tywyn Suburbs 1, Port Talbot Athletic 1
(replay) Port Talbot Athletic 1, Porth Tywyn Suburbs 0
Rhayader Town 3, Bangor City 0
Rhyl 2, Fflint Town United 2
(replay) Fflint Town United 1, Rhyl 1
(aet; 5-4 on pens.)
Total Network Solutions 2, Afan Lido 0
Treowen Stars 1, Pontardawe Town 2
bye - Ammanford

FOURTH ROUND
Inter CableTel 1, Pontardawe Town 1
(replay) Pontardawe Town 0, Inter CableTel 3
Total Network Solutions 2, Rhayader Town 1
Ammanford 1, Colwyn Bay YMCA 0
Port Talbot Athletic 2, Fflint Town United 0
Carmarthen Town 2, Caernarfon Town 0

Llanelli 1, Cwmbran Town 2
Conwy United 7, BP Llandarcy 0
Barry Town 0, Connah's Quay Nomads 1

QUARTER-FINALS
Ammanford 0, Conwy United 0
(replay) Conwy United 1, Ammanford 0
Total Network Solutions 1, Cwmbran Town 2
Connah's Quay Nomads 1, Inter CableTel 1
(replay) Inter CableTel 3, Connah's Quay Nomads 1
Carmarthen Town 1, Port Talbot Athletic 0

SEMI-FINALS
Carmarthen Town 1, Conwy United 0
Cwmbran Town 3, Inter CableTel 4

FINAL
09/05/99, Merthyr Tydfil
INTER CABLETEL 1 Poretta (116)
CARMARTHEN TOWN 1 Meredith (114)
(aet; 4-2 on pens.)
referee - Burge
INTER CABLETEL - Wager; Parselle, Wile, Brazil, Richards (Williams 79), Dyson, Davies, Porretta, Mardenborough, Evans (Tyler 108), Dyer (Misbah 62).
CARMARTHEN TOWN - Fitzgerald; Nicholas (Burrows 91), Jones, Barnhouse, Cable, Thomas, Rees (Vaughan 97), Rossiter, Nicholls, Williams, Meredith.

ABERYSTWYTH TOWN

CLUB DIRECTORY

Aberystwyth Town FC
The Lodge
Nat. Library of Wales
Aberystwyth
tel - (01970) 623520
fax - (01970) 617939
Year of Formation - 1884
Chairman - Donald Kane
Secretary - Rhun Owens
Manager - Barrie Powell
Stadium - Park Avenue (5,500)

MAJOR HONOURS
Domestic Cup - (1) 1900.

APPEARANCES 98/99

	P	Ap	(s)	Gls
Gavin ALLEN	A	6	(2)	2
Andrew CAREE	D		(2)	
Jim CLARKE (ENG)	D	2		
Martin CROMPTON (ENG)	D	16	(9)	1
Andy EVANS	A	16	(12)	4
Hayden FLEMING	D	15	(9)	
Mike FOSTER	D	13	(2)	
Martyn GRIFFITHS	M	19	(10)	4
Peter GRIFFITHS	M		(4)	
Chris HAMMOND (ENG)	M	8		2
Matthew HARRISON	M	2	(2)	1
Glyndwr HUGHES	M	21	(4)	9
Mark HUGHES	D	4	(3)	
Phil JOHNSON (ENG)	M	22		2
Martin JONES (ENG)	G	24		
Stuart JONES (ENG)	M	3	(7)	
Donald KANE (SCO)	D	16		1
Stuart KINNINMONTH	G	3		
Gareth KNOTT	M	5	(7)	2
Gari LEWIS	D	28		
Carl MAINWARING	A	7		5
Steve MELLOR (ENG)	M	1		
Kevin MORRISON (SCO)	A	18	(1)	10
Ryan NICHOLLS	A	7	(2)	1
Neil SIMON	D		(1)	
Aneurin THOMAS	D	22		1
Arron THOMAS	A		(1)	
Adrian TUCKER	G	5	(2)	
Leigh VICK	D	21	(9)	1
Jonathan WILLIAMS	A	31		9
Stephen WILLIAMS	A	17	(6)	4

LEAGUE RESULTS 1998/99

22/08/98	Afan Lido	H	2-1	Vick, Kane
29/08/98	Inter CableTel	H	1-1	Griffiths M.
09/09/98	Carmarthen Town	A	5-2	Nicholls, Williams J., Hughes G.,
				Johnson, Harrison
12/09/98	Cwmbran Town	A	1-0	Allen
19/09/98	Conwy United	H	3-1	Williams J., Johnson, Allen
26/09/98	Connah's Quay Nomads	A	0-0	
03/10/98	Caernarfon Town	H	1-1	Evans
09/10/98	Caersws	A	3-2	Evans, Hughes G., Williams J.
31/10/98	Total Network Solutions	A	0-0	
07/11/98	Newtown	H	5-0	Williams J. 2, Evans, Knott,
				Williams S.
14/11/98	Bangor City	A	2-1	Evans, Griffiths M.
28/11/98	Holywell Town	H	0-0	
05/12/98	Rhyl	A	0-1	
19/12/98	Barry Town	A	1-5	Hughes G.
26/12/98	Haverfordwest County	H	2-1	Williams J. 2
08/01/99	Inter CableTel	A	1-6	Knott
23/01/99	Conwy United	A	1-1	Morrison
27/01/99	Rhayader Town	H	2-1	Morrison (p), Williams J.
30/01/99	Connah's Quay Nomads	H	2-1	Morrison 2
06/02/99	Caernarfon Town	A	0-2	
19/02/99	Caersws	H	0-5	
05/03/99	Total Network Solutions	H	0-1	
10/03/99	Carmarthen Town	H	3-2	Williams S. 2, Hughes G.
13/03/99	Afan Lido	A	2-2	Griffiths M., Hughes D.
20/03/99	Newtown	A	1-1	Morrison
27/03/99	Bangor City	H	3-0	Crompton, Hammond, Morrison
30/03/99	Rhayader Town	A	2-0	Hammond, Mainwaring
03/04/99	Holywell Town	A	6-3	Morrison 2, Hughes G. 2,
				Griffiths M., Mainwaring
05/04/99	Haverfordwest County	A	6-2	Hughes G. 2, Mainwaring 2,
				Morrison, Thomas An.
10/04/99	Rhyl	H	2-1	Mainwaring, Williams S.
14/04/99	Cwmbran Town	H	1-3	Williams J.
24/04/99	Barry Town	H	1-1	Morrison (p)

AFAN LIDO

Afan Lido FC
56 Abbeyville Avenue
Sandfields Estate
Port Talbot
SA12 6PY
tel - (01639) 885638
fax - (01639) 872068
Year of Formation - 1967
Chairman - David Dale
Secretary - Phil Robinson
Manager - Mark Robinson
Stadium - Afan Lido Sports Ground (5,000)

APPEARANCES 98/99

	P	Ap	(s)	Gls
Michael COOK	D	9	(9)	
Steve COOK	D	2	(3)	
Gareth DEENEY	A	9	(2)	1
Paul EVANS	D	25	(1)	1
Greg HURLEY	D	30	(2)	1
Dean JOHNSTON	M	21	(1)	
Leighton JONES	D	18	(7)	
Karl LEWIS	M		(3)	
Phil LYONS	A		(1)	
Robertino MELI	M	1	(7)	
Lee MORGAN	D		(1)	
Tim O'CONNOR	A	2	(6)	
Shaun O'LEARY	M	23	(1)	1
Stephen PARRY	D	15	(5)	2
Mitch PATTON	A	32		11
Andrew PEARSON	A	15	(5)	5
Chris PIPER	A	13		1
Andy PITMAN (ENG)	M	31		2
Andrew RADFORD	M	8		
Geraint REYNOLDS	M	13	(10)	
Karl REYNOLDS	A	12	(6)	2
Andrew RICKARD	D	30		
Morys SCOTT	A	3	(2)	
James TAYLOR	A	7	(10)	1
Brian THOMAS	G	32		
John WAKELEY	M		(4)	
Gavin WELLINGTON	D		(4)	
Justin WILLIAMS	M	1	(3)	
Paul WISEMAN	M		(2)	

22/08/98	Aberystwyth Town	A	1-2	Patton (p)
29/08/98	Haverfordwest County	H	0-2	
08/09/98	Barry Town	A	2-0	Taylor, Patton
12/09/98	Inter CableTel	A	1-0	Pitman
18/09/98	Cwmbran Town	H	0-4	
26/09/98	Conwy United	A	0-2	
03/10/98	Connah's Quay Nomads	A	0-0	
10/10/98	Caernarfon Town	H	1-3	Patton (p)
07/11/98	Total Network Solutions	A	1-1	Patton (p)
14/11/98	Newtown	A	0-4	
28/11/98	Bangor City	H	0-2	
05/12/98	Holywell Town	A	0-0	
12/12/98	Rhyl	H	2-1	Parry, Evans
09/01/99	Haverfordwest County	A	1-1	Piper
16/01/99	Inter CableTel	H	0-2	
22/01/99	Cwmbran Town	A	4-1	Parry, O'Leary, Patton, Hurley
30/01/99	Conwy United	H	0-1	
06/02/99	Connah's Quay Nomads	H	1-3	Patton (p)
13/02/99	Caersws	A	1-2	Patton
20/02/99	Caernarfon Town	A	0-2	
27/02/99	Caersws	H	0-1	
06/03/99	Rhayader Town	A	1-1	Pearson
09/03/99	Barry Town	H	0-0	
13/03/99	Aberystwyth Town	H	2-2	Pearson, Deeney
20/03/99	Total Network Solutions	H	3-3	Pearson 2, Patton
23/03/99	Rhayader Town	H	2-0	Patton, Pearson
27/03/99	Newtown	H	0-2	
03/04/99	Bangor City	A	1-0	Patton
05/04/99	Carmarthen Town	H	1-1	Patton
10/04/99	Holywell Town	H	2-0	Reynolds K., Pitman
13/04/99	Carmarthen Town	A	1-1	Reynolds K.
17/04/99	Rhyl	A	0-2	

BANGOR CITY

CLUB DIRECTORY

Bangor City FC
Farrar Road Stadium, Farrar Road, Bangor LL57 3HU
tel - (01248) 712820   fax - (01248) 372132
Year of Formation - 1875
Chairman - Gwyn Pierce Owen
Secretary - Alun Griffiths
Manager - John King; Lee Williams
(99/00 - Meirion Appleton)
Stadium - Farrar Road (10,000)

MAJOR HONOURS
League Championship - (2) 1994, 1995.
Domestic Cup - (4) 1889, 1896, 1962, 1998.

APPEARANCES 98/99

	P	Ap	(s)	Gls
Mark ALLEN (ENG)	D	25	(4)	1
Sammy AYORINDE (NIG)	A	9		3
Mark CAMERON (ENG)	M	1	(6)	
Neil DAVIES (ENG)	A	2	(5)	
Lee DIXON (ENG)	D		(1)	
Martin FILSON (ENG)	D	3		2
Neil FISHER (ENG)	M	6	(4)	
Michael FOX (ENG)	D	3		
John GARNELL (ENG)	A	2	(3)	
Phil GIBNEY (ENG)	D		(1)	
Alan GLOVER (ENG)	M		(1)	
Ronnie GOULDBOURNE (ENG)	M	7	(2)	
Lee HARLEY (ENG)	M	12	(4)	
Darren HILDITCH (ENG)	A	15	(3)	
Noel HORNER (ENG)	D	8	(1)	
Steve JONES (ENG)	A	8	(3)	3
Paul LANGLEY (ENG)	M	12	(9)	
Arthur LLOYD (ENG)	D	8	(2)	
Danny McGOONA	M	5	(1)	
Mick McLOUGHLIN (ENG)	D	1		
Paul MOONEY (ENG)	D	23	(5)	5
Tommy MUTTON	A	21	(1)	8
Dave NORMAN	D	21		
Steve O'SHAUGHNESSY (ENG)	D	14		
Neil RIGBY (ENG)	D	21		
Neil RIMMER (ENG)	M	1	(2)	
Kevin ROBERTS	M		(1)	
Paul ROBERTS	A	9	(3)	1
Chris SHARRATT (ENG)	M	15	(1)	4
Daniel SHEPHERD	A	8	(10)	2
Jamie TAYLOR (ENG)	A	4		
Aaron THOMAS	A	4	(4)	1
Barry THOMAS	D	9	(8)	2
Gary TWYNEHAM	A	3		2
Neil WENHAM (ENG)	M	1	(6)	1
Gareth WILLIAMS (ENG)	D	3	(3)	
Lee WILLIAMS (ENG)	G	32		4
Robbie WILLIAMS	M	20	(1)	3
Scott WILLIAMS	D	16	(1)	1

LEAGUE RESULTS 1998/99

22/08/98	Caersws	A	0-2	
08/09/98	Connah's Quay Nomads	H	0-2	
12/09/98	Total Network Solutions	A	2-1	Allen, Ayorinde
19/09/98	Newtown	H	2-3	Williams L., Mooney
26/09/98	Haverfordwest County	A	0-0	
02/10/98	Holywell Town	A	1-1	Filson
10/10/98	Rhyl	H	4-1	Sharratt 2, Shepherd, Filson
17/10/98	Newtown	A	1-3	Mooney
31/10/98	Barry Town	H	0-3	
07/11/98	Carmarthen Town	A	2-1	Williams R., Jones
14/11/98				
14/11/98	Aberystwyth Town	H	1-2	Jones
28/11/98	Afan Lido	A	2-0	Williams L. (p), Williams S.
05/12/98	Inter CableTel	H	1-0	Williams L. (p)
12/12/98	Cwmbran Town	H	2-2	Mutton, Shepherd
18/12/98	Conwy United	A	1-3	Williams R.
26/12/98	Caernarfon Town	H	1-1	Jones
02/01/99	Caersws	H	0-1	
16/01/99	Total Network Solutions	H	2-1	Thomas B., Mutton
30/01/99	Haverfordwest County	H	3-0	Mooney, Roberts, Mutton
06/02/99	Holywell Town	H	5-2	Ayorinde 2, og (Hinchcliffe P.), Thomas B., Mutton
20/02/99	Rhyl	A	2-1	Twyneham 2
06/03/99	Barry Town	A	2-4	Mutton, Williams L.
13/03/99	Rhayader Town	H	0-1	
20/03/99	Carmarthen Town	H	4-0	Sharratt 2, Williams R., Thomas A.
27/03/99	Aberystwyth Town	A	0-3	
03/04/99	Afan Lido	H	0-1	
05/04/99	Caernarfon Town	A	0-1	
11/04/99	Inter CableTel	A	0-3	
20/04/99	Rhayader Town	A	0-0	
22/04/99	Connah's Quay Nomads	A	1-1	Mooney
24/04/99	Conwy United	H	1-3	Mutton
01/05/99	Cwmbran Town	A	4-2	Mutton 2, Mooney, Wenham

BARRY TOWN

Barry Town AFC
132 Westward Rise
Barry
Vale of Glamorgan CF62 6NQ
tel - (01446) 737188
fax - (01446) 701884
Year of Formation - 1912
Chairman - Paula O'Halloran
Secretary - Alan Whelan
Manager - Gary Barnett
Stadium - Jenner Park (6,000)

MAJOR HONOURS
League Championship - (4)
1996, 1997, 1998, 1999.
Domestic Cup - (3) 1955, 1994, 1997.

APPEARANCES 98/99

		P	Ap	(s)	Gls
Gary BARNETT (ENG)	M	27	(2)		3
Lee BARROW (ENG)	D	31			2
Danny CARTER (ENG)	M	20	(6)		5
Darren DAVIES	M	14	(10)		1
Mark DEMPSEY (IRL)	M	27	(3)		6
Andy DIBBLE	G	1			
Terry EVANS	D	28	(2)		
Jodie JENKINS	A	7	(17)		
Jon JONES	A	4			1
Richard JONES	M	28	(3)		14
Gary LLOYD	M	21	(2)		5
Lee MATTHEWS	M	1	(1)		
Paul MITCHELL (ENG)	D	26	(3)		1
Justin PERRY (ENG)	A	13	(13)		7
Chris PRIDHAM	M	9	(14)		1
John ROBERTS	G	3			
Tynan SCOPE (AUS)	G	3			
Gareth SHONE	M	13	(13)		2
Chris SLOAN (ENG)	A	3			4
Dave WELLS (NIR)	G	25	(3)		
Eifion WILLIAMS	A	22	(1)		28
Andrew YORK	D	26	(1)		1

LEAGUE RESULTS 1998/99

22/08/98	Cwmbran Town	A	4-0	Williams 2, Dempsey, Jones R.
29/08/98	Conwy United	H	1-1	York
08/09/98	Afan Lido	H	0-2	
12/09/98	Connah's Quay Nomads	A	3-0	Williams 2, Jones R.
19/09/98	Caernarfon Town	H	3-0	Williams 2, Jones R.
26/09/98	Caersws	A	4-2	Lloyd, Williams, Mitchell, Dempsey
03/10/98	Rhayader Town	H	7-1	Carter 2, Williams 2, Barnett, Jones R. (p), Perry
10/10/98	Total Network Solutions	A	2-1	Williams 2
31/10/98	Bangor City	A	3-0	Jones R. 2 (2p), Williams
07/11/98	Holywell Town	H	4-0	Lloyd 2, Dempsey, Williams
14/11/98	Rhyl	A	6-0	Lloyd 2, Williams 2, Carter, Jones R.
05/12/98	Haverfordwest County	H	2-0	Williams 2
12/12/98	Carmarthen Town	A	1-2	Barrow
19/12/98	Aberystwyth Town	H	5-1	Perry 2, Jones R. 2, Barnett
26/12/98	Inter CableTel	H	1-1	Williams
09/01/99	Conwy United	A	3-1	Williams 2, Pridham
16/01/99	Connah's Quay Nomads	H	1-0	Williams
23/01/99	Caernarfon Town	A	4-0	Williams 2, Shone, Jones R.
30/01/99	Caersws	H	5-2	Perry 2, Williams 2, Barnett
06/02/99	Rhayader Town	A	0-0	
20/02/99	Total Network Solutions	H	2-0	Barrow, og (Gallagher)
27/02/99	Newtown	A	0-0	
06/03/99	Bangor City	H	4-2	Jones R. 2, Carter, Shone
09/03/99	Afan Lido	A	0-0	
13/03/99	Newtown	H	1-0	Carter
20/03/99	Holywell Town	A	3-2	Williams 3
23/03/99	Cwmbran Town	H	2-1	Jones R., Dempsey
27/03/99	Rhyl	H	2-0	Dempsey, Perry
30/03/99	Carmarthen Town	H	6-2	Sloan 3, Dempsey, Jones J., Perry
06/04/99	Inter CableTel	A	2-1	Jones R., Sloan
10/04/99	Haverfordwest County	A	0-0	
24/04/99	Aberystwyth Town	A	1-1	Davies

CAERNARFON TOWN

CLUB DIRECTORY

Caernarfon Town FC
20 South Penrallt
Caernarfon
Gwynedd LL55 1NS
tel - (01286) 674045
Year of Formation - 1876
Chairman - Geraint Lloyd Owen
Secretary - John Watkins
Manager - Paul Rowlands
Stadium - The Oval (3,000)

APPEARANCES 98/99

	P	Ap	(s)	Gls
Mark AITKEN (ENG)	A	5	(8)	
Andrew BARR (ENG)	A	6	(5)	
Nicky BROOKMAN (ENG)	M	25	(4)	1
Peter BYRNE (ENG)	D	5		1
Scott CALDER (CAN)	D		(1)	
Dave COCKRAM (ENG)	A	1	(8)	
Phil DALEY (ENG)	A	22	(1)	7
Neil DAVIES (ENG)	D	12	(3)	1
Mark DEEGAN (ENG)	G	32		
Neil DOHERTY (ENG)	M	8		
Mark EDWARDS (ENG)	D	10	(4)	
Richard EVANS	A		(1)	
Steve FISHER (ENG)	A	30	(2)	5
Mike GARSIDE (ENG)	A	2	(1)	2
Eiddon GRIFFITHS	D		(2)	
Kevin HAGAN (ENG)	A	5	(2)	3
Derek HIGHDALE (ENG)	M	10	(1)	
Ian HORRIGAN (ENG)	M	14	(5)	1
Darren HUGHES	D		(2)	
Steve HUMPHRIES	M		(3)	
Steve HUNT (ENG)	M	6	(4)	1
Paul McANDREW (ENG)	D	21		
Tommy MARSDEN (ENG)	M		(3)	
Chris PICKERING (ENG)	D	24	(1)	1
Chris ROSCOE (ENG)	M	13	(6)	2
Paul ROWLANDS (ENG)	D	14	(6)	
Jason SADLER (ENG)	A	17	(8)	6
Mark SIMPSON (ENG)	M	3	(1)	
Robbie TYNAN (ENG)	M	30	(1)	4
Tony UNGI (ENG)	A	8	(9)	4
Steve WHITEHEAD (ENG)	D		(4)	
Emrys WILLIAMS	D	29		5

LEAGUE RESULTS 1998/99

22/08/98	Holywell Town	H	2-2	Tynan, Williams
29/08/98	Rhyl	A	1-0	Williams
08/09/98	Newtown	A	1-1	Ungi
19/09/98	Barry Town	A	0-3	
26/09/98	Carmarthen Town	H	3-2	Sadler, Fisher, Williams
03/10/98	Aberystwyth Town	A	1-1	Hagan
10/10/98	Afan Lido	A	3-1	Daley, Sadler, Roscoe
24/10/98	Inter CableTel	H	1-1	Brookman
31/10/98	Cwmbran Town	A	0-6	
07/11/98	Conwy United	H	1-1	Hunt
14/11/98	Connah's Quay Nomads	H	1-1	Sadler
28/11/98	Haverfordwest County	A	2-0	Horrigan, Ungi
05/12/98	Caersws	H	2-2	Ungi, Daley
12/12/98	Rhayader Town	A	0-2	
19/12/98	Total Network Solutions	H	2-1	Williams, Tynan
26/12/98	Bangor City	A	1-1	Garside
08/01/99	Rhyl	H	3-0	Tynan 2, Garside
23/01/99	Barry Town	H	0-4	
30/01/99	Carmarthen Town	A	0-0	
06/02/99	Aberystwyth Town	H	2-0	Sadler, Ungi
20/02/99	Afan Lido	H	2-0	og (Rickard), Davies
27/02/99	Inter CableTel	A	0-3	
06/03/99	Cwmbran Town	H	2-4	Fisher 2 (1p)
10/03/99	Newtown	H	3-1	Daley 2, Sadler
13/03/99	Holywell Town	A	2-1	Daley, Sadler
20/03/99	Conwy United	A	1-1	Fisher (p)
23/03/99	Connah's Quay Nomads	A	2-2	Fisher (p), Pickering
03/04/99	Haverfordwest County	H	2-0	Roscoe, Hagan
05/04/99	Bangor City	H	1-0	Daley
10/04/99	Caersws	A	2-3	Byrne, Daley
17/04/99	Rhayader Town	H	2-0	Hagan, Williams
24/04/99	Total Network Solutions	A	0-2	

CAERSWS

CLUB DIRECTORY

Caersws FC
3 Hafren Terrace
Caersws
Powys
tel - (01686) 688103
fax - (01686) 688103
Year of Formation - 1887
Chairman - Garth Williams
Secretary - Mike Jones
Manager - Mickey Evans
Stadium - Recreation Ground (4,000)

APPEARANCES 98/99

	P	Ap	(s)	Gls
Hugh CLARKE	A	21	(3)	6
Craig EDWARDS	M	4		1
Leighton EDWARDS	A	6	(11)	
Steven EDWARDS	A	23	(8)	2
Alex FLETCHER	D		(4)	
Antony GRIFFITHS	D	32		
Matthew GRIFFITHS	G	29		
Robert HAMER	A	27	(3)	1
Lee HARDING	M		(4)	
Mark HOWELLS	D	15	(14)	4
Marc HUGHES	M	25	(1)	1
Sean JEHU	M	27	(1)	13
Gary JONES	A		(20)	
Robert JONES	G		(1)	
Wyn JONES	M		(7)	
Geraint LEWIS	M	18	(5)	2
Kevin LLOYD	D	22		2
Garri POWELL	D		(1)	
Craig RICHARDS	D		(1)	
Steve ROGERS (ENG)	A	6	(4)	
Damon RUSSELL (ENG)	A	11		4
John SILLITOE (ENG)	G	3		
Tim STEEL	A	8	(2)	5
Andy THOMAS	D	29		1
Jason WEETMAN (ENG)	D	26		1
Andrew WHITTICASE	A	20	(5)	5

LEAGUE RESULTS 1998/99

Date	Opponent		Score	Scorers
22/08/98	Bangor City	H	2-0	Edwards C., Clarke
29/08/98	Holywell Town	A	0-0	
09/09/98	Total Network Solutions	A	1-2	Clarke
12/09/98	Rhyl	H	3-1	Howells, Russell, Jehu
26/09/98	Barry Town	H	2-4	og (Lloyd), Jehu
03/10/98	Carmarthen Town	A	1-0	Jehu
09/10/98	Aberystwyth Town	H	2-3	Russell, Hughes
01/11/98	Inter CableTel	A	0-6	
07/11/98	Cwmbran Town	H	1-3	Howells
14/11/98	Conwy United	A	1-2	Hamer
27/11/98	Connah's Quay Nomads	H	2-0	Russell 2 (1p)
05/12/98	Caernarfon Town	A	2-2	Jehu, Clarke
12/12/98	Haverfordwest County	H	4-4	Lloyd, Edwards S., Lewis, Clarke
19/12/98	Rhayader Town	H	0-0	
26/12/98	Newtown	A	0-4	
02/01/99	Bangor City	A	1-0	Lloyd
09/01/99	Holywell Town	H	3-2	Jehu 2 (1p), Clarke
16/01/99	Rhyl	A	1-1	Whitticase
30/01/99	Barry Town	A	2-5	Clarke, Jehu (p)
06/02/99	Carmarthen Town	H	1-2	Thomas
13/02/99	Afan Lido	H	2-1	Steel, Howells
19/02/99	Aberystwyth Town	A	5-0	Jehu 2, Steel 2, Weetman
27/02/99	Afan Lido	A	1-0	Edwards S.
06/03/99	Inter CableTel	H	0-2	
09/03/99	Total Network Solutions	H	3-1	Whitticase 3
20/03/99	Cwmbran Town	A	1-2	Steel
27/03/99	Conwy United	H	0-3	
02/04/99	Connah's Quay Nomads	A	0-0	
05/04/99	Newtown	H	1-1	Steel
10/04/99	Caernarfon Town	H	3-2	Jehu 3 (1p)
17/04/99	Haverfordwest County	A	1-1	Howells
24/04/99	Rhayader Town	A	3-1	Jehu, Whitticase, Lewis

CARMARTHEN TOWN

CLUB DIRECTORY

Carmarthen Town AFC
3 Maesdolau
Idole
Carmarthen SA32 8DQ
tel - (01267) 232432
fax - (01267) 2201116
Year of Formation - 1948
Chairman - Malcolm Williams
Secretary - Alan Latham
Manager - John Mahoney; Tomi Morgan
Stadium - Richmond Park (3,000)

APPEARANCES 98/99

	P	Ap	(s)	Gls
Richard ADAMS (ENG)	A	15	(12)	4
James ARCHER	M	1	(2)	
David BARNHOUSE	D	25	(1)	1
David BURROWS	D	7	(4)	
Paul BURROWS	A	20	(1)	9
Matthew CABLE	D	29		2
Robbie EVANS	A		(2)	
Steve EVANS	D	25	(1)	2
Robert FITZGERALD	G	25		
Gafin GRIFFITHS	A	1		
Gareth JAMES	M	3	(4)	2
Ieuan JOHN	D		(3)	
Gethin JONES	M		(1)	
Wayne JONES	D	18	(7)	2
Colin LOSS (ENG)	M	14		
Sion MEREDITH	M	8	(8)	3
David MORGAN	G	7		
Tommi MORGAN	A	2	(9)	2
Nigel NICHOLLS	D	20	(7)	2
Ryan NICHOLAS	A	5	(2)	3
Richard PARKER (ENG)	A	11		3
Gareth PHILLIPS	M	4		
Tony REES	A	23	(2)	6
Alan ROBERTS	M	2	(3)	1
Dean ROSSITER	M	21	(2)	2
Rhodri THOMAS	D	13	(2)	
Wyn THOMAS	M	15	(11)	
Malcolm VAUGHAN	M	18	(12)	
Steve WILLIAMS	M	20		1

LEAGUE RESULTS 1998/99

29/08/98	Cwmbran Town	A	0-2	
01/09/98	Inter CableTel	A	2-1	James, Williams
09/09/98	Aberystwyth Town	H	2-5	Burrows, Rees
12/09/98	Conwy United	A	2-1	Burrows, Adams
19/09/98	Connah's Quay Nomads	H	6-2	Burrows 2, Adams, Nicholson, Rees, James
26/09/98	Caernarfon Town	A	2-3	Cable, Burrows
03/10/98	Caersws	H	0-1	
10/10/98	Rhayader Town	A	0-1	
31/10/98	Newtown	A	0-0	
07/11/98	Bangor City	H	1-2	Burrows
14/11/98	Holywell Town	A	1-1	Barnhouse
28/11/98	Rhyl	H	1-2	Rees
12/12/98	Barry Town	H	2-1	Rossiter, Adams
19/12/98	Haverfordwest County	A	2-1	Adams, Burrows
02/01/99	Inter CableTel	H	0-1	
09/01/99	Cwmbran Town	H	1-1	Rees
23/01/99	Connah's Quay Nomads	A	2-0	Morgan T., Meredith
30/01/99	Caernarfon Town	H	0-0	
06/02/99	Caersws	A	2-1	Burrows 2
19/02/99	Rhayader Town	H	1-1	Cable (p)
27/02/99	Total Network Solutions	A	1-1	Rossiter
10/03/99	Aberystwyth Town	A	2-3	Roberts, Parker
20/03/99	Bangor City	A	0-4	
24/03/99	Total Network Solutions	H	1-0	Jones W.
27/03/99	Holywell Town	H	3-0	Meredith, Nicholls, Rees
30/03/99	Barry Town	A	2-6	og (Barrow), Nicholls
03/04/99	Rhyl	A	2-1	Morgan T., Parker
05/04/99	Afan Lido	A	1-1	Nicholas
10/04/99	Conwy United	H	2-1	Nicholls, Parker
13/04/99	Afan Lido	H	1-1	Jones W.
24/04/99	Haverfordwest County	H	3-1	Meredith, Rees, Evans S.
01/05/99	Newtown	H	1-0	Evans S.

CONNAH'S QUAY NOMADS

CLUB DIRECTORY

Connah's Quay Nomads FC
40 Brookdale Avenue
Connah's Quay
Clwyd CH5 4LU
tel - (01244) 831212
fax - (01244) 538084
Year of Formation - 1946
Chairman - T.R. Morris JP
Secretary - Rob Hunter
Manager - Nev Powell
Stadium - Halfway Ground (3,000)

APPEARANCES 98/99

	P	Ap	(s)	Gls
John ALLEN	A	4		
Mike CARROLL (ENG)	M	25	(5)	
Phil COLLISTER (ENG)	G	32		
Chris DAVIES	A	4	(13)	3
Neil DAVIES	A	3	(3)	1
Chris EDGE (ENG)	M	10	(1)	1
Dave EVANS (ENG)	D	1		
Neil FISHER (ENG)	M	4	(3)	
Steve FUTCHER (ENG)	M	24	(1)	3
Nicky HENDERSON (ENG)	D	7	(3)	
Carl HUGHES (ENG)	A	16	(3)	3
Jamie HUGHES (ENG)	A	28	(3)	16
Phil HUGHES	A		(7)	
Craig HUTCHINSON (ENG)	M	23	(1)	3
Jamie JARDINE (ENG)	D	22		
Paul JONES (ENG)	D	20	(4)	1
Jon KENWORTHY	M	24	(7)	
Ricky LAMPKIN (ENG)	M	2	(8)	
Richard LAUGHTON (ENG)	A	1	(5)	
Chris McGINN (ENG)	A		(1)	
Dave O'GORMAN	A	8		4
Stuart RAIN (CYP)	A	18	(7)	4
Carl SMYTH (ENG)	D	31		3
Andy THOMAS (ENG)	D	32		1
Barry THOMAS	D	6	(3)	
Darren WYNNE	M	12	(14)	
Gary WYNNE	D		(4)	

LEAGUE RESULTS 1998/99

22/08/98	Rhyl	A	2-1	Smyth, Davies N.
29/08/98	Rhayader Town	H	4-1	Hughes J. 3, Thomas A.
08/09/98	Bangor City	A	2-0	Edge, Davies C.
12/09/98	Barry Town	H	0-3	
19/09/98	Carmarthen Town	A	2-6	Hughes J. 2
26/09/98	Aberystwyth Town	H	0-0	
03/10/98	Afan Lido	H	0-0	
10/10/98	Inter CableTel	A	1-1	Davies C,
31/10/98	Conwy United	A	3-1	Futcher 2, Hughes J.
14/11/98	Caernarfon Town	A	1-1	Hughes J.
27/11/98	Caersws	A	0-2	
12/12/98	Total Network Solutions	A	0-2	
26/12/98	Holywell Town	A	0-0	
16/01/99	Barry Town	A	0-1	
23/01/99	Carmarthen Town	H	0-2	
30/01/99	Aberystwyth Town	A	1-2	Hughes J.
06/02/99	Afan Lido	A	3-1	Hughes J. 2, Rain
20/02/99	Inter CableTel	H	1-2	Hughes J. (p)
27/02/99	Cwmbran Town	A	1-2	O'Gorman
20/03/99	Haverfordwest County	A	0-1	
23/03/99	Caernarfon Town	H	2-2	Hughes J. 2
27/03/99	Haverfordwest County	H	3-1	Hutchinson, Davies C., Futcher
30/03/99	Conwy United	H	1-2	Jones
02/04/99	Caersws	H	0-0	
05/04/99	Holywell Town	H	4-2	Hughes C. 2, Smyth, Rain
10/04/99	Rhayader Town	A	0-2	
17/04/99	Total Network Solutions	H	2-3	og (Morris), Hutchinson
20/04/99	Rhyl	H	6-2	O'Gorman 3, Hughes J. 2,
				Hughes C.
22/04/99	Bangor City	H	1-1	Hughes J.
24/04/99	Newtown	A	0-1	
27/04/99	Cwmbran Town	H	1-0	Hutchinson
29/04/99	Newtown	H	3-2	Rain 2, Smyth (p)

CONWY UNITED

CLUB DIRECTORY

Conwy United FC
1 Tan-y-Maes
Glan Conwy
Conwy LL28 5LQ
tel - (01492) 573243
fax - (01492) 573243
Year of Formation - 1977
Chairman - Joe Davies
Secretary - Graham Rees
Manager - Nigel Roberts; Stan Allen
Stadium - Morfa Conwy (4,000)

APPEARANCES 98/99

	P	Ap	(s)	Gls
Graham AUSTIN (ENG)	A		(9)	
Ian BAMFORD (ENG)	G	16	(1)	
Geoff BLUNDELL (ENG)	M	1	(1)	
Terry BROWN (ENG)	M	5	(6)	4
Matt CORCORAN	A	26	(5)	6
Joe DONNELLY (ENG)	M	31		
Kevin ELLISON (ENG)	M	25	(3)	4
Danny EMBLETON (ENG)	G	10		
Gary FINLEY (ENG)	D	23		1
Carl FURLONG (ENG)	A	1		
Darren HILDITCH (ENG)	A	10		1
Martin IVISON (ENG)	M		(13)	
Bleddyn JONES	D		(1)	
Darren KELSEY (ENG)	D	4	(1)	
Mike KINSELLA (ENG)	G	1		
Gary LLOYD (ENG)	D	9	(6)	
Danny McGOONA	M	9	(9)	2
James McILVOGUE	A	22	(2)	8
Ian McLELLAN (ENG)	D	2	(4)	
Mike MALONEY (ENG)	M	26		2
Peter MELLOR (ENG)	D	8		
Mark PHILLIPS (ENG)	D	6		
Paul PHILLIPS (ENG)	M	1	(3)	
Chris SHORT (ENG)	D	26		
Antony SMITH (ENG)	M	23		2
Colin SMITH (ENG)	A	5	(13)	1
Mally TIDSWELL	D	24	(2)	1
John TONER (ENG)	A	22	(1)	20
Jason TURNER	G	5	(4)	
Lee WILLIAMS	A	2	(12)	
Robbie WILLIAMS	M	9		2

LEAGUE RESULTS 1998/99

29/08/98	Barry Town	A	1-1	Toner
08/09/98	Holywell Town	A	3-4	Toner, Corcoran, Maloney
12/09/98	Carmarthen Town	H	1-2	Williams R.
19/09/98	Aberystwyth Town	A	1-3	Toner
26/09/98	Afan Lido	H	2-0	Corcoran, Williams R.
03/10/98	Inter CableTel	H	3-0	Toner, Ellison, Corcoran (p)
10/10/98	Cwmbran Town	A	0-3	
24/10/98	Haverfordwest County	H	0-2	
31/10/98	Connah's Quay Nomads	H	1-3	Smith A.
07/11/98	Caernarfon Town	A	1-1	Toner
14/11/98	Caersws	H	2-1	McIlvogue, Toner
28/11/98	Rhayader Town	A	2-2	Toner, Smith C.
05/12/98	Total Network Solutions	H	3-3	Ellison, Toner, Corcoran (p)
12/12/98	Newtown	H	1-0	Toner
18/12/98	Bangor City	H	3-1	Finley, Toner, McIlvogue
09/01/99	Barry Town	H	1-3	Toner
23/01/99	Aberystwyth Town	H	1-1	Smith A.
27/01/99	Rhyl	H	2-1	Toner 2
30/01/99	Afan Lido	A	1-0	Corcoran
06/02/99	Inter CableTel	A	0-3	
20/02/99	Cwmbran Town	H	2-4	McGoona, McIlvogue
27/02/99	Haverfordwest County	A	3-1	McIlvogue 2, Ellison
10/03/99	Holywell Town	H	2-1	Toner 2
20/03/99	Caernarfon Town	H	1-1	Tidswell
27/03/99	Caersws	A	3-0	McIlvogue, Corcoran (p), Toner
30/03/99	Connah's Quay Nomads	A	2-1	Toner, McIlvogue
03/04/99	Rhayader Town	H	1-1	Toner
05/04/99	Rhyl	A	3-0	og (Simms), Toner, Maloney
10/04/99	Carmarthen Town	A	1-2	McIlvogue
13/04/99	Total Network Solutions	A	4-1	Brown 2, McGoona, Toner
20/04/99	Newtown	A	1-2	Brown
24/04/99	Bangor City	A	3-1	Brown, Ellison, Hilditch

CWMBRAN TOWN

CLUB DIRECTORY

Cwmbran Town AFC
30 Llanover Road Est
Blaenavon
Torfaen NP4 9HP
tel - (01495) 792557
fax - (01633) 863324
Year of Formation - 1955
Chairman - John Colley
Secretary - Karl McCarthy
Manager - Tony Wilcox
Stadium - Cwmbran (13,200)

MAJOR HONOURS
League Championship - (1) 1993.

APPEARANCES 98/99

		P	Ap	(s)	Gls
Mark AIZLEWOOD	D	12	(6)		
Jim BLACKIE	D	32		1	
Richard CARTER	D	1	(2)		
Micky COPEMAN	D	2	(6)		
Mattie DAVIES	A	24	(3)	20	
Mark EVANS	D	13	(9)		
Paul GILES	M	4		1	
Wayne GOODRIDGE	M	3	(2)		
Ben GRAHAM	D	12	(1)	1	
Wayne HEWITT	D	23	(2)	4	
Phil JAMES	M	20	(4)		
Ray JOHN	D	15			
Phil JOHNSON (ENG)	M	8	(2)	1	
Lee MATTHEWS	M	5	(5)		
Ian MITCHELL	A	1	(2)		
Adam MOORE	M	28		4	
Neil O'BRIEN	D	22		1	
Pat O'HAGAN	G	32			
Mark PARFITT	D	10	(2)	1	
Michael PATTIMORE	M	8	(8)		
Kevin PAYNE	M		(3)		
Chris PIKE	A	10	(19)	6	
John POWELL	M	2		1	
Chris SUMMERS	A	26		21	
Geraint TWOSE	M	2	(11)	2	
Chris WATKINS	A	13	(6)	3	
Russ WIGLEY	A	24	(3)	2	

LEAGUE RESULTS 1998/99

22/08/98	Barry Town	H	0-4	
29/08/98	Carmarthen Town	H	2-0	O'Brien, Davies
06/09/98	Rhyl	A	4-1	Davies, Parfitt (p), Pike, og (Lee)
12/09/98	Aberystwyth Town	H	0-1	
18/09/98	Afan Lido	A	4-0	Pike 2, Summers, Davies
26/09/98	Inter CableTel	A	1-0	Pike
03/10/98	Haverfordwest County	H	4-0	Summers 2, Davies, Moore
10/10/98	Conwy United	H	3-0	Davies 2, Summers
31/10/98	Caernarfon Town	H	6-0	Twose 2, Moore 2, og (Williams), Summers
07/11/98	Caersws	A	3-1	Blackie, Powell, Wigley
13/11/98	Rhayader Town	H	3-6	Summers, Davies, og (Barton)
28/11/98	Total Network Solutions	A	2-2	Summers, og (Morris)
05/12/98	Newtown	A	0-0	
12/12/98	Bangor City	A	2-2	Hewitt, Watkins
19/12/98	Holywell Town	H	4-0	Watkins 2, Hewitt, Summers
09/01/99	Carmarthen Town	A	1-1	Giles
22/01/99	Afan Lido	H	1-4	Pike (p)
30/01/99	Inter CableTel	H	0-0	
06/02/99	Haverfordwest County	A	1-2	Davies
20/02/99	Conwy United	A	4-2	Summers 2 (1p), Davies 2
27/02/99	Connah's Quay Nomads	H	2-1	Summers, Davies
06/03/99	Caernarfon Town	A	4-2	Davies 2, Graham, Summers
10/03/99	Rhyl	H	6-1	Summers 3, Wigley, Johnson, Davies
20/03/99	Caersws	H	2-1	Summers, Davies
23/03/99	Barry Town	A	1-2	Summers (p)
26/03/99	Rhayader Town	A	1-1	Summers
03/04/99	Total Network Solutions	H	0-4	
10/04/99	Newtown	H	3-0	Summers 2, Davies
14/04/99	Aberystwyth Town	A	3-1	Moore, Hewitt, Summers
24/04/99	Holywell Town	A	4-0	Davies 2, Pike (p), Hewitt
27/04/99	Connah's Quay Nomads	A	0-1	
01/05/99	Bangor City	H	2-4	Davies 2

HAVERFORDWEST COUNTY

CLUB DIRECTORY

Haverfordwest County AFC
Chapel Lane
Keyston
Haverfordwest SA62 4HW
tel - (01437) 710805
fax - (01437) 767125
Year of Formation - 1899
Chairman - Roger Cottrell
Secretary - Barry Vaughan
Manager - Mike Ellery
Stadium - Bridge Meadow (2,000)

APPEARANCES 98/99

		P	Ap	(s)	Gls
Adrian BARNSLEY	G	3		(1)	
David BURROWS	D	7	(5)		2
Jan CEGIELSKI	A			(7)	
Chris DAVIES	M	1		(5)	
Mike ELLERY	M			(6)	
Phil EVANS	D	23		(1)	
Richard EVANS	M	20	(2)		2
Neil FREDERICKSON	G	29			
Richard GAY	A	32			16
Mickey GEORGE	M	25	(4)		1
Jamie HARRIS	A	16			4
Andy JONES	A	23	(1)		4
Jason JONES	M	26	(4)		
John JONES	D	2		(1)	
Lee KISSICK	D	9		(7)	
Carl MAINWARING	A	7			1
Richard MOLYNEUX (ENG)	M	8	(15)		
Karl MUNROE (ENG)	D	10			
Mark OTTEN	D	19	(6)		
Gavin REES	D	15	(6)		
Jamie RICKARD	M	29	(1)		9
Morys SCOTT	A	4	(3)		
Neil SIMON	D	7	(3)		
Nigel STEVENSON	D	2			
Billy TIMOTHY	A	9	(16)		1
Paul WALKER	D	26	(2)		2

LEAGUE RESULTS 1998/99

22/08/98	Total Network Solutions	H	1-3	Walker
29/08/98	Afan Lido	A	2-0	Rickard, Gay
09/09/98	Rhayader Town	A	2-2	Gay, Mainwaring
12/09/98	Newtown	H	2-0	Jones A., Timothy
19/09/98	Inter CableTel	H	0-1	
26/09/98	Bangor City	H	0-0	
03/10/98	Cwmbran Town	A	0-4	
10/10/98	Holywell Town	H	7-2	Gay 3, Jones A., Rickard, George, Evans R.
24/10/98	Conwy United	A	2-0	Rickard, Burrows
31/10/98	Rhyl	H	5-2	Gay 4, Rickard
28/11/98	Caernarfon Town	H	0-2	
05/12/98	Barry Town	A	0-2	
12/12/98	Caersws	A	4-4	og (Griffiths A.), Gay, Burrows, Rickard
19/12/98	Carmarthen Town	H	1-2	Gay
26/12/98	Aberystwyth Town	A	1-2	Gay
02/01/99	Total Network Solutions	A	2-4	Gay, Jones A.
09/01/99	Afan Lido	H	1-1	Harris
16/01/99	Newtown	A	1-1	Harris
22/01/99	Inter CableTel	A	0-1	
30/01/99	Bangor City	A	0-3	
06/02/99	Cwmbran Town	H	2-1	Harris, Gay
27/02/99	Conwy United	H	1-3	Harris
06/03/99	Rhyl	A	2-1	Rickard 2
10/03/99	Rhayader Town	H	1-0	Gay
20/03/99	Connah's Quay Nomads	H	1-0	Jones A.
27/03/99	Connah's Quay Nomads	A	1-3	Evans R.
03/04/99	Caernarfon Town	A	0-2	
05/04/99	Aberystwyth Town	H	2-6	Gay, Walker
10/04/99	Barry Town	H	0-0	
17/04/99	Caersws	H	1-1	Rickard
24/04/99	Carmarthen Town	A	1-3	Rickard
01/05/99	Holywell Town	A	0-4	

HOLYWELL TOWN

CLUB DIRECTORY

Holywell Town FC
Bryn Awel, Holway Road, Holywell, CH8 7NH
tel - (01352) 714216   fax - (01352) 714216
Year of Formation - 1906
Chairman - Ernie Moore
Secretary - Carol Hughes
Manager - Vernon Keep
Stadium - Halkyn Road (4,000)

APPEARANCES 98/99

	P	Ap	(s)	Gls
Keven BLUNDELL (ENG)	A	1		
Brian CASLIN (ENG)	M		(2)	
Gareth CROFTS (ENG)	A	22	(4)	7
Neil DAVIES (ENG)	A	4	(2)	1
Paul DODD	M	3		
Peter DONNELLY (ENG)	A	1		
Craig DULSON (ENG)	M	16	(6)	4
Leigh EDWARDS	G	32		
Dave EVANS (ENG)	D	9		
Alan GLOVER (ENG)	M	6		
Alex GRIFFITHS	D	4	(7)	
Lee HARLEY (ENG)	M	7		1
Geoff HINCHCLIFFE	D	21		
Phil HINCHCLIFFE	M	24		
Darren HORNE	M	4	(10)	
Carl HUGHES (ENG)	A	13	(2)	1
Peter HUGHES	A	24	(7)	10
Darren JONES	A	2		
Lee JONES	D	25	(2)	1
Rob JONES	M	23	(2)	3
Steve JONES (ENG)	M	11		7
Vernon KEEP (ENG)	M	12	(8)	2
Kevin LANGLEY (ENG)	M	8	(1)	
Phil LANGLEY (ENG)	M		(1)	
Mike LEWIS	D	11	(3)	
Peter McNAY (ENG)	D	4	(2)	
Steve MANN (ENG)	D	12		
Chris MILROY	A	1	(3)	
Paul NELSON (ENG)	D	6	(3)	
Ian PARRY (ENG)	A	3	(2)	
Richard POWELL (ENG)	M		(1)	
John ROBERTS (ENG)	M	7	(3)	
Mike SCULLY (ENG)	M	8		
Jordan STONES	M		(2)	
Lee TAYLOR	A	5	(10)	
Danny WILLIAMS	A		(5)	
John WOODS (ENG)	D	1		
Kenny WOODS (ENG)	M	13	(11)	1
Mark WOODS (ENG)	M	9	(1)	

LEAGUE RESULTS 1998/99

22/08/98	Caernarfon Town	A	2-2	Jones R., Woods
29/08/98	Caersws	H	0-0	
08/09/98	Conwy United	H	4-3	Hughes P. 2, Crofts, Jones R.
12/09/98	Rhayader Town	A	3-1	Jones R., Dulson, Hughes P.
19/09/98	Total Network Solutions	H	3-3	Hughes P. 3
25/09/98	Newtown	A	0-4	
02/10/98	Bangor City	H	1-1	Keep
10/10/98	Haverfordwest County	A	2-7	Hughes P., Crofts
24/10/98	Rhyl	A	1-5	Dulson
07/11/98	Barry Town	A	0-4	
14/11/98	Carmarthen Town	H	1-1	Hughes P.
28/11/98	Aberystwyth Town	A	0-0	
05/12/98	Afan Lido	H	0-0	
12/12/98	Inter CableTel	H	1-2	Hughes C.
19/12/98	Cwmbran Town	A	0-4	
26/12/98	Connah's Quay Nomads	H	0-0	
09/01/99	Caersws	A	2-3	Dulson, Crofts
16/01/99	Rhayader Town	H	2-2	Hughes P., Crofts
23/01/99	Total Network Solutions	A	0-2	
30/01/99	Newtown	H	0-3	
06/02/99	Bangor City	A	2-5	Dulson, Jones L.
26/02/99	Rhyl	H	0-3	
10/03/99	Conwy United	A	1-2	Davies
13/03/99	Caernarfon Town	H	1-2	Jones S.
20/03/99	Barry Town	H	2-3	Jones S., Keep
27/03/99	Carmarthen Town	A	0-3	
30/03/99	Inter CableTel	A	1-5	Hughes P.
03/04/99	Aberystwyth Town	H	3-6	Jones S. 2, Harley (p)
05/04/99	Connah's Quay Nomads	A	2-4	Jones S. 2
10/04/99	Afan Lido	A	0-2	
24/04/99	Cwmbran Town	H	0-4	
01/05/99	Haverfordwest County	H	4-0	Crofts 3 (1p), Jones S.

INTER CABLETEL

CLUB DIRECTORY

Inter CableTel AFC (now - Inter Cardiff AFC)
48 Radyr Court Close, Llandaff
Cardiff CF5 2QG
tel - (01222) 552679   fax - (01222) 552679
Year of Formation - 1990
Chairman - Max James
Secretaries - John McTavish & C. Hicks
Manager - George Wood
Stadium - Leckwith (6,000)

MAJOR HONOURS
Domestic Cup - (1) 1999.

APPEARANCES 98/99

		P	Ap	(s)	Gls
Derek BRAZIL (IRL)	D	16			
David BURROWS	D	2	(2)		
William CLARKE	G	2	(1)		
Richard DAVID	D	23	(1)	1	
Neil DAVIES	M	25	(5)	3	
Simon DYER	A	20	(5)	11	
Lee DYSON (ENG)	D	23	(1)	1	
Paul EVANS	A	27		12	
Richard EVANS	D	5			
Paul GILES	M	5	(4)	3	
Jarred HARVEY	D		(6)		
Ray JOHN	D	2	(1)		
Jamie LAISTER	D		(1)		
Ian LOVELESS	G	1			
Steve MARDENBOROUGH (ENG)	A	24	(3)	7	
Samir MISBAH	D	5	(11)	2	
Chris MORGAN	D	1	(2)		
Jamie MURRAY	M	11	(4)	4	
Norman PARSELLE	M	15	(6)	1	
Dean PHILPOTT	D	14	(1)	2	
Chris PIPER	A		(5)		
Darren PORRETTA	M	11	(3)	2	
Paul RICHARDS	D	1	(5)		
Ronnie SINCLAIR (SCO)	G	2			
Gavin SMITH (ENG)	D	1	(4)		
Dean THRELFALL	G	1			
Simon TYLER	M	1	(6)		
Gary WAGER	G	26			
Sean WHARTON	A	12		4	
John WILE	M	20	(4)	3	
Chris WILLIAMS (ENG)	M	19	(5)		
Richard WILLIAMS	M	15	(7)	3	
John WILLS (ENG)	M	20			
Dai WITHERS	A	2	(3)		

LEAGUE RESULTS 1998/99

29/08/98	Aberystwyth Town	A	1-1	Dyer
01/09/98	Carmarthen Town	H	1-2	Wharton
12/09/98	Afan Lido	H	0-1	
19/09/98	Haverfordwest County	A	1-0	Mardenborough
26/09/98	Cwmbran Town	H	0-1	
03/10/98	Conwy United	A	0-3	
10/10/98	Connah's Quay Nomads	H	1-1	Philpott
24/10/98	Caernarfon Town	A	1-1	Dyer
01/11/98	Caersws	H	6-0	Murray 2, Evans P., Wharton, Dyer, Misbah
07/11/98	Rhayader Town	A	5-0	Dyer 2, Evans P., David, Wharton
14/11/98	Total Network Solutions	H	1-1	Wharton
28/11/98	Newtown	A	3-1	Davies 2, Williams R.
05/12/98	Bangor City	A	0-1	
12/12/98	Holywell Town	A	2-1	og (Hinchcliffe P.), Evans
19/12/98	Rhyl	A	2-1	Evans P., Parselle
26/12/98	Barry Town	A	1-1	og (Wells)
02/01/99	Carmarthen Town	A	1-0	Misbah
08/01/99	Aberystwyth Town	H	6-1	Williams R. 2, Evans P. 2, Mardenborough, Wile (p)
16/01/99	Afan Lido	A	2-0	Dyer, Evans P.
22/01/99	Haverfordwest County	H	1-0	Evans P.
30/01/99	Cwmbran Town	A	0-0	
06/02/99	Conwy United	H	3-0	Philpott, Dyson, Dyer
20/02/99	Connah's Quay Nomads	A	2-1	Porretta, Evans P.
27/02/99	Caernarfon Town	H	3-0	Davies, Mardenborough, Evans P.
06/03/99	Caersws	A	2-0	Porretta, Giles (p)
20/03/99	Rhayader Town	H	1-0	Giles
27/03/99	Total Network Solutions	A	3-1	Mardenborough 2, Evans P.
30/03/99	Holywell Town	H	5-1	Mardenborough 2, Murray 2, Giles
03/04/99	Newtown	H	0-2	
06/04/99	Barry Town	H	1-2	Dyer
11/04/99	Bangor City	H	3-0	Dyer 3
24/04/99	Rhyl	H	3-2	Wile 2 (2p), Evans P.

NEWTOWN

Newtown AFC
Latham Park
Newtown
Powys SY16
tel - (01686) 625337
fax - (01686) 623813
Year of Formation - 1875
Chairman - Keith Harding
Secretary - John Annereau
Manager - Brian Coyne
Stadium - Latham Park (4,000)

MAJOR HONOURS
Domestic Cup - (2) 1879, 1895.

APPEARANCES 98/99

	P	Ap	(s)	Gls
Mike BARTON	G	1		
Steve CLIFFORD (ENG)	A	10	(11)	5
Mark COMERFORD (ENG)	A	1	(5)	1
Lee DAVIES (ENG)	D	1	(8)	
Steve ECCLESTONE (ENG)	D	19		
Gareth EVANS	D	31		1
Martin EVANS	D	13	(14)	
Huw GRIFFITHS	D	2	(5)	1
Paul LINF (FNG)	M	21	(5)	
Kevin MORRISON (SCO)	A	5		2
Adam OWEN	M		(3)	
Richard PIKE (ENG)	M		(16)	
Robert PLANT (ENG)	G	11		
Colin REYNOLDS	D	27		1
Mark ROBERTS	M	29		3
Lee ROBINSON	M	1	(3)	
David ROSE (ENG)	G	1		
Scott RUSCOE (ENG)	M	30	(1)	4
Damon RUSSELL (ENG)	A	3	(11)	
Matthew SHORT	G	1		
Richard SIM	G	1		
Chris TAYLOR (ENG)	D	14		1
Aneurin THOMAS	D	4		
Mark THOMAS	D	26	(5)	1
Nicky WARD	A	23	(5)	13
John WHITLEY	D	1	(1)	
Justin WICKHAM (ENG)	A	32		5
Andy WITHINGTON (ENG)	G	17		
Jason YATES (ENG)	A	27	(3)	7

29/08/98	Rhayader Town	A	2-0	Morrison 2
29/08/98	Total Network Solutions	H	0-0	
08/09/98	Caernarfon Town	H	1-1	Wickham
12/09/98	Haverfordwest County	A	0-2	
19/09/98	Bangor City	A	3-2	Roberts, Clifford, Reynolds
25/09/98	Holywell Town	H	4-0	Ruscoe, Clifford, Yates, Ward
03/10/98	Rhyl	A	3-3	Yates, Ruscoe, Wickham
17/10/98	Bangor City	H	3-1	Wickham, Clifford, Comerford
31/10/98	Carmarthen Town	H	0-0	
07/11/98	Aberystwyth Town	A	0-5	
14/11/98	Afan Lido	H	4-0	Yates 2, Griffiths, Ward
28/11/98	Inter CableTel	H	1-3	Roberts
05/12/98	Cwmbran Town	H	0-0	
12/12/98	Conwy United	A	0-1	
26/12/98	Caersws	H	4-0	Yates, Ward 3 (1p)
02/01/99	Rhayader Town	H	1-0	Ward
09/01/99	Total Network Solutions	A	1-1	Ward
16/01/99	Haverfordwest County	H	1-1	Ward (p)
30/01/99	Holywell Town	A	3-0	Ward 2, Wickham
06/02/99	Rhyl	H	2-1	Ruscoe, Taylor
27/02/99	Barry Town	H	0-0	
10/03/99	Caernarfon Town	A	1-3	Evans G.
13/03/99	Barry Town	A	0-1	
20/03/99	Aberystwyth Town	H	1-1	Ward
27/03/99	Afan Lido	A	2-0	Clifford, Wickham
03/04/99	Inter CableTel	A	2-0	Yates 2
05/04/99	Caersws	A	1-1	Ward
10/04/99	Cwmbran Town	A	0-3	
20/04/99	Conwy United	H	2-1	Ruscoe, Clifford
24/04/99	Connah's Quay Nomads	H	1-0	Ward
29/04/99	Connah's Quay Nomads	A	2-3	Roberts, Thomas M.
01/05/99	Carmarthen Town	A	0-1	

RHAYADER TOWN

CLUB DIRECTORY

Rhayader Town FC
Bwthyn Llon, Hazelmere, Rhayader
tel - (01597) 811286   fax - (01597) 810076
Year of Formation - 1890
Chairman - M.A. Pugh
Secretary - Phil Woosnam
Manager - Mark Pound; Phil Woosnam; John Lewis
Stadium - Y Weirglodd (2,000)

APPEARANCES 98/99

	P	Ap	(s)	Gls
Steve ARTHUR	M		(1)	
Ben BANNON	M	2	(2)	
Mike BARTON	G	17		
Shaun BEDWARD (ENG)	A	11	(7)	2
Mark BENBOW (ENG)	A	2		
Romilly BROWN	M	21		1
Matthew BURTON (ENG)	M	4	(4)	
Justin CLARKSON	A	1		
Steve CORRIERI (ENG)	D	12	(1)	
Ryan DURHAM	D		(1)	
Steve ECCLESTONE (ENG)	D	1		
Marc EVANS	D	2	(3)	
Duncan GAZZILLO (ENG)	M		(1)	
Phil GREEN	A	1		
David GRIFFITHS	D	4	(3)	
Nicky GUY (ENG)	M	2		
Gareth HUGHES	M	7		
Wil HUGHES	M	6	(1)	
Anthony JENKINS	M	3		
Ian JONES	M	14		
Ian Tyrone JONES	D	5		
Karl JONES	M	1	(2)	
Paul JONES	D	2	(2)	
Richard JONES	A	19	(9)	4
JUNIOR (BRA)	A		(1)	
Ian LANCASTER (ENG)	M	20	(1)	1
John LEWIS	M		(2)	
Kevin LLOYD	M		(2)	
Callum McKENZIE (ENG)	M		(1)	
Dylan McPHEE	M	13	(8)	2
Chris MORGAN	D	18		
John MORRIS	D	25	(1)	4
Steve MORRIS	G	7		
Lyn OWEN	M	14	(4)	2
James PANNIERS (ENG)	G	4		
Mark PARFITT	D	14		1
Richard PARKER (ENG)	A	10		6
Kevin PAYNE	M	7		
Gavin PERRY	D	1	(2)	
Mark POUND (ENG)	A		(1)	
Matthew PRYCE	A	1	(2)	
Mark RIX (ENG)	D	1		
Chris ROBERTS	M	17	(7)	
Darren STARBOROUGH (ENG)	G	2		
Paul SUGRUE (ENG)	G	1		
Anthony THOMAS	M	8	(1)	
Dean THRELFALL	A	9		1
Jason TREHEARNE (ENG)	A	1		
Chris WATKINS (ENG)	A	13		2
Dave WEBLEY	A	9	(7)	1
Craig WILLIAMS	M	5	(10)	
Glen WILLIS	D	14	(9)	2
Andy WITHINGTON (ENG)	G	1		

LEAGUE RESULTS 1998/99

22/08/98	Newtown	H	0-2	
29/08/98	Connah's Quay Nomads	A	1-4	Brown
09/09/98	Haverfordwest County	H	2-2	Owen, Morris J.
12/09/98	Holywell Town	H	1-3	Parker
19/09/98	Rhyl	A	1-3	Willis
03/10/98	Barry Town	A	1-7	Parker
10/10/98	Carmarthen Town	H	1-0	Parker
07/11/98	Inter CableTel	H	0-5	
13/11/98	Cwmbran Town	A	6-3	Jones R. 2, Parker 2, Morris J., Bedward
28/11/98	Conwy United	H	2-2	Jones R., McPhee
12/12/98	Caernarfon Town	H	2-0	Parker, Willis
19/12/98	Caersws	A	0-0	
26/12/98	Total Network Solutions	A	0-1	
02/01/99	Newtown	A	0-1	
16/01/99	Holywell Town	A	2-2	Webley, Lancaster
23/01/99	Rhyl	H	1-2	Owen
27/01/99	Aberystwyth Town	A	1-2	Threlfall
06/02/99	Barry Town	H	0-0	
19/02/99	Carmarthen Town	A	1-1	Jones R.
06/03/99	Afan Lido	H	1-1	Morris J.
10/03/99	Haverfordwest County	A	0-1	
13/03/99	Bangor City	A	1-0	McPhee
20/03/99	Inter CableTel	A	0-1	
23/03/99	Afan Lido	A	0-2	
26/03/99	Cwmbran Town	H	1-1	Watkins
30/03/99	Aberystwyth Town	H	0-2	
03/04/99	Conwy United	A	1-1	Parfitt (p)
05/04/99	Total Network Solutions	H	0-0	
10/04/99	Connah's Quay Nomads	H	2-0	Morris J., Bedward
17/04/99	Caernarfon Town	A	0-2	
20/04/99	Bangor City	H	0-0	
24/04/99	Caersws	H	1-3	Watkins

RHYL

CLUB DIRECTORY

CPD y Rhyl FC
46 Clwyd Avenue, Prestatyn, Rhyl LL19 9NG
tel - (01745) 887792
Year of Formation - 1883
Chairman - John B. Williams
Secretary - Steve Harms
Manager - Adie Jones
Stadium - Belle Vue (4,000)

MAJOR HONOURS
Domestic Cup - (2) 1952, 1953.

APPEARANCES 98/99

	P	Ap	(s)	Gls
Simon ABERCROMBIE (ENG)	A	20	(1)	8
Danny BARTON (ENG)	A	7		3
Mattie BEATTIE (ENG)	M	1	(7)	
Phil CLENCH (ENG)	M	3	(4)	1
Lee CLOWES (ENG)	M	1	(2)	
Damien CURRIER (ENG)	A	3		
Gary CURTISS (ENG)	D	32		3
Lee DARNBOROUGH (ENG)	G	2		
Gareth DAVIES	A		(2)	
Nathan DAVIES	M	5	(6)	
Dean EARLY (ENG)	A	1		
Mark EDWARDS (ENG)	D	1		
Mike EDWARDS (ENG)	M	4	(4)	
Peter EVANS	M		(3)	
Steve GIBSON (ENG)	M	4	(2)	1
Leon GIERKE	A	7	(5)	1
Brian GRIFFITHS (ENG)	M	1		
Troy HADER (ENG)	A	8	(4)	2
Adrian JONES	M	18	(8)	4
Owen JONES	D	7	(2)	
Steve JONES (ENG)	A	4		
Steve B. JONES (ENG)	A	4	(1)	
Kevin LANGLEY (ENG)	M	15	(5)	1
Steve LEE (ENG)	D	7		
Jason LEIGHTWOOD	M	5	(2)	
Neil MARSH (ENG)	M	6		
Andy MEEHAN (ENG)	M	3		1
Scott MILLINGTON (ENG)	M	13	(11)	3
Lee MURPHY (ENG)	D	13		1
Dave NORMAN (ENG)	D	1		
Phil PATTERSON	D	13	(4)	
Stuart PICKTHALL	D	25	(4)	3
Lee PRIOR (ENG)	M	7	(1)	1
Mark RUTTER (ENG)	D	16		
Mike SCULLY (ENG)	M	3		
Mark SIMMS (ENG)	D	17	(1)	
Paul SMITH	G	23		
Tim STEEL	A	11	(2)	2
Leighton SUMNER	M	10	(1)	1
Lee THORNTON	G	2		
Gary URQUHART	A	12	(9)	3
Paul WALKER (ENG)	G	5		
Jamie WEBSTER (ENG)	D	12	(3)	1

LEAGUE RESULTS 1998/99

22/08/98	Connah's Quay Nomads	H	1-2	Webster
29/08/98	Caernarfon Town	H	0-1	
06/09/98	Cwmbran Town	H	1-4	Pickthall (p)
12/09/98	Caersws	A	1-3	og (Thomas)
19/09/98	Rhayader Town	H	3-1	Steel, Langley, Millington
26/09/98	Total Network Solutions	A	0-6	
03/10/98	Newtown	H	3-3	Gierke, Abercrombie, Murphy
10/10/98	Bangor City	A	1-4	Abercrombie
24/10/98	Holywell Town	H	5-1	Jones A. 2, Abercrombie 2, Steel
31/10/98	Haverfordwest County	A	2-5	Meehan, Abercrombie (p)
14/11/98	Barry Town	H	0-6	
28/11/98	Carmarthen Town	A	2-1	Urquhart, Jones A.
05/12/98	Aberystwyth Town	H	1-0	Clench
12/12/98	Afan Lido	A	1-2	Pickthall (p)
19/12/98	Inter CableTel	H	1-2	Millington
08/01/99	Caernarfon Town	A	0-3	
16/01/99	Caersws	H	1-1	Jones A.
23/01/99	Rhayader Town	A	2-1	Curtiss, Sumner
27/01/99	Conwy United	A	1-2	Prior
30/01/99	Total Network Solutions	H	0-3	
06/02/99	Newtown	A	1-2	Hader
20/02/99	Bangor City	H	1-2	Hader
26/02/99	Holywell Town	A	3-0	Curtiss, Pickthall (p), Urquhart
06/03/99	Haverfordwest County	H	1-2	Millington
10/03/99	Cwmbran Town	A	1-6	Curtiss
27/03/99	Barry Town	A	0-2	
03/04/99	Carmarthen Town	H	1-2	Abercrombie
05/04/99	Conwy United	H	0-3	
10/04/99	Aberystwyth Town	A	1-2	Barton
17/04/99	Afan Lido	H	2-0	Barton 2
20/04/99	Connah's Quay Nomads	A	2-6	Urquhart, Gibson
24/04/99	Inter CableTel	A	2-3	Abercrombie 2

TOTAL NETWORK SOLUTIONS

CLUB DIRECTORY

Total Network Solutions FC
5 Maes-y-Garreg
Llansantffraid, Powys SY22 6BD
tel - (01691) 828535
fax - (01691) 828441
Year of Formation - 1959
Chairman - Edgar Jones
Secretary - Tony Williams
Manager - Andy Cale
Stadium - Recreation Field (2,000)

MAJOR HONOURS
Domestic Cup - (1) 1996.

APPEARANCES 98/99

		P	Ap	(s)	Gls
Danny BARTON (ENG)	A	5	(7)	2
Mike BARTON	G	5		
Neil BREEZE	M		(1)	
Mark COATES	A	10		3
Damien CURRIER (ENG)	A	7	(9)	1
Tim EDWARDS	D	32		2
Gary EVANS	M	23	(5)	4
Ricky EVANS	M	19	(1)	3
Jamie FAIRHURST (ENG)	D	12	(8)	1
Mick GALLAGHER (ENG)	D	20		4
Arwel JONES	D	16	(3)	1
Ian LANCASTER (ENG)	M		(3)	
Ken McKENNA (ENG)	A	22	(2)	12
Neil MARSH (ENG)	M	16	(3)	1
Scott MILLINGTON (ENG)	M	6		1
Rob MORRIS (ENG)	D	14	(8)	
Paul MULLEN (ENG)	M		(3)	
Andy MULLINER (ENG)	G	26	(1)	
Steve O'SHAUGHNESSY	D	6	(1)	2
Dewi PARRY	D	25	(4)	
Gary POWELL	A	19	(9)	6
Darren RYAN (ENG)	M	25	(2)	4
Tony TOLLEY (ENG)	G	1		
James WATKINS (ENG)	M	15	(7)	
John WHELAN (ENG)	D	11	(5)	2
Gareth WILSON	A	17	(14)	4

LEAGUE RESULTS 1998/99

22/08/98	Haverfordwest County	A	3-1	McKenna, O'Shaughnessy (p), og (Rickard)
29/08/98	Newtown	A	0-0	
09/09/98	Caersws	H	2-1	Evans G., Ryan
12/09/98	Bangor City	H	1-2	Wilson
19/09/98	Holywell Town	A	3-3	McKenna, Edwards, O'Shaughnessy
26/09/98	Rhyl	H	6-0	Evans G., Edwards, Powell, Currier, Barton D., Whelan
10/10/98	Barry Town	H	1-2	McKenna
31/10/98	Aberystwyth Town	H	0-0	
07/11/98	Afan Lido	H	1-1	Wilson
14/11/98	Inter CableTel	A	1-1	Gallagher (p)
28/11/98	Cwmbran Town	H	2-2	McKenna, Marsh
05/12/98	Conwy United	A	3-3	McKenna 2, Powell
12/12/98	Connah's Quay Nomads	H	2-0	Ryan, Powell
19/12/98	Caernarfon Town	A	1-2	Ryan
26/12/98	Rhayader Town	H	1-0	Barton D.
02/01/99	Haverfordwest County	H	4-2	Evans R. 2 (2p), McKenna 2
09/01/99	Newtown	H	1-1	Powell
16/01/99	Bangor City	A	1-2	Evans G.
23/01/99	Holywell Town	H	2-0	Wilson, Ryan
30/01/99	Rhyl	A	3-0	Powell, Jones, Whelan
20/02/99	Barry Town	A	0-2	
27/02/99	Carmarthen Town	H	1-1	McKenna
05/03/99	Aberystwyth Town	A	1-0	Coates
09/03/99	Caersws	A	1-3	og (Jehu)
20/03/99	Afan Lido	A	3-3	Fairhurst, Powell, McKenna
24/03/99	Carmarthen Town	A	0-1	
27/03/99	Inter CableTel	H	1-3	McKenna
03/04/99	Cwmbran Town	A	4-0	McKenna, Gallagher, Evans G., Coates
05/04/99	Rhayader Town	A	0-0	
13/04/99	Conwy United	H	1-4	Evans R.
17/04/99	Connah's Quay Nomads	A	3-2	Gallagher 2 (2p), Coates
24/04/99	Caernarfon Town	H	2-0	Millington, Wilson

PROMOTED CLUBS

SECOND DIVISION FINAL TABLES 98/99

SOUTH (WELSH LEAGUE DIVISION ONE)

		Pd	W	D	L	F	A	Pt	GD
1	Ton Pentre	34	25	5	4	79	32	80	+47
2	**Llanelli**	**34**	**21**	**5**	**8**	**79**	**45**	**68**	**+34**
3	Rhondda	34	19	7	8	78	46	64	+32
4	BP Llandarcy	34	19	4	11	69	47	61	+22
5	UWI Cardiff	34	15	8	11	49	44	53	+5
6	Pontardawe Town	34	15	8	11	55	54	53	+1
7	Bridgend Town	34	14	10	10	76	48	52	+28
8	Maesteg Park	34	13	12	9	51	43	51	+8
9	Port Talbot Athletic	34	15	4	15	54	56	49	-2
10	Treowen Stars	34	12	10	12	57	52	46	+5
11	Goytre United	34	13	5	16	50	50	44	0
12	Cardiff Civil Service	34	12	4	18	41	64	40	-23
13	Aberaman Athletic	34	10	7	17	53	74	37	-21
14	Briton Ferry Athletic	34	9	9	16	46	66	36	-20
15	Cardiff Corinthians	34	9	8	17	51	70	35	-19
16	Porth Tywyn Suburbs	34	7	11	16	57	66	32	-9
17	Grange Harlequins	34	6	10	18	46	83	28	-37
18	Porthcawl Town	34	6	5	23	35	86	23	-51

N.B. Ton Pentre refused promotion for financial reasons; Llanelli promoted instead.

NORTH (CYMRU ALLIANCE)

		Pd	W	D	L	F	A	Pt	GD
1	**Flexsys Cefn Druids**	**30**	**22**	**3**	**5**	**105**	**36**	**69**	**+69**
2	Rhydmwyn	30	17	6	7	66	36	57	+30
3	Fflint Town United	30	14	6	10	60	44	48	+16
4	Oswestry Town	30	15	3	12	67	53	48	+14
5	CPD Glantraeth	30	13	7	10	57	47	46	+10
6	Cemaes Bay	30	12	9	9	53	48	45	+5
7	CPD Porthmadog	30	12	7	11	52	49	43	+3
8	Welshpool Town	30	11	9	10	47	39	42	+8
9	Llandudno	30	11	7	12	49	48	40	+1
10	Lex XI Wrexham	30	11	7	12	48	62	40	-14
11	Holyhead Hotspur	30	11	6	13	49	62	39	-13
12	Denbigh Town	30	11	4	15	53	66	37	-13
13	Ruthin Town	30	7	15	8	36	37	36	-1
14	Buckley Town	30	9	6	15	48	75	33	-27
15	Brymbo Broughton	30	8	7	15	28	43	31	-15
16	Mostyn	30	1	8	21	26	99	11	-73

CLUB DIRECTORY

Llanelli AFC
29 Pemberton Park
Llanelli SA14 8NN
tel - (01544) 756176
fax - (01544) 773847
Year of Formation - 1896
Chairman - Robert Jones
Secretary - Roger Davies
Manager - Leighton James
Stadium - Stebonheath Park (3,700)

CLUB DIRECTORY

Flexsys Cefn Druids FC
7 Lancaster Terrace
Acrefair
Wrexham
LL14 3HP
tel - (01978) 823027
Year of Formation - 1869
Chairman - Brian Beesley
Secretary - Ron Davies
Manager - Gareth Powell
Stadium - Plaskynaston Lane (2,500)

MAJOR HONOURS
Welsh Cup - (8) 1880, 1881, 1882, 1885, 1886, 1898, 1899, 1904.

YUGOSLAVIA

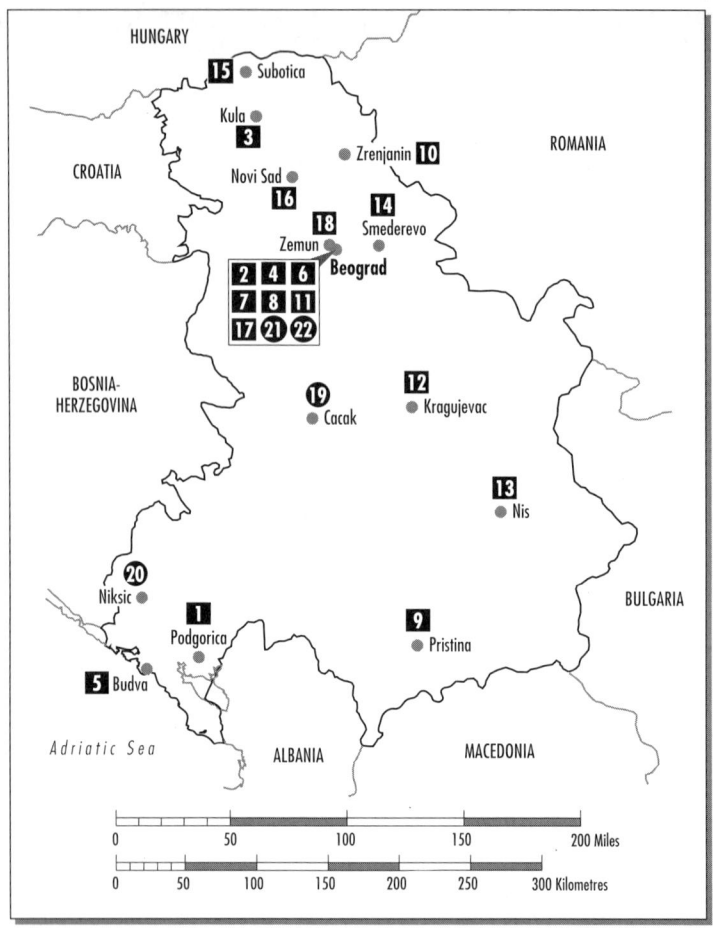

1	BUDUCNOST PODGORICA	1091
2	CRVENA ZVEZDA BEOGRAD	1092
3	HAJDUK KULA	1093
4	MILICIONAR BEOGRAD	1094
5	MOGREN BUDVA	1095
6	OBILIC BEOGRAD	1096
7	OFK BEOGRAD	1097
8	PARTIZAN BEOGRAD	1098
9	FK PRISTINA	1099
10	PROLETER ZRENJANIN	1100
11	RAD BEOGRAD	1101
12	RADNICKI KRAGUJEVAC	1102

13	RADNICKI NIS	1103
14	SARTID SMEDEREVO	1104
15	SPARTAK SUBOTICA	1105
16	VOJVODINA NOVI SAD	1106
17	ZELEZNIK BEOGRAD	1107
18	FK ZEMUN	1108
Promoted clubs		
19	BORAC CACAK	1109
20	SUTJESKA NIKSIC	1109
21	CUKARICKI BEOGRAD	1109
22	HAJDUK BEOGRAD	1109

EURO 2000 BID ALLOWED TO CONTINUE

Football grounded by NATO air strikes

FEDERATION DIRECTORY

Fudbalski Savez Jugoslavije
Terazije 35, 11000 Beograd
tel - (011) 3233447
fax - (011) 3233433

Year of Formation - 1919
President - Miljan Miljanic
Secretary - Branko Bulatovic

During the spring of 1999 football was low down on the priority list for the citizens of Yugoslavia. While NATO responded to the outrage in Kosovo by bombing Serbian cities, footballers joined the rest of their compatriots in the air-raid shelters and demonstration parades.

For two and a half months Yugoslav football was at a standstill. It would normally have been one of the busiest periods of the season, with titles to decide, Cups to win and important international matches to play. But, instead, all activity was suspended.

In the case of the domestic championship, the only option for the league adminsitrators was to abandon it completely. By March 20, when the NATO bombardment began, the Yugoslav First Division had reached round 24 of 36. With a third of the programme still to complete,

there was no chance of a re-start - even when the skies above Belgrade had been emptied of enemy aircraft. The constraints of the international football calendar made it impossible. So, on May 14 the Yugoslav Federation officially declared the championship over. A month later they confirmed that the team which had been leading the table at the time of the stoppage, Partizan Belgrade, had been proclaimed champions of Yugoslavia.

Had there been no official statement to this effect, Yugoslavia would not have been permitted to enter UEFA's 1999/2000 club competitions. But by nominating Partizan as the title winners, the country was assured of its place in the Champions' League as well as two berths in the expanded UEFA Cup.

Partizan might have taken the 16th championship title

LEAGUE CHAMPIONSHIP RESULTS 98/99

		1	2	3	4	5	6	7	8	9	10	11	12	13	14	15	16	17	18
1	Buducnost Podgorica		0-1			4-1	1-3	2-2		0-0			2-1	3-1	0-0	2-0	1-0	2-0	1-0
2	Crvena zvezda Beograd	4-0		2-0		3-0	1-1		2-2		2-1	3-1		4-0	0-1		1-0	4-0	5-1
3	Hajduk Kula	3-0			0-0	1-0		0-0		2-0	2-0		3-0	2-0	3-3	2-0		1-0	3-0
4	Milicionar Beograd	6-3	1-7			1-1	0-0	4-0	0-1	2-0		5-0		4-5		2-1	2-1	3-0	
5	Mogren Budva			2-2	1-0		0-0		0-3		1-2	0-2	1-0	0-0	1-1		0-0	2-2	1-0
6	Obilic Beograd	5-0		5-0	2-0			2-0		3-0	2-0		4-0	5-0	4-2	3-1		2-0	6-3
7	OFK Beograd	5-3	1-1	1-0	2-2	1-2	0-1		2-3	3-2		1-1	2-0				0-0	5-2	
8	Partizan Beograd	1-0	2-1	3-0		3-1	0-0			3-0		4-0	2-0	4-1		5-1	2-0	4-1	
9	FK Pristina		0-1	3-1	3-2	6-1	0-2	1-3	0-4		1-1	1-2		1-1			2-1	3-1	
10	Proleter Zrenjanin	1-1	2-1		0-1	2-2		1-0	0-1	2-0			3-0		1-0	3-1		2-2	2-1
11	Rad Beograd	2-1	1-1	1-0		1-0	0-2			1-1		2-1	2-0	1-1	1-0		1-0	2-0	
12	Radnicki Kragujevac		1-1	1-0	1-0			6-1	1-2	2-0	2-0	1-1		2-0	3-2	2-3			0-2
13	Radnicki Nis	1-0		1-1	4-1		0-2	0-0	0-0	3-1	1-2		2-2		0-0	0-2			0-1
14	Sartid Smederevo	0-0	1-1		1-0			0-1	0-2	3-0	2-1	1-0		1-3		2-1	0-3		3-0
15	Spartak Subotica		1-3	2-0	4-2	3-1	0-4	3-4	0-4	3-1	0-1	1-3					1-3		3-2
16	Vojvodina Novi Sad	2-0	1-2	3-1		3-0	0-1			4-1	1-1	8-1	1-0	1-0				3-2	5-1
17	Zeleznik Beograd			1-0	1-1		1-2	2-1	0-2		1-0	0-0	2-0	4-1	1-1	3-1			3-1
18	FK Zemun	3-2	0-3		1-0	2-0		1-0	1-2	3-0		1-0	1-3		1-1	4-2	0-2		

LEAGUE CHAMPIONSHIP FINAL TABLE 98/99

			Home				Away					Total						
		P	W	D	L	F	A	W	D	L	F	A	W	D	L	F	A	P	GD
1	Partizan Beograd	24	11	1	0	33	5	10	2	0	26	6	21	3	0	59	11	66	+48
2	Obilic Beograd	24	12	0	0	43	6	8	4	0	18	3	20	4	0	61	9	64	+52
3	Crvena zvezda Beograd	24	9	2	1	31	7	6	4	2	23	11	15	6	3	54	18	51	+36
4	Vojvodina Novi Sad	24	9	1	2	32	10	4	2	6	13	12	13	3	8	45	22	42	+23
5	Rad Beograd	24	8	3	1	15	7	3	4	5	11	19	11	7	6	26	26	40	0
6	Proleter Zrenjanin	24	7	3	2	19	10	3	2	7	10	19	10	5	9	29	29	35	0
7	Hajduk Kula	24	9	3	0	22	3	0	2	10	5	25	9	5	10	27	28	32	-1
8	OFK Beograd	24	5	4	3	23	17	3	3	6	12	22	8	7	9	35	39	31	-4
9	Sartid Smederevo	24	6	2	4	14	12	1	7	4	10	15	7	9	8	24	27	30	-3
10	Radnicki Kragujevac	24	7	2	3	22	12	2	1	9	11	31	9	3	12	33	43	30	-10
11	Milicionar Beograd	24	7	2	3	30	19	1	3	8	9	20	8	5	11	39	39	29	0
12	FK Zemun	24	7	1	4	18	15	2	0	10	12	32	9	1	14	30	47	28	-17
13	Zeleznik Beograd	24	7	3	2	19	10	0	2	10	10	33	7	5	12	29	43	26	-14
14	Buducnost Podgorica	24	7	3	2	18	9	0	2	10	10	33	7	5	12	28	42	26	-14
15	Mogren Budva	24	3	6	3	9	12	1	2	9	9	30	4	8	12	18	42	20	-24
16	Radnicki Nis	24	3	5	4	12	12	1	2	9	9	32	4	7	13	21	44	19	-23
17	FK Pristina	24	5	2	5	21	20	0	1	11	4	29	5	3	16	25	49	18	-24
18	Spartak Subotica	24	5	0	7	21	28	1	0	11	12	30	6	0	18	33	58	18	-25

in their history by default, but nobody could claim that they did not deserve it. Of the 24 matches they played, 21 resulted in victory and the other three were drawn. Additionally, Partizan set a new Yugoslav league record by winning each of their first 15 fixtures.

Remarkably, despite such superior statistics, Partizan still had company at the top of the table. Defending champions Obilic were also unbeaten at the 24-match cut-off point and stood just two points behind their city rivals with a total of 20 victories and four draws. In combination with their unbeaten run in the second half of the previous season, Obilic had also set a new Yugoslav First Division record of their own by going 46 games without defeat.

Everything was set up perfectly for an intriguing head-to-head showdown in the final third of the campaign.

No-one, however, will ever know how it would have turned out.

Obilic's frustration at missing out on a second successive title was exacerbated when UEFA decreed that the club would be denied access to the UEFA Cup because the club's head honcho, Zeljko Raznatovic (aka "Arkan"), had been indicted for war crimes by the United Nations. Earlier in the season Raznatovic had failed to accompany Obilic on their European assignments in Munich and Madrid for fear of being arrested; he sent his model wife Ceca instead. On the eve of the Champions' League qualifier away to Bayern Munich he also betrayed his military sensibilities by sacking the club's championship-winning coach Dragan Okuka for disobedience.

On the field Obilic were found out in Europe, going

NATIONAL TEAM RESULTS 98/99

02/09/98	Switzerland	H	Nis	1-1	Stankovic D. (51)
23/09/98	Brazil	A	São Luis	1-1	Milosevic (8)
18/11/98	Republic of Ireland (ECQ)	H	Belgrade	1-0	Mijatovic (63)
23/12/98	Israel	A	Tel-Aviv	0-2	
10/02/99	Malta (ECQ)	A	Ta' Qali	3-0	Nadj (22, 56), Milosevic (90)
08/06/99	Malta (ECQ)	H	Salonika (Greece)	4-1	Mijatovic (33), Milosevic (47, 90),
					Kovacevic D. (74)

TOP SCORERS

16 Dejan OSMANOVIC (Hajduk Kula)
14 Mihajlo PJANOVIC (OFK Beograd/
   Crvena zvezda Beograd)
13 Zoran RANKOVIC (Obilic Beograd)
   Sasa ILIC (Partizan Beograd)
12 Vladimir IVIC (Partizan Beograd)
   Antal PUHALAK (Spartak Subotica)
11 Milan BELIC (Vojvodina Novi Sad)
   Zoran TOMIC (FK Zemun)

down without much of a fight to both Bayern and, in the UEFA Cup, Atlético Madrid, but at home they were every bit as dominant as they had been during their 1997/98 triumph, with key players Nenad Grodzic, Dragan Sarac, Miroslav Savic and top scorer Zoran Rankovic maintaining their high level of consistency.

But anything Obilic could do, Partizan did better. Their storming start, which included a quartet of four-goal victories in August and a 2-1 home win over eternal rivals Red Star in September, left every other team bar Obilic chasing shadows. It was only when the top two came face to face, at the end of November, that Partizan's sequence of victories was brought to a halt. The summit meeting ended 0-0 and enabled Partizan to go into the winter break with a six-point lead.

Partizan dropped further points early in the spring to both Radnicki Nis and Red Star, but even though Obilic won all of their matches (without conceding any goals) during the same period, they could not completely close the gap. One more draw for Partizan would have done it as Obilic had the superior goal difference, but then the bombs began to fall on Belgrade and that was that.

40,000 spectators saw Partizan's final fixture against Red Star, but little did they know that it would be the last football match they would be attending for some time. There was, however, to be another Belgrade derby played before the season closed, and it came in the final of the Yugoslav Cup, which, unlike the league, managed to survive the war and be brought to a proper conclusion.

Partizan and Red Star both won their delayed semi-finals against, respectively, Obilic and Vojvodina Novi Sad, but the just-crowned champions came badly unstuck in the final, which again drew a 40,000 crowd. Two goals down early on, Partizan managed to draw level by half-time, but Red Star restored their lead from the penalty spot just after the hour mark and clinched their

INTERNATIONAL HONOURS

World Cup Finals appearances: 1930 (semi-finals), 1950, 1954 (qtr-finals), 1958 (qtr-finals), 1962 (4th), 1974 (2nd phase), 1982, 1990 (qtr-finals), 1998 (2nd round)

European Championship appearances (last 8), 1960 (runners-up), 1968 (runners-up), 1972, 1976 (4th), 1984

European Club Competitions
Champions' Cup   Crvena zvezda Beograd (1991)

DOMESTIC CUP 98/99

1/16 FINALS
CSK Celarevo 3, Partizan Beograd 4
FK Zemun 3, FK Loznica 2
Hajduk Kula 2, Borac Cacak 0
Radnicki Nis 4, Rad Beograd 2 (aet)
FK Becej 1, Spartak Subotica 2
Teleoptik Zemun 1, Sartid Smederevo 2 (aet)
Trajal Krusevac 1, Proleter Zrenjanin 2
Radnicki Kragujevac 1, OFK Beograd 0
Mladost Lucani 3, Rudar Pljevlja 0
Dinamo Pancevo 1, FK Pristina 1 (aet; 6-5 on pens.)
Crvena zvezda Gnjilane 1, Zeleznik Beograd 3
Sutjeska Niksic 1, Cukaricki Beograd 1
(aet; 3-5 on pens.)
Crvena zvezda Beograd 10, Mladost Podgorica 1
Buducnost Podgorica 2, Buducnost Valjevo 1
Obilic Beograd 5, Radnicki-Jugopetrol Beograd 1
Mladi Radnik Pozarevac 0, Vojvodina Novi Sad 2

1/8 FINALS
Partizan Beograd v Radnicki Kragujevac 2-0; 1-0
(Partizan Beograd 3-0)
Cukaricki Beograd v Obilic Beograd 0-1; 0-2
(Obilic Beograd 3-0)
FK Zemun v Mladost Lucani 0-0; 2-0
(FK Zemun 2-0)
Proleter Zrenjanin v Vojvodina Novi Sad 2-4; 2-1
(Vojvodina Novi Sad 5-4)

Zeleznik Beograd v Crvena zvezda Beograd 0-4; 1-7
(Crvena zvezda Beograd 11-1)
Spartak Subotica v Hajduk Kula 3-0; 0-2
(Spartak Subotica 3-2)
Rad Beograd v Dinamo Pancevo 3-2; 2-1
(Rad Beograd 5-3)
Buducnost Podgorica v Sartid Smederevo 2-2, 0-1
(Sartid Smederevo 3-2)

QUARTER-FINALS
Partizan Beograd 3 (Ilijev 8, Ilic 37, Krstajic 73),
FK Zemun 0
FK Zemun 1 (Celar G. 45), Partizan Beograd 4
(Ilic 6, Obradovic 48, Tomic 75, Krstajic 84)
(Partizan Beograd 7-1)

Sartid Smederevo 1 (Kljajc 52), Obilic Beograd 3
(Grozdic 15, Rankovic 45, Kovacevic 70)
Obilic Beograd 4
(Jelenkovic 15, Babeu 69, Vasiljevic 81, 90),
Sartid Smederevo 1 (Pantic 83)
(Obilic Beograd 7-2)

Spartak Subotica 0, Crvena zvezda Beograd 4
(Pantelic 13, Ognjenovic 16, 18, Micic 69)
Crvena zvezda Beograd 3
(Ilic 12, Williams 23, Micic 31),
Spartak Subotica 1 (Vukicevic 11)
(Crvena zvezda Beograd 7-1)

Vojvodina Novi Sad 1 (Bratic 62), Rad Beograd 0
Rad Beograd 1 (Batrovic 52),
Vojvodina Novi Sad 1 (Jankovic 34)
(Vojvodina Novi Sad 2-1)

SEMI-FINALS
Partizan Beograd 1 (Kezman 6), Obilic Beograd 0
Vojvodina Novi Sad 0, Crvena zvezda Beograd 2
(Skoric 33p, Drulic 70)

FINAL
26/06/99, Belgrade
CRVENA ZVEZDA BEOGRAD 4 Skoric (16, 62p),
Pjanovic (18), Gojkovic (86)
PARTIZAN BEOGRAD 2 Rasovic (37p), Kezman (45)
referee - Filipovic
CRVENA ZVEZDA BEOGRAD - Kocic; Dudic, Bjegovic,
Bunjevcevic, Vitalic; Miljkovic (Ilic 46), Skoric,
Boskovic B. (Micic 89), Gojkovic; Drulic, Pjanovic
(Bajcetic 85).
PARTIZAN BEOGRAD - Ilic R.; Rasovic, Krstajic,
Stojanoski (Ilijev 73), Savic; Stanojevic, Ivic, Ilic S.,
Tomic (Rankovic 73); Bjekovic, Kezman.

NATIONAL TEAM APPEARANCES 98/99

Coach - Milan ZIVADINOVIC	SUI	BRA	IRL	ISR	MLT	MLT	Cps	Gls
Ivica KRALJ (26/03/73) - FC Porto (POR)/Radnicki Kragujevac	G	G46	G	G84	G	G	26	-
Zoran MIRKOVIC (21/09/71) - Juventus (ITA)	D				D	D	34	-
Goran DJOROVIC (11/11/71) - RC Celta (ESP)	D	D	D		D	D	36	-
Sinisa MIHAJLOVIC (20/02/69) - Lazio (ITA)	D30		D		D		38	5
Slobodan KOMLJENOVIC (02/01/71) - MSV Duisburg (GER)	D46			D84			14	2
Slavisa JOKANOVIC (16/08/68) - CD Tenerife (ESP)	D46	D	D		D	D	43	8
Dejan STANKOVIC (11/09/78) - Lazio (ITA)	M		M	M77	M88	M61	12	3
Vladimir JUGOVIC (30/08/69) - Atlético Madrid (ESP)	M		M84				31	3
Dragan STOJKOVIC (03/03/65) - Nagoya Grampus 8 (JPN)	M46		M46			M77	72	13
Darko KOVACEVIC (18/11/73) - Real Sociedad (ESP)	A46	s57	s46	A	A70	A	28	4
Predrag MIJATOVIC (19/01/69) - Real Madrid (ESP)	A61	A75	A		A	A	39	18
Nisa SAVELJIC (23/03/70) - Girondins de Bordeaux (FRA)	s30				D		23	1
Predrag DJORDJEVIC (04/08/72) - Olympiakos (GRE)	s46			s53			2	-
Albert NADJ (29/10/74) - Real Oviedo (ESP)	s46	s46			M	M46	26	3
Kristijan DJORDJEVIC (06/01/76) - VfB Stuttgart (GER)	s46						1	-
Savo MILOSEVIC (02/09/73) - Real Zaragoza (ESP)	s46	A57	A77	A34	s70	s46	37	19
Ilija IVIC (17/02/71) - Olympiakos (GRE)	s61						1	-
Nenad SAKIC (15/06/71) - Sampdoria (ITA)	D						1	-
Miroslav DJUKIC (19/02/66) - Valencia CF (ESP)	D	D		D	D		29	1
Zoran NJEGUS (25/06/73) - Atlético Madrid (ESP)		M46					4	-
Nenad GRODZIC (03/02/74) - Obilic Beograd		M	s84	M	s88	s61	6	-
Dejan PETKOVIC (10/09/72) - Vitória Bahia (BRA)		M75					6	1
Jovan STANKOVIC (04/03/71) - RCD Mallorca (ESP)		M76	D	M53	M75		4	-
Dragan ZILIC (14/12/74) - Vojvodina Novi Sad		s46					1	-
Sasa CURCIC (14/02/72) - Crystal Palace (ENG)		s75					14	1
Nikola LAZETIC (09/02/78) - Vojvodina Novi Sad		s75					1	-
Dragan SARAC (27/09/75) - Obilic Beograd		s76		s34			2	-
Ljubinko DRULOVIC (11/09/68) - FC Porto (POR)		s77	M65		s77		19	1
Miroslav SAVIC (20/04/73) - Obilic Beograd				D			2	-
Goran BUNJEVCEVIC (17/02/73) - Crvena zvezda Beograd				M			1	-
Dejan SAVICEVIC (15/09/66) - Milan (ITA)				A53			52	19
Sasa KOVACEVIC (29/03/73) - Obilic Beograd				s53			1	-
Nikoslav BJEGOVIC (16/11/67) - Crvena zvezda Beograd				s65			1	-
Jovan GOJKOVIC (07/01/75) - Crvena zvezda Beograd				s77			1	-
Sasa ILIC (18/07/72) - Charlton Athletic (ENG)				s84			1	-
Vinko MARINOVIC (03/03/71) - Crvena zvezda Beograd				s84			1	-
Djordje TOMIC (11/11/72) - Partizan Beograd						s75	1	-

EUROPEAN CUPS 98/99

CHAMPIONS' CUP
● **OBILIC BEOGRAD**
Preliminary round ÍBV (ISL)
H 2-0 Juksic (18), Grozdic (65)
Lukic; Babeu, Savic (Zoric 46), Vargec, Zivkovic (Filipovic 81);
Serafimovic, Juksic, Grozdic, Sarac; Kovacevic, Manojlovic (Vasiljevic 61).
A 2-1 Vasiljevic (65), Grozdic (87)
Lukic; Babeu, Savic (Zoric), Vargec, Filipovic (Zivkovic); Serafimovic,
Juksic, Grozdic, Sarac; Kovacevic, Manojlovic (Vasiljevic).

Qualifying round FC BAYERN MÜNCHEN (GER)
A 0-4
Lukic; Babeu, Savic, Vargec, Zivkovic (Filipovic 66); Zoric, Juksic, Grozdic,
Sarac; Kovacevic (Manojlovic 62), Rankovic (Viciknez 72).
H 1-1 Sarac (67)
Lukic; Babeu, Savic (Ocokoljic 70), Mrkic, Zivkovic; Zoric, Serafimovic,
Grozdic, Sarac; Vasiljevic (Viciknez 65), Rankovic (Kovacevic 51).

CUP WINNERS' CUP
● **PARTIZAN BEOGRAD**
Qualifying round DINAMO BATUMI (GEO)
H 2-0 Bjekovic (17), Ilic (34)
Damjanac; Rasovic, Sabo, Gerasimovski, Duljaj; Trobok (Rankovic 71),
Ivic (Vukovic 64), Ilic, Stojisavljevic; Obradovic, Bjekovic (Kezman 73).
A 0-1
Damjanac; Rasovic, Savic, Sabo (Stojanoski 31), Duljaj; Trobok,
Ivic (Tesovic 68), Ilic, Stojisavljevic; Obradovic, Rankovic (Kezman 50).

1st round NEWCASTLE UNITED (ENG)
A 1-2 Rasovic (70p)
Damjanac; Rasovic, Savic, Stojanoski, Krstajic; Trobok, Ivic (Pazin 75),
Ilic, Tomic; Obradovic, Bjekovic (Stojisavljevic 85).
H 1-0 Rasovic (53p)
Damjanac; Rasovic, Savic, Stojanoski, Krstajic (Stojisavljevic 46); Trobok,
Ivic, Ilic, Tomic; Bjekovic (Tesovic 81), Kezman (Pazin 65).

2nd round LAZIO (ITA)
A 0-0
Damjanac; Rasovic, Savic, Stojanoski, Krstajic; Trobok, Ivic (Pazin 75),
Ilic, Tomic; Obradovic (Ilijev 64), Kezman.
H 2-3 Krstajic (18), Ilijev (85)
Damjanac; Rasovic, Savic, Gerasimovski, Krstajic; Trobok, Ivic (Ilijev 66),
Ilic, Tomic; Obradovic (Stojisavljevic 50), Kezman (Bjekovic 70).

UEFA CUP
● **CRVENA ZVEZDA BEOGRAD**
Preliminary round KOLKHETI 1913 POTI (GEO)
A 4-0 Ognjenovic (20), Acimovic (57, 73), Pantelic (63)
Jevric; Dudic, Pecelj (Vitakic 75), Bunjevcevic, Bjegovic; Ilic, Skoric,
Gojkovic (Slovic 70), Acimovic; Pantelic, Ognjenovic (Micic 61).
H 7-0 Pantelic (28), Ognjenovic (45p, 47), Gojkovic (54), Micic (57, 69, 90)
Jevric; Dudic, Pecelj, Bunjevcevic, Bjegovic; Ilic, Skoric, Gojkovic, Acimovic
(Ljubojevic 66); Pantelic (Micic 46), Ognjenovic (Slovic 66).

Qualifying round ROTOR VOLGOGRAD (RUS)
H 2-1 Skoric (61p), Ognjenovic (90p)
Jevric; Dudic, Pecelj, Bunjevcevic (Marinovic 46), Bjegovic; Ilic, Skoric,
Gojkovic, Acimovic; Pantelic (Micic 69), Ognjenovic.
A 2-1 Ognjenovic (74), Dudic (81)
Jevric; Dudic, Pecelj, Bunjevcevic, Bjegovic; Ilic, Skoric, Gojkovic, Acimovic;
Pantelic (Vitakic 75), Ognjenovic (Micic 84).

1st round FC METZ (FRA)
H 2-1 Ognjenovic (3), Drulic (12)
Jevric; Dudic, Bjegovic, Bunjevcevic, Adilson; Ilic, Skoric, Pantelic,
Acimovic; Drulic (Vitakic 68), Ognjenovic (Micic 83).
A 1-2 Marinovic (18)
(aet; 3-4 on pens.)
Jevric; Bjegovic (Dudic 78), Marinovic, Bunjevcevic, Adilson (Vitakic 75);
Ljubojevic, Skoric, Gojkovic (Micic 101), Acimovic; Pantelic, Drulic.

2nd round OLYMPIQUE LYONNAIS (FRA)
H 1-2 Skoric (58p)
Jevric; Dudic, Marinovic, Bunjevcevic, Bjegovic; Ilic, Skoric, Gojkovic,
Acimovic (Bajcetic 57); Pantelic, Ognjenovic.
A 2-3 Bunjevcevic (31), Acimovic (90)
Jevric; Dudic (Acimovic 60), Marinovic, Bunjevcevic, Bjegovic
(Adilson 46); Ilic, Skoric, Gojkovic, Vitakic; Pantelic (Micic 63),
Ognjenovic.

● **OBILIC BEOGRAD**
1st round ATLETICO MADRID (ESP)
A 0-2
Lukic; Babeu, Savic (Litera 68), Mrkic, Zivkovic; Zoric, Serafimovic
(Vargec 65), Grozdic, Sarac; Manojlovic (Rankovic 46), Kovacevic.
H 0-1
Lukic; Novic (Vasiljevic 70), Savic, Mrkic, Zivkovic; Zoric (Litera 65),
Juksic, Grozdic, Sarac; Kovacevic, Rankovic (Viciknez 46).

---

sixth Cup win of the decade with a killer fourth goal four minutes from time.

Although Red Star's return to European competition had already been secured through their league placing, victory was particularly sweet given the struggle they had endured in the championship. The Cup triumph was not enough, though, to keep coach Vojcin Lazarevic in his job. He had moved up from assistant following the sacking of Milorad Kosanovic in the wake of the team's UEFA Cup elimination by Lyon in the autumn, but the Red Star board chose to appoint Obilic coach Miloljub Ostojic as their new man for 1999/2000.

The Cup final was also the last hurrah for Partizan boss Ljubisa Tumbakovic, who, having led the club to no fewer than five championship titles and two Cups during his seven years in charge, was overdue a lucrative foreign assignment. That arrived from AEK Athens, who saw Tumbakovic as the man who could rival the incredible success of another Yugoslav coach, Dusan Bajevic, in the Greek championship.

Happily for Partizan, Tumbakovic was the only big name to leave. His successor, Miodrag Jesic, was able to take over the championship-winning side *en bloc*, and that meant another season in black and white stripes for the

PLAYERS OF THE SEASON

SINISA MIHAJLOVIC

There is some doubt as to whether, as Italian statisticians have claimed, Sinisa Mihajlovic has scored more free-kicks than any other player in the history of Serie A. But what is not open to question is his current standing as the one of the most dangerous set-piece experts in world football today. The 30-year-old Yugoslav international has an astonishingly accurate and powerful left-foot shot which he is not afraid to use from any distance up to 35 yards out. His first season with Lazio - and his seventh in Italy - was an absolute triumph. Although the team failed narrowly to win the Serie A title, they did capture the European Cup-winners' Cup by way of compensation. Mihajlovic was outstanding in both competitions although he reserved all his goals for the championship. There were eight in total - all of them, needless to say, from stunning free-kicks.

JOVAN STANKOVIC

One of the few newcomers to break into Yugoslavia's European Championship qualifying team, 28-year-old Jovan Stankovic earned his place with a succession of outstanding displays in the Spanish league for Mallorca. A nifty left-footed schemer, he likes to operate close to the touchline. Very accomplished on the ball, his speciality is the quick, inswinging cross that catches defenders out of position. Granted his first international cap in a friendly against Brazil in September 1998, he was chosen from the start for the opening Euro 2000 qualifier at home to Ireland, a match in which he provided the cross for the winning goal scored by Predrag Mijatovic.

MATEJA KEZMAN

Although still uncapped at senior level by the end of the 1998/99 season, Partizan Belgrade striker Mateja Kezman showed during the truncated season that he has the potential to become the next top-class star to emerge from Yugoslavia. It was the first season in the top flight for the 20-year-old striker from Zemun, and he adjusted remarkably quickly, earning himself hero worship from the Partizan fans after scoring the winning goal at home to arch-rivals Red Star and then finding the net in each of the next two meetings with Red Star, in league and Cup. Skilful and beautifully balanced, he can strike with both feet and is particularly dangerous when running at retreating defenders.

team's major stars such as Mateja Kezman, Sasa Ilic, Djordje Tomic and Vladimir Ivic. No big foreign bids came in for any of those players despite the publicity they attracted to themselves during the club's fine UEFA Cup run, which incorporated the elimination of Newcastle United and two impressive displays against eventual winners Lazio.

Surprisingly, only one of those Partizan players - Tomic - got a game for the Yugoslav national team during the season (compared with four each from Obilic and Red Star), but new coach Milan Zivadinovic showed little inclination to make significant changes to the team that had performed - or, rather, under-performed - for his predecessor Slobodan Santrac at the World Cup in France.

Six European Championship qualifiers were scheduled for Yugoslavia during the season, but, because of the Kosovo crisis, only half of them were actually played. For a long while during the NATO bombardment it seemed likely that Yugoslavia would be thrown out of the competition - as they had been on the eve of the Euro '92 finals - but UEFA, who were bound by no political ties to the contrary, stood by them and gave permission for them to complete their programme, albeit within an unfavourably condensed two-month period during the early autumn.

The matches called off at UEFA's behest were the two home games with Croatia and Macedonia originally scheduled for the end of March - the time when the NATO strikes began. Additionally, the Republic of Ireland decided unilaterally to veto the June 5 qualifier in Dublin.

Yugoslavia had begun their campaign with a delayed fixture against the Irish, from which they took three points courtesy of Predrag Mijatovic's winning goal. Two routine victories over Malta then followed, with the home fixture being transported to the Greek town of Salonika. Nine points out of nine looked promising, but there was still much work to do, and, in any case, the Yugoslavs were to have a new coach in charge for those final five games, with veteran Vujadin Boskov being appointed in July after Zivadinovic was found guilty of a breach of contract and sacked for negotiating a move to top Saudi Arabian club Al Nasr without the Federation's prior knowledge.

Boskov, a man of vast experience and accomplishment in European club football, seemed a sound and worthy choice, but he was the first to acknowledge on taking over that he had been plunged head-first into a race against time.

BUDUCNOST PODGORICA

CLUB DIRECTORY

FK Buducnost
Vaka Djurovica bb
81000 Podgorica
tel - (081) 41955/41560
fax - (081) 51651
Year of Formation - 1925
President - Marko Radunovic
Coach - Dimitrije Mitrovic; Petar Ljumovic;
Dragan Okuka
Stadium - FK Buducnost (15,230)

APPEARANCES 98/99

	P	Ap	(s)	Gls
Savo BARAC	M	1	(2)	
Albino CAMAJ	M	7	(7)	2
Zeljko CETKOVIC	A	3	(3)	
Adrian DJOKAJ	A	15	(1)	2
Hasam DJOKOVIC	M	3	(3)	
Goran DJUROVIC	M	20		
Igor DRAGICEVIC	M	10	(4)	
Branimir IVANISEVIC	A	17	(1)	2
Srdjan KJAJEVIC	G	5		
Zlatko KOSTIC	M	18		10
Darko LUBARDA	G	10		
Zoran MIJOVIC	D	21		
Slavisa MIRKOVIC	D	4	(2)	
Zeljko MRVALJEVIC	D		(1)	
Aleksandar NEDOVIC	M	15	(3)	1
Nikola NIKEZIC	M		(4)	
Srdjan NIKIC	A	13	(4)	3
Dejan OGNJENOVIC	D	11	(2)	
Zvonko PAVICEVIC	M	3	(5)	
Goran PERISIC	D	20		
Rade PETROVIC	A	2		
Milos PRODANOVIC	M	8		1
Marko RADONJIC	M	1		
Blazo RAOSAVLJEVIC	D	16		2
Zvonko RMANDIC	M	11		
Vladimir STANIC	A		(5)	
Zeljko TADIC	G	1		
Milan VRANJES	A	12	(3)	4
Miodrag VUKICEVIC	M	7	(9)	1
Miodrag VUKOTIC	D	2		

LEAGUE RESULTS 1998/99

07/08/98	Crvena zvezda Beograd	A	0-4	
16/08/98	Obilic Beograd	H	1-3	Nedovic
22/08/98	Sartid Smederevo	A	0-0	
29/08/98	OFK Beograd	H	2-2	Prodanovic, Vranjes
05/09/98	Vojvodina Novi Sad	A	0-2	
12/09/98	Radnicki Nis	H	3-1	Nikic 2, Kostic
19/09/98	FK Zemun	A	2-3	Kostic 2 (1p)
25/09/98	FK Pristina	H	0-0	
03/10/98	Rad Beograd	A	1-2	Raosavljevic (p)
17/10/98	Zeleznik Beograd	H	2-0	Kostic 2 (1p)
24/10/98	Proleter Zrenjanin	A	1-1	Djokaj
31/10/98	Spartak Subotica	H	2-0	Kostic 2
08/11/98	Partizan Beograd	A	0-1	
12/11/98	Mogren Budva	H	4-1	Vranjes, Djokaj, Camaj, Kostic
21/11/98	Hajduk Kula	A	0-3	
28/11/98	Radnicki Kragujevac	H	2-1	Camaj, Vranjes
05/12/98	Milicionar Beograd	A	3-6	Vukicevic, Nikic, Vranjes
24/02/99	Crvena zvezda Beograd	H	0-1	
27/02/99	Obilic Beograd	A	0-5	
03/03/99	Sartid Smederevo	H	0-0	
06/03/99	OFK Beograd	A	3-5	Kostic, Raosavljevic, Ivanisevic
13/03/99	Vojvodina Novi Sad	H	1-0	Ivanisevic
17/03/99	Radnicki Nis	A	0-1	
20/03/99	FK Zemun	H	1-0	Kostic

CRVENA ZVEZDA BEOGRAD

CLUB DIRECTORY

FK Crvena zvezda
Ljutice Bogdana 1a
11000 Beograd
tel - (011) 668213/660216
fax - (011) 661753
Year of Formation - 1945
President - Dragan Djajic
Secretary - Vladimir Cvetkovic
Coach - Milorad Kosanovic; Vojin Lazarevic
(99/00 - Miloljub Ostojic)
Stadium - Crvena zvezda (97,422)

MAJOR HONOURS
League Championship - (20)
1951, 1953, 1956, 1957, 1959, 1960, 1964,
1968, 1969, 1970, 1973, 1977, 1980, 1981,
1984, 1988, 1990, 1991, 1992, 1995.
Domestic Cup - (17) 1948, 1949, 1950, 1958,
1959, 1964, 1968, 1970, 1971, 1982, 1985,
1990, 1993, 1995, 1996, 1997, 1999.
European Champions' Cup - (1) 1991.
World Club Cup - (1) 1991.

APPEARANCES 98/99

	P	Ap	(s)	Gls
Milenko ACIMOVIC (SLO)	M	20	(2)	8
ADILSON dos Santos (BRA)	D	11	(1)	
Srdjan BAJCETIC	M	11	(3)	1
Nikoslav BJEGOVIC	D	12	(1)	
Branko BOSKOVIC	M	4	(2)	1
Goran BOSKOVIC	D	3		
Goran BUNJEVCEVIC	M	22		4
Goran DRULIC	A	15	(2)	7
Ivan DUDIC	D	18	(2)	
Jovan GOJKOVIC	M	19		8
Dejan ILIC	M	17		1
Dragoslav JEVRIC	G	21		
Aleksandar KOCIC	G	3		
Leo LERINC	M	5	(1)	
Darko LJUBOJEVIC	M	2	(4)	3
Vinko MARINOVIC	D	12	(1)	1
Dragan MICIC	A	7	(12)	4
Nenad MILJKOVIC	M		(3)	
Vladislav MIRKOVIC	D		(2)	
Perica OGNJENOVIC	A	9		3
Miodrag PANTELIC	A	10	(5)	3
Srdjan PECELJ	D	5	(1)	
Zeljko PEROVIC	D	1	(2)	
Mihajlo PJANOVIC	A	5		3
Dejan SAVICEVIC	M	3		
Dalibor SKORIC	M	16	(2)	3
Slobodan SLOVIC	A		(6)	
Milivoje VITAKIC	D	12	(3)	
WILLIAMS dos Santos (BRA)	A	1	(3)	

LEAGUE RESULTS 1998/99

07/08/98	Buducnost Podgorica	H	4-0	Acimovic, Gojkovic, Ognjenovic, Bunjevcevic
15/08/98	Sartid Smederevo	H	0-1	
29/08/98	FK Zemun	H	5-1	Pantelic, Skoric, Ognjenovic, Gojkovic, Ljubojevic
05/09/98	Rad Beograd	A	1-1	Drulic
09/09/98	Vojvodina Novi Sad	A	2-1	Gojkovic, Micic
12/09/98	Proleter Zrenjanin	H	2-1	Acimovic, Bunjevcevic
20/09/98	Partizan Beograd	A	1-2	Ljubojevic
25/09/98	Hajduk Kula	H	2-0	Ljubojevic, Acimovic
03/10/98	Milicionar Beograd	A	7-1	Gojkovic 2, Skoric, Acimovic, Bajcetic, Ognjenovic, Pantelic
16/10/98	Obilic Beograd	H	1-1	Gojkovic
24/10/98	OFK Beograd	A	1-1	Gojkovic
30/10/98	Radnicki Nis	H	4-0	Micic 2, Pantelic (p), Acimovic
07/11/98	FK Pristina	A	1-0	Drulic
11/11/98	Zeleznik Beograd	H	4-0	Gojkovic, Bunjevcevic, Ilic, og (Lucic)
21/11/98	Spartak Subotica	A	3-1	Drulic, Bunjevcevic, Skoric (p)
28/11/98	Mogren Budva	H	3-0	Acimovic 2, Marinovic
05/12/98	Radnicki Kragujevac	A	1-1	Micic
24/02/99	Buducnost Podgorica	A	1-0	Drulic
27/02/99	Sartid Smederevo	A	1-1	Drulic
03/03/99	Vojvodina Novi Sad	H	1-0	Boskovic B.
06/03/99	FK Zemun	A	3-0	(w/o)
13/03/99	Rad Beograd	H	3-1	Pjanovic 2, Drulic
17/03/99	Proleter Zrenjanin	A	1-2	Acimovic
20/03/99	Partizan Beograd	H	2-2	Pjanovic, Gojkovic

HAJDUK KULA

CLUB DIRECTORY

FK Hajduk
Svetozara Markovica 8
25230 Kula
tel - (025) 722812/723569
fax - (025) 722812
Year of Formation - 1925
President - Bogdan Rodic
Coach - Miroslav Vukasinovic; Risto Pavic
Stadium - Hajduk (10,000)

LEAGUE RESULTS 1998/99

08/08/98	OFK Beograd	H	0-0	
15/08/98	Radnicki Nis	A	1-1	Osmanovic (p)
22/08/98	FK Pristina	H	2-0	Mandic, Vuksanovic
29/08/98	Zeleznik Beograd	A	0-1	
05/09/98	Spartak Subotica	H	2-0	Mandic, Osmanovic
12/09/98	Mogren Budva	A	2-2	Stamatovic, Djedovic
19/09/98	Radnicki Kragujevac	H	3-0	Osmanovic 2, Miljanic
25/09/98	Crvena zvezda Beograd	A	0-2	
03/10/98	Sartid Smederevo	H	3-3	Miljanic, Markoski, Osmanovic
17/10/98	Vojvodina Novi Sad	A	1-3	Osmanovic
24/10/98	FK Zemun	H	3-0	Osmanovic 2 (1p), Stojakovic
31/10/98	Rad Beograd	A	0-1	
07/11/98	Proleter Zrenjanin	H	2-0	Osmanovic, Mandic
12/11/98	Partizan Beograd	A	0-3	
21/11/98	Buducnost Podgorica	H	3-0	Osmanovic 3 (1p)
28/11/98	Milicionar Beograd	H	0-0	
05/12/98	Obilic Beograd	A	0-5	
20/02/99	OFK Beograd	A	0-1	
27/02/99	Radnicki Nis	H	2-0	Osmanovic 2
03/03/99	FK Pristina	A	1-3	Markoski
06/03/99	Zeleznik Beograd	H	1-0	Osmanovic
13/03/99	Spartak Subotica	A	0-2	
17/03/99	Mogren Budva	H	1-0	Osmanovic
20/03/99	Radnicki Kragujevac	A	0-1	

APPEARANCES 98/99

	P	Ap	(s)	Gls
Sinisa ARSIC	M	1		
Slobodan BACIC	M	5		
Aleksandar BOGDANOVIC	A	1		
Dimitrije DIMITRIJEVIC	A	5	(1)	
Milenko DJEDOVIC	M	19	(2)	1
Goran DJORDJEVIC	M	8		
Goran DJUKIC	M	16		
Istvan DUDAS	G	23		
Sinisa IVANISEVIC	A	1	(1)	
Goran JOVANOVIC	M	4	(5)	
Zeljko KARANOVIC	D	21		
Aleksandar KIRKOV	M	3		
Nebojsa KLJESTAN	D	13	(3)	
Igor KOZOS	M		(2)	
Zoran KULIC	D	3	(4)	
Damir LOKNAR	G	1		
Nikola MALBASA	A	1	(2)	
Dragan MANDIC	D	22		3
Aleksandar MARKOSKI	M	17	(3)	2
Bojan MARKOVIC	D	4	(1)	
Ivica MILIVOJEV	M	5	(1)	
Dejan MILJANIC	M	8	(2)	2
Vukadin MILUNOVIC	M	1	(8)	
Dragan MOJIC	D	20		
Dejan NIKOLIC	D	5	(2)	
Dejan OSMANOVIC	A	21		16
Savo PAVICEVIC	M		(2)	
Zeljko RACIC	M	1	(4)	
Dalibor RADAKOVIC	A	3		
Uros STAMATOVIC	A	7	(9)	1
Aleksandar STOJAKOVIC	A	8	(6)	1
Darko STOJANOVIC	M		(5)	
Dejan STOSIC	M		(3)	
Vladica TASIC	A		(3)	
Zoran VUKSANOVIC	D	17	(2)	1

MILICIONAR BEOGRAD

CLUB DIRECTORY

FK Milicionar
Stari obrenovacki put 1A
11000 Beograd
tel - (011) 556/688/3548032
President - Stojan Misic
Coach - Stanislav Karasi; Slavko Radovanovic;
Djordje Gerum
Stadium - Milicionar (5,000)

APPEARANCES 98/99

	P	Ap	(s)	Gls
Petar ALEKSIC	M		(1)	
Sasa ANTIC	M	1	(6)	1
Aleksandar BOGDANOVIC	D	8	(4)	
Milivoje CIRKOVIC	D	19		2
Voja COSIC	D	15	(3)	1
Miodrag DJERISILO	D	8	(4)	
Nenad DJORDJEVIC	M		(1)	
Goran DJUKIC	D	6		
Milos DROBNJAK	D	15		3
Ivan GVOZDENOVIC	A	12	(1)	2
Stevan JAKOBA	M		(1)	
Pajo JANKOVIC	M		(4)	
Goran JEZDIMIROVIC	M	17		
Marko KNEZEVIC	D	4		
Goran KOLARIC	A		(2)	
Oliver KOVACEVIC	G	21		
Djordje KUNOVAC	A	1	(5)	
Nenad LALATOVIC	D	21		
Zoran LJUJIC	G	3		
Enes MALICI	M		(3)	
Radovan MARKOVIC	A	17	(3)	7
Nesko MILOVANOVIC	A	5	(2)	1
Marko MITROVIC	A	1	(4)	
Sinisa MULINA	M	22		10
Ratko NIKOLIC	A	5	(3)	
Konstantin OGNJANOVIC	A	15		7
Vladan PASIC	D	3		
Nedeljko PEROVIC	A		(5)	1
Milan RATKOVIC	A	3	(1)	
Mladen STANISIC	D	11	(4)	1
Perica STOJILJKOVIC	A	5		2
Vladan STOJAKOVIC	D	1	(1)	
Sergej TICA	M	6	(2)	
Zoran URUMOV	D	13		
Djordje ZAFIROVIC	A	6	(4)	1

LEAGUE RESULTS 1998/99

07/08/98	Obilic Beograd	H	0-0	
15/08/98	OFK Beograd	A	2-2	Ognjanovic 2
22/08/98	Radnicki Nis	H	4-5	Drobnjak 2, Mulina, Perovic
29/08/98	FK Pristina	A	2-3	Ognjanovic, Mulina
05/09/98	Zeleznik Beograd	H	3-0	Ognjanovic, Zafirovic, Stanisic
12/09/98	Spartak Subotica	A	2-4	Ognjanovic 2
19/09/98	Mogren Budva	H	1-1	Mulina
27/09/98	Radnicki Kragujevac	A	0-1	
03/10/98	Crvena zvezda Beograd	H	1-7	Stojiljkovic
17/10/98	Sartid Smederevo	A	0-1	
24/10/98	Vojvodina Novi Sad	H	2-1	Mulina 2
31/10/98	FK Zemun	A	0-1	
07/11/98	Rad Beograd	H	5-0	Markovic 3, Drobnjak, Stojiljkovic
11/11/98	Proleter Zrenjanin	A	1-0	Markovic
21/11/98	Partizan Beograd	H	0-1	
28/11/98	Hajduk Kula	A	0-0	
05/12/98	Buducnost Podgorica	H	6-3	Mulina 3, Gvozdenovic,
				Ognjanovic, Cirkovic
20/02/99	Obilic Beograd	A	0-2	
27/02/99	OFK Beograd	H	4-0	Markovic 2 (1p), Mulina, Antic
03/03/99	Radnicki Nis	A	1-4	Milovanovic
06/03/99	FK Pristina	H	2-0	Mulina, Markovic
13/03/99	Zeleznik Beograd	A	1-1	Cosic
17/03/99	Spartak Subotica	H	2-1	Gvozdenovic, Cirkovic
20/03/99	Mogren Budva	A	0-1	

MOGREN BUDVA

CLUB DIRECTORY

FK Mogren
Jadranski put b.b.
81310 Budva
tel - (086) 51128
fax - (086) 51613
Year of Formation - 1945
President - Miroslav Ivanovic
Coach - Dlobodan Halilovic
Stadium - Mogren (4,000)

APPEARANCES 98/99

	P	Ap	(s)	Gls
Zarko BELADA	D	20		1
Branko BOSKOVIC	M	8	(1)	
Dejan DIMIC	M	2		1
Dragan DJUKANOVIC	A	1		
Zoran DJURASKOVIC	M		(1)	
Vlatko DJURISIC	M	5		
Petar GUSIC	A	6		
Predrag JOVETIC	M		(1)	
Radovan KAVAJA	M	21		5
Jovan KLIKOVAC	M		(1)	
Goran KNEZEVIC	M		(3)	
Darko LJUBANOVIC	G	5		
Djeto LJUCOVIC	A	5	(1)	
Sefko MACIC	M	10	(4)	
Bojan MAGAZIN	M	7		
Milos MANOJLOVIC	D	3	(2)	
Milorad MARKELIC	D		(2)	
Milan MESTER	D	20	(3)	2
Vladislav MIRKOVIC	M	10	(5)	1
Igor MATIC	M	2		
Ivica MOMCILOVIC	M	7		
Nusret MURATBASIC	A	10	(2)	
Sead MURATOVIC	D	21		
Dusko OBADOVIC	D	14	(1)	
Marko PIMA	D	16		
Dejan PURIC	A	7	(2)	
Ilija RADJENOVIC	M		(5)	
Aleksandar RAKOVIC	A	6	(9)	1
Dejan ROGANOVIC	M	11	(3)	
Goran SIMOV	G	11		
Dejan SUSKAVCEVIC	G	8		
Dusan VLAISAVLJEVIC	D	6	(1)	
Nebojsa VOJVODIC	A	22		6
Zoran VUKCEVIC	A		(3)	
Milija ZIZIC	M		(4)	1

LEAGUE RESULTS 1998/99

08/08/98	Vojvodina Novi Sad	A	0-3	
15/08/98	FK Zemun	H	1-0	Vojvodic
22/08/98	Rad Beograd	A	0-1	
29/08/98	Proleter Zrenjanin	H	1-2	Vojvodic
05/09/98	Partizan Beograd	A	1-3	Mirkovic
12/09/98	Hajduk Kula	H	2-2	Kavaja, Rakovic
19/09/98	Milicionar Beograd	A	1-1	Belada
25/09/98	Obilic Beograd	H	0-0	
03/10/98	OFK Beograd	A	2-1	Mester, Kavaja (p)
17/10/98	Radnicki Nis	H	0-0	
24/10/98	FK Pristina	A	1-6	Vojvodic
31/10/98	Zeleznik Beograd	H	2-2	Kavaja (p), Vojvodic
07/11/98	Spartak Subotica	A	1-3	Mester
12/11/98	Buducnost Podgorica	A	1-4	Vojvodic
21/11/98	Radnicki Kragujevac	H	1-0	Kavaja
28/11/98	Crvena zvezda Beograd	A	0-3	
05/12/98	Sartid Smederevo	H	1-1	Kavaja (p)
20/02/99	Vojvodina Novi Sad	H	0-0	
27/02/99	FK Zemun	A	0-2	
03/03/99	Rad Beograd	H	0-2	
06/03/99	Proleter Zrenjanin	A	2-2	Vojvodic, Zizic
13/03/99	Partizan Beograd	H	0-3	
17/03/99	Hajduk Kula	A	0-1	
20/03/99	Milicionar Beograd	H	1-0	Dimic

OBILIC BEOGRAD

CLUB DIRECTORY

FK Obilic
Gospodara Vucica 189
11000 Beograd
tel - (011) 412085/412945
fax - (011) 412085
Year of Formation - 1924
President - Dragoslav Sekularac
Coach - Dragan Okuka; Miloljub Ostojic;
Dragoslav Sekularac
Stadium - Obilic (3,000)

MAJOR HONOURS
League Championship - (1) 1998.

APPEARANCES 98/99

	P	Ap	(s)	Gls
Kuzman BABEU	D	16	(2)	3
Zoran BIDZIC	M		(1)	
Veselin BOJIC	D		(3)	
Sasa BRANEZAC	A		(2)	
Predrag FILIPOVIC	D	2	(2)	
Nenad GROZDIC	M	23		7
Nebojsa JELENKOVIC	M	5	(10)	1
Zivojin JUKSIC	M	11		
Milorad KORAC	G	1		
Sasa KOVACEVIC	A	19	(3)	9
Nikola LAZETIC	M	6	(1)	2
Ivan LITERA	M	2	(9)	2
Nenad LUKIC	G	23		
Igor MANOJLOVIC	M	2		1
Nenad MLADENOVIC	M		(1)	
Sasa MRKIC	D	14		
Darko NOVIC	D	5	(1)	
Milan OBRADOVIC	D	3		
Predrag OCOKOLJIC	D	5	(10)	
Predrag POPOVIC	M		(2)	
Zoran RANKOVIC	A	22	(1)	13
Dragan SARAC	M	22		7
Miroslav SAVIC	D	22		1
Goran SERAFIMOVIC	D	4		
Darko VARGEC	D	12	(1)	
Aco VASILJEVIC	M	4	(1)	1
Sasa VICIKNEZ	M	2	(13)	6
Mihajlo VUJACIC	M		(1)	
Sasa ZIMONJIC	M	3	(2)	
Marjan ZIVKOVIC	M	17	(3)	2
Sasa ZORIC	M	19	(2)	5

LEAGUE RESULTS 1998/99

07/08/98	Milicionar Beograd	A	0-0	
16/08/98	Buducnost Podgorica	A	3-1	Vasiljevic, Rankovic, Kovacevic
21/08/98	OFK Beograd	H	2-0	Babeu, Grozdic
30/08/98	Radnicki Nis	A	2-0	Grozdic, Rankovic
05/09/98	FK Pristina	H	3-0	Viciknez 2, Grozdic
11/09/98	Zeleznik Beograd	A	2-1	Grozdic, Zivkovic
19/09/98	Spartak Subotica	H	3-1	Rankovic, Viciknez, Litera
25/09/98	Mogren Budva	A	0-0	
03/10/98	Radnicki Kragujevac	H	4-0	Rankovic, Viciknez, Zoric, Grozdic
16/10/98	Crvena zvezda Beograd	A	1-1	Kovacevic
24/10/98	Sartid Smederevo	H	4-2	Sarac 2, Rankovic, Kovacevic
31/10/98	Vojvodina Novi Sad	A	1-0	Grozdic
07/11/98	FK Zemun	H	6-3	Rankovic 2, Viciknez 2,
				Kovacevic, Grozdic
11/11/98	Rad Beograd	A	2-0	Kovacevic, og (Mutavdzic)
21/11/98	Proleter Zrenjanin	H	2-0	Zoric, Rankovic
28/11/98	Partizan Beograd	A	0-0	
05/12/98	Hajduk Kula	H	5-0	Zoric 2, Manojlovic, Savic, Litera
20/02/99	Milicionar Beograd	H	2-0	Lazetic, Rankovic
27/02/99	Buducnost Podgorica	H	5-0	Kovacevic, Zivkovic, Lazetic,
				Babeu, Rankovic
03/03/99	OFK Beograd	A	1-0	Sarac (p)
06/03/99	Radnicki Nis	H	5-0	Kovacevic 2, Sarac 2 (1p),
				Rankovic
12/03/99	FK Pristina	A	2-0	Rankovic, Sarac
17/03/99	Zeleznik Beograd	H	2-0	Kovacevic, Jelenkovic
20/03/99	Spartak Subotica	A	4-0	Rankovic, Sarac, Zoric, Babeu

OFK BEOGRAD

CLUB DIRECTORY

OFK Beograd
Mije Kovacevica 10
11000 Beograd
tel - (011) 765425/767045
fax - (011) 762364
Year of Formation - 1945
President - Ljubisa Samardzic
Coach - Djordje Serpak; Miodrag Jesic
Stadium - Omladinski (25,000)

MAJOR HONOURS
Domestic Cup - (4) 1953, 1958, 1962, 1966.

APPEARANCES 98/99

	P	Ap	(s)	Gls
Miodrag ANDJELKOVIC	A	4		2
Nenad BEGOVIC	M		(5)	
Aleksandar BRATIC	D	19		
Branko CVETKOVIC	M	1		
Igor DJOKIC	M		(1)	
Dejan DJURDJEVIC	M	17		1
Dusko DJURISIC	D	10	(6)	
Milan DRAGELJEVIC	D	15	(2)	
Dragan DRASKOVIC	G	23		
Srdjan GASIC	M		(10)	
Dragan ILIC	M		(2)	
Sasa KLJAJIC	M	4	(5)	
Zoran LONCAR	A	19		3
Zoran LUKIC	D	10	(9)	2
Slavko MATIC	M	16		
Goran MILOVANOVIC	M	2	(4)	2
Boban NIKOLOVSKI (MAC)	D	13	(3)	1
Vladimir PAVLOVIC	M		(1)	
Milorad PEKOVIC	A	19		5
Vladimir PETKOVIC	M	15	(5)	2
Sasa PETROVIC	G	1		
Mihajlo PJANOVIC	A	16		11
Bogic POPOVIC	M		(1)	
Milorad POPOVIC	D	2		
Dejan RADJENOVIC	M	20		2
Miftar RAMA	D	21		1
Vladimir RASIC	M		(3)	
Vladimir SANDULOVIC	D	5	(4)	
Aleksandar STANOJEVIC	D	12		2

LEAGUE RESULTS 1998/99

08/08/98	Hajduk Kula	A	0-0	
15/08/98	Milicionar Beograd	H	2-2	Pjanovic 2
21/08/98	Obilic Beograd	A	0-2	
29/08/98	Buducnost Podgorica	A	2-2	Stanojevic, Pjanovic
05/09/98	Radnicki Nis	H	2-0	Pekovic, Pjanovic
12/09/98	FK Pristina	A	3-1	Rama, Nikolovski, Pekovic
19/09/98	Zeleznik Beograd	H	5-2	Loncar 2, Petkovic, Pjanovic, og (Glavardanov)
26/09/98	Spartak Subotica	A	4-3	Pjanovic 3, Stanojevic
03/10/98	Mogren Budva	H	1-2	Loncar
17/10/98	Radnicki Kragujevac	A	1-6	Pjanovic (p)
24/10/98	Crvena zvezda Beograd	H	1-1	Radjenovic
31/10/98	Sartid Smederevo	A	1-0	Lukic
07/11/98	Vojvodina Novi Sad	H	0-0	
11/11/98	FK Zemun	A	0-1	
21/11/98	Rad Beograd	H	1-1	Radjenovic
28/11/98	Proleter Zrenjanin	A	0-1	
06/12/98	Partizan Beograd	H	2-3	Pjanovic 2
20/02/99	Hajduk Kula	H	1-0	Petkovic
27/02/99	Milicionar Beograd	A	0-4	
03/03/99	Obilic Beograd	H	0-1	
06/03/99	Buducnost Podgorica	H	5-3	Pekovic 2 (1p), Djurdjevic, Lukic, Andjelkovic
13/03/99	Radnicki Nis	A	0-0	
17/03/99	FK Pristina	H	3-2	Milovanovic 2, Pekovic
20/03/99	Zeleznik Beograd	A	1-2	Andjelkovic

PARTIZAN BEOGRAD

CLUB DIRECTORY

FK Partizan
Humska 1
11000 Beograd
tel - (011) 3227181/3229793
fax - (011) 3229906
Year of Formation - 1945
President - Ivan Curkovic
Secretary - Zarko Zecevic
Coach - Ljubisa Tumbakovic
(99/00 - Miodrag Jesic)
Stadium - Partizan (50,819)

MAJOR HONOURS
League Championship - (16) 1947, 1949, 1961,
1962, 1963, 1965, 1976, 1978, 1983, 1986,
1987, 1993, 1994, 1996, 1997, 1999.
Domestic Cup - (8) 1947, 1952, 1954, 1957,
1989, 1992, 1994, 1998.

APPEARANCES 98/99

	P	Ap	(s)	Gls
Nenad BJEKOVIC	A	13		1
Nikola DAMJANAC	G	24		
Igor DULJAL	M	7	(8)	
Marjan GERASIMOVSKI (MAC)	D	9	(4)	1
Sasa ILIC	M	23		13
Ivica ILIJEV	A	7	(8)	3
Vladimir IVIC	M	18	(2)	12
Mateja KEZMAN	A	17	(5)	6
Mladen KRSTAJIC	D	15	(2)	
Nenad MISKOVIC	M	1		
Goran OBRADOVIC	A	12	(3)	6
Predrag PAZIN	D	1	(4)	
Ljubisa RANKOVIC	A	3	(3)	
Vuk RASOVIC	D	17		6
Zoltan SABO	D	3		
Branko SAVIC	D	17	(1)	
Aleksandar STANOJEVIC	D	2	(1)	
Milan STOJANOSKI	A	16		
Dragan STOJISAVLJEVIC	A	8	(4)	1
Djordje SVETLICIC	M	6	(4)	
Darko TESOVIC	M	1	(2)	
Djordje TOMIC	M	18		3
Goran TROBOK (BOS)	M	23		2
Aleksandar VUKOVIC	M	3	(11)	3

LEAGUE RESULTS 1998/99

08/08/98	Radnicki Nis	H	4-1	Ilic 2, Vukovic, Trobok
16/08/98	FK Pristina	A	4-0	Ivic 2, Trobok, Gerasimovski
22/08/98	Zeleznik Beograd	H	4-1	Obradovic 3, Rasovic (p)
30/08/98	Spartak Subotica	A	4-0	Stojisavljevic, Ilic, Tomic, Obradovic
05/09/98	Mogren Budva	H	3-1	Ivic 2, Ilic
12/09/98	Radnicki Kragujevac	A	2-1	Kezman 2
20/09/98	Crvena zvezda Beograd	H	2-1	Tomic, Kezman
27/09/98	Sartid Smederevo	A	2-0	Rasovic, Ivic
04/10/98	Vojvodina Novi Sad	H	2-0	Ivic, Ilic
17/10/98	FK Zemun	A	2-1	Obradovic, Tomic
25/10/98	Rad Beograd	H	4-0	Rasovic (p), Ilijev, Vukovic, Ivic
31/10/98	Proleter Zrenjanin	A	1-0	Ilic
08/11/98	Buducnost Podgorica	H	1-0	Ilic
12/11/98	Hajduk Kula	H	3-0	Ilic 2, Ilijev
21/11/98	Milicionar Beograd	A	1-0	og (Drobnjak)
28/11/98	Obilic Beograd	H	0-0	
06/12/98	OFK Beograd	A	3-2	Rasovic 2 (1p), Obradovic
19/02/99	Radnicki Nis	A	0-0	
27/02/99	FK Pristina	H	3-0	Ivic, Vukovic, Ilic
03/03/99	Zeleznik Beograd	A	2-0	Ivic, Kezman
06/03/99	Spartak Subotica	H	5-1	Stojanoski, Ivic, Ilijev, Kezman, Ilic
13/03/99	Mogren Budva	A	3-0	Ivic, Bjekovic, Ilic
17/03/99	Radnicki Kragujevac	H	2-0	Rasovic, Ivic
20/03/99	Crvena zvezda Beograd	A	2-2	Kezman, Ilic

FK PRISTINA

CLUB DIRECTORY

FK Pristina
Gradski Stadion PF111
38000 Pristina
tel - (038) 26968
Year of Formation - 1922
President - Zvonimir Stevic
Coach - Zoran Colakovic; Timotije Davidovic
Stadium - Gradski (30,000)

APPEARANCES 98/99

	P	Ap	(s)	Gls
Veljko ALEKSIC	D	6	(3)	
Branimir BANJAC	M	8	(4)	1
Jugoslav BANJAC	A	1		
Predrag BOGOSAVLJEVIC	D	1	(2)	
Sasa BUKMIROVIC	A		(1)	
Nemanja DANCETOVIC	M	20		8
Milorad DEDIC	M	2	(4)	
Darko DINIC	A	3	(15)	1
Goran DJURKOVIC	D	22		1
Almir DRESKOVIC	M	12	(1)	
Prodrag GAJIC	M	3		
Nebojsa IVANOVIC	M	3		
Ljubisa IVIC	M	20		1
Ivica JANICIJEVIC	D	3	(3)	1
Dragan JOSIC	A	5	(4)	
Predrag JOVANOVIC	M	4	(5)	
Branko KOSTIC	M	3	(3)	
Srdjan MARJANOVIC	G	5		
Miodrag MOMCILOVIC	M	7		
Dejan MRVALJEVIC	D	21		
Goran NIKOLIC	D	15		
Miodrag NIKOLIC	D	6		
Ratko NIKOLIC	D	3	(2)	
Zoran PEROVIC	G	19		
Predrag POPOVIC	M	6		1
Nebojsa SELAKOVIC	A		(3)	
Darko SPALJEVIC	A	1	(9)	
Predrag TATOVIC	D	4		
Sasa TESIC	M	18		5
Sergej TICA	M	2	(1)	
Filip TRIVAN	A	19	(2)	3
Aleksandar VLAHOVIC	A	7		1
Slavisa ZDRAVKOVIC	D	15		2
Milan ZIVIC	M		(1)	

LEAGUE RESULTS 1998/99

08/08/98	Proleter Zrenjanin	A	0-2	
16/08/98	Partizan Beograd	H	0-4	
22/08/98	Hajduk Kula	A	0-2	
29/08/98	Milicionar Beograd	H	3-2	Zdravkovic, Dinic, Dancetovic
05/09/98	Obilic Beograd	A	0-3	
12/09/98	OFK Beograd	H	1-3	Dancetovic
19/09/98	Radnicki Nis	A	1-3	Tesic
26/09/98	Buducnost Podgorica	A	0-0	
03/10/98	Zeleznik Beograd	H	3-1	Djurkovic, Dancetovic, Trivan
17/10/98	Spartak Subotica	A	1-3	Janicijevic
24/10/98	Mogren Budva	H	6-1	Tesic 3, Dancetovic 2, Ivic
31/10/98	Radnicki Kragujevac	A	0-2	
07/11/98	Crvena zvezda Beograd	H	0-1	
11/11/98	Sartid Smederevo	A	0-3	
21/11/98	Vojvodina Novi Sad	H	2-1	Zdravkovic, Dancetovic (p)
28/11/98	FK Zemun	A	0-3	
05/12/98	Rad Beograd	H	1-2	Dancetovic (p)
20/02/99	Proleter Zrenjanin	H	1-1	Popovic
27/02/99	Partizan Beograd	A	0-3	
03/03/99	Hajduk Kula	H	3-1	Banjac B., Dancetovic, Vlahovic
06/03/99	Milicionar Beograd	A	0-2	
12/03/99	Obilic Beograd	H	0-2	
17/03/99	OFK Beograd	A	2-3	Tesic, Trivan
20/03/99	Radnicki Nis	H	1-1	Trivan

PROLETER ZRENJANIN

CLUB DIRECTORY

FK Proleter
Karadjordjev trg 100
23000 Zrenjanin
tel - (023) 64856/66550
fax - (023) 30430
Year of Formation - 1947
President - Stanko Ilic
Coach - Radivoje Draskovic
Stadium - Gradski (20,000)

APPEARANCES 98/99

	P	Ap	(s)	Gls
Stanoje DJOKIC	M	9	(9)	1
Ivan DJUROVIC	M		(1)	
Dragan JANJATOVIC	A	3	(8)	
Dragan JOVIC	A	18		10
Dusko KLINDO	A	2	(2)	1
Sinisa KUJUNDZIC	M	10	(4)	1
Zoran LISICA	D	21		1
Nenad LJUBENOVIC	M	8	(6)	
Predrag LUBURIC	D	16	(1)	1
Predrag MACANOVIC	A	20	(1)	1
Borko MARINKOVIC	M	13	(3)	1
Savo MARTINOVIC	M	1	(1)	
Dejan MILJKOVIC	M	2	(3)	
Nenad MIROSAVLJEVIC	M	16	(3)	4
Nenad MISKOVIC	D	15		1
Stevan NEDELJKOV	D	2		
Srdjan PJEVAC	M	8	(7)	
Ilija REJIC	M		(1)	
Jovo SIMANIC	D	21	(1)	3
Sasa TODIC	G	24		
Mirko TODOROVIC	M	18		1
Nenad TRAJKOVIC	D	9	(3)	1
Svetozar VUKASINOVIC	D	5		
Srdjan ZAKIC	D	14	(1)	
Milorad ZECEVIC	D	3	(3)	
Marko ZORIC	M	6	(4)	1
Djordje ZUZA	M		(2)	

LEAGUE RESULTS 1998/99

08/08/98	FK Pristina	H	2-0	Simanic, Trajkovic
15/08/98	Zeleznik Beograd	A	0-1	
22/08/98	Spartak Subotica	H	3-1	Jovic 3
29/08/98	Mogren Budva	A	2-1	Kujundzic, Zoric
05/09/98	Radnicki Kragujevac	H	3-0	Jovic 2, Mirosavljevic
12/09/98	Crvena zvezda Beograd	A	1-2	Mirosavljevic
19/09/98	Sartid Smederevo	H	1-0	Jovic
26/09/98	Vojvodina Novi Sad	A	1-4	Macanovic
03/10/98	FK Zemun	H	2-1	Simanic, Djokic
17/10/98	Rad Beograd	A	1-1	Klindo
24/10/98	Buducnost Podgorica	H	1-1	Luburic
31/10/98	Partizan Beograd	H	0-1	
07/11/98	Hajduk Kula	A	0-2	
11/11/98	Milicionar Beograd	H	0-1	
21/11/98	Obilic Beograd	A	0-2	
28/11/98	OFK Beograd	H	1-0	Jovic
05/12/98	Radnicki Nis	A	2-1	Miskovic, Lisica
20/02/99	FK Pristina	A	1-1	Mirosavljevic
27/02/99	Zeleznik Beograd	H	2-2	Jovic, Mirosavljevic
03/03/99	Spartak Subotica	A	1-0	Jovic
06/03/99	Mogren Budva	H	2-2	Todorovic, Simanic
13/03/99	Radnicki Kragujevac	A	0-2	
17/03/99	Crvena zvezda Beograd	H	2-1	Jovic, Marinkovic
20/03/99	Sartid Smederevo	A	1-2	og (Kljajic)

RAD BEOGRAD

CLUB DIRECTORY

FK Rad
Crnotravska bb
11000 Beograd
tel - (011) 663039/666884/664377
fax - (011) 662169
Year of Formation - 1958
President - Milos Dimitric
Coach - Cedomir Djoincevic
Stadium - Rad (13,000)

APPEARANCES 98/99

	P	Ap	(s)	Gls
Milos ALILOVIC	M	2	(6)	
Dejan BATROVIC	D	5	(3)	
Mirko BUNJEVCEVIC	M		(1)	
Sasa DJORDJEVIC	M		(3)	
Drazen DUKIC	D	16		
Jane GAVALOVSKI	M		(1)	
Stevo GLOGOVAC	D	22		1
Saudin HUSEINOVIC	A	16	(4)	3
Aleksandar JANJIC	A	6		3
Goran JERINIC	U		(3)	
Mile KNEZEVIC	D	6		
Djordje KUNOVAC	M	10	(1)	7
Stevica KUZMANOVSKI (MAC)	D	20		
Milan MARTINOVIC	M		(1)	
Zeljko MATIC	D	1		
Bosko MIHAJLOVIC	M	5	(14)	1
Zeljko MIJOVIC	D	7	(4)	1
Aleksandar MUTAVDIC	D	20		3
Ozren RADANOVIC	D	5	(2)	
Aleksandar RANKOVIC	D	4	(4)	
Milan SEVO	G	24		
Borislav STEVANOVIC	M	3	(1)	2
Dragan TOMIC	M	18	(3)	
Nebojsa TOPALOV	M	20	(1)	1
Dusan VIDOJEVIC	M	4	(17)	2
Nebojsa VIGNJEVIC	A	19		
Ede VISINKA	D	11	(1)	
Aleksandar ZIVKOVIC	D	20		1

LEAGUE RESULTS 1998/99

08/08/98	Zeleznik Beograd	H	2-0	Huseinovic, Kunovac
15/08/98	Spartak Subotica	A	3-1	Kunovac 2, Vidojevic
22/08/98	Mogren Budva	H	1-0	Mihajlovic
29/08/98	Radnicki Kragujevac	A	1-1	Kunovac
05/09/98	Crvena zvezda Beograd	H	1-1	Kunovac
12/09/98	Sartid Smederevo	A	0-1	
19/09/98	Vojvodina Novi Sad	H	1-0	Kunovac
26/09/98	FK Zemun	A	0-1	
03/10/98	Buducnost Podgorica	H	2-1	Mutavdzic, Glogovac
17/10/98	Proleter Zrenjanin	H	1-1	Kunovac
25/10/98	Partizan Beograd	A	0-4	
31/10/98	Hajduk Kula	H	1-0	Zivkovic
07/11/98	Milicionar Beograd	A	0-5	
11/11/98	Obilic Beograd	H	0-2	
21/11/98	OFK Beograd	A	1-1	Huseinovic
28/11/98	Radnicki Nis	H	2-0	Vidojevic, og (Gavrilovic)
05/12/98	FK Pristina	A	2-1	Mijovic, Mutavdzic
20/02/99	Zeleznik Beograd	A	0-0	
27/02/99	Spartak Subotica	H	1-0	Janjic
03/03/99	Mogren Budva	A	2-0	Huseinovic, Janjic
06/03/99	Radnicki Kragujevac	H	2-1	Topalov, Stevanovic
13/03/99	Crvena zvezda Beograd	A	1-3	Mutavdzic
17/03/99	Sartid Smederevo	H	1-1	Janjic
20/03/99	Vojvodina Novi Sad	A	1-1	Stevanovic

RADNICKI KRAGUJEVAC

CLUB DIRECTORY

FK Radnicki
17 Udarne divizije 21
34000 Kragujevac
tel - (034) 32974/331937
fax - (034) 762364
President - Tanasije Katanic
Coach - Zarko Olarevic; Slobodan Stasevic
Stadium - FK Radnicki (10,000)

APPEARANCES 98/99

	P	Ap	(s)	Gls
Dalibor ANTONIJEVIC	D	10	(2)	
Zeljko BUZIC	A	18	(1)	6
Pavle DELIBASIC	A	1	(2)	
Radojica DESPOTOVIC	D	14	(4)	1
Darko DIMITRIJEVIC	M		(5)	
Budmir DJUKIC	M	10	(9)	3
Milos FILIPOVIC	A	1	(1)	
Ranko GOLIJANIN	D	6		2
Velimir IVANOVIC	A	17		4
Sinisa JANJIC	G	16		
Slavoljub KIZIC	M	23		4
Ognjen KOROMAN	M	3	(6)	1
Ivica KRALJ	G	3		
Aleksandar MADZAR	A	2	(6)	1
Dejan MILICEVIC	M	5	(3)	
Dejan MILOSAVLJEVIC	D	18	(1)	
Zoran MILOSEVIC	D	11		
Goran MILOVANOVIC	A	9	(3)	4
Nesko MILOVANOVIC	A	6	(4)	3
Stevan PALASTI	M	1	(2)	
Nebojsa PANTOVIC	M	1	(1)	
Vladimir RADIC	M		(2)	
Zoran RADOSAVLJEVIC	M	22		2
Milan RISTIC	M	13	(7)	1
Dragan SPASIC	D	22		1
Goran SRETENOVIC	G	5	(1)	
Zoran STEVANOVIC	D	20	(1)	
Darko STOJANOVIC	M		(2)	
Dragan VELJOVIC	A		(2)	
Dejan ZERADJANIN	M	7		

LEAGUE RESULTS 1998/99

08/08/98	Sartid Smederevo	A	3-1	Milovanovic G. 2 (1p), Kizic
15/08/98	Vojvodina Novi Sad	H	2-3	Kizic, Buzic
22/08/98	FK Zemun	A	3-1	Madzar, Ivanovic, Koroman
29/08/98	Rad Beograd	H	1-1	Kizic
05/09/98	Proleter Zrenjanin	A	0-3	
12/09/98	Partizan Beograd	H	1-2	Kizic
19/09/98	Hajduk Kula	A	0-3	
27/09/98	Milicionar Beograd	H	1-0	
03/10/98	Obilic Beograd	A	0-4	
17/10/98	OFK Beograd	H	6-1	Milovanovic N. 3, Radosavljevic, Buzic, Spasic
24/10/98	Radnicki Nis	A	2-2	Golijanin, Buzic
31/10/98	FK Pristina	H	2-0	Golijanin, Ristic
07/11/98	Zeleznik Beograd	A	0-2	
11/11/98	Spartak Subotica	H	3-2	Milovanovic G. 2 (1p), Ivanovic
21/11/98	Mogren Budva	A	0-1	
28/11/98	Buducnost Podgorica	A	1-2	Djukic
05/12/98	Crvena zvezda Beograd	H	1-1	Radosavljevic
20/02/99	Sartid Smederevo	H	2-0	Despotovic, Ivanovic
26/02/99	Vojvodina Novi Sad	A	1-8	Buzic
03/03/99	FK Zemun	H	0-2	
06/03/99	Rad Beograd	A	1-2	Djukic
13/03/99	Proleter Zrenjanin	H	2-0	Buzic 2
17/03/99	Partizan Beograd	A	0-2	
20/03/99	Hajduk Kula	H	1-0	Djukic

RADNICKI NIS

CLUB DIRECTORY

FK Radnicki
Devete brigade bb
18000 Nis
tel - (018) 22016/25030/24445
fax - (018) 22016
Year of Formation - 1923
President - Dragan Pantelic
Coach - Bosko Antic; Ilija Dimoski;
Radmilo Ivancevic
Stadium - Cair (25,000)

APPEARANCES 98/99

	P	Ap	(s)	Gls
Perica ADZIC	M	12		2
Mirko ANDRIC	M	12	(2)	
Dejan DIMITRIJEVIC	M	10		1
Milan DINIC	A	3	(3)	
Petar DJENIC	D	20	(1)	
Dusan DJORDJEVIC	D	3	(6)	
Goran DJORDJEVIC	M	20	(1)	1
Zoran DJURDJEVIC	M		(1)	
Predrag FILIPOVIC	M	6		
Dragan GAVRILOVIC	D	14		1
Petar JEKIC	A	14	(2)	4
Bratislav JOVANOVIC	A	1	(1)	
Goran IOVANOVIC	M	14	(1)	
Darko KARAPETROVIC	M	1		
Igor MANOJLOVIC	A	7		1
Dragan MATIJEVIC	M		(1)	
Bojan MILENKOVIC	D	21		4
Bojan MILICEVIC	M	1	(3)	
Miroslav MILOSEVIC	D	4	(4)	
Dalibor MITROVIC	A	16		4
Goran MLADENOVIC	M	3	(3)	
Svetozar MURIC	M		(2)	
Milan PECELJ	D		(1)	
Ivan POLIC	A	18	(2)	1
Zarko RADONJIC	M	8	(9)	
Zoran RADOVIC	G	1		
Bratislav RISTIC	M		(5)	
Goran SIMOV	G	6		
Srdjan SOLDATOVIC	G	11		
Dragan STANKOVIC	D	20	(2)	
Dusan STANKOVIC	A	1	(3)	
Ivan STUPLJANIN	G	6	(1)	
Dragan VASILJEVIC	D	6		
Zoran VASKOVIC	M		(1)	
Mihajlo VUJACIC	A	5		1

LEAGUE RESULTS 1998/99

08/08/98	Partizan Beograd	A	1-4	Mitrovic
15/08/98	Hajduk Kula	H	1-1	Jekic
22/08/98	Milicionar Beograd	A	5-4	Milenkovic 2 (1p), Mitrovic, Polic, og (Mulina)
30/08/98	Obilic Beograd	H	0-2	
05/09/98	OFK Beograd	A	0-2	
12/09/98	Buducnost Podgorica	A	1-3	Mitrovic
19/09/98	FK Pristina	H	3-1	Gavrilovic, Milenkovic, Jekic
26/09/98	Zeleznik Beograd	A	1-4	Mitrovic
03/10/98	Spartak Subotica	H	0-2	
17/10/98	Mogren Budva	A	0-0	
24/10/98	Radnicki Kragujevac	H	2-2	Dimitrijevic, Jekic
30/10/98	Crvena zvezda Beograd	A	0-4	
07/11/98	Sartid Smederevo	H	0-0	
11/11/98	Vojvodina Novi Sad	A	0-1	
21/11/98	FK Zemun	H	0-1	
28/11/98	Rad Beograd	A	0-2	
05/12/98	Proleter Zrenjanin	H	1-2	Jekic
19/02/99	Partizan Beograd	H	0-0	
27/02/99	Hajduk Kula	A	0-2	
03/03/99	Milicionar Beograd	H	4-1	Djordjevic G., Adzic, Manojlovic, Vujacic
06/03/99	Obilic Beograd	A	0-5	
13/03/99	OFK Beograd	H	0-0	
17/03/99	Buducnost Podgorica	H	1-0	Adzic
20/03/99	FK Pristina	A	1-1	Milenkovic

SARTID SMEDEREVO

CLUB DIRECTORY

FK Sartid
Goranska 55
11300 Smederevo
tel - (026) 223319/224509
fax - (026) 223030
President - Branko Grujic
Coach - Branko Radovic; Bosko Antic
Stadium - FK Sartid (10,000)

APPEARANCES 98/99

	P	Ap	(s)	Gls
Sasa ANTUNOVIC	A	9	(5)	1
Dejan BATOS	D	10	(5)	
Sasa BRANEZAC	A	5	(5)	3
Radoslav BULIC	D	19		2
Dalibor CORLUKA	D	22		
Zoran CUGALJ	M		(1)	
Blaze GEORGIOSKI	M	11	(4)	1
Milan JOVIC	M	12	(6)	2
Predrag KATIC	A	20		7
Dusan KLJAJIC	D	19		
Sasa KOCIC	M	20		3
Blagoje LAZAREVIC	M		(2)	
Marjan MILOVANOVIC	A	2	(13)	2
Aleksandar PANTIC	M	16		1
Dejan PURIC	M		(2)	
Dejan RABRENOVIC	D	12	(1)	
Dejan RADOJKOVIC	M	1	(1)	
Mladen RANITOVIC	M		(3)	
Darko SAVIC	A	1	(2)	
Goran SERAFIMOVIC	D	2	(1)	
Dusan STAMENKOVIC	M	5	(3)	
Sasa STEVANOVIC	G	1		
Marko STOJIC	D	20	(2)	
Dragan VASIC	G	23		
Dejan VILOTIC	M	12		
Darko VOJVODIC	M	14	(2)	1
Goran VUCIC	M	8	(1)	

LEAGUE RESULTS 1998/99

08/08/98	Radnicki Kragujevac	H	1-3	Milovanovic
15/08/98	Crvena zvezda Beograd	A	1-0	Katic
22/08/98	Buducnost Podgorica	H	0-0	
29/08/98	Vojvodina Novi Sad	H	0-3	(w/o)
05/09/98	FK Zemun	A	1-1	Georgioski
12/09/98	Rad Beograd	H	1-0	Bulic
19/09/98	Proleter Zrenjanin	A	0-1	
27/09/98	Partizan Beograd	H	0-2	
03/10/98	Hajduk Kula	A	3-3	Katic (p), Kocic, Branezac
17/10/98	Milicionar Beograd	H	1-0	Pantic
24/10/98	Obilic Beograd	A	2-4	Branezac 2
31/10/98	OFK Beograd	H	0-1	
07/11/98	Radnicki Nis	A	0-0	
11/11/98	FK Pristina	H	3-0	Kocic, Bulic, Milovanovic
21/11/98	Zeleznik Beograd	A	1-1	og (Aleksic)
28/11/98	Spartak Subotica	H	2-1	Katic, Antunovic
05/12/98	Mogren Budva	A	1-1	Vojvodic
20/02/99	Radnicki Kragujevac	A	0-2	
27/02/99	Crvena zvezda Beograd	H	1-1	Katic
03/03/99	Buducnost Podgorica	A	0-0	
06/03/99	Vojvodina Novi Sad	A	0-1	
13/03/99	FK Zemun	H	3-0	Katic 2 (1p), Jovic
17/03/99	Rad Beograd	A	1-1	Katic (p)
20/03/99	Proleter Zrenjanin	H	2-1	Jovic, Kocic

SPARTAK SUBOTICA

CLUB DIRECTORY

FK Spartak
Lenjinov Park 10
24000 Subotica
tel - (024) 551035/551979
fax - (024) 551293/555016
Year of Formation - 1945
President - Milorad Stavljanin
Coach - Josip Duvandzic; Slobodan Kustudic
Stadium - Gradski (28,000)

APPEARANCES 98/99

	P	Ap	(s)	Gls
Nikola BASTA	A	8	(11)	1
Esad BRKIC	D	9	(4)	
Nebojsa COROVIC	D	2		
Ivica FRANCISKOVIC	A	16	(2)	1
Radoslav IGNJIC	D	6		
Dragan ILIC	A		(1)	
Dejan IVANISEVIC	A	1	(2)	
Aleksandar KOPUNOVIC	M	14	(8)	5
Ognjen KOROMAN	M	6		1
Milos KRUSCIC	D	10	(2)	
Zoltan KUJUNDZIC	G	11		
Miodrag LATINOVIC	U	17		1
Goran MARINKOVIC	M	17	(1)	1
Predrag MARKOVIC	D	13	(1)	
Ljubomir MORAVAC	G	1		
Viktor ORSAG	D	1	(2)	
Mladen PEROVIC	D	7		
Dejan PESIC	G	7		
Dejan POLJAKOVIC	M	13	(2)	2
Miljan PRIJIC	A		(2)	
Antal PUHALAK	A	20	(1)	12
Zolt RADIC	D	4	(4)	
Zoran RADULOVIC	A		(1)	
Jovan SARCEVIC	M	16		2
Branko SCEPANOVIC	D	7	(4)	
Alan SISKA	A		(2)	
Goran SOMODJI	D	4	(1)	
Zoran STJEPANOVIC	M	17	(5)	3
Davor STOJANOVIC	G	5		
Stanko SVITLICA	M	15	(1)	1
Nenad VUKCEVIC	A	11	(2)	2
Vasilije ZARKOVIC	M		(2)	
Zlatko ZEBIC	D	6	(2)	

LEAGUE RESULTS 1998/99

08/08/98	FK Zemun	A	2-4	Poljakovic, Puhalak
15/08/98	Rad Beograd	H	1-3	Basta
22/08/98	Proleter Zrenjanin	A	1-3	Stjepanovic
30/08/98	Partizan Beograd	H	0-4	
05/09/98	Hajduk Kula	A	0-2	
12/09/98	Milicionar Beograd	H	4-2	Puhalak, Sarcevic, Kopunovic, Poljakovic
19/09/98	Obilic Beograd	A	1-3	Svitlica
26/09/98	OFK Beograd	H	3-4	Kopunovic, Puhalak, Sarcevic
03/10/98	Radnicki Nis	A	2-0	Puhalak 2
17/10/98	FK Pristina	H	3-1	Franciskovic, Puhalak, og (Dreskovic)
24/10/98	Zeleznik Beograd	A	1-3	Puhalak
31/10/98	Buducnost Podgorica	A	0-2	
07/11/98	Mogren Budva	H	3-1	Puhalak 2, Stjepanovic
11/11/98	Radnicki Kragujevac	A	2-3	Kopunovic, Vukcevic
21/11/98	Crvena zvezda Beograd	H	1-3	Vukcevic
28/11/98	Sartid Smederevo	A	1-2	Kopunovic
05/12/98	Vojvodina Novi Sad	H	1-3	Stjepanovic
20/02/99	FK Zemun	H	3-2	Marinkovic, Puhalak, Latinovic
27/02/99	Rad Beograd	A	0-1	
03/03/99	Proleter Zrenjanin	H	0-1	
06/03/99	Partizan Beograd	A	1-5	Puhalak
13/03/99	Hajduk Kula	H	2-0	Kopunovic, Puhalak (p)
17/03/99	Milicionar Beograd	A	1-2	Koroman
20/03/99	Obilic Beograd	H	0-4	

VOJVODINA NOVI SAD

CLUB DIRECTORY

FK Vojvodina
Zarka Zrenjanina 8
21000 Novi Sad
tel - (021) 25481/421687
fax - (021) 20270
Year of Formation - 1914
President - Nenad Knezevic
Secretary - Svetozar Sapuric
Coach - Tomislav Manojlovic
Stadium - Gradski (22,000)

MAJOR HONOURS
League Championship - (2) 1968, 1989.

APPEARANCES 98/99

	P	Ap	(s)	Gls
Mirko ALEKSIC	M	12	(7)	1
Vlada AVRAMOV	G	1		
Milan BELIC	M	16	(1)	11
Igor BOGDANOVIC	A	6	(1)	4
Vidak BRATIC	D	17		1
Zoran CILINSEK	M	8		3
Dalibor DRAGIC	D	16	(1)	
Zdravko DRINCIC	A	7	(1)	4
Ronald HABI	M	7	(1)	
Zoran JANKOVIC	A	18	(1)	6
Mayro KARBAJAL	A	1		
Radovan KRIVOKAPIC	M		(2)	
Nikola LAZETIC	M	11	(1)	
Leo LERINC	A	8	(2)	3
Vladimir MATIJASEVIC	D	14		1
Milorad MRDAK	D	18	(1)	
Vladimir MUDRINIC	M	12	(3)	4
Uros PREDIC	M	3	(2)	1
Ivan RISTIC	D	3	(3)	
Milislav SECKOVIC	M		(3)	
Goran STOJILJKOVIC	A	2	(4)	
Darko SUSKAVCEVIC	D	14	(4)	
Jovan TANASIJEVIC	M	8	(1)	
Sreten VASIC	M	7	(9)	1
Boris VASKOVIC (BOS)	M	14	(8)	1
Ljubomir VORKAPIC	A		(3)	
Mico VRANJES	M	18	(1)	
Dragan ZILIC	G	23		

LEAGUE RESULTS 1998/99

08/08/98	Mogren Budva	H	3-0	Drincic 2 (1p), Mudrinic
15/08/98	Radnicki Kragujevac	A	3-2	Drincic 2 (1p), Vaskovic
29/08/98	Sartid Smederevo	A	3-0	(w/o)
05/09/98	Buducnost Podgorica	H	2-0	Jankovic, Lerinc
09/09/98	Crvena zvezda Beograd	H	1-2	Jankovic
12/09/98	FK Zemun	H	5-1	Belic 3, Cilinsek, Mudrinic
19/09/98	Rad Beograd	A	0-1	
26/09/98	Proleter Zrenjanin	H	4-1	Jankovic 2, Belic, Lerinc (p)
04/10/98	Partizan Beograd	A	0-2	
17/10/98	Hajduk Kula	H	3-1	Cilinsek 2 (1p), Lerinc
24/10/98	Milicionar Beograd	A	1-2	Belic
31/10/98	Obilic Beograd	H	0-1	
07/11/98	OFK Beograd	A	0-0	
11/11/98	Radnicki Nis	H	1-0	Bratic
21/11/98	FK Pristina	A	1-2	Jankovic
28/11/98	Zeleznik Beograd	H	3-2	Belic 3
05/12/98	Spartak Subotica	A	3-1	Vasic, Aleksic, og (Markovic)
20/02/99	Mogren Budva	A	0-0	
26/02/99	Radnicki Kragujevac	H	8-1	Bogdanovic 3, Predic,
				Matijasevic (p), Belic, Jankovic,
				Mudrinic
03/03/99	Crvena zvezda Beograd	A	0-1	
06/03/99	Sartid Smederevo	H	1-0	Mudrinic
13/03/99	Buducnost Podgorica	A	0-1	
17/03/99	FK Zemun	A	2-0	Belic, Bogdanovic
20/03/99	Rad Beograd	H	1-1	Belic

ZELEZNIK BEOGRAD

CLUB DIRECTORY

FK Zeleznik
Avalska bb
11250 Beograd
tel - (011) 577164
fax - (011) 577164
Year of Formation - 1930
President - Dragan Bulic
Coach - Baja Maric; Slobodan Dogandzic
Stadium - Zeleznik (10,000)

APPEARANCES 98/99

	P	Ap	(s)	Gls
Srdjan ALEKSIC	D	19		
Branko BOZOVIC	D	13		
Goran CVETKOVIC	G	3	(1)	
Igor CVETKOVIC	M		(1)	1
Vujica DRAGUTINOVIC	M	1		
Antonio FILESKI	G	5		
Radoslav GLAVARDANOV	M	9	(3)	1
Dragan ILIC	M	20		2
Vladan ISAILOVIC	A	3		
Predrag JOVANOVIC	M	5	(1)	
Sinisa LUCIC	D	11		
Zoran MAJSTOROVIC	M	17	(2)	7
Goran NEGIC	D	2		
Dragan NIKOLIC	M	9	(4)	
Sinisa NIKOLIC	A	2	(3)	
Sinisa NINKOVIC	D	10		
Slobodan PANIC	M	17	(4)	3
Dalibor PESTERAC	D	6	(1)	
Vladimir POPOVIC	D	13	(1)	
Sinisa PRERADOVIC	M	10	(4)	3
Vojin PROLE	G	14		
Miodrag RADULOVIC	M	1	(1)	
Ivan RAICEVIC	M		(2)	
Slobodan SLOVIC	M	7		
Srdjan SOLDATOVIC	G	2		
Sladjan SPASIC	M	4	(12)	1
Kristijan STOJANOV	M	1	(1)	
Boban STOJANOVIC	A	7	(4)	
Nenad STOJANOVIC	M	6	(3)	
Vladimir TINTOR	M	15	(3)	5
Milovan TODOROVIC	M	2	(4)	
Vladan VUKOVIC	D	22		1
Slobodan ZIVKOVIC	M	8	(2)	5

LEAGUE RESULTS 1998/99

08/08/98	Rad Beograd	A	0-2	
15/08/98	Proleter Zrenjanin	H	1-0	Majstorovic
22/08/98	Partizan Beograd	A	1-4	Tintor
29/08/98	Hajduk Kula	H	1-0	Majstorovic
05/09/98	Milicionar Beograd	A	0-3	
11/09/98	Obilic Beograd	H	1-2	Tintor
19/09/98	OFK Beograd	A	2-5	Ilic, Tintor
26/09/98	Radnicki Nis	H	4-1	Majstorovic 2, Glavardanov, Tintor
03/10/98	FK Pristina	A	1-3	Tintor
17/10/98	Buducnost Podgorica	A	0-2	
24/10/98	Spartak Subotica	H	3-1	Preradovic 2 (1p), Vukovic
31/10/98	Mogren Budva	A	2-2	Panic, Majstorovic
07/11/98	Radnicki Kragujevac	H	2-0	Panic 2
11/11/98	Crvena zvezda Beograd	A	0-4	
21/11/98	Sartid Smederevo	H	1-1	Ilic
28/11/98	Vojvodina Novi Sad	A	2-3	Cvetkovic I., Zivkovic
05/12/98	FK Zemun	H	3-1	Zivkovic, Preradovic, Majstorovic
20/02/99	Rad Beograd	H	0-0	
27/02/99	Proleter Zrenjanin	A	2-2	Zivkovic 2
03/03/99	Partizan Beograd	H	0-2	
06/03/99	Hajduk Kula	A	0-1	
13/03/99	Milicionar Beograd	H	1-1	Zivkovic
17/03/99	Obilic Beograd	A	0-2	
20/03/99	OFK Beograd	H	2-1	Majstorovic, Spasic

FK ZEMUN

CLUB DIRECTORY

FK Zemun
Ugrinovacka 80
11080 Zemun
tel - (011) 612949/618889
fax - (011) 193879
Year of Formation - 1946
President - Dusan Celar
Coach - Mile Tomic
Stadium - Gradski (15,000)

APPEARANCES 98/99

	P	Ap	(s)	Gls
Vladimir ANOKIC	M	6	(2)	
Sinisa BRANKOVIC	M	14	(2)	1
Dejan CELAR	D	3	(2)	
Goran CELAR	D	2	(5)	1
Petar CESTIC	D	8		
Bosko CVORKOV	M	19	(3)	4
Sinisa DJURIC	M	2	(7)	
Sreten DJUROVIC	D	5	(2)	
Milos DOBRIJEVIC	M	3		
Ranko GOLIJANIN	D	3		
Goran GRKINIC	A	1		
Marko GRUBELIC	M		(1)	
Predrag ILIC	M		(3)	
Djordje INDJIC	M	20	(2)	4
Nikola JOLOVC	D	15	(1)	
Mladen LAMBULIC	D	14		
Dusko LJUBICIC	M	13	(5)	
Igor MATIC	A	2		
Dragoslav MILENKOVIC	D	8		
Zoran MILJKOVIC	D	8		
Dragan MLADENOVIC	D	16	(2)	
Goran PETKOVIC	M		(1)	
Sasa PREGELJ	M		(2)	
Sasa RACA	D	22		2
Predrag RISTOVIC	G	19		
Dejan SARIC	M	14	(4)	6
Zoran SMILJANIC	D	7	(7)	1
Vladimir SUBERT	M	13		
Dejan TOMIC	M	2	(11)	
Zoran TOMIC	A	20	(1)	11
Djordje TOPALOVIC	G	5		

LEAGUE RESULTS 1998/99

08/08/98	Spartak Subotica	H	4-2	Indjic 2, Smiljanic, Tomic Z.
15/08/98	Mogren Budva	A	0-1	
22/08/98	Radnicki Kragujevac	H	1-3	Tomic Z.
29/08/98	Crvena zvezda Beograd	A	1-5	Tomic Z.
05/09/98	Sartid Smederevo	H	1-1	Tomic Z.
12/09/98	Vojvodina Novi Sad	A	1-5	Saric
19/09/98	Buducnost Podgorica	H	3-2	Tomic Z. 3
26/09/98	Rad Beograd	H	1-0	
03/10/98	Proleter Zrenjanin	A	1-2	Saric
17/10/98	Partizan Beograd	H	1-2	Cvorkov
24/10/98	Hajduk Kula	A	0-3	
31/10/98	Milicionar Beograd	H	1-0	Cvorkov
07/11/98	Obilic Beograd	A	3-6	Saric 3
11/11/98	OFK Beograd	H	1-0	Cvorkov
21/11/98	Radnicki Nis	A	1-0	Raca
28/11/98	FK Pristina	H	3-0	Indjic, Tomic Z., Cvorkov
05/12/98	Zeleznik Beograd	A	1-3	Brankovic
20/02/99	Spartak Subotica	A	2-3	Tomic Z. 2
27/02/99	Mogren Budva	H	2-0	Indjic, Saric
03/03/99	Radnicki Kragujevac	A	2-0	Raca, Celar G.
06/03/99	Crvena zvezda Beograd	H	0-3	(w/o)
13/03/99	Sartid Smederevo	A	0-3	
17/03/99	Vojvodina Novi Sad	H	0-2	
20/03/99	Buducnost Podgorica	A	0-1	

PROMOTED CLUBS

SECOND DIVISION FINAL TABLE 98/99

WEST

		Pd	W	D	L	F	A	Pt	GD
1	**Borac Cacak**	21	15	3	3	51	16	48	+35
2	**Sutjeska Niksic**	21	13	4	4	45	21	43	+24
3	Bane Raska	21	13	2	6	40	21	41	+19
4	Zeta Golubovci	21	10	7	4	30	20	37	+10
5	Zeleznicar Lajkovac	21	9	6	6	29	26	33	+3
6	FK Berane	21	10	3	8	30	29	33	+1
7	Rudar Pljevlja	21	11	0	10	26	25	33	+1
8	Lovcen Cetinje	21	10	2	9	27	31	32	-4
9	Javor Ivanjica	21	9	3	9	28	30	30	-2
10	Mladost Lucani	21	9	2	10	21	27	29	-6
11	FK Novi Pazar	21	8	4	9	29	32	28	-3
12	Buducnost Valjevo	21	8	4	9	31	39	28	-8
13	Mladi Radnik Pozarevac	21	7	6	8	31	29	27	+2
14	FK Loznica	21	8	3	10	28	32	27	-4
15	Celik Niksic	21	7	2	12	22	36	23	-14
16	Sloboda Uzice	21	5	4	12	21	27	19	-6
17	Crvena zvezda Gnjilane	21	4	3	14	23	42	15	-19
18	Sloga Kraljevo	21	3	2	16	15	44	11	-29

EAST

		Pd	W	D	L	F	A	Pt	GD
1	**Cukaricki Beograd**	21	14	5	2	62	18	47	+44
2	**Hajduk Beograd**	21	12	8	1	28	13	44	+15
3	Zvezdara Beograd	21	13	3	5	47	18	42	+29
4	Dinamo Pancevo	21	12	5	4	42	26	41	+16
5	Kolubara Lazarevac	21	11	6	4	47	19	39	+28
6	FK Novi Sad	21	10	6	5	38	20	36	+18
7	CSK Celarevo	21	11	3	7	40	27	36	+13
8	Mladost Apatin	21	11	1	9	43	21	34	+22
9	FK Vrbas	21	10	3	8	32	19	33	+13
10	FK Kikinda	21	8	2	11	38	33	26	+5
11	Radnicki-Jugopetrol Beograd	21	8	2	11	34	34	26	0
12	FK Bor	21	6	7	8	33	30	25	+3
13	Jedinstvo Paracin	21	8	1	12	22	32	25	-10
14	FK Beograd	21	6	5	10	29	33	23	-4
15	Napredak Krusevac	21	6	5	10	25	29	23	-4
16	FK Becej	21	6	4	11	27	34	22	-7
17	Palilulac Beograd	21	3	2	16	27	71	11	-44
18	Winer Broker Niska Banja	21	0	0	21	9	146	0	-137

CLUB DIRECTORY

FK Borac
Gradski bedem 6
3200 Cacak
tel - (032) 25458
fax - (032) 22302
Year of Formation - 1926
President - Dragan Kuzmanovic
Coach - Bozo Vukovic
Stadium - Gradski (12,000)

CLUB DIRECTORY

FK Cukaricki Beograd
Beogradskog bataljona 25
11000 Beograd
tel - (011) 551302
fax - (011) 3544819
Year of Formation - 1926
President - Aleksandar Mihajlovic
Coach - Milenko Kokovic
Stadium - Cukaricki (8,000)

CLUB DIRECTORY

FK Hajduk Beograd
Milana Rakica 48
11000 Beogrnd
tel - (011) 3406706
fax - (011) 417338
President - Stojak Golic
Coach - Djordje Gerum
Stadium - Hajduk (4,000)

CLUB DIRECTORY

FK Sutjeska
Trg Marsala Tita 1
81400 Niksic
tel - (083) 213426
Year of Formation - 1944
President - Brana Micunovic
Coach - Zarko Olarevic
Stadium - Gradski (18,000)

MAJOR SUMMER TRANSFERS 1999

PLAYER	OLD CLUB	NEW CLUB	PLAYER	OLD CLUB	NEW CLUB
● AUSTRIA			● BELGIUM		
Danijel BREZIC (SLO)	Rudar Velenje (SLO)	SC Austria Lustenau	Jan KOLLER (CZE)	KSC Lokeren	RSC Anderlecht
Leeroy ECHTELD (HOL)	RKC Waalwijk (HOL)	SC Austria Lustenau	Elonga EKAKIA (DRC)	KSC Lokeren	RSC Anderlecht
Harald KATEMANN (GER)	Fortuna Düsseldorf (GER)	SC Austria Lustenau	David BROCKEN	K Lierse SK	RSC Anderlecht
Alex PASTOOR (HOL)	KRC Harelbeke (BEL)	SC Austria Lustenau	Mike VERSTRAETEN	Germinal Beerschot Antwerpen	RSC Anderlecht
Markus SCHNEIDHOFER	SK Vorwärts Steyr	SC Austria Lustenau	Davy OYEN	PSV (HOL)	RSC Anderlecht
Goran STANISAVLJEVIC	SV Ried	SC Austria Lustenau	Stijn MEERT	KV Kortrijk	RSC Anderlecht
Muhammet AKAGÜNDÜZ	FCN St. Pölten	FK Austria Wien	Nikos KOUNENAKIS (GRE)	OFI (GRE)	RSC Anderlecht
George DATORU (NIG)	SK Vorwärts Steyr	FK Austria Wien	Kenny DE VUYST	KV Oostende	KSK Beveren
Mladen IVANCIC (CRO)	Rijeka (CRO)	FK Austria Wien	Jochen JANSSEN	KVC Westerlo	Club Brugge KV
Pawel SOBCZAK (POL)	Petrochemia Plock (POL)	FK Austria Wien	Philippe CLEMENT	Coventry City (ENG)	Club Brugge KV
Roman STARY	First Vienna FC	FK Austria Wien	Goëtan ENGLEBERT	K St.-Truidense VV	Club Brugge KV
Emmanuel AKWUEGBU (NIG)	RC Lens (FRA)	SW Bregenz	Philippe VANDE WALLE	KSC Eendracht Aalst	Club Brugge KV
Slobodan GRUBOR	SK Vorwärts Steyr	SW Bregenz	Sandy MARYENS	KAA Gent	Club Brugge KV
Thomas HICKERSBERGER	SK Vorwärts Steyr	SW Bregenz	Nikola JERKAN (CRO)	Nottingham Forest (ENG)	RSC Charleroi
Wolfgang OTT	SC Rheindorf Altach	SW Bregenz	Marjan MRMIC (CRO)	Varteks Varazdin (CRO)	RSC Charleroi
David PRATS (ESP)	FC Barcelona B (ESP)	SW Bregenz	Jean-François LECOMTE	K St.-Truidense VV	RSC Charleroi
Zoran TOMIC (YUG)	FK Zemun (YUG)	SW Bregenz	Zoran CILINSEK (YUG)	Vojvodina Novi Sad (YUG)	RSC Charleroi
Lars UNGER (GER)	Southend United (ENG)	SW Bregenz	Dimitri DE CONDE	R Standard Liège	RSC Charleroi
Martin AMERHAUSER	SV Salzburg	Grazer AK	Tomasz ROMANIUK (POL)	LKS Lodz (POL)	RSC Charleroi
Roger NILSEN (NOR)	Tottenham Hotspur (ENG)	Grazer AK	Warry VAN WATTUM (HOL)	Veendam (HOL)	KSC Eendracht Aalst
Ewald BRENNER	Grazer AK	LASK Linz	Geoffrey CLAEYS	RSC Anderlecht	KSC Eendracht Aalst
Hannes JOCHUM	FC Tirol Innsbruck	LASK Linz	Predrag FILIPOVIC (YUG)	Obilic Beograd (YUG)	KSC Eendracht Aalst
Saso UDOVIC (SLO)	Lausanne-Sports (SUI)	LASK Linz	Marcin ZEWLAKOW (POL)	KSK Beveren	R Excelsior Mouscron
Jens DOWE (GER)	FC Hansa Rostock (GER)	SK Rapid Wien	Michal ZEWLAKOW (POL)	KSK Beveren	R Excelsior Mouscron
Andreas LAGONIKAKIS (GRE)	Panathiniakos (GRE)	SK Rapid Wien	Alexandre TEKLAK	RSC Charleroi	R Excelsior Mouscron
Dejan SAVICEVIC (YUG)	Crvena zvezda Beograd (YUG)	SK Rapid Wien	Tamás SZEKERES (HUN)	MTK Hungária FC (HUN)	KAA Gent
Günter SCHIESSWALD	FK Austria Wien	SK Rapid Wien	Emil STERBAL (SLO)	Maribor Teatanic (SLO)	KAA Gent
Roman WALLNER	SK Sturm Graz	SK Rapid Wien	Tom VANDERVEE	Germinal Beerschot Antwerpen	KAA Gent
Herwig DRECHSEL	Grazer AK	SV Ried	Gunther SCHEPENS	Karlsruher SC (GER)	KAA Gent
Markus HIDEN	SK Sturm Graz	SV Ried	Eric JOLY	KV Kortrijk	KAA Gent
Christophe LAUWERS (BEL)	Toulouse FC (FRA)	SV Ried	Ole-Martin ÅRST (NOR)	RSC Anderlecht	KAA Gent
Andrzej LESIAK (POL)	SK Rapid Wien	SV Ried	Saso GAJSER (SLO)	Rudar Velenje (SLO)	KAA Gent
Marco VILLA (GER)	Borussia Mönchengladbach (GER)	SV Ried	Tarik KHARIF (FRA)	FC Metz (FRA)	KAA Gent
Christoph JANK	SK Vorwärts Steyr	SV Salzburg	Cédric CARREZ (FRA)	Lille OSC (FRA)	KAA Gent
György KORSÓS (HUN)	Györi ETO FC (HUN)	SK Sturm Graz	Anders CHRISTENSEN (DEN)	Naestved IF (DEN)	KAA Gent
Yorgos KOUTSOUPIAS (GRE)	OFI (GRE)	SK Sturm Graz	Zoran BAN (CRO)	R Excelsior Mouscron	KRC Genk
Gerald STRAFNER	SV Ried	SK Sturm Graz	Jesper JANSSON (SWE)	Stabaek IF (NOR)	KRC Genk
Imre SZABICS (HUN)	Ferencváros (HUN)	SK Sturm Graz	Ilir CAUSHLLARI (ALB)	Korotan Prevalje (SLO)	KRC Genk
Christoph FREUND	SC Kundl	FC Tirol Innsbruck	Filip HAAGDOREN	K Lierse SK	Germinal Beerschot Antwerpen
Paul HAFNER	ASK KLingenbach	FC Tirol Innsbruck	Marc DEGRYSE	KAA Gent	Germinal Beerschot Antwerpen
Peter PAWLOWSKI	LASK Linz	FC Tirol Innsbruck	Bram VERBIST	KAA Gent	Germinal Beerschot Antwerpen
			Andrei DEMKIN (RUS)	RSC Anderlecht	Germinal Beerschot Antwerpen

MAJOR SUMMER TRANSFERS 1999

PLAYER	OLD CLUB	NEW CLUB
Djordje SVETLICIC (YUG)	Partizan Beograd (YUG)	Germinal Beerschot Antwerpen
Vinko MARINOVIC (YUG)	Crvena zvezda Beograd (YUG)	Germinal Beerschot Antwerpen
Aleksandar MUTAVDZIC (YUG)	Rad Beograd (YUG)	Germinal Beerschot Antwerpen
Peter MAES	R Standard Liège	Germinal Beerschot Antwerpen
Blessing KAKU (NIG)	RWD Molenbeek	KRC Harelbeke
Kurt VANDOORNE	KV Kortrijk	KRC Harelbeke
Coen BURG	KVC Westerlo	K Lierse SK
Karel SNOECKX	KSC Lokeren	K Lierse SK
Patrick NIJS	KFC Lommelse SK	K Lierse SK
Charles DAGO (CIV)	Africa Sport (CIV)	KSC Lokeren
Sam-Dominique ABOUO (CIV)	ASEC Abidjan (CIV)	KSC Lokeren
Mladen DABANOVIC (SLO)	Rudar Velenje (SLO)	KSC Lokeren
Novica NIKCEVIC (SLO)	HIT Gorica (SLO)	KSC Lokeren
Jan KOZAK (SVK)	1.FC Kosice (SVK)	KSC Lokeren
Daniel SCAVONE	K Lierse SK	KFC Lommelse SK
Gert DAVIDTS	KV Mechelen	KFC Lommelse SK
Kresimir MARUSIC (CRO)	Northern Spirit (AUS)	KFC Lommelse SK
Louis GOMIS (SEN)	Etoile du Sahel (TUN)	KFC Lommelse SK
Mark FORD (ENG)	Burnley (ENG)	KFC Lommelse SK
Daniel CAMUS	KAA Gent	KV Mechelen
Benjamin DEBUSSCHERE	R Standard Liège	KV Mechelen
Sergei KULICHENKO (RUS)	FC Lantana Tallinn (EST)	KV Mechelen
Gunter VERJANS	Club Brugge KV	K St.-Truidense VV
Frédéric PIERRE	R Excelsior Mouscron	R Standard Liège
Laurent WUILLOT	RSC Charleroi	R Standard Liège
Daniel VAN BUYTEN	RSC Charleroi	R Standard Liège
Ariel GRAÑA (ARG)	San Lorenzo (ARG)	R Standard Liège
Filip SUSNJARA (CRO)	Osijek (CRO)	R Standard Liège
Mathieu MERTENS	Germinal Beerschot Antwerpen	KFC Verbroedering Geel
Georgica VAMESU (ROM)	RWD Molenbeek	KFC Verbroedering Geel
Bruno VERSAVEL	Herentals	KFC Verbroedering Geel
Miklós LENDVAI (HUN)	Ferencváros (HUN)	KFC Verbroedering Geel
István FERENCZI (HUN)	Zalahús ZTE FC (HUN)	KFC Verbroedering Geel
Cvijan MILOSEVIC	Germinal Beerschot Antwerpen	KVC Westerlo
Marc SCHAESSENS	Germinal Beerschot Antwerpen	KVC Westerlo
Ives SERNEELS	K Lierse SK	KVC Westerlo
Franky FRANS	RSC Charleroi	KVC Westerlo
Sidney LAMMENS	KV Oostende	KVC Westerlo
Björn DE CONINCK	Club Brugge KV	KVC Westerlo
Vedran PELIC (BOS)	Bosna Visoko (BOS)	KVC Westerlo

● CZECH REPUBLIC

PLAYER	OLD CLUB	NEW CLUB
Michal SLACHTA	FC Karvina	Banik Ostrava

PLAYER	OLD CLUB	NEW CLUB
Pavel SUSTR	Panseraikos (GRE)	Boby Brno
Patrik HOLOMEK	Synot Stare Mesto	Boby Brno
Petr BARTES	Tatran Postorna	Boby Brno
Martin HYSKY	Boby Brno	Bohemians Praha
Ludek KLUSACEK	Slovan Liberec	Bohemians Praha
Jan PEJSA	Slezsky Opava	SK Ceske Budejovice
Pavel PENICKA	FK Jablonec 97	SK Ceske Budejovice
Richard JUKL	SK Hradec Kralove	SK Ceske Budejovice
Martin OBSCITNIK	1.FC Kosice (SVK)	SK Ceske Budejovice
Frantisek KOUBEK	SK Hradec Kralove	Chmel Blsany
Jan VELKOBORSKY	FC Plzen	Chmel Blsany
Ivan VALACHOVIC	Petra Drnovice	Dukla Pribram
Zdenek JANOS	FK Jablonec 97	Dukla Pribram
Daniel SMEJKAL	KFC Uerdingen 05 (GER)	Dukla Pribram
Petr PIZANOWSKI	Sigma Olomouc	FK Jablonec 97
Karel HAVLICEK	SK Hradec Kralove	FK Jablonec 97
Marcel CUPAK	Sigma Olomouc	Petra Drnovice
Zdenek VALNOHA	Dukla Pribram	Petra Drnovice
Emil NECAS	Petra Drnovice	Sigma Olomouc
David KOTRYS	FC Karvina	Sigma Olomouc
Lukas DOSEK	Viktoria Plzen	Slavia Praha
Tomas DOSEK	Viktoria Plzen	Slavia Praha
Radek KREJCIK	Dukla Pribram	Slavia Praha
Michael STEFKA	Sigma Olomouc	Slezsky Opava
Robert NEUMANN	FK Jablonec 97	Slovan Liberec
Marian KLAGO	FC Nitra (SVK)	Slovan Liberec
Vladimir LABANT	Slavia Praha	Sparta Praha
Rene BOLF	Banik Ostrava	Sparta Praha
Libor SIONKO	Banik Ostrava	Sparta Praha
Michal KOLOMAZNIK	Boby Brno	FK Teplice
Martin FRYDEK	Bayer 04 Leverkusen (GER)	FK Teplice
David SOURADA	FC Karvina	FK Teplice
Miroslav MIKULIK	Banik Ostrava	Viktoria Zizkov

● DENMARK

PLAYER	OLD CLUB	NEW CLUB
Frank KROGSDAL	Aarhus Fremad	AGF
Ken MARTIN	Aarhus Fremad	AGF
Jens MELVANG	OB	AGF
Kenni SOMMER	Viborg FF	Esbjerg FB
Michael STENSGAARD	Southampton (ENG)	FC København
Jesper FALCK	AB	Herfølge BK
René TENGSTEDT	Fortuna Düsseldorf (GER)	Lyngby FC
Jesper THYGESEN	Brøndby IF	Silkeborg IF

MAJOR SUMMER TRANSFERS 1999

PLAYER	OLD CLUB	NEW CLUB	PLAYER	OLD CLUB	NEW CLUB
Ulrik BALLING	Aarhus Fremad	Vejle BK	Stéphane HENCHOZ (SUI)	Blackburn Rovers	Liverpool
Dick LAST (SWE)	IFK Göteborg (SWE)	Vejle BK	Vladimir SMICER (CZE)	RC Lens (FRA)	Liverpool
Jan LARSEN	Aarhus Fremad	Viborg FF	Aboubacar CAMARA (GUI)	Olympique Marseille (FRA)	Liverpool
Henrik STEEN PEDERSEN	Lyngby FC	Viborg FF	Sami HYYPIÄ (FIN)	Willem II (HOL)	Liverpool
			Erik MEIJER (HOL)	Bayer 04 Leverkusen (GER)	Liverpool
● **ENGLAND**			Mark BOSNICH (AUS)	Aston Villa	Manchester United
Thierry HENRY (FRA)	Juventus (ITA)	Arsenal	Christian ZIEGE (GER)	Milan (ITA)	Middlesbrough
Slilvio Mendes "SILVINHO" (BRA)	Corinthians (BRA)	Arsenal	Paul INCE	Liverpool	Middlesbrough
Oleh LUZHNYI (UKR)	Dynamo Kyiv (UKR)	Arsenal	Kieron DYER	Ipswich Town	Newcastle United
Stefan MALZ (GER)	TSV 1860 München (GER)	Arsenal	MARCELINO Elena (ESP)	RCD Mallorca (ESP)	Newcastle United
Davor SUKER (CRO)	Real Madrid (ESP)	Arsenal	Alain GOMA (FRA)	Paris Saint-Germain (FRA)	Newcastle United
George BOATENG (HOL)	Coventry City	Aston Villa	Franck DUMAS (FRA)	AS Monaco (FRA)	Newcastle United
David JAMES	Liverpool	Aston Villa	John KARELSE (HOL)	NAC (HOL)	Newcastle United
Najwan GHRAYEB (ISR)	Hapoel Haifa (ISR)	Aston Villa	Gilles DE BILDE (BEL)	PSV (HOL)	Sheffield Wednesday
David WETHERALL	Leeds United	Bradford City	Gerald SIBON (HOL)	Ajax (HOL)	Sheffield Wednesday
Andy MYERS	Chelsea	Bradford City	Simon DONNELLY (SCO)	Celtic (SCO)	Sheffield Wednesday
Neil REDFEARN	Charlton Athletic	Bradford City	Phil O'DONNELL (SCO)	Celtic (SCO)	Sheffield Wednesday
Gunnar HALLE (NOR)	Leeds United	Bradford City	Dean RICHARDS	Wolverhampton Wanderers	Southampton
Lee SHARPE	Leeds United	Bradford City	BRUNO LEAL (POR)	Sporting CP (POR)	Southampton
Matt CLARKE	Sheffield Wednesday	Bradford City	Kevin DAVIES	Blackburn Rovers	Southampton
Dean SAUNDERS (WAL)	SL Benfica (POR)	Bradford City	Stefan SCHWARZ (SWE)	Valencia CF (ESP)	Sunderland
Chris SUTTON	Blackburn Rovers	Chelsea	Carsten FREDGAARD (DEN)	Lyngby FC (DEN)	Sunderland
Didier DESCHAMPS (FRA)	Juventus (ITA)	Chelsea	Steve BOULD	Arsenal	Sunderland
Jes HØGH (DEN)	Fenerbahçe (TUR)	Chelsea	Thomas HELMER (GER)	FC Bayern München (GER)	Sunderland
Mario MELCHIOT (HOL)	Ajax (HOL)	Chelsea	John OSTER (WAL)	Everton	Sunderland
Gabriele AMBROSETTI (ITA)	Vicenza (ITA)	Chelsea	Chris PERRY	Wimbledon	Tottenham Hotspur
Mustapha HADJI (MAR)	RC Deportivo (ESP)	Coventry City	Willem KORSTEN (HOL)	Vitesse (HOL)	Tottenham Hotspur
Youssef CHIPPO (MAR)	FC Porto (POR)	Coventry City	Øyvind LEONHARDSEN (NOR)	Liverpool	Tottenham Hotspur
Robbie KEANE (IRL)	Wolverhampton Wanderers	Coventry City	Dominic FOLEY (IRL)	Wolverhampton Wanderers	Watford
Seth JOHNSON	Crewe Alexandra	Derby County	Des LYTTLE	Nottingham Forest	Watford
Esteban FUERTES (ARG)	Colon Santa Fé (ARG)	Derby County	Mark WILLIAMS (NIR)	Chesterfield	Watford
Kevin CAMPBELL	Trabzonspor (TUR)	Everton	Paulo WANCHOPE (CRC)	Derby County	West Ham United
Mark PEMBRIDGE (WAL)	SL Benfica (POR)	Everton	Stuart PEARCE	Newcastle United	West Ham United
Richard GOUGH (SCO)	San José Clash (USA)	Everton	Trond ANDERSEN (NOR)	Molde FK (NOR)	Wimbledon
Michael DUBERRY	Chelsea	Leeds United	Walid BADIR (ISR)	Hapoel Petach-Tikva (ISR)	Wimbledon
Danny MILLS	Charlton Athletic	Leeds United	Kelvin DAVIS	Luton Town	Wimbledon
Michael BRIDGES	Sunderland	Leeds United	Tore PEDERSEN (NOR)	Eintracht Frankfurt (GER)	Wimbledon
Eirik BAKKE (NOR)	Sogndal IL (NÖR)	Leeds United			
Darren HUCKERBY	Coventry City	Leeds United	● **FRANCE**		
Tim FLOWERS	Blackburn Rovers	Leicester City	Stéphane GUIVARC'H	Rangers (SCO)	AJ Auxerre
Phil GILCHRIST (SCO)	Oxford United	Leicester City	Cyrille MAGNIER	RC Lens	AJ Auxerre
Dietmar HAMANN (GER)	Newcastle United	Liverpool	Alexandre COMISETTI (SUI)	Grasshopper-Club Zürich (SUI)	AJ Auxerre
Sander WESTERVELD (HOL)	Vitesse (HOL)	Liverpool	Dan PETERSEN (DEN)	RSC Anderlecht (BEL)	SC Bastia

MAJOR SUMMER TRANSFERS 1999

PLAYER	OLD CLUB	NEW CLUB	PLAYER	OLD CLUB	NEW CLUB
Lilian NALIS	Le Havre AC	SC Bastia	Said CHIBA (MAR)	SD Compostela (ESP)	AS Nancy-Lorraine
Cyril EBOKI-POH	AS Cannes	SC Bastia	Laurent ROBERT	Montpellier HSC	Paris Saint-Germain
Jérôme BONNISSEL	RC Deportivo (ESP)	Girondins de Bordeaux	Godwin OKPARA (NIG)	RC Strasbourg	Paris Saint-Germain
Stéphane ZIANI	RC Deportivo (ESP)	Girondins de Bordeaux	Ali BENARBIA	Girondins de Bordeaux	Paris Saint-Germain
Laurent BATTLES	Toulouse FC	Girondins de Bordeaux	CÉSAR Augusto (BRA)	Portuguesa (BRA)	Paris Saint-Germain
Teddy RICHERT	Toulouse FC	Girondins de Bordeaux	CHRISTIAN (BRA)	Porto Alegre (BRA)	Paris Saint-Germain
Jean-Christophe ROUVIERE	Montpellier HSC	Girondins de Bordeaux	Edwin MURATI (ALB)	Fortuna Düsseldorf (GER)	Paris Saint-Germain
Eric DELOUMEAUX	FC Gueugnon	Le Havre AC	Franck GAVA	AS Monaco	Stade Rennais FC
Argemiro VEIGA (BRA)	FC Basel (SUI)	Le Havre AC	Grégory MALICKI	Chamois Niortais	Stade Rennais FC
Thomas DENIAUD	AJ Auxerre	Le Havre AC	Christian BASSILA	Olympique Marseille	Stade Rennais FC
Sébastien CHABBERT	AS Cannes	RC Lens	Lamine DIATTA	Olympique Marseille	Stade Rennais FC
Ferdinand COLY	LB Châteauroux	RC Lens	El Hadji DIOUF (SEN)	FC Sochaux	Stade Rennais FC
Jocelyn BLANCHARD	Juventus (ITA)	RC Lens	Jean-Guy WALLEMME	FC Sochaux	AS Saint-Etienne
Stéphane COLLET	RC Strasbourg	RC Lens	ALOÍSIO da Silva (BRA)	Goias (BRA)	AS Saint-Etienne
Charles-Edouard CORIDON	En Avant Guingamp	RC Lens	Alex DIAS (BRA)	Goias (BRA)	AS Saint-Etienne
Patrick BARUL	AS Cannes	RC Lens	Philippe MONTANIER	FC Gueugnon	AS Saint-Etienne
Olivier DACOURT	Everton (ENG)	RC Lens	Tchiressoua GUEL (CIV)	Olympique Marseille	AS Saint-Etienne
Joseph-Desiré JOB (CMR)	Olympique Marseille	RC Lens	Stéphane PEDRON	FC Lorient	AS Saint-Etienne
Redouanne EL OUARDI (MAR)	FAR Rabat (MAR)	RC Lens	Jean-Louis MONTERO	Fc Lorient	CS Sedan Ardennes
Pierre LAIGLE	Sampdoria (ITA)	Olympique Marseille	Eddy CAPRON	Stade Rennais FC	CS Sedan Ardennes
Tony VAIRELLES	RC Lens	Olympique Marseille	Laurent HUARD	Stade Rennais FC	CS Sedan Ardennes
Angelo HUGUES	FC Lorient	Olympique Marseille	Oumar DIENG	AJ Auxerre	CS Sedan Ardennes
ANDERSON da Silva (BRA)	FC Barcelona	Olympique Marseille	Pascal CAMADINI	FC Sion (SUI)	RC Strasbourg
Eric DECROIX	FC Nantes	Olympique Marseille	Joseph NDO (CMR)	Neuchâtel Xamax FC (SUI)	RC Strasbourg
Stéphane DALMAT	RC Lens	Olympique Marseille	Pierre NJANKA (CMR)	Neuchâtel Xamax FC (SUI)	RC Strasbourg
Stéphane TREVISAN	En Avant Guingamp	Olympique Marseille	Marin HAAS (AUT)	SK Sturm Graz (AUT)	RC Strasbourg
Sébastien PEREZ	SC Bastia	Olympique Marseille	Diego GARAY (ARG)	Newell's Old Boys (ARG)	RC Strasbourg
Eduardo BERIZZO (ARG)	River Plate (ARG)	Olympique Marseille	Luciano ZAVAGNO (ARG)	RC Strasbourg	A Troyes AC
Lilian MARTIN	AS Monaco	Olympique Marseille	Frédéric ARPINON	RC Strasbourg	A Troyes AC
Iván DE LA PEÑA (ESP)	Lazio (ITA)	Olympique Marseille	Samuel BOUTAL	SM Caen	A Troyes AC
Kaba DIAWARA	Arsenal (ENG)	Olympique Marseille	Farid GHAZI (ALG)	JS Kabylie (ARG)	A Troyes AC
Ibrahima BAKAYOKO (CIV)	Everton (ENG)	Olympique Marseille			
Pablo Ignacio CALANDRIA (ARG)	Huracán (ARG)	Olympique Marseille	● **GERMANY**		
Serhiy SKACHENKO (UKR)	Torpedo Moskva (RUS)	FC Metz	Berkant GÖKTAN	Borussia Mönchengladbach	Arminia Bielefeld
Christophe BASTIEN	AS Nancy-Lorraine	FC Metz	Markus WEISSENBERGER (AUT)	LASK Linz (AUT)	Arminia Bielefeld
Nicolas GOUSSE	Stade Rennais FC	FC Metz	Michael BALLACK	1.FC Kaiserslautern	Bayer 04 Leverkusen
Marcelo GALLARDO (ARG)	River Plate (ARG)	AS Monaco	Oliver NEUVILLE	FC Hansa Rostock	Bayer 04 Leverkusen
Marco SIMONE (ITA)	Paris Saint-Germain	AS Monaco	Bernd SCHNEIDER	Eintracht Frankfurt	Bayer 04 Leverkusen
Pablo CONTRERAS (CHL)	Colo Colo (CHL)	AS Monaco	Róbson PONTE (BRA)	Guarani (BRA)	Bayer 04 Leverkusen
Olivier SORLIN	ASOA Valence	Montpellier HSC	Vratislav GRESKO (SVK)	Inter Bratislava (SVK)	Bayer 04 Leverkusen
Patrice LOKO	FC Lorient	Montpellier HSC	Thomas BRDARIC	Fortuna Köln	Bayer 04 Leverkusen
Romain FERRIER	Girondins de Bordeaux	Montpellier HSC	Patrik ANDERSSON (SWE)	Borussia Mönchengladbach	FC Bayern München
Reynald PEDROS	Parma (ITA)	Montpellier HSC	PAULO SÉRGIO (BRA)	Roma (ITA)	FC Bayern München

MAJOR SUMMER TRANSFERS 1999

PLAYER	OLD CLUB	NEW CLUB	PLAYER	OLD CLUB	NEW CLUB
Roque SANTA CRUZ (PAR)	Olimpia Asuncion (PAR)	FC Bayern München	Stephan PASSLACK	Borussia Mönchengladbach	TSV 1860 München
Michael WIESINGER	1.FC Nürnberg	FC Bayern München	Martin MAX	FC Schalke 04	TSV 1860 München
Victor IKPEBA (NIG)	AS Monaco (FRA)	Borussia Dortmund	Ebbe SAND (DEN)	Brøndby JF (DEN)	FC Schalke 04
Fredi BOBIC	VfB Stuttgart	Borussia Dortmund	Niels OUDE KAMPHUIS (HOL)	FC Twente (HOL)	FC Schalke 04
Christian WÖRNS	Paris Saint-Germain (FRA)	Borussia Dortmund	Gerald ASAMOAH (GHA)	Hannover 96	FC Schalke 04
Giuseppe REINA	Arminia Bielefeld	Borussia Dortmund	Tomasz WALDOCH (POL)	VfL Bochum	FC Schalke 04
Otto ADDO (GHA)	Hannover 96	Borussia Dortmund	Marcelo BORDON (BRA)	FC São Paulo (BRA)	VfB Stuttgart
Sead KAPETANOVIC (BOS)	VfL Wolfsburg	Borussia Dortmund	Ioan Viorel GANEA (ROM)	Rapid Bucuresti (ROM)	VfB Stuttgart
Marijan KOVACEVIC (CRO)	VfL Wolfsburg	MSV Duisburg	Jens TODT	SV Werder Bremen	VfB Stuttgart
Michael ZEYER	VfB Stuttgart	MSV Duisburg	Pavel KUKA (CZE)	1.FC Nürnberg	VfB Stuttgart
Pavel DRSEK (CZE)	Chmel Blsany (CZE)	MSV Duisburg	Heiko GERBER	1.FC Nürnberg	VfB Stuttgart
Martin SCHNEIDER	Borussia Mönchengladbach	MSV Duisburg	Sean DUNDEE	Liverpool (ENG)	VfB Stuttgart
Torsten KRACHT	VfL Bochum	Eintracht Frankfurt	Dennis GRASSOW	1.FC Köln	SpVgg Unterhaching
Horst HELDT	TSV 1860 München	Eintracht Frankfurt	Oliver STRAUBE	Hamburger SV	SpVgg Unterhaching
Rolf-Christel GUIE-MIEN (CON)	Karlsruher SC	Eintracht Frankfurt	Ludwig KÖGL	FC Luzern (SUI)	SpVgg Unterhaching
Tibor DOMBI (HUN)	DVSC-Epona (HUN)	Eintracht Frankfurt	Frank BAUMANN	1.FC Nürnberg	SV Werder Bremen
Bachirou SALOU (TOG)	Borussia Dortmund	Eintracht Frankfurt	Jacek CHANKO (POL)	Stomil Olsztyn (POL)	SV Werder Bremen
Oumar KONDE (SUI)	Blackburn Rovers (ENG)	SC Freiburg	Jonathan AKPOBORIE (NIG)	VfB Stuttgart	VfL Wolfsburg
Andreas ZEYER	VfL Bochum	SC Freiburg	Jean-Kasongo BANZA (DRC)	CS Sfaxien (TUN)	VfL Wolfsburg
Niko KOVAC (CRO)	Bayer 04 Leverkusen	Hamburger SV	Marino BILISKOV (CRO)	Hajduk Split (CRO)	VfL Wolfsburg
Roy PRÄGER	VfL Wolfsburg	Hamburger SV	Christian BRAND	SV Werder Bremen	VfL Wolfsburg
Mehdi MAHDAVIKIA (IRN)	VfL Bochum	Hamburger SV	Markus FELDHOFF	Borussia Mönchengladbach	VfL Wolfsburg
René SCHNEIDER	Borussia Dortmund	FC Hansa Rostock	Dorinel MUNTEANU (ROM)	1.FC Köln	VfL Wolfsburg
Kai OSWALD	VfB Stuttgart	FC Hansa Rostock	Patrick WEISER	Stade Rennais FC (FRA)	VfL Wolfsburg
Kreso KOVACEC	Tennis Borussia Berlin	FC Hansa Rostock	Christian WÜCK	Karlsruher SC	VfL Wolfsburg
Magnus ARVIDSSON (SWE)	Trelleborgs FF (SWE)	FC Hansa Rostock			
Ali DAEI (IRN)	FC Bayern München	Hertha BSC Berlin	● **HOLLAND**		
Sebastian DEISLER	Borussia Mönchengladbach	Hertha BSC Berlin	Brian LAUDRUP (DEN)	FC København (DEN)	Ajax
Kai MICHALKE	VfL Bochum	Hertha BSC Berlin	Nikos MAHLAS (GRE)	Vitesse	Ajax
Kostas KONSTANTINIDIS (GRE)	Panathinaikos (GRE)	Hertha BSC Berlin	Aron WINTER	Inter (ITA)	Ajax
Marko REHMER	FC Hansa Rostock	Hertha BSC Berlin	Frank VERLAAT	VfB Stuttgart (GER)	Ajax
Jörgen PETTERSSON (SWE)	Borussia Mönchengladbach	1.FC Kaiserslautern	Stanley MENZO	K Lierse SK (BEL)	Ajax
Igli TARE (ALB)	Fortuna Düsseldorf	1.FC Kaiserslautern	Jan VAN HALST	FC Twente	Ajax
Slobodan KOMLJENOVIC (YUG)	MSV Duisburg	1.FC Kaiserslautern	John NIEUWENBERG	Sparta	Ajax
Thomas SOBOTZIK	Eintracht Frankfurt	1.FC Kaiserslautern	Jason CULINA (AUS)	Sydney Olympic (AUS)	Ajax
Jeff STRASSER (LUX)	FC Metz (FRA)	1.FC Kaiserslautern	Martijn REUSER	Vitesse	Ajax
Youri DJORKAEFF (FRA)	Inter (ITA)	1.FC Kaiserslautern	Pius IKEDIA (NIG)	ASEC Mimosas (CIV)	Ajax
Thomas HÄSSLER	Borussia Dortmund	TSV 1860 München	John BOSMAN	FC Twente	AZ
Thomas RIEDL	1.FC Kaiserslautern	TSV 1860 München	Krzysztof BOCIEK (POL)	NEC	FC Den Bosch
Filip TAPALOVIC (CRO)	FC Schalke 04	TSV 1860 München	Jan DE VISSER	SC Heerenveen	Feyenoord
Tomas VOTAVA (CZE)	Sparta Praha (CZE)	TSV 1860 München	Tomasz RZASA (POL)	De Graafschap	Feyenoord
Marcus PÜRK (AUT)	SK Rapid Wien (AUT)	TSV 1860 München	Dennis GERRITSEN	De Graafschap	Fortuna Sittard
Christian PROSENIK (AUT)	SK Rapid Wien (AUT)	TSV 1860 München	Dennis KRIJGSMAN	Sparta	Fortuna Sittard

MAJOR SUMMER TRANSFERS 1999

PLAYER	OLD CLUB	NEW CLUB	PLAYER	OLD CLUB	NEW CLUB
Arno SPLINTER	Ajax	De Graafschap	Marco ROCCATI	Perugia	Bologna
Harris HUIZINGH	FC Groningen	SC Heerenveen	Nicola VENTOLA	Inter	Bologna
Allan JEPSEN (DEN)	Hamburger SV (GER)	SC Heerenveen	Pierre Nlend WOME (CMR)	Roma	Bologna
Theo SNELDERS	Rangers (SCO)	MVV	José Marcelo ZÉ ELIAS (BRA)	Inter	Bologna
Ivica KRALJ (YUG)	FC Porto (POR)	PSV	Raffaele AMETRANO	Salernitana	Cagliari
Mark VAN BOMMEL	Fortuna Sittard	PSV	Davide CARRUS	Modena	Cagliari
Jan HEINTZE (DEN)	Bayer 04 Leverkusen (GER)	PSV	Daniele CONTI	Roma	Cagliari
Johann VOGEL (SUI)	Grasshopper-Club Zürich (SUI)	PSV	Bernardo CORRADI	Fidelis Andria	Cagliari
Eric ADDO (NIG)	Club Brugge KV (BEL)	PSV	Nicola DI LISO	Vicenza	Cagliari
Silvan INIA	FC Volendam	Sparta	Jason MAYELE (FRA)	LB Châteauroux (FRA)	Cagliari
Michael LANGERAK	AZ	Sparta	François MODESTO (FRA)	SC Bastia (FRA)	Cagliari
Sieme ZIJM	FC Zwolle	Sparta	Daniele ADANI	Brescia	Fiorentina
Steve GOOSSEN	Vitesse	Sparta	Abel BALBO (ARG)	Parma	Fiorentina
Bram MARBUS	Go Ahead Eagles	Sparta	Mauro BRESSAN	Bari	Fiorentina
Roy STROEVE	Emmen	Sparta	Enrico CHIESA	Parma	Fiorentina
Arjan VAN DER LAAN	Sparta	FC Twente	Angelo DI LIVIO	Juventus	Fiorentina
Scott BOOTH (SCO)	Borussia Dortmund (GER)	FC Twente	Predrag MIJATOVIC (YUG)	Real Madrid (ESP)	Fiorentina
Andy VAN DER MEYDE	Ajax	FC Twente	Paul OKON (AUS)	Lazio	Fiorentina
Frédéric PEIREMANS (BEL)	RSC Anderlecht (BEL)	FC Twente	Alessandro PIERINI	Udinese	Fiorentina
Jan VERLINDEN (BEL)	KV Mechelen (BEL)	FC Twente	Fabio ROSSITTO	Napoli	Fiorentina
Marinus DIJKHUIZEN	SC Cambuur Leeuwarden	FC Utrecht	Giuseppe TAGLIALATELA	Napoli	Fiorentina
Theo LUCIUS	PSV	FC Utrecht	Laurent BLANC (FRA)	Olympique Marseille (FRA)	Inter
Jamie FORRESTER (ENG)	Scunthorpe United (ENG)	FC Utrecht	Cyril DOMORAUD (FRA)	Olympique Marseille (FRA)	Inter
Pierre VAN HOOIJDONK	Nottingham Forest (ENG)	Vitesse	Fabrizio FERRON	Sampdoria	Inter
Victor SIKURA	Go Ahead Eagles	Vitesse	Vladimir JUGOVIC (YUG)	Atlético Madrid (ESP)	Inter
Pieter COLLEN (BEL)	KAA Gent (BEL)	Vitesse	Christian PANUCCI	Real Madrid (ESP)	Inter
Stefan NANU (ROM)	Rapid Bucuresti (ROM)	Vitesse	Angelo PERUZZI	Juventus	Inter
Dragoslav JEVRIC (YUG)	Crvena zvezda Beograd (YUG)	Vitesse	Martín RIVAS (URU)	Perugia	Inter
Nenad GRAZDIC (YUG)	FK Zemun (YUG)	Vitesse	Christian VIERI	Lazio	Inter
Marco GENTILE	FC Volendam	Willem II	Grigoris YEORGATOS (GRE)	Olympiakos (GRE)	Inter
Dmitriy SHUKOV (RUS)	Vitesse	Willem II	Cristiano ZANETTI	Cagliari	Inter
			Jonathan BACHINI	Udinese	Juventus
● **ITALY**			Andreas ISAKSSON (SWE)	Trelleborgs FF (SWE)	Juventus
Antonio BELLAVISTA	Treviso	Bari	Darko KOVACEVIC (YUG)	Real Sociedad (ESP)	Juventus
Carlo CARDASCIO	Lodigiani	Bari	Sunday OLISEH (NIG)	Ajax (HOL)	Juventus
Raphael CHUKWU (NIG)	Mamelodi Sundowns (SAF)	Bari	Edwin VAN DER SAR (HOL)	Ajax (HOL)	Juventus
Mattia COLLAUTO	Cremonese	Bari	Gianluca ZAMBROTTA	Bari	Juventus
Alessandro DEL GROSSO	Salernitana	Bari	Kennet ANDERSSON (SWE)	Bologna	Lazio
Matteo FERRARI	Lecce	Bari	Simone INZAGHI	Piacenza	Lazio
Diego Fernando MARKIC (ARG)	Argentinos Juniors (ARG)	Bari	Roberto Néstor SENSINI (ARG)	Parma	Lazio
Simone PERROTTA	Juventus	Bari	Diego SIMEONE (ARG)	Inter	Lazio
Giulio FALCONE	Fiorentina	Bologna	Juan Sebastián VERON (ARG)	Parma	Lazio
Gianluca PAGLIUCA	Inter	Bologna	Serhiy ATLEKIN (UKR)	Boavista FC (POR)	Lecce

MAJOR SUMMER TRANSFERS 1999

PLAYER	OLD CLUB	NEW CLUB
David BALLERI	Sampdoria	Lecce
Emiliano BILIOTTI	Ravenna	Lecce
Claudio BONOMI	Empoli	Lecce
Antonio CHIMENTI	Roma	Lecce
Gianluca COLONELLO	Perugia	Lecce
Alessandro DE POLI	Treviso	Lecce
Domenico DI CARLO	Vicenza	Lecce
Francisco LIMA (BRA)	FC Zürich (SUI)	Lecce
Cristiano LUCARELLI	Valencia CF (ESP)	Lecce

Christian Vieri - Lazio to Inter.

PLAYER	OLD CLUB	NEW CLUB
Riccardo MASPERO	Reggiana	Lecce
Angelo PARADISO	Napoli	Lecce
Matteo PIVOTTO	Chievo	Lecce
Alberto SAVINO	Brescia	Lecce
Diego DE ASCENTIS	Bari	Milan
Valerio FIORI	Piacenza	Milan

PLAYER	OLD CLUB	NEW CLUB
Gennaro GATTUSO	Salernitana	Milan
Pierluigi ORLANDINI	Parma	Milan
Mirko SADOTTI	Monza	Milan
Sérgio Claúdio SERGINHO (BRA)	FC São Paolo (BRA)	Milan
Andriy SHEVCHENKO (UKR)	Dynamo Kyiv (UKR)	Milan
Carlo TEODORANI	Cesena	Milan
Max TONETTO	Empoli	Milan
Márcio AMOROSO (BRA)	Udinese	Parma
Roberto BREDA	Salernitana	Parma
Marco DI VAIO	Salernitana	Parma
Giampiero MAINI	Bologna	Parma
Johnnier MONTAÑO (COL)	Quilnes (ARG)	Parma
Ariel ORTEGA (ARG)	Sampdoria	Parma
Michele SERENA	Atlético Madrid (ESP)	Parma
Stefano TORRISI	Atlético Madrid (ESP)	Parma
Johan WALEM (BEL)	Udinese	Parma
Pierpaolo BISOLI	Empoli	Perugia
Jorge BOLAÑO (COL)	Junior Barranquilla (COL)	Perugia
Alessandro CALORI	Udinese	Perugia
Daniele DAINO	Napoli	Perugia
Massimiliano ESPOSITO	Napoli	Perugia
Stefano GUIDONI	Verona	Perugia
Marco MATERAZZI	Everton (ENG)	Perugia
Mauro MILANESE	Inter	Perugia
Claudio RIVALTA	Cesena	Perugia
Héctor TAPIA (CHL)	Universidad Católica (CHL)	Perugia
Arturo DI NAPOLI	Empoli	Piacenza
Stefano MORRONE	Empoli	Piacenza
Flavio ROMA	Chievo	Piacenza
Roberto BARONIO	Lazio	Reggina
Ezio BREVI	Ternana	Reggina
Paolo FOGLIO	Verona	Reggina
Alessandro IANNUZZI	Lazio	Reggina
Mohammed KALLON (SRL)	Cagliari	Reggina
Arnauld MERCIER (FRA)	Fidelis Andria	Reggina
Giovanni MORABITO	Vicenza	Reggina
Nenad PRALIJA (CRO)	Hajduk Split (CRO)	Reggina
Enrique REGGI (ARG)	Gymnasia La Plata (ARG)	Reggina
Lorenzo STOVINI	Vicenza	Reggina
Salvatore VICARI	Palermo	Reggina
Francesco ANTONIOLI	Bologna	Roma
MARCOS Assunção (BRA)	Santos (BRA)	Roma
Giuseppe COLUCCI	Foggia	Roma

MAJOR SUMMER TRANSFERS 1999

PLAYER	OLD CLUB	NEW CLUB
Nesat GÜLÜNOGLU (TUR)	VfL Bochum (GER)	Roma
Sergei GURENKO (BLS)	Lokomotiv Moskva (RUS)	Roma
Cristiano LUPATELLI	Fidelis Andria	Roma
Amedeo MANGONE	Bologna	Roma
Vincenzo MONTELLA	Sampdoria	Roma
Alessandro RINALDI	Bologna	Roma
Francesco COCO	Milan	Torino
André CRUZ (BRA)	Milan	Torino
Djibril DIAWARA (FRA)	AS Monaco (FRA)	Torino
Erik EDMAN (SWE)	Helsingborgs IF (SWE)	Torino
Felice FOGLIA	Lucchese	Torino
Ilija IVIC (YUG)	Olympiakos (GRE)	Torino
Marcus LANTZ (SWE)	Helsingborgs IF (SWE)	Torino
Gustavo MENDEZ (URU)	Vicenza	Torino
Fabio PECCHIA	Sampdoria	Torino
Andrea SILENZI	Ravenna	Torino
JORGINHO Amaral de Castro (BRA)	PSV (HOL)	Udinese
Morgan DE SANCTIS	Juventus	Udinese
Stefano FIORE	Parma	Udinese
Massimo MARGIOTTA	Reggiana	Udinese
Roberto MUZZI	Cagliari	Udinese
Mauricio PINEDA (ARG)	RCD Mallorca (ESP)	Udinese
David PIZARRO (CHL)	Wanderers (URU)	Udinese
Olivier RENARD (BEL)	RSC Charleroi (BEL)	Udinese
Andrea SOTTIL	Atalanta	Udinese
Delio César TOLEDO (PAR)	Cerro Porteño (PAR)	Udinese
Marco ZAMBONI	Lecce	Udinese
Runar BERG (NOR)	Rosenborg BK (NOR)	Venezia
Massimo BORGOBELLO	Ternana	Venezia
Igor BUDAN (CRO)	Rijeka (CRO)	Venezia
Fabrizio CASAZZA	Torino	Venezia
Giuseppe CARDONE	Vicenza	Venezia
Hiroshi NANAMI (JPN)	Jubilo Iwata (JPN)	Venezia
Dejan PETKOVIC (YUG)	Vitória Bahia (BRA)	Venezia
ADAILTON Martins (BRA)	Paris Saint-Germain (FRA)	Verona
Giuseppe ANASTASI	Foggia	Verona
Aimo DIANA	Brescia	Verona
Marco FRANCESCHETTI	Sampdoria	Verona
Sébastien FREY (FRA)	Inter	Verona
Luca MEZZANO	Perugia	Verona
Emiliano SALVETTI	Cesena	Verona
Anthony SERIC (CRO)	Hajduk Split (CRO)	Verona
Robert SPEHAR (CRO)	AS Monaco (FRA)	Verona

PLAYER	OLD CLUB	NEW CLUB
● PORTUGAL		
Sergei OVCHINNIKOV (RUS)	SL Benfica	FC Alverca
VERISSIMO	Académica Coimbra	FC Alverca
JOSÉ ANTÓNIO	Leça FC	FC Alverca
Vasiliy KULKOV (RUS)	Krylya Sovetov Samara (RUS)	FC Alverca
JOSÉ CARLOS	Vitória Guimarães	CF Os Belenenses
FERNANDO MENDES	FC Porto	CF Os Belenenses
WILSON	Gil Vicente FC	CF Os Belenenses
GOUVEIA	SC Farense	CF Os Belenenses
Jesús SEBA (ESP)	GD Chaves	CF Os Belenenses
Carlos BOSSIO (ARG)	Estudiantes (ARG)	SL Benfica
Robert ENKE (GER)	Borussia Mönchengladbach (GER)	SL Benfica
MARCO FREITAS	FC Alverca	SL Benfica
MANICHE	FC Alverca	SL Benfica
SÉRGIO NUNES	União Leiria	SL Benfica
Ricardo ROJAS (PAR)	Estudiantes (ARG)	SL Benfica
JOSÉ SOARES	FC Alverca	SL Benfica
EMANUEL	Rio Ave FC	Boavista FC
FORMOSO	SC Braga	Boavista FC
Augustine AHINFUL (GHA)	Venezia (ITA)	Boavista FC
MOREIRA	Gil Vicente FC	Boavista FC
RICARDO SILVA	Gil Vicente FC	Boavista FC
BARROSO	Académica Coimbra	SC Braga
PEDRO LAVOURA	Académica Coimbra	SC Braga
JEAN PAULISTA (BRA)	SC Farense	SC Braga
ARLEY (BRA)	Vitória Guimarães	SC Campomaiorense
CAO	SC Salgueiros	SC Campomaiorense
MICKEY	Académica Coimbra	SC Campomaiorense
TIAGO	Sporting CP	CF Estrela Amadora
GAÚCHO (BRA)	Académica Coimbra	CF Estrela Amadora
DINO	UD Salamanca (ESP)	SC Farense
CARLOS FERNANDES	SC Campomaiorense	SC Farense
NUNO CAMPOS	SC Campomaiorense	SC Farense
VÍTOR MANUEL	SC Campomaiorense	SC Farense
TULIPA	CS Marítimo	SC Farense
LUÍS CAVACO	Boavista FC	SC Farense
PAULO LOPES	SL Benfica	Gil Vicente FC
RUI GUERREIRO	SC Braga	Gil Vicente FC
AURI (BRA)	Vitória Guimarães	Gil Vicente FC
CARLOS	Leça FC	Gil Vicente FC
ZÉ NANDO	Leça FC	Gil Vicente FC
Ilian ILIEV (BUL)	Levski Sofia (BUL)	CS Marítimo
Marius SUMUDICA (ROM)	Rapid Bucuresti (ROM)	CS Marítimo

MAJOR SUMMER TRANSFERS 1999

PLAYER	OLD CLUB	NEW CLUB
HILÁRIO	CF Estrela Amadora	FC Porto
ARGEL (BRA)	Santos (BRA)	FC Porto
RICARDO SILVA	União Leiria	FC Porto
RUBENS JÚNIOR (BRA)	Palmeiras (BRA)	FC Porto
RODOLFO	CF Estrela Amadora	FC Porto
RICARDO SOUSA	SC Beira Mar	FC Porto
PAULO FERREIRA	CF Estrela Amadora	FC Porto
DOMINGOS	CD Tenerife (ESP)	FC Porto
ALESSANDRO (BRA)	Santos (BRA)	FC Porto
ROMEU	CS Marítimo	FC Porto
DUDA (BRA)	Rio Ave FC	FC Porto
COSTA	Vitória Guimarães	Rio Ave FC
ARTUR JORGE	Boavista FC	Rio Ave FC
RUI FERREIRA	Gil Vicente FC	SC Salgueiros
CANDIDO	SL Benfica	SC Salgueiros
BASÍLIO ALMEIDA	Vitória Guimarães	SC Salgueiros
FIGUEIREDO	Sporting CP	CD Santa Clara
SÉRGIO	SC Braga	CD Santa Clara
LUÍS MIGUEL	SC Campomaiorense	CD Santa Clara
AMARAL	Vitória Setúbal	CD Santa Clara
LUÍS CARLOS (BRA)	SC Braga	CD Santa Clara
WANDERLEY (BRA)	GD Chaves	CD Santa Clara
CLAYTON (BRA)	Atlético Mineiro (BRA)	CD Santa Clara
PALADINI (BRA)	Flamengo (BRA)	CD Santa Clara
Peter SCHMEICHEL (DEN)	Manchester United (ENG)	Sporting CP
Mauricio HANUCH (ARG)	Independiente (BRA)	Sporting CP
TOÑITO (ESP)	Vitória Setúbal	Sporting CP
AYEW Kwame (GHA)	Boavista FC	Sporting CP
NUNO VALENTE	Sporting CP	União Leiria
Florin BATRÂNU (ROM)	Dinamo Bucuresti (ROM)	União Leiria
SOUSA	FC Porto	União Leiria
HERIVELTO (BRA)	CS Marítimo	União Leiria
PORTELA	CD Santa Clara	Vitória Setúbal
CARLOS MANUEL	FC Porto	Vitória Setúbal

● **SCOTLAND**

PLAYER	OLD CLUB	NEW CLUB
David PREECE (ENG)	Darlington (ENG)	Aberdeen
Eyal BERKOVIC (ISR)	West Ham United (ENG)	Celtic
Bobby PETTA (HOL)	Ipswich Town (ENG)	Celtic
Stilian PETROV (BUL)	CSKA Sofia (BUL)	Celtic
Dmitriy KHARIN (RUS)	Chelsea (ENG)	Celtic
Olivier TEBILY (FRA)	Sheffield United (ENG)	Celtic
Fabien LECLERCQ (FRA)	Lille OSC (FRA)	Heart of Midlothian

PLAYER	OLD CLUB	NEW CLUB
Nick COLGAN (ENG)	Bournemouth (ENG)	Hibernian
Fabrice HENRY (FRA)	FC Basel (SUI)	Hibernian
Dirk LEHMANN (GER)	Fulham (ENG)	Hibernian
Frédéric DINDELEUX (FRA)	Lille OSC (FRA)	Kilmarnock
Michael MOLS (HOL)	FC Utrecht (HOL)	Rangers
Dariusz ADAMCZUK (POL)	Dundee	Rangers

● **SPAIN**

PLAYER	OLD CLUB	NEW CLUB
Alejandro Díaz "ALEX"	CD Numancia	CD Alavés
Angel MORALES	Hércules CF	CD Alavés
Dan EGGEN (NOR)	RC Celta	CD Alavés
Javier MORENO	CD Numancia	CD Alavés
Meho KODRO (BOS)	CD Tenerife	CD Alavés
Raúl GAÑAN	CD Badajoz	CD Alavés
Cosmin CONTRA (ROM)	Steaua Bucuresti (ROM)	CD Alavés
Victor TORRES MESTRE	Girondins de Bordeaux (FRA)	CD Alavés
Joan "Nan" RIBERA	RCD Espanyol	CD Alavés
Arturo Igoroín "SIVORI"	CD Alavés	Athletic Bilbao
Eduardo ALONSO	UD Salamanca	Athletic Bilbao
Oscar VALES	RC Celta	Athletic Bilbao
Pablo ORBAIZ	CA Osasuna	Athletic Bilbao
Antonio Jiménez "TONI"	RCD Espanyol	Atlético Madrid
Carlos GAMARRA (PAR)	Corinthians (BRA)	Atlético Madrid
Gustavo DE LA PARRA	Atlético Madrid B	Atlético Madrid
HUGO LEAL (POR)	SL Benfica (POR)	Atlético Madrid
Juan CAPDEVILA	RCD Espanyol	Atlético Madrid
Veljko PAUNOVIC (YUG)	RCD Mallorca	Atlético Madrid
Jimmy Floyd HASSELBAINK (HOL)	Leeds United (ENG)	Atlético Madrid
Daniel García "DANI"	RCD Mallorca	FC Barcelona
Frédéric DEHU (FRA)	RC Lens (FRA)	FC Barcelona
Jari LITMANEN (FIN)	Ajax (HOL)	FC Barcelona
SIMÃO SABROSA (POR)	Sporting CP (POR)	FC Barcelona
Joaquín BORNES	RC Recreativo	Real Betis
Miroslav KARHAN (SVK)	Spartak Trnava (SVK)	Real Betis
Diego CROSSA (ARG)	Newell's Old Boys (ARG)	Real Betis
Benni McCARTHY (SAF)	Ajax (HOL)	RC Celta
Everton GIOVANELLA (BRA)	UD Salamanca	RC Celta
Gustavo LOPEZ (ARG)	Real Zaragoza	RC Celta
Jaime KAVIEDES (ECU)	Perugia (ITA)	RC Celta
Juan VELASCO	Sevilla FC	RC Celta
Mirko PANTELIC (YUG)	Paris Saint-Germain (FRA)	RC Celta
Pablo COIRA	SD Compostela	RC Celta
Pablo GONZALEZ	CD Numancia	RC Celta

MAJOR SUMMER TRANSFERS 1999

PLAYER	OLD CLUB	NEW CLUB	PLAYER	OLD CLUB	NEW CLUB
SERGIO Fernández	Sporting Gijón	RC Celta	OSCAR Alvarez	FC Barcelona	Real Oviedo
Mario TURDO (ARG)	Independiente (ARG)	RC Celta	Roberto LOSADA	CD Toledo	Real Oviedo
Alberto CELADES	FC Barcelona	RC Celta	Frédéric DANJOU (FRA)	AJ Auxerre (FRA)	Real Oviedo
CESAR Martín	Real Oviedo	RC Deportivo	Albert NADJ (YUG)	Real Betis	Real Oviedo
David Almazán "PIRRI"	Mérida CP	RC Deportivo	Fernando MORAN	CD Ourense	Racing Santander
IVAN Pérez	Girondins de Bordeaux (FRA)	RC Deportivo	Gonzalo COLSA	CD Logroñés	Racing Santander
JAIME Sánchez	Real Madrid	RC Deportivo	Gonzalo SUANCES	CD Ourense	Racing Santander
José Manuel COLMENERO	Sporting Gijón	RC Deportivo	Javier MANJARIN	RC Deportivo	Racing Santander
Manuel Menéndez "MANEL"	Real Oviedo	RC Deportivo	Marcelo ESPINA (CHL)	Colo Colo (CHL)	Racing Santander
Roy MAKAAY (HOL)	CD Tenerife	RC Deportivo	Sigurd RUSHFELDT (NOR)	Rosenborg BK (NOR)	Racing Santander
Slavisa JOKANOVIC (YUG)	CD Tenerife	RC Deportivo	Daniel BOUZAS	Albacete Balompié	Rayo Vallecano
VICTOR Sánchez	Racing Santander	RC Deportivo	GILMAR (BRA)	Real Zaragoza	Rayo Vallecano
Antonio VELAMAZAN	CF Extremadura	RCD Espanyol	QUINZINHO (ANG)	FC Porto (POR)	Rayo Vallecano
César SANTIS (CHL)	Union RCD Española (CHL)	RCD Espanyol	Jordi FERRON	FC Barcelona	Rayo Vallecano
Juan Luis MORA	Real Oviedo	RCD Espanyol	Kasey KELLER (USA)	Leicester City (ENG)	Rayo Vallecano
Mauro NAVAS (ARG)	Udinese (ITA)	RCD Espanyol	ROBSON (BRA)	Spartak Moskva (RUS)	Rayo Vallecano
Miklos MOLNAR (DEN)	Sevilla FC	RCD Espanyol	Gerhard POSCHNER (GER)	Venezia (ITA)	Rayo Vallecano
Pablo ROTCHEN (ARG)	Independiente (ARG)	RCD Espanyol	Elvir BALJIC (BOS)	Fenerbahçe (TUR)	Real Madrid
Sergio CORINO	UD Salamanca	RCD Espanyol	Iván HELGUERA	RCD Espanyol	Real Madrid
Pablo CAVALLERO (ARG)	Vélez Sarsfield (ARG)	RCD Espanyol	JULIO CESAR Santos	Real Valladolid	Real Madrid
Carles PUYOL	FC Barcelona	Málaga CF	MICHEL SALGADO	RC Celta	Real Madrid
Fernando SANZ	Real Madrid	Málaga CF	Steve McMANAMAN (ENG)	Liverpool (ENG)	Real Madrid
Kiki MUSAMPA (HOL)	Girondins de Bordeaux (FRA)	Málaga CF	GEREMI Njitap (CMR)	Gençlerbirligi (TUR)	Real Madrid
Pedro CONTRERAS	Real Madrid	Málaga CF	Nicolas ANELKA (FRA)	Arsenal (ENG)	Real Madrid
Roberto ROJAS	Real Madrid	Málaga CF	Victor BONILLA (COL)	Deportivo Cali (COL)	Real Sociedad
Ardijan DJUKAJ (YUG)	Buducnost Podgorica (YUG)	RCD Mallorca	Alfredo Lubeiras "FREDI"	Sporting Gijón	Sevilla FC
ARMANDO Alvarez	RC Deportivo	RCD Mallorca	Angel RODRIGUEZ	CD Numancia	Sevilla FC
DAVID Castedo	CF Extremadura	RCD Mallorca	Gabriel POPESCU (ROM)	Valencia CF	Sevilla FC
Germán BURGOS (ARG)	River Plate (ARG)	RCD Mallorca	Juan José VALENCIA	Athletic Bilbao	Sevilla FC
Iván César GABRICH (ARG)	CF Extremadura	RCD Mallorca	Marcelo OTERO (URU)	Vicenza (ITA)	Sevilla FC
Juan José SERRIZUELA	Lanús (ARG)	RCD Mallorca	Marcelo ZALAYETA (URU)	Juventus (ITA)	Sevilla FC
Alberto BELSUE	CD Alavés	CD Numancia	Nicolás OLIVERA (URU)	Valencia CF	Sevilla FC
Alejandro Castro "JANDRO"	Valencia CF	CD Numancia	Gerardo RABADJA (URU)	Puebla (MEX)	Sevilla FC
Domingo NAGORE	Athletic Bilbao	CD Numancia	Andrés PALOP	Villarreal CF	Valencia CF
Fabrice MOREAU (FRA)	Rayo Vallecano	CD Numancia	Daniel FAGGIANI (ARG)	Newell's Old Boys (ARG)	Valencia CF
Jorge PEREZ	Athletic Bilbao	CD Numancia	GERARD López	CD Alavés	Valencia CF
José Rojo "PACHETA"	RCD Espanyol	CD Numancia	Juan SANCHEZ	RC Celta	Valencia CF
Juan Ramón López MUÑIZ	Rayo Vallecano	CD Numancia	OSCAR García	FC Barcelona	Valencia CF
Rubén NAVARRO	Valencia CF	CD Numancia	"KILY" GONZALEZ (ARG)	Real Zaragoza	Valencia CF
Vicente Blanco "TITO"	Albacete Balompié	CD Numancia	Gabriel HEINZE (ARG)	Sporting CP (POR)	Real Valladolid
Constantin BARBU (ROM)	Rapid Bucuresti (ROM)	CD Numancia	LUIS GARCIA	FC Barcelona	Real Valladolid
Gert CLAESSENS (BEL)	Club Brugge KV (BEL)	Real Oviedo	Manuel TENA	Real Madrid	Real Valladolid
Juan GONZALEZ	Atlético Madrid	Real Oviedo	Juan Castaño "JUANELE"	CD Tenerife	Real Zaragoza

MAJOR SUMMER TRANSFERS 1999

PLAYER	OLD CLUB	NEW CLUB
Martin VELLISCA	UD Salamanca	Real Zaragoza
PIER Luigi Cherubino	CD Tenerife	Real Zaragoza
Marco LANNA (ITA)	UD Salamanca	Real Zaragoza

Nicolas Anelka - Arsenal to Real Madrid.

● **SWITZERLAND**

PLAYER	OLD CLUB	NEW CLUB
Jean-Pierre LA PLACA	FC Sion	FC Aarau
Pascal ZUBERBÜHLER	Grasshopper-Club Zürich	FC Basel
Ivan KNEZ (PER)	FC Luzern	FC Basel
Alexandre QUENNOZ	FC Sion	FC Basel
Raphael KEHRLI	BSC Young Boys Bern	FC Basel
Nenad SAVIC (YUG)	Neuchâtel Xamax FC	FC Basel
GÜNER Çetin (TUR)	Borussia Dortmund (GER)	FC Basel
George KOUMANTARAKIS (SAF)	FC Luzern	FC Basel
Didier THOLOT (FRA)	FC Sion	FC Basel
ITAMAR (BRA)	Rio Grande do Sul (BRA)	SR Delémont

PLAYER	OLD CLUB	NEW CLUB
FABINHO (BRA)	FC Wil	SR Delémont
TANIELTON (BRA)	Santa Cruz Recreativo (BRA)	SR Delémont
Samuel DRAKOPOULOS (GRE)	BSC Young Boys Bern	SR Delémont
Stefan HUBER	FC Basel	Grasshopper-Club Zürich
Marc HODEL	FC Zürich	Grasshopper-Club Zürich
Patrick ISABELLA	Neuchâtel Xamax FC	Grasshopper-Club Zürich
Eric VISCAAL (HOL)	De Graafschap (HOL)	Grasshopper-Club Zürich
Edin GAZIC (BOS)	Neuchâtel Xamax FC	Grasshopper-Club Zürich
Sven CHRIST	Grasshopper-Club Zürich	Lausanne-Sports
Jean-Philippe KARLEN	Servette FC Genève	Lausanne-Sports
Cédric HORJAK (FRA)	AS Saint-Etienne (FRA)	Lausanne-Sports
Lionel PIZZINAT	Servette FC Genève	Lausanne-Sports
Marcin KUZBA (POL)	AJ Auxerre (FRA)	Lausanne-Sports
David INGUSCIO	SR Delémont	FC Lugano
Eddy BAREA	Servette FC Genève	FC Lugano
Markus BRUNNER	FC Luzern	FC Lugano
Sergio BASTIDA (BOL)	FK Teplice (CZE)	FC Lugano
Michael HOY (FRA)	SR Delémont	FC Lugano
Bruno SUTTER	FC Wil	FC Lugano
Joël MAGNIN	Grasshopper-Club Zürich	FC Lugano
Patrick FOLETTI	FC Schaffhausen	FC Luzern
Sébastien LIPAWSKY	FC Sion	FC Luzern
Marcelo SANDER (BRA)	Friburguense (BRA)	FC Luzern
Alexander FREI	FC Thun	FC Luzern
David SENE	FC St. Gallen	Neuchâtel Xamax FC
Charles WITTL (GHA)	SK Rapid Wien (AUT)	Neuchâtel Xamax FC
Giuseppe MAZZARELLI	Grasshopper-Club Zürich	FC St. Gallen
Charles AMOAH (GHA)	FC Wil	FC St. Gallen
Fouzi EL BRAZI (MAR)	FUS Rabat (MAR)	Servette FC Genève
Matteo VANETTA	FC Sion	Servette FC Genève
Dan POTOCIANU (ROM)	FC Basel	Servette FC Genève
Léonard THURRE	Lausanne-Sports	Servette FC Genève
Carlos VARELA (ESP)	FC Basel	Servette FC Genève
Olivier BIAGGI	FC Sion	Yverdon-Sports
ABEDI (BRA)	FC Basel	Yverdon-Sports
ADAOZINHO (BRA)	Matsubara (BRA)	Yverdon-Sports
Thierry EBE	Etoile-Carouge FC	Yverdon-Sports
Marco PASCOLO	Nottingham Forest (ENG)	FC Zürich
Ivan QUENTIN	Neuchâtel Xamax FC	FC Zürich
Martin STOCKLASA (LIE)	FC Vaduz (LIE)	FC Zürich
Philippe DOUGLAS	Lausanne-Sports	FC Zürich
Mauro GIANNINI (ITA)	FC Lugano	FC Zürich
Mario FRICK (LIE)	FC Basel	FC Zürich